LET'S GO:

The Budget Guide to

EUROPE

1988

Ian Stewart Gibson
Editor

Judson A. R. Weaver
Assistant Editor

Written by Harvard Student Agencies, Inc.

ST. MARTIN'S PRESS
NEW YORK

Books are available in quantity for promotional or premium use. Write to Director of Special Sales, Patti Hughes, St. Martin's Press, 175 Fifth Avenue, New York, NY 10010, for information on discounts and terms, or call toll-free (800) 221-7945. In New York, call (212) 674-5151.

Distributed outside the U.S. and Canada by Columbus Books Ltd.

ISBN: 0-312-01455-4

First Edition
10 9 8 7 6 5 4 3 2 1

Let's Go: Europe is written by Harvard Student Agencies, Inc., Harvard University, Thayer Hall-B Cambridge, Mass. 02138.

ACKNOWLEDGMENTS

Spending an entire summer searching out synonyms for "good" gives one a real sense of the limits of the language; the quality of the contributions of Assistant Editor Jud Weaver and Managing Editor Daphne Bien are far past those limits. Jud's commitment and attention to detail are phenomenal—this book never would have happened without him. Daphne combined tremendous writing and editing skills with a real generosity of character.

The real stars of the show, though, are the researcher/writers; hearty individuals who spend their summers in hostels and on roofs, on buses, trains, and boats; without adequate rest, time, or pay. And they manage to write well-crafted descriptions of their travels. Mary Yntema did a magnificent job on Paris; thousands of next summer's travelers ought to toast an effort far and beyond the call of duty. It's worth shelling out 11 clams just for Steve Grover's superb accounts of London and Madrid. Heidi Sullivan's copy, complete with explanatory illustrations, was more thorough than I imagined possible. Peter Redfield traveled faster than a speeding bullet, throughout all of Scandinavia, penning great copy all the time. Rich Mintz, noted economist, Anglo-Saxon scholar, and *Let's Go* bard, contributed another year of tremendous work to our coverage of Great Britain. Charlotte Chiu brought her boundless enthusiasm to some difficult places, and broke the *Let's Go* record for postcard production. Peter Sagal endured illness and last-minute changes of plan to send back copy that I admired more frequently than edited, and Tim Screech truly stepped into the breech for us in Jordan. I hope that Joe Freeman and Jamie Cook enjoyed their North African travels nearly as much as I enjoyed their copy. Fellow Turkophile Robert Brooker made good coverage better. Gordon Burnes and Wade Stokes brought expertise to their Spanish assignments. Dennis Macray VW-bused it through Germany and the Alps, doing a great job, while Eric Fay and Z. Ben Robinson were a source of valuable insight into Eastern Europe. Fellow Funster inmate John Thompson's copy made grounds that I have frequently stomped sound new and interesting. Ellen Goodman's taste for the classical spiced her Peloponnese chapter. Chrystia Freeland's copy was always cause for excitement. Alix Cooper and Debbie Benor did justice to Ireland and Greece, respectively, and then both came back to lend a much appreciated hand in the basement. Astrid Tuminez, Corey Miller, David Fisher, Eily Pearl, Michael Ventre, Jess Bravin, Sue Stewart, and Kathy Kleiman wrote excellently wherever they went.

The fellow occupants of the little warren we call an office all went out of their way for this book on a regular basis. Chris Russ, David Stone, Kathleen Skerrett, Lee Sanders, and Liz Scarlett were all tremendously helpful from February onwards, and good friends to boot. Similarly, Alice Ma, Andrea Piperakis, Isabella Fu, Joe Barloon, Julianne Hunt, Lauri Hornik, Lynley Ogilvie, Marie Breaux, Mark Selwyn, and Rebecca Carpenter all put work into what became truly a group endeavour. Karen Baldeschwieler's work in the spring and Jake Roth's struggles against errant computers and cockroaches the size of small rabbits were also much appreciated. Bridget Keegan and Lisa Estreich, bearers of free meals, both made the office a cheery place during their tenure. We couldn't have done any of it without Ghen Maynard, the ringmaster of the *Let's Go* circus. Falak Kagda, Alisa Savetamal, and Liz Allard were among those who put in long hours at the computers, and Vlad Jenkins and Verónica Cortínez lent their impressive knowledge of Europe to the proofreading process. Special thanks also to Dr. Seuss, whose classic *One Fish Two Fish Red Fish Blue Fish,* published by Random House, Inc., provided an epigraph for both this volume and the summer.

Thanks to Diane Wachtell, Gideon Schor, Scott Campbell, and Bob Brennan; friends from *Let's Go*s past. And thanks to Ghen Maynard, Daphne Bien, Mark Denneen, and Bob Brennan for the tremendous job they did to ensure the well-being of *Let's Go*s future. Finally, thanks to Mike Foster and Jacqui Mackenzie, who lightened many a summer evening, and to Pete, who was always there to keep things in sufficiently ridiculous perspective. Suzy Reich proofread over half of the book, and that was the smallest of her contributions; from agonizing over the interview to typing in exchange rates at the eleventh hour, she was always there. My largest acknowledgment, though, goes to Mum and Dad, the real travelers in the Gibson family. This book is for them.

—Stewart Gibson

What a long, strange trip it's been. I'd like to thank Stewart most of all for making the summer bearable and productive. His knowledge, experience, and patience hold this book together. I would like to thank everyone at *Let's Go* for making this summer a great one. We all worked and played hard, side-by-side, for four months and somehow ended up with the entire *Let's Go* series. Most of all, Mom and Dad, Amanda, Nicole, Eric, Shawn, and Ralph provided the encouragement needed to complete this hog.

—Judson Weaver

Reykjavik
ICELAND
ATLANTIC OCEAN
NORW
Oslo
Glasgow
SCOTLAND
Edinburgh
North Sea
Belfast
IRELAND
Dublin
GREAT
BRITAIN
ENGLAND
DENMAR
WALES
Cardiff
London
NETH.
Hamburg
Amsterdam
Brussels
BEL.
Bonn
Paris
LUX.
Rennes
WEST
GERMANY
Munich
FRANCE
Bern
SWITZ.
Bordeaux
Lyon
Milan
Venice
Bilbao
PORTUGAL
Nice
Florence
Madrid
Corsica
Lisbon
Barcelona
SPAIN
Valencia
Majorca
ITALY
Malaga
Sardinia
Tangier
Mediterrane
Rabat
Fez
Tunis
ALGERIA
MOROCCO
TUNISIA
Marrakesh

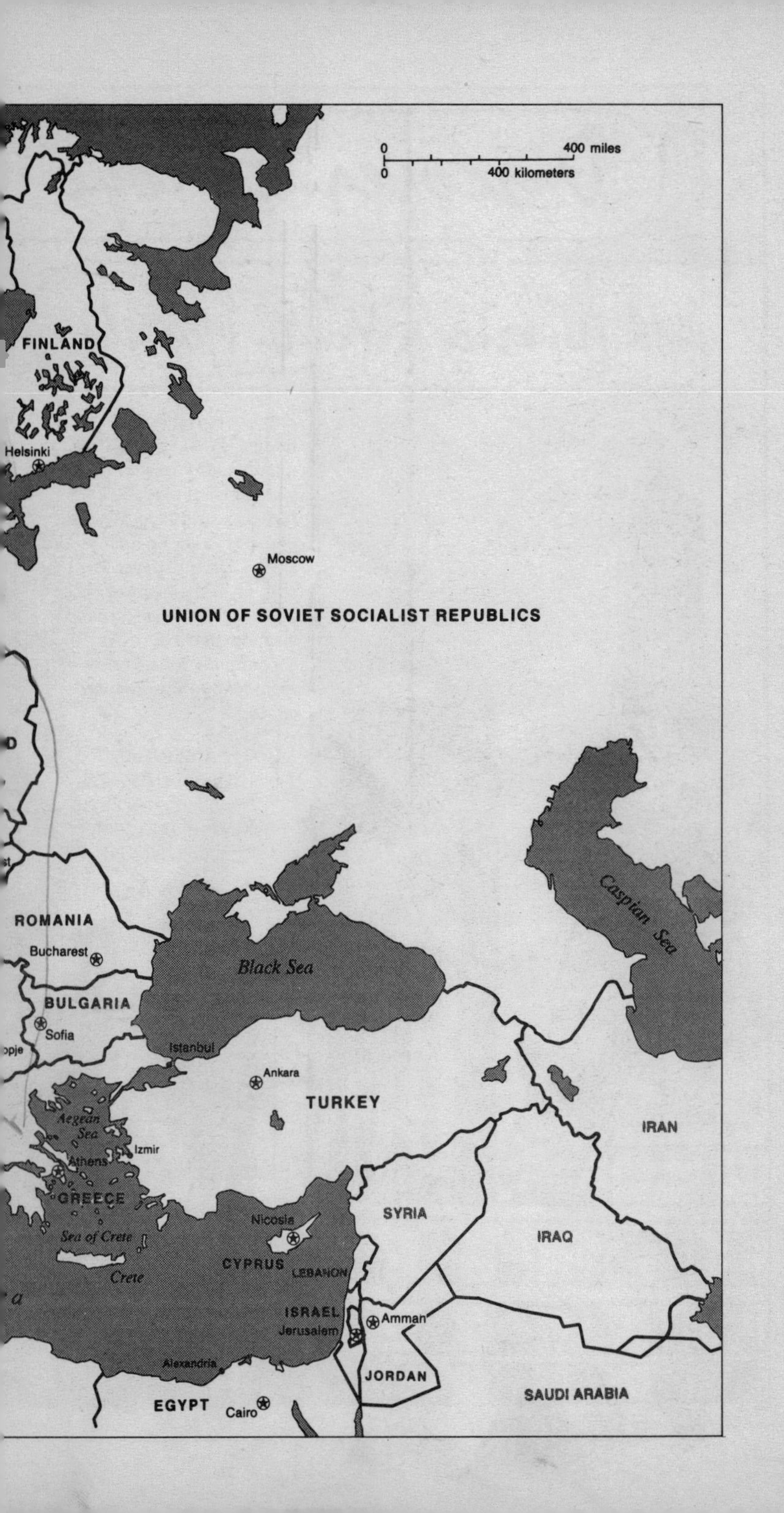

0
400 miles
0
400 kilometers
FINLAND
Helsinki
Moscow
UNION OF SOVIET SOCIALIST REPUBLICS
ROMANIA
Bucharest
BULGARIA
Sofia
Black Sea
Caspian Sea
Istanbul
Ankara
TURKEY
Aegean Sea
Izmir
Athens
GREECE
Sea of Crete
Crete
IRAN
SYRIA
IRAQ
Nicosia
CYPRUS
LEBANON
ISRAEL
Jerusalem
Amman
JORDAN
Alexandria
EGYPT
Cairo
SAUDI ARABIA

CONTENTS

Let's Go: Europe

From there to here,
from here to there,
funny things
are everywhere.
—Dr. Seuss

From the Sacred Oxen of Saqqara to the Sacred Carp of Şanliurfa, *Let's Go* guides you to the most interesting and beautiful attractions that Europe has to offer. Moreover, we help make your travels cheap and trouble-free—our researchers comb every country in Europe and collect information that will save you time and money. Researchers travel on a shoestring budget, so their concerns are the same as yours: eating, drinking, sleeping, seeing the sights and festivals, and enjoying the nightlife—all for as little as possible. They have provided detailed directions to out-of-the-way places where you can escape the crowds and relax with the locals. Their precise and honest appraisals will help you decide your style of travel, and then help you along the way.

Planning Your Trip will aid in tasks to be completed before you go: obtaining passport and visas, dealing with money matters, and packing. In Getting There, you'll find information about the different kinds of flights and ships traveling to Europe. Our Once There section provides information on transportation and accommodations in Europe, and will help you decide whether to invest in a railpass, a student card, or a hostel card before you go. For best results, combine this information with that in the specific country introductions; we include exchange rates and prices throughout so that you can match your plans to your resources.

Once you're in Europe, *Let's Go* can help you settle into unfamiliar territory. For smaller cities, we highlight sights and entertainment first, then provide information on the basics— tourist offices, accommodations, and food. For larger cities, each topic receives a special heading. Orientation and Practical Information describes the geographic location of the city and the various services available for visitors; Accommodations and Camping lists the locations and prices of hostels, budget hotels, and campgrounds; Food reviews a selection of restaurants and student mensas, cafes, and open-air markets; Sights explores the major attractions and unique offerings of the city; and Entertainment describes nightlife, cultural events, and festivals.

Let's Go: Europe has been called the bible of budget travelers. But if it is your bible, don't be narrow in your interpretation. Healthy skepticism will serve you better than blind faith. We don't pretend to have the last word in travel advice; in fact, one of our primary goals is to point out the myriad other sources of information about budget travel in Europe. For more detailed information you can also turn to the six regional *Let's Go* guides: *Let's Go: Britain and Ireland (including Scotland and Wales), Let's Go: France, Let's Go: Spain, Portugal, and Morocco, Let's Go: Italy (including Tunisia), Let's Go: Greece (including Cyprus and the Turkish Coast),* and *Let's Go: Israel and Egypt (including Jordan).* But don't forget to put *Let's Go* away occasionally and explore on your own. The most memorable discoveries will be those you make for yourself.

Planning Your Trip

Price Warning

We quote prices in effect in the summer of 1987, when our researchers were in the field; the exchange rates at the head of each chapter are based on the values of August 28, 1987. Inflation rates vary greatly throughout the countries in this guide, ranging from 5% in Great Britain to 130% in Yugoslavia.

For a successful trip, plan ahead. The amount of information available is amazing—peruse Useful Organizations and Publications in this introduction, and don't forget the National Tourist Offices listed in our appendix. A few hours of letter writing will yield a deluge of pamphlets and maps.

Consider writing an itinerary. Even if discarded upon arrival, it will force you to think about your priorities. Do you travel to see the sights or to meet people? To abandon civilization, or to learn about a particular culture? Don't be afraid to improvise—traveling should be a vacation, not a chore. The urge to see and do everything too often gets the better of travelers; remember that blitzing Rome in three days, or Scandinavia in a week, isn't seeing Europe. Spend some time away from the major tourist attractions . . . get out into the city streets, wander, soak up the sounds and smells. And instead of hopping from one capital to the next, spend a few days in a small town and in the countryside.

Think about whether you want to travel with someone, or on your own. Friends are a great source of energy and comfort, sharing in food and lodging costs and providing companionable security. However, steady traveling with one person or group may insulate you from the local culture. You may want to split up occasionally to explore on your own that which interests *you.* Solo travel additionally means more contact with the locals, which is always a boon to your understanding of a culture.

When should you travel? Late summer is high season throughout Europe, with great numbers of travelers making accommodations more expensive and more difficult to find. Also, there are fewer natives with whom to share your urban excursions—cities throughout Western Europe are effectively deserted during July and (especially) August, as locals leave to escape the onslaught of tourists. In the off-season, museum hours may be abbreviated and some hostels closed, but not having to share Europe with everyone who owns a backpack more than compensates.

Documents

Passports

You must have a valid passport to enter any European country and to reenter your own.

U.S. citizens may apply for a passport, good for 10 years (5 if you are under age 18), at any office of the U.S. Passport Agency, or at any Federal or State court or post office authorized to accept passport applications. If you have been issued a passport before, *and* your current passport is not more than 12 years old, *and* it was issued after your sixteenth birthday, you may renew your current passport by mail or in person. To do this, send in a completed application form, the fee (US$20 if 16 or 17 years old, US$35 if older), and your old passport. Otherwise, you must apply in person for a new passport. Parents may apply on behalf of children under age 13. Before applying, gather all of the following: (1) completed application form; (2) proof of U.S. citizenship (a certified copy of your birth certificate, naturalization or citizenship papers, or previous passport not more than eight years old are adequate proof); (3) one piece of identification bearing your signature and either your photo or description (a driver's license or similar ID will do); and (4) two identical photographs, 2" square on a white background, taken not more than six months before the application date. Your old passport will serve as both (2) and (3). The fees are US$42 if you are an adult (passport is valid for 10 years), US$27 if you are under age 18 (passport is valid for 5 years), and US$35 for a 10-year renewal. Processing usually takes about two weeks if you apply in person at the Passport Agency, usually much longer if you apply at a court or post office; file your application as early as possible to be on the safe side. If you wish, you may pay for express-mail return of the passport. In emergencies—providing you have proof of departure within five working days (e.g. an airplane ticket)—the Passport Agency will issue a passport while you wait (and wait, and wait); be sure to arrive in the office by 2pm. For more information, write to the **Bureau of Consular Affairs,** Passport Serv-

ices, Department of State, 1425 K St. NW, Washington, DC 20524 (tel. (202) 523-1462 or 783-8200).

Canadian citizens may apply by mail for a five-year, renewable passport from the **Passport Office,** Department of External Affairs, Place du Centre, 200 Promenade du Portage, Hull, Quebec, K1A 0G3 (tel. (819) 994-3500), or in person at one of their 19 regional offices. The current passport fee is CDN$21. More complete information can be found in the brochure *Canada Passport* and in the 40-page booklet *Bon Voyage, But—,* both free from the Passport Office.

British citizens may apply for a passport at any post office. The current price for a British passport is £10.

Australian citizens must apply in person at the local post office or at a Passport Office (these are usually located in the provincial capital). An Australian passport costs AUS$60 if you are 18 or older (good for 10 years) and AUS$30 if under 18 (good for 5 years).

New Zealanders must visit or write to the Office of Internal Affairs in Wellington (or to the local district office) for an application, which may be filed in person or by mail. The current cost of a New Zealand passport is NZ$30.

Losing your passport can be a nightmare: Getting a replacement may take weeks, your new passport will probably be valid for a limited time, and any visas will be irretrievably lost. To facilitate replacement of your passport should it be lost or stolen, get a photocopy of it showing its number, and date and place of issuance. Keep this information in a location separate from your passport or give it to someone with whom you will be traveling. In the event your passport is lost or stolen, notify your embassy/consulate and the local police immediately. To replace the passport, you'll need to prove your identity and citizenship. Proving your identity is usually not too hard—a driver's license or any photo ID will do. Proving your citizenship may be more difficult. The U.S. Passport Office recommends that you carry an *original* birth certificate (not necessarily the one issued at your birth, of course), or an expired passport, in a location apart from your other documents. It is always a good idea to photocopy all important documents and carry the photocopies separate from the originals.

Visas

Following a terrorist bombing on September 14, 1986, Prime Minister Jacques Chirac announced that beginning September 16, 1986, visas would be required of all visitors to France, except those from Switzerland and the European Common Market countries. Travelers should expect delays at all French borders.

A visa is an endorsement or stamp placed in your passport by a country's government, and permits you to visit that country for a specified purpose and a limited period of time. Before beginning the application process, check to see if your visas will be compatible: If you have an Israeli visa, you will not be able to obtain visas for East Germany and most Arab nations; check with the various consulates in your home country before you go. Don't postpone difficulties until the border stop. Instead, read the chapter introductions carefully and check out the problems; sometimes you can insist that the visa or entry stamp be placed on a removable page in your passport—Israel and Turkey provide this service, Egypt does not. As a rule, you will have to apply for visas in advance, at the embassy (or consulate) of the countries you plan to visit—visas are usually stamped into your passport so you will have to surrender your passport to an official at each foreign embassy or consulate; this can be awkward if you are applying while touring, so do it at the various consulates in your home country. It may take several weeks for each visa, especially if you are applying by mail, so begin the process early. For American citizens, the U.S. Department of State provides two free pamphlets, *Visa Requirements of Foreign Governments* and *Tips for Travelers.* Write to the **Bureau of Consular Affairs,** Passport Services, Department of State, 1425 K St. NW, Washington, DC 20524 (tel. (202) 783-8200 or (202) 523-4230). If you'd rather have someone else deal with this red tape, call **Visa Center, Inc.,** 507 Fifth Ave., Suite 904, New York, NY 10017 (tel. (212) 986-0924). The service charge varies with your passport's requirements; the average cost for an American is US$10 per visa. This is especially useful if you are seeking multiple visas in a small amount of time.

Most western European countries do not require American, Canadian, British, Australian, or New Zealander citizens to obtain visas for stays of less than three months; the sole exceptions are Spain, which requires visas of Australians and New Zealanders staying for more than four weeks, and Portugal, which requires a visa of all New Zealanders. Virtually all Eastern European countries require visas, for which you usually pay a fee. Czechoslovakia, Poland, East Germany, Bulgaria, Hungary, Romania, and the USSR demand advance application; Yugoslavia will issue a visa at its borders, but you're advised to get it beforehand to avoid delays. A visa for a day visit to East Berlin will be issued when you arrive at the checkpoint. Cyprus and Turkey do not require a visa; Tunisia requires one of Australians and New Zealanders; Israel and Egypt require one of American, British, Canadian, Australian, and New Zealander citizens, but will issue one at the border. Again, to avoid delays and refusals at the borders, apply for the visas in your home country *before you go.*

For more detailed visa information, see the various country chapters.

Youth and Student Identification

If you are a student, the **International Student Identification Card (ISIC)** will entitle you to discounts on museum admissions, local transportation, theater tickets, and on various other fees in thousands of spots throughout western Europe. When issued in the U.S., the card includes limited sickness and accident insurance. Cost is US$10 and all of the following must be supplied, whether you apply in person or by mail: (1) current dated proof of your full-time student status (a letter on school stationery signed and sealed by the registrar or a photocopied transcript will suffice); (2) a 1½" by 2" photo with your name printed on the back; (3) proof of your birthdate (only ages 12 and up are eligible) and nationality. When purchased in roughly the first half of the calendar year, it is valid until December 31 of the same year; when purchased in the second half, it's valid until December 31 of the following year. If you are about to graduate, get the card before you leave school and escape a few financial realities for another six months. Always pick up the annual *ID Discount Guide,* which lists some of the available discounts.

With the increase of phony or improperly issued ISICs, many airlines and some other services are requiring double proof of student status. It's a good idea to have a signed letter with the school seal from your registrar. Graduate students may find it particularly useful to have a letter of introduction stating their status.

If you're not a student, don't despair: The **Youth International Educational Exchange (YIEE) Card** is available to travelers under age 26; the card entitles you to many of the same benefits accorded ISIC holders. The card was piloted by the Federation of International Youth Travel Organizations, and is occasionally referred to as the FIYTO card. Your passport number, proof of birthdate, a photograph, and US$10 are needed to apply. For more information, and to receive their catalog, contact CIEE, Travel CUTS, Let's Go Travel, SSA, or FIYTO. (See Useful Organizations and Publications.) Don't assume that discounts are available only to students; in many cases, they apply both to seniors and to anyone under age 26.

The **International Union of Students Card (IUS)** is the YIEE card's Eastern European counterpart; it is *not* limited to students. The card entitles you to discounts of 25% on international trains within Eastern Europe and some other student discounts. You should be able to obtain an IUS card by presenting an ISIC or passport in most student travel offices in Eastern Europe; we list these offices under our Budget Travel listings in the country chapters. In 1987, the IUS was very difficult to obtain in Bulgaria and Romania.

Other Documents

Remember that if you want to get a **Eurailpass,** you must do so before you leave home; this is also true for some of the national rail cards (see By Train under Transportation in Europe). If you are planning to rent or lease a car, you should get an **International Driver's License** from your national automobile club (see By Car, Van, and Caravan).

Useful Organizations and Publications

National tourist offices, listed in the appendix, provide abundant free literature. Their business is to make every city and region look irresistible, so evaluate glossy brochures with care. Also, the more specific your request, the better your chances of receiving the information you need; many will even supply lists of campsites and youth hostels. Our listings below include such added resources as budget travel and accommodations services, work and study programs, various organizations and guidebooks for vegetarians, seniors, gay men and lesbians, and the disabled.

Useful Books

Bradt Enterprises, Inc.: 95 Harvey St., Cambridge, MA 02140 (tel. (617) 492-8776). Distributes a number of interesting imported guidebooks for travel in Europe.

E.P. Dutton, Inc.: 2 Park Ave., New York, NY 10016 (tel. (212) 725-1818). Publishes *The World Guide for the Jewish Traveler,* a guide to places of interest to Jewish travelers, including listings of kosher restaurants and synagogue addresses.

European Association of Music Festivals: 122, rue de Lausanne, 1202 Geneva, Switzerland (tel. (22) 32 28 03). Their booklet, *Festivals 1988,* lists the dates and programs of major music and theater festivals. Don't be discouraged by some high prices; student rates are often available.

Giovanni's Room: 345 S. 12th St., Philadelphia, PA 19107 (tel. (800) 222-6996). *Gaia's Guide* available for US$12.50 postpaid. This "international guide for travelling women" lists lesbian, feminist, and gay information numbers, publications, cultural centers and resources, hotels, and meeting places. Also available from **Gaia's Guide,** 9-11 Kensington High St., London WS, England; and **Open Leaves,** 71 Cardigan St., Carlton, Victoria 3053, Australia.

Bruno Gmünder: Lützowstrasse, 105, P.O. Box 30 13 45, D-1000 Berlin 30, West Germany. Publishes the 1987 *Spartacus Guide for Gay Men,* listing bars, restaurants, hotels, bookstores and hotlines in Europe. Readily available in the U.K. for £12.50.

John Muir Publications: P.O. Box 613, Santa Fe, NM 87504 (tel. (505) 982-4078). Distributes Rick Steves's *Europe 101: History, Art and Culture for the Traveler* (US$10), and (by the same author) *Europe Through the Back Door* (US$12).

Hippocrene Books, Inc.: 171 Madison Ave., New York, NY 10016 (tel. (212) 685-4371). Though geared to the U.K. citizen, *Baby Travel* (US$12) includes relevant tips concerning baby travel for everyone traveling in Europe. Everything from airline food to babysitting and toys.

North American Vegetarian Society: P.O. Box 72, Dolgeville, NY 13329 (tel.(516) 568-7970). The *International Vegetarian Handbook* (US$9) lists vegetarian restaurants, guesthouses, societies, and healthfood stores in Europe.

Routledge Rough Guides (Methuen Inc.): 29 W. 35th St., New York, NY 10001 (tel. (212) 244-3336). Publishes the various *Rough Guides,* covering Amsterdam and Holland, France, Greece, Morocco, Portugal, Spain, Tunisia, and Yugoslavia.

Travel and Accommodations Services

Let's Go Travel Services: Harvard Student Agencies, Inc., Thayer Hall-B, Harvard University, Cambridge, MA 02138 (tel. (617) 495-9649). Student ID cards, American Youth Hostel memberships (valid at all IYHF youth hostels), Eurail, etc. Use the order form in *Let's Go,* call or write for their "Bag of Tricks" discount and information packet.

Council on International Educational Exchange (CIEE): 205 E. 42nd St., New York, NY 10017 (tel. (800) 223-7402 or (212) 661-1450). Information on overseas budget travel, education, voluntary service and work opportunities. Will send its annual *Student Travel Catalog* for US$1, or you can pick it up free at one of their offices. ISIC and YIEE cards. Stocks *Work, Study, Travel Abroad: The Whole World Handbook* (US$8 plus US$1 postage), *The Teenager's Guide to Study, Travel and Adventures Abroad* (US$9 plus US$1 postage), and *Volunteer! The Comprehensive Guide to Voluntary Service in the U.S. and Abroad* (US$5.50 plus US$1 postage). Also *Summer Jobs in Britain* (US$9 plus US$1 postage), and *Emplois d'Eté en France* (US$11 plus US$1 postage). **Council Travel** is the budget travel division of CIEE, and has 23 offices throughout the U.S. The New York office is located at 205 E. 42nd St., New York, NY 10017 (tel. (212) 661-1450); the Los Angeles office at 1093 Broxton Ave., Los Angeles, CA 90024 (tel. (213) 208-3551); and the Chicago office at 29 East Delaware Place, Chicago, IL 60611 (tel. (312) 951-0565).

Student Travel Network (STN): 17 E. 45th St., Suite 400, New York, NY 10017 (tel. (212) 986-9470), offers low prices on flights to and around Europe.

Canadian Universities Travel Service (Travel CUTS): 187 College St., Toronto M5T 1P7, Ontario, Canada (tel. (416) 979-2406). Offices throughout Canada. Discount transatlantic flights from Canadian cities. ISIC, YIEE, and IYHF cards. Transalpino, Eurotrain, and Eurailpass. Canadian Student Work Abroad Programme. Their excellent newspaper, *The Canadian Student Traveler,* is available free at their offices, and at campuses across Canada.

STA Travel Ltd.: 74 Old Brompton Rd., London SW7 3LQ (tel. (01) 581 47 51) is a source of worldwide bargain flights and travel services, including accommodations, tours, and rail tickets.

Federation of International Youth Travel Organizations (FIYTO): 81 Islands Brygge, DK-2300 Copenhagen S, Denmark (tel. (01) 54 32 97). YIEE cards for anyone (not just students) under age 26. Free annual catalog lists over 4000 discounts available to cardholders.

Scandinavian Student Travel Service (SSTS): Hauchsvej 17, 1825 Frederiksberg C, Copenhagen, Denmark (tel. (01) 21 47 40). Student and youth flights worldwide. Sputnik tours to the USSR. Student Travel Network in New York (listed above) is their agent in the U.S.

SSA/STA: 220 Faraday St., Carlton, Melbourne, Victoria 3053, Australia (tel. (03) 347 69 11). ISICs and budget travel.

Student Travel: Courtenay Chambers, 2nd floor, 15 Courtenay Place, Wellington, New Zealand (tel. (04) 85 05 61). ISICs.

International Youth Hostel Association (IYHF): 9 Guessens Rd., Welwyn, Garden City, Herts. AL8 6QW, England (tel. (0707) 32 41 70). National hostel associations include **American Youth Hostels, Inc. (AYH),** P.O. Box 37613, Washington, DC 20013-7613 (tel. (202) 783-6161). IYHF cards, hostel handbooks, information on budget travel, and summer positions as group leaders. Distributes the *International Youth Hostel Handbook, Vol. 1: Europe and Mediterranean* (US$7.50). **Canadian Hostelling Association (CHA),** 333 River Rd., Tower A, 3rd floor, Vanier, Ontario KIL 8H9, Canada (tel. (613) 748-5638). IYHF cards and hostel handbooks. **British Youth Hostel Association (YHA),** Treveyan House, 8, St. Stephen's Hill, St. Albans, Herts. AL1 2DY, England (tel. St. Alban's 552 15). **Australian Youth Hostel Association,** 60 Mary St., Surrey Hills, Sydney, New South Wales 2010, Australia (tel. (02) 212 11 51). **Youth Hostel Association of New Zealand,** P.O. Box 436, Christchurch, 1, New Zealand (tel. 79 99 70).

U.S. Servas Committee: 11 John St., Room 706, New York, NY 10038 (tel. (212) 267-0252). An organization devoted to world peace and international understanding which has organized a worldwide network of people willing to host visitors.

Europ Assistance Worldwide Services, Inc.: 1333 F St., NW Suite 300, Washington, DC 20004 (tel. (800) 821-2828 or (202) 347-2025). A 24-hour hotline; offices in Brussels, London, Madrid, Munich, and Paris. Expertise in health and legal assistance, document recovery and cash advance, long-distance medical transport, insurance. Membership can be costly—it depends upon the length of your trip.

Information for Disabled Travelers

The accessibility of European countries varies greatly, as does the information available to *Let's Go.* If you are a disabled traveler, please send us information about your traveling experiences—as always, the more specifics the better. We recommend that you contact the organizations listed below, or the national tourist boards (see Appendix).

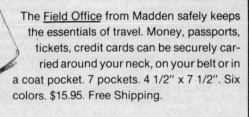

British, Dutch, French, and Italian national tourist boards provide directories on the accessibility of various accommodations and transportation services. In other nations, contact the various institutions, etc. directly rather than relying upon travel agents.

Rail is probably the most convenient form of travel. BritRail offers a discount card, conveys guide dogs free of charge, and (if you let them know in advance) will assure a comfortable spot for a wheelchair. The French national railroad offers a guide to stations equipped for wheelchairs (see below); all TGV (high speed) trains accommodate wheelchairs, and guide dogs travel free. Other trains have a special compartment and an escalator for boarding. Still, it's a good idea to contact the destination station about your arrival. In Italy, the law requires that wheelchairs be transported for free. However, the chair will be packed away with your luggage.

You should check with the country you are visiting regarding the customary six-month quarantine on all animals, including guide dogs. Owners must usually obtain an import license, have current certification of the animal's rabies, distemper, and contagious hepatitis inoculations, and a veterinarian's letter attesting to the dog's health.

American Foundation for the Blind: 15 W. 16th St., New York, NY 10011 (tel. (212) 620-2000). Information and ID cards for discounts to the legally blind.

Directions Unlimited: 344 Main St., Mount Kisco, NY 10549 (tel. (212) 829-5110 or (914) 241-1700; outside NY (800) 533-5343). Provides tours for the disabled.

Disability Press, Ltd.: Applemarket House, 17 Union St., Kingston-upon-Thames, Surrey KT1 1RP, England. Publishes the *Disabled Traveller's International Phrasebook,* a compilation of useful phrases in English, French, German, Italian, Spanish, Portuguese, Swedish, and Dutch.

Evergreen Travel Service: 19505L 44th Ave. W., Lynnwood, WA 98036 (tel. (800) 435-2288 or (206) 776-1184). Travel services include Wings on Wheels and White Cane tours.

Facts On File, Inc.: 460 Park Ave. S., New York, NY 10016. Publishes *Access to the World,* by Louise Weiss (US$13), which includes guides and travel tips on tours and organizations for disabled travelers.

Mobility International USA (MIUSA): P.O. Box 3551, Eugene, OR 97403 (tel. (503) 343-1284 (voice and TDD)). Membership costs US$20 per year. Information on travel programs, international workcamps, accommodations, access guides, organized tours, and opportunities for disabled travelers. Ask for the *Guide to International Educational Exchange, Community Service and Travel for Persons with Disabilities* (US$11 postpaid for members, US$13 postpaid for nonmembers). MIUSA has contacts in 25 countries.

Pauline Hephaistos Survey Projects Group: 39 Bradley Gardens, West Ealing, London W13 8HE, England. Distributes access guides to London, Israel, Paris, Brittany, Jersey, the Loire Valley, and the Channel ports (£3 each).

Travel Information Service, Moss Rehabilitation Hospital: 12th St. and Tabor Rd., Philadelphia, PA 19141 (tel. (215) 329-5715 ext. 2233). Provides information for disabled travelers on tourist sights, accommodations, and transportation. Nominal postage and handling fee charged for mailing information.

National Rehabilitation Board: 25 Clyde Rd., Ballsbridge 4, Dublin 4, Ireland (tel. (01) 68 41 81). Has an accommodations guide to Ireland, compiled in conjunction with the Irish Tourist Board.

Rehabilitation International USA (RIUSA): Travel Survey Department, 1123 Broadway, Suite 704, New York, NY 10010 (tel. (212) 620-4040). Distributes the *International Directory of Access Guides* (US$5).

Royal Association for Disability and Rehabilitation (RADAR): 25 Mortimer St., London W1N 8AB, England (tel. (01) 637 54 00). Information on travel in Britain; publishes *Holidays for Disabled People* (£6, including postage to the U.S.).

Theta Association: P.O. Box 8171, San Francisco International Airport, San Francisco, CA 94128 (tel. (800) 258-4382 or (415) 573-9701). Offers a large data base of information on facilities and services throughout the world.

Van Nostrand and Reinhold Co., Inc.: 135 W. 50th St., New York, NY 10020. Publisher of *A Travel Guide for the Disabled* (US$12), a comprehensive guide to Europe for the disabled.

L'Association des Paralysés de France, Délégation de Paris: 22, rue du Père-Guerin, 75013 Paris, France. Publishes the guide *Ou ferons-nous étape?*, listing hotels and motels in France with disabled access (70F, postage included).

Inter-Touring Service: 117 bd. Auguste Blanqui, 75013 Paris, France (tel. (45) 88 52 37). Rents cars equipped for the disabled.

Information for Senior Travelers

The following is a list of organizations that provide information on discounts and special services available to seniors. Don't forget that the International Youth Hostel Association sells IYHF cards to those over age 59 for US$10, half the regular membership fee. See Travel and Accommodations Services, above.

American Association of Retired Persons (AARP): 1909 K. St. NW, Washington, DC 20049 (tel. (202) 872-4700). For a US$5 annual membership fee, those 50 years and older and their spouses receive benefits from AARP Travel Services and become part of the Purchase Privilege Program, which includes member discounts for hotels, motels, car rental, and sightseeing companies in the U.S. and Europe. For an application, write to P.O. Box 38997, Los Angeles, CA 90230.

Bureau of Consular Affairs: Passport Services, Room 6811, Department of State, Washington, DC 20524. Free pamphlet, *Travel Tips for Senior Citizens,* has information on passports, visas, health, and currency.

E.P. Dutton, Inc.: 2 Park Ave., New York, NY 10016 (tel. (212) 725-1818). Publishes *The Discount Guide for Travelers Over 55.*

Elderhostel: 80 Boylston St., Suite 480, Boston, MA 02116 (tel. (617) 426-7788). You or your spouse must be 60 or over to join. Week-long programs in over 30 countries in the Americas and Europe cover varied subjects; a fee of US$195-225 covers room, board, tuition, and extracurricular activities.

National Association of Mature People: P.O. Box 26792, 2212 NW 50th St., Oklahoma City, OK 73126 (tel. (405) 648-1832). For people 40 and over. Membership (US$9.95) includes discounts on hotels, car rental, and group travel.

National Council of Senior Citizens: 925 15th St., Washington, DC (tel. (202) 847-8800). Information on discounts and travel abroad.

Pilot Books: 103 Cooper St., Babylon, NY 11702 (tel. (516) 422-2225). Distributes Paige Palmer's *The Senior Citizen's Guide to Budget Travel in Europe, revised edition* (US$4).

Money

If you stay in hostels and prepare your own food, you can expect to spend US$30 per day in more expensive countries, and as little as US$15 in less expensive countries. Transportation and eating regularly in restaurants will increase these figures. Hostels are undoubtedly the cheapest lodgings you'll find unless you're camping, particularly in northern Europe where the price of a hotel room can be prohibitive. In Mediterranean countries, couples or groups staying in hotels won't spend too much, but single rooms will increase expenses considerably. If you need more money, you can wire home (see Sending Money Abroad), but this will mean delays, costs, and snarls of red tape.

Currency and Exchange

We post the exchange rates valid in August, 1987; however, rates fluctuate, so check the financial pages of a national newspaper before planning your trip. Take our quoted figures as guides to prices—inflation and other changes will inevitably compromise their accuracy.

When exchanging money, it usually pays to compare rates. Banks usually have the best rates; they generally charge a commission, which can be as much as US$3 per exchange. To minimize your losses, convert fairly large sums at one time, though never more than you feel is safe to carry around. Contrary to popular belief, American Express does not offer a uniquely favorable rate, nor do they usually exchange their own checks commission-free. Carry bills or checks in small denominations, and save them for those occasions when you may be forced to exchange money at train station offices or, worse yet, at luxury hotels or restaurants, where rates can be appalling.

Before leaving home, check to see if you can import local currency into the countries you will be visiting. This is a serious crime in Eastern Europe and Tunisia. However, it is perfectly acceptable elsewhere, and taking US$50 or so, already changed, will save you time, hassles, and the misfortune of poor exchange rates at airports and stations. Indeed, every time you leave a country, consider buying some currency for your destination. Don't purchase more of a currency than you'll need in a particular country; every time you exchange you lose. You can exchange foreign bills when you leave a country, but will usually have to save coins for your next trip. Always save your exchange transaction receipts, as a number of countries will not let you buy back dollars unless you can prove that your holdings in their currency were originally in dollars. Many Eastern European countries require the receipts as evidence that you have made the mandatory daily exchange. Be honest and careful—black market dealings are a crime with potential jail sentences; at the very least, inaccurate receipts will necessitate further exchanges at your point of departure. The currency of an Eastern European country is worthless outside that country, and it's frequently illegal to export. For more specific information, check the Practical Information section of the introduction to each country.

Traveler's Checks

Nothing is likely to cause more headaches than money—even when you have it. Carrying large amounts of cash, even in a money belt, is just too risky. Traveler's checks are the safest and least troublesome means of carrying your funds.

Traveler's checks are sold by many agencies and banks, usually for the face value of the checks plus a 1% commission. American Express traveler's checks are perhaps the most widely recognized. Each agency listed provides refunds if your traveler's checks are lost or stolen.

To buy traveler's checks, consult your bank for the nearest vendor. Several companies offer toll-free numbers which provide refund information and check-purchase assistance. For **American Express** checks, call (800) 221-7282 in the U.S. and Canada; in the U.K., call toll-free 0 800 52 13 13; in Europe, call collect (44) 273 57 16 00. To reach **Citicorp,** call (800) 645-6556 from U.S. and Canada; from overseas, call collect (813) 623-1709. **Visa** is another option for traveler's checks. The number is (800) 227-6811 within the U.S. and Canada; from abroad, call collect (415) 574-7111. **Bank of America** sells its own traveler's checks; in the U.S. call (800) 227-3460; from Canada and abroad, call collect (415) 624-5400. Two others are **Thomas Cook Travel Agency** (in U.S. call (800) 223-2131; from Canada and abroad, call collect (212) 974-5696), and **Barclay's Bank** (in U.S. call (800) 221-2426; from Canada and abroad, call collect (415) 574-7111).

If your traveler's checks are lost or stolen, expect a fair amount of red tape and delay. To expedite a refund, be sure to separate your check receipts and keep them in a safe place. Record check numbers as you cash them to help you identify exactly which checks are missing. As an added precaution, leave a list of check numbers with someone at home. When you buy your checks, obtain a list of refund centers. Most importantly, keep a separate supply of cash or traveler's checks, perhaps in the same place you keep your receipts, for financial emergencies.

Should you buy your checks in dollars or in foreign currencies? If you'll be visiting several countries, buy your checks in U.S. dollars. Few currencies are as easily exchanged; British pounds run a rough second. You'll also save yourself the cost of repeated currency exchanges. But if you'll be spending most of your time in one country, it may be wise to purchase your checks in that country's currency. You will get a marginally lower exchange rate purchasing them at home than you would in Europe, but the convenience is usually worth it.

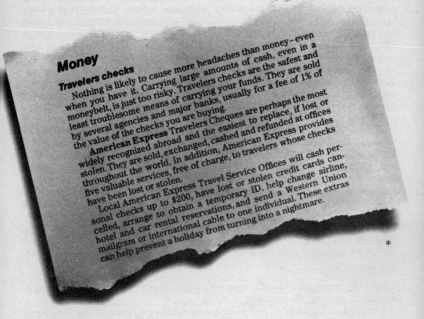

Credit Cards

Credit cards are of limited value for the budget traveler because low-cost establishments rarely honor them, but they can be invaluable in a financial emergency. A major credit card is an excellent insurance policy for your cash and traveler's checks. If you are a **Visa** cardholder, you can get an instant cash advance in local currency as large as your line of credit; this service is available from banks throughout Europe that honor the card. A quick transfusion of cash like this can tide you over if your traveler's checks or cash are lost or stolen; indeed, it may be your only source of cash for several days, as many traveler's check vendors will not cash a personal check and transatlantic money cables take at least 48 hours. For a Visa card application, write to Chase Visa, 802 Delaware Ave., Wilmington, DE 19850 (tel. (800) 433-3369). Visa is also installing automated teller machines throughout Europe that will accept their card.

American Express Travel Service (tel. (800) 528-4800) provides valuable services to cardholders. Most American Express offices will cash up to US$1000 worth of cardholders' personal checks in any 21-day period. They will also wire to replace lost or stolen credit cards. Another advantage of the American Express card is that it allows you to use American Express offices freely as mailing addresses; otherwise you will have to show American Express traveler's checks, or pay, to pick up your mail. Perhaps the greatest bonus for cardholders with American-issued cards is automatic access to the 24-hour help line, Global Assist. Global Assist provides information and money in cases of personal medical/legal emergency, visa and inoculation information, and sends urgent messages home. Cardholders with Canadian-issued cards can subscribe to a similar service; others should check with their national office. For more information on credit cards, contact American Express, 65 Broadway, New York, NY 10016.

If your income level is low, you may have difficulty acquiring a credit card; however, if someone in your family already has a card, you can get a joint-account card. American Express issues extra cards for US$25 each per year. There is usually no charge for a joint-account Visa.

Sending Money Abroad

Sending money overseas is a time-consuming, expensive, and often extremely frustrating process. Do your best to avoid it.

The quickest and cheapest way to have money sent is to have someone back home cable money through the local office of a large foreign bank whose home country you are visiting. These banks have plenty of branches throughout their country; they can often reach you in remote corners, and there is less chance of delay or mix-up with an in-house transaction. **Barclay's Bank** (International Transfer Department tel. (212) 412-3837), for instance, cables up to US$3000 to any of its English branches within two days for a US$15 fee.

You can also have money sent through a large commercial bank for roughly the same cost and with the same efficiency. The sender must either have an account with the bank, or take cash to one of its branches (some won't cable money for noncustomers). The destination bank may also charge you a fee to pick it up. Cabled money can arrive the same day, the next day, or within a week: It depends on the sophistication of the receiving bank system. The sender can sometimes specify whether the money is to be disbursed in local currency or in U.S. dollars. All information the sender gives, such as your passport number, and recipient bank name and address, must be exact if you want to avoid delays. In any case, the sender will receive no confirmation of whether or not the money has reached you.

Using a local bank to send money will be slower and more expensive, as these banks usually go through larger banks. It is possible to prearrange with your local bank to have them send you money at a specified time, but as the procedure is cumbersome, many banks will be reluctant to do this.

Sending money through **American Express** costs about the same as sending it through a bank. Usually the sender must have an American Express card, but certain offices will waive this requirement for a commission. The money is guaranteed to arrive within 72 hours at the designated overseas office, where it will be held for 14 days before being returned to the sender. It costs US$15 to send up to US$500, and US$30 to send up to US$1000, which is the limit for a single cable. US$200 will be disbursed in local currency, the rest in dollar traveler's checks. This service operates only between American Express offices proper, *not* their representative offices. In listings, *Let's Go* specifies which offices accept wired money.

Western Union offers convenient but expensive money cabling abroad. If the sender has a MasterCard or Visa credit card and is in the U.S., he or she can call Western Union's toll-free number, (800) 325-4176 or (800) 325-6000, and have them cable up to the credit limit of the card. If the sender doesn't have a card, he or she must go in person to a local Western Union office with cash or a cashier's check (no money orders accepted). Western Union serves most of Europe and North Africa, but there are a number of exceptions—check their coverage after deciding your travel plans. Rates for Europe vary, but in general are as follows: to send US$50 costs US$14, US$50-100 costs US$16, US$100-200 costs US$24, US$200-300 costs US$28, and US$300-500 costs US$35, and US$500-1000 costs US$43. Remember that the receiving bank will add its own service charge.

Finally, if you are an American and you suddenly find yourself in big trouble, you can have money sent to you via the **State Department's Citizens Emergency Center** (tel. (202) 647-5225). The center defines emergencies as cases of destitution, hospitalization, or death. For a fee of US$15 the State Department will send money within hours, or sometimes overnight, to the nearest consular office, which will then disburse the cash according to instructions. Unless the emergency is great, the department prefers to send sums not greater than US$500 to Europe, slightly more to North Africa. The sender must provide her or his name and address, the name of the recipient, and the nature of the emergency. If requested, the State Department will include a message with the money. The quickest way to have the money sent is to cable money to the State Department through Western Union or else drop off a certified check, bank draft, or money order at the Department itself. It will take more time and costs an extra US$25 to send money to the Department through a bank. The address is Citizens Emergency Center, Department of State, Room 4811, 2201 C St. NW, Washington, DC 20520.

Value Added Tax (VAT)

A form of sales tax, levied especially in the European Economic Community (EEC), VAT is generally part of the price paid on goods and services. Eastern European countries, Iceland, Portugal, and Morocco do not participate in the VAT refund scheme. The amount of tax (6-36%) varies from country to country and also usually according to the item purchased (necessities taxed less, luxuries taxed more); some countries set VAT at a flat rate. Overseas visitors not from the EEC can participate in a complex export scheme that exempts them from VAT on goods but not on services. Applying for the tax refund is only worth it, though, if you are purchasing an item worth over US$50. In some countries, stores are required to offer the refund, while in others offering a refund is optional. In some large luxury-oriented stores, the VAT may already be removed from the price—but check this carefully, as they may just be saying this to relieve themselves of the hassle.

When making your purchase, ask for a certificate of export or a VAT refund form (you will probably be asked to show your passport). If the store does not have one, the customs office or the post office usually will. The retailer will fill out the form—including where to mail it, what you bought, and how much it cost—and usually give you a reciept as well. Once you reach the border (or airport) customs office, have the form stamped to prove that you left the country. Also, be ready to present the items at the customs office, although they don't always ask. Be careful: Some countries set limits on how much time can elapse between when you make your purchase and when you leave the country (varying between 3 weeks and 3 months)—check at the customs office upon entering each country. Your best bet is to wait as long as you can to make your expensive purchases. Once home, mail the form and the receipt (if you were given one) back to the retailer. You will usually receive your refund in the form of a check in the currency of the country in which you made the purchase. Some stores offer a refund in your country's home currency, but you must request this, usually when you are making the purchase. The refund will usually only be sent to an address outside of the EEC. Often, making your purchase with a credit card will make it easier and faster for the retailer to give the refund—you're also more likely to be able to receive the refund in your home currency.

Prices quoted in *Let's Go* include VAT unless otherwise specified.

Health

Don't cut corners on health—few things are as disappointing as a trip ruined by illness or accident. Before you leave, check your insurance policy to see that it covers medical costs incurred while abroad. If you're a student, you may be covered by your parents' policy; if you're under a plan at school, find out if it includes summer travel—many do. If you're Canadian, the health insurance plan of your home province may apply while you're abroad, but the particulars vary from province to province; check with the provincial Ministry of Health or Health Plan Headquarters for details.

If your insurance policy does not extend overseas (Medicare, for example, does not cover European travel), you may want to purchase a short-term policy for your trip. An ISIC provides coverage of US$2000 for accident-related medical expense and US$100 per day to a maximum of 60 days for in-hospital sickness. CIEE (see Useful Organizations and Publications) also has an inexpensive plan called Trip Safe with options that cover medical treatment and hospitalization, accidents, and even charter flights missed due to illness. Be sure to check what kind of reimbursement your policy offers: reimbursement while you are still in Europe, or reimbursement when you return. Keep all receipts and statements from your doctors (try to have them written in English), and file an out-of-country claim when you return. If you will be spending a considerable amount of time in one country, look into its medical bureaucracy. See also the Insurance section of Planning Your Trip.

A compact first-aid kit will suffice for minor health problems. It should include bandages, tweezers, aspirin, antiseptic soap, antibiotic, a thermometer in a sturdy case, something for motion sickness, antihistamine, sunscreen, and a Swiss Army knife. If you wear glasses or contact lenses, take along an extra pair. Also, take a prescription with you, and make arrangements with someone at home to send you a pair if the need arises. Condoms (specifically to lessen the chances of contracting AIDS or other sexually transmitted diseases) are readily available throughout Western Europe. However, it is best to purchase condoms and other types of birth control at home for convenience and knowledge of manufacturer reliability. Women taking birth control pills should remember to take time zone changes into consideration.

The **Superintendent of Documents,** U.S. Government Printing Office, Washington, DC 20402, publishes a general information booklet called *Health Information for International Travel* (US$4.25). From Viking-Penguin, Inc., *How To Stay Healthy Abroad,* by Dr. Richard Dawood, has several excellent chapters on health for travelers in Europe. Write to Viking-Penguin, Inc., Attn. Direct Order Dept., 299 Murray Hill Parkway, East Rutherford, NJ 07073 or call (201) 933-1460 for more information.

Travelers who have a chronic medical condition requiring medication on a regular basis should consult their physician before leaving. Get a statement and/or prescription from your doctor if you'll be carrying insulin, syringes, or any narcotic drugs (just in case anyone asks). Make sure all prescriptions are legible, preferably typewritten. They should include the medication's trade name, manufacturer, chemical name, and dosage. Carry an ample supply of all medications, since matching your prescription with a foreign equivalent is not always easy. Check on immunization requirements for the places you're visiting, and have your vaccination records with you (typed on an index card for convenience) to facilitate entry at international ports.

Additional preparation can assure you skilled medical care from English-speaking doctors and can also alert you to health problems unique to your destination. Perhaps the most extensive health service for travelers is furnished by the **International Association for Medical Assistance to Travelers (IAMAT),** 417 Center St., Lewiston, NY 14092 (tel. (716) 754-4883). Membership in IAMAT (free, but donations are encouraged) provides you with a worldwide directory of English-speaking physicians whose services are available to you at reasonable, fixed rates. English-speaking doctors can also be located through embassies and consulates of English-speaking countries, and at American Express and Thomas Cook offices. Many of the first-aid centers and hospitals *Let's Go* lists for major cities can also provide you with medical care from an English-speaking doctor.

Travelers with a medical problem or condition that cannot be easily recognized (e.g. diabetes, allergies to antibiotics, epilepsy, heart conditions) should seriously consider obtaining a **Medic Alert identification tag.** This internationally recognized emblem communicates vital information in emergency situations. In addition to indicating the nature of the medical problem, the tag provides the number of Medic Alert's 24-hour hotline, through which attending medical personnel can obtain information about the member's medical history. Lifetime membership costs US$20; write to Medic Alert Foundation International, P.O. Box 1009, Turlock, CA 95381-1009 or call (800) IDALERT, that's (800) 432-5378.

Safety

Common sense and reasonable precautions should carry you through your trip more safely (and more enjoyably) than constant vigilance and paranoia. While traveling, steer clear of empty train compartments, particularly at night. Large cities require some extra caution. Even if you're familiar with the place, avoid public parks and bus and train stations after dark. Ask the managers of your hotel or hostel for advice on specific areas. And always carry enough change for a phone call, bus, or taxi.

If you are in a dormitory room, or if there are no locks on your door, sleep with all valuables on your person (a money belt is a good investment) or under your pillow—laying your pack alongside the bed is not enough. If you plan to sleep outside, or simply don't want to carry everything with you, try to store your gear at a train or bus station. By day, don't leave your valuables unattended, ever—a trip to the shower or the telephone could cost you a camera or wallet. Wear a moneybelt or neckpouch next to your skin, and don't take expensive jewelry on your trip. With most insurance agencies providing reimbursement only upon your return, theft could force a bitter and premature end to your travels.

Certain cheap accommodations may entail more risks than savings for solo travelers, and hitchhiking is rarely safe alone (see Hitchhiking under Transportation in Europe). Try to forego dives and city outskirts in favor of centrally-located university accommodations or youth hostels. Religious organizations which offer rooms are a very safe option.

Insurance

The following firms offer insurance against theft, loss, trip cancellation/interruption, and medical emergency. You can buy a policy directly from them or through a travel agent operating on their behalf. There are two basic points to remember in buying insurance. (1) Beware unnecessary coverage. Check whether your homeowners' insurance (or your family's coverage) provides against theft during travel. Homeowner's policies generally *will* cover against loss of travel documents such as passport, plane ticket, and railpass, for up to US$500. (2) To claim your insurance reimbursement, you will need to submit evidence. Insurance companies generally require a copy of the police report filed at the time of the theft before they will honor your claim. With medical expenses, you must prove that you paid the charges for which you are requesting reimbursement. One final point: Check the policy's time limits to make sure that you will be returning in time to secure reimbursement.

The Traveler's Insurance Co.: 1 Tower Square, Hartford, CT 06183-5040 (tel. (800) 243-3174; in CT (203) 277-2318). Trip cancellation/interruption, accident, baggage, and emergency medical evacuation coverage. Comprehensive coverage with "Travel Insurance Pak."

ARM Coverage, Inc.: P.O. Box 310, Mineola, NY 11501 (tel. (800) 645-2424). Comprehensive travel insurance package called "Carefree Travel Insurance," which includes loss of luggage coverage. Cancellation/interruption coverage can be purchased separately.

HealthCare Abroad: 243 Church St. W., Vienna, VA 22180 (tel. (800) 237-6615). One of the oldest firms in the field. Medical plan required; then choose optional trip cancellation, accidental death, and baggage protection plans. US$3 per day per person for medical plan, and 5% of total trip cost for trip cancellation coverage.

Mutual of Omaha Insurance Company: Mutual of Omaha Plaza, Omaha, NB 68175. Their **Teletrip** subsidiary (tel. (800) 228-9792) offers comprehensive accident insurance for travelers.

Drugs

Every year, hundreds of young travelers are arrested in foreign countries for illegal possession, use, or trafficking in drugs. Some countries—Turkey, Morocco, East Germany—are stricter and more severe in their treatment of those arrested on drug-related charges, but even reputedly liberal countries—the Netherlands and Denmark—contribute to the sorry statistics. Remember that you are subject to the laws of the country you are visiting. A helpful publication is *Travel Warning on Drugs Abroad,* available from the Bureau of Consular Affairs, PA room 5807, Department of State, Washington, DC 20520 (tel. (202) 647-1488). It covers everything you want to know about drug policy in every country in the world.

Even where drugs seem to be freely available, the openness can be an illusion. In Turkey, North Africa, and Israel, for example, dealers often work hand-in-hand with the police. Drug dealers are known to sell to a foreign visitor, head straight for the police, describe the patron in detail, collect a fee for information, and get the goods back when the buyer is arrested. *Never* bring anything across borders. International express trains are not as safe as they might seem; you may be searched entering a country that you'll be leaving a half hour later.

Your government is completely powerless should you be arrested in another country. Consular officers can only visit the prisoner, provide him or her with a list of attorneys, and inform family and friends. As a U.S. State Department bulletin dourly maintains, "U.S. officials cannot ask for or obtain different treatment for American citizens than that given to others under the laws of the country concerned. You're virtually "on your own' if you become involved, *however innocently,* in illegal drug trafficking."

The Canadian Department of External Affairs adds these cheery warnings: "The legal codes of some countries provide for *guilt by association* under which someone may be charged simply for being in the company of a person suspected or found guilty of a crime (e.g. trafficking in or possessing drugs) . . . ." Moreover, because drug offenses are particularly distasteful in some countries, extradition or expulsion may be spurned and a suspected drug offender brought to trial regardless of nationality.

Alternatives to Tourism

The view of the tourist is too often the view of an outsider gazing in from the periphery. If you are planning an extended visit to Europe, consider the alternatives of study or work—these are the most effective means of establishing a rich understanding of a country and its people. As a participant in the culture, you will gain a perspective unavailable to the average traveler. Moreover, after two or three months in Europe, the appeal of tourism may wear thin, and you will probably welcome the opportunity to see different cultures from another angle.

dy

There's so much information on foreign study that it's hard to know where to k first. Most American undergraduates enroll in programs sponsored by domes- universities and many colleges have offices to give advice and information on dy abroad. Talk to the counselors there and use their libraries. Opportunities study abroad range tremendously in expense, academic quality, living condi- is, degree of contact with local students, and exposure to the local culture and guage. Ask for the names of students who have recently participated in the pro- ms you are considering, and write or talk to them to help decide which program ts you.

f you have the gumption and have extensive language ability, consider enrolling ectly in a European university. This may be more rewarding and less expensive. ite to the embassy of the country of your interest; many put out literature de- bing their national university systems.

Bernan-Unipub: 4611F Assembly Dr., Lanham, MD 20706 (tel. (800) 233-0505). Publisher of UNESCO's *Study Abroad* (US$15).

Central Bureau for Educational Visits and Exchanges: Seymour Mews House, Seymour Mews, London W1H 9PE, England. Provides information on educational visits and exchanges.

Institute of International Education (IIE): 809 United Nations Plaza, New York, NY 10017 (tel. (212) 883-8200), offers a variety of resources on study abroad. Their free pamphlet, *Basic Facts on Foreign Study,* will help you get started. IIE also publishes annually *Academic Year Abroad* (US$20), describing 900 semester and year study programs; *Vacation Study Abroad* (US$20) details over 900 spring, summer, and fall study programs offered by U.S. colleges and universities, as well as by foreign and private sponsors.

Work

You won't get rich working in Europe, but there's no better way to become inti mately acquainted with a country and its people. Official sources may require wor permits (often available only if you can demonstrate a skill that local workers lack or Common Market membership, but if red tape entwines, don't despair. Lots c foreigners working in Europe get jobs without work permits. British citizens ca work legally in any country that is a member of the European Economic Commu nity.

If you're looking for skilled work or you want to avoid the uncertainty of an on the-spot search, plan in advance. The organizations listed below are of good repute but you might speak with former clients before you begin paying fees. **CIEE** (se below) will obtain a work permit for students in the U.K., Ireland, France, an Germany. While they will not locate a job for you, they will provide a handboo and staff in the host countries to help you find employment and housing. Canadia students should write **Travel CUTS** (see Useful Organizations and Publications for details about their Student Work Abroad Programme in Britain, Ireland France, Australia, New Zealand, and Japan.

Two programs secure employment for students in certain fields. **AIESEC, U.S.** 14 W. 23rd St., New York, NY 10010 (tel. (212) 206-1888), places qualified busines and economics students in management trainee positions, including marketing, ac counting, and computer science, in 57 countries worldwide. Positions pay a stipen to cover living expenses. Applications, accepted in early January, must come fron students at colleges with AIESEC membership. The **IAESTE Trainee Program** *c/o* Association for International Practical Training (AIPT), Park View Building Suite 320, 10480 Little Patuxent Parkway, Columbia, MD 21044 (tel. (301) 997 2200), offers on-the-job training in 47 countries for students in agriculture, enginee ing, computer science, math, and natural/physical sciences. You must have com pleted two years at an accredited four-year institution. Apply by December 10 for summer placement, otherwise six months in advance. (US$50 non-refundable fee.)

Positions as group leaders are available from **American Youth Hostels (AYH)** and the **Experiment in International Living (EIL).** AYH requires you to complete successfully their week-long leadership course (US$225) and to lead one domestic trip before leading one in Europe. Besides food and accommodations, leaders are compensated US$200 per trip plus US$3 per day. Write to National American Youth Office, American Youth Hostels, Inc., P.O. Box 37613, Washington, DC 20013-7613 (tel. (202) 783-6161). EIL has a rigorous application process; you must be at least 24, and have established leadership abilities, language fluency, and in-depth overseas experience. For a summer position, apply before December 1 to Summer Studies Abroad, The Experiment in International Living, Kipling Road, Brattleboro, VT 05301 (tel. (802) 257-7751 ext. 228). For a semester position, write to Semester Studies Abroad at the same address.

CIEE: (See Useful Organizations and Publications.) Distributes *Work, Study, Travel Abroad: The Whole World Handbook* (US$8 plus US$1 postage), which offers leads to overseas opportunities, although it does not list specific job openings. Also available are *Summer Jobs in Britain* ((US$9 plus US$1 postage), and *Emplois d'Eté en France* (US$11 plus US$1 postage).

Central Bureau for Educational Visits and Exchanges: Seymour Mews House, Seymour Mews, London W1H 9PE, England. Provides information on *au pairs,* holiday jobs, and volunteer work. Also publishes *Working Holidays* (£4.80 plus postage).

Writer's Digest Books: 1507 Dana Ave., Cincinnati, OH 45207 (tel. (800) 543-4644 for orders only; in OH (800) 551-0884). Distributes the *Directory of Overseas Summer Jobs* (US$12, postage included), which is a list of over 50,000 openings worldwide, volunteer and paid. They also carry *Work Your Way Around the World* (US$13, postage included).

Vacation Work Publications: 9 Park End St., Oxford 0X1 1HJ, England. A great source of books on working abroad. They carry *1988 Directory of Summer Jobs Abroad* (£4.95), *Work Your Way Around the World* (£6.95), *Working Ski Resorts—Europe* (£4.95), *The Directory of Work and Study in Developing Countries* (£6.95), and *The International Directory of Voluntary Work* (£5.95). Be sure to include £2 per book to cover airmail postage outside of England.

Volunteer jobs are readily available almost everywhere; in some countries, particularly in Eastern Europe, they're virtually your only hope. You won't make money—although you may receive room and board in exchange for your labor—but the work can be fascinating, and you're likely to meet European students. Volunteer opportunites include *kibbutz* work (see Israel chapter), archeological digs, community work, and workcamp projects. Write for CIEE's *Volunteer! The Comprehensive Guide to Voluntary Service in the U.S. and Abroad,* and the Central Bureau for Educational Visits & Exchanges' booklet, *Working Holidays.* Perhaps the most complete and up-to-date listings are provided by **Volunteers for Peace,** 43 Tiffany Rd., Belmont, VT 05730 (tel. (802) 259-2759), which publishes a free newsletter, as well as the *International Workcamp Directory* (US$7). In the past, this directory has publicized opportunities as diverse as reclaiming an abandoned island near Venice, repairing bicycles in Belgium for export to South African refugees, and excavating concentration camps in Germany. They also offer placement for workcamps in the Soviet Union.

If you don't plan for work in advance, you needn't lose all hope. An on-the-spot search offers flexibility. But without a work permit you may have to settle for menial work, poor conditions, low pay, and long hours.

Some jobs can be found anywhere in Europe. Ask at pubs, cafes, restaurants, and hotels. Youth hostels frequently provide room and board to travelers who are willing to stay a while and help run the place. You can also earn room and board as an *au pair.* These babysitting and household jobs abound in Great Britain, France, and to some extent in Germany and Scandinavia. Hiring male *au pairs* seems to be in vogue now, too. Look for ads in city newspapers and on bulletin boards. In non-English-speaking countries, your English-language ability may be an asset: Consider teaching English. Post a sign in markets or learning centers to the effect that you are a native speaker, and scan the classifieds of local newspapers, wh residents often advertise for language instruction.

Open your eyes also to jobs peculiar to a region or a season. Hikers who mer asked to sleep in a barn have found work on dairy or sheep farms in Great Brita Many travelers follow the grape harvest in the fall—mostly in France, but also Switzerland and Germany's Mosel Valley. In the winter, the Swiss leave resort w to foreigners who don't mind its menial nature. The best tips on jobs for foreign come from other travelers, so be alert and inquisitive in hostels and other yo hangouts.

Packing

Pack light. A tried and true method is to set out everything you *think* you'll n for your trip, eliminate half of it, and take more money. Remember that lots of l gage will mark you as a tourist, and a heavy bag will create extra transportat needs and costs. A large amount of luggage is both hard to keep track of and e to steal. The benefits of traveling light far outweigh the inconvenience of a limi wardrobe. Always test your luggage by trudging around the block with it a few tin *before* you leave. Having extra room for presents and other purchases is anot good reason to begin with a less-than-stuffed bag.

Decide first whether a backpack, light suitcase, or shoulder bag is most suita for your travels. If you plan to cover a lot of ground by foot, a sturdy backpa with several external compartments is hard to beat. The debate over the vari types of backpacks, however, continues unabated: Internal frames stand up to a line baggage handlers well and can often be disguised as shoulder bags; exter frames distribute weight better, and lift the pack a bit off your back. It's your choi but beware excessive economy—you could well find yourself collecting the pie of the frame after a transatlantic flight. Consider a light suitcase or a large shoul bag if you wish to travel less obtrusively. An empty, lightweight duffel bag pack inside your luggage will be much appreciated. Once abroad you can fill your lugg with your purchases and keep your dirty clothes in the duffel. Regardless of w you choose, a small daypack or haversack is indispensable for plane flights, sights ing, carrying a camera, and/or keeping some of your valuables with you.

To avoid being left with nothing if robbed, guard your money, passport, and ot important articles in a money belt or neck pouch and keep it with you at all tim The best combination of convenience and invulnerability is the nylon zippe pouch with belt which can be arranged to sit either outside or inside the waist your pants or skirt. Money belts should be available at any good camping sto

When deciding what type of clothing to pack, take into consideration the vari climates in which you'll be traveling. Good sources of worldwide weather inforn tion include encyclopedias, atlases, and major newspapers. Also, IAMAT (Inter tional Association for Medical Assistance to Travellers), 417 Center St., Lewist NY 14092, will send you a free World Climate Chart for the countries you reque These include recommended seasonal clothing and the sanitary conditions of lo water, milk, and food.

Women traveling in Muslim areas and in Orthodox regions of Israel should aware of the customs governing female dress. If you plan to visit a mosque, a sc to cover your face is recommended. In Israel, Egypt, and especially Jordan, opac material, long sleeves, and skirts to the ankle are a must. However, many excepti exist in heavily touristed areas, where Western culture has overridden local custo Wearing a swimsuit when not near the beach is acceptable only in these areas. M and women alike should note that bare shoulders and shorts above the knee forbidden in places of worship *all over Europe.*

Comfortable walking shoes or a good pair of running shoes are essential; ta two pairs in case one gets wet or disintegrates. In sunny climates, sandals or ot light shoes are great. For heavy-duty hiking, sturdy lace-up walking boots sho suffice. Make sure they have good ventilation—the new leather-reinforced ny hiking boots are lightweight, rugged, and dry quickly. A double pair of socks—li

absorbent cotton inside and thick wool outside—will cushion feet, keep them dry, and help prevent blisters.

Rain gear is very handy, and absolutely required in such regions as the U.K. Look for a lightweight rain poncho that will cover your pack completely when it's on your back. Ponchos can also serve well as ground cloths or impromptu lean-tos for campers.

Here's a checklist of other items you should consider taking: a pocketknife (a must—try to find one with a corkscrew, can-opener, roach clip, bottle opener, and scissors), emergency kit including tweezers, flashlight, needle and thread, string, waterproof matches, canteen or water bottle (sturdy plastic is best), small notebook and pen, traveler's alarm clock or alarm watch, plastic bags, rubber bands, and sturdy plastic containers. See our Camping section under Accommodations in this General Introduction for other equipment suggestions. Toiletries such as aspirin, razor blades, and tampons are available throughout Western Europe; but carrying a few extras, plus toilet paper, is probably a good idea if you're heading for Eastern Europe or North Africa.

In most European countries, electricity is 220 volts AC, enough to blow out any North American appliance. An adaptor only changes the shape of the plug—it's not enough if you want to use your appliance overseas. Travelers who wear contact lenses should note that their heat disinfection units will require a converter. You can purchase small converters for this purpose for about US$20. Converters must match the wattage of the appliance, and the current in the outlet: Check with the national tourist office of the country concerned for further details, or write to **Franzus Company,** 352 Park Ave. S., New York, NY 10010 (tel. (212) 463-9393), for their pamphlet *Foreign Electricity is No Deep Dark Secret.* Or avoid the issue entirely by not taking any electrical appliances.

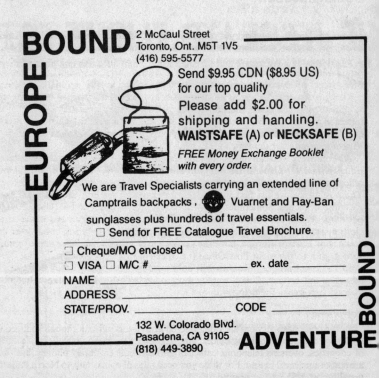

Foreign Languages

Perpetuated for years by English-speaking travelers, the myth that "they all speak English" is manifestly false, and very inconsiderate. Every time you ask a European a question in English, you are asking a favor that you probably would not be able to perform were he or she to visit your hometown. Keeping this in mind will help you to remember, as common courtesy, to ask "Do you speak English?" before launching into a question. Better yet, before you go, try to learn even a little about the foreign languages of the countries you'll be visiting. Attempts to speak the indigenous language will meet with happy—sometimes startled—approval from locals, and you'll come home with memories of warm encounters. Some Europeans may revel in your mistakes, but don't let occasional snubs or laughter put you off. Laugh with them at your own ignorance, and they will be more than happy to help you learn. Two weeks in a foreign country can be more fruitful than one year in a classroom at home.

English	*Hello*	*Goodbye*	*Please*	*Where is . . . ?*
Arabic	*marHaba*	*bikhaaTrak*	*dakhlak*	*wayn . . . ?*
French	*Bonjour*	*Au revoir*	*S'il vous plaît*	*Où est . . . ?*
German	*Guten Tag*	*Auf Wiedersehen*	*Bitte*	*Wo ist . . . ?*
Greek	*YAHsas*	*YAHsas*	*parakaLO*	*pou EEneh . . . ?*
Italian	*Buon Giorno*	*Arrivederci*	*Per favore*	*Dóve sta . . . ?*
Russian	*Zdrástvuytye*	*Prashcháytye*	*Pazhálusta*	*Gdyé . . . ?*
Spanish	*Hola*	*Hasta luego*	*Por favor*	*¿Dónde está . . . ?*

Communication

Mail

Receiving mail can be risky if you have no fixed address. Sending mail c/o American Express offices is reliable; most offices will hold your mail for 30 days for free if you have American Express traveler's checks or a card; even if you buy another brand of checks, you may want to buy some American Express checks for this purpose. Most offices will charge you a couple of dollars to pick up mail if you have neither an American Express card nor checks. The sender should underline and capitalize your last name, marking the envelope "Client Letter Service." There are offices in most large cities; a complete list is available for free; call Customer Service at (800) 528-4800. Ask for the booklet called *The Travel Companion* and allow at least one month for delivery.

Alternatively, you can have your mail sent to you c/o Poste Restante (the international phrase for General Delivery) in any city or town. In major cities, the post office handling Poste Restante is efficient, open long hours and (often) weekends. The post offices we list first in Practical Information sections are the main Poste Restante branches. Sometimes you will have to pay a minimal fee (US$0.10-0.40) per item. Again, the sender should underline and capitalize your last name. If the clerk insists that there is nothing for you, ask him or her to check under your first name. For Eastern Europe, have the sender put a "1" after the city name to make sure it goes to the main Post Office (i.e., Bratislava 1, Dresden 1).

In Eastern Europe, embassies will hold mail for you, though they don't like to advertise this service. This is usually more reliable than Poste Restante, but allow at least two weeks for delivery.

Telephone

In Europe, these services are often offered at the post office, although some countries have separate telephone offices; you pay after you make the call. In a number of countries, overseas telephone calls can also be made from pay phones, but these are sometimes hard to find. For these you need piles of coins; calls to North America usually cost US$3-4 per minute.

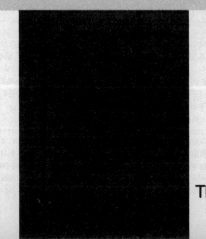

EurAide offers an answering service for travelers in Europe for a weekly or monthly fee. Anyone who wants to get in touch with you calls a "home base" in Europe and leaves a short message; you get the messages by calling the "home base" as often as you like throughout your trip. The big money-saving aspect is that your call to a European "home base" is much cheaper than an overseas call. For more information, contact EurAide, Inc., P.O. Box 2375, Naperville, IL 60565 (tel. (312) 420-2343).

International calling within Europe is relatively cheap, and is recommended for making reservations prior to arriving in a large city. Following is a list of the dialing codes for the countries covered by this book. It is not possible to dial the U.S.S.R. directly. First dial the international access code (usually listed in the booth), then the country code (from the list below), and then the number. For city codes, see the Practical Information section of that city.

COUNTRY	CODE	COUNTRY	CODE
Austria	43	Israel	972
Belgium	32	Italy	39
Bulgaria	359	Jordan	962
Cyprus	357	Luxembourg	352
Czechoslovakia	42	Morocco	212
Denmark	45	The Netherlands	31
Egypt	20	Norway	47
Finland	358	Poland	48
France	33	Portugal	351
East Germany	37	Romania	40
West Germany	49	Spain	34
Great Britain	44	Sweden	46
Greece	30	Switzerland	41
Hungary	36	Tunisia	216
Iceland	354	Turkey	90
Ireland	353	Yugoslavia	38

Telegrams to and from Europe are hardly a bargain; a 10-word telegram will cost approximately US$12.10. This really isn't cheaper than a short phone call—and 10 words by telegram simply can't match a three-minute phone call.

Getting There

By Air

It's very difficult to generalize about getting to Europe or offer exact fares; prices and market conditions fluctuate significantly from one week to the next. The best advice is to begin looking for a flight as early as possible. Remember: ISIC and YIEE cardholders (see Youth and Student Identification) are eligible for many reduced airfares worldwide—available from most travel agencies we list, and from many student travel agencies.

Flexibility is the best strategy. Direct regularly scheduled flights are ordinarily far out of any budget traveler's range. Consider leaving from a travel hub; certain cities—like New York, Atlanta, Dallas, Chicago, Los Angeles, San Francisco, Seattle, Vancouver, Toronto, and Montréal—are more competitive for flights than others. The savings realized on flights from these cities may more than pay for the feeder flight or gasoline you'll spend getting there.

A similar flexibility in destination is advisable, as fares to cities only 100km apart may differ by that many dollars, and will fluctuate significantly with time. Flying to London is usually the cheapest way across the Atlantic, though special fares to other cities may cost even less. Once in Europe, you should be able to arrange inexpensive ground transportation with private bus lines or by purchasing a BIGE ticket—see the following section Once There for more information.

Traveling to Europe on a one-way ticket may save you some money. European cities with consistently inexpensive transatlantic fares include London, Paris, and Amsterdam; see Budget Travel listings in the respective cities. Traveling without a return ticket also unchains you from the bondage of a circular itinerary.

If at all possible, consider traveling in the off-season; most major airlines maintain a steep multi-tiered fare structure that reaches its peak between mid-June and early September.

Finally, shop around. Have a knowledgeable travel agent guide you through the plethora of travel options. It's best to inquire at several places; travel agents are not all the same. Commissions are smaller on budget flights, so some travel agents may not search for the cheapest fare. In addition, check the Sunday travel sections of major newspapers, perhaps from several travel centers near you, for bargain fares. Student travel organizations such as CIEE in the U.S. or Travel CUTS in Canada (see Useful Organizations and Publications) are excellent sources of information; they specialize in budget travel and have specials unknown to regular travel agents or unavailable through the airlines. If you are eligible, ask about "youth fares:" round-trip discounts available to those aged 12 through 24 who purchase their tickets 72 hours before departure.

Whenever flying internationally, avoid last-minute problems by picking up your ticket in advance of the departure date and arriving at the airport several hours before your flight.

A **charter flight** is the most consistently economical flight option. You can book charters up until the last minute, but most summer flights fill up several months in advance. Later in the summer, charter companies find it more difficult to fill all their seats and either offer special reduced fares *or* cancel flights. Fares advertised in newspapers are usually the lowest possible; always read the fine print, and call around. Charter flights allow you to stay abroad up to one year, and also often allow you to "mix-and-match" arrivals and departures from different cities. Once you have made your plans, however, the flexibility ends. You must choose your departure and return dates when you book your flight, and if you cancel your ticket within 14 or 21 days of departure, you will lose some or all of your money. Travel insurance will usually not cover cancellations.

Although charter flights are less expensive, figure in the cost of being crowded, spending more time in airports, and experiencing delays. Ask a travel agent about the charter company's reliability. Charter companies reserve the right to cancel flights up to 48 hours before departure; they will do their best to find you another flight, but your delay could be days, not just hours. American charter operators are bonded with the U.S. government, so should they default or declare bankruptcy, your ticket should be refunded—eventually.

CIEE (see Useful Organizations and Publications) was among the first on the charter scene and offers flights from the U.S. to destinations all over the world. As one of the largest U.S. charter operators, their flights are extremely popular, so reserve early. Write, or call (800) 223-7402 (in NY (212) 661-1450). Other charter companies offering service to Europe include **Travac,** 989 Sixth Ave., New York, NY 10018 (tel. (800) TRAV-800 and (212) 563-3303); **Tourlite,** 1 E. 42nd St., New York, NY 10017 (tel. (800) 272-7600 and (212) 599-2727); **UniTravel Corp.,** P.O. Box 16220, St. Louis, MO 63105 (tel. (800) 325-2222 or (314) 727-6106); and **DER Tours,** 11933 Wilshire Blvd., Los Angeles, CA 90025 (tel. (800) 421-4343; in CA (800) 252-0606). In Canada, try **Travel CUTS,** 187 College St., Toronto M5T 1P7, Ontario, Canada (tel. (416) 979-2406), and **Wardair** (tel. (800) 237-0314 from the U.S.; various 800 lines in Canada).

Major airlines offer two options for the budget traveler: standby flights and APEX fares. The advantage of **standby** fares, which are generally sold only in the summer, is flexibility; you can come and go as you please. The disadvantages are that standby fares are roughly 20% higher than charter fares, and that flying standby can turn into a game of roulette as you and the rest of the masses gamble on winning the

few seats available. Most airlines allow you to purchase an open ticket in advance; tickets are also sold at the airport on the day of departure. In any case, the number of available seats is established only in the moments before takeoff. Call individual carriers to find out about the availability and price of standby fares. Most travel agents can issue standby tickets, but it's usually necessary to do your own research first, since many either don't know about or are reluctant to tell you about standby options. Canadians, ages 12 to 21, can receive a 40% youth discount flying standby from Canada on Air Canada.

More expensive still is the **Advanced Purchase Excursion Fare (APEX).** APEX provides you with confirmed reservations and allows you to arrive and depart from different cities. Reservations usually must be made 21 days in advance, with 7- to 14-day minimum and 60- to 90-day maximum stay limitations. To change an APEX reservation you must pay a US$50-100 penalty, and to change a return flight you must pay a US$100 penalty or upgrade your ticket, which will cost you well over US$100. For summer travel, book APEX fares early—by May you may have difficulty getting the departure date you want.

Yet another option is to try **Virgin Atlantic** (tel. (800) 862-4141), which offers regularly scheduled flights from New York to London for US$289 one way. If you have the flexibility to book one week or less in advance, you can take advantage of their Late Saver fares (New York-London US$258 one way). Peak-season competition for seats is fierce, so book early.

U.S. organizations that have been discount clearing houses for unsold airline, charter, and/or cruise tickets include **Air Hitch,** Suite 100, 2901 Broadway, New York, NY 10025 (tel. (212) 864-2000); **Last Minute Travel Club,** 132 Brookline Ave., Boston, MA 02215 (tel. (800) LAST-MIN, that is (800) 527-8646, or (617) 267-9800); **Worldwide Discount Travel Club,** 1674 Meridian Ave., Miami Beach, FL 33139 (tel. (305) 534-2082); **Discount Travel International,** Ives Building, Suite 205, Narberth, PA 19072 (tel. (800) 824-4000 or (215) 668-2182); and **Stand-Buys Ltd.,** 311 W. Superior, Suite 404, Chicago, IL 60610 (tel. (800) 255-0200 or (312) 943-5737). These organizations, which usually have a yearly subscription fee of

US$35-45, sell empty seats on commercial carriers and charters three weeks to a few days before departure. You may have to send money before you have your departure date and destination city confirmed. Check with them for further restrictions and liabilities—the cancellation fines are hefty. Contact these agencies early, as they often require a three- to five-week advance notice.

If you live on the West Coast of the U.S., budget travel to Europe can be tough. **European Tourist Information** (tel. (800) 621-1974) is a wholesale outlet specializing in flights from the West Coast to Europe. They arrange both charter and scheduled commercial flights. In 1987, E.T.I. offered charter seats from Los Angeles to Paris for US$500 round-trip.

Enterprising travelers who can travel light might consider flying to Europe as a courier. Couriers are people used by major companies to deliver parcels. You get a great fare price, and the company gets to use your luggage space (you are only allowed carry-on bags). The company sends a representative to the airport to pick up the parcel, so you need only drop it off before you can begin your trip. The company usually chooses your travel dates and times. **NOW Voyager** (tel. (212) 463-1616) is the major courier service; they arrange flights to London, Amsterdam, Madrid, and Milan. Membership costs US$45.

By Sea

If you can afford Cunard's **Queen Elizabeth II,** you probably don't need this book; you can still ply the waters in the grand old style between New York and Southampton, England or Cherbourg, France. In summer 1987, one-way fare per person (food included) for the five-day crossing was US$999 for a single, and US$799 per person for a double. For information, write Cunard Lines at P.O. Box 2935, Grand Central Station, New York, NY 10163 (tel. (800) 221-4770). **Polish Ocean Lines** has crossings between Montréal and London for US$640 one way, US$1090 round-trip. For information, contact McLean Kennedy Ltd., 410 St. Nicholas St., Montréal, Québec H2Y 2P5, Canada (tel. (514) 849-6111). In addition, freighters occasionally take on passengers for a transatlantic crossing, but it's not cheap. For a brief but complete list, write to **Ford's Travel Guides,** 19448 Londelius St., Northridge, CA 91324 (tel. (818) 701-7414). Ask for *Ford's Freighter Travel Guide.*

The myth that you can work your way to Europe aboard a cargo ship is just about that. In order to get a job as a crew hand, you must have "sailing papers" roughly equivalent to a union card; the only way to get these papers is to know someone in the industry.

Once There

Transportation in Europe

By Plane

Flying across Europe on regularly scheduled flights will empty your wallet quickly; rail and bus travel is almost always less expensive. Nearly all airlines cater to business travelers and set prices accordingly. Student fares and holiday charters are a happy exception to this rule; on high-volume routes between northern Europe and sun spots in Spain, Italy, Greece, and North Africa, budget fares are also frequently available (usually in spring and summer only). To find such fares, consult budget travel agents and local newspapers and magazines. The **Air Travel Advisory Board,** Morley House, Regent St., London, England (tel. 636 50 00), can put you in touch with the cheapest carriers to most destinations—for free. **STA Travel,** 74 Old Brompton Rd., London SW7 3LQ, England, and the **Council on International Educational Exchange (CIEE),** 51, rue Dauphine, *6éme,* Paris 75006, France (tel. 43 26 79 65), are the agencies to write to for inexpensive flights throughout Europe.

By Train

European trains retain the romance and convenience their North American counterparts have lost. Second-class travel is very pleasant, and compartments are excellent for meeting people of all ages and nationalities. Bring some food, as it's expensive on the train.

You may be tempted to save on accommodations by taking an overnight train in a regular coach seat. For your body's sake, don't do this often: Sightseeing through bleary, lead-lidded eyes is not fun. If you do, look for trains with compartments rather than airplane-style seating, and avoid trains that cross international borders. A sleeping berth in a bunkbedded *couchette* car, with linen provided, costs US$11. Be aware that sleeping train riders are the most prized prey of thieves; lock the door of your compartment if you can, and keep your valuables on your person while you sleep. You should also know that many compartments will not be single sex.

Ariel Publications, 14417 SE 19th Place, Bellevue, WA 98007 (tel. (206) 641-0518), publishes *How to Camp Europe by Train* (US$13), by Lenore Baken. This excellent book covers nearly all aspects of train travel, including sections on railpasses, packing, and specifics on rail travel in each European country.

If you're dying to know the time schedules for *every* train in Europe, eastern and western, write to **Forsyth Travel Library,** 9154 W. 57th St., P.O. Box 2975, Shawnee Mission, KS 66201 (tel. (800) FOR-SYTH or (913) 384-3440). Ask for the *Thomas Cook Continental Timetable* (US$18.45, first-class postage included). They also carry a wide range of travel maps. A free catalog is available.

Before you invest in a railpass, do some research to find out if it will save you money. Visit a travel agent and consult the current *Eurailtariff Manual.* Add up the second-class fares for the major routes you plan to cover and remember to deduct 30-50% if you're under age 26 and eligible for BIGE (see below); you may find it very difficult to make your railpass pay for itself in Belgium, Greece, Ireland,

Italy, Luxembourg, the Netherlands, Portugal, or Spain, where train fares are reasonable or distances short. However, if the sum comes close to the price of the pass, the convenience of avoiding ticket lines may be worth the difference. Just beware an obsession with making the pass pay for itself or you may return with little but blurred memories of train stations.

The various **Eurailpasses** are valid in Austria, Belgium, Denmark, Finland, France, West Germany, Greece, Ireland, Italy, Luxembourg, the Netherlands, Norway, Portugal, Spain, Sweden, and Switzerland; they are not valid in Great Britain and Northern Ireland. The pass gives you free travel on all trains except privately-run mountain railroads in Switzerland. You still have to pay a supplement for many express trains and for seat reservations (the only *guarantee* you can get for a spot on a train), usually US$1-2 each. The pass gives you free transit on many ferry routes, though you must pay a sizable supplement on the Italy-Greece boat in summer.

Travelers under age 26 can buy the **Eurail Youthpass,** validated the first time you use it, and good for one or two months of second-class travel (US$310 and US$400, respectively). If you are over 26, you must purchase the first-class **Eurailpass,** which is practically impossible to make pay off (15 days, US$280; varying periods to 3 months, US$760). Eurailpasses are officially available only outside of Europe; any good travel agent, as well as CIEE, Travel CUTS, and Let's Go Travel Services, can sell you one (see Useful Organizations and Publications). While Eurailpasses are not refundable, some provision has been made for their loss. When you get the pass, sign it immediately and detach the "Validation Slip." This part, coupled with a receipt from the agent of sale confirming issuance, will permit reissuance for US$5.

The **InterRail** pass entitles travelers under age 26 to one month's unlimited travel in an even wider area: In addition to the 16 countries covered by Eurail, InterRail is valid in Great Britain, Morocco, Yugoslavia, Romania, and Hungary. Holders receive only 50% reduction on travel within the country in which the pass is purchased, and on ferries between countries on the pass. InterRail is much cheaper than Eurail (one month £139), but you can only buy it in a European country in which you have resided for six months. This is an especially good pass for foreign students who wish to travel after their term of study. Some travelers have been known to obtain a pass by simply showing up at a train station ticket counter and asking politely, showing a passport stamp from a previous trip to Europe, or presenting any other evidence of your presence in Europe six months ago or earlier. However, you should know that any train conductor can demand to see your passport; if she or he is not satisfied that you obtained the pass legally, it can be confiscated. Good luck.

If you will be doing intensive traveling in one country, you might consider purchasing a national railpass, available in Great Britain, France, West Germany, Finland, Austria, Switzerland, Belgium, Italy, Poland, and other countries. Most require very hectic traveling to make them pay off. For information, check our country introductions or write to the national rail office, care of the national tourist office. A few countries, such as Turkey and Israel, offer regular reductions for students on their standard train tickets. On international rail travel within Eastern Europe, where no western European pass is valid, holders of the IUS card (see Documents) get a 25% discount.

BIGE tickets (known variously as **Transalpino, Eurotrain, BIJ,** and **Twen-tours** tickets), available for international trips and travel within France, save anyone under age 26 up to 55% on regular second-class fares. Tickets are valid for two months (tickets to Turkey and Morocco are valid for 6 months), and free stopovers in other countries along a direct route are allowed. For example, you can go from London to Istanbul for about £105, stop off in half a dozen countries along the way, and take up to six months. The only disadvantage of BIGE is that the places at which you can stop are limited to the ones along the specific route of your ticket. Tickets must be purchased from specified selling agents, usually student travel orınizations, located throughout Europe. *Let's Go* lists sales agents in many cities, ıd refers to all the varieties of BIGE tickets simply as "BIGE."

y Bus

In Israel, Morocco, Turkey, and Greece, bus networks are more extensive and ficient than train services. However, even in those countries covered by a good ain network, bus travel shouldn't be dismissed. You'll find that the bus is often gnificantly less expensive than the train; this is particularly true of Great Britain. us networks are also more comprehensive, reaching many places inaccessible by ain. Unfortunately, you'll also find it's generally much slower and less comfort- ıle.

Amsterdam, Athens, Istanbul, London, and Munich are centers for private bus ıes that offer long-distance jaunts across Europe and, from time to time, overland India. **London Student Travel** has year-round express coach services from Lon- ɔn to over 100 destinations in France, Greece, Italy, the Netherlands, Portugal, ɔain, and Switzerland, and summer services to Morocco, Turkey, and Yugoslavia. ɔr information, contact them at 52 Grosvenor Gardens, London SW1W 0AU, ngland (tel. (01) 730 34 02). **Miracle Bus,** 408 The Strand, London WC2, England el. (01) 379 60 55), also has competitive bus fares throughout Europe. **Europabus,** 'o German Rail, 747 Third Ave., 33rd floor, New York, NY 10017 (tel. (800) 223-)63 or (212) 308-6447), is a specialist in coach service to smaller European towns accessible by train. Try **Magic Bus,** Rokin 38, Amsterdam, The Netherlands (tel. 20) 26 44 34), for cheap, direct service between major European cities. See our uses listings in major cities for other major bus lines.

y Boat

Travel by boat is a scenic and relaxing alternative which is often overlooked. owns and villages along all the major rivers and lakes of Germany, Switzerland, ustria, and Scandinavia are connected by reasonably priced steamship services.

A Eurailpass usually entitles you to large reductions. The most famous routes are those of the Mosel, Rhine, and Danube riverboats.

Another part of Europe that can only be truly appreciated by boat is the Mediterranean. Boats here provide a welcome respite from the monotony of bus and train travel—skin pallid after hours in smoky second-class cabins recovers quickly under the Mediterranean sun. Some popular routes are from Genoa or Marseilles to Tunisia; from Venice to the Yugoslav coast or Greece; throughout the Greek islands; and from Greece on to Turkey, Cyprus, Israel, or Egypt. However, ferries are extremely crowded during July and August, particularly from Italy to Greece and from continental ports to the Balearic Islands and Sardinia. Advance planning and reserved tickets purchased from a travel agency can often spare you several discouraging days of waiting in uninteresting ports. Scores of firms are in operation, particularly along the Yugoslav coast and in the Greek islands, but smaller operations have frustratingly erratic schedules and work on a first-come, first-served basis. A good source of tickets and information on Mediterranean ferries is **Extra Value Travel, Inc.,** 437 Madison Ave., 26th floor, New York, NY 10022 (tel. (800) 223-1980 or (212) 750-8800).

By Car, Van, and Caravan

The advantages of travel by car speak for themselves. However, some aspects of car touring may be unpleasant. Gasoline is expensive almost everywhere in Europe (prices start at US$2 per gallon; call tourist boards for specific information), and unfamiliar laws and driving habits can make driving a truly frightening odyssey. Tolls in Europe also tend to be much more expensive than those in North America. Taxes are another important consideration: They can turn an apparently frugal venture into an unintended splurge; be sure the VAT tax is included when you ask for a price quote. Despite these problems, renting a car in Europe can easily be worth the money and trouble invested, particularly for groups of three or more. For periods of three weeks or less, the only option is to rent; for longer periods, leasing can be much cheaper. Leases are usually tax-exempt. Reputable agencies such as those listed below will inform you of these and other subtleties, so make your arrangements with them. It's often less expensive to make arrangements and pay for cars at home, rather than find an agency after arriving in Europe. Be sure to check minimum age requirements with each company.

Purchasing a car may save you several hundred dollars, especially if you would otherwise be leasing one for an extended length of time. You must order the car before leaving for Europe. In addition to the listings below, check with Peugeot, Saab, Volvo, and VW-Porsche-Audi—these manufacturers have their own transatlantic shipment plans. The car you import must comply with U.S. safety and emission standards; for information about regulations, write the U.S. Environmental Protection Agency, Public Information Center, 401 M St. SW, Washington, DC 20460 (tel. (202) 382-2080) for the pamphlet *Automotive Imports—Fact Sheet.* See Kemwel Group and Nemet Auto International below for new car purchase information.

If you are brave or know what you're doing, buying a used car or van in Europe and selling it before you leave can provide the cheapest wheels on the Continent. Be sure to check the different countries' import/export laws concerning used vehicles, registration, and safety and emission standards before buying. By sending US$6 to David Guterson, 13024 Venice Loop, Bainbridge Is., WA 98110 (tel. (206) 842-8469), you can get his booklet *Europe By Van,* which explains buying and selling a used van in Europe (may be helpful for other vehicles as well).

Another option is the motor caravan, a British term for a trailer. "Motor caravanning" encompasses car-and-trailer, car-and-tent, and outfitted bus arrangements. In addition to offering the advantages of car rental, motor caravanning spares you the cost and hassle of a daily search for lodgings. You can rent or buy caravans from various firms, and groups of four can rent outfitted minibuses economically. Prices vary drastically from season to season, and from country to country. Contact the firms listed here for catalogs.

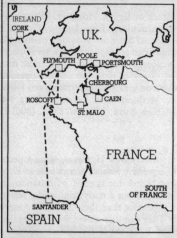

Whatever arrangements you make, be sure you know exactly what legal documents are involved in your transaction and what to do in case of an accident or breakdown. Car insurance in the form of the standard **International Insurance Certificate,** or "green card," is a prerequisite for driving in Europe. Most rental agencies include this coverage in their prices. If you buy or lease a car, you can obtain a green card through the dealer or from some travel agents. As for license requirements, the **International Driver's Permit,** available from the American Automobile Association (AAA) or the Canadian Automobile Association (CAA), will suffice anywhere; you'll need a completed application form, a valid driver's license, two recent passport-size photographs, and US$5. You must be at least 18 years old. This license is valid for one year, and you must carry your regular driver's license with you as well. If there's no AAA office near you, write to the main office at 8111 Gatehouse Rd., Falls Church, VA 22047 (tel. (703) 222-6713).

Kemwel Group: 106 Calvert St., Harrison, NY 10528-3199 (tel. (800) 468-0468). Very professional. Good rental prices (from US$89 per week). Discounts for students and faculty. Advance reservations get substantially lower rates. Rentals, leases, and purchases of most makes of cars in Europe. Camper rental also available.

Avis: Call (800) 331-2112 in the U.S. for information on international rentals. Ask about their "Supervalue Rate." You must reserve in advance *while in the United States.* Rates average US$125 per week plus tax, with unlimited mileage. No leasing plan.

Hertz Rent A Car: Call (800) 654-3131 in the U.S. for international reservations. Their "Affordable Europe" plan offers rates around US$100-250 per week with unlimited mileage; you must book at least 2 days in advance *from outside of Europe* and keep the car a minimum of 5 days. 10% discount for rentals over 21 days.

Europe by Car, Inc.: 1 Rockefeller Plaza, New York, NY 10020 (tel. (800) 223-1516 or (212) 581-3040). Economy cars US$100-140 per week, campers US$300-400 per week. 5% student and faculty discounts. Tax-free car leasing.

Foremost Euro-Car, Inc.: 5430 Van Nuys Blvd., Van Nuys, CA 91401 (tel. (800) 423-3111; in CA (800) 272-3299). Rents and leases throughout Europe; US$125-150 per week. Advance reservations a must.

Frances Auto Vacances: 420 Lexington Ave., New York, NY 10170 (tel. (212) 867-2625). US$129 per week for 3-week minimum lease (2-seat car); 2-door sedan US$84 per week for an 8-week lease. Pick up and return at several points in France, or in Geneva.

Nemet Auto International: 153-03 Hillside Ave., Jamaica, NY 11432 (tel. (800) 221-0177). One of the leading firms in European car purchase plans. Catalogs give full information on prices and shipping rates for a wide variety of European cars.

Auto Europe: P.O. Box 1097, Camden, ME 04843 (in U.S. tel. (800) 223-5555; in Canada (800) 237-2465). Car rentals, leases, and camper rentals throughout western Europe. Minimum age 21. Call or write for free catalog.

Hitchhiking

Some swear they'll never do it, others swear there is no other way. Whatever you views, hitching is the cheapest way to get around, and just about the most interest ing. Most drivers pick you up because they want someone to talk to; they'll ver likely converse about their own lives and countries, and will no doubt be intereste in finding out about yours. Indeed, a driver who has picked up a hitchhiker ha already shown hospitality, and may welcome you home for the evening.

Hitchhiking is much more common in Europe than in North America, and inf nitely safer. Nonetheless, keep all your belongings, and always your valuables an identification, in the passenger compartment with you and try not to ride in th back of a two-door car. A wedding ring or conservative dress will often ward o prospective suitors. Male-female couples will avoid hassles by letting the woma sit next to the door. Hitching at night has many drawbacks and should be a las resort: (1) Drivers will be leery of nocturnal thumbers (if you must, try to stan in a well-lit area), and potential attackers will have the advantage with less traffi and the cover of darkness. (2) You can get run over. In any case, if you start feelin uneasy about the ride for any reason, get out at the first opportunity or firmly de mand to be let off, no matter how unfavorable the spot appears for further hitching

Two women make very good time hitchhiking, and may be more comfortab than if thumbing alone. A man and a woman are an excellent combination. Bulleti boards may be a good way to find a hitching partner of the opposite sex. Two me itching together have difficulties, and three go nowhere; groups of men should consider splitting up and meeting at an agreed destination.

The lighter you travel, the better your luck will be. If you're traveling heavy, stack aggage compactly or even hide some of it. Once the driver halts you can usually nd space, but many vehicles will whip by if your baggage seems excessive. Dress eatly and keep your spirits up—you're more likely to get a ride that way. Anything ou can do to make yourself stand out, and seem interesting, wholesome, and harmess will help you. Never sit—standing makes you and your thumb more visible nd dynamic, and forces drivers to take your request more seriously. Don't take he term "thumbing" too seriously: Most Europeans use an open hand with and ithout meaningful motions. Walking while you hitch is not a good idea; your back aces the traffic, and drivers don't get the benefit of your dazzling smile. A sign is good idea; write in large, bold letters, and add "please" in the local language.

Where you stand is important. On secondary roads, pick a place where the driver an stop easily, return to the road safely, and have as much time as possible to look ou over as she or he approaches; never hitch on hills or curves. Throughout Europe, it's illegal to hitch on super-highways ("E" roads on most maps, "M" roads n Great Britain). Instead, you must stand on the highway entrance ramp, in front f the blue sign with a white pictograph of a bridge over a road which indicates he "legal" beginning of super-highway traffic regulations. In some countries, each ntrance ramp has a toll booth, in which case you must stand before it. Once on he motorway, it's best to have the driver let you off at roadside rest areas. This nay mean getting out some distance before your driver is to leave the road, but t will set you up well for a subsequent lift; presumably drivers are resting because hey're traveling long distances. While you're waiting at a rest area, you might actully approach drivers with license plates corresponding to your destination. If you're itching across several countries in one journey, it's wise to wait at a border, where raffic must slow down, and refuse any lifts that aren't going at least all the way cross the country. Getting in and out of town can be time-consuming; in general, on't waste time hitching when you're in range of a city bus.

In the Practical Information listings of many cities, we list the tram or bus lines hat will take you to strategic points for hitching out. You may also want to look t *Europe: A Manual for Hitch-hikers* (£5.95, airmail postage to the U.S. included), vhich provides directions for hitching out of hundreds of European cities; it also ates the various rest areas and entrance ramps. It's available from **Vacation Work ublications,** 9 Park End Street, Oxford OX1 1HJ, England. The *Hitchhiker's Guide to the Galaxy,* by Douglas Adams (Crown, 1980) might also be fun reading.

There are several organizations which link drivers with riders. Though you pay fee to both agency (about US$25 membership) and driver (per kilometer), you'll nd up paying significantly less than the equivalent rail fare, and may be more comortable about the drivers you meet. **Eurostop International** (called **Verband Der Deutschen Mitfahrzentralen** in Germany; **Allostop** in France) is one of the largest n Europe. Once in Europe, look them up in any large city.

Mopeds and Motorcycles

Mopeds (motorized bicycles) offer a wonderful and relatively inexpensive way o tour coastal areas and countryside, particularly where there's little automobile raffic. They cruise at about 35mph, and can be put on trains and ferries. However, nopeds can also be quite dangerous; wear a helmet, don't wear a backpack, and void riding in the rain or on rough roads. Other drawbacks of mopeds include the park plugs, which require frequent attention, and your luggage, which must be bsolutely minimal. Mopeds can be a good compromise between the high cost of ar travel and the limited range of bicycles, but long distances become *very* long vhen sitting upright on a motorized bicycle going 35mph. In general, rentals run JS$15-20 per day; try auto-repair and bicycle shops.

Nicholas Crane's *Cycling In Europe* (Oxford Illustrated Press, Haynes Publicaions), and *How to Tour Europe By Motorcycle: An Adventurer's Guide* (Motorbooks

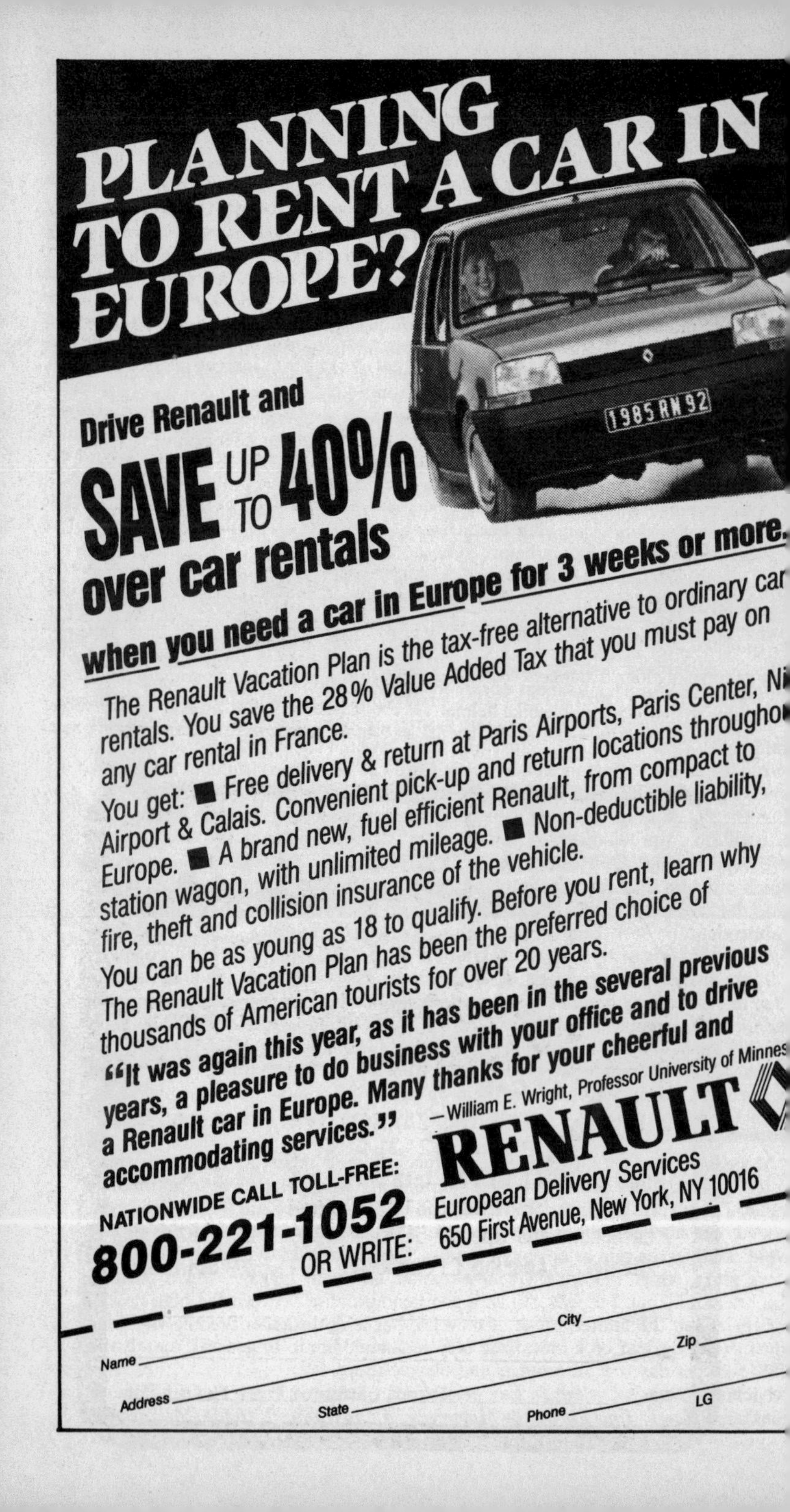
PLANNING TO RENT A CAR IN EUROPE?
1985 RN 92
Drive Renault and
SAVE UP TO 40%
over car rentals
when you need a car in Europe for 3 weeks or more.
The Renault Vacation Plan is the tax-free alternative to ordinary car rentals. You save the 28% Value Added Tax that you must pay on any car rental in France.
You get: ■ Free delivery & return at Paris Airports, Paris Center, Ni
Airport & Calais. Convenient pick-up and return locations througho
Europe. ■ A brand new, fuel efficient Renault, from compact to station wagon, with unlimited mileage. ■ Non-deductible liability, fire, theft and collision insurance of the vehicle.
You can be as young as 18 to qualify. Before you rent, learn why The Renault Vacation Plan has been the preferred choice of thousands of American tourists for over 20 years.
"It was again this year, as it has been in the several previous years, a pleasure to do business with your office and to drive a Renault car in Europe. Many thanks for your cheerful and accommodating services."
—William E. Wright, Professor University of Minnes
RENAULT
NATIONWIDE CALL TOLL-FREE:
800-221-1052
OR WRITE:
European Delivery Services
650 First Avenue, New York, NY 10016
Name
Address
City
State
Zip
Phone
LG

International, 1983), by Philcox and Boe, are two books that could be helpful in planning your tour.

Bicycles

Bicycling can bring rewards like no other form of transportation—try cycling down a deserted back road in the cool, early morning air and you'll see why. Only walking compares as a way of getting close to the countryside and the people. For information about touring routes, independent cyclists can consult national tourist offices or any of the numerous books about bicycle touring in Europe. *Bicycle Touring In Europe,* by Karen and Gary Hawkins (Pantheon Books, Random House, New York, 1980), is a helpful guide to outfitting yourself and your bike, while *Europe By Bike,* by Karen and Terry Whitehill (The Mountaineers Press, Seattle, 1987), is a great source of specific area tours.

Serious cycling is not the same affair as a Saturday afternoon jaunt around town. Remember you'll be pedaling not only yourself but also whatever gear you store in the panniers. Be sure the gear range on your bike is adequate; you'll need extremely low gears to get a loaded bike up a steep hill. Take some reasonably challenging day-long rides before you leave, both to get in shape and to assure yourself that you're not in over your head. Finally, have your bike tuned up by a reputable, well-equipped bike shop before you go.

It is possible to buy a bicycle in Europe, though the limited savings may not be worth the hassle. The best deals are to be found on components and on bicycles that would retail for US$350 and up in the U.S. To avoid import taxes when returning home with a bike, remember that used bikes aren't taxed while new ones are. Do buy proper touring equipment: Riding a bike with a frame pack strapped on it or on your back is about as safe as pedaling blindfolded over glare ice. The first thing to buy is a suitable bike helmet. At about US$31-55 for the best—a Bell Biker II or Bell Tourlite—it's a lot cheaper and more pleasant than having your head fixed.

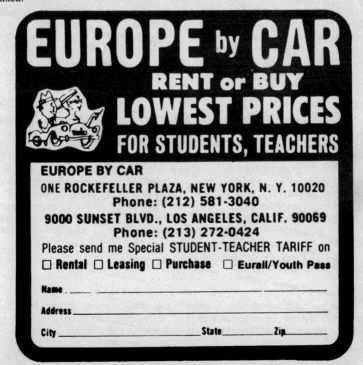

Fortunately, mail and telephone ordering has been perfected to a fine art in the U.S. Don't spend a penny before you scan the pages of *Bicycling* magazine for the lowest sale prices. **Bike Nashbar,** 4111 Simon Rd., Youngstown, OH 44512 (tel. (800) 345-2453; in Ohio (800) 654-2453), is the one company that really stands out. They almost always have the lowest prices, and when they don't, they cheerfully subtract 5¢ from the best price you can find. Call their toll-free number (open 24 hours) and the order will usually be on its way the same day. They regularly ship anywhere in the U.S. and Canada, and will also send things overseas. Their own line of products, including bicycles, is the best value.

Although you may not be able to build a frame or spoke a wheel, fixing a modern derailleur-equipped mount and changing a tire are things just about anyone can do with a few simple but specialized tools. Many books offer useful advice; *Understanding, Maintaining, and Riding the Ten-Speed Bicycle,* by Michael J. Lolin and Denise M. De la Rosa (from Rodale Press; tel. (800) 441-7761), is easy to read and includes tips on buying a bicycle and accessories (US$12).

To lessen the odds of not finding your bike where you left it, especially in large cities, your best bet is a U-shaped lock made by Citadel or Kryptonite. It's expensive (about US$30), but worth the money. Each company insures its locks against theft of your bike for one or two years.

Most airlines will count your bicycle as your second free piece of luggage (you're usually allowed two pieces of checked baggage and a carry-on piece). As an additional piece it will cost US$60-80 each way. Policies on charters and budget flights vary; check the airline's policy before buying your ticket. Perhaps the safest way to send your bike is in a box; you'll have to remove handlebars, pedals, and the front wheel, but this might spare your bicycle costly damage. Ferries often allow bike transport free.

If you'd like to explore several widely separated regions, it's easy to combine cycling with train travel. You can always ship your bike on trains, though the cost varies from a small fixed fee to a substantial fraction of the ticket price.

If you'd rather not travel exclusively on two wheels, you can rent a bike almost anywhere. A sturdy if unexciting one-speed model will cost US$6-8 per day; be prepared to lay down a sizable deposit. *Let's Go* lists bike rental shops in many cities and towns; where we have no listing, ask at the local tourist office. Some youth hostels (especially in France) rent bicycles for low prices. In many countries (including France and Belgium), train stations rent bikes and often allow you to drop them off elsewhere in the country without charge.

Hiking

Europe's most beautiful scenery is often accessible only by foot: Crete's Samaria Gorge, the Italian Alps, and Yorkshire's Pennine Way are but a few examples. *Let's Go* describes many daytrips for those who want to hoof it, but locals, hostel wardens, and fellow travelers are the best source of tips. Many European countries have hiking and mountaineering organizations; alpine clubs in Germany, Austria, Switzerland, and Italy, as well as tourist organizations in Scandinavia, provide inexpensive, simple accommodations in beautiful settings. Facilities are usually open to all.

Good books on hiking in Europe include J. Sydney Jones' *Tramping in Europe: A Walking Guide* (Prentice-Hall, 1984, US$8), Rob Hunter's *Walking in France* (Haynes, 1986, US$10), and Brian Spenser's *Walking in the Alps* (Hunter, 1986, US$7).

Accommodations

Hotels

Hotels are quite expensive in London, Switzerland, Austria, and northern Europe: Rock bottom for singles is US$12-15, for doubles US$16-20. In the rest of Europe, couples can usually get by fairly well (rooms with 1 double bed are generally cheaper than rooms with 2 twin beds), as can groups of three or four. Singles are scarce or expensive or both. Inexpensive European hotels might come as a surprise to those used to hotels in North America. A bathroom of your own is a rarity and costs extra when provided. Hot showers may also cost extra. Continental breakfast usually consists of a roll, jam, coffee or tea, and maybe an egg; in the United Kingdom and Ireland a larger meal is served. Pensions (guesthouses) are usually smaller and friendlier. The owners of these establishments are used to dealing with budget travelers and will often direct you to points of interest in the town and countryside. Unmarried couples will generally have no trouble getting a room together, though in a few countries (Ireland and Belgium, for example) couples under age 21 may occasionally encounter resistance.

If you wish to make reservations (at hotels or hostels) you can ensure a prompt reply by enclosing four International Postal Reply Coupons (available at any post office). Indicate your night of arrival and the number of nights you plan to stay. The hotel will send you a confirmation, and may request payment for the first night. Not all hotels accept reservations, and few accept dollar checks. You'll sacrifice spontaneity, but you may save yourself some tiring legwork and even some money; you're not likely to land any bargains by arriving at 8pm in a popular city.

Less expensive than hotels or pensions are rooms in private homes, available in many countries. Bookings are usually handled by local tourist offices. If you're traveling alone, this is an economical way to get your own room, and often you'll meet interesting families. Make sure, though, that the family doesn't live 20km out of town. Occasionally people will approach you in train stations to ask if you're looking for a place to stay. This may seem like a dangerous proposition, but don't be put off—it is a custom in many areas. You must, however, exercise some caution; women, for instance, are safer if they do not accept offers from men who approach them.

Don't assume that *Let's Go* is an exhaustive guide to budget accommodations in a given town. We have space to list only a few places; whenever you can, visit the local tourist office. Many distribute extensive listings free of charge, and will also reserve a room for a small fee. Further, note that we list high-season prices; if you're traveling in the off-season, you'll often pay less.

Hostels

Hostels can be the budget traveler's mecca. Prices are extraordinarily low—at US$3-10 for shared rooms, only camping is cheaper. Meals are frequently available, although these are likely to be bland. Many hostels have kitchen facilities, often with pots and pans. Most important, however, are the opportunities to meet other travelers from all over the world. You can find new travel partners, exchange stories, learn of places to visit. Most guests will be 17 to 25 years old, but hostels are rapidly becoming a resource for all ages. Some hostels, especially in northern Europe, are now open to families.

Quality does vary widely. Some hostels are set in strikingly beautiful castles and boats; others in run-down barracks far from the center of town. Rural hostels are generally more appealing than those in large cities.

Most hostels share certain disadvantages. The most common is an early curfew—fine if you're climbing a mountain the next morning, but a distinct cramp in your style if you're planning late nights on the town in Paris or Copenhagen. Conditions are sometimes spartan and cramped, there's little privacy, rooms are usually segregated by sex, and you may run into more pre-teen tour groups than you care to remember. Finally, there is often a lockout from morning to early afternoon, which means that you can't hang around all day or return for a siesta.

The most extensive line of hostels is that organized by the **International Youth Hostel Federation (IYHF)** (marked "IYHF" in our book); in most countries you must have a membership card to be eligible for IYHF hostel accommodations. (Exceptions include Israel, Sweden, and Yugoslavia where nonmembers pay higher rates; and Greece, where hostels are open to all.) The cost of membership varies by country, but is US$20 for ages 18 to 59 and US$10 for ages under 18 or over 59. A card will usually pay for itself very quickly, especially in the more expensive countries where hostels provide the only reasonably priced beds. Family cards are also available for one or two adults and all children under age 18 (US$30). Contact your local American Youth Hostel (AYH) office or the national headquarters (see Useful Organizations and Publications). *Let's Go* lists IYHF hostels in hundreds of cities and towns, but you may want to purchase the *International Youth Hostel Handbook. Volume I* has up-to-date listings on all hostels in Europe and the Mediterranean countries.

Sheet sleeping sacks are required at many of these hostels. Sleeping bags are often not allowed, although most hostels provide blankets. You can order a sleeping sack for about US$13 from Let's Go Travel Services or AYH (see Useful Organizations and Publications), or make your own by folding a sheet and sewing it shut on two sides.

In addition to the IYHF hostels, numerous other hostels offer inexpensive lodgings. These privately-owned dormitories are often found in major tourist centers, and throughout some countries—Ireland has many. No membership is required, and you won't always have to contend with early curfews or daytime lockouts.

Camping

While backcountry camping requires special skills and can be physically demanding, camping in campgrounds can be a pleasant experience for the novice. Camping not only costs less than sleeping indoors—it also gives you flexibility in finding a place to stay.

There are organized campgrounds in almost every European city, and in the countryside they're often beautifully situated by lakes, rivers, or the sea. While camping is best suited to travel by car, many campgrounds remain accessible by foot or by public transportation. Camping without a car won't be as convenient as staying in hostels or hotels, but the savings afforded by this cheapest of traveling styles may compensate for any inconveniences. Furthermore, a tent frees you from hostel regulations, drab cheap hotels, and, in most cases, the limitations of advance reservations.

Many campgrounds have showers, bathrooms, and a small restaurant or store; some have more elaborate facilities. Prices range from US$0.50-10 per person plus a similar amount per tent. *Europa Camping and Caravanning* (US$11), updated annually, is a detailed catalog of campsites in Europe. It's available through Recreational Equipment, Inc. (REI), P.O. Box C-88126, Seattle, WA 98188 (tel. (800) 426-4840). Another option is the German "encyclopedia of camping," *ADAC Camping Führer (1987),* in two volumes (readily available throughout Germany). Most national tourist offices have comprehensive listings of campgrounds, and regional lists are available at many local tourist offices. An **International Camping Carnet** (membership card) is required by some European campgrounds, but it can usually be purchased on the spot. In the U.S., it's available through the National Campers and Hikers Association, Inc., 4804 Transit Rd., Building #2, Depew, NY 14043 (tel. (716) 668-6242); the US$20 purchase price includes membership in the association. They also distribute a short bibliography of travel guides for campers and a list of camping stores in major European cities.

You won't be alone if you stick to organized campsites, and at some sites, you may not enjoy much peace and quiet. At urban campgrounds, Europeans arrive with trailers, radios, and cooking paraphernalia. The situation is aggravated by the limited room between tent spots. If you're searching for solitude, unofficial camping may be more your style. Sweden, Finland, and Norway permit you to camp for one night anywhere except on fenced land. And in many other countries, you can camp where you please in the countryside, so long as you are discreet and observe elementary courtesies, such as asking permission before setting up on a farmer's land.

Would-be campers without equipment will have to decide what they need and find the best possible gear at the lowest price. The advice given here is of the most general sort and you should spend some time perusing catalogs and questioning knowledgeable salespeople at outdoor stores before buying anything. There are many reputable mail-order firms; use them to gauge prices and order from them if you can't do as well locally. For the best deals, look around for last year's merchandise, particularly in the fall; tents don't change much, but prices may be reduced by as much as 50%. **Campmor,** 810 Rte. 17 North, P.O. Box 999, Paramus, NJ 07653 (tel. (800) 526-4784), offers a huge selection of equipment at attractive prices. **Cabela's,** 812 13th Ave., Sidney, NE 69160 (tel. (800) 237-8888), has great prices on high-quality equipment. For a wide range of the latest in camping gear, **Recreational Equipment, Inc. (REI),** P.O. Box C-88126, Seattle, WA 98188 (tel. (800) 426-4840 or (206) 431-5804), is the one. Great seasonal sales, too. Twenty-four hours, 365 days per year **L.L. Bean,** Freeport, ME 04033 (tel. (207) 865-3111), is a legend with plenty of its own equipment and some national-brand stuff.

If you're just starting out, you'll need the basics: sleeping bag, pad, and tent. If you'll just be camping in southern Europe during the summer, you can usually make do without the latter—and the view's much better. Choose your **sleeping bag** according to the weather in which you'll be camping. Most of the better bags—either down (lighter weight) or synthetics (cheaper, more water resistant and durable) have ratings for specific minimum temperatures; the lower the mercury, the higher the price. Anticipate the most severe conditions you may encounter, subtract a few degrees, and buy a bag. Not only will you waste money by buying one suitable for alpine winters when you'll be sleeping on roofs in Greece, but you'll spend more time perspiring than sleeping. Expect to pay at least US$25 for a lightweight synthetic bag to US$150 for a down bag suitable for use in below-freezing temperatures. **Sleeping bag pads** start at around US$10 for simple Ensolite pads to about US$50 for the best air mattress or hybrid such as the **Thermarest.**

Modern **tents** are remarkably clever and utterly unlike those canvas contraptions scouts seem so fond of. The best tents are "self-supporting," with their own frames and suspension systems, set up quickly, and do not require staking, though stakes are usually used to prevent movement. Up-to-date versions of simpler designs still require staking but are made of modern materials and have effective insect netting and integral floors just like the self-supporting ones. Backpackers and cyclists may wish to pay a bit more for a sophisticated lightweight tent and should get the smallest tent they can stand—some two-person tents weigh just over two pounds. Most major manufacturers, like **Eureka,** offer a wide range of tents, all of decent quality. Expect to pay at least US$40 for a simple two-person tent to US$150 for a serviceable four-person one. Be sure to buy a tent with a protective rain fly.

Other basics include a battery-operated **lantern** (never gas) for use inside the tent and a simple plastic **groundcloth** to protect the tent floor. Other accessories can dramatically increase comfort or decrease expenses. Fairly large, collapsible **water sacks** will significantly improve your lot in primitive campgrounds and weigh practically nothing when empty. **Campstoves** come in all sizes, weights, and fuel types, but none is truly cheap; consider your needs and style of travel before laying out US$35-125.

Alternative Accommodations

For a change from the routine, consider the wide range of alternative accommodations at your disposal, including student dormitories, religious institutions, and host networks.

Ask at local tourist offices of university/college towns whether student dormitories are available to travelers when school is not in session. These are often let to visitors for a nominal fee, usually comparable to youth hostel prices. Most dormitories are administered such that you won't have to share a room with strangers or endure stringent curfew and eviction regulations. Monasteries and convents are another possibility—many will open their doors to those seeking corporeal or spiritual relief, particularly in Italy. A letter of introduction from one of your clergy could facilitate matters.

There are a number of host networks which will help you find accommodations with families throughout Europe. **Servas** is devoted to promoting world peace and understanding among people of different cultures. Traveler members may stay free of charge in host members' homes in 80 countries. You are asked to contact hosts in advance, and you must be willing to fit into the household routine. Stays are limited to two nights, unless you are invited to stay longer. Membership costs US$45, and for a US$15 deposit you get a directory with short self-descriptions of host members. Write the U.S. Servas Committee at 11 John St., Room 706, New York, NY 10038 (tel. (212) 267-0252).

Sleeping in European train stations is a time-honored tradition. The romance does not survive the reality. While it *is* costless and very often tolerated by local authorities, it is neither comfortable nor especially safe. If you've ever slept with the lights on in a filthy room full of untrustworthy strangers talking loudly, you may know what it's like. Spending the night in an urban park is similarly cheap; your life may be too.

Customs: Returning Home

Returning home to the United States, you may bring US$400 worth of goods duty-free; you pay 10% on the next US$1000 worth. Duty-free goods must be for personal or household use and cannot include more than 100 cigars, 200 cigarettes (one carton), or one liter of wine or liquor (you must be 21 or older to bring liquor into the U.S.). The exemptions of persons traveling together may be combined. All items included in your duty-free allowance must accompany you; you cannot have them shipped separately. You can mail unsolicited gifts duty-free if they're worth less than US$50. However, you may not mail liquor, tobacco, or perfume into the U.S. If you mail home personal goods of U.S. origin, mark the package "American goods returned" in order to avoid duty charges. Spot checks are occasionally made on parcels, so it is best to mark the accurate price and nature of the gift on the package. If you send back a parcel worth over US$50, the Postal Service will collect the duty plus a handling charge when it is delivered. A useful resource on these regulations is the brochure, *Know Before You Go,* available from the **U.S. Customs Service,** P.O. Box 7407, Washington, DC 20044 (tel. (202) 566-8195). Different regulations apply to foreign nationals living in the United States.

Canadian regulations are similar. Any number of times per year, after you have been abroad at least two days, you can bring in goods up to the value of CDN$100, and once every calendar year, after you have been abroad at least seven days, you may bring in up to CDN$300 worth of goods. You cannot claim both the $100 and $300 allowances on the same trip, and the duty-free goods can include no more than 50 cigars, 200 cigarettes (one carton), two pounds of tobacco, or 1.1 liters of alcohol (you must be at least 16 years old to bring any tobacco products into the country, and liquor can be carried in only if you meet the age requirements of the province of your port of return). Anything above the duty-free allowance is taxed: 20% for goods which accompany you, more for shipped items. You can send gifts up to a value of CDN$40 duty-free but again, you cannot mail alcohol or tobacco. More detailed information is found in the pamphlets *I Declare* and *Bon Voyage, But—,* available from the **Canadian Department of External Affairs,** Ottawa, Ontario, K1A 0G2, Canada.

As an Australian citizen, your allowance upon returning home is 200 cigarettes (one carton), 250 grams of cigars *or* 250 grams of tobacco, and one liter of alcohol. You are allowed to bring in up to AUS$200 worth of goods duty-free; the next AUS$160 worth will be taxed at 20%. If you are under age 18, your allowance is AUS$100; the next AUS$80 will be taxed at 20%. You can mail back personal property; mark it "Australian goods returned" to avoid duty. You may not mail unsolicited gifts duty-free. For further information see the brochure *Australian Customs Information,* available from the **Department of Industry and Commerce,** Canberra, A.C.T. 2600, Australia.

New Zealand customs regulations are quite extensive and enforced very strictly. Only those aged 17 and older may bring tobacco or alcohol into the country. The concession is 200 cigarettes (one carton) or 250 grams of tobacco or 50 cigars or a combination of all three not weighing more than 250 grams. You may also bring in 4.5 liters of beer or wine, and 1.125 liters of spirits or liqueurs. Each person may bring goods up to a total value of NZ$500 duty-free. Children may claim this concession. However, goods must be intended for personal use or as unsolicited gifts. Persons traveling together may not combine individual concessions.

The U.S., Canada, Australia, and New Zealand prohibit or restrict the importation of firearms, explosives, ammunition, fireworks, controlled drugs, many plants and animals, lottery tickets, and obscene literature and films. To avoid problems in carrying prescription drugs, make sure the bottles are clearly marked and have a copy of the prescription to show the customs officer.

> *Let's Go* uses the terminology **B.C.E.** (Before Common Era) and **C.E.** (Common Era), which are the historical equivalents of B.C. (Before Christ) and A.D. (Anno Domini).

Helping Let's Go

We receive thousands of suggestions from our readers each year. We read *every* piece of correspondence, whether a 10-page letter or a postcard, and our researcher/writers use the information in putting together the next year's edition. (Please note that mail received after April 15, 1988, will probably be too late for the 1989 book, but will be retained for the following edition.) *Let's Go* does not want to list hotels, restaurants, or any other institutions that discriminate on the basis of race or religion. If you are witness to, or a victim of, such discrimination, please write and let us know. You may also complete the readership survey enclosed. To share your discoveries with our readers and help us improve *Let's Go,* please send a card or letter to:

To The Editor
Let's Go: Europe
Harvard Student Agencies, Inc.
Thayer Hall-B
Harvard University
Cambridge, MA 02138 U.S.A.

In addition to the invaluable travel advice our readers share with us, many are kind enough to offer their services as researchers. Unfortunately, the charter of Harvard Student Agencies permits us to employ only currently enrolled Harvard-Radcliffe students as research or as editorial staff.

Parting Words

Always remember, especially in out-of-the-way places, that you are a representative of your country and a guest in others'. Your hosts' impressions of your home country will be shaped to a great degree by their encounter with you. By talking with the people you meet you'll allow them to understand your country a little better. A little graciousness on your part may be repaid with an inordinate degree of hospitality. If you cannot take the time to learn the language, learn at least one phrase: *thank you.* The most important parting words we can give you are the parting words you should use to express your appreciation of European hospitality.

Arabic	*shukran*
Basque	*eskerrik asko*
Bulgarian	*blagodarya*
Catalan	*gràcies*
Czech	*děkuji*
Danish	*tak*
Dutch	*dank u wel*
Finnish	*kiitos*
French	*merci*
Gaelic	*go raibh maith agat*
German	*danke*
Greek	*efharisto*
Hebrew	*todah*
Hungarian	*köszönöm*
Icelandic	*tokk fyrir*
Italian	*grazie*
Luxembourgish	*merci*
Norwegian	*takk*
Polish	*dziękuję*
Portuguese	*obrigado*
Romanian	*mulţumesc*
Russian	*spasibo*
Serbo-Croatian	*hvala*
Spanish	*gracias*
Swedish	*tack*
Turkish	*teşekkur*

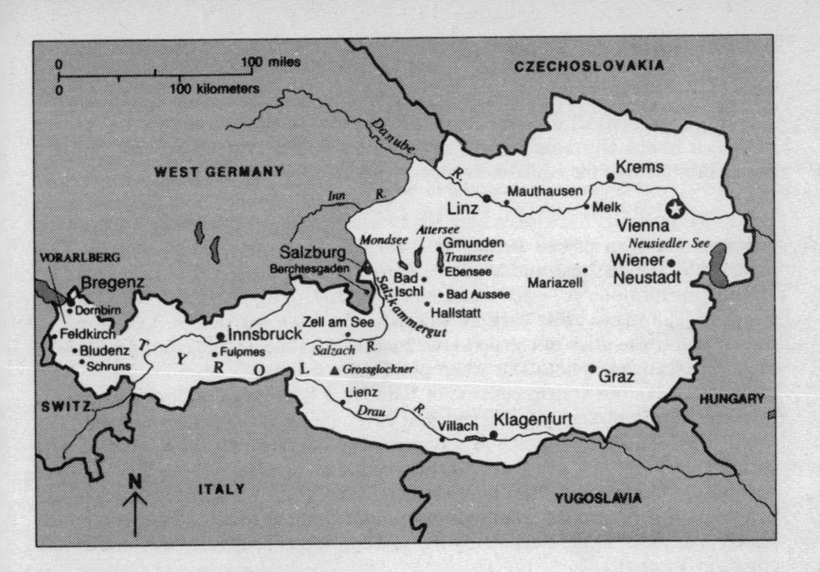

AUSTRIA

US$1 = 12.82 schilling (AS)	**10AS = US$0.78**
CDN$1 = 9.71AS	**10AS = CDN$1.03**
UK£1 = 20.83AS	**10AS = UK£0.48**
AUS$1 = 9.04AS	**10AS = AUS$1.11**

This small alpine country, more mountainous even than Switzerland, once held an empire that stretched from Venice to parts of France and included Northern Italy and much of Central Europe. Throughout the eighteenth and nineteenth century, Vienna was the undisputed capital of European music: Haydn, Mozart, Beethoven, Brahms, Schubert, Strauss, Mahler, and Schönberg are only the most illustrious of the great musicians who called Vienna their home (on a less refined note, *Silent Night, Holy Night* was also written here—by Austrian Francis Gruber).

Austrians are Germanic, and this land was once a frontier of Germanic culture ("Austria" derives from "Ostland" (East-land)—the lands east of Bavaria). When nationalism became the rage in the late nineteenth century, the Hapsburgs in Vienna began to lose their grip on their ethnically distinct hinterlands, and the Empire began to fall apart. World War I (itself initiated by a nationalist struggle within the Austro-Hungarian Empire) was the final straw, and the Treaty of Versailles left the new state of Austria a mere shadow of its powerful past. Sentiment for unification with Germany (*anschluss*) was strong, and Hitler had little difficulty engineering the rise of the Austrian Nazi sympathizers in the Depression-weakened Austria of the late 1930s. This part of Austria's past has recently come back to haunt it—the election of Kurt Waldheim to the Austrian Presidency sparked loud protest concerning crimes committed by Waldheim as a Nazi officer in Yugoslavia.

Transportation

Rail travel in Austria is expensive (Vienna-Innsbruck, 5½ hr., 570AS; Vienna-Salzburg, 3½ hr., 328AS). If you're not carrying Eurail or InterRail (3200AS), there are several options. For anyone under 26, the **Austria Ticket** is the best deal. It covers all second-class trains, post buses, and Danube steamers (in Austria), and gives reductions on other cruises and many cable cars. It costs 950AS for nine days,

1350AS for 16 days. The **Bundes-Netzkarte**—the over-26 version of the Austria Ticket—costs 1440AS for nine days, 1960AS for 16 days, and 3100AS for one month. It covers all trains, railway-operated boats, and Danube steamers, but not buses. Both tickets are available at major train stations and travel agencies in Austria.

Seniors (men over 65, women over 60) are entitled to half-price tickets in Austria, but must show an official **Reduction Card** (*Halbpreis-Karte für Senioren*). This card—valid for one year and available at major post offices and train stations for 160AS—entitles you to a 50% discount on trains, long-distance buses, Danube steamers, and many cable cars. Newlyweds who have married in Austria get to travel two-for-the-price-of-one up to two months after the wedding; bring your marriage certificate and photo IDs when purchasing tickets.

The Austrian bus system consists of **Bahn-** and **Post-buses** (orange and yellow, respectively). Both are very efficient and cover mountain areas not accessible by train. They cost about as much as trains; neither InterRail nor Eurail is valid. The occasional private bus company will take the passes, and the Austria Ticket covers post buses. All Austrian cities have excellent tram and/or bus systems; tickets are bought on board, or often from a *Tabak Trafik* booth at reduced rates. You must punch your ticket at the start of any trip (except tickets bought from Automat machines in Vienna).

Hitching varies in quality within Austria; generally it is easiest to get a ride on the well-traveled valley roads in the west. For longer inter-city routes, you could make things easier on yourself by contacting a **Mitfahrzentrale.** Companies charge roughly half the going rail fare to connect you with somebody traveling by car in your direction (Vienna-Salzburg 200AS versus 328AS by train; Vienna-Innsbruck 240AS versus 570AS by train). They have offices in Vienna and Innsbruck, and also make pairings for international trips. Beware of waiting lists during peak seasons.

The Danube flows down from West Germany through Austria, into Czechoslovakia and Hungary. Steamers and hydrofoils of the Austrian company **Erste Donau Dampfschiffahrts-Gesellschaft** sail upstream and downstream from Vienna, respectively. (For steamer routes and prices, see the Danube section.) Hydrofoils to Bratislava, Czechoslovakia and Budapest, Hungary are not cheap (Bratislava 490AS round-trip; Budapest 940AS round-trip), but they are fast and nicer than the trains. (Railpasses not honored on these routes.)

About 100 Austrian rail stations rent bikes from April to October. Bikes can be returned to any participating station, and cost 70AS per day—half price if you have a train ticket *to* the station from which you are renting, and have arrived on the day of rental. Pick up the list (*Fahrrad am Bahnhof*) of participating stations at any station. The eastern part of the country is flatter; the Salzkammergut and Tyrol reward effort with dramatic scenery. Tourist offices have regional maps of bike routes. **Austria Tourist Information,** the national tourist board, will give you a *Radfahren in Österreich,* a free, large, high-quality cycling map of Austria. Contact their office in Vienna, at Margaretenstr. 1 (tel. 58 72 00; open Mon.-Fri. 9am-5:30pm). Drivers may want to avoid *Autobahns* (E-roads) and some alpine roads, as tolls range as high as 5AS per kilometer.

Practical Information

Local tourist offices (*Verkehrsbüro* or *Verkehrsverein*) are uniformly very efficient, and most will help with room-finding. The Austrian Alps are as readily accessible as they are beautiful, thanks to the activities of various alpine associations. These organizations maintain more than 700 mountain huts, with a total of about 25,000 *Schlafplätze* (some mattresses where you can put your sleeping bag and yourself, others actual beds). Not much equipment is required for a tour that uses these mountain refuges; most serve meals, and all have some cooking facilities. Prices for an overnight stay vary from 50AS to 150AS, and no reservations are necessary; if they're crowded, you may end up sleeping on a cot, but you won't be turned away.

Before you begin a walking tour, ask at the local alpine society (which you can find in the phone book under "*Alpenverein*") about refuges along the route. The ordinary tourist office is another source for this information, as are the numerous branches of the *Alpine Auskunft* (mountain information) organization, also in the phone book. Topographic maps *(Alpenvereinskarten),* available in most bookstores, show hut locations.

Those planning extensive walking tours of the Austrian Alps may want to purchase a membership in the largest of the alpine associations, the **Österreichischer Alpenverein.** (375AS, ages under 26 250AS.) This will entitle you to a 30-60% reduction and preferential treatment at their refuges, all of which have beds. They have offices at Bäckerstr. 16, Vienna (tel. (222) 52 54 88), and at Wilhelm-Greil-Str. 15, Innsbruck 6020 (tel. (05222) 231 71). Even if you're only going for a day hike, find out about terrain and weather conditions. *Always* carry waterproof clothing and a little high-energy food, and wear decent footwear. If you get into serious trouble, use the *Alpinenotsignal* (Alpine Distress Signal), consisting of six audible or visual signals spaced evenly over one minute and followed by a break of one minute before repetition.

Western Austria is one of the world's best skiing regions. The areas around Innsbruck and Kitzbühel in the Tyrol are virtually saturated with lifts and runs. There's good skiing year-round on several glaciers, including the Stubaital near Innsbruck and the Dachstein in the Salzkammergut. All local tourist offices have extensive information on regional skiing. Youth hostels do not generally offer ski packages, but budget travel agencies in larger cities often do.

Communication should seldom be a problem; English is the most common second language, though in some remote regions you may encounter only German.

Banks throughout Austria are usually open Monday through Friday from 7:45am to 12:30pm and 2:15 to 4pm; in Vienna, most banks close at 3pm. Stores in Austria close Saturday afternoons and Sunday, while many museums take Monday off. Especially in the smaller towns, stores take most of the afternoon off for lunch, usually from noon to 3 or 4pm. Everything closes up tightly on religious holidays, which include Epiphany (Jan. 6), Assumption (Aug. 15), All Saint's (Nov. 1), and Immaculate Conception (Dec. 8); and on Austrian National Day (Oct. 26).

Poste Restante may also be addressed *Postlagernde Briefe.* You can make international phone calls at telephone centers (usually only in the larger cities), in most post offices, and from pay phones. For a police emergency anywhere in Austria, dial 133; to summon an ambulance, dial 144. When using a payphone, you must push the red button when your party answers.

Accommodations, Camping, and Food

Rooms in Austria are almost always spotless and comfortable. Hotels are very expensive; smaller pensions and *Gasthäuser* are within the budget traveler's range, usually under 200AS per person anywhere but Vienna. Family-run establishments often include breakfast as well. Look for *Zimmer frei* or *Privat Zimmer* signs wherever you go; they advertise rooms in private houses, which are usually inexpensive (100-150AS per person). Hostels are fairly numerous in Austria; most are open to nonmembers, though a 20AS markup is standard. Campgrounds are least expensive, charging about 25AS per person. A dense network of alpine refuges accommodates those enjoying the Alps (see Practical Information).

Unless you're a real connoisseur of *Wurst,* Austrian food will sit better in your stomach than on your palate. The exception is the heavenly cake and pastry sold in the *Konditoreien* (bakeries) and in cafes. *Sacher torte* is a chocolate cake with the barest hint of marmalade. Back on earth, try *Bauernschmaus,* a variety of meats served with sauerkraut and an enormous *Knödel* (a bread or potato dumpling). *Gulasch* (a spicy beef stew), especially in eastern Austria, is almost always a hearty and cheap way to get some real meat into your stomach. The east is also famous for its white wine. Both reasonably priced and dry is Grüner Veltliner's *Klosterneuburger.* The Austrian beers are outstanding; try *Stiegl Bier,* a Salzburg brew. Austria imports lots of Budweiser beer (the real Czechoslovak thing, not the American attempt), which is a good sampling for those not venturing east of Austria.

Vienna (Wien)

Overwhelmingly cultured, Vienna is among Europe's treasures. The Hapsburgs, once rulers of half the continent, shaped sprawling palaces and gardens, heroic statuary, and a legacy of cosmopolitanism. Today Vienna carries its worldliness with assurance, secure in its best traditions—the elegant cafes, the boys' choir, the Royal Lipizzaner horses. Still one of the musical capitals of the world, the city of Beethoven, Schubert, and Strauss is also home to excellent museums and a flourishing club and theater scene.

Orientation and Practical Information

Vienna is in eastern Austria, within a few dozen kilometers of the borders of Czechoslovakia and Hungary. The core of historic Vienna is the area south of the old Danube called the **Ring,** bound by the roughly circular belt of *Ring*-roads. *Bezirk* (district) numbers precede each street address. Generally, 1 is everything inside the Ring; districts 2-9 are arranged clockwise around it, and any number above that is a long way out. Two channels have been cut for the Danube.

The meeting of the Opernring, the Kärntnerring, and Kärntnerstrasse, the main shopping drag, marks a center of activity and transit. Just below ground lies **Opernpassage,** and the main tourist office—a woefully small booth. Three of the four U-Bahn lines intersect at nearby **Karlsplatz.**

Tourist Offices: 1 Opernpassage (tel. 43 16 08 13). Room-finding service, currency exchange, city tours, and ticket information. Pick up their *Wiener Musiksommer* pamphlet, with a complete list of concerts; the excellent *Vienna Live,* for recreational, dining, and shopping information; and the *Netzplan,* a free map of the rapid transit system. Open daily 9am-7pm. Also at Westbahnhof and Südbahnhof (each open daily until at least 10pm), at Franz Josefs Bahnhof (open daily until 9pm), at the ship station by the Reichsbrücke (open May-Sept. daily 8am-9pm), and at the airport (open daily 9am-11pm, 9am-10pm in winter). The city information office in the *Rathaus* provides information on cultural events, though their English is limited. Open Mon.-Fri. 9:30am-6pm. **Austrian National Information:** Österreich Information, Margaretenstr. 1 (tel. 587 20 00). Open Mon.-Fri. 9am-5pm.

Budget Travel: ÖKISTA, 9 Türkenstr. 4-6 (tel. 347 52 60). Flight and BIGE tickets, accommodations (no commission), and general help. Newsy bulletin boards with personal ads. Open Mon.-Fri. 9:30am-5:30pm. **ÖS Reisen** (Austrian Student Travel), 1 Reichstratstr. 13 (tel. 42 15 61), deals mostly with transportation. Cheap train, flight, and bus tickets. Open Mon.-Fri. 9:30am-5:30pm. BIGE tickets also sold at the **Verkehrsbüro,** 1 Opernring 5 (tel. 588 00). Open Mon.-Fri. 8:30am-5:30pm, Sat. 9am-noon.

American Express: 1 Kärntnerstr. 21-23 (tel. 515 40). Mail held. All banking services. Open Mon.-Fri. 9am-5:30pm, Sat. 9am-noon.

Currency Exchange: Banks are open Mon.-Fri. 8am-3pm. When banks are closed, all information offices will change money (until 7pm at Opernpassage, 10pm at Westbahnhof and Südbahnhof, and 9pm at Franz-Josefs Bahnhof, which only exchanges currency).

Post Office: 1 Fleischmarkt 19. Open 24 hours, as are the post offices at Westbahnhof, Südbahnhof, and Franz-Josefs Bahnhof. **Telephones** and telegraph also available at these 4 offices. Poste Restante at Fleischmarkt (send to Postlagernde Briefe, 1 Fleischmarkt 19, A-1010, Wien). **Postal codes:** Within the first district (ring) 1010, in the second 1020, in the third 1030, in the fourth 1040, etc. (i.e. a 2-digit number always preceded by a "1" and followed by a "0").

Telephones: 1 Börseplatz 1 (near the Schottenring). Open daily 6am-midnight. Telegraphs here as well. **Telephone code:** 0222. Push the red button on pay phones to connect.

Flights: The airport **Wien Schwechat,** 19km out of town, is connected by regular bus service (50AS) to Westbahnhof, Südbahnhof, and the City Air Terminal (at the Hilton Hotel in third *Bezirk.* U-Bahn: Landestrasse.). Both buses stop running at 7pm.

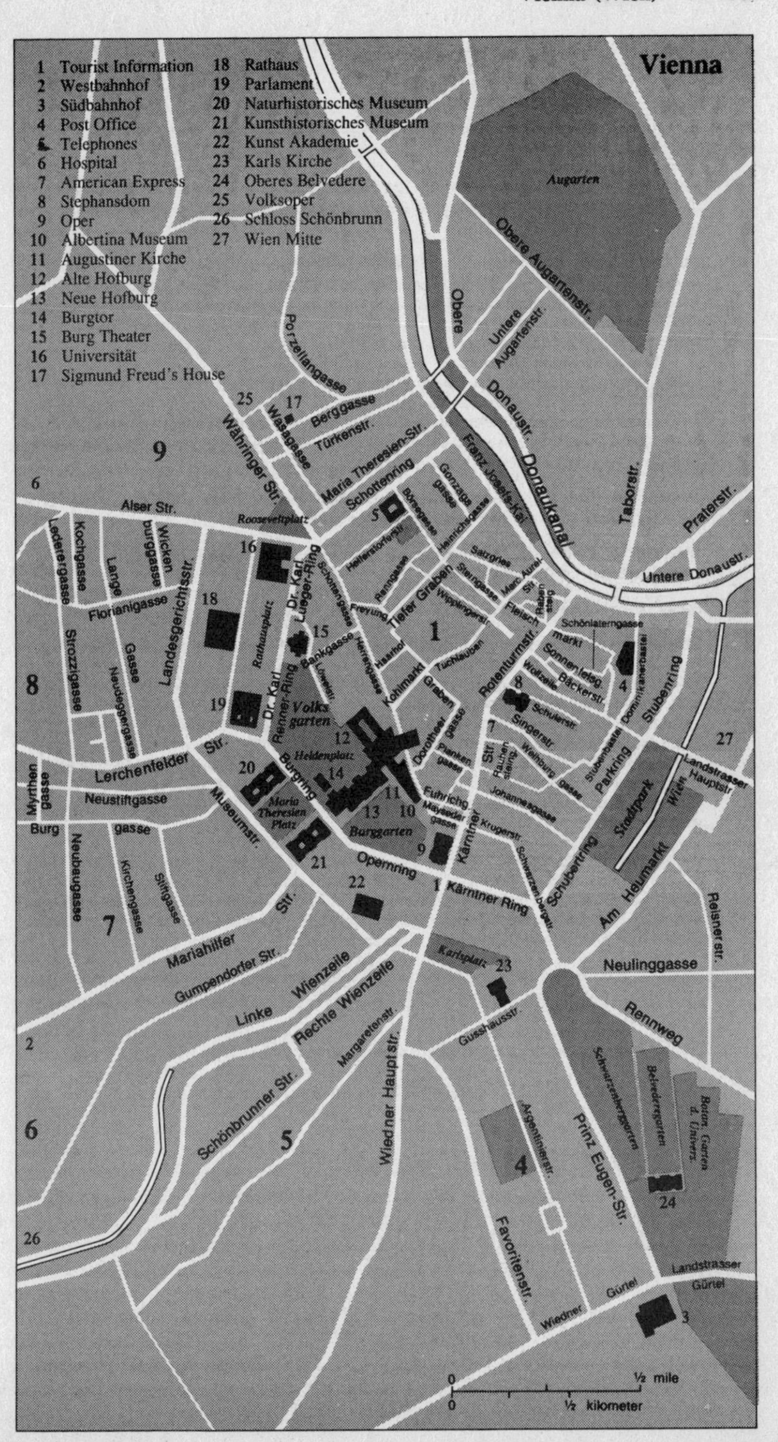
Vienna
1 Tourist Information
2 Westbahnhof
3 Südbahnhof
4 Post Office
5 Telephones
6 Hospital
7 American Express
8 Stephansdom
9 Oper
10 Albertina Museum
11 Augustiner Kirche
12 Alte Hofburg
13 Neue Hofburg
14 Burgtor
15 Burg Theater
16 Universität
17 Sigmund Freud's House
18 Rathaus
19 Parlament
20 Naturhistorisches Museum
21 Kunsthistorisches Museum
22 Kunst Akademie
23 Karls Kirche
24 Oberes Belvedere
25 Volksoper
26 Schloss Schönbrunn
27 Wien Mitte
Augarten
Obere Augartenstr.
Obere
Untere Augartenstr.
Donaustr.
Donaukanal
Franz Josefs-Kai
Porzellangasse
Berggasse
Türkenstr.
Maria Theresien-Str.
Schottenring
Währinger Str.
Alser Str.
Rooseveltplatz
Taborstr.
Praterstr.
Untere Donaustr.
Tiefer Graben
Rotenturmstr.
Stubenring
Landstrasser Hauptstr.
Stadtpark
Parkring
Am Heumarkt
Schubertring
Kärntner Ring
Kärntner Str.
Opernring
Burgring
Dr. Karl Renner-Ring
Dr. Karl Lueger-Ring
Volksgarten
Heldenplatz
Burggarten
Maria Theresien Platz
Museumstr.
Lerchenfelder Str.
Neustiftgasse
Burggasse
Landesgerichtsstr.
Florianigasse
Strozzigasse
Mariahilfer Str.
Gumpendorfer Str.
Linke Wienzeile
Rechte Wienzeile
Schönbrunner Str.
Wiedner Hauptstr.
Karlsplatz
Gusshausstr.
Neulinggasse
Rennweg
Prinz Eugen-Str.
Favoritenstr.
Argentinierstr.
Schwarzenbergplatz
Reisner str.
Landstrasser Gürtel
Wiedner Gürtel
½ mile
½ kilometer

Trains: There are 4 principal stations in Vienna. **Wien-Mitte,** in the center of town, handles commuter trains. **Franz-Josefs Bahnhof** has local trains, and 2 trains per day to Berlin via Prague (you need a Czechoslovakian transit visa, obtained in advance; unless you want to visit Czechoslovakia, it's easier to go through West Germany). Tram D (direction: Südbahnhof) will take you to the Ring. **Westbahnhof** sends trains to France, West Germany, Switzerland, the Netherlands, Belgium, the U.K., Bulgaria, Romania, Hungary, and western Austria. U-Bahn line 3 and tram #52 and 58 run to the Ring. **Südbahnhof** has trains to Italy, Yugoslavia, Greece, Czechoslovakia (through Bratislava), and (June-Sept.) Bulgaria and Hungary. Take tram D (direction: Nussdorf) to the Ring. Information (tel. 72 00). Open daily 6am-6pm.

Public Transportation: Vienna's huge public transportation system is thorough but complex; to exploit it properly, you should spend 5AS on a system map. The *Netzplan,* given free at tourist offices, shows rapid transit routes and a selection of tram routes. Buying a 72-hr. pass (92AS at transport and tourist offices) will simplify things, though it's not worthwhile if you plan to stick close to the center of town. Individual tickets cost 19AS; 65AS for a booklet of 5. Direct, necessary transfers are permitted. Tickets bought in booklets at Tabak-Trafik kiosks should be stamped at the start of a journey; singles sold by automat machines in U-Bahn stations need no validation. The best deal is an 8-day (Tage-Streifen) ticket for 200AS, which must be stamped for each rider every day. With this card, 4 people can ride for 2 days, 8 for 1, etc. The system shuts down shortly before midnight. Bus lines in the first district (marked "A") only run Mon.-Fri. 7am-8pm, Sat. 7am-2pm.

Boats: Boats dock at the Reichsbrücke on the New Danube; Take U-Bahn line 1 to get to the Ring. Daily trips on the Donau; railpasses valid.

Emergencies: Police (tel. 133); *Fremdenpolizei* headquarters at Bäckerstr. 13 (tel. 63 06 71). **Ambulance** (tel. 144); at night (tel. 55 00).

Medical Assistance: General Hospital, 9 Alserstr. 4 (tel. 48 00).

Embassies: U.S., Gartenbaupromenade 2 (tel. 514 51), off Parkring. **Canada,** 10 Karl-Lueger 1 (tel. 63 36 91). **U.K.,** 3 Reisnerstr. 40 (tel. 75 61 17). **Australia,** 4 Mattiellistr. 2-4 (tel. 52 85 80). **New Zealand,** 1 Lugeck 1 (tel. 52 66 36). **Spain,** 4 Argentinierstr. 34 (tel. 65 91 66). **Bulgaria,** 4 Schwindgasse 8 (tel. 65 64 44); 7-working-day visa wait. **Czechoslovakia,** 14 Penzingerstr. 11-13 (tel. 89 31 12); 3-hr. visa wait. **East Germany,** 13 Auhofstr. 28-30 (tel. 82 36 54); 1-week visa wait. **Hungary,** 1 Bankgasse 4-6 (tel. 63 26 31); 2-day visa wait. **Poland,** 13 Hauptstr. 42c (tel. 82 74 44); 2-week visa wait. **Yugoslavia,** Salmgasse 4 (tel. 712 12 05), 2-day visa wait. **Romania,** Prinz-Eugen Str. 60 (tel. 505 23 43), 2-day visa wait. Most open Mon.-Fri. mornings; visa applicants should arrive early—usually 8-9am—and as early in the week as possible.

Bookstores: Bücher Gerold, 1 Am Graben 31 (tel. 52 22 35), for the very latest. Open Mon.-Fri. 8:30am-6pm, Sat. 8:30am-12:30pm. **Shakespeare and Co.,** 1 Sterngasse 2 (tel. 66 43 76), for scholarly works and the arts; will take trade-ins. Open Mon.-Fri. 9am-6pm, Sat. 9am-1pm. **Penguin English Bookshop,** 1 Plankengasse 7 (tel. 52 37 01), has a wide selection of classics. Open Mon.-Fri. 9am-6pm, Sat. 9am-12:30pm.

Laundry: Wäscherei Miele, at the corner of 8 Lerchenfelderstr. and 8 Neudeggerstr. Open Mon.-Fri. 8am-6pm, Sat. 8am-midnight. Also at the corner of Porzellangasse and Seegasse. Open Mon.-Fri. 7:30am-6pm, wash and dry 90AS.

Hitchhiking: For Salzburg, go to the western end of the U4 subway and look for the highway that feeds into the *Autobahn* about 10km farther out. Southbound, try the traffic circle near Laaerberg (tram #67). **Mitfahrzentrale Wien,** 5 Franzensgasse 11 (tel. 56 41 74), matches drivers and riders.

Accommodations and Camping

In summer, you are strongly advised to reserve in advance. Late June, before the student dormitories open, is the worst time. Once you've exhausted all the student accommodations, you might turn to the **Zimmernachweis** service for help; there is one at each tourist office. They charge a nonrefundable fee of 25AS to set you up in a room, not always one of the cheapest. They also handle private homes (min. stay 3 days) in the 150AS range, but many of these are out in the suburbs. **ÖKISTA,** sometimes more price conscious (see Budget Travel), also finds rooms and does not charge commission. It may be best to avoid the fees and often lengthy lines at these agencies by calling hotels from the station yourself (most hotel proprietors speak English). If they are full, ask for suggestions—don't waste time tramping from hotel to hotel. For other reasonable suggestions, turn to the "*Saisonhotels*" section of the Vienna hotel pamphlet, or the "Accommodations" page of the tourist office's *Vienna Live.* The tourist office also has a listing of dormitories and youth hostels in *Wien Herbergen.* Reject offers of rooms or short-term apartment rentals made at the station. These deals often have hidden costs, and, being illegal, leave the duped party no recourse.

Hostels and Dormitories

Catholic College Association, Ebendorferstr. 8 (tel. 48 35 87), owns 5 dormitories with clean, adequate rooms available to anyone for about 160AS per person. Open July-Sept. Call ahead.

Myrthengasse (IYHF), 7 Myrthengasse 7 (tel. 93 63 16), just outside the Ring off Burggasse. From Westbahnhof there are two options: Take tram #52 or 58, get off at Zollergasse, and take bus #13A to Kellermanngasse; or, take tram #8 to Burggasse, then bus #48A to Neubaugasse, walk back about 50m, and it's on the first road on the right. About a 25-min. trip. A beautifully renovated building with enthusiastic management. All the amenities, including convenient location. Reservations essential. Members 130AS, nonmembers 160AS. Breakfast included. Check-in 7:30am-midnight. Lockout 9am-1pm. Luggage storage open all day. Midnight curfew. Facilities for the disabled (elevators, showers). Open year-round.

Hütteldorf-Hacking (IYHF), 13 Schlossberggasse 8 (tel. 82 15 01). Out of the way but entirely worth it. Tower design (great view) and a huge, sunny yard. From Südbahnhof take U-Bahn line 1 to Karlsplatz, then U-4 to Hütteldorf, cross the footbridge and follow the signs. From Westbahnhof, take tram #58 to Hietzing, then the U-4 to Hütteldorf, or take the S-50 train (Eurailpasses valid) to Hütteldorf (last train, 10:15pm). Whichever way, a 30- to 40-min. trip. May have space when others are full. Members only. 110AS. Sheets, showers, and breakfast included. Check-in 7am-11:30pm. Lockout 9am-4pm. Curfew 11:45pm. Open year-round.

Brigittenau (IYHF), 20 Friedrich-Engels-Platz 24 (tel. 33 82 94 or 33 82 46). Your last choice among the hostels. Big and adequate, but a 35-min. bus ride from the center, and often filled with raucous pre-teens. Take tram #8 from Westbahnhof to Nussdorfstr., then bus #34A or 35A to Friedrich-Engels-Platz. From Südbahnhof, take tram D to Liechtenwerder Platz, then bus #34A or 35A. Members 130AS, nonmembers 160AS. Sheets, showers, and breakfast included. Check-in 6-10pm. Lockout 9am-4pm. Midnight curfew. Open year-round.

Porzellaneum der Wiener Universität, 9 Porzellangasse 30 (tel. 34 72 82). From Südbahnhof, take tram D towards Nussdorf, get off at the Fürstengasse stop. From Westbahnhof, take tram #5 to Franz-Josefs Bahnhof, then tram D (direction: Südbahnhof) to Fürstengasse. A 15- to 20-min. trip. Nice and quiet, with renovated rooms, a lovely courtyard, and a considerate staff. 125AS per person, in singles or doubles. Sheets and showers included. Kitchen facilities. No curfew. Open July-Sept. Often full, so call ahead.

Haus Pfeilheim, in the Hotel Avis, 8 Pfeilgasse 6 (tel. 438 47 62). From Südbahnhof, take bus #13A up Strozzigasse. From Westbahnhof, take tram #8 to Lerchenfelderstr., then tram #46 to Strozzigasse. Walk left onto Pfeilgasse. A 20-min. trip. Sparkling new rooms in a good location, run by helpful students of the Hotel Academia. A large, bare facility with 400 beds. Singles 190AS, doubles, triples, or quads 165AS. Breakfast included. Check-in 24 hours. Open June-Aug.

Hostel Zöhrer, 8 Skodagasse 26 (tel. 43 07 30), just off Alserstr. Take bus #13A from Südbahnhof, tram #5 from Westbahnhof, tram #43 or 44 from along the ring. Dingy showers but big, sunny dorm rooms. Often has space when others are full. 110AS. Sheets, showers, and kitchen use included. Breakfast 20AS. Check-in 9:30am-10pm. No curfew.

Hotels and Pensions

To reserve a room it is usually sufficient to call a few days ahead, but the truly cautious may feel better writing.

Pension Kraml, 6 Brauergasse 5 (tel. 587 85 88), just off Gumpendorferstr. Take bus #57 along Gumpendorferstr. From Westbahnhof, walk down Mariahilferstr., take the third right onto Otto-Bauer-Str., first left, and first right. A 15-min. trip. Tidy, comfortable, new, and run by a friendly family. The hallways and larger rooms are better-kept than the singles. Singles 210AS, doubles from 380AS. Doubles with shower 590AS. 120AS per extra person. Breakfast included. Call first, as it's often full.

Pension Wild, 8 Lange Gasse 10 (tel. 43 51 74), just outside the Ring, very close to Pfeilgasse. From Westbahnhof, take tram #52 or 58 Mariahilferstr., and then U-Bahn 2 to its terminus at Lerchenfelderstr.; Lange Gasse is 1 block up on the right. From Südbahnhof, take U-Bahn

1 to Karlsplatz, then U-Bahn 2 to Lerchenfelderstr. A 15- to 20-min. trip. Unspectacular rooms, but a good location. Kitchen facilities and nice young management. Singles 190AS, doubles 330AS, triples 450AS. Breakfast 30AS.

Hotel zum Goldenen Bären, 9 Türkenstr. 27 (tel. 34 51 11), just outside the Ring, close to the Danube canal. From Südbahnhof, take tram D to Schlichgasse. From Westbahnhof, take tram #52 or 58 to the Ring, then tram D. A 20-min. trip. Singles 150AS, doubles 250AS, 80AS per extra person. Shower 35AS. Often full, so reserve.

Pension Columbia, 8 Kochgasse 9 (tel. 42 67 57), just off Alserstr. From Südbahnhof, take tram D to Schottenring, then tram #43 or 44 down Alserstr. From Westbahnhof, take tram #52 or 58 to the Ring, then tram D, then #43 or 44. A 25-min. trip. An elegant Viennese experience; large rooms with lots of light in a polished building. Doubles 470-510AS, triples 630-690AS, quads 760-820AS, the more expensive rooms with private shower. Some singles (290-310AS) Nov.-March only. Breakfast (until noon) included.

Pension Adria, 8 Wickenburggasse 23 (tel. 42 02 38), near the university. Central location and luxurious rooms: armchairs, radios, and some TVs. Take tram D from Südbahnhof, or catch it along the Ring. At Schottenring take tram #43 or 44, or walk a few blocks up Alserstr. A 20-min. trip. Singles from 350AS, doubles 400-600AS, triples 800AS, quads 1000AS. Breakfast included. Reservations recommended.

Irmgard Lauria, 7 Kaiserstr. 77-78 (tel. 96 31 53 or 93 41 52), an easy walk from Westbahnhof. Modern rooms with TVs and dishes. The owner may meet you up at the station. Doubles 450AS, with shower 600AS. "Family rooms" (4-6 people) 150AS per person, with private shower 180AS. Discounts on stays of 3 or more nights. Nearby and run by the same family is **Franz Schubert,** Esterhazygasse 32 (tel. 56 85 31). Newly renovated. Student room with TV and no breakfast 200AS; rooms (2-5 persons) with breakfast served in the room 350AS. Open mid-Feb. to Oct. daily until 8pm.

Camping

Campgrounds are all out in the suburbs. Prices are about 44AS per person plus 42AS per tent for the first night. **Wien-West I and II,** at Hüttelbergstr. 40 and 80 (tel. 94 14 49 and 94 23 14), respectively, are the most convenient (both in the fourteenth *Bezirk* about 6km out of the city center). I is open from June through September, II year-round. II also has four-person bungalows to rent (312AS). For either, take U-Bahn 4 to the end, then switch to bus #52B.

Food

Viennese cuisine derives from the city's former imperial position, and its specialties betray the influence of Eastern Europe; try *Serbische Bohnensuppe* (Servian bean soup) and *Goulash* (spicy beef stew). Even the famed *Wiener Schnitzel* (fried pork or veal with bread crumbs) is something of an import, having originated in Milan. *Wurst* stands offer tasty and inexpensive fare: a good, mildly spicy variety is *Debrecziner* (18AS). Remember that Vienna is world-renowned for its desserts—unbelievably rich, although you may not be after you pay for them.

Preparing your own fare is an enjoyment here with hundreds of small, specialized markets. For supermarket convenience and prices, try any **sparmarkt** or **supermarkt** outside district 1.

Restaurants

Sobieski, 7 Burggasse 83, a 5-min. ride on bus #48 from the Burgring. Superb meals in a friendly, romantic atmosphere. Unobtrusive and kind host. The *menu* (*Schnitzel* with soup; or meat with sauce, noodles, and soup) is a real bargain at 45AS. Open Mon.-Fri. 11am-10pm.

Budra, 1 Naglergasse 1, in the heart of Vienna. A fine combination of formal atmosphere and good food. Cold entrees for 45AS, and warm entrees and meat dishes for 60-70AS. Try the spiced rice with meat (60AS), or the mixed meat dish, farmer's style (70AS). Open Wed.-Mon. 11:30am-2:30pm and 6:30pm-12:30am. Live gypsy music Wed.-Mon. at 7:30pm.

Gasthaus Schmidt, 7 Neubaugasse 52. From the Burgring, take bus #48A until it stops at Neubaugasse—a 5-min. ride. You'll stand in line for an hour, but the bigger-than-your-plate *Schnitzel* for 48AS is hard to resist. Open Mon.-Sat. 11:30am-2pm and 5:30-10pm. Closed 3 weeks in Aug.

Tunnel, 8 Florianigasse 39. Take the U-2 to Landesgerichtstr. and walk opposite the *Rathaus.* A 3-story student pub with tasty meals at very low cost (25-70AS), live music, and lots of locals. Open daily 11am-2am.

Rembetiko, Porzellangasse 38. Take tram D to Fürstengasse. Outstanding meat, fish, and Greek specialties (65-130AS). Try their pork *souvlaki,* served with rice, vegetable, fries, and *tzaziki,* for 65AS. Lunch *menu* (meat and soup) 58AS. Open daily 11:30am-3pm and 5:30pm-midnight.

Ring Restaurant, Währingerstr. 33-35. Take tram #37, 38, 40, or 41 from Schottenring. Sleek interior and scrupulously prepared vegetarian dishes. The dinner *menu* (soup, stuffed vegetables, and potatoes) is 105AS. Open daily 9am-11pm. Up Währingerstr. 2 blocks is the **Vegetarian Restaurant,** with a solid daily *menu* for 84AS. Open only for lunch Mon.-Fri. 11:30am-2:30pm.

Trzesniewski, 1 Dorotheergasse 1 (tel. 52 32 91). A famous stand-up sandwich restaurant. (Franz Kafka used to pick up a bite here.) They've been serving open-face delicacies for over 75 years. Sandwiches (the size of tea sandwiches) around 6AS. Open Mon.-Fri. 9am-7:30pm, Sat. 9am-1pm.

Cafes and Konditoreien

The cafe is an integral part of Vienna's unhurried charm. Go to the counter to choose a piece of cake before sitting down; either you'll pay for it immediately and give your receipt to the server when you order beverages, or you'll at least know what to ask for. The server, in any case, brings you your pastry. Coffee can be ordered in any number of ways: *Schwarzer* is black, *Brauner* has a little milk, *Melange* is light, and *Mazagron* is iced and contains rum. The many outdoor cafes along Kärntnerstrasse are great for people-watching but expensive. On the other hand, cafes outside the mainstream (generally beyond the Ring) may sell sweets gone stale; the freshest stuff is often where the people are.

Sperl, 6 Gumpendorferstr. 11, hasn't been altered since the days when the Vienna art nouveau circle gathered here—marble tables, mahogany chairs, mirrors, chandeliers, and ornate ceilings. A trip to the turn of the century. Coffee 25AS, cake 22AS. Open Mon.-Sat. 7am-llpm.

Cafe Hawelka, 1 Dorotheergasse 6, just off Graben. Formerly a hangout for artists, intellectuals, and radicals. Trotsky may—or may not—have been a regular. After 10pm, ask for *warme Büchteln,* sweet rolls filled with preserves. Open Wed.-Mon. until 2am.

Demel, 1 Kohlmarkt 14. The most famous bakery in Austria. Take tram #52 or 58. Cakes arranged like jewels amid mahogany and brass. Shoot your budget to hell and send your taste buds to paradise. Salads about 100AS, cold meals 70-170AS, hot meals 75-155AS, cake 42AS. Open Mon.-Sat. 9am-7pm, Sun. 10am-7pm.

Hotel Sacher, 1 Philharmoniker str. 4, behind the Staatsoper. This historic sight has been serving its world-famous *Sacher Torte* (a delicious chocolate-peach cake, 45AS) for years. Open until 11:30pm.

For the best ice cream, stand in line at **Eissalon Schwedenplatz,** Franz-Josef-Kai 17, right next to the canal. Their product is considerably less sweet than elsewhere. (Open late March-Sept. Mon.-Sat. 10am-11pm, Sun. noon-11pm.)

Sights

Individual museum tickets usually cost 15AS, and 150AS will buy you a book of 14. On Friday mornings, admission to municipal museums is free. Admission to the national museums is always free for students, and on Saturdays and Sundays from September through April for the general public. To distinguish between national and municipal museums, pick up the pamphlet *Museums Vienna* at the tourist office.

Begin exploring Vienna at the Gothic **Stephansdom,** in the center of the city on Stephansplatz. This magnificent cathedral is covered with sculpture, and its smoothly tapering, lace-in-stone spire has become a symbol of Vienna. Next to an elevator ascending the north tower is the entrance to the catacombs, the final resting place of the Hapsburg family. Young people of all nationalities can be found outside the cathedral on the benches all day and into the evening. Once you've surveyed the city, walk down **Kärntnerstrasse,** the main shopping street, to the **Staatsoper,** 1 Opernring 2, home of the Vienna State Opera. You can take a tour of the glittering gold, crystal, and red-velvet interior. Check the side of the Staatsoper house for listings of rehearsals and tours. (Tours July-Aug. daily at 10am, 11am, 1pm, 2pm, and 3pm; Sept.-Oct. and May-June daily at 1pm, 2pm, and 3pm; Nov.-April daily at 2pm and 3pm. Admission 30AS, students 20AS.)

From the Staatsoper, follow Opernring around to the squat, Roman-looking **Burgtor,** which marks the entrance to the enormous complex of the **Hofburg** (Imperial Palace). The staggering concave facade is one of Fischer von Erlach's greatest works. The steps provide a splendid view of heroic statuary against a background of city spires. Inside is the **National Bibliothek,** 1 Josefsplatz 1 (tel. 533 70 26), with spectacular rooms adorned with frescoes and various temporary exhibitions. (Open May-Oct. Mon.-Sat. 10am-4pm; Nov.-April Mon.-Sat. 11am-noon.)

Next door, in the carriageway covered by a huge dome, is the entrance to the grand gilt rooms of the **Imperial Apartments.** (Open Mon.-Sat. 8:30am-4pm, Sun. 8:30am-12:30pm. Tours 25AS, students 10AS.) Normally housed here also, the **Schatzkammer** (royal treasury) is scheduled to re-open in 1988; the crown jewels and other treasures are temporarily on display in the Kunsthistorisches Museum (see below). The section of the palace known as the **Stallburg** (enter from Josefsplatz) houses some of Vienna's most famous residents, the Royal Lipizzaner stallions of the **Spanish Riding School** (Spanische Reitschule). Their performances are always sold out; you must reserve tickets six months in advance. (Write to Spanische Reitschule, Hofburg, A-1010 Wien. If you reserve through a travel agency, you'll pay a hefty surcharge. Write only for reservations; no money will be accepted. Tickets 200-600AS, standing room 135-150AS.) Watching the horses train is almost more fun. (Mid-Feb. to late Feb. Mon.-Sat. 10am-noon; March-June, Sept.-late Oct., and Nov. to mid-Dec. Tues.-Sat. 10am-noon, except when the horses tour. Tickets sold at the door from about 8:30am. Admission 40AS, children 10AS. No reservations.) True enthusiasts may want to make the pilgrimage to the breeding farm at Bieber, near Graz. The other part of the Stallburg contains a special gallery, **Neue Gallerie,** part of the Kunsthistorisches Museum.

From the palace, walk across the **Volksgarten,** with its hundreds of labeled varieties of rose, to reach the impressive, sculpture-adorned **Parliament** building—a true gilded lily of neoclassicism. Just up Karl-Renner-Ring is the **Rathaus,** an intriguing remnant of late nineteenth-century Neo-Gothic with Victorian mansard roofs.

Just south of the palace on Maria-Theresien-Platz is the magnificent and famous **Kunsthistorisches Museum,** home to one of the best art collections in the world, including entire rooms of prime Breughels, Vermeer's *Allegory of Painting,* and numerous works by each of Rembrandt, Rubens, Titian, Dürer, and Velásquez, to name but the most famous. Cellini's famous golden salt cellar is here, and there is a superb collection of ancient art, an entire Egyptian burial chamber, and vast numbers of antique musical instruments and weapons. (Open Tues.-Fri. 10am-6pm, Sat.-Sun. 9am-6pm. Tours on Tues. and Fri.; reserve 2 weeks in advance by calling (0222) 93 44 48. Admission 45AS, students 20AS.)

The **Museum Moderner Kunst** (Museum of Modern Art) in Liechtenstein Palace at 9 Fürstengasse 1, has a strong collection of mostly American art, including works by Frank Stella, Andy Warhol, Roy Lichtenstein, and Julian Schnabel. Take tram D. (Open Wed.-Mon. 10am-6pm. Admission 30AS, students 15AS.) Special exhibits are held at the **Museum des 20. Jahrhunderts** (Museum of the Twentieth Century), 3 Schweizer Garten, near Südbahnhof. (Open Thurs.-Tues. 10am-6pm. Admission 30AS, students 15AS.)

If you still have an appetite for art after these, visit the **Albertina,** 1 Augustinerstr. 1 (tel. 52 42 32). This is perhaps the best drawing collection in the world, with 200,000 original etchings and prints and 20,000 drawings and watercolors, including works by Dürer, Michelangelo, Rembrandt, and Rubens—though only facsimiles of the real treasures are displayed. Prince Charles had a special showing of the originals; if you're feeling royal, you can write to request one yourself. (Open Sept.-June Mon.-Tues. and Thurs. 10am-4pm, Wed. 10am-6pm, Fri. 10am-2pm, Sat.-

Sun. 10am-1pm; July-Aug. Mon.-Sat. only. Free.) Vienna's Old Masters are collected in the **Akademie der Bildenden Künste** (Academy of Fine Arts), 1 Schillerplatz 3 (tel. 58 81 60), which contains Hieronymus Bosch's *Last Judgment* and works by Rubens. (Open Tues. and Thurs.-Fri. 10am-2pm, Wed. 10am-1pm and 3-6pm, Sat.-Sun. 9am-1pm. Guided tours Sun. at 10:30am. Admission 10AS, students free.)

Set aside some time to visit the **Österreichische Gallerie,** housed in the **Belvedere Palace.** The building itself, designed by Lukas von Hildebrandt, is one of the world's finest baroque creations. The lower Belvedere, 3 Rennweg 6, contains Austrian medieval art, with Romanesque and Gothic wood sculptures. The upper palace, 3 Prinz-Eugen-Str. 27 (tel. 784 15 80), across the splendid park, holds everything from about 1700 on. Skip the *Biedermeier* galleries and go straight to the glorious third floor and its unmatched collection of Vienna's own *Jugendstil* (art nouveau). Works by Klimt, Schiele, and Kokoschka abound. (Open Tues.-Sun. 10am-4pm. Admission 30AS, students 15AS.)

If the *Jugendstil* grabs you, you might visit the **Österreichische Museum für Angewandte Kunst** (Museum of Applied Arts), 1 Stubenring 5 (tel. 72 56 96), the oldest museum of applied arts in Europe. You'll see glass, crystal, china, furniture, rugs, and much more, from the Middle Ages to the present. (Open Tues.-Wed. and Fri. 10am-4pm, Thurs. 10am-6pm, Sun. 10am-1pm. Admission 30AS, students 15AS.) Lovers of *Jugendstil* should also obtain *Art Nouveau in Vienna,* an excellent pamphlet prepared by the tourist office, with color photos and discussion of the style's top addresses in town. Request the *Jugendstil* map as well. One creation that no one will miss is Otto Wagner's **Pavilion** at Karlsplatz, the major U-Bahn station. Wagner's **Kirche am Steinhof,** Baumgartner Höhe 1, has a splendid interior; take bus #48A to the end of the line. (Open Sat. from 3pm.)

The **Naturhistorisches Museum** (Natural History Museum), Maria-Theresien platz, has interesting exhibits on nature from the prehistoric to the present. (Open Wed.-Mon. 9am-6pm. Admission 30AS, students 15AS.)

Vienna's other great palace is **Schloss Schönbrunn,** 13 Schönbrunner Schlosstr. (tel. 83 36 46), located in an enormous garden west of town and reached by U-Bahn 4. The interior is breathtaking: Ornaments covered with 14-carat gold leaf, porcelain tile stoves, and crystal chandeliers are among the collection. The obligatory 40-room tour is surprisingly interesting, and often includes gossip on the private lives of Maria Theresa, Emperor Franz Josef, the young Marie Antoinette, and Napoleon; tours in English are frequent. (Open May-Sept. daily 9am-noon and 1-5pm; Oct.-April daily 9am-noon and 1-4pm. Admission 50AS, students 20AS.) The surrounding park is lovely for strolling or picnics. (Open 6am-dusk.)

Vienna has been home to its share of famous people, none more controversial than **Sigmund Freud.** His former house at 9 Berggasse 19 is now a small memorial. (Open Mon.-Fri. 9am-1pm, Sat.-Sun. 9am-3pm. Admission 30AS, students 15AS.) Musical figures also merit homage here; you can visit houses once occupied by or otherwise connected with Schubert, Strauss, Mozart, Beethoven, Haydn, and Brahms. *Museums Vienna* lists all homes open to the public. The graves—some honorary—of these and other notables are in the **Zentralfriedhof** (Central Cemetery), 11 Simmeringer Hauptstr. 234. Take tram #71. (Open May-Aug. daily 7am-7pm; March-April and Sept.-Oct. daily 7am-6pm; Nov.-Feb. daily 8am-5pm.)

On Sunday afternoons, visit **Türkenschanz Park** in the eighteenth *Bezirk* for a stroll, complete with *Dackels* (dachshunds) on the leash and peacocks on the well-tended lawns. The **Prater** is a huge forest and park between the city and the Danube, where you can spin on the *Riesenrad,* an ancient, huge ferris wheel cherished as a symbol of the city—you might recognize it from the latest James Bond flick.

Entertainment

Music and Theater

If yŏu are visiting Vienna for its music, it's best not to do so in summer, as th **Staatsoper** and the **Wiener Sängerknaben** (Vienna Boys' Choir) vacation durin July and August. The Sängerknaben sing 9:15am mass each Sunday during the res of the year at the **Burgkapelle** (Royal Chapel) of the Hofburg. (Tickets 50-120AS Reservations recommended at least 2 months in advance; write to Verwaltung de Hofmusikkapelle, Hofburg, Schweizerhof, A-1010 Wien. Do not enclose money Tickets may be picked up at the Burgkapelle on the Fri. before the mass 11am-noon or on the Sun. of the mass by 9am. Unreserved seats sold starting at 5pm on th preceding Fri.; max. of 2 tickets per person. Standing room free.) Sunday Hig Masses in the major churches (Augustinerkirche, Michaelerkirche, Stephansdom are accompanied by choral or organ music that approaches the celestial. The Staat soper is commonly sold out; get in line on the west side early (about 4:30pm) fo standing room (*Stehplätze* 15-20AS, sold only on day of performance).

The **Theater an der Wien,** 6 Linke Wienzelle 6, opens with musicals in mid-July and the **Wiener Kammeroper** performs all summer in Schloss Schönbrunn. The **Ar kadenhofkonzerte** are fine orchestral concerts held in the courtyard of the *Rathaus* The setting is memorable, the programs familiar, and the tickets reasonable, bu buy them at the *Rathaus* to avoid a service charge and arrive early to nab goo seats. (July-Aug. Tues.-Thurs. at 8pm. Admission 100AS.) On Wednesday and Sat urday summer evenings, there are festive combined tours/concerts at Schönbrunn be there at 7:15pm for the tour, 8:15pm for the music (130AS). The Belvedere offer free samplings of music by all the famous Viennese composers Monday at 5pm i summer, while Strauss (Tues. 5pm) and jazz (Fri. 5pm) are performed *gratis* in fron of the *Rathaus.* Organ concerts held in the Stephansdom (Wed. 7pm) and Straus concerts in the Stadtpark (daily 4-6pm and 8-10pm) are also free. See the pamphlet *Wien Programm* and *Wiener Musiksommer* for more ideas. For any event (suc as the Staatsoper or Volksoper) that requires advance planning, write to the touris office for schedules, but not for reservations.

English theater is offered at the theater on Josefgasse and at the **Internationa Theater,** Porzellangasse 8—look for the posters around the city. English cinema plays at two locations on the Ring: the **Schottenring Kino,** Schottenring 5 (tel. 34 52 36), and the **Burg Kino,** Opernring 19. (Last show usually around 8:30pm.)

Heurigen and Nightlife

Vienna is almost as famous for its *Heurigen* as for its art and music. *Heuriger* are unique to Vienna—they began when Empress Maria Theresa, in a fit of largesse allowed the local wine-growers to sell and serve their wine in their homes at certai times of the year. The traditions of the *Heurigen*—outside seating at picnic tables a sprig of pine hung over the door, and mugs of wine—continue with gusto. Th mood is festive and informal; in some places, you can carry out food served inside or bring a picnic. Only wine produced on the property is served. The feast of Mar tinas on November 11 is the official turning point: Any wine left over then from last year's crop becomes "old" wine, no longer authentic *Heurigen*—so there is al ways a huge effort to spare the wine this fate by consuming it. You might want to know (since Austrian wine can be very *süss,* or sweet) that the word for "dry" is *trocken.*

Heurigen are out in the northern, western, and southern suburbs, where grape are grown. **Grinzing** is the largest *Heurigen* area, but the atmosphere and the wine are better in **Nussdorf** (tram D from the Ring), in **Sievering** (tram #38 and change to bus), and in **Salmannsdorf** (tram #38, and change to #35). One of the bes *Heurigen* is in Beethoven's home in **Heiligenstadt** (tel. 37 12 87). Take tram #37 to the last stop, walk down Wollergasse and through the park, take a right, then your first left on Pfarrplatz. Ask the tourist office for its extensive list. *Heurigen* are all usually open daily 4pm-11pm. Wine is about 80AS per liter.

There are some wonderful *Weinkeller* (wine cellars) downtown as well. **Zwölf Apostel Keller,** 1 Sonnenfelsgasse 3 (tel. 52 67 77), has many levels—the lowest is the liveliest. This is one of the best Viennese cellars, with great atmosphere and lots of locals. (Open Aug.-June 4:30pm-midnight.) **Esterhazykeller,** 1 Haarhof, off Naglergasse (tel. 63 34 82), is the cheapest and perhaps the best *Weinkeller* in Vienna; a quarter liter is 19AS, and food is inexpensive. Try the *Grüner Veltliner* wine from Burgenland. (Maria Theresa granted the concession for this cellar on the condition that it close at 9pm; although the Empress is no longer in a position to enforce her mandate, the hours are still 10am-1pm and 4-9pm.)

Vienna has a fast-paced, modern nightlife as well. *Falter-Zeitschrift,* a local newspaper, is the best source of information on the evening scene; in summer they have partial English coverage in the entertainment section. Explore the "Bermuda triangle" district around the Seitenstettengasse and Rabensteig, or the area around the Schonlaterngasse; both are very active. **Peter's Beisl,** 1 Rauhensteingasse 12 (tel. 513 39 40), is a casually hip bar. (Open Sun.-Thurs. 5pm-2am, Fri.-Sat. 5pm-4am.) **Manhattan,** Laimgrubengasse 3 (tel. 572 90 74), is a relaxed bar for gay men. (Open 8pm-4am.) **Why Not?,** 1 Tiefer Graben 22 (tel. 66 11 58), is a plush disco and bar for gay men and lesbian women. (Open 9pm-4am.) The **Tunnel** (see Food) has good music and casual atmosphere until 2am. **U4,** Schönbrunner Str. 222, is one of Vienna's biggest, hottest discos. It's at the Meidling-Hauptstrasse stop on U-Bahn 4, not far from the center of town. *Wien Live, for Young People* contains lists of hot spots including bars, discos, and cafes. Remember that the subway closes just before midnight.

Near Vienna

South and west of Vienna is the famous **Wienerwald** (Vienna Wood). It was in this beautiful forest that Viennese forces decisively defeated invading Turks in 1683. Take tram #38S to the Grinzing terminus and continue by bus #38A to Kahlenberg, where you have a view of the city and the Danube; wander off into the dense woods on well-marked trails.

Just outside the village of **Mauthausen** stands the site of an extermination camp for thousands of victims of the Third Reich. The guided tour evokes images that do not easily disappear. Take an early morning train from Vienna's Westbahnhof to St. Valentin, then switch to the 10-minute train to Mauthausen—about a two-hour trip each way.

If you are heading west, you might visit **Mariazell,** the most important religious pilgrimage site in Austria. The town is a delight and offers hills to climb as well as a spectacular view from the cable car. From Westbahnhof go to **St. Pölten** (1 hr.), then switch to a smaller train to Mariazell (2 hr.). The **Jugendherberge (IYHF)** is at Fischer-von-Erlach-weg 2 (tel. (03882) 26 69). (65AS. Showers included. Breakfast 25AS. Open mid-May to mid-Oct.)

The Danube (Donau)

The "blue Danube" is largely the invention of Johann Strauss's ¾ imagination, but this mighty, muddy-green river still merits a cruise. The **Erste Donau Dampfschifffahrts-Gesellschaft (DDSG)** runs ships daily from May to September; check with them, travel agencies, or tourist offices for more facts. They have offices in Vienna (Handelskai 265, by the Reichsbrücke bridge; tel. 26 65 36), Linz (Nibelungenbrücke; tel. (0732) 27 00 11), and Passau (Im Ort 14a, Dreiflusseck; tel. (0851) 330 35). Cruises run from Vienna to Greim, passing Krems and Melk *en route,* and between Linz and Passau, on the German border. East of Vienna, hydrofoils run to Bratislava, Czechoslovakia, and Budapest, Hungary.

All fares have shot up to astronomical levels. Fortunately, Eurailpass and Austria Tickets are valid on the cruises from Vienna to Greim and Linz to Passau, West

Germany, while InterRail gets a 50% discount. Everyone pays full fare for the eastward hydrofoils.

The trip between **Linz** and **Passau** is neither very expensive nor terribly exciting (6½ hr. upstream, 5 hr. downstream; 125AS one way, 156AS round-trip). There are **IYHF youth hostels** in **Linz** (Stronglhofweg 3; tel. (0732) 644 34; 85AS) and **Passau** (Veste Oberhaus; tel. (0851) 413 51; 8DM; open April-Oct.).

By far the prettiest part of the river is the stretch between Krems and Melk, along the Vienna-Greim route. Vine-covered and forested hills capped by abbeys and ruined castles line the riverbanks. Possible trips are Krems to Melk (3 hr. upstream, 1¾ hr. downstream; 190AS one way), or Vienna to Krems (5 hr. upstream, 3½ hr. downstream; 260AS one way, 390AS round-trip). This route is particularly well served; take the train to Krems (1 hr. from Vienna) or Melk (2 hr. from Vienna) and walk down to the dock. You can also sail from Vienna to Melk (8 hr. upstream, 5½ hr. downstream; 450AS one way, 900AS round-trip). Only Danube die-hards will want to make the full Vienna-Greim run (12 hr. upstream, 10 hr. downstream; 580AS one way, 1160AS round-trip).

Krems, one hour by train northwest of Vienna, is an expanding city with a number of pretty churches. Climb the covered stairway to the fifteenth-century **Piaristenkirche,** a light Gothic structure with baroque altars. Stroll through the old **Stein** section of town, upriver from the boat landing. The pedestrian zone was renovated in medieval style, with pastel seventeenth-century houses lining the wonderfully quiet Steiner Landestrasse. The **Fremdenverkehrsamt** (tourist office) (tel. (02372) 26 76) is just down Wichnerstr. from Südtirolerplatz; they have suggestions for affordable rooms. (Open May-Aug. Mon.-Fri. 8:30am-noon and 1:30-7pm, Sat. 9am-noon; Sept.-April Mon.-Fri. only.) The **Jugendherberge (IYHF),** Kasnerstr. 6 (tel. 42 17), near Südtirolerplatz, is in a clean if depressing school building. (70AS. Breakfast 20AS. Check-in 5-9pm.) Right by the marina is **Camping Donau,** on the Danube. (25AS per person, 25AS per tent. 3-night min. stay. Open mid-April to mid-Nov. daily 7:30-10:30am and 4:30-7:30pm.)

Melk, upstream, has the good humor to purvey its own shameless copy of the *Mozartkugeln,* namely the *"Original Melker Kugel."* The gold-leafed angels and capitals of the baroque **Benediktinerstift** are resplendent. The hourly tours afford fascinating instruction in how a large monastery functioned. (Open Mon.-Sat. 9am-5pm, Sun. 9:15am-5pm. Free. Tours in German 30AS, students 15AS. English tour begins daily at 11:15, or by arrangement for groups.) You might also bike, hike, or hitch 5km out of town to see the **Schallaburg,** one of the finest Renaissance castles in the German-speaking countries. It's worth the walk to see the architecture, but there's not much inside. Take Kirschengraben out of town and turn left under the Autobahn, or take the post bus "Schallaburg" from the train station. The **tourist office,** Rathausplatz 11 (tel. (02752) 23 07), is in the center of town. (Open July to mid-Aug. daily 9am-6pm; mid-April to June and mid-Aug to mid-Oct. Wed.-Mon. 9am-noon and 3-6pm; mid-Oct to mid-April Mon.-Fri. 7am-noon and 1-4pm.) Melk's **Jugendherberge (IYHF),** Abt-Karl-Str. 42 (tel. (02752) 26 81), to your right as you leave the station, is spotless and friendly, but busy. (95AS. Sheets, showers, and breakfast included. Check-in 5-9pm. Lock-out 9am-5pm. Curfew 10pm. Open Feb.-Nov.) For private lodgings, go to **Gasthof Goldener Stern,** Sterngasse 17 (tel. (02752) 22 14). (Doubles 300AS, triples 450AS. Showers 15AS. Breakfast included.) There's a good restaurant downstairs. (Open year-round daily 7am-1am.)

The Vorarlberg

A bewildering dialect, fierce independence, and a beautiful natural setting are the special charms of this westernmost region of Austria. The scenery varies dramatically from the shores of the Bodensee in the west to the alpine hamlets of the east. There the Arlbergtunnel, nearly 10km long, connects the region with Innsbruck and the Tyrol.

Bregenz and the Bodensee Plain

Classy little Bregenz sustains a resort mood without pandering to tourists. The tourist office, Inselstr. 15 (tel. (05574) 233 91), distributes brochures for a walking tour of the Oberstadt. They can also book you a room in a private home (130-150AS) for a 10AS fee. Ask for their guest card, which entitles you to various reductions (10-30%) on boats, cable cars, and museums. (Open July-Aug. Mon.-Fri. 9am-noon and 2-7pm, Sat. 9am-noon and 4-7pm, Sun. 4-7pm; May-June and Sept. Mon.-Fri. 9am-noon and 2-7pm, Sat. 9am-noon and 4-7pm, Sun. 4-7pm; Oct.-April Mon.-Fri. 9am-noon and 2-6pm, Sat. 9am-noon.) To get to the **Jugendherberge (IYHF),** follow the signs uphill and east from the train station for 10 minutes; the hostel is near the base of the Pfänderbahn cable car at Belrupstr. 16a (tel. (05574) 228 67). (85AS. Sheets 18AS. Breakfast included. Check-in 5-7pm. 10pm curfew. Open April-Sept.) A short distance out of town towards the hills is **Pension Merz,** Landstr. 4 (tel. (05574) 25 68 05). Simple rooms with breakfast cost 160AS per person in summer, 140 AS per person in off-season. **Camping** is most economical at **Gasthof Lamm** (tel. (05574) 317 01), out the Mehrerauerstr. (30AS per person, 20AS per tent. Open April to mid-Oct.)

Boats make scenic crossings to Konstanz in West Germany (190AS) every day, as well as to closer towns along the shore. Ask at the tourist office for schedules. The **Vorarlberg Tourist Office,** Römerstr. 7 (tel. (05574) 22 52 50), will fill you in on mountain trips and hiking. You can take the **Pfänderbahn** (tel. (05574) 221 60) cable car straight out of Bregenz and ascend 1064m for a view of Lake Constance. (56AS up, 40AS down, 80AS round-trip. Open daily: April 9am-7pm, May 9am-8pm, June and Sept. 8:30am-8pm, July-Aug. 8:30am-10:30pm, Oct.-March 9am-6pm.) From here, climb a few hundred meters for a view of the snowbound Alps. Further east lie some of Europe's finest winter playgrounds.

From July 22 to August 23 1988, the **Bregenzer Festspiele** brings opera, ballet, musicals, and classical and chamber music to town. Performances take place on a huge floating stage, while the audience sits in an ampitheater on shore. It's best to write ahead for tickets (150-1100AS) to any of the tourist offices in the region or to Bregenzer Festspiele, Postfach 119, A-6901 Bregenz Austra. There's plenty of outdoor entertainment, from folk dancing to chamber concerts on the water, all *gratis.* In inclement weather, check out the **Folklore Evenings** at Anton-Schneider-Str. 1 (May-Oct. Tues. from 8pm; 70AS, with guest card 50AS).

Some 10km south of Bregenz lies **Dornbirn,** the largest town in the region, but a boring place with no cheap rooms. Nevertheless, you must stop here to hike the famous **Rappenlochschlucht** gorge, one of the most dramatic natural formations in Europe. Although it is accessible by bus, the most enjoyable way to get to the gorge is by cable car: Take the **Karrenbahn** cable car to the rim and then hike one hour downhill into the gorge, where you can sun yourself and even take a surreptitious swim in the tumbling stream which carved the gap. (Cable car 48AS one way. Open May-June and Sept. Mon.-Fri. 9am-6pm, Sat.-Sun. 8am-6pm; July-Aug. Mon.-Fri. 9am-6pm, Sat.-Sun. 8am-6:30pm.) For a longer hike (about 3 hr.), go from the top of the cable car over to the mountain village of **Ebnit** and then return by bus. Down in Dornbirn, the **Verkehrsverein** is in the *Altes Rathaus* (tel. (05572) 621 88), on Rathausplatz. They'll find you a room for around 150AS per person; singles will cost 20AS extra, as will stays of less than three nights. (Open Mon.-Fri. 8am-noon and 1-6pm, Sat. 9am-noon.)

The Arlberg

About 70km east of Dornbirn are the mountain villages of the Arlberg. Trains run several times per day from Bregenz or Dornbirn. **Stuben,** on the West side of the Arlberg tunnel, has several inexpensive hotels, while farther north are the classy resorts of **Lech** and **Zürs.** Ski slopes connect the towns of **St. Christoph** and **St. Anton** on the eastern side of the tunnel. Several hotels run ski week packages which include six days of instruction, ski pass, and accommodations with two meals per day. These run from 2235AS to 4000AS. Call or write to the **main tourist office** in Lech (tel. (05583) 216 10), Verkehrsamt Lech, A-6764 Lech, Austria for information on hiking as well as skiing. The Arlberg ski pass (305AS per day, 1620AS per week) entitles you to some of the best slopes in Austria, including the famous **Valluga** summit. For the weather and a snow report, call (05583) 18.

Innsbruck

Ancient capital of the Tyrol, Innsbruck was once a coveted strategic point which controlled travel between Italy and Germany via the Brenner Pass. Today it is the center of Austria's winter activities, and occasionally of the world's alpine interest, having hosted the Winter Olympic Games in 1964 and 1976. More than 150 cable cars and chairlifts and an extensive network of mountain paths radiate from Innsbruck, making the stunning surrounding Alps equally accessible for winter skiers and summer hikers.

Orientation and Practical Information

The *Altstadt,* center of the city, is an easy 10-minute walk from the train station, or you can take tram #1 or 3 or any of a dozen buses.

From the budget traveler's point of view, Innsbruck is one of the most organized cities in Europe. The first-class treatment starts at the train station, where a **youth waiting room** offers travelers a bulletin board for messages, a washroom, and a friendly place to collect oneself. (Open July-early Aug. Mon.-Fri. 1-5pm; early Sept.-June Mon.-Fri. 11am-7pm, Sat. 10am-2pm; closed early Aug.-early Sept.) There or at any tourist office you can get a copy of the indispensable pamphlet *Innsbruck—for Young People,* which includes a city map, information, and listings of cheap accommodations. You can join **Club Innsbruck** at no charge if you have registered at any Innsbruck accommodation for three or more nights; membership provides you with discounts on the city's various cable cars and museums, free bike tours, and the opportunity to participate in the club's hiking program, run from June through September (ask at the *Verkehrsverein*).

Tourist Office: Verkehrsverein, Burggraben 3 (tel. 267 71), on the edge of the *Altstadt.* Large and quite helpful. Free room reservations and a message board. Open Mon.-Fri. 8am-5:30pm, Sat. 9am-noon. Expects to move by 1988—ask at the train station.

Budget Travel: ÖKISTA, Josef-Hirn-Str. 7/2 (tel. 289 97), open Mon.-Fri. 9:30am-5:30pm. **Tiroler Landesreisebüro,** corner of Wilhelm-Greil-Str. and Boznerpl. (tel. 349 85), open Mon.-Fri. 8:30am-12:30pm and 2-6pm.

American Express: Brixenstr. 3 (tel. 224 91), near the station. Mail held. All banking services. Also a great map for finding out-of-the-way addresses. Open Mon.-Fri. 9am-5:30pm, Sat. 9am-noon.

Currency Exchange: At the station, daily 9:15am-1:30pm and 3:15-7:45pm. Poor rates. Also at the tourist office, Mon.-Fri. 8am-5:30pm, Sat. 9am-noon.

Post Office: Maximillianstr. 2 (tel. 267 61), just down from the Triumpharch. Open 24 hours. Send Poste Restante to Postlagernde Briefe, Brunecker Str. 1-3, 6020, Innsbruck. Office by the train station open Mon.-Fri. 7am-9pm, Sat. 7am-9pm, Sun. 9am-noon.

Telephones: At either of the above post offices. **Telephone code:** 05222.

Public Transportation: Excellent tram and bus system, though almost unnecessary in this compact city. One ride 14AS, 10-ticket book 90AS.

Ski and Bike Rental: Schischule Innsbruck, Burggraben 17 (tel. (05222) 223 10). Open mid-June to mid-Sept. Mon.-Fri. 9am-noon and 2-6pm, Sat. 8:30am-noon. Or, rent bikes at the train station in nearby Hall (70AS per day, 35AS per day with Eurail or InterRail) and return them to any train station in Austria.

Emergencies: Police (tel. 133); headquarters at Kaiserjägerstr. 8 (tel. 267 21). **Ambulance** (tel. 144).

Medical Assistance: University Hospital, Anichstr. (tel. 723).

Laundry: Laundromat at Amraserstr. 15 (tel. 413 67), on the far side of the train tracks. 77AS per load, including soap. Open Mon.-Fri. 10am-6pm.

Hitchhiking: Mitfahrzentrale, Brixnerstr. 3 (tel. 323 43), pairs drivers and riders.

Accommodations and Camping

Budget accommodations flourish in Innsbruck, but they fill up in July and August—book one day ahead. If you get stuck, ask the *Verkehrsverein* for their list of private rooms (100-170AS per person, including breakfast) in town and in nearby **Igls.** If you plan to be in Innsbruck over the Christmas holiday, it's essential to write ahead: Many establishments close for two weeks at this time.

Hostel Innsbruck (IYHF), Reichenauerstr. 147 (tel. 461 79). Large, modern, and often overcrowded. Take bus R or O to one stop beyond Campingplatz. Members only. 120AS the first night, 90AS thereafter; 5AS less for ages under 19. Linen and breakfast included. Lockout 10am-5pm. Check-in 5-10pm. 11pm curfew. Closed Dec. 24-26.

Hostel Torsten-Arneus Schwedenhaus (IYHF), Rennweg 17b (tel. 258 14), along the river. Guests rave about this spotless and friendly hostel. Great location—you can take bus C from the station to the Handelsakademie stop, or walk for about 15 min. Members only. 55AS; 5AS less for ages under 20. Sheets 20AS. Breakfast 30AS. Check-in 5-7pm. Lockout 9am-5pm. 10pm curfew. Open July-Aug.

MK (IYHF), Sillgasse 8a (tel. 313 11). Close to the station with friendly, flexible management, and a hopping cafe next door. Members only. 90AS the first night, 80AS thereafter; 5AS less for ages under 19. Linen and breakfast included. Check-in 7:30-9am and 5-11pm. Lockout 9:30am-5pm. 11pm curfew. Open Easter holiday for 1 week, Christmas holiday for 2 weeks, and July-early Sept.; call for exact dates.

St. Paulus, Reichenauerstr. 72 (tel. 442 91), on the R bus line. Simple but efficient. 45AS per night plus 15AS for linen in dorms. Breakfast 20AS. Check-in 5-10pm. Lockout 9am-5pm. 10pm curfew. Open mid-June to mid-Aug.

Studentenpension Technikerhaus, Fischnalerstr. 26 (tel. 821 10). Cheerful single, doubles, and triples. Take bus B from the station. 103AS per night. No breakfast. Reduction with student ID. Open July-Aug.

Haus Schwarz, Lindenbühelweg 12 (tel. 855 35). Attractive rooms and an indoor pool (10AS extra, pool open May-Oct.). Take bus A from the railroad station to Grosser Gott (runs until 11pm), or bus H to Graner-Stein and take the next left. Or call ahead and they may pick you up at the station. 150-170AS per person in singles or doubles. 20AS per person extra for 1-nighters.

Camping: Campingplatz Reichenau, Reichenauerstr. (tel. 462 52). Take bus R or O from train station. 50AS per person. Open May-Oct. **Campingplatz West,** bus LK (tel. 841 80). Same price. Also open May-Oct.

Food

An indoor **market** takes place Monday through Saturday (8am-6pm) in the Markthalle along the Inn behind the *Altstadt.*

Gasthof Lamm, Mariahilferstr. 10 (tel. 831 56), on the river opposite the *Altstadt.* Succulent meals in a casual, bar-like atmosphere for 80-100AS. Their specialty, fresh trout, is often affordable. Open Wed.-Mon. 11:30am-2pm and 6-10pm.

Gasthof Gruber, Innrain 22 (tel. 218 21). A neighborhood place with an outside terrace and countryside atmosphere. About 55AS for a small meal, 95AS for a larger meal with meat and vegetables. Open 6:30am-3pm and 6pm-midnight.

Lewisch, Bienerstr. 19 (tel. 260 43), a short walk down Inginieur Etzel Str., or take line #1 to Bundesbahndion. A neighborhood place with antlers on the wood-panelled walls. Not much English, but *gulasch* for 30AS, large hamburgers with salad for 40AS, and beer or coffee. Open Mon.-Fri. 9am-midnight.

Nordsee, Burggraben 15. Smoked and fried fish sandwiches are the best bargains. Open Mon.-Fri. 9am-6pm, Sat. 8:30am-noon.

University Mensa, Herzog-Siegmund-Ufer, basement of the new university. Lunches 50AS. Open Sept.-June 11am-6pm.

Sights and Entertainment

The **Altstadt** is the center of Innsbruck, and the **Goldenes Dachl** (Golden Roof) is both the center of the *Altstadt* and the city's emblem. It once served as a vantage point for spectators during the medieval tournaments held in the square below. Inside the building is the **Olypiamuseum** (tel. 209 48), which commemorates the 1964 and 1976 Winter Games with relics (don't miss Franz Klammer's skis) and video tapes of the competition. (Open daily 10am-5:30pm. Admission 20AS, students 10AS; covers the nearby *Stadtturm* tower.) Just to the left as you face the Goldenes Dachl, notice the incredibly elaborate stucco work on the **Helbinghaus.** Equally elaborate but grander is the **Hofburg** (Imperial Palace), Rennweg 1 (tel. 271 86), right next to the old town. It was initially built around 1500 under Emperor Maximillian I in the Gothic style; after his death Empress Maria Theresa rebuilt it in rococo style. Guided tours pass through the private chapel, the banquet hall, and several rooms of paintings. (Tours mid-May to mid-Oct. daily 9am-4pm; mid-Oct. to mid-May Mon.-Sat. 9am-4pm. Admission 20AS, students 5AS.)

Next door is the imperial chapel, the **Hofkirche,** at Universitätsstr. 2. The two dozen intricately detailed, larger-than-life bronze statues which surround the tomb of Maximillian I make the visit worthwhile. (Open May-Sept. daily 9am-5pm; Oct.-April daily 9am-noon and 2-5pm.) The entry ticket (15AS, students 7.50AS) will also admit you to the interesting collection of the **Tiroler Volkskunstmuseum** (Tyrolian Handicrafts Museum), next door at Universitätsstr. 2. Old implements and costumes, and exquisitely carved complete rooms from old houses offer a brief introduction to Austrian culture. (Open Mon.-Sat. 9am-noon and 2-5pm, Sun. 9am-noon.) Lovers of Gothic art shouldn't miss the **Tiroler Landesmuseum Ferdinandeum,** Museumstr. 15 (tel. 220 03), a few blocks from the *Hauptbahnhof.* The collection includes beautifully colored, delicately etched stained-glass windows, a few outstanding altars and paintings, and an array of works ranging from impressionism to modern realism. (Open May-Sept. Tues.-Sat. 10am-5pm, Sun. 9am-noon; Oct.-April Tues.-Sat. 10am-noon and 2-5pm, Sun. 9am-noon. Admission 14AS, students 7AS.)

From the **Triumphbogen** (triumphal arch), stroll down broad Maria-Theresien-Str. and enjoy the striking view of the **Nordkette** (Northern Range). The **Dom zu St. Jakob,** in the old city, has an altar decorated with Lukas Cranach's *Virgin and Child,* and above, beautiful *trompe l'oeil* ceilings. Other attractions in Innsbruck include the famed **Alpine Zoo,** which displays all vertebrate species indigenous to the Alps (open daily 9am-5pm; admission 36AS, students 18AS); and the collection of armor and paintings at **Schloss Ambras.** For the zoo, take bus Z towards Hungerburg; and for the castle, bus K or tram #3 in the opposite direction.

The mountains around the city offer a much grander view than the *Stadtturm.* At **Hafelekar,** after a gondola ride, you can enjoy panoramas of the Inn Valley, the city beneath, and the somber mountain chains of the Tyrolean Alps. Go first to **Seegrube,** the midway station, and then to the mountain station Hafelekar, only a few minutes from the summit. (143AS for ascent, 216AS round-trip.) Even **Hungerburg,** at the base of the cable car, offers a splendid view of the city below. You can walk up by way of **Buchsenhausen Schloss,** or take tram #1 to the base of the cog railway.

St. Nikolaus Kellerei, Innstr. (tel. 856 25), just downstream from St. Nikolaus Gasse, is a good place to work on your Austrian dialect over a large glass of wine (15AS); no English spoken. (Open Mon.-Thurs. 9am-noon and 3-8pm.) If you prefer beer, go to **Löwenhaus** (tel. 254 79), Rennweg 5, a great restaurant-cum-beer garden where *schinken-spätzle* (68AS) is the specialty (open daily 9am-midnight). At **Zipfer Braustube,** Maria-Theresien-Str. 9 (tel. 280 88), in the center of town, beer costs 24AS and hot appetizers go for around 70AS. (Open daily 9am-midnight.) Dancers should try **Club Filou** (tel. 21 54 12), in the *Altstadt* at Stiftsgasse 12—never a cover, and open daily from 6pm to 4am. **Treibhaus** is a sort of student hangout/regional cultural center at Angerzellgasse. There are over 20 bars open past 2am.

During July and August, Innsbruck sponsors musical performances at **Ambraser Schloss** (every Tues. at 8:30pm; tickets 90-180AS), concerts in the churches, and occasionally outdoor jazz festivals. Check with the *Verkehrsverein* on times and prices.

Near Innsbruck

Igls, a small resort village outside Innsbruck, will live up to your expectations of Alpine Austria—the streets are lined with picturesque chalets with hand-carved hearts on their shutters. Igls makes a fine base for hiking; call the **tourist office** (tel. (05222) 771 01) for information. The ride up the **Patscherkofel** in Igls offers a panoramic view of the city below for the lowest price among the area's mountain lifts. (104AS up, 71AS down, 142AS round-trip; 20% off with Eurail, InterRail, or Austria Ticket.) To get to Igls from Innsbruck, take bus J from the station (23AS) or tram #6.

A daytrip from Innsbruck up the **Stubai Valley** may be the most rewarding of your activities while in Innsbruck. The mountain villages you will encounter—**Fulpmes** and **Neustift,** for example—are highly touristed, but offer the chance to assemble a picnic before setting off on foot. In this area, you can't miss—you're sure to encounter lots of roaming cows and beautiful scenery. Take the "ST" line from Innsbruck station (38AS one way). Buses also travel up the valley, crossing the *Europabrücke*—a 200-meter-high bridge—en route.

At the very top of the valley, you can ski year-round on the magnificent **Stubaigletscher.** Many private groups and pensions in Innsbruck offer package deals for a day's skiing; decide whether the convenience they offer is worth paying a little more (usually about 100AS). Also, know that many packages are reluctant to refund your money if your plans change. To do it yourself, take the post bus #1 (leaving the train station at 7:25am) to the last stop (about 80 min., 130AS round-trip). Here, buy a daypass (June-Sept. 225AS; Oct.-May 275AS) and ride the gondola to the top station, where you can rent equipment (180AS per day). In Innsbruck, check at ÖKISTA for cheap ski deals. Four lifts are always open, with many more running in winter. There's a self-service restaurant on the summit with meals for 60 to 100AS. If you want to spend some time at one of the more remote resorts scattered about the Tyrol, contact the **Tiroler Fremdenverkehrswerbung,** Boznerpl. 7 (tel. 207 77; open Mon.-Fri. 8am-12:30pm and 1:30-5pm).

Kitzbühel

One and a half hours by train from Innsbruck, Kitzbühel is the St. Moritz of Austria. Wealthy visitors displaying fancy cars and fancier fashions fill the streets in the winter. Site of the first cable car in Austria, Kitzbühel challenges skiers and hikers with an ever-ascending network of lifts and runs, while catering to the less hearty with its mountain meadow walks. Pick up a town map at the train station and then head for the **Verkehrsbüro,** Hinterstadt 18 (tel. 22 72), a 15-minute walk. They'll give you more maps, and help you find a hotel, pension, or private room. They also sponsor a free guest card—which you receive at your lodgings—giving reductions on sports facilities, cable cars, car tolls, and guided mountain tours. (Open late Dec. to mid-March and July-Aug. Mon.-Fri. 8:30am-noon and 3-6:30pm, Sat. 8:30am-noon and 4-6pm, Sun. 4-6pm; mid-March to June and Sept.-Dec. closed Sat. afternoons and Sun.) Opposite the *Verkehrsbüro* is **Reisebüro Eurotours** (tel. (05356) 31 31), where you can exchange money. (Open Mon.-Fri. 8am-noon and 3-6:30pm, Sat. 8am-noon and 4:30-6:30pm, Sun. 10am-noon and 4:30-6:30pm.) A superb place to stay is the **Schmidinger-Rupinger Pension,** Ehrenbachgasse 13 (tel. (05356) 31 34), about a 20-minute walk from the train station—follow the main street, Josef-Pircht, through the old city, "Vorderstadt," until Ehrenbachgasse is on your right. This pension is a gem, with a delightful breakfast room, very friendly service, and spacious, fresh, clean rooms with balconies overlooking the Austrian Alps. (160AS, plus or minus 20AS, depending on the season. Breakfast included. Reservations welcomed.) The **Jugendheim Seereith,** Schwarzseestr. (tel. 23 60), is out of the way; take a bus from the train station which heads toward Seereith and to the stop, "Schwarzsee"; the hostel is 150m on your left. (Dec.-March 230AS; April-Nov. 220AS. Breakfast, lunch, and dinner included. Check-in 5-10pm.) For *Zimmerfrei,* wander down Ehrenbachstr. An inexpensive and pleasant restaurant, the **Glockenspiel,** is located on a side street off Vorderstadt at Hinterstadt 13. They have an outdoor cafe and serve meat dishes for approximately 110AS; simple Tyrolian meals are 90 to 100AS. (Open daily 10am-3am.) The **HüberbräuS-tübel** Restaurant, Vorderstadt 18, right in the city's hub, is cheerful, with an outdoor cafe overlooking the main center. Smaller meals (spaghetti and pizza) cost approximately 70AS, large hot *menu* meals are around 95AS. (Open daily 8am-midnight.) The **post office,** where you can make long-distance phone calls, is on Josef-Pircht-Str. Poste Restante is held here; send to Lagernd Post A-6370 Kitzbühel. The **telephone code** for Kitzbühel is 05356. (Post office open Mon.-Fri. 8am-noon and 2-7pm, Sat. 8-11am.) There's a coin-operated **laundry** at Josef-Herold-Str. 19. (130AS per load. Open Mon.-Fri. 10am-5pm, Sat. 10am-midnight.) For groceries, shop at the **Sparmarkt,** Vorderstadt Str., below the Park Hotel. (Open Mon.-Fri. 8am-6pm, Sat. 8am-noon.)

To get to some of the lower hiking trails and meadow walks, ride the **Hahnenkammbahn** or the **Kitbüheler-Horn** (Nov.-April 110AS; May-Oct. 100AS, with guest card 80AS. Open 8am-noon and 1-5:30pm.) Or climb up yourself; descent is always free. There is also great hiking and skiing in the towns surrounding Kizbühel, all accessible by post bus (20AS) from the station. Get a map (*Panoramakarte*) from the tourist office, or at each individual office: In **Oberndorf** (tel. (05352) 29 27); in **Reith** (tel. (05356) 54 65); in **Kirchberg** (tel. (05357) 23 09); in **Avrach** (tel. (05356) 46 22); and in **Jochberg** (tel. (05355) 52 29). Prices in these towns are considerably lower than in Kitzbühel. The fantastic Kitzbühel ski area is connected with all the towns listed above and, of course, Kitzbühel. A ski pass for one day is 290AS (prices go down after the first day). Downhill ski rental runs 150AS for the first day, and lessons run 330AS per day. Ask at the tourist office about ski packages—one week of lodging, ski instruction, and ski passes (approx. 3245AS). Call (05356) 25 00 for more information.

Lienz

No less rich in mountain attractions than its neighbors to the north, Lienz is nonetheless quiet and captivating, unhurried in its charm. Situated in the jagged Dolomites of the eastern Tyrol, the city is approximately three hours by train from Innsbruck or Salzburg. Trains to or from Innsbruck pass through Italy; the Austria Ticket is only valid on bus service to or from Innsbruck. The **Verkehrsamt,** Hauptpl. 9 (tel. (04852) 28 80), issues a free guest card which you pick up at your lodgings, good for various reductions. They also find rooms (150AS) for free. (Open July to mid-Sept. Mon.-Fri. 8am-noon and 2-6pm, Sat. 9am-noon; mid-Sept. to June Mon.-Fri. 8am-noon and 2-6pm.) They may be closed for renovation, in which case go to the main **Verkehrsamt,** Albin-Egger-Str. 17 (tel. (04852) 47 47), about a 10-minute walk west of the train station. Ask here for information about the special winter ski package, *Schipauschale.* (Open July to mid-Sept. Mon.-Fri. 8am-noon and 2-6pm; mid-Sept. to June daily 8am-6pm.) Just as helpful is the travel agency **Bundschuh,** Boznerstr. 2 (tel. 33 68). They have currency exchange, and will also give you a list of private rooms starting at 130AS. For hiking information, visit the **Alpenverein** office on Waltherpl. (tel. (04852) 489 32; open Mon.-Fri. 8am-noon).

Lienz has a wonderful **Jugendherberge (IYHF),** spotless, rustic, and directly on the fierce River Isel at Linker Iselweg 22 (tel. (04852) 33 10). From the station, cross the river and walk upstream 10 minutes. (102AS the first night, 76AS thereafter. Linen and breakfast included. Check-in 6-10pm. 10pm curfew. Open July-Aug.) For private lodgings, take advantage of the lists of private rooms, or wander away from the center looking for *Zimmerfrei* signs. For a little luxury, go to **Gasthof Goldener Stern,** centrally located at Schweizergasse 40 (tel. 21 92). You will receive a warm welcome and find spacious rooms in a beautiful, rustic house (155AS, with shower 180AS). Cheap but spartan, **Gasthaus Bahnhof,** Bahnhof platz 3 (tel. (04852) 23 76) charges 130AS per person, including breakfast. For great local food (70-100AS) in a garden or vaulted tavern, visit **Gasthof Neuwirt** (tel. (04852) 21 01), between Schweizergasse and the river. (Open daily 7am-11pm.)

Above Lienz is the **Schloss Bruck,** home of the **East Tyrolian Regional Museum,** which houses everything from Roman remains and local artifacts to carved Christmas *crèches.* Buses run from the train station (12AS one way; take the bus for Matrei), or it's a 25-minute walk. (Open June-Sept. daily 10am-5pm; April-Oct. Tues.-Sun. 10am-5pm.) For a not too arduous four- to five-hour hike, take the Hochsteinbahnen chairlift, which starts near the castle (110AS one way for both halves, 100AS with guest card), then climb **Hochstein** (2057m), and descend to the valley. The **Zettersfeld** chairlift (110AS round-trip, 100AS with guest card) provides access to hiking on the Zettersfeld peak (1930m). And from Boznerstrasse 2, buses run to another good hiking base, the **Lienzer Dolomitenhutte** (hut) in the mountains above town. (Daily at 8am, 1pm, and 4:30pm, 1 hr., 90AS round-trip.)

Some 14 ski lifts operate betwen November and April. (Ski passes cost 230AS, children 170AS; prices go down after the first day.) The **Lienzer Dolomiten Skischule,** at the Zettersfeld lift (tel. 56 90), offers lessons for 320AS per day. Cross-country skiing and rental is also available.

Outside Lienz begins the scenic **Grossglocknerstrasse,** one of the highest mountain roads in Europe. You'll pass **Grossglockner** peak, which at 3797m is the highest mountain in Austria. Stop at Franz-Josefs-Höhe, at the foot of the mountain, and take the Gletscherbahn (50AS round-trip) for a beautiful view of the glacier, or hike the 2.5-kilometer path through Gamsgrube to a spectacular waterfall, **Wasserfallwinkel.** For hiking information on Grossglockner call the road's special information bureau at (04824) 22 12 or 22 13. The road often closes in the winter and visibility can be poor at any time of the year. Those hitchhiking or driving to Innsbruck might take the **Gerlosstrasse,** which will take you past the **Krimmler Waterfalls** and the Tyrol's **Ziller Valley.** The road toward Kitzbühel is scenic, but the **Felbertauerntunnel** takes a 180AS toll. In Heiligenblut, there is a new **IYHF youth hostel** at Hof 36 (tel. (04824) 22 59; 100AS per night; open Dec.-Sept.).

Salzkammergut

East of Salzburg lies the Salzkammergut, an area of peaks and lakes, small villages, and abandoned salt mines. You can choose between bustling resorts and quiet, isolated towns, have your fill of water sports or take a solitary swim. And there is probably no better place for some relaxed hiking, cycling, or camping—the region offers a near-perfect combination of easy access, 2000km of footpaths, 12 cable cars and chairlifts, and loads of hostels. Winter brings a soft blanket of snow to the valleys and downhill skiing to the slopes. The tourist office in each town has information on winter sports.

The Vienna-Salzburg rail line skirts the northern edge of the Salzkammergut. At Attnang-Puchheim, 50km east of Salzburg, a spur line begins its way south through Gmunden, Ebensee, Bad Ischl, Obertraun, and Bad Aussee to Steinbach. If you're hitching, traveling by bus, or have your own wheels, you can enter directly from Salzburg, along Highway 158. Within the region there is a dense network of **post buses.** Most routes are covered 4 to 12 times per day. Ask at the Salzburg kiosk for a comprehensive schedule, or call for information: Salzburg (06222) 712 10; Gmunden (07612) 46 05; Mondsee (06232) 26 69; Bad Ischl (06132) 31 13; Bad Aussee (06152) 20 50. The pamphlet *Wandern mit dem Postauto* (*Hiking with the Postbus*), available at the main bus stations in these towns, details hikes that coincide with the post bus network. There is also a less complete network of **Bahnbuses;** their schedule is available at local rail stations. If hitching from Salzburg, take bus #4 to Gnigl, and come into the Salzkammergut at Bad Ischl.

Two-wheeled transportation is a lot more fun, but only if you get a good bike—some mountain passes top 1000m. For the less energetic, a moped is tempting. Just remember that your luggage must be minimal. (See Salzburg for rental agency addresses.) Finally, economical ferries serve each of the larger lakes. The **Wolfgangsee** line is operated by the Austrian railroad, so railpasses are valid; on the **Attersee** and **Traunsee** lines, Eurailpass holders receive a discount.

Hostels abound in the Salzkammergut. Most cater to school groups, yet all but the one in St. Wolfgang keep beds open for individuals. A few, such as Obertraun, are downright luxurious. Even hostels supposedly open year-round take short unofficial breaks during the slow spring and fall seasons. If hostels are full or closed, you can turn to the **Zimmernachweis** (room-finding service) in every town, or look for *Zimmerfrei* signs. **Camping** areas dot the region, but many are trailer-oriented; away from large towns, you can usually camp anywhere discreetly without trouble. Hikers can capitalize on dozens of **cable cars** in the area to gain altitude before setting out on their own, and almost every community has a local trail map publicly posted and/or available at the tourist office. At higher elevations there are many **alpine huts,** but check carefully at the tourist office for their opening hours or you may find yourself stuck up the mountain.

Western Salzkammergut

Highway 158 connects Salzburg and Bad Ischl, and bus service is good. **St. Gilgen,** on **Lake Wolfgangsee,** is one of the area's prettiest towns, easily reached by post bus from Salzburg and Bad Ischl (hourly). The **youth hostel** in St. Gilgen, Mondseerstr. 7 (tel. (06227) 365), has fine accommodations in a newly renovated building for 85AS per person. The **Verkehrsverein** (tel. (06227) 348) in the *Rathaus* has information on alternative budget accommodations. (Open July-Aug. Mon.-Sat. 8:30am-6pm, Sun. 9am-noon; Sept.-June Mon.-Fri. 9am-noon and 1-5pm.) Dominating the Wolfgangsee is the **Schafberg.** The Austrian Railroad runs a *Schafbergbahn* (a cog-wheel train) up to the breathtaking 1783-meter summit, from which it's an easy three-hour hike back into town. (Open May-Oct. 168AS round-trip, railpasses valid.) A steamer runs from St. Gilgen to the base of the cog (April-Oct., 38AS each way, free with Eurailpass); ask for the schedule at the *Verkehrsverein.*

Over the Schafberg lies the **Mondsee,** the warmest of the Salzkammergut's lakes. The town of Mondsee is close to the *Autobahn* and not especially memorable, but the lakeshore is full of wonderful spots to stop and take a swim. The **Jugendgästehaus (IYHF),** Krankenhaustr. 9 (tel. (06232) 24 18), is luxurious. (85AS. Showers and breakfast included. Check-in 5-10pm. 10pm curfew. Open mid-Jan. to mid.-Dec.) The **Verkehrsverein** (tel. (06232) 22 70) lies halfway between the church and the lake at Dr.-Franz-Müller-Str. 3. (Open July-Aug. Mon.-Fri. 8am-7pm, Sat.-Sun. 9am-7pm; Sept.-June Mon.-Fri. 8am-noon and 2-6pm, Sat. 9am-noon.)

Next to the Mondsee is the **Attersee,** the largest lake in the Salzkammergut, and the only one lacking a major town. At the southern end in little **Weissenbach,** the Austrian Young Socialists operate a reasonably-priced **Europa-Camp** (tel. (07663) 220); membership is not required. A ferry service links the small villages around the Attersee, and the lake is easily accessible from Mondsee, Bad Ischl, and Gmunden.

Northern and Eastern Salzkammergut

Gmunden, a large and bustling resort town with a fine view down the **Traunsee,** is the northern gateway to the Salzkammergut; trains run frequently from Salzburg via Attnang-Puchheim. To reach the center of town from the train station (tel. (07612) 42 07), take any tram (12AS) from opposite the train station; all run to town. The friendly **Kurverwaltung** (tourist office) is at Am Graben 2 (tel. (07612)

43 05), the first road on the left from the terminus of the tram. Be sure to pick up their *Welcome to Gmunden* pamphlet, which contains lists of lodgings and a city map. (Open May-Sept. Mon.-Fri. 8am-noon and 2-6pm, Sat. 9am-noon; Oct.-April Mon.-Fri. 8am-noon and 2-6pm.) There's also a Tourist Information kiosk (tel. 49 46) right on the lake.

The **Jugendgästehaus Wunderburg,** Wunderburgstr. 12, is for large groups only. A good place for private lodgings is tiny **Haus Platzer,** Lehengasse 6 (tel. (07612) 59 45), just off the Esplanade along the lake right before the Oberbank. The place is run by a kind couple who speak only German and the rooms are cozy, comfortable, and clean. (100AS per person in singles or doubles. Showers 15AS, bath 20AS. Breakfast included. Open year-round.) A **Campingplatz** is also on the lake at Traunsteinerstr. 259 (tel. (07612) 30 60), to the left of town as you face the lake. (41AS per person, 18AS per tent; bed in a cabin 61AS. Showers 20AS. Open May-Sept.) Gmunden holds a festival from late July to mid-August every year. Ask at the tourist office for tickets and information.

From mid-May through mid-September, ferries will take you around the Traunsee (100AS round-trip), or to **Ebensee** (45AS), the lake's southernmost town. From Bad Ischl, buses run north to Ebensee (hourly). The **Familie Eder** ferry company (tel. (07612) 52 15) has more information. You can also take Highway 145 along the western edge of the lake. On your way, pause at **Traunkirchen** (the train stop is Traunkirchen Ort); its village church has an eighteenth-century carved pulpit depicting the Miracle of the Fishes. In Ebensee, 4km farther, a newly renovated **Jugendherberge (IYHF)** (tel. (06133) 698) sits on the far side of town at Rindbachstr. 15. (60AS. Linen 20AS. Breakfast 20AS. Other meals 40AS. Check-in 5pm. 10pm curfew. Open year-round.) The **Fremdenverkehrsverband** (tourist office), Hauptstr. 34 (tel. (06133) 80 16), is by the indoor pool beside the train station. (Open July-Aug. Mon.-Fri. 8am-noon and 2-5pm, Sat. 8am-noon; Sept.-June Mon.-Fri. only.) From a station on the edge of town, the Feuerkogel cable car makes the 1625-meter ascent to a nearby summit (140AS round-trip). From here, trek or take the chairlift up to **Alberfeldkogel** (1708m).

South of Ebensee is **Bad Ischl,** the cultural and geographical center of Salzkammergut. From here you can continue south to the more isolated upper valley; the town is also the major junction to the western Salzkammergut. The **Kurverwaltung** (tourist office), Bahnhofstr. 6 (tel. (06132) 35 20), will help you find a room in a private home or pension from 100AS per person (no commission). They're quite helpful, and also have information on summer opera (July-Aug. 110-360AS) and free outdoor concerts (May-Sept.). (Open in summer Mon.-Fri. 7:30am-noon and 1-6pm, Sat. 8am-noon and 1:30-5pm, Sun. 9-11:30am; in winter Mon.-Fri. 7:30am-noon and 1:30-5:30pm, Sat. 8am-noon and 1:30-5pm.) The **Jugendherberge (IYHF)** (tel. (06132) 65 77) is at Am Rechensteg 5, in the center of town. (80AS. Showers 20AS. Breakfast included. Lunch and dinner available. Check-in 5-10pm. Flexible 10pm curfew. Open year-round.) **Pfarrheim,** Auböckplatz (tel. (06132) 348 38), beside the post office, is a non-IYHF youth hostel in a basement with two 20-bed rooms. (40AS. Sheets 10AS. Showers included. Check-in 6-10pm. No lockout. 10pm curfew. Open June-Aug.)

About 15km south of Bad Ischl by post bus, crammed between the **Hallstättersee** and steep cliffs broken by a waterfall, **Hallstatt** swells with picture-taking opportunities—you may recognize it from some of Austria's stunning travel posters. Site of one of the richest prehistoric finds north of the Alps (including more than 2000 graves dating from as far back as the early Iron Age (800 B.C.E.), Hallstatt and its lake are surprisingly undisturbed, a truly special place.

If you arrive by train, get off at **Obertraun,** across the lake—but at the stop marked "Hallstatt." Ferries cross the lake after each train's arrival (15AS); the 5-kilometer walk around the southern end of the lake is pleasant and takes you past the best camping and swimming spots. The Hallstatt **tourist information** is in the **Prähistorisches Museum,** off Seestr. (tel. (06134) 208). (Open May-Aug. Mon.-Fri. 8am-6pm, Sat.-Sun. 10am-4pm; Sept.-Oct. and March-April Mon.-Fri. 8am-noon and 2-5pm; Nov.-Feb. Mon-Fri. 8am-noon.) The nicest and least expensive lodging is at the **TVN Naturfreunde Herberge,** Kirchenweg 36 (tel. (06134) 428), an unofficial hostel with clean, airy rooms, and a mountain stream rushing past. (130AS. Breakfast included. Restaurant with great meals for 50-80AS. No curfew. Open year-round.) For privacy, try any of the many homes with *Zimmerfrei* signs, or go to comfortable **Haus Sarstein,** Gosaumühlstr. 83 (tel. (06132) 217), on the lake. (150AS per person. Showers 10AS. Breakfast included.) The **Jugendherberge (IYHF),** Salzbergstr. 22 (tel. (06134) 279), offers the bare, dingy minimum: a bed and WC, but no showers. Look for the kindergarten sign. (52AS. Sheets 20AS. Breakfast 20AS. Flexible 10pm curfew. Open May-Sept.) **Camping** is at Höll, Lahnstr. 6 (tel. (06134) 329), near the bus stop. (25AS per person, 20AS per tent, 4AS tax.) The best deal in town on food is the **Gasthof Weisses Lamm,** in the center at Dr.-Morton-Weg 166. Casual and pleasant, the two-course *menus* (90-100AS) include dessert. (Open mid-May to Sept. daily 10am-midnight; Oct. to mid-May Wed.-Mon. Hours vary.) For a memorable meal, dine along the lake at **Bräugasthof,** Seestr. 20; pan-fried trout is 110-130AS, meat meals 100-120AS. (Open May-Oct. daily 8am-9pm.)

At the end of the lake, in Obertraun itself, the **Jugendherberge (IYHF),** Winkl 26 (tel. (06131) 360), is truly luxurious. (94AS. Showers and breakfast included. Lockout 9am-noon. Flexible 10pm curfew. Closed 1 week in early Sept. and Dec.) Here, too, are spectacular ice caves, such as the **Rieseneishöhle.** (Open May to mid-Oct. daily 9:30am-5pm. Admission 50AS.) These are accessible by the **Dachstein** cable car (90AS round-trip).

For information on winter and summer skiing, contact the **Skischule Zavner,** in Hallstatt at Markt 51 (tel. (06134) 246).

Salzburg

Protected by forested mountains, Salzburg is a city of enchantment whose voice is expressed in the sublime music of favorite son Wolfgang Amadeus Mozart. Purists may be offended by the city's exploitation of the composer, manifested most brazenly in the *Mozartkugeln,* an orgiastic confection of marzipan, hazelnut nougat, and bittersweet chocolate, wrapped in foil paper bearing Mozart's pensive image. Still, the age that produced Mozart also built the beautiful castles and churches of Salzburg, and spawned a love of music that lives on today in Salzburg's countless concert series and annual summer festival.

Orientation and Practical Information

Salzburg lies at the border of Austria and West Germany. The **Salzach River** separates the old town from the new town and the train station. The old town, concentrated and expensive, centers around **Residenzplatz,** and is largely a pedestrian zone. The (relatively) new town centers around **Mirabellplatz** and **Markartplatz,** a 15-minute walk south of the train station.

Tourist Offices: The train station kiosk at platform #10 (tel. 717 12) will give you a free map and find you a room for 10AS and a 50AS refundable deposit. Open July-Aug. daily 8am-10pm; Sept-June daily 8am-8pm. Branches at Auerspergstr. 7 (tel. 807 20) by the Kongresshaus, and at Mozartplatz 5 (tel. 34 62 or 34 63). Auerspergstr. open July-Aug. Mon.-Fri. 7:30am-6pm. Mozartplatz open July-Aug. daily 8am-10pm; May-June and Sept.-Oct. daily 9am-7pm; Nov.-April daily 9am-6pm. Ask for their excellent youth-oriented pamphlet, *Salzburg für die Jugend.*

Budget Travel: Young Austria, Alpenstr. 108a (tel. 25 75 80). Open Mon.-Fri. 8am-5:30pm. **ÖKISTA,** Hildmannplatz 1a (tel. 467 69). Open Mon.-Fri. 8:30am-5:30pm. Both have good travel discounts.

American Express: Mozartplatz 5 (tel. 425 01). Mail held. All banking services. Open Mon.-Fri. 9am-5:30pm, Sat. 9am-noon.

Currency Exchange: Banking hours are Mon.-Fri. 8am-noon and 2-4:30pm; currency exchange at the station open daily 8am-8pm.

Post Office: Poste Restante, unless letters are specifically addressed to another location. Open 24 hours for all services. In town, try Residenzplatz 9 (tel. 84 41 21 16). Open Mon.-Fri. 7am-7pm, Sat. 8-10am. **Postal code:** A-5020.

Telephones: At the train station post office. Open 24 hours. At Residenzplatz daily 7am-7pm. **Telephone code:** 0662.

Public Transportation: Buses, the routes of which are indicated on all maps, are excellent. 12AS per ride, 45AS for a book of 5 rides, 36AS for a 24-hour pass.

Emergencies: Police (tel. 133); headquarters at Alpenstr. 90 (tel. 295 11). **Ambulance** (tel. 144).

Medical Assistance: Hospital, Müllner-Hauptstr. 48 (tel. 31 51 80).

Pharmacies: Open Mon.-Fri. 8am-12:30pm and 2:30-6pm. Closed pharmacies post name and address of nearest open pharmacy.

Bike Rental: At the station (tel. 715 41) for 70AS per day, 35AS with train ticket. Motorbikes are available at **Zweirad Schmidt,** Alpenstr. 122 (tel. 288 22). 360AS per day with 800AS or a credit card as deposit. Open Mon.-Fri. 8am-noon and 1-6pm, Sat. 8am-noon.

Bookstore: Buchhandlung Alpenverlag, Rudolfs-Kai. Open Mon.-Fri. 8am-noon and 2-6pm, Sat. 8am-noon.

Laundry: Wäscherei Constructa, Kaiserschulzenstr. 10, opposite the station. 79AS per load. Open Mon.-Fri. 6:30am-8pm, Sat. 6:30am-1pm.

Hitchhiking: Towards Innsbruck, Munich, or for any part of Italy but Venice, go first to the German border; take bus S from the train station. For Vienna or Venice, take bus #2 from the train station, get off at Mirabellplatz, cross the street and take bus #4 (direction: Liefering) to the *Autobahn* entrance. Bus #4 can also be picked up in other parts of town. The **Mitfahrzentrale** is at W. Philharmoniker gasse 2 (tel. 84 13 27). Open Mon.-Thurs. 8am-5pm, Fri. 8am-6pm.

Accommodations and Camping

Ask for the tourist office's list of private rooms (*not* the hotel map). During the summer festival (late July-Aug.), hostels fill up by mid-afternoon; if you're arriving later, call ahead. The youth pamphlet has information on hostels in the suburbs.

Hauerspergstrasse (IYHF), Hauerspergstr. 27 (tel. 750 30), close to the train station. Staff occasionally disappears from the office; just wait. Clean if sterile. 95AS. Sheets and breakfast included. Laundry 40AS per load. Check-in all day, but usually filled by 2pm. IYHF advance booking voucher necessary for reservations. No lockout. Curfew 11pm. Open July-Aug.

Bayrische Aussicht (IYHF), at Glockengasse 8 (tel. 762 41), is in a quiet spot but can be chaotic—particularly the showers. Walk to the foot of the Kapuzinerberg (mountain) from the train station. 80AS. Sheets, showers, and breakfast included. Check-in 5-10pm. 10pm curfew. Open April-Sept.

Naturfreundehaus, Mönchesberg 19 (tel. 84 17 29), towers over the old town from the top of the Mönchesberg; the view is staggering. Take bus #1 to Astättengasse and then take the elevator built into the cliff (15AS round-trip). For convenience to the old town, an unbeatable choice. 85AS in dorms. Sheets 85AS. Breakfast 40AS. Curfew 11pm. Open May-Sept. Popular, so call ahead.

Institut St. Sebastian, Linzer Gasse 41 (tel. 713 86). Elegant and spacious, with a large recreation room and friendly management. Dorm beds 120AS. Sheets 10AS. Doubles and triples 340AS and 450AS respectively. Sheets and showers included. Breakfast 25AS. No curfew or lockout. Reception open year-round Mon.-Fri. 8am-10pm, Sat.-Sun. 5-10pm.

International Youth Hotel, Paracelsusstr. 9 (tel. 796 49). Walk up Gabelsbergerstr. Lots of English-speakers; not even the staff is Austrian. Clean and roomy. *Sound of Music* shown daily. Bar/cafe with tasty meals 60AS, evening happy hour, and the right music (open until midnight). 90AS in dorms, doubles 120AS, quads 100AS; all prices per person. Sheets 15AS. Showers 10AS. Breakfast 25-40AS. No curfew or lockout. Open 24 hours for check-in, but reservations recommended. Open year-round.

Zum Junger Fuchs, Linzer Gasse 54 (tel. 754 96). A real bargain. Clean rooms and well situated in the new town, near the old. Singles 180-200AS, doubles 280-300AS. Showers 15AS.

Haus Moser, Kasern Berg 59 (tel. 53 32 33), a few kilometers out of town in a semi-rural area. Take bus G from Mirabellplatz to Kasern and then walk 5 min. up the hill, or take any northbound train from the main station to the first stop, Salzburg-Maria Plain, then walk up the hill. If you call from the main station, they may pick you up. Quaint rooms, beautiful location on the side of a mountain, and a friendly English-speaking hostess. 150AS per person in singles, doubles, or triples with use of showers and filling breakfast. Nearby, at #64, is **Haus Lindner** (tel. 53 32 54). Nice English-speaking family will pick up guests at station. Doubles 300AS, triples 420AS, quads 560AS. Breakfast included. Just down the street at #44 is the much smaller **Germana Kapeller** (tel. 53 32 14), with a charming owner who likewise will pick up guests at the station. Doubles 300AS, triples 450AS. Breakfast included.

Camping: Most convenient at **Stadtcamping Fallenegger,** Bayerhamerstr 14a (tel. 711 69), about 4 blocks behind the station. 55AS per person, 15AS per tent. Open May-Oct. Reservations advised July-Aug.

Food

The open-air **market** is held Thursdays from 6 to 11am by St. Andrew's Church. Be sure to sample the amazing variety of giant pretzels available at the stand on **Kapitelplatz** by the Dom.

Pitterkeller, Rainerstr. 6 (tel. 785 71), just south of Max-Ott-Platz. A local restaurant with meat, cold, and vegetarian dishes for 70-95AS. Accordion player April-Oct. after 7pm (12AS surcharge). Open daily 10am-11:30pm.

Bärenwirt, Müllner-Hauptstr. 8, near the Augustiner Kloster. Traditional Austrian food in a warm setting off the main tourist drags. Meals 70-100AS. Open daily 10am-midnight, though hours may vary.

Augustiner Bräustüble, Augustinergasse 4-6 (tel. 312 46). The first brewery in Salzburg, with several beer halls. You can assemble an inexpensive lunch or dinner at the many small stores and delis in the building, and wash your meal down with a liter of excellent beer (34AS). The boisterous atmosphere quiets down late in the evening. Open daily 3-11pm.

Stieglkeller, Festungsgasse 10. A fine beer garden at the base of the Mönchesberg. Hefty meals 70-140AS, beer 23AS. A nice view over the old town from the large terrace. Folk dancing Sat. and Wed. after 8:15pm (100AS). Open May-Sept. 10am-10pm.

Sights

Salzburg's impressive hills rise straight out of the old town. The most conspicuous hilltop fortification is the **Hohensalzburg,** Mönchesberg 34, built over the centuries on an ancient Celtic and Roman site. The **Rainermuseum** inside the fortress displays the archbishop's weaponry and instruments of torture, mainly from the thirteenth to fifteenth centuries. (Tours July-Aug. 9am-5:30pm; May-June and Sept. 9am-5pm; April and Oct. 9:30am-4:30pm; Nov.-Feb. 9:30am-3:30pm; March 9:30am-4pm. 30AS, students 15AS.) The funicular from Festungsgasse costs 13AS one way, 21AS round-trip.

For splendor of another sort, visit the **Schloss Mirabell** and its **Gardens,** in the new town on Rainerstrasse. Prince-Archbishop Wolf Dietrich built this wonder in 1606 for his mistress Salome Alt; it was embellished in the 1720s by architect Lukas von Hildebrandt. You can wander around the extravagant rosebeds and lawns of the **Zwerglgarten.** (Open in summer until 10pm; in winter until 6pm.) The frequent chamber music concerts (180-240AS) held in the *Schloss* offer a chance to inspect the baroque excesses of the interior, including the gorgeous Angel staircase. (Staircase also open daily 8am-noon and 2-5pm.) The tourist office has a pamphlet of performances and dates.

Back in the old town lies the archbishop's own palace, the **Residenz,** Residenzplatz 1. You can visit both the main baroque rooms and the art gallery. (Open for tours in German July-Aug. every 20 min. 10am-noon and 1-3:40pm; Sept.-June at 10am, 11am 2pm, and 3pm. Tours 20AS, students 10AS.) Your time is perhaps better spent on the collection of works by Rembrandt, Rubens, Breughel, and Titian in the **Residence Gallery.** (Open daily 10am-4pm. Admission 20AS, students 15AS; combined admission to Residenz and Gallery 30AS.)

Salzburg's powerful bishops and monks left behind some spectacular ecclesiastical architecture as well. The **Dom,** completed by the Italian Santino Solari in 1628, is a standard baroque edifice, but it was the first of its kind north of the Alps. Master architect Fischer von Erlach left Salzburg a more exciting baroque legacy: Overlooking Markartplatz, the simple concave facade of his **Dreifaltigkeitskirche** (Trinity Church) belies the glories of its interior; don't miss the altar of gilded clouds and cherubim. The larger **Universitätskirche** on Universitätsplatz is generally considered von Erlach's masterpiece.

A slightly different brand of baroque graces the elaborate interior of **St. Peter's.** Behind this Benedictine church is the small graveyard where Liesl's boyfriend Rolf blew the whistle on the von Trapp family in the *Sound of Music.* Here also is the entrance to the **Katakomben** (catacombs), St. Peter-Bezirk 1, where Christians worshiped in secret as early as 250 C.E. (Open May-Sept. daily 10am-noon and 1-5pm, tours in English every ½ hr.; Oct.-April daily 11am-noon and 1:30-3:30pm, tours hourly. Admission 8AS, ages 17 and under 7AS.)

To learn about Mozart and his life, go to his **Geburtshaus** (birthplace) at Getreidegasse 9. The street itself is worth a look; the guild signs and painted wall decorations are much as they were at the time of Mozart's birth. The house exhibits pictures, letters, and stage sets for the various operas Mozart wrote. (Open May-Sept. daily 9am-7pm; Oct.-April daily 9am-6pm. Admission 30AS, students 20AS.) Mozart's **Wohnhaus** (residence), Markartplatz 8, was badly damaged in air raids, and is now the site of a museum relating to his work of 1773-1780. (Open June-Sept. Mon.-Sat. 10am-4pm. Admission 20AS, students 10AS. Combined admission to Geburtshaus and Wohnhaus 40AS, students 25AS.)

For a little peace and a wonderful view of the city, wander the footpaths on the east side of the Mönchesberg. You can either descend by the elevator built into the mountain, or go the long way and emerge at **Hildmannplatz**—a great walk.

South of the city lies the fantastic **Schloss Hellbrunn,** a one-time bishop's pleasure palace ringed by a world-famous alpine **zoo,** a large park, and trick fountains that do things you'd never think possible. (Open April daily 9am-4:30pm; May to mid-Sept. daily 9am-5:30pm; mid-Sept. to Oct. 9am-4:30pm. Admission (including the park and fountains) 39AS, students 19AS.) The zoo is open year-round; take bus H from the station. (Admission 30AS, students 15AS. Open April-Sept. 9am-5pm; Oct.-March daily 9am-4pm.)

Entertainment

The **Salzburger Festspiele** (summer music festivals) run from late July to the beginning of September. Detailed programs are available in December from Direktion der Salzburger Festspiele, Festspielhaus, Salzburg, or from an Austrian national tourist office. The few tickets still available by summer are sold at the Festspielhaus box office. Travel agencies in Salzburg add a 20% service charge to the ticket price. Opera seats go for 400-2400AS, concert seats for 100-1000AS. Standing room is available for 50AS and up. At **Marionetten Theater,** Schwarzstr. 24, the lighthearted performance is accompanied by tapes of past festival opera performances (tickets 200-350AS).

In an effort to cater to youth, Salzburg sponsors the **Szene der Jugend/Club 2000** festival, which coincides with the Festspiele. It offers a little bit of everything—check at Waagplatz 1a (tel. 426 23) for information. Tickets cost 30-120AS. The city constantly offers music in all its churches and palaces—you should never have trouble finding a performance in Salzburg.

Peterskeller, just outside the entrance to St. Peter's graveyard, is the oldest restaurant in Salzburg and a fun place to sample wine in a medieval atmosphere. (Open Easter-Sept. daily 9am-midnight; Oct.-Easter Tues.-Sun. 9:30am-midnight.) The **Felsenkeller,** around the corner in the Toscaninihof, dispenses wine in a damp, coin-studded cellar built right into the cliff. Look for the huge iron door 5m into the mountain; the crowd inside is mainly local and quite friendly. (Open Sun.-Fri. 2:30pm-1am, Sat. 10:30am-1am.) For a younger scene, try any of the clubs off Neumayrplatz, or linger in one of the bars along Giselakai. Always packed, **Bazillus,** Imbergstr. 3, has a terrace right on the river. (Open in summer daily 5pm-2am; in winter daily 5pm-1am.)

Near Salzburg

If you want to see what the Alps look like inside, visit one of the many **Salzbergwerke** (salt mines) around the Salzkammergut. The closest are at Bad Dürrnberg near Hallein, accessible by rail or bus. They're quite an experience—you wear traditional miner's clothes, slide down passages in the dark, take a miniature train ride, and sometimes a raft ride on the salt lakes is included. The cable car ride to the entrance provides an outstanding view, and at the mines you'll be treated to a 1½-hour tour. (Open May-Oct. daily 8am-5pm. 130AS includes round-trip cable car, tour, and museum.)

BELGIUM

US$1 = 38.46 francs(BF)	**10BF = US$0.26**
CDN$1 = 28.57BF	**10BF = CDN$0.35**
UK£1 = 61.53BF	**10BF = UK£0.16**
AUS$1 = 26.82BF	**10BF = AUS$0.37**

Stretching from the lowlands along the North Sea to the wooded hills of the Ardennes, Belgium displays a thoroughgoing charm, dignity, and order. Until the nation's independence in 1830, the rulers of France and the Hapsburg Empire fought to secure its strategic ports and fertile lands. The vast graveyards around Ypres are painful reminders of a past torn by two world wars. Don't rush through this small country at the crossroads of Europe; its turbulent history has left in its wake more cultural variety than one might expect.

The Roman Empire extended as far north as modern-day Brussels, and Germanic Franks conquered the lands to the north. The ancient dichotomy is still apparent today: The economy of the northern provinces rests upon industry and commerce, while the rolling hills of the Ardennes are primarily farmland. Flanders was cut off from its Protestant neighbor to the north when the revolt of the United Netherlands against the Spanish crown stalled at the present-day border; Flemish, the language of Flanders, is a variant of Dutch. The Walloons, to the south, speak French, while a small German-speaking community lives in the east of the country. Language remains a point of contention; after centuries of French as the only official language, Flanders today is defiantly Flemish-speaking. It is diplomatic to approach people in the north with English rather than French.

Belgium has many treasures to tempt the visitor: The extraordinarily well-preserved guildhouses and romantic canals of Bruges, the youthful energy and Renaissance splendor of Ghent, the Rubens masterpieces that seem to fill Antwerp, the gentle Ardennes countryside around Namur, the modern bustle of Brussels, and of course famous Belgian chocolates, waffles, and beer. Last but not least, Belgium is perhaps the worst place in Europe in which to commit a crime; both Georges Simenon's Maigret and Agatha Christie's Hercule Poirot hail from Belgium.

Transportation and Practical Information

Belgium's train network is one of the most comprehensive and reliable in Europe. Prices on Belgian trains are low (Namur-Brussels 185BF; Brussels-Bruges 325BF; Bruges-Ghent 130BF), if only because the country is small; at its widest point, Belgium is only four rail hours across. Each station offers a variety of **Un Beau Jour/Een Mooie Dag** tickets entitling you to 50% off same-day returns. The **B-Tourrail "5/17" Pass** allows five days of unlimited second-class travel on all Belgian trains during a 17-day period—a value only if you'll be seeing a great deal of the country. (Available May to mid-Sept.; 1600BF.) If you're planning to visit Luxembourg and the Netherlands as well, the **Benelux Tourrail Pass** may be worthwhile. It covers five days' travel in all three countries during a 17-day period (2490BF, ages under 26 1790BF; available April-Oct.; inquire at any travel agency). A **Half-fare Card** (500BF for 1 month) is also available. Both Eurail and InterRail passes are valid on all Belgium trains and intercity buses.

Like the Netherlands, Belgium is a cyclist's delight. The land is flat, intercity distances are short, and roads have special bicycle lanes. Sixty train stations rent bikes; you can return a bike at any of 150 rail stations. Bikes cost 105BF per day, 90BF per day for three more days, or 150BF per day without a rail ticket; tandems cost 250BF, 215BF, and 350BF, respectively. Pick up the brochure *Train et Vélo/Trein en Fiets* at any station.

Hitching on secondary roads in Belgium is generally good; on motorways it's illegal. If you're planning to traverse Belgium in one swoop, wait at the border and don't accept any ride that isn't going all the way across the country; there are no rest areas on the highways, and drivers leaving major cities are remarkably indifferent. Use a bilingual sign: "please" is *s.v.p.* in French, *a.u.b.* in Flemish. **Taxi Stop** has offices in major cities and links travelers with Belgian drivers to destinations all over Europe. To become a member costs 500BF (otherwise, it's 300BF per trip), and to become a member of **Eurostop** (see General Introduction) costs another 200BF. In addition, you pay 1BF per kilometer.

Belgium's dense network of efficient tourist offices ensures hassle-free travel throughout the country. Their services are supplemented by those of *Infor-Jeunes/Info-Jeugd,* a nationwide information service that caters to young people. Services vary from town to town, but you'll almost always find friendly people to help with medical or legal problems, work or study in Belgium, and short- or long-term accommodations. *Bulletin,* an English-language weekly, lists everything from movies in English to job opportunities.

Major national holidays in Belgium include Ascension Day (the sixth Thurs. after Easter), Whit Monday (the seventh Mon. after Easter), July 21, and August 15.

Public telephones take two 5BF coins. Direct-dial international calls can be made from any public telephone, but bring a sack of coins. You're better off going to the RTT (telephone and telegraph) office, which is separate from but usually near the main post office. In an emergency, anywhere in Belgium, dial 900. To reach the operator for phone calls within Belgium, dial 997, and for numbers outside of Belgium, dial 904.

Accommodations, Camping, and Food

Hotels in Belgium are expensive, with rock-bottom prices of 400BF for a single or 600BF for a double. You can avoid bankruptcy by staying in any of the 31 IYHF hostels, which charge 240-280BF per night (350-550BF in Oostende and Brussels) and are usually clean and comfortable; IYHF cards are required (these cost 360BF). Pick up *Budget Holidays* at any tourist office for complete hostel listings. Also look for unofficial hostels and student hotels. Campgrounds charge about 90BF per night. The pamphlet *Camping*, with complete listings and prices, is available free at tourist offices.

Belgian cuisine has earned a reputation of being amongst the best in Europe. Seek out these regional specialties: *carbonnades flamandes* (beef stewed in beer), *boudins Liège* (sausage), *waterzooi* (chicken and vegetables stewed in a mustard sauce), after-dinner cheeses, and chocolate truffles. Eels, mussels, rabbit, and pigeon are cooked in dozens of ways. If the national cuisine leaves you unimpressed, you should at least respect Belgium's brewing prowess. Choose from 30 to 45 different varieties of beer in any saloon—a total of 355 varieties are made in Belgium. Light *(blonde)* pils costs as little as 30BF, and dark beers cost about 50BF. Be sure to sample one of the excellent Trappist beers, originally brewed in Cistercian monasteries. *Gueuze* beer is made from local wheat and ferments in the bottle, while *Kriek* is made from cherries.

Brussels (Bruxelles, Brussel)

Brussels could be called the "capital of capitals." In the sixteenth century, it was declared the capital of the Spanish Low countries. In the nineteenth century, it (and The Hague) were declared the capitals of the Netherlands. And today it is the capital of Belgium, known to be the world capital of the comic strip, and also the headquarters for NATO, countless multinational corporations, and the European Parliament. But you won't find monumental architecture to go with the city's titles; the magnificence of the Grand' Place and several fine museums compensate, but Brussels is for the most part an acquired taste.

Orientation and Practical Information

Tourist Brussels is roughly bounded by Gare du Nord in the north, Brussels Park in the east, the Palais de Justice in the south, and the Bourse (stock exchange) in the west. Gare Centrale and the Grand' Place share the center.

Brussels and its suburbs are officially bilingual. Since most Bruxellians speak French (the city is estimated to be 75% Walloon), and since French is more familiar to most travelers than is Flemish, *Let's Go* uses French when giving street names and other information.

Tourist Offices: National, 61, rue du Marché aux Herbes (tel. 513 90 90), near the Grand' Place. Pick up the helpful *What's On* brochure. They will make hotel reservations anywhere in Belgium, but a deposit is required. Open June-Sept. Mon.-Fri. 9am-8pm, Sat.-Sun. 9am-7pm; Oct. and March-May daily 9am-6pm; Nov.-Feb. Mon.-Sat. 9am-6pm, Sun. 1-5pm. Also a branch at the airport (tel. 722 30 00); open daily 6am-10pm. **T.I.B. (Tourist Information Brussels),** in the town hall on the Grand' Place (tel. 513 89 40). Brochures, free room reservations; theater, opera, and ballet tickets. Open April-Sept. Mon.-Sat. 9am-6pm, Sun. 9am-5pm; Oct.-March Mon.-Sat. 9am-6pm.

Budget Travel: Acotra World, 51, rue de la Madelaine (tel. 512 55 40). Room-finding service (free), budget flights, and tickets for the highly recommended **Chatterbus** tours. Open Mon. 10am-6:30pm, Tues.-Wed. and Fri. 8am-6:30pm, Thurs. 10am-8pm, Sat. 10am-4:30pm.

American Express: 2, pl. Louise (tel. 512 17 40). Mail held and all banking services. Open Mon.-Fri. 9am-5pm, Sat. 9am-noon.

Currency Exchange: Mediocre rates but long hours at Gare du Nord (daily 7am-11pm), Gare Centrale (daily 8am-9pm), and Gare du Midi (daily 7am-11pm).

Post Office: In the tall building on pl. de la Monnaie, through the door marked "Galeries" and up the escalator. Open Mon.-Fri. 9am-8pm, Sat. 9am-noon. Poste Restante open same hours. Branch at Gare du Midi, 48a, av. Fonsny, open 24 hours.

Telephones: 17, bd. de l'Impératrice, near Gare Centrale. Open daily 8am-10pm. Also at Gare du Midi, 1D, av. Fonsny. Open Mon.-Fri. 9am-5pm, Sat. 8am-noon and 12:30-4pm. Public phones take 2 5BF coins (min.). **Telephone code:** 02.

Flights: Trains (20-min. trip) to **Brussels International Airport** leave Gare Centrale 9 and 39 min. after each hr. (daily 5:39am-11:09pm), and stop at the Gare du Nord. 70BF. Information (tel. 720 71 67).

Trains: There are 3 major stations in Brussels. Almost every domestic and international train stops at **Gare Centrale,** and many stop at either **Gare du Nord** or **Gare du Midi** as well. Gare Centrale is near the Grand' Place, the tourist office, and Acotra, but a 15-min. walk from most budget accommodations. Gare du Nord is convenient to several hostels, though little else. Avoid Gare du Midi and the seedy neighborhood surrounding it. Information (tel. 219 28 80).

Buses: Information (tel. 521 00 07).

Public Transportation: The **Metro** covers most of the city. All public transportation—buses, Metros, trams—costs 35BF; transfers are free if you request a *transit* when you buy your ticket. A 24-hour pass is available for 140BF; a 5-trip punch card costs 140BF; a 10-trip card costs 210BF. All are available in any Metro station or T.I.B., as well as at Gare du Midi and Gare Centrale. Public transportation runs 6am-midnight.

Emergencies: Police or **Ambulance** (tel. 900 or 901). **First Aid** (tel. 906).

Medical Assistance: Free Clinic, 205, chaussée de Wavre (tel. 511 66 99). Open Mon.-Fri. 9am-7pm. 24-hour standby medical services (tel. 479 18 18 or 648 80 00).

Pharmacy: All pharmacies post locations of 24-hour pharmacies.

Crises: SOS-Jeunes, 27, rue Mercellis (tel. 512 90 20). Psychological help and friendly assistance in any kind of crisis; 24-hour telephone service. Also **Infor-Jeunes,** 27, rue du Marché aux Herbes (tel. 512 96 02 or 512 32 74), near the national tourist office. Open Mon.-Fri. noon-6pm.

Embassies: U.S., 27, bd. du Régent (tel. 513 38 30). **Canada,** 6, rue de Loxum (tel. 513 79 40). **U.K.,** 28, rue Joseph II (tel. 219 11 65). **Australia,** 6, rue Guimard (tel. 231 05 00). **New Zealand,** 47-48, bd. du Régent. **Spain,** 19, rue de la Science. (tel. 230 03 40).

Women's Center: YWCA, 94, av. Brugmann (tel. 343 51 33).

Gay Center: Brussels Homocentrum, 16-18, rue des Riches Claires (tel. 512 62 20). Open Wed. noon-2pm and 10pm-midnight, Fri.-Sat 10pm-1am.

Bookstores: Replace lost copies of *Let's Go* at **Granado Paperbacks,** 71-75, bd. Adolphe Max (tel. 219 50 34), a huge but expensive English bookstore. Also try 8, bd. Anspach.

Comicstrips: Strips & Trips, 113, chaussée de Wavre (tel. 512 40 78). Open until 9pm. For addresses of more comicstrip places, ask at the tourist office.

Laundry: Salon Lavoir, 5, rue Haute, around the corner from the IYHF youth hostel. Open Mon.-Fri. 8am-6pm.

Hitchhiking: For Antwerp and Amsterdam take tram #52 from Rogier to the terminus, or even better, bus B.H., F.K., or B.M. from Gare du Nord and get off at Nieuwe Haachtsesteeweg, right by the E10 *autoroute.* For Liège and Cologne, take tram #90 or 23 from Rogier to Diamant to reach the E5. For Ghent, Bruges, and Oostende, take bus #85 or tram #62 from the Bourse. South to Namur and the Ardennes, take Metro 1B direct to Demey for the E40. To Paris, take tram #52 to terminus Drogenbos for the E19. **Taxi-stop** is at 27, rue du Marché aux Herbes (tel. 512 10 15). Open Mon.-Fri. 9am-6pm.

Accommodations and Camping

Brussels has a wealth of cheap hostels, but hotels are expensive. Most hostels have singles and bunk doubles. Remember that the tourist office and Acotra will help you find a place.Acotra's airport branch (tel. 720 35 47; daily 8am-1pm) and **Infor-**

Jeunes at track 4, Gare du Midi (open 12:30-7:30pm) can also help with accomodations.

Bruegel (IYHF), 2, rue du St. Esprit (tel. 511 04 36), in an alley behind Notre-Dame-de-la-Chapelle. From Gare Centrale, go out the back exit and take a right on bd. de l'Empereur. About a 10-min. walk. A huge hostel brimming with fine facilities and noisy adolescent tour groups. Dorm beds 330BF; singles 550BF, in doubles 450BF, in quads 375BF. All prices per person. Linen 80BF. Hot showers and breakfast included. No kitchen facilities. Dinner 210BF. Lockout 10am-3pm. Midnight curfew. Open year-round.

Sleep Well, 27, rue de la Blanchisserie (tel. 218 50 50). Metro: City 2. From Gare du Nord, walk to pl. Rogier and continue straight to rue Neuve, and take the first left. Clean, friendly, and centrally located. Beds in "sleep-ins" (huge dorms) 170BF (June-Aug.); dorms 270BF, singles 430BF, doubles 380BF, rooms with 4-6 beds 330BF. All prices per person. Linen 50BF. Showers (5-11pm only) and breakfast included. No kitchen facilities. Rooms closed 10am-5pm, but lounge and luggage storage open. 1am curfew April-Oct.; 11:30pm Nov.-March. Open year-round. If your name contains the letters of "Sleep Well" you get 50% off one night, and if your passport number has the number 27 in it, you get 25% off.

CHAB, 8, rue Traversière (tel. 217 01 58). Metro: Botanique. From Gare du Nord, take tram #62 to rue Traversière or walk 10 min.; from Gare Centrale take bus #65 or 66 and get off at rue du Méridien. Big clean rooms and a grassy courtyard. Very friendly. Kitchen and laundry facilities. Beds in "sleep-ins" 220BF, smaller dorms 280BF, singles 520BF, doubles 420BF, triples and quads 370BF. All prices per person. Linen 60BF. Showers and breakfast included. 1am curfew Mon.-Thurs; 2am Fri.-Sun. Open year-round.

Maison Internationale, 205, chaussée de Wavre (tel. 648 85 29 or 648 97 87), out of the center, near Gare du Quartier Leopold. Metro: Porte de Namur. Take bus #38 or #37 from Gare du Nord (bus #37 from Gare Centrale). Call the hostel at 648 97 87 if there's several of you, and they'll send a van to the train station or airport. Almost always has room. Singles 340BF, doubles 290BF. All prices per person. Showers and breakfast included. For 200BF you can pitch a tent in their garden. Open year-round 7am-12:30pm.

Hotel Pacific, 57-59, rue Antoine Dansaert (tel. 511 84 59). 5 min. from the Grand' Place. Metro: Bourse. A pleasant 1-star hotel with elegant old sinks in each room. Singles 520BF, doubles 750-950BF, triples 950BF, quads 1200BF. Showers 100BF. Check-in 11am-midnight.

Residence Osborne, 67, rue Bosquet (tel. 537 92 51). Metro: Pl. Louise. High ceilings, bathtubs, and a friendly British proprietor. Singles 540-815BF, doubles 900-1250BF, triples 1200-1450BF, quads 1420BF. Breakfast included.

Camping: Other than the camping option at the Maison Internationale, campgrounds are inconveniently located outside Brussels. Try **Beersel** at Steenweg op Ukkel 75 (tel. 376 25 61), in Beersel. 30BF per person plus 20BF per tent. Showers 20BF. Open year-round. Take tram #55 from Nord-Bourse, then change to bus U.H. Closer and better-equipped is **Paul Rosmant,** Warandeberg 52 (tel. 731 07 74), in Wezembeek-Oppem. 85BF per person, 45BF per tent. Open April-Sept.

Food

The cost of eating out in Brussels ranges from expensive to extremely expensive. You'll do best at the city's ubiquitous *frites* stands and snack-bars. There are daily **markets** at place Ste. Catherine (7am-5pm), place Emile Bockstael (7am-2pm), and place de la Chapelle (7am-2pm); and **GB** supermarkets on rue Marché aux Poulets (open Sat.-Thurs. 9am-8pm, Fri. 9am-9pm) and in the "City 2" shopping center, 50m from the Sleep Well. Restaurants usually have a *plat du jour* for 200-300BF.

La Canette, 1, rue de la Madelaine, down the hill directly across from Gare Centrale. A Greek restaurant. Try the *meze* platter (200BF) or the luscious *moussaka* (290BF). Open Mon.-Fri. 11:30am-3pm and 6pm-1am, Sat.-Sun. 6pm-3am.

Chez Léon, 18-20, rue des Bouchers, just off the Grand' Place. Deep in the tourist maelstrom, but fun. Anything from hamburgers to mussels to more sophisticated Belgian cuisine (255-545BF). Open daily noon-midnight.

Restaurant Hotel Hacht, 12, rue de la Montagne. Great omelettes and chicken dishes (180-325BF). Open daily 8am-1am.

Sights and Entertainment

One pleasant aspect of sightseeing in Brussels is the Bruxellians' willingness to show their city. The tours offered by **Le Bus Bavard/De Babbelbus** (alias the **Chatterbus**) are excellent (and in English) and range from 220BF (Brussels on foot) to 920BF (evening in Brussels; 820BF for students and hostelers). For information and reservations call 512 55 40.

You'll see what Victor Hugo meant by "the most beautiful square in the world;" the **Grand' Place,** a magnificent collection of guildhalls and public buildings, teems with visitors day and night. If the facades of the guildhalls are not enough, visit the fifteenth-century **Town Hall** on the *place.* (Open Tues.-Fri. 9:30am-5pm, Sun. 10am-4pm. Earliest tour in English starts around 10:45am. Admission 50BF.) Not far away is Brussels's second sight, the **Mannekin-Pis,** a fountain of a small boy urinating, three blocks behind the town hall on the corner of rue de l'Etuve and rue du Chêne. The story goes that the mayor of Brussels promised to build a statue in the position that his lost son was found; another says the statue commemorates a boy who saved the city by ingeniously extinguishing the fuse which had been lit to blow up the Town Hall.

Brussels has several good art museums. The **Musée d'Art Ancien,** 3, rue de la Régence, has a huge collection of early Flemish masters, including Breughel's enigmatic *Fall of Icarus* and *Census in Bethlehem.* (Open Tues.-Sun. 10am-noon and 1-5pm. Free.) Next door is the recently renovated **Musée d'Art Moderne.** This architectural showpiece houses the best of nineteenth- and twentieth-century Belgian modernists. (Open Tues.-Sun. 10am-1pm and 2-5pm. Free.) The **Musées Royaux d'Art et d'Histoire,** 10, parc du Cinquantenaire, cover a wide variety of periods and genres. Here you'll find Roman torsos missing their heads, Syrian heads missing their torsos, ancient floor mosaics, colorful Egyptian caskets with protruding wooden feet, Chinese porcelain, and tapestry exhibits; not to mention a sampling of Belgian toys, bicycles, and old vehicles. There's also a **museum for the blind** here, with an emphasis on exhibits on touch and sound. (Metro: Merode. Open Tues.-Fri. 9:30am-12:30pm and 1:30-4:45pm, Sat.-Sun. and holidays 10am-4:45pm. Free.) **Autoworld,** 11, parc du Cinquantenaire, houses the largest collection of automobiles in Europe, with vintage cars dating back to 1894. (Open April-Oct. 10am-6pm; Nov.-March 10am-5pm. Admission 200BF.

Brussels, like Barcelona, is one of Europe's top addresses for art nouveau architecture, a style that was considered radical in its day (1900-1920), but is currently in vogue. For a taste of art nouveau, try out the cafe/restaurant/bar **De Ultieme Hallucinatie,** 316, rue Royale (tel. 217 06 14), for music and a dance hall in a classy atmosphere. (Restaurant open Mon.-Sat. noon-2:30pm and 7:30-10:30pm; cafe open Mon.-Fri. from 11am, Sat. from 4pm. Take tram #92 or 94.) The tourist office has a brochure listing neighborhoods in which the style abounds. Baron Victor Horta is art nouveau's greatest representative in town, and you can visit his house, the **Musée Horta,** at 25, rue Américaine; take bus #54, or trams #18, 32, or 92. (Open Tues.-Sun. 2-5:30pm. Admission 50BF.)

Those with a taste for the bizarre should visit the house of one **Vallobra** (his full name), 147, rempart des Moines. This is not a public museum with regular hours: If you show up and Vallobra is there, he'll give you a delightful tour.

There's a **flea market,** with real junk, on place du Jeu de Balle. (Daily in summer, Sat.-Sun. in winter.) This square is in the **Marolles,** an area of narrow streets and old houses. Finally, be sure to visit **St. Michael's Cathedral,** the city's most impressive Gothic edifice, and walk the length of the **Galerie St. Hubert,** Europe's oldest shopping arcade.

The **Cinema Museum,** 9, rue Baron Horta (tel. 513 41 55), shows two silent movies a night with piano accompaniment. (Open 5:30-10:30pm. 30BF for a 2-hr. stay. Metro: Gare Centrale, or take train #92, 93, or 94.) For more decibels for your dollar walk down rue des Dominicains, near the center of town, where you'll find a string of nightclubs/discos/bars. For live jazz try **Travers,** 11, rue Traversière (tel. 218 40 86; open Mon.-Sat. from 9pm), or **The Brussels Jazz Club,** 13, Grand'

Place (tel. 512 40 93; open Tues.-Sat., featured performer 11pm-2am, cover charge 150BF). From June through September there are nightly concerts outdoors on the **Grand' Place, place de la Monnaie,** and in the **Parc de Bruxelles.** Pick up a calender of events at the tourist office. For more information about cultural events in Brussels (music/dance/theater/opera) call **BBB Agenda** (tel. 512 82 77).

Near Brussels

Twenty minutes away by train you can find relief from the Bruxellian brick and bustle in medieval **Leuven.** Pedestrians rule the streets of this university town, and nearly every corner has its bookshop or cafe. Pick up a map (5BF) at the **tourist office,** Naamsestraat 1a (tel. (016) 23 49 41). (Open April-Sept. Mon.-Fri. 8:30am-5pm, Sat.-Sun. 10am-noon and 2-5pm; Oct.-March Mon.-Fri. 8:30am-5pm.)

The **Stadhuis** (town hall) is a contender for the most sculpture-laden Gothic building in Europe (although the statues are a nineteenth-century afterthought); the recently cleaned facade, adorned with bright flowers and flags, is endearing. Across from the Stadhuis is **St-Pieterskerk,** a fifteenth-century church with a collection of paintings by Dirk Bouts, including his *Last Supper,* a richly colored masterpiece. (Open Tues.-Sat. 10am-noon and 2-5pm, Sat.-Sun. 2-5pm. Admission 20BF.) If you thought Brussels's Mannekin-Pis was cute, you'll enjoy **Fonske** behind St-Pieterskerk. The name is a diminutive which combines "Alphonse" and "*Fons Sapientiae*" (fountain of wisdom); Fonske diligently pours knowledge into his brain, though he misses when the wind blows. Several blocks down Naamsestraat is the **Groot Begijnhof,** a lovely "city within a city." At one time a convent, its restored houses and narrow streets are now used by university students. The **university,** where Erasmus once studied, is the focus for much youthful activity.

The **Wiering** on Wieringstraat, between Naamsestraat and Brusselsestraat, is an excellent place to meet students. **De Blauwe Schuit,** off Vaarstraat near the fish market, is just about as welcoming and popular. More pubs pouring Belgium's finest cluster around **Oude Markt.**

Napoleon was finally caught with both hands in his shirt at **Waterloo,** south of the city. Climb the **Lion Mound** for a superb view of the plains (open May-Aug. daily 8:30am-12:30pm and 1:30-7pm; Sept.-Oct. and March-April 9:30am-12:30pm and 1:30-5pm; Nov.-Feb. 10am-12:30pm and 1:30-3pm), and visit the **Commemorative Museum** in nearby Caillou (open in summer daily 10am-7pm; in winter daily 3-6pm; admission 15BF). Bus W leaves for Waterloo from pl. Rouppe in Brussels (every ½ hr.), or you can take the train (direction: Charleroi).

Bruges (Brugge)

Bruges, the capital of Flanders, is Europe's sleeping beauty. Five hundred years ago, this wealthy Renaissance town slipped quietly to rest as accumulating silt from the River Zwin cut it off from the sea and its livelihood. Antwerp quickly assumed the discarded role of economic capital, and Bruges was pronounced dead. But in 1907, a second seaport—Zeebruges—was connected to the town, and Bruges—its youth preserved by long slumber—awoke from obscurity. Today it is the best-preserved example of northern Renaissance architecture in Europe; the beauty of its romantic canals and remarkable facades is matched only by its art. Bruges is a museum pulled inside out, displayed with a loving touch and subtlety that most curators can only dream of.

Orientation and Practical Information

Bruges can easily be visited as a daytrip from Ghent, Antwerp, or Brussels, but you'll probably want to be here after dark, when the tourist buses are gone and the buildings and canals are beautifully illuminated (May-Sept. daily dusk-midnight). Bruges is ringed by a highway and a canal; several other canals flow through the town. The center of town is the **Markt,** a beautiful square presided over by the remarkable **belfort** (belfry). The train station lies just outside the ring, directly south of the Markt.

Tourist Office: Markt 7 (tel. 33 07 11), beneath the belfry. Very helpful office provides a map (5BF) and a good list of pubs and cafes, makes hotel reservations, and books tickets for special events. Open April-Sept. Mon.-Fri. 9:30am-6:30pm, Sat.-Sun. 10am-noon and 2-6:30pm; Oct.-March Mon.-Fri. 10am-1pm and 2-6pm, Sat. 10am-1pm and 2-6pm.

Youth Information Center: J.A.C., Kleine Hertsbergestr. 1 (tel. (050) 33 83 06), with information on cheap accommodations, meals, travel, and youth clubs.

Currency Exchange: Regular banking hours are Mon.-Fri. 9am-noon and 2-4:45pm, Sat. 9am-noon. Weekends, the tourist office will change money April-Sept. Sat. 2-6pm, Sun. 10am-12:30pm and 2-6pm; Oct.-March Sat. 2-6pm.

Post Office: Markt 5. Open Mon.-Fri. 9am-6pm. **Postal code:** 8000.

Telephones: Stationsplein, next to the train station. Open Mon.-Fri. 9am-noon and 12:30-5:15pm. **Telephone code:** 050.

Trains: To get to the Markt and the tourist office from the station, go left through the park, past the equestrian statue of King Albert, to 't Zand Sq., and then right on Zuidzanstraat. Information (tel. 38 23 82), open daily 7am-10pm.

Ferry Information: Daily ships and jetfoils leave for England from Oostende and Zeebrugge, easily accessible by train from Bruges. Tickets for the ferries can be purchased in travel agencies, at the ports, or in the Oostende train station. **Townsend-Thoresen,** with offices at Natiënkaai 5, Oostende (tel. (059) 70 76 01), and the Car Ferry Terminal, Doverlaan 7, in Zeebrugge (tel. (050) 54 22 22), runs daily ships between Oostende and Dover, Zeebrugge and Dover, and Zeebrugge and Felixstowe. (5-day round-trip 1690BF, one way somewhat more than half that.) Check the Youth Information Center or JEST in Antwerp for BIGE or bus tickets from Belgium to London.

Bike Rental: At the station (tel. 38 58 71). 150BF per day, 105BF with railpass or train ticket; if you rent for 3 or more days, 130BF and 90BF per day respectively. **Koffieboontje,** Hallestraat 4 (tel. 33 80 27), off the Markt next to the belfry, rents for 200BF per day, 120BF for the second and subsequent days, 680BF per week; less for students and children, and Sept. through mid-April. Tandems cost about double. 500BF deposit or passport.

Emergencies: Police or **Ambulance** (tel. 900). Police headquarters at Hauwerstraat 3 (tel. 33 77 33), off 't Zand Sq.

Laundry: Belfort, Ezelstraat 51, next to the Snuffel Sleep-In. Open daily 7am-10pm. **Ipsomat** is a few doors to the left of Bauhaus International Youth Hostel. Open daily 7am-10pm.

Hitchhiking: For Brussels take bus #5 or 7 to St. Michiels, or pick up the highway behind the station.

Accommodations, Camping, and Food

The tourist office has an efficient reservation counter, but there's usually a line. Try to arrive before noon. Bruges has a number of fine private hostels.

Europa Jeugdherberg (IYHF), Baron Ruzettelaan 143 (tel. 35 26 79). Take bus #2 to Steenbrugge. An equally inconvenient distance from the station and the center of town. Conditions have improved with a new annex, but still somewhat factory-like. Members only, 280-320BF, but nonmembers can purchase an International Guest Card for 80BF. Sheets 80BF. Showers and good breakfast included. Lockout 10am-5pm. 11pm curfew in main building, none in annex. Open year-round except 3 weeks in Dec.

Bauhaus International Youth Hotel, Langestraat 135-137 (tel. 33 61 75), a 15-min. walk from the Markt. Bus #6 from the station. Bar, cafe, and very comfortable beds. Changes money and distributes free town plans. 280-295BF. Showers and breakfast included. No lockout. 2am curfew weekdays; 4am weekends. Open year-round.

Snuffel Sleep-In, Ezelstraat 49 (tel. 33 31 33), a 10-min. walk from the Markt, or take bus #3, 8, 9, or 13 from the station. A fun house. Happy-hour (8-9pm) with 20BF beers. Call before noon to reserve a place. Dorm beds 280BF. Showers and breakfast included. Ask about working from 9:30am-noon in exchange for a free night's stay. No lockout. Curfew Fri.-Sat. 2am, Sun.-Thurs. 1am. Open year-round.

Bruno's Youth Hotel, Dweersstraat 26 (tel. 34 02 32). Pleasant and clean, with a bar even more elaborate than at Snuffel and Bauhaus. Dorm beds 295BF. Showers and breakfast included. Kitchen facilities available. No lockout. No curfew. Open year-round.

Huyse Elckerlyc, Hauwerstraat 23 (tel. 33 62 26), off 't Zand Sq. near the station. Clean and very comfortable; nice common area with cheap drinks. Popular, so call ahead. Singles 475BF, doubles 800BF, triples 1200BF, quads 1600BF. Showers and good breakfast included. 1am curfew. Open July-Aug.

Camping: St. Michiels (tel. 38 08 19), southwest of town off the road to the *autoroute.* Take bus #7 from Markt or the station. A large campground; crowded but well-kept. Hot showers (50BF), a well-stocked store, and a restaurant. 65BF per person, 40BF for children, 80BF per tent. Reception open 9-11:30am and 12:30-9pm. Open year-round.

You can get a terrific sit-down meal at the **Ganzespel,** Ganzestraat 37, a residential street off Langestraat. It's a coffeehouse-restaurant frequented by young people and has a very reasonable 180-215BF *menu du jour.* (Open Wed.-Sat. noon-2:30pm and 6-10pm, Sun. noon-10pm.) **The Lotus,** near the Markt at Wapenmakerstraat 5, has a pleasant cafe-style atmosphere and serves a fine vegetarian *plat du jour* (around 150BF). (Open noon-1:30pm, closed Aug. 1-15.) The **market** in Bruges takes place Saturday mornings until 1pm at 't Zand Square, and Wed. mornings at Burg Square.

Sights and Entertainment

The best way to see the town is on foot; the tourist office has excellent suggestions for walking tours. For an overview of the city's circular perimeter, climb the 366 steps of the *belfort* on the Markt; go early to avoid the hordes. (Open April-Sept. daily 9:30am-12:30pm and 1:30-6pm; Oct.-March daily 9:30am-noon and 2-5pm. Admission 50BF, students 40BF.) The fourteenth-century **Stadhuis** (town hall), on nearby Burg Sq., is a good example of flamboyant Gothic architecture. (Open April-Sept. daily 9:30am-noon and 2-6pm; Oct.-March daily 9:30am-noon and 2-5pm. Admission 30BF.)

Many Flemish masters worked in Bruges; some of their masterpieces, including van Eyck's and Breughel's, are housed in the excellent **Groeninge Museum** on Dijverstraat. (Open April-Sept. daily 9:30am-noon and 2-6pm; Oct.-March Wed.-Mon. 9:30am-noon and 2-5pm. Admission 80BF, students 50BF.) Next door is the **Gruuthuse Museum,** housed in the fifteenth-century residence of a wealthy family which massed its fortune by levying taxes on "gruut," an herb used to make beer before barley and hops were introduced. Edward IV of England had such a good time at the Gruuthuse's that he made Louis Gruuthuse the Earl of Winchester. The museum today is filled with a collection of historic weapons, musical instruments, pottery, lace, and coins. Don't miss the wooden bust of Charles V as a young man, in the first room. (Open April-Sept. daily 9:30am-noon and 2-6pm; Oct.-March Wed.-Mon. 9:30am-noon and 2-5pm. Admission 80BF, students 50BF.) The **Church of Our Lady** contains the only Michelangelo to leave Italy during the master's lifetime, a soft and touching *Madonna and Child;* there is also a fantastically ornate wood pulpit. (Open April-Sept. Mon.-Fri. 10-11:30am and 2:30-5pm, Sat. 10-11:30am and 2:30-4:30pm, Sun. afternoons only; Oct.-March Mon.-Sat. 10-11:30am and 3-4:30pm, and Sun. 2:30-4:30pm. Free.)

In medieval Belgium, women who didn't want to become nuns but who nevertheless appreciated the secluded life resided in *beguinages.* Bruges's **begijnhof,** with its tiny homes and grassy courtyard, is one of the prettiest; Benedictine nuns live here now, but you can still visit and tour one of the old homes. Nearby is the aptly named **Minnewater** (Lake of Love), where Bruges seems even more picture-perfect than usual. On Kruisvest, just off Langestraat, are three **windmills;** you can inspect the interior of the **St. Janshuismolen.** (Open May-Sept. daily 9:30am-noon and 1:30-6pm. Admission 20BF.)

Bruges is renowned for its lace, and a visit to the **Kantcentrum** (lace center) on Balstraat is interesting. (Open Mon.-Sat. 10am-noon and 2-6pm, Sun. 2-5pm. Admission 40BF.) Around **Walplein** you can see weavers (no relation) making lace by hand. You'll do best to buy lace, as well as other Bruges specialties, on weekend afternoons at the busy **flea market** on the canal bank in front of the museums.

There are innumerable late-night cafes around the old town; the best are far from the water's edge. **Vlissinge,** on Blekerstraat, claims to be the oldest in Europe. **De Versteende Nacht,** Langestraat 11, has jazz concerts (Tues.-Thurs. and Sun. 7pm-2am, Fri.-Sat. 7pm-4am). The rollicking **Cactus,** St. Amandsstraat 13, on a side street off the Markt (open Mon.-Fri. noon-2pm and 7pm-1am, Sat.-Sun. 7pm-1am) and **(Ma) Rica Rock,** 't Zand Sq., are other good places.

A wonderful place to spend an evening is the **Marionette Theater,** Sint-Jakobstraat 36 (tel. 33 47 60), which produces four full-blown puppet operas each summer. Shows take place Thursday, Friday, and Saturday nights at 8pm from April through September, and Monday through Saturday at 8pm during July and August. (Ticket office open performance days 10:30am-12:30pm, 2-5pm, and 7-8pm. You can also buy tickets at the tourist office. Admission 250BF, students 200BF.) During the **Festival van Vlaanderen** (July 25-Aug. 8), the entire town comes alive with the famous **International Fortnight of Music.** Pick up the monthly program *Agenda Brugge* at the tourist office for a schedule of local events.

Near Bruges

A beautiful 30km bike trip runs along Canal Bruges-Sluis to **Damme;** according to legend, this is the birthplace of Tijl Uilenspiegel, who inspired Richard Strauss's symphonic poem. You can **camp** in Damme at **Hoecke,** Damse Vaart Oost 10 (tel. (050) 50 04 96). (58BF. Open March-Nov.) From April through September you can also take an excursion boat from Bruges to Damme, leaving Noorweegse Kai at 10am, noon, 2pm, 4pm, and 6pm. (100BF, ages 65 and older 90BF.)

The North Sea coast of Belgium is spattered with towns that are loved largely for their beaches. You can return a rented bike and take the train back to Bruges from stations at Knokke, Blankenberge, Zeebrugge, or Oostende. There are two **IYHF youth hostels** in Oostende; **De Ploate,** Langestraat 82 (tel. (059) 70 54 84), is only five minutes from the station; **De Branding,** Raversijdestraat 20 (tel. (059) 50 12 77), is closer to nicer beaches. There are also campgrounds all along the coast: **De Vuurtoren,** Heistlaan 202, in Knokke (tel. (050) 51 17 82; open mid-March to mid-Oct.; 70BF per person, 40BF per child, 80BF per tent, 80BF per caravan); **Bonanza,** Polderlaan 74, in Blankenberge (tel. (050) 41 50 00; open year-round; 90BF per person, 45BF per child, 150BF per tent, 40BF per car); and **Townsend Thoresen,** Bredeweg 115, in De Haan (tel. 23 44 75; open mid-April to Sept.).

Ghent (Gent)

Thanks to the textile industry, fourteenth-century Ghent became the second-largest continental city north of the Alps, preceded only by Paris. Though the city has lost some of its Renaissance splendor, modern Ghent combines some of the beauty of Bruges with the liveliness of Antwerp. Let's go? **Ghent** went.

Practical Information

Tourist Offices: East Flanders Tourist Office, Koningin Maria-Hendrikaplein 64 (tel. 22 16 37), across the square to the left as you exit the station. Maps and lists of hotels and restaurants (including prices). Open Mon.-Fri. 8:30am-noon and 1:15-4:30pm. **Municipal Tourist Office,** in the crypt of the town hall on Botermarkt (tel. 24 15 55). Same services, with more emphasis on Ghent itself. Very informative walking-tour booklets (30BF) and maps (20BF) of the city. Open Easter-Sept. Sun.-Thurs. 9am-8pm, Fri.-Sat. 9am-9pm; Oct.-Easter daily 9am-noon and 2-5pm.

Budget Travel: JEST/Acotra, Overpoorstraat 47, at Stalhof (tel. 21 21 47). BIGE tickets and helpful advice. Open May-July Mon.-Fri. 10am-6pm, Sat. 10am-2pm; Aug.-April Mon.-Fri. 10am-6pm. **Taxi-stop,** Onderbergen 51, (tel. 23 23 10). Matches drivers with people looking for a ride and books cheap last-minute flights and budget bus tickets. Open Mon.-Fri. 10am-6pm, mid-June to mid-Aug. also Sat. 10am-1pm.

Post Office: Korenmarkt 13. Open Mon.-Thurs. 9am-6pm, Fri. 9am-7pm, Sat. 9am-noon.

Telephones: Keizer Karelstraat 1. Open Mon.-Fri. 8am-8pm, Sat. 8am-noon and 12:30-4pm, Sun. 11:15am-7:15pm. **Telephone code:** 091.

Trains: Tram #1 runs between **Sint-Pietersstation** and Korenmarkt, the center of the old city. Frequent trains to Bruges, Brussels, and Antwerp. Information (tel. 22 44 44).

Public Transportation: Public transportation is both efficient and necessary in this sprawling city. Tram and bus tickets cost 29BF; an 8-ride ticket is 130BF in the train station, 170BF on the train or bus; 24-hr. passes cost 105BF, while 48- and 72-hr. passes cost 150BF and 200BF, respectively.

Emergencies: Police or **Ambulance** (tel. 900). Police headquarters (tel. 23 24 25).

Laundry: St. Jacobsnieuwstraat 85. Open Mon.-Sat. 8am-10pm. On Sun. try **Miele Wassalon** at Dampoorstraat 58. Open daily 6am-10pm.

Hitchhiking: Ghent lies at the intersection of the E40, connecting Brussels and Germany with Oostende, and the E17, linking Paris and Amsterdam. From the train station, walk down Burggravenlaan and cross the railroad tracks.

Accommodations, Camping, and Food

The best cheap-and-clean lodgings in Ghent are at the **university.** Between mid-July and mid-September, 1000 spotless singles are available in student dormitories. (400BF. Sheets, showers, towel, and breakfast included.) Contact the main reservations office at Stalhof 6 (tel. 22 09 11), the second large building on the right off Overpoorstraat (reception open 24 hours). The rest of the year, try **La Lanterne,** Prinses Clementinalaan 140 (tel. 20 13 18), an immediate right from the station. (Singles 500BF, doubles 700BF, with shower 800BF. Breakfast included.) Another option is **De Fonteyne,** Goudenleeuwplein 7 (tel. 25 48 71), one block from the tourist office. (Singles 410BF, with shower 470BF; doubles 680BF, with shower 760-870BF. Breakfast included.) **Camping Blaarmeersen,** Zuiderlaan 12 (tel. 21 53 99), is 15 blocks or a bus ride (#85 or 86) northwest of Sint-Pietersstation (75BF per person, plus 90BF per tent. Open March to mid-Oct.)

The best deal for meals is the modern, multi-level **University Restaurant** on 49 Overpoortstraat near Citadellaan; a full meal costs around 120BF for lunch and 100BF for dinner. (Open Mon.-Fri. 11:30am-2pm and 6-7:30pm.) During the school year (Oct.-June), there is another university restaurant at 45 St. Pietersnieuwstraat. **De Appelier,** Citadellaan 47, has vegetarian *menus* for 85-210BF. (Open Sun.-Fri. 11:30am-2pm and 5:30-8pm.) There is a good grocery store at St. Jacobsnieuwstraat 119 (open Mon.-Sat. 9am-6:30pm), but buy your fruits and vegetables at the **Groentenmarkt.** (Open Mon.-Fri. 7am-1pm, Sat. 7am-7pm.)

Sights and Entertainment

To appreciate Ghent's heritage of commercial splendor, visit **Sint-Michielsbrug** (St. Michael's Bridge). Bordering the canal are the **Graslei** and the **Koornlei,** both lined with guildhalls (fifteenth to seventeenth century meetingplaces of artisans; each trade had its own hall). This area was the town's medieval harbor. A bit farther north along Canal Sint-Veerleplein stands the forbidding **Gravensteen** (Castle of the Counts of Flanders), a grim fortress replete with grisly medieval dungeon paraphernalia. (Open April-Sept. daily 9am-6pm; Oct.-March daily 9am-4pm. Admission 40BF, students 20BF.)

Although the thirteenth-century **Sint-Niklaaskerk** has long been closed for restoration, you can visit the large and impressive **belfort** (belfry) and **cloth hall.** Here you can also attend the audio-visual presentation *The Ghent Experience,* an excellent introduction to the city's past and present. (Open daily April-Oct. 9:20am-6:30pm; Nov.-March Tues.-Sat. 9:20am-4:20pm. Admission 40BF, students 20BF. English-language presentations Nov.-March Tues.-Sat. at 10:40am and 3:40pm; April-Oct. daily at 10:40am, 2:30pm, and 5:10pm.) Also interesting is the **Stadhuis** (town hall) on the corner, a strangely handsome juxtaposition of Gothic and Renaissance architecture. Another block down on Limburgstraat lies **Sint-Baafskathedraal,** a fine edifice dating from the fourteenth to sixteenth centuries. The real gem here is Jan van Eyck's *Adoration of the Mystic Lamb,* a magnificent polyptych (a series of paintings on oak wood panels) worth the trip to Ghent alone. (Open April-Sept. Mon.-Sat. 9:30am-noon and 2-6pm, Sun. 1-6pm; Oct.-March Mon.-Sat. 10:30am-noon and 2:30-4pm, Sun. 2-5pm. Admission to the cathedral is free, but it's 40BF to see the *Mystic Lamb.*)

Also worth a visit are the **Museum voor Schone Kunsten** (Museum of Fine Arts) and the **Museum van Oudheden** (Museum of Antiques). The former, located in the lovely Citadel park, has a good Flemish collection and an outstanding exhibit of modern works by Belgian artists. The latter occupies the **Van de Bijloke Abbey,** Godshuizenlaan 2, and has a fine exhibition on local social history and beautiful reproductions of monastery and guildhall rooms. (Both museums open Tues.-Sun. 9am-12:30pm and 1:30-5:30pm. Admission 40BF, students 20BF.)

Nightlife is most interesting when the university is in session. Students meet in the cafes and discos near the university restaurant on Overpoortstraat. **Dulle Griet,** Vrijdagmarkt 50, serves 250 brands of beer and often has live jazz. Ghent actively participates in the **Festival van Vlaanderen,** a major music festival held in Flemish towns from late July through early November. Nocturnal boat trips on the **River Lys** (July-Aug. Sat.) depart from the Recollettenlei (law courts) at 8pm and return at 1am (200BF, children 120BF).

Antwerp (Antwerpen)

Antwerp's appeal derives from its unique mix of styles and peoples. First there's the no-nonsense part of town around Centraal Station; the shipping, diamond, and garment industries are headquartered here. Then there's the art and culture that wealth has bought throughout the centuries: Flemish Old Masters, particularly native son Rubens, are well-represented here. Finally, there are the smoky streets of the immense port on the Scheldt River, which connects Antwerp to the North Sea.

Orientation and Practical Information

Antwerp lies 40km north of Brussels on the Amsterdam-Brussels-Paris rail line. **Grote Markt** and **Groenplaats** at the end of **Meir** are the important squares in Antwerp.

Tourist Offices: Information Pavilion, Koningin Astridplein (tel. 233 05 70), directly in front of Centraal Station. They will supply a hotel list, make hotel reservations, and sell an indispensable city map (10BF). The well-conceived walking-tour brochure (with English translation) is worth 30BF. Open Mon.-Fri. 8:30am-8pm, Sat. 9am-7pm, Sun. 9am-5pm. **Municipal Tourist Office,** Gildekamersstraat 9 (tel. 232 01 03), off Grote Markt. Same services as above. Open Mon.-Fri. 8:30am-6pm, Sat.-Sun. 9am-5pm. **Provincial Tourist Office,** K. Oomsstraat 11 (tel. 216 28 10), provides information about excursions around Antwerp province. Open Mon.-Fri. 10am-6pm.

Budget Travel: JEST, Pieter van Hobokenstraat 20 (tel. 232 55 52). General travel information and youth tickets. Open Mon.-Fri. 10am-6pm.

American Express: Frankrijklei 21 (tel. 232 59 20). Mail held. All banking services. Open Mon.-Fri. 9am-5pm, Sat. 9:30am-12:30pm.

Currency Exchange: Desk at Centraal Station open daily 8am-11pm.

Post Office: Main office for Poste Restante on Groenplaats. Open Mon.-Fri. 9am-5pm, Sat. 9am-noon. Also a branch across from the train station on Pelikaanstraat 16. Open Mon.-Fri. 9am-6pm. **Postal code:** 2000.

Telephones: Jezusstraat 1. Open daily 8am-8pm. **Telephone code:** 03.

Trains: Centraal Station, in the eastern part of town, is a 15-min. walk from the old town and most of the sights.

Public Transportation: Trams and buses cost 30BF; purchase an 8-ride ticket for 144BF at the train station and in underground tram and subway stops. The tourist offices also offer **Toeristenkaart** deals: The 85BF version is an all-day pass that expires at midnight; the 135BF pass is valid 24 hr.; the 150BF pass 48 hr.

Emergencies: Police or **Ambulance** (tel. 900). Police headquarters, Oudaan 5 (tel. 231 68 80).

Medical Assistance: St. Elizabeth Hospital (tel. 231 48 80).

Consulates: U.S., Nationalestraat 5 (tel. 232 18 01). **U.K.,** Lange Klarenstraat (tel. 232 69 40).

Bookstores: For English books, try the **Club** on Carnotstraat, around the corner from Centraal Station (open Mon.-Fri. 9am-6pm, Sat. 9am-noon); or **Boekhandle** at Eiermarkt 23, near the Groenplaats.

Youth Information Center: Centrum voor Jeugdtoerisme, Dambruggestr. 78 (tel. (03) 233 99 14); **Jeugd-Info-Antwerpen,** Apostelstr. 20-22 (tel. (03) 232 27 28), for information about budget accomodations, meals, youth clubs, and general advice.

Laundry: Wassalon Soek, Van Den Nest Lei 5, one block from the New International Youth Home.

Hitchhiking: For Germany, the Netherlands, and Ghent, take bus #20 from the train station to the big interchange outside town. For Brussels and other points south, take tram #2 to the intersection of Jan Devoslei and Jan van Rijswijklaan.

Accommodations, Camping, and Food

Be aware that some of the cafes around the train station that advertise "rooms for tourists" rent lodging by the hour.

Jeugdherberg Op-Sinjoorke (IYHF), Eric Sasselaan 2 (tel. 238 02 73). Take tram #2 or 15 to Camille Haysmanslaan and follow signs. Far from center, but beautiful and modern. Kitchen facilities, luggage lockers, and washing machines. Members 280BF, nonmembers 360BF. Sheets 80BF. Breakfast included. Lunch 95BF, dinner 190BF. Lockout 10am-5pm, but can leave luggage. Midnight curfew and 8am wake-up.

New International Youth Home, Provinciestraat 256 (tel. 230 05 22). Take tram #11 from Centraal Station or walk 15 min.: Left down Pelikaanstraat, and another left onto Provinciestraat (the fifth underpass under the railroad tracks). A cheery, comfortable, clean place with friendly management. Flowers on the breakfast table, and a large TV lounge. Uncrowded dorms 280BF. Singles 500BF, doubles 790-830BF, triples 1140BF, quads 1460BF. Breakfast included, but no kitchen facilities. No lockout. No curfew (but pick up a key).

Boomerang Youth Hotel, Volkstraat 58 (tel. 238 47 82), a block from the Royal Art Gallery. From Centraal Station, take bus #23. People keep coming back, and no wonder: This is a palatial townhouse with outdoor barbecue, terrace, library, and brutal tropical cocktails at night. Dorm beds 260BF. Doubles 650BF, triples 900BF, quads 1040BF. Sheets 80BF. If you can break the Boomerang parallel bar dip record you stay for free. Kitchen facilities, but the 220BF meals are the best in town (reserve before 5pm). No lockout or curfew, but ask for a key if you'll be carousing.

Camping: Jan van Rijswijcklaan, on Vogelzanglaan (tel. 238 57 17), and **De Molen,** on St. Annastrand (tel. 219 60 90). Both 30BF per person, 30BF per tent. Both open April-Sept.

In the **Jewish District,** along Pelikaanstraat, are fine kosher butchers and restaurants. Try **Kleinblatt,** Provinciestraat 20, Antwerp's best kosher bakery. For bread, cold cuts, cheese, and other grocery items, the **Grand Bazaar** at the corner of Shoenmarkt and Groenplaats has a wide selection and good prices. (Open Mon.-Thurs. and Sat. 9am-6pm, Fri. 9am-9pm.) **De Ware Jacob,** Vlasmarkt 19, is popular among locals; its 295BF *menu* includes soup, entree, dessert, and beer. (Open daily noon-2am.) Or try **'t Steen,** one of the many fine seafood restaurants on Suikerrui near the harbor; a veritable bucketful of mussels with fries costs 350BF, and the *menu* of the day costs 300BF. **Korenaai,** Oude Koorn Markt 73, serves ravioli (95BF), lasagne (125BF), and pizza (160BF). And although you probably didn't come to Belgium for Chinese food, there are few places better than the little take-out place at **Schelde Straat 80,** just off Volkstraat; dinner for two (600BF) is enough to feed two army battalions. (Open Mon.-Tues. and Thurs.-Sat. noon-2pm and 5-11pm, Sun. noon-11pm.)

Sights and Entertainment

Start with a walk through the **oude stad** (old city), beginning at Grote Markt, where the **Stadhuis** (town hall) stands as a magnificent example of Renaissance architecture. (Open Mon. 9am-noon, Tues.-Thurs. 9am-3pm, Fri. noon-3pm, Sat. 9am-4pm. Admission 20BF.) The nearby **Kathedraal van Onze-Lieve-Vrouw,** Groenplaats 21, has a spectacular Gothic tower; its interior is richly decorated with stained glass and Flemish masterpieces, most notably Rubens's *Descent from the Cross* and *Exaltation of the Cross.* The Emperor Charles V said of the cathedral: "This splendid building is worth a kingdom. It should be carefully kept in a case and shown to the people only once a year." (Open April to mid-Oct. Mon.-Fri. noon-5pm, Sat. noon-3pm, Sun. 1-4pm; mid-Oct. to March Mon.-Fri. noon-4pm, Sat. noon-3pm, Sun. 1-4pm. Admission 30BF.) From the **Zuiderwandelterras** (south promenade), admire the cathedral and the **Steen,** a beautiful story-book fortress that dates from the twelfth century.

The **Plantin-Moretus Museum,** Vrijdagmarkt 22, is three blocks southwest of Groenplaats. Plantin turned printing into an art during the sixteenth century, and most of his tools and presses are here on display. The picturesque courtyard and Rubens paintings also recommend the visit. (Open daily 10am-5pm. Admission 50BF, students 20BF.) The little-known **Mayer van den Bergh Museum** at Lange Gasthuisstraat 19 is home to Breughel's *Mad Meg,* among other works. (Open Tues.-Sun. 10am-5pm. Admission 50BF, students 20BF.)

Save time to visit **Rubens Huis,** Wapper 9 (off Meir), one of the best museums of its kind in the world. Rubens lived and worked for nearly 30 years in this sumptuous house, and even built it himself. His garret is exquisitely furnished and richly stocked with art treasures. (Open daily 10am-5pm. Admission 50BF, students 20BF.) The **Royal Art Gallery,** Leopold De Waelplaats 1-9, has one of the best collections of the Old Flemish Masters (from the fourteenth to seventeenth centuries) in the world, especially Memlinc, van Eycks, and van der Weydens, as well as some monumental Rubens canvasses. Natural lighting and the originality of its exhibit designs have made this gallery a model for many others. (Open Tues.-Sun. 10am-5pm. Free.)

If the Old Masters begin to overwhelm, visit the serene sculpture garden of **Middelheim,** an estate about 30 minutes from Groenplaats via bus #26. In August, an outdoor jazz festival is held. (Open June-July 10am-9pm; closing time gets ever-earlier until it's at 5pm in Dec. Free.)

Few tourists get to **Cogels Osylei,** an avenue in the southeastern part of Antwerp with an uninterrupted procession of art nouveau mansions, each one seeming to outdo the one before it in architectural fantasy. There are several more dazzlers on the adjacent streets, especially **Transvaalstraat** (don't miss #59). Take tram #11 from Korte Nieuwstraat at Melkmarkt.

Antwerp has other gems—most of the world's diamonds pass through the city. Visit the **Vieligheidsmuseum** at Jezusstraat 28-30 (open Wed.-Sun. 10am-5pm; demonstrations Sat. 2-5pm; free), and then stop by **Sidiam,** Lange Herentalsestraat 29, and watch laborers polishing and cutting stones. (Open Mon.-Fri. 10am-noon and 1-4pm; closed August 1-14. Ring the bell and don't be shy. Free.)

Most of the good bars in Antwerp are within a few blocks of Grote Markt. The **Pelgrim,** Pelgrimsstraat 15, is an old wine cellar where a decent bottle costs less than 300BF. Elbow-benders also congregate at **Het Grote Ongenorgen,** Jeruzalemstraat 9, an unassuming alley off Lange Koepoorts; they claim to stock between 750 and 1200 different kinds of beer in their hot, crowded hall. Antwerp's **cinemas** usually show films in the original language. Many are located in the area bordered by Centraal Station, De Keyserlei, Frankrijklei, and Gemeentestraat. For movie listings, call cine info at 231 78 00. For a list of events, pick up the monthly guide *Antwerpen* at the tourist office.

Namur and the Ardennes

Situated in the green Walloon heartland at the confluence of Rivers Meuse and Sambre lies Namur, gateway to the Ardennes Forest and a great base for exploring the provinces of Namur, Liège, and Luxembourg. Castles, caves, and kayaks greet those who flee the city for a few days. Trains link the larger towns, and buses, though infrequent, cover the rest. There are a few **IYHF youth hostels** (at Beverce, Tuliff, Logne, and Champion) and many official campsites. To get a list of farmers who let campers stay on their property and use their facilities (usually for 120BF per person plus 25BF per tent), check with the **Fédération du Tourisme de la Province de Namur,** 3, rue Notre Dame (tel. (081) 22 29 98; open Mon.-Fri. 8am-noon and 1-5pm).

Namur itself is pleasant despite the 20 sieges it's undergone. Climb or take the *téléférique* (runs daily April to mid-Sept. 10am-6pm; mid-Sept. to Nov. 11 weekends only; 90BF one way; 120BF round-trip) to the city's immense **citadel.** In summer, guides lead visitors through the castle's torch-lit underground passages. (Open daily 10am-6pm. Tours given sporadically April-June; daily late June-Sept. Admission 110BF.) Of Namur's 13 museums (including a strawberry museum in nearby Wepion), perhaps the most interesting is the **Musée de Croix,** 3, rue J. Saintraint, a handsome eighteenth-century mansion and former monastery. (Tours Wed.-Mon. at 10am, 11am, 2pm, 3pm, and 4pm. Admission 50BF.) For a complete list of museums and excursions, as well as accommodations information, visit the **tourist office,** pl. Leopold (tel. 22 28 59), in the pavilion—up av. de la Gare, to the left as you leave the train station. (Open June-Sept. Mon.-Sat. 9am-7pm, Sun. 10am-6pm; Oct.-May Mon.-Fri. 9am-noon and 2-5pm, Sat. 9am-noon.) For youth travel information and general tips on Namur and its surroundings, consult **Infor-Jeunes** (tel. 71 47 40), in Namur's medieval belfry. (Open Fri. 10am-1pm and 2-5pm, Sat. 10am-noon.) The **telephone code** for Namur is 081.

You'll feel at home in the **auberge de jeunesse (IYHF),** 8, av. Félicien Rops (tel. 22 36 88). Facilities are ordinary (dorm beds, hot showers included), but the energy is boundless. Breakfast runs until 10am, so you can sleep a little later. You can make collect calls and exchange money here, do your laundry for 90BF, and consult their library of tourist information. A bed and good breakfast runs 285BF; fantastic dinners are 210BF. (Use of kitchen 20BF. Camping with breakfast and hot shower 175BF. Nonmember supplement 80BF/night. Sheets 90BF. Midnight curfew.) To reach the hostel, take bus #3 or 4, or walk 40 minutes along the River Meuse; the train station information office usually has the hostel's own map and set of directions. **Les Quatre Fils Ayman,** the nearest campground, is 12km away at 5, chaussée de Liège (tel. 58 83 13), in Lives-sur-Meuse; **Les Trieux,** 99, rue des Tris (tel. 44 55 83), in Malonne, is another "wilderness" option. If you don't take advantage of the hostel feast, try the 250BF *menu du jour* at **Le Rimbaud,** 58, rue de la Croix. (Open daily noon-2pm and 6pm-midnight.) Or try **Café/Friterie St. Aubain,** 2, pl. St. Aubain, with meals for 225 to 300BF. (Open daily 11am-10pm.)

The countryside around Namur is great for daytrips. You can rent a bike at the train station and wheel 10km along route 22 to **Floreffe,** which has a pleasant thirteenth-century abbey (open March-Dec. Mon.-Fri. 11am-6pm, Sat. 11am-8pm; Jan.-Feb. Fri.-Sat. only; admission 60BF, children 40BF), as well as perpetually cool caves. If cycling is not your speed, hop a Charleroi-bound train, or bus #931 or 950. At **Dinant** you can wander through extensive **grottoes** (open May-Aug. 10am-5pm; April and Sept.-Oct. 11am-4pm; tours last 45 min.; admission 140BF), and peer at the region's most striking architectural feature—an indescribably bizarre bulb atop a late Gothic church outlined against the cliff and severe citadel above it. Dinant can also be reached by frequent trains from Namur; its **tourist office** is at 37, rue Grande (tel. (082) 22 28 70).

A descent of the **River Lesse** by kayak from Houyet to Anseremme makes an exciting diversion. The river winds through the Ardennes and passes some striking cliffs and a massive chateau just before Anseremme. Unless you plan to paddle on a summer weekend, same-day reservations are usually possible. The hostel will call for you, or try **Ansiaux** (tel. 22 23 25), **Libert** (tel. 22 24 86), or **Lesse-Kayaks** (tel. 22 31 20). You must arrive in Houyet before 11am, and you should bring clothes to change into at the end of the journey. Two-person kayaks cost 500BF; solo boats command 400BF. At **Han-sur-Lesse,** you can do much the same thing underground—tour boats ply the subterranean river which courses through extensive caves below the town. (Open in summer daily 9:30-11:30am and 1-5:30pm, July-Aug. until 6pm, in winter until 3:30pm. Closed Jan.-Feb. 235BF, children 135BF.) Han-sur-Lesse is a pleasant cycle from Namur, or a rail-and-bus journey: Take the train to Jemelle and a coach from there.

BULGARIA

US$1 = 0.87 leva (Lv) | **1Lv = US$1.14**
UK£1 = 1.42Lv | **1Lv = UK£0.70**

For 500 years the most secure European possession of the Ottoman Empire, Bulgaria today may seem to some just a similarly secure pawn of a new empire. Yet the country's close relationship with the Soviet Union—Bulgaria is widely held to be the Soviet Union's closest ally in the Eastern Bloc—is a lot more willing than "iron curtain" imagery might suggest. Tied to Russia by a common Eastern Orthodox Christianity and a Slavic language similar enough to Russian that citizens of the two countries can just about understand one another, Bulgaria is also indebted historically to the only European power that was sympathetic to its nineteenth-century struggle for independence from the Ottomans. From the statue of Czar Alexander II in Sofia's Parliament Square to the posters that everywhere express fraternity with the Soviet Union, Bulgaria gives the traveler an interesting perspective on Eastern European politics.

During the early Middle Ages, the powerful Bulgarian Kingdom stretched from the Black Sea to the Adriatic, and was a bridge between the intellectually and artistically vital Byzantine Empire and the northern Slavic nations. A brilliant flowering of Slavic Orthodox monasteries produced the Cyrillic alphabet and some great literature before it was crushed by the Turkish invasion in the fourteenth century. The Ottomans valued this region only for its agricultural output, and for over five centuries ruthlessly turned Bulgaria into a nation of peasants. Nonetheless, the nineteenth century witnessed a "National Revival" of Slavic identity and massive anti-Turkish rebellions. In towns like Plovdiv, Veliko Turnovo, and Koprivshtitsa, as in isolated monasteries, you can sense the flavor of this period from beautiful traditional architecture.

For most of the period of post-war Soviet hegemony, Bulgaria has been ruled by Todor Zhivkov. Zhivkov's economic programs have brought the country a steadily increasing standard of living—though you'll probably find his stated intent to make Bulgaria "the Japan of the Balkans" a little far-fetched. A darker side of Bulgaria's recent history is its handling of its Turkish ethnic minority—widespread imprisonments in the southern province of Kurdzhali are alleged.

Planning Your Trip

Visas for Bulgaria must be obtained in advance. In the United States they are available from the Bulgarian Embassy, 1621 22 St. NW, Washington, D.C. 20008 (tel. (202) 483-5885); their embassy in Canada is at 325 Steward St., Ottawa, Ontario. In 1987, fees were US$14 plus US$3 for postage. You must send your passport to be returned with the visa about one week later. In East European capitals, Bulgarian visas take seven to ten days to process, although you *may* be able to get a transit visa more quickly. Get a visa for the maximum stay (30 days), because you pay nothing extra, and visas are difficult to extend. If you must extend your visa, go to the passport office (located in each district). It is possible to shortcut the visa application process by buying accommodations vouchers. One of the best deals is available from Sunwaves Travel on Voukourestiou 16 in Athens, two blocks from the Bulgarian Embassy. (Two nights of a private room in Sofia at US$13.50 per night, and you get a visa overnight for US$27.) Even if you have a visa, check into vouchers in various countries before you come. The same double can cost US$10 if you buy it in West Germany, US$20 in Greece, and US$30 in Sofia.

Bulgaria has no minimum daily exchange requirements, though to pay for accommodations or international train tickets, you will need to produce an exchange receipt that shows that you've obtained leva legally.

When you cross the border you will be given an exit card (also called "statistical card") which will be stamped every night by the establishment at which you stay. Since many Western travelers pass through Bulgaria on transit visas, some border guards may stamp you "transit;" check your passport after their formalities.

Transportation and Practical Information

Public transportation in Bulgaria is adequate but crowded, and costs about 3Lv per 100 kilometers. The train system is very thorough; direct trains run between Sofia and all major towns. Service is especially good to Plovdiv (4Lv), Bourgas (12Lv), and Varna (14Lv). Trains come in three categories: *Ekspresen* (Express), *Brzi* (fast) or *Putnichki* (slow). Opt for express, which, unlike the others, often runs on schedule. To buy a ticket in advance, you must go to the office designed for that purpose, located usually in the town center, where lines can be several hours long in high season. You can buy the ticket at the train station only two hours before departure (although you can try earlier if there are no lines). In small cities where there is no separate office, tickets cannot be purchased in advance. Buying your ticket on the train will cost up to 100% more.

Buses usually cover distances of less than 100km and are much less reliable. For both buses and trains, if the idea of having a seat for the trip appeals to you, buy tickets a day in advance and make sure a seat reservation is included. Some useful words include: *vlaka* (train), *aftobus* (bus), *garata* (station), *peron* (track), *bilet* (ticket), *pristigane* (arrival), and *zaminavane* (departure). For longer distances, Balkan Air domestic shuttle flights are not that expensive (about 50-100% more than ground transport), and will save you a lot of aggravation. Seats can be booked at Balkan Air Offices only on the day of travel.

Hitchhiking is not bad; expect to wait about half an hour for a ride. In a country filled with signs proclaiming peace in three different languages, you can get a ride with a sign promoting peace and disarmament that you otherwise might not get. About half of the rides have space for only one passenger. Women may encounter sexual advances when hitchhiking. Open the door to signify your intent to leave and get out at the first opportunity.

Practical Information

Balkantourist is the national tourist bureau, with offices throughout the country. The generally helpful staff exchanges money and books private rooms.

One *leva* (Lv), the standard monetary unit, is divided into 100 *stotinki* (st). Despite outdated signs everywhere proclaiming the contrary, the exchange rate *does not* increase after you have stayed two days. By changing money illegally on the street (US$1 = 3-4Lv), you can cut your expenses in half. You will be approached, chiefly in Sofia, but be careful not to be swindled in black market transactions. Any Bulgarian bill not dated 1962 or 1974 is worthless—check carefully. Many tourists effectively turn themselves in by trying to spend this money in a train station or Balkantourist office. A word of caution: If caught changing an amount less than 100Lv, you are slapped with a fine three times the amount you changed; for an amount above 100Lv, you will spend time in jail—no exceptions.

Regardless of how you change money, don't get more *leva* than you need. You're entitled to up to 50% of a traveler's check's value in hard currency. If one exchange booth doesn't have change in hard currency, find another that does. Balkantourist officials will assure you that when you depart the country, "someone" will appear on your train to re-exchange *leva.* Though it's illegal to export Bulgarian currency, this person very rarely appears.

The International Union of Students (IUS) card, the Eastern European version of the ISIC, is not sold to Westerners. If you want to try your luck at ORBITA, the youth travel agency, it helps to bring a friend with an IUS card at which you can point.

Russian is the only really useful foreign language. Bulgarians can understand Russian if spoken slowly and illustrated with gestures. Few Bulgarians know English, other than professionals who use it on the job. Many people may know a few basic words of German and some know a little French; some tourist services offer only German. It's important that you learn the Cyrillic alphabet, as signs will otherwise be incomprehensible. Russian-English dictionaries and phrasebooks can be found all over Bulgaria for about 1Lv.

Bulgarian head movements for "yes" and "no" are the reverse of the West's—a minor detail that can lead to endless misunderstandings. Complicating matters is the willingness of some Bulgarians to reverse their gestures when dealing with Westerners. Ignore head movements altogether and confirm everything with *da* (yes) or *ne* (no). The final straw is that "ne" means "yes" next door in Greece.

Women will not encounter much harrassment, although they may receive sexual advances when hitchhiking. A firm refusal is usually sufficient. Look very angry so that your gut reflex to shake your head won't be interpreted as a "yes, yes!"

Sanitary napkins can be purchased in drugstores, but toilet paper is often unavailable.

Accommodations, Camping, and Food

ORBITA runs youth **hostels** which are open to Westerners by reservation only. Groups of five or more may be able to book them in advance from Sofia.

Hotels in Bulgaria are classed by stars. The rooms in one-star hotels are identical to those in two- and three-star hotels, but have no private bath. They cost about US$15.50 for singles, US$22 for doubles, but are available to Westerners in very few cities. More likely you will pay US$24 for singles and US$36 for doubles.

Private rooms are available, notably in Sofia (singles US$22, doubles US$24). In some other cities, private rooms cannot be let if hotel rooms are available, or are actually hotel rooms in disguise. Be wary about accepting illegal offers for cheap private rooms—for each night's accommodations, the hotel, campground, or (for private rooms) Balkantourist must give you a stamp on the back of your "statistical card;" if you cannot account for stampless nights when leaving the country, you may face a 200Lv fine. These cards are not always checked scrupulously; the more stamps you have, the less likely it is that they'll be tallied.

Campgrounds are crowded and afford encounters with Eastern European backpackers (2.50Lv per person, 2.50Lv per tent). Comfortable wooden bungalows are available at nearly every campground, but may be full (16Lv for 2 people). All large towns have campgrounds nearby. Freelance camping is popular, but remember the 200Lv fine for stampless nights.

Grabbing food from kiosks is cheap, but grocery shopping is tiresome and restaurants average 5Lv per meal. Kiosks sell *kebabches* (small hamburgers, 75st), hot dog rolls, and breads baked with cheese inside (40st). In stores you can purchase bread, cheese, sausage, and yoghurt (*kisselo mleko*d). A few types of fruits and vegetables are also available. Fruit juice is a rarity, but delicious fruit-flavored sodas will quench your thirst.

Bulgarians work wonders with vegetables. *Chopska salada* is available in almost all restaurants; this addictive salad of tomatoes, peppers, and cucumbers is covered with *siren,* grated white goat cheese. *Appetit* is a hot pepper salad. *Kiopolou* and *imam bayalda* are vegetable dishes based on eggplant. A *guvetch* is a mixed vegetable stew with onion, eggplant, peppers, beans, and peas. Try *tarator* as well—a cold soup made with yoghurt, cucumber, and garlic.

Eat carefully. Don't drink the unpasteurized milk unless heated. Don't eat the hamburgers if undercooked, or yoghurt if too sour. The food in self-service restaurants may mildly irritate your stomach. Water is generally safe to drink.

Sofia (Sofija)

Those who arrive in Sofia from one of Europe's hotter, dustier, or more crowded cities may very briefly think they have entered paradise. The center of town is a grid of enormously wide *bulevarts* paved with yellow bricks, and the quiet pedestrians don't even begin to fill the streets. For the most part, Sofia has been built over the last 100 years, though a few medieval churches compete with an even smaller number of mosques (left over from the Turkish occupation) for a spiritual presence in the city. National Revival architecture from the turn of the century lurks in small enclaves north of Lenin Square. Watch for small palaces and public buildings which look like a cross between German baroque and Russian Imperial ideals; most are surrounded by massive, squared-off modern monuments. Sofia is a great place to see socialist architecture: The party house facing Lenin's statue across Lenin Square is one of the best Stalinist monsters loose outside of Moscow. The perfectly straight streets outside the city's center are lined for miles with identical apartment buildings.

Orientation and Practical Information

Sofia lies in far western Bulgaria, 50km from the Yugoslav border, and about 500km southeast of Belgrade. Domestic train routes branch out in all directions toward the country's borders. International lines run to Belgrade, Thessaloniki and Athens, Istanbul, and Bucharest. Buses shuttling back and forth between Istanbul and northern Europe will let you off here.

Lenin Ploshtat (Lenin Square) is the center of Sofia. The central district is surrounded by a ring road which changes names as it circles the city. Incoming roads intersect this ring; the most important is **Vitosa Georgi Dimitrov,** which runs approximately south-north through the center of town before bending around to reach the train station at the northern end of the city. At right angles to Georgi Dimitrov run **Bulevart Stambolijski** and **Dondukov Ulitsa,** two other major thoroughfares. Get a street map in the Roman alphabet from Balkantourist or a newsstand, and practice transliterating the Cyrillic signs.

Tourist Offices: Balkantourist, Dondukov Ul. 37 (tel. 88 44 30). Take tram #1, 7, 9, or 15 from the train station to Lenin Pl., walk up the boulevard to the left of the Sheraton Hotel, and fork left onto Dondukov. Accommodations, bookings, and maps. The train station office is basically just an exchange booth, but the tellers speak English and are very helpful. Both offices open daily 7am-10:30pm.

Budget Travel: ORBITA, Bul. Stambolijski 45a (tel. 87 95 52), 5 blocks from Lenin Pl., in the opposite direction from the party house. Westerners may have difficulty getting an IUS. In 1987 this office was closed and another open in the ORBITA Hotel: take tram #9 south past the Palace of Culture to the intersection with Anton Ivanov and look behind Hotel Vitoša. Open Mon.-Fri. 8:45am-12:15pm and 1-5:30pm.

American Express: Interbalkan, in the Grand Hotel Balkan, Lenin Pl. 1 (tel. 83 11 35). Currency exchange, and checks sold and replaced, but no wired money accepted. Mail service as well, but unreliable.

Currency Exchange: Balkantourist offices and all large hotels. Open daily 7am-10pm.

Post Office: General Gurko Ul. 2, at the park west of Lenin Pl. Poste Restante here, but unreliable. Open 7am-8:30pm.

Telephones: International office across from the post office, but direct calls only (no collect). Open 24 hours. For local calls buy tokens at the phone office or at a newspaper kiosk (5st). Pick up the receiver, drop the coin, and hope.

Flights: Aeroport Sofija (tel. 45 11 13 for domestic flights, tel. 72 24 14 for international), about 10km out of town, roughly to the northeast. Municipal buses #84 and 284 run regularly. **Bulgarian Balkan Airlines'** main in-town office is at Pl. 12 Narodno Subranie (tel. 88 44 93). Another office conveniently located 2 blocks west of Lenin Pl., at 19 Leggae (tel. 88 09 49). Open Mon.-Fri. 7:30am-9pm, Sat.-Sun. 8am-2pm. Tickets also sold at the Palace of Culture ticket office.

Trains: Sofia's central train station is north of the center on Pl. Marks i Engels. Trams #7 and 15 travel to Lenin Pl. For information, tickets, and couchette reservations for international departures, visit the main office at General Gurko Ul. 5 (tel. 87 07 77). To purchase international tickets, you must present an exchange receipt that shows you have legally acquired leva; there are exchange booths near the ticket windows. For domestic routes, the ticket-issuing office is nearby at 8 Slaveikov Ul. The window at the station sells tickets, but no couchettes. Both offices open daily 8-11:30am and noon-4pm, though mid-afternoon hours are erratic. Information (tel. 31 11 11). To Athens US$35, Beograd US$20, Bucharest US$10, Budapest US$47, Istanbul US$27. Terrific deals can be found at the **Rila Agency,** inside the **Comprehensive Ticket Office,** under the Palace of Culture (take bus #72, 76, 104, or 304, or tram #9). You can buy a ticket to Budapest traveling the scenic route through Romania (transiting through Bucharest, Brasov, and Cluj-Napoca) that is valid for 2 months and costs only 20Lv. 25% discount on rail travel in East European countries for IUS cardholders. International tickets can be purchased only with Western currency or leva exchanged that day.

Public Transportation: The tram system is very cheap (6st). Tickets are bought at kiosks near stops and self-validated on board.

Emergencies: Officially it's **Police** (tel. 166) and **Ambulance** (tel. 150). Both lines ordinarily staffed by monoglots; try calling an embassy, ordinarily on call around the clock. The motorist assistance line (tel. 146) may be your last resort for finding someone who speaks German or English.

Pharmacy: The one at Alabin 29 is open 24 hours.

Embassies: U.S., Bul. Stambolijski 1a (tel. 88 48 01), 3 blocks from Lenin Pl. Will hold mail without fuss; most reliable option. Library with periodicals and TV tapes. Open Mon.-Tues. and Thurs.-Fri. 9am-5pm, Wed. 9am-1pm. **U.K.,** Bul. Tolbukhin 65 (tel. 88 53 61), 3 blocks northwest of the Palace of Culture. Open Mon.-Thurs. 8:30am-12:30pm and 1:30-5pm, Fri. 8:30am-1pm. Travelers from **Canada, Australia,** and **New Zealand** should contact the British Embassy. **Czechoslovakia,** Bul. V. Zaimov 9 (tel. 44 62 81), 9 blocks west of Balkantourist. Visas issued in 10 minutes, Mon., Wed., and Fri. 10-11:30am. Need 2 photos and Western cash: Americans US$15, Australians US$12, Canadians US$8, Britons US$21, and New Zealanders US$10. **Hungary,** September 6 St. 57 (tel. 66 20 21). Visas issued overnight for US$14.

Poland, Khan Kroum St. 46 (tel. 88 51 66). Visas take 2 or 3 days and cost US$20 (US$15 for students). **Romania,** D. Polyanov St. 10 (tel. 44 33 81). Visas issued in 1 hr. for US$20, but not necessarily every day.

Accommodations, Camping, and Food

Balkantourist at Dundukov can book private rooms for around US$22 per single and US$25 per double. They will quote you a price of US$30 and US$40 respectively, and then give you 10 and 20 leva back. The procedure changes day to day and may take up to three hours in the morning when they are busy. Best to go at night. Don't accept any "cheap private room" offers in the station until you read the Planning Your Trip section of the chapter introduction. Two one-star hotels are conveniently located on Georgi Dimitrov on the tram route from the train station to Lenin Ploshtat. **Hotel Sredna Gora** (tel. 83 53 11) at #60 charges 20Lv for a single and 34Lv for a double. **Hotel Edelvais** (tel. 83 54 31) is one block down and across the street and charges the same price.

Campgrounds are cheaper but an hour away by public transportation. **Camping Cherniya Kos** (tel. 57 34 79) is 11km southeast; take tram #5 from behind the National Museum of History, then a bus. Set on a wooded slope, this campground has the most comfortable bungalows in Bulgaria. (3Lv per person, 3Lv per tent, 16Lv for a double in a bungalow.)

Finding cafe-like *mehani* is much easier than finding restaurants. The self-service restaurants on Vitoša, south of Lenin Pl. are filling, but the food may irritate your stomach. (Meals 4-5Lv.) There is an **open-air market** at Georgi Kirkov Ul. 1 (not very far from the train station), where vegetables, fruit, and cheese are sold at very low prices. Arrive at 7am to avoid the lines; most of the good stuff is gone before noon.

Bulgarska Gozba, Bul. Vitoša 34 (tel. 87 91 62), a few blocks south of Lenin Pl., has an intimate setting and is the best place to sample Bulgarian cuisine. Entrees cost about 6Lv. (Open 11:30am-3pm and 5-10pm.) One block south of the National Museum of History on Knjaz Boris is **Epma** restaurant, where you can eat a full meal for 5Lv (they even have ice cubes!). (Open 11:30am-3pm and 5:30-10:30pm.)

Sights and Entertainment

Two "medieval" churches, **St. George's Rotunda** and **St. Sophia,** were originally constructed in the fourth and sixth centuries, respectively. St. George's is in the courtyard of the Hotel Balkan and will be closed several years for restoration. St. Sophia, the city's namesake, is several blocks behind the party house, with the ever-burning flame of the **Tomb of the Unknown Soldier** flickering just beside it. Across the square from St. Sophia is the massive **Alexandur Nevsky Church,** erected in the early twentieth century to the memory of the 200,000 Russians who died in the 1877-78 Russo-Turkish war. The icons by the altar offer an interesting comparison of the styles of different East European and Russian painters, but the main attraction is downstairs in the **crypt:** an enormous collection of painted icons and religious artifacts from the past 1000 years. (Crypt open Wed.-Mon.) In an underpass in Lenin Ploshtat is the tiny fourteenth-century **Church of Saint Petka Samardjiyska,** which contains some interesting frescoes; despite its small size, this is one of Sofia's nicest churches. (Admission 1.20Lv.)

If you can manage it, visit the **Georgi Dimitrov Mausoleum,** on September 9 Ploshtat, on a national holiday and observe the huge, solemn crowds as they wait to view the gloriously lit, plasticized remains of this pre-World War II hero of Bulgaria's Communist Party. Dimitrov leapt to international revolutionary stardom in 1933 when he conducted his own defense while being tried in Germany for setting fire to the Reichstag. He spent the later part of the 1930s developing close ties with the Soviet Communist Party. (Open Wed.-Thurs., and Sun. 3-6pm.)

Be sure to visit Sofia's outstanding **National Museum of History,** guarded by two bronze lions, off Lenin Ploshtat. This outstanding panorama of Balkan history since prehistoric times merits a half-day's tour. All exhibits are labeled only in Bulgarian;

pick up the English guidebook for 4Lv. (Open Tues.-Thurs. and Sat.-Sun. 7:30am-5:30pm, Fri. 2:30-5:30pm.) Each Bulgarian town has its **Museum of the Revolutionary Movement in Bulgaria;** Sofia has the biggest, at Bul. Ruski 14. Here you can see the personal items of almost every dead party member in Bulgaria. Included are shaving soap, toothbrushes, even underwear and pajamas. The **Archeological Museum,** located where Bul. Vitoša meets Lenin Pl., houses relics from the Thracian, Greek, Roman, and Turkish settlements in Bulgaria, as well as religious articles from the Bulgarian Kingdom. On the other side of Lenin Pl. is the **Banya Bashi Mosque** (now a museum), worth a look for those whose itineraries don't include Turkey. (All museums open erratically Tues.-Sun. 10:30am-6:30pm.)

Sofia shuts down early—there's not much to do after 10pm and most of the city seems to wander rather aimlessly through the streets. Try the **Disco** underneath the Palace of Culture, but go around 9pm; it closes at 11pm (cover 1Lv). You can also purchase tickets to see one of Bulgaria's fine performing arts companies. Arrange these through Balkantourist or any of the fancy hotels north of Lenin Ploshtat.

The Mountains

The **Stara Planina** bisects Bulgaria horizontally from Sofia to Varna. The Rila and Pirin Mountains are south of Sofia, and the less interesting Rhodopi Mountains center around the resort of Pamporovo, south of Plovdiv. Trails throughout the country are uncrowded, but because most of the mountains have not been developed as tourist centers, hotels are scarce and transportation indirect. Trains take you to the hills, and buses to the feet of most mountains. Before you go, look for a map in Sofia at kiosks or bookstores. During winter, the slopes of Mt. Vitoša and Pamporovo are the most popular and best equipped ski areas. Transportation from Sofia and Plovdiv is easy, with additional buses provided in high season (Nov.-March).

Rila Monastery

The **Rila Monastery,** 120km south of Sofia, is the largest and most famous monastery in Bulgaria. Founded by the hermit Ivan Rilski in the tenth century, it kept alive the arts of icon painting and manuscript copying during the Turkish occupation. The Kurdalis destroyed the monastery in the eighteenth century, but it was rebuilt during the National Revival period and is now considered the finest architectural monument of that era. The 1200 frescoes on the central chapel and surrounding walls resemble an outdoor art gallery. Try to make one of the services, at 6:30am and 5pm.

To reach the monastery from Sofia, take one of the frequent trains to the Kocherinovo station (12km from Kocherinovo Town); buses run to the monastery every half hour. Alternatively, take a bus from the **Ovča Kupel** station in Sofia (tram #5). To hitchhike, take tram #5 to highway E79. **Camping Bor** is 1km beyound the monastery (US$2.50 per person, US$2.50 per tent. 3-person bungalows 16Lv).

Because of its proximity to Sofia, the Rila is the most crowded of Bulgarian mountain ranges, but the hiking is superb. One great route is from Malyovitsa to the Rila Monastery. Take tram #14 or 19 in Sofia to stop Nadleza, and then a bus to Samokov (2 per hr.). Buses from Samokov to Malyovitsa leave at 11:30am, 1:40pm, and 4:10pm.

A possibility for those with lots of time is the three-day hike to Rila via **Mt. Musala,** the highest in Bulgaria (2925m). The hike begins in **Borovec,** a mountain resort accessible from Samokov. **Hizha Yastrebets** is two hours along the trail from Borovec, but try to make it to **Hizha Musala,** which is above the tree line and affords splendid views.

Koprivshtitsa

With its picturesque museums and cottages, Koprivshtitsa is among the most enchanting villages in Bulgaria. It was here in April 1876 that Todor Kableshkov drafted his momentous "letter of blood" announcing the April uprising against the Ottoman rule. The Turks savagely quashed the insurgency, but their brutality sparked an international furor which led to the Russo-Turkish War of 1877, and Bulgarian independence. Koprivshtitsa today has some brilliant examples of architecture from the National Revival. Several houses have been converted into museums which showcase Bulgarian handicrafts. Balkantourist has not printed any maps, but you can buy an informative book about the town at the bookstore in the town center (open 8am-noon and 3-5:30pm). There is a brochure (in French and Russian) which provides a small map.

You will see two types of cottages. The first are the sturdy half-timbered houses from the early nineteenth century with open porches, high stone walls, and sparse ornamentation; such are the **Benkovsky House,** the eminent poet **Dimcho Debelyanov's House,** and the building of the restaurant **Diado Liben.** The second, more common type features enclosed verandas, delicate woodwork, and exhibitions of folk traditions. The **Oleskov** and **Doganov Houses** exemplify this style. You can buy a comprehensive admission ticket at entrances to the houses. (30st, students 15st. Generally open 7:30am-noon and 1:30-5:30pm.)

Four fast trains per day connect Sofia with Koprivshtitsa station, 15km away. A bus (every 1 or 2 hr.) takes you to the town. If hitchhiking, take tram #3 out of Sofia; the last 12km from the highway to Koprivshtitsa may be short on cars during the week.

Balkantourist is in the brown house facing the river behind the restaurant enclave in the center. (Open daily 10am-noon and 4-9pm.) Ask about private rooms here or at Hotel Koprivshtitsa, directly across the river, up the steps and on your right. So-called private rooms for Westerners are not in Bulgarian homes, but in nice bungalows (doubles only, 24Lv). **Hotel Koprivshtitsa** (tel. 21 82) has singles for 25.60Lv, and doubles for 32.50Lv. If you come on a weekend, everything may be full. Some maps show a non-existent campground. **Restaurant Diado Liben,** in the blue house across the river from the town center, serves grilled specialties and *sirene potrakiiski* (cheese with sausage) for 4Lv. There is a **cafeteria** inside the restaurant complex in the town center. The small outdoor **market** is a few minutes beyond the bus station.

Plovdiv

Highly industrialized Plovdiv seems to be merely a sprawl of gray apartment complexes, until you wander up the Three Hills into the rambling stairway-streets of the **old town.** Here Bulgarian Revival houses hang their beamed, protruding upper stories over the cobblestones, windows stare down into alleyways at impossible angles, and churches and mosques hide in secluded corners.

To see the old town, start at the **Djoumaya Mosque** on Vasil Kolarov, and wander up Maksim Gorki. Stop by the **Icon Exposition,** on the right (open 9am-12:30pm and 2-6pm), and continue a little farther to the **National Ethnographic Museum.** Housed in an exquisite townhouse characteristic of the National Revival, it contains a well-presented collection of artifacts from this period. (Open Tues.-Sun. 9am-noon and 1:30-5pm.) The most interesting and colorful baroque houses are down the hill from here, through the Roman gate. The **Georgiadi House** has exhibits from the War of Liberation. Plovdiv's **Archeological Museum,** in a square off Sesti Septemvri St. near the river, holds a collection of gold goblets from the fourth century B.C.E. (Open Tues.-Sun. 9am-12:30pm and 2-5:30pm.)

Inquire at Balkantourist about tickets for the **Plovdiv Chamber Music Festival** in June or July, or the many diverse performances in the city's two theaters. On a hot summer day, the poolside bar of the **Novotel Plovdiv,** on the far side of the River Maritsa, near Bul. Dimitrov, is the best place to get wet.

Plovdiv lies 150km southeast of Sofia, on the main road and rail lines between Istanbul and Bourgas. Trains connect Plovdiv with the capital about every hour (4Lv).

The **Balkantourist** office, 34 Moskva Bulevard (tel. 538 48) is gracious, but cannot offer you a private room (singles US$21, doubles US$25) if any rooms are available in the expensive hotels. To reach the office from the train station, take tram #102 to Moskva Bd., the ninth stop. Walk back one block, and Balkantourist is within sight on your right. (Open daily 7am-9pm.) The **Hotel Bulgaria,** 13 Patriarch Euthymius St. (tel. 260 64), is the cheapest hotel in town (singles US$25, doubles US$36). You will probably have to settle for **Trakia Camping** (tel. 55 13 60), 4km west of town, or **Maritsa Camping** (tel. 23 34 23), 5km farther. For Trakia, take bus #102 from train station to the large telephone center, then catch bus #4. You have to hitchhike to Maritsa.

For food, try along **Ulitsa Nektarev,** which begins downhill from the Ethnographic Museum; you'll find three restaurants with garden terraces and comfortable interiors. The first, at #19, has *nadinitsa* (sausage with vegatables and bread) or pork cutlets for less than 2Lv. Its neighbors are more expensive but offer more variety. For cheaper fare, try the **self-service cafeteria** at the intersection of Vasil Kolarov and Maksim Gorki. (Open Mon.-Fri. 6am-9pm, Sat. 6am-4:30pm.)

North of Plovdiv (28km) is the **Bachkovo Monastery,** second largest in the country after the Rila Monastery. Take a bus from the main bus station to Asenovgrad, where you can catch a bus to the monastery.

Veliko Turnovo

Dramatically set on the steep banks of the River Jantra, Veliko Turnovo was the capital of the powerful Second Bulgarian Kingdom. Amid the ruins of the palaces of Bulgarian tsars and patriarchs are fragments of mural paintings and mosaics that testify to the flowering of this center of medieval culture.

Veliko Turnovo is half an hour by train south of Gorna Oryahovitsa, which is on the main rail line connecting Sofia and Varna. From the train station (1km from center), take bus #4 up the steep bank to the center of town and walk 15 minutes down Vasil Levskii to Balkantourist. Trams #7 and 11 run from Balkantourist and the town center to the old town.

The ruins of the fortress **Tsarevetz** litter the top of a large hill. There's enough here to keep the summer youth brigades employed in restoration work for decades. As you wander to or from the fortress, stop at the **Archeological Museum,** off Ivan Vasov Ul., which contains wonderful Thracian pottery, a fine collection of medieval crafts from the Turnovo ruins, and copies of the most famous frescoes in Bulgarian medieval churches. (Open, unreliably, Tues.-Sun. 8am-noon and 1:30-5:30pm.) Also worth a stop is the **Museum of the Bulgarian Renaissance,** on T. Rakovski off Dimitrii Blagoev, with an interesting collection of folk costumes. (Open Wed.-Mon. 8am-noon and 1:30-5:30pm.) You can see twentieth-century depictions of Veliko Turnovo over the ages at the municipal **art museum,** situated on the peninsula within the river's bend. (Open Tues.-Sun. 10am-6pm.) The village of **Arbanassi,** 4km northeast of Veliko Turnovo, has several beautiful merchant houses dating from the seventeenth and eighteenth centuries, when the town was a flourishing commercial center; take a bus from the old bus station, just uphill from the main one. **Preobrazhenski Monastery,** 7km north of town on a hill high above the Jantra, has frescoes by Zographe and Dosperski, the two greatest Bulgarian painters of the nineteenth-century. Take bus #10 (direction: Samovodene), then walk 2km uphill from the bus stop.

Balkantourist, at the intersection of Vasil Levskii and Histo Botev (tel. 281 65), provides a useful brochure. (Open Mon.-Sat. 8am-noon and 1-6:30pm.) Private rooms are generally unavailable to Westerners. The cheapest lodging is **Motel Sveta Gora** (tel. 204 72), 2km west of town. (Bungalows 16Lv, doubles only. 3Lv per tent and 1.50Lv per person.) Take bus #14 across from Balkantourist. The **Hotel ORBITA** was shut in 1987, so your only option may be the **Hotel Etur** (tel. 268 51), on Histo Botev just before the park. (Doubles 36Lv.)

Many cafes and restaurants dot Dimitar Blagoev, but nothing to write home about. **Mexaha,** in the small square where Georgi Dimitrov becomes D. Blagoev, is a fine place to sample *shishlik* (lamb kebab), served with a hot loaf of homemade bread. (Meals 4Lv. Open Thurs.-Tues. 4pm-midnight.) There's a **market** at the intersection of Vasil Levskii and Dimitrii Ivanov.

Black Sea Coast

In summer the crowded Black Sea coast reveals more about Eastern European swimsuit fashion than Bulgarian culture. Varna and Bourgas are the principal transportation centers. Train travel from Sofia is excruciatingly long, crowded, and slow (14Lv), so consider flying (28Lv). Very crowded buses run quite often and stop at most points of interest. The Kometa line runs a hydrofoil between Albena, Varna, Nesebăr, Bourgas, Sozopol, Primorsko, and Michurin. Service is frequent, fast, and not much more expensive than the bus; Varna to Bourgas is only 5.20Lv (2 sailings per day), but tickets sell out three days in advance. If you are alone, hitching is no problem; couples may have to wait longer. Hitching to the coast from Sofia will probably require several days.

The areas south of Bourgas have rapidly become one of the biggest resort areas for students and families from all the socialist countries. Poles, East Germans, Russians, and many others occupy no less than 15 campgrounds along the stretch between Bourgas and Ahtopol. During the summer all cheap accommodations, including campgrounds, may be full. If possible, make reservations a few days in advance, preferably from Sofia. Usually the campgrounds are so chaotic that if you're told there is no room, you can walk in unnoticed and sleep wherever you find space. Private rooms, rarely available, are US$20 per double including a 5Lv food voucher.

Sozopol, an hour south of Bourgas by bus, is one of the most beautiful towns along the coast, and rests on the site of an ancient Greek harbor now occupied by the Soviet Navy. There are no hotels, and private rooms are only available for a minimum of three nights (11Lv, including a 6Lv food voucher); otherwise, there are campgrounds a few kilometers away. **Primorsko,** yet another hour south, has a **Student Village** and an **International Youth Camp.** Both require groups of five or more, and reservations made through ORBITA in Sofia. Others can stay at the campground nearby and still use the beach and restaurant facilities of the two complexes.

The areas north of Bourgas cater more to the family package-vacation crowds, making it much harder to find cheap lodgings.

Varna is the third largest city in Bulgaria, and impossibly crowded in summer. **Balkantourist,** Arram Gačev 33 (tel. 223 89), is across the street from the train station. (Open daily 7am-10pm.) If you hitchhike in, take bus #48 from the center intersection of Karl Marx and Dimitar Blagoev. A few stops later is the hydrofoil port. **Hotel Moussallah** at 3 Moussallah (tel. 239 25) is the cheapest in town. Cape Galata is 6km away and has no bungalows. In the summer everything is booked and people sleep in the park next to the train station; check your luggage at the *garderoba* across the street from the train station. (Open 5-10:30am, 11am-6:30pm, and 7-11pm.) At the orange kiosks to the far right near Intourist, 6-inch pizzas are only 80st.

Nearby is the **Alazha Rock Monastery.** The chapel and cells are all hewn into the rock. From Varna take bus #99 from Center to Directia (40st), and another bus to the monastery.

Seven buses per day (3Lv) run to Bourgas from the main bus station in the northwest of town. Take tram #22 or 41 from the train station and ask for the *autogara.* North of Varna, campgrounds and students take over once again. The student village at **Albena** accepts groups on the same basis as the two near Bourgas.

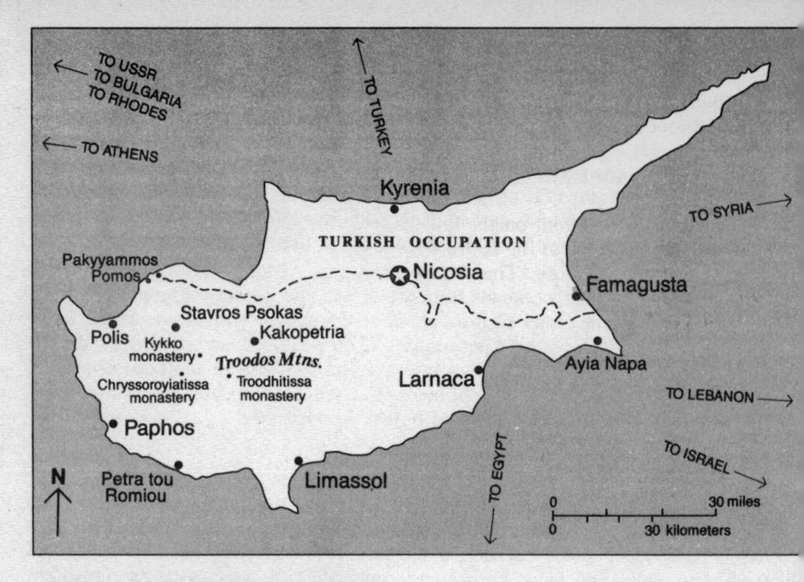

CYPRUS

US$1 = C£0.48 (Cyprus pounds)	**C£1 = US$2.08**
CDN$1 = C£0.36	**C£1 = CDN$2.75**
UK£1 = C£0.79	**1C£ = UK£1.28**
AUS$1 = C£0.34	**1C£ = AUS$2.94**

The Mediterranean island of Cyprus sparkles with remote mountain monasteries, crusader castles, ancient mosaics and temples, and fine sandy beaches. Though long influenced by Greece, Cyprus reflects both its proximity to the Middle East and its century-long occupation by the British in its food, architecture, and culture. Many Cypriots speak and understand English, and many signs in the south are in both the Greek and Roman alphabets. Cyprus is not cheap, but a budget holiday is not out of the question.

You should know something about the political situation in Cyprus before you go. Cyprus had been independent for only 14 years when, in 1974, Turkish forces invaded the island in support of the Turkish Cypriots, who felt that they were being treated as second-class citizens and that a coup in process put them in imminent danger. Turkey has occupied the northern part ever since, and in November, 1983, that sector declared itself a sovereign state. Unlike the Turkish Cypriots, who seem content with the current stand-off, most Greek Cypriots are anxious to reunite the island.

All the information we give on Northern Cyprus is in a separate section at the end of this chapter.

Getting There

The third largest island in the Mediterranean after Sicily and Sardinia, Cyprus can be reached by boat from Italy, Greece, and the Middle East. Boats frequently change their names and routes, so check ahead of time—especially during the off-season. Limassol is visited by the *Vergina* and the *Paloma* (Piraeus, Iraklion, and Haifa), and the *Sol Phryne* (Piraeus, Rhodes, and Haifa). You can also sail to Larnaca on the *Empress* and the *Sunny Boat* from Jounieh, Lebanon.

By air, Cyprus is accessible from Greece or Egypt as well as other European and Middle Eastern countries on **Olympic Airlines, Egypt Air, Cyprus Airways,** and other commercial lines. Flights on Cyprus Air to Tel Aviv from Larnaca cost C£89, students C£49; to Athens C£98, students C£41—it's cheaper to buy your ticket in Athens.

The only crossing point on the long, heavily fortified border between southern and northern Cyprus is at the **Ledra Palace Hotel,** Markos Drakos Ave., just west of the city walls in Nicosia. The checkpoint is open Monday through Friday from 8am to 6pm, and closed weekends and Islamic holidays. Leave your name and passport number with the Greek Cypriot police stationed there; cross over to the Turkish side and you will be issued a permit for C£1. It's easy (though technically illegal) to visit any area in nothern Cyprus but you must be back in southern Cyprus at 6pm, or you'll have trouble with the southern Cypriot authorities. You *cannot* visit Greek Cyprus if you enter the island on the Turkish side.

Transportation

Getting around is easy between the bigger cities, but more difficult in more remote areas. Buses and service (shared) taxis run regularly on weekdays (until 7pm) between Limassol, Paphos, Larnaca, and Nicosia. There are also shared taxis from Paphos to Polis, and from Larnaca to Agia Napa. Service taxis generally cost C£1.15 to C£1.75 between the four major cities, while buses, slower and less frequent, cost about half as much. Reserve a place in a taxi by calling the offices listed under major cities. Hitching in Cyprus is very common, especially on secondary roads not served by public transportation; you should have little problem getting a ride. Cypriots drive on the left side of the road.

Practical Information

Tourist information bureaus are all extremely helpful and efficient. They can arrange accommodations for you, but you'll find better deals on your own.

The main unit of currency is the Cyprus pound (C£), divided into 100 cents. Since the cent was introduced only recently to replace the mil (one-thousandth of a pound), many prices are quoted in mils or, to further complicate matters, in shillings, a term left over from the British occupation. There are 10 mils to a cent, and five cents to a shilling.

Official banking hours are 8:30am to noon, but nearly all banks in the four major cities provide an afternoon tourist service in summer (usually 4-7pm). Stores are open Monday through Saturday from 8am to 1pm, and on Monday, Tuesday, Thursday, and Friday from 4 to 7pm as well. Museums and archeological sites are open Monday through Saturday afternoon. Most places are closed on Christian Holidays, including Orthodox Easter (May 31-April 2 in 1988), Archbishop Makarios III Day (Jan. 19), the Cypriot National Holiday (April 1), Labor Day (May 1), the anniversary of the death of Archbishop Makarios III (Aug. 3), and Independence Day (Oct. 1). Two Greek national holidays, on March 25 and October 28, are also honored.

Overseas calls can be dialed direct from nearly all public phones if you have enough 10¢ pieces. Country codes are posted in all phone booths and in the phone books. For information dial 191 or 192. For information on international calls, dial 194, and for the international operator, 198.

Greek is spoken in the southern part of Cyprus, and most people speak English. The Popular Bank of Cyprus distributes a free booklet listing useful Greek phrases as well as helpful practical information. The weather in Cyprus runs from 16-17°C in the winter to 30-33°C in the summer. The sea is generally too cold for swimming from December through March (15-17°C).

Cyprus is rich in folklore and tradition, and hosts a number of festivals every month. A general list of the major activities can be obtained by writing to the **Cyprus Tourism Organization** (in the U.S.: 13 East 40th St., New York, NY 10016; in Cyprus: 18 Theodotou St., Nicosia). Once in Cyprus, you can obtain a copy of *This Month's Principal Events* from any tourist information office.

Accommodations and Food

Cheap, clean hotels in Cyprus are few and far between. Be sure to get a copy of the *Cyprus Hotels and Tourist Services Guide* from the tourist office; it does not list all of the cheap hotels (many are unofficial), but does provide approved prices at government-regulated hotels and pensions. If you are charged a price higher than the one listed in the booklet, register a complaint with the nearest tourist office. Nicosia, Limassol, Paphos, and Troodos all have IYHF youth hostels, and hostel cards are not required. There are only a few formal campgrounds, but you can sleep on beaches and in forests. In the Troodos area, try staying in the monasteries; they're free and you'll be exposed to an interesting facet of Cypriot culture.

Cypriot food has much in common with Greek, Turkish, and Middle Eastern cuisine. Cooks often grill meat over charcoal, and restaurants everywhere sell cutlets and steaks. Try *meze,* a platter of about a dozen appetizers for two to four people, and *kleftiko,* lamb roasted in spherical charcoal ovens. The *souvlaki* is similar to Greek *yiro,* but the sandwich is larger, the lamb drier, and the sauce absent. *Sheftalia,* grilled ground meat with onions, is also served in a pita pocket. Try some *Iranie* from a cart on the street. This Turkish drink, made of yogurt with mint and salt, is supposed to make you sober no matter how drunk you are. Drink up.

Southern Cyprus

Limassol

Limassol, the port of entry for most passenger ferries, is an unattractive introduction to an otherwise beautiful island. Rapid growth from a sudden influx of refugees and lack of foresight in urban planning have led to the construction of an endless row of concrete blocks stretching east along the coast. It is nonetheless a convenient base for excursions to the rest of the island.

Orientation and Practical Information

The **new port** is about 5km southwest of the center of town. Bus #1 runs from the port to the center (7 per day, last at 5:35pm, 20¢). A taxi from the port into town should cost C£1.50-2. If you are headed directly for one of the other major towns, call the appropriate service taxi (see below) and you will be picked up at the port at no extra charge.

Cyprus Tourism Organization Office: 15 Spiro Araouzos St. (tel. 627 56), on the waterfront, 1 block east of the castle. A wise first stop. The capable and helpful staff can answer all questions, suggest daytrips, and provide maps, bus schedules, and general information for the entire island. Open in summer Mon. and Thurs. 8am-1:15pm and 4-6:15pm, Tues.-Wed. and Fri.-Sat. 8am-1:15pm; off-season Mon. and Thurs. 8:15am-1:30pm and 3-5:30pm, Tues.-Wed. and Fri.-Sat. 8:15am-1:30pm. Another small office is open at the port when boats arrive.

American Express: A.L. Mantovani and Sons, 130 Spiro Araouzos St. (tel. 620 45). Open for financial transactions Mon.-Fri. 8:30am-noon; for mail collection Mon.-Fri. 8am-1pm and 3:30-6:30pm.

Post Office: Archbishop Kyprianou St., 1 block inland from St. Andrew St. Open Mon.-Tues. and Thurs.-Fri. 7:30am-1pm and 4-6pm, Wed. and Sat. 7:30am-1pm.

Telephones (CYTA): Corner of Markos Botsaris and Athens St. Open daily 7am-7:30pm. **Telephone code:** 051.

Bus Stations: KEMEK terminal, corner of Irene and Eroseos St. (tel. 632 41). Buses to Nicosia (Mon.-Sat. 12 per day 6am-4:30pm, 75¢) and Paphos (Mon.-Sat. 4 per day 6:30am-3:15pm, 75¢). **Lefkaritio terminal,** 107 Spiro Araouzos St., near the waterfront. Buses to Larnaca (Mon.-Sat. 8 per day 6am-4pm, 65¢).

Service Taxis: Karydas, 129 Spiro Araouzos St. (tel. 620 61). **Kypros/Akropolis,** 49 Spiro Araouzos St. (tel. 639 79). **Kyriakos,** 9 Pateur St. (tel. 641 14). **Makris,** 166 Hellas St. (tel. 655 50). Karydas, Kypros/Akropolis, and Kyriakos run taxis to Nicosia (in summer daily every ½ hr. 6am-7pm; off-season 6am-6pm; C£1.50). Akropolis and Makis run taxis to Larnaca (in summer daily every ½ hr. 6am-7pm; off-season 6am-6pm; C£1.30). All the companies except Akropolis go to Paphos (every hr. 6am-6:30pm, C£1.50).

Bicycle and Motorbike Rentals: All shops near the luxury hotels at the eastern edge of town, on the shore road. A motorcycle license is required, but the police station will issue a temporary Cypriot license. Motorbike C£3-4 per day. If you plan to rent long-term, you'll do better for quality and price in Paphos.

Emergencies: Police headquarters at Gladstone and Leondios St. (tel. 756 11), next to the hospital. **Medical Assistance:** Hospital at Leondios St. (tel. 631 11).

Accommodations and Food

For the most part budget accommodations in Limassol, clustered near the bus station, are cheap but of low quality. Hotel apartments at the east end of town are nicer and more expensive.

The **youth hostel (IYHF),** is at 120 Ankara (Angira) St. (tel. 637 49), a few blocks west of the castle; the entrance is on a small alley off Ankara St. (the sign on Ankara St. is easy to miss). Andreas, the manager, is friendly and helpful. (First night C£1.85, breakfast included; C£1 for each additional night, plus 60¢ for breakfast. Hot showers 35¢, cold showers 20¢. 11pm curfew, but they'll show you where the key is.) **Guest House Ikaros,** 61 Eleftherias St. (tel. 543 48), decorated with family heirlooms and guarded by a porcelain collie, is cleaner, greener, and friendlier than other places in town. (C£2 per person. Showers included.) **Guest House Stalis,** 59 Eleftherias St. (tel. 681 97), is dingy but tolerable. (Doubles C£3, quads c£1. All prices per person.) Both of the latter rent bicycles and motorbikes.

Food in Limassol is mediocre, especially at the restaurants on the waterfront and in the town center. However, the **kebab house** on Spiro Araouzos St., opposite the tourist office, serves excellent *souvlaki* and *sheftialia* for 80¢. **Lefteris,** at Gladstone and Anexartisia St., also serves good *kebab* for 80¢. If you can navigate a menu in handwritten Greek, visit the **Popular Restaurant,** Kanaris St., near the city bus station. Good, filling meat dishes go for about C£1.25, bean stews for 80¢, and salads 40¢. The **market,** also near the bus station, is open Mon.-Fri. 7am-1pm.

Sights

Limassol Castle is about all there is to see in Limassol. At this thirteenth-century Frankish structure, Richard the Lion-Hearted married Berengaria of Navarre. The Lusignan dynasty leased the castle to the Templar Knights, who thickened the walls and covered the Gothic windows in the early fourteenth century. Later the Knights of St. John converted the great Western Hall into a Gothic church and the chapel into a series of prison cells. (Open in summer Mon.-Sat. 7:30am-1:30pm; off-season Mon.-Sat. 7:30am-1pm. Admission 30¢.) The **Archeological Museum,** Byron St., across from the Curium Palace Hotel, houses a small collection; most notable is the fourth-century head of Aphrodite in the north room. (Open in summer Mon.-Sat. 8am-1:30pm and 4-6pm, Sun. 10am-1pm; off-season Mon.-Fri. 7:30am-2pm and 3-5pm, Sat. 7:30am-1pm and 3-5pm, Sun. 10am-1pm. Admission 30¢.)

If you want to see what today's Limassol is all about, visit the **KEO factory,** Franklin Roosevelt St., a five-minute walk west (right, if facing the water) of the castle. The free tours (Mon.-Fri. 10am) close with complimentary glasses of wine and beer. The city's long, stone beach is nothing to write home about, but **Dassoudi Beach,** 3km to the east, is better. Take bus #6, 13, or 25 from the market (on Kanaris St.).

Kourion, 12km west of Limassol, actually lies within the British Sovereign Base Area, which includes all of the Akrotiri Peninsula. A **Sanctuary to Apollo** (8th-century B.C.E.) and a **stadium** (2nd-century C.E.) are both west of the main settlement. The ruins of the town itself lie just to the south of the highway. The impressive **theater,** which commands an expansive view of the Mediterranean, hosts the Shakespearean Festival in June, occasional concerts during the summer, and weekend theater in September. Ask the tourist bureau in Limassol for more information.

Troodos Mountains

The Troodos mountain range, halfway between Nicosia and Paphos, is one of the most beautiful parts of Cyprus. Tiny villages, breathtaking Byzantine churches, and remote monasteries dot the mountainsides, and the surrounding forests of flat-topped pines provide a welcome escape from the summer heat. The best time to visit in the summertime is during the week, when crowds are thin. During the winter, Mt. Olympos, the highest point in Cyprus, is capped with snow, providing slopes for thousands of skiers.

Public transportation to and from the Troodos area and between villages within Troodos is infrequent and nonexistent, respectively. Motorbike rental is cheapest in Paphos (C£2 a day for small bikes, C£4 for large). However you choose to travel, be careful: The roads throughout the region are single-laned and have many blind curves. Get a map from the tourist office—it's excellent and free.

Platres will most likely be your first stop in the Troodos region, as it is the most accessible by public transportation from Limassol and Nicosia. The **tourist office,** to the left of the parking lot, is extremely helpful. (Open Mon., Wed.-Thurs., and Sat. 8:30am-1pm.) In town, one block from the fountain/parking lot, is the nice (but not splendid) **Splendid Hotel** (tel. 214 25). All rooms have balconies and private showers. (Singles C£7, doubles C£10.) The best place to stay is the **Pafsilypon Hotel** (tel. 356 48). Andreas, the proprietor, makes sure the rooms are clean. To get there, bear right at the fork in the town and go one block up the hill. (C£3.50 per person, C£5 in Aug. English breakfast included.)

Picturesque **Kakopetria,** on the main road from Nicosia to Troodos, is the most popular town in the northern part of the mountains. Buses to Kakopetria travel from Constantza Bastion in Nicosia (Mon.-Fri. 9 per day 6:15am-6pm, 55¢). The oldest section of the village, with its mudbrick houses overlooking a river, is being preserved by the government; in the rest of the village slick new pubs and "rustic" hotels cater to vacationers. If you come on a weekday before August, you can stay in the **Rialto Hotel** (tel. 24 38), where singles are C£5, doubles C£10 with breakfast, or at the **Hekali** (tel. 25 01), where singles are C£7, doubles C£11, breakfast included. Elsewhere, you pay nearly twice this. Kakopetria and its smaller neighbor, **Galata,** have five interesting Byzantine churches between them. The most beautiful, **Agios Nikolaos tis Stegis,** 2 or 3 miles southwest of Kakopetria on a dirt road, features Byzantine frescoes and a unique protective roof.

Ten miles northeast of Kakopetria, the tiny Byzantine church at **Asinou** stuns its visitors with the gorgeous frescoes that cover every inch of its interior. To visit the church, find the priest in the nearby village of Nikitare (ask in the village cafes), and take him with you in a taxi (C£1.50 round-trip). Ten miles southeast of Kakopetria is the church of **Panayia tou Arakou,** another repository of beautiful twelfth-century frescoes. At each of these places it is appropriate to leave a small donation at the door.

Many visitors overlook the accommodations in the monasteries. Not only are they free, but they'll show you how rich and alive the Greek Orthodox Church is in Cyprus. Donations are always welcome and women are not permitted to enter in shorts or short skirts. Services are held daily at sunrise and are well worth waking up for, especially if you've never been to one—the monks will also appreciate your attendance. On the eastern slopes of the Troodos range, the **Monastery of Macheras** (knife), lies 26 miles south of Nicosia. From Nicosia, take the Nicosia-Agros road

9 miles to the village of Kato Deftera and turn left for Pera; the monastery is about 12 miles farther.

Hens, cats, monks, and a donkey make their home in the modern **Trooditissa Monastery,** 3½ miles from Platres on the Prodromos-Platres road. Dedicated to the Virgin Mary, the monastery was built specifically to house a miracle-working icon of her; the name Trooditissa literally means "she who is resident of Mt. Troodos." (Open daily 6am-noon and 2-8pm; no overnight guests accepted mid-June to mid-Sept.)

Kykko Monastery, in the northwestern part of the mountains, enjoys more wealth and fame than any other monastery on the island. Enter its palatial courtyard and you may think you've wandered into a large luxury hotel by mistake; but because hotels have been complaining about business, Kykko has now restricted itself to taking in Greek Orthodox pilgrims. Founded in the eleventh century, Kykko today consists mainly of structures built in the early nineteenth century. As for its treasures, one of St. Luke's three great icons of the Virgin Mary sits just to the left of the church altar—half-covered by a curtain, completely covered with silver plate, and ensconced in a mother-of-pearl shrine. Kykko gained new fame in this century because of its role in the Cypriot struggle for independence, and because it was the monastic home of Archbishop Makarios III. The monastery was used as a communication and supply center. The grave of Greek Cyprus' patriarch is just 2km away; ask at the monastery for directions. Kambos buses, departing from opposite the KEMEK station in Nicosia, run to Kykkos (Mon.-Fri. at 12:15pm, C£1).

Between Troodos and Prodromos soars **Mt. Olympos** (6401 ft.), the highest peak on the island—on a clear day you can see to the ocean. From January through March, you can alternate sunbathing in Limassol with skiing on the mountain's north face. If you'll be skiing for a while, it's probably cheaper to become a member of the Cyprus Ski Club (about C£15, plus C£8 inscription fee). The three lifts on the mountain cost members about C£4 per day and C£20 per week, while nonmembers must pay roughly double. Ski rentals and lessons have similar discounts for members. There are no accommodations at the mountain, only restaurants.

Nicosia (Lefkosia)

Capital of Cyprus, Nicosia sits astride the north/south border (or "Green Line"); like Berlin, Nicosia is a divided city.

Orientation and Practical Information

The easiest way to orient yourself in this city is by the Green Line running east-west at the north end of the city. The **Laiki Yitonia (Old City),** within the circular Venetian walls, is sliced in half by this divider. From Eleftheria Square, Evagoras Street leads southwest into the **New City,** much busier than the old.

Cyprus Tourist Organization Office: Laiki Yitonia, within the city walls (tel. 442 64). Route maps and a complete list of village buses. Open Mon.-Sat. 9am-2:30pm, Mon. and Thurs. also 4:30-6:30pm.

Post Office: Constantinos Paleologos Ave., just east of Eleftherias Sq. within the walls. Open in summer Mon.-Tues. and Thurs.-Fri. 7:30am-1pm and 4-6pm, Wed. and Sat. 7:30am-1pm; off-season Mon.-Tues. and Thurs.-Fri. 7:30am-1:30pm and 3:30-5:30pm, Wed. and Sat. 7:30am-1pm.

Telephones: CYTA, 1 Museum Ave. (tel. 47 71 11), around the corner from the museum. Open 24 hours.

Bus Stations: KEMEK, 34 Leonides St. (tel. 46 39 89). To Limassol (in summer 12 per day 5:45am-4:30pm; off-season Mon.-Fri. 8 per day 6:15am-4pm; 75¢) and Platres (at 12:15pm, C£1). Also route maps. **Lefkaritis,** 6 Stassinos Ave. (tel. 44 25 66), just east of Eleftherias Sq. outside the city walls. To Larnaca (Mon.-Fri. 12 per day 6:15am-5:45pm, 55¢). **Solea**

Bus, Constantza Bastion, 200m east of Eleftheria Sq. To Kakopetria (Mon.-Fri. 4 per day 6:15am-6pm, 55¢). The tourist office has a complete list of buses.

Service Taxis: Makris (tel. 46 62 01), **Akropolis** (tel. 47 25 25), **Kypros** (tel. 46 48 11), and **Kyriakos** (tel. 44 41 41), are all located on Stassinos Ave., which runs east along the city walls from Eleftherias Sq. **Karydas,** 8 Homer Ave. (tel. 46 22 69), is nearby. All run to Limassol (C£1.50), and all continue to Paphos (an additional C£1.50); Makris, Akropolis, and Kyriakos travel to Larnaca (C£1.15).

Emergency: Police (tel. 199). Police headquarters at Archbishop Makarios III Ave. (tel. 40 35 35).

Medical Assistance: Hospital between Hilon and Homer St. (tel. 45 11 11), near the municipal gardens.

Embassies: U.S., Dositheos and Therissos St. (tel. 46 51 51), near the Hilton Hotel, just off Archbishop Makarios III Ave. Take bus #16, 50, 55, or 58. **British High Commission,** Alexander Pallis St. (tel. 47 31 31), west of the old city. **Australian High Commission,** 4 Annis Comninis St. (tel. 47 30 01), corner of Stassinos Ave. **Egypt,** 3 Egypt Ave. (tel. 46 51 44). 1-day wait for visas. Visa section open Mon.-Fri. 9am-noon; arrive early. **Syria,** Androcleous and Thoukidides St. (tel. 47 44 81). 24-hour visa wait (or less); bring 2 photos. Visa section open Mon.-Fri. 9am-1pm.

Accommodations and Food

Nicosia is not known for the cleanliness of its budget accommodations. Moreover, the staffs of Nicosia's "cabarets" tend to frequent a number of the cheaper places. Except where noted, all the hotels listed below are within the walls of the Old City.

Youth Hostel (IYHF), 13 Prince Charles St. (tel. 44 48 08), opposite the Asty Hotel. About a 25-min. walk (or bus #27) from the center of town. Members C£2.15, nonmembers C£2.25. Sheets, cold showers, and breakfast included; C£1.75 after the first night. Lockout 10am-4pm. 11pm curfew.

Tony's Furnished Flats, 13 Solon St. (tel. 46 67 52). Friendly, efficient, and helpful. Small, respectable rooms have fan, radio, and thermos. Pleasant roof gardens. Singles C£4-7, doubles C£8-10, triples C£11.50-15. A/C C£1.80. Good English breakfast included.

Hotel Delphi, 24 C. Pantelides Ave. (tel. 47 52 11), just west of Eleftherias Sq. Nice place in a lively location. All rooms have balconies and tolerable private bathrooms. Singles C£4, doubles C£7. Breakfast 50¢.

The cafes and restaurants in the Old City, on the slate pathway around the tourist office, serve some of the town's tastiest and most reasonably priced meals, and they're usually uncrowded until mid-August. The **Paphia Aphrodite Bar and Restaurant** serves fish *meze* (assorted fish appetizers) for C£3, *kalamari* (squid) or octopus for 75¢, and swordfish for C£2. There's a great **estiatorio** at 40 Arsinoes St., in the heart of the old city near the Green Line (roast chicken or pork with potatoes and salad, C£1.25). Buy your own provisions at the **market** at Dhigenis Akritas and Kalipolis St.

Sights

The **Cyprus Museum** enjoys international renown for its display of artifacts collected from excavations throughout Cyprus—everything from Neolithic stone vases to Roman idols. (Open in summer Mon.-Sat. 8am-1:30pm and 4-6pm, Sun. 10am-1pm; off-season Mon.-Sat. 7:30am-2pm and 3-5pm, Sun. 10am-1pm. Admission 40¢.)

Nicosia's other important sights lie within the walls of the Old City. The **Archbishop's Palace** represents a combination of the Vatican and the White House; the Greek Orthodox Church is almost the government in Cyprus. The **Byzantine Museum,** next door, has the largest collection of icons on the island, and one of the finest in all of Europe. (Open Oct.-April Mon.-Fri. 9am-1pm and 2-5pm, Sat. 9am-1pm; May-Sept. Mon.-Fri. 9:30am-1pm and 2-5:30pm, Sat. 9am-1pm. Admission 40¢.) Next to and in front of the Byzantine Museum is the seventeenth-century **St. John's Church,** adorned with eighteenth-century frescos; look to the left of the archbishop's throne for the picture depicting the discovery of the tomb of St. Barnabas at Salamis.

Down Koreas St. from the palace you'll find the unusual monument to the Cypriot struggle for freedom. Designed by the Greek artist Falireas, the monument depicts 14 Cypriots, each representing a period of the island's history, as they are released from jail by soldiers and overseen by a religious figure.

Under restoration, the **Konak Mansion,** also known as **The House of Hajigeorgakis Karnessios,** 18 Patriar Gregory St., is just around the corner from the archbishop's complex and is worth a peek. A famous Turkish dragoman—an interpreter for the Turks and Greeks—lived in this once luxurious eighteenth-century structure. There's a colorful **botanical garden** adjacent to the museum behind the Garden Cafe (enter on Homer Ave., adjacent to the museum). The aviaries here contain most of the island's indigenous bird species.

Ten miles southwest of Nicosia are the royal tombs of **Tamassos,** where an ancient Cypriot kingdom thrived on agriculture and copper mining. The site contains houses, the remains of a temple of Aphrodite-Astarte, and two elaborately carved sandstone tombs from 650-600 B.C.E. (Open in summer daily 9am-noon and 4-7:30pm; off-season 9am-1pm and 4-6:30pm.)

Paphos

Paphos has everything you could ask for in a vacation spot: ancient buildings, gorgeous mosaics, good restaurants, and, in the surrounding countryside, superb beaches, ruined cities, and isolated villages. Furthermore, even in the middle of summer, there is a cool breeze blowing off the sea.

The mosaic floors of the **House of Dionysus** are unquestionably the most dazzling of Paphos' ancient treasures. Discovered accidentally in 1962 by a farmer ploughing his fields, the superbly preserved mosaics once covered 14 rooms of a large Roman villa. (Open in summer 7:30am-7:30pm; off-season 7:30am-dusk. Admission 40¢.) The **Odeon,** a small, roofed semi-circular theater constructed in the second century C.E., can accommodate 3000 spectators and is periodically used for theatrical and musical performances. (Contact the tourist office for information.) The **Archeological Museum,** Grivas Diogenes Ave. in Ktima-Paphos, houses a fine array of Bronze Age pottery and tools, and Classical sculpture. (Open in summer Mon.-Sat. 8am-1:30pm and 4-6pm, Sun. 10am-1pm; off-season Mon.-Sat. 7:30am-2pm and 3-5pm, Sun. 10am-1pm. Admission 30¢.)

Just south of the town center at 1 Exo Vrysi St. is the private **Ethnographical Museum,** in the residence of the Eliadeses. The admission (50¢) includes a guided tour in English conducted by Mrs. Eliades, the museum's effervescent curator. (Open in summer Mon.-Sat. 10am-1:30pm and 4-7pm; off-season 9am-1:30pm and 3-5:30pm.)

The city of Paphos is divided into two sections: the upper, called **Ktima-Paphos,** and the lower, **Kato-Paphos,** about a mile to the south. Today most shops, budget hotels, and services are located in Ktima-Paphos; luxury hotels, holiday villas, and nightclubs jam Kato-Paphos. The **Cyprus Tourism Organization,** 3 Gladstone St. (tel. 328 41), has a helpful staff. (Open Mon. and Thurs. 8am-1:15pm and 4-6:15pm, Tues.-Wed. and Fri.- Sat. 8am-1:15pm; afternoon hours in winter 2-4pm.) Ask for Tasos at **Psomas Rentals,** Poseidonas St. (tel. 355 61), across from the Paphos Beach Motel; tell him *Let's Go* sent you, and he may give you an extra-special deal on bike and motorbike rentals.

Paphos' handful of cheap hotels are reasonably priced and, for the most part, tolerably clean. The **IYHF youth hostel,** 37 Eleftherias Venizelou Ave. (tel. 325 88), is on a quiet residential street northeast of the town center (signs point the way). (C£2 per night. Breakfast included. Lockout 10am-4pm. Open year-round 7:30am-10pm.) **Paphos Palace Hotel,** 10 Grivas Diogenes Ave. (tel. 323 46), on Kennedy Sq., is spacious and clean. (Singles C£9. Breakfast 80¢.) Cheaper and almost as clean is **Hotel Trianon,** 99 Archbishop Makarios III Ave. (tel. 321 93). (Singles C£3, doubles C£5. Breakfast 50¢.)

Most restaurants are in Kato-Paphos and are outrageously overpriced. One good deal with nice ambience is **Yacinthus,** Ayra Napee St., next to the Kato-Paphos post office. Open for dinner, it serves delicious, large, and reasonably priced salads (85¢-C£1.20), hamburgers with chips (C£.90), and omelettes (C£.80). In Ktima-Paphos, the most reasonable restaurant is **Trianon,** Archbishop Makarios III Ave. (most dishes C£1.60, *mousaka* C£1.25, *afelia* C£1.40).

Near Paphos

Some 15 miles out of Paphos along the Limassol-Paphos road is **Petra tou Romiou,** the mythical birthplace of Aphrodite. There are no ancient ruins here, just a good, albeit rocky, beach, surrounded by stunning rock formations, which the signposts call the "Rocks of Venus." Five miles closer to Paphos, near the modern village of Kouklia, lie the ruins of the great **Temple of Aphrodite** and **Paleopaphos** (Old Paphos), once the capital of a kingdom encompassing nearly half of Cyprus. The temple was the religious center of the island and a destination for pilgrims from all parts of the Roman world.

North of Paphos, the lovely village of **Pegia** lies tucked in the hills. Rent a motorbike so you can fully appreciate the road, which runs along a mountain ridge with rolling hills on one side and the sea on the other. A few kilometers from Peyia is the lovely beachside village of **Agios Georgios** (St. George). There are barely four buildings there, excluding the chapel, and two of them are hotels. Down a dirt road from Agios Georgios is **Lara Beach,** one of the longest in Cyprus. One restaurant is the only thing here, so unless your visit coincides with the boat excursion from Paphos, you should be pretty much alone with the sand, trees, and turtles.

Larnaca

Unless you're flying in or out of Cyprus or passing through on your way to the lovely area around **Agia Napa,** try to avoid Larnaca.

The biggest tourist attraction is the dirty town beach, which somehow manages to satisfy the hordes of vacationers who bake on it every day. Tourist buses travel northeast to less crowded beaches. (Buses leave from the Sun Mall Hotel at the north end of Athens Ave.; in summer every ½ hr. 7am-7pm, 20¢.) Next to Barclay's Bank, by the tourist office in King Paul's Sq., is the private **Museum of the Pierides Foundation,** founded by and located in the former home of the collector Demetrios Pierides. The collection includes everything from Bronze Age ceramic milk pots with carved cows' udders to Cypriot costumes. (Open Mon.-Sat. 9am-1pm. Donations requested.) At the southern end of the port is **Scala,** where you'll find a small **medieval fortress** set precipitously on the water's edge. (Open in summer Mon.-Sat. 7:30am-7pm; off-season 7:30am-5pm. Admission 30¢.) The first left north of the fortress leads to the **Church of St. Lazarus,** built over the tomb of St. Lazarus, first Bishop of Cyprus, who came to Cyprus from Palestine after he was resurrected by Christ. (Open April-Aug. daily 8am-12:30pm and 3:30-6:30pm; Sept.-March daily 8am-12:30pm and 2:30-5pm.)

The **Cyprus Tourism Organization Office,** on King Paul Sq. (tel. 543 22), provides maps and information for the entire island. (Open in summer Mon. and Thurs. 8:15am-1:30pm and 4-6:15pm, Tues.-Wed. and Fri.-Sat. 8am-1pm; off-season Mon. and Thurs. 8:15am-1:45pm and 3-5:30pm, Tues.-Wed. and Fri.-Sat. 8am-1pm.) Another office in the airport is open 24 hours. **Esmeralda,** 33 Hermes St. (tel. 539 69 or 212 21), has clean rooms, but the bathroom and kitchen could use a good scrub. The friendly owner will pick you up at the airport for free if you give him a call. (C£2 per night.) **St. Lazarus Inn,** at the corner of Dionissou St. and St. Lazarus Sq. (tel. 263 22), is clean, pleasant, and reasonable: Take one of the sunny rooftop rooms. (Singles C£5, with bath C£6, doubles C£7, with bath C£8, triples C£9.)

Beach Forest Camping (tel. 224 14), 5 miles northeast of Larnaca on the road to Agia Napa, lies on a pleasant pebbly beach. You can hitch, take a taxi (C£1.30), or catch the tourist beach bus from the Sun Mall Hotel at the north end of Athens Ave. (in summer every ½ hr. 7am-7pm, 15 min., 20¢). (25¢ per person, C£1.50 per tent; they will supply tents at no added cost. Open April-Oct.) Most of Larnaca's nearly indistinguishable restaurants are on the waterfront.

Northern Cyprus

Northern Cyprus uses Turkish lire.

If you speak with Cypriots living in the southern part of the island, they'll sadly admit that some of the most beautiful parts of their tiny homeland are in the northern 40% of Cyprus, occupied by the Turkish Army since the summer of 1974. If you arrive in one of the southern cities, it is impossible to spend the night on the Turkish side of the island or continue on to the Turkish mainland; border guards won't let you carry luggage across the border. You can, however, visit for a day, provided that you return by 6pm.

The only place in southern Cyprus where it is possible to cross the border is at the **Ledra Palace Hotel** (now occupied by the United Nations), just outside the walls on the western side of Nicosia. To get to the border (opens at 8am) from Eleftheria Square, follow the walls of the old city along Stassinos, Homer, Egypt, and Marcos Drakos Avenues. At United Nations Square, take the right fork.

Taxis in northern Nicosia will take you to you to other parts of the island, but remember to allow yourself plenty of time to get back by 6pm. The border is closed on weekends and on Christian and Islamic holidays. Don't purchase any gifts while you're in Turkish Cyprus; you are technically forbidden to bring anything back.

One of the best student deals around is **Cyprus Turkish Airlines'** flight from Istanbul to Nicosia's Ercan Airport (49,000TL one way, students 16,000TL); you can fly from Izmir for the same price. You can also travel overland to the Mediterranean ports of Taşucu or Mersin. Boats sail from **Taşucu** to Girne (Kyrenia) (in summer daily at 10am; in winter at least 2 per week; 6 hr., 10,000TL, students 8000-9000TL). There are two ferry companies, **Liberty** (tel. Taşucu 12 49; Girne 528 66; Lefkoşa 718 98), and **Ertürk** (Taşucu 10 33; Girne 523 08), sailing on alternate days; the latter offers the larger student discount. A more expensive and less pleasant trip is from the larger port of **Mersin** to Famagusta. The Friday sailing continues to Lattakia, Syria. The Famagusta-Lattakia leg costs non-Turks about $25. (Western currency only; no student discount.) Student discounts of 10% apply on all other fares.

Should you wish to visit Greece later, you must get a removable visa so that the passport itself will not be stamped. This can be obtained at any of the three Turkish Federated State of Cyprus consulates in Turkey. They are in Ankara at Incirli Sok. 20, Gaziosmanpaşa (tel. 28 05 47); in Istanbul at Büyükdere Cad. 99, Kuğu Is Hani, Kat. 6, Daire 9, Mecidiyeköy (tel. 173 29 90); and in Mersin at Atatürk Cad., Hamidiye Mahallesi, Yilmaz Apt. #3, (tel. 162 28).

The **telephone code** for Northern Cyprus is 905. The country has its own **postal system,** and Turkish Cypriot stamps must be used (postage rates are cheaper than in Turkey). All mail going to Cyprus should be suffixed with "Mersin-10, Turkey." Finally, the north of Cyprus uses the Turkish lire as currency, but as there is a flourishing black market trade with the south, many are eager to accept Cypriot pounds, pounds sterling, or U.S. dollars. You should easily get 10-20% above the official rate if you change money on the black market—it *is* illegal, though, so be careful.

Should you need consular help in Northern Cyprus, you're out of luck, because no one but the Turks themselves recognizes this "republic." There is a representative from the British Embassy who crosses every weekday from 9am to 1pm, who can be found at the old British High Commission; walk along Osman Paşa Ave., which runs parallel to the Green Line, and turn left at the army camp into Mehmet Akif Ave. The building is on your right.

Lefkoşa (Nicosia)

Entering Lefkoşa from the south, you'll probably feel as if you have traveled much farther than 200m. You'll notice a change in the atmosphere as soon as you pass within the walls: The buildings look a little older, the shops more cluttered, and people on the street will probably pay more attention to you.

The monumental **Selimiye Mosque,** formerly the St. Sophia Cathedral, is decidedly the most impressive building in Lefkoşa. Beneath its ribbed vaulted archways, flying buttresses, and ornate carvings, the kings of Cyprus were crowned. It was converted into a mosque in the sixteenth century under Ottoman rule. If you can find Mustafa Biyikli, the caretaker, he'll give you a friendly, detailed tour of the place in English (a few hundred lire will suffice for the tour). There is a small covered **market** next to the mosque; try *sucuk,* a candy made by dipping a string of almonds into boiled grapes. The **Turkish Cyprus Ethnographic Museum,** Mevlevi Tekke, on Kyrenia Ave., contains tombs of important Mevlana dervishes and sheiks as well as a fascinating exhibit of traditional Ottoman dress and artifacts. (Open in summer Mon. 7:30am-2pm and 3:30-6pm, Tues.-Fri. 7:30am-2pm; off-season Mon.-Fri. 7:30am-2pm. Admission 100TL.)

Across the street from the old British High Commission is Lefkoşa's **tourist office** (open April-Sept. Mon.-Fri. 8am-2pm; Oct.-March Mon.-Fri. 8am-1pm and 2:30-5pm). **Kumarcilar Khani** is an ancient inn which serves as a tourist office; this is likely to be far more convenient. On the right, you'll pass the small, simple **Arabahmet Mosque,** built in the early seventeenth century, and if you continue in this direction, you'll pass through most of the city's shopping district. Kyrenia Ave., on the left, leads to **Atatürk Square** and its Venetian column, taken from Salamis as a symbol of Venetian rule on the island. This is the main square in Lefkoşa, containing a **post office,** a few travel agencies, and the English bookstore, **Rustem's,** just south of the square at 22-24 Kyrenia Ave. Shared taxis wait here. The road continuing to Selimiye runs roughly parallel to the Green Line. For **police** dial 713 11; for **first aid** 734 41. The city's **telephone code** is 020.

The area around Selimiye Mosque contains some cheap pensions. Directly behind the mosque is **Marmara Pansiyon,** Selimiye Camii Arkasi, which is clean for Lefkoşa and cheap. (2000TL per person.) From behind the mosque, make a left onto Kirlizade and then a right on to Haydarpaşa St. to get to **Anadolu Pansiyon,** 26 Haydarpaşa Sok. (tel. 729 03; 2000TL per person, showers included.) On the other side of town on Girne Cad., down the block from Atatürk Square in the old city, are some cheap, good restaurants; try **Antalya Restaurant** at #73.

To visit the city's lesser sights (such as the Mehmet II Library, the Sarayonu Mosque, the Arabahmet Mosque, the Lapidary Museum, and the Bedesten Church), you must ask for a guide at the Kumarcilar Khani. Regular opening times are impractical, since there are so few tourists. The guide simply unlocks doors for you, and you pay only the regular 100TL admission fees.

Girne (Kyrenia)

Girne may be the most appealing harbor town on the island. The newer part of the city, dominated by the luxury Dome Hotel, is not so memorable, but the old port nearby retains an idyllic setting, with a castle at one end, and unobtrusive cafes and stone buildings surrounding the rest of the harbor.

Practical Information, Accommodations, and Food

If you come by boat from Taşucu you can walk up from the picturesque harbor to the main street, **Humiyet Caddesi,** on which lie all the shops, restaurants, and the bus station. The **post office** (open in summer Mon. 7:30am-2pm and 3:30-6pm, Tues.-Fri. 7:30am-2pm and 4-6pm, Sat. 8:30am-12:30pm) and **telephones** (open Mon.-Fri. 7:30am-9:30pm, Sat.-Sun. 8am-6pm) are 100 yards away from the bus station square, on the main coastal road to the east. Messages in English and advertisements for apartments for rent are posted on a tree outside the post office. The **police** are just off the square on the street that leads down the hill to the castle, past the supermarket. The **tourist office** (tel. 521 45) is by the harbor. They speak English and supply maps, transportation schedules, and other printed information. (Open May-Aug. Mon 7:30am-6pm, Tues.-Fri. 7:30am-2pm; Sept.-April Mon.-Fri. 8am-5:30pm.) From the bus station, Kambos service taxis go to Magosa about every hour. Minibuses go to Lefkoşa very frequently, as soon as they fill. Every hour, buses go to Güselyurt.

The **O.T.E.M. Hotel,** right above the tourist office (tel. 522 27), is for students studying hotel management and one of the best accommodation buys on the island. It's big, usually empty, and a tad institutional. Rooms with more character, but without breakfast or bathroom, can be found at the **Set Pension** (tel. 538 45), next to the mosque, just above the harbor. Three kilometers outside Girne, right on the beach, is **Riviera Motel Camping** (tel. (081) 533 69), with camping, bungalows, a restaurant, and a private beach.

Back in town, restaurants on the harbor are ridiculously expensive, but you can eat cheaply on Humiyet Cad. Both **Ziya Baba,** next to the medieval tower, and **Ali Baba** (no relation), down the street 50 yards on the right, serve good stew-type Turkish food. Farther down by the tourist office, diagonally across from the Anadolu Hotel, is **Little Arif,** with a pleasant garden behind the street (*şiş* 1000TL). At 22 Hurriyet Ave., you can get interesting, reasonably-priced food at the **Orphan Restaurant.** Don't miss the tall glasses of ice-cold, fresh-squeezed orange juice at the little stall at 57 Humiyet Cad., across from the Bristol Hotel.

Sights

The preeminent sight in Girne is the huge **medieval castle** at the harbor's mouth. Built by the Byzantines with material plundered from the ruins of the now nonexistent Roman city, it was fortified by the Lusignans and refortified by the Venetians. On the left side of the courtyard (if facing the water) are dungeons with deep pits in the center. The scraps from the royal family's dinner were dumped from above so the prisoners were forced to grab at the flying food; their final punishment came when they reached too far and fell into the pit. The **Shipwreck Museum** contains the well-preserved skeleton of a Greek merchant vessel that sunk over 2000 years ago. Directly above the harbor is a modern **Folk Art Museum** in a 300-year-old building.

CZECHOSLOVAKIA

US$1 = 5.49 koruny (kčs) **10kčs = US$1.82**
UK£1 = 8.95kčs **10kčs = UK£1.18**

A textbook might explain Czechoslovakia simply in political terms—a federative republic consisting of two peoples, the Czechs and the Slovaks—but native writer Milan Kundera comes closer to the truth in his *Book of Laughter and Forgetting.* The western Czechs (Bohemians and Moravians), with their strong urban intelligentsia, are ethnically and socially different from the more traditional countryside population of Slovakia; still, these differences have not become preeminent political issues despite successive conquests and foreign domination. From the Magyars in the early tenth century to the Holy Roman Empire and the Hapsburgs—and, in recent times, Nazi Germany and the Soviet Union—foreign powers have determined the country's internal affairs. The 1960s witnessed a flourishing of democratic socialism under Alexander Dubček, which culminated in 1968 in the so-called "Prague Spring" but was cut short when Soviet tanks fraternally rolled in.

The placards and neon signs proclaiming "With the Soviet Union Forever" were raised by the government to stress its commitment to the status quo. Today this slogan ironically represents the sentiments of those who would like the current government to adopt Gorbachev-style reforms. Gustav Husák's government has recently had to cope with the problems of an industrial economy pressured by East Asian competition, and with one of the most active dissident groups in the Eastern Bloc. Husák is old and in poor health, and analysts see a struggle shaping up between the reform-minded Lubomír Strongal and the more conservative Vasil Bilák. Gorbachev, who was cheered in the streets when he visited in April 1987, may have been putting his influence behind the path to reform when he obliquely said that the difference between himself and Dubček was "nineteen years."

While Czechoslovakia's turbulent history is reflected in the several thousand castles spread throughout the land, the sheer beauty of its countryside should take your mind off politics. Glorious Prague is one of the great Gothic and baroque cities of Europe. A Victorian ambience pervades the spas of Karlovy Vary (Karlsbad) and Mariánské Lázně (Marienbad). And Bratislava, only a few dozen kilometers east of Vienna, welcomes travelers to its medieval castles and monuments.

Planning your Trip

All visitors to Czechoslovakia must have a visa before they arrive; these are available from any Czech diplomatic mission. For a visa application, write to **Čedok,** the state tourist company (see our appendix for the location nearest you), or the **Czechoslovak Embassy,** 3900 Linnaean Ave. NW, Washington, D.C. (tel. (202) 363-6315); the application will outline fees. In Canada, obtain a visa at the **Consulate General of Czechoslovakia,** 1305 Pine Avenue, West Montréal, Québec, H3G 1B2 (tel. (514) 849-4495). The process takes two to three weeks in North America. At a Czech embassy in Europe, the process is ordinarily completed overnight or while you wait; we list Czech embassies in London, Vienna, Belgrade, and Eastern European capitals.

Your visa must bear a stamp indicating where you've spent each night of your stay in Czechoslovakia. If you use official accommodations—including all those listed in this chapter—this will ordinarily be done for you. If you make your own arrangements to stay in private homes, you need to register with the local police. Visa forms are not always checked scrupulously, but if they are, you may be forced to recount all the trans-Czechoslovakian overnight trains you took.

You must exchange DM30 into Czechoslovak koruny per day that your visa is valid (in 1987, US$16 per day). You'll be given a receipt, which you must produce when purchasing international transportation tickets, when paying for most forms of lodging, and most importantly, *when leaving the country.* If you lose your receipt, you will be required to purchase as many koruny again as you did upon entering. Should you decide to prolong your stay in Czechoslovakia, you can extend your visa at the local police station for 60kčs, but *first* you must exchange the required amount of money for each additional day; take the bank receipt to the station.

The exchange rate for the 30DM per day (or equivalent) is set by the government. But there is talk of abolishing the mandatory daily exchange requirement in 1988 and aligning the exchange rate to the current black market trade. Be extremely careful about offers to exchange money on the black market, or less frequent offers to buy any Western-made possessions. You can get into serious trouble if you're caught making the transaction or attempting to leave the country without objects you declared on your way in. If you decide to assume the risk of such exchanges, insist on double the official rate and be discreet. Also, watch out for being cheated. In the fall of 1985, Czechoslovakia introduced new 1000kčs notes, in a bright, pretty blue; any 1000kčs notes from before 1985 are without value. Some marketeers will add a zero (or two!) by hand to notes' denominations. If you fall for this one, don't tell anybody.

The cheapest way to visit Czechoslovakia is to participate in the series of **Volunteer International Work Camps** for students, which CKM, the student travel bureau, has instituted. Two- to three-week programs take place in July and August. There are camps all around the country with various projects—archeological work, trail maintenance in the Tatry Mountains, and study-discussion camps in Prague. Room and board are paid for, and workers are exempt from the mandatory currency exchange. It's an excellent way to meet students from all over (English is the common language). There are 29 camps, with 20 to 25 spaces each for foreigners. Make arrangements several months in advance through CIEE or Volunteers for Peace (see the General Introduction).

Transportation

Rail travel is cheap in Czechoslovakia; train tickets cost only 14 to 30kčs per 100km, depending on the speed of the train. The faster trains, used for international and long distance routes, are the *expres;* the *rychlík* (fast) trains cost as much as *expres,* while the few *spěšný* (semi-fast) trains cost less. Avoid the slow train, *osobný,* and trains passing through major towns around commuting hours. Tickets can be bought on the train, but find the conductor before s/he finds you; if you don't, you face a 100kčs fine. Don't continue your train trip farther than your ticket stipulates without disembarking to buy a ticket for the extra distance—otherwise you forfeit your first ticket, and pay for the entire extended trip.

Seat reservations (*místenka,* 4kčs), are a good idea on popular lines, and are obligatory on all international trains, even if you're not traveling beyond the border. On international routes, booking at least a day in advance is recommended; tickets must be purchased and reservations made at Čedok offices. You'll be required to pay in Western currency for the portion of your trip outside Czechoslavakia. You can circumvent this requirement by buying a regular Czech domestic ticket as far as the border, and then purchasing a German or Austrian domestic ticket (or using your railpass) once you're out of Czechoslovakia. Neither Eurail nor InterRail is valid in Czechoslovakia, but IUS cardholders are entitled to a 25% discount on international journeys within Eastern Europe.

Buses are often a faster, if more expensive, alternative to rail travel. Inside the country, **ČSAD** is the company you'll have to deal with; terminals are known as *autobusové nádraží.* On major routes, trains are usually more frequent than buses. Buy your bus ticket at least one day in advance to guarantee yourself a reserved seat.

Many young people hitchhike in Czechoslovakia. Since Czechs begin the work day very early, the best hitching hours are from 6 to 8am; after 9am, leaving most cities will be difficult.

Terrain and roads throughout Czechoslovakia are satisfactory for cycling. Unfortunately there are no bicycles available for rent; you may, however, bring your own across the border. Unless you read Czech you won't understand the youth magazine *Mladý svět,* which publishes information on cycling tours. Air travel in Czechoslovakia is prohibitively expensive.

Practical Information

Čedok, the state tourist company, has an effective monopoly on the tourist industry in Czechoslovakia. They handle almost everything—international transportation tickets, almost all hotels and campgrounds, and local information—and they're the place you're most likely to find English speakers. Be insistent with them; at times, it seems that they're under explicit instructions to withhold information and force you to spend more money than you need to. **CKM** is the youth and student travel bureau. They issue the IYHF card and the IUS card, the Eastern European version of the ISIC. They're a prime source of help and information and a good place to find English speakers. Look also for **Information** and **TIS** offices, both of which cater more to individual travelers than either Čedok or CKM.

The Czech and Slovak languages are closely related. Russian is every student's mandatory second language, but they are reluctant to use it; German is the most common third. Older people speak German throughout Bohemia, in most of Moravia, and in parts of Slovakia, and German is spoken in all large cities and resorts. You are strongly advised to know some German—if not Czech—or to travel with someone who does. English-Czech dictionaries are quite cheap (30kčs) and easily available. The *Say It In Czech* phrasebook will also prove indispensable: Pick it up at home, as it's unavailable in Czechoslovakia.

National holidays are New Year's Day (Jan. 1), Easter Sunday and Monday, International Workers' Day (May 1), Anniversary of Soviet Liberation (May 9), and Christmas (Dec. 25-26). On holidays, most shops close but most restaurants stay open (except Dec. 24, when everything is closed).

You can have mail sent to your embassy, Čedok offices, or American Express, but allow *at least* two weeks. Embassies are probably most reliable.

For emergencies it's wise to make use of your country's embassy in Czechoslovakia; local police may not understand English.

The **country code** for Czechoslovakia is 42.

Accommodations and Camping

In July and August, CKM converts student dormitories in major university towns into youth hostels *(junior-střediska),* with very comfortable two- to four-bed rooms costing 45kčs per person with a hostel or student card, 93kčs without. CKM also has seven permanent, year-round Junior Hotels. These usually cost 45kčs for IYHF members, and have B-hotel rates (see below) for nonmembers. CKM facilities give priority to groups, but there is often space for independent travelers. Even in Prague, the addresses of CKM facilities change annually; the current IYHF handbook usually has the correct locations and opening days, but it's wise to pick up a reliable list at the first CKM office you visit.

Private homes are the next cheapest accommodations option. Čedok and Pragotur act as agents for local residents with spare space. In Prague, Čedok has access only to 20 private rooms, so Pragotur is considerably more convenient. Outside of Prague, ask at Čedok offices. Fees are payable at the office, and average about 110kčs for singles and 180kčs for doubles. Facilities are generally excellent, though apartments are often a healthy commute from the city center. You may be approached by people offering space in their homes. This practice is not illegal and is your only opportunity in the country to bargain, but remember that you must register with the police.

Hotels in Czechoslovakia are grouped into the categories A, B, and C, according to price and quality. Except in the countryside, the government has been closing class C hotels. Class B singles cost about 160kčs and doubles are about 240kčs, including breakfast. Prices vary somewhat, according to the city's popularity.

Camping is available everywhere and is very inexpensive, though most campgrounds are open only during the summer. Čedok offices overseas and Čedok and CKM offices within Czechoslovakia should be able to supply you with a list of sites. The book *Ubytování ČSR* lists comprehensively the hotels, inns, hostels, huts, and campgrounds in Bohemia and Moravia; it is in Czech, but not too difficult to decode. Bookstores also sell a fine hiking map of the country, *Soubor turistických Map* (8.50kčs), with an English key.

Food

The cheapest food is found at a stand-up *bufet,* also called *samoobsluha* (self-service). A *hostinec* is also inexpensive; it caters to a steady clientele of beer drinkers, and is one of the best places to meet people. A *pivnice* is a beer hall, a *vinárna* a wine bar, usually specializing in fine Slovak wines; both are good places to eat. *Kavárny* and *cukrárny* serve exquisite pastry. Expect to pay 30-40kčs at a medium-class restaurant, and 40-80kčs at the best places.

Meals in Czechoslovakia traditionally consist of soup *(polévka),* a main meat-and-vegetable dish, and a drink. *Knedliky* are the fluffy bread dumplings that accompany everything; *kyselé zelfi* (sauerkraut) is also often served.

There is no question of what to drink; Czech beer is among the world's best. The most famous are *plzeňský Prazdroj* (Pilsner Urquell) and *Budvar* (the original Budweiser). At 2.50-7kčs per half liter, it is the best bargain around. *Slivovice* (plum brandy) is at its best here in the country that parented it. Other popular liquors are *Borovička* (made of juniper berries), *Becherovka* (herbs), and *Myslivec,* very popular with students.

Prague (Praha)

Prague is one of the most spectacular of all European cities. Because Czechoslovakia was not of major strategic importance in either of the great wars of the twentieth century, Prague escaped the ravages which leveled comparable cities such as Dresden. The so-called "city of a hundred spires" is largely unblemished by elephantine Stalinist architecture, and the River Vltava is incomparably majestic. Prague's residents have assumed the air of their respectable city; you'll find no pandering to tourism here.

Orientation and Practical Information

Prague straddles the River Vltava in western Czechoslovakia. Direct rail and bus service links the city with Vienna to the southeast, Berlin to the north (6 hr. by rail), Munich to the southwest, and Warsaw to the northeast.

You'll have a hard time finding a free map at the train station; instead, go to a *tabak* stand and buy the excellent, indexed *plán města* (12kčs, in book form 30kčs; also available at bookstores).

The **Staré Město** (old town) lies with **Josefov,** the old Jewish quarter, inside a 90-degree bend of the river. In the former are Prague's busiest commercial streets and squares. The center of downtown action is **Václavské náměstí** (Wenceslaus Square), Prague's widest boulevard; at its northern end the major shopping street **Na příkopě** begins. The huge plaza **Staroměstské náměstí** joins the old town with Josefov. Across the renowned **Karlův most** (Charles Bridge) from these districts is **Malá Strona** (lesser town), above which is **Pražský hrad** (Prague Castle), the city's principal landmark. Most architectural monuments are concentrated near the castle and in the old town. The **Nové Město** (new town), established in 1348 by Charles IV, lies south of the old town, back on the east side of the river.

Tourist Offices: Čedok, Na příkopě 18 (tel. 212 71 11). Information, travel services, and so on. Arrive before 8:30am if you want to buy a train ticket without waiting 1 hr. or more. Open June-Sept. Mon.-Fri. 8:15am-4:15pm, Sat. 8:15am-2pm, closed Sun.; Oct.-May Mon.-Fri. 8:15am-4:15pm, closed Sat.-Sun. April-May occasionally open Sat. 8am-noon. **CKM,** main office in Junior Hotel Praha, Žitná 12 (tel. 29 85 89). Open Mon.-Fri. 8-10am and 1-4:30pm. Information, IYHF, ISIC, and IUS cards also available at Jindřisská 28 (tel. 26 85 07). Open Mon. and Wed. 10am-noon and 2-6pm, Tues., Thurs., and Fri. 10am-noon and 1-5pm. IUS cards sold only Tues. and Thurs. 2-4pm (IUS cards also sold at IUS, see below). **Pražská informačni služba** (Prague Information Service), Na příkopě 20 (tel. 54 44 44), is less crowded than Čedok; especially good for theater and concert listings. Open April-Oct. Mon.-Fri. 8am-8pm, Sat. 8am-noon; Nov.-March 8am-7pm, Sat. 8am-noon. Try to get a copy of *The Month in Prague,* full of pertinent information.

Budget Travel: Not really a concept in this country, but an IUS card will get you 25% off international train tickets within Eastern Europe. The world headquarters of the **International Union of Students** is in Prague at Pařižká 25, across from the Intercontinental Hotel. Card sold for 40kčs upon presentation of an ISIC card and one photo. Open Mon.-Fri. 12:30-4pm.

American Express: Represented in Czechoslovakia by **Čedok,** Na příkopě 18 (tel. 212 71 11), the first desk as you enter. Mail held (at the Overseas Department counter), US$ traveler's checks sold to cardholders, and lost or stolen checks replaced. Will cash cardholders' personal checks, but this may take up to 24 hours, since they call your bank; the cash advances they provide cardholders are easier. Open same hours as Čedok (see Tourist Offices).

Currency Exchange: Possible at Čedok, banks, and Interhotels. The several Interhotels on Václavské nám. will change money on weekends and in the evening; they are also great for English-speaking help in general, and for mailing things.

Post Office: Jindřišská 14. Poste Restante held, but embassies are more reliable. Open 24 hours. At the main train station (hlavní nádr.). Open Mon.-Fri. 8am-8pm, Sat. 8am-1pm.

Telephones: At the post office. Open 24 hours. **Telephone code:** 2.

Trains: There are 4 train stations in Prague; it's impossible to discern a simple pattern in the destinations they serve. Always ask about your point of departure—the information may not be volunteered. The main station, **Praha hlavní nádraží,** figures in most international routes and many domestic ones. For information and help with accommodations, you'll have to ride the Metro to the tourist offices. Baggage storage in the basement (15kg limit, 2kčs per day, open 24 hours); lockers 1kčs (usually full); clean showers 8kčs. **Praha střed** is nearby on Hybernská, and serves only domestic routes; their information office is often less hectic than that at the main station. **Praha-smíchov** and **Praha-holešovice** are across the river; the first serves mainly domestic routes, the second serves domestic as well as many northwest/southeast transit trains. If you speak Czech, or know someone who does, call train information (tel. 24 44 41 or 26 49 30).

Buses: ČSAD has 3 terminals *(Autobusové nádraží)* in town. The central one is **Praha-Florenc** (tel. 22 14 45) on Křižíkova behind the Praha střed railway station (Metro: Sokolovská); the staff at the Informace desk speak only Czech. Open Mon.-Fri. 6am-8pm, Sat. 6am-2pm, Sun. 6am-4pm.

Public Transportation: Prague is a pleasant city to roam about on foot, but for longer distances the Metro, tram, and bus systems are quite convenient. Bus routes are frequently shifted for street repairs. The 3 lines of the **Metro** are very fast, as are its escalators and killer doors. Tickets, good for all forms of transportation, cost 1kčs each; purchase them at newspaper stands, *tabak* shops, restaurants, railway stations, and the orange *automat* machines in all Metro stations. Stock up on tickets, as they are not easily available in residential suburbs or at night. You must punch your ticket on boarding and, since they are not transferable, punch a new one when switching vehicles; the only exception is the Metro, which allows a one-way journey for 90 min. The primary system, including the Metro, closes at midnight; thereafter night trams and buses, often with different routes than their daytime counterparts, operate. These run about every 40 min. Night trams are numbered 51-58, night buses 500-510; look for their midnight blue signs at transport stops. By 1988 1- and 3-day passes should be available. Information, not necessarily in English (tel. 22 92 52).

Emergencies: Ambulance (tel. 333). **Medical Emergency** (tel. 155). No English spoken; try calling your embassy. **Police** headquarters at Olšanská 2: Come here to register if you're staying in a private home, or, with luck, to get a visa extension. Often long lines. Take Metro A to Flora, then walk down Jičinská and right onto Olšanská; the station is about 200m on your right. Or take tram #9, 10, or 21. Open Mon.-Tues. and Thurs.-Fri. 8am-noon and 12:30-3:30pm, Wed. 8am-noon.

Embassies: U.S., Malá Strana, Tržište 15, code 125 48 (tel. 53 66 41-9, ext. 229 for consular services), in the former Colloredo Schönborn Palace, where Kafka worked as a librarian. Open 8am-1pm and 2-4:30pm. **Canada,** Hradčany, Mickiewiczova 6, code 125 33 (tel. 32 69 41). **U.K.,** Thunovská 14, code 125 50 (tel. 53 33 47). Travelers from **Australia** and **New Zealand** should call the British Embassy. All embassies will hold mail—a valuable service considering the lines at Čedok and the post office. **Bulgaria,** Krakovská 6 (tel. 26 43 10). **Hungary,** Mičurinova 1 (tel. 36 50 41). **Poland,** Valdštejnská 8 (tel. 53 69 51); consular section Václavské nám. 19 (tel. 26 54 41).

Laundry: Jungmannova 16. Open Mon.-Fri. 8am-6pm.

Hitchhiking: To hitch to the east, take tram #9 or 21 to the last stop. To hitch south, take the Metro C to Pražskeho povstáni, then go left 100m, crossing Náměsti hrdinů to 5 Května, also known as highway D1. To hitch west—towards Munich—take tram #15 down Plzeňská to the Motol district, or tram #2 or 25 to Chomutov. To hitch north, take tram or bus to Kobyliské nám., then bus #175 up Horňátecká. Always hitch *before* the roads become highways—highway hitching is illegal.

Accommodations and Camping

Finding a room in Prague is suitably Kafkaesque: The city has 8000 beds for an annual 3,000,000 visitors. Hostels and hotels change category or go out of business frequently and unpredictably, and may have vacancies that only Čedok has access to. Arrive early, as places fill up quickly, especially on weekends and in July and August, and lines at Čedok and Pragotur are often long. Call the hostels before turning to the accommodations services, as these services do not always mention dorm space. You'll need some luck, though, since large groups have priority at hostels. Go to Pragotur for private rooms.

If you arrange to stay in someone's home, you must register with the police; even though most people who will approach you are reluctant to have you do so, since they subsequently pay tax. The procedure is not difficult, but it is time-consuming. Go to the registration office at Olšanska 2 (see Police, under Emergencies, above). If you stay at any of the official places below, you will automatically be registered.

Phone reservations might seem the solution, but they are rarely accepted *and* honored. The Čedok offices in New York and London will make official reservations (only London for private rooms). Čedok requires a deposit, and all services are best contacted at least two weeks in advance. Travel agencies abroad will work with Čedok for you, but at a price.

Particularly in the high season (Easter-Nov.), you may have trouble getting even a B hotel room. The best strategy in this case is to be at Čedok or Pragotur at 5pm, when forfeited reservations become available.

In despair, remember: Prague *is* worth it.

Accommodations Services

Čedok and Pragotur will help you navigate Prague's lodging morass, though you'll pay a commission and spend time in their often-long lines. Be sure to ask Čedok about their hostels. If you resign yourself to a hotel, insist on something close to the city center.

Čedok, Panská 5 (tel. 22 56 57 or 22 70 04). The cheapest places Čedok regularly offers are B hotels. (Singles 200kčs; doubles 300kčs, with shower 405kčs. Breakfast included.) During July and Aug., Čedok also arranges stays in "luxury" student dormitories, many inconveniently distant. (Doubles 248kčs.) Even in the morning, you will more likely find a room through someone on the street than through this office. Open April-Nov. Mon.-Fri. 9am-10pm, Sat. 8:30am-8pm, Sun. 8:30am-5pm; Dec.-March Mon.-Fri. 9am-8pm, Sat.-Sun. 8:30am-2pm.

Pragotur, U Obecního domu 2 (tel. 231 72 81), a side street off Nám. republiky, 1 block north of the Prašná Brána. Metro: Nám. republiky. They do not "own" hotel spaces as Čedok does, but their lines are shorter, and they do handle C-class hotels and CKM hostels. They also book rooms in private homes. Rooms are often far from the center of town, but cheaper and infinitely less sterile than downtown hotels. Doubling or tripling up with other people waiting to get a room may speed things up. For private rooms there is often a 3-day minimum stay. (130-250kčs per person, commission 5kčs per day.) Open Mon.-Sat. 7:30am-8:30pm.

CKM, Žitna 12 (tel. 29 99 41). Not an accommodations service (hence no lines), but the place to ask about affordable hostels (members 45kčs, nonmembers 93kčs).

Hostels (Studentska Kolej)

The one permanent characteristic of hostels in Prague is their state of flux. Locations may change from one summer to the next, and prices certainly will. CKM contracts with student dorms only in March, so on-the-spot inquiries are the only sure method. Opening dates also vary, but they usually run from early July to late Aug. It's always a good idea to check with the latest IYHF handbook, or with CKM. Hostels are usually much more interesting than hotels, since they're popular with Eastern European students, and are usually impeccable. Čedok hostels are considerably more expensive (doubles only, 248kčs), and are more likely to have space. These can be booked only at Panská 5 in Prague (be there around 9:30am), or through travel agents abroad. Couples can stay together.

In 1989 CKM will open the 304-bed Junior Hotel Vltava, which will be open year-round and should ease the squeeze.

Koleje všcht, Jižní město. Metro: Budovatelău, then bus #154 to 2nd or 3rd stop; ask for *Všcht.* Far from the center, but very comfortable. CKM hostel (see above). Singles 60kčs. Open July.

Koleje VŠZ, Kamýcká ul. (tel. 34 41 98). Take Metro A to Leninova, then bus #107 or 147 to Kamýcká (in Suchdol district); look for the big *VŠZ* sign. A ½-hr. trip from the station. Large rooms with kitchenettes. CKM hostel. Open Aug.

Správa Kolejí University Karlovy, Větrnik (tel. 35 52 75). Take Metro A to Hradčanská, then tram #1 or 18 for 6 or 7 stops to Petřiny. Čedok's largest hostel: 300 beds. Comfortable rooms and quiet location. Singles 238kčs, doubles 248kčs. Open July-Aug.

TJ Dukla Karlin, Malého (tel. 22 20 09). Behind the Praha-Florenc *autobusová nádraži* (bus terminal). Metro: Sokolovská. Bunk beds for the first ten arrivals; cots in a gymnasium for the rest. Not elegant at all, but there's usually room here. 45kčs. Check-in 6pm-midnight; check-out 8am.

Tourist Hotel TJ Dolní Měcholupy, Na Paloučku 223. Metro: Želivskeho, then bus #229 to Měcholupska. Singles 65kčs; doubles and triples also available.

C Hotels

There are few C hotels in Prague. Singles are practically impossible to find.

Národní dům, Bořivojova 53 (tel. 27 53 65). Take tram #26 to Nám. sladkovského and walk south one block. Its dorm-style accommodations are often filled by groups. Doubles 210kčs, triples 315kčs, quads 357kčs.

B Hotels

Try first at CKM's **Junior Hotel Praha,** Žitna 12 (tel. 29 99 41). Take the Metro to Nám. pavlova and walk back one street. Formerly a CKM hostel, it is convenient and comfortable. (Singles 217kčs, doubles 326kčs, triples 403kčs.) If this fails, see if Čedok or Pragotur can put you up in one of their hotels.

Camping

Theoretically, Pragotur lists the city's seven campgrounds, but they may tell you there's no space, or that they no longer have the brochure, *Praha Camping.* Be insistent, ask for the addresses, and call the campgrounds yourself—German is always spoken, and sometimes English. The best facilities and most space are at the **Sokol Dolní Počernice,** Dolní Počernice, Nad rybníkem (tel. 89 90 34). Take tram #9 to the end of the line, then bus #109 and ask for the campground. Bungalow singles 67kčs, doubles 134kčs. Tent singles 22kčs, doubles 44kčs.

Food

Cheap *pivnice* (beer halls) and *vinárny* (wine cellars) are all over town, usually with very good local specialties, and always with posted menus (in Czech, of course, but at least they can give you an idea of prices). The food is usually better in *vinárny,* the best of which are often underground. Sausage and butcher shops often have grilled meats, and some provide beer and a place to stand. These are generally even cheaper than stand-up *bufets;* look for *jídelna* (eatery) signs (most open 11:30am-2pm). For a light snack or a quick lunch, the numerous window stands selling tasty *párek v rohlíku* (sausage in a small roll with mustard) for 2.50kčs are a fine deal; there are many squares in Prague where half the people are eating sausages and the other half are waiting to buy them. *Smažený sýr* (fried cheese) and *bramborák* (a potato omelette) are other Prague favorites.

Many rate Prague's pastries above Vienna's; you be the judge. The best *cukrárny* (bakeries) are on Vodičkova, 2-4 blocks off Václavské nám. *Zmrzlina* (ice cream) is scrumptious. Crowds flock to the **Italská Zmrzlina** (Italian ice cream) shop on Vodičkova near Karlovo nám.

U Schnellů, Tomášská 2, in Malá Strana. Clean and cheery, with meat and potato dishes 20-45kčs. Don't miss their *Däbelské toasty,* a filling, spicy meat and bean stew over bread (8kčs). Open daily 11am-10:30pm.

U Prince, Staroměstské náměstí. Touristy, but one of the best inexpensive restaurants in the old town square. Fine food in attractive surroundings. Main dishes 15-35kčs. Open daily 9am-10pm; terrace on the square open 10am-8pm.

Obecní Dům, Nám. republiky 1090, near the Powder Tower. Cafe on one side, restaurant on the other, both serving tasty meals for 20-50kčs. The *Jugendstil* decor in the restaurant is in a class by itself. Friendly waiters, but you may have to fight for their attention. Open daily 7am-11pm; cafe terrace open April-Oct. daily 11am-8pm.

Arbat, Na přikopě 29. Russian food served fast. Meals for less than 20kčs. Open daily 7:30am-11pm.

Hotel Pařiž, u. Obecniho Domu č.l. (tel. 232 20 51). Parisian art deco elegance. An affordable splurge—turn down the hors d'oeuvres to keep the price reasonable. Menu in English.

Maÿur, Štěpánska 61, off Václavské nám. (tel. 236 99 22), 2 doors from British Airways. An uncanny combination: simply delicious Indian food served with a touch of Old World elegance. Worth a splurge. Dinner here costs 50-75kčs. Reservations recommended. Open Mon.-Sat. noon-4pm and 6-11pm.

Vegetarka, Celetná 3, just off Staroměstské nám. The only vegetarian restaurant in town. Good food in a bland atmosphere. Menu changes daily. Main courses around 15kčs. Open for lunch only.

Automat Koruna, at the corner of Na příkopě and Václavské nám. One of a number of downtown self-service restaurants. Not the finest cuisine, but very cheap. Watch what locals order to avoid disappointment. Open Mon.-Fri. 6am-10pm, Sat. 9am-7pm, Sun. 8am-6pm.

Sights

Prague grew up as five independent towns and was not united by central administration until 1784. The Stare Město (old town) was the first and most important, but the Jewish village, Josefov, was not far behind, winning its own banner and government in 1358. Hradčany, across the river, was the royal city, crowned by the sprawling Gothic castle. Beneath it Malá Strana (lesser town) rose on the seventeenth-century ambitions of the local gentry; Italian architects built its splendid palaces and gardens. Once the Hussite stronghold, Nové Město was repeatedly destroyed in religious wars. Its rich nineteenth-century fronts and spacious squares are now the commercial center of Prague.

Between Staré Město and Nové Město is the central boulevard, Václavské náměští, a favorite meeting place of Czech and foreign students in the days of the liberalization; in 1968 and 1969, it was the site of mass demonstrations. **Staroměstské náměstí** is the city's most famous square, dominated by the **Old Town Hall,** which grew from the original fourteenth-century tower to include several neighboring buildings. Townspeople as well as tourists gather on the hour to see the famous clock with 12 peering apostles and a bell-ringing skeleton. A statue of Czech theologian and leader **Jan Hus** occupies an appropriate position in the center of the square. Across from the Town Hall is the **Tyn Church,** once a center of the Hussite movement. The difference between the two towers is intentional: one represents Adam, the other Eve. Between Maiselova and the church is Franz Kafka's former home, sometimes marked with a plaque. (Hardcore Kafka devotees can visit the writer's final resting place at the Jewish Grave Yard right outside the Želivskeho Metro station.) A short detour down Jilska will bring you to the **Bethlehem Chapel,** where Jan Hus preached to his loyal congregation from 1402 until his death at the stake.

Walk southeast down Václavské nám. to reach the **National Museum** at Vitězného Unora 74. Its mammoth collection includes meteorites, textiles, precious stones, and skeletons still on the ground as they were discovered—don't miss the horse and rider. (Open Mon. and Fri. 9am-4pm, Wed.-Thurs. and Sat.-Sun. 9am-5pm. Admission 5kčs, students 2.50kčs.) Follow Vitězného Unora north to Hybernská 7, the **Lenin Museum.** Sometimes called the "People's House," this and the **Klement Gottwald Museum,** Rytířská 29, are Prague's two centers of communist history. Exhibit captions in Czech only. Read the comments in the guest book before you leave. (Klement Gottwald Museum open Tues.-Sat. 9am-5pm, Sun. 9am-3pm. Admission 1kčs.)

Josefov, the traditional Jewish quarter around Parižská and U. St. Hřbitova, lost much of its population to Nazi death camps during World War II, when it was emptied and used for storage. All that remains can be seen in the scattered buildings of the **Státní Židovské Muzeum** (State Jewish Museum), off Hřbitora, which includes five synagogues, a cemetery, and a collection of Jewish artifacts from Bohemia and Moravia. The fascinating underground **Staronová Synagogue** is the oldest in Europe; parts date back to 1270. Succeeding generations have added new layers to the nearby Jewish cemetery, which now crowds 12,000 tombstones within its walls. Most of the exhibits were collected during World War II at Hitler's direction so that a museum of "decadent" Jewish culture could be founded in Prague after the war. A unique collection of children's drawings and poems from the wartime Terezin ghetto has also survived. (Open in summer Sun.-Fri. 9am-5pm; in winter 9am-4:30pm. Admission 5kčs, students 3kčs.) In the vicinity of the Jewish quarter, tucked away on a little street (Anežská ulice) is a branch of the National Gallery in **St. Agnes convent** with a collection of nineteenth-century Czech painting. (Open Tues.-Sun. 10am-6pm).

Karlův most (Charles Bridge) is the most impressive of the Vltava bridges, with 30 baroque statue groups. Look for legendary hero Jan Nepomuk being drowned from the bridge for guarding his queen's confidences, or for the French noblemen coming to the rescue of despondent Christians imprisoned by Turks. Climb the Gothic **defense tower,** on the Malá Strana side, for the best view over Prague's red roofs, the bridge, and the river. (Open daily 10am-6pm. Admission 2kčs, students 1kčs.) For an afternoon on the water, rent a rowboat at the northeast corner of **Slovansky ostrov** (island). (Weather permitting, open mid-May to mid-June and mid-Aug. to mid-Sept. daily 10am-7pm; mid-June to mid-August Mon.-Fri. 10am-7pm, Sat.-Sun 9am-7pm. 3kčs per hr.) Either Slovansky ostrov or the larger **Střelecky ostrov** (accessible from Máje Most) serves as a pleasant, shaded retreat.

The **Malá Strana** (lesser town) is rich in palaces, ornate gardens, and grand baroque churches. The greatest of all is certainly **St. Nicholas's Church,** built by the Jesuits in the eighteenth century and considered the highest achievement of Czech baroque art. Nearby on Karmelitská ulice rises the more modest **Church of Our Lady Victorious,** repository of the world-famous statue of the Infant Jesus of Prague, a Spanish Renaissance work. A modest gate on Letenská ulice (off Malostranské nám. opens onto the **Valdštejnská zahrada** (Wallenstein Garden), one of Prague's best kept secrets. This tranquil seventeenth-century baroque garden, adorned with frescoes and statues, is enclosed by old buildings which look splendidly golden on sunny afternoons. (Open May-Sept. daily 9am-7pm.) If you poke around, you'll come upon still more anonymous gardens. Five are open to the public in this part of town. Venture, for example, through the gate at Karmeliská 25 into the ascending and descending planes of splendor beyond.

It is possible to spend entire days wandering about the edifices which comprise the **Pražský hrad** (Prague Castle), up Nerudova ulice. All the styles of architecture that have made Prague so astonishingly beautiful are well represented at Pražský hrad. The castle itself houses the **Národní Galerie** (National Gallery), which contains an excellent collection of woodcuts and paintings, including works by Dürer and Breughel (open Tues.-Sun. 10am-6pm). The **Katedrála sv. Vita** took 600 years to build; it was not completed until the 1930s. The brilliance and purity of the massive stained-glass windows are astounding, and the tombstones inside are nothing short of extraordinary. To the right of the high altar stands Christ and four angels, a three-meter-high baroque bonanza of glistening silver. Nearby, the **Starý královský palác** (Old Royal Palace) offers a whole array of Gothic designs. Higher up is a tiny street carved into the fortified wall, **Zlatá ulička** (Golden Lane), where the court alchemists are supposed to have worked. At #21, now a tiny bookstore, Kafka wrote for a time in 1917. (Buildings open April-Sept. Tues.-Sun. 9am-5pm; Oct.-March Tues.-Sun. 9am-4pm. Admission for each building 2kčs, students 1kčs. Golden Lane free. For more information on the entire complex, go to the Informačni středisko behind the cathedral.) The **Petřínské sady,** the gardens on the hills to the south, dominated by a model of the Eiffel Tower, offer a soothing escape from the city. The **Múzeum Mozart,** Mozartova 169, is housed in Villa Bertramka, an old but beautifully restored farmhouse that was Mozart's home in 1787. (Open Tues.-Fri. 2-5pm, Sat.-Sun. 10am-noon and 2-5pm.)

A half-hour walk south of Nové Město, untouched by tourists, is the quiet fortress **Vyšehrad.** This is Czechoslovakia's most revered landmark: Here the legendary Princess Libuše is said to have prophesied Prague's glory. There remain on the mount above the river a Neo-Gothic church, a Romanesque rotunda, and the Vyšehrad Cemetery. (Complex always open.) Take tram #3, 17, or 21, or Metro C to Gottwaldova. The subway stop is a sight itself, with a spectacular panorama of Prague.

Entertainment

The area around **Václavské náměstí** has a number of places with dance floors. **Cafe Luxor** at #41 is a traditional meeting place for younger crowds (Cover 25kčs. Reservations required.). The best way to enjoy Prague at night is to head to a *pivnice* or a *vinárna.* Head out early since places close up around 11pm.

U sv. Tomáše, Letenská 12. A crowded beer hall with a cheerful atmosphere. Open daily 11am-3pm and 4-11pm.

Reduta, Národní 20. A good jazz club, an easy place to meet artists and intellectuals.

U Fleků, Křemencova 11. Prague's answer to the German beer house, with occasional turn-of-the-century-style cabaret shows and great brown ale. Open daily 9am-11pm.

Cafe Slavia, Národní and Smetanov nábř., opposite the National Theatre. Smoky hangout of literati, punks, and rockers. Open daily 8am-midnight.

U Kalicha, Na bojišti 12. Serves first-rate Pilsner Urquell beer; this classic Czech pub is immortalized in Jaroslav Hašek's *The Good Soldier Schweik.* Open daily 11am-11pm.

Every year from mid-May to early June, the **Prague Spring Festival** draws musicians from all over the world; outdoor concerts take place in courtyards all over the city. Tickets (15-80kčs, some standing room available) can be bought at **Sluna,** Panská 4, Cerná ruže Arcade (tel. 22 12 06). For a list of exhibitions, concerts, museums, and films, pick up a copy of *The Month in Prague* at Prague Information Service or Pragotur, and, during the summer, the monthly brochure *Prague Cultural Summer.* The star tourist attraction in town is the **Laterna Magika,** Národní 40 (tel. 26 00 33). Their clever integration of film, drama, and dance might be a little too cute for some, but the show regularly attracts a large international audience. (Performances Mon.-Fri. 8pm, Sat. 5 and 8pm. Tickets 25-35kčs. Box office open Mon.-Sat. 2:30-6pm. Often sold out in summer 2 weeks in advance.)

Near Prague

The Central Bohemian hills surrounding Prague are the backdrop for 14 castles, some built as early as the thirteenth century. A half-hour train ride (10kčs) from Praha-Smíchov station brings you to **Karlštejn,** Charles IV's walled and turreted fortress. The chapel is decorated with inset precious stones and a stunning collection of apocalyptic paintings attributed to the famous medieval painter Nikolaus Wurmser. There is a **campsite** not far away, on the left bank of the River Berounka. **Konopiště** in Benešov (take the bus from Praha-Florenc station) is a Renaissance palace with a luxurious interior preserved from the days of Prince Ferdinand's hunting trips.

Bohemia

Definitely worth a visit is **Karlovy Vary** (Karlsbad), whose guest list reads like a roster of nineteenth-century notables. Goethe, Schiller, Gogol, Beethoven, Metternich, and even Marx took the waters here. Today people still throng to the town to cure their ailments and to enjoy the air of Victorian luxury and grandeur. The main sight is the crowd; get into the spirit by buying the proper narrow mug and drinking some of the local specialty. The cheapest place to stay in Karlovy Vary is the attractive **Junior Hotel Alice** at ul. Pětiletky 147 (tel. 248 48). Set in a pretty wooded area, the hotel is a bit out of town, but the walk to the center is lovely (a good deal of it along the path of the traditional constitutional walk). From the train station take bus #11 to the market place, and then bus #7 about nine stops. Try to reserve at least one month in advance. (IYHF members and students 45kčs, others 140kčs.) For B hotels, **Čedok,** Tržiště 23 (tel. 261 10 or 267 05), recommends making reservations three to four months in advance. To get to Čedok from the train station take bus #11 into town, walk left from the bus terminal down

Varšavská, cross the river, and follow it to the right for 20 minutes, or take bus #2 from the marketplace to the end of the line. (Open mid-May to Sept. Mon.-Fri. 9am-6pm, Sat. 9am-noon, closed Sun.; Oct. to mid-May Mon.-Fri. 9am-4pm, Sat. 9am-noon, closed Sun.) ČSAD buses to Karlovy Vary leave almost every hour from Prague's Praha-Florenc station (39kčs). Trains run from Praha střed (6-7 per day, 3½hr., 43kčs).

Mariánské Lázně (Marienbad), 40km south of Karlovy Vary (2 hr. by mountain train, 8kčs), is another spa famed among ailing European gentry and their raucous offspring. The town is a stately park, designed and landscaped by a man who was a genius in his field, Václav Skalník. It was here also that Goethe experienced his love for the beautiful Ulrika von Levetzow, expressed in his famous *Marienbader Elegie.* Venture into the dark surrounding forests for a constitutional and you'll feel rejuvenated. Take the waters at the Maxim Gorki Colonnade; like magic, the faucets go on and off when you wave your hand over them. There is a fountain concert every hour.

The **Čedok** office is in the center of town; take bus #5 from the station and get off at the sixth stop. Don't count on much assistance, though: The one English-speaker will tell you that it's simply not profitable to arrange short stays for small parties. End of conversation. Be tough; don't leave until they have at least suggested a few hotels likely to have space. By far the best place to stay is CKM's beautiful **Junior Hotel Krakonoš** (tel. 26 24), about 5km from town in a gorgeous wooded location. (IYHF members and students 45kčs, others pay 281kčs for doubles.) From the train station take bus #5 six stops to the Hotel Excelsior, and then bus #12 to the top of the mountain. It's smart to reserve one month in advance. If they're full, obsolete, out to lunch, or otherwise unavailable, you'll have to compete for a room in town with the hordes who come to take the waters. It won't be fun. There are several B-category hotels on the main street. (Singles 130-200kčs, doubles 200-300kčs.) As in Prague, you'll have the most luck securing lodgings either early in the morning or shortly after 5pm (sometimes 6pm) when no-shows become no-shows. Staying at private homes is out of the question in Mariánské Lázně; these rooms are reserved for nationals of socialist countries. You have two choices for dining: picnic meals or hotel restaurants, which are fairly uniform in price and setting (full meals 60-100kčs). Don't leave the spa without trying the *lázeňskě oplatky,* huge circular wafers which taste quite good in their *čokoládové* (chocolate) variety.

Mariánské Lázně is on the Prague-Nuremberg rail line. Trains leave for Mariáské Lásně from Prague's main station (4 per day, 3½hr., 43kčs).

Plzeň, 80km southwest of Prague, is famed as the birthplace of beer, and for its home brew, *Plzeňsky Prazdroj* (Pilsner Urquell), arguably the best beer in the world. Czechoslovakia is one of the world's top five beer-drinking nations, and much of it flows from this town. To visit the brewery, you must make reservations 14 days in advance. You can, though, try the town's best at **Restaurace Prazdroj,** U Prazdroja ul. 1 (tel. 35 60 8), right outside the brewery gates. Say "Prazdroj" and the people will point in the right direction. To spend the night (in a hotel, not a bar), contact **Čedok,** at the corner of Sedláckova and Arešovská. (Open Mon.-Fri. 9am-noon and 1-5pm, Sat. 9am-noon.) The **Hotel Plzeň,** Žižkova 66 (tel. 27 26 56), has singles for 125kčs. Take streetcar #1 or 4 from the center of town. The **Bíla Hora autocamping** (tel. 356 11) has bungalows for 220kčs per person. Plzeň lies conveniently on the Prague-Munich line.

Bratislava

Just outside the sphere of Ottoman conquests, Bratislava became the Hungarian capital in the sixteenth century, but it continually resisted both German and Magyar domination, holding firmly to its Slavic language and culture. Today the capital of Slovakia, Bratislava is an easy-going city with an attractive old town and a friendly populace.

Orientation and Practical Information

Bratislava is on the banks of the Danube, a mere 64km east of Vienna. Hydrofoils, trains, and buses connect the city with Budapest and Vienna. Traveling by rail to Prague (6 hr.), you may have to change at Brno.

To get to the compact center of town from the tram station, take tram #13. Tickets (1kčs) are available throughout town from orange *automat* machines. There's a very helpful English-speaking staff at the train station information office.

Tourist Offices: Čedok, 13 Štúrová (tel. 520 02). Currency exhange, help with accommodations, international tickets, and general information. Open mid-May to mid-Sept. Mon.-Fri. 9am-6pm, Sat. 9am-noon, closed Sun.; mid-Sept to mid-May Mon.-Fri. 9am-5pm, Sat. 9am-noon, closed Sun. **CKM,** Hviezdoslavovo nám. 16 (tel. 33 16 07), in the old town near the river. Check here first for help with accommodations. Open Mon.-Fri. 1-4pm, closed Sat.-Sun. **BIPS,** Leningradská 1 (tel. 33 44 15). Information about the city, especially cultural events. Open Mon.-Fri. 8:30am-6pm, Sat. 8:30am-1pm, closed Sun. All tourist offices are within easy walking distance of one another.

Budget Travel: Buy the IUS card at **CKM** if you're a student and will be making any international journeys in Eastern Europe.

Currency Exchange: At Čedok or any fancy hotel.

Post Office: Kolárska 14. **Telephone** here. Open 24 hours. **Telephone code:** 7.

Trains: The main station, **Hlavna stanica,** is at the northern end of town. Take tram #13 (direction: *centrum*) to Nám. kammene, the center of town; Čedok and most sights are nearby.

Buses: ČSAD Autobusové stanica, at Mlynské nivy. Take bus #215 or 218 to the center of town. Information (tel. 632 13).

Hydrofoils: Buy your tickets at **Slovakoturist,** Nálepkova 13. Open Mon.-Fri. 8am-noon and 2:30-4:30pm. No tickets sold at the dock or on board.

Consulates: Poland, 22 Obrancov Mieru (tel. 476 30); **Hungary,** Palisady 60 (tel. 33 56 01); **Bulgaria,** Kuzmányho la (tel. 33 89 03); **Romania,** F. Králá 11 (tel. 405 22); **USSR,** Godrova 4 (tel. 33 14 25); **East Germany,** Palisady 47 (tel. 33 78 87); **Yugoslavia,** Holubyho 9 (tel. 33 49 33).

Hitchhiking: To hitch to Vienna, cross the new Danube bridge and walk down Viedenská cesta. The same road will take you to Hungary via Györ; that direction is more difficult. To hitch to Prague, take bus #104 from the center up Pražská ul. to the Patronka stop.

Accommodations and Camping

Make it clear to Čedok and CKM that you want inexpensive student accomodations. If they send you to a hotel, ask them to call ahead and make sure there is room. For information on the location of this year's **CKM Youth Hostel** call 32 10 14 or 32 19 68.

Hotel Sputnik (CKM), Ul. Drieňová 14 (tel. 23 43 40). If you can't get a room in a private home, this is the hotel of choice. Students 45kčs; others 218kčs in singles, 328kčs in doubles. Reservations recommended. Take tram #8 from the train station to the 8th or 9th stop (look for a small lake on your left). The hotel is across the lake. Open year-round.

Motel Zlaté Piesky, Ul. Vajnorská, in suburban Trnávka (tel. 651 70 or 660 28). Take tram #2, 4, or 10, then bus #32 for 3 stops. Campground and bungalows near a popular river beach. Open year-round.

Palace, 1 Poštová (tel. 33 36 56), has the cheapest singles (160kčs) in town. Take tram #13 five stops from the main train station.

Food

Dining well is almost inevitable in Bratislava: grilled meats of various kinds and Slovak wine are the local staples. Don't neglect the city's countless *cukráreni,* with sumptuous pastry for 3-5kčs and homemade ice cream *(zmrzlina)* for 2kčs.

Slovanské Reštauracie, Šturová 3, in the arcade. Excellent food, and menu in English. Their soups are delicious. You'll spend 40-50kčs per person; the heaping Slovak platters for 2 are a great deal (75-100kčs). Open Mon.-Fri. 11am-3pm and 5:30-10pm, Sat. 11am-4pm.

Vináreň Vel'kí Františkáni, Františkáni, Dibrivova 10, in the old town near Nám. 4 Aprila. Good Slovak food in an old monastery. The waiters loosen up after 10pm, when they'll sit and drink with their customers. Meals from 26kčs.

Stará Sladovňa, Cintorínska 32. An old malt house converted into an enormous beer hall and restaurant complex. Meals from 35kčs. Open daily 10am-10pm.

Vináreň Tokaj, Ul. Ursulinská 1, off Leningradská. Sweet Tokay wine and raucous gypsy music make this a delightful Hungarian establishment. Open Tues.-Sat. 11am-3am.

Reduta, Fučíkova 7, near the Danube in the center of town. Specializes in pork dishes *(bravcové)* for 30kčs. Usually open Mon.-Sat. 10am-10pm.

Sights

The imperial residential interiors of the **Bratislavský hrad** (Bratislava Castle) were lost to fire during the Napoleonic wars, but its gardens still offer a splendid view of the new bridge over the Danube and of the hills of three different countries. (Open Tues.-Sun. 9am-5pm. Admission 4kčs, students 1kčs.) From Castle Hill you can descend the streets of the **Staré Město** (old town) to the **Dóm sv. Martina,** the early Gothic coronation cathedral of 10 Hungarian kings and eight queens. Around every corner in the old town you'll find different branches of the Mestské Múzeum (City Museum). The **Mirbach Palace** houses changing collections of modern Slovak paintings as well as a beautiful series of seventeenth-century English tapestries based on Greek myths. Take time to listen to the recorded description of the tapestries' mysterious discovery in Bratislava. The baroque **Old Town Hall** is home to a museum of Bratislav history, including a frightening exhibit of devices of torture and execution. The best preserved section of the town wall is the **Michalskà veža,** a tower embellished in a baroque style and now full of ornamental weapons. The **Franciscan Church** at Nám. Dibrivova 1 is an amazing hybrid of Gothic, Renaissance, and baroque styles.

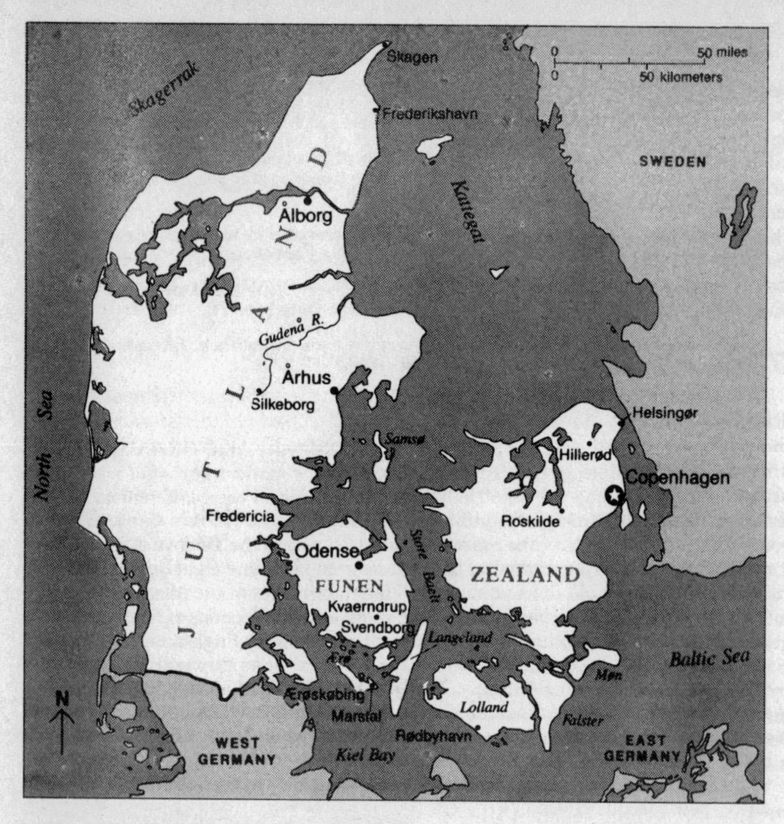

DENMARK

US$1 = 6.99kr	**10kr = US$1.43**
CDN$1 = 5.29kr	**10kr = CDN$1.89**
UK£1 = 11.38kr	**10kr = UK£0.88**
AUS$1 = 4.98kr	**10kr = AUS$2.01**

"Ah yes, the little country..."
—Karen Blixen, *Out of Africa*

Once the name "Dane" struck fear into hearts all over Europe, but today the Viking past lives mainly in tourist shops and brochures. Life is comfortable and calm; people rarely jaywalk and evening coffee or tea is a ritual. With its snug farmhouses and clean cities, Denmark sometimes resembles the peaceful shire of J.R.R. Tolkien's *The Hobbit.*

Under the Kalmar Union, lasting into the sixteenth century, the Danish crown ruled an empire extending across the northern sea, including Norway, Sweden, Iceland, and parts of Germany. Strategically positioned at the northern tip of continental Europe, Denmark was the bridge across which first Christianity, then the Protestant Reformation, and finally the socialist experiments of the late nineteenth century crossed into Scandinavia. The legacy of these experiments persists—Denmark today is a model welfare state, with extensive guaranteed social services. Prime minister Paul Schlüter's Conservative government has recently cut back some of these services, an action which the liberal press has defended as an economic necessity. Other contemporary issues include the Danish ties to the EEC and growing racism against guest workers and political refugees.

Danes joke that if you stand on a carton of beer you can see from one end of the country to the other, but it's neither quite that flat nor that small. Though Copenhagen may be Denmark at its best, save time for visits to the rich countryside, where beech trees sway in the clean constant sea-breeze. This simple beauty is reflected in Danish design; noted architects include Arne Jakobsen, Kaj Fisker and Jørn Utzon. In literature, Hans Christian Andersen, Søren Kirkegaard, and Isak Dinesen (Karen Blixen) are names of international stature.

Transportation and Practical Information

The quiet countryside and superb network of bicycle paths make Denmark a cyclist's paradise. Bicycles can be rented for 30-45kr per day from tourist offices, ubiquitous bicycle rental shops, and a few railway stations in North Zealand (Helsingør, Hillerød, Klampenborg, and Lyngby). A 100kr deposit is ordinarily expected. For faster travel, and during the rain and snow season (Oct.-March), a reliable network of trains, buses, and ferries efficiently connects all points in Denmark. Eurail and InterRail passes are valid on all state-run routes. The **Nordturist Ticket**, available at any train station in Scandinavia, permits 21 days of unlimited second-class rail travel in Denmark, Sweden, Norway, and Finland for 1550kr. The pass is also good on all **DSB** ferries (those operated by the national railways) and on Copenhagen's city trains. The **Nordisk Ungdomskort** permits one month of unlimited rail travel in Scandinavia for those 26 and under (you must pay 50% of fares within the country of purchase), but is technically sold only to Scandinavians. The **DIS Rejsebureaus** (travel bureaus) offer student discounts on round-trip train tickets within Denmark. For more information on travel in Denmark, visit the **InterRail Center** at Copenhagen Central Station.

You will find a tourist office (*turistbureau*) in almost every Danish town. They can usually help with accommodations, bike rental, and travel information. Regular banking hours in Denmark are Monday through Wednesday and Friday from 9:30am to 4pm, Thursday 9:30am to 6pm. In pay phones, local calls require a minimum of 0.50kr, long distance calls 1kr. A beep means that you have 10 seconds to insert another coin. You must dial the area code before the number, even when you're calling within the area. For access to an international operator, dial 0039. In an emergency anywhere in Denmark, dial 000 (no coins needed). The **country code** for Denmark is 45.

Accommodations, Camping, and Food

There are 84 **IYHF youth hostels** (*vandrerhjem*) scattered throughout Denmark; they generally include rooms for families, and are well-run and pleasant. All charge members 35-45kr, depending on facilities and the number of occupants per room. Nonmembers pay a 15-20kr supplement. Cards (90kr) and an official hostel guide are available at **Danmarks Vandrerhjem,** Vesterbrogade 39, 1620 Copenhagen V (tel. 31 36 12). (Open Mon.-Fri. 9am-4pm.) You do not have the right to pitch a tent anywhere in Denmark; you must either get permission from the landowner or stay at one of the many official campgrounds, costing 22-28kr per person per night. The mandatory camping pass is available at all campgrounds (21kr) and good for one year. The **Dansk Camping Union,** Gammel Kongvej 74, Copenhagen (tel. (01) 21 06 00), offers good advice and a list of campgrounds in Denmark. Tourist offices in many cities can find you a room in a private home (generally about 80kr for singles, 175kr for doubles, breakfast included). The rooms are frequently pleasant, you will usually have access to a kitchen, and you'll get to meet a Danish family; homes are sometimes quite far from the city center.

Danish food is generally simple and filling. For lunch, many Danes eat *smørrebrød*, open-faced sandwiches with a variety of toppings. For a proper *smørrebrød* meal, start with *sild* (pickled herring), then sample cold sausage, eggs, vegetables, shrimp, and delicious mayonnaise salads before ending with cheese. You can try these at numerous take-out shops for about 10kr, or make your own for less. Danish breads (*brød*) are fantastic; try the dark, heavy *rugbrød,* sold in cubes, *groubrød,* made with almost no flour and all whole grains, and tasty *trekornsbrød. Frikadeller* (spicy meatballs) is perhaps the national dish. The pastry standard of Denmark is not the Danish but rather *wienerbrød* (Vienna bread). Sample yours at any place marked with the sign *bageri* or *konditori.* Milk products are excellent; yogurt comes in many varieties and is quite cheap. Cheese (*ost*) is consumed in enormous quantities; *blåost* (blue cheese), *havarti, danbo,* and *flødeost* (cream cheese with herbs) are especially popular. Danish beer is some of the best in the wold. Tuborg and Carlsberg are favorites, while the Elephant has a kick like . . . three guesses.

Copenhagen (København)

With its expansive parks, waterways, and lively pedestrian streets, the Danish capital is among the most youthful and exuberant cities in northern Europe. Students, sailors, and visitors from all over the world mix on the streets, drinking beer at outdoor cafes, and performing music on the sidewalks. The city is both exciting and pastoral; you can walk through crowded plazas or bike along shaded avenues. Copenhagen is free-spirited enough to make room for Christiania—a tax-exempt experimental living project and bastion of '60s counter-culture.

Orientation and Practical Information

Copenhagen lies on the Danish island of **Zealand.** Just across the sound (Øresund) lies Malmö, Sweden, and rail connections to points throughout Scandinavia, Germany, and the rest of Europe. Copenhagen is also connected by regularly scheduled ferries to Oslo, Norway, and Malmö and Helsingborg, Sweden.

Copenhagen's **Hovedbanegården** (Central Station) lies conveniently close to the city's main sights. **Tivoli** and **Rådhuspladsen** (the square in front of City Hall) are a few blocks to the right as you walk out the main entrance; the tourist office and the pedestrian district are a little farther in the same direction. The heart of the old city is bisected by the longest pedestrian thoroughfare in the world: the **Strøget.** The districts of Vesterbro, Nørrebro, Østerbro and Christianshavn fan out from the center.

Tourist Offices: Danmarks Turistråd, H. C. Andersens Blvd. 22 (tel. 11 13 25), in the Louis Tussaud's Wax Museum building. To the right on Rådhuspladsen coming from the train station—turn left on Bernstorffsgade, right on Vesterbrogade. Everything you need to know about Copenhagen and the rest of Denmark: a free map, the helpful *Copenhagen This Week,* and *After Midnight,* a nightlife guide. Open May-June and Sept. Mon.-Sat. 9am-6pm, Sun. 9am-1pm; July-Aug. Mon.-Sat. 9am-8pm, Sun. 9am-1pm; Oct.-April Mon.-Fri. 9am-5pm, Sat. 9am-noon, closed Sun. **Værelseanvisning,** in Central Station, is a room-finding service (see Accommodations).

Budget Travel: Use It, the travel division of Huset, Rådhusstræde 13 (tel. 15 65 18). All kinds of travel assistance, from bed-finding to help with lost passports. Ride boards, message boards, flash reports on state of accommodations, free luggage storage, mail held. Get their map and a copy of their guide *Playtime.* Open mid-June to mid-Sept. daily 10am-8pm; mid-Sept. to mid-June Mon.-Fri. 10am-5pm. **Transalpino/BIGE** sells tickets at Skoubogade 6 (tel. 14 46 33). Open Mon.-Fri. 9:30am-6pm, Sat. 10am-1pm. Reduced train and plane fares are also available at **DIS,** Skindergade 28 (tel. 11 00 44). 25-35% discounts on round-trip tickets within Denmark available to students under 25. Open Mon.-Fri. 9:30am-6pm, Sat. 10am-1pm. **Spies,** Nyropsgade 41 (tel. 12 35 00), and **Tjæreborg,** Rådhusplads 75 (tel. 11 41 00), often have cheap charters to southern Europe.

American Express: Amagertorv 18, on the Strøget (tel. 12 23 01). Mail held. All banking services. Open Mon.-Fri. 9am-5pm, Sat. 9am-noon.

Currency Exchange: Regular banking hours are Mon.-Wed. and Fri. 9:30am-4pm, Thurs. 9:30am-6pm. Change money at Central Station daily 7am-10pm; at Tivoli office daily noon-11pm; or at the airport daily 6:30am-10pm.

Post Office: At Tietgensgade 37, behind Central Station. Open Mon.-Fri. 9am-7pm, Sat. 9am-1pm. **Poste Restante** held here. Station branch open Mon.-Fri. 9am-9pm, Sun. 10am-4pm. **Postal code:** 1570.

Telephones: At Købmagergade 37. Open daily 9am-10pm. **International information:** 0039. **Information in Denmark:** 0038. **Telephone code:** 01.

Flights: Bus #32 (32 min., 10.50kr) and the SAS bus (20 min., 21kr) connect **Kastrup Airport** with Rådhuspladsen.

Trains: All trains check in at **Hovedbanegården** (Central Station), in the center of town. There is an **InterRail Center** in the station for all holders of BIGE, InterRail, or Eurail passes. You can relax in a special lounge, wait for late-night connections, make phone calls, get information, take free showers, and store luggage. Open June-Sept. daily 7am-1am.

Ferries: Those arriving by ferry can reach Rådhuspladsen or Central Station aboard the buses just across the street from the pier.

Public Transportation: Copenhagen is served by a fine network of S-trains (subway) and buses. A ticket on one is honored on the other. A **KlipKort** (clip card) allows travel on any bus or train in North Zealand (60kr for a 10-clip card). You must punch your KlipKort into the red box beside bus drivers or the yellow boxes on train platforms; all transportation within Copenhagen itself is in a single zone and will cost 6kr, or one clip. The **Copenhagen Card** allows unlimited free travel on buses and trains as far as Helsingør, Roskilde, and Køge; discounts on ferries to Sweden; and free admission to nearly all sights (including Tivoli). Available for 70kr (1 day), 120kr (2 days), or 150kr (3 days) at the tourist office, large train stations, travel agencies, and hotels. Buses and trains run approximately Mon.-Sat. 5am-12:30am, Sun. 6am-1am; night buses run until about 2:30am.

Bike Rental: Dan Wheel, Colbjørnsensgade 3 (tel. 21 22 27). 30kr per day, 140kr per week, plus 100kr deposit. Open Mon.-Fri. 9am-5:30pm, Sat.-Sun. 9am-2pm. **Copenhagen Cycle,** Gothersgade 157-159 (tel. 14 07 17). 30kr per day, 125kr per week, plus 100kr deposit. Open Mon.-Fri. 9am-noon and 1-5:30pm, Sat. 9am-1pm.

Emergencies: Police or **Ambulance** or **Fire** (tel. 100); no coins needed for public phones.

Medical Assistance: Open to foreigners, **Kommunehospitalet,** Øster Farimagsgade 5 (tel. 15 85 00). Take bus #14 from Rådhuspladsen or #40 from Central Station. Free treatment for sudden illness or unexpected aggravation of chronic disease.

Pharmacies: Look for the word *"Apotek."* **Steno Apotek,** Vesterbrogade 6c (tel. 14 82 66). Open 24 hours. After 8pm, ring for entrance; 10kr fee on purchases.

Information for the Disabled: Handicapped Access, Hans Knudsenplads 1a (tel. 18 42 55). Information on disabled-accessible museums, hotels, etc. Open Mon.-Fri. 9am-4pm.

Embassies: U.S., Dag Hammerskjölds Allé 24 (tel. 42 31 44). **Canada,** Kristen Bernikowsgade 1 (tel. 12 22 99). **U.K.,** Kastelsvej 40 (tel. 26 46 00). **Australia,** Kristianiagade 21 (tel. 26 22 44). Travelers from **New Zealand** should contact the British Embassy.

Bookstore: The Book Trader, Skindergade 23. Open Mon.-Wed. 10:30am-5:30pm, Thurs.-Fri. 10:30am-7pm, Sat. 10am-3pm. Cheaper second-hand English books available on carts outside most bookstores; try those around the University: **Arnold Busck,** Fiolstræde 24, or **Harcks Antikvariat,** Fiolstræde 34. Huset and Sleep-In also have books to trade.

Laundry: Just about everywhere; look for the sign *"møntvask."*

Hitchhiking: To hitch to Helsingør and Sweden, take bus #6, 24, or 84 to Hans Knudsenplads. For southern Denmark and Germany, take the S-train to Ellebjerg Station, and hitch west on Folehaven (Ring 11). For Funen and Jutland, take the S-train to Taastrup Station and go to Roskildevej. Hitching is not easy; try Use It's ride boards.

Accommodations

Copenhagen has plenty of hostels and campgrounds, and a few inexpensive hotels. The city is popular, though, so avoid the high season crunch (mid-June to late Aug.) by calling ahead at least a day in advance. Huset is always up-to-date on space available. If you arrive late at night, stop by Central Station's Værelseanvisning (see Private Homes and Hostels below).

Hostels

Bellahøj Vandrerhjem (IYHF), Herbergvejen 8 (tel. 28 97 15). Set on a park and small lake in the quiet Bronshøj section of the city, a 20-min. bus or bike ride from Rådhuspladsen. Good facilities, but somewhat large and impersonal. Take bus #2 (direction: Bronshøj) to Fuglsang Allé, or night bus *(natbus)* #902. Avoid the large basement dormitories. 344 beds fill up quickly. No cooking facilities. Members get priority. Members 40kr, nonmembers 58kr, linen 27kr, breakfast 27kr. Reception closed 10am-noon. Curfew 1:30am. Open Jan.-Nov.

Copenhagen Hostel (IYHF), Sjællandsbroen 55 (tel. 52 29 08). Take bus #46 from Central Station or #37 from Holmens Bro (direction: Valby-Toftegårdsplads) to Sjællandsbroen. Very modern, with laundry and cooking facilities. Members 40kr, nonmembers 58kr (including "guest card"). No curfew. Check-in 1-4pm. Open Jan. to mid-Dec.

Lyngby Vandrerhjem (IYHF), Rådvad 1 (tel. (02) 80 30 70). S-train line A toward Holte, stop at Lyngby, then bus #187 to Rådvad. The most distant of the 3 official hostels but easy to find. Big and clean with laundry facilities. No kitchen facilities. Members 40kr, nonmembers 58kr, breakfast 31kr. Reception open 7am-noon and 4-9pm. Open mid-May to Aug.

Sleep-In, Per Henrik Lings Allé 6 (tel. 26 50 59). Take bus #1, 6, or 14 to Idrætsparken, or S-train lines A, B, or C to Nordhavn. Co-ed dorms, no curfew, great atmosphere, a bit noisy. The best last-minute place; they'll virtually always find you a spot to hang your backpack. 55kr, breakfast included. Lockout noon-4pm. Open late-June to Aug.

Vesterbro Ungdomsgaard, Absalonsgade 8 (tel. 31 20 70). Excellent location makes it worth the price, though it's a little gritty. Avoid the 60-bed dorm room. 70kr, buffet breakfast 15kr. Reception always open. No curfew. Open early May-Aug.

International University, Olfert Fischersgade 40 (tel. 15 61 75). Walk or take bus #10 towards Emdrup to Sølvgade. Rather dark and crowded, but comfortable enough, good location, and unbeatable price. 30kr. Lockout 11am-5pm. Curfew 1am.

Private Homes and Hotels

Central Station's **Værelseanvisning** (tel. 12 18 80) will find you a room in a private home or hotel for an 11kr fee per bed. Private home prices are 80-100kr in a single, 150-210kr in a double. Hotel prices start at 170kr and 260kr respectively. Huset can often do significantly better for price.

Jørgensens Hotel, Rømersgade 11 (tel. 13 81 86), in a quiet area about 20 min. from Central Station. The cheapest in town: singles 125kr, doubles 160kr. Also a mixed basement dorm for 60kr; sleeping bag required, sheet rental 25kr. Reception open until 1:30am.

Søfolkenes Mindehotel, Peder Skramjgade 19 (tel. 13 48 82), conveniently located near Nyhavn. Friendly, clean, and comfortable. Singles 185kr, doubles 325kr. Breakfast included. Open year-round.

Camping

Camping, as usual, is the cheapest way to stay, though in Denmark you must buy a camping pass from any campground (21kr); these are good for one year.

Bellahøj Camping, Hvidkildevej (tel. 10 11 50), 5km from the center. Take bus #2 or 8 from Rådhuspladsen to "Camping" stop. 26kr. Open June-Aug.

Absalon Camping, Korselalsvej 132 (tel. 41 06 00), 9km away in nearby Rødovre. Take S-train line B to Brøndbyøster. 28kr. Open year-round daily 7am-10pm.

Food

Eating cheaply in Copenhagen is fairly easy if you avoid sit-down restaurants. Picnic in a park or by the harbor on take-out *smørrebrød* (from 10kr), or make your own. Avoid the pedestrian district and Tivoli, which tend to overcharge. Look for supermarkets **Irma** and **Brugsen,** both of which have several outlets in the center of town. An open **market** flourishes on Israels Plads near Nørreport Station for much of the year; take advantage of it or the many fruit stalls on **Strøget.**

Univesitets Caféen, Fiolstræde 2. Smoky and wood-paneled; Copenhagen University's student pub. Outdoor cafe in the summer. Sandwiches 16kr, meals 32kr. Open Mon.-Sat. 10am-5am, Sun. 5pm-5am. Cafe open in warm weather daily 11am-8pm or 10pm.

Restaurant Vista, Vesterbrogade 40. Plain and run-down, feels like a pool hall. Amazingly cheap: large 2-course meals from 27.50kr. Open daily 9am-11pm.

Spisehuset, Rådhusstræde 13. Part of Huset and therefore "in;" nice atmosphere and fresh healthy food. All-you-can-eat lunch 60kr, sandwiches 20kr. Open noon-3:30pm and 5-11pm.

Det Grønne Køkken, Larsbjørnsstræde 10. Hidden away on the 3rd floor of an old building, this vegetarian haven offers an all-you-can-eat buffet 49kr noon-5pm and 9-10pm and 69kr 5-9pm. Open Mon.-Sat. noon-10pm.

Smørrebrød, Gothersgade 10. Scrumptious open-faced sandwiches 15kr. Open daily 8am-4pm. Their location at Vesterbrogade 6 is open 4pm-5am.

Café Smukhe Marie, Knabrostræde 19. Copenhagen's only crêperie has fresh food and an artsy herbal atmosphere. Meals from 30kr. Desert crêpes from 14kr. Open Mon.-Fri. 5-9pm, Sat.-Sun. 11am-11pm.

Papas, Kultorret 14. Candles line the staircases and romantic Italian music resounds. In summer, you can sit outside. Full meals, including appetizer, dessert, and entree, 115kr. But no need to splurge; pizza is only 40-44kr. Open May-Aug. Mon.-Sat. 11am-midnight, Sun. noon-midnight; Sept.-April Mon.-Sat. 11am-midnight, Sun. 2pm-midnight.

Sights

Copenhagen is best seen on foot or by bike. From late March to mid-October, the tourist office conducts six guided walking tours of different parts of the city, including the canals, Rosenborg castle and gardens, Christianshavn, and the city center. (2-hr. tours 15kr, except Rosenborg castle 30kr.) For complete information, request *Copenhagen on Foot* at the tourist office. **Use It** publishes the more freely structured *Copenhagen by Bike* and *Copenhagen by Bus.*

Many things in Copenhagen—the pedestrian drag, Strøget; Central Station; Tivoli; and bus connections—converge at **Rådhuspladsen.** The Rådhus itself is worth a peek, as the interior features a bewildering melange of architectural styles. (Open Mon.-Sat. 10am-5pm. Free.)

Tivoli, Copenhagen's happy amusement park, will draw you into its carnival atmosphere. Most people go in the evening; the grounds are romantically illuminated, concerts and shows (most free) are in full swing, and there are closing fireworks Wednesday, Saturday, and Sunday. In the morning and early afternoon, the crowd is primarily Danish—people eating huge cones of soft ice cream, others crowded around a roulette wheel, kids on the famous (but overrated) roller coaster. Be sure to eat before entering, or the roller coaster won't be the only thing that takes you for a ride. (Open May to mid-Sept. daily 10am-midnight. Admission 23kr.)

A walk down **Gammel Strand** onto **Slotsholmen** island takes you to the **Folketinget** (Parliament), **Børsen** (Stock Exchange), **Christianborg Palace,** and the excellent **Thorvaldsen's Museum,** housing his sculptures and collection of paintings and antiques. (Open May-Oct. daily 10am-4pm; Nov.-April Wed.-Mon. 10am-3pm. Free.)

Further to the southeast lies **Christiania,** the experimental "free community" founded in 1971 by youthful squatters. A source of continuing controversy, Christiania accepts visitors, and you can wander through its workshops and houses. Always ask before taking pictures, and remember that hash is still illegal in Denmark. Nearby, the twisted tower of **Frelsers Kirkes Tårn** offers a good view of the city from its spiral stairs. (Open Mon.-Sat. 9am-4:30pm, Sun. noon-4:30pm. Admission 10kr.)

Head north of the city to **Kastellet,** an old fortress-turned-park, and catch a glimpse of forlorn **Den Lille Havefrue**—Hans Christian Andersen's *Little Mermaid*—through hordes of camera-clickers. Close by, the **Frihedsmuseet,** in Churchillparken, offers a fascinating depiction of Denmark's resistance movement during World War II. (Open in summer Tues.-Sun. 10am-4pm; in winter Tues.-Sun. 11am-3pm. Free.) Walk back towards the city along the harbor past **Amalie Garden** to the official residence of the royal family, **Amalienborg Palace.** You can't visit inside the palace, but you'll probably enjoy the Changing of the Guard at noon on the brick plaza. **Nyhavn,** a canal lined with yachts and colorful brick buildings, was once the rough sailor district. Now its trendy cafes serve expensive fish dinners under yellow umbrellas. **Kongens Nytorv,** the port at the terminus of Nyhavn, is the departure point for harbor and canal boat tours. (May to mid-Sept. 10am-5pm. 24kr with a guide, 18kr without. Boats also leave from Gammel Strand.) Kongens Nytorv also marks the ritzy endpoint of **Strøget;** the **Royal Theatre** here is home of the world-famous **Royal Danish Ballet.** Also worth a visit is the **Statens Museum for Kunst** (Royal Museum of Fine Arts), off Sølvgade, in the Botanical Gardens. **Rosenborg Castle** contains the crown jewels. (Open June-Aug. daily 10am-3pm; Sept. to mid-Oct. daily 11am-3pm; mid-Oct. to May Tues. and Fri. 11am-1pm, Sun. 1am-2pm. Admission 18kr.)

Beer enthusiasts will want to make a pilgrimage to the city's breweries: **Carlsberg,** Carlsbergvej 140 (tel. 21 12 21; take bus #6 from Rådhuspladsen; tours Mon.-Fri. 9am, 11am, and 2:30pm), and **Tuborg,** Strandvegen 54 (tel. 29 33 11; take bus #1; tours Mon.-Fri. 8:30am-2:30pm). Both offer unlimited free beer or soda at the end of the tour.

One of Copenhagen's greatest attractions extends far beyond the borders of Denmark. **American Pictures** is Dane Jacob Holdt's photographic exploration of the American underclass, complemented by music, interviews, and commentary. The four-hour presentation is shown daily at 6pm at Købmagergade 43 (tel. 12 44 12), and is well worth the 40kr admission.

Entertainment

Nighttime in Copenhagen offers a wide range of options. Most bars and discos on Strøget are packed and designed for mass consumption. Kogens Nytorv contains fancier establishments—many of them private—and chic cafes where Copenhageners meet over espresso or exotic drinks. Nyhavn, once the site of tattoo parlors and rowdy sailor brawls, is mellow these days but makes a refreshing walk between nightspots. The tourist office and Use It distribute *After Midnight,* a guide to Copenhagen's nightlife. Use It also has a comprehensive gay and lesbian guide to the city. Be sure to visit bars in the outskirts, where the beer is cheaper and the atmosphere friendly.

Huset, Rådhusstræde 13. Entertainment and everything else. **Musikcafe'n** has rock, funk, soul, reggae; open nightly 9pm-2am. Cover Sun.-Thurs. 35-60kr, Fri.-Sat. 40kr, includes admission to **Foyerscenen,** with live jazz. The blue-haired crowd meets at **Barbue,** with live music Wed.-Thurs. 9pm-2am, disco Tues. and Fri.-Sat. 9pm-2am. Cover 15-30kr, discounts for railpass holders.

Alexandra, Nørregade 1. Big, fun, hi-tech disco with laser shows, videos, and concerts. Open Fri.-Sat. 11pm-6am.

Jazzhaus Montmartre, Nørregade 41 (tel. 11 46 67). The best of the jazz clubs, featuring internationally known artists and excellent local bands. Open Sun.-Thurs. 8pm-2am, Fri.-Sat. disco 8pm-4:30am. Cover 30-110kr.

Heering Café, Pilestræde 19-25. A mod drink and chat spot done in rose and murals. Popular with young Copenhageners. Espresso 12kr, white wine 18kr per glass. Open Sun.-Tues. 10am-2pm, Wed.-Thurs. 10am-3am, Fri.-Sat. 10am-5am.

Pan Club, Knabrostræde 3. Has a reputation as one of the finest gay/lesbian clubs in Europe. Open nightly 10pm-5am (Thurs. women only). Cover 55kr.

Loppen, 32 Bådmandsstræde, just through the entrance of Christiania, features rock, jazz, and funk. Open Thurs.-Sat. 9pm-3am. Cover 30-50kr.

Streets, pubs, and concert halls all over town celebrate the world-famous **Copenhagen Jazz Festival,** in July; make accommodation reservations early. In May watch for **Karneval,** a cultural import from Brazil that sends thousands of Scandinavians dancing into the streets for three days.

Near Copenhagen

The entire island of Zealand is a suburb of Copenhagen—no place is much more than an hour away by bus or train. Castles, museums, beaches, and forests, are all within easy reach. **Roskilde,** an hour west of Copenhagen on the S-train (3 *KlipKort* clips (18kr) or a 28kr ticket), is home to much Danish history; King Harald Bluetooth made this his capital and evangelical seat in 980. The **Viking Ship Museum** houses five ships that were sunk to bar the entrance of enemy fleets. (Open April-May and Sept.-Oct. daily 9am-5pm; June-Aug. daily 9am-6pm; Nov.-March daily 10am-4pm. Admission 16kr, students 8kr.) Danish royalty is still buried in the **cathedral;** their tombs vary from lavish white marble baroque monuments to the simple, austere lines of modern times. Concerts are given on the Rasphaëlis organ (ca. 1550) every Saturday at noon from June through August. Roskilde's twelfth-century wall is still standing, and the **tourist office** (tel. (02) 35 27 00), near the cathedral, can suggest walking tours around the lovely old quarter. A large vegetable, fruit, and flower market transforms Roskilde on Wednesday and Saturday mornings. In early July Roskilde plays host to one of the largest music festivals in northern Europe, with rock, jazz, and folk bands from all over the world.

Bike or take the train (1 *KlipKort* clip (6kr) or a 7kr ticket) to **Fredensborg Castle,** spring and autumn residence of the royal family. When Queen Margrethe is in residence there is a colorful changing of the guard. The park is free and open year-round from 9am to 5pm. (Castle open July daily 1-5pm.) Admission 6kr. If you find yourself in the hostel at **Lyngby** don't despair; there is plenty to see in the area. The hostel itself borders **Dyrehaven,** a large park on the former royal hunting ground. In the middle of the park lies **Eremitageslotten,** a small castle with a large view. On Dyrehaven's southern edge, near **Klampenborg** on the S-train line, is **Bakken,** Copenhagen's other amusement park. While the atmosphere cannot compare to Tivoli, admission is free and the old wood roller coaster gives a fantastic ride. Just north of Lyngby, in **Sorgenfri,** you find **Frilandsmuseet,** the excellent open-air museum containing over 100 authentic old buildings from around the country. (Open mid-April to Sept. daily 10am-5pm; Oct. 1-14 Tues.-Sun. 10am-3pm; mid-Oct. to mid-April Sun. 10am-3pm. Admission 10kr.) For easy transportation rent a bike at the Lyngby Station (tel. 87 01 65; open 8am-7pm).

The most spectacular castle in all of Denmark rises in **Hillerød,** 40 minutes north of Copenhagen on the S-train (3 *KlipKort* clips (18kr) or a 28kr ticket). Moated **Frederiksborg Slot** (ca. 1560) features lovely gardens, brick ramparts, and the world's first elevator throne. Concerts are given on the famous **Esaias Compenius organ** (ca. 1610) in the chapel Thursdays at 1:30pm. (Castle open May-Sept. daily 10am-5pm; Oct. daily 10am-4pm; April daily 11am-4pm; mid-Jan. to March daily 11am-3pm.)

Humlebæk, 30km north of Copenhagen, is the site of **Louisiana,** Denmark's museum of contemporary art. Named after the three wives of the estate's donor, all called Louisa, the museum contains works by Picasso, Chagall, and Magritte, and hosts excellent temporary exhibits. Stretched along a knoll overlooking the sea, the remarkable building itself is well worth a trip. (Open Thurs.-Tues. 10am-5pm, Wed. 10am-10pm. Admission 25kr, plus special exhibition prices.) Continuing in the same direction you find **Helsingør**—Elsinore in Shakespeare—the site of the heavily fortified **Kronborg.** Erroneously known as Hamlet's Castle, Kronborg was actually built to collect tolls from passing merchant ships. While smaller than Fredriksborg, the castle is certainly nothing to sneeze at. (Open May-Sept. daily 10am-5pm; April and Oct. daily 11am-4pm; mid-Jan. to March daily 11am-3pm.)

Bornholm

East of Denmark and south of Sweden, Bornholm is a popular vacation spot of Scandinavians and Germans. The expansive sand beaches of the southern coast are reputedly the best in northern Europe, while the northern coast's scenic hills and cliffs harbor fishing villages that double as artists' havens.

From June through September two **ferries** per day run from Copenhagen to Rønne, Bornholm's main city; fewer ferries run the rest of the year. You need no reservations for deck passage (129kr one way); just come to the terminal next to Nyhavn one hour before departure. In summer, ferries sail from Ystad, Sweden (2-5 per day, 2½ hr., 180kr round-trip), with bus and ferry connections from Copenhagen's Central Station (90kr one way). Call Bornholmerbussen (tel. (02) 97 98 99) for information and reservations.

Rønne, on Bornholm's western coast, lacks the charm of smaller fishing villages, but its **tourist office** (tel. (03) 95 08 10), to the left of the ferry terminal, can help you plan your stay on the island. They book rooms in private homes. (Open late June-Aug. Fri.-Mon. 8am-9pm, Tues.-Thurs. 8am-5pm; Sept.-late June daily 9am-5pm.)

Rønne's **vandrerhjem (IYHF)** is in a quiet woodsy area. (39kr. Reception closed noon-4pm. Open Jan.-Oct.) Meals are cheap at the cafeteria above Kvickly, on the *torvet* (square). (Open Mon.-Thurs. 11am-6:45pm, Fri. 11am-7:45pm, Sat. 11am-1:45pm.) You can rent **bikes** at Havnegade 11, near the tourist office.

For white sand beaches and good windsurfing, visit **Dueodde,** on Bornholm's southeastern tip. The beach, the hostel, and four ice cream stands are what Dueodde is all about. Tan beach bums pack the **Dueodde Vandrerhjem and Camping (IYHF)** (tel. (03) 98 76 49). As indicated by the name, camping is also available. (Rooms 39kr. Kitchen facilities. Open May-Sept.) About 6km north is **Balke Strand,** the best known beach on Bornholm.

Gudhjem, on the northern coast, is also worth a visit. Like everything else, the **tourist office** (tel. (03) 98 52 10) is on the harbor. (Open Mon.-Fri. 9am-5pm, Sat. 9am-noon.) The **Vandrerhjem St. Jorgens Gård (IYHF)** (tel. (03) 98 50 35), right by the harbor and across from the bus stop, has a great kitchen. (40kr. Check-in 4-5pm, or call for reservations. Open April-Oct.) There is a small beach about 1km away, to the right of the harbor. North of town, **Sletten Camping** has a beautiful view of the sea.

On the northwest point of Bornholm lies **Hammerhaus,** a spectacular crumble of stone which is northern Europe's largest castle ruin. One kilometer away, on a cliff overlooking the sea, is the village of **Sandvig.** You can stay at **Vandrerhjem Sjølban,** Hammershusvej 94 (tel. (03) 98 03 62). (40kr. Reception closed noon-4pm. Open mid-March to Oct.)

Funen (Fyn)

Funen is Denmark's garden. Colorful flowerbeds grace nearly every household, and the variety of wild flowers in the sparsely populated coastal areas is enchanting. The north of the island is largely farmland, while the south features rolling green hills and expansive beaches. Rent a bike at one of the tourist offices, and explore the half-timbered villages along your route by the sea.

Birthplace of Hans Christian Andersen, **Odense** will inspire you to write fairy tales of your own. Tiny thatched-roof houses line cobblestoned streets, and swans really do swim in green waterways among weeping willows. At **H. C. Andersens Hus,** Hans Jensens Stræde 39-43, you can learn about the author's eccentricities and listen to recordings of his stories in English. (Open June-Aug. daily 9am-6pm; April-May and Sept. daily 10am-5pm; Oct.-March daily 10am-3pm. Admission 15kr.)

The **tourist office** (tel. (09) 12 75 20), in the City Hall, a few blocks south of the station, will provide information on Odense and Denmark, exchange currency at bank rates when banks are closed, and book you a room in a private home (singles 100-150kr, doubles 200kr). They also have a **Meet the Danes** program; with a day or two of advance notice, they'll arrange an evening of tea and conversation with a Danish family who shares your interests. Follow Jernbanegade, to the right of the station, all the way to Vestergade, and turn left. (Open mid-June to Aug. Mon.-Sat. 9am-8pm, Sun. 10am-noon and 6-8pm; Sept. to mid-June Mon.-Fri. 9am-5pm, Sat. 9am-noon.) **Vandrerhjem Kragsbjerggården (IYHF)** (tel. (09) 13 04 25) is in a picturesque, old yellow building. Take bus #6 across from the town hall. (39kr. Open March-Nov.) **DSB,** the public transportation company, operates a free, popular sleep-in one week a year, usually in July; contact the tourist office or DSB at the train station. (Open 8am-midnight.) You can camp at Hunderup Skov on Odensvej (29kr per person), next to **Fruens Bøge,** the lovely park which accommodated H. C. Andersen in his weirder moods, and which has the best ice cream stand in town.

Den Fynske Landsby (Funen Village) is a very good open-air musuem just south of the city. Evenings it puts on the *Hans Christian Andersen Play,* a fairy tale enacted by children from Fame—yes, the local theater school. (30kr, mid-July to mid-Aug.) For good meals (50kr), try cafe **Amfita** in the factory-turned-art-and-culture-center, **Brandt's Klædefabrik.** (Open daily noon-10pm.) The center is alive both day and night in the summer, with exhibits and street performances. For a beer head to Franck-A, Jernbanegade 4, where all types meet over low wood tables.

1988 will make Odense's 1000th anniversary; be sure to check with the tourist office for information, as major celebrations are planned. In early July, look for the **Midtfyns** festival, which brings local and international rock, jazz, and blues to **Ringe,** near Odense.

South of Odense in **Kværndrup** is **Egeskov Slot,** a beautiful Renaissance moated castle. It is still inhabited, but you can visit the gardens, and a museum of antique cars, airplanes, and carriages. (Open July-Aug. daily 9am-6pm; May-June and Sept. daily 10am-5pm; April and Oct. Sat.-Sun. only 10am-5pm.)

Svendborg is the best base for longer stays on Funen and for bicycle trips to the islands just south of it. Outdoor cafes line the *torvet* (town square), which lies between a sixteenth-century farmhouse and a lovely brick church. On this square, up the hill from the train station, you'll find the **tourist office** (tel. (09) 21 09 80); they'll give you a map of the best beaches and find you a room in a private home. (Open July Mon.-Fri. 9am-5pm, Sat. 9am-2pm, Sun. 10am-noon; Aug.-June Mon.-Fri. 9am-5pm, Sat. 9am-noon, closed Sun.) You may want to take home a picture of **Vandrerhjemmet Søro (IYHF),** Christiansmindevej 6 (tel. (09) 21 26 16), in its park-like surroundings above the sailboat-filled Svendborg Sound. Take bus #201 or 209 (6kr) from the train station, or walk 3km to the right of the station or ferry terminal. (Members only, 39kr. Open mid-March to Oct.) **Fåborgvej Camping,** Ryttervej 21 (tel. (09) 21 36 10), is closest to town. (29kr. Open mid-May to Aug.) The nicer **Carlsberg Camping,** Sundbrogvej 19 (tel. (09) 22 53 84), across the sound on the island of Tåsigne, has a great view. (29kr. Open May-Aug.) You can rent a bike at **Sydfyns Cykleludlejning-ninz,** Gerritsgarde 10 (tel. (09) 21 03 71). (35kr per day. 100kr deposit. Open daily 9am-1pm and 2-5pm.) **Underground Icecream,** Kattesundet 10, features puff pastry quiche, salad and great 100% natural ice cream.

The tiny islands of the **Funen Archipelago**—Thurø, Hjortø, Drejø, and Skarø—feature old villages, fragrant wildflowers, and the wide open sea. Thurø is connected to Funen by a bridge (you can take a bus); the other three are accessible by three or four ferries per day from Svendborg. Round-trip to Skarø or Drejø is 40kr plus 10kr for a bike. Camping on the beach is permitted.

AErø

One of the most important islands south of Funen, AErø is delightful. Its quaint little towns are popular with Danish and German tourists, but only old churches and windmills dot the gently rolling farmland.

AErøskøbing, the main town, is a beautiful seventeenth-century time capsule, complete with hollyhocks, cobbled lanes, and tiny half-timbered houses. The **tourist office** (tel. (09) 52 13 00) is located near the church on the *torvet* (main square). They find rooms in private homes for a 5kr fee. (Singles 80kr, doubles 150kr. Breakfast included.) (Open in summer Mon.-Fri. 9am-5pm, Sat. 10am-noon and 1-3pm, Sun. 10am-noon.) The **youth hostel (IYHF),** Smedevejen 13 (tel. (09) 52 10 44), is about one kilometer outside town on an old farm. (42kr.) **AErøskbrug Camping** (tel. (09) 52 18 54) is 10 minutes to the left as you leave the ferry on the waterfront. (29kr per person, 4-person huts 70kr. Open May to mid-Sept.) You can rent a bike at the campground or at the gas station on Pilebækken 7. **AErøhus,** Vestergaden 38, serves very good meals. (Open Feb.-Dec. daily 7:30am-11pm.)

Frequent **ferries** run from Svendborg and cost 35kr one way. A round-trip ticket (70kr) is also good on trips from Marstal to Rudkøbing (on Langeland), and Søby to Fåborg (on Funen). Purchase tickets on the ferry.

Marstal, on AErø's east coast, is also worth a visit. The friendly **tourist office,** Kirkestrand 29 (tel. (09) 53 19 60), on the *torvet,* rents bikes and finds rooms in private homes. (Open mid-June to mid-Aug. Mon.-Fri. 9am-5pm, Sat. 10am-3pm, Sun. 10am-noon; mid-Aug. to mid-June Mon.-Fri. 9am-noon and 1-4pm.) You may want to stay at the incredibly comfortable **Mejerigården,** with an excellent kitchen, airy rooms with private bath, and beautiful decor. Contact the tourist office. The **youth hostel (IYHF),** Færgestræde 29, is down by the harbor, a 10-minute walk to the left of the ferry. (43.50kr. Open year-round.) **Camping** (tel. (09) 53 10 60) is down Havnegaden past the hotel, near the best beach in town. (26kr. Open May-Aug.) **Hotel Marstal** on Dronningstræde, to the right as you leave the ferries, offers good reasonable meals.

Frequent **buses** run between Marstal and AErøskøbing (12kr), though biking is the preferred form of transport. Ferries run between Marstal and Rudkøbing, on Langeland (35kr one way), with bus connections to Svendborg and the real world.

Jutland

Homeland of the Jutes (who made history when they hitched up with the Angles and conquered England), the Jutland peninsula is Denmark's largest land body and the only one connected to continental Europe. Low hills and occasional forests make for a slightly more interesting typography than that of the islands. **Legoland,** a huge amusement park, contains a 14-meter-high Sitting Bull, the space shuttle *Columbia,* and an Amsterdam canal. Take a bus from Vejle or Varde to **Billund,** an hour north of Fredericia. (Open May-Sept. daily 10am-8pm. Admission 35kr.)

Three ferries per week run from **Esbjerg,** on the west coast, to Newcastle, England (830kr one way). For student and off-season discounts inquire at **DFDS,** A/S Englandskajen, DK-6700 Esbjerg (tel. (05) 12 48 00).

Århus

For some reason unknown to the Danes themselves, the residents of Århus are the traditional butt of many Danish jokes. But don't be misled. Århus is the cultural and student center of Jutland, the closest thing Denmark has to a college town.

Visit **Den Gamle By** (old town), a unique cultural history museum with more than 60 original buildings from the sixteenth through the nineteenth centuries arranged into a believable village. (Open June-Aug. daily 9am-5pm; Sept.-May 1-2 hr. less.)

Two thousand years ago, the people living near Århus sacrificed some of their own and threw them into nearby bogs. The bodies have been miraculously preserved, and one, **Grauballemanden,** is on exhibit at the **Moesgård Museum.** Take bus #6 from the train station to the end. (Open April to mid-Sept. daily 10am-5pm; mid-Sept. to March Tues.-Fri. 10am-5pm.) When you're finished with the museum, buy the informative pamphlet (3kr) on the **Prehistoric Trackway**—an open-air museum of re-created prehistoric settings that leads through the Moesgård behind the museum all the way down to the excellent sand beach (about 3km). Bus #19 will bring you back from the beach to the Århus station (summer only).

In September, watch for the **Århus Festuge,** a week-long celebration of theater and music. The helpful **tourist office** is in the town hall (tel. (06) 12 16 00), one block from the train station. They run a **Meet the Danes** program, through which you can meet a Danish family; make arrangements at least one day in advance. Their 25kr tourist card includes a 2½-hour comprehensive tour of Århus, and city bus travel for 24 hours. The office will also book accommodations for free. (Open mid-June to Aug. daily 9am-9pm; Sept. to mid-June Mon.-Fri. 9am-5pm, Sat. 9am-noon.) The **IYHF youth hostel** is 3km from the city center on Østreskovvej (tel. (06) 16 72 98), in the quiet forest of Risskov, only five minutes from the town beach. Take bus #1 or 2 to the terminus at Marienlund and follow signs to the hostel. (40kr. Breakfast 27kr. Curfew 11pm. Open mid-Jan. to mid-Dec.) There are several campsites south of town. **Blommehaven,** Ørneredevej 15 (tel. (06) 27 02 07), in Marselisborg Forest, is the nicest, laid out in terraces down Århus Bay, and near a beach. Take bus #19 from the rail station directly to the grounds, or bus #6 to Hørhavej. (27kr. Open mid-April to mid-Sept.)

Århus is loaded with student bars and cafes. During the academic year, the cheapest lunches are served at the university; stop by the **Matematiske Fakultet. Casablanca,** Rosengade 12, has cafe fare and an international atmosphere. Try the street **Skolegade** for reasonable food of several varieties. The **Second Hand English Bookstore,** Mørksgade 7, sells—guess what? (Open Mon.-Thurs. 11am-5:30pm, Fri. 11am-6pm, Sat. 10:30am-1pm.)

Silkeborg

An hour west of Århus by train is Silkeborg, one of Denmark's loveliest towns. Located in the lake district, it offers many possibilities for canoeing and hiking. The **tourist office,** on the main square at Torvet 9 (tel. (06) 82 19 11), will give you a city map and suggestions for tours along the district's numerous canals and lakes. (Open late June-Aug. Mon.-Fri. 9am-5:30pm, Sat. 9am-3pm, closed Sun.; Sept.-late June Mon.-Fri. 9am-5pm, Sat. 9am-noon, closed Sun.) The **Vandrerhjemmet Åbo (IYHF),** Åahavevej 55 (tel. (06) 82 36 42), has a large green lawn running to the edge of a duck-filled canal. Walk left from the train station to the end of the street, turn left, then take the first right. (37kr. Open Jan.-Nov.) For camping, **Indelukket** (tel. (06) 82 22 01) is closer, but **Århusbakkens** (tel. (06) 82 28 24) is nicer.

The **Silkeborg Cultural Museum** is inhabited by the Tollund Man and the Elling Girl, two more bog people. (Admission 8kr. Open mid-April to Oct. daily 10am-5pm; Nov. to mid-April Wed. and Sat.-Sun. noon-4pm.) The **Silkeborg Museum of Art,** Gudenåvej 7-9, contains an exceptional array of paintings and ceramics by Asger Jorn and the Cobra group. (Admission 10kr. Open April-Oct. daily 10am-5pm; Nov.-March Sat.-Sun. noon-4pm.) **Cyclekompagniet,** Vestergade 18 (tel. (06) 82 09 29), rents bikes for 35kr per day; canoes and boats are available at **Kanoterminalen,** Remstrupvej 39-43 (tel. (06) 82 35 43).

Northern Jutland

Åalborg, two hours north of Århus, features the "merriest street in Scandinavia," **Jomfru Ane Gade,** complete with over 20 restaurants, cafes, and jazz clubs. The **Åalborg Vanderhjem (IYHF),** Skydbanevej 50 (tel. (08) 11 60 44), is a veritable hotel, if priced to match (50.50kr. Kitchen, laundry. Open Jan. to mid-Dec.). The nearby campsite, **Strandparken** (tel. (08) 12 76 29), lies next to a swimming pool. (25kr per person. Open May 15-Sept.)

The self-proclaimed busiest ferry terminal in the world, **Frederikshavn** is otherwise uninteresting. Ferries leave here for Gothenburg, Sweden (6 per day, 3¼ hr., 126kr one way, free with railpass), as well as Oslo and other points in Norway (several per day, 216kr one way, 50% reduction with railpass). Ferries are less frequent and cheaper in the off-season. The **IYHF youth hostel,** Buhlsvej 6 (tel. (08) 42 14 75), is a 15-minute walk from the station and harbor. It's friendly but packed in summer. (39kr. Open Feb. to mid-Dec.) **Nordstrand Camping** (tel. (08) 42 93 50) is a beautiful campsite on the beach; take bus #2 to Skagensvej, then walk (and walk) along Skagensvej to Nordstrand. (Mid-June to mid-Aug. 29kr per tent; otherwise 22kr. Open April-Sept.)

More impressive is **Skagen,** which lies among the dunes at Denmark's northernmost tip. The town, well known for its mid-nineteenth-century artists' colony, is accessible by bus #79 or railway from the Frederikshavn train station (60kr round-trip, railpasses not valid). The **tourist office** is at Sct. Laurentii Vej 18 (tel. (08) 44 13 77; open Mon.-Sat. 9am-5pm). Ask for their free map and guide to Skagen. They can also arrange accommodations in private homes. The bus from Frederikshavn stops right in front of the **IYHF youth hostel** in Gammel Skagen at Hojensvej 32 (tel. (08) 44 13 56). This hostel is outstanding, even for Denmark. Call ahead for reservations. (39kr. Open mid-March to Oct.) Campsites, most open April through September, are scattered all over the area; **Østerklit Camping,** 53 Flagbakkevej (tel. (08) 44 31 23), charges 27kr per person. Works of the Skagen painters are on display in the *Skagen Museum,* in *Anchers Hus* and in *Drachmanns Hus.*

Keep going north—by bus, bike, or thumb—to the point of Skagen, and the white sandy beaches of Denmark's northernmost tip.

EGYPT

US$1 = 2.17 Egyptian pounds (LE)	**LE1 = US$0.46**
CDN$1 = LE1.64	**LE1 = CDN$0.61**
UK£1 = LE3.62	**LE1 = UK£0.28**
AUS$1 = LE1.54	**LE1 = AUS$0.65**

While it may seem confusing, the culture of Egypt is no more complex than that of any other place that has been continuously civilized for 5000 years. Monumental painting and sculpture, not to mention an advanced literature, were old news to the ancient Egyptians when the Greeks were just another tribe of Neolithic cave-men. In more relatively recent times, the Arabs made Egypt and its capital, Al-Qahirah, into one of the greatest centers of culture and learning in the medieval world. Modern Egypt tries to juggle the awesome weight of history and the impossible demands of widespread poverty and overpopulation. After 30 years of military autocracy and war, the Egyptian Republic is determined to partake of the peace and especially the prosperity of the Western world.

Egypt is caught between the fiery rhetoric of Arab nationalism and the pacific moderation required of respectable nations; so far, moderation has won out. Continuing the "open door" policy of his assassinated predecessor Anwar el-Sadat, President Hosni Mubarak has welcomed foreign aid and investment while soundly rejecting the recent upsurge of Islamic fundamentalism. For the tourist, this means that on every street corner you will be happily and loudly welcomed by Egyptians—some of whom will be eager to get their own share of foreign aid. But even in the slums of Cairo the streets are safe—the traditional society and the still-authoritarian government guarantee security.

The Nile *is* Egypt and has been since the introduction of agriculture in the area at least 6000 years ago. From the first cataract at Aswan to the Mediterranean Sea, the mighty river meanders some 1200km through the Egyptian countryside to bring water to an otherwise parched land. Until the completion of the Aswan Dam in 1971, the annual flooding of the Nile dictated the rhythm of Egyptian life, inundating its valley and delta each summer with the water and silt which supported Egypt's concentrated population. The river, now regulated by elaborate irrigation systems, remains the lifeblood of a country that still thrives on agriculture. Recently, for the first time in its history, Egypt has had to import food to survive.

Flanking the Nile Valley are the deserts. On one side of the road are lush groves of date palms, fig, banana, and mango trees, and fields of sugar cane, corn, and squash; on the other side, a few feet away, desolate sand dunes stretch as far as the eye can see. **Lower Egypt** includes the Delta and Cairo vicinity, while **Upper Egypt** is the whole Nile Valley to the south. To the east is the **Eastern Desert,** facing the Red Sea coast and its ports, Suez, Hurghada, and Safaga. Only a few oases interrupt the **Libyan Desert** as it spreads westward into the Sahara. The lightly touristed **Sinai Desert** has only recently been restored to Egypt.

For a good historical and cultural survey of Egypt past and present, consider *Nagel's Encyclopedia Guide to Egypt.* Detailed travel and sightseeing coverage is provided in *Let's Go: Israel and Egypt.*

Planning Your Trip

All visitors to Egypt must have a visa, valid for three months from date of issuance and for 30 days' stay within the country. Visas can be obtained at all points of entry for a fee of about LE19; American nationals pay only LE4 for their visas. Egyptian diplomatic missions can also supply visas, usually on-the-spot or within 24-48 hours, for a similar fee (averaging about US$20).

Sinai-only visas are valid for one week and are issued at the Israeli border. Travelers are allowed to visit the Gulf of Aqaba and Mount Sinai. Sinai travelers should note that currency exchange facilities are rare; it's wise to change what you'll need at the border.

Travelers arriving overland from Israel should know that an Egyptian entry stamp from Taba or Rafah on the Israeli border is proof that you've been in Israel; most Arab nations will not admit anyone documented to have been in Israel.

Once in Egypt, all foreigners must register with the local police within seven days. A fine of LE25 is imposed for late registration. Only expensive hotels can be counted on to do this for you; to register in person, go to the second floor of the **Mugaama Building** on the south side of Tahir Square in Cairo, or to any local police station.

Getting There

Egypt can be reached by land from Israel, by sea from Jordan and Greece, and by air from Athens, London, and other points in Europe. Buses run regularly between Jerusalem or Tel Aviv and Cairo. Municipal bus #15 can be taken from downtown Eilat, Israel to the Egyptian checkpoint at Taba, which is connected by daily buses to other points in the Sinai and to Cairo.

The ferry that travels from Athens to Alexandria via Rhodes is more expensive than comparable flights. More affordable are the boats that connect Aqaba, Jordan's port, with Nuweiba (US$20), on the Sinai's Aqaba coast, and the seedy port of Suez (US$58), on the Egyptian mainland. Boats also sail between Alexandria and Syria, Tunisia, and Algeria.

Flying to Egypt is inexpensive, especially from Athens (US$90-100, with student discount US$58-60) or London (£120-140). Airplane tickets purchased in Cairo have an 85% surcharge; purchase any tickets before arriving in Egypt.

Transportation

For longer trips, such as to Upper Egypt, it's best to stick to trains. There are large student discounts on most train fares; you receive as much as 35-40% off some fares, though the reduction on air-conditioned sleeper berths to the south is only about 10%. First-class sleeper fare is LE114 to either Luxor or Aswan, but a second-class sleeper is almost as comfortable and only LE71.40. A reclining seat in first class, also air-conditioned, is LE15 to Aswan and LE11 to Luxor. Second- and third-class seats are 50% and 75% less expensive, respectively, but significantly less comfortable. Purchase tickets and seat reservations three days or more in advance; Thursday evenings and Fridays are particularly difficult times to travel or purchase tickets. You should arrive at the station two hours before departure.

Service (shared) taxis run between every major town or village in the Nile Valley and take much less time than the train for short distances. They're comfortable and cheap, at just over 1pt per kilometer. Beware, though, that the drivers typically drive like lunatics.

Buses are a better alternative, especially between major cities. Private companies run comfortable, air-conditioned buses between Cairo, Alexandria, Marsa Matruuh, the Canal cities, and points in Upper Egypt.

Car rentals in Egypt cost about US$22 per day plus 7¢ per km over 100km. Flying in Egypt is expensive (Cairo-Aswan LE95.70), though only by Egyptian standards. Perhaps the most romantic way to travel in Egypt is to charter a *felucca* (sailboat) to sail between Luxor and Aswan (about a 5-day voyage) for about LE120. If you split the cost among four to six people, this is a good deal. Hitchhiking is not done in Egypt; thumbers are expected to pay the equivalent service taxi fare.

Practical Information

EGAPT, the national tourist organization, maintains offices in all major Egyptian cities. EGAPT's efforts are complemented by those of the **tourist police,** whose officers wear police uniforms with red armbands. They're the people you should turn to with problems of theft, fraud, and so forth.

Though not the hottest place in the world, Egypt is certainly the hottest place regularly visited by tourists. Fortunately, it is among the driest, and your body's cooling system will work miraculously well in the low humidity. Even in midsummer, air temperatures (around 90-100°F) should not cause major difficulty. The main problem is the relentless sun. Bring a wide-brimmed hat and plenty of sunscreen and lip protection, which you should use liberally. Always carry a large canteen of water with you, or expect to spend a lot of money for liquids. You can buy a large bottle of Baraka (mineral water) for 35pt. Under no circumstances should you consume salt tablets, which may accelerate dehydration. A sightseeing schedule that keeps you out of the midday sun will keep you happier as well.

Egypt is a developing land without the medical facilities and sanitation taken for granted in the West. Before you go, make sure that your inoculations against typhoid, tetanus, and diphtheria are up-to-date. Get a shot of gamma globulin for protection against hepatitis as well. If you plan on traveling in the Delta region, you should take chloroquine tablets (500mg) once a week starting two weeks before you go and continuing for six weeks after you leave. These tablets are available in Cairo, but not at every drugstore; it's easier to buy them abroad. The most common health complaints are dysentery and diarrhea. Cholera and trachoma are rare, but amoebic dysentery has the potential for real harm. It is very important that you avoid contact with Nile water. Bilharzia, a parasite that can penetrate skin, predominates in the more stagnant regions of the Nile. The bug can affect the liver and vision, and is very difficult to treat. If you're splashed with Nile water, wipe it off immediately. Tap water is reputedly safe in Cairo, Alexandria, Luxor, and Aswan, but this assessment ultimately depends on the sensitivity of your stomach. To be on the safe side, stick to bottled water. As far as solid food goes, it's generally safe to eat anything that has been recently cooked, generally unsafe to eat anything raw—except fruit that you can peel. If you experience diarrhea, two local remedies are often effective: fresh yogurt, and lemon or lime juice with a small amount of salt added. Be sure to drink plenty of liquid. If sickness persists, consult a physician or pharmacist. (Note that the drug Enterovioform has been banned throughout North America and Europe.)

No matter how poor or pressed for cash you feel, you will seem rich to Egyptians. Everyone from perfume vendors to professional beggars will solicit you as you walk down the street, and children will incessantly pester you for *baksheesh.* You should know the protocol of *baksheesh;* its most common form is a tip in return for some service. Somewhere between 25 and 50pt is usually in order, so always keep small change with you. A second type of *baksheesh* is the giving of alms—for which you are also likely to be solicited frequently. A more annoying, but less frequent potential drain on your finances is the tourist hustler. Refuse all goods and services offered to you near tourist areas.

Islam is the religion of most Egyptians. An understanding of its basic tenets and customs will help you avoid misunderstanding—and perhaps more serious problems—while traveling here. The basic requirements of Islam are an acceptance of one God and the prophethood of Muhammad, regular prayer (5 times per day), fasting during the month of Ramadan, a ritual visit to Mecca, and charity. Islam is also a sense of community and identity based on the concept of a world-wide Muslim state (*ummah*). Lately, Islam has assumed a strong political dimension. Many Muslims see the rapid influx of Western culture as a threat to their religious and cultural identity. You should be careful not to offend standards of behavior and morality. During Ramadan (April 18-May 18 in 1988), eating and drinking are forbidden during the day and many museums, shops, banks, government offices, and small restaurants change their schedules.

Travelers in Egypt should dress conservatively; bare legs or shoulders are unheard of among Egyptians, and are offensive to many. Solo women may be uncomfortable among Egyptian men. Ignoring catcalls or harassment is advisable; repeated advances are best quelled with harsh public outrage.

Money matters are more complex here than in most countries. Banks, which are all open Monday-Thursday 8:30am-1:30pm, Sunday 10am-noon, will provide you with a dated receipt every time you change money. Such receipts are requested if you need to purchase a plane ticket and at some hotels—note that you should keep the receipt even when changing money at the high tourist rate.

Currency exchange in Egypt is somewhat complicated. The official rate (US$1 = LE1.30) is only used by travelers to buy international transportation. For all other purchases, change money at the tourist rate (US$1 = LE2.20), available at all banks. The infamous black market, once the scourge of the Egyptian economy, has been made obsolete by the institution of this new, very advantageous rate. The Egyptian pound is broken down into 100 piasters.

Arabic is a complicated language, but even the simplest effort to learn it will be wildly appreciated and encouraged with impromptu lessons. Just about everyone you're likely to encounter will speak some words of English, and those that don't will try to help you find someone who can.

Communicating with the outside world from Egypt is always a problem. Collect calls are not possible. To make an international call, it's best to go to a major hotel. Local calls can be made at some train stations, at telephone-and-telegraph offices, and at some street kiosks, but patience and perseverance are necessary. The **telephone code** for Egypt is 20.

Accommodations, Camping, and Food

Most budget travelers stay in low-range hotels (LE6-10 per person per night). Youth hostels, which are in all the major cities, are very dirty, but passable if you're pinched for piasters (LE1-3 per night). In big cities like Cairo, good, clean accommodations are often in small complexes at the top of office buildings. They're usually marked with small signs in English at street level. Bargaining works best in the summer, when business is slow. Agree to pay the 20% tax requested only if the management can show you that they are accredited—otherwise the money is just pocketed. Most budget places under LE10 do not have air conditioning, but many can provide you with a fan. Camping happens only on the beaches of the Sinai and Hurghada.

For most travelers in Egypt, food and health are closely related. Eating from street stands may not always be safe, though it *will* be cheap—well under a pound for a meal. Fortunately, good restaurant food is rarely too expensive, even for the budget traveler. Entrees of *kebab, kushari* (macaroni, rice, lentils, and tomato sauce), and *samak* (fish) cost LE4-5. Even the best restaurants tend to serve colorless and bland food. Beer (LE2-3) is available at good restaurants, but is served only indoors. A cup of hot tea (20-25pt) is easy to come by anywhere and is usually safe; most places keep the water boiling all day. Fruit should be peeled before consumption.

Cairo (Al-Qahira)

Intense and inscrutable, Cairo is the cultural center of the Arab world and the intellectual focus of Islam. For the budget traveler, Cairo is an outstanding find—one of the world's least expensive capitals, yet one of the most fascinating. Countless traffic jams and construction sites tell of the frenetic pace of Cairo's modernization over the last three decades. Amidst the chaos, however, remarkable monuments of the city's previous inhabitants survive. The 4500-year-old pyramids south of Cairo are hard to miss, but the unequalled treasure of Cairo resides in its superb Islamic architecture and its bizarre concatenation of old and new.

Orientation and Practical Information

Cairo straddles the River Nile a few hundred kilometers upstream from Alexandria. As you will no doubt be reminded as you try to cross the street, or to sleep at night, or to take a train, bus, taxi, subway, or city bus, Cairo is the transportation center of Egypt. Trains, buses, and service taxis come and go frequently direct from Cairo to the most distant points in the country, and buses connect the city with Israel; flights from London, Athens, and other points in North Africa and the Middle East land at Cairo International Airport.

Cairo is large. Moreover, street names are not always transliterated. **Tahrir Square** is the center of Cairo; buses leave here for every pocket of the city and its suburbs. **Talaat Harb Street,** still known as Sulayman Pasha Street, runs off Tahrir Square, and **Adly Street** runs north of Talaat Harb Street just a few blocks up from Tahrir Square. This modern district contains most of the city's travel agents and tourist offices, as well as many inexpensive hotels. Many of Cairo's foreign embassies and banks are in **Garden City,** an optimistic project in pastoral urban planning now almost as crowded as the rest of Cairo; its maze of curvy streets lies south of Tahrir Square. Farther south, the city becomes steadily more impoverished as it reaches the squalor around **Old Cairo.** Some 3km east of Tahrir lie the numerous Islamic monuments, narrow streets, and dense population of **Islamic Cairo,** the germ of the modern city. Across the river are the upscale neighborhoods of **Dokki, Mohandiseen,** and **Gizah,** which fade into the slums of **Boulaq** to the west. **Zamalek Island** on the Nile is still one of Cairo's wealthiest and quietest neighborhoods.

Tourist Offices: 5 Adly St. (tel. 92 30 00). Walk up Talaat Harb St. past Talaat Harb Sq. (a.k.a. Suleyman Pasha Sq.), then turn right and walk several blocks on Adlai Pasha St. (about 2km from Tahrir Sq.). Free map. Questions answered with a smile and, at times, slightly outdated information. Open daily 9am-7pm; Ramadan daily 9am-5pm. Other offices at the airport and Giza pyramids (tel. 85 02 59).

American Express: 15 Kasr el Nil St. (tel. 75 07 03), 3 blocks north of Tahrir Sq. Mail held. Most banking services (cardholders cannot cash personal checks). Best place in Egypt to have money or mail sent. Open daily 8am-4:30pm; Ramadan daily 9am-3:30pm. Letter service closed Fri. Also at the Hilton (open until 10pm), Meridien, Sheraton, and Marriot Hotels.

Currency Exchange: Bank of America, at 106 Kasr el Aini, in Garden City (tel. 357 73 33), and Sharia Sheikh Rihan St., is the easiest place to get cash advances with a MasterCard or Visa. **Bank Misr** at the Nile Hilton is open 24 hours for currency exchange.

Post Office: Ataba Sq. Open Sat.-Thurs. 8am-7pm, Fri. 8am-noon. Telegrams taken in the building across the street. Other post offices open Sat.-Thurs. 8:30am-3pm; Ramadan 9am-1pm.

Telephones: Adly St. near Ataba Sq., also on Alfi St., Ramsis St., and Tahrir Sq. All open 24 hours. International calls are easiest from business service offices in the Meridien, Sheraton, and Nile Hilton, though there is a 25% surcharge; open 24 hours.

Flights: Bus #400 connects **Cairo International Airport** with Tahrir Sq. (the last stop); look for a red and white bus toward the rear of the parking lot directly in front of the terminal. The 1-hr. ride costs 10pt (service 24 hours). Taxi fare is LE5, regardless of party size; you might have to bargain. Limousines have posted rate of LE8.50.

Trains: All rail traffic in Egypt passes through **Ramsis Station,** on Ramsis Sq. A black and white taxi to or from Tahrir costs 50pt; walking, it's about 30 min. For travel to Luxor or Aswan, buy tickets from the ticket office on platform #11; second-class sleeper are sold at the Wagons-Lits office just inside the entrance to the station. Buy both several days in advance.

Buses: Midaan Ahmad Hilmi, behind Ramsis Station, for Aswan, Luxor, Hurghada. **Midaan Tahrir,** behind the Nile Hilton, for Alexandria and Marsa Matruuh. **Abbesiya Station,** in Abbesiya, for Israel and the Sinai. To get here take the yellow and green bus from in front of the Nile Hilton (50pt), or a black and white taxi (LE1).

Service Taxis: Private taxis which follow set routes; they leave when full. Often dangerously driven. **Tahrir Sq.:** Taxis to Alexandria. **Ulali Sq.,** across the street to the west of Ramsis Station: Shared taxis to the Canal cities and the Israeli border. **Ahmed Hilmi Sq.,** behind and to the north of Ramsis Station: Taxis to the Delta. **Giza Sq.,** Al Ahram St., west of the Giza Bridge, reached by buses #6 and 803 from Tahrir Sq.: To al-Fayyum and points south. Fare is usually about twice the third-class train fare, though never posted. Ask other people at the station or watch what others pay; drivers may quote tourists an inflated price.

Public Transportation: Buses in Cairo are extremely crowded and uncomfortable, but very cheap and very regular. They rarely come to a full stop. Watch Cairenes for pointers on jumping off a moving vehicle and clambering onto buses already impossibly crowded. Fare is always 10pt. Bury your wallet and valuables securely on your person. The new **metro** runs north-south, connecting Maadi and Helwan in the south to the northern suburbs by way of major stations at Ramses and Tahrir Sq. Also crowded, but cheap and efficient.

Taxis: Collective black and white taxis are very cheap (35-40pt for 1-2km) and much more comfortable than buses. To hail a taxi, pick a major thoroughfare headed in the general direction you wish to travel, stand on the side of or in the street, stretch out your arm as anything black and white approaches (whether or not there are already passengers inside), and scream your destination as the driver slows down (they never stop to chat). Drivers rarely negotiate a price in advance. If they ever propose a price, hop back out and try again. If they try to talk price at the end of the journey, again, ignore them. Pay what you think is reasonable upon arrival; for journeys of 2km or less, 50pt is usually sufficient, then add about 15pt per km thereafter. 1LE should suffice for any destination in Cairo; add more for extra people and late night rides. *Never* hail the more expensive monochromatic Peugeot taxis—these are off-duty service taxis interested in your business only because they know you don't know what you're doing. New meters have recently been installed in all taxis, and since the official rates have been increased, chances are the driver will turn the meter on, particularly if you are the only one using the cab. If the meter is already running, or if the driver doesn't turn it on, the only way to avoid being overcharged is to know what you're doing and how much to pay.

Emergencies: Police (tel. 122). **Ambulance** (tel. 123). **Police Registration** at the Mugamma, the large curved building on Tahrir Sq.

Medical Assistance: Anglo-American Hospital, Botanical Garden St., Geziera-Zamalek, next to the Cairo Tower (tel. 340 61 62, -63, or -64). For emergencies use **As-Salaam International Hospital,** Corniche al-Nil, Maadi (tel. 350 71 95 or -96). Bring enough cash to pay at time of treatment.

Pharmacy: Gomhouria, at the corner of Ramsis St. and 26 July St. (tel. 74 33 69). Open 24 hours.

Embassies: U.S., 5 Latin America St. (tel. 355 73 71). **Canada,** 6 Muhammad Fahmi al-Sayed St., Garden City (tel. 354 31 10). **U.K.,** Ahmed Ragheb St. (tel. 354 08 50). **Australia,** 1097 Corniche el-Nil (tel. 354 50 44). Citizens of **New Zealand** should contact the British Embassy. **Jordan,** 6 Gohaina, Dokki (tel. 44 55 66). Open Sat.-Thurs. 9am-2pm. **Sudan,** 3 al-Ibrahimi St., Garden City (tel. 54 50 43). Open Sat.-Thurs. 8:30am-3pm. **Israel:** 6 Ibn al-Malek St., in Dokki (tel. 72 60 00).

Cultural Centers: American Cultural Center, 4 Ahmed Ragheb St. (tel. 55 73 71, ext. 336), across from the British Embassy. Library and occasional free films and lectures. Open Mon. and Wed. 10am-8pm (4pm in summer), Tues. and Thurs.-Fri. 10am-4pm. **The American University in Cairo,** 113 Kasr el-Aini, opposite Tahrir Sq. Pleasant garden and cafeteria. Very good bookshop with Egyptian and American novels, also foreign periodicals and T-shirts. Open 9am-3pm.

Bookstores: Anglo-Egyptian, 165 Muhammad Farid St. (tel. 91 43 37), and **Shady,** 29 Abdel Khalek Sarwat St. (tel. 74 86 18), have the best selection of English books. For books on Egypt, visit the Hilton's bookstore. Foreign periodicals are available at kiosks along Talaat Harb Sq.

Accommodations

Many of Cairo's inexpensive hotels are hidden on the upper floors of downtown office buildings. The higher the floor, the quieter it will be at night. The uppermost floors, however, can be without running water, especially at night. There are a number of inexpensive hotels along **Talaat Harb Street** near the train station, and in **Ataba Square,** north of Talaat Harb St. along Adly St.

Youth Hostel (IYHF), 135 Abdel Aziz al-Saud St. (tel. 84 07 29). From Tahrir Sq., follow the river south along the Corniche. Cross the channel that branches from the river by the Hotel Meridien, and continue to the large bridge (University Bridge) over the main river. A long walk, so you might want to take bus #8 or 900 from Tahrir Sq. and get off just before it crosses University Bridge. From Ramsis Station, take bus #95. Wall-to-wall bunks in spartan but clean rooms with pleasant river-view balconies. Be extremely careful with valuables. Often very crowded. Members LE2.50, nonmembers 3.50. They no longer sell hostel cards to non-Egyptians. Reception and rooms closed 10am-2pm, also 6-8pm during Ramadan. 11pm curfew. Open year-round.

Tulip Hotel, 3 Talaat Harb Sq. (tel. 76 27 04), near Groppis pastry shop. Reception on 3rd floor. Helpful manager. Not particularly quiet, but adequate rooms. Singles with bath LE12.50, doubles with bath LE15. Breakfast included.

Everest Hotel, Ramsis Sq. (tel. 74 27 07), the tallest building immediately south of the train station, topped by an Egypt Air sign. Reception on 15th floor. Not recommended for solo women. Singles LE4, with bath LE7.50; doubles LE6.10, with bath LE9.25.

Pensione Roma, 169 Muhammad Farid St. (tel. 91 10 88 or 91 13 40), 1 block east of Sharif St. off Adly St. A genuine step up. Comfortable, reasonably clean rooms. Singles LE6, doubles LE11.20. Doubles with bath LE14.50. Breakfast included.

New Hotel, 21 Adli St. (tel. 74 70 33). Rooms quite clean. Singles with bath LE11.50, doubles with bath LE21.55. Extra bed LE3. Breakfast included.

Anglo-Swiss Pension, 14 Champollion St. (tel. 75 14 97). Roomy. Family atmosphere. Clean beds and hot water. Singles LE6.75, doubles LE12.66, with bath LE14. Breakfast included.

Grand Hotel, 17 26th of July St. (tel. 75 77 00 or 75 76 28). Excellent location. Comfortable, air-conditioned rooms. Quiet and safe for women. Singles LE15, with bath LE22; doubles LE21.10, with bath LE29.90. Breakfast included.

Windsor Hotel, 19 Alfy Bey St. (tel. 91 52 77). Ornate and clean, with an atmosphere of faded glory. Singles with bath LE21, doubles with bath LE28. A/C LE1 extra. Breakfast included. Mr. Doss, the manager, offers a 25% discount to *Let's Go* readers; this might also be available at the **Lotus Hotel,** 12 Talaat Harb St.

Food

If you only want to fill your stomach, you can do so for as little as 10pt, although taste and sanitation may be wanting. The cheapest grub in town is probably *fuul* and *taamiyya* (beans and fried vegetable paste); there are literally hundreds of *fuul* restaurants in Cairo. Another inexpensive alternative is *kushari,* a mixture of macaroni, rice, lentils, and fried onions with tomato sauce costing only 25pt; *kushari* shops, scattered all over the city, are easy to spot by the conical piles of rice displayed in their windows.

There are several fruit-juice stands on Kasr el-Aini Street and Talaat Harb Street, a few blocks off Tahrir Square. They will squeeze you a delicious glass of mango, orange, strawberry, banana, guava, or sugar cane juice for 25-35pt.

Zaina Cafeteria-Restaurant, 32 Talaat Harb St., next to the Oxford Guest House. A popular midtown eatery with food on display at the counter. Complete meals LE2-3; 12% less if you eat at the counter. Open 8:30am-10pm.

Felfela, 15 Hoda Sharawi St., off Talaat Harb St. Specializes in Egyptian food: *fuul* 40pt, *taamiyya* 40pt, kebab LE4. Tacky "folk" decoration, with turtles and alligators in aquariums.

Z-Cafeteria Restaurant, 3 Tahrir Sq., 100m from American University. Counter service or tables upstairs. Fast and courteous service. *Shwarma* sandwiches 40pt, meals LE3-6. Open 10am-9pm.

El Dahaan, Maydan al-Husayn, at the end of al-Muski. Very good *kebab, kofte,* and grilled meat LE17.50 per kilo (¼ kilo is plenty). Open noon-11pm.

Alfy Bey Restaurant, 3 Alfy St. Old-fashioned atmosphere. Very clean. Excellent Egyptian food for LE4-6. Open 11:30am-9:45pm.

Lappas, 17 Kasr el-Nil St. Popular rendezvous of intellectuals. Reasonably good selection of pastries and snacks. Macaroni served for lunch (50pt).

Dumyati, Falaki Sq., near the pedestrian overpass about 4 blocks east of Tahrir Sq. One of the best and most popular *fuul* restaurants in Cairo. *Fuul, taamiyya,* salads, bread, and *mahalabiyya* (resembling rice pudding) about LE1. Open 11am-10pm.

Tahrir Patisserie, a newly renovated storefront on Tahrir St. 1 block east of the square. Delicious, spicy *fatir* (a pizza made with flaky dough) for LE2.50. Open until 11pm.

Sights

The **Egyptian Museum,** just off Tahrir Sq. northeast of the Nile Hilton, is the world's preeminent warehouse of pharaonic remains. Despite the poor layout and labeling, the museum's collection is, both quantitatively and qualitatively, simply extraordinary. The **Tutankhamen (King Tut) Collection,** which toured the world, is stacked on the upper floor. (Open Sat. and Tues.-Thurs. 9am-3pm, Fri. 9-11:15am and 1:15-3pm. Admission LE3, students LE1.50.)

Before plunging into Islamic Cairo, consider visiting the recently renovated **Museum of Islamic Art,** off Ahmad Mahar Sq. at the corner of Port Said and Muhammad Ali St. The Museum is about ½km west of Bab Zuwayla, so it is easily incorporated into a trip to Islamic monuments. (Open Sat.-Thurs. 9am-4pm, Fri. 9-11am and 1:30-4pm. Admission LE2, students LE1.) Mosques have sporadic hours, but are usually open daily from 9am to 3pm, a few hours shorter during Ramadan. Do not enter the mosques at prayer time or on Fridays. *Baksheesh* of 50pt-LE1 to the guard who admits you or gives you a tour is customary. Appropriate dress means no bare shoulders or legs, and for women, no trousers; head covering for women is recommended but not required. All visitors should remove their shoes before entering the mosque.

A walk through Cairo's medieval Islamic district will reveal splendid mosques and monuments representing some of the finest ninth- to seventeenth-century Islamic architecture found anywhere in the world. From Tahrir Sq., take bus #63 or 66 or walk east from Ataba Sq. to Husayn Sq. along al-Azhar St. On Husayn Square you'll see the modern **Mosque of Sayyidna Husayn** and the Fatimid **Mosque of al-Azhar.** Established in 972, al-Azhar is the world's oldest university and an unrivaled institution for Islamic theological studies. (Admission LE1.) Al-Muizz Street connects **Bab al-Futuh** and **Bab Zuwayla,** the northern and southern eleventh-century Fatimid gates. A walk between these two gates is a good introduction to Cairene Islamic architecture and urban planning. Next to Bab al-Futuh is the recently renovated Fatimid **Mosque of al-Hakim** (900-1010); its outstanding minarets have trapezoidal bases projecting into the streets. Farther south on al-Muizz St. is the very small Fatimid **Mosque of al-Aqmar;** its ornate facade exhibits numerous keel arched niches.

Continue down on al-Muizz Street, and you'll see on your right three impressive Mamluk constructions: The **Mosque of Sultan Barquq,** the **Madrasah of Sultan al-Nasir Muhammad,** and the **Complex of Sultan Qalaun,** the last distinguished by its "Romanesque" facade. Farther down, at the intersection of al-Azhar St. and al-Muizz St., stand two imposing Mamluk structures: the **Madrasah of Sultan al-Ghori,** and the **Mausoleum of al-Ghuri,** which has lost its huge dome. The spectacular Fatimid gates of Bab Zuwaylla mark the location of the **Mosque of al-Muayyad.** Go through the gate and turn left on Darb al-Ahmar St., which will lead you through a maze of mosques to Muhammad Ali Square, from where you can easily reach the **Citadel.** Within its walls is the Ottoman Mosque of Muhammad Ali, crowned by a host of silver domes. (Admission LE2, students LE1.) Among the largest complexes located at Muhammad Ali Square are the Mamluk **Mosque of Sultan Hasan** (1356) and the **Rifa'i Mosque,** built in 1912. The former is considered the most monumental and ambitious project of Mamluk architecture. (Admission LE1.)

If you see only one mosque in Cairo, let it be the **Mosque of Ibn Tulun,** the largest, oldest (879), and most harmonious of the city's Islamic monuments. With sweeping contours, vast courtyard, intricate inscriptions and superb lacy stucco decoration, and an original helicoidal minaret modelled after the minaret of the Great Mosque of Samarra (Iraq), the mosque is a remarkable blend of simplicity and grandeur. (Admission LE1, students 50pt.) Next door is **Bayt al-Kritiliyya,** also called Gayer-Anderson House, a delightful Ottoman mansion refurbished in the 1930s by Mayor Gayer-Anderson, a British art collector. It contains European and Oriental furniture, and a large collection of painting and porcelain. (Open Sat.-Thurs. 9am-3:30pm, Fri. 9-11am and 1:30-3:30pm. Admission LE1, students 50pt.)

To the south, **Old Cairo** harbors many fine Coptic churches, among them **al-Muallaqa, Abu Serga, Ste. Barbara,** and the **Ben Ezra Synagogue.** The **Coptic Moseum,** next to the Roman fortress of Babylon, houses the world's finest collection of Coptic art. To reach Old Cairo, take the commuter train from Sayyida Zaynab Station to Mari Girgis, or take bus #92, 134, 140 or 94 from Tahrir Sq. to the end of the line. (Churches open Sat.-Thurs. 9am-4pm, Fri. 2-4pm. Admission LE2, students LE1.)

Stretching between Sayyidna al-Husayn and al-Muizz St. in Islamic Cairo is one of the largest bazaars in the world, the **Khan al-Khalili.** Haggling is expected here, as are phenomenal variations in quality and honesty. Whether or not you're in the market for one, see the weekly **Camel Market** at Imbaba. Camels, many veterans of 30-day trans-Sudan treks to the beginning of the road north at Aswan, are sold every Friday between 5 and 10am, with the liveliest trade happening from 7 to 9am. To reach the market take a taxi to the Imbaba Airport or bus #167.

Near Cairo

No words can describe the **Pyramids** at Giza. The first pyramid as you approach the site, the **Pyramid of Cheops** (2690 B.C.E.) soars 137m from the desert floor. A crawl through the narrow passageways to the **King's Chamber** affords a sensual appreciation of the pyramid's gargantuan mass. The highlight of the expedition is the tall and narrow **Gallery,** with walls 9m high. To get away from the hawkers and self-proclaimed pyramid experts, walk over to the **Pyramid of Chephren,** one meter shorter and 40 years younger than Cheops. The third in line is the **Pyramid of Mycerinus,** a comparative pygmy at only 66m. Hewn out of solid rock, the **Sphinx** reclines for a length of 80m, casting bemused eyes upon intrigued camera-clickers. The pyramids are crumbling, and the stair-like appearance is quite deceiving. Each night, a number of tourists bribe the guards and climb them anyway; each year, a number of foolhardy die.

To reach Giza from downtown Cairo, take bus #8 or 900 (5pt), or the minibus (25pt) from in front of the Mugamma building on Tahrir Square. There is no "entrance" to the pyramids, so they can be seen for free at any time. Their interiors are open daily 9am-4pm; a comprehensive admission is LE3. If you can survive without crawling through the smelly, crowded, hot interiors, the best time to visit is after 4pm.

Saqqara

Many of Egypt's oldest pharaonic monuments are clustered 32km south of Cairo at Saqqara, burial ground of the pharaohs during the most glorious days of the Old Kingdom (3100-2181 B.C.E.). The royal necropolis, spanning a 7-kilometer stretch of the desert, teems with fabulous funerary monuments. There is, unfortunately, no easy way to get to Saqqara. The cheapest option is to take a minibus from Giza Square, near the pyramids, as far as the Abu Sir turn-off (25pt), and hitch or walk from there. It's more convenient to take a tour (LE15-20) operated by various hotels and travel agents, but for the same price you can hire a camel or horse, with guide, at the Giza pyramids and trek to Saqqara past otherwise inaccessible sights, including the pyramids at **Abu Sir** and the sun temple of **Abu Gurab.** Another alternative is to take the train from Ramsis Station to the town of al-Badshin, then catch a cab (about LE2).

The mountainous **Step Pyramid** of Pharaoh Zoser dominates Saqqara. Built around 2650 B.C.E., it is the oldest stone structure built on such a grand scale. Just south, the **Pyramid of Unas** (c. 2300 B.C.E.) houses the celebrated **Pyramid Texts,** the earliest known example of decorative hieroglyphics in a pharaonic tomb chamber. Beneath a nearby shanty lie three of Egypt's deepest burial chambers, the so-called **Persian Tombs.** A dizzying spiral staircase drills its way 25m into the ground to the burial area. About 1½km from the Step Pyramid you'll find the **Tomb of Ti,** with bas-reliefs illustrating many scenes of Egyptian everyday and ceremonial life. Inside the nearby **Serapeum** are the **Tombs of the Apis Bulls,** where 25 **sacred oxen** were embalmed and placed in enormous sarcophagi. Returning toward the entrance area, stop and explore some of the 30 rooms which comprise the **Tomb of Mereruka,** northeast of the Step Pyramid. The portrayal of wildlife discovered inside has enabled scientists to reconstruct Egyptian fauna from the time of the pharaohs. The adjoining **Tomb of Ankhma-hor** pictures a Sixth Dynasty (c. 2200 B.C.E.) circumcision and other surgical operations.

Alexandria (El Iskandariya)

To the Western ear the very phonetics of the word are exotic and enticing—Alexandria. Append images of Alexander the Great, who founded the city in 332 B.C.E., Queen Cleopatra, who frolicked with Marc Antony on the beaches, and Napoleon, whose lesson in French language and culture the city has yet to forget, and the perception of Egypt's second capital grows complete. Alexandria today faces problems of grime, decay, and overpopulation, and virtually all relics of the age when Alexander's city was the center of Hellenistic civilization have vanished. Although Shakespeare, Shaw, or even Lawrence Durrell would never recognize the place, the comfortable climate and laid-back way of life make it a respite from the pressure cooker of Cairo.

Alexandria pins down the northwest corner of the Nile delta, 225km from Cairo. Expensive ferries sail here from Athens and Cairo once per week. Trains, buses, and service taxis keep the city well connected to Cairo (about LE3-4 each). Buses travel either the boring Desert Road or the dangerous Delta Road; taxis, unfortunately, zoom along the latter only. The city is laid out in a narrow strip along the coast, about 20km long and 2 to 3km wide. Central Alexandria consists of two harbors separated by a peninsula. The modern port, the **Western Harbor,** handles all commerce and passenger traffic. Downtown centers around **Sa'ad Zaghloul Square,** on the **Eastern Harbor,** and **Ramli Station Square,** which adjoins Sa'ad Zaghloul's southeast corner. Sa'ad Zaghloul is the main terminus for all intercity and municipal buses, and Ramli is the center for the city's tram network. Arriving by train or shared taxi, you'll find yourself at **Masr Station,** six blocks south of Sa'ad Zaghloul Square.

The most famous remnant of ancient Alexandria is an unimpressive granite column mistakenly known as **Pompey's Pillar.** Actually, it was raised for the third-century emperor Diocletian, in gratitude for his not massacring the rebellious population. Take tram #16 from Orabi Sq. and get off when you see the pillar on Karmuz St. A few blocks west are the **Kom al-Shokafa Catacombs,** eerie tombs cut into rock and decorated with remarkable bits of sculpture and reliefs. Just northwest of the train station is the white marble **Roman Amphitheater.** (All open daily 9am-4pm; Ramadan daily 9am-2pm. Admission to each 50pt, students 25pt.) Just north of Horriya St. and east of Safia Zaghloul St., the **Greco-Roman Museum** is an excellent introduction to Ptolemaic culture. (Open Sat.-Thurs. 9am-4pm, Fri. 9-11:30am and 1:30-4pm. Admission LE1, students 50pt.) Gleaming **Fort Qayit Bey,** at the northeastern tip of the peninsula, dominates the Eastern Harbor; within its imposing white walls are a naval museum and a model of Alexandria's ancient lighthouse, from whose remains the fort was built. Take tram #15 from Ramli Station (2pt). (Open daily 9am-3pm. Admission LE1, students 50pt.)

To register your passport or extend a visa, go to the **Passport Office,** 28 Talaat Harb St. (tel. 80 34 48), opposite the Leroy Hotel, on the corner of Falak St. (Open Sat.-Thurs. 8am-1pm and 7-9pm, Fri. 10am-1pm and 7-9pm.) The well-informed staff of Alexandria's **tourist office,** Nabi Danial St. (tel. (03) 80 76 11), on the southwest corner of Sa'ad Zaghloul Sq., distributes copies of *Alexandria By Night By Day,* which includes a good map and a train schedule. (Open daily 8am-6pm; Ramadan daily 9am-4pm.) The main office of the **tourist police** (tel. 86 38 04) is in Montaza Palace, but there's a convenient branch office (tel. 80 79 85), above the tourist office in Sa'ad Zaghloul Square.

There are a number of small **hotels** (LE3-5 per person) on the streets running south from the waterfront near Sa'ad Zaghloul Square. Think twice before staying here, though, as people have complained about bugs. Martyrs in search of the local **IYHF youth hostel,** 32 Port Said St. (tel. (03) 597 54 59), near Chatby Beach, should take any eastbound tram from Ramli Station to St. Mark's College, a red and white domed building; the hostel lies opposite the college grounds. It's crowded, colorless, and noisy. (Foreigners LE2.05. Members only, but you can buy a guest card for LE3 more per night.) Much more comfortable is the breezy **Hotel Leroy,** 25 Talaat Harb St. (tel. (03) 80 90 99), a few blocks west of Sa'ad Zaghloul Sq., on the top floors of an office building, with fairly clean rooms, some with balconies. (Singles LE9.50, doubles LE15. Breakfast included.) The amiable **Hotel Acropole,** 1 Gamal al-Din Yassin St., fifth floor (tel. (03) 80 59 80), a block west of Sa'ad Zaghloul Sq., is one of the best deals in town, but it fills early. (Rooms LE4 per person. Breakfast included.) **Hotel Marhaba,** 10 Orabi Sq. (tel. (03) 80 09 57), near the colonnade of the Tomb of the Unknown Soldier, is the best around. (Singles LE12, doubles LE16.50. Hot showers and breakfast included.)

Muhammad Ahmed Fuul, two blocks south of Sa'ad Zaghloul Sq., serves great *fuul* and *taamiyya,* with bread and salads, for about 35pt. **Elite Restaurant,** 43 Safia Zaghloul, a block north of Horriya St., has good French and Greek food, as well as great pizzas (LE1.50) and salads (50-60pt). **Restaurant Denis,** just off the waterfront three blocks east of Ramli Station, is justifiably famous for its seafood, pulled daily from the Mediterranean. Choose your own fish in their kitchen. (Sold by weight, so dinner can run anywhere from LE4 to LE8.)

While the seaside **corniche** charms downtown pedestrians, Alexandria's best **beaches** lie far from the main squares. Many Egyptians recreate at **Montaza** and **Ma'amura,** both a 30-minute ride on bus #129 (10pt), or an air-conditioned double-decker (25pt) from the main waterfront squares downtown. At Montaza you can also visit the grounds of **Montaza Palace,** a bizarre pink edifice that once belonged to King Farouk. (Admission 80pt.) About 25km east of downtown Alexandria are the white sand beaches and excellent seafood restaurants of **Abu Qir** (take bus #129 from El-Manshiya Sq.), with inexpensive **camping** facilities at **Abu Qir Camp** (tel. 97 14 24).

Marsa Matruuh

Marsa Matruuh, 300km west of Alexandria, is in the middle of nowhere. But this small city, built around a perfect white sand bay, is worth a major detour. It's one of the most charming places in the country—even if everything in town *is* named after German field marshall Erwin Rommel, the legendary "Desert Fox." The charms of the town have yet to be discovered by foreign tourists, but Egyptians come here in droves, many of them aboard the air-conditioned buses that leave Alexandria's Sa'ad Zaghloul Square. (4-6 per day, 4¾ hr.; Blue Line LE6, Golden Rocket LE8, and a slow non-air-conditioned bus LE3.50.) Many of these vacationers also make reservations for this popular route a few days in advance—in Alexandria at the ticket office on Sa'ad Zaghloul Sq., and in Marsa Matruuh at the bus station office one street west of Alexandria St., at the inland end. Direct buses also run from Cairo's Tahrir Square each morning (8 hr., LE10-12). A new sleeper-train service from Cairo attests to the increasing popularity of Marsa Matruuh among upper-crust Cairenes. (June-Oct. 3 per week, first-class LE21.25, second-class LE11. Book ahead.)

Magnificent beaches are practically the only sights in Matruuh. Five kilometers of soft sand rim the crescent-shaped bay adjacent to the town. The **Beach of Lovers** caps the western horn of the bay, while **Rommel Beach** arcs around the peninsula at its eastern side. They're accessible on foot, by surf kayak (available at the Hotel Beau Site, LE4) or by bike (LE1 per hr. from Galeh St., 1½ blocks west of Alexandria St.). Farther afield, you'll find windy **Cleopatra's Beach** to the west, and flat **Ubayyad Beach.** Twenty kilometers west of town awaits the finest jewel, **Agiiba Beach,** where a sandy cove hugs cliffs pocked with caves. To reach the western beaches from the bus station, take a taxi or microbus (LE2-3), or the public bus (50pt). Transportation stops at 5pm.

Decent hotel beds are becoming expensive in Marsa Matruuh. Piaster pinchers might want to find the bland, bare **youth hostel**—if they can. It's a two-story concrete cube west of Alexandria St., 1km inland of the big mosque on the corniche. (LE1. Members only; guest card available.) The best of the cheap hotels in town is the **Hotel Gazalah,** off Alexandria St. about five blocks inland. It's clean and caters to foreigners (LE3.50 for a bed in a shared room). The **Cairo Hotel** on Tahrir St. west of Alexandria St. is the runner-up (LE3). As is the case all along Egypt's western Mediterranean coast, freelance **camping** is possible with permission from the local police. Hardy men can sleep in crowded dorm rooms along Alexandria St. (Beds LE1.)

Many inexpensive restaurants vie for customers on Alexandria St., but the champion is tiny **Hani El Onda Restaurant,** Nasser St. (Meals LE1-3.) The busy, more expensive season in Marsa Matruuh runs from May through October; the off-season is very slow—and very cheap.

Isolated, beautiful **Siwa Oasis** is 300km to the south. For more information on Siwa, check *Let's Go: Egypt and Israel* or Ahmed Fakhry's *Siwa Oasis,* both available at The AUC Bookstore in Cairo.

Hurghada (Ghardaka)

In fleabag hotels and second-class train compartments, travelers debate whether Hurghada belongs on a Egyptian itinerary. The affirmative team consists of temple-weary snorkeling enthusiasts, who appreciate Hurghada's relaxed pace and low prices, and can't get enough of its brilliant, teaming submarine world. The negative eam contends that a town whose port lies several kilometers down the street, whose eaches are rocky and windblown, and whose buildings are universally charmless r under construction, should never be called a seaside resort. You decide.

Buck-toothed trigger fish, iridescent parrot fish, sea cucumbers, giant clams, and million others perform in a big circus just off the coast of barren, mountainous lesert. Boat trips are necessary to reach the best reefs. The trip to **Geftun Island** s the most popular, and is an all-day affair (LE10 including two snorkeling stops nd lunch). Seats on all the boat excursions must be reserved the night before. If ou're low on cash, you can find fairly intriguing reefs on your own—try near the heraton beach and off the coast at the northern end of town.

You can **camp** for free at the beach, with permission from the **Frontiers Office** ear the big northern mosque. (Take along your passport and 40pt. Open Sat.-Thurs. 10:30am-2pm and 7-9:30pm, Fri. sporadically.) The cheapest and most popular places to stay are the various **tourist flats** scattered around town (most charge LE2.50 per person). The **Hurghada Happy House,** al-Dhar Mosque Sq. (tel. 405 40), 50m uphill from the bus station, has clean bathrooms and large rooms with fans. Retired sea-captain Muhammad Awad is a friendly fellow who (like all guides) will rent mask and snorkel for LE1 per day and arrange snorkeling trips to the reefs. Ask about his special trip to the awesome "House of the Sharks."(LE3-4 per person for minibus, 10am-5pm.) If you don't want to buy any of the seaside knick-knacks in his Red Sea Wonderland or stay at his place, at least stop by for a chat. He knows the reefs, the water, the fish, and the latest travel information. (Happy House open late Aug.-June.) Also try the **Happy Home** next door, the **Sunshine House Hotel** (tel. 405 40) down the street on the main avenue coming up from the port and bus station, and the **Nefertiti House** (tel. 400 83) near the more expensive Global Hotel at the northeastern corner of town. To sleep near the beach, head 4km south on the coastal road to **Moon Valley** (tel. 400 74), where minimal bungalows for two persons look out onto turquoise waters. You can take a local bus (25pt) or a minibus (50pt) to get there. (LE20 for 2 people, with a private bath. Tasty breakfast and dinner included.)

All boat captains and all vacationers spend the evening on the **Red Sea Restaurant's** roof garden (full meals under LE5). Along Hurghada's lively central streets, **Restaurant Happyland** offers fish or chicken with soup, pita, and veggies (LE1.75). Dinners at **Moon Valley** cost LE4 for non-guests.

Buses to Hurghada are hot and crowded; reserve a seat in advance. There is service from Cairo's Ahmed Himli Station, near Ramses Station (7:30am, LE8; 8pm A/C, LE10; 20 hr.), Qena and Luxor (6am and noon, LE4), and Suez (6am, 7½ hr., LE4.50). Return schedules are comparable. Service taxis from Luxor, Qena, and Suez cost roughly the same, and can be more convenient. Boats to Sharm El Sheikh, in the Sinai, operate only when 20 people ask local captains for the service. (Several boats per week in winter, LE25-30 per person.) Seven people in a service taxi to Sharm El Sheikh should pay about LE20 per person.

Sinai Desert

Long the stage for Arab-Israeli enmity, the Sinai has finally been excused from duty as the Middle East's largest battlefield. Tourism on the peninsula has dwindled since the Sinai was returned to Egypt in 1982, leaving it relatively unmarred by developers and tour groups. Jagged mountains, exquisite coral reefs, and a rich religious history make the Sinai a budget traveler's dream: remote, inexpensive, and spectacularly beautiful, tempting for a short stopover or a month-long immersion.

The Sinai is most easily approached on the way to or from Israel. **Buses** leave the Egyptian/Israeli border at Taba, near Eilat, and travel the full length of the Aqaba Coast to Sharm el Sheikh. (Bus #15 leaves from opposite Eilat's central bus station for the border.) Coming from Cairo, catch a bus at Abassiya Station, 5km northeast of Ramses Station. Daily buses run from Cairo to Sharm el Sheikh, St. Catherine's Monastery, Nuweiba, and on to Taba. Direct buses also run to the

Nuweiba ferry and to Dahab. There are daily connections to all of these points fro
Suez, too. The Sinai is also reached by **boat** from Jordan; daily service connec
Nuweiba with the Jordanian port of Aqaba. (Arrive early for visas, available at th
boat.) Once in the Sinai, notoriously irregular buses will provide the best mea
of transportation. Two daily buses link the towns on the Aqaba Coast, and dai
buses also run between Nuweiba and St. Catherine's. Bus fares between one tow
and the next run LE1.50 to 5; shared taxis, when you can find them, cost the sam

Don't try to **hitchhike** in the Sinai; the roads are almost always deserted, ar
the heat will knock you out before you know it. Temperatures can top 100°F, s
you must make some concessions to the brutal sun. Drink more fluids than yo
think you could possibly need, always carry water, and don't simply be guided b
your thirst, since heat can dehydrate you imperceptibly. Don't exert yourself exce
sively, keep your head covered, and unless you have a very good base tan, wea
a shirt, especially while snorkeling.

Inexpensive beds are rare in the Sinai, so be prepared to **camp** on the peninsula
beautiful beaches; it rains only a few times each decade, so a sleeping bag shoul
suffice. Tap water is not always potable, but mineral water is sold everywhere (5(
75pt per bottle). Bring toilet paper with you, and guard it with your life. Conside
bringing your own snorkeling gear—though you can rent it in all three dive town
rates are high (LE4-5 per day for mask, fins, and snorkel) and quality mediocr

Aqaba Coast

The Aqaba Coast, running from Taba to Ras Muhammad, has the most spectacu
lar underwater scenery in the world, while the desert interior to the west expose
ridge after ridge of jagged mountains. **Nuweiba,** the first settlement south of Taba
is the most expensive of the coastal beachtown trio. The tourist village contains eve
rything of interest except the ferry, 8km to the south. To reach the best snorkelin
territory, walk south from the tourist village and enter the water where the wave
are breaking. There is a toilet-and-shower pavilion on the main beach, as well a
a good fish restaurant. The only cheap place to sleep is the beach. (LE1 on the mai
beach, free elsewhere.) Nuweiba, along with Dahab, is the place to arrange a **came
trek** into the desert with a Bedouin guide (ask anyone). Treks cost about LE12 pe
day per person, and will go just about anywhere into the wilderness interior.

Dahab, the next town south of Nuweiba, is an oasis of swaying palms, roamin
camels, and frolicking Bedouin children, all at the foot of a row of stark, dauntin
mountains. To get to the **Bedouin village** from the modern town and bus stop (abou
30 min.), take a taxi or walk toward the twin white water towers of the MFO base
and follow the dirt road that begins on the inland side of the camp. The larges
reefs begin at the northern edge of the cove, but there is an equally beautiful spo
at the southern edge. Though the Bedouin village lacks toilets and electricity, yo
can rent a palm-frond hut (for 1-3 people, LE1), or camp on the beach. The bes
food is in the Bedouin village at **Tota's Cafe,** with spaghetti, soup and salad, an
other Sinai rarities. Back in the modern village are a dive shop, a kiosk, and a
expensive hotel and restaurant.

There are no swaying palm trees or charming Bedouins at **Na'ama Bay,** but wha
this broad, barren cove lacks in exotic atmosphere it makes up for in submarin
splendor. This part of the coast claims better diving than either Dahab or Nuweiba
and Na'ama is the perfect place from which to explore it all. The **Near Gardens**
at the northern end of the bay, and the **Far Gardens,** a half-hour walk beyond, are
a medley of leafy coral and splendiferous fish. There are even better dive sites farthe
away, such as world-famous **Ras Muhammed;** you can reach these through one o
the dive shops' daily excursions. (Transport and snorkeling gear LE10. Full scuba
gear LE40.) It is illegal to sleep on the main beach at Na'ama, but you can sack
out elsewhere—walk south over the hill to the beach below the MFO base, or nort
around the rocks. Otherwise, fork over LE3 to **Beach Camping,** at the center o
the bay. Na'ama's **supermarket** has an extraordinary variety of goods for the Sina
(including fresh produce), and the **snack bar** next door serves good meals.

Sharm el Sheikh, 7km south of Na'ama, has an **IYHF youth hostel** at the top of the hill across from the bus stop. (LE2. Closed 9am-2pm. 11pm curfew; 10pm in winter.) At the junction at the bottom of the hill are a **hospital** and a **police station.** The southern Sinai's only **post office,** two **banks,** and a feeble attempt at a supermarket line the town's main square at the top of the hill. The **bus station** is behind the green metal fence halfway up the hill. Here you can and should buy advance tickets for Cairo; note that Cairo-bound buses don't serve Na'ama. About 1km southwest of the junction is the **passport office.** Beyond these basic services and the hostel, there is nothing of interest in Sharm el Sheikh.

Mount Sinai and Saint Catherine's Monastery

You might call this vast mountainous desert region God forsaken—if you didn't know its history. **Mount Sinai** (Gebel Musa) is revered by Jewish, Christian, and Muslim believers alike as the peak upon which Moses spoke to God and received the Ten Commandments. The monastery was founded in 342 C.E. when Helena, mother of Emperor Constantine, had a small chapel built next to what was believed to be the famous Burning Bush through which God first spoke to Moses (Exodus 3:1-22). Emperor Justinian ordered the construction of a splendid fortified basilica and monastery which would allow Christians to live in the desert without fear of persecution. The precautions worked: **St. Catherine's Monastery,** at the base of the mountain, is presently the oldest unrestored example of Byzantine architecture in the world. (Only the chapel and gruesome ossary are open to the public, Mon.-Thurs. 9:30am-12:30pm.)

The **"camel path"** to the top of Mt. Sinai (2285m) begins directly behind the monastery. The 3000 **Steps of Repentance,** allegedly built by a single monk to fulfill his pledge of penitence, also lead to the summit, but they're arduous by day and treacherous by night. The two- to three-hour ascent is most comfortably made in the late afternoon or early evening; bring a flashlight and a sleeping bag as the summit is chilly.

The most popular place to sleep is on top of Mt. Sinai, where you can enjoy the sunrise and a spectacular view of the desert as it stretches toward the Red Sea. The good people at the monastery will watch your bags for the night, and you can use their showers. The monastery also runs a **hostel,** or you can camp at the **Katrine Tourist Camp,** 1km below the village and 1km from the monastery. **Zeitouna Camping** has toilets, hot showers, and reasonable prices, but is inconveniently situated 4km east of town. There are two **restaurants** in the village, on the main road where the buses stop, and the pink **bakery** sells delicious hot *pitah.* Ask for Sheikh Musa if you'd like to arrange a **camel trek** into the surrounding wilderness.

Luxor

Built on the site of ancient Thebes, capital of the United Kingdom of Upper and Lower Egypt during the New Kingdom (1555-1090 B.C.E.), the town of Luxor displays some of the country's most mammoth and impressive monuments. The temples of Luxor and Karnak, with their overwhelming array of gateways and forests of gigantic columns, are only a part of Luxor's historical and artistic wealth. Across the Nile are yet more monumental temples, as well as Luxor's famous tombs. The city deserves its reputation as Upper Egypt's capital of the hustle, the hassle, and the hard-sell. But comfortable accommodations, world-class sights, and occasional glimpses of Egyptian hospitality make Luxor a worthy host.

Orientation and Practical Information

Luxor has custody over the site of bygone Thebes, once the metropolitan home to one million Ancient Egyptians. The town faces the temple-studded West Theban plain across the Nile. **Sharia al-Mahatta** (Station St.) runs perpendicular to the Nile, east-west from the train station to riverside Luxor Temple. **Sharia el-Nil** (Nile St.), soon to sport an Aswan-style *corniche,* runs north-south along the east bank of the Nile. The third main thoroughfare, **Sharia al-Karnak** (Karnak St.) runs parallel to and one block away from the Nile between Luxor Temple and Karnak Temple, 3km to the north.

Tourist Office: In the tourist bazaar next to the New Winter Palace Hotel (tel. 822 15), just south of Luxor Temple. Very helpful staff. The free *Upper Egypt Night and Day* has a train schedule and lousy map. Open daily 8am-2pm and 5-8pm.

American Express: Sharia el-Nil (tel. 828 62), at the entrance to the Old Winter Palace Hotel. Mail held and checks sold, but no wired money accepted. (Cairo the nearest office to accept.) Open daily 8am-9pm.

Telephones: Behind the New Winter Palace Hotel.

Flights: Airport: (tel. 820 77), 5km northeast. Take a taxi (LE3) or the Egypt Air shuttle (50pt). **Egypt Air,** (tel. 820 40), next to Old Winter Palace Hotel, serves Cairo (about US$50) and Aswan.

Trains: If you're returning to Cairo, make reservations the day you arrive. Trains to Cairo (6 per day with air-conditioned seats; 13 hr.; first class LE12.55, second class LE5.85), to Aswan (3 per day with air-conditioned seats; 5 hr.; first class LE5.50, second class LE2.05).

Buses: Intersection of Sharias al-Karnak and al-Mahatta. Express air-conditioned bus to Cairo (2 per day, 12 hr., LE10). Several buses per day to Esna (75pt), Edfu (LE1.25), Kom Ombo (LE1.50), Aswan (LE2.50), and Qena (75pt). To Hurghada (2 per day, 4 hr., LE4).

Service taxis: Sharia al-Karnak, near Luxor Museum. To Qena (1 hr., LE1), Esna (45 min., 60pt), Edfu (1½ hr., LE1.25), Kom Ombo (2-3 hr., LE1.50), and Aswan (3-4 hr., LE3-3.50).

Police: Tourist Police, Sharia el-Nil (tel. 821 20), in the tourist bazaar. Open daily 8am-midnight. Branch in train station. **Luxor Police** (tel. 820 06), just north of Luxor Temple off Sharia al-Karnak. **Passport Office,** Sharia el-Nil (tel. 823 18), next to ETAP Hotel. Register your passport or extend a visa here. Open Sat.-Thurs. 9am-2pm and 5-9pm. Come in the morning for visa business.

Bike Rental: Many shops charging LE1-2 per day. New Karnak Hotel obliges early morning requests (LE1.50 per day). Bikes are great for cruising Luxor streets in peace, and exploring West Thebes.

Accommodations and Food

Inexpensive hotels with variable sanitary facilities line both Sharia al-Mahatta and Sharia al-Karnak. Just start knocking on doors. Several homey **pensions** cluster west of the train station around Television Street. Summer rates (May-Oct.) can be as much as 50% lower than winter rates. The cheapest hotels raise prices only in December and January.

Youth Hostel (IYHF), Sharia al-Karnak (tel. 821 39). Relatively clean but a bit inconvenient—about halfway between Luxor and Karnak Temples (north of the service taxi station). Closed in 1987, but scheduled to reopen in 1988. Used to get very hot in summer; maybe they'll install air conditioning.

Negem El Din Pension, Sharia Ramses (tel. 823 52), next to the railway tracks. Basic rooms, moderately clean, and inexpensive. Pleasant garden. Stove, fridge, and wash basin available. The only drawback is the noise from the midnight train horns. LE2 per person in summer; LE3 in winter. Air-conditioned rooms 50pt extra. Omelette breakfast LE1.

New Karnak Hotel, opposite the train station (tel. 824 27). Clean, comfortable, with friendly management. Popular, so call ahead. Singles LE4, doubles LE5, with bath LE6.

Nile Hotel, Nefertiti St. (tel. 823 34), 200m north of Luxor Temple off the Nile. For those in search of air conditioning and carpeted comfort. Singles LE10, doubles LE15. Winter rates LE3-4 higher. Breakfast included.

Most of the inexpensive restaurants in Luxor huddle around the train station. The cheapest filling meal in town is in the **kushari restaurant** on your left as you walk down Sharia al-Mahatta from the train station. (15pt for a regular bowl, 30pt for a large plate.) For variety, try **New Karnak Restaurant,** next to the hotel of the same name. (¼ roast chicken LE1, rice with tomato sauce 25pt.) At the **Amoun Restaurant,** just north of Luxor Temple, a full meal costs LE2.50.

Sights

The graceful columns of **Luxor Temple** rise in the heart of Luxor town. The temple's interior is comprised of a blend of architectural styles from the New Kingdom through the Roman era, but holds together beautifully—especially at night when the dark, silky Nile moves silently past the illuminated interior. (Open in summer daily 6am-10pm; in winter daily 7am-9pm; Ramadan daily 6am-6:30pm and 8-11pm. Admission LE2, students LE1; no student discount in the evening.) The even more sumptuous **Karnak Temple,** dedicated to Amun, is the greatest monument to Thebes's ancient glory. Its **Great Hypostyle Hall,** a convocation of 134 colossal columns, is large enough to accommodate Paris's Notre Dame. (Open sunrise-6pm; in winter sunrise-5pm; in midsummer sunrise-7pm. Admission LE3, students LE1.50.) A melodramatic sound-and-light show draws crowds to Karnak every night. (Shows in English on Mon., Wed., and Sat. at 7pm, Fri. at 9pm. Admission LE5.) Halfway between the Luxor and Karnak Temples along the Nile is the **Luxor Museum,** Egypt's most aesthetically pleasing museum. (Open in summer daily 5-10pm; in winter daily 4-9pm; Ramadan daily 10am-2pm. Admission LE2, students LE1.)

Just across the river from Luxor (4 ferries per hr., 10-25pt), **West Thebes** overflows with a fabulous array of tombs, temples, and monuments stretched across seven square kilometers of desert. The **necropolis** is best explored in a series of short early morning visits, before the onslaught of sun and tour groups; arrive as near to opening time (6am) as possible. Plan your excursion carefully, as tickets for the sights are sold only at kiosks on the western bank of the river, several kilometers away from the sights themselves. There are two ticket kiosks, located far apart: The non-student kiosk is on the west bank next to the northern ferry dock; the student kiosk is 3km inland, near the necropolis. Separate admission tickets are sold in advance for each sight. (LE1 per antiquity except the Valley of Kings, which is LE5; students half-price.) Cycling is the most economical way to get around; rent a bike in Luxor before crossing the Nile. For groups, taxis are most reasonable; small cabs (1-4 passengers) charge LE10 for a five-hour tour, large cabs (5-8 passengers) are LE15. Last but not fast, plodding along on the back of a donkey offers the most picturesque, and in summer the most sizzling, alternative. (Don't pay more than LE2 per donkey, plus LE4 for the guide.) However you go, bring plenty of water and a flashlight—many of the tombs are dark.

The most magnificent site in West Thebes is the famed **Valley of the Kings,** about 8km from the West bank of the Nile, where the tombs are richly illuminated with painted decorative carvings. Don't miss the famous **Tomb of Tutankhamen** (#62), where King Tut's gilded coffin still lies, or the **Tomb of Seti I** (#17), the necropolis' largest and most ornamental burial chamber. The **Tomb of Amenhotep II** (#35) is perhaps the most beautiful; its interior was never plundered. On the left as you enter the valley, you'll see the **Tomb of Ramsis IX** (#6), celebrated for its depiction of the spirit's journey to the underworld. (All tombs open daily 6am-6pm.)

A number of imposing mortuary temples rest in West Thebes, the finest of which is three-tiered **Deir el Bahri,** erected by Queen Hatshepsut. Nearby, the **Ramasseum** houses a chunk of the enormous colossus which provided Shelley with the inspiration for his poem *Ozymandias.* Ruins of administrative buildings and the mortuary temple of Ramses III, the richest pharoah ever, constitute **Medinet Habu.** The crowded enclosures of the **Tombs of the Nobles** comprise over 300 tombs in all, with nine burial chambers of particular interest. The **Valley of the Queens** houses four outstanding tombs for wives and sons of the most powerful pharaohs, though they're now open only sporadically.

Near Luxor

Several well-preserved pharaonic and Ptolemaic temples overlook the Nile in Upper Egypt, easily accessible as day trips from Luxor. Go early to avoid scampering about ruins in the midday sun.

One hour north by taxi is the bustling town of **Qena** (60pt), the stopping-off point for the antiquities at **Dendera** and **Abydos.** The **Temple of Hathor** at Dendera, dating from the first century B.C.E., is graced with a massive hypostyle hall composed of 18 papyrus-shaped columns emblazoned with the cow-goddess's face. Take a shared taxi from Qena (20pt) to within 1km of the temple and walk the rest along the paved road that leads across a field. (Open daily 6am-6pm. Admission LE2, students LE1.)

A 1½-hour ride beyond Qena, near the village of **Al-Balyana** (LE2) is the famed **Temple of Seti I,** dedicated to Osiris and notable for its delicately painted murals and exquisite bas-reliefs. Constructed upon the site of the ancient city of Abydos, this imposing structure also houses the "King's List," a lengthy inscription which has enabled scholars to pinpoint the sequence of pharaohs from Menes of Memphis to Seti I. (Open daily 7am-6pm. Admission LE1, students 50pt.)

South of Luxor, and easily visited in a single daytrip, are the temples at **Esna** and **Edfu.** The first-century **Temple of Khnum** at Esna is a charming structure dedicated to the deity Khnum, who was believed to have fashioned humanity from clay on a great potter's wheel. (Open 7am-6pm. Admission LE1, students 50pt.) The lively **camel market** (daily 3-4pm) and the unspoiled village streets are themselves worth the trip (30 min., 50pt). From Esna it is a 45-minute bus or taxi ride to Edfu (75pt), home of Egypt's largest and best-preserved pharaonic temple, the **Temple of Horus,** one of the Ptolemies' last major attempts at monument building. (Open 7am-6pm. Admission LE2, students LE1.)

Aswan

Just downstream from the first cataract along the Nile, Aswan flourished as the frontier town of Egypt. A gateway to the desolate lands of Nubia (now inundated by Lake Nasser, a product of the High Dam), Aswan has the warmest and driest climate in Egypt and has consequently been developed as a winter resort. It has perhaps the cleanest and most picturesque streets and boulevards, and the lively evening *souk* (market) provides ample entertainment. The great numbers of Nubians in the city and its surrounding villages contribute to Aswan's warmhearted spirit and African élan. The city's riverside *corniche,* overlooking an archipelago of small fertile islands, is one of the most enchanting settings on the Nile. But around Aswan, the river Nile suddenly ceases to be sandwiched by green fields, coursing instead through the stark landscapes of the desert.

The southernmost city in Egypt, Aswan is 890km upstream from Cairo. To travel that distance, reserve a *wagon-lit* (first class, 2 per day, 16 hr., LE114; second class, 1 per day, 18 hr., LE71.40; second class needs to be booked at least a week in advance) or a seat on an air-conditioned train car (5 per day, 18-20 hr.; first class LE15.50, second class LE7.00). **Egypt Air** flies from Cairo (2-4 per day in summer, many more in winter; LE95.70). Frequent shared taxi, bus, and train service links Aswan to Luxor (220km north, LE3-4), Esna, Edfu, and Kom Ombo. Aswan's transportation hubs cluster in the northern half of the city.

You'll need at least three days to take in Aswan and the nearby attractions, including Abu Simbel. **Elephantine Island,** in the Nile opposite Aswan, draws visitors with its views of the Nubian landscape and minor pharaonic ruins at the northern tip. (Sites and archaeological museum with mummies open daily 8am-4pm, in summer 8am-5pm. Admission LE1, students 50pt.) **Kitchener's Island** (Geziret al-Nabatat or Botanical Island), Aswan's most enchanting spot, is one unbroken botanical garden where African and Asian species blossom in profusion. (Island open to tourists 8am-sunset. Admission 50pt.) On the west bank of the Nile, the impressive, modern **Mausoleum of Agha Khan** enshrines a deceased leader of the Ismaili sect. (Open Tues.-Sun. 9am-5pm. Dress respectfully. Free.) Directly inland from the mausoleum, **Dayr Amba Samaan** (Monastery of St. Simeon) is probably the best-preserved Coptic monastery in Egypt. Built in the sixth and seventh centuries and abandoned in the thirteenth, the monastery sits on a terrace carved into the steep hill. Rent a camel for LE2 (1 camel carries 2 people) and save yourself a 30-minute walk through stifling desert heat. (Open daily 9am-6pm. Admission LE1, students 50pt.) You can reach all of the above sights by hiring a *felucca* (sailboat). (Official rate for a 4-hr. trip to Elephantine, Kitchener's, and the west bank sites is LE8, regardless of the number of passengers. Add LE2 to include St. Simeon.) Two local ferries cross from Aswan to Elephantine Island. (4 per hr. 6am-9pm, 25pt for foreigners.)

The helpful **tourist office** (tel. 232 97) is four blocks west of the train station, one-half block in from the *corniche,* but is obscured by a small park. (Open daily 9am-2pm and 6-8pm; Ramadan daily 9am-3pm.) The **IYHF youth hostel,** 96 Sharia Abtal el Tahrir (tel. 223 13), is by the train station; the entrance for foreigners is at the side of the building. (Large, crowded rooms. Members 60pt, nonmembers 70pt. Lockout 10am-2pm.) If you're tired of the hostel scene but are pinched for piasters, try the amiable **Marwa Hotel,** (no phone), across the street and next to the cinema, with shabby but adequate rooms with fans for LE1 per person. To get to the well-managed **Rosewan Hotel** (tel. 244 97), turn right as you leave the train station, head past a gas station, and take the next left; the hotel is on the right in the middle of the following block. Women may feel most comfortable here. (Large rooms with fans. In summer, singles LE3, with shower LE4; doubles LE4, with shower LE6; triples LE7.50. 25% more Oct.-May.) The **Molla Hotel,** Kelanie St. (tel 222 78), 3 tangled blocks in from the Aswan Moon Restaurant and the *corniche,* is clean and comfortable for the price, with conscientious management and fans in every room. (Beds in shared room LE1.50; singles LE2; doubles LE3, with bath LE4; triples LE4.50. Oct.-May prices hiked 40%.) Money to spend? Try the **Ramsis Hotel,** Sharia Abtal al-Tahrir (tel. 240 00), near the bus station. The spacious, spotless rooms, are all air-conditioned with private bathrooms. (May-Oct. singles LE6, doubles LE9, triples LE13. In winter add LE4.)

For Aswan's tastiest cheap meals, head for the unassuming **El Madena Restaurant,** Sharia al-Suq, 2½ blocks south of the train station. A chicken or meat dish with rice, potatoes, salad, bread, and zesty tahina goes for LE1.65. Along the *corniche,* **Monalisa, Aswan Moon,** and **El Shati** all offer excellent afternoon and evening meals in their riverside cafes for about LE2. Sample their fresh juices and delicious ice cream. Sip tea in the evening market on Sharia al-Suq at **Al Nasr Club.** (The *souk* is liveliest 8-10pm.)

Near Aswan

Ten kilometers south of the town looms Egypt's most recent exercise in monumentalism, the controversial **Aswan High Dam,** completed in 1971. Three kilometers wide and 100m high, with enough room on the top for a two-lane highway, the dam powers the nation. Its planners justified the tragic inundation of Nubia and the loss of the Nile's rejuvenating silt with praise for the project's flood-controlling capacities and its ensuring a steady source of water for irrigation. For LE10 to 15, a **service taxi** is yours for a day, and you can visit **Philae,** the **Unfinished Obelisk,** the **Fatimid Tombs,** and Aswan's great granite quarries. Otherwise, take the train to Saddel-Ali and walk to the dam.

Make every effort to see the island of **Philae,** a collection of ruins situated in the backwaters of the original **Aswan Dam,** completed in 1910. The Ptolemaic **Temple of Isis,** a collection of pylons and colonnades, focuses on a small inner sanctum. Its reliefs are all easily decipherable, with portrait after portrait of the deities Osiris, Isis, and Horus. Take the Hazan bus to the old Aswan Dam and then walk east along the shore to the spot where boats depart for the island. (Open daily 7am-6pm;

Ramadan daily 7am-4pm. Admission LE3, students LE1.50. Boats to the island cost LE6 and can take up to 8 people.)

Forty kilometers north of Aswan is **Kom Ombo,** home of the most romantically situated pharaonic ruin along this stretch of the Nile. The **Temple of Sobek and Horus,** perched above the banks of the gliding river, is as unique for its location as for its symmetrical construction. Erected in honor of the gods Sobek the Crocodile and Horus, a sun god represented as a falcon, or a falcon-headed man, the temple was built in a mirror-like configuration: Not wanting to offend either god, the diplomatic priests of Kom Ombo ordered everything to be built in tandem. (Open daily 6am-6pm. Admission LE1, students 50pt.) Take a taxi, bus or train from Aswan for 50pt-LE1.

Nothing but lake, lunar landscape, and spectacular **Abu Simbel** lie in the desert 274km south of the High Dam. The Great Temple of Abu Simbel, hewn out of a cliff, features four gargantuan statues of its builder Ramses II staring majestically into the rising sun. Together with the nearby **Temple of Hathor,** dedicated to Nefertari, Ramses's beloved wife, the Great Temple was taken apart in large blocks and moved to higher ground when rising Lake Nasser threatened to engulf the site. This UNESCO project cost US$36 million and involved the construction of a hollow mountain. (Admission LE6.50, students LE3.50. Includes a guided tour.)

Buses for Abu Simbel leave from the Aswan bus station every morning at 8am. They arrive at the temple at 11:30am and leave at 2:30pm to arrive in Aswan at 6pm (LE8 each way); bring snacks and water. Purchase your ticket at the station at least one day in advance. Egypt Air flies out to Abu Simbel from Aswan several times per day for a whirlwind tour; the round-trip costs a whopping LE84.90.

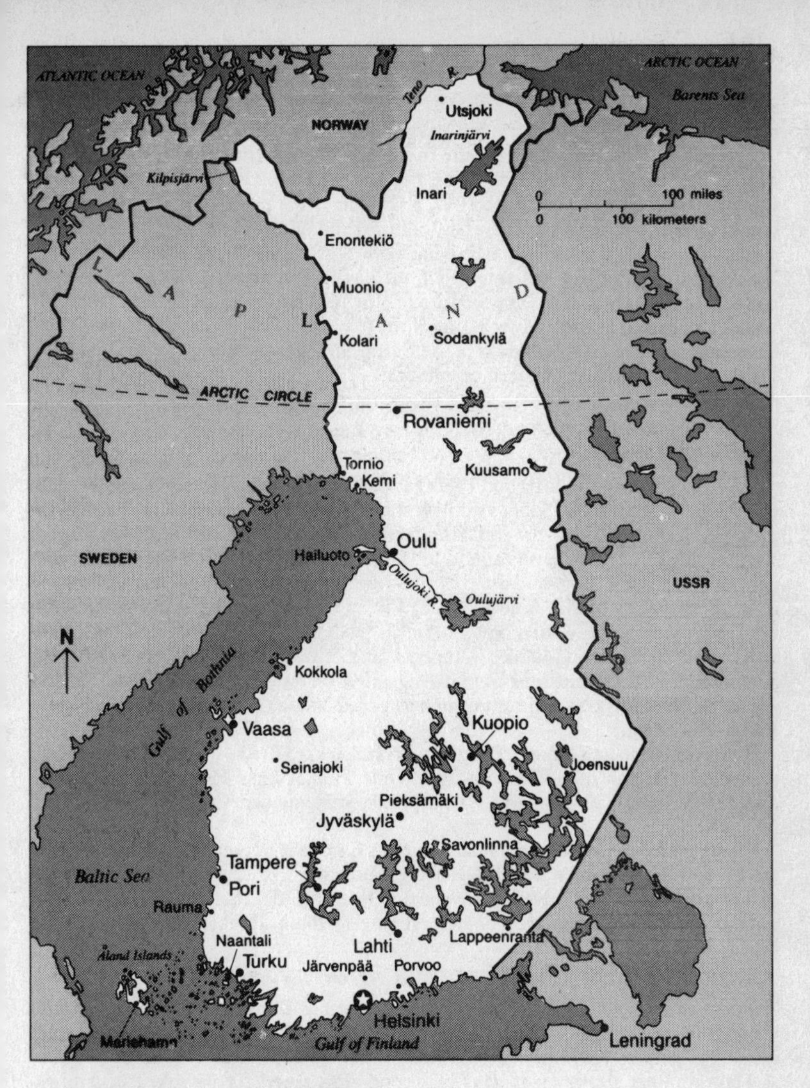

FINLAND

US$1 = 4.35 markka (mk)	**1mk = US$0.23**
CDN$1 = 3.33mk	**1mk = CDN$0.30**
UK£1 = 7.18mk	**1mk = UK£0.13**
AUS$1 = 3.13mk	**1mk = AUS$0.32**

Between the Scandinavian peninsula and the Russian wilderness rests an expanse of trees, water, and clear air, inhabited by an unusual people. The Finns have perfected the art of living in harmony with nature, and exult in their unspoiled land. Their enthusiasm is reflected in the aesthetic honesty of Finland's acclaimed architects and textile designers, in village market displays, and in the cool, clean lines of Helsinki's neoclassical center. To themes of comfort and simplicity, the Finnish environment adds a drama of opposing extremes, where darkness disappears in summer and winter daylight seems but passing fancy.

Finland's culture and language are markedly different from those of either Sweden or Russia, yet for centuries these neighbors have played political catch with Finland. Independent only since 1917, a portion of the population is still Swedish speaking, and Finland's strongest ties, political and otherwise, are with the Scandinavian countries. Successfully surviving both Soviet and German attacks during World War II, Finland has emerged from physical devastation with strong economic and military policies appropriate to a neutral nation at an ideological crossroads. The Finns see themselves as one of the few neutral countries in Europe—they have long declined representation in the European Parliament because of what they see as that body's clear Western orientations. They maintain strong economic and diplomatic relations with both the EEC countries and the USSR.

Getting There

Even deck passage on **Silja** and **Viking Lines** will allow you to travel from Sweden to Finland in high style. Silja's two new ships, *Svae* and *Wellamo,* have bunk beds in large sleeping rooms. Several Silja ferries depart daily from Stockholm. (To Turku 115mk or 152 Swedish kronor, to Helsinki 180mk or 240kr. Free with Eurailpass and Nordturist from mid-June to mid-Aug. Students and InterRail passholders 25% off; mid-Aug. to mid-June 50% off.) **Viking Line** sails Kapellskär-Mariehamn-Naantali twice per day each way (105mk), Stockholm to Helsinki (175mk), and Stockholm to Turku (140mk); (students and Eurail, InterRail, or Nordturist passholders 25% off mid-June to mid-Aug., 50% off mid-Aug. to mid-June). There are many other less traveled routes such as Umeå-Vaasa (50-80mk), and Sundsvall-Vaasa (60-100mk).

Polferries connect Gdánsk, Poland, with Helsinki (370mk; students or InterRail passholders 220mk mid-May to Aug.), while **Finnjet** links Helsinki with Travemünde, Germany (530mk peak, 410 off-peak, students and InterRail passholders 50% discount).

Flying between Helsinki and many cities in Europe is not terribly expensive with the **Finnair International Youth Discount.** Those aged 26 and under who book no earlier than one day in advance are entitled to a 66% discount; you'll save lots of time at the least (Copenhagen 535mk, Brussels 910mk, Paris 1130mk).

Transportation and Practical Information

Trains in Finland cover the country as far north as Kemijärvi. They are fast and very comfortable, but quite expensive: Helsinki-Oulu (680km) is 150mk, and Helsinki-Tampere (187km) is 51mk. Both Eurail and InterRail (975mk) are valid. A **Finnrail Pass** allows eight days of second-class travel for 390mk, and entitles you to free seat reservations. (15 days 550mk, 22 days 700mk.) The **Nordturist** pass (called **Pohjolaa Junalla** in Finland) allows 21 days of unlimited travel in Denmark, Sweden, Norway, and Finland for 935mk. Seat reservations cost 8mk on both express trains *(pikajuna)* and others, though they are usually unnecessary. *Erikoispikajunat* are special express trains requiring a reservation, though this can usually be purchased just before departure (13mk, except 20mk on the Botnia Express to Tampere). A bed in a sleeping car (all doubles) costs more than most youth hostels. (Sun.-Thurs. 46mk, Fri.-Sat. 56mk.) It's a good idea to reserve them a day in advance, especially on Friday night trains.

A multitude of private bus companies, as well as the public postal line, service all corners of the country. Fares are standard, and roughly equal to train fares, though express buses charge a 5mk surcharge. The **Bussilomalippu** pass offers 1000km of travel within two weeks for 210mk, and earns a 20% reduction on train trips over 75km. Pick up a nationwide bus schedule at tourist ofices and bus stations.

Finnair flights are relatively cheap, and will save you lots of time: Helsinki-Rovaniemi takes one hour and costs 278mk. In addition, there is a 50% year-round

Youth Discount for those under 24, and a 50% discount for everyone on specified round-trip flights called "red routes." The **Finnair Holiday Ticket** gives you 15 days of unlimited air travel for US$260.

Hitchhikers often delight in Finland—the people are friendly and the roads good, though experiences and weather can vary. To facilitate wanderings by thumb, purchase one of the series of GT maps which cover the whole country thoroughly. Good maps for hiking and boating are available at Karttakeskus, Eteläesplanadi 4, in Helsinki (on Market Square).

Cycling is an excellent way to travel around Finland or to enjoy a daytrip. You can usually rent bikes at campgrounds and bike shops, and occasionally at youth hostels and tourist offices; 25mk per day is normal. Tandems are also available.

Stores close early—4 to 5pm Monday through Friday and around 1pm on Saturday. This is especially true in the countryside. In cities, the largest supermarkets may be open until 8pm, but only Monday through Friday. Kiosks sell basic food, snacks, and toilet articles usually until 9pm, sometimes 11pm.

Local calls cost 1mk for a surprisingly short time, so always keep extra coins on hand—most payphones take only 1mk coins. Rates (domestic and international) drop at 10pm and on weekends. Call 920 20 for international information, 920 23 for price estimates, 920 22 to place a collect call, and 000 in emergencies.

Not an Indo-European language, Finnish is virtually impenetrable to foreigners. Nouns change their endings to indicate meanings such as "to" and "in;" watch out for town names that modify their form on train schedules, etc. Many Finns speak English, but older people, especially in remote areas, often do not. Swedish is the official second language and, especially in the south and along the western coast, many signs are in both languages. "M" and "N" on bathroom doors mean "men" and "women" respectively.

You haven't been to Finland until you've been in a Finnish **sauna,** a national invention and passion. A few public communal saunas remain in larger cities, costing 15-20mk per person. Finns use small birch twigs to slap their skins and thus improve their circulation; the leaves are wonderfully scented.

Accommodations, Camping, and Food

Youth hostels are definitely the cheapest accommodations with a roof. There are 160 hostels in Finland, 40 of which stay open year-round; many summer hostels are housed in school dormitories. Prices are based on a four-star system and range from 22mk to (rarely) 100mk. The nicest hostels often include saunas. If you don't have your own sheets, you'll have to buy paper ones for 20mk; sleeping bags are accepted. The **Finnish Youth Hostel Association** (Suomen Retkeilymajajärjestö) is located at Yrjönkatu 38B, Helsinki (tel. (08) 69403 77). As in Sweden and Norway, you may camp anywhere, though it's customary to pitch your tent out of sight of homes. A network of official campgrounds covers the country, offering many amenities, occasionally saunas. They range in price from 10 to 50mk per night.

A Finnish *baari* is not a bar, but a cafe which serves food, coffee, and occasionally beer. *Kahvilas* also serve food, and are often a bit nicer. *Ravintola* is a restaurant, which often turns into a place to dance or drink beer toward the end of the evening. If so, you are not required to dine, but you must usually pay a cover charge (10mk and up), and tip the person at the door a few marks. The standard minimum age is 18, but some places range all the way up to 24; age is usually checked carefully. Prices for alcohol are quite high. Service is included in the bill in Finland, so you need not tip (the bill is often rounded up). *Grillit* are Finnish fast-food stands; patronized mostly late at night, they offer hamburgers, sausages, and *lihapiirakat* (meat pies).

As in Scandinavia, lunch is the cheapest meal, and almost all restaurants offer special fixed menus. In northern Finland it is not uncommon for this special to be an all-you-can-eat buffet (25-40mk), and occasionally lunch hours extend well into the afternoon.

Marketplaces exist in most towns, but you'll actually find the large department store supermarkets cheaper. Keep an eye open for a large K sign; Alepa and Valintatalo stores can be especially cheap. A twisted pretzel symbol denotes a bakery.

Finland abounds in regional specialties. Often you can try these from a *Finlandia Menu,* offered at restaurants throughout the country. There are dozens of ways of serving fish, from *silli,* Baltic herring, to *lohi,* salmon (if you can afford it). In midsummer, salmon is often made into soup. *Karjalan piirakat* are a Karelian specialty, but you can find these small rice porridge pies in any store. *Kalakukko,* an east Finnish specialty, is a bread filled with fish and meat, also found all around Finland. Staples of the Finnish diet include *ruisleipa,* the deliciously strong Finnish rye bread, delicious cheeses, and *viili,* a yogurt-like product that slides off your spoon. In July and August, forests are full of blueberries, lingonberries, cranberries, and, in the far north, Arctic cloudberries—though the last are not to be picked by visitors.

Åland Islands (Ahvenanmaa)

Geographic and cultural stepping stones in the Baltic, the Swedish-speaking Åland (pronounced Oh-lant) Islands form a bridge between Finland and Sweden. When Sweden ceded Finland to Russia in 1809, Åland went with it. Finland gained its independence in 1917, but refused to grant the Ålanders' desire to be part of Sweden. Since 1951, though, Åland has been an autonomous territory within Finland, and the islanders vigilantly minimize Finnish influence. Only Swedish is spoken here, and Finns who wish to live in Åland must demonstrate their knowledge of Swedish. For the visitor the islands may seem an unlikely spot for controversy, their gentle landscape better suited for leisurely hikes, bike rides, and basking in the sun.

The **Viking** and **Silja Lines** sail daily between Mariehamn, Åland's capital, and Stockholm and Turku. (To Turku 70mk or 94 Swedish kr, to Stockholm 45mk or 60kr.) Viking offers a 50% discount to students and holders of Eurail, InterRail, and Nordturist from mid-August to mid-June, and a 25% discount from mid-June to mid-August. Silja offers students a 25% discount from mid-June to mid-August (excluding Fri. night departures), and InterRail passholders a 50% discount year-round; you're entitled to free boat passage with Eurailpass or Nordturist. The **Birka Line's** *Princessen* sails daily between Stockholm and Mariehamn for 22.50mk (June-Dec.), and the **Eckerö Line** sails from Eckerö, on Åland, to Grisslehamn in Sweden, with bus connections to both Mariehamn and Stockholm (24.50mk, students and journalists 15.50mk). Inter-island ferry traffic is considered an extension of the road system and is free, although there is a 30mk fee whenever the border of the Turku archipelago is crossed.

Åland is great for biking. The **Geta, Saltvik,** and **Sund** districts in the north are hilly and offer spectacular fjord scenery, remnants of Stone Age settlements, the thirteenth-century **Kastelholm Castle** and its historical museum, and **Jan Karlsgården**, an open-air museum. To the east, **Lemland** and **Lumparland** have flatter terrain. From Långnäs, ferries shuttle to and from the more distant island clusters of Brändö, Kumlinge, Sottunga, Föglö, and Kökar, where tourist traffic is even lighter. The tourist office's *Cykla På Åland* brochure is in Swedish, but can be helpful in planning itineraries. For bike rental, most convenient is **RoNo Rent** (tel. 128 21), right across from the ferry terminal, with branches in Österhamn and Västerhamn. (19mk per day, 95mk per week. Also rent mopeds, boats, etc . . . . Open June-Aug. daily 9am-noon and 1-6pm; May and Sept. call for arrangements.)

Åland's only towns are Mariehamn and Eckerö, 30 miles apart. Both are pleasant, a fact known by too many vacationers. In Mariehamn, **tourist information** is at Storagatan 18 (tel. (928) 165 75), five minutes north on Havsgatan from the Viking/Silja terminal. The helpful staff can give you maps and a copy of *Ålandstrafiken,* containing transportation schedules for all traffic to, from, and within the islands. *Åland* magazine (in English) is also full of useful information. (Open June-Aug. daily 9am-6pm; Sept.-May Mon.-Fri. 9am-5pm.) For help with rooms, cross the park to **Ålandsresor,** Norra Esplanadgatan 1 (tel. (928) 121 40). This office handles booking for all the islands; whether in town or on the outer islands, you can always call them for help, though you won't escape the 20mk fee. (Open Mon.-Fri. 9am-5pm, Sat. 9am-1pm.) To make advance reservations from Helsinki, visit Ålandresor's office at Bulevardi 3 B 14 (tel. 60 50 88).

Hotels in Åland are expensive, but rooms to let are much more common here than in Finland proper. Ålandsresor can set you up with a room for a 20mk fee (singles 80mk, doubles 50-70mk, triples 48-60mk; all prices per person). The room situation improves on the more remote islands, and you may be able to find bed and breakfast in a pension for about 100mk per person. Campgrounds often rent cottages for considerably less than more sophisticated accommodations (2 persons 140mk, 3 for 165mk, 4 for 190mk). Freelance camping is not permitted in Åland without the landowner's say-so, but the 10 campgrounds are not as expensive as on the mainland (5-9mk per person, 5-9mk per tent), and on islands without them you should have no difficulty getting permission.

Åland's only **youth hostel (IYHF)** (tel. 384 70) in Eckerö may be closed in 1988. If it isn't, then take the Eckerö bus (14mk) from the Mariehamn bus station and ask the driver to drop you off at the hostel. (35mk. Open June-Sept.) In **Djurvik,** on the way to Eckerö, there is a reasonable hotel, a bit closer to Mariehamn but difficult to reach. You must take the bus to Gottby (9km), then walk 4-5km to the hotel; the light traffic makes hitching difficult. Once there the trek will seem worthwhile: **Djurviks Gästgård** (tel. 324 33) sits on a secluded inlet with wonderful fishing and swimming. Call ahead or contact Ålandsresor. (Singles 95mk, doubles and triples 80mk per person. Breakfast available.)

Campground Gröna Udden (tel. 110 41) is only 10 minutes from downtown Mariehamn (walk down Skillnadgatan), located on the water, with swimming nearby. (9mk per person, 9mk per tent. Open June-Aug.) Even cheaper is **Hummelvik** in Eckerö (tel. 383 11). Take the bus to Handelslagan and walk 2km. (5mk per person, 5mk per tent.)

Budget restaurants are scarce in tourist-conscious Mariehamn, but there's a **market** at the corner of Norragaten and Ålandsvägen. (Open Mon.-Fri. 9am-8pm, Sat. 9am-5pm, Sun. 10am-4pm.) Just downstairs, **Pizzeria Oasen** offers an ample lunch special for 25mk. (Open Mon.-Fri. 11am-midnight, Sat.-Sun. 1pm-midnight; lunch special 11am-7pm.) Mariehamn's cafes offer a chance to compare Finnish and Swedish varieties of pastry in old-fashioned settings. Sample the famous *Ålands pannkaka,* a large pancake spiced with cardamon, often served with marmalade and whipped cream. Try **Amanda Kaffestuga,** Norragatan 15, or **Cafe Katrina,** at Torgatan across from the marketplace. (Open Mon.-Fri. 9am-7pm, Sat. 9am-5pm, Sun. noon-5pm.)

Turku

The country's oldest city, Turku evolved from a trading outpost into Finland's first capital and premier town. In 1812 time overtook Turku, and the government shifted to Helsinki to be closer to the new ruler, Alexander I of Russia. Fifteen years later the university followed suit, and as a final blow 2500 wooden buildings burned to the ground in the worst fire in Scandinavian history. Today both Helsinki and Tampere are larger cities, but Turku retains a stronger link with Finland's past. Completed in 1300, the massive, white, vaulted **cathedral** speaks of a time when Turku was the center for the spiritual and commercial colonization of the Finnish hinterland. (Open June-Aug. Mon.-Fri. 9am-7pm, Sat. 9am-3pm, Sun. 2:30-4:30pm; Sept.-May Mon.-Fri. 10am-4pm, Sat. 10am-3pm, Sun. 2:30-4:30pm. Concerts in summer Tues. at 8pm. Free.) Small-town charm lingers along the banks of the Aura and in the gardens behind the **Turku Art Gallery.** (Open Mon.-Sat. 10am-4pm, Thurs. 10am-4pm and 6-8pm, Sun. 10am-6pm. Admission 8mk, students 5mk.) **Luostarinmäki,** at Luostarinkatu 1, across the river from Market Sq., is a good crafts museum. (Open May-Sept. daily 10am-6pm; Oct.-April daily 11am-

3pm. Admission 3mk). The intriguing **Wäinö Aaltonen Museum,** Itäinen Rantakatu 38, houses works by the renowned Finnish sculptor. (Open Mon.-Fri. 10am-4pm, Sat. 10am-4pm, Sun. 10am-6pm. Admission 3mk, children 2mk.) The **Sibelius Museum,** at Piispankatu 17, contains many original Sibelius scores and an interesting collection of musical instruments. (Open May-Sept. daily 11am-3pm; Oct.-April daily noon-3pm. Admission 5mk, students 1.50mk.)

Eight-hundred-year-old **Turku Castle** owes its impressive proportions to the town's days as the seat of the Grand Duchy under the Swedish crown. Today, its restored interiors are a tasteful combination of medieval artifacts and modern design. Besides ducal chambers and banquet halls, the castle houses a fine **Historical Museum** featuring a fascinating collection of ethnic objects and folk art. (Open May-Sept. daily 10am-6pm; Oct.-April daily 10am-3pm. Admission 3mk.)

The friendly **Central Tourist Office** is at Käsityöläiskatu 3 (tel. 33 63 66). (Open June-Aug. Mon.-Fri. 8am-5pm; Sept.-May Mon.-Fri. 8:30am-4pm.) You can also get help with accommodations from the tourist office at the station (open June-Aug. Mon.-Fri. 9:30am-7:30pm, Sat.-Sun. 9:30am-2:30pm), or the harbor information office (desk at Silja Line open daily 7:30am-12:30pm and 6-9:30pm). Another office is downtown at Aurakatu 4 (tel. 152 62), near the city hall. (Open Mon.-Fri. 8:30am-8pm, Sat. 8:30am-6pm, Sun. 8:30am-3pm.)

As in the rest of Finland, accommodations in Turku are relatively expensive. The city hostel may save you; **Kaupungin Retkeilymaja (IYHF)** is at Linnankatu 39 (tel. (921) 165 78), by the River Aura, 1km toward the harbor from Market Sq. Take bus #1 from the harbor or Market Sq. It's friendly, comfortable and clean, with a nicely equipped kitchen. (40mk. Check-in 3pm-midnight. Lockout 10am-3pm. Open year-round. Call ahead in July and Aug.) **Matkakievari Matdustajokodit,** Läntinen Pitkäkatu 8 (tel. (921) 32 72 08), near the train station, offers the next cheapest bed (singles 110mk, doubles 150mk, triples 190mk). **Camping Ruissalo** (tel. (921) 30 66 49), 12km out, has good facilities: a sauna, beach, and water slide. Take bus #8 from Market Sq. (2 per hr., 6.20mk). (Open June-Aug.)

Visit the elaborate indoor market, **Kauppahalli,** at Eerikinkatu 16, and sample mouth-watering pastries, breads, and various regional specialties. (Open Mon.-Fri. 8am-5pm, Sat. 8am-2pm.) Regular markets are open until 8pm weekdays. For vegetarian food try **Verso** located in a peaceful old wooden house by the river, at Linnankatu 3a. You can get full plate of tasty fare for 30-35mk, or delicious soup and salad for 22-28mk. (Open Mon.-Fri. 11am-4pm.) If you tire of pizza, eat surrounded by antiques in the timbered attic of **Ravintola Ja Kahvinuone Lyra,** Humalistonkatu 4. An old singers' guild, it serves good large meals for 25-50mk. (Open June-Aug. daily noon-7pm; Sept.-May Sat.-Sun. only.)

Turku has a fine collection of cafes and evening spots. **Mämeenportti,** Hämeekatu 7, is a favorite with students. (Open Mon.-Sat. 10:30am-1am, Sun. 4pm-1am.)

Near Turku

The sea has long exercised a telling influence on the area around Turku. Take an excursion to one of the islands or small coastal villages to see first-hand its importance to the archipelago; wherever you go, trade and fishing will be part of the present as much as of the past.

Naantali makes a pleasant boat trip from Turku, though buses cost about half as much and run frequently. Boats depart from near the bridge at Auransilta. (Mon.-Fri.at noon, Sun. at 11am and 2pm. 25mk round-trip.) Although the village is a popular excursion spot, it has preserved the charm of old wooden buildings, narrow streets, and long history. Naantali's **tourist office** is at Tullikatu 12 (tel. 75 53 88). (Open Mon.-Fri. 8:30am-3:30pm.) **Naantali Yacht Harbor Tourist Information** is at Mannerheiminkatu 2 (tel. (921) 75 53 92). (Open June 12-19 daily 9am-8pm; June 20 to Aug.10 daily 9am-10pm; Aug. 11-31 daily 11am-6pm.) The **Naantali Music Festival,** held each year in late June, features good performances of classical music. On **Sleepyhead's Day** (July 27), the town hosts Finland's largest festival: The highlight occurs in the early morning, when a well-known guest or resident is woken by surprise and thrown into the sea.

Rauma, about 100km north of Turku, is Finland's best preserved medieval community, famous for seafaring, lace making, and an incomprehensible dialect. Rauma is most easily reached by bus from Turku (10 per day, 1½ hr., 32mk one way). Hitching is quite easy as well. The **Rauma Museum** in Market Square will give you an idea of the area's history. (Open Tues.-Fri. 10am-4pm, Tues. 10am-4pm and 6-8pm, Sat. 10am-2pm, Sun. 11am-5pm.) Look into the fifteenth-century **monastery church,** still in use at the corner of Isopoikkikatu and Luostarinkatu. The **Rauma Lace Festival,** held in late July, celebrates the craft with exhibits, music, and plays. The **tourist office,** Eteläkatu 7 (tel. (938) 22 45 55), is down Nortamonkatu from the bus station. (Open June-Aug. Mon.-Fri. 8am-4pm, Sat. 10am-1pm; Sept.-May Mon.-Fri. only.) It's worth spending the night here just for the **IYHF youth hostel** (tel. 22 46 66). Situated on the water, the old wooden building is 1km down Osmonkatu from the train station. (32mk. No breakfast, but kitchen and sauna available. Open mid-May to Aug.)

Helsinki

Approach Helsinki from the sea, and you meet neoclassical buildings of serene lines and pastel colors, and a marketplace overflowing with strawberries and salmon. The city has grown with attention to harmony, and new and old mesh in calm elegance. In summer many residents abandon Helsinki for their country cottages, but in winter the capital comes alive with theater, political institutes, and some 20,000 university students.

Orientation and Practical Information

Helsinki is on a peninsula at the southern tip of Finland. Ferries connect the city with Stockholm, Travemünde, Germany, and Gdańsk, Poland. To get your bearings, take a round- (or, rather, figure-8) trip aboard tram #3T, which you can catch on Aleksanderinkatu—between the tram station and Market Square—or along Mannerheimintie, the main drag starting near the post office. (Quatrilingual commentary May-Aug. Mon.-Fri. 10am-3pm and 6-8pm, Sat.-Sun. 9am-8pm.) All streets have both a Finnish and Swedish name—we list the Finnish.

Tourist Offices: Kaupungin Matkailutoimisto, Pohjoisesplanadi 19 (tel. 169 37 57), next to Market Sq. Friendly, helpful advice, and a free phone for calling accommodations. Open mid-May to mid-Aug. Mon.-Fri. 8:30am-6pm, Sat. 8:30am-1pm, closed Sun.; mid-Sept. to mid-May Mon. 8:30am-4:30pm, Tues.-Fri. 8:30am-4pm, closed Sat.-Sun. **Hotellikeskus** (Hotel Booking Center), Asemaaukio 3 (tel. 17 11 33), between the post office and the train station. Primarily room-finding (10mk fee for a private room, 5mk for a hostel bed), but also city maps, youth hostel lists, and useful brochures. Very friendly. Open in summer Mon.-Fri. 9am-9pm, Sat. 9am-7pm, Sun. 10am-6pm; in winter Mon.-Fri. 9am-6pm. **Finnish Tourist Board,** Asemapäällikönkatu 12b (tel. 14 45 11). Take bus #17 on Mikonkatu (about 15 min.). Useful information on the whole country, including a list of campsites. Open in summer Mon.-Fri. 8am-3:15pm; in winter Mon.-Fri. 8am-4:15pm. **Finnish Youth Hostel Association,** Yrjönkatu 38 (tel. 694 03 77), on the south side of the bus station. Come here if you plan to hike—the helpful staff arranges accommodations in all refuges in Lapland. They also have lists of hostels throughout the country. Open Mon.-Fri. 9am-4pm. **Forest Council of Finland,** Erottajankatu 2 (tel. 616 31), near Eteläesplanadi, behind Stockman's department store. Maps and lists of free huts in Finland's wilderness; excellent camping and hiking advice. Call **Helsinki Today** (tel. 058) for a recording in English of tourist events. **News in English** (tel. 040).

Budget Travel: Travela, Mannerheimintie 5 (tel. 62 41 01), in the first block on the right as you exit the train station. Sells student IDs, including the IUS card (for students traveling to Eastern Europe), BIGE tickets, and other money-saving deals. Arranges English tours to Leningrad (4 days, 835mk) and Moscow (5 days, 1280mk). 7- to 10-day wait for visas. Open Mon.-Fri. 9am-5pm.

American Express: Travek Travel, Katajanokan Pohjoisranta 9-13 (tel. 66 16 31), behind the Uspensky Cathedral, east of Market Sq. Mail held, currency exchange and check sales, but no wired money accepted. Open Mon.-Fri. 8am-4:30pm.

Currency Exchange: Most banks open Mon.-Fri. 9:15am-4:15pm. Rates and fees the same at the train station as in banks, except after 4pm when they charge 4mk for exchanges of 50-199mk. Open daily 11:30am-6pm. Also at the airport (open 6:30am-11pm), and at Olympic Harbor (open daily 9am-noon and 3-6pm).

Post Office: Mannerheimintie 11 (tel. 195 51 17), next to the station. Open Mon.-Fri. 9am-5pm. Poste Restante open Mon.-Sat. 8am-10pm, Sun. 11am-10pm. Stamps available in railway station booth Mon.-Fri. 7:15am-8pm, Sat.-Sun. 10am-8pm. **Postal code:** 00100.

Telephones: Mannerheimintie 11, next to the post office. Open daily 7am-11pm. **Telephone code:** 90.

Flights: Sirola Company bus #615 runs frequently between the airport and platform #12 in the train station (5:25am-11:50pm, 9mk). The Finnair bus is more expensive and leaves you in a less convenient location, at the Finnair terminal at Töölankatu 21. Information: Tel. 41 04 11.

Trains: In the center of town. Service throughout the country and to the Soviet Union. Information: Tel. 65 94 11.

Buses: Long-distance buses depart from the square between Salomonkatu and Simonkatu. Purchase tickets on board or in the train station. Information: Tel. 60 21 22.

Ferries: A short walk along the pier will bring you to Market Sq. Tram #3T runs to the center of town.

Public Transportation: Trams and buses run until about 1:15am, though the Metro stops Mon.-Fri. before 11pm. 5.80mk for 1 hr. of travel, with free transfers. **10-trip tickets** are 47mk. The **Tourist Ticket** (37mk) allows unlimited use of trams, buses, and some ferries for 24 hours. Both available at Hotellikeskus. The **Helsinki Card** entitles you to free public transportation and free admission to some museums, as well as discounts at various hotels, restaurants, and stores. At 55mk for 1 day, 75mk for 2 days, and 90mk for 3 days, it probably won't pay for itself.

Bike Rental: At the Olympic Stadium youth hostel. 25mk per day, tandem 30mk per day.

Emergencies: Police (tel. 002); headquarters at Olavinkatu 1 (tel. 694 06 33). **Ambulance** (tel. 000).

Medical Assistance: Meilahti Hospital, Haartmaninkatu 4 (tel. 47 11), receives foreigners. Take tram #4 north on Mannerheimintie to Nordenskiöldinkatu, then left up Messeniuksenkatu. Buses #14 and 18 go direct.

Embassies: U.S., Itöinen Puistotie 14b (tel. 17 19 31). **Canada,** Pohjoiesplanadi 25b (tel. 17 11 41), on the corner of Fabianinkatu. **U.K.,** Uudenmaankatu 16-20 (tel. 64 79 22). **USSR,** Tehtaankatu, (tel. 66 18 76). Travelers from **Australia** and **New Zealand** should contact the British Embassy.

Bookstore: Academic Bookstore, Keskuskatu 1, has a huge selection of books in English. Open Mon.-Wed. and Fri. 9am-8pm, Thurs. 9am-7pm, Sat. 9am-4pm.

Public Sauna: Pietkarinkatu 14 (tel. 66 26 98), near Kaivopusto Park. 20mk. Birch twigs 12mk. Open Wed.-Fri. 2-7pm, Sat. 2-5pm.

Laundry: Look for the words "Itsepalvelu Pesula." Facility at Suonionkatu 1, near the Nuorisotoimiston hostel, is open Mon.-Fri. 8am-5pm, Sat. 8am-1pm.

Accommodations

Hostels in Helsinki span the range of price and quality. In July and August they are often crowded, so it is wise to call ahead. Hotels are uniformly expensive; if you find yourself stuck inquire at Hotellikeskus about special summer rates (from 200mk per double).

Retkeilymaja Academica (IYHF), Hietaniemenkatu 14 (tel. 44 01 71). Walk 10 min. down Mannerheimintie to Arkadiankatu, then turn left via Lapuank to Hietaniemenkatu; or take bus #18 or tram #3T. A conveniently located university dormitory. Clean, comfortable rooms with kitchen facilities and showers. Pool and sauna (extra fee). Singles 110mk, doubles 55mk, triples 35mk. All prices per person. Open June-Aug.

Stadionin Retkeilymaja (IYHF), Pohjoinen Stadionintie 3b (tel. 49 60 71), in the Olympic Stadium complex. Take tram #3T or walk 25 min. from the train station. Enormous, crowded, and noisy. Announcements blasted on loudspeakers. Kitchen and TV room. Dorm beds 27mk, doubles 76mk, triples 96mk. Small breakfast 17mk. Lockout 10am-4pm. 2am curfew; late fee of 2mk after 11pm. Open year-round.

Nuorisotoimiston Retkeilymaja, Porthaniankatu 2 (tel. 709 95 90), 3 min. north on Siltasaarenkatu from Hakaniementori. From the station, take tram #3B, 7, or 10; from Market Sq., tram #1 or 2. Get off at Hakaniemi Sq. Small and friendly; run by Helsinki's youth organization. TV room and excellent kitchen facilities. Fills up, so call for reservations. 30mk. Sheets 10mk. Open mid-May to Aug.

Hotel Satakuntatalu, Lapinrinne 1 (tel. 694 03 11). A cozy, clean summer hotel near a park. Phone in every room. Singles 145mk, doubles 210mk, triples 270mk, quads 330mk. 10% discount with student card. Open late May to mid-Aug.

Rastila Camping (tel. 31 65 51). Large, large, and large. 7km from the center; take the metro to Itäkeskus and then catch bus #90, 90A, or 96 (one 5.80mk ticket covers all). Good facilities. 20mk per person; families 40mk. Open mid-May to mid-Sept.

Food

Beat the high cost of sustenance with produce and fish at **Market Square,** near the port (open mid-May to mid-Sept. Mon.-Fri. 6:30am-2pm and 3:30-8pm; mid-Sept. to mid-May 6:30am-2pm only), and in the nearby indoor **Market Hall** (open Mon.-Fri. 8am-5pm, Sat. 8am-2pm). Don't overlook the best ice cream in town, sold at **Fazer** sweet shops—the one at Kluuvitatu 3 dishes out some wonderful stuff. Markets at the railway station metro entrance are open Mon.-Sat. 10am-10pm, Sun. noon-10pm.

Palace Cafe, Eteläranta 10, above the Palace Hotel. Abundant lunch specials: an entree, vegetable, dessert, bread and butter, and drink for 25mk. Eat on the terrace and enjoy the great view of the harbor and Market Sq. Open Mon.-Fri. 7am-5pm. Lunch served 10:30am-1:30pm.

Helsinki School of Economics Student Cafeteria, Runeberginkatu 14, near the Academica hostel. Light lunches (14-18mk) during the summer, full meals the rest of the year. Open in summer Mon.-Fri. 8:30am-2pm; in winter Mon.-Fri. 10am-6pm.

Kasvis, Korkeavuorenkatu 3, 10 min. south of Eteläesplanadi. Tasty vegetarian meals in an oh-so-mellow atmosphere. Soups 18-22mk, filling meals 20-39mk. Open Mon.-Fri. 11am-6pm, Sat.-Sun. noon-5pm. **Succis Konditoria,** across the street, serves scrumptious *korvapuusti* (coffee bread) for 5mk, and a wide assortment of teas for 4mk in a bamboo and palm tree setting. Open Mon.-Fri. 7:30am-9:30pm, Sat. 10am-6pm, Sun. 10am-9pm.

Bulevardin Kahvisalonki, Bulevardi 1. The place to enjoy a fruit pastry (7.50mk) and coffee (5mk). Open Mon.-Fri. 8am-10pm, Sat. 10am-10pm, Sun. 10am-9pm.

Kreisi, Bulevardi 7 (tel. 61 10 81). Really crazy. Settings range from a sauna to a dungeon. Make a request when you call for reservations. Dinners 42-90mk. Open Mon.-Sat. 11am-midnight.

Troikka, Caloniukesenkatu 3 (tel. 44 52 29). The tsars never had it so good. Antique icons and tapestries cover the walls of this Russian restaurant, one of Helsinki's best. Dinners from 49mk. Reservations are a good idea. Open Mon.-Sat. 11:30am-midnight.

Sights

The handsome neoclassical buildings surrounding **Senate Square** were designed almost singlehandedly by German architect Carl Ludwig Engel in the early nineteenth century, just after Helsinki replaced Turku as Finland's capital. The crowning piece is the **Lutheran Cathedral.** (Open Mon.-Sat. 9am-7pm, Sun. noon-7pm.) Elsewhere in the city, the bold, simple creations of the city's great twentieth-century architects—notably Aalto and Saarinen—blend with the clean neoclassical lines. The five self-guided walking tours, with map available at the tourist office, are an excellent introduction to Helsinki's architecture, though they've mistakenly omitted the **Temppeliaukio Church**—a modern masterpiece built into a hill of rock. From the National Museum, go down Aurorankatu, and turn right on Temppelikatu. (Open Mon.-Sat. 10am-9pm, Sun. noon-3pm and 6-9pm.) The striking **Jean Sibelius Monument,** dedicated to Finland's most famous composer, consists of hundreds of steel pipes sculpted by Eila Hiltunen. The monument is in Sibelius Park on Mechelininkatu; take bus #18 from the train station.

The **Kansallismuseo** (National Museum), Mannerheimintie 34, has wonderful displays of Finnish culture, from Gypsy and Lapp costumes to *ryijy* (rugs woven for use on boats and sleighs). (Open daily 11am-4pm, Tues. also 6-9pm. Admission 5mk, free Tues.) Finnish mastery of graphic and industrial design is well-documented at the **Finnish Design Center,** Kasarmikatu 19b, next to the Finlandia Mall (open Mon.-Fri. 10am-5pm, Sat. 10am-3pm, Sun. noon-4pm), and at the **Museum of Applied Arts,** Korkeavuorenkatu 23, south of Eteläesplanadi. (Open Tues.-Fri. 11am-5pm, Sat.-Sun. 11am-4pm. Admission 5mk, students 3mk.) The **Art Museum** of the Ateneum, Kansakoulukatu 3, is the largest in Finland, featuring Finnish art from the eighteenth century to the present. (Open Mon.-Tues. and Thurs.-Fri. 9am-5pm, Wed. 9am-8pm, Sat.-Sun. 11am-5pm. Admission 3mk.)

The islands surrounding Helsinki make excellent daytrips. The sandy beaches and smooth rocks of **Pihlajasaari** make it a popular summer spot for tanning Finns. Boats leave from Merisatama (1 per hr., more when sun shines; 6mk one way). **Seurasaari,** connected to the mainland by a causeway, is a lovely place to picnic, swim, and walk. Its open-air museum of old Finland includes a smoke house. Take bus #24 from inside the Swedish Theater to the last stop. (Open Thurs.-Tues. 11:30am-5:30pm, Wed. 11:30am-7pm. Admission 5mk, students 2mk, free Wed.) An old fortress and great beaches await you at **Suomenlinna.** Ferries leave from Market Square twice per hour.

Entertainment

Most action occurs in the area between the train station, Mannerheimintie, Pohjoiesplanadi, and Mikonkatu—a warren of restaurants and shops that makes for good people-watching. Alternatively, wander aound **Hakariementori.** Every summer there are free outdoor concerts in the city's numerous parks. Afternoons, all kinds of music resound on the leafy **Esplanadi.** About once a month from May to September huge open-air rock concerts are held in Kaivopuisto featuring Finland's biggest bands; information is available in *Helsinki This Week* or at the tourist office. All the arts, from opera to avant-garde mixed-media creations, are represented in the two-week **Helsinki Festival** in late August. Showtimes at Helsinki's movie theaters are generally 6 and 8pm.

Finland is one of the few countries in Europe where the drinking age—18 for beer and wine and 20 for alcohol—is enforced. Still, ID is checked less stringently—and admission is usually cheaper—on weeknights. Tickets to some discos sell out before the evening begins, so it's a good idea to pick up tickets beforehand at **Tiketti,** Keskuskatu 7 (tel. 66 01 24), off Pohjoiesplanadi. (Open Mon.-Fri. 10am-5pm.)

Café Metropol, Mikonkatu 17, near the station. The place for live rock—very, very popular. Open daily noon-2am.

Botta, Toolonkatu 3 (tel. 44 69 40), behind the National Museum. A favorite of students and young sailors. Choose your entertainment: everything from a swinging dance floor to a sing-along room with piano and hammocks. Cover Mon.- Thurs. 15mk, 35mk live band. Fri.-Sun. 35mk. Open Mon.-Thurs. 8pm-1am, Fri.-Sun. 8pm-2am.

Juttutupa, Säästöpankinranta 6 (tel. 753 10 33). From the train station, go north on Siltasaarenkatu, then left after the bridge (15 min.). A roving accordion player plays polkas in this beer hall. Open daily 9am-2am.

Arkadia, Fredrikinkatu 43 (tel. 694 02 75). A disco with 2 dance floors. Something of a meat market. Cover Mon.-Thurs. 15mk, Fri.-Sun. 30mk. Open daily 7pm-2am.

Gambrini, Iso Roobertinkatu 3 (tel. 64 43 91), 2 blocks south of the beginning of Mannerheimintie. Helsinki's most popular gay bar. Open 8pm-1am.

Kosmos, Kalevankatu 3 (tel. 60 77 17), across Mannerheimintie from Stockman's department store. For the self-proclaimed artsy; have you anything to say about Björn Wesckström's use of texture? Expensive—espresso 14mk, desserts 21mk. Open Mon.-Fri. 11am-1am.

Alko, next to the university, and other locations. The state-run liquor store—the place to beat the cost of 15mk beers in Helsinki's bars. Open in summer Mon.-Thurs. 10am-5pm, Fri. 10am-6pm; in winter also Sat. 9am-noon.

Near Helsinki

Finnish composer Jean Sibelius spent the last 43 years of his life at **Ainola** in **Järvenpää.** Hidden amid the trees is his unassuming home and garden, where he and his wife lie buried. Buses to Tuusula pass the site (every ½ hr. from Helsinki bus station, 15mk). Alternatively take local train R, H or T from the station. (Open May-Aug. Thurs.-Tues. 10am-6pm, Wed. noon-8pm; Sept. Thurs.-Sun. 11am-5pm. For information call 28 73 22.)

Porvoo, Finland's oldest town after Turku, is great for a respite from the relative bustle of Helsinki. There is a splendid **Retkeilymaja (IYHF)** at Linnakoskenkatu 1 (tel. (915) 13 00 12). (Open early Jan.-late Dec.) The helpful **tourist office** is on Rauhankatu (tel. (915) 14 01 45), the fourth right across the bridge from Mannerheiminkatu. To reach the city, 50km from Helsinki, sail aboard the *M/S J.L. Runeberg* (departures Wed. and Fri.-Sun. at 10am; 3 hr., 75mk one way, 95mk round-trip), or take a much less expensive bus from the Helsinki bus station (20mk).

Lake District

Half water, half pine-covered land, southeastern Finland's Lake District is an ideal place to commune with nature. Many Finns have summer houses here, where they swim, hike, bike, and canoe after the seven-month winter. The main towns (Lappeenranta, Jyväskylä, Savonlinna, Joensuu, and Kuopio) are useful bases, but none is nearly as thrilling as the stretches of water and forest under an enormous sky. Spend a few days here and you'll begin to appreciate Finland's vast uninhabited countryside.

Boats, though expensive, are a good way to see the Lake District. A very popular route is the 12-hour sail between Kuopio and Savonlinna on Lake Kallavesi. Boats depart Tuesday through Saturday mornings from both towns, and you can break up the journey into shorter segments. (Full trip 200mk one way, 270mk round-trip; more expensive Sat.-Sun.) Contact **Roll-Laivat Oy** (tel. (971) 12 67 44) in Kuopio for details. The 10-hour trip from Jyväskylä to Lahti is somewhat cheaper (149mk one way). All tourist offices have boat timetables, and often make reservations. There are many sightseeing boats as well—just go down to the harbor and choose your trip length and price. Bikes can be rented at several youth hostels in the region for about 25mk per day or 100mk per week. Elsewhere, tourist offices will help you find rentals. Trains and buses connect the major towns with frequent service, and hitching along the country roads is quite good.

Make a point of spending some nights in the country. Rooms in farmhouses can almost always be arranged through tourist offices, or you can stop at one of the area's hostels. Possibilities also include wilderness huts, which are free of charge, and camping, either in the many campgrounds or on open land.

Savonlinna can be reached from Helsinki (3-4 trains per day) or Kuopio (2 trains per day).

Jyväskylä

Jyväskylä is famous as the home of Alvar Aalto, the acclaimed Finnish architect. Here, surrounded by endless forests and lakes, Aalto drew inspiration from nature. Unfortunately, his genius did not permeate all of Jyväskylä, and most of its buildings are pretty dull. Still, equipped with a map, you'll be able to find Aalto's gems amid the mediocrity. **Aalto Museum,** at Seminaarinkatu 7, near the corner of Vapaudenkatu and Hannuksenkatu, will help you follow the development of Aalto's style. The building itself is one of his designs. (Open Wed.-Sun. noon-6pm, Tues. noon-8pm. Admission 5mk, students 2mk.) You can visit the worthwhile **Museum of Central Finland** next door with the same ticket. The nearby **University of Jyväskylä,** also largely designed by Aalto, occupies an isolated campus strewn with large pine trees overlooking a lake.

Hiking, canoeing, and biking are especially good in Jyväskylä; the **tourist office** can give you maps and advise you on an itinerary and accommodations along the way. Visit them at Vapaudenkatu 38 (tel. (941) 29 40 84), just up Asemakatu and then left. (Open Mon.-Fri. 8am-6pm, Sat.-Sun. 10am-6pm.) Their branch at the train station is open in summer (8:45am-12:30pm and 1:30-8pm).

The **Amis Summer Hotel,** Sepänkatu 3 (tel. (941) 61 29 20), is clean and conveniently located, just behind the bus station as you come from the center. (Singles 90mk, doubles 150mk, quads 40mk per person. Sheets 15mk. Breakfast 22mk. Open June-early Aug. 7am-9:30pm.) The newly renovated youth hostel **Laajari (IYHF),** is much farther from the center (tel. (941) 25 33 55). (39mk in dorms, 80mk in doubles. Sheets 15mk. Kitchen facilities available. Open year-round.) **Tuomiojärven Camping** (tel. (941) 29 40 86) is 2km north of the city on a lake. (22mk per person; family 48mk. Open June-Aug.) For lunch, **Pizzeria Nr. 1** at Kauppakatu 8 and 14 has a good lunch special (Mon.-Fri. 11am-2pm) for 26mk, including a drink, salad, and coffee. Asemakatu, the street perpendicular to the train station, has several **markets,** most open Mon.-Fri. 9am-8pm, Sat. 8am-6pm.

Trains from Turku (3 per day) and from Helsinki (7 per day) make Jyväskylä easy to reach. Trains from the north come via Seinäjoki (change in Tampere) or via Kuopio (change in Pieksämäki; a bit longer, but much more scenic). Buses connect Jyväskylä to towns throughout the Lake District.

Savonlinna

When Finland was part of the Russian empire, the Petersburg aristocracy turned Savonlinna into a fashionable resort. Today Savonlinna is one of the primary tourist towns in Scandinavia, and its attractions have grown beyond the sheer beauty of its clean lakes and pine forests.

The renowned **Opera Festival** in July is the centerpiece of a host of high quality cultural events. If you are not interested in opera, the town will be disappointing during much of July, when masses of tourists make accommodations impossible to find. But if you *are,* then Savonlinna is the place to be. Tickets to performances cost 200 to 320mk and should be ordered as early as the preceding October. Write to Opera Festival, Poistokatu 1, SF-57130 Savonlinna. Resale tickets are sold at 4pm the day of the show at the ticket office, Puistokatu 5 (tel. (957) 244 84); be there at 2pm to beat the crowds. A concert and chamber opera series is held in the **Retretti Arts Center;** two or three performances resound every afternoon in the wonderful acoustics of an underground cave. (Tickets 30mk, students 20mk; inquire at the Opera Festival ticket office.) The 1½km of caverns blasted out of pure rock house paintings and sculpture amid shimmering reflecting pools. Light in Art is the theme of an exhibition projected for 1988. Rettreti (the retreat) has its own stop on the rail line between Savonlinna and Helsinki (July only); or take the Finnair bus from the marketplace. (Open mid-May to Aug. daily 10am-8pm; Sept. 1-21 daily 10am-7pm; Feb. to mid-May Tues.-Thurs. and Sun. 11am-7pm. Admission 35mk, students 20mk.)

In town, stroll past the wooden houses of **Linnankatu,** the town's oldest street, and through the surrounding park. Then cross the moat to **Olavinlinna Castle,** the impressive fortress in the lake. You can creep up the winding, steep stairways to visit defense passages, bedrooms with medieval privies, and finally—through a hole in the ceiling—the munitions room. (Open daily 10am-5pm. Admission 10mk.)

The staff at the **tourist office,** Puistokatu 1 (tel. (957) 134 92), can help you find accommodations—not an easy task in July. (Open June-Aug. daily 8am-10pm; Sept.-May Mon.-Fri. 9am-4pm.) **Savonlinna Hospiz,** Linnekatu 20 (tel. (957) 224 43), is reasonable and convenient. (Dorm beds 40mk. Breakfast 20mk. Open June-Aug.) All the IYHF hostels charge members 38mk, nonmembers 48mk. **Retkeilymaja Malakias (IYHF),** Pihlajavedenkuja 6 (tel. (957) 232 83), is 1½km from town, near the beach. Take bus #2, 3 or 4. (Open June to mid-Aug.) **Retkeilymaja Mertamalakias (IYHF),** Otavankatu 6 (tel. (957) 206 85), is 2km away. (Open in July.) **Youth Hostel Uuorilinna (IYHF)** (tel. (957) 228 64) is only open two weeks at the end of August. **Vuohimäki Camping** (tel. (957) 71 223) is 7km out, but there is bus service twice per hour. (25mk per site. Open late May-late Aug.)

Savonlinna's restaurants are quite expensive. Visit the lakeside **Market Square** for good deals on vegetables and fruits. Otherwise, try **Pizzeria Terazza,** Olivinkatu 44, on the second floor, or **Pizzeria Capero,** Olivinkatu 51, with pizza and salad for 25mk. (Open Mon.-Fri. 8am-10pm, Sat. 10am-6pm, Sun. noon-6pm.)

Savonlinna can be reached by train from Helsinki (3-4 per day) or Kuopio (2 per day). There are two train stops: Savonlinna and Savonlinna-Kauppatori. The latter is more convenient, unless you want to leave luggage or buy a ticket; it's right in the center of town near the tourist office.

Near Savonlinna

The stretch of land and water between Savonlinna and Kuopio offers many worthwhile stops. One of the most special is the isolated farmhouse **Pohjataival (IYHF)** (tel. (972) 664 19), 12km from Heinävesi, with its own steamboat pier. Here you can stay amid the cows, ducks, and dogs which roam the premises. (27-38mk per night. Meals, sauna, and rowboats available. Open year-round.)

Biking is particularly attractive in the hilly **Heinävesi** region. Heinävesi's **Koulukeskus Hostel** (tel. (972) 610 29), in a school building up the road from the lake, costs 27mk per night. **Rantasalmis Hostel** (tel. (957) 811 24) runs 32mk per night, with breakfast 15mk; there's a sauna right on the lake. Both are accessible by boat or land transportation from Savonlinna and Kuopio. **Valamo Monastery** offers overnight stays in a beautiful setting, though it can get crowded. About 35km from Heinävesi along the Savonlinna-Kuopio boat route, it can also be reached by bus. You can stay in the guest house for 50mk per night, and a restaurant serves meals for 35-50mk. Guests are asked to observe certain rules (no shorts or photographs, for example). (Open year-round.) A visit may give you some insight into monastery life; you may also meet some of the young Finns who are completing their compulsory period of social service here.

Kuopio

North of Savonlinna lies Kuopio, at once an industrial center and a major resort. In this particularly odd mixture of old and new, you can both meet working Finns and stroll peaceful old pedestrian ways lined with wooden buildings. Kuopio features the **Orthodox Church Museum,** Karjalankatu 1, the only one of its kind in the West, with a remarkable collection of icons, illustrated bibles, and music books brought from the territories ceded to the Soviet Union after World War II. (Open May-Aug. Tues.-Sun. 10am-4pm; Sept.-April Mon.-Fri. 10am-2pm, Sat.-Sun. noon-5pm. Admission 5mk.) Kuopio's **Open-Air Museum,** Kirkkokatu 22, presents old-fashioned living quarters and trade exhibits from 1780 through 1930. Walk up Puijonkatu away from the station and turn left. (Open mid-May to mid-Sept. Thurs.-Tues. 10am-5pm, Wed. 10am-7pm. Admission 3mk.)

The **tourist office** is at Haapaniemenkatu 17 (tel. (971) 12 14 11), next to Market Square and the town hall. (Open June to mid-Aug. Mon.-Fri. 8am-6pm, Sat. 8am-2pm; mid-Aug. to May Mon.-Fri. 8:30am-4pm.) Their branch at the train station (tel. (971) 11 52 44) has less information, but longer hours. (Open Mon.-Sat. 7:50am-7:45pm, Sun. 7:50-11:25am.)

Both youth hostels are busy in summer and rather far from town. **Retkeilymaja Tekma (IYHF),** Taivaanpankontie 14 (tel. (971) 22 29 25), 5km from town, has pleasant woody surroundings. Take bus #5 from Market Square. (2 per hr.). (Members 32-38mk, nonmembers 42-48mk. Breakfast 19mk. Open early June to mid-Aug.) **Jynkän Retkeilymaja (IYHF)** (tel. (971) 31 23 61), is 8km from town. Take bus #20 from the bus station. Rooms in this old house are inexpensive, but the facilities—sauna, canoe rental— are a bit pricey. (Member 27mk, nonmembers 37mk. Open March to mid-Oct.) Kuopio's best beach is at **Rauhalahti Camping** (tel. (971) 31 22 44), 7km from town. They also rent bikes, mopeds, canoes, and boats. (45mk per person. Open mid-May to Aug.)

Kuopio's **marketplace** is lively and colorful, with crafts, flowers, and delicious traditional foods. This is the place to sample *kalakukko,* Finnish bread with fish in the middle. At 7am you can buy hot *munkki*-pastries for 3mk, and then sit in one of the outdoor cafes where the old folks of Kuopio watch the day start. (Open Mon.-Fri. 7am-3pm, Sat. 7am-2pm.) If you arrive too late to visit Market Square, visit the **evening market,** at the end of Kauppakatu on the passenger harbor. (Open June-Aug. daily 3-10pm.) A good reasonable restaurant is **Taverna Traviata,** Kirkkokatu 40-42, with a lunch special of soup, an entree, bread and butter, drink, and dessert for only 26mk. (Open Mon.-Fri. 11am-8pm, Sat.-Sun. 11am-7pm. Lunch served 11am-1pm.) **Sampo,** Kauppakatu 13, has a typical *muikku* (fish) dinner in a bar-like atmosphere (31mk). (Open daily 9am-12:30pm.) As well as the outdoor stalls, Market Square also has several grocery shops, open until 8pm weekdays.

Four daily trains link Kuopio to Helsinki; two also run to Jyväskylä, and there are connections to Kajaani and Oulu in the north.

Kajaani

At the northern edge of Finland's vast armada of lakes lies **Kajaani,** a quiet town straddling a river. Pause here before heading farther north to Lapland or Kuusamo, and spend some time fishing in the center of town. Wander down Linnankatu to the remains of Kajaani's **castle.** Built in 1666, it was razed by the Russians in 1717. Today it forms the center of a bridge that connects the town over the river. The **tourist office** (tel. (986) 15 55 17), is at Kauppakatu 24, in the center of town. (In 1988 it may move to Pohjolankatu 16. Open mid-June to mid-Aug. Mon.-Fri. 8am-8pm, Sat. 9am-2pm; mid-Aug. to mid-June Mon.-Fri. 9am-5pm.) A summer branch is at the train station.

Retkeilymaja Kajaani (tel. (986) 257 04) is a 1½-kilometer hike from the train station. (Bed 50mk, doubles 90mk. Open June-Aug.) The **campground** (tel. (986) 227 03) is closer and right on the river, but almost as expensive. (40mk per site. Open June-Aug.) For pleasant atmosphere and reasonable food try **Kahvila Millatuulia,** Kappalatu 24, by the tourist office. (Main dishes from 28mk. Open Mon.-Fri. 8am-6pm, Sat. 8am-4pm, Sun. noon-6pm.) There are several grocery shops on the same street; **Palvelemme** is open from 8:30am to 7:30pm.

The rail line from Oulu to Kuopio and Helsinki passes through Kajaani, and there are 3-4 trains per day in each direction. The nearby village of **Paltaniemi** offers the tranquillity of woods and nearby Lake Oulujärvi, as well as an eighteenth-century wood church with remarkable ceiling paintings. Hourly buses make the trip to Paltaniemi from Kajaani (5mk).

Oulu

Once the leading tar exporter in the world, and still one of Finland's busiest ports, Oulu is northern Finland's center of commercial and cultural life. For a great overview of the city, take bus #7 or 13 (4.50mk) to the **observation tower,** 4km from the city center. (Admission 5mk.) The **cathedral,** downtown, is the hub of Evangelical Lutheranism in Finland. (Open June-July daily 10am-7pm; Aug.-May daily noon-1pm.) The tar bourgeoisie, who brought prosperity to Oulu in the eighteenth and nineteenth centuries, built large, ornate wooden houses in the **Rantakatu** area, down by the river behind **City Hall.** Ski back in history during the **Tar Ski Race,** a national festival held annually for nearly 100 years; the world's oldest cross-country ski race is open to everyone. Finland's rock musicians congregate here for a weekend in mid-July for the annual **Kuus Rock Festival.** For information, call (931) 54 15 41.

There are tourist offices at the bus and train stations, but go to the **Municipal Tourist Office,** Kirkkokatu 2a (tel. (981) 153 30), where the staff is humorous and helpful. (Open June-Aug. Mon.-Sat. 9am-6pm, Sun. 9am-4pm; Sept.-May Mon.-Fri. 9am-4pm.) The only inexpensive accommodation is at **Retkeilymaja Välkkylä (IYHF),** Kajaanintie 36 (tel. (981) 22 77 07), in the park-like campus of Oulu university. The hostel features spacious quads with showers and kitchenettes, indoor pool and sauna for 5mk, and a popular disco. (Members 38kr, nonmembers 48kr. Open June-July.) **Nallikari Camping** (tel. (981) 34 35 16) has the best beach in the vicinity. Take bus #5 from the cathedral. (16mk per person for tents, 140mk for cabins.) Pizza is the cheapest alternative to fresh bread, fish, cheese, and fruit from the marketplace; also try the large shopping center between the railway station and youth hostel (stores open Mon.-Fri. 9am-8pm, Sat. 9am-6pm).

Four or five trains per day leave south to Helsinki and north to Rovaniemi.

Kuusamo and the Karhunkierros

For foaming rapids and bottomless gorges, visit **Kuusamo,** near the Finnish-Soviet border. You can reach it via Highway 20, which passes Finland's southernmost fell, **Syöte,** along the way (2 buses per day from Oulu, 4 hr., 72mk). From Kuusamo, Highway 81 takes you northwest to Rovaniemi and Lapland. Trains leave Helsinki daily for Taivalkoski, where buses connect with Kuusamo (3-4 per day, 1 hr., 24mk).

The town has little to offer except information on hiking through the unspoiled countryside. The **tourist office,** Kaiterante 22 (tel. (989) 119 11), and the travel agency **Kuusamon Lomat Oy,** Kitkantie 20 (tel. (989) 126 62), offer expert advice.

The grandest trail in the region is **Karhunkierros** (the Bear's Ring), an 82-kilometer hike. You can buy a map of Karhunkierros at the tourist office or bookstores in Kuusamo and find your way through forests and bogs, over suspension bridges, and past the Kuitaköngäs and Jyrävä waterfalls. There are free huts every 10km or so, but they fill up quickly in July and August—it's a good idea to carry a tent. You can also stay overnight at **Myllykoski,** a two-room restored mill. Sneakers will do for most of the trail, though you may want rubber boots for the boggy stretches. Most importantly, bring food and mosquito repellent—there are only two places where you can buy supplies along the way, but there are pests waiting to make a meal of you with every step. If you want to fish, you'll need the appropriate licenses, available at tourist offices and campgrounds. The route begins on the Sallantie road, which you can reach by bus from the center of Kuusamo (Mon.-Fri. 2 per day, Sat.-Sun. 1 per day), and continues through Oulunka National Park and Kitka Cape to Juuma and Virkkula. If you complete the whole circuit—you should count on four to six days—you will emerge at Ruka, from where a bus will return you to Kuusamo (4-5 per day).

If you have less time, consider the 32-kilometer **Bear's Walk,** which takes you through the old villages of Vuotunki and Määttälänvaara. There are also many possibilities for one-day hikes along the trail, including a walk to the **Ristikallio Cliffs,** a unique gorge 5km off the Salla road; a hike to Kiutaköngäs lying in Oulanka National Park, 2km from the road; or the 3-kilometer trail beginning at Juuma village and going to the Myllykoski and Jyrävä rapids.

Those tired of roughing it will appreciate the nearby youth hostels. **Salmilampi retkeilymaja** (tel. (989) 811 16), in Heikkala Tauno, is 3km from the end of the hike at Ruka, and 26km from Kuusamo (4-5 buses per day). (33-38mk. Open year-round.) **Kuusamon Kansanopisto (IYHF)** (tel. (989) 221 32) is open June to mid-

August (32-37mk), while **Etlä-Kuusamon Lamapalvelu (IYHF)** (tel. (989) 221 32), in Käsmä, 29km from Kuusamo, is open year-round.

Lapland (Lappi)

For a different sense of space and time, for untouched fells rising against a clean northern sky, for vast herds of reindeer and mosquitoes, visit Lapland, Europe's greatest wilderness. In the south, near Tornio, you will find spectacular river rapids and whitefish. To the north lies 80-kilometer-long Inarinjärvi (Lake Inari), with countless islands, and, even farther north, the steep tundra slopes of the **Teno River Valley.** Continue beyond Kolari and Sodankylä to the true fell-and-bog of northern Lapland. The highest mountains rise around Enontekiö, while rocky cliffs line the shores of Lake Pakasaivo.

The hot sun never sets on Lapland during the two- to three-month summer. In winter, temperatures hit the opposite extreme and the sun may not rise for 50 days. But Kaamos, this period of the year, is not insufferably dark. Rather, the combination of clear sky, moon, and white snow produces an eerie blue light, and in December and January, the green, red, and yellow streaks of the Northern Lights illuminate the sky. March to mid-May is ideal for skiing, and there are facilities and rental outlets at almost every tourist center (Saariselkä, Pallas, Ylläs, and Ounasvaara, near Rovaniemi). In summer, experienced guides lead hiking expeditions from the same places. Independent excursions are recommended only for experienced groups. Hikers should plan their routes around the mountain huts run by the Finnish Youth Hostel Association.

Most of the *Same* (Finnish Lapps) and *Kolttas* (originally Russian Lapps) live in the four northernmost parishes of Sodankylä, Enontekiö, Inari, and Utsjoki. Both wear costumes of deep blue felt with bright bands of green, red, and yellow, and decorative embroidery. At least 800 families still make a living off of reindeer herding. Don't neglect to sample the local delicacies—*poro* (reindeer meat), *lohi* (salmon), and *siika* (whitefish), as well as liqueurs and desserts made from Arctic *hilla* (cloudberries) and *karpalo* (cranberries).

Rovaniemi

Capital of Finnish Lapland and home to Europe's Santa Claus, Rovaniemi propagates its tourist image shamelessly. You'll find reindeer meat in every restaurant and a Santa Claus Village just north of the city on the Arctic Circle. Such contrivances notwithstanding, the city makes a good base for exploration, and it is easily reached by rail or plane from Helsinki (Finnair youth fare 278mk one way). From the bus and train stations, turn left and right respectively onto Rantakatu, which becomes Hallituskatu; follow it until the end and turn left on Valtakatu for three blocks to find the **tourist office** at Aallonkatu 2c (tel. (960) 162 70). They find rooms in private homes (50-90mk), distribute *Rovaniemi This Week,* and issue licenses to herd reindeer. (Open June-Aug. Mon.-Fri. 8am-7pm, Sat.-Sun. 10am-7pm; Sept.-May Mon.-Fri. 8am-4pm.) The branch at the train station (tel. (960) 222 18) is open June-Aug. only (Mon.-Sat. 7:30am-noon and 2:30-6pm, Sun. 7:30am-noon). Rovaniemi's **IYHF youth hostel,** Hallituskatu 16 (tel. (960) 106 44), is nice but lacks kitchen facilities. Turn right from the station, go up the hill, through the large intersection, and down Hallituskatu. (Members 33mk, nonmembers 43mk. Small breakfast 18mk. Check-in 7:30-10:30am and 4-10pm. Open year-round.) Just across the river from the center of town, **Ounaskoski Camping** (tel. (960) 153 04) has an excellent location and a friendly staff (25mk per person; families 50mk. Open June to mid-Aug.). The tourist office has a list of restaurants, including prices. Not far from the station, **Ravintola Lapinpaula,** Hallituskatu 24, serves a mean buffet lunch for 28mk (open daily 10am-1am). There are several large markets; **Markkina market** is closest to the station (open Mon.-Fri. 9am-8pm, Sat. 8am-6pm).

Northern Lapland

If you set out for Lapland, plan ahead, since bus connections can sometimes be difficult. From Rovaniemi, there are two hitching/bus routes to the north: Highway 79 leads to Muonio in the northwest, Highway 4 to Inari in the north. At the information office in the Rovaniemi train station, you may obtain a timetable for bus connections from Rovaniemi to as far as the North Cape in Norway via Ivalo, Inari, and Karasjok (2 per day, 152mk to Karasjok), and to Kautokeino via Muonio and Enontekiö (Sun.-Fri. 1 per day, 98mk to Enontekiö, 133mk to Kilpisjärvi). Note that there are two bus lines in the north: the slow postal bus and the faster **JM Eskelisen Lapin Linjat Oy.** Both have the same fares. When traveling to Norway or Sweden, remember the one-hour time difference.

The areas north of Inari and around Enontekiö meet and even exceed the most dramatic visions of untouched tundra and nightmarish mosquitoes. Close to Lake Inari, the town of **Inari** is both a tourist spot and an old Lapp center. There is a well-kept and friendly **retkeilymaja (IYHF)** (tel. (997) 512 44) right in the center of the village. (38mk in doubles. Open June to mid-Sept.) **Inari Opisto** (tel. (997) 510 24) operates as a summer hotel (50mk per person, 75mk in doubles). In addition to its seven official **campsites,** Inari offers plenty of surrounding wilderness. For information visit the helpful English-speaking staff at **Näkäläjärvi,** a souvenir shop and cafeteria. (Open in summer 8am-11pm; in winter shorter hours.)

Get acquainted with *Same* culture at the **open-air museum** just 200m north of the center of Inari. (Open June-July 8am-10pm; Aug. 8am-8pm; Sept. 1-20 9am-4pm. Admission 7mk, students and children 3mk.) From here you can hike 7km to the **Pielppajärvi Wilderness Church,** built in 1760. People used to come from miles around to worship here, but it is now usually deserted. Travelers may stay in the two huts at the church site.

Lapland's magic zone begins 30 to 40 kilometers north of Inari; boreal forest changes into endless slopes covered with dwarf birches. Whether you hitch, take the bus, or drive, you must take the road from the border town of **Karigasniemi,** 98km from Inari, to Utsjoki. Winding along the **River Teno,** famous for its salmon and sport fishing, you will see the Norwegian tundra on the far side of the river and beautiful sand beaches and more tundra on the Finnish side. Only a few Lapp villages, several herds of reindeer and sheep, and a few attentive mosquitoes interrupt the wilderness. Karigasniemi has a **retkeilymaja (IYHF)** (tel. (997) 611 88) right in the center of town. Ask to stay in one of the small huts. (27mk. Open year-round.)

Up the other route from Rovaniemi is **Enontekiö,** a major Lapp center in the "arm" of Finland. You can reach it from Inari (go southwest to Kittilä, then north), or from Karigasniemi (via Kautokeino in Norwegian Lapland). The route from Tornio, on the Gulf of Bothnia, to Enontekiö (Highway E78) is especially beautiful. There is a **retkeilymaja (IYHF)** (tel. (996) 510 16) in the center of town. They'll put you up in cottages (each with a kitchen) for 35mk, and let you use the sauna for a fee. About 150km north of Enontekiö, in Finland's most mountainous region and practically in Norway, is the town of **Kilpisjärvi.** You can stay at the **retkeilykeskus** (tel. (995) 777 71).

Hiking in this part of the world is a true adventure. From Kilpisjärvi, the path to the top of **Saana Fell** (1029m) begins right behind the Excursion Center (about 4 hr.). This is the edge of uninhabited wilderness; you should carry a map and compass at all times. Another hike leads from Kilpisjärvi across the gently rounded peaks of the **Malla Nature Reserve** and the **Three Countries Frontier,** where Finland, Norway, and Sweden meet on the shores of a lonely lake. For more information on nearby regions, turn to the Norway and Sweden chapters.

FRANCE

US$1 = 5.88 francs (F)	**1F = US$0.17**
CDN$1 = 4.55F	**1F = CDN$0.22**
UK£1 = 9.88F	**1F = UK£0.10**
AUS$1 = 4.35F	**1F = AUS$0.23**

Visas are required of all visitors to France, except those from Switzerland and EEC countries. To avoid long waits at the French embassies in European capitals, procure your visa from a French consulate before leaving home.

Although Paris is the highly centralized administrative center of France, it is certainly not typical—France is a quilt made from an extraordinary variety of provincial fabrics. The north combines the smog of Lille with the history and viniculture of the Champagne region. The headlands, cliffs, and fertile countryside of Normandy inspired the impressionists, while the Celtic population of Brittany has retained its regional language, music, and passion for independence. The Loire Valley blossoms with the architecture of the French Renaissance, while the snow-capped Alps offer beauty of a natural kind. The friendly Midi to the south has a special flavor, with its red-roofed, white-walled houses and luminous, bright skies, while the Côte d'Azur is so attractive that it has ruined itself.

The first French were the Gauls, a Celtic people familiar to many from Goscinny's *Astérix* books. While Getafix's secret potion enabled Astérix, Obelix, Dogmatix, and crew to keep the Romans permanently at bay, the real story was different: All Gaul was secured by the Romans, from Julius Caesar's conquest to the transfer of the imperial capital to Constantinople in the third century C.E. Violent feudal strife was the rule of the day until Charlemagne, a Frank, conquered most of Europe from his capital at Aix-la-Chapelle. This empire, the Carolingian, fell apart soon after Charlemagne's death, and throughout the Middle Ages the Kings of France struggled to unite the country against the destructive forces of famine, plague, the English, and a powerful nobility. The years from 1515 to 1789 are the period of large things beginning with "R:" the Renaissance, the Reformation and the Wars of Religion, the Rise of the Bourbon monarchy, and the subsequent Revolution.

The last climaxed on July 14, 1789 with the storming of the Bastille. The guillotine was kept working overtime during the ensuing Reign of Terror, and by 1799 almost everyone of note in French politics had fallen victim to its stroke. A young Corsican officer named Napoleon Bonaparte stepped into the power vacuum, and Europe was never again to be the same. For 15 years French armies terrorized the continent, until Napoleon met his Waterloo and left nineteenth-century France to the hands of a series of more-or-less constitutional governments. After World War II, Charles de Gaulle proclaimed the Fourth Republic, which lasted until the political crisis provoked by Algerian independence in 1958. De Gaulle returned as leader of the Fifth Republic, and so remained until his resignation following the violent student riots and general strikes of the summer of 1968. Georges Pompidou and Valéry Giscard d'Estaing, two politicians in the conservative Gaullist vein, took turns leading France until the election of François Miterrand in 1981.

Miterrand's Socialist goverment effected sweeping changes in the first two years of office: banks and industries were nationalized, the work-week shortened, the minimum wage raised, and political power decentralized. Economic difficulties, however, forced a retreat from these positions and steadily undermined support for the Socialists. In 1986 the Socialists lost control of the government, but Miterrand (whose personal popularity was, and is, still high) remained President: *Cohabitation* began. Right-wing Prime Minister Jacques Chirac took office determined to press his power to the fullest and calling for an "irreversible break with Socialism," but the crippling transport and utilities strike in the winter of 1986/87 suggests that the French are not so decided. To follow the twists and turns of French politics, pick up a paper; *Le Figaro* leans to the right, *Le Monde* to the left.

Transportation

The **Société Nationale de Chemins de Fer (SNCF)** is one of Europe's most efficient and extensive rail networks. Their premier offering, the **France Railpass,** comes in three varieties: four days of travel within a 15-day period; nine days within a month; and 16 days within a month. Days of use need not be consecutive. Extra goodies include one or two days' free Métro, bus, and RER train travel in Paris, free transfer to and from Orly or Roissy airports, and discounted car rentals. The catch is the price: US$69 for four days, US$130 for nine, and US$170 for 16. The pass must be purchased outside France; in the U.S., contact SNCF at 610 Fifth Ave., New York, NY 10020.

Further cards offer cost-cutting help which applies only to specified periods. "Blue periods" are periods of minimum train traffic, usually Monday afternoon through Friday morning and Saturday afternoon to Sunday afternoon; "white periods" coincide with heavier train use (most other times), while other holidays are "red periods." The **Carte Jeune** (150F) entitles those aged 12-25 to a 50% reduction on blue travel undertaken between June and September. The **Carré Jaune** (150F), offers those aged 12-25 savings on any four one-way trips within a one-year period: 50% off during blue periods, 20% off during white. A **Carte Vermeil** (85F) entitles women and men over 60 to essentially the same discounts as a Carte Jeune. These passes can be obtained at most large train stations or from SNCF, Paris-Tivoli, 20, rue de Longchamp, 75016 Paris. Bring a photo when you make your purchase.

Always remember to validate your train ticket (*compostez votre billet)* by inserting it in the orange machine at the entrance to the platforms; otherwise, you may be fined over and above the price of a regular ticket. All Eurailpass and France Railpass holders must validate their passes before boarding their first train. Seat reservations for longer trips will prevent you from having to stand from Calais to Cannes, and are especially recommended for international trips. If traveling on an overnight train, you may want to reserve a couchette (70F) for sleeping.

SNCF's pamphlet *Guide du train et du vélo* offers details on combining cycling and railroading in France; bikes cost 30F apiece when transported on trains, and they often take three days to arrive. The **Train + Vélo** program allows you to rent bikes at 219 train stations throughout France and return them to other stations. Rates and deposit vary; usually around 45F per day.

Cycling is an excellent way to see the countryside. French roads, with a wealth of well-paved minor routes, are generally fine for cyclists. Avoid the main roads (marked in red on Michelin maps) in favor of the secondary roads (marked in yellow) or the local roads (marked in white). Excellent touring regions include the Loire Valley, Normandy, Brittany, Provence, the Vosges, the Massif Central, and the somewhat mountainous Jura.

French buses are useful mainly for filling in the gaps in the train system; they are usually slower and cheaper. The bus station, usually by the train station, is called the *gare routière.*

You're likely to have the best luck hitching on secondary roads and in regions that see few foreigners. In general, the larger the city, the more difficult it is to hitch out of. **Allostop** is a nation-wide service that brings together drivers and riders to share the expenses of a car trip. They charge 60F for long trips, 30F for short trips, plus 16 centimes per kilometer, or 150F for a year's membership, which entitles you to use their services for free (you still pay the 16 centimes per km). Their office in Paris (84, passage Brady, 10*ème,* 75010) can give you the addresses of offices throughout the country.

Practical Information

For the forseeable future, France will require visas of everyone except Swiss and EEC nationals. These should only take between one and three days to process for citizens of English-speaking countries, but lines at consulates becomes very long as summer nears. There are consulates in the U.S. in Boston, Chicago, Detroit, Houston, Los Angeles, Miami, New York, New Orleans, Puerto Rico, San Francisco, and Washington D.C.: in Chicago at 737 N. Michigan Ave. (tel. (312) 787 53 59); in Los Angeles at 8350 Wilshire Bd. (tel. (213) 535 10 00). In Montréal the consulate is at Pl. Bonaventure (tel. (514) 878 43 81); in Ottawa at 42 Sussex Dr. (tel. (613) 232 17 95); in Vancouver at 736 Granville St., suite 1201 (tel. (604) 681 43 45). In London, the consulate is at 29 Wrights Lane (tel. (01) 937 12 02); in Sydney at 31 Market St., 5th floor, Sydney, NSW, 2000 (tel. (02) 261 57 79); and in Wellington at 1 Willeston St., Box 1695 (tel. (04) 72 02 00).

The extensive French tourism support network revolves around **syndicats d'initiative** and **offices de tourisme.** There's no essential difference between the two: Either will help you find accommodations (usually for a small fee) and outfit you with other information.

Everything you've heard about the politeness of the French may prove true if you address people in English without a prefatory "*Parlez-vous anglais, Madame/Monsieur?*" Even the simplest of efforts to speak French will be appreciated and encouraged, especially in less touristed areas. A healthy appreciation of the importance of *politesse* will break down a great many barriers. Be lavish with your *Monsieurs, Madames,* and *Mademoiselles,* and greet people with a friendly *bonjour.*

Just about everything closes in France from noon to 2pm. The traditional Monday closing seems to be on the wane, particularly in large cities and for larger stores, and food stores remain open on Sunday mornings. Many museums close on Tuesday.

To operate payphones, even if you just need an operator or an emergency number, you'll need to insert a 1F coin. Most pay phones take ½F, 1F, and 5F coins. International calls, which can be made from any pay phone, require 19 plus a country code. When you are running out of money, a small circle on the upper left-hand corner of the box should flash to let you know, but sometimes it doesn't. The expression for a collect call is "en PCV" (ON-PAY-SAY-VAY). Payphones are gradually being replaced by *télécarte* phones, operated by credit cards that you can purchase at post offices and train stations.

Anywhere in France, dial 10 for an operator, 12 for directory assistance, 15 in medical emergencies, 17 for police help, and 19 33 11 for the international operator.

Accommodations and Camping

Auberges de jeunesse (youth hostels) cover France, ranging from well-kept, centrally-located buildings to run-down barracks. Most are affiliated with IYHF, but are not always strict about requiring membership cards. If you just show up, wardens may often let you stay one night, or make you pay a 10-20F supplementary charge. Typical charges are 32-64F per person, with breakfast often 11F more (not usually required).

The quality of hotels in France generally matches their standardized rating, a scale of one to four stars. Our listings are generally one-star or unclassified. Rock-bottom hotels start at about 45F for singles, 50F for doubles, without private bath or breakfast. Often, rates are the same for single- and double-occupancy. Showers, if not included in the room (often they are not), can cost anywhere from 10 to 22F. Be sure to inquire whether the breakfast or meals at the hotel are *obligatoire*. Breakfast (12-22F) almost always means continental breakfast: coffee, tea, or hot chocolate, with bread, jam, and sometimes *croissants*.

Campgrounds, plentiful in France, are also rated on a star system. Michelin's *Camping and Caravanning in France* details the best sites. The **Club Alpin Français** maintains a network of mountain huts in upland regions.

Tourist offices list local *gîtes d'étape* (rural bed and breakfasts) or *chambres d'hôte* (guest rooms). Most *syndicats* in rural areas have a list of *campings à la ferme*—small campsites located on private farms, where you can buy all sorts of wonderful fresh produce.

Food

The French take food seriously, and lunch is just about the most important event of the day; hence the almost sacred noon-2pm break taken by just about everybody. In restaurants, fixed price full meals (called *menus*) are served from about 45F up. Exert caution when ordering *à la carte* (paying for each item separately); *l'addition* (check) may exceed your weekly budget. The *plat du jour* (plate of the day) is often the best choice; the ubiquitous *coq au vin* (chicken cooked in red wine) and *steak/frites* are reasonable alternatives. Even cheaper are the *sandwiches* you can buy at most French *bars* or *brasseries;* for 8-12F you get a foot-long baguette with cheese or meat inside. Service is usually included *(compris);* if not (*service non compris,* or *s.n.c.*), a tip of roughly 15% is appropriate. Cafes are a forum for continuous conversation, but you pay for the right to sit and watch the world go by. In a cafe, a *croque monsieur* (grilled ham and cheese) or *madame* (with the addition of an egg on top) is the classic order (15F), though omelettes may be more filling. Order at the bar *(comptoir);* drinks and food are always 10-30% more if served in the dining room *(salle)* or outside *(sur la terrasse).*

France offers a fragmented array of small specialty shops in which to still pangs of hunger. A *charcuterie* or *traiteur* is a delicatessen of one sort or another, the best place to partake of *pâtés* and *aspics. Boulangeries* sell bread and some pastries, while *pâtisseries* sell pastries and some candy, and *confiseries* candy and some ice cream. *Crêmeries* sell hundreds of varieties of wonderful French cheese; *boucherie* means butcher shop; *épiceries* are grocery stores. *Supermarchés* exist in growing numbers. For convenient shopping, look for **Félix Potin, Uniprix, Prisunic,** or **Monoprix,** where prices are lower and knowledge of French less essential. Local markets *(marchés)* are picturesque, animated, and often of better quality. Some towns hold them once or twice per week, while others, with covered *halles,* have them every morning, usually ending around noon.

Café comes black; *café crème* or *au lait* (with warm milk) can be ordered *grand* (large) or *petit* (small); large is very large. A favorite morning drink is *chocolat chaud* (hot chocolate). A *demi* of *pression* will get you a half-liter of unremarkable beer; a few bottled imported beers are usually available. Wine, *blanc* (white) or *rouge* (red), may be what you'll drink the most of in France. Tart *vin ordinaire* is quite cheap and usually good; many grocery stores have a large keg of local wine from

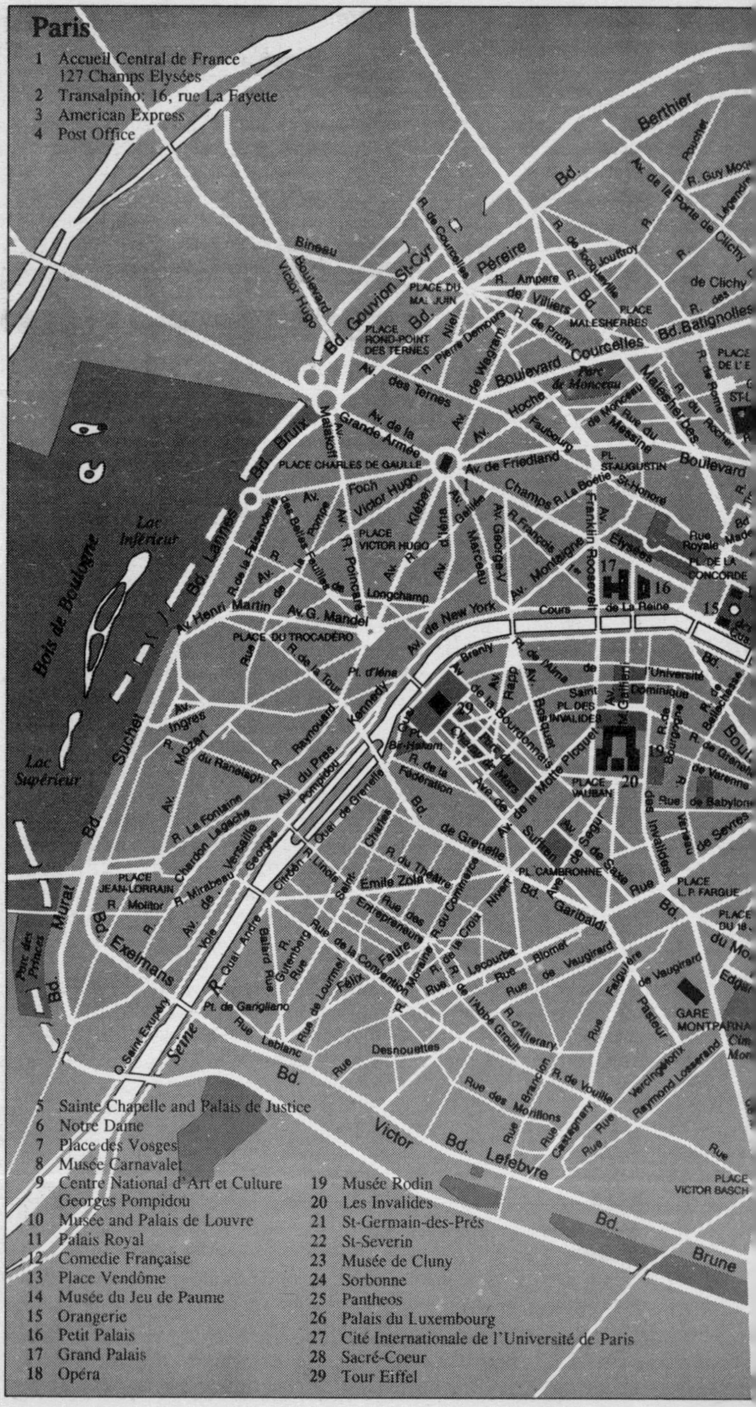
Paris
1 Accueil Central de France
127 Champs Elysées
2 Transalpino: 16, rue La Fayette
3 American Express
4 Post Office
5 Sainte Chapelle and Palais de Justice
6 Notre Dame
7 Place des Vosges
8 Musée Carnavalet
9 Centre National d'Art et Culture
Georges Pompidou
10 Musée and Palais de Louvre
11 Palais Royal
12 Comedie Française
13 Place Vendôme
14 Musée du Jeu de Paume
15 Orangerie
16 Petit Palais
17 Grand Palais
18 Opéra
19 Musée Rodin
20 Les Invalides
21 St-Germain-des-Prés
22 St-Severin
23 Musée de Cluny
24 Sorbonne
25 Pantheos
26 Palais du Luxembourg
27 Cité Internationale de l'Université de Paris
28 Sacré-Coeur
29 Tour Eiffel
Bois de Boulogne
Lac Inférieur
Lac Supérieur
Parc des Princes
Parc de Monceau
PLACE CHARLES DE GAULLE
PLACE DU TROCADÉRO
PLACE VICTOR HUGO
PLACE DU MAL JUIN
PLACE RONDPOINT DES TERNES
PLACE MALESHERBES
PL. ST-AUGUSTIN
PL. DE LA CONCORDE
PL. DES INVALIDES
PLACE VAUBAN
PL. CAMBRONNE
PLACE L. P. FARGUE
PLACE JEAN-LORRAIN
PLACE VICTOR BASCH
GARE MONTPARNA
Champs Elysées
Seine
Bd. Lefebvre
Bd. Victor
Bd. Brune
Bd. Exelmans
Bd. Murat
Bd. Suchet
Bd. Lannes
Bd. Gouvion St-Cyr
Bd. Pereire
Boulevard Courcelles
Bd. Batignolles
Bd. Garibaldi
Bd. de Grenelle
Av. de la Grande Armée
Av. de Friedland
Av. Foch
Av. Victor Hugo
Av. Kléber
Av. d'Iéna
Av. Marceau
Av. de New York
Av. G. Mandel
Av. Henri Martin
Av. Montaigne
Av. de Suffren
Av. de Ségur
Av. de la Motte Picquet
Rue de Vaugirard
Rue de Sèvres
Rue de Babylone
Rue de Grenelle
Rue de l'Université
Rue St Dominique
Rue de la Convention
Rue Lecourbe
Rue du Théâtre
Emile Zola
Rue Royale

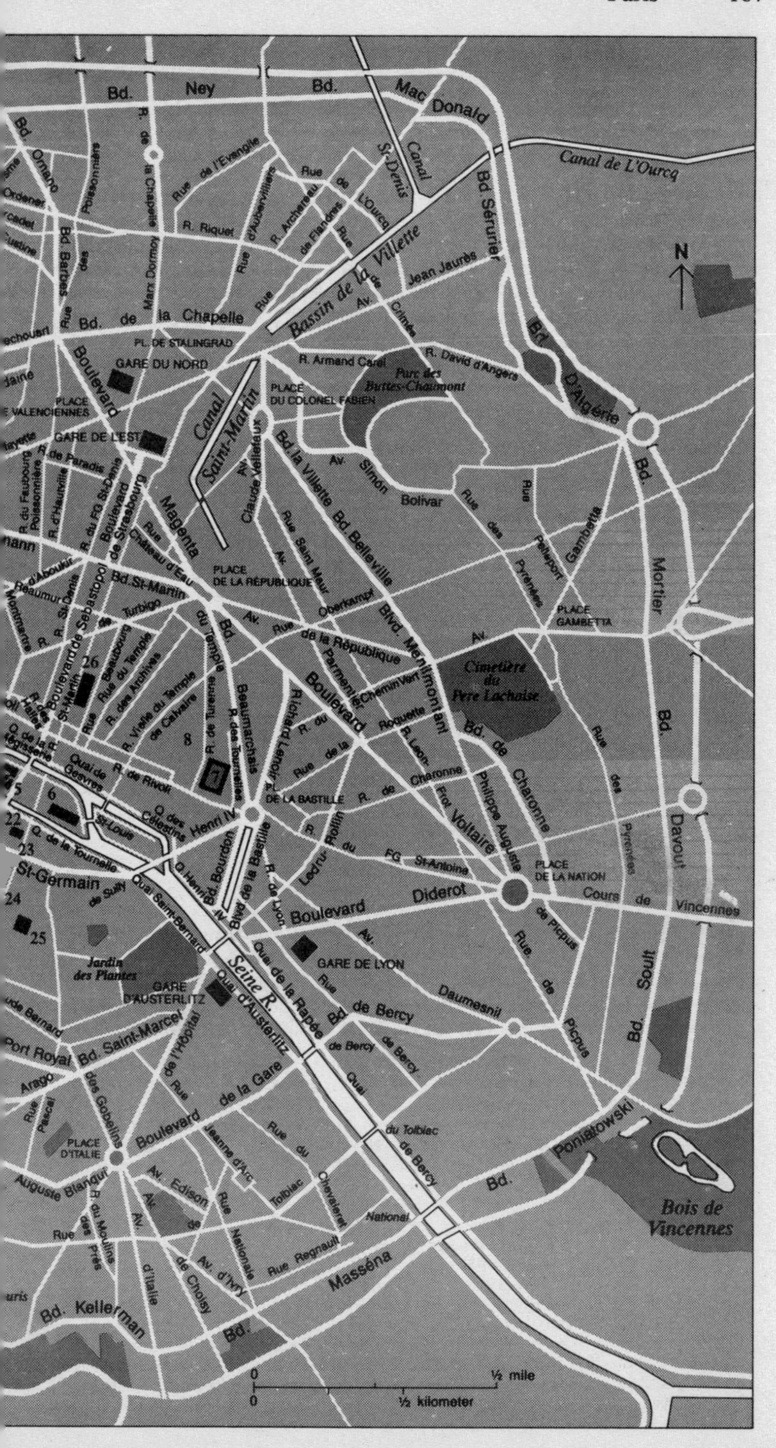
Bd. Ney
Bd. Mac Donald
Canal de L'Ourcq
Canal St-Denis
Bd Sérurier
Bassin de la Villette
Av. Jean Jaurès
Bd. de la Chapelle
PL. DE STALINGRAD
GARE DU NORD
GARE DE L'EST
PLACE DE VALENCIENNES
Canal Saint-Martin
PLACE DU COLONEL FABIEN
Parc des Buttes-Chaumont
Bd D'Algérie
Boulevard Magenta
PLACE DE LA RÉPUBLIQUE
Bd. Belleville
Bd. la Villette
Av. Simon Bolivar
Rue Gambetta
Bd. Mortier
PLACE GAMBETTA
Av. de la République
Cimetière du Père Lachaise
Blvd. Ménilmontant
Boulevard Voltaire
Bd. de Charonne
Bd. Davout
PLACE DE LA BASTILLE
PLACE DE LA NATION
Cours de Vincennes
Boulevard Diderot
GARE DE LYON
Av. Daumesnil
Bd. de Bercy
Bd. Soult
Seine R.
Jardin des Plantes
GARE D'AUSTERLITZ
Bd. Saint-Marcel
Boulevard de la Gare
PLACE D'ITALIE
Bd. Poniatowski
Bois de Vincennes
Bd. Masséna
Bd. Kellerman
N
0 ½ mile
0 ½ kilometer

which you can drain a bottle. For more expensive wine, the descriptions "*appellation controlée*" and "*mise en bouteille au domaine*" or "*au château*" indicate ascending levels of quality.

Paris

Steeped in history right down to its sewers, Paris is a shrine, an advertising slogan, or a vague longing for (sexual, political, artistic) liberation before it is anything so mundane as the hometown of three million people. The city has always considered itself, with some reason, the capital of Western civilization. In the spirit of its great tolerance, the city has harbored thinkers, rabble-rousers, artists, and eccentrics as diverse as Robespierre, Curie, Wilde, Sartre, Picasso, Ho Chi Minh, Hemingway, and Khomeini. Paris is predominantly the product of efficient nineteenth-century urban design, but its architecture, as its art, music, and theater, ranges from the classical to the avant-garde and beyond. If Paris, self-conscious symbol of history, newness, culture, civilization itself, did not exist, we would have to invent it.

Orientation and Practical Information

Paris is in northern France, 200km and two to three rail hours from the English Channel (La Manche), a similar distance from Belgium, and no more than 12 hours from any point in the country. As you might imagine, it's a major travel hub for trains, buses, and flights throughout France and Europe.

Paris is divided into 20 *arrondissements,* or districts. The numbers rise clockwise in a rough spiral from the first or *premier* district around the Louvre and the west end of the Ile de la Cité to the newer *arrondissements* on the city's outskirts. We give the *arrondissement* with every address: *5ème* means *cinquième,* or fifth. The city is cut in half by the River Seine, which flows from east to west; **Rive Gauche** (Left Bank) lies to the south, and **Rive Droite** (Right Bank) to the north. Traditionally, the Left Bank has had a bohemian, artsy character; the student areas of the Sorbonne, the Latin Quarter (*5ème*), and around the Odéon in St-Germain (*6ème*) are all here, although most of St-Germain and the neighboring *7ème* are pricey. Across the river lie the *grands boulevards* of the Right, and districts such as the *16ème* and the Faubourg St-Honoré—very elegant, or as the French would say, *BCBG (bon chic bon genre).* If you are staying in Paris for more than a few days, consider investing in a copy of the *Plan de Paris par Arrondissements,* a collection of maps of each *arrondissement* with a complete street index and other useful information. Unless you have a hankering to explore Paris's suburbs (*banlieue*), the 38F edition should suffice. Paris's efficient Métro (abbreviated here as "Mo.") will whisk you from one quarter to the next (see Public Transportation below).

Tourist Offices: Bureau d'Accueil Central, 127, av. des Champs-Elysées, *8ème* (tel. 47 23 61 72). Mo. Etoile. Very helpful, also very crowded. Handles Paris and all of France. Room reservations made here; 14F commission on 1-star hotels, but free for hostels. Will make reservations in 40 other French cities, though not more than 7 days in advance (20F). Open daily 9am-8pm. Branches at Gare du Nord (tel. 45 26 94 82), Gare de l'Est (tel. 46 07 17 73), Gare de Lyon (tel. 43 43 33 24), Gare d'Austerlitz (tel. 45 84 91 70), and (May-Sept.) the Eiffel Tower (tel. 45 51 22 15). **Accueil des Jeunes en France (AJF),** 119, rue St-Martin, *4ème* (tel. 42 77 87 80), right in front of the Pompidou Center. Mo. Rambuteau. Commission-free room-finding, maps, gracious Parisian advice, and general good cheer. Open Mon.-Sat. 9:30am-7pm, closed Sun. Other offices at 16, rue du Pont Louis-Philippe, *4ème* (tel. 42 78 04 82), Mo. Hôtel de Ville or Pont-Marie (open Mon.-Fri. 9:30am-6:30pm, also Sat. in summer); arrival hall next to Agence de Voyages SNCF in the new building at the Gare du Nord (tel. 42 85 86 19), Mo. Gare du Nord (open June-Sept. daily 8am-10pm; April-May and Oct. Mon.-Fri. 9:30am-6:30pm), and at 139, bd. St-Michel, *5ème* (tel. 43 54 95 86), Mo. Port Royal (open June-July 31 Mon.-Fri. 9:30am-6:30pm). **Centre d'Information et de Documentation Jeunesse (CIDJ),** 101, quai Branly, *15ème* (tel. 45 66 40 20). Mo. Bir-Hakeim. Information on camping, touring, and sports, all in French. Some information on lodgings. Part-time job possibilities posted weekday mornings (scarce for non-French). Open Mon.-Fri. 9am-7pm.

Budget Travel: Council on International Education Exchange (CIEE), 51, rue Dauphine, *6ème* (tel. 43 26 79 65). Mo. Odéon. Sells cheap charters, BIGE tickets, and ISICs (32F). Another branch at 16, rue de Vaugirard (tel. 46 34 02 90). Mo. Odéon. If you have lost your CIEE ticket, go to their new office at 31, rue St-Augustin, *2ème* (tel. 42 66 20 87). Mo. Opéra. All open Mon.-Fri. 10am-6:30pm, Sat. 10am-1pm and 2:30-5pm. **Centre Franco-Americain Odéon,** pl. de l'Odéon, *1er* (tel. 46 34 16 10). Mo. Odéon. CIEE's work and study center for American students in Paris. If you want to work in France and are enrolled full-time in an American university, come here as soon as you arrive in France to get working papers (US$82 (550F) for up to 3 months). Open Mon.-Fri. 9am-6:30pm. The **Accueil des Jeunes en France** office, rue St-Martin, also sells BIGE tickets. **Maison de France,** 8, av. de l'Opéra (tel. 42 96 10 23). Mo. Palais-Royal. Friendly and efficient, with information on vacations anywhere in France, tailored to your budget. Open Mon.-Fri. 9am-7pm. **Office de Tourisme Universitaire,** 137, bd. St. Michel (tel. 43 29 12 88). Mo. Port-Royal. A French student travel agency much like CIEE. Open Mon.-Fri. 10am-6:30pm, Sat. 10am-5:45pm.

American Express: 11, rue Scribe, *9ème* (tel. 42 66 09 99), right across from the Opéra. Mo. Opéra or Auber. Mail held; free if you have an AmEx card or AmEx traveler's checks, 5F otherwise. All banking services. Financial services open Mon.-Sat. 9am-5pm; other services, including mail and money orders, open Mon.-Fri. 9am-5:30pm. Mobbed in summer, especially Fri., Sat., and Mon. Count on a 3-day wait for wired money.

Currency Exchange: All 6 train stations have late exchange: Gare du Nord daily until 10pm, Gare de Lyon until 11pm. The bank at 154, av. des Champs Elysées is open Sat.-Sun. 10:30am-6pm. The one at #115 has a better rate, and is open Sat. 8:30am-8pm and July-Sept. Sun. 10:15am-6pm. **Le change de Paris,** 2, rue de l'Admiral Coligny, *1er* (across from the Louvre). Open daily 10am-7pm. Rates at train stations tend to be poorer. Banks close at noon or 1pm on the eve of major holidays.

Post Office: 52, rue de Louvre, *1er,* first floor. Mo. Louvre. Unless otherwise directed, Poste Restante will end up here. Open 24 hours. Only urgent telegrams, and no mailings over 2kg outside normal business hours. Long lines Sat. and Sun.

Telephones: At the main post office. Also open 24 hours. No collect calls to the U.S. on Sun. You can make long-distance calls from any phone: Call 191 for the U.S. or Canada, 19 61 for Australia, 19 64 for New Zealand; for calls within France, dial 16—no city code. Buy a *télécarte* at a rail station ticket window, post office, or *tabac,* as coin-operated phones are scarce and will cost you more per call. No rebates, so when you leave town (few machines use them outside of Paris) pass it on.

Flights: Two airports serve Paris. Most international flights land at **Aéroporte Roissy-Charles de Gaulle** (tel. 48 62 22 80), 23km northeast of Paris. The cheapest and fastest way to get into town is Roissy Rail, a bus-train combination to Mo. Gare du Nord, Châtelet, St-Michel, and Luxembourg. Roissy Rail leaves from Aérogare 1, gate 30, arrival level; Aérogare 2A, gate A5; and Aérogare 2B, gate B6. (4 per hr., about 35 min., 25.70F.) Another option is RATP bus #350 to Gare de l'Est from Aérogare 2A, gate A5; Aérogare 2B, gate B6; or Aérogare 1, *boutiquaire* level (2 per hr., 50 min., 6 Métro tickets); or bus #351 to pl. de la Nation, leaving from the same *aérogares* and gates (2 per hr., 40 min., 6 Métro tickets). The Air France bus leaves from Aérogare 2A, gate A5; Aérogare 2B, gate B6; and Aérogare 1, gate 34, arrival level,for Mo. Porte Maillot (5 per hr., 35F). Charters usually fly into **Aéroporte Orly Sud** (tel. 48 84 32 10), about 10km from the city. A shuttle bus will take you from gate H to the Orly Rail terminal, where the RER leaves for a number of Left Bank depots (4 per hr., 20F). The RATP Orly bus will drop you at Mo. Denfert-Rochereau (4 per hr., 6 Métro tickets). Another option is the Air France bus from gate J to Mo. Invalides (5 per hr., 28F). All of this transport runs roughly 6am-11pm.

Trains: General train information (tel. 45 82 50 50), not necessarily in English, daily 8am-8pm. **Gare du Nord** (tel. 42 80 03 03) is for Channel ports, Belgium, Holland, northern Germany and Berlin, and Scandinavia. In this station at night, drugs and prostitution abound, although in the day it is perfectly safe. **Gare de l'Est** (tel. 45 82 50 50) handles traffic to and from eastern France (Champagne, Alsace, Lorraine), Luxembourg, parts of Switzerland (Basel, Zürich, Lucerne), southern Germany and Austria. **Gare de Lyon** (tel. 43 45 92 22) is a southern gateway, with trains to Provence and the Côte d'Azur, parts of Switzerland (Geneva, Lausanne, Berne), Italy, and Greece. **Gare d'Austerlitz** (tel. 45 84 15 20) pushes buggies southwest toward Bordeaux, the Pyrénées, the Loire Valley, Spain, and Portugal. **Gare St-Lazare** (tel. 45 65 60 60) waves good-bye to those bound for Normandy. And at the **Gare de Montparnasse** (tel. 45 38 52 29), trains roll in and out from and to western France, including Brittany, Versailles, and Chartres. Every train station is also a Métro stop; if you're traveling *through* Paris, you'll have to use the Métro; neither Eurail nor InterRail is valid, and ticket sellers will accept only francs.

Buses: Most international buses arrive at **Gare Routière Internationale,** 8, pl. Stalingrad (tel. 42 05 12 10), in the northeastern section of the city. Mo. Stalingrad. Many charter buses or bus-and-ferry companies will drop you off and pick you up wherever they like—normally close to their own offices.

Public Transportation: The Paris subway, or **Métro,** is quick and efficient. There are 13 lines in the system. Lines are distinguished by color only on maps—not on the signs in the station. Connections are called *correspondances.* Tickets anywhere within the city cost 4.70F, but it's more economical to buy a *carnet* of 10 for 28.20F; don't buy tickets anywhere but the official station booth. If you plan on using the Métro a lot, you may want to invest in a *carte orange,* which comes in two flavors: *coupon hebdomadaire* (valid Mon.-Sun. regardless of what day you buy it, 46F), and *coupon mensuel* (valid from the first to the last day of the month, 162F). Both allow unlimited travel on the Métro and buses—just bring a picture when you buy it. Another variety of the *carte hebdomadaire* allows you 2 trips per day per week, starting from the station in which you purchased it (25F). The special *Billets Paris Sesame* are a worse deal (2 days 53F, 4 days 83F, 1 week 138F). If you're staying in Paris for a short time, get a *Formule 1,* valid for Métro, bus, and RER. 19F per day for 2 zones (the most you'll likely need); no photo necessary. There is no need to ride first class on the Métro; "1" and "2" are marked on the cars. Class distinctions exist only 9am-5pm; at all other times, anyone can ride first class. Hold onto your ticket until you pass the point marked "*Limite de Validité des Billets.*" Also, any *correspondances* you make to the **RER** (Réseau Express Régional, rapid train to the suburbs, often very convenient within central Paris) require that you insert into a turnstile your validated (and uncrumpled) ticket. Buses use the same tickets as the Métro, but on trips crossing 2 zones (refer to the route map on buses) you'll need 2 tickets, both of which must be validated in the machine by the driver's seat. Buses usually take longer than the Métro, but you'll see more of the city. Buses worth riding from start to finish include #21, 30, 52, 56, 67, 82, 95 and 96. The Métro starts at 5:30am, and the last trains leave the stations at the *portes de Paris* (i.e. Porte d'Orléans) for the center between 12:40am and 12:55am. (Check the poster on every platform called *Principes de Tarification* for specifics on each line.) Buses run until 8:30pm, *autobus du soir* until 12:30am, and a few *autobus de nuit* run all night. Schedules are available at the RATP office, 53ter, quai des Grands-Augustus, *6ème* (tel. 43-46-14-14). Mo. St.-Michel. Open daily 6am-9pm, year-round. The exceptionally friendly and useful **Services Touristiques de la RATP,** is at place de la Madeleine, *8ème* (tel. 42-65-31-18). Mo. Madeleine. Open daily 7:30am-7pm, year-round.

Taxis: Hail one, or call a radio cab (tel. 42 03 99 99 or 42 00 67 89). You pay for the time it takes to reach you. Cabs are most expensive 10pm-6:30am, and from the airports. For the going rates, dial 42 02 22 22.

Emergencies: Police (tel. 17); headquarters at 9, bd. du Palais, *4ème* (tel. 42 60 33 22). Mo. Cité. **Ambulance** (tel. 45 67 50 50). **Fire** (tel. 18). **SOS Médecins,** 24-hour emergency medical help (tel. 47 07 77 77). **Lost property: Bureau des Objets Trouvés,** 36, rue des Morillons, *15ème.* Mo. Convention. Open Mon. and Wed. 8:30am-5pm, Tues. and Thurs. 8:30am-8pm, Fri. 8:30am-5:30pm.

Medical Assistance: Hôpital Franco-Britannique de Paris, 48, rue de Villiers, Levallois-Perret (tel. 47-58-13-12). Mo. Anatole France. Consultations 80F, with specialists 150F, Sun. and holidays 180F, 8pm-8am 222F. For birth control, contact the **Mouvement Français pour le Planning Familial,** 4, square Irénée, *11ème* (tel. 48 07 29 10). Mo. St-Ambroise. Open Mon.-Fri. 2-6pm, year-round.

Pharmacy: Pharmacie Dhéry, 84, av. des Champs Elysées, *8ème* (tel. 45 62 02 41). Mo. George V. Open 24 hours. On the Left Bank: **Drugstore St.-Germain,** 149, bd. St.-Germain, *6ème* (tel. 42 22 92 50). Mo. St.-Germain or Mabillon. Open daily 9am-2am.

Crises: SOS Crisis Help Line (tel. 47 23 80 80), staffed daily 3-11pm. English speaking assistance. You name it, they'll point you in the right direction. **Rape: SOS Viol** (tel. 05 05 95 95); you can call free from anywhere in France. Open Sept.-June Mon.-Fri. 10am-7pm; irregular hours July and Aug., but they have an answering service. **Drug Problems:** Tel. 45 74 00 04, open 24 hours.

SOS Homosexualité: 3bis, rue Clairault, *17ème* (tel. 46 27 49 36). Mo. La Fourche. Pastor Doncé is a polyglot, author, activist, and friendly font of information on various services, clubs, discothèques, bookstores, and other aspects of gay and lesbian life in Paris. He's also a *Let's Go* fan. Usually open daily 10am-1pm. In the same building, **Permanence Lesbiennes** has a hotline Sat. 3-7pm (tel. 46 27 49 36), and sponsors various activities.

Embassies: U.S., 2, av. Gabriel, *8ème* (tel. 42 96 12 02). Mo. Concorde. For lost passports, go to the **Office of American Services,** 2, rue St-Florentin (tel. 42 96 12 02, ext. 2613), 3 blocks away. **Canada,** 35, av. Montaigne, *8ème* (tel. 47 23 01 01). Mo. Franklin Roosevelt. **U.K.,** 35, rue du Faubourg-St-Honoré, *8ème* (tel. 42 66 91 42). Mo. Concorde or Madeleine.

Australia, 4, rue Jean Rey, 15*ème* (tel. 45 75 62 00). Mo Bir-Hakeim. **New Zealand,** 7ter, rue Léonard-de-Vinci, 16*ème* (tel. 45 00 24 11). Mo. Victor-Hugo. **Czechoslovakia,** 18, rue Bonaparte, 6*ème* (tel. 43 54 26 18). Mo. St-Germain-des-Prés. **Poland,** 5, rue de Talleyrand, 7*ème* (tel. 45 50 21 48). Mo. Varenne. **Hungary,** 5bis, av. Foch, 16*ème* (tel. 45 00 41 59). Mo. Charles-de-Gaulle-Etoile. **Bulgaria,** 1, av. Rapp, 7*ème* (tel. 45 51 85 90). Mo. Ecole-Militaire. **Rumania,** 5, rue de l'Exposition, 7*ème* (tel. 45 51 83 80). Mo. Ecole-Militaire. **Spain,** 13, av. George V, 8*ème* (tel. 47 23 61 83). Mo. George V. Australians and New Zealanders need to pick up a visa here.

Bookstores: Shakespeare and Company, 37, rue de la Bûcherie, 5*eme* (no tel.), just across from Notre Dame. A unique and wonderful Parisian institution, more than 60 years old. A Lost Generation haunt. Library upstairs. Open daily noon-midnight. **Brentano's,** 37, av. de l'Opéra, 2*ème*. Mo. Opéra. Emphasis on American publications, and a large display of guidebooks (including *Let's Go*) at reasonable prices. Open Mon.-Sat. 10am-8pm. **W.H. Smith,** 248, rue de Rivoli. Mo. Concorde. More British publications and a bit cheaper, but a smaller selection of guidebooks. Open Mon.-Sat. 9:30am-7pm.

Libraries: Bibliothèque Publique Information, at the Centre Pompidou (tel. 42 77 12 33). Many books in English. Open Mon.-Fri. noon-10pm, Sat.-Sun. 10am-10pm. If you have your own books and need only a quiet place to read, the historic **Bibliothèque Mazarine,** 23, Quai de Conti, 6*ème*. Mo. Pont-Neuf, stocks perfect silence, handsome old tomes in the walls, and scholars (maybe even a *Let's Go* researcher) at work. You can obtain a free *carte d'entrée* good for 6 visits by applying to the library (bring ID and 2 photos). Open Mon.-Fri. 10am-6pm. Closed first 2 weeks in Aug.

Laundry: Check the phone book under *laverie automatique* for the closest. In the Latin Quarter, 63, rue Monge (tel. 47 07 68 44). Mo. Monge. About 24F.

Public Baths: Beat the high cost of hotel showers at 8, rue des Deux Ponts, 4*ème* (tel. 43 54 47 40). Mo. Pont-Marie. Showers, soap, and towel 4.35F. Check under *Bains Douches Municipaux* in the phone book for other addresses. All open Thurs. noon-7pm, Fri. 8am-7pm, Sat. 7am-7pm, Sun. 8am-noon.

Hitchhiking: Thumbing out of Paris is difficult, and can be unsafe. Toward the east (Strasbourg, Munich), take the Métro to Porte de Charenton and walk along bd. Massena to catch the A4. Toward the north (Brussels, Cologne, Berlin), catch the Métro to Porte de la Chapelle, right next to the A1. Toward the west (Rouen, Mont St-Michel, St-Malo), take the Métro to Porte de St-Cloud, and walk up bd. Murat towards pl. de la Porte d'Auteuil, where the A13 begins. Towards the south, take the Métro to Porte d'Orléans, walk down av. de la Porte d'Orléans, and turn left to a number of *autoroutes:* A16 goes to Lyon, the French Riviera, Switzerland, Italy, and Barcelona; A10 to Bordeaux and Madrid; A11 branches off A10 towards Brittany. If you have a little money and want to save some time, try **Allostop-Provoya,** 84 passage Brady, 10*ème* (tel. 42 46 00 66). Mo. Strasbourg-St-Denis. They will match you with a driver going your way for 60F if your trip is longer than 300km, 30F if it is shorter, plus 16 *centimes* per km. If you plan to use this service more than 2 or 3 times, it pays to spend the 120F for a year's worth of rides. Eurostop International membership 30F more (see General Intro: Hitching).

Accommodations

Trying to find accommodations in Paris may be your least pleasant experience here. During summer, empty rooms are scarce and patient hotel owners even more so. It's hard to emphasize enough how much easier the task will be if you search early in the day. We do not list Paris's five IYHF youth hostels; they are either booked up to half a year in advance, or so distant that transportation costs make them less economical. *Foyers* are similar to hostels; they cost a bit more (but less than singles in a hotel), have smaller rooms and fewer rules than hostels, and are generally fun—full of youth groups and young travelers from around the world.

Most *foyers* won't accept reservations, but nearly all hotels will; take advantage of this courtesy. To reserve on your own before you embark, write to the hotel of your choice and specify date of arrival, length of stay, and type of room desired. The hotel will then send a confirmation, generally asking for one night's deposit. The whole process shouldn't take more than a month, but be sure to tell the hotel that you must receive confirmation before leaving. Few places are keen on phone reservations; improve your chances by proposing a time, before noon, by which you'll arrive.

Remember that the Accueil des Jeunes en France (see Tourist Offices under Practical Information) will find you a room in one of its *foyers* or in a cheap hotel for free, and that the tourist offices will do the same for a small fee. These services will save you much aggravation.

Foyers

Breakfast and linen are included, and showers are free and unlimited. Call, or better still go in the morning before 10am. AJF foyers will call around for you to their facilities, but get to one of their offices early.

Hôtels de Jeunes (AJF): Central Office at 119, rue St.-Martin, *4ème* (tel. 42 77 87 80), Mo. Rambuteau. Open Mon.-Sat. 9:30am-7pm. Go here to book a place in any of their *foyers* (bookings free), or you can try going directly to one of the foyers between 8 and 9:30am. There are three: **Le Fauconnier,** 11, rue du Fauconnier, *4ème* (tel. 42 74 23 45), Mo. St-Paul or Pont-Marie; **Le Fourcy,** 6, rue de Fourcy, *4ème* (tel. 42 74 23 45), Mo. St-Paul; **Maubisson,** 12, rue des Barres, *4ème* (tel. 42 72 72 09), Mo. Pont-Marie. These *foyers* are all located in pleasant historic buildings in the Marais district, close to one another and the sights. Le Fauconnier is the nicest, while Le Fourcy is the only one of the three with lockers (all AJF residents can use them; 150F deposit, 5F per day.) The English-speaking staff is basically friendly. Each *foyer* is 72F per night, breakfast and shower included. No daytime lock-out; no curfew. Maximum stay (usually) 5 days. AJF gives priority to groups, which, unlike individuals, can make reservations in advance. AJF runs a restaurant, **La Table d'Hôte,** 16, rue du Pont-Louis-Philippe. (Lunch and dinner 40F; you must reserve for the meal.) AJF also runs the **Résidence Bastille,** 151, av. Lédri Rollin, *11ème* (tel. 43 79 53 86), Mo. Voltaire, which costs slightly less and has a few singles. 64-67F per night in 2- to 4-bed rooms, 72F per night in singles, showers and breakfast included. Reception open 8am-10:30pm, hostel closed noon-2pm. Open year-round. **Résidence Luxembourg** is open July-Sept. only, and has the same prices. Neither have curfews. Less snazzy than the Marais establishments, these two are nevertheless well-located, and apt to be less crowded. Most will hold spots reserved by phone for an hour or two. You cannot occupy your room on the first day until 2:30pm. No families accepted.

Centre International de Paris (BVJ), Paris Louvre, 20 rue Jean-Jacques Rousseau, *1er* (tel. 42 36 88 18), Mo. Louvre; **Paris Opéra,** 11, rue Thérèse, *1er* (tel. 42 60 77 23), Mo. Pyramides; **Paris Les Halles,** 5 rue du Pélican, *1er* (tel. 42 60 92 45), Mo. Palais Royal; **Paris Quartier Latin,** 44, rue des Bernardins, *5ème* (tel. 43 29 34 80), Mo. Maubert. Right in the center of things, these 4 youth centers are very friendly and comfortable. No individual reservations accepted; arrive by 9am or call. Crowded, small, but spotlessly clean multi-bedded rooms and a few singles (75F per night, showers and breakfast included). Quartier Latin lets singles only to students who are studying in Paris and have applied in writing. Paris Louvre has a restaurant with meals for 45F, and a *demi-pension* option for 110F; Quartier Latin has kitchen facilities (though no pots). Each has a flexible maximum stay of 3 days, except Quartier Latin. Each is open daily 6am-2am, year-round.

Centre International de Séjour de Paris (CISP). Ravel, 6, av. Maurice Ravel, *12ème* (tel. 43 43 19 01), Mo. Porte de Vincennes. Go right on bd. Soult, left on av. Courteline, and right on av. Vincent d'Indy, which turns into av. Maurice Ravel (10-15 min. from Metro). Singles and doubles 106F, rooms with up to 5 beds 80F, dormitory beds 67F. A big place with excellent facilities, but on the edge of nowhere. Bar, restaurant, and access to a pool (meals 37F and 43F, use of pool 9.30F for CISP guests). Breakfast and showers included. **Kellerman,** 17, bd. Kellerman *13ème* (tel. 45 80 70 76), Mo. Porte d'Italie. Same prices for beds and restaurant; no pool, but facilities for the disabled. Located in a park. Both give priority to groups, but take families and individuals. No individual reservations; phone reservations only 1 or 2 days ahead. Reception open 6:30am-1:30am, year-round. No curfew.

Y & H Hostel, 80, rue Mouffetard, *5ème* (tel. 45 35 09 53), Mo. Monge. Ideally located and cheap. Rooms are crowded with 2, 3, or 4 beds. The atmosphere is informal and . . . well, youthful and happy. Though the building is old and run-down, the rooms are clean and the management friendly. 57F per night, showers included. No breakfast. Reserve by mail with 1 night's fee or arrive by 10am. Hostel and reception open 8-11am and 5pm-1am. Curfew 1am.

Foyer Franco-Libannais, 15, rue d'Ulm (tel. 43 29 47 60), Mo. Cardinal-Lemoine or Luxembourg. Excellent location. Good chance of finding a room in July and Aug., when the students leave. The rooms are large and pleasant, and the showers clean. Reservations only 15 days in advance; you must pay for the whole stay. Singles 100F, with shower 110F; doubles 135-170F. Students pay 20F less on rooms, 15-20F less on rooms with shower. 10% reduction if you stay 15 days or longer. Open 8am-midnight. No curfew.

Association des Etudiants Protestants de Paris (AEPP), 46, rue de Vaugirard, *6ème* (tel. 46 33 23 30 or 43 54 31 49), Mo. Luxembourg or Odéon. Across from the Jardin du Luxembourg. Friendly, international atmosphere and lots of facilities. 5-day minimum stay and 3-week maximum (flexible). No reservations; arrive by 10am. Rooms with 4-6 beds 54F per person, doubles 65F per person, singles 70F. Showers and breakfast included. Reception open Mon.-Fri. 9am-noon and 3-7pm, Sat. 9am-noon and 6-8pm, Sun. and holidays 10am-noon. Doors close at 10pm, but guests get a key.

Maison des Clubs UNESCO, 43, rue de la Glacière, *13ème* (tel. 43 36 00 63), Mo. Glacière. Friendly, English-speaking staff and some of the nicest *foyer* rooms in Paris. Only groups can make reservations. Individuals show up at 9:30-10am to check for vacancies. 5-day maximum stay (flexible). Singles 100F, rooms with 2-4 beds 73F, breakfast included. Doors close at 12:30am and don't open until 7am.

Maison Internationale des Jeunes, 4, rue Titon, *11ème* (tel. 43 71 99 21), Mo. Faidherbe-Chaligny. 150 beds. Rooms with 2-8 beds for ages 18-30. Floors generally single-sex, but expect coed showers. 4-day maximum stay (flexible). Reservations not accepted, so come early in the morning. 75F per night, including a good shower and a meager breakfast. Open 8am-10pm. Loosely enforced lock-out 10am-6pm. Curfew 1am.

Foyer International d'Accueil de Paris, 30, rue Cabanis, *14ème* (tel. 45 89 89 15), Mo. Glacière. Monolithic, modern, and clean. More like a high-rise apartment than a *foyer.* You can make reservations, but not more than a month in advance. No minimum stay. 3 rooms have facilities for the disabled. Not the friendliest in the world. Singles 90F, with shower 105F; doubles 78F, with shower 90F. Breakfast 15F, meals 42F. Curfew 2am.

Foyer International des Etudiantes, 93, bd. St. Michel, *6ème* (tel. 43 54 49 63), Mo. Luxembourg. The *foyer* to stay in, though from Oct.-June it accepts only women at the University of Paris. Both sexes accepted July-Sept. Across from the Jardin du Luxembourg, with an astounding view of the city from the terrace. Many facilities, including kitchenettes on each floor. Reservations in writing should be made 2 months ahead, and followed by 150F and confirmation. You can try calling or visiting at around 9:30am to see if there are any no-shows. Singles 114F, doubles 78F. Showers and breakfast included. Doors close Sun.-Fri. 1:30am-6am, open all night Sat.

Hotels

As we've said, if you're traveling with someone (or several people) you don't mind sleeping with, you'll do better in a hotel. Expect to pay at least 70-80F for a single, but only 20-25F more for a single-bedded double; two-bed doubles are rare and cost considerably more. In less expensive hotels, few of the rooms come with private bath, though there are bidets and sinks with hot and cold water. Showers are always available, usually for 10-20F extra.

Rooms disappear quickly after morning check-out (generally 10am-noon), so try to arrive early. If you can't, consider spending your first night in a *foyer* or in whatever AJF or the tourist office can find for you, and look for a better place the following morning. In summer, hotels in the Latin Quarter are usually packed by early afternoon; those on the Right Bank are more likely to have vacancies. In any case, it's easier to use one of the accommodations services. Many *hôteliers* will try to unload their more expensive rooms on you, so be sure to check the price list (which must be posted inside by law) and ask about cheaper rooms.

The Left Bank

Hôtel Nesle, 7, rue de Nesle, *6ème* (tel. 43 54 62 41), Mo. Odéon, off rue Dauphine. "You'll either love it or hate it" says Mme. Renée, the owner. Once a bastion of psychedelic design, the Nesle has been redecorated in an eclectic mix of styles (Egyptian, Indian, Victorian...). Breakfast with incense and Arab music persists. Mme. Renée continues to welcome *Let's Go* users with open arms. Many guests leave their doors open in the evening and mingle. Co-ed rooms. No reservations, so go early. Singles 70-80F, doubles 80F, with shower 140-186F. Breakfast 18F (Mon.-Sat. only). Showers 10F.

Hôtel de Médicis, 214, rue St-Jacques, *5ème* (tel. 43 29 53 64 or 43 54 14 66), Mo. Luxembourg. An excellent small hotel, especially for longer stays. Although the rooms are old and one of the showers smells, the prices, Mme. Rault, her husband, and the 2 big Dalmatians are all great. 3-day minimum stay. Telephone reservations recommended. Singles 59-70F, doubles 75-97.50F, triples 115F. Less for extended stays. Showers 10F.

Hôtel de Nevers, 3, rue de l'Abbé-de-l'Epée, *5ème* (tel. 43 26 81 83), Mo. Luxembourg, on a side street of rue Gay-Lussac. Attractive rooms overlooking the Panthéon, and cheerful management. Reservations accepted by phone. Singles 90F, doubles 110F, with shower 160-230F. Extra beds 25F. Breakfast 15F. Showers 20F.

Hôtel d'Orient, 43, rue Abbé-Grégoire, *6ème* (tel. 45 48 23 23), Mo. St-Placide. Near the Jardin du Luxembourg. A pink interior perhaps once considered elegant. Run by a delightful older woman. Singles 70F, doubles 120F, triples and quads 260F. Showers 8F. Breakfast included.

Hôtel de Cujas, 18, rue de Cujas, *5ème* (tel. 43 54 58 10), Mo. Luxembourg. A good choice on a street with many hotels. Large, with a good chance of finding a room. Far from spotless. Reservations not accepted in summer. Singles 60F, with shower 90F; doubles 145F, with shower 160F; triples with shower 185F. Showers 10F. Open all night, year-round.

Delhy's Hotel, 22, rue de l'Hirondelle, *6ème* (tel. 43 26 58 25), Mo. St-Michel. On a wee street between place St-Michel and rue Gît le Coeur, this hotel has been recently refurbished. Reasonably priced compared to many others in this excellent location. Singles 60-80F, doubles with shower 150-200F. Breakfast 18F. Showers 15F. Written reservations a month in advance are recommended, but if there is space you can reserve a day or two ahead by phone.

Hôtel du Commerce, 14, rue de la Montagne-Ste-Geneviève, *5ème* (tel. 43 54 89 69), Mo. Maubert. Tiny rooms, narrow halls, and peeling paint, but cheap and a great location. The old woman at the desk is Balzacian. No reservations. Singles 67F, doubles 78F, with shower 100F. Showers 13F, baths 23F. No breakfast.

Hôtel Marignan, 13, rue du Sommerard, *5ème* (tel. 43 54 63 81), Mo. Maubert. On a quiet street between bd. St-Germain and rue des Ecoles. One of the best deals in this central area. Multi-lingual staff offers useful sightseeing information. Popular, so reservations a month ahead are suggested (they will sometimes help you find another room). In summer, 3-night stay required. Singles 100F, doubles 180F, triples 255-270F, quads 300-340F. Showers and breakfast included. Rates 20F lower Nov. to mid-March.

Île de la Cité

Hôtel Henri IV, 25, place Dauphine, *1er* (tel. 43 54 44 53), Mo. Pont-Neuf or Cité. On a lovely square behind the Palais de Justice. The lower floors are some 400 years old, and the whole building is deliciously beset with the problems of age. The rooms are small and a bit faded, the walls thin, and the washrooms and showers can be reached only by an outside staircase. English-speaking managers, whom some people consider rude and inflexible. Overwhelmingly popular: during the summer you must reserve a month or two in advance. Singles 78F, doubles 105-130F, triples 142-160F. Showers 17F. Breakfast included.

The Right Bank

Hôtel de Nice, 42bis, rue de Rivoli, *4ème* (tel. 42 78 55 29), Mo. Hôtel-de-Ville. Slightly more expensive, but cleaner and more cheerful than most. Reservations must be made at least 3 weeks in advance and followed by a letter of confirmation including 1 night's payment. Rooms overlooking the square are the quietest. Singles 100-180F, singles and doubles with shower 165F, singles and doubles with bath and toilet 270F. Showers 16F. Breakfast included. Curfew midnight or 2am (depending on who's on the shift).

Hôtel Rivoli, 2, rue des Mauvais-Garçons, *4ème* (tel. 42 72 08 41), Mo. Hôtel-de-Ville. On a small street off rue de Rivoli past the BHV (Bazar de l'Hôtel de Ville) department store. Nicely renovated. The rooms can be noisy, but they're clean and attractive. Run by a helpful proprietor, cute children, and three tropical birds. Singles 75F, with shower 80F; doubles 110F, with shower 140F; triples 140-180F. No reservations. Breakfast, usually in your room, 15F. Showers 15F. Curfew 1am (flexible).

Hôtel Picard, 26, rue de Picardie, *3ème* (tel. 48 87 53 82), Mo. République or Filles du Calvaire. Excellent hotel, run by an efficient and pleasant manager. Rooms are large, clean, and very modern. Extremely popular, so arrive early. Reservations should be made at least 2 weeks in advance, although if there's space, same-day phone reservations are accepted. Singles or doubles 100F, with shower 175F. Delicious breakfast with unlimited bread and coffee 20F. Showers 15F. Extra beds 50F.

Grand Hôtel Malher, 5, rue Malher, *4ème* (tel. 42 72 60 92), Mo. St-Paul. Good location on a small street that connects the Jewish quarter with rue de Rivoli. One of the most picturesque hotels around, in an old building with lace curtains. An elderly French couple, their son, and a dog keep the place in shape. Some rooms are being redone and will become more expensive. Singles 60-75F. Doubles 100F, with shower 150F, with bath and toilet 250F. Triples 150F, with bath and toilet 300F. Breakfast, which can be brought up to rooms on first three floors, 16F. Showers 12F.

Hôtel Chancelier Boucherat, 110, rue de Turenne, *3ème* (tel. 42 72 91 28), Mo. Filles-du-Calvaire. Extremely friendly staff. The neighborhood, a bustling garment district by day, becomes uncomfortably quiet at night. Specially recommended for groups of 3 or 4. Small singles 112F, with shower 181F; doubles 129F, with shower 198F; triples 166F, with shower 264F; quads 183F, with bath 281F. Showers 12F. Breakfast 15F.

If the above neighborhoods prove fruitless, try some of the less expensive residential or commercial areas. Perfectly adequate accommodations dot the area around the quiet place des Abbesses, between seedy Pigalle and the touristy, overpriced heights of Montmartre in the *18ème.* The farther out you go, the better chance you'll have of finding something. All neighborhoods are well-connected to the center of town, and since each *arrondissement* is a self-sustaining community, you shouldn't have trouble finding a local bar, cafe, or *épicerie*—or staying away from other tourists.

Food

Eating in Paris should always be a pleasure. Parisians have developed gastronomy as highly as any other aspect of civilization, and even on a budget you can join in this culinary celebration, eating well for 50F and unforgettably for 80F. If mealtime means a paper bag and a bench, you can enjoy delicious cheeses, quiche, and fresh fruits. Some very cheap French restaurants hide in corners of the city, but other inexpensive choices, especially in the Latin Quarter, represent a dizzying range of cuisines—Greek, Italian, Vietnamese, and North African, often crammed together on one small street. For the best deals, look for *menus à prix fixe;* three-course meals, with drink (*boisson*) sometimes included. *Service compris* means the service is included in the price; if the menu says "S.N.C." *(service non compris)* you'll be charged 15% gratuity. For a snack, buy a crepe (about 14F) from one of the many stands around the city, especially common near Montparnasse.

Cafes provide snacks, light meals, telephones, and toilets. Prices are higher if you sit at a table, and in cafes on major streets or near major sights. Colorful open **markets** are everywhere, and offer an array of excellent food. Convenient to the Latin Quarter is the market on rue Mouffetard, and near Place de l'Odéon is the market on rue de Buc. Most markets are open Mon.-Sat. 8am-6pm, with an afternoon break. Prices often go down before closing, but otherwise are similar to those in stores. The French style of shopping is ideal for picnics; store owners are used to people buying a slice of pâté or enough salad for two. In most markets and specialty shops, you point (never touch) and the salesperson fetches. *Epiceries, boulangeries,* and other small stores seldom close before 7pm (after a mid-afternoon break). Small shops are closed Monday, when you'll have to wander the aisles of the Prisunic or Monoprix supermarkets.

At university restaurants (usually closed on weekends and in summer), you can get an institutional three-course meal for only 18F; you will ordinarily be asked to show an ISIC. A complete list of *restaurants universitaires* (affectionately dubbed "Resto-U") is available from **CROUS,** 39, av. Georges Bernanos, *5ème* (Mo. Port Royal; open year-round Mon.-Fri. 9am-5pm); there is a restaurant there. The most popular among students is **Albert Châtelet,** 10, rue Jean Calvin, *5ème* (Mo. Censier-Daubenton; open Sept.-June Mon.-Fri. 11:30am-2pm and 6:30-8:25pm). The **Alliance Française,** 101 bd Raspail, *6ème* (tel. 45 44 38 28; Mo. Notre-Dame-des-Champs) has better-than-average student food. (Lunch (noon-2pm) 20F, dinner (6-9pm) 25F. Open year-round Mon.-Fri.)

Left Bank

Le Petit Vatel, 5, rue Lobineau, *6ème,* between rue de la Seine and rue Mabillon. Mo. Odéon or Mabillon. What can you say about a restaurant that is just steps from the Senate and some of Paris's fanciest shops and serves hearty main dishes for 21F? An institution among students, this place offers a changing *carte* with black bean soup or curried rice for 12F, turkey or grilled beef for 21F, a vegetarian plate for 23F, and cheese or cake for 12F. Cider, beer, or wine 6-8F. Open Mon.-Sat. noon-3pm and 7pm-midnight, Sun. 7pm-midnight. Closed 1 week in Aug.

Restaurant des Beaux-Arts, 11, rue Bonaparte, *6ème.* Mo. St-Germain-des-Prés. Across from the Ecole des Beaux Arts, and around the corner from where Oscar Wilde died and Jorge Luis Borges lived. Great traditional food at great prices: *menu* 46F, *service et boisson compris.* Zut! Also recommended are the *Poissons au gratin* (fish and cheese casserole), *boeuf bourguignon,* and *tarte maison.* Open daily noon-2:30pm and 7-10:45pm.

Aux Charpentiers, 10, rue Mabillon, *6ème.* Mo. Mabillon. A small restaurant frequented by students. *Plat du jour* 46-50F, *service et boisson non compris.* The Greek-style mushrooms are very popular (32F). Open Mon.-Sat. noon-3pm and 7-11:30pm.

Les Incroyables, 9, rue Gregoire de Tours, *6ème.* Mo. Odéon. Very good selection, if a little expensive. 60F *menu* offers *entrées* such as *terrine aux foies de volailles* (chicken liver pâté), various salads, *soupe à l'oignon gratinée,* and main dishes such as *caneton au muscadet* (duckling cooked in wine). *Boisson non compris.* Open daily noon-2:30pm and 7-11pm.

L'Acropolis, 59/61, rue St. André des Arts (in the cour de commerce). Mo. Odéon. An attractive Greek restaurant in an old passage leading into an even older courtyard. *Menu* 49.50F, *service et boisson compris.* Open Sept.-July Tues.-Sat. noon-2pm and 7-10:30pm.

Zéro de Conduite, 64, rue Monsieur-le-Prince, *6ème.* Mo. Luxembourg. A favorite among Parisians, with checkered tablecloths and goofy posters. Extensive 55F *menu, boisson non compris,* features among other things *estouffade de boeuf* (beef stew). Main course 45-79F, *plat du jour* 35-41F. Open Sept.-July noon-2:30pm and 7-10:30pm.

Saigon Luxembourg, 50, rue monsieur-le-Prince, *6ème.* Mo. Luxembourg. The portions may be small, the choices few, and the decor less than sparkling, but a 34.50F *menu* (including asparagus and crab soup, chicken chop suey, and rice) is all that's needed to distinguish this place. If you're hungry, order *à la carte;* shrimp and crab dishes cost 30.44F. Open daily noon-2:30pm and 7-10pm.

La Cochonaille, 21, rue de la Harpe, *5ème.* Mo. St. Michel. Right in the middle of everything. Serves traditional food, with, as its name implies, an emphasis on pork dishes. Varied 3-course *menu* 66.70F, 2 courses 49.50F. Open daily 11:30am-3pm and 7pm-midnight.

Koutouki, 13, rue Xavier-Privas, *5ème.* Mo. St. Michel. On one of the tiny food- and people-filled streets off rue de la Huchette. Representative of the many fairly cheap Greek restaurants in the area. 40F 2-course *menu, boisson non compris.* Open daily noon-11pm.

Place de la Contrescarpe and **rue Mouffetard** are filled with inexpensive, attractive restaurants. A market street teeming with stalls and shoppers by day, rue Mouffetard is an international diner's paradise by night.

La Sousie, 5, rue du Sommerard, *5ème.* Mo. Maubert- Mutualité. A truly *sympa* place, with two 45.50F *menus* including an excellent salad bar, fresh, tasty main dishes, and dessert. *Boisson non compris.* Also—a reasonable fondue: 85F for 2 people. Open Mon.-Sat. 11:45am-2:30pm and 6:30-11pm.

Aux Savoyards, 14, rue des Boulangers, *5ème.* Mo. Jussieu. A homey place on a narrow twisting street. Traditional 3-course *menu* is a good value at 50F, *service et boisson compris.* Popular with the university crowd. Open Sept.-July Mon.-Fri. noon-2:30pm and 7-10:30pm, Sat. noon-2:30pm.

Microlimano, 29, rue Descartes, *5ème.* Mo. Cardinal Lemoine. An extremely pleasant Greek restaurant with music and outdoor tables. The 45F *menu* is delicious, although selection is limited. *Boisson non compris.* Open daily noon-3pm and 7pm-midnight.

Le Tire Bouchon, 47, rue Descartes, *5ème.* Mo. Cardinal-Lemoine. A tiny place, always very crowded. Well-prepared, fresh, French food. *Steak au fromage, mousse au chocolat,* and mouth-puckering fresh lemon sherbet included in the 39F *menu* (*boisson et service compris* only during lunch). Open Mon.-Thurs. 4pm-1am, Fri.-Sun. 10:30am-3pm and 6pm-1am.

Crêperie de la Mouff, 9, rue Mouffetard. *5ème.* Mo. Cardinal-Lemoine. A bit expensive, but a fine place to begin the happy study of crepes. From 10F for the lowly dessert *crêpe au beurre et sucre,* to 45F for *crêpe au saumon fumé* (with smoked salmon). *Bol* of cider 10F, ½ pitcher 18F.

Right Bank

Mèlodine, 42, rue Rambuteau, *3ème.* Mo. Rambuteau. Near the Centre Pompidou. A very decent *self* (cafeteria) with 3-4 dishes that change daily, good salads, cheeses, and desserts, and an area for non-smokers. *Steak-frites* served with a very tasty sauce. Main dishes 16.80F-38.70F. Whole meals 45F. Open daily 10am-10pm.

La Coquillière, 12, rue Coquillière, *1er.* Mo. Louvre or Les Halles. As close to Les Halles as you can get at these reasonable prices. 59F *menu* includes *moules marinieres* (mussels in butter), *assiette de crudités,* or *terrine de campagne* (pâté), followed by roast trout or chicken, and then ice cream, chocolate mousse, or tart. *Boisson non compris.* Open 24 hours.

Le Petit Goulot, 20, rue de Roule, *1er.* Mo. Louvre. 64F *menu* (54F at lunch) features attractive entrées like *mousse de canard* (duck mousse), or *terrine de saumon au coulis de tomates* (salmon pâté with purée of tomato sauce), and main dishes like *gratin de turbot* (turbot baked in cheese) and *rôt de porc aux aromates* (roast pork with spices). Expensive, with dessert and drink not included, but in an unpretentious, cozy atmosphere. Open Sept.-July Tues.-Sat. noon-2:30pm and 7-10:30pm.

Aquarius, 54, rue Ste-Croix-de-la-Bretonnerie, *4ème.* Mo. Hôtel-de-Ville. Small vegetarian restaurant near the AJF and BVJ foyers. Organically grown vegetables (*légumes biologiques*) with no preservatives. Salads 10-24F, vegetable tarts 24F, and other prepared dishes such as *quenelles de soja* (soybean patties). 37F *menu* available noon-2pm and 7-10pm only. No smoking and no liquor. The bread is excellent, and can be purchased at the front of the store. Open Sept.-July Mon.-Sat. noon-10pm; Also at 40, rue de Gergovie, *14ème* (tel. 45 41 36 88; Mo. Pernety). Open Mon.-Sat. noon-3pm and 7-10pm.

Mexico Linda, 105, rue Veille du Temple. Mo. St-Sebastien-Froissart. Near the AJF and BVJ foyers, and behind the Picasso Museum. A new Mexican restaurant with nice owners and a very cheap *menu* at 40F, *service et boisson compris.* Open Mon.-Sat. noon-3pm and 7:30-10pm, Tues. and Sat. to 11pm.

L'Esterel, 8, rue Tardieu, *18ème.* Mo. Abbesses. Extremely attractive and friendly atmosphere. 40F *menu, service et boisson compris.* Try the house specialty *roule de jambon "Esterel"* or traditional food such as *lapin à la moutarde* (rabbit in mustard sauce). Open daily 7pm-1am.

Casa Miguel, 48, rue St-Georges, *9ème.* Mo. St-Georges. Entered by Guinness as the cheapest restaurant in the Western world, but much more than a gimmick. Started in 1949 by Maria and Miguel Codina, refugees from Franco's Spain, Casa Miguel has since been serving cheap food as a labor of love (check out the inspiring quotations in the window). Small place (max. 32 people served per night) and small portions. For 5F (no joke), you get an appetizer, main course, and cheese, *boisson et service compris.* Fri. is fish day. For an extra 1.50F you get a dessert. Open Mon.-Sat. noon-1pm and 7-8pm, Sun. noon-1pm. Closed for 1 week at the end of July, beginning of Aug.

Le Chartier, 7, rue du Faubourg-Montmartre, *9ème.* Mo. Montmartre. The selection is extensive and the food reasonably priced and very good, hence the crowds at lunch and dinner. *Menu* 59F, *service et boisson compris.* **Le Dronot,** 103, rue de Richelieu, *2ème* (Mo. Richelieu-Druoot) and **Le Commerce,** 51, rue de Commerce, *15ème* (Mo. Lamotte-Picquet) are both under the same management as Le Chartier. All open daily 11am-3pm and 6-9:30pm.

Sights

Sightseeing in Paris seems a little redundant: the whole city is a sight. And Paris so avidly aquires new attractions that sometimes it's hard to know whether to visit a well-preserved relic or this year's monument to newness. Take time to appreciate aspects of the city missed from the top of the Eiffel Tower or in chasing between well-known sights. To begin with, the city's design itself deserves your attention: largely the product of planner Baron Haussmann under Napoleon III, it balances awesome monuments linked by great boulevards with the quiet squares and alleys of older neighborhoods. Originally settled by the Parisii tribe in the third century B.C.E., and expanded as a Roman outpost called Lutetia after the first century C.E., early Paris was concentrated on the Ile de la Cité. The city began to develop its current shape when Hugh Capet, Count of Paris, bacame King of France (987) and made Paris his capital. King Phillip Augustus (1180-1223) confirmed the basic segregation of functions that still characterizes the city: political and ecclesiastical authority on the Ile de la Cité, academic life on the Left Bank, and commerce on the

Right Bank. Bouts of urban planning and renewal after uprisings in 1789, 1848, and 1871 added the distinctive boulevards.

The Ile de la Cité and the Ile St-Louis are the only two remaining of the original eight islands in this part of the Seine. On the **Ile de la Cité,** the **Cathédrale de Notre-Dame** (Mo. Cité), built from 1163 to 1330 according to the plans of Bishop Maurice de Sully, remains the geographical heart of Paris and of France; all distances in the country are measured from its *parvis* (front porch). Stop for a look from quiet **place René Viviani** on the Left Bank; then cross to the island for a look at its interior. Climb the cathedral's south tower (22F, students 12F) and visit the crypt (open daily 10am-5:30pm; admission 22F, students 12F). The cathedral, with its flying buttresses and looming interior, is impressive, but the jewel in the crown of Parisian architecture is the Gothic **Ste-Chapelle,** located inside the courtyard of the Palais de Justice at the western end of the island and accessible from bd. de Palais. The lower, darker chapel was intended for servants, the magnificently ornate upper one for the nobility. This upper chapel is adorned with 15 partially restored thirteenth-century stained-glass marvels portraying biblical scenes. In summer, inexpensive concerts are held in this chapel; ask at the ticket office outside for information. (Open April-Sept. daily 10am-6pm; Oct.-March daily 10am-5pm. Admission 21F, ages 18-25, and everyone on Sun., 11F.) During the French Revolution, Marie Antoinette, Robespierre, and many others on the way to the guillotine were imprisoned in the **Conciergerie,** located in the same complex of buildings as the Ste-Chapelle (enter from quai de l'Horloge). (Open daily 10am-5:30pm. Admission 22F, students, and everyone on Sun., 12F.)

The **Pont-Neuf,** or New Bridge is, of course, the oldest in Paris. Built in the late sixteenth century, it connects the Cité to both the Right and Left Banks. Also on the western point of the island is ship-like **Place du Vert-Galant,** piloted by the famous 1818 statue of Henry IV, the first Bourbon king of France. The sensible monarch from Navarre earned this spot in the very core of Paris. A Protestant sympathizer, he was offered the French throne in 1593 on the condition that he embrace Catholicism, and he memorably explained his change of heart: *Paris vaut bien une messe* ("Paris is well worth a Mass").

A footbridge leads from the Ile de la Cité to the peaceful **Ile St-Louis,** whose calm streets are lined with modest but dignified eighteenth-century houses that fetch the highest prices of any Parisian real estate. From the quai d'Orléans you'll have one of Paris's best views of the Notre-Dame.

Paris is home to art and artists of all generations; hence there are museums of all kinds. Pick up the bimonthly *Musées, Monuments, Expositions de Paris et de l'Île-de-France,* available for free from the tourist office and at the Hôtel de Sully, 62, rue St-Antoine, 4*ème* (tel. 48 87 24 14). The colossus of art museums, the **Musée du Louvre,** 1*er* (Mo. Louvre), is on the Right Bank. Most famous amid its massive collection are Leonardo da Vinci's *Mona Lisa,* the third-century *Winged Victory,* and the second-century *Venus de Milo.* But the Louvre is far more than these three works. The sculpture collection on the ground floor of the Pavillon de Flore is comprehensive, as is the array of Egyptian, Greek, and Roman artifacts on the first floor of the main museum. Painting on the second and third floors is organized by school: Spanish, Italian, Flemish, Dutch and English. The building itself originated as a fortress in 1214, and was transformed by various monarchs into a royal palace, until 1871, when it began its present duty.(Open Wed.-Mon. 9:45am-5pm or 6:30pm—different rooms close at different times. Admission 20F, students 10F; free and mobbed Sun.) Also in the Louvre, the **Musée des Arts de la Mode,** 109, rue du Rivoli, 1*er* (Mo. Palais-Royal), is a chronologically arranged presentation of French fashion, including 8000 costumes and more than 30,000 accessories. (Open Wed.-Sat. 12:30-6:30pm, Sun. 11am-5pm. Admission 25F, students 18F.) All self-respecting French presidents want to leave their imprint on Paris; Mitterand has commissioned architect I.M. Pei to build a glass pyramid as the Louvre's main entrance. As with most major construction projects in Paris in the last hundred years, debate has raged over Pei's pyramid: Opponents claim that this ultra-modern geometric extravagance would clash with the Louvre's traditional architecture, and that its large dimensions (20m high) would interrupt the view that extends from the Louvre and the Carrousel past the obelisk on place de la Concorde to the Champs-Elysées and the Arc de Triomphe.

The **Jardin des Tuileries** (Mo. Concorde or Tuileries), a pleasant park where geometry has transformed nature, extends from the Louvre to **Place de la Concorde,** where Louis XVI, Marie Antoinette, and Robespierre lost their heads during the Reign of Terror (1793-1794). At the far end of the gardens are the **Jeu de Paume,** whose impressionist collection is now at the new Musée d'Orsay, and the **Musée de l'Orangerie,** which houses a small but distinguished collection of impressionist and early twentieth-century art. (Open Wed.-Sun. 9:45am-5:15pm. Admission 15F, students, and everyone on Sun. 8F.)

Some of Paris's finest treasures glow in quiet removal from the hurly-burly of the city in the **Marais,** a district that harbors a combination of past elegance, ethnic diversity, and chic young artists and intellectuals. **Place des Vosges** (Mo. St-Paul), Paris's oldest square, was conceived by Henry IV to house himself and his queen Marie de Medici. Victor Hugo lived at #6, where the **Maison de Victor Hugo** now displays a collection of sketches by the author, furniture of his design, and his old military decorations. (Open Tues.-Sun. 10am-5:40pm. Admission 7F, students 3.50F; free Sun.) The *hôtels particuliers,* elegant town houses for which the area is famous, were erected during the seventeenth century, and decorated by the famous artists of the time. The Hôtel Carnavalet at 23, rue de Sévigné, site of the famous literary *salons* of the Marquise de Sévigné, is now the **Musée Carnavalet** (Mo. St-Paul), dedicated to the social history of Paris since the Renaissance. Fans, miniature guillotines, and the *objets d'art* of lovers George Sand and Frederic Chopin are among the highlights of this excellent collection of artifacts and curiosities. (Open Tues.-Sun. 10am-5:40pm. Admission 20F, students 10F; free Sun.) In the Hôtel Salé, the **Musée Picasso,** 5, rue de Thorigny, *3ème* (Mo. St-Paul), contains 203 paintings, 158 sculptures, 88 ceramics, 1500 drawings, and the artist's collection of primitive art, given to the government in lieu of inheritance taxes. Each room has been carefully set according to Picasso's different periods, and provided with excellent explanations. The free audiovisual presentation is a good introduction to some of Picasso's main works. Allow yourself a complete day if you want to see this outstanding museum properly; the cozy cafeteria is inexpensive. (Open May-Sept. Thurs.-Mon. 9:45am-6pm, Wed. 9:45am-10pm; Oct.-April Thurs.-Mon. 9:45am-5pm, Wed. 9:45am-10pm. Admission 21F, ages under 25 and over 60 11F.) The **rue des Rosiers,** the heart of the Marais, is the old Jewish section of the city.

Right next to the Marais in the old market and artisan neighborhood of Les Halles is the **Centre National d'Art et de Culture Georges Pompidou** (Mo. Rambuteau), often called the **Beaubourg.** Conceived as a cultural center where arts of all kinds might coexist and influence one another, the building itself is a work of incessantly debated artistic worth. Much of Paris's collection of modern art has been moved to the **Musée National d'Art Moderne,** within the Pompidou. Also in the center are a library, movie theater (especially classic and avant-garde films), plays, and numerous rotating exhibitions. (Open Mon. and Wed.-Fri. noon-10pm, Sat.-Sun. 10am-10pm. Admission to the complex is free. Separate admission to major exhibits usually 10-15F. Musée National d'Art Moderne 20F, ages 24 and under 15F. Day pass to all exhibits 45F, ages 24 and under 40F.) The Pompidou ticket also entitles you to visit the little-known **Atelier Brancusi,** at the corner of rue Rambuteau and place Pompidou—definitely worth a visit. (Open Mon., Thurs., and Sat. 2:45-5:45pm.) A few hundred yards away is the **Forum des Halles** (Mo. Les Halles), an immense subterranean shopping complex with branches of Paris's fanciest stores. If you're alone, avoid the area at night; it is patrolled by police and terrifying dogs, and drug addicts hang around here. Les Halles and the surrounding streets are home to a number of chic restaurants, popular bars, fashionable cafes (Cafés Costes and Beaubourg), and funky clothing stores (Creeks). For a change from art museums, try the **Musée de l'Holographie** at *niveau* (level) 1 in the Forum des Halles: A short movie (in English) explains how holographs are made. (Open Tues.-Sat. 10:30am-7pm, Sun.-Mon. 1-7pm. Admission 25F, students 19F.)

Farther west on the Right Bank, you'll find the *grands boulevards.* The chic reputation of the **avenue des Champs-Elysées** stems from its cafes, luxurious shops, and spectacular view. Usually thronged with tourists in the summer, it becomes a rallying point for Parisians in the winter. The **Arc de Triomphe,** ordered by Napoleon and completed in 1836, is the world's largest triumphal arch and a symbol of France. Climb to the top for a grand view. (Open daily 10am-5:30pm. Admission 22F, ages 24 and under 12F). The 12 tree-lined avenues that radiate from the Arc de Triomphe take you through some of the more affluent residential *arrondissements* of the Right Bank. North of Place de la Concorde is the severe **Madeleine Church,** worth a detour for a closer look. Within hailing distance along the *grands boulevards* is the **Opéra,** nearly as grand outside as it is inside. Consider getting a seat in the *paradis* (high balcony) for a performance; though you won't see the entire stage, you'll have an excellent view of the remarkable Chagall ceiling. Following rue de la Paix, you'll encounter **Place Vendôme,** the most dignified and elegant of all, with its prestigious banks, *parfumeurs,* and jewelers. The story goes that Baron Rothschild, instead of lending his friends money, would allow them to stroll next to him around Place Vendôme for a few minutes—next morning the fortunate souls would be certain of credit at the most prestigious banks.

North of here Romanesque-Byzantine **Sacré-Coeur** perches high on Montmartre; sit on its steps and watch dusk fall. For an even better view of the city, head to the top of the dome. (Church and dome open daily 9am-6pm. Church free; dome 6F, students 3F.) Some people prefer the view from the top of the **Tour Eiffel** (Mo. Bir-Hakeim), no longer the world's tallest free-standing structure as it was upon its completion for the 1889 World Fair, but certainly a symbol of Paris and France. (Open daily 9:30am-11:30pm. Admission first level by foot 7F, by elevator 11F; second level by foot 15F, by elevator 27F; third level by foot 15F, from ground 42F.) Eastward toward the fashionable residential districts is the huge **Bois de Boulogne** (Mo. Porte Dauphine), frequented by prostitutes at night, but a nice place to stroll. Rent a boat on the **Lac Inférieur** or take pictures at the lovely **Bagatelle** flower garden. The **Musée National des Arts et Traditions Populaires,** 6, route Mahatma Ghandi (Mo. Sablous), at the north end of the Bois, is a fascinating exploration of the traditional clothing, work, and ritual of the people of France. (Open Wed.-Mon. 10am-5:15pm. Admission 15F, students and on Sun. 8F.) If you go to the **Sewers** *(Egouts de Paris),* at the corner of Pont de l'Alma and quai d'Orsay (Mo. Alma-Marceau), make sure you wear shoes that won't slip. Sewers are sewers, even in Paris—don't expect the aroma of Chanel. (Open Mon., Wed., and last Sat. of each month 2-5pm. Admission 8F.)

The greatest attraction on the Left Bank is undoubtedly the new **Musée d'Orsay,** 62 rue de Lille Feme (RER Musée d'Orsay), opened in December 1986. Housing all the old favorites from the Jeu de Paume impressionist collection, the Orsay does nothing less than exhibit the idea of the second half of the nineteenth century in the western world. The museum is in the old Gare d'Orsay, which, when finished in 1840, was as fine an expression of the spirit of the new as was the Eiffel Tower 50 years later. Highlights of the exhibit include the French impressionists in the huge Gallery K, the art nouveau exhibits in Galleries U-X, and the exhibit on the early history of film-making in the unlettered gallery at the southwest corner. The museum seriously lacks English documentation, and the historical exhibits are largely meaningless without a knowledge of French. You might take one of the hour-long tours in English (led by very good guides; Tues. and Thurs. at 11:15am). The museum is open Tues.-Wed. and Fri.-Sat. 10:30am-6pm, Thurs. 10:30am-9:45pm, Sun. 9am-6pm. Ticket sale stops 45 minutes before closing. (Admission 21F, ages under 25 and over 60, and everyone on Sun., 21F.)

Two other interesting museums occupy the Left Bank. At the **Musée Rodin,** 77 rue de Varenne, *7ème* (Mo. Varenne), the best of Rodin's works are displayed in a lovely eighteenth-century *hôtel* and a surrounding garden. (Open July-Sept. Wed.-Mon. 10am-5:45pm; Oct.-June Wed.-Mon. 10am-5pm. Admission 15F, ages 18-25, and over 60, and Sun., 7.50F; ages under 18 free.) In the Latin Quarter, the **Musée de Cluny,** 24, rue du Sommerard, *5ème* (Mo. Odéon or St-Michel), is Paris's museum of medieval artifacts. The building was built in the fifteenth century as a private mansion next to the ruins of the Roman *thermes* (baths). Its most famous exhibits are the *Lady and the Unicorn* tapestries, but a number of lesser works are also worth seeing. (Open Wed.-Mon. 9:45am-12:30pm and 2-5:15pm. Admission 15F, students 7.50F, Sun. 8F.)

If you've had enough of museums, join the children sailing toy boats in the fountain and the seniors playing *pétanque* in the **Jardin du Luxembourg** between the bustle of St-Germain and Odéon. In the middle of the Latin Quarter is the **Arènes de Lutèce,** a small Roman site in a quiet park. Just a couple of blocks away is the splendid **Jardin des Plantes** (Botanical Garden), whose formal flower beds and zoo inspired post-Impressionist Henri Rousseau's jungle fantasies. At the vivarium, pay homage to the axolotls, slimy creatures with near-human hands. (Open daily July-Sept. 9am-6pm; Oct.-June 9am-5pm. Admission 20F. Park open daily 7am-8pm.) The nearby **Tour Montparnasse** broke the city's polished surface, but it's a sleek building nonetheless. Take advantage of its view—from the highest terrace in Paris. (Open daily 9:30am-11:30pm. Admission 29.50F, students 22F.)

No visit to Paris is complete without a pilgrimage to and perhaps a picnic in the **Père Lachaise Cemetery** in the 20 *arrondissement* (Mo. Père Lachaise), the resting place of Molière, Chopin, Oscar Wilde, Edith Piaf, and Jim Morrison. (Open March 16-Nov. 5 Mon.-Sat. 7:30am-6pm, Sun. 9am-5pm; Nov. 6-March 15 Mon.-Sat. 8:30am-5pm, Sun. 9am-5pm.) At least four times larger than the Beauborg, the newly opened **Cité des Sciences et de l'Industrie,** 30, av. Corentin-Cariou, 19*ème* (tel. 40 05 70 00; Mo. Porte de la Villete), is the best science museum in France, with innovative and participatory exhibitions, and excellent audiovisual presentations. (Open Tues. and Thurs., Fri. 10am-6pm, Wed. noon-9pm, Sat.-Sun. noon-8pm. Admission 30F, ages under 25 and over 60 23F. Planetarium 15F extra.)

Boat trips along the Seine on large *bateaux mouches* leave the Pont d'Alma (10am-noon and 2-7pm, 1½ hr., 25F). From 8 to 10pm the boats don huge spotlights. All are packed with tourists, but the view is lovely.

For more than a few days in Paris, dig into a copy of *Let's Go: France.*

Entertainment

Whether you decide to splurge on a fancy meal or wine bar, or just spend the evening wandering around, Paris's excitement is bound to infect you. Check the weekly magazines *Pariscope, l'Officiel des Spectacle,* or 7 *à Paris,* and the English-language monthly *Passion,* for complete listings of dance, theater, concerts, etc. The tourist office has a list of current festivals. The student organization, **COPAR,** 39, av. Georges Brenanos, 5*ème* (tel. 43 29 12 43; Mo. Port-Royal), has some discounted tickets for plays (list available), and many concerts. They will accept any student ID. (Open Sept.-July Mon.-Fri. 9am-4:30pm.) You can get tickets for plays, festivals, and all sorts of concerts at **Alpha Fnac: Spectacles,** with three different offices: 136, rue de Rennes, 6*ème* (tel. 45 44 39 12; Mo. Montparnasse-Bienvenue); 26 av. de Wagram, 8*ème* (tel. 47 66 52 50; Mo. Charles de Gaulle-Etoile); and Forum des Halles, 1-7, rue Pierre Lescot, 1*er* (tel. 42 61 81 18; Mo. Châtelet-Les Halles). Their *carte alpha* (40F per year) and *carte fnac* (100F per 3 years) entitles you to 40% off all classical music and theater tickets. (Open Tues.-Sat. 10am-7pm.)

For free entertainment, stroll around place St-Michel. Place St-Germain also can be relied on for good music and sometimes even street theater, as well as excellent people-watching. Nearby place Furstemberg is a romantic spot. In the summer come here to listen to guitar and French folk music. Les Halles, especially around the Pompidou center, fairly bursts with interesting street performances in the evening, especially fire-eating and mime. It is, however, a rough area, getting rougher after 10pm.

While large crowds on the left bank ensure that the streets are relatively safe, elsewhere the city should be approached with care. Stay away from the *quais* and the Bois de Boulogne late at night. Also avoid the Gare du Nord and Pigalle, especially if you are alone. Metro stations and trains are perfectly safe, but don't hang around. The conductor sits in the first car.

Concerts, Jazz, and Discos

Music can come cheaply in Paris. Besides entertainers in the Métro and musicians in front of the Centre Pompidou, most jazz clubs let you listen as long as you like for the price of one drink. A number of churches hold classical concerts during the summer: **Notre-Dame** has free organ concerts with well-known musicians Sundays at 5:45pm, the **American Church** has free concerts Sundays at 6pm (Sept.-June only), and the **Ste-Chapelle** hosts concerts a few times per week during the summer. (For information about all church concerts, call 43 29 68 68.)

Night clubs and discos that are "in" (or even in business) change radically from year to year. The area along the Seine between **rue St-Jacques** and **rue Bonaparte** (Left Bank) is the old standby, especially for jazz clubs and bars. The big discos tend to be on the Right Bank. The newest hot spot is the Bastille, in particualar the rue de Lappe.

New Morning, 7 and 9, rue des Petites-Ecuries, *10eme* (tel. 45 23 51 41); Mo. Château d'Eau). Probably the current great jazz club in a great jazz town, the New Morning is known for its fine acoustics. Prices change with shows—not cheap. Open Tues.-Sat. from 9:30pm.

Le Petit Journal, 71, bd. St-Michel, *5ème* (tel. 43 26 28 59; Mo. Luxembourg). A *sympa* (pleasant) place—small jazz cafe with very French decor. Past performers include the Claude Bolling trio and Bill Coleman. First (required) drink 75F, 40F thereafter. Open Sept.-July Mon.-Sat. 10pm-2:30am.

Slow Club, 130, rue de Rivoli, *1er* (tel. 42 33 84 30) Mo. Châtelet. Big bands and traditional jazz in a setting that hasn't changed in years. Cover 50F, weekends 62F. Drinks from 18F. Open Tues.-Thurs. 9:30pm-2am, Fri. 9:30pm-3am, Sat. 9:30pm-4am.

Chapelle des Lombards, 19, rue de Lappe, *11ème* (tel. 43 57 24 24; Mo. Bastille). On the street it's in to be on. Jazz, African, and salsa in a cave. Cover 65F, weekends 80F. Open Tues.-Sat. 10:30pm-4am.

Chez Felix, 23, rue Mouffetard, *5ème* (tel. 47 07 68 78; Mo. Monge). 2 different levels. On the top you can eat, and in the caves underneath you can sway to excellent Brazilian beat. Tues.-Thurs. first (required) drink 70F, 50F thereafter, Fri.-Sat. first 2 drinks 90F each, 50F thereafter. Open Sept.-July Tues.-Sat. 8pm-5am; music 11pm-dawn.

Scala de Paris, 188 bis, rue de Rivoli, *1er* (tel. 42 60 45 64; Mo. Palais-Royal). A place with everything: 3 balconies, dance floor, little sitting rooms, and video rooms. Cover 80F, women free except Fri. 50F, Sat. and holidays 80F. Sat.-Sun. 2:30-7pm reserved for ages 13-18 (no alcohol served); admission 40F. Open daily 10:30pm-dawn.

Le Palace, 8, Faubourg Montmartre, *9ème* (tel. 42 46 10 87; Mo. Montmartre). The funkiest disco in Paris; room for a few thousand on multi-level dance floors, moving to the beat of an awesome sound system. Dancing teas and rollerskating afternoons. Sometimes rock concerts are held here. Don't even think about eating at its new, very trendy, very expensive restaurant Le Nouveau Privilége. Cover 100F. Open Tues.-Sun. 11pm-dawn.

Les Bains, 7, rue de Bourg l'Abée, *3ème* (tel. 48 87 01 80; Mo. Les Halles or Réaumur-Sébastopol). One of the livelier places in Paris, with good music. Very *branché.* A turn-of-the-century facade conceals what used to be the municipal showers that Proust used to use. You may see famous models and artists here. First drink 100F. Open Tues.-Sun. midnight-5am.

Le Sept., 7, rue Ste-Anne, *1er.* Mo. Pyramides. Well-known gay (male) disco, always full. Walls plastered with mirrors. 70F. Open Wed.-Mon. 11pm-dawn; disco open after midnight.

Katmandou, 21, rue de Vieux-Colombier, *6ème* (tel. 45 48 12 96; Mo. St-Sulpice). A very chic lesbian bar which sometimes admits accompanied men. Some say the best lesbian bar in Paris: you can have up to 50 dancing partners in summer. First drink 80F. Open at management's discretion; call ahead to check.

Bars, Cafes, and Wine Bars

The difference between a café and a bar is subtle. Apparently a café is a room encased with plate-glass windows, open to the world passing by, and a bar a room that is closed and dim, but you can order the same things at both. The essential difference is cultural: While the French go to a café for a quick cup of coffee on their way to someplace else, a bar is a destination in itself.

La Closerie des Lilas, 171, bd. du Montparnasse, *6ème* (tel. 43 54 21 68; Mo. Montparnasse-Bienvenue). Historically one of the most famous places in Paris. Frequented by young artists and writers throughout the 19th century (including Hemingway; see the inscriptions on the tables). Fashionable and extremely beautiful, but can be hard to find a spot. Large selection of drinks 17-70F. Open year-round daily 10am-2am.

Pub St-Germain-des-Prés, 17, rue de l'Ancien Comédie, *6ème* (tel. 43 29 38 70; Mo. Odéon). Perhaps the largest pub in Europe with 7 rooms, 100 types of whiskey, 450 different types of bottled beer (24 on tap). 3 underground rooms look like opium dens, and are the most fun: Popular and '40s music is played and the place is generally packed with French youth. Drinks and ice cream only downstairs, expensive full meals upstairs. *Dégustation:* 8 small glasses of different beers (including Belgian cherry and apple) 35F, other beers from 18F. Open year-round 24 hours.

Café Pacífico, 50, bd. du Montparnasse, *6ème* (tel. 45 48 63 87; Mo. Montparnasse-Bienvenue). Always full of young people; lots of Americans. There are 3 such Mexican restaurants in Europe (Paris, London, and Amsterdam), and all are successful. Main dishes around 60F, *service et boisson non compris.* Brunch (noon-4pm) 80F and 100F. During the week (until 3pm) you get a free buck fizz (champagne and orange juice). Also a wide variety of cocktails from 29.50F. Don't miss the daily happy hour (6-7pm) when you get snacks and drinks for half-price. Open year-round Mon. 3pm-2am, Tues.-Sun. noon-2am.

La Coupole, 102, bd. du Montparnasse, *14ème* (tel. 43 20 14 20; Mo. Vavin). One of the most famous cafes in Paris, cited by authors all the way from Harold Robbins to Henry Miller. Still quite a "scene," full of Beautiful People who come to spend their monthly allowances eating oysters. Dancing in the basement. Sandwiches from 16F (cheese) all the way to 102F (*foie gras*). *Plats* 45-95F, dessert 27-42F, coffee 8-29F. Open Sept.-July daily 8am-2am.

Café Costes, place des Innocents, 4-6, rue Berger, *1er* (tel. 45 08 54 39; Mo. Les Halles). The Café as Art Form: Part I. Opened in 1986 in the heart of les Halles, designed by Philippe Stark and consequently *trés branché* (ever since Stark was commissioned by Mitterand to design his wife's room at Palais de L'Elysée, he has become the last word). A prime people-watching spot; expect to be checked out for how you are dressed. *Nobody,* my dear, sits on the side away from the Fontaine des Innocents. Coffee 11F, beer 18F, sandwiches start at 18F. Open year-round daily 8am-2am.

Café Beaubourg, 100, rue St-Martin, *4ème* (tel. 48 87 63 96; Mo. les Halles). The Café as Art Form: Part II. Across from Café Costes, this café was opened by the other Costes brother in spring 1987, and is maybe even a bit more chic. Coffee 10F, sandwiches 16-23F. Open year-round daily 8am-2am.

Wine bars have become increasingly popular in Paris, partly due to the invention a few years ago of a machine that pumps nitrogen into the bottle as wine is poured out, thus preserving the wine once it is open. This means you can buy very rare and expensive wine by the glass, wine which you would never be able to afford by the bottle.

Taverne Henri IV, 13, place du Pont Neuf, *1er* (Mo. Pont-Neuf). A traditional and friendly oak tavern long known to Parisians for its extensive wine list and its delicious *charcuteries* served with *Poilâne* bread. A plate of bread and *rillettes* (minced pork) only 18.40F, a selection of *charcuteries* up to 46F. Wine by the glass 14-44F. Open mid-Sept. to mid-Aug. Mon.-Fri. 11:30am-9:30pm.

Bistrot à Vins, rue Léon-Frot, *11ème* (Mo. Charonne). Charming owner and a lively atmosphere. Great harvest party each 2nd or 3rd Sat. in Sept. Open Aug.-June Tues.-Sat. 9am-7:30pm.

La Boutique des Vins, 33, rue de l'Arcade, *8ème* (Mo. Madeleine). Run by Françoise Dupuy, Paris's first woman wine bar owner. Food is delicious, but expensive; stick to the *plats du jour* (35-120F). Open Mon.-Fri. 11am-3pm and 7pm-midnight.

Cinema and Theater

Paris may well be the film capital of the world, and film may be the capital of Paris's entertainment world. As well as screening the latest European and American big-budget features, Paris's cinemas show classics from all countries, avant-garde and political films, and little-known or forgotten works. Ever since the New Wave crested, French interest in American movies has been nothing short of phenomenal; in fact, many American films play here that have not been shown in U.S. cinemas for years. Big-studio films run in large, expensive theaters on the Champs-Elysées, while more artsy offerings play in the little theaters on the side streets of the Left Bank.

The three entertainment weeklies give showtimes and theaters. Films are listed by several schemes: alphabetically under "new films," "first-run," and "others"; by genre; and by cinemas in each *arrondissement.* Film festivals are listed separately. The notation "V.O." (for *version originale)* after a non-French movie listing means that the film is being shown in its original language with French subtitles, while "V.F." (for *version française)* means that it is dubbed. Occasionally during the peak tourist season, French movies will be shown with English subtitles. Almost all cinemas grant card-carrying students a 10F discount off their regular 30-45F admission, but only on weekdays and sometimes only before 5pm. In many cinemas, prices are several francs lower on Mondays. In almost all Parisian theaters you will be greeted by an usher who tears your ticket, escorts you to your seat, and expects a tip of 1F.

Government-subsidized theaters include the **Opéra-Comique** (Mo. Richelieu-Drouot; open Aug.-June), the **Comédie Française** (Mo. Palais Royal; open Sept.-July), and the **Opéra** (Mo. Opéra; open Sept.-late July Wed.-Mon.). All sell rush tickets to students for around 40F. If you're homesick, go to **Galerie 55,** "The English Theater of Paris," 55, rue de Seine (tel. 43 26 63 51). Mo. Odéon.

The **Théâtre Shakespeare** (tel. 42 27 39 54), in the Bois de Boulogne (bus #244 from Porte Maillot, puts on Shakespearean plays during the summer; from late June to early July the plays are in English. (Admission 80F, students 40F.) Otherwise try the **Théâtre de la Ville,** pl. du Châtelet, with dance, poetry, and *spectacles* for 20-50F (discount for students at Sat. matinees). Superb performances of Ionesco's *La Cantatrice chauve* (The Bald Soprano) and *La Leçon* have been playing at the **Théâtre de la Huchette** (tel. 43 26 38 99) non-stop for almost 30 years. Tickets are on sale Mon.-Sat. 7-9:30pm at 120F for both shows (80F with student ID), 80F for one show (60F with student ID). Shows Mon.-Sat. 7:30pm (*La cantatrice chauve)* and 8:30pm (*La Leçon*).

Near Paris

Versailles, the magnificent palace of the Sun King, Louis XIV, embodies his absolute power. Disliking Paris for its association with the power struggles of his youth, Louis XIV turned his father's small hunting château into his royal residence and capital. The court became the center of noble life and status. Be sure to see the **Grand Trianon,** a royal guesthouse built for the king by Mansart; the **Petit Trianon,** Marie Antoinette's toy palace, and **Le Hameau,** the hamlet where the Queen amused herself by pretending to live the peasant life. You can reach Versailles by RER line C (4 per hr., 35 min., 20F round-trip); more cheaply by taking the Métro to Pont de Sévres and transferring to bus #17 there; or by catching the train at Gare St-Lazare (4 per hr., ½ hr., 18.40F round-trip). From Versailles *rive droite* you can catch the special bus to the château. (Main palace open Tues.-Sun. 9:45am-5pm. Admission 20F, students and everyone Sun. 10F. Grand Trianon open same hours. Admission 18F and 9F, respectively. Petit Trianon open Tues.-Fri. 2-5pm. Admission 10F and 5F. Combination tickets to both Trianons 18F and 9F.)

Fontainebleau is older than Versailles, and more appealing in many respects. For eight centuries, all sovereigns contributed to the widening of what started out as a medieval castle—Napoleon called it *la maison des Siècles* (the house of centuries), an allusion to its rich mixture of styles. The park and forest, beloved by the impressionists, are especially beautiful. Take the train from Gare de Lyon (4 per hr. 10am-midnight, 40 min.). (Palace open Wed.-Mon. 9:30am-12:30pm and 2-5pm. Admission 20F, Sun. 10F.)

The unforgettable **Cathédrale de Chartres,** spared by bureaucratic inefficiency after being condemned during the Revolution, survives today as one of the most sublime creations of the Middle Ages. The dark vault glows with rich "Chartres blue" stained glass, which relates human history from Adam and Eve to the Last Judgment. Malcolm Miller—the man who, for the last 25 years, has brought the cathedral to life for English-speaking visitors—gives outstanding tours. (Open daily April-Sept. 7:30am-7:30pm; Oct.-March 7:30am-7pm. Free tours at noon and 2:45pm.) Also of interest at Chartres is the **Centre International du Vitrail** (stained glass center), 5, rue Cardinal Pie. (Open Wed.-Mon. 10am-6pm. Admission 10F.) For a map and help with accommodations, stop by the helpful **office de tourisme,** right in front of the cathedral (tel. 37 21 54 03). (Open May-Oct. Mon.-Sat. 9:30am-12:30pm and 2-6:30pm, Sun. 10am-noon and 3-6pm; Nov.-April Mon.-Sat. only.) The pleasant **auberge de jeunesse (IYHF),** 23, av. Neigre (tel. 37 34 27 64), is 2km south of the station—past the cathedral, and over the river by the Eglise St-André (follow the signs). (30F. 11pm curfew. Open year-round.) **Au Pain de France,** 14, av. Jehan de Beauce, has beautiful glazed-fruit tarts and a full *menu* (most entrees 30-45F). (Open daily 10am-10pm.) Frequent trains run from Gare Montparnasse to Chartres (11 per day 7:19am-8:30pm, 50 min., 98F round-trip).

Normandy (Normandie)

Inspiration to the impressionists, fertile Normandy is a land of rolling countryside, jagged coastline, and soaring cathedrals. The Vikings or Norsemen (a term later corrupted to "Normans") seized the region in the ninth century, and invasions have twice since put Normandy on the map of world history; in 1066 when William of Normandy conquered England, and centuries later when, on D-Day, June 6, 1944, Allied armies landed on the Normandy beaches and started on the road to the liberation of Europe.

Famous for its produce and dairy products, Normandy supplies a large percentage of France's butter. Try the creamy, pungent *camembert* cheese, but be sure it's ripe (soft in the middle). The province's traditional drink, *cidre,* is a hard cider that comes both dry (*brut*) and sweet (*doux*). *Calvados* is apple brandy aged 12 to 15 years, and it ranks with the finest, most lethal cognacs.

Rouen

Victor Hugo dubbed Rouen the city of 100 spires, the most famous of which are the needles, gargoyles, and gables of the **cathedral.** Reading like a textbook of twelfth- through sixteenth-century Gothic architecture, the facade so fascinated Monet that he took it as one of his few architectural subjects. (Open daily 10am-noon and 2-6pm.) Behind the cathedral is **St-Maclou,** a fine example of the later, flamboyant Gothic style. Its charnel house, **Aitre St-Maclou** (turn left into 186, rue de Martinville), with its cloister of macabre wood carvings, has also been preserved. Equally exquisite are the park and the light-filled **Abbey of St-Ouen,** the scene of Joan of Arc's recantation and avowal to heresy. She eventually met her end at the stake on **place du Vieux Marché** in the center of town; a cross near the modern, boat-shaped **Eglise Jean d'Arc** marks the spot. In the center of Rouen, pedestrian precincts with cafes and restaurants radiate from the town's favorite monument, the **Gros Horloge,** a fourteenth-century clock tower and Renaissance gatehouse. The **Monument Juif,** an eleventh-century Jewish synagogue, is completely underground, accessible only by guided tours conducted by the *syndicat.* (Sat. at 2pm; 20F, 15F if under 25 or over 65.)

From Rouen's train station, walk straight down rue Jeanne d'Arc and turn left on rue Gros Horloge for pl. de la Cathédrale and the **syndicat d'initiative** (tel. 35

71 41 77), where the English-speaking staff will book rooms for 9F. (Open Easter to mid-Sept. Mon.-Sat. 9am-12:30pm and 1:30-7pm, Sun. 9am-12:30pm and 2:30-6pm; mid-Sept. to Easter Mon.-Sat. 9am-noon and 2-7pm.) Rouen's **auberge de jeunesse (IYHF)** is at 17, rue Diderot (tel. 35 72 06 45), 2km from the train station on the left bank of the Seine. Take bus #12 to rue Diderot or walk straight from the station down rue Jeanne d'Arc across the bridge, and left on av. de Caen to rue Diderot. (47F. Breakfast and linen included. Curfew 11pm.) From June through September, you can get a single for 33F at the Cité Universitaire, in Mont St-Aignan, well out of town (take bus #10 from the center). You will need a student ID and an extra photo; contact **CROUS,** 3, rue d'Herbouville (tel. 35 98 44 50) for specifics. **Hôtel Normandya,** 32, rue du Cordier (tel. 35 71 46 15), has attractive rooms and a soft spot for *Let's Go* users. (Singles and doubles 70F.) The cozy **Hostellerie du Vieux Logis,** 5, rue de Joyeuse (tel. 35 71 55 30), rents singles and doubles for 60-70F. Make reservations.

Local specialties include *paté de canard* (duck paté), *poulet sautée à la crème* (chicken in a rich cream sauce), and *tripes à la Normandaise* (intestines). A **market** fills place du Vieux Marché every day except Monday, and gourmet *traiteurs* line the streets. The Hostellerie proposes a huge 50F *menu* (including wine and coffee) in a terrific atmosphere. (Open 12-1pm and 7-8pm. Make reservations for dinner.) One of Rouen's liveliest restaurants is the **Bar des Fleurs,** pl. des Carmes, with *menus* at 57F and 80F and live music occasionally. (Seatings daily 7-9pm.) Creperie **Ty Breiz,** 5, rue du Père Adam, has the best crepes and *galettes* (whole wheat dinner crepes); a 38F *menu* includes three courses and cider. (Open Tues.-Sat. noon-1:30pm and 7pm-midnight; *menu* not served after 10pm.) **Les Flandres,** 5, rue des Bons-Enfants, has a simple and unpretentious atmosphere with a filling 52F *menu* and 32F *plats du jour.* (Open Mon.-Fri. noon-1:30pm and 7:30-9:15pm, Sat. noon-1:30pm.)

Rouen is easily accessible from Paris's Gare St-Lazare (1 per hour, 70 min., 74F) and from Dieppe (every 1-2 hr., 40 min., 38F). It is a convenient stopover for those traveling between Paris and London via either Dieppe or Calais.

Norman Coast

The road from Dieppe to Le Havre passes through some of Normandy's most spectacular countryside, between white cliffs and fertile interior. Hitching is not a good idea since roads are not well traveled. Cyclists should keep in mind that the roads become more hilly as you approach the coast.

Dieppe is a channel port with frequent crossings to Great Britain. After a look at its lively quays and its beach, boardwalk, and faded Victorian hotels, head west out of town up the steep white cliffs for a panoramic view of the coast. The **auberge de jeunesse (IYHF),** is a 25-minute hike from the station on rue Louis Fromager (tel. 35 84 85 73). From the station, turn left, then right four blocks later on rue de la République, then a sharp left onto rue Gambetta, right onto av. Jean Jaurès, and finally left on Fromager; you've still got a way to go. (About 35F. Lockout 9:30am-5:30pm. Closed mid-Dec. to early Jan. and Feb. 10-25.) Eight kilometers to the west of Dieppe is **Varengeville-sur-Mer,** the quiet town where Georges Braque spent much of his life; he is buried in the village cemetery under a tombstone that he created. The church, on the end of a rocky promontory, is graced with windows he designed. Nearby is the **Parc Florale des Moutiers,** a botanical garden. Farther inland at **Miromesnil** lies the beautiful **Château de Miromesnil** where Guy de Maupassant was born in 1850. Call ahead (tel. 35 04 40 30) for guided tours (May to mid-Oct. Wed.-Mon. 2-6pm; admission 12F).

Fécamp is an important deep-sea fishing port and resort, famous for its massive, harmonious **Abbatiale de la Trinité,** with a nave as long as that of Paris's Notre Dame. An **auberge de jeunesse (IYHF)** overlooks town from rue du Commandant Roguigny (tel. 35 29 75 79). (35F. Curfew 11pm. Open July to mid-Sept.) Fécamp is accessible by train and bus from Le Havre and Dieppe.

Claude Monet was inspired by the two natural arches hewn out of cliffs that frame the harbor at **Etretat,** the next coastal resort. The **syndicat d'initiative,** pl. de la Mairie (tel. 35 27 05 21), can help you year-round with information and accommodations. Etretat has no hostel, but is accessible by bus from Le Havre. **Le Havre** is France's largest transatlantic port, the base for ferries serving Rosslare and Cork, Ireland, and Southampton and Portsmouth, England. **Townsend Thoresen Car Ferries,** quai de Southampton (tel. 35 21 36 50), serves Portsmouth year-round. Take bus #3 from the train station or the Hôtel de Ville. **Irish Continental Lines,** route du Môle Central (tel. 35 21 55 02), serves Rosslare (year-round) and Cork (summer). Both Eurail and InterRail passes are honored on this crossing, making it the cheapest way from the Continent to Ireland for passholders. Take bus #4 from the train station or Hôtel to stop "Marceau." If you have to stay over, avoid the areas near the port and the train station. Try the hostel-like **Union Chrétienne de Jeunes Gens,** 153, bd. de Strasbourg (tel. 35 42 47 86), with 37F singles; the place also has an appetizing cafeteria (*plats du jour* 14-23F). If they're full, try your luck at the pleasant **Hôtel Jeanne d'Arc,** 91, rue Emile-Zola (tel. 35 41 26 83), centrally located off rue du Paris. (Singles 65F, doubles 75F.) The **office de tourisme** is across the bridge. (Open Mon.-Sat. 9am-12:15pm and 2-7pm.)

Honfleur, the next town to the west, was an important base for sixteenth- and seventeenth-century expeditions to the New World. Today, painters explore the colors and forms of its picturesque port. The **Musée Eugène Boudin,** rue de l'Homme du Bois, houses a rich collection of contemporary paintings from the Saint-Siméon school. (Open mid-March to Sept. Wed.-Mon. 10am-noon and 2-6pm; Oct.-Dec. and mid-Feb. to mid-March Mon. and Wed.-Fri. 2:30-5pm, Sat.-Sun. 10am-noon and 2:30-5pm. Admission 10F, students 7F.) The two parallel naves of the church of **Ste-Cathérine** seem to resemble a boat's upturned hulk—a reminder of Honfleur's maritime history. The charming staff of Honfleur's **syndicat d'initiative,** 33, cours des Fosses (tel. 31 89 23 30), near the bus station, will help with accommodations. (Open Mon.-Sat. 9am-noon and 2-6pm; after Easter also Sun. 10am-noon.)

Cabourg is perhaps the most well known *fin-de-siècle* resort on the Norman coast. Visit the impressive casino and the grand hotel facing the sea across promenade Marcel Proust, so named because the author frequently sojourned here. Many scenes of his *Remembrance of Things Past* seem to take place in a Cabourg renamed Balbec. The **syndicat d'initiative** in the Jardin du Casino (tel. 31 91 01 09) can direct you to area campsites (open daily 9am-noon and 2-6pm), or try the **L'Oie Qui Fume,** 18, av. de la Brèche-Buhot (tel. 31 91 27 79), with a few rooms for 70F and an obligatory 15F breakfast. (Open Feb.-Dec.)

Bus #20 (bus Verts du Calvados) serves the coast west of Le Havre all the way to Cabourg and then on to Caen.

Caen, Bayeux, and the D-Day Beaches

Despite Allied bombing during World War II, **Caen** has preserved its architectural treasures. The favorite city of William the Conqueror, Caen was especially blessed by a proliferation of religious architecture in the eleventh century. Perched above the city center, the **Abbaye-aux-Dames** and its twin church, the **Abbaye-aux-Hommes,** are finely carved examples of Romanesque architecture. In the town center the assertive remains of William's **château** have lush gardens and two noteworthy museums, the **Musée des Beaux Arts,** with paintings by Rubens, van der Weyden, and Perugino, and the **Musée de Normandie,** devoted to local crafts and folk art. (Both open March-Oct. Wed.-Mon. 10am-noon and 2-6pm; Nov.-Feb. Wed.-Mon. 10am-noon and 2-5pm. Admission 4F, students 2F, free Sun.) Beneath the château, the thirteenth-century **Church of St-Pierre** has a majestic bell tower and a richly ornate Renaissance front. The **office de tourisme,** pl. St-Pierre (tel. 31 86 27 65), will help with room-finding and is well-informed on the city and the region.

(Open July-Aug. Mon.-Fri. 8:45am-7:30pm, Sat. 8:45am-7pm, Sun. 10am-noon and 2-4:45pm; Sept.-June Mon.-Sat. 8:45am-12:15pm and 2-7pm.)

The **Auberge de Jeunesse Foyer Robert Rème (IYHF)**, 68bis, rue Restout (tel. 31 52 19 96), is a modern hostel with an excellent cafeteria and game room facilities. Take bus #3 towards Grâce de Dieu from the train and bus station to Armand Marie stop. (49.50F per person. Welcome hours 5-10pm. Open April-Sept.) More convenient is the **Hôtel Demolombe,** 36, rue Demolombe (tel. 31 86 18 99), between pl. St-Pierre and the Abbaye-aux-Hommes. (Singles and doubles 53-63F. Showers 12F.) **Hôtel de la Paix,** 14, rue Neuve-St-Jean (tel. 31 76 18 99), near the château, is especially friendly to *Let's Go* users, and has comfortable rooms. From the *syndicat,* take a left onto rue St-Pierre, then a right through the underpass. (Singles and doubles 89F. Obligatory breakfast 16F.) Several inexpensive *crêperies* and *brasseries* can be found around rue du Vaugeux and av. de la Libération, near the château. **La Couscoussière,** 12 rue de Vaugueux, serves *couscous* starting at 37F. (Open noon-2pm and 7-11pm.)

Caen is linked by train to Paris (17 per day, 2 hr., 120F), Rouen (5 per day, 1½ hr., 87F), and Cherbourg (8 per day, 1½ hr., 72F). Take any bus except #4 from the station to the tourist office.

Beautiful and ancient **Bayeux** is an excellent visit in itself, and also an ideal embarkation point for the D-Day beaches. The town is renowned for its **Tapisserie de Bayeux** (Bayeux Tapestry), which tells the story of the Norman invasion of Britain in 1066. The captions are in Latin, but the audio-visual exhibition will help you understand the tapestry. Actually a linen embroidery, the work was commissioned for Bayeux's cathedral, and is now housed in a renovated seminary on rue de Nesmond. (Open June-Sept. daily 9am-7pm; Oct. to mid-March daily 9:30am-12:30pm and 2-6pm; mid-March to May daily 9am-12:30pm and 2-6:30pm. Admission 17F, students 10F.) Nearby is the splendid **cathédrale.** Outside, Gothic spires crown older Romanesque towers, while inside, light pours through Gothic stained glass to illuminate Romanesque arches a century older. (Open in summer daily 8am-7pm; in winter daily 8am-noon and 2-7pm.)

The **office de tourisme,** 1, rue des Cuisiniers (tel. 31 92 16 26), will make hotel reservations for the price of a phone call, find rooms in private homes, and change money when banks are closed. (Open July to mid-Sept. Mon.-Sat. 9:30am-12:30pm and 2-6:30pm, Sun. 10am-12:30pm and 3-6:30pm; mid-Sept. to June open Mon.-Sat. only.) The coziest place to stay is **Family Home,** 39, rue Générale-de-Dais (tel. 31 92 15 22), off rue de la Juridiction, with billowing quilts and a rural ambience. Make reservations. (IYHF members 65F, nonmembers 85F. Showers and a magnificent breakfast included. Bikes for rent. 35F per day. Open daily 7am-7pm.) Staying here earns you the privilege of indulging in their sublime dinner—countless dishes and unlimited wine (55F). The **Centre d'Accueil,** chemin de Boulogne (tel. 31 92 08 19), has modern singles for 58F (showers and breakfast included).

Nine kilometers north of Bayeux on the D516 is **Arromanches,** easternmost of the **D-Day beaches.** Its fascinating **Musée du Débarquement** displays superb miniature models of the Allied artificial harbor. (Open daily 9am-5:45pm. Admission 14F, students 8F.) **Omaha Beach** lies to the west. The **American Cemetery** is in St-Laurent; the **Canadian Cemetery** is at Bény-sur-Mer-Reviers, near Courseulles. Bus Verts #74 travels to Arromanches and other points east (Mon.-Sat. 2 per day); to Port-en-Bessin and points westward, take bus #70 (3 per day). You may find, however, that bike travel proves easier and more reliable in this region.

Mont Saint-Michel

Shrouded in a vast and airy solitude, Mont St-Michel appears to define timelessness. An ancient abbey and beautiful cloister balance precariously on the jutting rock, surrounded by military fortifications and a *ville basse* that developed to serve medieval pilgrims. Modern tourists throng the narrow streets in summer, but the view down to the bay and its surging tides is unforgettable. Admission to the abbey buildings is by guided visit only. (French tours every 15 min.; English tours daily at 10:30 and 11:30am and 1, 2:30, 3:30, and 4:30pm. 23F, ages 18-25 13F, under 18 3F; half-price Sun.) The two-hour *visites conférences* (French only) are a special treat; they allow you to walk atop a flying buttress and creep inside the deepest crypts. (Tours daily at 10 and 11am and 2 and 3pm. 29F.) Watching the tide rush in to envelop the Mont at 2m per second is an extraordinary sight. Try to time your visit with the highest tides—36-48 hours after the new and full moons respectively—especially those in March, April, September, and October. You must be on the Mont two full hours ahead of time, as the causeway becomes impassable. Mont St-Michel is as stunning illuminated at night as it is during the day. (July-Sept. nightly; Oct.-June high-tide nights, and during festivals.)

To get to Mont St-Michel, take a train to **Pontorson** (through Poligny rather than Rennes) and board the connecting STN bus to the Mont (6 per day, 18F round-trip). You can rent a **bike** at Pontorson train station (open daily 8am-noon and 2-8pm), but it'll cost you 45F per day. Most hotels and restaurants on the Mont are priced out of sight for the budget traveler, although the **Hôtel de la Croix Blanche,** rue Grande Pontorson (tel. 33 60 14 04), is reasonable with singles at 70F, doubles 90F. (Open April-Oct; call ahead.)

In Pontorson, stay at the **Hôtel de l'Arrivée,** pl. de la Gare (tel. 33 60 01 57), with singles starting at 52F, doubles at 92F. The **Hôtel de France,** 2, rue de Rennes (tel. 33 60 29 17), is less appealing but occupies a stately building (singles 40-70F, doubles 115F).

The **auberge de jeunesse** at 15, rue du Jardin des Plantes (tel. 33 58 06 54) in Avranches, across the bay from the Mont and accessible by train from Pontorson, is especially recommended. From September through May, the hostel may be full of young French workers. (38F. Breakfast included. Curfew 10pm, but keys available.) The **auberge de jeunesse (IYHF)** at Pleine Fougères (tel. 99 40 29 80), is 5km (only 1 bus per day) from Pontorson on rue de la Gare. (30F. Open July-Aug.)

Brittany (Bretagne)

This sea-battered peninsula has long tugged away from France, intent on its own direction. Though the tug is gentler today, Brittany and France have long been distinct. Brittany, ethnically and linguistically Celtic, resisted affiliation with France until the sixteenth century. The traditional ambivalence is especially evident in the region's folk music, whose featured instrument, the *biniou,* resembles the bagpipe. Bretons maintain these cross-Channel ties with cultural festivals, such as Lorient's *Festival Interceltique* in early August. The largest and most publicized celebration of Breton culture is Quimper's *Festival de la Cornouaille,* in the second half of July.

While there are plenty of summer resorts and soft sandy beaches here, a wilder beauty is never far away. The wave-beaten cliffs of the Cap Fréhel are spectacular, while farther west, ancient *menhirs* (prehistoric stone obelisks) dot the high, windy headlands of the Côte Sauvage on the Quiberon peninsula. A retreat to the wooded Argoat interior provides a tranquil break from the crowds on the coast.

Many hotels and a few entire towns only open their doors to tourists from about June to mid-September. Fortunately, there are a number of IYHF *auberges de jeunesse* in the region that remain open most of the year. The **Association Bretonne des Relais et Itinéraires (ABRI)** or any of the larger tourist offices can supply you with a list of *gîtes d'étape* in the region, shelters in rural settings where travelers can spend the night for only 22F (off-limits to motorists). Brittany is one of France's best loved vacation spots; during July and August, reservations are recommended.

Ubiquitous *crêperies* offer the famed regional specialty: crepes of ground wheat flour *(froment)* with sweet fillings, and the darker buckwheat variety *(sarasin)* wrapped around eggs, cheese, or sausage. These are accompanied by *cidre bouché,* hard cider, or by the non-alcoholic *cidre doux,* while such delectable seafood meals as *coquilles St. Jacques, saumon fumé* (smoked salmon), and *moules marinières* (mussels in a white-wine-based cream sauce) are served with *Muscadet,* a dry white wine from the vineyards around Nantes.

The main rail lines are Rennes-Brest in the north, and Rennes-Redon-Quimper and Redon-Nantes in the south. Private bus lines connect other towns, but their services are infrequent and expensive. This leaves cycling as the best and most common means of travel. Many youth hostels, including those at Dinan, St-Brieuc, Lannion, Quimper, and Rennes, rent bikes to IYHF members for about 30F per day. A number of train stations rent bikes for 35-45F per day; these are listed in the free pamphlet *Train et Vélo,* available at SNCF stations. It's possible to rent a bike and then return it to a different station. Hitching is a little easier in Brittany than in the rest of France. Stick to the major roads, such as the D786. The quickest hitching returning to Paris is via Avranches in the north and Nantes, Angers, and Le Mans in the south, rather than the less-developed road through Rennes.

Rennes

In 1720, a drunken carpenter knocked over his lamp and set most of Rennes ablaze. The resultant loss of most of the medieval town hasn't left much to look at, but Rennes is the gateway to the Breton Peninsula. Stop here to pick up excellent travel information on the way west, and to rest yourself on the way back east.

The **syndicat d'initiave** on Pont de Nemours (tel. 99 79 01 98) has lists of all the youth hostels, hotels, and campgrounds in Brittany, as well as maps of most of the larger cities. From the train station, follow rue Jean Janvier to the canal and turn left. You can also visit **ABRI,** 3, rue des Portes Mordelaises (tel. 99 31 59 44)—devoted to helping you discover the region on foot, bicycle, or horseback, they provide lists of travel shelters, bike routes, etc. The **Centre d'Information Jeunesse Bretagne,** in the Maison du Champ de Mars, has leaflets on almost every aspect of traveling and living in Brittany. The **post office** is on pl. de la République—they also exchange currency. (Open Mon.-Fri. 8am-7pm, Sat. 8am-noon.) There's an **Allostop** office (they match riders with drivers) at Maison du Champ de Mars, 6, Cours des Alliés. (Open July-Aug. Mon.-Fri. 1:30-5pm, Sat. 9am-noon; Sept.-June Mon.-Fri. 3-6:30pm, Sat. 9am-noon.)

Rennes's **auberge de jeunesse (IYHF)** is at 10-12, Canal St-Martin (tel. 99 33 22 33). Walk west from the center to the canal d'Ile de Rance, then follow quai St-Cast/bd. de Chézy along the canal; the hostel is just after rue St-Malo. (43F per night in 1-2 bed rooms; 32F in 3-4 bed rooms. Showers in every room. Reception open Mon.-Fri. 8am-11pm, Sat.-Sun. 8-10am and 6:30-11pm.) Otherwise, **Hôtel Magenta,** 35, bd. Magenta (tel. 99 30 85 37), has singles for 78F, doubles for 88F. Magenta branches to the left from in front of the train station. A **market** is held daily from 7am to 6pm at rue Jules-Simon and bd. de la Liberté. For a sit-down meal, try the *crêperies* in the old quarter and on rue St-Melaine; **Le Boulingrain,** at #25, is a particularly good value. (Open Mon.-Fri. noon-11pm, Sun. 6-11pm.)

Trains run from Rennes to Paris (10 per day, 3½ hr., 173F), Caen, Nantes, and Brest. Call 99 65 50 50 for information. Buses run throughout Brittany, but if you have a choice, take the train—it's cheaper and faster.

Northern Coast

St-Malo and Dinan

Once a town of privateers and merchants, St-Malo is now a fashionable summer resort, popular with the young, and lively at night. The **vieille ville** (old town) is its main attraction, encircled by high granite walls and surrounded by magnificent beaches on three sides. When the tide is out, you can walk to the **Fort National** or the **Ile du Grand Bé,** where the writer Chateaubriand is buried. To tour the ramparts—and you must—look for the sign "Accès aux Ramparts" near **Porte St-Vincent,** the main gate to the old town. To find the few houses that are not reconstructions, explore **rue Pelicot,** which ends at the **cour la Houssaye,** and the seventeenth-century house of Duchesse Anne de Bretagne.

St-Malo's **office de tourisme** is located on the Esplanade St-Vincent, just outside the Porte St-Vincent. (Open July-Aug. Mon.-Sat. 8:30am-8pm, Sun. 10am-6:30pm; Sept.-June Mon.-Sat. 9am-noon and 2-6:30pm.) To reach the tourist office and the entrance to the old city, turn right as you exit, cross bd. de la République, and head straight down av. Louis-Martin (10-15 min.). Red buses #2 and 3, and the purple-coded #4, run from bd. de la République (turn right and right again from the station) to St-Vincent, near the center (every 20 min., 5.70F).

Finding a hotel room in St-Malo in July and August is not hard—it's impossible. Even the huge modern **auberge de jeunesse (IYHF),** 37, av. du Père Umbricht (tel. 99 40 29 80), is often full, so you are likely to end up in their **annex** (open mid-July to Aug.) on av. de Moka (tel. 99 56 31 55). Take the red #2 bus to Courtoisville and continue along av. du Père Umbricht. To reach the annex from the station, follow av. Jean Jaurès and turn left onto av. de Moka. (Main hostel 31F; annex 26F. Check-in 8-10am, 5-7pm, and 8-10pm.) With a reservation or a little luck you might find a room at **Hôtel Le Vauban,** 7, bd. de la République (tel. 99 56 09 30). (Singles and doubles 70-100F. Showers 8F. Breakfast 15F.) Even without forethought or luck, you'll find good cheap food downstairs at Le Vauban. (*Ménus* from 35F.) In the old town the **Créperie Chez Chantal,** 2, pl. aux Herbes, has filling crepes (9-28F). The youth hostel serves full meals for 32F.

All train journeys to St-Malo require a change at Rennes; Gare Montparnasse is the Parisian gateway to the city (6 per day, 5 hr., 202F). The pavilion on the Esplanade St-Vincent houses the offices of practically all bus and ferry services; inquire about sailings to the Channel Islands, daytrips to Mont St-Michel (see Normandy), and transportation to other points in Brittany.

Dinan, 35km southwest of St-Malo, calls itself Brittany's best preserved medieval town, and the superlative is apt. The precipitous cobblestone streets and gabled fifteenth- and sixteenth-century houses of the **vieille ville** stand 66m above the Rance Valley. Rue du Jerzual and rue du Petit Fort are especially lovely. Also in splendid condition is the **Château de Dinan,** a short and lovely walk from the post office along **Promenade des Petits-Fossés.** The heavily fortified fourteenth-century **donjon** houses an excellent museum displaying polychromed religious statuettes and medieval weapons and artifacts. Next door in the chilly dungeon of the **Tour de Coëtquen** reposes a collection of *gisants* (tomb sculptures). (Chateau and museum open June-Aug. daily 9am-noon and 2-7pm; Sept.-Oct. and March-May Wed.-Sun. 9am-noon and 2-6pm; Nov.-Feb. Wed.-Sun. 2-5pm. Admission 6F.) With its churches, gardens, and ramparts, Dinan has far more to see, and far fewer people trying to see it, than its overcrowded neighbors to the north.

The **office de tourisme,** 6, rue de l Horloge (tel. 96 39 75 40), is a 15-minute walk from the station. Bear left across pl. du 11 Novembre 1918 onto rue Carnot, then right onto rue Thiers, which brings you to pl. Duclos. Head up the hill to the left on rue du Marchix and turn left at the sign for the *office de tourisme.* Cross a square and take rue Ste-Claire to rue de l'Horloge. (Open June-Sept. daily 9am-6pm; May daily 9am-noon and 2-6pm; Oct.-April Tues.-Sat. 9am-noon and 2-6pm.) The **auberge de jeunesse (IYHF)** (tel. 96 39 10 83), in a forested setting a half-hour's walk downhill from the train station, is a friendly place with excellent facilities. From the main exit of the train station, turn left, left again across the tracks, and follow the signs. (32F. Breakfast 10F.) **Hôtel du Théâtre,** 2, rue Ste-Claire (tel. 96 39 06 91), in the heart of the *vieille ville,* has small but pleasant rooms. Follow directions for the tourist office. (Singles 55F, 2-bed doubles 85F. Showers included.) **Hôtel-Restaurant de l'Océan,** pl. du 11 Novembre 1918 (tel. 96 39 21 51), opposite the station, is also recommended. (Singles and doubles 70F. Showers 15F. Open Nov.-Sept.) The **campsite** behind the youth hostel (above) is in a lovely spot near a stream. A closer site is the **Camping Municipal,** 103, rue Châteaubriand (tel. 96 39 11 96). If you're facing the post office and pl. Duclos, rue Châteaubriand is to your right.

The **Crêperie des Artisans,** 6, rue du Petit Fort (tel. 96 39 44 10), has four-course *menus* (crepes and *galettes*) at 29F and 39F. (Open April-Sept. daily noon-10:30pm.) Down the hill, the restaurant **La Kabylie,** 48, rue du Petit Fort, serves excellent *couscous* for 43-69F. (Open June-Aug. daily noon-2pm and 7-10pm; Sept.-May Wed.-Sun. only.)

Dinan is accessible by train from Rennes, which is on the Paris-Brest and Paris-Quimper lines (Dinan to Rennes via Dol, 8 per day, 1½-2 hr., 49F). Less frequent service connects Dinan to St-Brieuc (Mon.-Sat. 3 per day, Sun. 2, 1 hr., 40F) and St-Malo (7 per day, change at Dol, 1¼ hr., 31F). From July to September, buses run three times per day to and from St-Malo (26F).

Côte d'Emeraude and Côte de Granite Rose

These two geographic divisions of Brittany's northern coast are fascinatingly diverse, sweeping around rugged windswept points of rock to serene coves and sandy beaches. Adventurers will love the windswept magnificence of **Cap Fréhel** on the Côte d'Emeraude. The **Auberge de Jeunesse Plévenon** (tel. 96 61 91 87), 4km from the Cap, will offer you a tent or a bed inside. (Camping 20F per person. Beds 32F. Open July-Aug.) The impressive **Fort La Latte** is perched nearby. CAT runs buses from St-Brieve to Le Vieux-Bourg (3 per day, 31.50F); from here you're on your own—the Cap is 5km northeast on the D34A. (Don't take the bus to Fréhel; it's nowhere near the Cap.) Across the Baie de la Frênaye from the Fort is the **Pointe de St-Cast,** 2km north of the bus stop in St-Cast, worth a stop for its views of the Breton coast. Buses arrive from St-Brieuc (2 per day, 31.50F). Mme. Grouazel, the friendly director of **Camping de la Ferme de Pen-Guen** (tel. 96 41 92 18), will fetch you from the bus stop for the price of the gas (about 6F).

To the west, the Côte de Granite Rose has unique rock formations and wonderful, secluded beaches. The fishing town of **Paimpol** makes a good base for daytrips to the pastoral **Ile de Bréhat.** Boats (10 min., 16F round-trip) leave every 30 minutes in summer, about every two hours in winter, from **Arcouest,** reached by a bus from the Paimpol train station (10 per day, 20 min., 9F). There's an **auberge de jeunesse (IYHF)** in Paimpol (tel. 96 20 83 60), 25 minutes on foot from the station; turn left on av. Général de Gaulle, right at the first light, left at the next light, and then follow signs for "Kerraoul." (32F. Nightly feast also 32F.)

The stretch of coast from **Perros-Guirec** to **Trébeurden** is beach-laden and beautiful. A spectacular cliff path, the **Sentier des Douaniers** leads from Perros's beach to the Pors Rolland at **Ploumanach.** Ploumanach's **Pointe de Squewell** and the **Gréve Blanche** at **Trégastel,** 3km farther, are famous for the strange beauty of their wind-carved rocks. You can tour the area from Trébeurden, accessible by bus from Lannion's train station (2-3 per day, 10.50F, with luggage 12F). Lannion is equipped with an **auberge de jeunesse (IYHF)** as well, at 6, rue du 73ème Territorial (tel. 96 37 91 28). From Lannion, take a train to Plouaret (7-9 per day, 11.80F) and then to **Morlaix,** a short train ride east on the main Paris-Brest line. Morlaix's **auberge de jeunesse (IYHF)** is located at 3, route de Paris (tel. 98 88 13 63), about 20 minutes from the station.

From Morlaix, trains run north to **Roscoff,** a small resort and the departure point for ferries to Cork, Ireland, and Plymouth, England. **Brittany Ferries** (tel. 98 62 22 11) sends boats to Plymouth (mid-May to mid-Sept. 2 per day; late July-early Aug. 3 on Sun.; March to mid-May and mid-Sept. to Oct. Sat.-Thurs. 1 per day; Nov.-Feb. 1 per week.) The trip takes 5-6 hours. (Jan.-March 290F; April-June and Oct.-Dec. 290-300F; July-Sept. 300-322F. Ask about round-trip discounts.) The same company runs ferries to Cork. (Mid-June to mid-Sept. 2 per week; March to mid-June and mid-Sept. to Oct. 1 per week. High season 530F on deck, 550F in an airplane seat; otherwise 410F, 438F.) Accommodations in Roscoff are expensive, but **Hôtel les Arcades,** rue Admiral Réveillère (tel. 98 69 790 45), rents singles for 64F and doubles for 84F. (Open April-Sept.)

If you're in Roscoff, don't miss the rustic **Ile de Batz.** The island's **auberge de jeunesse (IYHF)** is located straight up the hill from the dock at Créac'h ar Bolloc'h

(July-Aug. tel. 98 61 76 98; Sept.-June tel. 98 02 30 02). Call in advance to reserve a place. (Beds 26-32F. Camping 13F. Open April to mid-Nov.) Ferries serve the island regularly from Roscoff. (July-Sept. 1 per hr. 8am-8pm; Oct.-June 1 every 1½ hr.; 18F round-trip, with bicycle 20F.)

Up the Monts d' Arrée south of Morlaix, **Huelgoat** is a small, friendly town on a lovely lake. Grottoes, *menhirs,* and jumbled heaps of granite boulders freckle this corner of the *Argoat* (wooded country). Here you can stroll along well-marked paths through hilly forests, or bicycle to tiny villages where the Breton language is alive and well. Within walking distance from Huelgoat are the **Roche Tremblante** (a 137-metric-ton boulder that can be moved if you know the secret), the **Grotte du Diable** (more a space between heaps of boulders than a cave), the solitary obelisk **menhir de Kerampeulven,** and many other curiosities.

Inquire at the **office de tourisme,** off pl. Aristide-Briand (tel. 98 99 72 32), for information. (Open July-Aug. Mon.-Sat. 10am-noon and 2-6pm.) During the rest of the year, inquire at the **mairie** (mayor's office), next door. (Open Mon.-Fri. 8:30am-noon and 1:30-5:30pm, Sat. 8:30-noon.) The cheapest place around is the **gîte d'étape,** which offers 22F dorm beds and kitchen facilities in a dusty, partially remodeled village school house. From the bus stop in the village of Locmaria-Berrien, one stop beyond Huelgoat on the bus from Morlaix, walk up the hill for about 1km to a *café/épicerie,* and turn right past the eighteenth-century church and seventeenth-century oaks; the *gîte* and the village pay phone are on the right. Obtain the key at the *mairie* (open Mon.-Fri. 8am-noon and 2-5pm) located just behind the *gîte.* Otherwise (Sat.-Sun. roughly 9am-9pm, and Mon.-Fri. 5-9pm), the key may be found at the *café/épicerie* (tel. 98 99 73 74). In town the **Hôtel l'Amorique,** 1, pl. Aristide-Briand (tel. 98 99 71 24), has simple, fairly large rooms with comfortable mattresses. (Singles 52F, doubles 63F, triples 93F.) The often crowded but pleasant **Camping Municipal du Lac,** rue de Brest, is open year-round. **Aux Amis Routiers,** on the road to Carhaix, at the intersection with the D769, 3½km from town, serves a seven-course lunch for 43F. (Open Mon.-Fri. noon-2pm.) For lighter fare try **Crêperie des Myrtilles,** pl. Aristide-Briand, with a 32F three-crepe *menu.* (Open July-Aug. daily noon-9:30pm; April-June and Sept.-Oct. open Tues.-Wed. and Fri.-Sun.; Nov.-March open Fri.-Sun. only.)

SNCF buses run from Morlaix to Huelgoat twice per day during the week (around 8am and 6pm), three times on Saturday (extra bus around 2pm), and twice on Sunday (morning bus leaves at about 10am). The one-hour trip (25F, railpasses valid) ends at pl. Aristide-Briand, near the tourist office.

Brest and The Crozon Peninsula

At the very end of the Breton peninsula, **Brest** is an industrial port with little in the way of tourist attractions but for an excellent youth hostel and good railway connections. The **hostel** is at Le Moulin Blanc, rue de Kerbiant (tel. 98 41 90 41), about 4km from the station. Take bus #7 from the train station to Port de Plaisance. It has superb facilities and is a two-minute walk from a large, sandy beach. (32F; bike rental 30F per day.) Rue de Siam (which becomes rue Jean Jaurès) is the place to stock up on stores.

From Brest, a 2½-hour boat ride brings you to **Ile d'Ouessant,** a ruggedly beautiful island where you're likely to see more sheep than people. Because of its isolation, the island developed a Breton subculture found nowhere else, including elaborate ceremonies for those lost at sea and a tradition of women proposing marriage to men. Boats dock at **Port du Stiff,** where you can rent bicycles for the day; the island's town, **Lampaul,** is a 45-minute stroll across to the south-western coast. There the **syndicat d'initiative** (tel. 98 48 85 83) will give you a map of the island and information on the four hotels in town. Boats leave from Brest to the island. (June to mid-Sept. daily; mid-Sept. to June Wed.-Mon.; 62F one way, 102F round-trip.)

Brest is the easiest place to start a trip to the **Crozon Peninsula,** with its steep, jagged cliffs and ancient *menhirs.* Daily boats run from Brest to Le Fret (leave Brest 8:30am and stop at Le Conquet at 9am), with connecting buses to Camaret, Crozon, and Morgat. **Aútocars Douguet** runs buses from Brest to Crozon and Camaret (Mon.-Fri. in the morning and in the afternoon; Sat. morning only; 41F to Camaret). Four SNCF buses per day (railpasses valid) run from Quimper to Camaret via Crozon and Morgat.

Camaret, though overpriced, is the best base from which to explore the peninsula. Three-and-a-half kilometers away on the D8 towers the **Pointe de Penhir,** whose cliffs, violent seas, and isolated rock masses are a staggering sight. Farther north, the road passes the **Alignements de Lagatjar,** some 100 *menhirs* arranged in intersecting lines and ending in a Stonehenge-like circle. The D355 leads to **Pointe des Espagnols,** another spectacular point with superb views.

Prices on the peninsula are as steep as the cliffs. The best way to find indoor accommodation is to inquire at the tourist offices about *chambres d'hôtes* (bed and breakfast in rural settings; transportation usually required) or about *gîtes d'étape* (22F dorm space with facilities; transportation required, cars prohibited). Camaret's **syndicat d'initiative** is on quai Kleber (tel. 98 27 93 60), near the bus stop. (Open mid-June to mid-Sept. Mon.-Sat. 9:30am-12:30pm and 2:30-6:30pm, Sun. 10am-noon; mid-Sept. to mid-June call the mayor's office at 98 27 94 22.) **Hôtel Vauban,** on quai Styvel (tel. 98 27 91 36), has comfortable rooms, some with a view of the port. (Singles and doubles 110F. Showers 10F. Breakfast 16.50F; ordinarily required, but you may be able to talk your way out of it. Open mid-March to mid-Oct.) The **Hôtel du Styvel,** also on quai Styvel (tel. 98 27 92 74), is similarly attractive. (Singles and doubles from 110F. Showers 25F. Breakfast 15F. Open April-Sept.)

Happily, there are plenty of campgrounds in the area. **Camping Municipal de Lannic** (tel. 98 27 91 31) is close to the center of Camaret, off rue du Grounach. (5.85F per person, 4.50F per tent. Showers 5F. Open June to mid-Sept.) Close to Crozon's SNCF station is the two-star **Camping Pen-Ar-Ménez** (tel. 98 27 12 36), off noisy rue de la Marne. (10F per person, 11.50F per tent. Showers included. Open April-Sept.) The campsite rents bikes (25F per day), as does **Melamar** (tel. 98 27 95 29), a garage across from the church on the quai in Camaret (35F per day).

Southern Coast

La Cornouaille

Quimper is the capital of the Breton homeland of la Cornouaille, whose original inhabitants came from Cornwall in England, supposedly from the Court of King Arthur at Tintagel. One of Brittany's biggest folk festivals, the **Festival de la Cornouaille,** is held between the third and fourth Sundays in July. The action usually begins on the Tuesday after the third Sunday, and includes concerts, films, street musicians playing anything even remotely Celtic, parades in traditional costumes, and plays in the Breton language. The youth hostel is usually full during festival week, but otherwise has lots of space.

Quimper is readily accessible by train from Paris (7-10 per day, 6½ hr., 263F), Rennes (119F), or Nantes (124F). From the train station turn right and follow av. de la Gare to the river; cross the bridge and turn left on bd. Amiral de Kerguélen, then right on rue du Rois Gradlon for the **Cathédrale St-Corentin,** the tourist office, and the *vieille ville.* A number of private bus lines connect Quimper to surrounding towns; ask at the **office de tourisme,** 3, rue du Rois Gradlon (tel. 98 95 04 69), for schedules, or poke around the parking lot next to the train station where most buses stop and schedules are posted. (Tourist office open July-Aug. Mon.-Sat. 8:30am-8pm, Sun. 9:30am-noon, longer during festival week; Sept.-June Mon.-Sat. 9am-noon and 2-6pm.)

Quimper's **auberge de jeunesse (IYHF),** 6, av. des Oiseaux (tel. 98 55 41 67), has clean but crowded dorms. (30F. Limited camping space, 13F. Check-in 8-10am and 6-8pm. No lockout.) Near the train station, the **Hôtel de Cornouaille,** 46, rue Aristide-Briand (tel. 98 90 05 05), has comfortable rooms and a friendly staff. (Sinles 68F, doubles 75F, with shower 114F. Showers 12F.) A two-star **municipal ampground,** right next to the youth hostel, offers woodsy sites. (3.50F per person, F per tent.) For rural accommodations nearby, ask at the tourist office for lists f *chambres d'hôtes* and *gîtes d'étape.*

The westernmost point of all France is the **Pointe du Raz,** with truly awe-aspiring cliffs. The Pointe is accessible by CAT/TV buses from Quimper (Mon.-at. 4 per day, 2 Sun.) Catch the bus at signpost #3 in the big parking lot next SNCF station. All buses also stop at (and on Sun. they *only* stop at) 5, bd. Kergué-en.

Quiberon Peninsula (Presqu'île de Quiberon)

The Presqu'île de Quiberon is a long, narrow peninsula—too narrow, it seems, o support its armies of summertime tourists. The principal town, **Quiberon,** is an xpensive madhouse in July and August, with nothing to see and too many people rying to see it. The main reason to come is to use the youth hostel as a base for xploring the idyllic Belle-Ile or the barren, windy Côte Sauvage.

Quiberon is accessible by rail in July and August only, when trains run from uray on the Quimper-Rennes line (4 per day, 40 min., 18F). Buses run year-round rom Auray (5-7 per day, 1½-2 hr., 26F). The **office de tourisme,** 7, rue de Verdun tel. 97 50 07 84), has complete bus and ferry schedules. (Open July-Aug. Mon.-at. 9am-7pm, Sun. 10am-noon and 5-7pm; Sept.-June Mon.-Sat. 9am-12:30pm and -6:30pm.) The **auberge de jeunesse (IYHF),** 45, rue de Roch-Priol (tel. 97 50 15 4), is a 1½-kilometer walk from the station (turn left and follow the signs); with little luck you may find a bed under a tent or even an indoor spot, but otherwise ou'll have to camp in the spacious lot out back. (Indoor bed 30F, tent beds 26F. Camping 13F. Office open 8:30-10am and 6-10pm. Bike rental 25F per day.)

Ferries leave for **Belle-Ile** from Port-Maria (tel. 97 50 06 90) every few hours rom late June through August. From September to mid-June departures are four o six times per day (45 min., 32F each way, bikes 27F). To explore the island's igh cliffs, small creeks, and flowered pastures, you can rent bikes for 28F per day rom **Louis Banet** (tel. 97 31 84 74), near the docks. (Open 9am-noon and 2-7pm.) At the **tourist office** near the gangplank, 3F buys you a helpful map. The closest oints of interest are the fishing port of **Sauzon** (8km down the D30), the rock for-mations at **Pointe des Poulains** (follow the D30 west from Sauzon for 1km and turn ight on the D25 for 2km), and the **Grotte de l'Apothicaire** (follow the D30 west rom Sauzon for 3½km).

Tour the **Côte Sauvage** by following the D186 along the west side of the Quiberon Peninsula. Don't swim where *baignades interdites* (swimming prohibited) is post-ed—the waters are genuinely treacherous. Hitching around the peninsula is quite easy.

Nantes

"Nantes, ça bouge!" is the slogan here, and even a short stay shows that this is ndeed a city on the move. Nantes bears many resemblances to Paris: Wide boule-vards mark the boundaries between administrative *arrondissements,* and opulent architecture testifies to a wealthy past. Under the rule of the great Ducs de Mont-fort, François I and II, Nantes was firmly established as the administrative center of Brittany.

The Gothic vaults of Nantes's **Cathédrale St-Pierre** soar higher above worship-ers' heads than the arches of Notre-Dame, thanks to the lightweight white Vendée stone of which they are made. (Open to visitors daily 8:45am-noon and 2-7pm.) Behind the cathedral on rue Malherbe (off rue Henri IV), the **Chapelle de l'Immaculée** has an eerie aerial virgin in place of a spire.

Nearby, Nantes's heavily fortified fifteenth-century **château** is surrounded by a moat and an emerald-green strip of lawn. Built by François II, it was the birthplace of Duchesse Anne de Bretagne, queen to two successive kings of France; now tw museums remain in residence. The **Musée des Arts Populaires Régionaux** hous an excellent collection of colorful Breton costumes, period rooms, and some fir carved-oak furniture. The **Musée des Salorges** is a nautical museum of great intere to sailors, armchair or otherwise. (Château and museums open July-Aug. dail 10am-noon and 2-6pm; Sept.-June. Wed.-Mon. 10am-noon and 2-6pm. Entry t the courtyard and ramparts free. Ticket for all museums 7.50F, students 4F; fr Sat.-Sun.).

Two blocks from the cathedral on rue Clemenceau is Nantes's **Musée des Beau Arts,** with fine paintings by Rubens, Courbet, de la Tour, Ingres, and the early Ita ian painters. (Open Wed.-Mon. 10am-noon and 1-5:45pm, Sun. 11am-5pm. Admi sion 5F, students 2.50F; free Sat.-Sun.) For a lark, visit the **Musée Jules Vern** which tries to recreate the imaginative world of Captain Nemo and other Verr characters. (Open Wed.-Sat. 10am-noon and 2-5pm, Sun. 2-5pm only. Admissic 5F; free Sat.-Sun.)

Ile Feydeau, between allée Turenne and allée Tuouin, was at one time an islan here wealthy sea merchants spent the spoils of the triangular slave trade on lavis houses. Walk down **rue Kervegan** for the best view. Even more stately is eighteent century **place Royale** and **rue Crébillon,** leading to **place Graslin.** A place of pilgrin age for Corbu-buffs is Le Corbusier's **Cité Radieuse,** embodying a unified concep tion of suburban life. Take bus #31 from the Commerce stop on cours Frankli Roosevelt. Although residences and centers of the **Université de Nantes** are sca tered through the city, the area north of rue Crébillon seems to be most populi in the evening, and rue Scribe has a multitude of bars and cafes to catch the lat night crowd. Every evening at 10pm you can hear a live jazz ensemble at **Le Ti Break,** 1, rue des Petites Ecuries. (Open Mon.-Sat. 10pm-3:30am.)

The **Maison de Tourisme** (tel. 40 47 04 51) is on place du Commerce, down cour John Kennedy from the station. (Open Mon.-Fri. 9:30am-7pm, Sat. 10am-6pm For information on budget travel, visit **CROUS,** at 14, rue Santeuil (tel. 40 73 7 84; open Mon.-Fri. 10am-12:30pm and 1:30-5:30pm). **ABRI,** 7, rue de la Clavuri (tel. 40 20 20 62), organizes cycling tours of Brittany. Ask about their *gîtes d'étap* (travel shelters). (Open Tues.-Fri. 2:30-7pm, Sat. 10am-1pm.)

To get to the modern **auberge de jeunesse (IYHF),** 2, pl. de la Manufacture (te 40 20 57 25), take a right onto bd. de Stalingrad as you leave the station, then left into the Manufacture complex (15-min. walk). Or take the tram from the statio to stop "Manufacture." Kitchen, TV room, and friendly staff. (33F. Sheets 10I Breakfast 9.50F. Open year-round daily 7-10am and 6-11pm.) The **Centre Jea Macé,** 90, rue du Préfet Bonnefoy (tel. 40 74 55 74), at the corner of rue Sully, i accessible by bus #12 from the SNCF station to pl. Maréchal Foch. They rer clean, if dimly lit, doubles and triples for 40F per person, and there's also a reasor able restaurant (breakfast 10F, other meals around 25F). You can camp at **Campin du Val de Cens,** 21, bd. du Petit Port (tel. 40 74 47 94), 3km from town. Buse #42, 43, 54, and 55 run from pl. du Commerce. (8.70F per site, 6.40F per person.

The **market** in Nantes happens in place du Bouffay (Tues.-Sun. 9am-1pm). Fc the crepes that made Nantes famous (or something like that), go to **Crêperie Jaun** 1, rue des Echevins, off pl. du Bouffay. The *pavé nantais* crepe (32-36F) is as del cious as it is huge, and vice versa. **Le Mangeoire,** 16, rue des Petites Ecuries, i run by a friendly bunch who serve up a good 46F *menu.* (Open Tues.-Sat. noor 1:30pm and 7:30-9:30pm.)

Frequent **trains** link Nantes to Paris (3-4 hr., 181F), Bordeaux, and Quimpe and trains run in July and August to Quiberon.

Near Nantes, **La Baule** boasts that it has the most beautiful beach in Europ and it may well be right. A smooth curve of sand stretches for miles along the coas washed by gentle, warm waves. Relaxation seems to be the town's main industr and it is expensive and busy in summer. **Trains** connect Nantes to La Baule (July Aug. 6 per day; Oct.-June 8-10 per day; 1 hr., 47F). There are two train station La Baule les Pins, east of the center in a quiet area close to camping, and La Baul Escoublac, close to the busy center. Avenue Georges Clemenceau runs from th train station to pl. de la Victoire, where you will find the **office de tourisme** (tel. 40 24 34 44). (Open July-Aug. daily 9am-7:30pm; Sept.-June Mon.-Sat. 9am-12:30pm and 2:15-6:30pm.) From here, av. du Général-de-Gaulle runs down to the beach. You'll probably want to also.

Loire Valley (Pays de la Loire)

The Loire isn't just another pretty river. Along its banks, as along the Rivers Loir, Indre, and Cher, rise the dignified, magnificent, and much-praised châteaux. Under a prosperous and united France, the valley's fortresses were transformed into country residences of the nobility; transfixed, like Narcissus, by pools made to reflect their beauty. Don't miss the most flamboyant—Chambord—or the most beautiful—Chenonceau—but be sure to explore some of the others. Blois and Cheverny merit a visit for their gilded interiors; Azay-le-Rideau and Villandry for their settings and exteriors; Angers for its episodic tapestries.

Almost by definition, the most spectacular châteaux are often the most secluded and the least accessible. To see all the major châteaux will take five or six days. Trains between Blois and Tours stop at Amboise and Chaumont; those between Tours and Angers stop at Langeais and Saumur. Azay-le-Rideau, Chenonceau, and Chinon are accessible by train from Tours as well. Four of the nicest châteaux—Ussé, Villandry, Cheverny, and Chambord—can be reached only by bike, tour bus, or thumb. Bus tours lasting nine (full-day excursion, around 100F) or five hours (half-day excursion, 70F) depart from both Tours and Blois, usually visiting two to four castles. Admission fees are not included, but will be half-priced. Visit the *syndicats* in Tours or Blois for tickets and information.

Unquestionably the best way to see this beautiful valley is by bike. Distances are relatively short, and the terrain is not that challenging. Train stations at Amboise, Blois, Chinon, Langeais, and Tours rent bikes for 45F per day, with a 250F deposit, and you can often drop a bike off at a different station (inquire where you rent). For more expensive, better quality rentals consult the local *syndicats.* Hitching to the isolated châteaux, such as Chambord and Chenonceau, is challenging. Fortunately, many châteaux rise near well-traveled roads, so a ride can be possible despite the sea of tourist-packed cars slowly passing you by.

The Loire valley boasts particularly appealing **IYHF auberges de jeunesse** in Chartres, Blois, Chinon, Saumur, and Beaugency; those in Tours, Amboise, and Angers are less distinguished. Ask any *syndicat* for the blue book listing hours and prices for all the region's attractions, and the green book listing the area's abundant campsites. Blois, Amboise, and Chinon make comfortable bases for day trips—Tours is most convenient but less appealing than these smaller towns.

The Loire's culinary specialties will soothe those weary after a day of cycling. Local cheeses, such as creamy sweet *Port Salut* and savory *fromage de chèvre* (goat's cheese), go well with the light and rosé wines of Anjou, Saumur, and Vouvray, as do trout and pike from the area's rivers. *Veal escalope,* thinly sliced veal and mushrooms cooked in wine, is a local favorite. Picnic grounds are abundant.

Angers

Angers's massive stone walls, guarding the western gateway to the château region, once daunted potential attackers. Today they cringe in the face of urban onslaught. Since their construction, the 17 formidable towers have been truncated and toppled (during the Wars of Religion), and the deep moat's waters replaced with formal gardens. Inside, in a modern gallery, the enormous **Tapestries of the Apoca-**

lypse relate serially the *Book of Revelations.* This tour-de-force of medieval art, spun in gold and wool thread, covers enough square footage to carpet a small street. After your visit, don't miss the free *dégustation* at the **Maison du Vin de l'Anjou** at 5bis, pl. Kennedy, across the street from the château entrance. (Château open April-June 9am-noon and 2-6:30pm; July-Sept. 9am-6:30pm; Oct.-March 9:30am-noon and 2-5:30pm. Admission 22F; students, and everyone on Sun. 12F.)

Angers's prominent **Cathédrale St-Maurice** is noted for its unique Angevin vaulting and elegant four-part arrangement, both of which merge the best of Gothic loftiness and Romanesque simplicity. For the only good views of the cathedral, go to the **Montée St-Maurice** (steps leading down to the river Maine) or to one of the towers of the château.

Either of Angers's two **syndicats d'initiative** will find you a room for a 5F fee; one is across from the château, and another is adjacent to the train station. (Open July-Oct. daily 9am-7pm; Nov.-June Mon.-Sat. 10am-noon and 2-5pm.) There is an **auberge de jeunesse (IYHF)** on rue Darwin (tel. 41 48 14 55), 4km from the station. Take bus #6 to "Bull." (30F per person. No lock-out. Curfew 11pm. Open July-Aug.) The friendly, clean **La Coupe d'Or,** 5, rue de la Gare (tel. 41 88 45 02), is one of the best deals near the train station. (Rooms 65-80F.)

The pedestrian district around place Romaine abounds with appetizing eateries. **La Treille,** 12, rue Moutault, off pl. St-Croix, has a fresh, original 49F *menu* and an a la carte selection that includes vegetarian tarts and salads (25-30F), *brochettes* (39F), and good *au gratin* dishes (33F). (Open Mon.-Sat.) **A la Petite Marmite,** 22ter, rue Denis-Papin, has regional specialties on a 45F *menu.* (Closed latter half of July.)

Tours

Although less quaint than its smaller neighbors, Tours draws more tourists than any other Loire town. Its bustling modern streets and extensive *vieille ville* contain plentiful accommodations. More importantly, Tours is a treasure chest of bus and train connections to nearby châteaux.

If you have time to kill in Tours, tour the **old quarter.** From the two remaining massive towers of the **Basilique St-Martin,** walk along rue du Change to place Pimereau, where you'll see several fifteenth-century wooden houses. To the east, **Cathédrale St-Gatien** has beautiful thirteenth-century windows whose blues are subtly different from those at Chartres; above, tall and simple arches lend a look of incredible height to the nave. (Closes at 8pm in summer, 5:30pm in winter; closed daily noon-2pm. Admission 12F, students 6F.) Tours's large **Office de Tourisme,** pl. Maréchal-Leclerc (tel. 47 05 58 80), is in front of the train station. The office provides a supermarket of services, and the friendly staff speaks English. (Open in summer Mon.-Sat. 9am-7pm, Sun. 9am-6pm; in winter Mon.-Sat. 9am-noon and 2-6pm.) After hours, pick up town information and a hotel list from the vending machine (1F) outside the office.

Even in high season, you shouldn't have much trouble finding inexpensive lodgings in Tours. Tours's **auberge de jeunesse (IYHF)** (tel. 47 25 14 45), 5km from town and accessible via buses #2 and 6 from pl. Jean Jaurès (turn left as you exit the station), is dusty with fetid kitchen facilities but a lively atmosphere. (30F. Lock-out 10:30am-5pm. Midnight curfew. Open Feb.-Nov.) Hotels can be more comfortable: Try rue Blaise Pascal, rue Vaillant, or rue Palissy, all a backpack's throw from the train station. **Hôtel Bretagne,** 8, rue Blaise-Pascal (tel. 47 05 41 43), is cheerful and the best place on the street. (Singles 60-75F, doubles 75-100F. Breakfast 12F.) **Hôtel Grammont,** 16, av. de Grammont (tel. 47 05 55 06), has clean, quiet rooms and a warm, English-speaking management. (Singles 79F, doubles 85F, with shower 105F. Breakfast 16F.) **Hôtel Vendôme,** 24, rue Roger-Salengro (tel. 47 64 33 54), one block off av. Gramont, has singles for 65-68F, doubles for 90F.

Appetizing, inexpensive restaurants abound on rue Colbert and in the old quarter around place de la Lamproie. **Aux Trois Canards,** 16, rue de la Rotisserie, has elegant, candle-lit dinners for 25-50F, and a 4-course 39F *menu,* service and wine included. Join young local workers at **Le Foyer,** 16, rue Palissy, where the student discount brings the price of four courses down to 27F. (Open daily noon-1:15pm and 7-8pm. Closed Sat.-Sun. in Aug.)

Near Tours

Graceful **Chenonceau,** perhaps the loveliest château of all, arches effortlessly over the languid river Cher. The palace was built for Diane de Poitiers, Henri II's mistress, who was exuberantly evicted by Henri's wife, Catherine de Medici, after the king's death. By day, you can walk through the well-renovated interiors on your own, soothed by soft Renaissance music, or row under the arches of the dance gallery. In summer, make an effort to stay until night, when an unforgettable *son et lumière* performance fills the woods with soft light and gentle music. (Château open in summer daily 9am-7pm; in winter daily 9am-noon and 2-4:30pm. Admission 25F, students 15F. *Son et lumière* show summer nights at 10 and 10:45pm, 20F.) The only reasonable accommodation in the town of Chenonceau is the comfortable, two-star **Hostel du Roy,** (tel. 47 23 90 17), four minutes from the château. (Singles 75F, doubles 90F. Showers included.) Four trains per day (¾hr., 23.50F) travel to the town (the castle is 2km from the station) from Tours; you'll have to stay here to see the sound-and-light show.

More easily accessible by train from Tours is the pastoral **Azay-le-Rideau,** a beautiful château raised on one of a series of islands in the River Indre. Lolling trees and a picturesque moat surround the castle's white stone towers, fairy-tale battlements, and Renaissance *loggia.* Unfortunately, the crowds and required tours (in French only) can be unpleasant. (Château open daily July-Aug. 9:15am-6:30pm; Oct.-early Nov. 9:15am-noon and 2-5pm; early Nov.-Jan. 9:30am-noon and 2-4:45pm. Admission 16F, students 9F.) In Azay-le-Rideau, rent a 10-speed bicycle at **Le Provost,** 13, rue Carnto (tel. 47 43 30 94), to make the peaceful half-hour ride to green **Villandry.** (Bicycles 25F per day. Shop open Tues.-Sat. 9am-noon and 2-7pm.) At Villandry, the star attractions are the fantastic formal gardens, three terraces of sculpted shrubs and flowers; the château is less interesting. (Open mid-March to Sept. daily 9am-6pm; Oct. to mid-March daily 9am-noon and 2-6pm. Admission 16F, students 11F; 5F less if you skip the château.)

Ussé, surrounded by the thick woods of the Forêt de Chinon, is also an easy bike trip from Azay. The inspiration for *Sleeping Beauty,* this château is still inhabited by a marquis. (Open March-Nov. daily 9am-noon and 2-6pm. Admission 30F, students 18F.) Just west of Tours is the feudal and forbidding **Langeais.** Notice the stone slabs along the upper fortifications which, when drawn back, reveal holes for hurling boiling oil, pitch, and other nasty things at attackers. "Fetchez la vache!" Trains run from Saumur (22.50F) and Tours (17.60F).

Further from Tours is the delightful town of **Chinon.** Its ruined château is the perfect place to let your mind recreate the past, and the several wine-tasting establishments in the *vieille ville* are ideal for indulging in the present. Chinon also has a modern **auberge de jeunesse** on rue Descartes (tel. 47 93 10 48), a five-minute walk from the station. (29F per night, sheets 10F. Closed 2-6pm; reception open 6-10:30pm.)

About 30km northwest of Chinon, a massive fourteenth-century chteau cuts an imposing profile above the town of **Saumur.** (Open July-Aug. daily 9am-6:30pm and 8:30-10:30pm; off-season 9am-noon and 2-6pm. Admission 16F, students 13F). There's an **auberge de jeunesse** (tel. 41 67 45 00) on Ile d'Offard, between the station and town center, with a great view of the chteau. (32F per night, sheets and breakfast 11F each. Reception open 8-10am and 5-10pm.)

Blois

Blois, with winding, hilly streets, a restored old quarter, a château, and a comfortable rural hostel, is a picturesque base for château-hopping.

The **Château de Blois** was constructed over a period of four centuries, which explains the almost humorous juxtaposition of different architectural styles. While many châteaux seduce you from afar and bore you once you're inside, Blois makes good its promise. Here are the finest interiors in the Loire: red brick, gilted blue and gold beams, black and orange tiles, and green monogrammed wallpaper. (Open April-Aug. 9am-6:30pm; shorter hours off-season. Admission 20F, students 10F.) Apart from its château, Blois has attractive churches and gardens. The **Abbaye St-Lomer** impresses inside and out, a tinted hodgepodge of Renaissance and Gothic. Don't miss the old quarter around the **Cathédrale St-Louis.**

The **Office de Tourisme,** 3, av. Jean Laigret (tel. 54 74 06 49), will change money and book rooms for a 5F fee. (Open in summer Mon.-Sat. 9am-noon and 2-7pm, Sun. 10am-1pm and 4-7pm; in winter Mon.-Sat. 9am-noon and 2-6pm.) Ask here about guided bus tours to Chambord and Cheverny (July-Aug. daily; 60F) and to Chenonceau and Amboise. Accommodations in Blois fill up fast, so arrive before noon or call ahead. The homey and rustic **auberge de jeunesse (IYHF)** (tel. 54 78 27 21), is 5km from the station and surrounded by forest. Take bus #70 from pl. Valin by the river. (26F. Lock-out 10am-6pm. Open March to mid-Nov.) The friendly and comfortable **Hôtel du Bellay,** 12, rue des Minimes (tel. 54 78 23 62) is in a quiet, old neighborhood. (Singles and doubles 89F. Showers 10F. Avoid the meager 18F breakfast.) There are many hotels across the river on av. Wilson, including **Hôtel la Sologne,** 20, av. Wilson (tel. 54 78 02 77; singles 50F, doubles 57F, triples 77F. Closed Sat. night in off-season).

Cheap restaurants are hard to find in Blois; try **Les Glycines,** 54, rue Foulérie (tel. 54 79 17 95), which is a tad cheaper than others of its kind; they serve good pizza for 25-38F and salads from 22F. For 58F, **Hôtel de la Gare,** across from the train station, offers a wonderful four-course *menu.* Don't let the tacky exterior scare you—the food is delicious and filling.

You can rent a bicycle for touring the nearby countryside at the station (1-speeds for 36F per day plus a 200F deposit), but you can find a greater selection at **Atelier Cycles,** 44, levée des Tuileries (tel. 54 74 30 13) for 35F and 45F per day plus a passport as deposit. (Open daily 9am-10pm year-round.)

Near Blois

White, plump **Chambord,** built by François I for his frequent hunting trips to nearby forests, is the largest and most extravagant of the châteaux on the Loire, with a melange of dormers and arcades that are magically harmonious when viewed from a distance. Access to the expansive grounds is free and unlimited. Bask in the lush wildlife preserve, but beware the few tusked boar that still roam the forest. The château's beautifully restored interior, noted for its intriguing double-helix staircase, is as remarkable as the surrounding grounds. (Open daily 9:30am-noon and 2-6pm. Admission 22F, students 12F.) Chambord is accessible by bike or thumb from Blois, but there is no regular bus service, only excursion trips. Take the D956 south for 2-3km and turn left onto the D33 for 11km, direct to Chambord.

Cheverny, served by a few local buses from Blois, soothes with stately classical lines and one of the most comfortable interiors of all the châteaux, probably because it has been kept in the family for three centuries. (Open 9am-6:30pm in summer; closed from noon-2pm in off-season. Admission 19F, students 10F.) To hitch to Cheverny from Blois, follow the D956 south.

Amboise is accessible by frequent trains between Blois and Tours. The **Château d'Amboise** is in a highly-decorated Italian Renaissance style, but lacks the magic of its neighbors. Leonardo da Vinci spent his last years here, under the patronage of François I; his reburied bones rest in the flamboyant **Chapelle St-Hubert.** The required tour (in French) includes the chapel, the Logis du Roi, and best of all, the Tour des Minimes, a giant five-story spiral ramp for bringing horses and carriages into the château from the river below. (Open in summer daily 9am-noon and 2-7pm; in winter 9am-noon and 2-6pm. Admission 20F, students 10F.)

Perhaps the most underrated of all the châteaux in the area is the compact **Chaumont-sur-Loire,** which, with its towers and drawbridge, is a masterpiece of the Renaissance, combining both the elegance of a château and the solidity of a fortress. The château is best known for its luxurious *écuries* (stables).(Open April-Sept. daily 9-11:20am and 1:30-5:20pm; shorter hours in off-season. Admission 21F, students 11F.) Chaumont is accessible by train from Blois (8 per day, 10 min., 9F). The train station lies in Onzain, 2km north of Chaumont, across the river.

Orléans

In 1429, Joan of Arc won Orléans, then the most important city in France after Paris, from the English. Whether she would want to do the same today is questionable. Orléans has grown into an industrial center of no interest to the traveler except as a gateway to the châteaux. To pass time in town, visit the **Cathédrale de la Ste-Croix,** noted for its stained-glass windows depicting events from the life of Joan of Arc, as well as for the only Carolingian floor mosaic in France. (Open daily 8am-noon and 2-7pm.) The **Centre Jeanne d'Arc** in place de Gaulle features period costumes and an audiovisual re-creation of the siege of Orléans. (Open May-Oct. Tues.-Sun. 10am-noon and 2-6pm; Nov.-April Tues.-Sun. 2-6pm.) When you tire of churches and museums, take bus S from place Albert I*er* to the **Parc Floral,** a blissful garden with fields of purple and white irises and a potpourri of tulip beds. (Open April 1-Nov.11 daily 9am-6pm. Admission 12F, students 6F.)

The **Office de Tourisme,** bd. Aristide Briand (tel. 38 53 05 95) sponsors walking tours of the city and books accomodations for 6F in Orléans and 20F outside the Loiret region. (Open June-Aug. Mon.-Sat. 9am-7:30pm, Sun. 9am-12:30pm and 3-6:30pm; Oct.-May Mon.-Sat. 9am-noon and 2-7pm.) There's a simple, homey **auberge de jeunesse** on rue Faubourg Madeleine on the west side of town (tel. 38 62 45 75); take bus B (*direction* Paul-Bert) from in front of the train station. (29F per person, reception open 7:15-9:30am and 5:30-10:30pm.) Both **Hôtel Coligny** (80, rue de la Gare, tel. 38 53 61 60) and **Hôtel Touring** (142 bd. de Châteaudun, tel. 38 53 10 51) have pleasant rooms for 60-70F in a quiet neighborhood 10 minutes north of the station. Creperies are plentiful in the pedestrian district of the *vieille ville;* try **Le Viking** at 235, rue de Bourgogne (tel. 38 53 12 21).

Southwestern France

The wide southwest is among the least-visited corners of France. Fertile plains surround Bordeaux while the dramatic coastline farther south is the stronghold of the fiercely independent Basques. The beaches of the Côte Basque are distinguished by their rough surf and violent conditions, but nearby Biarritz is well-known as the Monte Carlo of western France, an old-style elegant resort that has raised the *grande promenade* to an art. Inland, the Pyrénées rise steeply, running past the renowned pilgrimage spot of Lourdes then jumping over the tiny state of Andorra before reaching the Mediterranean. In summer, the Pyrénées are a particularly pleasant alternative to the crowded French Alps. The ancient *langue d'oc*—the language of Provençal courtly literature—united the lands stretching from Provence to the Pyrenees, including the Catalan region of Roussillon and the area around Toulouse. Spanish influence persists here, and Languedoc, almost totally dependent on its vineyards for revenue, has remained a rustic area rippling with hills and vines.

Bordeaux

When Eleanor of Aquitane married Henry Plantagenet in the twelfth century, her sizeable dowry included the port city of Bordeaux. The marriage soured Anglo-French relations for the next three centuries, but brought Bordeaux great prosperity as the production of wine became economically important. Wine still flows, but Bordeaux is now a sprawling and rough city under the makeup of several attractive shopping arcades and handsome eighteenth-century riverfront facades. The city is also within striking distance of the immensely enjoyable Dune du Pilat, a gargantuan mountain of silken sand that brings out the acrobat in everyone.

Orientation and Practical Information

Bordeaux is situated 40km inland from France's Atlantic coast, about 200km north of the Spanish border. The city is directly accessible from Paris Austerlitz, Nantes, La Rochelle, Angoulême, and Tours. The city is crowded with tourists in the summer and pickpockets all year; be careful with your valuables. **Rue Ste-Catherine** is part pedestrian and connects **place de la Victoire** with **place de la Comédie,** the other main square.

Tourist Offices: Syndicat d'Initiative, 12, cours du XXX Juillet (tel. 56 44 28 41). Take bus #7 or 8 from the train station and get off near the corner of cours de l'Intendance and cours du XXX Juillet. Large, crowded office with decent maps, hotel and camping information, and a daily tour of nearby vineyards, with several tastings (85F, students 50F). Open July-Aug. Mon.-Fri. 9am-7:30pm, Sat. 9am-7pm, Sun. 9am-4pm; Sept.-June Mon.-Sat. 9am-12:15pm and 1:45-6:30pm, closed Sun. **Centre d'Information Jeunesse d'Aquitaine,** 5, rue Dufour-Dubergier (tel. 56 48 55 50). Reams of information about campgrounds, hostels, and activities in the area.

Currency Exchange: On Sat. try the post office, open 8am-noon, or the Banque Franco-Portugaise, 10, rue Claude Bonnier (tel. 56 98 73 93), open 9am-12:30pm and 2-5:30pm. On Sun., the **Thomas Cook** at the train station (tel. 56 91 58 80) is open 8am-8pm.

American Express: 14, Cours de l'Intendance. Open Mon.-Fri. 8:45am-noon and 1:30-6pm.

Post Office: 52, rue Georges-Bonnac. Open Mon.-Fri. 8am-7pm, Sat. 8am-noon.

Trains: Gare St-Jean (tel. 56 92 50 50). Take bus #7 or 8 for the tourist office. To Paris (10-14 per day, 4½-5½ hr., 259F), to Poitiers (10-14 per day, 2½ hr., 124F), and Nantes (5-8 per day, 4 hr., 180F). To Arcachon and buses for Dune du Pilat (12-16 per day, 45 min., 38F; June-Sept. special 52F round-trip deal available).

Buses: Citram, 14, rue Fondaudege (tel. 56 81 18 18), is the principal regional carrier. Inquire at the *syndicat* for smaller bus companies.

Emergencies: Police (tel. 17); headquarters at 87, rue Abbé de l'Epée (tel. 56 90 92 75). **Ambulance** (tel. 56 96 70 70).

Medical Assistance: Hospital/Clinic St-André, 1, rue Jean Burguet (tel. 56 96 83 83).

Consulate: U.S., 22, cours Maréchal Foch (tel. 56 52 65 95).

Accommodations, Camping, and Food

The *Accueil* bureau (*quai* #1 in the train station) will provide you with a map and a list of accommodations in town.

Auberge de Jeunesse (IYHF), 22, cours Barbey (tel. 56 91 59 51), 10 min. from the station. Bear right onto cours de la Marne and then turn left on cours Barbey. Huge and gray, but decent. Members 29F, nonmembers 32F. Breakfast 12F. Reception open 7:30-9:30am and 6-11pm, but you can leave luggage all day. Strict 11pm curfew.

Maison des Etudiants, 50, rue Ligier (tel. 56 96 48 30). Take bus #7 or 8 from the train station (6F) to stop Bourse du Travail, then continue in the same direction on cours de la Libération to rue Ligier, on the right. Or walk right from the station onto cours de la Marne to pl. de la Victoire; pick up cours Aristide-Briand (straight across the *place*) which becomes cours de la Libération; look to right for rue Ligier (30 min.). Women only Oct.-June, but men as well July-Sept. Friendly staff and plenty of rooms. Singles: students 40F, *Carte Jeune* holders 45F, others 47F.

Hôtel-Bar-Club Les 2 Mondes, 10, rue St-Vincent-de-Paul (tel. 56 91 63 09). Turn left from station and right onto rue St-Vincent-de-Paul. Spacious, clean, bright rooms. Singles and doubles 70F. No communal shower available. Singles with shower 80F, doubles with shower 100F. Breakfast 15F.

Camping: Try **Camping les Gravières,** Pont-de-la-Maye, in Villeneuve D'Ornon (tel. 56 87 00 36). 12.50F per person, 11F per tent. Open 8am-11pm.

Place St-Michel, between *centre ville* and the station, clutches a handful of what could be the cheapest restaurants in France. **La Perla,** 3, rue Gaspard Philippe, offers a 4-course meal for 26F, wine included. (Open Mon.-Sat. 10:30am-1:45pm and 6:30-8:45pm.) Only slightly more expensive (32F, wine included) is the four-course *ménu* built around the delicious house *couscous* of **Bar-Café de la Grosse Cloche,** 29, rue St-James. (Open daily noon-2pm and 7:30-9:30pm.) For a memorable splurge, try friendly **La Flambée,** 26, rue du Mirail. (*Ménus* start at 90F. Open Mon.-Sat. noon-2pm and 7:30-10pm.)

Sights

Perhaps the most remarkable feature of the **Cathédrale St-André** is the wide variety of flying buttresses that encircle it. Come here for free organ concerts in the summer (in off-season concerts cost 30-50F). Adjacent to the **Church of St-Michel** is the equally beautiful, free-standing bell tower; if you ever wondered what Flamboyant Gothic was all about, this is it. Also not to be missed is Bordeaux's Romanesque representative, the twelfth-to-thirteenth century **Church of Ste-Croix,** with its richly ornamented facade. The **Musée des Beaux Arts** (near the cathedral) has a fine collection, including works by Delacroix, Corot, Renoir, and Matisse. (Open in summer Wed.-Mon. 10am-noon and 2-6pm, in winter until 5pm. Admission 5F, students 3F; free Wed. and Sun.)

The **Maison du Vin,** 1, cours du XXX Juillet, across the street from the *syndicat,* offers free tastings of regional wines. (Mon.-Fri. 10:30-11:30am and 2:30-4:30pm, Sat. 10:30-11:30am.) Both **Magnum,** 3, rue Gobineau, and the **Vinothèque** are close to the *syndicat* and will gladly sell you a Bordeaux red in the 10-10,000F range.

Near Bordeaux

Visiting the châteaux where wine is produced requires an advance phone call at the very least. Call the **Syndicat d'Initiative St-Emilion** (tel. 57 24 72 03) for tours of that town's wine cellars and underground church, or enlist the help of the Bordeaux *syndicat.* St-Emilion may be reached by Citram bus from Bordeaux (5-7 per day, 1¼ hr., 32F one way).

Trains leave Bordeaux's Gare St-Jean for Arcachon, the first leg of the imperative day trip to the **Dune du Pilat.** Bikes may be rented either at the Arcachon station or at **M. Judlin,** 104, cours Lamarque (tel. 56 83 11 88). Buses leave from the Arcachon station for Pyla-sur-Mer (about 24 per day, last return around 7:45pm, 40 min., 6.70F one way), which is a 10 to 15-minute walk from the Dune; continue in the direction the bus was traveling, climbing to the left. When you get to the Dune, kick off your shoes and prepare to lose yourself in a mountain of sand.

Toulouse

Toulousains know their city as "La ville rose," an epithet that describes its brick architecture as well as its warmth and vibrancy. France's fourth largest city, Toulouse is home to a student population that is almost a third the size of the entire city. Its traditionally large immigrant population has included Spaniards in the 1930s, Central European Jews in the 1940s, and North Africans more recently. As polished as Paris in some neighborhoods, its close squares and lively cafes can still impart the intimacy of a smaller town.

Toulouse has an important collection of distinctive churches—if you've seen one, you haven't seen them all. The **Basilique St-Sernin** on rue du Taur is the largest and maybe most majestic Romanesque cathedral in France. (Open daily 8am-noon and 2-7pm. Guided tours at 3pm.)

Down the street, the **Eglise Notre-Dame-du-Taur** is named for Toulouse's first priest, who was martyred by being tied to a bull's tail and dragged to death. **Les Jacobins,** rue Lakanal, is an example of southern Gothic architecture and has a cloister and a **Museum of Contemporaray Art** in the old rectory. Church open June-Sept. Mon.-Sat. 7:30am-9pm, Oct.-May 2-7pm. The **Musée des Augustins,** rue de Metz, near rue Alsace-Lorraine, is an unsurpassed depot of Romanesque and Gothic sculpture in a well-designed display. (Open Mon. and Thurs.-Sat. 10am-noon and 2-6pm, Wed. 10am-noon and 2-10pm, Sun. 10am-noon. Admission 5F; free entry and concerts at 8:30pm on Wed.)

Take the time to linger in the pedestrian rue St-Rome and the places du Capitôle, President Wilson, and St-Georges. Duck into the courtyards of *hôtels particuliers*—gardened mansions, often dating from before the seventeenth century. The opulence, particularly of the **Hôtel d'Assezat** and the gaudy **Hotel de Pierre,** is an indicator of the city's prosperous past.

The **syndicat** is on pl. du Capitôle, in the Donjon (tel. 61 23 32 00). They change money when banks are closed, make hotel reservations in Toulouse or other cities, and offer guided tours of the city. (Open Mon.-Fri. 8-11:45am and 1:30-5:15pm. Currency exchange open June-Sept. Mon.-Sat. 9am-7pm, Sun. 9am-1pm and 2-5:30pm; Oct.-April Mon.-Sat. 9am-6pm.) The **Auberge de Jeunesse Villa des Rosiers,** 125, rue Jean Rieux (tel. 61 80 49 93), is friendly but remote and a little rundown. (32F per night. Breakfast 10F.) Call **CROUS** (tel. 61 21 13 16) to find out which *cité universitaire* will be open this summer. (Singles 45F per night, 675F per month.) **Hôtel des Arts,** 1bis, rue Cantegrol, and rue des Arts (tel. 61 23 36 21) is the best of the town's cheap hotels, run by a delightful young couple who speak English and will help find you a room if they are full. (Doubles 80F. Breakfast 18F.)

There are daily **markets** at the pl. du Capitôle, the bd. de Strasbourg (Tues.-Sun. mornings), and in Les Halles, on the ground floor of the Parking Victor Hugo. Check the rue St-Rome, its continuation the rue des Filatiers, and their side streets for cheap, interesting restaurants. The **Place du May,** 4 rue du May, with a terrace and jazz music, is a good choice. (Good 35F *menus.*)

Near Toulouse

The peaceful towns of Albi and Castres are each an hour's train ride from Toulouse through the low, forested hills and valleys of the **Montagne Noire.** The enormous **Basilique Ste-Cécile,** a fortified yet graceful red brick structure, towers over **Albi.** Inside the church hide rich Italian frescoes, and Burgundian and Gothic statuary. The nearby **Eglise** and **Cloître St-Salvy,** with its fragrant garden, provides an intimate contrast to the imposing cathedral. Albi was the childhood home of Henri Toulouse-Lautrec; the **Musée de Toulouse-Lautrec,** in the Palais de la Berbie, today holds the world's best collection of his work. The complete collection of his posters, together with 600 other works, embody his candid vision of the underlife of Paris in the 1890s. (Open in summer daily 9am-noon and 2-6pm; otherwise daily 10am-noon and 2-5pm. Admission 12F, students 6F.) Be sure to visit the manicured gardens behind the Palais for a lovely view over the River Tam and the Pont Vieux.

The **syndicat d'initiative,** 19, pl. Ste-Cécile (tel. 63 54 22 30), is helpful and has accommodations information. The **Maison des Jeunes et de la Culture,** 13, rue de la République (tel. 63 54 20 67), is a good deal, but assertive regulars may make women feel uncomfortable. Dorm rooms 21F. The **Hôtel la Régence,** 27 av. Maréchal-Joffre (tel. 63 54 01 42), opposite the station, is tasteful, with rooms from 70F. Camp at **Parc de Caussels** (tel. 63 54 38 87), 2km east of Albi, on the route de Millan. **La Pastaciutta,** 11bis, rue de la Piale, has fresh pasta with rich sauces for 25F, or try **Chez Jean-Louis,** 1bis, rue Toulouse-Lautrec, for jazz background music and a four-course meal at 38F. (Open Tues.-Sun. noon-2am.)

Nearby, the medieval town of **Cordes** juts high above the fertile valley of the River Cerou. The walled city was a haunt of Jean-Paul Sartre and is now one of southern France's most lively communities of artists and artisans, many of whom contributed to the town's renovation. Hotels here are exorbitant, but Cordes makes a good afternoon excursion from Albi. Ask at the Albi **syndicat,** pl. de la Halle (tel. 63 56 00 52), for minibus schedules, take the train to Vindrac-Cordes and walk 4km to the town, or try thumbing the 25km.

Castres was the home town of the assassinated socialist and pacifist leader Jean Jaurès, a beloved national hero whose name is on streets in virtually every French city. Visit **Musée Jean Jaurès,** in the Palais de l'Eveché; it is a tribute that vigorously evokes political France at the turn of the century. Across the corridor is the **Musée Goya,** with an extensive collection of Spanish paintings and three series of Goya engravings. (Open in summer Tues.-Sat. 9am-noon and 2-6pm, Sun. 10am-noon and 2-6pm; in winter until 5pm. Admission 5F, students 4F.) The **syndicat d'initiative,** pl. de la République (tel. 63 59 92 44), will help you find a room. (Open April-Sept. Mon.-Sat. 9am-noon and 2-7pm; Oct.-March Tues.-Sat. 9am-noon and 2-7pm.) **Hôtel Perigord,** 22, rue Emile Zola (tel. 63 59 04 74), has unusually fine rooms in the center for 60-75F. **Hôtel Carcasses,** 3, rue d'Augue (tel. 63 35 37 72), is family-run and generous. So is the restaurant, which serves a 55F *menu.* For food, also try **Les Sarrasines,** 34, rue Villegoudon, for crêpes and salads in a quiet loft. (Open Tues.-Sun. noon-midnight.) The tourist office can provide information on local festivals.

Carcassonne

Carcassonne's medieval fortress-city is a child's toy castle grown to life-size proportions. The **Cité,** with its bristling towers and battlements, was begun in Gallo-Roman times. It played an important role in Languedoc's unsuccessful effort, lasting until 1209, to remain independent of northern France. The exterior wall was completed under Louis IX (St-Louis). By the mid-nineteenth century, villagers had so thoroughly pillaged the walls for building materials that only truncated ruins remained. But rising interest in medieval France spurred the rebuilding of the Cité, directed by architect/restorer Viollet-le-Duc. For the best castle-roving, visit the Cité in early morning or at night. The **Basilique St-Nazaire,** on the south side of the Cité on rue Dame Carcas, combines a northern Gothic transept and apse with a much older Romanesque nave. The stained glass is generally considered among the finest in southern France. Near the Basilique, an **amphitheater** hosts a music festival in July and a week-long jazz festival the second week in August. In June, the city celebrates its medieval history with the **Troubadours** festival of epochal music and theater. The entire Cité returns to the Middle Ages during the **Médiévales** festival in August, during which actors dressed as medieval townspeople talk to visitors, display crafts, and pretend nothing has changed in 1000 years.

Reaching the Cité from the train station involves a strenuous 3-kilometer walk uphill, or you can take the black #4 bus (every ½ hr. until 6:53pm). The **syndicat d'initiative** (tel. 68 25 07 04), 15 bd. Camille-Pelleton, is reached from the train station via av. Jean-Jaurès. (Open June-Sept. Mon.-Sat. 9am-12:30pm and 1:30-7pm; Oct.-May 9am-noon and 2-6:30pm.) It **changes currency** when banks are closed (5F commission). There is an annex in the *porte narbonnaise,* within the Cité. (Open July-Aug. daily 9am-7pm; June and Sept. daily 9:30am-12:30pm and 1:30-6:30pm.) Most of Carcassonne's inhabitants live in the *ville basse,* the ordinary town at the foot of the Cité. You, however, can inhabit history by staying at the clean, pleasant **auberge de jeunesse (IYHF)** on rue Vicomte Trencavel (tel. 68 25 23 16. 44F. Breakfast included. Midnight curfew in the summer, 10-11pm in winter. Open Feb.-Nov.). In the *ville basse,* the **Hôtel de l'Octroi,** 106, av. Géneral LeClerc (tel. 68 25 29 08), has crisp, appealing rooms. (Singles 58F, doubles 62F, with shower and toilet 130F, triples 105F. Showers 10F. Breakfast 10F.) **Hôtel St-Joseph,** 81, rue de la Liberté (tel. 68 25 10 94), has large rooms and friendly management. (Doubles 60F, with shower 100F, triples 100-120F. 4 people 110F, with shower 130F. Breakfast 12F.)

The Cité's restaurants are surprisingly inexpensive. For the simplest food, try **La Taverne Médiévale,** 4-7, rue Cros Mayrevieille, a wood-beamed cafeteria with a 35F *menu.* (Open daily 11:30am-3pm and 6:30-10pm.) Most restaurants offer an almost identical 55F *menu,* which includes the hearty *cassoulet,* a regional specialty with beans and meat. At **Le Sénéchal,** 6 rue Viollet le Duc, you'll have to pay a little bit more (*menu* with wine 65F), but it's worth it. (Open Wed.-Mon. noon-2pm and 7-9:30pm.) **Au Bon Pasteur,** 29, rue Armagnac, is in the *ville basse,* far enough away from tourists to serve an honest meal in a relaxed environment. Friendly, English-speaking owner. (Open noon-2pm and 7:15-9:30pm.)

Périgord-Quercy

If you relish uncovering some of France's better hidden secrets, Périgord-Quercy is the place to go. For nature buffs, there arelandscapes of wooded hills, serene river valleys, and dramatic cliffs, as well as the spectacular crystal caverns of Padirac and the Grotte du Grand-Roc. Of somewhat more recent origin are the prehistoric cave paintings, colorful and sophisticated, of Les Eyzies. In the first century the Romans left their mark on Périgueux; some thousand years later Byzantine-Romanesque churches appeared in Périgueux and Souillac, a fortified bridge was erected in Cahors, and a medieval town, recently restored, sprang up in Sarlat. The coming of the Hundred Years' War with England prompted construction of the fortified towns, known as *bastides,* near Périgueux. Pleasant, pastoral villages such as Brantôme (just north of Périgueux), Beynac, Carsac, La Rocque-Gageac, and Rocamadour are found along, or high above, the region's many rivers.

Public transportation in Périgord and Quercy is not good. Driving and biking are best, and many *sentiers de grande randonnée* (clearly marked long-distance footpaths) form an extensive network connecting such cities as Limoges, Les Eyzies, Sarlat, Souillac, Cahors, and myriad points in between. Périgueux's helpful **syndicat d'initiative,** 1, av. de l'Aquitaine (tel. 53 53 10 63), runs bus tours from mid-June to mid-September to the Dronne Valley and Brantôme (Wed., 90F); Sarlat, Domme, La Rocque-Gageac, and Beynac (Thurs., 85F); the *bastides* (Thurs., 96F); and the re-creation of the no-longer-visitable Lascaux Caves, known as Lascaux II (Fri., 96F). Call the day before; also ask for the free guide *La Fête en Périgord,* with information on practically everything, including bike rentals in numerous towns.

Périgueux is a convenient and remarkably uncrowded starting point with lots to see, most notably the **Cathédrale St-Front,** with its myriad Byzantine domes and spires, and first-century **Tour Vésone.** For both women and men, the **Foyer des Jeunes Travailleurs,** off bd. Lakanal (tel. 53 53 52 05), is the cheapest place to stay. (42F. Showers and breakfast included. Check-in 6-8pm.) The **Hôtel des Voyageurs,** 22, rue Denis-Papin (tel. 53 53 17 44), opposite the train station, is run-down and showerless, but has lots of room. (Doubles 50-56F.) Other places, more expensive and of higher quality, are next door at #18 and 20. The nearest campground is **Barnabé-Plage** (tel. 53 53 41 45), in Boulazac, 1½km away; take the city bus (*direction:* Cité Belaire) from the station or from cours Montaigne. (9.20F per person, 7.20F per tent. Open year-round.)

For lunch, join the locals at **Lou Campagnard,** 2, rue Lammary. The filling five-course *menu* including wine costs only 40F. (Open Mon.-Sat. noon-2pm.) Meet younger locals at the **Phoebus,** 11, rue Notre Dame, with a savory 40F *menu,* good salads (18-25F), and foreign beers. (Open May to mid-Oct. daily 10:30am-2am.) Frequent trains (tel. 53 09 50 50) run from Périgueux to Bordeaux.

Four trains per day connect Périgueux to **Les Eyzies-de-Tayac** (30-45 min., 28.50F), where numerous caves conceal fascinating prehistoric paintings and carvings, and spectacular stalagmites and stalactites. The caves are whoppingly popular;

from July to mid-September get here by about 8am to buy your ticket (take the 7:14am train from Périgueux) and be prepared to kill time before your guided visit starts. The best artwork is in the **Grotte de Font-de-Gaume.** Some excellent carvings are found in the slightly less popular **Grotte des Cambarelles.** (Both open April-Sept. Wed.-Mon. 9am-noon and 2-6pm; Oct.-March Wed.-Mon. 10am-noon and 2-4pm.) One-and-a-half kilometers from town, the **Grotte du Grand-Roc** is a crystal palace. (Open mid-March to June and mid-Sept. to Oct. daily 9am-noon and 2-6pm; July to mid-Sept. daily 9am-6:30pm. Admission 27F, ages 6-12 11F.)

Bikes may be rented at the Les Eyzies station and at the **syndicat** (tel. 53 06 97 05) in pl. de la Mairie. Hotels in Les Eyzies are expensive, and booked solid from July through September. Fortunately, you can find cheap and comfortable lodgings at the idyllic *gîte d'étape,* **Ferme des Eymaries,** route de St-Cirq (tel. 53 06 94 73). From the center of town head out on the route de Périgueux, cross the train tracks and the river Vézère, and look immediately for the route de St-Cirq on your left; take this for 1½km, turn right just before more train tracks, and follow the signs for 1km. (28F. Breakfast 13F. Dinner by advance phoning 45F. Open April-Oct. daily 6am-10pm.) Campers can try **Camping La Rivière** (tel. 53 06 97 14), on the route de Périgueux. (12F per person, 10F per tent. Hot showers 2F. Canoes rented at river. Open mid-March to Oct.)

Twenty kilometers north of Les Eyzies in **Montignac** is the exhibit **Lascaux II,** a skillful re-creation of the contents of the Lascaux caves. (Open July-Aug. daily 9:30am-7pm; Feb.-June and mid-Sept. to mid-Dec. Tues.-Sun. 10am-noon and 2-5:30pm. Buy tickets at 9am on pl. Tourny. Admission 28F.) Montignac may also be reached by bus from Brive.

The handsomely restored medieval quarter of **Sarlat** is jammed with vacationers in summer, but the **Cathédrale St-Sacerdos,** the enigmatic **Lanterne des Morts,** and the promise of good biking, hiking, and swimming nearby are real temptations. Buses (railpasses valid) connect Sarlat to Souillac (4-5 per day, 45 min., 21F) and trains run to Périgueux. Rent a bike for 45F per day and enjoy swimming in the River Dordogne, 7km away. The **Hôtel Marcel,** 8, av. de Selves (tel. 53 59 21 98) is recommendable. (Singles and doubles from 70F, with showers 95-110F.) Camp at either **Les Accacias** (tel. 53 59 29 30; open Easter-Sept.) or **Rivaux** (tel. 53 59 04 41), both on the D47, 2½km from town. Stop by the **syndicat d'initiative,** pl. de la Liberté (tel. 53 59 27 67), and pick up the free and useful booklet *Informations Générales.* Daytrips from Sarlat could include **Souillac** (by bus) with its Byzantine-Romanesque **Eglise Abattiale,** or the tiny village of **La Rocque-Gageac** (by bike), huddled between the river and a high cliff and considered one of the most beautiful villages in France.

Another dramatic collaboration of nature and artifact is at **Rocamadour,** a town carved into the sheer face of a cliff. The miraculous setting befits a town famous for its marvels and holy revelations—for centuries Rocamadour has been one of Europe's main centers of pilgrimage. From the town's one street climbs **L'Escalier des Pélérins;** some pilgrims still kneel on each of its 216 steps. This leads to the **Cité Religieuse,** a complex of chapels including the **Chapelle Miraculeuse,** housing the venerated Notre-Dame de Rocamadour and the **Chapelle St-Michel** (tip the guide 1-2F), where the supposed sword of Roland and the rock in which it is lodged hang above the door. Perched precariously at the top of the cliff—and reached by more zigzagging steps—is the fourteenth-century **château.** Its buildings are private, but its ramparts, commanding exceptional views of the valley below, are open to the public. (Open mid-July to Aug. 9am-7pm; April to mid-July and Sept.-Oct. 9am-noon and 2-7pm. Admission 5F.)

Rocamadour is most easily reached via Brive-la-Gaillarde, to the north; trains runs 4-5 times per day (30-45 min., 31F). If you are coming from Sarlat or Souillac, take a bus to St-Denis-Prés-Martel (Mon.-Sat. 2-3 per day, 1 Sun. in July-Aug. only, 45 min. from Souillac), and then a train (3-4 per day, 15 min., 14F). In summer a van shuttles you the 5km from the train station to L'Hospitalet (7F), or you can hitch pretty easily. The walk from L'Hospitalet along the path through the Porte de l'Hôpital affords a stunning view of Rocamadour and the valley. The **office de**

tourisme at L'Hospitalet (tel. 65 33 62 80) can help with indoor accommodations, or try the **Relais du Campeur** (tel. 65 33 63 28) at L'Hospitalet. (12F per person, 12F per tent. Open April-Sept.) In general, hotels are expensive and booked in summer.

Fifteen kilometers from the village of Rocamadour and 10km from the station is the **Gouffre de Padirac,** an extensive system of caverns and crystal formations toured by boat along an underground river. (Open April-Oct. daily.) Excursions leave from Souillac and Rocamadour once per week from mid-June to mid-September—contact the *syndicat.* Cyclists can head for the **auberge de jeunesse (IYHF),** pl. du Monturu (tel. 55 91 13 82), in **Beaulieu-sur-Dordogne,** about 30km northeast of Padirac. (30F. Open Easter-Oct. Bicycle rental 30F per day.)

Provence

In this favored province of the Romans, the hills are colored with lavender, mimosa, and grapevines, and the air is redolent of the *herbes de provence*—thyme, rosemary, and sage—which grow wild over the hills. The vibrant, almost magical quality of the region inspired medieval troubadours in their musical verses of courtly love, and later attracted artists such as Cézanne, Picasso, and van Gogh.

Some of the best-preserved Roman structures in the world are here, vying with medieval towns for attention. The area's Latin influence asserts itself in Provençal cuisine, with its abundance of garlic, tomatoes, and olive oil. Seafood and fish soups such as *bouillabaisse* are specialties, as is *pistou,* a rich vegetable soup seasoned with basil. Summer brings bullfights, festivals, and concerts, often staged in old arenas and palaces.

Avignon

In 1309 the popes beat a hasty retreat from Rome to Avignon, both to escape the regional warfare of the Italian peninsula and to placate the powerful French kings. Six popes later, Rome regained its pontiffs, but not before Avignon's extravagant **Palais des Papes** had been built. This medieval white stone fortress, with touches of a Gothic cathedral, lost much of its splendor when it served as a barracks during the French Revolution. Guided tours in English leave daily at 10:45am and 3:45pm, though from April to September you may explore on your own with the aid of a free English pamphlet. (Open July-Aug. daily 9am-6pm; Sept.-June daily 9am-noon and 2-6pm. Admission 20F, students 12F, including tour.) Nearby is the **Petit Palais,** which once housed cardinals and now has an impressive collection of Italian primitive and Renaissance painting. (Open daily 9:15-11:50am and 2-6pm. Admission 14F, students 7F; 3F more to see the temporary special exhibits. March-Oct. free Sun.) Beside the Palais is the **Cathédrale Notre-Dame des Doms,** and overlooking them all is the sprawling garden, **Le Rocher des Doms.** The bridge that you can see below, ending abruptly in midstream, is the twelfth-century **Pont St-Benézet,** the "Pont d'Avignon" of nursery rhymes.

From early July through early August, not even the stern ramparts of Avignon can hold back the thousands who come from around the world for the celebrated **Festival d'Avignon.** Tickets to this explosion of dance, mime, film, and theater—everything from Gregorian chants to all-night readings of the *Odyssey*—cost 100-200F (no student discounts available) and are available from the **syndicat d'initiative,** 41, cours Jean Jaurès (tel. 90 86 24 43; open July-Aug. Mon.-Sat. 9am-8pm, Sun. 11am-6pm; Sept.-June Mon.-Sat. 10am-6pm). Tickets are also sometimes sold just before the performance. There are also about 50 fringe or "off" events performed each day in tiny basements and theaters (tickets 50-80F, available at the door), and in the main streets you can watch performers and spectators from all over the world.

Festival visitors will probably continue to sleep in the streets, in the station, and along the Rhône, illegal as it may be. If you want to abide by the law, it's wise to reserve ahead or arrive very early in the day. The *syndicat* distributes a list of *foyers,* and the branch at the train station (tel. 90 85 56 68; for reservations tel. 90 82 05 81) also books rooms for visitors. (Open same hours as city office except also July-Aug. Sun. 10am-5pm.) Try **Bagatelle** (tel. 90 86 30 39), in the huge campsite on the Ile de la Barthelasse, with dorm beds for 34F per night—sign in at the cafeteria. Take bus #10 (4.50F) from the train station, or it's a 25-minute walk. The **Squash Club,** 32, bd. Limbert (tel. 90 85 27 78), is 50F for bed, sheets, and breakfast, or 40F for bed only. From the main station walk 45 minutes along the walls or take bus #2. **Association Jeunesse Accueil (AJA),** on the route de Nîmes in Les Angles (tel. 90 25 00 49) sets up large tents with beds during the festival (14F), and also has some indoor dorm beds (20F). From porte de l'Oulle, cross pont Daladier and walk along the *ancienne rue de Nîmes* (3km), or take bus #10 from the post office. Women can try **Foyer des Jeunes Comtadines,** 75, rue Vernet (tel. 90 86 10 52), near the station, with singles for 80F, and doubles or triples at 60F per person. For hotels, try the **Hôtel le Parc,** 18bis, rue Agricol-Perdigurer (tel. 90 82 71 55) with doubles 67.70F, with shower 110F. (Breakfast 15F.) Also try the **Hôtel Central,** 31, rue de la République (tel. 90 86 07 81), with a small terrace shielded from the busy street. (Singles 82.50F, doubles 99F, with shower 154F, triples and quads 138F. Breakfast 17.50F.) If you can't find a room, it's an easy commute to Nîmes, Orange, or Arles.

The *syndicat* distributes *Avignon Pratique,* which includes a list of restaurants costing less than 60F. The restaurants and cafes on shaded rue des Teinturiers are popular meeting places during the festival. The area around rue Thiers and rue Philonarde has several inexpensive places, but women might not want to walk here alone at night. Tuesday through Saturday mornings, a huge indoor market convenes in **Les Halles** on pl. Pie. **Le Pain Bis,** 6, rue Armand-de-Pontmartin, is mostly vegetarian and offers a 42F *plat du jour,* 54F with dessert. There are some tables on the street. (Open Mon.-Fri. noon-2:30pm and 7pm-midnight.) **Tache d'Eucre,** 22 rue des Teinturiers (tel. 90 85 46 03), is a pleasant *café théâtre* with a terrace for watching the pedestrian traffic. 45F *plat du jour,* with dessert. (Open daily noon-2pm and 7-10pm, later during festival.) **La Ciboulette,** 1bis rue du Portail Magnaneu (tel. 90 85 09 95), off rue des Lices, has a 43.90F *menu,* which includes a fresh, interesting *cruditée* bar.

Near Avignon

Half an hour north of Avignon by train (26F) is the restful town of **Orange,** which has two internationally known monuments left from its days as the Roman city of Aurasio—an imposing **triumphal arch** and the best preserved **Roman theater** in France.

Vaison-la-Romaine, located among the idyllic, fragrant hills and vineyards of the **Vaucluse,** has partially excavated Roman villas, a medieval city, and a hillside castle. The **syndicat** is on place du Chanorine Santel (tel. 90 36 02 11). The **Centre Culturel à Couer Toîe** (tel. 90 36 00 78), about 1km down av. César Geoffrey, rents rooms with two and three beds for 76F per person, breakfast included. There is an excellent **auberge de jeunesse (IYHF)** (tel. 90 46 93 31) with a pool in Seguret, 8km away and a request stop on the bus line. (Bed and breakfast 55F, doubles 42F.) Vaison is 75 minutes by bus (26.50F) from Avignon's *gare routière* (across from the train station).

Also within easy distance by bus is the heavily touristed village of **Fontaine-de-Vaucluse,** where the Italian poet Petrarch spent 16 years after meeting Laura in Avignon. One of the largest springs in the world and a large, funnel-shaped cave set among towering hills don't compensate for commercialism truly run amok. There is a simple **auberge de jeunesse (IYHF)** (tel. 90 20 31 65) on a rural site 1km out of town. (32F, breakfast 10F. Kitchen facilities available. Lockout 10am-5pm. Open Jan.-Nov.) Much more pleasant is the authentic stone village of **Gordes,** named one of the *beaux villages* of France. It has a medieval castle and the graceful twelfth-century **Abbaye de Senanque** is only 3km away. Buses leave Cavaillon (15km away), which is well connected to Avignon. If you're feeling fit, rent a bike in Cavaillon from **Cycles Roen** (tel. 90 71 45 55). Finally, there are buses (½ hr., 15F) from Avignon to **Châteauneuf-du-Pape,** where you can taste the celebrated wine at countless *caves.*

Arles

Arles is a welcoming city with international flavor: its main sights are Roman; its most famous resident, Vincent van Gogh, Dutch; and its food and entertainment slightly Spanish. Every summer, festivals attract international dancers, guitar players, and photographers. Still, the town is above all proudly Provençal; plaques on statues and monuments are inscribed in the regional tongue, and the proud **Fête de la Tradition** on July 2-4 celebrates Provence—residents dress in local costume, bonfires blaze in the streets, and a *reine* (queen) is crowned every four years.

Once known as the "Little Rome of Gaul," this sun-baked town preserves **Roman baths,** a beautiful **Arènes** (Roman Arena), now used for bullfights, and an incomplete but evocative **Théâtre Antique.** The **Church of St-Trophime** and its adjoining cloister, with a carved portal of the Last Judgment and beautiful capitals in the courtyard, are well worth a visit. The **Musée d'Art Chrétien** has one of the world's richest collections of early Christian sarcophagi; don't miss the **Crypte aux Portiques** underneath. The **Musée Réattu** exhibits contemporary art, as well as paintings of the Camargue by Henri Rousseau. The museum takes greatest pride in its 57 Picasso drawings, completed in 1971 and donated by the artist to the city he visited so often. (All of Arles's monuments and museums are open daily May-Sept. 8:30am-7pm; Oct.-April erratically 9am-noon and 2-5pm. Individual admission 4-6F; occasional student discounts. If you plan to visit most sites, purchase a *billet global* for 33F, students 22F.)

A van Gogh museum and cultural center is planned for 1988, but in the meantime, the tourist office leads a tour called "on the traces of van Gogh" (twice per week in the summer, 2 hr.; 20F, students 10F). You can best find van Gogh in the sunflower and olive tree-covered countryside on the way to St. Rémy (22km), the site of the sanatorium where he willingly stayed. Four buses run to St. Rémy per day, or you can rent a bike at **Cycles Montuori** (tel. 90 96 01 54; 45F per day) or at the train station.

Throughout July the **Rencontres Internationales de la Photographie** offer both internationally acclaimed photography exhibitions and public workshops with masters of the art. Soon after the photography festival, the city starts up its dance and music **Festival,** with international performances in the Théâtre Antique and a fair amount of dancing in the streets. The **office de tourisme,** bd. des Lices (tel. 90 96 29 35), has festival information, currency exchange, and an accommodations service (4F). (Open April-June daily 9am-8pm; July-Sept. daily 8am-8pm; Oct.-March Mon.-Sat. 9am-6pm.)

Inexpensive hotels cluster around place du Forum and place Voltaire, but they fill up fast in July and August. The clean, modern **ALAJ youth hostel** is on rue Foch (tel. 90 96 18 25), a few blocks behind the tourist office. (Bed, breakfast, sheets, and showers 43.50F per night. 11:30pm curfew. Open March-Oct.) Good hotels include **Hôtel du Musée,** 11, rue du Grand Prieuré (tel. 90 96 04 49), opposite the Musée Réattu, with friendly English-speaking owners and a flowered courtyard. (Doubles 75F, with shower 100F. Large breakfast 15F.) **Hôtel Mistral,** 16 rue du Dr-Fauton (tel. 90 96 12 64), has very worn rooms but excellent prices and is next to the best nighttime cafés. (Singles 40F, doubles 60F. Showers 5F. Breakfast 14F.)

A busy **market** is held Wednesday mornings along bd. Combes, and a more elegant, equally entertaining one takes place Saturday morning along the length of bd. des Lices. After buying provisions, cross the street to the **Jardin d'Eté** for a picnic. The popular **Lou Gardian,** 70, rue 4 de Septembre, attracts more tourists than locals, but the food is good nonetheless. (*Menu* 43F, wine included. Open Mon.-Sat. noon-1:45pm and 7-9:45pm. In summer, reservations or early arrival suggested.) **Vitamine,** 16 rue du Dr-Fauton, has fresh, creative salads and pasta. Photographers show their work on the walls during the festival. **Le Passage,** Quai Max Dormoy, is a movie theater/bookstore/art gallery/restaurant with a 45F *menu* (wine not included) and films in the original language. (Open for meals noon-2pm and 7-10pm.)

Aix-en-Provence

The gentle grace and dignity that one associates with life in the unharried Midi can still be found along the shaded boulevards of Aix. The **cours Mirabeau** is the focus of this ambience; spend some time sipping *anisette* and watching the passing crowds. One side of the street is lined with cafes and bookshops, the other with some of the best preserved *hôtel* facades in France, creations of gracefully carved doorways and wrought-iron balconies. Behind the *cours,* narrow streets meander between unexpected squares and moss-covered fountains.

If you can stir from the comfortable cafes, you'll see Aix's worthwhile sights. The **Cathédrale St-Sauveur** features an impressive mixture of constructions, from a fourth-century baptistery to an elegant thirteenth-century cloister. The **Musée Granet** has a striking collection of Roman sculpture, a large number of Dutch and French works, and eight paintings by native son Cézanne. (Open July-Aug. daily 10am-noon and 2-6pm; Sept.-June Wed.-Mon. 10am-noon and 2-6pm. Admission 15F, students 10F.) The **Musée des Tapisseries** houses a small but excellent collection of tapestries. (Open Wed.-Mon. 9:30am-noon and 2:30-6:30pm; in winter, 10am-noon and 2-6pm. Admission 13F, students 8F.) Cézanne's *atelier,* a short walk out of town at 9, av. Paul Cézanne, is as he left it in 1906, but may not prove to be very interesting except to devotees. (Open June-Sept. Wed.-Mon. 10am-noon and 2:30-6pm; Oct.-May 10am-noon and 2-5pm. Admission 6F, students 4F.) An unusual collection can be found in the **Fondation Vasarely,** a vast, defiant monument to Op-Art. It's at 1, av. Marcel Pagnol, next to the youth hostel; take bus #8 or 12 from the city center. (Open Wed.-Mon. 9:30am-12:30pm and 2-5:30pm. Admission 18F.)

Accommodations are expensive and hard to find during the **Music Festival** in July, but the **office de tourisme,** pl. du Général de Gaulle (tel. 42 26 02 93), can give you a list of hotels or book a room for 2F. (Open Oct.-June daily 8am-7pm; July-Sept. Mon.-Sat. 8am-10pm, Sun. 8:30am-12:30pm and 6-10pm.) They'll also change money (Mon.-Sat. 9am-noon and 1:30-5:30pm, Sun. 9am-noon). There is a modern, crowded **auberge de jeunesse (IYHF),** 3, av. Marcel Pagnol (tel. 42 20 15 99), 2km from the station; take bus #8 or 12 (look for the Vasarely building). (42F. Sheets 10F. Breakfast included. 11pm curfew.) For a more sedate environment closer to the center, try the **Hôtel des Quatre Dauphins,** 54, rue Roux Alphéran (tel. 42 38 16 39), near the Musée Granet. (Doubles 78F and up. Showers 7F. Breakfast included.) **Hotel Vigouroux,** 27, rue Cardinale (tel. 42 38 26 42), near pl. des Dauphins, is run by a friendly, English-speaking owner. (Doubles 90F, with shower 110F. Showers 10F. Breakfast 16F.) **Le Feliberge** (tel. 42 92 12 11) is a campsite in Puyricard, 3km from Aix. Buses run from cours Sextius Mon.-Sat. every half hour. (30F per night.)

There is *couscous* (40-55F) at **Djerba,** rue Rifle-Rafle, off pl. des Prêcheurs. **La Tour de Pise,** 10, rue Victor Leydet, 1 block from cours Mirabeau, is a popular place with good spaghetti for 30F and a 56F *menu* with French food. (Open Mon.-Sat. noon-2pm and 7-11pm.)

Trains run hourly from Aix to Marseille (27F); you must change there for most destinations. Four buses per day run to Avignon (53F one way, 79.60F round-trip).

French Riviera (Côte d'Azur)

Picture a sun-blessed garden of earthly delights where hills covered with mimosa, cypress trees, and white villas watch over rugged coastline, palm-lined beaches, and a deep azure sea. Then obscure this vision with miles of shameless developments packed with hordes of vacationers, and you'll get a rough idea of the French Riviera. The attractions of the *côte* today are still ambrosial, but you may find yourself wishing fewer people had discovered them.

The sunshine and scenery of the coast have always attracted writers and artists; memories of Renoir, Matisse, and Picasso linger around Nice, as do those of Cole Porter and F. Scott Fitzgerald at Cap d'Antibes. The area now offers some of the world's most tastefully conceived museums of modern art, and is a center for jazz in the summer.

By day, sample the diverse beaches: *Calanques* (mini-fjords) form protective coves for swimming or sunning. All the beaches are topless and many are bottomless as well, so you can pursue your "St. Tropez tan" without harassment. The largest cities are the worst for beaching, but centers like Nice make inexpensive bases for daytrips to smaller places.

Accommodations are very tight in summer and youth hostels may be booked months in advance. If stuck, join the crowds that sleep outside train stations and on the beaches. The police may abruptly wake you up while thieves will wish you a good night's sleep. Stay close to other people and guard your valuables, or, better yet, lock them up at a bus or train station. Organized campsites also abound; most are well-equipped and near the beach.

The Côte d'Azur is conveniently compressed—all the towns are on a straight line, and both trains and buses connect coastal resorts frequently, quickly, and inexpensively. Hitching in summer is awful.

Marseille

Marseille's reputation as a tough town is not entirely unfounded, but while caution is definitely advised, you shouldn't let the hint of danger keep you away. Alexandre Dumas called the port "the meeting place of the world," and along its quays the French mix with North Africans, gypsies, Indians, and sailors from the four corners of the globe. The center of town is the **Vieux Port,** flanked by fortresses. Running straight out of the port is Marseille's main artery, **La Canebière,** a turbulent, crowded thoroughfare affectionately known to English sailors as "Can o' beer." Between La Canebière and the station are the narrow, dusty streets of the North African quarter. This area can be dangerous at night, as can the streets directly across La Canebière.

The **Jardin du Pharo,** at the mouth of the Vieux Port, contains a castle built by Napoleon III for Empress Eugénie, with excellent views of the harbor and city. The view from the top of the **Basilique de Notre Dame de la Garde** takes in the Pomègues and Ratonneau Islands, Château d'If, the city, and its surrounding mountains (take bus #60). North of the port, on av. Robert Schumann, is the **Ancienne Cathédrale de la Major,** which has a Romanesque reliquary from 1122, a delicate ceramic relief by Luca Della Robbia, and a fifteenth-century altar dedicated to Lazarus. Here you'll also find the tomb of Bishop Xavier of Belsunce, who devoted himself to the suffering Marseillais and Marseillaises during an eighteenth-century plague. (Open Wed.-Mon. 9am-noon and 2-6:30pm.)

Motorboats run from quai des Belges to **Château d'If** (15 min., 30F round-trip), which was immortalized by Alexandre Dumas in *The Count of Monte Cristo.* The tourguides are willing to play along with the tale and will point out the hole through which the Count escaped. Along bd. Michelet (en route to the *calanques*) is Le Corbusier's **Cité Radieuse,** designed in the early 1950s. It embodies many of the architect's theories on modern, efficient, moderately priced housing and, with its 2000 citizens, aspires to be a united city-within-a-city.

The **office municipal de tourisme,** 4, La Canebière (tel. 91 54 91 11), near the Vieux Port, offers a free accommodations service. Sight-seeing tours leave in summer daily at 9:30am (70F). Turn left from the station steps and walk along bd. d'Athènes. (Open July-Aug. Mon.-Thurs. 9am-12:30pm and 2-6:30pm, Fri.-Sat. 9am-6pm.) In July and August additional offices operate at the train station (Mon.-Sat. 7:30-11am and 3-7:30pm) and in the Vieux Port (Sun.-Thurs. 12:30-8pm). **BIGE** tickets are available at **Vovac,** 8, rue Bailli-de-Suffren (tel. 91 54 31 30), at the corner of quai des Belges in the Vieux Port. (Open Mon.-Fri. 9:30am-12:30pm and 2:30-6:30pm, Sat. 9:30am-1pm.) There are a number of **consulates** in Marseilles: U.S., 9, rue Armény (tel. 91 54 92 00); Canada, 24, av. du Prado (tel. 91 37 19 37); U.K., also at 24, av. du Prado (tel. 91 53 43 32).

Both IYHF hostels lie far from the center: take bus #6 or 8 from cours Joseph Thierry to the **Auberge de Jeunesse de Bois-Luzy (IYHF),** 76, av. de Bois-Luzy (tel. 91 49 06 18); take the Métro to pl. Castellane and then bus #19 to Les Gatons Plage for the **Auberge de Jeunesse Bonneveine (IYHF),** 47, av. J. Vidal (tel. 91 73 21 81). Both charge 42F per night, breakfast included. The cheapest hotels are along rue des Dominicains or rue Bernard de Bois, but many are seamy; you're better off at places near the station—look along place des Marseillaises, boulevard Maurice Bourdet, or rue Breteuil. The area around cours Julien is good for cheap eats; rue Longue des Capucins and vicinity is the place to go for North African food, but don't go alone late at night. Marseille's varied nightlife is catalogued in *Le Petit Futé,* sold at newsstands, and in *Marseille Poche,* available at the tourist office.

Marseilles is a transportation hub, with trains to Paris (9 per day, 375F), Toulouse, Barcelona, and Nice. Buses run all along the coast; they're usually cheaper than the train. **SNCM,** 61, bd. des Dames (tel. 91 56 32 00) has information on ferries to Corsica and North Africa. **Allostop,** 1, pl. Gabriel Déri (tel. 91 56 50 51), matches riders with drivers. (Open Mon.-Fri. 3:30-6:30pm and Sat. 10am-noon.)

St-Tropez

St-Tropez is preceded—and exceeded—by its risqué reputation. It is a pretty little port dwarfed by showy yachts and cruised by the well, if barely, dressed. St-Tropez is accessible by bus (39F from St-Raphael, 70F from Toulon); call 94 97 62 77 for information. An alternative that doesn't involve the abominable summer traffic is to take the boat from St-Raphael (40F one way, 75F round-trip); call 94 95 17 46 for information.

A minibus leaves from Place des Lices every 20 minutes for the fabled beaches (5F, last leaves at 5:25pm). **Sodetrav** runs less frequent buses to Pamplonne and Tahiti beaches. Hitching is poor; rent your own wheels at **Louis Mas,** 7, rue Joseph Quaranta (tel. 94 97 00 60; open Mon.-Fri.). (Bicycles 38F per day, 500F deposit; mopeds 60F per day, 1500F deposit.) The **Plage des Salins** has the greatest amount of free swimming space, while the celebrated **Plage de Tahiti** is studded with private clubs.

Camping is the best idea here, since hotels are out of the budget range; the **syndicat d'initiative,** quai Jean-Jaurès (tel. 94 97 41 21) has a list of sites. **La Croix du Sud,** route de Pamplonne (tel. 94 79 80 84; 14F per person, 28F per tent), and **Les Tournels,** route du Phare de Camarat (tel. 94 79 81 38; 34F per person, tent included), are large sites, but reservations are recommended for summer. The nearest **auberge de jeunesse (IYHF)** is over 20km away in **la Garde-Freinet** (tel. 94 43 60 05), and only reached by one bus per day. It's also very small; call ahead to avoid disappointment. (40F per night. Breakfast included.)

Restaurants are as expensive as everything else in St-Tropez. **La Flo,** rue de la Citadelle, has outdoor seating and salads and *plats du jour* for 25-40F. (Open daily noon-midnight.) **Crêperie Bretonne,** quai F.-Mistral, serves crepes (16-28F) in a wine cellar. Still anyone on a budget will probably become familiar with the **Codec** supermarket one block above the port. Be warned that the snack bars on the beach charge more than decent restaurants in less self-conscious places.

Cannes

Cannes is a citadel of stand-offish opulence, the showiest jewel on the Riviera's necklace. It sparkles with sumptuous villas and flaunts a sandy beach that, like most things in Cannes, is painstakingly maintained and artificially improved. The heart of the town is the **promenade de la Croisette,** a long and lavish palm-fringed boulevard by the sea. On one side are palatial luxury hotels; on the other are beaches whose every parasol-studded inch is private. Don't despair, however; there is some public beach space on la Croisette, and more if you walk west past Port Canto. The famed **Cannes Film Festival** (May 8-20 in 1988) is—you guessed it—only for insiders.

The **syndicats d'initiative** at the station (tel. 93 99 19 77) and at 1, promenade de la Croisette (tel. 93 39 24 53) will make hotel reservations. (Both open daily 9am-8pm.) **Hôtel le Bourgogne,** near the station at 13, rue du 24 Août (tel. 93 38 36 73), is dull but clean. (Singles 70F, doubles 85F, with shower 130F. Breakfast 14F. Showers 11F.) **Hôtel National,** 8, rue de Maréchal-Joffre (tel. 93 39 91 92), is ideally located in the pedestrian district. (Singles 80F, doubles 95F, triples 170F. Showers 10F. Breakfast 15F.) **Hôtel des Roches Fleuries,** 92 rue Georges-Clemenceau (tel. 93 39 28 78), is a touch classier and has kind owners. (Singles 90F, doubles 120F, with shower 170-190F. Showers 15F. Breakfast included.)

For camping, try one of the 10 sites around Mandelieu, just west of Cannes. **Camping Les Pruniers,** La Pinède, on the N559 (tel. 93 49 92 85), isn't gorgeous, but you're likely to find space. (70F for 2 people.) Take the St-Raphael bus to La Napoule (8 per day, 10 min., 6.30F), or the less frequent train. In Cannes-La Bocca, try **Caravaning Bellevue,** 67, av. M Chevalier (tel. 93 47 28 97). (52F per person, tent included. Open Jan.-early Dec.) The rue Meynadier is an insomniac pedestrian street with several affordable restaurants, including **Au P'tit Creux,** #82, which serves hearty *couscous* (43F). (Open daily noon-3pm and 7pm-late.) Also try **Chez Mamichette,** 1 rue St-Antoinne, off the western end of the rue Meynadier and rue Félix-Fauré. This cozy place offers fondue for 42F and a 56F *menu.* (Open Mon.-Sat. noon-2pm and 7-10pm.) Daily outdoor **markets** are held in place Gambetta and rue Forville until 12:30pm.

Near Cannes

The **Corniche d'Estérel,** southwest of Cannes between **La Napoule** and **St-Raphael,** offers some of the most spectacular scenery on the coast, with jagged red-clay mountains and sheltered coves. Trains bypass some of the best bits, so take a local bus from pl. de l'Hôtel de Ville in Cannes.

Mougins, set on a hill near Cannes, is a peaceful anomaly on this most developed of Europe's coasts. Buses leave from near the train station in Cannes (every hr., 15 min., 8F). **Antibes,** halfway between Cannes and Nice, is a glamorous old resort with a beautiful *vieille ville,* port, and long beach. It is worth a trip just for the **Musée Picasso,** which exhibits work Picasso produced in the area, as well as art by his contemporaries. The museum, perched above the sea in a dazzling restored castle with a sculpture garden, is a work of art itself. (Open in summer Wed.-Mon. 10am-noon and 3-7pm; in winter Wed.-Mon. 10am-noon and 2-6pm. Admission 15F, students 8F; free Wed. Dec.-May.) You can spend the night at the **Relais International de la Jeunesse,** bd. de la Garoupe (tel. 93 61 34 40), in an old villa by the ocean at Cap d'Antibes. Take the bus (direction Eden Roc) from pl. de Gaulle in Antibes. (43F. Sheets 8F. Breakfast included. Meals 35F.)

There are 10 campsites near the train station at **Biot** (20 min., 15F from Nice). **Le Logis de la Brague,** off the N7 on Port de la Brague (tel. 93 33 54 72), is likely to have room. (Open May-Sept.) **Camping Les Mimosas** (tel. 93 33 52 76) is well-equipped and spacious, but popular, so reserve ahead; it's off the N7 on bd. des Groules. (Open April-early Sept.) In Biot, the **Musée National Fernand Léger** houses Léger's cubist renditions of mechanized modern life. (Open in summer Wed.-Mon. 10am-noon and 2-6pm; in winter 10am-noon and 2-5pm. Admission 15F, students, and everyone on Sun., 8F.)

Nice

Nice weathers its storm of tourists each summer with all the usual accoutrements of a Riviera town—casual affluence, an ample beach, museums, flowery avenues—but lacks the affected aloofness of its neighbors. Furthermore, Nice is blessed with reasonably priced hotels, good public transport within the town and to all points on the coast, and a population accustomed to visitors.

Orientation and Practical Information

Nice is well-connected to all points on the Côte d'Azur, and makes a good base for Riviera exploration—and exploring is recommended for beachgoers, since Nice's beach is thin and rocky. The city is also very well served by trains from afar, with frequent direct trains to and from major points in Spain, Italy, Switzerland, and, of course, Paris.

The majestic **promenade des Anglais** sweeps along the coast. The pedestrian zone west of **place Masséna** swarms with boutiques, busy restaurants, and all varieties of tourists. The *vieille ville* (old town), tucked untidily into the southeastern pocket of Nice, is also limited to pedestrians.

Tourist Office: Syndicat d'Initiative, av. Thiers (tel. 93 87 07 07), beside the station. Hotel reservations made after 10am (10F, non-refundable). Open July to mid-Sept. daily 8:30am-8pm; Oct.-June Mon.-Sat. 8:45am-12:30pm and 2-6pm.

American Express: 11, promenade des Anglais (tel. 93 87 29 82). Mail held. All banking services. Long lines in summer. Open May-Oct. Mon.-Fri. 9am-noon and 2-6:30pm (financial services close at 6pm), Sat. 9am-noon; Nov.-April Mon.-Fri. only.

Currency Exchange: Office Provençal, 17, av. Thiers (tel. 93 88 56 80), across the street from the train station, charges no commission. Open daily 7am-midnight.

Post Office: Main office at 23, av. Thiers. **Telephones** here. the office at pl. Wilson, rue de l'Hôtel des Postes, has longer hours (Mon.-Sat. 8am-10pm, Sun. 8am-7pm). Poste Restante, and telephones (7am-midnight).

Trains: Every 20 min. to Cannes (23F), every ½ hr. to Monaco (12.40F). 6 per day to Paris via Marseille (7½ hr., 447F). Showers 14F; bring your own towel and soap or you'll pay almost as much again. Information (tel. 93 87 50 50).

Buses: Gare Routière, promenade du Paillon (tel. 93 85 61 81), off av. Jean Jaurès. Frequent buses along the coast in both directions.

Public Transportation: Station Centrale, 10, av. Felix Fauré, near pl. Masséna. Information and *carnets* of 5 tickets. (27.50F; a paltry saving on individual tickets at 6.50F each.)

Bike and Moped Rental: Ets Arnaud, 4, pl. Grimaldi (tel. 93 87 88 55), near the pedestrian zone behind Hôtel Meridien. Bikes 40F per day, 700F deposit; mopeds 65F per day plus 25F for gas (enough for round-trip to Monaco), 1250F deposit. Reductions for longer periods.

Pharmacy: 7, rue Masséna (tel. 93 87 78 94). Open 7:30pm-8:30am.

Emergencies: Police (tel. 17). **Ambulance** (tel. 93 83 01 01).

Crises: Rape (tel. 93 52 17 81). 24 hours.

Bookstore: The English Bookshop, 4, rue Congrès, near the Croisette. A decent selection. Open Mon.-Sat. 9:30am-12:30pm and 2-6:30pm.

Laundry: Laverie Self-Service, 8, rue Belgique, near the train station. Wash, dry, and soap 25F. Open daily 7am-11pm.

Accommodations

There never seem to be enough hotels to accommodate the waves of travelers that come in on the morning trains, so try to book in advance. If not, arrive early to get a place in line at the tourist office reservations desk, which opens at 10am. Most inexpensive hotels are clustered around the train station. Two youth hostels are located so far away from town that they do not always fill up, but call before going anyway. If you sleep on the beach, put everything you own in a locker at the station and hide the key. Don't sleep in the shadows under the promenade des Anglais; city cleaners come during the night, hosing bottles and debris onto the rocks below. Sleep in groups, for added safety, whether at the beach, or at the train station—the latter is generally less dangerous. In both places, you will probably be kicked awake in early morning by the *gendarmes.*

International House for Young People, 22 rue Pertinax (tel. 93 62 02 79). Near the train station. A no-nonsense place run by a generous man who sincerely cares about his guests. Kitchen facilities. No curfew. Bed in coed dorm 40F, quads 45F, in doubles 50F. Owner will put down a mattress if the hostel fills (35F).

Auberge de Jeunesse (IYHF), route Forestière du Mont-Alban (tel. 93 89 23 64), 4km away. Take bus #5 from the train station to pl. Masséna (or walk), then take #14 from bd. Jean-Jaurès (leaves every 25-40 min., last at 7:50pm, 6.50F). About 45 min. on foot. A small hostel with an unpleasant manager but kind co-workers. (Bed, breakfast, and shower 40F. Required sheet rental 10F. Lockout 10am-6pm. 11pm curfew, 1am in summer.)

Relais International de Jeunesse, av. Scudéri at Cimiez (tel. 93 81 27 63). Take bus #15 from pl. Masséna. An unofficial hostel run by students. Luggage must be kept in a common storage room. 43F. Breakfast included. Midnight curfew.

Hôtel Belle Meunière, 21, av. Durante (tel. 93 88 66 15), a 2-min. walk from the station. Run by a helpful, friendly family. Pretty garden. Doubles 104F, with shower 129F. Shared rooms 60F per person. Showers 10F. Breakfast 13F. Open Feb.-Nov.

Hôtel les Orangers, 10bis, av. Durante (tel. 93 87 51 41), across from Belle Meunière. Large rooms with kitchenettes. Run by a young English-speaking couple who will help you find room in a comparably-priced hotel if they're full. Singles 50F, with kitchenettes 70F. All other rooms with kitchenettes. Doubles 80F, with shower 120F, triples with shower 180F, quads with shower 240F. Showers 10F. Breakfast 12F. Open Dec.-Oct.

Hôtel Novelty, 26, rue d'Angleterre (tel. 93 87 51 73). Enthusiastic owner enjoys meeting students and is modernizing the hotel. Singles 67F, doubles 94F, with shower 119F. Showers 10F. Breakfast with unlimited orange juice 14F.

Hôtel Montreuil, 18bis, rue Biscirra (tel. 93 85 95 90), off av. Jean Médecin. Small. Friendly management. TVs in rooms. Singles 80F, doubles 110-120F. Showers included. Breakfast, by request, 15F.

Hôtel Rialto, 55, rue de la Buffa (tel. 93 88 15 04), 2 blocks from the ocean. Rooms with kitchenettes. Singles 90F; doubles 110F, with shower 135F; triples with shower 145F.

Food

Although the restaurants along rue Masséna are best left for after-dinner drinking, ice-cream eating, and people-watching, the pedestrian streets of the nearby *vieille ville* hide some interesting and inexpensive restaurants. The wide **cours Saleya** is busy in the morning with a market and at night with crowded cafés and restaurants. If you can afford to spend, try fresh fish soup (*bouillabaisse*), the specialty of the Côte, at the restaurants here. A **mini-market** two blocks to the left of the train station on rue Thiers is open until midnight. Restaurants around the station have inexpensive but unexciting food. Much better meals can be had at **Chez Davia,** 11bis, rue Grimaldi, a short walk from pl. Masséna, off bd. Victor Hugo. The lovely

Italian proprietor offers four- and five-course *menus* for 43F and 55F; Sunday is duck and rabbit. (Open Thurs.-Tues. noon-2pm and 7-10pm.) Near the station, try **Le Saëtone,** 8, rue d'Alsace-Lorraine with 38F and 42F *menus* featuring regional dishes such as *soupe au pistou.* (Open Thurs.-Tues. 11:45am-2pm and 6-9pm.) **Restaurant de Paris,** 28, rue d'Angleterre, has tasty 28F, 38F, and 49F *menus.* (Open Tues.-Sun. 5:30-11pm.) **L'Auberge "In,"** 7, rue Gioffredo, near pl. Wilson, is vegetarian. (*Plat du jour* 35F, *menu* 50F. Open Mon.-Sat. noon-2pm and 7:30-9:30pm.)

Sights and Entertainment

Nice's long thin beach and bronzing guests are what people have come for. In fact, the best strands are elsewhere on the Riviera; **Villefranche-sur-Mer** and **Cap d'Ail** are only 10 minutes away by train (7.20F and 13.80F, respectively). Other fine beaches are farther afield.

Nice's *vieille ville* (old town) is an unusual blend of glitter and a Mediterranean-medieval quarter of tiny streets and outdoor markets. For a spectacular Riviera panorama, climb up to the top of the **château.** (Gates close at 8pm.)

Nice does have several outstanding museums. The **Musée Matisse,** on av. des Arènes-de-Cimierez, displays a comprehensive collection spanning Matisse's long and varied career, from impressionist-inspired oils of the 1890s to simple cut-outs and line drawings of the 1950s. Take bus #15. (Open May-Sept. Tues.-Sat. 10am-noon and 2:30-6:30pm, Sun. 2:30-6:30pm; Oct. and Dec.-April Tues.-Sat. 10am-noon and 2-5pm, Sun. 2-5pm.) The collection of the **Musée National Marc Chagall,** av. du Docteur Ménard, includes vivid depictions of biblical themes, a stained-glass auditorium, and an outdoor cafe. The museum is a pleasant walk from town, or a short ride aboard bus #15. (Open July-Sept. Wed.-Mon. 10am-7pm; Oct.-June Wed.-Mon. 10am-12:30pm and 2-5:30pm. Admission 22F; students, and everyone on Sun., 11F.)

From July 10 to 20, the **Jazz Parade** takes place at the Jardins des Arènes-de-Cimierez, near the Matisse Museum; some of the top European and American jazz musicians play simultaneously on three stages for seven hours each day. If you happen to be on the Côte in February, stop in for Nice's **Carnaval,** a festive time of fireworks and parades.

Near Nice

Northwest of Nice is **St-Paul,** a cobblestoned village with sixteenth-century ramparts. The town is now an artists' colony; galleries and studios line its narrow streets. The **Fondation Maeght,** 1km from the center of town, has a thoughtfully presented modern sculpture garden that includes pieces by Miró, Calder, and Giacometti, and an indoor gallery with rotating exhibits and permanent displays of work by Braque, Matisse, Chagall, and others. (Open July-Sept. daily 10am-7pm; Oct.-June daily 10am-12:30pm and 2:30-6pm. Admission 25F, students 20F.) Buses for St-Paul leave Nice's *gare routière* hourly (14.70F one way).

The **Monaco** of legend glitters with majestic wealth and playboy glamor, its streets graced with royalty and its casino crowded with debonair spies. In reality, Monaco—likened by Chekhov to "a luxurious water-closet"—is a concrete jungle clogged with gaudy hotels. The **Casino** is free but will usually refuse you admission if you're wearing jeans or sneakers or if you're under 21. (Slot machines open at 10am; the *salle américaine* blackjack, craps, and roulette tables at 4pm. Admission 50F.) To fathom the principality's wealth, count the Rolls-Royces and Ferarris outside the celebrated **Hôtel de Paris.** When you leave the station, bear uphill to the right to see the **palace** and the narrow streets of **Monaco-Ville.** Bear right through la Condamine, the harbor district, for racier **Monte-Carlo.** The least expensive hotels and restaurants are near the station. You can stay at the excellent **Centre de Jeunesse Princess Stephanie,** av. Prince Pierre (tel. 93 50 75 05). It's a bright, clean, converted villa with friendly staff and good facilities, including a kitchen. (35F per night. Breakfast included. No reservations. Open 7-10am and 2pm-1am.) Frequent trains link Nice and Monaco (20 min., 12.50F).

Menton, not far from the Italian border, sports all the Riviera accessories, including casino, beaches, gardens, and an appropriately tangled old quarter, but lacks the crush of other towns its size. The **Musée Jean Cocteau** on the promenade du Soleil next to the *vieille ville* has an extensive collection of works in various media by the brilliant *cinéaste.* (Open mid-June to mid-Sept. Wed.-Sun. 10am-noon and 3-6pm; mid-Sept. to mid-June Wed.-Sun. 10am-noon and 2-5:30pm. Free.) The **auberge de jeunesse (IYHF),** on the plateau St-Michel (tel. 93 35 93 14), is a strenuous walk up a cascade of steps, but worth it for the view; there are camping facilities as well. (43F, tents 39F. Breakfast included. Open April-Aug.) Menton is on the Riviera coastal rail line, east of Nice.

The Alps

Dorothy Parker called them "beautiful, but dumb," and indeed these timeless snowy peaks will bore no one with details of their history. After museum corridors and enervating urban centers, this most imposing, most startling, and most spectacular of European landscapes will refresh and exhilarate. Crowned by the grandeur of Mont Blanc, Europe's highest peak, the mountains include gentler, greener areas of pastures, Alpine flowers, and villages set next to cascading waterfalls.

The region is divided into the **Savoie,** including the Mont Blanc massif, and the **Dauphiné** country, where the modern capital of Grenoble is located. Trains link Grenoble, Chamonix, Chambéry, Aix-les-Bains, and Annecy to each other and to other parts of France, Italy, and Switzerland; a thorough bus system reaches even the most remote villages. When you reach the base of the mountains, cable cars or your feet will take you further. Hostels and campgrounds abound, and unofficial camping is also possible. Many towns maintain chalet dormitories; in less accessible spots, the **Club Alpin Français** runs refuges. Get a list at one of their offices: 136, av. Michel-Croz, Chamonix (tel. 50 53 16 03), 38, av. due Parmelan, Annecy (tel. 50 57 02 22), or av. Félix Vialet, 32, Grenoble (tel. 76 87 03 73).

While in the Alps, be sure to sample trout from cold mountain streams, ham, and *eau de vie,* distilled from every kind of fruit. The best local cheeses are *reblochon* and *pomme de Savoie;* the best regional wines are *roussettes.* And you may want to indulge in at least one warm pot of *fondue savoyarde* (made from local Savoy cheese, white wine, and garlic), and one round of *raclette,* a concoction of melted cheese, potato, and beef.

Annecy

Nowhere else in France do an emerald lake, an embracing string of steep mountains, and a photogenic medieval town get along so well as in Annecy. Hordes of vacationers, French and otherwise, come to enjoy the lakeside beaches and cobblestone streets of the *vieille ville* at the edge of the River Thiou. Stroll along the flower-dotted canals around the **Palais d'Ile,** on a tiny triangular island in the middle of the river, and climb up to the castle, also a museum, for a splendid view of the lake. (Open Tues.-Sun. 10am-noon and 2-6pm. Admission 7F, students 3.50F.) The pure lake waters are great for swimming. The **Champs de Mars** is the busiest strand. Cruiseboats crisscross the lake; get tickets and information at the dock. There are rowboats and pedalboats for rent all around the lake.

The upper part of the lake is surrounded by quiet, picturesque towns, many with their own châteaux. The most beautiful is the **Château de Montrottier;** take the Crolard bus from the train station to Lovagny. (Open Easter to mid-Oct. Tour 15F, students 8F.) Nearby are the **Gorges du Fier;** the wild torrent of water cutting through cliffs and crashing on the rocks below is spectacular.

The first two weeks in July, the **Festival de la Vieille Ville** draws mobs to Annecy for indoor and outdoor concerts and performances; most of the events are free. In the evening, entertainment can be sought in the casino, at impromptu street concerts, or in cafes and bars along the canal.

In July and August, especially during festivals, rooms are few and expensive. The **maison du tourisme,** pl. de la Libération, Bonlieu (tel. 50 45 00 33), will counsel you on lodging. (Open mid-May to Sept. daily 9am-noon and 1:45-6:30pm; Oct.-early May Tues.-Sat. 9am-noon and 1:45-6:30pm, Sun. 1:45-6:30pm.) The best accommodations are in the **Maison des Jeunes (MJC),** 52, rue des Marquisats (tel. 50 45 08 80), with a gorgeous view of the lake. Take bus #1 from the station, or take a walk. (Beds in shared doubles, triples, and quads 55F. No curfew, but reception closes at 8:30pm.) The **Auberge de Jeunesse La Grande Jeanne (IYHF),** on the route de Semnoz (tel. 50 45 33 19), is pleasant enough, but a grueling 45-minute walk uphill (follow the signs from the tourist office). (June-Sept. 40F; Oct.-May 32F. No curfew.) On the road to the youth hostel is the oft-mobbed **Camping Le Belvedere** (tel. 50 45 48 30; open March to mid-Oct.). The five lakeside campgrounds in Albigny help absorb the overflow. (Take a Voyages Crolard bus from Annecy's *gare routière.*) **Hôtel Savoyard,** 41, av. de Cran (tel. 50 57 08 08), in a residential area behind the train station, is comfortable and cheery. (Doubles 80F, triples 100-110F. Showers 8F. Breakfast 14F.)

Lakeside picnics are the most affordable way to enjoy a meal. There are many restaurants clustered in the *vieille ville* offering *menus* for 45-60F. **Au Lilas Rose,** passage de l'Evêché, on a narrow street off the river, serves everything from pizza (27F) to fondue (45F per person). (Open daily 11:45am-2:30pm and 6:45-11pm.) For a light meal, try **Tarte Julie,** pl. Ste-Claire, serving sweet and salted homemade pies (17-23F; open daily 10am-10pm). There are **open-air markets** on pl. Ste-Claire (Tues., Fri., and Sun. mornings) and on bd. de Taine (Sat. mornings). At other times, try the **Prisunic** supermarket on pl. Notre-Dame.

Chamonix

Chamonix is a slightly profaned altar from which to worship the alpine gods, ranged above in an astonishing pantheon which includes **Mont Blanc.** The cog railway from St-Gervais prepares you for spectacular scenery as it winds over gorges and waterfalls, past forests, and towards the peaks. Chamonix includes a complex of villages in the valley, most of them easily accessible by foot or Chamonix Bus. Directions and location are often expressed in altitudes—Chamonix is at 1035m, and most everything else is up the mountain.

The **office de tourisme** at pl. de l'Eglise (tel. 50 53 00 24) has a free room-reservation service as well as information on camping, climbing, and weather conditions; they also sell maps with all trails clearly marked. (Open daily 8:30am-noon and 2-7pm.) In the same building is a **currency exchange** (open Sat.-Sun. 9am-noon and 2-7pm). Next door, the **Maison de la Montagne** (tel. 50 53 22 08) has a climbing and skiing school and a guide service; upstairs in the **Office de Haute Montagne** you can get specific information on trails and mountain refuges.

Hotels in town are expensive, but the numerous chalets on the periphery are fun and cheap. The **auberge de jeunesse (IYHF)** in Les Pélerins (tel. 50 53 14 52) is a barracks, but the setting is beautiful. Take the bus from Chamonix in the direction of Les Houches; if you are coming by train, get off at Les Pélerins, cross the river, and walk uphill 600m. (Members 40F, nonmembers 58F. Breakfast and evening campfires included. Open Dec.-Sept.) On av. du Bouchet is the **Chalet le Chamoinard** (tel. 50 53 14 09), with homey four-to-six-bed coed rooms and kitchen facilities. (39F. Sheets 10F.) The **Chalet Ski Station,** 6, route des Moussoux (tel. 50 53 20 25), left of the *téléphérique* du Brévant, has large dorm rooms and showers, though no kitchen. (33F. Sheets 8F. Showers 6F.) The tourist office dispenses a map with campsites marked; **Les Rosiers,** on route de Praz (tel. 50 53 10 42), is the closest. (Open year-round, reservations required in winter.) Although illegal, many people pitch their tents for free in the Bois du Bouchet.

Le Fer à Cheval, 118, rue Whymper, serves the best fondue in the valley (34F per person; open noon-midnight). The **Brasserie Natimale,** 3, rue du Dr. Paccard, serves a 68F *menu* and is lively at night. Restaurant prices will soon drive you to the supermarket; **Supermarché Payot Pertin** is at 117, rue Vallot.

One of Chamonix's most rewarding hikes is to **Lac Blanc,** a turquoise lake encircled by jagged peaks and Alpine flowers. To get there, take a 25-minute walk along the Bois du Bouchet to le Praz, and then board the *téléphérique* for La Flégère (22F one way, 33F round-trip). From there you can hike two hours to the lake, often ice-covered even in July. (This should give you an idea of what clothing to bring.)

Chamonix has some of the most breathtaking *téléphériques* anywhere. Get under way as early as you can—crowds and clouds usually gather by afternoon. The dazzling **Aiguille du Midi** is the highest in the world. The simplest trip takes you to Plan de l'Aguille (24F one way, 33F round-trip), but most continue to Aiguille du Midi (70F one way, 100F round-trip). Summer skiers (rentals available throughout Chamonix) can go to the next stop, Gare Helbrouner, in Italy (110F one way, 160F round-trip; bring your passport). Be sure to bring very warm clothes and a lunch.

The huge **Mer de Glace** glacier can be reached by a special cog railway next to the train station (28F one way, 41F round-trip); otherwise it's a not-very-strenuous one-hour hike.

Burgundy (Bourgogne)

Beautiful, sparsely populated countryside envelops Burgundy's many monasteries, cathedrals, and castles, but the region is most renowned for the forty million bottles of wine it produces annually. Burgundy was a center of monastic organization in medieval times, and the religious orders that constructed the monumental abbeys at Tournus, Cluny, and Vézelay also planted the golden vineyards which now cover the hills. Their wines were originally reserved for liturgical celebrations, but are now an integral part of the region's gastronomy, imparting flavor to *boeuf bourguignon, coq au vin,* and Dijon's famous mustard. Other regional specialties include *gougère* (a soft bread made with *pâté à choux* and cheese), *escargots* (snails cooked in lots of butter and garlic), and *quenelles* (little dumplings made with anything from fish to veal).

Dijon

> *Oh, the beautiful city! There are at least a hundred spires!*
>
> —King Francis I

Dijon's aura of grace and history is reminiscent of its days as capital of a duchy that rivaled even the crown of France in wealth and influence. Many of the turrets and steeples that so inspired Francis I in 1515 are still visible today. On a cool summer night, when the streets are deserted, the rows of elegant *hôtels particuliers* (mansions) silhouetted against the darkening sky seem frozen in the seventeenth century. But Dijon is not inanimate: Its compact and well-restored *vieille ville* lends itself to aimless wandering and people-watching, and its prominent university keeps the ancient city young.

Dijon's greatest attraction is undoubtedly the **Musée des Beaux Arts,** occupying a wing of the splendid **Palais des Ducs de Bourgogne.** Second only to the Louvre among French museums, it houses paintings from all periods as well as the *salles des gardes,* these dominated by the impressive tombs of Philippe le Hardi and Jean sans Peur. (Open Mon. and Wed.-Sat. 10am-6pm, Sun. 10am-12:30pm and 2-6pm. Admission 7.80F, students and everyone on Sun. free.) On the other side of the Palais is the **Tour Philippe le Bon,** which provides a wonderful view of Dijon. (Open daily 9:30am-1:30pm and 2:30-5:30pm. Admission 5F, students and everyone on Sun. free.) The **Church of Notre-Dame** has a gargoyle-bedecked facade. More austere, the facade of the **Cathédrale St-Benigne** is an excellent sample of Burgundy's early Gothic. Its huge and beautifully sculpted ninth-century crypt contains the remains of St-Benigne. The fine Gallo-Roman collection of the **Musée Archéologique** is housed under the thirteenth-century arches of the adjacent monastery.

For a complete list of the more than 50 *hôtels particuliers* still standing, visit the **office de tourisme,** pl. Darcy (tel. 80 43 42 12), a five-minute walk down av. Maréchal-Foch from the train station. (Open April-Oct. Mon.-Sat. 9am-noon and 2-8:30pm, Sun. 10am-noon and 2-7pm; Nov.-March. Mon.-Sat. 10am-noon and 2-6pm, Sun. 10am-noon and 3-7pm.) The cheapest accommodations in Dijon are at the **auberge de jeunesse (IYHF),** 1, bd. Champollion (tel. 80 71 32 12), a large, modern, and often noisy edifice popular with tour groups. To reach it, take bus #5 from pl. Grangier to Epirey, the terminus, or take bus #4 from the station to bus #5. During May and June, the **Foyer International d'Etudiants,** 1, av. Maréchal Leclerc (tel. 80 71 51 01), rents rooms to travelers. This clean and cheerful dormitory is accessible via bus #4 (*direction:* Grezille); get off at Parc des Sports. (Singles 45F.) Vacant university dormitories offer space from July to September. Take bus #9 to **Résidence Universitaire Mansard,** on bd. Mansard (tel. 80 66 18 22), or two stops farther to **Résidence Universitaire Montmuzzard,** on bd. Gabriel (tel. 80 65 45 45). (Singles 51F.) Hotels in the center fill quickly in summer. The **Hôtel du Théâtre,** 3, rue des Bons Enfants (tel. 80 67 15 41), is a bit out of the way, so it may have rooms when others don't. (Singles 65F, with shower 68F; doubles 80F, with shower 88F.) **Camping du Lac** (tel. 80 43 54 72), 2km out of town toward the Natural History Museum, at av. Albert 1*er,* is clean and on the lake, but usually packed in summer. (4.25F per person, 2.25F per tent.)

The best way to sample Burgundy's fabulous wines is with a gourmet meal—something easy to come by in Dijon. **Au Bec Fin,** 47, rue Jeannin, is outstanding, with a 42F *menu* at lunch, and 54F or 69F *menus* at dinner; the latter lists a superb *galantine de volaille.* (Open Mon.-Sat.) Otherwise, pick up vital vittles at any of the food shops along rue de la Liberté. To hasten the ruination of your liver, try **Le Messire Bar,** 3, rue Jules-Mercier, in the town center.

From June to November, Dijon becomes a festival town; the brochure *Un Petit Guide de la Vie Musicale en Bourgogne* has a list of the concerts played during the **Festival des Nuits de Bourgogne** and during **Un Été Musical.** On a Sunday in early September, the week-long **Festival International de Folklore** culminates in Dijon's traditional **Fête de la Vigne,** a festival honoring Burgundy's vineyards.

Near Dijon

In the center of the vineyards of the Côte d'Or lies **Beaune,** a proud, prosperous winemaking town. The **Hôtel-Dieu,** built by Nicholas Rolin in the fifteenth century as a hospital for the poor, is a landmark of Burgundian architecture. (Open late June-early Sept. daily 9am-6:45pm; early Sept.-late June 9-11:40am and 2-6pm. Admission 13F, students 9F. Tours (45 min.) every 15 min. in French only. Free pamphlet in English on your way in.) Beaune is famous for its ancient *caves* and *dégustation* (tasting) of local wines. A particularly tantalizing option is a visit to the **Marché aux Vins,** near the Hôtel-Dieu. For 25F you are given a glass and about one hour to sample 37 of Burgundy's finest wines. Bring bread to clear your palate and your head. The **office de tourisme,** opposite the Hôtel-Dieu (tel. 80 22 24 51), provides a list of other *caves* in Beaune and the surrounding area. Buses run along the *route de vin* (8 per day, 1 hr.).

Farther to the south, the little town of **Tournus** preserves one of the finest examples of early Burgundian Romanesque style at the **Abbatiale St-Philibert.** The oldest part of the church is the ninth-century narthex; the nave, with its five transverse barrel vaults, is unique to this church. The **office de tourisme** is on pl. Carnot (tel. 85 51 13 10). Tournus is a good point of departure to the surrounding countryside, dotted with small villages, each with its own Romanesque church. These churches reflect the artistic and religious influence of the once powerful and brilliant abbey of **Cluny,** about 35km to the southwest. The Cluny **syndicat d'initiative,** 6, rue Mercière (tel. 85 59 05 34), has plenty of information on local sights and wines. (Open March-Oct. daily 9am-noon and 2-6:45pm.)

Vézelay

Perched high atop a hill overlooking a lush checkerboard of forest, mountains, and pastures, tiny Vézelay is famous for its twelfth-century **Basilique de la Madeleine,** considered the finest Romanesque structure in France; you can spend hours in the narthex and nave examining the figures on the stone capitals. The tympanum over the central portal inside the church represents Christ after the Resurrection. If you can negotiate the long and ancient stairway, climb to the top of the tower for an extraordinary view of the Morvan countryside (2F). To reach Vézelay from Paris or Dijon, take the train to Laroche-Migenne and change for Avallon. Buses run from Avallon and Sermizelles twice per day (Mon.-Sat.). Sermizelles is closer, and the bus there usually connects directly with trains from Laroche. The Avallon and Vézelay tourist offices have schedules, or call Cars de la Madeleine (tel. 86 33 25 67). Hitchhiking is fairly easy as well.

Vézelay is a good base for exploring **Avallon** and **Semur-en-Auxois** (a bus circulates between these 2 towns), and for hiking in the beautiful **Parc Naturel de Morvan.** Bus and train information as well as brochures on the park, are available from the **syndicat d'initiative,** next to the basilica. (Open Mon.-Tues. and Thurs.-Sat. 10am-1pm and 2-6pm, Sun. 10am-1pm.) Stay at the friendly and rustic **Centre de Rencontres Internationales Pax Christi,** rue des Ecoles (tel. 86 33 26 73), off the main street. (35F, breakfast included. Lunch and dinner 30F. Open July-Aug.) Vézelay's **auberge de jeunesse (IYHF),** route de l'Etang (tel. 86 33 24 18), is located on a rural site 600m out of town. (32F. Lockout noon-5pm. Curfew 10:30pm. Open mid-June to mid-Sept.) Camping is available next door. (7F per person, 1F per tent. Also open mid-June to mid-Sept.)

Lyon

Historically renowned for its silk exchange and medieval fairs, Lyon is France's second largest city. Many travelers think of it as just a huge train station, and miss the flavor of one of Europe's gastronomic capitals. The heart of Lyon lies on a spit of land between the Rivers Rhône and Saône, and is split by rue Victor Hugo; this artery runs from Perrache, Lyon's main train station, to place Bellecour and then continues as rue de la République to Terreaux. Part-Dieu, on the east bank of the Rhône, is the city's financial district. The *vieille ville,* on the west bank, is a neighborhood of seventeenth- and eighteenth-century houses and cobblestone lanes. Many of the houses have neat architectural quirks: The wincing gargoyle on the top of 11, pl. Neuve St-Jean, or the *traboule* (a passageway from one house to another) from 1, rue de Boeuf to 24, rue St-Jean are but a few examples. For a suggested walking tour of the old town, pick up the free pamphlet distributed by the tourist office; their free map is fine for street navigation.

Best seen from across the Saône, the **Cathédrale St-Jean** rises amid red tiles and gray stone. It's noted for its strongly articulated nave and flamboyant rose window; don't miss the fourteenth-century clock in the north transcept. From pl. St-Jean, take the funicular up to the **Fourvière esplanade** from which you can gaze down onto the urban sprawl.

The **Musée des Beaux Arts,** in the Palais St-Pierre, is known chiefly for its Spanish and Dutch masters, impressionists, and early moderns. (Open Wed.-Mon. 10:45am-6pm. Free.) The **Musée des Marionettes** in the Hôtel Gadagne displays the well-loved Lyonnais Guignol, a light-hearted puppet invented by an unemployed silk worker. The tourist office can supply you with a more complete museum list.

The **office de tourisme** is on pl. Bellecour (tel. 78 42 25 75), behind the flower market, two Métro stops from Gare Perrache, or a 10-minute walk along rue Victor Hugo. (Open in summer Mon.-Fri. 9am-7pm, Sat. 9am-6pm; off-season Mon.-Sat. 9am-6pm.) French-speakers should ask for the valuable city guide, *Le Petit Paume.* There are also branch offices at Perrache and Part-Dieu train stations. Lyon's **auberge de jeunesse (IYHF),** 51, rue Roger Salengro (tel. 78 76 39 23), is a lively, sociable place with a snack bar/dance floor upstairs. Take the Métro to Bellecour and bus #35 to Georges Lévy; after 9pm, take bus #53 from Perrache to Etats-Unis Viviani and walk 500m along the train tracks. From Part-Dieu take bus #36 to Viviani Joliot-Curie. A good place to look for grape-picking jobs in September. (32F. Breakfast 10F. No lockout, but reception closed noon-5pm. 11:30pm curfew. Open year-round.) The **Residence Benjamin Delessert,** 145, av. Jean Jaurès (tel. 78 72 86 77), is a dormitory with comfortable beds. From Perrache, take any bus that goes to J. Macé and walk under the train tracks for 5 to 10 minutes; from Part-Dieu, take the subway to Marcé. (Singles 55F, doubles 100F.) **Hôtel Croix-Pâquet,** 11 pl. Croix-Pâquet (tel. 78 28 51 49), in Terreaux, has simple but comfortable rooms. (Singles 65-75F, doubles 90F. Showers 15F. Breakfast 15F.) For **camping,** try huge **Dardilly** (tel. 74 69 80 07). Take bus #19 from the Hôtel de Ville (*direction:* Ecully-Dardilly) to the Parc d'Affaires stop.

In Lyon, people don't eat—they dine. Restaurants on rue Mercieère, near place Bellecour, aren't as picture-perfect as their counterparts in the old town, but meals average only 40-50F. **Titi Lyonnais,** 2, rue Chapponnay, 3*ème,* serves a 65F *menu* with a wide choice of dishes. (Open Tues.-Sat. noon-1:30pm and 7:30-9:30pm, Sun. noon-1:30pm.) **Garioud,** 14, rue de Palais-Grillet, off rue de la République, serves truly great *cuisine lyonnaise;* choose from *menus* at 79F, 148F, and 178F. (Open Mon.-Fri. noon-2pm and 7:30-10pm, Sat. 7:30-10pm.) And of course, whatever you eat, wash it down with a local Beaujolais or a white burgundy from the neighboring Mâcon villages.

Lyon is a major rail center, with frequent connections to Paris, Switzerland, Italy, Germany, the Côte d'Azur, and Spain. Gare Perrache is the more convenient of Lyon's two train stations; Gare Part-Dieu is in the center of the city's commercial district. **BIGE** tickets are sold at Gare Perrache. (Open Mon.-Fri. 9am-noon and 2-7pm, Sat. 1-6pm.) Hitching is rumored to be dismal; for Paris, take bus #2, 5, 19, 21, 22, or 31 to Pont Monton and the N6. Better still, get in touch with **Allostop,** 8, rue de la Bombarde (tel. 78 42 38 29).

Alsace and Champagne

Alsace, long a political shuttlecock, has spent half of the last hundred-odd years under German dominion. German influence in language and cuisine is strong, but Alsatians are also French in customs and orientation. Strasbourg, the capital, is a gracious university city and the seat of the European Parliament. The Route du Vin, a ribbon of wine-producing villages, threads the lakes, valleys, and wooded slopes of the Vosges region, as well as Colmar, a town of well-preserved Alsatian houses. The Vosges is ideal for hiking, camping, and cross-country skiing, with hundreds of miles of marked trails and overnight shelters along the way. Maps and guides are available from Club Vosgien, 4, rue de la Douane, 67000 Strasbourg (tel. 88 32 57 96).

Champagne, the region between the Alsatian borderlands and Paris, is known the world over for its bubbly. You may be shocked to learn that you have seldom or never drunk real champagne, which must by French law be vinted from the grapes of the region and produced according to the rigorous and time-honored *méthode champenoise.*

Strasbourg

Sophisticated Strasbourg impressed both Goethe and Rousseau—a feat probably not duplicated by any other place. Today the city is a symbol of reconciliation between nations: In 1955 it was chosen as the seat of the European Parliament. Cosmopolitan Strasbourg nonetheless remains thoroughly Alsatian in appearance, with its half-timbered houses, covered bridges, and flower-lined canals.

Start a tour at the **cathedral,** whose light, open spire rises 160m above the historic core of Strasbourg. While you wait for the delightful play of the **horloge astronomique** (astrological clock) at 12:31 Strasbourg mean time, be sure to see the **Pilier des Anges** (doomsday column), one of the high points of Gothic sculpture; both are in the south transept. Across from the cathedral are the elegantly gilded eighteenth-century **Château des Rohan,** housing a porcelain, archeology, and fine arts museum, and the **Maison de l'Oeuvre Notre-Dame,** a huge collection of medieval and Renaissance art. For folklore, visit the **Musée Alsacien,** 23, quai St-Nicolas. The **Ancienne Douane** (old customs house) by the river on rue de la Douane, shelters the pleasant **Musée d'Art Moderne,** with a good collection of paintings and sculpture by Klimt, Chagall, Arp, Klee, and many of the impressionists. (All museums open April-Sept. Wed.-Mon. 10am-noon and 2-6pm; Oct.-March Mon. and Wed.-Sat. 2-6pm, Sun. 10am-noon and 2-6pm. Admission to the Château des Rohan 5.40F, students 2.60F; all other museums 3.80F, students 2F.)

During the summer, there are folklore and music programs, and a walk along the quays of **La Petite France** (the old quarter) is best on a warm summer night. In early June, Strasbourg hosts an **International Festival of Music.**

The main **office de tourisme** is at pl. Gutenberg (tel. 88 32 57 07), right in the center of the old city. (Open in summer daily 8am-7pm; in winter Mon.-Fri. 9am-12:30pm and 2-6pm, Sat. 9am-noon, closed Sun.) Room-finding services (5F) are available here and also at the branch offices across from the train station (tel. 88 32 51 49), and at the German border (Pont de l'Europe). Strasbourg has quite a few budget hotels, though the good ones fill fast in summer. In 1988 there will be three hostels in Strasbourg. The **Auberge de Jeunesse René Cassin (IYHF),** 9, rue de l'Auberge de Jeunesse (tel. 88 30 26 46), has one of the best hostel bars in France, a complete game room, good meals, and a campground. Take bus #3, 13, or 23 from the covered bus stop on rue de Vieux-Marché-aux-Vins. (Dorm beds 42F, singles 85F, doubles and triples 65F. Breakfast included. Camping 22F per person including breakfast. Meals 30F each. Open 7am, all day, year-round.) The sparkling **CIARUS, Centre International d'Accueil de Strasbourg,** 7, rue Finkmatt (tel. 88 32 12 12), is 10 minutes by foot from the train station. Take rue du Maire-Kuss to the canal, and then a left onto rue Finkmatt. (Singles 40-97F. Breakfast 13F, lunch and dinner 36F.) Finally, the **Auberge de Jeunesse du Parc du Rhin (IYHF),** rue des Cavaliers (tel. 88 60 10 20), will open its doors in 1988. Take bus #11 from the train station, get off at Pont-du-Rhin. (Singles 130F, doubles 140F, triples 180F. Sheets and breakfast included. Lunch and dinner 40F. Open daily 7am-midnight.) The **Hôtel au Cycliste,** 8, rue des Bateliers (tel. 88 36 20 01), is a pleasant riverside place near the Eglise Ste-Madeleine. (Singles from 68F, doubles 75F and 80F. Showers 10F. Breakfast 12.10F.) **Hôtel Patricia,** 1a, rue de Puits (tel. 88 32 14 60), behind Église St-Thomas, is in a central location between *La Petite France* and the cathedral. (Singles 68F, doubles 77F. Breakfast 15F.)

Be sure to try the delicious Alsatian cuisine. You can't miss **Au Pont St-Martin,** 13-15, rue des Moulins, an enormous, three-tiered riverside restaurant that caters to tourists and locals alike. The location in *La Petite France* is great, and a three-course *ménu* is only 40F. For excellent regional food, go to **Restaurant d'Quetsch,** 6, rue du Faisan. Their *plat du jour* costs 45F. (Open Sept.-July Mon.-Sat.) **Restaurant de la Place,** 16, rue des Tonneliers, is cheaper: An appetizer, the *plat du jour,* and coffee or tea, cost only 34F Monday through Friday at lunchtime. (Open Mon.-Sat. 11:45am-2pm and 7pm-1am.)

To hitchhike to Paris, take bus #2, 12, or 22 to route des Romains; for Colmar and the E9 south, try bus #3, 13, or 23 to bd. de Lyon, and then follow signs for Colmar to the highway ramp.

Near Strasbourg

Ringed by vineyards and overshadowed by the craggy Vosges, **Colmar** is a good slice of Alsatian lifestyle. The recently-restored tanners' lodgings and **"La Petite Venise"** preserve the feeling of a medieval town. The extraordinary **Musée Unterlinden,** on pl. Unterlinden, preserves a large collection of medieval religious art in a former Dominican convent. Among a collection famous for its primitive Alsatian masters, Grünewald's *Issenheim Altarpiece* is especially worthy of a pilgrimage. (Open April-Oct. daily 9am-6pm; Nov.-March daily 9am-noon and 2-6pm. Admission 15F, students 7F.) The annual **Alsatian Wine Festival** is held here in August, with plenty of beer kegs and free wine tasting. The end of August and beginning of September bring the **Jours Choucroute** (Sauerkraut Days), two weeks filled with feasting, dancing, wine and beer, and plenty of you-know-what.

The **Maison des Jeunes** (Centre Internationale de Séjour), 17, rue Camille Schlumberger (tel. 89 41 26 87), is a short walk from the station in a pleasant residential neighborhood close to the center of town. (Dorm beds 29F. Check-in after 2pm. Curfew 11pm.) Colmar is 30 minutes south of Strasbourg by train.

Reims

Pounded to rubble during World War I, Reims has been tenaciously reconstructed into a graceful city. The **Cathédrale de Notre-Dame,** on pl. du Cardinal Luçon, is a Gothic masterpiece crowned and ornamented with several dream-like Chagall windows. From Clovis to Charles X, 25 kings of France were crowned beneath its vaulted roof. The **Plais du Tau** next door, once the Episcopalian archbishop's palace, now houses medieval sculptures and dazzling cathedral treasures. (Open in summer daily Wed.-Mon. 10am-noon and 2-6pm; in winter Wed.-Mon. 10am-noon and 2-5pm. Admission 11F, students 9F.) To the east lies the **Basilique St-Remi,** a Gothic renovation of a Carolingian Romanesque church reputed to contain the tombs of France's earliest kings. The **Musée St-Denis,** once an ancient abbey, has a fine Corot collection, portrait sketches by the Cranachs, elder and younger, and some other fine French works. (Open in summer Wed.-Mon. 10am-noon and 2-6pm; in winter Wed.-Mon. 10am-noon and 2-5pm. Admission 7F.)

Reims's **cité souterraine** of champagne *caves* is its underground life; get a brochure with maps and hours of the different cellars from the tourist office. The most interesting *caves* (and perhaps the best wines) belong to **Taittinger,** 9, pl. St-Niçaise (tel. 26 85 45 35). The only *cave* still winning visitors' hearts by giving free samples of the bubbly brew is **Mumm,** 34, rue du Champs-de-Mars (tel. 26 40 22 73).

By the summer of 1988 the **office de tourisme** should be located in the ruins of the old chapterhouse, next to the cathedral, at 2, rue Guillaume de Machault. (Open Mon.-Sat. 10am-6pm, closed Sun.) Stay at the sparkling **Centre International de Séjour (IYHF),** 1, chausée Bocquaine (tel. 26 40 52 60), opposite parc Leo Lagrange, a 15-minute walk from the station; turn right on bd. Général Leclerc on the far side of the gardens in front of the station, cross a bridge (rue de Vesle), and take the first left, beside the Maison de Culture. (Singles 63F, rooms with 2 or 3 beds 60F. Breakfast included.) Cheaper though less convenient singles are to be found in vacant university dormatories during July and August through **CROUS,** 34, bd. Henri Vasnier (tel. 26 85 50 16). (Students 26F, others 34F. Office open Mon.-Fri. 8:30am-noon and 1:30-5pm.) The **Hôtel d'Alsace,** 6, rue Général-Sarrail (tel. 26 47 44 08), is pleasant and close to both the station and the sights. (Singles and doubles 69F, with shower 116F. Breakfast 16.50F.) **Hôtel Linguet,** 14, rue Linguet (tel. 26 47 31 89), has been newly renovated. (Singles 65F, doubles 70F. Breakfast 16F.)

Place Drouet d'Erlon is crammed with *brasseries* serving *ménus* for around 45F. **Le Flamm' Steak,** 17, rue Libergier, south of the cathedral, has tasty crepes and regional dishes with *ménus* from 38-65F. (Open Tues.-Sun.) **Ancien Pavillon,** 2, bd. Jules César, off pl. de la République, is a sure bet in a country atmosphere, with a 43F *ménu* and beef kidneys flambéed in cognac. (Open Mon.-Fri. noon-2pm, Sat. 7-10pm.)

Near Reims

"Brothers, brothers, come quickly! I am drinking stars!"

—Dom Perignon

There are no great cathedrals in **Epernay,** but the golden *caves* under avenue de Champagne are enough to inspire worship. Several firms, unlike their Reims competitors, offer free samples. The best tour is at **Moët et Chandon,** 20, av. de Champagne. For information about other *caves,* and lodging, consult the **office de tourisme,** 7, av. de Champagne (tel. 26 55 33 00), off pl. de la République. The **MJC Centre International de Séjour,** 8, rue de Reims (tel. 26 55 40 82), only three minutes from the station, has beautiful modern rooms. (62F per person in singles to quads. Breakfast included. Good cafeteria for lunch and dinner.) **Hôtel du Progrès,** 6, rue des Berceaux (tel. 26 55 24 75), is conveniently located. (Singles 70F, doubles 85F.)

The seventeenth-century mansions of **Châlons-sur-Marne** were built with blocks of chalk alternating with brick—an old *champenois* method. The **syndicat d'initiative,** 3, quai des Arts (tel. 26 65 17 89), provides a guide to parks, canals, and several fascinating old churches, including the **Cathédrale St-Etienne,** with its unique Châlons—green stained glass. The **auberge de jeunesse,** rue Kellerman (tel. 26 68 13 56), is unattractive and open only in summer, but Châlons is an easy day trip by rail from Reims or Epernay. (Hostel 32F. Curfew 10pm.)

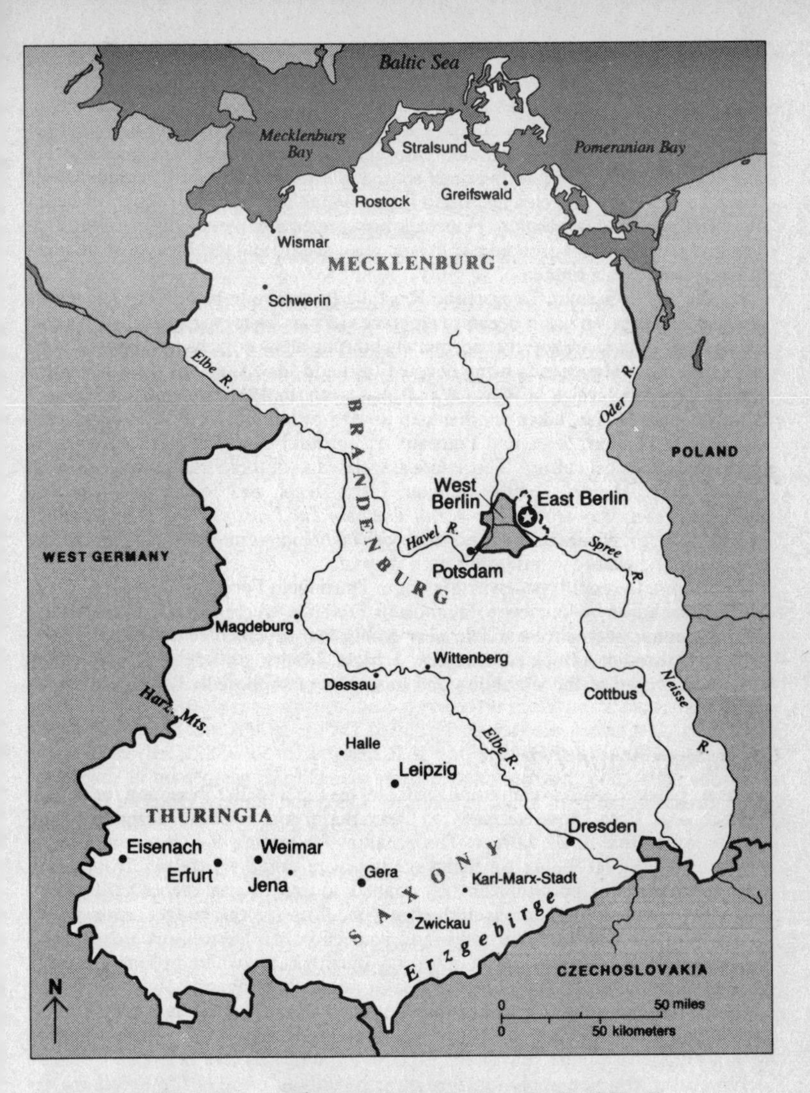

EAST GERMANY

US$1 = 1.82 Ostmarks (M) — **1M = US$0.55**
CDN$1 = 1.37M — **1M = CDN$0.73**
UK£1 = 2.95M — **1M = UK£0.34**
AUS$1 = 1.30M — **1M = AUS$0.77**

The most industrialized of the world's socialist countries, East Germany is in many ways a weather vane for their future. Many economic reforms have anticipated Gorbachev's *perestroika,* and the dual influence of Western and Eastern media has afforded East Germans a unique perspective on a divided world. On the other hand, East Germany's conservative leadership rules over a social and political environment that is repressive even by Eastern European standards. Two issues at center stage of East German politics are the country's relationship to its German sibling and its response to the winds of political change blowing from Moscow. West Germany currently puts a lot of money into East Germany's sophisticated industrial economy, and relations have warmed since 1984, when East German leader Erich Honecker abruptly canceled his trip to Bonn. As to the possibility of countenancing more criticism and opposition, Honecker has seemed completely disinterested thus far—the East German economic ship is in good shape, and the Party sees no point in fixing what isn't broken.

As the small German Democratic Republic (pop. about 17 million) has grown in self-confidence, so has it begun to embrace German history. Especially now that the country's massive project of adequately housing all its citizens nears completion, more and more attention is being devoted to the historic shape of the inner cities. Ornate Dresden, leveled in World War II, has, with the 1985 reopening of Semper's famous Opera House, taken another step toward reclaiming its old contours. Leipzig, Erfurt, Weimar, Jena, and Potsdam are splendid examples of the richness of Germany's classical culture. The names associated with these small towns—Martin Luther, Bach, Handel, Goethe, Schiller, Liszt, Hegel, and Nietzsche—have long since made their way around the world. The play *The Prussians Are Coming,* which ran to rave reviews in Berlin (and may still be doing so in 1988), addresses East Germany's newfound relationship with its past.

Don't miss the countryside villages of the Thuringian Forest and Elbe River Valley. Visit a church in Annaberg-Buchholz or Freiburg, where you might hear a classic Silbermann organ; cross a field near Königstein or Lilienstein above the Elbe; or traipse through a flock of hens near Schloss Pillnitz, outside of Dresden. You may be surprised at the variability and humanity of supposedly featureless socialism.

Planning Your Trip

Visiting East Berlin on a day visa is simple; see the East Berlin section for details. Transit visas from West Germany to West Berlin are similarly straightforward; they're issued free at the border. The penalties for leaving the city limits of East Berlin or getting off the transit highway are severe, and laws are rigidly enforced. East Germany is by no means an easy country to tour; tourist offices hardly exist, and strict currency regulations add extra difficulties for the budget traveler. Yet if you have the will, there's a way—and your effort will be well-rewarded.

To go outside of *Bezirk* Berlin or to stay overnight anywhere in East Germany you must obtain one of three types of visas: tourist, camping, or visitor's. Camping visas are the only remotely inexpensive option, unless a relative in East Germany invites you to visit, in which case you can obtain a visitor's visa. Those traveling with a tourist visa must stay at the expensive Interhotels (see below).

Whichever visa you apply for, deal directly with an office of the **Reisebüro der DDR** at any one of the five main border crossings: **Helmstedt** (near Hannover), **Heerleshausen** (near Fulda), **Rudolfstein** (near Hof), **Gudow** (near Hamburg), or **East Berlin,** Alexanderplatz 5. At Reisebüro window #13 in Berlin, they will arrange for your accommodations and take your Western currency; window #12 will then issue you a visa (no wait).

You must reserve accommodations in advance, pay DM15 for a visa, and exchange DM25 into Ostmarks (at a rate of 1 to 1) for each day you plan to spend in the country. Arranging accommodations means laying out a day-by-day itinerary; ask for the special "Internationale Campingplätze" booklet to know where you may camp. For Interhotels, you pay at least 100M per person per night, and you pay at the tourist office in advance of your trip. This fee is above the mandatory 25M per day exchange. If you camp, you pay 25M per person per day in advance—that sum, too, above the mandatory daily 25M. Expect, then, to spend at least 50M (US$27) per day. You should bring camping equipment, but many campgrounds have inexpensive bungalows to let; arrive early. Flexible officials may simply stamp a list of campgrounds (in the different *Bezirk* in which you want to stay) on your voucher without any specification of where you stay and when. Otherwise—and this is the norm—you must stay in the specified campsites on the dates specified on your voucher. The only drawback with the camping visa is that the campgrounds are often far from the town centers.

Before you are let into East Germany, your pack might be searched. The main problem is printed matter, so use some discretion and leave behind political books and newsweeklies. Pornography or graphic action/adventure magazines will almost certainly get you into trouble. Also declare all your foreign currency and valuables when you enter. Save all exchange receipts; the government wants to prevent any black market activity, so it is worthwhile to make sure that your figures tally, even if no one checks in the end.

Don't try to import or export Ostmarks. You are not allowed to change any of the mandatory DM25 *per diem* amount back into hard currency when you leave. You can, however, deposit it *(deponieren)* at the border when you leave in exchange for a receipt which you can cash back into Ostmarks on another visit. Any hard currency you exchange beyond the mandatory 25M *per diem* amount you can cash back at the border if you can present your receipt.

Transportation

Train travel is inexpensive (Leipzig-Dresden 12.20M in second class), but often crowded; always make a seat reservation (1M) at least two hours prior to departure. Express trains *(Schnellzüge)* are much faster and cost only 3M extra. Don't bother waiting at the ticket counter if the lines are long; you can skip the line, ask for a *Bestätigung* (an affidavit certifying that you were not able to buy the ticket at the station), and pay 1M extra aboard the train. Railpasses are not valid in East Germany, nor on the West Germany/West Berlin corridor.

The best way to see the country is by car—rent one in the West. Particularly if you plan to camp, this will save you a great deal of inconvenience. Driving in the DDR is not restricted if you have a valid overnight visa. If you have a transit visa or a day visa for Berlin, you can buy gasoline only with Western currency and only at Intertank stations; ask for a map that shows their locations. Gas prices are almost identical to those in the West, and many stations have diesel and unleaded fuel. Traffic regulations are enforced with a vengeance and hefty fines. People with transit and day visas must pay the fines in Western currency. It's illegal to honk your horn (except in emergencies) or to ride in the front seat without a seat belt.

Hitchhiking is illegal in East Germany, as is inter-city cycling for foreigners.

Practical Information

If you run out of Ostmarks, you can exchange currency at specified banks, special *Wechselstellen* (exchange offices), at any Reisebüro der DDR, or in most Interhotels.

The International Union of Students (IUS) card is the Eastern European equivalent of the ISIC; ask at a **Reisebüro der DDR** about obtaining one, though it may be enough just to tell officials at tourist sights that you're a student. Also of great value is the booklet *77 Praktische Tips für Besuche in der DDR,* available at **DER Reisebüros** in West Germany.

After having your English grammar corrected by West German bus drivers, the lack of English speakers in East Germany may come as a bit of a shock. Traveling here is of course possible without a knowledge of German, but may be much less rewarding.

Food

Restaurants, pubs, and cafes in the DDR always seem to be filled with a *gemütlich* hum. There are not nearly so many of them as there are in the West, and they're surprisingly inexpensive, so they're often full. Adopt slightly irregular eating hours to avoid long waits. There are sometimes lines at bakeries and groceries, but you can usually stock up with a minimum of fuss. Nearly everything is painfully cheap. Local specialties include pork steaks, sausages, and beefsteak tartar, usually served with homefries, steamed vegetables, and a side of sauerkraut. For a snack, grab a sausage and beer to go at a *Schnellimbiss* (fast-food stand). If you are vegeterian, you'll have a rough go of it, but many places serve a *Käseplatte* (cheese plate with bread).

Berlin (East)

Like other European capitals, East Berlin offers historical treasures, a wealth of theater and music, and some of the finest museums in the world. While the architectural heritage of nineteenth-century Germany lines Unter den Linden, also note the city's distinctly post-war repudiation of its past: the futuristic Alexanderplatz, the sterile apartment buildings, and the mirrored Palast der Republik. East Berlin may lack the spontaneity and funkiness of Kreuzberg, yet the challenge to life in the fast lane represented by its silent, lumbering concrete structures overwhelms the traveler with questions, opinions, and reflections.

Orientation and Practical Information

Day-visiting East Berlin is easy. You can enter the city any day of the week between 7am and 8pm, and must leave by midnight. No exceptions. It is possible to extend your one-day visa once you're in East Berlin (see the Budget Travel listing below).

There are two points at which foreigners can cross from West to East Berlin: **Checkpoint Charlie,** at Friedrichstrasse and Zimmerstrasse (U-Bahn: Kochstrasse), for pedestrians and drivers; and **Bahnhof Friedrichstrasse** (U-Bahn 6 or S-Bahn: Friedrichstrasse), for pedestrians only.

Formalities take 15 to 90 minutes; weekends are generally the busiest times. If you arrive before 9am, however, you can usually get through promptly. Crossing at Bahnhof Friedrichstrasse and so taking the S-Bahn through the intricate security precautions of the wall lets you viscerally experience the post-war division of Europe, but crossing at Checkpoint Charlie is usually quicker. If you are traveling with a resident of West Germany or West Berlin, you have no choice: You must cross at Friedrichstrasse. Unless you have subsequently changed your visa status, you must leave East Berlin from the same border checkpoint at which you entered. The day visa costs DM5, payable only in Western currency; you are also required to change DM25 into Ostmarks. The exchange rate is one to one, and prices are lower than those in West Berlin. If you take your car into East Berlin for the day, you'll have to pay a DM10 street tax—again, only in Western currency. Do not bring in any East German currency or printed material of a political nature.

When you cross the border, you may have to fill out a customs declaration *(Erklärung),* which lists all Western currencies and gifts of value that you are taking into the country. When you leave, you fill out the back side of this sheet with the amounts of moneys you still possess and articles purchased in the DDR. If you pay out any Western currency while in East Germany, whether changing money at a bank or buying tickets or other items, get a stamped confirmation *(Bestätigung),* which the police may request when you leave. You're not supposed to take East German currency back out with you, but you can deposit it at the border for another visit.

If you'd like to arrange a longer visit to East Berlin or the DDR, see the Budget Travel listing below.

Both border checkpoints are on Friedrichstrasse, formerly one of Berlin's grand commercial streets. To **Unter den Linden,** walk straight ahead about half a mile from Checkpoint Charlie, or walk under the train tracks away from the river for three blocks from Bahnhof Friedrichstr. East down Unter der Linden will bring you first to Museumsinsel and Marx-Engels-Platz, and then to Karl-Liebknecht-

Strasse and Alexanderplatz. Along the river Spree, just beside the distinctive, red Rathaus, are the twin spires of the Nikolaikirche, and the Nikolaiviertel, the reconstruction of Berlin's medieval city center.

Tourist Offices: Informationszentrum am Fernsehturm, underneath the TV tower next to Alexanderplatz (tel. 212 46 75). The monthly *Wohin in Berlin* (0.30M) is worthwhile. Open Mon. 1-6pm, Tues.-Fri. 8am-6pm, Sat.-Sun. 10am-6pm. The Palasthotel has a **Zentraler Besucherdienst** which sells theater tickets. Open Mon. 1-7pm, Tues.-Fri. 10am-1pm and 2-7pm, Sat. 10am-1pm. The **Reisebüro der DDR** (see Budget Travel) may also be of some help.

Budget Travel: Not really a concept in East Germany. To obtain a visa for a longer stay in East Germany, visit the **Reisebüro der DDR,** Alexanderplatz 5 (tel. 215 44 02). The *Ausländer Dienst* desk upstairs is the place to book hotel rooms, buy camping vouchers, make visa arrangements, and change money. They also sell tickets to the Fernsehturm, reservations for the Lindencorso nightclub, and tickets for the *Weisse Flotte* boat excursions. Open Mon.-Fri. 8am-7pm, Sat.-Sun. 10am-7pm. Downstairs, the office sells train tickets, city bus tours, and tickets for most cultural events (10% markup). Very long lines. Open Mon., Wed., Fri. 9am-5:30pm, Tues. and Thurs. 9am-7pm; every 4th Sat. of the month 9am-noon.

Currency Exchange: At the Reisebüro, Alexanderplatz 5; at Bahnhof Friedrichstr.; or at Ostbahnhof. The tiny bank at Friedrichstr. by Checkpoint Charlie has the longest hours: open daily 8am-11:30pm. Also at the airport, Flughafen Berlin-Schönefeld: open daily 7am-10pm.

Telephones: Go back to the West for international calls. **Telephone code** (from West Berlin): 0372. You can call directly to West Berlin for 1M but not all payphones take 1M pieces.

Trains: Ostbanhof (Hauptbahnhof) is East Germany's major rail station. Information: national (tel. 495 31), international (tel. 495 41). You can also buy tickets in West Berlin's Bahnhof Zoo. **Bahnhof Lichtenberg** serves many destinations in the DDR and other East European countries.

Public Transportation: East Berlin's efficient system allows you to travel to all parts of the city with relative ease. Travel on the tram, bus, or U-Bahn costs 0.20M; you must buy a new ticket each time you change to a new U-Bahn line or a new bus. Drop change into the pay-box aboard the bus or in the station, pull the lever on the pay-box, and tear off a ticket; once aboard, you must validate this ticket. S-Bahn rates are determined by distance traveled; they range from 0.20M *(Preisstufe I)* within the downtown area to 1M *(Preisstufe 7)* for longer distances. You can buy a 24-hour pass (1M for S-Bahn only, 2M for all forms of transit anywhere in the city; available at most stations), but it's probably not worthwhile.

Emergencies: Police (tel. 110). **Ambulance** (tel. 115).

Medical Assistance: If you can't make it back to West Berlin, try the emergency room of **Rettungsamt Berlin,** Marienburgerstr. 41-46 (tel. 282 05 61).

Embassies: U.S., Neustädtische Kirchstr. 4-5, 108 Berlin-Mitte (tel. 220 27 41), just off Unter den Linden. **U.K.,** Unter den Linden 32-34 (tel. 220 24 31). Travelers from **Canada** and **Australia** should contact the British Embassy, or, preferably, their missions in West Berlin. **New Zealand** nationals should also contact the British Embassy. For travel to other East European countries, it's best to contact their tourist offices, not their embassies. **Bulgaria** (Balkantourist), Unter den Linden 40 (tel. 229 20 72). **Czechoslovakia** (Čedok), Strausberger Platz 8 (tel. 439 41 13). **Hungary** (Ibusz), Karl-Liebknecht-Str. 9 (tel. 212 35 59). **Poland** (Orbis), Warschauerstr. 5 (tel. 589 45 30).

Cultural Centers: American Library, next to the U.S. Embassy, Neustädtische Kirchstr. 4. Open Mon.-Fri. 10am-5:30pm. **Centre Culture Française,** Unter den Linden 41. French movies, plays, music; lending and periodical library. Open Mon. 1:30-6:30pm, Tues.-Fri. 10:30am-6:30pm.

Bookstores: Das Internationale Buch, Spandauerstr. 4, on the corner of Unter den Linden. Perhaps the best place to spend your excess East German currency. Wide collection of German and Russian books. Upstairs, works of Marx, Engels, and Lenin are available in handsome hardbound English editions relatively cheaply. Open Mon.-Fri. 9am-7pm., Sat. 9am-1pm. **Kunstsalon,** Unter den Linden 41, is another great place to unload Ostmarks. Inexpensive posters, art books, classical music recordings, and sheet music. Next to the Komische Oper. Open Mon. 1-7pm, Tues.-Fri. 10am-7pm, Sat. 9am-1pm.

Accommodations and Camping

Berlin has no shortage of **Interhotels,** but a room for less than 100M is just about nonexistent. If you must, book at the **Reisebüro der DDR** (see Budget Travel under Practical Information). The cheapest legitimate alternative (roughly 60M) is the **Christliches Hospiz,** Auguststr. 82 (tel. 282 53 21). The best bet for the budget traveler is camping. The only Inter-camping area in *Bezirk* Berlin is **Berlin-Schmöckwitz,** on Lake Krossinee. Getting there without a car is not easy. Take the S-Bahn (direction: Königswusterhausen) and get off at Grünau, then take tram #86 to Altschmöckwitz (last stop). Then take bus #E25 (every 40 min., last bus 7:36pm) to the first stop. Count on at least 90 min. one way for the full trip (25M per person).

Food

Most people in East Berlin for a daytrip will have money to eat and drink well—a welcome relief from cheese and tomato sandwiches in the west. The problems are the crowds and the wait at normal meal times (noon-2pm and 6-8pm), but you can usually find something without waiting too long. Sit wherever there are free chairs, as you seldom get your own table. Tip by rounding up at least 10%. There are plenty of restaurants around Alexanderplatz and the Nikolaiviertel, but it's worth wandering in Prenzlauerberg, a largely reconstructed area of the city just north of the center.

Morava, Rathauspassage 5, right at Alexanderplatz. Good Czech food in a nice atmosphere. Try their *paniertes Schweinschnitzel mit Käse* (breaded pork chop cooked with cheese) for 8M. Beer (2.50M) expensive by DDR standards. Open Sun.-Thurs. 11am-midnight, Fri.-Sat. 11am-1am.

Gastmahl des Meeres, corner of Spandauerstr. and Karl-Liebknecht-Str., across from the Palasthotel. Centrally located. Meals, primarily seafood, for 7-8M. Open daily 11am-7pm.

Café am Palast, on Karl-Liebknecht-Str., just across the Spree from the cathedral, down the street from Gastmahl des Meeres. Expensive by East German standards, but still tasty and affordable; lines infrequent. Try steak with pineapples on toast (14.70M), *Apfelstrudel* (2M), and a pot of cocoa (2.50M).

Imbiss, along the Rathauspassage, next to the Fernsehturm. A host of cubicles representing the East Berlin equivalent of fast food. The lines move quickly, the food isn't bad, and everything is incredibly cheap. Broiled chicken goes by weight—a whole one usually costs around 5M. *Bratwurst* 1.15M. On beer mugs and soft drink glasses you submit hefty deposits of 2M and 1M respectively.

Zur letzten Instanz, Waisenstr. 14/16 (tel. 212 55 28). A little tricky to find: in a little alley a few blocks behind the Rathauspassage, toward the river. Popular and wonderfully atmospheric old-Berlin pub and restaurant. You might want to phone ahead.

Alt-Cöllner Schankstuben, Friedrichsgracht 50. Follow the Spree along the south side of Museumsinsel. A nice place to stop for a beer or *schnitzel.* Old-fashioned atmosphere.

Probierstube, 11 Sophienstr. A little wine bar in a scenic restored street near the Sophienkirche. Open Mon.-Fri. 8am-1pm and 3-7pm. If it's full, try the larger beer garden just up the street, on the corner of Grosse Hamburger Str.

Sights

East Berlin harbors evidence of an historic Berlin that seems almost entirely missing on the western side. But keep an eye out for the post-war city: Names such as Liebknecht, Luxemburg, and Thälmann on streets and squares; the emphasis given to classic poets Heinrich Heine and Georg Büchner in bookstores, parks, and statuary; the monuments to revolutionaries and to the victims and resisters of fascism. If you don't recognize many of these new names, ask an East Berliner.

Whichever cross-over point you choose, your first view of Berlin will be **Friedrichstrasse,** which is slated to emerge as Eastern Europe's most luxurious commercial thoroughfare. All but the most famous buildings along Unter den Linden have been destroyed, but towards downtown, the eighteenth-century buildings have been carefully restored to their original Prussian splendor, and the famous statue of Frederick the Great atop his horse looks on. The first massive building to your left is the **Deutsche Staatsbibliothek.** Walk into the courtyard and read Brecht's wonderful poem *Questions of a reading worker* (in German). Beyond the library is **Humboldt Universität,** where Hegel and Fichte worked. Next door, the old "New Watch House," designed by the famous Prussian architect Friedrich Schinkel, is today the somber **Monument to the Victims of Fascism and Militarism.** Both a commemoration of the victims and a fearful warning against the crimes of fascism, it gives you an idea of how concrete war and peace are for the Germans. The honor guard in front changes on the hour, with the full ceremony on Wednesdays at 2:30pm. Across the way is **Bebelplatz,** the site of Hitler's notorious book burnings, now named for the old Social Democratic Party leader, August Bebel. The building with the curved facade is the **Alte Bibliothek.** On the other side of the square is the handsome **Deutsche Staatsoper,** fully rebuilt from original sketches by Knobelsdorf. The most striking of the monumental buildings is the **Zeughaus,** now the **Museum of German History.** From the museum you can enter the courtyard and see the tormented faces of Andreas Schlütter's "Dying Warriors"—so prophetic of Prussia's fate.

Berlin's most impressive ensemble of eighteenth-century buildings is a few blocks south of Unter den Linden at **Platz der Akademie,** graced by the twin cathedrals of the **Deutscher Dom** and the **Französischer Dom.** Enclosing the far end of the square, the classical **Schauspielhaus,** designed by Schinkel, is Berlin's most elegant concert space and hosts many international orchestras and classical performers. The square around these buildings is being rebuilt with cafes and shops.

Unter den Linden, as it crosses the bridge, opens out onto Marx-Engels-Platz. To the right is the **Altes Museum** with a big polished granite bowl in front, and the multiple domed **Berliner Dom** (Berlin Cathedral). The cathedral's interior is being restored, but it is possible to visit. (Open daily 10am-noon and 1-5pm. Admission 1.55M, students 0.80M.) Behind the Altes Museum lie three other enormous museums, and the ruins (now being restored) of a fourth. The ensemble, a spectacular jungle of pediments, porticoes, and colonnades, is known as **Museumsinsel** (museum island).

Crossing another bridge brings you to the **Marx-Engels-Forum** (not Platz), a park and "conceptual memorial" consisting of steel tablets engraved with images of worker struggle and protest, centered on a twin statue of Marx and Engels. Behind the forum you will see the twin spires of the **Nikolaikirche,** and the single tower of the **Rotes Rathaus,** Berlin's famous town hall. The Nikolaikirche is Berlin's oldest building, dating from about 1230. A small museum inside has exhibits from the early history of the city. (Open Mon. 10am-5pm, Thurs. 10am-6pm, Fri. 10am-4pm, Sat. 10am-6pm and Sun. 10am-5pm. Admission 1.05M, students 0.50M.) The reconstructed city kernel about the church is very popular and crowded, and features a range of historic buildings including the Knoblauchhaus and Ephraim-Palais. Another early church, the fifteenth-century **Mariankirche,** stands on the wide open plaza before the **Fernsehturm** (television tower), which offers fabulous views of both Berlins and some very expensive food. (Open April-Oct. daily 8am-11pm; Nov.-March daily 9am-11pm; open the 2nd and 4th Tues. of each month 1-11pm only. Tower admission 3M, students 1.50M; telecafé admission 5M, students 2.50M.) Just beyond the tower is the new **Alexanderplatz,** the modern center of town. Still a favorite meeting spot for Berliners, it has become a much quieter and less chaotic place than in Alfred Döblin's troubled times.

Northeast of Alexanderplatz is **Sophienstrasse,** a beautifully restored street on the yard in the baroque **Sophienkirche.** Two reminders of Berlin's great Jewish community lie nearby. At the end of Grosse Hamburgerstrasse as it intersects with Oranienburgerstrasse are the remains of the **Alter Jüdishe Friedhof.** Destroyed by the Nazis, it is now a quiet park. A single marker has been replaced on the grounds, that of the famous philosopher Moses Mendelsohn. Down Oranienburgerstrasse, at #31, is the burnt-out shell of Berlin's major synagogue. Torched by Nazis on

Kristallnacht, November 9, 1938, it has been left unrestored. A sign on the side of the building reads simply "Never forget this."

Take Oranienburgerstrasse farther down to Friedrichstrasse and bear right to reach the **House of Bertolt Brecht,** Chausseestr. 125. If you understand German you might want to take a guided tour which is sometimes given in a flamboyant Brechtian style. (Open Tues.-Fri. 10am-noon, Thurs. also 5-7pm, Sat. 9:30am-1:30pm.) Just before Brecht's house, the **Dorotheenstädtische Friedhof** contains the graves of a dazzling host of German luminaries, including Brecht, Fichte, and Hegel. (Open 10am-7pm.) From there you might want to head eastward into the residential district of Prenzlauerberg, which appears much the way it did in pre-war Berlin.

The powerful **Soviet War Memorial,** at S-Bahnhof Treptower Park, is a mammoth promenade built with marble taken from Hitler's Chancellery. The Soviets dedicated the site in 1948, honoring the soldiers of the Red Army who fell in World War II, and adorned massive granite slabs along the walk with quotations from Stalin. The memorial sits in the middle of **Treptower Park,** a spacious wood ideal for picnics. The neighborhood adjoining the park is known for its pleasant waterside cafes and handsome suburban mansions (most now divided among several families or used by one of the Academies).

An enjoyable way to take in the city is by boat. The **Weisse Flotte ship service** can take you on a journey around the city's waterways. For reservations, check with the **Verkehrspavillion Treptow** at the dock (tel. 271 23 27), just by the Treptower Park S-Bahn station.

Museums

The collections of the three museums on the Museumsinsel are astoundingly broad. When buying tickets, always ask for the student price; you'll be asked only rarely to present an IUS card, but note that the ISIC is *not* recognized in the DDR.

Pergamonmuseum, Kupfergraben (tel. 220 03 81), Museumsinsel. One of the world's great museums, the scale of its exhibits is mind-boggling: the Babylonian Ishtar Gate, the Roman Market Gate of Miletus, and one of the ancient wonders of the world, the majestic Pergamon Altar. These were all shipped to Berlin by zealous archeologists and reassembled in huge halls. The museum also houses extensive collections of Greek, Assyrian, Islamic, and Far Eastern Art. Open Wed.-Thurs. and Sat.-Sun. 9am-6pm, Fri. 10am-6pm. Admission 1.05M plus 0.20M mandatory baggage check.

Nationalgalerie, Bodestr. 1020 (tel. 220 03 81), Museumsinsel. An excellent collection of German expressionist art, with works by Feininger, Kokoschka, and the Brücke school. Open Wed.-Thurs. and Sat.-Sun. 9am-6pm, Fri. 10am-6pm. Admission 1.05M, students 0.50M.

Bodemuseum, Monbijou-Brücke (tel. 220 03 81), Museumsinsel. A world-class exhibit of Egyptian art, as well as late Gothic wood sculptures and fifteenth- to eighteenth-century paintings. Open Wed.-Thurs. and Sat.-Sun. 9am-6pm, Fri. 10am-6pm. Admission 1.05M, students 0.50M.

Museum für Deutsche Geschichte, Unter den Linden 2 (tel. 200 05 91). A detailed exhibit recounting the history of the earth from the advent of *homo sapiens* to the coming of socialism. The major East German presentation of its historical self-understanding. Open Mon.-Thurs. 9am-7pm, Sat.-Sun. 9am-4pm. Admission 0.60M, students 0.30M.

Altes Museum, Lustgarten, next door to the Berliner Dom. Belies its name with an exhibit of twentieth-century paintings, largely of the socialist-realist school. On its eastern side, accessible by a smaller, difficult-to-find door is the **Kupferstichkabinett,** a stellar collection of lithographs and drawings by various Renaissance masters, including many Dürers and the sublime illustration Botticelli drew for the *Divine Comedy.* Open Wed.-Thurs. and Sat.-Sun. 9am-6pm, Fri. 10am-6pm. Lithograph and drawing section open Mon.-Thurs. 9am-noon and 1-5pm, Fri. 10am-noon and 1-5pm. Admission 1.05M, students 0.50M.

Otto Nagel Haus, Märkisches Ufer 16-18 (tel. 279 19 73). A collection of proletarian art from the Nationalgalerie. It includes works by Käthe Kolwitz, and an exciting collection of photomontage by the famous satirist John Herzfeld. Open Mon.-Tues., Thurs., and Sun. 10am-6pm, Wed. 10am-8pm. Admission 1.05M, students 0.50M.

Entertainment

Nightlife

The local population gathers in neighborhood *Kneipen,* cafes, or *Weinstuben.* To hunt for *Bierkneipen,* head north across the river from Bahnhof Friedrichstrasse to the bars around the intersections of Friedrichstr. with Oranienburgerstr. and Wilhelm-Pieck-Str., or try Prenzlauerberg. Remember that daytrippers must leave East Berlin by midnight.

Kleine Melodie, Friedrichstr. 127. A lively discotheque. Cover 2.50M. Open Mon. and Wed.-Thurs. 9pm-4am, Fri.-Sat. 8pm-4am, Sun. 9pm-3am.

Französische 47, Französischestr. 47, near the French Cathedral. On Tues. and Fri.-Sat., they have disco dancing; Wed., German music; the 3rd Thurs. of each month, jazz. Open Tues. and Thurs. 7pm-midnight, Fri.-Sat. 8pm-2am.

Prenzlauer Café, Prenzlauer Allee 27. A trendy disco. Jazz Wed. evenings. Cover 1.60M. Open nightly 7:30pm-1am.

Alextreff Tanz Café, Rathauspassage, across from the Fernsehturm, and **Jugendtanz** at the base of the Fernsehturm. Both very popular dance spots among locals, but a somewhat sterile atmosphere. The latter is dominated by a teenage crowd. Long lines. Open nightly 6:30pm-midnight.

Milch-Mix-Mocca Bar, Karl-Marx-Allee 35. An odd but enticing ice-cream bar. Huge, with a merry crowd. The only alcohol is liqueurs. Open daily until midnight.

Operncafé, Unter den Linden 5, and **Café Linden Corso,** Unter den Linden 17, are pretentious establishments that cater to tourists and the East German elite. Dancing in the evenings (cover 2.60-3.10M). Both have "night bars" that stay open until 4 or 5am. Also popular among the young. Both open Mon.-Fri. 9am-6:30pm and 7:30pm-midnight, Sat.-Sun. 9am-6:30pm and 7:30pm-midnight.

Theater and Music

Cultural activity is one of East Berlin's strong points; in many of the houses listed below, you'll find more West Berliners than Easterners.

Theater listings are available in the monthly pamphlet *Kultur in Berlin,* available in West Berlin. In this brochure, as in its Eastern equivalent *Wohin in Berlin,* you'll also find notices of concerts in the courtyard of the old Arsenal, on the Schlossinel Köpenick, or in the parks. Tickets for most, but not all, cultural events are available at the *Zentralbesucherdienst* at the Palasthotel, at Karl-Liebknecht-Str. and Spandauerstr. (tel. 212 52 58), or at window #1 of the **Reisebüro der DDR.** If you know what you want, go to the auditorium yourself and avoid the 10% commission charged by these offices. Unfortunately, most theaters close from at least mid-July to late August.

Metropol Theater, opposite Bahnhof Friedrichstr. (tel. 200 06 51 or 207 17 39). Site of larger theatrical reviews, and popular and classical concerts. Tickets are hard to come by; try stopping by the theater at 6pm on the night of a performance.

Deutsche Staatsoper, Unter den Linden 7, (tel. 205 40). The leading opera company of Berlin, East and West. Ballet and classical music, too. Tickets 3-15M. Box office open Mon.-Sat. noon-6pm, Sun. 4-6pm, and 1 hr. before performances.

Berliner Ensemble, Bertolt-Brecht Platz, (tel. 288 80). Turn left out of Bahnhof Friedrichstr. and cross the river. The famous theater established by Brecht still specializes in his plays, and is the country's leading stage. Tickets 1-12M. Box office open Mon.-Fri. 11am-1:30pm and 2-6pm, Sat.-Sun. 1 hr. before performances. Closed early July-early Sept.

Deutsches Theater, Schumannstr. 13a-14 (tel. 287 12 25). The place for classical drama: Goethe, Schiller, Shakespeare (in German), etc . . . . Also a smaller theater, **Kammerspiel** (tel. 287 12 26), which stages newer and sometimes highly controversial plays.

Maxim-Gorki-Theater, Am Kastanienwäldchen (tel. 207 17 90), just off Unter den Linden. The place to see the best contemporary East German works.

Die Distle, Degnerstr. 9 (tel. 376 51 74), and Friedrichstr. 101 (tel. 207 12 91). A cabaret for political satire. Box office open Tues.-Fri. 3-7pm.

Das Schauspielhaus, Platz der Akademie. Grosser Konzertsall (tel. 227 21 29); Kammermusiksaal (tel. 227 21 22). The home of the Berliner Symphonie Orchester. Opulent.

Komische Oper, Behrenstr. 55-57 (tel. 220 27 61). Its post-war reputation was developed by its famous director, Felsenstein; some consider it better than the Staatsoper. The repertoire isn't all comic.

Potsdam

If you're in Berlin (East or West), you should definitely find time to visit Potsdam, city of Frederick the Great and palatial seat of the Prussian empire. Don't, however, try to visit Potsdam on your East Berlin day visa. It's not worth the risk, and it's not that difficult to arrange an overnight visa. Being caught in Potsdam without a valid visa can mean a serious fine. If you're driving to Potsdam from West Berlin and have advance visa arrangements, note that it is much quicker to cross the border at Drewetz than to go over Checkpoint Charlie.

The 600-acre **Sanssouci Park** houses four baroque palaces and countless exotic pavilions. The largest of the royal quartet is the **Neues Palais,** the royal family's summer residence. Inside is the nineteenth-century *Grottensaal,* a glittering reception room whose ribbed walls are plastered with seashells and semi-precious stones. The palace also houses a luxurious cafe (open 10am-6pm) and a theater, open all summer, with afternoon and evening performances. The original royal domicile, **Schloss Sanssouci,** is perhaps the best place to judge the vagaries of rococo taste. Next door, the fabulous **Bildergalerie** sports a gilded ceiling and works by Caravaggio, van Dyck, and Rubens. (Admission 0.50M.) **Schloss Charlottenhof,** a prime example of early Romanticism is designed to blend in with its landscaped gardens and grape arbors. Nearby lie the **Römische Bäder.** (Admission 0.50M.) Overlooking the park from the north, the pseudo-Italian **Orangerie** is famous for its *Raffaelsaal* with 67 dubious copies after the master. The palace tower offers an excellent view of the park and cityscape. The most bizarre of the park's pavilions are its "oriental" houses: The **Drachenhaus** is around the corner from the Orangerie, while the **Chinesisches Teehaus** is a gold-plated opium dream. The baroque Buddha on the roof looks like Neptune with a parasol. (All palaces open March-Sept. daily 9am-5pm; Oct.-Feb. daily 9am-4pm; all closed the 2nd Sun. of each month. Admission 1.05M, students 0.50M; extra admissions noted above.)

Potsdam's second major park, the **Neuer Garten,** also contains several royal residences. The most worthwhile is **Schloss Cecilienhof,** site of the 1945 signing of the Potsdam treaty, which sealed the political fate of modern Germany. The exhibit on the Potsdam conference assumes a strikingly neutral political tone on the issue of East-West relations. (Open May-Sept. daily 8am-5:15pm; Oct.-April daily 9am-4:15pm. Admission 1.05M, students 0.50M.)

The area around the **Alter Markt** is dominated by the classical dome of the **Nikolaikirche.** (Open Mon. 2-5:30pm, Tues.-Sat. 10am-5:30pm, Sun. 11:30am-5:30pm.) All that remains of the original city palace that once occupied this site is the Orangerie. The national **Filmmuseum** within features historical exhibits and daily films, primarily Eastern European, with an occasional West German or American feature. (Museum open daily 10am-5:30pm. Admission 1.75M, students 1M. Stop by or check with the tourist office for film times. Matinees 0.75M, evening shows 1.50M.) Across from the Marktplatz, at the base of the Lange Brücke, **Weisse Flotte boats** (tel. 210 90) depart for various destinations.

The **Brandenburger Tor,** Potsdam's monumental arch, rises above regal Platz der Nationen. From here, **Klement-Gottwald-Strasse,** a charming cobblestone street lined with restaurants and shops, leads down to the nineteenth-century **Peter-Pauls-Kirche.** One block before the church, Friedrich-Ebert-Strasse leads left to the red-brick **Dutch Quarter.** One block farther is the **Nauener Tor,** a gate designed to mimic the appearance of an English castle. The sumptuous if somewhat decrepit mansions along **Hegelallee** hint at Potsdam's former grandeur. Follow Hegelallee two blocks to reach the graceful **Jägertor,** another of the triumphal gateways into the downtown area.

The **tourist office,** Friedrich-Ebert-Str. 5 (tel. 211 00), has information on local happenings, as well as a modest city map. (Open Mon. and Wed.-Fri. 9am-1pm and 2-5pm, Tues. 10am-1pm and 2-6pm.) The best source of information in English is the staff of the **Hotel Potsdam,** across the street on Lange Brücke (tel. 46 31). (Rooms 95M per person.) Most budget travelers will find themselves at **Intercamping-platz Riegelspitze,** 5km outside of the village of Werder, on the other side of Lake Havel from Potsdam. Bus D-31 runs from Potsdam Hauptbahnhof to the campground. (7.50M per person, 6M per tent.)

The main neighborhood for eating in Potsdam is in front of the **Stadttor,** at the head of Klement-Gottwald-Str. Here you'll find the fancy **Restaurant Am Stadttor;** the main salon is usually booked solid, but the upstairs **Speisebar** offers entrees for 4-5M. (Both open until 9pm.) Across the street, **Gastmahl des Meeres,** Klement-Gottwald-Str. 72, offers seafood dishes for 7-8M. (Open Mon.-Fri. 9am-6pm, Sat.-Sun. 10am-3pm.) **Bolgar,** nearby at Klement-Gottwald-Str. 36, specializes in Bulgarian cuisine (5-7M). In the Sanssouci area the only hot food is at the **Gaststätte Charlottenhof,** Geschwister-Scholl-Str. (Entrees 4-6M. Open 9am-6pm.)

Weimar

Weimar epitomizes the paradoxical sway of German history, encompassing both the darkest elements of its barbarism and the extraordinary range of its humanism. Birthplace of the Bauhaus, the city where Germany's first republic was founded, and site of Buchenwald, Weimar has been home to Cranach, Wieland, Goethe, Schiller, Herder, Liszt, and (not emphasized by officials) Nietzsche.

Before you visit any sights, stop by the **Zentralkasse** (next to the tourist office on Marktstr.) for admission tickets. Most individual museum tickets cost 1.05M; many are available only here and not in the museums. You can also buy a six-museum pass for 3.05M. (All museums listed below, except the Schillerhaus, are open Tues.-Sun. 9am-1pm and 2-4pm; Schillerhaus open Wed.-Mon. 9am-1pm and 2-4pm.) The city's cultural events also fall under this office's cultural monopoly; check here for theater and concert tickets. (Open Mon. 10am-12:30pm and 1:30-5pm, Tues.-Fri. 9am-12:30pm and 1:30-5pm, Sat.-Sun. 8:30am-12:45pm and 1:45-4:30pm.)

Not only one of Germany's greatest poets, but also an active botanist, geologist, government officer, and artist, Goethe is Weimar's local hero *par excellence.* **Goethehaus,** Frauenplan 1, where he resided from 1782 until his death in 1832, gives a chronological account of his life—note the Marxist treatment of *Faust.* The house's rear chambers, set now as Goethe prescribed in his will, reveal the image the poet wished to reserve for posterity, while the six front rooms show how Goethe presented himself to his contemporaries.

A good English guide, *Goethe's House on the Frauenplan at Weimar,* explains all the exhibits (3M). Down Frauentorstrasse, the cobbled **Marktplatz** is presided over by the pseudo-Gothic **Rathaus,** and the colorful Renaissance facade of the **Lucas Cranach Haus,** where the famous painter spent his final years. Adjoining the Marktplatz is the handsome **Herderkirche,** where the philosopher of the same name once preached regularly. The **Kirms-Krackow Haus,** Jakobstr. 10, documents the life and times of Herder, offering a well-developed Marxist perspective on the *Sturm und Drang* literary movement, the most turbulent and rich period of German literary history. Retrace your steps to the Marktplatz, crossing over Frauentorstrasse; **Schillerstrasse,** a picturesque, shop-lined pedestrian zone crammed with antiques and bookstores, will appear on your right one block up. At the end of the street, the **Schillerhaus,** Schillerstr. 12, former residence of the playwright, complements the Goethehaus, complete with originally penned drafts, early editions of plays, and a biographical chronicle of the life of Goethe's friend and sometime literary rival.

Around the corner, the pair are reconciled in stone before the **Deutsches Nationaltheater,** where their works were first performed. The contemporary repertoire is varied, but still features performances of the classic works. The **Wittumpalais** and **Wielandmuseum,** located across the square at Am Palais 3, devotes itself to the life of the poet Wieland.

On the far side of the Marktplatz, inside the Schloss is the **Schlossmuseum,** Burgplatz 4. The first floor is devoted to Cranach, the upper floors contain a collection of minor nineteenth- and twentieth-century works, as well as a Bauhaus exhibit that details the history of some of the work of this famous school, once located in Weimar. The display shows the remarkable extent to which these few designers determine, even now, our everyday environment. The neighboring **Park an der Ilm,** landscaped by Goethe, contains numerous worthwhile pavilions in eighteenth-century style. **Goethes Gartenhaus,** Corona-Schröter Str., provided some of his finest moments of inspiration. At the edge of the park is the **Franz Liszt Haus,** Marienstr. 17, where the composer spent the last years of his life. The instruments and furnishings are supposed to be original, but given Liszt's torrid love-life, the small single bed seems unlikely. The conservatory he founded, now the *Hochschule für Musik "Franz Liszt,"* holds an international seminar annually during the last two weeks of July, accompanied by daily concerts. **Schloss Belvedere** at the park's end, the summer residence of the royal family, houses a rococo museum. (Open May-Sept. Tues.-Wed. 9am-1pm and 2-5pm, Fri. 10am-1pm and 2-5pm, Sat.-Sun. 9am-noon and 2-6pm.) The Belvedere Express bus leaves from the Goetheplatz (Mon.-Fri. every hr. on the ½hr. 12:30-6:30pm, Sat.-Sun. every 30 min.).

Also south of the town, the **Historischer Friedhof** contains, among other notable memorabilia, the **Tombs of Goethe and Schiller** and the **Denkmal der Märzgefallenen,** designed by Bauhaus-founder Gropius to honor those killed in the 1919 revolution, the truncated political moment between World War I and the Weimar Republic when Germany almost became independently socialist. The monument's completion in 1923 led to the Bauhaus's expulsion from Weimar.

Bus #1 connects Weimar's train station with Goetheplatz in the center of town. From there, the **tourist office,** Marktstr. 4 (tel. 21 73), is not far away. Walk out Geleitstr. until you come to the Herderkirche, then walk right along Dimitroffstr. to the marketplace; you'll find the office around the block to your right. (Open Mon. 10am-noon and 1-5pm, Tues.-Fri. 9am-noon and 1-5pm, Sat. 8:30am-noon, closed Sun.)

A popular tourist destination, Weimar does not lend itself to a spontaneous trip. The hotels, hostels, and campgrounds are often full; you might have to take a room in one of the small towns nearby. The bother of the daily trip may be worth the chance to become familiar with one of these small, historic spots. The best of the Interhotels is **Hotel Elephant,** am Marktplatz (tel. 614 71), with comfortable accommodations and a superb location. (Rooms 100M per person.) If you want to try to wrangle permission for a non-Interhotel establishment, look into one of the four youth hostels in Weimar, all in the south part of town. The people at **Maxim Gorki,** Zum Wilden Graben 12 (tel. 31 71), have been relatively receptive to foreigners; you might also try **15 August,** Humboldstr. 17 (tel. 40 21), or **Ernst Thälmann,** Windmühlenstr. 16 (tel. 20 76). **Albert Kuntz Hostel** (tel. 672 16), is at Weimar-Buchenwald, about 8km out of town. The closest international campsite, **Campingplatz Weissensee am Terrassenbad,** is more than two hours away; take the train to Erfurt, then to Sommerdä, and then a bus to the village of Weissensee. The campground is about 2km by foot from the central bus stop.

The **Elephantkeller** on the Markt (*not* the expensive hotel-restaurant upstairs) has inexpensive, well-prepared food. (Open Mon. and Sat. 11:30am-8pm, Tues.-Fri. 11:30am-10pm.) For a fantastic, though slightly expensive, meal, go inside the Hotel Elephant to the downstairs **Restaurant Belvedere;** highly recommended is their *Kalbsteak Sankt Gallen* (lamb with cheese sauce, 13.55M) and their *Thüringer Bachforelle* (local brook trout, priced by weight). (Open Sun.-Fri. 6:30am-midnight, Sat. 6:30am-1am, last hot orders 10:45pm.) **Weimarhalle,** Schwanseestr. 3, is a bit hidden in a courtyard and popular with locals. (Meals 3-6M. Open Thurs.-Sun. 9am-11pm.)

Near Weimar

Follow Ernst-Thälmann-Strasse directly north of town to reach the chilling remains of the Nazi concentration camp **Buchenwald,** also accessible by bus from the train station. The Nazis' largest center for holding political prisoners, Buchenwald is charged with questions of the political and moral responsibility for fascism. The heart-wrenching display raises in particular the issue of the role of capitalism in Hitler's rise. Agree or disagree with the interpretation, you may leave feeling less smug about your own moral ascendancy. The heavy thoughts are further burdened by the lonely bell tower on the hillside and a stark monument by East Germany's leading sculptor, Fritz Cramer. Films documenting the camp's history are shown daily at 10am and 1pm.

Jena, a few dozen kilometers east of Weimar, was once home to Germany's premier university, today known as Friedrich Schiller Universität. At the turn of the nineteenth century, the Romantic movement sunk its first roots into German soil here under Hölderlin, Schlegel, Novalis, and Tieck, while philosophers Schiller, Hegel, Fichte, and Schelling argued for a new conception of intellectual and political freedom. The **Schiller-Gedenkstätte,** on Schillergässchen, is housed in the philosopher-poet's original residence, where he dwelt from 1789 to 1799. (Open April-Oct. Tues.-Sun. 11am-2pm.) The **Optisches Museum,** Karl-Zeiss Platz 2, pays tribute to Karl Zeiss, who launched the city's economy and its most renowned industry: high quality optical equipment for microscopes, glasses, cameras, and telescopes. (Open Tues.-Fri. 9am-12:45pm and 1:15-5:30pm, Sat. 9am-12:15pm and 12:45-4pm.) The **University Tower** features a Panorama Cafe which lives up to its name. **Erfurt,** about a half-hour train ride west of Weimar, is the beautiful Thuringian merchant city where Marx's classic "Erfurt Programm" was first presented. **Tourist information** is available near the train station at 37 Bahnhofstr. (tel. 262 67). The **Krämer Brücke,** like the Ponte Vecchio in Florence, is a fourteenth-century bridge lined with merchant stalls and antiquarian shops.

Leipzig

Leipzig is famous for books and music. The university (founded in 1409) stands for an illustrious tradition of learning that embraces the names of Leibnitz, Lessing, and Nietzsche, among others. Book merchants have translated all this local learning into a thriving industry; the *Altstadt* is still crammed with bookstores, and three major international book fairs take place here annually. Leipzig's reputation as a city of music was launched in 1723 when Johann Sebastian Bach settled here. The handsome churches he filled with the sound of his early works are well-preserved. Today, the *Leipzig Gewandhaus Orchester,* under conductor Kurt Masur, ranks as one of the world's finest. The **Gewandhaus** was destroyed in the war, but the new hall has been built with modern acoustic technology. The orchestra is often on tour, and when it's at home, tickets are tough to come by.

The **Museum der Bildenen Kunsten,** Georgi-Dimitroff-Platz 1, has a fabulous collection of old masters' as well as recent artists' works. (Open Tues.-Fri. 9am-6pm, Sat. 9am-5pm, Sun. 9am-1pm. Admission 1.50M, students 0.80M.) The fortified towers of the **Neues Rathaus** dominate the *Altstadt* in the south. Nearby, just off the Marktplatz, is the **Thomaskirche** where J. S. Bach served as cantor. Bach's grave lies just in front of the altar. Mozart and Mendelssohn also performed in this church, and Richard Wagner was confirmed here. Next door, the **Bach Gedenkstätte** (Bach Memorial), Thomaskirchof 16, chronicles Bach's work and years in Leipzig, 1723-1750. (Open Tues.-Sun. 9am-5pm.) The heart of the city throbs within the **Marktplatz,** a colorful cobbled square guarded by the charming **Altes Rathaus.** Inside, the **Museum für Geschichte der Stadt Leipzig** recounts the history of the city. (Open Tues.-Sun. 9am-5pm. Admission 1M, students 0.50M.) Behind the Altes Rathaus, on Nikolaistr., the 800-year-old **Nikolaikirche** hosted many premieres of Bach's works, including the *St. John Passion.* Continuing away from the Marktplatz, take Universitätstr. to reach the modern **Karl-Marx Universität.** Small morsels of the pre-war university, embedded in bits and pieces about the campus, are all that remain of the original institution.

From Karl-Marx-Platz, in front of the university, take tram #15 to Messegelände to reach the **Russische Kirche,** a gold onion-domed memorial erected in 1912 in honor of the Russian dead of the Battle of Nations (Völkerschlacht) of 1813. Follow Semmelweisstr. two blocks farther and turn left to reach the **Deutsche Bücherei,** housing a small exhibit on the history of alphabets and books. (Open Mon.-Sat. 9am-4pm. Free.) The **Völkerschlachtdenkmal,** the most grandiose of the over 70 monuments in Leipzig commemorating the heroes of the Battle of Nations, towers in the Sudfriedhof. To the north of the *Altstadt* lies the eighteenth-century **Gohliser Schlösschen,** a delicate urban palace of modest proportions.

Leipzig's **tourist office** is at Sachsenplatz 1 (tel. 795 90). From the train station, walk through Platz der Republik and bear right past the Interhotel. They sell a small booklet containing a map of sights, and a list of restaurants and hotels (0.50M). If you read German, pick up the excellent *Atlas Stadtführer* (8.90M) as well. If they try to force you into a fancy hotel, request **Hotel Merkur,** which is definitely the best. Otherwise, try the **Intercamping-platz** in Auensee, a 30-minute commute; take tram #11 or 28 from the Hauptbahnhof to Wahren and follow the signs. (Camping in summer 16M per person; in winter 13M per person. Huts and bungalows only slightly more expensive. Closed to foreigners in 1987, but things may change for 1988.)

The best food buy around is the Italian fare at the **Restaurant Milano,** in the Hotel Merkur complex on Gerberstr. (Pasta dishes 10-15M. Open 11am-11pm.) **Burgkeller,** Naschmarkt 1-3, next to the Altes Rathaus, is Leipzig's oldest restaurant. The upstairs dining hall serves the best food, but it's usually packed or closed. Downstairs is a great place for breakfast (4.50M), and there's usually room. There's also a lively bar on the premises. **Auerbachs Keller,** Mädlerpassage, just off Grimmaischestr., is famous as the setting of one of the scenes in Goethe's *Faust;* the interior wall frescoes depict scenes from the play. (¼ chicken 5.50M. Open 9am-10pm.)

Dresden

Standing on one of the bridges spanning the Elbe and looking toward Dresden, you see ornate story-book spires and domes, the baroque Dresden of legend. The equally legendary destruction of the royal Saxon seat is also visible; the palace and the vaulted Frauenkirche are by and large the rubble that British and American bombing raids left them in. Dresden, though, remains East Germany's *Kunststadt,* its artistic and architectural gem. From the terrace and galleries along the river to the stately suburbs lush with fruit trees, Dresden has the feel of quiet elegance and culture. The number of artists who continue to live here attests to this abiding magnetism.

The exquisite baroque palace **Zwinger** now contains half of Dresden's museums. The **Gemäldegalerie Alte Meister** is one of Europe's oldest and best painting collections; its star piece is Raphael's *Sistine Madonna.* (Open June-Sept. Tues.-Sun. 9am-6pm; Oct.-May Tues.-Sun. 10am-4pm. Admission 1.55M, students 0.80M.) The **Historisches Museum** is an ornamental collection of weaponry. (Open March-Oct. Thurs.-Tues. 9am-5pm; Nov.-Feb. Thurs.-Tues. 9am-4pm. Admission 0.80M, students 0.50M.) The **Porzellansammlung** traces the history of Dresden's famous porcelain. (Open Mon.-Thurs. 9:30am-4pm, Sat.-Sun. 9am-4pm.) On the hour, inside the palace courtyard, the sky-blue porcelain bells of the *Glockenspiel* gate chime. The northern wing of the palace, a later addition, was designed by Gottfried Semper, revolutionary activist and master architect. Semper's famed Opera House, the **Semper-Oper,** echoes the robust style of the palace wing. Its painstaking restoration, both inside and out, has made it the major Dresden attraction, and the company now housed in it gains in reputation each day.

Across the street from Zwinger are the ruins of the old residential **Palace of Saxony's Electors and Kings.** The decrepit complex—being restored piece by piece—embraces the reconstructed **Katholische Hofkirche** (Catholic cathedral), which allows an interesting comparison with the **Protestant Kreuzkirche** (Protestant church) on the Altmarkt. The **Kreuzchor,** one of the world's most famous boys' choirs, sings in the latter. On the wall of the alley leading to the main entrance of the Catholic cathedral is the *Fürstenzug* (Procession of Kings), a pictorial in porcelain tiles tracing the rule of Saxony since the Middle Ages. Around the corner, the medieval **Stalhof** was once the stables of the Saxon royal family. (Open 9am-4pm.)

From the Catholic cathedral, the sixteenth-century **Brühlsche Terrasse** offers a beautiful view of the River Elbe (best at sunset). Turn right at the end of the terrace to reach the **Albertinum,** another of Dresden's fabulous museum complexes. The **Gemäldegalerie der Neuen Meister** presents a collection of nineteenth- and twentieth-century works, including Gauguins and Monets. The **Grünes Gewölbe,** one of Dresden's premier tourist attractions, is a dazzling display of priceless coins and gem-studded treasures. Note the carved cherry pit with over 180 miniature heads. (Open June-Sept. Fri.-Wed. 9am-6pm; Oct.-May Fri.-Wed. 10am-4pm; often very long lines, so arrive at least 15 min. before opening. Admission 2.05M, students 1.05M.)

From the Albertinum, a walk to the Neumarkt will take you to what was once Germany's most splendid Protestant church. The ruins of the **Frauenkirche,** now covered with trees and vegetation, have been left as a memorial to the city's destruction. Jog south to the beginning of Ernst-Thälmann-Str. where the **Landhaus,** an eighteenth-century neoclassical palace, houses the **Museum für Geschichte der Stadt Dresden.** The exhibit contains some sobering photos of the city from 1945. (Open Mon.-Thurs. and Sat. 10am-6pm, Sun. 10am-4pm. Admission 1.05M, students 0.40M.)

Paradoxically, Dresden's **Neustadt** is now the oldest part of the city; it escaped the worst of the bombing. In front of the Catholic church, the picturesque Georgi-Dimitroff Brücke spans the Elbe to the **Goldener Ritter,** a gleaming gold-plated statue of Friedrich August II. The pedestrian **Strasse der Befreiung,** a cobbled, tree-lined avenue of shops and restaurants, extends from the river bank back to **Platz der Einheit,** still surrounded by handsome nineteenth-century mansions. Readers of Vonnegut can take tram #10 from the Hauptbahnhof to the slaughterhouses *(Schlachthofringe);* little-changed since they were pressed into service as a camp for prisoners of war.

Dresden's **tourist office** is at Pragerstr. 10-11 (tel. 495 50 25), a five-minute walk from the train station in the pedestrian zone. (Open April-Sept. Mon.-Sat. 9am-8pm, Sun. 9am-2pm; Oct.-March Mon.-Sat. 9am-6pm, Sun. 9am-2pm.) There are five campgrounds in *Bezirk* Dresden. The closest and best is **Campingplatz Moritzburg,** although it's still a good hour away by bus and on foot. From the Hauptbahnhof take the Moritzburg or the Moritzburg/Radeburg bus and get off at Sonnenland. (Camping 10M per person, 6M per tent.) If you book hotel accommodations, you'll probably stay in one of the three Interhotels on Pragerstrasse. If you're very lucky, you may be able to convince the authorities to let you sleep at either the **Jugendherberge Rudi Arndt,** Hubnerstr. 11 (tel. 47 06 67), out Juri-Gagarinstr., which begins behind the main station, or the **Jugendherberge Schloss Eckberg,** Bautznerstr. 134 (tel. 544 03), accessible by tram #11.

For a filling meal head for the **Kügelgenhaus,** Str. der Befreiung 13 in the Neustadt, a fine restaurant stuffed with historical mementos. Try the *Broilerspiese auf Curryreis* (skewered barbecued chicken with curried rice) for 6.65M. (Open daily 11am-midnight. *Bierkeller* downstairs open daily 5pm-midnight.) **Restaurant Elbflorenz** in the Hotel Astoria at Ernst-Thälmann Platz, is a little expensive by DDR standards, but truly delicious. Try their daily Saxon soup special (4-7M), often a meal in itself. The *Schweinekeulensteak* (10.90M) and *Prager Schnitzel* (10M) are both excellent pork dishes. (Open daily 6-11am for breakfast, 11:30am-midnight for serious eating.) **Restaurant im Kultur Palast,** at the corner of Ernst-Thälmann-Str. and Galeriestr., serves uninspiring food, but is conveniently located, inexpensive, *and* open to the general public, most of whom seem to show up; arrive at odd times. The 4-6M entrees include a salad bar. (Open 11am-8pm.) For over-priced ice cream and a great view, try the **Café am Goldenen Ritter.**

If possible, take in a performance at the sumptuous **Semper-Oper.** Tickets are sold at the *Theaterkasse* in the Dresden tourist office, and through the **Reisebüro der DDR** in Berlin. The opera company is on vacation from mid-July through early September. For more pedestrian entertainment, try **Alt Dresden,** Dr. Fr. Wolf Platz right by Bahnhof Neustadt, a friendly evening hangout with great cheese platters. (Open until midnight.) **Tonne,** on Schiessgasse, behind the Albertinum, is a popular jazz club/wine cellar in the basement of a ruined building—the stuff punk club owners in West Berlin dream of. (Closed in summer, erratic schedule otherwise.)

Dresden is two hours and 150km south of Berlin, on the main Prague-Berlin rail line. Most trains use **Dresden Hauptbahnhof,** on Leninplatz, at the end of Prager-str.; a number of trains leave from a second station, **Bahnhof Neustadt,** at Dr. Fr. Wolf Platz, across the river. Trams #3 and 11 connect the two stations.

Near Dresden

Dresden lies in the fertile Elbe River valley and the countryside around the city is the most beautiful in East Germany. The area is Europe's northernmost wine-growing region, and Meissner wine is respected beyond East Germany's borders. Several kilometers down-river from Dresden, around the resort city Bad Schandau, the striking, hilly landscape is known as **Sächsische Schweiz** (Saxon Switzerland). The Bastei, Lilienstein, and Königstein are tall sandstone cliffs standing watch above the river. Take the train (or a Weisse Flotte boat) south toward Bad Schandau (or Prague) and get out at the town of **Königstein.** The fortress on the cliff is a spectacular medieval compound, protected by thick walls and impervious gates. It now houses museums on themes ranging from weaponry to porcelain, but don't let these occupy all your time here: Wander about, take the ferry across the river to the Lilienstein, or climb among the cliffs.

You can also take a train or boat trip upstream to **Meissen.** Crowded with narrow, hilly streets and teetering sixteenth- and seventeenth-century homes, Meissen brims with treasures from the eleventh century, and even older ruins. Towering above the city is the *Albrechtsburg,* a grand fortress, palace, and cathedral from which this royal Saxon city was spiritually and physically guarded. (Open daily 9am-5pm. Admission 1.05M.) Deservedly famous for its architecture, its Elbe setting, and its wine, Meissen is best known for its precious porcelain. It is here that August the Strong, Elector of Saxon and King of Poland, had built Europe's first porcelain factory, the source of its renowned Dresden china. You can tour the **Staatliche Porzellanmanufaktur** at Leninstr. from April 1 to October 31. (Open Tues.-Sun. 9am-noon and 1-4pm. Admission 1.05M.)

A short train or bus ride north from Dresden takes you to the royal hunting lodge **Moritzburg** (open Wed.-Sun. 9am-7pm; admission 2.05M, students 1.05M). The enormity of the palace, which sits in the middle of a artificial lake, is a lot more than you'd expect from a hunting lodge.

WEST GERMANY

US$1 = 1.82 Deutschmarks (DM)
CDN$1 = DM1.37
UK£1 = DM2.95
AUS$1 = DM1.30

DM1 = US$0.55
DM1 = CDN$0.73
DM1 = UK£0.34
DM1 = AUS$0.77

West Germany has risen from the ashes of World War II with a vengeance. The cities that were left in rubble in 1945 will amaze you with their shiny surfaces and sleek efficiency. Not only have cathedrals, town halls, and palaces been rebuilt stone by stone; skyscrapers have sprung up, subways have been tunneled, and every mechanized wonder imaginable has been installed.

Away from the modern metropolises, along the byways of rural areas, the old image of Germany as a land of half-timbered villages set between hills survives. Spend some time in the peaceful Harz Mountains, wandering in the hills of the Black Forest, or sailing down the Rhine. Munich is one of Europe's most enjoyable and lively cities, and you can satisfy your *Wanderlust* only an hour away in the Bavarian Alps. A bit farther north, the towns along the Romantic Road have preserved much of their late-medieval appearance. Heidelberg, Tübingen, and Freiburg in the southwest have long contributed to Germany's illustrious university tradition. Finally, for a completely different sort of landscape, explore the rolling countryside and sandy coasts of the north, or experience the casual cosmopolitanism of West Berlin and the irony of The Wall, a barrier which physically tries to close the politically open German question.

Transportation

Germany's train system is one of Europe's best and most expensive (a one-way ticket Munich-Hamburg is DM164 second-class). "D" trains are faster than "E" trains, and "IC" (inter-city) trains are speedier still, but you must pay a supplement *(Zuschlag)* for a second-class seat. (DM5 when bought from an *Automat,* DM6 on the train.) The supplement includes a *Platzkarte* (seat reservation), which normally costs DM3.50. Railpass holders are exempt from these supplements. The German Rail **Touristenkarte** entitles you to four days of unlimited second-class travel for DM164, nine days for DM246, or 16 days for DM339. Unlike international railpasses, it also gets you a reduced ticket to West Berlin through East Germany. The **Juniortouristenkarte,** available to those under 26, entitles you to nine days of unlimited second-class travel for DM165, or 16 days for DM215. Anyone under age 23 and students under 27 can buy a one-month **Tramper-Monats Ticket** for DM228—designed for German youth, but nothing prohibits its use by foreigners. Good for unlimited second-class travel on the federal railroad (Deutsche Bundesbahn-DB), the railroad-run buses (Bahnbusse), and the S-bahn (tram), it also includes the IC *Zuschlag.* Bring a photo and your passport or other proof of age, and a student ID. The **Junior-Pass,** available to people aged 18-22 and students under 27, is valid for one year and merits a 50% reduction on all rail tickets; price is DM110. The **Taschengeld-Pass** offers the same deal for everyone between 12 and 17 (DM40), and the **Familien-Pass** offers the same discount for families, single parents with children under 18, and married couples (DM130). **Rail Europ F** (DM20) is also for families and good for one year of travel in 14 countries. One adult pays the normal fare, the rest of the family pays half-price, children under 12 get 75% off. Women over 60 and men over 65 years of age, regardless of nationality, can purchase a **Senioren-Pass** (DM110) valid one year for a 50% discount on the regular fare. All these passes are available at major train stations throughout Germany. **Transalpino/BIGE** and **Twen-Tours** tickets (40-50% off) are available to those under 26, for *both* domestic and international trains.

Eurail and InterRail passholders get free passage on the S-bahn (tram), and on German bus lines run by the railroad (marked *Bahn*). This includes the popular Romantic Road bus as well as hundreds of smaller lines. In small towns these buses often serve as municipal lines. Both railpasses are valid on most ships operated by the KD (Köln-Düsseldorf) line, which sail on the Rhine and Mosel rivers. (On the hydrofoils railpasses only receive a 50% discount.) Railpasses are also valid for the ferry from Puttgarden to Rødby, Denmark. Anyone with a railpass or ticket can rent a bicycle at one of the over 270 rental shops in rail stations throughout West Germany for DM5 per day (half the standard rate). Most stations offer this service from April to October only, but some offer it the entire year. Generally you can return the bicycle to any train station that rents. For more information, pick up the brochure *Fahrrad am Bahnhof* from any train station; it includes a bicycle map and a list of train stations that rent. You can forward your bicycle by train; bring it to the station three days before you want it shipped. (DM28-41 for 200-900km. Insurance costs DM3 per DM500 insured.)

Hitching is easy and legal anywhere except on the *Autobahn.* The heavily traveled, more scenic secondary roads, *Bundesstrassen,* are good bets. Once you get a ride, figure out how far the driver is going in your direction and ask to be let off at the last rest-stop (*Tankstelle,* shown on nearly all road maps) before he or she leaves the highway. Because the *Autobahn* network crosses and splits so frequently, a sign is particularly important.

Mitfahrzentralen are offices in 40 cities that bring drivers and riders together. If you seek either a ride or riders, call the *Mitfahr* in your departure or destination city. The rider pays the driver a set fee when the two meet at the *Mitfahr* office. In addition, the *Mitfahr* charges a DM5-20 commission, which gives the riders complete insurance coverage and thus protects the driver. Write to the head office, Verband Deutscher Mitfahrzentralen e.V., Dieffenbachstr. 39, 1000 Berlin 61, Federal Republic of Germany, for a list, or check the yellow pages (*Gelbe Seiten)* under "Mitfahrzentrale."

In general, the **S-Bahn** (tram) and the **U-Bahn** (subway) that run within cities are expensive—but so phenomenally efficient that you can literally set your watch by them. Most German transport networks operate on a sort of honor system. Often you must get your ticket beforehand at an automat and then validate (*entwerten*) it in one of the little boxes either in the station or on board. Periodically an official (in civilian clothes) will come through and check for tickets. If you didn't buy one, or have one that isn't validated, you must pay a DM40 fine. Multiple tickets (*Streifenkarte*) will save you money if you stay in a town for any length of time.

Practical Information

Tourist offices, known as *Verkehrsamt* or *Verkehrsverein,* will always book rooms, and are uniformly helpful and efficient.

English is the most common second language, especially among tourist office personnel, hotel proprietors, and young people.

Currency exchange (*Wechsel*) is usually found in train stations (open 7am-11pm). Banks are generally open from 9am to noon and from 2 to 4pm. Most post offices are open Monday through Friday from 8am to 6pm, Saturday from 8am to noon. Those in train stations and airports, and the central offices in large cities, are normally open longer. For Poste Restante, inquire after *Postlagernde Briefe.*

Local phone calls cost DM0.20 for eight minutes. Short rapid beeps are the busy signal, longer-spaced beeps the ringing. Phones with green signs can be used for international calls. Dial 01188 for national information (a toll call), 00118 for international information (toll-free), and 0114 for an operator—use this for collect calls (*R-Gespräche*). With newer phones, keep an eye on the red-lit numbers, as you'll be cut off immediately if the amount reaches zero. If you use DM5 or DM1 coins, your change will not be returned after you complete your call. However, if you don't hang up, then press the green button and wait for the dial tone, you can make another call. In most areas, standard emergency numbers are used: Police (tel. 110), Ambulance (tel. 112). For long-distance calls, it is easiest to go to the post office (*Postamt*). In many cities, the phones are open most of the night.

Shops are generally open Monday through Friday from 8:30am to 6pm, and Saturday until noon. In some smaller towns stores close from noon to 3pm for *Mittagspause,* and might stay open later on the first Saturday of each month *(langer Samstag).*

Accommodations and Camping

Rooms can always be booked for DM1 or 2 through the local tourist office, usually located at the main train station *(Hauptbahnhof)* in the larger cities or at the marketplace *(Marktplatz)* in smaller towns. *Hotels* are expensive, while *Pensionen,* their less elegant, but equally comfortable counterpart, are more reasonably priced. In smaller towns, look for *Gasthäuser,* cozy family-run establishments, and *Fredenzimmer,* small rooms at the tops of pubs and restaurants which are often the best value. Rooms in a private home *(Zimmer Frei)* are usually a few marks less, but are often unavailable (or more expensive) for one-night stays; the same holds true for many rural pensions. In big cities, beware accommodations so far out in the suburbs that the expense of public transportation eats up your savings. Unmarried couples will not have problems, except perhaps in rural parts of the south.

Germany has one of the most extensive IYHF youth hostel *(Jugendherberge)* systems in Europe. Signs for hostels read "DJH." Bed and breakfast normally cost DM9-14 for "juniors" (under 25), and 2 or 3 marks more for "seniors" (25 and over); sheet rental, sometimes compulsory, costs DM2.50-3.50. Priority is given to visitors under 27 until 7pm; in Bavaria this is an absolute maximum age. A hostel card is usually mandatory; you can buy it at most hostels (DM30). Some hostels allow nonmembers to stay overnight if they purchase a guest card (DM4). Curfews at German hostels are normally early, between 9:45pm and midnight. At many hostels one meal is obligatory, and breakfast is usually cheapest (DM3-4).

Campgrounds are everywhere, and usually only a few marks per person; ask at local tourist office for the most convenient sites. Freelance camping on public land is *verboten*—high fines are levied.

Food

Unless you experiment, German food may seem monotonous and unappetizing. Staples of the German diet include pork *(Schwein)*, veal *(Kalb)*, sausage *(Wurst)*, and potatoes *(Kartoffeln)*. Vegetarians can almost always find omelettes and salad *(Salatteller)*, but outside of big cities there are few vegetarian restaurants. German breakfasts *(Frühstück)* are light and simple, consisting of coffee and buttered rolls. The main meal, *Mittagessen*, is served at noon. At about 4pm, you may notice the streets becoming deserted as people head for the *Konditorei* for *Kaffee und Kuchen* (coffee and cake). You will have little difficulty becoming accustomed to this tradition; German pastries and coffee are delicious. The final meal, *Abendbrot*, is usually light and simple—typically including bread, cheese, and cold cuts. Everyone knows about German beer, but don't neglect German wine, especially from the Rhine and Mosel valleys.

In a restaurant or *Gaststätte* (a simpler, less expensive restaurant), order from the *Tageskarte* (daily menu). All restaurant prices include tax and service *(Mehrwertsteuer und Bedienung)*. If you wish to express gratitude for especially good service, it's customary to round up the bill a mark or two. For inexpensive food, go to the *Schnell-Imbisse* (fast food stands) or try a department-store cafeteria or *Mensa* (dining halls located at most universities, open to anyone with student ID). *Mensa* food is usually unappetizing, but filling. In most larger German cities, Yugoslavian, Turkish, and Greek restaurants are common and relatively inexpensive. And don't forget the outdoor markets: They sell fruits and vegetables by the bushel, and often sweets and smoked meat and sausages as well. Supermarkets usually open from 8am to noon and from 2 to 7pm.

Northern Germany

This region has a history of prosperity which began with the medieval Hanseatic League, and a tradition of fierce independence as well. Hamburg, an immense port and Germany's second largest city, is a bustling metropolis; Bremen and Lübeck present the visitor with a better preserved medieval heritage. The beautiful Lüneburger Heide, a mist-shrouded moorland, is especially enjoyable in August and September, when the heather turns bright purple. Farther north lie the East Frisian Islands and the Baltic and North Sea coasts, which offer beautiful sandy beaches and windswept dunes.

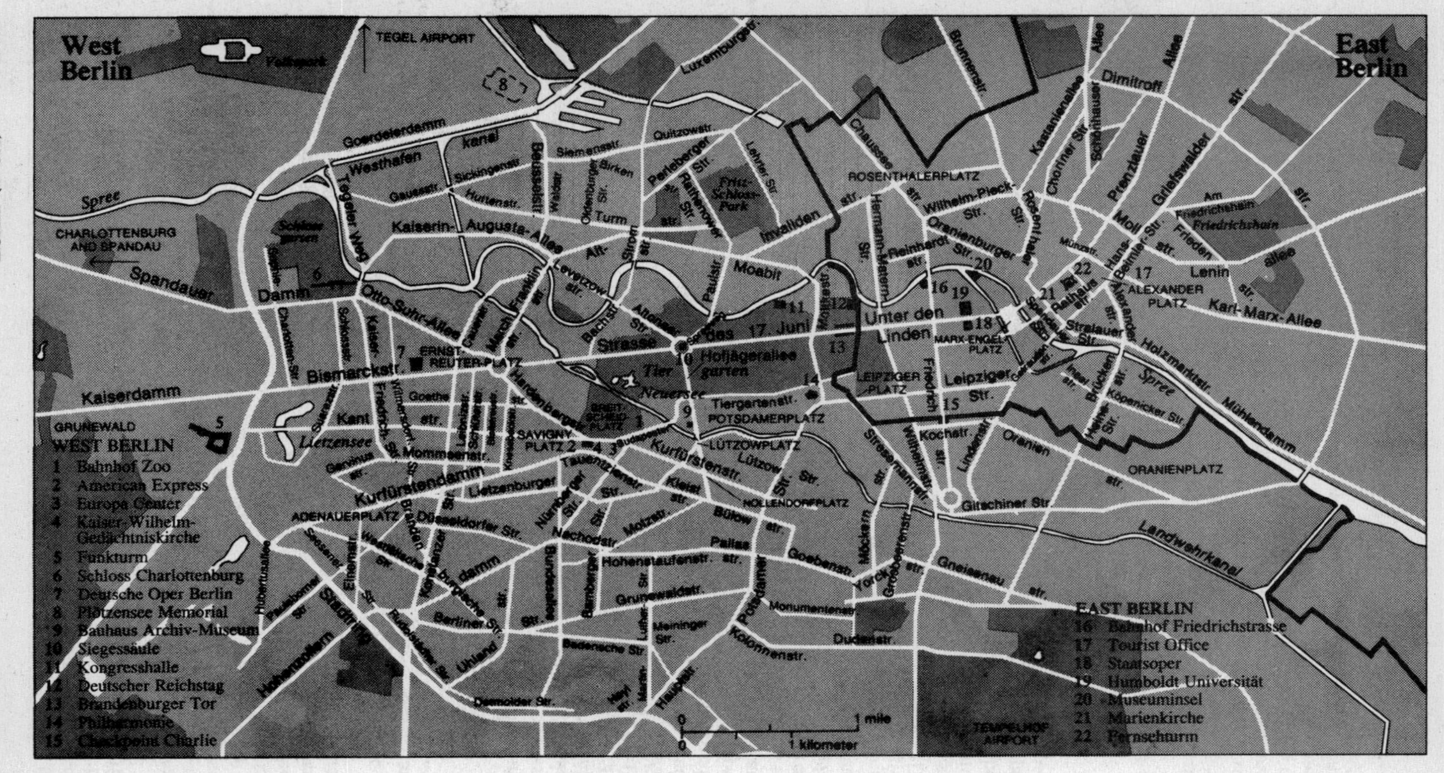
West Berlin
East Berlin
TEGEL AIRPORT
CHARLOTTENBURG AND SPANDAU
TEMPELHOF AIRPORT
WEST BERLIN
1 Bahnhof Zoo
2 American Express
3 Europa Center
4 Kaiser-Wilhelm-Gedächtniskirche
5 Funkturm
6 Schloss Charlottenburg
7 Deutsche Oper Berlin
8 Plötzensee Memorial
9 Bauhaus Archiv-Museum
10 Siegessäule
11 Kongresshalle
12 Deutscher Reichstag
13 Brandenburger Tor
14 Philharmonie
15 Checkpoint Charlie
EAST BERLIN
16 Bahnhof Friedrichstrasse
17 Tourist Office
18 Staatsoper
19 Humboldt Universität
20 Museuminsel
21 Marienkirche
22 Fernsehturm
0 1 mile
0 1 kilometer
Kaiserdamm
Bismarckstr.
Kurfürstendamm
Unter den Linden
Karl-Marx-Allee
Landwehrkanal
ALEXANDER PLATZ
POTSDAMERPLATZ
LEIPZIGER PLATZ
ERNST-REUTER-PLATZ
ADENAUERPLATZ
SAVIGNY PLATZ
LÜTZOWPLATZ
ROSENTHALERPLATZ
ORANIENPLATZ
GRUNEWALD

Berlin (West)

Berlin is, above all else, a modern city. Green and white police vans with their white-clad officers seem to be actively anticipating the twenty-first century as they slowly cruise the Kreuzberg streets or line up somewhere in preparation for one of Berlin's frequent demonstrations. The naive Berlin of Heinrich Zille's turn-of-the-century ink drawings or the risqué voyeurism of the Weimar 1920s is gone, replaced by the techno-decadence of the side streets off the Kurfürstendamm. West Berlin lacks the royal ministries and monuments that give so much shape to other European capitals; Prussia's grandeur lies in East Berlin. West Berlin did wind up with the ruins of Gestapo and SS headquarters, but that sort of history is harder to work with.

In Berlin more than in any other European city, contemporary history pervades art, theater, and daily life. West Berlin itself, in fact, is as divided as East and West Berlin: While the chamber of commerce proclaims the city's world-class cosmopolitanism, alternative movements warn how dark a politics of forgetfulness and enthusiasm can be. After the Revolution of 1918, the frenzy of the Weimar Republic, two World Wars, an Allied occupation, and a wall isolating it from its mainland, Berlin finds itself struggling with jittery single-mindedness to shape its troubled legacy into a workable future.

Orientation and Practical Information

Railpasses are not valid for the journey from West Germany across East Germany to West Berlin. Trains cross the border at Hof, Helmstedt, Gutenfürst, Büchen, and Probstzella. The trip lasts 2-4 hours and costs DM42-70; a BIGE ticket can save you DM10-15. The necessary East German transit visa is issued without charge on the train. Excellent train connections link Berlin to all major West German cities at least three times per day.

If you're traveling by car and are not a German citizen, you will have to pay DM5 for a transit visa; you must also have an oval national identification sticker on your car. While in transit through East Germany, expect very strict enforcement of traffic regulations. *Don't* leave the transit road or stop anywhere but at Intertank rest areas; you'll be caught immediately (helicopters cruise the highway routes) and questioned for hours.

Hitchhiking to Berlin is quite good, since just about everyone is traveling directly from the border to the city. In the very rare event that you encounter a driver who is stopping somewhere in East Germany, politely refuse the offer; hitchhiking is absolutely forbidden within East Germany.

Flying to West Berlin is quite economical; the German government subsidizes service by British Airways, Air France, and Pan Am. Any student may fly standby from most major German cities; the price-worthiest international route is Berlin-London. Prices are regulated, so all three airlines offer the same fares. East Germany beats even these subsidized fares with service to Schönefeld Airport in East Berlin, but most flights originate in other Eastern European capitals. If you do fly into Schönefeld, transit visas are issued on the bus from the airport to West Berlin.

The commercial district centers around **Bahnhof Zoo** and **Breitscheidplatz,** where you'll find the ruined Kaiser-Wilhelm-Gedächtniskirche (Berlin's second most famous symbol), as well as the boxy tower of Europa Center and the main tourist office. Bahnhof Zoo is Berlin's major train station and the central point of Berlin's subway and surface rail systems. A star of streets radiates out from Breitscheidplatz. Toward the west run **Hardenbergstrasse, Kantstrasse,** and the great commercial boulevard of modern Berlin, the **Kurfürstendamm,** popularly known as the "Ku'damm." Half a mile down Hardenbergstrasse is Steinplatz and the enormous Berlin Technical University. Half a mile down Kantstrasse is **Savignyplatz,** home to many cafes, restaurants, and pensions.

The **Berlin Wall** is a little removed from all this action. The first place to find it is by the Reichstag building and the Brandenburg gate, at the eastern end of Berlin's large urban park, **Tiergarten.** Several miles to the south and east, along the wall's snaking course, is **Checkpoint Charlie,** the famous, but not so heavily used, crossing point to East Berlin. Heading south again, away from the wall, puts you in **Kreuzberg.**

Berlin is insulated in more than just a political sense. The **Landwehrkanal,** the **Havel,** and its various lakes—from the popular Wansee in the south to the Teglersee in the north—form a crescent around the western edge of the city. The Landwehrkanal runs from Tiergarten, by the Nationalgalerie, then through the length of Kreuzberg.

Tourist Offices: Verkehrsamt Berlin, in the Europa Center on Budapesterstr., 2 min. east of Bahnhof Zoo (tel. 262 60 31). An extensive selection of free maps and brochures on Berlin, including complete hotel and pension listings; rooms found for DM2. Their leaflet *Tips für Jugendliche* lists inexpensive accommodations. Open daily 7:30am-10:30pm. **Branch offices** at Bahnhof Zoo and at Autobahn control points Staaken and Dreilinden, all open daily 8am-11pm. **Informationszentrum Berlin,** Hardenbergstr. 20 (tel. 31 00 40), is just across from the train station. Mainly historical and political information, but also *Berlin for Young People,* an invaluable English booklet. Open Mon.-Fri. 8am-7pm, Sat. 8am-4pm.

Budget Travel: ARTU Reisebüro, Hardenbergstr. 9, near Bahnhof Zoo. Additional offices near U-Bahn: Dahlem-Dorf at Takustr. 47 (tel. 831 50 94), and in Kreuzberg at Mariannenstr. 49 (tel. 618 57 33). Issues IUS, the student card for socialist countries. Hardenbergstr. branch open Mon.-Tues. and Thurs.-Fri. 9:30am-6pm, Wed. 10:30am-7pm, Sat. 10am-1pm. Other branches same hours, but closed 2-3pm.

American Express: Kurfürstendamm 11, 2nd floor (tel. 882 75 75). Mail held. All banking services. Open Mon.-Fri. 9am-6pm, Sat. 9am-noon.

Currency Exchange: At Bahnhof Zoo, on Hardenbergstr. Open Mon.-Sat. 8am-9pm, Sun. 10am-6pm. Berliner Bank in Tegel Airport is open daily 8am-10pm.

Post Office: In the Bahnhof Zoo, D-1000 Berlin 12. Open Mon.-Fri. 8am-6pm, Sat. 8am-noon. Poste Restante kept here at window #9, just around the corner. Open 24 hours.

Telephones: At Bahnhof Zoo. Open 24 hours. **Telephone code:** 030.

Flights: Flughafen Tegel is West Berlin's main airport, connected to Bahnhof Zoo by bus #9. **Flughafen Tempelhof** is rarely used. **Flughafen Schönefeld,** in East Berlin, is connected by bus to the western sector's central bus station.

Trains: The sprawling **Bahnhof Zoo** is Berlin's principal station.

Buses: ZOB, the central bus station, is by the Funkturm, near Kaiserdamm. U-Bahn: Kaiserdamm. Information (tel. 301 80 28).

Public Transportation: The transit system is as indispensable and efficient as it is expensive. The **U-Bahn** (subway), **S-Bahn** (commuter rail network—use it to cover long distances quickly), and an extensive bus system cost DM2.30 per ride or DM10.50 for a 5-ride *Sammelkarte.* Each ticket entitles you to 2 hours' travel in one direction with unlimited changes. At Bahnhof Zoo U-Bahn station, you can buy 1-day (DM8), 2-day (DM16) or 4-day (DM32) **Touristenkarte** passes. It's also a good idea to buy a *Liniennetz* map, which shows the bus and subway routes in detail (DM2). The system shuts down 1-4am.

Emergencies: Police (tel. 110); headquarters at Tempelhofer Damm 3. **Ambulance** (tel. 31 00 31). **Sexual Assault Hotline** (tel. 251 28 28), open Tues. and Thurs. 6-9pm, Sun. noon-2pm.

Medical Assistance: The tourist office has a list of English-speaking doctors.

Pharmacies: When closed, each *Apotheke* posts a sign directing you to the nearest open pharmacy.

Consulates: U.S., at Flughafen Tempelhof (tel. 819 50 19 or 819 55 23). **Canada,** Europa Center (tel. 261 11 61). **U.K.,** Uhlandstr. 7-8 (tel. 309 52 93). Eastern European visas are processed more quickly in East Berlin.

Cultural Centers: Amerika Haus, Hardenbergstr. 22-24. The library has English-language books and periodicals. Open July and Aug. Mon.-Fri. 11:30am-5:30pm; Sept.-June Mon., Wed., and Fri. 11:30am-5:30pm, Tues. and Thurs. 11:30am-8pm. **British Center,** at Hardenbergstr. 20, next door. Open year-round Mon.-Fri. 11:30am-5:30pm.

Bookstores: Great selection of English books at **Marga Schoeller Bücherstube,** Knesebeckstr. 34, between Savignyplatz and the Ku'damm. Open Sun.-Fri. 9am-5:30pm, Sat. 9am-2pm; first Sat. of month 9am-6pm. Secondhand English books bought and sold at **Sesenheimerstrasse 15,** U-Bahn: Deutsche Oper. Very sporadic hours. For books on Berlin, go to **Kultur Zentrale Buchhandlung,** Budapesterstr. 44, across from the Gedächtniskirche. Open Mon.-Sat. 10am-11pm. For German readers **Autorenbuchhandlung,** Carmerstr. 10, on Savignyplatz, has a very literary selection and frequent readings. **Literaturhaus Berlin** is wonderfully set in an old mansion at Fasanenstr. 23, complete with garden cafe and frequent readings. The selection is a bit too tony for its own good. Berlin's Käthe Kollwitz museum is next door, just a short walk from the Ku'damm.

Laundry: Haupstrasse 151, open 6am-midnight; **Uhlandstrasse 53,** open 6am-10:30pm; and **Kantstrasse,** by Savignyplatz, near Schlüterstr.

Hitchhiking: To hitch west to Hannover or south to Munich, go to Dreilinder; take the S-Bahn toward Wannsee to the end of Kronprinzessinweg, then switch to line 18 right to the checkpoint. To hitch north to Hamburg, take bus #94 to checkpoint Staaken. Don't be intimidated by the huge crowd of hitchhikers; someone gets picked up every few minutes. **Mitfahrzentrale** has offices at Kurfürstendamm 227 (tel. 882 76 06) and Arndtstr. 42 (tel. 693 60 95). Berlin has numerous other Mitfahrzentrale not belonging to the national chain; see *Zitty* magazine for addresses and phone numbers.

Accommodations and Camping

Though you can almost always find a room in Berlin, in summer you should book ahead. The pensions and hotels listed below accept phone reservations. You can also make reservations by writing any hotel or pension directly, or by writing to the **Verkehrsamt,** Europa Center, 1000 Berlin 30, at least two weeks before you arrive, stating precisely how much you're willing to spend. For DM2 they will try to find a room for you on the spot, but late on summer weekend evenings they may be dry. If you arrive in the middle of the night, visit the **Bahnhofsmission** in Bahnhof Zoo, where a nurse will give you directions to the dorm at Franklinstr. 27. (Bunks start at DM15.)

Hostels and Dormitories

These hostels fill quickly, especially in summer and on weekends.

Jugendgästehaus (IYHF), Kluckstr. 3, 1000 Berlin 30 (tel. 261 10 97). Bus #29 from Kurfürstendamm toward Oranienplatz takes you to the door. Central location, newly renovated, and friendly management. Members only. DM18.50. Breakfast included. If you arrange in advance, you can sometimes stay out an hour past the midnight curfew. Open year-round.

Jugendherberge (IYHF), Bayernallee 36, 1000 Berlin 19 (tel. 305 90 11). Take U-Bahn #1 to Neu-Westend, then walk south along Preussenallee. Members only. Juniors DM15.70, seniors DM17.70. Breakfast included. Check-in all day. Lockout 9am-noon. Midnight curfew. Open year-round.

Jugendherberge Wannsee (IYHF), Badeweg 1, 1000 Berlin 38 (tel. 803 20 34). Fine facilities and a nice location, near the Strand Bad Wannsee beach. Take the S-3 tram to Nikolassee station; from there it's a 10-min. walk toward the beach. Far from the center, so likely to have space. Members only. DM19.20. Breakfast included. Midnight curfew. Open year-round.

Jugendherberge Ernst Reuter (IYHF), Hermsdorfer Damm 48-50, 1000 Berlin 28 (tel. 404 16 10). U-Bahn #6: Tegel, then bus #15 headed for Frohnau; get off at the 4th stop. Similarly remote, so also likely to have space. Nice management. Juniors DM15.70, seniors DM17.70. Breakfast included, dinner DM5.20. No lockout. Midnight curfew. Open year-round.

Jugendgästehaus am Zoo, 1 Berlin 12, Hardenbergstr. 9a (tel. 312 94 10). Very central location. A little more expensive than an IYHF hostel. Singles DM30, doubles DM50, triples DM70. With more beds DM20 per person. Breakfast DM6.

Studentenhotel Berlin, Meiningerstr. 10, 1000 Berlin 62 (tel. 784 67 20). U-Bahn: Rathaus Schöneberg. From Bahnhof Zoo, hop on bus #73, get off at Rathaus Schöneberg, and walk across Martin-Luther-Str. Decent dormitory accommodations in a green, quiet neighborhood. Beds in a double room DM27, in a quad DM25. Showers and breakfast included. No curfew. Reservations recommended. If they're full, they're usually quite helpful about recommending secluded pensions in the neighborhood.

Studentenwohnheim Schlachtensee, Wasgenstr. 75, 1000 Berlin 38 (tel. 80 10 71). U-Bahn #2: Krumme Lanke, then bus #3 to the corner of Potsdamer Chaussee and Wasgenstr. A university dormitory open to travelers mid-July to mid-Sept. and mid-Feb. to April. Distant, but with kitchen facilities and very cheap. Singles DM10; admission DM5, linen rental DM5. Reception open Mon. and Fri. 9-11am, Tues. and Thurs. 9-11am and 2-3pm.

Hotels and Pensions

Berlin really does have pension rooms for under DM40 per person—it just takes some searching. The farther from the center of town you're willing to stay, the better your chances of finding a good deal. The area around Savignyplatz is a good place to start looking.

Charlottenburger Hof, Stuttgarterplatz 14 (tel. 324 48 19). U-Bahn: Willemsdorferstrasse. Good location only 4 min. from Ku'damm. Very clean rooms with funky pictures. A great buy. Singles DM35-45, small doubles about DM60, triples DM85, quads DM100-110. Breakfast DM5.

Pension Kreuzberg, Grossbeerenstr. 64, 1000 Berlin 61 (tel. 251 13 62). U-Bahn: Möckernbrücke. From Bahnhof Zoo, bus #19 will take you right to their door—get off at the Grossbeerenstr. stop. Huge rooms. For *Let's Go* readers the prices are whatever it says in the book. This is what it says in the book: Singles DM36, doubles DM60, triples DM75, quads DM88. Showers included. Breakfast DM7.

Pension Fischer, Nürnbergerstr. 24a, 1000 Berlin 30 (tel. 24 68 08). Right across the street from U-Bahn: Nürnbergerstrasse. Comfortable rooms with clashing decor. Singles DM30-35, doubles DM45-50. Showers included.

Hamburger Hof, Kinkelstr. 6 (tel. 333 46 02), in the old quarter of Spandau. Easily accessible, right next to the U-Bahn: Altstadt Spandau. A tiny, comfortable hotel with only 15 beds, but so far from the action that they usually have room. Singles DM35, doubles DM72. Showers and breakfast included.

Pension am Savignyplatz, Grolmanstr. 52, 1000 Berlin 12 (tel. 313 83 92). Large, sumptuously furnished rooms, but a sometimes difficult management. Singles DM35, doubles DM58. On the 5th floor, a few doubles for DM50 and triples for DM75. Breakfast DM7.

Pension Knesebeck, Knesebeckstr. 86 (31 72 55). Large rooms, some with running water. Singles DM40-45, doubles DM70-80. Breakfast included.

Camping

There are four major sites in Berlin: **Kladow,** Kampnitzer Weg 111 (tel. 365 27 97; bus #94, 35); **Haselhorst,** Pulvermühlenweg (tel. 334 59 55; U-Bahn: Haselhorst); **Kohlhasenbrücke,** Neue Kreis-Ecke Stubenrauchstr. (tel. 805 17 31; U-Bahn: Oskar-Helene-Heim; then bus 18); and **Dreilinden,** Albrechts Teerofen (tel. 805 12 01; directions as to Kohlhasenbrück, then a 20-min. walk.). All charge DM6 per person, DM4-5 per tent, and are open year-round, except Kohlhasenbrück which is open April-Sept. All are far from the center.

Food

Berlin's restaurant scene is as international as its population; German cuisine oughtn't be one of your priorities here. *Berliner Weissbier* is one local specialty; natives swear by this concoction of beer and fruit syrup. Around Savignyplatz are a number of inexpensive Turkish and Greek eateries. At Savignypassage 8, **Corfu** hops until 3am serving *gyros* with pita bread (DM4) and basic Greek dishes such as *pastitsio* (DM9) and *mousaka* (DM12). Around the corner, at Bleibtreustr. 50, by Kantstr., **Meyhave** features inexpensive Turkish delicacies, Middle Eastern music, and great banana juice (DM2.50).

Mensa of the Free University, corner of Habelschwerdter Allee and Thiel Allee. U-Bahn #2: Thielplatz. Reputedly one of the best in Germany. Meals from DM1.20, ISIC required. Open year-round Mon.-Fri. noon-2pm.

Mensa of the Technische Universität, Ernst-Reuter-Platz. U-Bahn #1: Ernst-Reuter-Platz. Much more conveniently located than the above. You must buy a meal ticket before collecting your food. Technically, you have to be a student here—usually, no questions asked. Meals of four levels of complexity: DM1.40, DM2, DM2.40, and DM2.90. Open year-round Mon.-Fri. 11:15am-2:30pm.

Simsalat, Ansbacherstr. 11, just north of the Wittenbergplatz U-Bahn station. A salad bar that charges DM1.70 per 100g. After 800g (DM13.60) you can take as much as you want. Open Mon.-Sat. 8:30am-midnight.

La Batea, Krummestr. 42. U-Bahn #1: Deutsche Oper. Good Latin American food for DM7-15. The daring can try the bread with hot sauce (DM1). Open daily noon-1am.

Cour Carré, Savignyplatz 5. Delicious French food in a lovely wine garden, enclosed by high shrubbery. Meals DM10-20. Open daily noon-1am.

Dicke Wirtin, Carmerstr. 9, around the corner. Serves large bowls of thick soup and stew for DM2-5. Homey atmosphere. Open Mon.-Sat. noon-4am, Sun. 5pm-4am.

Cafe Voltaire, Stuttgarterplatz 14. Trendy but inexpensive cafe. Great breakfasts 5am-3pm, warm meals noon-5am. Try the *Rasta Pasta* (DM8). Open 24 hours.

Tegernseer Tönnchen, Mommsenstr. 34, near Wilmerdorferstr. A thoroughly delightful Bavarian restaurant. For a real mountain of food order the *Grosse Schlachtplatte,* an assortment of Bavarian *Wurst* (DM13.80). 3-course daily *menus* DM11.90-13.50. The *Zigeunerschnitzel* (pork chop with peppers and spicy sauce) is a huge quantity of food (DM14.20). Also features a wide selection of beers (DM2.20-4). Open noon-midnight.

Zillemarkt, Bleibtreustr. 48. Always a popular cafe, with soups, salads, and dessert crepes. Large outdoor garden, board games, and pool tables. Open daily 8am-2am.

Schwarzes Cafe, Kantstr. 148, near Savignyplatz. A hopping cafe with many young people and hip music. Always serves breakfast: Omelettes start at DM8.50. Open 24 hours (except closed Mon. 8pm-Tues. 8pm).

Z, corner of Fidicinstr. and Friesenstr., near Chamissoplatz in Kreuzberg. A friendly Greek restaurant in a part of Berlin that too many people miss. Lots of food and an ouzo aperitif, DM12-14. Open noon-1am.

Sights

Architecture, Monuments, and Parks

A grim reminder of the devastation caused by World War II, the **Kaiser-Wilhelm-Gedächtniskirche** has lost some of its didactic force in the giddy neon of the Ku'damm and Europa Center. To the north and east, toward what was the center of old, unified Berlin, spreads Berlin's lush **Tiergarten,** a vast landscaped park formerly used by the Prussian monarchs as a hunting ground. In the heart of the Tiergarten, the **Siegassäule** victory column celebrates Prussia's campaign against France in 1870. (Open April-Nov. Mon. 1-6pm, Tues.-Sun. 9am-6pm. Admission DM1, students DM0.50.) Climb to the top for a sweeping view of the monuments beyond the wall. Former entrance into the center city, the **Brandenburger Tor** is today flush with the **Berlin Wall.** Just to the north sits the **Reichstag** building, the seat of the unified German empire's parliament. In August 1914 Karl Liebknecht's famous "Nein!" was the only vote in its halls against the impending First World War. In November 1918, Philipp Scheidemann declared a German Republic from one of its windows, while down the street Liebknecht simultaneously announced the creation of a German Socialist Republic, bringing the tragic November Revolution to a head. The building, which Hitler burned in February 1933, today holds an exhibit on German history (see Museums).

If you want a glimpse of how heavy Berlin's history can be, go to an empty field at the intersection of Kochstrasse and Wilhelmstrasse. (From U-Bahn Kochstr., facing Checkpoint Charlie, it is a few blocks to your left.) A plain sign, in German only, marks the field as the site of the headquarters of Hitler's Gestapo and SS. The wall, which cuts sharply in front of the field, contributes to the starkness of the setting. Climb up on the platform on the other side of the lot and look north into the desolation of what was once Berlin's busiest square, Potsdamer Platz. The small mound marks the air raid shelter where Hitler committed suicide on April 30, 1945. Once the main street of Berlin's newspaper district, Kochstrasse was the site of the most dramatic struggles of the 1918-1919 Revolution, the defeat of which helped pave Hitler's rise to power. Breathe in deeply—rarely can one sense the consequences of history so vividly.

Indispensable for a sense of Berlin's counter-culture is a visit to **Kreuzberg.** Get off at U-Bahn #6 or 7: Mehringdamm and wander around anywhere—particularly interesting is the area around Chamissoplatz, bordered by Bergmannstrasse and Fidicinstrasse. At night there are many counter-culture and punk pubs on Yorckstrasse, which heads west from the intersection with Mehringdamm. The east end of Kreuzberg (U-Bahn #1: Schlesiches Tor) boasts a particularly vital Turkish and Balkan neighborhood and a view of the river Spree as it flows along the wall. Note the political slogans painted wherever you turn.

Schloss Charlottenburg, the vast baroque palace built by Friedrich I for his wife Sophie-Charlotte, stands on the outskirts of town amidst spacious landscaped gardens. The ornate **Knobelsdorff Wing** is the most lavish of the palace suites. From Ernst-Reuter-Platz, take Ott-Suhr-Allee northwest to Spandauer Damm, or take bus #54 from Bahnhof Zoo. (Open Tues.-Sun. 9am-4pm. Admission to the entire palace complex (*Sammelkarte*) DM5.50, students DM3. Admission to the Knobelsdorff Wing alone DM3, students DM1.50.) **The Palace Gardens** (open Tues.-Sun. 9am-9pm) surround the **Royal Mausoleum** (open April-Oct. 9am-noon and 1-5pm); **Belvedere,** an eighteenth-century residence housing a porcelain exhibition; and the **Schinkel Pavilion,** with furniture designed by Schinkel (open Tues.-Sun. 9am-4pm).

A somber monument to the victims of Nazism, the **Gedenksstätte Plötzensee Memorial** exhibits documents recording death sentences of "enemies of the people" (including the officers who unsuccessfully attempted to assassinate Hitler in 1944) in the former execution chambers of the Third Reich. Literature on the monument is available in English at the office. Take bus #23 from S-Bahn: Tiergarten to Goerdelerdamm, and follow Hüttingpfad 200m away from the Kanal, along a tall brick wall. (Open March-Sept. daily 8am-6pm; Feb. and Oct. daily 8:30am-5:30pm; Nov. and Jan. daily 8:30am-4:30pm; Dec. daily 8:30am-4pm. Free.)

In the southern suburb of Dahlem, Berlin's **Botanischer Garten** is a delight, especially the tropical greenhouses. Take bus #19 from the Ku'damm to Potsdamerstr., then bus #48 south. (Open daily 9am-sunset. Admission DM2.) The renowned **Zoo,** across from the Europa Center, houses an exotic collection of fauna as well as the spectacular **Aquarium,** Budapesterstr. 32. (Zoo open April-Sept. daily 9am-7pm; March daily 9am-5:30pm; Oct.-Feb. daily 9am-5pm. Aquarium open daily 9am-6pm. Comprehensive admission DM6.50, students DM5.50.)

Museums

Dahlem Museum, Arnimallee 23-27. U-Bahn: Dahlem-Dorf. A huge complex of 7 museums, each worth a half-day's visit. Particularly superb are the **Gemäldegalerie,** a fantastic collection of Italian, German, Dutch, and Flemish Old Masters (including 26 Rembrandts); the **Museum für Ostasiatische Kunst,** collecting Japanese, Korean, and Chinese art; the **Museum für Völkerkunde** (Ethnography), with magnificent Mayan and Incan treasures; and the **Museum für Indische und Islamische Kunst.** All open Tues.-Sun. 9am-5pm. Free.

Schloss Charlottenburg, U-Bahn 2: Sophie-Charlotte-Platz, contains several museums. The **Ägyptisches Museum,** situated just across Spandauer Damm from the main entrance to the castle, houses a fascinating collection of ancient Egyptian art, including the 3300-year-old bust of Queen Nefertiti. The **Antikenabteilung,** across the street, contains a fabulous collection of Greek, Roman, and Etruscan jewelry and ceramics. Both open Sat.-Thurs. 9am-5pm. Free.

The Kunstgewerbemuseum, Tiergartenstr. 6, next to the Philharmonic and Nationalgalerie, displays ceramics, porcelain, and various handicrafts in wood, silver, and gold. Open Tues.-Sun. 9am-5pm. Free.

Nationalgalerie, Potsdamerstr. 50. Take Bus #29 from the Ku'damm. This handsome building, designed by Mies van der Rohe, has a remarkable collection of expressionist works, as well as exhibits of contemporary art. Open Tues.-Sun. 9am-5pm. Free.

Bauhaus Archiv-Museum, Klingelnhöferstr. 13. Take bus #29 to Lützowplatz. The shimmering modern building designed by Walter Gropius, former director of the famous school, displays exemplary works by Bauhaus members (among them, Kandinsky and Klee), including paintings, housewares, graphics, textiles, and furniture. Open Wed.-Mon. 11am-5pm. Admission DM3, students DM1; free Mon.

Akademie der Künste, Hanseatenweg 10, in an area of town near Tiergarten that was built by an international group of architects in the late 1950s. U-Bahn: Hansaplatz. A modern building with changing exhibits, concerts, and experimental theater.

Brücke Museum, Bussardsteig 9. From the Zoo, take bus #A60 to the corner of Clayallee and Pücklerstr. An impressive collection of works by the German expressionist *Brücke* school, which flourished in Dresden and Berlin from 1909 to 1913. Open Wed.-Mon. 11am-5pm. Admission DM3, students DM1.50.

The Reichstag, near Brandenburg Tor. Take bus #69 from the Zoo. A fascinating exhibit of German history from 1800 to 1949. If you're headed to East Berlin, you may wish to compare the history recounted here with the chronicle offered in the Museum für Deutsche Geschichte. Open Tues.-Sun. 10am-5pm. Free.

Entertainment

Berlin is a happening city. The best guides to theater, cinema, nightlife, and the extremely active musical scene are the biweekly magazines *Tip* (DM3) and the more underground *Zitty* (DM2.50). Listings are usually comprehensible to non-German speakers. *Berlin Program* (DM2.50) lists more "cultural" events, and includes good theater information. *Berlin von hinten* is the best guide to gay life.

As if there weren't enough going on already, Berlin is always throwing festivals. There is an international **Film Festival** (late Feb.-March) and a **Theater Festival** (May). In mid-July, **Bachtage** (Bach Days) offer an intense week of classical music; every Saturday night in August **Sommer Festspiele** turns the Ku'damm into a multifaceted concert hall with punk, steel drum, and folk groups competing for attention. The high points of the festive year are the fabulous **Berliner Festwochen,** lasting almost the whole month of September and drawing the world's best orchestras and soloists, and the **Berliner Jazztage** in November. For more information on all these events (and tickets for the last two, which are always sold out long in advance), write to Berliner Festspiele, Budapesterstr. 48-50, 1000 Berlin 30.

Nightlife

No place in the German-speaking world hops, shakes, and shouts at night as much as Berlin; things are happening until 4am every night with a vengeance that is a matter of municipal pride. Mainstream activity centers around two areas to the north and south of the Ku'damm. To the north it is a bit more inviting and young: the middle point is Savignyplatz and it includes Grolmanstr., Knesebeckstr., Bleibtreustr., and Schlütterstr., as well as Steinplatz, along Carmerstr. to the north. The area to the south of Ku'damm centers on Ludwigkirchplatz, and is roughly bordered by the Ku'damm, Fasanenstr., and Pariserstr. up to Adenauerplatz.Perhaps the best plan is just to head into one of these areas and get lost. Check the listings in *Berlin for Young People* and *Tip* for information on the characters of different nightspots.

Metropol, Nollendorfplatz 5 (tel. 216 41 22). U-Bahn: Nollendorfplatz. *The* place in town to dance the night away. Live band or disco music; admission varies accordingly. Rather chic. Popular with, but not dominated by, gay people. Usually the music goes until 4am.

Abraxas, Kantstr. 1, between U-Bahn Wilmersdorfenstr. and S-Bahn Savignyplatz. Jazz, soul, funk, and Latin American. A major hot spot. Open Tues.-Sun. 10pm-5am. Fri.-Sat. there is a DM6 cover which includes 1 drink.

Ex, Mehringhof, Gneisenaustr. 2a. Hangout for the people from the Green Party, etc. Piped-in music. Occasional concerts.

Loretta im Garten, Lietzenburgerstr. 89, near Knesebeckstr. A lively German beer garden, complete with ferris wheel, disco, outdoor food stands, all kinds of beer, and all kinds of people having all kinds of fun. Beer DM3.50. Open all night.

Go In, Bleibtreustr. 17 (tel. 881 72 18). Live folk, blues, cabaret. Nightly starting at 8pm. Admission varies according to performer.

Quasimodo, Kantstr. 12a. A basement pub, with live jazz and rock, and a lively crowd. From 8pm. Cover charge.

Das Wirtschaftswunder, Yorckstr. 81. A Kreuzberg club with tongue-in-cheek streamlined '50s decor. Serves drinks from 2:30pm until late.

Yorck-Schlösschen, Yorckstr. 15. Enjoyable pub with live music (sometimes) late in the evening (now and then a punky crowd). In an old Kreuzberg tenement. During the day, pleasant garden in front. Open daily 9am-5am.

Quartier Latin, Potsdamerstr. 99 (tel. 261 37 07). International jazz and rock groups, tending to punk and reggae. Ticket cost varies according to group. Box office open nightly from 7pm. Also advance ticket sales for rock concerts around town.

Theater and Music

Berlin is world-renowned as a center of experimental theater; however, many of the city's 20 to 30 theater companies vacation during July and August. Still, on any night in Berlin you can choose from 100 different films, many in the original, subtitled versions. (O.m.U. next to a movie listing means it is subtitled.) To purchase theater tickets, go to **Theaterkasse Centrum,** Meinekestr. 25 (tel. 882 76 11); **Sasse,** Kurfürstendamm 24, (tel. 882 73 60); or **Ottfried Laur,** Hardenbergstr. 7 (tel. 313 70 07). (All open Sept.-June Mon.-Fri. 9am-noon and 3-5:30pm, Sat. 9am-3:30pm; July-Aug. Mon.-Fri. 9am-3pm.)

Philharmonie, Kemperplatz, 1000 Berlin 30 (tel. 261 43 83). Take bus #29 from Ku'damm to Potsdamerstr. and walk 3 blocks north. The big yellow building is as acoustically perfect within as it is unconventional without, and the Berlin Philharmonic is one of the very best. Especially when von Karajan conducts, it's almost impossible to get a seat, but check an hour before concert time or (preferably) write far in advance. Here and at the Oper you can also stand out front just before the performance with a small sign saying "*Suche Karte;*" invariably a few people can't come at the last moment.

Deutsche Oper Berlin, Bismarckstr. 34-37, 1000 Berlin 10 (tel. 341 44 49). U-Bahn #1: Deutsche Oper. Box office open daily 10am-2pm, and 90 min. before performances. Tickets cannot be reserved on weekends. You can get student reductions, up to 50% off depending on the price of the ticket, 10 min. before performances. Tickets start at DM5. Performances usually begin at 7:30pm.

Das Schillertheater, Bismarckstr. 10 (tel. 319 52 36), by U-Bahn: Ernst-Reuter-Platz. The country's leading stage for both classical and modern plays. Followed closely by the **Schlosspark Theater,** Schlossstr. 48 (tel. 791 12 13). U-Bahn: Rathaus Steglitz.

The Freie Volksbühne, Schaperstr. 24 (tel. 881 37 42), U-Bahn #2 or 9: Spichernstr., and the **Renaissance Theater,** Hardenbergstr. 6 (tel. 312 42 02), U-Bahn #1: Ernst-Reuter-Platz. Both are slightly less expensive than the above, and boast excellent repertory companies.

Tanzfabrik, Möckernstr. 68 (tel. 786 58 61). U-Bahn #1 or 7: Möckernbrücke. Modern dance performances, as well as a general center for dance-related workshops. Ticket office open Mon.-Thurs. 10am-1pm and 5-8pm. Tickets DM10, students DM8. Daily performances starting at either 8pm or 8:30pm.

Greater Berlin

In summer, clear your head in the **Grunewald,** a 745-acre birch forest. While there, visit the **Jagdschloss,** a royal hunting lodge now housing a worthwhile exhibit of European paintings, including works by Rubens, van Dyck, and Cranach. (Open Tues.-Sun. 10am-6pm. Admission DM2.50, students DM1.50.) **Bachtage** (Bach Days) concerts are held during the summer in the Schloss at 6pm. (Tickets DM5.) To reach the Jagdschloss and Grunewald take bus #A60 to the Brücke Museum and follow Pücklerstr. into the forest.

The breezy waters of the Wannsee, Tegler See, Niederneuendorfer See and Heiligensee lap the city from all sides, connected to one another by narrow canals. From **Wannsee,** tour boats sail to Tegeler Weg and Charlottenburg (Sat.-Thurs., leaving at 4:30pm, DM6.50). Other ships sail to Spandau (DM6) and Kladow (DM2.10) daily between 12:42pm and 5:17pm (tel. 391 46 93 or 391 70 10 for information). Wannsee also offers lengthy stretches of sandy beach along Havelufer Promenade. To reach Wannsee, take the triangle bus from either the Wannsee or Nikolassee U-Bahn stations to Strand Bad Wannsee (for the beach) or to the end of Nikolskoer Weg (for the boats).

The suburb of **Tegel** is a popular destination for Berliners on summer weekends. Lined with numerous old houses, the broad pedestrian strip **Alt Tegel** runs through the heart of the district, ending at the waters of the Tegeler See, where one can relax in a waterfront cafe or hop a boat. U-Bahn: Alt Tegel.

The grandiose **Olympia Stadion,** erected for the 1936 Olympic Games, is the spot where Hitler watched Jesse Owens's gold medal victories. (Open 6am-sunset. Admission DM0.50. U-Bahn: Olympia Stadion.)

Spandau Citadel is notorious as the prison where Nazis convicted of war crimes served their sentences. The twelfth-century fortification now houses an historical exhibition. (Open Tues.-Fri. 9am-4pm, Sat.-Sun. 10am-4pm. Historical tours Sat. 2-5pm, Sun. 10am-5pm. Admission DM2, students DM1. Tour DM1. U-Bahn #7: Altstadt Spandau.)

Lübeck

Capital of the Hanseatic League and completely surrounded by rivers, Lübeck is the best preserved town in the unspoiled countryside around Hamburg. (40 min. from Hamburg; frequent trains.) A centuries-old tradition of Baltic trade continues today, and Lübeck's historic merchant houses illustrate the civic pride and fine artisanry of its past.

Much of the small inner city of old Lübeck has remained intact. The core of this historic town is the **Rathaus,** a striking thirteenth-century structure of glazed black bricks which serves as a backdrop for the colorful fruit and flower market. You might want to try the famous *Lübecker Marzipan,* available across the street at I.G. Niederegge; flavors run the gamut from milk chocolate to kiwi. North on Marktplatz is **St. Marienskirche,** a moving reminder of the tragedy of World War II. The church was partially destroyed during a bombing raid, when its gigantic bells plunged from the steeple and shattered. The townspeople restored the beautiful brick structure and its soaring ceilings, but left the kaputt bells embedded in the stone floor as a remembrance. (Open daily 9am-6pm.) Behind the church at Mengstrasse 4 is the **Buddenbrookhaus,** once owned by the family of Thomas Mann. The organ inside the beautiful **Jacobikirche,** farther north on Breitestrasse, is one of the oldest in Germany; its baroque pipes have been used to good effect in many famous recordings. (Open Tues.-Sun. 11am-6pm; ½ hr. of organ music every Sat. at 5pm.) The well-preserved houses of sea captains adorn **Engelsgrubestrasse,** opposite Jacobikirche; explore **Berrahn's Gang** at #73, and **Hellgrüner Gang** at Engelswisch 28, off of Engelsgrube, and look for footprints of cats and dogs who stepped on the freshly-laid brick 800 years ago. Between the inner city and the train station is **Holstentor,** one of the four gates built in the fifteenth century to guard the entrance to Lübeck. The Holstentor also appears on the back of a DM50 bill.

The **Touristbüro** (tel. (0451) 723 00) in the train station will exchange currency or book a room for DM3. (Open Mon.-Sat. 9am-1pm and 3-8pm, Sun. 10am-noon.) The **Verkehrsverein,** Am Markt 1 (tel. (0451) 723 00), next door to the post office, will sell you a brochure (DM0.50) that includes a small map; the free hotel list contains a similar map. (Open Mon.-Fri. 9am-6pm, Sat. 9am-2pm, Sun. 10am-noon.) The **Folke-Bernadotte-Haus (IYHF),** Am Gertrudenkirchhof 4 (tel. (0451) 334 33), is often full of school groups. One meal obligatory per day; kitchen available. (Members only, but membership cards are available. Juniors DM8.80; seniors DM10.80.

Sheets DM2-3.50. Breakfast DM4. Check-in 8-9am and 1:30-11:30pm. Closed 9-11:30am. Curfew 11:30pm. Open mid-Jan. to mid-Dec.) More attractive is the **Sleep-Inn,** in an 800-year-old house at Grosse Petersgrube 11 (tel. (0451) 789 82). Run by the YMCA but open to anyone, this clean, friendly place is right in the old area of town (a 10-min. walk from the train station), and has rooms with 10 beds. (DM11 per person. Sheets DM3.50. Breakfast 4.50DM.) Reception open Mon.-Fri. 8-11am and 5pm-midnight.) **Hotel Schönwald,** Chasotstr. 25 (tel. (0451) 641 69), at the corner of Gneisenaustr., is quiet, pleasant, and cheap. Take bus #3 (direction: Schlutup) and get off at Königstrasse; change onto bus #4 or 14 until Gneisenaustrasse stop. Call first during the summer; if there's space you might get picked up from the train station. (Singles DM29-35, doubles DM58-65. Breakfast included.) **Camping** is possible all along the shore of the Travemünde delta. The nearest campsite is in the village of **Ivensdorf,** 15 minutes away by bus (DM3) on the road to Travemünde. (DM4 per person, DM10 per tent. Showers included. Tel. (04502) 26 67.)

For good seafood, visit **Fischgaststätte Lück,** Hüxstr. 42, with an unpretentious atmosphere and tasty local specialties (DM10-18). (Open Mon.-Sat. 10am-3pm.) **Formosa Wang,** Hüxtertorallee 25, has a DM9 lunch special featuring soup, main course, and rice. (Open Tues.-Sun. noon-3pm and 5:30-11pm; no lunch special on Sun.) Try the pub at Grosse Burgstr. 13, where a 0.4 liter pils costs DM2. (Open daily at 9am.)

Hapag-Lloyd Reisebüro, Am Kohlmarkt 7-15 (tel. (0451) 15 01 74; open Mon.-Fri. 9am-6pm, Sat. 10am-1pm), has information on daytrips to Rostock in East Germany from Travemünde (about DM79.50 per person). The **Mitfahrezentrale,** Grosse Gröpelgrube 11 (tel. (0451) 778 25), is located next to the Heiligen Geist Hospital. (Open Mon.-Fri. 2:45-6pm, Sat. 10:30am-1pm.)

For ferry travel to Scandinavia and Poland, take the train from Lübeck to "Lübeck-Travemünde-Skandinavienkai" (15-min. ride; frequent trains). Across the street on the wharf is the friendly, information-packed **Nordische Touristik Information** (tel. (04502) 66 88; open June-Aug. daily 9am-8pm; Sept.-May Mon.-Fri. 8am-5pm). The **Jugendfreizeitstätte Priwall (IYHF),** buried away in Travemünde on Mecklenburger Landstr. 69 (tel. (04502) 25 76), can be reached only by a ferry which runs frequently. To reach the ferry, go past Nordische Touristik Information to the light, and then stay right until you reach the dock. Clean, basic rooms. (Juniors DM7.50, seniors DM9.50. Sheets DM2. Breakfast DM3.20. Check-in 11am-10pm. Open April to mid-Oct.)

Hamburg

Hamburg, a centuries-old trading city, juxtaposes the swank shopping promenades of Spitalerstrasse and Jungfernstieg and the seamy sexuality of the city's notorious Red Light District. Though badly damaged in World War II, much of the copper-roofed brick architecture so characteristic of northern Germany survives, while lovely parks and lakes give rise to Hamburg's claim that it—not Stockholm—is the Venice of the north. An active cultural life lends further vitality to this port city.

Orientation and Practical Information

Tourist Offices: Main office in the Bieberhaus (tel. 24 87 00), 100m left from the Kirchenallee exit of the train station. Their free *Hamburg Guide* lists entertainment and cultural events and includes a map. Open Mon.-Fri. 7:30am-6pm, Sat. 8am-3pm, closed Sun. Room bookings (DM3) at the branch in the station open daily 7am-11pm, and at the airport office. (Open daily 8am-11pm.) Concert information tel. 115 15, opera and theater tel. 115 16, day-to-day events tel. 115 17. Another branch at the St. Pauli Landungsbrücken. Open daily 9am-6pm.

Budget Travel: SSR Reiseladen, Rothenbaumchaussee 61 (tel. 410 20 81), near the university. BIGE and student discounts. Open Mon.-Fri. 9am-6pm, Sat. 9am-noon.

American Express: Rathausmarkt 5 (tel. 33 11 41). Mail held. All banking services. Open Mon.-Fri. 9am-5:30pm, Sat. 9am-noon. Financial services available Mon.-Fri. 10am-1pm and 2-5:30pm, Sat. 9am-noon.

Currency Exchange: Decent rates and small service charges at the Hauptbahnhof station. Open daily 7:30am-10pm.

Post Office: At the train station (Kirchenallee exit). Postlagernde Briefe also here. Open 24 hours.

Telephones: At the train station post office. (Open Mon.-Sat. 6:15am-10:45pm, Sun. 7am-10:45pm.) **Telephone code:** 040.

Flights: Tel. 508 25 57. Buses leave for Fuhlsbuttel airport outside the Kirchenallee exit of the train station (every 20 min. 5:17am-9:17pm, 30 min., DM8).

Trains: The **Hauptbahnhof** handles most traffic. **Dammtor** station is across the Kennedy/Lombardsbrücke, and **Altona** station is in the west of Hamburg.

Ferries: Hapag-Lloyd, Jungfernstieg, on the Alster (tel. 328 41), has connections to England. Hamburg-Harwich runs March 21-June 12, and Sept. 7-Oct. 24 (Sun.-Wed. DM120, Thurs.-Sat. DM138); and June 13-Sept. 6 (Sun.-Wed. DM152, Thurs.-Sat. DM174. Ages 4-15 get a 50% discount; students under 26 and seniors get a 25% discount.) Also information and tickets for boats to Scandinavia. (Open Mon.-Fri. 9am-6pm, Sat. 10am-1pm.)

Public Transportation: The efficient public transportation system (buses, U-Bahn, and S-Bahn) costs DM1.80-3.80 depending on distance traveled. Rail passes are valid on the S-Bahn, or you can buy a day ticket (DM7) from an orange automat or at the tourist office. The day ticket is valid for the U-Bahn and the S-Bahn, Mon.-Fri. 9am-4:30pm, Sat.-Sun. all day; children under 12 ride free with day ticket holders. A 24-hour ticket valid for the entire public transportation system costs DM12.50. Public transportation shuts down around 1am, after which only a few buses stay in service.

Emergencies: Police (tel. 110); headquarters at Kirchenallee 46, opposite the train station. **Ambulance** (tel. 112).

Hitchhiking: To Berlin, Copenhagen, and Lübeck take S-Bahn line 1 to Wandsbeker Chaussee, then walk along Hammerstr. until the Hamburg Horn, a large rotary (and dangerous traffic spot) at the base of the *Autobahn.* For points south, take S-Bahn line 3 (direction: Harburg) to Veddel, and walk 5 min. to the *Autobahn.* **Mitfahrzentrale,** Johanniswall 5 (tel. 33 19 14), needs 24-hour notice to arrange domestic rides, 3 days for international. Open Mon.-Fri. 8am-7pm, Sat. 9am-2pm, Sun. noon-4pm. **Mitfahrzentrale for Women,** Grindelallee 43 (tel. 45 05 56).

Laundry: Testorp, Tieloh 19-25. (Tel. 61 16 61).

Accommodations, Camping, and Food

Rooms are generally expensive; expect to pay at least DM30 per person. A wealth of small, inexpensive pensions line **Steindamm, Bremer Weg,** and **Bremer Reihe** just north of the train station. Check out your hotel before you accept a room—half the pensions along this strip are of questionable repute. To help the search, pick up a *Hotelführer* (DM0.50) from the tourist office.

Jugendherberge auf dem Stintfang (IYHF), Alfred-Wegener-Weg 5 (tel. 31 34 88). Take S-1, S-2, or S-3 from the main station to Landungsbrücke. Walk uphill from there—a fantastic view. Juniors DM13.40, seniors DM15.40. (Nonmembers add DM4.) Sheets DM3.50. Breakfast included. 3-day maximum stay. Curfew 1am. Kitchen facilities.

Horner-Rennbahn (IYHF), Rennbahnstr. 100 (tel. 651 16 71), is strict and a bit far from things. Take U-3 to Horner-Rennbahn, then walk 10 min. or take the bus toward Wandsbek (DM 2.80). Juniors DM20.50, seniors DM22.50. Sheets and breakfast included. Midnight curfew. Reception open 7:30-9am, 1-6pm, and 6:30pm-midnight. Closed Jan.

MUI, Budapesterstr. 45 (tel. 43 11 69). Geared toward young people. Clean rooms and a friendly atmosphere. Singles DM25, larger rooms DM20 per person. Showers DM5. Breakfast DM5.50.

Kolpinghaus St. Georg, Schmilinskystr. 78 (tel. 24 66 09). A modern *Jugendgästehaus* with an international guestlist. Leave train station through the Kirchenallee exit, go left, and turn onto Lange Reihe; follow until Schmilinskystr., then turn right. (10-min. walk.) Singles

DM30-33, doubles DM52-56, triples DM72-76, quads DM94-98. Breakfast included. Reception open 24 hours. Open year-round.

Hotel-Pension Terminus, Steindamm 5 (tel. 280 31 44), near Hauptbahnhof. Better than it looks at first. Friendly service and clean rooms, but avoid the few closet-sized singles. Singles DM30-45, doubles DM60-70, triples DM80-97, quads DM100-120, quint DM105-150.

Hotel-Pension Nord, Bremer Reihe 22 (tel. 24 46 93). Cheerful, almost luxurious rooms with a fantastic breakfast included. Good for a splurge. Singles DM40, doubles DM65, triples DM97.50, quads DM120. Showers DM3. Open year-round.

Camping: Buchholz, Kielerstr. 374 (tel. 540 45 32); **Anders,** Kielerstr. 650 (tel. 570 44 98). Take S-3 to Eidestedt and walk 15 min. DM4.50 per person, DM6-9 per tent. Reception open 8-10am, 4-8pm. **Camping Info.** (tel. 239 92 46).

Walk along St. Paul's Quai (Landungsbrücke) for small fish restaurants. **Fischerhaus,** at St. Pauli Fischmarkt 14, is cozy and has great service. (Meals DM11-30. Open daily 11am-11pm.) **Vegetarische Gaststätte,** on a terrace overlooking the Rathausplatz, has been serving delicious, inexpensive vegeterian dishes for 95 years. (Salads DM4.60-15.70, meals DM9.90-14.25; also a quick-service cafe downstairs. Open Mon.-Fri. 11:30am-6:45pm, Sat. 11:30am-3pm, first Sun. of month 11:30am-5pm.) For a typical, local restaurant/bar try the music- and smoke-filled **Max und Konsorten** on Spadenteichstrasse: simple, tasty, and inexpensive meals for DM5.50-11.50. The university area around **Rentzelstrasse** and **Grindelhof** has many small, student-oriented restaurants and a **mensa** at Schlüterstr. 7, which serves lunch Monday-Friday (DM1.50-5; ID required, but usually no questions asked).

Sights

Ships come from all over the world to the **Hamburg Hafen,** the largest port in West Germany. A grand tour of the port by **Hadag** steamer (tel. 37 68 00) runs every half hour from pier #2. (Tours in German only. In summer Mon.-Sun. 9am-6pm; in winter Sat.-Sun. only. DM11, children DM5.50.) Tours in English leave the harbor from pier #1. (Mid-March to Oct. at 11:15am, 1:15pm, 3:15pm, and 5:15pm daily. Tours last 1 hr. DM14, ages under 14 ½ price.) For more information call 56 45 23.

The city center is dominated by the richly ornamented **Rathaus,** a nineteenth-century monstrosity. Tours pass through the several gorgeous rooms still used for receptions and meetings. (Open Mon.-Fri. 10am-3pm, Sat.-Sun. 10am-1pm. Tours given in German, English and French. Admission DM1.) Close by is the equally imposing **St. Michaeliskirche,** on the Ost-West-Strasse; climb the massive spire of this lovely baroque church for the view. (On foot DM1.80, elevator DM3. Open in summer Mon.-Fri. 9am-4pm, Sun. 11:30am-4pm; in winter Mon.-Fri. 10am-4pm.) Across Ost-West-Strasse from the *Michel,* the colloquial term for Hamburg's church, is **Grossneumarkt,** a large square that comes alive with outdoor cafes on summer nights.

One block north of the train station, the enormous **Hamburger Kunsthalle,** Glockengiesserwall 1, holds a fine collection of paintings and drawings ranging from the Gothic to the present. (Open Tues.-Sun. 10am-5pm. Admission DM3, students DM0.70.) One block in the other direction, on Steintorplatz 1, is the **Museum für Kunst und Gewerbe,** an extremely well-designed collection of handicrafts, china, and furnishings ranging from medieval items to art nouveau rooms; Near and Far Eastern works are also displayed. (Open Tues.-Sun. 10am-5pm. Admission DM4, seniors and college students DM2.) The beautiful **Planten un Blomen** (Public Gardens) cultivate beds of fragrant roses and other flowers. (Open daily 7am-11pm.) You can rent sailboats at a wharf along An Der Alster, on the wide part of the Alster basin (DM20 per hr.). The **Holstenbrauerei** (brewery), Holstenstr. 214 (S-Bahn: Holstenstrasse) is open for touring Mon.-Fri. 8am-6pm, but call first (tel. 38 10 10).

Pöseldorf, north of the city center, is a charming quarter of ritzy homes, small cafes, boutiques, and antique stores (U-Bahn: Hallerstr.). The **Hanse Viertel,** between Rathausplatz and Jungfernstieg, is thick with shops, art galleries, and auction houses, while the area around **Sternschanze** has a slightly less upscale feel; a **flea market** is often held on Saturdays. South of here, the three squares Gänsemarkt, Rödungsmarkt, and Grossneumarkt are all lined with cafes and *Kneipen;* at night there's a lot of door-to-door bar-hopping. (U-Bahn: Feldstr.) An entirely different atmosphere—and smell—reigns in the **Fish Market,** along the River Elbe at St. Pauli, which comes alive on Sunday mornings (6-9:30am) as the North Sea catch is brought in. Although the scent of smoked fish prevails, other foods, such as breakfast waffles and doughnuts, lend their aromas. (U- or S-Bahn: Landungsbrücken.) A wealth of second-hand shops await in the **Karo Viertel** (U-Bahn: Messehallen).

Entertainment

Hamburg's infamous **St. Pauli** district extends along the harbor between Nienstedten and Wedel (S-Bahn: Reeperbahn). This area includes the notorious **Grosse Freiheit** (translated "great freedom"), the most concentrated block of sleaze in Europe, as well as respectable discotheques and beer halls. If you visit, do so at night—there's *nothing* to see during the day. **Grosse Freiheit 36,** a bar and disco with live music, on the Reeperbahn, is popular with young people and relatively free of prostitutes. (Cover DM10, with reduced prices for drinks.) **Gestern & Heute,** Kaiser-Wilhelmsstr. 55, never closes. **The Front,** Heidenkampsweg 1, is a gay disco. (Open Wed. and Fri.-Sat. 10pm-3am.) The **Cotton Club,** Alter Steinweg 10 (tel. 34 38 78), has a different traditional jazz band every night at 8:30pm. (Open Mon-Sat. 8pm-midnight.)

Hamburg's rainy climate will often send you looking for a cafe. **Cafe Schwarze Wiege,** Bundesstr. 15 (tel. 45 83 18), has piped-in jazz in a slick atmosphere. **Gröninger Braukeller,** at the corner of OstWeststr. and Brandstwieter, is a very cozy pub which has been brewing its own beer for centuries. (Open Mon.-Fri. 11am-1am, Sat. 5pm-1am.) When the sun is shining, try **Paolino,** Alsterufer 2, on the banks of the Alster. (Open Tues.-Sun. noon-3pm and 6pm-midnight. S-Bahn: Dammtorbahnhof.)

Szene and *Oxmox,* available at newsstands, contain reviews and listings of events (DM4). The *Hamburg Guide* is available free from the tourist office.

Near Hamburg

Flensburg, close to the Danish border and not far from Hamburg, is a graceful old harbor town and a good base for exploring the Baltic coast. For more information, call the **Verkehrsverein,** Norderstr. 6 (tel. (0461) 230 90; open Mon.-Fri. 9am-6pm, Sat. 10am-1pm).

East Frisian Islands

While most visitors head for fairy-tale villages and boisterous beer halls, work-weary Germans flock to these seven islands for healthful sea air and a warm, sunny climate. Despite their popularity, the East Frisian Islands provide a peaceful escape from the densely populated German mainland. Auto traffic is forbidden on all the islands except Borkum and Norderney (where it is highly restricted), and the soothing North Sea surf is always within walking distance.

Oldenburg, not far from Bremen (25 min., with frequent trains), serves as the jumping-off point for most trips. The **tourist office** is in the fifteenth-century *Lappanturm* tower at Langestr. 3 (tel. (0441) 250 96). Rooms (DM28.50 and up) are booked for free. (Open Mon.-Thurs. 9am-1pm and 2-6pm, Fri. 9am-1pm and 2-5:30pm, Sat. 10am-1pm.) For extensive information on the islands (and free copies of brochures you'd pay for at the tourist office), visit the **Fremdenverkehrsverband Nordsee-Niedersachsen-Bremen,** Bahnhofstr. 19-20 (tel. 145 35), in a small alley. (Open Mon.-Tues. 8am-5pm, Wed.-Thurs. 8am-5:30pm, Fri. 8am-1pm.) The city's modern **Jugendherberge (IYHF),** is on Alexanderstr. 65 (tel. 871 35). (Members only: juniors DM11.50, seniors DM13.50. Linen DM2-3.50. Breakfast included. Reception open 7-10pm. Open year-round.) For information about camping, call (0441) 328 28.

Norderney, the most accessible of the islands, is the oldest German North Sea spa; it can be reached from the mainland city of Norddeich Mole. The ferry costs DM9.50 one way, DM13.50 round-trip day excursion, DM19.50 regular round-trip (rail passes not valid). On the island, the **tourist office,** Am Kurplatz (tel. (04932) 89 10), will find you a room in a pension (DM30) or a private home (DM22, for longer stays) for a hefty DM5 fee. (Open in summer Mon.-Fri. 8am-1pm and 3-6pm, Sat. 8am-noon, Sun. 9:30am-12:30pm; off-season Mon.-Sat. only.) Norderney's two **Jugendherbergen (IYHF)** are both crowded; write in advance to reserve space. The hostel at Südstr. 1 (tel. 24 51), is for members only. (Juniors DM7.50, seniors DM9.50. Linen DM2-3.50. Obligatory breakfast DM3.50; if you stay more than one night, all 3 meals are obligatory (DM12.70). Reception open 8:30-9am, 5-5:30pm and 9:45-10pm. No sleeping bags.) The other hostel is at In der Dünen 56 (tel. 25 74), quite far from the ferry; rent a bike while in town. Open March-Oct., it has the same prices as the Sdstr. hostel, but you can camp during the summer (DM4.15 per tent). At both hostels, an island tax is added (DM4.50, ages under 21 DM0.75). **Camping Booken** (tel. 448) is expensive, but the best alternative when the hostels are full. (DM8 per person, DM8 per tent; children ½ price. Showers DM1. Reception open 9:30-10:30am and 5-6pm.)

Borkum, the largest and westernmost of the islands, affords fine wandering possibilities. Unfortunately the 2¼-hour boat trip costs DM20 round-trip day excursion, DM40 regular round-trip from Emden on the mainland. For transportation information call (04921) 89 07 22. You can make room reservations at the **Verkehrsbüro** am Bahnhof (tel. (04922) 30 32 95), with private rooms beginning at DM20. **"Insel-Camping"** is at Hindenburgstr. 114 (tel. 10 88), about 15 min. from the island's train station.

Ships that follow the tides serve all the other islands; be careful not to get stuck overnight. Times and fares are available at any Bundesbahn station. Juist is accessible from Norddeich. To reach Baltrum, take the bus from the Norden train station to Nessmersiel, where you connect with the ship. For Langeoog, take the bus from the Esens train station to Bensersiel, and the ship from there. For Spiekeroog take the bus from Esens to Neuharlingersiel. For Wangerooge, take the train from Wilhelmshaven to Carolinensiel, and then the ship.

Bremen

A longtime member of the Hanseatic League, Bremen has preserved much of its medieval heritage while capitalizing on such modern assets as the Beck's Beer brewery. And the charismatic port city is always inviting its visitors back; many believe that if you walk up to the statue of the fabled Brementown musicians and say "Guten Tag" to the mule, you will some day return.

Another old belief is that as long as the giant stone **Statue of Roland** on Markplatz stands, Bremen will not die. The fabulous **Rathaus,** begun in the 1200s but expanded and decorated as the town grew wealthier, is one of the best examples of north German architecture. (Free tours March-Oct. Mon.-Fri. 10am, 11am, and noon; Sat.-Sun. 11am and noon; Nov.-Feb. Mon.-Fri. 10am, 11am, and noon.) The impressive **St. Petri Dom,** begun in 1042, rather miraculously survived World War II. (Open Mon.-Fri. 9am-5pm, Sat. 9am-noon, Sun. 2-5pm. Admission to climb the tower DM1, seniors and ages under 10 DM.50.) In the basement of St. Petri is the **Bleikeller,** where in 1695 the mummified corpses of workers who had fallen from the roof of the cathedral were discovered. The mummies have been on exhibition for almost three centuries. Several years ago a tourist broke a thumb off of one of the mummies as a souvenir; she was so beset with the mummy's curse that she soon mailed the thumb back to Bremen. (Bleikeller open May-Oct. Mon.-Fri. 9-11:45am and 1-4:45pm, Sat. 9-11:45am. Admission DM2, ages under 12 DM1.)

Near Marktplatz you'll find the beautiful, narrow, cobblestoned **Böttcherstrasse,** lined with boutiques and galleries. Hidden among them is the fifteenth-century **Roselius House** (tel. 32 19 11), which now houses medieval art. (Open Mon.-Thurs. 10am-4pm, Sat.-Sun. 11am-4pm. Admission DM2.50, students DM1.50.) Farther on Böttcherstr., the **Glockenspiel** plays themes from the *Song of Roland* at noon, 3pm, and 6pm. From here you can follow the footprints on the street to **Schnoorviertel,** a cobblestone pedestrian zone. For a pleasant stroll or a picnic, visit the beautiful park surrounding the **Mühle am Herdentor.** The **Kunsthalle** contains a fine collection of paintings and sculpture ranging from the Renaissance to the present; the early twentieth-century German art is especially strong. (Open Tues. 10am-9pm, Wed.-Sun. 10am-5pm. Admission DM5, seniors and students DM2.50, families DM10; tours are an additional DM1.)

The **Verkehrsverein** (tel. (0421) 363 61), right across from the train station, finds rooms for DM3. (Open Mon.-Thurs. 8am-8pm, Fri. 8am-10pm, Sat. 8am-6pm, Sun. 9:30am-3:30pm.) The **post office** and the **telephone office** are at Domsheide 15, near the Markt. (Open Mon.-Fri. 8am-6pm, Sat. 8am-1pm.) Bike rentals are available in **Fahrradstation ADFC** (tel. 30 21 14), to your left as you exit the station, for DM8.50 per day. (Open Wed.-Mon. 9am-6pm.) The **Mitfahrzentrale** bureau is at tel. 720 11. The clean, modern **Jugendherberge (IYHF),** Kalkstr. 6 (tel. 17 13 69), has a rooftop patio overlooking the Weser River. From the station follow Bahnhofstr. to Herdentor; go right at Am Wall and then left on Bürgermeister-Smidt-Str., then right along the water to the hostel. (Juniors DM8, seniors DM10. Linen DM2-3.50. Breakfast DM3.50-4.50. Check-in Mon.-Fri. 1:30-10pm, Sat.-Sun. 4:30-10pm.) **Camping** is quite far out of town, at Am Stadtwaldsee 1 (tel. 21 20 02); take bus #22 or 23 (about 15 min.) to the last stop, then walk along Kuhgangweg to Anwieseck and turn left. (DM5.50 per person, DM8 per tent. Open March-Oct.)

In the *Rathaus* visit Bremen's famous **Ratskeller** (the oldest in Germany, 1408) to sip a glass of one of the 600 varieties of German wine. The *menus* (DM15-25) make a good splurge, but Monday through Friday at lunchtime the *Touristenteller* plate is more economical (DM10.65, glass of wine included). (Open daily 10am-midnight.) At the corner of Wachtstr. and Marktstr., right off Marktplatz, is elegant **Restaurant Friesenhof.** (Summer *menu* DM13.75-22.95, fish meals DM12.90-23.90, steak DM19.80-26.50. Lunch, 11am-3pm, DM8.50. Open daily 11am-midnight.) All the action is along **Ostertorsteinweg,** just east of the old city. Several reasonably priced Greek and Chinese restaurants line Ölmühlenerstrasse, near the hostel.

Lüneburger Heide

South of Hamburg stretches the flat, heather- and birch-covered Lüneburger Heide. Bicycling here from one mist-shrouded town to the next during the still, morning hours makes for a tranquil break between visits to the bustling ports of Schleswig-Holstein. **Lüneburg** is a cobblestoned old city tucked among birch trees on the banks of the River Ilmenau. The Gothic **Michaeliskirche** on Johann-Sebastian-Bach-Platz in the *Altstadt,* is an impressive brick church built in 1418 on a foundation of salt; since then, the massive pillars have warped due to this insecure foundation. The **Verkehrsverein** (tel. (04131) 245 93) is in the **Rathaus** on Waagestr.; from the train station take Lünertorstr. which turns into Lünerstr., then go left onto Bardowickerstr. (Open May-Sept. Mon-Fri. 9am-1pm and 2-6pm, Sat. 9am-12:30pm, Sun. 9am-12:30pm; Oct.-April Mon.-Sat. only.) There's a fruit and vegetable market every Wed. and Sat. morning in front of the Rathaus. The **Jugendherberge (IYHF)** is at Soltauerstr. 133, a 30-min. walk from the Verkehsverein, or take bus #1. (Tel. 418 64. Members only: juniors DM7.50, seniors DM9.50. Sheets DM2-3.50. Breakfast DM3.50-4.90. Bike rental DM5 per day. Curfew 10pm.) **Campingplatz Rote Schleuse** is 5km south of Lüneburg on the Ilmenau (tel. (04131) 79 15 00). At night, the pubs of Lüneburg's **Stintmarkt** come alive, especially in summer, when tables are set up in the street along the Ilmenau.

Celle, some 80km from Hamburg, is a fine base for exploring the region. Opposite the Verkehrsverein is the **Herzogschloss** (Duke's Castle), built in 1670. (Tel. 123 73. Tours daily 10am-noon and 2-4pm. Admission DM1, ages under 14 DM.50.) One of the castle's most famous residents was Caroline-Mathilde, who was married to the King of Denmark in 1766 for political reasons. Six years later her love affair with the King's minister was discovered; he was executed and she was given asylum in the Herzogschloss. (Open Sun.-Fri. 10am-4pm, Sat.10am-12:30pm.) The **Bomann Museum** has exhibits on the folk culture of the region. (Open Mon.-Sat. 10am-5pm, Sun. 10am-1pm. Admission DM1, students and children DM0.50.) You can rent bikes at the **Verkehrsverein,** Schlossplatz 6a (tel. (05141) 230 31), for DM8 per day. They will reserve rooms (from DM25) free of charge. Pick up a copy of *Jahresveranstaltung,* which lists concerts and musical productions for the year. (Open mid-May to mid-Oct. Mon.-Fri. 8am-6pm, Sat. 9am-1pm and 2-5pm, Sun. 10am-noon; mid-Oct. to mid-May Mon.-Fri. 8am-5pm, Sat. 10am-noon.) There is a stark but clean **Jugendherberge (IYHF)** at Weghausstr. 2 (tel. (05141) 532 08); go left along the tracks from the station as far as you can, then left on Bremer Weg (30 min.), or take bus #3. (Juniors DM7.50, seniors DM9.50. Showers included. No sleeping bags. Sheets DM2. Breakfast DM3.50. Check-in 5-7pm. Curfew 10pm.) **Walsrode,** between Hamburg and Celle, makes a fine excursion with its colorful **Vogelpark Am Rieselbach** (tel. (05161) 20 15), a menagerie of exotic birds. Cycle here; transportation from Celle is poor. (Open mid-March to Nov. daily 9am-7pm. Admission DM10, students and children DM6.)

Central Germany

Goslar

On the northern edge of the Harz, Goslar was once the beat of the Roman emperors. Today the town, perhaps the prettiest in central Germany, appears uniformly medieval. The stone walls and churches and the *Fachwerkhäuser* (shingled houses peculiar to the region) complement each other well. Goslar is accessible by train from Bremen (5 per day), Göttingen (4 per day), and Hannover (12 per day).

The **Kaiserpfalz,** Kaiserbleek 6, is a massive Romanesque palace from which the Holy Roman emperors exercised sporadic control over feuding German states in the eleventh and twelfth centuries. The interior of the great hall is decorated with nineteenth-century murals, designed to remind Bismarck's Second Reich of the mythical heritage left by the first. (Open May-Sept. daily 9:30am-5pm; Nov.-Feb. 10am-3pm; March-April and Oct. 10am-4pm. Admission DM2.50, students DM1.25.)

Below the palace is the **Domvorhalle,** all that remains of the cathedral that collapsed 150 years ago. (Open June-Sept. Mon.-Sat. 10am-1pm and 2:30-5pm, Sun. 10am-1pm; Oct.-May daily 10:30am-noon. Admission DM0.60, students DM0.30.) To reach the **Markt** (market held every Tues. and Fri. morning) from the train station, take Rosentorstr., then fork left down Fischemäkerstrasse. Here, the **Glocken und Figurenspiel** plays at 9am, noon, 3pm, and 6pm; its wooden figures celebrate both knights in armor and the miners who made the area prosperous. The **Neuwerkkirche,** a pure Romanesque church, preserves its original thirteenth-century apse paintings and eerie stone motifs. (Open April-Oct. Mon.-Thurs. 9:30-11:30am and 2:30-4:30pm, Sat. 9:30-11:30am and 2-4pm; Nov.-Dec. Mon.-Fri. 9:30-11:30am.)

The **Mönchehaus** at the corner of Jakobistr. and Mönchestr. is an outstanding small museum of modern art in an ancient house. (Open Tues.-Sat. 10am-1pm and 3-5pm, Sun. 10am-1pm. Admission DM2.50, students and children DM1.)

The **Kur- und Fremdenverkehrsgesellschaft,** Markt 7 (tel. (05321) 2846) can find rooms (DM23 and up, with reductions for longer stays) for a fee of DM3. (Open

Mon.-Fri. 9am-1pm and 2-5pm, Sat. 9am-12:30pm.) The **Jugendherberge (IYHF),** Rammelsbergerstr. 25 (tel. (05321) 222 40) is in the hills behind the Kaiserpfalz. No bus runs from the station to the hostel; pick up a map from the tourist office, and look for the sign at the bottom of Rammelsbergerstrasse. If you're of college age, don't expect to be consistently treated politely. (Members only; juniors DM7.50, seniors DM9.50. Linen DM2-3.50. Breakfast DM3.50, one meal obligatory. Camping half hostel prices. Check-in 6-7pm; closed 9:30-11am. Curfew 9:45pm.) Call to see if there's room at the **Pension Alscher,** Klosterstr. 9a (tel. (05321) 225 74), behind the station; go up Tappenstr. and turn left at the third intersection (10-min. walk). (Singles DM25, doubles DM24 per person. Extremely generous breakfast included.) **Campingplatz Sennhütte,** Clausthalerstr. 28 (tel. 225 02), 3km out of town along the B241, is equipped with a restaurant and sauna. (DM4 per person, DM3.50 per tent. Showers DM1. Open year-round.)

Reasonably priced eateries cluster in the pedestrian zone at the center of town. **Balkan-Grill im Weissen Schwan,** Münzstr. 11, opposite the Markt off a corner of Schuhhof, offers reasonable Yugoslavian and German fare (DM11 and up) in an old half-timbered house. (Open daily 11:30am-3pm and 5:30pm-midnight.) A bit farther from the Markt, **Restaurant Christall,** Bäckerstr. 106, serves meals from DM7. (Open Mon.-Sat. 11am-11pm, Sun. 11am-3pm; in winter closed Mon.-Sat. 3-6pm.)

Near Goslar

The delightful village of **Hahnenklee,** with its pretty Norwegian stave church, is a great base for further exploration of the Harz. To get there, and for a good view of the Harz, take the frequent post bus #1 (about every hr. until 8:45pm) from Bahnhof Goslar (direction: Hahnenklee Bockswiese; DM3.50). To reach the modern, pleasant **Jugendherberge (IYHF),** Steigerstieg 1 (tel. (05325) 22 56), get off at the Bockswiese stop. (Juniors DM7.50, seniors DM9.50. Breakfast DM3.50; large lunch DM4.50-7, dinner DM4.80. Check-in 5pm and 9:45pm; closed 9:30-11:30am. Curfew 10pm.) The excellent **Campingplatz am Kreuzeck** (tel. 25 70) is also on the post bus route; get off the bus 2km before Hahnenklee. (DM5.50 per person, DM8.50 per tent. Open year-round.)

Harz Mountains

In densely populated central Germany, the wooded Harz Mountains offer tourists and natives alike a peaceful escape from the blandness of reconstructed cities. The range stretches from Goslar in the north to the health resort Bad Sachsa in the south, where the border with East Germany cuts an ugly gash pocked with land mines and guard towers. After a sobering view of the border from a town such as Hohegeiss, cheer up in the beautiful forests and lakes of this mountain region. In winter there is also cross-country and downhill skiing, skating, and tobogganing.

Most of the mountains fall within the **Naturpark Harz.** Maps of hiking trails are available at many shops; the DM6.80 version is adequate. The **Harzer Verkehrsverband** in Goslar at Markstr. 45 (tel. (05321) 200 31) has more detailed information. Be sure to pick up their indispensable *Grüner Faden für den Harz-Gast* pamphlet, which lists the castles, ruins, churches, caves, ski areas, celebrations, and more in the Harz region. Equally important is their *Jugend und Freizeitheime im Harz und im Harzvorland* pamphlet, a complete list of youth hostels and student centers in the area. (Open Mon.-Thurs. 8am-5pm, Fri. 8am-2:30pm.)

Braunlage is a good base from which to explore the mountains. The **Kurverwaltung,** Elbingeröderstr. 17 (tel. (05520) 10 54), can help with accommodations. (Open Mon.-Fri. 7:30am-12:30pm and 2-5pm, Sat. 10:00am-noon.) After hours, the large board outside the office lists prices, addresses, and availability of pensions and hotels in Braunlage. Sport shops in town rent skis, boots, and poles for about DM20 per day. The **Jugendherberge (IYHF),** Von-Langen-Str. (tel. 22 38), is practically in the woods. Take bus #2422 (Goslar-Braunlage) to the **Wienerwald** restaurant stop (a cheap place to eat), and follow the signs. (Juniors DM7.50, seniors DM9.50. Sheets DM2-3.50. Breakfast DM3.50. Check-in 5-7pm. Lockout 10-11:30am. Curfew 10pm. Open year-round.) Camping **Ferien vom Ich,** Am Campingplatz (tel. (05520) 413), is located in the forest, toward Bad Lauterberg. (DM4 per person, DM3 per tent. Open year-round.)

The Harz Mountains offer more than 1000km of hiking trails. Many towns offer guided hikes; these trips are offered most frequently from May to August in Bad Harzburg (*Kurverwaltung,* tel. (05322) 30 44; from Goslar train station, take bus line #2407 or the train for a 15-min. ride; both leave approximately every hr. until 8:30pm); Bad Lauterberg (*Kurverwaltung,* tel. (05524) 40 21); and St. Andreasberg (*Kurverwaltung,* tel. (05582) 10 12; bus #2402 runs from Goslar train station to both these towns). You can rent ski equipment in **St. Andreasburg** at **Sportgeschäft Pläschke,** Dr. Willi Bergmannstr. 10 (tel. (05582) 260) for about DM15 per day, or from **H. Diegner** on Schützenstr. 38 (tel. (05582) 13 02) for about DM15 per day. Inexpensive, stark, and crowded lodgings abound on Am Gesehrstrasse; there are several pensions (beginning at DM17) along Auf der Höhe Strasse.

For more specific advice, the office of the **Alpenverein** in any major city can help. The Goslar office is at Schuh-und-Sport Deckert, Fischemäkerstr. 1. For members, there might be two to three hikes and one rock climb per week from Goslar. Come prepared for rain; mists add to the mystery of these wonderful mountains, but make a hike miserable if you're not prepared to fight back. Call (05321) 401 24 for a daily Harz weather report, tourist information, and information on snow conditions.

Hannover

Hannover, the capital and transportation center of Lower Saxony, is no great shakes, but you may find it convenient to stop here on your way to or from the Harz Mountains. While in town, take the elevator up the tower of the stately **Rathaus,** Trammplatz 2, (open in summer only, 10am-5pm; DM1.50, students DM0.50) for a view of the **Maschsee,** Hannover's artificial lake. (In summer, boats for rent and cruises.) Hannover's prize is the **Grosser Garten Herrenhausen** (U-bahn: Herrenhäuser Gärten), a palace set in a painstakingly well-kept baroque garden. Music, theater, and ballet are performed from May-Sept. For ticket information, call 168 75 93, or ask at the tourist office (tel. 168 28 00). For wheelchair reservations, call 168 75 92.

The information center in the train station can provide you with a map of Hannover, but the main **Verkehrsbüro** lies across the S-bahn tracks, at Ernst-August-Platz 8 (tel. (0511) 168 23 19; after 6pm tel. 168 28 01). They'll find you a room for DM3, and can suggest a walking tour. (Open Mon.-Fri. 8:30am-6pm, Sat. 8:30am-noon.) To reach the **Jugendherberge (IYHF),** Ferdinand-Wilhelm Fricke Weg 1 (tel. 32 29 41), take Bus #24 toward Stadionbrücke. (Juniors DM8, seniors DM10; nonmembers add DM4. Linen DM2-3.50. Breakfast DM3.50-4.90. Curfew 11:30pm. Camping also available: juniors DM4, seniors DM5.) The peaceful **Naturfreundehaus in der Eibenriede,** Hermann-Bahlsen-Allee 8, is only a 15-min. walk away from Hannover's zoo. From the station, take Stadtbahnlinie #3 and 7 toward Lahe and Fasanenkrug to the Spannhagengarten stop. From there, it's a 10-min. walk down Hermann-Bahlsen-Allee. (Members: singles DM24, doubles DM19 per person. Nonmembers: singles DM30.50-36. Doubles DM22.50 per person. Sheets, shower, and breakfast included.) For a beer garden atmosphere, with occasional live music, head to **Bavarium,** Windmühlenstr. 3 (tel. 32 36 00), across from the opera house. (Dishes DM8-20. Open July-Aug. Mon.-Sat. 11am-midnight.) The traditional drink of Hannover's 450-year-old **Schützenfest** (a huge beer festival held annually during the first week of July, with parades, bands, floats and fireworks) is the *Lüttje-Lage.* Without spilling, one must drink from two glasses (stacked one atop the other) at the same time—one glass contains dark beer, the other, Schnaps. It's as dangerous as it sounds.

Göttingen

Since the establishment of Europe's first free university here in 1737 (until this time, all universities had been run by men appointed by the state), Göttingen has been the home of some of Germany's most brilliant minds. In the eighteenth century, it was immortalized by the poets of the *Göttinger Hain,* in the nineteenth it graduated Otto von Bismarck, and in this century it was a gathering place for Max Planck and others who originated the quantum theory of physics.

The most notable of Göttingen's churches is the Gothic **St. Johannis;** the two magnificent octagonal towers, begun in 1320, give the plain exterior of the church the appearance of a fortress. (Tower open Sat. 2-4pm only; church open 11am-noon and for mass.) The twelfth-century 72-meter tower of **St. Jacobi** dominates the town. (Both the church and the tower closed except on Fridays at 6pm for the weekly organ concert.) At the corner of Obere Maschstr. and Untere Maschstr. a graceful monument commemorates the synagogue burned on *Kristallnacht* in 1938. Walk along Lange Geismarstr. from the corner of Kurze Geismarstr. to see an impressive block of *Fachwerkhäuser* (half-timbered houses). The **Rathaus,** a reminder of the town's wealth as a member of the Hanseatic League from 1351 to 1572, is best appreciated from the outside, where two lions made in Kassel in 1795 hold shields showing the municipal arms. Free tours of the city depart from the statue of Gänseliesel (which students at the University kiss upon getting their doctorates) in front of the *Rathaus.* (April-Oct. Wed. and Sat. 3pm.)

The **Verkehrsamt** (tel. (0551) 560 00) opposite the train station has a room-finding service (DM3) with places for DM34 and up; they also have city maps and hiking and hostel information. (Open Mon.-Fri. 9am-6pm, Sat. 9am-1pm.) Another branch (tel. (0551) 540 00) is located in the *Rathaus.* (Open April-Oct. Mon.-Fri. 9am-6pm, Sat. 9am-4pm, Sun. 10am-4pm; Nov.-March Mon.-Fri. 9am-6pm, Sat. 9am-1pm.) There's a pleasant, modern **Jugendherberge (IYHF)** at Habichtsweg 2 (tel. (0551) 576 22); from the *Bahnhof* take bus #8 or 11 to Theaterplatz, then bus #6 or a 30-min. walk left on Berliner Str. to the hostel. (Juniors DM8, seniors DM10. Sheets DM2-3.50. Hot showers included. Breakfast DM3.50. Reception open 8-9am and 4-10pm. Hostel closed 9-11:30am; lockout 9am-4pm. Curfew 11:30pm. Open year-round.) Of the several **University Mensas,** the most convenient is on Wilhelmsplatz. (Open mid-April to mid-July and mid-Oct. to mid-Feb. Mon.-Fri. 11:30am-2pm.) Both the **Nord Mensa,** Grisebachstr. 10, and **Zentralmensa,** at the University, are open year-round. (Nord Mensa open Mon.-Fri. 11:30am-2pm; Zentralmensa open Mon.-Fri. 11:30am-2:15pm, Sat. 11:30am-2pm.) For dinner, try the Yugoslavian specialties (DM8.50-16.50) at **Balkan Sonne,** Paulinerstr. 10, behind the *Rathaus.* (Open daily noon-3pm and 6pm-midnight.) Vegetarian fare flourishes at **Estragon,** Angerstr. 8, with meals for DM4.50-12. (Open Mon.-Fri. 6-11pm, Sat.-Sun. noon-3pm.)

To find some students who aren't studying, parole the pedestrian zone. **Pegasus,** Weender Str. 39 (tel. 424 26), is a bar with outdoor seating, sometimes featuring live music. (Open daily until 11:40pm.) **Zum Altdeutschen,** Prinzenstr. 16 (tel. 565 45), is similarly popular among students. (Open Mon.-Thurs. 1pm-2am, Fri.-Sat. 1pm-3am, Sun. 6pm-2am.) The **Kleiner Ratskeller,** Jüdenstr. 30 (tel. 573 16), is a pub frequented by students of all nationalities.

Hannoversch Münden

Wedged between steep, wooded hills at the junction of the Werra and Fulda Rivers, Hannoversch Münden has a setting whose beauty few other towns in Germany can rival. The town is easily accessible by train from Göttingen (35 min.) or Kassel (20 min.), yet the half-timbered medieval houses of the nationally famous *Altstadt* remain refreshingly tranquil.

Walk through the **Altstadt** (old town) to admire the beautiful fourteenth-century *Fachwerkhäuser.* The **Rathaus** and its ornate facade is a leading example of the Weser Renaissance style which arose in this area of Germany around 1550. To reach the Rathaus from the train station, go down Bahnhofstr. to the end, then turn right in the pedestrian zone. For a view of the wooded valley, cross the Fulda and follow the signs to **Tillyschanze,** an old stone tower up on a hill. (Open May-Sept. daily 10am-6pm. Admission DM1, children DM0.50.) The **Naturpark Münden** surrounds the town with numerous wooded trails.

The **Verkehrsbüro** (tel. (05541) 753 13), in the *Rathaus,* finds private rooms (DM15 and up) and hotel rooms (DM25 and up) free of charge. (Open May-Sept. Mon.-Fri. 8:30am-5pm, Sat. 8:30am-12:30pm; Oct.-April Mon.-Thurs. 8:30am-12:30pm and 1-4pm, Fri. 8:30am-12:30pm.) On Saturday and Sunday, help is available at the *Auskunftsschalter* in the same building. The very friendly **Jugendherberge (IYHF),** Prof.-Oelkers-Str. 8 (tel. 88 53), is located just outside the town limits on the banks of the Weser off the B80. It's a 35-min. walk, or you can take bus #5203 from the station. (Mon.-Fri. 10 per day 6:35am-7:40pm, Sat. 6 per day, Sun. and holidays only 1 per day; railpasses valid.) (Juniors DM7.50, seniors DM9.50. Sheets DM2.50-3.50. Breakfast DM3.50. Check-in 9am and 11:30am-10pm. Curfew 9:45pm. Open year-round.) **Gasthaus zur Hafenbahn,** Blume 54 (tel. 40 94), down Langestr. from the *Rathaus* and across the bridge, offers simple but clean rooms at DM23 per person, showers and breakfast included. Good food (DM3.50-17.50) is also available. (Open Tues.-Sun. 9am-10pm. Closed end of July.) You can pitch your tent conveniently at **Campingplatz Tanzwerder** (tel. 122 57), 10 minutes from the train station, on an island in the River Fulda off Pionierbrücke. Unaccompanied teens (12-18 yrs.) need written permission from their guardian to camp. (DM4.50 per person, DM3 per tent. Office open daily 7am-1pm and 3-10pm. Open April-Sept.)

The paths along the Weser River which lead to the Tillyschanze continue on towards the Reinhardswald. (Maps of this forest area at the youth hostel, DM7.50.) For more information, inquire at the Verkehrsbüro in the *Rathaus.*

Marburg

The Brothers Grimm compiled their fairy tales and legends in the forests surrounding Marburg, a town tucked away in the rolling hills of central Germany. From a distance the town looks ageless, as if its medieval castle were still vigilant. But this university center buzzes with political activity. The bars in the *Altstadt* (walk across the bridge opposite the train station, and turn left onto Elisabethstr.) and the cafes on Steinweg are good places to meet students. The tradition of opposition in Marburg is at least as old as the Reformation; the town was the site of the first Protestant university in Europe, founded at the behest of Luther himself.

Climb up the seemingly endless narrow staircases of the old city or take bus #16 from Rudolfsplatz (3 per hr., 10 min.) to the **Landgrafenschloss.** Most of the castle remains unrestored, but even the few rooms open are worth the climb. Visit the *Disputationsraum,* which in 1529 served as the site of a famous religious debate between Martin Luther and Ulrich Zwingli. (Open May-Oct. Tues.-Sun. 10am-1pm and 3-6pm; Nov.-April Tues.-Sat. 10am-1pm and 3-5pm, Sun. 3-5pm. Free.) The **Elisabethkirche,** one of the earliest Gothic churches in Germany, houses some exceptional early medieval art. Cross the bridge opposite the train station and take a left. The reliquary for the bones of the church's namesake, a widowed duchess turned altruist, is remarkably ornate. (Open Mon.-Sat. 9am-6pm, Sun. 11am-noon and 12:30-6pm. Tours Mon.-Fri. 3pm, Sat. 4pm, Sun. 11am and 3pm. Admission to the art treasures DM2, students DM1.) Many of the houses with parti-colored flags are university fraternities. Stop in one or two and ask to see their old fencing equipment; well into the nineteenth century these frats fought regular duels to defend their pieces of sidewalk.

Marburg, with relatively few tourists, is served by frequent trains from Frankfurt (1 hr.) and Kassel (1-1½ hr.). The friendly **Verkehrsamt** (tel. (06421) 20 12 62), just to the right of the train station, will find you a private room for DM15-20 or a pension or hotel room for DM30 and up, free of charge. (Open April-Oct. Mon.-Fri. 8am-12:30pm and 2-5:30pm, Sat. 9:30am-noon; Nov.-March Mon.-Fri. 8:30am-12:30pm and 2-5pm.) The **Jugendherberge (IYHF),** Jahnstr. 1 (tel. (06421) 234 61), is a 20-minute walk along the river; take a left as you exit the train station. (Juniors DM11.80, seniors DM13.80. Linen DM3.50. Breakfast included. Reception open 5-8pm. Curfew April-Oct. 11:30pm, Nov.-March 10pm.) A more pleasant alternative with clean, fresh rooms and a friendly proprietor is **Gästehaus Einsle,** Frankfurterstr. 2a (tel. (06421) 234 10), near Rudolfsplatz; walk a few blocks up Am Grün until the street changes names. (DM35 per person. Breakfast included.) The country inn **Hotel Sonnengold,** Zur Hainbuche 2 (tel. (06424) 14 83), has pleasant and inexpensive rooms, but is way out of town. (Singles DM22, doubles DM40. Showers and breakfast included.) Barren **Camping Lahnaue** (tel. (06421) 213 31) is along the Lahn River; take bus #1 toward Sommerbad. (DM3 per person, DM3 per tent. Showers DM1. Open year-round.)

Alter Ritter, Steinweg 44, has good food and friendly service in a casual atmosphere. Their cold meals with salad cost DM9-12.50, and a daily *menu* runs DM9.80-18. (Open Mon.-Fri. 11am-2:30pm and 5:30pm-midnight, Sat.-Sun. 11am-5pm.) **Futterkiste,** Frankfurterstr. 2a, serves Afghan fare, including vegetarian dishes, for DM9-15; their lunch special is DM6. (Open Mon.-Thurs. 11:30am-2pm and 5pm-1am, Fri.-Sat. 5pm-1am, Sun. 11:30am-2pm and 5pm-midnight.) For beer and/or students, try **Destille,** Steinweg 23.

The excellent **Filmkunsttheater,** Steinweg, shows a new film every day; most are dubbed in German. If you're in Marburg in the summer, ask at the Verkehrsamt for a program of the summer concerts which take place on the open-air stage in the Schlosspark.

Frankfurt am Main

Frankfurt is not charming—no one expects it to be—but it is well-equipped with an airport and trains to get you someplace that is. After being leveled in World War II, Frankfurt poked its head up out of the debris and has been living and breathing money ever since.

The **Römerberg** is the historic center of Frankfurt. Still in the throes of a massive reconstruction project, the area will someday combine archeological excavations, historic burghers' houses, and modern shops. Nearby at Grosser Hirschgraben 23, the **Goethe House,** Frankfurt's most treasured museum, conveys a sense of the Goethe family's opulence; the portraits on the fourth floor trace the author's family history. (Open April-Sept. Mon.-Sat. 9am-6pm, Sun. 10am-1pm; Oct.-March Mon.-Sat. 9am-4pm, Sun. 10am-1pm. Admission DM3, college students and disabled DM2, younger students DM1.50.)

Frankfurt has several fine new museums, all next to one another along Schaumainkai, renamed Museumsufer, on the south side of the River Main between the Alte Mainbrücke and the Friedensbrücke. Sculpture, handicrafts, anthropology, the German postal system, German cinema, German architecture, and the fine arts are all celebrated. But the most unexpected pleasure in Frankfurt is the **Palmengarten,** a huge collection of over 3000 orchids and 1600 kinds of cacti, spreading over acres of greenhouses, gardens, and fountains. To reach it, take tram #19 to Palmengartenstrasse. (Open daily 9am-dusk. Admission DM4, DM6 on holidays; students and ages under 18 DM1.50, DM3 on holidays; disabled free, DM2 on holidays.)

Frankfurt's **tourist office** is at the head of platform #23 in the Hauptbahnhof (tel. (069) 23 10 55). They find rooms for DM3, pass out free maps, and sell the *Frankfurter Woche,* a booklet with listings of accommodations, sights, and concerts (DM0.50). (Open April-Oct. Mon.-Sat. 8am-10pm, Sun. 9:30am-8pm; Nov.-March Mon.-Sat. 8am-9pm, Sun. 9:30am-8pm.) There is another office at the airport, offering the same services, and a third in the Hauptwache-Passage (tel. 212 87 08; open Mon.-Fri. 9am-6pm, Sat. 9am-2pm). For hostel lodgings, try the **Haus der Jugend (IYHF),** Deutschherrnufer 12 (tel. (069) 61 90 58). Take the very frequent bus #46 from the station to Frankensteinerplatz. (Juniors DM14.60, DM11.70 after first night; seniors DM17.30, DM14.40 after first night; nonmembers DM3 extra, DM1.50 when there are free beds. Linen and breakfast included. Lockout 9am-1pm.) A *Jugendkino* (tel. (069) 43 26 26) on the premises shows movies from Disney to current hits every Friday at 4pm. (Admission DM4.) A nice alternative is **Pension Backer,** Mendelssohnstr. 92 (tel. (069) 74 79 92), in a pleasant part of town near the university and the Palmengarten. Take tram #19 (direction: Ginnheim) to Siesmayer/Mendelssohnstr. or the U-bahn to Westend. (Singles DM25-35, doubles DM50. Showers DM3. Breakfast included.) Adjacent to the station (go right from the southern exit, across from track #1) is **Pension Lohmann,** Stuttgarterstr. 31 (tel. 23 25 34), a cozy, clean place. (Singles DM34, doubles DM58. Showers DM3. Breakfast included. Closed July.)

The seamy streets radiating from the train station are lined with cheap snack stands and fast-food places (the number of McDonald's are testimony that Frankfurt was located in the American Zone of Germany after World War II; don't despair, there is a German city to be found). For a better selection, cross the river to **Sachsenhausen.** The area between Brückenstr. and Drei-Eichenstr. is home to dozens of inexpensive Hessian and foreign eateries.

The 12-minute S-Bahn connection between the **airport** and train station (lines #14 and 15) is simple and frequent (DM3.10 from a blue automat; Eurail and InterRail valid). If you're hitchhiking to Munich, take bus #36 or 960 from Knostablerwache headed south until you see the *Autobahn.* For all other directions, take tram #13 or 61 to Stadion, and continue in the same direction along Mörfelder Landstr. **Mitfahrzentrale,** Gutleutstr. 125 (tel. (069) 23 02 91), is to the right of the train station. (Open Mon.-Fri. 8:30am-6:30pm, Sat. 8:30am-2pm, Sun. noon-4pm.) The prices outside do not include a booking charge of DM2-25.

The Rhinelands

Mainz to Koblenz

This is the Rhine of legend, with robber castles, steep vineyards, and the famed **Lorelei Cliff,** marked by a flag near St. Goar where fair sirens once lured passing river travelers to their death on the rocks below. Every twist of the river brings another castle ruin into view.

KD Line river steamers sail from April 4 to October 25; regular and express boats and hydrofoils head up and down the river between Köln and Mainz several times per day, with stops in all or most of the small villages. Eurail is valid for free passage on the regular boats; Eurail holders must pay a surcharge for express boats, and half-price for the hydrofoil. InterRail and Tramper-Monat tickets are not valid. Train ticket for a corresponding stretch are interchangeable with KD tickets; a small charge may apply. Try at the tourist offices to get an English copy of the fiendishly complicated boat schedule. Children under 4 ride free with KD, and those under 14 for half-price. If you are a senior (over 60) you ride for half-price on Mondays, and for free on your birthday!

Mainz, the center of the Rhine Valley, is a city you'll likely see at some point in your cruise. Try to stop at the **Gutenberg Museum,** Liebfrauenplatz 5 (tel. (06131) 12 26 40 or 12 26 44), in a magnificent Renaissance building, where you can see a Gutenberg Bible, surrounded by woodcuts, copper engravings, and lithographic prints. Handpresses, printing machines, and the first newspaper printing-press are also on display. (Open Tues.-Sat. 10am-6pm, Sun. 10am-1pm. Free.) Also worth seeing is the massive **Martinsdom,** an eleventh-century cathedral of red stone. (Open April-Sept. Mon.-Fri. 9am-6:30pm, Sat. 9am-4pm, Sun. and holidays 1-2:45pm and 4-6:30pm; Oct.-March Mon.-Fri. 9am-5pm, Sat. 9am-4pm, Sun. 1-3pm and 4-5pm. Entrance on the Markt.) On the hill directly above the cathedral rises **Stephanskirche,** with its impressive Chagall windows. (Open daily 10am-noon and 2-5pm.) The **tourist office** (tel. (06131) 23 37 41), just down the street opposite the train station, reserves rooms for DM2; unfortunately, the town has few inexpensive ones. (Open Mon.-Fri. 9am-6pm, Sat. 9am-1pm.) Inexpensive meals (DM3-5) are available at the **University Mensa;** take bus #16 or 17 from the main train station to Friedrich-von-Pfeiffer-Weg, cross the footbridge, and continue down the street as it curves left. (Open Mon.-Fri. 11am-2:30pm, Sat. 9am-noon.) Food is also reasonable in the **Altstadt.** *Wiener-Schnitzel* with salad and fries runs about DM19, *Schwein-Schnitzel* with salad and fries about DM11.50, salad dishes with ham and eggs about DM10.50. Mainz's **IYHF youth hostel** (tel. (01621) 853 32), with 220 beds, is at Am Fort Weisenau—take bus #1 or 22 from the station to Viktorstift stop (direction: Weisenau). (DM17.10, linen and breakfast included. Reception open 5:15-10pm. 11:45pm curfew. Open year-round.) Mainz has Germany's second largest **Fasching festival** (late Feb.-early March.), climaxing on "Rose Monday" with a huge parade featuring bands, chariots, flags, costumes, and floats. Vendors sell cognac and schnapps to the singing and dancing crowds, and there are all-night costume balls before the festival ends on Wednesday morning.

Farther downstream lies **Rüdesheim,** celebrated for its wines. Rüdesheim lacks the charm of most Rhine villages, yet it is overrun with visitors. The **Verkehrsamt** (tel. (06722) 29 62) is at Rheinstr. 16, on the river across from the docks. Ask for *Welcome to Rüdesheim,* a bulletin telling you everything you'd ever want to know about the city. (Open May-Oct. Mon.-Fri. 8:30am-12:30pm and 1:30-6pm, Sat.-Sun. 2-6pm; Nov.-April Mon.-Fri. only.) The **Jugendherberge Am Kreuzberg (IYHF)** (tel. (06722) 27 11) is easily accessible by helicopter. Otherwise it is a 30-minute hike into the hills. Follow these directions unless you would fain be lost in vineyards. From the tourist office go down Christophelstr., and turn right on Oberstr.; continue to Am Eibinger Tor, then head upwards to the hostel. The reward is a postcard-view of the Rhine and the vineyards, and, of course, the trip back down. (Juniors DM11.50, seniors DM13.50. Breakfast included, dinner DM5-6.50. No kitchen facilities. Check-in 5-7pm. 11:30pm curfew. Open year-round.) If you don't feel like trekking to the hostel, seek the tourist office's help: They'll find rooms starting at DM18, breakfast included. The most convenient **camping** is on Hindenburg Allee (tel. (06722) 25 28), on the river a bit downstream. (DM4.70 per person, DM4.30-6.30 per tent. Open May-Sept.) To capture what Rüdesheim is all about, elbow your way through the **Drosselgasse:** Beer, wine, and music spill out of the town's bars. Make sure to try a glass of white Riesling wine (about DM4; wine tasting sessions up to DM8.50). This region (Rheingau) produces wines with a more assertive character than the sweeter, softer Moselle wines. Of the many winery tours in Rüdesheim, the best is conducted at **Asbach-Uralt,** where the most popular German brandy is produced; you can see the distillery and the bottling sections, and also sample wines. You must be at least 18 to join in the fun. Go to Am Rottland 6 (across from the train station), or call (06722) 123 61. Tours generally take place Monday through Thursday from 9 to 11am and from 1 to 3pm, Friday 9 to 11am only. Next-door to Asbach-Uralt is the **Brömserburg,** one of the oldest castles on the Rhine, now a wine museum. (Open daily 9am-5:30pm. Admission DM2.50, ages under 18 DM1.50.) The tourist office has information about rides over Rüdesheim to the **Niederwald** in either a cable-car or a chair-lift. On the first Saturday in July, the annual "Rhine on Fire" fireworks festival takes place along the river. The Verkehrsamt sells tickets (DM25 per person) for boat rides from Rüdesheim to Trechtingshausen, which afford great views of the festivities and the lighted castles along the Rhine. Boats leave at 8pm and return at midnight.

For an overnight stop, and perhaps a hike in vineyards high above the Rhine, **Bacharach** is by far the most inviting town in the valley. The **Verkehrsamt,** Oberstr. 1 (tel. (06743) 12 97), is in the *Rathaus,* a right from the train station, and has information on how to forward your luggage if you want to hike or bike down the Rhine. (Open Mon.-Fri. 8:30am-noon and 1:30-5pm.) The super **Jugendherberge Stahleck (IYHF)** (tel. (06743) 12 66), in a renovated castle overlooking town, thunders with *Kinder,* but the view is worth the trip even if you don't stay. (Juniors DM7.50, seniors DM9.50. Linen DM2.50. Breakfast DM4. No kitchen facilities. Check-in 5-7pm. 9:50pm curfew. Open year-round.) The **pension** at Spurgasse 2 charges DM18, breakfast included. **Camping** (tel. (06743) 17 52) is on the river bank south of town. (DM4.50 per person, DM4 per tent. Showers DM1.50. Open year-round.)

Along the Rhine itself, there are hostels in **Lorch** (Schwalbacherstr. 54; tel. (06726) 307), **Oberwesel** (Auf dem Schönberg; tel. (06744) 83 55), **St. Goar** (Bismarckweg 17; tel. (06741) 388), and **St. Goarshausen** (Auf der Loreley; tel. (06771) 619). Take the train to St. Goarshausen and visit **Burg Katz** and **Burg Maus,** both on the east bank. Crossing the river shouldn't be a problem; there are no bridges, but ferries abound.

Koblenz is a prosperous, somewhat staid town at the corner of the Rhine and the Moselle (known as *Deutsches Eck).* The **Verkehrsamt** (tel. (0261) 313 04) is just across from the train station. Pick up their encyclopedic city plan, which lists everything from pensions to miniature golf courses. They book rooms for DM2. (Open mid-June to mid-Oct. Mon.-Sat. 8:30am-8pm, Sun. 1:30-7pm; May to mid-June and mid- to late Oct. Mon.-Fri. 8:30am-6pm, Sat. 9am-2pm; Nov.-April Mon.-Thurs. 8:30am-1pm and 2:15-5pm, Fri. 8:30am-1pm and 2:15-4:30pm.) From June through September there is also an office at the docks. Perhaps the nicest thing about Koblenz is its **IYHF youth hostel** (tel. (0261) 737 37), in the Ehrenbretstein fortress across the river. Call before you go, as it's often full; take bus #8, 9, or 10 (DM2.20) to the Ehrenbretstein stop, and then take the chairlift (in operation Easter-Nov. 1 10am-5pm; June 15-Aug. 31 10am-6pm) to the hostel (with an IYHF card, roundtrip DM3). To get there by foot (about 1 hr. from the train station), cross the Rhine, and follow the signs. (Juniors DM9, seniors DM11. Breakfast DM4. Reception opens at 4pm. 11:30pm curfew. No sleeping bags allowed. Open year-round.) There is **camping** (tel. (0261) 827 19) just across the Rhine from Deutsches Eck (another ferry ride, DM0.60). (DM3.75 per person, students DM2.75, DM3.75 per tent. Showers DM1. Open April to mid-Oct.) All ships depart from the docks near this corner; to reach the wharf from the station take bus #1. You can do your laundry at **Wash-Center,** Löhrstr. 117. (Open Mon.-Sat. 6am-midnight. 6kg wash including detergent DM5.) And who knows? An advertisement for the laundromat shows a happy couple asking, "Guess where we met?"

Cologne (Köln)

This fourth-largest German city, a center for industry and transportation, has an extremely rich cultural tradition. Founded by the Romans in 38 B.C.E., Cologne became an important medieval archbishopric whose religious power was matched by the stature of its religious scholars. Albertus Magnus and Thomas Aquinas studied and taught in Cologne, and Duns Scotus is buried here. During World War II, 95% of Cologne was demolished, but the city miraculously recovered and now is an attractive and lively center of European art.

You can't say you've been to Cologne until you've seen the the **Kölner Dom,** and you can't help but see it. This breathtaking cathedral, with its brilliant stained-glass windows, was begun in 1248 and completed only in 1880. It is justly famous as one of the world's purest expressions of High Gothic architecture. (Organ concerts mid-June to Sept. Tues. at 8pm.) Across the square from the cathedral in Roncalliplatz 4, is the **Römisch-Germanisches Museum** (tel. (0221) 221 44 38), which displays artifacts from the original Roman colony. (Open Tues. and Fri.-Sun. 10am-5pm, Wed.-Thurs. 10am-8pm. Admission DM3, students DM1.) The **Wallraf-Richartz-Museum/Museum Ludwig,** in a new building on Bischofsgartengasse behind the cathedral, is a must for art enthusiasts. One section displays twentieth-century art, including expressionist and Russian constructivist works; the pop art of Warhol and Liechtenstein is also well-represented. The other section exhibits paintings dating from the fourteenth to nineteenth centuries. (Open Tues.-Thurs. 10am-8pm, Fri.-Sun. 10am-6pm. Admission DM3, students DM1.)

A host of twelfth- and thirteenth-century churches, and several more in ultra-modern post-war style, dot the streets of Cologne. The friendly **Verkehrsamt** (tel. (0221) 221 33 45), across the street from the main entrance to the cathedral, will give you a city map, and book a single for DM2, a double for DM3. (Open May to mid-Oct. Mon.-Sat. 8am-10:30pm, Sun. 9am-10:30pm; mid-Oct. to April Mon.-Sat. 8am-9pm, Sun. 9:30am-7pm.) You can exchange money in the train station daily 7am-8pm. The **Mitfahrzentrale** in Cologne is located on Saarstr. 22 (tel. (0221) 23 34 64). You can wash your clothes at the **laundry** on Brüsselerplatz, or at the youth hostel if you're a guest.

Rooms in Cologne start at about DM30 in pensions (breakfast included); it might be easiest to book through the tourist office, particularly during the trade fairs in spring and autumn. The **Jugendherberge (IYHF),** Siegesstr. 5A (tel. (0221) 81 47 11), is a 20-minute walk from the station; cross the Hohenzollernbrücke behind the cathedral, and continue straight to the Deutz train station; the hostel is across the street. You can also take the train or S-bahn from the Hauptbahnhof one stop to Deutz. (Often full. Juniors DM12.90, seniors DM14.90; nonmembers add DM4. Linen DM3.50. Mandatory breakfast included. Check-in from 12:30pm. 11:30pm curfew. Open year-round.) When full, they will send you to a nearby **hotel** where bed and breakfast cost DM25. More luxurious but less convenient (and usually packed) is the **Youth Guest House (IYHF),** An der Schanz (tel. (0221) 76 70 81), on the Rhine north of the cathedral by the Zoo bridge; take U-Bahn #16 or 18 (direction: Ebertplatz) to the Boltonsternstrasse stop, or walk (30 min.) along the Rhine on Konrad-Adenauer-Uferstr. (DM21.50. Breakfast, showers, and sleep-sack included. Check-in 11am-midnight. Open year-round.) **Hotel Henn,** Norbertstr. 6 (tel. (0221) 13 44 45, a 10-minute walk from the train station down Komodienstr. and Zeughauserstr., has comfortable rooms with a charming proprietor. (Singles DM34, doubles DM52, triples DM72. Showers DM3. Breakfast included. Open year-round.)

Inexpensive food—and just about anything else—can be obtained along **Hohe Strasse,** the main pedestrian shopping district by the cathedral. For local color try the traditional Cologne pub-restaurant **Brauhaus Sion,** Unter Taschenmacher 5-7, with meals for DM8-16. (Open daily 10am-midnight.) **Früh,** Am Hof 12, right by the cathedral, is another traditional Cologne pub, outdoor cafe, and restaurant. Satisfying meals cost DM7-20. (Open daily 10am-11:45pm.)

Near Cologne

Still officially only the provisional capital of West Germany, **Bonn** has developed since the war into a pleasant university and diplomatic town. Anything else? Beethoven was born here.

On the open expanse of Münsterplatz, the **Münster** presents a stark Romanesque exterior that contrasts pleasantly with the painted capitals and arches of the interior. **Beethovens Geburtshaus,** Bonngasse 20, houses various mementos and musical instruments, and even huge metal funnels Beethoven stuck in his ears, in the days before hearing aids. (Open April-Sept. Mon.-Sat. 9am-1pm and 3-6pm, Sun. 9am-1pm; Oct.-March Mon.-Sat. 9:30am-1pm and 3-5pm, Sun. 10am-1pm. Admission DM3, students DM1.) Most of the government buildings, including the **Bundeshaus** (Parliament), **Villa Hammerschmidt** (Seat of the President), and **Bundeskanzleramt** (Seat of the Chancellor), are located outside the city center. You can tour the Bundeshaus, Görresstr. 15 (tel. (0228) 16 27 79), when its not in session. To attend a session, you must apply in advance to your embassy in Bonn. The **Markt** is a hive of activity summer long. Music and theater on the stage in front of the old pink **Rathaus** vie for your attention with street performers and vegetable hawkers. Behind the *Rathaus,* the **Städtisches Kunstmuseum** exhibits a super collection of expressionism and German contemporary art. (Open Wed. and Fri.-Sun. 10am-5pm, Tues. and Thurs. 10am-9pm. Free.)

The **Verkehrsamt,** Münsterstr. 20 (tel. (0228) 77 34 66), 100m from the train station, will book rooms free of charge; accommodations start at about DM30 per person. (Open Mon.-Sat. 8am-9pm, Sun. 9:30am-12:30pm.) The **Jugendherberge (IYHF)** (tel. 28 12 00) is located in the woods on Venusberg, far from the center of town; take bus #21. Clean, modern, and pleasant, it often accommodates large groups. (Juniors DM12.90, seniors DM14.90. Linen DM3.50. Breakfast included. Lunch or dinner DM6. Check-in until 8pm. 11:30pm curfew.) If you're staying more than one day, buy a strip of 8 bus tickets for DM7. You need 2 tickets per ride, and otherwise you'll pay DM2.20 a pair. For inexpensive meals, try the **University Mensa,** Nassestr. 11, a 15-minute walk from the train station along Kaiserstr. (Open Mon.-Sat. 8am-8pm. Lunch DM1.90-2.60 with student ID, DM4.75-5.45 without, but usually no questions asked. Open year-round. July 20 to mid-Sept. closed Sat. and no dinners served.) **Casa Pedro,** Heerstr. 67, offers Spanish food for DM4-12.50. Bonn's **Mitfahrzentrale** is at Herwarthstr. 11a (tel. (0228) 69 30 81). You can wash your clothes at the **Wasch Center** at the corner of Breite Str. and Kölnstr. (Open Mon.-Sat. 7am-11pm.)

One hour west of Cologne lies **Aachen** (Aix-la-Chapelle), from where Charlemagne ruled the newly formed Holy Roman Empire in the early ninth century. His unique **Dom** in the center of the city circle is one of the world's best-known cathedrals. Remarkable for its central octagonal dome, inspired by Byzantine architecture, the cathedral also boasts a fifteenth-century Gothic choir with stained-glass windows. Inside, Charlemagne's throne is a simple chair of marble slabs, perched high above the main apse. Don't miss the breathtaking jeweled crowns, reliquaries, altar paintings, and hand-carved crosses in the **Schatzkammer** (treasury). There are music concerts in the cathedral every Thursday evening from June 25 to August 27. (Cathedral open mid-April to mid-Oct. Mon.-Sat. 10:30am-10pm, Sun. 12:30-7pm; mid-Oct. to mid-April Mon.-Sat. 10:30am-7pm, Sun. 12:30-7pm. *Schatzkammer* open Mon. 9am-1pm, Tues.-Sat. 9am-1pm and 2-5pm, Sun. 10:30am-1pm and 2-5pm; mid-April to mid-Oct. Tues.-Wed. and Fri.-Sat. until 6pm, Thurs. until 10pm. Admission DM3, students DM2. Tours in German leave every hr. on the ½ hr. from the *Schatzkammer,* visiting sections off-limits to the general public; DM2.) The fourteenth-century **Rathaus** on Marktplatz near the cathedral is an impressive monument to the former glory of Aachen. On the northern facade statues of 50 German sovereigns hold court. (Open Mon.-Fri. 8am-1pm and 2-5pm, Sat. 10am-1pm.) An English pamphlet describing the exterior and interior of the *Rathaus* is available across the street at the friendly **Verkehrsverein,** Markt 39-41 (tel. (0241) 334 91), which also reserves rooms for a DM3 fee. (Open Mon.-Fri. 9am-6:30pm, Sat. 9am-1pm.) Pensions start at DM20. There's another Verkehrsverein opposite the train station (tel. 253 12). (Open Mon.-Fri. 9am-6:30pm, Sat. 9am-1pm.) **Campingplatz,** Pass Str. (tel. (0241) 15 54 95) costs DM3.50 per person, DM3 per tent. Showers DM1.50. Take bus #1, 3, 11, 13, or 21 (direction: Bushof). The **Katakomben Studentenzentrum,** Pontstr. 74-76, has good, inexpensive food; breakfast (9-11:30am) with coffee, bread, jam, cheese, or ham is DM5.10-6; lunch (11:30am-3pm) runs DM4.20-7.50; dinner (7-10:30pm) meat dishes are DM4.50-8. **Heidekrug,** Bondelstr. 9-21, also has tasty, inexpensive meals. There's a **Mitfahrzentrale** in Aachen at Roermonderstr. 4 (tel. 15 54 00).

Mosel Valley (Moseltal)

The Mosel River carries much less commercial traffic than the Rhine, but the region's excellent wines and flower-laden towns attract droves of tourists. Though it's no longer possible to travel the entire 200-kilometer stretch from Koblenz to Trier by boat, you can take ships of the **KD Line** from Koblenz to Cochem, change to the train from Cochem to Bernkastel-Kues, and continue by boat to Trier. Ships, however, do not run frequently; from June 15 to October 5 ships sail on Mondays, and from July 18 to August 29 they also sail on Thursdays and Saturdays. For more information about the KD Line, call (0221) 208 82 88. Eurail is valid for free passage and InterRail is good for a 50% discount on the KD ships, but neither are valid on Moselbahn buses.

Some of Germany's most famous vintages come from the steep slopes lining the river between Cochem and Bernkastel-Kues. On any summer weekend, several *Weinfeste* enliven the area with flowing festivities and brass bands in traditional costume. The vineyards were planted by the Romans, who believed wine was medicine; Roman soldiers were punished if they didn't drink their daily quota of one liter. Tourist offices can arrange wine-tasting tours of local cellars; be sure to ask for the list of wine festivals along the Mosel. But set out into the countryside, too. The entire valley lends itself to excellent biking or boating—traffic is light and camp sites abundant. Some train stations will rent you a sturdy, heavy one-speed for DM5 per day if you have a train ticket, Bundesbahn bus ticket, or railpass (DM10 otherwise). You can drop off the bike at another train station at no extra charge; you can also have your luggage sent ahead.

About 35km upstream from Koblenz perches **Burg Eltz,** reached by a steep walk from Münden or a gentler climb from Moselkern (the train stops at both). Eltz is a fine place to start a Mosel expedition, and also makes a pleasant daytrip from Koblenz. This castle displays every architectural style from the eleventh to the seventeenth centuries. Because the buildings have never been harmed, the original arabesques and religious frescoes still cover the walls of rooms filled with sixteenth-century furniture; the state room is decorated with a vast Gobelin tapestry. (Open April-Oct. Mon.-Sat. 9am-5:30pm, Sun. and holidays 10am-5:30pm. Admission DM5.50, students and children DM3.50. Tours (every 10-15 min.) last about 45 min. English written translations are available.)

Clinging to the steep walls of the Mosel Valley and flanked by vineyards, **Cochem** is dominated both by its majestic **Burg** and by the busloads who come to view it. The castle is a feudal fantasy of nineteenth-century restorers: Originally built in the eleventh century and destroyed by the French in 1689, it was rebuilt in a style that missed the mark by 200 years. (Open mid-March to mid-Nov. daily 9am-5pm. Tours on the hour, in English if requested. Admission DM3.50, students and children DM1.50.) From April 1 to Novermber 1 every Sunday after dark (ask at the Verkehrsamt for exact times) there is a presentation of *Sleeping Beauty* at the Burg. The castle is illuminated and the tale is recited with musical accompaniment. Cochem itself is a charming hillside maze of streets lined with interesting shops and cafes. Wander down the scenic flower-lined promenade, or climb or take the *Sesselbahn* (chairlift) on Endertstrasse (DM4 one way, DM6 round-trip) to **Pinnerkreuz,** named after Pinn the shepherd, who fell to his death here while looking for his sheep. (Chairlift runs daily April-Oct. 9:30am-7pm.)

The **Verkehrsamt** (tel. (02671) 39 71) is in the heart of Cochem; from the train station go to the river and turn right; the tourist office is on Endert Platz next to the bridge. (Open Mon. 9am-1:30pm and 2-6pm, Tues.-Fri. 9am-6pm, Sat. 10am-3pm, Sun. 10am-noon.) They'll book rooms for DM2, but you shouldn't need help—*Zimmerfrei* signs abound along **Endertstrasse** and **Oberbachstrasse;** try #42, where the proprietor charges DM20. The **IYHF youth hostel** is on Klottenerstr. (tel. 86 33) in Cond; either take the bus toward Freibad which leaves at a quarter to each hour from Endert Platz (DM1.50), or walk 30 minutes across the Mosel bridge and turn left onto Bergstr., which turns onto Klottenerstr. (Juniors DM8, seniors DM10. Sheets DM2.50. Breakfast DM4. No sleeping bags. Check-in 3-3:30pm and 5-6pm. If you arrive earlier you can leave your luggage (no locks available), and use the showers and the kitchen. 10pm curfew. Open year-round.) Camping is just below the hostel, or at **Camping Schausten** (tel. (02671) 75 28) on Endertstr. farther out of town; buses toward Endertstr. leave from the train station. (DM3.50 per person plus DM4-5 per tent. Open Easter-Nov.)

Solid food, including *Schweineschnitzel* and steak, can be found at cozy **Zum Onkel Willi,** Endertstr. 39 (DM5-16.50); clean rooms are also available. (DM30-35, breakfast included.) (Restaurant and rooms open daily 8am-1am.) On the other side of the Mosel, in **Cochem-Cond,** there is a pool (open daily 8am-8pm; DM6), a sauna (open Mon.-Fri. 2-10pm, Sat.-Sun. 10am-7pm; DM14), and camping at the **Freizeitzentrum,** near the youth hostel. About 24km north of Cochem, on the other bank, lies **Brodenbach,** with a **Jugendherberge (IYHF)** at Moorkamp 7 (tel. (02605) 33 89). (Juniors DM7.50, seniors DM9.50. Sheets DM2.50. Breakfast DM3.20. Check-in 5-10pm. Open year-round.)

Ten kilometers farther upstream lies **Beilstein,** "the Sleeping Beauty of the Mosel." Privately run buses leave Cochem frequently for Beilstein (DM6.80 round-trip). From May to October, Cochem's local boat excursion company **Mosel-Personen-Schiffahrt** (tel. (02673) 15 15) also runs to Beilstein. (Excursions daily at 10:30am, 1:15pm, 2:30pm, and 4pm. DM10 one way, DM14 round-trip, railpasses not valid.) This is one sleepy little town: A tourist brochure lists the 1956 re-filming of the German film *If We Were All Angels* as the city's most recent significant event. The half-timbered houses and crooked streets are more attractive and draw less tourist traffic than their counterparts in Cochem. Beilstein is famous for the fine woodcarving of the baroque **Karmelitenkirche,** and for the ruins of the **Burg Metternich,** destroyed by the French in 1683. **Cafe Klapperburg,** by the steps leading to the church, serves as a **tourist office** in summer (tel. (02673) 14 17; open daily 8am-5pm).

Claiming both banks of a beautiful bend in the Mosel, **Traben-Trarbach** offers a look at the area's hillside vineyards and medieval cellars of the area's wine industry. Looming above the town are the ruins of **Grevenburg Castle,** a pleasant half-hour hike from the Mosel on the Trarbach bank. The **Verkehrsamt** (tel. (06541) 90 11) is at Bahnstr. 22 in Traben, inside the *Altes Rathaus.* They'll find you a room in a pension or private home for as little as DM15-20 per person (no service charge). Pick up the useful *Willkommen in Traben-Trarbach* pamphlet, and a *Wanderkarte* (hiking map; DM4.80) to guide you along the area's excellent trails. (Open June-Aug. Mon.-Fri. 8am-12:30pm and 2-5:30pm, Sat. 2:30-5:30pm; Sept.-May Mon.-Fri. only.) Sample local wines in any of the *Weinkelleren,* which charge DM3 to 5 for a glass; **Weingut Carl Emert,** Am Bahnhof, 14a (tel. (06541) 63 06) has exceptional wine, as well as an interesting tour. (Open daily 10am-10pm, but call first.) During the **Wine Festival,** on the second and last weekends in July, you can indulge in even more white wine tasting. The modern **Am Hirtenpfädchen Hostel (IYHF),** off Kövenigerstr. (tel. 92 78) comes with ping pong table, TV room, and pinball machines. The hostel is a 20-minute walk from the center; cross the bridge to the train station, turn right, take your second left onto Obere Kaiserstr., and then a right onto Kövenigerstr. (Juniors DM8, seniors DM10. Linen DM3.50. Breakfast DM4; dinner DM5.20-6.20. 11pm curfew.) The cheapest pension in town is on the Trarbach side of the Mosel; **Gasthaus Beitzel,** Schottstr. 2-4 (tel. 92 33), charges DM30-38 for doubles with breakfast. The adjacent restaurant, although dark and small, has delicious and reasonably priced food. *(Schnitzel* with soup, salad, and fries DM9; other meat dishes DM8.50-10.50. Open Tues.-Sun. 8am-2pm and 5pm-1am.) **Pension Bartz,** Wildbadstr. 161 (tel. (06541) 23 49), has a friendly proprietor who asks DM20-25 per person for excellent rooms, breakfast included. It is a 25-minute haul from the train station. Cross the bridge and take a right onto Brückenstrasse; follow this main road (which frequently switches names) through the Weihertorplatz onto Wildbadstrasse.

Bernkastel-Kues sells itself as one of the most picturesque towns along the Mosel, and is accordingly overpriced and overblown. Yet the real life of the Mosel Valley continues unperturbed just beyond the walking range of the average tourist. The **tourist office** is along the river at Gestade 5 (tel. (06531) 40 23), across from the KD Line dock. They book rooms for free, and might help you find work picking grapes if you write in advance. (Open Mon.-Fri. 8am-12:30pm and 2-5:30pm, Sat. 9am-noon and 2:30-5:30pm.) Kues was the birthplace of philosopher and cardinal Nicolaus Cusanus. The **hospital** he founded over 500 years ago, at Cusanusstr. 2, is now a nursing home. It also houses Cusanus's personal manuscript collection. (Open Sat., but call (06531) 22 60 beforehand.) Karlstrasse twists out of the famous **Bernkastler Marktplatz** (to the right, facing the Rathaus), past one of Germany's narrowest houses, and on through vineyards to **Burg Landshut,** the ruined summer castle of the archbishops of Trier. The castle is now a pleasant restaurant with a great view of the town. Dishes cost DM6 to 24. (Open daily 11am-9pm.) On the next hill, a 10-minute walk up, is the **IYHF youth hostel** (tel. 23 95), with terrific views. (Juniors DM7.50, seniors DM9.50. Linen DM2.50-3.50. Showers included. Breakfast DM4; dinner or lunch DM5.20-6.20; one meal obligatory. 10pm curfew.) Both Burg Landshut and the hostel are accessible by the Burg-Landshut Express (every hr. on the hr. 10am-5pm). Along the Mosel River are **Campingplatz Kueser Werth** (tel. 82 00), where you can rent bikes and boats, and **Camping Schenk** (tel. 81 76).

Trier

Far upstream on the Mosel, almost on the Luxembourg border, lies Trier, Germany's oldest city. Founded by Augustus in 15 B.C.E., the city served for a short time in the fourth century as the capital of the decaying Western Roman Empire. The magnificent sandstone fortress **Porta Nigra,** built in 115 C.E., was once an important part of the city's defenses. Adjacent to it is the **Städtisches Museum,** which conveys the art and history of Trier through paintings by local artists, portraits of the archbishops of Trier, Gothic sculptures, and a large model of the city in 1800. (Open June-Sept. daily 9am-5pm; Oct.-April Tues.-Sun. only. Admission DM2, students DM1.) Within and around the Porta Nigra you can see vestiges of Roman ingenuity, including the baths, amphitheater, and Pfalzel (summer residence of the emperors). (Open April-Sept. daily 9am-1pm and 2-6pm; Oct. daily 9am-1pm and 2-5pm; Nov. and Jan.-March Tues.-Sun. 9am-1pm and 2-5pm. Admission DM2 each, DM6 for entire complex; students, seniors, disabled, and ages under 18 half-price.)

Trier's **Dom,** the oldest Christian church in Germany, was embellished by each successive age as the city's prestige grew. Romanesque apses, early Gothic vaulting, and rococo frippery were gradually integrated into the massive Roman structure. Part of the religious complex was completely replaced by the **Liebfrauenkirche,** Germany's first Gothic church, with brilliant stained-glass windows. (Dom and Liebfrauenkirche open Nov.-March daily 6am-noon and 2-5:30pm; April-Oct. daily 6am-6pm. Tours of the Dom Mon.-Fri. and Sun. at 2pm, DM1.)

A visit to the **Karl-Marx Haus,** Brückenstr. 10 (tel. (0651) 430 11), will bring you back from Roman times to the near present. Marx's birthplace is now a virtual shrine, containing an interesting if somewhat disorganized account of his life and work. (Open April-Oct. Mon. 1-6pm, Tues.-Sun. 10am-6pm; Nov.-March Mon. 3-6pm, Tues.-Sun. 10am-1pm and 3-6pm. Admission DM2, students DM1.) **Tourist information** (tel. (0651) 754 40), next to the Porta Nigra, will book rooms for DM2, but the map they charge you for is free at the train station. (Open May-Aug. Mon.-Sat. 9am-6pm, Sun. 9am-1pm; Sept.-Oct. daily 9am-6pm; Nov.-April Mon.-Fri. 9am-5pm, Sat. 9am-1pm.)

The **IYHF youth hostel,** Maarstr. 156 (tel. 410 92), is a large, modern building by the Mosel. Take bus #2 to Kaiser-Wilhelm-Brücke, ½km downstream from the hostel. By foot, go out the station, up Theodor-Heuss-Allee, turn right at Paulinstr., then left onto Maarstr. (Maarstr. is cut off by Zurmaienerstr.; you must continue beyond it to the hostel.) The location is inconvenient and noisy, but on the river. (Juniors DM13, seniors DM15. Nonmembers add DM4. IYHF cards available, DM20. Sheets DM3.50. Breakfast included. 11:30 curfew.) The **Jugendhotel Kolpinghaus,** in Hotel/Restaurant Warsberger Hof at Dietrichstr. 42 (tel. 751 31), is one block off Hauptmarkt. Rooms are clean and simple. (Singles DM20-26, doubles DM40-50.) Adjoining the Jugendhotel and slightly more elegant is **Hotel Kolpinghaus** (tel. 751 31). (Singles DM26, doubles DM45-52. Reception open until 10pm. 11pm curfew.) **Camping Schloss Monaise,** on Monaisestr. (tel. 862 10), has taken over the grounds of an eighteenth-century castle. Take the bus from the station toward Zewen. (DM3 per person, DM3 per tent. Washing machines DM2-5.)

Flower and fruit stands crowd the **Simon Haupt Markt. Oen der Beiz,** Viehmarktplatz 8, serves excellent meals. They have an English menu, but daily specials (DM7-20) are listed in the local *Trierer* dialect. (Open Mon.-Fri. 11am-2:30pm and 5pm-1am, Sat.-Sun. 11am-1am.) The new university campus in **Tarforst** has daily *menus* (open Mon.-Sat. for lunch; DM2-5.50), along with some impressive modern architecture. Take bus #1 from the train station until you see a blue building (about 10 min.).

Saarland

Although the Saarland has yo-yo'ed between France and Germany throughout its history (most recently, in 1957, the inhabitants voted to become part of Germany once again), it has never suffered an identity crisis. Its philosophy, unlike its nationality, has remained consistent throughout the years: Eat and drink well. The Saarland's cuisine is lauded as a gourmet mixture of French and German dishes; a few specialties include *Metzelsupp* (soup with sausage), *Dibbelabbes* (a grated-potato soufflé), and *Hooriche,* or *Stracke* (potato dumplings). The Saarland is also one of Germany's premier wine-growing regions, and is second only to Bavaria among the German provinces in per capita beer consumption. Fewer rainy days than any other province in Germany and a slower pace of life make West Germany's youngest federal state well-suited for its many spa clinics. Spots of interest are connected by footpaths through the woods, including part of the Black Forest (main loop 253km; Moselgau loop 42km; Bliesgau loop 73km). Bring your own bike—train stations in the Saarland have none to rent.

Capital of the Saarland, **Saarbrücken,** a mining town since Roman times, was home to Friedrich Joachim Stengel, a busy little architect who worked for Prince Wilhelm-Heinrich. Stengel's works include the **Ludwigskirche** on Ludwigsplatz, **St. Johann Basilika,** and the **castle, old Rathaus,** and **Erbprinzenpalais** on Schlossplatz. Step inside the old Rathaus and visit the **Abenteuer Museum** ("Museum of Adventure"). Here you can meet and talk with Heinz Rox-Schulz, "the King of the Globetrotters," a man who has lived amongst pygmies, gurus, and yogis, looked for Bigfoot, sailed down the Amazon, and ridden across America on a horse. He also organizes excursions and horseback-riding trips. (Museum open Tues.-Wed. 9am-1pm, Thurs.-Fri. 3-7pm, first Sat. in month 10am-2pm. Admission DM2, children DM1.)

The **Deutsch-Französischer Garten,** Deutschmühlental (tel. 534 37), is an expanse of meadows and rose gardens jointly maintained by Germany and France, symbolizing their relatively newfound friendship. Take bus #15 or #16 from the train station. (Open daily 8:30am-midnight. Admission DM2, students and children DM1.) For information about a boat ride down the Saar River (April 15-Oct.) call 87 51 92 (Mon.-Fri. 8am-noon). **The Stadtgalerie,** St. Johanner Markt 24 (tel. 300 17 51), features exhibits by modern artists (including video art) and different music and cabaret programs. (Open Tues.-Sun. 11am-7pm. Free.) The **Giesskanne,** a jazz cellar, is located on Am Steg 3 (tel. 368 09), and most of the student bars are found in Nauwieser Square, near the town hall. For movies, try **Stadtkino Camera,** Berliner Promenade 7 (tel. 39 92 97). The radio station orchestra performs three times per week—call 60 20 for more information. Saarbrücken's most popular annual events include the **Non-Traditional French Theater** (a week in May), the **Altstadtfest** (summer), and the one-week-long **Max-Ophüls film festival** in January. (For information about these events, call 300 14 02.)

The **Verkehrsverein,** located on Trierer Str. 2 (tel. 365 15), finds rooms and sells maps of the city (DM1). From the train station, head straight (about 200m), then look right. (Open Mon.-Fri. 7:30am-8pm, Sat. 7:30am-4pm.) The **Jugendherberge (IYHF)** is on 31, Meerwiesertalweg (tel. 330 40). Take bus #15 or 16 from Bahnhofstr. to the Prinzenweiher stop, or walk 30 minutes: right onto Bahnhofstr. from the Verkehrsverein, left onto Dudweilerstr., and finally right onto Meerwiesertalweg. (Juniors DM8.50, seniors DM10.50. Sheets DM2.50-3.50. Obligatory breakfast DM3.50. Check-in 4-5:30pm and 7:30-11pm. 11:30pm curfew.) Camp at **Campingplatz Burbach,** Mettlacher Str. (tel. 761 21), for DM3 per person, DM2.50 per tent. (Check-in until 10pm; closed 2-5pm.) **The Mitfahrzentrale** in Saarbrücken is at Rosenstr. 31 (tel. 679 81).

Trains run from Saarbrücken to Cologne and northern Germany via Trier, to Paris via Metz, and to the Black Forest and southern Europe via Strasbourg. Saarbrücken's **telephone code** is 0681.

Northwest of Saarbrücken is the county of**Merzig-Wadern.** The **Verkehrsverein** is in Merzig, Poststr. 12 (tel. (0681) 738 74). Merzig ("where the man lives with the wolves") features findings from early Roman settlements; in **Nennig** (part of the town of **Perl,** near Luxembourg) you can visit a Roman villa with a beautiful mosaic floor. In **Orscholz** you can visit the **Cloef Viewpoint,** and at the **Dreiländereck,** where Luxembourg, France, and West Germany border one another, all three countries are in view.

West of Saarbrücken is **Saarlouis.** The **Verkehrsverein** is at Kaiser-Wilhelm Str. 4-6 (tel. (06831) 44 44 10). Saarlouis was built by Louis XIV in 1680 as a military installation, and moats and remains of fortresses from the time of the Sun King are still extant. Saarlouis is the twin city to Eisenhüttenstadt in the DDR, the first partnership of its kind between West and East Germany. Connections to East Germany are also especially strong in the town of Neunkirchen, the birthplace of Erich Honecker, leader of the DDR.

Baden-Württemberg

This densely populated region hosts the mysterious wilderness of the Swabian Jura and the Black Forest; the charming university towns of Heidelberg, Freiburg, and Tübingen; and Baden-Baden, a nineteenth-century spa-cum-gambling resort. The food here is especially good; wild *Himbeeren* (raspberries) and *Johannisbeeren* (currants) are sold in outdoor markets, and *Schwarzwälder Schinken* (Black Forest ham) is deservedly famous. Be sure to sample the Swabian delicacies: *Maultaschen* (meat wrapped in noodles and cooked with one of a variety of sauces), *Spätzle* (a heavy Swabian pasta served with practically everything), *Wildschweinbraten* (roasted wild boar), and *Hirschbraten* (roast stag).

Heidelberg

Heidelberg is Germany's archetypal university town. Founded in 1386, the university is the country's oldest, and it throbs with student life, except in late summer. Then tourists throng the streets, Heidelbergers take off, bookstores give way to souvenir shops, and the city's traditional flavor becomes increasingly commercialized. Still, you can always escape to the town's restful surroundings which provided the inspiration for W. Somerset Maugham's *Of Human Bondage.*

Orientation and Practical Information

To get in, out, and around the city, buy a 36-hour ticket for the streetcars and buses (DM6) at the **HSB Verkauf-Stelle,** located opposite the side entrance to the station; single rides are expensive at DM2.

Tourist Office: Just outside the train station (tel. 277 35). Busy but extremely helpful. Open Mon.-Thurs. 9am-7pm, Fri. 9am-9pm, Sat. 9am-7pm, Sun. 10am-6pm.

Budget Travel: HS Reisebüros, am Bismarckplatz (tel. 271 51). Special student deals; any type of student card will do. Open Mon.-Fri. 8am-12:30pm and 2-6pm, Sat. 9am-noon.

American Express: Friedrich-Ebert Anlage 16 (tel. 290 01). Mail held. All banking services. Open Mon.-Tues. and Thurs.-Fri. 8:30am-5:30pm, Wed. 9am-5:30pm, Sat. 9am-noon. Banking services closed noon-2pm.

Post Office: Diagonally to the right across from the station. Open Mon.-Fri. 8:30am-6pm, Sat. 8:30am-noon. **Telephones** open Mon.-Fri. 7am-9pm, Sat. 7am-6pm, Sun. 10am-noon. **Telephone code:** 06221. **Postal code:** 6900.

Trains: From the station, take tram #1 to Bismarckplatz, bus #34 to Kornmarkt, or bus #11 to Universitätsplatz.

Bike Rental: At station. DM10 (DM5 with railpass). Open April-Sept. Mon.-Fri. 6:30am-7pm, Sat. 7:30am-5pm, Sun. 10am-5pm.

Emergencies: Police, Rohrbacherstr. 11 (tel. 52 09). Dial 110 for all types of emergencies, including medical.

Bookstore: Braun Gustav, Sofienstr. 3, has the best selection of English books. Open Mon.-Fri. 9am-6pm, Sat. 9am-2pm.

Laundry: Wasch Hansel, Riemerstr. 50 (tel. 243 23). DM9 for a large load of laundry, soap included. Open Mon. and Wed.-Fri. 8am-6:30pm, Tues. and Sat. 8am-1pm.

Hitchhiking: For all directions, walk to the end of Bergheimerstrasse. **Mitfahrzentrale,** Kurfürstenanlage 57 (tel. 246 46), 200m from the station. Open Mon.-Fri. 9am-6pm, Sat. 10am-2pm, Sun. and holidays noon-2pm.

Accommodations, Camping, and Food

Heidelberg's cheap hotels—there aren't many—fill quickly in summer, so it's advisable to call or write ahead. The tourist office will help you search for a room but they may not always be able to make a reservation. If you arrive in the evening during July or August, try the listings in Kirchheim, 20 minutes from downtown (see Sonne and Goldene Rose/Erna below).

Jugendherberge (IYHF), Tiergartenstr. 5 (tel. 41 20 66). Take bus #11 from Bismarckplatz or the station; after 8pm, take tram #1 to the Hospital of Surgery, and then bus #11. The hostel is the first stop after—and in many ways an extension of—the Zoo. Noisy, crowded, disorganized, especially in summer. Hostel card mandatory. Juniors DM11.70, seniors DM13.70. Breakfast included. 11:30pm curfew. Open year-round.

Jeske Hotel, Mittelbadgasse 2 (tel. 237 33). From the station take bus #34 to the Kornmarkt. Central location and the friendly, efficient Frau Jeske attract many students. DM16 per person in rooms with 2-5 beds. Showers DM2. No curfew.

Hotel Krokodil, Kleinschmidtstr. 12 (tel. 240 59). A good alternative to the Jeske Hotel. Dorm beds DM18. Singles DM35-55, doubles DM60-70. Showers included.

Pension Elite, Bunsenstr. 15 (tel. 257 34), between the station and the center of town. Cozy, spacious rooms with a helpful and friendly owner. Small, so book ahead. Singles DM40, doubles DM65.

Futterkrippe, Hauptstr. 93 (tel. 256 56). Clean, pretty rooms in a central location. Singles DM45, doubles DM75. Breakfast included.

Grimminger, Heinrich-Fuchs-Str. 1 (tel. 39 09 38). Several rooms, only 5 min. from downtown. Take street cars to Leimen/Boxberg and get off at the end of Rohrbacherstr. Singles DM35, doubles DM68. Large breakfasts.

Sonne Hotel, Schmitthennerstr. 1 (tel. 721 62), in Kirchheim, a 20-min. ride from the center. Take bus #42 to Albert-Fritz-Str. Spotless, charming, and very quiet. Singles with private shower DM30, doubles with shower DM45. Breakfast included.

Goldene Rose, Hegenich Str. 10 (tel. 712 56), in Kirchheim. A small cafe where you pick up your room key for the sumptuous **Hotel Erna** (tel. 72 09 87) just down the street. From bus stop #2 in front of the Hauptbahnhof, take bus #7007 to Kirchheim. Rooms are fabulously clean, large, luxurious, and almost always available. Singles DM40, doubles DM70. Price includes large breakfast served in Goldene Rose.

Camping: Haide (tel. (06223) 21 11) is between Ziegelhausen and Kleingemünd. Take bus #35, get off at the Orthopedic Clinic, and cross the river. DM4 per person, DM4 per tent.

The more expensive **Camping Neckertal** (tel. (06223) 80 25 06) is on the other side of the river, near the Orthopedic Clinic.

Many of Heidelberg's larger restaurants are expensive, but a number of small snack bars, pubs, and restaurants cater to the student population.

Zum Goldenen Hecht, Am Brückentor, by the Alte Brücke. An old pub with mythical German scenes painted on the walls. Locals frequent here. Good, filling meals from DM10, plus a lively bar that remains open until midnight.

Essighaus, Plöck 97, parallel to Hauptstr. Wonderful complete dinners from DM8 in a cozy atmosphere. Open daily until midnight. **Südpfanne,** up Hauptstr. (past Weinmarkt), serves excellent food from DM10.

Mensa der Universität, building #304 in the new university complex near the Jugendherberge. Hard to find, and mediocre once you do. Open Mon.-Fri. 9am-5:30pm. ISIC required.

Roter Ochsen, Hauptstr. 217, open Mon.-Sat., and **Zum Sepp'l,** Hauptstr. 213, open daily, are two historic student pubs—more of attractions than places to eat. Both serve food until 11pm.

Sights

The **Heidelberger Schloss** is perhaps at its most magnificent when illuminated at night. On the first Saturday evening in June, July, and September, the town holds festivals complete with fireworks set off from the castle. If you don't mind crowds, the show can be a lot of fun. To view the interior of the castle, you must take a guided tour. (Open daily 9am-5pm. Admission DM4, students DM2.) The tour includes a visit to the **Fass,** reputedly Germany's largest wine barrel. (Separate admission to the Fass DM1, students DM0.50.) The **Apothekenmuseum,** also in the castle, features a seventeenth-century laboratory. (Open daily 10am-5pm. Admission DM1.50, students DM0.50.) The castle gardens and terraces, always open, offer a tremendous view of the town and valley. From here you can hike further into the mountains or take a cable car up to **Königstuhl.** The funicular *(Bergbahn)* runs from Kornmarkt to the castle (DM2) and on to Königstuhl (DM4) every 20 minutes from 7am-7:25pm in summer, and 9:50am-6pm in winter.

In town, most sights are clustered near the **Marktplatz,** a cobbled square surrounded by picturesque buildings. Notice **Hercules' Fountain,** where witches and heretics were burned in the fifteenth century. Here you'll find the two oldest structures in Heidelberg: The fifteenth-century **Heiliggeistkirche** and the **Haus zum Ritter,** a charming Renaissance mansion that has been converted into a fancy hotel. The stately Heidelberg **Rathaus** overlooks the far end of the square. From the Marktplatz take Hauptstrasse west for more sightseeing; five blocks down, the **Universitätsplatz,** centered about a stone lion fountain, is the former headquarters of the Alte Universität. In the **Student Prison,** Augustinerstr., students were jailed between 1778 and 1914. (Open Mon.-Sat. 9am-5pm. Admission DM0.60, students DM0.40.) At Hauptstr. 97, the **Kurpfälzisches Museum** is crammed with artifacts such as the jawbone of "Heidelberg man," one of the oldest humans yet discovered, works of art by Van der Weyden and Dürer, and a spectacular Gothic altarpiece by fifteenth-century sculptor Tilman Riemenschneider. (Open Tues.-Sun. 10am-5pm. Admission DM1, students free.)

Along the river, below the Kurpfälzisches Museum, stand the handsome **Kongresshaus** and the turreted **Marstall,** a former prison that now houses a student mensa. The best view of these buildings is from the far side of the river. Cross the Neckar over the elegant **Karl-Theodore-Brücke** (Alte Brücke) with its twin towers. From the far end, clamber up the **Schlangenweg,** a winding stone stairway to the **Philosophenweg**—a famous pedestrian walkway where Hegel once indulged in afternoon promenades. The path traverses one side of the 400-meter **Heiligenberg** and affords spectacular views of the town, especially at sunset. At the top of the Heiligenberg lie ruins of the twelfth-century **St. Michael Basilika,** the thirteenth-century **St. Stephan Kloster,** and an **amphitheater** built under Hitler in 1934 on the site of an ancient Celtic gathering place. From May through September, the

Rhein-Neckar-Fahrgastschiffahrt, in front of the Kongresshaus, runs cruises up and down the Neckar. (Adults DM5-12, children DM3-8, depending on length of cruise.) Climb the wooded **Königstuhl** or take the *Bergbahn* to enjoy a view of the city.

Heidelberg's **Faschings Parade** struts through the city in early March, and the **Spring Festival** begins at the end of May and continues for two weeks. A **wine festival** is held in mid-September, and the **Christmas market** runs from late November to December 22. The **Holy Ghost Church** has organ concerts by international musicians (July-Aug., Mon.-Thurs. 6:30-7pm, Fri. 9pm, Sat. 9pm, Sun. 11:30am.)

At night, check out the bars and pubs along the Hauptstrasse; **Club 1900,** Hauptstr. 117, has good music and dancing.

Near Heidelberg

Heidelberg is a good base from which to explore the medieval towns of the Neckar Valley, and the cathedral sites of Speyer and Worms. If you take bus #7007 from the train station in Heidelberg (leaves from stop #3, Eurail and InterRail valid), you can comfortably explore the fabulous landscaped gardens of Schwetzingen Palace and the Speyer cathedral in one afternoon. The eighteenth-century palace is only a block away from the Schwetzingen train station. Once the home of the Prince Elector, its spacious grounds contain a mosque, ruins, Roman aqueduct, and Chinese bridges—all eighteenth-century fakes.

From Schwetzingen, bus #7007 continues on to **Speyer.** The events which inspired the *Nibelungen Saga* took place here in 600. This bishop's town is also famous for its massive, four-towered Romanesque **Dom.** The cathedral's gargantuan but simple interior harbors a **crypt** in which several holy Roman emperors are entombed. (Open April-Sept. Mon.-Fri. 9am-6pm, Sat. 9am-4pm, Sun. 1:30-4:30pm; Oct.-March Mon.-Sat. 9am-noon and 1:30-5pm, Sun. 1:30-4:30pm. Free; crypt admission DM1, students DM0.50.) Speyer's **wine museum** houses the oldest vintage in the world: Rome 300 C.E. The **tourist office,** on Marktplatz, just up the street facing the cathedral, can provide you with a list of accommodations. (Open Mon.-Fri. 9am-noon and 2-5pm.)

Martin Luther protested the abuses of the Church, in 1521, at **Worms.** Religious monuments have long made this town a destination for pilgrimages. The elaborate **Dom St. Peter** is perhaps one of the most striking cathedrals in Germany. Partially damaged in World War II, it has been rebuilt with the stones of the original structure. Don't overlook the beautiful baroque facade of the **Dreifaltigkeitskirche** (Church of the Holy Trinity), across from the tourist office at Maximilianstr. 11. The **Stadtinformation,** across from the cathedral, provides a map with a walking tour of the town.

For centuries Worms has been an important destination for Jewish pilgrims. Here is the **synagogue** housing the yeshiva of Rabbi ben Yitzhak Shlomo (Rashi), the most famous commentator on the Talmud. There is also an adjacent **ritual bath.** Worms was a medieval center for European Jews, but today its Jewish quarter, concentrated around Judengasse and the synagogue, is virtually abandoned—only two Jewish families live here, and the synagogue is used most by American soldiers stationed nearby. The **Rashi House Jewish Museum,** next to the synagogue, documents and chronicles the history of the community. Just beyond the walls is **Liebfrauen Kirche,** the original source of inspiration for the name of the regional wine *Liebfrauenmilch,* and still a loyal sentinel over the vineyards.

Worms is only an hour from Heidelberg by train.

Baden-Baden

Tucked between vineyards and the Black Forest, Baden-Baden is famous for its costly *Kur,* a therapeutic treatment in the town's natural springs. Wealthy Europeans (and more recently, North Americans) come here to flaunt their wealth. The

Augustaplatz is great for wandering about and wondering at the turn-of-the-century villas. Surrounded by a vast garden of rose bushes, fir trees, and small waterfalls, the **Kurhaus** complex houses the Casino and Trinkhalle. A devastating fire destroyed much of the Kurhaus in the spring of 1987, but it should be rebuilt by early 1988. For a taste of what *Kur* is all about, drink from the springs in the **Trinkhalle,** but don't blame us. (Open daily 10am-5:30pm. Admission DM3, students DM1.50.) Begun in 1855 by Frenchman Edouard Bénazet, the **Casino** is the most luxurious in the world, with interior rooms designed as copies of Versailles. (Tours May-Sept. daily 9:30am-noon; Oct.-April daily 10am-noon. Admission DM2.) Attendance during gambling hours is a little more complicated: You must be at least 21 and present a foreign passport. Technically, students are not admitted, but you can get in without obligation to play if you wear coat and tie or evening dress, and pay the DM5 admission. Minimum bets are DM5; the maximum is only DM50,000.

The most impressive place to "take the waters" is the 150-year-old **Roman Bathhouse,** at Römerplatz 1 (tel. (07221) 27 51). In this elegantly restored building you will enjoy two fabulous hours of steam, saunas, massage, hot and cold pools, and so forth. (Admission DM25; DM20 on Sat. or with a guest card. Open Mon. and Wed.-Sat. 8am-10pm, Tues. 8am-4pm; last admission 2 hr. before closing time.) The modern **Caracalla-Therme** was named after the Roman Emperor Caracalla, the first to discover the healing qualities of the town's springs. (Open daily 8am-10pm. Admission DM15 for 2 hr., each additional ½ hr. DM3; DM20 for 4 hr. Saunas and a visit to the inhalatorium included.) Hitch a ride up Alter Schlossweg to the **Altes Schloss** perched high above the town. This twelfth-century castle has a panoramic view of Baden-Baden, the Rhine plane, and the Vosges Mountains. (Open Tues.-Sun. 10am-8pm.)

The **Kurverwaltung,** Augustaplatz 8 (tel. (07221) 27 52 00), behind the fountain, offers information and room-finding assistance. (Open Mon.-Sat. 9am-10pm, Sun. 10am-10pm.) The accommodations situation is rosy, thanks to Baden-Baden's luxurious **Jugendherberge Werner Dietz (IYHF)** Hardbergstr. 34 (tel. (07221) 522 23). Get off bus #1 or 3 at Grosse Dollen Str. (the 4th or 5th stop) between the station and town (don't go to the tourist office first or you'll have to backtrack), and follow the signs. There are family apartments and disabled facilities, plus a public swimming pool just across the street. (Usually packed in the high season; no phone reservations. Juniors DM11.70, seniors DM13.70. Sheets DM3. Breakfast included. Open in summer 8am-11:30pm; in winter 8am-10pm. Admission to pool DM1.) Otherwise, try **Hotel zum Felsen,** Geroldsauerstr. 43 (tel. 716 41). Take bus #1 or 3 to Brahmsplatz, then walk 10 minutes. The elegant rooms have private baths and the owner is very friendly. (Singles DM44, doubles DM70. Showers and breakfast included. Open Tues.-Sun. 10am-midnight.) To reach the cheerful **Gasthaus Kühler Krug,** Beuernstr. 115 (tel. (07221) 723 38), take bus #1 or 17 from the station or the center to the Sauerbosch stop. (DM30 per person in singles, doubles, and triples. Private showers in some rooms.) The **Gasthaus zum Engel,** Ooser Hauptstr. 20 (tel. (07221) 616 10), rents simple and inexpensive rooms. (Singles DM22, doubles DM44. Breakfast included.) The closest campsite is **Campingplatz Adam** in Bühl-Oberbruch (tel. (07223) 231 94); take the train to Bühl and walk 1km. (DM6.50 per person, DM7 per tent. Open year-round.)

Ristorante Romano, in the pedestrian zone at Lange Str. 45, has mediocre but cheap pizza (DM6.50 and up). **Restaurant Dubrovnik,** near the *Kurverwaltung* at Maria-Victoriastr. 1, offers good Yugoslavian and German cuisine (DM10-18). In **Bratwurstglöckle,** Steinstr. 7 (tel. (07221) 29 68), just above the *Rathaus,* locals munch on large meat dishes for DM9.50-14.50. (Open Wed.-Mon. 10am-midnight.) The **Pils Stube Rondo,** Langestr. 49, near the Alter Bahnhof, stays open until 1am. (Meals DM5.90-10.)

Trains arrive at **Baden-Oos** station, about 8km from town. Take bus #1 or 3 (DM1.90) into town, and get off at Augustaplatz (15-min. ride); leave backpacks at the train station, as there are no lockers in the city center.

Black Forest (Schwarzwald)

The Black Forest is the Germany of fairy tales and storybooks. Stretching west of the Rhine from Karlsruhe to Basel, the region received its name from the thick stands of evergreens covering its steep hillsides. Under their canopy it is often eerie and dark, but on the open hillsides the light is brilliant and the air clear. This heavily Catholic area retains most of its traditional customs. Many families continue to live in farmhouses which combine living quarters with space for animals in one large structure.

The most beautiful route through the Black Forest is the stretch from northern Waldkirch to southeastern Hintergarten. Along this way you can see over the heights, beyond to the Alps, and down into the Rhine Valley. You can also stop at the towns of St. Peter and St. Märgen, both known for their traditional lifestyle.

The main access points to the Black Forest are Freiburg to the southwest, Baden-Baden to the northwest, and Stuttgart to the east. Public transportation is good in this mountain region: Rail lines run from Lörrach, Freiburg, Offenburg, and Baden-Baden in the west to Donaueschingen, Villingen-Schwenningen, Freudenstadt, and Stuttgart in the east. The most beautiful connection is the **Höllental** route leading out of Freiburg to the Titisee lake. Bahn and Post buses cover all major roads, but often run only two to four times per day. The hiking trails of the Schwarzwald are used in the winter for cross-country skiing, and there are downhill slopes at Feldberg and at Schwarzwaldhochstrasse.

Northern Black Forest (Nördlicher Schwarzwald)

Though the hills are lower, the forest cover is often more dense here than in the south—the northern Black Forest looks truly black—and there is good hiking. For information, the Kurverwaltung in Baden-Baden (tel. (07221) 27 52 00) or Freudenstadt (tel. (07441) 60 74) are the most helpful; much of the area's transportation runs between these two towns.

Freudenstadt is a beautifully situated town with arcaded streets and a lovely seventeenth-century church. The town is a *Kur* town, so the emphasis is on relaxation. A good place to get some is the large **Panorama Bad** complex on Ludwig-Jahn-Str. It has 6 pools for swimming, sunning, and relaxing. (Unlimited admission DM6, students DM4.50. Open Mon.-Fri. 9am-9pm, Sat.-Sun. 9am-8pm.) The **Kurverwaltung** (tel. (07441) 60 74) is at Lauterbadstr. 5, in the center of town. (Open April-Oct. Mon.-Fri. 9am-noon and 2:30-5pm, Sat.-Sun. 10am-noon; Nov.-March Mon.-Fri. 9am-noon and 2:30-5pm.) **Gasthof See,** Forststr. 17 (tel. (07441) 26 88), near the Stadtbahnhof (station), has pretty rooms. (Singles DM30, with bath DM37; doubles DM60, with bath DM74.) Behind the station is **Gasthaus am Dobel,** Gottlieb-Daimlerstr. 71 (tel. (07441) 68 18), a student sport house next to a soccer field; it resembles a luxurious hostel with bright doubles, triples, and quads. (DM22 per person. Breakfast included. Open Tues.-Sun. 10am-2pm and 5pm-midnight.) The **Jugendherberge (IYHF),** Eugen-Nägele-Str. 69 (tel. (07441) 77 20), across town, toward the stadium, has kitchen facilities. (Juniors DM7, seniors DM9. Sheets DM3.50. Mandatory breakfast DM3.60; lunch DM6.20, dinner DM5.50. Check-in 5-10pm. Flexible 10pm curfew. Open year-round.) **Camping** (tel. (07441) 28 62) is at Langenstadt, 3km west of town on the B28 highway. (DM4.50 per person, DM3.50 per tent, DM2.50 per car. Open May-Sept.) Eat at the **Anuschka-Grills,** Lossburgerstr. 15 (steaks and cafeteria-style meals DM6 and up; open 9am-10pm).

You can rent bicycles at **Haus Schierenberg,** Lauterbadstr. 43 (tel. (07441) 60 74), and at the **Bahnhof** (tel. (07441) 45 54). Check the activities board in the *Kurhaus* for a list of events and guided trips.

Buses run between Freudenstadt and Baden-Baden along the scenic 55-kilometer Schwarzwaldhochstrasse (B28). You might consider a hike along part of the accompanying trail, the **Westweg,** which runs along the spine of the mountains and offers a continuous view of the Rhine Valley, France, and the Vosges Mountains. At the crossing just beyond Alexanderschanze, about 17km north of Freudenstadt, and 300m off the main road, is a large, popular **Jugendherberge (IYHF)** (tel. (07804) 611). Pleasantly isolated, it is the perfect base for hiking in summer and cross-country or downhill skiing in winter (ski rental DM6 per day). (Juniors DM7.50, seniors DM9. Sheets DM3. Breakfast DM4.50; bag-lunch DM5.50.)

About 13km toward Baden-Baden is the small settlement of **Ruhestein,** accessible by public transportation only from June to September. From here the Westweg leads over Seiblesecke and the Mummelsee to **Unterstmatt,** traversing the **Hornisgrinde** (1164m), the highest peak in the area. Famous in German folklore, the **Mummelsee** is not very large but is extremely deep; legends tell of an evil sea king who lives in its depths, and von Grimmelshausen mentioned the lake in his *Simplicissimus.* Past the Mummelsee, you can leave the Westweg in Unterstmatt and continue to Baden-Baden by bus. Farther along the road in **Plättig/Bühlerhöhe** there is a pleasant little **Naturfreundehaus** (tel. (07226) 238). Look for the signs—it's about 2km off the road. (DM7.50. Sleep-sack DM2. Breakfast DM5. 10pm curfew. Open Wed.-Mon.) Routes to the east of Freudenstadt are less interesting. If you're traveling south, your best bet is to head toward Freiburg along the B294. **Alpirsbach,** about 20km south of Freudenstadt, has a **Jugendherberge (IYHF)** at Reinerzauer Steige 80 (tel. (07444) 24 77), only 15 minutes from the train station. (Juniors DM7, seniors DM9. Sheets DM3. Breakfast DM3.60. 10pm curfew.)

Southern Black Forest (Südlicher Schwarzwald)

The highest part of the Black Forest, the Hochschwarzwald, feels like the roof of Germany. With rounded mountaintops covered with bright green pasture, crisp air, high-altitude valleys, dark woods, and centuries-old farms, the Hochschwarzwald is at once satisfyingly remote and hospitable. The best source of information is the **Freiburg tourist office,** Bertoldstr. 45 (tel. (0761) 313 17), which has great hiking advice. The tourist offices of all the local towns will provide maps and information. Get a bus schedule (Fahrplankarte #2) from the station in Freiburg for the **Panorama Strasse** between Freiburg and Titisee.

St. Märgen, at the top of the Glottertal Valley, is perhaps the prettiest village of the entire region. Look for the two bulbous towers of the church: The *Rathaus* next door has a **Kurverwaltung** office (tel. (07669) 10 66) with a room-finding service. (Open July-Sept. Mon.-Fri. 8am-12:30pm and 2-5pm, Sat. 10am-noon; Oct.-June Mon.-Fri. 8am-noon and 2-5pm.) St. Märgen is an official *Luftkurort* ("air convalescence area") known for its healthful climate; hiking here is pure pleasure. The Kurverwaltung's small pamphlet *Wanderführer* is helpful. The 13km Zweribachfälle trail leads past a splendid waterfall with a magnificent view. In winter, the center for cross-country skiing in this area is the **Thurnerspur,** just outside town. Equipment is available; call the **Blockhaus** (tel. (07669) 10 20), or ask at the tourist office. You may want to hike the 2km east to **Gasthaus Steinbach-Hirschen** at Mooshöhe 1 (tel. (07669) 246), where a room with breakfast is about DM22, and an inexpensive restaurant serves meals downstairs (DM8-11). The **Gästehaus Böckmann,** Raukhofstr. 18 (tel. (07669) 290), has clean rooms with views of the valley. (Single with breakfast and shower DM25. Open daily 9am-7pm.) You can find private rooms for as little as DM14 through the tourist office.

Just 8km from St. Märgen is the village of **St. Peter,** famous for its Benedictine abbey which perished in the early nineteenth-century "secularization" that robbed southern Germany of a large part of its Catholic cultural heritage. Peter Thumb was the architect of the medium-sized church whose simple outer appearance belies an interior with wonderfully frescoed ceilings. The village's **Kurverwaltung** (tel. (07660) 274), just opposite the church, will help with accommodations and offer free guided hikes. (Open Mon.-Fri. 7:30am-noon and 1:30-5pm.) Rent bicycles from **Kiosk Kunert,** Roterweg (tel. (07660) 458). **Pension Schwär,** Schweighofweg 4 (tel. (07660) 219), has simple rooms (DM22 per person; showers and breakfast included). Camp at **Steingrubenhof** (tel. (07660) 210), about 1km out of town; ask the driver of the Glottertal bus to let you off at *Haldenweg* or *Steingrubenhof.* Buses leave Freiburg's main train station about every half hour and arrive approximately 30 minutes later in St. Peter. From St. Peter to Freiburg, buses leave approximately every 45 minutes.

On the way to Freiburg from St. Peter lies the tiny village of **Glottertal,** home to some of Germany's most famous restaurants. Two of them, **Hirschen** and **Engel,** offer special deals for students. (Less than DM20 and DM15, respectively.)

Next to the Glottertal is the famous **Höllental,** tortuous and narrow. Emerging from the top of the valley are the twin towns of **Titisee,** particularly popular with senior travelers, and **Neustadt.** Although the lake is heavily touristed and the town is expensive, the dense forests flanking the lake are worth visiting. You can rent boats on the Titisee for DM7-12 per hour, or guided boats will take you on a 25-minute tour for DM4.

The **Titisee tourist office** (tel. (07651) 81 01) is in the *Kurhaus* about three blocks from the lake. (Open July-Aug. Mon.-Fri. 8am-noon and 1:30-5:30pm, Sat. 10am-noon and 3-5pm, Sun. 10am-noon; Sept.-June Mon.-Sat. only.) The **Neustadt tourist office** is on Kurbadstrasse in the Sebastian-Kneipp-Anlage (tel. (07651) 206 69). **Jugendherbergen Veltishof (IYHF),** Bruderhalde 27 (tel. (07652) 238), is at the far end of the lake in Titisee. The small rooms are a bit crowded, but comfortable. (Juniors DM11.20, seniors DM13.20. Breakfast DM3.90. Check-in 5-7pm. Open year-round.) If Veltishof is full, try **Jugendherberge Rudenberg,** Haus Nr. 6 (tel. (07651) 76 30), in Neustadt. (Juniors DM8, seniors DM10. Sheets DM3. Breakfast DM3.90.) Wake up by the smooth water of the Titisee at **Campingplatz Weiherhof** (tel. (07652) 14 68), about 1km out of town. (DM5 per person, DM4 per car, DM4.50 per tent. Clean bathroom and shower facilities. Open 8am-10pm.) Bicycle rental is available at the stations in both towns. In Titisee, call (07651) 82 98; in Neustadt, call (07651) 14 15. Ask at the tourist office for a fishing permit always handy when biking in Titisee and Neustadt.

In the winter, you can ski at **Feldberg,** 20km southeast of Titisee. Rentals are available. There is a small youth hostel at **Altglashütten (IYHF),** Am Sommerberg 26 (tel. (07655) 206), in Feldberg. (Juniors DM7.50, seniors DM9.50. Sheets DM3. Breakfast DM3.90. Open year-round 10am-9pm.)

Tucked into a Black Forest valley, the small town of **Triberg** is home of the highest waterfall in Germany; to convince yourself, pay DM2 (students DM1) and walk to the top. Reward yourself later with a piece of *Schwarzwälderkirschtorte* (Black Forest cake; about DM5.50) in the cafe at the foot of the thundering falls. A **Jugendherberge (IYHF)** (tel. (07722) 41 10) is about 20 minutes away by foot (40 minutes from the station); follow the signs up the hill to **Am Hofeck,** Rohrbacherstr. 35. This beautifully situated hostel has a friendly host and about 6 beds per room. (Juniors DM7.50, seniors DM9.50. Breakfast DM3.60. 10pm curfew. Open May-Oct.) In **Gutach** is the **Vogtsbauernhof,** a collection of genuine fifteenth- and sixteenth-century buildings that is now a folk museum. (Open April-Oct. daily 8:30am-5pm. Admission DM3, students DM1.50.) Triberg and Gutach are both on the train line from Offenburg.

The Kaiserstuhl

Easily accessible from Freiburg, this hilly region overlooks the Rhine and Alsace. Slower and quieter than the rest of the Black Forest, the Kaiserstuhl (Emperor's Chair) is famous for its delicious white wines, especially *Gutedel* and *Müller-Thurgau.* There are few more pleasant places to hike: Every square meter of its gently rolling hills is covered with fragrant vines.

The main town of the area is **Breisach,** on the Rhine. Here is a veritable city on a hill, its *Münster* (cathedral) crowning an astonishing mixture of medieval fortifications and private homes. **St. Stephen's Cathedral** may seem rather ugly from the outside, but it is deservedly famous for its huge and elaborately carved birchwood altar. The altar's top curves ever so slightly forward, a reminder of the bet made by woodcarver Hans Loi that an altar could be built taller than its chapel. The prize for his success was the mayor's daughter, and there was a happy ending for all but the class-conscious mayor. Group tours can be arranged for DM5 per person at the tourist office; the Freiburg office sometimes also arranges trips here.

The **ZBW,** or **Zentralkellerei Badischer Winzergenossenschaften** (tel. (07667) 822 70), is Europe's largest wine cellar and bottling facility; you can witness methods used to produce the more than 500 distinctive wines of the region. The three-hour tour takes you through the enormous production facilities, the underground cellars (on an automatic railway), and finally to the optional wine-tasting session, which costs only DM4. Call ahead to register. Find out from the tourist office about tours of other wine cellars. To sample the region's many wines, drink your way down the **Badische Weinstrasse,** which runs through one wine-growing village after another. Public transportation is sparse, so you may want to rent a car or hitchhike. Rail lines do run from Freiburg to most of the towns surrounding the Kaiserstuhl. The free guide, *Wanderwege am Kaiserstuhl,* lists hikes around this region.

The **Fremdenverkehrs-Gemeinschaft,** Werd 9 (tel. (07667) 832 27), has information on the entire region. In the same room, the **Verkehrsbüro** (tel. (07667) 832 27) will help you find private rooms for DM18-25, breakfast included. (Both offices open Mon.-Fri. 8:30am-12:30pm and 1:30-5:30pm, Sat. 8:30am-noon.) Breisach's **Jugendherberge (IYHF)** (tel. (07667) 76 65) is fabulously located on Münsterbergstr. 30-32, right below the cathedral and next to a medieval gate. (Juniors DM7, seniors DM9. Sheets DM2. Mandatory breakfast DM3.90. Free view of France. Check-in 5-5:30pm and 7:30-8:30pm. Open year-round.) The **Kaisersthler Hof,** Richard-Müller-Str. 2 (tel. (07667) 236), charges DM30 per person, breakfast included. (Open Tues.-Sun. 10am-9pm.) In **Bahlingen,** stay in the **Gaststätte Bad-Silberbrunnen** (tel. (07663) 12 54). Rooms with showers and breakfast DM20-25. **Camping** (tel. (07667) 285) is available at **Münsterblick** in the Hochstetten part of Breisach, 2km from the center. (DM4 per person, DM3 per tent. Open in summer.) **Hotel Post,** Neutorstr. 1, serves a pleasant, inexpensive lunch. Otherwise, you'll have to eat at the hostel or hit the grocery stores (open daily 11am-3pm and 6-9pm).

Freiburg im Breisgau

The metropolis of the Black Forest, Freiburg is a cosmopolitan university town with a rich cultural tradition. The town was largely destroyed in a single bombing attack in World War II, but its citizens have painstakingly recreated the architecture and public spaces. The continuing strength of local custom is evidenced in the daily **Münsterplatz** market, in outdoor chess games (played on a life-size set in the park), and in the warm welcome accorded all visitors. Although it's a university town, Freiburg does not roll up its sidewalks in summer, and the yearly events—the wine festival during the last weekend in June, the **Narrenfest** (the fools' festival, traditionally known as *Fasnacht*) in mid-February, and the **Christkindl** markets during December—contribute to the city's vitality.

Follow the **Bächle,** small streams in the middle of the streets, to the *Altstadt.* These served as the sewage system for the medieval town. Here rises the magnificent **Münster,** built in the thirteenth century on the site where Bernhard of Clairvaux proclaimed the Crusade of 1146. One of few buildings to survive the war, it is a splendid mixture of high and late Gothic styles. (Open Mon.-Sat. 10am-noon and 2-6pm, Sun. 1-6pm. Admission DM1, students free.) The tower is well worth climbing, both to enjoy the view and to admire the architecture at close range. (Open March-Nov. Tues.-Sat. 10am-5pm, Sun. 1-5pm. Admission DM1, students DM0.80.) The tower bells, which toll on the hour, are also worth a look. The **Schwabentor,** two blocks from the Münster, offers a similarly beautiful view—as well as a chair lift.

The **Augustiner Museum,** Salzstr. 32 (tel. (0761) 216 33 01), located in a thirteenth-century cloister, is an intimate museum with medieval art and artifacts and a fascinating exhibit on Freiburg's history. Classical music concerts are held here during the summer; see the tourist office for a schedule. (Open Tues.-Sun. 10am-5pm, Mon. 10am-8pm. Free.) Just behind Augustinerplatz are two of Freiburg's five gates, the well-restored **Schwabentor,** and **Martinstor. Erasmus' house,** as red and gold as the *Rathaus,* stands on Gauchstrasse. Here is where he spent the last years of his life. Note the interesting combination of the new and the old architecture in the **Rathaus.**

The staff at the **Freiburger Verkehrsamt,** Rotteckring 14 (tel. (0761) 216), two blocks downtown of the train station, is enthusiastic, and will help you find a room for DM3. *Privatzimmer* are cheaper but usually available only for stays of three or more days. (Open Mon.-Wed. and Sat. 9am-6pm, Thurs.-Fri. 9am-9pm, Sun. and holidays 10am-noon.) The adjoining travel agency has BIGE. At Universitätstr. 15 is an excellent travel **bookstore** which sells guides to the Black Forest. (Open Mon.-Fri. 9am-6pm, Sat. 10am-1pm.)

The **Jugendherberge Ottilienwise (IYHF)** (tel. (0761) 676 56) is at Kartäuserstr. 151. Take tram #1 (direction: Littenweiler) to the Römerhof stop, walk down Fritz-Geige-Str., cross the river, and turn right. It's enormous, modern, and sterile, but with a private shower for every two rooms. (Juniors DM8.50, seniors DM10.50. Sheets DM3. Mandatory breakfast DM3.90. Reception open 7am-11:30pm. 11:30pm curfew. Open year-round.) To reach the **Hotel Schemmer,** Eschholzstr. 63 (tel. (0761) 27 24 24), turn right from the train station and cross over the tracks, then go down the stairs of the bridge past the church. (DM25-30 per person with showers and breakfast.) The **Gasthaus Hirschen,** Breisgauerstr. 47 (tel. (0761) 821 18), is a bit out of town. Take tram #1 to the end and walk for about five minutes. This cozy establishment, run by the Baumgartner family since 1740, has comfortable, clean rooms for DM27-30 per person, showers and breakfast included. The cafe in the backyard serves meat, soup, and salad for DM13. **Camping** is at Kartäugerstr. 99 (tel. (0761) 350 54), near the hostel at Hirzberg; get off the tram at Messeplatz. (DM5 per person, DM3.50 per tent. Open April-early Oct.)

Thanks to its students, Freiburg has a plethora of cheap eateries. The best feature of these *Stuben* and restaurants is their wide selection of excellent local wines (about DM4 per glass). The tangy, rich flavor of Baden whites is well worth the price; all are available during the several Black Forest wine festivals held here throughout the year. During the harvest celebrations in October, be sure to try the traditional *Zwiebelkuchen,* an onion pie designed to complement the *Neuwein,* the newly-pressed wines. One particularly good place for wine is **Zum Deutschen Haus,** Schusterstr. 40. (Open Mon.-Fri. 10am-noon and 4:30pm-midnight, Sat. 10am-midnight.) **Zum Grossen Meyerhof,** Grundwäldestr. 1-7, serves local specialties for only DM10-15. (Open daily 9am-midnight.) How about a restaurant that specializes in toasts? The **Toast Reich Toasteria,** Münsterplatz 14 (tel. (0761) 379 33), has nearly 50 types of sandwiches and toast (DM6-15). The **Pizzeria Milano,** Schusterstr. 7, has light meals and stays open daily until 10pm. (Pizzas from DM6.) Freiburg's **University Mensas** won't let you starve. One which looks like a giant aquarium is two blocks down Rempartstr. west of the Martinstor; the other is on the main campus north of Albertstrasse. You must buy tickets at lunchtime for both lunch and dinner (student ID required; non-students will pay up to DM7 for a meal. But one of the students wandering around will probably be glad to sell you a ticket for DM3. (Rempartstrasse open Sept.-June 11:45am-2pm and 5:30-7:30pm; July-Aug. 11:45-2pm. Albertstrasse open Sept.-June 11:45am-2pm.) If the idea of spending an evening sitting in *Gemütlichkeit* over beer or wine doesn't appeal to you, the **"LP"** on Schiffstr. bops.

Freiburg public transport costs DM2, with special tourist deals available; the 24-hour ticket (DM5) is valid on all public transportation; the weekend ticket (DM6.50), and the 4-day ticket (DM13) are valid on all buses and trams. **Hitchhiking** out of Freiburg shouldn't be a problem. To go north, take tram #2 or 5 (direction: Zähringen) to the last stop and walk back some 50m; south, catch tram #1 to Landwasser, and then bus #36 (direction: Hochdorf) to Kandelblickstr.; west, take tram #1 to Padua-Allee, and then bus #31 or 32 to Hauptstr.; east, take tram #1 (direction: Littenweiler) to Lassbergstr., and then bus #18 (direction: Strandbad) to Strandbad. The **Mitfahrzentrale,** Belfortstr. 55 (tel. (0761) 367 49), is open Mon.-Fri. 9am-6pm, Sat. 8:30am-1pm, Sun. 11am-2pm.

Tübingen

One third of Tübingen's residents are affiliated with the city's 500-year-old university. The students leave in August and September, but at other times you will find Tübingen crowded with young people and quite short of tourists.

The winding streets and gabled houses of the town center contain the lovely fifteenth-century **Stiftskirche** (open daily 9am-5pm) and the **Tübinger Stift,** the seminary where Hegel once studied. Wander through the narrow streets of the old city and inspect the **Rathaus,** with its ornately painted nineteenth-century facade. Although you cannot enter the **Hohentübingen Castle** in 1988 because of restoration work, you can still view the old town from its great balcony (a 10-min. walk from the train station; cross the Alleenbrücke, take a right onto Neckarhalde, and the castle will be on the left). Stroll (or row) along the sleepy Neckar River for a panoramic view of the old city and the **Hölderlinturm** (tower) on the north bank. Hermann Hesse fans can look for the red house in which Hesse was an apprentice bookbinder, on Holzmarkt by the Stiftskirche. Worth a side trip is the beautiful Cistercian abbey of **Bebenhausen.** To visit its peaceful cloisters, take the bus marked "Stuttgart" from bay #9 at the train station (a 10-min. ride). (Abbey open Mon.-Fri. 8-11am and 2-4pm, Sat.-Sun. 10-11am and 2-4pm.)

Relax at the **Uhlandbad,** a cheap alternative to the Black Forest *Kurs.* Across from the tourist information, the pool is open September through July (Tues., Thurs.-Fri., and Sat. 8am-8pm, Sun. 8am-noon). Admission for all facilities DM3.50.

To reach the **Verkehrsverein** (tel. (07071) 350 11), walk from the train station through the underground passage and the park to Uhlandstr., turn right, and you'll see the sign at the intersection. For DM2.50, they will find you a room. (Open May-Oct. Mon.-Fri. 8:30am-6:30pm, Sat. 8:30am-5pm, Sun. 2-5pm; Nov.-April Mon.-Fri. 8:30am-6:30pm, Sat. 8:30am-12:30pm.) A kiosk in front of the station offers a map of the city. (Open daily 7am-6:30pm.)

The **Jugendherberge (IYHF),** Gartenstr. 22/2 (tel. (07071) 230 02), is very nice and just downriver from the main bridge on the old town side. (Juniors DM11.40, seniors DM13.40. Sheets DM3. Breakfast included. Open 5-8pm and 9-9:45pm. 11:30pm curfew. Open year-round.) The only private lodgings in the town which are not astronomically expensive or light-years away, are the clean, comfortable rooms at **Gasthof Ritter,** am Stadtgraben 25 (tel. (07071) 225 02). After crossing the bridge, continue for about five or ten minutes, then turn left. (Singles DM35, doubles DM55-60. Breakfast included.) The inexpensive restaurant inside serves large cold plates for DM10 and meat entrees for about DM15. **Camping** is available at Rappernberghalde, on the river (tel. (07071) 233 43). Go upriver from the old town, or left from the station, across the river on the Alleenbrücke, and left again. (DM5.50 per person, DM5 per tent. Open April to mid-Oct. daily 8am-1pm and 3-10pm.) The **University Mensa,** at the corner of Wilhelmstr. and Keplerstr., offers some meals for DM2.40, and large meat entrees for DM12. (Open late Aug.-late July Mon.-Thurs. 11:30am-1:30pm and 5:30-8pm, Fri. 11:30am-1:30pm and 5:30-7pm. Student ID required.) The restaurant at **Hotel am Schloss,** Burgstr. 18, near the castle at the top of the hill, is elegant and cozy, with delicious meals for DM10-20. The **Restaurant zum Kiess,** Karlstr. 1, near the tourist office, has reasonable prices for Schwabian specialties (DM7-10). The **Restaurant/Cafe Museum,** on Wilhelmstr., is a good deal at lunchtime, with specials including main dish, salad, and side-orders for DM9-11. (Both open Tues.-Sun.)

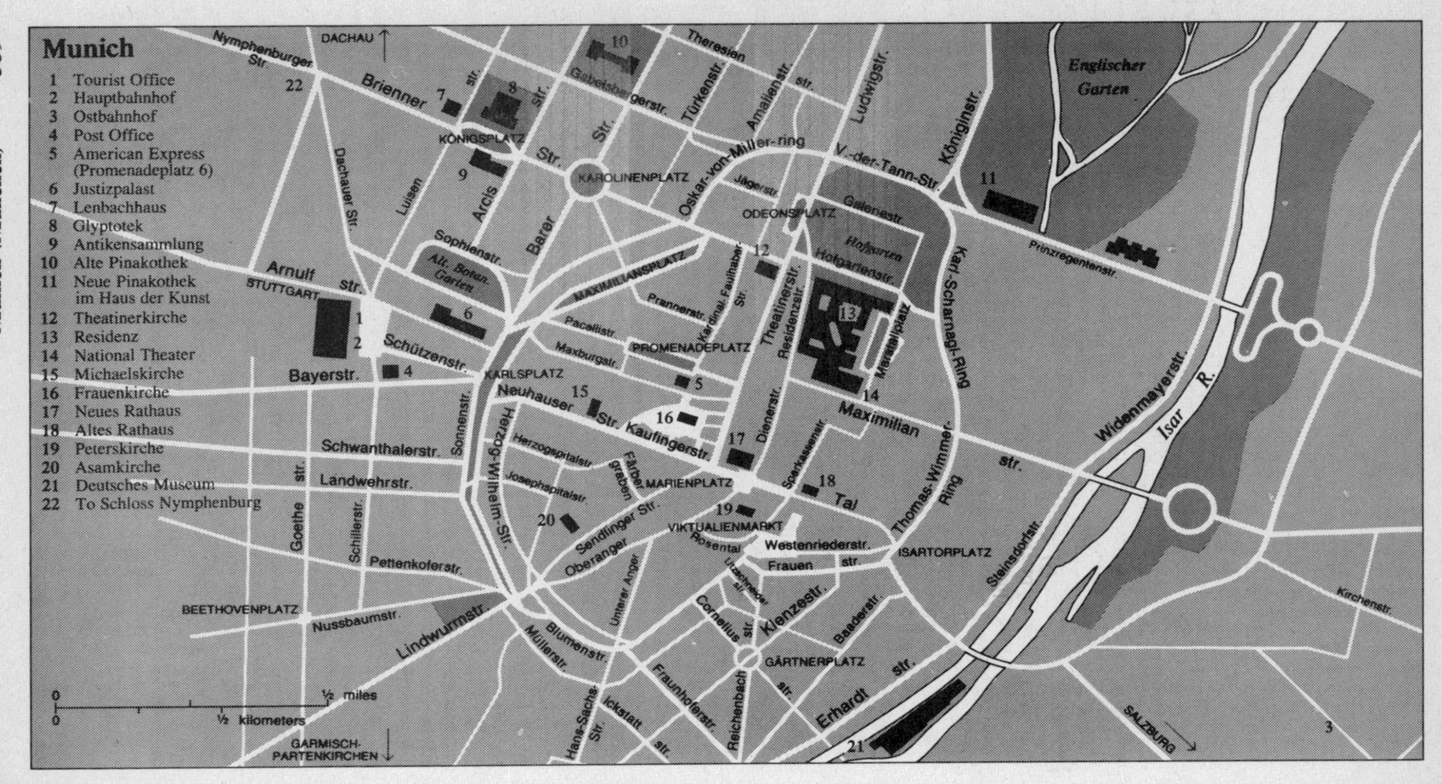
Munich
1 Tourist Office
2 Hauptbahnhof
3 Ostbahnhof
4 Post Office
5 American Express (Promenadeplatz 6)
6 Justizpalast
7 Lenbachhaus
8 Glyptotek
9 Antikensammlung
10 Alte Pinakothek
11 Neue Pinakothek im Haus der Kunst
12 Theatinerkirche
13 Residenz
14 National Theater
15 Michaelskirche
16 Frauenkirche
17 Neues Rathaus
18 Altes Rathaus
19 Peterskirche
20 Asamkirche
21 Deutsches Museum
22 To Schloss Nymphenburg
0 ½ miles
0 ½ kilometers
DACHAU
GARMISCH-PARTENKIRCHEN
SALZBURG
Englischer Garten
Isar R.
Nymphenburger Str.
Brienner str.
KÖNIGSPLATZ
Arcis Str.
Barer Str.
KAROLINENPLATZ
Theresien str.
Gabelsbergerstr.
Türkenstr.
Amalienstr.
Ludwigstr.
Königinstr.
Oskar-von-Miller-ring
V.-der-Tann-Str.
ODEONSPLATZ
Galeriestr.
Hofgarten
Hofgartenstr.
Prinzregentenstr.
Karl-Scharnagl-Ring
Marstallplatz
Theatinerstr.
Residenzstr.
Dachauer Str.
Luisen
Sophienstr.
Alt. Botan. Garten
Arnulf str.
STUTTGART
Schützenstr.
Bayerstr.
KARLSPLATZ
MAXIMILIANSPLATZ
Prannerstr.
Kardinal-Faulhaber-Str.
Pacellistr.
Maxburgstr.
PROMENADEPLATZ
Neuhauser Str.
Kaufingerstr.
Dienerstr.
Maximilian str.
Widenmayerstr.
Sonnenstr.
Schwanthalerstr.
Landwehrstr.
Goethe str.
Schillerstr.
Pettenkoferstr.
Herzog-Wilhelm-Str.
Herzogspitalstr.
Josephspitalstr.
Färbergraben
MARIENPLATZ
Sparkassenstr.
Tal
Thomas-Wimmer-Ring
Sendlinger Str.
Oberanger
VIKTUALIENMARKT
Rosental
Westenriederstr.
Frauen str.
ISARTORPLATZ
Steinsdorfstr.
BEETHOVENPLATZ
Nussbaumstr.
Lindwurmstr.
Unterer Anger
Müllerstr.
Blumenstr.
Cornelius str.
Klenzestr.
Baaderstr.
GÄRTNERPLATZ
Hans-Sachs-Str.
Ickstatt str.
Fraunhoferstr.
Reichenbach str.
Erhardt str.
Kirchenstr.

Bavaria (Bayern)

Munich (München)

Home to the sound of clinking beer mugs and Bavarian music, Munich is just what some people have come to Germany to find. In addition, though, Munich features world-class museums, beautiful parks and architecture, and a uniquely liberal attitude that has made the city a cultural capital of Germany. The beautiful public buildings and monuments which have survived the war testify to the imperial aspirations of the Wittelsbach family, rulers of Bavaria from the twelfth to the early twentieth century. An odd mix of proud traditionalism and avant-garde culture will keep you interested and active at all hours—and the town does stay up until all hours, with its 80,000 students and earthy Bavarian *gemütlichkeit.* Particularly riotous times occur during Munich's many carnivals, starting with *Fasching* (early Jan. to mid-Feb.), and continuing full-tilt until the famous *Oktoberfest,* which lasts from the third Saturday in September through the first Sunday in October.

Orientation and Practical Information

From the **Hauptbahnhof,** Schützenstrasse leads toward **Karlsplatz** and Munich's famed **Marienplatz.** From the Marienplatz, the pedestrian area extends north to **Odeonsplatz** (past the Residenz), where a broad boulevard, first Ludwigstrasse, then Leopoldstrasse, leads north through **Schwabing,** Munich's student district. Close by is the enormous **Englischer Garten.** To the southeast of the Marienplatz, small shops and restaurants fill the districts along the **Isar,** Munich's river.

Munich's public transport system operates from about 5am to 1am. Eurail and InterRail passes are valid for any S-Bahn (suburban) train. Single rides on the U-bahn, on *Strassenbahn* (trams), and on buses cost DM2.30, but buy a blue 5- or 10-ride *Streifenkarte* (DM4.50 or DM9) from an automat or at most *Tabak* shops. To ride legally, you must fold over 2 stripes and cancel the second—never less than two. You can travel up to two hours on any vehicle in any one direction with unlimited changes across up to two zones—more zones, more stripes cancelled. For trips within one zone, a red 5-stripe *Kurzstreifenkarte* is a bargain at DM3. Again, always cancel two stripes. Stripe tickets are available from bus drivers, blue automats at U- and S-Bahn stations, and shops with a white K in the window. Consider the DM6.50 24-hour ticket, good for the entire metropolitan system; much less confusing, it is also available at blue automats, and in shops displaying a white K. Weekly or monthly tickets *(Zeitkarten)* are also available, in the Starnberger wing of the station or at Im Tal 70. We often mention the closest public transport stops for convenience's sake, but don't assume you *must* take the subway—many things are quite centrally located.

Tourist Office: Fremdenverkehrsamt, opposite track #11 in the main station (tel. 239 11). A must, but a 15-30 min. wait in the summer. They book rooms (DM3) and sell accommodations lists (DM0.30). Invest in the following: a DM0.30 map (adequate); *Munich for Young People,* invaluable at DM0.50; and the *Monatsprogram* for DM1.30, listing all current museum hours, cultural events, and other information. Open June-Aug. daily 8am-11pm; Sept.-May Mon.-Sat. 8am-11pm, Sun. 1-9:30pm. Recorded **museum and gallery information** (tel. 23 91 74). Recorded information on **sights and castles** (tel. 23 91 75). **EurAide Inc.** (tel. 59 38 80), in the station, will comb Munich to get you the best deal in accommodations, but you pay DM10. Open May-Oct. daily 8am-8pm; Nov.-April daily 9am-5pm.

Budget Travel: ASTA-Reisen, Amalienstr. 73 (tel. 28 07 68), near the university. Sells concert tickets too. Open Mon.-Fri. 9am-6pm. **Transalpino-Reisen,** Schwanthalerstr. 2-6 (tel. 55 71 65), near Karlsplatz. BIGE tickets. Open Mon.-Fri. 9am-6pm, Sat. 9am-1pm. **Jugendreise-center,** Arnulfstr. 6-8 (tel. 59 22 20), beside the station. Generally open Mon.-Fri. 9am-6pm, Sat. 9am-1pm.

American Express: Promenadeplatz 6 (tel. 219 90), 2 blocks north of Neuhäuserstr. Mail held. All banking services. Open Mon.-Fri. 9am-5:30pm, Sat. 9am-noon. Banking services Mon.-Fri. 9am-5pm only.

Currency Exchange: To your right as you enter the station. Open daily 6am-11:30pm.

Post Office: Directly opposite the station (tel. 559 84 06). Open Mon.-Fri. 8am-6pm, Sat. 8am-1pm, Sun. 11am-noon. Poste Restante open daily 7am-11pm; send mail to Lagernde Briefe, 8000 München 32. Telecommunications services open 24 hours. **Postal code:** 8000. **Telephone code:** 089.

Flights: Airport information (tel. 92 11 21 27). Buses connect Riem airport and the Hauptbahnhof every 15 min. (20-30 min., DM5).

Trains: All trains arrive at **München Hauptbahnhof.** Information (tel. 59 29 91).

Bike Rental: Lothar Borucki, Hans-Sachs-Str. 7 (tel. 26 65 06), near the Sendlinger Tor. DM10 per day, DM50 per week. Open Mon.-Fri. 9am-1pm and 3-6pm, Sat. 9am-noon. Also at the southern entrance to the Englischer Garten on summer weekends. DM5 first hr., DM3 thereafter, DM15 all day. If you're staying at the Tent (Jugendlage Kapuzinerhölzl), you can get a cheap bike there.

Emergencies: Police (tel. 110). **Ambulance** (tel. 22 26 66).

Medical Assistance: Check with the U.S. or British consulate for their list of English-speaking doctors. The main **university clinic** is across the river on Ismaningerstrasse. VD checkups at the **Gesundheitshaus,** Dachauerstr. 90.

Pharmacy: Bahnhof Apotheke (tel. 59 41 19), on the outside corner of the station, is open Mon.-Sat. 8am-6:30pm. 24-hour service rotates among the city's pharmacies—call 59 44 75 for recorded information.

Consulates: U.S., Königinstr. 5 (tel. 230 11). **Canada,** Maximilliansplatz 9 (tel. 55 85 31). **U.K.,** Amalienstr. 62 (tel. 39 40 15).

Bookstores: In this university city, every bookstore has a few English books, but visit the overflowing **Anglia Bookshop,** Schellingstr. 3 in Schwabing (tel. 28 36 42). Open Mon.-Fri. 9am-6:30pm, Sat. 9:30am-1pm.

Laundry: Wäscherei at Klenzestr. #18 and 39.

Swimming Pool: Indoors at the **Olympia Schwimmhalle** (tel. (30613) 390). Take U3 or U8 to Olympic Village or bus #36, 41, 43, 44, 81, 84, or 184. Open Mon. 10am-9:30pm, Tues.-Sun. 7am-9pm. Outdoor pools too, but the Englischer Garten is much more fun.

Hitchhiking: Watch the bulletin boards in the *Mensa* at Leopoldstr. 13. Otherwise, try these routes: *Autobahn* Salzburg (Ell), for Salzburg-Vienna and Brenner-Italy, take S-Bahn to Ostbahnhof, then bus #95 to Ramersdorf. For Stuttgart, Karlsruhe, France, and England, take U1 to Rotkreuzplatz, then tram #12 to Amalienburgstrasse station, then bus #73 or 75 to Blutenburg station; or take S2 to Obermenzig, then bus #73 or 75. For Nuremburg and all points north, take U6 to Studentenstadt and walk 500m to Frankfurter Ring (Outer Ring) *Autobahn* entrance. For Switzerland, take tram #16 to the last stop (Gondrellplatz). For *Autobahn* Garmisch-Partenkirchen (E6), take U3 or U6 to Westpark, from there with bus #33 to Luisse-Kiesselbach-Platz. Two agencies put drivers and passengers in contact: **Mitfahrzentrale,** Lämmerstr. 4 (tel. 59 45 61), near the train station, and **Känguruh,** Amalienpassage (tel. 28 01 24). They will arrange for you to ride along for a reasonable price. Open Mon.-Fri. 8:30am-12:30pm and 2-6pm, Sat. 8:30am-noon.

Accommodations and Camping

Munich attracts crowds year-round and cheap hotels are often filled by early afternoon. Several of Munich's hostels allow arrivals and check-in all day, so don't put off your search until 5pm. Those planning to sleep in the tempting Englischer Garten should be wary of occasional police checks. If you have a railpass, Augsburg's hostel (30-45 min. by train) remains a viable fallback. Remember, Bavarian IYHF hostels have a 27-year age limit.

Hostels and Camping

Jugendlage Kapuzinerhölzl, In den Kirschen (tel. 141 43 00). Cheap and very popular. Accommodations in a large circus-style tent, ("the Tent"). Take U1 to Rotkreuzplatz, get on tram #12 (direction: Amalienburgstr.), and hop off at Botanischer Garten. DM5 gets you a foam pad, blankets, a dry spot on the floor, jet-johns, a shower, hot tea, and enthusiastic management. Check-in 5pm-9am. Somewhat flexible 23-year age limit. 3-night maximum stay. No curfew. Open late June to early Sept.

Jugendherberge Burg Schwaneck (IYHF), Burgweg 4-6, 8023 Pullach (tel. 793 06 44). A ½-hr. commute: Take S7 to Pullach (last train 10:40pm) and follow the signs (begin on Margaretenstr.). The bizarre appearance of this renovated castle (130 beds) encourages frolic and lunacy. Busy in summer; try calling 9-9:30am the day of your arrival. DM10 in 6-8 bed rooms, DM11.20 in quads. Sheets DM1. Breakfast included. Reception open 5-11:30pm. Curfew 11:30pm. Open year-round.

Jugendgästehaus München (IYHF), Miesingstr. 4 (tel. 723 65 50). A ½-hr. commute: Take U8 or U1 to Sendlinger for bus #57 to the Thalkirchen (Tierpark) stop, and then walk down Frauenbergstr., turn left on Münchenerstr., and left again for hostel. Huge, modern, clean, and quiet. DM15 in large dorms, DM17 in quads, DM19 in doubles, DM22 in singles (very hard to get in summer). Sheets and breakfast included. Reception open 7am-1am; rooms available after 3pm.

Jugendherberge (IYHF), Wendl-Dietrich-Str. 20. (tel. 13 11 56). Take U1 to Rotkreuzplatz; enter on Winthirplatz. The biggest and worst of Munich's hostels. Neither rooms nor bathrooms very clean. DM10.60, ages 25-27 DM12.60. Sheets DM2.50. Breakfast included. Dinner DM5.60. Lockout 8:30am-6pm. Reception open Feb.-Nov. 6-9am and noon-1am. Curfew 1am.

CVJM (YMCA), Landwehrstr. 13 (tel. 55 59 41), 2 blocks south of the station. Clean, comfortable rooms for either sex. Singles DM34-36 for 1-2 nights, DM32.50-34.50 for 3-6 nights, DM31-33 for 7 or more nights; doubles DM31.50, DM30, DM28.50; triples DM28.50, DM27, DM25.50. All prices per person. Breakfast included. Popular, so call ahead. 14% VAT for ages over 27. Reception open year-round 8am-12:30am. Curfew 12:30am.

Campingplatz Thalkirchen, Zentralländstr. 49 (tel. 723 17 07). Large and crowded. Located in the Isar River Valley Conservation Area; take the S-Bahn (Eurailpasses valid) from Hauptbahnhof to Siemenswerke, or take U3 or U6 south to Implerstr., then bus #57 to Thalkirchen stop (the last). DM4 per person, DM1.70-4 per tent. Showers DM1. Laundry and a cheap restaurant (meals 2-6DM). Open mid-March to late Oct.

Hotels and Pensions

Munich in high season (July-Aug. and *Oktoberfest*) is simply very crowded. Private rooms as well as hostel beds should be booked in advance, and in any case pensions will come very dear—when the city is full, finding singles under DM35 or doubles under DM60 is near impossible. If the situation seems tight, the tourist office's DM3 fee will be money well spent, but they don't handle the cheapest places.

Pension am Kaiserplatz, Kaiserplatz 12 (tel. 34 91 90). U3 or U6 to Münchener Freiheit. A friendly, family-run pension where every room is a late-Victorian surprise. Singles DM35, doubles DM65. Showers and breakfast included.

Hotel Westend, Landsbergerstr. 20 (tel. 50 40 04). A 10-min. walk from the station down Bayerstr. or take tram #19 or #29 to the Ford dealership. A large, clean, well-managed hotel only 2 blocks from the *Octoberfest* grounds. Singles DM35, doubles DM70. Breakfast included.

Pension Scheel, Isabellastr. 31 (tel. 271 36 11). Take U8 to Hohenzollernplatz, or tram #18 to Kurfürstenplatz. Well-furnished, spacious rooms. Singles DM35, doubles DM56-60. Showers DM1.

Hotel-Pension Am Markt, Heiliggeiststr. 6 (tel. 22 50 14), off Viktualienmarkt right in the center of town. Cheerful rooms in an elegant atmosphere. Rates from DM45 per person in singles and doubles. Showers and breakfast included.

Pension Frank, Schellingstr. 24 (tel. 28 14 51). U3 or U6 to Universität. A curious combination of backpackers and business people. Spacious, clean rooms. Singles DM40, doubles DM70. Showers DM3. Breakfast included.

Food

Munich's special food attraction is the vibrant **Viktualienmarkt,** the area just south of Marienplatz, with its colorful array of bread, fruit, meat, pastry, cheese, wine, vegetable, and sandwich shops. (Open Mon.-Fri. 6am-6:30pm and Sat. 6am-noon.) Try *Münchener Weisswrstl,* a pork sausage served with zesty *sauerkraut,* and don't miss out on a huge *Brezel* (salted pretzel), which should be washed down with one of the local beers. Don't be tempted to dine in the beer halls; prices are better at the stands set up outside.

University Mensas serve reasonable food—they'll take any student with ID. The two most central are at Arcisstr. 17 (near the Pinakotheks) and Leopoldstr. 15 in Schwabing. The lunch *menu* is DM2.30, and includes soup and salad. Other meat dishes, such as pork or *Wiener Schnitzel,* cost DM3.15 and DM4.20 respectively, and include 3 selections of vegetables or salad. (Open Nov.-July Mon.-Thurs. 9am-4:45pm, Fri. 9am-3:30pm.)

Zum Bögner, Im Tal 72, near the *Rathaus.* A big, bustling place, with a great atmosphere and every Bavarian specialty under the sun. Excellent pork and beef dishes from DM9. Try the *Bauernschmaus* for a little of everything (DM15). Open daily 9am-midnight.

Gaststätte Stadt Kempten, Dreifaltigkeitsplatz, right off the Viktualienmarkt. Rub elbows with the locals while enjoying inexpensive Munich specialties (DM9-DM13). Open daily 6:45am-10pm.

Isabellahof, Isabellastr. 4, near the cemetery in Schwabing. Large, tasty helpings of Serbian food; the *Isabellaplatte* (DM27) has several different meats with peas, potatoes, and salad and that are enough for 3. Other meat dishes for DM10. Open Mon.-Fri. 11:30am-3pm and 6-11:30pm, Sat.-Sun. 11:30am-11:30pm.

Naturastüberl, Heiliggeiststr. 16. A quaint, casual, vegetarian restaurant connected to a health food store. Noodles with a vegetable sauce DM9.80, *Müsli* DM6.90, soups DM4.50. Open Mon.-Fri. 9:30am-6:15pm.

Cafe Rischart, Marienplatz. A spectacular family-run cafe. Browse through the candy, cakes, and breads in the ground floor cafe, and sample the melt-in-your-mouth *Rischartwürfel* (chocolate cake with a whippped cream layer) in the upstairs cafe. Cakes about DM4. Large tasty breakfast, including coffee with whipped cream, DM8. Open Mon.-Fri. 8:30am-7pm, Sat. 8:30am-6pm.

Sights

A large number of Munich's wonders are within walking distance of **Marienplatz,** the city's main square. Here you'll see the **Altes Rathaus** (Old Town Hall), and the Neo-Gothic **Neues Rathaus** with its famous *Glockenspiel.* Crowds gather to watch the elaborate mechanized show of jousting knights and dancing coopers. (May-Oct. daily at 11am, noon, 5pm, and 9pm; Nov.-April daily at 11am.) Near Marienplatz are two of Munich's oldest churches. **Peterskirche** was founded in the eleventh century and has a breathtaking interior with elaborate gold statues, a spectacular gold altar, and numerous frescoes. **Frauenkirche** is more austere, with brick towers and stained-glass windows. (Both open daily 6am-6:30pm.) Take Neuhäuserstrasse to the outstanding Renaissance **Michaelskirche,** or walk toward Sendlinger Tor to the **Asamkirche,** which concentrates all the energy of Bavarian baroque in its tiny interior. To appreciate the optical illusions and dramatic lighting, go when you can get beyond the ornate grill at the back of the sanctuary (Mon.-Fri. 4-5:30pm).

The enormous **Residenz** of the Wittelsbach dukes, Max-Joseph-Platz 3, contains dozens of magnificent rooms built from the fourteenth to the nineteenth centuries. There are also the state collections of Egyptian art and coins, portraits of the Wittelsbachs, Far Eastern porcelain, and more. Housed separately in the Residenz is the ducal **Schatzkammer** (treasure chamber), currently closed for renovation. Even more impressive is **Schloss Nymphenburg,** the royal summer residence. A baroque wonder set in a lovely park, the palace contains a host of unexpected treasures, including a two-story granite marble hall decorated with stucco and frescoes, Brussels tapestries, a Chinese lacquer cabinet, and King Ludwig's "beauty gallery"—whenever he saw what he thought to be a particularly beautiful Munich woman, he would have her portrait painted and "collect" her. Take U1 to Rotkreuzplatz, and then tram #12 (direction: Amalienburgstr.). (Main palace open April-Sept. Tues.-Sun. 9am-12:30pm and 1:30-5pm; Oct.-March 10am-12:30pm and 1:30-

4pm. The various pagodas, pleasure palaces, and so forth have separate but similar hours. Admission to main palace DM2, to entire complex DM15, students DM1 less; wander the grounds for free.)

Munich is one of the world's great museum cities, with several stunning collections. Take tram #18 or the S-Bahn to Isartor, where the **Deutsches Museum** (tel. 217 91), one of the most important museums of science and technology in the world, fills an entire island in the River Isar with displays on just about anything ever invented on this planet. Highly recommended are the planetarium (DM1) and the daily electrical show, which will warm the heart of any would-be mad scientist. (Open daily 9am-5pm. Admission DM5, students DM2.)

The city's best-known art is at the **Alte Pinakothek,** Barerstr. 27, and at the **Neue Pinakothek,** just across the street. Take U-Bahn 8 to Königsplatz or tram #18. The older museum holds an extensive collection of great northern European and Italian art, including a number of Dürers and Rubens, and Albrecht Altdorfer's elaborate *Battle of Alexander.* The ultra-modern quarters of the newer museum house an array of eighteenth- and nineteenth-century works. (Both open Tues. 9am-4:30pm and 7-9pm, Wed.-Sun. 9am-4:30pm; Alte Pinakothek also open Thurs. 7-9pm. Admission to each DM4, to both DM7, students DM1 at either; free Sun.) The **Haus der Kunst** occupies the former quarters of the Neue Pinakothek, Prinzregentenstr. 1 (tel. 22 26 57), in the Englischer Garten. These galleries contain a splendid collection of twentieth-century works, including those of Beckmann, Kandinsky, Schmidt-Rotluff, and Nolde. (Open daily 9am-6pm. Admission DM3, students DM1; free Sun.) In the western wing of this building, the **Staatsgallerie Moderner Kunst** (tel. 29 27 10) holds some 400 paintings and sculptures dating from the beginning of the twentieth-century to the present. (Open Tues.-Sun. 9am-4:30pm, Thurs. also 7-9pm. Admission DM3, students free; free Sun.)

Lenbachhaus, Luisenstr. 33, just off Königsplatz, houses an extensive collection of early Kandinsky and the *Blaue Reiter* school (later Kandinsky, Münter, Klee, and others), which revolted against the style of late nineteenth-century painting typified by Lenbach. (Open Tues.-Sun. 10am-6pm. Admission DM6, students DM3; free Sun.) Just around the corner, facing one another on the Königsplatz, the **Glyptotek,** Königsplatz 3 (tel. 28 61 00), and the **Antikensammlung,** Königsplatz 1 (tel. 59 83 59) hold Germany's best collection of antique art, especially Greek and Roman sculpture. (Both open Tues.-Sun. 10am-4:30pm; Glyptotek Thurs. until 8:30pm, Antikensammlung Wed. until 8:30pm. Admission to each DM3.50, to both DM6, students half price; free Sun.)

Munich has many other museums, but by now you'd probably rather head to the **Englischer Garten,** one of Europe's largest city parks and Munich's summer playground; the green stretches north for several miles from Prinzregentenstrasse. In summer, thousands of Müncheners soak up the sun in the nude, swim, drink in the beer gardens, meet people, and relax.

Entertainment

Munich offers every type of nocturnal diversion, from cafes in Schwabing to rowdy beer halls. Pick up the *Young People's Guide to Munich* and the *Monatsprogram* (the city's monthly calendar) from the tourist office.

The six great Munich beers are *Augustiner, Hacker-Pschorr, Hofbräu, Löwenbräu, Paulaner-Thomasbräu,* and *Spaten-Franzinskaner.* With a little footwork you can try them all—each brand supplies its own beer halls. Most are closed Monday. In business since 1859, the **Hofbräuhaus am Platzl,** Platzl 9 (tel. 22 16 76), two blocks from Marienplatz, is patronized largely by tourists. After 7pm, live Bavarian music adds to the boisterous ambience. Beer is served by the *Mass,* which is just over a quart (or liter); meals cost DM10 and up. (Open daily 10am-midnight.) The **Mathäuser-Bierstadt,** am Stachus (tel. 59 28 96), near Karlsplatz, is the largest "beer city" in the world and has several distinct divisions, each with its own atmosphere. (Open daily 8am-midnight.) For outdoor Stein-hoisting, nothing can beat the **Chinesischer Turm** beer garden, secreted away in the Englischer Garten. The cafes, discos, and beer gardens in this area are great places to meet students all year, and are usually open until 1am.

Beer is only the beginning of nightlife in Munich. The **Schwabing** district, particularly the electric **Leopoldstrasse,** provides distraction enough for a month of Saturday nights. Along the crowded streets you'll find cafes, sidewalk chess clubs, cabarets, discos, bars, and galleries. Many discos are located along **Occamstrasse,** while jazz and songwriters' spots are spread all over. For avant-garde jazz, check the **Loft,** Kirchenstr. 15 (tel. 47 58 16), where the music is mixed with a gallery, studio, and an artsy crowd. (Call ahead; hours and prices vary.) Free (for the price of a beer, that is) classical music is offered Monday through Friday at the **Gaststätte Mariandl,** Goethestr. 5, right off Beethovenplatz. Get there a bit before 8pm; Wednesdays are often the most fun because members of the audience join in the proceedings. Munich's rock concert hall is the **Alabama Halle** on Schleissheimerstr. 418 (tel. 351 30 85), located on the north edge of town (tram #12 or 13 to Südetendeutschestrasse stop). For smaller rock clubs, check bulletin boards and posters around the university. Well-known popular artists often perform at the Olympic stadium, on the northern edge of town. Check brochures and listings for dates and ticket information.

The city has a vast range of concert and theater offerings; the tourist office's monthly program covers them very thoroughly, providing instructions (in German) on getting tickets. Standing room (DM8) and reduced-rate tickets to the **Bavarian State Opera** are sold at Maximillianstr. 11 (tel. 22 13 16), behind the Opera House or, starting one hour before the performance, at the opera. (Box office open Mon.-Fri. 10am-12:30pm and 3:30-5:30pm, Sat. 10am-12:30pm.) The **Staatstheater,** Gärtnerplatz 3 (tel. 201 67 67), offers everything from opera to operettas and musicals; standing room tickets start at DM8. Take U-Bahn 1 or 8 to Fraunhoferstr., tram #18 or 20, or bus #52 or 56. (Open Mon.-Fri. 10am-12:30pm and 3:30-5:30pm, Sat. 10am-12:30pm.) Munich's **Opera Festival** runs throughout July as does a concert series in the Nymphenburg and Schleissheim palaces.

Visitors to **Oktoberfest** enjoy games and shopping booths, amusement park rides, delicious foods, and, of course, hundreds of beers. The Oktoberfest runs from the third Saturday in September to the first Sunday in October.

Near Munich

Large glacial lakes in the area are among the favorite holiday spots of Müncheners. Take S-Bahn #6 out to the old resort town of **Starnberg** or the S5 to **Herrsching** on the Ammersee. Herrsching is the start of one of the many *Wanderwege* (hiking paths) established by the transit system in connection with the S-Bahn. Ask at the tourist offices at either Herrsching (tel. (08152) 374 44) or Starnberg (tel. (08151) 132 74) for more information.

The nineteenth-century German poet Heinrich Heine wrote: "Once they burn books, they'll end up burning people." This eerily prophetic statement is posted at **Dachau,** Germany's first concentration camp, next to a photograph of one of Hitler's book burnings. Though most of the buildings were destroyed in 1962, walls, gates, and crematorium remain from the original site. The horrible memory of Dachau is further preserved in photographs and on film in the museum, the two reconstructed barracks, and the several memorials and chapels on the grounds. Take S-Bahn #2 toward Petershausen, get off at Dachau, and catch bus #722 (DM1.50) in front of the station to the *Gedenkstätte* (memorial), about a 20-minute ride. (Open Tues.-Sun. 9am-5pm. Free.)

Bavarian Alps

South of Munich, the land becomes mountainous and the accents even thicker as you head into the Bavarian Alps. Trains travel throughout the region.

Garmisch and **Partenkirchen** were once two small, unassuming Bavarian villages. Today they make up one large and enjoyable resort at the foot of the **Zugspitze,** Germany's highest mountain. Though there are a lot of people in Garmisch the combined town is quiet and peaceful. There are two ways up the peak. The first is to take a cog railway from the **Zugspitzbahnhof** (about 50m behind the main station at Garmisch) via Grainau to the stop Hotel Schneefernerhaus, then a cable car, "Gipfelseilbahn," to the top, "Zugspitze"; the entire trip takes 80 minutes. (DM47 round-trip, DM6 discount with Eurail.) Another cable car, "Eibseeseilbahn," which runs from Eibsee to the summit, also costs DM47. Tickets are interchangable and include the cog railway between the two base stations, so you can go up one and down the other route.

Back down in Garmisch, the **Verkehrsamt der Kurverwaltung** is to your left as you leave the station, at Bahnhofstr. 34 (tel. (08821) 180 21; open Mon.-Sat. 8am-6pm, Sun. and holidays 10am-noon). *Zimmerfrei* are available; the tourist office can recommend places but cannot make reservations. The map they offer shows trails in the immediate vicinity of Garmisch, but invest in a *Kompass Wanderkarte* map, available throughout town (DM4). One very pleasant hike is up to **Partnachklamm** gorge, a dramatic gash 250m deep. An **IYHF youth hostel** (tel. 29 80) is located at Jochstr. 10 in Burgrain, 4km out; take bus #6 or 7 from the train station (DM1.20). (Juniors DM10, seniors DM12. Reception open 7-10am and 5-10pm. 10pm curfew. Open mid-Nov. to mid-Oct.; closed Dec. 26-28.) Be warned that the church bells across the street toll three to four dozen times every morning at 6:30am. **Camping** (tel. 31 80) is out highway B24; take the blue and white bus from the station towards Eibsee/Grainau and get off at Schmelz. (DM6 per person, DM5 per tent. Open Easter-Sept.) **Ski Rental** is available at the **Olympia-Ski Schule,** Reintal Str. 15 (tel. (08821) 713 19). Five days of equipment costs DM100.

Füssen, at the foot of the Romantic Road 100km from the Bodensee and Munich, is easily accessible from both. From the Bodensee take a train from Lindau to Kempten, and then a bus to Füssen. Trains leave almost hourly from Munich and usually switch at Kaufbeuren en route to Füssen (a 55-min. ride). From Füssen to Garmisch, catch a bus in front of the train station. Füssen is crowded with visitors, but you'll want to join them for two good reasons—the famous Bavarian *Königsschlösser* (castles): **Hohenschwangau** and **Neuschwanstein.** These castles illustrate the legends of medieval Germany better than any fairy tale or heroic epic, though not by reason of their authenticity; they are products of King Ludwig II's nineteenth-century fascination with Wagner's medieval mystical world. Neuschwanstein, the inspiration for the Disneyland castle, is the more impressive. Both are about 5km out of Füssen itself and accessible by the bus marked "Königsschlösser," which departs from the *Bahnhof* more or less hourly (DM2). When you get off the bus in Hohenschwangau village, you still have a steep 1-kilometer climb to the Neuschwanstein castle. Tours in English are usually swamped, so come in the morning, preferably on a weekday. Hohenschwangau, nearby but less spectacular, has the same hours and prices and fewer people. (Both open early April-Sept. 9am-5:30pm, Oct.-March 10am-4pm; admission DM6, students DM3.) The castles can also be visited as a daytrip from Garmisch. Buses leave in front of the Garmisch train station at 8am and 12:10pm, arrive about three hours later, and return from the castles at 4:50pm and 5:30pm (free with Eurail, otherwise DM12.80 one way, DM21 round-trip).

The town of Füssen is relatively deserted during the day—maybe everyone is up at the castles. In the center of town is a modest edifice, called simply the **Hohes Schloss.** Go out of your way to wander up to its courtyard at least for a few minutes; the inner walls are decorated with superb *trompe l'oeil* windows and towers. Just below the castle and also worth a brief stop is the wonderful little baroque **St. Mangkirche** (1701). The **König Ludwigweg** is a marked trail that leads north through the mountains from Füssen toward Steingaden, about 20km away. There are also ships on the **Forggensee,** fun for a day's excursion (June-Sept.).

The Füssen **Kurverwaltung** (tel. (08362) 70 77) is on the Augsburger-Tor-Platz, about a three-minute walk from the station; go left, toward the center of town. They can give you advice on hiking and help find you a *Zimmer* for about DM25 per person. (Open July-Aug. Mon.-Fri. 8am-noon and 2-6pm, Sat. 10am-noon and 4-6pm, Sun. 10am-noon; Sept.-June Mon.-Fri. 8am-noon and 2-6pm.) Füssen's **IYHF youth hostel,** Mariahilfer Str. 5 (tel. (08362) 77 54), is near the railway tracks. To find it, turn right outside the station and follow the train tracks away from town—a 15-min. walk. (Juniors DM10.70, seniors DM12.70. Sheets DM3.50. Breakfast included. Check-in 5-7pm. 10pm curfew.)

About a half hour north of Füssen by bus is the **Wieskirche,** a tiny yet world-famous pilgrimage church. A bus, departing at 1:05pm from the Füssen *Bahnhof,* will take you directly to the church (DM8); other buses will drop you about 2km away. The Wies, as it is called, is one of the world's most extravagant rococo buildings, built in 1749 to commemorate the miracle of a wooden statue of Christ which appeared to be crying. Designed, constructed, and frescoed by Dominikus Zimmerman and his brother, the church packs an incredible richness of decoration into a small building. Notice, for example, the "upside down" arches around the choir and the superb frescoes on the ceiling; you can stare for hours, and people come from around the world to do just that. (Open daily 8am-7pm.)

A good deal farther east, close to Salzburg and the Austrian border, lies **Berchtesgaden,** a beautiful town set high in the Alps. The friendly people in the **Kurdirektion** opposite the train station (tel. (08652) 50 11) can help with rooms and advice. Ask for their *Berchtesgadener Land: General Information* pamphlet, which lists sights, concerts, and other activities. (Open in summer Mon.-Fri. 8am-6pm, Sat. 8am-5pm, Sun. 9am-3pm; in winter Mon.-Fri. 8am-5pm, Sat. 9am-noon.) Don't miss a chance to visit the salt mines (tel. 40 61), where you get to dress up in an old salt miner's outfit, slide down snaking passages in the dark, and go on a raft ride on a salt lake. (Tour 1½ hr. Open May to mid-Oct. daily 8am-5pm; mid-Oct. to April Mon.-Fri. 12:30-3:30pm. Admission about DM11.)

Berchtesgaden is remembered as the site of **Kehlstein** (tel. (08652) 29 69), Hitler's retreat. If you'd like to visit, take the RVO bus from the Berchtesgaden post office to Obersalzberg-Hintereck (every ½ hr., DM5.20 round-trip, Eurail not valid). There you must switch to a private bus (DM13) which takes you to the Kehlstein parking lot. From the parking lot you can either climb (½ hr.) or take a lift (DM3) up to the house. (Open May-Oct.) Berchtesgaden's **IYHF youth hostel,** Gebirgsjägerstr. 52 (tel. (08652) 21 90), in the Strub district, has a great backyard view. Take the orange bus from opposite the train station to the last stop, Kaserne Stube (15 min.), or ask at the tourist office for exact pedestrian directions. (Members only. DM8.50. 10pm curfew.) **Camping** is possible at several locations: the most convenient are **Grafenlehen** (tel. 41 40) and **Mülleiten** (tel. 45 84), both in Berchtesgaden's Königsee district toward the lake. The former charges DM9.50 per tent plus occupant, the latter DM13.

Lake Constance (Bodensee)

The largest lake in the German-speaking world, the Bodensee is an Alpine watersports paradise, busy all summer with Germans, Austrians, Swiss, and whatever you call people from Liechtenstein. **Lindau,** on the northeastern shore, is a splendid medieval town; it's situated on an island, and linked to the mainland by two causeways. The **tourist office** (tel. (08382) 50 22), opposite the train station, provides maps and brochures, and can help you find a room for DM3. (Open April-Oct. Mon.-Fri. 8am-12:30pm and 2-7pm, Sat. 9am-12:30pm, Sun. 3-6pm; Nov.-March Mon.-Fri. 8am-noon and 2-5pm.)

The **IYHF youth hostel** (tel. 58 13) is on the mainland at Herbergsweg 11, reached from the station by bus #2 or 6—get off at the Hallenbad stop and walk one block down Bregenzerstr. (Juniors DM11, seniors DM13. Breakfast included. Open Jan. 5-Dec. 15.) Private rooms for a single night are hard to get. Check with the tourist office; they often have rooms in Oberreitnau, 6km inland on bus line #7. On the island, try **Gästehaus Lädine,** in der Grub 25 (tel. 53 26), with clean rooms and a cheerful proprietor. (Singles DM32, doubles DM60. Showers and breakfast included.) **Camping** (tel. 722 36) is 4km down Bregenzerstr., on the lake at **Lindau-Zech;** take bus #3 or 6 from the station (2 per hr.). (DM6 per person plus DM7 per tent. Warm showers included. Open May-Sept.) **Restaurant Helvetia,** right on the harbor, serves excellent fish dishes for about DM25. The charming old **Gasthof Goldenes Lamm,** at Paradiesplatz, offers well-prepared German fare for DM12-20.

Ships on the Bodensee are operated by German national railways, so Eurail and InterRail entitle you to discounts on scheduled trips. For a three- to four-hour trip on the lake, take the ferry west to **Konstanz** (about 6 boats per day, DM12.80 one way). This lively modern city has a small university (5600 students) and retains pieces of its medieval past. The helpful **tourist office** (tel. (07531) 28 43 76) is right next to the train station at Bahnhofplatz 6. (Open Mon.-Fri. 8:45am-6pm, Sat. 10am-1pm and 4-6pm, Sun. 4-6pm.) The office lists boat trips on which InterRail and Eurail are valid. You can rent boats from the shop behind the station (DM9 for first hr., DM3.50 for each additional hr.). (Open daily 10am-7pm.)

Accommodations in Konstanz are expensive, so try the **IYHF youth hostel,** Allmanshöhe 18 (tel. (07531) 322 60), in an old, forbidding cylindrical tower. (Juniors DM10.70, seniors DM12.70. Breakfast included. Try to register before 6pm. 10pm curfew. Open March-Oct.) **Haus Antoinette,** Seestr. 15 (tel. (07531) 623 51), on the waterfront, has cozy rooms. (Doubles with bath DM50. Breakfast included.) Try the **University Mensa** for a DM2.30 lunch with a lake view. Take bus #9 from the station. (Open year-round Mon.-Fri. 8am-7pm, Sat. 8am-1pm. No student ID required.)

The Lindau-Konstanz ferry stops at Mainau and Meersburg.

The **Flower Island of Mainau** is a blessing to the senses—a palace and church surrounded by flowering gardens and exotic plants. The island and its attractions are open to visitors Easter through October from 10am to 5pm. (Admission DM7, students DM4.)

Meersburg, perched precariously on a hill, is a lovely medieval town graced by Germany's oldest **castle** (tenth century), in which the German poet Annette von Droste-Hülshoff spent her last year. (Open March-Oct. 9am-6pm. Admission DM5, students DM4.) Next door is the baroque **Neues Schloss,** whose terrace commands a beautiful view of the Bodensee. (Open April-Oct. daily 10am-1pm and 2-6pm. Admission DM5, students DM4.)

Continue west along the lake shore to reach the town of **Unteruhldingen.** Here, a group of Bronze- and Stone-Age dwellings, originally perched on pilings in the lake, has been reconstructed. (Open April-Sept. daily 8am-6pm; Oct. daily 9am-5pm; Nov. and March Sat.-Sun. 9am-5pm. Admission DM4, students DM3.) Lodging is available at the **IYHF youth hostel,** Alte Nussdorferstr. 26 (tel. (07551) 42 04), in nearby Überlingen. (Juniors DM11.70, seniors DM13.60. Sheets DM3. Breakfast included. 10pm curfew. Open year-round.)

Romantic Road (Romantische Strasse)

From the Alps to the vineyards of Franconia (Franken), walled cities and flamboyant palaces dot the rolling hills of western Bavaria. The German tourist industry has brought commerce and fame to this hodgepodge of charming backwaters and baroque extravagances by christening it the Romantische Strasse. Many consider this heavily-touristed way to be too packaged for its own good, but the towns retain some of their medieval flavor in the evenings, after the tour buses have gone.

The best transportation along the road is the Bundesbahn's **Europabus,** which runs twice per day from mid-March to early November. The central stretch is between Würzburg and Augsburg where the routes change slightly; some buses stop at Würzburg, while one continues to Wiesbaden (a spa town near Frankfurt); at

Augsburg, one route extends to Füssen, while another goes to Munich. The bus does make 45-minute stops in a few places but you can give yourself more time by starting with the earlier bus, stopping in a town that strikes your fancy, and catching the later bus which usually follows about an hour behind. Be warned, though, that the Europabus occasionally skips stops, leaving passengers stranded in tiny medieval walled towns. The towns, not the landscape, are the charm of the trip, but, with the exception of Würzburg, all are very small; unless you plan to hike or rest, rarely will there be more than an afternoon's activity to occupy you.

Trains connect few of the towns along the Romantic Road. Train and bus fares are usually identical. The entire trip, from Wiesbaden to Füssen, costs DM97; Würzburg to Augsburg costs DM50. Eurailpass covers the bus, while InterRail gets a 50% discount. Students under 26 receive a 10% discount. You can switch buses as often as you like, but you will be charged DM2 for each piece of luggage; leave the stickers on to avoid paying repeatedly. Free reservations are necessary in summer, especially on weekends. Call the **Touring Büro** in Frankfurt (tel. (069) 790 32 40) three days in advance. You can also go there for information, or to the Munich office in the north wing of Starnberger station. Other Europabuses cover similar routes—the **Bürgenstrasse,** for example, runs along the lovely Neckar valley between Rothenburg and Heidelberg. (See Near Heidelberg for more information.)

Würzburg

Würzburg immortalizes eighteenth-century Germany's passion for baroque buildings with Balthasar Neumann's **Residenz,** a 10-minute walk from the train station down Kaiserstrasse and Theaterstrasse. Magnificent in scale and splendor, the palace was completed and lavishly decorated by Tiepolo. During the second half of June, the **Mozartfest** takes place in its Kaisersaal. (Tickets from DM10, available at the Congress Centrum Verkehrsamt). The entire palace is worth viewing; ask for directions to the rooms not included in the guided tours. The gallery often hosts special exhibitions, and the **Residenzhofkirche** is simply magnificent. (Open April-Sept. Tues.-Sun. 9am-5pm; Oct.-March Tues.-Sun. 10am-4pm. Admission DM3.50, students DM2.50, ages under 15 free.) Just down Hofstr. from the Residenz stands the magnificent **Cathedral of St. Kilian.** Notice the three Riemenschneider sculptures on the right side of the transept. (Open after Easter, daily 10am-noon and 2pm-5pm.) Next door, the **Neumünster** has a graceful eighteenth-century baroque facade and a Riemenschneider *Virgin and Child* inside.

Across the river, the thirteenth-century **Marienburg Fortress** dominates the town. You can make the taxing climb in about 20 minutes, or take bus #9, which runs every half hour (9:43am-5:43pm, May-Sept. only) from the western end of the Alte Mainbrücke bridge. (Open April-Sept. Tues.-Sun. 9am-5pm; Oct.-March Tues.-Sun. 10am-4pm. Admission DM1.50, students DM1, ages under 15 free.) The fortress also houses the **Mainfränkisches Museum,** with a large collection of Riemenschneiders. (Open April-Oct. daily 10am-5pm; Nov.-March daily 10am-4pm. Admission DM2.50, students DM1.) On the adjoining hill, the **Frankenwarte Käppele** commands a tremendous view of the city. Return to town via the elegant fifteenth-century **Mainbrücke,** adorned with statues of the 12 German saints. At the far end of the bridge, the **Rathaus,** begun in 1816, is a patchwork of different structures and architectural styles. Also worth a visit are the sixteenth-century structures of the **Alte Universität,** dominated by the stately tower of the newly-renovated **Neubaukirche.**

The helpful **Verkehrsamt** (tel. (0931) 374 36), in front of the train station, will find you a room (DM30 approx.) for a DM2 fee. (Open Mon.-Sat. 8am-8pm.) A second tourist office will open in 1988: **Verkehrsamt Würtzburg-Palais am Congress Centrum** (tel. (0931) 373 35; open Mon.-Thurs. 8am-5pm, Fri. 8am-noon). Würzburg's **IYHF youth hostel,** Burkarderstr. 44 (tel. (0931) 425 90), is convenient to the center of town, near the large Romanesque basilica of St. Burkard. Disabled access. (Juniors DM16, seniors DM18. Breakfast and sheets included. Curfew 1am. Open year-round.) The **Gasthof zum Goldenes Fass,** Semmelstrasse 13 (tel. (0931)

546 66), three blocks from the station toward the Residenz, has singles DM30, doubles DM55. Showers DM5. Breakfast included. The centrally located **Gasthaus Kirchlein,** Textorstr. 17 (tel. (0931) 530 14), has singles DM30, doubles DM50. Breakfast included. Showers DM5. If you don't mind the revelers downstairs, the best deal is the **Gehrings-Bierstube,** Neubaustr. 24 (tel. (0931) 525 45), halfway between the Residenz and the Fortress. (Singles DM30, doubles DM45. Showers DM3. Breakfast included.) Campers should take tram 3 to Heidigsfeld, then walk 3km toward Winterhausen to **Campingplatz Kalte Quelle** (tel. (0931) 70 55 98) on Winterhäuserstr. (DM4.50 per person, DM5 per tent. Open year-round.)

Cheap university food is available during the school year at the **mensa** in the **Studenthaus** on the corner of Friedrich-Ebert-Ring and Münzstrasse. (Open noon-2pm. Student ID required.) For a standup meal at a super price, try the **Bistro-Grill,** Kaiserstr. 27 (tel. (0931) 168 23), where *schweineschnitzel* and salad costs DM7.20. (Open Mon.-Sat. 9am-6pm.) Behind the marktplatz at Domstr. 14, **Sternbäck** sells baked potatoes with more than 20 types of toppings (DM2.50-4.80). Polish your palate with the region's famous *Frankenwein* at Würzburg's oldest *Weinstube,* **Weinhaus zum Stachel,** Gressengasse 1, just off Marktplatz. If you have the energy, climb up to one of Würzburg's hillside beer gardens, **Burggaststätten Schänke zur Alten Wache** and **Gutsschänke Schützenhof.**

In 1988, Würzburg will host the 57th Mozartfest during the last two weeks of June, and the 30th *Winzerfest,* or Wine Festival, will be at the end of September. Buses leave the Domplatz for the **Veitschöchheim Castle** (tel. (0931) 915 82) whose superbly groomed palace grounds have been converted into a public park. (Open April-Sept. Tues.-Sun. Admission DM2.50, students DM1.50.) The Veitshöchheimer Personenschiffahrt Company (tel. (0931) 556 33) runs boat cruises from the **Alten Kranen** and the **Weisser Kiosk** along the waterfront. Europabuses down the Romantic Road depart daily at 9am and 10:15am next to the station.

Rothenburg, Dinkelsbühl, and Nördlingen

The main attractions along the Romantic Road, these medieval towns seem to adopt English as their first language during the summer. Again, to get the most out of them, stay a night or two; rooms are not hard to come by, and you have to share the town with far fewer tourists of the tourbus variety.

Rothenburg-ob-der-Tauber, 50km south of Würzburg, is a gem of sixteenth-century German architecture. Next door to the **Rathaus,** the **Rattrinkstube** is where the mayor saved the town in 1631 by draining a mug containing almost a gallon of wine, thereby placating a general who was about to destroy Rothenburg. Don't miss Tilman Riemenschneider's carved wooden *Altar of the Holy Blood* in the **St. Jakobskirche;** note that the figures are curiously grouped around Judas. The **tourist office** (tel. (09861) 404 92), in the Rattrinkstube, will book you a room (DM26-32), or you can stay at one of two **IYHF hostels: Rossmühle,** Mühlacker 1 (tel. (09861) 45 10), or **Spitalhof,** in a medieval courtyard on Spitalgasse (tel. (09861) 78 89). Each costs DM7 and are open year-round.

Dinkelsbühl, 40km south of Rothenburg, is full of the half-timbered houses that you came to Germany to see. The town really comes into its own with the colorful, nine-day **Kinderzeche,** a celebration of the town's rescue during the Thirty Years' War by children who pleaded with the Swedish king to spare the town. Visit the **St. Georgskirche,** with more Riemenschneider School wood carvings, and walk down **Nördlingerstrasse,** where none of the old houses are perfectly rectilinear—medieval superstition held that houses with 90° angles were homes of demons. The **Verkehrsamt,** Segringerstr. 2 (tel. (09851) 30 13) can help you with accommodations and sell you a town map. There is an **IYHF hostel** at Koppengasse 10 (tel. (09851) 509). (Open Jan.-Oct.)

The walled city of **Nördlingen,** yet further south, is marginally less touristed than its neighbors to the north. The tower of the **St. Georgskirche** affords a great view of the circular town, and of the circular meteor crater, the Ries, the largest of its kind in the world. For a closer look at the walls, walk along the completely preserved parapet; a full circle of the town takes about an hour. The **Verkehrsamt** (tel. (09081) 841 16), next door to the Rathaus, can provide a list of pensions in town or book you somewhere for a few marks. Rooms run only DM20-27 per person, so it's a shame to stay in the drab youth hostel.

Augsburg

Founded by Augustus 2000 years ago, Augsburg today is a trove of festivals, museums, and eighteenth-century rococo architecture. Augsburg is 50km northwest of Munich and connected by frequent trains. From the Königsplatz, down Bahnhofstrasse from the station, walk down Bgm-Fischer Strasse to the well-preserved medieval **Augsburg Guildhouse.** Head down Dominikanerstrasse toward the onion-shaped domes of **St. Ulrich's Cathedral,** but stop at #15, the **Dominikanerkirche,** which houses the **Roman Museum.** (Open Oct.-April Tues.-Sun. 10am-4pm; May-Sept. 10am-5pm. Free.) Follow Am Schwall Strasse to the remains of the old city wall, through which Oberer Graben Strasse leads to the large **Fuggerei** complex, the welfare housing for those who built the city. (Open March-Oct. daily 9am-6pm. Admission DM1, students DM.50.)

Augsburg has an **IYHF youth hostel,** Beim Pfaffenkeller 3 (tel. (0821) 339 09); take bus #2 from the Bahnhof to *Stadtwerke.* They are often full during the summer, so call ahead. (Juniors DM7.50, seniors DM9.50. Sheets DM2. Breakfast DM3. 11pm curfew. Open Feb.-Dec.) To get to **Campingplatz am Autobahnsee** (tel.(0821) 70 75 75), take bus #23 to Hammerschmiede, then walk 1km to the Autobahnsee, across Mühlhauserstr. (DM5. Open year-round.) An **outdoor market** is at Függerstr. 12. (Open Mon.-Fri. 7am-6pm, Sat. 7am-1pm.) The **Europabus** for the Romantic Road stops in Augsburg. The **Mitfahrzentrale,** Branderstr. 36 (tel. (0821) 41 46 55), is open Monday through Friday from 9am to 5pm. If you're in Augsburg in the summer, don't miss the annual **Bürgerfest** (June 24-July 17).

Nuremberg (Nürnberg)

The medieval painter Albrecht Dürer lived and worked in Nuremberg's well-preserved *Altstadt,* and the modern industrial city has made a name for itself as the toy capital of the world, as the renowned Christmas markets confirm. But the darkest pages of Nuremburg's history are those for which it is infamous; the site of Hitler's annual *Parteitagen* in the 1930's, Nuremburg fittingly accommodated the Nazi war crime trials.

From the station, cross the street in front of the Bahnhof and enter the old city at the *Königstor.* Walk straight down Königstrasse, across the Pegnitz river, until you arrive at the pastel and gold **Schöner Brunnen** fountain, in the Marktplatz. Also here is the **Frauenkirche,** a pocket-sized Gothic church with beautiful stained-glass windows. (Open Mon.-Sat. 9am-5pm, Sun. 12:30pm-6pm.) Every day at noon you can watch the antics of Emperor Karl IV and his seven elector-princes on the church clock. From Marktplatz walk toward the river and **St. Lorenzkirche.** The most spectacular work in the church is the **Engelsgruss,** a large, free-hanging wooden circle over the main altar with a lovely Annunciation scene in its center. (Open Mon.-Sat. 9am-5pm, Sun. 2-4pm.)

The **Kaiserburg** (Emperor's Fortress), begun in 1040, is one of the most beautiful in central Europe. Tours of the interior (conducted in German) are offered every five to 10 minutes, or you can simply check out the view from **Sinwellturm** tower. (Complex open April-Sept. daily 9am-5pm; Oct.-March daily 9:30am-noon and 12:45-4pm. Admission DM3, students DM2, DM1 to tower.)

Just below the castle is the **Dürer House,** a perfectly preserved structure from the mid-fifteenth century. The Dürer memorabilia is interesting, and the house is noteworthy as a representation of wealthy medieval family life. (Open March-Oct. Tues. and Thurs.-Sun. 10am-5pm, Wed. 10am-9pm; Nov.-Feb. Tues., Thurs., and Fri. 1-5pm, Wed. 1-9pm, Sat.-Sun. 10am-5pm. Admission DM3, students DM1.)

From here, a walk straight down Albrecht-Dürer-Strasse will bring you to Nuremberg's **Toy Museum** on Karlstrasse. Its amazing collection of models and toys will be on display at the **Spielzeug-Paradies Vedes,** Sigmundstr. 220 (outside town toward Würzburg), for the first half of 1988 while the museum is renovated. The museum will reopen on Karlstrasse after June 1988. (Open Tues.-Sun. 10am-5pm. Admission DM3, students DM1.) The world-famous Nuremburg Christmas Market runs from November 25 through December 24, 1988.

Across the river and down to Kornmarkt is the **Germanisches Nationalmuseum,** with a rich collection of medieval art and an outstanding ensemble of antique musical instruments. The two high points of the museum are its stunning collection (upstairs) of works by early German masters (including a magnificent series by Dürer), and its extensive array (downstairs) of wood sculpture, with several Tilman Riemenschneider masterpieces. (Open Tues.-Sun. 10am-5pm, Thurs. 8-9:30pm as well. Admission DM3, students DM1.)

Spend a sobering afternoon exploring Nuremberg and the relics of World War II with the help of the booklet *Nuremberg 1933-45,* distributed (free) at the tourist office. The legacy of the war is still visible in the monolithic structures begun by Albert Speer, Hitler's confidante and architect, which loom over the Party Congress area. The former **Nuremberg Rally Grounds** are scattered about the area now occupied by **Dutzendteich Park.** The two most conspicuous legacies of the parade grounds are the broad **Great Road** and Hitler's circular **New Congress Hall,** erected in 1935 and currently used for storage.

Nuremberg's **tourist offices** (tel. (0911) 20 42 56) are helpful and friendly: One is in the main train station (open Thurs. and Sat. 9am-8pm, Fri. 9am-9pm); the other is downtown on Marktplatz (open Mon.-Sat. 9am-1pm and 2-6pm, Sun. 10am-1pm and 2-4pm). The **Jugendherberge Kaiserstallung (IYHF),** Burg 2,(tel. (0911) 22 10 24), is one of Europe's finest. Built into the Imperial castle which towers over the city, the hostel is comfortable, clean, and well-managed. Double rooms are available if you and your significant other happen to have the same last name. (Juniors DM16, seniors DM18. Breakfast and sheets included. 1am curfew. Open year-round.) Should the hostel be full, head to the **Jugendhotel,** Rathbergstr. 300 (tel. (0911) 52 90 92), 20- to 30-minutes out of town. Take tram #2 to its last stop, then bus #41 to Felsenkeller. (DM20.50-30, depending on the degree of privacy and amount of sanitary equipment you require. Open year-round.) **Camping,** Zeppelinstr. 56 (tel. (0911) 40 84 16), is behind the soccer stadium; take the U-Bahn south to Messenzentrum. (DM5 per person, DM5 per tent. Open May-Sept.) Cheery **Pension Brendel,** Blumenstr. 1 (tel. (0911) 22 56 18), is a five-minute walk from the station; go two blocks along Gleissbühlstrasse and turn left. (Singles DM35, doubles DM65. Breakfast and showers included.) In the heart of the old town is **Pension Altstadt** at Hintere Ledergasse 2-4 (tel. (0911) 22 61 02), with modern, well-furnished lodgings. (DM34 per person. Breakfast included. Showers DM3. Closed last 2 weeks in August.) Nearby **Pension Fischer,** Brunnengasse 11 (tel. (0911) 22 61 89) has singles DM32, doubles DM60. Showers DM2. Breakfast included.

Rostbratwurst, a mild sausage, is the thing to eat in Nuremberg, and one of the best places to do so is the tiny **Bratwurst-Häusle,** with its smoking chimney, just below St. Sebalduskirche. Larger groups might go to **Bratwurstherzle,** Brunnengasse 11, where you can get 12 *wurst*—enough for 2 or 3—for DM12. (Open daily 9am-9pm.) The **Mensa** of the Erlangen-Nürnberg university is located in the historic *Weinstadel* building, at Maxplatz near the river. (Open Mon.-Fri. 11:30am-2pm; closed mid-Aug. to mid-Sept. Student ID required; buy a coupon from a student.) Spend the evening sampling the wines of Frankenland at **Trödelstuben,** Trödelmarkt 30, on the small island in the river; look for the bottle collection outside the door. (Open Mon.-Sat. 3-11pm.)

To hitch north and west from Nuremberg, walk out Rothenburgerstrasse, reached by U-Bahn. For Munich and points southwest, walk 20 minutes along Bahnhofstrasse and then Regensburgerstrasse to Hainstrasse. Take tram #8 to Erlenstegen for Bayreuth and Berlin. **Mitfahrzentrale,** Allersbergstr. 31a (tel. (0911) 44 69 66). (Open Mon.-Fri. 9am-6pm, Sat. 8:30am-1pm, Sun. 11am-2pm.)

Bamberg

Once the pride and joy of Emperor Heinrich II, last of the Saxons, Bamberg has been adding architectural treasures to its peaceful natural setting ever since Heinrich bought the farm in 1024.

The **Altes Rathaus** sits in the middle of the Regnitz River like an anchored ship. This building is half *Fachwerk* (timber and plaster) and half baroque frescoes, with a rococo tower between. Cross the river to get a good look, then go up Dominikanerstrasse and climb the steps of the **Domplatz,** the center of ancient Bamberg.

The **Dom** itself, begun in 1004, started out Romanesque and ended up Gothic. The four almost perfectly matched towers give it a fairy-tale air; the interior design is equally unusual. Rounded choirs form both ends, so there is hardly a front or back to the church. Inside is the mysterious horse-and-rider statue called the *Bamberg Reiter,* as well as a famous wooden altar by the master carver Veit Stoss, and the Emperor's own grave, carved by Tilman Riemenschneider. (Normally open daily 9am-6pm. Organ concerts every Saturday 12-12:30. Free.) Across the square looms the enormous bulk of the **Neue Residenz** palace. From the **rose garden,** the town is just a sea of roofs, and to the left you can see the **Michelsberg.** (Neue Residenz open April-Sept. daily 9am-noon and 1:30-5pm; Oct.-March daily 9am-noon and 1:30-4pm. Admission DM2.50, students DM1.50.) Back in town, go by Judenstrasse 14 to see the baroque facade of **Böttingerhaus,** just below St. Stephen's. Downriver is **Concordia House,** a stunning baroque stone mansion built on the banks of the Regnitz. Visit the **Fränkisches Brauerei-Museum,** at Michaelsberg 10f, to see how beer was brewed in the twelfth century. (Open Mon.-Fri. 1pm-4pm. Admission DM2, students DM1.) The tourist office runs two-hour guided walking tours of the town (in German only). (April-Oct. Mon.-Sat. at 2pm; DM6, students DM3.)

Arriving at the train station, walk straight down Luitpoldstrasse, right on Obere Königstrasse, then left across the bridge to the **tourist office** at Hauptwachstr. 16 (tel. (0951) 210 40). (Open in summer Mon.-Fri. 8am-6pm, Sat. 8:30am-12:30pm; in winter Mon.-Fri. 8am-5pm, Sat. 8:30am-12:30pm.) On the Domplatz, the entrance to the **Historisches Museum** doubles as a tourist office. The main office has a free room-finding service; after hours, this is handled by **Hotel Straub,** Ludwigstr. 31 (tel. (0951) 258 38), to your right as you leave the station.

Wolfsschlucht (IYHF), Oberer Leinrittstr. 70 (tel. (0951) 560 02), on the river, is cheerful and clean. Take bus #1, 2, 6, or 12 to Schönleinsplatz, switch there to bus #16 or 28 toward Bug, and ask the driver to let you off "Am Regnitzufer." (Juniors DM11, seniors DM13. Breakfast included. Curfew 9:45pm. Open Feb. to mid-Dec.) **Stadion (IYHF),** Pödeldorferstr. 178 (tel. (0951) 123 77) is a newly opened hostel, near the stadium, in a residential part of town. Take bus #2 to *Stadion.* Call ahead, as the hostel often has groups. (Juniors DM10, seniors DM12. Breakfast included. Registration 5:30pm-7pm. Curfew 9:30pm. Open April-Sept.) **Campingplatz Insel** (tel. (0951) 563 20) is also in Bug, about 4km from town. Follow the Buger Hauptstrasse or take bus #16 from the center of town. (DM5 per person, DM5 per tent.) The **Maiselbräustübl,** Obere Königstr. 38 (tel. (0951) 255 03) has rooms for DM24 per person, showers DM4, breakfast included, and good dinners for about DM8. **Zum Wilden Mann,** Untere Sandstr. 9 (tel. (0951) 564 62), rents well-furnished and surprisingly large rooms (DM25 per person in singles and doubles. Showers included).

The university **Mensa,** centrally located at Ausstr. 37, just off Grüner Markt, offers the cheapest meals in town at about DM3. Any student ID will do. (Open Nov.-July daily noon-2pm.) The **Hofbräuschänke,** Dominikanerstr. 10, serves a local specialty, *Fränkisches Schweinekotelette* (pork chop cooked with apple slices) for DM12.50, as well as Greek food. (Open daily 10am-midnight.) Blow your refreshment budget on Bamberg's specialty, *Rauchbier,* a spicy, smoke-flavored beer traditionally consumed at **Das Schlenkerla,** Dominakanerstr. 6, across the Untere Brücke. This venerable institution, founded in 1678, has the cheapest brew (½ liter DM2.50), and you can accompany it with hearty Bavarian specialties. (Open Wed.-Mon. 9:30am-midnight). Other prime hangouts are the **Weinkeller** in the Ringvogelhaus on Judenstrasse, or the **Spezialbierkeller** on Stephansberg. Stop at **Cafe Abseits,** Pödeldorferstr. 39 (tel. (0951) 470 80), for a good breakfast (DM3.80) or a drink in the outdoor courtyard. (Open daily 9am-1am.) For good music and dancing visit the **Downstairs Disco,** Langestr. 16, one block from the Grüner Markt. (Open nightly 10pm-3am.)

Bayreuth

Summer visitors descend from all corners of the world onto the small town of Bayreuth, capital of German opera and Bavaria's dramatic and musical center. The city's name has become irrevocably associated with that of Richard Wagner. The world-famous **Bayreuth Festspiele,** a Wagner extravaganza, takes place every summer in the theater which Wagner planned and built before his death. (Festival late July-late Aug., 1988.) Tickets, especially for the *Ring der Niebelungen,* are extremely difficult to get; some opera lovers remain on the waiting list up to eight years. (Tickets DM15-DM200.) Those turned away may be consoled by a tour of the **Festspielhaus** theater. (Open daily 10-11:30am and 1:30-3pm; irregular hours during rehearsal and performance season. Admission DM2.) Wagner's house, **Ville Wahnfried,** is also open to the public, at Richard-Wagner-Str. 48. (Open daily 9am-5pm. Admission DM3.50 during the festival, otherwise DM2.50, students always DM1.) Wagner's compositions are performed daily here at 10am, noon, and 2pm. The ticket window sells an excellent English guide with translations of the captions on all the museum's exhibits (DM3). Behind the house in the lush park lies the grave of Richard and Cosima Wagner, while next door is the **Jean Paul Museum,** dedicated to the famous novelist/philosopher who prophesied the nineteenth-century flowering of German opera. (Open June-Sept. daily 9am-noon and 2-5pm; Oct.-May Mon.-Fri. 9am-noon and 2-5pm, Sat. 10am-1pm.) The **Markgräfliches Operahaus,** on Operastr., was Princess Wilhelmina's (Frederick the Great's sister) attempt to construct the eighteenth century's most sumptuously adorned and technically sophisticated opera house. (Open April-Sept. Tues.-Sun. 9-11:30am and 1:30-4:30pm; Oct.-March Tues.-Sun. 10-11:30am and 1:30-3pm. Admission DM2, students DM1.) Just down the street lies Wilhemina's palace, the **Neues Schloss,** Ludwigstr. 21, with guided tours in English. (Open in summer Tues.-Sun. 10-11:20am and 1:30-4:30pm; in winter Tues.-Sun. 10-11:20am and 1:30-2:50pm. Admission DM2, students DM1.)

The **tourist office,** Luitpoldplatz 9 (tel. (0921) 220 11), to the left and about four blocks from the train station, provides a free map of the city, a list of hotels, and information about the surrounding areas. For information on the summer's cultural events, get the thorough and free monthly pamphlets *Bayreuth Veranstaltungen* and *Godrom's Festspielmagazin.* (Open Mon.-Fri. 8:30am-6pm, Sat. 9am-noon.) Although rooms are often booked and prohibitively expensive during the festival period, there are some reasonable places at other times. A 10-minute walk from the train station toward St. Georgen will take you to the **Gasthof Hirsch,** St. Georgen 26 (tel. (0921) 267 14), with rooms for DM24 per person, showers DM2. Breakfast included. The best value is probably **Pension Schindler,** Bahnhofstr. 9 (tel. (0921) 262 49), with large and comfortable rooms. (DM25 per person in singles and doubles. Showers DM3. Breakfast included.) To get to Bayreuth's spacious and modern **IYHF Youth Hostel,** Universitätsstr. 28 (tel. (0921) 252 62), take bus #4 from the Marktplatz to the last stop. (Juniors DM8, seniors DM10, sheets DM2.50. Breakfast DM3.50. Curfew 10pm. Open Feb. to mid-Dec.) For a good hearty meal, try the **Porsch,** Maximilianstr. 63 (tel. (0921) 646 49), where you can get a *Schlacht-*

platte of fresh meats, with *kraut* and potatoes for DM7.50; ½ liter beer DM2. (Open Mon.-Sat. 11am-10pm.)

East Bavaria (Ost Bayern)

Extending east of Munich from the hilly Czechoslavak border to the Alps along the Austrian border, this corner of Germany is one that few travelers put on their itinerary. Regensburg, on the Danube, is one of Germany's best-preserved medieval towns, while Passau, 125km downstream, also merits a visit. The region's biggest attraction may be the unpopulated Bavarian Forest, east of the Danube, on the Czechoslovak border.

Bavarian Forest (Bayerischer Wald)

Central Europe's largest range of wooded mountains, the Bavarian Forest, provides excellent opportunities for nature walks, mountain climbing, and cross-country skiing. The Danube was Germany's easternmost border for centuries, which accounts for the relative lack of development. For information contact the **Bayerischer Wald Park Verwaltung,** Freyunger str. 2, 8352 Grafenau (tel. (08552) 20 77), or the offices in **Amberg,** Raseliushaus, 8450 Amberg (tel. (09621) 102 33); **Weiden,** Marktplatz (tel. (0961) 814 11); **Landshot,** Rathaus, Altstadt 315 (tel. (0871) 230 31); and **Straubing,** Rathaus (tel. (09421) 163 07).

The towns of **Cham, Deggendorf,** and **Regen** can all be reached by train (Cham from Regensburg or Nuremberg via Schwandorff, Deggendorf and Regen from Regensburg or Munich via Plattling). Buses run from Regensburg and Straubing to Cham and from Passau and Straubing to Deggendorf and Regen. The **Lindenhof (IYHF),** Herbergsweg 2 (tel. (08553) 300), is at **Waldhäuser** in the heart of the Forest. Take the bus from Spiegelau or Neuschönau. (Juniors DM7, seniors DM9.) **Mauth** has a hostel at Jugendherbergstr. 11 (tel. (08557) 289), accessible from Passau. (Juniors DM7, seniors DM9. Open Jan.-Oct.) **Camping** is on the edge of the national forest at **Wistlberg,** 1km north of Finsterau, and at **Klingenbrunn,** 2km south of the train station.

Regensburg

This medieval city, built around a Roman fortress dating from the second century C.E., is as well-preserved as any in Germany. Begin your visit at the gothic **Altes Rathaus,** where the **Imperial Diet Museum** is housed. (Open Mon.-Sat. 9:30am-4pm, Sun. 10am-noon. Admission DM2, students DM1.) Down Fischgasse the **Steinern Brücke** has spanned the river since 1146. Two blocks upriver, at Keplerstr. 5, is the **Kepler Memorial House,** where the famous astronomer used to live. (Open Tues.-Sat. 10am-3pm, Sun. 10am-noon. Admission DM2, students DM1.) Pass through the **old city gate** near the bridge to walk back into town, to the **Cathedral of St. Peter.** (Open daily 9am-6pm. Admission DM1.50, including tour.) From the cathedral, any street running toward the train station will take you to the **Diocese Museum.** Romanesque, Gothic, and Baroque sculptures, graphics, paintings, and twelfth-century textiles are on display here. (Open April-Oct, Tues.-Sun. 10am-5pm; Nov. and Jan.-March Sat.-Sun. 10am-4pm, Dec. Tues.-Sun. 10am-4pm. Admission DM2, students DM1.) For exhibits on the city's Roman history, try the **Regensburg City Museum,** at Dachauplatz 1. (Open Tues.-Sat. 10am-4pm, Sun. 10am-1pm. Admission DM2, students DM1.) Buy a ticket from the tourist office for admission to most museums and sights. (DM4, students DM2.)

The **tourist office,** on Rathausplatz, Landshuterstr. 13 (tel. (0941) 571 86), finds rooms, provides maps, and sells tickets to events. (Open Mon.-Fri. 8:30am-6pm, Sat. 9am-4pm, Sun. 9am-noon.) For the best budget accommodations, go to the **IYHF youth hostel** at Wöhrdstr. 60 (tel. (0941) 574 02). Cross the bridge at St. Georgen Platz and turn right onto Wöhrdstr. or take bus #5 to Weichs. (Open Jan. to mid-Dec. Juniors DM8, seniors DM10. Sheets DM3.50. Breakfast DM2.90.

Curfew 11:30pm.) At the **Peterhof,** Fröliche-Türken-Str. 12 (tel. (0941) 575 14), a single with breakfast starts at DM26. The **Landshuter Hof,** Landshuterstr. 23 (tel. (0941) 511 53), a 10-minute walk to the right of the station, is clean and comfortable. (Singles with breakfast DM24, doubles DM42. Open Tues.-Sun.) **Camping** is available at Weinweg 40 (tel. (0941) 268 39), about 2km out of town. Go to the *sport anlage* or take bus #6 to the end of the line. For reasonably priced food, try any of the restaurants along the river on Keplerstr. or Thundorferstr. At the **Wurst Kuchl,** Fröliche-Türken-Str., a plate of 12 wurst and sauerkraut (enough for 2 big eaters) costs DM10.50. (Open Mon.-Fri. 8am-7pm, Sat. 8am-3pm.) Trains leave for Passau every hour; train station information is open until 7:30pm daily.

Passau

Passau guards the Austrian border from a bluff at the confluence of the Danube, Inn, and Ilz Rivers. The **Three Rivers' corner** presents a spectacular view of the rivers from a peaceful park. The **Cathedral of St. Stephen** houses the largest organ in the world. Across the Danube, the **Veste Oberhous** (take bus #9 from Rathausplatz) contains an impressive collection of art and historical exhibits.

The **tourist office** is at the Nibelungenhalle, the first right from Bahnhofstr. (tel. (0851) 334 21). The **Jugendherberge (IYHF),** Veste Oberhaus 125 (tel. (0851) 413 51) is the safest bet for getting a bed in this crowded town. Take bus #9 or walk up the hill. (Juniors DM8, seniors DM10. Breakfast DM2.90. Closes at 10pm.) Or try the pensions along Neuberger Strasse and Ludwigstrasse. **Dreiflüsse-Camping** (tel. (08546) 633) is 8km west of town in **Passau-Irring.** (DM5 per person, DM3-7 per site.) **Zeltplatz der Faltbootabteilung,** Halserstr. 34 (tel. (0851) 414 57), is behind the youth hostel. (DM4, ages under 17 DM2.50.) Trains to the Bavarian Forest and Austria depart every half hour from the Haupt Bahnhof.

GREAT BRITAIN

US$1 = 0.61 pounds (£)	**£1 = US$1.63**
CDN$1 = £0.47	**£1 = CDN$2.15**
AUS$1 = £0.44	**£1 = AUS$2.27**
NZ$1 = £0.39	**£1 = NZ$2.58**

Britain's history has long been shaped by its isolated but strategic position off the continent of Europe. This northwestern outpost of the Romans (who had to wall out the Celtic tribes they couldn't subdue) was overrun by seagoing Germanic tribes in the first centuries of this era. Their new kingdoms were subsequently Christianized by missionaries from continental Europe, and the new Christians barely fought off another wave of pre-Christian Germanic invaders before themselves falling to the Normans.

And so the story goes; each group that has come to these isles has absorbed something of the cultures that were here before. Celts, Saxons, Angles, Jutes, Danes, Normans, Irish, Scots, Welsh, Flemings, Huguenots, Jews, Africans, West Indians, Pakistanis, and Indians—all have contributed to the British peoples. The stereotypical Briton is master of the unseen and the unsaid, of all those intangible, indefinable gifts—taste and irony, grace, and wit—that go with the slightly crooked eyebrow or the bemused tone. But today's British are masters of much more—from *tandoori* chicken to microprocessing.

Britain is a kaleidoscope of multicolored bits, but the country can also be divided fairly neatly along regional lines. Industrial northern England, for instance, is traditionally on the political left, and local authorities in the north are publicly at odds with Margaret Thatcher's Conservative government, which they blame for the continuing economic decline. As you get even farther from London, the Iron Lady becomes even less popular—in Scotland, where a third of the manufacturing jobs have disappeared and unemployment doubled since Thatcher came to office, the Conservative Party governs despite having won only a fifth of the vote. In the Home Counties, on the other hand, the Jaguars in driveways seem all that is out of place in a setting of Tudor houses, clipped hedges, and affable Anglican pastors that could have been lifted out of P.G. Wodehouse.

Under Victoria in the latter half of the nineteenth century, Brittania ruled the waves—the sun never set on the Empire, and a rigid social stratification (chronicled by writers as disparate as Dickens and E.M. Forster) was the order of things at home. Two World Wars destroyed both the Empire and much of that social inequality: The post-war Labour government established a welfare state that saw working-class Britons receive adequate education, health care, and housing for the first time. Lately, under Margaret Thatcher, the high public-sector spending that financed social services has been severely cut back. Reactions have been mixed, but always strong: To the white-collar workers making payments on their new house, car, and VCR, she is the brilliant architect of Britain's economic miracle; to the over three million unemployed, the tenants of deteriorating public housing in the inner cities, and nearly all of Britain's large minority population, she is best described by words that we can't print in this book. As the June, 1987 general election showed, the former group is larger; Thatcher won an historically unprecedented third term against Labour leader Neil Kinnock and the soon-to-be-merged-into-one-party-with-perhaps-a-coherent-platform SDP/Liberal Alliance. Follow the vicissitudes of British politics in one of the quality dailies (i.e., not the papers with topless women on the third page): *The Times* is right of center, *The Guardian* is left of center, *The Independent* is boring, and *The Daily Telegraph* is excellent for wrapping fish.

Britain is often the cheapest gateway to Europe from either North America or Oceania; check with budget travel agencies listed in the Getting There section of the General Introduction.

For more coverage of Britain than we have space for here, turn to *Let's Go: Britain and Ireland.*

Getting There

The cheapest way to reach Britain from continental Europe is to swim the English Channel; this requires extraordinary physical condition and stamina and has been tackled by only a handful of budget travelers. Frequent ferries and hovercrafts connect Great Britain with various ports. The most frequent service is from Calais and Boulogne in France to Dover and nearby Folkestone (both about 2 hours southeast of London by rail), and there is also service from Oostende, Dieppe, Le Havre, Cherbourg, Santander, Hamburg, the Hook of Holland, and several Scandinavian ports, as well as Dublin, Rosslare, and Roscoff in Ireland. Fare between Calais or Boulogne and Dover is about £13. Oostende-Dover is about the same. The Dover-London rail fare adds £8.40 to these prices; thumbing from Dover to London is quick. Budget-bus deals often compete with these prices; coaches originate in Paris, Brussels, and Amsterdam, and continue through to London. These are usually cheaper than the comparable BIGE train fare. Flights to London, especially from Paris, may be economical, but remember to add the cost of transportation from the airport to the city center. Needless to say, the situation is complicated; your cheapest option depends on whether you have a railpass or a willing thumb, and on your pre-Britain itinerary. It's best to consult a budget travel agent in Paris, Brussels, or Amsterdam.

Transportation

Rail transport in Great Britain is readily available and expensive: Prices outpace most of those on the continent and Eurail is not valid (though InterRail is). But though individual tickets are costly, British Rail offers a huge and perplexing variety of passes, reductions, and discounts. The best deal is the **Young Person's Railcard** (£12), which gives 33% off any British Rail ticket. The card is valid for an entire year and is available at most rail station. You'll need proof that you're under 24 or a student at least 15 hours per week, 20 weeks of the year (ISIC acceptable), plus two photos. Railcards are also available for seniors (ages 60 and over) and for disabled travelers; these cards are also £12 but entitle the holder to an even greater discount of 50% off some fares. **Intercity Savers,** available to everyone, are cheap return fares offered between many large cities, saving about 30% (savings are smaller for Fri. departures, Sat. departures July-Aug.). Discount programs are also offered on regional rail travel. These change every year, so always ask.

Regional **Rail Rover** tickets offer a week's travel within one of nine regions of Britain for £18-42. The **All Line Rail Rover,** covering all of England, Wales, and Scotland, is £125 for a week, £199 for two weeks. These may be purchased at main-line stations within the regions concerned; normal railcard reductions apply. A **BritRail Pass** offers eight days of unlimited second-class travel for US$149, two weeks for US$225, three for US$285, and a month for US$335. The corresponding **Youth Pass** (for ages 16-25) costs US$20-50 less across the board. Both must be purchased outside Britain. With either, you'll have to travel a lot to get your money's worth.

Make yourself familiar with British train nomenclature: the expression for one way is "single;" round-trip is "return," and "period return" is a round-trip ticket that must be used within a specified time (usually 30 days).

Express coaches (long-distance buses) are cheaper than trains and often almost as fast. The **National Express/Scottish Citylink** intercity coach network covers most of Britain; a **Student Coach Card** (£3.50; ISIC and photo required) nets you 33% off their already low fares.Foreign citizens can purchase a **Britexpress Travelcard** which offers five or ten separate days of unlimited travel between 60 major towns in England, Wales, and Scotland. The card costs £28 for five days, £45 for 10 days (ages under 26 pay £22 and £35, respectively). The Britexpress pass is available from travel agents abroad or from the National Express office at Victoria Coach Station, Buckingham Palace Rd., London SW1 9TP.

Even cheaper local buses cover more territory more slowly. Some local authorities publish regional timetables in booklet form to help you make sense of the various and competing companies' routes. Regional **Explorer, Wayfarer,** or **Day Rambler** tickets (about £3) cover a day's unlimited travel on one company's routes or the routes of all companies in a region.

Hitchhiking in Great Britain is among Europe's best. Lorry (truck) drivers are always on the road. Early morning is the best time for finding long rides. Singles have the best luck since most lorry cabs are two-seaters, but couples don't have much trouble. Sundays are more difficult since fewer lorries are on the road, and small highland roads can be terrible. The best hitching is just off "roundabouts" (rotaries) and intersections. In parts of Britain, even major roads are narrow, and some roads are bordered by high hedges or stone banks; if you're hitching on such a road, be sure to stand at a point where the road widens. The fastest hitching is on "M" roads or "motorways" where you must hitch on entrance ramps or, better at the exits to the "services," the gas station/restaurant complexes strung all along the road at intervals of about 20 miles.

Perhaps the finest way to see Britain is on foot. Villages are usually only a couple of miles apart, and in areas of high tourist traffic virtually every village has one or two places that will put you up for the night. Pick up a large-scale Ordnance Survey map of the area you plan to cover; it will help you find the footpaths that aren't signposted.

Practical Information

There are independent local tourist offices everywhere in Great Britain; any will book you a room in a bed-and-breakfast, and most post a list after hours. Tourist offices are also excellent sources of information on local hiking routes and sights.

There are few of the old pay-on-answer 10p payphones left. New payphones come in two flavors; those that are coin-operated (2p, 5p, 10p, and 20p), and those that operate with an electronic Phonecard, purchased in denominations from £2 to £20 at post offices. If the display flashes "999 calls only," find another call box. Rates fall after 6pm. To make international calls cheaply, find a credit card phone or a call box that accepts 50p or £1 coins (bring a lot of them), or convince a friendly B&B proprietor to let you use the phone (the operator will tell you the exact rate you're being charged so that you can reimburse the proprietor). Directory assistance is 192; the operator is 100. The national emergency number is 999.

Given the cost of admission to many British sights and monuments, investing in a pass or two may pay off. **English Heritage** controls many English monuments; their pass costs £8 (seniors and ages under 16 £4). It's available at any of their properties, or at Building 1, Vision Way, Victoria Rd., Ruislip, Middlesex. If you plan to visit **National Trust** properties, consider their pass (£14.50), available from National Trust Membership Department, P.O. Box 30, Beckenham, Kent. The British Tourist Agency's *Historic Houses, Castles, and Gardens in Great Britain* can help you choose your sights judiciously.

Accommodations and Camping

Hospitality, not tourism, is Britain's stock in the visitor trade. Bed and breakfasts fill the country, offering a room and breakfast in someone's home for £7-10 (£12-14 in London). You can usually be sure of a clean room, a wholesome atmosphere, and a sustaining English breakfast.

The British and Scottish Tourist Boards publish *Where to Stay* books. **Tourist Information Centres** in each town have a list of accommodations and campsites. They will also find you a room (70p-£1 fee), and often book rooms in other towns (£1.50 fee). Most B&Bs will accept a telephone reservation, but few will keep the room past noon without a deposit. B&Bs are usually clumped together; *Let's Go* suggests areas of town or streets in which to look. Usually, if a place is full, the owner has her or his own referral system. In very small towns, you can ask at the pub or the post office for people offering B&B. When tourist offices close, they usually put a list of vacancies in their window.

Youth hostels are priced according to your age and their class. British hostels charge seniors and juniors (ages under 20) £2.50 and 2 Simple, £3.50 and 2.80 Standard, and £4.10 and 3.80 Superior. We list two prices per hostel throughout this chapter: Seniors, then juniors. Rates are higher in London. "Simple" hostels may not have showers. The main disadvantage of hostels is their 11pm curfew (11:30pm in London, and later in Scottish urban hostels); the daytime lockout (10am-5pm) can be a drag if you're in the middle of nowhere and it's raining. Finally, most hostels close during the off-season (from 1 month to as long as 9 months). You must own or rent a sheet sleeping sack, though in Scotland a pillowcase and a clean sleeping bag may be sufficient. You should book ahead in high season. Many hostels in Great Britain, especially rural ones, require chores of their guests. The *England and Wales YHA Guide* and *Scotland YHA Guide* are invaluable for finding hostels, checking closing dates, and learning details of access.

Camping can be a wet proposition in any British season, but it may also give you the most freedom. British campsites are very civilized, with facilities ranging from flush toilets to lounges. You usually have to put up with an adjacent caravan site. Farmers will frequently let you camp on their land, sometimes for a small fee, but you should always ask before pitching your tent.

Self-catering accommodations are growing in popularity. Flats, cottages, and caravans are rented by the week; they can be very economical if you (and friends) plan to stay in one place for a while. The tourist office has a list of these in each town.

Food

> *English cooking, like the English climate, is a training for life's unavoidable hardships.*
>
> —R.P. Lister

"If you want to eat well in England," wrote Somerset Maugham, "eat breakfast three times a day." The bad reputation of English cuisine is redeemed by the acknowledged splendor of English breakfasts. This famous repast, still served in many B&Bs, consists of tea or coffee, orange juice, cereal, eggs, bacon, sausage, toast, butter, marmalade, grilled tomatoes and mushrooms, and, in winter, porridge.

But if English breakfasts have the best reputation, the rest of English cuisine is not all boiled blandness. This is a nation of meat-eaters, and the best native dishes are roasts—beef, lamb, and Wiltshire hams. Vegetables are the weakest part of the meal, and are often overcooked; ask for salads instead. Desserts are exceedingly sweet, but even if you shy away from sugar, you should try an English pudding. "Boiled in a pail, tied in the tail of an old bleached shirt, so hot that they hurt," some of the best varieties are Christmas pudding, treacle tart, Spotted Dick, and steamed castle pudding, all served with thick jams, syrups, or custard. Crumpets, scones, shortbread, Jaffa cakes, and rich Dundee fruitcake are all creations of the English sweet tooth—and are scrumptious.

For lunch, pub grub is fast and filling. Hot meals vary from Cornish pasties (meat and vegetable wrapped in pastry) and toad-in-the-hole (sausages dipped in batter and baked) to steak and kidney pie with vegetables. The ploughman's lunch is inexpensive (£1-3): cheese, bread, pickle, chutney, and a tomato or two. Ironically, the ploughman's lunch is not traditional country fare but the product of a 1960s advertising campaign. Fish and chips are traditionally showered with vinegar and salt.

The best supermarket chains are Asda, Safeway, Sainsbury, and Co-op. As an alternative to English food, try Asian, Greek, and Indian cuisines. The last is especially worth a try; English restaurants (especially those in London and the larger cities) serve some of the best curries outside India. Remember that the usual 15% VAT surcharge is now levied on hot take-out foods.

England may be surrounded by water, but tea is what keeps it afloat. Tea (the drink) is the preferred remedy for exhaustion, ennui, a rainy morning, or a hot afternoon. English tea is served strong and milky; if you want it any other way, say so in advance. "Tea" is also a meal. Afternoon high tea as it is still served in northern England includes cooked meats, salad, sandwiches, and dessert. Cream tea, a specialty of Cornwall and Devon, includes toast, shortbread, crumpets, scones, and jam, presented with the essential feature—clotted cream. The afternoon tea that you will find served in London hotels is quite expensive (£5 or more) and often disappointing. Most British take less elaborate tea breaks every day, mornings ("elevenses") and afternoons at 4pm.

If tea remains the focus of family life, the pub is where individual and community come together, a place to catch the latest news or gossip, air an opinion, or relax with your mates. Sir William Harcourt was right when he said in 1872: "As much of the history of England has been brought about in public houses as in the House of Commons." As a passerby you may not see much local history in the making but you'll learn a lot about local life.

The pub's importance as a social institution is reflected in its careful furnishing. Many pubs are much more comfortably and expensively built than their North American counterparts, with old and often intricately-carved mahogany walls and velvet-covered benches. To sample the flavors of several different pubs, try an evening pub-crawl. Some of the larger cities put out pub guides (available in bookstores) and CAMRA publishes a guide to real ale pubs (34 Alma Rd., St. Albans, Herts. AL1 3BR; £4.50 plus postage). For information on pubs throughout Britain, stop by the Pub Information Centre, 93 Buckingham Palace Rd., London SW1 (tel. (01) 222 32 32).

British laws on pub licensing originated at the beginning of the nineteenth century. They were not so much an expression of social reform or even social morality as of industrialization. Drinking had been part of the rhythm of labor and recreation in pre-industrial England, but the factory system required workers to be as punctual and sober as the machines they operated. Although exact times vary from pub to pub, the most common hours are from 11am to 3pm and 5:30 to 11pm. The hallowed cry of the publican taking the last orders—"Hurry up, please, it's time"—means that you have 10 minutes to empty your glass. Beer—not wine or cocktails—is the standard pub drink. Except for the few individually-controlled "free houses," most pubs are little more than franchise operations for the six largest breweries. Most beer today is drawn under pressure and artificially carbonated, but a consumers' movement called the Campaign for Real Ale (CAMRA) has sprung up to fight for the retention of old-style beer. Real ale, which is fermented in the bottle or cask without machine carbonation, may taste slightly bitter and flat to those used to modern methods of production. Youngs and Fullers are widely available brands, and Ruddles, Sam Smith, and Tetleys, although less common, are worth looking for. North of the border, Bellhaven is the ale of choice. Those who don't drink alcohol shouldn't pass up the pub experience; cider, a fermented apple juice served either sweet or dry, is one alternative to beer. Cidona, one of the non-alcoholic ciders, and fruit juice is widely available.

London

When a man is tired of London, he is tired of life;
for there is in London all that life can afford.
—Dr. Samuel Johnson

Of all capitals, London lives deepest in the imagination of the English-speaking world. In nursery rhymes and songs we absorb London before we are aware it exists, and when we finally approach the city, it presents an odd homecoming, an eerie *déjà vu.* There are the red double-deckers, the bobbies and impassive guards at Buckingham, Westminster Abbey, and the notes of Big Ben, sounding as we have come to believe all bells should toll. We see these things with satisfaction.

Yet there is much to surprise. London is not quaint. London is not a museum, though you could spend all of your time going from one to the next. It is a booming, urban sprawl, with traffic snarls, porno shops, and an astonishingly international population. Visit the monuments of our semi-shared culture, the grave of Chaucer, or the pub where the captain of the Mayflower drank; but don't miss contemporary London, with its active theater, music, international cuisine, punks and peers, and everyone in between.

Orientation and Practical Information

London engulfs the surrounding country to an extent matched not even by Paris. When London became the world's largest city 200 years ago, Britain as a whole lagged well behind the population of most European countries. Even London's apparent population decline during the last 35 years is largely misleading. The growth outward continues, and many people simply live and commute from beyond the 10-mile wide "Green Belt" (thrown up in the '50s around the perimeter of London's 620 square miles as an attempt to halt London's sprawl).

London is divided into boroughs, precincts (or neighborhoods), and postal code areas. Both the borough name and postal code prefix appear at the bottom of most street signs. London has grown mostly by absorbing nearby villages or "cities"—a "city" meaning any town with a cathedral; this is reflected in borough names like "City of Westminster" and "City of London" (or simply "The City").

Central London, bounded roughly by the Underground's Circle Line, contains most major sights. East of the center is **The City**—London's financial center—and further east is the **East End,** ethnically diverse and working-class. The vaguely defined **West End** incorporates the understated elegance of Mayfair, the crowded shopping streets around Oxford Street, the touristy glitter of Piccadilly Circus, the theaters around Leicester Square, the exotic yet squalid labyrinth of Soho, and the chic, rehabilitated market in Covent Garden. In the middle of this zone is London's official center, Charing Cross, as well as its unofficial center, Trafalgar Square.

South of the West End is the *precinct* of **Westminster** (part of the *borough* of Westminster), the royal, political, and ecclesiastical center of England: Buckingham Palace, the Houses of Parliament, and Westminster Abbey. Southwest of the West End are gracious **Knightsbridge, Chelsea,** and **Kensington,** home to London's poshest shops and most expensive restaurants, and **Belgravia,** peppered with embassies and aristocrats.

Northwest of the West End, tidy terraces overlook the streets bordering Regent's Park, yielding in the southwest to the deteriorating squares of Paddington, Bayswater, and Notting Hill Gate, home to large Indian and West Indian communities. Northeast of the West End, **Bloomsbury** harbors the British Museum, London University colleges, and plenty of art galleries and specialty bookshops. Between the West End and The City lies Holborn, the center of legal activity, and Fleet Street, a warren of journalists. Trendy residential districts stretch to the north, including **Hampstead,** with its enormous heath and fabulous views of the city.

Trying to reach a specific destination on foot in London can be frustrating. Numbers often go up one side of a street and down the other. One road may change names four times in fewer miles and a name may designate a street, lane, square, and row in different corners of the city. A good map is essential. For a day's walk, London Transport's free map will do, but those staying a week or longer ought to buy a London street index. *London A to Z* (£1.60-4) is the traditional favorite, and Nicholson's *Streetfinder* is also good (£1.75-4.50). Price variations due to differences in level of detail. The *Ordnance Survey ABC London Street Atlas* (£2.50) is excellent.

Informative **London Walks** are daily guided tours with themes varying from the staid ("Westminster—1000 Years of History") to the macabre ("1880s East End Murders—Jack the Ripper"). Tours last from 1½-2 hours, with no advance reservations needed. (£2.25, students £2.) London Walks also sponsors three-hour historic **pub crawls.** Schedules for activities are available from tourist offices or from London Walks, 139 Conway Rd., Southgate, London N14 7BH (tel. 882 27 63). **Streets of London,** 32 Grovelands Rd. (tel. 882 34 14), also sponsors guided walks around the city, with topics like "Shakespeare's London," "Dickens' London," and "Haunted London" (which ends at a pub with a poltergeist). Each tour has a different startpoint—call the above phone number. (£2.50, students £2.25.) Do it yourself with a copy of Mary Cathcart Borer's *London Walks and Legends* (£1.50). The *London Silver Jubilee Walkway* guide (50p) is available from tourist offices; the route passes the big sights and some lesser-known treasures. For daytrips out of

0
1 mile
0
1 kilometer
Regent's Park
Maida
Randolph
Ave.
Hall Road
Vale
Ave.
St. John's Wood Rd.
Park
Rd.
Elgin
Ave.
Sutherland
Warwick Ave.
Clifton Gdns.
Blomfield
Rd.
Frampton St.
Rossmore
Rd.
Stanhope St.
Harrow Rd.
PADDINGTON
St. Mary's
Terrace
Hall
Place
Church St.
Broadley St.
Bell St.
MARYLEBONE
Marylebone
Rd.
Gloucester
Baker
Marylebone High
St.
Devonshire
Pl.
Park
Harley
Portland
Pl.
Gt.
Portland
NOTTING HILL
Bishop's Bridge
Rd.
PADDINGTON
St.
Praed
Edgware
Crawford St.
Dorset St.
ST. MARYLEBONE
Seymour
Place
Rd.
George
St.
Place
Wimpole
St.
Marylebone Lane
Gloucester Ter.
Westbourne Ter.
Sussex Gdns.
Queensway
Leinster
Ter.
Craven Hill
Sussex
Pl.
Sussex
Hyde Park
St.
Seymour
St.
Wigmore
St.
Oxford
Hanover
Sq.
New Bond St.
Davies
Bayswater
Rd.
Green St.
Upper Brook
St.
Audley
Grosvenor St.
Berkeley
Sq.
Dover
BAYSWATER
Lancaster
Gate
26
MAYFAIR
Kensington Gardens
Hyde Park
Curzon St.
Piccadilly
1
Hyde Park
Corner
Green Park
KENSINGTON
Kensington
2
Rd.
Constitution Hill
3
Exhibition Rd.
Ennismore
Gdns.
Trevor Pl.
KNIGHTSBRIDGE
Grosvenor
Halkin
St.
Chapel
St.
Wilton
Prince
Consort Rd.
Gloucester
Queen's
4
6
5
Brompton Rd.
Hans
Rd.
Sloane
St.
Pont
Belgrave Pl.
Buckingham Palace Rd.
Cornwall
Gdns.
Cromwell
Rd.
Thurloe Pl.
Walton
Cadogan
Sq.
Milner St.
BELGRAVIA
St.
Elizabeth
St.
EARL'S
COURT
Collingham
Rd.
Ashburn
Pl.
Rd.
Gate
Harrington
Rd.
Pelham St.
Sloane Ave.
Cadogan
St.
Sloane
Sq.
Ebury
PIMLICO
Elystan St.
Draycott P.
Rd.
Rd.
Brompton
Onslow
Gdns.
Sydney St.
Cale St.
Pimlico Rd.
Warwick Way
The Little
Boltons
The Boltons
Drayton Gdns.
Cranley Gdns.
Rd.
Old Church St.
Dovehouse
St.
King's
Smith St.
Chelsea
Bridge Rd.
Ebury Bridge
Sutherland St.
Old
Radcliffe
Gdns.
Gilston
Rd.
Beaufort
St.
CHELSEA
Oakley St.
Flood St.
Royal Hospital Rd.
Grosvenor
Church
Rd.
Chelsea
Embankment
Fulham
Rd.
Cheyne
Walk
River
N
King's
Battersea Park

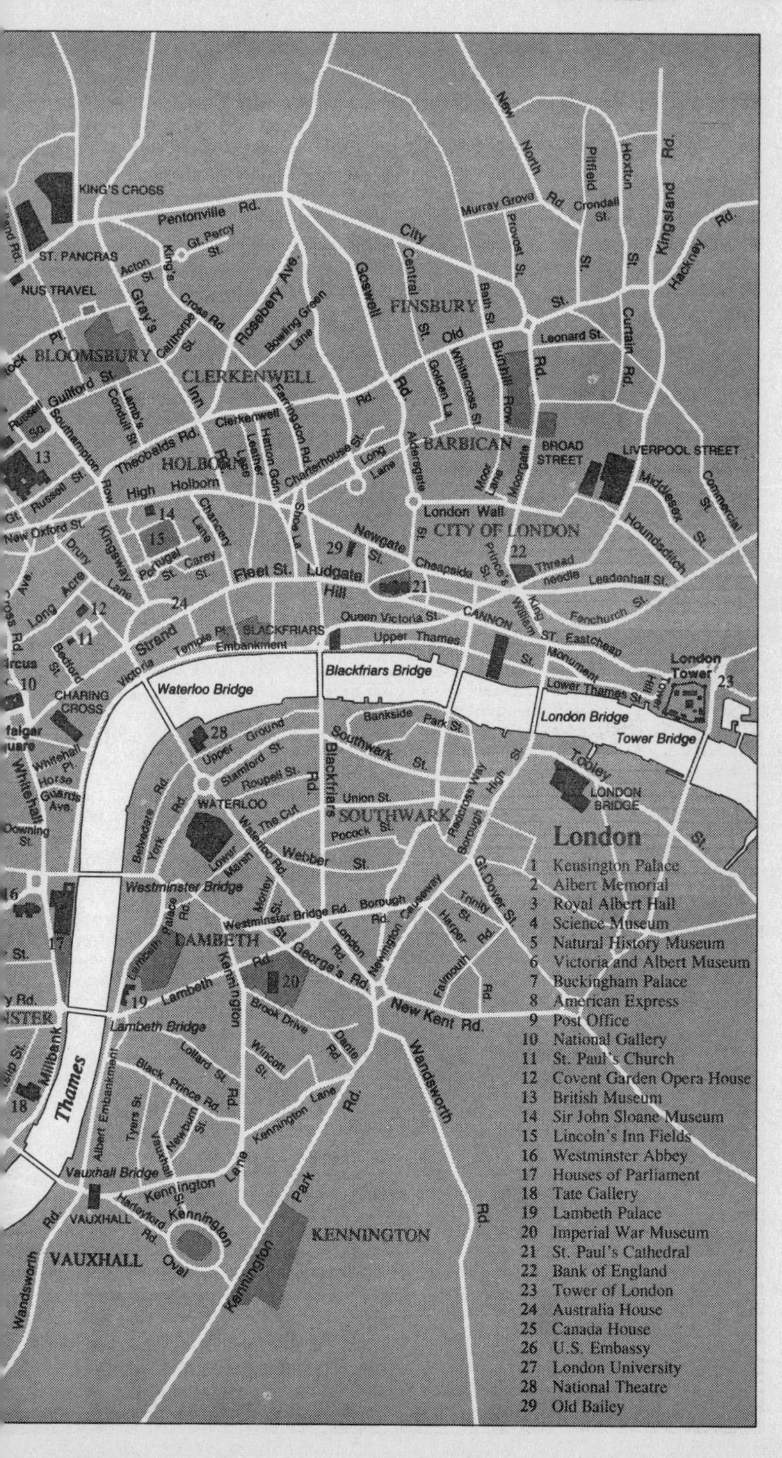
London
1 Kensington Palace
2 Albert Memorial
3 Royal Albert Hall
4 Science Museum
5 Natural History Museum
6 Victoria and Albert Museum
7 Buckingham Palace
8 American Express
9 Post Office
10 National Gallery
11 St. Paul's Church
12 Covent Garden Opera House
13 British Museum
14 Sir John Sloane Museum
15 Lincoln's Inn Fields
16 Westminster Abbey
17 Houses of Parliament
18 Tate Gallery
19 Lambeth Palace
20 Imperial War Museum
21 St. Paul's Cathedral
22 Bank of England
23 Tower of London
24 Australia House
25 Canada House
26 U.S. Embassy
27 London University
28 National Theatre
29 Old Bailey
KING'S CROSS
ST. PANCRAS
NUS TRAVEL
Pentonville Rd.
BLOOMSBURY
CLERKENWELL
HOLBORN
FINSBURY
BARBICAN
BROAD STREET
LIVERPOOL STREET
CITY OF LONDON
BLACKFRIARS
CANNON ST.
CHARING CROSS
WATERLOO
SOUTHWARK
LONDON BRIDGE
LAMBETH
VAUXHALL
KENNINGTON
Thames
Waterloo Bridge
Blackfriars Bridge
London Bridge
Tower Bridge
Westminster Bridge
Lambeth Bridge
Vauxhall Bridge
London Tower
City Rd.
Goswell Rd.
Old St.
Fleet St.
Ludgate Hill
Strand
Cheapside
London Wall
Newgate St.
High Holborn
Kingsway
New Oxford St.
Queen Victoria St.
Upper Thames St.
Lower Thames St.
Fenchurch St.
Leadenhall St.
Houndsditch
Middlesex St.
Commercial St.
Moorgate
Southwark St.
Blackfriars Rd.
Union St.
The Cut
Webber St.
Westminster Bridge Rd.
Borough Rd.
St. George's Rd.
New Kent Rd.
Kennington Rd.
Kennington Lane
Kennington Park Rd.
Kennington Oval
Albert Embankment
Millbank
Whitehall
Tooley St.
Kingsland Rd.
Hackney Rd.
Wandsworth Rd.

London, **British Rail** offers day-returns (after 9:30-10am) that cost only slightly more than the one-way fare. **Green Line** suburban buses are cheaper still (students travel at half-fare), but slower; they are best for shorter trips to places like Hampton Court or Windsor (tel. 668 72 61 for information). For £3.95 you can enjoy unlimited Green Line travel for a day. Most of the routes originate on Buckingham Palace Rd. or on Eccleston Bridge, two roads alongside Victoria Station. For longer distances, **National Express,** Buckingham Palace Rd. (tel. 730 02 02), also has many cheap day-returns.

London is an extremely inexpensive—and complicated—travel center. For information on London's three airports, eight train stations, numerous bus companies, and countless budget options, see our Budget Travel and transportation listings below.

Tourist Offices: Tourist Information Centre, Victoria Station. Run by the London Visitor and Convention Bureau. Information and accommodations service (£3) for London and England. Open daily 9am-8:30pm. Another LVCB center at Heathrow Central Tube station. Telephone inquiries (tel. 730 34 88) Mon.-Fri. 9am-5:30pm. **City of London Information Centre,** in St. Paul's Churchyard (tel. 606 30 30). Tube: St. Paul's. Open Mon.-Fri. 9:30am-5pm, Sat. 9:30am-1pm, closed Sun. **Kidsline** (tel. 222 80 70) answers queries on children's events.

Budget Travel: London is *the* place to shop for cheap bus, plane, and train tickets to North America, Africa, Asia, and Australia. When they start running budget flights to the moon, this'll be the place to get those too. The travel sections of *Time Out* and *LAM* magazines are good places to look, or go to one of the agencies below:

STA Travel, 74-78 Old Brompton Rd. Tube: South Kensington. Also at 117 Euston Rd. Tube: Euston. Call 581 10 22 for intercontinental travel, 581 82 33 for European travel. Make this your first stop on a budget travel hunt. A helpful and knowledgeable staff will sell you cheap flights to everywhere imaginable.

Transalpino: 3 London offices: 71-75 Buckingham Palace Rd., SW1 (tel. 834 96 56 or 834 62 83; Tube: Victoria); 214 Shaftesbury Ave., near the British Museum, WC2 (tel. 836 00 87 or 836 00 88; Tube: Tottenham Court Road); and 117 Euston Rd., NW1 (tel. 388 22 67; Tube: Euston). Each sells discounted tickets for students under 26. Unless you are going to Ireland, you need a passport as proof of age. Ask about their Holland specials (2 for the price of 1). Same-day and next-day bookings. Offices open daily 8am-8pm.

London Student Travel: 52 Grosvenor Gardens, SW1 (tel. 730 34 02). Tube: Victoria. Competitive rail, coach, and air fares all over the Continent and beyond. No age limit for many of their offers. Open Mon.-Fri. 9am-6pm, Sat. 10am-1pm, longer hours May-July.

Miracle Bus: 408 The Strand, WC2 (tel. 379 60 55). Tube: Charing Cross. Competitive coach and air fares to Europe; more destinations than Euroways. Open Mon.-Fri. 10am-6pm, Sat. 10:30am-1:30pm.

YHA Travel, 14 Southampton St., WC2 (tel. 836 85 41). Tube: Covent Garden or Charing Cross. Youth travel services. Great selection of travel guides (*Let's Go* and more), maps, and sports and camping equipment. Less information available about student discounts than at other agencies listed above. Open Mon. and Wed.-Sat. 9:30am-5:30pm, Tues. 10am-5:30pm.

American Express: 6 Haymarket, SW1 (tel. 930 44 11). Tube: Piccadilly. Mail held. All banking services. Currency exchange open Mon.-Fri. 9am-5pm, Sat. 9am-6pm (June-Sept. 9am-8pm), Sun. 10am-6pm. Message and mail pickup in basement, open Mon.-Fri. 9am-5pm, Sat. 9am-noon. Leaving a message costs 20p. Other offices with similar services near Westminster Cathedral (Tube: Victoria), opposite Harrods (Tube: Knightsbridge), and in the Oxford St. Selfridges (Tube: Bond St.).

Currency Exchange: Best rates at banks, not Thomas Cook or *bureaux de change.* Banks with long hours at both Heathrow and Gatwick Airports. Bank next to platform #8 in Victoria Station open daily 8am-9pm. **Thomas Cook,** near Terminus Place outside Victoria Station, open daily 6am-10pm. **Berkeley Safe Deposit,** outside Victoria Station, open daily 8am-midnight. **Trafalgar Square post office** operates currency exchange Mon.-Sat. 9am-9:30pm. *Bureau de change* with longest hours and worst rates (5% commission when changing dollars to pounds) at Piccadilly Circus, open daily 9:30am-11pm. Every *bureau de change* recognized by the London Tourist Board must display its exchange and commission rates. Stay away from **Chequepoint**—the rates are bad.

Post Office: Mail addressed simply Poste Restante, London, is delivered to: Chief Office, King Edward Building, on King Edward St. (tel. 239 30 49). Tube: St. Paul's. Open Mon.-Fri. 8am-7pm, Sat. 9am-12:30pm. Probably more convenient to have your mail sent to Trafalgar

Sq. Branch Office, 24-28 William IV St., London WC2N 4DL. Tube: Charing Cross. Open Mon.-Sat. 8am-8pm, Sun. 10am-5pm.

Telephones: You can make international calls from the British Telecom office, 1A Broadway (tel. 222 44 44; open 9am-7pm), near St. James's Park Tube, or from specially designated booths ("Intercontinental"). Directory information for London (tel. 142); for the rest of Britain and Ireland (tel. 192); operator (tel. 100); international operator (tel. 155). **Telephone code:** 01.

Flights: Heathrow Airport (tel. 759 43 21) is the world's busiest airport. The easiest way to reach central London from Heathrow is by **Underground** (about 55 min.). A single ticket into the city costs £1.70, but you can save money by buying a one-day **Travelcard** for £2. To reach **Victoria Station,** transfer at Earl's Court or Gloucester Road to a District line or Circle Line train heading east. At Victoria, you'll find a blue **Tourist Information Centre** with an accommodations service, a currency exchange office, and information about transportation connections (see Getting Around London, below). London Regional Transport's **Airbus** goes from Heathrow to central points, including hotels, in the city (1-2 hr., depending on traffic; £3, children £1.50), as does a **Green Line** bus. The bus is more convenient that the Underground if you have a lot of luggage. If you arrive after midnight, you can still avoid the £10-23 taxi fare by taking night bus #N97 from Heathrow bus station to Piccadilly Circus (every hour just before the hour until 5am). Most charter flights land at **Gatwick Airport** (tel. 668 42 11). From there, you can take a **BritRail** train to Victoria Station (45 min., £4.50). Avoid taxis, since they take twice as long and cost over twice as much. **Green Line** (tel. 668 72 61) coach #777 (departure times vary before 7am and after 6pm, but are at 10 'til the hour and 20 past the hour 7am-6pm) travels between Gatwick and Victoria in 70 minutes. (£3 one way, £5 round-trip.) From **Stansted Airport** in Essex (tel. (0279) 50 23 80), 1 hr. north of London, coaches are coordinated with incoming flights (£3).

Trains: If you are leaving London by train, be certain to find out from which of the eight major stations your coach departs. Call 834 23 45 for information on all **British Rail** departures to continental Europe, or one of the phone numbers below for information on trains destined for the regions listed. The London subway system, called the **Underground** or **Tube,** stops at stops bearing the same names as the train stations. **King's Cross Station** (tel. 278 24 77 or 837 42 00): East and northeast England, Scotland (including Edinburgh) via east coast; **Charing Cross Station** (tel. 928 51 00): France and southeast England; **Liverpool St. Station** (tel. 283 71 71 or 247 76 00): Northern Europe, East Anglia, and Essex; **Paddington Station** (tel. 262 67 67 or 723 70 00): West and Southwest England, Ireland, South Midlands, and South Wales; **Euston Station** (tel. 387 70 70 or 387 94 00): Ireland, North Midlands, North Wales, northwest England, and Scotland (including Glasgow) via west coast; **St. Pancras Station** (tel. 387 70 70 or 387 94 00): North Midlands; **Victoria Station** (tel. 928 51 00): France, Northern Europe, south and southeast England, and Gatwick; **Waterloo Station** (tel. 928 51 00): South and southeast England.

Buses: National Express has service to most of Great Britain. The main depot is **Victoria Coach Station** at the corner of Buckingham Palace Rd. and Elizabeth St. (tel. 730 02 02). Tube: Victoria. Just across Buckingham Palace Rd. is the **Green Line** depot (tel. 668 72 61), for buses to London suburbs. Private coach companies are frequently the best deal for long-distance trips (to the North, to Scotland, to Ireland). **Miracle Bus,** 408 The Strand (tel. 379 60 55), Tube: Charing Cross, and **Euroways,** 52 Grosvenor Gardens (tel. 730 82 35), Tube: Victoria, have scheduled coaches to Paris, Greece, and other continental destinations. Check the back of *Time Out* magazine for information.

Ferries: Sealink has offices in the major rail stations listed above. The one in Liverpool Street Station (open Mon.-Sat. 8am-8pm, Sun. 8:30am-8pm; advance bookings Mon.-Sat. 8am-6pm only) is less crowded than the one near platform #2 at Victoria Station (tel. 834 23 45; open daily 8am-6pm, Sat. same-day ticket service only). They're good for information; but for the cheapest channel crossing, consult one of the budget travel agents listed above. Transalpino train tickets are usually the best deals for those under 26; other travelers might do better with a bus package (see Buses above). As always, shop around and check *Time Out* and *LAM.* Dover-Calais or -Boulogne is the cheapest port-to-port crossing, but unless you're traveling to France or Spain, Oostende in Belgium is likely to be a more convenient continental gateway.

Taxis: London taxi fares are reasonable, possibly less than the Tube for short distances and for parties of 4 or more. Cabbies literally know every street in Greater London. Distances are great in this megalopolis, and drivers are accustomed to a 15% tip. Hail your own, or call for a radio-dispatched taxi (tel. 286 48 48, 272 30 30, 286 60 10, or 286 61 28). Women traveling alone may prefer "Ladycabs" (Mini Cab Service), with women-only cabbies (tel. 254 35 01 or 254 33 14), Sun.-Fri. 8am-1am, Sat. 8am-2am.

Public Transportation: The **Underground** (or **Tube**) is fast, efficient, and usually about 50p per trip (fares range 30p-£1.50). Transfers are free. The Tube opens about 6am and closes about midnight. You must buy your ticket before you board and save it for handing to a guard at your final destination; delinquents pay again. To avoid queues and constant coin-scrounging, arm yourself with a **Travelcard,** which allows you unlimited use of both the Tube and London's famous buses. It's available for 1 day (£1.70), 3 days (£3), or 7 days (£5). Two passport photos are needed for the 7-day card. Red double-deckers are the regular city buses; the single-decker Red Arrows are expresses. Within London Transport's central zone (bounded roughly by the Underground's Circle line), the fare is a standard 50p; journeys outside this zone cost 70p-£2.40. Pick up a **London-Wide Bus Map** (free) from any Tube station or Travel Information Centre (Euston, King's Cross, Victoria, Oxford Circus, Heathrow, Piccadilly Circus, and St. James's Park). Also get a schedule for the **night bus** routes; these can save your life after midnight, when other forms of transport have turned into pumpkins. London Transport's 24-hour phone information line (tel. 222 12 34) can advise you on all routes.

Bike Rental: Dial-a-Bike, 18 Gillingham St., W1 (tel. 828 40 40). Tube: Victoria. Rents 3- and 10-speed bicycles from £5-7.50 per day, £ 20-30 per week. £40 deposit, ouch. Must leave a driver's license or passport. Open in summer Mon.-Fri. 9:30am-6pm, Sat. 9:30am-5pm; in winter Tues.-Fri. 9:30am-6pm, Sat. 9:30am-1pm.

Moped Rental: Scootabout Ltd., 59 Albert Embankment, SE1 (tel. 582 00 55). Tube: Vauxhall. From £10.95 per day, £ 54.50 per week. Minimum driving age in Britain is 17, but you can ride a moped if you're 16 or over.

Car Rental: London is not the place to go spinning about in your Mini—parking is impossible, traffic deplorable, and when it's all said and done you could have biked, bused, Tubed, or walked more quickly and cheaply. Obstinate? Then try **Cartel Car Rentals,** 16 Warner St., Mount Pleasant, EC1 (tel. 278 60 01). Tube: Farringdon or Chancery Lane. From £17.25 per day plus insurance; 200 free miles, then 5p per mile. From £96.60 per week plus insurance and unlimited mileage. Open Mon.-Fri. 8:30am-5:30pm, Sat. 9am-1pm. Must be over 21.

Baggage Storage: Bishop and Sons' Depositories, 10-12 Belgrave Rd., SW1 (tel. 821 81 51), near corner of Belgrave Rd. and Eccleston Sq. About 2 blocks from Victoria rail, Victoria Tube, and Victoria coach stations. Safe, secure, and only £2.46 per item (large backpacks inclusive). Minimum charge of £4.92 (2 items).

Legal Trouble: Release, 1 Elgin Ave., W9 (tel. 289 11 23; 24-hour emergency tel. 837 56 02 or 603 86 54). Tube: Westbourne Park. Advice and referrals; specializing in drug arrests. Also psychiatric and abortion referrals. **Law Centres Federation,** 18 Warren St., W1 (tel. 387 85 70). Tube: Warren St. 25 London offices providing free legal help.

Emergencies: Police or **Ambulance** (tel. 999), no coins required.

Medical Assistance: In an emergency, you can be treated at no charge in the casualty ward (emergency room) of any hospital. The National Health Service has no further obligations to foreigners, so you will probably have to pay for non-emergency medical care, although for less than in North America. Try the **Royal Free Hospital,** Point St., NW3 (tel. 794 05 00), or the **Chelsea Hospital for Women,** Doverhouse St., SW3 (tel. 352 64 46). **Family Planning Association,** 27-35 Mortimer St. (tel. 636 78 66), for contraceptives, pregnancy tests, and abortion referrals. Tube: Oxford Circus.

Pharmacy: Boots has a 24-hour pharmacy on the northeast side of Piccadilly Circus.

Haircare: Cheapest reliable places are the many hairdressing schools. Prices are rock bottom and students experienced. **London College of Fashion,** 20 John Prince's St. (tel. 493 07 90; Tube: Oxford Circus), is the cheapest in town. Free haircuts for men, £1-3 for women. Open Sept.-June.

Crises: Call or visit the **Samaritans,** 3 Hornton Place (tel. 283 34 00), if you're feeling suicidal, lonely, despairing, or just need someone to talk to; phones answered 24 hours. Tube: Kensington High St. The **London Rape Crisis Centre,** P.O. Box 69 (tel. 837 16 00), can also be reached any time of the day or night. If you're absolutely broke, try the **Salvation Army,** 101 Queen Victoria St. (tel. 236 52 22), for shelter. Tube: Mansion House or Blackfriars.

Women's Center: A Woman's Place, Hungerford House, Victoria Embankment (tel. 836 60 81). Tube: Embankment. Information clearinghouse, some rape and abortion referral, and minimal accommodations listings. Emergency center listings for the rest of England. Open Mon.-Fri. noon-7pm, Sat. noon-6pm.

Disabled Travelers' Information and Sevices: London's help for the disabled has recently been decentralized. **Federation of London Dial-A-Ride** (tel. 482 23 25), **GLAD** (Greater London Association for the Disabled) tel. 247 01 07.

Gay Centers: Gay Switchboard (tel. 837 73 24). 24-hour advice and support service for men and women. **London Lesbian and Gay Centre,** 67-69 Cowcross St. (tel. 608 14 71), is the largest in Europe: bar, cafe, disco, bookshop, women-only floor. Tube: Farringdon. Open Tues. 6pm-midnight, Wed.-Thurs. and Sun. noon-midnight, Fri.-Sat. noon-2am. *Time Out* magazine has comprehensive gay listings.

Embassies and High Commissions: U.S., 24 Grosvenor Sq. (tel. 499 90 00). Tube: Bond St. **Canada,** Canada House, Trafalgar Sq. (tel. 629 94 92). Tube: Charing Cross. **Australian High Commission,** Australia House, The Strand (tel. 438 80 00). Tube: Aldwych. **New Zealand High Commission,** New Zealand House, Haymarket (tel. 930 84 22). Tube: Piccadilly Circus. **Bulgaria,** 186 Queen's Gate (tel. 584 94 00). Tube: South Kensington. **Czechoslovakia,** 28 Kensington Palace Gardens (tel. 727 39 66). Tube: Gloucester Rd. **Hungary,** 35 Eaton Pl. (tel. 235 71 91 or 235 40 48). Tube: Sloane Sq. **Poland** (tel. 580 43 24). **Spain,** 24 Belgrave Sq. (tel. 235 55 55), for Australians and New Zealanders traveling there. Tube: Knightsbridge.

Hitchhiking: For Cambridge, Tube to Turnpike Lane (Piccadilly Line), then bus #144, 217, or 231 to Great Cambridge Roundabout, then A10. For Canterbury and Dover, bus #53 to Blackheath (Shooters Hill Road), then A2 to M2. For Edinburgh, bus #16a to M1, then M18, finally A7. For Lake District, bus #16a to Kilburn, then bus #16 to Staples Corner, then M1 to M6. For Oxford, Tube to Hanger Lane (Central Line), then walk along Western Ave. to A40, and take A40 to M40. For South Wales, bus #23 from Marylebone Rd. to M4, or Tube to Chiswick Park (District Line), then walk along Chiswick High Rd. to the roundabout (A315) to M4. Remember that drivers cannot stop along Motorways (M roads), nor can you walk along them. Women hitching alone out of London are taking a big chance.

Accommodations and Camping

London's popularity assures most hotels a steady stream of customers; the hospitality and delicious breakfasts of English B&Bs are best experienced outside the capital. Fortunately, hotels in London will often charge reduced weekly rates or even rent by the bed in large "shared" rooms. Reservations are highly recommended for June through August. Write to the hotel of your choice well in advance, stating date of arrival and probable length of stay, and include one night's payment as deposit; some hotels accept personal checks in foreign currencies, though others demand traveler's checks. Call about availability and find out what the exact procedure is. London offers an enormous range of accommodations; consider staying in a private hostel or a University Hall of Residence.

For longer stays, renting a room in a private home or sharing an apartment ("flat") may be more economical. Room-locating agencies such as **Universal Aunts,** 250 King's Rd. (tel. 351 57 67; Tube: Sloane Sq. or South Kensington), will find you lodgings for a week or more for a fee equivalent to a week's rent. Also check newspapers, and bulletin boards at the University of London Student Union for by-the-week and long-term accommodations. The **University of London Student Union** accommodations office will find long-term accommodations (2 week minimum) for students from mid-June through mid-August. You must visit them in person, with a valid ID, at 1 Malet St. (tel. 636 28 18). (Tube: Goodge St. or Russell Sq.)

YHA Hostels

London's seven YHA (IYHF) hostels are as encumbered with rules as with people. Each closes for part of the day, and allows a maximum stay of four consecutive nights in all London hostels (counted as 1 in this context); most observe strict curfews. Maximum stay rules can be stretched if there is space, but this is unlikely in summer.

Although much space is booked in advance by groups, all hostels try to keep some beds free for individual travelers. For July and August, you should reserve a bed by writing in advance; otherwise be sure to arrive before breakfast. It is always a good idea to call in advance. All London hostels require international membership cards. These are available for £6, often at the hostels and always at YHA London Headquarters, 14 Southampton St. (tel. 836 85 41). Tube: Covent Garden. (Open Mon.-Sat. 9:30am-6pm.)

The standardized cost per night in all London IYHF/YHA hostels is seniors (ages 21 and over) £5.50, juniors (ages 16-20) £4.50, and youths (ages 5-15) £3.75. They all require sleep sacks and will rent one to you for 50p-£1.

Holland House (King George III Memorial Youth Hostel), Holland Walk, Kensington, W8 (tel. 937 07 48). Tube: Holland Park or High Street Kensington. Restored Jacobean mansion on the east side of Holland Park, where Londoners play cricket while befuddled squirrels and hostelers look on. Daily pick-up soccer games. Hostel is bright and clean, with kitchen and laundry facilities. Breakfast £1.70, evening meals £3-4. Large lockers (20p) in video-monitored room which is open throughout the day. Dorms, though, are locked 10am-5pm. Reception open 7am-midnight.

Carter Lane, 36 Carter Lane, EC4 (tel. 236 49 65). Tube: St. Paul's or Blackfriars. A stone's throw from the cathedral. Clean and friendly, but very crowded. Some *very* large rooms with as many as 21 bunkbeds. Pure bedlam at dinner time: school children seem to ricochet off the walls. Laundry facilities, midnight curfew, no limit to length of stay, surprisingly quiet study area. Lockers fitting large backpacks included in the price. Reception open 7-10am and 11:30am-midnight. Dorms locked 10am-1pm.

Earl's Court, 38 Bolton Gardens, SW5 (tel. 373 70 83). Tube: Earl's Court. A converted town-house in a busy reisdential neighborhood. The best self-catering kitchen facilities of all the London hostels, but the toilet paper is as abrasive as sandpaper. Staff answers your questions with robot-like aloofness. Small, key-operated lockers won't fit large backpacks and cost 50p every time opened. Breakfast £1.70, but not worth it. Lockout 10am-5pm. Midnight curfew. Show up at hostel's doorstep at 8:30am to get a bed.

Hampstead Heath, 4 Wellgart Rd., Hampstead, NW11 (tel. 458 90 54). Tube: Golder's Green, then ¼-mile walk along North End Rd. Inconvenient, but beautiful location is less bustling than central hostels. Cooking and laundry facilities, TV room. Optional breakfast £1.60. Reception open 7am-11:30pm. Lockout 10am-5pm. No curfew! Hallelujah! Open daily year-round.

Highgate, 84 Highgate West Hill, N6 (tel. 340 18 31). Tube: Archway, then ¾-mile walk up Highgate Hill and Highgate High St. Or take bus #210 or 271 from the Tube to Highgate Village and walk down South Grove. Beautiful neighborhood: out of the way, but well worth it. Breakfast £1.60. Reception open 5-11:30pm. Dorm closed 10am-5pm. Open Feb. 16-Dec. 14.

Wood Green, Brabant Rd., N22 (tel. 881 44 32). Tube: Wood Green, then walk 2 min. west on Station Rd; ½hr. from central London. 157 single rooms. Good kitchen facilities. No curfew. All-night security guard. Dorms locked 10am-5pm. Open at Easter time (March 30-April 24 in 1988) and July 13-Sept. 18.

White Hart Lane, All Saints Hall Residence, White Hart Lane, N17 (tel. 885 32 34). Tube: Seven Sisters, then BritRail to White Hart Lane (50p); or BritRail direct from Liverpool St. Grimy neighborhood reminiscent of Coketown in Dickens's *Hard Times.* Food in local stores costs 25-40% less than in central London. No showers—all bathtubs. Small clothes cabinets in rooms. Evening meals available. Laundry facilities. Reception open 7-10am and 5pm-midnight. Dorms locked 10am-2pm. No curfew. Open July 13-Sept. 11.

Private Hostels

The following places are less likely to be full of schoolchildren, don't require membership cards, don't have curfews, and tend to be less attached to their rule boards. None is the Ritz, but all offer accommodations of roughly the same standard as the IYHF hostels. All are open year-round.

The Ritz, by the way, is on Picadilly St. (tel. 493 81 81). Tube: Isn't that the underground conveyance in which poor people ride? Just take the Rolls. Ever-so-posh, and we hear that the rooms are clean, but no kitchen facilities and no lockers for your backpack. Singles £135, doubles £160, suites £350-650.

Astor Museum Hostel, 27 Montague St., WC1 (tel. 580 53 60), off Bloomsbury Sq. Tube: Holborn, Tottenham Court Road, or Russell Square. Central hostel at the above address, and an annex around the corner at 18 Little Russell St. Check in at the former and avoid the latter; it's bleak, mildewy, malodorous, and breakfast isn't as good. Two basement showers service 27 people, but the hostel does have a young, international clientele, a buoyant staff, and is in a terrific location (close to British Museum, Soho, and Picadilly). Free safe for storage of valuables. 5-bed dorm rooms £8.50 per person in central hostel, £8 per person in annex. Doubles £12 per person in central hostel. Weekly rates Oct.-April. Reception open 24 hours.

Central University of Iowa Hostel, 7 Bedford Pl., WC1 (tel. 580 11 21), near the British Museum. Tube: Holborn or Russell Square. Slanted floors may have you rolling out of bed. Water pressure so weak that showering takes 20 min. Laundry and kitchen facilities, TV room. £8 per person per night in 4-bed dorm, £9 in 2-bed. All-you-can-eat continental breakfast included. Reception open 9am-1pm and 3-10pm. Open late May-Aug. Write as soon after April 1 as possible.

Repton House, 31 Bedford Pl., WC1 (tel. 636 70 45). Grim, with distinct *eau de mildew* creeping through the halls. Laissez-faire management. Still, dorm prices hard to beat in this area: 8-bed rooms £9 per person. Singles £18, doubles £28-36, triples £36-42. Continental breakfast included. Open mid-June to early Aug.

Fieldcourt House, 32 Courtfield Gardens, SW5 (tel. 373 01 52). Tube: Gloucester Rd. Several readers have written us about thefts here. In a grand old Victorian home. Comfortable and exceptionally clean. Lockers (which are allegedly not at all fail-safe), laundry facilities, study, and TV rooms. £10 linen deposit. Singles £13, double bunks £10.50 per person, 10-bed dorm rooms £8.50 per person.

Maranton House Hostel, 14 Barkston Gardens, SW5 (tel. 373 57 82). Tube: Earl's Court. Snappy manager keeps the place clean. Noon checkout; £5 key deposit. English breakfast £3 extra. Small dorm rooms £8 per night, singles £12, doubles £18.

Ridgemont Hotel, 65 Gower St., WC1 (tel. 636 11 41). Lovingly maintained by conscientious proprietor. For special pampering, tell them you were referred by *Let's Go.* Singles £16, doubles £25, triples £33, quads £40, shares £14 per person.

Regency House Hotel, 71 Gower St., WC1 (tel. 637 18 04). Clean, quiet, and cool-looking, with garden. Efficiently run, with attention to security. Book 1 week in advance to be certain of a room. Singles £20, doubles £30, shares £15 per person; in winter singles £16.

Bluedaws Hotel, 133-135 Sussex Gardens, W2 (tel. 723 60 40 or 262 63 14). Clean, fresh-smelling rooms. Singles £15, doubles £23, triples £27, shares £8 per person. Continental breakfast included.

Dashwood House, 6 Pembridge Sq. (tel. 229 78 48). Tube: Notting Hill Gate. Residential hostel for women only, run by Christian Alliance. Beautifully-kept building in peaceful, leafy square. Rooms institutional but comfortable. Singles £8.50, doubles £13.80.

Redcliff Student Hotel, 21 Redcliffe St., SW5 (tel. 373 46 36). Tube: Gloucester Road or Earl's Court. A young crowd is "sardined" into this far-from-lavish hotel. Front door and bedrooms with lock and personal key. £6.50 per person in 6-bed dorms, £7.50 in 4-bed dorms. Reception open 8am-midnight. No curfew or lockout.

London Student Hotel, 14 Pennywood Rd., SW5 (tel. 373 46 33). Tube: Earl's Court. Spartan accommodations, dingy staircases. £10 per person in 4-bed dorms. Singles £17, doubles £22. Some doubles almost spacious. No curfew or lockout.

Rees Hotel, 22 Argyle St., WC1 (tel. 637 62 00). Tube: King's Cross/St. Pancras. In a weathered neighborhood. A nearby junk-filled lot has been facetiously labelled "Argyle Community Garden" by a spray painter. But who can argue with £7 B&B per person in small dorms (6-bed maximum)? 50p deposit for shower key. Noon checkout time hours later than all hostels. Laundry and kitchen facilities.

Tonbridge School Clubs, Ltd., 120 Cromer St. (tel. 837 44 06). Tube: King's Cross/St. Pancras. The price is right, but only for the strong-hearted. Weather-beaten patrons; men sleep in basement gym, women in karate-club hall. Blankets and foam pads provided, hot showers, TV lounge. No safe place to leave packs during the day. Student ID required. £2 per night. Arrive 10pm-midnight; leave by 10am.

Halls of Residence

While not rock-bottom cheap, university dormitories are better equipped than similarly-priced hotels. Most have space only during the summer (mid-July through Sept.) and are good places to scout for single rooms. Write to the Bursar in advance.

King's College, part of the University of London, controls summer bookings for the first seven halls listed below. They include continental breakfast, cooking and laundry facilities, and have no curfew. Singles cost £16 from July-Sept., £14 during the off-season (Easter inclusive) at the first four halls listed below. The other three halls cost £12.50 per night year-round because they're less central. A £5 deposit is required for each week reserved.

Lightfoot Hall, Manresa Rd., SW3 (tel. 351 24 88). Tube: Sloane Square or South Kensington. From South Kensington, take bus #14 or 49, or simply walk toward the Thames. Great location just off King's Rd. Rooms are institutional, but pleasant.

Queen Elizabeth Hall, Campden Hill Rd., W8 (tel. 937 54 11 ext. 255). Tube: High Street Kensington. Walk north 1 block from the Tube station. By far the nicest of the 7 King's College halls. In a timelessly quaint location.

Wellington Hall, Vincent Sq., Westminster, SW1 (tel. 837 47 40). Tube: Victoria. From Tube station walk 1 long block along Vauxhall Bridge Rd. to Rochester Row to Vincent Sq.

Ingram Court, 552 King's Rd. (tel. 351 24 88). Tube: Fulham Broadway, then 10-min. walk. One of the most popular halls. Green lawn with pond in the middle. No charge for use of tennis courts. Laundry facilities.

King's College Hall, Champion Hill, SE5 (tel. 733 21 66). Britrail to Denmark Hill. Out of the way.

Halliday Hall, 64-67 Southside Clapham Common, SW4 (tel. 673 20 32). Tube: Clapham. Also out of the way.

Malcolm Gavin Hall, Beachcroft Rd., SW17 (tel. 767 31 19). Tube: Tooting Bec. Not London's nicest neighborhood.

John Adams Hall, 15-23 Endsleigh St., WC1 (tel. 387 47 96), off Tavistock Square. Tube: Euston Square. Elegant London University building; some rooms have small balconies overlooking street. Most rooms are singles. Laundry facilities, TV lounge, Ping-Pong table, and quiet reading room. English breakfast included. The 3-course dinner (£4) is unappetizing. Open at Easter time and July to mid-Aug. Book well in advance, then confirm in writing; usually no deposit required. Singles £12.65, doubles £21.27. Reception open Mon.-Fri. 8am-1pm and 2-11pm, Sat.-Sun. 9am-1:30pm and 5:30-10pm.

Passfield Hall, 1 Endsleigh Pl., WC1 (tel. 387 35 84 or 387 77 43). Tube: Euston. London School of Economics hall in a green area around the corner from John Adams Hall. A real party because of the large number of long-term residents. Rooms vary tremendously in size, but all have high ceilings and desks. Laundry and cooking facilities. Singles £11, doubles £18. Open July-Sept. (rooms scarce July and early Aug.), Christmas (mid-Dec. to mid-Jan.), and 1 month around Easter.

International Lutheran Student Centre, 30 Thanet St., WC1 (tel. 388 40 44 or 388 48 21). Tube: King's Cross/St. Pancras. Kitchen and dining room on each floor. Laundry room and 2 nice TV rooms. Elevator service. Most rooms available July-Aug. only. Singles £9.30 per night, £44.78 per week. Doubles £8.80 per person per night, £42 per person per week. Non-students pay 10% more. English breakfast included.

Queen Alexandra's House, Kensington Gore, SW7 (tel. 589 36 35 or 589 40 53), on southwest corner of Albert Hall, near Kensington Gardens. Tube: South Kensington. Women only. Ornate and intriguing Victorian building. Extremely welcoming, and run with a touch of class. Cozy rooms full of character (some with window seats). Kitchen and laundry facilities, sitting room, and sunny dining hall. Singles £12.50. English breakfast. Rooms available July 1-Aug. 21; reservations suggested for long stays.

International Student House, 229 Great Portland St., NW1 (tel. 631 32 23), at the foot of Regents Park. Tube: Great Portland Street. A thriving metropolis, with its own films, discos, study-groups, expeditions, parties, and mini-market. 300 beds in doubles and singles, 43 flats. Singles £12.30, doubles £20.60, triples £34.

Methodist International House, 4 Inverness Terrace (tel. 229 51 01), just north of Kensington Gardens. Tube: Bayswater. Christian orientation, but it's open to all. Slightly faded rooms are big, clean, and comfortable, with solid furniture. Lots of regulations, but friendly. Laundry facilities. Singles £13.25 per night, £82 per week; doubles £24.50 per night, £150 per week; triples and quads £11.20 per person, £68 per person per week. £10 key deposit. Breakfast and dinner included. Open July-early Sept.

Bed and Breakfast Hotels

The number of B&Bs in London is staggering, but most are about as distinct as blades of grass, providing functional facilities, a TV lounge, and indifferent service, and often congregating in slightly tawdry areas. It may be wisest to choose simply on the basis of location. Scan the neighborhood descriptions below for a general idea.

Victoria and Earl's Court

These areas represent the bargain basement of budget B&Bs—with the emphasis on base. Near Victoria Station, patrol Belgrave Road, St. George's Drive, or Warwick Way for unimpressive but acceptable lodging at around £10-16 per person (more for singles). Earl's Court is even less tranquil. Penywern Road and Earl's Court Square are good areas to try for prices comparable to Victoria. The following suggestions stand out for quality and/or price.

The Beaver Hotel, 57-59 Philbeach Gardens, SW5 (tel. 373 45 53). Ward and June would be comfortable here, despite small rooms and a TV lounge straight off a *Dark Shadows* set. Lots of groups, but quiet. English breakfast. Singles £17, doubles £26, with bath £36, triples (none have baths) £32. Parking £2 per day.

Windsor House Hotel, 12 Penywern Rd., SW5 (tel. 373 90 87). Clean. Glows with funkadelic paint. Singles £15, doubles £22, triples £30, quads £40. May have cheap dorm rooms come winter. Reception open 24 hours.

Merlyn Court Hotel, 2 Barkston Gardens (tel. 370 16 40). A cut above the rest in the area—light and pleasant, with high Victorian ceilings. Overlooks a quiet garden. Owner's golden retriever is a sweetheart. Singles £18-22, doubles £27-32. Shares £10 per person in 4-bed room, but you must be traveling with your roommates.

London Tourist Hotel, 15 Penywern Rd., SW5 (tel. 370 43 56). Quiet and clean, but a little worn. Garden in back. Obliging, soft-spoken manager brightens considerably if you mention Maine or Massachusetts. Continental breakfast with eggs. Singles £15, with shower £19; doubles with shower £28. In winter, 7 nights for the price of 6.

York House Hotel, 28 Philbeach Gardens, SW5 (tel. 373 75 19), on a quiet crescent. Not posh, but not ratty either. Efficient management. TV lounge. Singles £15, doubles £25, triples £33, quads £36. Reduced rates in winter. English breakfast included.

Kensington and Chelsea

The Royal Borough of Kensington and Chelsea is awfully nice and thus not a haven for budget B&Bs. The odd exceptions to this rule are particularly pleasant, though.

Vicarage Hotel, 10 Vicarage Gate, W8 (tel. 229 40 30). Tube: High Street Kensington. Dignified, friendly, newly renovated, and very clean. A cozy TV lounge, with cushions and old photographs. Around the corner from Kensington Palace. On a sidestreet with minimal traffic. Singles £16.50, doubles £29.50, triples £36, quads £42. English breakfast included.

Abbey House Hotel, 11 Vicarage Gate, W8 (tel. 727 25 94). Tube: High Street Kensington. Guests return year after year, drawn by ebullient innkeepers, a superb location, and an English breakfast without par. Recently renovated rooms are as grand as the entrance hall. All rooms have color TV. Singles £18, doubles £30, triples £40, quads £48. To reserve a room, call 1 week in advance or send a personal check for the first night.

North of Hyde Park

Squashed between Paddington Station, Hyde Park, and Kensington, this area is crowded with sad, slightly decrepit B&Bs. There is hardly a building in Norfolk Square and Sussex Gardens that does not proclaim itself a hotel. Talbot Square and Princes Square are similar hunting grounds. As you travel west, the hotels become less seedy and more serene.

Coleman Lodge Hotel, 32 Craven Hill Gardens, W2 (tel. 723 59 88 or 402 14 57). Tube: Bayswater. Not as attractive as the Rena next door, but overlooks the same peaceful square. Cooking facilities and bar. Singles £15; doubles £20, with shower £26; triples £9 per person; quads £8.50 per person.

Rena Hotel, 34 Craven Hill Gardens, W2 (tel. 723 35 25). Tube: Bayswater or Queensway. Clean, pleasant, and friendly, with kitchen. Singles £15, doubles £18, triples £9 per person, quads £8.50 per person. Extra for rooms with private shower.

Leinster Hotel Group, 7-11 Leinster Sq., W2 (tel. 229 96 41). Tube: Bayswater. Looks like a lost Holiday Inn, and caters largely to groups. Rooms are basic, but pleasant and clean; some discounts on long-term stays. Singles £13, doubles £24, triples £34, quads £46.50. Private bath or shower £3 extra. Continental breakfast.

Lords Hotel, 20-22 Leinster Sq., W2 (tel. 229 88 77). Tube: Bayswater. Well kept, with more character, but less friendly management than the Leinster. Halls have high ceilings: basic rooms are clean and pretty, some with balconies. Singles £14, with shower £17.50; doubles £21, with shower £23. Continental breakfast.

Talbot Hotel, Talbot Sq., W2 (tel. 402 72 03) Tube: Paddington. No English breakfast; no breakfast at all in fact, but you'd be hard pressed to find cheaper singles. Singles £9 per night, £56 per week; doubles £15, shares £7. £5 key deposit.

Bloomsbury

Bloomsbury remains unusually gracious, diverting, and often surprising, exempt from the bustle and chaos of central London. For a couple of extra pounds, lodgings near the British Museum put you within walking distance of Soho, Piccadilly, and The City. Lots of comfortable hotels in the range of £15-20 per person line Gower Street, though you should ask for a room away from the busy thoroughfare. Cartwright Gardens is a step up in price and comfort. Elegant Bedford Place is the nicest street in the area. The farther north and east in Bloomsbury, the less charming the accommodations.

Jesmond Hotel, 63 Gower St., WC1 (tel. 636 31 99). Cozy, clean rooms. Welcoming owners. TV lounge. Singles £17, doubles £26, triples £35. Tasty English breakfast included.

Gower House, 57 Gower St., WC1 (tel. 636 46 85). Carpeting neither worn, mildewed, nor plaid (what a difference!). Singles £18, doubles £28, triples £39, quads £48. English breakfast included. Deposits (non-refundable) paid by personal check are accepted if they arrive well before you do.

Hotel Crichton, 36 Bedford Pl., WC1 (tel. 637 39 55 or 637 39 57). Roomier than most, with color TV and telephones in every room. Many rooms overlook a quiet green yard. Singles from £20, doubles £33.50, triples £39.50. Good English breakfast included.

St. Margaret's Hotel, 26 Bedford Pl., WC1 (tel. 636 42 77 or 580 23 52). Classy and spiffy—fresh daisies on breakfast tables, small but elegant rooms. Competent and friendly management. Worth the extra pence. Singles £22.50, doubles £34.50, triples £45, quads £60. To book in advance, send personal check for first night; U.S. dollars OK.

Camping

Camping in London is not the smartest idea—for one thing, you won't be *in* London. The time and cost involved in shuttling in and out might be better spent on a cheap (and rain-proof) hostel. If you're determined to rough it, check the options below. For other suggestions and information on tent rental, contact the Victoria Station tourist office.

Hackney Camping, Millfields Rd., Hackney Marshes, E5 (tel. 985 76 56). Bus #38 or 55 from Victoria via Piccadilly Circus, or bus #22 from Piccadilly Circus. A wide expanse of flat green lawn in the midst of London's rundown East End. Luggage storage, cafe, laundry facilities. No caravans. £1.60 per person plus tent, 60p per car. Open June-Aug. 8am-11:45pm.

Tent City, Old Oak Common Lane, W3 (tel. 743 57 08). Tube: East Acton, or take bus #7 from Oxford Circus or Tottenham Court Rd., or bus #177 from Waterloo Station. Former army tents, each filled with 30 or more bunk beds. Also space for visitors with tents. Laundry facilities, baggage lock-up, snack bar. £3 per person. Open June-Sept. daily 24 hours.

Food

London offers a tantalizing range of both foreign and English specialties. With Indian, Lebanese, Greek, Chinese, Thai, Italian, West Indian, African, and American food readily available and relatively inexpensive, the city has few rivals when it comes to diversity.

If you taste no other foreign cuisine while in London, eat an Indian meal (consisting of *mulligatawny* soup; *keema nan,* partially leavened bread stuffed with minced meat; *tandoori,* or curried beef, lamb, or chicken; and *pilau,* rice). You don't have to look far for an Indian restaurant, but meals are £1-3 cheaper on Westbourne Grove between Queensway and Hereford Rd. (Tube: Bayswater) than in Piccadilly and Covent Garden.

Afternoon tea is a long-standing British tradition. Avoid the touristy places that announce "Devon cream teas"—head instead for the authentic and expensive all-you-can-eat pastry tea at **Harrod's** (£5.50; Tube: Knightsbridge), the elegant sandwich and pastry repast on the Promenade at the **Dorchester Hotel** (£6.50; Tube: Marble Arch), or the scone and sandwich spread at **Liberty's** (£4-6; Tube: Bond Street). All are offered around 3:45-5:30pm.

If you are making your own meals, try supermarkets instead of little corner shops; they're cheaper. **Safeway** stores are on King's Rd., Edgeware Rd. (not too far from Paddington), and in the Brunswick Shopping Centre opposite the Russell Square Tube stop. **Sainsbury** has a branch on Victoria Rd., not far from Victoria Station. **Apollo Food** stores are expensive but they stay open until 11pm, with branches at Victoria, Charing Cross, and Tottenham Court Road.

Victoria, Kensington, and Chelsea

Chelsea Kitchen, 98 King's Rd. Tube: Sloane Square. Our readers rave about this place, and with good reason. Cheap, filling, artsy restaurant frequented by Sloanes (English preppies, more or less). You can easily eat lunch for £2, dinner for £3. Open Mon.-Sat. 8am-11:45pm, Sun. 11:30am-11:45pm.

Chelsea Pot, 356 King's Rd. Tube: Sloane Square. Same great value as the Chelsea Kitchen. Chicken cacciatora or baked gammon (ham) steak for under £3. Open daily noon-11:30pm.

Luba's Bistro, 6 Yeoman's Row. Tube: Knightsbridge, a few blocks down from Harrod's. Big portions of Russian specialties £3-5. BYOB. Open Mon.-Sat. noon-3pm and 6pm-midnight.

Bamboo Kitchen, 305 King's Rd. at Beaufort St. Tube: Sloane Square. Cheap Chinese take-away; no seating. *Chow mein* or curry with fried rice £2.30. Open Mon.-Sat. noon-11:30pm, Sun. 5-11:30pm.

Texas Lone Star Café, 154 Gloucester Rd. Texas re-created in London: nachos, entree, and a Lone Star (the official beer of Texas) £7; £2.95 minimum after 7pm. Very popular with U.S. expatriates and some lost Londoners. Open Mon.-Sat. noon-11:45pm, Sun. noon-11:30pm.

Hard Rock Café, 150 Old Park Lane. Tube: Hyde Park Corner. Jimi Hendrix's guitar hangs over the bar in this veritable rock museum. High-quality burger, fries, and shake £6-7. Arrive before 5pm to reduce wait.

North of Hyde Park

Khan's, 13-15 Westbourne Grove. Tube: Bayswater. Most Indian restaurants are cemetery quiet, but not Khan's. Great *tandoori.* Good-sized meals £2.50-6.50. Try the *keema nan* (Indian bread stuffed with minced meat). Open daily noon-3pm and 6pm-midnight.

Geale's, 2 Farmer St. Tube: Notting Hill Gate. Efficient service, nice rustic atmosphere, and consummately crisp fish and chips from £2.80. Often a wait—sit it out in the bar upstairs. Open Tues.-Fri. noon-3pm and 6-11:30pm, Sat. noon-3pm and 6-11pm.

Tootsie's, 115 Notting Hill Gate. Tube: Notting Hill Gate. Excellent burgers (£2.40-3.90), chips, ice cream, and coffee. Open Mon.-Sat. noon-midnight, Sun. noon-11:30pm.

Notting Hill Coffee House, 215 Kensington Church St. Tube: Notting Hill Gate. No-nonsense food. Welsh rarebit £1.10, cod fillet with fries £2.50. Open daily 8am-8pm.

Kremps American Pasta Joint, 80 Heath St. Tube: Hampstead. As much as you can eat in one hour of 9 different types of pasta (£3.20). Open Mon.-Fri. 6-11:30pm, Sat. noon-12:30am, Sun. noon-11:30pm.

Bloomsbury and Northeast

The Fryer's Delight, 19 Theobald's Rd. Tube: Holborn. One of the best chippies around, so it's always crowded with Londoners. Fish or chicken with chips £2. Popular with British Library scholars. Open Mon.-Sat. noon-11pm.

Conduit Coffee House, 61 Lamb's Conduit. Tube: Russell Square. Cute 6-table coffee house. Good breakfast or cheap take-away sandwiches (40-80p). Breakfast 95p-£1.50, lunch £1.60-2.50. Open Mon.-Fri. 7am-5:30pm.

Great Nepalese Restaurant, 48 Eversholt St. Tube: Euston. They're right; great. Huge dinner of *mulligatawny* soup, *keema nan,* and curried chicken, lamb, or beef for under £5.50. Nepalese pop plays in the background. Ask for Govind as your waiter—he's all smiles. Open daily noon-3pm and 6-11:45pm.

Cranks Health Foods, 9-11 Tottenham St. Tube: Goodge Street. Large portions of excellent food served in a bright, cheerful room. Many choices £1.25-1.75, large salad £2.85. Open Mon.-Fri. 8am-8pm, Sat. 9am-8pm.

Quack's Wholefood and Take-Away, 33 Theobald's Rd. Tube: Holborn. Daily vegetarian specials. Stuffed eggplant £1, high-protein pizza 80p, tofu burgers 50p, and delicious fruit breads (honey-apricot) 50p. Open Mon.-Fri. 8am-6pm.

The Gurka, 23 Warren St. Tube: Warren Street. Tempting treats from Nepal. *Thurpa* (hot noodle soup) and *nan* (potato and herb bread) make great starters at 85p; mutton *moghlai* or lamb *karahi* £3.25. Open daily noon-2:45pm and 6-11:45pm. Other location: 339 Euston Rd. (Tube: Euston).

My Old Dutch Pancake House, 131-132 High Holborn St. Tube: Holborn. 101 varieties of giant Dutch pancakes, thinly cooked, with a 1½-ft. diameter. Popular toppings include ham, chicken, salami, and curry. £2-4. Open daily noon-midnight.

Diwana Bhel Poori House, 121 Drummond St. Tube: Warren Street. Quick, slick, and tasty Indian vegetarian food in a clean and airy restaurant. Try *samosas* or *thali* (an assortment of vegetables, rices, sauces, breads, and desserts made to be shared). Meals £2.50-4. BYOB. Open daily noon-11pm. Another branch at 50 Westbourne Grove (Tube: Bayswater). **Gupta Confectioners,** across the street at 100 Drummond St., has tongue-teasing take-away sweets and savories at ½ the sit-down price. Open Mon.-Sat. 11am-7pm, Sun. noon-7pm.

The City of London and the West End

Blooms, 90 Whitechapel High St. Tube: Aldgate East. London's finest kosher restaurant, with good salt (corned) beef and chopped liver sandwiches (£1.20-2.10). Popular on Sun. mornings. Open Sun.-Thurs. 11am-10pm, Fri. 11am-3pm.

Stockpot Restaurant, 40 Panton St. Tube: Piccadilly. Both floors always packed because of delicious food at rock-bottom prices. Salads with salmon, smoked mackerel, or chicken £1.50-2. Try their tasty chicken madras and scrumptious hot custard puddings. A great meal for less than £2.70. Open Mon.-Sat. 8am-11:30pm, Sun. noon-10pm. Additional locations: 50 James St. (Tube: Bond Street or Marble Arch), open Mon.-Sat. 11am-10:30pm; 6 Basil St., near Harrod's (Tube: Knightsbridge), open Mon.-Sat. 11:30am-10:30pm.

Fatso's Pasta Joint, 13 Old Compton St. Tube: Leicester Square or Tottenham Court Road. All you can eat of 1 of 9 types of pasta with 1 of 11 kinds of sauce for £2.60. No time limit, but deal only good Sun.-Thurs. Fast-beat pop music keeps your fork twirling. A young crowd packs this place. Open Mon.-Thurs. noon-midnight, Fri.-Sat. noon-1am, Sun. noon-10:30pm.

Food For Thought, 31 Neal St. in Neal's Yd. Tube: Covent Garden. Perennial line at noon for a very good reason. Generous servings of vegetarian food straight from the pot in a tiny downstairs restaurant with plants everywhere. Sweetcorn chowder (£1), layered lentil roast with apple sauce (£1.50). £2.50 will fill you up. Take-away after 3pm. Open Mon.-Fri. noon-8pm.

Diana's Diner, 39 Endell St. Tube: Covent Garden or Tottenham Court Road. Huge servings of typical English fuel food: eggs, bacon, toast, steak and kidney pie, and vegetables. Everything homemade. Breakfast about £1.75, lunch £2-4, take-away lunch £1.50-3. Vegetarian specialties daily. Outdoor seating during summer. Open Mon.-Fri. 7:30am-7pm, Sat. 9am-2pm.

Porter's, 17 Henrietta St. Tube: Covent Garden. It's delightful, it's delicious, and it destroys your budget. But worth a splurge to taste how fine British food *can* be. Huge assortment of lovely hot pies with traditional crusts (turkey-chestnut, steak-mushroom, lamb-apricot, fish). All £3.50. Roast beef and Yorkshire pudding lunch on Sat. and Sun. £4.25 (£3 minimum). Open Mon.-Sat. noon-3pm and 5-11:30pm, Sun. 5:30-10:30pm.

Pubs

"Would that I were an alehouse in London! I would give all my fame for a pot of ale."
—Shakespeare, Henry V, Act III

London's 700 pubs are as colorful and historic as their counterparts in the country, but in London the clientele varies widely from one neighborhood to the next. Avoid pubs within a half mile of train stations. They prey upon naïve tourists by charging 20-40p extra for an ale. For the best pub prices, head to the East End or, better yet, head south of the Thames. Not only do pints cost under £1, but dancing and loud bursts of drunken laughter are not uncommon.

Many London pubs offer a choice of as many as a dozen ales and two ciders—all are similarly potent. A few pints of cider and you'll be bronze and list (drunk), as the cockneys say. Don't overlook pubs as a source of sustenance: They offer cheap, standard British fare.

In 1987, Parliament repealed a 1915 liquor law requiring English pubs to close from 3-6pm. This means that pubs are now open daily 11am-1am. Cheers!

Dirty Dick's, 202-204 Bishopgate. Tube: Liverpool Street. Pub "decorated" with cobwebs and stuffed cats. Not comforting to know that Jack the Ripper stalked these streets.

Museum Tavern, 49 Great Russell St. Tube: Tottenham Court Road. A scholar's pub directly opposite the British Museum. The Star Tavern which formerly occupied this site was a rendezvous for some of Casanova's exploits. 13 beers on tap.

Sherlock Holmes, 10 Northumberland St. Tube: Charing Cross. A replica of Holmes's den at 221B Baker St. Relics include the head of the *Hound of the Baskervilles.*

The Three Kings, North End Rd., next to West Kensington Tube station. Dubbed "the real ale capital of the world" by some of its more enthusiastic patrons. Lively and fun.

Saint Stephen's, 10 Bridge St. Tube: Westminster. Members of Parliament down ales here until a bell is rung to call them back to vote.

Ye Olde Cheshire Cheese, 145 Fleet St. Samuel Johnson's old stomping ground. Now "sinister street" journalists' favorite watering hole. Sawdust on the floor changed twice daily.

Prospect of Whitby, 57 Wapping Wall, London Docks. Tube: Tower Hill, then walk east along the Thames. 600-year-old tavern where diarist Samuel Pepys used to imbibe. American and English jazz groups every Tues.-Sun. night.

Elephant and Castle, South Lambert Place. Tube: Elephant and Castle. Nightly drag shows. Comfortable open-air drinking.

Sights

London is a city of walkers. Some sights are (relatively) isolated, but most can be seen on an easy wander around the city. Beware of yielding to London Transport's unlimited travel tickets—you don't see anything from the Tube, and even the double-decker buses—a sight in themselves—can't substitute for on-foot explorations.

A particularly rewarding walk can start from Piccadilly Circus and its infamous statue of Eros. **Piccadilly Road** is lined with exclusive shops, including **Fortnum and Mason,** long famous for its extraordinary food hampers and morning-suited clerks. A proper English tea is served upstairs, while downstairs is an American soda bar straight out of the 1920s. Almost across the street is the **Royal Academy of Arts,** where you should be prepared for anything. During the Summer Exhibition, spectators vote for their favorites among the previous year's art. (Open daily 10am-6pm. Admission £2.60, students £1.75.) A little farther along the street is **Green**

Park, so named for the absence of flower beds. Follow any of its paths across miniature meadow and woodlands; they all converge at **Buckingham Palace.** (Check at the tourist office, as the Changing of the Guard occurs at different times in different seasons.)

The Mall is the wide, processional road that leads from the Palace up to **Admiralty Arch** and Trafalgar Square. To its right are the lovely gardens of **St. James's Park,** complete with pelicans. Tourists and pigeons crowd **Trafalgar Square** where the great stone lions appear unperturbed. The **National Gallery,** on the square to the left, has one of the best collections of European painting in the world. Da Vinci's *Virgin of the Rocks* and Velázquez's *The Toilet of Venus* are here. (Open Mon.-Sat. 10am-6pm, Sun. 2-6pm. Free.) The **National Portrait Gallery** is on Charing Cross Rd., tucked behind this enormous edifice—many English schoolchildren learn their history in this crammed panorama of public personalities. (Open Mon.-Fri. 10am-5pm, Sat. 10am-6pm, Sun. 2-6pm. Free.) **Charing Cross Road** is itself famous for bookshops, and leads into the theater district of **Leicester Square.**

To the right of Trafalgar Sq. is **Whitehall,** where you'll find many of London's political monuments. **Downing Street,** home of the Prime Minister, is on the right, and in the middle of the road is the **Cenotaph,** a monument to Britain's war dead and site of the annual Remembrance Sunday service. Whitehall ends at **Parliament Square,** home of Big Ben, Westminster Abbey, and the sprawling Houses of Parliament. To watch bicameralism in action—debates are noisy and lively—contact your embassy or tourist office about obtaining a pass, or join the long lines. (The waiting list list at the U.S. Embassy in the summer of 1987 was 1 month long.) Strictly speaking, **Big Ben** is neither the tower nor the clock, but the 13½-ton bell, cast while a similarly proportioned Sir Benjamin Hall served as Commissioner of Works. Church and state tie the knot in **Westminster Abbey,** coronation chamber to English monarchs for the past 682 years, also site of Poet's Corner and the Tomb of the Unknown Soldier. Be sure to ask the story surrounding the Stone of Scone—although paying the extra fees to see the coronation throne is a dubious investment. (Westminster Abbey open Mon.-Fri. 9am-4pm, Sat. 9am-2pm and 3:45-5:45pm. Free; to see royal chapels, Coronation Chair, and Poet's Corner £1.50, students 75p. All parts of abbey free Wed. 6-7:45pm. Photography permitted Wed. 6-7:45pm only.) Abbey Guided Super Tours are excellent. They depart from the Enquiry Desk in the nave Mon.-Fri. at 10am, 11am, 2pm, 2:30pm, and 3pm. Tours cost £3.50. To book, inquire at the desk, call 222 51 52, or write to Super Tours, 20 Dean's Yd., London SW1P 3PA.

Along the river on Millbank, the **Tate Gallery** houses the best of British art—Blake, Constable, Gainsborough, Turner, Hogarth, the Pre-Raphaelites—plus such modern favorites as Picasso, Dalí, Chagall, Arp, and Mondrian. (Open Mon.-Sat. 10am-6pm, Sun. 2-6pm. Free.) The Tate is about ½ mile up the Thames from Parliament Square.

Sundays from 11am to dusk is the best time to hear soapbox orators at **Speaker's Corner** (Tube: Marble Arch), but **Hyde Park** is relaxing on any day. Pick up an ice cream from one of the vendors by the **Serpentine,** or stroll over to **Kensington Gardens**—an elegant reminder of Edwardian England—for model yacht racing at its best. When the nearby **Albert Memorial** was unveiled it was considered a great artistic achievement, but early in this century the cluttered monument became the symbol of all that was unacceptable about Victoria's reign. The **Royal Albert Hall,** across the street, resembles nothing so much as an older woman's pudding bowl hat, complete with lace trim. Just around the corner, Exhibition Road contains the **Science Museum;** the **Natural History Museum,** where dinosaurs stand tall; and the **Victoria and Albert Museum,** which has been described as "the nation's attic"—ask where the original Winnie-the-Pooh is on display. (Science and Natural History Museums open Mon.-Sat. 10am-6pm, Sun. 2:30-6pm. Joint admission £2.50, students £1.20. Free Mon.-Fri. 4:30-6pm, Sat.-Sun. 5-6pm. Victoria and Albert Museum open Mon.-Thurs. and Sat. 10am-5:50pm, Sun. 2:30-5:45pm. Free.)

The **City of London** is an enclave unto itself; its boundaries are guarded by small and snarling silver griffins. The **Tower of London** has a fascinating history and the

Beefeaters are all blessed with the gift of storytelling. (Tube: Tower Hill. Open March-Oct. Mon.-Sat. 9:30am-5pm, Sun. 2-5pm; Nov.-Feb. Mon.-Sat. 9:30am-4pm. Admission includes all Tower sights, including the Crown Jewels. Adults £4, children £2, ages under 5 free.) Throughout the City are scattered other pieces of history, among them the **Temple of Mithras** on Victoria St., and 24 Christopher Wren churches interspersed with the stone and steel of modern skyscrapers. Look into some smaller churches, such as The Strand's **St. Clement Danes** of "Oranges and Lemons . . . " fame or **St. Magnus Mary** on lower Thames St., and then head for Wren's masterpiece, **St. Paul's Cathedral.** Be sure to visit the graves of Wren, Nelson, and Wellington in the crypt; from there it's a dizzying climb to the top of the dome, which offers a good view. (Open Mon.-Fri. 10am-4:15pm, Sat. 11am-4:15pm. Admission to church nave 85p, to ambulatory 50p, to crypt 75p, to galleries 90p. Guided 90-min. tours Mon.-Sat. at 11am, 11:30am, 2pm and 2:30pm. Tours cost £4.) The City has been ravaged by plague, destroyed by the Great Fire of 1666, rebuilt according to the designs of Sir Christopher Wren, demolished by the Blitz in 1940, and rebuilt again along corporate lines. The **Museum of London,** which is constantly adding to its collection, can fill you in on the whole story. (Open Tues.-Sat. 10am-6pm, Sun. 2-6pm.)

Covent Garden—historic meeting place of Henry Higgins and Eliza Doolittle—still has its grand opera house, but much of the wonderfully tattered old market has been transformed into a characterless and expensive shopping center. Nearby **Soho** is a chaotic jumble of the exotic and the tacky, a maze of porno palaces punctuated by restaurants and shops. Sequestered to the north is **Bloomsbury**—eccentric, erudite, disorganized, and serene. The area is known for its literary (Virginia Woolf et al.) and educational (the University of London) connections. Here is the **British Museum,** displaying the Empire's plunder and treasures: the Rosetta Stone, the Elgin marbles, thousands of manuscripts (including *Beowulf* and a *Magna Carta*), and the world's oldest mummy. Karl Marx studied in the Reading Room. (Open Mon.-Sat. 10am-5pm, Sun. 2:30-6pm. Free.)

Fleet Street is home to most members of the British press; close by are the **Inns of Court,** which have controlled access to the English bar since the thirteenth century. Across the green from Lincoln's Inn is the fantastically cluttered **Sir John Soane Museum,** 13 Lincoln's Inn Fields (tel. 405 21 07), which brings Holbeins, an ancient Egyptian sarcophagus, and much more under one roof. (Open Tues.-Sat. 10am-5pm. Lecture tour Sat. at 2:30pm. Free.) Across the park is the **London School of Economics** and **Dickens's Old Curiosity Shop** (Tube: Holborn).

If your feet begin to ache, then hop on the **Culture Bus** (tel. 629 49 99), which loops around major London sights all day long. There are 37 stops; passengers get on and off wherever they please. Buses run every 30 minutes during the week and every 20 minutes on weekends. You can board at any stop. (1-day ticket £4, ages under 16 £2. 3-day ticket £8, ages under 16 £4. One-day tickets purchased after 1pm can be used for all of the following day.)

The above paragraphs, of course, can barely scratch the surface of London. For a more comprehensive treatment of the city's offerings, invest in a copy of *Let's Go: Britain and Ireland. Nicholson's Student London* (£1.75) and *Nicholson's Visitor's London* (80p) are both useful, as is Nicholas Saunders's *Alternative London* (£3.50).

Entertainment

For guidance through London's amazing cultural network, consult *Time Out* or *City Limits* (both 80p-£1). These have exhaustive and entertaining listings on every type of activity, from opera to political meetings to jogging clubs.

Theater in London is generally excellent and runs the gamut from West End to fringe, lunchtime, open-air, and children's productions. Seats can cost as little as £1.50, and student standby puts even the best seats within reach. An "S" or "concessions" in the theater listings of *Time Out, City Limits,* the *Guardian,* or the *Evening Standard* means that unsold tickets will be sold to students for £3-4 just before the performance. It's wise to arrive early, though—lines often start forming an hour or so in advance. For performances in the **National Theatre,** on South Bank (tel. 928 22 52; Tube: Embankment), standby tickets (£4.50-5.50) go on sale at 10am on the day of performance. Ask about the excellent backstage tours. The **Barbican Centre** (tel. 628 22 95 or 628 97 60; Tube: Barbican or Moorgate), the London home of the Royal Shakespeare Company, takes part in the student program, offering tickets for £5-13.50. The **Leicester Square Ticket Booth** on Leicester Sq. sells half-price tickets to selected plays on the day of the performance. (Mon.-Sat. noon-2pm for matinees, 2:30-6:30pm for evening performances; get in line early. £1 booking fee.) Some of the major theaters, including the **Aldwych** and the **Royal Court,** maintain a "fringe" stage to encourage experimental works and new artists. Watch for productions at the **Young Vic,** the **Triangle,** and the **Lyric** theaters, as well as at the **Institute of Contemporary Arts.** From July through October, Regent's Park has open-air Shakespeare productions (tel. 486 24 31; Tube: Baker Street). Tickets run £5-10, student standby tickets £4 one hour before performance. Ring and check on availability before heading to theater. Avoid ticket agencies; they take 20% commission.

Few cities rival London's musical preeminence and diversity. Most of its classical music is staged at the acoustically refined **Royal Festival Hall** and at its smaller siblings, the **Queen Elizabeth Hall,** the **Purcell Room,** the **Barbican Hall,** and at the small, elegant **Wigmore Hall. Kenwood House** and the **Crystal Palace Concert Bowl** have low-priced outdoor concerts on summer weekends; Kenwood is particularly beautiful. Many churches sponsor free concerts. Opera is performed at **Covent Garden** and the **London Coliseum.** The Coliseum and **Sadler's Wells** are the homes of London's premier ballet companies. The **Proms** (Henry Woods Promenade Concerts), held nightly mid-July through mid-September, are the most popular and endearing feature of the London music scene. The orchestras and soloists are first-rate, and lining up for long hours for standing room in the gallery and arena of the Royal Albert Hall has been a cult phenomenon among young Londoners for almost a century. The foyer of the **National Theatre** on South Bank always has a varied schedule of free concerts—everything from Irish folk to John Cage. You can order drinks from the bar and enjoy a great view of the Thames; you don't need a theater ticket to get into the foyer. All the big names in rock come through London at some point or another. Ticket offices and record shops have full listings of concerts.

Ronnie Scott's, 47 Frith St. (tel. 439 07 47; Tube: Leicester Square), is London's most famous jazz club. (Open Mon.-Sat. 8:30pm-3am, music 9:30pm-2am. Admission £10.) **The Marquee,** 90 Wardour St. (tel. 437 66 03; Tube: Piccadilly), helped Mick Jagger and company get started, but punk rock now dominates the scene. (Open daily 7-11pm. Admission £4-7, sometimes free, student rates available.) **The Rock Garden,** 6-7 Piazza, Covent Garden (tel. 240 39 61; Tube: Covent Garden), features local rockers nightly. U2, the Talking Heads, and the Police played here before hitting stardom. (Open Mon.-Sat. 8pm-3am, Sun. 8pm-12:30am. Admission Sun.-Thurs. £3, Fri.-Sat. £5.) The **Hippodrome,** Charing Cross Rd. (tel. 437 43 11; Tube: Leicester Square), does a wild light show with a deafening sound system. Mon. is gay night. (Open Mon.-Sat. 9pm-3am. Admission Mon.-Thurs. £6, Fri.-Sat. £10.) The **Camden Palace** disco, 1A Camden Rd. (tel. 387 04 28; Tube: Camden Town), draws a more British crowd. The palace is an ornate theater converted into a disco. Two huge stuffed acrobats—one male, one female—swing overhead. Surprisingly, the dancers below remain oblivious to the antics overhead. (Open Mon.-Sat. 8:30pm-3am. Admission Mon.-Thurs. £4, Fri.-Sat. £5.) **Heaven,** Villiers St. (tel. 839 38 52; Tube: Charing Cross), is possibly one of the best gay discos in Europe, but it admits only men. (Open Tues.-Fri. 10:15pm-late, Sat. 10:30pm-very late. Tues. and Fri. are for club members only. Admission Tues.-Fri. £3.50, Sat. £4.50-5.50. Free admission Fri. before midnight.) *Time Out* and *City Limits* list music by club and by type, and include a brief review of the place and the artist.

During late June and early July, half of London goes to **Wimbledon** (Tube: Southfields). Admission to the grounds costs £5 (£3 after 5pm); an important tennis match costs as much as £13. Lines are very long, and finals matches are sold out ages in advance. In the middle of June, a sort of pre-Wimbledon goes on at **Queen's Club,** Palliser Rd. (tel. 385 34 21; Tube: Barons Court). Seats are easier to obtain there. Football (i.e. soccer) is a rowdy, raucous, religious obsession in Britain. Should you decide to attend a match, buy a seat ticket, since the "terraces," where the faithful stand, often break out in violence. Tournament matches are played at **Wembley;** half a dozen other fields are scattered around the city, all accessible by Tube. (**Arsenal F.C.,** Tube: Arsenal; **Chelsea F.C.,** Tube: Fulham Broadway; **Tottenham Hotspur F.C.,** Tube: oops—ask at the tourist office.) The Valhalla of rugby is **Twickenham.** A day at **Lord's** or the **Oval** will expose you to the ritualized quality of cricket; games last three to five days, and *are* more exciting than watching grass grow.

Near London

The transport system that encouraged London's urban sprawl now makes it easy to escape the urban scene. **Highgate** and **Hampstead Heath** are both on the underground lines—if Hyde Park seemed a small bit of green, these two areas will reassure you that there is an English countryside. Karl Marx and George Eliot are buried in the Highgate Cemetery. **Windsor Castle** is a popular tourist haunt. Homesick North Americans can enjoy a Baskin-Robbins ice cream in the castle's shadow; others might cross into **Eton,** England's foremost public (that is, very private) school where students (all male) still wear formal top hat and tails. **Hampton Court,** another train ride from London, is a former royal residence now largely converted into an excellent art museum. Its grounds contain the famous maze—a hedgerow labyrinth—and Henry VIII's tennis courts.

Southeastern England

Canterbury

For hundreds of years, the most heavily traveled road in England was that between London and Canterbury, the pilgrimage route to the shrine of England's favorite saint, the martyr Thomas à Becket. The **Cathedral,** where he was murdered in 1170, is a magnificent building, embellished and expanded by the archbishops of many generations. (Guided tours of the cathedral Mon.-Fri. at 11:30am, 12:30pm, 1:30pm, and 2:30pm. £1.) The rest of the city is filled with the monuments of religious orders: **St. Augustine's Abbey,** near the medieval city wall, **Eastbridge Hospital,** on St. Peter's St., and the gatehouse of **Greyfriars,** on the River Stour, are all reminders of the powerful religious community of medieval Canterbury and the constant threat and annoyance it posed to the temporal rulers at Westminster.

Canterbury's **Tourist Information Centre,** 13 Longmarket (tel. (0227) 45 54 90), provides a reliable accommodations service (70p in Canterbury, £1.75 out of town). (Open June-Aug. Mon.-Sat. 9:30am-6:30pm, Sun. 10am-4:30pm; Sept.-Nov. and March-May Mon.-Sat. 9:30am-5:15pm; Dec.-Feb. Mon.-Sat. 9:30am-4:30pm.) Rooms, especially singles, are not plentiful in Canterbury; arrive by midday or call for reservations. New Dover Road has the highest concentration of B&Bs (not the cheapest in town), as well as Canterbury's **IYHF youth hostel,** 54 New Dover Rd. (tel. (0227) 46 29 11). (£3.85. Curfew 11pm. Open July-Aug. daily; Feb.-June and Sept.-Dec. Mon.-Sat.) **Mrs. Wainwright,** 7 South Canterbury Rd. (tel. (0227) 663 96) is full of stories and loves young people. (Singles £6.50-7.) **Mrs. M. Durham,** 39 Whitstable Rd. (tel. (0227) 615 13) runs a very reasonable little place. (Singles £8.50, doubles £17.) **St. Martin's Touring Caravan and Camping Site,** Bekesbourne Lane (tel. (0227) 46 32 16), off the A257, the route to Sandwich, is 1½ miles east of the city center. (£2.10 for 2 people and tent. Open Easter-Sept.)

Bakeries and sweet shops fill the streets around the cathedral, but you'll have to satisfy your cravings before 6pm. **Alberry's,** 38 St. Margaret's St., has quiche, pizza, and vegetarian dishes. (£2-4. Open Mon.-Sat. noon-2:30pm and 6:30pm-midnight.) For burgers and huge quantities of fries and salad, try **Caesar's Restaurant,** 46 St. Peter's St. (burgers £3.20).

The brochure *Kent for Walkers,* available at the tourist office, guides you to the North Downs Way and other trails in the area.

Dover

Chances are you'll find yourself among the 14 million travelers who pass through Dover each year on trips between Britain and the continent. Besides the famed **White Cliffs,** best viewed from sea, Dover harbors an imposing clifftop castle and relics of Britain's Roman past. The **Roman Painted House,** New St., is a remarkably well-preserved Roman town house with over 400 square feet of wall paintings and an exhibit on the Roman occupation. (Open April-Oct. Tues.-Sun. 10am-5pm. Admission 80p.) On the grounds of **Dover Castle** you can enter the empty **Pharos,** the only Roman lighthouse still extant. The castle's impressive medieval keep and underground works may be explored as well. (Open April-Sept. daily 9:30am-6:30pm; Oct.-March daily 9:30am-4pm. Admission £2.)

Dover's **Tourist Information Centre,** on Town Wall St. (tel. (0304) 20 51 08), will give you a list of the city's B&Bs or book you in one for £1. (Open daily 9am-6pm.) There's a **youth hostel (IYHF)** at Charlton House, 306 London Rd. (tel. (0304) 20 13 14. Lockout 10am-5pm. Curfew 10:30pm.) If you arrive late, look for B&Bs with the lights on along Folkestone Road, next to the station. There's camping at **Hawthorne Farm,** Martin Hill (tel. 85 26 58), near the Martin Hill railway station between Dover and Deal. (£5.20 per tent, no charge per person. Open March-Oct.)

Trains for Dover Priory leave from Waterloo, Charing Cross, and Victoria Stations in London. Some continue to Dover Western Docks; otherwise, courtesy shuttle buses, timed to coincide with sailings, run between the Priory station and the various ports. Listen for announcements as you get off the train.

Near Dover

Sandwich and Deal are just north of Dover along the coast, and make excellent daytrips. **Sandwich** is filled with sagging medieval houses, and the Roman fortress at **Richborough** is just a mile away on the Canterbury road. **Deal** boasts three nearby castles, but is now chiefly a seaside resort. No big deal. Bus and train connections are simple from either Canterbury or Dover.

Rye is one of the most attractive towns in England, with its picturesque cobblestoned streets and half-timbered houses. Henry James lived in Rye for 18 years, and his home, **Lamb House,** on West St., is now a museum. (Open Wed. and Sat. 2-6pm. Admission £1.) Walk down **Mermaid Street** for a taste of old Rye, and visit the **Rye Museum,** housed in the thirteenth-century Ypres Towers, for background information on Rye's dashing history as a smuggler's port. (Open Easter to mid-Oct. Mon.-Sat. 10:30am-1pm and 2:15-5:30pm, Sun. 11:30am-1pm and 2:15-5:30pm. Admission 75p.) Rye's **tourist office,** on Cinque Port St. (tel. (0797) 22 22 93), books rooms for 60p. (Open in summer Mon.-Fri. 8:30am-1pm and 2-6:30pm, Sat. 10:30am-1pm and 2-5pm; in winter Mon.-Thurs. 9am-1pm and 2-4:30pm, Fri. 9:45am-12:45pm and 2-4:30pm.) Don't miss having a drink in the splendid **Mermaid Inn.** The best place to dine is the **Peacock** on Lion St.; their country pâté and enormous salads are worth a splurge. (Meals £4-5. Open until 9:30pm.) Frequent trains run from London and Dover (change at Ashford), or try hitching or cycling along the A20 and A259 from Dover.

Sussex Coast

Brighton, with its pier, promenade, and pebbly beach, offers all the colorful and tacky delights of an English seaside holiday town. *Don't* miss the *Pavilion,* a fantasy that defies description. The **Tourist Information Centre,** Marlborough House, 54 Old Steine (tel. (0273) 237 55), can help you find accommodations for a £1 refundable deposit. (Open Easter-Oct. Mon.-Fri. 9am-6:30pm, Sat.-Sun. 9am-6pm; Nov.-Easter Mon.-Fri. 9am-6:30pm, Sat.-Sun. 9am-5pm.) The nearest **youth hostel (IYHF)** is in Patcham (tel. (0273) 55 61 96), 4 miles north along the A23; take a bus from Old Steine to Patcham. (£6, including a meager breakfast. Open July-Aug. daily; Sept.-Dec. and Feb.-June closed Wed.; closed Jan.) The **Meeting House Restaurant** on Meeting House Lane has good food for about £2.50. (Open daily 8am-6pm.) The **Royal Oak,** 46 St. James St., offers live folk music on weekends.

The countryside itself is the star attraction in Southern England. Before setting out, invest in a detailed guide, such as *South Downs Way* (£3.95); the pamphlet *Along the South Downs Way and on to Winchester,* available at the Arundel Tourist Centre (90p), outlines possible hikes as well as local accommodations. Try the rewarding hike to **Firle Beacon,** one of the highest points on the Downs. The **Ramblers Association** conducts hikes in the region and offers information and advice; contact them at 1-5 Wandsworth Rd., London SW8 2LJ.

At **Arundel,** two hours from London by train, the magnificently furnished castle, home of the Dukes of Norfolk, has weaponry, suits of armor, and a fine art collection. (Open April-May and Sept.-Oct. Mon.-Fri. 1-5pm; June-Aug. noon-5pm. Admission £2.60.) The helpful **tourist office,** 61 High St. (tel. (0903) 88 24 19), has an accommodations service (85p) as well as hiking information on the region. (Open in summer Mon.-Fri. 9am-1pm and 2-6pm, Sat. 10am-6pm; in winter Mon.-Fri. 9am-1pm and 2-5pm.) The local **youth hostel (IYHF),** at Warningcamp (tel. (0903) 88 22 04), outside town, is a fine place to collect tips on hiking in the Downs. From the train station turn right on the Worthing Rd. (away from Arundel), take the first left, then look for signs. (£3.45. Open March-June and Sept.-Jan. Mon.-Sat.; July-Aug. daily.) Have tea at **Belinda's** in town, or rent a boat (£5 per hr., £18 per day) and sail down the River Arun for an ale at **The Black Rabbit.**

Chichester has something for devotees of all eras: a graceful eleventh-century cathedral, a second-century Roman palace, and an excellent Festival Theatre. The **cathedral** merits a visit for its juxtaposition of the modern and the medieval; there's a Chagall window in the south aisle. (Open in summer daily 7am-7pm; in winter daily 7am-6pm.) Built in 75 C.E., the **Roman palace** at nearby **Fishbourne** is one of the most magnificent Roman ruins in England. A number of mosaic floors have been preserved, and there is also an excellent if exhausting museum. Take bus #700 from the west side of South St. (Open May-Sept. daily 10am-6pm; April 10am-5pm; March, Oct., and Nov. 10am-4pm. Admission £1.50, students £1.) The **Chichester Festival Theatre,** founded by Sir Laurence Olivier, is perhaps the best place outside of London to see English theater. The festival runs from mid-May to mid-September; four plays are produced each season. (Tickets £7-11; student tickets, sold day of performance, 50% off.)

The **Tourist Information Office,** in St. Peter's Market on West St. (tel. (0243) 77 58 88), 100 yards from the City Cross, will help you locate a B&B. (Open Easter-Sept. Mon.-Sat. 9:15am-5:15pm, Sun. 10am-4pm; otherwise Mon.-Sat. only.) **Mrs. Bates,** 7 Lyndhurst Rd. (tel. (0243) 78 69 67), is recommended. (£9.) For camping, take the Lavant bus to the **Goodwood Racecourse** near the A286 (tel. (0243) 77 44 86). (Open Easter-late July and early Aug.-Sept. £2.50.) **Nicodemus Restaurant,** 14 St. Pancras, serves creative Italian food. (£3.50-5. Open Mon. 7-10:30pm, Tues.-Sat. noon-2pm and 7-10:30pm.)

Chichester is southwest of Arundel, and is reached by Southcoast Express buses and, from London, by hourly trains from Waterloo and Victoria (1½ hr., £8.40 one way, £8.90 day return).

Winchester

When Winchester missed being capital of England in the thirteenth century, it missed urban problems as well—it remains an idyllic cathedral town. The great **cathedral** is an interesting mix of Norman and Gothic styles. (Open daily 7:30am-8pm, with guided tours 11am and 3pm. Evensong Mon.-Tues. and Thurs.-Sat. 5:30pm.) Walk past the cathedral to reach **Winchester College,** England's oldest public school, complete with black-robed scholars and fourteenth-century buildings. (Excellent tours April-Sept. Mon.-Sat. 11am, 2pm, and 3:15pm; Oct.-March Sun. 2pm and 3pm. £1, students 50p.) For a superb view, stroll across the river up **St. Giles Hill,** site of medieval fairs and public executions.

Winchester's **tourist office,** Guildhall, Broadway (tel. (0962) 654 06), helps with accommodations and runs inexpensive (£1) guided tours of the city. (Open June-Sept. Mon.-Sat. 9:30am-6pm, Sun. 2-5pm; Oct.-May Mon.-Sat. 9:30am-6pm. Tours June-Oct. Mon.-Sat. 10:30am and 2:30pm, Sun. 3pm; July-Aug. also 7pm.) The beautiful **youth hostel (IYHF),** 1 Water Lane (tel. (0962) 537 23), is worth a visit, whether you want to stay or not. Located in an eighteenth-century watermill on the River Itchen, it is now protected by the National Trust. (Open to tourists Tues.-Sat. 3-4:30pm. Free. Hostel opens for guests at 5pm. £3.45. Closed Jan.) For bed and breakfast, try **Mrs. Farrell,** 5 Ranelegh Rd. (tel. (0962) 695 55), down St. Cross Rd., or **Mrs. Tisdall,** 32 Hyde St., off Jewry St. (tel. (0962) 516 21). (Both £9.) Camping is at **Morn Hill Caravan Site,** Alresfon Rd. (tel. 698 77); take bus #67 or 67a. (Tent and 2 people £4.50.)

Spy's wine bar, Great Minster St., next to the Close, has large servings for £3-4, and doesn't overcook the vegetables. (Open Mon.-Sat. 11:30am-2:30pm and 6-11pm.) **Blue Dolphin Fish Restaurant,** 154 High St., sells fish and chips for £1.25. (Open Mon.-Thurs. 10:30am-11pm; Fri. 10:30am-midnight; Sat. 10am-midnight.) **The Wykeham Arms** has the best pub food in town.

Not far from Winchester is **Chawton,** the home of Jane Austen. Here she wrote *Pride and Prejudice, Emma, Northanger Abbey,* and *Persuasion;* her house is filled with memorabilia. Bus #214 runs to Chawton three times per day. (Open April-Oct. daily 11am-4:30pm; Nov.-March Wed.-Sun. 11am-4:30pm. Admission 85p.)

Winchester is 60 miles southwest of London and easily accessible by train from London's Waterloo Station (hourly, 1 hr., £8 one way, £8.60 round-trip). Buses also run from London's Victoria Station (7 per day, 2 hr., £6 one way, £9 period return). To get to the center of town from the train station, walk down City Rd. to Jewry St., or take any local bus (map and schedule in train station).

Salisbury and Stonehenge

Few places can compete with Salisbury Plain when it comes to piling up stones. Thirteenth-century **Salisbury Cathedral** piles up 7000 tons of them to form the tallest spire in England—and one of the most audacious. Ask the friendly cathedral guards to show you the buckling pillars near the choir and the architectural tricks in the cathedral's design. The guided tours take you up into the cathedral's dizzying heights for a look into the "underside" of medieval architecture. (Cathedral open Aug.-June daily 8am-6:30pm; July daily 8am-8:30pm. Guided tours £1 Mon.-Fri. 11am and 2:30pm.) You can see one of the four surviving copies of the *Magna Carta* in the delicately designed **Chapter House,** next to the cathedral. (Open Mon.-Sat. 10am-5pm, Sun. 1-5pm.)

The **Tourist Information Centre** on Fish Row (tel. (0722) 33 49 56), will book you a bed for £1. (Open June-Sept. Mon.-Sat. 9am-5pm, Sun. 11am-5pm; Oct.-May Mon.-Sat. 9am-5pm.) A list of accommodations is posted outside when the office is closed. There is a **youth hostel (IYHF)** at Milford Hill House (tel. (0722) 275 72) which also allows **camping** out back. From the center of Salisbury, walk down Endless St. to Milford St., turn left, and walk up the hill. (Beds £3.45, camping

£1.85. Open March-Jan.) **Ron and Jenny Coats,** 51 Salt Lane (tel. (0722) 274 43), love students. (Dorm beds £3.45.) They'll point you to friends of theirs if they're full. **Mo's,** 62 Milford St., is a classy little hamburger joint. (Burgers £2.75-3.15.)

For its time, **Stonehenge** was an extraordinary technological achievement, and this strange cluster of prehistoric monoliths has intrigued scientists ever since. A visit to the "rough-hewn giants" can be a humbling experience, if you're willing to share your mystical space with a few other like-minded pilgrims. Ordinarily, you can walk around the roped-off area quite near the stones; in winter, on some Tuesdays and Fridays in good weather, they will take the ropes down to allow a close-up view. From any perspective, the stones are awe-inspiring. (Site open daily 9:30am-6:30pm. Admission £1.30.)

Buses run from Salisbury's Endless St. about every two hours, beginning at 8:55am, and from the railway station three times per day. The last direct bus back to Salisbury leaves Stonehenge at 6:08pm (£1.99 round-trip). Buses leave every 15 minutes for Amesbury, from where it's an easy 2-mile stroll to Stonehenge. You should also be able to hitch along the busy A345 to Amesbury. Rent bicycles at the Milford Hill hostel. (£3.50 per day, £2.50 per ½ day.) The pubs and spectacular scenery along the route will compensate for the hilly terrain. Try to avoid a visit during the summer solstice, when huge numbers of self-proclaimed druids assemble around the monument, arousing reactions ranging from annoyance among the townspeople to police brutality.

The West Country

The sea laps and pounds at the coast of the West Country, the peninsula that extends 200 miles southwest of Bristol and Southampton. Wetter than London in winter, but often the warmest place in Britain in summer, this region of foggy moors, wooded valleys, and downy green hillsides is one of the most beautiful in England. As you move westward, the scene changes: The rolling Mendip Hills of Avon and Somerset are replaced by the stark moorlands of Devon and the cliffside fishing villages and broad, sandy beaches of Cornwall.

Beauty and sun attract scores of tourists each summer, but many visitors come in search of the past. Reminders of former occupants abound—Norman castles, Roman ruins, and Stone Age and Bronze Age burial mounds are found throughout the region. Some former residents have left only legend behind: Tintagel is said to be King Arthur's birthplace, and nearby Camelford the site of his last battle.

Bath

A visit to Bath remains *de rigueur,* even if this elegant Georgian city is now more museum than resort. In its eighteenth-century Golden Age, Bath was a social circus under the direction of ringmaster Beau Nash; newly affluent gentry came to town to drink, bathe, gamble, dance, and hunt for a suitable spouse. An explosion of building accommodated them, and Bath today is one of Europe's premier examples of an eighteenth-century planned city.

Orientation and Practical Information

Bath is served by direct rail lines from Bristol and London Paddington. From the west, north, and south, you may have to change at Bristol. Coaches duplicate most rail routes to the city, and are often less expensive.

The River Avon circles Bath, encompassing most places of interest.

Tourist Office: Tourist Information Centre, Abbey Churchyard (tel. 628 31). Useful miniguide 20p; other leaflets and guided tours free. *This Month in Bath* lists current events, hours, and admission prices. Open Easter-Sept. Mon.-Sat. 9:30am-7pm, Sun. 10am-4pm; Oct.-Easter Mon.-Sat. 9:30am-5pm.

Post Office: New Bond St. **Postal code:** BA11AA. Open Mon.-Thurs. 9am-5:30pm, Fri. 9:30am-5:30pm, Sat. 9am-1pm. **Telephones** at the post office. **Telephone code:** 0225.

Trains: Bath Spa Station (tel. 630 75). To reach the tourist office, walk up Manvers St. and turn left into the Abbey Churchyard. For Oxford, change at Reading; for Devon and Cornwall, at Bristol.

Buses: Manvers St. Station (tel. 644 46), near the train station.

Emergencies: Police or **Ambulance** (tel. 999).

Accommodations, Camping, and Food

Bath is mobbed in summer, especially August; if possible, make reservations. Pulteney Road (by the railroad bridge), Pulteney Gardens, and Lime Grove are all lined with B&Bs.

Youth Hostel (IYHF), Bathwick Hill (tel. 656 74), in a hillside mansion 1 mile east of city center (uphill, so take bus #18 from bus station or Orange grove roundabout.) Often fills in summer, so call ahead and arrive early. £3.85, £3.15. Lockout 10:30am-5pm. Curfew 10:30pm.

YMCA International House, Broad St. Pl. (tel. 604 71), an easily missed street between Broad St. and Walcot St. Much better location than the IYHF and no curfew. Heavily booked in summer. Dormitory beds £6, with sheets £7; beds in singles £8.15, doubles £7.65. Continental breakfast included, cooked breakfast 50p extra.

The Shearns, Prior House, 3 Marlborough Ln. (tel. 31 35 87). Great location near Royal Victoria Park and Royal Crescent; take bus #14 or 15 (last bus 10:30pm) from the bus station. Warm, wonderful proprietors treat you like family. £7.50.

The Limes, Mrs. Ellis, 1 Pulteney Rd. (tel. 31 10 44). Musty, but homey and well furnished. £7.50 per person in singles or doubles.

Mr. and Mrs. Farrar, 9 Raby Place (tel. 641 24), at the foot of Bathwick Hill. Good view from the top floor, but weak showers. £9.

Camping: Newton Mill Touring Center (tel. 33 39 09), 3 miles from Bath on the A36/A39. Bus #5 leaves bus station every 12 min.; get off at Newton Road. Laundry and showers. £2.65 per person.

For fresh fruits and vegetables visit the **Guildhall Market** between High St. and Grand Parade. There are a half-dozen bakeries along Union St. and Milsom St. An excellent selection of health foods fills **Harvest Wholefoods** at 27 Walcot St. (open Mon. 11:30am-5:30pm, Tues.-Sat. 9:30am-5:30pm). **Huckleberry's** has good, if small, vegetarian meals for £2-3. (Open Mon.-Sat. 9am-6:30pm and 7-10:30pm; last orders 10pm.) Try **The Cellar Bar** at the Huntsman, North Parade, for good pub meals from £1.50. **The Pump Room** at the Roman Baths has concerts and coffee in the morning (Mon.-Sat. 10am-noon), and concerts and cream tea in the afternoon (in summer daily 2:45-5pm; in winter Sun. only).

Sights and Entertainment

The best of Bath's Georgian heritage reposes graciously in the residential northwest part of the city. Walk up **Gay Street** (a continuation of Barton St.) to **The Circus,** a full circle of Georgian townhouses. Number 17 was home to the painter Thomas Gainsborough for 16 years; the late Prime Minister William Pitt had #7 and 8 built for himself. Leave The Circus on Brock Street for the renowned **Royal Crescent,** the premier accomplishment of John Wood the younger. Number 1 is a superbly restored Georgian house. (Open March-Dec. Tues.-Sat. 11am-5pm, Sun. 2-5pm; last admission 4:40pm.)

The **Assembly Rooms,** Bennett St., are on the other side of The Circus; these rooms staged *the* social events in England during the late eighteenth century. They now contain the most comprehensive **Museum of Costume** in Britain, with excellent hourly guided tours. (Open March-Oct. Mon.-Sat. 9:30am-6pm, Sun. 10am-6pm; Nov.-Feb. Mon.-Sat. 10am-5pm, Sun. 11am-5pm. Admission £1.40, ages 5-16 85p, under 5 free. Ticket including Roman Baths £2, ages 5-16 £1.15.)

Most of the remains of the **Roman Baths** are in the museum, which has the finest collection of Roman artifacts in Britain. From the Abbey Churchyard entrance, follow the stream to the hot spring source, and then go out to the large open-air pool where tours start every half hour. Upstairs from the Baths is the **Pump Room,** the room to which hot spring water was, and still is, pumped for drinking purposes. (Baths and pump room open March-June and Sept.-Oct. daily 9am-6pm; July daily 9am-7pm; Aug. daily 9am-7pm and 8:30-10:30pm; Nov.-Feb. Mon.-Sat. 9am-5pm, Sun. 10am-5pm. Admission to baths £2, ages 5-16 £1.15. Pump room free.) A beacon for disoriented tourists, **Bath Abbey** stands solidly by the Pump Room, looming over the busy Abbey Churchyard. The technical advances of Gothic architecture allowed the Abbey's builders to pierce one entire wall with magnificent windows; the effect has earned the church its nickname, "Lantern of the West." (Open Mon.-Sat. 9am-5:30pm, Sun. depending on services. 50p donation collected at door.)

The Crystal Palace, 11 Abbey Green, is a quiet, pleasant pub with an outdoor patio. **The Grapes** on Westgate St. draws the student crowd; the **Regency Bar** on Sawclose features rock videos; **Moles Club** on George St. is the choice for live bands; and The Green Room at **The Garrick's Head,** behind the Theatre Royal, is a relaxed gay pub.

Somerset

Somerset County, southwest of Bath, is rich in farmland, cathedrals, and legend. While many tourists come to view the prehistoric remains in the Mendip Hills, others choose to concentrate on the towns that lie just south of them—Wells and Glastonbury. The best way to tour is by bike or by the area's excellent bus service. Be sure to try Somerset's famous "scrumpy," a deadly, delightful, thick apple cider.

Wells

A lovely and compact market town, Wells is the smallest cathedral city in England. Dominating the town, the **Cathedral Church of St. Andrew** is the hub of one of the best surviving examples of a whole cathedral complex—complete with princely **Bishop's Palace** and **Chapter House.** The cathedral's striking west front still bears almost 300 separate pieces of medieval sculpture. Nearby **Vicar's Close** is the oldest intact street of houses in Europe.

The **tourist office** off the Market Place (tel. (0749) 725 52) will sell you an accommodations list (25p) or book a room (80p). (Open April-Oct. Mon.-Fri. 9:30am-5:30pm, Sat.-Sun. 10am-5pm; Nov.-March. Mon.-Fri. 10am-4pm, Sat. 10am-1pm. The nearest **youth hostel (IYHF)** is 6 miles away in the town of Cheddar (tel. (0934) 74 24 94), off The Hayes. (£3.40, £2.60. Open April-Sept. daily; Nov. and Jan.-March Tues.-Sat.) In Wells, try Chamberlain Street or St. Andrew Street for B&Bs. Cheerful **Mr. and Mrs. Coles,** 29 Chamberlain St., take good care of you for £8. **The Old Poor House,** 7a St. Andrew St. (tel. (0749) 750 52), is rich in hospitality; guests are treated like kin. (£9.50) **Richmond House,** 2 Chamberlain St. (tel. (0749) 764 38), has a tastefully furnished common area, huge rooms, and huge breakfasts. (£9-10.)

The River Yeo carves the **Cheddar Gorge** on its hurried way down from the Mendip Hills. For the best view of the Gorge, climb the 322 steps of **Jacob's Ladder** (40p, seniors and children 25p). Bus #125 or 126 runs hourly from Wells to Cheddar, and hitching the six miles on the A371 is easy.

Glastonbury

The acknowledged birthplace of Christianity in England, Glastonbury was reportedly visited by Jesus with Joseph of Arimathea. The ruins of **Glastonbury**

Abbey, the oldest abbey in the British Isles (founded 678), still outline the original walls. In 1191 monks here dug up a coffin that allegedly contained the remains of King Arthur and Queen Guinevere; they later reinterred it in front of the high altar. Enter the abbey grounds from the Market Cross. (Open daily 9:30am-sundown. Admission 80p.) According to another Arthurian legend, **Glastonbury Tor,** the mythical island of Avalon, is the place where the second coming of the Messiah will occur. Don't hold your breath, but the grassy mound has become a popular pilgrimage site anyway. From a height of 525 feet (a half-hour trek from town), you can view the Wiltshire Downs, the Mendips, and on a really clear day, the Bristol Channel. On your way back down, you'll pass **Chalice Well,** where Arthurian legend places the burial site of the Holy Grail (or Chalice Cup), and where Christian tradition says the water runs red with Jesus' blood. (Open March-Oct. daily 10am-6pm; Nov.-Feb. daily 1-3pm. Admission 30p, children 10p.) Nearby, in the Abbey Barn on Chilkwell St., is an exceptional **Rural Life Museum.** (Open Easter-Oct. Mon.-Fri. 10am-5pm, Sat.-Sun. 2-6pm. Admission 60p.)

The **Tourist Information Centre** (tel. (0458) 329 54) is on Northload St. off the central square. (Open April-Oct. Mon.-Sat. 9:30am-5pm. Accommodations service 60p, free list.) **Tor Down Accommodation,** 5 Ashwell Lane (tel. (0458) 322 87), at the base of Glastonbury Tor, a bit of a walk from the town center, is pleasant with great breakfasts (£9.50-10.50). **Tamarac,** 8 Wells Rd. (tel. 343 27 or 320 36) is central and friendly and serves a full English breakfast. (£9; doubles only.) Camp at the **Ashwell Farm House,** Edgarley End, off Ashwell Lane (tel. (0458) 323 13). (£1.50 per person with tent.) The closest **youth hostel (IYHF)** is four miles away in Street (tel. (0458) 429 61), reached several times per day by bus. You can hitch to Street and walk the remaining two miles uphill on the B3151 to Ivythorne Hill. (£2.30, £1.90. Open April-Oct. Wed.-Mon.) For lunch, try the excellent vegetarian cafe **Rainbow's End** on High St. (open Sept.-June Mon.-Tues. and Thurs.-Sat. 10am-4:30pm; July-Aug. Mon.-Sat. 10am-4:30pm), or the wholefood **Assembly Rooms Cafe** across the street (open daily 9am-6pm).

Devon and the West Country Moors

The county of Devon lies between Cornwall and Somerset, roughly 60 miles from Land's End. Spectacular cliffs and sandy beaches comprise Devon's north coast; inland, the green farm country, snug in tidy walled quadrants, rolls gently toward the south coast's beautiful coves, estuaries, and seaside resorts. The county also contains all of Dartmoor and part of Exmoor, two of England's most beautiful National Parks. Devon's "cream teas" consisting of fresh scones, clotted cream, and jam, are famous throughout England. Land in Dartmoor and Exmoor is privately owned, and you must have permission to camp.

Exeter

Exeter is a good base for excursions to Dartmoor, though bus connections are erratic. The town itself was heavily bombed during World War II and was subsequently rebuilt as a modern city, but the finest buildings in town survived the war. The intricate medieval stone figures on the west front of Exeter's **cathedral** open onto the longest stretch of Gothic stone vaulting in the world. The cathedral **library** displays the **Exeter Book,** which medievalist **R.B. Mintz** has called the richest surviving treasury of Anglo-Saxon poetry.

The **tourist office,** behind the coach station on Paris St. (tel. (0392) 724 34), has information on the coast and on Dartmoor and Exmoor. They also find accommodations (75p) and give out a free list. (Open Mon.-Fri. 9am-5pm, Sat. 9am-1pm and 2-5pm.) The **youth hostel (IYHF),** 47 Countess Wear Rd., Topsham (tel. (0392) 87 33 29), is exceptionally well-equipped, and very popular despite its location two miles from town; take bus #K or T from High St. (£3.85, £3.15. Open Feb.-Nov.) Closer to town and more relaxed is the **Clock Tower Guest House,** 16 New North

Rd. (tel. (0392) 524 93; quads £4, singles and doubles £7.50, continental breakfast included). For B&Bs, try St. David's Hill or New North Road; expect to pay from £8. The nearest campsite is **Cat and Fiddle Leisure Park** (tel. (0392) 87 50 08), four miles east on the A3052. (Tents £4.) **Herbie's** on North St. is an excellent vegetarian restaurant (open Mon. 11am-2:30pm, Tues.-Fri. 11am-2:30pm and 7-10:30pm, Sat. 10am-4pm and 7-10:30pm). **The Milk Maid** on Catherine St. has cheap, good food, and fresh ice cream.

The tourist office has information about Devon General buses #359-361 and #X38/9, which stop in Dartmoor year-round.

Plymouth

Devon's largest city and a transportation hub, Plymouth suffered major damage in World War II, and was rebuilt from the ground up. The hilly **Hoe,** with its seafront esplanade, substitutes for a beach; nearby, the old **Barbican** quarter by the harbor bears a plaque where the *Mayflower* set sail for the New World in 1620. Near the city center on Catherine St. is the oldest Ashkenazi (Eastern-European-rite) **synagogue** in the English-speaking world, dating from 1762. Plymouth's nightlife is the liveliest in the southwest; **Union Street** leads past discos and dance-halls to the immense **Academy,** which holds 1500 revelers (open Tues.-Sat.).

The **tourist office** on Royal Parade (tel. (0752) 26 48 49) books accommodations for 60p and has a free map and list of places to stay. (Open year-round Mon.-Thurs. 9am-5pm, Fri. 9am-4:30pm; also June-Sept. Sat. 9am-4pm; Oct.-Nov. and April-May Sat. 9am-noon.) Take bus #3A or 4A to the **youth hostel (IYHF),** Devonport Rd., Stoke (tel. (0752) 56 21 89). (£3.85, £3.15. Open March-Oct. daily; Dec.-Jan. Wed.-Sun.) The **YWCA** on Lockyer St. at Notte St., just south of the city center (tel. (0752) 66 03 21), admits women and men. (Singles £7.21, doubles £6.54, 4-bed dorm £4.59. Continental breakfast included.) The Hoe area, especially Citadel Road, is teeming with B&Bs from £8. **Riverside Caravan Park,** Longbridge Rd., Marsh Mills (tel. (0752) 34 41 22), allows tent camping for £5.50 (tent and 2 people). Take bus #20 or 21 to the junction of the A38 and A374. Fresh produce, dairy products, and wholefoods are available from the stalls in the **Plymouth Market** on New George St. (open Mon.-Tues. and Thurs.-Sat. 7am-5:30pm, Wed. 7am-4pm).

Dartmoor

Between Exeter and Plymouth, Devon's neat, lush pastureland gives way to the strange, desolate beauty of **Dartmoor National Park.** Craggy granite tors reach upward from barren plateaus, the variegated moorland rolls and sweeps, and you can hike for miles without encountering another person. Dartmoor has the largest array of Bronze Age ruins in England, most free of fences and tourist mobs.

The best source of information is the *Dartmoor Visitor,* an annual free publication that lists places to visit, guided walks, and campsites. Get yours at the Exeter or Plymouth tourist office or at any of these **National Park Information Centres:** in **New Bridge,** at Spitchwick Common (tel. Poundsgate 303); in **Okehampton,** on Main St. (tel. (0837) 30 20); in **Parke,** on the Haytor road (tel. (0626) 83 20 93); in **Postbridge,** in a car park off the B3212 (tel. (0822) 882 72); in **Princetown,** in the Town Hall (tel. (0822) 894 14); in **Steps Bridge** (tel. (0647) 520 18); and in **Tavistock,** The Guildhall, Bedford Sq. (tel. (0822) 29 38). Only Parke is open year-round; the others are open April to November (usually daily 10am-5pm, but call first).

If you hike on your own, be sure to have strong shoes, rain gear, a large-scale Ordnance Survey Map (about £2.50 at any bookstore or information office), and a compass you know how to use. Dartmoor is renowned for its capricious weather, and is unsafe for lone, inexperienced walkers. Be sure to stay on paths across farmland, close all gates you open, and keep the water supplies pure for livestock.

In July and August, the Transmoor Link bus #82 runs from Exeter to Plymouth through the middle of the park. The various bus passes available aren't a good value because of the infrequency of service. From September to June, buses from Exeter and Plymouth reach only the outskirts of the park (Moretonhampstead, Steps Bridge, Okehampton, Tavistock), a long way from the high moor. Hitching is slow.

All the information centers have local accommodations lists, and the Okehampton and Tavistock offices will book accommodations. There are several **IYHF youth hostels** in the area. The hostel at **Bellever** (tel. (0822) 882 27) is secluded 1 mile southeast of Postbridge village. (£3.40, £2.60. Open April and June-Oct. Tues.-Sun.; Nov.-March Fri.-Sat.) The hostel at **Gidleigh** (tel. (06473) 24 21) is 3 miles west of Chagford village, the nearest bus stop, in a wooden hut on a tiny farm. (£2.30, £1.90. No showers. Open April-Sept. Fri.-Wed. No phone bookings.) The hostel at **Steps Bridge** (tel. (0647) 53 24 35) is a cabin with funky wardens in a wooded area 1 mile southwest of Dunsford village; the Exeter-Moretonhampstead bus stops at the hostel gates. (£2.30, £1.90. Evening meals. Open April-May and Sept. Thurs.-Mon.; June-Aug. Wed.-Mon.) There is also a hostel at **Dartington** (tel. (0803) 86 23 03), between Dartmoor and Torbay, 19 miles from Bellever. (£2.30, £1.90. Open April-May and Sept. Fri.-Tues.; June-Aug. Fri.-Wed.) Farmhouse **B&Bs** are scattered along most roads, as are **campsites.**

Exmoor

In a last, frenzied defiance of its seeming fate—to roll verdantly and gently evermore—the county of Devon gathers up its northeast coast and plunges into the sea. Such is the northern boundary of Exmoor, which Devon shares with Somerset. The park's landscape includes wooded combes and stunted heath; if you're lucky, you'll spot a herd of hardy Exmoor ponies or a rare red deer.

From the west, the best approach to the park is via Exeter to **Barnstaple.** Trains run from Exeter to Barnstaple every two hours (1 hr., £6.60 day return), but coaches are cheaper (5 per day, 2 hr., £2.90 day return). From the north and east, go through Taunton to **Minehead,** served by hourly buses and the less frequent West Somerset Railway. From Barnstaple, **North Devon Bus** (tel. (0271) 454 44) serves **Ilfracombe,** a lovely coastal town. **Country Bus** (tel. (07695) 21 20) serves **Lynton** via **Blackmoor Gate,** a good starting point for a hike on the high moor. From Minehead, Country Bus serves Lynton and Dunster; **Scarlet Coaches** (tel. (0643) 42 04) serves **Porlock Weir** on the coast and **Dulverton** on the high moor.

Start with a copy of the *Exmoor Visitor,* an exhaustive free publication detailing virtually everything to see and do in the park and including also a detailed list of B&Bs (from £8), guesthouses, and campgrounds. It's available at the Exeter and Plymouth tourist offices as well as the information centers within the park. The **National Park Information Centres** can also supply you with large-scale Ordnance Survey maps, bus timetables, and detailed guides to the coastal path (£1-1.75). They're located in **Dulverton** (tel. (0398) 236 65), at the south end of the park (open July-Sept. daily 10am-5pm; Oct.-March Mon.-Fri. 10am-noon and 2-4pm; April-June Mon.-Fri. 10am-4:30pm); in **Dunster,** the Steep Car Park (tel. (0643) 82 18 35); **Lynmouth,** the Esplanade (tel. (0598) 525 09); **Combe Martin,** Cross St., off King St. (tel. (027188) 33 19); and **Countisbury,** 1 mile east of Lynton on the A39 (tel. (05987) 321). The first two are open April-October daily 10am-5pm, the latter two April-September daily 10am-5pm. The **Tourist Information Centres** in the area are in **Barnstaple,** Holland St., the second right down from the bus station (tel. (0271) 727 42; open April-Sept. Mon.-Sat. 10am-7pm; Oct.-March Mon.-Sat. 10am-6pm); in **Minehead,** on the corner of Bancks St. and the Parade (tel. (0643) 26 24; open year-round Mon.-Sat. 2-5pm; also April-Oct. Mon.-Sat. 9am-1pm); in **Ilfracombe,** on the Promenade (tel. (0271) 630 01; open April and Oct. Mon.-Fri. 9:30am-5pm, Sat. 2-5pm, Sun. 10am-noon; May-June Mon.-Fri. 9:30am-5pm, Sat. noon-5:30pm, Sun. 10am-noon; July-Sept. Mon.-Fri. 9:30am-5:30pm, Sat. noon-6pm, Sun. 10am-noon; Nov.-March Mon.-Fri. 9:30am-4pm); and in **Lynton,** the Town Hall (tel. (0598) 522 25; open April-Sept. Mon.-Sat. 10am-4:30pm).

B&Bs line the streets in coastal towns, and there are many farmhouse B&Bs on roads in the park; expect to pay £7.50-8.50. Campsites are plentiful along the coastal roads. **IYHF youth hostels** are strung out along the **Somerset and North Devon**

Coast Path. They are in **Instow** (tel. (0271) 86 03 94; £3.40, £2.60; open Jan.-Feb. Sat.-Wed.; April-Aug. Sat.-Thurs.; March and Sept.-Oct. sporadically); in **Ilfracombe** (tel. (0271) 653 37; £3.85, £3.15; open April-July and Sept. Tues.-Sun.; Aug. daily); in **Lynton** (tel. (05985) 32 37; £3.40, £2.60; open late March to Sept. Wed.-Mon.; Oct.-Dec. Thurs.-Mon.); in **Exford** (tel. (064383) 288; £3.85, £3.15; open Feb.-March and Oct.-Nov. Tues.-Sat.; April-Sept. Mon.-Sat.); and in **Minehead** (tel. (0643) 25 95; £3.40, £2.60; open Jan.-March and Oct. Tues.-Sat.; April-Aug. Mon.-Sat.). The hostels are a full day's walk from one another. Also along the path are **Selworthy,** a thatched-roof village now owned by the National Trust, the 100-foot dunes at **Saunton Sands,** and **Porlock,** where Samuel Taylor Coleridge dreamed the fantastical incidents of "Kubla Khan."

Exford and **Dulverton** are quiet towns from which to explore the interior of the park. Three miles out of Exford is the 500-acre **Westermill Farm** (tel. 238), for tent camping with showers. Take Porlock Rd., fork left after ¼ mile, continue 2½ miles to sign on tree, and fork left.

In Dulverton, stay at the **Berry House** (tel. 236 17), run by Mr. and Mrs. Clarke. Take the first right after the bridge as you leave Dulverton toward Bampton. Check the window of **Kemps News Agents** on High St. for other B&Bs. The lovely walk from Dulverton to Exford along the River Exe passes a prehistoric slate bridge.

Cornwall

Cornwall languishes at the end of England, bathed year-round by salty winds. Some tropical plants grow here, tourists bask on sandy beaches, and seabirds and wildflowers thrive on the craggy cliffs of the spectacular Southwest Peninsula Coast Path. **IYHF youth hostels** in the area are spaced about a day's bicycle ride apart (5-25 miles—the terrain is quite hilly), and are often easily accessible from the coast path as well. If you're hosteling, try to book ahead by at least several days during the summer, and by as wide a margin as possible in August; popular hostels, such as Newquay and Tintagel, often fill up by mid-June. The resort towns—especially St. Ives and Newquay—swarm in summer with British and foreign tourists.

Trains serve Penzance, Falmouth, St. Ives, and Newquay (call British Rail at (0752) 22 13 00). **Cornwall Busways** (tel. (0736) 694 69) serves these towns year-round, and many smaller ones in summer, though schedules are somewhat erratic. If you plan daytrips, check timetables carefully for returning buses. Hitching along the coast roads is often decent. If you'll be here a few days, get a **Cornish Rover** railpass (3 days £10, 7 days £15) or an **Explorer** ticket for the bus network (£2.80 per day); the **Key West** ticket (£12) is good on buses in both Devon and Cornwall for 1 week.

Falmouth, an old port on the southern coast, is guarded by Henry VIII's **Pendennis Castle** atop rocky Pendennis Head. (Castle open mid-March to mid-Oct. Mon.-Sat. 9:30am-1pm and 2-6:30pm, Sun. 2-6:30pm; mid-Oct. to mid-March Mon.-Sat. 9:30am-1pm and 2-4pm, Sun. 2-4pm; April-Sept. also Sun. 9:30am-1pm. Admission 75p, seniors 55p, children 35p.) An **IYHF youth hostel** is right on the grounds (tel. (0326) 31 14 35; £3.40, £2.60; open Feb.-Oct. daily; Nov. to mid-Dec. Mon.-Fri.). Nearby **Gyllyngvase Beach** and **Swanpool Beach** are broad, sandy, and mobbed. Trains to Falmouth stop at three stations, including The Dell Station (near the town center) and Falmouth Station (near the youth hostel). Buses stop on The Moor beside the **tourist office** (tel. (0326) 31 23 00), which has a free list of B&Bs and books rooms for 85p. (Open May-Sept. Mon.-Sat. 9am-5pm; Oct.-April Mon.-Fri. 9am-5pm.) On your own, try Melvill Road or Avenue Road, near The Dell Station and the beaches, or Dracaena Avenue and Marlborough Road. Camping is at secluded **Tremorvah Tent Park** on Swanpool Rd. (tel. (0326) 31 21 03; £1.80 per person). **The Laughing Pirate** has a great selection of beers; the **Cavalier Tavern** near the hostel has a great view.

The ferry from Falmouth to **St. Mawes** costs £2.50 return; have a look at the fort there, then hitch up the A3078 to Pendower Beach for a lazy afternoon. Alternatively, hike south from Falmouth along a particularly dramatic segment of the coast path to Lizard Point (or hitch; bus service is infrequent). The **youth hostel (IYHF)** in the tiny village of **Coverack** (tel. (0326) 28 06 87), on the east edge of the Lizard peninsula, offers a great view of the harbor. (£3.40, £2.60. Open April-Oct. Tues.-Sun.) The **Blue Anchor Pub** in nearby Helston serves some of the best homemade brew ("spingo") in the Southwest.

Penzance, as in *Pirates of,* is the bustling transit hub of the **Penwith** peninsula, the very tip of Cornwall. Penwith has plenty of sandy beaches and quaint fishing villages, but be prepared for company almost anywhere you go in summer. Penzance is on a direct rail route from London and Exeter, and is a convenient base for exploring the rest of Penwith. The **tourist office** (tel. (0736) 622 07), near the station, books accommodations (75p, free list) and can tell you about the area. The **youth hostel (IYHF)** (tel. (0736) 626 66), in an eighteenth-century smuggler's mansion 1½ miles from the train station, is crowded but romantic; walk up Market Jew St., continue on Alverton St., then turn right on Castle Horneck Rd. (£3.85, £3.15; open March-Jan. daily except some days in Dec.) If the hostel is full, try the well-located **YMCA,** on Alverton Rd. (tel. (0736) 650 16), about ½ mile from the hostel back toward town. (£3.45-4.85 in small dorm.) The B&Bs on Morrab Road, off Alverton St., are convenient and reasonable (about £8.50). For a bland campsite, try **Mounts Bay Holiday Centre,** Eastern Green (tel. (0736) 647 18; £1.60 per tent, £1.60 per person).

Buses run from Penzance to **Land's End,** which is just that. For a great hike, get off the bus at Sennen Cove, a gorgeous spit of silver sand 1 mile away along the coast path. **St. Michael's Mount** is a Norman monastery-turned-castle on a rocky mound about 400m off the coast of **Marazion,** 2 miles east of Penzance. At low tide, you can walk to St. Michael's Mount and visit the castle; at high tide, there's a ferry (45p). Buses to Marazion are frequent, or you can walk along the beach. Three miles west of Penzance, **Mousehole** (pronounced "Mow-zel") is a relatively unspoiled fishing village whose steep and twisting streets provided abundant storage space during Cornwall's lengthy smuggling history. The **Minack Theatre** in **Porthcurno** hosts outdoor performances on a dramatic cliffside arena overlooking the ocean.

If you've traveled to Cornwall along the south coast, return along the north; this coast includes not only some of England's most beautiful cliff scenery, but some of its finest beaches as well. **St. Ives,** situated on a breathtaking bay 10 miles north of Penzance, has been a center for artists since Whistler came to town in 1880, but now doubles as a crowded tourist resort. The **Tourist Information Centre,** The Guildhall, Street-An-Pol (tel. (0736) 79 62 97), can help find you a room (75p commission) or provide a free accommodations list. The closest IYHF and YMCA are in Penzance; bus service between Penzance and St. Ives is frequent. Get a delicious Cornish pasty or saffron bun, reputedly Cornwall's best, from the tiny **Ferrell's Bakery** on Fore St., and then try some fresh-caught local fish (and chips) at the nearby **Dolphin Fish Bar.**

Newquay is one of England's most popular beach spots. There is little of historical interest here, just British young folk who come to sunbathe along the 7 miles of beaches and to enjoy the swinging nightlife, supposedly the liveliest in Cornwall. Newquay's beachside **youth hostel (IYHF),** Alexandra Court, Narrowcliff Rd. (tel. (0637) 87 63 81), is very popular and often full during July and August. (£3.85, £3.15. Open Jan. to mid-April Tues.-Sat.; mid-April to June and Sept. Mon.-Sat.; July-Aug. daily.) The town is packed with B&Bs, many of which are also full in July and August; the **Tourist Information Centre,** Morfa Hall, Cliff Rd. (tel. (0637) 87 13 45), has an accommodation service (50p) and free accommodations lists.

Tiny **Tintagel,** near the edge of nowhere, isn't worth a visit unless you're a King Arthur nut with a vivid imagination. If you're set on it, one bus per day runs from Plymouth, via Bodmin.

Central England

Oxford

An undeniable allure surrounds a university which has educated men and women—mostly men—for eight centuries. And this university casts a mysterious spell; it seems a soft, sheltered world, full of verdant nooks, gentle riverbends, prim shops, and buildings eerily haloed at twilight or daybreak. Yet the crew team's latest victories are chalked elatedly onto dormitory archways, and students spill bitter and lager into themselves and onto one another until 10:30pm every evening. There is a noticeable contrast between the "dreaming spires" and secluded courtyards of the colleges, and the congested streets of the city. Oxford houses a year-round jumble of students, tourists, and locals, as well as enough buses and bicycles for a town 10 times its size.

Orientation and Practical Information

The center of the town is Carfax, where Queen Street, High Street, St. Aldates Street, and Cornmarket Street intersect. The colleges lie generally north, east, and south of Carfax; the bus and train stations, west. The rail station is a 10-minute walk from the center; turn left out of the station driveway and head down Park End St., cross the river, bear right on New Rd., and then bear slightly left onto Queen St. to Carfax and the tourist office.

Tourist Office: St. Aldates St. (tel. 72 68 71). Accommodations service 80p. The excellent *Welcome to Oxford* guide has a map and opening times of all colleges and museums. Open June-Sept. Mon. and Wed.-Sat. 9am-5:30pm, Tues. 9:30am-5:30pm, Sun. 10:30am-1pm and 1:30-4pm; Oct.-May Mon.-Sat. only. Accommodations desk closes ½ hr. earlier. When the office is closed, but before 10:30pm, call Mrs. Tong, Secretary of the Oxford Association of Hotels and Guesthouses, for help in finding lodgings (tel. 24 29 91). No fee. Excellent **walking tours** daily every ½ hr. 10:30am-3:30pm (£2, children £1). **Ticket office** on premises (tel. 72 78 55) open Mon.-Fri. 10am-5pm.

Budget Travel: Oxford Student Travel Centre, 13 High St. (tel. 24 20 67). Very energetic, knowledgeable staff. International discount tickets. Open Mon.-Fri. 9:30am-5:30pm, Sat. 10am-3pm.

American Express: Keith Bailey Travel, St. Aldates St. (tel. 79 00 99), a few doors from the tourist office. Mail held and checks sold. Open Easter-Sept. Mon.-Fri. 9am-5:30pm, Sat. 9am-5pm, Sun. 10am-3pm; otherwise Mon.-Sat. only.

Currency Exchange: A Bureau de Change in the train station is open daily 8am-7:30pm.

Post Office: St. Aldates St. Open Mon.-Tues. and Thurs.-Fri. 9am-5:30pm, Wed. 9:30am-5:30pm, Sat. 9am-12:30pm. **Postal code:** OX1 1DY.

Telephones: Several at Carfax. **Telephone code:** 0865.

Trains: Information (tel. 72 23 33 or 24 95 51). Station is ½ mile west of town. Trains from London's Paddington Station (every hr.); from Stratford (change at Leamington Spa; every 2 hr.).

Buses: Gloucester Green Station, George St., 5 blocks west of Cornmarket St. 2-3 buses to London per hr. Cheaper than the train.

Bike Rental: Pennyfarthing, 5 George St. (tel. 24 93 68), near Carfax and stations. £5 per day, £9 per week for 3-speeds; £25 deposit. Open Mon.-Sat. 8:30am-5:30pm. Get free *Cycling in Oxford* booklet from any bike shop.

Emergencies: Police or **Ambulance** (tel. 999).

Women's Center: 35 Cowley Rd. (tel. 24 59 23). Phone answered Mon.-Sat. noon-4pm.

Arts Center: Old Fire Station Arts Centre, 40 George St. (tel. 72 26 48). Bulletin boards, galleries, and cafe.

Accommodations and Camping

B&Bs line the main roads leading out of town, usually requiring a bus ride or a 20-min. walk from the center. Try the 200 to 300 addresses on **Iffley Rd.,** or 250-350 **Cowley Rd.** Expect to pay at least £11 per person, and book ahead (especially for singles) in summer.

IYHF youth hostel, Jack Straw's Lane (tel. 629 97), 2½ miles from the center. Take green City Nipper minibus from Carfax. Kitchen, lounge, and a small store. Lockout 10am-5pm. Strict 10:30pm curfew (10pm in winter).

YWCA, Alexandra Residential Club, 133 Woodstock Rd. (tel. 520 21). Very long walk past top of Cornmarket St., or bus #420 or 423. Women ages 16 and up only. Bunks £5, less for longer stays.

Micklewood, 331 Cowley Rd. (tel. 24 73 28), about 1 mile from city center (take any Cowley bus). Large, clean, and comfortable rooms (each with TV), and a gracious proprietor. £11.

Kings Guest House, 363 Iffley Rd. (tel. 24 13 63). Large rooms; nice garden and proprietors. £9-10.50.

Camping: Oxford Camping International, 426 Abingdon Rd. (tel. 24 65 51). Take bus to Red Bridge car park. Laundry and warm showers. £1.50 per tent, £1.80 per frame tent, 90p per person. Open year-round.

Food

Oxford sprouts innumerable bright, new restaurants and cheap cafes to divert students from unappetizing college food. For standard pub fare, try one of the pubs listed under Entertainment. The **Covered Market** between Market St. and Carfax is the best place for fresh produce and deli foods, and also offers several inexpensive cafes.

Arts Centre Cafe, 40 George St., upstairs. Plants on the windowsill, mellow music on the stereo. Interesting entrees (smoked mackerel pie) with salad and potato from £2.75; 3 side salads £1.25. Open Mon.-Fri. 9am-7:30pm, Sat. 9am-5:30pm.

Alfredo's, 3a St. Michael's St. A triple-decker restaurant popular with students. Pizza and pasta from £2.50. Open daily noon-2:30pm and 6-10:30pm, Thurs.-Sat. until 11pm.

Munchy Munchy, 6 Park End St. Stark wooden decor redeemed by spirited cooking and a genial proprietor. About 5 different dishes each day, all Indonesian or Malaysian, each about £3.50. Open Tues.-Sat. noon-2:30pm and 5:30-10pm.

Sights and Entertainment

Since 1167, Oxford University has educated countless poets, prelates, and prime ministers; many of them studied at **Christ Church,** the wealthiest, largest, and most famous of Oxford's colleges. It has its own expansive backyard, **Christ Church Meadows,** as well as a **picture gallery** housing several da Vincis and a Rubens. Its chapel is Oxford's **cathedral.** (College open Mon.-Sat. 10:30am-1pm and 2-5:30pm, Sun. 2-5:30pm. Admission 50p, students and seniors 20p. Gallery admission 40p.) Walk along High St. to **Magdalen College,** widely considered the prettiest college. Magdalen (pronounced "maudlin") has its own deer park, rural trails (Addison's Walk), and a legacy of arty flamboyance reminiscent of alumnus Oscar Wilde. Nearby **Queen's College** (look for the statue of Queen Caroline above the gate) exhibits a statelier beauty. **New College** on Holywell St. is known for its chapel, containing a striking statue by Epstein and a painting by El Greco; its spotless garden, bordered by the craggy turrets of the old city wall; some disarming gargoyles; and cloisters quieter than a graveyard. **St. Catherine's** (left at the end of Holywell St., then bear right), a glassy and glacial geometric compound designed in 1964 by Danish architect Arne Jacobsen, is a break from traditional Oxonian architecture; as is **Keble College,** a quiet haven in patterned red brick up Parks Rd. These and other colleges are usually open in the afternoon; the tourist office can fill you in on exact opening times.

In four massive edifices on Catte St. is the intimidating **Bodleian Library,** a home for lost scholars that transports its books on an intricate subterranean railway system. The exhibition inside is like a miniature British Museum, with everything from first editions of Shakespeare to Aztec scrolls to locks of Shelley's hair. (Open Mon.-Fri. 9am-5pm, Sat. 9am-12:30pm.) Across the street is the equally intimidating **Blackwell's bookstore** (open Mon. and Wed.-Sat. 9am-5:30pm, Tues. 9:30am-5:30pm). Next to the Bodleian on Broad St. is Christopher Wren's **Sheldonian Theatre,** an architectural jewel which hosts the pomp and splendor of Oxford's graduation ceremonies. (Open mid-Feb. to mid-Nov. daily 10am-4:45pm; mid-Nov. to mid-Feb. daily 10am-3:45pm. Admission 30p, children 5p.) Up Parks Rd. is the **University Museum,** a great glass-roofed natural history exhibition with a working beehive. (Open Mon.-Sat. noon-5pm. Free.) On Beaumont St., you'll find the **Ashmolean Museum,** with a casual but outstanding collection of Italian, French, and English art as well as ancient curiosities. (Open Mon.-Sat. 10am-4pm, Sun. 2-4pm. Free.) Follow Beaumont St. to its end and visit **Worcester College's** shimmering lake. Back down St. Aldates St., on Pembroke St., is the excellent **Museum of Modern Art.** (Open Tues.-Sat. 10am-6pm, Sun. 2-6pm. Free.) The miles of entertaining historical displays in the **Museum of Oxford,** St. Aldates St., will fill you in on what you've missed on your tour. (Open Tues.-Sat. 10am-5pm. Free.)

When you've tired of the colleges, head to the end of High St. and across Magdalen Bridge to the funky neighborhood along **Cowley Road,** where you'll see a fascinating clutter of alternative lifestyles, Marxist bookshops, jumble shops, and scruffy wholefood and ethnic restaurants. The **women's center** is also nearby.

A favorite pastime here is **punting** (propelling a boat with a pole) on the river. Punts and rowboats can be rented at Folly Bridge (at the end of St. Aldates St.) or Magdalen Bridge (at the end of High St.) for £4 per hour.

Among Oxford's best pubs is **The Turf,** 4 Bath Pl., off Holywell St. Inside, it's rambling, medieval, and cozy; outside, its labyrinth of small courtyards is particularly inviting on warm nights. Special beers, punches, and country wines tempt visitors; fill up on their great salad buffet (noon-10pm). **The Chequers,** off High St., near Carfax, is unassuming and serves good food, while **The Bear,** at Alfred St. and Bear Lane, is a dyed-in-the-wool Oxford landmark with a great collection of ties hanging on the walls (it's Christ Church College's local). **The King's Arms,** Holywell St., is the university's unofficial student union, the crowded site of every student rendezvous; **The Perch,** in Binsey, serves drinks and Sunday lunch in its lovely garden.

Much at Oxford happens behind closed doors. Look at the invaluable *Oxford This Week* poster, check the tourist-office boards, or pick up *What's On in Oxford* for 50p. Especially worthwhile are various summer college productions staged in the magical gardens and cloisters; concerts at the antique **Holywell Music Rooms;** or double bills, changing weekly, at the **Penultimate Picture Palace** off Jeune St. Away from the university, the **Jericho Tavern** on Walton St. features local jazz and rock bands. Yearly events include the **May Day** celebrations, the **Summer in Oxford** festival in July and August, and **Eights Week** at the end of May, when the best and brightest gather on the river banks to nibble strawberries, gulp champagne, and watch rowers clash.

Near Oxford

Winston Churchill was born at **Blenheim Palace,** an immense mansion set 8 miles away in acres of parkland in **Woodstock.** Take the express coach (£1.20 single) or a local bus to Woodstock, or walk past the roundabout and hitch north on the A34. (Open mid-March to Oct. daily 11am-6pm. Admission £3.90, children £1.90.) Churchill is buried at nearby **Bladon.**

The countryside around Oxford is ideal for the lazy cyclist; every few miles of gently sloping road reveal still another picturesque Cotswold village. Pick up an Ordnance Survey map and explore at random, or visit **Burford,** 15 miles from Oxford, a favorite haunt of Charles II and Nell Gwynn.

Cotswolds

The Cotswolds rise almost imperceptibly from the grassy meadows of the upper Thames until they offer sweeping views across the Severn Valley and the Vale of Evesham. This is England bedecked in its finest greenery and scenery, and the wealthy buy summer homes here to enjoy the serenity.

Many Cotswolds villages were first established during Saxon times, but it was the development of the wool trade that brought prosperity to the area; the name "Cotswold" is a variant of "the hills of the sheepcotes." During the Middle Ages wool merchants in the area enjoyed wealth unknown in the rest of England, reflected in their opulent wood churches and honey-colored limestone houses.

Walking is one of the best ways to see the Cotswolds. The **Cotswold Way** follows the western escarpment of the Cotswold hills along 97 miles of gorgeous countryside. Its waymarking is clear and comprehensive; color-coded arrows painted on gates and trees highlight the entire route. Consult the Ramblers' Association's *Cotswold Way Handbook* (60p), or Mark Richards's *Cotswold Way: A Walker's Guide* (£1.50), which contains 1:25,000 maps of the route. The entire walk takes about eight days, but detours to local sights beckon frequently, and you may choose to hike a shorter segment. One of the busiest, most attractive, and most visited villages along the way is **Broadway.** An important coach stop on the old London to Worcester route, Broadway's restored Tudor, Jacobean, and Georgian buildings are roofed with traditional Cotswold tile or thatch. Broadway Beacon affords grand views across the Midland Plain.

Three miles east of Broadway, beautiful **Chipping Campden** was once the capital of the Cotswold wool trade; the town is currently famous for its "Dover Games" in late May and early June, highlighted by the brutal "sport" of shin-kicking. This activity was prohibited from 1852-1952, but has since been enthusiastically revived. Beautiful views abound from 1000-foot **Bredon Hill** where, as A.E. Housman wrote, "larks fly high." A few miles southwest lie the **Slaughters, Upper** and **Lower;** don't be alarmed—you'll be perfectly safe in these tranquil villages. The Cotswolds are littered with prehistoric and Roman ruins—take a look at the amphitheater in **Cirencester.** If nature is more your thing, visit the **Wildfowl Trust** reserve in Slimbridge (tel. (0453) 893 33).

The spa town of **Cheltenham,** on the northwestern edge of the Cotswolds, is the center of the area's burgeoning tourist trade. The **Tourist Information Centre,** Municipal Offices, Promenade (tel. 52 28 78), has maps and information on the entire region, as well as a book-a-bed-ahead service (£1 for the Cotswolds). Local buses serve the larger towns in the region, but rural transportation is sparse; ask at the tourist office, which can also recommend hikes. The **train station** is a bus ride or a 15-minute walk west of the town center. Trains run regularly from London Paddington.

Most small towns have a number of guesthouses, usually in the £8-10 range. Campgrounds are common; pick up a list at an area tourist office, or get the landowner's permission to pitch your tent in an open field. **IYHF youth hostels** dot the area, at Charlbury (tel. (0608) 81 02 02); Cleeve Hill (tel. (024267) 20 65), 4 miles northeast of Cheltenham; Duntisbourne Abbots (tel. (028582) 682), 5 miles northwest of Cirencester; Inglesham (tel. (0367) 525 46); Slimbridge (tel. (045389) 275), 4 miles from Cotswold Way; and Stow-on-the-Wold (tel. (0451) 304 97 or 307 40).

Stratford-upon-Avon

In Stratford today, the diverse nature of human characterand expression that Samuel Johnson so praised in hometowner William Shakespeare's plays lives on in flying elbows and crushed toes as tourists jostle for photo space. But away from the crowds, you may be surprised to discover that Stratford is quite lovely, full of old houses and well-kept gardens.

The five Shakespeare houses are run by the Birthplace Trust. You can enter them individually (£1-1.50) or buy a ticket (£4.50) that admits you to all. The **Birthplace** on Henley St. is a set of bare rooms filled with indifferent pots and a few stray manuscripts. (Open April-Oct. Mon.-Sat. 9am-6pm, Sun. 10am-6pm; Nov.-March Mon.-Sat. 9am-4:30pm, Sun. 1:30-4:30pm.) **New Place** on Chapel St. was Stratford's grandest house when Shakespeare bought it for £60. It is comfortably dark-timbered and airy; the beautiful gardens can be easily seen from Chapel Lane. **Hall's Croft,** on Old Town Rd., home of Shakespeare's daughter, is grander still, and also has lovely gardens. (New Place and Hall's Croft both open April-Oct. Mon.-Sat. 10am-6pm, Sun. 2-6pm; Nov.-March Mon.-Sat. 9am-4pm.) **Anne Hathaway's Cottage** is convenient to **Warwick Castle,** a photographer's dream and perhaps England's finest medieval castle. The castle's magnificent battlements loom over gracious, meandering grounds, with plenty of places to picnic. (Castle and grounds open March-Oct. daily 10am-5:30pm; Nov.-Feb. daily 10am-4:30pm. Admission £3.75.) If the footpath doesn't appeal there is a Midland Red bus from Stratford to Warwick (express #X57, every 1-2 hr., 15-20 min.; slower buses run more frequently). There is also frequent train service from Stratford to Warwick (£2.10).

Mary Arden's House, where Shakespeare's mother spent her childhood (in Wilmcote, 3 miles away by local train or bike, or accessible by footpath from Hathaway's Cottage), is relatively tranquil, evocative, and pretty. (Open April-Oct. Mon.-Sat. 9am-6pm, Sun. 10am-6pm; Nov.-March Mon.-Sat. 9am-4pm.)

Perhaps the least tarnished and most moving sight in Stratford proper is **Holy Trinity Church,** where Shakespeare lies buried under a humble slab and two menacing couplets he devised to ward off grave robbers. As authentic as the Birthplace Trust properties and less overrun is **Harvard House** on High St., an unassuming Tudor home filled with simple period furniture.

The **Royal Shakespeare Theatre's gallery** is a museum of props and costumes that would-be thespians can play with. (Open Mon.-Sat. 9am-6pm, Sun. noon-5pm. Admission 60p, students 35p.) Don't miss an opportunity to see the **Royal Shakespeare Company** in its main theater or in the theater's more intimate, experimental appendage, **The Other Place.** The new **Swan Theatre,** farther down on Waterside, has been specially designed for RSC productions of plays written by other Elizabethan playwrights. Be sure to book ahead (tel. 29 56 23) for regular tickets (£5-14); 24-hour information tel. 691 91. Once in Stratford, try lining up for cancellations (by 9:30am) or infrequent £4 student standby seats (1-2 hr. before curtain). You may be able to get standing-room tickets (£2); check on the day of the performance.

Stratford's **Tourist Information Centre,** 1 High St. (tel. (0789) 29 31 27; recorded information tel. 675 22), will help you find a room; a list is posted after hours. (Open March-Oct. Mon.-Sat. 9am-5:30pm, Sun. 2-5pm; Nov.-Feb. Mon.-Sat. 11am-4pm.) To reach Stratford's large, attractive **IYHF youth hostel,** Hemmingford House, Alverton (tel. 29 70 93), walk 2 miles along Wellesbourne Rd., or catch the hourly bus #158 from the bus station; line up before the reception opens at 5pm. (£3.65. Curfew 11pm.) For B&Bs, it's best to make reservations, especially in summer. The best places to look are along **Grove Road, Evesham Place,** and **Evesham Road. Strathcona,** 47 Evesham Rd. (tel. 29 21 01), is pleasant and well-run, but a bit noisy (£9). **Lemarquand,** 186 Evesham Rd. (tel. 20 41 64), offers big rooms and breakfasts (£9). If a search in this area fails, try **Shipston Road,** across the river, or the tourist office's accommodations service (90p). Campers should find **The Elms** (tel. 29 23 12), 1 mile east of town on the B4056. (Tent and one person £1.50, extra people £1 each. Open April-Oct.)

Food in Stratford is generally expensive and bad. **Kingfisher,** 13 Ely St., is your basic chippie (£1-2). The **Windmill Inn,** Church St., is one of the more reasonably priced places in town: ploughman's lunches only £1.70, fish and meat dishes £2-2.50. (Open Tues.-Sat. noon-2pm and 5:30-8pm, Sun.-Mon. noon-2pm.)

Stratford is 2¼ hours by rail from London Paddington (£11.60 one way, £12.40 day return), and 1½ hours from Oxford (£6 one way, £6.50 day return). Buses run to and from London's Victoria Coach Station (2¾ hr., £7.50 one way or day return, £10 period return). The "Shakespeare Connection" can get you back to London after a night at the theater (£10.20 one way, £11.10 day return); contact **Guide Friday,** Civic Hall, 14 Rother St. (tel. (0789) 29 44 66), to reserve a space.

East Anglia

Bound to the North Sea by an intricate web of marshes, rivers, and streams, East Anglia's flat green expanses take on an oceanic aspect of their own. The peat marshes of the southern Fens and the brooks and tributaries of the northern Broads are a haven for wildlife, while cycling along the by-roads will take you through medieval villages with stark Norman churches, rambling stately homes, and thatched cottages smothered in rose trellises.

Cambridge and Norwich are the best centers for touring the region. The **Anglia Ranger Ticket** is good for unlimited train travel throughout the region (£15 for 2 days, £22 per week). Buses cover the areas that trains don't; an **Explorer** bus ticket (£2.70) gives you unlimited travel for one day on all buses in East Anglia. Cyclists and hikers will delight in the fact that East Anglia enjoys the lowest annual rainfall of any region in Britain and that it is almost completely flat; bike rental in most towns is about £3 per day and £15-17 per week. Hitchhiking may be the best bet in this region of gracious motorists and capricious bus schedules.

Cambridge

Cambridge is the quintessential university town—brimming with students, bicycles, and bookshops. The academic rivalry between Oxford and Cambridge is ancient and tireless, but Cambridge undoubtedly surpasses Oxford in setting. The town exudes a rural charm, and the university takes full advantage of the River Cam, cultivating the riverside gardens and meadows of the Backs.

Orientation and Practical Information

The names of Cambridge's two main streets change every few blocks. The main shopping avenue starts at Magdalene Bridge and is known progressively as Bridge Street, Sidney Street, St. Andrew's Street, and Regent Street; the other, the main drag through the university, is known alternately as St. John's Street, Trinity Street, King's Parade, and Trumpington Street. **Market Square** lies between the two.

Tourist Office: Tourist Information Centre, Wheeler St. (tel. 32 26 40 or 35 89 77, ext. 371; evenings and weekends tel. 35 33 63), a block south of the marketplace. Piles of leaflets and listings for all of East Anglia. Open March-Oct. Mon.-Fri. 9am-6pm, Sat. 9am-5pm, Sun. 10:30am-3:30pm; Nov.-Feb. Mon.-Fri. 9am-5:30pm, Sat. 9am-5pm. Information and tickets for Cambridge events at the ground floor box office in the **Central Library,** Lion Yard, in the Grafton shopping mall off St. Andrew's St.

American Express: Abbot Travel, 25 Sidney St. (tel. 35 16 36). Mail held, checks cashed and sold, but no wired money accepted. Open Mon.-Sat. 9am-5:30pm.

Post Office: 9-11 St. Andrew's St. Open Mon.-Tues. and Thurs.-Fri. 9am-5:30pm, Wed. 9:30am-5:30pm, Sat. 9am-12:30pm.

Telephones: At 1 Regent St. **Telephone code:** 0223.

Trains: Frequent trains from London's Liverpool St. Station (1 hr., £7.10 one way, £7.90 day return). Last train returns to London at around 10pm. Buses #180, 181, 185, and 186 run from the station to the town center (2km).

Buses: Drummer St. Station is 2 blocks east of Market Sq. Coaches to London's Victoria Coach Station every 2 hr. (2 hr., £6.50 one way or day return).

Bike Rental: Howes Cycles, 104 Regent St. (tel. 35 03 50). £2.50 per day, £5 per week. Open at 9am—get there promptly. Otherwise, the tourist office has a list.

Emergencies: Police or **Ambulance** (tel. 999). Police headquarters at Parkside (tel. 35 89 66).

Accommodations, Camping, and Food

The tourist office will find you a room for a 95p fee, or offer you their list with addresses and telephone numbers; after hours, a list is posted in the window. **Tenison Road,** near the train station, and **Jesus Lane,** closer to the town center, are good places to look.

Youth Hostel (IYHF), 97 Tenison Rd. (tel. 35 46 01); enter on Devonshire Rd. Large, super-clean, and modern; always crowded in summer. Laundry and kitchen facilities, and bikes for hire. £3.85, £3.15. Lockout 10am-1pm. Curfew 11:30pm. Open mid-Jan. to mid-Dec.

Mrs. Spalding, 56 Jesus Ln. (tel. 35 38 58). Very friendly, with high standards. Well worth it. £8.50, £8 in top floor rooms.

Mrs. V. M. Day, 72 Jesus Ln. (tel. 35 69 61). Very kind proprietor. Large, pleasant rooms (bathtubs, no showers) and a big breakfast. £8.50.

Mrs. Owen, 65 Jesus Ln. (tel. 606 48). Nice family house with big rooms. £8.

Ellensleigh, 37 Tenison Rd. (tel. 648 88). Mrs. Marchant runs a convivial, good-value house, and dishes up a big breakfast. Singles £12, doubles £20.

Mrs. Connally, 67 Jesus Ln. (tel. 617 53). The proprietor's cheerfulness is reflected in her bright orange decor. Doubles £16.

Camping: Highfield Farm Camping, Long Rd., Comberton (tel. (0223) 26 23 08), 2½ miles west on A45. Take bus #118 or 119 from Drummer St. Not particularly scenic. £3.60 per tent. Open April-Oct.

For fresh fruit and vegetables, shop at the **outdoor market** in Market Square. (Open Mon.-Sat. 8:30am-5pm.) For vegetarian and wholefood groceries, visit **Arjunam,** 12 Mill Rd. (open Mon.-Sat. 9:30am-6pm) and **Natural Selection,** 32 Regent St. (open Mon.-Sat. 9am-6pm).

Like many university towns, Cambridge has a variety of inexpensive restaurants. **Varsity,** 35 St. Andrew's St., is a quiet Greek restaurant with delicious chicken and lamb dishes for £3-4. **Crusts Wine Bar and Restaurant,** 21 Northampton St., is full of students, and great for lunch (£1.50-2.50) or dinner (£3-6). (Open Mon.-Sat. 11am-2pm and 5-11pm.) **Nettles,** 5 St. Edward's Passage, is a tiny place specializing in vegetarian fare under £2. (Open Mon.-Sat. 10am-8pm.) The **Taj Mahal,** 37-39 Regent St., is one of the most popular Indian restaurants in Cambridge, with meals £4-8. (Open daily noon-3pm and 6pm-midnight.)

Sights and Entertainment

The pamphlet *Cambridge: A Brief Guide for Visitors* includes basic information about the colleges and various museums, and provides a street map (available at the tourist office for 25p). If you're staying in Cambridge for more than a couple of days, invest 90p in the *Official Guide,* available at the tourist office and in bookshops. It covers the sights, entertainment, and history of Cambridge, and tells about places of interest outside the city. *The Citizen's Guide* (25p), available at 51 New Market Rd., lists and discusses virtually every shop and service in Cambridge. The tourist office runs a tour of the town at 6:30pm, and excellent walking tours that concentrate on four of the major colleges—well worth £1.85.

Oldest and most picturesque of the university's colleges are those that lie between Trinity Street-King's Parade and the River Cam. On the other side of the river are the elegant gardens and meadows of the **Backs,** where Cantabrigian scholars go to think. If you have time for only a few colleges, try to see **King's, Trinity, Queen's, Christ's,** and perhaps **Jesus.** Remember that they are closed to the public between exams and graduation (mid-May to mid-June). While wandering through Christ's, visit the gardens (open Mon.-Fri. 2-4pm). The other college known for its sculpted flora is **Clare** (open Mon.-Fri. 2:30-4pm). At King's College, visit the impressive **King's College Chapel,** begun by Henry VI and finished by Henry VII. Be sure to see the Renaissance wood screen, the magnificent stained glass, and Rubens' *Adoration of the Magi* over the altar. (Chapel open vacations Mon.-Sat. 9:30am-5:45pm, Sun. 10:30am-5:45pm; otherwise Mon.-Sat. 9am-3:45pm, Sun. 2-3pm and 4:30-5:45pm.) **St. John's College** is worth a visit for its Bridge of Sighs, which resembles Venice's, and **Trinity** for its library, designed by Sir Christopher Wren.

Perhaps the best way to enjoy Cambridge is to rent some form of river transportation. **Scudamore's Boatyards** at Magdalene Bridge (tel. 35 97 50) rents by the hour: £3.60 for punts, £3.40 for rowboats, £3.20 for canoes. Go on a weekday or after 4:30pm to avoid bumper-punting, or try the more tranquil route from the boatyards at Silver Street to Grantchester Meadows.

Cambridge is most lively during the three eight-week terms that university is in session: Michaelmas, from early October through early December; Lent, from mid-January to mid-March; and Easter, from mid-April through the first week of June. Not surprisingly, Cantabrigian pubs are most crowded during those six months. **The Cambridge Arms,** King St., is a thriving pub that used to be a brewery. **Portland Arms** on Chesterton Rd. occasionally has live music. The **Eagle Hotel** on Benet St. has welcomed sages from Shakespeare to Crick and Watson, who told the world of DNA. On the river, try the **Anchor** or the **Mill,** both near the Silver St. Bridge.

Cambridge hosts much drama, particularly during term-time. The **Arts Theatre Club** is at 6 St. Edwards Passage (tel. 35 20 00); £2.60 standby tickets are sold one hour before most Friday and Saturday performances. (Students £1 off at other times. Box office open Mon.-Sat. 9:30am-8pm.) For enthusiastic performances throughout the year, try the **Amateur Dramatic Club** on Park St. (tel. 35 95 47), with seats only £1.50-1.90. Each summer the **Cambridge Festival** includes an extensive and varied series of musical concerts (some free) and special exhibits during the last two weeks of July, ending in a large folk festival. Tickets (£1.50-10) are available from the Central Library Box Office in Lion Yard (tel. 35 78 51).

Near Cambridge

Fifteen miles north of Cambridge, **Ely Cathedral** stands in tribute to the piety of its founder, St. Etheldreda, seventh-century Queen of Northumbria. (Open Mon.-Sat. 7:30am-7pm, Sun. and in winter 7:30am-6pm.) Hourly trains roll from Cambridge to the town of Ely (30 min.), as do three daily buses (40 min.).

Located 25 miles east of Cambridge, the little village of **Bury St. Edmunds** owes its name to Edmund, the Saxon king interred there. Its four-square street plan is lined with historic buildings, from the Georgian **Athenaeum,** where Charles Dickens gave readings so enthusiastic that he endangered his health, to the ruins and lovely garden of the eleventh-century **abbey.** Buses from Cambridge serve Bury daily every two to three hours. Thumbers should find the A143.

Norwich and the Broads

Norwich's medieval title of "Second City" has been revived with tongue in cheek for the annual **festival** in July, and the city's architectural offerings—a cathedral, castle, and host of churches—coupled with a vital commitment to the arts, bring Norwich close to the top of any traveler's list. Visit the square **castle,** now an excellent art museum (open Mon.-Sat. 10am-5pm, Sun. 2-5pm; admission 60p), and the soaring **cathedral** (open daily 7:30am-7pm), but don't ignore Norwich's contemporary offerings. **Premises,** Norwich's art center, in Reeve's Yard off St. Benedict's (tel. (0603) 66 03 52), stages a variety of performances, runs workshops, and has an excellent cafe. (Open Mon.-Sat. noon-6pm, also Thurs.-Sat. 7-10pm.) The **Theatre Royal,** Theatre St. features debuts of London-bound shows and a variety of performing artists. (Open Mon.-Sat. 10am-9pm, Sun. 10am-4pm.)

The **tourist office,** Guildhall, the westward continuation of London St. (tel. (0603) 66 60 71), has a long list of events and a free list of accommodations. (Open June-Sept. daily 9:30am-6pm; Oct.-May Mon.-Fri. 9:30am-5:30pm, Sat. 9:30am-1pm.) The **IYHF youth hostel,** 112 Turner Rd. (tel. (0603) 276 47), is modern and clean and has an elegant common room. (£3.85. Open April-Oct. daily; March and Nov. Thurs.-Mon.) To reach the hostel, take bus #19 or 20 from Castle Meadows to the Earl of Leicester pub. Look for B&Bs along roads to the west of the city center, especially **Unthank Rd.** and **Earlham Rd.** (£8-10). Rail service to London and Cambridge is fast and frequent (but check schedules on Sun.), and the **Anywhere Bus Ticket** (£2.70) will take you through the surrounding area for a day.

The **Norfolk Broads,** a network of channels and tributaries through flooded peat bogs, spreads from just east of Norwich to the English Channel. Much of the land is nature reserve; decaying windmills and miles of wild, unspoiled country are all you'll find here. For information on sights and tours, call or visit the **Hoveton Information Centre,** on Station Rd. in Wroxham (tel. (06053) 22 81), 7 miles northeast of Norwich; take bus #717 or 718 from Norwich. (Open Easter-Oct. Tues.-Sat. 10am-6pm.) The **tourist office** (tel. (0553) 76 36 44), in **King's Lynn,** a medieval trading city on the banks of the Great Ouse River, has information on nature reserves and beaches to the north; it is located at the corner of Queen St. and St. James St. (Open May-Sept. Mon.-Thurs. 10am-1pm and 2-5pm, Fri. 10am-1pm and 2-4:30pm, Sat. 10am-4pm; Oct.-April Mon.-Sat. only.) Buses and trains run regularly to Lynn from Cambridge and Norwich; those from Norwich are cheaper and faster. Just down the street is an **IYHF youth hostel** (tel. 77 24 61); its rustic setting in a sixteenth-century priest's house and its heavenly down comforters make it an excellent place to bed down for a night or two. (Open July-Aug. daily; April-June and Sept. Fri.-Wed. £3.35.)

Southwest of Norwich, the city of **Harwich** is a major port for ferries to the Netherlands. **Sealink** offers one day sailing and one night sailing to Hook of Holland (£20 single; £5 extra in economy berth at night). Call (0255) 50 40 41 for information. If you plan to continue to Scandinavia, ask about bargain *Scanbridge* fares.

North England

Sliced by the Pennine Mountains, the North is a region of natural boundaries that have historically prevented the easy exchange of goods and ideas. England's spine is constantly massaged by hikers trekking along the Pennine Way, the longest of England's long-distance footpaths. The Lake Country, Britain's most famous "wilderness," is a lot less wild than when it fired the imagination of Wordsworth, but a region of fresh mountain streams and misty hillsides nonetheless. Although this is probably the area most responsible for British food's bad name, try tasty local produce like Wensleydale cheese or Craster kippers (smoked herring) from Northumbria.

BritRail's **North West Rover** (£24) and **North East Rover** (£30) offer a week of unrestricted regional rail travel. **Wayfarer, Explorer,** or **Day Rambler** tickets, good for a day's bus travel within a certain region or on a certain company's lines, are available in many areas (£3).

Cheshire and Derby

Lying just south of the Merseyside/Manchester/Yorkshire Riding industrial heartland, the counties of Cheshire and Derby are surprisingly attractive. Chester, the capital of Cheshire, is a well-preserved medieval town just across the Mersey from Liverpool's sprawl. Chester is also a likely point of entry into North Wales; trains run to Holyhead and into Snowdonia, via Colwyn Bay and Bangor, and Crosville runs buses along the coast to Caernarfon. The Peak District National Park is England's most accessible wilderness, nonetheless beautiful for the large numbers of cityfolk who hike its trails every summer weekend.

While *Let's Go: Europe* doesn't cover them, the industrial cities of this region were the engine room of Britain at its Greatest, and are beginning to market this heritage for the visitor. Bradford, Leeds, Sheffield, and Stoke aren't of much interest, but **Liverpool** and **Manchester** are the capitals of an England that gets precious little mention by the tourist authorities. Liverpool in particular is interesting; Beatles fans will surely want to visit Abbey Road and Penny Lane, and soccer fans can see the consistently best soccer in Britain at Anfield or Goodison Park—the terraces can be dangerous.

The delightful jumble of Roman, medieval, and modern that is **Chester** is totally encircled by a high **city wall** broken by only seven gates. Past and present mingle gracefully; walkways join two-tiered black-and-white timbered buildings (Chester's unique "rows") to modern shopping centers. Just outside Newgate, part of Britain's largest **Roman amphitheater,** seating 7000, was excavated in 1960. The **Grosvenor Museum,** 27 Grosvenor St. (tel. 216 16), concentrates on Chester's Roman period. (Open Mon.-Sat. 10:30am-5pm, Sun. 2-5pm. Free.) The **Chester Visitor Centre** (tel. 31 89 16), houses a life-size reconstruction of a Chester street in the 1850s (open daily 9am-9pm; free). The **cathedral** has Norman arches in the north transept and a branch of Barclays Bank in the west wing.

Chester's main **tourist office** is in the Town Hall (tel. 401 44, ext. 2111 or 2250; open June-Sept. Mon.-Sat. 9am-5:30pm, Sun. 10am-4pm; Oct.-May Mon.-Sat. only), and there's another branch in the Chester Visitor Centre (tel. 31 31 26). Several B&Bs for £10 are along Hoole Road near the train station; try **Alexandra Lodge,** 1 Hamilton St., at Hoole Rd. (tel. 31 98 60), near the third traffic light from the railroad bridge. Chester also has an **IYHF youth hostel,** 40 Hough Green (tel. 68 00 56), 1½ miles from town; take bus #16, 17, B2, or B4. (£3.40, £2.60.) Stop at **Needham's** on Lower Bridge St. for greaseless fish and chips (open Mon.-Sat. 11:30am-2:30pm and 5-8pm), or try **Sidoli** on Northgate St. for pasta, pizza, or homemade ice cream (open Mon.-Sat. 10am-10:30pm, Sun. 2-5pm for ice cream only). **The Falcon** and **Ye Olde King's Head** are restored seventeenth-century houses turned pubs on Lower Bridge St.

Between Manchester and Sheffield, the **Peak District National Park** rises out of rolling pastureland and gentle river valleys. At higher elevations, especially in the northern park, the landscape is bleak peat moorland; in the valleys sheep frolic on the riverbanks, fenced in by drystone walls built without mortar. Since major cities are so close, public transport into and through the park is excellent, and it actually improves on Sundays. There is easy rail and bus access from Manchester and Sheffield, and also bus access from Nottingham.

There are **National Park Information Centres** and **tourist offices** in **Ashbourne** (tel. (0335) 436 66); **Bakewell** (tel. (062981) 32 27); **Buxton** (tel. (0298) 51 06); **Castleton** (tel. (0433) 206 79); **Edale** (tel. (0433) 702 07); **Fairholmes; Hartington; Matlock Bath** (tel. (0629) 550 82); and **Torside.** Hartington and Torside are open summer weekends only; the rest are open daily in summer and weekends in winter, with Bakewell, Buxton, Edale, and Matlock Bath open weekdays in winter as well. There are over twenty **IYHF youth hostels** in the park, including **Bakewell,** Fly Hill (tel. (062981) 23 13; £3.40, £2.60; open Jan.-March and Nov.-Dec. Fri.-Sat.; April-Aug. and mid-Sept. to Oct. Fri.-Wed.); **Buxton,** off Harpur Hill Rd. (tel. (0928) 22 87); £3.40, £2.60; open April-Oct. Mon.-Sat.; Nov. to mid-Dec. Tues.-

Sat.); **Castleton** (tel. (0433) 202 35; £3.40, £2.60; open Feb.-Dec. daily); **Edale** (tel. (0433) 703 02; £3.85, £3.15; open Jan.-Feb. and Nov.-Dec. Fri.-Sat.; March-Oct. daily); and **Matlock,** 40 Bank Rd. (tel. (0629) 29 83; £3.40, £2.60; open Jan.-March Wed.-Sun.; April-Oct. Tues.-Sun.). The region is also rich in B&Bs (about £8) and campsites.

In the southern park, the former spa town of **Buxton** still keeps its swimming pool filled with spa water; just outside of town, **Poole's Cavern** is near a nature trail through **Grin Low Woods.** (Cavern open Easter-May and Oct. Thurs.-Tues. 10am-5pm; June-Sept. daily 10am-5pm.) A mile out of town in a landscaped garden, the **Brook Cottage** B&B (tel. (0298) 20 24) is worth the walk (£7.50). To the east, **Bakewell** still holds the Monday livestock market that it has held since 1330. In Bakewell, try **The Mount** B&B on Yeld Rd. (tel. (06981) 21 98), with a fine flower garden (£10). Farther south, in **Matlock Bath,** a **cable car** will take you up to the Heights of Abraham for some superb views (£2.95 round-trip). The **Peak District Mining Museum** is also in town. (Open Feb.-Nov. daily 10am-5pm; Dec.-Jan. Sat.-Sun. 11am-4pm. Admission 80p; students, seniors, and children 40p.) The **Tor View** guest house near the cable car (tel. (0629) 562 62) is a bargain at £7.50.

In the northern park, the village of **Edale** is at the southern terminus of the **Pennine Way** footpath to the Scottish border. Nearby **Castleton,** in the shadow of **Peveril Castle's** ruins, has four caverns where the town's characteristic Blue John stone is quarried. At **Speedwell Cavern,** you tour by boat. (Open year-round daily 9am-5pm. Admission £2, children £1.50.) From Castelton, you can see **Mam Tor,** known as "Shivering Mountain." **Hathersage** was the model for the village of Morton in *Jane Eyre.*

York

Graced by the heavenly Minster and bridges arching over the Rivers Ouse and Foss, York will gently lure you into its ancient, rose-colored precincts. Its magnificent thirteenth-century walls arch over the four chief gates to the city: Micklegate, Bootham, Monk, and Walmgate. Mind you—in York, the streets are called "gates," the gates are called "bars," and the bars are called "pubs." Whatever you call them, York's enchanting mazes are crammed with sightseers in July and August, but the city is well worth exploring despite the crowds.

Orientation and Practical Information

Fast and frequent **Intercity 125** trains will take you from London's King's Cross Station to York in 2 hours (£29-37 Saver return). Trains also depart frequently for Edinburgh via Durham and Newcastle (2½ hr., £34-42 Saver return). National Express Rapide coaches will get you from London Victoria to York in 4½ hours (£15 single or day return). If hitching from London, take the A1, then pick up the A64 between Leeds and York.

The **Tourist Information Centre,** in the De Grey Rooms off Exhibition Sq. (tel. 217 56), near the Minster, offers useful leaflets, including a free accommodations list with map, and *What's On,* with information on entertainment in York. Their booking service costs £1.25. (Open June-Sept. Mon.-Sat. 9am-8pm, Sun. 2-5pm; Oct.-May Mon.-Sat. 9am-5pm.) There is also a branch office in the railway station. (Open Mon.-Sat. 9:30am-8pm, Sun. 11am-6pm.) York's **telephone code** is 0904.

Accommodations, Camping, and Food

B&Bs cost £9 or more unless you book ahead for one of the cheaper places, which fill up quickly. Fortunately, there is usually room at one of the hostels.

IYHF Youth Hostel, Haverford, Water End, Clifton (tel. 531 47). Take bus #17 to Clifton Green, or walk 1 mile from Exhibition Sq. down Bootham to Clifton. Large, superior-grade hostel. £3.85, £3.15. Curfew 10:30pm. Open Feb. to mid-Dec. daily.

Bishophill House Youth Hostel, 11-13 Bishophill Senior Rd. (tel. 259 04). Probably the best inexpensive place to stay in York; always has room. TV lounge, bike rentals, and only a 10-min. walk from Exhibition Sq. Reasonably clean. Bed in large dorm £3, in small dorm £4.50, singles £7. Continental breakfast 80p, English breakfast £1.70. 24-hr. access.

International House, 33 Bootham (tel. 228 74). Centrally located. Fills up quickly. TV room. £4. Hot showers included. No breakfast or cooking facilities. No curfew; £2 key deposit.

If you're hunting for B&Bs on your own, try **Haxby Road** in Bootham, or the **Mount** area down Blossom St. near the railway station. The **Queen Anne Guest House** at 24 Queen Anne Rd., near Bootham (tel. 293 89), charges £8.50 for very clean rooms. **South View Guest House,** 114 Acomb Rd. (tel. 79 65 12), has large rooms and small prices (£7.50). Take bus #5, 5A, 7, or 7A to West Bank, Acomb. Camping is at **Bishopthorpe,** 3 miles south of York off the A64 (tel. 70 44 42). (£2.50 for tent and 4 people. Open May-Sept.)

Just off King's Square is an open-air **market.** Down Low Petergate at #75, you'll find **Yates,** a cafe and bakeshop. **York Wholefood,** 98 Micklegate, is a good-value wholefood restaurant (open Mon.-Sat. 10am-4pm and Thurs.-Sat. 7:30-10pm) above a well-stocked wholefood shop (open Mon.-Wed. 9am-5:30pm, Thurs.-Sat. 9am-10pm). **The King's Manor,** Exhibition Sq., serves a cheap lunch (from £1.30) in a charming seventeenth-century dining room (open Mon.-Fri. noon-2pm); and **St. William's Restaurant,** 3 College St., in a cobbled courtyard next to the cathedral, serves morning coffee, lunch, and tea. (Open Mon.-Sat. 10am-5pm; lunch served noon-7:30pm.) **Lew's Place,** King's Staithes, near Ouse Bridge, has large portions and delicious meals for £3.20-5. **Kooks,** 108 Fishergate, offers a lively atmosphere with games at every table. (Open Tues.-Fri. noon-3pm and 7pm-midnight, Sat.-Sun. 7pm-midnight.) For pub grub, see Entertainment below.

Sights

A promenade along the city's medieval walls starts at **Bootham Bar,** near the tourist office, and continues toward **Monk Bar.** This is the most beautiful part of the wall, with glimpses of the Minster through the trees. At **Walmgate Bar,** take a look at one of the few remaining "barbicans," a double-gate device which gave city defenders a second crack at the enemy.

The magnificent **Minster** (an old name denoting mission center) is estimated to contain more than half the medieval stained glass in England. The Great East Window, spanning an area larger than a tennis court, is the largest stained-glass window in the world. In July 1984, a fire broke out in the south transept, the oldest part of the cathedral, completely destroying the roof; the rest of the Minster was unharmed and is open to visitors. Ascend the 275 steps of the **Lantern Tower** (£1, children 50p) for a broad panorama. (Minster open daily at 7am-8:30pm; suggested donation 80p. Tower open daily 10am-6pm.) Outside, refresh yourself in the nineteenth-century **Yorkshire Museum Gardens,** off Museum St., where you will find the multi-angular tower of the first-century Roman wall and the ruins of **St. Mary's Abbey.** You can picnic and watch a game of bowls on the green in the northern corner. The **museum** itself has exhibits on York's Roman past. (Open Mon.-Sat. 10am-5pm, Sun. 1-5pm. Admission £1.50; students, seniors, and children 75p.) A host of historic buildings lies behind the Minster, including the magnificently preserved and furnished **Treasurer's House.** (Open April-Oct. daily 10:30am-5pm. Admission £1.30, children 60p.) You can also ramble through the narrow **Shambles,** once the butcher's quarters, and visit the **Whip-ma-whop-ma-gate,** York's shortest street.

The huge **Castle Museum,** Castlegate, is a must. Endowed primarily with the vast collection of Dr. Kirk, a nineteenth-century physician who often accepted antiques, relics, and "bygones" in lieu of a fee, it's one of the best folk museums anywhere. Visit **Kirkgate,** a cobbled reconstruction of a Victorian street, and the **Half Moon Court,** its Edwardian counterpart, complete with a pub. You can also learn about the history of the kitchen, the bathtub, and the vacuum cleaner. (Open Mon.-Sat.

9:30am-5:30pm, Sun. 10am-5:30pm. Admission £2.25; students, seniors, and children £1.15.)

Across from the Castle Museum is **Clifford's Tower;** a remnant of York Castle, it was the site of the worst anti-Jewish uprising in English history. York's Jews, besieged by their fellow citizens, committed communal suicide here in 1190. (Open late March and early Oct. Mon.-Sat. 9:30am-6:30pm, Sun. 2-6:30pm; April-Sept. daily 9:30am-6:30pm; mid-Oct. to mid-March Mon.-Sat. 9:30am-4pm, Sun. 2-4pm. Admission 75p, students and seniors 55p, children 35p.) The **National Railway Museum** is on Leeman St., behind the station. (Open Mon.-Sat. 10am-6pm, Sun. 11am-6pm. Admission £1.50; students, seniors, and children 75p.)

The tourist office arranges a free walking tour; meet across from the office in Exhibition Sq. (April-Oct. daily at 10:15am and 2:15pm; June-Aug. also at 7pm.)

Entertainment

York's pubs are noted as much for their atmosphere as for their food. The **Nags Head,** Micklegate, serves decent pub grub from £1.60, or try **The Lowther,** King's Staith, for a riverside atmosphere. The most popular drinking, eating, and socializing spot must be the **Black Swan Inn** on Peasholme Green, once the home of Martin Bowes, twice Lord Mayor of London and goldsmith to Queen Elizabeth I. Fine local and guest folk talent performs upstairs on Thursday nights. The **Olde Starre** on Stonegate St., dating from the seventeenth century, is the most venerable of York public houses. **Oscar's Wine Bar and Bistro** in Little Stonegate serves good mixed salads, and has jazz and swing every Monday night from 10pm on. The leaflet *Historic Pubs,* available at the tourist office, is a worthwhile investment if you're interested in doing more pub-crawling.

For outdoor entertainment of all kinds, take a weekend afternoon to visit **King's Square,** where musicians, politicians, and evangelists all compete for your loyalty. The **Theatre Royal,** St. Leonard's Pl. (tel. 235 68), performs classical and modern plays; student seats are available Monday through Friday (£1.50). The **Arts Centre York,** Mickelgate (tel. 271 29), hosts avant-garde theater and classical and folk concerts on its intimate sunken stage. For a peek into supernatural York, join the **Ghost Walk** (£1.20), leaving Monday through Friday at 8pm from the Angler's Arms on Stonegate (£1.50).

Yorkshire Dales

The unique topography of this huge upland area extends from the famous moors and foothills of the southwest, through Airedale, Ribbledale, Wharfedale, Wensleydale, and Swaledale, encompassing the Pennine Hills and surrounding valleys. From Malham up to Alston Moor in Cumbria, waterfalls and rushing rivers have carved steep-sided limestone valleys and gorges ("scars" to the locals) out of bog and moor, leaving high, humpbacked hills careening downward in vast swaths of green, brown, and purple.

The Dales are a hiker's paradise. The **Pennine Way** and the **Dales Way** slice through the National Park area, where the **National Park Information Centres** can give you up-to-date information on weather, equipment, and the best travel routes. They can be found at Aysgarth Falls (tel. (09693) 424); Clapham (tel. (04685) 419); Malham (tel. (07293) 363); Hawes (tel. (09697) 450); Sedbergh (tel. 0587) 201 25); and Grassington (tel. (0756) 75 27 48). The center in Grassington, on Hebden Rd. across from the station, is the most comprehensive. To explore the area's lesser-known corners, use a reputable guide such as Wainwright's *Walks in Limestone Country.*

Unfortunately, the Dales are difficult to reach. The only place in the Dales served by BritRail is Skipton; local buses cover everything else, but the only frequent services are to Grassington and Malham. Pick up timetables for **West Yorkshire Road Car** (tel. (0423) 660 61) and **Pennine Motor Services** (tel. Gargrave 215), the major operators, at park or tourist offices. Both companies offer **Explorer** tickets good fc a day's travel (£3), but since they don't honor each other's, it's hard to plan a rout that makes the tickets worthwhile. **IYHF youth hostels** are everywhere in the Dale: **Hawes** (tel. (09697) 368), **Keld** (tel. (0748) 862 59), and **Malham** (tel. (07293) 321 hostels along the Pennine Way are closed on weekdays except in the summer, s call ahead. **Ingleton Hostel** (tel. (0468) 414 44), on the edge of the Northern Park is a link hostel for the Lake District, so make reservations here as well. Quiete hostels include **Dacre Banks** (tel. (0423) 78 04 31), a simple school building in Nid derdale (£2.39, £1.90; open April-Aug. Tues.-Sun.), and **Linton** (tel. (0756) 75 2 00), a seventeenth-century rectory on the Skipton-Grassington bus route (£3.40 £2.60; open March and Oct. Tues.-Sat.; April-Sept. Mon.-Sat.; Nov.-Feb. Fri.-Sat.) A relatively new association, **Dalesbarns,** offers cheap accommodation in converte barns (£3). Pick up a leaflet at a National Park Centre for more information. Man pubs and farmhouses in the Dales have B&Bs for £7-8; check at local post office for information. National Park offices have a complete list (25p).

In the southern part of the Dales district, you'll find **Grassington** and **Bolton Abbey** settled along the River Wharfe. The abbey, once a peaceful monastic site now serves as a crowded swimming hole in the summer. A West Yorkshire bus from Skipton stops at Bolton Abbey.

At **Malham** you'll find the great limestone cliffs of Malham Cove, a small lak called Malham Tarn, and Gordale Scar, a dramatic gorge that inspired Turner. I you don't have your own hiking plans, join the thousands of tourists on the road into the gorge. In town are the **Malham Youth Hostel** (Skipton, North Yorkshire tel. (07293) 321), a **Park Information Centre,** and the **Buck Inn,** a pub popular with hikers.

Another popular part of the Dales lies on the western edge of the region not fa from **Ingleton.** Here, the popular **Three Peaks Walk** (24 miles) takes in Whernside Pen-y-Ghent, and Ingleborough. **Dent,** a bit to the north, is one of the most provin cial villages in Yorkshire. In this wool-spinning hamlet, the "Terrible Witches o Dent" won their name by spinning seven strands at once, a feat that required super natural talents.

Base your exploration of **Wensleydale** and **Swaledale** in **Hawes,** where there is a **youth hostel** on Lancaster Terrace. Nearby is **Hardraw Force,** the highest water fall in England, accessible only through a pub. (Too bad.) **Aysgarth Falls** to the east is also a beautiful spot. To the east of Aysgarth is **Bolton Castle,** where Mary Queen of Scots, was once held prisoner. The ruins of **Jervaulx Abbey** lie near Masham. **Richmond,** to the east in Swaledale, is a quiet market town on the River Swale with a **Georgian Theatre Museum** (open May-Sept. 2:30-5:30pm; admission 60p).

North York Moors

If cathedral crowds have finally gotten to you, the strange and peaceful beauty of the North York Moors may provide the respite you need. The **North York Moors National Park** is a stretch of open heather and moorland to the north of York, reaching out to the dramatic windswept coast. The park is encircled by the towns (clockwise from northwest to southwest) of Guisborough, Whitby, Scarborough, Pickering, Helmsley, and Thirsk.

British Rail's Esk Valley line runs through the northern part of the park from Darlington via Middlesbrough to Whitby (£1.20 one way). At Grosmont, it connects with the North Yorkshire Moors Railway, the only way to reach scenic spots in Newtondale Gorge. The railway ends in Pickering, from where there are buses to other areas of the park. Another British Rail line connects York with Scarborough. Hitching around the park is always difficult. The best way to travel is to hike the park's long-distance footpaths. The **Lyke Wake Walk** (40 miles), the **White Rose Walk** (40 miles), and the **Cleveland Way** traverse the area; all are broken by hostels. The **National Park Information Centre,** Moors Centre, Danby Lodge (tel.

(0287) 606 54; open Easter-Oct. daily 10am-5pm; Nov.-Easter Mon.-Sat. 10am-5pm, Sun. noon-4pm), ½ mile from the Danby rail station, has maps and guides, including the indispensible *North York Moors Visitor* (20p).

Good touring bases with plenty of B&Bs and tourist offices are **Pickering,** a pretty market town 25 miles northeast of York, and **Goathland,** located in the park center, with some scenic walks to waterfalls and across moorland. Near Goathland is **Wheeldale Hostel (IYHF)** (tel. (0947) 863 50; £2.30, £1.90; open March-Oct. Thurs.-Tues.). Other IYHF hostels in the park are at **Helmsley** (tel. (0439) 704 33; £3.40, £2.60; open Nov.-Feb. Fri.-Sat.; March and late Oct. Tues.-Sat.; April-Sept. Mon.-Sat.); **Lockton,** near Levisham (tel. (0751) 603 76; £2.30, £1.90; open March and Oct. Fri.-Sat.; April-Sept. Wed.-Mon.); **Malton** (tel. (0653) 20 77; £3.40, £2.60; open March and Oct. Mon.-Sat.; April-Sept. Tues.-Sun.); **Osmotherly** (tel. (060983) 575; £3.85, £3.15; open Feb. Thurs.-Mon.; March to mid-April, mid-Sept. to Oct., and early Dec. Wed.-Sun.; mid-April to June Mon.-Sat.; July-Aug. daily): **Thixendale** (tel. (0377) 882 38; £2.30, £1.90; open April-Sept. Wed.-Mon.); and **Westerdale** (tel. (0287) 604 69; £3.40, £2.60; open March and Oct. Tues.-Sat.; April-June Tues.-Sun.; July-Aug. daily).

Bram Stoker found inspiration for *Dracula* in **Whitby,** where the skeletal remains of **Whitby Abbey** still haunt the town from above. A wolf supposedly leapt off a boat from Transylvania, ran up the 199 steps to the abbey, and disappeared into the crowded graveyard from which Dracula would later terrorize the town. The **IYHF youth hostel** at Whitby (tel. (0947) 60 28 78), is right next to the abbey. (£3.40, £2.60. Open April-June and Sept.-Oct. Wed.-Mon.; July-Aug. daily.)

A bus ride (#93, 258, or 287), or a hitch down the coast brings you to the cliffside fishing village of **Robin Hood's Bay,** a fantastic location at sunrise. You'll find an IYHF hostel at nearby **Boggle Hole** (tel. (0947) 88 03 52; £3.85, £3.15; open Jan.-Feb. and Nov. Tues.-Sat., March-Oct. daily). The **Lyke Wake Walk** ends 3 miles away at Ravenscar, while the **Cleveland Way** winds clockwise around the perimeter of the park and down the coast, where it terminates just above Scarborough. The **IYHF youth hostel** (tel. (0723) 36 11 76) at Scarborough is in a converted water mill. (£3.40, £2.60. Open Nov.-Feb. Fri.-Sat.; March and Oct. Fri.-Tues.; April-June Fri.-Wed.; July-Aug. daily.)

Lake District

Embrace me then, ye hills, and close me in.
—William Wordsworth, *The Recluse*

Literary pilgrims will soon see why Wordsworth thought the Lakes the most exquisite place in England; climbers on Helvellyn and harrowing Honister Pass will better understand the romantic notion of beauty in *The Lap of Horror.* Dramatic in places, the Lake District is alternately a pastoral patchwork of hill farms dotted with mortarless stone cottages. If you're seeking the lonely vistas for which the Lakes are famous, remember that you'll share your interest in solitude with quite a few others; head to Scotland for more isolated countryside.

The major lakes are ranged like spokes of a wheel with Grasmere as the hub. Windermere, Ambleside, Grasmere, and Keswick are good bases, with transport connections and knowledgeable tourist offices, but you should try to get up to the villages in the hills, especially in the more remote northern and western areas.

Windermere has rail service (with direct trains from London in the summer), and the BritRail pass gets you free rides on Lake Windermere ferries as well. Trains from all over run to Oxenholme, then connect to Windermere seven times per day. From York, **Mountain Goat** (tel. (09662) 51 61) runs a bus (Mon., Wed., and Fri.-Sat., summer only) via Skipton, Keighley, and Ingleton. **Ribble** (tel. (0539) 332 21) runs an hourly bus connecting Lancaster, Windermere, Ambleside, Grasmere, and Keswick (a £3 Explorer ticket will let you ride all day), and Mountain Goat serves smaller towns such as Buttermere and Borrowdale. (If you want to be picked up at an intermediate stop, call in the morning to alert the company, or wave your arms wildly at their minibus.)

But the best way to get around in the Lake District is to walk. Public footpaths are everywhere, and they are easily identifiable. Take a good Ordnance Survey map, compass, and waterproof clothing. Any of the tourist offices can give you detailed advice on hiking and camping in the area. The Lake District **National Park Information Service** has a camping advisory number (tel. (09662) 55 55) and an up-to-date weather report (tel. (09662) 51 51). Tourist offices and National Park Information Centres have a comprehensive series of guides, *Walks in the Countryside,* for 10p each.

The Lakes have the highest density of youth hostels in the world—27 at last count—but you should still phone ahead in July and August. The Lakeland **Regional YHA Office** in Windermere (tel. (09662) 23 01) is staffed by a helpful bunch who will call around to see which hostels in the area have beds on any particular night. Pick up their *Youth Hostels in Lakeland* (£1), which includes hiking and cycling routes and practical information. B&Bs run £8-10, and fill up at an alarming rate during the summer.

Windermere

Windermere and its sidekick **Bowness** on Lake Windermere are starting points for most tourists, and hence quite crowded. The Windermere **Tourist Information Centre,** on Victoria St. (tel. (09662) 45 61), next to the train station, has a free booking service and posts an accommodations list after hours. (Open April-Oct. daily 10am-8pm.) The office on the pier in Bowness, also a National Park Information Centre (tel. (09662) 56 02 or 28 95), has information on boat rental and lake cruises. (Open April-Oct. daily 9:30am-7pm; Nov.-Dec. Mon.-Fri. 1-4pm, Sat.-Sun. 10am-12:30pm and 1:30-4pm.) Near the rail station, **Lakeland Leisure** (tel. (09662) 47 86; open daily 9am-5pm) will rent you a bike (£3 per day); if you're on foot, head out Birthwaite Rd. to Queen Adelaide's Hill for a nice view.

The nearest **IYHF youth hostel** is 2 miles north of Windermere in Troutbeck Bridge (tel. (09662) 35 43), on the way to Ambleside; from the Ambleside bus route it's a ¾-mile walk. (£3.85, £3.15. Open mid-March to mid-Sept. daily; mid-Feb. to mid-March and mid-Sept. to Oct. Wed.-Mon.) There are several B&Bs on Cross Street and Oak Street. You can camp at **Park Cliffe,** Birks Rd. (tel. (0448) 313 44), north of Windermere on the A592, for £4.35. The **Hedge-Row Vegetarian Restaurant** in Bowness is open daily from noon to 2pm and from 6 to 10pm.

Ambleside and Grasmere

Ambleside is a pleasant resort town, slightly less frenetic than Windermere, while Grasmere is an exquisite lakeside spot. The easy hike between the two is breathtaking. The Ambleside **tourist office,** on Church St. (tel. (0966) 325 82) has a free accommodations service. The **Ambleside Youth Hostel (IYHF),** is 1 mile south of the village on the Windermere road (tel. (0966) 323 04). A former hotel on the shores of Lake Windermere, it is the country club of hostels. (£4.50, £3.70. Open mid-March to mid-Sept. daily; Jan. to mid-March and mid-Sept. to Dec. Thurs.-Tues.) For B&Bs, try **Thorneyfield,** Compston Rd. (tel. (0966) 324 64), at £9.50 per person, or **3 Cambridge Villas,** Church St. (tel. (0966) 323 07) next to the tourist office, from £8. **Sheila's Cottage,** on the Slack off the Market Place, offers traditional meals and sumptuous cakes in a warm atmosphere, and the **Harvest Vegetarian Restaurant** on Compston Rd. serves up hearty casseroles and transcendental coffee. (Open July-Sept. daily; Easter-June and Oct. Fri.-Wed.; Jan.-March Fri.-Sat.)

Walk to **Elterwater Youth Hostel (IYHF)** in Langdale (tel. (09667) 245); from here you can ascend the **Langdale Pike.** (£3.40, £2.60. Open March-Sept. Tues.-Sun.; Feb. and Oct.-Nov. Wed.-Sun.) **Hawkshead Hostel** (tel. (09666) 293; £3.40, £2.60; open mid-March to mid-Sept. daily; mid-Feb. to mid-March and mid-Sept.

to Oct. Mon.-Sat.) is another lovely walk from Ambleside. At nearby Sawrey, you can visit the **Beatrix Potter Museum,** complete with original drawings by this whimsical author of children's books. Hawkshead village was the boyhood home of William Wordsworth. Nearby is **Tarn Hows,** a stunning spot in itself, but the walk there is even more beautiful. The **Wildlife and Forestry Museum** at Grizedale (tel. (022984) 373) holds daily nature walks during the summer.

Grasmere, 4 miles north of Ambleside, is a lovely village inundated by those on the Wordsworth trail. Open to the public are **Dove Cottage** (£2.50), where William and Dorothy lived from 1799 to 1807, and **Rydal Mount** (£1.50), the poet's final home. His simple grave lies in the village churchyard. For a true Wordsworth experience, walk around lovely Grasmere and Rydal Water. There are two **IYHF youth hostels** in the villages: **Butharlyp How** (tel. (09665) 316), just down the road to Easdale (£3.85, £3.15; open mid-March to mid-Sept. daily; mid-Feb. to mid-March and mid-Sept. to Oct. Tues.-Sun.), and **Thorney How** (tel. (09665) 591), farther down the Easdale road—right at the fork, then left (£3.40, £2.60; open mid-March to mid-Sept. daily; mid-Sept. to mid-March Wed.-Mon.).

Keswick and Environs

Keswick, in the northern Lake District, is a bit more relaxed than the Windermere towns and is set in more dramatic scenery. Climb 1½ miles to the Bronze Age **Castlerigg Stone Circle** and you'll find yourself surrounded by peaks which mirror the arrangement of the stones. **Skiddaw** in the north and **Helvellyn** to the south are good climbs, or you can walk through the pass to Buttermere and catch the bus back. Vacationers throng **Derwentwater** (the lake), but you can escape them all by taking the ferry around the lake or by flexing your muscles in a rowboat. **Derwentwater Youth Hostel (IYHF)** is 2 miles south of Keswick (tel. (059684) 246), with a 100-foot waterfall on the grounds (£3.85, £3.15; open mid-March to mid-Sept. daily; mid-Feb. to mid-March and mid-Sept. to Oct. Mon.-Sat.). For camping, try **Dalebottom Holiday Park** (tel. (0596) 721 76), 2 miles south on the Ambleside road (£3.50).

From Keswick, hike, hitch, or bus up into the hills. Cumberland buses serve **Borrowdale** (south via the beautiful east side of Derwentwater) and **Cockermouth** (north via Bassenthwaite Lake). From **Seatoller** at the end of the valley, you can climb harrowing **Honister Pass** from Borrowdale (note the "YOU HAVE BEEN WARNED! . . . " signs) to Buttermere, and catch the bus for Keswick or Cockermouth.

Durham

On a small island created by a hairpin bend in the River Wear stands **Durham Cathedral,** founded in 995 as a shrine for St. Cuthbert's bones and then rebuilt a century later. In its architectural innovation, the new cathedral heralded the coming of the Gothic age; in its power and beauty, it enshrined the faith of its Norman builders. The entire city of Durham clusters around the structure which Sir Walter Scott described as "half church of God, half castle 'gainst the Scot." The bones of the Venerable Bede are in a simple stone tomb in the Galilee Chapel; fragments of St. Cuthbert's carved coffin are in the **treasury** (admission £1, children 20p), along with some fine manuscripts. Climb the **tower** for a superb view (50p). (Cathedral open June-Aug. daily 7:15am-8pm; Sept.-May 7:15am-5:45pm. Treasury open June-Sept. Mon.-Sat. 10am-5pm, Sun. 2-5pm; Oct.-May daily until 4:30pm.) Across the **Palace Green** is **Durham Castle,** a Norman fortress accessible only by guided tour (95p, children 45p). It's now a university residence, so if you look like a male university student you may be able to walk in. The fourteenth-century **Great Hall** and **Black Staircase** contain some marvelous woodcarving, and students still worship in the Norman **chapel.** In summer you can spend the night here for £10.50 B&B, and eat a three-course evening meal in the Great Hall for £4.40. (Call (091)

374 38 65 for information.) Both sides of the **River Wear** are criss-crossed with lovely wooden footpaths—you can buy a 10p walking map at the **tourist office,** The Market Place (tel. 384 37 20; open May-Sept. Mon.-Sat. 10am-6pm, Sun. 2-5pm; Oct.-April Mon.-Sat. 10am-5pm), but it's not really necessary. Just follow the river all the way around this majestic peninsula city.

Most of Durham's cheap accommodations are a mile or so out of the city center. The **IYHF youth hostel** often moves from year to year; in 1987 it was at the Gilesgate Sixth Form College on Providence Row. (£3.40, £2.60. Open late July-Aug. only.) **Gluck Auf,** a guest house at 6-7 Prospect Terrace (tel. 384 25 47), is run by a friendly proprietor who charges £7, £6.50 after the first night. Take bus #49, 49A, or 50 and get off at Neville's Cross post office, or walk 1 mile out Crossgate; the house is just past the second traffic light, on the right. Camp at **Coal Hole Caravan Park,** 1½ miles east of town toward Sherburn (tel. 386 33 94; £4 for tent and 2 people).

Try the cheap eats at **House of Andrews,** down the alley at 73 Saddler St. (open April-Dec. daily 9am-9pm; Jan.-March daily 9am-5:30pm), or **Pimlico's Vegetarian Restaurant** next door (open Mon.-Sat. 10am-5pm; lunch served 11:45am-2pm). **The Gallery,** off Silver St., serves lunch by the river (Mon.-Sat.). Durham holds an elaborate **Folk Festival** (call 384 44 45 for information) in the first week of August. This is the only time you can camp for free along the banks of the river; pitch your tent early.

Durham lies on the **Intercity 125** rail line, with frequent trains running from London (3¼ hr., £39 Saver return), York (1 hr., £12 Saver return), and Newcastle (15 min., £2.20 cheap day return). Coach service is also fairly good; five per day make the 4¾-hour trip to London (£18 one way, but ask about special offers). The Tynelink Express runs hourly to Newcastle (40 min.; £2 day return).

Durham's **telephone code** is 091.

Wales

Rarely will you sense so strongly as in Wales a perseverance nourished by the countryside's beauty and harshness. Indeed, it took Norse pirates two centuries to subdue this land of lush valleys, rugged mountains, and weather-beaten shore. Llewelyn, Prince of Wales, the first and only native to rule his country, was removed in the thirteenth century by English monarchs, who have fought intermittently ever since to maintain their sway over Wales. The country's many castles and Offa's Dyke, built in the eighth century as a boundary between Wales and England, are visible reminders of Wales's struggle to assert its distinctiveness and independence from England. Wales has long been a stronghold of Labour Party politics, and in the 1987 elections it overwhelmingly voted against Thatcher and for favorite son, Neil Kinnock.

Welsh culture has waxed and waned at intervals over the centuries, with its most dramatic resurgence during the last decade. Bilingualism is now the rule in all schools, with the odd result that many children speak better Welsh than their grandparents, who were forbidden to speak it. Welsh language prevails outside the south, though virtually all Welsh speak English as well. A good, recent social history is Gwyn A. Williams's *When Was Wales?* (Pelican Books).

Hiking is perhaps the best way to see Wales. Offa's Dyke Path and the Pembrokeshire Coastal Path can easily be broken into smaller segments. Tourist offices in these regions will help you plan short- and long-term journeys; they often stock local walking guides (10-50p) and Ordnance Survey maps (£2-3), essential for more extensive hiking. Always leave your itinerary with someone; it's easy to get lost in the foggy hills and dales of Wales. Sturdy shoes, a reliable and detailed map and compass, and proper clothing and rain gear are absolutely necessary.

YHA youth hostels are both your best and worst accommodations option. Though the best buy (junior hostelers pay £1.90-3.15, others £2.30-3.85), they are also the least accessible and most crowded. Many can be reached only by foot or bridle path, so always call (before 10am or after 5pm). For directions and closing days, buy the *YHA Handbook* for England and Wales at any hostel (£1.50). Welsh hostels tend to be more relaxed than those in England; many lack showers, but you'll find the curfews less strict and the wardens friendlier. Outside of Brecon Beacons National Park, there is no organized wilderness camping in Wales. Almost all land, including that in parks, is privately owned; politely ask the farmer or landowner if you may pitch your tent.

Though expensive, **British Rail** serves certain parts of Wales. One line runs along the northern coast (Chester to Holyhead); a second covers the southern coast from Newport to Fishguard; and a third, centered on Shrewsbury, serves mid-Wales. The steam-powered "little trains of Wales" cover parts of the country untouched by British Rail, though they are even more expensive. Bus service is cheaper than the train and reaches more destinations. Each region offers its own economy fares—usually £3 per day or £15 per week of unlimited travel. **National Welsh** and **Crosville** are the largest bus companies. Regional schedules (15-50p) are worthwhile if you plan to use buses extensively. Buses rarely operate on Sunday. Hitching is risky business in Wales, since even in summer cars are infrequent in many regions; North Wales is a bit better in this regard. Pick up a *Wales Tourist Map,* which shows the main roadways.

South Wales

Forested mountains and coastal cliffs defy the image created by the scarred mining valleys of central South Wales. For the best scenery, stay north of the coast until Pembrokeshire, where industry thins out and the land reasserts itself.

Wye Valley and the Brecon Beacons

Crossing the Severn from Bristol on the M4, you will quickly reach **Chepstow,** with its long narrow castle guarding the mouth of the Wye Valley. The **Chepstow Youth Hostel (IYHF)** is just past the first roundabout on the A466 to Monmouth (tel. (02912) 26 85); take the first left. (£3.85.) A bit farther along is the **Chepstow Race Course,** one of the busiest in Britain.

Beginning in Chepstow is **Offa's Dyke Path,** running along the 180-mile-long ditch dug by the Saxons to keep the Welsh in their own land. This varied path—well-trodden in some places, strenuous in others—follows the Welsh-English border past Monmouth to Llangollen and the north coast, and can easily be broken into shorter bits. One of the most popular of these is the 17-mile section known as the **Wye Valley Walk,** which runs along the wooded banks of the winding River Wye to Monmouth. The trail passes close to **Tintern Abbey** (admission £1), a majestic twelfth-century Cistercian monastery that inspired Wordsworth's famous poem, *Lines Composed a Few Miles Above Tintern Abbey.* Ask at the abbey about the half-hour hike to **Devil's Pulpit,** from which the Nasty One is said to have tempted Tintern's monks. If not walking, take bus #69, passing Tintern every two hours (except Sun.), or hitch along the A466. If you do hike all the way to the market town of Monmouth, stay at the **Priory Street Hostel (IYHF)** (tel. (0600) 51 16).

Brecon Beacons National Park encompasses the Brecon Beacons, the Black Mountains, and the spectacular waterfall country around Ystradfellte. Topped by the windswept Pen-y-fan peak (2900 ft.), the **Beacons Ridge** has steep northern slopes, but dips away gently to the south. The best trails into the Beacons themselves start with the small roads leading southward from **Llanfaes,** across the Usk from Brecon. Head for **Cwm Llych** for waterfalls and mountain lakes. The **Black Mountains,** farther east, known for their uncompromising solitude, are excellent for ridgewalking. Information on the park is available from the **National Park Informa-**

tion Centre in Brecon at Watton Mount (tel. Brecon 44 37; open Easter-Sept. Mon.-Sat. 9:30am-1pm and 1:30-5pm). If you're really serious about getting up into the park, visit the **Mountain Centre** in Libanus (tel. Brecon 33 66), about five miles south of Brecon, where you'll find competent advice and a great view of the Beacons. (Open May-Aug. daily 9:30am-7pm; Sept.-April slightly curtailed hours.) **Llwyn-y-Celyn Youth Hostel** (tel. (0874) 42 61; open Mon.-Sat.), two miles south of Libanus off the A470, and the **Ty'n-y-Caeau Youth Hostel** (tin-uh-kay-uh), a mile out of Brecon, (tel. (087486) 270), are good bases for exploring the mountains. Brecon itself has an ample number of B&Bs, and a lovely **cathedral** up the hill from the town center.

Abergavenny, connected to Brecon by a frequent bus (#21), is the nearest rail stop, as well as an excellent base for touring the Black Mountains. The **Tourist Office,** 2 Monk St. (tel. 32 54), can help you find a room. (Open Easter-Sept. Mon.-Sat. 9:30am-5:30pm; in Aug. open Sun. as well.) You can look yourself along Monmouth Road or Brecon Road, across town. **Ivy Villa,** 43 Hereford Rd. (tel. 24 73), is a good deal. (£8.) **Clam's,** Lion St. (tel. 44 96), has lovely soups, desserts, and afternoon tea (£1.40). (Open Mon., Wed., Sat. 10am-4:30pm, Thurs. 10am-2:30pm, Fri. 10am-10pm.) The **Swan Hotel,** Cross St., has excellent, piping hot pub grub. (Open noon-2pm and 6-10pm.)

Cardiff

The only urban center in a region of small villages, Cardiff leads Wales in extremes of wealth and poverty. The Butes, an illegitimate line of the royal Stuarts, made its enormous fortune from the shipping industry in the nineteenth century. Today, working-class Cardiff is a center of labor activism and Welsh nationalism.

Cardiff Castle, in the middle of the city, preserves an ornate Victorian interior within its Roman walls and Norman keep. (Open in summer daily 10am-5pm; in winter daily 10am-4pm. Admission and guided tour £2, last tour 1 hr. before closing.) The **National Museum of Wales** asserts Cardiff's status as a repository of Welsh culture. The Mining Gallery and the collection of French impressionist paintings alone merit a visit. (Open Tues.-Sat. 10am-5pm, Sun. 2:30-5pm. Free.) At nearby St. Fagan's (bus #32 runs hourly from Cardiff's central station), the 20 reconstructed traditional buildings of the **Welsh Folk Museum** house artisans demonstrating the crafts of rural Welsh life. (Open Mon.-Sat. 10am-5pm. Admission £2.)

Cardiff has a **youth hostel (IYHF)** on Lake Rd. West (tel. (0222) 46 23 03), 2 miles from the city center (take bus #82 from the central station). If it's full, the **Cathedral Road** area is your best bet for cheap, clean bed-and-breakfast accommodations. **Coniston House,** 11 Dyfrig St. (tel. (0222) 322 49), just off Cathedral Road, is run by a very cheerful woman. (£9.) The **Tourist Information Centre,** 8-14 Bridge St. (tel. (0222) 272 81), can help you look for others. Just off Cathedral Rd., at 77 Pontcanna St., you'll find **77 Diner,** popular with students for its hero sandwiches (£3.80). When the university is in session (roughly Oct.-May), there's lots to do at night; drop by the **Student Union** (tel. (0222) 39 64 21) for the word on what's hot. The **Chapter Arts Center,** on Market Rd. off Cowbridge (tel. (0222) 39 60 61), has everything from live music to theater and cinema. You should also tap into some Brains S.A. (Special Ale), brewed in the city, and known as Brains Skull Attack. Try some—you'll see why.

Bus and train routes from Birmingham, Bristol, London, and points throughout Wales converge here.

Dyfed

At the northern extreme of Dyfed County, **Aberystwyth** is the fading grandparent of **Cardigan Bay** resorts. The real action centers on the **University College of Wales** up the hill, where Welsh nationalism brews in classroom and pub alike. After visiting the **National Library of Wales,** with its collection of Welsh books and manuscripts (open Mon.-Fri. 9:30am-6pm, Sat. 9:30am-5pm), try the **Cooper's Arms** on Northgate St., or the **Angel,** on Great Darkgate St., for organized and impromptu folk music and jazz. Or head up the hill again to the **Aberystwyth Arts Centre,** housing the very active **Theatre-y-Werin.** Room-finding help is available at the **Tourist Information Centre,** 13 Eastgate St. (tel. 61 21 25), but accommodations shouldn't be a problem, even in the summer. South Marine Terrace, Rheidol Terrace, Bridge Street, and Cambrian Street, all offer **B&Bs** for £8-10. There's an **IYHF youth hostel** (tel. Borth 498), nine miles north in Borth, accessible by train and bus. Student restaurants line Bridge Street and Pier Street. **Trains** and **Crosville Buses** run north to Machynlleth for connections to the north and east; only the buses run south to Cardigan and Fishguard. The Day Rover bus pass (£2.90) is good for one day's unlimited travel on all Crosville buses north of Cardigan (Weekly Rover £5.90, Monthly Rover £19.90).

Ferries leave **Fishguard** for Rosslare, Ireland at 3am and 3pm year-round. (Additional departures June 19-Sept. 14 daily at 6am; July 16-Sept. 13 Thurs.-Sun. at 5:45pm.) Trains are timed to connect with ferries. Check ahead with **Sealink** (tel. (0348) 87 28 81) or the **Tourist Office** (tel. (0348) 87 34 84; open April-Oct. daily 9:30am-5:30pm). The latter will help you find a place to stay, or wander down **Vergam Terrace,** on the main road from Fishguard town square to the harbor. The **Pwll Deri Youth Hostel (IYHF),** is five miles away on Strumble Head (tel. (03485) 233). Book in advance during the summer. If you're stranded in town for an hour or more, walk the **cliff path** for some splendid scenery.

The **Pembrokeshire Peninsula** is home to some of the country's finest coastal scenery: magnificent cliffs and sheltered beaches, natural sea arches, and islands teeming with wild birds and breeding seals. Most of the coast is protected by the **Pembrokeshire Coast National Park,** which has information offices in most towns. The 180-mile **Pembrokeshire Coast Path,** beginning at Saundersfoot, near Tenby, and ending at St. Dog Maels, near Cardigan, covers the best scenery. Avoid the heavily-industrialized area near Milford Haven, and concentrate on the stretches at Cemaes Head near Poppit Sands, or those between Marloes Sands and St. David's.

The coast is lined with a series of well-spaced **IYHF youth hostels.** All are small, removed from town, and relaxed. They are **Pentlepoir** (tel. Saundersfoot 81 23 33), outside Tenby; **Marloes Sands** (tel. Dale 257), near the Dale Peninsula; **Broad Haven** (tel. Broad Haven 688), on St. Bride's Bay; **St. David's** (tel. (0437) 72 03 45); **Trevine** (tel. Croesgoch 414); and **Pwll Deri** (tel. St. Nicholas 233). Near the end of the trail is **Poppit Sands** (tel. Cardigan 61 29 36).

The best coastal scenery is found near **St. David's,** the smallest city in Britain. It is a city by virtue of having a **cathedral**—a remarkable structure whose elegant Norman nave slopes precariously thanks to a thirteenth-century earthquake. Don't miss the exquisitely carved wooden roof and misericords. The giant, fortified **Bishop's Palace** across the way was built by the wealthy Bishop Gower as a monument to himself. The **National Park Information Centre** (tel. (0437) 72 03 92) has information on accommodations; try **Redcliffe House,** 17 New Street (tel. (0437) 72 03 89) for bed and breakfast. Camping information and booklets detailing walks (10p) are also available. Try *St. David's: Caerfai-Porthclais* or *Whitesands to St. David's Head.*

Area rail and bus lines meet in **Haverfordwest.** To get to town from the railway station, walk downhill to the roundabout, past the bus station, then over the bridge onto High Street. The **Tourist Office** and **Pembrokeshire Coast National Park Information Centre** share an office at 40 High St. (tel. (0437) 31 10), which stocks excellent annotated plastic strip maps of the path (15p each), as well as information on pony-trekking (£6-10 per day) and fascinating boat trips to the islands. Their *Pembrokeshire Coast Path Accommodations* (70p) lists scores of cheap tent sites, often in superb locations on the coast, and consolidates area bus information.

Tucked between cliff and beach on lovely Carmarthen Bay, **Tenby's** pastel-colored houses crowd narrow streets which twist down to the sea. Regular buses connect Tenby with Cardiff and Swansea. B&Bs line Warren Street (near the rail station), or you can try **Sunnybank,** Harding St. (tel. (0437) 40 34), with bright and clean rooms for £7 per person. **Tourist Information** (tel. (0437) 24 02) at The Croft, above North Beach, also has listings. Good vegetarian meals are offered at **Plantagenet Restaurant** on Quay Hill.

North Wales

Here is the Wales the world imagines—castles guarding misty valleys, rivers, waterfalls, and jagged mountains of granite and slate. The variety of landscape contained in this relatively small area is delightful; an easy afternoon of travel can take you from seaside peninsulas and rolling greenery onto mountainsides thick with conifers. Hills laced with ancient stone walls rise above modern village centers, and a 10-minute hike and a twist of a valley can release you into gorgeous isolation.

You'll get the strongest sense of a separate Welsh culture in the north. Welsh is widely spoken here. Aberffraw, on the Isle of Aglesey, was the country's medieval capital, and Harlech Castle, taken from Edward I in the thirteenth century by the Welsh rebel Owain Glyndwr, was the center of Wales' last royal court. Anti-English sentiment can still run high; at its worst a few years ago, vacant English summer cottages were burnt and the English portions of the bilingual road signs were plastered out with mud.

Two rail lines serve the area: one from Holyhead to Chester, the other from Pwllheli to Aberystwyth. They are connected via the narrow-gauge steam engine from Llandudno Junction to Blaneau Ffestiniog to Porthmadog. Extensive bus service radiates from Bangor west along the north coast to Conwy and Llandudno, north to Holyhead on the Isle of Anglesey, southwest to Porthmadog and Pwllheli on the Lleyn Peninsula, and southeast into Snowdonia. The best way to explore the area is to buy a Crosville Bus Weekly Rover ticket (£6), which gives you a week of unlimited travel in the county of Gwynedd (to all the places listed below, except Llangollen). Bed and breakfasts share duty with 16 youth hostels; tourist offices in every town will find you accommodations.

Snowdonia National Park

The mountains of **Snowdonia National Park,** covering the western half of North Wales, rise unexpectedly from the English flatlands and sweep as startlingly into the Cambrian coast. **Snowdon** itself, at 3560 feet, is the highest, barest, most precipitous peak in Great Britain, south of Scotland. Hiking and walking information, as well as exhibits on the natural history of the area, are available at the **visitor centres** run by the National Park (centers in Llanberis, Betws-y-Coed, Harlech, Dolgellau, Bala, Blaenau Ffestiniog, Conwy, and Aberdyfi). Transportation to, and between, the villages nestled among the Snowdonias is made easy by the summertime Crosville Bus Sherpa service.

The **IYHF youth hostels** in this area are well-tailored to the needs of climbers and walkers, but are often full during the summer. **Pen-y-Pass** (tel. (0286) 87 04 28) is YHA's luxurious mountain center, located in a dramatic pass at the foot of the extremely difficult Pyg approach to Snowdon. **Capel Curig** (tel. (0690) 42 25), or **Lledr Valley** (tel. (0690) 62 02), and **Idwal Cottage** (tel. (0248) 600 25) are also set, though less dramatically, in the heart of the Snowdonias. The hostels of **Llanberis** (tel. (0286) 87 02 80) and **Snowdon Ranger** (tel. (0286) 853 91) are near main walking routes up Snowdon. If you're not up to the climb, take the **Snowdon Mountain Railway** from Llanberis (£9). The **Snowdonia Forest Park Campsite,** located 1 mile from Beddgelert, makes another good base for hiking (accessible by Sherpa bus). For all hikes in the Snowdonias, safety precautions and common sense are essential; be sure to talk to a ranger or visitor center before heading uphill. After climbing Snowdon you might tackle the peaks of the **Glyders,** approached from the opposite side of Llanberis Pass.

Llanberis is also the site of the **North Wales Quarry Museum,** housed in an old slate-finishing plant on the edge of Llwyn (Lake) Padarn. For breakfast, lunch, dinner, or an enormous mug of tea, go to **Pete's Eats** in Llanberis, the local climber's cafe. Of the two quarries in Blaenau Ffestiniog, **Gloddfa Ganol** is more authentic.

At the southern edge of the park, the market town of **Machynlleth** (Ma-HUN-hleth), situated in a lovely forested valley, is connected to Shrewsbury by BritRail. The **tourist office** (tel. 24 01), on the site of Owen Glendower's fifteenth-century parliament, books accommodations. (Open Easter-Sept. 10am-6pm; Oct.-Easter 10am-5pm.) The area's main attraction, just 3 miles north by bus, is the innovative **Centre for Alternative Technology,** featuring windmills and conservation exhibits. (Open mid-July to mid-Sept. daily 10am-1pm and 2-7:30pm; otherwise 10am-1pm and 2-5:30pm. Admission £2.20.) The center runs an excellent vegetarian restaurant, the **Quarry Shop Cafe,** in the center of town.

About 10 miles down the coast south of Porthmadog is **Harlech,** a lovely town with an uncrowded 4½-mile beach and spectacular **Harlech Castle.** The third of Edward I's great Welsh castles, it was built in a concentric plan with a massive double gateway. Views of Snowdonia and the Lleyn Peninsula from the castle walls are superb. The town has a helpful **tourist office** on High St. (tel. (0766) 78 06 58), and the small, simple-grade hostel **Pen-y-Garth (IYHF)** is right in town (tel. (0766) 78 02 85; £2.30). From Harlech, there are frequent buses south through Barmouth to **Dolgellau** (Dole-geth-lee), a small market town built entirely of stone at the bottom of craggy Calder Idris in southern Snowdonia. There is a legend that if you spend the night alone on Idris, you will return either blind, mad, or a poet. A good base for the climb, which is a full day's excursion even for serious hikers, is the **IYHF youth hostel** at **Kings** (tel. (0341) 42 23 92).

Lleyn Peninsula and Northern Coast

The Lleyn Peninsula juts 50 miles into St. George's Channel. Towns here purport to be beach resorts, but don't be surprised if you find Porthmadog, Pwllheli, and Abersoch lashed by rain and wind. In any event, they are indigenously Welsh, and at least partially spared the crush of tourists that pressures the northern coast. Porthmadog is connected to Blaenau Ffestiniog by the small-gauge **Ffestiniog Railway,** whose 13-mile course passes some of the most spectacular scenery in Great Britain (8-11 per day, £6.20 round-trip). The **Porthmadog Tourist Information Centre** on High St. (tel. 29 81) provides guides for town walks as well as listings of B&Bs in the £7-8 range.

Pwllheli, 8 miles from equally peaceful **Criccieth** and its castle ruins, is the peninsula's transportation center, with buses to London (1 per day), Bangor via Porthmadog and Caernarfon (every 2 hr.), and Aberdaron (5 per day). The **tourist office** is on Maes Sq. (Open June-Sept. daily 10am-6pm.) B&Bs average £7 per person; try the **Bank Street Guest House** (£7.50, including a huge breakfast). Food in Pwllheli is best in pubs and hotels. For a quick meal, the **Sparta Cafe** on Maes Sq. serves delicious meat pies for 90p. The best place for a beach day is **Morfa Nefyn** on the northern side of the peninsula (accessible by bus).

Perched on the edge of its bay, **Caernarfon** lures visitors with Wales' grandest Edwardian **castle,** dating from 1283. Here, Edward I employed every trick of slits and passageways he had picked up on his Middle Eastern travels during the Crusades; the result proved virtually impregnable. (Open mid-March to mid-Oct. daily 9:30am-6:30pm; otherwise Mon.-Sat. 9:30am-4pm. Admission £2, ages under 16 £1.) The **Segontium,** remains of an ancient Roman fort and accompanying displays, occupies a hill half a mile away on Beddgelert Road. On a less historical note, the graceful **Aber Bridge** by the castle leads to a quiet walk along the edge of the strait.

Tourist information (tel. (0286) 22 32) in the castle car park offers accommodations services; B&Bs are plentiful along **North Penrallt** or **Beddgelert Road** (also known as Constantine Road). On the latter is **Gwelfor** (tel. (0286) 768 08), with a little family noise but a delightful owner. (£8 per night.) You can camp for £2.50 at **Cadnant Valley Park** (tel. (0286) 31 96) on Llanberis Road. For a good meal and lively local color when drinking begins, try the **Black Boy Inn** just off the square.

Bangor is the transportation hub for North Wales, and a pleasant university town to boot. The **tourist information center,** Theatre Gwynedd, off Deiniol Rd. (tel. 35 27 86), will arm you with information on all of North Wales. **Crosville Buses** (tel. (0248) 37 02 95) leave from Garth Rd. station. (Office open Mon.-Fri. 9am-1pm and 1:30-4:30pm, Sat. 9-11:30am. Schedules are posted on the office window.) The **Tany y Bryn hostel (IYHF)** (tel. (0248) 35 35 16) is 1km from town; walk toward the sea on Deiniol Rd., then on the A5 toward Llandegai. (Open March-Jan. Often full in summer—call ahead.) For private accommodations, try the B&Bs along Garth Road.

Holyhead, on the Isle of Anglesey, is a one-horse town from which **ferries** leave to Ireland. **B&I** ferries (tel. (0407) 502 22) run twice per day (year-round) to Dublin; round-trip fares cost £27-48, depending on the season and day of the week (Fri.-Mon. £13 more expensive). **Sealink** ferries (tel. (0407) 46 04) also sail twice per day, and prices are similar. The morning boats of both companies sail *very* early (3:15am and 5:30am). Tickets for both companies are sold at the train station. Ask about BritRail Pass, InterRail Pass, or YHA card discounts. B&B vacancies are posted nightly at the **tourist office,** Marine Sq. (tel. (0407) 26 22)—a caravan near the ferry dock. Buses run from Bangor to Holyhead (Mon.-Sat. every hr., Sun. 3 per day).

Conwy's castle was once one of the finest along the coast, and is still encircled by the intact town wall. **Ty Bach,** Britain's smallest house, is here as well, with a mere 72 inches of frontage on the quay. **Aberconwy House** on Castle St., the oldest dwelling in town (14th century), and the Elizabethan **Plas Mawr,** around the corner on High St., are both architecturally interesting. Conwy's **tourist office** is on Castle St., just down from where the bus lets you off. (Open Feb.-Oct. daily 10am-6pm.) A visit to Mrs. Hughes' **Llwyn Guesthouse,** 15 Cadnant Park (tel. (0492) 59 23 19), is recommended, as is a stay at the **Meifod Guest House** next door (tel. (0492) 59 37 82). Both charge £8.

Llandudno Junction, across the bridge from Conwy, is gateway to the beautiful **Vale of Conwy,** where you'll find the lush **Bodnant Gardens** and many campsites and footpaths along the route to tiny Betws-y-Coed. This is a fine place to cut across to the western coast; get bus timetables from tourist offices and bus depots.

Halfway to Shrewsbury, **Llangollen** is not served by train, but you can hitch there along the A5 or take the frequent buses from Chester or Chirk. Nestled amongst wooded hills in the Vale of Llangollen, this is an emphatically Welsh town. The large stones perched on the hill are the ruins of **Dinas Brân** (Crow Castle). Two miles west on that side of the river lies the **Vale of Crucis** with its ancient, roofless **abbey.** Closer to town is **Plas Newydd,** home of the two eccentric "Ladies of Llangollen." The interior of this half-timbered house, where Wordsworth once visited the Ladies to compose some poems, is a masterpiece of woodcarving. The first-rate **tourist office** is in the town hall (tel. (0978) 86 08 28), two blocks from the bridge. (Open Easter-June daily 10am-6pm; July-Sept. daily 9am-7pm; Oct.-Nov. daily 10am-4pm.) The **IYHF youth hostel** is 1½ miles away (tel. (0978) 86 03 30) in a gorgeous former mansion. (£3.25.) The town fills to bursting during the **Llangollen International Musical Eisteddfod,** which takes place each year in early July. Performers from all over the world compete at outdoor concerts of music and dance.

Scotland

"When God made time, he made plenty of it." This Scots proverb captures the easy-going nature of the people who inhabit one of the most breathtakingly beautiful lands of Europe. The past is alive and important in this ancient kingdom of ruined castles and strong traditions, where the ewes are still separated from the rams in

the strictly Presbyterian northwest, and people still smile and greet the passer-by. Today most of the people in Scotland are crowded into the narrow belt of land running southwest from Aberdeen to Glasgow, and too many of them live in deprived conditions typical of decaying northern Britain.

Although united with England in 1707, Scotland maintains a distinct identity, with its own school, church, and judicial systems, most of which are based in the ancient capital of Edinburgh. Distinct, too, is Scotland's famous heritage of kilt, clan, and bagpipe, although that owes more to the romanticism of Sir Walter Scott than to actual fact. After having ruthlessly suppressed the Highland culture in the eighteenth century, Romantic Britain "discovered" the noble Gaelic-speaking Highlander as an attractive alternative to its often ignoble industrial present. This discovery did not, however, extend to returning the Highlands to the clans, and so hills and glens remain the deserted wilds that you see today.

These wilds are staggeringly beautiful. The majestic mountains and glens, volcanic in origin, were shaped to their present rugged form by a series of glaciers. Humans finished the work by destroying the forests hundreds of years ago, and today every chiselmark of nature is visible. Although the highest of the peaks, Ben Nevis, barely tops 4400 feet, treeless slopes and precipitous rises from loch to summit make these mountains breathtaking.

Early August through mid-September is heather time in Scotland, and whole mountains erupt in purple. May and June are probably the best months to visit: The tourists are few, the softly-colored primroses are in bloom, and the weather is best. But don't count on the weather; it's often soggy, and you should prepare accordingly. You will need warm woolen clothing, a slicker (preferably light and stowable), and a hat. In more remote areas, waterproof overpants and boots will prove a blessing.

During July and August, parts of the western coast and the inner islands can feel like an international zoo. By all means don't linger in the big tourist centers like Inverness, Oban, and Fort William. Use them as transportation bases and absorb the flavor of the smaller villages. Go to a *Ceilidh* (rhymes with "daily") dance or to a weekend folk festival; look for a bagpipe competition or a **Highland Gathering** in an out-of-the-way place. The best festivals take place in June: the **Burns Festival** in Ayr, Orkney's **St. Magnus Festival,** and **Border Ridings** throughout the Borders. July brings the **Glasgow Folk Festival,** and August, the renowned **Edinburgh International Folk Festival.**

There is no way to rush through the Highlands or islands, so relax. Only a few railway routes snake their way north; some smaller towns and islands have but a few buses or boats passing through each week; some remote areas are served only by post buses. Be sure to invest a pound in *Getting Around the Highlands and Islands,* an exhaustive timetable. This is exciting cycling country, if the weather doesn't dampen your enthusiasm; bikes can be rented in almost every town and transported to your starting point by train for half-fare. Hitching is excellent except in heavily-touristed areas.

The **Freedom of Scotland ticket** allows unlimited travel on the railways for £42 for one week, £66 for two weeks. The **Highlands and Islands Travelpass** allows unlimited travel on most rail, boat, and bus routes, and is available for 7 or 14 days (March-May and Oct. £30 and £50 respectively; June-Sept. £49 and £75). Neither gives you your money's worth unless you're moving like crazy, and if you can't spare the time to explore a heathered moor or share a few pints in a rural pub, you're wasting your time here.

Hiking is rewarding, but the undomesticated countryside can be extremely dangerous. You can't rely on cairns or well-marked paths to guide your way, and you can *never* predict when the mist will come down. Blizzards are possible even during July. Never go up a mountain without sturdy, well broken-in boots, a one-inch or 2½-inch **Ordnance Survey Map,** plus a compass you know how to use, adequate waterproof gear and clothing to withstand freezing temperatures, and an emergency food supply. A friend and some mosquito repellent will also come in handy. Leave a planned route and timetable at the hostel, croft, or nearest mountain rescue station. For more details on walking and mountaineering in Scotland, consult a respectable guide, such as Poucher's *The Scottish Peaks* (£8), or the Scottish Tourist Board's *Scotland for Hillwalking* (£1.75). Mid-August to mid-October is deer-stalking season, so consult the hostel warden or innkeeper before heading for an area where hunters might be.

Camping in Scotland is the cheapest way to spend the night; proper gear is necessary. Most private sites cost about £2-3 per night and are oriented toward caravanners; you might prefer simply to camp beside the road. Pick up a copy of *Camping and Caravan Sites in Scotland* (£1.50) at any tourist office. IYHF (SYHA) youth hostels are often ideally located for hikers, but call ahead if you're traveling in the summer; they fill up fast. Charges are £2.15-3.45 per night; sheets (or sheet sleep-sacks) and membership cards are required. All hostels rent cotton sleep-sacks and temporary membership passes, but, if you'll be hosteling regularly, it's more economical to buy your own and to join. For £10, foreigners can join IYHF at the Edinburgh and Stirling offices and at many of the larger hostels. Most hostels are closed by October and don't reopen until March, April, or May.

Edinburgh

Capital of the medieval kingdom of Scotland, Edinburgh is arguably the most beautiful city in Northern Europe. Still the center of Scotland's autonomous judicial, ecclesiastical, and administrative establishments, Edinburgh has become neither too civilized to be cold nor too large to be unattractive. Medieval alleyways cluster around an imposing castle, elegant eighteenth-century townhouses sweep around lush parks, and culture thrives.

Practical Information

Tourist Office: 3 Princes St. (tel. 557 27 27), in Waverley Market, next to the Waverley train station. Efficient if busy accommodations service (75p). Good information on all of Scotland. Open July-Aug. Mon.-Sat. 8:30am-9pm, Sun. 11am-9pm; May-June and Sept. Mon.-Sat. 8:30am-8pm, Sun. 11am-8pm; Oct.-April Mon.-Fri. 9am-6pm, Sat. 9am-1pm.

Budget Travel: Student Travel Centre, Potterow Union, Bristo St. (tel. 668 22 21), at Edinburgh University. Open Mon.-Fri. 9am-5:30pm.

American Express: 139 Princes St. (tel. 225 78 81). Mail held. All banking services. Open Mon.-Fri. 9am-5pm, Sat. 9am-noon.

Currency Exchange: When banks are closed, go to the train station. Open Mon.-Sat. 8:30am-9:30pm, Sun. 10am-8:30pm.

Post Office: 2 Waterloo Place (tel. 550 82 00), at the corner of Princes and North Bridge St. Open Mon.-Fri. 9:30am-5:30pm, Sat. 9:30am-noon.

Public Transportation: Buy ticket (20-50p) on bus; correct change needed.

Train Station: Waverley Station (tel. 556 24 51). Ticket office open whenever trains run. Baggage check 70p, showers £1.

Bus Station: Scottish Citylink, St. Andrew's Sq. (tel. 556 84 64). Information desk open Mon.-Sat. 8am-8:30pm, Sun. 9am-5pm.

Emergencies: Police or **Ambulance** (tel. 999).

Consulates: U.S., 3 Regent Terrace (tel. 556 83 15). **Australia,** 80 Hanover St. (tel. 226 62 71). **Canada** (in Glasgow; tel. (041) 248 30 26).

Laundry: 108 Bruntsfield Place, near the Bruntsfield youth hostel. Many throughout the city.

Hitching: For points south (except Newcastle and the northeast of England), take bus #4, 15, or 79 to Fairmilehead and then the A702 to Biggar. For Newcastle, York, and Durham, take bus #48 to Musselburgh and the A1. For Glasgow and the North, take bus #18 or 20 to Barnton.

Telephone code: 031.

Accommodations and Camping

Though room-finding should not be difficult except during the Festival, and not impossible even then, the tourist office will be happy to help (75p). Try Minto Street, Mayfield Gardens, and Craigmillar Park, to the south; Hartington Place and Leavington Terrace to the west; and Pilrig Street or Ferry Road to the north. The **Merlin Guesthouse,** 14 Hartington Place, has airy rooms for £11 single; and the **Robertson Guest House,** at #5, has similar rooms and prices. Both are open year-round, and reduce rates by about £2 from September to May.

High Street Youth Hostel: 8 Blackfriars St. (tel. 557 39 84), the first right walking downhill on the Royal Mile after the South Bridge intersection; very central. This friendly, clean establishment fulfills Edinburgh's long-standing need for an unofficial youth hostel. Free movie videos every night. 10-30 bunk beds per room. Kitchen facilities. May-Sept. £3.80, Oct.-April £3.30. Curfew Mon.-Fri. 1:30am, Sat.-Sun. 2:30am, during the Festival 3am.

Youth hostel (IYHF), 17-18 Eglinton Crescent (tel. 337 11 20), and 7-8 Bruntsfield Crescent (tel. 447 29 94). For the former, take bus #3, 4, or 12 to Haymarket; for the latter, bus #11, 12, 15, or 26 from Princes St. Though both are pleasant, Bruntsfield, across from a park, is smaller and nicer. Both £3.50. Both open their doors at 2pm and are usually full in summer by 3pm; they can, however, direct you to one of several temporary hostels. 11:45pm curfew, extended to 2am in summer. Both open year-round.

Pollock Halls of Residence, 18 Holyrood Park Rd. (tel. 667 19 71), behind the Royal Commonwealth Pool. 1500 large singles in modern college buildings. Bus #14, 21, or 33 from Princes St. to the pool. B&B £12.80, students £7.30. Generally booked by groups during the Festival. Open July-Sept.

YWCA: 14 Coates Crescent (tel. 225 36 08). A B&B for £7 in a shared room, £8.50 for a single. 11pm curfew, or ask for a key for special events. Women only.

Food

Edinburgh's cuisine is generally tailored to the genteel patron of the arts; you're not likely to get cheap food, friendly atmosphere, *and* traditional Scottish fare all in one restaurant. The posh establishments that do serve Scottish treats will blow your budget for a week, but you can get such delights as *cock-a-leekie soup* or *haggis,* that famous dish made from sheep's pluck, at reasonable prices in local cafes and groceries. Pub lunches are usually good values (£1.50-2 for an entree with vegetable and 1 or 2 salads).

Old Sailor's Ark, 4 New St. Just off High St. near Canongate in a big hall behind an obscurely marked door. If you want to fill up cheaply, this is the place to come. For breakfast, 75p gets you 2 fried eggs, 2 large sausage patties, black pudding, beans, a roll, a bowl of porridge, and a mug of tea; similar price and quantity for lunch. Open Mon.-Fri. 8:30-10am and noon-2pm; take-aways 11am-noon.

Teviot Row House, Bristo Sq. The Student Union, open Oct.-June to those with student ID. Hot full meal for £2.50. During the festival, it becomes the **Fringe Club,** a restaurant open to all, and prices go up by about 50%. Open 10am-7:30pm.

Lachana Vegetarian Restaurant, 3 Bristo Pl., near the university. A delicious all-you-can-eat buffet (hot dish, soup, salad, and dessert) for £2.50. Open Mon.-Thurs. noon-2:30pm and 5-8pm, Fri. noon-2:30pm. Or try **Seeds,** 53 West Nicolson St. Heaping plate of vegetarian curry £1.50; good teas. Open Mon.-Sat. 10am-8pm.

Lillig's, 30 Victoria St., off George IV Bridge. Coffees, baked goods, a bar, and filling meals with a German twist. Knockwurst platter with big helpings of potato and green salad £2.10. Open Mon.-Sat. 11am-11pm.

Henderson's Salad and Wine Bar, 94 Hanover St. Wide selection of salads (average £2.40 per plate, 60p per portion) and wines, all served in a warm atmosphere; live guitar and piano nightly from 8pm. Open Mon.-Thurs. 8am-11pm, Fri.-Sat. 8am-midnight.

The Waterfront, Old Waiting Room, Dock Place, in Leith (Edinburgh's port). Take bus #16 and ask to get off at the bridge over Leith Water; the restaurant is on the left bank of Leith

Water as you face the sea, tucked away behind a parking lot. Nautical motif and delicious seafood barbecues that will set you back £5 but are worth every penny. Open Mon.-Sat. 6-9pm, bar until 11pm.

Sights

Unquestioned centerpiece of the city, **Edinburgh Castle** looms into view around street corners for miles around. From its windows, when the mist is not too heavy, you can see all the way across the Firth of Forth to Fife. Eleventh-century **Queen Margaret's Chapel,** the oldest building in Edinburgh, is contained within the castle walls. (Castle open Mon.-Sat. 9:30am-6pm, Sun. 11am-6pm.) On your way there, you'll pass the medieval dwelling called **Gladstone's Land,** the oldest house on the Royal Mile, preserved as it was in the fifteenth and sixteenth centuries (open Mon.-Sat. 10am-5pm, Sun. 2-5pm. Admission £1.50, students 75p), and **Lady Stair's House,** a seventeenth-century townhouse containing memorabilia of Scotland's literary trinity of Robert Burns, Sir Walter Scott, and Robert Louis Stevenson. (Open June-Sept. Mon.-Sat. 10am-5pm, Sun. 2-5pm. Free.) Next view the **High Kirk of St. Giles,** whose open-work spire is supported by a crown of flying buttresses. The final lap of the Mile includes **Canongate Tolbooth,** where you can learn how to trace your Highland ancestry (if you have any) through the tartans. Save **Holyrood Palace** for last; worth special attention are the **Music Room** and the **Northwest Tower,** where Mary Queen of Scots' secretary, David Riccio, was stabbed to death before her eyes. Bus #6 or 45 will take you to the palace. (Open June-Aug. Mon.-Sat. 9:30am-5:15pm, Sun. 11am-4:15pm; Sept.-May Mon.-Sat. 9:30am-5:15pm. Admission £1.20, students 60p.)

Of Edinburgh's constellation of galleries, two are especially notable. The **National Gallery,** on the Mound, has a collection of Old Masters including Raphael's Bridgewater *Madonna.* (Open Mon.-Fri. 10am-5pm and Sun. 2-5pm.) The **National Gallery of Modern Art,** on Belford Rd. (take bus #3), houses pieces by Henry Moore, drawings by Picasso and Rouault, and rotating monthly exhibits. (Open Mon.-Sat. 10am-5pm, Sun. 2-5pm. Both museums free.) The **City Art Centre** and **Fruitmarket Gallery,** both around the corner from the train station on Market St., hold excellent exhibits of modern and traditional painting.

One of the best ways to enjoy Edinburgh is to walk through its elegant Georgian neighborhoods. From Charlotte Square, laid out by young architect James Craig in the 1790s, walk west across Queensferry Street and through the West End to Palmerston Place. Turn right, passing the huge Gothic **St. Mary's** Anglican cathedral, and follow the road downhill past Douglas Gardens to Belford Bridge. Here, various small alleys and stairs head off to your right to the medieval village of **Dean,** clustered in the ravine of Leith Water hundreds of feet below the Georgian townhouses of the New Town. A pathway leads east along Leith Water from Dean to **Stockbridge,** a quaint community full of students, coffeeshops, and good pubs. From here, any one of a number of buses will take you back up the hill to Princes Street.

For a sweeping view of Edinburgh, climb **Arthur's Seat,** an extinct volcano (823 ft.) located in Holyrood Park. Another view is from **Calton Hill,** well past the east end of Princes St., where you can also get a close-up look at Edinburgh's folly, the unfinished shell of what the city elders intended to build into a replica of the Parthenon; money ran out midway through the first row of columns.

Entertainment

Even without the *Complete Edinburgh Pub Guide* (Edinburgh University Student Publications, 1 Buccleuch Pl.), you'll be well-watered no matter where you land. A good place for live blues and jazz bands is **Preservation Hall,** 9 Victoria St., a large New Orleans-style hall. (Music starts nightly at 9pm; no cover except Fri.-Sat. after 9:30pm, £1.) Two especially good student bars are the traditional **Pear Tree Pub** on West Nicolson St, with its large outdoor courtyard, and **Greyfriars Bobby,** both of which are open (and crammed) late. Greyfriars Bobby was a loyal dog who refused to leave his owner's grave, in the yard of Greyfriar's Kirk, for years. Lucky travelers may catch performance artist **Peter Blumberg** doing his skillful interpretations of the canine hero. Look for him in pubs, bakeries, or the phone booths in the National Library. The **Cafe Royal** on West Register St., off Princes St., is perhaps the most beautiful around, with old wood and stained glass.

You'll find drama at the **Traverse Theatre** on West Bow (tel. 226 26 33), and at the **Royal Lyceum Theatre,** Grindlay St. off Lothian Rd. (tel. 229 96 97). **Usher Hall,** Lothian Rd. (tel. 228 11 55), holds concerts of the Scottish National and Chamber Orchestras, while **Ripping Records,** 91 South Bridge (tel. 226 70 10), has information on and tickets for more contemporary musical performances. The best cinema in town is the **Filmhouse,** 88 Lothian Rd. (tel. 228 26 88), showing a selection of classic and critically-acclaimed films. Tickets run from £2, but student discounts (50p) are available for early afternoon shows. *The List,* available at most bookshops, will let you know what's on.

The Edinburgh Festival and its satellites—the Fringe Festival, the Jazz Festival, the Film Festival, and the Military Tattoo—transform the city and transfix their audiences. Thousands of the culture-minded congregate here, and the city does its best to keep them happy—museum hours are extended and special exhibitions are arranged in addition to the festivities. In 1988, the festival will be held August 14 to September 3. Tickets are on sale by mail starting in May, and the Festival Box Office, 21 Market St., Edinburgh EH1 18W, opens in early June for counter sales; you can book by phone with a credit card, except on the day of a performance (tel. 226 40 01). During the year, the office is open Mon.-Fri. 9am-5pm, Sat. 10am-noon; during the festival, the box office is open Mon.-Sat. 9am-6pm, Sun. 10am-5pm. Prices for musical and theatrical events can go as high as £15, but many plays and concerts cost only £5-7. Performances are often sold out well in advance, but sometimes you can buy unsold tickets at half-price on the day of the performance; go to the booth at the bottom of The Mound from 1 to 5pm.

Around the established festival has grown an even larger **Fringe Festival,** now with over 400 amateur and professional companies presenting theater, music, poetry, dance, mime, opera, revue, and various exhibitions. Ticket prices average about £3, and occasionally there are student discounts. For tickets and a comprehensive program, write the **Fringe Festival Office,** 180-182 High St., Edinburgh EH1 1QS (from abroad, include £1.67 postage for the program). Telephone or over-the-counter bookings can be made at the office, starting in late July (tel. 226 52 57; open year-round Mon.-Sat. 10am-5:30pm, Sun. 10am-4pm). Both festivals run clubs where performers and visitors can hang out. Membership fees are about £5 for the three weeks.

Progress in contemporary cinema is represented in the **International Film Festival,** and a **Jazz Festival** has also recently swung into gear. Film information is available from The Filmhouse, 88 Lothian Rd., Edinburgh EH3 9BZ (tel. 228 63 82). The box office is open in early August; no phone or postal bookings are accepted. For jazz information, contact the Information Centre, 116 Canongate (tel. 557 16 42). The **Military Tattoo,** a fantastic spectacle of bagpipes and drums, is performed almost every night on the Castle Esplanade during Festival time; for tickets (£3.50 and up) write or stop by the office, 22 Market St., Edinburgh EH1 1QB (tel. 225 11 88).

Glasgow

Edinburgh may have more historical attractions and tourists, but Glasgow is the real center of work-a-day Scotland. You'll find the people here friendlier, and the city generally far more energetic. Five-hundred-year-old Glasgow University is perched on a hill overlooking Kelvingrove Park; its 40,000 students make the city one of the liveliest in Britain. For year-round arts events, performances, and energetic pub-crawls, Glasgow is the place to visit. Those fearful of the city's industrial reputation will find central Galsgow surprisingly fresh, clean, and interesting.

Glasgow's underground system, recently redone, circles the center of the city (35p flat fare). The cooperative **Tourist Information** (tel. 227 48 80) is at 35 St. Vincent Place, adjacent to George Square. (Open June-Sept. Mon.-Sat. 9am-9pm; Oct.-May Mon.-Sat. 9am-5pm.) The areas east of Glasgow Cross and near the docks on the south bank of the Clyde can be dangerous.

The cheapest lodgings are in the **youth hostel (IYHF),** 10 Woodlands Terrace (tel. 332 30 04), which is next to Kelvingrove Park, one of the nicest areas in town. It's just a short walk from the art gallery and university: Take Sauchiehall St. west to Charing Cross, then follow the hostel signs, or from Buchanan Bus Station, walk about six blocks up Renfrew St. to the footbridge over the motorway; on the other side, turn right, take the steps past Claremont Terrace, and then turn left onto Woodlands Terrace. (£3.40. Check-in before 11:30pm. 2am curfew.) You'd be well advised to use the tourist office's accommodation service (40p plus a 30p deposit); B&Bs are widely dispersed and not that numerous. If you go it alone, try Hillhead Street (Hillhead underground stop), especially the **Chez Nous Guesthouse,** at #33 (tel. 334 29 77), with lots of singles for £11, doubles £18. In any event, there will almost certainly be a clean, bright room in **Queen Margaret Hall,** 55 Bellshaugh Rd. (tel. 334 21 92), at the university (B&B singles £11, students £7.50).

Inexpensive Indian and Chinese restaurants abound on Sauchiehall Street, in the center of town, and around Byres Road, near the university. **Shish Mahall,** Gibson St., off Byres Rd., is Stu's favorite, with chicken and vegetable curries from £2.95. (Open daily 11:45am-11:30pm.) The **Third Eye Centre,** 350 Sauchiehall, has a good vegetarian menu (hot dishes start around £1.20) and an interesting bookstore and art gallery. **The Grosvenor Café,** Ashton Lane, behind Byres Rd., is a student hang-out with excellent values on hamburger-type grub (cheesburgers 47p, homemade soup 34p; open Mon.-Fri. 9am-7pm, Sat. 9am-6pm). The **University Refectories** across from the library at Glasgow University offer wholesome, inexpensive grub, and you don't have to be a registered student (Oct.-May).

Even if you're just in Glasgow to catch a train, visit **Kelvingrove Park.** Lounge about by the Kelvin River, or wander the leafy paths, discovering the park's odd statues and fountains. In the southwest corner of the park is the **Glasgow Art Gallery and Museum,** where you'll find Rembrandts and Monets, an arms-and-armour display, and Van Gogh's portrait of a Glaswegian art dealer. (Open Mon.-Sat. 10am-5pm, Sun. 2-5pm. Free.) Towering at the north end of the park is the central building of **Glasgow Uniersity,** near which is Byres Road, the place to begin your nighttime activities. The popular **Byres Road pub crawl** usually begins at **Tennents Bar** by University Road, and then continues down towards the River Clyde—the path is long an' the ale is strong. **Oblomov** is a gorgeous pub, with oriental rugs for tablecloths, a colorful poster montage on the ceiling, and jazz on the speakers. **Nico's,** on Sauchiehall St., West End, is a lively, hectic place, where people pour through the French windows that open onto the street. More information on nightlife can be found in *The List,* which you can buy at most newsstands.

Every Saturday and Sunday at London Rd. and Gallowgate (east of the city center), is the Glasgow **Barras,** billed as the largest open-air market in the world. South of town (5km) is the beautifully wooded **Pollok Park** (buses #23, 45, or 57), site of the **Burrell Collection,** a fascinating personal collection amassed from William Burrell's travels in the Orient. (Open Mon.-Sat. 10am-5pm, Sun. 2-5pm. Free.)

Near Glasgow: Arran

Two hours southwest of Glasgow by train and ferry lies the rugged island of Arran, the most accessible Scottish island. Trains and buses connect Glasgow and the harbor at Ardrossan, where frequent ferries (1 hr., £5 round-trip) leave for **Brodick,** Arran's largest village and only tourist trap. Rising above the curving, sandy bay at Brodick is the peak of **Goatfell,** from which you can see north to the ridges of the Castles and south down the coast to Holy Island. This fairly strenuous climb averages five hours round-trip, from Brodick to the cold and windy peak and back. Fifteen miles away, at the north end of the island, is **Lochranza,** as idyllic a Scottish village as you could imagine, with one store, one pub, one castle, and one **youth hostel (IYHF)** (tel. Lochranza 631). This is the best base for exploring the gentle headlands of the **Cock of Arran** and the island's central peaks. At the southern end of the island, where peaks and ridges give way to meadows and beaches, there's a **youth hostel (IYHF)** at **Whiting Bay** (tel. (07707) 339).

Highlands and Islands

The northwest of Scotland, where the mountains meet the sea, contains some of the most spectacular scenery in Britain. From the lochs of Argyll and the silver sands of Morar to the crags of Glen Coe and Torridon, not much has changed since Bonnie Prince Charlie landed at Glenfinnie to rally the Highland clans and reclaim his family's crown. The misty Cuillin mountains of the Isle of Skye and majestic Ben More of the Isle of Mull would be quite recognizable to Messrs. Boswell and Johnson, were they to retrace the steps of their eighteenth-century tour through the Hebrides. The Outer Hebrides, which were too remote for the two old gentlemen to visit, are unearthly, lonely places unviolated by tourist crowds.

Travel is a lot easier now than in Johnson's day; **Caledonian MacBrayne** holds a monopoly on ferry services to almost all the inner and outer isles, and trains leave Glasgow for Oban (the Highlands' main port) and Fort William (the Highlands' main resort) three or four times per day in summer. Buses are the cheapest (and slowest) way to go; check the **Scottish Citylink** schedules for inexpensive fares on runs such as Glasgow-Oban and Glasgow-Fort William (30% off with student coach cards, obtainable at major bus stations for £3). Throughout the region, buses frequently run only once or twice per day, and very seldom on Sunday. *Getting Around the Highlands and Islands* (£1.75 at any tourist office) is indispensable; it lists all the public transit systems in the region, though transport sometimes runs at its own sweet pace. Don't try to see everything; pick one place, settle down, and explore. Rent a bike and cycle down one-lane roads, or walk across the bogs and *machair* (spongy wild grass).

Inverness

Inverness is Scotland's busiest tourist trap and the transportation center of the Highlands, a city full of backpackers all looking for the quickest way out. The castle in town, contrary to lore, is not where Macbeth murdered King Duncan; the actual site is a moat-and-drawbridge dream, **Cawdor Castle,** 12 miles east of town. (Open May to mid-Sept. daily 10am-5:30pm. Admission £2.20.) Five buses per day from Inverness travel to Nairn via Culloden (the site of Bonnie Prince Charlie's decisive defeat) and Cawdor. If the weather is good, the best thing to do is rent a bike at **Ness Motors,** King St. (tel. 22 28 48), for £2.50 per day, and cycle down the south side of **Loch Ness.** Start at the riverbank in town and stick close to the water. The suburbs give way shortly to beautiful farm country; after 5 miles you'll reach **Dores,** at the head of the loch, where you can pony-trek or rent a rowboat. The ruins of **Urquhart Castle** are across the loch. This is where most sightings of the famous **monster** have occurred.

The **Tourist Information Centre** (tel. 23 43 53) is at 23 Church St. (Open in summer Mon.-Fri. 9am-8pm, Sat. 9am-6pm, Sun. 2-6pm; in winter Mon.-Fri. 9am-5:30pm.) The **train** and **bus stations** are just a few blocks away, and the **post office** is one block away on Queensgate. Arrive early in the day during high season to assure yourself of a bed in your price range. The tourist office will find you one for free, or give you an accommodations list with map. (Take it—it's the only free map you'll get.) The **IYHF youth hostel** on Castle St. and Old Edinburgh Rd. (tel. (0463) 23 17 71) is comfortable and convenient, but in summer the queue forms before the 2pm opening time. If it's full, ask the warden to direct you to the overflow hostel, a cheap B&B, or free camping near town. If you're absolutely stuck, the **Wayside Hotel,** across the road from the hostel, will give you a dingy room for

£5.50 (£7.50 B&B), or a mattress on which to put your sleeping bag for £4.50. The areas around **Argyll St.** and **Old Edinburgh Rd.** have a high concentration of B&Bs.

Oban and Fort William

Oban, despite being the major ferry port for the islands, is a pleasant place. If you tire of the bustling pier, you can sit overlooking the bay from the amphitheater arches of **McCaig's Folly** (built in the 18th century to employ masons) or walk 15 minutes north out of town to the crumbling tower of **Dunollie Castle,** from which you can see the mountains of Mull. The **IYHF youth hostel,** on the Esplanade (tel. Oban 620 25), has a beautiful view of the bay. (£3.45. Check-in 7-11am and 2-11:45pm. Open early March-early Nov.) **Jeremy Inglis,** 21 Airds Crescent (tel. Oban 630 64; nights and evenings tel. 650 65), has a similarly priced and very welcoming B&B. (£4.25. Shower and kitchen privileges included.) The **tourist office,** Argyll Sq. (tel. 631 22), is one of Scotland's best, and books accommodations for free. (Open in summer Mon.-Fri. 9am-9pm, Sat. 9am-6pm, Sun. 2-6pm; off-season Mon.-Fri. 9am-5:15pm.) Most visitors leave from the Oban pier for **Mull,** the largest of the southern isles. Ferries leave several times per day in summer for **Craignure** (£3.30 round-trip) from where you can bus to **Tobermory,** the island's largest town, or **Fionnphort.** There's an **IYHF youth hostel** (tel. (0688) 24 81) in Tobermory, among the colorful houses overlooking the bay. (£2.35. Open March 21-Sept.) If you want to climb **Ben More,** the main trail begins on the west coast at Dishig, but you'll have to hitch or call A.J. McColl (tel. (06803) 321) to get there. The cliff-side coast road (B8073), which winds past scores of off-shore islands, is itself worth a look. The less energetic can visit the alluringly situated **Duart Castle,** near Craignure, and **Torosay Castle,** a graceful Victorian mansion close by. Hitch or cycle through the mountainous scenery by Loch Scridain and Ben More to **Fionnphort,** where you can catch a ferry to the sacred isle of **Iona**—one of the shining lights of culture in Britain during the Middle Ages. The Iona community continues to maintain an alternative spiritual center in the old abbey. Inexpensive accommodation (£5) is sometimes available in the abbey (tel. (06817) 314). Oban's book-a-bed-ahead service can reserve you a B&B (£7-9), or you can ask landowners for permission to camp.

Fort William no longer has a fort, but it could do with one to keep the tourists away in the summer season. Mountaineers are drawn by the challenge of **Ben Nevis** (4406 ft.), the highest mountain in Britain. The main tourist path starts just up Glen Nevis past the town park. Count on seven hours round-trip. The **tourist office** books accommodations. (Open in summer Mon.-Sat. 9am-9pm, Sun. 2-6pm; off-season Mon.-Thurs. 9am-5:30pm, Fri. 9am-5pm.) At the base of the Ben Nevis trail, in the lush valley of Glen Nevis, the pleasant **Glen Nevis Youth Hostel (IYHF)** (tel. (0397) 23 36), is often full of hikers, so call ahead. You can camp for free farther up the valley. **McTavish's Kitchen** in town will fill you up cheaply; the self-service restaurant in the **Nevisport** mountain shop has similar prices. Try the famous raisin bread from the **Ben Nevis Bakery. Lochaber,** the area west of Fort William, is stunningly beautiful. The famous "Road to the Isles" winds to **Mallaig** through mountains and past lochs to the Silver Sands of Morar, white beaches that would look more at home in the Caribbean. No buses take this route, but there are even better views from the train. (June-Sept. Mon.-Sat. 4 per day; Oct.-May 2 per day; £6 day return.) Three miles north of **Arisaig** station, the **Garramore Hostel (IYHF)** (tel. Arisaig 268; £3.25) sits not far from the Morar beaches. From Mallaig you can catch the frequent ferry to Skye.

Hebrides

The **Isle of Skye** is the most touristed of the Hebrides, and its scenery merits the publicity. You'll discover the craggy **Black Cuillin Hills,** volcanic peaks which blast straight up into the swirling clouds, ignoring such conventions as foothills. At the northern and southern ends of the island are the lush peninsulas and bays near Staffin and Armadale. The island also has a rich history of intrigue between the warring MacLeod and MacDonald clans. Skye is easily reached by ferry from Mallaig (£1.80) or Kyle of Lochalsh (33p). Transportation on the island is not readily available; bus service is infrequent and expensive, and hitching unreliable. Try biking, hiking, or renting a car. Skye's four **hostels** are in ideal locations, though they're often full. **Glenbrittle** (tel. (047842) 278) is in the heart of the Cuillins, accessible only to hikers or those with their own transportation. (Open late March-Sept.) **Uig Hostel (IYHF)** (tel. (047042) 211), overlooking the bay at the northern peninsula, is the least crowded and is accessible by bus or by ferry from the outer isles. The wardens run frequent trips to *ceilidhs* (KAY-LEES; parties) and keep the folk music going all day long. (Open late March-early Nov.) **Broadford** (tel. (04712) 442) is the most centrally located, near mountains and beaches. (Open late March-early Nov.) **Armadale** (tel. (04714) 260), on the southern tip, is a mile away from the Mallaig ferry and provides a good base from which to tour the lush **Sleat Peninsula.** (Open late March-Sept.)

Trotternish, the untouristed northern arm of the island, is watched over by the ruins of the MacDonalds's **Duntulm Castle,** near the **Quirang,** a dramatic rock escarpment overlooking Staffin Bay. Four miles north of overtouristed Dunvegan Castle lies Coral Bay, where you can find miniature shells on the beach. Rock climbers shouldn't miss the challenge of the Cuillins to the south. There are many easily accessible walks out of **Sligachar,** where there's a large campsite, a small store, and a hotel. The main path here leads over an old bridge and through a river valley between the peaks. On a sunny day, take the difficult bike trip from Broadford to Elgol for a spellbinding view of the Cuillins across the sea.

Several smaller islands are accessible from Skye. From Sconser, take the ferry to **Raasay** (Sat. only; year-round), a long, narrow island with an **IYHF youth hostel** (no phone and few restrictions; open mid-May to Sept.). Ferries run from Mallaig and Arisaig to **Rum** (Mon. and Wed.-Sat.; May only), a nature preserve managed by the National Trust. Rooms for stays of more than a few days (tel. Rum 26; £5 per night) are available in a castle built in 1901. The small communities of **Muck** and **Eigg** are also worth a visit.If the Inner Hebrides aren't remote enough, then the **Outer Hebrides,** 40 miles into the Atlantic, are what you're looking for. The scenery in these Outer Isles, with the exception of Harris's weird volcanic hills, is initially unremarkable. But there's a timelessness on these desolate islands that you won't find anywhere else in Britain. The pure sunlight, unfiltered by smoke and dust, the Atlantic mists, the unpopulated moors, lochs, and *machair* meadows will all draw you into a tranquil lifestyle that becomes hard to leave. The islands are best visited between late April and October; the rest of the year accommodations are a little hard to find and the weather is fearsome. This is the last stronghold of both the Gaelic language and the Free Church, whose strict observation of the Sabbath makes travel impossible and food, drink, and accommodation difficult to find on Sunday.

To get here, hop on the ferry at Oban (for Castlebay on Barra and Lochboisdale on South Uist), at Uig on Skye (for Lochmaddy on North Uist and Tarbert on Harris), or at Ullapool (for Stornoway on Lewis). **Caledonian MacBrayne** operates all ferries year-round. Its main Highland office is in Oban (tel. (0631) 622 85). An **Island Hopscotch** ticket will take you through all the islands at a reduced rate. A good route is to start in Oban and take the ferry to the Uists (a breathtaking 6-hour journey that takes you past most of the Inner Hebrides), work your way up to Harris and Lewis, and then return to Skye.

Starting from the south, the Hebrides run in a string from Barra, South Uist, Benbecula, North Uist, to the largest island, which is divided into Harris (the southern third) and Lewis. There are seasonal **tourist offices** (May-Sept.) on the southern group at Castlebay (tel. 336), Lochboisdale (tel. 286) and Lochmaddy (tel. 321), all open for ferry arrivals. On North Uist there is an **IYHF youth hostel** at Lochmaddy (tel. 368; £3.15; open mid-May to Sept.); when the rain and wind pour off the Atlantic, the warden opens early so you can dry off by the woodstove. Travel is by several infrequent post buses, but hitching is a definite alternative. The southern group's most spectacular feature is the beach on the western coast, which stretches uninterrupted for nearly 40 miles. There are numerous archeological and historical sites, rich with atmosphere, but virtually undistinguishable from the surrounding landscape. It's worth reading up on the island's history; there will be no crowds to spoil your contemplation of the site of a Celtic university, or the areas where fugitive Bonnie Prince Charlie hid from government troops. Try Alistair McLean's *MacDonald for a Prince,* or *The World of an Island* by Philip Coxon. The *Outer Hebrides Leisure Map* will show you the location of every standing stone and bird preserve. On these islands, as well as on Harris, there are several **independent hostels** run by the Gatliff Trust—rudimentary accommodations in old crofts. Very well run by friendly wardens, with bunks, peat fires, and cooking facilities. Get their green leaflet at the ferry port tourist offices when you arrive.

Northernmost in the chain, "The Long Island" of **Harris/Lewis** is divided by the mountainous **Forest of Harris,** in which there is not a single tree. These once impassable mountains, formed by volcanic gneiss, give Harris the most singularly weird landscape in Scotland. Open hills, softened by a piebald carpet of *machair* and wildflowers, make for great off-trail rambling. During the Highland Clearances, crofters were forced from the lush west coast to the rocky east, where they developed the "lazybed"—a combination of seaweed and peat laid on bare rock—to compensate for the lack of arable land.

Lewis is better known for its Celtic ruins, most famous of which are the **Stones of Callanish.** This Stonehenge-like circle of stones tracks the movements of the moon in the same way Stonehenge follows the sun, but the Lewis monument is spared Stonehenge's tour buses and popsicle stands. The best way to Callanish and other ruins is on the bus (£4) run by the Stornoway tourist office. Off this route, at the northern tip of the island, is the Butt of Lewis, where a lighthouse stands above a pounding surf. **Stornoway,** the island's largest town, is a dull ferry port (boats to Ullapool in the northwest) where there's a **tourist office** (tel. Stornoway 30 88; open year-round 9am-5:30pm and for ferry arrivals). The tiny **fish and chip shop** on Church St. is one of the best in Scotland. There is also a **tourist office** in **Tarbert** (tel. (0859) 20 11) on Harris (same opening times). B&Bs are often in the middle of nowhere, so book ahead at the tourist offices. The **Stockinish Youth Hostel (IYHF)** (no phone; £2.35; open mid-May to Sept.) is 8 miles south of Tarbert along "the Golden Road;" one to two buses run daily. This is a gorgeously peaceful place with few restrictions; there are no showers but always an open peat fire. Ask about hikes in the area. Gather mussels and periwinkles from nearby beach rocks (boil fresh 3 times, 10 min. per time, butter and salt and a needle for dipping; delicious).

The Northwest

Stretching from the craggy Torridons to Cape Wrath, site of the highest and northernmost seacliffs in mainland Britain, the Northwest is regarded today as Britain's last great wilderness. The landscape overwhelms the few villages and narrow, thinly traveled roads; the region's oddly-shaped mountains—most notably Suilven and Liathach—are set apart from each other on great expanses of moor. It's a beautiful area, almost menacing in its loneliness and grandeur.

Hitching can prove difficult, as many of the coastal roads are single-lane and the few cars that do pass are often full. The weather is predictably cold, even in summer. Public transport north of Kyle is sketchy, though you can make day by day progress on post bus connections. You'll need your own transport or a lot of time. The *Getting Around the Highlands & Islands* guide (£1.50), available at all tourist offices, is a must.

Plockton, once a fishing village, is now a crafts center. The annual **Plockton Regatta** is held in the quiet bay each July. The **campsite** a mile outside town is a costly £2.50 per night, but farmers generally allow campers if permission is asked. Farther north on the coast is **Applecross,** a small village isolated from the rest of the mainland by a massive mountain range. The most spectacular way to get to Applecross is to take the route up **Bealach-Na-Ba Pass** from Kirshorn. On a clear day, the isles of Rhum and Skye are visible from the top. The volume of summer traffic over this pass makes hitching possible. When leaving, take the coastal road, which offers equally spectacular scenery. Buses run from Kirshorn to Applecross via Shieldaig and the coastal road (Mon.-Sat. 1 bus per day).

The mountains surrounding **Torridon** contain some of the oldest rock formations in Europe, providing a great variety of terrains and surfaces for climbers and hill walkers. At the junction into the village (where there's a shop/post office) the **ranger station** can give you information on hikes in the area. Nearby is a modern **IYHF youth hostel** (tel. Torridon 284; £3.45; open early March-early Nov.), which, if full, has a small campground on the side. Right behind is the ragged ridge of **Liathach** (3456 ft.), perhaps the mightiest and most imposing of all Scotland's mountains. Buses run to Torridon from Strathcarron, on the Inverness-Kyle rail line, and from Kinlochewe.

Ullapool is the only town of any size along the northwest coast and is the main ferry link to Stornoway on the Isle of Harris. There is an **IYHF youth hostel** adjacent to the pier (tel. (0854) 22 54), and the helpful **Tourist Information Centre** (tel. (0854) 23 15) can book you an inexpensive B&B for a 40p fee. (Open Mon.-Sat. 9am-6pm.) Buses leave Ullapool for Inverness (Mon.-Sat. 2 per day) and **Lochinver,** a quiet, sheltered village surrounded by imposing seas and unbroken wilds. Behind the town is the curious mountain **Suilven,** rising above the wet moors. For those who want to see Scotland at its most remote the **Achmelvich Youth Hostel (IYHF)** (no phone) is 4 miles west of town (£2.20; open mid-May to Sept.); a post bus runs twice per day to the turn-off, 1½ miles from the hostel. Ask about camping and using hostel facilities. Bare knuckles of rock glisten through the grass here and rock-trapped water forms lochs at every level of every tiny gulley. Ask the hostel warden where to find **One Man's Castle,** built in 1959 as a retreat for its since-vanished architect.

Farthest north, 15 miles from Cape Wrath, is **Durness,** where there's an **IYHF youth hostel** (tel. (097181) 244) 1 mile outside town at Smoo. (£3.15, £2.85. Open May 15-Oct. 1.) Iris MacKay (tel. (097181) 343) runs a ferry and mini-bus out to **Cape Wrath.** Also in this area are the enormous **Smoo Caves** (ask at the hostel or tourist office) and some empty sand beaches.

Orkney Islands

The Orkneys are quiet, slow-paced islands just off the northern coast of Scotland. Released from Danish dominion only 500 years ago, Orkney maintains a cultural distinctiveness. It is a land of fertile valleys and rolling, cloud-topped hills, with a life as soothing as the landscape.

Two ferries serve Orkney: one into Stromness from Scrabster, near Thurso (£8.50 one way), the other into Brunswick from John O'Groats (May-Sept.; £7 one way, £9 round-trip). Bus service is relatively frequent on the Mainland (the largest of the Orkneys), and hitching is almost guaranteed. A timetable for all buses and boats within the archipelago is available from the **Kirkwall Tourist Office,** Broad St. (tel. Kirkwall 28 56), or try at the Stromness P&O ferry office.

Stromness looks as if it has just slid down the hillside and lost half its houses to the harbor—bayfront buildings, with their private piers, project into the water. **Victoria Street,** narrow and paved with flagstones, is the main street and looks medieval. In fact, Stromness dates only from the late eighteenth century, when it became a port of call for transatlantic shipping. The **IYHF youth hostel** is open from mid-May to mid-September. You may prefer **Mrs. Brown's Hostel** on Victoria St. (tel. Stromness 661; £3). In mid-July, the town becomes an all-night party during **Stromness Shopping Week.**

Ferries from Stromness reach the **Isle of Hoy,** with its dramatic cliff scenery. There are two IYHF youth hostels here, both often deserted. **Hoy Hostel,** open from May to mid-September, is next to the church, a mile up from the Moaness pier; **Rackwick Hostel** is 6 miles away by a tiny village and beach of the same name—about halfway to the Middle of Nowhere. The entire island of Hoy is a must-see if you visit the Orkneys. **Ward Hill** (1565 ft.) has a sweeping view of all the Orkney's; the **Old Man of Hoy,** a 450-foot rock stack that was finally climbed in 1966, is the dramatic remnant of an ancient sea-arch; the cliff path along **St. John's Head** has some of the best cliffs in Britain—you can watch great skuas divebomb the seagulls (or you, if you stray near their nests); and the **Dwarfie Stane,** a 5000-year-old tomb hewn from solid rock, is one of two of its kind in Britain.

Fifteen miles east of Stromness back on the Mainland is **Kirkwall,** the shopping, fishing, and cultural center of the Orkneys, not to mention the capital. The red sandstone **Cathedral of St. Magnus** was started in 1137; it is almost entirely in Norman style, although the building was begun by the Norse Earl Rognvald, and finished well into the Gothic period. The best time to visit Orkney is at the summer solstice, when the sun never really sets, and the big **St. Magnus Festival** inspires the islanders to four days of traditional music, drama, and poetry.

Shetland Islands

The Shetlands, three times closer to Bergen (Norway) than to London, are Britain's northern outpost. North Sea oil brought big business to Shetland—the terminal at Sullom Voe now handles half the United Kingdom's oil—and Lerwick harbor is often full of large fish-processing ships from as far as the Soviet Union. But despite all this, moors and bird sanctuaries are still a much stronger presence than industry.

If you've ever doubted the pleasures or rigors of bird-watching, have a look at the great skuas divebombing ornithologists, or search for colorful, rabbit-sized puffins. Human life is also interesting and unique on the Shetlands; given to Scotland 500 years ago as the dowry of a Danish princess, Shetland was barely integrated into Britain before the twentieth century. The local dialect, with its liberal smattering of Norse-derived words and its lilting accent, is a potent reminder of Shetland's Nordic heritage. **P&O Ferries** operate between Lerwick and Aberdeen daily, leaving both ports at 6pm (£30.50). If 14 hours in a reclining seat doesn't appeal to you, you can book a berth for an extra £4-5. There is also service between Lerwick and Bergen and, weekly, between Stromness (Orkney) and Lerwick. For details, contact P&O Ferries, P.O. Box 5, Jamiesons Quay, Aberdeen, Scotland AB9 8DL (tel. (0224) 57 26 15).

The friendly folk at the **Shetland Tourist Organization** at Market Cross in Lerwick will tell you all you need to know and book you a bed for free. A must for getting around is the **Inter-Shetland Transport Timetable** (30p), which has information on all boats, buses, and planes. Ferries are heavily subsidized and cheap. Hitching is excellent on the A970, except north of Voe where the traffic thins drastically.

Lerwick, where ferries arrive, is the most convenient base. There is a recently upgraded and friendly **IYHF youth hostel** at Isleburgh House (tel. Lerwick 21 14; £3.15, £2.85). There are four new official campsites on the island (see the tourist office); to freelance camp, check with the landowner. In Lerwick, the **Viking Cafe** on Commercial Rd. has bacon and egg rolls for 80p (open Mon.-Sat. 8am-7pm); **Tatties and Point** at Market Cross serves stuffed baked potatoes for £1.

Lerwick is the site of the annual **Up-Helly-Aa Festival,** held at the winter solstice. An enthusiastic torch-lit revival of the Shetlands' Viking heritage, the festival ends with the torches being put to a Viking galley, which then burns merrily out into the harbor. Look over the harbor from **Fort Charlotte,** a Cromwellian relic (free), or, for a better view, take the ferry (5 min., 25p) to the isle of **Bressay** and walk up the conical **Ward of Bressay.** The **Isle of Noss** (dinghy service from Bressay) is a well-populated bird sanctuary; a good place to look—and look out—for skuas, puffins, and gulls. **Jarlshof,** near Sumburgh, at the southern tip of the mainland, is a large pre-historic site. **St. Ninian's Isle,** off the southwest coast, is connected to the Mainland by a tombolo—a crescent white sandbar, washed by waves on both sides. **Mousa Isle,** off the east by ferry, is the site of "the world's best preserved Iron Age broch."

The northern islands are a little less accessible. **Esha Ness** is worth exploring for its cliffs and weird volcanic formations, which include drongs and rocky fangs that jut from beneath the sea. Remote **Yell** and **Unst** feature nothing but quiet and bird life. **Mr. A. Fraser** runs a **private hostel** on Unst at Crosbister Uyeasound. (Tel. 237 or 259; £2-3 per night. Open April-Oct.)

Back on the Mainland, **Wormadale Hill,** near Whiteness, has a gorgeous view down the west coast past scores of uninhabited isles. Farther north, another walk with good views of the northern islands begins at the intersection of the A970 and the B9075 and continues up **Scalla Field.**

GREECE

US$1 = 139 drachma (dr)	**100dr = US$0.72**
CDN$1 = 105dr	**100dr = CDN$0.95**
UK£1 = 226dr	**100dr = UK£0.44**
AUS$1 = 97.5dr	**100dr = AUS$1.03**

As seductive as Circe, Greece must be handled with the same mixture of caution, admiration, and cunning. Some areas of Greece are more heavily visited than anywhere else in Europe, while others, only 30 minutes away, remain beautifully deserted. Neon-lit tourist strips, timeless classical temples, mobbed beaches, and pristine mountainsides—the Greeks pack it all into the largest little country around.

In one sense, Greece is an aggressively western country that groups its noisy capital with London, Paris, and Rome. As proud guardian of the classical inheritance, the Greek personality considers western civilization a home-spun export. Yet to step into Greece is to walk east—into stalls lined with Byzantine icons, past Orthodox priests trailing long dark robes, and through space carved by mystical *bouzouki* music. All the same, Greece is unceasingly hostile toward Turkey, its closest Eastern neighbor. For four centuries, Ottomans ruled Greece, instilling a tenacious sense of national will and a profound dislike for things Turkish. The dirty little secret of the children of Hellas, however, is that they have learned much from the Turks. Cafes crowd with men drinking coffee that in other places is called Turkish, eating sweets they would never recognize as Turkish delight. For the most part, women are excluded from these places as they are from public life in general; much of the Muslim concern for female modesty has infiltrated traditional Greek culture and made widows' weeds standard garb.

Greece has only in the last 15 years begun to recoup from a battering century that included Nazi occupation, mass starvation, civil war, and military rule. Most villages did not see their first automobiles and electric lights until the 1960s. Greece today still faces severe problems: Despite its recent entry into the Common Market, per capita income and productivity are only half the EEC average, and inflation rages. Consequently, color-coded Greek politics are volatile, fiery, and loud. ΡΑΣΟΚ, the green or socialist party, is currently in power; Prime Minister Papandreou has made a name for himself as the outspoken leader of the U.S.'s most difficult NATO ally. Perennial issues of contention include the presence of U.S. military bases and high levels of U.S. military funding to Turkey. The conservatives (blues), called ΟΝΝΕΔ or simply ΝΔ, are the main opposition; the Communist reds (KKE) are the smallest of the three parties. Each party apparently feels that it proclaims its patriotism best by defacing the mother country with huge political slogans painted on anything that doesn't move. Hopefully the Parthenon will continue to escape the ravages of Greek politics, but you can never tell.

If at all possible, come to Greece in the off-season. The tourists are gone, accommodations are cheaper and easy to find, and the Greeks are more relaxed, more receptive. You can sightsee all day without having to retreat from the afternoon heat. And you can still get your tan on Crete, which offers almost year-round swimming.

For more comprehensive coverage of Greece than we can offer here, turn to *Let's Go: Greece.*

Getting There

Whether or not you have a railpass, one of the less expensive ways to reach Greece is by train. Border-to-border fare for the length of Yugoslavia is very cheap, and InterRail is valid. The journey is long, and not necessarily comfortable. From Venice or Vienna, expect a 36-hour trip, and enormous crowds in summer; if you can't get a seat reservation for the time that you hope to travel, *wait* until you can. Buses are even cheaper, but a real marathon; **Euroways Eurolines,** 52 Grosvenor Gardens, Victoria, London (tel. 730 82 35), runs from London to Athens for £75.

Certainly the most popular way of getting to Greece is by ferry from Italy. Boats travel primarily from Brindisi to Corfu (10 hr.), Igoumenitsa (11 hr.), and Patras (20 hr.). From Patras, buses leave for Athens frequently and also for points throughout the Peloponnese. With a ticket to Patras, you can stop over in Corfu, provided you indicate your intention prior to embarkation (they must write "S.O. Corfu" on the ticket). No stopovers are permitted on tickets to Igoumenitsa.

If you plan to travel from Brindisi in the summer, make reservations and arrive at the port well before your departure time. Waiting to buy your ticket in Brindisi is a risky proposition; if you find yourself forced to do this, buy from an accredited office, not from the "representatives" hanging around the train station. If you don't check in at least three hours ahead of time, you risk losing your reservation and possibly your ticket. Get an embarkation pass at the main office of the line you are traveling, then take the pass to the police station on the second floor of the maritime station to have it stamped. The major lines in Brindisi are **Adriatica,** Staz. Marittima, 2nd floor (tel. 238 25); **Hellenic Mediterranean Lines,** corso Garibaldi, 8 (tel. 285 31); **Fragline,** c/o Italmar, corso Garibaldi, 96/98 (tel. 297 71); **Adriatic Ferries,** c/o Pattimare, p. E. Dionisi, 11 (tel. 265 48). Other lines change names and owners from year to year and usually operate only during high season. Brindisi-Patras deck class fares for students (ages 17-30 with ISIC, up to 26 with FIYTO or IYHF card) range from L45,000 to L55,000. During peak season (mid-July to mid-Aug.), fares rise about 30%. Non-student fares are about 10% higher than above on the average, regardless of season. Eurail is honored on Adriatica and Hellenic Mediterranean Lines, but passholders must pay a L14,000 supplement in order to travel on the boat, and passage is always contingent on available space. InterRail passholders receive a 30% discount from Fragline and other lines, though it may be necessary to wait until you arrive in Brindisi to purchase a discounted ticket. In 1987, Fragline was the best deal for those without passes.

On some lines it is possible to arrange group rates through travel agents. Makeshift groups can secure a 10-15% discount per person, plus a free trip for the enterprising leader. Bicycles travel free on most lines. Everyone must pay a L6000 embarkation tax. There is no reason to spend money on anything more plush than deck class; in summer you'll actually be more comfortable on deck than those who've paid extra to spend the night in an airplane-style seat in a large, smoke-filled cabin.

From October through April, boats also travel from Bari, a much more attractive city than Brindisi. The fare is about the same. More expensive boats run from Ancona and Venice in Italy, and from points along the Yugoslav coast. Two boats steam weekly from Haifa, Israel to Greece, and a number of small lines connect Turkey's Aegean coast with islands in the northeast Aegean and Dodecanese (usually US$20-25; most run only in summer). Finally, boats run twice per month from Odessa (USSR), stopping in Bulgaria, Istanbul, and Piraeus.

Flying from northern European cities is an extremely popular way of getting to Greece. Watch for special package fares offered by travel agents or advertised in newspapers, especially from London, Amsterdam, and major cities in Germany and Scandinavia. These are often the cheapest deals available, even if you must take a package including a few nights in a hotel. In addition, you may be able to fly aboard charters to island destinations otherwise inaccessible by direct flight.

Transportation

Train service in Greece pales in comparison with that in the rest of Europe—service on the scarce train routes is slow and infrequent. Both Eurail and InterRail passes are valid. **OSE,** the national network, offers a 20% discount to those under 26. They also sell touring cards for unlimited travel for 10, 20, or 30 days (also valid on OSE buses).

Bus service, however, is widespread, regular, and cheap. Little blue signs marked with white buses or the word "ΣΤΑΣΣΙΣ" indicate bus stops, but drivers usually stop anywhere if you signal. Let the driver know ahead of time if you want to get off; if your stop is passed, yell *"Stassis!"*

Hitching is satisfactory in Greece, at least along the main roads. To do well, be out by 6am, though in the interior cars are so few that all effort may prove unrewarding. It helps to have a sign with your destination written on it, in both Greek and English. Women are usually safe alone, but as always, caution is advised.

Biking is impractical. Mountainous terrain and unpaved roads work against you. Rent a moped instead; the flexibility you'll gain may be worth it.

Traveling among the Greek islands, you'll come to know and love Greek ferries. Though sailings are frequent in summer, the hows and whys of ferry travel are rather complicated. Direct connections between all but the major islands are very infrequent. No matter where you're trying to catch a boat, you'll find that schedules, not prices, will exasperate you endlessly. The regulated prices do not vary, but wild competition ensues nevertheless, so that you'll have to visit several—or all—agencies in town to find out about your choices. No Greek ferry agent has ever breathed a word about the competition's schedule (or even their existence). In Piraeus, the situation is considerably better, since GNTO publishes a schedule—but it loses meaning as the summer progresses. Keep an ear to the ground for boat strikes. An option for faster, more expensive sea travel is the hydrofoil.

Olympic Airways operates efficient and cheap flights between many islands. Short hops are particularly economical, and don't cost much more than ferries. These flights, however, are often booked weeks in advance during the summer.

Practical Information

All over Greece you'll encounter the **Greek National Tourist Organization (GNTO,** also known as **EOT)** and the **Tourist Police** (*Touristiki Astinomia*). The first runs offices designed to inform and assist tourists; the police are really intended only to enforce Greece's extensive tourist protection laws, though they often double as a tourist office where GNTO is unavailable. Tourist information is available in English 24 hours a day by calling 171.

Aside from perhaps a few unsolicited propositions (usually harmless), women traveling Greece are relatively safe. If you find yourself in an emergency, the Greek word for "Help" is "*vo-EE-thee-a.*" Don't be afraid to use it. For both sexes, modest dress is required at monasteries (no shorts, short skirts, or revealing tops) and at some archeological sites (no bathing suits).

Language, both the spoken and non-verbal varieties, will be a concern in Greece. Relatively few Greeks speak English and most tourists will find the Greek alphabet an additional confusion. Be sure to learn its characters, or carry a chart, so that you can transliterate the most basic signs. And because so few visitors bother to do so, any effort to learn a little Greek will go a long way. If you're really stuck, try to find someone of high school age; most young Greeks speak a little English. Even more important to know is Greek body language, which can lead to endless misunderstandings. To say no, Greeks silently close their eyes or click their tongues while lifting their heads and/or eyebrows. To indicate a positive, they tilt and bow the head in one motion. A hand waving up and down which seems to mean "stay there" means "come." Be careful waving goodbye; doing so palm forward could be taken as an insult.

Greece's telephone company is **OTE;** their offices are usually open from 7:30am to 3pm in small towns, and from 7:30am to 10pm in larger towns. In cities, OTE offices are open 24 hours, but you must bang on the door after midnight. For an English-speaking operator, dial 162. Post offices are generally open Monday through Friday from 7:30am to 2:30pm; be especially persistent if you're inquiring after Poste Restante; it may be filed under your last name, first name, or randomly. Normal business hours in Greece include a break from about 2 until 5:15 or 5:30pm, with evening hours usually on Tuesday, Thursday, and Friday. Haggling is often effective, especially in small establishments. Banks are normally open Monday through Thursday from 8am to 2pm, Friday 7:45am to 2pm. The major national holidays in Greece, during which all banks and shops are closed, are New Year's Day, Ephiphany (Jan. 6), Shrove Monday (Feb.), Good Friday, Easter Sunday, National Holidays (March 25 and Oct. 28), Labor Day (May 1), The Assumption of the Virgin Mary (Aug. 15), and Christmas and Boxing Day (Dec. 25-26).

Accommodations, Camping, and Food

Lodging in Greece is a great bargain. The country's two dozen or so youth hostels are loosely run and cost about 400dr per night. Curfew is usually midnight or 1am, and IYHF membership requirements are not rigorously enforced. Hotels are also reasonable, particularly since bartering is common; expect to pay 1200 to 2000dr for a double without bath in a C, D, or E class hotel, plus 100 to 150dr for a shower, possibly hot. GNTO or Tourist Police offices invariably have a list of inexpensive accommodations, with prices.

Don't stay just in hotels, though—in many places, *dhomatia* (rooms to let) are an attractive and perfectly dependable option. You should expect to pay around 600dr per person, and although you may lack locks or towels, the possibility of sharing coffee at night or some intriguing conversation is worth the trade. Very often you'll be approached by locals as you enter town or disembark from your boat; don't hesitate to go along and see their rooms before you decide. Greece has plenty of official campgrounds but freelance camping, practiced discreetly, is widely tolerated. Under the warm, dry skies of Greece, this may prove to be your favorite way to spend the night, but only if you remember to bring mosquito spray. Traditional settlements scattered throughout Greece can provide both shelter and a taste of indigenous culture. Double rooms in cottages range from 1000 to 5000dr. Check with the GNTO for more information.

If there's an art to Greek cuisine, it's ingenuity, for the people have managed to do well by the sparse yield of a dry and stony land. A meal without olive oil is unthinkable; pine resin has been put to use in the everyday wines *retsina* and *kokkinelli.* You'll find that the quality and price in *tavernas* varies astonishingly little—few meals are particularly good or bad, cheap or expensive.

Breakfasts are usually light. Coffee is a vestige of Turkish rule, syrupy sweet and so strong it comes in miniature doses with a glass of water; many travelers prefer to order it *metrio* (with a medium amount of sugar) or *sketo* (without sugar). Standard (instant) coffee goes by the catch-all name of Nescafé. Specify *zesto* (hot) or *me gala* (with milk). A *frappé* is an iced coffee, shaken until it's frothy. Greek pastries, with their heavy honey base, are delicious. *Baklava* is a honeyed strudel, filled with chopped nuts; *galaktobouriko* is similar but comes with a creamy filling; and *kataifi* consists of nuts and cinnamon rolled up in a kind of shredded wheat.

Choriatiki is a "peasant's salad" of cucumbers, tomatoes, onions, and olives with a wedge of tangy feta cheese—filling lunch for about US$1. Dinner is a leisurely and late affair; some restaurants don't even open until 9pm. Menus are often multilingual; if not, head for the kitchen and browse—it's accepted (even encouraged) in most places. It's always a good idea to ask the price before ordering. Start your meal with a salad or *lathera*—any vegetable, usually beans, eggplant, or zucchini marinated in oil, tomato sauce, and oregano. Meat, whether lamb *(arni),* beef *(moschári),* or pork *(hiriní),* is relatively expensive. Cheaper entrees are chicken *(kotópoulo),* spiced meatballs *(soutzoukákia),* or stuffed tomatoes, peppers, or eggplant *(tomato, pipéri,* and *melitzána gemistá).* Fish and shellfish are fresh on the islands, though expensive; an affordable option is fried squid *(kalamari).*

Athens (Athina)

Elegant, serene, immaculate—Athens is none of these. Modern Athens is a crowded labyrinth of squat concrete structures, bristling with television antennae and inundated with clamorous traffic. Here the classical temples and Byzantine churches seem anomalous structures. These monuments, whose heft alone has protected them from the passage of time, stand as ageless spectators of the equally immortal Athenian society. The ancient potters whose wares now fill Athens' glorious galleries have their modern counterparts in the artisans near the Plaka. And the fervor of the earliest democrats is mirrored in the graffiti and posters on the walls of the city's buildings.

Don't sacrifice time on the coast of Crete or in the mountains of the Peloponnese for the urban jungle of Athens. But while you're here, brave the crowds and dust and enjoy what the city has to offer.

Orientation and Practical Information

Athens is connected to northern Europe by rail and bus, to North Africa and the Middle East by ferry, and to every continent by air. **Platia Syntagma** (Syntagma Square) is the focal point for tourists: Here you'll find the tourist office, the Ameri-

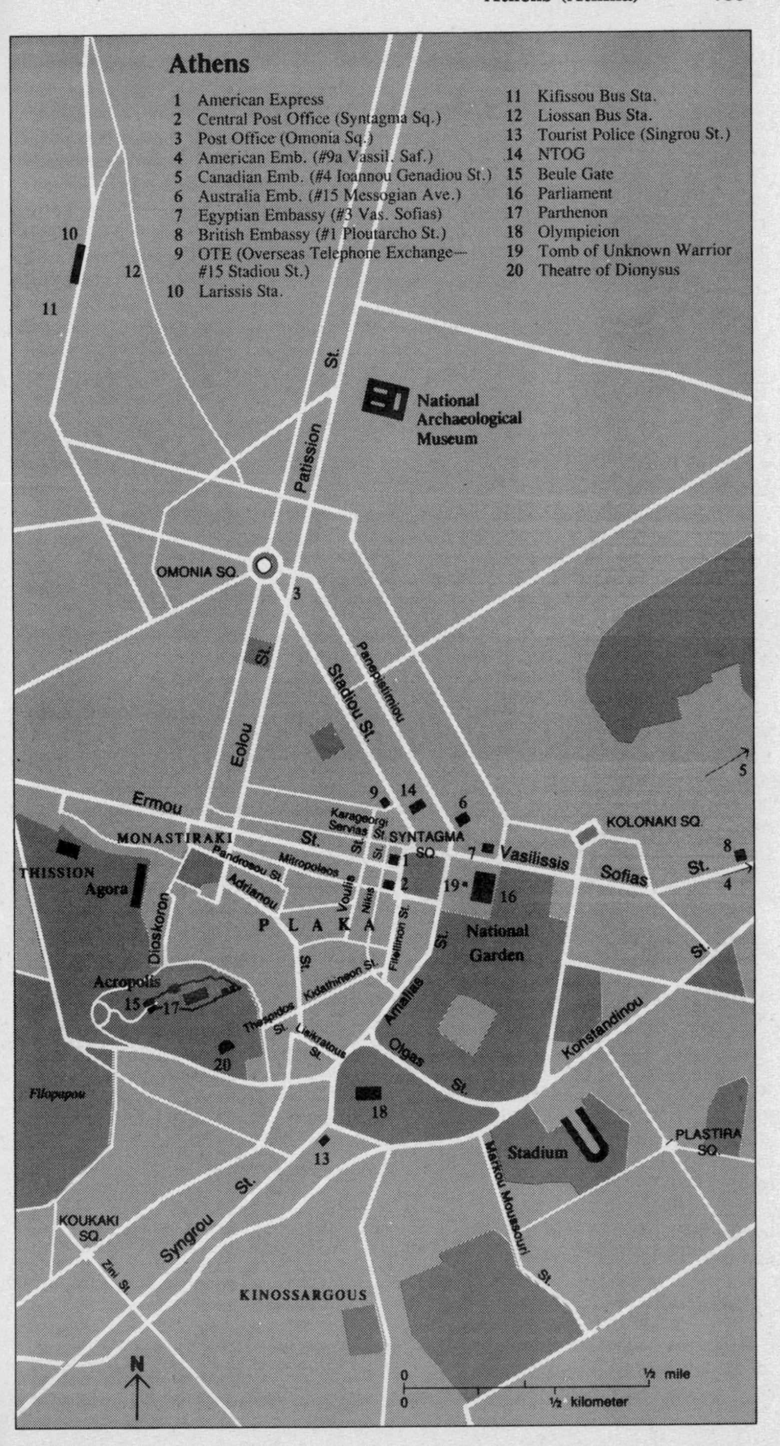
Athens
1 American Express
2 Central Post Office (Syntagma Sq.)
3 Post Office (Omonia Sq.)
4 American Emb. (#9a Vassil. Saf.)
5 Canadian Emb. (#4 Ioannou Genadiou St.)
6 Australia Emb. (#15 Messogian Ave.)
7 Egyptian Embassy (#3 Vas. Sofias)
8 British Embassy (#1 Ploutarcho St.)
9 OTE (Overseas Telephone Exchange—#15 Stadiou St.)
10 Larissis Sta.
11 Kifissou Bus Sta.
12 Liossan Bus Sta.
13 Tourist Police (Singrou St.)
14 NTOG
15 Beule Gate
16 Parliament
17 Parthenon
18 Olympieion
19 Tomb of Unknown Warrior
20 Theatre of Dionysus
National Archaeological Museum
Patission St.
OMONIA SQ.
Eolou St.
Stadiou St.
Panepistimiou
Ermou
MONASTIRAKI
THISSION
Agora
SYNTAGMA SQ.
Vasilissis Sofias St.
KOLONAKI SQ.
PLAKA
National Garden
Acropolis
Filopapou
Stadium
PLASTIRA SQ.
KOUKAKI SQ.
Syngrou St.
KINOSSARGOUS
Konstandinou
Olgas St.
Amalias St.
Markou Mousouri St.
N
½ mile
½ kilometer

can Express office, budget travel outlets, Parliament, the top hotels, the most expensive cafes, the most important banks, and the most traffic. Next to Parliament is the **National Garden,** which contains the **Zappeion** area, nightlife center for Athenians. The **Plaka,** between Syntagma and the mile-high **Acropolis,** is a labyrinth of narrow streets lined with trees, stores, restaurants, and cafes. Ermou Street leads from Syntagma to **Monastiraki,** another old section, home of the Athens flea market. Adjacent to the flea market is the **Agora,** marketplace and administrative center of classical Athens and the site of major archeological work. About 15 minutes from Syntagma to the north—down Stadiou or Panepistimiou Street—is **Platia Omonia,** the crass, noisy, "downtown" of the modern metropolis. South of the Acropolis, divided by Leoforos Singrou, are the **Koukaki** region to the west, and the **Kinossargous** region to the east. **Piraeus,** the seedy port, is a subway ride to the southwest.

A good map is invaluable in Athens. The best is free at Tourist Police offices. Important public transportation routes (buses, trolleys, subway) are also marked on the map; all fares are 30dr. Taxis charge 23dr per kilometer plus 25dr upon entrance. There is a minimum charge of 130dr.

This Week in Athens, available at the GNTO, is a valuable pamphlet of addresses and phone numbers (60dr). The daily *Athens News* and the monthly *Athenian* magazine are good for sights and cultural information.

Tourist Offices: Greek National Tourist Organization (GNTO), 2 Karageorgi Servias St. (tel. 322 25 45), inside the National Bank on Syntagma Sq. Boat schedules to the islands and a list of campsites throughout the country. They will help with accommodations. Often very crowded; arrive before 10am to beat the mob. Open Mon.-Sat. 8:30am-7:30pm. Another office, open 24 hours, is in the east terminal of the airport. **Tourist Police,** headquarters, 7 Singrou St. (tel. 171 in emergencies; 923 92 24 otherwise). Usually very helpful. Go to them if you think a hotel owner is cheating you. Open daily 8am-9pm. Train station office (tel. 821 35 74) open daily 7am-11pm; airport office (tel. 981 40 93) open 24 hours.

Budget Travel: Most offices are on Nikis and Filellinon Sts., off Syntagma Sq. Athens is a major bargain travel center for those going anywhere, any way. Flights to India and North America for less than US$250, to Australia for US$500-550. Well worth shopping around. **Magic Bus,** 20 Filellinon St., is regularly very knowledgeable. Open Mon.-Fri. 9am-7pm, Sat. 9am-2pm.

American Express: Syntagma Sq. (tel. 324 49 75). Mail held. All banking services. Open Mon.-Fri. 8:30am-5:15pm, Sat. 8:30am-1pm. Bank open Mon.-Thurs. 8:30am-2pm, Fri. 8:30am-1:30pm, Sat. (with horrendous lines) 8:30am-12:30pm.

Currency Exchange: National Bank on Syntagma Sq. is open latest—daily until 8pm.

Post Office: Central Post Office, 100 Eolou St., on Omonia Square. Another office on Syntagma Square. Poste Restante held 1 month; specify Omonia or Syntagma. Both open Mon.-Fri. 7:30am-8:30pm, Sat. 7:30am-3pm, Sun. 9am-2pm. Parcel post at 4 Stadiou St.

Telephones: OTE, 85 Patission St. (main branch). Open 24 hours. Also at 15 Stadiou St. Open 7am-11:30pm. **Telephone code:** 01.

Flights: East Air Terminal serves foreign and charter flights. Take the yellow bus leaving every 15-20 min. for Leoforos Amalias at Syntagma (80dr); to return to the airport take bus #018 from Syntagma. 25-min. journey. **West Air Terminal** serves all Olympic Airways flights. Bus #133 leaves for Syntagma from the road outside the gates (every 20 min., 30dr). To return, take bus #133 from Othonos on Syntagma. 20-min. journey.

Trains: Larissis Station, take yellow trolley #1 from Deligiani St. to Syntagma. **Information** (tel. 522 43 02 or 362 44 02).

Buses: Kifissou Station serves all of Greece except Delphi and much of central Greece. To reach Syntagma, take bus #051 to the end of the line on Agios Konstandinou (30dr), walk up the hill 2 blocks to Omonia Sq., and take any of the trolleys (#1, 2, 4, 5, 11, and 12) going up Stadiou St. (30dr). **Liossion Bus Station** serves Delphi, Evia, Lamia, and Larissa; take bus #024 at Omonia Sq. (30dr).

Ferries: All dock at **Piraeus.** No reason to linger. To reach Syntagma, walk left (facing inland) along the waterfront to Rousvelt St., take the subway to Monastirion (30dr), turn right up Ermou St., and walk for 5 min. Alternatively, take green bus #040 from Vassileos Konstandinou across from the Public Theater (every 10 min. when on schedule, 30dr). Bus runs

24 hours. From Athens, catch the subway at Monastiraki; bus #040 leaves from Filellinon St. off Syntagma Sq. Boat schedules available at the tourist office.

Emergencies: Tourist Police, 7 Singrou St. (tel. 171). English spoken. Greek-speakers can phone the **Municipal Police** (tel. 100). **Medical Emergency** (tel. 166).

Medical Assistance: Red Cross First Aid Center, 21 Tritis Septemvriou St. (tel. 150), 3 blocks north of Omonia Sq., on the left.

Pharmacies: English spoken at 4 Filellinon St. (tel. 822 62 65). Open Mon. and Wed. 8am-2:30pm, Tues. and Thurs.-Fri. 8am-2pm and 5:30-8:30pm. Check the *Athens News* for pharmacies open weekends.

Embassies: U.S., 91 Vassilissis Sofias (tel. 721 29 51). **Canada,** 41 Ioannou Genadiou St. (tel. 723 95 11). **U.K.,** 1 Ploutarchou St., at Ypsilantou St. (tel. 723 62 11). **Australia,** 15 Messogion Ave. (tel. 775 76 50). **New Zealand,** 15-17 An. Tsoha St. (tel. 641 03 11). **Egypt,** 3 Vassilissis Sofias (tel. 361 86 12); visa window around the corner on Zalokosta St. Bring one photo (1300dr, one-day wait). Open Mon.-Fri. 9:30-11:30am. **Jordan,** 14 Philikis Esparias, Kolonaki (tel. 72 84 84).

Bookstore: Eleftheroudakis, 4 Nikis St., sells new and used books in English, as well as the *Let's Go* series. Open Mon., Wed., and Sat. 8:50am-2:30pm, Tues. and Thurs.-Fri. 8:50am-1:30pm and 5:30-8:30pm.

Laundry: Angelou Geronta St., in the Plaka. Wash 200dr, dry 200dr, soap 50dr. Open Mon.-Sat. 8am-4pm. Also at 9 Psaron St. (tel. 522 82 19), off Karaiskaki Sq. near Larissis Station. 120dr/kg to do it yourself, 150dr/kg to have it done. Open Mon.-Fri. 8:30am-4pm, Sat. 8:30am-2pm. The Greek word for laundry is *plintirio,* but most places say "Laundry" or "*Aytomata.*"

Hitchhiking: Hitchhiking out of Athens is almost impossible. For Yugoslavia and central Europe, you'll have the most luck if you go to the truck parks at the cargo wharves in Piraeus and hold a sign. For northern Greece, take the subway to the last stop (Kifissia), walk up to the town's central square, take the bus to Nea Kifissia, walk to the National Road (Ethniki Odos), and start praying.

Accommodations and Camping

Accommodations in Athens are among the cheapest in any European capital. A clean, pleasant double with use of a shower shouldn't cost more than 2000dr, while rock-bottom—and rock-hard—rooftop floor spaces go for as little as 300 to 400dr per person; make sure you have a foam pad. In July and August, accommodations fill up as early as noon. If you arrive late, the farther you venture from Syntagma Square, the better your chances of finding a place.

If you come on the train from Patras, you'll be accosted by swarms of hotel hawkers. Some lure travelers to abysmal fleabags far from the center and charge exorbitant prices. Have the hawker point out the place on a map, and agree on a price before leaving the station. Most of the places we list are in the Plaka area, near most things of interest; many places in Piraeus are seedy, and places near the train station are a half-hour walk from the center of town.

Thisseos Inn, 10 Thisseos St. (tel. 324 59 60). Walk down Perikleous from Syntagma and turn right onto Thisseos. Kitchen facilities, lounge, and terrace. Dorms 600dr per person, doubles 1800dr, triples 2100dr.

Festos, 18 Filellinon St. (tel. 323 24 55), 3 blocks straight down Filellinon from Syntagma. Noisy, dusty, and stuffy, but cheap. Fills fast. Dorms 600dr per person, singles 1000dr, doubles 1300dr, triples 1650dr, quads 2000dr.

Students' Inn, 16 Kidathineon St. (tel. 324 48 08), in the heart of the Plaka, right off Filellinon from Syntagma. Clean but noisy. Reading lamps over all the beds. Singles 1000dr, doubles 1600dr, triples 2100dr. Breakfast 200dr in garden.

Hotel Tempi, 29 Eolou St. (tel. 321 31 75). Walk down Ermou St. from Syntagma and turn right on Eolou. Clean and well-furnished. Laundry facilities and a book exchange. Singles 1100dr, doubles 1750dr, triples 2400dr; roof (mattress available) 400dr.

Hotel Ideal, 39 Eolou St. (tel. 321 31 95). Right down the street from the Tempi and its big rival. Clean and comfortable rooms. Singles 1100dr, doubles 1750dr, triples 2300dr.

Hotel Hermion, 66 Ermon St. (tel. 321 27 53). Clean and quiet. Friendly and patient management speaks little English. Singles 1100dr, doubles 1600dr, triples 2250dr.

Art Gallery Pension, 5 Erechthiou St. (tel. 923 83 76), in Veikou. Take trolley #1 or 5 from Syntagma to the corner of Veikou and Drakou. Expensive but great. Very friendly. Singles 2250dr, doubles 3000dr, triples 3750dr. Prices 10% more for one-night stay.

Youth Hostel #5 Pangrati, 75 Damareos St. (tel. 751 95 30), in Pangrati. Take trolley #2, 11 or 12 to Pangrati plaza, then walk down Imitou 2 blocks, take a left on Frinis and the first right on Damareos. Go down Amalias and left on Olgas; continue 1 block past the Stadium, go right on Eratosthenous, then tackle the 14 blocks to Damaseos. Quiet, in a lively residential area. Laundry facilities. Dorms 400dr per person. Midnight curfew, but key available.

Athens Connection Hostel, 20 Ioulianou St. (tel. 821 39 40). From the train station take Filadelfias St., which becomes Ioulianou St., and go past the little park when it seems as though the street has ended; the sign outside says "Athens Hostel." From Syntagma, take trolley #2, 4, 11, or 12 to Patission. Lively and popular. Mixed reactions to management. Doubles 1600dr, quads and quints 700dr per person. Avoid the basement rooms.

Iokasti's House, 65 Aristotelous St. (tel. 822 66 47 or 823 40 11). Follow the directions to the Athens Connection Hostel but turn right off Ioulianou at Aristotelous. Clean, comfortable, and friendly. Singles 900dr, doubles 1600dr, triples 2100dr; roof 500dr.

Food

Though Athens does not rank among the world's culinary capitals, you can e reasonably well and inexpensively here. A meal with beer or wine should cost abo 550dr per person and if you eat take-out food from the many *psistaria* (outdo snack stands), it should be considerably less (250dr). Wherever you eat, be certai that you're not being charged for any *bouzouki* entertainers that might voluntee themselves. If you prefer to prepare your own meals, visit the huge **outdoor mark** on Athinas St., between Evripidou St. and Sofokleous St. The Plaka is full of mo estly priced restaurants serving decent meals.

Eden Vegetarian Restaurant, 3 Flessa St., in the Plaka, a block up Adrianou. Tasty dishes and various vegetable pies for about 200dr. Open Wed.-Mon. noon-midnight.

Restaurant Gardenia (sign in Greek), 31 Zini St., in Koukaki, south of Filopapou Hill. Authentic, inexpensive, and delicious Greek fare. Pasta 90dr, veal with vegetables 280dr, stuffed meatballs 200dr; 80dr for table. Open for lunch and dinner.

Kostanoinos Athanasias Velly's Restaurant (no sign), Varnava Sq., Plastira. Take trolley #2, 4, or 12 to Plastira Sq. Walk 3 blocks down Proklou St. to the grassy park in Varnava Sq.; restaurant is between Stilponos and Pironos St. A real treat. Authentic, delicious, and cheap, in a residential district. No English spoken; you'll have to point. Fish 185dr, meatballs 80dr, spaghetti 68dr, Greek salad 50dr. Open for dinner.

Sights

Both a fortress and a temple in the past, the famed **Acropolis** ("high city") migh ily overlooks the Aegean Sea and the Attic plain. During Athens's Golden Age (th second half of the fifth century B.C.E.), four glorious buildings were constructe on this summit: the **Parthenon,** the **Temple of Athena Nike,** the **Propylaea** ("monu mental gates"), and the **Erechtheum.** Despite the ravages of time, earthquakes, po lution, and present reconstruction, the Parthenon's harmony, monumental size, an grace remain breathtaking. Visit the site in the early hours of the morning or evenin to avoid the heat and the hordes. While there, stroll through the **Acropolis Museum** which houses the famous karyatids (columns in the shape of women) of the Erech theum. (Acropolis open Mon.-Sat. 7:30am-7:30pm, Sun. 8am-4:45pm. Museum open same hours Mon. and Wed.-Sun., Tues. noon-5:45pm. Admission to Acropoli and museum: 400dr, students 200dr.)

At the base of the Acropolis are the **Agora,** the **Temple of Hephaistos,** and th adjacent **Agora Museum,** housed in the reconstructed **Stoa of Attalos.** The Agor contains the ruins of the administrative center and marketplace of ancient Athens (Complex open in summer Mon.-Sat. 7:30am-7:30pm, Sun. 8am-6pm; in off-seaso

Mon.-Sat. 9am-3pm, Sun. 9:30am-2:30pm. Admission 150dr, students 80dr.) Another significant site, sometimes overlooked, is the **Olympeion** (Temple of Olympian Zeus), behind **Hadrian's Arch.** The temple was the largest attempted in classical Greece, as attested to by the immense remaining columns. (Open Mon.-Sat. 8:45am-3pm, Sun. 9:30am-2:30pm. Admission 100dr, students 50dr.)

As might be expected, one of the world's finest collections of classical sculpture, ceramics, and bronzework is found in Athens' **National Archeological Museum.** Pieces that would shine elsewhere are lost in this sea of magnificence. The room in the center of the museum contains treasures from the tombs of Mycenae, a civilization predating that of Socrates and Euripides by some 800 years. The rest of the ground floor is arranged chronologically in a clockwise series of rooms. Upstairs are the Santorini frescoes, from that island's Minoan civilization, the vase collection, and the spectacular numismatic collection. (Museum open Tues.-Sun. 8am-3pm. Admission 400dr, students 200dr. Numismatic collection open Tues.-Sat. 7:30am-1:30pm, Sun. 9am-2pm. Free.)

The **Byzantine Museum,** 22 Vassilissis Sofias, in an elegant Florentine building, holds an extensive collection of Byzantine icons, frescoes, and mosaics. (Open Tues.-Sat. 8am-7pm, Sun. 8am-6pm. Admission 150dr, students 80dr.) The **Benaki Museum** houses Anthony Benaki's extraordinarily eclectic personal collection. Particularly noteworthy are the two El Greco canvasses, Benaki's oriental pieces, and the exhibit of regional Greek costumes. (Open Wed.-Sat. 8:30am-2pm. Admission 100dr, students 50dr.) The Byzantine period is also represented in Athens by the numerous churches which dot the Plaka, many of them in the most unlikely places. A particularly good example is **Kapnikaria Church,** on the corner of Ermou and Eolou Sts.

For more justice than we can do Athens here, turn to *Let's Go: Greece.*

Entertainment

The **Plaka** is Athens' center for cafe-sitting, though any resemblance to Greek culture or prices is purely accidental. Singers, comedians, and acrobats frequent an outdoor stage at the **Zappeion**—free if you stand, expensive if you sit in a cafe. The **Monastiraki** region is wonderful for browsing or shopping; the indoor/outdoor market has everything one could desire. The **National Garden** is the quickest and easiest escape from the noise and fumes of the city. If you are dead set upon dancing, consult *This Week in Athens* (available at the GNTO) for nightclub locations. English-language movies, many of them shown outdoors, are listed in the *Athens News.*

The best summertime alternative to cafes and carousing is the **Athens Festival,** held annually from June through September. Featured are classical theater productions held in the **Odeon of Herodes Atticus,** a restored Roman amphitheatre dating from 170 C.E., the Greek Philharmonic Orchestra, and a varied slate of visiting artists and companies. The festival office is at 4 Stadiou St.

Fun-loving Athenians congregate at the restaurants and cafes in **Glyfada** or **Voula,** both along the water's edge. (Take bus #122 from Olgas St., 40 min.) You can swim at Voula or Glyfada during the day and enjoy a stroll and a Nescafé *frappé* in the evening. The last bus to Athens leaves Glyfada at 11:30pm.

Near Athens

The **Temple of Poseidon** awaits you on **Cape Sounion,** some 65km from Athens. The clifftop view of the Aegean seems the only setting appropriate to the cult of the Sea God. Bring your swimsuit for some excellent swimming off the Apollo Coast. A bus leaves from 14 Mavromateon St. (every hour, 2 hrs., 310dr).

The superb mosaics in the monastery at **Daphni** awe visitors as they stand beneath the second-largest Byzantine dome in the world. (Open Mon.-Sat. 9am-3pm, Sun. 9am-2:30pm. Admission 200dr.) Daphni also hosts a popular all-you-can-drink **wine festival** from mid-July to the end of August. (Daily 7pm-12:30am; 200dr, students 100dr.) Buses #853, 864, 873, and 880 travel to Daphni from Eleftherias Square (35 min., 30dr).

The breathtaking ancient site of **Delphi** once held the ancient world enthralled. Its solemn oracle was law; its sacred springs carried Apollo's blessings. Much of the Delphic complex remains on its steep lookout over the Gulf of Corinth—a vantage point more than noble enough to offset the mobs that journey here like pilgrims of old. There are several buses a day from 260 Liossion St. in Athens; take bus #024 from Omonia Sq. (3 hr., 860dr). If you have a railpass, take the train to Levadia and catch the Delphi bus from there (300dr). Between Levadia and Delphi, at the turn-off to Distomo, get off the bus and beg, borrow, or steal a ride to the monastery of **Ossios Loukas** (there are also very infrequent direct buses from Levadia). The multicolored brown stone buildings look like gingerbread cake, and are decorated with Byzantine mosaics second only to those of Daphni. Ten kilometers before Delphi the bus stops in **Arachova,** a delightful Greek "alpine" village stacked up on the slopes of Mt. Parnassus, and unspoiled except for a touristy main street. Delphi's delightful **IYHF youth hostel** (tel. 822 68) charges 500dr for a bed and 350dr for the roof when beds are full. There is **camping** 3km away (tel. 289 44; 250dr per tent, 220dr per person). Delphi's best food for the money is at **Taverna Vakhos,** next to the hostel.

Northern Greece

For unspoiled mountains, canyons, and lakes, for Hellenistic reminders of Alexander the Great's empire, and for Byzantine treasures, head north. Less touristed than most other parts of Greece, the four northern provinces—Thessaly, Epirus, Macedonia, and Thrace—contain some of the country's most spectacular scenery.

Thessaly is crowned by **Mount Olympos,** home of the ancient Greek gods and Greece's highest peak (2917m). Olympos can be scaled in a moderate two-day climb, leaving from **Litohoro** and staying overnight at either of two hostel-like **refuges** run by Greece's mountaineering clubs, SEO and EOS. In town, stay at **IYHF youth hostel** (tel. 813 11; 350dr). Climbing season, during which the hostels and refuges are open, runs from late May to September.

Southwest of Olympos is **Meteora,** where Orthodox monasteries cling to the top of 600-meter-high rock formations that could only have been imagined by Dr. Seuss. Beginning in the eleventh century C.E., monks created Byzantine cloisters to escape the secular world and its marauding infidels. Today the few monks and nuns who remain spend much of their time managing crowds of visitors. Lodging can be found in the nearby town of **Kalambaka** at the **Hotel Astoria** (tel. 222 13), where clean dorm rooms and doubles run 600dr per person. *Tavernas* with outdoor tables ring the town square; try the **International.** Two campgrounds and the **Hotel Kastraki** (tel. 222 86; singles 700dr, doubles 1200dr) are a couple of kilometers closer to Meteora at Kastraki.

West of Kalambaka, heading toward the coast, is the village of **Metsovo,** in the mountainous province of Epirus. Metsovo's immediate surroundings make excellent stomping grounds; from Agios Nikolaus follow the footpath down to the dirt road that contiues to the village of Anilio. From here you can take the high roads to the right and venture into gorgeous pines. Metsovo's cheapest hotel, the **Athenai** (tel. 418 25), offers perfectly adequate rooms. (Singles 900dr, doubles 1600dr if bargained; hot showers 100dr.) Paying more will get you a big boost in quality at the **Hotel Egnatia** (tel. 419 00), 100m up the main road. Here the charm of Metsovan furnishings really stands out with chandeliers, stone floors, colorful hand-woven wall hangings, a warm hearth, and fine woodwork. (Singles 1800dr, doubles with private bath 2300dr.) The *taverna* attached to the Athenai, just off the main square, serves the best (and cheapest) food in town.

Farther west is **Ioannina,** with a mosque, now a museum, and other remnants of Ottoman domination. A couple of hours away on the coast is the tiny port of **Parga,** whose pine trees and sandy coves are dominated by a medieval fortress.

Just north of Ioannina is the spectacular **Vicos-Aoos National Park,** comprising the canyons of the Vicos and Aoos Rivers and the remote village of **Zagoria,** built entirely of gray stone and slate and regarded as a national treasure. Hiking and free-lance camping in and above the gorges will assure you that there *is* a beautiful Greece without tourists. Bus rides along winding roads will take you to either **Papingo** or **Monodendri;** beautiful hikes lead into the hills from both. The main road past Monodendri runs for 7km through amazing rock formations before arriving at a precipice overlooking the Vicos. *Xenonon,* comfortable guesthouses, are available in most towns. (Usually 800dr per person, hot showers included.) At the one or two restaurants in each village, try the *pita,* a feta-cheese pie. The most convenient base for this area is **Konitsa** (4 buses per day run from Ionnina, 1 hr., 300dr.). Here you can stock up on provisions and stay in the hotel **Egnatia** (singles 800dr, doubles 1600dr; big, old-fashioned bathtubs). From here, a footpath leads through the Aoos River Gorge to a monastery where you can lodge (1½-hr. hike).

The city of **Thessaloniki,** once an important cultural center of the Byzantine Empire, has numerous churches with outstanding mosaics and frescoes. Its **Archeological Museum** houses opulent artifacts from the important Macedonian finds at Vergina. (Open in summer Mon. and Wed.-Sat. 8am-7pm, Sun. 9am-2pm; in winter Mon.-Fri. 8am-3pm. Admission 300dr, students 150dr.) The city has abundant inexpensive lodgings clustered at the western end of Egnatia St., and an **IYHF youth hostel,** 44 Alex Svolou St. (530dr). The restaurants in the downtown area a couple of blocks off the waterfront are filling and cheap.

Thirty-eight kilometers west of Thessaloniki is **Pella,** capital of ancient Macedonia and birthplace of Alexander the Great. The ruins, including remarkably creative mosaic floors, are a mere javelin toss from the road along which buses to Edessa from Thessaloniki pass every hour. To the east you'll find gorgeous sandy beaches on the pristine peninsula of **Sithonia,** particularly at the east coast towns of **Vourvourou, Kalamitsi,** and **Paradissos,** the aptly named western port.

Male readers who want to experience the ascetic life at the monasteries and hermit caves on **Mount Athos** (**Agion Oros** or the Holy Mountain), should procure a letter of recommendation from their embassy in Athens or consulate in Thessaloniki, then a permit from the Ministry of Northern Greece, Platia Dikitirou, Thessaloniki (tel. 27 00 92). During July and August, this should be done at least two weeks in advance because only 10 visitors are permitted to enter the Mount each day. Once you have a permit, catch a bus from Thessaloniki's KTEL/Halkidikis Station to **Ouranopolis,** where you may need to spend the night; the **Hotel Ouranopolis** (tel. 712 05) is the cheapest in town (doubles 2000dr). From Ouranopolis, catch a boat to Daphni, whence buses continue to Karyes, the capital of the Mount, where you'll pass through a few formalities. Lodging in any of the 20 monasteries on the peninsula is free; hiking is the only means of transportation. Women (as well as the female of any species) are barred from the peninsula but can view the monasteries, including the more spectacular cliff-hangers to the south, from excursion boats sailing from Ouranopolis (departures at 10:30am, 1400dr).

The Peloponnese

Red and brown in the Arcadian high ground, eternally green through Elysian fields, and streaked everywhere with veins of grey rock on their unhurried course to the southernmost spear of Mani, the Peloponnese is perhaps the most beautiful region in Greece. The cities of Patras, Tripolis, and Kalamata are of little interest, but Nafplion, Corinth, Epidavros, and Mycenae are rich in classical ruins and legend, and along the southern coast you'll find the Aegean Sea at its least developed. You'll probably enter the Peloponnese by sea from Italy to Patras or by land from Athens to Corinth. The train system is limited, but buses run almost everywhere; buses leave Athens from 100 Kifissou St. Hitching is difficult the farther south you venture. The Peloponnese is not quite as fixed for tourism as the islands. This means few hostels, flexible hotel pricing, and ample opportunity to see Greek life lived as if you weren't there.

Argolis and Corinthia

"Where'er we tread 'tis haunted, holy ground," intoned Byron of this mountainous region of the Peloponnese pitted with some of the ancient world's most stunning ruins. Corinth, Mycenae and Epidavros recall more than the heyday of the Greek city states; at their fringes whisper the legends of Oedipus Rex and the House of Atreus.

The first stop for most visitors to the Peloponnese from Athens is **Korinthos (Corinth),** a town twice destroyed by earthquakes and rebuilt with squat, concrete houses. The ruins of Ancient Corinth are 7km from town; follow either the road to Patras or that to Argos and look for signs. Don't miss the elaborate and well-preserved **Fountain of Peirene** or the columns of the **Temple of Apollo,** sixth-century B.C.E. monoliths that keep a quiet vigil over the city's Roman ruins. Also worth a peek are the mosaics from the site—found now in the **museum** (whole site open Mon. and Wed.-Sat. 8:45am-3pm, Sun. 9:30am-2:30pm. 300dr, students 200dr). The Turko-Venetian fortress of Acrocorinth towers 525m over the classical site; you can hitch, take a taxi directly from Corinth, or make the tough one-hour hike up. Buses leave on the hour for Ancient Corinth from the main station on the corner of Koliatsou and Ermou Streets (60dr), returning on the half hour. If you must stay in Corinth, try the **Hotel Bellevue** on the waterfront. (Singles 800dr, doubles 1200dr). Buses to Corinth from Athens leave from 100 Kifissou Street (hourly 7:30am-9:30pm, 460dr). Returns are from the corner of Ermou and Koliatsou Streets.

Nafplion, a little over an hour from Corinth by bus (from the station at Aratou and Ethnikis Anistassis St.), is the best base for seeing the northeast Peloponnese. A charming port, Nafplion has an out-of-the-way **IYHF youth hostel** (tel. 247 20; 300dr), and many reasonably priced hotels which appear on the large map available in shops by the bus station. Try the **Hotel King Otto** (tel. 275 85), a beautiful old house two blocks behind Syntagma Square. (Singles 1300dr, doubles 1800dr, triples 2100dr. Breakfast 240dr.) There are also gorgeous doubles to let for around 1500dr in the hilltop streets behind the Hotel Leto.

Every summer evening Nafplion's port has a fruit fest—vendor's carts spill over with pears, apricots, and peaches. On Staikpoulos St. behind Syntagma Square try **To Koutouki** or **O Khelmos** restaurants. For a workout, climb the nearly 900 steps to the **Palamidi Fortress.** (Open Mon.-Sat. 8am-5:30pm, Sun. 10am-3pm. Admission 200dr, students 100dr.) Or take a small boat to the medieval island-fortress of **Bourtzi** (100dr round-trip) and pretend you're swimming.

Nafplion has good bus connections to Mycenae (160dr), Tiryns (70dr), and Epidavros (170dr). **Mycenae** was the most powerful city in Greece from 1600 to 1100 B.C.E., and was once ruled by Agamemnon, commander of the Greek forces during the Trojan War. His wife Clytemnestra murdered him on these palace stones as the House of Atreus grieved yet again. Most of the treasures from the excavation are in the Athens Museum, but the **Lion's Gate** and the **Beehive Tombs** are among the most celebrated archeological finds in modern history. To see the imposing Mycenaean walls, head for the monstrous fortress at **Tiryns.** In **Epidavros,** visit the ruins of the **Sanctuary of Asclepius** as well as the miraculously well-preserved **theater,** which had a seating capacity of 14,000. In July and August on weekend evenings you can see classical drama (in Greek) at the theater. Tickets for shows in this acoustic marvel start at 200dr for upper tier seats and may be purchased at the theater four hours before the performance (usually 9pm), or at Olympic Airways, 2 Bouboulinas St., Nafplion.

Patras

Don't jump ship when in Patras. Do your business—then get out quickly. Everything you'll need is on the waterfront. Leaving the customs house, make a right for the bus station and continue (with the water on your right) to the train station. The youth hostel is 1½km in the other direction. Notoriously slow **trains** run to Athens (5-6 per day, 5 hr., 545dr), Kalamata, and Olympia. For Delphi take the train to Ceradia. You can leave luggage at the train station (50dr per day). **Buses** run to Athens (every hr., 4 hr., 1130dr) and Kalamata. There is an **OTE** at the customs house (open daily 7:20am-10pm) as well as a **post office.** The **tourist police,** 40 Othonos Amalias St. (tel. 22 09 02), across from the train station, know the ferry schedules backwards. For **ferry tickets,** go to one of the general ticketing offices like **Manolopulous,** 35 Amalias St. (tel. 22 36 21), one block before the train station (open 8am-9pm). To Brindisi on Flavia Lines, deck fare with a Eurailpass is 1200dr, with InterRail (or if you're under 28) 3000dr, without pass 5600dr, students 4400dr. Everyone pays the port tax of 400dr at the agency. In summer, boats depart at 5pm and 9pm; in off-season at 9pm only. Get to the port two hours early in summer. Sadly, there are no railpass, student, or youth discounts to the Ionian Islands. Boats sail to Corfu at 9pm (10 hr., 1600dr), and to Cephalonia and Ithaca at 1:30pm and 9pm in summer, 1:30pm in off-season (4-5 hr., 935dr).

Stay at the crowded but adequate **IYHF youth hostel,** 68 Iroon Polytechniou St. (tel. 42 72 78). Beds 500dr, roof space 350dr. Open 24 hours. Other inexpensive lodgings hole up in the shabby buildings on Agiou Andreou St., one block from the waterfront along the main square. The **Hotel Delphi** (tel. 27 30 50) rents comfortable rooms (singles 850dr, doubles 1200dr, triples 1680dr). While waiting for your boat, climb the stairs to the Venetian *kastro* (on the street leading from the long pier by the train station).

Western Peloponnese

From Pirgos, trains (5 per day, 45 min., 100dr) or buses (hourly, 45 min., 150dr) will take you to **Olympia,** the religious sanctuary that hosted the ancient Olympics. While the ruins proper may not grab you, the divine groves and streams nearby will. (Open Mon.-Sat. 7:30am-7pm, Sun. 8am-6pm. Admission 300dr, students 150dr.) The gleaming **New Museum** opposite the ruins brings it all to life. (Open Mon. and Wed.-Sat. 7:30am-7pm, Sun. 8am-6pm. Admission 300dr, students 150dr.) Inside is Praxiteles' statue of Hermes, with lines so subtle the god's expression changes from each angle. The modern town is touristed but tasteful. In the center of town is a 50-bed **youth hostel** (tel. 225 80; 400dr per night; sheets 100dr; breakfast 140dr). **Camping Diana** (tel. 223 14), just above town, costs 300dr per person plus 250dr per tent. Otherwise find one of the scores of rooms to let, or stay at the **Hereon** (tel. 225 49) with singles 1000dr, doubles 1290dr (try bargaining). The **Hotel Pelops** can be an incredible bargain when business is slow. Most rooms to let are on Spiliopoulou St., parallel to the main road.

To the south, **Pylos** is an attractive town, both for its fertile setting and low prices. Take the bus (120dr) to the Mycenaean remains of **Nestor's Palace.** Nearby is Chora, which has a good museum. In Pylos, stay at the **Navarino** (tel. 222 91), with singles for 1000dr, doubles for 1200dr. With a little effort you should be able to find a double in the outer streets for 1000dr.

Quieter and even more beautiful is a trio of towns to the south—**Methoni,** with the ultimate Venetian fortress sprawled lazily beside its long sandy beaches, where you can stay at the **Iladision** (tel. 312 25) or in a private house; **Koroni,** farther to the east, where you can stay at the **Diana** (tel. 223 12); and, in the middle, the tiny fishing village of **Finikoundas.** All can be reached from **Kalamata,** the bustling capital of Messinia. If you get stuck here, stay at the **Hotel Nevada** (tel. 824 29) or at the **Hotel Avra** (tel. 827 59). From the bus or train station grab a #1 city bus and get off when it turns left on the water. For prime fruit go to the **new market** across from the bus station.

Laconia (Southeastern Peloponnese)

Time has done what the combined might of Hellenic civilization could not—it has tamed the ferocious Spartan spirit. Modern **Sparta** is a tidy town that will deny you nothing except great ruins. The Spartans considered monumental architecture a luxury that made strong citizens flaccid. Though they didn't indulge, Byzantium did only 5km. away in **Mystra,** where three tiers of tiled churches and ghostly palaces stagger up a steep hillside. (Open Mon.-Sat. 8:45am-3pm, Sun. 9:30am-2:30pm. Admission 300dr, students 150dr.) Sparta is an agreeable and convenient place to stay, or you can camp at **Camping Mystra** (tel. (0731) 227 24) between Sparta and Mystra. (300dr per person, 250dr per tent. Open year-round.) In Sparta, **Hotel Anessis** (tel. (0731) 210 88), across from the stop for buses to Mystra, is run by a kind woman. (Singles 1000dr, doubles 1300dr.) Around the corner is the clean **Hotel Sparti** (tel. (0731) 285 91; 700dr per person in doubles and triples. To reach either, turn left out of the main bus station onto Pelaeologou St. and then right onto Lykourgou. **Hriso Klithi,** Lykourgou St., has great pizza (450dr; open daily 8am-2am). You can reach Sparta by bus from Tripolis (1 hr., 320dr) or Kalamata (2 hr., 320dr). The latter trip takes you over a spectacular road.

The really adventurous can plunge south into the lower reaches of the **Mani,** the middle peninsula of the southern Peloponnese, known for a bloody past of family vendettas and savage piracy; known today for its repressive social mores. The entire region is stark—the mountains are utterly barren, the beautiful coastline is jagged and deserted, and the abandoned towns feature hooded and inhospitable fortress-towers. In the beautiful beach town of **Kardamili,** stay at the **Hotel Dioscouri** (tel. 734 97) or on the beach. From **Areopolis,** you can make daytrips to **Gerolimenas** and to the famous lake caves of **Pirgos Dirou,** known as *Ta Spilia.* For a place to stay in Aeropolis, take Kapetan Matapa Street off the main square and you'll see a sign ("11 rooms") on the left.

For one of the most spectacular hikes in Greece, continue south from Gerolimeras (15km) past the tower-houses of **Vathia** to **Porto Kagio**—wild, secluded, and unspoiled. The **Glyfatha Caves** near Pirgos Dirou are among the most splendid natural sights in Greece. (Open June-Sept. daily 8am-5:30pm; Oct.-May daily 8am-3pm. Admission 500dr.) The ticket includes a 30-minute boat ride through the cave and some dry land exploration. The organization here is as bureaucratic as the caves are wonderful: Visitors are admitted in turn according to the serial number on their ticket; you may have to wait 2 to 3 hours (don't arrive after 4pm or you won't get in). You can wait on the beach next to the caves, but numbers are called out in Greek so be careful not to miss your turn. Inside, the dense forest of stalactites and stalagmites compensates for all the inconvenience. Buses come here from Gythion, Areopolis, and sometimes Sparta; allow a full day for the expedition.

The capital of the Mani is the picturesque port of **Gythion.** You can swim off the wooded islet nearby, or in many of the desolate rocky coves to the southeast. **Rooms to let** are along the waterfront on the far right as you face the sea. **Andreako** (tel. (0733) 228 29), next door to the Port Captain's Office, has great sea views and comfortable, clean rooms. (Singles 1000dr, doubles 1300dr, triples 1600dr. Showers included.) The **Kranai** (tel. (0733) 222 49) and the **Aktaion** (tel. (0733) 222 94) are both centrally located (singles 1000dr, doubles 1500dr). There are two very nice campgrounds: **Gytheio Beach** (tel. (0733) 234 41; open year-round), and **Mani Beach** (tel. (0733) 234 50; open mid-April to mid.-Oct.); both charge 250dr per person plus 200dr per tent. Boats from Gythion connect with Piraeus (via Kythira and Monemvassia) on Fridays at 3pm and with Crete on Mondays and Thursdays. Contact **Rozakis Travel Agency** (tel. (0733) 222 29) on the waterfront for schedules.

Just off the easternmost peninsula of the Peloponnese is **Monemvassia,** a ruined city atop a huge rock that rises straight from the sea. A medieval village, still inhabited, climbs up the rock to a church at the summit. Stay overnight in the new town on the mainland at the **Akrogiali** (tel. (0732) 612 02) or the **Likeneion** (tel. (0732) 612 09). The **Aktaion** is more expensive (tel. (0732) 612 34) but has balconies and—a rarity in Greece—screens. Buses connect Monemvassia with Sparta (3 per day,

430dr) and Gythion (1 per day, 330dr). Flying Dolphin hydrofoils link the town with Piraeus (1 per day, 4 hr., 2580dr).

Ionian Islands

Greener and less touristed than the Aegean islands, this archipelago possesses a unique blend of Byzantine tradition and Renaissance culture. Most of the islands lie off the west coast of Patras. It's possible to hop from Cephalonia to Ithaka to Corfu, but Zakinthos is reached only by ferry from Killini on the Peloponnese. You can stop in Corfu en route between Brindisi, Italy and Patras, Greece.

Corfu (Kerkyra)

In Corfu Town, British palaces sit pretty on an esplanade modeled on the Rue de Rivoli in Paris. Behind are the shuttered alleyways of a little Venice. Such a pastiche only makes sense on this island of extremes—ravishing seascapes and ruined beaches, dense olive groves and rudely commercialized villages.

Ferries from Patras and Italy dock in Corfu Town's new port. Follow the water to your left to get to the old town where you'll find an informative **GNTO** in the palace (tel. 302 98). (Open mid-May to mid-Oct. Mon.-Sat. 8am-1:30pm and 6-8pm, Sun. 9am-noon; late Oct.-early May Mon.-Fri. 8am-1:30pm.) As you disembark from your ferry, you'll be besieged by hoteliers. You can usually get a good bargain on a room this way, but agree on a price before you leave the dock area, and find out exactly where the room is located—Corfu is a big island, and some accommodations are quite remote. Corfu's isolated, crowded, rowdy **IYHF youth hostel** is 4½km north on the main road from the port (tel. (0661) 912 02); take bus #7 from Platia San Rocco to Kontokali (2 per hr., 20 min.). (500dr. Cold showers included.) The best place to stay in Corfu Town is the **Hotel Cyprus,** 13 Agion Pateron (tel. (0661) 300 32), near the National Bank on Voulgareos St. It's hard to find, but immaculate, friendly, and quiet. (Beds in hall 600dr, doubles 2000dr.) Nearly all the cheap hotels and restaurants in town are clustered around the little road beginning to the right of the **Hotel Constantinoupolis** (tel. (0661) 398 26), which has decent rooms. (Singles 1250dr, doubles 2200dr.) **Hotel Elpis,** 4, 5H Parados N. Theotoki St. (tel. 302 89), in an alleyway opposite 128 N. Theotoki St. (in the Old Port), has clean, quiet, and well-kept rooms. (Singles 900dr, doubles 1400dr, triples 2000dr. Showers 100dr. Add 10% for stays of under 2 days.) Closer to the new port is the **Hotel Europa** (tel. 393 04), which is very popular among backpackers. (Doubles 200dr). The hotel rents mopeds for 800dr, motorcycles for 1800dr. In the evenings have a drink on the Esplanade and watch the cricketers play at being civilized. **Pizza Pete,** 19 Arseniou St., serves vegetarian and pizza specials (500-700dr). (Open April-Oct. daily 9am-midnight.)

KTEL buses leave frequently from New Fortress Square in Corfu Town for most of the island's major spots (some are reached by city buses from Platia San Rocco); it's easier but more dangerous to travel by moped. You can rent one almost anywhere for 1000dr per day. A trip west will take you to **Paleokastritsa,** with its white-washed mountaintop monastery. Ask for the *monopati* (footpath) to the bella vista promontory. Also here are the beautiful beaches of **Glyfada** and **Pelekas** and the nearby nudist beach **Moni Mirtidon.** (Plain old topless sunbathing is the rule on just about all of Corfu.) Pelekas swings at night and has several more inexpensive pensions, notably **Jimmy's** and **Alexandros'.** (Both 1000dr per person.) Nearby are the breathtaking cliffs of **Agios Gordios,** arguably Corfu's most spectacular beach and the site of the **Pink Palace,** a combination summer camp/fraternity/hotel that's amazingly popular among North Americans. (1600dr per person, 1900dr for a cot on the terrace. Breakfast, dinner, and disco included.)

A trip north will take you to the great sand beaches at **Roda, Kharoussades,** and **Sidari.** These are crowded near towns, but become significantly quieter between them. There is a good **campground** at Kharoussades. You can camp freely on Sidari beach's sandstone cliffs. From Sidari, walk the 3½km west to catch the sunset in Peroulades. For relatively secluded shores, head down the southwest coast of Corfu to the beaches of **Vitalades** and **Agios Giorgios.**

Ithaca (Ithaki)

Was it really for this small, steep, rocky place that Odysseus pined? Ithaca doesn't seem up to being Western literature's primal home, but visit the island's northern villages and coves and you'll understand at least a degree of Odysseus' homesickness. Though Homeric sleuths aren't Ithaca's only tourists, they can do their hunting in a peace unheard of on most islands.

Ferries run from Nidri and Vasiliki on Lefkas via Fiscardo and Cephalonia. There is also a ferry from Patras on the mainland to Vathi on Ithaca via Sami on Cephalonia. Another ferry departs from Astakos on the mainland to Vathi, and continues to Agia Efemia on Cephalonia. You can also catch that ferry on its way back to Vathi from Agia Efemia. Be sure to check boat schedules with travel agencies at your port of embarkation.

The main town of **Vathi** is a cluster of shops and houses situated in the middle of a horseshoe-shaped harbor. All the hotels here are expensive. The **Hotel Mentor** lets its roof for 300dr per person including bathroom and sunset. Check for *dhomatia* at Polyctor Tours (tel. 331 20), or camp out on the nearby beach (generally tolerated by the police). Along the same street as the post office is an excellent *taverna* with inexpensive grilled meat dishes.

Those with a poetic imagination and sturdy walking shoes will want to climb up to the "Cave of the Naiads" where, so it is said, Odysseus hid his treasure when he returned home; bring a flashlight or you'll only see the entrance. The site of Odysseus' palace is farther north in Stavros. Ask for the village schoolteacher's wife; she has the key to a museum erected on the alleged site. The winding 6km walk from Frikes to **Kioni** will tempt you with quiet coves and small pebble braches. Kioni's only bar is the island's best.

Cephalonia

If Corfu whets your appetite for islands, visit rugged Cephalonia, larger and far less touristed. In summer, **Ionian Lines** links Patras and Cephalonia daily, non-stop (2 per day, 4 hr., 970dr). Boats from Corfu and Brindisi stop here every day in July and August on their way to Patras. All boats leave you on the east coast of the island in **Sami,** a tranquil port town. Though smaller and duller than the capital town, Sami has a beach and is closer to the gorgeous northern part of the island. Stay at the **Hotel Kyma** (tel. 220 64; singles 1300dr, doubles 1900dr, showers 80dr), or take a cot on the roof of the **Hotel Melissani** (tel. 224 64) for 600dr per person. Otherwise head for the main town of **Argostoli,** the island's transportation center. You'll find a helpful **GNTO** on Vallianou St. (tel. 228 47; open Mon.-Fri. 9am-2pm and 5-8pm, Sat.-Sun. 10am-2pm), and a surprisingly interesting **Historical and Cultural Museum** (open Mon.-Fri. 8:30am-2pm and 6:30-8:30pm, Sat. 10am-noon; admission 100dr, students free). Hotels here are expensive; the nicest budget place, the **Hotel Allegro** (tel. 222 68) charges 2000dr for doubles without bath, 2430dr with bath. There are many cheaper rooms to let: **Emilia Dionisatou** (tel. 287 76) and **Denis Vassilatos** (tel. 286 05), across from each other at 18 and 16 Avilhos St., rent immaculate doubles with terraces, free showers, and kitchen facilities (2000dr in high season). Both Sami and Argostoli have superior campgrounds (350dr per person, 200dr per tent), though Argostoli's is a 3-kilometer trek.

Take the trip north to the fishing town of **Fiskardo,** the only village left intact after the 1953 earthquake. On the way you'll pass the sensational beaches at **Agia Kyriaki** and **Myrtos** as well as the little town of **Assos,** joined by a narrow isthmus to an island with a Venetian fortress. You can stay here at the Assos Snack Bar (doubles 1600dr). There are only two buses per day, but mopeds can be rented for 1000dr in either Argostoli or Sami.

Saronic Gulf Islands

In ancient times, no matter how many people crowded the shores of the Saronic Gulf Islands, the higher rocky interior of each remained gloriously quiet. That's why you'll find the sanctuaries built as far from the teeming shore as possible. Note that the islands farther from Athens are more pristine.

To find inexpensive lodgings search the streets and alleys on the hills above the main towns for "rooms to let" signs (650-750dr per person). Consult the tourist police and larger tourist agencies for assistance, but also query the younger Greek children, who often serve as prowling *hôteliers* on behalf of their parents. Freelance camping, technically illegal, is common in the hills and beside quieter beaches. If you arrive on a weekend you'll have a difficult time finding lodging.

The **Argosaronicos Line** runs ferries from Piraeus to each of the islands, stopping at points in between. They also run the "Flying Dolphin" hydrofoils from Zea Marina in Piraeus (at least 30% more expensive). For information on hydrofoils, call 452 71 07; on regular boats, call the Port Authority of Piraeus at 451 13 11.

Only 1½ hours by ferry from Piraeus, **Aegina** is the busiest of the islands. The port is one of the better places to stay on the island, as well as being the center of its bus system. A bit off the tourist circuit, the **Temple of Aphaea** is magnificently well-preserved and offers a panoramic view. Take the Agia Marina bus. (Open daily 10am-5pm. Admission 200dr, students 100dr.)

Much nicer is the lush island of **Poros.** While blessed with superb beaches, this lovely island is not without its drawbacks; during July and August the number of tourists daily exceeds the native population of 5000. **Family Tours** and the **Takis Travel Bureau,** both on the waterfront, can help you find accommodations, mostly private double rooms, for about 1400-1800dr, but pension owners will probably accost you before you arrive at either of these places. The **tourist police** are on Agiou Nikolaou (tel. 224 62), 100m to the right of the ferry landing. (Open mid-June to Sept. Mon.-Fri. 8am-2:30pm.) **Neorion Beach** is 3km to the left, as you face inland; if you don't want to walk, take one of the small boats which travel back and forth frequently. The main sight on Poros is the **Monastery of Zoodochos Pigis,** a scenic bus or boat ride from town (20 min., 30dr). History buffs and connoisseurs of spectacular views should rent motorbikes and trek up to the scant ruins of the **Temple of Poseidon** at the top of the mountain. A short caïque ride across to the Peloponnese brings you to **Galatas** and sandy beaches of **Plaka** and **Aliki.** Walk 1km to **Lemonodassos** and its dense lemon groves. **Cardassi Taverna** serves fresh-squeezed lemonade. In the other direction from Galatas awaits an extensive flat plain of cultivated flowers—perfect for cycling. Poros offers the best low-priced food in the Gulf; try **Caravella** and its neighbor **Lagoudera,** a short walk to the right along the wharf. **Ferries** run between Poros and Piraeus daily (3 hr., 550dr).

Sailing into the port of **Hydra** is like breaking into a painting. The artist has created a perfectly balanced port town with Venetian-style houses set in perfect opposition and colored every shade of white, blue, and brick red. In a stroke of sheer brilliance, the artist also omitted automobiles and motorbikes. Go on, pinch yourself—Hydra is real.

The **tourist police** (tel. 522 05) are open 24 hours and will find private double rooms for 500-700dr per person. Walk up the street beside the marble clock tower to find them. Stay among the friendly owner's personal antique collection at **Raphalia's Mansion** (tel. 525 84), on the harbor. Ask at the pharmacy above the tourist police. (1200dr per person.) Also try **Rooms Spiros** (tel. 524 24) on the eastern edge of the harbor and up a flight of stairs, or **Pension Douglas** (tel. 525 99) on the water. Both have spacious doubles for 1800dr. Hydra's accomodations fill quickly, so call ahead. The village of **Vlihos** has a good pebble beach. **Ferries** run between Hydra and Piraeus daily (3½ hr., 610dr).

In the southernmost currents of the Saronic Gulf is **Spetses,** almost completely covered in pines. John Fowles taught English here and centered his novel *The Magus* on the island. Unfortunately, the once-sleepy isle has recently been discovered, especially by Britons. From the harbor you can see the tourist bureaus and the only cheap hotel: the **Saronikos** (tel. 726 46). (Singles 1100dr, doubles 1400dr. Showers 150dr.) The **Takis Travel Office** (tel. 722 15), at the left of the wharf, has most of the rooms in town, including the cheapest, at its disposal. The **tourist police** (tel. 731 00), straight up from the dock on Botassi St., are open 24 hours, and are helpful with accommodations. The **bank** and **OTE** are side-by-side facing the water on Santou St. (Bank open Mon.-Thurs. 8am-2pm, Fri. 8am-1:30pm; in summer also Mon.-Fri. 7-9pm. OTE open Mon.-Fri. 7:30am-10pm.)

A bus leaves three times per day for the excellent beaches of **Anargyri** and **Paraskevi** (120dr round-trip; boats to Anargyri 200dr round-trip). One of the great mysteries of life is why the best caves remain empty, but they do, and they're yours for the price of a motorbike tour. (You can also hike the island's 28-km perimeter.) **Ferry** service between Spetses and Piraeus is often only once per day (5 hr.).

Cyclades

Once upon a time, the Cyclades were remote Greek islands with lovely secluded beaches and sleepy port towns. Then, travel magazines began advertising them as ideal getaways, magical paradises far from the hustle and bustle of the city. Now, each summer, the Cyclades are jammed to the hilt with tourists.

Despite the crowds, the Cyclades are still what Greek islands are supposed to be, with whitewashed houses, winding narrow streets, abundant flowers, and tiny, jewel-like churches. Shutters and doors, painted blue and green, harmonize with the sky and sea. By contrast, the land is brown, rocky and dry, and many islands (especially Ios) suffer from a shortage of water. Travel in the off-season for a taste of authentic Greek culture, but if it's nightlife you're after, you'll find nothing compares with the Cyclades in summer.

Once you pick up a ferry schedule from the GNTO in Athens, you won't have trouble picking up boats to the Cyclades. The main islands are served frequently during the summer; islands mentioned in this chapter are connected one to the other at least four times per day. In the off-season service is reduced, and even in summer, bad weather can show what a capricious beast the ferry system is.

Mykonos and Delos

When Narcissus drowned, gazing at his reflection in a pool of water, his spirit is said to have been reincarnated on the island of Mykonos. While archeologists have yet to unearth substantial proof of his existence, one visit will alleviate all doubts—Narcissus and his followers are alive and well on Mykonos. Some may feel a bit out of place on this most consistently popular of the Cyclades islands. This is an epicenter of chic international social life—gay and straight.

Mykonos is 5½-7½ hours from Piraeus (1910dr), with daily connections in summer to all the other major Cyclades. Most D-class hotels are unaffordable in high season (May-Oct. here), charging about 1000dr for singles (if you're lucky) and 1800dr for doubles; prices drop at least 20% in the off-season. In high season, grab the first person who tries to rent you a room, as accommodations are scarce and get scarcer as the day goes on. Unofficial **camping** is popular on the large beaches (Paradise, Super Paradise, and Elia); there is also an official **campsite** on Paradise Beach. (250dr per person.) For dinner, **Nikes Taverna** serves authentic hearty meals; **Antonini Taverna** is also an affordable choice.

For most visitors the word "beach" is synonymous with the famous nude **Paradise Beach,** and the mostly gay nude **Super Paradise Beach** nearby. Take a bus to Plati Yialos (40dr) and a boat from there (50dr to Paradise, 70dr to Super Paradise), or a more expensive boat direct from the harbor in town. For nightlife, go to **Apollos** (lively and straight), **Pierros** (always happening and mostly gay), or the **Windmill** (inexpensive and mixed). The **Irish Bar** near Pierros and **Seagull Bar,** near Apollos, are more relaxed sit-down bars.

The nearby island of **Delos,** legendary birthplace of Apollo and his twin sister Artemis, was one of the great spiritual centers of the ancient world. Extensive ruins cover the island, but they can only be visited on a daytrip from Mykonos or Naxos, as there are no accommodations on the island. Boats leave the dock by the Tourist Police at 9am, returning at 12:30pm sharp. (3-hr. visit, 600dr round-trip. Admission to site 300dr, students 150dr.)

Paros and Naxos

Paros has taken its place among Santorini, Mykonos, and Ios as one of the Cyclades' most popular islands. A haven for young backpackers in its own right, Paros' role as a hub for Aegean ferries adds to the crowds. **Parikia,** the main port of the island, has two redeeming features: an active nightlife and the wonderful old stone church of **Panagia Ekatontapiliani.** Nearby is the **Valley of the Butterflies,** where (in summer) brightly colored moths dot the bushes and trees. The **Hotel Dina** (tel. 213 25) is the best place to stay. It's quiet, immaculate, and well-located off the main shopping street. (Doubles with private showers 2200dr.) The **Hotel Parko** (tel. 222 13) has singles for 1500dr, doubles 2200dr, triples 3000dr, showers included (35% less in off-season). The **Oasis** (tel. 213 83), on the same street and one of the nicest places in town, has doubles for 4000dr, triples 4500dr. There are a number of **pensions** east of town, most charging 1400-1600dr for doubles, 1800-2100dr for triples. Since all accommodations are full from late July through mid-August, sleeping on the island's beaches is quite common, and fairly safe from the long arm of the law anywhere but Parikia. There are also official campsites such as **Koula** (tel. 220 82), near town, **Kolybithras Beach** (tel. 515 95), and **Parasporas** (tel. 219 44), 2km south of Koula. (All 250dr per person, plus 250dr per tent.) **Chryssi Akti** (Golden Beach) is a short bus ride away. Also worth a visit is the adjacent island of **Antiparos** with its stalactite caves. **Piso Livadi** and **Naoussa** are quieter towns in which to base a stay on Paros. Paros is six hours from Piraeus by ferry (2-3 per day, 1200dr) and in summer is connected to all the neighboring islands by frequent ferry service. Olympic Airways offers **flights** between Paros and Athens (10 per day, 5290dr).

Naxos is the land of Ariadne, daughter of King Minos of Crete. This island is the largest and least spoiled of the major Cyclades. A foray into **Naxos Town,** also called Chora, will take you through the old market section; it's often impossible to tell whether you are indoors or out as you wander through the narrow alleys half-covered with archways.

On the waterfront across from where the boats dock is a **Tourist Information Center** (tel. 233 28 or 233 29; open mid-March to Oct. daily 8am-11pm). There are numerous **pensions** up the small hill behind the OTE office. (Beds 600dr, roof spots 300dr.) In the old market section, near the Venetian *kastro,* directly uphill from the port (look for arrows pointing there) is the **Hotel Dionyssos** (tel. 223 31). (Dorms 400dr, doubles 1600dr, showers included.) Walk all the way down the waterfront to get to the **National Bank of Greece** (open in summer Mon.-Thurs. 8am-2pm, Fri. 8am-1:30pm). Around the corner and up the hill is the **post office** (open Mon.-Fri. 7:30am-2pm). Further along is the **Rental Center,** an outlet for cheap rooms, motorbikes, excursions, and information. Down the hill past the Rental Center, beaches for **freelance camping** extend south for miles: **Agia Anna,** a 30-minute walk or short bus ride (hourly) from town, is the nicest.

Naxos' splendid interior is easily traversed by bus or, with some difficulty, by moped. The main road across the island passes through the pristine towns of **Chalki** and **Apiranthos,** arcadian olive groves, and terraced hillsides that seem to hark from Asian paintings. Near Chalki, on the road to Moni, the eighth-century church **Panagia Drossiani** is well worth a sidetrack. The road ends in the pleasant beach town of **Apollon** on the west coast. Don't miss the 10m-high *kouros* (sculpture of an idealized male figure) outside of town.

Solitude-seekers should know that some of the least-touristed Cyclades are just east of Naxos. Daily ferries sail for rugged **Amorgos,** home of the dramatic **Kho-**

zoviotissa Monastery, perched on a cliff face. The monastery's charter bears the signature of wily Byzantine Emperor Alexis Comemnus, who gave the word "byzantine" its modern connotation. The tiny islands of **Shinoussa, Koufonissa,** and **Donoussa** have ferry service every couple of days, and rarely see visitors.

Ios

Dionysian revelry is reborn on Ios, where life is a perpetual party and the summer population is largely Scandinavian or Australian. If your idea of paradise is to lie on a beach all day and drink and dance all night, this is your island. For the sunset and jazz or classical music, try **Ios Club;** for discos go to **Scorpio's** or **Fanari's.** There is good rock at **The Friend,** and **Alex's Bar,** at the top of the village, has tequila specials for 100dr. Just above Alex's, good, cheap food is served next to the old windmills overlooking the town.

Cut into the hillside, the village of **Ios** is a tumble of houses connected by labyrinthine of winding whitewashed alleys. The many **rooms to rent** start at about 1000dr for doubles, 1200dr during July and August. Ask for **Damvakari Katerina,** near the top of the village, for beds and a great roof. (Beds in shared rooms 500dr. Cold showers included.) Just behind the post office are pleasant pensions run by **Anna Mettou** (tel. 414 45) and **George Stavraki** (tel. 914 86). (Doubles 1300dr, triples 1650dr.)

If you try to sleep on one of the town beaches in Ios, the police may confiscate your passport and fine you. But gorgeous **Milopatos Beach,** the center of all daytime activity, has two crowded **campgrounds;** the cheaper one is at the far end of the strand.

Santorini (Thira)

Formed by the massive volcanic eruption which gave rise to the Atlantis legend and is believed by many to have destroyed the Minoan civilization on Crete, Santorini is the most striking island in the Aegean. The island is actually the outer rim of a sunken volcano, its entire eastern coast a succession of small towns perched on high cliffs.

Larger ferries land at **Athinios** harbor, where you can strike a deal for a room with the homeowners who meet every boat. Try for one of the small towns near **Thira,** the island's dramatically situated capital, or near beautiful **Perissa Beach.** In Thira, you'll find the **tourist police** (tel. 226 49), on 25th of March St., next to the Olympic Airways office. You can stay at the 100-bed **youth hostel (IYHF),** 400m north of town (look for signs). It's a great deal—400dr per person, 350dr on the roof, egg breakfast 180dr. You can also free-lance camp on Perissa Beach. The numerous travel agents in the town square will book rooms and excursions, check bags, and change money. **Santorama Travel** (tel. 231 80, 231 21, or 231 77) and **Domingos Tours** are especially good.

Like Perissa, **Kamari Beach** has black sand, but it's lined with hotels. If clothes are not your style, head for **Monolithos** where you can camp under the trees. Dividing Perissa from Kamari is a small mountain topped by the remains of **Archaia (Ancient) Thira,** with Greek and Roman ruins and a great view. More fascinating are the excavations at **Akrotiri,** a late Minoan city preserved virtually intact under layers of volcanic rock. The famed frescoes of Akrotiri are in the Athens Museum. (Open daily 8:30am-2pm.) Guided bus tours and infrequent public buses will take you to most of these sights, or you can climb to Ancient Thira from Kamari. This all-day trek via the hilltop **Monastery of Porfitas Elias** pays off when you catch the view. Even more stunning is **Ia,** a small village clinging to the rocky point of land at the northern tip of the island, 300m above the sea—a great place to enjoy the sunset.

Western Cyclades

A more laid-back scene prevails in the western Cyclades: **Milos, Kimolos, Sifnos,** and **Serifos.** Don't plan on finding a room here in summer, but prepare to unroll your sleeping bag under a fragrant cedar on a beautiful beach: Ask fellow campers about public showers, or politely offer a local pension proprietor 100dr.

People come here for the scenery, not any particular "sights." One side effect of the calm atmosphere is that ferries are less frequent than those in the eastern Cyclades. Several boats per week hit all the western Cyclades, and others branch in from Ios and Santorini en route to Piraeus. Sifnos also has daily service to Paros and Naxos.

Sporades

Lush and beautiful, with thickly wooded interiors and jagged cliffs, the Sporades are greener, cooler, and generally less touristed than the famed Cyclades. This said, no one would call the Sporades undiscovered, and July and August bring droves of tourists, most notably to Skiathos and Skopelos. A hydrofoil now connects all four of the Sporades, so you can travel to and from Skyros without going to Kimi.

Ferry information for the Sporades is difficult to come by. It's a good idea to stop at **Alkyon Travel,** 98 Akadimias St., Athens (tel. 362 20 93) before setting out; information, even on the islands, is either scarce or unreliable. Getting to the Sporades usually involves travel to the charming town of **Kimi,** on Evia. (5 buses per day from Liossion Station, 3½ hr., 900dr). The **Kimi Hotel** (tel. (0222) 408) is cheap and comfortable (singles 800dr, doubles 1300dr). All buses going to Kimi should continue on to the port area, Paralia Kimi. From there a ferry travels daily to Skyros (700dr). Boats leave Kimi for Skiathos (4½ hr., 1638dr), Skopelos (3¾ hr., 1451dr), Alonissos (3 hr., 1330dr), and Volos (2503dr), Monday at 6:30pm and Friday at 11am; in summer boats operate four times per week. There are also weekly ferries to Limnos (1023dr) and Kavala (1657dr). You can go directly to Skiathos from Athens on any day via Alkyon buses which connect with ferries at Agios Konstantinos (1900dr), or from Volos by ferry (2-3 per day, 800dr). Ferries arrive in Skopelos from Skiathos three times per day (386dr) and continue on to Alonissos (452dr). Hydrofoils also connect the Sporades with Agios Konstantinos and Volos for 60-70% more.

Busy, cosmopolitan, and expensive, **Skiathos** earns the title, "Mykonos of the Sporades." Single rooms are extremely difficult to find in late July and August; homes advertising "rooms to let" have the cheapest rates. **Yolanda Constantinidou,** George Pandra St. (tel. (0424) 223 64) and **Maria Papagiorgiou,** just off Grigoriou before Christina's Bar (tel. (0424) 215 74) are two proprietors worth knowing. (Doubles 1400dr.) Solo travelers, here and elsewhere, have to double up or convince the proprietor to set up a cot for about 700dr. For dinner, try the lamb dishes at **Taverna Stavros** on Evangelistrias. Many travelers spend the night dancing at **Charlie O'** or the ultra-chic **BBC.** Have a drink at any of the bars along Polytechniou Street, or at the **Adagio Bar,** with classical music.

A bus runs about every half-hour along Skiathos's only paved road to the 60 beaches on the southern coast. The same bus route also passes the island's only two campgrounds; **Aselinos Camping,** a 20-minute walk from the road, is nicest. (200dr, 100dr per tent.) At the end of this line, **Koukounaries** and the nearby, nude, **Krassa,** feature pine trees, golden sand, and big crowds. Head north to **Mandraki,** or east to the coves, for the same pines and sand, freelance camping, and few companions.

Skopelos, Skiathos' most immediate neighbor, is less inundated by tourists. During the summer crush, more and more tourists are discovering Skopelos—sometimes out of necessity, as there are accommodations here. For the lowest prices, seek out private rooms, or try **Hotel Stella** (tel. (0424) 220 81), east of town on the waterfront. (Doubles 1400dr.) Room-booking agencies collect large commissions.

Consider making the four-hour round-trip hike from Glossa to **Agios Ioannis,** a chapel topping a sheer cliff that emerges from clear Aegean waters. There's a beach here, too. The best beaches are **Velanio,** accessible by bus and a good spot for camping; and **Limnonari,** reached by taking a bus from either Glossa or Skopelos to Agnondas, and then a small boat.

Alonissos is the least populated of the four major islands. The ferry leaves you in **Patitiri,** where **Ikos Travel** will help with rooms and information, and exchange money. Take the uphill hike to the old town of Alonissos (½ hr.), or trek to the beaches—**Chrisimilia** is among the best.

Skyros is the most beautiful and interesting of the Sporades; its strong island culture has survived increasing tourism. Try to get a room in a traditional home (about 600dr per person); interior decorating has been a major folk art here since the island's upper class started to purchase decorative items from pirates. **Freelance camping** is possible 1km out of the village on one of the best beaches in the Sporades; the local bugs will welcome you enthusiastically. If *you* want food, try the delicious **Kabanera,** tucked away in the maze of streets; or the vegetarian and meat specialties at **Sisifus,** right up the street from the bus stop.

Skyros Travel runs boat and bus excursions around the island (400-800dr). In town, visit the **Monastery of St. George,** the **Archeological Museum,** and the fascinating **Faltaits Museum,** to the left of the Rupert Brooke statue. The interior is a model of a traditional Skyrian home. In the craft shop in the basement you might meet Manos Faltaits, founder of the museum, and author of the informative book *Skyros* (500dr). Rent a motorbike (1500dr per day with gas) at either the **Trahanas** house, third right from the bus stop, or try **Cosmos** rental, across from the bank. (Maps are available at Skyros Travel.)

Crete (Kriti)

The Cretan landscape is alternately abundant and austere: barren mountain ranges in the interior, treacherous passes and gorges, great expanses of olive and citrus trees, and isolated villages along the Libyan Sea. Visitors have been known to succumb to Crete for weeks, some not budging from a cove or deserted beach, others exploring the incredible array of old cities, ruins, and mountains.

Cretans have much to be proud of. The Minoan Period of Crete's history, from 2600 to 1400 B.C.E., represented the first great flowering of European civilization, as demonstrated by the art and frescoes discovered among the impressive palace remains at Knossos, Phaestos, Malia, and Kato Zakros. After nearly two millennia of continually resisted foreign subjugation by the Romans, the Byzantines, the Venetians, and the Turks, Crete was unified with Greece in 1913.

Most of the present-day invaders (tourists) converge on Crete's major cities and stick to the eastern half of its easily accessible northern coast. Don't make this mistake. The rest of the island—rugged, windblown, and delightfully secluded—is where you should be.

Iraklion, the port of entry for most visitors, is connected by ferry with Piraeus (2 per day at 6:30pm and 7:30pm, 12 hr., 1780dr) and Santorini (mid-July to mid-Sept. 1 per day, off-season 3-5 per week, 5 hr., 1080dr; by hydrofoil 2½ hr., 1960dr). A boat from Piraeus passes through Gythion (on the Peloponnese) and Kythera en route to Kastelli at the western end of the island (2 per week, 1820dr). Three ferries also connect Agios Nikolaos on Crete, with Kasos, Karpathos, Halki, Rhodes, Milos, Folegandros, Anafi, and Santorini; the *Vergina* and the *Paloma* sail weekly via Iraklion from Athens to Cyprus and Israel (Iraklion-Cyprus 7000dr, Iraklion-Israel 8500dr). Jet-setters can fly to Crete from Athens (several flights per day, day 6630dr, night 4980dr), Rhodes, Mykonos, Santorini, Karpathos, Kassos, Paros, and Thessaloniki.

Central Crete

It is unfortunate that so many visitors see **Iraklion** first—compared to the rest of Crete it's overdeveloped and ugly. Its main attraction is the **Archeological Museum** off Eleftherias Square. The museum is one of the finest in Greece, housing an enormous number of Minoan artifacts from excavations throughout the island. (Open June-Oct. Tues.-Sat. 8am-7pm, Sun. 8am-6pm; Nov.-May Tues.-Sun. 8am-5pm. Admission 400dr, students 200dr.) Relax gratis in the museum's palm tree garden. Across the street is the office of the **Greek National Tourist Organization (GNTO),** with maps of the city, hotel lists, and bus and ferry schedules for the entire island. (Open Mon.-Sat. 7:30am-6pm, Sun. 7:30am-2pm.)

Most of Iraklion's cheap accommodations are clustered on or around **Handakos Street,** which runs between the waterfront and Venizelou Square. From the port, turn right after disembarking and right again at the old city walls, then walk along the waterfront about 700m until you pass the Xenia Hotel; Handakos is to your left. The crowded **IYHF youth hostel,** at #24 (tel. (081) 28 62 81), has an 11:30pm curfew. (400dr, no card required. Open year-round.) **Rent Rooms Mary,** at #69 (tel. (081) 28 11 35), is more humane and charges 1200dr for doubles, 1500dr for triples. The **Hotel Ideon Andron,** 1 Perdikari St. (tel (081) 28 36 24), is also cheap and quiet. From Venizelou Sq., walk down Dedalou St. to Perdikari, the first left. (Singles 900dr, doubles 1400dr, triples 1800dr.) For food, head to the **open-air market** on 1866 St., just off Venizelou Sq. There you can either assemble a picnic (try the fresh yogurt) or sample one of the 10 colorful *tavernas* on **Theodosaki Street,** the first left as you enter the market.

Bus #2 travels from Venizelou Sq. to **Knossos,** 6km south. Here is the liberally reconstructed mytho-historical palace of King Minos and his Minotaur, and the ancient capital of the Minoan civilization. (Open daily 8am-7pm. Admission 400dr, students 200dr.) Ten buses per day travel from Hania Gate in Iraklion to the Greco-Roman ruins at **Gortys,** where a stone wall is inscribed with one of the earliest examples of Greek law. (Open Mon.-Sat. 8:45am-3pm, Sun. 9:30am-2:30pm. Admission 200dr, students 100dr.) The same bus continues to the Minoan ruins at **Phaestos** (2 hr., 390dr). Purists will appreciate this site; the various layers of palaces dating from four successive periods have been left more or less untouched. (Open June-Oct. Mon.-Sat. 8am-7pm, Sun. 9am-6pm; Nov.-May Mon.-Sat. 10am-4pm, Sun. 9am-2pm. Admission 250dr, students 150dr.) At the end of this route are the sandy beach and spacious caves at **Matala.** The grottoes surrounding the town were used by the Minoans as tombs, by the Germans as hideouts, and are now unofficial summer homes for young foreigners. The caves above the central harbor are fenced off, but those above the town to the south are inhabitable and usually not patrolled by the police. Most budget travelers stay legally at **Matala Camping** (150dr per person, 150dr per tent), or at one of Matala's dozen expensive pensions. (Doubles average 1400dr.) You'll want to avoid the tinsel and tourists of Agia Galini, but consider continuing west to **Plakias.** There is a superb sandy beach here and two lively **IYHF youth hostels,** one in Plakias itself, and another 20 minutes uphill at **Myrthios.** (Both 350dr, no card required; Plakias open March-Dec., Myrthios year-round.)

Keep an eye open for **Daphne,** the party nymph, who sometimes frolics in the waves near here.

Western Crete

Rethymnon, 81km west of Iraklion, is an enchanting slice of Crete's past. The Venetian and Turkish influences seen all over northern Crete are most evident in this charming town, with its minarets, narrow winding streets, and imposing Venetian **Fortezza.** The **youth hostel (IYHF),** 41 Tombasi St. (tel. (0831) 228 48), is cheerful, relaxed, and crammed in summer. (350dr, no card required. No curfew.) **Paradisos Hotel,** 35 Ig. Gavril St. (tel. (0831) 224 19), across from the park, has singles for 900dr, doubles for 1400dr, triples for 1700dr. **Elizabeth Camping,** 3km east of town (tel. (0831) 286 94), charges 300dr per person, 250dr per tent; buses run frequently from the bus station.

The blend of Ottoman and Venetian architecture continues in the lively harbor town of **Hania,** where narrow streets and fading mansions have captivated travelers for years. The **tourist office** is in the converted mosque at the eastern end of the harbor. (Open Mon.-Fri. 9am-7:30pm, Sat.-Sun. 9am-3pm.) The **youth hostel (IYHF),** 33 Drakonianou St. (tel. (0821) 535 65), is far from the center of town; take the Agios Ioannis bus from the market and get off at the fifth stop. (350dr. No curfew.) The helpful management of the **Hotel Fidias,** 6 Sarpaki St. (tel. (0821) 524 94), charges 550dr per person for singles, doubles, and triples. **Pension Kydonia,** 16 Isodion St. (tel. (0821) 571 79), offers singles for 600dr. The harbor area is the place for a seafood dinner and an evening promenade. Try **Faka's** behind the Customs House to the east where you can have boiled octopus for 350dr and dine with the locals. **Café L'Amour,** a health bar on Platia 1866 near the bus station, has yogurt boats for 350dr.

One of the few "musts" in Crete is a hike through **Samaria Gorge,** a spectacular ravine that cuts through heavy forests and sheer granite cliffs. (Open officially May-Oct.) Buses run from Hania via Omalos to **Xyloskalo** at the mouth of the gorge daily at 6:15, 7:30, 8:30, 9:30am, and 4:30pm (1½ hr., 280dr). The 18-kilometer hike takes five to seven hours and ends at **Agia Roumeli** on the southern coast. Boats sail east to Loutro and busy **Chora Sfakion** (1¼ hr., 450dr), where buses return to Hania. If you have the energy, you'll do much better to hike along Crete's unspoiled southwest coast. A spectacular coastal path leads past **Marble Beach** (4½ hr.) and the tiny village of **Finix** (5½ hr.) to the charming port of **Loutro** (6 hr.). From there, another path continues east past two coves to **Sweetwater Beach** (2 hr.) and Chora Sfakion. **Sougia** and **Paleochora,** to the west of Agia Roumeli, are likewise beautiful, though more crowded.

Eastern Crete

Northern European families and package-tourists flock to **Malia** and **Agios Nikolaos** like flies to garbage. Avoid these overdeveloped resorts if you can. If you do come here, visit the compact ruins of the **Palace of Malia,** one of the four great cities of Minoan Crete, and spend the night elsewhere. The crowded **IYHF youth hostel** (tel. (0841) 228 23), two blocks from the bridge over the "bottomless lake" in Agios Nikolaos is casual and friendly, and has seaside views. (Members and nonmembers 350dr. No curfew. Open year-round.) Try to make it inland to **Tzermiado** on the **Lassithi Plain,** a stunning patchwork plateau irrigated by hundreds of sail-rigged windmills. In Tzermiado, try **Kourites** (doubles with bath 1800dr) or the **Hotel Kri-Kri** (singles 800dr, doubles 1000dr). Near Tzermiado at **Psychro** sinks the **Dikteon Cave,** where Rhea supposedly gave birth to Zeus. Buses frokm Iraklion's Terminal A run to Psychro and Tzermiado at 8:30am and 2:30pm (430dr).

Sitia, at the eastern end of the island, is a hospitable harbor town with a good **IYHF youth hostel** (tel. (0843) 226 93) at 4 Therissou St. (Members and nonmembers 350dr. No curfew. Open year-round.) From here it's an easy trip east to **Vai,** a palm-lined beach where accommodations are nonexistent and camping is forbidden on the main beach. In the coves to either side, nude sunbathers relax undisturbed and camping is allowed. Though the beaches of the southeast coast pale beside their more westerly counterparts, the 5km of black sand at **Myrtos** are a wonderful exception. Pension rooms here are reasonable, usually costing about 1000dr for doubles. Myrtos is best reached by bus from Ierapetra, an offensive resort 15km to the east.

Northeast Aegean and Dodecanese

Strung along the coast of Turkey, Lesvos, Chios, and Samos are the main islands in the northeastern Aegean group; **Lesvos** is popular, especially the towns of **Plo-**

mari, in the south, and **Molyvos,** dominated by a Genovese fortress. Coming from the main port of Mitilini, the bus stops at Molyvos' **tourist office,** which can find you a private room for 700dr per person. But **Petra,** 5km to the south, is quieter and as scenic; get a room managed by the **women's collective** by the bus stop, and enter the daily life of a Greek family. You can camp at the excellent beach at **Eressos** (south of Molyvos), a popular gathering place for lesbian travelers during the summer. Boats run daily to Lesvos via Chios from Piraeus (14 hr., 1800dr).

On **Chios,** bizarre, ornamental architecture in the well-preserved towns of **Pirgi** and **Mesta,** and the impressive **Monastery of Nea Moni** (16km from Chios Town, accessible by bus only on Sun. mornings) lend the island a medieval aura. The helpful **tourist office** in Chios Town (tel. (0271) 267 43) is the best place to start searching for rooms. (Open daily 4:30am-1:30pm and 5:30-9pm.) They also rent motorbikes, a convenient and economical way to see the island (1500dr per day for a 2-seater). The closest beach is sandy **Karfas,** serviced by frequent buses during the summer, but the stunning black volcanic beach at **Emborio** is quieter. Boats leave daily for Piraeus, and also for Çeşme, Turkey (3 per week, 4000dr one way, 5500dr round-trip).

Samos is perhaps the most beautiful and certainly the most touristed island of the area, although it's quiet compared to the islands of the Dodecanese and Cyclades. Ferries make the 12-hour trip from Piraeus (1752dr) at least once per day in summer, and there are summertime connections south to Patmos and the other Dodecanese islands from **Pythagorion,** on the south coast. Boats to the Dodecanese may not run at all in winter. Boats from Piraeus arrive at Samos Town, and **Samos Tours** (tel. (0273) 277 15), right at the end of the ferry dock, has all the information you'll need. The best place to stay in town is the clean, cheap, and very friendly **Pension Ionia** (tel. (0273) 287 82) at about 800dr per person. Try to phone ahead during July and August; if they can't squeeze you in, they'll try to direct you somewhere else. The beaches along the northern coast between Samos Town and picturesque **Kokkari** are numerous and beautiful, and, with the exception of Kokkari, uncrowded. **Chrissi Ammos** on the southern coast is especially nice after 4pm, when the excursion buses go back to Samos Town.

Samos is the main transit point to **Ephesus** on the Turkish coast, the site of perhaps the most extensive classical ruins in the Mediterranean (see Turkey). Government regulations require that you buy a ticket that includes a tour of Ephesus, whether you want it or not (1500dr, 2500dr round-trip). There is also a Turkish port tax of US$7, US$14 if you stay overnight (other currencies are accepted at a less advantageous exchange rate).

A legendary aura permeates **Rhodes,** despite the absence of the Colossus and the annual inundation of tourists both in the capital city of **Rhodes** and in Lindos. The island holds unparalleled medieval architecture, impressive ancient ruins, and splendid beaches and coves. The best beaches are along the east coast towards Lindos, at **Faliraki, Tsambika, Haraki,** and Lindos itself. Five kilometers north of Faliraki is **Kalithea,** one of the few places at the north end of the island where you can camp undisturbed. On the northern coast, there are the ruins of an ancient town at Kamiros, and farther west, the majestic hilltop castle at Monolithos. The interior and southern half of the island are quieter, subsisting on agriculture rather than the tourist trade.

The city of **Rhodes** is dominated by the massive, and beautifully restored **Crusader Castle** of the Knights of St. John. Start an exploration of the medieval city from the **Hospital of The Knights,** on Argykastrou Square, an imposing fortress that houses the **Archeological Museum.** (Open Mon. and Wed.-Sat. 8am-7pm, Sun. 8am-6pm. Admission 300dr, students 150dr.) **Ippotou Street,** which heads uphill from the square, is the historic **Avenue of The Knights,** on which the different national orders of the Crusaders kept their "Inns." At the top of the street stands the castle itself, an impregnable fortress complete with moats, drawbridges, and colossal battlements. Another part of the city worth a visit is the **Chora;** from Kleovolou Square as you leave the palace, turn left onto Orfeos St. The exclusive reserve of Turks and Jews during the Ottoman rule, the Chora harbors the **Mosque**

of Suleyman (open unreliably Sat.-Thurs. 10am-12:30pm; no shorts or bare shoulders), and the **Turkish baths,** on Arionos Square (open Mon.-Sat. 5am-7pm; bath 150dr Mon., Tues., and Thurs., 50dr Wed. and Sat.).

Though the modern **new town** is packed with hotels and expensive shops and restaurants catering to package tours, the **old city** of Rhodes is both interesting and cheap, dotted with small pensions and inexpensive restaurants. The local **tourist office** is on Rimini Sq. (tel. 248 88), near Mandraki, the port area. The **GNTO** is a few blocks up the street. Stay at the friendly and international **Steve Kefalas' Pension,** 60 Omirou St. (tel. 243 57). (Cots on roof 400dr, bed in large room 700dr.) Alternatively, try **Pension Apollon,** 28c Omirou St. near Steve's (tel. 358 14), or the **Dionisos Pension,** 75 Platanos St. (tel. 220 35). Both have places outside or on the roof for 300dr, rooms 600-700dr per person. The cheapest eating establishment is the **Belmore Inn,** 46 Amerikis St. (tel. 323 64), in the New Town. The place is small but portions are large and worth the trek. A good place in the Old Town is **Coralli,** 13 Ippodamou St.

The Crusader fortress, ancient acropolis, steep whitewashed streets, and sandy beach of **Lindos** have attracted huge crowds and high prices. But visit anyway. If you can't find a pension (look along Apostolous Pavlou St.), you can camp with mosquitos and other backpackers on the beach, where there are free showers. The walk up to the **acropolis** will tax your legs not nearly as much as the donkey ride up will tax your wallet; if you head down the other side of the hill, you can sun in relative solitude on the large rocks by the sea.

There are **ferries** from Rhodes to all of the Dodecanese islands, to Athens (2000dr), and to Marmaris in Turkey. Rhodes is also a stopping point for boats traveling from Piraeus to Cyprus and the Middle East. These go four times per week, arriving in Cyprus one day later and Haifa or other Middle East destinations 12 hours after that. For tickets and schedules go to **Triton Tours,** 25-27 Plastira St. (tel. 216 90; open Mon.-Fri. 9am-1:30pm, 5:30-8:30pm, Sat. 9am-1:30pm). There are regular **flights** in summer from Rhodes to Athens, Crete, Kos, Santorini, Mykonos, Karpathos, and Kassos. Various European charters also fly into Rhodes's airport.

On **Kos** you'll find varied classical and Hellenistic ruins, and some good, though crowded, beaches; the most popular is at **Tingaki,** 10km west of **Kos Town,** crowded and notable only for its boisterous nightlife. For accommodations, inquire at the **tourist office** or **tourist police,** next to each other on the waterfront. Try **Pension Alexis,** 9 Irodotou and Omirou St. (tel. 287 98), the first right off Megalou Alexandrou St. (Doubles 2000dr, triples 2300dr.) The main archeological sites are in town and at **Asklepion,** Hippocrates' school of medicine, 5km away. A good place to hike is among the five mountain villages of **Asfendiou.** For a quieter beach town than Kos itself, try **Kardamena** on the southern coast, where you can stay at **Hotel Stelios** (tel. 912 10; doubles 1600dr). Two boats per day travel from Kos to Bodrum, Turkey (3000dr).

Patmos, northernmost of the Dodecanese islands, is where St. John wrote the Book of Revelations in a cave in the hills. The **monastery** dedicated to him is one of the most impressive in Greece, squatting above the charming and labyrinthine village of Chora. Stay in the pleasant port of **Skala,** or camp for 250dr per person at the well-appointed campsite at **Meloi Beach,** 1½km from Skala and well-signposted.

The rest of the Dodecanese are substantially quieter than these islands. **Kalymnos** and **Leros** are on the main ferry route to Piraeus and are thus a little busier; for quiet, friendly islands as yet relatively untouristed, try **Nissiros,** with the dormant volcano of Polyvotis, or **Tilos,** even quieter, with long empty beaches at **Livadia** the port, and on the other side of the island at Erestos. Both Nissiros and Tilos are served by the frequent ferries between Rhodes and Kos. Avoid staying in **Symi.** The harbor is picturesque and the **Panormitis Monastery** at the other end of the island (accessible only by boat) is imposing, but the island is tainted by the commercialism of Rhodes, without its appeal.

Karpathos, south of Rhodes, is more isolated, and features **Olymbos,** a traditional town with two working windmills and women in traditional garb, and the pretty, stony beach at Vananda. Both are accessible from the small port of **Diafani** in the northern part of the island; the main administrative port is **Karpathos** in the south. In Karpathos Town stay at **George's Pension** (tel. 224 79) up the stairs to the left off Dimokratia St. (Doubles 1000dr, triples 1500dr.) The beautiful, nearly deserted beaches of **Ahata** and **Amopi** are perfect for camping and nude bathing. The island is served by boats sailing from Rhodes to Crete; sailings are infrequent during the winter, and always at the mercy of the weather in this, the roughest stretch of the Aegean.

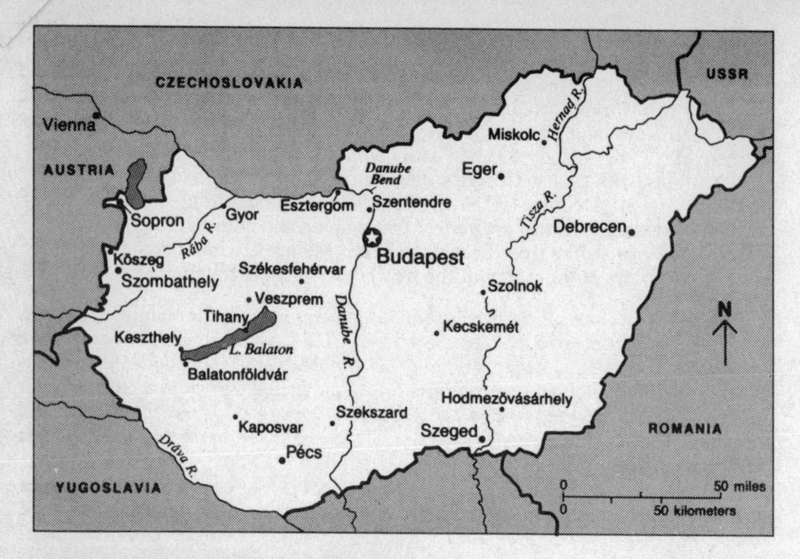

HUNGARY

US$1 = 47.7 forints (Ft)
UK£1 = 77.8Ft

10Ft = US$0.21
10Ft = UK£0.13

A trip to Hungary is the perfect way to ease your way into Eastern Europe. The government welcomes tourists, and tries to spare them the bureaucratic hassles and restrictions you might encounter elsewhere. Furthermore, competing tourist offices can always find you a room, making spontaneous budget travel a breeze. Perhaps most important, Hungary is *cheap;* prices of US$4-6 for a room or US$4 for a three-course meal are unheard of anywhere else in continental Europe.

Always on the fringe of powerful empires, Hungary has a history of successive occupations. Overrun by the Mongols in the thirteenth century, Hungary was occupied from 1540-1700 by the Turks. Thereafter ruled by the Hapsburgs, Hungary joined with Austria to form the Austro-Hungarian Empire in 1867. When that empire fell apart after World War I, Hungary became an independent state. But even in the shadows of foreign powers, the Magyars have always been successful in preserving their own lifestyle. Twice in recent times they've rebelled against foreign domination: in 1944, against the Nazis, and again in 1956, in opposition to the Soviet-backed government. Though Soviet tanks crushed the more recent revolt, driving 200,000 Hungarians into exile, the result was ultimately a compromise.

Communist Party leader János Kádár has developed a uniquely progressive brand of socialism, proclaiming that all who were not against the system could be with it. A new economic system, dubbed "goulash communism" by some wits, incorporated many features of the Western market economy, and the country enjoyed remarkable economic prosperity throughout the '70s. It probably won't strike you as much like Marxism, though: BMWs and bag people are both common sights on the streets of Budapest. However, with Kádár getting old and the economy slowing down under the weight of a high foreign debt, changes may be in the offing. Ferenc Havasi, a proponent of further Westernization, and Karoly Grosz, a more orthodox Marxist, are both poised to contest the leadership in the post-Kádár era.

Despite the country's political turmoil (or perhaps because of it), Hungarian culture has flourished. Hungary's contribution to the music world includes nineteenth-century composer Ferenc (Franz) Liszt, as well as twentieth-century geniuses Zoltán Kodály and Béla Bartók. The country's many musical groups are respected worldwide, and theater and film also thrive; evenings are spent at a play, or watching the visual poetry of film directors like Miklós Jancsó. Victor Vasarely, the father of pop art, is one of Hungary's sons.

Although much of the country's architecture and landscape makes it undeniably Central European, Hungary has something Mediterranean about it. Maybe it's the food: At least three varieties of paprika give you a choice of ways to set your mouth on fire, and there's a fine selection of wines to cool you back down. Maybe it's the way people drive. Even a boxy East German sedan turns into an Italian sports car with a Hungarian behind the wheel.

With a fifth of Hungary's population and a seemingly limitless supply of things to see and do, Budapest dominates the country. The capital does not, however, have a monopoly on cultural attractions, and you shouldn't let it monopolize your attention. None of the provincial centers is more than a three-hour train ride from Budapest, making even daytrips very feasible. In Györ, Pécs, and Szeged, life slows down. Western travelers are less common in these parts and so are met with greater interest and hospitality.

Try the beaches around Lake Balaton or consider visiting some of the smaller towns. In 1526, Mohács, in the south along the Danube, was the site of the final battle leading to Turkish domination of Hungary; today a park occupies the battlefield, poignantly commemorating the Magyars' inglorious defeat with life-size wood sculptures representing both the combatants and their fallen. Kalocsa, upriver between Mohács and Budapest, is famous mostly for its paprika fields, which in autumn resemble a flaming sea. Szombathely, on the Austrian border, has Roman ruins, plus a recently discovered sanctuary of the Egyptian goddess Isis. The hot and dry eastern Great Plain, or Puszta, is the source of Hungary's famous horses, as well as much of its folklore; the Hortobágy National Park preserves the area's varied wildlife.

Planning Your Trip

All visitors to Hungary arriving by rail or boat must have a visa, obtained in advance from a Hungarian embassy or consulate. Those who fly or drive can get a visa at the border (for a somewhat higher fee), but auto travelers will avoid two-hour lines by applying in advance. The standard tourist visa is good for 30 days (but can be extended), and is valid for entry up to three months from the date of issue. Most Hungarian diplomatic missions in Europe will issue a visa overnight for a fee of about US$10; same-day service is often available, at a US$5 surcharge. In bordering countries, visas are issued on the spot, without a surcharge. Visa procedures by mail in North America take about two weeks. Write to IBUSZ (see our appendix) for an application, which explains requirements and fees, or contact a Hungarian mission directly: Consulate General of the Hungarian People's Republic, 8 E. 75th St., New York, NY 10021 (tel. (212) 879-4126); Hungarian Embassy, Consulate Section, 3910 Shoemaker St. NW, Washington, D.C. 20008 (tel. (202) 362-6730); in Canada: Hungarian Embassy, 7 Delaware Ave., Ottawa, Ontario K2P 0Z2 (tel. (613) 234-8316 or 232-1711); in Great Britain: Consulate General, 35 Eaton Pl., London SW1 (tel. 235 71 91); and in Australia: Hungarian Embassy, 79 Hopetown Circuit, Yarruluma A.C.T. 2600 (tel. (6162) 82 32 26), or at 351/a Edgecliff Rd., Edgecliff, Sydney, N.S.W. 2027 (tel. (612) 323 78 59).

IBUSZ offices abroad (see our appendix) are very helpful and efficient, and will usually send you information on particular areas or topics of interest. Ask for the tremendously helpful booklet *Travel Information Hungary.*

Getting There and Getting Around

Transportation in Hungary is very centralized—when entering or leaving it's easiest to go through Budapest. The Danube hydrofoil is the most enjoyable, though most expensive, way to go—it's fast and comfortable, with beautiful scenery. The trip between Vienna and Budapest costs about US$50 (departures daily in summer, 5 hr.). Boat travel from Bratislava in Czechoslovakia is much less expensive, but sometimes tickets are difficult to come by in Hungary. One-way second-class rail fare from Vienna to Budapest is about US$24, less for travelers under 21. If you're making an excursion from Vienna to Budapest and back, buy a round-trip youth ticket in Vienna, as no student or budget tickets to the West are sold in Budapest. Eurailpass holders can travel free as far as the Austrian-Hungarian border; Inter-Rail is valid throughout both Austria and Hungary. It is possible to take a bus into Hungary, but conditions are cramped and the border crossing takes much longer than on a train. Hitchhiking across the Austrian border is not difficult as there is considerable traffic on the main highway between Vienna and Budapest (E5). The distance can easily be covered in five hours. Avoid crossing the border on foot.

Trains in Hungary are slow, but reliable and inexpensive. *Személyvonat* are excruciatingly slow; *gyorsvonat* cost twice as much, and move at least that much more quickly. All of the larger provincial towns are accessible by the express rail lines (*sebesvonat*). It's best to purchase both international and domestic train tickets at IBUSZ offices (where there's usually an English-speaker), since lines at the train station can stretch to unbearable lengths. If you do go to the station, do so early in the morning or late at night; international trains should be booked a day in advance. Since most people at the ticket windows do not speak English, have everything clearly written out before you get to the front of the line. For all international train journeys you have to pay the portion beyond the Hungarian border in Western currency.

If you're headed for another socialist country, remember that an IUS student card will get you a 25% reduction on train tickets. Train journeys between socialist countries are much cheaper than those between East and West. Keep this in mind when planning your trip; for example, you can save by traveling from Budapest to Split via Belgrade instead of Vienna.

An option when leaving Hungary is the national airline **Malév.** Though normally not cheap, Malév offers special standby fares to most cities for people under 25—roughly a third of the regular cost. You can purchase standby tickets one business day in advance at the Malév office in Vörösmarty tér. Malév also gives a 25% discount on all flights to those under 25.

The extensive bus system is cheap but crowded. It provides some direct connections between provincial cities where the train system would force you to go back to Budapest first, but otherwise will not save you any time. The main bus station at Engels tér. in Budapest has schedules and fares posted. You can sometimes flag down intercity buses on the road.

Either IBUSZ or Tourinform can provide a guide to cycling in Hungary, which includes maps, suggested tours, repair shops, and recommended border crossing points. Write to the **Hungarian Nature-lovers' Federation (MTSZ),** 1065 Budapest, Bajcsy-Zs. u. 31, or the **Hungarian Cycling Federation,** 1146 Budapest, Szabó J. u. 3, for more information.

Hitchhiking is feasible, but only on the main roads. Cars are small, so you should hitch alone or with one other person at most. Most Hungarians are up and on the road early (6am).

Practical Information

Unlike other countries in Eastern Europe, Hungary does not require a minimum daily currency exchange of its Western tourists. Change money only as you need it, as it's quite difficult to reconvert forints into Western currency. Be especially careful not to convert much money on your first exchange; you may be surprised how inexpensively you can live in Hungary. All Hungarian banks, tourist offices, and train stations offer the same official rate of exchange. The black market is no longer a hot item in Hungary for tourists—expect no more than 10Ft per U.S. dollar above the official exchange rate. The small rewards aren't worth the risks. You should, however, bring some Western cash—some purchases (e.g., international train tickets) must be made with Western currency.

Visitors must register with the local police in each town they visit. If you stay in official accommodations, your visa form will be stamped and formalities taken care of for you. However, if you make arrangements to spend the night in the home of a private citizen, you should register at the police station and have your visa stamped there. Though these forms are seldom checked rigorously as you're leaving the country, violators can be fined.

Perhaps the best word for foreigners to know is **IBUSZ,** the Hungarian national travel bureau. IBUSZ has offices throughout the country, each with a friendly multilingual staff. Among other things, IBUSZ can make room arrangements, change money, sell train tickets, and charter tours. IBUSZ can provide much written material about the country; be sure to pick up the excellent pamphlet *Travel Information Hungary,* which contains just about all the practical information you'll ever need. Budapest IBUSZ offices can give you listings of the tourist offices throughout the country, give you information about other cities, and even make reservations for you in hotels outside Budapest. **Express,** the national student travel bureau, handles student accommodations and tours, sells bus tickets, and changes money. You can purchase an IUS card from them upon production of an ISIC or passport and 100Ft. In most towns Express handles youth hostel accomodations. **Tourinform,** Petöfi Sńdor u. 17-19 (tel. 17 98 00, open Mon.-Fri. 7am-9pm, Sat. 7am-8pm, Sun. 8am-1pm) is an information service with one central location in Budapest (near Déak tér.). They won't find you a room, but they can answer questions about Budapest and the rest of Hungary. Their staff can often be particularly helpful as interpreters, expediting tourists' dealings with all sorts of agencies.

Hungarian (*Magyarul*) is probably one of the more exotic languages you'll ever encounter; it's related to Finnish and Estonian, but only distantly. Many older people and restaurant staff know German, while many younger people know English, but don't count on getting by without learning a little Hungarian. Buy a phrase book before you arrive and learn the pronunciation chart; many words sound very different from how they look. Hungarians will appreciate your efforts. Phrase books, such as *Berlitz Hungarian for Travellers,* and dictionaries (try the *Tourist's English-Hungarian Dictionary*) can be bought in Budapest's foreign language bookstores, or at gift shops in the large hotels. Also note that Hungarians always put the surname before the proper name; this is useful to know when decoding street names. Hungarians call their country *Magyarország.*

Western periodicals are available in Hungary in many newspaper shops and in large hotels, but are expensive. The Hungarians put out an English language daily called *Daily News* (7Ft), with a balanced mix of Western and socialist-bloc wire-service articles.

General business hours in Hungary are Monday-Friday 10am-6pm (7pm for food stores), Thursday until 8pm. Banks close around 2pm on Friday, and on Saturday virtually everything is closed after 1pm. Nothing is open on national holidays; besides the Christian holidays, the main ones are April 4, May 1, August 20, and November 7. Post offices are open Monday-Friday 8am-6pm, and Saturday 8am-2pm. Pay phones take a 2Ft piece for every three minutes. Lift the receiver, deposit the money, and dial. It may take a couple of tries before your call goes through—don't give up. To call abroad from Hungary dial 00, then the country code and number. The **country code** for Hungary is 36.

If you should fall ill, you can contact the U.S. and British embassies for lists of English-speaking doctors in Budapest.

Accommodations and Camping

Hungary offers a range of accommodations with a variety of prices. Your best bet is to find a room in a private home through the paying-guest service *(fizetö-vendégláto szolgálat)* at IBUSZ or one of the local tourist offices. These rooms cost 250-500Ft per night, plus a slight commission for the first night. Conditions in private rooms vary greatly, but many are quite comfortable. If you are displeased with your room, go back to the paying-guest service and they'll assign you another. By IBUSZ rules, you are not allowed to occupy your room until 5pm of the first day, so find a place to stow your bags until then. You'll be expected to be out of your room by noon.

Even cheap hotels are expensive (750-1000Ft), and full in summer. **Express** offers a number of inexpensive student hotels, open year-round, as well as hostels open during July and August. Hostels are numerous and usually quite large, so it's unlikely that you'll be crowded out. Go to an Express office to book a space in one of their hostels, since locations sometimes change annually. Express offices can also give you a complete listing of all hostels in the country.

Hungary also offers a number of "tourist hotels" which are similar to youth hostels but don't require IYHF membership. Prices per person per night run 50-70Ft. Make reservations at any of the country's tourist offices.

You can legally accept private offers of accommodation, but you must register with the local police (see Practical Information). In larger cities you may be approached on the street; in small towns, look for the sign *Szoba Kiadó* or *Zimmer frei.*

There are over 100 campsites in Hungary, priced from 50-115Ft per day. You can often rent four-person bungalows for 275-500Ft, but you must pay for every space, whether or not it is filled. Most sites are open from May to September. Discounts are offered at the beginning and end of the season (10%), to those with an FICC card (20%), and to those with an ISIC or IUS card (up to 50%). For information and maps, write or visit the **Hungarian Camping and Caravanning Club** in Budapest.

In March, during Hungary's spring festival, hotel prices and the prices of many other services offered by tourist offices are substantially reduced.

Food

Magyar cuisine is among the best in Europe, specializing in fantastic concoctions of meat, spices, and fresh vegetables. In Hungarian restaurants, called *vendéglö* (or *étterem*), paprika is the predominant spice. You might begin your meal with *gulyás,* a beef soup seasoned with paprika, or with the addicting *meggyleves* (sour cherry soup). Close to what we call goulash is *pörkölt,* a pork or beef stew, again with paprika. Stuffed cabbage and stuffed peppers *(töltött káposzta* and *töltött paprika)* are other typical entrees. *Gombas risz,* a rice dish with giant fried mushroom caps, is a common meatless dish. If you really want to splurge, go with some friends and order a whole roast wild pig (*vaddisznó*). Fresh fruits and compotes are the lightest desserts, but don't pass up a chance to try the superb *rétes;* Hungarians claim that the Austrians stole the recipe and called it *strudel.* Especially good are *almasrétes* (apple) and *makosrétes* (poppy-seed). Don't leave Hungary without sampling the sinfully rich pastries. One specialty is *dobostorta,* about 10 layers of mocha filling topped with a hard caramel coating. Another is *Gundel palacsinta,* crepes with a walnut and currant filling, covered with chocolate-rum sauce and flambéed. *Somlói galuska* is a fantastically rich and delicious concoction of chocolate, nuts, and cream, topped with an orange-rum sauce. Hungarians like to savor their meals, so be prepared to spend a couple of hours.

For faster but more prosaic food, a *büfé* or a *bisztro,* where you'll find more Hungarians, offers reasonable full meals for about 50Ft and up. For pastry and coffee, look for a *cukrászda.* Coffee is served espresso-style.

Hungarians are proud of their wines, and with good reason. The most famous are the red *Egri Bikavér* (the "Bull's Blood of Eger"), the white *Tokaji* wines, and the whites of the Balaton region. Feel free to experiment, though, as most Hungarian wines are quite good and rarely more than 60Ft per bottle at a store, 100Ft at a restaurant. Fruit brandies, most notably apricot, cherry, and pear, are a national specialty; you can try them in most cafes and bars. Local beers are good and tend to be strong; if you don't specifically request Hungarian beer you may be served a more expensive import. Stick to imports when it comes to liquor, though.

For a change from heavy restaurant fare, try buying your own food at a local grocery store (*csemege*) or supermarket (ABC-*áruház);* for produce, go to a *közért* or to the local markets. Shopping at these stores is an excellent way to glimpse everyday Hungarian life. Vegetarians will find these stores a necessity, as virtually every restaurant item has meat in it.

Budapest

Sitting atop three hills and straddling one of Europe's greatest rivers, Budapest is majestic. A tribute to Magyar adaptability, Budapest successfully combines the ostensibly incompatible traits of a socialist capital and a lively Western city. Throughout the city severe edifices of the new order stand beside ostentatious monuments of the late Hapsburg Empire.

Budapest was created officially only in 1873, by the joining of three ancient towns, Buda, Obuda, and Pest. Nonetheless, the city has always been an enormously important part of Hungarian national life. Few other cities have been destroyed by invasion so many times and rebuilt with such dedication. In spite of the scars of 1956, the city's atmosphere is anything but grim. Best of all, travelers can enjoy Budapest's vitality and elegance for next to no money.

Orientation and Practical Information

Budapest is situated in northwestern Hungary, about 250km downstream from Vienna. Regular trains and excursion boats connect the two cities. Budapest also has direct rail links to Belgrade to the southeast, Prague to the northwest, and other major cities throughout Eastern Europe.

Buda lies on the west side of the River Danube; Pest is on the east. Buda's medieval character dates from its days as the Magyar capital, while Pest is the heart of the modern city, filled with businesses, shops, museums, and restaurants. Addresses in Budapest are always given with their district number, a Roman numeral. The numbering system has no apparent logic, so pick up a street map from a newsstand or Trafik Shop (14Ft). Central Buda is I, and downtown Pest is V.

Pest is based loosely on a set of ring streets (*körút*) and avenues (*út*) emanating from the Erzsébet bridge. The first ring starts at the Szabadság bridge as Tolbuhin körút, becoming Múzeum körút and then Tanács körút, but never quite making it to the Chain bridge (lánchid). The next ring starts at Margit bridge as Szt. István körút and then becomes Lenin körút, József körút and Ferenc körút before meeting the Petöfi bridge. The final ring stretches from the Árpád bridge almost all the way over to Összekötö bridge as Róbert Károly körút, Hungaria körút, and Könyves Kálmán körút.

The main avenues are **Kossuth út,** which becomes Rákóczi út, running from the Erzsébet bridge to Keleti train station; **Bajcsy-Zsilinsky út,** running from Engels tér to Nygati station; and **Népköztarsaság út,** which runs from Engels tér to the Millenium monument.

Hungarian officials and tourist staffs are very helpful and usually quite friendly, but nearly always slow; arrive as early in the morning as possible for any bureaucratic dealings.

Tourist Offices: IBUSZ, V, Felszabadulás tér 5 (tel. 18 68 66). Budapest's principal source for all sorts of information. Arranges private accommodations and hotel rooms, changes money, and sells train tickets. Open Mon.-Fri. 8am-7:45pm, Sat. 8am-4:45pm, closed Sun. Branch offices in all train stations are open daily 8am-8pm. A branch at Pétöfi tér 3 (tel. 18 57 07) is open 24 hours. **Tourinform,** VII, Rákóczi út 52 (tel. 17 98 00), is *the* place to go with problems and unanswered questions; they also have loads of information in English on all of Hungary. Open Mon.-Sat. 8am-8pm, Sun. 8am-1pm. **Hungarian Camping and Caravanning Club,** VIII, Üllöi út 6 (tel. 33 65 36), has information on sites for the entire country. Open Mon.-Fri. 8:30am-5pm, Sat. 8:30am-1pm. Foreign-language information (tel. 17 22 00).

Budget Travel: Express, V, Szabadság tér 16 (tel. 31 77 77). Room and hostel reservations, IUS cards (100Ft), and travel discounts and excursions offered. Open Mon.-Fri. 8am-8pm, Sat. 9:30am-8:30pm, Sun. 10:30am-5:30pm. Branches in the train stations are the most helpful and are open 24 hours in summer; come at odd hours to avoid a long wait.

American Express: IBUSZ, Petöfi tér 3 (tel. 18 48 48). Mail held, checks sold and replaced, but no wired money accepted. Nearest office that can accept is in Vienna.

Post Office: Offices next to Keleti and Nyugati railway stations are open 24 hours. Mail is best sent to your embassy.

Telephones: International calls are best made at V, Petöfi Sándor u. 17. **Telephone Code:** 1. International calls can also be made from red pay phones.

Flights: Ferihegy Airport is easily reached by Volán bus, which runs daily 5am-11pm to and from Engels tér (½ hr., 20Ft). Youth standby tickets can be purchased at the Malév office at V, Dorottya u. 2, on Vörösmarty tér.

Trains: Keleti palyaudvar or **pu.** (East Station) handles international and domestic traffic in all directions. **Nyugati pu.** (West Station) is the starting point for trains to Romania, Czechoslovakia, Yugoslavia, and other points in Eastern Europe, as well as to some Hungarian towns. **Déli pu.** (South Station) carries passengers to Lake Balaton and the southwest, as well as to Austria. All 3 stations are on the Metro. International and domestic tickets may be purchased at IBUSZ (see Tourist Offices) or at **MAV Hungarian Railways,** VI, Népköztársaság u. 35 (tel. 22 80 49 or 22 80 56), open Mon.-Sat. 9am-5pm. Foreign-language information about domestic trains (tel. 22 78 60); international traffic information (tel. 22 40 52). Both answered 6am-9pm.

Buses: Main Station is on V, Engels tér. Schedules and fares are all posted here, though some buses depart from the new **Népstadion Station.**

Hydrofoils: For information and ticketing, **MAHART International Boat Station,** V, Belgrád rakpart 2 (tel. 18 17 58), near the Erzsébet bridge; or **IBUSZ** main office, Tanacs Krt. 3/c (tel. 42 31 40). Arrive 1 hr. before departure for customs and passport control.

Public Transportation: The Metro is quick and easy to use, and along with the extensive bus and tram service, will take you almost anywhere you want to go. All Trafik Shops and the occasional sidewalk vendor sell yellow tram and Metro tickets *(villamos jegy)* for 2Ft and blue bus tickets for 3Ft. Last run is sometime between 11pm and midnight, depending on the line; times are posted. Details can be found in the pamphlet *Public Transportation in Budapest* and in the *Budapest Guide,* both available from IBUSZ or Tourinform. Day passes are available, but it is probably more economical to buy individual tickets.

Taxis: Call **Fötaxi** (tel. 22 22 22) or **Volántaxi** (tel. 66 66 66), or hail one with its "taxi" light lit. Taxi prices are very reasonable.

Emergencies: Police (Rendörség), officially (tel. 07), but call or visit **KEOKH,** the Foreign Nationals Office, Népköztársaság u. 12 (tel. 11 58 89), for English-speaking assistance or to extend your visa. Embassies are on 24-hour call. **Ambulance:** Tel. 04.

Embassies: U.S., V, Szabadság tér 12 (tel. 12 64 50, after hours 32 93 74). **Canada,** II, Budakeszi u. 32 (tel. 38 77 11). Take bus #22 from Moszkva tér. **U.K.,** V, Harmincad u. 6 (tel. 18 28 88). **Australia,** V, Apaczai Csere J. u. 12-14 (tel. 18 81 00). **New Zealanders** are represented by the British Embassy. **Bulgaria,** VI, Népköztársaság u. 115 (tel. 22 08 24). **Czechoslovakia** (Consulate), XIV, Népstadion u. 24 (tel. 63 66 00). **Poland,** VI, Gorkij fasor 16 (tel. 22 84 37).

Bookstores: For literature, grammars, dictionaries, and travel books, in a variety of languages, try the bookstore at V, Váci u. 32 (tel. 18 27 18), off Kossuth L. and a couple of blocks from Erzsébet híd. Open Mon.-Wed. and Fri. 10am-6pm, Thurs. 10am-8pm, Sat. 9am-1pm. If they don't have what you want, have them direct you to another shop; there are a number in this area. For maps, also try the shop at V, Petöfi Sándor u. 2 (tel 18 31 36).

Laundry: Mosószalon, József Nador tér 9 and Városház u. 3. 69Ft to wash up to 5kg. Both open Mon.-Fri. 7am-7pm, Sat. 7am-3pm.

Swimming Pool: Szabadság Pool, XIII, Népfürdó u. 36. Take bus #133 from Marx tér.

Hitchhiking: To hitchhike south to Szeged and Belgrade, take tram #2 out Soroksári u. to the end of the line; switch to bus #23, then bus #66. To go east to Debrecen and Romania (E15), take the Metro to the end, then change to either tram #50 or bus #35 out Vörös Hadsereg u. To go west to Györ and Vienna or southwest to Lake Balaton and Zagreb, take bus #12 from Moszkva tér out Budaörsi u., then switch to bus #72. The highway M7 splits a few kilometers outside Budapest with E5 heading west and E96 going south.

Accommodations and Camping

It is not difficult to find an inexpensive room in Budapest, even in July and August—though the city sometimes fills on summer weekends. The best value is to find a room in a private home through a paying-guest service. It's important to arrive early for one of these rooms, as the nicest, cheapest, and most convenient to the town center are usually given out first. Prices vary with agency, location, and facilities; expect to pay 150-250Ft per person, single or double. If you have trouble finding a room, Tourinform can help by calling the various agencies to see who has space available.

To meet other students, especially Eastern European ones, get a room in a hostel set up in vacant university dormitories during July and August. Go directly to an Express office (see Budget Travel listing under Practical Information) for a reservation; don't trek out to a hostel, as many are booked in advance by groups. Express can also book reservations for any hostel in the country, with advance payment. Hostels cost about the same as a room in a private home.

Hotel rooms, which can be arranged through IBUSZ, cost at least 700Ft.

Private Accommodations Service

No significant difference exists between the agencies listed below. IBUSZ has one of the largest room collections, but may fill first since it's the best known. When lines at the station office are long, a trip to one of the city branches may prove a faster alternative.

IBUSZ, at any of the locations listed under Tourist Offices in Practical Information. Try them first; they have over 3000 listings and an exceptionally helpful staff.

Budapest Tourist, with 4 locations: V, Roosevelt tér 5-6 (tel. 17 35 55), open Mon.-Sat. 8am-10pm, Sun. 9am-5pm; Baross tér 3 (tel. 33 65 87), near Keleti pu., open Mon.-Sat. 8am-9pm, Sun. 2-8pm; VI, Marx tér, in the underground passage beneath Nyugati pu. (tel. 32 49 11), open Mon.-Sat. 8am-7pm; and at Déli pu. (tel. 15 42 96), open daily 8am-9pm. More rooms than IBUSZ; a good bet in a crunch.

Cooptourist, V, Kossuth Lajos tér 13-15 (tel. 12 10 17), and VI, Marx tér (tel. 12 36 21), in the underground mall near Nyugati pu. Open Mon.-Fri. 8:30am-1pm and 2-7pm.

Volántourist, V, Október 6 u. 11-13 (tel. 12 96 49).

UTAS Tours, Münnich Ferenc u. 19 (tel. 11 40 25). Branch in Keleti pu.

Camping

There are two main campgrounds in the Budapest area. Both are large and rarely full; both are open from May to mid-October.

Hárs-hegy, Hárshegy u. 5 (tel. 15 14 82). Take bus #22 from Moszkva tér. A 3-star campground. Good cheap restaurant. 35Ft per person, 50Ft per tent. 4-person bungalows 360Ft.

Római Camping, Szentendri u. 189 (tel. 88 71 67). A 1-star campground. Take the Metro to Batthyány tér, then watch signs for the green HEV suburban-railway trains. 20Ft per person, 30Ft per tent.

Food

Eating cheaply is easy in Budapest. The city is full of inexpensive restaurants (*bisztros,* grills, *büfés,* self-service, and *eszpresszos*) which serve simple meals with good soups for under 50Ft. You needn't stick to the cheaper restaurants, though, as many elegant Budapest establishments may well be within your budget. Almost all Class I and Class II (I. and II. *osztályu*) restaurants offer a fixed-price meal (*menü*) at lunch (noon-3pm), and some have one at dinner. Such a meal costs 40-100Ft at a Class II restaurant and about 150Ft at a Class I restaurant; meals ordered á la carte average 100Ft and 170Ft, respectively.

Many restaurants feature gypsy music; though a nice touch, this is a sure sign of a tourist establishment. Similarly, restaurants located right on the Danube tend to cater to foreigners, and may overcharge the unsuspecting. Though many restaurants have menus printed in German, only the most expensive (or most touristed) have them in English.

The listings below are just a sampling of what Budapest has to offer. Try out the *vendéglö* or *bisztro* in your neighborhood for a taste of Hungarian life. You can buy your own food from the truly overwhelming spread at Budapest's **Nagyvásárcsarnok** (Great Market Hall), IX, Tolbuhin krt. 1-3. This feast for the senses is best in late summer, when the pepper harvest comes in. (Open Mon. 7am-5pm, Tues.-Thurs. 6am-6pm, Fri. 6am-7pm, Sat. 6am-3pm and 6-11pm.)

Restaurants

Büfé (Self-Service), II, Margit u., at the foot of the Margit bridge on the Buda side of the Danube. Simple food at rock-bottom prices; full meals for about 40Ft.

City Grill, Váci u. 20, next to the Hotel Taverna (other locations as well). Fast-food joint. English understood.

Csülök Csárda, VIII, Berzsenyi u. 4, off Baross tér, opposite from Keleti pu. (down from the Hotel Hungaria). Enter through wine cask doorway. A popular neighborhood spot with tasty fare and good service. Meals from 75Ft. Open daily 11am-11pm.

Fehér Galamb, I, Szentháramság 9/11, just down the street from Mátyás Cathedral. Excellent food (80-130Ft); gypsy music, too. Very romantic wine cellar in the same building. Open daily noon-midnight.

Emke Kalocsa Csárda, VII, Lenin krt. 2, at Metro (red line) stop Blaha Lujza tér. An unabashedly touristy place that nevertheless offers well-prepared national dishes (listed in English), and an energetic and varied folk program. Open daily noon-1am, music from 9pm.

Kárpátia, V, Karoly M. u. 4-8, just off Felszabadulás tér. A Class I establishment serving excellent Hungarian and international fare. Try the cold fruit soup (*hideg gyümölcsleves*) for 26Ft or the venison ragout (125Ft) and grilled meats.

Szondi, VI, Lenin krt. 97, in the Hotel Béke. Elegant and gracious, this deluxe restaurant offers superb and interesting meals, from turtle soup (100Ft) and crêpes caviar (40Ft) to salmon (220Ft) and roasted goose liver (385Ft). Excellent wines and desserts, too. The place for a splurge. Open nightly 6pm-midnight.

Wine and Pastry

A. Regi, I, Országház u. 17. A deep, dark, ancient stone wine cellar, one of Budapest's many *borok* (wine cellars which often serve meals). Open until 11pm.

Vörösmarty (Gerbeaud) Cukrászda, V, Vörösmarty tér 7. For the best pastry east of Vienna. Formerly the meeting place of Budapest's literary elite, this cafe retains its 19th-century elegance. Service, however, can be excruciatingly slow—bring a long book. Open daily 9am-10pm.

Ruszwurm, I, Szentháromság u. 7, near Mátyás Cathedral. This excellent confectionery has been in business since 1827 and is decorated with furniture from that period. Open daily 10am-8pm.

Hungária, Lenin krt. 9-11. This sumptuously decorated coffee house was a favorite hang out for artists, writers, and journalists at the turn of the century. Open daily 10am-midnight.

Sights

Buda, and particularly its **Várhegy** (Castle Hill) section, is the richest part of the city for historical and architectural monuments. Unfortunately, as so much of Buda's history has been violent, most buildings have been reconstructed a number of times. Enter old Buda through Vienna Gate in the north, and wander through the quaint **Fortuna útca,** lined with baroque town houses, or along **Táncsics Mihály útca** in the old Jewish commercial sector. Don't miss the excavated foundation of the old **synagogue** at #26. Continue to the central square in front of magnificent

Mátyás Cathedral, where the Hungarian kings were crowned. Romanesque when it was first built in the thirteenth century, the cathedral was turned into a mosque by the Ottomans in the fifteenth and sixteenth centuries, and finally restored in Neo-Gothic style in 1903. Check out the beautiful painted walls and curiously avant-garde window at the rear of the church, and the artistic and royal treasures in the south porch. Organ concerts are held regularly at 8pm. In front of the cathedral stands the colonnaded twentieth-century **Halászbástya** (Fishermen's Bastion); from here you get perhaps the most spectacular view of the Danube, with its series of bridges and sprawling Pest beyond. While you're in the area, step into the **Budapest Hilton Hotel,** which incorporates part of a seventeenth-century Jesuit college and a thirteenth-century abbey in its modern design.

Continue walking south along the top of the hill, and you'll soon come to the **Royal Palace,** for hundreds of years the residence of Hungarian monarchs. Originally built in the thirteenth century, the palace has undergone sieges by Tatars, Turks, and Nazis, as well as those during the War for Hungarian Independence (1848-9). The fighting in 1944-5 left the palace and most of Castle Hill in ruins; notice the bullet holes in the facades, remnants also of the 1956 uprising. During post-war reconstruction, extensive excavations revealed artifacts from even the earliest palaces; these can be seen in the **Budapest History Museum** located in Wing E of the palace. Other museums in the palace include the **Hungarian National Gallery** (Wings B, C, and D of the palace), and the **Museum of the Hungarian Workers' Movement.** The National Gallery contains work of Hungarian artists from the eleventh century to the present. The permanent exhibit at the Workers' Museum (Wing A) is interesting to those who can read Hungarian. Check the foyer for the museum's temporary exhibits; some excellent artists display their work here. (All 3 museums, like all major sights in Budapest, are open Tues.-Sun. 10am-6pm. Admission 5-10Ft; students, and everyone on Sat., free.) From the **Citadella** and the Soviet **Liberation Monument** on **Gellért-hegy** there are breathtaking views.

Still in Buda, take the bus or streetcar up Szilagyi Erzsébet fasor from Moszkva tér. In front of the round Hotel Budapest you can catch a **cog-railway** which takes you to the top of Szabadság-hegy, where you can catch the **Pioneer Railway,** run entirely by schoolchildren. Ask where to get off for the János-hegy **chairlift** (*libegő*), which will take you back down the hill.

Pest, the commercial center of the capital across the river, bustles with activity. Its heart is the **Inner City,** an old section once surrounded by walls, now centered in the popular pedestrian zone of Váci u. and Vörösmarty tér. Pest's river bank is lined with modern luxury hotels, up to the nineteenth-century Neo-Gothic **Parliament** building at Kossuth tér.

Just north of the Parliament, the Margit hid (bridge) crosses to the lovely mid-Danube island of **Margitsziget.** The island is a municipal park, off-limits to private cars, with thermal baths and shaded terraces.

On Hösök tér, you'll find the **Szepmuveszeti muzeum** (Museum of Fine Arts), displaying a fine collection of European drawings, one of the best collections of Spanish painting outside Spain, and works by Italian and Flemish masters. Not all the exhibits are open at once, so check the schedule ahead of time. Across the square lies the **Múcsarnok** (Art Gallery), where temporary exhibits of Hungarian and international art are mounted. Some of these are excellent; check with Tourinform or IBUSZ to see what's on. The **Millenium monument** on Hösök tér shows off 1000 years of Hungarian leaders and national heroes. The **Városliget** (City Park) behind the monument contains a permanent circus, an amusement park, and the Széchenyi Baths where you can play chess in the water.

If you are at all interested in Hungarian history, the **National Museum,** Muzeum körút 14-16, is an absolute must. Be sure to buy the English guidebook (15Ft), as most of the labels are in Hungarian. Set majestically by themselves in a huge room are the crown, scepter, and orb of the Hungarian kings (returned to Hungary from the United States in 1978). The **Jewish Museum,** Dohány u. 2, commemorates the history of Hungary's Jews. (Open April-Oct. Mon. and Thurs. 2-6pm, Tues. and

Fri. 10am-1pm.) The **Medieval Jewish Tabernacle** is at Táncsics Mihály u. 26. (Open April-Oct. Tues.-Fri. 10am-2pm, Sat.-Sun. 10am-6pm.)

If you're not going to get to Turkey, Budapest is the next best place for a Turkish bath. There are a number of medicinal baths, built during the 150 years of Turkish rule. Try the **Gellért** baths, XI, Kelenhegyi u. 4-6, or the **Hotel Thermal,** on Margit Island, for a bath and massage (usually about 50Ft). Women should check out a bath before going there, as sexual harassment has been known to occur. A reputable bath has both male masseurs and female masseuses, and will often have alternate days for the two sexes; **Király** bath, I, Fö u. 85, is one such.

Entertainment

Budapest is a city of concerts—both indoor and outdoor. The **Budapest State Opera** and the city's **Philharmonic Orchestra** are world famous. Look for performances under János Ferencsik, or attend the **Györ Balet,** directed by Ivor Markó. Performances are held in Budapest almost every evening from September through June. During the summer season, there are still plenty of opportunities to see a concert, theater, or opera performance, especially in one of the many open-air arenas. The **Hilton Hotel Courtyard** (opera); **Margitsziget Theater** (opera and Hungarian music concerts); **Zichy Mansion Courtyard,** III, Fö tér 1 (orchestral concerts); and the **Mátyás Cathedral** (organ and other recitals) are but a few of the many possibilities. Folk-dance performances are given at the **Buda Park Theater,** XI, Kosztolányi Dezsö tér. Tickets are cheap and available at box offices; the central booking office for all theater performances is at Népköztársaság u. 18. For open-air performances, try the ticket office at Vörösmarty tér 1.

The **Budapest Spring Festival,** in late March, provides an excellent chance to see the best in Hungarian art and music. **Budapest Music Weeks** (Sept. 25-Oct. 25) is another major music festival.

Hungary has an outstanding cinematic tradition; most notable among its directors are Miklós Jancsó (*The Round-Up, The Red and the White*) and István Szabó (*Mephisto, Colonel Redl*). Cinemas abound in Budapest, showing the latest Hungarian and foreign films. The English-language *Daily News* lists movies with an English soundtrack.

One popular student spot is the **Casino** on Margitsziget. The island is particularly alive from 10pm to 1am, when the strains of live rock music drift across the spas and fountains along the Danube.

The best student clubs are the **Vár Klub,** located at XI, Irinyi József u. 42; **MKKE Klub,** at Dimitrov tér 8 on the University of Economics campus; and the **"E" Klub,** situated at the Technical University. Despite their limited schedules in the summer, they are good places to meet Eastern European students. You have to become a member of the club in order to attend, but any university student can help you with the formalities.

Just about all of Budapest's happenings are listed in the monthly cultural guides, *Coming Events in Budapest* and *Programme in Hungary.* Both are available in any hotel or tourist office.

Danube Bend (Dunakanyar)

Forty kilometers north of Budapest, after its long trek east, the Danube makes a broad, sweeping turn to the south between the Börzsöny Mountains and the Visegrád Mountains. Known as the Danube Bend, this area is one of Hungary's most pleasant (and most touristed). The river's cool waters rush past green hills dotted with quaint old towns such as Szentendre, Visegrád, and Esztergom.

Boats leave Budapest daily at 6:45am, 7am, 7:30am, and 2pm from the Vigado tér dock, and steam upriver to Visegrád (3½ hr., 38Ft) and Esztergom (4½ hr., 46Ft), making short stops along the way. Tickets can be bought the day of departure, but avoid lines by buying a day in advance. For information and tickets contact

Dunatours, Bajcsy-Zsilinszky u. 17 (tel. 31 45 33), in Budapest. This office will also arrange hotel, hostel, and camping accommodations.

Boats on the Danube connect with towns served by bus and rail systems: the suburban railway (HEV) starts from the underground terminal in Bathyany tér and runs as far as Szentendre (14Ft), while buses from Engels tér serve all towns on both banks.

On the west bank appears the village of **Szentendre,** nestled in the foothills of the Visegrád Mountains. In the seventeenth century the town was setled by Serbian merchants and is today distinguished by a mixture of Serbian and Greek Orthodox architectural styles. This is most apparent in the **Blagovestenska Church** on the main square. Since the turn of the century, Szentendre has been an important artists' colony, with a unique, almost Mediterranean atmosphere. Exhibitions of previous and current art works are held at the **Kis Galéria** and the **Szentendre Picture Gallery** on Marx tér. The **Kovács Margit Muzeum,** on Washtagh György u., off Görög u., houses a unique collection of entertaining ceramic sculptures by twentieth-century Hungarian artist Margit Kovács. (Open Tues.-Sun. 9am-7pm. Admission 5Ft, students free.) Up the hill at the foot of the red tower of the Serbian Cathedral is a private collection of Serbian and Greek Orthodox religious art. (Admission 4Ft.) The **Czóbel Museum,** on top of Church Hill, exhibits the works of Hungarian impressionist painter Béla Czóbel. For bathing in the area, head for **Szentendre Island,** reached by ferry every 15 minutes. Dunatour's **Idegenforgalmi Hivatal,** Somogyi-Bacsó part 6 (tel. (26) 113 11), on the Danube, is both a tourist office and a room-finding service. (Open June-Aug. Mon.-Thurs. 8am-6pm, Fri. 8am-3:30pm, Sat. 8:30am-1:30pm, Sun. 9am-noon; Sept.-May Mon.-Fri. 8am-noon, closed Sat.-Sun. Singles 60-150Ft, doubles 120-320Ft.) The local **campground** is on Pap Island (tel. (26) 109 67). (Open May-Sept.)

A few kilometers upriver is the village of **Visegrád.** Walk (50 min.), hitch, or take a bus (10 min.) up the hill. The stone **fortress** at the top was constructed by King Béla IV to resist the Mongol onslaughts of the thirteenth century. The security afforded by this stronghold convinced the Anjou Kings of Hungary to build a **Royal Palace** just down the hill; the excavated remains of this legendary building at Fö u. give an idea of its former grandeur. In July the ruins are the site of a jousting tournament. Contact Dunatours for the exact dates. Visegrád offers inexpensive dining and lodgings. Hotels, with up to six beds in a room, are crowded in the summer, but cheap; the one at Széchenyi u. 7 is good. Get the local **tourist office,** Fö u. 3A (tel. (26) 283 30), to find you a hotel or private home; the latter is likely to be more comfortable. (Hotel rooms 100Ft. Rooms in private homes 200-250Ft.) There is a **campground** at the Mogyoró-hegy excursion center. (Tent and occupants 110Ft.) **Diofo Étterem,** Fö u. 59, on the embankment, is a good fish place popular with locals.

Esztergom, the capital of medieval Hungary, is home to some of the oldest and most magnificent monuments in the country. On **Várhegy** (Castle Hill), overlooking the Danube, are the remains of a once-magnificent Romanesque **Royal Palace.** The **cathedral**—you can't miss it—is the biggest in Hungary and the center of the country's Catholic church. The **treasure room** contains the coronation cross upon which all the kings of Hungary, the last one in 1916, swore their oath. (Admission 5Ft.) From the cupola you can look across the river into Czechoslovakia. The **Christian Museum,** at the foot of the hill, houses an exceptional collection of Hungarian and Italian religious artwork. The country-town atmosphere of this one-time capital city can be sensed at an early-morning **market** on Petöfi Sándor u. There are a number of parks on the island and an excellent restaurant with Danube fish specialties, **Úszófalu Halászcsárda.** The **Komtourist office** is at Széchenyi tér 13 (tel. 484). (Open Mon.-Fri. 7am-3:30pm, Sat. 7-11:30am.) The youth hostel **Hotel Fürdö** is at Bajcsy-Zsilinszky u. 14 (tel. 292; singles 230Ft, doubles 700Ft). For **camping,** go to the Vadvirág site on Bánomi dülö (tel. 174).

Györ

Halfway from Budapest to either Vienna or Bratislava lies Györ. A border garrison against the Turks, Györ was overrun more than once. The town took its present shape in the eighteenth and nineteenth centuries and today is Hungary's third-largest industrial town. Györ's expansive and well-preserved old town is now an enormous pedestrian zone.

From the train station, walk past the turn-of-the-century Jugendstil **town hall** and down Lenin út. Several blocks down at Alkatmány u. take a right to see the baroque **Széchenyi tér,** the former market place. Or go left to **Köztársaság tér** (Republic Square) and on to the Györ **cathedral.** The present market place on the river becomes a colorful bazaar Wednesday and Friday mornings. From the end of June to mid-July each year, Györ hosts theater, ballet, and musical performances during its **summer festival.**

A five-minute walk from the train station, the **IBUSZ** office, Tanácsköztársaság u. 29-31, can find you a private room. (Open Mon.-Wed. 8am-4pm, Thurs. 9am-6pm, Sat. 7am-1pm; singles 200Ft, doubles 300-360Ft.) **Ciklámen Tourist,** Aradi Vertanuk u. 22 (tel. 961 15 57 or 961 67 01) across from the town hall, can also help you in your room search. (Open Mon.-Wed. and Fri. 8am-4pm, Thurs. 10am-6pm, Sat. 8am-1pm.) Györ **camping,** at Kiskut-liget (tel. 189 86), has bungalows for 260Ft. Take bus #8 from the station.

In the dungeon of the sixteenth-century castle on Köztársaság tér, try the **Vaskarkas** (Iron Rooster) Tavern (meals 150Ft).

Sopron

Free from the noise and jumble of Budapest, the lovely town of Sopron, on the Austro-Hungarian border, is only a few hours by train from Vienna. Spared of invasion and occupation by the Turks, Sopron once served as Northern Europe's gateway to Byzantium and was thus an important military and commercial center. The old town lies in the circular area encompassed by **Lenin körút** and **Ogabona tér.** The heart of the old town is the **Fö tér,** where you'll find Sopron's distinctive **Fire Tower,** whose different sections trace the area's Roman, Norman, Renaissance, and baroque influences. The little streets off the Fö tér are all good areas to explore. At the far end of the inner city near Széchenyi tér is the **Franz (Ferenc) Liszt Palace of Culture,** where ancient Roman stone displays can be seen in a Gothic cellar. During the **Sopron Festival Weeks** (June-July), the town offers a wide range of opera, ballet, and concerts, some set in the nearby **Fertörákos Quarry** caverns.

The terminus for trains from Vienna is Gysev pu. From here walk up Mátyás Király út past Széchenyi tér to Lenin körút. The **IBUSZ** office is at Lenin körút 31 (tel. (99) 132 81). They can provide a town map, and book rooms in private homes. (Open Mon.-Fri. 7:30am-1pm and 1:30-4pm, Sat. 7:30am-12:30pm. Singles 200Ft, doubles 300Ft.) If IBUSZ can't help, try **Ciklámen Tourist,** Ogabona tér 8 (tel. 120 40), with brochures on the town and a supply of private rooms. (Open Mon.-Thurs. 7:30am-4pm, Fri.-Sat. 7:30am-8pm, Sun 8am-1pm.) If you arrive in the evening, go to the **Hotel Pannonia,** Lenin körút 75. They can change money and find you a room. The **Lövér Campground** is located at the south end of town, on Köszegi u. Take any bus going to the Lövér Szálló and ask the driver to let you off at the camping.

For traditional Hungarian cuisine in an unconventional setting, try **Szélmalom,** set on a hilltop with a great view. From Lenin körút walk down Otvos u., which becomes Magyar u., to Semmelweis u. (Live music after 8pm.) In a more pedestrian milieu, but with food just as good, is **Tramini,** a family-style restaurant on Lenin körút, two blocks from the IBUSZ office. Or try **Várkerület,** a block from the Pannonia Hotel on Lenin körút.

Near Sopron

Twenty kilometers from Sopron, in the small town of **Fertöd,** stands the magnificent rococo **Eszterházy Palace,** once the seat of the Holy Roman Empire and the place where Haydn produced most of his great works. In the castle's **Ceremonial Hall,** concerts are performed by an array of international musicians; check at the Sopron IBUSZ office for bus information and show times. Buses leave Sopron from the station on Lackner út about every 30 minutes (45 min., 28Ft).

Tucked in the shadows of ancient parapets and towers, **Köszeg** is an enchanting little town deep in the alpine foothills near the Austrian border. It is accessible by morning bus from Sopron, or from Budapest by train through Szombathely. Köszeg saw its heyday in the Middle Ages, when its castle played a crucial role in battles against Turkish invaders. Even today, Köszeg's central Jurisich tér retains its medieval cityscape; **St. James Church** is one of the country's most significant Gothic treasures. The green hills outside town are ideal for wandering and relaxing.

The **Savaria Tourist Office,** Várkör u. 5 (tel. 195), is on Köszeg's main square; walk up Rákóczi Ferenc from the train station. They'll place you in a private home (rooms 220Ft), or direct you to one of the town's two tourist motels (50Ft fee). **Irottkö Restaurant,** Köztársaság tér 4, is good, and **Kulacs Restaurant,** Beke u. 14, 1½ blocks from Irottkö, is better, but costs more.

Pécs

The extended Turkish occupation of Pécs has given it a Mediterranean flavor; note the minarets and former mosques. Before the arrival of the Turks, Pécs was home to Hungary's first university (1367), and today the city is known as the museum and cultural capital of Hungary.

For a city its size, Pécs encompasses a surprisingly wide range of religious traditions. On Kossuth tér you can visit the **synagogue,** while on Széchenyi tér is the **Mosque of Pasha Ghazi Kasim.** Originally the St. Bartholomew's church, this building was converted into a mosque in the sixteenth century and has now been reconverted. The beautifully restored romanesque Pécs **cathedral** completes this religious trilogy.

Pécs is a paradise for museum addicts. Birthplace of abstract pop artist Victor Vasarely, the town has a **Vasarely museum** (located between the Dom tér and Hunyadi út) filled with the artist's dizzying works. On Pannonius u., the **Csontváry museum** houses the work of native artist Tidvar Csontváry Kosztka. For something in the Kandinsky vein, try the **Martyn Ferenc museum,** just down the street from the Vasarely museum.

For a retrospective on Pécs try the **Jakowli Hassan museum,** Rakoczi u. 2, which documents the Turkish era of Pécs's history, or the **Varosörteneti és Munkasmozgalmi museum,** Felsö Malom u. 9, which covers the rest of the city's history and its workers' movement.

Mecsek Tourist, Széchenyi tér 9 (tel. 133 00), can arrange private accommodations (singles 120-160Ft) or put you up in one of its campsites (bungalows 250-450Ft, tents 65-90Ft; open Mon. 8:30am-4pm, Tues.-Fri. 8:30am-6pm, Sat. 8:30am-1pm). **IBUSZ,** Széchenyi tér 8 (tel. 121 48), also arranges private rooms (singles 150Ft, doubles 200-250Ft; open Mon.-Fri. 8am-4:30pm, Sat. 8am-noon).

The **Bástya Sörözö,** Landler Jenö út behind the cathedral, has good food and atmosphere, or try **Pizzeria Ételbár** on Hunyadi út just above Széchenyi tér.

Szeged

In Hungary Szeged conjures up images of salami, spicy fish soup, and sweet paprika. Thanks to a flood in 1879 which wiped out the city, almost everything had to be rebuilt. As a result, Szeged is Hungary's only planned city.

The grateful survivors of the flood decided to build the neo-romanesque **Votive Church** that dominates the city's skyline. Between July 20 and August 20 every year, this church is the backdrop for the town's open-air theater festival. Behind the Votive Church is the less imposing **Serbian Church** with its precious orthodox icons. In the center of town is **Széchenyi tér,** containing the yellow **town hall,** restored to its present eclectic form following the deluge. Walk along the Vörösmarty u. side of the square to see the lavish art nouveau **gyógyszertár** (pharmacy) building.

Szeged Tourist, Victor Hugo u. 1 (tel. 117 11), or on Klauzal tér, will find you private rooms (singles 105-150Ft, doubles 140-266Ft; open daily 9am-7pm). **IBUSZ,** Klauzal tér 2 (tel. 111 88), provides its usual services including room finding. **Express** is at Kígyó u. 3 (tel. 113 03).

Eger

Although much of eastern Hungary is a dusty plain, the northeast is a haven of rolling hills and vineyards. Eger, the country's red-wine capital, lies at the southern edge of this region, just a three-hour train ride from Budapest. The center of Eger is **Dobó István tér.** North of the square is one of the most famous historical monuments in all of Hungary, **Castle Eger.** Built following the 1241 Mongol invasion, this fortress was the site of the 1551 battle with the Ottomans in which István Dobó and his men turned back the Turkish invasion. Today, it is revered by most Hungarians as an ancient symbol of their pride and independence; inside, museum exhibits document the historical significance of the battle. (Undergoing renovations, but open May-Aug. Tues.-Sun. 7am-5pm.) Facing the castle, turn left down Dobó István u. until you see the graceful lines of the town's **minaret,** a remnant from the days of Turkish rule.

Despite Eger's historical significance, most foreigners know the city as the home of the wonderfully potent wine *Egri Bikavér.* The southern part of the town (walk through the **Népkert Park** and out Uttörö u.) shelters more than 2000 private wine cellars, as well as the large Borkatakomba State Wine Cellar. Ask for the restaurant **Ködmön** and sample the wine with *töltött borju,* a fine veal dish. In the center of town, the restaurant **Kazamata** is unbeatable for its wine list, fish dishes, and wonderful cave-like interior under Eger's neoclassical cathedral.

The bus and train stations are both within easy walking distance from the heart of town. From the train station, follow signs to *centrum;* reaching the end of Lenin út, turn right, then take the first left onto the main Széchenyi u. Just off this street, within the Bajcsy-tömb courtyard area, is the **IBUSZ** office (tel. (36) 114 51); they'll give you a map and find you a room in a hotel, bungalow, or private home. **Egertourist,** Bajcsy-Zsilinszky u. 9 (tel. (36) 117 24), and **Cooptourist,** Hibay Karoly u. 22 (tel. (36) 119 98), can also help you find a room. (Each should cost 150-250Ft.) **Buttler-Ház,** Kossuth Lajos u. 26 (tel. 228 86), offers hostel conditions. (Singles 50Ft, doubles 190Ft.) The nearest **campground** is 3km north of the city at Rákóczi u. 79; take bus #1a from the center. (Tent and occupants 30Ft. Open May-Sept.)

Near Eger

Eger's charm derives partly from its proximity to the **Bükk Mountains,** a small, densely forested range with a national park and numerous hiking trails. For camping, try the area at Szilvásvárad, near the beautiful Szalajka valley (open May-Sept.; 75Ft for tent and occupant). The IBUSZ or Egertourist office in Eger has information and maps.

Beyond the Bükks, near the Czechoslovak border, is the village of **Aggtelek.** Here, accessible by frequent bus from Eger and Miskolc, are the **Baradla Caves,** among the most spectacular in Europe. Hour-long tours start from Aggtelek and Jósvafo, about 6km east. Longer six-hour tours require a little more effort but are also more rewarding. With stalagmites reaching 25m and lakes 2km in length, the caves are overwhelming in size alone. The ornamental lights in some sections and the occasional performances held in the "Concert Hall" make this a fantastic natural sight. The local youth hostel, **Hotel Cseppkö,** can also be found at the caves, 3km from the Jósvafo-Aggtelek train station. (Doubles 280Ft.)

Northeast of Eger lies Hungary's other great wine town, **Tokaj.** Best reached by bus or rail via Miskolc, Tokaj is a pleasant side trip from one of the larger towns. Set upon a hill, the village is worthwhile for its warm, genuine atmosphere, lovely surroundings, and, of course, delicious golden wine. The abundance of wine cellars enables the visitor to sample the many varieties of *Tokaj*—if you're lucky, even the rare and expensive *Tokaj essencia.* **Borsod Tourist,** at Óvár u. 6, can provide both information and accommodations.

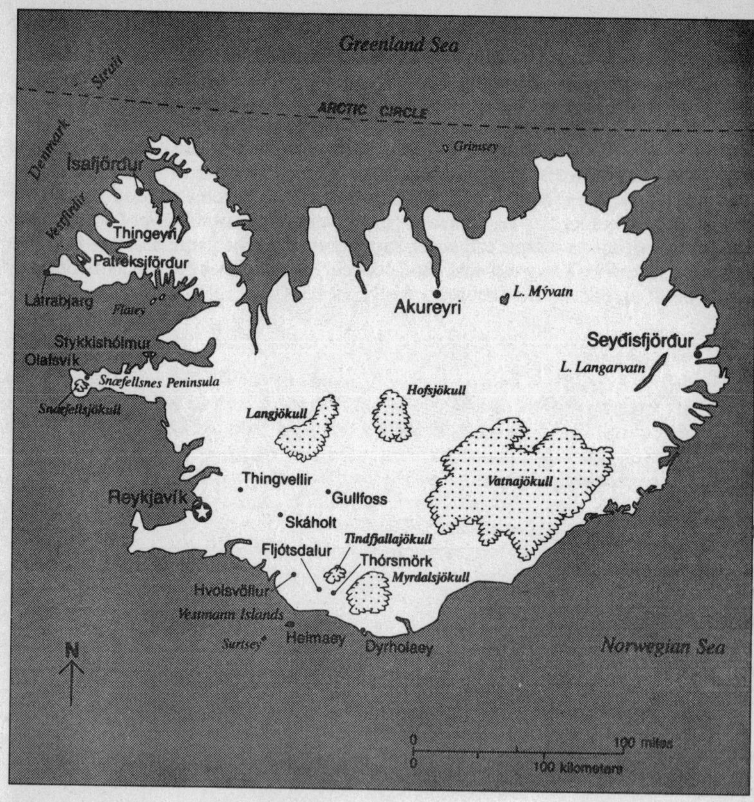

ICELAND

US$1 = 38.5 krónur (kr)
CDN 1 = 29.4 kr
UK£1 = 64.1kr
AUS $1 = 27.6kr

10kr = US$0.26
10kr = CDN$0.34
10kr = UK£0.16
10kr = AUS$0.36

Iceland is not a myth; it is a solid portion of the earth's surface.
—Pliny Miles, nineteenth-century traveler

Miles was wrong on both counts. Iceland's mythic landscape—crafted by the shifting plates of the mid-Atlantic ridge and weirdly backlit by the summer's perpetual sun—is one of Europe's best-kept secrets, kept safe by forbiddingly high prices. Arriving in Iceland is tantamount to landing on the moon; chances are you've not experienced anything like its weather, its scenery, or its expense.

Iceland's tumultuous geological history has left a legacy of unique natural beauty. Volcanoes stand decapitated in the northern Mývatn District. Glaciers carve gorges in the volcanic rock of the central desert. Frost and storms have splintered the coastline around Vestfirðir District. Eruptions nearly destroyed the Vestmann Islands only 12 years ago. And coffee costs more than a dollar a cup.

While Iceland's volcanoes were erupting, fuming Norwegians were fleeing the oppression of King Harold the Finehaired; they settled the island in 874, displacing a few Irish monks. Fifty-six years later, the settlers founded the Althing, the world's first legislature. Despite Norwegian and Danish rule, the Althing has met for over 1000 years, and remains a symbol of Iceland's strong egalitarianism. Independent since 1944, Iceland continues to be a political frontier, electing the world's first woman president in 1980. The Icelandic feminist party holds a strong position in Parliament. Tales of life during Iceland's early days are recorded in its sagas, epic stories transmitted orally for centuries; most were recorded in script by the end of the thirteenth century. *Njal's Saga, Grettir's Saga,* and the prose and poetic *Eddas* tell tales of bloody feuds, foreign wars, plague, and famine; the Icelandic literary tradition is carried on by Nobel laureate Halldór Laxness.

Getting There and Getting Around

Getting to Iceland is surprisingly easy. **Icelandair** (tel. (800) 223-5500 from U.S.) flies daily from New York, Baltimore, Boston, Chicago, and Orlando via Reykjavík to Luxembourg. The stopover in Iceland is free, and fares are competitive, though not the lowest. During peak-season (early June to mid-Aug.), round-trip APEX fares to Luxembourg range from US$599 from New York to US$669 from Orlando. Regular fares, for those who purchase fewer than 21 days in advance or stay in Europe more than 90 days, are about US$100 more. Icelandair does not have service from Canada, nor any standby fares that allow stopovers in Iceland. From late May to early September the **Smyril Line** ferry *Norröna* sails weekly between Seyđisfjörđur (Eastern Iceland), the Faeroe Islands, the Shetland Islands, Bergen (Norway), and Hanstholm (Denmark). Fares vary (Denmark-Iceland about US$200 one way), but it's best to buy the ticket all the way to your final destination. For information and prices, contact Smyril Line (in Iceland: Skógarhlid 6, Reykjavík (tel. (91) 258 55); in Denmark: Kronprinsesse Sofies Vej 23, DK-2000 Copenhagen (tel. (01) 87 30 00); in Norway: Engelgården, Nye Bryggen, N-5000 Bergen (tel. (05) 32 09 70).

Travel within Iceland is slow unless you fly, and very expensive unless you hitch. For hitchers, sparse traffic, bad roads, and capricious weather can be heartbreaking. Problems are somewhat alleviated in summer, when fellow travelers stop frequently, but even when they stop, they are usually not traveling far. The coastal Highway #1, a two-lane road of some 1000 miles, circles the island. Roads are relatively safe for cycling as traffic is light. Hitchers and cyclists alike should absolutely avoid the unpaved and virtually untraveled roads of the interior. Bicycles can be hired at **Tjaldaleigan** (Rent-a-Tent), Hringbraut (tel. 130 72), by the bus station in Reykjavík. (Open Mon.-Fri. 10am-noon and 1-6pm, Sat.-Sun. 10am-2pm and 6-8pm.) Information on road conditions is available from the **Vegagerd Rikisins** (Highway Department), Borgartun 5-7, 105 Reykjavík (tel. (91) 210 00).

Next to hitching and cycling, the cheapest way to travel around Iceland is by public bus. The 420-kilometer trip to Akureyri, for example, is about 1500kr. Buses connect most major Icelandic towns, though not always very frequently. They are comfortable, but slow (Reykjavík-Akureyri, 9 hr.; Reykjavík-Ísafjörđur, 13 hr.); in remote regions, more agile, compact Rovers are used. Be careful, as sporadic schedules can leave you stranded for days—especially in the off-season (Sept. to mid-June). An **Omnibus Passport** entitles you to a specified period of unlimited travel on all inter-city and municipal buses (1 week 5800kr, 2—7500kr, 3—9600kr, 4—10,800kr). The **Full Circle Passport** (4800kr) is good from June through mid-September and allows you to circle the island at your own pace, though you must remain on Highway #1. You cannot, for example, use it to visit the western fjords. Both passes entitle users to 10-15% discounts at campgrounds, youth hostels, and on ferries. Contact the bus station in Reykjavík, or write to BSI-Travel, BSI-Bus Terminal, Vatnsmýrarveg 10, Reykjavík, Iceland.

Don't even think about renting a car in Iceland. Rates begin at 1200kr per day plus 12kr per kilometer plus 23.5% sales tax.

The only really quick way to travel in Iceland is by propeller plane; Icelandair laces the country with frequent flights. One-way connections can cost three or four times the bus fare, but flight packages make this extravagance more feasible. An **Air Rover Ticket** (30 days, 9400kr) covers the route Reykjavík-Ísafjörður-Akureyri-Egilsstaðir-Höfn-Reykjavík in any order. Icelandair also offers a variety of other special discounts. If you paid full fare for your ticket to Iceland, all domestic flights are free. If your ticket is already a discounted fare, you receive a 33% discount on all internal flights (though only one discounted return trip), provided you buy these tickets at the same time as your ticket to Iceland. This only applies to those whose final destination is Iceland, not those on a stopover. Another offer is the **Iceland Airpass**—four flight coupons for 5000kr. Students are entitled to 25% off, and standby tickets (50% reduction) are sold 30 minutes before departure. The **Air/Bus Rover** allows you to ride one way to a destination and fly the other (Reykjavík-Akureyri 3607kr). In the winter, Icelandair offers several package tours with hotel accommodations in Reykjavík.

Although safe, propeller plane flight in Iceland is not for anyone with even a slight fear of flying. Whimsical weather may ground your flight at any time. Do not fly to the Vestmann Islands or the western fjords the day before you are to leave Iceland—you might get stuck overnight.

Although it requires time, the cheapest and most rewarding way to see Iceland is to hike. Well-defined trails are rare, but almost any area of the country is suitable for walking. Spartan huts scattered throughout the interior are marked on most maps, and can provide refuge from the unpredictable and often severe weather. Never venture out without a four-season sleeping bag, a sturdy, wind-resistant, waterproof tent, more provisions than you think you'll need, a compass, and an accurate, detailed map. A 1:250,000 map of the particular region in which you are traveling is recommended; a 1:1,000,000 map is sufficient for planning your trip. Both are readily available from tourist offices, travel agencies, newsstands, or at bus and air terminals. Broad valleys with rivers draining from glaciers are often impossible to cross—the streams change in course and depth from day to day, snow and ice are present year-round, and the interior is sparsely populated. Before departing Reykjavík, leave an itinerary with the tourist office or **The Society for the Prevention of Accidents** (Slysavarnafèlag Islands), Gradagarđi 14 (tel. 27000). In emergencies call the **Life-Saving Association** at (91) 111 50.

These concerns make travel with one of Iceland's several excellent tour groups an attractive option. Four of the best are: **Outdoor Life Tours** (Útivist), Lækjargata 6a, Reykjavík (tel. 146 06); the **Icelandic Touring Club** (Ferđafélag Islands), Öldugötu 3, Reykjavík (tel. 195 33); and the England-based **Dick Phillips,** Whitehall House, Nenthead, CA9 3PS, England (tel. (498) 814 40), or **Fljótsdal,** Fljótshlíđ, 801 Ranga, Iceland (tel. (99) 984 98). All four specialize in week-long hiking and riding tours. Dick Phillips integrates Icelanders and Europeans in an eight-day riding tour of the Loneburg plateau for about 17,550kr. Útivist tours are often much shorter and much cheaper (as little as 1560kr, as short as one day). To join an organized tour, talk to the people at **Sagaland Travel Agency,** Lautasvegur 2, 101 Reykjavík (tel. 271 44). The best guidebook on Iceland is David Williams's *Iceland: The Visitor's Guide.*

Practical Information

The weather in Iceland, especially the rain, is a decisive ingredient in the island's mystique; it is also the scourge of hikers, campers, walkers, indeed anyone who sets foot outside. Summer and winter, Icelandic weather is utterly unpredictable. Fortunately, it is confined within a fairly narrow and endurable range; the Gulf Stream keeps the mercury from traveling far below freezing or much beyond 60°F. The month of July tends to be the warmest, and hence, the best month to travel. Bring watertight, lightweight clothing that can be layered according to temperature. Rain jacket, woolen sweaters, and sturdy shoes are a must any time of the year. Finally, carry a bathing suit with you at all times, as the warm springs are great for swimming year-round.

The midnight sun is a dazzling part of the eerie, other-worldly effect Iceland manages to conjure. Darkening at an infinitely slow pace, the sky passes through hues not seen farther south. Only the northern half of the island is subject to truly perpetual sunlight during the summer. In Reykjavík, the sun does dip below the horizon for several hours (between about 3am and 5am), even on the summer solstice (June 21). Similarly, the darkness in winter breaks between about 11am and 3pm.

The **Iceland Tourist Bureau,** at Reykjanesbraut 6, Reykjavík (tel. 258 55), near the bus station, is supplemented by a network of independent local tourist offices in nearly every substantial town, as well as an ever-growing number of youth hostels which are excellent sources of information. Tourist offices produce a flood of tourist brochures in English, all free. The most comprehensive is *Around Iceland.* Pick up yours when you arrive.

The Icelandic language is part of the Northern Germanic family, but it has changed little in 1000 years due to isolation; it is not easily understood, even by other Scandinavians. Fortunately, most Icelanders speak English and often several other foreign languages.

On Independence Day (June 17), festivals occur all over Iceland—the best of them in Reykjavík. Regular business hours in Iceland are Monday through Friday from 9am to 6pm and Saturday from 9 or 10am until noon. Many shops are closed Saturday; all but cafes and newsstands are closed Sunday. Banks are open Monday through Friday from 9:15am to 4pm, Thursday until 6pm, and are closed Saturday and Sunday.

All post offices and youth hostels will hold mail. International calls may be made at telephone offices (usually connected to post offices), or by dialing 90 (09 for operator assistance) and then the country code. The **country code** for Iceland is 354. An **ambulance** can be summoned at any time by dialing 111 00 (in Hafnarfjörður, 511 00). A **doctor** can be reached at 812 00 (8am-5pm); after hours call a **hospital** at 212 30 (Reykjavík, Kópavogur, and Seltjarnarnes), 513 28 (Hafnarfjörður, Gardabaer, and Bessastadahr), or 66 62 01 (Mosfellssveit). Finally, remember that you must have your original exchange receipt to reconvert leftover cash.

Not only is Iceland the most expensive country in this book, it also suffers high inflation. Prices quoted should be 20-30% higher by 1988.

Accommodations and Camping

There are about 70 organized campsites in Iceland—a list is available at most tourist offices, travel agencies, and hostels. They charge 80kr per person and 80kr per tent, and are, for the most part, located in sizable towns where free camping is illegal. In the countryside, you may camp anywhere without charge; however, if you want to camp on fenced property, Icelandic law and common courtesy require that you get permission from the landowners. Occasionally, a sign reading *Tjaldstoedi bonnud* will tell you that camping is forbidden. Two formidable problems face campers in Iceland. The first is the weather: Iceland's polar winds and chilling rain can quickly cave in an exposed tent. Second, you cannot build a campfire; Iceland has no firewood and it is illegal to burn any of the sparse vegetation. You can rent all kinds of camping gear (from a gas stove at 180kr per day to a 4-person tent at 400kr per day) from **Tjaldaleigan** on Hringbraut directly across from the bus station in Reykjavík (tel. 130 72; open Mon.-Fri. 9am-noon and 1-6pm, Sat. 10am-2pm). You can save on the camping gear if you buy either a Full-Circle Ticket or an Omnibus Passport. For smaller camping items, try **Sport Magasin** on Óðinsgata.

There are 19 **IYHF youth hostels** (*farfuglaheimli*), usually of the highest quality. All provide hot showers and cooking facilities. (Members 370kr, nonmembers 470kr.) The more remote hostels close sporadically, so call ahead. The second option is the network of 14 **hotel eddas,** closed schools which provide *svefnpokapláss* (sleeping-bag accommodations) for 450kr-600kr from mid-June through August. Hotel eddas usually provide all the facilities of a well-equipped hostel. Many **farms** rent spare rooms to travelers. These accommodations vary in quality, but most are as comfortable as hostels or hotel eddas (around 750kr, breakfast included). The comprehensive *Hosteling in Iceland* and *Icelandic Farm Holidays* are available at most travel agencies in Reykjavík. If you come in the winter, be warned that few hostels and hotels remain open.

Food

Grocery stores and bakeries have to be the basic source of food for a shoestring traveler in Iceland, but even in these, prices are a drain on one's budget. **Kaupfélagid** is Iceland's bargain supermarket. Seafood is predictably the least expensive commodity. A meal of haddock still costs less than 120kr, and the habit-forming sardines and herring are only 40kr a tin. Icelandic specialties are good buys and deserve to be tried. *Skyr,* a milk product, is thicker and less tangy than yogurt. *Harðfiskur,* dried haddock, tastes better than it smells; Icelanders often eat it with butter. Among reasonably priced baked goods is the unavoidable Scandinavian flatbread. Purchase of a cup of coffee usually allows unlimited refills. Tipping is unnecessary and indeed tantamount to an insult.

There is a ban on all alcoholic beer in Iceland, and no pubs exist. Keflavík International Airport has a duty-free shop where you are allowed to buy 12-24 cans of Icelandic Polar Bear, or 6 liters of imported beer. Wine and liquor are served in restaurants and may also be purchased in state liquor stores (open Mon.-Fri. 9am-noon and 1-6pm). You must be over 20 to purchase alcohol in Iceland.

Reykjavík

The northernmost capital in the world, Reykjavík is not just the smoky bay suggested by its Icelandic name. Brightly painted roofs alternate with colorful shop windows, and children feed ducks and swans in the city's intimate lake, Tjörnin. Tucked under snow-striped Esjufjall, the city looks across Faxa Bay to jagged rows of black cliffs and shadowy mountains farther inland. Neither a bustling metropolis nor a village, Reykjavík is the seat of Iceland's only university, home to half its population, and its window to the outside world.

Orientation and Practical Information

International flights arrive at Keflavík Airport, 50km southwest of Reykjavík. **Loftleider** buses, which meet each flight, connect this airport with the Hotel Loftleider at Reykjavík Airport, from which intra-Icelandic flights depart (170kr or US$5 currency accepted). There, pick up a city map, and proceed into town either by hourly city bus #5 (28kr) or on foot (20 min.). The route leads down **Hringbraut,** past the national tourist office to Sóleyjargata, then past the lake (Tjörnin) to the center of town. Hitching all the way from the international airport is possible in good weather, but is not always the best idea; you may be stranded with no prospect of catching a bus for 24 hours.

Many flights leave Keflavík at shockingly early hours. Buses run from the Hotel Loftleider two hours before each scheduled departure. As city buses to the hotel may not run early enough, you may need to walk or arrange the day before for an early-morning cab to the hotel.

Tourist Offices: Municipal, in a booth at Austurstræti and Lækjartorg (tel. 100 44), at the beginning of the pedestrian street and marked "i." For Reykjavík and all Iceland. Comprehensive city-bus route map. Open July-Aug. Mon.-Fri. 9am-5pm, Sat. 10am-2pm; Sept.-June Mon.-Fri. only. **Ferðaskrifstofa Ríkisins** (Iceland Tourist Bureau), Skógarhlíð 6 (tel. 258 55), not far from the entrance roads to the municipal airport. Iceland's national tourist office. Free lists of hostels, hotels, restaurants, transportation schedules, and maps. Accommodations service. Books organized tours. Open June-Aug. Mon.-Fri. 8am-6pm, Sat.-Sun. 8am-2pm; Sept.-May Mon.-Fri. 9am-5pm.

Budget Travel: Iceland Student Travel, Hringbraut (tel. 168 50), next door to the National Museum. Discount plane, boat, and bus tickets. 25% off domestic and international flights with ISIC.

American Express: Útsýn Tourist Agency, Austurstræti 17 (tel. 266 11). Mail held. Traveler's checks cashed after banking hours. No wired money accepted. Open Mon.-Fri. 9am-5pm.

Currency Exchange: Banks open Mon.-Wed. and Fri. 9:30am-4pm, Thurs. 9:30am-6pm.

Post Office: Póstur, Pósthússtræti 5 (tel. 260 00), in the center of town. Open Mon. 8am-5pm, Tues.-Fri. 9am-5pm, Sat. 8am-3pm. Branch at the bus station open Mon.-Fri. 9am-7pm.

Telephones: Símstöðin, Austurvöllur Sq., in the city center. Also telegrams. Open Mon.-Sat. 9am-7pm, Sun. 11am-6pm. **Telephone code:** 91.

Flights: Flugvöllur, Keflavík Airport, for international flights. **Reykjavík Airport** (domestic), beside Hotel Loftleider, behind bus station off Hringbraut (tel. 251 00 or 266 22 for reservations; tel. 260 11 for flight information). You can't get to the airport from the hotel, but must either walk around to Thoragata (25 min.) or take bus #5 or 17.

Buses: Umferðarmiðstöðin, Hringbraut (tel. 223 00), near the domestic airport. Handles all long-distance bus service. Terminal open daily 7:30am-11pm. Luggage storage open Mon.-Fri. 7:30am-9:30pm, Sat. 7:30am-2:30pm; 28kr per day, 64kr per week (cheaper at the Laufásvegur hostel).

Public Transportation: Strætisvagnar Reykjavíkur. (S.V.R.). Fare 28kr. The driver can give you a free transfer good for 45 min. Service Mon.-Fri. 7am-midnight, Sat. 7am-1am, Sun. 10am-midnight.

Taxis: BSR, Lækjargata 4b (tel. 117 20).

Emergencies: Police (tel. 111 66). **Ambulance** (tel. 111 00).

Medical Assistance: Borgarspítalinn, Slyadeild (tel. 812 00). Take bus #7 from Lækjartorg.

Embassies: U.S., Laufásvegur 21 (tel. 291 00). **Canada,** Skúlgata 20 (tel. 253 55). **U.K.,** Laufásvegur 49 (tel. 158 83). Travelers from **Australia** and **New Zealand** should contact the British embassy.

Bookstores: Fornbókaverslunin, Laufásvegur 4. English books and used paperbacks for half-price. **Almenna Bókafélagið,** on Austurstræti. The town's largest. Has detailed maps for hiking and driving. Both open Mon.-Thurs. 9am-6pm, Fri. 9am-7pm, Sat. 9am-2pm; in winter Sat. 9am-noon.

Women's Alliance (*Kvennalistinn),* Vallarstræti 4 (tel. 137 25). Meeting place for feminist and lesbian groups. Open Mon.-Fri. 2-6pm.

Laundry: Called *thvoltahúsið.* Try Thvoltahúsið Fönn, Skelfunni 11, (tel. 822 20).

Hitchhiking: Take bus #10 to the eastern edge of town.

Accommodations and Camping

Hostels in Reykjavík are friendly and cozy, and offer by far the cheapest beds in town. Hotel prices are steep: at least 1600kr for a single and 2200kr for a double. Rooms in private homes are available at the tourist office for 1250-1800kr.

Reykjavík Youth Hostel (IYHF), Laufásvegur 41 (tel. 249 50), in the center. From the domestic airport, walk along Flugvallarbraut, turn left on Hringbraut and then right on Laufásvegur. Social life centers around the well-equipped kitchen. The warden offers travel advice, sells tours of the countryside, rents bikes, changes traveler's checks, and stores luggage (10kr per piece per day, 40kr per week). Members 370kr, nonmembers 470kr. Required sheets 90kr. Open mid-Jan. to mid-Dec. 8-11am and 4-11pm.

Reykjavík Youth Hostel (IYHF), Sundlaugavegur 34 (tel. 381 10), farther from the center. A new hostel, tends to have more families and kids. Members 370kr, nonmembers 470kr. Required sheets 90kr. Open late May-early Jan.

Salvation Army Guest House (Gestaheimilið), Kirkjustræti 2 (tel. 133 03), 1 block north of the lake adjacent to the center of town. Friendly and airy. Singles 800kr, doubles 1100kr, triples 1300kr. Six-bed rooms 300kr per person with sleeping bag, 400kr without.

Camping: (tel. 869 44), a 25-min. walk from the city center. Walk up Lækjargata toward the harbor until you come to Skúlgata. Walk along Skúlgata to Borgartun (about 1 mile); the campground is on the right, just past the swimming pool. Alternatively, take bus #5. Comfortable, convenient, and cheap. Hot running water, electrical outlets, and adjacent to the city's best swimming pool. 80kr per person plus 80kr per tent. No reservations accepted. Open May-Sept.

Food

More so than in other cities, local specialties will help you save money in Reykjavík. Oranges are a splurge, while caviar is a staple. Typical dishes include *svið* (the meat from the sheep's head), *hangikjöt* (hang-dried meats), and *kinnir* (the fleshy meat from fish cheeks). You can pick up these delicacies at **Tómas,** Laugavegur 2, a small local shop, or at the **Kaupfélagið** supermarket at Skeifunni 15. There is a market, **Viður,** and several good bakeries on Austrustræti, and a healthfood store, **Korn Markaðurinn,** on Klapparstígur.

Svarta Pannan, Hafnarstræti 17. Locals congregate to eat fish (140kr) and fries (60kr) while enjoying a view of the harbor. Open daily 11am-11:30pm.

Jurtafaedi af Matastofa N.I.F.I., Laugavegur 20b. A vegetarian haven on a side street; cafeteria meals 250-350kr. Open Mon.-Fri. noon-2pm and 6-8pm.

Restaurant Hornid, Hafnarstræti 15. Beautiful food for beautiful people. Pizza from 340kr, omelettes 320kr. Open daily 9am-11:30pm.

Hef-Inn Restaurant, Laugavegur 74. Clean cafe. Salad from 100kr, soup 120kr. Near many other restaurants. Open daily 10am-10pm.

Café Hressó, Austurstræti. Chic and flashy, but a centrally located place to people-watch. Coffee 70kr, soup 120kr. Open daily 8:30am-11:30pm.

Sights and Entertainment

Treasured fragments of the world of the sagas are housed in the **Thjóðminjasafnið** (National Museum), on Hringbraut at its junction with Suðurgata, just off the southern edge of the lake. The museum packs a millenium of history into a few well-arranged rooms on two floors—from the disintegrating iron swords of the tenth-century Norse settlers to models of boats from the heroic fishing age of the nineteenth century. The second floor of the museum serves as Iceland's **National Gallery of Art,** which displays works by contemporary Icelandic artists. (Both open June-Aug. daily 1:30-4pm; Sept.-May Tues., Thurs. and Sat.-Sun. 1:30-4pm. Free.) The audacious, organ-shaped **Hallgrímskirkja** (Hallgrims Church) dominates both the hill at the top of Skólavörðustígur and Reykjavík's cityscape. The church has been under construction since World War II. Calder's statue just outside depicts Leif Eyríksson riding imaginary waves in his marble ship. From the tower there is a spectacular view of Mount Esja and Reykjavík's green and red rooftops. (Open Tues.-Sat. 10am-noon and 2-6pm, Sun. 2-6pm. Admission 100k.)

Farther from the center but definitely worth a visit are two open-air museums. The large, contemporary sculptures of Asmundur Sveinsson are on display in the garden and workshop at **Asmundarsafn.** (Open Tues, Thurs., and Sat. 2-4pm; garden open 24 hours.) Old Icelandic houses, some not larger than a room, illustrate the country's history at **Arbær Open-Air Museum.** (Take bus #10. Open June-Aug. Tues.-Sun. 1:30-6pm; Sept.-May exteriors only.)

Stopping at one of Reykjavík's **swimming pools** is a must. As you enjoy the hedonistic pleasures of warm water and steam, you'll be exposing yourself to an integral part of Icelandic culture: Swimming is a ritual here. Icelanders use the pools year-round; underground hot springs heat the water even in the dead of winter. **Breiðholti** is one of the most popular swimming complexes. (Open Mon.-Fri. 7:30am-8:30pm, Sat. 7:30am-5:30pm, Sun. 8am-5:30pm. Admission 45kr. Towels and suits 60kr.) **Icelandic sweaters** are cheaper here than in most parts of the world, but will still cost you around 2000kr. Hafnarstræti has the largest concentration of stores. Shop around. For a unique audio-visual experience go to the **Volcano Show;** the show presents over two hours of documentary films on Iceland's volcanoes and landscape, as well as commentary by the filmmaker. (Tues-Sat. 8pm. Admission 350kr, no discounts.)

Near Reykjavík

Even if you have only two days in Iceland, you ought to get out of Reykjavík. Iceland's countryside is probably like nothing you've ever seen: Within a day's trip from the city lie monumental glaciers, basalt caves, jagged fjords, historical and saga sites, lakes, and exotic wildlife. Organized tours can be arranged through most travel agents, tourist offices, and hostel wardens, a good option for those short on time and long on money—one-day tours cost at least 1500kr.

Thingvellir, an hour's drive east of Reykjavík, provides spectacular evidence of the continuing evolution of Iceland. Here plates pull apart to create the **Almannagjá Valley.** It was in 930, on the sheer basalt cliffs bordering this valley, that Iceland's first settlers created the **Althing,** their famous open-air parliament. Thingvellir makes a good base for hiking explorations of the Icelandic countryside and for row-boat rides on windy **Lake Thingvellir.** (Open mid-May to mid-Sept.) The **Thingvellir National Park** runs an attractively situated campground from which you can climb extinct volcanoes for spectacular views. (First night 160kr, each additional night 100kr. Open early May-early Sept.) The park has an **information center** (tel. (99) 26 25; open June-Aug. daily 9am-11:30pm). The National Park staff offers free guided hikes Wed.-Mon. 9am-8pm. According to the legend, witches were drowned in the waterfalls **Drekkingarhulur** and **Thingvallar** nearby. A public bus leaves the Reykjavík bus station for Thingvellir at 2pm each day, and begins the return trip at 5pm (190kr one way).

Gizur the White, chieftain of **Skálholt,** converted Iceland to Christianity. The resulting literacy gave rise to the Icelandic sagas. A place for learning, Skálholt was the seat of the main bishopric in Iceland from 1056 to 1800. The present concrete **church** dates from 1962 and takes the place of legendary churches three times its size. The crypt houses Bishop Páll Jonsson's stone coffin, mentioned in the thirteenth-century sagas and unearthed in 1954. Skálholt organizes a series of summer concerts in July and August, and operates a summer hotel. Food and coffee are served all day in the **school house** (tel. (99) 68 71 or 68 70). Regular buses to Skálholt leave from Reykjavík daily at 9am and 1pm (360kr).

An ideal base for exploring the surrounding geothermal region is **Laugarvatn** (Hot Spring Lake). You may swim in the lukewarm waters of the lake, but you *must* try the free **sauna,** next to the beach, which is nothing but a wooden shelter built over the hot spring. (Open Mon.-Fri. 11am-9pm, Sat.-Sun. 10am-noon.) A 10-kilometer hike northeast of Laugarvatn leads to the steaming plumes around **Geysir,** etymological parent of this geological phenomenon. Geysir itself, which can shoot as high as 60m, has been inactive for years, but is sometimes made to spout through the addition of soap, a trick that breaks the surface tension of the water. These eruptions are announced in the papers and tourist offices. The smaller **Strokkur** nearby, reputedly the world's most active geyser, spouts every 10 minutes. Right opposite Geysir, the **Hotel Geysir** (tel. (99) 69 20), has sleeping-bag accommodations (400kr). On Saturdays and Sundays, the hotel's restaurant features a delicious Icelandic smørgåsbord for 350kr. Buses to Gullfoss and Geysir via Skálholt leave Reykjavík's bus station daily at 9am and 11:30am, returning from Gullfoss at 2:30pm and 5pm (3½ hr., 900kr round-trip). The unlikely by-product of a geothermal plant, the **Blue Lagoon** lies near Keflavík on the Reykjanes Peninsula. A dip in its steaming waters offers solace to the skin (100kr). Buses leave Reykjavík at 10:30am and 6:30pm, returning at 1pm and 9pm (1 hr.; 380kr round-trip).

Snæfellsness Peninsula

This long, thin arm of Iceland juts to the west, 120km north of Reykjavík. It is a region of small fishing villages, gentle mountains, and tasty mineral springs. In the sixteenth century, bishop Oddur Einarsson wrote about Snæfellsness's naturally carbonated waters, comparing them with fine ale. The largest and most famous spring, **Raudamelur,** lies off the main Snæfellsness road. Turn right past the Haffjardara River; the spring is a 15-minute walk from the road. **Snæfellsjökull,** an extinct conical volcano, watches over the peninsula from its western tip. Known in the sagas as the den of Bardi the half-troll, Snæfellsjökull was more recently immortalized as the entrance point to the inner world in Jules Verne's *Journey to the Center of the Earth.* Should you wish to attempt a similar journey, take the bus to **Ólafsvík,** right below the cone. Buses leave Reykjavík Monday through Thursday at 9am, Friday and Sunday at 7pm, and Saturday at 1pm; the bus from Ólafsvík to Reykjavík leaves daily at 5:30pm (830kr one way). For bus information in Ólafsvík, call (93) 63 12.

To climb the mountain, walk back along the road east of town. Cross the gate past the "Ólafsvík Verið Velkomin" sign and turn right up a dirt road. This becomes a narrower path and continues across the peninsula toward its southern shore. When the ice cap is clearly visible on the right, climb over gradual lava slopes and snow to the summit. The not-so-steep walk takes about three hours. You'll probably have to spend the night in Ólafsvík; the campground is just outside the town.

To the east, accessible by bus from Reykjavík and Ólafsvík, lies **Stykkishólmur,** near Helgafell. (Bus from Reykjavík 740kr one way.) The grand **Norwegian House,** built in 1828, is one of the oldest buildings in Iceland. From Stykkishólmur, you can catch the ferry *M.S. Baldur* north to the western fjords. The fare to Brjánslækur is 600kr and includes a stop on the island of Flatey. Schedules vary daily and seasonally, so check at Skipagerð Ríkisins in Reykjavík (tel. 288 22) before setting out. (In Stykkishólmur call (93) 81 20, in Brjánslækur call (94) 20 20.)

Western Fjords (Vestfirðir)

Reaching into the Greenland Sea like a ragged claw, Vestfirðir is Iceland's most isolated coastal region. Inlets mirror rugged cliffs veined with snow, and wooly rams graze on verdant slopes. The western fjords may be everything you came to Iceland to see. The only problem is getting there.

Buses connect Reykjavík and Vestfirðir (in summer 2 per week, 13 hr., 1850kr one way). The ride winds along the rugged northern shore, and is a spectacular and efficient way of seeing the fjords. Flights (2 per day, 2120kr one way) are no less spectacular, but much briefer (40 min.). Once you reach the fjords, you will still be at the mercy of infrequent buses if you want to see the outlying areas. Hitching is slow.

If you seek a secluded peninsula, make a trip to **Ísafjörður,** a fishing port walled in by the cliffs of Eyrarfell and Ernir. The airport is 5km from town across the shallow bay, and accessible by bus (80kr) or thumb. Cheap accommodations here are limited. The **hótel edda, Ísafjörður** (tel. (94) 41 11), has sleeping-bag accommodations for 600kr. In winter, there is skiing at **Paradis Skidamanna.** From mid-January through April, you can stay at the *svefnpokapláss.* Four kilometers south of town, at Tungadalur, there is free **camping** in a valley surrounded by waterfalls. The campground features restrooms, hot water, and buses to town twice daily. (Open mid-June to Aug.) There is a **Kaupfélagið** (supermarket) in the center of town, in addition to several restaurants.

Ísafjörður is an ideal starting point for exploring the region's stunning scenery. Though busy, the **tourist bureau,** Hafnarstræti 4 (tel. (94) 35 57), will bend over backward for you. An 11-hour boat tour of the **Ísafjarðarjúp** fjord system (tel. (94) 42 00) leaves at 8am every Tuesday (June to mid-Oct., 1300kr). A five-hour abridged version leaves Friday at 8am (650kr). You can hop from Suðureyi to Holt to Thingeyri to Patreksfjörður aboard **Ernir Aviation Company's** mail plane. (Departures Mon.-Fri. at 10am, 1700kr.) The tourist office can help you combine boat and bus along the fjords. The only way to get directly from Ísafjörður to Akureyri is by plane (a whopping 3622kr each way); to take the bus, you must backtrack as far as Borgarnes.

Thingeyri is about 70km south of Ísafjörður, along a gravelly road, which rises around the calm and hilly Dýrafjörður. A half-hour walk from town is **Sandar,** a cone-shaped mountain of brown rock; it's very steep, but the ascent is safe and quick. At the summit a compass identifies all the highest peaks in the vicinity. During the summer, sleeping-bag accommodations are available at **Núpsskólin** (tel. (94) 82 53), an old school on the north side of Dýrafjöður. You may camp for free in the protected area in inner Dýrafjörður or stay at a renovated farmhouse (tel. (94) 82 29).

Patreksfjörður derives its name from St. Patrick, bishop of the Hebrides, whose foster son landed here at the time of Iceland's settlement. The fishing town presides over the westernmost fjords, looking over a broad inlet toward gentle mountains and winding sandy rivers. Stay at **Gistihús Erlu,** Urðargata 2 (tel. (94) 12 27), or at the campsite just out of town. The imposing cliffs of **Látrabjarg,** 50km west of Patreksfjörður, fall away to an oceanic wilderness that extends all the way to the Arctic. The isolated settlement of **Breidavik**—12km from Látrabjarg and 50km from Patreksfjörður—overlooks a beautiful golden bay. It has a **youth hostel (IYHF)** (tel. (94) 11 00) and a **farm** (tel. (94) 15 75) that offer sleeping-bag accommodations and serve breakfast and other meals. Call before hitching out; traffic is naturally very light on this dead-end road. When you make it, you'll be rewarded by the sight of the black gulls and black-throated geese that reel around the cliffs of Iceland's westernmost point.

Akureyri and the Mývatn District

Set at the head of the imposing Eyjafjörður, hugged by ice-topped basalt mountains, Akureyri lies in one of Iceland's most fertile valleys. Although the country's second city is 150km nearer the pole than Reykjavík, days tend to be warmer and drier here. Akureyri is a good base for touring the north and, in particular, the active volcanic region of Lake Mývatn, 100km to the east.

Akureyri is relatively easy to reach. It is the northernmost stop for traffic on Highway #1, and buses connect it with Reykjavík. (1 per day, 9 hr., 1500kr one way.) Hitching is feasible since there is regular commerce between Reykjavík and Akureyri, but be prepared for an overnight trip. The easiest way to reach Akureyri is by plane. Icelandair schedules six 55-minute flights each day from Reykjavík (2275kr one way). The extra cost may be worth the convenience for those without bus passes. Walk, hitch, or take a taxi (650kr) from the airport into town (4km).

Akureyri is a great source of information about the surrounding wilderness. You can tour this picturesque town in half a day. Climb to the top of the town for vistas of fjord and mountains, and stroll through the **Botanical Park** to see an impressive array of arctic plants. (Open in summer daily 9am-10pm. Free.) The **Folklore Museum,** Adalstræti 58, displays items of historical interest (open mid-June to mid-Sept. daily 1:30-5pm), while the **Museum of Natural History,** Hafnarstræti 81, contains a unique collection of Icelandic birds and plants (open June to mid-Sept. Sun.-Fri. 11am-2pm; mid-Sept. to May Sun. only 1-3pm). The **municipal pool** is near the campground on Thorunnarstræti. (Open July-Aug. Mon.-Fri. 7am-9pm, Sat. 8am-6pm, Sun. 8am-3pm; June-Sept. Sun. until noon. Admission 60kr.)

The friendly **youth hostel (IYHF),** Stórholt 1 (tel. (96) 236 57), just off Glerargáta about 10 min. north of the center, has small doubles, triples, and quads. (Members 370kr, nonmembers 470kr. Alcohol forbidden. No lock-out. Open year-round.) There is another **youth hostel (IYHF)** at Lónsa (tel. (96)250 37), further north along the same road. (Members 370kr, nonmembers 470kr; open May-Oct.) Several guesthouses also offer sleeping-bag accommodations (450kr; list at tourist office). The cheapest place to spend the night in Akureyri is the campground on Thorunnarstræti (tel. (2) 33 79; 80kr per person plus 80kr per tent; open mid-June to Aug.). The **Sulnaberg Cafeteria,** at Hafnarstræti and Kaupvangsstræti, serves good plain food, but also try the food shops downtown. There is a **KEA supermarket** in the center and another near the campground.

The helpful **tourist office,** Rádhústorg 3 (tel. (96) 250 00), has brochures that will arouse your wanderlust for northern Iceland. (Open Mon.-Fri. 9am-5pm.) In

July and August it has a branch on Hafnarstræti, the walking street. The most spectacular destination is **Lake Mývatn,** where the scenery is both bizarre and beautiful. The 2-kilometer-wide **Huerfjall** crater dominates the skyline, and tall mountains of ash rise nearby. The first Apollo astronauts trained around the **Namafjall** crater—the terrain resembles that of the moon. Strange lava formations known as "black castles" spike a jagged area called **Dimmuborgir,** and behind the hills lies an intensely active geothermal field now being harnessed to generate electricity. Here the ground steams madly and sulfurous pits burp and spit blue sludge. When exploring this area, take heed of the many warning signs and stick to the brown soil, or you may drop through the thin crust to the boiling sulfur pit below (destroying the geyser and ruining your day).

Regular one-day excursion bus tours of the Mývatn area leave from Rádhústorg in Akureyri daily at 8:15am and from the airport daily at 9am (1800kr). A regular bus leaves Akureyri for Skútustadaskóli on Lake Mývatn's southern shore (2½ hr., 920kr round-trip). In Skútustadaskóli you can stay at the *svefnpokapláss* (tel. 441 11; open mid-June to Aug.). From there it is a 16-kilometer hike around to **Reykjahild** and its campground on the northeastern shore. On the way you'll pass by the lava fields of Dimmuborgir.

Southern Coast

Less other-worldly than the interior, Iceland's southern coast would be the star attraction of most countries. Waterfalls, lava fields, glaciers, cliffs, and volcanoes provide rich terrain for hiking, while the shoreline, bordered by grassy cliffs and black sands, offers equally captivating scenery. Hundreds of sheep wander over the green slopes, and precipices highlight the region you'll pass as you travel south and east along Highway #1. Three bus routes connect Reykjavík with points on the southern coast: Reykjavík-Höfn (mid-June to Aug. 1 per day; Sept.-Dec. and April to mid-June 3 per week); Reykjavík-Thórsmörk (mid-June to Aug. 1 per day); and Höfn-Egilsstadir (June to mid-Sept. 6 per week). Schedules and fares vary; inquire at the bus station in Reykjavík (tel. (91) 22 300) or at the bus company **Austurleid** (tel. (99) 81 45).

Easily reached by bus (670kr) or thumb is **Vík,** the district's main village, crowned by a little church on a hilltop. Rare Icelandic plants cover slopes above the village. Beyond the beach is **Reynisdrangar,** an odd cluster of stone formations. Iceland's colorful, sagacious puffins cavort in the breakwater 200 yards from Vík. Within walking distance of the village is **Dýrholaey.** Here at the southernmost tip of Iceland, wind and waves have battered a hole in the cliffs large enough for boats to pass through if the tides are right. The view from these cliffs includes seagulls nested in rocks and lava formations, and the great glacier of Mýrdalsjökull towering inland. Five kilometers from the road to Kerlingardalur and 10km east of Vík is the **Reynisbrekka Hostel (IYHF)** (tel. (99) 71 06); call from Vík and the warden will pick you up at the bus station in Vikuskafi. (Bus from Vík daily at 3pm.) The hostel has clean, modern rooms and a cozy TV room. (Members 370kr, nonmembers 470kr. 10% discount for bus pass holders. Open June to mid-Sept.) Flights to the Vestmann Islands and one-day visits to the Faeroe Islands can be arranged from the youth hostel. More conveniently located in the center of Vík, the **Leikskalar Community Center,** off the main road in a white building ornamented with green window sills, offers sleeping-bag accommodations during the summer.

Farther east is the **Vatnajökull** glacier, larger than all the glaciers of continental Europe combined. It's the centerpiece of spectacular **Skaftafell National Park.** The town of Skaftafell is on the Reykjavík-Höfn bus route (1160kr one way); from mid-June through August you can also take the longer "Behind the Mountains" bus route leaving Reykjavík Monday, Wednesday, and Saturday at 8:30am and reaching Skaftafell at 7:30pm. Once here, you can camp or stay at the farmhouse **Bolti** at the top of the hill (tel. (97) 86 26). A number of well-marked trails lead into the forests and snow-capped ridges, but don't try to conquer Iceland's highest peak,

Öræfajökull (2119m), without adequate preparation. It's farther than it looks; and even in July, hikers can bring home frostbitten hands as a memento of their trip up the slopes.

Vestmann Islands (Vestmannaeyjar)

One night in 1973 the residents of **Heimaey** woke up to an unusually graphic demonstration of Iceland's volcanic underpinnings. A nocturnal eruption forced the fishing fleet to evacuate the island's 5300 inhabitants, and extended the island some 30m into its own harbor. Today, the brightly painted, reconstructed village looks like a Lego town among the island's peaks. Soaring cliffs, rare arctic seabirds, and frequent local celebrations make a visit to the Vestmann Islands worth the time and expense. Icelandair flies three times per day in summer from Reykjavík to Heimaey (1483kr one way). You can also arrive by ferry: A bus (200kr) leaves Reykjavík's bus station daily at 11am and connects with the ferry at Thorlakshöfn. (Ferry 600kr; inquire at the tourist office or youth hostels in Reykjavík about special round-trip discounts.)

The harbor in Heimaey is striking. Jagged green mountains enclose the town, separating the harbor from the sea. The **Vestmann Islands Natural History Museum** houses a unique aquarium where you can come face to face with all kinds of strange Icelandic sea creatures. The curator, Fridrik, has fascinating sea stories to tell. (Open May-Sept. daily 11am-5pm.) Wander through the gray lava desert east of town, or follow the footpaths to the summit of **Eldfell** for an incredible view. Outside town lies **Helgafell,** a volcano which last erupted in 3000 B.C.E. The lush **Herjólfsdalur Valley** is the scene of the three-day National Festival, held on the first weekend in August, a non-stop jamboree of entertainment and dancing.

The **Vestmannaeyjar Hostel (IYHF),** Faxastigur 38 (tel. (98) 23 15), offers brand-new lodgings. (Members 370kr, nonmembers 470kr. Open year-round.) The youth hostel also runs a very good **camping site** in Herjólfsadalur.

Fljótsdalur and Thórsmörk

A good place to begin your own trips into the wilderness is the **IYHF youth hostel** at Fljótsdalur (tel. (99) 84 98), which offers some of the finest views of glaciers and snowcapped peaks in the country. Take the bus to Hvolsvöllur (370kr), and be prepared for a 27-kilometer walk up the left fork of the main road past town. The hostel is the last farmhouse on the road. On some nights in the summer it is fully booked by groups, so call ahead for reservations. (Open mid-April to mid-Oct.) The warden is English and has a fine library of English publications on Iceland. He can also direct you to interesting destinations nearby—the icecap **Tindfjallajökull,** numerous waterfalls, and sites featured in *Njal's Saga* (Hliđarendi, Thórólfsfell, and Einhyrningur). This place is remote; beware of the River Markarfljöt, which can only be crossed by bridge. Be sure to bring several days' worth of food—you'll want to explore.

Ten kilometers from the Fljótsdalur hostel is **Thórsmörk.** The name means "Home of the God Thor" and, indeed, here you'll find an earthly paradise graced by bizarre lava formations, huge green canyons, and plummeting waterfalls. This pristine valley is bordered to the south by the Mýrdalsjökull glacier, which you can ascend by several routes. Regular buses leave Reykjavík daily at 8:30am, and Friday also at 8pm (1600kr round-trip). Weekend bus tours are run year-round by both Ferđafélag Islands and Útivist; it's quite a ride. The tour includes transportation, two nights at one of two well-furnished mountain cabins, and guides if desired. Those arriving on foot from the hostel can stay in the **Ferđafélag Islands** hut for a small charge.

IRELAND

US$1 = 0.68 pounds (£)	**£1 = US$1.46**
CDN$1 = £0.52	**£1 = CDN$1.93**
UK£1 = £1.11	**£1 = UK£0.90**
AUS$1 = £0.48	**£1 = AUS$2.08**

For centuries, Ireland was the mysterious Western fringe of what Europeans knew of the world. Abruptly rising mountains in the southwest, the bleak wind-swept sheets of Connemara stone, and the rocky crags of the Wicklow range offered few comforts to Ireland's early settlers. While heavy winter seas battered the periphery of the island, a tumultuous history unfolded ashore. Seafaring missionaries arriving in the fifth century were greeted by clans of warring Celts, though within a century of their arrival, a written language had developed and Christianity began to replace older religions. The Celtic Kingdoms of Connaught, Leinster, Munster, and Ulster shared the island until Henry II inaugurated a new age in Irish history by seizing the island for the English throne.

In this new era, the crucial and unfortunate fact of Ireland's existence was its proximity to England. Protestant settlers, Cromwell's Puritan army, and anti-Catholic Penal Laws were typical of England's policy toward its neighbor to the west. The road to independence was forged by Daniel O'Connell in the 1830s; by the turn of the century, nationalist Fenians increasingly agitated for home rule. Following the abortive proclamation of the Irish Republic in Easter 1916, a five-year-long Anglo-Irish War ended in the partition of the island into the Irish Free State and Northern Ireland, a partition that remains (and remains in bloody contention) to this day.

Ireland is most beautiful where green earth meets gray sea, so a good plan is to stick to the coast. The near-tropical greenery of the Beara Peninsula and the heathered rocks of Donegal are two aspects of this beauty. Examine the tar and canvas-hulled *curraghs* (traditional fishing boats), or sit by a turf fire and smell the sage of the Irish fields. To see the county at its most traditional, head to the *Gaeltacht* (Irish-speaking areas), found mainly in the more remote coastal areas of Counties Kerry, Dingle, Galway, Mayo, and Donegal. Though road signs and shop names are printed in Irish, just about everyone speaks English.

A good guide to Ireland's archeological sites is *Irish Art and Architecture from Prehistory to Present,* by Harbison, Potterton, and Sheehy (£11). Robert Kee's *Ireland—A History* (£7.34) gives a concise historical overview of the nation, while *Irish Tales and Sagas,* by Vlick O'Connor, is an illustrated selection of Ireland's rich folklore (£6). The richness of Ireland's English-language literature is extraordinary; choose a traveling companion from amongst the works of W.B. Yeats, James Joyce, Flann O'Brien, or Padraig O'Donnel. Ben Forkner's Futura Press edition of *Modern Irish Short Stories* is a good selection of the best of recent Irish writing.

For more thorough coverage of Ireland, Chris Russ says pick up a copy of *Let's Go: Britain and Ireland.*

Getting There and Getting Around

Eurail and InterRail passholders receive free boat passage between Le Havre or Cherbourg (France) and Rosslare in southeastern Ireland (otherwise about US$80). **B&I** and **Sealink** ferries make several runs per day between Holyhead (North Wales) and Dublin, and between Fishguard (South Wales) and Rosslare. Fares average UK£25 one way, UK£40 round-trip, with a 25% discount for IYHF members and a 50% discount for Travelsave stamp holders (see below); discounts are only valid at certain times of the week—check when you buy your ticket. Students and anyone under age 26 should consult USIT offices in London and Paris or budget travel offices throughout England—other bargains are available, especially on combined rail or bus and ferry tickets from major British cities. From Great Britain north of Manchester, the cheapest way to Ireland is usually to cross from Stranraer, Scotland to Larne, Northern Ireland, and then train or bus to Dublin. Flights from London to Dublin are reasonable due to a recent price war between Aer Lingus and Ryan Air. Direct flights from North America to Ireland are way out of the budget traveler's range.

Prohibitively expensive trains connect most large cities to Dublin but not to one another. The expression for one way is "single;" round-trip is "return," while "period return" is a round-trip ticket that must be used within a specified time. Buses adhere vaguely to their schedules, and they go to more destinations, but they are also quite expensive.

Affixed to your ISIC card, the CIEE **Travelsave stamp** (sold for £5.50 at USIT offices) entitles students to a 50% discount on all rail and bus travel in Ireland (except on local runs costing less than £2). **Rambler tickets** for eight days of second-class rail or bus travel (£49), eight days of rail *and* bus travel (£62), 15 days second-class rail or bus (£73), or 15 days rail *and* bus (£90), aren't really worth it unless you want to zip around the country at breakneck speed. Eurailpasses are valid on trains and Expressway buses in the Republic. If you bought your InterRail pass in Great Britain, you must also pay half-price in Ireland, and vice versa.

Hitchhiking in Ireland is usually a snap; friendly drivers offer frequent and safe rides. Your thumb will consequently face great competition, but on main roads, progress is nearly always steady and you usually can hitch across the country in less than a day.

Cycling is one of the best ways to explore remote areas. Tourist offices have a national listing of bicycle rentals (£3.50 per day is the going rate). In addition, many travelers cover beautiful areas thoroughly by taking long-distance hikes over the gorgeous terrain. Youth hostels frequently lie within 20 scenic miles of one another.

Practical Information

The excellent **Irish Tourist Board (Bord Fáilte)** operates a network of offices throughout the country, many of which will book rooms for you (locally, 50p; in another telephone area code, £1.50). They sell a variety of maps, including Ordnance Survey maps (£3), indispensable for hikers. A series of free information sheets succinctly summarizes information on everything from cycling to castles to traditional music. The free *Calendar of Events* will clue you in on which towns and events to head for (or avoid). For planning trips to Ireland's myriad medieval ruins, invest in one of the many available guides to national monuments. *Ireland Guide* (£3.50) is a hefty, comprehensive book complete with maps, pictures, and historical anecdotes. Youth hostels are also likely to be fine sources of information. **USIT** is Ireland's extremely helpful student travel organization.

It's rare that you'll encounter someone who doesn't speak English, but learning a few words of Ireland's native tongue is diplomatic; look for a teach-yourself book, available almost everywhere.

Fickle summer temperatures range from a 50°F low to a 80°F high and warm sunshine can suddenly yield to damp, chilly weather. Keep a rain poncho or umbrella handy and carry a warm sweater, or buy a rich *bainin* sweater, the traditional outerwear of western fisherfolk. (As each family had its own design, the intricate raised patterns on the sweaters were used to identify drowned fisherfolk when they washed up on shore.)

Ireland has nine annual bank holidays: New Year's Day (Jan. 1), St. Patrick's Day (March 17), Good Friday and Easter Monday, first Mondays in June and August, last Monday in October, Christmas Day (Dec. 25) and St. Stephen's Day (Dec. 26). In Northern Ireland, Good Friday and St. Patrick's Day are not holidays, and July 12 and 13 are. Also check for local half-day holidays, when banks and stores close down. English coins (though not the £1 coin) are accepted in Ireland, but not vice versa. Sterling pounds are worth more than Irish "punts." As you spend, watch out for VAT, added to just about everything but raw food, clothing, and transport. Many prices already include VAT, unless specifically mentioned. Foreigners are eligible to have the VAT refunded on purchases that are shipped home. (See VAT in the General Introduction.)

The green-fronted post offices are labeled in Irish—*Oifig an Phoist.* Some contain the old, low-cost public phones. (Press the "A" button when you make a connection and expect a few frustrating moments; if no one answers, push "B" for coin return.) Newer phones have a miniature rampway on top; line up your coins, and they'll automatically feed into the phone as needed. Dial 10 for the operator (and to make international calls), 190 for directory assistance. Dial 999 anywhere in the country in an emergency.

Though contraceptives are legal, religious opinion keeps them out of many pharmacies, especially in rural ones.

Accommodations, Camping, and Food

Make a point of hosteling while in Ireland. In addition to the 55 hostels run by **An Óige,** the Irish IYHF association, there are scores of independent hostels, most costing £3.50 and without the institutional atmosphere, curfews, membership, requirements and daytime lockouts that can make hostelling a drag. Several of these independent hostels have banded together in the **Independent Hostel Owners (IHO)** association, which sells a guide to their member hostels for 50p, available at any of their hostels or at their information office, the North Strand Hostel, 49 North Strand Rd., Dublin 3 (tel. (01) 36 47 16). Also procure a copy of the *Irish Budget Hostel Guide* (30p), listing a dozen more hostels, from Isaac's, 2-4 Frenchman's Lane, Dublin 1 (tel. (01) 74 89 21). An Óige's rural hostels are generally clean, friendly, and relaxed by IYHF standards. They charge £3 from June through September, £2.50 in other months, £1 more in the large cities. Their head office is at 39 Mountjoy Sq., Dublin (tel. (01) 36 31 11). You must have a membership card to stay in Irish IYHF hostels; nonmembers can buy them at the city hostels or the main office for £6. The An Óige guide costs £1. Many hostels are open year-round; check in the respective guides to be sure.

Expect to pay £8-10 for lodging in bed and breakfasts. Showers are sometimes an extra 50p, but many owners generously offer tea and biscuits or sandwiches upon your arrival, or at night. Camping can be a soggy proposition in the Emerald Isle. *Caravan and Camping Parks* (£1)lists all approved sites; most charge £3.50-4.50 per tent, depending on season. Unofficial campgrounds are less expensive (£2 or so), and farmers often permit short-term camping for free, but be sure to ask first. Bord Fáilte's *Farmhouses, Town and Country Homes* (£1.50) lists many B&Bs (with phone numbers), and is a worthwhile investment.

The staples of Irish food—wholemeal bread, porridge, potatoes, milk, and fresh fish—are all tasty and filling, though the routine may become tedious. Doing your own shopping is generally a better idea than eating at unremarkable and surprisingly expensive restaurants. Wholewheat bread and white soda bread both keep for days, Irish dairy products are addictive, and you can buy (or catch) fresh fish all along the coast.

Ireland's wonderful pubs embody the Irish ethos of generosity, lively talk, and good spirits, but they close at 11:30pm (10pm on Sun.), and also for "holy hour" during the afternoon in Dublin, Cork, and Limerick. The standard Irish beer is Guinness, a rich dark brown stout (it grows on you). Irish coffee—strong, laced with Irish whiskey, sweetened with brown sugar, and dolloped with whipped cream—can make you jocose, bellicose, lachrymose, and comatose, all in a single afternoon. Linger and listen to the lilt of conversation—some of the country's best literature hangs in the smoky air. Ask for directions to a singing pub, where groups of varied talents perform traditional music and folk songs. In the larger towns, pubs also host jazz concerts, theater, and poetry readings.

Dublin

Ireland has never taken well to cities. The Irish lived on farmsteads for centuries, isolated as the island they inhabited and happy to be so. Ireland's capital, originally Baile Atha Cliath ("town at the mouth of the hurdle fjord"), was little more than a crossing on the Liffey before the advent of Norse traders in the ninth century.

Long an adopted child, founded and built up by foreigners, Dublin finally came into its own at center stage of the Irish nationalist drama. The movement that had surfaced in the nineteenth century gained popular support after the Easter Rising of 1916, when a small group of Irish nationalists occupied the General Post Office and were subsequently shot by the British; bullet holes are still visible in the facade of the imposing building.

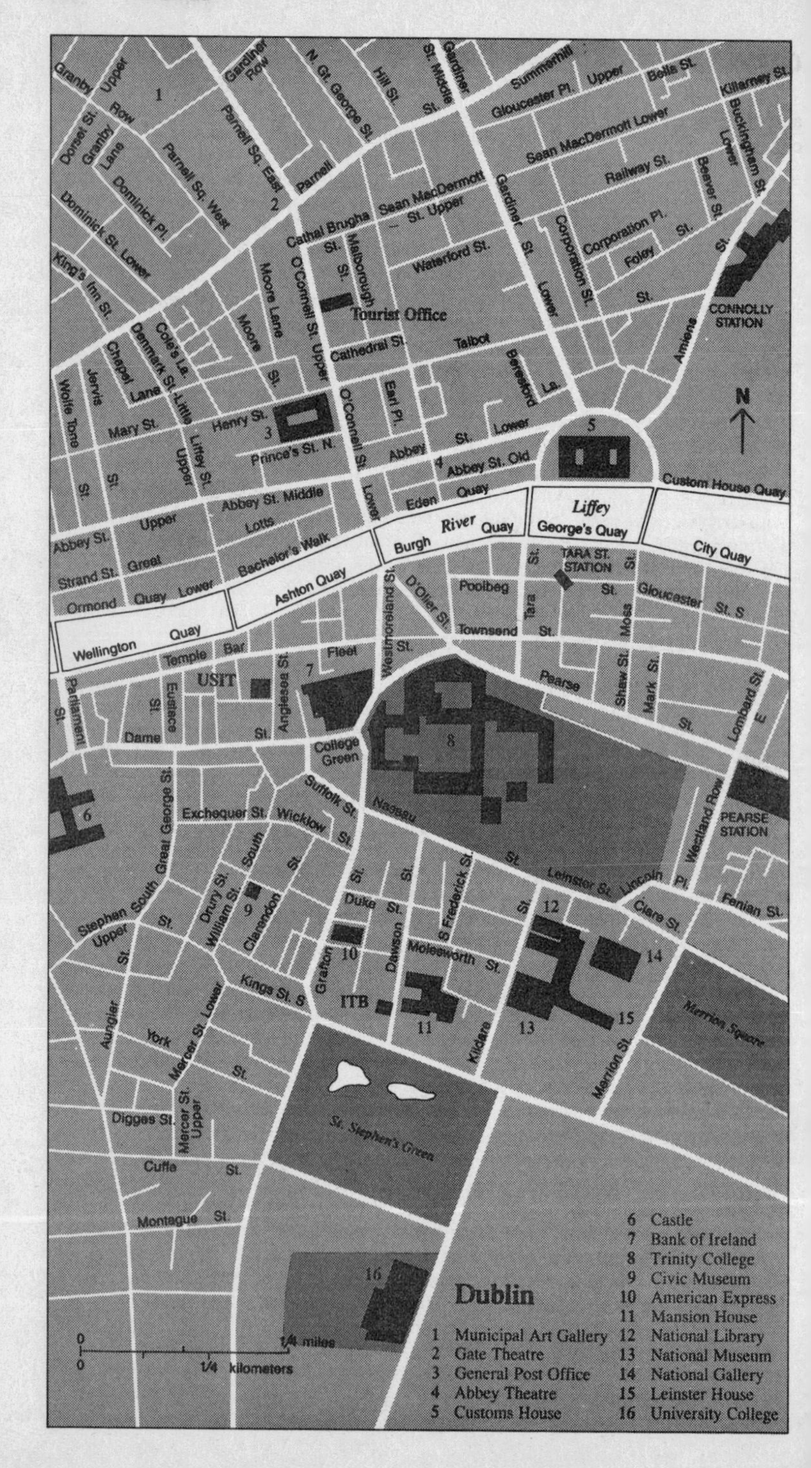
Dublin
1 Municipal Art Gallery
2 Gate Theatre
3 General Post Office
4 Abbey Theatre
5 Customs House
6 Castle
7 Bank of Ireland
8 Trinity College
9 Civic Museum
10 American Express
11 Mansion House
12 National Library
13 National Museum
14 National Gallery
15 Leinster House
16 University College
N
0 1/4 miles
0 1/4 kilometers
Tourist Office
USIT
ITB
CONNOLLY STATION
TARA ST. STATION
PEARSE STATION
Liffey
River
St. Stephen's Green
Merrion Square
Custom House Quay
George's Quay
City Quay
Burgh Quay
Eden Quay
Bachelor's Walk
Ashton Quay
Wellington Quay
Ormond Quay Lower
Temple Bar
Dame St.
College Green
Westmoreland St.
D'Olier St.
Pearse St.
Nassau St.
Grafton St.
Dawson St.
Kildare St.
Merrion St.
Leinster St.
Clare St.
Lincoln Pl.
Westland Row
Fenian St.
Molesworth St.
Duke St.
Kings St. S
South William St.
Drury St.
Clarendon St.
Wicklow St.
Exchequer St.
Suffolk St.
Great George St. South
Stephen St. Upper
Aungier St.
York St.
Mercer St. Lower
Mercer St. Upper
Digges St.
Cuffe St.
Montague St.
O'Connell St. Upper
O'Connell St. Lower
Abbey St. Middle
Abbey St. Upper
Abbey St. Lower
Abbey St. Old
Henry St.
Mary St.
Talbot St.
Cathedral St.
Earl Pl.
Moore St.
Moore Lane
Parnell St.
Parnell Sq. East
Parnell Sq. West
Gardiner St.
Gardiner St. Lower
Sean MacDermott St. Upper
Sean MacDermott Lower
Gloucester Pl. Upper
Summerhill
Amiens St.
Townsend St.
Tara St.
Moss St.
Gloucester St. S
Poolbeg
Lombard St. E
Mark St.
Shaw St.
Fleet St.
Anglesea St.
Eustace St.
Parliament St.
Liffey St. Upper
Strand St. Great
Jervis St.
Wolfe Tone St.
Capel St.
Denmark St. Little
Dominick St. Lower
Dorset St.
Granby Row
Beresford St.
Corporation St.
Railway St.
Beaver St.
Buckingham St. Lower
Foley St.
Waterford St.
Marlborough St.
Cathal Brugha St.
Hill St.
N. Gt. George St.
Gardiner Row

Orientation and Practical Information

Dublin is situated on the east coast of Ireland, across the Irish Sea from Liverpool and northwest of Holyhead. It is the hub for road and rail traffic throughout the country.

Tourist Office: 14 Upper O'Connell St. (tel. 74 77 33). Well-staffed. Accommodations service 50p plus 10% deposit for Dublin, £1.50 for elsewhere in Ireland. **Currency exchange.** Open March to mid-Sept. Mon.-Sat. 9am-5pm; late Sept.-Feb. Mon.-Fri. 9am-5:15pm. Offices also at **Baggot St. Bridge,** open May-Oct. Mon.-Fri. 9am-5:15pm; **Dublin Airport,** open daily 8am-8pm; and **Dun Laoghaire** (near ferry terminal), open daily 7am-8pm. **Youth Information Centre,** at Sackville House, Sackville Place (tel. 78 68 44), behind Clery's on O'Connell St. A new and quiet library. A wealth of resources (some free literature) on travel and accommodations (no bookings). Helpful, well-organized staff, and bulletin boards advertising youth organizations and special-needs groups. Open Mon.-Wed. 9:30am-6pm, Thurs.-Sat. 9:30am-5pm.

Budget Travel: USIT, 7 Anglesea St. (tel. 77 81 17), off Dame St. The Irish student travel agency. Cheap flights and ferries, ISIC and IYHF cards, visas, Travelsave stamps, InterRail passes. Billboards have information on everything from accommodations to concerts. Also books B&Bs.

American Express: 116 Grafton St. (tel. 77 28 74), just up the street from Trinity Gates. Mail held. All banking services. Open Mon.-Fri. 9am-5pm, Sat. 9am-noon.

Post Office: General Post Office, O'Connell St. Site of the 1916 rebellion, now a playground for pickpockets. Open Mon.-Sat. 8am-8pm (packages until 7pm), Sun. 10:30am-6:30pm (no packages).

Telephones: In the post office. Open same hours. **Telephone code:** 01.

Flights: From **Dublin Airport** (tel. 37 99 00), you can take a special coach (£2.50) to Busáras, the main bus station, situated behind the Customs House on Store St.; local bus #41A or 41C (85p) will bring you to Eden Quay in the city center.

Trains: Heuston Station (tel. 77 18 71) is Dublin's main station, with service to Cork, Limerick, Waterford, and Tralee (County Kerry), Galway, and Westport. Bus #24 connects it with the city center. **Connolly Station** (tel. 74 29 41) is a secondary station, just behind Busáras and the Customs House on Amiens Rd. Service to Belfast, Sligo, Wexford, and Rosslare. Both stations, in conjunction with **Pearse Station,** on Westland Row directly behind Trinity College (tel. 77 65 81), serve suburban lines.

Buses: Busáras, Store St. (tel. 74 29 41), directly behind the Customs House (down to the right of O'Connell St. Bridge, looking from south side), is the central station for expressway and provincial buses. A much more extensive network of destinations than rail. Get Travelsave Stamp from USIT for 50% off all fares. Call 78 77 77 for information on all national buses, city buses, and trains.

Ferries: B&I or **Sealink** ferries from Liverpool or Holyhead. For more information, call both B&I (tel. 77 82 71) and Sealink (tel. 80 88 44). Arriving by B&I ferry, catch bus #53 to the center. Buses #7, 7A, 8 and 46A provide city-bound service from the Sealink ferry dock in **Dun Laoghaire** (pronounced "Dun-leary").

Public Transportation: Buses run 6am-11:30pm; fare 45-85p. Buy tickets from the bus conductor. Information (tel. 78 77 77). Unlimited bus travel for 1 week £8; bus and train £9.50. Buy these tickets from **CIE,** 59 Upper O'Connell St. The *Dublin District Timetable* (50p) gives schedules and stops. **Dublin Area Rapid Transit (DART)** trains cost the same as buses and run north-south from Howth to Bray.

Bike Rental: USIT Rent-A-Bike, 58 Lower Gardiner St. (tel. 72 59 31). £3 per day, £18 per week. £30 deposit. Open Mon.-Sat. 9am-6pm.

Emergencies: Police or **Ambulance** (tel. 999). Police headquarters at Harcourt Sq. (tel. 73 22 22).

Crises: Rape (tel. 61 49 11). **Samaritans,** 66 S. William St. (tel. 77 88 33). **FLAC,** 49 S. William St. (tel. 79 42 39), for free legal advice.

Gay Centers: Gay Health Action (tel. 71 09 39). **Tel-a-Friend** (tel. 71 06 08). Sun.-Fri. 8-10pm, Sat. 3:30-6pm; Thurs. women only.

Embassies: U.S., 42 Elgin Rd. (tel. 68 87 77). **Canada,** 65-68 St. Stephen's Green (tel. 78 19 88). **U.K.,** 33 Merrion Rd. (tel. 69 52 11). **Australia,** Fitzwilton House, Wilton Terrace (tel. 76 15 17). **New Zealanders** should contact the British Embassy.

Laundry: Avon Laundrette, 2 Belvedere Rd., off Dorset Rd. Open daily 9:30am-6:30pm. **Launderland,** 145 Rathmines Rd.

Accommodations and Camping

Check with USIT for summer accommodations at **Trinity Hall** (tel. 97 17 72), a University of Dublin dormitory with large, well-furnished rooms on Dartry Rd., Rathmines (£9.50).

Hostels

Morehampton House (IYHF), 78 Morehampton Rd., Donnybrook, Dublin 4 (tel. 68 03 25). A large, well-situated hostel, 10 min. from the city center. Bus #10 from O'Connell St. Members only, £3.50. Lockout 10am-5pm. Midnight curfew.

Mountjoy Square Youth Hostel (IYHF), 39 Mountjoy Sq., Dublin 1 (tel. 36 31 11). Right above the *An Oige* office. Bus #3, 11, 16, or 16a. Same rates and rules as Morehampton House.

Scoil Lorcáin Youth Hostel (IYHF), Eaton Sq., Monkstown (no phone). 5 miles south of Dublin and 1 mile north of Dun Laoghaire, near *Comhaltas Ceoltoiri Eireann* headquarters. Take bus #7A or 8. In a school that serves as a supplementary youth hostel July-Aug. Same rates and rules as Morehampton House.

Dublin Tourist Hostel (Isaac's), 2-4 Frenchman's Lane (tel. 74 93 21), near Busáras under the railway line. Also known as "The Happy Rambler." Large, renovated dorms. Bike hire, kitchen, cafe. £3.50. Hot showers included. Midnight curfew.

Young Traveller, St. Mary's Place, off Dorset St., on Western Way, Dublin 7 (tel. 30 50 00). Immaculate small dorms. A very congenial place. £7.50. Breakfast included.

The North Strand, 49 North Strand Rd., Dublin 3 (tel. 36 47 13). Take bus #20B, 30, or 54. Nice hostel, run by well-informed and friendly proprietors. Quiz Patrick O'Donnell about independent hostels throughout the country. Hot showers and kitchen available. Car park. £3.50. No curfew.

Bed and Breakfast Hotels

There are hundreds of B&Bs in Dublin; the tourist office can book you a place (50p plus 10% deposit), or give you a list. The following, in the suburbs, are a sampling of the best.

Mrs. S. Doyle, 35 Seafort Ave., Sandymount (tel. 68 98 50). Take bus #2 or 3 from Clery's, O'Connell St. Near the sea. Singles available. £9. Open year-round.

Mrs. A. Lawlor, 95 Iona Rd. (tel. 30 90 52), 5 min. from the city center, 10 min. from the airport and ferry. Take bus #11, 11a, 16, or 16a. £11. Open March-Nov.

Mrs. B. O'Neill, 6 Whitworth Parade, Drumcondra (tel. 30 47 33), on a quiet cul-de-sac off St. Patrick's Rd. Take bus #3, 11, 13, 16, 16a, 41, or 41a. £8.50. Showers 75p. Open April-Oct.

Mrs. D. Farrell, Thaddeus, 83 Cyprus Grove Rd., Templeogue (tel. 90 34 29). Take bus #15b, 49, 54, or 65. £7.50. Showers 75p. Open year-round.

Camping

Cromlech Caravan and Camping Park, Killiney Hill Rd. (tel. 82 68 82), in Ballybrack. Take bus #46 from Dublin or #46A from Dun Laoghaire. A well-equipped site. 50p per person, £4 per tent. Open mid-April to mid-Sept.

Shankill Caravan and Camping Park (tel. 82 00 11), near Cromlech, in Shankill. Take bus #45, 45a, or 84 from Dublin. 50p per person, £4 per tent. Open Easter to mid-Sept.

Food

Pub grub is wholesome and filling, and usually available anywhere in the city. In the northside, Moore Street and Thomas Street **markets** provide fruit and vegetables daily. Henry Street nearby is lined with bakeries and restaurants.

Frankie's Food Co., O'Connell St., across from Eason's Bookstore. Tasty fast food. The staff is friendly; "even the auld ones luv it." Self-service. Irish stew, fish and chips, bangers and mash. £2.50-3.50. Open daily 9:30am-11pm.

Dinty Moore's, 21 D'Olier St., near O'Connell St. Bridge. Inconspicuous and down-to-earth, with generous helpings. Fish and chips £1.95. Whole-day meals less than £2.50. Also takeaway. The ultimate student hangout. Open Mon.-Fri. 8:30am-6pm, Sat. 9am-6pm.

Murphy Doodles, Suffolk St., downstairs beside 18th Precinct. Cheap wholesome fare. Triple-decker sandwich £1.95. Salads, quiche, and pasta. Self-service. Open Mon.-Sat. 10am-11pm.

Runner Bean, Nassau St. A grocery store. Vegetables and homemade breads, some packaged foods, fruits and nuts.

Bewley's, Grafton St., Westmoreland St. and South Great George St. *The* classic Dublin cafeterias, going way back. Extensive bakeries in the front, seating in the back. Outstanding coffee, pastries, and lunches. Open Mon.-Sat. 7:30am-6pm.

Sights

Start your exploration of Dublin's handsome eighteenth-century Georgian architecture at **Trinity College,** the *alma mater* of Swift, Berkeley, Burke, Moore, and Wilde. Slip through the gate at the top of Westmoreland St. and walk in the quiet, cobbled yard to the impressive **Old Library.** Notable for its staircase and plaster work by German architect Cassels, the library has a fine collection of Egyptian, Greek, Latin, and Irish manuscripts. Its pride is the high, wood-vaulted reading room, where two volumes of the eighth-century *Book of Kells* are on display. (Open Mon.-Fri. 9:30am-4:45pm, Sat. 9:30am-12:45pm. Admission April-Oct. £1, students and seniors 80p; Nov.-March free.) Trinity College students offer vigorous two-hour guided tours around the city (£3); tours begin at noon and 3pm at Trinity's main entrance.

Stroll through the university grounds and leave by the back gate to reach the **Dail** and **Seanad,** the Irish houses of parliament, located since 1922 in the magnificent Leinster House on Kildare St. (Not open to public.) Parliament's former headquarters at **Old Parliament House** (now the Bank of Ireland) is another striking example of Georgian architecture.

The **National Museum,** Kildare St., is the world's best aggregation of Irish cultural artifacts. Here you can see Celtic goldwork, the Tara brooch, and a stirring exhibit on the 1916 uprising. Connected to the main building is the **Division of Natural History,** which houses exhibits on Ireland's wildlife. (Both museums open Tues.-Sat. 10am-6pm, Sun. 2-5pm. Free.) Across the street, the **National Library** is important mainly as an Irish cultural research center. (Open mid-Aug. to mid-July Mon.-Thurs. 10am-9pm; mid-July to mid-Aug. Mon.-Fri. 10am-5pm, Sat. 10am-1pm.) Just around the corner on Merrion Square is the **National Gallery,** which houses an excellent series of Rembrandts, an interesting modern collection, and a few rooms displaying portraits of modern literary greats including Brendan Behan, Frank O'Connor, James Stephens, George Bernard Shaw, and John Millington Synge. (Open Mon.-Wed. and Fri.-Sat. 10am-6pm, Thurs. 10am-9pm, Sun. 2-5pm. Free.)

Stroll to nearby **St. Stephen's Green,** frequented by pedestrians, punks, and pensioners alike. On the park's north side, the **Mansion House** on Dawson St. has been the residence of the Lord Mayor of Dublin since 1715. It was here that the Declaration of Independence was signed in 1919 and the Anglo-Irish Truce adopted in 1921. The **Dublin Civic Museum,** 58 South William St., has interesting exhibits on Ireland's history. **Dublin Castle** has an impressive history and reveals some superb plasterwork and floorwork in the rooms of the **State Apartments.** (Open Mon.-Fri.

10am-12:15pm and 2-5pm, Sat.-Sun. 2-5pm. Admission 75p, students 50p.) On the Liffey, visit the **Customs House** and the **Four Courts,** marvels of eighteenth-century architecture. **Phoenix Park,** the largest enclosed park in Europe, hosts a variety of activities, from horse racing to rock concerts.

Entertainment

The best entertainment in Dublin shows nightly in its many pubs. **McDaid's,** Harry St., was Brendan Behan's creation. Recently renovated, it attracts a hip crowd. James Joyce made **Mulligan's,** Poolbeg St., **Davy Byrne,** 21 Duke St., and the **Bailey,** also on Duke St., famous. Both **O'Donaghue's,** near Baggot St. (always packed), and the ancient, well-kept **Brazen Head,** Bridge St., off Merchant's Quay, Dublin's oldest public house, entertain patrons nightly with live traditional music. **Ryan's,** on Parkgate St., is well known for its dark, enclosed "snugs." **Keogh's,** on South Anne St., off Grafton St., also has a few of these worn, secure shelters.

The **Abbey Theater,** Lower Abbey St. (tel. 74 45 05), founded by W.B. Yeats and Lady Gregory, provides a cultural alternative to bar-hopping. Other well-known theaters include **The Gate,** Cavendish Row; **Project Arts Centre,** 39 East Essex St.; **The Gaiety Theater,** South King St.; and the **Olympia Theatre,** Dame St. Call the **Theater Booking Office** at 47 Nassau St. (tel. 77 84 39) for information, prices, and tickets. *In Dublin* (85p; published bi-weekly) has information on all cultural happenings in Dublin.

June 16 is **Bloomsday** in Dublin. Check with the tourist office for ways to join Joyce aficionados commemorating *Ulysses'* hero Leopold Bloom and his 19-hour odyssey across the city. Recharting his course with a helpful map (50p) actually takes 30 hours—complete with appropriate drinking and debauching—but fall in with this crew and you'll fall into bed more than a mere visitor to Joyce's city.

Rugby season starts in September; home games are played in **Landsdowne Stadium.** Gaelic football and hurling championships are in abundance during the summer months. Don't miss the wild shrieking and roaring of the **All-Ireland Finals,** played in early September in **Croke Park,** Phibsboro.

Near Dublin

North of the city, the **Hill of Howth** presents an impressive view of Dublin Bay, with the Mourne Mountains to the north and the Wicklow Hills to the south. Howth's rhododendron gardens and cliff walks are added attractions (take bus #31). Also north of the city, visit extravagant **Malahide Castle** in Malahide. (Open April-Oct. Mon.-Fri. 10am-12:45pm and 2-6pm, Sat. 11am-6pm, Sun. 2-6pm; Nov.-March Mon.-Fri. 10am-12:45pm and 2-5pm, Sat.-Sun. 2-5pm. Admission £2, students £1.35.)

Other worthwhile daytrips north are to **Kells,** the site of the extensive ruins of St. Columcille's Monastery, and to **Newgrange,** a Celtic burial chamber. South of Dublin, sandy beaches and resort towns stretch down into Wicklow. Windswept **Sandycove** harbors **Joyce's Martello Tower and Museum,** where the man himself lived briefly. (Open May-Sept. Mon.-Sat. 10am-1pm and 2-5pm, Sun. 2:30-6pm. Admission 80p, students 60p.) You can swim farther south off the beaches of White Rock Strand at Killiney—walk to the top of **Killiney Hill** for a splendid view.

County Wicklow

People tout it as "The Garden of Ireland," but Wicklow's wild, powerful beauty has little in common with genteel flowerbeds. With lofty granite summits and lush valleys enclosing waterfalls and wooded glens, Wicklow has an ancient and spellbinding allure.

Glendalough, the area's geographical and spiritual center, cradles two lakes, a pine-tree forest, and the ruins of an ancient monastic settlement. A St. Kevin's bus (tel. 81 81 19) runs daily at 11:30am from the Royal College of Surgeons in Dublin.

The Wicklow Mountains have hiking trails throughout the range. Before embarking on any such adventure, get Ordinance Survey maps from the **tourist office** (tel. (0404) 679 04) in **Wicklow Town,** the town hall in **Bray** (tel. (01) 86 71 28), or the main tourist office in Dublin, on Abbey St. (open June-Sept.). There are several **IYHF youth hostels** through the Wicklow range that provide bases for foot tours. These are in **Glendalough** (tel. (0404) 51 43), **Ashford** (tel. (0404) 42 59), **Aghavannagh** (tel. (0402) 61 02), **Blessington** (tel. (045) 672 66), and **Valleymount** (tel. (045) 567 11). Try to reserve beds in advance; all bookings must be made through the Dublin office (tel. (01) 36 31 11). B&Bs are easy to find in this area for around £8-9. If you have difficulty, try the tourist offices. The most central camping in the mountains is at **Roundwood** (tel. (01) 81 81 63), but if you're stopping in Wicklow, try **Silver Strand** (tel. (04) 29 34), south along the coastal road.

Wicklow provides much more than **Lugnacullia,** Ireland's third-highest mountain. Check out the harmonious **Glen of the Downs,** enjoy the roar of the waterfall at **Devil's Glen,** or simply relax in the beautiful **Mount Usher Gardens,** near Ashford. **Brittas Bay, Silver Strand,** and **Jack's Hole** provide the best beaches.

On the road leaving Bray past the Town Hall, hitch southwest to **Enniskerry.** From there, visit the sprawling 14,000-acre **Powerscourt Demesne,** with its formal garden and splashing waterfall. The mountains are best viewed and explored from the old British military road as it wanders through desolate **Glencree, Sally Gap,** and back down to **Laragh.** Otherwise, hitch right down the Wexford road (N11) to the sunny southwest.

Cork City (Corcaigh)

As Ireland's second city, Cork carries a chip on its shoulder. The good-natured rivalry with Dublin permeates all aspects of life, especially sports and drinking. Since its seventh-century foundation, "Rebel Cork" has endured a history of oppression and rebellion: The city has been invaded by the Anglo-Normans, besieged by Cromwell, and burned in the 1919-1921 War of Independence.

Practical Information

Tourist Office: Grand Parade, on the corner of S. Mall St. (tel. 27 32 51). Informative and friendly staff. Accommodations service 50p. Open in summer Mon.-Sat. 9am-7pm, Sun. 3-5pm; in winter Mon.-Fri. 9:15am-5:30pm, Sat. 9:15am-1pm.

Budget Travel: USIT, University College, Students' Union, Boule Library (tel. 27 39 01). Well-staffed. Travel bargains and ferry information. Open June-Sept. Mon.-Fri. 10am-4:30pm; Oct.-May Mon.-Fri. 9:15am-4pm.

American Express: Casey Travel Ltd., 60 South Mall, around the corner from the tourist office (tel. 20 12 13). Mail held, checks sold and replaced, but no wired money accepted. Open Mon.-Fri. 9:30am-12:30pm and 1:45-5:30pm, Sat. 9:30am-1pm.

Post Office: Oliver Plunkett St. (tel. 50 86 55). Open Mon.-Sat. 9am-6pm.

Trains: Kent Station, Lower Glanmire Rd. Information (tel. 50 44 22).

Buses: Parnell Pl., 2 blocks from Patrick's Bridge. Information (tel. 50 44 22).

Ferries: Brittany and **Irish Continental** ferries (France), and **Swansea/Cork** ferries (Wales) all arrive/depart at the **Ringaskiddy** terminal, 9 miles out on Cloyne Rd.

Bike Rental: Try **USIT** (see Budget Travel) or **Kilgrew's Ltd.,** 30 N. Main St. (tel. 27 34 58). £3.50 per day, £21 per week. Some youth hostels also have rentals.

Emergencies: Police or **Ambulance** (tel. 999).

Medical Assistance: Cork Regional Hospital (tel. 464 00).

Telephone Code: 021.

Accommodations and Food

Cork is full of B&Bs; the areas with the highest concentration include **College Road, Western Road,** and **Kinsale Road.**

Youth Hostel (IYHF), 1-2 Redclyffe, Western Rd. (tel. 432 89), by the university. Take bus #8, or walk along by Lancaster Quay. Nice location but often full. £4.

Cork Tourist Hostel, 10 Belgrave Pl. (tel. 50 55 62), off Wellington Rd., near bus and train stations. A fine independent hostel. Hot showers, kitchen, car park. £3.50. No curfew.

Mrs. M. Smythe, Ashford House, Donovan's Rd. (tel. 27 63 24). A comfortable old house, opposite the college. £9. Open Feb.-Dec.

Mrs. S. O'Brien, Swansea House, 2 Woburn Pl., Lower Glanmire Rd. (tel. 50 14 41). An old 3-story house in an iffy neighborhood beside the railway station. £8.

Halpin's, 14 Cook St., offers the best in cheap, filling food. **Canty's Bar,** 6 Pembroke St. (tel. 205 66), has freshly made meat sandwiches (£2.50-3). Nights, **Sir Henry's,** S. Main St., is *the* wild student hangout. **Old Vic's,** Cook St., is similarly popular but more subdued. Traditional music lovers should drop by **De Lacy's,** on Oliver Plunkett St.

Sights and Entertainment

Visit the Gothic **Cathedral of St. Finbarr** and **St. Anne's Church** for the 200-year-old bells and the view from the tower. Cork hosts the well-attended, one-week **International Film Festival** in June. Get a schedule at the tourist office. Both hurling and Gaelic football are played at **Pairc Ui Chaoimh,** Marina. The **Guinness Jazz Festival** comes to Cork in late October.

Four miles outside Cork is the infamous **Blarney Castle,** where with some acrobatics you can kiss the **Blarney Stone** and acquire the gift of gab. (Open May Mon.-Sat. 9am-7pm, Sun. 9:30am-5:30pm; June-July Mon.-Sat. 9am-8:30pm, Sun. 9:30-5:30pm; Aug. Mon.-Sat. 9am-7:30pm; Sept. Mon.-Sat. 9am-6:30pm; Oct.-April Mon.-Sat. 9am-sundown, Sun. 9:30am-sundown. Admission £2, students and seniors £1.50, children £1.) Kiss or no kiss, the castle is quite interesting and the surrounding area is beautiful. Buses run to Blarney from Cork (every hr., £2 round-trip).

Western Cork

South and west of the town of Cork, the roads narrow, the population thins, and the fresh sea air carries the scents of kelp and wild summer honeysuckle across hilly pastures and dense thickets. From east to west, the first seaside town is sleepy **Kinsale** with connections to Cork by bus (5 per day, £3.20). Accommodations in town are nothing to shout about, but the **Kinsale Youth Hostel (IYHF)** (tel. (021) 77 23 09) in Summer Cove, 1½ miles out of town, has a wonderful view. (Bring food from town.) **Mrs. Priors,** Carraig Ban, Sandycove (tel. 77 43 44), 2 miles out of town, offers attractive and immaculate rooms plus a good breakfast for £9.50. (Open June-Aug.) The **Blue Haven,** Pearse St., serves good fish lunches for £3-4. For an evening pint and a little music try **The Spaniard** or **The Shanakee.**

There are no buses running west along the coast from Kinsale, and hitching is slow, but a bus does run from Cork to **Skibbereen,** where you'll find a **tourist office,** North St. (tel. (028) 217 66). (Open July-Aug. Mon.-Sat. 9am-8pm; Sept.-June Mon.-Fri. 9:15am-5:30pm.) Head from Skibbereen southwest to **Baltimore,** an easy 8-mile hitch or bus ride (Mon.-Sat. 3 per day). The pace is slow in this old pirate town, and nowhere is it more relaxed than **Rolf's Hostel** (tel. (028) 202 89), where you can get a clean bed, use of a good kitchen, and a piping hot shower for £3.50. (Open year-round.) Ask at the hostel about boats to nearby **Sherkin Island** (15 min., £2 round-trip) and the slightly more distant **Clear Island** (45 min., £6 round-trip), where you can camp near almost deserted beaches. Alternatively, there is an **IYHF**

youth hostel on Clear (no tel.; open year-round), or a good B&B at **The Island House** (tel. (028) 203 14) on Sherkin (£9).

West Cork stretches three fingers out into the Atlantic: Mizen Head, Sheep's Head, and (longest and best of all) the **Beara Peninsula.** Each offers peace, quiet, peace, quiet, and more peace; plus a few sandy beaches. The road from Adrigole to Lauragh across the Beara Peninsula cuts through the Caha Mountains at Healy Pass, where the persistent hitchhiker or the very fit biker will enjoy some of southwestern Ireland's finest views at every switch and turn of the narrow road. Several independent hostels have sprouted along the southern rim of the Beara Peninsula. No public transport serves these three peninsulas.

West Cork is as beautiful inland as along its shoreline. For positively idyllic days, stay at the **Shiplake Hostel,** near Dunmanway (tel. (023) 457 50). Few accommodations of any sort are this homey. (£3. Showers 30p.) Dunmanway is on the bus route from Cork to Glengariff.

Kerry

In overcrowded Kerry, dark green and gray mountains dotted with wandering sheep tumble into narrow gorges cut by rushing water. **Kenmare,** a small town south of Killarney, makes a good base for exploring the Ring of Kerry. A **tourist office** (tel. (064) 412 33), banks, and eating places are all situated on its wide Main Street. Nearby Henry Street is filled with grocery stores and intimate pubs. Opposite the **post office** on Henry St. is the warm, comfortable **Fáilte Hostel** (tel. (064) 410 83), a wonderfully clean and well-run independent hostel. (£4.50, continental breakfast included. Showers 50p. Open year-round.) If you must stay overnight in tourist-infested **Killarney,** the **Súgán Kitchen Hostel,** Lewis Rd. (tel. (064) 331 04), is the place to go. (£3.50. Showers 50p. Delicious 3-course meals £5, cheaper soups equally good. Midnight curfew.)

The **Black Valley Youth Hostel (IYHF)** (tel. (064) 323 00) is a perfect place from which to explore the **Upper Lake** and the dramatic **Gap of Dunloe.** The hostel lies about 2 miles northwest of Lord Brandon's cottage, the southern entrance to the Gap, and about 15 miles up Killarney Rd. from Kenmare. The nearby **Macgillicuddy's Reeks** present some of Ireland's most challenging climbs. In the event of a mountaineering accident, contact the **Kerry Mountain Rescue Team** at the Killarney Police Station (tel. (064) 312 22). In the southern and northern foothills of Carrauntoohil Mt. respectively, the **Mountain Lodge,** Bridia Valley, Glencar (tel. (066) 601 34), and the **Corrán Tuathail Hostel (IYHF)** (tel. (064) 443 38) offer accommodations for about £3.

The road running around the perimeter of all this is the famous **Ring of Kerry,** which extends 112 miles through coastal towns with plentiful, though expensive, B&Bs. (£9-10.) On the north coast, **Glenbeigh** contains a marvelous beach and the **Hillside House Hotel** (tel. (066) 682 28). **Cahirciveen** has a **tourist office** (tel. (0667) 21 41), banks, food stores, bike rental, and little else. At the western end of the ring, an **IYHF youth hostel** in **Ballinskelligs** (tel. (0667) 91 09) is a good launching pad for the **Skellig Rocks,** steep crags offshore with a monastic settlement perched atop. The **Carrigbeg Hostel** (no phone), in Caherdaniel, is near the wonderfully expansive Derrynane Beach as well as the abbey where Daniel O'Connell is buried. The hostel accepts no one in a car. (£3. Open April-Sept.)

Buses run only along the northern edge of the ring from Killarney to Cahirciveen (Mon.-Sat. 2 per day), but **CIE** in Killarney and Tralee runs a tour daily in summer (£8, students £6).

North of Killarney, it's an easy hitch to **Tralee,** a town whose sole redeeming feature is the bus connection to **Dingle Town,** in the heart of the Dingle Peninsula. (Hitching is difficult.) Though touristed, this Irish-speaking fishing village retains an inviting atmosphere. Stay in one of the high-quality B&Bs on **Dykegate Street** (£8.50), or try the private **Westlodge Hostel** (tel. (066) 514 76) by the pier (£3.50). The 30-mile road around the peninsula makes for a breathtaking day of cycling, with its striking beaches, scattered monastic ruins, and the oceanside cliffs of **Slea Head.** Rent a bike at **Moriarty's** on Main St. (tel. (066) 513 16). Or continue to **Dunquin,** where you can catch a ferry out to the ascetic **Blasket Islands,** uninhabited for much of the year. Dunquin's **IYHF youth hostel** (tel. (066) 561 21) lies north of town on Ballyferriter Rd. For splendid views of mountain valleys and Dingle Bay, hitch back toward Tralee by the narrow **Conor Pass.** Cloghane and Brandon, small villages off the road, offer beautiful if somewhat strenuous paths up **Mt. Brandon,** Ireland's second-highest peak.

Counties Limerick and Clare

Give Limerick County a miss. Its uninteresting farmlands and even less interesting capital city will encourage you to move on. If for some reason you end up in Limerick City, ask the **tourist office,** in The Granary, Michael St. (tel. (061) 317 22), to find you accommodations. (Open Mon.-Fri. 9am-5:30pm, Sat. 9:30am-1pm.) The **IYHF youth hostel,** 1 Perry Sq. (tel. 31 46 72), just around the corner from the **bus and train station,** usually has room. (£4 per person. Open year-round.) If the hostel is full, look into the B&Bs on Ennis Rd. across the River Shannon.

Clare County is much more interesting, with an often stunning coastline and a consistently reliable traditional music scene. The 700-foot **Cliffs of Moher** plunge dramatically into the choppy, cold Atlantic; the observation point is tourist-packed, but you can walk along the cliffs for miles. Base yourself in **Liscannor** to the south, at either the **Liscannor Village Hostel** (tel. (065) 813 85), close to the old town center, or the **Old Hostel** (no phone), closer to the cliffs. (Both £3.50.) Or continue on up to **Doolin,** where the accordion and bodhran can be heard almost every night in the pubs. The **Doolin Hostel** (tel. (065) 740 06), has by far the best facilities (shop, currency exchange, and tourist information point right in the hostel), while the smaller **Rainbow Hostel** (no phone) and **Tomo's Hostel** (tel. (065) 742 14) are more relaxed.

Just to the north begins the **Burren,** a landscape of bizarre limestone formations and exquisite wildflowers. The excellent **Bridge Hostel** (tel. (065) 761 34) in Fanore, on the coast north of Doolin, will start you out. (£3.50. Open April-Oct.) The warden runs trips to local **caves** (£3.50 for 2½ hr.); don't explore the caves on your own, as they are extremely dangerous. Also don't go to the popular Ailwee Cave; it's a rip-off at £2.20. Another good base is **Johnston's Hostel,** Main St., Kinvara, on the northeastern edge of the Burren (in Co. Galway), with an extremely congenial proprietor. (£3.50. Open May-Sept.)

Transportation in the area is scanty. Buses run from Galway, Limerick, and Ennis to points along the coast, as well as to **Lisdoonvarna,** a spa town about 5 miles from Doolin. A post bus runs from the Ennis post office to Liscannor and Doolin. You're best off on a bicycle.

Galway Town

Galway was originally a Norman port, but the charter it received from King Richard II of England gave it the status of an independent city-state ruled by the "Tribes of Galway." Perched at the edge of Ireland's second-largest *Gaeltacht,* the town meanders between river and sea, full of old merchant houses, odd leaded windows above stone doorways, and aged stone walls set off by modern storefronts.

Wander down Shop Street past Eyre Square and **Lynch's Castle,** an elegant stone mansion that's now the Allied Irish Bank. Walking up the banks of the Corrib River toward **Salmon Weir Bridge,** you can hang over the rail to watch salmon struggle upstream to their spawning grounds. Summer kicks the town into action with the **Galway Races** in late July, a week's medley of horseflesh, high society, and charming cutthroat bookies. The **Arts Festival** in August attracts performers from all over

Ireland. Throughout the year, you can hear traditional music at many of the pubs, including **Púcán** on Forster Street and **Clogs** on Dominick Street.

The **tourist office** (tel. (091) 630 81), off Eyre Square (follow the signs), is full of accommodations and transportation information. (Open Mon.-Sat. 9am-6:45pm.) One block away is the **train** and **bus station** (tel. 621 41; office open July-Aug. daily 9:15am-6pm; Sept.-June Mon.-Sat. 9:15am-6pm). For student travel bargains, walk to University College Galway, where there's a **USIT** office (tel. 246 01) in the New Science Building (open Mon.-Fri. 10am-1pm and 2-5pm). The **post office** is on Eglinton St. (open Mon.-Sat. 9am-6pm), and there's a **Rent-A-Bike** at Ballalley Lane, Eyre Square. (New bikes £3 per day, £18 per week, £10 deposit. Open daily 9am-6pm.) Galway's **telephone code** is 091.

Galway has no fewer than three independent hostels. **Corrib Villa** (tel. 628 92), down Eglinton St. past the post office, is convenient and clean, with wonderful proprietors. (£3.50. Hot showers 20p.) Farther away, the **Galway Tourist Hostel,** Gentian Hill (tel. 251 76), is friendly, crowded, clean, and a bit battered. Take bus #2 to Knocknacarra, and walk along the road from the terminus, with the sea on your left, for about 300 meters. (£3.50.) **Mary Ryan's Hostel,** 4 Beechmount Ave. (tel. 233 03), in Highland Park, is even smaller. Be sure to call ahead. Take bus #2 to Taylor Hill Convent and walk 100 meters or so. (£3.50.) The town abounds with B&Bs, but they are far flung throughout the suburbs, and often full. You may want to use the tourist office's 50p accommodations service. **Mrs. O'Sullivan,** 4 Lower Canal Rd. (tel. 647 96), is in a nice neighborhood on the university side of the river. (£9.) **Mrs. Lydon,** 8 Lower Abbeygate St. (tel. 649 14), is right in the middle of town, but noisy as a result. (£8.50.) Stock up on food at the **Roches Stores** supermarket near Eyre Square. **Shop Street** has the most bakeries and groceries. For lunch, try the **Tigh Neachtain,** 17 Cross St., or the **Hungry Grass** next door.

A worthy sidetrip from Galway is south to **Gort,** where W.B. Yeats bought sixteenth-century tower house **Thoor Ballylee** as a summer retreat. Lady Gregory used to live at **Coule Park,** now a national forest and wildlife park. Buses en route to Limerick stop here; it's also an easy hitch from Galway.

Connemara and the Aran Islands

Famous for unspoiled shoreline and rugged, mountainous interior, the **Connemara** region stretches northwest from Galway. The green valleys of the eastern edges yield to the grays and purples of stone, sky, and sea that merge to the west. The main road from Galway to Clifden heads through the heart of Connemara's inland wilderness. Just off the road 8 miles east of Clifden is the **Ben Lettery Hostel (IYHF)** (tel. (095) 346 36), an ideal base for hill walkers and climbers. (Members £2.50, nonmembers £3.) Ask at the hostel, which doubles as a stretcher post in case of emergency, for advice on routes to the surrounding **Twelve Bens** of Connemara.

Clifden, at Connemara's Atlantic edge, is an over-touristed place somewhat redeemed by the spectacular countryside along Sky Road, which heads out of town. Until you do the same, stay at the **Clifden Hostel and Camping** (tel. (092) 460 89), the red house on the beach road. (£3.50. Open Feb.-Nov.) There's a **tourist office** on Market St. (tel. (095) 211 63), next door to a **bike rental** shop (open June-Sept. Mon.-Fri. 9am-6pm, Sat. 9am-1pm and 2-6pm).

August brings the **Connemara Pony Show;** the shaggy beasts share the stage with traditional arts and crafts. If Clifden gets too busy, head south to **Roundstone** or north to **Letterfrack.** Boat trips leave from nearby Cleggan for the beautiful white strands of the island of **Inishbofin.** The views around the **Killary Harbor Youth Hostel (IYHF)** (no phone) inspired Wittgenstein to the completion of his major work, the *Philosophical Investigations*—see if the view inspires you to particularly profound postcards. (Members £2.50, nonmembers £3.)

The southern coast of Connemara cradles Galway's **Gaeltacht,** a must for anyone with an interest in Irish language, music, and folk traditions. *Curragh* races and small festivals are held at **Spiddal** and **Carraroe** in the summer, while spoken English is as scarce as the grass on the barren islands of **Lettermore** and **Lettermullen.** The **Indreabhán (Inverin) Youth Hostel (IYHF)** (tel. (091) 931 54), on the coast road, provides a convenient resting spot for travelers heading to or from **Rossaveal.**

Ferries depart from Rossaveal for the **Aran Islands,** 30 miles from Galway Town. Fares on the *Rose of Aran,* the *Queen of Aran* and the *Dun Aengus* are £7 one way, £12 round-trip (students £6 and £10)—cheaper (and quicker) than from Galway Town. Buses are timed to connect with ferries. The Aran Islands' rugged granite rocks blend into the traditional lifestyle of fishing communities immortalized in J.M. Synge's *Riders of the Sea.* On **Inishmore,** the largest of the islands, **Kilronay** is a convenient base. There are many B&Bs; the **tourist office** (tel. (099) 612 63; open June to mid-Sept.) will be glad to book you in one. The **Aran Hostel** (tel. (099) 612 48), right on the waterfront, is crowded but friendly. (£3.75. Refundable key deposit £3. Open April-Oct.) Hike away from the tourists toward the center of Inishmore along the spectacular coast to **Dun Aengus,** a cliffside fortress. Other ruins abound. Camping is free in unofficial sites, £2 in official ones with water and toilets. If the landscape intrigues you, hop aboard the frequent boats to **Inishmaan** or **Inisheer** and partake of their even more traditional mode of life. Go when it's sunny to enjoy Inisheer's sandy beach, or any time to enjoy Inishmaan, the most culturally active of the Aran Islands.

County Mayo

For the most part a flat and barren peat bog buffetted by Atlantic tempests, Mayo rises towards its southern border into the dramatic scenery of Connemara. An eighteenth-century planned town, **Westport** sits at the base of island-speckled **Clew Bay,** haunt of the sixteenth-century pirate chieftain Grace O'Malley (Granváille). Set aside an afternoon to hike up **Croagh Patrick,** the holy mountain where St. Patrick supposedly fasted and prayed. Pilgrims honor him by climbing this mountain on the last Sunday in July, but you can ascend the wide rocky path by yourself on any clear day. Although the summit is often shrouded in mist, the slopes offer striking views of the bay. If you decide to stay near town, walk one mile west on the Louisburgh Rd. to the **Granary Hikers' Rest** (tel. (098) 259 03), a somewhat primitive independent hostel, or a mile further to the friendly **Summerville Hostel** (tel. (098) 259 48). Both charge £3.50. Westport B&Bs may be booked through the **tourist office,** North Mall (tel. (098) 257 11; open June-Sept. Mon.-Sat. 9am-6pm; Oct.-May Mon.-Fri. 9am-5:15pm).

Several buses per day cross the bridge from the mainland to the beaches and mountains of **Achill Island.** Stay at **The Valley House** (tel. (098) 472 04), a musty mansion with adjoining pub in Dugart on the northwestern tip of the island (£3.50), or more conveniently at the very spartan **Wayfarer Hostel** (tel. (098) 432 66), on the beach in **Keel,** the administrative center of the island.

Just off the Westport-Galway road, the village of **Cong** sits astride the two lakes of Lough Mask and Lough Corrib. At one time the seat of the early medieval Kings of Connaught and an important monastic settlement, the town today is worth a stop for its lakeside scenery. One of Ireland's finest hostels, the **Cong Hostel** (tel. (092) 460 89), a mile from Cong on the Galway Rd., has extremely friendly and informative proprietors, a large kitchen, good showers, a free rowboat, and comfortable beds—all for £3.50. For private lodgings, try the **White House** (tel. (092) 460 16), on a pleasant side street in the middle of the village (£9). The little booklet, *The Glory of Cong* (£2 in stores, or on loan from the hostel), provides a comprehensive guide to the area—from limestone caves to early Christian churches to Oscar Wilde's family home.

County Sligo

William Butler Yeats spent his childhood summers in Sligo, and landscaped his poetry with its countryside. But this was already an area rich in mythic tales and the remains of early warfare between Connaught and Ulster—cairns, dolmens, passage graves, ring forts (pick up a copy of *Prehistoric Sligo* (25p) for more on these). **Knocknarea** and **Ben Bulben** mountains, Sligo County's main sights, are worth exploring. Their hulking, seemingly decapitated forms dominate the skyline. Knocknarea, which looms over Strandhill, is a particularly easy climb. The 40-minute walk offers spectacular coastal views; on the summit you'll see an 80-foot-high cairn, the rumored grave of the strong-minded Maeve of Connaught (the woman on the £1 note), who led a war against Ulster's warrior hero Cuchulainn to win a brown bull.

Sligo town is pleasant and friendly, graced by the winding River Garavogue. Its most prominent ruin is the **Dominican Abbey** (ca. 1250), with well-preserved cloister and pillars. The **County Museum** contains one of the finest collections of modern Irish art in the country, and numerous first editions of Yeats. (Open Tues.-Sat. 10:30am-12:30pm and 2:30-4:30pm. Free.) The writer's simple grave lies 4 miles north of town in Drumcliffe Churchyard, an easy hitch in the summer (or take the Donegal bus). Close by, the **Yeats Country Hostel** (tel. (071) 631 17) is a friendly place with its own pub. (£3.50 per night.)

Conveniently located right in Sligo, the **White House Hostel** (tel. (071) 451 60) is pretty and cozy. (£4, including toast and tea for breakfast.) Several of Sligo's B&Bs line Wolfe Tone Street across from the train station, or you can walk over to Quay Street to visit **The Anchor** (tel. (071) 429 04; £8 per person). For accommodations bookings (50p), free maps, and general information on the area, visit the well-run **tourist office** on Temple St. (tel. 612 01; open June Mon.-Sat. 9am-6pm; July-Aug. Mon.-Sat. 9am-8pm, Sun. 9am-5pm; Sept.-May Mon.-Fri. 9am-5pm, and Sat. 10am-1pm). For light meals, try **Lyon's Cafe** on Quay St., or **Kate's Kitchen** on Market St. (Both open Mon.-Sat. 9am-6pm.)

Sligo is a great place to catch traditional music and theater. The town is afire during the **Yeats Summer School's** two-week August session, with productions of Yeats's plays, poetry readings, and concerts of traditional Irish music. Try to see a show at the **Hawks Well Theatre** (tel. 615 26), which has rapidly become the drama center of the northwest. (Box office open Mon.-Sat. 10am-6pm. Tickets around £3.50, students £2.) For traditional music, try **McLynn's** on Market St., **Feehily's** on Bridge St., or the Tuesday night meetings at the **Sligo Trades Club** on Castle Street.

County Donegal

Mountainous and barren even by Irish standards, the northernmost Irish county is a land of silent peat bogs, fierce sea winds, and cliffs of staggering proportions. Tourists do visit Donegal, but outside the main towns of Donegal and Letterkenny, the vastness of the elements easily absorbs them. Ignore the wind-driven rain and spend some time hiking or fishing in this, Ireland's most primitive wilderness.

Donegal town is an unfortunate necessity—avail yourself of the tourist office, laundrette, and supermarket, then move on. The friendly **tourist office** (tel. (099) 211 48), in a caravan just out of town on the Sligo road, will book accommodations for 50p. (Open June and Sept. Mon.-Sat. 10am-6pm; July-Aug. Mon.-Sat. 9am-7pm, Sun. 10am-1pm and 2-5pm.) Stay more cheaply at the well-appointed **Ball Hill Hostel (IYHF)** (tel. (073) 211 74), 3 miles out of town off the Killybegs road on a lonely headland, or at the equally friendly **Bridge End Hostel** (tel. (073) 22 30), on the Killybegs road just as it leaves town. (£3.50. No curfew.) There really aren't any good restaurants in Donegal, but the **Foodland** supermarket on the Diamond stocks a much wider variety than the average Irish food store. **Eleanor's Laundrette,** Upper Main St., charges £1.50 per wash, 30p per drying cycle. (Open Mon.-Sat. 9am-6pm.

They cut hair, too.) Just a few doors away is **O'Donnails,** the town's best pub. (Music Thurs.-Sat. nights.)

Frequent buses run west to **Killybegs,** a bustling fishing port, and thence to **Glencolumbkille,** at the end of the peninusula (July-Aug. Mon.-Sat. 3 per day; Sept.-June Mon.-Sat. 1 per day). You can stay at the new **Hollybush Hostel** (tel. (073) 311 18; £3.50) in Killybegs, at the fine **Derrylahan Hostel** (tel. (073) 380 79; £3, showers 30p), 3km west along the coast road from Kilcar, or 3km further west at the dilapidated **Carrick Hostel (IYHF)** (tel. Carrick 73; £3). From Carrick you can start a day-long trek up to the cliffs of **Slieve League,** Europe's highest at almost 2000 feet. The path signposted to Bunglass, *not* the one to Slieve League, affords better views and gets you to the summit just the same. Continuing along the cliffs, you eventually come back to the road at the beautiful beach of Malin Beg, from which another 4-mile walk will get you to the **Dooey Hostel** (no phone), near Glencolumbkille. (Open year-round.) A bed in the slightly worn-out lower house costs £3.50, with metered showers and cooker, while one in the nicer four-bed apartments is £4 with showers and cooker included. The **Folk Museum,** at the bottom of the path to the hostel, is well worth a visit. (Open June-Aug. Mon.-Sat. 10am-6pm. Free.)

The road from Glencolumbkille north to Ardara is spectacular, though a real workout for bikers. Hikers might want to stick to the north coast of the peninsula; every headland discloses another stretch of some of Ireland's most dramatic coastal scenery. North of Ardara rise the **Derryveagh Mountains,** completely unspoiled hiking territory with **IYHF youth hostels** at **Crohy Head** (tel. (075) 213 30), 5 miles from Dungloe, **Aranmore Island** (no phone; open May-Sept.), 10 miles north of Crohy Head, and **Errigal** (tel. (075) 311 80), near the village of Dunlewy, about 15 miles inland from Dungloe.

Letterkenny serves as purgatory to the four heavenly peninsulas to the north: **Horn Head, Rosguill, Fanad,** and **Inishowen.** The **tourist office** in Letterkenny (tel. (074) 211 60) is open year-round and can give more information.

Northern Ireland

British pounds (£) are used in Northern Ireland.

The six provinces in Ulster, which have comprised troubled Northern Ireland since 1920, are as beautiful as any in Ireland. The lake county of Fermanagh and the wondrous north coast and southeast glens of Antrim make Northern Ireland worth at least a stopover. This is a land full of Celtic heritage: Sagas tell of pagan warriors battling upon the hillsides, and legend claims that it was near Downpatrick that St. Patrick founded the first Christian church in Ireland. Northern Ireland is also a haven for festivals, folk customs, and distinctive traditional music. Well-known festivals include the **Ould Lammas Fair** at Ballycastle on the last Monday and Tuesday of August, and Belfast's **Queens University Arts Festival** in November.

Most of Northern Ireland is quite safe, and the area welcomes visitors, since it gets so few. The violence is concentrated in the slums of Derry and Belfast, and you should maintain a healthy distance from any of the security forces—don't camp in a field next to a border outpost, for instance. It's also a good idea to avoid Northern Ireland entirely during the marching "season" (July 12-Aug. 12), traditionally a time of sectarian hostility. The Northern Irish appreciate questions, but morbid curiosity and ready-made solutions are not welcome.

Three ferry companies connect Northern Ireland to Britain. **Sealink** crosses from Stranraer in Scotland to Larne (2 hr., £11.80, students £8.20). For information and reservations contact Sealink, 24 Donegal Pl., Belfast (tel. 22 51 30). **Townsend Thorenson** (tel. Larne 42 31) runs ferries between Cairnryan in Scotland and Larne for about the same price. **Belfast Car Ferries** (tel. 22 68 00) has overnight service from Liverpool to Belfast (£30), and connects Belfast to the Isle of Man. Travelers from Scotland or the north of England to the Irish Republic should look into BIGE tickets via Stranraer and Larne. **Britrail Pass** holders pay for the Sealink crossing, but the pass is valid on Northern Ireland Railways. The National Express Student Coach Card is valid on Ulsterbus.

Outside Belfast hitching is as safe and easy as anywhere in the Republic. By agreement of **Northern Ireland Railways,** the 50% discount of a CIE Travelsave stamp applies to all trains in Northern Ireland. You can use your Travelsave stamp on CIE buses which pass through the North as they travel between two points in the Republic. For example, the cheapest way to get to Enniskillen from Dublin (if you have the Travelsave stamp) is to pay half-price to Ballyshannon and then get off in Northern Ireland en route. Northern Ireland offers a **Rail Runabout ticket,** good for seven consecutive days of travel. The **Ulsterbus Company** offers frequent service to all parts of Northern Ireland; its **Freedom of Northern Ireland Ticket** also allows travel for seven consecutive days (£16). The **Northern Ireland Tourist Board (NITB)** and local borough councils offer plenty of information centers throughout Northern Ireland.

Although British pounds are used in Northern Ireland, don't take away any of the notes issued by Northern Irish banks—they are very hard to use in the rest of the UK. Ironically, they're no problem to change in the Republic.

Calls to the Republic are international, while those to Great Britain are domestic.

Belfast

Although you definitely wouldn't want to live there, Belfast isn't a bad place to visit. The main sights, stores, and entertainment extend from the center city to the elegant **Queens University** area. The **Tourist Information Centre,** 48-52 High St. (tel. 24 66 09), gives away an excellent map with bus routes. (Open June-Sept. Mon.-Fri. 9am-5:15pm, Sat. 9am-noon, closed Sun.; Oct.-May closed Sat.-Sun.) Their pamphlet, *Belfast's Civic Festival Trail,* suggests a good walking tour of the city. Rest your feet (and oil your throat) in the Victorian splendor of the **Crown Liquor Saloon**—Britain's only licensed National Trust monument. In the Botanic Gardens, the **Ulster Museum** holds an interesting collection of contemporary art and the dazzling treasures of a Spanish Armada shipwreck. (Open Mon.-Fri. 10am-4:50pm, Sat. 1-4:50pm, Sun. 2-4:50pm. Free.)

West Belfast, separated from the rest of the city by the motorway, is a horrible and dangerous place—the troubles aside (and they are very much center stage in this part of Northern Ireland), this is one of the most economically depressed spots in Europe. Seven miles to the east of Belfast, the **Ulster Folk and Transport Museum** is a meticulously reconstructed open-air exhibit spread over 180 acres of parkland. The museum will fascinate anyone interested in the history of Irish rural society. Ulsterbus (blue bus) #1 (Belfast-Bangor) stops right by the entrance. (Open May-Sept. Mon.-Sat. 11am-6pm, Sun. 2-6pm; Oct.-April Mon.-Sat. 11am-5pm, Sun. 2-5pm. Admission 50p.)

Belfast's **IYHF youth hostel,** Saintfield Rd. (tel. 64 78 65), is a good 3 miles southeast of the city in Newtownbreda. Take bus #83 from Donegall Sq. East. (£3-3.50. Open early Jan. to mid-Dec.) More pleasant but open only during university holidays (mid-March to mid-April and mid-June to mid-Sept.). is **Queen's University Halls of Residence,** Malone Rd. (tel. 38 16 08), where rooms, kitchen, TV room, and showers cost £2.55 for students enrolled in a British university, £2.80 for non-British students, £5.80 for non-students. Walk from the center (about 30 min.) or take bus #71 from Donegall Sq. East. The university area is the best place to look for B&Bs; try **Mrs. Davidson,** 81 Eglantine Ave. (tel. 66 71 49; £8; showers included).

Good places to eat are clustered around Shaftesbury Square at the bottom of Malone Road. Try **Spud's,** 23 Bradbury St., which serves great burgers (£1.09 for the New Yorker) daily until 3am. If you look reasonably student-like, you can have a cheap lunch at the **Student Union Refectory.** (Open year-round Mon.-Fri.) The **Botanic Inn,** Malone Rd., known as "the Bot," is popular with students and does good pub grub.

The **Arts Theatre,** Botanic Ave. (tel. 32 49 36), puts on the best of the city's drama, but closes in July and August, as does the **Queen's Film Theatre,** a good repertory cinema attached to the university. The cultural scene in Belfast blossoms in November of each year, when the city stages the **Belfast Festival at Queen's,** a two-week treasure trove of attractions from opera to the Royal Shakespeare Company to fine jazz and traditional music. A program is available from Festival House, 8 Malone Rd., Belfast, BT9 SBN (tel. 66 76 87).

Glens of Antrim and Causeway Coast

North of Belfast, the nine deep and richly green Glens of Antrim stretch from high moorlands to the rocky coast. The villages of Glenarm, Carnlough, and Waterfoot each stand at the seaside mouth of a glen, all beckoning with beaches and accommodations. **Glenarm Glen,** the farthest south, holds the art galleries and pubs of **Glenarm,** as well as nearby Glenarm Forest. Just north on the A2, **Carnlough** boasts both the merry and musical **Black's Pub,** and Jim McKillop, an Irish fiddle champion and instrument maker. **Waterfoot,** Antrim's broadest glen, is only 8 miles farther; in July it hosts the **Glens of Antrim Feis,** one of Ulster's major music and dance festivals.

You might find it practical to base yourself in the town of **Cushendall;** the somewhat untidy **Moneyvart Youth Hostel** (tel. Moneyvart 344) is a 15-minute walk north of town. (Open Jan.-Nov.) **Mrs. K. Quinn** runs a small, friendly B&B on Chapel Rd. (tel. Cushendall 716 10; £7.50). The **tourist office** (tel. Cushendall 714 51; open July-Aug. Mon.-Sat. 10am-6pm), is also on Chapel Rd., in the parlor of a private home at #11. Soaring above the town is flat-topped **Tieveragh Hill,** in which many of the "little people" are believed to live. Nearby, you can see **Ossian's Grave,** a megalithic tomb which supposedly contains the remains of the bard Ossian, son of Finn the Warrior. You'll find **Pat's Bar** between Cushendun and Cushendall; and in Cushendall is **Joe McCullum's** at 23 Mill St. This tiny, centuries-old pub is the best on the coast.

Even a short trip to Northern Ireland should include the acclaimed **Causeway Coast.** The name stems from one of Ireland's most impressive natural sights, **The Giant's Causeway.** A series of perfectly-shaped basalt columns supposedly built by the giant, Finn McCool, these columns form a honeycomb pathway into the sea. The cliff path leading east from this volcanic pathway is the most spectacular part of the Causeway, winding among dramatic basalt formations and deep coves; at the head of the Causeway is a **National Trust Information Centre** where you can inquire about walks and learn the area's history.

The Causeway's biggest **tourist office** is in **Portrush** in the Town Hall (tel. 82 33 33; open Easter-Sept. Mon.-Sat. 9am-8:30pm, Sun. 2-6pm). Portrush is an over-touristed arcade center worth visiting only to get information and to catch bus #172 from Dunluce Ave., which runs east along the coast as far as Ballycastle. (Mon.-Sat. 4 per day, 2 Sun. Bus stops at all towns and sights, or when flagged down.) Nearby **Portballintrae** is lovely, and convenient to both Dunluce Castle and The Causeway. Stay with **Mrs. Jackson,** 82 Ballaghmore Rd. (tel. Bushmills 312 75; £6.50. Open April-Sept.). Don't miss the chance to tour the **Bushmills Distillery,** home of the excellent whiskey of the same name. (Tours Mon.-Fri. 10:30am, 11:30am, 2pm, and 3:30pm. Call Bushmills 215 21 in advance.)

Five miles short of the Causeway, the ruins of **Dunluce Castle** are perched on a cliff with good beaches not far away in either direction. The closest hostel is **Whitepark Bay (IYHF)** (tel. Bushmills 317 45; £3; open Jan.-Nov.); a larger one is in **Ballycastle,** at 34 North St. (tel. 623 37; open Feb.-Dec.). Whitepark Bay is a gorgeous stretch of white sand and cliffs; from the Ballycastle hostel you can see out to Fair Head, and to Rathlin Island where the Scottish king Robert the Bruce lived in exile. For B&Bs in Ballycastle, try the **Atlantic Guest House,** The Promenade (tel. (02657) 624 12), at £8. This seaside town of parks and rose gardens is where the **Ould Lammas Fair** is held, on the last Monday and Tuesday of August.

Fermanagh County

As you travel between Northern Ireland and the west coast of the Republic, the lakes of **Fermanagh** are a logical and attractive stopping point. **Upper and Lower Lough Erne** form a lake district far larger and much quieter than their English counterpart. **Enniskillen,** a busy and attractive town on an island at the southern end of Lower Lough Erne, is a comfortable touring base. There is a very helpful tourist office in town at the **Lakeland Visitor Centre** (tel. Enniskillen 231 10; open July-Aug. Mon.-Fri. 9am-7pm, Sat.-Sun. 10am-1pm and 2-5pm; Sept.-June Mon.-Fri. 9am-5pm). **Mrs. Mulhern,** 19 Sligo Rd. (tel. 248 89), offers the least expensive B&B in town, at £7.50 for a single (open April-Sept. only), or take an Enniskillen-Kesh bus to Lisnarrick for the **Castle Arendale Youth Hostel** (tel. 281 18; open Jan.-Nov.). Camping is available next door (tel. 213 33; £1.25 per person). **The Vintage** is a pub popular with young folks; go to **Pat's** near the Town Hall for traditional Irish atmosphere.

The nearby **Marble Arch Caves,** by the bordertown of **Belcoo,** have been recently opened to visitors and are well worth a visit. (Open June Mon.-Sat. 11am-6pm, Sun. 11am-6:30pm; July-Aug. Mon.-Sat. 11am-7pm, Sun. 11am-7:30pm; Sept.-Oct. Mon.-Sat. 11am-6pm, Sun. 2-6:30pm. Last tours leave 1½ hr. before closing. Admission £2.25, students £1.25.) Belcoo is an easy ride through the predominantly flat countryside, but there's nowhere in town to rent bikes. Numerous companies run short cruises on the island-dotted lower lake (from £2)—check at the tourist office. Serious hikers should consider tackling the Fermanagh stretch of the 23-mile **Ulster Way,** a forest path leading from Belcoo to Lough Navar. A descriptive pamphlet is available at the Enniskillen tourist office.

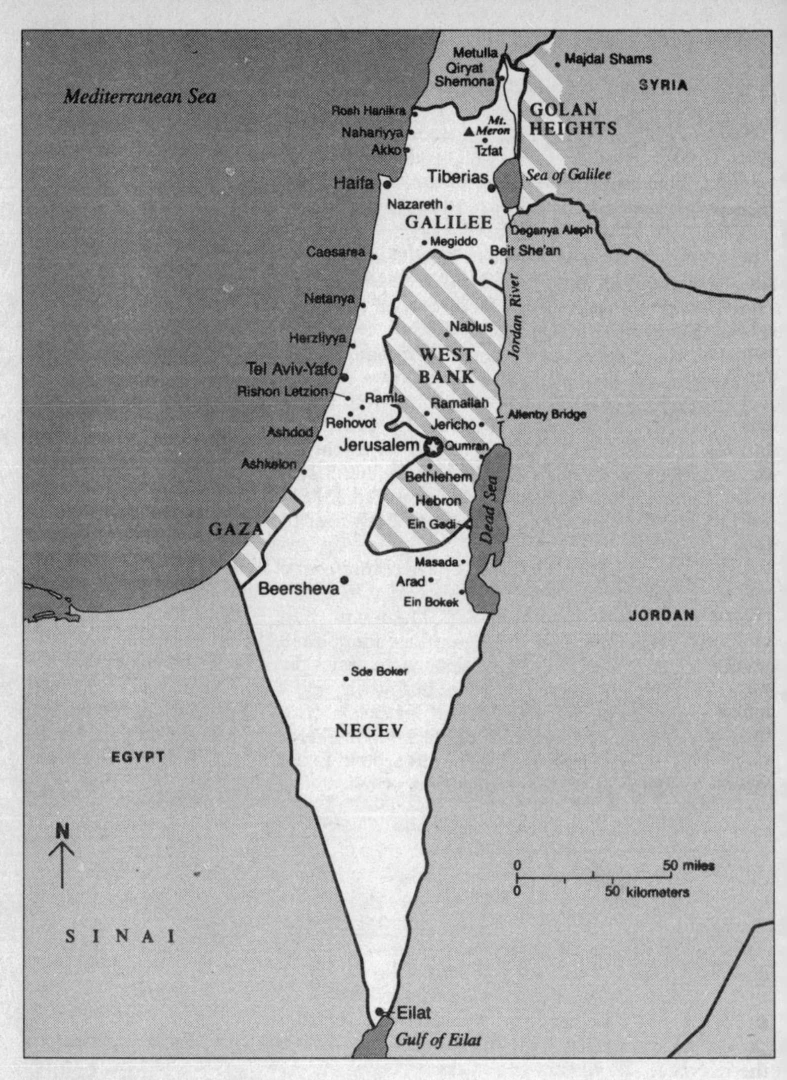

ISRAEL

US$1 = 1.61 shekels
CDN$1 = 1.20 shekels
UK£1 = 2.59 shekels
AUS$1 = 1.14 shekels

1 shekels = US$0.62
1 shekels = CDN$0.83
1 shekels = UK£0.39
1 shekels = AUS$0.88

Each of the Biblical prophets had different divine revelations: Ezekiel witnessed a valley filled with dry bones resurrected to life, Amos envisioned hills dripping with wine, and Jeremiah saw a seething pot in the distance. So it is with Israel—this embattled country has long been a land of conflicting personal visions.

As the birthplace of Jesus, the land promised by God to the Jews, and the site of the place from which Muhammad ascended to heaven, Israel has been the site of holy wars from Biblical times, through Roman conquests and Crusader battles, to the present day.

Modern Zionism—the effort to create a Jewish state in the Biblical land of Israel—was founded in the 1870s by Theodor Herzl, an Austrian journalist. Spurred by the nationalism and socialism of the late nineteenth century, the early Zionist pioneers reclaimed fertile soil from the desert, resuscitated the then-dead Hebrew language, and built a society around it. In the process they too were transformed: The native-born Israeli is nicknamed *sabra*—a cactus fruit—tough and prickly on the outside, tender and sweet within. Sharing this land are 700,000 Palestinian Arabs whom many observers consider a disenfranchised people. The Palestinian question has contributed to the outbreak of six wars and to countless acts of terrorism, and, most recently, to the conflict in southern Lebanon and the bloody battle for Beirut.

To some (most notably, the U.S.) the innocent victim of fanatical Arab belligerence, to others a quasi-apartheid pariah with little respect for international law, the tiny state of Israel is in the news more than any other country, of any size. Upon its declaration of independence in May of 1948, Israel was attacked by the Arab nations surrounding it. Since independence, Israel has been involved in four wars with its neighbors: the 1956 Sinai campaign, in which Israel, in collaboration with the U.K. and France, wrested control of the Sinai and the Suez Canal from Egypt; the 1967 Six Day War, in which Israel pre-emptively struck against Syria, Jordan, and Egypt and gained the West Bank; the 1974 Yom Kippur War, a bloody and indecisive campaign of attrition; and the 1982 Lebanon campaign, in which the Israelis occupied strife-torn Lebanon as far north as Beirut, forcing the P.L.O. to move its headquarters to Tunisia (they have since moved to Yemen). To fund these wars, Israel has matched the petrodollar resources of the Arab World with massive influxes of U.S. military and non-military aid. Even so, by 1984 the economy was in a shambles, with wages that were not nearly keeping pace with the 400% inflation rate. The government fell, and elections in the summer of 1984 produced in no clear victor. A coalition between Labor and Likud, the two main parties, was formed, with Shimon Peres (of the former) and Itzhak Shamir (of the latter) to share the responsibilities of top office. The marriage has not been a happy one—the acrimony reached a feverish pitch early in the summer of 1987 with a split on the issue of the proposed Jordanian peace plan. Israel's foreign relations remain as unstable as its domestic policies—the large number of soldiers you'll see carry guns, a situation the Israelis take for granted but that you may find disconcerting.

Israel today faces more questions than can be satisfactorily answered—moral questions about the nation's responsibilities to the displaced Palestinians; intellectual questions about whether Judaism must now be defined in national, religious, and/or ethnic terms; and practical questions regarding the extent to which Israel should be governed by traditional Jewish law. But regardless of your opinions on the relevance and importance of these issues, you will likely be dazzled with the country's unique ethnic, geographical, and historical diversity.

For such a small country, Israel generally surprises tourists with its varied landscape. One passes quickly from the mountainous Golan Heights in the north, through the agricultural plains of the Galilee, past the miles of Mediterranean beach, and into the partially reclaimed Negev desert in the south. Jerusalem has been a center of pilgrims for centuries, but the coastal plain from Tel Aviv north to Haifa is Israel's most industrialized and populated area. The West Bank, to the north, east, and south of Jerusalem, contains a volatile Palestinian population and a number of controversial Jewish settlements. Since the Israeli withdrawal from the Sinai in 1982, the crowded resort of Eilat is the only Israeli city on the Red Sea.

For historical background on the land and people of Israel, the works of Solomon Grayzel are both authoritative and elegant, though tedious at times. For a more complex sociocultural analysis, try Raphael Patai's books, *The Jewish Mind* and *The Arab Mind.* Saul Bellow's *To Jerusalem and Back* is a thoughtful, personal evaluation of modern Israel, and journalist Lawrence Meyer's *Israel Now* is also an excellent and very readable introduction to the country. For a lighter look at tourists' experiences in the Holy Land, try Mark Twain's *The Innocents Abroad. In the Land of Israel,* by Amos Oz, a prominent Israeli author, contains interviews with native Israelis, including West Bank residents, and *Arab and Jew: Wounded Spirits in a Promised Land* by David Shipler, is an exceptionally readable examination of Israeli society today. For an in-depth budget guide to Israel with more detailed coverage than we can provide here, turn to *Let's Go: Israel and Egypt.*

Getting There

Three ferries connect Europe to Israel: two out of Athens and one from Venice. The **Stability Line's** *Vergina* travels weekly between Piraeus and Haifa, departing Piraeus Thursday evening and stopping in Iraklion (Crete) and Limassol (Cyprus) before arriving in Haifa on Sunday morning. It returns to Greece the same evening. For students or those under 26, deck-fare for the full trip is about US$75, plus US$10 per stopover (US$10 less in Oct., April, and May.) **Sol Maritime Services** operates two boats. The *Sol Phryne* has fares and schedules similar to the *Vergina,* calling in Rhodes and Limassol on its way to Haifa. The *Sol Olympia* makes the slow, expensive voyage from Venice to Haifa (via the Yugoslav coast and Athens) every 10 days. Of the three, only the *Phryne* maintains service year-round; the *Vergina* runs April through October 30, and the *Olympia* January 1 through October 16.

Air travel from Europe presents a quicker alternative. London and Athens are the two cheapest hubs for service to Israel. During the summer of 1987, one-way fares from London and Paris to Tel Aviv were as low as US$160. Consult our Budget Travel listings in your departure city for student, youth, and budget fares. Flights returning to Europe are similarly priced.

There are two overland routes to Israel—from Egypt and from Jordan. The border crossings between Israel and Egypt are at Rafiah, on the Mediterranean, and at Taba, south of Eilat. Coming to Israel via Jordan is somewhat complicated; see the Jordan chapter for details, and remember that political circumstances could close this route.

You should know that if you plan to travel to Jordan (or most other Arab or African countries) from Israel, your passport must be free of evidence that you've been in Israel. When you enter Israel, you may request to have your entry visa stamped on a separate piece of paper that you can later remove from your passport. Countries that don't admit travelers with Israeli-stamped passports will also not admit travelers with Egyptian-Israeli border entry stamps in their passports.

Transportation

Distances are short in Israel, and fairly inexpensive buses go almost everywhere. **Egged** runs most of the country's buses, except in Tel Aviv, where **Dan** buses run. Inter-city buses leave from the Central Bus Station *(Tachanah HaMerkazit).* To avoid the pre- and post-Sabbath jams, remember that from Friday afternoon until Saturday after sunset buses do not operate anywhere in Israel, except Haifa. Early Sunday mornings (until 8:30am) tend to be crowded with soldiers returning to base. Cities with large Arab populations have independent, Arab-owned buses which run all week.

For the trip to Eilat, reserve seats a day before departure. Make sure the ticket vendor has affixed a sticker with the date and your seat number to the back of the ticket. For other trips, don't bother to buy a ticket before boarding the bus; you can pay the driver and avoid waiting in line. Students get 10% off all inter-city fares. Unlimited travel passes are available, but given the price—US$35 for one week, US$55 for two—you'll have to zoom around to make them worthwhile.

There is limited train service in Israel. Prices are somewhat lower than buses, and there's a 25% student discount. The best service is on the express trains between Haifa and Tel Aviv, where the journey takes less time than the bus trip. Otherwise trains are slower and much less frequent than buses and not worth the savings.

The fastest way of getting around is by *sherut* (shared taxi). Running between the large cities, or between a city and its suburbs, these leave as soon as they fill up. On the road, they will beep as they go by and you can hail them. To Eilat, there's a fixed schedule, and you must buy a ticket two days in advance. A *sherut* taxi costs about 20% more than the same trip on a bus. Make sure that the car you get into is a *sherut* taxi and not a regular taxi, which charges a good deal more. *Sherut* taxis operate on Saturdays and late at night when buses are not running, but prices during these times are 20% higher.

In a country where hitchhiking was once common practice, most people no longer risk it because of an increasing number of grisly incidents. The government prohibits women soldiers from hitching; civilian travelers should take their cue from this. With bus fares as reasonable as they are, we really don't recommend it. A car of your own is great, but rental rates (from US$40 per day) and gas prices are astronomical. Furthermore, driving in Israel is an aggressive, dangerous art.

If you are one of the determined few who try cycling through Israel, be aware that cyclists are an unfamiliar phenomenon on Israeli roads, and are treated by drivers as another obstacle in the way of their progress. Cycling during the summer is possible, but it's wise to keep your head covered and carry plenty of water.

Accommodations and Camping

Because of the high prices of hotels in Israel, we list very few, preferring the network of IYHF youth hostels, and the unofficial hostels in larger cities. You can obtain a list of IYHF hostels from the office of the **Israel Youth Hostel Association,** at 3 Rehov Dorot Rishonim St., P.O. Box 1075, Jerusalem 91009 (tel. (02) 22 16 48); they also sell IYHF cards (US$14). Hostels are listed on the back of the invaluable Israel Survey map, available free at any Israel Government Tourist Organization (IGTO) office. Most IYHF hostels accept reservations; they have no age limit, but a few limit stays to three nights. IYHF hostels are generally more expensive than unofficial hostels; prices run about US$7.50, with breakfast included. Nonmembers typically pay about US$1 extra. Many hostels are closed from 9am to 5pm, or at least during the afternoon.

In beach resorts such as Nahariya or Eilat, or seasonal resorts such as Tzfat, there are private rooms to let. You'll be accosted at the bus station by agents of the various hoteliers. Prices and quality vary considerably, but a private room in a pension might run US$15 or more during July and August. Always ask to see a room, inquire about facilities (bathrooms, showers, use of kitchen), and get a price set in advance.

The Israel Survey map also lists campgrounds with full facilities in areas of natural beauty, starting at around US$4 per person in summer, US$2.50 in winter. You may prefer to pick your own site. In the north and east, though, think before you hammer in your tent stakes—check with the local tourist office. Lastly, be warned that robberies are frequent, particularly near cities.

Practical Information

Everyone celebrates a different sabbath in Israel. The Jewish sabbath (*Shabbat* in Hebrew) begins Friday night at sundown and ends Saturday night at sundown. National offices and services (including Egged buses) close down. As a rule of thumb, Jerusalem is the most observant of Shabbat, while Haifa and Eilat are the least. Tickets for museums or restaurant meals can often be purchased a day ahead of time and used on Saturday. Arab buses, stores, and restaurants are often closed on Friday, but operate all day Saturday. Almost everything is open Sunday.

The major Jewish holidays are Rosh HaShana (Sept. 12-13 in 1988) and Yom Kippur (Sept. 21 in 1988). For these days and the week in between them, many shops and offices work reduced hours. The major Islamic holiday is Ramadan (April 18-May 18 in 1988); many restaurants close between dawn and dusk and it is disrespectful to eat during daylight hours in Arab areas.

Although inflation in Israel was once the highest in the world, it is now down to single digits and the exchange rate has remained stable. As the shekel has stabilized, people have been less anxious to purchase American dollars and it's no longer profitable to change money on the black market.

The Israel Survey map gives the telephone number and location of the **Israel Government Tourist Organization (IGTO)** offices in all major towns and cities; there may also be municipal tourist information offices in some cities. Offices are generally quite helpful, though they seldom offer room-finding services.

Neither Hebrew nor Arabic are written in Roman characters, but street signs are always translated into English and most Israelis speak at least a little English; those who don't often speak French or German. There are two English-language newspapers, the daily *Jerusalem Post,* and *Al Fajr,* a weekly Palestinian journal. "The Voice of Peace" plays tunes in English all day.

There are public telephones everywhere, but many of them are out of order. The best bet for a working phone is the post office; after these try Egged stations and hotels. Phones use tokens *(ossimonim),* bought at the post office, hostel, hotel desk, or newsstand. Wait for a dial tone, then put a few *ossimonim* in the slot and dial the area code. Pause (you'll hear a click) before dialing. When you connect, the *ossimonim* will start dropping into the phone—keep an eye on the little window to make sure there are enough. At the end of your call, lift up the small lever to regain any left-over tokens. Useful numbers are: Information (14), Police (100), First Aid (101), and Fire (102). Dial 18 or (03) 62 28 81 for an overseas (collect) operator. It is impractical to make an international call direct from a pay phone; you must go to a main post office with metered phones, or to a luxury hotel, the latter of which will charge an exorbitant commission. The **country code** for Israel is 972. Post offices are generally open Sunday through Thursday from 7:45am to 12:30pm and again from 4 to 6pm; on Friday, offices are open only in the morning. Banks are usually open Sunday through Friday from 8:30am to 12:30pm, and Sunday through Tuesday and Thursday from 4 to 6pm. Shops usually close around 1pm and reopen at 4pm, sometimes staying open until 9pm. Grocery shops are closed Tuesday afternoons.

The **Chevra Le Haganat HaTeva** (Society for the Protection of Nature in Israel) sponsors outings from walking tours of a city to weekend tours of the Golan. An SPNI outing of a few days is a worthwhile use of your time when first arriving in Israel, especially as it isn't hard to come out of a tour with friends and places to stay all over the country. Visit or write the organization at 4 HaShfela St., Tel Aviv (tel. (03) 38 25 01), near the Central Bus Station; 13 Helena HaMalka St., Jerusalem (tel. (02) 24 95 67); or 8 HaMenachem St., Haifa (tel. (04) 66 41 35).

A unique fact of Israeli life is its agricultural collectives: *kibbutzim,* communal settlements in which all work and profits are shared equally by members; and *moshavim,* in which members own their own plots of land but share machinery and facilities. The socialist Jewish movements of Eastern Europe at the turn of the century created these agricultural communities. Idealistic young men and women went to Palestine to pump out the swamps and plant fields in the desert; many of the first leaders of Israel, including David Ben-Gurion and Golda Meir, were from *kibbutzim.*

Today the *kibbutz* movement has grown and diversified. Some are exploring industry and international marketing. Many are also moving children from the communal children's houses to their parents homes, in strong contrast to the original kibbutz ideology of child-rearing. Three major kibbutz movements exist: Kibbutz Artzi is the most socialist, Kibbutz Takam is traditional, and Kibbutz HaDati is the most religious. Of special interest are Kibbutzim Lotan and Yahel, founded by the Reform Movement, and Kibbutz Hanaton, founded by the Conservative Movement. Kibbutz Nes Amim is a Christian kibbutz.

The best way to get a feeling for kibbutz life is to work on one. This involves a commitment of at least one month of hard work and early hours. Kibbutz members, used to parades of foreign volunteers passing through the kibbutz for a month or two, may not reach out to you unless you make the initial effort to meet them.

Volunteering opportunities have recently become a little more restricted, but if you do want to volunteer, visit the offices of the **kibbutz associations'** in Tel Aviv. Each office represents the ideologies of Israel's various political parties—ask the Tel Aviv tourist office for addresses. All charge a US$15 registration fee. You must be between the ages of 18 and 32 and have a medical certificate stating that you are in good health and capable of doing agricultural work in a hot climate. Before you commit yourself, do some advance intelligence work; it's a good idea to visit the kibbutz and talk to some of the volunteers. Volunteers generally work six six-hour days per week with several days off per month, receiving a small monthly allowance of pocket money (US$20-25) along with some other benefits.

Many *kibbutzim* also offer an *ulpan,* a Hebrew language class combined with slightly reduced volunteer work duties. The *ulpan* may also include classes on Israeli and Jewish history and culture, and trips around the country. These programs normally require a commitment of 4½ to 6 months, though there are some shorter programs in the summer.

Working on an archeological dig is another popular way to earn your keep. In March, the Ministry of Education and Culture (Department of Antiquities and Museums, P.O. Box 586, Jerusalem 91004) publishes a list of excavations open to summer volunteers. The cost ranges from free to US$30 per day, room and board included. This option is available only in the summer, and you should reserve well in advance. There may be other digs continuing in the off-season; contact the Department of Antiquities and Museums, Rockefeller Museum, Jerusalem (tel. (02) 28 51 51); ask for Karen.

Black-market employment is available, principally in youth hostels, both IYHF and private. A normal agreement consists of four hours of general cleaning in exchange for room, part or full board, and possibly a small stipend. Similar positions are sometimes available at the Field Schools of the Society for the Protection of Nature. It is also often possible to get cleaning or restaurant work at luxury resort hotels, most likely in Eilat; these usually pay room and board plus about US$150 a month. All of these jobs are filled on a first-come, first-served basis; you must show up ready to work.

Food

Thanks to the diverse ethnic background of Israeli society, every kind of cuisine is available, from Eastern European to Middle Eastern, and from American-style fast food to Chinese. When shopping for your own food, rely on the excellent and inexpensive dairy products and fruit and vegetables; milk, bread, and a few other staples are subsidized by the government and thus kept extremely cheap.

The standard inexpensive street food is a *felafel* sandwich, flat pita bread stuffed with balls of ground chickpeas deep-fried in oil, with various salads, french fries (called chips), and *tahina* (a white sauce made from sesame seeds) or red *harif* (hot) sauce. Another popular option is *shwarma,* chunks of spiced lamb with salad in a pita. Pizza runs a close third. You will see fruit juice sold everywhere for 75¢ a glass. If you ask for soda you'll get soda water. There are numerous native wines, most not up to European standards. The two most common beers are *Maccabee,* a lager, and *Goldstar,* slightly stronger and cheaper. *Nesher* is a very sweet, syrupy malt beer. If you ask for coffee, you'll get a small cup of strong, muddy Turkish coffee; if you want something resembling American coffee, ask for *nes,* or *nes kafeh,* and you'll get instant coffee. If you want it with milk, ask for it *eem halav.*

When eating in restaurants it is important to be aware that many follow the Jewish laws of *kashrut* relating to food preparation. This means that a dairy restaurant won't serve meat (except fish), and a meat restaurant won't provide butter for your bread or cream for your coffee.

A good option for a cheap, good meal in any town is the Egged self-service (cafeteria-style) restaurant in the Central Bus Station. *Be careful* to observe the signs indicating which tables are only for non-meat meals.

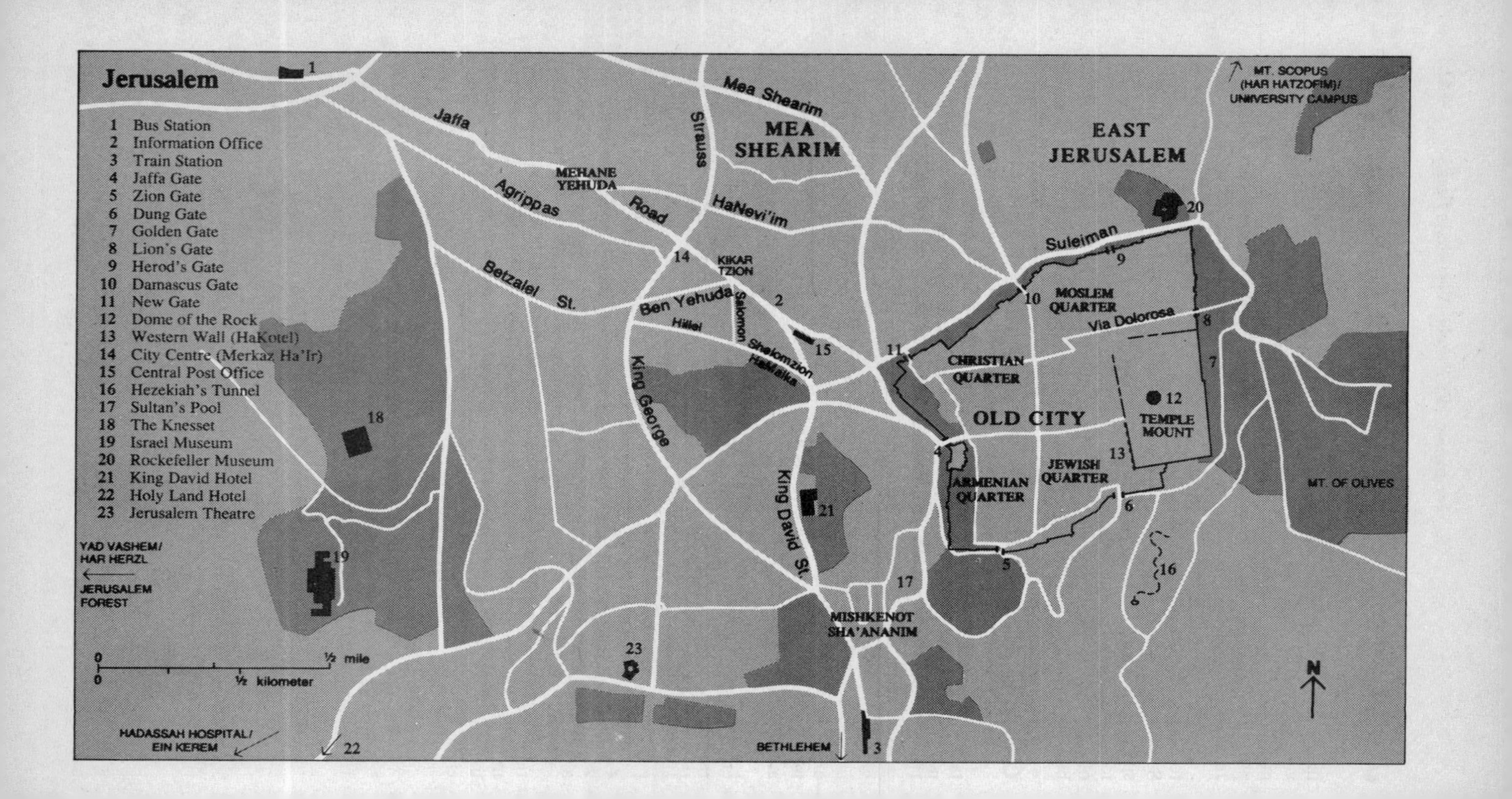
Jerusalem
1 Bus Station
2 Information Office
3 Train Station
4 Jaffa Gate
5 Zion Gate
6 Dung Gate
7 Golden Gate
8 Lion's Gate
9 Herod's Gate
10 Damascus Gate
11 New Gate
12 Dome of the Rock
13 Western Wall (HaKotel)
14 City Centre (Merkaz Ha'Ir)
15 Central Post Office
16 Hezekiah's Tunnel
17 Sultan's Pool
18 The Knesset
19 Israel Museum
20 Rockefeller Museum
21 King David Hotel
22 Holy Land Hotel
23 Jerusalem Theatre
YAD VASHEM/
HAR HERZL
JERUSALEM
FOREST
HADASSAH HOSPITAL/
EIN KEREM
BETHLEHEM
MT. SCOPUS
(HAR HATZOFIM)/
UNIVERSITY CAMPUS
EAST
JERUSALEM
MEA
SHEARIM
Mea Shearim
Jaffa
Strauss
MEHANE
YEHUDA
Agrippas
Road
HaNevi'im
KIKAR
TZION
Betzalel St.
Ben Yehuda
Hillel
Salomon
Shelomzion
HaMalka
King George
King David St.
Suleiman
MOSLEM
QUARTER
Via Dolorosa
CHRISTIAN
QUARTER
OLD CITY
TEMPLE
MOUNT
ARMENIAN
QUARTER
JEWISH
QUARTER
MT. OF OLIVES
MISHKENOT
SHA'ANANIM
0 ½ mile
0 ½ kilometer
N

Jerusalem (El Khuds, Yerushalayim)

On Fridays, the Muslim merchants of the Old City close their shops and move in waves through labyrinthine alleys toward their mosques. On Saturdays, the fervently religious Hasidic Jews of the Mea She'arim sector barricade their streets to guard the sanctity of Shabbat. On Sundays, the inhabitants of the Armenian Quarter put down their tools to attend churches along the Via Dolorosa, the road on which Jesus carried the cross to Calvary.

To Muslims, Jerusalem is the "furthest sanctuary" from which Muhammad rose to heaven, and the third holiest city of Islam; to Jews, it is the site of the First and Second Temples and the symbol of their national identity; to Christians it is the site of Christ's crucifixion and resurrection. Each people has brought a new set of ideas to Jerusalem; each has added a layer to the Old City. From the foundations of the First Temple to the Roman streets, from Crusader churches to the modern buildings of the New City, each group has left its mark.

Orientation and Practical Information

Jerusalem is connected to all major points in Israel; frequent buses and *sherut* taxis connect the city with Tel Aviv, and buses run to the Dead Sea, to Eilat, and north to the Sea of Galilee. Buses and *sherut* taxis also connect to the Allenby/King Hussein Bridge and West Bank cities.

Until 1860 there was only the walled **Old City** of Jerusalem. The Old City is divided into the four quadrants laid out by either the Mamelukes or the Ottomans after the expulsion of the Crusaders 800 years ago: the **Christian, Armenian, Jewish,** and **Muslim** Quarters. Today, the Christian Quarter, largest after the Muslim Quarter, is predominantly Muslim Arab; Jews, Armenians, and Christians represent only a small minority of the Old City's population.

East Jerusalem, a densely populated Arab quarter, is tucked up against the northern walls. The **New City,** more commonly known as **West Jerusalem,** is the administrative/commercial center, and the seat of Israel's national government. Its central thoroughfare is **Jaffa Road** (Dereḥ Yafo), stretching, for the traveler's purposes, from the Central Bus Station to **Jaffa Gate,** the main western entrance to the Old City. Mid-way between the bus station and Jaffa Gate, the **downtown** area extends over the intersection of HaMeleḥ George Street, Jaffa Road, and Ben Yehuda Street. To reach the Old City from the downtown area, hop aboard bus #20, which travels along Jaffa Road through West Jerusalem.

The tourist office hands out free maps of Jerusalem that include public transportation routes. If you will be staying more than a few days in Jerusalem, invest in the more thorough map "Prepared by the Survey of Israel" (US$1), available at the bookstores listed below. You might also purchase *Footloose in Jerusalem,* a set of eight self-paced walking tours, available only at Steimatzky's.

Tourist Offices: Israel Government Tourist Office (IGTO), 24 HaMeleḥ George St. (tel. 24 12 82), in the New City. The branch office inside Jaffa Gate in the Old City is more helpful (tel. 28 22 96). Both open Sun.-Thurs. 8:30am-5pm, Fri. 8:30am-2pm. **Municipal Information Office,** 17 Jaffa Road. (tel. 22 88 44). More helpful and less crowded than the IGTO. Ask about free walking tours (Sat. at 10am). Open Sun.-Thurs. 9am-12:30pm, Fri. 9am-noon. **Christian Information Center,** inside Jaffa Gate to the right (tel. 28 76 47). Infinitely patient and helpful, this staff provides almost the same information as the IGTO. This is the place to write or visit for tickets to the Christmas Eve midnight mass in Bethlehem. Open in summer Mon.-Sat. 8:30am-12:30pm and 3-6pm; in winter until 5:30pm. **Lifshitz Information Center,** (tel. 28 18 27), above the Cardo in the Jewish Quarter. Information on the Jewish sights in the Old City. Open Sun.-Thurs. 9am-6pm, Fri. 9am-1pm.

Budget Travel: ISSTA, 5 Eliashar St. (tel. 22 72 57). From the Old City, turn right off Jaffa Road 1 block north of Zion Sq., where you'll see a bright yellow ISSTA sign. Cheap flights to London, Cairo, North America, and Europe. Open Sun.-Tues. and Thurs. 8:30am-1pm and 3-6pm, Wed. and Fri. 8:30am-1pm.

American Express: Meditrad Ltd., 27 HaMeleḥ George St. (tel. 22 22 11). Mail held, checks sold, and cardholders' personal checks cashed, but no wired money accepted. The nearest place to have money cabled is in Cairo. Open Sun.-Tues. and Thurs. 8:30am-1pm and 3:30-6pm, Wed. and Fri. 8:30am-1pm.

Post Office: 23 Jaffa Rd. Open Sun.-Thurs. 8am-6pm, Fri. 8am-1pm. Poste Restante open Sun.-Thurs. 8am-1pm and 4-6pm, Fri. 8am-noon.

Telephones: Koresh St., behind the post office building. Open Sun.-Thurs. 7am-9pm, Fri. 7am-2pm. For collect calls from a pay phone, dial (03) 62 28 81. **Telephone code:** 02.

Flights: There are always plenty of *sherut* taxis waiting outside **Ben-Gurion Airport** to take you to Jerusalem; bargain, and don't pay more than US$7-10 per person. For transport from Jerusalem to the airport, call **Nesher,** 21 HaMeleḥ George St. (tel. 23 12 31), a day or more in advance, and confirm the night before. Show up at their office (US$4); for US$2 more, one of their *sherut* taxis will pick you up at your hotel or hostel. For **flight Information** call (03) 971 24 84.

Trains: Station is at Kikar Remez (tel. 71 77 64), near the intersection of Bethlehem and HaMeleḥ David St. The trip to Haifa via Tel Aviv is slower than by bus, but cheaper and a beautiful ride.

Buses: Egged Central Bus Station, (tel. 52 82 31), at the western end of Jaffa Rd. Most city buses stop here. To reach the HaMeleḥ George/Jaffa Rd./Ben Yehuda intersection, cross the street (via the tunnel) and catch bus #5, 6, 13, 14, 18, 20, 21, or 35; buses#13 and 20 continue to the Old City. Extremely frequent service to Tel Aviv, Haifa, and other major cities (Eilat, 4 per day). *Sherut* taxis to Tel Aviv are run by **HaBirah,** 1 HaRav Kook St., and **Kesher-Aviv,** 12 Shammai St. The **Arab Bus Station** on Sultan Suleiman St., between Herod's and Damascus Gates, serves points south on the West Bank. A second **Arab Bus Station** on Nablus Rd. (Dereḥ Sheḥem) handles traffic to the northern West Bank. *Sherut* taxis to West Bank destinations also leave from Nablus Rd.

Public Transportation: Jerusalem has a good, if confusing, municipal bus system. Buses run Sun.-Thurs. until midnight, Fri. until 3pm. Fare is US$0.30. The tourist office map has information on bus routes. Buy a 25-ride ticket for the price of 20, available on any bus.

Emergencies: Police (tel. 100); headquarters at the Russian Compound, off Jaffa Rd. **Ambulance** (tel. 101).

Medical Assistance: For first aid and emergency assistance, look for **Magen David Adom** next to the Central Bus Station or inside Dung Gate in the Old City. **Yad Sarah** (tel. 24 42 42) offers free assistance to disabled travelers.

Crises: Rape (tel. 24 55 54), staffed 24 hours. **Mental Health Hotline** (tel. 22 71 71).

Consulates: U.S., 18 Agrar St. (tel. 23 42 71). **U.K.,** 19 Nashashibi St., at Sheik Jarrah St. (tel. 28 24 81).

Bookstores: Yalkut, 1 Helena HaMalka St., has the best selection of used English books. Open Sun.-Thurs. 8am-7pm, Fri. 8-11am. **Sefer VeSefel,** 2 Ya'Avetz St. near the corner of 49 Jaffa Rd. (third door on the right and up the stairs), also has a good selection, as well as a nice patio and cafe with the best ice cream in Israel. Open Sun. 9am-7pm, Mon.-Thurs. 8am-11pm, Fri. 9am-1:30pm. **Steimatzky's,** at 5 HaMeleḥ George St., 39 Jaffa Rd., and on the Cardo in the Old City. Specializes in new books; the place to look for *Let's Go* books. The **SPNI bookstore,** 13 Helena HaMalka St., has the best maps of Jerusalem and Israel.

Swimming Pool: Emek Refaim St. (tel. 63 20 92). Take bus #4 or 18 south from the center of town. Open daily 8am-5pm. Sun.-Fri. US$1.60, Sat. US$4.

Laundry: Superclean Geulah, 1 Eter Yoldot St., is the closest to the Old City. Walk west from the intersection of Mea She'arim and Strauss; it's the first alley on the left. Closes early on Fri.

Accommodations

Many of the hostels in the Old City are clean and comfortable, but others are wretched; look before you choose. Women may feel uncomfortable on Old City streets at night. Places in the New City generally offer comfort and safety, but less atmosphere. East Jerusalem has the cheapest accommodations, but at the cost of diminished safety and convenience. All hostels that we list are open year-round.

New City

Bernstein Youth Hostel (IYHF), corner of Keren HaYesod St. and Agron St. (tel. 22 82 86). Booked solid by groups from July to mid-Aug. A large, clean hostel with excellent facilities—coffeehouse, reading room, daytime luggage check, courtyards, clean rooms. Members US$6.50, nonmembers US$7.50. Check-in 7-9am and 5-7pm. 11pm curfew, with 20-min. grace period.

Beit Shmnel (IYHF), 13 HaMeleḥ St. (tel. 20 34 55). Brand new, with courtyard, kitchen, and disabled access. Make reservations, especially in summer. Dorm beds, members US$8, nonmembers US$9; singles US$18 and 19; doubles US$24 and 26. Breakfast included.

Edison Youth Hostel, 2 Belilius St., corner of Yeshayahu (tel. 23 21 33). From Jaffa/HaMeleḥ George walk up Strauss and left onto Hanevi'im and right onto Yeshayahu. Crowded but friendly. The staff will often help you find a job. US$4.40. No curfew.

Hotel Zefania, 4 Zefania St. (tel. 28 63 84). Walk up Strauss to Meah She'arim Rd. (where Strauss turns into Yehezkel), then walk 3 blocks to Zefania. Take bus #4 or 9 from the city center, or #27 or 39 from the bus station. A converted apartment building in an ultra-orthodox neighborhood. Management requests modest dress. Clean, large rooms, nice sitting room. Dorm beds US$3.15, singles and doubles US$12. No curfew.

International Youth Hostel, 35 Ussishkin St., in Shimon Peres' neighborhood. Take bus #17 from the Central Bus Station, or bus #19 from Jaffa Gate. US$3.30. 12:30am curfew.

King George Hostel, 15 HaMeleḥ George St. (tel. 22 34 98), between Jaffa Rd. and Ben Yehuda St. New regime; the 1960s throwbacks are gone. Kitchen, lounge, no lockout. US$4.40.

Old City

Christ Church Hospice, El Khattab Rd. (tel. 28 20 82), inside Jaffa Gate next to the post office. Safe, pretty, and in a great location. Well-kept, with a peaceful courtyard. Dorm beds US$8, newly renovated doubles US$23. Breakfast included. Lockout 10am-4pm. 11pm curfew.

Lutheran Youth Hostel, St. Mark's Rd., (tel. 28 21 20). From the Jaffa gate, cross the square, turn right onto al-Khattab, left onto Maronite Convent Rd., and right onto St. Mark's. Best facilities in the Old City—beautiful garden courtyard, well-equipped kitchen. US$5. Check-out 9am, check-in 9:30am; rooms closed until noon. Strict 10:45pm curfew.

Citadel Youth Hostel, St. Mark's Rd., (tel. 28 62 73), just before the Lutheran Hostel. Clean and airy, in a newly renovated building. Great management. Small kitchen. US$3.15. Midnight curfew.

Al Ahram Hostel, al-Wad Rd. (tel. 28 09 26). Enter Damascus Gate and bear left on al-Wad Rd. Fairly clean, with hot showers and a kitchen. Beds on the covered roof US$2.60, beds in dorm US$3.30; doubles US$12.60. Midnight curfew.

Ecce Homo Convent, Eastern Via Dolorosa (tel. 28 24 45). Turn left onto Via Dolorosa from al-Wad Rd. For women only. An excellent, spotless place. Beds in partitioned spaces US$11. Filling breakfast included. Lockout 10am-noon. 10pm curfew.

JOC Inn and Teahouse, 21 al-Khanka St. (tel. 28 28 65). Bear right from Damascus Gate onto Suq Khan Ez-Zeit, then right onto al-Khanka. An attractive place with small but clean rooms. Dorm beds US$3.15. Midnight curfew.

East Jerusalem

The hostels listed below are within a block of Damascus Gate. Women should expect hassles, especially at night.

Ramsis Youth Hostel, 20 HaNevi'im St. (tel. 28 48 18). Clean, large-windowed rooms and nice beds—with purple sheets. Good kitchen facilities. Dorm beds US$3.75, singles US$9.40, doubles US$12.50. 11pm curfew.

Faisal Youth Hostel, 4 HaNevi'im St. (tel. 28 21 89). Quite clean and spacious. Great view of the Old City. Floor mattresses US$3.15. Dorm beds US$3.75. Doubles US$9.45.

Palm Hotel, 6 HaNevi'im St. Pleasant and well-run, with Christian atmosphere. No unmarried couples. Beds US$3.75. Lockout 10:30am-2:30pm. 11:30pm curfew.

Food

Jerusalem's diverse populace assures variety in restaurant fare. The best deals are found at self-service *felafel* places, where you can stuff your pita with as much salad as you want. In the New City, these places are clustered along HaMeleh George St. between Jaffa Rd. and Ben Yehuda St. **Merkaz HaFelafel HaTeymani,** 48 HaNevi'im St., and **Meleh HaShwarma VeFelafel,** at the corner of HaMeleh George and Agrippas, are two of the best for *felafel* and *shwarma* (roast lamb in pita), respectively. For sit-down restaurants, the area inside Damascus Gate in the Old City and the neighborhood surrounding the **Mahane Yehuda Market,** which runs between Jaffa Rd. and Agrippas St., are best. *Hummus* (chickpea dip) is another tasty Middle Eastern staple—try **Abu Shakri** or **Linda's,** both in the Old City near the Damascus Gate.

To prepare your own food, try the **markets** on David St. in the Old City, and at Mahane Yehuda, between Jaffa Rd. and Agrippas St. in the New City. If you really want to save money, stroll through the meat market to the west of Mahane Yehuda—after looking at the dangling ex-animals, you won't want to eat for days.

On Friday afternoon and all day Saturday, when the New City shuts down, you'll find the food stores on Salah el-Din—the main street extending north from near Damascus Gate in East Jerusalem—alive and well.

Abu Ali Restaurant, off Salah el-Din. Great Middle Eastern food for about US$4.

Sova, 3 HaHistadrut St. Hefty, tasty, filling fish, chicken, meat, and potato stews. Self-service and inexpensive. Open Sun.-Thurs. 11am-4pm, Sat. 11am-2pm.

Off the Square, 6 Yoel Salomon St., off Zion Sq. Extensive menu, including vegetarian dishes. Garden seating. Open Sun.-Thurs. noon-midnight, Fri. 11am-2pm, Sat. sundown-midnight.

Poondak HeHalav, 17 Bezalel St. Sweet or savory blintzes US$4-5. Open Sun.-Thurs. noon-midnight, Fri. 9am-4pm, Sat. sundown-midnight.

Sights

Jerusalem speaks through a tremendously rich past, and its color and diversity are best appreciated by those who learn something of this history. **The Society for the Protection of Nature in Israel, Archaeological Tours and Seminars,** and **Walking Tours Ltd.** all offer tours of the city, most of them two to three hours long and costing US$4-7. The tourist office distributes schedules and descriptions of the routes. Saturdays at 10am, a **free tour** (organized by the city government) leaves from 32 Jaffa Rd. The tour lasts three hours and can be very crowded. The renowned **Jeff Seidel** leads free tours of Jewish historical and religious sites (Sun.-Tues. and Thurs. at 3pm, Sat. an hour before sunset; meet at the palm tree to your right as you face the Western Wall).

A good way to start touring the **Old City** independently is to walk the ramparts of its walls, built by Suleiman the Magnificent in 1542. One ticket is good for two days and four entries, so you can climb down for sightseeing and re-enter at another gate. Purchase your tickets (US$1.25, students US$1) at the entrance to Jaffa or Damascus Gates, and don't pay any of the "guards" who solicit above. Women should not walk alone, even in broad daylight. From the ramparts you'll have a gorgeous view of the Temple Mount, consisting of the golden (actually aluminum and bronze) **Dome of the Rock** and the adjacent **al-Aqsa Mosque.** The Dome of the Rock is built over the spot from which Muhammad rose to heaven, and where Abraham offered to sacrifice Ishmael. (Both open Sat.-Thurs. 8am-3pm. Admission US$3.30, students US$2.70.) The most colorful approach to the Mount is from Jaffa Gate, down through the **shuq** (market) on HaMeleh David St. and straight (follow the signs) to the plaza in front of the **Western Wall** ("HaKotel HaMa'aravi" in Hebrew, also known as the Wailing Wall). This wall is part of the retaining wall of the **Temple Mount (Har HaBayit),** the holiest site in Judaism. A good deal of the Herodian wall is still underground, and much of what is visible was added by the Crusaders and by Moses Montefiore, a British Jew who sought to rebuild Jerusalem in the 1860s—it's not difficult to distinguish between the different sections. The notes crammed between the stones are hand-scrawled entreaties to God. Steps to the right (as you face the wall) lead to the Muslim shrines above.

When you leave the Temple Mount complex, bear left and go up the modern stairs leading to the **Jewish Quarter,** with its artists' galleries and modern apartment houses. Since 1967, constant archeological discovery has hampered restoration of the Quarter, razed during the 1948 War and the subsequent years of Jordanian rule. A soaring white arch marks the site of the **Hurva Synagogue,** once the religious center of the Jewish Quarter. Just north of the Hurva is the newly excavated **Cardo,** Jerusalem's main street during Roman and Byzantine times. East on Tiferet Yisrael Rd. is the **Burnt House,** whose perfectly preserved remains testify to the Roman destruction of the Second Temple and upper city in 70 C.E. Descend into its cavernous underground remains for a sound and light show (Sun.-Thurs. at 9:30 and 11:30am, and 1:30 and 3:30pm; admission US$1, students US$0.55). The **Yishuv Court Museum,** 6 Or HaḤaim St., near the southern end of the Cardo, has exhibits of life in the Jewish Quarter before its destruction in 1948. (Open Sun.-Thurs. 9am-4pm. Admission US$1.50, students US$1.30.)

Explore the Christian Quarter from St. Stephen's Gate. If you enter the Old City here, you'll be near the first station of the **Via Dolorosa** (Path of Sorrow); each successive station marks another incident on the path Jesus took to his crucifixion. **Church of the Holy Sepulchre,** one of the most venerated structures in Christiandom, has been built and rebuilt on the site of the crucifixion. (Open daily 4am-7pm.) An unwitting testimony to sectarian strife, the church is divided into many denominational jurisdictions, squabbling over which keeps renovation in a state of limbo. The Holy Sepulchre itself, Jesus' tomb, is on the ground floor. Up the stairs to the right is **Golgotha** (Calvary), where he was crucified. Every Friday afternoon at 3pm (July-Aug. 4pm), according to tradition the day and hour Jesus died, priests lead a procession of pilgrims along Via Dolorosa, starting at St. Stephen's Gate.

The best place to orient yourself in the Old City is the **Citadel** (or Tower of David), to the right of Jaffa Gate. From its summit there is a panoramic view of the entire city; the interior has been developed into a cultural center containing ethnographic exhibits on every group in the city. (Open Sat.-Thurs. 8:30am-4:30pm, Fri. 8:30am-2pm. Sat.-Thurs. at 9:30pm there is an English-language sound and light show.)

South of the Citadel, the **Armenian Compound** (just outside Zion Gate) is a self-contained community complete with schools, soccer fields, printing press, and seminary. Visitors are allowed to enter the sumptuous **St. James Cathedral** (open during services Mon.-Fri. 3-3:30pm, Sat.-Sun. 2:30-3:15pm); the rest of the compound is off limits. To learn more about the history of this private residential community, visit the **Mardigian Museum,** to the left off Armenian Patriarchate Rd. (Open Mon.-Sat. 10am-5pm. Admission US$0.60.)

The Old City's **Arab Market,** which extends along David St. and its continuation, HaShalshelet St., offers everything from crowns of thorns to Bedouin dresses. Check quality scrupulously, and *bargain*—start by offering a third of the quoted price. The **Armenian Market,** around Muristan St., is both less chaotic and more authentic than its Arab counterpart. Food, spices, and sweet shops abound on **Khan-Ez-Zeit St.,** the right fork as you enter the city from Damascus Gate.

West Jerusalem is as interesting as the Old City, but not so overwhelming. **Meah She'arim,** populated entirely by orthodox Hasidic Jews, is the only true example of a European Jewish *shtetl* remaining in the world. Conservative dress is required in this area; this means long trousers for men and long skirts (no trousers) and shoulder covering for women. To reach Mea She'arim from Jaffa Gate, walk along Shivte Yisrael St.

The **Israel Museum,** in addition to its interior galleries and lovely **Billy Rose Sculpture Garden,** houses a fascinating **Biblical and Archeological Museum** as well as the famed **Shrine of the Book,** which houses the Dead Sea Scrolls. These are the most significant recent find in Biblical archeology. To reach the museum, take bus #9, 16, or 24. (Open Sun.-Mon. and Wed.-Thurs. 10am-5pm, Tues. 4-10pm,

Fri.-Sat. 10am-2pm. Admission to museum US$2; to museum and shrine US$3.50, students US$1.60. Tickets for Sat. must be purchased on Fri. Free English tours Sun.-Mon. and Wed.-Fri. at 11am, Tues. at 4:30pm. Free English tour of the Shrine of the Book Sun. at 1:30pm and Tues. at 3pm.) The **Knesset,** Israel's parliament, is five minutes away. (Knesset meets Mon.-Tues. 4-7pm, and Wed. 11am-1pm. Admission to visitors' gallery requires a passport. Free tours Sun. and Thurs. 8:30am-3:30pm.)

In East Jerusalem, visit the **Garden Tomb,** on the right side of Nablus Rd., down from Damascus Gate. An "alternate" site of Jesus' crucifixion, the Tomb is surrounded by an oasis-like garden. (Open Mon.-Sat. 8am-12:30pm and 2:30-4pm.) Nearby, right across from Herod's Gate on Suleiman St., the **Rockefeller Archeological Museum** records the history of Palestine from Carmel Man 100,000 years ago. (Open Sun.-Thurs. 10am-5pm, Fri.-Sat. 10am-2pm. Free tours Sun. and Fri. at 11am.) East of the museum is the **Mount of Olives.** The cemetery holds great religious significance for Jews, while Christians revere the Mount of Olives as the site of many events of Jesus' last days in Jerusalem. This is the location of the **Garden of Gethsemane,** where Jesus was betrayed by Judas. A climb through the Kidron Valley, past the **Basilica of the Agony**—with its sparkling mosaic facade of Jesus blessing all nations—and up the Mount of Olives, with stops at the **Russian Orthodox Church of Mary Magdalene** (open Tues. and Thurs. 9am-noon and 2-4pm) and the **Basilica of Dominus Flevit** ("The Lord wept"; open daily 8-11:45am and 3-5pm), climaxes with a picture-perfect view of Jerusalem from the Intercontinental Hotel.

Several major sights lie on the outskirts of Jerusalem. Buses #13, 18 and 20 travel to **Yad VaShem,** the chilling museum documenting the Holocaust. (Open Sun.-Thurs. 9am-4:45pm, Fri. 9am-1:45pm. Free.) Bus #21 goes to the **Holyland Hotel,** with its sprawling, dramatic scale model of Jerusalem at the time of the Second Temple. (Open in summer daily 8am-5pm; in winter 8am-4pm. Admission US$1.50, students US$0.65.) Bus #19 or 27 will take you to the **Hadassah Medical Center,** housing a synagogue adorned with the famous **Chagall Windows,** one for each of the 12 tribes of Israel. (Free tours Sun.-Thurs. at 8:30am, 9:30am, 10:30am, 11:30am, and 12:30pm, Fri. at 9:30am, 10:30am, and 11:30am.)

For a pleasant half-day excursion, take Egged bus #36 or an Arab bus toward Jericho, and get off in the town of **Bethany,** 4km outside Jerusalem. There you can visit a first-century tomb, reputed to be the site where Jesus raised Lazarus from the dead.

If you have the time to do more justice to Jerusalem than we can here, turn to *Let's Go: Israel and Egypt, including Jordan,* Sarah Fox Kaminker's *Footloose in Jerusalem,* or Nitza Rosovsky's *Jerusalem Walks.*

Entertainment

Jerusalem nightlife tends to be easygoing and pleasant—not hip and hopping. **Tzavta,** 38 HaMeleḥ George St. (tel. 22 76 21), offers a variety of entertainers and evening moods, ranging from bluegrass to religious folk-rock. (Admission US$2-3 with student ID.) **Pargod,** 94 Betsalel St. (tel. 23 17 65), is a lively jazz club; call for showtimes. At **The Courtyard,** off 27 Yafo St., you'll find several popular drinking spots where travelers mingle, and which remain open Friday nights. There is Israeli folk dancing (*rikudei 'am)* on Saturday and Tuesday evenings at the **International Cultural Center for Youth,** 105 HaRav Herzog St., and in the **Liberty Bell Gardens** on Saturdays during the summer. The new **Jerusalem Cinemateque,** Hebron Rd. (tel. 71 53 98), screens repertory films (Fri. afternoon, and Sat., Mon., Tues., and Thurs. nights) and has a wonderful terrace cafe. For listings of theater performances, concerts, and folk dancing, check *Events in the Jerusalem Region, This Week in Jerusalem* (both available at the tourist office), and the Friday supplement to the *Jerusalem Post.* Finally, be sure to walk (in a group, to be safe) the walls of the Old City, particularly the South Wall, with its beautiful view of the illuminated Western Wall.

Galilee (HaGalil)

The Galilee—northern and northeastern Israel—is the land of the Bible, and like the Bible it bears witness to spiritual attainments and bloody conflicts. **Tzfat** (Safed), once the home of the Cabbalists (Jewish mystics), is today one of Israel's four Jewish "holy cities," along with Jerusalem, Hebron, and Tiberias. The old quarter is best appreciated on Friday evenings, when its streets are closed to traffic and dozens of Ḥasids make their way to synagogue amid the chants of evening prayer. Be sure to visit the two sixteenth-century Caro and Ha'Ari synagogues (don't take cameras on Fri. night or Sat. and always dress modestly). The **Artist's Quarter,** a labyrinth of cobbled alleys, holds serendipitous discoveries at the ends of alleys, in shops, and at the **General Exhibition** of Tzfat's artists' work. (Open in summer Sun.-Thurs. 9am-6pm, Fri. 9am-4pm; in winter Sun.-Thurs. 9am-5pm.) The **Ethiopian Folk Art Gallery,** Oleh Hagardom, is worth seeing, even if you cannot afford the steep prices. The cool, shady **park** at the top of the hill on which Tzfat is built contains the meager ruins of a Crusader citadel; at the summit stands a memorial to the fallen of the 1948 War. Shlomo Bar-Ayal's city tours bring Tzfat's past to life; check at the tourist office for details (US$5 per person).

Mild summers make Tzfat popular, so cheap accommodations are scarce in high season. You may be approached at the bus station about staying in a pension in town; alternatively, look for "rooms to let" signs along Reḥov Yerushalayim. The **Beit Benyamin Youth Hostel (IYHF)** (tel. (06) 93 10 86) is modern, comfortable, and rarely full. Take bus #2, 2A, or 6 from the bus station. (Members US$7.50, nonmembers US$8.50.) There's a **swimming pool** just beyond the bus station, off Dereḥ Ha'Atzmaut (open Sun.-Fri. 7:30am-4pm, Sat. 8:30am-4pm; admission US$1.20, students US$0.85).

The trip from Tzfat to the **Sea of Galilee** (also known as the **Kinneret)** is beautiful, but the 1000-meter descent brings an unwelcome increase in heat and humidity. (The sea, actually a fresh-water lake, is 200m below Mediterranean Sea level). **Tiberias** (Teveriya), the major town on the lake, is the best place to base yourself for a tour of the area. The **IGTO,** 8 Al Hadef St. (tel. (06) 72 09 92), a few blocks toward the sea from the bus station and to your left up the hill, can help with accommodations. (Open Sun.-Thurs. 8am-6pm, Fri. 8am-2pm.) Although crowded with vacationers year-round, Tiberias claims several of the best hostels in the country, and fierce competition keeps room prices reasonable. Prices in hotels and private hostels increase by a few dollars per night during August and September. The **Meyouhas Hostel (IYHF)** (tel. (06) 72 17 75), one block east of the bus station on HaYarden St., is modern, appealing, and large, but generally full in summer. (Members US$7.50, nonmembers US$8.50.) **Nahum Hostel** (tel. (06) 72 15 05) is cheaper and friendlier. Walk towards the lake on HaYarden St., turn right on HaGalil St., and bear right on Tavor St.; you'll see the sign. (Dorm beds US$3, doubles US$10.50.) **Maman Hostel** (tel. (06) 79 29 86), 100m up the hill from Nahum's, offers similar amenities for a similar price; they also rent bicycles for US$5 per day. All three have air conditioning. The **Castle Inn Hostel** (tel. (06) 72 11 75) has kitchen facilities and a great location on the wharf next to the Plaza Hotel. (Beds US$4.) During the summer there's an **information center** (tel. (067) 520 56) at the south end of the lake where the road from Beit She'an forks east-west. Pick up information on the campgrounds that ring the lake. (Open June-Sept. daily 9am-5pm.)

For a quick, cheap meal, choose one of the numerous felafel stands along HaYarden Street. **Maman Restaurant,** on HaGalil St. at the corner of Bibass, offers good Middle Eastern food at reasonable prices. St. Peter's fish, unique to the Sea of Galilee, may be sampled at one of the many rather expensive restaurants lining the seaside esplanade.

Beaches in Tiberias all charge admission, usually about US$4. All have restaurants and picnic areas, and most rent kayaks or windsurfers. **Blue Beach,** to the north, runs a disco in the evening during the summer, starting at 8:30pm. (You'll have to leave the beach when it closes at 5:30pm and pay again if you want to dance.) The **municipal beach,** to the south (bus #2 or 5), charges only US$2.50.

Check out the Roman hot baths at **Tiberias Hot Springs,** 2km south of town aboard bus #2 or 5; they offer massage and indoor and outdoor mineral pools. On the northwest shore of the lake are some of Christianity's most holy sites: the **Mount of Beatitudes,** where Jesus delivered the Sermon on the Mount, has a stunning church built by Mussolini. Take any bus from Tiberias to Tzfat or Qiryat Shmona and get off two stops after the bus turns uphill away from the lake, at the sign marked "Hospice of the Beatitudes." The mosaic-floored **Church of the Multiplication of the Loaves and Fishes** and the **Church of the Primacy,** where Jesus made Peter "shepherd of his people," are both at Tabgha, l2km west of the ancient town of **Capernaum** (Kfar Naḥum). Buses running to the Mount stop here before they turn uphill.

Just south of the churches is the **Karei Deshe Youth Hostel (IYHF)** (tel. (06) 72 06 01), with a private beach and campground. (Members US$7.50, nonmembers US$8.50. Breakfast included. Camping US$5 per person.) Call first, as the hostel may be closed in 1988.

Nazareth (Natzeret), the home of Jesus, disappoints many travekers. If religion doesn't interest you, pack your bags. The major sight is the **Basilica of the Annunciation,** built in 1966 on the spot where, according to tradition, the angel Gabriel announced to Mary that she would bear the Son of God. Also worth visiting is the **St. Gabriel Greek Orthodox Church,** built in 1750 C.E., just past **Mary's Well** on Paul VI St. The **GTIO** on Casa Nova St., near the intersection with Paul VI, is five minutes from the bus station. Stay at the **Religieuses de Nazareth Hospice,** Casa Nova St. (tel. (06) 55 43 04; US$3 per person), or the **Sisters of Charles Borromeus Hospice,** behind the Carmelite Convent (tel. (06) 55 44 35; US$10 per person).

South and east of Nazareth is the **Jezreel Valley** ('Emeq Yizre'el), home to some of Israel's oldest and richest **kibbutzim.** On Sunday nights during the summer at 8:30pm, the kibbutzniks and townspeople from the Beit She'an valley gather for folk dancing at **Gan HaShlosha (Saḥne) Park,** 6km northwest of the town of Beit She'an. The park, one of the most beautiful and popular in Israel, features a waterfall and three natural swimming pools. One kilometer farther toward Afula is the ancient synagogue of **Beit Alpha,** within the grounds of Kibbutz Hephzibah, with a beautiful sixth-century mosaic floor. Don't be misled by the sign for Kibbutz Beit Alpha, 1km back toward Beit She'an. Several kilometers away from Afula, on the same road, **Beit She'an** itself is the site of an unreconstructed Roman amphitheater and a new set of large-scale excavations.

Ten kilometers southeast of Afula, 1km north of the junction where the bus lets you off, stands the massive *tel* (mound) of **Megiddo,** site of the biblical Armageddon. The *tel* is well-labeled and the small museum at its base guides the visitor through the remnants of the 20 civilizations that have settled at this Galilean crossroads.

Halfway between the Sea of Galilee and Beit She'an is **Belvoir** (Koḥav HaYarden), a twelfth-century Crusader fortress commanding a majestic view of the entire area (hence the name). If you want to visit the site, you'll have to walk or hitch the 6km uphill from the main road to the castle.

Haifa (Ḥefa)

The breeze that blows out of Haifa Bay and up the face of Mt. Carmel has lifted the ancient dust from this steeply terraced city. Haifa is clean and spacious, proud of its modernity and progressive spirit. This city may lack the trappings of a more traditional Middle Eastern atmosphere, but its stately residential neighborhoods, natural beauty, and surrounding artists' colonies and Druze villages offer an interesting introduction to the modern state of Israel.

Orientation and Practical Information

Haifa, Israel's principal port and the port of entry for passenger ferries, is on the Mediterranean coast about 100km south of the Lebanese border and due west of the Sea of Galilee.

Rising from the sea, Haifa divides into three tiers of ascending beauty and affluence: the bustling **downtown** or **port** section, a rough neighborhood where the bus and train stations are located; the **Hadar** district, home to most businesses, restaurants, and hotels; and **Carmel,** a collection of beautiful homes and ritzy hotels crowning the Mount. Buses will save your strength; become familiar with them, as the city map fails to show Haifa's topographical tortures.

Tourist Offices: Israeli Government Tourist Organization, 20 Herzl St. (tel. 66 65 21). Take bus #10 or 12 from the port, #21 or 28 from the bus station. Quite helpful, with plenty of maps and schedules. Open Sun.-Thurs. 8:30am-4pm. Also in the **Passenger Hall** (Sun.-Fri.) to greet ship arrivals. There are 4 **Municipal Information Offices:** Central bus station branch open Sun.-Thurs. 9am-4pm, Fri. 8am-1pm. Useful information is posted when office is closed. **Society for the Protection of Nature in Israel,** 8 Menahem St. (tel 66 41 35). Maps and information about guided nature tours and hikes.

Budget Travel: ISSTA, 28 Nordau St. (tel. 67 02 22). Open Sun.-Tues. and Thurs. 8am-1pm and 4-7pm, Wed. and Fri. 8am-1pm.

American Express: Meditrad, Ltd., 2 Kikar Khayat (tel. 66 50 69), off HaAtzmaut St. Mail held and checks sold, but no wired money accepted. Open Sun.-Tues. and Thurs. 8am-4pm, Wed. and Fri. 8am-1pm.

Currency Exchange: Banks close Mon., Wed., and Fri. at 12:30 or 1pm. First International Bank closes Tues., Thurs., and Fri. afternoons.

Post Office: 19 Sderot HaPalyam, near the port. Open Sun.-Thurs. 7am-4pm, Fri. 7am-2pm. Also branches at the central bus station; at Shabtai Levi and HaNevi'im St. in Hadar; and at 1 Palmer in the port. Poste Restante only at Palyam Branch.

Telephones: At the HaPalyam post office. Same hours. **Telephone code:** 04.

Trains: Station is at Bat Gallim, behind the central bus station. Frequent trains to Tel Aviv. Also to Jerusalem (1 per day at 7am) and Nahariya. Information (tel. 53 12 11) open daily 8am-7pm.

Buses: Central Bus Station, Dereh Yafo, at the start of the main road to Tel Aviv. Bus #271 to Akko runs daily, including Sat. Bus #900 and 901 to Tel Aviv; last bus Fri. 5pm. Bus #940 and 966 to Jerusalem; last bus Fri. 3:15pm.

Ferries: The terminal is at the port, next to the train station. Departures for Cyprus, Crete, and Athens. Buy tickets at **Kaspi Travel,** 67 HaAtzmaut St. (tel. 36 74 44), and **Multitour,** 55 HaNamal St. (tel. 66 35 70).

Emergencies: Police (tel. 100); headquarters at 28 Dereh Yafo.

Magen David Adom First Aid: Tel. 101.

Crises: Rape (tel. 38 26 11). Open 24 hours.

Consulates: U.S., 12 Yerushalyim St. (tel. 67 06 15), in Hadar. Emergencies only; all other business will be referred to Tel Aviv.

Bookstores: For new and used English books, try **Beverly Book,** 7 Herzl St., ½ block from HaNevi'im St. Open Sun.-Mon. and Wed.-Thurs. 9am-1pm and 4-7pm, Tues. and Fri. 9am-1pm. Also **Steimatzkys** in Hadar and Carmel.

Accommodations and Food

There are few budget hotels in Haifa, and most of the youth hostels are inconveniently (but beautifully) located outside of town.

Carmel Youth Hostel (IYHF), south of the city at Hof HaCarmel (tel. 53 19 44). Take bus #43 directly to the hostel (last bus 6:20pm), or bus #45 from the bus station (last bus 11:30pm) to the road below the hostel and follow the signs uphill for 20 min. (dangerous at night). Near the beach; great view. Single rooms: members US$7.50, nonmembers US$8.50. Reception open 5-7pm. No curfew.

Bethel Tourist Hostel, 40 HaGeffen St. (tel. 52 11 10), a few blocks west of the Haifa Museum. Take bus #22 from the central bus station. Clean, friendly, centrally located, and very popular. The only drawback is the strict 10pm curfew. US$4.50 in a dorm bed. Lockout 9am-5pm, but you can leave your luggage and return to register at 5pm. Reception open Sun.-Thurs. 5-10pm, Fri. 4-10pm.

Talpiyyot, 61 Herzl St. (tel. 67 37 53). In a great location, with fans in the clean, bright rooms. Singles US$16, doubles US$25. Breakfast on the balcony included.

Nesher Hotel, 53 Herzl St. (tel. 64 06 44); also in a good location in Hadar. Air conditioning and fans. Nice breakfast buffet. Singles US$16, doubles US$30; try bargaining.

Eden Hotel, 8 Shemaryahu Levin St. (tel. 66 48 16), in Hadar. Hot in summer; not as nice as those listed above. Singles US$13.50, doubles US$25.

Inexpensive lodgings in Haifa may be scarce, but cheap food abounds. It's easy to survive on *felafel, borekas, tiras* (corn on the cob, sold from street vats), *shwarma,* and other Middle Eastern stand-up specialties. **HaNevi'im Street** in the Hadar district, particularly around HeḤalutz St. is the place to search: Just follow your nose. Especially good restaurants in this area are **At Benny's,** 23 HeḤalutz St., and **Farm Foods,** 30 Herzl St. **Bis-Bo Sandwich Bar,** 25 HaNevi'im St., bills itself as "the only American-style deli in Haifa." Hardly, but worth a try anyway (burgers US$1.40 and up). **Bagel Nosh,** 135 Sderot HaNassi, in Merkaz HaCarmel, offers salads, bagels, and light dinners. There is an outdoor produce **market** west of Kikar Paris between Nahum and Nathan St., and an enormous **supermarket** in the basement of the Mashbir Department Store, just off the corner of Herzl and Shemaryahu Levin St. On Fridays, many of the pricey cafes in the Carmel remain open, and on Saturdays, **Rimini's,** 20 HaNevi'im St., in Hadar, is open.

Sights and Entertainment

Haifa Tourism Development Association, 10 Aḥad HaAm St. (tel. 67 16 45), just off HaNevi'im St., offers a great three-hour walking tour of the city every Saturday at 10am (free); the tour begins at the corner of Sha'ar and Yefe Nof St. On HaTsionut Ave., the beautiful **Baha'i Temple,** whose stone structure was built in 1909 and golden dome added in 1953, is set in elaborate gardens overlooking the harbor. The temple houses the body of Siyyid Ali Mohammed, who heralded the future arrival of a prophet who would introduce a new world religion. Across the street from the temple is the large white **Universal House of Justice,** where the Baha'i leaders are elected every five years (not open to tourists). To reach the temple, take bus #23, 25, 26, or 32 from HaNevi'im and Herzl St. (Temple open daily 9am-noon; gardens open daily 9am-5pm. Free. No shorts allowed.) Take off your shoes before entering, and as a measure of courtesy don't turn your back as you leave; walk out the doorway backward.

Elijah's Cave, honored by Christians, Jews, and Moslems alike, is where the prophet hid during his flight from King Ahab. It is interesting more for those who come to worship than for the shrine itself. Look for the stairs across from the National Maritime Museum on Allenby Rd. (Open in summer Sun.-Thurs. 8am-6pm, Fri. 8am-1pm; in winter Sun.-Thurs. 8am-5pm, Fri. 8am-1pm. Free.) A few hundred meters above the cave is the **Stella Maris Carmelite Monastery,** used as a hospital for Napoleon's army when he attacked Turkish Akko in 1799. The monastery houses a beautiful chapel with a grotto to light candles to Elijah and a painted dome ceiling. (Open daily 8:30am-1:30pm and 3-6pm. Free. No shorts allowed.) Buses #25 and 26 run to the monastery. Near the caves, at 198 Allenby Rd., are the **National Maritime Museum** and the **Clandestine Immigration and Naval Museum.** The latter commemorates the daring smuggling of immigrant Jews into Palestine during British Mandate. Take bus #43 or 44 from the Central Station. (Clandestine Immigration Museum open Sun. and Tues. 9am-4pm, Mon. and Wed.-Thurs. 9am-3pm, Fri. 9am-1pm. Admission US$0.65.) A cable car passes over this area, starting down the street from the museums and running to the monastery. (Open Sun.-Thurs. 9am-midnight, Fri. 9am-2pm and 8pm-1am, Sat. 10am-midnight.)

In Hadar, the **Haifa Museum,** at 26 Shabtai Levi St., has an excellent collection of archeological finds from the area, as well as an interesting body of ancient and modern Israeli art and folk costumes. (Open Sun.-Thurs. 10am-5pm, Sat. 10am-2pm. Admission US$2.50; the ticket is also good for the Prehistory, Japanese Art, and National Maritime Museums.) The tiny **Museum of Japanese Art** at 89 HaNassi Ave. has a delightful array of paintings and miniatures. (Open Sun.-Thurs. 10am-1pm and 4-7pm, Sat. 10am-2pm.)

Some of Israel's most impressive modern architecture is found in Haifa: the colossal **Dagon** on the waterfront, a grain storage silo that looks like a latter-day Crusader fortress, and the two universities **Haifa University** and the **Technion.** From **Eshkol Tower** at Haifa University, you can survey most of Israel. Haifa also has lovely public gardens and protected forests; try the **Carmel Forest Reserve** or the **Sculpture Garden,** up HaTsionut Ave. from the Baha'i Temple.

Carmel Beach, reached by bus #44 or 45, is free, but **Hof HaShaket Beach,** on the north coast past the Dagon Silo, is more convenient and worth the US$1.50 admission.

Asked once about the city's sparse entertainment, Haifa's first mayor is reputed to have pointed to the round-the-clock factories and said "There is our nightlife." But all is not so laborious. The **Technion** has frequent students-only programs of folkdancing, disco, and films; call 23 41 48 for information. Most nightlife offerings are in the Carmel, where **Beit Rothschild,** 138 Sderot HaNassi, has disco, folkdancing, and occasionally jazz. Nearby at Sderot HaNassi 104, you'll find the **Haifa Cinemateque,** with nightly screenings of English films, and the beautiful **Haifa Auditorium,** where the Israel Philharmonic and numerous other musicians perform regularly. **Little Haifa,** 4 Sha'ar HaLevanon, is a popular bar. Call 64 08 40 for tape-recorded events information. Of course there's always cafe-sitting and people-watching in the Carmel; Yefe Nof Road and Bat Gallim are particularly popular.

Near Haifa

Less than 25km south of Haifa are the two Druze villages of **Daliyat el-Carmel** and **Isfiya.** The Druze religion was founded in 1017 by an Egyptian chieftain who drew on the strands of messianism, gnosticism, and incarnation then current in Islam. Due to a long history of persecution, the Druze are very secretive about their faith, but it is known that their most holy prophet is Jethro, Moses' father-in-law, and that the Prophet Elijah also plays an important role. The Druze have preserved their ethnic and religious identity for 900 years, although they speak Arabic and have always lived among Muslims and Christians. Of the 16 Druze villages built in the late seventeenth century, 14 were destroyed by the Egyptian Pasha in 1830, and only two remain. Today Israel has a Druze population of 60,000, with 17,000 in the Carmel. Isfiya, the smaller of the two villages, also has a minority Christian population, some of whom can trace their ancestry to Crusaders. The inhabitants of both villages are overwhelmingly hospitable, and may well invite you into their homes. The **bazaar** at Daliyat el-Carmel is most active on Saturday. To reach the villages, take bus #92 or #93 from the bus station, or a bus to Haifa University and then a *sherut* taxi from Sderot Abba Khoushy. On Saturday, catch a *sherut* from Shemaryahu Levin St., at the corner of Herzl St. **Mukhraqa,** 4km from Daliyat, is the site at which Elijah killed 450 priests of Ba'al. From the roof of the Carmelite monastery here, you have a spectacular view of the valley in all directions.

Akko, 20km north of Haifa, is centuries apart from its cousin across the bay. The minarets, fortifications, and alleys of a 200-year-old Turkish settlement are surrounded by a rapidly encroaching new town. More interesting than either is the ancient **Crusader City** buried beneath old Akko and only partially excavated; eerie, half-lit rooms are linked by a network of tunnels. After seeing the entrance halls, courtyard, knights' halls, and administrative center, you pass through a 65m long tunnel (no place for the claustrophobic) to the guard post and the exit. Across from the Crusader City is the **Mosque of el-Jazzar,** (admission US$1), built by el-Jazzar in the late eighteenth century, after Napoleon bombed the original mosque of Akko. The courtyard incorporates Roman columns taken from Caesarea, 50km down the coast.

There are three *caravanserai* (ancient inns on the caravan route) in the old city, the most impressive of which is the **Khan el-Umden,** with its handsome two-tiered colonnades. The huge **Crypt of St. John,** originally a Christian basilica, is one of the oldest examples of Gothic architecture in the world; an escape tunnel, Al Bosta, begins near the third column. The **Citadel** was the main British Mandate prison, from which members of the Irgun (the Jewish resistance group) staged an incredible escape; appropriately, the Citadel now houses the **Museum of Heroism.** Renowned as the most impregnable port in the east (even Napoleon's siege of 1799 failed), Akko remains above all a city of battlements and bastions. A walk along the **Moat Gardens** walls, across the parking lot from the Mosque and Crusader City, provides a view of Haifa to one direction, and the roofs and minarets of old Akko to the other.

Akko's **Municipal Information Office** (tel. (04) 91 02 51) is at the entrance to the subterranean city, on el-Jazzar St. The **Municipality** building, 35 Weitzman St., is also a good source of information. The excellent **Akko Youth Hostel (IYHF),** opposite the old lighthouse (tel. (04) 91 19 82), is in a 200-year-old Moorish building with clean, spacious rooms. To get there, take any bus to the old city; or walk left from the bus station, right at Ben Ami St., and left onto Weitzman St. Once in the old city, cross your fingers and follow your nose through the market to the hostel on Salach Ravtziri St. (Members US$7, nonmembers US$8.50; ages under 18 US$0.50 less. Breakfast included.)

Just outside the Land Gate is **Walls Beach.** About a 15-minute walk south is **Nof Argamon** beach. (Open June-Oct. 8am-6pm. $2.50.) A free, unguarded beach is a little farther. Watch out for jellyfish in July. Buses #251 and 271 run from Haifa to Akko; *sherut* taxis also make the trip.

Nahariya, 10km north of Akko and the northernmost town on the Israeli coast, is one of the country's premier beach resorts. The **Rehayim Youth Hostel,** 6 Wolfson St. (tel. 92 05 57), is the best place to stay. (US$4.40. Sheets US$1.25.) Otherwise try the many rooms to let on Jabotinsky Street—the **Kalman Hotel,** at #27, is particularly good. Buses #270 and 271 run from Haifa through Akko to Nahariya.

Tel Aviv

Tel Aviv may lack the sense of history that distinguishes much of the Middle East, but it makes up for lack of ancient charm with cosmopolitan bustle. From the colorful Kerem HaTemanim (the Yemenite quarter) to the glittering nightlife of Dizengoff Circle, the vigor of twentieth-century Israel is evident everywhere.

Orientation and Practical Information

Tel Aviv basks in perpetual sunshine on Israel's Mediterranean coast. You'll likely pass through here at some point—Israel's principal international airport is near the city, and everyone traveling from Egypt or Haifa to Jerusalem must change here. Tel Aviv is big; become familiar with the efficient network of public buses. Street numbers run east from the sea and from south to north.

Tourist Office: Israel Government Tourist Organization, 7 Mendel St. (tel. 22 32 66), off Ben Yehuda St. For maps and hotel lists. Open Sun.-Thurs. 8:30am-5pm, Fri. 8:30am-2pm.

Budget Travel: ISSTA, 109 Ben Yehuda St. (tel. 24 71 64). For budget flights. Open Sun.-Tues. and Thurs. 8:30am-6pm, Wed. and Fri. 9am-1pm.

American Express: Meditrad Ltd., 16 Ben Yehuda St. (tel. 29 46 54). Mail held, traveler's checks sold, cardholders' personal checks cashed, but no wired money accepted. (Nearest office that can accept wired money is in Cairo.) Open Sun.-Tues. and Thurs. 8:30am-1:30pm and 3:30-6pm, Wed. and Fri. 8:30am-1pm.

Post Office: Main branch at 132 Allenby Rd. **Poste Restante** kept 2 blocks east at 7 Mikve Yisrael St. Both open Sun.-Thurs. 8am-6pm, Fri. 8am-2pm.

Telephones: At the Mikve Yisrael post office. Same hours. **Telephone code:** 03.

Flights: Ben-Gurion Airport is 22km southeast. Egged bus #475 to the airport leaves every 20 min. from Finn St., near the bus station; United Tours Bus #222 leaves every hr. from HaYarkon St. and the central train station. Airport departure tax US$10.

Trains: Trains to Haifa leave from the **Central Railway Station,** Arlosoroff St., near Haifa Rd. Trains to Jerusalem leave at 8:15am from **Benei Beraq Station.** Information (tel. 25 42 71).

Buses: Most intercity buses leave from the **Central Bus Station** on Solomon St. in the southern part of town. Take city bus #4 from Ben Yehuda, #5 from the youth hostel and Dizengoff, #46 from Yafo; many other city buses stop here as well. Buses leave from the seven islands outside the information and ticket counter. If traveling to a major city, avoid the chaos within the station by purchasing tickets at the small booths on the islands, or on the bus if your departure point is a block or more from the station.

Sherut Taxis: To Jerusalem, from Solomon St. opposite the Central Bus Station. To most other major cities in Israel, from Allenby Rd. and Kikar HaMoshavot, 3 blocks west of the Central Bus Station. *Sherut* taxis run Fri. evening and Sat., but often charge 20% more.

Public Transportation: 4 urban bus lines are particularly important for travelers: #4 runs from the bus station up Allenby Rd. and Ben Yehuda St., through the heart of downtown Tel Aviv; #5 travels from the bus station along Dizengoff St. and turns around 2 blocks from the youth hostel; #10 runs down Ben Yehuda St. to the old port town of Yafo; and #27 goes from the bus station to Tel Aviv University and the Diaspora Museum. Information (tel. 43 24 14).

Emergencies: Police (tel. 100). **Ambulance** (tel. 101).

Crises: Rape (tel. 23 48 19), open 24 hours. **Telephone Counseling** (tel. 25 33 11).

Embassies: U.S., 71 HaYarkon St. (tel. 65 43 38). **Canada,** 220 HaYarkon St. (tel. 22 81 22). **U.K.,** 192 HaYarkon St. (tel. 24 91 71). **Australia,** 185 HaYarkon St. (tel. 24 31 52). Travelers from **New Zealand** should contact the British Embassy. **Egypt,** 54 Basel St. (tel. 22 41 52). Visa section open Sun.-Thurs. 9-11am; get there early and bring your passport, 2 photos, and US$12.

Bookstores: Steimatzky's, 103 Allenby St., has the largest selection in Israel. **Pollard's Used Books,** 36 King George St., has good used paperbacks.

Laundry: 45 Bograshov St. and 51 Ben Yehuda St. Both open Sun.-Mon. and Wed.-Thurs. 8am-7pm, Tues. and Fri. 8am-1pm.

Accommodations and Food

Tel Aviv's **IYHF youth hostel** is in the northern part of the city at 32 Benei Dan St. (tel. 45 50 42). Take bus #5 from the bus station to Pinkas St., make a left onto Brandeis St., then a right at the end of Brandeis. (Members US$8.50, nonmembers US$9.50; ages under 18 US$1.50 less. Breakfast included. Lockout 9am-5pm. Flexible 11pm curfew.) **The Greenhouse,** 201 Dizengoff St. (tel. 23 59 94), is Tel Aviv's best hostel. (Beds in 4-bunk rooms US$7 in summer, US$6 in winter. No curfew.) **Hotel Yosef,** 15 Bograshov St. (tel. 28 09 55), off Ben Yehuda downtown (bus #4 from the Central Bus Station), is cramped but friendly, and has a nice bar. (Dorm beds US$4, "roof-top lounge" US$3. Flexible 1am curfew.) **Mash House,** 4 Trumpeldor St. (tel. 65 76 84), is right on the beach between Herbert Samuel and HaYarkon St. (Singles US$7, doubles US$12, apartments US$18; all with baths and kitchen.) The **Top Hostel,** 84 Ben Yehuda St. (tel. 23 78 07), *not* to be confused with The Hostel at #60, is large and clean. (Dorm beds US$4.50, private rooms with shower US$14. 1am curfew.)

The cheapest and most colorful place to eat in Tel Aviv is the **Shuq HaCarmel** (Carmel Market), where a half-dozen felafel stands compete feverishly to sell you a US$1 pocket filled with your choice of their huge variety of vegetables. (No fixed hours, but usually Sun.-Thurs. 10am-7pm, Fri. until mid-afternoon.) The market, which extends westward from Kikar Magen David, is also the place to shop for fresh produce. An extremely diverse collection of restaurants—Italian, Balkan, Chinese, North African, and Middle Eastern—line **Dizengoff Street** and the streets nearby. For Yemenite food, try **Zion Gamliel** at 12 Peduyin St. The best seafood is at the Old Port in Yafo; try **Fisherman's Restaurant,** right on the wharf at Ha' Aliyah HaShniyah St. For a splurge, visit **Pirozki,** 265 Dizengoff St.; their Russian meals and salads are outstanding. (Salads US$3.50-4.50.) Nearby, **Banana,** 334 Dizengoff St., serves creative vegetarian food (US$5).

Sights and Entertainment

The **Beit Hatfusot** (Diaspora Museum), located on the Tel Aviv University campus in Ramat Aviv, provides ambitious, thought-provoking documentation of the definitive event of Judaism: the Diaspora and subsequent centuries of exile. Take bus #25 from Yafo, the Carmel Market, or the youth hostel; or #27 from the bus station. (Open Sun.-Tues. and Thurs. 10am-5pm, Wed. 10am-7pm. Admission US$2.50, students US$1.50.)

The **Tel Aviv Museum,** 27 Sderot Shaul HaMeleḥ, has fancy, split-level galleries and a fine collection of Israeli and international modern art. Take bus #18 or 19. (Open Sun.-Thurs. 10am-2pm and 5-9pm, Sat. 11am-2pm. Admission US$1.75, students US$1.50.) The admission ticket also entitles you to visit the changing exhibits at the **Helena Rubinstein Pavilion,** 6 Sderot Tarsat. From the Tel Aviv Museum, turn right on Shaul HaMeleḥ, left on Ibn Govirol, right on Dizengoff, and left on Tarsat. (Open Sun.-Thurs. 10am-1pm and 5-7pm, Sat. 11am-2pm.)

Yafo, south of Tel Aviv, is one of the world's oldest ports. The center and its crumbling Arab stone buildings were empty for years after 1948, but have recently been restored. Now Old Yafo is an artist colony, full of galleries and cafes. Outside this area are interesting neighborhoods and the exotic **Shuq HaPishpishim** (flea market). The view of Tel Aviv and the ocean from the **HaPisga Gardens** is magnificent. To get to Yafo, take bus #10 from Ben Yehuda St., or #42 or 46 from the bus station.

Most visitors to Tel Aviv bake on the beach by day and party by night. The **Colosseum,** at Kikkar Atarim, the **Penguin,** 43 Yehuda HaLevi St., and **Liquid,** 18 Montefiore St., are three of the most popular, if youngish, discos. (Cover US$5-10. Open Sat.-Sun. and Tues.-Thurs. from 10pm, though usually empty until midnight.) Until then, watch the evening parade from one of the cafes on Dizengoff Street. **The Backyard** and **Long John Silver's,** off Dizengoff Circle near the Ester Cinema, offer a friendly atmosphere and a mostly English-speaking crowd. **HaShoftim,** at the intersection of HaShoftim and Ibn Gvirol St., is popular among young bohemian Israelis.

The tourist office distributes *Tel Aviv Today,* a weekly bulletin on concerts and cultural events throughout the area.

Dead Sea (Yam HaMelah)

Early Christian settlers distraught with the complete absence of life in the sea's warm and heavily salted waters coined the name. At 400m below sea level, the Dead Sea is the lowest point on earth; the view to the barren hills which soar above makes even a short visit worthwhile. In the summer, the heat and humidity will be unbearable unless you stay in one of the two air-conditioned hostels. Aside from the hostel cafeterias, there are no inexpensive food stores, so bring provisions and *lots of water.* The area is served by buses from Jerusalem, Tel Aviv, and Eilat.

Because of the high salt and mineral content, swimming is quite an experience—you actually have to struggle to keep your feet down. There are organized beaches along the coast at **Qulya, Ein Feshka** (Ein Tzukim), **Ein Gedi, Ein Boqeq,** and **Newe Zohar,** all with very necessary showers to wash off the salt. For even better (though fresh-water) swimming, climb the path to the hidden oasis at **Ein Gedi.** The lushest vegetation around surrounds a waterfall, natural pools, and the cave where David hid from King Saul. The biblical image that springs to mind, though, is the Garden of Eden, especially for those who plunge into the sweet water pools after baking off the Dead Sea salt in the fierce sun. The **IYHF youth hostel** at **Ein Gedi** (tel. (057) 841 65) is clean, with cheap food and 200 beds. (Members US$7.50, nonmembers US$8.50. Breakfast included; dinner US$4.80.) **Ein Gedi Camping,** a bit further south, charges about US$4.50 per person.

Masada, 20km south of Ein Gedi, is one of the most remarkable archeological sites in Israel, as well as a symbol of the Jews' struggle for freedom. The huge fortress, originally built as a resort by King Herod, was the scene of the last holdout of the Jews against the Romans. When defeat was imminent, the defenders committed mass suicide rather than surrender. There are two trails and a cable car to the top. (Sun.-Thurs. every ½ hr. 8am-3:30pm, Fri. 8am-1:30pm. US$2.80 one way, US$4.20 round-trip; students US$1.50 and US$2.25.) Arrive early (gates open at 4:30am) to climb and watch the sunrise. Camping on the rock is no longer allowed, and the prohibition is enforced. The **Taylor Youth Hostel (IYHF)** at the base of the site (tel. (057) 843 49) charges members US$8, nonmembers US$9. (Breakfast included; dinner US$4.80. Reservations recommended.)

Negev Desert and South Coast

The desert has rules of hospitality, and the Bedouin are friendly to those who set out to explore here. In the summer, this region gives new dimension to the word "hot," and the areas near the Dead Sea are especially humid. Drink at least a gallon of liquid every day and try to avoid physical exertion between noon and 3pm.

Beersheva, once a frontier town on the northern edge of the desert, is now a city of 120,000. On Thursdays, however, hundreds of Bedouin, both semi-settled locals and deep-desert nomads, still gather to sell their wares behind the municipal market on the road to Eilat. This Bedouin market is open from 6am to 2pm; arrive early and bargain vigorously for the best deals. The **Negev Museum,** 18 Ha'Atzmaut St., has exhibits taken from excavations in the area; a visit will make trips to the sites themselves that much more interesting. The enormous **Bet Yatziv Youth Hostel (IYHF),** 79 Ha'Atzmaut St. (tel. (057) 774 44), is 500m from the center of town; bus #13 runs from the station. (Members US$7.50, nonmembers US$8.50. Breakfast included; huge dinners US$5, US$7 on Fri. Reception always open. No curfew.) For a lighter meal, try the snack bar on the corner of Keren Kayemet LeYisrael and HeHalutz St. Join Ben-Gurion University students on Trumpeldor and Smilansky Streets every night (including Fri.) for live entertainment at **Little Beersheva's, The Alley,** and **Chaplin's.** Beersheva is a transportation hub for southern Israel, with hourly bus connections to and from Jerusalem, Tel Aviv, Ashqelon, and Eilat.

About 60km north is **Bet Guvrin,** a kibbutz built in 1949 on a site once fortified by the Romans who gave it the Greek name of Eleutheropolis. This is an area of striking natural beauty, with dozens of caves, many molded into beautiful bell-shaped abodes by the Phoenicians. Make the half-hour trip to the top of **Tel Maresha,** which offers views of the Mediterranean and the Dead Sea. Frequent buses leave Beersheva for Qiryat Gat; once there it's an easy hitch to Bet Guvrin.

The house of David Ben-Gurion, Israel's first Prime Minister, is on the lush kibbutz of **Sde Boqer,** 40km south of Beersheva. (Open Sun.-Thurs. 8am-3pm, Fri. 8am-noon, Sat. 9am-1pm. Free.) Five kilometers south, on a hill overlooking the desert, are the spectacular ruins of **Avdat,** a Nabatean city from the first century B.C.E. (Open daily 8am-5pm. Admission US$1, students US$0.75.) The small modern community of **Mitzpe Ramon,** 86km south of Beersheva, overlooks the awe-inspiring **Mahtesh Ramon** (Ramon Crater), the largest natural pit in the world—300m deep by 8km wide by 40km long. Overlooking the crater is a **visitors center,** with a museum and audio-visual show (admission US$2.40). Across from it, the brand new **Mitzpe Ramon Youth Hostel (IYHF)** (tel. 884 43) charges US$8.50, including breakfast (dinner US$4.80). Bus #392 continues from here to Eilat. The **Field School of the Society for the Preservation of Nature in Israel,** 3km outside Mitzpe Ramon, will provide you with maps and hiking information. Call 886 16.

The coastline stretching south of Tel Aviv has good beaches at Bat Yam, Palmahim, Ashdod, Nizzanim, and Ashqelon. All are easily reached by bus from Tel Aviv. This area is extremely hot and humid during the summer. From the central bus station in **Ashqelon,** bus #4, 5, or 7 will take you to the **Israel Government Tourist Office** (tel. 324 12), located on Zephania Sq. in Afridar. Bus #3 and 9 run to the **National Park,** where you'll find beautiful beaches, Roman ruins, and campgrounds.

Eilat

Three decades ago, Eilat was an unremarkable town far from everything else in Israel. It began to grow when the 1956 war opened the Red Sea to Israeli shipping, and mushroomed when the capture of the Sinai gave the city sufficient elbow room to become Israel's premier playground. In recent years Eilat has succumbed to the decadence brought by thousands of sunworshipers from all over the world. Some Israelis call it "the end of the world," and swear off it as "another country." Nevertheless, hideous hotels and tourist restaurants cannot completely obscure Eilat's tremendous natural assets—the rugged desert landscape behind the town, and the spectacular underwater world just offshore.

Orientation and Practical Information

Eilat is divided into three sections. The town itself lies on the hills above the sea; **Lagoon Beach,** below and east, has luxury hotels and a public beach; and **Coral Beach** and the ports, ancient and modern, lie to the south. The **Government Tourist Office** (tel. 722 68), across the street from the Central Bus Station on HaTmarim Bd., is extremely useful. (Open Sun.-Thurs. 8am-6pm, Fri. 8am-1pm.) The **telephone code** in Eilat is 059.

If you plan to take the bus to or from Jerusalem or Tel Aviv, buy your ticket a day or two in advance, and be sure to get a seat number attached to the ticket. Even with a reservation, you need to be aggressive in line and in claiming your seat. To get to the Egyptian border, take bus #15 across the street from the Central Bus Station and get off at the Israeli checkpoint. For travel to the Sinai simply bring your passport. If you plan on going on to Cairo, you must procure an Egyptian visa at the **Egyptian Consulate,** 34 Deror St. (tel. 761 15; open Sun.-Thurs. 9am-2pm). One Egyptian bus per day leaves from the border and travels down the Aqaba coast. Before you hit the beach or head south, equip yourself with head-covering and a couple of canteens, as the dry heat can dehydrate you quickly. Get these at the department store next to the bus station, where you may also want to invest in a snorkel and mask.

Accommodations, Camping, and Food

The cheapest air-conditioned accommodations in Eilat cost around US$5 per person. Choose carefully among the numerous apartment-hawkers who besiege travelers at the bus stop; there are some good deals. Rooms should come equipped with cooking facilities—insist on this before setting off with a peddler.

Freelance camping, though unsafe, abounds on Eilat's public beaches. Sleeping is tolerated everywhere, but tent pitching is allowed only east of Sun Bay Camping, south of the Red Rock Hotel, and on the beach at Taba, 8km south of Eilat on the Egyptian border. The last is the safest and cleanest beach. Two official alternatives do exist.

Youth Hostel (IYHF), corner of Elot and Arava St. (tel. 732 58), across from the Red Rock Hotel. A/C. Members US$8, ages under 18 US$7.50; nonmembers add US$1. Breakfast included. Closed 9am-5pm. Midnight curfew.

Please
Place
Stamp
Here

REI®
DEPT. 2660
P.O. BOX C-88127
Seattle, WA 98188-0127

...when you order a Eurailpass

$25
WORTH
OF
GOODIES!

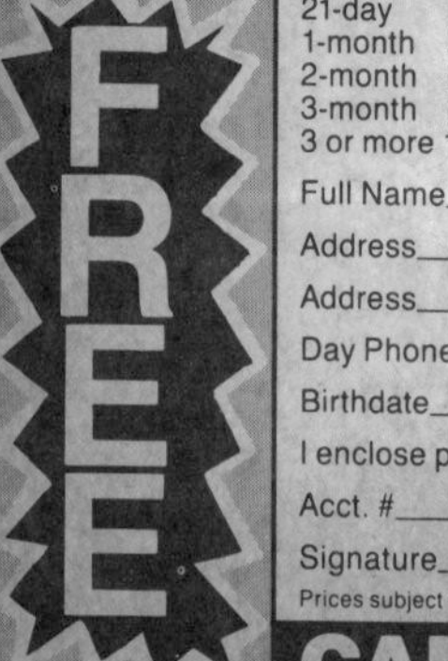

Order by phone or send a check. Normal delivery, 14 days. Stree[t] addresses only. 5-day rush service, only $5 extra.

1988 Eurail Pass

	1st-Class Adult	Youth (12-25) 2nd-Class
15-day	☐$298	N/A
21-day	☐$370	N/A
1-month	☐$470	☐$320
2-month	☐$650	☐$420
3-month	☐$798	N/A

1988 Britrail Pass

	1st-Class	2nd-Class	Youth (12-25
8-day	☐$230	☐$166	☐$139
15-day	☐$350	☐$249	☐$209
22-day	☐$440	☐$319	☐$269
1-month	☐$520	☐$369	☐$309

3 or more 15 day Saverpasses ☐$210 *(Oct. '87 – Mar. '88 2 pass minimum!)*

Full Name______________________________

Address______________________________

Address______________________________

Day Phone ( )______________ Eve Phone ( )______________

Birthdate______________ Departure Date from U.S.______________

I enclose payment by: ☐Check ☐Credit Card ☐RUSH Service $5.0(

Acct. #______________________ Exp. Date______________

Signature______________________________

Prices subject to change.

CALL 1-800-4-EURAIL NOW!

Max and Merran's Youth Hostel, Ofarim St. (tel. 714 08). From the bus station, walk on HaTmarim Blvd. across Hativat HaNegev, take the first right, and turn left just before the end of the street. Much cleaner and brighter than any other place in Eilat, with reliable air conditioning. Friendly to boot. Cooking facilities and 2 refrigerators. US$5. Excellent US$1.25 breakfast optional. Closed 9-11am for cleaning. Midnight curfew.

Shalom Hostel, Hativat HaNegev St. (tel 765 44), across the street from the back lot of the bus station. Brand new, air-conditioned, spacious dorm rooms (US$6.50 per person), and the most coveted doubles in Eilat (US$25). Continental breakfast included. No curfew.

Camping: Sun Bay Camping, 750m from the Jordanian border (tel. 731 05); take bus #1A. Sites US$3.15 per person. **Yigal's Camping** is across the street from the Coral World Underwater Observatory; take bus #15 to the last stop. Sites US$2.50 per person.

Eilat has dozens of restaurants, but none are memorable. **The Fisherman House,** off Coral Beach, serves all the fish, chips, salad, and bread you can eat for US$7; all-you-can-eat of the varied salad offerings for US$3.75. The restaurant in the bus station is good for a cheap, filling meal.

Sights and Entertainment

Twenty-five kilometers north of Eilat is **Timna Valley,** a national park full of geological oddities and ancient mining sites. It's accessible by thumb, rented car, or organized tour from Eilat. Farther north at Kibbutz Yotvata is the **Hai Bar Biblical Nature Reserve,** a wildlife refuge constructed to repatriate a number of species native to the region in biblical times.

Eilat's number one sight is underwater. A venture into the ocean will reward you with an incredibly colorful world of coral and exotic fish. The best diving is at **Coral Beach Nature Reserve** (take bus #15; US$2.40 entrance fee); you can rent snorkel, mask, and fins for US$3 per day at the entrance to the reserve. For more secluded swimming, head for **Taba** (bus #15, last stop).

If you don't swim, take bus #15 to the **Coral Island World Underwater Observatory and Aquarium,** where a submerged chamber allows you to examine the reefs up close. The complex might also be of interest to divers, as aquarium tanks contain and identify many of the fish to be met in underwater forays. (Open Fri. 8:30am-3pm, Sat.-Thurs. 8:30am-4:30pm. Admission US$6.30.)

The Red Lion Pub at the new Tourist Center roars nightly until 2am. Discos abound in major hotels.

West Bank

The West Bank was not updated in the summer of 1987; all prices and information date from 1986 and are likely to have changed.

The towns of the West Bank give a physical immediacy to the Bible. In a cave in Hebron lie the bones of Abraham and Sarah, Isaac and Rebecca, Jacob and Leah; a candle-lit grotto in Bethlehem marks the birthplace of Jesus; and Jericho is the site of Joshua's tumbling wall. Yet the territory west of the River Jordan could easily be described as godforsaken. A barren mixture of chalk-white and brown, this land where legend places the Garden of Eden has been desiccated by the sun.

Occupied by Israel during the 1967 (Six-Day) War, the West Bank is in a curious state of limbo, neither granted autonomy, nor returned to Jordan, nor annexed outright by Israel. In a mortar shell, the dispute is this: The Palestinian Arabs, displaced almost four decades ago from their homeland, and forced to live under military rule, are demanding a land of their own. The Israelis, provoked by the hostility of the Palestinian Liberation Organization and Syria, fear that to pull out of the West Bank would be to guide the knife to their own throats. Eager to establish a friendly and stable buffer, the Israeli government used to encourage Jewish settlement in the Occupied Territories and has recently leaned towards a negotiated settlement with the relatively moderate Jordanians rather than the West Bank residents themselves. The volatile mixture of Jewish settlers and resentful, often impoverished Palestinian Arabs has repeatedly burst into violence.

Jerusalem provides relative safety, cheap accommodations, and convenient bus connections. Ramallah, and especially Bethlehem and Jericho, are quite safe to visit or to stay in overnight. Arab buses provide frequent, convenient, and diplomatic service to all West Bank towns from stations in Jerusalem: Damascus gate station for Jericho, Bethlehem,and Hebron; Nablus Road Station, one block west, to Ramallah and Nablus; buses to the south stop at Jaffa Gate. Arab buses operate from about 5am to 6pm. Shared taxis serve the same routes from similar stations, are speedier for long distances, cost two or three times as much as buses, and usually travel back to Jerusalem until 8pm. More comfortable but less colorful Egged buses travel some of the same routes, but they are sometimes targets for stonings or even bombings.

Knowledge of a few Arabic phrases demonstrates a sensitivity which will help eliminate mistrust caused by the Israeli occupation. If you know any Hebrew, pretend you don't. Using the Arabic name for Jerusalem (El Khudz) will also win friends. Respect the customs of the largely Muslim populace: Men should wear long trousers and a shirt; women should wear a long skirt and a long-sleeved shirt. Women might think twice before traveling alone on the West Bank. During Ramadan (April 18 to May 18 in 1988), many restaurants on the West Bank are closed until sundown.

Bethlehem, Herodion, and Hebron

Suburban but beautiful Bethlehem, about 20 minutes by bus from Jerusalem, contains the massive **Basilica of the Nativity,** built on the site of Jesus' birth. Stairs lead down to a grotto where a silver star marks the spot. The church was built by Emperor Constantine in 326 C.E. and improved during the Crusades. (Open daily 7am-6pm; Franciscan procession daily at noon or 1pm.) A few minutes east of the basilica, along Milk Grotto St., stands **Milk Grotto Church,** where the Holy Family hid while fleeing from Herod into Egypt. (Open daily 8-11:45am and 2-5pm.) On the northern side of town, along Star St., the **King David Cinema** shows a tasteful film on the life of Jesus (4 per day, US$6); the **Well of David** graces the parking lot. Sacred to Jews, **Rachel's Tomb** lies at Manger St. and the road to Hebron, 3km north of Manger Square. Jacob's second wife died here while giving birth to Benjamin (Genesis 35:18-20). Expectant mothers still travel here to pray for a safe delivery. (Open Sun.-Thurs. 8am-5pm, Fri. 8am-1pm.)

For a map of Bethlehem and transportation information, visit the **tourist office** on Manger Sq. (tel. 74 25 91). (Open in summer Mon.-Fri. 8am-5pm; in winter Mon.-Fri. 8am-4pm.) The hospitable **Franciscan Convent Pension** (tel. 74 24 41), just beyond the Milk Grotto Church, has clean, quiet rooms with panoramic views. (Dorm beds about US$5, singles US$12, doubles US$22. Breakfast included. Gates close at 8pm.) **St. Joseph's Home** (tel. 74 24 97), ½km north of Manger Sq. and next to King David's Well, offers similar rates and cleanliness.

The cheapest hotel in town is the **Al-Andalus** (tel. 74 13 48) on Manger Square. (Singles US$15, doubles US$30. Breakfast included. US$5 per person for heat in winter.) **Ramat Raḥel Camping** (tel. 71 57 12) is just 4km to the north on the road to Jerusalem; walk or take bus #7. (US$4 per person. Bungalow places US$9, breakfast included.) Felafel stands surround Manger Square, and the covered **market** just uphill and southeast of Manger Square offers cheap produce. For more substantial meals, try the **Ruins Al-Atlal Restaurant** on Milk Grotto St. Buses #22, 47, and 60 connect Bethlehem with the Damascus Gate station in Jerusalem (½ hr., US$0.75).

Herodion, 11km southeast of Bethlehem, is one of the Holy Land's most dramatic archeological sites. Atop a spectacular volcano-like peak stands Herod's greatest achievement, its massive battlements enclosing a splendid palace and bathhouse. (Open Sat.-Thurs. 8am-6pm, Fri. 8am-5pm. Admission US$0.80, students US$0.40.) To reach Herodion from either Jerusalem or Bethlehem, take Arab bus

#47 to Beit Sahur (US$0.75); from Bethlehem, take a minibus from Cafe Salim near Manger Square to Beit Sahur. From there catch bus #52 or 62 (infrequent), or continue past Shepherd's Fields on the road from Beit Sahur and hike or hitch 7km from the marked turn-off. Also southeast of Bethlehem is the colossal cliffside **Mar Saba Monastery,** founded in the fifth century. English-speaking monks will tell visitors (men only) about the monastery every day but Sunday until about 4pm. Take bus #60 from Bethlehem to Abudiye village and walk the remaining 6km (last bus returns from Abudiye at 4pm); *sherut* taxis will make the journey to Herodion or Mar Saba for US$10 and US$13 round-trip, for a carload of as many as six persons.

In a cave in **Hebron,** 40km south of Bethlehem, three great religious traditions converge over the haunting tombs of the Biblical patriarchs and matriarchs. Jews, Muslims, and Christians revere their common prophets at the **Cave of Machpelah,** the burial site of Abraham and Sarah, Isaac and Rebecca, Jacob and Leah, and Adam and Eve. The tombs are housed in a combination citadel, mosque, church, and synagogue. The massive outer walls contain Herodian remains as well as layers from succeeding generations. (Open Sun.-Thurs. 7am-7pm, Sat. 11:30am-7pm. Closed Fri. to non-Muslims.) The **market** in Hebron is one of the largest and most interesting on the West Bank. Hebron is predominantly Palestinian Arab, and its inhabitants are unusual, even on the West Bank, for the fierceness of their resentment. The proximity of the controversial Jewish settlement of Qiryat Arba fuels these flames. Arab bus #23 serves the city from the Damascus Gate station (US$0.80); taxis to Jerusalem cost US$1.50.

Jericho and Nablus

Forty kilometers east of Jerusalem, Jericho is a magnificent oasis city, and one of the world's hottest spots. It is worth a trip to Jericho if only to take in the beautiful desert landscape of the Judean wilderness on the road from Jerusalem. Rent a bike and visit the **Tel el Sultan** (ancient city) 1½km northwest of town. There's not much to see, but these 7000-year-old ruins are the basis of Jericho's claim to being the oldest city in the world. (Site open Sat.-Thurs. 8am-5:30pm, Fri. 8am-4:30pm. Admission US$0.70, students US$0.35.) Across from its walls, famous for tumbling at the blare of Joshua's trumpet, flows the **Ein el Sultan** (Elisha's Spring). The source of Jericho's lush greenery, the spring was supposedly desalinated by the prophet at the behest of the local population (II Kings 2:19-22).

From ancient Jericho, peddle north for 2km, then turn right, doubling back toward town on Qasr Hisham St. Next to this intersection, 3km north of Jericho's main square, lies ruined **Hisham's Palace.** An outstanding example of early Islamic architecture, it features beautifully preserved mosaics. (Open April-Sept. Sat.-Thurs. 8am-5pm, Fri. 8am-4pm; Oct.-March Sat.-Thurs. 8am-4pm, Fri. 8am-3pm. Admission US$1.50, students US$.80.) Looming above ancient Jericho to the west is the **Qarantal** (Mount of Temptation), where Satan reportedly visited the fasting Jesus after his baptism in the nearby River Jordan. You can climb to the Greek Orthodox monastery on the face of the mountain, where an ancient Greek inscription describes the event. (Open in summer Mon.-Sat. 8am-5pm; in winter 7am-2pm and 3-4pm.)

Virtually the only place to stay in Jericho is the **Hisham's Palace Hotel** (tel. 24 14) on Ein es Sultan St. (US$5-10 per night depending on when you ask.) Halfway between Jerusalem and Jericho is the **Mosque of Nabi Musa,** revered by Muslims as the final resting place of Moses (open only during Muslim prayer times; closed in April to non-pilgrims). Ask the bus driver to let you off at the dirt road that leads from the eastbound side of the Jersualem-Jericho highway. Reach Jericho from Jerusalem on Arab bus #28 from Damascus Gate (US$1), or on Egged buses #961 or 963 between Jerusalem's Central Station (US$1.75) and Tiberias. Shared taxis cost about US$2.

Many Palestinians look upon **Nablus,** largest city in the West Bank, as the intellectual and administrative capital of their nation. After strolling through the intriguing central **market,** head 3km down the road to Jerusalem to reach **Jacob's Well.** Featured in the New Testament, the well dates from the time when Jacob bought the surrounding patch of land to pitch his tents (John 4:6-42). Access to the well is through the Greek Orthodox convent (open Mon.-Sat. 8am-noon and 2-5pm). Nearby, a guarded Jewish shrine (until recently held by Muslims) encloses **Joseph's Tomb.** (Open daily 6am-6pm.) Nablus is the Biblical Shekhem; just above town on wooded **Mount Gerizim,** according to the Samaritans, Abraham offered to sacrifice his son Isaac.

Spending the night in Nablus can be unsafe for non-Arabs. If you're stuck, try the **Palestinian Hotel** (tel. 700 40), 300m west of the bus and taxi stops, up Ghirnata St. (Singles and doubles US$10.)

Nablus can be reached by Arab buses from Jerusalem's Nablus Road Station (2½ hr., US$2.50). Shared taxis from the nearby stand are more comfortable and speedier (1 hr., US$4).

The underrated archeological site of ancient **Sebastiya** (or **Samaria),** 11km northwest of Nablus, features an impressive array of Israelite, Hellenistic, and Roman ruins, including a **Roman theater** more interesting than the one at Caesarea. (Open Sat.-Thurs. 8am-5pm, Fri. 8am-4pm. Admission US$1.15, students US$0.85.) The modern hillside village of Sebastiya below is home to a twelfth-century Crusader cathedral, since converted to a mosque. Coming from Nablus, hail one of the numerous taxis to Sebastiya village (US$0.80 per person).

ITALY

US$1 = 1315 lire(L)
CDN$1 = L990
UK£1 = L2143
AUS$1 = L934

L1000 = US$0.76
L1000 = CDN$1.01
L1000 = UK£0.47
L1000 = AUS$1.07

Massive medieval walls still encircle most Italian cities with protective arms of rough hewn stone. In past centuries they insulated the cities from the confusion and violence of the outside world, encouraging the development of highly original artistic and architectural styles, dialects, and customs. Though the asphalt and steel of the twentieth century have long since broken the rough stone seal, a proud individualism persists in each city, expressing itself in everything from wine to politics.

Part and parcel of this individualism is a deep-seated respect for the past, and every town jealously guards its unique artistic and historical heritage. In fact, the past is so lovingly preserved that one could travel through the rich expanse of Italian history end to end.

The trip would begin beneath the grassy hills of Tarquinia, in the brightly painted tombs of the Etruscans; this highly developed civilization ruled central Italy centuries before the beginning of the Common Era. Next stop would be Sicily where the Greeks honored their gods with soaring temples of white marble. The Romans are everywhere, in the monumental coliseums and arches of Rome and Verona, and the volcanically embalmed towns of Pompeii and Herculaneum. Somber early Christian churches, sparkling with Byzantine frescoes, distinguish Ravenna as a treasure-house of early medieval culture. San Gimignano bristles with the forbidding towers of the later Middle Ages. Swing by Florence for a taste of Italian Renaissance at its most intoxicating, and visit the hills of Lombardy to imagine yourself at the side of Camillo di Cavour, swelling with hope and pride for the as yet unborn Italian nation.

On the way, you'll see the equally vast diversity of Italy's natural treasures: the rugged hills of Lazio, the beaches and papyrus groves of Sicily, and the seasoned, cypress-clad Tuscan landscape. Farther north are the vast, cool lakes and towering mountains of Lombardy and the Dolomites. Any trip would reveal the vast differences between regions and between individual cities, rooted in divergent histories and dissimilar geography. Choose a few regions, and explore them patiently. Get to know the people and their customs, in addition to the monuments. Savor the exquisite traditional and regional food and wines, and adjust your schedule to include the time-honored *siesta* and after-dinner stroll (*passeggiata*).

Since the fall of Mussolini and the fascists, Italy has seen no less than 47 governments, the result of an electoral system which gives unusual power to even the smallest of parties and thus necessitates the formation of unwieldy coalitions. The Christian Democrats and the Socialists are perennially the strongest parties. A two-month-long political crisis in the spring of 1987 saw a coalition involving these two and three smaller parties collapse, only to be replaced at the June elections by a coalition of the exact same five. Giovanni Goria, a Christian Democrat and, at 44, the youngest post-war Prime Minister, may inaugurate a new era of stability, but the smart money is against him. Despite the chaotic political scene, Italy is doing very well, thank you—the country recently passed Britain in GNP and enjoys an inflation rate of only 4%, and analysts estimate that the *economia nera* (unofficial economy) accounts for fully a quarter of the country's wealth. The most popular dailies are, on a spectrum from left to right, *L'Unitá, La Repubblica,* and *Il Giornale.*

Italy has long inspired writers, native and foreign. Dante's *Divine Comedy* is one of the most powerful and revolutionary works ever written. The *Decameron* of Boccaccio is a deft blend of folktales, teeming with bawdy friars, righteous maidens, and fierce knights—all of whom are strikingly human. Equally true to life, Alessandro Manzoni's *I Promessi Sposi (The Betrothed),* is a portrait of Italy at the height of the *Risorgimento.* More recently still, Luigi Pirandello put pen to *Sei Personaggi in Cerca d'Autore (Six Characters in Search of an Author),* and Italo Calvino wrote *Se una Notte d'Inverno un Viaggiatore (If On a Winter's Night a Traveler).* Some of Italy's most compelling tales are on celluloid rather than paper: Vittorio de Sica's film, *The Bicycle Thief* (1948), heads dozens of lists of history's top ten, and Rossellini's *Voyage to Italy* (1953) and Fellini's *La Strada* (1954) are other classics of international stature.

For a comprehensive budget travel guide with more detailed coverage than can be offered here, turn to *Let's Go: Italy.*

Transportation

Italian trains are cheap and the network is very comprehensive. A *locale* stops at nearly every station, the *diretto* is only slightly more direct, and the *espresso* is considerably faster. The *rapido* is very swift, but requires a *supplemento* (Eurailpass and InterRail holders exempt); this can be purchased ahead of time or on the train. Second-class fares are refreshingly cheap—about US$29 from Venice to Rome. The *Biglietto Chilometrico* is good for 20 trips amounting to 3000 kilometers and can be used for two months by as many as five people. The ticket can be purchased for US$93 at any Italian rail station. If you plan to do much train traveling here, pick up the *Nuovo Orario delle Ferrovie,* a book published twice yearly with complete lists of state train lines, hours, and prices (L2200 at newsstands).

Intercity buses are often preferable to trains on shorter hauls off the main rail lines, especially when the geography—the hills of Umbria and Tuscany, for example—prevents trains from pulling directly into town. City buses cost L400-600, and tickets are available in *tabacchi* stores and most newsstands. Tickets must be validated on the bus. The *autostrade* (super-highways) are fast and relatively uncrowded (except in Aug.), but gas and tolls are expensive, and Italian drivers will rattle all but the most confident. Hitching *(autostop)* is strictly prohibited on the *autostrade;* wait in front of toll booths, with a clearly-lettered sign indicating your destination. If time is not of the essence, thumb the primary road system, which offers more contact with Italy and Italians alike. Bicycling is a popular national sport but not always pleasant. Bikers have to use the main roads (bike trails are rare), drivers are often reckless, and the terrain challenges even the most fit, particularly in Tuscany, Umbria, and the mountainous north.

Touring Club Italiano maps are invaluable for drivers, hitchers, and bikers. Detailed regional maps are available free in most tourist offices.

Practical Information

Italian tourist offices, usually able to help with room-finding, come in two varieties: the **Ente Provinciale per il Turismo (EPT),** in the largest cities, and the **Azienda Autonoma di Turismo** nearly everywhere else. These offices are generally friendly and well-informed on local matters, and make a good first stop in any city.

Any knowledge of Spanish, French, Portuguese, or Latin will help you understand spoken and written Italian. Most tourist office staff speak at least some English, but elsewhere you may have to struggle along in Italian. Any attempt at Italian, no matter how bungling, is likely to be warmly and enthusiastically received.

Italy's cathedrals are religious institutions and not museums. Don't visit during mass, and be sure to cover legs and shoulders; you may want to carry a shirt and trousers or a skirt and shawl in a daypack. The more neatly and conservatively you dress, the better treatment you'll receive everywhere.

Italian men have a tarnished reputation, one not entirely deserved of course. Women may encounter unwanted male attention; obliviousness will deter all but the most persistent. No response at all is generally more effective than a show of anger or disgust.

Festivals are a significant aspect of life in Italy. Events such as the **Palio** of Siena (July 2 and Aug. 16), the **Carnival** in Venice (early March), and the bizarre **Corsa dei Ceri** held in Gubbio (May 15), have age-old histories and rituals. August, especially the weeks around the 15th, is vacation month for most Italians, who head for the beaches and mountains and leave the cities closed up and empty.

Summers are humid and hot in the north, dryer and hotter with every step south; everywhere early afternoon is good for nothing but a snooze (*siesta*). Winters are ferocious in the Alps and cold and damp in Venice, Florence, and Rome, but Sicilian waters are swimmable year-round.

Just about everything closes from 1 to 3 or 4pm. Food shops remain closed until 5 or 5:30pm in the summer. Museum hours vary, but most are open from 9am to 1pm and some again from 4 to 7pm. Monday is the *giorno di chiusura* (day of closure) for most museums, so plan your itinerary accordingly. In general, banks are open from 8:30am to 12:30pm and 2:30 to 4pm.

Payphones are most often available at bars and *tabacchi* stores, where *gettoni* are also sold. These tokens cost L200, and are often used just like L200 coins. Most phones also take L200 and L100 coins. One is enough for local calls; on intercity calls, deposit eight or more, as unused tokens will be returned (push the button insistently). A card, rather than *gettoni* or coins, is used to operate some new public phones; cards can be bought from machines usually placed next to the phone. International and collect calls are best made from the offices of **SIP** and **ASST,** the state phone companies, usually located near the main post office or train station. Every town has at least one bar with a *telefono a scatti*—talk first, pay later—which can be used for international calls. *Fermo posta* is the Italian term for Poste Restante.

Accommodations and Camping

The Italian hostel federation **(AIG)** has dozens of youth hostels *(ostelli della gioventù)* scattered across the country; there are proportionately more in the north. A complete list is available from most EPT and CTS offices and from many of the hostels. Prices average about L11,000 per night including breakfast, with dinners usually available for L6000 more. Only some hostels require IYHF cards, though there is an occasional extra charge (about L2000) for nonmembers. Cards can be purchased at many hostels for L15,000. Hostels are the best place for solo travelers, as single rooms are relatively scarce in hotels. But 11pm to 1am curfews, daytime lockouts (no *siesta*), and out-of-the-way locations detract from the charm of hostels; and two or more people can often stay almost as cheaply in a hotel.

One-star accommodations, be they hotel, *albergi, pensioni,* or *locande,* are the best budget option. Prices fluctuate with the region, but a good deal is L15,000 per single and L23,000 for a double (L5000 more is not outrageous). By law the price must be posted on the door; if it isn't, get it in writing from the management. Always check to see if the tax (IVA), breakfast, and shower privileges are included and/or mandatory, as these can mount up to an unexpectedly high bill. For doubles, specify *due letti* (2 beds) or a *letto matrimoniale* (double bed). A triple should cost no more than 135% the price of a double. A private bath usually costs at least L5000 extra, but if there is an extra charge for showers, two or three people traveling together may save money in a room *con bagno* (with bath).

Tourist offices always have a list of their town's hotels. The prices they cite are sometimes wildly inaccurate. Make sure you get information on *pensioni* and *locande* too, as they are sometimes listed separately. While you're at it, ask about *camere libere,* rooms to let in private residences; they sometimes cost significantly less. An even better value found in most large cities are the *Protezione della Giovane,* dorms run by religious orders for women travelers only. Quality is high, and beds average only L8000, but there are usually curfews.

Camping spots tend to be loud and modern and may run as high as L6000 per person plus L6000 per tent. No all-inclusive guide to Italian campsites exists at present, but the *Euro Camping* guide to Italy and Corsica is a good start and widely available (L8500).

Whether you seek roofed or *all'aperto* accommodations, try to reach your destination before noon to begin looking. Especially during the summer and in the major tourist centers, the best and cheapest rooms vanish quickly after 11am. If you must arrive late, consider calling to make a reservation the day before you arrive, or take what the local room-finding service gives you for the first night, then hunt yourself the next day.

Food

Mangia, mangia did not become one of the Italian phrases best known to English-speakers by accident. The production, preparation, and loving consumption of food is a central part of Italian culture. While comparatively expensive, Italian food is more than worth it; so eat, eat.

Breakfasts are light; *colazione* usually means a *cappocino* (a warming mixture of coffee and hot, frothy milk) and a *brioche* (pastry). Ordering a *caffè* will get you a black, strong *espresso.* You can have this potent brew softened with milk by requesting a *caffè macchiato* ("spotted coffee"). For simple, hearty fare, try *alimentari* stores; they often make a mean sandwich *(panino),* with fresh local *salami* and slices of excellent Italian cheese—*groviera, Bel Paese, provolone,* or the divinely rich *parmigiano* (parmesan). Local markets *(mercato)* offer these delicacies also, along with the freshest produce around, although supermarkets are often cheaper. *Rosticcerie* (grills) offer delicious roast meats (a whole chicken goes for about L9000, great for a group), and take-out pasta dishes for about L3500. A *tavola calda* is a cheap, sit-down option, as is the student *mensa* in every university town. *Pizzerie* come in simple, stand-up and more expensive sit-down varieties; and the local *forno* (bakery) often sells hot pizza by the slice (about L800), as well as cookies and local savory specialties (from onion-covered *schiacciata* to cheese-filled *focaccia).*

Osterie, trattorie, and *ristoranti* are, in roughly ascending order, fancier and more expensive. The hours you can count on finding them open are 12:30-2pm and 7-10pm (later in the south). Menus in smaller restaurants are often incomplete or nonexistent; ask for the *piatti del giorno* (daily specials). A *menù turistico,* when offered, usually runs only L9000-12,000 for a full meal, but almost always features a limited variety of dishes. Virtually every sit-down establishment in the country charges *pane e coperto* (bread and cover charge). Make sure this isn't too far above the L1000-1500 average, and check to see whether service is included *(compreso).*

A full meal consists of an *antipasto* (appetizer); a *primo piatto,* pasta or soup; a *secondo piatto,* meat or fish with a vegetable *(contorno)*—usually followed by salad, fruit, and/or cheese. The north is famous for meat dishes with delicate cream sauces and a host of variations on standard pasta: rice is most popular in Lombardy; *polenta,* made from corn, and *gnocchi,* with potato flour, in Froili and the Veneto. Central Italy, and Emilia Romagna in particular, is the best place for serious eating, with tangy cheeses, superb produce, and rich meat-and-mushroom sauces. Seek and devour the *pasta all'uovo* (egg pasta) in all its delectable shapes: long, flat *tagliatelle, lasagne,* and meat-filled *tortellini.* As one travels south, spice and tomatoes play an increasingly significant role. By the time you reach Naples, the standard pasta dish beads the brow with sweat. Pastries and sweets get progressively sweeter, reaching an all-time glucose high in the fanciful *marzipan* of Sicily.

Italian wines also change as you move south. Beginning with the delicate white *Asti Spumante* from Piedmont and *Soave,* from Verona, local wines get redder and earthier on the way south. Roman wines are full-bodied, the *falerno* of Naples (famous since the classical period) even more so, and Sicilian *Marsala* tastes like middleweight sherry. In the middle is the *Chianti* region of Tuscany, where some of the world's best red wine is produced. There are numerous exceptions to the north-south rule—the rich, red *barbera d'asti* from Piedmont, the golden *Est! Est!! Est!!!* from Lazio, and numerous light, aromatic Sicilian wines. Restaurant house wines usually offer everything but a label and high price tag. Although *birrerie,* with a dizzying assortment of brews on tap, are everywhere, Italian beer leaves something to be desired. Drink *Peroni* or *Wührer* only if there are no imports in sight.

Bars are a good place to sample wines, eat breakfast, and stop for snacks. They also serve a colorful collection of Italian liqueurs. Try *grappa,* the ice-clear fire water of the Dolomites flavored with different fruits, and *sambuca,* a sweet Roman potation served with coffee beans in it. Remember, though, that sitting down at a table will double the price of anything you order. The *Mona Lisa* notwithstanding, Italy's greatest contribution to civilization is *gelato* (ice cream). Watch for the *produzione propria* (homemade) sign. Also great on hot summer days are *granite* ("Italian ices") and *frullati* (cool fruit shakes).

Northern Italy

Falling from Alpine heights to the expanse of the Po valley, this relatively small region is home to some of Europe's most compelling attractions. Dozens of Renaissance cities each preserve beautiful *palazzi* and *piazze;* everyone seems decked out in the latest fashion; and the food is superb, even by Italian standards. The region of **Lombardy** has a history of affluence; Milan today is a European financial capital and Mantua, Cremona, and Pavia are repositories of centuries of high culture. **Liguria,** stretching along Italy's Mediterranean coast, is an equally attractive and less costly alternative to the French Riviera. Giuseppe Mazzini and Giuseppe Garibaldi, who with Cavour make up the trinity of Italian unification, were Ligurians. Flat, humid **Emilia Romagna** is the breadbasket of Italy, but lays claim as well to Europe's oldest university (in Bologna), and some of its best-preserved Byzantine art (in Ravenna). And then there's Venice—and who can say more?

Milan (Milano)

It is said that for every church in Rome, there is a bank in Milan. But besides being Italy's wealthiest city, Milan is also its most fashionable. The city's most recent contributions to the nation's culture are the *paninari,* teenage preppies named after the fast-food *panini* they prefer to traditional pasta. Preening themselves atop their Vespa scooters in front of cafes throughout the country, they represent all that Milan holds dear: money, modernity, fashion, and flair.

Orientation and Practical Information

Milan lies in the heart of northern Italy, and is linked by rail to all major cities in Italy and Europe. The city is huge, but manageable if you familiarize yourself with the historic center and the area around the huge **Stazione Centrale,** a frightening collusion of art deco and Fascist bombast. The center of the city is the unmistakable fairytale Gothic **duomo** (cathedral), and its elegant commercial counterpart, the lofty **Galleria Vittorio Emanuele II.** Like many *Milanesi,* you probably won't be able to afford lodgings in this area, but the **Metropolitana Milano (MM)** makes getting around quick and easy. Be warned that Milan closes down with a terrific vengeance during August; if you visit then, expect to find a nearly deserted city.

Tourist Offices: APT, at 3 locations, all with free room-finding services and city maps. **Stazione Centrale** (tel. 669 05 32), open in summer Mon.-Sat. 9:15am-12:30pm and 2-6pm. **Piazza del Duomo** (tel. 80 96 62), open Mon.-Fri. 9am-12:30pm and 1:30-6pm, Sat. 9am-12:30pm and 1:30-5pm. **Linate Airport** (tel. 74 40 65), open Mon.-Fri. 9am-4:30pm.

Budget Travel: Centro Turistico Studentesco, via S. Antonio, 2 (tel. 86 38 77). Open Mon.-Fri. 9am-6:30pm (until 5pm for airline tickets), Sat. 9am-12:30pm.

American Express: Via Brera, 3 (tel. 855 71), beyond p. Scala. Will hold mail. All banking services. Open Mon.-Fri. 9am-5pm, Sat. 9am-noon.

Currency Exchange: At Stazione Centrale, **Banca Nazionale delle Comunicazioni** (tel. 669 02 53) has standard rates. Open Mon.-Sat. 8am-9pm, Sun. 8am-2pm.

Post Office: Via Cordusio, 4, near p. Duomo. General services at window #30, Poste Restante at window #34. Open Mon.-Fri. 8:15am-8pm, Sat. 8:15am-1pm. **Postal Code:** 20100.

Telephones: ASST, in the post office. Open 24 hours. Also **SIP** in the Galleria Vittorio Emanuele II. Open daily 8:10am-9:30pm. **Telephone code:** 02.

Flights: Buses to and from intercontinental **Malpensa Airport** (tel. 86 80 28) run in connection with scheduled flights (1 hr., L6000). If you're on a charter, check a day or two in advance at the **Doria Agency** (tel. 669 08 36) in Stazione Centrale about reserving a seat; buses leave just outside. They also can tell you about scheduled buses (every 20 min. 5:40am-9:20pm, adults L3000, children L1000) to and from **Linate Airport** (tel. 74 85 22 00), where domestic and European flights land; it's cheaper and just as convenient to take city bus #73 from p. S. Babila (on MM1).

Trains: Stazione Centrale, Porta Garibaldi, and **Lambrate** all lie on MM2; most trains use Centrale. Information (tel. 675 00).

Buses: Intercity, at p. Castello and the nearby streets. For points throughout Italy, the largest company is **Autostradale,** p. Castello, 1 (tel. 80 11 61).

Public Transportation: The 2 efficient lines of the **Metropolitana Milano** serve much of the city; buses fill the gaps. Information in the MM stop at p. Duomo (tel. 87 54 94). A L700 ticket is good for 75 min. of surface travel and 1 subway ride. Day passes, available at major stations, cost L2800.

Emergencies: Police (tel. 113); *Questura* at via Fatebenefratelli, 11 (tel. 622 61, ext. 327). **Ambulance** (tel. 77 33).

Medical Assistance: Ospedale Maggiore Policlinico, via Francesco Sforza, 35 (tel. 58 16 55).

Pharmacy: In the Stazione Centrale (tel. 669 07 35). Open 24 hours.

Consulates: U.S., largo Donegami, 1 (tel. 65 28 41, after hours 21 41 05). **Canada,** via Vittor Pisani, 19 (tel. 669 74 51, after hours 669 80 60). **U.K.,** via San Paolo, 7 (tel. 80 34 42, after hours 21 41 05). **Australia,** via Turati, 40 (tel. 659 87 27). **Spain,** via Monte Rosa, 3 (tel. 48 23 37). Call after-hours numbers only in truly dire circumstances.

Bookstore: American Bookshop, via Camperio, 16 (tel. 87 09 44), near largo Cairoli, has the best selection in Milan, including *Let's Go* guides. Open Tues.-Fri. 9:30am-7pm, Sat. 9:30am-1pm and 2-7pm, Mon. 2-7pm.

Laundromat: Via Tatino, 17 (tel. 204 21 23), off via Boscovitch near corso Buenos Aires. MM1: Lima. Open Mon.-Fri. 8am-12:30pm and 3-7pm. About L10,000 for 5kg of clothes.

Hitchhiking: For Bologna, Rome, and Florence, take tram #13 from via Mazzini, near p. Duomo, to piazzale Corvetto. To go north, take tram #14 from largo Cairoli (on MM1) to viale Certosa. For the Riviera and Genoa, start hitching at p. Belfanti, near the Romolo end-station of MM2.

Accommodations

After Venice and Florence, Milan is probably the most expensive place to stay in Italy. Inexpensive rooms lie east and south of Stazione Centrale (MM1: Loreto); try around p. Aspromonte, along corso Buenos Aires, and near viale Tunisia.

Ostello Piero Rotta (IYHF), viale Salmoiraghi, 2 (tel. 36 70 95), 30 min. from the station. MM1: QT8. Clean and modern but the staff can be brusque. Members L11,500, nonmembers L14,000, sheets and breakfast included. Flexible 3-day maximum stay. Check-in 7-9am and 5-11pm. Midnight curfew. Open year-round.

ACISJF, corso Garibaldi, 121a-123 (tel. 659 52 06), near Stazione Garibaldi. MM2: Muscova. Women only. Extremely secure. L12,000. Breakfast L1500, filling meals L8000. Curfew 10:30pm, midnight on Sat.

Hotel Valley, via Soperga, 19 (tel. 669 27 77), 2 streets to the left, running parallel to the train station. Modern and clean. Singles L21,000, doubles L31,400. Showers L2000.

Albergo Canna, viale Tunisia, 6 (tel. 22 41 33). MM1: Porta Venezia. Large, well-kept rooms and an obliging proprietor. Singles L25,000-26,000, doubles L38,000-40,000. Two other *pensioni* in the same building are marginally more expensive but have downright luxurious rooms (6th floor) or amazingly friendly owners (3rd floor).

Pensione Dante, via Dante, 14 (tel. 86 64 71). MM1: Cairoli or Cordusio. *Centralissimo.* Clean and well-run. Singles L25,000, doubles L35,000. Showers included.

Pensione Cantore, corso Genova, 25 (tel. 835 75 65). 10 min. on foot from p. Duomo, or MM2 to Cadorna, then bus #19. Personable proprietors, decent neighborhood—a good choice. Singles L23,000, doubles L36,500, all with bath. Usually closed 2 weeks in Aug.

Food

Milanese specialties include *riso gallo* (rice with saffron) and *cazzoeula* (a mixture of pork and cabbage). Though the obvious areas (around the Duomo, near the station) tend to be overpriced, cheaper options abound. To present mass starvation during the August exodus, Milan's civic leaders operate a huge open-air cafeteria in **Parco Sempione** near the Arco di Pace, where school-system chefs prepare the world's finest institutional food. (Full meals L8000, including wine. Open daily noon-2pm and 7:30-9:30pm.) Also check the newspaper *Il Giornale Nuovo* for listings of open restaurants. The largest **markets** are around via Faucher or viale Papiniano on Saturdays and Tuesdays, and along via Santa Croce on Thursdays; the **Fiera di Sinigallia,** Milan's oldest market, fills via Calatafimi all day Saturday.

After dinner, indulge in one of the exotic flavors at **Viel,** Milan's most famous *gelateria,* on via Luca Beltrami, off largo Cairoli. (Open Thurs.-Tues. until 2am.)

Trattoria da Bruno, via Cavalotti, 15 (tel. 70 06 02), off corso Europa. MM1: Duomo or S. Babila. Popular with locals. Better food than your L9500 can buy elsewhere. Open Mon.-Fri. noon-2pm and 7-9pm, Sat. noon-2pm. Closed Aug.

Spaghetteria di Via Solferino, via Solferino, 3 (tel. 87 27 35). The variations on spaghetti are amazing. Daily specials. Try the *assagini:* 6 "little tastes" of spaghetti in different sauces at L1000 each. Open Mon.-Sat. 7:30pm-midnight. Closed Aug.

Trattoria da Carmela, via Garibaldi, 127 (tel. 65 02 37). MM2: Moscova. No inspired flourishes but wholesome food, friendly service, and the best prices in the city. Open Mon.-Sat. noon-2:30pm and 5-8:30pm. Closed Aug.

Mergellina, via Molino delle Armi, 48 (tel. 837 07 80), off corso di Porta Ticinese. Walk or catch bus #15 or 19 along via Torino. Terrific pizzas L4300-6000. Cover L1500. Open Thurs.-Sat. 11am-3pm and 7pm-1am; Wed. 7pm-1am. Open only part of Aug.

Rosticceria Peck, via G. Cantù, not far from the Duomo. A Milan tradition. Perfect for a quick stand-up meal. Understandably expensive but only if compared to other delis. Open Tues.-Sat. 8am-1pm and 3:30-7pm. Open in Aug.!

Sights

Start with the **Duomo,** a 600-year-old tribute to Milanese extravagance. Stylistically, it's a mixture of flamboyant French, stolid Italian Gothic, and virtually posthumous neoclassicism; the individual gables, pinnacles and belfries could keep your eyes and your camera occupied for hours. After a look at the stained-glass and rose windows inside, ascend to the roof and stroll among the 135 pinnacles and 200 statues. (Cathedral open daily 7am-7pm. Free. Roof open June-Sept. daily 9am-5pm; Oct.-May daily 9am-4:30pm. Admission L2000 for the stairs, L3000 for the elevator.)

Beside the Duomo is the true center of Milan, the colossal **Galleria Vittorio Emanuele II,** a giant iron-and-glass arcade over a city block that houses Milan's best cafes and shops; at its far end is piazza della Scala. As you enter the *piazza,* **La Scala,** the world-famous opera house, lies to your left. Inside, the greatest opera stars in the world, from Caruso to Pavarotti, have made international debuts—indeed, being invited to sing here remains the mark of success in the opera world. To see the lavish, many-tiered hall, you must enter through the **Museo alla Scala** (tel. 805 34 18), which houses operatic and theatrical memorabilia. (Open June-Sept. Mon.-Sat. 9am-noon and 2-6pm, Sun. 9:30am-noon and 2:30-5pm; Nov.-March Mon.-Fri. 9am-noon and 2-5pm, Sat. 9am-noon and 2-4pm, Sun. 9:30am-noon and 2:30-5pm; April Mon.-Sat. 9am-noon and 2-5pm. Admission L3000.)

Via Verdi leads to via Brera and the **Pinacoteca di Brera,** one of Italy's finest museums. This seventeenth-century *palazzo* houses Raphael's *Marriage of the Virgin* as well as works by Caravaggio, Bellini and Piero della Francesca. (Open Tues.-Sat. 9am-2pm, Sun. 9am-1pm. Admission L4000.) The **Museo Poldi Pezzoli,** on via Manzoni, houses an outstanding private collection. It's worth visiting as much for its silverware, embroideries, and china as for its collection of art, which includes more works by Bellini and Piero della Francesca. (Open Tues.-Wed. 9:30am-12:30pm and 2:30-6pm, Thurs.-Sat. 9:30am-12:30pm and 2:30-5:30pm, Sun. 9:30am-12:30pm. Admission L3000.)

The **Castello Sforzesco** (MM1: Cairoli) is the huge fifteenth-century castle of the Sforza, Milan's powerful Renaissance dukes. The beautifully arranged sculpture collection includes Michelangelo's *Pietà Rondanini.* (Open Tues.-Sun. 9:30am-12:15pm and 2:30-5:30pm. Free.) Behind the castle is the vast **Parco Sempione,** the site of free open-air concerts in summer and a great place for a picnic.

Leonardo da Vinci created his *Last Supper* for the refectory wall of the **Basilica of Santa Maria delle Grazie** (MM1: Sant'Ambrogio). Despite damage sustained from bombing, flooding, and natural decay, and despite the scaffolding erected for restoration of the fresco, it's clear why it is counted among the world's most moving works of art. (Open Tues.-Sat. 9am-1:30pm and 2-6:30pm, Sun.-Mon. 9am-1:30pm. Admission L4000.) The adjacent church is best known for Bramante's decorative and colorful tribune, added in 1492.

The **Basilica of Sant'Ambrogio,** another building worth a special visit, served as a prototype for medieval churches throughout Lombardy. The ninth-century high altar still retains its dazzling decoration of silver and gold enriched with enamels and gems.

Entertainment and Shopping

Milan is perhaps Italy's most entertaining city—there are always a thousand things going on. Visit the **Comune di Milano** office (tel. 87 05 45), Galleria V. Emanuele II at the corner of p. della Scala, for a wealth of information on all things cultural in Milan. Pick up their monthly publication *Spettacoli a Milano* (Performances in Milan). Every Thursday Milan's two leading papers, *Corriere della Sera* and *La Repubblica,* sum up the city's cultural offerings in slick magazine-type inserts which include information about performances at **La Scala** (tel. 80 91 26; regular season Dec.-June, fewer shows in summer and Sept.). Gallery seats are available from L10,000—you won't see much, but the sound is magnificent. (Box office open Tues.-Sun. 10am-1pm and 3:30-5:30pm, on performance days unsold gallery seats and standing room available after 5:30pm.)

Cinema Porpora, via Porpora, 104 (tel. 23 03 85), and **Cinema Mexico,** via Savona, 2 (tel. 47 98 02), show films in English. Two established rock clubs are **Prego,** via Besenzanica, 3 (tel. 407 56 53), and **Rolling Stone,** corso XXII Marzo, 32 (tel. 73 31 72). Admission is L10,000, more on live-music nights. (Each open Thurs.-Sun. until 2am.) For jazz, Milan's leading spot remains **Le Scimmie,** via Ascanio Sforza, 49 (tel. 839 18 74; open Wed.-Mon. nights until 2am). If you want dance action, prepare to drop L15,000-20,000 at a nightclub such as **USA,** via B. Cellini, 2 (tel. 70 29 38; open Wed.-Sun. 11:30pm-3am). Of Milan's several gay discos, **Nuova Idea,** via de Castilla, 30 (tel. 689 27 53), is the largest and best-known. (Cover L8000-10,000. Open Tues. and Thurs.-Sun. 9:30pm-1 or 2am.)

Fashion—designing it, buying it, and flaunting it—is Milan's lifeblood. **Corso Buenos Aires** is the acknowledged haunt of clothes horses with limited budgets. The **Fiera di Sinigallia** market (Sat. on via Calatafini; MM2: Sant'Agostino) will reward the truly assiduous shopper with the best bargains in Milan. Even if you don't want (can't afford) to buy, stroll down via Monte Napoleone and peek into the headquarters of greats like Armani and Versace. Devotees of trendier fashion can pay homage at **Fiorucci's** original shop at Galleria Passerella, 1 (tel. 70 80 30), at the corner of corso V. Emanuele (MM1: San Babila).

Mantua (Mantova)

Mantua was one of Europe's great Renaissance courts, home of the lavish Gonzaga dynasty. During their 400-year reign, the Gonzaga filled the center of town with their palaces, churches, and towers, and attracted some of the most important artists of the Renaissance to their court. Mantua is about two hours southeast of Milan by train. The train station is a 10-minute walk along corso V. Emanuele and corso Umberto from the center of town.

The **Church of Sant'Andrea** is one of the most brilliant creations of architect Leon Battista Alberti. Its ensemble of a single barrel-vaulted nave, perpendicular side chapels, and domed crossing served as the prototype for European church-building for the next 300 years. The immensity of its interior seems even more staggering when compared to the intimate *piazza* in front and the small houses along the side.

In nearby p. Sordello rises the **Palazzo Ducale,** one of the largest and most sumptuously decorated palaces in Europe. Its more than 500 rooms include a series of miniature chambers designed for court dwarves. Displayed in the Camera degli Sposi (marriage chamber) are Andrea Mantegna's famed frescoes of the Gonzaga family (1474). His use of vanishing perspective lines makes the frescoes appear to be an extension of the space of the room; this was the first decoration of the Renaissance to exploit optical illusion. (Open Tues.-Sat. 9am-6pm, Sun. 9am-2pm. Admission L6000.)

At the southern end of town is the **Palazzo del Tè,** built in the early sixteenth century as the Gonzaga family's suburban villa. Romano decorated the rooms of the palace with an extraordinary cycle of frescoes based on classical themes. The frescoes in the giant's room depict *Jove's Victory Over the Mad Presumption of the Giants,* a terrifying apocalypse of billowing clouds and falling columns. Before leaving the palace grounds, visit the delightful **Casino della Grotta,** to the left at the end of the garden. The palace is on viale delle Aquile, off viale Risorgimento. (Open Tues.-Sat. 9:30am-12:30pm and 2:30-5pm; April-Sept. open until 5:30pm; July-Aug. open Sun. 9am-12:30pm as well. Admission L2500, students L1500.)

The friendly, well-informed **EPT** (tel. 35 06 81) is on p. Mantegna. (Open Mon.-Sat. 8:30am-1pm and 3-6:30pm, Sun. 9am-12:30pm.) Mantua has an outstanding youth hostel, the **Ostello Sparfucile (IYHF)** (tel. 37 24 65), in a beautifully restored but slightly uncomfortable sixteenth-century castle. Take bus #2, 6, or 9 from p. Cavallotti. (L7500 per night. Breakfast included. Open April to mid-Oct. On-site camping available July-Aug.) Otherwise try the cordial **Locanda La Rinascita,** via Concezione, 4 (tel. 32 06 07). (Singles L18,000, doubles L28,000.) The **Albergo Roma Vecchia,** via Corridoni, 20 (tel. 32 21 00), off via Roma, has large, sparsely-furnished rooms. (Singles L17,000, doubles L28,000.)

For cheap sit-down meals go to the **Centro Ristorante Sociale,** p. Virgiliana, 57; they have a *menu* for L8000. (Open Mon.-Fri. noon-2pm). The similarly priced **Self-Service Nievo,** via Nievo, 8, off via Verdi, is less appetizing, but stays open for dinner. (Open Sept.-July Mon.-Fri. 11:30am-2pm and 7:30-10pm.) **Al Quadrato,** p. Virgiliana, has huge, excellent pizzas (L4500) and other tasty dishes (L8000). (Open Tues.-Sun. noon-2pm and 7:30pm-1am.) **Trattoria al Lago,** p. Arche, 5, serves delicious filling meals with a touch of class. Fixed *menu* L11,000. (Open Tues.-Sun. noon-3:30pm and 7:30pm-midnight.)

Mantua's **telephone code** is 0376, and the **postal code** is 46100.

Finale Liguria

Sandy white beaches, an abundance of really good places to eat, a beautiful youth hostel, and not too many Gucci-garbed visitors make Finale the best place to stay on the Riviera di Ponente. Trains leave hourly for Genoa (L4200) and Ventimiglia (L3500). Get maps and change your money at the **Associazione Alberghi e Turismo,** p. Vittorio Veneto, 29 (tel. 69 23 47), across from the **train station.** The **post office** is on via Concezione, along the beach. The **telephone code** is 019. The **police** are at via Brunaghi, 68 (tel. 69 26 66), and the **hospital** at the summit of viatella Pineta (tel. 69 07 95).

The **IYHF youth hostel,** via Generale Caviglia (tel. 69 05 15), is the best place to stay. From the station turn left onto via Torino then head up the endless (321 steps!) staircase on your left past the Esso station. You will be treated royally in this castle; the staff are very friendly. (L7000 per night, showers and breakfast included. Curfew 11:30pm; daytime lock-out 9:30am-5pm.) Try via Rossi and via Roma, inland from the waterfront, for food. Eat great *panini* and listen to rock at **Paninoteca Pilate,** via Garibaldi, 67 (tel. 69 22 20). (Open Sept.-June Thurs.-Tues. 10:30am-2pm and 4-8pm; June-Aug. daily 10:30am-2pm and 4pm-midnight.) For a splurge, climb up via XXV Aprile then go past the hospital on via tella Pineta; you can enjoy full meals including wine for about L18,000 on the terrace of **Trattoria Beppi.**

Genoa (Genova)

If Calabria is the toe of Italy, and Rome is the knee, then Genoa is just about the crotch. Yep. A busy, heavily industrialized port, Genoa falls far short of the artistic marvels of Venice or Florence. On a more positive note, Genoa is accessible: By rail Milan is one and a half hours north, Florence three hours south, and the French border two hours west. There are two main train stations: **Stazione Principe** (tel. 26 26 33) to the west near the port, and **Stazione Brignole** (tel. 56 20 56) farther east. From Principe, **via Balbi** leads to piazza Nunziata. Via Fiume connects Brignole to **via XX Settembre** which eventually leads into **piazza de Ferrari.** North of p. de Ferrari is p. Fontane Marose, off of which runs via Garibaldi. Here you'll find the palazzi **Bianco, Rosso, Municipale, Potestà,** and **Paroti** which are splendid in their own right and house many of the Flemish and Dutch masterpieces amassed by the merchant Genovese.

There is a helpful **tourist office** at via Roma, 11 (tel. 58 14 87; open Mon.-Thurs. 8am-2pm and 4-6pm, Fri. and Sat. 8am-1pm). The main **post office** is on via Dante, off p. de Ferrari. (Open Mon.-Fri. 8:15am-8pm; Sat. 8am-1pm.) Want to reach out and touch someone? **SIP** telephone service is in the same building (open daily 8am-11:50pm). For **police emergencies** call 112; the general **emergency** number is 113. **Ospedale San Martino** is at viale Benedetto XV, 10 (tel. 353 51); for an ambulance call 59 59 51. Genoa has a **U.S. consulate,** p. Portobello, 6 (tel. 28 27 41), and a **British** one, via XII Ottobre, 2 (tel. 56 48 33). The **telephone code** is 010 and the **postal code** is 16100.

Women staying in Genoa should take advantage of the **Casa della Giovane,** p. Santa Sabina, 4 (tel. 20 66 32), near p. Nunziate. Clean and cheap rooms cost L7000, shower and breakfast included. Curfew is 10:30, but this is plenty late for Genoa. Across from the Casa, **Albergo Fontane,** via della Fontane, 12 (tel. 20 24 27), has run-down rooms and a slightly forbidding exterior, but the courtyard and modern bathrooms compensate. (Doubles L22,000, with shower L25,000.) Rooms near Stazione Brignole are a tad more expensive, but may be worth it for the far more pleasant neighborhood. From the station walk down via de Amicis to your right; at the first intersection (p. Brignole) go right again, cross the tracks, and go up via Gropallo. The large, ornate building to the left at #4 houses several *pensioni.* Genoa's youth hostel was closed in 1987. The nearest hostel is now the **Ostello Villa Cesare de Franceschini,** about 2km outside of Savona (15 min. by train west of Genoa) in Conca Verde.

Genoese cuisine, drawing on the abundant riches of the sea, is fantastic. *Pesto,* a Ligurian sauce made from basil, oil, parmesan, and nuts, is delicious. *Ravioli* are said to originate here as are *pansotti,* similar to ravioli but smaller and served with a walnut sauce. Full-course meals in Genoa are cheaper than in most cities. The best place to eat is **Cucina Casalinga da Maria,** vico Testa d'Oro, 14r (tel. 57 10 80), off via XXV Aprile. Fixed *menù* for lunch and supper, including wine and cover, only L6,500. (Open Sun.-Thurs. noon-2:30pm and 7-9pm, Fri. noon-2:30pm.)

Riviera di Levante

Charming hamlets are scattered throughout the Riviera di Levante region, clinging to the cliffs along the coast. The two principal areas to explore are the **Portofino** peninsula (about ½ hour by train east of Genoa) and the **Cinque Terre** area (immediately west of La Spezia). In July and August you'll need reservations or amazingly good fortune to find a place for the night.

Base your exploration of the Portofino Peninsula in **Santa Margherita di Ligure.** Frequent trains run from Genoa. Keep an eye open for the flowering white Margherita bush: In full bloom it looks like it's covered with giant snowballs. On a bleary morning you may think the weather gods have a nasty sense of humor. If basking in the town's friendly atmosphere is not enough, hit the beach. The best beaches are a 10-minute train trip east in Lavagna.

The **tourist office** is at via XXV Aprile, 26 (tel. 28 74 85). Turn right from the train station onto via Roma and when you arrive at largo Giusti turn right again. Get maps, look for rooms, and change money here. (Open Oct.-June Mon.-Sat. 8:15-11:45am and 3:15-5:45pm; July-Sept. Sun. 9:15-11:45am.) Stay at the **Corallo,** via XXV Aprile, 20 (tel. 28 67 74), about 3 blocks from the tourist office. (Singles L14,000, with shower L16,900; doubles L27,000, with shower L35,000; showers L3500; breakfast L5000.) **Hotel Fasce,** via Luigi Bozzo, 3 (tel. 864 35), off corso Matteotti, is slightly more expensive but everything from showers to breakfast to washing machines is included and the rooms sparkle with newness. (L20,000 per person.) Buy bread, cheese, meat, and produce along corso Matteotti; on Fridays from 8am to 1pm the shops spill out onto the corso. For a night out try **Trattoria Baicin,** via Algeria, 9 (tel. 867 63), off p. Martiri della Libertà. Full meals cost around L15,000 for meat, L18,000 for fish; wine L5000 per liter. (Open daily noon-4pm and 6:30-11pm.)

Camoglie is a contraction of *Case moglie* (Wives' homes), from times when Camoglie's women were left home alone while their husbands went out to sea. You can see the daily catch of Camoglie's fishing fleet being landed from 4 to 6pm at the port. Reach Camoglie by train (L600) or by bus (L1000) from Santa Margherita. More isolated than Camoglie is **San Fruttuoso,** a green gem of a village at the western corner of the peninsula. There are no trains or buses to San Fruttuoso but you can take a boat from Camoglie (L4000) or from Portofino (L3500). Intrepid trekkers can make the three-hour hike from Camoglie or the two-hour hike from Portofino.

West of Santa Margherita, the region of **Cinque Terre** stretches out to the peninsula at whose end lies the village of **Portovenere.** Portovenere is a world apart: It's full of labyrinthine alleyways, multi-colored homes, and cats that crawl out from the most unexpected crannies. The Cinque Terre (literally "Five Lands") are five villages: Monterosso (the farthest from La Spezia), Vernazza, Corniglia, Manarola, and Riomaggiore (the closest). All five are renowned for their picturesque surroundings and fine wines: Scia Che Tra (a smooth, sweet, full wine, almost like a port) and Cinque Terre (a dry white). Bus P from outside the La Spezia train station goes to Portovenere and frequent trains run from La Spezia to Monterosso. **In Tur** and **Linea Pozzale** run ferries to Portovenere and Cinque Terre from La Spezia's *molo* (dock). (L3500 one way, L6000 round-trip.) For more information on transport in the region, ask the tourist office in La Spezia.

La Spezia itself is newer, more crowded, and less pleasant than the smaller towns to the immediate west. The nearest **IYHF youth hostel** (tel. (0585) 202 88) is at **Marina di Massa,** south of La Spezia. The hostel has friendly management and is in a splendid setting (L6500; showers L500); the Carrara-Avenza train station is a 3-kilometer walk away. The most accessible **campground** in the area is Campeggio Maralunga, v. Carpanini, 61 (tel. (0187) 96 65 89), off via Tagliata in **Lerici.** Get there by taking bus L from outside the La Spezia train station.

Venice (Venezia)

In Italo Calvino's *Invisible Cities,* Marco Polo admits to Kublai Khan that all his descriptions of fabulous cities are but feeble attempts to capture one city—Venice. Indeed, perhaps no city is as fabulous as this construction built upon pilings, this labyrinth poised over a lagoon.

Venice has been called "the drawing room of Europe," and indeed for centuries the city was a sanctuary for ideas and idealists, a crossroads of the Byzantine and Roman worlds. The great thinkers and traders left in their wake an extraordinary visual feast of color, texture, and form—from the elegant *palazzi* that line the Grand Canal to the world-famous paintings that fill Venetian galleries.

For the past two centuries—since Napoleon's armies toppled the none too steady government of the Republic—Venice has been more museum *cum* amusement park than erudite salon. Venetians seem to have painlessly adapted to this change of status. Foreigners flocked to the city when it was a thriving mercantile center, and continued to come while Venice spent its accumulated wealth in a spree of partying and gambling. Now they come to pay homage to the splendor of the city (perhaps to capture some small piece of it on Kodak film), and Venetians continue to welcome them with more warmth than is to be found anywhere else in Italy. So buck the alarming trend of foregoing Venice altogether. As Mary McCarthy has observed, the tourist Venice *is* Venice. Don't you want to be a part of the magnificent pile of marble on the lagoon?

Orientation and Practical Information

In summer, Venice is every bit as busy as you've heard it is, but crowds are only really a problem in piazza San Marco and along the road between the *piazza* and the train station. In winter, Venice becomes misty and mysterious, often cloaked by heavy fog, sometimes dusted with snow. The *acque alte* (high waters) occasionally submerge the city under several feet of water. Platforms are raised above all the major thoroughfares, but a pair of rubber boots may prove a good investment. Ask at the tourist office for current information, or check the signs posted at all *vaporetto* stops.

Situated at the northern tip of the Adriatic, Venice is connected by ferry to ports in Yugoslavia, Greece, and the Middle East, and by rail to major cities throughout Europe. A good indexed map is absolutely essential in this city, though it's small defense against getting temporarily lost. The red map *Edizioni Foligrat Mestre-Venezia* is the best (L4000).

The main part of Venice is divided into six *sestieri,* or districts: **San Marco, Castello, San Polo, Santa Croce, Cannaregio,** and **Dorsoduro.** Within each section, there are no individual street numbers, but one long sequence of numbers (roughly 6000 per *sestiere*) which wind their tortuous way through the district with no apparent logic. This makes it almost impossible to find a particular address knowing only the name of the *sestiere.* However, every building is located on a "street"—*fondamenta, salizzada, calle, via, campo, piazza, piazzale*—and *Let's Go* supplies these whenever possible. Always be sure you're looking in the proper *sestiere;* some street names are duplicated. Yellow signs posted all over town will direct you to and from piazza San Marco, the Rialto Bridge, the train station (*ferrovia*), and piazzale Roma. Boats plow across the lagoon regularly to Venice's two principal islands, **la Giudecca** and **Lido di Venezia.**

The **Canale Grande** (Grand Canal), Venice's main waterway, is shaped like an inverted "S," with the train station at one end and **piazza San Marco** at the other. The canal can be crossed on foot at only three points. The **Ponte Scalzi,** just outside the train station, links the *sestieri* of Cannaregio and Santa Croce. **Ponte Rialto** links the east end of Cannaregio with San Polo. The **Ponte Accademia** links the districts of San Marco and Dorsoduro. The remaining district, Castello, extends to the east of the piazza San Marco.

For current information on nightlife, events, museums, *vaporetti,* and train and plane schedules, pick up the free booklet *Un Ospite di Venezia* at any of the tourist offices; or shell out L5000 for the more comprehensive monthly *Marco Polo,* sold at newsstands. Also available at newsstands is *Venezia in Jeans,* a booklet catering to young and budget travelers. An English edition should be out in 1988.

Tourist Offices: An office in the **train station** (tel. 71 50 16), and a less crowded one in the **bus station,** p. Roma (tel. 522 74 02). Room reservations and little else. L10,000 deposit is deducted from your bill at the hotel. If the line is intimidating and your Italian is functional, you may find a room faster on your own. Both open daily 8am-7:30pm. Another office on **piazza San Marco** (tel. 522 63 56), under the arcade at the opposite end of the *piazza* from the church. No accommodations help. Open Mon.-Sat. 9am-2pm and 3-7pm. A fourth office on the Lido, at viale Santa Maria Elisabetta, 6a (tel. 76 57 21). Also no accommodations service. Open Mon.-Sat. 9am-2pm.

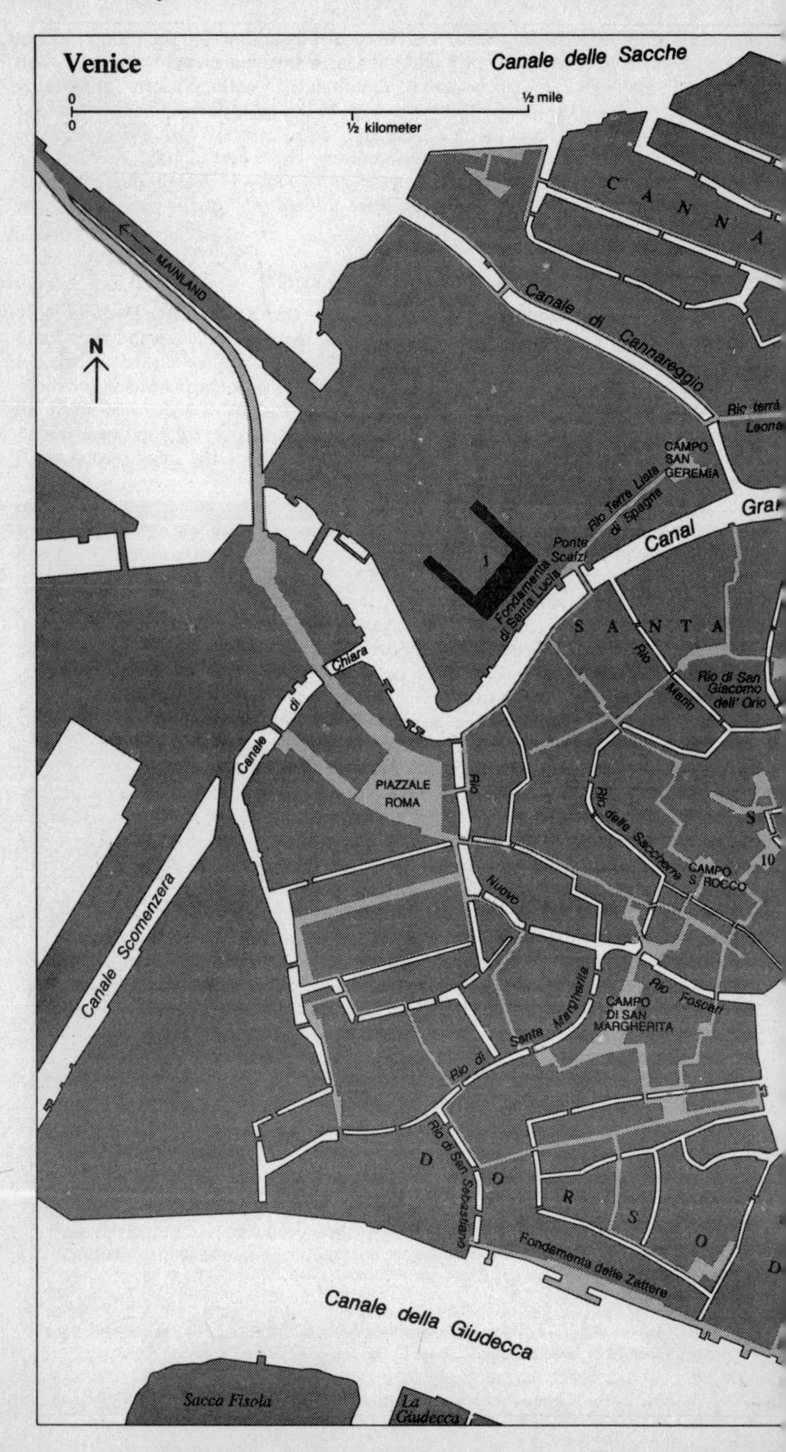

Venice
Canale delle Sacche
0
½ mile
0
½ kilometer
MAINLAND
N
C A N N A
Canale di Cannareggio
Rio terrà
Leone
CAMPO
SAN
GEREMIA
Rio Terra Lista
di Spagna
Ponte
Scalzi
Canal
Gra
1
Fondamenta
di Santa Lucia
S A N T A
Rio
Marin
Rio di San
Giacomo
dell' Orio
Chiara
di
Canale
PIAZZALE
ROMA
Rio
Rio della Sacchere
S
10
CAMPO
S. ROCCO
Nuovo
Canale Scomenzera
Rio Foscari
CAMPO
DI SAN
MARGHERITA
Rio di Santa Margherita
Rio di San Sebastiano
D
O
R
S
O
D
Fondamenta delle Zattere
Canale della Giudecca
Sacca Fisola
La
Giudecca

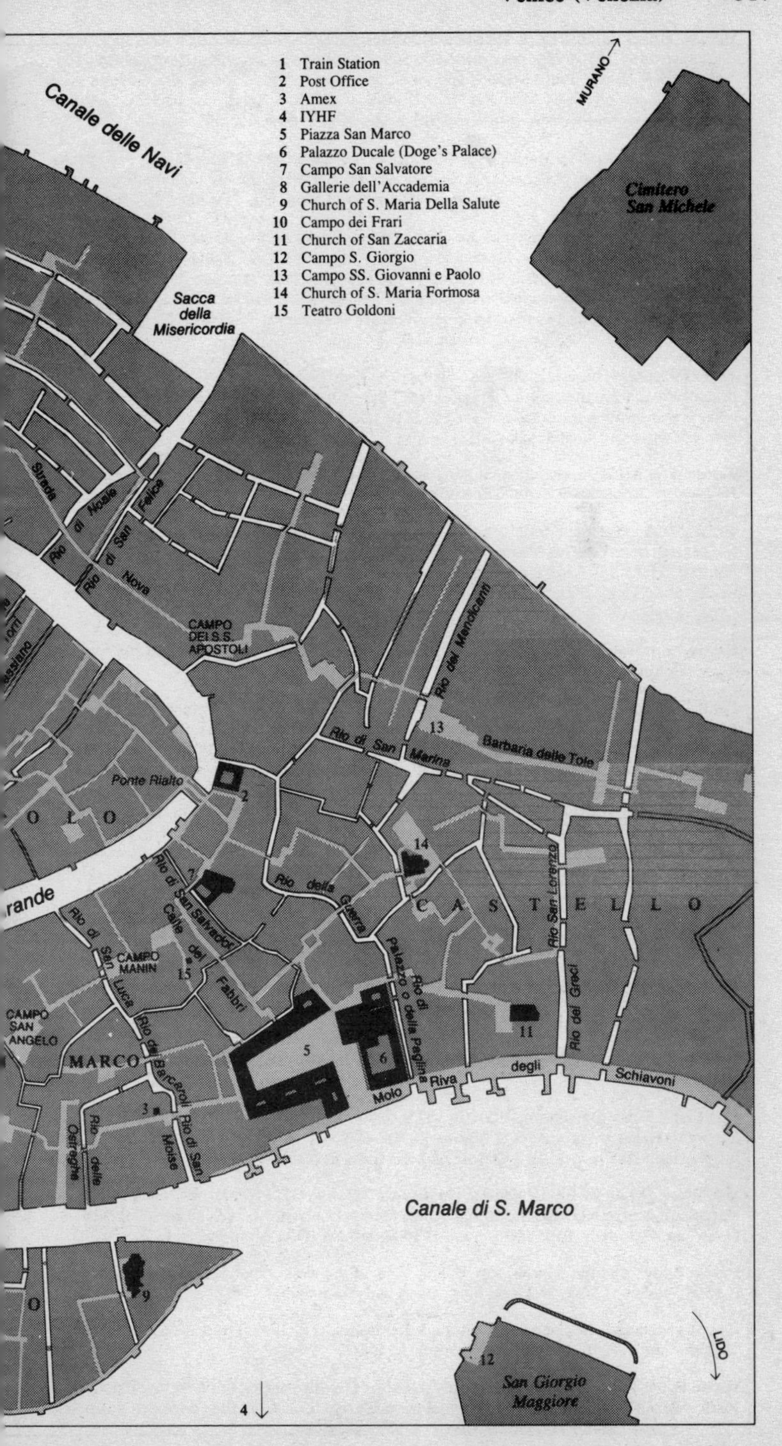
1 Train Station
2 Post Office
3 Amex
4 IYHF
5 Piazza San Marco
6 Palazzo Ducale (Doge's Palace)
7 Campo San Salvatore
8 Gallerie dell'Accademia
9 Church of S. Maria Della Salute
10 Campo dei Frari
11 Church of San Zaccaria
12 Campo S. Giorgio
13 Campo SS. Giovanni e Paolo
14 Church of S. Maria Formosa
15 Teatro Goldoni
MURANO
Cimitero San Michele
Canale delle Navi
Sacca della Misericordia
Strada Nova
Rio di Noale
Rio di San Felice
CAMPO DEI S.S. APOSTOLI
Rio dei Mendicanti
Rio di San Marina
Barbaria delle Tole
Ponte Rialto
Rio della Guerra
C A S T E L L O
Rio San Lorenzo
Rio dei Greci
Rio di San Salvador
Calle dei Fabbri
Rio di San Luca
CAMPO MANIN
CAMPO SAN ANGELO
MARCO
Rio dei Barcaroli
Palazzo o della Paglina
Rio di
Molo
Riva degli Schiavoni
Rio delle Ostreghe
Moise
Rio di San
Canale di S. Marco
LIDO
San Giorgio Maggiore

Budget Travel: CTS (Centro Turistico Studentesco), Dorsoduro, 3252, on the fondamenta Tagliapetra (tel. 70 56 60), near campiello Squellini, due west of campo Santa Margherita. Vaporetto: S. Tomà. Budget tickets and an accommodations service with shorter lines than at the train station. Open Mon.-Sat. 7am-12:30pm and 3:30-6:30pm. For BIGE tickets also try **ATG,** Dorsoduro, 3856, just across the bridge. Open until 7:30pm.

American Express: San Marco, 1471 (tel. 520 08 44), on salizzada San Moisè, a few blocks west of p. San Marco. Mail held. All banking services. L3500 charge for mail inquiry by non-card holders. Open Mon.-Sat. 8am-8pm. Mail pick-up Mon.-Fri. 9am-6pm, Sat. 9am-1pm.

Currency Exchange: When banks are closed, try any travel agency, some of which are open Sun. in summer. **Romeatour,** Cannaregio, 134a, is on the lista di Spagna. Also a **bureau de change** on campo San Zulian, near San Marco. If all else fails, grin and bear the wretched rates at the **Ufficio Informazioni** in the station. The **Banca d'America e d'Italia,** via 22 Marzo, across the bridge from American Express, gives cash advances on Visa cards. Normal banking hours are Mon.-Fri. 8:30am-1:30pm and 2:45-3:45pm.

Post Office: Main branch at salizzada Fontego dei Tedeschi, near the eastern end of the Rialto bridge. Poste Restante (ask for **Fermo Posta**) here. Open Mon.-Sat. 8:15am-7pm. Another office is just through the arcades at the end of p. San Marco. Open Mon.-Fri. 8:10am-1:40pm, Sat. 8:30am-noon. **Postal code:** 30124.

Telephones: ASST, in the same building as the main post office. Open daily 8am-8pm. **SIP,** on piazzale Roma open daily 8am-9:30pm. **Telephone code:** 041.

Trains: Make sure your train is going all the way to **Venezia-Santa Lucia.** Many through trains serve only **Venezia-Mestre,** several miles across the lagoon on the mainland. Information (tel. 71 55 55). **Luggage storage** at Santa Lucia is to the far right as you come off the tracks; always a long line. To Florence (4½ hr., L12,700), Milan (3½ hr., L13,200), Bologna (2 hr., L7800).

Buses: In p. Roma. Frequent buses to the villas on the Riviera del Brenta and connections to the Dolomites. Information (tel. 528 78 86).

Public Transportation: The only motorized vehicles in Venice travel on water. Efficient *vaporetti* ply the Canale Grande and travel to the outlying islands. L1500 for the slower boats (*accelerato*) and L2000 for faster ones, plus a L300 surcharge if you buy on board. Many maps, including the tourist office's, have all *vaporetto* lines and stops marked. Line #5 circumnavigates the city both clockwise (*destra*) and counter-clockwise (*sinistra*); lines #1 and 2 both sail the Grand Canal out to the Lido. A 24-hour pass (calculate carefully whether it's worth it) costs L8000. A **Carta Venezia,** which also costs L8000, is valid for 3 years (you'll come back!), and gives 60% reductions on all lines. This is worthwhile for visits of 4 days or more. Bring a passport photo to the ACTV office at the S. Angelo *vaporetto* stop. (Open Mon.-Sat. 8:30am-1pm.) Listen for news of rather frequent strikes (*scioperi*).

Police: Tel. 113. Headquarters (*questura*) on fondamenta San Lorenzo. Their **Ufficio Stranieri** (Foreigners Office) can be reached at 520 07 54.

Hospital: Ospetati Riuniti Ciuili di Venezia, campo SS. Giovanni e Paolo (tel. 520 56 22).

Medical Emergency: Ambulance (tel. 523 00 00).

Pharmacies: Call 192 to find out who currently has the rotating 24-hour duty, or look it up in *Un Ospite di Venezia.*

Consulate: U.K., Dorsoduro, 1051 (tel. 52 272 07), near the Accademia bridge. The **U.S.** has a representative at via dei Pellegrini, 42 (tel. (040) 91 17 80) in Trieste, but the nearest full-fledged office is in Milan. **Canada** and **Australia** also have consulates in Milan.

Bookstore: Il Libraio a San Barnaba, Dorsoduro, 2835a (tel. 522 87 38), on fondamenta Gherardini, off campo San Barnaba, has a good selection of classics as well as books on Venice. Open Jan.-Oct. daily 10:15am-1pm and 3:15-8pm; Nov.-Dec. Mon.-Sat. only.

Public Baths: Albergo Diurno, San Marco, 1266, at the west end of p. San Marco. Showers (L1900), toilets (L300), and long lines. Open daily 7am-8pm.

Laundry: Lavaget, in Cannaregio on fondamenta Pescaria, 1269. Open Mon.-Fri. 8:15am-12:30pm and 3-7pm, Sat. 8:15am-12:30pm. L11,000.

Hitchhiking: The only place to leave a car in Venice is in the parking lots near piazzale Roma. Plant yourself (and your sign) just before the bridge that leads from the *piazzale* to the mainland. Take the first ride you get to the entrance of the *autostrata* in Mestre and all will be well; hitching from this mammoth interchange is as good as anywhere else in Italy.

Accommodations and Camping

Venice is unbelievably crowded in summer, and priced accordingly. Singles run about L25,000, doubles L45,000. If possible, make a reservation. A letter in English with a one-night deposit is standard. Most proprietors are reluctant to hold a cheap room; despite your written pleas to the contrary, expect to be offered a room with private bath (L7000 or more extra) and mandatory breakfast (L4000 per person).

Without a reservation, start phoning around the night before you get to Venice. Find a place that will hold a room until 10am the next day, and be on the doorstep well before the agreed-upon hour. The tourist office at the train station is a good place to begin your quest for a bed—as always, be early. You might consider bypassing Venice altogether for the first day; stay in either Padua, Vicenza, or Verona, and spend your first afternoon looking for suitable accommodations in Venice. If you're considering staying outside Venice for your entire visit, remember that only Padua (½ hr. by train) is suitable.

Hostels and dorms run by religious orders are often cheaper and invariably have more vacancies than cheap hotels. Women will almost always find a place at one of the dormitories run by nuns. Unfortunately, all these institutions are on the tranquil island of Giudecca, which can only be reached by *vaporetto* (L1500).

A recent tightening up of regulations prohibits unofficial camping on the steps of the train station. If night is falling and you still haven't found a place, try looking in Mestre, a nearby bedroom community.

Hostels and Student Accommodations

Ostello Venezia (IYHF), fondamente di Zitelle, 86C (tel. 523 82 11), on the Giudecca. Take *motoscafo* #5 (*sinistra*) from the station, #5 (*destra*), or #8 from S. Zaccaria, near S. Marco. Get off at Zitelle and walk to your right. An spotlessly clean renovated *palazzo.* The 30-bed rooms can get hectic. Members only, though cards (L15,000) are available at the desk. Singles L11,000. Sheets and breakfast included. Meals L7000. Try to reserve in person before 9:30am; people start queuing in summer at 3 or 4pm for the 6pm opening. 11pm curfew.

Istituto Cannosiano, fondamente del ponte Piccolo, 428 (tel. 52 21 57), also on the Giudecca. Take boat #5 to Sant' Eufemia, and walk to your left. Women only. Kind nuns and a pleasant garden. L10,000 per person. Lockout 9am-4pm, but very flexible. 10:30pm curfew.

Foresteria Valdese, Castello, 5170 (tel. 528 67 97); the closest *vaporetto* stop is S. Zaccharia. From campo S. Maria Formosa take calle lunga S.M. Formosa. L16,000 in small (8-16 people) dorm rooms. Breakfast included. Check-in 9:30am-1pm and 6-8:30pm (occasionally someone is there 1-6pm). Lockout 10am-1pm. No curfew.

Archie's House, Cannaregio, 1814b, S. Leonardo (tel. 72 08 84), where S. Leonardo meets campiello Anconetta. Clean and orderly. L15,000 per person in 3-, 4-, and 5-bed rooms. Hot showers L500, cold L300. No lockout. No curfew.o lock-out.

Foresteria S. Fosca, Cannaregio, 2372 (tel. 71 57 75). From the station, walk down Lista de Spagna and Rio T.S. Leonardo to campo S. Fosca, then walk away from the Grand Canal, across a bridge. Friendly atmosphere. L11,000 per person, plus an initial L2000 fee. Reception open 10am-noon and after 6pm. Lockout 10am-6:30pm. 11pm curfew Open July 15-Sept. 15.

Istituto San Giuseppe, Castello, 5402 (tel. 522 53 52). From piazzetta dei Leoncini left of S. Marco, take calle dei Specchieri to campo S. Zulian, then go right on campo de la Guerra over the bridge, and left immediately. Unmarried couples should be discreet. Write a month or so ahead (in summer) with 1-night deposit. 5- and 6-bed rooms L18,000 per person. Call ahead; sometimes closed in the middle of the day. 11pm curfew. Closed Easter and Christmas.

Domus Civica, S. Polo 3082 (tel. 522 71 39), on the corner of calle Chiovere and calle Campazzo, between the Friari Church and piazzale Roma. Women only. Great management. Singles L20,000, doubles L34,000. Daytime lockout. 11:30pm curfew. Open June-July and Sept. to mid-Oct.

Istituto Ciliota, S. Marco, 2976 (tel. 520 48 88), in calle delle Muneghe, off calle delle Botteghe and campo Morosin (*vaporetto* #2 to S. Samuele). Near major sights, yet off major thoroughfares. Friendly nuns run the show. Singles L24,000, with shower L28,000; doubles L40,000 (solo travelers can opt for one bed in a double), with shower L46,000. Breakfast L5000. 11pm curfew. Phone reservations accepted; an especially good idea in June. Open mid-June to Oct.

Suore Mantellate, Sant' Elena, calle Buccari, 10 (tel. 522 08 29). Take *vaporetto* #1 or 2 to Sant' Elena and walk across the park, or walk east along the sea from S. Marco (about 45 min.). A leafy neighborhood outside of tourist's Venice. Large rooms and yet more friendly nuns. L27,500 per person in doubles or triples. Breakfast included. Open Sept.-July.

Hotels

Locanda Antica Casa Carettoni, Cannaregio, 130 (tel. 71 62 31), down the lista di Spagna to the left of the station. Homey atmosphere and wonderful rooms for this part of town. Singles L21,000, doubles L38,000. Showers included. Phone reservations accepted. Open March-June; closed one week in Aug.

Locanda Rossi, Cannaregio, 262 (tel. 71 51 64), off calle delle Procuratio. Quiet location off to the left of rio Terrà Lista di Spagna. Rooms are spotless and sterile. Singles L26,500, with shower L38,000; doubles L42,500, with shower L60,000. Showers L2000. Breakfast (L4500) is mandatory for the first few nights. Phone reservations accepted. Open Feb.-Dec.

Locanda Ca' Foscari, Dorsoduro, 3888 (tel. 522 58 17), at the foot of the calle Crosera just east of calle Larga Foscari. The small sign is easy to miss. Singles L24,000, doubles L37,000. Rooms reserved by phone held until noon. Open Feb.-early Nov.

Locanda Montin, Dorsoduro, 1147 (tel. 522 71 51). From campo S. Barnaba go south through the passageway Casin dei Nobili, across the bridge and right on the fondamenta Lombardo, then around the corner onto fondamenta di Borgo. Worth finding; on a sunny canal. Singles L22,000, doubles L35,000. Showers included. Open Feb.-Dec.

Locanda Sturion, San Polo, 679 (tel. 523 62 43), on calle Sturion, the fourth right off fondamenta del Vin (along the Grand Canal) going south from the Rialto bridge. Large, clean rooms. The view of the Grand Canal from the dining room graces many a postcard. Singles L28,000, doubles L48,000. Showers L1000. Breakfast included.

Locanda Stefania, Santa Croce, 181a (tel. 520 37 57), on fondamenta Tolentini. Turn right after crossing the station bridge, then left at the first canal, and look for the little lantern. Uncomfortable beds, but the frescoed building and the nifty neighborhood adequately compensate. Singles L20,000, with bath L30,000; doubles L35,000, with bath L50,000. Phone reservations accepted. Open mid-Dec. to mid-Nov.

Casa Petrarca, San Marco, 4393 (tel. 520 04 30). From campo San Luca go south on calle dei Fuseri, take the second left, then turn right onto calle Schiavone. All is sweetness and light from the wicker furniture to the hospitality of the English-speaking proprietor. Singles L25,000, doubles L38,000-40,000. Showers L2000, but they're usually on the house. Phone to reserve.

Locanda San Samuele, San Marco, 3358 (tel. 522 80 45). On salizzada S. Samuele, leading out of the *campo* of the same name, just beyond campo Morosini. Rooms are cramped and dingy but the management is very kind and the prices are terrific. Two singles at L24,000, doubles L32,000, with bath L47,000. Showers L2000.

Pensione Casa Verardo, Castello, 4765 (tel. 528 61 27). Take Rimpetto la Sacrestia across the bridge, out of campo S. Filippo e Giacomo. Some weird touches (the dusty rose-colored plastic covering the walls in the front hall), some inspired ones (the well-polished antique furnishings). Singles L23,000, doubles L35,000. Showers L2000. Breakfast (optional) L4000. Phone reservations accepted, but not much English spoken. Open Feb.-Dec.

Locanda Sant' Anna, Castello, 269 (tel. 520 42 03). Take via Garibaldi, which becomes Fondamenta Sant' Anna (right side of the canal), then go left across the bridge at calle Crociera, and right at corte del Bianco. *Vaporetti* #1 and 4 will take you to Giardini near via Garibaldi. Spotless rooms and accommodating family are well worth the hike. This neighborhood lives up to its billing as the most authentically "Venetian" in the city. Singles L25,000, doubles L39,500, with bath L57,000. Showers L2500. Breakfast (optional) L4500. Might be closed in Nov. Phone reservations accepted.

Camping

Prices are outrageous—unless you're with two or more companions, you'll stay more cheaply in a hotel. The **Litorale del Cavallino**—one long row of campgrounds on the beach—is a peninsula about 25 minutes southeast of p. San Marco by *vapo-*

retto #15. Try **Marina di Venezia,** via Hermada (tel. 96 61 46), and **Ca' Pasquali,** via Fausta (tel. 96 61 10). Marina charges L5500 per person and L15,000 per tent; Pasquali is a few pennies cheaper. Both are open unreliably from May through September. Avoid sleeping at the beach on the Lido; if the thieves don't get you, the sand ants definitely will. **San Nicolò,** on the Lido, is a rustic site about 45 minutes from p. San Marco and 15 minutes from the beach. Take bus A to the left from the *vaporetto* stop. (L3000 per tent, L2500 per person.)

The many places that offer beds for travelers with sleeping bags are cheaper. **La Fusina** (tel. 96 90 55) is by far the best deal. (L7000 for a bunk in an 8-person bungalow.) To reach Fusina take bus #4 (L600) from piazzale Roma to Mestre and then take #13 from in front of Supermarket Pam. Boat #16 from the Zattere in Venice (L2000) is faster; the last one leaves at 11:45pm. In the summer the City of Venice also conscripts several elementary schools to use as dormitories. Open to tourists from mid-June through August, these generally charge L10,000 for a place inside and L3000 for hardier types willing to sleep under the stars. A L2000 membership fee may be charged for the first night. The tourist office has a list of the schools open.

Food

Most restaurants in Venice are prohibitively expensive. Venetians subsist on *panini* (small grilled sandwiches) and other good bar food, consumed standing (prices triple if you sit down). Avoid restaurants between the train station and San Marco; instead, prowl the Dorsoduro quarter between the Accademia and the Frari. Cover *(coperto)* charges are regularly twice as high in Venice as elsewhere in Italy; as much as L3000 per person is not unusual.

Fresh produce and fish are sold Monday through Saturday in **open air markets** on campo Santa Margherita and every morning in the bustling **Rialto** market. One of the best deals in town is the nameless **supermarket** on fondamenta Zattere, 1492, near the S. Basilio *vaporetto* stop (on the way to the hostel or Fusina); they charge 30% less than any other place. (Open Mon.-Sat. 9am-noon and 3:30-7:30pm.) The best *gelato* in Venice is uncontestably **Nico,** Dorsoduro, 922, on fondamenta Zattere, near the *vaporetto* stop of the same name; don't miss the rich chocolate and whipped cream *gianduiotto,* a Venetian specialty. (Open Fri.-Wed. until 10:30pm.) **Geleteria Santo Stefano** on campo Santo Stefano is also a good vantage point for the evening *passeggiata* (stroll). (Open Sat.-Thurs. 7:30am-11:30pm.)

Trattoria della Dona Onesta, Dorsoduro, 3922, on the calle of the same name, off calle Crosera, between campo San Pantalon and the Frari. Definitely worth finding. A family-run place with excellent, if simple, full meals for about L15,000. Open Sept. to mid-Aug. Mon.-Sat. noon-3:30pm and 6-11pm.

Cantina Do Spade, San Polo, 860, on the sottoportego delle Do Spade. Hard to find; tucked away under an archway before the Do Spade bridge (the first one south of campo Beccarie). A winery (L1200-1600 per glass) with sumptuous sandwiches (L800-1500). Open Sept.-July Mon.-Sat. 9am-1pm and 5-8pm. **Cantina Do Mori** is a similar place just down the street at #429. Open mid-Sept. to mid-Aug. Mon.-Sat. 9am-1pm and 5-9pm. A few hours spent in either of these *cantine* is as revealing of Venetian culture as diligently visiting 100 museums—and a lot easier on the feet.

Leon Bianco, San Marco, 4153, on salizzada S. Luca, near the Rialto and just off the campo S. Luca. Tasty food eaten standing at marble counters. *Risotto* and other hot dishes around L3500, and the usual array of snacks L1000-2000. Open Mon.-Sat. 8am-8pm.

Osteria al Mascaron, San Marco (tel. 522 59 95), on calle longa Santa Maria Formosa, east of the *campo* of the same name. Old Venetians linger here all afternoon to play inscrutable card games; the young and hip hang out in the evenings. Pasta L4000-5000. Main courses (fish only) L7000-12,000. Open Sept. to mid-Aug. Mon.-Sat. 11am-3pm and 6-11pm.

Da Gianni, Dorsoduro, 918, on fondamenta Zattere, near Gelateria Nico. The beautiful setting on a raft on the canal justifies the slightly higher prices; pizza is the best deal (L3500-7000). Open Feb.-Dec. Thurs.-Tues. noon-3pm and 6:30-10:30pm.

Mensa dell' Architettura, Santa Croce, 2553, on calle Magazen, on the north side of the Frari complex. Boisterous atmosphere. L6000 buys a filling cafeteria meal. Open mid-Sept. to June Mon.-Sat. noon-1pm and 6-8:30pm.

Sights

No monument is as memorable as the city itself, so use the major sights only as an excuse for wandering. Venice revolves around **piazza San Marco.** Housing the body of an evangelist was the last word in civic prestige in the Middle Ages, so the Republic set about acquiring one. Two merchants smuggled the body of Saint Mark out of Alexandria by burying it under a consignment of pork which they gambled (correctly) would put off the Muslim customs officials—thus did St. Mark become the patron saint of Venice in the eleventh century. The *pièce de résistance* of the mosaic-covered **Basilica di San Marco,** the church erected to house the saint, is the **Pala D'Oro,** a glittering gold Byzantine bas-relief. (Open Mon.-Sat. 9:30am-5:30pm, Sun. 1:30-5:30pm. Admission L500.) The same ticket admits you to the **treasury,** a dazzling collection of gold and relics. Upstairs in the **Galleria della Basilica** you can see the four powerful Hellenistic bronze horses which Venice stole from Constantinople; those standing on the loggia are reproductions. (Open daily 9:30am-5:30pm. Admission L500.) The **Torre dell' Orologio** (clock tower), left of San Marco, is a pretty arrangement of sculpture and sundials. The two bronze Moors on top still strike the hour. You can ascend the brick **campanile** in front of San Marco for a great view of the whole city. (Closed in 1987; only St. Mark can say if it will reopen in 1988. Tel. 523 18 79.) Toward the sea, the *piazza* opens into the **piazzetta San Marco,** with the two symbolic columns of Venice at the far end, topped with the winged lion and Neptune. The **Palazzo Ducale** (Doge's Palace), next to San Marco, faces Sansovino's famous and exquisite **Libreria** across the open space. Visit the palace for a mass display of Titians, Veroneses, and Tintorettos, as well as the armor museum and the **Ponte dei Sospiri** (Bridge of Sighs), which leads out to the prison. (Open daily 8:30am-7pm. Admission L5000; seniors, children, and students L3000.) Public bathrooms—rare in p. San Marco—are clean and located near the exit; save your ticket for access.

The **Accademia** displays the best of Venetian painting. The collection includes a superb Bellini *Madonna,* Giorgione's enigmatic *Tempest,* and Tintoretto's magnificent cycle depicting the life of St. Mark. Go on a bright day, as all the lighting is natural. (Open Mon.-Sat. 9am-7pm, Sun. 9am-1pm. Admission L4000.) For a very different idea of art, visit the **Collezione Peggy Guggenheim,** Dorsoduro, 701, in her magnificent canal-side *palazzo* east of the Accademia off fondamenta Venier. All the major names of modern art are here. (Open April-Oct. Mon. and Wed.-Sun. noon-6pm, Sat. 6-9pm; Nov.-March Sun.-Fri. noon-6pm, Sat. 6-9pm. Admission L5000; free Sat.)

Another area especially rich in art surrounds the Gothic **Basilica dei Frari** (*vaporetto:* San Tomà). The basilica holds a moving wooden sculpture of St. John by Donatello, Bellini's *Madonna and Saints,* and Titian's dramatic *Assumption.* (Open daily 9am-noon and 2:30-5:30pm. Admission L300.) For yet more art, check with the tourist office about the 1988 edition of *Venice Biennale,* an exhibition of international art staged every other year. The *scuole* of Venice were a combination of guilds and fraternities. In addition to providing welfare services for their members the *scuole* were a collective pride so potent that their "clubhouses" became some of the most ornate edifices in a city known for its opulence. The richest *scuola* of all was the **Scuola Grande di San Rocco** (across the campo at the end of the Frari), which houses 56 Tintorettos. The *Crucifixion* panel takes in so large a scene that half the people in the painting aren't even aware of the central event. (Open in summer daily 9am-1pm and 3:30-6:30pm; in winter Mon.-Fri. 10am-1pm and 3:30-6pm. Admission L5000.)

Across the Giudecca canal are two churches designed by the great Renaissance architect Palladio—**San Giorgio Maggiore** on the Isola di San Giorgio, and the **Chiesa del Redentore** on Giudecca itself, built at the end of one of the many plagues which struck Venice. Both can be viewed from **Church of Santa Maria della Salute,** a baroque extravaganza commemorating yet another plague savior, at the tip of Dorsoduro. Alternatively, take *vaporetto* #5 or 8 from p. San Marco.

Don't miss a *vaporetto* ride along the Canale Grande. Coming from the station you'll see the **Palazzo Vendramin-Calergi** and the **Ca' d'Oro** on the left bank, and the **Ca' Pesaro** on the right. After you pass under the elaborate stone **Ponte Rialto,** you'll see the **Ca' Foscari** on the right.

North of Venice stretches the **lagoon.** With a *vaporetto* ticket (L8000) you can visit the glass museum at **Murano;** the fishing village of **Burano;** and **Torcello,** an island with an enchanting Byzantine cathedral. The mudflats (*barreme*) that the ocean reveals at low tide give some idea of the very real sweat and strain that went into the construction of the Ethereal City. The **Lido** separates the Venice lagoon from the Adriatic. Its long sandy beach is very popular, though the water is filthy.

There's much more to this maze of stone and color than we can cover here. For a more thorough treatment of the city, pick up a copy of *Let's Go: Italy,* or Mary McCarthy's *Venice Observed.*

Entertainment

Perhaps the most entertaining evening activity in Venice is a tour of the Grand Canal at twilight; board the slow *vaporetto* at either end. **Gondolas** are indeed romantic, but probably out of reach—the official rate begins at L50,000 per hour. Travel the Venetian way is not altogether impossible. During the day, residents use *traghetti* to cross the Grand Canal between bridges. Look for a street that dead-ends onto the canal (marked "calle del traghetto") and pay L300 for a one-minute ride.

Concerts and exhibitions take place in the city's beautiful palazzi. Check *Un Ospite di Venezia, Marco Polo,* or with the EPT for details. At night, cafes and strolling are much more popular than dancing, but if you must, the **Club 22** at lungomare Marconi, 22, on the Lido, is a good disco.

Venice's most colorful festival is the **Festa del Retentore,** a no-holds-barred display of fireworks on the third Satuday of July. Venice's annual **International Film Festival** brings the world's best cinema to the city for the last week of August and the first week of September. (The EPT has schedules. Tickets begin at L4000.) July 1988 will be Venice's turn to host the **Old Republic's Maritime Regatta,** a boat race between Pisa, Genoa, Amalfi, and Venice; all that remains of the ancient rivalries between these four great Italian naval powers. On the first Sunday in September, the city holds its **Regatta Storica,** a series of pell-mell gondola races down the Grand Canal preceded by a procession of elegantly decorated boats. **Carnevale,** a wild period of costumed celebration and dancing in the streets, takes place during the 10 days prior to Ash Wednesday.

Padua (Padova)

Padua, a university town for some 600 years, has been home to many famous Italian intellectuals. Dante, Petrarch, and Galileo are just three illustrious predecessors of the 40,000 students who continue to enliven this small city.

Down corso Garibaldi (bus #3 or 8 or 10 min. on foot) lies the center of town; on the way you'll pass the **Cappella degli Scrovegni,** Padua's artistic highlight. Giotto designed the building itself, then executed the magnificent cycle of frescoes on the lives of the Virgin Mary and Christ. (Open April-Sept. daily 9am-12:30pm and 2:30-5:30pm; Oct.-March Mon.-Sat. 9:30am-12:30pm and 1:30-4:30pm, Sun. 9:30am-12:30pm. Admission L2000.) Next door is the **Church of the Eremitani,** with the fragments of Mantegna's brilliant frescoes that survived the last war.

Piazza delle Erbe and piazza della Frutta surround Padua's famous food market, the **Salone.** Take via Antenore, then turn down via del Santo to get to the **Basilica di Sant' Antonio,** a potpourri of a half-dozen major architectural styles. Sant' Antonio's tongue and jaw are preserved in a heart-shaped reliquary in the apse of the church; most of the pilgrims who visit Padua specifically to pray are inclined to kiss the toe of his sarcophagus. (Open April-Sept. daily 6:30am-7:45pm; Oct.-March daily 6:30am-7pm. Free.) Padua erupts in celebration during the week-long **Festa di Sant' Antonio** in late June. On the piazza del Santo, don't miss Donatello's imposing equestrian statue of **Gattemelata,** a mercenary general. Cast in the same pose as the famous Marcus Aurelius, this is the first great bronze of the Renaissance. Also on the *piazza* is the **Oratorio di San Giorgio,** where Giotto's students studied his art and decorated the walls, and the **Scuola del Santo,** which contains a sixteenth-century tribute to the saint in frescoes, and includes four early Titians. (Both open daily 9am-noon and 2:30-6:30pm. Admission to both L500.)

The **APT** (tel. 277 67), in the train station, is useful for maps and help with rooms. (Open Mon.-Sat. 9:30am-12:30pm and 3:30-8pm, but don't count on it.) Cheap rooms are plentiful in Padua, but during the summer they fill quickly with overflow travelers from nearby Venice (trains every ½ hr., ½ hr. journey, L1800 one way). Venice is so unbelievably packed that many people come here first, and spend their first day searching for suitable inexpensive accommodations in Venice. Unless the sentimental value of sleeping near a canal is worth the extra L10,000-30,000 Venetian hoteliers will extort, consider staying in Padua.

If you arrive in town late, check the vacancy board outside the tourist office. The friendly, crowded **Ostello Città di Padova,** via Aleardi, 30 (tel. 283 69), is clean and attractive. From the station, take bus #3, 8, or 18. (L9500. Breakfast included. 11pm curfew. Open year-round.) Two good *pensioni* are located on via Papafava, just across the canal, north of the hostel. **Albergo Pavia** at #11 (tel. 66 15 58) offers a cozy family atmosphere (singles L17,500, doubles L26,000), while **Pensione Pace** at #3 (tel. 253 52) has doubles for L26,000. Both are extremely popular, and should be reserved a week in advance. You can also try any of the places around the piazza del Santo. (They average singles L16,000, doubles L28,000.)

Padua has several **university mensas.** During the summer only the larger ones, at **via San Francesco, 122,** and at the top of **via Marzolo** are likely to be open. (Full meals L6000, ISIC not necessary. Open noon-2pm and 7-9pm.) But try to go to **Ristorante Vecchia Padova,** via Zaborella, 41, for lunch (noon-2:30pm)—gourmet food and cheerful cafeteria atmosphere for L10,000 or so. Avoid it at night, or else just have pizza, since prices go up. A good *trattoria* is **Al Pero,** via Santa Lucia, 72, with full meals for about L11,000. (Open Sept.-July Mon.-Sat. noon-2pm and 6:30pm-12:30am.)

Padua's **telephone code** is **049,** and the **postal code** is **35100.**

Verona

Set amid endless vineyards and cypress groves, this melange of Roman ruins, pink *palazzi,* and fanciful sepulchers is irresistably romantic. Shakespeare set *Romeo and Juliet* here, and would likely be amused to know that his imaginary lovers have become Verona's hottest tourist attraction. More entertaining than the balconies and palaces fancifully plastered with Shakespearean couplets are the operas and ballets performed during the summer festival. These take place nightly during July and August, in Verona's 22,000-seat **Roman Arena.** Even unreserved seats, usually available the day of performance, cost L15,000, but the staging and productions are imaginative, and the traditional candlelighting during the overture is unforgettable. Take along water and a cushion—these extravaganzas often last five hours. Tickets are available under arch #6 of the arena (tel. 235 20; open Mon.-Sat. 9am-12:20pm and 3-6:20pm), or by mailing a certified check to Ente Lirico, Arena di Verona, p. Brà, 28, 37121 Verona. Be sure you're getting seats in the arena, and not in the **Teatro Romano** (tel. 93 91 11), across the river, which stages jazz, ballet, and more Shakespearean plays. (Tickets from L8000.)

The train station, on the Milan-Venice line, is a 20-minute walk or a L600 bus ride (#2) south of Verona's center, **piazza Brà.** You can't miss the almost perfectly preserved Roman Arena here. Up via Mazzini from the Arena is **piazza delle Erbe,** where hokey trinkets are sold amid the Renaissance *palazzi* of former Veronese merchants. Through an arch on the right are **piazza dei Signori** and the **Tombs of the Scaligeri,** the peculiar Gothic remnants of the della Scalla, Verona's medieval tyrants. The equestrian statue of Cangrande I, head of the Scala clan, a glorification of raw power, is in the museum of the **Castelvecchio.** Badly damaged during the last war, the castle has been carefully restored, and offers spectacular views of the River Adige from its ramparts. (Open Tues.-Sun. 7:30am-7:30pm. Admission L5000.) Along the south riverbank is **Chiesa di San Zeno Maggiore,** a Romanesque church noted for the bronze panels of its door and its Mantegna altarpiece. This painting was removed by Napoleon to Paris, and again by thieves in 1973. None the worse for wear, Mantegna's spatial compositions draw the viewer into the scene; pay L200 to have the altarpiece lit. For the incurable romantic, there is **Juliet's House** at via Cappello, 23. (Open Tues.-Sun. 7:30am-7:30pm. Admission L2000.) What the Veronese call **Romeo's House,** via Arche Scaligere, 2, is now a bar.

The helpful but harried **tourist office** is just behind the arena at via Dietro Anfineatro, 6 (tel. 59 28 28). (Open Mon.-Sat. 9am-12:30pm and 3:30-6pm.) To get to the **Ostello Verona (IYHF),** salita Fontana del Ferro, 15 (tel. 59 03 60), take bus #2 across Ponte Nuovo to p. Isolo, then take a right on via Ponte Pignolo, walk three blocks, then left, right, and left again. Our researchers wax eloquent about this place, a frescoed fifteenth-century villa with sparkling bathrooms and sympathetic management. (L9500. Camping in a shady park for L6500, breakfast included. 3-course dinner L7000. 11pm curfew, extended if you're at the opera. Common room open all day. Open year-round.) Other student accommodations include: **Istituto Don Bosco,** via Provolo, 16 (tel. 59 13 00; open July-Sept.), with 100 beds for L8000 apiece, and **Casa della Giovanne,** via Pigna, 7 (tel. 59 68 80), where women only can stay for L10,000-12,000 per night. Both have a 10:30pm curfew, with exceptions for the opera. On the hotel front, clean and cheerful **Locanda Catullo** (tel. 227 86) is a bargain at L13,000 for singles, L24,000 for doubles. **Camping** is at **Romeo e Giulietta,** strada Bresciana, 54.

For amazing pizza and a young local crowd, go to **Pizzeria Farina,** corte Farina, 4 (tel. 59 10 32), off via Quattro Spate. Eat in the pretty courtyard outside rather than amidst the orange and blue tartan theme inside. Pizzas L3000-5000, and no cover! (Open Tues.-Fri. noon-2:45pm and 6-11pm, Sat.-Sun. 5pm-1am.) Across the river is **Trattoria al Cacciatore,** via Seminario, 4, with a fine *menù* for L10,000. (Open Mon.-Fri. noon-3pm and 6-10pm, Sat. noon-3pm.) **Trattoria Ropeton,** just below the hostel at via S. Giovanni in Valle, 46, is a great place for a quiet splurge. (L15,000. Open Wed.-Mon.)

Verona's **telephone code** is **045;** the **postal code** is **37100.**

Bologna

People have strained themselves over the years inventing nicknames for wondrous Bologna: *la Dotta* (the learned), for being the home of Europe's oldest university, an institution that still attracts tens of thousands of students; *la Grassa* (the fat), for being a gastronomic marvel with more, and better, restaurants than many world capitals; and finally, *Bologna Rossa,* on the strength of its leftist politics. Stroll among the endless miles of porticos which grace the burnt-orange buildings, and catch the energy which hums quietly in the streets.

From the train station, walk down the elegant galleries of via dell'Indipendenza to the main east-west street, via Ugo Bassi. Straight ahead are piazze Nettuno and Maggiore, where the crowd gathers under the Corinthian columns of the **Palazzo del Podestà,** shifting in the afternoon with the shade to the steps of the **Basilica of San Petronio,** a huge Gothic structure which would have been "even bigger than St. Peter's in Rome had the Pope not intervened." Fortunately, Jacopo della Quercia had already completed his spectacular doorway. In the fountain outside, the bronze *Neptune and Attendants* (Giambologna) splash happily. The two towers to the west on **piazza di Porta Ravegnana** attest to times when Bologna was dominated by rival coalitions—neighborhoods were organized around towers built by the most powerful families. Now they are considered the symbols of the city. You can climb the taller of the two (taller because the other tipped so badly that its upper portion broke off) for a great view of Bologna and the Po Valley. (Open daily 9am-6pm. Admission L2000.)

Down via Santo Stefano, the triangular **piazza Santo Stefano** opens into a complex of Romanesque churches unrivaled in their austere beauty. The most spectacular of the four small churches that make up the **Basilica of Santo Stefano** is the round **Santo Sepolcro,** where San Petronio, patron of Bologna, is buried under a carved pulpit. In the courtyard behind is the **Basin of Pilate** in which that judge is supposed to have absolved himself of responsibility. Don't miss the cloisters behind the **Church of the Crucifixion** next to Santo Sepolcro, or the arches of the **Church of San Vitale,** the oldest in the group. The **Church of San Domenico** is a few blocks away. Here Saint Dominic, contemporary of Saint Francis and founder of the Dominican order, is buried under a marble monument with statuettes by Michelangelo and Nicolò dell'Arca, and four softly molded reliefs by Nicola Pisano. (Most churches are open early morning-noon and 4-6pm.)

The **Pinacoteca Nazionale,** via delle Belle Arti, 56 (tel. 22 37 74), is one of Italy's best galleries, containing an outstanding collection of Bolognese painting as well as a number of Renaissance masterworks. (Open Tues.-Sat. 9am-2pm, Sun. 9am-1pm. Admission L2000.)

Thanks to its enormous student population, Bologna enjoys an booming nightlife. Try hanging out at the **Black Lady** on p. Giuseppe Verdi, where huge crowds gather during the academic year. (Open Mon.-Sat. 8am-2am.) Watch the posters in p. Verdi for information on the frequent concerts; Bologna is the center of Italy's new-wave music scene. Unfortunately, entertainment is pretty scarce in July and August, when everyone just takes to the streets.

Bologna's **Informazione Azienda Turistica (IAT),** in the train station (tel. 37 22 20), dispenses maps and information, and helps with room-finding; a list of accommodations is posted after hours. Ask for *A Guest in Bologna,* a free booklet with listings of museums, exhibits, and concerts. (Open Mon.-Sat. 9am-7pm, Sun. 9am-1pm.) The main office in Palazzo Comunale has more exhaustive information. (Open same hours.) The **telephone code** for Bologna is 051.

Bologna's **Ostello (IYHF),** via Viadagola, 14 (tel. 51 92 02), is 6km out of town. Take bus #93 (Mon.-Sat. until 8:15pm) or bus #19 (Sun and Aug.1-24). (Members L10,500, nonmembers L13,000. Breakfast included. Check-in 7-9am and 5-11:30pm.) Hotels are expensive: Expect to pay L23,000 for a single and L36,000 for a double, L5000 less in winter. Near the station, try **Pensione Marconi,** via Marconi, 22 (tel. 26 28 32). **Pensione Cattani,** via Cattani, 7 (tel. 23 17 92), off via dell'Indipendenza, has more singles than other *pensioni.* The very nice **Pensione Neva** is at via L. Serra, 7 (tel. 36 98 93), off via Matteotti across the tracks behind the station.

It seems as if every street in Bologna has two *trattorie* and three *pizzerie;* quality runs high and prices moderate to high. Try all the pasta and the various sausages. **Pizza Altero,** via dell'Indipendenza, 33, is strictly take-out, crowded, and delicious. Slices only: L800-1500. (Open Sept.-July Mon.-Sat. 8am-midnight.) **CAMST,** at via A. Righi , is a *rosticceria* (take-out) from 10:30am to 3pm and 5:30 to 9pm, and a *tavola calda* (self-service) from 11:30am to 2:30pm and 6:30 to 9:30pm, but always tasty and reasonable; *primi* are L3000 to L5000, *secondi* L5500 to L7000, and the wine is cheap. **Trattoria Da Danio,** via S. Felice, 50, has classic pasta dishes and local sausage; try *cotechio.* (Open Sept.-July Mon.-Sat. noon-2:30pm and 7:30-10pm.) More expensive but worth it is **Trattoria Buca San Petronio,** at via dei Musei, 2, with outdoor tables on a charming covered street. (Pasta dishes L5000, *secondo* L7500-9000.) A little more expensive is the **Ristorante Franco Rossi,** via Donzelle, 1, just off via dell'Indipendenza; if there's one place in Italy to splurge for a meal, this is it. (Pasta dishes L10,000, *secondi* L18,000 and up; cover charge L5000.)

Parma

Parma, so elegant, so wealthy, so conveniently located on the Bologna-Milan rail line, is one of the most enjoyable stops in Emilia Romagna. The harmonious **Duomo** (cathedral) contains two medieval masterpieces: the moving *Descent from the Cross,* and the *Episcopal Throne,* by Benedetto Antelami, Parma's medieval master sculptor. The brilliant Correggio painted the interior of the cathedral's dome, and also that of the **Church of San Giovanni Evangelista.** Antelami also adorned the exterior of the **battistero** (baptistry) with bas-reliefs of fantastic animals, Biblical allegories, and the *Labors of the Months.* (Churches open daily 7:30am-noon and 3:30-7pm.) Nearby, the **Palazzo Pilotta** houses the **Galleria Nazionale di Parma,** with works by Correggio, Parmigianino, da Vinci, the Holbeins, van Dyck, Murillo, and many others. (Open Mon.-Sat. 9am-2pm, Sun. 9am-7:30pm. Admission L3000, ages under 18 or over 60 free.)

Via Garibaldi, Parma's main street, runs from the station to the center of town. The **Ente Provinciale per il Turismo,** p. Duomo, 5 (tel. 347 35), provides a good map and information on Parma and its province. If you have a maple leaf, display it prominently, as one of the staff is Canadian. The **Ostello Cittadella (IYHF),** via Passo Buole (tel. 58 15 46), is housed inside a seventeenth-century fortress. Take bus #9 or 10 from the station or bus #6 from the center. (L7500. Check-in all day. 11pm curfew. Open April-Oct.) The **Albergo Stella d'Italia,** via Albertelli, 10 (tel. 28 56 24), near the station, is cheap but not great. (Singles L11,000, doubles L18,500.)

Sample great sandwiches at **Da Walter,** borgo Palmina, 2/B, off Strada Farini; then wash them down with local *lambrusco.* (Open Mon.-Fri. noon-2:30pm and 7-8:30pm.) Parma is Italy's acknowledged gastronomical capital and **La Filoma,** via XX Marzo, 15, is one of the city's best. Full meals run L35,000-40,000, but you can order only one course and still be in the black. (Open Sept.-July Mon.-Sat. 12:30-2:30pm and 7:30-10:30pm.)

Parma's **telephone code** is 0521, and the **postal code** is 43100.

Ferrara

The court of Ferrara was the aesthetic capital of the northern Italian Renaissance city-states. The despotic d'Este dukes ruled from 1294 to 1598, and patronized such poets as Ariosto and Tasso, as well as the painters Pisanello and Mantegna. Today, the melancholic long streets of the Addizione Erculea, lined with deserted *palazzi* and gardens, combine with the medieval core of Ferrara to make up one of the most hauntingly romantic towns in Italy. Bassani's *The Garden of the Finzi-Contini* and de Sica's film version are both set here.

The towered and turreted **castello** dominates Ferrara; the awesome brick complex stands exactly in the center of town. The Ducal Apartments contain richly frescoed rooms—the *Salone dei Giochi,* the *Loggetta degli Aranci*—while the **Cappella di Renata di Francia** is filled with opulent Lombardesque ornamentation. (Open Tues.-Sun. 9am-12:30pm and 2:30-5pm. Free guided tours hourly.) The **Duomo,** a short distance away, is an interesting compendium of styles; one contributor was Biagio Rossetti, the architectural master-mind of Duke Ercole's schemes. The **Museo del Duomo** houses numerous examples of the Ferrarese school of painting, including Jacopo della Quercia's masterful *Madonna della Melagrana* (Madonna with a Pomegranate). (Church open Mon.-Sat. 6:30am-noon and 4-7:30pm, Sun. 7:25am-1pm and 4-7:45pm. Museum open Mon.-Sat. 10am-noon and 4-6pm. Donations accepted.)

On the fringes of the city center stand the numerous and beautiful d'Este *palazzi.* The EPT has complete lists of the salons and galleries you can visit. Don't miss the museum complex of the **Palazzo Massari,** with its many fine arts collections. (Open 9am-1pm and 4-7pm. Admission L2000, students usually free.) The **Palazzo**

Schifanoia, via Scandiana, 23, contains the *Saloni dei Mesi,* the most accurate and vivid depictions of Quattrocento courtly life in Italy. (Open daily 9am-7pm. Admission L1500, free the second Sun. and Mon. of each month).

The **Informazioni Azienda Touristica** in the Palazzo Municipio, near the castello, is very friendly. The **Ostello Estense (IYHF),** via Benvenuto Tisi Garofalo, 5 (tel. 210 98), is off via Ariosto. (L6200. Open Feb. to mid-Dec.) The **Albergo Nazionale,** corso Porta Reno, 32 (tel. 352 10) near the *duomo,* is a good deal. (Singles L15,000, doubles L33,000.) Take bus #3 to **Camping Estense,** via Porta Catena (tel. 527 91). (L2350 per person, L3770 per tent). **Pizzeria Antica Ferrara** offers cheap pizza and snacks, in addition to reasonably-priced dinners (L12,000). (Open Sept.-July Tues.-Sun. 11am-3pm and 5pm-1am.)

Tuscany and Umbria

Tuscany has been congratulating itself for its civic spirit, land, food, and above all, its art, for 700 years. Tuscans have never completely accepted the concept of Italian unity and they have never really had to. Their landscape forms the classic background of much of Italian painting, and Tuscan, the language of Dante, Petrarch, and Machiavelli, is today's textbook Italian. Tuscany, the Tuscans can say with understandable confidence, *is* Italy.

Umbria is the self-proclaimed green heart of Italy, carelessly bypassed by speedsters on the Florence-Rome highway. Its marvelously preserved medieval hill towns preside over misty fields and olive groves, inspiring twentieth-century travelers much as they did St. Francis, Perugino, Giotto, and Signorelli.

Florence (Firenze)

Florence is as vital and beautiful today as when its merchants and bankers were known throughout Europe. Florentines such as Michelangelo, Cellini, and Guicciardini set standards of Renaissance culture, and the Medici court became Italy's artistic and intellectual standard-bearer. The fruits of the city's rebirth are still evident in its seemingly endless array of museums, churches, and *palazzi.* But more remains of Florence's incomparable heritage than stones and paint—the city's indomitable spirit today ensures the liveliness and sophistication of Florentine life.

Orientation and Practical Information

All roads may lead to Rome, but every railpass seems to lead to Florence. Happily, once in Florence, all roads definitely lead to the **duomo,** whose giant profile dominates the city and is an unmistakable reference point. The center of town lies between the *duomo* and the pedestrian **Ponte Vecchio,** the principal bridge across the **River Arno.** The **Oltrarno** is the primarily residential section of Florence on the opposite side of the river. The train station lies down via de' Cerretani (which becomes via de' Panzani). Car-free via Calzaiuoli connects the *duomo* with **piazza della Signoria,** the center of street nightlife. You won't need to use Florence's public transit system unless you're camping or hosteling; most pensions and sights are within a 15-minute walk of the *duomo.*

Two sequences of street numbers are used: red indicates a commercial building, blue/black a residential one (including most pensions). Here, as in Florentine publications, commercial addresses are denoted by a numeral followed by an *r.*

Tourist Offices: Azienda Autonoma di Turismo, via Tornabuoni, 15 (tel. 21 65 44). From the station, walk across p. Unità and along via de' Panzani; second right onto via Rondinelli which becomes via Tornabuoni. Central and efficient with free map; no accommodations service. Open Mon.-Sat. 9am-1pm. **Ente Provinciale per il Turismo (EPT),** via Manzoni, 16 (tel. 247 81 41). Come here with complaints about hotels. Open Mon.-Fri. 8:30am-1:30pm and

4-6:30pm, Sat. 8:30am-1:30pm. **Summer office,** via Santa Monaca, 2, in the Oltrarno; staffed by university students. Open in summer Mon.-Fri. 8-11am and 4-7pm. Also at the train station, by track #16. Open in summer daily 9am-9pm. Other transient offices appear around the *duomo* and the Palazzio Vecchio.

Accommodations Service: Informazioni Turistiche Alberghiere (ITA), in the train station. Will find rooms for L1500-1800 commission. Often a very long line. Open April-Oct. daily 8am-9:30pm; Nov.-March daily 9am-6:30pm. **ACISJF,** in the station, down track #16. Usually less crowded than ITA. Open Sept.-July Mon.-Sat. 10am-12:30pm and 1-4pm.

Budget Travel: Centro Turistico Studentesco e Giovanile, via dei Ginori, 11*r* (tel. 26 35 70), near San Lorenzo. Open Mon.-Fri. 9:30am-1pm and 4-7pm, Sat. 9am-12:30pm; Oct.-May Mon.-Fri. 9am-12:30pm and 3-5:30pm.

American Express: Universalturismo, via Guicciardini, 96*r* (tel. 27 87 51). Exchange service and check replacement downstairs, mail pick-up upstairs. No wired money accepted. Open Mon.-Fri. 9am-6pm, Sat. 9am-1pm.

Currency Exchange: Try to change money at banks (open Mon.-Fri. 8:20am-1:20pm and 2:45-3:45pm). **Cassio di Risparmia di Firenze** banks are open Sat. afternoon. The **Esercizio Promozione Turismo,** via Condotta, 42*r,* near p. Signoria, changes after banking hours for a large commission. Open Mon.-Sat. 10am-7pm, Sun. 10am-6pm. Change at the **Ufficio Informazioni** in the station only if you absolutely have to. Open daily 7:20am-1:20pm and 2:35-8pm.

Post Office: Via Pellicceria, off p. della Repubblica. Poste Restante at windows #23 and 24. Open Mon.-Fri. 8:15am-7pm, Sat. 8:15am-noon. **Postal code:** 50100.

Telephones: ASST in the post office and at Via Cavour 21*r.* Both open 24 hours. Lines are sometimes shorter at **SIP** in the station. Open daily 7:30am-9:30pm. **Telephone code:** 055.

Trains: Most trains arrive at **Santa Maria Novella** station, near the center of town, though some stop only at **Campo di Marte** station, on Florence's east side; bus #19 connects both stations 24 hours per day. Trains to Milan, Venice, Bologna, and Rome. Information (tel. 27 87 85) open daily 7am-9:50pm.

Buses: LAZZI, via della Stazione, 1-6*r* (tel. 21 51 54). For Lucce, Pisa, and Pistoia. **SITA,** via Caterina da Siena, 15*r* (tel. 21 14 87), just outside the train station. For Siena and Arezzo.

Public Transportation: ATAF information booth in the train station; also at p. del Duomo, 57*r.* Buy tickets (L600 for 1 ride, L700 for 70 min.) at *tabacchi.* Route map posted at the booth in the station.

Emergencies: Police (tel. 113); **Ufficio Stranieri,** for foreigners (English-speaking personnel 9am-2pm), at via Zara, 2 (tel. 497 71).

Medical Assistance: Misericordia, p. del Duomo, 20 (tel. 21 22 22). **Tourist Medical Services,** via Lorenzo il Magnifico, 59 (tel. 47 54 11), for 24-hour house calls.

Pharmacy: Farmacia Comunale (tel. 26 34 35), by track #16 in the station and **Molteni,** via Calzaiuoli, 7*r* (tel. 26 34 90), are both open 24 hours.

Consulates: U.S., lungarno Vespucci, 38 (tel. 29 82 76). **U.K.,** lungarno Corsini, 2 (tel. 28 41 33).

Bookstores: Paperback Exchange, via Fiesolana, 31*r.* Buy, trade, or get cash for your books. Open March-Nov. Mon-Sat. 9am-1pm and 3:30-7:30pm; Nov.-March Tues.-Sat. only. For the widest selection of new books, try **Seeber,** via Tornabuoni, 68*r.* Same hours, though closed 2 weeks in mid-Aug.

Public Baths: Albergo Diurno, outside train station. Showers L4000. Open Mon.-Wed. and Fri.-Sat. 6am-8pm, Sun. 6am-1pm.

Hitchhiking: For the A-1 to Bologna and Milan or the A-11 to the Riviera and Genoa, take bus #29, 30, or 35 from the train station to the feeder near Peretola. For the A-1 to Rome and for the Siena extension, take bus #31 or 32 from the station to exit 23.

Accommodations and Camping

Reservations (*prenotazioni*) are a good idea, especially in summer and at Easter. Virtually any hotel will accept a reservation with one night's deposit, and some will accept a phone reservation 12 to 72 hours in advance. Agree on the time (usually

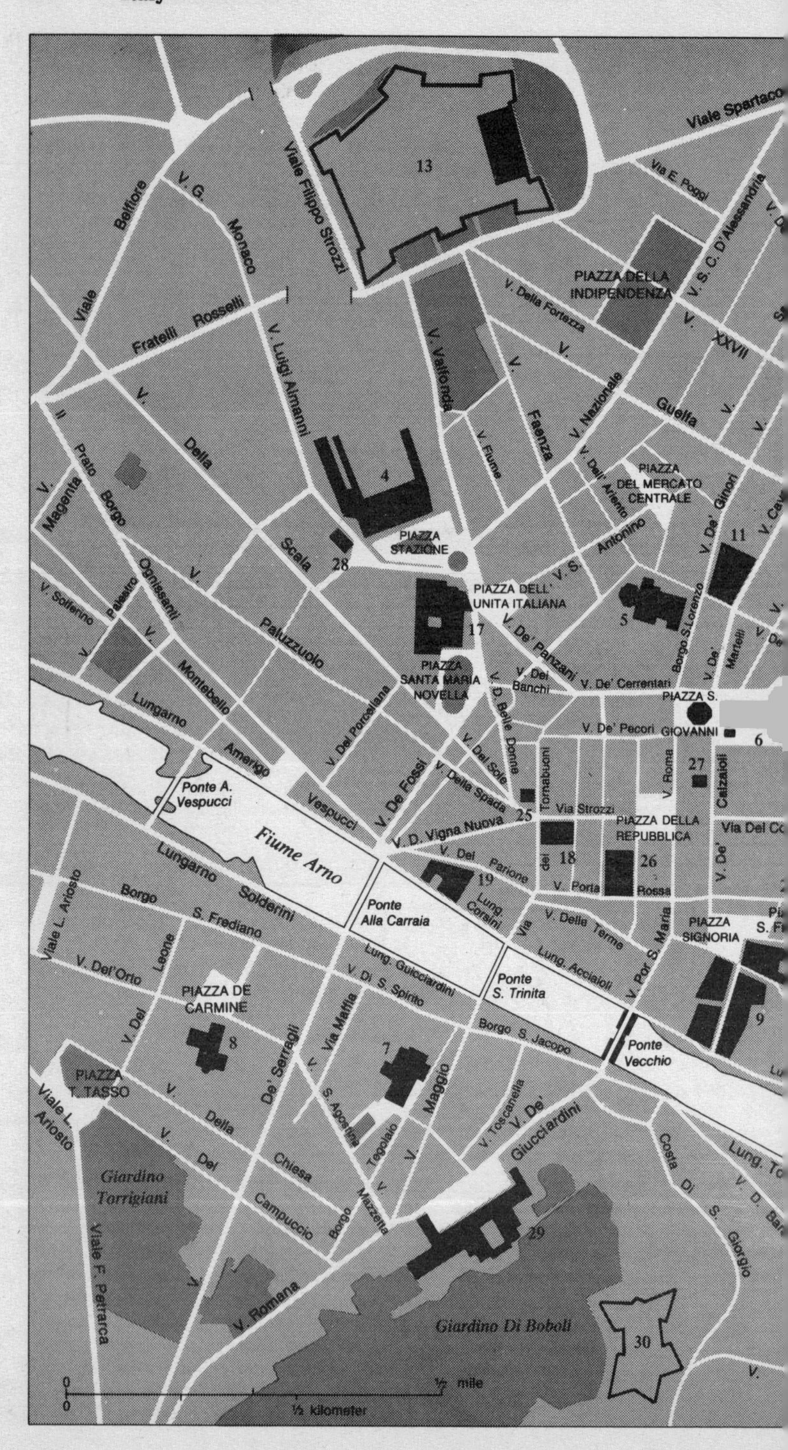

13
Viale Spartaco
Via E. Poggi
V. S. C. D'Alessandria
Viale Filippo Strozzi
V. G. Monaco
Viale Belfiore
Viale Fratelli Rosselli
V. Luigi Alamanni
V. Valfonda
V. Della Fortezza
PIAZZA DELLA INDIPENDENZA
V. XXVII
V. Nazionale
V. Faenza
V. Guelfa
V. Fiume
V. Dell' Ariento
PIAZZA DEL MERCATO CENTRALE
V. De' Ginori
11
4
PIAZZA STAZIONE
28
V. Della Scala
Il Prato
Borgo Ognissanti
V. Magenta
V. Solferino
V. Palestro
V. Montebello
V. Palazzuolo
V. S. Antonino
PIAZZA DELL' UNITA ITALIANA
17
V. De' Panzani
5
Borgo S. Lorenzo
V. De' Martelli
PIAZZA SANTA MARIA NOVELLA
V. Dei Banchi
V. De' Cerretani
PIAZZA S. GIOVANNI
6
Lungarno Amerigo Vespucci
V. Del Porcellana
V. D. Belle Donne
V. De' Pecori
V. Del Sole
V. Della Spada
V. De Fossi
Tornabuoni
V. Roma
27
Calzaioli
Ponte A. Vespucci
Fiume Arno
25
Via Strozzi
PIAZZA DELLA REPUBBLICA
Via Del Co
V. D. Vigna Nuova
V. Del Parione
18
26
19
V. Porta Rossa
Lungarno Soderini
Borgo S. Frediano
Viale L. Ariosto
Ponte Alla Carraia
Lung. Corsini
Via V. Delle Terme
PIAZZA SIGNORIA
V. Del'Orto
V. Leone
Lung. Guicciardini
V. Di S. Spirito
Ponte S. Trinita
Lung. Acciaioli
V. Por S. Maria
9
PIAZZA DE CARMINE
8
V. Del
Via Maffia
7
Borgo S. Jacopo
Ponte Vecchio
PIAZZA T. TASSO
V. Della Chiesa
De' Serragli
V. S. Agostino
Maggio
V. Toscanella
V. De' Guicciardini
Viale L. Ariosto
V. Del Campuccio
V. Tegolaio
Costa Di S. Giorgio
Lung. To
Giardino Torrigiani
Borgo
Mazzetta
29
V. D. Bar
Viale F. Petrarca
V. Romana
Giardino Di Boboli
30
0
½ mile
0
½ kilometer

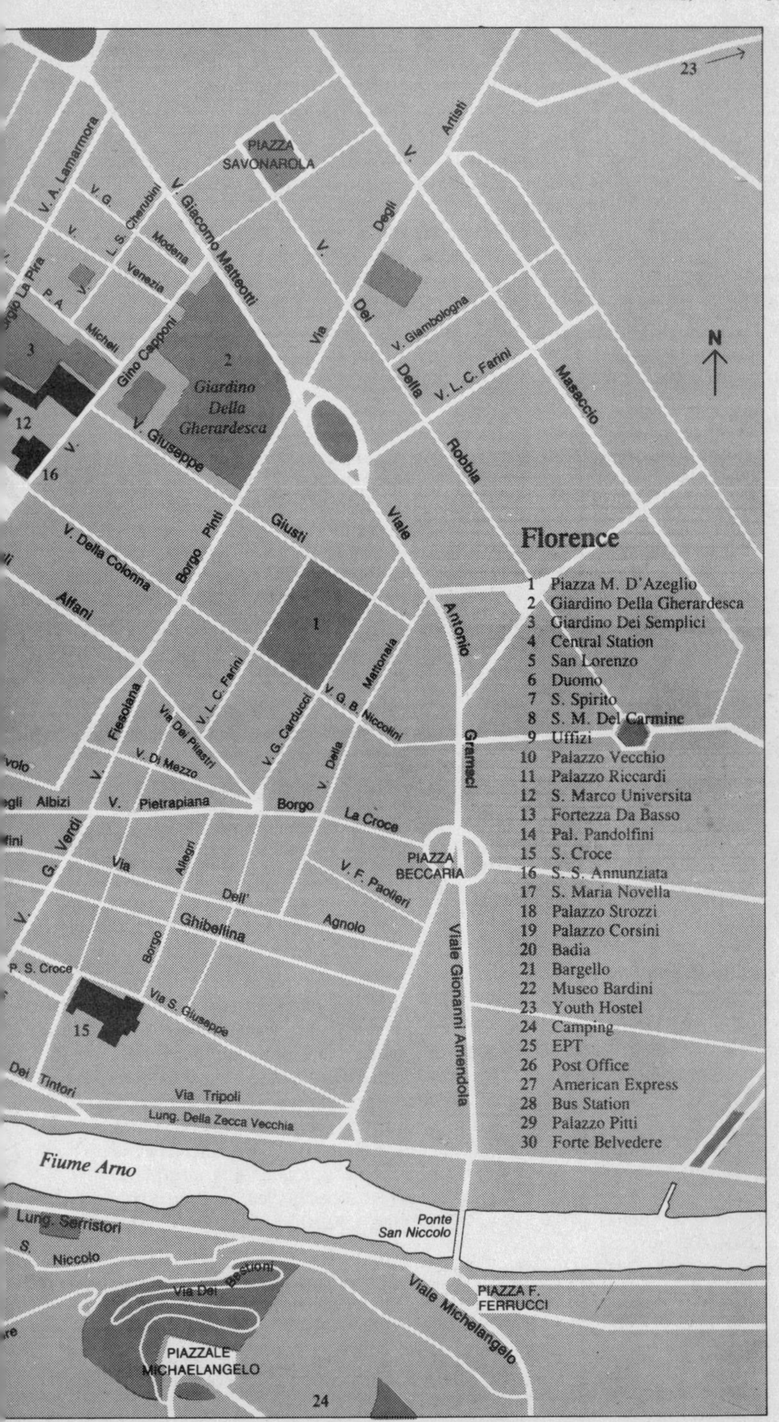
Florence
1 Piazza M. D'Azeglio
2 Giardino Della Gherardesca
3 Giardino Dei Semplici
4 Central Station
5 San Lorenzo
6 Duomo
7 S. Spirito
8 S. M. Del Carmine
9 Uffizi
10 Palazzo Vecchio
11 Palazzo Riccardi
12 S. Marco Universita
13 Fortezza Da Basso
14 Pal. Pandolfini
15 S. Croce
16 S. S. Annunziata
17 S. Maria Novella
18 Palazzo Strozzi
19 Palazzo Corsini
20 Badia
21 Bargello
22 Museo Bardini
23 Youth Hostel
24 Camping
25 EPT
26 Post Office
27 American Express
28 Bus Station
29 Palazzo Pitti
30 Forte Belvedere
N
PIAZZA SAVONAROLA
V. A. Lamarmora
V. G.
V. L. S. Cherubini
Modena
Venezia
P. A.
Micheli
V. Giacomo Matteotti
V. Degli Artisti
Via Dei Della Robbia
V. Giambologna
V. L. C. Farini
Masaccio
Gino Capponi
Giardino Della Gherardesca
V. Giuseppe Giusti
Viale Antonio Gramsci
Borgo Pinti
V. Della Colonna
Alfani
V. Fiesolana
Via Dei Pilastri
V. L. C. Farini
V. G. Carducci
V. G. B. Niccolini
Mattonaia
V. Della
V. Di Mezzo
Albizi
V. Pietrapiana
Borgo La Croce
PIAZZA BECCARIA
V. F. Paolieri
G. Verdi
Via Dell' Agnolo
Allegri
Ghibellina
Borgo
P. S. Croce
Via S. Giuseppe
Viale Gionanni Amendola
Dei Tintori
Via Tripoli
Lung. Della Zecca Vecchia
Fiume Arno
Ponte San Niccolo
Lung. Serristori
S. Niccolo
Via Dei Bastioni
Viale Michelangelo
PIAZZA F. FERRUCCI
PIAZZALE MICHAELANGELO

before noon) when you will arrive; otherwise, a nervous proprietor might give the room to someone else. Without a reservation, be sure to begin looking early (before noon), or reconcile yourself to the offerings of an accommodations service (see Practical Information). If you arrive much after noon, consider taking whatever they will give you and spend your first evening or morning in Florence looking for a more suitable place. If you are charged more than the price posted on the door of your room, complain to the EPT. During summer you should expect your host to insist that you take breakfast.

In past years, the city of Florence has run an *area di sosta* at Villa Favard (6km out of town), which provides a canopied spot to sling a sleeping bag, plus showers and toilets—all for free. The *area* may be open for the summer of 1988; inquire at the tourist office. Couples especially should avoid camping or parking in secluded areas around the city, due to the prowlings of "Cicci, the Monster of Scandicci," a serial murderer, who has struck annually over the past eight years: Twice the victims have been foreign couples camping.

Hostels

Ostello Europa-Villa Camerata (IYHF), viale Augusto Righi, 2-4 (tel. 60 14 51). In a beautiful, if remote, old building, 30 min. from the station on bus #17b (exit by track #5). Opens at 2pm, and fills fast. Members L11,000, nonmembers L13,500. Sheets and breakfast included. Midnight curfew. Reservations by mail only.

Ostello Santa Monaca, via Santa Monaca, 6 (tel. 26 83 38), near the Carmine Church in the Oltrarno. Take bus #36 or 37 from p. Santa Maria Novella to the first stop across the river. Or walk 10 min. from the *piazza:* take via de' Fossi (which begins diagonally across the *piazza* from the church), cross the Ponte alla Carraia and continue on via de' Serragli; the third right is via Santa Monaca. L11,000. Kitchen privileges and a trickle of hot water. Sheets L1500 extra. Arrive 9:30am-1pm (especially in summer), sign the list, drop any ID in the box, then return between 4-4:30pm to register. Strict midnight curfew. No reservations accepted.

Pensionato Pio X-Artigianelli, via de' Serragli, 106 (tel. 22 50 44). Same directions as for the Santa Monaca, except get off the bus at the second stop across the river. Much quieter than its neighbor, but only 36 dorm-style beds and a slow turnover, so arrive very early. L10,000 with 2-day min. stay. Midnight curfew. No reservations. Open July-Sept.

Istituto Gould, via de' Serragli, 49 (tel. 21 25 76), near the Santa Monaca. Extremely clean, friendly, and quiet; well worth the L17,000 per person for doubles. Arrive Mon.-Fri. 9am-1pm and 3-7pm only. No curfew. Often filled with local students from Oct.-June. Reservations by prepayment only; write 3-4 months in advance.

Hotels

Near the Railroad Station

Veer left when leaving the station and you'll find yourself in the heart of the allegedly "budget" *pensione* district—accompanied by nearly everyone else who has just arrived in Florence. **Via Nazionale, via Faenza, via Fiume,** and **via Guelfa** are the best places to look for a room. This area is convenient to the train station, and nothing else. Moreover, it's a jungle of indifferent proprietors, 10am evictions, and midnight lockouts. One exception is the area directly across from the station's main entrance, p. Santa Maria Novella (behind the church); it's also close to the station, convenient to the city center, far more pleasant, and generally cheaper.

The six *pensioni* at **via Faenza, 56** are all reasonably clean and well-run; try the **Merlini** first. Singles L20,000-21,500; doubles L30,500-31,500, with bath (at Merlini) L40,000.)

Hotel Apollo/Tony's Inn, via Faenza, 77 (tel. 21 79 75 or 28 41 19). The friendly and linguistically able owners offer 20 unique rooms, most with large private baths. Singles L32,000, doubles L55,000; L2000 less without bath. Breakfast included. Midnight curfew.

Albergo Sampaoli, via S. Gallo, 14 (tel. 28 48 34). 14 renovated rooms overseen by one of the city's most charming proprietors. Singles L23,000, doubles L32,000, with bath L40,000. Showers L2000. No curfew. No reservations accepted.

Soggiorno Caterina, via di Barbano, 8 (tel. 48 37 05), 1 block from p. dell'Indipendenza (walk out via Nazionale). A giant step up from any place nearby. Quiet, friendly and clean. Doubles L40,000, with bath L45,000. All with breakfast and showers. No curfew. Phone reservations accepted.

Pensione Ausonia e Rimini, via Nazionale, 24 (tel. 49 65 47), near p. dell'Indipendenza. *Let's Go* readers get a 5% discount (10% Jan.-March). Singles L26,000, doubles L37,900, triples L51,000-65,000. Breakfast included.

Locanda La Romagnola/Soggiorno Gigliola, via della Scala, 40 (tel. 21 15 97). 2 blocks from the station, to the right. Friendly, and likely to have room. Singles L20,000, doubles L30,000. Showers L2000. Breakfast L5000. Midnight curfew.

Pensione La Mia Casa, p. Santa Maria Novella, 23 (tel. 21 30 61). A touch of disorder only adds to the charm in this antique-filled seventeenth-century *palazzo.* The kind owner, bar, free showers, and great prices make this one of the most popular places in town. Singles L20,000, doubles L28,000, triples L37,000. Midnight curfew. Phone reservations usually held until 3pm.

Albergo Universo, p. Santa Maria Novella, 20 (tel. 21 21 84). Unspectacular, but 54 clean rooms make it a good bet. Singles (some closet-sized) L24,000, doubles L40,500, triples L56,500, quads L75,500. Breakfast included. No curfew. Phone reservations sometimes accepted.

Near the *duomo*

If you can drag yourself farther from the station, you'll probably enjoy Florence more and pay less. The area between the *duomo* and river has some great deals. None of the following is more than a 20-minute walk from the station, but call first or leave your pack at the station, as they are small and dispersed.

Hotel Colore, v. dei Calzaiuoli, 13 (tel. 21 03 01), just off p. del Duomo. Small rooms and low prices in an absolutely central location. Singles L21,000; doubles L32,000, with shower L38,000. **Locanda Aldini,** (tel. 21 47 52), 1 floor down, has more spacious rooms but higher prices due to the mandatory breakfast. Doubles L40,500. Showers L3000. Phone reservations usually held.

Soggiorno Brunori, via del Proconsolo, 5 (tel. 26 36 48), off p. del Duomo. Comfortable rooms and friendly people in a great location. Doubles L31,500, with bath L40,000. Showers L3000. Breakfast L6000. Midnight curfew. Phone reservations sometimes accepted.

Soggiorno Bavaria, borgo degli Albizi, 26 (tel. 234 03 13), off via del Proconsolo. Average rooms, clean and quiet. Run by the owners of the Ausonia e Rimini (see Near the Railroad Station): same 5% discount for *Let's Go* readers. Singles L26,500, doubles L41,000, triples L54,000. Showers and breakfast included. No curfew. Reserve by phone several days in advance.

Pensione Davanzati, via Porta Rossa, 15 (tel. 28 34 14), between p. della Signoria and via Tornabuoni. Fine location and prices, but cramped rooms. Singles L20,000, doubles L30,000. Showers L2000. No curfew. Phone reservations usually accepted.

Pensione Rigatti, lungarno Diaz, 2 (tel. 21 30 22), on the river at Ponte alle Grazie. The elegant salons, lush gardens, and impeccable standards in this *palazzo* make it the most beautifully appointed *pensione* you are ever likely to see. Singles L38,000, with bath L46,000; doubles L60,000 with bath L72,500. Breakfast included. The soft-spoken proprietor speaks English and locks the door at 1am. Reserve up to 6 months ahead.

In the Oltrarno

Places on this side of the river are marginally farther from the city's sights and services, and generally more expensive than those in town. So what? They're also almost uniformly quieter and more comfortable.

Pensione Adria, p. Frescobaldi, 4 (tel. 21 50 29), just across Ponte Santa Trinità. Sunny surroundings overlooking the Arno. Singles L27,000, doubles L42,000. Breakfast included. No curfew. Reservations accepted.

Pensione La Scaletta, via Guicciardini, 13 (tel. 28 30 28), just across the Ponte Vecchio. Gracious management and a glorious rooftop terrace. Singles with bath L45,000, doubles L58,000, with bath L70,500. Breakfast included. No curfew. Telephone reservations sometimes accepted.

Pensione Sorelle Bandini, p. Santo Spirito, 9 (tel. 21 53 08). Old-world elegance and amicable people on the top floor of a large *palazzo.* Beautiful sun-filled *loggia.* Often booked by groups, but worth trying. Good English spoken. Doubles L49,500, with bath L58,000. Showers and breakfast included. No curfew. Reservations accepted.

Camping

Camping Italiani e Stranieri, viale Michelangelo, 80 (tel. 681 19 77), near piazzale Michelangelo. Take bus #13 from the station. An excellent view, one you'll share with *many* others. May tell you they're full if you phone, but if you show up with your pack, they'll always offer you a space. L4300 per person, L5000 per tent. Open April-Oct.

Camping Villa Camerata, viale A. Righi, 2/A (tel. 61 03 00), near the youth hostel. Take bus #17B from the station. L3600 per person, L3200 per tent. Open April-Oct.

Food

Florentine food, like all things Florentine, is done with style. Restaurants in the city are generally outstanding, though few are cheap. To help defray food costs, try the fare at the city's numerous *rosticcerie* and *gastronomie;* do-it-yourselfers should go to the enormous **Mercato Centrale,** near San Lorenzo, for supplies. (Open June-Sept. Mon.-Sat. 8am-1pm; Oct.-May Mon.-Sat. 6:30am-1pm and 4-8:30pm.)

No day in Florence would be complete without a dish of *gelato.* Two *gelaterìa* are particularly outstanding: **Gelateria Vivoli,** via Isole delle Stinche, 7, behind the Bargello, has flavors so rich and true, you'll almost forget it's ice-cream (open Sept.-July Tues.-Sun.); **Triangolo delle Bermude,** via Nazionale, 61*r,* serves unusual flavors including rose, whiskey, and peanuts (open Tues.-Sun. 8am-midnight).

Trattoria, via Palazzuolo, 69*r.* People stand in line for their excellent, filling, fixed-price meals for less than L10,000. Open Sept.-July Sun.-Fri. 11am-3pm and 7pm-midnight. For a similar deal and more Italians, try **Trattoria da Giorgio** at #100*r.*

Pizzeria-Ristorante I Ghibellini, p. S. Pier Maggiore, 8, off borgo degli Albizi. Lots of tourists, outdoor tables on a quiet piazza. Everything is outstanding. Full meals from L17,000. Open Thurs.-Tues. noon-4pm and 7pm-12:30am.

Le Colisée, via Cavour, 52*r.* Creative cold cuisine at excellent prices—great for a snack or light lunch. Open Sept.-July Mon-Sat. 7am-10pm.

Trattoria Da Za-Za, p. Mercato Centrale, 26*r.* Excellent food and lots of locals. Meals from L12,000. Open Mon.-Sat. noon-2:30pm and 7-10pm. Closed most of Aug. **Trattoria da Mario,** two doors down, is similarly good. *Primi* L1700-2600, *secondi* L4000-6500. Open Sept.-July Mon.-Sat. noon-3pm.

Trattoria Le Mossacce, via del Proconsolo, 55*r,* between the *duomo* and the Bargello. Affordable and delicious. Good *menù* L12,000. Open Mon.-Fri. noon-3pm and 7-10pm. Closed most of Aug.

Sights

Hundreds of years of art can't be fully appreciated in a few days. Take your time, and remember that most important sights close at 2pm, and on Sunday and Monday.

Begin with the incomparable **Uffizi;** this collection is one of the best in the world. It houses the best of the Italian Renaissance—Giotto, Cimabue, Filippo Lippi, Paolo Uccello, Piero della Francesca, Botticelli, Leonardo da Vinci, Michelangelo, Raphael, and Titian—plus some superb examples of northern art, including Rubens, Rembrandt, and Dürer. Unfortunately, crowds can be a real problem, so try to come very early or during the lunch hour. (Open Tues.-Sat. 9am-7pm, Sun. 9am-1pm. Admission L5000.) Vasari designed the Uffizi, and incorporated a secret **corridor** (tel. 21 83 41) between Palazzo Vecchio and Palazzo Pitti in the Oltrarno; the corridor runs through the Uffizi and over the Ponte Vecchio, and displays more art, including a special collection of artists' self-portraits. (Open Wed., Fri., and Sun. at 9:30am by appointment only. Admission included in Uffizi fee.)

Piazza della Signoria, dominated by the mass of the **Palazzo Vecchio,** was the original setting for Michelangelo's *David,* but this and a number of his other works (including the unfinished *Prisoners* series) are now located in the **Accademia,** via Ricasoli, 60. (Open Tues.-Sat. 9am-2pm, Sun. 9am-1pm. Admission L4000.) Get here before 9am to avoid the crush. Near the Palazzo Vecchio on via del Proconsolo lies the **Museo Nazionale,** containing the best of Florentine sculpture. Housed in the **Bargello**—the medieval palace of the chiefs of police—the collection includes works by Donatello, Michelangelo, Giambologna, and Cellini. (Open Tues.-Sat. 9am-2pm, Sun. 9am-1pm. Admission L3000.)

The symbol of Florence for centuries, the **duomo** stands at the heart of the city, down via del Proconsolo from p. della Signoria. Begun in 1299, the huge building has always said more about Florentines' civic pride than about their piety. The masterful octagonal dome which Brunelleschi built to span a crossing no one else could attempt was a marvel of the fifteenth century. If you climb the dome for the view, you'll be able to examine first-hand the ingenious double shells which Brunelleschi employed; be sure to explore the church's echoing interior as well. The *duomo* is a house of worship, and those in immodest attire (bare shoulders or legs) will be turned away. (*Duomo* open daily 7am-noon and 2:30-6pm. Free. Dome open Mon.-Sat. 8:30am-12:30pm and 2:30-5pm. Admission L3000.) The much older **Battistero** (Baptistery), just in front of the *duomo,* is famous for its bronze doors, the southern set by Andrea Pisano, the others by Ghiberti, whose naturalistic style enabled him to beat Brunelleschi in their famous 1401 competition. (Interior open daily 9am-12:30pm and 2:30-5:30pm.) Next to the *duomo* stands the brightly-colored **Campanile,** or "Giotto's Tower." (Open in summer daily 9am-7pm; in winter 9am-5pm; last climbers admitted 40 min. before closing. Admission L3000.) Most of the *duomo's* sculpture is housed in the nearby **Museo dell'Opera del Duomo.** The collection includes an unfinished *Pietà* by Michelangelo; the figure of St. John is a self-portrait in stone. (Open March-Oct. Mon.-Sat. 9am-8pm, Sun. 10am-1pm; Nov.-Feb. Mon.-Sat. 9am-6pm, Sun. 10am-1pm. Admission Mon.-Sat. L3000; free Sun.)

In many ways, the churches of Florence are its museums. Lorenzo il Magnifico, the great Medici political boss and patron of the arts, is buried in the **Basilica di San Lorenzo,** one of the great creations of the early Renaissance architect Brunelleschi. To the left of the church entrance, you'll find access to the **Biblioteca Laurenziana,** whose rooms, designed by Michelangelo, are among the most important sources of mannerist architecture. (Open Mon.-Sat. 9am-5pm. Free.) Through the market at the opposite end of the basilica you'll find the **Cappella dei Principi** (Princes' Chapel). Michelangelo's simple, unfinished **New Sacristy,** the final resting place of Lorenzo and Giuliano de' Medici, stands in sharp contrast to the gaudy, ornate chapel that shelters it. (Open Tues.-Sat. 9am-2pm, Sun. 9am-1pm. Admission L4350.) Michelangelo used the walls of a basement room beneath the New Sacristy as a sketch pad. You must ask for a supplementary ticket (free) to *la sala di Michelangelo* when purchasing the regular admission, and then approach one of the guards standing in front of an unmarked door in a corner of the New Sacristy.

Near the Accademia, the **Museo del San Marco** has a series of monks' cells decorated by Fra Angelico, who was nearly canonized for his unique shade of blue. (Open Tues.-Sat. 9am-2pm, Sun. 9am-1pm. Admission L3000.) Masaccio's *Holy Trinity* may be seen in the Dominican **Basilica di Santa Maria Novella.** In its **Spanish Chapel** are the famous Bonaiuti frescoes depicting the history of the Dominican order. (Open Mon.-Thurs. and Sat. 9am-7pm, Sun. 8am-1pm. Admission L3000.) To grasp Masaccio's revolutionary representation of three-dimensional space on a two-dimensional surface, walk over to the **Church of Santa Croce** to see the spectacular but flatter frescoes Giotto painted a century earlier. Afterwards, stop next door to see Brunelleschi's **Pazzi Chapel** in Santa Croce's cloister. (Open March-Sept. Thurs.-Tues. 9am-12:30pm and 3-6:30pm; Oct.-Feb. until 5pm. Admission L2000.) Florence's most remarkable frescoes are those by **Carmine,** in Oltrarno; the finest panels depict the *Rendering of the Tribute Money* and *The Expulsion from Paradise.*

Strewn about the city in all their outsized glory are various *palazzi,* grand palaces that reflect the architectural magnificence of the Renaissance. The **Palazzo Medici,** just around the corner from the *duomo,* was one of the first of the genre. Where the Medici led, others quickly followed: High points of the building boom that ensued include the huge **Palazzo Strozzi,** in many ways the quintessential Tuscan *palazzo,* with its rustified stonework and carefully articulated facade. The facade of the **Palazzo Rucellai** was Alberti's characteristically unique contribution. Across the **Ponte Vecchio,** with its assortment of expensive jewelers, souvenir stands, and international flotsam, is the **Palazzo Pitti,** another onetime Medici stronghold, which now contains several fine museums, most notably the **Galleria Palatina.** (Open Tues.-Sat. 9am-2pm, Sun. 9am-1pm. Admission L4000.) Behind the palace are the **Giardini Boboli,** magnificent gardens that slope uphill toward the **Forte Belvedere,** which regularly hosts outstanding traveling sculpture exhibitions. (Gardens open May-Aug. daily 9am-6:30pm; March-April and Sept.-Oct. 9am-5:30pm; Nov.-Feb. 9am-4:30pm. Fort open in summer daily 9am-8pm; in winter until dusk. Accessible along via Costa San Giorgio. Free. Admission to Belvedere exhibitions varies.) The views of the city from the Forte and **piazzale Michelangelo** at the summit of the hill are stunning.

For a broad analysis of the art and times of the Florentine Renaissance, consult Jacob Burckhardt's definitive work *The Civilization of the Renaissance in Italy,* Mary McCarthy's *The Stones of Florence,* or *Let's Go: Italy.* Benvenuto Cellini's *Autobiography* is an easily read account of the times of a famous Florentine artisan and desperado.

Entertainment

Crowds thread their way through Florence's streets every evening in fair weather. Florentines and tourists alike congregate on the steps of the *duomo,* along via Calzaiuoli, on piazza della Signoria, on the Ponte Vecchio, and on piazzale Michelangelo. Those who like to move a bit faster may enjoy dancing at **Space Electronic,** via Palazzuolo, 37 (open in summer nightly 9:30pm-1:30am; in winter Tues.-Sun.; cover L12,000, L2000 less with a copy of this book), or the **Red Garter,** via dei Benci, 33*r* (open nightly 8:30pm-1am; one-drink min.). **Tabasco,** p. S. Cecilia, 3*r,* near p. della Signoria, is Florence's most popular gay disco. (Open Tues.-Sat. 9:30pm-1am. Cover Tues.-Thurs. L10,000, Fri.-Sun. L15,000.) The **Astro Cinema,** opposite Gelateria Vivoli on p. S. Simeone, shows films in English (Tues.-Sun. at 8pm and 10pm; admission L5000).

After warming up with the **Scoppio del Carro** festival on Easter Sunday, Florence enjoys another fireworks-filled celebration on June 24, the **Feast of St. John,** the city's patron saint. June also brings the traditional games of **Calcio Storico in Costume,** an archaic, hilarious form of soccer, played in historical dress (usually June 16, 24, and 28). More contemporary tastes are satisfied at the **Florence Film Festival,** held from May 24 to June 7 at the Forte Belvedere. Noteworthy musical events occur all year. Most important in summer is the **Estate Fiesolana,** which takes place in early June, July, and August, filling the old Roman theater in Fiesole with concerts, opera, theater, ballet and movies—tickets are reasonable (L6000 and up). Pick up the schedule from the EPT in Florence. Bus #7 runs to Fiesole from Florence's train station (30 min.). In July the summer season at the **Teatro Comunale** offers ballet and concerts in the courtyard of the Palazzo Pitti, and the international music festival, **Maggio Musicale Fiorentino,** takes place in May and June. For tickets, visit the box office at corso Italia, 16. (Open Tues.-Sun. 9am-1pm. Seats L15,000-40,000.)

Siena

In an area well-known for its art, Siena stands as a living masterpiece, a tribute to the gentle care and creativity of its builders and inhabitants. In few other places does an entire town come together as harmoniously as Siena; the city's medieval perfection extends even to harmony with the red clay hills from which the color "burnt sienna" gets its name. Today, great care is taken to see that all modern buildings meld gracefully into the medieval landscape. Furthermore, much of Siena's historic center is closed to automobiles, protecting the red buildings from discoloration (some would claim the town's potent pigeon population more than makes up for it), and lending an air of quiet to the heart of the town.

Siena lies off the main rail lines. Change at Chiusi if coming form Rome (L12,700), or at Empoli if taking a non-direct train from Florence (L4900) and the north. Any bus across the street from the station will take you into town. Express **SITA** buses, often faster than the train, link Siena with Florence (1 hr., L5400) and Rome (3½ hr., L13,700). Siena's **telephone code** is 0577.

Siena's **Duomo,** though less imaginative than its Florentine counterpart, is meticulously crafted. Nicola Pisano's pulpit, with scenes of the life of Christ, is remarkably expressive for its period. (Open April-Oct. daily 9am-7pm; Nov.-March daily 8am-5pm.) The **Battistero** (baptistry), at the back of the church (separate entrance), contains a font by Jacopo della Quercia, and Donatello's *Herod's Banquet,* an important work in the development of perspective. The **Museo dell' Opera della Metropolitana,** next to the cathedral, has some fine sculpture by Pisano, as well as Duccio's splendid *Maestà,* considered to be the culmination of Sienese painting. (Open in summer daily 9am-7:15pm; in winter daily 9am-1:45pm. Admission L3000.) If you're intrigued by this pictorial school, take in the exceptional collection of the **Pinacoteca,** via San Pietro, 29. (Open Tues.-Sat. 8:30am-7pm, Sun. 8:30am-1pm. Admission L3000.) The striking, shell-shaped **piazza del Campo** is the locus of Sienese living day and night. At the bottom of the shell is the **Palazzo Pubblico,** the most elegant Gothic palace in Tuscany. The interior is filled with more Sienese painting; climb the stairs to the tower for a spectacular view of the city. (Open April-Sept. Mon.-Sat. 9am-6:30pm, Sun. 9am-1pm; Oct.-March daily 9am-1:30pm. Admission L4000, students L2000.)

The **Azienda Autonoma di Turismo** (tel. (0577) 28 05 51) is at p. del Campo, 55; the friendly staff will offer you a map, help find rooms, and decipher transportation schedules. (Open Mon.-Sat. 9am-12:30pm and 3:30-7pm; July-Sept. also open Sun.) Try to visit Siena on July 2 or August 16 for the **Palio,** when the city erupts with night-long celebrations and colorful processions in fifteenth-century costume. The central event is a traditional horse race around the p. del Campo, jammed for the occasion by tens of thousands of people. Get there a day early to see some of the test races and to choose a *contrada* to root for; and don't miss the winning district's torch-light procession through the city the night after the race. The race is held around 7pm; the best seats are at the top of the *piazza* near the fountain, but these cost about L100,000. Infield standing-room is free, though the area is cut off from about 4pm on, and you can't leave for four or five hours. For both tickets and a list of hotels and *pensioni,* write to the tourist office by March; don't arrive without a reservation or you'll sleep in the streets.

Siena is extremely popular at any time of the summer, and has a limited number of inexpensive rooms and very few singles; arrive by noon or book ahead, particularly in July and August.

There is an excellent hostel, the **Ostello della Gioventù "Guidoriccio" (IYHF),** via Fiorentina, 17 (tel. 522 12), in Località lo Stellino, about 2km from the center of town. Take bus #10 or 15 across from the station or p. Matteoti. If coming from Florence by bus, get off at the stop just after you see the large blue sign announcing that you've entered Siena. (Members only. L10,700. Breakfast included; dinner L7000. 11pm curfew.) The **Albergo Tre Donzelle,** via delle Donzelle, 5 (tel. 28 03 58), off p. Il Campo, is a great value at a great location. (Singles (very few) L19,1000, doubles L32,500, triples L43,500. 12:30am curfew. Telephone reservations accepted and recommended.) Next door, **Albergo Nuove Donzelle,** via delle Donzelle, 1-3 (tel. 28 80 88) is not the nicest, but it's hospitable, and the price is right. (Singles L17,300, doubles L29,700, triples L40,200, quads L50,600. 12:30am curfew. Phone reservations held until noon.) **Albergo Centrale,** via Calzoleria, 24 (tel. 28 03 79), off p. Tolomei, is a clean, cavernous building that is likely to have space. (Doubles L36,300, triples L45,000. 12:30am curfew. Reservations only with deposit.) The **Al-**

bergo Chivsarelli, viale Curtatone, 9 (tel. 28 05 62), is a slowly deteriorating villa with palm trees and a garden. (Singles (very few) L24,500, with bath L35,300, doubles with bath L53,000. No curfew. Pre-paid reservations preferred.)

Siena has a wide selection of sinfully rich pastries, most notably the *panforte,* a dense conglomeration of honey, almonds, and candied fruit. Sample the large selection at **Bar Pasticceria Nannini,** via dei Banchi di Sopra, 22-24. The **Enoteca Italia** in the **Fortezza Medicea** are old dungeons put to use as wine cellars; a perfect place to throw you when you can't pay the astronomical bill. Get cafeteria-style grub at **Il Barbero,** p. Il Campo, 80-81. (Salad bar L2500, 5-course meal L1500. Open daily noon-2:30pm and 7-10pm.) Cheaper still, the **Mensa Universitaria,** via Sant' Agata, 1, is tucked away in a courtyard beneath Sant' Agata. (Meals L6000. Open Sept.-July noon-2pm and 6:45-9pm.) **Ristorante Torrido,** via Diacceto, 1, off p. Indipendenza, is where the locals come for good, reasonably priced meals. (*Primo* L2500-4000, *secondo* L7500-9000. Open Sun.-Fri.)

San Gimignano

The hilltop town of San Gimignano is a nice change from the urban closeness of Pisa or Siena. If you can avoid the place on weekends, its modest artistic and historical significance, combined with its stunning panoramas of the surrounding vineyards, might just make San Gimignano one of your favorite places in Italy.

San Gimignano has no train station, but **TRA-IN** buses connect it with Florence and Siena every 1-2 hours (L4100). Change buses at Poggibonsi. Poggibonsi is also the nearest rail station (located on the Empoli-Siena line), 20 minutes by bus from San Gimignano.

San Gimignano bristles with the tall fortress-towers of its medieval nobility. Only 15 of the original 72 still stand, reminders of the medieval factionalism and civil war which tore the city apart and put the warring Guelphs and Ghibellines, the Italian version of the Hatfields and McCoys, in their graves. Most of the surviving towers surround **piazza della Cisterna,** named after the thirteenth-century cistern in its center. Nearby **piazza del Duomo** is fronted by the **Collegiata Cathedral,** whose interior is covered with fourteenth-century frescoes. Ghirlandaio's work in the **Chapel of Santa Fina** (off the right aisle) is superb, and also shows how the town's towers once looked. The **Palazzo del Popolo** next door houses the **Museo Civico,** with a *Maestà* by Lippo Memmi, out of place amid frescoes of hunting scenes, and a radiant Lippi *Annunciation.* From the *palazzo,* climb to the top of the **Torre Grossa,** the highest tower in town. (April-Sept. daily 9:30am-12:30pm and 3:30-6:30pm; Oct.-March Tues.-Sun. 9:30am-12:30pm and 2:30-5:30pm. Comprehensive admission L2500.) At the other end of town, Gozzoli's fabulous fresco *Cycle of the Life of St. Augustine* in the **Church of Sant' Agostino** is worth seeing.

Budget accommodations are limited. The **Ostello del Chianti (IYHF),** via Roma, 137 (tel. (055) 807 70 09) is a one-hour bus ride away in Tavernelle Val di Pesa (change in Poggibonsi). (L6300 per night; membership required.) In town, the rooms at the **Convento di Sant' Agostino** on p. Sant Agostino (tel. (0577) 94 03 83) are comfortable and the cloister beautiful, but they fill quickly; reserve one month in advance by writing to the *Padre Superiore.* **The Associzone Pro Loco** on p. del Duomo has a list of private rooms to let (singles L20,000, doubles L25,000-35,000). The **Accomodations Service "La Rocca,"** via dei Fossi, 35A (tel. (0577) 94 03 87) also finds rooms in private homes for L2500 (open 9am-1pm and 3-9pm), as does the **Agenzia d'Affari "Simona,"** via S. Giovanni, 95 (tel. (0577) 94 00 26). **Camp** at **Il Boschetto,** at Santa Lucia (tel. (0577) 94 03 52), 2½km out of town (L2420 per person, L1210 for small tent).

Dining is costly and you'll pay 70% more for an outside table. Shop at the **open-air market** Thursday and Saturday morning in p. del Duomo. **Le Vecchie Mura,** via Piandornella, 15, provides great food at reasonable prices (L15,000 for complete meal) in a medieval setting. (Open Wed.-Mon. noon-2:30pm, 7-9:30pm.)

Pisa

In the minds of most tourists, Pisa is a one-dimensional (and leaning) town. But the city-state of Pisa once rivaled Genoa and Venice as a maritime republic, emulated Padua and Perugia as a university town, and developed a distinctive style of Romanesque architecture. Today Pisa relies on the tide of tourists who flow into the city every morning, and is the world's leading manufacturer of plastic Leaning Tower replicas.

The most important monuments are concentrated in the **piazza del Duomo.** The baptistery, cathedral, Leaning Tower, and Camposanto shine like carved ivory, rising out of a broad expanse of emerald green grass. The **duomo** contains Giovanni Pisano's masterful pulpit, with its violently dramatic Gothic reliefs. (Open daily 7:45am-12:45pm and 3-6:45pm.) Next door, the **battistero** houses another expressive pulpit, the first Gothic sculpture in Italy (1260), by Giovanni's father, Nicola. (Open daily 9am-12:50pm and 3-6:50pm.) You can make your unbalanced way to the top of the **Torre Pendente** (Leaning Tower), from which local boy Galileo Galilei dropped a variety of objects in his attempt to understand gravity. If you are prone to claustrophobia, acrophobia, vertigo, or uncontrollable urges to jump, don't venture up the 294 steps. (Open Easter-Sept. daily 9am-7pm; Oct.-Easter 9am-5pm. Admission L4000.) The adjoining **Camposanto** has some haunting frescoes by Benozzo Gozzoli. (Open in summer daily 8am-6:40pm; in winter 9am-5pm. Admission L2500.) The **Museo delle Sinopie,** across the street, displays elegant sketches of the frescoes. (Open in summer daily 9am-12:45pm and 3-6:45pm; in winter until 5:30pm. Admission L1000.)

The **EPT office** off p. del Duomo will provide maps and help with accommodations. (Open Mon.-Sat. 9am-noon, 3-6pm.) The places listed below are likely to have room, but you might find a cheaper place if you ask the EPT to call around for you. The **Albergo Gronchi,** p. Arcivescovado, 1 (tel. (050) 227 32), is just off p. del Duomo (singles L19,000, doubles L31,000). **Albergo Helvetia,** v. Don G. Boschi, 31 (tel. 412 32), is around the block from Gronchi, and is simple and clean (singles L20,000, doubles L31,000, with bath 38,000). Midnight curfews at both. **Albergho Milano,** via Mascagni, 4 (tel. 231 62), is around the block to the left as you leave the *stazione.* (Singles L20,000, doubles L31,000, triples L42,000, quads L53,000. Curfew 1am.) The **Casa della Giovane,** via Corridoni, 31 (tel. 227 32) is a ten-minute walk following an immediate right turn from the station, and has beds for women only at L14,000 per night, including breakfast (reception closes midnight). **Camping Torre Pendente** is just outside the gates at viale delle Cascine, 86 (tel. 56 17 04; L6000 per person, L3000 per tent.) Pisa's cheapest meals cost L2100 at the **Mensa Universitaria** on via Martiri off p. dei Cavalieri; stand at the foot of the stairs and get tickets from someone with extras. (Open Oct. to mid-July Mon.-Fri. noon-2pm and 7-9pm, Sat.-Sun. noon-2pm.) For real food go to **Da Stelio,** p. Dante, 11, where a hearty meal will run L12,000. (Open Mon.-Sat.)

Perugia

Perugia, the capital of Umbria, has it all: the beauty of a medieval hill town, the energy of a major university city, a rich artistic tradition, inexpensive food and lodging, and a central location for explorations throughout the regioin. Halfway between Rome and Florance, Perugia is a three-hour train ride from either.

The **piazza IV Novembre,** at the opposite end of corso Vannucci from p. d'Italia, sports a towering double-basined fountain, adorned with sculptures and bas-reliefs by Nicola and Giovanni Pisano. The dramatic **Palazzo dei Priori,** with its colored marble and widening steps, adds grace to the setting. The palace houses the frescoed **Sala dei Notari** and the **Galleria Nazionale dell' Umbria,** with works by Perugino, Duccio, Piero della Francesca, and Fra Angelico. (Open Tues.-Sat. 9am-2pm, Sun. 9am-1pm. Admission L4000.) Next door are the delicate frescoes of the **Collegio**

del Cambio, created by Perugino in collaboration with his pupil Raphael. (Open Tues.-Sun. 9am-12:30pm and 2:30-5:30pm. Admission L1000.) The **Museo Archeologico Nazionale dell' Umbria,** next to the Church of San Domenico near via Cavour, emphasizes the Etruscan origins of the town. (Open Mon.-Sat. 9am-2pm, Sun. 9am-1pm. Admission L2000.) The **Rocca Paolina,** a sixteenth-century fortress down via Marzia, is also the gateway to Perugia's underground city, **via Baglioni Sotteranea.** On top are the lush **Giardini Carducci,** offering a splendid view of the quilt-like countryside around Perugia; at night it becomes *the* place in Perugia to take your *amore.* Off via della Prome is the **Arch of Augustus,** the largest extant piece of Etruscan stonework.

The **Azienda di Promozione Turistica,** corso Vannucci, 94a (tel. 233 27), near p. d'Italia, has information on the city and region, as well as accommodations listings. (Open Mon.-Sat. 8:30am-1:30pm and 4-7pm, Sun. 9am-1pm.) The cheapest place to stay is the independent youth hostel, **Centro Internazionale Accoglienza per Giovani,** via Bontempi, 13 (tel. 228 80), off p. Danti by the *duomo.* (Bunks L8000. Sheets L1000. Lockout 9:30am-4pm. Strict midnight curfew.) If you're not into the hostel scene, try the **Pensione Paolo,** via della Canapina, 5 (tel. 238 16), with very friendly management and beautifully furnished rooms. (Singles L16,000, doubles L21,000. Reservations recommended.) At the **Albergo Etruria,** via della Luna, 21 (tel. 237 30), off corso Vannucci, the rooms have less character than the twelfth-century entranceway, but are large and quiet nonetheless. (Singles L17,200, doubles L23,100. Showers a whopping L3,500.)

Dining in Perugia is both good and cheap—a rare combination in Italy these days. The best deal is at **Trattoria la Botte,** via Volte della Pace, 31, off via Bontempi behind p. Danti, where a filling *menu* costs L6,500. A slightly classier spot, near the foreigners' university, is **Trattoria Fratelli Brizi,** via Fabretti, 75. (L13,000 *menu.*) At **Pizzeria Medio Evo,** via Baldo just off corso Vannucci, L4000 gets you thicker-crusted pizza than usually found in Italy. Top it off with excellent and inexpensive gelato at **Gelateria 2000,** via Luigi Bonazzi, 3, or **Gelateria Veneta,** corso Vanucci, 20, both right off the main drag.

Perugia is connected to towns throughout Umbria and to Rome and Florence by bus and train; city buses regularly connect the station in the valley with piazza d'Italia in the center of town (L500). Perugia's **telephone code** is 075.

Near Perugia

Perugia is the only reasonably-priced place to stay in Umbria. Nevertheless, daytrips to any of a half-dozen towns in Umbria are a delight, almost as much for the beautiful vistas along the way as for the towns themselves.

Gubbio, north of Perugia, seems almost forgotten by time—a medieval period piece sprung from the forested Umbrian cliffs. In the main piazza della Signoria you can view the **Palazzo dei Consoli,** a beautiful pre-Renaissance structure with superb detailing. Inside is the **Museo Civico,** which contains the Tavole Eugubine, seven rare and remarkable bronze tablets from the third through first centuries B.C.E., written in the long-dead Umbrian language. (Open May-Sept. 9am-12:30pm and 3:30-6pm; Oct.-April 9am-1pm and 3-5pm. Admission L2000, students L1500.) The Renaissance **Palazzo Ducale** and the rosy Gothic **Duomo** face each other at the top of the town. (Open Tues.-Sat. 9am-2pm, Sun. 9am-1pm. Free.) To immerse yourself in Gubbio's architecture, walk along via dei Consoli, via Vantaggi, via Gabrielli, and via del Popolo, all lined with medieval *palazzi.* A cable car climbs **Monte Ingino,** which affords a marvelous view of the Apennines.

Every May 15, the **Festival of the Ceri** brings an unusual sort of revelry to the usually sleepy city. Teams of men in traditional garb carry the *ceri,* giant wooden structures of uncertain origin, on a mad race through the streets. The last Sunday in May is highlighted by the **Palio della Balestra,** or crossbow competition, in which Gubbio's archers take on arch-rival Borgo S. Sepolcro; municipal officials join in the fun by dressing up in their medieval outfits, making the place look like a deck of playing cards come to life.

The **Azienda Autonoma di Turismo** is at corso Garibaldi, 6 (tel. (075) 927 36 93), next to the Communist Party offices in p. Oderisi. (Open Mon.-Sat. 8:30am-1:30pm and 3-7pm (3-6pm in winter), Sun. 9:30am-12:30pm). If you must spend the night in Gubbio, the **Hotel Oderisi,** via Mazzatini, 2 (tel. (075) 927 37 47), is nothing to shout about, but probably has space. (Singles L19,000, with bath L25,000; doubles L29,000, with bath L36,000.) Outstanding pizza is available for L3500 to L6500 at **Pizzeria Il Bargello,** via dei Consoli, 37; or try **Trattoria San Martino,** via dei Consoli, 8, near p. Bruno, for meals starting at L15,000.

ASP buses cover the gorgeous countryside between Gubbio and Perugia (10 per day, 1 hr., L6000 round-trip). The nearest train station is at Fossato di Vico on the Rome-Ancona line; buses run to Gubbio regularly (L1600).

Assisi

Assisi is pervaded with a serenity and beauty that overcomes all—even the tasteless knickknacks of the town's booming tourist trade. In the evenings and at mealtimes, the hordes retire, leaving silent the steep, narrow streets. This seems a fitting birthplace for the gentle, meditative St. Francis, founder of the Franciscan Order and one of the best known figures of Catholicism. Soon after his death in 1226, the greatest Florentine and Sienese painters came to Assisi to decorate the **Basilica di San Francesco** in his honor; they left a spectacular concentration of frescoes illustrating the story of St. Francis' life. The lower church contains additional work by the early Italian masters, including Cimabue, Simone Martini, Pietro Lorenzetti, and members of Giotto's school. (Open in summer 8am-7pm; in winter 8am-12:30pm and 2-8pm. English-language Mass Sun. at 8:30am.) A one-hour hike through Porta di Cappuccini up a steep hill will take you to the **Eremo delle Carceri,** the hermitage where St. Francis went on retreat. (open in summer 6:30am-8pm; in winter 6:30am-5pm.)

Tourist officials say they expect a youth hostel to open by 1988; check with **Azienda di Promozione Turistica,** p. del Comune 12 (tel. 81 25 34), for an update, or for other help with lodgings. (Open April-Oct. 9am-1pm and 4-7pm; Nov.-March Mon.-Sat. 9am-noon and 3:30-6:30pm.) Several houses along the main street leading uphill from the Basilica di San Francesco offer *camere libere* for about L15,000 per person. In town, try the **Albergo La Rocca,** via Porta Perlici, 25 (tel. 81 22 84), near the *duomo.* (Singles L14,000, doubles L23,000, with bath L32,000. Showers L2500.) **Locanda Anfiteatro Romano,** via Anfiteatro, 4 (tel. 81 30 25), is off p. Matteotti, behind the *duomo.* (Singles L17,000, doubles 23,100.) For food, consider the pleasant **Pallotta,** via S. Rufino, 4, near p. del Comune. (Meals about L15,000. Open Wed.-Mon.) The **Ristorante-Pizzeria** at via Italia, 34, serves pizza for around L4000. (Open Tues.-Sun.)

Assisi sits on the Foligno-Terontola rail line, about 45 minutes down the tracks from Perugia (L2000); from Florence change at Terontola; from Rome or Ancona change at Foligno. Assisi is also connected by bus to Perugia and other Umbrian towns. Assisi's **telephone code** is also 075.

Rome (Roma)

Fifteen hundred years ago Saint Ambrose advised Saint Augustine, "When you are in Rome, live as the Romans do." Good advice endures; instead of racing around the city to see a bunch of monuments, enjoy a cup of coffee at an outdoor cafe in the piazza Venezia, attend mass at St. Peter's, buy fruit in Trastevere, dine late, or stroll from the Spanish Steps to the piazza del Popolo. To Romans, their city is not a museum, but a practical home. Locals hang their laundry on priceless build-

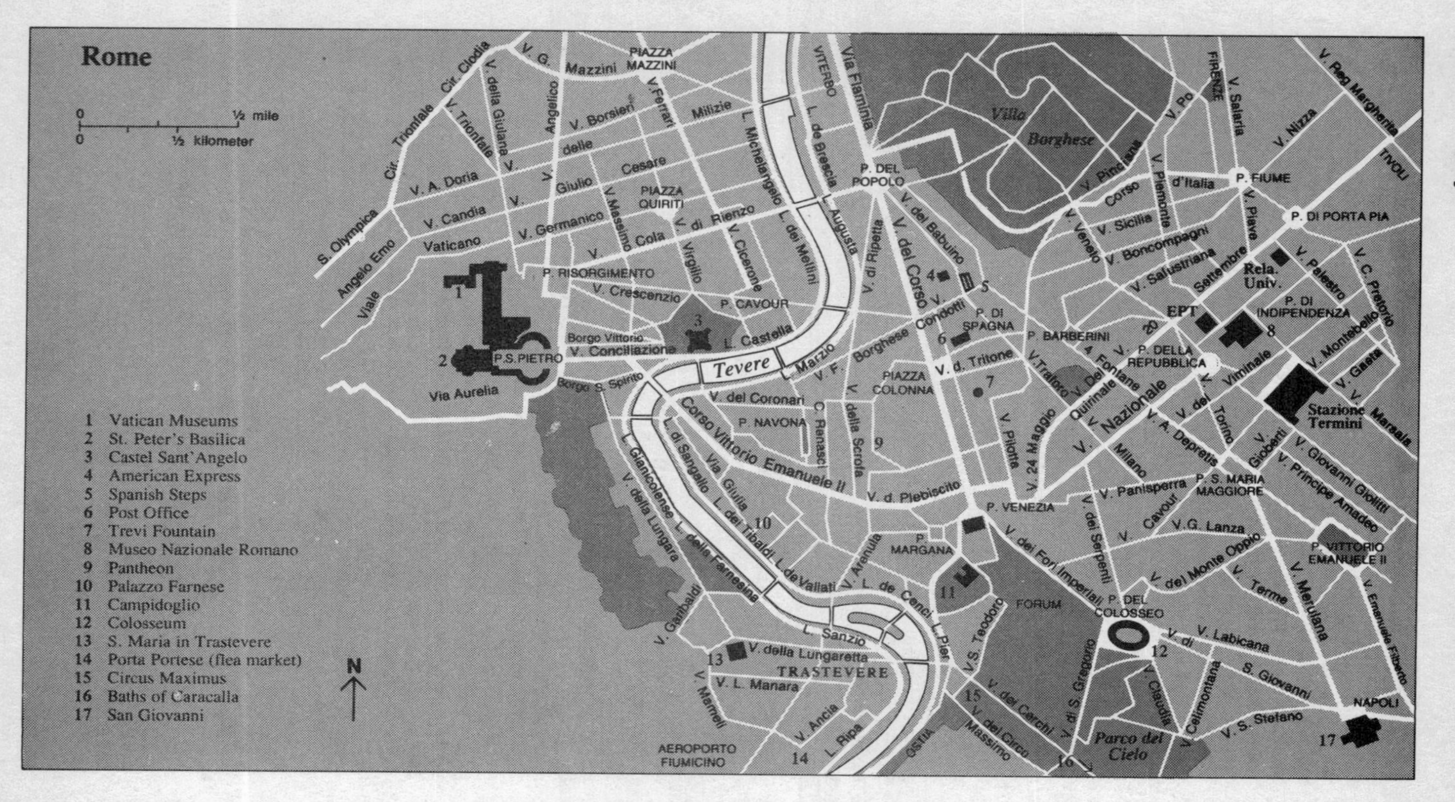
Rome
0 ½ mile
0 ½ kilometer
1 Vatican Museums
2 St. Peter's Basilica
3 Castel Sant'Angelo
4 American Express
5 Spanish Steps
6 Post Office
7 Trevi Fountain
8 Museo Nazionale Romano
9 Pantheon
10 Palazzo Farnese
11 Campidoglio
12 Colosseum
13 S. Maria in Trastevere
14 Porta Portese (flea market)
15 Circus Maximus
16 Baths of Caracalla
17 San Giovanni
N
Villa Borghese
Tevere
TRASTEVERE
Stazione Termini
FORUM
Parco del Cielo
Rela. Univ.
EPT
V. del Corso
V. Nazionale
V. Merulana
Corso Vittorio Emanuele II
Via Flaminia
Via Aurelia
V. Conciliazione
V. Veneto
V. del Babuino
V. d. Tritone
V. d. Plebiscito
V. dei Fori Imperiali
V. Cavour
V. Labicana
P. DEL POPOLO
P.S.PIETRO
P. RISORGIMENTO
P. CAVOUR
P. VENEZIA
P. DI SPAGNA
P. BARBERINI
P. DELLA REPUBBLICA
P. DI INDIPENDENZA
P. FIUME
P. DI PORTA PIA
P. S. MARIA MAGGIORE
P. VITTORIO EMANUELE II
P. DEL COLOSSEO
P. NAVONA
P. MARGANA
PIAZZA COLONNA
PIAZZA MAZZINI
PIAZZA QUIRITI
NAPOLI
AEROPORTO FIUMICINO
OSTIA

ings, while movies and soccer games are projected on vast screens in the majestic *piazze.*

Orientation and Practical Information

No longer defined by the Seven Hills, Rome sprawls over a large area between the hills of the Castelli Romani and the beach at Ostia. Even so, the city can be managed on foot; from Termini, the main train station, almost everything you'll want to see is in a compact area to the west. To the northwest is the plush area of glossy shops and glassy-eyed tourists around **piazza di Spagna** and **via Veneto,** and above them, Rome's largest park, the **Villa Borghese;** southwest are most of the Roman remains, including the Forum, Palatine, and Colosseum; due west is the **old city;** and across the **River Tiber** are **Vatican City** and the **Trastevere** quarter.

When it comes to schedules, Rome is mystifying and frustrating. Some generalizations are possible: most shops and offices are open Monday through Friday from 9am to 1pm and 3:30 to 7:30pm, and often Saturday mornings. On Monday mornings in winter, most shops are closed. Food stores are closed on Thursdays throughout the year. Many monuments and sights close by 2pm. The city really rolls up the sidewalks on weekends; in particular, don't forget to change money on Friday morning, because only the *cambio* in Termini and American Express are open the next day, and lines are long.

Rome in August is much like the Sahara Desert—lots of dry wind and no people. All but the cats desert Rome for the beaches and mountains, and it's difficult to find much of anything—including restaurants—open.

Tourist Offices: Ente Provinciale per il Turismo (EPT), office in Stazione Termini, between tracks 1 and 2. Open daily 9am-7pm. Headquarters 10 min. away at via Parigi, 5, off p. della Repubblica. Open May-Sept. Mon.-Sat. 8:30am-1pm and 2-7pm; Oct.-April Mon.-Sat. 8:30am-1pm and 4-7pm. At either, grab a street map and give the accommodations service a try, though they call inexpensive places only for the truly persistent. Better to give the number of a place you've selected and ask them to call for you. Also available are the useful pamphlets *Roma Giovane* (in English, *Young Rome*) and *Qui Roma,* which list current events and hours. **Italian Youth Hostels Association (AIG),** lungotevere Marescialio Cadorna, 31 (tel. 396 00 09). No beds here but plenty of helpful advice and lists of hostels throughout Italy. Definitely worth a visit.

Budget Travel: Centro Turistico Studentesco (CTS), via Genova, 16 (tel. 47 99 31). Discounts, BIGE tickets, and an accommodations service for Rome *and* other Italian cities. Open Mon.-Fri. 9am-1pm and 4-7pm, Sat. 9am-1pm. BIGE tickets also sold from the Transalpino booth at **Termini aisle #6.** Open daily 8:30am-9:30pm. Rome is *not* a bargain-travel center for flights; some cheap long distance bus tickets are available at CTS.

American Express: p. di Spagna, 38 (tel. 676 41). Mail held. All banking services. Go early in the morning and not at all on Sat. to avoid huge lines. Open Mon.-Fri. 9am-5:30pm, Sat. 9am-1pm. To replace lost or stolen cards or checks, call 54 79 81 (24 hours).

Currency Exchange: Avoid weekend exchange; only American Express and the *cambio* in the station are open Sat., the latter on Sun. (though erratically). Very long lines.

Post Office: Main office in p. San Silvestro. Open Mon.-Fri. 8:30am-8pm, Sat. 8:30am-noon. Fermo Posta held here, but to mail packages heavier than 1kg, go to p. dei Caprettari near the Pantheon. Vatican post office, p. San Pietro, is faster and much more reliable. Open Mon.-Fri. 8:30am-7pm, Sat. 8:30am-6pm. No Fermo posta here.

Telephones: ASST, next to the main post office. Open 8am-midnight. Also at Termini. Open 24 hours. **SIP** (domestic calls only), via Santa Maria. Open 8am-9:45pm. **Telephone code:** 06.

Flights: International and domestic flights touch down at Aeroporto Leonardo da Vinci, usually referred to as **Fiumicino.** Take the Acotral bus to Stazione Termini (4 per hr., 1 hr., L5000); catch the bus for Fiumicino on via Giovanni Giolitti (to the right of the station as you face Termini). Many charters arrive at **Ciampino;** take the Acotral bus (1 per hr., L700) to the Subaugusta stop on Metro line A.

Trains: All trains come and go from **Stazione Termini,** the center of all Rome's transportation. Practically a city itself, with information, money exchange, baggage storage, ticket agencies, bars, over-priced restaurants, day hotels, barber shops, and even an aquarium. Watch for pickpockets and cardboard-waving children. Brindisi trains leave at 7:15am, 9:05am, 1:05pm, 6:15pm, and 10:25pm. BIGE agents can sell you a Greece ticket, as can the **Hellenic Mediterranean Lines,** via Umbria, 21 (tel. 474 01 41), near via Veneto.

Buses: Compagnia Italiana di Turismo (CIT), p. della Repubblica 64 (tel. 479 44 11), sells bus tickets to destinations all over Italy. They speak no English. Open Mon.-Sat. 6:30am-8pm, Sun. 6:30am-3:30pm. Ask at CTS if you can't make yourself understood here.

Public Transportation: Rome's perpetually slow-moving traffic may convince you that the best transportation is your feet. However, the **ATAC** bus system is cheap and efficient. Buy bus tickets (L700; L6000 for 10 rides) at *tabacchi* (kiosks) or at the occasional corner vending machine. Regular buses run until around midnight; infrequent night service continues until 5:30am. A bus route map (L1000) is available at the ATAC kiosk in the piazza in front of Termini. For longer hauls, take the **Metropolitana** (L700; L6000 for 10 rides); its two lines intersect at Termini. Trains run until 11:30pm.

Emergencies: Police (tel. 113). Police headquarters for foreigners *(Ufficio Stranieri)* in the *Questura* at via Genova, 2 (tel. 46 86); English speakers available 24 hours.

Medical Assistance: Policlinico A. Gemelli, largo A. Gemelli, 18 (tel. 330 51, emergencies 338 37 30 or 33 05 40 36). **V.D. Clinic,** via dei Fratte de Trastevere, 34.

Pharmacies: Dial 19 21 for listings of all-night places. Recording in Italian.

Crises: The Samaritans, in the Chiesa di San Silvestro on p. San Silvestro (tel. 678 92 27). English-speaking help for despair and suicide. Available daily 4:30-10:30pm.

Embassies: U.S., via Vittorio Veneto, 119a (tel. 46 74). **Canada,** via G. B. Rossi (tel. 85 53 41). **U.K.,** via XX Settembre, 80a (tel. 475 54 41). **Australia,** via Alessandria, 215 (tel. 84 12 41). **New Zealand,** via Zara, 28 (tel. 85 12 25).

Bookstores: Economy Book Center, via Torino, 136 (tel. 474 68 77). A treasure trove of English and American books. Used and discounted books, trade-ins taken. Open Oct.-June Mon. 3:30-7:30pm, Tues.-Sat. 9:30am-7:30pm; July-Sept. Mon.-Fri. 9:30am-7:30pm, Sat. 9:30am-1:30pm. **American Book Shop,** via della Vite, 57 (tel. 679 52 22). Also an excellent selection. Open Mon. 4-8pm, Tues.-Sat. 9am-1pm and 4-8pm; July-Aug. open Mon. morning, closed Sat. afternoon.

Laundry: The Italian word is *lavanderia.* Try **Lavaservice,** via Montebello, 11. Open Mon.-Fri. 9am-7pm, Sat. 9am-1pm. **Via dei Serpenti, 131,** 1½ blocks off via Cavour. Open Mon.-Fri. 8am-1pm and 3-7:30pm. A load of 3-4kg costs L10,000.

Hitchhiking: North toward Florence, take bus #319 to p. Vescovio and then #135 onto via Salaria (get off near the *autostrada*). South toward Naples, take Metro line A to Anagnina (last stop) on via Tuscolana, right in front of the *autostrada.*

Accommodations and Camping

Though full of tourists in July and August, Rome is also full of *alberghi* (hotels), *pensioni,* and *locande.* Prices aren't always posted, the best places are usually full, proprietors can play hard-to-get, singles seem to exist only in your imagination, and the dearth of elevators (if you do find one, it's likely to be coin-operated, requiring hard-to-find L10, 50, and 100 coins) makes trudging around an exhausting experience. Try to make reservations, even if only by phone (agree on a time by which you'll arrive). Otherwise, *arrive early.*

The tourist offices and budget travel agents will usually help you find a place, but they usually won't deal with the cheapest places.

Hostels and Institutions

Roman hostels are not much cheaper than private accommodations, and their curfews and evictions—shortly following sunset and sunrise—may cramp your style. Solo travelers should note that many *pensioni* near the station rent by the bed.

Ostello del Foro Italico (IYHF), viale delle Olimpiadi, 61 (tel. 396 47 09), miles from town. Take Metro line A to Ottaviano or bus #492 to the last stop, and transfer to bus #32. Not worth the trip. L11,000. Max. stay 3 nights. Curfew 11pm.

Protezione della Giovane, via Urbana, 158 (tel. 46 00 56). For women only. Take via d'Azeglio on the left from Termini; it becomes via Urbana after a few blocks. L10,000. Curfew 10pm.

University Housing, via Cesare de Lollis, 24/B and viale del Ministro degli Affari Esteri, 6. Contact EPT (tel. 46 37 48) or AIG (tel. 396 00 09) for more information. L12,500 for B&B. Open late July to mid-Sept.

Hotels and Pensions

Near the Station

The area around the station is packed with inexpensive hotels. Though the *pensioni* themselves are often clean, comfortable, and friendly, the neighborhood can be depressing and a little dangerous. Some hotels and restaurants in this area raise their prices at the sound of a foreign voice; they give themselves away by asking more than L18,000 per person. Whichever direction you head, leave your pack at the station (L800).

The area to the right as you exit Stazione Termini, surrounding via Montebello, is quieter and less shabby, but farther from the major sights.

Pensione Papá Germano, via Calatafimi, 14a (tel. 48 69 19). Friendly English-speaking owners run the best budget *pensione* in Rome. Often full, so try before 11am. Single beds L12,000, single rooms L15,000. Showers included. Nov.-March, also doubles L30,000, with showers L35,000.

Pensione Katty, via Palestro, 35, 3rd floor (tel. 475 13 85). At L10,000 per person in triples, L24,000 for doubles, this is about as cheap as it gets.

Pensione Cina, via Montebello, 114, 4th floor (tel. 46 40 32). Clean rooms, and one of the few places with reading lights on night tables. L12,000 per person in triples, L1000 extra for a stay of only 1 night.

Pensione Cervina, via Palestro, 55 (tel. 49 10 57). Friendly management, large rooms. L12,000 per person in multi-bed rooms; singles L16,000, showers L1000. On the 3rd floor, **Pensione Restivo** (tel. 49 21 72) is nicer but costlier. Clean singles L20,000, doubles L30,000.

Pensione Lachea, via Martino della Battaglia, 11 (tel. 495 72 56). Very friendly proprietor. Singles L20,000, doubles L30,000, triples L45,000.

Pensione Stella, via Castelfidardo, 51 (tel. 475 46 32). Clean rooms for the right price. Singles L20,000; doubles L33,000, with bath L50,000.

Pensione Danubio, via Palestro, 34 (tel. 474 36 08), and **Pensione Positano,** via Palestro, 49 (tel. 49 03 60), are nice splurges. Singles (only at Danubio) L24,000; doubles L40,000, with bath L45,000.

Hotel Floridia, via Montebello, 45 (tel. 475 70 64). Lots of space. Singles with private toilet and shower L23,000, doubles L43,000.

Petit Hotel Asmara, via Castelfidardo, 31 (tel. 474 28 94). L14,000 per person in triples, singles L20,000, doubles L28,000. Lots of space, no curfew.

The area to the left as you leave the station, surrounding via Principe Amedeo, is home to scads of budget hotels, though the neighborhood, especially around p. Vittorio Emanuele, is run-down and somewhat unsafe at night.

Soggiorno Pezzotti, via Principe Amedeo, 79 (tel. 73 46 33). The best bargain on the street. Pleasant clean rooms and an obliging proprietor. L14,000 per person. Showers included. Reservations not accepted.

Pensione di Rienzo, via Principe Amedeo, 79a, 1st floor (tel. 73 69 56). Also **Pensione Cotorillo** on the fifth floor (731 60 64). Both rickety but bearable; English spoken. At Rienzo, singles L21,000, doubles 32,000. At Cotorillo, singles L20,000, doubles L28,000. Showers included.

Pensione Tony, via Principe Amedeo, 79d (tel. 73 69 94). Very clean and friendly. Doubles L32,000. Showers L1500. Doubles with shower L37,000. Flexible midnight curfew. Reservations recommended.

Pensione Terni, via Principe Amedeo, 62 (tel. 474 54 28), to the left as you enter the building. Spacious, well-decorated rooms. Singles L20,000; doubles L30,000, with bath L35,000. On the right side of the building is **Pensione Fiorini** (tel. 46 50 65), almost as nice and a little cheaper. Singles L21,000, doubles L32,000. (You may skip breakfast for a L2000 reduction.)

Pensione Morgana, via Turati, 37 (tel. 73 48 74). Dozens of rooms of varying condition and price, with a very friendly English-speaking management. From L15,000 per person in triples and quads to L55,000 for a double with private shower.

Near the Center

Rome gets more expensive as you travel away from the center. Higher prices, though, get you out of the backpackers' ghetto and closer to the action.

Pensione Navona, via dei Sediari, 8 (tel. 686 42 03), 2 short blocks from the southeast corner of p. Navona, in the happeningest hangout of the old city. Singles L28,600, doubles L47,200, triples and quads L22,000 per person. Breakfast included. Reservations strongly recommended.

Albergo Sole, via del Biscione (tel. 654 08 73), behind S. Andrea della Valle. Large and cheap for this part of town; no surprise, it's a run-down building with inattentive management. Singles L18,000, doubles L30,000, triples L45,000. Reservations accepted.

Pensione Fiorella, via del Babuino, 196 (tel. 361 05 97), less than a block from p. del Popolo. Great location and amiable management. Singles L22,400, doubles L39,400. Breakfast included. Reservations not accepted.

Pensione Irene, via del Lavatore, 37 (tel. 679 11 31), near the Trevi fountain. Spare but clean rooms at a decent price for this location. The management can be less than helpful. Singles L14,500, doubles L25,700, triples 34,000. Showers L2000. Reservations not accepted.

Albergo Palermo, via del Gambero, 21 (tel. 679 18 25), 1 block east of via del Corso, in the heart of Rome's most trendiest area, near p. di Spagna. Tiny, dark and dirty rooms, some with makeshift wiring and lighting and primitive plumbing. But hey, some rooms even have balconies, and the view almost compensates for the 6-story climb. Singles L15,900, doubles L32,000. Showers L1500.

Pensione Parlamento, via delle Convertite, 5 (tel. 678 78 80), 1 block from the Chamber of Deputies. Nice rooms in a central location. Singles L32,000, doubles L42,000. Reservations recommended.

Pensione Zurigo (tel. 35 01 39) is the best of the several *pensioni* at via Germanico, 198, near the Vatican. No singles, but doubles at L33,000. Single beds in crowded rooms L15,000. Reservations accepted. **Pensione Nautilus** (tel. 31 55 49) has doubles for L34,000, while doubles at **Residence Guiggioli** (tel. 31 52 09) go for L37,000, triples with bath L50,000. Reservations accepted.

Camping

The closest and best campground is **Flaminio,** via Flaminio (tel. 327 90 06), 8km out of town. Take Metro line A to Flaminio, then bus #202, 204, or 205. (L6100 per person, L2900 per tent. Open April-Oct.) **Capitol Campground,** via di Castelfusano (tel. 566 27 20), in Ostia Antica, is 3km from the ruins and has a swimming pool and tennis courts. (L4600 per person, L2250 per tent. Open year-round.) Take the train from the Piramide Metro station to Ostia Antica, then walk or hitchhike the 3km; or take the train to Lido Centro and bus #5 to the site. Closer to Rome is **Nomentano,** via della Cesarina (tel. 610 02 96), at the corner of via Nomentana. (L5800 per person, L2900 per tent. Open March-Oct.) Take bus #36 from Termini and transfer to bus #337 at p. Sempione.

Those who enjoy living won't sleep out in Rome; if such is unavoidable, store your bags and sleep in the train station, with your money kept under your clothes. The larger your group, the less likely you'll be victimized.

Food

A Roman evening—Vermouth or Campari at a sidewalk cafe, followed by dinner, and then coffee at another cafe—is one of the city's great contributions to civilization. This ritual lasts from about 7pm to midnight, and tends to obscure eating itself.

When looking for a restaurant, walk away from hotels, menus in English, and main streets. There is no hard and fast rule, but generally, *trattorie* near Termini are likely to be poor values; similar places around **piazza Navona** or in **Trastevere** are a better bet. You can find a good *menu turistico* for about L12,000-18,000, or enjoy a more imaginative meal for L14,000-25,000. A sandwich shop or **pizzeria rustica** can fill you up quickly and inexpensively. For provisions, go to the neighborhood *alimentari* (many bake their own breads), the local outdoor markets throughout the city, or the huge **market** at p. Vittorio, not far from the train station. Ice cream is best sampled at the elegant but expensive **Giolitti,** via degli Uffici del Vicario, 40, the trendier **Gelateria della Palma,** via della Maddalena, 20 (both near the Pantheon), or almost anywhere you see a *produzione propria* (homemade) sign.

Ristorante da Nazzareno, via Magenta, 35, to your right as you leave Termini. Despite the multilingual menus and bow-tied waiters, it's good and reasonably priced. *Menu* L12,000, pasta L4000. Open Thurs.-Tues. noon-3:30pm and 7-10:30pm.

Trattoria Angelo, via Principe Amadeo, 102. *Menu* for L15,000; *penne all'arrabbiata* (L4000) is especially good. Open Thurs.-Tues. 11am-3:30pm and 6:30-11pm.

Osteria con Cucina de Andreis Luciano, via Giovanni Amendola, 73-75. Earthy, cheap, and hardly a tourist in sight. No *menu,* but a full meal with pasta, salad, wine, water and half a chicken will run you under L10,000. Open 11am-3pm and 7-10pm.

Restaurant Monte Arci, via Castelfidardo, 33. A step up in price, but everything on the menu is delicious. Try the *lasagne* or *spaghetti con le vongole* (with clams). *Menu* L15,000. Open Thurs.-Tues. noon-3pm and 7-11:30pm.

Hostaria Botte di Frascati, largo di Chiavari, 85, off corso Vittorio Emanuele near p. Navona. A creative menu, and slightly lower prices than other eateries in this fashionable part of town. *Pasta* L3500-5000, *secondi* L3500-7000. Open Thurs.-Tues. 12:30-3pm and 6:45-11pm.

Pizzeria Baffetto, via del Governo Vecchio, 114, near the Chiese Nuova on corso Vittorio Emanuele. Great pizza, but poor service.

Mario's, via del Moro, 53, in Trastevere. Lots of cheap, ho-hum food. *Menu* L9000, *pasta* L2500-3800. Open Sept.-July Mon.-Sat. noon-4pm and 7pm-midnight.

Sights

Many museums close on Monday, and Tuesday through Sunday by 2pm; the Catacombs, St. Peter's and the Vatican museums, the Forum, and the Colosseum are exceptions. Be prepared as well for some disappointments; almost every major sight is at least partially obscured by scaffolding or some kind of restoration work. In 1987 the Arch of Constantine, the Sistine Chapel, and the Column of Trajan were among the innumerable sights covered by green canvas. Many museums are free the first and third Saturday and second and last Sunday of each month. Churches are usually open from early in the morning to around noon, and frequently reopen for a couple of hours around 4pm. When visiting churches, dress modestly—no bare shoulders or legs.

Rome is a baroque city plastered onto an ancient metropolis, and the results are cluttered, grandiloquent, and magnificent all at once. Its builders, including many great popes, did not work so much with stone and paint as with space itself, and the city's treasures are not just buildings or paintings, but the great squares and streets—piazza Navona, the Campidoglio, piazza del Popolo, piazza di Spagna, and piazza San Pietro.

Nowhere do interior and exterior chime so grandly as at the **Vatican,** the great center of the Catholic Church. The entrance to the **Vatican Museums** is at the end of via Tunisi, a 10-minute walk from the Ottaviano stop on Line A. Select one of the four tour routes—"D" winds past Egyptian mummies, through miles of extravagantly decorated corridors full of treasures. Classical sculpture, including the *Laocoön* and *Apollo Belvedere,* decorates the elegant **Belvedere Courtyard.** This and the other courtyards were designed by Bramante, the first great Renaissance architect. From the windows you can glimpse the manicured splendor of the private **Vatican**

Gardens, and catch the most impressive perspective of St. Peter's. All routes lead to the breathtakingly frescoed **Raphael Stanze** (rooms) and ultimately to the **Sistine Chapel** and Michelangelo's fresco masterpieces—the *Last Judgment* on the end wall, and the spectacular ceiling. Once out of the Sistine Chapel, don't rush past the **Pinacoteca;** Raphael's *Transfiguration* alone is worth the stop. (Museums open Easter week and June-Aug. Mon.-Fri. 9am-5pm, Sat. 9am-2pm; Sept.-May Mon.-Fri. 9am-2pm. Admission L7000, ages 24 and under L4000. Open, free, and mobbed on the last Sun. of every month 9am-2pm. Last visitors admitted 1 hr. before closing.)

Back outside, approach the **Basilica di San Pietro** (St. Peter's) through Bernini's stunning colonnades, a high point of baroque design. St. Peter's, built on an early Christian site, was the product of centuries of confused and competing efforts. Begun by Bramante under Julius II, the project was carried on by da Sangallo, Michelangelo, Raphael, and finally Maderna, who added the present facade. The stupendous dome was Michelangelo's final great achievement; only he was able to solve the problem of its construction. To appreciate the result and thoroughly inspect the structure it crowns, make the strenuous climb to the top. Inside, Michelangelo's *Pieta,* carefully restored after a 1970 vandal's attack, glows behind bullet-proof glass. Downstairs, the grottoes harbor the tombs of St. Peter and his successors. (St. Peter's open in summer daily 7am-7pm; in winter 7am-6pm. Free. Grottoes (free) and dome (L2000, elevator halfway L500) close 1 hr. earlier in summer.) Mass is conducted several times per day, with a particularly beautiful vespers service Sunday at 5pm. The Pope grants public audiences in p. San Pietro on Wednesdays: usually at 10am when he's in residence at the Vatican (Sept.-May), 11am when he's staying at Castel Gandolfo, south of Rome (June-Aug).

Across the River Tiber from the Vatican lie most of the visible remnants of ancient Rome. Unfortunately, far too few remain standing, for the same Church which erected so many beautiful buildings concertedly destroyed the monuments left by its pagan predecessors. Enter the Roman **Forum,** once the center of the Empire, from via dei Fori Imperiali just behind the Vittoriano monument. The Forum contains dozens of significant monuments, including the **Curia,** where the Senate met; the reputed **Tomb of Romulus,** Rome's legendary eponym and founder; the **Imperial Rostra,** from which politicians orated; and the **Arch of Titus,** which features the famous frieze of Roman legionaries carrying off the great Menorah and other booty from the Jewish Temple at Jerusalem. At the far end of the Forum, the **Palatine Hill** houses a complex of imperial palaces surrounded by parks and gardens. The largest and most impressive structure here is the **Palace of Domitian,** divided into the Domus Flavia (official palace), the Domus Augustana (private residence), and the Stadium. (Forum and Palatine open Mon. and Wed.-Sun. 9am-1 hr. before sunset. Admission L5000.) At the southern base of the Palatine is the **Circus Maximus;** you can still see the markings of the start and finish lines for the chariot races once held here. Further south stands the **Domus Aurea,** the splendid dwelling built for Emperor Nero; it was closed for restoration in 1987, but may be open again by 1988.

Dominating the heart of ancient Rome, the **Colosseum,** erected in 80 C.E. by Emperor Titus, stands as the city's grandest symbol. Used as a quarry by the popes through the eighteenth century, it was hallowed as a site where Christian martyrs perished—actually, only pagan gladiators died in the games. (Open 9am-1hr. before sunset. Free, access to upper levels L3,000.) The **Museo Nazionale Romano,** near Termini, has some of the most striking classical sculpture in Rome. (Open Tues.-Sat. 9am-2pm, Sun. 9am-1pm. Admission L4000.)

The best preserved monument of the ancient city is the **Pantheon,** erected in 120 C.E. as a monument to all the gods (*pan*=all, *theion*=gods), and only surviving through its consecration as a church in 609. This remarkable circular building is as impressive as any in Rome, from any century. The Pantheon lies between piazza Navona and via del Corso. (Open Tues.-Sat. 9am-2pm, Sun. 9am-1pm. Free.) From this elegant structure, it's a short walk to the seventeenth-century and the finest baroque space in Rome, **piazza Navona,** today the setting for summer festivals and political rallies. At night, it's one of the liveliest spots in the city.

Michelangelo left his mark on Rome's secular face in his masterful redesign of the **Campidoglio** (Capitoline Hill), off piazza Venezia— it's easily recognized by the adjacent tastelessness of the huge, white **Vittoriano,** the nineteenth-century monument King Victor Emanuel II erected to himself. From the back of the piazza, behind Rome's City Hall (the central building), is a great daytime view of the Forum. On the piazza are the **Musei Capitolini,** home to an extraordinary collection of classical sculpture and Renaissance painting. (Museums open Tues.-Sat. 9am-2pm, Sun. 9am-1pm; Tues. and Thurs. also 5-8pm, Sat. also 8:30-11pm. Admission L3000.)

Renaissance Rome is at its enigmatic finest in **Vecchia Roma,** or Old Rome, which surrounds the **campo dei Fiori.** The **Gesu,** on nearby corso Vittorio Emanuele, is the parent church of the Jesuit order. Back toward the station, at the intersection of via Barberini and via XX Settembre, the **Church of Santa Maria della Vittoria** houses Bernini's *St. Theresa in Ecstasy.* The exquisite rendering of the saint swooning with physical and spiritual delight is unforgettable. (Church open irregulary in summer.) **San Pietro in Vincoli,** on via Cavour near the Colosseum, contains Michelangelo's tremendous statue of Moses, one of few significant art works in the city dealing with an Old Testament subject. You can attend Mass at any of a score of neighborhood churches scattered throughout the city, or at the huge pilgrim basilicas of **Santa Maria Maggiore** (down via Cavour from the station), **San Giovanni in Laterano,** with its remarkable cloister (down via Meraluna from Santa Maria Maggiore), and **San Paolo fuori le Mura** (at the Basilica San Paolo stop of subway line B). These churches defined the far outskirts of Rome as late as the sixteenth century—the city had shrunk so from its ancient size.

Many of the Renaissance and baroque **palazzi** (mansions), built by papal "nephews" (sons, in reality) or other relatives, today serve as galleries. The **Galleria Borghese** sits in Rome's largest park and houses Bernini's greatest early sculpture and a large collection of Titians and Caravaggios (some parts of the villa will be closed in 1988). The fine art collection of the **Palazzo Barberini** in via Quattro Fontane, near the Barberini Fountain, is one of the best labeled and most attractive in Rome. (Open Tues.-Sat. 9am-2pm, Sun. 9am-1pm. Admission L3000. Some areas will be closed in 1988.) Of the other palazzi-cum-galleries, the **Spada,** near the campo dei Fiori (open Tues.-Sat. 9am-2pm, Sun. 9am-1pm; admission L2000) and the **Doria** (open Tues. and Fri.-Sun. 10am-1pm; admission L2000, L2000 more for tour of the private apartments) are the most important. The **Palazzo Farnese** is closed to the public indefinitely.

The **Catacombs** are mysterious monuments to the Christianity that existed before it became the official faith of Rome. Thousands of pre-Constantinian Christians are buried in underground labyrinths that stretch as far as 20km. The greatest concentration rests along the old Appian Way, one of the oldest Roman roads still in use. Reach them by the #118 bus from the Colosseum down via Appia Antica. The catacombs of **San Sebastiano, Santa Domitilla,** and **San Callisto** are next to each other (open 8:30am-noon and 2:30-5pm; San Sebastiano closed Thurs., Santa Domitilla closed Tues., San Callisto closed Wed. Required tour L3000.) Jewish catacombs contemporary with those of the Christians also exist along the Appian Way, but these for some reason are not operated as a tourist attraction. A different sort of posthumous attraction is the **Protestant Cemetery,** off the Pyramide stop on Metro line B. Behind Roman tribune Caius Cestius' tomb—a marble pyramid jutting out of the medieval city wall—are the graves of Keats and Shelley, carefully tended in the garden-like cemetery (open 8am-noon and 3:20-6pm; donation requested). The **Synagogue of Rome,** lungotevere Cenci, built following the nineteenth-century emancipation of the Jews, offers a startling contrast to the baroque ornament that characterizes most of the city. Designed in a sort of Babylonian revival style, the building houses a museum that chronicles Rome's Jewish history. (Synagogue open Sat. Museum open Sun.-Fri. 10am-2pm. Both free.)

For people-watching, try the **Spanish Steps** or less orthodox hangouts at piazza Navona and campo dei Fiori. Another favorite is the **Trevi Fountain,** which dominates its tiny piazza. Try to visit the fountain at night, as water pressure is often turned down drastically during the day. By all means throw your coin in and make a wish—stranger things than a return trip to Rome have happened. **Trastevere,** on the far bank of the River Tiber, is a quarter of meandering streets, innumerable *trattorie,* and impromptu celebrations in its many *piazze.* Perched above Trastevere sits **San Pietro in Montorio,** home of one of Italy's smallest but most exquisite buildings, the **Tempietto.** This circular jewel was one of Bramante's finest creations, and first awakened his contemporaries to the possibility of recapturing the glory of Roman architecture.

For more than a few days in Rome, invest in a copy of *Let's Go: Italy,* which does a capital job on the Eternal City.

Entertainment

Roman entertainment is communal, public, and outdoors—concerts under the stars, street fairs with acrobats and fire-eaters, and crowds that assemble with cheerful aimlessness all over the city. Check *La Repubblica* or other newspapers for specific events; the tourist office is a good source for calendars of events, many of which are printed in English. The magazine *Settimana a Roma* (This Week in Rome), available at newsstands for L3000, lists concerts, plays, and special events with prices and times. Of special note are the operas in the ancient **Baths of Caracalla** in July and August. The outdoor acoustics don't compare to an opera house, but the extravagant productions are great fun. *Aida,* Verdi's Egyptian opera, is a perennial favorite, with a cast of over 200, complete with chariots and horses. Buy tickets (L15,000-40,000) at the opera house, p. Beniamino Gigli, 1 (tel. 46 17 55). The one Roman cinema which does not dub out English is **Cinema Pasquino,** on vicolo del Piede in Trastevere; the movies will be several months behind American screens and cost about L5000. (Open Sept.-July.)

For jazz, the *dolce vita* atmosphere of **Musica Inn,** lungotevere dei Fiorentini, 3 (tel. 654 49 34), or the **Centro Jazz St. Louis,** via del Cardello, 13a (tel. 48 34 24), are good bets. Other clubs include **Folkstudio,** via Sacchi (tel. 589 23 74; closed in summer). Dancing the night away comes very dear in Rome: count on L15,000-25,000 cover at **Histeria,** via Giovannelli, 12 (tel. 86 45 87; open Fri.-Sat.), or **Acropolis,** via Luciani, 52 (tel. 87 83 60). Gay clubs include **Angelo Azzurro,** via Cardinal Merry del Val (tel. 580 04 72), and the elegant **L'Alibi,** via Monte Testuccio, 44 (tel. 578 23 43), near the Piramide.

In late July, Trastevere hosts the **Festa Noantri;** every night for 10 days, viale Trastevere closes to traffic and becomes a brightly lit row of food and junk stalls, jugglers and fun fairs. Perhaps the best time to appreciate the vigor of Christianity in Rome is during **Holy Week,** when every church hosts concerts and High Mass; the Pope traditionally conducts the Way of the Cross in the Colosseum on Good Friday. Also in spring are the antique and art festivals of via del Coronari and via Margutta, and the flower festival on the Spanish Steps (when they take the photos for the postcards).

Near Rome

A pleasant daytrip from Rome takes you to the archeological site of **Ostia Antica;** you can eat your picnic lunch in Ostia's restored amphitheater. Arrive before noon to visit the site's museum, which houses a fine collection of artifacts recovered from the excavation. Bring lunch and have a picnic in Ostia's restored amphitheater. Trains leave from the Pirimide stop on Metro line B (L700). Admission to the site, including the museum, is L4000. (Open Tues.-Sun. 9am-1 hr. before sunset.)

When Rome's heat, noise, and dirt get to be too much, escape to **Tivoli,** an hour outside the city; three buses per hour leave from via Gaeta near p. d. Cinquecento (L3400 round-trip). The sixteenth-century **Villa d'Este** is a dazzling and splashy park overflowing with fountains and waterfalls, some trickling, others torrential, some shaped like Catherine-wheels, others like cataracts. The house and gardens are beautiful and restful, and another good spot for a picnic. (Open Tues.-Sun. 9am-

1 hr. before sunset. Admission L5000.) A similar park that's slightly less well-manicured is the **Villa Gregoriana,** across town. (Open Tues.-Sun. 9:30am-1 hr. before sunset. Admission L750.) Just outside of Tivoli is the **Villa Adriana,** where the Emperor Hadrian reconstructed the architectural wonders of his far-flung empire. (Open same hours as Villa d'Este. Admission L4000.)

The Roman countryside is a far cry from the hustle and bustle of the city proper; just outside the road that rings the city lie peaceful towns such as **Frascati,** justly famed for its wine. Acotral buses run from the Subaugusta stop on Metro line A (every ½ hr.; L1000). Hitchhike up the hill to the Roman ruins at Tusculum, then down the other side to the pleasant hamlet of **Grottaferrata,** 3km from Frascati. This town's Romanesque eleventh-century **abbey,** inhabited by the Greek Orthodox monks of St. Niles, is particularly beautiful. You can catch the bus back to Rome from here (last at 9pm; L1000).

Southern Italy

Southern Italy, known as the *Mezzogiorno* (midday) region, is significantly poorer than the industrialized North. The problem of bringing the South up to Northern levels of housing, health care, and employment has been at the top of the agenda of Italian politics for a generation, but little has been achieved. Outside of the impoverished cities, though, it's debatable whether Southern Italians would want to trade the leisurely pace of their sun-baked villages for the more hectic pace of the North. This lifestyle of slow evenings sipping coffee and long, long meals, even more than splendid beaches and a rich inheritance of classical ruins, is the Mezzogiorno's prime attraction.

Naples (Napoli)

Many travelers hear that Naples is a dirty, dangerous city not worth visiting. Nonsense. It is the heart of Southern Italy, overflowing with energy. The Mafia has earned the city its infamous reputation, but tourists are rarely targets for anything more than petty thievery and pickpocketing. Neapolitans feel a cultural and communal identity that separates them from the rest of Italy; their passionate loyalties begin with the family, and often end with the city. Ignore Naples' honking horns and garbage-filled streets, stuff your money belt under your clothes, and enjoy.

Orientation and Practical Information

Naples is on the west coast of Italy, two hours south of Rome. The city is one of Italy's most important ports, with regular sailings to Sicily, Tunisia, and Sardinia. Naples is also a hub for rail lines, with service to and from Rome, Calabria, Sicily, and the Adriatic coast.

Tourist Office: Ente Provinciale per il Turismo (EPT), in the train station (tel. 26 87 79). Open Mon.-Sat. 8:30am-8pm. Main office, via Partenope, 10a (tel. 40 62 89), reached by bus #150 or tram #1. Open Mon.-Fri. 8:30am-2:30pm, Sat. 8:30am-noon. Offers the invaluable guide *Qui Napoli (Here's Naples).* Other booths open irregularly at the port (tel. 32 39 77), Stazione Mergellina (tel. 68 51 02), and the airport (tel. 780 57 61). **Azienda di Turismo,** p. Gesù Nuovo (tel. 32 33 28). Open Mon.-Sat. 9am-3pm.

American Express: Ashiba Travel, p. Municipio, 1 (tel. 32 27 86). Mail held and checks sold. No wired money accepted. Open Mon.-Fri. 9am-1pm and 3-7pm, Sat. 9am-1pm.

Currency Exchange: At the Stazione Centrale; bad rates, of course, but open Mon.-Sat. 24 hours, Sun. until 9pm.

Post Office: p. Matteotti, just off via Toledo on via Diaz. Open Mon.-Sat. 8am-8pm, Sun. 8am-noon.

Telephones: At the train station. Open 24 hours. An office in Galleria Umberto is less crowded. Open Mon.-Sat. 8am-9:30pm. **Telephone code:** 081.

Trains: From **Stazione Centrale** take bus CS or CD to p. Dante, near the historic center and university district; or bus #150 or 106 to p. Municipio, the center of the modern city, to the bay (Riviera di Chiaia), and to Mergellina. The Metropolitana will whisk you to p. Cavour, p. Amadeo, Mergellina, and the funicular to Vomero. Information (tel. 26 46 44). All public transportation costs L600.

Emergencies: Police or **Ambulance** (tel. 113).

Consulates: U.S., p. della Repubblica (tel. 66 09 66). **U.K.,** via Crispi, 122 (tel. 20 92 27).

Accommodations and Food

Naples's only youth hostel is the **Ostello Mergellina (IYHF),** salita della Grotta, 23 (tel. 761 23 46), two quick rights from Mergellina metro stop. (L10,000. Sheets and breakfast included. 11pm curfew. Open year-round.) Neapolitan hotel managers are a mixed breed; some are scrupulously honest, others simply don't care about cleanliness, service, or comfort. If you have any complaints about your hotel, call the EPT (tel. 41 98 88). The best place to stay is in the university area, near piazza Dante. It's safer than piazza Garibaldi, similarly priced, and the rooms are cleaner. **Soggiorno Imperia,** p. Miraglia, 386 (tel. 45 93 47) has large well-furnished rooms. (Singles L12,000, doubles L20,000. Showers included.) **Allogio Fiamma,** via Francesca del Guidice, 13 (tel. 31 38 82), is another one of Naples' best *pensioni.* (Doubles L25,000. Showers included.) Dozens of cheap *pensioni* are clustered around piazza Garibaldi. **Albergo Casanova,** via Venezia, 2 (tel. 26 82 87) is the most comfortable and cleanest of these. (Singles L12,000, doubles L26,000, with bath L30,000. Showers L2000.) **Albergo Fiore,** via Milano, 109 (tel. 33 87 98), is not the most elegant, but it's clean and safe. (Singles L10,000-15,000, doubles L20,000. Showers L2000.) **Hotel Ginevra,** via Genova, 116 (tel. 28 32 10), boasts clean rooms and a delightful proprietor. Call ahead. (Singles L13,000, doubles L24,000, with bath 28,000. Showers L2000.) In the higher priced Mergellina area on the waterfront, the most affordable place you'll find is **Pensione Muller,** 7, via Mergellina (tel. 66 90 56). (Doubles with bath L40,000.)

One of Naples's greatest attractions is its cuisine. *Spaghetti alle vongole* (with clams) and *alle cozze* (with mussels) are local favorities, as is *fritto di pesce* (battered and deep-fried fish). *Crocche* are potato knishes, cheap and available everywhere. Pizza, of course, is what put Naples on the map. The best eating places are near piazza Dante and down by the bay in Mergellina. **Pizzeria Bellini,** strada Santa Maria Constantinopoli, 8, near p. Bellini, just east of p. Dante, is a favorite of Neapolitans; try *linguine al cartoccio,* a delicious mix of seafood and pasta. (Open Mon.-Sat.) In Mergellina, **Birreria Gloria,** p. Sannazzaro, 70, is a nifty little joint with entrees ranging from L4000-7000 (open Tues.-Sun.) Around piazza Garibaldi, **Avellinese da Peppino,** via Silvio Spaventa, 31-35, offers friendly service and good seafood (open Sun.-Fri.), while **La Brace,** via Silvio Spaventa 14-16, has a 20-year-old prodigy pizza-maker who's made quite a name for himself (open Mon.-Sat.). Don't miss eating a pizza cooked in one of the domed ovens of the Spaccanapoli. There are dozens on the via Vicaria Vecchia (right after the intersection of via del Duomo) and along via Tribunali. One of the cheaper is **Pizzeria da Gennarino,** via Capuana alla Medelena, 1-2; *pizza Napoli* (with cheese and mushrooms) goes for L3500 plus a 10% service charge. (Open Thurs.-Tues.)

Sights

Begin with the world-famous **Museo Nazionale Archeologico** (Metro: Piazza Cavour); it's worth a trip to Naples just to see these treasures. The museum contains all the frescoes and jewelry excavated from Pompeii and Herculaneum, as well as outstanding sculpture and ceramics. (Open Tues.-Sat. 9am-2pm, Sun. 9am-1pm. Admission L4000.) On a hill overlooking the city, beside a large park, stands the **Museo di Capodimonte;** take bus #110 or 127. The highlight of the museum is the fabulous **Galleria Nazionale,** which features artists ranging from Simone Martini to Massacio to Raphael. (Open Tues.-Sat. 9am-2pm, Sun. 9am-1pm. Admission L4000.) The **Museo San Martino,** located in a Carthusian monastery on the hill of San Elmo, consists of weighty exhibits documenting the art, history, and life of Naples since the sixteenth century. To reach the museum, take the funicular from via Toledo near Galleria Umberto. (Open Tues.-Sat. 9am-2pm, Sun. 9am-1pm. Admission L3000.) The ornate rooms of the **Palazzo Realè,** on p. del Plebiscito, illustrate the lifestyle of the city in a more glorious era. (Open Tues.-Sat. 9am-2pm, Sun. 9am-1pm. Admission L3000.) The neighboring **Galleria Umberto** is an exquisite iron and glass arcade of shops, offices, and cafes.

The airy calm of the leafy hillside residential district of **Vomero** is a respite from downtown Naples (take a funicular up). The **Villa Floridiana** is situated on a knoll remarkable for its camelias, pine trees, and terrace overlooking the bay. (Grounds open 9am-1 hr. before sunset.)

Near Naples

The area south of Naples has spectacular offerings—Roman ruins, Greek temples, and the Amalfi coast. The eruption of **Mount Vesuvius** in 79 C.E. covered Herculaneum (Ercolano) in mud, and Pompeii (Pompei) in ashes. Both sites are accessible by the Circumvesuviana train line running from the lower floor of the Stazione Centrale.

Herculaneum (L1200 round-trip) is the smaller but better preserved site. (Open daily 9am-6pm. Admission L4000.) **Pompeii,** about 20km to the southeast, offers an extraordinary vision of Roman life in the first century (take the line to Pompeii; L3000 round-trip). From the train station, walk straight to the Church of the Madonna of Pompeii and turn right. (Site open year-round daily 9am-1 hr. before sunset. Admission L5000.)

The **Gulf of Salerno,** separated by the Amalfi Peninsula from the Bay of Naples, is rich in both scenic and archeological offerings. An hour south of Salerno by train are three well-preserved Greek temples at **Paestum.** Frequent buses run along the sheer cliffs of the sun-bleached Amalfi Coast between Sorrento and Salerno, making stops at **Positane, Praino,** and **Amalfi.** Hitching is easy. You can camp at **Tranquilità,** just outside of Praino, on the road to Amalfi (tel. 87 40 84). (Tents L10,000, L1500 per person; July-Aug. L4000 per person.) **Hotel Tramonto D'Oro,** by the church on the road to Amalfi (tel. (089) 87 40 08) is a luxury hotel built into the cliffs that sometimes rents interior rooms at reduced prices (L20-25,000 per person. Breakfast and use of roof-top pool included.) Next door, the **Trattoria San Gennaro da Vittoria** sells tasty homemade *Gnocchi alla Sorrentina* for L3500.

Girthed by spectacular cliffs, the islands of **Capri, Ischia,** and **Procida** beckon. They can be reached through Sorrento, Salerno, and Pozzuoli, but Naples is usually the most convenient port of departure; boats depart from the Molo Beverello at the end of p. Municipio. The largest ferry lines run about eight boats per day to Capri and Ischia (90 min., L9200 round-trip) and four per day to Procida. In winter, ferries run half as often. Stay high up in the gardens of the **Ana Capri** region of Capri at **Villa Eva** (tel. 837 20 40). Follow the signs from the bus stop (L15,000 per person).

Brindisi

There is only one reason to stop in Brindisi: It is the port of departure for most of the ferries from Italy to Greece, and to Dubrovnik in Yugoslavia. The closest that this city comes to splendor is the view of the sunset over the stern of your ship as you finally get under way.

Brindisi is served by **Adriatica,** Stazione Marittima (tel. (0831) 238 25), **Hellenic Mediterranean Lines,** corso Garibaldi, 8 (tel. (0831) 285 31), **Fragline,** c/oItalmar, corso Garibaldi, 96-98 (tel. (0831) 297 71), **Adriatic Ferries,** c/oPattimare, p. E.

Dionisi, 11 (tel. (0831) 265 48), and **Ionis,** c/oPattimare, p. E. Dionisi, 11 (tel. (0831) 265 48). You can buy your tickets either from one of the numerous travel agencies between the train station and the port, or from the ticket offices at the port itself, where you must go anyway to get a boarding pass and pay port taxes. Although an agency may sell you a student or railpass ticket without requiring proper ID, the port ticket office *will* ask to see ID. Fragline had the lowest rates in 1987. Adriatica and Hellenic Mediterranean Lines are the only companies that give a discount to Eurailpass holders. Remember to save L6000 for port taxes, and, if you have a Eurailpass, L14,000 for the supplement. Check in at the embarkation office at least two hours before departure, or else you may lose your reservation and ticket. Allow plenty of time for late trains, and for the 1-kilometer walk to the port from the station. **Trains** leave Rome for Brindisi five times per day.

If you want to eat while waiting for the evening ferry, stay away from the mediocre restaurants that crowd corso Garibaldi on the way to the port. **Spaghetti House-Osteria Cucina Casalinga,** via Mazzini, 57, not far from the station, will fill you with an excellent meal from L6000-10000 (open Mon.-Sat. 9am-9pm). **Albergo Venezia,** via Pisanelli, 6 (tel (0831) 254 11), is a little messy, but adequate. (Singles L15,000, doubles L25,000. Showers included.) The **Ostello della Gioventù Casale (IYHF)** (tel. 41 31 00) is 3km from Brindisi; take bus #3 or 4. No card required. (L7000, breakfast included. Curfew 11pm.)

Sicily (Sicilia)

Clinging to the edge of Europe, Sicily is far removed from the Italy most travelers visit: Palermo is geographically as close to Tunis as it is to Naples, and spiritually as far from Milan as it is from the moon. Sicily has suffered invasion by almost every Mediterranean civilization of the past 2500 years. All the conquerors have left their mark—the ancient Greeks with temples and theaters, the Romans with bridges and aqueducts, the Saracens with mosques and towers, and the Normans with churches and castles. Negligent Spanish domination provoked Sicilians to take the law into their own hands: Thus one of Italy's most enduring institutions—the Mafia. Time and again Sicilians have been reminded of the destructive forces beneath the surface of their island's rugged landscape, as earthquakes and the eruptions of Mt. Etna, Europe's largest active volcano, have devastated the land.

Trains from Rome and points north meet the ferry at Villa San Giovanni; there is another ferry at Reggio di Calabria. Both go to Messina. **Tirrenia** and **Grandi Traghetti** lines both serve the Genoa-Palermo route three times per week (23 hr., deck fare L60,500). Tirrenia also sails from Naples to Palermo (10½ hr., L32,700). Tirrenia also has weekly service to Tunis from Trapani (deck fare L64,700 in high season) and Palermo (L105,300). Reservations for the high season should be booked well in advance, either in Italy or at **Extra Value Travel,** 5 World Trade Center, New York, NY 10048 (tel. (212) 750 88 00).

Once on the island, take your time; some major sights can be reached only by local trains. For more independence, a car or motorcycle beats hitching hands down—there are simply not enough cars on major roads. There is only one hostel on the island, and campgrounds are expensive; you may want to try freelance camping.

Sicilian food is highly spiced and the wine strong. Palermo is heavy on pasta-seafood combinations and pizza, while Trapani borrows such dishes as *couscous* from nearby North Africa. *Melanzane* (eggplant) and *frutti di mare* (seafood) are popular items, and famous sweets like *cannoli* (cream-filled pastry tubes) and *cassata* (multi-flavored ice cream with bits of fruit) finish the large meals here splendidly.

Palermo

People and buildings in Palermo are tightly crammed into every nook and cranny. The main street is barely wide enough for two lanes of traffic and the overflow of people and goods from shops and markets renders the narrow sidewalks impassable. Historically the center of commerce, government, and church in Sicily, Palermo is in every sense the island's capital.

Get maps and pamphlets from the **APT,** p. Castelnuovo, 34 (tel. 58 38 47). (Open Mon.-Fri. 8am-8pm, Sat. 8am-2pm.) They also have branches at the train and maritime stations. (Open same hours.) Stroll along via Roma up to Corso Vittorio Emanuele, admiring the various squares and the exuberant cathedral. The **Palazzo dei Normanni** (Palace of the Normans) is an extraordinary fusion of styles. (Open Mon.-Tues. and Thurs.-Sat. 9am-1pm and 3-5:30pm, Wed. 9am-1pm, Sun. 9-10:20am, 11-11:30am, and 12:15-1pm.) The **Church of San Giovanni degli Eremiti,** around the corner, is now semi-ruined, but its pink domes shield an exotic cloister garden. (Open Mon.-Sat. 9am-7pm, Sun. 8:30am-2pm.) The **Museo Archeologico,** off via Roma at p. Olivella, contains the famous metopes (part of a Doric frieze) from the Greek temple of Selinus. (Open Mon., Wed.-Thurs. and Sat. 9am-1:30pm, Tues. and Fri. 9am-1:30pm and 3-5pm, Sun. 9am-12:30pm. Admission L2000.) The **National Gallery of Sicily,** housed in the Palazzo Abatellis, has a superb collection of paintings and sculpture. Take bus #3 or 24; the entrance is at via Alloro 4. (Open Tues.-Sat. 9am-1:30pm, Sun. 9am-12:30pm. Admission L2000.) The area's greatest mosaics, however, lie in nearby **Monreale** (take bus #9 or 8/9 from p. XIII Vittime; L500). Here, the cathedral combines Norman architecture with Sicilian and Arabian motifs, and features a breathtaking mosaic depiction of the Old and New Testaments. (Open Mon.-Sat. 7:30am-noon and 3-6:30pm, Sun. 7am-12:30pm.) The **Benedictine Cloister** next door frames a refined garden with imaginative medieval columns and capitals. (Cloister open Mon.-Sat. 9am-7pm, Sun. 9am-1pm. Admission L2000.)

For a good, cheap room in Palermo, try **Albergo Odeon,** via E. Amari, 140 (tel. 33 27 78), next to the Teatro Politeana. (Singles L12,000, with bath L16,000; doubles L22,000, with bath L26,000.) An excellent buy is **Albergo Pretoria,** via Maqueda, 124 (tel. 33 10 68), with large rooms and friendly management. (Singles L15,000, with bath L19,000, doubles L24,000, with bath L33,000.) **Albergo Rosalia Conca d'Oro,** via Santa Rosalia, 7 (tel. 616 45 43), is closer to the station. Turn left off via Roma as you head toward town. (Singles L16,000, doubles L25,000.)

For a truly Sicilian dining experience, visit **Osteria Lo Bianco,** via E. Amari, 104, off via Roma near p. Castelnuovo. *Pasta con sarde al forno* (spaghetti with sardines and fennel) runs L2500 and *pesce spada* (swordfish) runs L2500. No service or cover. (Open Mon.-Sat. noon-3pm and 7-10pm.) **L'Uccelleria,** via Volturno, 108, behind the Teatro Massimo up via Maqueda, serves a full meal for only L1300. (Open Mon.-Sat. 1-3:30pm.) In the mornings, don't miss the massive **open-air market** off via Maqueda. Most of Palermo's nightlife occurs outside the city proper in nearby **Mondello;** take bus #6, 14, or 15 from via della Libertà or the station, and get off at Mondello Paese. There you can join the strolling crowds of young Italians sampling fish from seaside kitchen stalls and eating *gelato.*

Agrigento

Among Sicily's classical remains, the **Valley of Temples** at Agrigento shares top honors with Syracuse. Although early Christians damaged most of the sites and turned the Temple of Concord into a basilica, enough remains to give you a feeling for the Greek design. The helpful **tourist office** is on the ground floor of the Banco di Sicilia building between p. Marconi and piazzale Roma, near the train station. (Open Mon.-Sat. 8:30am-1:30pm and 4:30-7:30pm.) Bus #10 leaves p. Marconi (in front of the train station) every half hour for both the Valley of Temples and the excellent beach at S. Leone. In the midst of the temples is the **Museo Archeologico Nazionale,** which has a fine collection of Greek vases. (Open June-Sept. Tues.-Sat. 9:30am-1:30pm and 3:30-5pm; Oct.-May Tues.-Sun. 9:30am-1:30pm. Free.)

The temples are lit nightly; it's worth staying over to witness the spectacle, although Agrigento can be seen as a daytrip from Palermo (2½ hr. by train, L6900). **Albergo Gorizia,** via Bocciere, 39 (tel. 201 05), between #283 and 285 on via Atenea, has small rooms. (Singles L11,000, doubles L18,000. Showers L2000.) **Concordia,** via S. Francesco, 11 (tel. 562 66), has modern rooms but is in one of the less attractive parts of town. Take via Pirandello from the bottom of p. Moro. (Singles L14,000, with bath L18,000, doubles L30,000, with bath L36,000.) **Paninoteca Manhattan,** Salita M. Angel, 9, up the steps to the right off via Atenea coming up from p. Moro, has well-endowed sandwiches. Try the *Rockefeller* with tuna, pepper, lettuce, tabasco, *insalata russa,* and a dousing of whiskey (Ll3,300). (Open Mon.-Sat. 8:30am-3pm and 5:30pm-midnight.)

Syracuse (Siracusa)

The Hellenic city of Syracuse was once rivalled only by Athens. Founded in 734 B.C.E. by Corinthians attracted to its splendid harbor and natural spring water, the city reached the height of its power during the fifth and fourth centuries B.C.E., especially under the rule of the tyrant brothers Gelon and Hieron I. Today, the many well-preserved reminders of its ancient glory make Syracuse a city of lingering charm and romance.

Go to the island of **Ortigia,** across the bridge on corso Umberto, for the **Temples** of **Apollo** and **Athena.** The latter, now part of the city's cathedral, has a richly embellished baroque facade, added in the eighteenth century. Across the street is the building which until recently housed the national museum. Its holdings are now in storage awaiting the opening of the **Museo Landolino** (scheduled for summer 1988) in the archeological area of the new city. It will become the new resting place of some exceptional Greek vases, and the famous *Venus Andiomene,* a first-century B.C.E. Roman copy of a Greek statue. (Will be open daily 9am-1pm. Admission L2000.) Another museum in the elegant **Palazzo Bellomo,** on via Capodieci, has a superb collection of painting and sculpture, including Antonella da Messina's *Annunciation* (1474). (Open daily 9am-1pm.)

For the big sights, travel across town to the **archeological park.** (Open Mon.-Sat. 9am-2 hr. before sunset, Sun. 9am-1pm. Admission L2000.) Here is the **Greek Theater** (fifth century B.C.E.) where Aeschylus' *Persians* was first performed; the same park contains the **Paradise Quarry,** now a shady park. The most impressive sight in the area is the **Orecchio di Dionisio** (Ear of Dionysius), a giant artificial grotto with an earlobe-shaped entrance, whose echo supposedly allowed the tyrant Dionysius to overhear conversations of prisoners in the lower room. Nearby are the covered **Roman Amphitheater** (second century C.E.), and the enormous **Altar of Hieron II** (241-215 B.C.E.), used for public sacrifices, both carved from solid rock.

There is an independent **youth hostel** at via Epipoli, 45 (tel. 71 11 18), near the Castello Eurialo, about 8km from Syracuse. Take bus #9, 10, or 11 to Belvedere (L8000. Showers L1000). **Gran Bretagna,** via Savoia, 21 (tel. 68 76 5), is the most charming and best-situated hotel in the city. Many of the differently shaped rooms have views of the sea, and some have huge nineteenth-century frescoes. (Singles L19,000, doubles L31,000-35,000. Showers L2000. Breakfast included.) Convenient to the archeological park, the **Casa del Pelligrino,** v. del Santuario, 33 (tel. 653 79) is a boarding house for divinity students that is also open to the public. (L10,000 per person.) **Trattoria Natoli,** via G. di Natale, 10, off corso Gelone on the way to the archeological park, is about the only reasonable restaurant in the city. (Pasta dishes L2500-3500. Open Tues.-Sun. noon-2:30pm and 7-10pm.)

Beachcombers can venture 18km on bus #34 from Foro Siracusano park to the long, sandy beach of **Fontane Bianche,** or ride 8km on bus #35 to the more popular

Arenella beach. Southwest of Syracuse by SAIS or AST buses (from p. delle Poste and v. Trieste in Syracuse; L2300) is the village of **Noto,** crammed full of anomalously large palaces and churches. Take a walk down corso Vittorio Emanuele for a sampling of fine baroque structures worked in soft golden rock.

Lipari Islands (Isole Eolie)

The Lipari (or Aeolian) Islands are seven volcanic islands that lie off the Sicilian coast north of Milazzo. They feature spectacular scenery and have become one of the major centers of Sicilian tourism. **Lipari,** the largest of the islands, has a picturesque town of the same name. Its pastel-colored houses hug a small promontory crowned by the walls of a medieval *castello.* Inside the castle walls you'll find the beautiful **Ostello Lipari (IYHF).** (Tel. 981 15 40. L6000. Breakfast L2000; meals L7500-9000. Kitchen facilites. IYHF card usually not necessary. Open March-Oct.) **Vulcano,** only 20 minutes and L1200 away by ferry (L2000 for more frequent hydrofoils), features thermal springs and a sulfur bath. From the boat dock, **Porto di Levante,** climb the snaking path to the crater for a breathtaking view. **Stromboli** is the most dramatic and frightening of the islands: It consists of a volcanic cone fissured with scars and a town of lush vegetation and beautiful beaches (4½ hr. and L7100 from Lipari). Plan to stay overnight here: An evening spent watching the explosions of its fiery lava fountains is unforgettable. Infrequent ferries make a quick excursion almost impossible anyway. The climb to the crater takes four to five hours. Recent disasters have made it technically mandatory to hire a guide; this law isn't enforced, but it has been implemented with reason. Guides leave daily in the summer from in front of **Il Gabbiano** restaurant at **Fico Grande** beach at 6:30pm (L15,000 per person). Bring some plastic to place on the wet ground underneath your sleeping bag, a heavy sweater (particularly in winter), plenty of food and water, and a flashlight with an extra set of batteries (the path is not lit). The sleeping area is indicated by stones. Lipari is reached by ferry from the city of Milazzo (L5900), on the Messina-Palermo train line, and also connected to Messina by frequent bus, or from Naples (L42,000).

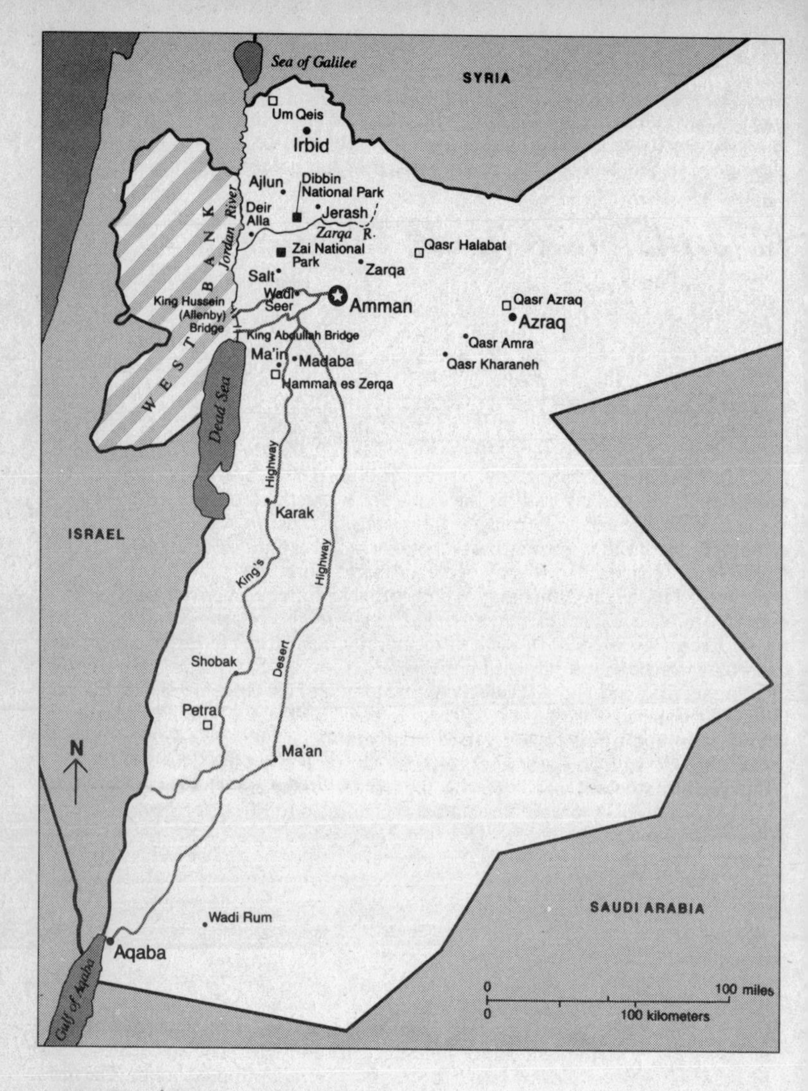

JORDAN

US$1 = 0.34 dinar (JD)	**1JD = US$2.91**
CDN$1 = 0.26JD	**1JD = CDN$3.83**
UK£1 = 0.56JD	**1JD = UK£1.76**
AUS$1 = 0.24JD	**1JD = AUS$4.17**

History and hospitality thrive best in the world's hottest spots, claim the Bedouin. Jordan proves their point. Here, the heat fueled by thousands of years of political and religious activity has forged an unparalleled array of historic monuments. Recent travelers have tended to let political thermometers scare them away from Jordan's ancient civilizations. Yet Jordanian hospitality has always warmed the weary traveler's soul. "*Ahlan wa Sahlan,*" runs the Bedouin greeting, "Welcome, twice welcome."

Travel is expensive, but to those willing to sacrifice dollars to the Arabian desert sands, Jordan offers wonders. Biblical sites abound; the Roman ruins at Jerash are more extensive than in any other Roman province; Crusader castles were built grander than any others to protect the sacred city of Jerusalem and the rich caravan routes between Egypt and Mesopotamia; the Nabateans chiseled Petra, the world's strangest city, into a stunning red rock outcrop amid desert sands; and an extraordinary variety of fish frequent the stunning reefs around the southern port of Aqaba. Amman, Jordan's capital and transportation hub, is pleasant if unexciting.

The history of Jordan is immense. Excavated inscriptions reveal that one of the world's first literate societies flourished here before the Children of Israel made their way back from captivity in Israel. During the time of the Old Testament, Amman (then Ammon) was capital of the Ammonites; the Edomites lived farther south, and the Moabites down by Petra. Jordan controlled the major trade routes between Egypt and Europe, and this led to Hellenizing influences from the third century B.C.E. To the Hellenes, Amman was *Philadelphia,* the City of Brotherly Love.

The Romans took Jerusalem in 63 B.C.E.; Roman remains in the entire area of the Holy Lands attest to the money they spent forcing their culture on the indigenous civilizations. When the Roman Empire officially adopted Christianity, churches were built on the east bank of the Jordan river; some 8% of the population is still Greek Orthodox Christian. The Byzantine era ended in the region in the seventh century C.E. when Muslim Umayyad forces secured the area.The **Umayyads** built palaces and castles whose remains are scattered from Azraq to Jerusalem, but when they moved their seat of government from Damascus to Baghdad, the prosperity of the region declined. The arrival of Crusaders in the closing years of the eleventh century left little impact except for a number of fantastic castles dotting the roads leading to Jerusalem. The legacy of the Ottoman Empire is more visible, although they concentrated their attention on Jerusalem rather than Jordan.

Only with the Ottoman involvement on the losing side in the World War I did Arab emancipation become feasible, and the Arab Revolt of 1916 (in which Laurence of Arabia took part) resulted in a degree of freedom. Jordan, as a British Mandate, took its current shape at that time. Jordan's support of the Allies in World War II earned it the status of Emirate under the rule of the present king's grandfather, Abdullah. Later the ruler was upgraded to king and the country became, as it is still, the Hashemite Kingdom of Jordan.

Jordan's neighbor to the East, Palestine, was granted independence from its British Mandate in 1948. The U.N. partitioned Palestine into Jewish and Arab autonomous regions, and the ensuing war was responsible for the emergence of the state of Israel. In 1950, the remnant of Palestine that had been neither deemed Jewish by the U.N. nor occupied by Israeli forces assimilated itself into Jordan. The fusion was voluntary but not without trouble, and a malcontent youth assassinated the king in Jerusalem in 1951. As the home of the majority of Palestinians who have left Israel since 1948, Jordan has always played a central role in the Arab-Israeli conflict. Jordan truly got the short end of the stick in 1967, when a war precipitated primarily by the less moderate regimes in Egypt and Syria resulted in the Israeli occupation of the West Bank, a region that had provided Jordan with 50% of its GNP. Aside from material loss, the 1967 war also resulted in a massive influx of Palestinian refugees; in the three or so years that followed, the PLO was to prove more of a menace to the Jordanian government than to the Israeli.

In 1970, a state of virtual civil war had developed, pitting the Jordanian army against the PLO irregulars, and in 1971 King Hussein expelled the PLO, to the vociferous condemnation of other Arab states. Jordan did not take part in the 1973 War, and has since been a voice of moderation in the region. In early 1987, Hussein gave up attempts to draft a joint peace plan proposal with Yasir Arafat and closed Arafat's Amman office, announcing that he was "unable to cooperate" with the PLO. A Jordanian-sponsored peace plan has since met with optimistic response from the U.S. and from Israeli Labor leader Shimon Peres, but has been rejected by new Israeli Prime Minister Itzhak Shamir.

For more thorough coverage of Jordan than we can offer here, consult the Jordan section of *Let's Go: Israel, Egypt, and Jordan.*

Planning Your Trip and Getting There

A visit to Jordan requires a sensitivity to the etiquette of conflicting national claims. Read on.

Visitors to Jordan must have a visa; these are issued at the Syrian border and at Aqaba, or in advance at any Jordanian embassy or consulate. Visas are *not* issued at the King Hussein/Allenby Bridge, the span across the River Jordan that links the West Bank with Jordan proper. If you travel to Jordan via Israel, you *must* obtain a visa *before* you reach Israel.

Though Jordan and Israel have been in a declared state of war since 1967, it is possible to travel between the two countries. As far as the Jordanian authorities are concerned, when you cross the King Hussein/Allenby Bridge from the West Bank, you are coming from occupied Jordan. However, since Jordan does not recognize the existence of Israel, your passport must be free of any evidence that you've *ever* been there. "Evidence" includes an Israeli entry stamp, a visa to Egypt or elsewhere issued in Israel, or an Egyptian entry or exit stamp from either Taba or Rafiah. On request, Israeli authorities will give you an entry stamp on a separate document; Egyptian authorities do not offer this convenience.

The King Hussein/Allenby Bridge is open Sunday through Thursday from 8am to 2pm; Friday from 8am to noon. Arrive as early as possible to be sure to get through. Occasionally political or religious events close the bridge; taxi and bus drivers keep abreast of the latest developments. To reach the King Hussein/Allenby Bridge from Jerusalem, take a *sherut* (shared taxi) from the stand north of Damascus Gate (US$5.50). From Amman, catch a shared taxi from Abdali Station (1.700JD), or, much safer, reserve a seat on the daily JETT bus (6:30am, 1 hr., 2.500JD; see Amman Practical Information). Once you've passed into the West Bank, you can catch a shared taxi to destinations throughout Israel. The Shaheen Arab Bus Company provides air-conditioned transport to Jerusalem roughly on the hour between 11am and 3 or 4pm (to Jerusalem US$3, to Jericho US$1.30, to Hebron US$4). You can pay for transportation in the West Bank with Jordanian dinars. When crossing into Jordan, it's wise to bring some dinars with you; exchange facilities at the border are unreliable.

The step-by-step process of crossing between Jordan and the West Bank is painful for Palestinians, who must endure heavy permit fees, strip searches, and rough treatment from both sides. For most foreigners (with the possible exception of Arabs and Jews from any country), the searches are mild, the officers respectful, and the waiting rooms air-conditioned. Upon leaving the West Bank, foreigners have to pay an exit fee to the Israeli authorities (US$20). Exiting Jordan, you'll have to show a West Bank permit, issued at the Jordanian Ministry of Interior in Amman (see below, and see Amman Practical Information).

The bridge is not considered an international border by Jordan, so you will *not* receive a Jordanian entry stamp in your passport, although you will receive a hand-held permit. It may be tricky to receive a permit to recross the bridge to the West Bank when you get to Amman. A good strategy: Don't keep your hand-held entry permit in an obvious place (it can prevent you from receiving a West Bank permit), and try leaving the "port of entry to Jordan" blank, or fill in "El Khuds." Although travelers do successfully cross from Israel to Jordan and back to Israel, you shouldn't stake too much on being able to duplicate the feat. If you can't get the permit to return to the West Bank (attempt it twice if possible), you'll have to leave Jordan by air, or by one of the daily ferries sailing from Aqaba to Nuweiba or Suez in Egypt (see Aqaba). Travelers hoping to visit Israel, the West Bank, and Jordan in a single trip will find it most convenient to begin in Jordan and leave Israel until last.

Syria is open to tourists except (as of 1987) Britons, but does not play by Jordan's rules when it comes to the West Bank. If you don't have a Jordanian entry stamp, they assume that you've entered at the King Hussein Bridge, and that therefore you've been in Israel. You can obtain a Jordanian entry stamp by taking the ferry from Aqaba to Nuweiba, Egypt, and back. (Boats leave Aqaba daily at 11am and 4:30pm; 4 hr., 16JD round-trip.) Please note that while this Aqaba-Nuweiba-Aqaba ferry scheme shows the Syrians that theoretically you've never been in Israel, it is *not* a foolproof way of getting the Jordanians to let you shuttle back to the West Bank; some official at the Ministry of the Interior may have the record of your entry at the King Hussein Bridge.

Traveling from Jordan to Israel (and back if you want to) is a simple process if, as explained above, you have not arrived from Israel on this trip. Again, the Jordanian authorities are simply allowing you to visit more of Jordan. For a permit to visit the West Bank and return (if so desired) within a month, go to the Ministry of Interior, Gamal Abdel Nasser Sq. in Amman; processing takes three working days. (See Amman Practical Information for details.)

Other than the King Hussein/Allenby Bridge, there are three overland routes into Jordan: Ferries sail twice per day from Nuweiba to Aqaba (4 hr., US$20); buses travel regularly from Ankara in Turkey, stopping in Antakya, (US$25); and buses and service taxis connect Damascus and Amman several times per day.

Transportation

A dense network of service taxi and minibus routes substitute for trains and coaches in Jordan's populous regions. With patience, travelers can find inexpensive public transportation to all but the most remote destinations. Azraq Oasis, the desert castles, and Wadi Rum are among the places not served by public transport.

Service (shared) taxis are identifiable by the white squares on their doors. They run specific routes in Amman and between the central transport terminals in the larger cities. In Amman, they cost 100fils; a ride from Amman to Aqaba may cost up to 2.650JD. Service taxis are the most convenient and comfortable way to travel, but they rarely run in the evenings and the long-distance ones may make only two or three trips per day (they won't depart until all 5 seats are full). Fares run about 10 fils per kilometer.

Buses cost about 40% less than taxis, but are slower and less frequent. Fortunately, both forms of transport usually share the same station, so you can choose the earliest departure; a 20-minute wait is fairly typical. If they have room, both can often be flagged down in transit, especially along rural routes. JETT private buses run longer hauls. (See Amman Practical Information for schedules and fares.)

If you're not under time pressure, hitchhiking is perhaps the best way to travel—and certainly one of the best ways to meet Jordanians. It's commonly practiced; waits of more than 30 minutes are rare. Hitching is better in the north than the rural south. Women should avoid hitching alone, and all hitchers should respect the local dress codes: no bare legs or shoulders (women may wear pants and need not cover their heads). Car rental is expensive (7.500JD per day plus 30fils per km).

Practical Information

At most major tourist sites, Jordan's friendly **tourist police** provide information and assistance. Elsewhere, ask locals; most Jordanians are very approachable and eager to help, and do not expect anything in return. Though English is widely spoken, any attempt to use even a few words of Arabic will be very warmly received. Script Arabic is quite complicated, but it's a good idea to learn the number system (which can be easily done by looking at car licence plates).

Ninety percent of Jordanians are Muslim, and many take Ramadan, the holy month of daytime fasting, very seriously. Banks, government offices, and most sights maintain their normal schedules; however, shops keep shorter hours, public transportation is reduced, and almost all restaurants except those in fancy tourist hotels remain closed until sunset. Jordanians can be arrested for eating or drinking on the street during the day, and foreigners wishing to avoid ill will should abstain from public displays of consumption. In 1987, Ramadan runs from April 18 to May 18, and is followed immediately by the Id-al-Fitr, three days of feasting and celebration. The Feast of Sacrifice, in the first week of August, also sees public transportation very busy and some offices closed.

You can quickly find the limit of Jordanians' voluminous hospitality by toying with their social customs. Shorts and bare shoulders on either sex make many Jordanians very uncomfortable, and dramatically increase the likelihood of unwanted attention. Everyone should exercise caution with the fierce Arabian sun. It's wise to wear a broad-brimmed hat and light, loose clothing. Always carry and drink much more water than you think you need.

The Jordanian dinar (JD) is divided into 1000fils, 10 of which is commonly called a piaster. All bills and coins are written in Arabic and English. There is no black market. Jordanian banks are normally open daily from 9am to 12:30pm, though foreign banks remain open as late as 5pm, and money exchange shops, offering similar rates to those at the banks, don't close until around 9pm.

You can avoid hours of waiting to place overseas calls from telephone offices in Amman and Aqaba by paying a 20% surcharge for using phones at fancy hotels. To place a local call (50fils), ask a shopowner; public phones (10fils) are virtually non-existent and/or broken. Collect calls are difficult to place except at large hotels in Amman; try the Intercontinental Hotel between Second and Third Circles. An airmail letter to North America costs 240fils, an aerogram 160fils; mail between Jordan and North America takes one to two weeks. Poste Restante operates at the central post office in Amman and in the larger cities. American Express offices also hold mail; they are located in Amman, Irbid, and Aqaba.

Accommodations, Camping, and Food

In Amman and Aqaba, you should expect to pay a minimum of 2JD for a decent bed. In outlying regions, camping is virtually the only alternative to the expensive Government Rest Houses. (Singles about 5.500JD, doubles 6.600JD.) Though there are virtually no organized sites, you can camp just about anywhere; the tourist police will often suggest a safe spot. Invitations to private homes are quite common, especially for men traveling alone or modestly clad couples. Jordan lacks youth hostels entirely.

Though you should exercise caution with Jordanian food, most places, even street stands, are safe for the Western digestive system. Fruits and vegetables, however, should be thoroughly washed or peeled. If you develop diarrhea or stomach discomfort, stick to bland foods; yoghurt may help. Municipal water is safe; bottled water runs 200fils per liter.

Amman

Like Rome, Amman was built on seven hills *(jebels).* Unlike Rome, it *was* built in a day—or perhaps two. Before 1948, Amman was a tiny village; since then, on two separate occasions, Jordan's population doubled in less than a week, with most of the growth in the capital. After the wars of 1948 and 1967, refugees streamed across truce lines to claim the citizenship only Jordan was willing to extend. Now during every work week Amman's population nearly doubles with the influx of workers from the surrounding areas. The result is a collage of loud, hectic markets, shining boulevards with elite housing and tourist hotels, and the measured calls to prayer of *muezzins.*

Orientation and Practical Information

Amman is just about every traveler's first stop in the country. The Y-shaped downtown area centers on the dome-less Al-Husseini Mosque, with 500-meter branches extending west along **King Faisal Street,** northeast to the Roman Amphitheater, and southeast to the kaleidoscopic vegetable and meat market. To the west, Shaaban Street and Prince Mohammed Street climb **Jebel Amman,** one of the original seven hills. Most of the embassies, government offices, and restaurants are strung out here, along the eight numbered traffic circles that lead away from downtown. To the northwest, **King Hussein Street** winds past **Abdali Station,** surrounded by more cheap hotels and the JETT station, before climbing to the ritzy residential district of **Shmeisani.** To the south, the checkered dome of the Abu Darwish Mosque neighbors **Wahadat Station** on Jebel Ashrafieh Talal. Even with a good map of the city (available at the Ministry of Tourism), you'll often need to ask directions.

Tourist Office: Ministry of Tourism, Jebel Amman, 1 block west of Third Circle (tel. 64 23 11). Posters, tourist literature, and free, quality maps of Jordan and Amman. Open Sat.-Thurs. 8am-2pm.

American Express: International Traders, across from the Ambassador Hotel in Shmeisani (tel. 66 10 14). Mail held and traveler's checks sold but not cashed. No wired money accepted. Open Sat.-Thurs. 8am-noon and 3-6pm.

Currency Exchange: Banks open Sat.-Thurs. 9:30am-12:30pm; foreign banks sometimes open later. Authorized currency exchange shops on the streets remain open until 8 or 9pm and give similar rates as banks, though some won't take traveler's checks. Exchange office at the airport open daily 7am-7pm.

Post Office: Prince Mohammed St., on the west side of downtown. Poste Restante here. Open daily 8am-8pm.

Telephones: As you exit the post office, all the way around the corner to the left, then 50m uphill. Open daily 8am-11pm. Arrive before 10pm to place overseas calls. Collect calls only from large hotels. For **information** dial 12. **Telephone code:** 06.

Flights: Bus #31b (100fils) connects **Queen Alia Airport** with Abdali Station in northern Amman. JETT buses (500fils) travel to the JETT station 1km north of Abdali. Service taxis are the cheapest trip downtown (70fils). Regular taxis 5JD. Currency exchange open to meet all flights.

Collective Buses and Service Taxis: Abdali Station, King Hussein St., 2km northwest of downtown, serves points north (Jerash, Ajlun) and King Hussein Bridge. **Wahadat Station,** 3km southeast of downtown or Jebel Ashrafieh, serves points south (Madaba, Aqaba, Karak; Ma'an—transfers there to Wadi Musa for Petra).

JETT Buses: Office on King Hussein St. (tel. 66 41 46 or 66 41 47), 600m northwest (uphill) from Abdali Station. Daily air-conditioned buses to King Hussein Bridge (connecting JETT minibus to the West Bank), Petra, and Aqaba. Buses to King Hussein Bridge and Petra leave early in the morning. Also to Damascus, Syria. Reserve one day in advance. Office open daily 6:30am-8pm.

Public Transportation: Service taxis run fixed routes to most destinations for under 100fils. Buses (60fils) cover similar routes. There are no central stations, so you'll have to ask where they start, or walk along a main street in the direction you want to go until you reach a bus stop: 4 red poles covered by a canopy. Service taxis with room (rare) can also be flagged down at these stops. Regular yellow taxis are expensive, even when they use their meters (insist on this), but are the only alternative to walking after buses and service taxis retire around 7 or 8pm (a couple of hours earlier on Fri.).

Car Rental: Arabian Rent-a-Car (AVIS), Intercontinental Hotel (tel. 64 13 50), between Second and Third Circles.

Emergencies: Call the American Embassy (tel. 64 43 71, 24 hours) and ask them to call for police or ambulance. Officially, it's **Police** (tel. 63 91 41), **Ambulance** (tel. 193 or 77 51 11), and **Medical Emergency** (tel. 63 03 41, 211, or 37 17).

Pharmacies: *The Jordan Times* lists all-night pharmacies. Contraceptives are not available.

Embassies: U.S., midway between Second and Third Circles on Jebel Amman (tel. 64 43 71). **Canada,** off Abd al-Karim al-Khattabi St. in Shmeisani (tel. 66 61 24). **U.K.,** at Third Circle on Jebel Amman (tel. 64 12 67). **Australia,** at Fourth Circle on Jebel Amman (tel. 67 32 46). **New Zealand** nationals should get in touch with the British Embassy. **Egypt,** Jebel Amman (tel. 62 95 26), just west of the American Embassy. For visas, bring one photo and

4.500JD. Regularly massive lines; better to get your visa before leaving home. **Syria,** walk up from Third Circle on Jebel Amman toward the Holiday Inn, take a left at the 5-way intersection, then your first right (tel. 64 13 92). Bring the following for a visa: (1) a letter of recommendation from your embassy, (2) a passport, free of any evidence that you've ever been to Israel and with a Jordanian entry stamp, (3) 2JD, and (4) 2 photos. **Iraq** and **Lebanon** are closed to independent travelers.

Ministry of Interior: At the southwest side of Gamal Abdel Nasser Circle (Ministry of Interior Circle), Jebel Hussein. 3½km northwest of downtown, about 2km northwest of Abdali Bus Station on King Hussein St., at intersection with Queen Noor St. Take bus #53-61, or service taxi #6 from downtown. For West Bank permits, bring 1 photo and two 50fil revenue stamps from a post office. Processing takes 3 working days. Open Sat.-Thurs. 8:30am-2pm; get there in the morning.

Bookstores: University Bookstore, on Jebel Luweibdeh near Khalaf Circle, and **Amman Bookstore,** on Prince Muhammad St. off Third Circle on Jebel Amman, have English paperbacks and books about Jordan.

Hitchhiking: To hitch south on the Desert Highway to Petra and Aqaba, walk 1km west on King Talal St. from the Hussein Mosque to Misdar St., which leads south and out of town. To hitch to Madaba, Karak, or points south on the more scenic King's Highway, try for a ride south from Seventh Circle. Service taxis to Madaba aren't that expensive, and increase your chances of getting a long-distance ride south. Hitch north to Jerash from Eighth Circle.

Accommodations

Budget accommodations cluster downtown around the Al-Husseini Mosque. The cheapest unclassified hotels (1.30-2JD) are regularly filled with guest workers, and are neither a good value nor very clean; solo women may be uncomfortable in (and sometimes are excluded from) these places. The following hotels are safe and beds are always clean, but washing facilites are often poor and showers often cost 250fils extra. Shared rooms (3-5 people) are the norm. Couples often cannot share a room unless married. Double beds do not exist.

Cliff Hotel, King Faisal St. (tel. 242 73), downtown, at the base of King Hussein St. On the 3rd floor, above a cafe. Cheap, small, and friendly, with some surprising amenities: Flush sit-down toilet, sinks in each room, reliable luggage storage. Often filled. Singles 1.500JD, doubles 2.500JD. Beds in shared room 1.350JD.

Bader Hotel, Prince Mohammed St. (tel. 63 76 02), a few blocks up from the post office, downtown. A particularly safe place with friendly management. Women can stay here alone. Will guard your pack for a few days. Singles 2.200JD, doubles 3.850JD.

Al-Monzer Hotel, King Hussein St. (tel. 63 32 44), next to Abdali Station. Clean, quiet rooms and a family atmosphere. Good for single women and couples. Singles 3JD, doubles 5JD.

Abassi Palace Hotel, al-Amaneh St. (tel. 63 85 05), a few blocks (east) behind the al-Husseini Mosque. Safe place where the owner's son speaks English. Singles 3JD, doubles 5JD, triples 6.500JD.

Canary Hotel, (tel. 23 62 37), up the steep hill across from Abdali Station. Air-conditioned rooms and breakfast in the garden. Best place to splurge. Singles 4.500JD, doubles 7JD. 10% service charge.

Food

Downtown is full of cheap street stands. Corn-on-the-cob, salads, breads, cheese, vegetables, and all sorts of meat on a spit are available in the vast markets near the al-Husseini Mosque, by the bus stations, and in the area 1½ blocks south of the stretch between First and Second Circles. *Felafel* sandwiches, stuffed with chopped meat and who knows what else, are a budgetarian staple (100fils each). Most restaurants are open until 9pm; some close for a few hours in the afternoon. During Ramadan, only the fancy restaurants in tourist hotels remain open.

Cairo Restaurant, dowtown near main market. From al-Husseini Mosque, walk 100m southeast and look left for a side street full of golden roasted chickens. Big, bright, orange, and Egyptian. Speedy and friendly service. Cheap feasts: ½ roasted chicken 600fils, *fasula* (bean soup), *fuul* plates (in morning) 200fils, salad 150fils. Open 5am-11pm.

Salaam Restaurant, on King Faisal St. near the al-Husseini Mosque. No English sign. Don't let the ambience put you off; a good chicken dinner for about 1JD more than compensates.

The Jordan Restaurant, opposite the post office, above a sweetshop. Full dinners for 750fils.

Sights

You can take in Amman's handful of outstanding attractions in one afternoon; they're all located downtown. It's hard to miss the second-century B.C.E. **Roman Theater,** the 6000-seat arena around which the city has grown for the last 2000 years. Below the theater's first floor, you'll find the **Folklore Museum** in the south, and the **Museum of Costumes and Jewelry** on the north. Consider the exhibits a prelude to the folk life and culture of the Palestinians, Circassians, and Bedouins you'll meet elsewhere in the country. (Both museums open Wed.-Mon. 9am-5pm; costume museum also open Tues. 9am-5pm. Theater gates close 5:30pm. Admission to each 250fils, students 150fils.) To the west of the theater sit the ruins of the **nymphaeum,** the old Roman fountain. The area beyond the theater has been converted into a pleasant square with a cooling fountain.

The streets facing the theater take you up **Jebel Qala'a** (Citadel Hill) to Amman's **acropolis,** the site of the ancient city; an **Ummayyad Palace** stands beside the ruins of Roman fortifications and a temple to Hercules. Don't miss the magnificent view of the city from the top of Jebel Qala'a. The **Archeological Museum** here presents a sample of findings from excavations throughout Jordan. (Open Wed.-Thurs. and Sat.-Mon. 9am-5pm, Fri. 10am-4pm. Admission 250fils).

Near Amman

The only stretch of sand along Jordan's **Dead Sea** shore lies an hour and a half from Amman. The peculiar buoyancy of this briny sea attracts quite a few Jordanian floaters. The **Dead Sea Rest House** (tel. (05) 57 29 01) charges 250fils for admission, but it offers fresh-water showers (250fils) and an air-conditioned restaurant (fish 1.750JD, beer 750fils). It's safe to sleep on their rock-hard beach, where you'll witness the world's lowest-altitude sunset.

From Amman's Abdali Station, take a morning service taxi bound for the King Hussein Bridge (1.700JD) as far as South Shuna (Shuneh Nimrin on some maps). There Jesus exalted the budget traveler, saying: "It is easier for a camel to pass through the eye of a needle than for a rich man to enter the kingdom of heaven" (Matthew 19:24). A collective minibus also runs to South Shuna from the Ras al-Ain area in southcentral Amman, near Jerusalem St. (200fils). From South Shuna, minibuses shuttle to a village near the Dead Sea Resthouse (about 120fils; last connection at 5pm).

Jerash

The northern town of **Jerash** has the most extensive ruins of any provincial Roman city. Excavations begun in 1925 have uncovered so much that a visit to Jerash is akin to immersion in a Roman bath of antiquities. And while your imagination is spirited away by the columns, theaters, temples, and gates, remember that 90% of ancient Jerash still lies beneath your feet. From the lonesome **Triumphal Arch** built for Emperor Hadrian in 129 C.E., walk north past the **hippodrome** to the main entrance and visitor's center. These lie next to the highway to Amman, just southwest of the modern town. Pass through the ancient walls into the oval-shaped **Forum of Ionian Columns.** The breathtaking **South Theater** is up the hill to the west, while the elegant **Street of Columns** runs for nearly half a kilometer to the north, passing the huge **Temple of Artemis** and numerous other structures.

The yellow booklet (500fils) distributed by the **visitors center** includes a more-than-adequate map and explanation of the sites; don't miss their scale model of ancient Jerash. Walking, talking guides cost 2JD per group (any size). In July the 12-

day **Jerash Festival** fills the ancient city with dance, folklore, and handicrafts. (Admission to most events 2-3JD.) The site closes after the nightly **sound and light show** (1JD), which lasts for the hour and a half following sunset. The **tourist police** at Jerash will ordinarily help you find a free place to camp. The nearest indoor accommodations are 8km southwest of Jerash at the **Government Rest House,** on the road between Jerash and Dibbin National Park. (Singles 5.750JD, doubles 7JD.) Buses (250fils) and service taxis (420fils) connect Jerash Abdali Station in Amman, 50km to the south. Hitching is easy.

The twelfth-century **Qalat al Rabadh** castle looms 1300m over the small town of **Ajlun,** 25km and an easy hitch west of Jerash. Built in response to Crusader castles elsewhere in the region, the fortress is a fine example of Islamic military architecture. The hike up takes almost an hour and features panaramic pastoral views; faster taxis (1JD round-trip) begin on the town's main circle. If you care to spend the night, camp out on the peak or bed down at the expensive **Hotel Rabadh** on the road up. (Singles 6.600JD, doubles 8.800JD.)

Kings' Highway

If you have a car or can hitch and chase minibuses for a couple of days, consider taking the slow route south. The Kings' Highway meanders up and down the rugged canyons which carve through the highlands between Amman and Petra. Anyone visiting Jordan should overcome the minor difficulties of transportation along this road, and travel the length of it. With luck, Amman to Petra is a day's bus and hitch.

In **Madaba,** town of mosaics, visit prominent **St. George's Church,** where priests and caretakers shuffle across a famous sixth-century mosaic map of Palestine. A helpful **Government Rest House** (no beds) is across the street. Other more lively Byzantine mosaics are preserved in the more northerly **museum.** (Open Wed.-Thurs. and Sat.-Mon. 9am-5pm, Fri. 10am-4pm. Admission 250fils.) Northwest of Madaba (10km) is the Biblical **Mount Nebo** where Moses got his first and last look at the Holy Land (Deuteronomy 34). On top, the **Memorial to Moses** houses baptismal fonts and mosaic floors of a Byzantine church. Three hours and 100km south await the mammoth ruins of the **Crusader Castle** at **Karak,** built by Baldwin I to control the triangular trade between Egypt, Syria, and Saudi Arabia. The **Rest House** beside the castle offers a panoramic view, meals (lunch or dinner 1.750JD), singles for 4.500JD, and doubles for 7JD. There is also a **tourist office,** above the **Castle Hotel** (2JD per bed; free showers). The first of the seven castles that Baldwin built is two hours farther south at **Shobak.** The isolated ruins surrounded by a deep natural moat make a romantic spot to camp. North of Karak are the panoramic gorges of Wadi Mujib. Southwards there is another choice of roads: continue along the Kings' Highway to Petra and Aqaba, or take the Jordan Valley Highway, served by buses to Aqaba (JD3; from there you can return to Petra). Those traveling the Jordan Valley Highway must get a permit by showing their passports, as the road is on the Israeli border. Permits are available from police (while you wait, and free) and at bus stations. Hitching is not allowed on the Jordan Valley Highway.

Petra

For more than a mile, you walk in reverent silence through a narrow breach in ochre and amber cliffs. Turning the last corner, you face a towering sculpture, raw red mountains impossibly fashioned by human hands into delicate features. This is the **Khazneh,** the Roman treasury, a prelude to the unreal, purplish city that Nabateans and Romans carved into the canyons beyond. Like Johann Buckhardt, who rediscovered Petra in 1822, you will want to spend days exploring temples and royal tombs carved in cliffs in the far corners of Petra. Unlike that Swiss explorer, you can reach the ancient city on a daytrip from Amman (see below). Today, as always, it's worth the trip to Jordan just to visit Petra.

The Nabateans settled this area in the seventh century B.C.E., and flourished on the trade between the Nile and Euphrates civilizations. Secure in their easily defended capital at Petra, the compulsive sculptors of Nabatea carved huge monuments dedicated to Dushara, god of strength, and Al-Uzza, the goddess of water and fertility. They first drew on Egyptian architecture for ideas, then turned to Greece and Rome; the only truly Nabatean style survives in the crow step staircases climbing the faces of many of the monuments—and even that idiosyncrasy has links with Assyria. The Nabateans kept their independence until 106 C.E., when the Romans entered Petra and began to improve even further on a city that fascinated them. At its height Petra may have housed an incredible 20 to 30,000 people, but following brief Byzantine, Arab, and Crusader occupations, the city was left to the slow decay of time and desert earthquakes.

Once in the valley, you'll see the purple **Roman Theater** to your left, and just before it the staircase up to the **High Place,** where sacrifices were performed. To the right is the long line of magnificent **Royal Tombs.** Ahead, the Roman **Street of Columns** passes the **Nymphaeum** and triple-arched **Temenos Gate** on its way to the **Nabatean Temple.** Behind the temple, the **Zib Faraon** (Pharaoh's Phallus) marks the entrance to the old Roman city; across the street an American team is excavating the workshops of the **Temple of the Winged Lions.** Many of the finds from this and other excavations are housed in the **Petra Museum** at the foot of nearby Jebel Habis. (Museum open Sun.-Thurs. 9am-5pm, Fri. 10am-4pm.) At the top of the mountain (20 min.) is the **Qasr Habis** (Crusader Castle). The huge **ed-Deir** (monastery) is past the **Lion's Tomb,** about half an hour to the west. From the monastery you can see across the Wadi Araba and spot **Jebel Harun,** the highest peak in the area. At the summit, a white church reportedly houses the **Tomb of Aaron.** On excursions into Petra, it's wise to bring plenty of water and your own food; the **Nabatean Shop** is overpriced, and the cliffside **Forum Restaurant** is downright expensive (meals 2.500JD).

The entrance to Petra, 5km west of the Kings' Highway, lies 2km below the main traffic circle in Wadi Musa village. Admission is 1JD for adults. Poorly enforced opening hours are 5am to 6pm (it's worth getting in to see the colors of the stones change at sunrise), but you can slip in for illicit camping until 8pm or later. The **tourist police** or staffers at the rest house next to the entrance gate can point out safe places for free camping outside Petra. The renovated **Government Rest House** (tel. 830 11) asks a steep 5JD for single-, and 7.700JD for double-occupancy of their bungalows or hotel rooms. Meals here are 1.500-2JD. The best cheap lodging is just outside Petra itself in Wadi Musa ("The Vale of Moses"), so-called because the spring that appears there is said to have been miraculously produced by Moses to slake the thirst of the Children of Israel returning from Egypt. The **Mousa Spring Hotel** (no tel.) is clean and friendly, with a good restaurant (1.500JD for a full meal), and free hot showers. A free shuttle bus takes you from hotel to Petra and back. (2JD per bed.) Negotiate a lower price for a mattress on the roof.

Wadi Musa and Petra lie 270km south of Amman and 130km north of Aqaba. **JETT buses** travel once per day from Amman (leave at 6:30am, return at 3pm, 4½ hr., 3JD one way). Book at least one day in advance. **Service taxis** from Amman's Wahadat Station usually wait for a while in Ma'an (5 hr., 2.650JD). From Aqaba, minibuses make the trip to Wadi Musa daily (2 hr., 1-1.500JD).

Aqaba

To some, Aqaba may seem an uninteresting port town that doubles as a swinging Arabian winter resort. Others have been swimming.

Legions of brilliantly colored fish romp through a fantasyland of coral in the waters surrounding Aqaba. The best beaches and snorkeling can be found between the ferry terminal, 10km south of town, and the Saudi Arabian border. Rent equipment at most luxury hotels along the *corniche* northwest of town. (2JD per day for equipment, 2.500JD including transportation at Aquamarina Club next to Aqaba Hotel.)

A number of inexpensive hotels and most services cluster around Municipality Square; the cheapest sleeps are on the mattresses on the roof of the decent **Jerusalem Hotel** (tel. 31 48 15; roof 700fils, singles 1.500JD, doubles 2.500JD). The best cheap place for solo women is the **Red Sea Hotel** (tel. 31 21 56), just northwest of Municipality Sq. (singles 2.500JD, doubles 4JD). Spoil yourself with air-conditioning and a private beach at the **Aqaba Hotel,** 1km west of town. (Singles 8JD, doubles 9.200JD.)

Fish may be the main source of entertainment in Aqaba, but they're not the dietary staple. **Sinbad's Fish Restaurant,** on the beach, is one of the few places that serves fresh fish. (Meals 2JD.) For land-based fare, visit the festive, inexpensive **Cafeteria Mohandes,** 250m north of Municipality Sq., on the road to Amman. *Hummus malakma* (with meat, tomatoes, and cucumber) costs 820fils; *fuul* with *tahina* is 240fils. (Open daily 6am to 1 or 2am.) The nearby **Ali Baba Restaurant,** 2 blocks west of Municipality Sq., offers tasty fare on a tacky outdoor patio. (Spaghetti 770fils, beer 400fils. Open daily 6am-1am.)

Aqaba sends a constant stream of cargo-laden trucks up the 335km to Amman; hitching is good. **Service taxis** make the trip from their stand just southeast of Municipality Sq. (To Amman 3-4JD. To Ma'an 1JD, transfer at Petra. Daily minibus to Petra 1JD.) Hitch a ride to Amman with a truck, or catch a comfortable **JETT** bus from the station, 1km west of town on the *corniche* past the Miramas Hotel. (5 per day 7am-4pm, 4½ hr., 3JD.)

Jordanian National Lines (in Amman tel. 78 27 82) send two ferries per day (at 11am and 4:30pm) from Aqaba to Nuweiba on the Sinai in Egypt (2¾ hr., deck class 7.500JD; arrive 1 hr. early for customs). At least one ferry per day heads for Suez—a grueling and expensive cruise. Save yourself hours and have Egyptian visas issued before leaving home; the nearest office that issues them here is in Amman. In Aqaba, purchase tickets from any agency; in Amman, at the JETT station.

Near Aqaba

To experience the awesome rusty crags and desert expanses of **Wadi Rum,** you'll have to hitchhike or rent a car. Buses or taxis along the Desert Highway can drop you at the turn-off, 25km north of Amman; from there it's fairly easy (easier in spring than in summer) to hitch the 30km to the headquarters building of the picturesque **Bedouin Desert Camel Corps,** cowering in the heart of the stupendous Wadi. With the Desert Police HQ as your base, you can camp, hike, or take a camel or jeep ride (2-8JD) to explore the peaks, spring, and sand dunes of the area. To reach and explore Wadi Rum independently, rent a car from **Khaled El Qedreh Rent-A-Car** (tel. 48 18), 600m north of the east side of Municipality Sq. in Aqaba. (4.500JD per 24 hr., 36fils per km. Open 8:30am-1:30pm and 2:30-5:30pm.)

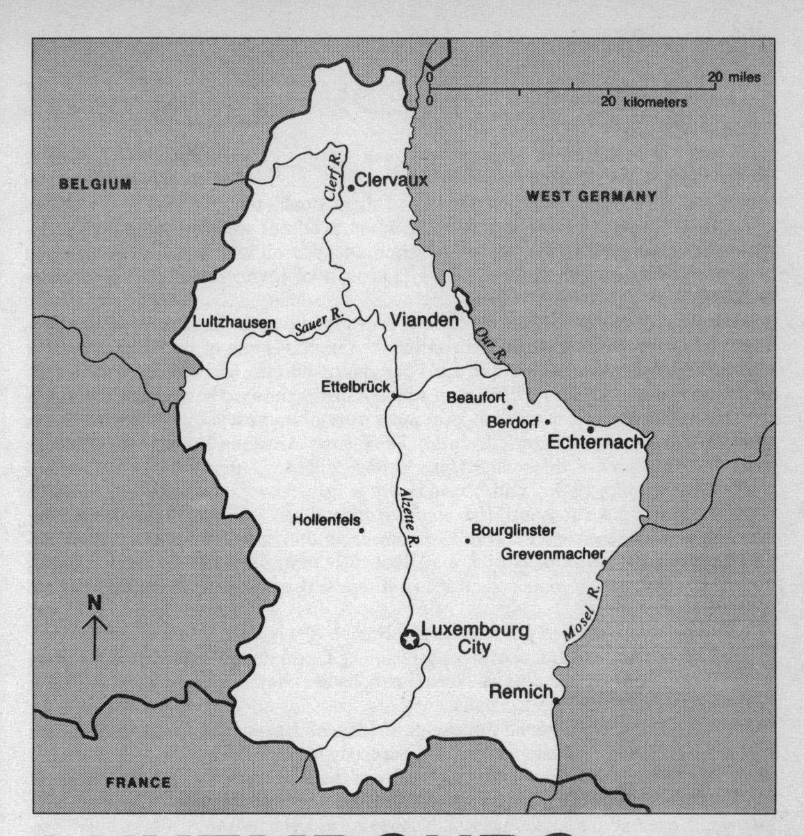

LUXEMBOURG

US$1 = 37.0 francs (LF) — **10LF = US$0.27**
CDN$1 = 28.6LF — **10LF = CDN$0.35**
UK £1 = 61.7LF — **10LF = UK£0.16**
AUS$1 = 26.9LF — **10LF = AUS $0.37**

Tiny Luxembourg has been a pawn in the European chessboard of power and politics, but it has been a pawn of the seventh rank. For centuries, Luxembourg has held an importance which belies its size, and which has kept the heavy pieces surrounding it watchful and wary. Founded in 963, it was first named *Luclinburhuc,* or "little castle." By the time successive waves of Burgundians, Spaniards, French, Austrians, and Germans had receded, the little castle had become a bristling armored mountain and the countryside was saturated with fortresses: Others could no longer afford to ignore Luxembourg. Only after the last French soldier returned home in 1867, and the Treaty of Paris restored its neutrality, did Luxembourg cultivate the image of a peaceful Grand Duchy. Today Luxembourg is a European financial center, and home to banks from all over the world.

Luxembourg's embattled history shows in the scarred fortifications of its capital, and in the steep citadels and fortresses that dot the landscape. From the wooded and hilly Ardennes in the north to the fertile vineyards of the Mosel Valley in the south, its unspoiled countryside delights worn-out travelers and adventure-seekers alike. Hike, boat, fish, cycle, or camp—or just savor the landscape as you enjoy the fine local wine.

Transportation and Practical Information

Luxembourg is only 2600km square, so there's not very far to go. Both Eurail and InterRail will whisk you across the country by rail *or* bus; you pay about 3-4LF per kilometer independently. All train and bus stations sell **Billets Reseaux** good for unlimited second-class train and bus travel. (Not valid for buses running within the city.) A one-day ticket—worthwhile only on long round-trips—is 217LF; a five-day ticket (658LF) is good for any five days in a 15-day period. A **Benelux Pass,** good for unlimited travel in Belgium, the Netherlands, and Luxembourg, costs 2390LF for any five days in a 17-day span, and only 1790LF for ages under 26. (This is a good deal—it's not that much more expensive than a one-way ticket from Luxembourg to Amsterdam.) On weekends, all trains and buses are half price. Bicycles are permitted on any train for 18LF (regardless of distance). Hitching is generally fair—distances are short, but traffic is light.

The tourist office network in Luxembourg is exhaustive. Every town of substantial size (over a few thousand) has an office, providing local and national information. Most are open from 10am to noon and from 2 to 6pm. The youth hostels are also great sources of information, and frequently offer discounts on guided tours. The hostel association maintains trails (well-marked with white triangles) between each of their houses.

The official language of Luxembourg is French, the most commonly spoken language Luxembourgeois (a bewildering fusion of German and French). But nearly every Luxembourger is trilingual, speaking polished German, French, and Luxembourgeois. Many also speak English.

Most banks are open Monday through Friday 9:30am to 5pm, most shops Monday through Friday 9:30am to 6pm and Saturday 9:30am to noon. However, many shops close at noon for two hours, especially in the countryside where even the post offices close. These untouristed towns lock up early; after 6pm only the taverns may be open. Luxembourg francs are worth the same as Belgian francs; you can use Belgian money in Luxembourg, but not vice versa. Some restaurants accept French and German money, but you'd be wise to change your money at a bank, where rates are better.

Accommodations, Camping, and Food

There are 10 IYHF hostels in Luxembourg, charging 140LF for ages under 26 and 180LF for everyone else (20LF higher in the capital). Breakfasts are 70LF, packed lunches 85LF, and dinners 170LF (with dessert). You pay 15LF less to stay if you eat a meal at the hostel. Most require sheets and charge 60LF if you don't have your own; all require membership. Members over 35 will only be given a spot if there is one available. There is a network of hiking trails in Luxembourg connecting all the youth hostels, and all hostels (except the one in Grevenmacher) have kitchens for members.

Hotels in Luxembourg are generally expensive, especially in the heavily touristed towns of Echternach, Clervaux, Vianden, and Remich. Fortunately, the situation is alleviated by an immense number of campgrounds; amenities vary, but most have hot and cold running water. Two people with a tent can expect to pay around 200LF.

The food in Luxembourg is heavily influenced by French cuisine. Still, enjoy such independently created specialties as *treipen* (black pudding), *quenelles* (calf's liver dumplings), and, in season (April-Sept.), fried trout or crayfish. The local Mosel wines, white and sparkling, are as excellent as the local beers.

Luxembourg

Poised at the edge of two steep gorges, the city of Luxembourg is one of the most physically dramatic capitals in Europe. The country's rolling landscapes penetrate the city, and medieval walls and spires share the skyline with prosperous international banks and office complexes.

Practical Information

Tourist Offices: Grand Duchy National Tourist Office, Pl. de la Gare, in the Luxair office (tel. 48 11 99), to the right as you leave the train station. Information on city and country, walking tours, lists of accommodations and sights, and free hotel reservations. Open July to mid-Sept. daily 9am-7:30pm; mid-Sept. to June daily 9am-noon and 2-6:30pm. A branch office at **Place d'Armes** (tel. 228 09), in the center of town, offers identical services, and also posts a list of concerts outside. Open July to mid-Sept. Mon.-Fri. 9am-1pm and 2-8pm, Sat. 9am-1pm and 2-7pm, Sun. 10am-noon and 2-6pm; mid-Sept. to June Mon.-Sat. 9am-1pm and 2-6pm.

Budget Travel: SOTOUR, 15, pl. du Théâtre (tel. 226 73 or 46 15 14). BIGE and other deals. Open Mon.-Fri. 8am-6pm, Sat. 10am-4pm.

American Express: 6-8 rue Origer (tel. 49 60 41), a short walk from the train/bus station. Mail held. Traveler's checks cashed, sold, and replaced, but no wired money accepted. Open Mon.-Fri. 9am-1pm and 2-5pm, Sat. 9am-noon.

Currency Exchange: Long hours and mediocre rates in the train station. Open Mon.-Sat. 8:30am-9pm, Sun. 9am-9pm. Better rates at banks.

Post Office: 38, pl. de la Gare. Open daily 6am-10pm. Poste Restante open daily 6am-8pm.

Telephones: 25, rue Aldringen. Open Mon.-Fri. 7am-8pm, Sat. 7am-7pm.

Flights: Bus #9 (25LF plus 25LF for luggage) is cheaper than the Luxair bus (120LF), and runs the same airport-hostel-train station route.

Trains: Gare CFL, av. de la Gare, near its intersection with av. de la Liberté. In the southern part of the city, a 20-min. walk from the city center. Bus #9 runs between the railway station, the hostel, and the airport. Pick it up on your right as you leave the station, in front of the Luxair office. **Buses** also run from this station.

Public Transportation: Buy a punch card at the railway station; 10 municipal bus rides for 175LF.

Emergencies: Police (tel. 49 49 49); headquarters at rue Glesner. **Ambulance** (tel. 012).

Medical Assistance: Call 012, the 24-hour access number for physicians/pharmacists (English spoken).

Embassies: U.S., 22, bd. E. Servais (tel. 401 23). **U.K.,** 14, bd. Roosevelt (tel. 298 64). Travelers from **Canada, Australia,** and **New Zealand** should contact the British Embassy.

Laundry: 3, pl. Strasbourg. Open Mon.-Tues. and Thurs.-Fri. 8am-7pm, Wed. 2-6pm, Sat. 8am-6pm.

Accommodations, Camping, and Food

The affordable hotels are near the station; the older and more scenic part of town is across the ravine, but you pay for the view. Rooms along rue Joseph Junck are inexpensive too, but it's an undesirable area. Remember that the tourist office can help you find a room (no service charge).

Auberge de Jeunesse (IYHF), 2, rue du Fort Olizy (tel. 268 89), 6km from the airport, 15 min. from the train station, accessible by bus #9 from both. Located in the Vallée d'Alzette off rue Sigefroi in the northeast section of town. Modern and well-equipped, if crowded and strict. Members only. Ages under 26 160LF, ages 26 and older 200LF. Sheets 60LF. Breakfast 70LF, dinner 170LF. Check-in 3-10pm. Lockout 9am-2pm. Strict midnight curfew. Open year-round. You can rent bikes for 300LF for the first day, 150LF each day thereafter.

Hotel Carlton, 9, rue de Strasbourg (tel. 48 48 02). Ornate lobby, clean rooms, cheerful management. Shoebox singles 600LF, larger doubles 1380LF. Breakfast included.

Hotel Atlas, 30, rue du Fort Neipperg (tel. 48 72 55), the first right off pl. de la Gare as you leave the station. Slight ambience of decay. Singles 800LF, doubles also 800LF.

Camping: Kockelscheuer (tel. 47 18 15). Adults 70LF, ages 15-18 55LF. 100LF per tent. Disabled access. Open Easter-Oct.

Luxembourg isn't a city for the budget eater. Your best option is to shop at grocery stores. The many *charcuteries* sell *wirstchen* (fried sausages) for 55LF and quiche for 80LF. For traditional Luxembourgeois fare try **Le Papillon,** 9, rue Origer, halfway between the train station and the center of town, with lunch *menus* for 220LF, and dinner *menus* for 250-400LF. Also consider **Ems,** 30, pl. de la Gare, or **Da Gennero,** 13, rue du fort Elisabeth.

Sights and Entertainment

The city of Luxembourg is worth a day of sightseeing, and the tourist office has a well-organized walking guide to the major sights. Easily the most impressive of these is the **Casemates Bock,** the oldest part of the town fortress. A masterwork of tunnels and storerooms, the Bock casemates sheltered 35,000 people from bombs during World War II. Over 13 miles of passageways remain open today. From the entrance at rue Sigefroi, near chemin de la Corniche, explore its corkscrew staircases and catch tremendous views through the loopholes. (Open March-Oct. 10am-6pm. Admission 30LF.) The streets nearby are the oldest in town. **St. Michael's Church** has stones laid in 987. The earliest section of the facade of the **Grand-Ducal Palace** is a magnificent example of the Spanish Renaissance style. The multilingual tours are mandatory, and tickets (80LF) must be bought in advance at the tourist office. (Open mid-July to Sept. Mon.-Tues. and Thurs.-Sat. 10am-5pm.) The streets below and to the west of the **Musées de l'État** drop among gardens into the ravines. (Open Tues.-Fri. 10am-noon and 1-5pm, Sat. 2-6pm, Sun. 10am-noon and 2-6pm. Free.) When you tire of the crowded old city, head for the parks along the shaded River Pétrusse or, for a change of pace, visit the Portuguese and Italian quarter along **rue St-Ulric** in the Alzette ravine. You can hear guitarists, bands, and choirs in the evening at **place d'Armes.** *La Semaine à Luxembourg,* available at the tourist office, lists the week's events.

Countryside

The wooded Ardennes and shallow rivers of Luxembourg's countryside will entice you away from the city quickly and permanently. From the train stations in Luxembourg and Ettelbrück, you can take the brown CFL buses to the smaller towns (Luxembourg-Echternach every hr., 121LF; Ettelbrück-Echternach 2 per hr., 110LF; Echternach-Vianden 2 per day, 116LF; Vianden-Ettelbrück 9 per day, 64LF). Railpasses are valid. Make sure your bus is direct, or your progress will be slow.

Ettelbrück is perhaps the best base for exploring the countryside; stay at the **IYHF youth hostel,** promenade de l'Alzette (tel. 822 69), a 25-minute walk south of the station (head left from the station, keep heading left through the main part of town, and follow the signs). This place often has room when nearby hostels are booked solid. (Members 140LF, nonmembers 180LF. Reception open 5-11pm, but luggage can be left from 2pm. Closed mid-Feb. to mid-March, early Nov.-early Dec., and several other weekends.) **Camp** in Ettelbrück at **Kalkesdelt** (tel. 821 85) for 80LF per person, 80LF per site. Open Apr.-Sept.

As you work your way into the countryside, you'll find hostels, in addition to those below, at **Beaufort** (6, rue de l'Auberge, tel. 860 75); **Bourglinster** (2, rue de Gonderange, tel. 781 46); **Grevenmacher** (Grueverek, tel. 752 22); **Hollenfels** (2, rue du Château, tel. 307 37); and **Lultzhausen** (tel. 894 24).

Echternach

Festivals, medieval buildings, and magnificent scenery attract visitors to Echternach. The **tourist office** in the **Basilica** coolly coordinates it all (tel. 722 30). (Open July-Aug. daily 9am-noon and 2-6pm; Sept.-June Mon.-Sat. only. From the bus station head left through the pedestrian zone and follow the signs.) In early June, the acclaimed month-long **Festival of Music, Dance, and Art** begins. The tourist office has standby seats, available to students half an hour before performances (150LF; otherwise 300-800LF). Concerts are held in the **Benedictine Abbey,** founded in honor of St. Willibrord, whose bones are in the crypt. The **IYHF youth hostel,** 9, rue Andre Duchscher (tel. 721 58), charges the usual. (Sheets 60LF. Breakfast 70LF, dinner 170LF. Reception open 5-11pm, but you can leave luggage earlier.) The cheapest alternative to the hostel is **Bon Accueil,** 3, rue des Merciers (tel. 720 52), which has spacious rooms. (Singles 500-580LF, doubles 850-950LF. Breakfast included.) The cheaper of the town's campsites are both near the bus station: **Camp officiel** (tel. 722 72), charges 80LF per person, 80LF per site (disabled access; open March 25-Oct. 20), and **Terrain Myers** (tel. 720 12), costs 45LF per person, 50LF per site.

Near Echternach lies the region called Little Switzerland. To explore its hills or the River Sûre, pick up the tourist office guide (60LF); it describes 12 walks (3-30km) in the vicinity. Or just climb rue Gibraltar for a stunning view. Another alternative is to wind up through forested ravines from Echternach to the small farming town of **Berdorf** (6km, letter "G" on the map), then take the CFL bus back. The trail plunges deep into the hills and then follows the rugged **Gorge du Loup,** offering spectacular views.

Vianden

Vianden, the refuge of expatriated Victor Hugo and romantics everywhere, spills down a steep hill beneath a severe ninth-century **chateau.** Dutch tourists crowd the riverside parades, and Dutch dishes are served in the restaurants, all because Vianden is the ancestral home of the formidable Orange-Nassau dynasty, rulers of Holland and (in the person of William III) England. The **tourist office** (tel. 842 57) is in the **Victor Hugo House,** on rue de la Gare, beside the bridge over the River Our. (Open April-Nov. daily 9:30am-noon and 2-6pm; Dec.-March Thurs.-Tues. only.) The town's friendly **IYHF youth hostel,** 3 Montée du Château (tel. 841 77), is a healthy walk from the tourist office: Cross the bridge on Grand' Rue, walk up the hill until you reach 85, Grand' Rue, then make a left up the steep alley. (Reception open from 5pm, but downstairs room open for luggage storage all day.) A list of rooms to rent in private homes (200-400LF) is kept at the tourist office. There are three campsites on the River Our: **Camp op dem Deich** (tel. 843 75) costs 85LF per person, 90LF per site (open April 18-Sept. 27); **Camp du Moulin** (tel. 845 01) costs the same (open May 27-Aug. 31); and **Camp de l'Our** (tel. 845 05) costs 80LF per person, 80LF per site, plus 30LF for showers (disabled access; open May 1-Sept. 15). All three campsites are easily reached by bus. Europe's largest hydroelectric plant, the **Barrage,** stands 1km upstream; the view of the chateau from here or from the top of the *télésiège* route (a giddy 110LF round-trip ride on a chairlift) is stunning. The chateau itself, undergoing reconstruction at a snail's pace, is floodlit on summer nights. (Open in summer daily 9am-7pm; in Oct. 10am-4:30pm. Admission 80LF.)

Clervaux

Clervaux, perched on one of the northernmost hillsides of the Ardennes, is distinguished by a twelfth-century **castle;** once the property of the crusading counts of Lannoi, it guards a bend of the River Clerve. Damaged in the Battle of the Bulge, which raged here through December 1944, this castle is still undergoing restoration—if you want more castles, clay miniatures fill the interior of this one. (Open April-Sept. daily 10am-5pm. Admission 30LF, students 15LF.) The **tourist office,** just outside the castle gate, can suggest rewarding hikes (tel. 920 72). (Open July-Aug. daily 10am-noon and 2-6pm; April-Sept. Mon.-Sat. 2-5pm.) There is no hostel in Clervaux, but **Camp Officiel** (tel. 920 42) is open from April to mid-November. (100LF per person, 80LF per site.) Hotels are less expensive in nearby **Troisvierges**—try **Hotel Hornung** at 4, rue d'Asselborn (tel. 982 26), with singles 420-500LF and doubles from 850LF. The restaurant at the **Hôtel des Nations,** across from the station, has a *menu du jour* for about 220LF.

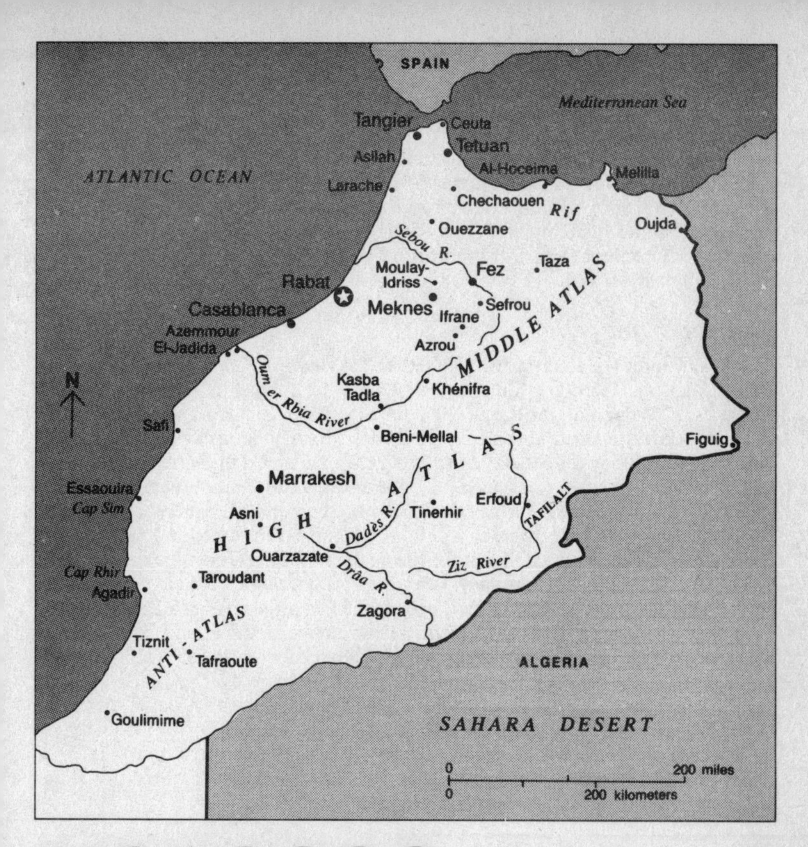

MOROCCO

US$1 = 7.90 dirhams(dh) **10dh = US$1.26**
UK£1 = 13.18dh **10dh = UK£0.76**

The Strait of Gibraltar separates not just Spain and Morocco but two worlds. You can't just sightsee in Morocco. With every step your senses are barraged; the crowds, the animals, the droning, wailing prayers, the pounding desert sun. It's all routine to Moroccans, but boggling to most Westerners. Hashish is everywhere, yet alcohol is taboo to devout Muslims. Hustlers threaten to form a barrier from other natives who are at once infinitely curious and unnervingly timid. The hoods and veils, the smells, songs, and smoke, the abject poverty and the abandoned wealth of colonialism—all conspire to inspire in this paradise of paradox.

The mountains and high plateaus of Morocco have been settled since time immemorial by Berber tribesmen, but the coastal towns have seen a parade of foreign rulers, including Phoenicians, Carthaginians, and Romans. Then Idris Ibn Abdullah founded an Islamic empire that was to stretch far north into Spain. Europeans reconquered the Iberian peninsula in the fifteenth century, and by the nineteenth had completely turned the tables: Morocco was divided into two protectorates, one Spanish, the other French. A nationalist movement rallied around Sultan Mohammed V after World War II, and French Morocco won independence in 1956. Spanish Morocco did not win independence until 1969, and relations betwen Morocco and Spain are still soured by the issue of anti-Muslim discrimination in the Spanish sovereign enclaves at Ceuta and Melilla. Sultan Hassan II (Mohammed's successor) has bigger problems, however—an 11 year-old war against Algerian-backed Polisario guerillas in the Western Sahara rages unabated to this day. Affected regions are far from the itinerary of any traveler, in the arid southwest of the country.

For more detailed coverage of Morocco than we offer here, try *Let's Go: Spain, Portugal, and Morocco,* or the *Rough Guide to Morocco.* Other good, if less useful, traveling companions are Edith Wharton's *In Morocco,* or anything by Paul Bowles or Mohammed Mrabet.

Getting There

You can enter the country through either Tangier or Ceuta ("Sebta" in Arabic). From Algeciras there are four ferries per day to Tangier in summer (2½ hr., 2080ptas; 20% discount for Eurail, 30% for InterRail), and three per day in winter. From Algeciras to Ceuta there are 6-12 ferries Monday-Saturday and 3-5 on Sunday, depending upon the season (2 hr., 1100ptas). Tangier is the better port of entry, as it is better connected to other parts of Morocco than Ceuta. Ceuta may be less shocking to a Westerner, but getting across the border here can be a nightmare. If you have trouble at the border, don't go back to Spain; wait for a few hours to see if the official is replaced. To make the customs officer happy, look respectable, be polite, and have plenty of money. Bearers of passports with Israeli or South African stamps are theoretically refused entry, but this almost never happens.

In more theory, the **Trans-Mahgreb Railway** connects Rabat and Tunis, but the line is often disturbed or unusable because of the conflict over the Spanish Sahara. It's cheaper to fly between Tunis and Morocco than to go overland anyway, since you have to change 1000 dinar (US$250) in order to cross the Algerian border in either direction. Any Westerner who's not driving a car will be turned away; it's possible to hitch a ride with engineers and construction workers returning to oil drill sites. Hang around the tourist office in Oujda if you want to try this route. Crossing *into* Morocco from Algeria presents no problems.

Transportation

Trains are faster, more expensive, and more comfortable than buses, but the **ONCF** network is limited to two routes: Tangier-Rabat-Casablanca-Marrakesh, and Casablanca-Rabat-Meknes-Fes-Oujda. Buses are more frequent and connect all cities, but are much less comfortable for long hauls. **CTM,** the national bus line, is best, with fares that work out to about 12dh per 100km. There are countless other private lines; buses are often overcrowded, but are usually the only way to get to smaller villages. Baggage that is too big to put on the overhead shelf will be put on the roof of the bus (about 2dh per bag). Many routes, especially in the south, run only once or twice per day, and you may find yourself stranded if you get off during the journey. Another thing to consider is whether your bus is en route or originates in the city where you board. Many of the former arrive full, and you could be delayed hours waiting for a place.

Collective taxis and *grand taxis* are often very reasonable. Sometimes they are the only choice for traveling between cities, and often cost only 5-10dh more than bus service. Most cut-rate car rental agencies are based in Casablanca and Agadir. Hitching is erratic, even on well-traveled roads, not to mention dangerous. Moreover, truck drivers often demand more money than buses traveling the same route.

Within cities, *buses urbaines* never cost more than 2.20dh, and *petit taxis* are very cheap—fares usually run between 4 and 10dh. Always ask the driver to use the meter. Taxis are prohibited by law from carrying more than three people, and there is a 50% surcharge after 8pm.

Practical Information

Many towns have both a state-run tourist office and a semi-private *syndicat d'initiative.* Many are nothing more than staffed brochure stands, but some will change money for you when banks are closed. Black-market money transactions are never any more profitable than official exchanges and are perilous to boot—hustlers have a full bag of tricks with which to rip you off.

Morocco's brief term as a French protectorate left a lasting imprint; French remains the official commercial language and is spoken widely. Still, you should learn a few words of Arabic. Even a simple *shokran* (thank you) will be rewarded with an appreciative smile.

Morocco is a poor country with few good jobs and staggering unemployment. When a service is performed for you, a small tip is always appreciated and may be the key required to open locked gates. At every tourist spot in Morocco, you will be approached and told that you need a **guide.** Such guides are illegal and often incompetent, but a good one can show you places you may never find otherwise. Guides also keep other hustlers and pesky kids out of your way. If you hire a guide, fix the price beforehand. Make it clear that you want to go sightseeing—not shopping, smoking, or anything else—and know where you and your belongings are at all times. Never go shopping with a guide—they make a healthy commission on anything you buy.

As a general rule, don't go with anyone who is very insistent on showing you around. This doesn't mean that every local is out to swindle you, but you should be wary of strangers who approach you without invitation or offer you something you don't want. People whom you approach are far more likely to give accurate information. If you refuse someone's services, his persistence depends on many things. In large cities the "guides" will often wish you a good vacation and move on, while in a more rural area they may have nothing better to do than tag along. Your attitude in refusing the guide's offers also has a great deal to do with the way you are received. Don't be frightened or too adamant without provocation. A simple question or compliment on the city can transform the person from a predator into your impromptu protector. This is in fact a good strategy when dealing with all Moroccans: A visitor who's interested is far less likely to be alienated or harrassed than one consumed by paranoia. To refuse all invitations to share a meal or a few hours is to miss perhaps the most satisfying way to spend time in Morocco.

Ten to twenty dirhams is a fair price for two to three hours with a guide. Beware of the "Berber money" trick; the notion that "Berber money" is five times as valuable as regular dirhams is pure fiction. Official guides can be engaged through tourist offices for 25 to 40dh per half day. These guides tend to be less personable and more expensive than the locals. Don't be fooled by street hustlers posing as official guides; the real guides who work with the tourist office have numbered bronze badges and can only be engaged through the office.

Solo travelers may encounter the challenge of their lives in Morocco. Those unfamiliar with the language and culture may sorely miss the cultural buffer a travel companion can provide, as well as the assurance found in numbers. A companion can help you deal with the hustlers, decipher maps or street signs, and accompany you on forays into the *medina*s. There have been reports of abuses committed on solo travelers, regardless of gender, and caution is therefore advisable if you're bent on braving it by yourself.

Very few women travel alone here. Common sense and cultural sensitivity are the best means of coping with unpleasant situations and avoiding threatening ones. Emulate the dress of local women as much as possible. Look as if you know where you're going—an air of confidence and composure can work wonders. If a situation becomes genuinely threatening, a tirade (in any language), especially in the presence of onlookers, is effective.

Although **marijuana** *(kif)* and **hashish** *(hash* or *chocolate)* are plentiful and often openly smoked, *drugs are not legal,* and, especially in the north around the Rif Mountains, there are road checks. In the Rif, where it's all grown, these laws are not rigidly enforced, but caution is still advisable. As you walk down almost any street, you'll be surrounded by hustlers murmuring "hashish, hashish." Say you don't smoke, and never admit to already having something. Many Moroccan dealers double as police officers—*caution* is the key word.

Morocco's **climate** often surprises visitors who prepare for blistering heat but encounter chilly nights, ocean breezes, and snow-covered mountains. It's wise to bring a wool sweater and a pair of long pants or a long skirt wherever you plan to be in the country. Winters are warmer inland than on the coast, and July and August are much hotter off the seashore. Only in the Atlas Mountains are winters truly wintry, but hot, dry days can be followed by cool and even cold desert nights throughout the country and the year. The southern region and the Sahara are suffocating during the summer. Be sure to bring plenty of bottled water wherever you go in these areas. Try to live in "inverted time"—be active in the early morning and late evening and rest during the hot afternoon.

Most Moroccan cities are made up of two parts: the *medina,* which usually is the old walled portion of the city, and the *ville nouvelle,* which consists of more modern buildings. The *medina* is usually the only area of interest to the tourist: It is where one finds artisans's shops, cultural attractions, and the most inexpensive accommodations and food. Because of the narrow, winding alleyways, the *medina* is often more intimidating than the *ville nouvelle,* but both areas are equally dangerous late at night. There's no law in Morocco against walking down the middle of the street after dark.

During the month-long Islamic holiday of **Ramadan,** pious Muslims will not smoke, eat, or drink between sunrise and sunset. Travel during the day is easier since there are fewer people about, but it's wise to abstain from any public displays of consumption. Each evening during Ramadan is marked by a flurry of activity in cafes, restaurants, and streets. Ramadan in 1988 will be from April 18 to May 18.

Using the local telephones is usually not worth the bother. International telephones are located at the main post offices (PTT). For emergency aid in any city, phone the police (tel. 19).

Accommodations, Camping, and Food

Morocco is a tremendously cheap place to travel. Inflation is negligible; after a good year, prices may even go down. Because things are so cheap, campgrounds may not be worth the trouble of lugging your gear around; charges are generally 5dh per person plus 3dh per tent. Moroccan IYHF youth hostels (there are 9) charge 10dh but vary tremendously in quality. On the other hand, they're an excellent place to meet other travelers, an especially important consideration here. As a rule, the cheapest hotels are in the *medina;* 15 to 20dh per person is a good rate for a budget room, but remember that an extra 10 to 20dh may get you a large, comfortable room in a modern hotel, often in a newer part of town. Showers cost 2 to 5dh; in cheaper places hot water is often available only at certain times, if at all. *Hamman* (public Turkish baths) or *bain-douches* (public showers) run 2.50 to 3dh, and are a good source of hot water. Always be sure to carry toilet paper with you; getting used to the holes-in-the-ground that prevail in holes-in-the-wall will be trouble enough. Neat dress and an obvious camera might gain you admission to the cleaner restrooms of modern hotels.

Couscous is the national dish of semolina grain covered with saffron-flavored chicken, beef, lamb, or fish, and cooked with onions, fruits, beans, and nuts. Local restaurants invariably serve meats roasted or smothered in a *tajine,* a fruit and vegetable stew with olives, prunes, or artichokes. You can always enjoy a steaming bowl of *harira,* a soup of chicken, chickpeas, and assorted spices, for 2 to 6dh, and you can find *brochettes* and *kefta* (balls of delicately-seasoned ground meat) for about .60-1.50dh per skewer. Briny olives (at only 1dh per kg.), roasted almonds, and cactus-bud innards are great snack foods. A "complete" or "standard" restaurant meal will include an entree, salad or *harira,* vegetables, and an orange or yogurt for dessert. If tip is not automatically included, 10% is ample.

Although only introduced in the eighteenth century by the English, the ritual of tea preparation, using sprigs of fresh mint and great quantities of sugar, dominates the daily routine of contemporary Moroccan life. You may find that a glass of tea will slake your thirst better than any cold drink. If you're lucky enough to be invited to a traditional rural feast, scoop up mouthfuls of food with pieces of bread, or shovel with the middle three fingers of your right hand (never the left, which is saved for a later stage of the digestive process).

For the sake of your health, drink *Sidi Ali* or *Sidi Harazem,* heavily chlorinated mineral water sold everywhere at 2.20-4dh per 1½-liter bottle. If the bottle isn't completely sealed, it's tap water. Although the water is reputedly safe in the north, unpurified water and uncooked vegetables are likely to wreak havoc on your bowels. In general, peel all fruit and wash everything thoroughly. A one-day fast is generally the best cure for diarrhea; local remedies (yogurt, or lemon or lime juice with salt) can also be effective. Over-the-counter remedies are also commonly available.

Tangier

While most people who visit think Tangier is a decent if uninteresting place, there is a vocal minority who give it a bad rep. Don't believe the horror stories you hear, and take Mark Twain's curse of "that African perdition called Tangier" with a grain of salt. You'll find that Tangier is not entirely unappealing: Throbbing drums in the *kasbah* conjure up images of remote oases in deepest Sahara, while Parisian-style cafes around the corner add a cosmopolitan twist.

Orientation and Practical Information

Hustling freshly-arrived foreigners have become a formidable industry in Tangier. Be polite but firm with anyone eager to accompany you, and particularly cautious if you venture into the *medina* or *kasbah* at night. Unwelcome—and sometimes dangerous—incidents do occur with alarming frequency in Tangier, and many of them begin under circumstances that seem innocent enough.

From the port, the train station is the large, white building to the left; buses leave from the chaotic square in front of the train station. Don't be "guided" onto the wrong bus; confirm the destination with the driver. For long distances try to take the CTM bus or the train. Don't give your baggage to anyone but the ticket taker, and offer a 1 to 2dh tip.

Tourist Office: 29, bd. Pasteur (tel. 329 96). Turn left on av. d'Espagne in front of the port, take Salah Eddine Ayoubi, turn left on rue Anoual and follow it as it curves sharply to the right; at the end of the street make 2 left turns onto bd. Pasteur. Or take a *petit taxi* from the port (3dh). Very sketchy maps. Train, bus, car, and ferry information. Open July-Aug. Mon.-Sat. 8am-noon and 4-7pm; Sept.-June Mon.-Sat. 8:30am-noon and 2:30-6:30pm; Ramadan Mon.-Sat. 8am-2pm.

American Express: Voyages Schwartz, 54, bd. Pasteur (tel. 334 59). Mail held, cardholders' personal checks cashed. Open Mon.-Fri. 9am-12:30pm and 3-7pm, Sat. 9am-12:30pm; Ramadan until 6pm.

Currency Exchange: Any major hotel will change money at all hours (check along bd. Pasteur). Avoid travel agencies near the port entrance.

Post Office: 33, bd. Mohammed V, the continuation of bd. Pasteur. Open Mon.-Thurs. 8am-3:30pm, Fri. 8:30am-12:30pm, Sat. 8-11:30am; Ramadan Mon.-Sat. 9:30am-4pm.

Telephones: In the post office. Open 24 hours.

Trains: Av. d'Espagne (tel. 312 01), to the left as you leave the port. 6 per day to Rabat (60dh) and Casablanca (78dh). Connections to Meknes (53dh) and Fes (64dh) at Sidi Kacem and Sidi Slimane, and to Marrakesh (128dh) at Casablanca.

Buses: In the chaotic square near the port. **CTM** (tel. 324 15), on the right coming from the port, has several buses per day to Rabat (51.35dh), Casablanca (67.95dh), and points in between. Other companies around the square are less expensive but have no fixed schedules.

Ferries: Algeciras in Spain is served 6 times per day (7:30am-8:30pm, 2½ hr., 170dh). Seasonal boats also reach Málaga and Tarifa. Book at **Agence de Voyage Hispamaroc,** bd. Pasteur at El Jabha Eloutania. To Gibraltar by hydrofoil (Mon.-Tues. and Fri. 2 per day, 1 hr., 140dh) and by ferry (Mon., Wed., and Fri.-Sun. 6 per day, 2½ hr., 190dh).

Emergencies: Police (tel. 19). **Ambulance** (tel. 15).

Medical Assistance: Hôpital Kortobi, rue Garibaldi (tel. 310 73).

Consulates: U.S., rue El Ouachaq (tel. 359 04). **U.K.,** 9, rue Amérique du Sud (tel. 358 95). Cannot do anything for drug offenders.

Bookstores: Librairie des Colonnes, 54, bd. Pasteur, for maps and guidebooks, mostly in French. **Epicerie de la Grande Poste,** 48, bd. Mohammed V, for foreign periodicals and *Gauthey Edition* maps of major Moroccan cities (20dh).

Accommodations and Food

Accommodations in the *medina* are cheaper and closer to the port but less comfortable and safe than those in the new city. There's a good range of places in the *medina* along **rue Mokhtar Ahardan** (formerly rue des Postes), off the Petit Socco. To get there from the port, make a U-turn around the CTM office and head west along rue de Cadiz until you come to a set of stairs on the left, just before the lower gate to the *kasbah;* go up the stairs. **Pension Palace,** at #2 (tel. 392 48), has a gracious management and clean, airy rooms around a tiled courtyard. (20dh per person.) **Hotel Olid,** at #12 (tel. 313 10), is clean, comfortable, and hospitable. (Singles 37-50dh, doubles 48-60dh.)

In the new city, look for the strip of hotels along **rue Salah Eddine Ayoubi** (formerly rue de la Plage). From the train station, head east along av. d'Espagne and take the first right. **Pension Miami,** at #126 (tel. 329 00), is the most palatable of this bunch, with a balcony on each floor and washbasins for clothes. (Singles 30dh, doubles 40dh. Showers 4dh.) **Hotel Paris,** 42, bd. Pasteur (tel. 381 26), is the best deal in the new city. Rooms, several of which have balconies, are spacious and sparklingly clean. (Singles 69dh, doubles 81dh, all with private showers.)

The least expensive meals are to be found in the one-person stalls of the *medina.* **Restaurant Aladin** offers *harira, tajine de kefta,* dessert, and bread for 20dh. At nearby **Restaurant Andalus,** six sizzling brochettes, salad, and dessert run 20dh. Both are located on rue du Commerce, an alley off rue Jamaakebir at the junction of the Petit Socco and rue Mokhtar Ahardan. **Restaurant Ahlen,** 8, rue Mokhtar Ahardan, is more comfortable, with generous portions and a wide selection; try the lamb *couscous* (15dh). In the new city, rue Salah Eddine Ayoubi is lined with the inexpensive restaurants. **Restaurant Africa,** at #83, is an airy place with a 25dh *ménu.*

For a treat try **Palace Mamounia,** just inside the *medina* at 6, rue Semmarine (tel. 350 99), between the Grand Socco and the Petit Socco. Waiters decked out in traditional garb serve a variety of tasty dishes off the *ménu touristique* (60dh). Acrobats balancing trays of burning candles on their heads complete the scene. (Open daily 8am-11pm.)

Sights

As any hustler will tell you, the *medina* (old city) is Tangier's most interesting sight, but you'll find more activity (and fewer dead rats) farther south. Don't buy *anything* when accompanied—your "friend" will get a 30% commission on the already inflated price.

Once the city's market, the **Grand Socco** is today a noisy square cluttered with fruit and honey-drenched parsley stands. Go through the **Bab Fahs** and, keeping to your left, walk up rue d'Italie and its steeper continuation, rue de la Kasbah. At the top, a right through the **Porte de la Kasbah** brings you to rue Riad Sultan. Along it are the **Jardins du Sultan,** where you can see artisans weaving carpets. (Open in summer Mon.-Sat. 8am-2pm; in winter 8:30am-noon and 2:30-6pm.) To the right as you exit the garden is **place de la Kasbah,** with a lookout promontory offering a fine view of the Spanish and Moroccan coasts. With your back to the promontory, walk straight ahead and then to the right toward the towering octagonal minaret of the **Mosquée de la Kasbah.** Directly opposite the mosque is the entrance to **Darel-Makhzen,** a palace begun during the reign of Moulay Ismail, and later enlarged. It now houses the superb **Musée des Arts Marocains,** as well as the **Musée des Antiquités.** The Moroccan arts exhibit features a good collection of Fes ceramics, Berber and Arabic carpets, copper and silver jewelry, and old Andalusian musical instruments. Especially noteworthy is the Roman mosaic, *The Navigation of Venus,* excavated at Volubilis. (Entire complex open in summer Wed.-Mon. 9am-noon and 3-6pm. Admission 3dh per museum.)

Near Tangier

Asilah spells relief. Only 46km south of the tension of Tangier, the golden beach and gleaming white Portuguese-style *medina* make this the perfect place to slip gently into Morocco. Though not without handicraft shops and self-appointed guides, the town remains a peaceful base from which to explore the beaches and ruins of the northwest coast.

Among the cheapest digs in town are the clean rooms and cozy terrace at the **Hotel Marhaba,** 9, rue Zallakah (tel. 71 44), outside the entrance to the *medina.* (Singles 15dh, doubles 37dh.) Even nicer are the immaculate little rooms at the **Hotel Sahara,** 9, rue Tarfaya (tel. 71 85). (Singles 32dh, doubles 46dh. Hot showers included.) For a bit more you can settle into the lush, carpeted rooms at the **Hotel El Makhazine** on av. Mellila (tel. 70 90); top-floor windows overlook the waterfront. (Singles 93dh, doubles 113dh, both with private bath.) Campgrounds abound in Asilah; north of town, **Camping Sahara** costs about 12dh per person and has access to a beautiful beach.

The tiny Berber restaurants that line **avenue Hassan II** along the walls of the *medina* will fill you up for 8-10dh. Otherwise, splurge at Asilah's best restaurant, **La Alcazaba,** on rue Zallakah, where shrimp in garlic sauce goes for 22dh and addictive pickled anchovies fly off the 18dh *plat du jour.*

Asilah is served by hourly buses from Tangier (5.50dh); the seven daily trains stop an inconvenient 2km outside of town. The **telephone code** in Asilah is 91.

Tetuan

In Djibliya, the local Berber dialect, "Tetuan" means "open your eyes." Take their advice and be on the lookout for both the charms and the wiles of Morocco's second gateway. Though the pace of life is somewhat less hectic and the *medina* more enchanting than in Tangier, Tetuan is by no means a typical Moroccan town.

Orientation and Practical Information

Ceuta is a Spanish holding in Morocco where ferries from Algeciras unload their intrepid cargo. At the port there is a **tourist office** (tel. 51 13 79; open Mon.-Fri. 8am-noon and 4-6pm). To reach the border from Ceuta, take local bus #7 from pl. de la Constitución (33ptas). Customs can take upwards of 90 minutes. Team up with four other travelers for a shared *grand taxi* from the border to Tetuan (12-15dh per person).

Tetuan is second only to Tangier for hustlers and guides, and most station themselves around the bus station and the entrance to the *medina* at pl. Hassan II. Be polite but firm, and watch out for pickpockets.

Tourist Office: 30, av. Mohammed V (tel. 70 09). Turn left as you exit the upper floor of the bus station, then right onto bd. Sidi Mandri. 3 right turns up is av. Mohammed V; the office is a few blocks to the left. No maps, but the staff is helpful. Open Sept.-June Mon.-Fri. 8:30am-noon and 2:30-6:30pm; July-Aug. Mon.-Fri. 8am-3pm; Ramadan Mon.-Fri. 10am-3pm.

Currency Exchange: Banque Marocaine (B.M.C.E.), pl. Moulay el Mehdi. Open daily 9am-8pm.

Post Office: Pl. Moulay el-Mehdi, just above av. Mohammed V. Service is best before 11am. Open same hours as tourist office, as well as Sat. 8:30am-noon.

Telephones: Behind the post office. Open daily 8am-8:30pm. **Telephone code:** 096.

Buses: Long-distance, bd. Ouadi al-Makh, near bd. Sidi Mandri. Service by several bus companies. Buy your ticket early, ask for a numbered seat, and don't pay extra for baggage. **CTM** (tel. 62 63) has buses for Tangier (hourly, 8dh, change there for trains to Rabat, Fes, and Marrakesh), Fes (2 per day, 36.80dh, 8 hr.), Chechaouen (4 per day, 9.50dh, 2 hr.), and Rabat (2 per day, 33.70dh, 6 hr.). Other companies serve many more destinations including Oued Laou (3 per day) and Ceuta (hourly). A special shuttle service to the beaches at Cabo Negro, Mdiq, Restinga-Smir, and Martil leaves July-Aug. about every 15 min. from the main station and from behind an old green and white palace on the road to Ceuta, a few blocks from the main bus station. (2dh to any beach.) Not all the buses serve all the beaches, so ask the driver.

Taxis: Shared taxis to Tangier (12dh per person) leave from av. Moulay Abbas, 2 blocks down and one to the right from the bus station.

Emergencies: Police, tel. 19; headquarters at the corner of bd. Sidi Mandri and bd. Generalissimo Franco, 1 block above av. Mohammed V.

Medical Assistance: Hospital (tel. 19) at bd. Sidi Mandri and bd. Generalissimo Franco, 1 door above the police station.

Accommodations and Food

There are scads of cheap hotels (12dh per person) in and around the *medina,* but most are crawling with cockroaches and hustlers. **Pensión Iberia,** 12, pl. Moulay el-Mehdi (tel. 36 79), at the head of av. Mohammed V, just above the B.M.C.E. bank, is the best deal in town—safe, clean, and only 16.21dh per person. You can have neither Moroccan guests nor hash in the rooms. **Hotel Trébol,** 3, bd. Yacuub el-Mansour (tel. 20 93), uphill and on the right from the lower level of the bus station, is convenient and clean. (Singles 38dh, doubles 52dh. Showers included.) Just up the street and to the right, at #20, **Hotel Príncipe** (tel. 27 95), is even cheerier, and a better value, with singles for 35dh and doubles for 48dh.

The cheapest food is in the *medina.* Pass through the entrance across from Pensión Central on pl. Hassan II and take the first left to find a series of small, cheap places. Back in the new city, the cheapest and fastest meals are the sandwiches at **Bocadillas Chatt,** av. Mohammed Torres, the corner opposite Restaurant Zarhoun, which are large, well stuffed and only 5dh. (Open daily 5am-11pm.) The best deal in town is at **Restaurant Moderno,** 1, pasaje Achach, between av. Mohammed V and av. Mohammed Torres (go through the marble-tiled alley from pl. Hassan II). Try the house specialty, *tajine de kefta,* a meatball and egg concoction (15dh) popular with the locals. The **Café la Unión,** across the pasaje, is a good place to meet Moroccans or play pachisi.

Sights and Entertainment

Although too tough to be typical, Tetuan's *medina* may be one of the most appealing you'll see. Official guides from the tourist office cost 30dh per half day, but tend to be jaded. Set out on your own or hire an unofficial guide (agree in advance on 10-20dh), but don't buy anything while accompanied. The main access to the *medina* is at pl. Hassan II, but if you go through Bab an-Nawadir near Moulay el-Mehdi, you'll find yourself in the teeming market area. Of particular interest are the flea market and the various *souks* where Berbers come down from the Rif Mountains to sell their crafts. A climb to the top of the *medina* will reward you with a splendid view of the whitewashed city and surrounding mountains. Before leaving, visit the ornate **Brisha Palace,** or the **Mellah el-Bali**—the old Jewish quarter—and the "new" (300-year-old) section on **Calle Israel,** where a few Jews remain.

Outside the walls of the *kasbah,* across the street from the Bab el-Okla, is the **Escuela de Arte,** which houses an interesting historical and folkloric museum.

(Open Mon.-Fri. 8:30am-noon and 2:30-5:30pm, Sat. 8:30am-noon. Admission 3dh.) Potters, coppersmiths, tile-makers, and other artisans work on the patio outside. Their handicrafts can be purchased at the **Exposition Artisanale,** 6, Derb Seffar; it's a good idea to wait a few days to develop some understanding of quality and haggling. The **Ensemble Artisanal,** a few blocks down the road to Ceuta, has a blanket and carpet workshop where you can watch these works of art being created. (Open Mon.-Fri. 9:30am-1pm and 3:30-7pm, Sat. 9:30am-1pm.)

In the evenings, strollers gravitate toward **place Hassan II.** Drink tea at the tables in the square or wander into a cafe; at the one adjacent to the Pensión Central, locals sample the hash harvest from the nearby mountains.

Near Tetuan

Chechaouen, (Chaouen), a peaceful mountain town some 80km (2 hr.) south of Tetuan, has long been popular with young folk. This undoubtedly has something to do with its strategic location on the edge of the lush *kif* (marijuana) fields of the Rif Mountains. But Chechaouen's fresh mountain air makes it a great escape from the hassles of Tetuan and Tangier, even if you prefer rolling hills to rolling paper.

Stay at the **Hotel Salaam,** 39, rue Tarik Ibn Ziad (tel. 62 39). From the bus station, walk through the market, take a left at Hotel Magou, then turn right and follow rue Tarik Ibn Ziad as it climbs up beside and around the *medina.* Authentic Moroccan decor and cosmic views from the terrace restaurant make this place a bargain. (Singles 35dh, doubles 46dh.) The best place in the *medina* is **Hotel Andaluz,** 1, rue Sidi Salem (tel. 60 34; 7-14dh per person, 5dh to sleep on roof). Also friendly and slightly more conveniently located is **Pension La Castellana,** 4, rue Sidi Ahmed Bouhali (tel. 62 95; 7dh per person, 2dh to sleep on roof). For cheap fare and reggae music, try **Restaurant Azhar,** down the steps from the post office (*tajine,* 12dh).

Chechaouen is easily accessible by bus from Tetuan (hourly 7am-6pm, 2 hr., 9.50dh).

Fes

Fes is sorcery, a cauldron of activity that's been simmering since medieval times. This city is probably everything you've come to Morocco for—the ringing hammers on sheets of brass, the squawksof chickens bandied about upside-down, the throaty voices in perpetual skirmish, the droning wail of prayer criers from countless minarets, the thicket of bodies in the needle-narrow streets, the mouth-watering aroma of brochettes on open grills, the whiffs of hash, the stench of tanning lye and donkey droppings, the sweet scents of cedar shavings and freshly-cut mint leaves.

Orientation and Practical Information

The orderly boulevards of the uninteresting *ville nouvelle* are a very long walk from the old city. Take a *petit taxi* (5dh), or the bus (1.10dh) which connects the private bus station at **Bab Boujeloud,** the main entrance to the *medina,* with the junction of avenue Hassan II and avenue Mohammed V in the *ville nouvelle.* The older city is divided into two discrete fortified sections. **Fes-el-Bali (Old Fes)** can be traversed along rue Tala Kebira, which runs southwest-northwest from Bab Boujeloud to the Karaouiyne Mosque. As you leave the *medina* through Bab Boujeloud, you meet avenue des Français, which leads to the entrance to **Fes-Jdid (New Fes)**—not the same as the *ville nouvelle.* South of this entrance is the grande rue de Fes-Jdid, a dead end. Here, rue Bou Ksissat leads (to the right) to the Royal Palace at place des Alaouites.

Tourist Offices: Office National de Tourisme, av. Hassan II at pl. de la Résistance. From the CTM terminal walk down bd. Mohammed V and turn right onto av. Hassan II. From the train station walk along rue Chenguit, bear left at pl. Kennedy, then turn left onto av. Hassan II. Helpful staff speaks English and dispenses maps and brochures. Open July-Sept.

15 Mon.-Fri. 8am-2pm; in winter Mon.-Fri. 8:30am-noon and 2:30-6:30pm; Ramadan Mon.-Sat. 10am-4pm. **Syndicat d'Initiative,** pl. Mohammed V. Also helpful but not as well-stocked. Open Mon.-Fri. 8:30-11:30am and 4:15-6pm; Ramadan Mon.-Fri. 10am-3pm.

Post Office: At av. Hassan II and bd. Mohammed V, in the *ville nouvelle.* Open July to Sept. 15 Mon.-Fri. 8am-3pm; Sept. 16 to June Mon.-Thurs. 8:30-noon and 2:30-6pm, Fri. 8:30-11:30am and 3-6pm; Ramadan Mon.-Fri. 9am-2pm. **Telephones** in main post office. Open daily 8am-8pm. Enter from the side on bd. Mohammed V. **Telephone code:** 06.

Currency Exchange: Les Merinides in the Borj Nord (tel. 425 25). Open daily 6-10pm.

Trains: Av. des Almohades (tel. 250 01), at rue Chenguit. 8 trains per day to Casablanca (change for Marrakesh; 66dh) and Rabat (47dh). 9 per day to Meknes (11.40dh). 3 per day to Tangier (only direct connection at 1:10pm, 64dh).

Buses: CTM, bd. Mohammad V (tel. 220 41), at rue Ksar el-Kebir. To Rabat (7 per day, 36.10dh), Casablanca (7 per day, 53dh), Marrakesh (2 per day, 53.85dh), Meknes (4 per day, 9.65dh), Tangier (1 per day, 47.30dh), and Tetuan (1 per day, 42.25dh). **Private buses** leave when full from the **Gare Routière,** Bab Boujeloud (tel. 335 29).

Taxis: Key stands for *petit taxis* are at the post office, *syndicat,* Bab Boujeloud, and, in case you emerge from a wrong end of the *medina,* Bab Guissa. After 8pm Sept. 16-June, 8:30pm July-Sept. 15, a ride will cost 50% more than the meter shows.

Bookstore: English Bookstore of Fes, 68 av. Hassan II, near pl. de la Résistance. Novels, guidebooks, phrasebooks, maps—and a helpful English-speaking staff. Open Mon.-Fri. 8:30am-12:30pm and 3-7pm.

Accommodations and Camping

In the *ville nouvelle* the best inexpensive accommodations are concentrated on or just off the western side of bd. Mohammed V between av. Slaoui, near the CTM station, and av. Hassan II, near the post office. Accommodations in Old Fes cluster around Bab Boujeloud. Though rooms are cheaper here, the hustlers outnumber even the cockroaches, and bargains don't come without serious haggling.

Auberge de Jeunesse (IYHF), rue Compardon (tel. 240 85). From the tourist office walk 4 blocks along bd. Chefchaouni, turn left to the street below, and look for the whitewashed walls or the sign. Reasonably clean rooms, toilets, showers, and a small kitchen. Hot water in winter only. Members 10dh per night, nonmembers 12.50dh. IYHF card available on the spot for 75dh (bring 2 photos). Open daily 8-9am, noon-3pm and 7-11pm.

Hotel Excelsior, 107, rue Larbi el Kaghat (tel. 256 02). From the main post office, 3 blocks up bd. Mohammad V, on the right. Clean, carpeted rooms, and sanitary toilets and showers. Singles 54dh, doubles 69dh. Showers included, but hot water in winter only.

Hotel Jeanne d'Arc, 36, av. Slaoui (tel. 212 23), up the next street on the right. Plain but clean rooms, and adequate facilities. Singles 30dh, doubles 40dh. Showers included, but hot water in winter only.

Hotel Renaissance, 47, rue Abdekrim el-Khattabi (tel. 221 93), near pl. Mohammed V. Reasonably clean rooms; those with balconies overlooking the street are less musty. Singles 22dh, doubles 33dh. Pit toilets and no showers.

Hotel du Jardin Public, 153, Kashah Boujeloud (tel. 330 86), a small alley as you approach Bab Boujeloud from outside the *medina.* Winding hallways surround a small, airy lobby. So-so showers and pit toilets. Singles 25dh, doubles 35dh. Hot water 4dh (on tap in winter only).

Hotel Erraha (tel. 332 26), 1 block from the Bab, on the right as you approach. Very clean for the *medina.* Helpful proprietor speaks mostly Arabic. Singles 25dh, doubles 35dh. Showers and clean tiled toilets included.

Food

In the *ville nouvelle,* restaurants cluster on the little streets to either side of bd. Mohammed V. A few blocks down this street from the post office on the left is rue Kaid Ahmed, with a fine nameless restaurant at #45. Steaks, liver, *tajines,* or half a dozen *brochettes* cost only 15dh. Old Fes eateries are situated—where else?—just inside Bab Boujeloud.

Restaurant Chamonix, 5, rue Kaid Ahmed, off the right side of bd. Mohammed V from the CTM. Clean if plain. Very filling *couscous à la Fassi,* with *salade marocaine* and dessert for 35dh. A gaudy color blowup of its French namesake covers one wall.

Restaurant des Voyageurs, 41, bd. Mohammed V (tel. 255 37), near the CTM Station. Try the *menu touristique:* lamb *tajine almondine* with *pastilla* and dessert, all delicious and a bargain at 45dh. Service charge 10%. Open daily noon-4pm and 6pm-midnight.

Restaurant Bouayad, 26, rue Serrajine, in Old Fes, on the right as you enter the Bab. Student *menu* 17dh, *menu* for public 40dh. Open 24 hours, even during Ramadan.

Sights

The life-size maze that is the **medina** (old city), 15km in circumference, is the largest and most difficult to navigate in Morocco. If you hire a guide just once in this country, do it here. You can hire an official guide before noon at either tourist office; a morning tour costs 30dh for up to 10 people (*not* per person). The greatest attraction of a guide is the guarantee that the other guides and hustlers will stay away for the rest of the day. Tell your guide you wish to see the sights and refuse to enter any shops with him—the price goes up 30% to include his commission. Don't allow your camera or other valuables to be carried, and don't tour after sunset. Try to have an idea of where you are at all times; one of the oldest hustler's tricks is to threaten to abandon you if a large wad of dirhams is not forthcoming. If you're without guide and armed with a decent map, consider saving Bab Boujeloud until the end of your visit; this will keep the hustlers who hang out there from descending on you from the start. Get off the bus just before Bab Boujeloud and enter the *medina* from a side entrance, or descend through Bab Boujeloud on the heels of a tour group and try to blend in until you leave the hustlers behind. If you get lost in the *medina,* ask people to point you back to the Bab. Shopkeepers are usually reliable sources of information, while would-be "guides" may misinform you.

Entering the *medina* through Bab Boujeloud, bear left immediately onto shop-lined, bamboo-shaded rue Tala Kebira. Nearby to the left is the **grain market.** Three right-hand blocks farther along is the entrance to **Medersa Bou Inania,** the finest Qur'anic university in Morocco. Built under the Merinid Dynasty in the middle of the fourteenth century, its beautifully carved white plaster walls and *mirhab* remain in remarkably good condition. As you leave the main entrance of the *medersa,* turn right and immediately right again into the first alley. This leads to rue Tala Seghira, a secondary artery which runs mostly parallel to rue Tala Kebira but bows in to meet it at Bab Boujeloud. When you reach rue Tala Seghira (the second street on the left), veer left and walk until you see the inconspicuous rue Guerniz. Going right down the long stone steps of rue Guerniz, take the first left down more steps, jog slightly to the right but continue straight down, make the first left (into an alley with more steps), and bear right into the covered alley. In this area of town is the **leather tannery,** a fascinating factory of vats and tubs filled with reeking colored dyes and skins.

The **Zaouia de Moulay Idriss** contains the tomb of Moulay Idriss II, who made Fes the capital of Morocco in 808. The cedarwood portal is decorated with faded geometric patterns. With your back to the entrance, walk left; soon you'll encounter a colorful **belt market** where an impressive array of embroidered and tassled goods are set out before you. Continuing across rue Rhabbet el-Kaiss, you'll find on your left the fourteenth-century **Medersa Attarine.** Behind the superb bronze doors lie intricately carved plaster walls topped by a cedarwood mantle and a splendid fountain. The austere prayer hall is open to all. Continuing in the same direction, you'll find the huge wooden doors and heavy iron-ring knockers of the main entrance to the **Karaouiyne Mosque,** the largest mosque in Morocco. Although the most exquisite parts of the interior are off-limits, the view through the front portal is still a treat. With your back to the front portal of the Karaouiyne, follow rue Bou Touil as it angles to the right towards place Seffarine. Here, dozens of artisans equipped only with simple tools, cut, hammer, and chisel sheets of copper into works of art. On the left stands the thirteenth-century **Medersa Seffarine.**

From Bab Boujeloud you can also make your way to the fountain at place Batha and turn right up the next street, where you'll find the entrance to the **Dar Batha Museum of Moroccan Arts.** The wide collection includes ancient calligraphed Qur'ans, wild Moroccan musical instruments, and colorful Berber carpets. (Open Wed.-Thurs. and Sat.-Mon. 8am-noon and 3:30-6:30pm, Fri. 4-6pm. Admission 3dh.)

Meknes

Meknes is an exercise in monumentality. Founded in the tenth century by the Meknassa tribe, it is a city of colossal gateways, ramparts, palaces, mosques, and *madrasahs* (Qur'anic schools). The spacious parks and crisp lines of the city contrast sharply with those of labyrinthine Fes, and the *medina* is a smaller, tamer—but nonetheless fascinating—version of its cousin 60km east.

The main reason to visit Meknes is the **Dar el-Kebira (Imperial City),** the largest palace in the world. It was the brainchild of dictator Moulay Ismail, who chose the city as his capital in 1672. Though the palace now lies in shambles, the ruins testify to the megalomaniacal power of this man. You'll enter the palace through **Bab El Mansour;** once inside, keep to the right and then turn left just before the next gate. Here, to the right, you'll find the emerald green roof of the **Salle des Ambassadeurs.** Ask the guard to unlock the door leading to the **Christian Dungeon,** and descend the stone steps through a narrow passageway into a dark chamber where the sultans kept the 60,000 slaves who built the place. (Open Sat.-Thurs. 8:30am-noon and 3-6pm. Admission 3dh.) As you leave the dungeon, walk through the arch ahead to the left. Here stands the mosque that houses the **Tomb of Moulay Ismail.** Not surprisingly, the egomaniacal Moroccan "Sun King" built himself a dazzling edifice in which to rest. This building, with its orange walls surmounted by a bright green tile roof, is the only mosque in Morocco open to non-Muslims. Visitors must dress modestly—cover everything but your head. From the prayer area (the room with the fountain), you can peek through the door on the right at the impressive mausoleum itself; only Muslims may enter. (Open Sat.-Thurs. 8am-1pm and 3-7pm, Fri. 3-7pm. Admission 3dh. Closed in 1987 for repairs.)

The best place to stay in town is the **Hôtel du Maroc,** 103, av. Berbrahin (tel. (05) 307 05), just off av. Roumazine, which leads from the bridge toward Bab El Mansour. Clean, friendly, and safe, with rooms overlooking a pleasant garden. (Singles 20dh, doubles 30dh.) If you're determined to stay in the distant and ugly *ville nouvelle,* try **Hotel Majestic,** 19, av. Mohammed V (tel. (05) 220 35), next to the small train station, with gracious management and almost-spotless rooms. (Singles 57dh, doubles 76dh; rooms with private shower 16dh more.) The best belly-filling bargains come from the one-person stalls along **rue Dar Smen,** right in front of Bab El Mansour. Otherwise, ask to sit in the plush *salon marocain* in the touristed but tasty **Rotisserie Oumnia,** across av. Roumazine from the Apollo Cinema. 30dh *ménu.*

The old town is separated from the modern *ville nouvelle* by the **Oued Bouffekane,** a long river valley about ½km wide. You can cross it on foot along av. Moulay Ismail, or catch a city bus (#5, 7, or 9) from the **CTM bus station** at 47, bd. Mohammed V (tel. (05) 225 83) to Bab El Mansour. Near the CTM terminal is the small **el-Amir Abdelkader** train station on rue d'Alger, two blocks from bd. Mohammed V; be sure to get off here rather than the bigger station on av. de la Basse. **Private buses** to the Middle Atlas and other destinations leave when full from the pink stone building at the foot of the hill below Bab El Mansour. The friendly **tourist office** on place Administrative (tel. (05) 244 26) can supply you with a decent map. (Open July to mid-Sept. Mon.-Fri. 8:30am-2:30pm; mid-Sept. to late May Mon.-Fri. 8am-noon and 2:30-6:30pm; Ramadan Mon.-Fri. 10am-4pm.)

Rabat

A clean and orderly anomaly in the context of the nation it represents, Rabat is just what you'd expect of a modern capital and national showpiece. The *medina* is lively, but just about rectilinear in layout; by royal fiat, the city is hustler- and hassle-free. With more European clothes, newspapers, and attitudes, Rabat has little of the traditional atmosphere of Fes or Marrakesh.

Orientation and Practical Information

Rabat is much easier to navigate than other Moroccan cities. Two arteries are key: **avenue Mohammed V** runs north-south from the Grande Essouna Mosque past the train station and the post office right through the *medina;* perpendicular is **avenue Hassan II,** which heads east along the *medina*'s southern walls toward Rabat's sibling city, Salé, and west into the route de Casablanca, where the "central" bus station is inconveniently located.

Tourist Offices: Office National Marocain du Tourisme (ONMT), 22 rue el Jazair (tel. 212 52). Far away, but very helpful. From the train station walk up av. Mohammed V to the Grande Essouna Mosque, turn left on av. Moulay Hassan, and 7 blocks later (on the right-hand side of the street) bear right into rue el-Jazair. Open Mon.-Fri. 8:30am-noon and 2:30-6:30pm; Ramadan Mon.-Fri. 10am-4pm. **Syndicat d'Initiative,** rue Patrice Lumumba (tel. 232 72), is more centrally located. From the post office, cross av. Mohammed V and bear right along rue Al Kahira, then walk a few blocks. Open same hours as the **ONMT.**

Currency Exchange: Hôtel Tour Hassan, 34, av. Abderrahman Annegai (tel. 214 01). Official bank rates. Open daily 8am-7pm.

Post Office: av. Mohammed V, at rue Soekarno. Open Mon.-Fri. 8:30am-noon and 2-6:45pm. **Telephones** and Poste Restante are across the street; open 8am-midnight. **Telephone code:** 07.

Trains: av. Mohammed V (tel. 232 40), at av. Moulay Youssef. Departures for Tangier (5 per day, 47dh), Casablanca (15 per day, 19dh), and Fes (8 per day, 37.50dh). Change in Casablanca for Marrakesh (6 per day, 47dh).

Buses: route de Casablanca (tel. 751 24), at pl. Mohammed Zerktouni. Far from the town center. Pay 10dh for *petit taxi,* or 2.20dh for bus #30 from av. Hassan II near rue Mohammed V. All intercity bus companies operate out of here. Tickets for CTM buses sold at windows #14 and 15; their buses run to Tangier (4 per day, 41dh), Tetuan (2 per day), Marrakesh (3 per day, 67dh), Meknes (5 per day, 23dh), Fes (4 per day, 33dh), and Casablanca (12 per day, 11.40dh).

Emergencies: Police (tel. 19), headquarters on rue Soekarno, 2 blocks off av. Mohammed V.

Medical Assistance: Hôpital Avicenne (tel. 728 71), at the southern end of bd. d'Argonne (also known as av. Ibn Sina), in the district of Souissi, just south of Agdal. 8dh by *petit taxi.* Morocco's best emergency medical care, free of charge.

Embassies: U.S., 2, av. de Marrakesh. Look for the flag over bd. Tarik Ibn Ziyad. 24-hour phone (tel. 622 65). **Canada,** 13 Zankat Joafar Essadik, Agdal (tel. 713 15). **U.K.,** 17, bd. Tour Hassan (tel. 209 05). Travelers from **Australia** and **New Zealand** should contact the British Embassy. **Algerian** consulate, 12, rue d'Azrou; open for visas Mon.-Fri. 9am-1pm.

Accommodations, Camping, and Food

Accommodations in Rabat run the gamut in price and quality. The few that are both pleasant and inexpensive are often full, so it's a good idea to reserve ahead, especially during July when students from all over the country descend upon the city to take their *bac* (high school final exams). **Hôtel Marrakesh,** 10 rue Sbahi (tel. 277 03), is the best deal in town, and one of the few enticing establishments in the *medina,* if a bit noisy. (25dh per person. Cold showers 2dh.) Enter the *medina* on av. Mohammed V and turn right after three blocks. The hotels just off av. Mohammed V as you walk from the train station toward the *medina* are also comfortable. **Hôtel Splendide,** rue Ghazza (tel. 232 83), has spacious, almost spotless rooms, some overlooking a courtyard. (Singles 45dh; singles with hot shower and doubles without 76dh; doubles with shower 91dh.) Take the seventh right from the station. **Hôtel Central,** 2, rue Al Basra (tel. 673 56), is a bit cheaper, with clean, spacious rooms. From the train station, walk two blocks down av. Muhammad V, then turn right. (Singles 45dh, doubles 54dh. Hot showers 7.50dh.) **Camping de la Plage,** on the beach across the River Bou Regreg in Salé, has running water, toilets, and a shop. Take bus #6 from av. Hassan II near av. Allal Ben Abdallah to Salé's Bab Bou Haja (2.20dh), and follow the signs. (8dh per person. Cold showers free.)

Inside the *medina,* several inexpensive places to eat line **avenue Mohammed V** and **avenue Hassan II.** Just through the walls is a square filled with food stalls, grills, and tables, where 12dh will buy you a meal of veal cutlet, salad, and bread. **Restaurant El Bahia** is built into the walls of the *medina,* to your right as you approach from av. Mohammed V. The lavish *salon marocain* upstairs has embroidered sofas and excellent food at budget prices (*tajine* 17dh). On Friday they feature a special seven-vegetable *couscous* for 17dh. **Restaurant Taghazout,** 7, rue Sebbahi, (tel. 256 47) off av. Mohammed V (to the right), is a fine place; if you peek through the service window, you can watch your succulent lamb (14dh) or tripe (14dh) roasting over the glowing charcoal pit. In the new city, **Restaurant Ghazza,** across from the Hotel Splendide, has a sign that says "sandwich" though in fact they have everything but. (*Omelette aux crevette* with vegetables 20dh; *filet du Merlan* 21dh.)

Sights

Begin sightseeing at the eighteenth-century **Essouna Grande Mosque** at the intersection of av. Mohammed V and av. Moulay Hassan. Below a handsomely carved wooden mantle, gold-trimmed windows grace the building's white plaster walls. Above, a minaret towers over the green shingle roof. Avenue Moulay Hassan leads to the soft salmon-pink Almohad **Bab er-Rouah,** "the Gate of the Winds." Walk back through the Bab and turn right through the wall at the first gate onto the tree-lined promenade leading to the **Dar el-Makhzen** (Royal Palace). Most of the present palace, a sprawling villa with another green shingled roof, postdates the French occupation. Outside Bab Zaers, a road leads to the impressive fourteenth-century stone gate of the **Chellah,** an Arab necropolis that struck Edith Wharton as "like a desert traveler's dream in his last fever." (Open daily 8am-7pm. Admission 3dh.) Try to time your sightseeing so that you arrive at either the Chella or the Oudaias Kasbah at sunset, when the view over the **River Bou Regre** is most stunning.

On the other side of town along avenue Abi Ragrag (near the Pont Moulay Hassan to Salé) stands the **Mausoleum of Mohammed V,** the tomb of the popular king who led the country from French and Spanish colonial domination to independence. A flight of marble steps draws you up to the entrance, flanked by royal guards who stand for hours on end in rapt anticipation of the daily blowing of horns and lowering of flags at 5pm. (Open daily 8am-8pm. Free.) In front of the mausoleum stands the huge **Hassan Tower,** the unfinished minaret of the Almohad mosque. All that remains today of what was in the twelfth century the largest mosque in the world, is a grid of columns intimating its original proportions.

Near the mausoleum, the Pont Moulay Hassan connects Rabat to the adjacent town of **Salé,** also accessible via rowboats from the nearby Ramp Sidi Maklouf (1dh). The *medina* of Rabat's riverside neighbor offers enchanting *souks* and a living medieval city free of tourist emporiums and hustlers. South of Rabat are the fantastic beaches of **Temara.** Take a collective taxi or bus #17 from bd. Hassan II near av. Mohammed V to Temara (2.20dh), and then walk 3km west.

Marrakesh

Marrakesh is intense. From the midsummer temperatures of over 90°F that prostrate tourists to the Djemaa's cacophonic circus of snake charmers, musicians, dancers, acrobats, medicine men, gamblers, peddlers, hustlers, and hash vendors; Marrakesh is intense. Gateway to the desert, Marrakesh's reddish-pink streets and alleys throng with *djellaba-* and *gandura*-clad Berber tribespeople, Arab artisans, French expatriates, Western tourists, Blue People from the Sahara, and troops of merchants and performers from Mali, Niger, and Mauritania.

Try to visit Marrakesh in the winter; most of the hustlers are on holiday and the temperatures are mild (though they drop significantly at night). If you do visit in the summer, try to make the **Folklore Festival** (June 3-19).

Orientation and Practical Information

The center of excitement and activity is the **Djemaa el-Fna** area. Most commercial services are along **avenue Mohammed V,** which runs from the **Koutoubia Minaret** near the Djemaa to the **Guéliz** (new city); bus #1 runs this route (1.20dh) and so do *petite taxis* (3dh).

Tourist Offices: Office National Marocain du Tourisme (ONMT), av. Mohammed V, at pl. Abdel Moumen ben Ali (tel. 302 58, but the phone is only ornamental). Bus #1 stops here. A laissez-faire attitude towards tourism, but the free brochures have good maps of the *souks* in the *medina.* English spoken. Official guides 30dh per ½ day, 50dh per day. Open July-Aug. daily 8am-2:30pm; Sept.-June daily 8am-noon and 2-6pm; Ramadan daily 9am-3pm. **Syndicat d'Initiative,** 170, av. Mohammed V (tel. 330 97), 2 blocks towards the Djemaa el-Fna from the tourist office. Has huge binders full of useful information. Open July to mid-Sept. Mon.-Fri. 9am-1:30pm and 4-7pm, Sat. 9am-1:30pm; mid-Sept. to June Mon.-Fri. 8am-noon and 3-6pm, Sat. 8am-noon.

American Express: Voyages Schwartz, rue Mauritania, 2nd floor (tel. 328 31). Rue Mauritania meets av. Mohammed V across from the *syndicat;* it's the last building on the left of the first block. Mail held, checks sold and replaced, but no wired money accepted. Open Mon.-Fri. 9-11:30am and 3-4pm.

Currency Exchange: The quickest place to change money in the Djemaa el-Fna is the **SGMB Bank** on rue Bab Aganaou, 2 blocks down from the post office. Open daily 8am-2pm and 4-8pm.

Post Office: Pl. du XVI Novembre, off av. Mohammed V. Open Mon.-Sat. 8am-9pm. Also in Djemaa el-Fna, open July to mid-Sept. Mon.-Sat. 8am-2pm; mid-Sept. to June Mon.-Sat. 8am-noon and 3-6pm.

Telephones: At both post offices, but quicker and more pleasant at the Djemaa el-Fna office. Open Mon.-Sat. 8am-2:30pm. **Telephone code:** 04.

Flights: The airport (tel. 303 38) is 5km out of town. No public buses; taxis cost 3dh. **Royal Air Maroc,** 197, av. Mohammed V (tel. 319 38).

Trains: The station is on av. Hassan II, 2 blocks from pl. de l'Empereur Haile Selassie. To reach the Djemaa, take a left down av. Hassan II to pl. du XVI Novembre, then go right on Mohammed V. To Casablanca (7 per day, express at 7:25am, 97dh). Daily train to Meknes and Fes. The "Marrakesh Express" used to run from Marrakesh to the small coastal town of Essaourra, but now only a bus makes the journey.

Buses: The new station is not marked on maps: It's outside the walls of the *medina* by Bab Doukkala. CTM, Satas, and private companies operate here. To reach the Djemaa, walk down rue Mohammed el-Mellah to pl. de la Liberté, then left on av. Mohammed V (20-min. walk). Or take a *petite taxi* (5dh) or bus #8 (1.20dh).

Collective Taxis: Leave from Bab Aganaou.

Medical Assistance: A doctor is on call at the pharmacy near the Hotel Marrakesh, down the road from the post office. Open until 10pm.

Accommodations

Apart from the youth hostels and the overpriced campgrounds, which are far from the *medina* but close to the train station, all cheap accommodations are within a stone's throw of the Djemaa el-Fna. Which is the right place to be.

Auberge de Jeunesse (IYHF), rue El Jahid (tel. 328 31), in the Quartier Industriel, 5 min. from the train station. Cross av. Hassan II, walk to the right, and take the first left; continue as straight as possible, passing railroad tracks, Tony Bar Terminus, rue Ibn el-Qadi, and a cluster of wandering streets. The hostel is to the right when you come to a vacant lot full of eucalyptus trees. Exceptionally clean, with a courtyard and terrace. Members only, 12dh. Cold showers included.

Hôtel CTM, facing the Djemaa el-Fna (tel. 423 25), up and to the right of where the taxis let you off, next door to the defunct bus station. The least expensive of the comfortable hotels in the neighborhood; a great bargain. Fabulous view of the Djemaa from the terrace. Singles 29dh, with bath 68dh; doubles 42dh, with bath 81dh; triples 55dh. Showers 2dh.

Hôtel de la Jeunesse, 56 Derb Sidi Bouloukate (tel. 436 31). The cleanest and friendliest of the dozen or so budget hotels lining this street, a narrow alleyway through the first arch on your right as you face the Hotel CTM on Djemaa el-Fna. Singles 20dh, doubles 30dh, triples 40dh. Cold showers included.

Hôtel des Amis, Riad Zitoune el-Kedim (tel. 425 15). Facing the bus station in the Djemaa, walk left through an arch onto Riad el-Kedim; it's immediately to your right. A modest place. Singles 20dh, doubles 30dh.

Hôtel de France, 197, Riad Zitoune el-Kedim (tel 430 67), a bit farther along (not to be confused with the Hôtel de France overlooking the Djemaa). Clean bathrooms. Singles 25dh, doubles 30dh. Cold showers 2dh, hot 3dh.

Hôtel du Haouz, 66, av. Hassan II, (tel. 319 89), halfway between the train station and the PTT. Singles 40dh, with bath 50dh; doubles 52dh, with bath 60dh; triples 72dh, with bath 79dh.

Food

For cheap food, eat in the stalls of the Djemaa. The number of eating places increases threefold in the evenings, as food vendors set up stalls and benches. Some of them have a wide selection; delicious *tajine, couscous,* and other main courses usually go for about 10dh.

Cafe-Restaurant-Hotel de France, pl. Djemaa el-Fna. Standard 35dh *menu,* but their *salone marocaine*—with pillows, chandeliers, and carved ceilings—is the coolest place around during the day. In the evening, their rooftop restaurant offers the best view of the square. Open daily 8am-midnight.

Café-Restaurant Marocain, pl. Djemaa el-Fna, farther along toward the *souks.* You'll recognize it by the yellow four-leaf grille pattern. Simple fare at rock-bottom prices: soup, salad, *brochettes,* omelette, bread, and beverage for 12dh. Open daily 8am-11pm.

Restaurant Étoile de Marrakech, rue Bab Aganaou, near the Djemaa. Comfortable upstairs dining, also a *terrasse panoramique.* Daily *menu* 25dh. Fantastic *tajine de kefta aux oeufs* (14dh) and a wide selection of juices (almond, lemon, apple, grapefruit) for 3.50dh. 10% service charge. Open daily 11am-11pm.

Café-Restaurant Oriental, rue Bab Aganaou, a little farther down the street. Similar fare and prices. Open daily 11am-11pm.

Restaurant Gharnata, Derb el-Arsaa Zitoun Djidid, and **Dar es Salam** on Riad Zitoune el-Kedim, are both in refurbished palaces. Come for the ambience rather than for the food: Meals run upwards of 90dh. Open daily 10am-11pm.

Sights

The **Djemaa el-Fna** ("Assembly of the Dead") is anything but what its name suggests. A hot and crowded market by day, the Djemaa really gets rolling at sunset when the entertainers invade; keep a pocketful of change handy if you want to take pictures. Almost every tour of Marrakesh begins at the twelfth-century **Koutoubia Mosque,** with its magnificent minaret presiding over the Djemaa. The minaret, crowned by a lantern of three golden spheres, is the oldest and purest surviving example of the architecture of the Almohads, who made Marrakesh their capital (1130-1213) and whose realm extended from Spain to present-day Tunisia. (Entrance for Muslims only.) At the northern end of the *medina,* feast your eyes and cool off at the ornate **Medersa Ben Youssef,** the largest Qu'ranic school in the Mahgreb. (Open in summer Tues.-Sun. 8am-noon and 3-7pm; in winter Tues.-Sun. 8am-noon and 2-6pm; Ramadan 8am-noon only. Free, but tip the guards.) Even more lavish are the dazzling **Saadian Tombs,** modeled upon the interior of the Alhambra in Granada. The old **Palace el Bedi** is today the site of the annual **Folklore Festival.** Close by, at the southeastern edge of the *medina,* the nineteenth-century **Bahia Palace** is the only royal palace in Morocco open to tourists (when the royal family is not in residence). It has elaborate cedar doors and ceilings, restful fountained gardens, and its own battalion of corny guides. (Open in summer daily 9:30am-1pm and 4-7pm; in winter daily 9:30-11:45am and 2:30-6pm. Free, but tip the guards.) To escape the relentless midday sun, wander in the lush **Manara Gardens** in the new city and lounge in the charming lakeside pavilion, or visit the extensive **Agdal Gardens,** south of the *medina.*

High Atlas

The High Atlas range jumps out of the Sahara in dramatic contrast to the dry monotony of the plain. The highest mountain in the range, **Mount Toupkal** (4167m), is also the highest peak in North Africa. Buses leave the Marrakesh bus station on the hour for **Asni** (2½ hr., 8dh per person, 3dh per pack), where you can stock up on food for an assault on the mountain. The **auberge de jeunesse (IYHF)** is about 100m to your right as you face the front of the market. A marvelously calm place with families of ducks, cows, and donkeys in its shade-filled yard, the hostel itself is reason enough to stay in Asni. (10dh.) You can continue to **Imlil** either by the blue truck that leaves every couple of hours (12dh), or by the town taxi, if you can round up a group of five (12dh each). In Imlil, the Club Alpin Français runs a **refuge** with good cooking facilities and bunk beds. (18dh, students and IYHF members 12dh.) Here you'll want to buy a topographic map of Toupkal. Leave your luggage here if you haven't already deposited it in Asni, and continue on foot to the Club's **Refuge Louis Neltner** (3207m), a five- or six-hour hike. (19dh, students 14dh.) Here you can consult with the innkeeper El Haj Lahcen Benaomar about the climb to the summit, which should take another day. Be wary of terrain, weather, and your own physical limitations, and take adequate cold-weather clothing and more than enough supplies. Don't drink stream water without either boiling it or using purification tablets as it is infested with the parasite *giarrdia.* Guides' services (which are recommended) cost 40-50dh per day.

A 75-kilometer trip from Marrakesh along sinuous roads will bring you to Oukaimeden, a mountain resort boasting the highest ski lift in Africa (3200m). Take a bus (6dh) or collective taxi (8dh) to the village of Ourika, then hitch the remaining 32km.

The narrow, verdant **Ourika Valley** (33km from Marrakesh) forks off from the road to Oukaimeden at Arbalou and stretches southeast to the tiny village of **Setti-Fatima.** To get here, take the S513 toward Oukaïmeden and turn left after the ramshackle synagogue, or catch one of the many buses that leave from outside the Bab er-Rob in Marrakesh (7dh).

THE NETHERLANDS

US$1 = 2.04 guilders (f)	**f1 = US$0.49**
CDN$1 = f1.54	**f1 = CDN$0.65**
UK£1 = f3.33	**f1 = UK£0.30**
AUS$1 = f1.45	**f1 = AUS $0.69**

Lolling cows, dike-rimmed fields, and horizons of limitless expanse are easy to find in modern-day Holland, the more familiar name for the Netherlands. Following its independence as the seven United Provinces in the 1580s, the Republic of the Netherlands embarked on major commercial enterprise; the Dutch East and West Indies Companies (the people who bought Manhattan from the Indians) traded as far afield as Java, parts of Africa, and the Caribbean. The Dutch were Europe's arms-makers and bankers in the seventeenth century, and cities such as Haarlem, Delft, Leiden, and Utrecht thrived. Known as the "Golden Age" of Dutch history, this was an era of considerable wealth and generous toleration—thousands of Europe's Jews and religious and political dissidents fled here to escape persecution. A remarkably open intellectual forum for its day, Holland attracted great minds such as Descartes and Spinoza, but it was in the art of painting that Holland most brilliantly distinguished itself. Hals, Steen, van Ruisdael, ter Borch, Vermeer, and

Rembrandt, the greatest of the bunch, all lived and painted in seventeenth-century Holland.

Holland faded from the limelight during the eighteenth century, occupied by the French and then gradually modernized by nineteenth-century monarchs. Under the Nazi occupation, the Dutch resistance distinguished itself in its efforts on behalf of Dutch Jews. Today Dutch politics are among the most liberal in Europe, and Holland is a center of the European peace movement. Get your hands (and yourself) on one of Holland's 9.5 million bicycles and take a trip into the quiet countryside. The best area for viewing Holland's tulips, which bloom in April and May, is the region between Oegstgeest, Noordwijkerhout, De Zilk, and Hillegom. Annual flower exhibitions are held in the town of Lisse. The Netherlands has reclaimed almost one fifth of its land from the sea; thus the canals, which drain the polders. In winter the canals sometimes freeze, at which time hundreds strap on their skates and indulge in one of the country's favorite pastimes.

Transportation

Travel in Holland is trouble-free. Amsterdam is a convenient base for daytrips to almost any point in the country. The Netherlands Railways, **Nederlandse Spoorwegen (NS)**, operates an efficient network—up to four trains per hour travel between major cities. A round-trip ticket is cheaper than two one-way trips (Amsterdam-Utrecht f8.10 one way, f14.90 round-trip), but is valid only on the day of issue. Those without a Eurail or InterRail pass can take advantage of special day-excursion rates and rover tickets, available at all train stations. **Day-excursions** to points all over the country are offered during the spring and summer months, entitling users to reduced train fares and discounts on tourist attractions. If you have a railpass, you can still save money by buying an "attraction ticket" at the departure or arrival station.

There are also various **Rail Ranger tickets,** which offer unlimited second-class train travel within the country. (3-day tickets f79.50, 7-day f109.50, 30-day f400. Available year-round.) You must travel almost constantly to make these pay; the one-month ticket starts to pay after the 3150th kilometer—approximately 45 journeys between Amsterdam and Delft. The one-day **multi-Ranger (Meer Man's Kaart),** which costs f73 for two persons (f88 for 3, f102 for 4, f116 for 5, and f130 for 6), is a better deal. Families can purchase a four-day **Family Ranger** ticket *(Gezinstoerkaart),* between July and August, valid for four days of travel within a 10-day period (f140). An excellent deal for those who are also traveling in Belgium and Luxembourg is the **Benelux-Tourrail** card, valid from mid-March to October, which can be used on any five days in a 17-day period, at a cost of f140 (f99 if you're aged 12-25). Those under 26 can buy BIGE tickets at most train stations or at **NBBS,** Holland's student travel organization.

Holland has a national public transportation fare system: Rides are bought in strip tickets *(strippenkaart)* valid anywhere in the country. Bus and tram drivers will sell you a one-hour ticket (f2.60), a two-strip ticket (f1.75), a three-strip ticket (f2.60), or a 10-strip ticket (f8.65). At public transportation counters, post offices, and certain tobacco stores, you get 15 strips for only f8.65. The country is divided into zones and the number of strips you need depends on the number of zones through which you will be traveling. The base charge is always one strip; from Amsterdam to Edam, for instance, you go through six zones, so you need seven strips. You can have the bus driver validate two 10-strip tickets (f17.30) as a day-ticket, good for unlimited travel anywhere in the country. Finally, you can combine unlimited use of public transportation with your Rail Ranger tickets by paying a surplus of f5.25 for the day pass, f10 for the 3-day pass, and f19.75 for the 7-day pass.

Cycling is the best way to see the country. Distances between cities are short, the countryside is flat, and most streets have separate bike lanes. One-speed bikes are widely available for about f7 per day and f35 per week (often with reduced rates for longer periods), and a deposit of f50 to f200. Three-speed bikes can be rented at a higher cost, though the absence of hills makes them unnecessary. Eighty different train stations in Holland rent bicycles for f4.25 per day, plus deposit of f50 to f200, upon presentation of your rail ticket (f7 without a rail ticket). You can also rent tandems for f20 per day (f300 deposit). It is best to reserve a bicycle a day ahead by calling the station. All the telephone numbers are included in the booklet, *Fiets en Spoor.*

Hitchhiking is fairly good, except out of Amsterdam, where competition is vigorous. Try the suggested spots (see Practical Information for Amsterdam), or take a suburban bus for a couple of zones in your intended direction and start away from the crowds. Hitching is not allowed on the national motorway; stick to the entrance ramps or the service stations along the highway. The free map of Holland distributed by the tourist offices gives a complete list of these stations.

Practical Information

The **VVV** are tourist information offices, found even in the smallest villages. They can be very helpful, but charge for almost everything they distribute. **VVV** offices in the large cities provide the normal services, and also make reservations for cultural performances anywhere in the country. The VVV, as well as museums themselves, sells the **Museumkaart** (Museum card), good for free or reduced admission to over 250 museums throughout the country, and discounts on various cultural events. The card is also a way to beat long lines in front of the more popular museums. (f21, ages under 26 f8.50, ages 65 and over f13.50. Valid for the entire calendar year in which it is purchased.) Also available to persons under 26 is the **Cultureel Jongeren Paspoort** (*CJP,* Cultural Youth Passport), which includes a Museumkaart and merits reductions on many cultural events and cover charges at clubs. It remains valid from September to September of the following year, costs f15, and can be obtained in Amsterdam at the **Amsterdam Uit Buro (AUB),** Leidseplein 26, and at most VVV offices. Don't forget to bring a passport-size photograph.

A wide variety of centers, coffeehouses, and crisis telephone lines exist for women in Holland, particularly in Amsterdam and the university towns. Gay men have many services available to them; a complete listing can be found in *Man to Man,* an annual publication available either in bookstores or directly from the publisher at Spuistr. 21, Amsterdam (f7). Disabled travelers should obtain the VVV's free and thorough pamphlet, *Holiday in Holland for the Handicapped.*

Remember that drugs are not legal in this country, despite what you may hear or smoke. Although the soft drug scene is given little attention by the police, possession of less than 30 grams of hashish is subject to fines, and possession of more than this is a serious offense.

The climate is a typical maritime one, which means that you can expect rather warm, but not hot, summers, and fair amounts of rain in the spring and fall, when it can also be quite cool.

Although a sizable number of Dutch persons speak English extremely well, you'll gain their respect by at least trying some words in the native tongue. Dutch is quite similar to German.

The unit of currency is the guilder (f), equal to 100 cents. Other coins in circulation are the *stuiver* (5 cents), *dubbeltje* (10 cents), *kwartje* (25 cents), and *rijksdaalder* (f2.50). The beautifully colored notes come in denominations of f5, f10, f25, f50, f100, and f1000. Banks are open Monday through Friday from 9am to 5pm and generally also on Thursday from 6 to 8pm or 7 to 9pm. Post offices are generally open Monday through Friday from 9am to 5pm; they exchange money at good rates. Most shops and supermarkets are open Monday afternoons, Tuesday through Friday from 9am to 6pm, Saturday 9am to 5pm, and generally also Thursday or Friday from 6pm until 9pm. Most museums are open Tuesday through Sunday from 9am to 5pm. National holidays are December 25 and 26, New Year's Day, Good Friday (only banks close), Easter Sunday and Monday, April 30 (the Queen's birthday), Ascension Day, and Whit Sunday and Monday. You can make international calls from any telephone booth. Payphones take 25¢, f1, and f2.50 coins. For operator assistance dial 008 (numbers within Holland), 0018 (numbers within Europe), 0010 (collect calls within Europe), and 0016 (calls outside of Europe).

Accommodations and Camping

Holland receives millions of visitors every year; in high season, rooms may be hard to find in cities and resort areas. The VVV, with their ubiquitous f3.50 bed-finding fee, can nearly always find you a place, and sometimes will even book ahead in other cities (same fee). The VVV also supplies a free list of accommodations. A room in a private home costs about two thirds as much as a hotel, but these are not available everywhere—check with the local VVV. The best values in Holland are the 43 youth hostels, in three grades, with the standard price of f16.75 for bed and breakfast. Some hostels charge a tourist tax of f0.25-1 per night, and hostels in Amsterdam, Rotterdam, and the Hague charge a supplement of f0.75 per night from June through August. Seven hostels are open year-round, 24 are open March/April through September/October, and 12 only in the summer. The **NJHC** (Dutch youth hostel federation) provides the VVV with lists, or you can obtain the useful Dutch-language guide (with symbols easily understood by all) *Jeugdherbergen,* which has full descriptions of the hostels. Both are free of charge. Contact the NJHC at Prof. Tulpplein 4, Amsterdam (tel. (020) 26 44 33). (Open Mon.-Fri. 9am-5pm.) Youth hostel cards are available at hostels for f25 (bring a passport photo). Nonmembers have the option of paying an extra f5 per night for a Guest Card stamp; six stamps and the card becomes a valid membership card. Cycling from one hostel to another is an easy and excellent way to see the Dutch countryside; most hostels sell maps of bike routes. About half the hostels have cooking facilities for guests. Camping is possible in all parts of the country, but many sites are crowded and trailer-ridden during summer. The VVV has lists of campgrounds.

Food

Dutch food is hearty and uncomplicated: plenty of meat, potatoes, bread, cheese, and milk. Slices of cold meat and fresh cheese on bread make up a typical breakfast. At lunch, you can have *broodjes,* open-faced sandwiches with cheese, ham, liver, shrimp, eel, steak tartare, or *haring* (herring). Try also *poffertjes* (small round pancakes), *pannekoeken* (like heavy crepes), *zuurkool* (pickled cabbage), and smoked eel. Dutch cheeses are not limited to *Gouda* and *Edam;* have a nibble of *Leyden* and the creamy *Kernhem,* too. Sweets include delicious chocolates and the ever-popular Dutch licorice, *drop.*

If you are in one of the many university towns in Holland, you can eat cheaply and plentifully at student *mensas.* At dinner, reap the benefits of Holland's colonial past: *Rijsttafel* is an Indonesian specialty comprising up to 20 or 25 different dishes, such as curried chicken or lamb with pineapple, all served on a mountain of rice. It is widely available in Indonesian restaurants all over the country. You can also try Surinamian food—another legacy of Dutch colonializing. Vegetarians may want to buy a copy of *Lekker en Gezond Eten in Nederland en België,* a complete Dutch-language guide to restaurants and macrobiotic shops in the Netherlands and Belgium, available in most such stores (f4.50). The names and symbols can be easily interpreted.

Beer doesn't only mean Heineken and Amstel—there are many less well-known brands. Before dinner, sample *jenever,* an excellent Dutch liqueur sometimes flavored with orange, lemon, or cranberry and served in tiny, fluted glasses. Specify *jong* (young) or *oud* (old), which is heavier, more perfumed, and more potent.

Amsterdam

Every summer, Amsterdam greets torrents of young travelers from all over the world with a beguiling combination of ease and exuberance. On warm evenings, the Leidseplein fills with foreign crowds and strains of jazz and blues until the early

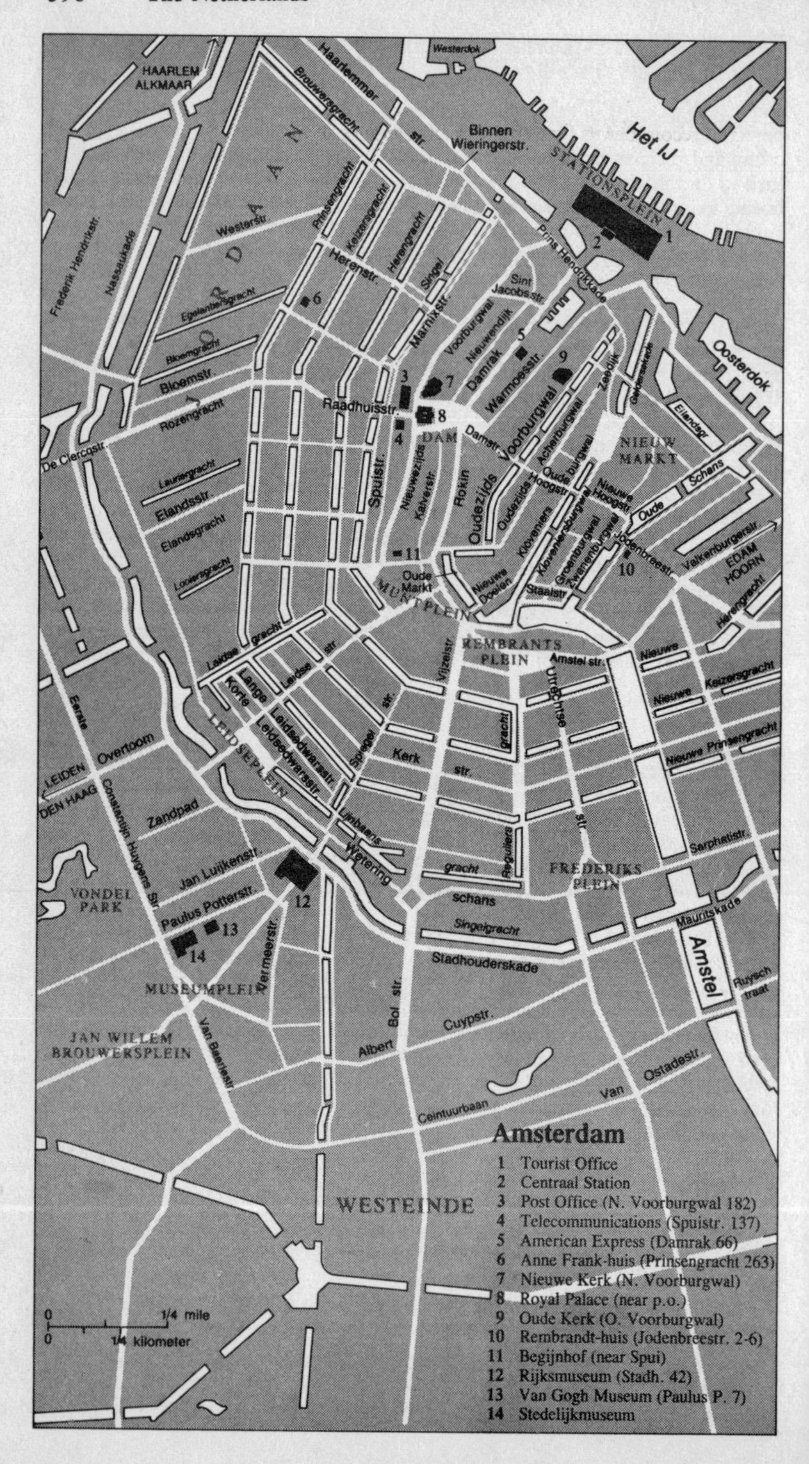
Amsterdam
1 Tourist Office
2 Centraal Station
3 Post Office (N. Voorburgwal 182)
4 Telecommunications (Spuistr. 137)
5 American Express (Damrak 66)
6 Anne Frank-huis (Prinsengracht 263)
7 Nieuwe Kerk (N. Voorburgwal)
8 Royal Palace (near p.o.)
9 Oude Kerk (O. Voorburgwal)
10 Rembrandt-huis (Jodenbreestr. 2-6)
11 Begijnhof (near Spui)
12 Rijksmuseum (Stadh. 42)
13 Van Gogh Museum (Paulus P. 7)
14 Stedelijkmuseum
Het IJ
Westerdok
Oosterdok
HAARLEM
ALKMAAR
Haarlemmer
str.
Brouwersgracht
Binnen
Wieringerstr.
STATIONSPLEIN
Prins Hendrikkade
JORDAAN
Westerstr.
Prinsengracht
Keizersgracht
Herengracht
Herenstr.
Singel
Frederik Hendrikstr.
Nassaukade
Egelantiersgracht
Bloemgracht
Bloemstr.
Rozengracht
Raadhuisstr.
De Clercqstr.
Sint
Jacobsstr.
Marnixstr.
Voorburgwal
Nieuwendijk
Damrak
Warmoesstr.
Voorburgwal
Zeedijk
Geldersekade
Eilandsgr.
DAM
Damstr.
NIEUW
MARKT
Schans
Oude
Achterburgwal
Oude
Hoogstr.
Nieuwe
Hoogstr.
Oudezijds
Rokin
Spuistr.
Nieuwezijds
Kalverstr.
Lauriergracht
Elandsstr.
Elandsgracht
Looiersgracht
Kloveniersburgwal
Groenburgwal
Zwanenburgwal
Jodenbreestr.
Valkenburgerstr.
EDAM
HOORN
Herengracht
Oude
Markt
Nieuwe
Doelen
Staalstr.
MUNTPLEIN
REMBRANTS
PLEIN
Amstel str.
Nieuwe
Nieuwe Keizersgracht
Nieuwe Prinsengracht
Utrechtse
str.
Vijzelstr.
Leidse gracht
Leidse str.
Lange
Korte
Leidsedwarsstr.
Spiegel
str.
Kerk
str.
gracht
Eerste
Overtoom
LEIDSEPLEIN
LEIDEN
DEN HAAG
Constantijn Huygens Str.
Zandpad
Lijnbaans
Wetering
gracht
Reguliers
FREDERIKS
PLEIN
Sarphatistr.
schans
Singelgracht
Mauritskade
Amstel
Ruysch
traat
Jan Luijkenstr.
VONDEL
PARK
Paulus Potterstr.
Stadhouderskade
Vermeerstr.
MUSEUMPLEIN
JAN WILLEM
BROUWERSPLEIN
Van Baerlestr.
Albert
Cuypstr.
Bol str.
Van
Ostadestr.
Ceintuurbaan
WESTEINDE
0
1/4 mile
0
1/4 kilometer

morning hours. Outdoor concerts at Vondelpark complement the interior pleasures of the city's many museums. Amsterdam granted asylum to English royalists *and* parliamentarians during the seventeenth century and pioneered the dispensing of controlled amounts of methadone and heroin to junkies, but the city has recently begun to reconsider its long tradition of tolerance in light of the steadily worsening crime and drug addiction centered in the Nieuwmarkt. Lest the picture begin to look too grim, remember that the old Amsterdam of tree-lined canals and renovated houses is an open-air museum left largely untouched for over 400 years.

Orientation and Practical Information

Canal-laced Amsterdam, situated at the base of the IJsselmeer—the former sea which the huge Afsluitdijk has turned into a lake—is a major world transportation center. Budget flights to all over the world, especially southeast Asia, can be found here. No point in the country is more than a few hours away by train, and there's also frequent service to cities throughout Europe.

Emerging from the train station, you will face roughly south onto **Damrak,** an important thoroughfare that splits the oldest parts of the city and leads to the **Dam,** its main square. Parallel streets and canals ripple out from the center of the city; in order, the main streets, next to the canals of the same name, are **Singel, Herengracht, Keizersgracht,** and **Prinsengracht.**

Unless you need to cross town in a hurry, Amsterdam is best seen by foot or bike. The names of streets change unpredictably; it's a good idea to buy a *Falk Plan* (f2.90) at the VVV. *Use It* (free at the VVV), includes a map, information on inexpensive accommodations, an index of youth agencies, and news about Amsterdam.

Amsterdam's police pay little attention to the small-scale soft drug scene, but they are cracking down on the hard drug trade. You should beware particularly of street dealers. Hash is sometimes laced with harder drugs, or is of poor quality—sometimes just wax. Never make an appointment for a deal; you are simply asking to be robbed. For information on the legal ins and outs of the Amsterdam drug scene, call 26 51 15 (Mon.-Fri. 9:30am-5pm). Anyone with drug-related health problems (addiction, overdose) should call 555 55 55.

Tourist Offices: VVV, Stationsplein 10, in front of Centraal Station (Mon.-Sat. 9am-5pm, tel. 26 64 44; Sun., tel. 22 10 16). Well-staffed office will find accommodations, change money (at less than optimal rates), sell tickets, and plan excursions. They charge for most of these services and the lines are long, but a visit is worthwhile. Open April-Oct. daily 9am-11:30pm; Nov.-March daily 9am-6pm. A **branch office,** Leidsestr. 106, offers the same services. Open Easter-Sept. daily 9am-10:30pm; Oct.-Easter Mon.-Fri. 10:30am-7pm, Sat. 10:30am-9pm, Sun. 10:30am-6pm.

Budget Travel: NBBS, the Dutch student travel outfit, Dam 17 (tel. 23 76 86 for a recording; visit in person for assistance). The first place to go for budget flights. Sample round-trip fares: Bangkok f1189, Hong Kong f1923, Singapore f1575, New Delhi f1539. Also information on budget trains and buses. Open mid-May to mid-Aug. Mon.-Fri. 9:30am-5:30pm, Sat. 10am-4pm; otherwise closes Sat. at 3pm. **Transalpino,** Rokin 44 (tel. 23 99 22), for Transalpino/BIGE travel. Open Mon.-Fri. 9am-5:30pm, Sat. 10am-4pm. **Magic Bus,** Rokin 38 (tel. 26 44 34 for bus information, 26 48 44 for flight information). Cheap long-distance travel from Holland to destinations all over Europe. One-way fares: Budapest f200, Zagreb f150 (ages under 26 f135), Athens f215 (ages under 26 f195), Tangier via Paris f355. Open Mon.-Fri. 9:30am-5:30pm, Sat. 10am-4pm. **Budget Bus,** Rokin 10 (tel. 27 51 51), also has good deals. Open Mon.-Fri. 9:30am-5:30pm, Sat. 10am-4pm.

American Express: Damrak 66 (tel. 26 20 42). Mail held. All banking services. Cash traveler's checks here: The rate is good, and there's no commission, as long as you accept guilders. Open April-Sept. Mon.-Fri. 9am-5pm, Sat. 9am-5pm, Sun. 11am-4pm (for currency exchange only); Oct.-March Mon.-Fri. only.

Currency Exchange: Change Express, Damrak 86. Commission of 3%; f10 maximum. Open daily 8am-midnight.

Post Office: Nieuwezijds Voorburgwal 182, behind the Dam. Open Mon.-Wed. and Fri. 8:30am-6pm, Thurs. 8:30am-8:30pm, Sat. 9am-noon. Poste Restante open same hours. Branch offices open Mon.-Fri. 9am-5pm.

Telephones: At the main post office. Open daily 24 hours. Use the rear entrance, Spuistr. 137, during off-hours. **Telehouse,** Raadhuisstr. 48-50 is also open 24 hours. Payphones take 25 cents, f1, and f2.50 coins. (One 25-cent coin is the min. for a local call.) **Telephone code:** 020.

Flights: Birds from all over roost at **Schiphol Airport.** A new train line connects Centraal Station and Schiphol in 16 min. (f4.40 one way). Charter information (tel. 511 06 66); all other flights (tel. 511 04 32).

Trains: All trains arrive at and depart from **Centraal Station,** Stationsplein 1, in the center of town, opposite the tourist office. For train information and reservations, get a number at the booth, then wait inside the office until you're called. In summer, expect waits as long as 1 hr. Open Mon.-Fri. 8am-10pm, Sat.-Sun. 9am-8pm. International information open Mon.-Fri. 8am-8pm, Sat.-Sun. 9am-5pm.

Buses: Private coaches come and go from various offices and pick-up spots throughout the city; consult one of the budget travel agents listed above.

Public Transportation: Most tram lines radiate from Amsterdam's Centraal Station. Trams stop running at midnight; get a separate schedule for the *nachtbussen* (night buses). You can buy tickets to be validated on board (*strippenkaart*) and day-passes (*dagkaart Amsterdam*) on board trams (10-strip tickets and day-passes each f8.65). Go to offices of the **Gemeentelijk Vervoers Bedrijf (GVB),** Amsterdam's public transportation company, for multiple-day passes and cheaper tickets and day-passes. The GVB office on Stationsplein (tel. 27 27 27) can also help you with information and the handy flyer *Welcome.* Open Mon.-Fri. 7am-10:30pm, Sat.-Sun. 8am-10:30pm.

Lost and Found: Waterlooplein 11 (tel. 559 80 05). Open Mon.-Fri. 11am-3:30pm. On bus, tram, metro: GVB main office, Prins Hendrikkade 108-114 (tel. 551 49 11). Open Mon.-Fri. 8:30am-3:30pm. On trains: Centraal Station (tel. 557 85 44). Open daily 7am-10pm.

Taxis: Fares start at f3.80 and are then f2.23 per km or min., more at night. Call 77 77 77 or look for a taxi stand. **Water Taxis** (tel. 75 09 09) run, you guessed it, on the canals.

Bike Rental: All train stations rent bikes (f6-7 per day, f30-35 per week), but don't expect anything fancy. **Koender's,** Stationsplein 12 (tel. 24 83 91), charges f7 per day, f30 per week. Open Mon.-Fri. 8am-10pm, Sat.-Sun. 8am-10pm. **Heja,** Bestevaerstr. 39 (tel. 12 92 11), is f7 per day, f35 per week; 3-speeds f9 per day, f45 per week. Open Mon.-Fri. 9am-12:30pm and 1:30-6pm, Sat. 9am-1pm; in summer also open Sat. 6-6:30pm and Sun. 9-9:30am and 6-6:30pm. All require a f50-200 deposit. **Ena's Bike Tours** (tel. (015) 14 37 97) runs 8-hr. tours that include visits to a cheese farm, windmill, lake, and pub (f37.50). Tours begin at Amstel Station June-Aug. daily at 10am; call for reservations and information. Take the metro or tram #12 to Amstel Station, then follow the blue signs to the Bicycle Depot.

Camper Rental: Braitman and Woudenberg, Droogbak 4 (tel. 22 11 68), near Centraal Station, rents 4-person campers. Mid-June to mid-Aug. f850; Sept.-May f700. Deposit f1000. Must reserve in advance. Open Mon.-Fri. 9am-5pm, Sat. 11am-3pm.

Emergencies: Police (tel. 22 22 22); headquarters at Elandsgracht 117 (tel. 559 91 11). **Ambulance** (tel. 555 55 55).

Medical Assistance: For hospital care, try **Academisch Medisch Centrum,** Meibergdreef 9 (tel. 566 91 11), Metro: Holendrecht; or **Onze Lieve Vrouwe Gasthuis,** Eerste Oosterparkstr. 179 (tel. 599 91 11). For free emergency medical care, daily 5pm-midnight, visit the **Kruispost,** Oudezijds Voorburgwal 129 (tel. 24 90 21). **Central Medical Service** (tel. 64 21 11) can give you the names of pharmacists, doctors, and dentists on duty 24 hours. **Sexually Transmitted Disease Clinics** are at Groenburgwal 44 (tel. 22 37 77), open Mon.-Fri. 8am-noon, and at Van Oldenbarneveldtstr. 42 (tel. 84 21 05 or 84 49 57), open Mon.-Fri. 1-3pm. Both are free and confidential. **Aletta Jacobshuis,** Overtoom 323 (tel. 16 62 22), offers birth control and pregnancy tests. Open Mon.-Thurs. 9am-4pm and 7:30-9pm, Fri. 9am-4pm; call weekends for morning-after pills. **AIDS Hotline** (tel. 24 42 44 or 24 42 45), Mon.-Fri. 3-8pm.

Crises: Rape, 24-hour hotline (tel. 25 34 73). **Drug counseling** is available at Binnenkant 46 (tel. 24 47 75), 10 min. from Centraal Station, near the Oosterdok. Open Mon.-Fri. 10:30am-5pm. There's an open house on hard drugs for everybody Thurs. 8-11pm. For serious drug problems, go to the "Red Attic," Valckenierstr. 2 (tel. 555 53 49), near Weesperplein. Open Mon.-Fri. 2-4pm. If you need someone to talk to, call 16 16 66, Mon.-Fri. 9am-3am, Sat.-Sun. 24 hours. For general problems, call **SOS Luisterlijn** (tel. 76 12 01).

Consulate: U.S., Museumplein 19 (tel. 64 56 61). **U.K.,** Koningslaan 44 (tel. 76 43 43). Citizens of **Australia, Canada,** and **New Zealand,** should contact their diplomatic representatives in The Hague. The numbers are (tel. (070) 63 09 83), (tel. (070) 61 41 11), and (tel. (070) 46 93 24), respectively.

Women's Centers: Vrouwenhuis, Nieuwe Herengracht 95 (tel. 25 20 66), near the university. Open Sept.-June Mon.-Fri. 2-5pm. For psychological help (tel. 25 01 50), Mon.-Thurs. 9am-noon and 8-11pm, Fri. 9am-noon. **Blijf van mijn lijf** (tel. 94 27 58) is an organization for women threatened by violence.

Gay Centers: COC, Rozenstr. 14 (tel. 26 30 87 or 23 40 79), is the main source of information. Open Mon.-Sat. 1-5pm, Sun. 3-7pm. There is also a pub open Wed.-Sun. 8pm-midnight. The gay/lesbian guide *Man to Man* (f7) has a "gay map" listing bars, shops, saunas, etc. Help for victims of attack or discrimination available Wed. and Sun. 8pm-midnight (tel. 24 63 21). **Gay Switchboard** (tel. 23 65 65) is a 24-hr. telephone service with information and advice for lesbians and gay men.

Bookstores: Athenaeum Boekhandel, Spui 14 (tel. 23 39 33), has a wonderful variety of English books. Open Mon. 1-6pm, Tues.-Fri. 9am-6pm, Sat. 9am-5pm. **Xantippe,** Prinsengracht 290 (tel. 23 58 54), is a women's bookstore with books in the original languages. Open mid-July to mid-Aug. Tues.-Thurs. 1-6pm, Fri. 10am-6pm, Sat. 1-5pm; mid-Aug. to mid-July Tues.-Fri. 10am-6pm, Sat. 10am-5pm. **Intermale,** Spuistr. 251 (tel. 25 00 09), is a gay bookstore. Open Mon.-Sat. noon-6pm. At **The Book Exchange,** Kloveniersburgwal 58 (tel. 26 62 66), you can get up to 2/3 of the original value of your books in books, or up to 40% in cash. Open Mon.-Fri. 10am-6pm, Sat. 10am-5pm. **The Open Book,** Prinsengracht 42, also deals in used English paperbacks; you get 50% off the price of exchange books, 20% off new books, or cash. The **American Discount Book Center,** Kalverstr. 158, is open daily 10am-10pm. There's also a **book market** at Oudemanhuispoort, Mon.-Fri. 11am-4pm.

Swimming Pools: Outdoor, Van Galenbad, at the corner of Jan van Galenstr. and Orteliuskade (tel. 12 80 01). Open June-Aug. daily 10am-5pm. f3.25, ages 65 and over f2.10, ages under 18 f2.80. **Indoor and Outdoor,** De Mirandabad, De Mirandalaan 9 (tel. 42 80 80), has deluxe artificial waves, and costs f3.90. Take tram #4 or 25.

Laundry: Look for a *Wasserette* sign, or try Rozengracht 59 (open daily 7am-8pm), or Oude Doelenstr. 12 (open Mon.-Fri. 8:30am-7pm, last start 6pm, Sat. 10am-4pm). Or you can leave your wash at the **Happy Inn,** Warmoesstr. 30 (tel. 24 84 64), and have it washed, dried, and folded for you. f8-10 per load, plus tip. Open Mon.-Sat. 9:30am-8pm.

Hitchhiking: To Utrecht, central and southern Germany, and Belgium, take tram #25 to the end and start at the bridge. To Groningen and northern Germany, take bus #56 to Prins Bernhardplein or the Metro to Amstel and start along Gooiseweg. To the airport, Leiden, and The Hague, take tram #16 or 24 to Stadionplein and start on the other side of the canal on Amstelveenseweg. To Haarlem, Alkmaar, and Noord Holland, take bus #22 to Haarlemmerweg and start from Westerpark. The **International Lift Center,** Nieuwe Zijds Voorburgwal 256, 1st floor (tel. 22 43 22), brings riders and drivers together for destinations all over Europe. Riders pay a f5-25 fee, plus 5 cents per km for gas. Open Easter-Oct. Mon.-Fri. 10am-7pm, Sat. 10am-4pm, Sun. noon-3pm; Nov.-Easter Mon.-Fri. 10am-5pm, Sat. noon-4pm, Sun. noon-3pm.

Accommodations and Camping

Amsterdam is a zoo of rooming possibilities. The city is packed from late June to mid-September, but you can always find a bed at one of the many hostels and student hotels. The following listings are divided into institutional hostels, private hostels, houseboats, hotels, and campgrounds. Institutional hostels generally have curfews, single-sex dorms, and a young clientele. Private hostels are freer, often dirtier, have private rooms and coed dorms, and are often more expensive. In both places, it's wise not to leave valuables while you're out, though many provide lockers, some big enough for backpacks. Houseboats are usually friendly, without curfews, priced by the bed, and generally inexpensive. It's best to reserve ahead or arrive early in the day. The VVV will book rooms for a fee of f3.50 per person, but they do not list the cheapest places, and you must insist on low-budget accommodations.

At the station, you'll undoubtedly be accosted by people offering all kinds of lodging. These deals are mostly above board, but exercise caution and search out the homekeepers or small hotel and boat owners, mostly women, amid all the professional hawkers.

All the accommodations we list include showers. Many serve a "Dutch breakfast," usually consisting of meats, cheese, bread, and coffee or tea, but quality varies. "Continental breakfast" is the standard rolls and coffee.

Avoid sleeping in Amsterdam's streets and squares; it's illegal, unsafe, and you won't win popularity points with the citizens. The almost-penniless should try the Sleep-In (see Camping) or the Christian Youth Hostels.

Institutional Hostels

Jeugdherberg Vondelpark (IYHF), Zandpad 5 (tel. 83 17 44). Take tram #1, 2, or 5 from the train station to Leidseplein, then walk 5 min. (follow the signs). Nice location on a back street overlooking Vondelpark, but often lots of school groups. Medium-sized bunk-bedded dorms. Members only, f16.75 (June-Aug. f17.50); IYHF cards sold (f25, or you can purchase a Guest Card, f5 per night). Cards also available at NBBS offices. Sheets f5. Breakfast included. Dinner f11.50. Kitchen facilities. Curfew 2am May-Oct., 1am Nov.-April. Open year-round.

Jeugdherberg Stadsdoelen (IYHF), Kloveniersburgwal 97 (tel. 24 68 32). A large and pleasant building between the Dam and Rembrandtsplein. Take tram #4, 9, 16, 24, or 25 to Muntplein. Similar to Vondelpark. Members only, f16.75 (June-Aug f17.50). Sheets f5. Breakfast included. Kitchen facilities. Free lockers. Reception open until midnight. Curfew 1:30am. Open mid-March to Oct.

Christian Youth Hostel Eben Haëzer, Bloemstr. 179 (tel. 24 47 17), 1 street from Rozengracht. Take tram #13 or 17 to the Marnixstr. stop. Tiny dorms with nice views; a bargain. Ages 18-35 only, but sometimes they're flexible. f13.50. Breakfast included. Dinner f5-6. Midnight curfew, Fri.-Sat. 1am.

Christian Youth Hostel "The Shelter," Barndesteeg 21-25 (tel. 25 32 30), off the Nieuwmarkt. Same rates and curfew hours as Eben Haezer, but a bit larger and near the Red Light District.

Private Hostels

Hotel Kabul, Warmoesstr. 38-42 (tel. 23 71 58), a 5-min. walk from Centraal Station, in the Red Light District. Huge, clean, efficient, and friendly. Late-night bar (happy hour 10-11pm), and meals for f10. Has a safe for valuables (f1) and free lockers in the room. Rooms with 4 beds f25-26—down to f19 in a 10-bed room. Doubles f55-75, triples f85. Breakfast f6. No curfew.

Euphemia Budget Hotel, Fokke Simonszstraat 1-9 (tel. 22 90 45), in a quiet area. Take tram #16, 24, or 25. A very safe place. Doubles f70, triples f75. Breakfast f5-6. Open year-round.

't Ancker, De Ruijterkade 100 (tel. 22 95 60). From the back exit of Centraal Station walk to your right 80m. Doubles (f70) and well-kept dorm rooms for 3-10 persons (f30) offer good views of the harbor, some with balcony. Oct.-March f25-27.50 per person. All-you-can-eat breakfast included. Happy hour 8-9pm. All Dutch drinks and beer f1.50. No curfew. Open year-round. The **Anvo,** Anna Vodelstr. 4-6, near the Vondelpark, is nearly identical.

International Budget Hotel, Leidsegracht 76 (tel. 24 27 84), near the Leidseplein. Take tram #1, 2, or 5. A friendly, relaxed spot with a '60s atmosphere. Doubles f60, quads f90. Free lockers. Kitchen facilities. Reception open 9am-11pm. No reservations taken in the summer, so get there early. No curfew. Open year-round.

Adam & Eva Youth Hotel, Sarphatistr. 105 (tel. 24 62 06), a bit far from the center, in a quiet area. Take the subway to Weesperplein. Friendly people and a cozy common room. f16.75 the first night, f16 after that. Sheets f5 first night only. Free safe. Breakfast included. No curfew in summer; winter curfew 3am. Open March-Dec.

Hotel My Home, Haarlemmerstr. 82 (tel. 24 23 20), 10 min. from Centraal Station. Not the nicest of neighborhoods. Turn right onto Prins Hendrikkade and cross the Singel Bridge. It's best to reserve ahead. Beds in doubles and quads f30 per person. Breakfast included. No curfew. Open year-round.

Bob's Youth Hostel, Nieuwezijds Voorburgwal 92 (tel. 23 00 63), not far from the Dam or Centraal Station. Take tram #1, 2, 5, 13, or 17. Lots of people, punked-out atmosphere, and good music. f17. Breakfast included. Curfew 3am. Open year-round.

Houseboats

Houseboats behind the train station vary in quality, many with tiny rooms and even tinier breakfasts. The best bet is to walk to your left from the station to the **Oosterdokskade** (about 4 min.), in front of the post office, where there are several boats offering good deals.

Osca, (tel. 27 12 50). June to mid-Sept. doubles f55, quads f22.50 per person; mid-Sept. to May doubles start at f45, quads at f17.50 per person. No curfew. Reception open 8am-midnight.

Holland Floatel, (tel. 24 07 65). Beds in 4-bed dorms f20, doubles f25-35 per person; off-season 4-bed dorms around f15, doubles f20-25 per person. Breakfast f4-6. Happy hour 6:30-7:30pm. No curfew. Closed Jan.-March.

Hotelboat Sonja, has rooms with 2 (f27.50) or 4 beds (f25); off-season 2-bed rooms f25, 4-bed rooms f22.50 per person. Breakfast f4.50-6. No curfew. Open year-round.

Hotels

Hotel van Onna, Bloemgracht 102 (tel. 26 58 01). Take tram #13 or 17 from Centraal Station. A well-kept place. Not the cheapest, but a good value. Reservations recommended. Singles, doubles, triples, and quads all f42 per person. Big breakfast included.

Hotel Bema, J. W. Brouwersplein 19b (tel. 79 13 96), across from the Concertgebouw. Take tram #16. Spacious and spotless rooms in a building near the museums. Personable owner. Good for a splurge. Make reservations. Singles f45, doubles f70-90; triples, quads, and quints all f30 per person. Breakfast included.

Hotel Casa Cara, Emmastr. 24 (tel. 62 31 35). Not far from the Vondelpark, in a nice neighborhood. Take tram #16 or 2, or nightbus #74. Singles f40, doubles with shower and toilet f80. Breakfast included. Best to reserve ahead.

Hotel Acro, Jan Luykenstr. 44 (tel. 62 05 26), **Hotel Fita,** Jan Luykenstr. 37 (tel. 79 09 76), and **Hotel Museumzicht,** Jan Luykenstr. 22 (tel. 71 29 54), all have singles f50-70 and doubles f80-100, in a nice area near the museums.

Hotel Pax, Raadhuisstr. 37 (tel. 24 97 35), **Hotel Ronnie,** Raadhuisstr. 41b (tel. 24 28 21), and **Hotel Westertoren,** Raadhuisstr. 35b (tel. 24 46 39), are located near the Dam Square in nice old buildings, but are rather small. Singles go for f30-50, doubles f55-80. Be sure to reserve in advance.

Camping

Sleep-In, s'-Gravesandestr. 51-53 (tel. 94 74 44). Take the Metro to Weesperplein, or bus #56 or tram #9 from the station (or night bus #76). Popular with those on extremely tight budgets—hip atmosphere, but watch your belongings. Only f11 per night if you have your own sleeping bag, f3.50 more for sheets. Breakfast roll f2. Dinner (for guests only) f9-13. Closed noon-4pm but open all night. Open late June-early Sept., and Easter.

Camping Zeeburg, Zuider-IJdijk 44 (tel. 94 44 30), next to the Amsterdam Rijncanal. There is a direct ferry connection with Centraal Station, or you can take bus #22. Youth-oriented, with regular performances by bands. Also information on cultural and political events. f4.25 per person, f1 per tent. Showers f1. Open mid-April to Oct.

Gaasper Camping, Loosdrechtdreef 7 (tel. 96 73 26), in the idyllic Gaasper Park., 20 min. from Centraal Station by Metro (Gaasperplas) or night bus #75. Call ahead or check with the VVV. Large and fully equipped. f4.50 per person, f3.25-5 per tent. Showers f1. Washers and dryers f8.50. Open year-round.

Amsterdamsche IJsclub, IJsbaanpad 45 (tel. 62 09 16; June-Aug. tel. 79 67 47). A huge, hectic place near the Olympic Stadium—take tram #16 or 24. f4.25 per person, f3 per tent. Open April-Sept.

Food

Dutch food may not bring you to the height of gustatory delight, but it is filling. You can eat good meat-and-potatoes fare with locals for about f12-20 at one of the many *eetcafés* found all over Amsterdam, especially in the Jordaan. Dinner is usually served from 5:30 to 9pm, at which time establishments go back to serving beer.

There are many international cuisines represented in the city, the fruit of the Dutch colonization and extensive trading over the centuries. Surinamian, Indonesian, Chinese, and Indian food may best be sampled in the Red Light District around the Nieuwmarkt, and off Dam Square, on streets such as Hartenstraat. Indonesian *rijsttafel* (rice table)—20-25 dishes of chicken, curry, chutney, raisins, beef, nuts, shrimp, coconut, and a variety of hot sauces, all heaped onto mountains of rice—is as good as it sounds. Tourist restaurants on Damrak are uniformly overpriced. There are several good mensas (student cards not required) in Amsterdam and snack food is plentiful. *Automatiek* are reasonably priced, and ubiquitous grillrooms serve *shwarma,* the Middle Eastern lamb and garlic pita. *Frikandel* (fried sausage) usually costs as little as f1.50. Indonesian *saté,* skewered meat in peanut sauce, is also readily available. Bakeries sell inexpensive lunch options such as cheese croissants and magnificent breads. Unusual bakeries cluster along Utrechtsestraat south of Prinsengracht. Food in the local street **markets** is your cheapest option. The huge and bustling market on Albert Cuypstraat, near the Heineken brewery, is open Monday through Saturday from 9am to 6pm, as is the one on Ten Katestraat in the Oud-West section of Amsterdam. Ask at the VVV for their *Marktstad* brochure, listing the hours and addresses of all the regular street markets. There is a **supermarket** at the corner of Nieuwmarkt and Bloedstr. (open Mon. 1-6pm, Tues.-Fri. 9am-6pm, Sat. 8am-5pm), and at DeClercqstr. 5-7 (more expensive, but open Mon.-Fri. 6pm-1am, Sat. 1pm-midnight, Sun. 6pm-midnight).

Mensa Tangram, Damstr. 3 (tel. 24 83 54), a university mensa just off Dam Square. Bland but generous meals including fruit for only f5.25. Open Mon.-Fri. 5-7pm. More appetizing fare (from f8.50) is available in the *eetcafé* downstairs (open Mon.-Sat. 7-9:30pm, Sun. 6-9pm), where there is also a snack bar (open Mon.-Sat. 4-7pm). Open year-round.

Mensa de Weesper, Weesperstr. 5 (tel. 22 40 36), a university mensa beyond Waterlooplein. Much better food in a less frenzied atmosphere. The excellent *standaarddagmenu* (menu of the day; f7.50) is served Mon.-Fri. 5-7:15pm. Open late Aug.-June.

H'88, Herengracht 88 (tel. 24 44 46), a university mensa near Brouwersgracht. The traditional run-down, graffiti-smeared student hangout, where a nondescript but fun meal will set you back f5.25. Open for meals Mon.-Fri. 5-7pm. The bar keeps jumping until 4am. Open late Aug.-June.

de Eettuin, tweede Tuindwarsstr. 10 (tel. 23 77 06), in the heart of the Jordaan off Tuinstraat. Noteworthy among *eetcafés.* Full salad bar. Open daily 5:30-11:30pm. Other cafes worth mentioning include **de Doffer,** Runstr. 12 (tel. 22 66 86), 5 min. from the Leidseplein, off Prinsengracht, and **de Reiger,** Nieuwe Leliestr. 34 (tel. 24 74 26), 1 block from Bloemgracht. Both open Sun.-Thurs. until 1am, Fri.-Sat. until 2am.

Bojo, Lange Leidsedwarstr. 51, near the Leidseplein. Indonesian fare for f10.50-15, *rijsttafel* at f12-14.50 per person. Open daily 5pm-5:30am.

Ling Nam, Binnen Bantammerstr. 3. Indonesian and Chinese dishes, including *rijsttafel* (f14.75-24.75 for 1 person, f51.50 for 2), chicken specialities (f16.75 and f17.75), and vegetarian dishes (f13.75-17.50).

Cantharel Eethuisje, Kerkstr. 377 (tel. 26 64 00), just off Utrechtsestr. Dutch cuisine—dishes f8.95-17.95—as well as *schnitzel, entrecôte,* and lamb entrees at f17.50. Open Mon.-Sat. 5-10pm.

The Pancake Bakery, Prinsengracht 191 (tel. 25 13 33), a long block down from the Anne Frank Huis. Crowded with local and out-of-town pancake-seekers. Nice setting. More than 50 varieties of this classic Dutch supper f6-15; omelettes f8.95-11.95. For a killer dessert, try the *kirsch* or *mokkakaramel* pancakes. Open daily noon-9:30pm.

Toi Toi, Nes 102 (tel. 26 39 70), 300m from Dam Square. A small vegetarian restaurant with a f10 daily *menu.* Open Mon.-Fri. noon-10pm, Sat.-Sun. 2-10pm. Lunch served until 5pm, dinner until 9:30pm.

Beit Hamazon, Anjeliersstr. 57, 2nd floor (tel. 27 42 55). Israeli vegetarian specialties in casual surroundings. Dishes f11.50-14.50. Open daily 5-10pm.

Egg Cream, Sint Jacobstr. 19, off N.Z. Voorburgwal. Stirred up by a lively crowd. Daily vegetarian specials for f10.50 and less. English spoken. Open daily 11am-8pm.

The Golden Temple, Utrechtsestr. 126, near Frederiksplein. An American in an Indian outfit runs this relaxed vegetarian restaurant. Entrees f10.50-18; all-you-can-eat salad bar f15. Open Mon.-Sat. noon-9pm, Sun. 5-9pm.

Poffertjeskraam, next to the Westerkerk, the well-known church in the Jordaan. Sample the traditional *poffertjes* (small pancakes) amid shiny copper and wood.

De Blauwe Hollander, Leidsekruisstr. 28. Dutch food, including *schnitzel,* roast veal and roast beef f12.50-17.50. Open daily 5-10pm.

Mouwes Strictly, Sandwiches and Delicatessen, Utrechtsestr. 73 (tel. 23 50 53), is a kosher restaurant. No warm meals served on Sat.

Sights

Amsterdam's former town hall, **Het paleis op de Dam,** represents the city's thriving commercial activities during the seventeenth century. The great Atlas, on top, carries the world on his shoulders—at a time when Dutch merchants sailed the seven seas, Amsterdam didn't think small. (Open mid-June to Aug. daily noon-4:40pm. Admission f1.50.)

The **Rijksmuseum,** on Museumplein at Stadhouderskade 42, has a magnificent collection of Dutch art. On display are some of the finest works of Hals, Ruysdael, van Dyck, ter Borch, Steen, Vermeer, and Rembrandt. The Rijksmuseum is huge, but the exhibit of Dutch art is well-selected, manageable, and explained in an introductory slide-show every 20 minutes. There are hordes of visitors all summer, especially in front of Rembrandt's *The Night Watch,* so try to arrive early. (Open Tues.-Sat. 10am-5pm, Sun. 1-5pm. Admission f6.50, ages under 18 and over 64 f3.50; free with Museumkaart or CJP (see chapter introduction), which may be bought at entrance.)

If the crowds at the Rijksmuseum or Dutch seventeenth century landscape art make you see red, head for the nearby **Stedelijk Museum,** Paulus Potterstr. 13. Its collection of modern art is very broad, stretching from French impressionists and post-impressionists including Monet, Bonnard, Cézanne, and Matisse, to German expressionists such as Heckel and suprematists such as Malewitch. More contemporary figures also figure prominently, especially in the museum's unusual temporary exhibits. (Open daily 11am-5pm. Admission f7.50, ages under 17 and over 64 f5; f2.50 with Museumkaart or CJP.) There's also the renowned **Van Gogh Museum,** at Paulus Potterstr. 7, with an elegant arrangement of the artist's work as well as paintings and Japanese prints that he collected. A Deadhead pilgrimage takes you from the Melkweg to the *Skelet met Brandende Sigaret,* exhibit F.212, on the top floor. (Open Tues.-Sat. 10am-5pm, Sun. 1-5pm. Admission f6.50, ages under 17 and over 64 f3.50; free with Museumkaart or CJP.) For a very different museum experience, try the **Tropenmuseum** (Museum of the Tropics), Linnaeusstr. 2, near the Oosterpark, a presentation center devoted to the people and problems of the Third World. (Open Mon.-Fri. 10am-5pm, Sat.-Sun. noon-5pm. Admission f5, ages under 18 and 65 and over f2.50; free with Museumkaart or CJP.)

A visit to the **Anne Frank Huis,** Prinsengracht 263, is profoundly moving. In the attic of the annex to the house, hidden away behind a bookcase, the young Jewish girl and her family hid from the Nazis; her diary is now famous. The house now serves as a center for the city's anti-fascist and anti-racist movements. (Open Mon.-Sat. 9am-5pm, Sun. 10am-5pm. Admission f5, ages 10-17 and those with CJP f2.50.) **Rembrandt Huis,** Jodenbreestr. 4-6, is the home where the master lived, worked, and taught until it was confiscated by the city for taxes. The building contains 250 of Rembrandt's etchings and drypoints, as well as many of his tools and plates. (Open Mon.-Sat. 10am-5pm, Sun. 1-5pm. Admission f2.50, ages 10-16 f1.50; free with Museumkaart and for ages under 10.)

Less well known is the **Joods-Portuguese Synagogue** (Portugese Synagogue), at Jonas Daniël Meijerplein, near Waterlooplein. A handsome seventeenth-century building with elegant gold candelabra, dark wooden benches, and enormous arched windows, the synagogue was founded by Portuguese Jews expelled from their country. (Open Mon.-Fri. 10am-12:30pm and 1-4pm, Sun. 10am-1pm. Free.) Next door at Jonas Daniël Meijerplein 2-4 is the **Joods Historisch Museum,** with exhibits on the history and culture of the Jewish people. (Open daily 11am-5pm. Admission f5; free with Museumkaart.)

Two small museums will allow you to experience what the Amsterdam *grachtenhuis* (house on a canal) was like. The first, **Museum Amstelkring "Ons Lieve Heer op Solder"** ("Our Lord in the Attic"), O.Z. Voorburgwal 40, in the Red Light District, houses a hidden church. (Open Mon.-Sat. 10am-5pm, Sun. 1-5pm. Admission f3, over 65 f2, free with Museumkaart or CJP.) The second, **Museum van Loon,** Keizersgracht 672, shelters a beautiful garden. (Open Mon. 10am-5pm. Admission f3.50, students and ages over 65 f3.) The ever-popular **Heineken Brewery,** van der Helstraat 30, gives half-hour tours which conclude with free beer sampling. (Tours given at 9am and 11am. f1 admission donated to UNICEF. Free Delft mugs if it's your birthday.) Amsterdam is considered one of the diamond capitals of the world. The largest diamond ever (the Cullinan) was polished in Amsterdam, and the smallest diamond in the world was also cut in Amsterdam; several factories give tours (but no free samples). The **Amsterdam Diamond Center B.V.,** Rokin 1 (tel. 24 57 87) gives tours Fri.-Wed. 10am-5:30pm, Thurs. 10am-8:30pm. You can buy wooden shoes and watch regular demonstrations of clog-making by hand at **'t Klompenhuisje,** Nieuwe Hoogstr. 9a (tel. 22 81 00), daily 11am-6pm.

Built as a district for artisans during Amsterdam's heyday in the seventeenth century, the **Jordaan** is the most intimate part of the city. You can explore many quiet streets and discover dozens of cafes, shops, and gabled homes in this artists' quarter. It is bounded roughly by Prinsengracht, Brouwersgracht, Marnixstraat and Lauriergracht.

The **Red Light District,** near the Oude Kerk around Oudezijds Voorburgwal and Zeedijk, has sailors' bars, sex shops, and real red lights. The bars are cheaper here than in other parts of the city, but hang on to your wallet. Beware also of the street prostitutes, who are not legal—unlike those in the windows. The Zeedijk is pretty dangerous at any hour, and the whole area dangerous after midnight.

For a refuge from Amsterdam's crowded sights and seamy streets, find the **Begijnhof,** a beautifully maintained grassy courtyard surrounded by eighteenth-century buildings; walk down Kalverstraat and turn onto Begijnensteeg, a small side street between Kalverstraat 130 and 132. Another place to escape the bustle is **Vondelpark,** a good place for picnicking and people-watching; the last vestiges of the counter-culture have floated here from the Dam, replete with frisbees, yoga, and hash.

Entertainment

Cafes and Bars

Amsterdam's residents know their cafes: They choose their beer spots with care, and take time to break them in. The nicest cafes are the old dark, wood-paneled *bruine kroegen* (brown cafes) of the Jordaan. Most cafes in Amsterdam stay open until 1am during the week, 2am on weekends.

Cafe de Prins, Prinsengracht 124, **Cafe Twee Prinsen,** Prinsenstr. 27, and **Cafe de Prinses,** Prinsengracht 98. This family of princely cafes is especially popular with paupers and students.

Cafe de Pels, Huidenstr. 25. Intimate and comfortable, popular among students.

Cafe Smalle, Egelantiersgracht 12. Pleasant, with outdoor tables and a canal view.

Françoise, Kerkstr. 176. Quiet and a bit expensive; decorated with women's art. Open Mon.-Sat. 9am-6pm.

Schaakcafe Het Hok, Lange Leidsedwarsstr. 134. Join the locals in a game of chess, backgammon, or cards. Also try the **Chesshouse Gambit,** Bloemgracht 20. Both open daily until midnight.

Le Shako, 's-Gravelandse Veer 14 (tel. 24 02 09), near Amstel, is a popular mixed gay bar. Open daily 10pm-3am.

Downtown, Reguliersdwarsstr. 31 (tel 22 99 58). A coffee shop for gay men. Open daily 11am-9pm.

Nightlife

There's a concentration of clubs on Leidseplein and Rembrandtplein; most are open later than the cafes.

Melkweg, Lijnbaansgracht 234a, (tel. 24 17 77). A multi-cultural center and a legend that manages to retain a very special alternative atmosphere, despite the crowds. In an old factory off Leidseplein, directly across from the police station. Admission (f7.50-17.50) buys access to excellent live music, theater, films, and, not to be forgotten, the snack bar with its space cakes (hash brownies) and balls (f5); you'll only need a *slice* to float away. Open Wed.-Thurs. and Sun. 7pm-2am, Fri.-Sat. 7pm-4am.

Paradiso, Weteringschans 6-8 (tel. 26 45 21). Some of the foremost international punk, new-wave, and reggae bands play here. Admission f7.50-20, depending on the band. Open Wed.-Sun.

De IJsbreker, Weesperzijde 23 (tel. 68 18 05), a bit far from the center. This hub of classical music attracts avant-garde ensembles. You can also eat and drink here. Admission f12.50; CJP holders f10. Open Sun.-Thurs. 10am-1am, Fri.-Sat. 10am-2am.

Bimhuis, Oude Schans 73-77 (tel. 23 33 73). Home to the best jazz and improvised music performances. Concerts Thurs.-Sat. at 9pm; workshops Mon.-Wed. Admission f10-15, depending on program; CPJ holders and ages over 64 receive a f2.50 reduction. There is also a cafe open Mon.-Thurs. 8pm-2am, Fri.-Sat. 8pm-3am.

De Kroeg, Lijnbaansgracht 163 (tel. 25 01 77), has late-night jazz and salsa sessions starting at 10:30pm.

Maloe Melo, an old garage at Lijnbaansgracht 160 (tel. 25 33 00). Blues. Open Mon.-Sat.

De Stip, Lijnbaansgracht 161 (tel. 27 96 92). Live pop music starting at 11pm. Open Mon.-Sat. 10pm-4am.

The String, Nes 98 (tel. 25 90 15), near Dam. A good folk cafe. Open daily from 8pm. Free.

Dancing

Most nightclubs in Amsterdam charge a membership fee in addition to entrance, so they can be expensive for a one-shot affair. There are many discos on Prinsengracht, near Leidsestrasse, and on Lange Leidsedwarsstrasse, but these tend to be expensive.

Odeon, Singel 460 (tel. 24 97 11), just off Leidsestr. Probably the best place to dance, despite its small floor. Open Thurs.-Sun. 11pm-5am, Admission Thurs. and Sun. f2.50, Fri.-Sat. f7.50, f5 with CJP.

Mazzo, Rozengracht 114 (tel. 26 75 00), is a new wave disco. Cover f5. Open Sun.-Thurs. 11pm-4am, Fri.-Sat. 11pm-5am.

Dansen bij Jansen, Handboogstr. 11, is a disco popular amongst students (officially, a student ID is required). Happy hour Sun.-Wed. 11pm-midnight. Open Sun.-Wed. 11pm-4am, Thurs. 11pm-5am, Fri.-Sat. 11pm-5:30am.

Homolulu, Kerkstr. 23 (tel. 24 63 87). A mixed gay disco, but popular with everyone. No cover; inexpensive drinks. Happy hour Mon.-Fri. 10pm-midnight. Open Sun.-Thurs. 10pm-4am, Fri.-Sat. 10pm-5am.

S'Jivon, Kerkstr. 346, near Amstel, is exclusively lesbian. Open Tues.-Sun. 11pm-2am.

Theater, Dance, and Music

VVV puts out *This Week* (f1), with comprehensive cultural listings. From June through August, there are free performances Wednesday through Sunday at the **Vondelpark Openluchttheater** (tel. 73 14 99); jazz and folk concerts dominate, but experimental and children's theater, political music, reggae, mime, and pop are also typical fare. Check posters at park entrances. In June, the **Holland Festival** of dance, drama, and music is devoted to a single theme or country, with performances by major Dutch and foreign cultural groups. The **Shaffytheater,** Keizersgracht 324 (tel. 23 13 11), coordinates a festival of small theater companies in the first two weeks of July. (Tickets f10-15.) During this same period, the annual **Dutch National Ballet Festival** is held at the **Stadsschouwburg,** the municipal theater at Leidseplein 26 (tel. 24 23 11; tickets f15-32.50). The National Ballet also holds occasional choreography workshops (f12.50). You can make reservations for any cultural event, in person only, at the **Amsterdams Uit Buro (AUB),** Leidseplein 26 (tel. 21 12 11; open Mon.-Sat. 10am-6pm). The larger tourist bureaus in Holland (VVV I) also have ticket-reservation services.

There is English-speaking theater in winter (continuing into early summer), Wednesday through Sunday evenings, at the **Art Theater** (tel. 24 01 08; tickets f17.50, with CJP f12.50). Also try the **Bellevue,** Leidsekade 90 (tel. 24 72 48; seats f20, seniors and CJP holders f15). In July and August, frequent English-language performances and cabarets are given at the theater/café **Suikerhof,** Prinsengracht 381 (tel. 22 75 71; open Wed.-Sat. from 5pm, Sun. from 2pm). Films in Amsterdam are shown in the original languages; most cinemas are near Leidseplein.

There are frequent organ concerts during the summer at **Oude Kerk,** Oude Kerksplein 23 (tel. 24 91 83), **Westerkerk,** (where Rembrandt is buried) Prinsengracht 281 (tel. 24 77 66), and **Nieuwe Kerk,** where Dutch monarchs are sworn in (they're not crowned), at Dam Square (tel. 26 81 68). Prices are f5-7.50.

Near Amsterdam

When you tire of free and easy Amsterdam, explore the surrounding countryside. Trains are expensive, so buy a cheap day return or get a one-day bus pass (f17.30 for all destinations). **Alkmaar,** 45 minutes by train (4 per hr.) from Amsterdam, holds an open-air **cheese market** every Friday from 10am to noon from mid-April through mid-September. Cheeses are tasted, weighed, displayed, and carried in an elaborate ritual; get there early to beat the huge crowds.

Edam, also known principally for its cheeses, is a town rich in history and atmosphere. The fifteenth-century **Grote Kerk,** or **St. Nicolaaskerk,** is the largest three-ridged church in Europe and has 30 superb stained-glass windows. Since Edam is not on the train line, you'll have to take the NZH bus from opposite Centraal Station in Amsterdam (7 strips). Rent a bike at **de Smederij,** Voorhaven 115 (tel. (02993) 721 55) for f7.50 and cross to the island of **Marken,** connected to the mainland by causeway. The **Marken Museum,** at Kerkbuurt 44-47, is especially worthwhile (open Easter-Oct. Mon.-Sat. 10am-4:30pm, Sun. noon-4pm; admission f1.50), and the nearby **church** has a traditional solemn Sunday service. To get to the island take bus #110 to Volendam. For the return trip take bus #111. Wherever you go sample the *broodje haring,* open-faced sandwiches with delicious little morsels of herring.

Hoorn is an old whaling town that attached its name to the tip of South America. Walking around here is enjoyable: The canals are lined with brightly painted facades. Each Wednesday morning during July and August there is a full **market** with old-time Dutch costumes, dancing, and food. Hoorn is quickly reached by train, and is on the line between Amsterdam and Enkhuizen. You can also take a direct bus (Mon.-Sat. 2 per hr., Sun. 1 per hr. until 9:55pm, 11 strips) or bus #114 to Edam (2 per hr., 7 strips).

Haarlem

Haarlem, 20km from Amsterdam, quietly entices visitors with its melodious organs, historical facades, and romantic canals. Fans of the dominant Dutch soccer teams of the late '70s might like to know that Haarlem is reportedly the birthplace (in 1879) of Dutch soccer. Even if you find that last tidbit completely uninteresting, you should enjoy the many attractive seventeenth- and eighteeenth-century *hofjes* (almshouses for elderly women), red-brick structures with grassy courtyards. Especially charming are **Hofje van Loo,** on Barrevoetestrant 7, and **Hofje van Bakenes,** on Bakenessergracht, just before Appelaarssteeg as you come from the station (enter through the door with the "ANWB" sign, but remember that the *hofjes* are private property). You can pick up a brochure describing the *hofjes* at the VVV.

From the station, Kruisweg leads to the **Grote Markt** (marketplace), and the beautiful medieval **Stadhuis** (town hall), originally the thirteenth-century hunting lodge of the Count of Holland. (You might be able to visit the lavishly furnished interior—ask at the reception desk.) Also located on the Grote Markt is the **Grote Kerk** (formerly St. Bavo's Cathedral). The cathedral houses the Müller organ, which Mozart played when he was 11 and the organ was 28. (Church open Mon.-Sat. 10am-5pm. Admission f1.50, students f1. Organ recitals April-late Sept. Sat. 3-4pm; May-Oct. Tues. 8:15-9:15pm and Thurs. 3-4pm. Free.) From the church, walk down Damstraat to the **Teylers Museum,** Spaarne 16—Netherland's oldest. Teyler was an enlightened eighteenth-century cloth merchant who bequeathed his fortune to promote the arts and sciences. The museum lets you see what people in 1788 thought a museum should be; a blend of scientific instruments of the era, fossils, coins, paintings, and superb drawings, including works by Raphael and Michelangelo. (Open March-Sept. Tues.-Sat. 10am-5pm, Sun. 1-5pm; Oct.-Feb. closes at 4pm. Admission f3, ages 65 and over f1.50; free with Museumkaart and CJP.)

Frans Hals, the great portraitist, was a resident of Haarlem, and is now buried in the Grote Kerk. The **Frans Hals Museum,** Groot Heiligland 62, is set in a seventeenth-century almshouse. (Almshouses (for men) differed from *hofjes* in that they were staffed by someone who did the cooking and washing—it was believed that women could look after themselves.) The museum contains Hals' lively group portraits (including the *Corporation Pieces*) as well as an original dollhouse from 1750, silver from Haarlem's silversmiths, and modern and contemporary art. (Open Mon.-Sat. 11am-5pm, Sun. 1-5pm. Admission f4, ages under 18 and over 64 f2; free with Museumkaart and CJP.) Throughout 1988 the museum will be celebrating its 375th birthday with events, special evening hours, etc. Ask at the tourist office for specifics. Also visit the **Corrie Ten Boomhuis,** better known as **The Hiding Place,** Barteljorisstraat 19, where Corrie Ten Boom and her family hid Jewish refugees during World War II. The refugees were never found, but the entire Ten Boom family was taken away to concentration camps and Corrie was the only one to survive. (Open Mon.-Sat. 10am-4:30pm.) Note that this and the Franz Hals Museum are two of the few in Holland open on Monday—a good day to visit Haarlem. Another good day to visit is Saturday, when a beautiful **flower market** fills the Grote Markt (9am-4pm).

The **VVV,** Stationsplein 1 (tel. (023) 31 90 59), can sell you an excellent map of Haarlem. (Open April-Aug. Mon.-Sat. 9am-6pm; Sept.-March Mon.-Fri. 9am-6pm, Sat. 10am-4pm.) The **Jeugdherberg Jan Gijzen,** Jan Gijzenpad 3 (tel. (023) 37 37 93), is 3km from the station; take bus #6 or 2 (direction: Haarlem-Nord). The hostel is often full, so reserve ahead. (f16.75. Breakfast included. Open March-Oct.) The VVV can book you a room at a B&B for around f25 plus a fee of f3.50. Across the Grote Markt from the Stadhuis, **Hotel Carillon,** Grote Markt 27 (tel. (023) 31 05 91), is a good value. (Singles f37.50, doubles f70, triples f99. Breakfast included.) Farther from the center of town are **Hotel Fehres,** Zijlweg 299 (tel. (023) 27 73 68; singles f35, doubles f70, triples f105; breakfast included), and **Zijlhoeve,** Zijlweg 159-161 (tel. (023) 32 59 09), with singles for f35 (breakfast included). You can camp at **De Liede,** Liewegje 17 (tel. (023) 33 23 60). Take bus #80 (direction: Amsterdam) from Tempeliersstraat (f3.75 per person, f3.75 per tent).

You can eat cheap filled pancakes (from f6) at **La Maison de Poupée,** Gierstr. 66 (open Sun.-Fri. 5-9pm), and **Pannekoekhuis De Smikkel,** Kruisweg 57 (open Tues.-Sat. 11:30am-8pm, Sun. 2-8pm). The **Stads Cafe,** Zijlstraat 56-58 (tel. 32 52 02), serves Dutch cuisine and has a daily menu (*dagschotel*) for f8.75. (Open Mon.-Wed. 5:30-8:30pm, Thurs.-Sun. 5:30-9:30pm.)

Haarlem is easily accessible from Amsterdam by train (4 per hr.) or by bus #80 from Marnixstr., near Leidseplein (2 per hr.). Night bus #86 runs from Amsterdam's Marnixstr. to Haarlem at 1:45am and 2:30am, but no night bus runs from Haarlem to Amsterdam.

Near Haarlem

Haarlem is only 10 minutes away by train from **Zandvoort** beach; south of here, between *paal* (wooden posts) #68 and 71, is a popular nudist beach. **Bloemendaal** beach, accessible by bus #81 (1 per hr.) from the Haarlem train station, is more peaceful. During April and May, over five million bulbs flourish at the magnificent **Keukenhof** garden. Take bus #50 or 51 toward Lisse from the Haarlem train station. (Admission f7.50.) A tremendous international flower auction is held year-round in the nearby town of **Aalsmeer;** visitors can watch from a special gallery. From Haarlem, take bus #140. (Open Mon.-Fri. 7:30-11am; the most active bidding is between 8 and 9am.) The **Frans Roozen Gardens** bloom with 500 different types of flowers and plants; summer flower shows are free. Bus #90 (direction: Vogelenzang) stops in front of the gardens. (Open July-Oct. daily 9am-5pm; tulip show April-May daily 8am-6pm.) Bus #50 or 51 south of Haarlem runs past some of Holland's famous flower fields. Daffodils bloom early to late April, hyacinths mid-to late April, and tulips late April to late May. In nearby Spaarndam, you can see the statue of **Hans Brinker,** the little boy who (according to the 19th-century children's story) put his finger in the hole in the dike and saved Holland.

Leiden

The University of Leiden is Holland's oldest, a gift of William the Silent in 1574. Museums of all kinds draw visitors to this town southwest of Amsterdam and near The Hague—there are no less than 11 to choose from. The **VVV,** Stationsplein 210 (tel. (071) 14 68 46), across the street from the station, sells maps (f0.50) and museum brochures. (Open April-Aug. Mon.-Sat. 9am-6pm; Sept.-March Mon.-Fri. 9am-5:30pm, Sat. 10am-4pm.)

The **Rijksmuseum voor Volkenkunde** (National Museum of Ethnology), Steenstraat 1, bursts with colorful artifacts from the Dutch East Indies. The Buddha room, with five huge bronze representations, is world-famous. (Open June-Sept. Tues.-Sat. 10am-5pm, Sun. 1-5pm; Oct.-May Tues.-Sat. 11am-5pm, Sun. 1-5pm. Admission f3.50, ages under 18 and over 64 f2; free with Museumkaart and CJP.) The **Rijksmuseum van Oudheden** (National Antiquities Museum), Rapenburg 28, contains the complete, beautifully restored Egyptian Temple of Taffeh, which the Dutch energetically rescued from the reservoir basin of the Aswan Dam and opened to the public in 1979. Besides Egyptian sarcophagi and mummies, the collection includes Greek, Roman, and Etruscan artifacts; and a fascinating exhibit on the prehistory of the Netherlands. (Open Tues.-Sat. 10am-5pm, Sun. 1-5pm. Admission f3.50, ages under 18 and over 64 f2; free with Museumkaart and CJP.)

The **Hortus Botanicus** at Rapenburg 73 is one of the oldest botanical gardens in Europe, and a perfectly scented place to relax. (Garden open April-Sept. Mon.-Sat. 9am-5pm, Sun. 10am-5pm; Oct.-March open Sun.-Fri. only, and reduced hours for hothouses. Admission f0.50, seniors f0.25; free with Museumkaart and f0.25 with CJP.) You can visit a Dutch windmill and see its complicated wooden gear system at the **Molenmuseum "De Valk,"** 2de Binnenvestgracht 1, built in 1743 and in operation until 1945. (Open Tues.-Sat. 10am-5pm, Sun. 1-5pm. Admission f2.50, ages under 17 and over 64 f1.25; free with Museumkaart and CJP.) Other museums in Leiden are devoted to subjects ranging from clay tobacco pipes to photographs and cameras.

Leiden is short on budget accommodations, but you can try **Pension Witte,** Witte Singel 80 (tel. (071) 12 45 92), with singles for f30, doubles f56. (Breakfast included. Open Dec.-Oct.) **Pension Bik,** nearby at Witte Singel 92 (tel. (071) 12 26 02), is also reasonably priced. (Singles f32.50, doubles f57.50. Breakfast included. Open Nov.-Sept.) **Pension In de Goede Hoek,** Diefsteeg 19a (tel. (071) 12 10 31), near the Stadhuis, is friendly and has large rooms with TVs. You can use the kitchen, and coffee and tea are free. (Singles f28.50 for one night, otherwise f26; doubles f42.) The VVV occasionally books rooms in private homes (about f25). **Jeugdherberg De Duinark,** Langevelderlaan 45 (tel. (02523) 729 20), in Noordwijk, is 18km from town. Take bus #60 from the Leiden train station. (f16.75. Breakfast included. Open April-Oct.)

Anybody can eat at the two university mensas. **Augustinus,** Rapenburg 24, serves meals for f4.75. (Open Sept.-June Mon.-Fri. 5:30-7:15pm.) **De Bak,** Kaiserstr. 23-25, has vegetarian dishes for f4.40. (Open Mon.-Fri. 11am-2pm and 5-7pm. Closed last week of July and first week of Aug.) **De Hooykist,** Hooigracht 49, is a cozy, good *eetcafé.* (Meals f12.50-20; open daily 5-11pm.) The **Azië,** Stationsplein 24, next to the VVV, is reputed to be one of the best Chinese-Indonesian restaurants in the country. (Dishes f14-23, *rijsttafel* for two f45-50. Open daily 11am-11pm.) The renovated area near Pieterskerk harbors some quiet, pleasant coffee shops.

Trains leave for Leiden from Amsterdam's Centraal Station (4 per hr., 30 min.).

The Hague (Den Haag)

Although Amsterdam is the capital of the Netherlands, the seat of government is The Hague. Here the streets are broader, the buildings grander, and even the roses in the parks seem more stately. This cool city of diplomats also harbors the royal residence and the International Court of Justice, which meets at the Peace Palace. Scheveningen, a popular beach and nightlife spot northwest of the city, will give you a break from The Hague's hauteur, as will the parks, the pedestrian areas, and Kijkduin, a seaside resort in the south of the city.

Practical Information

Tourist Offices: VVV, Kon. Julianaplein 30 (tel. (070) 54 62 00), next to Centraal Station. Will sell you a map (f1), and book you a room (f3.50). Open April to mid-Sept. Mon.-Sat. 9am-9pm, Sun. 10am-5pm; mid-Sept. to March Mon.-Sat. 9am-8pm, Sun. 10am-5pm. A second office at Zwolsestr., next to the Europa Hotel, in Scheveningen. Open April to mid-Sept. Mon.-Sat. 9am-9pm, Sun. 10am-5pm; mid-Sept. to March Mon.-Sat. 9am-6pm.

Budget Travel: NBBS, Schoolstr. (tel. 46 58 19). Open April-Sept. Mon.-Fri. 9:30am-5pm, Sat. 10am-2pm.

American Express: Venestr. 20 (tel. 46 95 15). Mail held. All financial services. Open Mon.-Fri. 9am-5pm, Sat. 9:30am-12:30pm.

Post Office: Nobelstr. and Prinsenstr., open Mon.-Fri. 8:30am-7pm, Thurs. 8:30am-8:30pm, Sat. 9am-noon. Telex, telegram, and international **phone** services also. **Area code:** 070.

Train Stations: There are two, **Holland Spoor** and **Centraal Station.** To get from Holland Spoor to Centraal Station and the VVV, take a *stoptrein* or tram #9 or 12. Information (tel. 82 41 41).

Public Transport: Information (tel. 82 41 41). Day-tickets cost f8.65.

Bicycle rental: At both Holland Spoor (tel. 89 08 30) and Centraal Station (tel. 85 32 35). f6 per day, f200 deposit. Cycling maps available at the VVV (from f1).

Emergencies: Police (tel. 22 22 22); headquarters at Burg-Patijnlaan 35 (tel. 10 49 11).

Embassies: U.S., Lange Voorhout 102 (tel. 62 49 11). **Canada,** Sophialaan 7 (tel. 61 41 11). **U.K.,** Lange Voorhout 10 (tel. 64 58 00). **Australia,** Koninginnegracht 23-4 (tel. 64 79 08). **New Zealand,** Mauritskade 25 (tel. 46 93 24).

Laundry: Sütmüller, Hoefkade 978 (tel. 80 78 22), near Holland Spoor.

Accommodations and Food

Budget accommodations are scarce in The Hague; less expensive are Delft and Rotterdam (at least 4 trains per hr. to both). In The Hague itself, private homes are a good idea (from about f25; ask at the tourist office). The beautifully situated **Jeugdherberg Ockenburgh (IYHF),** Monsterseweg 4 (tel. (070) 97 00 11), 8km out of town, in Kijkduin, is accessible by bus #122, 123, or 124 from Centraal Station. (June-Aug. f17.50; Sept.-May f16.75. Breakfast included.) In Scheveningen, try **'t Seehuys,** Zeekant 45 (tel. (070) 55 95 85), a hostel on the coast. Take tram #11 from Holland Spoor or tram #7 from Centraal Station to its terminus, and turn right while facing the sea; it's a two-minute walk. (Dorm beds f17.50, with breakfast f21, doubles with breakfast f23.50 per person.) **Pension Centrale,** Haagsestr. 61 (tel. (070) 54 16 53), also in Scheveningen, has a delightful proprietor. (Singles f31, doubles f52. Breakfast included.) You can camp a half mile from the beach at **Ockenburgh,** Wijndaelerweg 16 (tel. (070) 25 23 64). Take tram #3 from Centraal Station. (f3.60 per person, f11 per site. Open April to mid-Oct.)

Eating in this city of diplomats may require an expense account. Join ordinary citizens in the covered market at **Markthof,** Spuistr., a few blocks from Binnenhof, along Grote Marktstr. (Mon. 11am-6pm, Tues.-Wed. and Fri.-Sat. 9am-6pm, Thurs. 9am-9pm.) Or go to Scheveningen to sample *broodje haring* at any of the stalls along the promenade (about f3). **Het Pannekoekhuisje,** Strandweg 17 (tel. 54 78 74), serves filling pancakes from f7. (Open April-Sept. 11am-midnight; Sept.-March 11am-8pm.) More of a sight than a food alternative is the fish auction held at Visafslagweg (Mon.-Sat. 7:30-9am).

Sights

The **Binnenhof** is the Netherlands's Parliament, and one look is enough to make you want to enter a career in Dutch politics; have a look at the **Ridderzaal** (Hall of Knights). (Open Mon.-Sat. 10am-4pm; last guided tour starts at 3:55pm. Admission f1.50-4.50, depending on tour. Book ahead at (070) 64 61 44.) Just outside the north entrance of the Binnenhof, the **Mauritshuis,** a seventeenth-century mansion, houses a splendid collection of Dutch paintings, including Rembrandt's *De Anatomieles van Professor Tulp* (The Anatomy Lesson) and Vermeer's *Lady with a Turban.* (Open Tues.-Sat. 10am-5pm, Sun. 11am-5pm. Admission f6.50, seniors and ages 18 and under f3.50; free with Museumkaart and CJP.)

Lovers of the abstract will appreciate the largest collection of Mondriaans in the world, at the **Haags Gemeentemuseum,** Stadhouderslaan 41. (Open Tues.-Fri. 10am-5pm, Sat.-Sun. noon-5pm. Admission f3, seniors and ages 9-16 f1; free with Museumkaart and CJP.) If you thought the real Holland was small, you should see the scaled-down version at **Madurodam,** Haringkade 175, the plum of The Hague's tourist industry. Here you'll find chest-high models of every famous building and monument in Holland. At night, this nether-Netherlands lights up, and you can watch a Lilliputian procession. Take tram #1 or 9 from Centraal Station, or bus #22 from the center of town. (Open March 26-May daily 9am-10pm; June-Aug. daily 9am-10:30pm; Sept. daily 9am-9pm; Oct. daily 9am-6pm. Admission f8.)

The **Haags Filmhuis,** Denneweg (tel. 45 99 00), features oldies and the best of current movies; all films are shown in their original language. **Café La Valletta,** Nieuwe Schoolstr. 13a (tel. 64 45 43), is a jazz cafe nearby. There are lots of **bars** in Scheveningen along Gevers Deynootweg, Gevers Deynootplein, and Strandweg. In the summer, **fireworks** explode from the pier at the beach in Scheveningen every Friday night, and in mid-June the beach hosts the **International Fokker Kite Flying Festival.** For a complete listing of music, theater, festivals, and exhibitions pick up the brochure *Info* from the VVV.

Near The Hague

The largest port in the world, **Rotterdam** was completely destroyed during World War II: A cubist commemorative sculpture by Zadkine rises on the Blaak. **Spido,** Willemsplein (tel. (010) 413 54 00), offers tours of the huge port. Take the subway to Leuvehaven. (Open April-Sept. daily 9:30am-3:30pm. March and Oct. tours at

10am, 11:30am, 1pm, and 2:30pm. Tours from f11.) Rotterdam has some great humorous architecture: A paper clip stands near Binnenhaven (take a train south and you'll see it on your right), and an upright pencil (actually an apartment building) rises on the Blaak. In the same vein are the **cube houses;** take the subway to Blaak and follow the "*Cubuswoning*" sign. (Open April-Oct. Mon.-Fri. 10am-5pm, Sat.-Sun. 11am-5pm. Admission f2.50.)

Get a free map of Rotterdam's public transportation network at the **VVV** booth in the train station. (Open Mon.-Sat. 9am-midnight, Sun. 10am-midnight.) Their main office is at Stadhuisplein 19 (tel. (010) 413 60 00). (Open April-Sept. Mon.-Thurs. and Sat. 9am-6pm, Fri. 9am-9pm, Sun. 10am-6pm; Oct.-March Mon.-Thurs. and Sat. 9am-6pm, Fri. 9am-9pm.) The **Jeugdherberg (IYHF)** is at Rochussenstraat 107-109 (tel. (010) 436 57 63); take the subway to Dijkzigt. (June-Aug. f17.50; Sept.-May f16.75. Breakfast included.) **Bagatelle,** Provenierssingel 26 (tel. (010) 467 63 48), at the other side of the station, and **Simone,** Nieuwe Binnenweg 162a (tel. (010) 436 25 85), both rent singles for f30 and doubles for f60. **De Eend,** Mauritsweg 28, serves good meals for f10. (Open Mon.-Fri. 5:30-7:30pm.) Near the cube houses overlooking the old port, **Plan-C Theatercafé,** Slepersvest 1 (tel. (010) 412 43 52), combines theatricals with nourishment from f11.50. (No performances June-July.) In old Deltshaven, **Bla-Bla,** Piet Heinsplein 35, offers vegetarian dishes for f16-18. Rotterdam also has many fine cafes: **Dizzy,** 's-Gravendijkwal 127, attracts jazz lovers; **Melief Bender,** Oude Binnenweg, is an old favorite of beer drinkers; and **Mateloos,** Nieuwe Binnenweg 105, is a gay new wave cafe.

To the south of The Hague lies **Schiedam,** a town which at one time had 20 of the largest windmills in Europe, most operating to help produce gin. Today, four of those windmills are still operating, and two can be visited, including **"De Noord,"** Noordvest 38, the tallest windmill in Europe. (Tours Sat. 10:30am-4:30pm. Tel. 473 30 00.)

Regular ferries run between ports near The Hague and England: **North Sea Ferries** (tel. (01819) 555 00) sails from Benelux Haven, Europoort to Hull; and **Sealink** and **Hoek-Harwich** (tel. (01747) 39 44) sail from Hoek van Holland to Harwich. A one-way second-class ticket with Hoek-Harwich costs f90 for adults (ages 14 and older), f45 for children (ages 4-13) and f63 for seniors (men over 65 and women over 60). Bikes cost an additional f20-35.

Delft

To offset the introduction of Chinese porcelain three centuries ago, Delft potters conjured up their blue-on-white china. You can gawk at the high-priced plates in the boutique (or "bluetique") at **Royal Delftware De Porceleyne Fles,** Rotterdamseweg 196, in South Delft, where there are also hourly painting demonstrations. Take bus #60. (Open April.-Oct. Mon.-Sat. 9am-5pm, Sun. 10am-4pm; Nov.-March Mon.-Fri. 9am-5pm, Sat. 10am-4pm.) **De Delftse Pauw,** Delftweg 133, in the northern reaches of the city, is the main factory and offers tours as well. Take tram #1. (Open April to mid-Oct. daily 9am-4pm; mid-Oct. to March Mon.-Fri. 9am-4pm, Sat.-Sun. 11am-1pm. Free.) Both places have seconds at 25% off. The tour guides will tell you—if the prices don't—how to distinguish the real Blue from the imitations.

Delft has two important churches. Prince William I of Orange, who liberated the Dutch from the Spanish yoke, is buried in the **Nieuwe Kerk;** the remains of Vermeer—but none of his paintings—are in the **Oude Kerk.** (Nieuwe Kerk open April-Sept. Mon.-Sat. 9am-5pm; Oct.-March Mon.-Sat. 10am-noon and 1:30-4pm. Oude Kerk open April-Sept. Mon.-Sat. noon-4pm. Admission f2 to one church, seniors f1.25; f3 to both, seniors f2.) Also in town is **Het Prinsenhof** at Sint Agathaplein. Housed in a fifteenth-century convent and once the home of William of Orange (until he was assassinated here in 1584), this museum contains a fine collection of tapestries and paintings. In mid-October, the museum sponsors an antique fair famous throughout Holland. (Open June-Aug. Mon. 1-5pm, Tues.-Sat. 10am-5pm,

Sun. 1-5pm; Sept.-May Tues.-Sun. only. Admission f3.50; free with Museumkaart and CJP.)

You can get a complete pamphlet on Delft (f2.50), as well as hiking and cycling maps for the area, from the **VVV,** Markt 85 (tel. (015) 12 61 00). (Open April-Sept. Mon.-Fri. 9am-6pm, Sat. 9am-5pm, Sun. 11am-3pm; Oct.-March Mon.-Sat. only.) Delft has a half-dozen good, friendly pensions, all about the same price and all quite near the train station. **Van Leeuwen,** Achterom 143 (tel. (015) 12 37 16), is run by a delightful woman. (Singles f30, doubles f55. Breakfast included.) From mid-June through August, the cheapest place to stay is in student flats. Inquire at the room office, floor 9, of **Student Flats Krakeelhof,** 9 Jacoba van Beierenlaan (tel. (015) 13 59 53 or 14 62 35). To get here, turn right onto van Leeuwenhoeksingel as you leave the station, turn right again at the end of the street, go under the tunnel, and walk to the first traffic light. You'll see the bright, modern buildings ahead of you, surrounded by a moat. (Singles f15, after 7 nights f11, doubles f25. Bring your own sleeping bag.) Delft also has a **municipal campground** on Hoflaan, in the recreation area of Delftse Hout (tel. (015) 57 05 15). (f3.45 per person, f2.80 per tent.) To reach the site, take bus #60 from the station (to stop Korftlaan) or #133 (to stop Hoflaan).

There is a large **general market** every Thursday from 9am to 5pm on the marketplace in the town center (and a **flower market** at the same time on Hippolytusbuurt, next to the canal). On Saturdays, a **fruit and vegetable market** takes place on the Brabantse Turfmarkt. The largest **mensa** (tel. (015) 78 47 27) is on the university campus in town at Nieuwelaan 76. (f4.50 meals. Open year-round Mon.-Fri 12:15-1:15pm and 5-7:15pm.) **Alcuin,** Oude Delft 57 (tel. (015) 12 34 15) has long tables. (Basic meals f5. Open Sept.-July Mon.-Fri. 5:30-7:15pm, Sun. 6-7pm.) Along the same street at #123, **Eettafel Tyche** (tel. (015) 12 21 23) offers similar meat-and-potatoes fare. (Open Aug.-June Mon.-Sat. 5:15-7:15pm.) Otherwise, try **Stadspannekoeckhuys,** Oude Delft 113-115 (tel. (015) 13 01 93), for good, filling pancakes for f7 to 9.75. (Open in summer daily noon-8pm; in winter Tues.-Sun. only.) You can try the sandwich that was voted the best *broodje* in the Netherlands at **Kleyweg's Stads Koffyhuis** (tel. (015) 12 46 25), just down the street at #135. (Open Mon.-Fri. 9am-7pm, Sat. 9am-6pm.)

Delft is one hour southwest of Amsterdam by train, with connections at The Hague, Leiden, and Haarlem (2 per hr., about f15). For train or bus information in Delft, call (070) 82 41 41.

Utrecht

Utrecht is both the geographical center of Holland and one of its major university towns. National demonstrations often start here, and book and print shops dot tiny streets throughout the old town. If you arrive by train don't linger in **Hoog Catharijne,** the huge modern shopping complex around Centraal Station, but strike out across it towards Utrecht's older quarters.

In the seventeenth century, a hurricane separated the **Domtoren,** an imposing tower, from its **cathedral.** Don't let the 465 steps to the tower put you off—the view is splendid. The cathedral's chapel and enormous clocks are also fascinating. (Open April to late Oct. Mon.-Fri. 10am-5pm, Sat.-Sun. noon-5pm; late Oct. to March Sat.-Sun. noon-5pm. Mandatory tours every hr. until 4pm. Admission f1.50.) Across the street is the **Kloostergang,** part of the cathedral's Gothic cloister. (Open April to late Oct. Mon.-Fri. 10am-6pm, Sat.-Sun. 11am-6pm; June-Aug. also open Thurs. until 9pm; late Oct. to March Mon.-Fri. 10am-5pm, Sat.-Sun. 11am-5pm. Free.) The **Centraal Museum,** Agnietenstr. 1, is a five-minute walk on Korte Nieuwstr. and Lange Nieuwstr. Here you can marvel at a ninth-century Viking ship and paintings of the *Utrechtse* school, sixteenth- and seventeenth-century artists who, influenced by Caravaggio, became veritable masters of chiaroscuro (technique where the emphasis is not so much on color as on the division between light and shadow). (Open Tues.-Sat. 10am-5pm, Sun. 2-5pm. Admission f2.50, children and seniors f1.25; free with Museumkaart and CJP.) **Het Catharijneconvent,** Nieuwe Gracht 63, contains the largest collection of medieval art in the Netherlands. (Open Tues.-Fri. 10am-5pm, Sat.-Sun. 11am-5pm. Admission f3.50, ages under 18 and seniors f2; free with Museumkaart or CJP.)

Utrecht has few cheap hotels; the **VVV** will help you find lodgings for the usual fee. Visit their booth in the station (open Mon.-Sat. 9:30am-5:30pm), or the very friendly main office, Vredenburg 90 (tel. (030) 31 41 32), across the street at the end of the shopping mall. (Open April to mid-Sept. Mon.-Wed. and Fri.-Sat. 9am-8pm, Thurs. 9am-9pm, Sun. 10am-3pm; mid-Sept. to March Mon.-Sat. 9am-6pm.) They might find you a B&B (about f25 per person), but the best budget accommodations are probably at **Jeugdherberg Rhijnauwen (IYHF),** Rhijnauwenselaan 14 (tel. (03405) 612 77), a converted country house in a gorgeous rural setting. Take bus #40 from Utrecht's Centraal Station to Bunnik, and walk for about 10 minutes. (Members f16.75, nonmembers f21.75. Breakfast included. Open year-round.) For private lodgings, try the **Hotel Domstad,** Parkstr. 5 (tel. (030) 31 01 31), on the other side of town. (Singles f40, doubles f62. Breakfast included. Midnight curfew.) **Camping De Berekuil,** Ariensiaan 5-7 (tel. (030) 71 38 70), is not far from the center of town: take bus #57 from the station to the Veemarkt stop. (f3.90 per person, f3.90 per tent. Open April-Oct.) There is also a **Sleep-Inn,** Jansveld 51 (tel. (030) 31 53 26), where you can spend the night for f10. (Open 9pm-1am.)

In the evenings, **Zeezicht,** Nobelstr., just off Janskerkhof, attracts many people. Every Tuesday night (except July-Aug.) at 9:30pm, there's live music. You can also have a snack or dinner (f9.50-15.75) in this colorful cafe. (Open Mon.-Thurs. 8am-1am, Fri.-Sat. 8pm-2am, Sun. 11am-1am.) On the same street are two inviting pubs with old brown interiors: **De Kneus,** Nobelstr. 303 (open Sun.-Thurs. 4pm-2am, Fri.-Sat. 4pm-3am), and **'t Pandje,** Nobelstr. 193 (open daily 10pm-3am). **Theatercafé 't Hoogt,** Hoogt 4, near Neude, is an artist's cafe with two experimental cinemas and a small theater. (Open daily 3pm-1am, Sat. 3pm-2am.) **Café De Baas,** a co-op at Lijnmarkt 8, just across the canal from the Domtoren, offers good meals from f8.50. (Open Tues.-Sat. 6-8:30pm.) The two main student mensas, open to everyone, are **Veritas,** Kromme Nieuwe Gracht 54, and **Unitas,** Lucasbolwerk 8. Both offer meals for f5-7. (Open mid-Aug. to late June Mon.-Fri. 5-7:30pm.) On the wharf below the street at Oude Gracht 123 you'll find **De Werfkring,** a cozy hole-in-the-canal-wall vegetarian restaurant. (Open Mon.-Sat. noon-2:30pm and 5-8pm.) You can try spicy Surinamian specialties at **Pomo,** Wittevrouwenstr. 22, for f9.50 to 21.50. (Open Tues.-Sat. 2-10pm, Sun. 4-10pm.) Later, **Disco De Roze Wolk** attracts an artsy and gay crowd to its own hole-in-the-canal-wall below Oude Gracht 45. (Open Sun. and Wed.-Thurs. 10pm-4am, Fri.-Sat. 10pm-5am. Free.)

West of Utrecht, in Kamerik, **Wilhelminahoeve,** Mijzijde 6 (tel. (03481) 12 00), is where some of Holland's famous cheeses are produced. There are free demonstrations of cheese-making. (Year-round Mon.-Sat. 8am-6pm.)

Arnhem and the Hoge Veluwe National Park

Rebuilt after extensive World War II bombings, Arnhem, 100km southeast of Amsterdam (2 trains per hr., 70 min.) is now one huge outdoor shopping center with little to offer. Well worth the journey, however, is the Hoge Veluwe National Park, a 13,000-acre preserve of woods, heath, and dunes providing a welcome oasis of wilderness in the densely populated Netherlands. Clusters of white bikes crop up every few hundred meters; these are for the free use of park visitors—just hop on one and leave it at another station. The **Rijksmuseum Kröller-Müller** is one of the finest modern art museums in Europe, with a scintillating collection of 276 van Goghs and superb paintings by Seurat, Mondriaan, Braque, Gris, and many others. The museum's beautiful garden is filled with an astonishing variety of modern sculpture, including Jean Dubuffet's *Jardin d'Email* and pieces by Maillol, Moore, and

Lipchitz. The museum lies deep inside the park, a 35-minute walk from the nearest entrance. (Admission to the park f6, children f3; gains you entrance to the museum as well.) From June through August, and at selected times throughout the rest of the year, bus #12 ("Hoge Veluwe") leaves from the Arnhem train station; you can get on and off as often as you wish (1 per hr. 10:10am-4:10pm, f5.80 round-trip.) At other times, take bus #107 to Otterlo and hitch or walk 25 minutes from there. (Park open 8am-sunset; museum open April-Oct. Tues.-Sat. 10am-5pm, Sun. 11am-5pm; Nov.-March Tues.-Sat. 10am-5pm, Sun. 1-5pm.)

The **VVV,** Stationsplein 45 (tel. (085) 42 03 30), can help you with accommodations. (Open late May-early July Mon.-Fri. 9am-6pm, Sat. 10am-4pm; early July-early Sept. Mon.-Fri. 9am-8pm, Sat. 10am-5pm; early Sept-late May Mon.-Fri. 9am-6pm, Sat. 10am-2pm.) There is a modern **IYHF Jeugdherberg** at Diepenbrocklaan 27 (tel. (085) 42 01 14), in a rural setting. Take bus #3 toward Alteveer and ask the driver where to get off; then go up the steps. (f16.75, tax f0.50. Sheets f0.50. Breakfast included. Midnight curfew. Open year-round.) **Pension Parkzicht,** Apeldoornsestr. 16 (tel. (085) 42 06 98) is about 15 minutes from the station. (Singles f40, doubles f70. Breakfast included.) The camping **Kampeercentrum,** Kemperbergerweg 771 (tel. (085) 43 16 00), is accessible by bus #11 (direction: Schaansbergen). (f4 per person. Open March-Oct.) The **Old Inn,** Stationsplein 39a (tel. 42 06 49), is a cafe/restaurant with a f10.75 *menu* (Mon.-Fri. only). (Open daily noon-10pm.) **Nola Rae,** Dijkstr. 9, is a vegetarian restaurant with a relaxing outside terrace.

Charlemagne's 1000 year-old residence, the **Valkhof,** is in nearby **Nijmegen** (4 trains per hr. from Arnhem's Centraal Station, 20 min.). The star attraction here is the **St. Nikolaaskapel,** where a friendly guard will provide elaborate information. (Open in summer daily 1-5pm.) At the Grote Markt, you'll find **De Waag,** a handsome seventeenth-century edifice.

Wadden Islands (Waddeneilanden)

Wadden may mean "mudflat" in Dutch, but it is the plentitude of sand on these five islands that attracts so many Dutch and German vacationers. Sand and solitude together are not hard to find so long as you avoid the most popular beaches and villages, particularly on the biggest islands of Texel and Terschelling.

You can visit **Texel,** the southernmost and largest island, on a daytrip from Amsterdam if you time things right. Take the train to Den Helder (2 per hr., 70 min.), then bus #3 from the station to the ferry. Crossings are timed to follow bus arrivals (last boat back at 9pm, f9.25 round-trip). Bus service on the island is reliable but expensive; it's best to rent a bike (f6 per day) at the ferry landing and cycle between the island's three major villages—**Den Burg,** the largest, **De Koog,** by the beach and the most crowded, and **De Cocksdorp,** at the northern end of the island. The crowds thin out as you go south toward Den Hoorn. There are two popular nudist beaches, one south of Den Hoorn and the other on the west coast off De Cocksdorp. Birdwatching is excellent on Texel; you can only visit the nature reserves on a guided tour organized by the State Forest Department. (f1.50. Offered March-Aug.) You must book ahead of time at the Natuur Recreatie Centrum, Ruyslaan 92, De Koog (tel. (02228) 741). (Open Mon.-Sat. 9am-noon.) The Netherlands Society for the Promotion of Nature Reserves also offers excursions; contact C. Boot in De Waal, Polderweg 2 (tel. (02220) 25 90; 7-8pm only).

There are two **IYHF youth hostels** in Den Burg. **Panorama,** Schansweg 7 (tel. (02220) 21 97), is larger and more picturesque. **De Eyercoogh,** Pontweg 106 (tel. (02220) 29 07), is newer and cleaner, if more sterile. (Both f17.60. Breakfast and tourist tax included. Both open April-Oct.) The **VVV** in Den Burg, Groeneplaats 9 (tel. (02220) 47 41), as well as its branch office in De Koog, at Dorpsstr. 35, provides information about the island's 17 **campgrounds** and several farms where you can camp. (Den Burg office open in summer Mon.-Fri. 9am-6pm, Sat. 9am-5pm, Sun. 4-7pm; off-season Mon.-Sat. only. De Koog office open Easter-Oct. Mon.-Sat.

10am-6pm. In June, Texel holds **Ronde Van Texel,** the largest catamaran sailing race in Europe.

The four other islands (the Westfriese Islands) all have extensive dunes and wildlife sanctuaries. **Schiermonnikoog** and **Vlieland** are the most deserted. Schiermonnikoog's **VVV,** Reeweg (tel. (05195) 12 33), will help you find a room in a private home (f25-30 per person). Even in off-season, it's a good idea to reserve ahead. **Terschelling** and **Ameland** are more frequented. There are **IYHF youth hostels** (each about f16.75 per night) on three of the islands: **Hanskedune,** van Heusdenweg 39 (tel. (05620) 23 38), overlooks the sea, 2km from the boat landing on Terschelling (open April-Oct.); **De Kleine Grie,** Oranjeweg 59 (tel. (05191) 41 22 or 41 33), is in Hollum on Ameland (open April-late Oct.); **Rijsbergen** is at Knuppeldam 2 (tel. (05195) 12 57), near the center of the town on Schiermonnikoog (open July-Aug.). To reach Terschelling or Vlieland, take the main train line to Leeuwarden (1 per hr. from Amsterdam, 2½ hr.), then the bus to Harlingen (2 per hr., 25 min.), where you catch the ferry to either island (May-Sept. 3 per day; Oct.-April 2 or 3 per day; 2 hr., f29.60 round-trip, bikes f9.50). To reach Ameland, take bus #66 from Leeuwarden (8-11 per day, 50 min.), or the one from Groningen (April-Sept. 4-9 per day, 1 hr. 40 min.) to Holwerd and the ferry (June-Aug. 8-11 per day; Sept.-May 4-6 per day; 45 min., f11.50 round-trip). You get to Schiermonnikoog from Lauwersoog (3-5 per day, 40 min., f11.50 round-trip), itself reached by bus #51 from Leeuwarden (3-5 per day, 75 min.) or bus #63 from Groningen (3-5 per day, 1 hr.).

Groningen

Groningen, in the extreme northeast of Holland, was long a wealthy Hanseatic city carrying on a profitable trade in the Baltic and North Seas. The city is known as "the town of the horse;" note the beasts in front of the train station, in front of **St. Jozefkerk** at the corner of Radesingel and Rademarkt, and in place of the rooster on the weathervane of the **Martini Tower.** If lifeless representations aren't good enough, visit Groningen on August 28, when its annual festival is celebrated with, among other events, a horse show.

The **tourist office,** Naberpassage 3 (tel. (050) 13 97 00), signposted from the station, sells a map of the town with a walking tour (f0.50). (Open Mon.-Fri. 9am-5:30pm, Sat. 10am-4pm.) There's no youth hostel in Groningen, but the VVV can book you a room (f3.50 fee) at a B&B. (f22.50 for 1 night, f20 per night for longer stays.) **Camping Stadspark** is at Campinglaan 6 (tel. (050) 25 16 24; open March 15-Oct. 15).

The cheapest meal in Groningen is found at **Vera,** a university mensa at Oosterstr. 44. (Open only during the school year; meals around f5.) **A market** is held at Vismarkt every Tuesday, Friday, and Saturday. Groningen's 17,000-strong university population keeps the town lively. In the summer, join the townspeople in a stroll down Herestraat, taking in the street performers. Cafes abound here and on Grote Markt; pubs line Poelstraat off of Grote Markt, and you can find a cinema and cafe in the **Filmmuseum,** Ged. Zuiderdiep 139 (tel. (050) 14 06 59). In August, free pop concerts are held Sundays in the Stadspark (for information call (050) 14 02 78).

NORWAY

US$1 = 6.67 krone(kr)	**1kr = US$0.15**
CDN$1 = 5.05kr	**1kr = CDN$0.20**
UK£1 = 10.86kr	**1kr = UK£0.09**
AUS$1 = 4.74kr	**1kr = AUS $0.21**

Norway is Europe's great encounter with nature, its park and northern frontier. Here deep blue fjords cut a long and varied coast beneath stark waterfalls and the windswept emptiness of the tundra. Don't be blinded by spectacular train rides, the midnight sun, or Europe's northernmost point—take the time to get off the tourist-trodden route and *walk*. You won't be disappointed.

Once a spattering of farming homesteads among the ragged mountains of the northwestern sea, Norway was first united and ruled in the tenth century by Harald Hårfagre (Harold the Fair-haired). In 1030 Kong Olav den Hellige (Olav the Holy) fought at the Battle of Stiklestad, enabling the formal introduction of Christianity to Norway. During the Middle Ages, the Norse were best known for terrorizing their neighbors, but they were also among the most intrepid of explorers, sailing across uncharted waters to Iceland, Greenland, and the New World. The medieval Norwegian court included Icelandic saga-folk, who chronicled their age and pre-Christian myth in richly metaphoric poetry and action-filled sagas. Reminders of the medieval age are scattered throughout the land in the form of rune stones, stave churches, and preserved Viking ships. Customs and language vary with the landscape in Norway, as settlements were cut off from one another by rough mountains. Out of this isolation with nature sprang a dramatic imagination, documented in the works of Munch, Hamsun, Ibsen and Grieg.

While a feast for the eyes, Norway is no fun for the pocket. Prices are high even compared to the rest of Scandinavia, and in a land that sells half a cucumber there are simply no bargains.

Transportation

Transportation in Norway is difficult to sort out, with a confusing and very expensive array of boats, buses, trains, and planes to choose from. Pick up a copy of *Rutehefte for turister* at any tourist office. This booklet lists the major routes, schedules, and fares, but is by no means complete, especially as regards local buses and boats. *NSB lomme ruter* includes the most important train routes; free copies are at all train stations.

Trains in Norway often require reservations (12kr on all express trains); it is recommended that you purchase them a day in advance for night trains leaving the country. Second-class sleeping berths are comfortable but pricey (70kr); these should also be reserved in advance. **Norges Statsbane (NSB)** offers a series of services, significantly reducing the base second-class fare of roughly 75kr per 10km. The **Midtukebillett** (mid-week ticket) is valid for unlimited travel during a period of seven days, toward a specified destination. The ticket may be purchased any day of the week, but you cannot commence (or recommence) your trip on Friday or Sunday (295kr). Travelers on a **Minigruppebillett** (mini-group ticket) obtain a 25% discount; it can be used by two to nine persons traveling together (minimum 100km one way). If you plan to travel extensively in Scandinavia, you might want to investigate the **Nordturist Ticket,** available at any train station, which allows 21 days of unlimited second-class travel in all Scandinavian countries (1420kr). Eurail and InterRail (1490kr) are both valid in Norway.

Most of NSB's rail lines run through beautiful, untouched scenery and are attractions in themselves. Best known is the Oslo-Bergen railway; the 12-mile Flåm line is another engineering masterpiece. Train service from Oslo to Trondheim covers two parallel routes—the Dovre line crossing the Dovre Mountains, and the Røros line. From Dombås on the Dovre line, the spectacular Rauma line leads to Åndalsnes. The Sørlands line runs along the south coast between Oslo and Stavanger. In the north is the Nordland line, Norway's largest railway, covering the distance from Trondheim to Bodø. (Watch for the stone cairns marking the Arctic Circle.) The Ofoten line from Narvik runs eastward into Sweden and then south. To reach points between Bodø and Narvik or north of Narvik, you must rely on expensive buses and ferries.

Buses go everywhere in Norway, and are the only means of transportation to some areas—most notably, to the inland fjord district on the western coast, and the mountain plateaus of Finnmark. Buses in Norway are expensive, and you must inform the bus driver of whatever discounts you qualify for. In 1987, InterRail, Eurail, and Nordturist received a 50% discount on only some boats in the Western fjords, and no buses. In the Nordland region between Bodø and Narvik, InterRail earns a similar discount on buses, but otherwise there are **no** reductions, and student rates are restricted to those who study in Norway.

Water transport comes in two general varieties: slow and cheap car ferries and fast and expensive passenger boats. In addition, the legendary *Hurtigrute* coastal steamer fleet links towns along the coast as it has for centuries. Boats, leaving daily, make the week-long trip from Bergen all the way to Kirkenes, near the Soviet border, stopping at about 25 towns along the way. The legend comes at a price; regular round-trip fare during the summer, including meals and berth, is 8250kr. If you are under 26 you can get a three-week pass that allows unlimited stopovers for 1200kr.

Hitchhiking is particularly convenient in northern Norway and the fjord areas in western Norway, where there are no trains. Many Norwegians are partial to hitchhikers and may show you remarkable hospitality. However, keep in mind that distances are large; it helps to have a tent and a flexible itinerary. Try to find a ride before or during a ferry trip, or you may get stuck at the landing. A sign or a flag can also be helpful. Oslo's Municipal Youth Information Office brings drivers and riders together. (See Practical Information under Oslo.)

Budget travelers often overlook the possibility of flying. SAS's network reaches Oslo, Bergen, Stavanger, Haugesund, Trondheim, Bodø, Evenes, Bardufoss, Tromsø, Alta, Lakselv, Kirkenes, and Longyearbyen. Often, flying makes for the cheapest (not to mention fastest) means of transit to many places. If you are under 26 you can get a 50% reduction on all flights within the country when you fly standby. All ISIC holders (regardless of age) get a 25% reduction on a ticket with seat reservation; without a seat resrvation the reduction is 50%, the same as youth standby. Within Norway, a family reduction of 50%, also on special prices, is given to the accompanying spouse and children under 26. **Minipris** (mini-price) is valid for round-trip flights; you may leave any day but must spend at least one Saturday night at your destination. International tickets must be bought two weeks before departure. The reduction ranges from 35 to 50%.

Practical Information

Well-informed independent tourist offices *(turistinformasjon)* are found in nearly all towns throughout Norway. During the summer they have extended opening hours, including Sundays. Otherwise tourist information hours are the same as ordinary business hours, roughly Monday through Friday from 8am to 3:30 or 4pm. Banks are open Monday through Friday from 8:15am to 3:30pm, until 5pm on Thursdays; from mid-May to August all banks close at 3pm, except Thursdays when they close at 5pm. Note that as in most of Scandinavia, large post offices also exchange money and are often open late in the afternoon and on Saturday mornings. Stores conduct business Monday through Wednesday and Friday from 9am to 5pm, Thursday until 7pm, Saturday until 1pm. Legal holidays, when all offices and shops are closed, include New Year's Day, Maundy Thursday (April 16), Good Friday and Easter Monday (April 17 and 20, respectively), Labor Day (May 1), Constitution Day (May 17), Ascension Day (May 28), Whit Monday (June 8), and Christmas.

Telephoning within and outside Norway is expensive. When calling internationally, dial without interruption first the international prefix 095, next the country code, then the long distance code, and finally the local telephone number. Codes can be found in the Oslo Telephone Directory 1A on pages 13-15. For operator assistance dial 093 (English- and German-speaking), 092 (French), 091 (Nordic). Pay phones only take 1kr coins and generally demand at least 2; place them in the slot on top of the phone, then dial. When someone answers, the coins will drop.

You're not likely to encounter a language barrier in Norway; most Norwegians understand and speak English. Nevertheless, an effort on your part to approach someone in Norwegian is likely to be met with a warm smile.

For a few weeks on either side of the summer solstice (June 21), Norway north of Bodø experiences the midnight sun. We note the time frame for perpetual sunlight in particular sections. It's wise to check weather forecasts before heading north. The best time to visit Norway is between May and August. For skiing, come just before Easter, when the winter has loosened its grip somewhat, and the sun returns after months of darkness.

Accommodations, Camping, and Food

Camping is the best way to take advantage of this country's scenery, but more important, it is the only way to beat the high cost of accommodations. As in Sweden and Finland, you have the right to camp wherever you like for one night as long as you are in a rural area and well-removed from buildings; further, you must leave absolutely no trace of your presence when you go. If you are planning to hike or camp in Norway, be sure to take advantage of **Den Norske Turistforening** (Norwegian Mountain Touring Association); their Oslo office is particularly helpful. They provide maps and information, and maintain a series of mountain huts *(hytter)* throughout the country, many with provisions or cooked meals. Yearly membership (145kr, ages under 21 95kr) is required for lodging at some huts. A *hytte* generally costs 45-85kr per night for members; huts are open to nonmembers as well at a 30kr surcharge. For unattended huts, you must obtain the entrance key (deposit required) at a DNT or tourist office before heading out. DNT huts are open during Easter, and from the end of June to the beginning of September. In the high season (mid-July to mid-Aug.), the huts are crowded with hikers of all ages. You can pick up a list of DNT huts and appropriate maps at any DNT office.

From Kristiansand in the south to Honningsvåg in the north, some 90 youth hostels (*ungdomsheiberger*) are scattered throughout Norway. These youth hostels, which serve all ages, are among Europe's finest, and a great bargain by Norwegian standards (generally 60kr; 85kr where breakfast is required, and 15kr more without an IYHF card). Pick up a list at any tourist office. Unfortunately, only a few are open year-round.

Most tourist offices in Norway can book you a room in a private home; these usually run 100-150kr for a single, 150-200kr for a double. Those traveling in groups should remember that campgrounds usually have huts at 160-250kr, suitable for two to four people.

The high cost of food may be your biggest problem, and markets and bakeries your dearest friends. Watch for *smørgåsbord* breakfasts and lunches (30-50kr). These assortments of cold cuts, herring, eggs, cheese, bread, crackers, jam, and milk, can last you until evening. On the famous flatbread crackers (*flatbrød* or *knekkebrød*), try some national cheeses (*ost*): *jarlsberg* and *geitost,* a sweet peanut-butter-colored goat cheese. Fish in Norway is excellent and relatively inexpensive. Sample the local delicacies, or try *fersk sild* and *spekesild* (fresh and salted herring) and *torsk* (cod). Especially recommended are *stekt ørret* (fried trout), served with sour cream and delicious poached or smoked *laks* (salmon). A traditional main dish is *rømmegrøt,* a porridge made of sour cream, flour and milk, and served with sugar and cinnamon. For a quick meal, get a *pølse med lompe,* the Norwegian equivalent of a hot dog, served in a small, somewhat thick potato cake, and available at most kiosks and street grills.

Beer is heavily taxed, and quite expensive. *Pilsner* is the standard, while *Brigg* has a low alcohol content. An especially strong brand is *Export.* In the winter months and especially during Christmas, *Gløgg* is a very popular Scandinavian drink, made from red wine, boiled water, raisins, almonds, and various spices. Eating out is normally very expensive in Norway. Many restaurants, however, have daily specials from 60kr. Tips—except at the more expensive restaurants—are included in the bill. Self-service *kafeterias* are normally cheaper than table-service restaurants and trendy cafes. Usual hours are 9am to 9pm daily. In most Norwegian restaurants, alcohol is served only after 3pm and never on Sundays.

Oslo

At the end of the long Oslofjord, framed by the shoreline and surrounding hills, Oslo enjoys an enviable location. Compared to the rest of the world, the city seems as much a park as an urban center; depending on the season, people sail on the sea or ski in Nordmarka, the surrounding near-wilderness. Compared to the rest of Norway, Oslo appears shockingly cosmopolitan, with tall buildings, cafés, museums, and a constant swirl of people and traffic. What you get is a little of both—natural beauty and urban culture, sunlit islands and Munch's *Scream.*

Orientation and Practical Information

Karl Johans gate, running from the Central Station to the Royal Palace (Slottet), is Oslo's principal boulevard and a useful line of orientation. From early morning on, it bustles with musicians, sunbathers, and lunchbreakers.

Tourist Offices: Main office is in the Rådhuset (City Hall) at the end of Universitets gate (tel. 42 71 70), just off Karl Johans gate. Enter on the harbor side. Collect a city map, an *Oslo Guide* with current hours and practical information, and the more detailed *Oslo This Week.* Open May 20-Sept. 15 Mon.-Fri. 8am-5pm, Sat.-Sun. 9am-3pm; Sept.16-May 19 Mon.-Fri. 8am-3:30pm, closed Sat.-Sun. The **information office** at Central Station is open May-March daily 8am-11pm. **Ungdomsinformasjonen (Oslo Municipal Youth Information Office),** Akersgaten 57 (tel. 42 66 67). An extremely helpful staff will fill you in on what's really happening, and will match would-be hitchhikers with drivers. Open Mon.-Fri. 11am-5pm. **Den Norske Turistforening (DNT):** Roald Amundsens gate 28 (tel. 41 80 20), by the National Theater. A must if you plan to do any hiking or camping in Norway (see chapter introduction). Membership cards, hiking maps, and lists of *hytter* (huts). Open Mon.-Wed. and Fri. 8:30am-4pm, Thurs. 8:30am-6pm, closed Sat.-Sun. **NUH (Norwegian Youth Hostels),** Dronningens gate 26 (tel. 42 14 10), 2 blocks from Karl Johans gate. Not only an up-to-date list of hostels, but also a student travel service. Open Mon.-Wed. and Fri. 8:30am-4pm, Thurs. 8:30am-5pm, Sat. 9am-1pm. **Skiforeningen (Ski Society),** Kongleveien 5 (tel. 14 16 90), in VM-Huset, Holmenkollen. Information on downhill and cross-country skiing throughout the country. Open June-Aug. Mon.-Fri. 8am-3pm; Sept.-May Mon.-Fri. 8am-4pm.

Budget Travel: Universitetssenteret, Blindern (tel. 45 50 55). Low cost trains and planes, coastal steamers, boats to Britain and Iceland, and more. Open Mon.-Fri. 8:30am-4pm.

American Express: Winge Reisebyrå, Karl Johans gate 33 (tel. 42 91 50). Mail held. Traveler's checks sold and replaced, but cardholders' personal checks not cashed. No currency exchange and no wired money accepted. Open Mon.-Fri. 8:30am-5pm.

Currency Exchange: At Central Station. No extra commission, normal rates and longest hours. Open June-Sept. daily 7am-11pm; Oct.-May Mon.-Fri. 8am-noon and 1:30-8:30pm, Sat. 8am-7pm, Sun. 8am-noon.

Post Office: Dronningens gate 15 (tel. 40 78 23); entrance at corner of Prinsens gate. Open Mon.-Fri. 8am-8pm, Sat. 9am-3pm. Poste Restante open Mon.-Fri. 8am-8pm.

Telephones: Kongens gate 21; entrance on Prinsens gate. Open Mon.-Fri. 8am-10pm, Sat. 8am-9pm, Sun. 10am-9pm. Telegrams as well. **Telephone code:** 02.

Flights: White SAS buses run between **Fornebu Airport** and the Air Bus Terminal (tel. 41 49 91), seaside at Central Station. Frequent service daily 6am-9:30pm. Municipal bus #31 runs to Fornebu from various points in the city (roughly the same fare).

Trains: Oslo Sentralstasjon (Central Station, Oslo-S) is the newly remodelled terminus for trains from Bergen, Trondheim, and all foreign points. Pick up a city map here at the information office or Innkvartering office. If you come from Tønsberg and Skien on the south coast, you'll arrive at **Vestbanen** (Oslo-W). To get to Vestbanen from Central Station, walk up Karl Johans gate toward the royal palace, then turn left towards the port. Information (tel. 42 19 19). Open daily 7am-11pm. Seat reservation (tel. 41 60 70).

Ferries: Passenger ferries arrive a 15-min. walk from the center. To Kiel, Germany (Jahre Line; tel. 41 95 70) daily at 1:30pm (575kr). To Fredrikshavn, Denmark (Stena Line; tel. 41 22 10) June 26-Aug. 10 daily at 8:30pm (316kr, students 216kr); variable departure time during rest of the year (174kr, students 126kr). To Copenhagen (DFDS; tel. 42 93 50) daily at 5pm (460kr). Fares are lower Sept.-May.

Public Transportation: Oslo Sporveier, Kirkeristen, Dronningens gate 27 (tel. 41 70 30), near Stortorvet (Main Square). Open Mon.-Fri. 8am-7pm, Sun. 10am-3pm. Though Oslo is easily explored on foot, you'll probably need to use public transportation during your stay. All forms (bus, tram, subway, and ferry) cost 12kr per trip (6kr in the inner circle), so it can become an expensive activity. The 24-hour **Turistkort** is good for unlimited travel (40kr at any ticket counter). The **maxi-card** (12 trips, 120kr) and the **mini-card** (4 trips, 40kr) also provide some savings. The **Universal Card** may be the best deal if you are staying in town for any length of time (2 weeks 160kr, 1 month 295kr). It can bought at most Narvesen kiosks, and at ticket counters in subway and train stations. The **Oslo Card** entitles you to free public transportation, admission to many museums, extras in restaurants, admission to the municipal baths, price reductions in gift shops, and a 50% discount on travel to Oslo from any point in Norway. It can be purchased at hotels and camping sites, the Tourist Information Center in the City Hall, and the Accommodations Center at Central Station. (1-day card 70kr, 2-day 100kr, 3-day 130kr.)

Bike Rental: Den Rustne Eike, Oscars gate 32 (tel. 44 18 80), behind the Royal Palace. 60kr per day, 300kr per week. Deposit 500kr. Open Mon.-Fri. 8am-4:30pm, occasionally Sat. 10am-2pm.

Emergencies: Police (tel. 002). Police headquarters at Grølandsleiret 44 (tel. 66 90 50). **Ambulance** (tel. 003). **Fire** and **Accidents** (tel. 001).

Medical Assistance: Oslo Kommunale Legevakt, Storgata 40 (tel. 20 10 90). 24-hour emergency care. **Oslo Røde Kors,** Fr. Stangs gate 11-13 (tel. 44 39 80), entrance Gabels gate. Open Mon.-Fri. 7:30am-4pm, Sat. 7:30am-1pm.

Pharmacy: Look for the word *Apotek.* **Jernbanetorvets Apotek** (tel. 41 24 82), in front of Central Station, is open 24 hours.

Women's Centers: Kvinnehuset, Rådhusgata 2 (tel. 41 28 64), at the end of Dronningens gate. **24-hour help line** (tel. 35 00 48).

Embassies: U.S., Drammensveien 18 (tel. 44 85 50); take tram #1, 2, or 9, bus #27, 29, or 30. **Canada,** Oscars gate 20 (tel. 46 69 55), near Bislett Stadium; take tram #2 or 11. **U.K.,** Thomas Heftyes gate 8 (tel. 56 38 90). Travelers from **Australia** and **New Zealand** should contact the British Embassy.

Laundry: Look for the word *Myntvaskeri.* **Majorstua Myntvaskeri,** Vibes gate 15 (tel. 69 43 17). Open Mon.-Fri. 9am-8pm, Sat. 9am-3pm.

Hitchhiking: Leaving Oslo by thumb can be difficult. If heading south, try outside West Station, where access to the roads is not yet limited and stopping is still allowed. If traveling north, take bus #30 or 31 to Sinsenkrysset, the main intersection of north-bound highways. Check first at the Youth Information Center ride-board.

Accommodations and Camping

Cheap accommodations are not easy to find in Oslo, but if you take the time to check around you may come up with something. Ask at the **Innkvartering** accommodations office in Central Station and at the **Youth Information Center,** which maintains a list of cheap alternatives you won't hear about elsewhere. Innkvartering can book rooms in private homes for stays of two or more nights. (Singles 100kr, doubles 175kr; 10kr fee.) Singles are limited, so you may have to double up. *Pensjonater* (pensions) are normally less expensive than hotels but fill up quickly; call ahead to make reservations. Many hotels lower their prices from late June to mid-Aug. and offer special deals during some holidays.

Bjerke Studentheim (IYHF), Trondheimsveien 271 (tel. 64 87 87). Take bus #30 or 31 to Bjerkebanen; the hostel is in a tall building about 100m back toward town from the bus stop. A university dorm with modern, immaculate doubles and triples. Members 60kr, nonmembers 80kr. Open 5-11pm, but call 8-11am to leave your name, since it fills fast. 11pm curfew. Open mid-June to mid-Aug.

Haraldsheim (IYHF), Haraldsheimveien 4 (tel. 15 50 43). Take tram #1 or 7 (direction: Sinsen) to the end of the line, or local train to Grefsen from Central Station. Oslo's largest hostel, with 6-bed rooms and good facilities (washing machines, kitchen, cafe with relatively cheap meals). Great view of Oslofjord and the city. Members 88kr, nonmembers 95kr. Breakfast included. Closed 10am-4pm. Midnight curfew. Open year-round, often booked in summer.

Cochs Pensjonat, Parkveien 25 (tel. (02) 60 48 36), entrance on Hegdehaugsveien. Not luxurious, but right behind the Royal Palace. Rather primitive kitchen facilities. One of Oslo's cheapest. Singles 150kr, doubles 220kr.

KFUM, Møllergata (tel. (02) 42 10 66). The cheapest spot in town (55kr). Kitchen, showers, luggage storage. Open mid-July to mid-Aug. 7:30-11am and 5pm-midnight.

St. Katarinahjemmet, Majorstuveien 21B (tel. 60 13 70). Take tram #1 to Valkyrie Plass. Nice rooms. Run by nuns; men accepted. Singles 150kr, doubles 240kr. Breakfast 35kr.

Camping: Ekeberg Camping, Ekebergveien 65 (tel. 19 85 68), about 3km from the center, with a marvelous view. Take tram #9 or bus #24 from in front of Central Station. 30kr for a tent site. Open June 20-Aug. 20. **Bogstad Camping** (tel. 50 76 80). Take bus #41 from Nationaltheatret to Bogstad. Tent sites and chalets. A wonderful lake nearby. Open year-round. Free camping is permitted in any of the large wooded areas north of town as long as you stay away from public areas. One easily accessible spot is the forest at the end of the Sognsvann subway line.

Food

Appetites will be a major inconvenience in Oslo. Restaurant prices are high, though you can find specials which may beat the prices in standard cafeterias. Oslo abounds in bakeries, few of which are disappointments. When buying food, look for the less expensive supermarket chains—**Irma, Bonus,** and especially **Rimi.** There is a Rimi on Rosenkrantz gate, two blocks toward the harbor off Stortings gate; others are on Bogstadveien, and on Bydgoy Alle. **Jens Evesen** supermarket, in the subway station at Grønland, is open daily until 10:30pm. Surprisingly, many nightclubs have cheap, filling lunches for as little as 35kr; check the Entertainment section.

Frokostkjelleren, Karl Johans gate 47, is the best of the 2 student cafeterias downtown, located in the easternmost of the 3 university buildings (entrance on Universitets gate). No ID needed. Open Aug. 20-June 19 Mon.-Fri. 8am-8pm. The other cafeteria is **Aulakjelleren,** in the central building of the university. Open same hours. Both are very reasonable.

Vegeta Vertshus Frisksportrestaurant, Munkedamsveien 3B, off Stortings gate. Cozy basement. Daily special from 49kr; fabulous all-you-can-eat buffet 85kr (not only vegetarian). Open daily noon-11:30pm; meal service ends at 10pm.

Torgstova, Karl Johans gate 13. Eat cheap food while enjoying the view. Typical Norwegian fare from 35kr. Open daily.

Carl Johan Bistro, Karl Johans gate 37. Quite fancy, but specials from 45kr. A good way to fill up is the all-you-can-eat salad bar (50kr, only 25kr if ordered with an entree). Open Mon.-Sat. 11am-11pm.

Maxim Cafe, Teatergata 3. Pleasant courtyard and lots of color. Coffee, beer, desserts, and light meals from 20kr. Open Mon.-Fri. 11am-1am, Sat.-Sun. noon-1am.

Papa Sigolo, Fredensborgveien 13. Expensive, but large portions and excellent food make this Turkish import worth the splurge. Dishes from 88kr; all-you-can-eat salad bar 25kr. Open daily 3-11pm.

Lofotstuen/Dahl's Kro, Kirkeveien 40. Northern Norwegian fare. Omelettes 40-60kr. Suze's favorite. Mon.-Fri. 11am-7pm, Sun. noon-6pm.

Sights

Start your wanderings in Oslo at the **Rådhuset** (City Hall). An avant-garde sensation when built in 1950, it houses a series of murals painted by Henrik Sørensen to celebrate Oslo's 900th anniversary. These depict life from the innocence of nudity to the complexity of urban development and the tragedy of the Nazi occupation of Norway. (Open Jan.-March Mon.-Sat. 11am-2pm, Sun. noon-3pm; April-Sept. Mon.-Thurs. 10am-3pm, Sat. noon-3pm. Free guided tours in English June-Aug. at 10am, noon, and 2pm.) From the Rådhuset, stroll down the wharf to your left toward **Akershut Castle and Fortress,** built in 1300 and transformed into a Renaissance palace by Christian IV; it's now used for state occasions. The grounds are ideal for a picnic, and there is a fine view of Oslo from the bluff. Explore the castle, with its underground passages, banquet halls, dungeons, and courtyards. (Open May to mid-Sept. Mon.-Sat. 11am-4pm, Sun. 12:30-4pm; mid-Sept. to Oct. and April 15-30 Sun. 12:30-4pm. Admission 5kr.) The moving **Resistance Museum** in the fortress documents the Nazi occupation and the work of the Resistance movement. (Open May-Sept. Mon.-Sat. 10am-4pm, Sun. 11am-4pm; Oct.-April Mon.-Sat. 10am-3pm, Sun. 11am-4pm. Admission 10kr, children 3kr.)

From the Rådhuset you can head toward the island of **Bygdøy;** take the ferry from pier #3 or bus #30 or 31 from Nationaltheatret. The island's treasures include the **Folkemuseum,** an open-air museum with a collection of houses from different parts of Norway; and the the **Old Town,** where you can find Ibsen's study. (Open mid-May to Aug. Mon.-Sat. 10am-6pm, Sun. 11am-6pm; Sept. Mon.-Sat. 11am-4pm, Sun. noon-5pm; Oct. to mid-May Mon.-Sat. 11am-4pm, Sun. noon-3pm. Admission 15kr in summer, 8kr in winter.) There is folk dancing here every Sunday at 5pm; see *Oslo This Week* for further information. At the **Viking Ship Museum,** view vessels from the ninth century C.E. preserved right down to the smallest details. (Open May-Aug. daily 10am-6pm; Sept. daily 11am-5pm; April and Oct. daily 11am-4pm; Nov.-March daily 11am-3pm. Admission 5kr, students 2.50kr.) Thor Heyerdahl's craft *Ra I, Ra II,* and *Kon-Tiki* have their own museum on the island, and are accompanied by an entertaining recollection of his adventurous trips. (Open mid-May to Aug. daily 10am-6pm; off-season closes 1-3 hr. earlier. Admission 7kr, students and children 3kr.) If the weather gods allow, take a dip in the refreshing water of Huk beach, Oslo's most popular, located a kilometer or so from the Viking Ship Museum.

The beautifully arranged **Munch Museum,** Tøyengata 53 (tel. 67 37 74), contains an outstanding collection of the artist's paintings, woodcuts, and lithographs. On Tuesday at 8pm, concerts in the museum often feature the works of another Norwegian artistic hero, Edvard Grieg (check *Oslo This Week*), and on summer Thursday evenings at 6pm there is an excellent English-speaking guided tour of the museum. Take bus #29 from Roald Amundsens gate or the subway to Tøyen. (Open Tues.-Sat. 10am-8pm, Sun. noon-8pm. Admission 10kr, students 5kr. Free mid-Sept. to mid-May.) The **Nasjonalgalleriet** (National Gallery), Universitets gate 13 (tel. 20 04 04), devotes several rooms to Munch's work and also features other excellent nineteenth- and twentieth-century Norwegian and European artists. (Open Mon.-Tues. and Fri. 10am-4pm, Wed.-Thurs. 10am-4pm and 6-8pm, Sat. 10am-3pm, Sun. noon-3pm. Free.)

The stone figures of **Vigeland Park** (also called **Frognerpark**) depict with strength and simplicity the cycle of life; the park itself is an immense recreation area of grassy knolls, duck ponds, and tennis courts. The famous obelisk of writhing, squirming human bodies is Gustav Vigeland's vision of the depravity of humanity. Go in the early morning when the park is deserted. Take tram #2 or bus #20 from Nationaltheatret, or walk up the enjoyable Hegdehaugsveien, with its markets, cafes, and shops. The **Vigeland Museum,** Nobels gate 32, displays more sculptures, as well as drawings and woodcuts. During summer months, concerts are held in the forecourt every Sunday morning and Wednesday evening. Take tram #2 from Nationaltheatret to Frogner plass. (Open May-Oct. Tues.-Sun. noon-7pm; Nov.-April Tues.-Sun. 1-7pm. Free.)

The other Vigeland Museum only recently found its way into the tourist brochures. Constructed by Emanuel Vigeland, younger brother of Gustav, the **Emanuel Vigeland Museum,** Grimelundsveien 8, at Slemdal, features a fresco entitled *Vita.* The entrance inscription reading "All that God has created is pure . . . " is a key to understanding the provocative mural. Don't miss the side room displaying some of Emanuel's early paintings and drawings of stained-glass windows. Take the Holmenkollen subway from Nationaltheatret to Slemdal; from there it is a 10-minute walk to the red brick building. (Open Sun. noon-3pm. Free.)

For a great view of Oslofjord and the city, take the subway from Nationaltheatret to the last stop on the Frognerseteren line and walk to the **Tryvannstårnet** (radio tower); in season you can pick wild blueberries along the way. From the top of the tower you will realize the extent of the wilderness surrounding Oslo—over half the area is forest, with Oslo occupying just a small patch beside the Oslofjord. (Tower open June-July daily 9:30am-10pm; May and Aug. daily 10am-8pm; Sept. daily 10am-6pm; Oct.-Feb. Sat.-Sun. 10am-4pm. Admission 11kr, students 6kr.) It's a 20-minute walk from the tower down to the world-famous ski jump **Holmenkollen,** the broken fishhook on the Oslo skyline. (Admission 11kr, students 6kr.) Beside the ski jump is the **Ski Museum,** describing the history of skis with specimens up to 4000 years old. (Open May-June daily 10am-7pm; July daily 9am-9pm; Aug.-Sept. daily 10am-7pm; Oct.-April daily 10am-4pm. Admission 11kr, children 6kr.) Annually in March, Norway's greatest ski event takes place during the **Holmenkollendays.** The event comprises various cross-country races during the week and concludes with the jumping competition on Sunday, when 60,000 Norwegians come to watch the best ski jumpers in the world. In mid-June, the Holmenkollen arena transforms into **Sommerkollen,** a summer festival featuring a classical concert with the Oslo Philharmonic Orchestra, ballet performances, and jazz concerts. The end of summer is marked with **Oslodagene** (Oslo days), a week-long program of various cultural activities, including theater performances and concerts. For information, inquire at **Theatersentralen,** Youngstorget 5 (tel. 41 85 60). (Open Mon.-Wed. and Fri. 9am-4pm, Thurs. 9am-5pm.)

If you've only a little time to spend in Norway but want to experience some of the country's wondrous natural beauty, take the Sognsvann subway from Nationaltheatret to the end of the line, and walk up the road a few minutes. You'll find yourself on the shores of a quiet lake, surrounded by towering evergreens and misty waterfalls. In the winter, ask at the tourist office about cross-country ski rental.

Entertainment

For a delightful and inexpensive evening, take a ferry to one of the islands in the inner Oslofjord—**Hovedøya, Langøyene,** or **Gressholmen.** Boats leave from the piers in front of City Hall and from **Vippetangen,** reached by bus #18 (18kr round-trip, free with transport pass). In summer, Hovedøya sometimes hosts rock concerts; otherwise you can visit the ruins of an old monastery. Langøyene offers Oslo's best beach. The evening cruise is especially pleasant, as the lights of Oslo and the summer sun form a shimmering backdrop to the waves.

A stroll on Karl Johans gate on a weekend night is exciting and free, though slaking your thirst with a beer in one of the outdoor cafes will cost 30-35kr. The street abounds with musicians, acrobats, actors, and scores of people. Oslo's "parade" has also moved seawards with the renovation of **Aker Brygge,** an old wharf extending from the port below City Hall. The new complex hosts everything from small restaurants and boutiques to the **Black Box Theater,** which shows avant-garde plays. On a warm summer night the wharf bustles with people; the place is trendy, and the prices are steep.

Night cinema runs every Friday and Saturday at **Klingenberg,** Roald Amundsens gate; foreign films are shown in their original version with Norwegian subtitles. Admission to afternoon shows is 50% less. Consult the newspapers for times and prices of movies.

Café Fröhlich, Drammensveien 20, right next to the American Embassy. Students meet here for drinks and talk. Meals from 50kr. Frequent music, cover 15-30kr. Open Tues.-Thurs. noon-2am, Fri.-Sat. 7:30pm-2am.

Hot House, Pilestredet 15 (tel. 20 22 27), has live jazz and blues every night. Popular and a good place for a meal, too; *Steinbit* (fish) for 65kr. Cover Sun.-Mon. and Thurs. 15kr, Wed.-Thurs. 30kr, Fri.-Sat. 50kr. Open 11:30am-2am.

Creml, Rosenkrantz gate 11. Ritzy variation on a Kremlin motif. One of Oslo's hottest clubs; also has a pleasant atrium. Open daily 11am-4am.

Barock, Universitets gate 26. Expensive restaurant by day, expensive discotheque by night. Very fashionable. Club open 10pm-3am.

Southern Coast

While the scenery of Norway's southern coast may not be as spectacular as that farther to the west or north, hundreds of little islands and great beaches make up for the lack of drama. Despite the frequent ferries connecting Larvik and Kristiansand with Denmark that make this area one of Norway's most accessible, foreign tourists are relatively scarce. To many Norwegians, however, the area is synonymous with summer and holiday, and in July vacationing northerners pack most of the coastal towns. Two train lines run south from Oslo, one looping through Tønsberg to Skien and the other extending through Kristiansand to Stavanger.

Tønsberg is Norway's oldest town, mentioned in Snorre Sturluson's *Edda* in the ninth century. Only 90 minutes by frequent train from Oslo's West Station, the town makes an easy daytrip. Climb **Slottsfjellet** tower above the hostel for a wonderful vista of islands, clear water, and undulating blue mountains; for centuries this hill was the area's stronghold during recurrent battles. (Open Mon.-Sat. 11am-6pm. Admission 5kr.) **Vestfold Fylkesmuseum** (tel. (033) 129 19), just down the hill, is a collection of restored farmhouses. (Open mid-June to Aug. Mon.-Sat. 10am-7pm, Sun. 1-7pm. Admission 5kr.) From the harbor at the foot of the hill, the 75-year-old *Kysten* steamship departs daily at noon throughout the summer for a 3½-hour cruise around the nearby islands of Tjøme and Nøtterøy, provided there are at least 20 passengers. (Operates July 1-20 and Aug. 3-31. 70kr.) Tønsberg's old downtown area is well-preserved, with wooden houses and a lively market on the square. (Open Mon.-Fri. 8:30am-4pm, Sat. 8:30am-1pm.) The **tourist office,** Honnørbryggen (tel. (033) 148 19), on the quay, can tell you all about activities and places to eat, sleep, and swim. (Open July daily 10am-6pm; June 15-30 and Aug. 1-15 daily 11am-6pm; Aug. 15-June 15 daily 11am-3pm.) The superb **IYHF youth hostel** is a short walk from the station on Dronning Blancas gate (tel. (033) 128 48). (Members 75kr, nonmembers 90kr. Breakfast included. Open June-Aug.) **Vægteren** serves Norwegian meals (around 65kr), beer, and wine, in a warm traditional dining room. (Sandwiches 25-35kr, occasional live music in the evenings.)

Just 20km south of Tønsberg lies the resort town of **Tjøme,** with myriad camping and swimming facilities. Take bus #2 from the bus station on the harbor near the tourist office. For camping information, visit the Tjøme **tourist office** on Kirkebakken. (Open in summer Mon.-Sat. noon-5pm.) Those without a tent can rent room for four people in a *hytte* (200-400kr per night). Contact **Tjøme Hytter** (tel. 903 10).

Two-and-a-half hours south of Oslo lies **Larvik.** The **tourist office,** on Storgata (tel. (034) 826 23), just across from the station, will help you find accommodations in *hytter* or pensions. (Open late June-early Aug. Mon.-Sat. 8am-6pm, Sun. 3-6pm; early Aug.-late June Mon.-Fri. 8:30am-4pm.) **Hovland Camping** (tel. (034) 144 22) is about 1km northeast of town. (40kr per tent. Open June 15-Aug. 1.) Ferries to Frederikshavn (Denmark) leave the pier nearby two to three times per day in summer (6 hr., 235kr). If you're heading farther west, you might pay a brief visit to **Skien,** which has somewhat belatedly laid claim to native son Henrik Ibsen with a trio of museums. **Kragerø,** a little farther south, has an **IYHF youth hostel** (tel. (036) 818 66), right by the sea. (Members 104kr, nonmembers 119kr. Breakfast included. Open late June to mid-Aug.)

The **Sørlandet** part of the southern coast stretching from Risør in the east (200km south of Oslo) to Flekkefjord in the west, is Norway's premier holiday region during the summer months. Whitewashed wooden houses surround natural harbors filled with the soft sounds of traditional wooden *snekke* boats. The heavily wooded inland once formed the basis for an extensive foreign trade; stories have it that large parts of Amsterdam rest on wooden poles from these forests. **Arendal,** easily accessible by train from Oslo, Kristiansand, or Stavanger, is a good place to start exploring. The **town hall** of **Tyinholmen** is one of Norway's largest wooden buildings; the restored houses nearby are also well worth a stroll. For a guided tour of the area, inquire at the **tourist office,** Nedre Tyholmsvei 14 (tel. (041) 221 93). (Open in summer daily 9am-3pm.) The **Aust-Agder Museum** (tel. (041) 224 22), located at the Langsae Farm, a short ride out of town, has archeological evidence of Viking expeditions to Iceland and the Middle East. (Open late June to mid-Aug.; hours vary.) From June to August, the express steamer *Veslestril* sails between Oslo and Arendal, stopping at major ports along the way.

Twenty kilometers farther south from Arendal, accessible aboard Kristiansand buses (17kr), lies **Grimstad,** Arendal's smaller rival. For six years this little town was the home of **Henrik Ibsen;** he wrote his first play here in 1850. The houses where Ibsen worked and lived still stand; **Reimannsgården,** in Vestergade, is where he spent the first four years. It now houses art exhibitions. The other house, at Henrik Ibsens gate 14, is now a museum containing the writing desk where he secretly wrote poetry. (Open June-Aug. Mon.-Sat. 10am-3pm, Sun. noon-3pm. Admission 5kr, including entrance to the town/maritime museum in the same building.) A 3-kilometer walk east of town, the **Fjære Church** is an impressive stone structure dating from the twelfth century. The churchyard contains a huge obelisk honoring Terje Vigen, the legendary fisherman who rowed in an open boat to Denmark to fetch corn for his starving family, and who was later immortalized in Ibsen's epic *Terje Vigen.* (Open June-Aug. 9am-4pm.) Both the **tourist office** at **Torskeholmen** (tel. (041) 430 01; open in summer daily 10am-3pm) and **Due's Reisebyrå** (open Mon.-Fri. 9am-4pm, Sat. 10am-1pm) can provide more information on the town. **Bie Camping** is 500m east of the church. (5.50kr per person, 25kr per tent. Open May-Oct.) On a peninsula across the fjord, **Marivold Camping** (tel. (041) 408 46) has its own little beach; take the Rønnes bus from Grimstad bus terminal.

At the southern tip of Norway, about six hours from Oslo, is **Kristiansand,** the largest town on the coastline between Tønsberg and Stavanger. Though not a scenic village, it has good ferry connections to Hirtshals and Hanstholm (Denmark), and Harwich (England). Connections to Hirtshals are most frequent (3 per day, 4 hr., 236kr); the ferry to Harwich departs on Tuesday at 3pm (June 17-Aug. 21 only, 600kr). For schedule information, call (042) 265 00. **Roligheden Youth Hostel (IYHF),** Marvikveien 98 (tel. (042) 949 47), 3km from the train station, charges members 85kr, nonmembers 98kr, breakfast included. (Lockout 10am-4pm. Open May-Aug.) Across the street, **Roligheden Camping** (tel. (042) 947 59) is only a stone's throw away from the cool blue waters of **Bertesbukten** (Bertha's Bay). (15kr per person, 20kr per tent. Open June-Aug.) Further north of town a new youth hostel, **Atlanten (IYHF)** (tel. (073) 711 04), charges members 45kr, nonmembers 60kr.

At the end of the southern rail line lies **Stavanger,** an oil boomtown surrounded by clear blue sea. The **Mosvangen Youth Hostel (IYHF)** (tel. (04) 53 29 76 or 53 38 38) is one of Norway's nicest. (Members 95kr, nonmembers 110kr. Open year-round.) The **YMCA Interrailpoint,** Rektor Berns gate 7 (tel. (04) 53 28 88) is cheaper, though (50kr). If you come this way, visit the spectacular **Pulpit Rock,** a cliff plunging almost 1000 feet into the Lysefjord. From Stravanger, take a frequent ferry to Tau and hike two hours to the top. You can also catch a boat to Bergen; several hydrofoils leave daily (326kr, 235kr with railpass), as well as a slower ferry (150kr).

Oslo-Bergen Railway

An engineering marvel and the source of much political debate in the 1870s, the Oslo-Bergen run is one of the most thrilling rail trips in Europe. Fjords, glaciers, and tundra beckon on either side as the train roars around hairpin curves blasted from solid rock. Three or four trains per day make the six-hour run. For some this area will be too spectacular to view merely from a train window; many stop in one of the mountain villages along the rail line. **Geilo,** mid-way between Oslo and Bergen, is one of the best alpine centers in Europe, yet it is nearly deserted in summer. **Bakkegaard Pensjonat** (tel. (067) 850 08), a five-minute walk down the hill from the station, is extremely welcoming. Run by a friendly couple, it is especially geared toward families and groups of three or more. (Open year-round.) Geilo also has a good **IYHF youth hostel** (tel. (067) 853 00), 300m from the station. (Members 68kr, nonmembers 83kr. Open mid-June to mid-Sept. and Dec.-April.) Scattered along the tracks near the highest point on the Oslo-Bergen run, **Finse,** at the foot of the **Hardangerjøkulen Glacier,** is the gateway to wonderful hiking trails. DNT has a *turist hytte* only a few yards from the Finse train station. (DNT members 50-65kr, nonmembers 95kr. Open mid-Feb. to late May and late June to mid-Sept.) DNT also offers great guided tours of the glacier. (65kr per person per day, 250kr for groups of 4 or more; count on an extra 75kr for the recommended safety gear.)

For more spectacular scenery, visit **Voss,** birthplace of the legendary American football player Knute Rockne. A 90-minute train ride from Bergen, Voss lies on the shores of a mountain-cradled lake. The **Voss Youth Hostel (IYHF)** (tel. (055) 51 22 05) is perhaps the most popular youth hostel in Norway. No one even seems to mind the extravagant price—the hostel's sauna, rowboats, and beautiful lakeside location compensate quite well. (Members 72kr, nonmembers 87kr. Open Jan.-Oct.) If the Voss hostel is full, you might try **Mjølfjell Youth Hostel (IYHF)** (tel. (055) 181 11), an hour away by train. (Members 50kr, nonmembers 65kr. Open early March to mid-Sept.) There are several excellent hiking routes in the Voss area; especially recommended is a two-hour walk around the lush **Byrveden Valley.** Pick up maps and hiking information from the Voss **tourist office** at the Tinghus (tel. (05) 51 17 16), five minutes east of the train station; bear right when the road forks at the church. (Open June-Aug. Mon.-Sat. 9am-7pm, Sun. 2-6pm; Sept.-May Mon.-Fri. 9am-4pm.)

Bergen

Clinging tenaciously to the hills surrounding its deeply indented fjord, Bergen's stunning scenery sets it apart from most cities in the world, while its Germanic heritage sets it apart from most of Norway. Once the capital of Norway, Bergen has always played a leading role in the nation's history. Perhaps the best time to visit Bergen is during May and June, when the insistent rain lets up.

Orientation and Practical Information

Squeezed between mountains and bounded by water, the center of town stretches between the railway station, the harbor **Bryggen,** and **Torgalmenningen,** the main square.

Tourist Offices: In the pavilion on Torgalmenning (tel. 32 14 80), a 10-min. walk up Kaigaten from the train station. Pick up the *Bergen Guide,* with information on hours and sights. Open late April-late May Mon.-Sat. 8:30am-8pm, Sun. 9:30am-8pm; late May-early Sept. Mon.-Sat. 8:30am-10pm, Sun. 9:30am-10pm; early Sept.-early Dec. Mon.-Sat. 10am-3pm; late Jan.-late April Mon.-Fri. 10am-3pm. **DNT,** C. Sundts gate 3 (tel. 32 22 30), designs walking routes and provides information on the area's mountain lodges. Open Mon.-Wed. and Fri. 9am-4pm, Thurs. 9am-6pm.

Budget Travel: Universitetenes Travel Bureau, in the Studentsamskipnaden, Parkveien 1 (tel. 32 11 60 or 32 64 00), 10 min. from Torgalmenning. Up to 50% off on flights to Copenhagen and Stockholm for students under 26. 10% reduction on steamers to Newcastle, England. Open Mon.-Fri. 8:30am-3pm.

American Express: Winge Travel Bureau, Christian Michelsen gate 1-3 (tel. 32 10 80). Mail held and checks sold and replaced, but will not cash personal checks or accept wired money. Open Mon.-Fri. 8:30am-4pm, Sat. 8:30am-1pm.

Currency Exchange: At the tourist office when banks are closed.

Post Office: In the green building with the clock on Småstrand gate, 1 block from the Torget. Open Mon.-Wed. and Fri. 8am-5pm, Thurs. 8am-7pm, Sat. 9am-1pm.

Telephones: Starvhuse gate 4, across Rådhus gate from the post office. Open Mon.-Sat. 8am-9pm, Sun. 10am-9pm. **Telephone code:** 05.

Trains. Information (tel. 31 96 40 or 31 93 05). Open Mon.-Fri. 8am-10:30pm.

Buses: Strømgaten 8 (tel. 32 67 80). Service to neighboring areas of Bergen and the Hardangerfjord district.

Ferries: Smyril Line, Engelgården, at the Bryggen (tel. 32 09 70). During summer, service to the Shetland Islands (740kr), Faeroe Islands (930kr), and Iceland (1510kr, 1-week round-trip 3430kr). 25% student discount. Departure Thurs. at 3pm. **Fred Olsen Line,** Engelgården. To Hirtshals via Stavanger (290kr). Departures Fri. and Mon.; sails Jan. 16-June 10 and Aug. 28-Dec. 31. **Norway Line,** Slottsgaten 1 (tel. 32 27 80). To Newcastle May 23-June 16 and Sept.-Oct. 16 (495kr); June 20-Aug. 31 (825kr). Departures 2-3 times per week, 100kr cheaper Tues.-Wed.

Public Transportation: Fare is 9kr; with a transfer ticket you can use as many buses as you can flag down in an hour. 48-hour passes (for municipal buses only) available at the tourist office (35kr).

Emergencies: Police (tel. 002).

Medical Assistance: Accident Clinic, Lars Hilles gate 30 (tel. 32 11 20). Open 24 hours.

Laundry: Jarlen Vascoteque, Lille Øvere gate 17, near the funicular. Open Mon.-Fri. 10am-8pm, Sat. 9am-3pm.

Accommodations, Camping, and Food

Montana Youth Hostel (IYHF), Johan Blyttsveien 30 (tel. 29 29 00), halfway up Mt. Ulriken, 4km from the center. Take bus #4 to Lægdene. Reservation recommended; you may apply at the **IYHF Information Office,** Strandgaten 4 (tel. 32 68 80), near the Torget. Members 72kr, nonmembers 87kr. Breakfast 30kr. Open May 13-Oct. 8.

YMCA, Kalfarsveien 8 (tel. 31 32 75), a 10-min. walk from the center, up Kong Oscars gate near the train station. Definitely the cheapest place in town. 45kr on the floor, no mattresses available. Fine lounge, kitchen; cozy atmosphere. Open July 7-Aug. 15 daily 7-10:30am and 5-11:30pm.

Fagerheim's Pension, Kalvedalsveien 49a (tel. 31 01 72), a little over 1km from the center. Follow Kong Oscars gate, keeping to your right. Comfortable old wooden buildings. Singles 110kr, doubles 170-200kr.

Camping: Bergenshallen Camping, Vilhelm Bjerknesveien 24 (tel. 28 28 40), within the town limits. Take yellow bus #3 from outside the post office. May have new location in 1988. 40kr per tent, no charge per person. Open June 24-Aug. 10.

Sundt City, across from the tourist office, has a basement supermarket. Other than that, boring cafeterias are often your only chance for a cheap, warm meal. Watch for special offers in even the most expensive places.

Kaffistova, right across from the Torget. 3 floors—food, view, and decor get nicer and prices higher as you ascend. The 1st floor is a standard fast-food cafeteria (open Mon.-Sat. 8am-10pm, Sun. 11am-10pm). The 2nd floor has a pleasant cafeteria (50-60kr). On the 3rd floor you can partake of a copious Norwegian *smørgåsbord* for 125kr. (Open Mon.-Sat. 2-9pm.)

The Tudor Cafe, 7 Torget. A dark pub offering sandwiches from 17kr.

Ristorante Martini. Pizza and Italian staples from 42kr. Nice atmosphere and exceedingly friendly staff. Open daily 4pm-3am.

Enhjøringen, at Bryggen on the 2nd floor (tel. 32 79 19). A wonderful place for an evening out and a good spot to sample Norway's excellent seafood. Try the immense all-you-can-eat seafood lunch for 125kr; other dishes just as expensive. You may need a reservation in the evening. Open nightly until 11pm.

Sights and Entertainment

Bergen's most sensuous spot is the **Torget,** at the foot of the harbor—your nose will tell you what's being sold. Here you can choose fish from open tanks and watch traders net, weigh, and clean the creature you've chosen. (Open Mon.-Sat. 7:30am-3pm.) Looking toward the right side of the harbor from the Torget you'll see the pointed gables of **Bryggen's** roofline. This row of heavy-timbered medieval buildings, typical of Hanseatic architecture, has survived half a dozen disastrous fires since its construction in the sixteenth century. It now features restaurants, offices, and arts-and-crafts workshops. Housed in one of the best-preserved buildings, the **Hanseatic Museum** presents an interesting picture of commercial activity during those times. (Open June-Aug. daily 10am-4pm; May and Sept. daily 11am-2pm; Oct.-April Mon., Wed., Fri., and Sun. 11am-2pm. Admission 6kr, children 3kr.)

Starting from Torget or Bryggen, explore the jungle of houses on the slopes of **Mt. Fløien.** A steep hike above these houses will reward you with increasingly spectacular views of Bergen and the fjord beyond. On Saturday in spring and summer, listen for the sound of the *Buekorps,* small troops of young boys marching on the hill to the beat of their drums. The **Mt. Fløien Funicular** up Vetridsalmenningen, two minutes from Torget, will spare you the effort of the ascent (20kr round-trip). Paths at the top take you through a pine forest to a quiet lake.

Bordering **Little Lundgårdsvatnet,** the large pond with the fountain in the middle, the **Rasmus Meyer's Collection** offers a good cross-section of Norwegian naturalists, impressionists, and expressionists. (Open mid-May to mid-Sept. Mon.-Sat. 11am-4pm, Sun. noon-3pm; mid-Sept. to mid-May Wed.-Mon. noon-3pm. Admission 5kr.) Daily at 4pm from June 1 through September 10, there is an hour-long program with an introduction to the museum's fine Munch collection, followed by a performance of the piano works of Edvard Grieg. The composer lived for 22 years at **Troldhaugen,** beautifully situated on Nordås Lake. To reach his former home, take the bus to Hop (15 min., 14kr) from platform #14 or 15 at the bus station, then walk 20 minutes. (Open May-Sept. daily 10:30am-1:30pm and 2:30-5:30pm. Admission 6kr.) From late June to early August, you can hear Grieg's works played on his own grand piano (Wed. at 8pm and Sun. at 1pm).

The stretch from **Fjøsanger** to **Løvstakken** (500m) is beautiful for hiking; take the bus from platform #17. The steep, tree-lined path leads through Langeskogen, a small, idyllic wood. At the top awaits a thrilling panorama of Bergen and the surrounding coastline. Also a quick bus trip from downtown is **Gamle Bergen** (Old Bergen), a collection of wooden buildings from the last century which have been recreated as a village. Of the 40 old houses, 23 are now inhabited by artists and painters; the other 17 are open to the public via guided tours. Take city bus #1 or 9 (direction: Lønborg) from Vagsalmenning to the first stop past the tunnel. (Houses open May 11-June 14 and Aug. 18-Sept. 7 noon-6pm; June 15-Aug. 17 11am-7pm. Admission 15kr, students 5kr.)

For a lively evening, drop by **Hulen,** Olav Ryes vei 47, near the Student Center. This informal, student-run club is in an old air-raid shelter beneath Nygårdsparken. (Open Tues.-Sat. until 12:30am, with live music Tues.-Thurs. Cover 30kr; 25kr for a ½ liter of beer. Minimum age 20.) **Wesselstuen** is a fun place, popular with students during the winter. Up around the corner are Bergen's new hotspots; stop in at the **Café Opera,** a relaxed, stylish corner-cafe with regularly changing art exhibitions, the **Café Henrik,** or the intriguing **Café Chagall.** (All 3 open Mon.-Sat. noon-1am, Opera also open Sun. noon-1am, Henrik and Chagall Sun. 6pm-1am.)

From May 21 to June 1, the annual **Bergen International Festival** presents its 15-day program of music, ballet, folklore, and drama. Tickets are hard to come by, but try calling the ticket office (tel. 32 04 00); uncollected tickets are sold half-price on the day of performance.

Near Bergen

Bergen is a good departure point for fjord trips, though it might be cheaper to start from Voss on the Bergen-Oslo train line. The express boat from Bergen to Flåm, a tiny village at the end of the Aurlandsfjord, off the Sognefjord, costs 340kr (50% off with InterRail). From here you can take the steep 45-minute train ride to **Myrdal** on the Oslo-Bergen rail line; this 20-kilometer stretch of rail is among the most impressive in Norway. Consider walking the same route; the six-hour hike is inspiring, with misty waterfalls around every bend in the seldom-traveled road. From Bergen, express boats also make the five-hour trip through low fjords and open sea to **Stavanger** (3 per day, 326kr, 235kr with InterRail, Nordturist, or IYHF/ISIC cards).

Fjords

The entire Norwegian coastline is a maze of islands and peninsulas formed by deep fingers of water known as fjords. After the last Ice Age, the glaciers retreated and ocean water flooded the river valleys, creating these beautiful inlets. All are spectacular and pristine, lined by sheer mountains whose slopes plummet straight into the sea. Fjord prices are just as steep, and will similarly cut into your pockets.

Transportation is expensive, and Eurail, InterRail, and Nordturist passes draw 50% reductions on only a few buses, ferries, and boats. The longest and deepest of the fjords is **Sognefjorden,** with projections going every which way. An easily accessible departure point for Sognefjorden is **Flåm,** on the Oslo-Bergen Railway. You can also board the ferry at **Aurland,** a more picturesque village 7km across the water. From Aurland a marked hiking trail runs to Finse on the Oslo-Bergen Railway (about 3 days). Flåm has a hostel, **Heimly (IYHF)** (tel. (05) 63 22 41; members 53kr, nonmembers 68kr), and both Flåm and Aurland have **campgrounds.** From Flåm you can either return to Bergen by boat (340kr, railpass valid) or stop at Balestrand (94kr, same reduction).

A vacation spot good enough for Kaiser Wilhelm, **Balestrand** is the place to enjoy a swim in the fjord. Stop in at the **tourist office** (tel. (056) 912 55), near the bus station and quay. (Open mid-May to Sept. 20 daily 8:30am-12:30pm and 3-6pm; Sept. 21 to mid-May daily 9am-4pm.) The **Balestrand Youth Hostel (IYHF)** (tel. (056) 913 03) is in the Krinsjå Hotel, a five-minute walk up the hill and to the left. (Members 70kr, nonmembers 85kr. Open mid-June to Aug.) Balestrand has many pensions: **Bøyum** (tel. (056) 911 14), next door to the hostel, has cozy rooms (singles 115kr, doubles 150kr). **Sjøtum Camping** (tel. (056) 912 23) is only 500m down the coastal road. (Sites 20kr plus 9kr per person, 4-person huts 110kr, Open June-Aug.) **S-laget** (tel. (056) 913 06), between the quay and the hostel, rents bikes (40kr per person) and fishing equipment (5kr per hr., 30kr per day). The **Svingen Kafe** next to the tourist office has fish and chips for 18kr. The nearby village of **Vik** holds one of the oldest stave churches in Norway; take the ferry to Vangsnes and continue by bus (34kr). A well-planned ferry-bus combination leaves Balestrand around noon to cruise the **Fjærland Fjord** to Mundal. Buses meet the ferry and transport you to the base of the glacier, where blue ice hangs ominously overhead. The ferry returns to Balestrand around 6pm. Purchase the all-inclusive ticket (6 hr., 103kr) at the tourist office. (Accessible to disabled travelers.)

Leaving Balestrand, you can head back to Bergen (2 express boats per day, 4½ hr., 280kr, 50% off with railpass), or head out by bus or thumb. Route 51 takes you through the glaciers and snow of the Jotunheimen Mountains. Along the road you can stop at the **Skjolden Youth Hostel (IYHF)** (tel. (056) 866 15), located on a beautiful river. (40-55kr. Open June-Aug.) The 9am ferry to Fjærland has connections to Stryn in Nordfjord and Geiranger farther north.

Jotunheimen Mountains

The Jotunheimen are Norway's great mountains, with peaks which soar over 2000m. The area is laced with trails of varying difficulty, and huts abound. A spectacular bus ride from **Otta** on the Oslo-Trondheim rail line to **Sogndal** on the Sognefjord crosses the main massif of the Jotunheimen once per day.

Near **Turtagro,** the first mountain stop on the road north, is one of the premier rock-climbing areas in Norway. It's four hours to **Fannaräkhytta** (2069m), the highest hut in the DNT system, right on a glacier. The path is steep but well-maintained, and the view from the top is fantastic.

From the next stop, **Sognefjellhytta,** trails lead around a lake and over gentle slopes toward the higher summits. Hikes up **Glittertind** (2418m) or its sibling summit **Galdhöpiggen** (2469m) start from Röysheim. You can stay in the **Gjuvasshytta** and head from there to the glaciers with a guide.

Perhaps the most central and accessible point of departure for hiking in the Jotunheimen Mountains is **Gjendesheim.** Travel by train to Fagernes, and then by bus the rest of the way across the Valdresflya mountain road. Gjendesheim may also be reached by bus from Otta on the Oslo-Trondheim rail line, or through Vågamo on Route 55. From Gjendesheim you can hike west along a lake to the huts at **Memurubu** (6 hr.) and **Gjendebu** (10½ hr.). A boat also travels the lake, but, if you take it, you will miss much.

Nordfjord

Twisting over 100km into Norway's west coast, Nordfjord is one of the most attractive and accessible fjords in the area. Boats sail six or seven times per week from Bergen; the express service stops in Måløy (5 hr., 331kr, railpass reduction) while the more leisurely regular voyage continues all the way to Stryn (19 hr., 300kr, railpass reduction).

Set against mountains at the end of the fjord, **Stryn** is a small but busy town. The communication center of the region, it has good bus connections to both Hellesylt (3 per day, 44kr, no reductions) and Balestrand (2 per day, 123kr, no reductions). The **tourist office** next to the bus station gives information on trips to the **Briksdal** glacier nearby. (Open June-Aug. 10am-5:30pm. In winter travel agents dispense skiing information 8am-4pm.) The **IYHF youth hostel** (tel. (05) 77 11 06) will get you in shape, requiring a hefty hike up the hill behind town. (Members 50kr, nonmembers 65kr, doubles 60-75kr. Lockout 10:30am-4pm. Open June-Aug.) **Betal Camping** (tel. (05) 77 11 36) is closer. (7kr per person, 28kr per tent. Open mid-March to mid-Nov.)

Nearby **Hornindal,** the deepest lake in Europe, offers excellent hiking by its dark waters. There is a campground at **Grodås,** near Stryn (tel. (05) 77 95 15; open mid-May to Sept.).

Geirangerfjord

Resist the temptation to stay snuggled under your fluffy *dyn* (Scandinavian down comforter) and take the early morning bus from Balestrand or Stryn to the Geirangerfjord, the most stunning of all Norwegian fjords. From June through August, several daily ferries (1 hr., 20kr) connect the tiny towns of Hellesylt and Geiranger, at opposite ends of the fjord. The intervening 20km of green-blue water reflect stunning cliffs and cascading waterfalls. Watch for the drama of the **Seven Sisters,** the **Suitor,** and the **Bride's Veil.** In the tough years of the late 1700s, many families left this isolated valley for America; today you can see clusters of abandoned farms along the mountain walls. Bring some old bread, and the seagulls will follow you from one end of the fjord to the other, eating out of your hand.

Geiranger is visited by many tourists, but is definitely worth seeing—preferably from the top; the hike up and view down from **Dalsnibba** (1500m) is unforgettable. The Geiranger **tourist office** (tel. (071) 630 99), just up from the landing, provides camping and hiking information. (Open June-Aug. daily 10am-5:30pm.) The **Valldal Youth Hostel (IYHF)** (tel. (071) 575 11), in Valldal, is accessible by bus or hitching (members 40kr, nonmembers 55kr; open June-Aug.), though it might be easier to stay in Hellesylt. Geiranger has no less than five campgrounds; the nearest is **Geiranger Camping** (tel. (07) 16 30 68; 20kr per tent, 8kr per person).

Despite its location at the end of the world-famous Geirangerfjord, **Hellesylt,** with its own tiny beach and bath-house, remains unspoiled. A millennium ago, Vikings gathered near the **rune stone** on a field not far from the town center. A church was built near the stone, but was destroyed by a 1727 blizzard; today, the stone stands alone again on the field. Hellesylt has a long tradition of tourism; in the last century, passengers of cruise ships were led by pony from Hellesylt to Øye through the extremely narrow **Norangsdalen.** At the turn of this century, a huge avalanche dammed up the valley and formed a lake. Today backpackers stride along the old tow path, and farm buildings can still be seen below the surface. (Road closed during winter.) The friendly **Hellesylt Youth Hostel (IYHF)** (tel. (071) 651 28), up the hill to the right of the ferry landing (take the shortcut along the waterfall), has a beautiful view of the fjord. (Members 50kr, nonmembers 65kr. Lockout 10am-4:30pm. Open June-Aug.) The **tourist office** (tel. (071) 650 52) will provide hiking maps. (Open mid-June to late Aug. daily 8:30am-5:30pm.) Hellesylt is the base for mountain hiking in some of the wildest and most beautiful scenery in Norway. Obtain a detailed map at DNT in Oslo or Bergen, and inquire about suitable trips at the information office or the youth hostel.

The Geirangerfjord can also be reached by bus from Åndalsnes—up the Trollstigen (open June-Aug.) and down to Valldal. From Valldal, take a ferry over to Eidsdal and continue by bus via the **Ørnevegen** (Eagle's Highway) down to Geiranger; the driver stops at some especially scenic spots along the way (see Romsdal Valley and Ålesund).

Romsdal Valley and Ålesund

Connecting with the Oslo-Trondheim railway, the Rauma line runs three times per day from Åndalsnes to Dombås, through the Romsdal Valley, a spectacular two-hour stretch of narrow canyon bounded by 1000m walls. Just outside Åndalsnes on your left, you'll see the enormous **Romsdalhorn,** a beehive-shaped mountain popular with rock climbers. (Parachuting from Romsdalhorn was banned in 1986 after a fatal accident.) Also notice the awe-inspiring **Trollveggen,** the highest vertical rock face in northern Europe; it curves out over the valley with a drop of more than 1000m. Åndalsnes can also be reached from Geiranger by bus, including a ride down the spectacular Trollstigvegg mountain road (2 per day, 78kr, no reductions).

Åndalsnes is overshadowed by the surrounding scenery, but makes a good base for further explorations. The friendly **tourist office** (tel. (072) 216 22), a little brown hut to the left and across the bridge from the train station, can suggest hiking routes, rent you a bike (10kr per hr., 40kr per day), and book you a room in a private home (singles 130kr, doubles 150-180kr). (Open June-Aug. daily 9am-9pm.) The **IYHF youth hostel** (tel. (072) 213 82), 1½km outside town on E69, is airy, modern, and pleasant. (Members 50kr, nonmembers 65kr. Huge breakfast 30kr. Open mid-May to Sept.) **Åndalsnes Camping** (tel. (072) 216 29), 2½km outside town, has two- to four-person huts (60-100kr; 25kr per tent, 7kr per person). The **kafeteria,** down towards town from the hostel, has a salad bar (25kr) and filling meals (35-45kr).

From Åndelsnes you can reach **Ålesund** by bus (3 per day, 94kr) or thumb. After burning to the ground in 1904, Ålesund was rebuilt and lavishly embellished with the help of Germany's Kaiser Wilhelm II. The Norwegian architects who supervised the rebuilding were heavily influenced by Jugendstil, a German variant of the turn-of-the-century art nouveau movement. Today the town offers a coherent collection of this architectural style.

The **tourist office** (tel. (071) 212 02) is in the city hall building, just across the street from the bus station. Ålesund has no youth hostel and cheap accomodations are hard to find. **Centrum Hospits,** Storgata 24 (tel. (071) 217 09), has cozy rooms and hospitable proprietors (singles 160kr, doubles 260kr). **Camp Prinsen** (tel. (071) 452 04), 5km outside town next to a popular beach, has huts for 140 to 340kr and rooms for 120 to 200kr. Camping is 40kr per tent, 8kr per person. **Peppermøllen,** Kirkegaten 1, has good daily specials from 50kr and a student atmosphere. (Open daily 11am-1am.)

The **Ålesund Museum,** in the center of town, illustrates the city's rich past with ship models and vintage clothing. (Open Mon.-Sat. 11am-3pm, Sun. noon-3pm.) For a view of old Åldesund, the harbor, and the mountains beyond, walk up the 173 steps to **Aksla.**

Birdwatchers will enjoy the island of **Runde,** a sanctuary for more than 500,000 birds; several ferries travel daily between Ålesund and Runde. There's an old Viking site on **Giske.**

Dovrefjell and Rondane

The old, soft slopes of the mountain ranges of Dovre and Rondane are excellent areas for hiking. Great vistas open ahead of you, as only low alpine flora covers the ground. Both areas have national parks—the park in Dovrefjell is famous for its musk oxen, from which you should keep your distance. For more information on hiking and where to find (and avoid) oxen, contact the DNT office in Oslo; they have a comprehensive network of huts in this region.

Dombås, at an end of the beautiful Rauma Valley line from Åndalsnes, is also a major mid-way stop on the Oslo-Trondheim railway. You can stay at the **Dombås Youth Hostel (IYHF)** (tel. (062) 410 45), up the hill from the train station. Turn right, away from the city, on the main street. (Members 50kr, nonmembers 65kr. Lockout 10am-4pm. Open June-Aug. and Easter week.) Another excellent base for hiking is **Hjerkinn,** a 40-minute train ride north. Start your exploration here or from **Kongsvoll,** 10km north. A 4½-hour walk will take you to the DNT hut in **Reinheim,** from where you can conquer the imposing snow-covered Snøhetta (5 hr. up and down). A day's hike from Reinheim will bring you to Gautåseter, via Grønbakken and Hjerkinn. DNT's **Grimsdalshytta,** the gateway to Rondane, is only another day's hike from there.

Trondheim

The most important city in Europe—above the 62nd parallel—Trondheim is the natural stopping point between Oslo and destinations above the Arctic Circle. As the medieval capital of Norway, it holds its share of museums, markets, and waterways, but it's not worth more than a short visit. From the train station, walk across the bridge and continue six blocks on Søndregate, turn right on Munkegate, and continue to the main square, where you'll find the **tourist office** (tel. (075) 114 66). They'll book you a room in a private home (singles 120kr, doubles 190kr, 20kr fee). (Open June-Aug. Mon.-Sat. 9am-8pm, Sun. 1-6pm; Sept.-May Mon.-Fri. 9am-4pm, Sat. 9am-1pm.) The **IYHF Trondheim Youth Hostel,** Weidemannsvei 41 (tel. (07) 53 04 90), is large and clean, but plain. From the train station, walk up Søndregate, turn left on Olav Tryggvasonsgate and follow it over the bridge and four blocks up the hill. Bus #3 from Munkegate, down the street from the statue of King Olav, saves you the 20-minute walk. (Members 90kr, nonmembers 105kr. All-you-can-eat breakfast included. Lockout 10:30am-3pm. Open early Jan. to mid-Dec.) **Singesaker Sommerhotell,** Rogertsgate 1 (tel. (07) 52 00 92), has a grill, pool table, piano, and TV room. (Singles 150kr, doubles 250kr. Open mid-June to mid-Aug.) **Trondheim Camping** (tel. (07) 88 61 35), 10km from town, is large and often crowded. Take bus #44 from the bus station to Sandbakken, the last stop. (40kr per tent.)

For a treat after a week of bread and cheese, go to **Ravnkloa fish market,** at the end of Munkegate by the water. Try the cold *fiskekaker* (fish cakes) in **Fiskebrygga,** the shop next door. (Open Mon.-Fri. 8:30am-4:30pm, Sat. 8:30am-1:30pm.) **Café Paparazzi,** Nodregate 4, is loud but has reasonable specials from 40kr. (Open Mon. 10:30am-6pm, Tues.-Thurs. 10:30am-11:30pm, Fri.-Sat. 10:30am-3am.) The market **Bunnpris,** across from the train station, is open Mon.-Fri. 10am-8pm, Sat. 9am-6pm. In front of the tourist office rises the statue of **Olav Trygvasson,** who founded

Trondheim in 997. Today, he watches over an outdoor market with fresh fruit and vegetables. (Mon.-Fri. 9am-4pm, Sat. 9am-1pm.)

Another Viking king of Trondheim, Olav Haraldsson, became Norway's patron saint after he fought to introduce Christianity to the country. A steady stream of pilgrims to Trondheim prompted the construction of **Nidaros Cathedral,** Scandinavia's largest medieval structure. (Open mid-June to Aug. Mon.-Fri. 9:30am-5:30pm, Sat. 9:30am-2pm, Sun. 1:30-4pm. Admission 7kr, students 3kr.) Walk up the many stairs to the tower: The view of Trondheim is definitely worth the 2kr admission. Tram #1 from Prinsengate to the last stop will take you to the fascinating **Ringve Museum of Musical History.** Knowledgeable guides demonstrate instruments of different periods and regions. Displays range from a one-stringed Ethiopian violin to the ornate Mozart Room. (Tours in English daily at noon, 2pm, and 3pm, plus 7:30pm on Tues. and Wed. Admission 20kr, students 10kr.) The best Norwegian artists are represented at the **Trondelag Art Gallery,** next to the cathedral. (Open Tues.-Fri. 11am-6pm, Sat. 11am-3pm, Sun. 11am-4pm. Old films Wed. at 8pm.) On a sunny day, stroll through the park around **Kristiansten Fortress,** built in 1681. (Open June-Aug. Mon.-Sat. 10am-3pm, Sun. 10am-2pm. 5kr.) Or hop on a ferry to **Munkholmen,** a nearby island which has served duty as a prison, abbey, and fortress and now as a quiet beach and picnic spot. (17kr round-trip.)

Bodø

Norwegian rail service comes to an end in Bodø, a pretty harbor town that valiantly advertises itself as "more than just the middle." The **tourist office,** Sandgate 4a (tel. (081) 212 40), is next to the bus station, about five blocks towards the center from the train station. (Open June-Aug. Mon.-Fri. 9am-4:30pm, Sat. 10am-1:30pm, closed Sun.; Sept.-May Mon.-Fri. 9am-4pm, closed Sat.-Sun.) A summer branch office at the train station has evening hours. To get to the **IYHF Flatvold Youth Hostel** (tel. (081) 256 66), turn right on Sjøgate from the bus drop-off point, or left from the ferry landing and train stations; walk to the traffic circle, turn left, and walk 10 minutes to the traffic light. The hostel is excellent, with kitchen and laundry facilities, but avoid the 35kr styrofoam breakfast. (Members 65kr, nonmembers 80kr. No lockout. Open June 20 to mid-Aug.) **Bodøsjøen Camping** is 3km from town, right by the airport (tel. (081) 229 82). (40kr per tent; 2-person hut 130kr, 4-person 230kr. Open year-round.) Follow the directions for the youth hostel, but turn right at the traffic circle. **Koch Department Store,** Storgate 5, has a market on its ground floor and good meals in its fourth-floor cafeteria. (Daily special from 37kr. Sandwiches from 16kr.)

In Bodø, you can see the midnight sun from early June to mid-July. For the best view, walk up the road to the top of **Mt. Ronvik,** 1½km from the hostel or 3km from the center of town. Don't stop at the end of the road, but climb the hill to your right and avoid the crowd. From the top, you can watch the sun dip for a few minutes behind the Lofoten Wall, the distant, foggy outline of the island chain. Don't miss the largest maelstrom in the world, **Saltstraumen,** only 33km from town. This wild, whirling phenomenon occurs during high tide, when immense volumes of water from two fjords clash and swirl. Ask at the tourist office for tidal and transport timetables. **Kjerringøy,** an old coastal trading center 30km from town, recently opened as a highly reputed outdoor museum; there are several buses and ferries per day. Several of Knut Hamsun's stories are set in this village. If you plan to head north to Narvik, consider stopping in **Fauske,** 60km east of Bodø on the train line. Though tiny, it does have a **tourist office** (tel. (081) 433 03; open in summer mid-June to Aug. Mon.-Fri. 9am-7pm, Sat. 9am-2pm; in winter Mon.-Fri. 9am-3pm). The **IYHF youth hostel** (tel. (081) 447 06) is about ½km from the station on E6 towards Bodø. (Members 58kr, nonmembers 73kr. Open mid-June to mid-Aug.) **Lundhøgda Camping** (tel. (081) 439 66) is 3km further from town (35kr per tent).

Rago National Park offers hiking for every degree of enthusiasm and ability. You can hike within the park, or from here or Sulitjelma all the way to Jokkmokk or

[K]vikkjokk in Sweden. Keys for the huts strung along the park trails can be obtained [a]t the campground in Fauske. In the winter both Fauske and Bodø offer good skiing; [S]**tanemoen** and **Skarmoen** are nearby sites. Inquire at the tourist offices for condi[ti]ons and accommodations.

Bodø is, as advertised, the gateway to the Lofoten Islands. The *Hurtigrut* coastal [s]teamer sails north at 3pm daily from April to September, reaching Stamsund [(]169kr) and Svolvaer (181kr). In addition, there are daily ferries to Værøy (72kr) [a]nd Røst (85kr).

InterRail draws a 50% reduction throughout the Nordland area, including Bodø, [F]auske, the Lofoten Islands, and Narvik. Nordturist does the same only on the [F]auske-Narvik run, and Eurail gives no reduction anywhere. The only cheap alter[n]ative is hitching, which can be slow.

Lofoten Islands

Yes, there are enchanted islands and they are called the Lofotens. Jagged green [a]nd gray mountains shelter farmlands, fjords, sheep, and a few fortunate travelers. [F]rom a distance, their ghostly outline forms the **Lofoten Wall,** a moving sight in [e]ither sun or mist. Fisherfolk toil 20 hours a day from February through April, [w]hen boats from all over Norway turn up to hunt the spawning *skrei* (Arctic Ocean [c]od). From May on, life is more relaxed; you can live cheaply in *rorbu,* cottages [o]ccupied only during the Lofoten fishing season, and catch mackerel or salmon from [y]our doorstep. The tradition of living in *rorbu* dates to 1120, when King Øystein [o]rdered them built for the fisherfolk, who formerly had only the upturned hulls [o]f their rowboats to sleep in. These waterside lodgings, peculiar to the Lofotens, [r]un about 40 to 70kr per person per night, based on four-person occupancy. Larger [s]*jøhus* rent beds for about the same price. The brochure *Nordland 1987: Nord-Norge* [O]*vernatting* lists all *rorbu, sjøhus,* and other accommodations including camp[g]rounds.

The Lofoten's beauty comes at the price of transportation. The coastal steamer [s]tops at both Svolvær and Stamsund in the Lofotens, but the fare between the two [i]s 60kr. Express catamaran service runs from Narvik to Svolvær daily at varying [t]imes (4 hr., 188kr). Bus service is cheaper, crossing on the frequent car ferry at [S]**kutvik** (156kr). InterRail passes draw a 50% reduction between Narvik and [S]volvær and on the Lofotens themselves. R19, often called **Lofotenvegen** (the Lofo[t]en Road) runs from Fiskebøl to Å, and binds the four northern islands together. [B]uses travel the islands' length several times per day (Stamsund-Svolvær 61kr). The [t]wo southern islands, Værøy and Røst, can be reached either by ferry from Bodø [o]r from Reine, a village south of Stamsund.

Meet the smell of flowers, fish heads, and ship-engine oil in **Svolvær,** communica[t]ions and transport hub of the Lofotens. From March through June, thousands of [c]leaned cod dry on triangular racks in the open air, awaiting export. For suggestions [o]n excursions to mountain and sea, visit the **tourist office** (tel. (088) 710 53), right [o]n the dock. They also book *rorbu* and *sjøhus.* (Open in summer daily 9am-3pm [a]nd 6-10pm; in winter Mon.-Fri. 9am-4pm.) The **IYHF youth hostel** (tel. (088) 707 [7]7) charges an incredible 99kr, including a plastic breakfast. Svolvær's two *sjøhus* [a]re a better deal; **Svolvær Sjøhuscamping** (tel. (088) 703 36) and **Marinepollen** [S]**jøhus** (tel. (088) 718 33) both go for 70kr a bed. The best deal of all is free camping [o]n a beach 2km north of town, with running water and an ancient toilet. Northeast [o]f Svolvær lies spectacular **Trollfjorden:** On each side of the 2-kilometer long fjord, [p]recipitous cliffs dive almost vertically into the sea. Two boats cruise Trollfjorden [(]130kr per person, occasional 50% youth discount); inquire at the tourist office. The northbound *Hurtigrut* coastal steamer also passes through the fjord. For a [w]eekend in late July, the Lofotens rock with **Troilltampen:** Rock bands, folksingers, [d]ancers, and jazz artists perform in Kalle. For tickets call (088) 719 13. There is [c]ontinual bus access from Svolvær.

Stamsund is perhaps the best-known of the Lofotens' small villages, with its famous **Justad Rorbucamping Youth Hostel** (tel. (088) 891 66). Travelers from all over the world come planning to stay the night, and remain for months. A rare sense of community quickly develops; people sunbathe on smooth rocks together, sit around a wood-burning stove, and cook and share their day's catch of fish. The benevolent ruler of this island utopia is Roar Justad, who will recommend hiking trails and lend you his rowboats. Call in advance for reservations. (45kr. Bikes 25kr. Mopeds 70kr. Free fishing. Rooms for groups and families available.)

Flakstad, the next island south, may be reached from Stamsund; take the bus (3 per day) via Leknes to the ferry crossing at Lilleeidet to Napp (hourly). The island of Flakstad has a cruciform red-painted church built of Russian driftwood in 1780. Summer concerts are given here weekly from early July through early August. **Nusfjord,** farther south, was cited in 1975 as one of the best-preserved fishing villages in Norway.

On the island of Moskenes, **Sund** and **Reine** are well worth a visit. Sund has a small local fishing museum displaying old boats, engines, and various other curiosities. A cheap, lovely fjord cruise sails from Reine to Rostad, Kirkefjord, Engelsnes, Vindstad, Tennes, and back to Reine. (Mon.-Fri., 1¾ hr.)

Most distant and rustic of the Lofotens are Værøy and Røst. **Værøy** is sanctuary to thousands of seabirds, including the famous puffin. Another curiosity is the almost extinct *lundehund,* which hunts puffin on the precipices. You can stay at the **Værøy Youth Hostel (IYHF)** (tel. (088) 953 28). (50kr. Open June to mid-Sept.) The southernmost of the Lofoten Islands, **Røst** lies as a last reminder of land before the open ocean, and as a røost for the very rare sea eagle. Røst also has an **IYHF youth hostel** (tel. (088) 961 09), 500m from the boat landing. (50kr. Breakfast 30kr. Open May-Sept.)

Narvik

The journey to and from Narvik is more memorable than the town. Majestic snow-capped peaks pierce the clouds above and shimmer in the fjord below. The train through Kiruna in Sweden, the bus north to Alta or south to Bodø, the hydrofoil to Svolvær—all offer Scandinavian scenery at its most thrilling. If your sole interest is the midnight sun, check the forecast before you head north or this rainy, cloudy city may disappoint you. The **tourist office,** Kongensgate 66 (tel. (082) 433 09), is up the hill to your right from the train station (below the bus station). The knowledgeable staff can book you a room in a private home (singles 100kr, doubles 170kr, fee 10kr), and provide transport information for northern Norway. (Open in summer Mon.-Sat. 9am-9pm.) The **Nordkalotten Youth Hostel,** Havnegate 3 (tel. (082) 425 98), is by the harbor, through the town, and down the hill from the tourist office. (90kr. Buffet breakfast included. No curfew, but closed 10am-4pm. Open year-round. Reservations recommended, especially if you are coming by the evening train.) Guest house **Breidablikk,** Tore Hundsgate 41 (tel. 414 18), has a phenomenal view over the fjord. (Singles 160kr, doubles 220kr. Breakfast 45kr.) Two kilometers from town is **Narvik Camping** (tel. 458 10), with cabins for up to six, and crowds of campers. (Tent 35kr. Open year-round.) **Narvik Dampbakeri,** Dronningate 53, offers delicious light sandwiches and baked goods. For a good lunch, try **Café Aveny,** Kongensgate 36. There is also a **market** between the train station and tourist office. From late May to mid-July, the mountains are crowned 'round the clock by the midnight sun; even later in the summer there is little need for streetlamps at night. At **Teknisk Skole,** tables and chairs are provided for you to admire the view overlooking two fjords. Beginning at the Malmen Sommerhotel just above Teknisk Skole, hike up the mountain for a more panoramic view. Also near the hotel is Narvik's **Gondolbaner** (cable car); the beautiful 15-minute ride and the view from the summit are almost worth the 30kr round-trip fare. (Open June-Aug. daily 10am-late.) A bit hidden, across the square and behind the Mobil station, is the **Ofoten Museum,** Narvik's museum of cultural history, with exhibits ranging from hunting and fishing gear to domestic crafts to railroad construction. (Open Mon.-Fri. 10am-2pm.) Head down Kongensgate to the Swedish Church and Seaman's Center; its **reading room** has current international newspapers and magazines.

Tromsø and Finnmark

At the northernmost edge of Europe, you might expect a wilderness of ice. But because of the Gulf Stream, the ports are ice-free, even in the middle of winter. From late November to late January, however, the sun never rises in these Arctic regions, and it can become extremely cold. On cloud-free nights one may see the Aurora Borealis (northern lights) flame across the sky, transforming white and dark into exquisite colors. By March, days are longer than in the south of Norway, and from mid-May to late July, daylight remains around the clock. Though chilly at night, the Arctic can be sweltering with mid-day summer temperatures inland reaching into the 90°sF. Accompanying the heat are swarms of mosquitoes; life can be miserable for campers without protective netting and insect repellent (a local product, "3 × 6," seems to be effective).

Very little in northern Norway dates from before World War II. In 1944, retreating Germans torched and bombed houses, bridges, churches—anything and everything of value in their path—in their determination to leave a wasteland for advancing Russian troops. The post-war rebuilding effort produced stark buildings, which stand in sharp contrast to the pine forests and fjords.

Visiting the area requires a good deal of time and money. Both buses and boats are expensive and offer reductions only if you study in Norway. Consider flying youth standby. Hitchhiking is the only cheap transport and can be surprisingly successful, though traffic is light and distances long. Try to have a sign and a tent. The youth standby fares offered in Sweden—150 Swedish kroner from Stockholm to any point in Sweden—may make that option the cheapest way up to Lapland/Finnmark.

On your way up or down the coast, you may want to stop in **Tromsø,** 200km from Narvik. One of the few Arctic towns to escape the German swath of destruction in 1944, Tromsø is now the administrative, commercial, and educational center for northern Norway. Visitors feed pigeons outside the old **cathedral,** one of the largest wooden churches in Norway. (Open Tues.-Sat. 1-4pm.) Perhaps more striking are the clean white lines of the modern **Arctic Cathedral,** across the bridge in Tromsdalen. Wander down Storgata to the **marketplace** for a sight of strawberries, cherries, and all the other things you haven't eaten for weeks.

The **Tromsø Museum** features ethnographic exhibits on the independent cultures of Lapland. (Open June-Aug. daily 11am-3pm; Sept.-May Mon.-Fri. 11am-3pm. Admission 5kr.) The new **Polar Museum,** next door, has exhibits on everything from seals to the expeditions of Amundsen. (Open daily 11am-5pm. Admission 15kr.) For a sweeping view of the city and the midnight sun (roughly May 21-July 23), take the cable car to the top of Tromsdalstind; reach the cable car station aboard bus #28. (Cable car runs daily 10am-5:30pm and 10pm-12:30am, weather permitting. 35kr.)

The friendly **tourist office,** Kirkegate 2 (tel. (083) 847 76), is right by the harbor and bus station. (Open mid-June to mid-Aug. Mon.-Fri. 9am-8:30pm, Sat. 9am-5pm; mid-Aug. to mid-June Mon.-Fri. 9am-4pm.) The staff will find you a room in a private home for a 15kr fee. (Singles 100kr, doubles 150kr.) The **Elverhøy Youth Hostel (IYHF)** (tel. (083) 853 19) is a large converted student dorm. Walk a ways uphill or take bus #24. (Members 60kr, nonmembers 75kr. Lockout 10am-5:30pm. Open late June-late Aug.) Closer but more expensive is **Park Pensjonat,** Skolegate 24 (tel. (083) 822 08), with spacious and pleasantly furnished rooms. (Singles 175kr, doubles 225kr. Showers 10kr. Breakfast 40kr.) **Tromsdalen Camping** (tel. (083) 351 57) has its share of bumps and bare ground, but still undercuts the competition. Walk across the river to Tromsdalen, 20 minutes from the town center. (Cabins from 150kr. Tents 35kr. Open year-round.) Next to the open air market is **Domus,** a large indoor store with an inexpensive salad bar.

Tromsø is known in Norway for its nightlife. **Prelaten,** Sjøgata 12, is a cafe by day (lunch from 11am; salads 30kr, full meals 43kr), and a jazz club by night (Mon.-Sat. 7pm-4am). The trendy go to **Paletten,** a restaurant and rooftop cafe. Turn left on Storgata from the cathedral; the entrance is three doors down from the intersection of Storgata and Strandskittet, on the left side of the street. (Open Mon.-Thurs. 11am-1am, Fri.-Sat. 11am-4am, Sun. noon-1am.)

Tromsø is linked to the rest of the coast by the coastal steamer as well as by frequent buses. The northbound steamer leaves daily at 5pm, while the southbound arrives at 4:45am. The friendly **politi** (police station) is at Sjøgata 1 (tel. (083) 850 80), on the right, up the street from the pier and the tourist office. (Open 24 hours.) Three buses per day run between Narvik and Tromsø (5 hr., 204kr, no discounts), while one leaves north to Alta (6 hr., 226kr).

North and east of Tromsø begins the long tundra stretch of **Finnsmarksvidda,** Europe's largest uninterrupted wilderness. **Alta,** a coastal town north of Tromsø, is an important point for connecting buses in all directions. Though the settlement is basically one long street, it's worth stopping just to fish in the **River Alta;** one of the best salmon rivers anywhere. At **Hjemmeluft,** just outside the center of town, are 6000-year-old rock carvings. You can stay at the **IYHF Frikirkens Elevheim** (tel. (084) 344 09). (Members 65kr, nonmembers 80kr. Open late June to late Aug.) The **Campground** (tel. (084) 303 60) is a good 5km out of town, towards Hammerfest. (30kr per tent, 160kr for 4-person hut.)

From Alta, catch a bus (111kr) to **Hammerfest,** Europe's northernmost town. The coastal steamer stops here for one hour—just the right amount of time. The midnight sun is best seen from **Salen,** a short but steep hike up the hill from the **tourist office** (tel. (084) 121 85), on the left, up the street from the pier. (Open June-Aug. Mon.-Fri. 8am-6pm, Sat.-Sun. 10am-3pm; Sept.-May Mon.-Fri. 8am-3pm.) Several marked hiking and skiing trails begin at Hammerfest. A brochure with map (*Turstier og Løyper*) is available from the tourist office. The only cheap accommodation is the **campground** (tel. (084) 110 10), 1½km from the center (50kr per tent. Open June-Sept.).

The most popular destination in Finnmark is a barren cliff, originally named Kringskanes and now world-famous as **Nordkapp** (North Cape). While not actually Europe's northernmost point (that's Knivskejellodden, directly west), Nordkapp is the site of choice for thousands of tourists who make a pilgrimage to this windy cliff. Though packed with people at all times, the cafeteria and souvenir shop are kept in a limited area, and there is plenty of space for solitude and contemplation of the rough landscape and the midnight sun (roughly May 11-July 31). Before heading up, inquire about the weather forecast. Nordkapp loses much appeal in mist.

You reach Nordkapp from **Honningsvåg,** which is on the same island. Travel to Honningsvåg by steamer is expensive (Kirkenes 467kr, Tromsø 485kr, Hammerfest 187kr)—youth standby from Tromsø is actually cheaper (415kr). The bus from Alta costs 160kr, and transit from Narvik or Tromsø is a two-day affair. There is also service to Hammerfest twice per day (137kr). If you are hitching, beware of the Kåfjord-Honningsvåg ferry—you can get stuck at the landing for hours. If you would like to visit Nordkapp during the winter, call the **Nordkapp Turistheim,** N-9763 Skarsvåg (tel. (084) 752 19), where you can arrange transportation by motor sleigh. The trip between Honningsvåg and Nordkapp can be made by bus (4 per day; 85kr round-trip, including a 15kr "Nordkapp fee") or by thumb. The **IYHF Nordkapp Youth Hostel and Camping** (tel. (084) 751 13) is a 8km up the same road (10kr by bus). Reservations are recommended. (40kr in hostel, 30kr per tent. Open April 15-Aug. 20.) In Honningsvåg, the **tourist office** (tel. (084) 728 94) has transport information for all of Finnmark. (Open Mon.-Fri. 8:30am-6pm, Sat.-Sun. 11am-1pm.) Just above the tourist office is the interesting **Nordkapp Museum,** with friendly tours in English. (Open mid-June to mid-Aug. Mon.-Sat. 11am-3pm and 6-8pm, Sun. 6-8pm; mid-Aug. to mid-June Mon.-Sat. 11am-3pm.)

On the way down from Nordkapp, think of going inland and crossing into either Sweden or Finland. Travel in Lapland can take even more time than on the coast, as buses run infrequently and traffic is very light. A major bus route does run between Honningsvåg through Russenes and Lakselv to **Karasjok.** Karasjok has an interesting **Lapp Museum,** up the hill from the bus station, displaying old *Sami* tools, a mountain tent, and colorful costumes. (Open mid-June to late Aug. 10am-6pm; otherwise noon-3pm. Admission 10kr, students 2kr.) Karasjok's white wooden church is the oldest in Finnmark, built in 1807. The cozy youth hostel **Karakroa Motell and Camping** (tel. (084) 664 46) is up the hill near the ski lift. Ask about gold panning possibilities. (50kr. Open year-round.) **Karasjok Camping** is just down the street away from town (130-200kr in 4-bed huts. 25kr per tent, 8kr per person. Open early June-Aug.). There is plenty of freelance camping nearby—but watch for mosquitoes. Karasjok's tourist office-cum-travel agency is in the center of town: **Lapplandsturer A/S,** Finlandsveien 5 (tel. (084) 667 72), can suggest hiking tours and has all the transport information you'll need (open year-round). From Karasjok, you can continue on to Lake Inar and Rovaniemi in Finland (2 buses per day, 8 hr., 152 Finnish marks). When reading bus schedules, remember that Finland is one time zone ahead.

From Alta, take the bus south (1 per day) to the modern Lapp capital of **Kautokeino,** where *Sami* (Lapp) culture is perhaps the most authentic. Stay at the **IYHF Alfreds Kro og Overnatting** (tel. (084) 561 18; 41kr; open year-round). During Easter weekend, Kautokeino hosts concerts, theater, exhibits, games, and a reindeer race on a frozen river at noon on Easter Eve. Make reservations well in advance. From Kautokeino, continue south to **Enontekio,** Finland; from there connections can be made to Karesuando and Kiruna on the Swedish rail line. Probably the most interesting and rugged portion of Finnmark is between Kautokeino and Karasjok, off scrabbly Route 92. Buses run several times per week, and there are many mountain huts in the area; inquire at local tourist offices or the Oslo DNT. Connections also exist from Tromsø to Kilpisjärvi and Rovaniemi, Finland. For further information on nearby regions, turn to the Finland and Sweden chapters.

POLAND

US$1 = 270 złoty (zł) **100zł = US$0.37**
UK£1 = 440zł **100zł = UK£0.23**

Poland, the largest, most populous, and (in the last 10 years, anyway) most newsworthy of the Eastern European nations, has historically had the misfortune to occupy the flattest piece of land between Asia and Europe. Knights of the Teutonic Order, Mongols, Swedes, Russians, Prussians, French, Nazis, and Soviets have all marched along this highway across central Europe, and the country has all but ceased to exist on four separate occasions. Since 1944, Poland has been a single-party Communist state, but one with a Church and underground press that are more active than in any other Warsaw Pact country. In 1980 the independent Solidarity (Solidarność) trade union was formed, and the organization remains the main rallying point for Poland's disaffected. Economic ills caused the Solidarity strike, and the economic pressures levied by the U.S. and the IMF have recently caused leader Wojciech Jaruzelski to repeal the martial law imposed in 1980 and countenance an unprecedented (though, Solidarity warns, still insufficient) degree of political pluralism.

Planning Your Trip

In order to enter Poland, you must obtain a visa in advance from a Polish embassy or consulate. The fee is US$16 for a single-entry, US$30 for a multiple-entry visa.

Visa applications are available at some travel agencies or from any Polish consulate. Their addresses include: Polish Consulate General, 233 Madison Ave., New York, NY 10016 (tel. (212) 889-8360); Polish Consulate General, 1500 Pine Ave., Montréal, Québec; also in Chicago, Toronto and Washington, D.C. In Britain, contact the embassy in London. Australians should contact the embassy in Canberra (tel. 73 12 11); Polish representatives to New Zealand are located in Sydney, Australia (tel. 32 98 21). We also list Polish missions in London, Paris, Berlin (East and West), Vienna, and throughout Eastern Europe. Plan for your visa well ahead of time, as it may take several weeks. In addition to a visa, there is a minimum currency exchange requirement of US$15 per day (US$7 per day for students under 24 and individuals born in Poland). It's easiest to accomplish this by sending a certified check or money order to ORBIS, the official Polish state travel bureau. They will issue you a voucher which can be traded for złoty at the border. (You can also change Western currency at the border, if you don't have a voucher.)

Your visa will be valid for entry for three months from its date of issue, and for as many days as you've exchanged money. It's quite difficult to extend your visa once in Poland; it's impossible to get your money back should you shorten your trip.

When you enter Poland, you will be asked to declare how much money you have, and theoretically, your resources will be checked as you leave the country; it's important to be honest and to keep *all* exchange receipts, since any Western currency in excess of what you entered with is subject to confiscation. In other words, if you plan to "forget" to declare all your money when you enter in hopes of trading it on the black market (see Practical Information), you should follow through with those plans. And if some of your cash has "disappeared," you've presumably been trading on the black market. Finally, remember that it's illegal to import or export złoty—give it away.

Though private individuals may often offer accommodations at a wonderfully low price, you are required to have a stamp on your visa stating where you've slept each night. If you choose to stay in "unofficial" accommodations, you ought to register with the police. Again, we state the law, not the rigor with which you'll be checked at the border. Customs inspections can range from a cursory glance to a real hassle, so it is best to keep all receipts, including those for large purchases in Western currency at special stores.

Transportation

Travel around Poland is slow, crowded, confusing, and cheap (second-class train Warsaw-Gdańsk about US$3). Trains (PKP) run frequently and reach almost every town, but are slow and sometimes late. There are three types of domestic trains and fares. The few *Expresowy* (express) require a 60zł seat reservation *(miejscówka). Pośpieszne* (direct) move about as fast as express trains, but don't require reservations and consequently become very crowded, especially at peak times (early morning and late afternoon). *Osobowe/normalne* (local commuter trains) are the most commonly used and the cheapest—about 35% less than direct/express fares. Crowded in Poland means *crowded;* we advise traveling first class (50% markup), in a couchette (320zł), or getting a reservation whether or not it's mandatory. Until the day of departure, you can arrange for a couchette or make a reservation at an ORBIS office. If you're reading this a few hours before your train is leaving (and you'll need that much time), figure out from the posted schedule which train you want, write down the destination, type of train (*osobowy* are printed in black, *pośpieszne* in red with "Ex" in front of the number), day, and time on a piece of paper to hand to the clerk, make sure you're in the right line—and bring a good thick book. You can ordinarily buy your ticket aboard the train for a 50zł surcharge, though you must find the conductor before he or she finds you. **Polrais** passes can be purchased at travel bureaus (such as ORBIS) for periods of 8, 15, or 21 days, or one month. The prices are rather high (a 15-day first-class pass costs US$84, second-class US$56; a one-month first-class pass costs US$108, second-class

US$72), so unless you plan to do the grand tour of Poland, gather your strength to wait in line and buy tickets as needed. Avoid lines by buying tickets late at night or very early in the morning. To buy a train ticket to points abroad, you must change Western currency at ORBIS, and then pay with złoty. This amount is in addition to the official minimum daily currency exchange. IUS cardholders are entitled to 25% discounts on international fares.

The slow and crowded buses are not recommended except for very short excursions. The exception is in the mountainous southern regions (Kraków to Zakopane) where buses are more efficient and regular than trains. All bus tickets include seat reservations; advance tickets, which are crucial for popular routes such as Kraków-Zakopane, can be bought only at ORBIS. In the country, PKS markers indicate bus stops, but drivers will often stop elsewhere if you flag them down. Fares are generally the same as rail prices.

The domestic airline, LOT, makes any point in the country less than an hour or two away. Fares are no bargain (Warsaw-Kraków 11,000zł), but students can fly standby for half-fare. You must register at the airport the day of departure (1 hr. before flight time). Mid-day and mid-week flights are best.

Although local hitchers are expected to pay depending on the length of the ride (about 50zł for every 50km), drivers usually refuse payment from foreigners. The *Hitchhike Book* available from PTTK (valid May-Sept.) includes an insurance policy, an ID card, a tourist information book, and vouchers that qualify your drivers for prizes and compensation, but it is not necessary for successful hitching. Get an early start and wave at any approaching vehicle. You may stand on any road in the country.

Don't rent a car in Poland; most are in primitive condition. If you have your own, you'll save time: Roads are not bad, although you won't encounter many high-speed highways. Gas stations are rare—any time you see a long line of cars ahead, it's probably for gas; they are usually open from 7am to 5pm. They sell only 94 octane, *not* 98 (super). If your car is very fuel-sensitive, you might want to buy an additive in the West. Consider bringing an extra tank to limit the time you spend in line. Foreigners must pay for gas with special coupons available at ORBIS offices and at currency exchange counters in hotels. There is no limit to the number of coupons you may buy, but they must be paid for in Western currency (10-liter coupon US$6.50). Traffic laws are strictly enforced, and Western tourists are primary targets.

Taxis are cheap, but make sure you're in an official vehicle (in Warsaw, look for "919" on the door), and insist that the driver use the meter. Meters are currently set so that you pay three times the amount shown. You may be asked to pay for the driver's return trip if you travel outside the city. At night, fares are increased 50%.

Practical Information

The black market in Poland is not a dark secret. On the contrary, it is a normal aspect of life for many Poles, who all have the right to possess foreign currency. It is common for Poles to approach foreigners on the street with a greeting of "change money?" Although nearly everyone participates, remember that these transactions are illegal—even if relatively few people are ever caught. If you need a lot of złoty or will be in Poland for some time, look for someone who seems like a normal person (grandmotherly types are the safest), and hope for the best. Since you must account for every dollar spent in Poland (see Planning Your Trip), you'll need to underdeclare your resources when you enter the country. The going rate is about 900-1000złoty to one U.S. dollar.

ORBIS is the Polish state travel bureau. They have offices in most major hotels, and in several other locations throughout major cities. They're usually good for maps and general information on the city, and also exchange currency and sell international train tickets. They'll help you find accommodations, though only in luxury hotels. **ALMATUR** is the Polish student travel organization. Their staff, often students themselves, can also help with maps and information. Perhaps most important, they sell the IUS card, the Eastern European version of the ISIC; this card brings discounts on international trains and ferries, at ALMATUR hotels, and at many Polish museums.

Language will be a major problem for travelers in Poland, especially in smaller towns. Some older people speak German (mostly in western Poland), students generally know a little French or English, and most people understand some Russian. If you do speak Russian, it's advisable to first address the person in English and make it clear that this is your first language, and *then* propose Russian. By all means, try to learn a little Polish before you go. A minimal effort on your part will be repaid many times in warm appreciation from Poles. Try to buy a pocket dictionary before you arrive. You'll leave a treasured gift if you present it to a Polish friend when you go. Any of the standard ones will do, or a phrase book such as Berlitz. A note on some of the letters: ć and cz = soft and hard "ch"; similarly, ś and sz = soft and hard "sh"; ź, ż, and rz (in all but a few words) = "zh" as in "pleasure"; ę = "i" as in French "vin" or "e" as in English "bet"; ą = "o" as in French "mon"; ó = "oo" as in "cool"; y = "i" as in "bit"; ci = "chee"; zi = "zhee"; si = "she"; c = "ts"; ł = "w"; ń, ni = "ny" as in "canyon"; and w = "v". Other letters are more or less as in English. Good luck!

Money may be exchanged at any bank or hotel reception desk, and at ORBIS and ALMATUR offices. Traveler's checks cannot be used directly in Poland can be exchanged or cashed in their original currency at any bank; normal banking hours are Monday through Friday from 8am to 4pm.

Large department stores are usually open from 9am to 8pm and ordinary shops 6am to 7pm. Most of Poland's more than 300 museums are open Tuesday through Sunday from 10am to 4pm. Legal holidays in Poland are New Year's Day (Jan. 1), Easter, International Worker's Day (May 1), National Day (July 22), All Souls' Day (Nov. 1), and Christmas (Dec. 25). Museums are ordinarily closed the day following a holiday as well.

Mail to and from Poland is unreliable. Have friends send letters, well in advance, to an ORBIS or ALMATUR office, or to your embassy. Telephone calls to the rest of Europe and to North America can be arranged at any main post office, but you have to wait there until the call goes through—which could be a full day. Between midnight and 7am calls can go through in a matter of minutes. Charges cannot be reversed. There are two kinds of public telephones in Poland: small, local ones that accept only 5zł coins and larger ones that accept 5zł, 10zł, or 20zł pieces. Some public phones can be used to call those countries in Western Europe with which Poland has direct connections, but it is better to go to the post office (*poczta*), which has intercity and international phones.

Accommodations and Camping

Every time you stay in official accommodations of any kind, the amount you pay will be recorded on the back of your currency-exchange receipt. If you cannot show a currency-exchange receipt, you will have to perform another currency exchange, no matter how many złoty you have in your pocket. This means that you must officially exchange enough to cover *all* of your accommodations, the only expenditures recorded in this way. You are also registered every night that you stay in an official place, and your visa will be so marked. You probably won't be hassled if you're missing a few nightly stamps (perhaps you took an overnight train), but remember that you are breaking Polish law.

The best options are the **International Student Hotels** (ISH—also known as ALMATUR Hotels), run by ALMATUR in university dormitories during July, August, and occasionally the first half of September. The exact locations of ALMATUR Hotels usually change from one summer to the next. We give addresses of hotels if they seem to be permanent, but it's hard to tell, so ask for the current location at the tourist office or ALMATUR office. If you plan to stay in these hostels, the first thing you'll need is an ISIC or IUS card. Then you should buy ALMATUR vouchers *before* you apply for a visa, because every set of nine vouchers bought frees you from the currency exchange requirement. These vouchers cost US$7 for students with ID, US$10 for others (up to age 35)—the price for one night in an ALMATUR hostel. Be sure to bring your vouchers with you or send them when applying for the visa to avoid the currency exchange requirement. In Poland, you can buy vouchers at any ALMATUR branch office, and at some ORBIS offices. Vouchers can be purchased in the United States from Wegiel Tours, 1985 Main St., Springfield, MA 01103, or from ORBIS, 500 Fifth Ave., New York, NY 10036. In Britain this can be done at POLORBIS Travel, Ltd., 82 Mortimer St., London W1N 7DE. ISHs are generally quite comfortable, with two-, three-, and four-bed rooms, snack bars, dining rooms, and clubs or discos. The main problem is that they're nearly always full; in Gdańsk, Warsaw, and Kraków, reservations are highly recommended. ALMATUR vouchers guarantee you a place as long as you arrive before 2pm. If you do not have vouchers, and if the hostel is not yet full, the local ALMATUR office can call and reserve a place. If you are willing to set out an itinerary, any ALMATUR office will make reservations for your entire trip (for a small fee).

Vouchers may be exchanged for many other ALMATUR services, such as horseback riding, sailing, renting bikes, etc. If you decide you want a little more luxury, present your vouchers at any ALMATUR office and they can arrange for rooms at hotels of different classes, at less than the standard price (usually about twice the price of a hostel bed). Unused vouchers are refundable in Polish currency.

International-federation youth hostels are generally very crowded and not very comfortable or modern, but very cheap—no more than 300zł per night. The **PTSM** office in Warsaw (see Warsaw Practical Information) can give you a list of their hostels throughout the country.

The only other form of lodging that does not consume the daily exchange requirement is **camping.** Sites average 200zł per person, about 500zł with car. In addition to tentsites, bungalows are often available; a bed here ranges from 500 to 1000zł depending on its size. There is an excellent map which lists campgrounds throughout Poland *(Polska Mapa Campingów).* It's available in larger bookstores, some tourist information offices, and definitely at the National Auto Club (Polski Związek Motorowy) at Jerozolimskie 63 in Warsaw. ALMATUR also runs a number of campsites in the summer; ask for a list at one of their offices. Also try the **Polska Federacja Campingów** in Warsaw at Ul. Królewska 27a. (Open Mon.-Fri. until 3 pm.)

If your budget is not so tight, you can try **PTTK,** which runs a number of hotels called **Domy Turysty,** where you can stay in multi-bed rooms for 1200-1500zł. Finally, every town has a **Biuro Zakwaterowań,** which arranges stays in private homes. In summer, only Category I rooms are available: singles 2800zł, doubles 4300zł. In the off-season, ask for a Category II room: singles 2000zł, doubles 3000zł. You book and pay at the *Biuro,* and, as always, the amount is marked on your currency-exchange receipt. You may be able to get around this somewhat by paying for only one night at the *Biuro* and then arranging to stay on privately with your host, but remember that you won't then be registered.

When all inexpensive possibilities are exhausted, you can go the unofficial route and find a private room for yourself. Many people moonlight by offering space in their homes. This is illegal, which is not to say it isn't done. Waiters and hotel receptionists often have friends who can put you up; otherwise, try standing with a puzzled look in the entrance to a room-finding service or a tourist office. The going rate is around 1000zł. Many people live in newly built commuter settlements an hour or more out of town; watch for *Osiedle* in the address, which means that you will be in the suburbs.

Food

The U.S. Department of State for Eastern Europe and Yugoslavia has stated that food currently available in Poland is not in any way contaminated by fallout from the 1986 Chernobyl disaster.

Some foods are rationed in Poland, but you'll eat the most interesting meals in the extremely inexpensive self-service cafeterias found in every Polish city. The best cheap food is found in the *bar mleczny* (milk bars), which sell everything but meat. Try *chłodnik*, a cool soup with a fresh vegetable and sour cream base. You should also try *naleśnik* (pancake) and *placki ziemniaczane* (potato pancakes, sometimes served with mushrooms). Another meal is *pierogi leniwe* (dumplings with cottage cheese). Most milk bars are open daily from 7am to 8pm.

Among the Polish specialties served at sit-down restaurants are *bigos* (stewed cabbage with various assortments of meat and spices), *golonka* (pig's leg cooked in vegetables and served with horseradish sauce), and *kotlet schabowy* (pork chop served with vegetables—often listed first on the menu). Another favorite Polish dish is *kaczka* (roast duck) served with plums and apples. When in Gdańsk, try the *węgorz* (eel), especially tasty when fried.

Never order wine unless you are sure of the quantity and price. Since all wines are imported, they are extremely expensive; most places list by the glass, not by the bottle. Probably the most popular wines are the white Hungarian *Riesling* and the red Hungarian *Egri Bikaver.* Polish beer is not the best, but try to find *Żywiec* or *Okocim.* If you want your beer cold you must say so. Polish vodka, on the other hand, is a national specialty, although the very best is made for export and available only in Pewex, a store where Western and Polish export-quality goods can be purchased with Western currency. The most popular are *Żubrówka* and *Czysta Wyborowà. Żytnia* is the best of the pure vodkas. Tea and coffee are drunk in glasses, and never with milk.

Entertainment

Fryderyk Chopin's *Polonaises* may be the pinnacle of Polish musical accomplishment, but today more than ever Poland is one of the world's foremost music centers, with 19 permanent orchestras, eight major opera companies, and several excellent ballet troupes. When you add to this major music competitions and dozens of festivals such as the **International Jazz Jamboree** and the **Warsaw Autumn Festival of Contemporary Music** (both in Sept.), Poland becomes a music-lover's paradise.

You may have a difficult time finding your favorite Andrej Wajda films, but many English-language films are shown in the original with subtitles. Movie, theater, cabaret, and opera listings are in every daily newspaper, as are the hours of all museums.

Warsaw (Warszawa)

Tall, narrow buildings with somewhat faded but colorful facades line the cobblestone streets of Warsaw's *stare miasto* (old town). With much of the rest of the city, the *stare miasto* was almost completely destroyed by the Nazis, and painstakingly restored after the war. Buildings that never existed rose according to plans found in old archives, and others were rebuilt down to the last detail. This lovely quarter stands in direct contrast to modern Warsaw, with its broad streets and plain towers. Here the city's green enclaves, small and large, nicely offset the drab gray. Considering that Warsaw's population dropped by two-thirds during World War II, its reconstruction is a great monument to Polish perseverance and staunch nationalism.

Orientation and Practical Information

Warsaw lies in central Poland, about 150km from the Soviet border. It is Poland's principal transport hub for both flights and trains; several leave daily for Berlin, Paris, Vienna, and Eastern European capitals.

The *śródmieście* (city center) and most major points of interest lie on the west bank of the **River Wisła,** which bisects the city. Within sight of the main train station is the intersection of **ul. Marszałkowska** and **ul. Jerozolimskie,** the center of downtown Warsaw. Walk down al. Jerozolimskie to the next major street, **Nowy**

Świat. A right on Nowy Świat takes you down embassy row and eventually to Łazienki and Willanów palaces; a left takes you to the old town. A good map is essential for getting around. Try the *Ruch* stand in a large hotel, the National Auto Club just outside of Warsaw Centralna at ul. Jerozolimskie 63, or one of the Western embassies.

Tourist Offices: ALMATUR (administrative office), ul. Kopernika 15 (tel. 26 35 12). Perhaps the best place in the country for information. The director is extremely helpful and fluent in English. Open July-Aug. Mon.-Fri. 8:30am-8pm, Sat. 10am-6pm, Sun. 10am-4pm; Sept.-June Mon.-Fri. 8:30am-4:30pm, closed Sat.-Sun. To reserve a spot in the International Student Hostel, buy vouchers, ask general questions, buy an IUS card, or exchange currency, go to the Travel Office at ul. Kopernika 23. A good place to send Poste Restante (**postal code** 00-364). Open same hours as adminstrative office. **ORBIS** (main office), ul. Bracka 16 (tel. 26 02 71), off al. Jerozolimskie. Domestic and international train and plane tickets. Arrive very early to avoid horrendous waits. Open Mon.-Fri. 8am-7pm, Sat. 8am-5pm, closed Sun. For international train tickets, go to the Travel Office at Marszałkowska 142 (open same hours as main office). Information in English at the Foreign Tourist Information counter (open Mon.-Fri. 8am-6pm). **PTSM,** the Polish youth hostel federation, ul. Chocimska 28 (tel. 49 81 28), near pl. Unii Lubelskiej, has the current list of all Polish youth hostels. Open Mon.-Fri. 8am-3pm.

American Express: ORBIS, Marszałkowska 142 (see Tourist Offices). Only if you've lost checks; wired money not accepted. Replacing checks takes a couple days. The **Narodowy Bank Polski,** Plac Powstańców Warszawa 4, reputedly sells traveler's checks. Send mail to ALMATUR or your embassy. Nearest full-service offices are in Hamburg and Vienna.

Currency Exchange: All hotels and tourist offices change at the same rate. Hours vary; usually until 5pm in hotels.

Post Office: At Swiętokrzyska and Jasna. The last place to have mail sent. Try ALMATUR or your embassy first. If it is here, it will be at counter #12. Open daily 8am-10pm. **Postal code:** 00-001.

Telephones: At the post office. Open daily 8am-10pm. Lines may be shorter—and rates higher—at big hotels. **Telephone code:** 022.

Flights: From the international terminal of **Port Lotniczy Warszawa-Okęcie,** take bus #175 to the city center (after 11pm, bus #611); you must buy bus tickets at the *Ruch* stand in the departure hall. Taxis downtown should be 400zł. From the domestic terminal, take bus #114 (9zł).

Trains: Most trains use **Warszawa Centralna** in the center of the city. Some international trains arrive at the **Warszawa Gdańska,** on the northern side of the city. To get downtown, take train #15, 31, or 36, or bus #116, 122, or 132 from the stop in front of the station.

Public Transportation: Bus and tram lines are shown on the standard city map. Fare 9zł; some express buses are 27zł. You must buy tickets at a *Ruch* stand; there are no conductors on buses or trains. Once in the bus or tram, cancel the ticket. If you are caught with no punched ticket, you'll be fined 3000zł.

Taxis: Official taxis can be recognized by the "919" and license-plate number on their doors. Others are less scrupulous.

Emergencies: Police (tel. 997); headquarters (tel. 26 24 24). **Ambulance** (tel. 999).

Medical Assistance: Ul. Hoża 56 (tel. 28 24 24).

Embassies: U.S., al. Ujazdowskie 29-31 (tel. 28 30 41); entrance around the corner at ul. Piękna 12. **Canada,** ul. Matejki 1-5 (tel. 29 80 51). **U.K.,** al. Róż 1 (tel. 28 10 01). **Australia,** ul. Estońska 3-5 (tel.17 60 81). Citizens of **New Zealand** should contact the British Embassy. **Bulgaria,** al. Ujazdowskie 33-35 (tel. 29 40 71). **Czechoslovakia,** ul. Koszykowa 18 (tel. 28 72 21). **Hungary,** ul. Chopina 2 (tel. 28 44 51). **Romania,** ul. Chopina 10 (tel. 21 59 83). Note: the visa sections of the Eastern European embassies are open mornings only. With the exception of Bulgaria, you should be able to get a visa on the spot.

Cultural Centers: Klub Międzynarodowej Prasy i Ksiazky, ul. Nowy Świat 15-17. Current Western newspapers, a cafe, and loads of interesting characters. Open Mon.-Fri. 10am-9pm, Sat. 11am-7pm. More low-key is the **American Embassy library.**

Bookstore: MPik Universus, ul. Gagarina, near the university, has books in English.

Laundry: At Mordechaja Anielewicza and Karmelicka. Take bus #180 north from Marszał kowska. Bring your own soap. Open Mon.-Fri. 8am-8pm, Sat. noon-8pm, but get there early.

Hitchhiking: Coupon book and directions out of town available at the **Autostop Bureau,** ul. Narbutta 27a (tel. 49 62 08), and at **ALMATUR,** ul. Krakowskie Przedmieście 24, at the university. Available erratically at other ALMATUR offices.

Accommodations and Camping

There are quite a few cheap beds in Warsaw, but in summer vacationing Poles occupy many of them. The ALMATUR student hostels are open only in summer, but their Travel Office can usually get students a discounted room somewhere in the city throughout the year. Take advantage of ALMATUR's guarantee to find you lodgings if you arrive before 2pm.

Schronisko Młodzieżowe (IYHF), ul. Smolna 30 (tel. 27 89 52). Take bus #175 or 158, or tram #8, 22, or 24 from downtown. Crowded and not exactly immaculate. Members 200zł, nonmembers 250zł. Lockout 10am-5pm. Curfew 10pm.

Schronisko Młodzieżowe (IYHF), ul. Karolkowa 53a (tel. 33 88 29), less centrally located. Take tram #5, 22, or 24. Only slightly better than the ul. Smolna hostel. Members 260zł, nonmembers 330zł. Members given preference. Lockout 10am-5pm. Curfew 10pm.

International Student Hostel (ALMATUR), location changes annually; call or visit the ALMATUR Travel Office (see Practical Information). Usually less hectic and more comfortable than the hostels, but no less popular; make reservations and purchase vouchers at any ALMATUR office in the country, or arrive in the city early and buy vouchers at the Travel Office before setting out to the hostel. Open July-Aug.

Syrena, ul. Krucza 17 (tel. 28 75 40, 21 78 64, or 28 80 61). From the central train station go left up al. Jerozolimskie 2 long blocks to ul. Krucza. They find rooms in private houses, sell inter-city bus tickets, and may be able to help with theater tickets. Singles 3000zł, doubles 4000zł. Open Mon.-Fri. 8am-8pm, but the earlier the better.

Dom Turysty (PTTK), ul. Krakowskie Przedmieście 4-6 (tel. 26 30 11). Turn left up Nowy Świat, 1 block beyond ul. Krucza. Within walking distance of the station. Hardly a bargain. Beds in a 6-bed dorm 4400zł, in quads 6600zł, in doubles and triples 6300zł. Often booked.

Camping: Camping Gromada, ul. Zwirki i Wigury (tel. 25 43 91), at ul. Rokitnicke. Go right as you leave the station; at pl. Zawiszy, go left on Raszyńska. Or take bus #175 (direction: airport). 300zł per person, no charge per tent. Bungalows 2500-3500zł. Open June-Aug.

Food

Many of Warsaw's best restaurants are concentrated on or around the **Rynek Starego Miasta,** the market square of the old town. Of course, very few Poles can afford these places; Warsaw's proletarian cafeterias are infinitely more colorful and *very* cheap. Even if your tour of Eastern Europe goes only as far as Poland, you can travel to Poland's neighbors through Warsaw's restaurants. Get Russian food at **Tamara,** ul. Marszałkowska 115; Czech at the **Praha,** ul. Marszałkowska 9; Hungarian at the **Budapest,** ul. Marszałkowska 21-25; Romanian, at the **Bucuresti,** ul. Marzałkowska 45-49; and Bulgarian at the **Sofia,** on Plac Powstańców Warszawy.

Zodiak, behind WARS department store and next to the round PKO bank on the northeast corner of the Marszałkowska-Jerozolimskie intersection. One of the most popular cafeterias in the city. Full meals for less than 250zł. Open daily 8am-9pm.

Familijny, ul. Nowy Świat 39. Good soups 30-60zł, served at small tables with red-checkered tablecloths. Open Mon.-Fri. 7am-8pm, Sat. 9am-6pm, Sun. 9am-5pm.

Kamienne Schodki, Rynek Starego Miasta 26, tucked away at the corner of the old market where stone stairs descend to the river. Famous for its *kaczka* (roast duck), though sometimes only chicken is available. Big portions. Full meal about 650zł. Open daily 10am-10pm.

Bazyliszek, (tel. 31 18 41) Rynek Starego Miasta 5. Gets its name from the "basilisk," a legendary monster of medieval Warsaw that killed with its gaze. Don't be scared off. This elegant restaurant is one of Warsaw's best. Main dishes 1000-1500zł; stay away from the wine unless you are ready to spend twice as much. Reservations and neat dress recommended. Open daily noon-midnight.

Blikle, ul. Nowy Świat 35. For breakfast, gorge on the best donuts and pastries in the city. A very popular place, run by the same Swiss family since the 1870s. Open mid-July to mid-June.

Telimena, Krakowskie Przedmieście 25. Lovely, small cafe with outdoor tables. Great pastries, but no full meals. Open 9am-midnight.

Sights

The best place to begin seeing Warsaw is the top of the **Pałac Kultury,** on Marszałkowska, a 30-story "Stalin Gothic" monolith that many Poles would like to give back. Just before the look-out platform is a series of 1945 photographs that may help you appreciate 1988 Warsaw. (Open Mon.-Sat. 9am-2:30pm and 4-7:30pm, Sun. 9am-1pm and 2-8pm. Admission 30zł.) The reconstruction job was huge, and restoration already completed in the **stare miasto** (old town) is amazing. All the buildings on the **Rynek Starego Miasta** (Market Square) have reappeared in detail. The house on the corner at #31 is the oldest in the old town, and includes a sixteenth-century sculpture of Saint Anne. From the square, follow ul. Krzywe Kolo to the **Barbakan,** a rare example of sixteenth-century Polish fortification. To the north lies the **nowe miasto** (new town), actually the second-oldest district in the city, elegantly restored to its eighteenth- and nineteenth-century glory. Nobel prizewinner Marie Skłodowska-Curie was born at ul. Freta 16; her home has since been converted into a **museum.** (Open Tues.-Sat. 10am-4:30pm, Sun. 10am-2:30pm.) The polished **Rynek Nowego Miasta** lies farther along this street. For a beautiful view of the old and new towns take the Śląsji-Dąbrowski bridge to the other side of the Vistula. Warsaw's commercial district lies southwest of the old town along Marszałkowska. Here, at Jerozolimskie 3, is the **Muzeum Narodowe** (National Museum), with excellent collections of eighth- through twelfth-century Coptic and medieval art, as well as Polish art from the last two centuries. (Open Tues. 10am-8pm, Thurs. noon-6pm, Wed. and Fri.-Sat. 10am-4pm, Sun. 10am-6pm.) Most museums cost 35zł, and students are entitled to a 50% discount.

Many of Warsaw's important sights lie along the 4-kilometer **Trakt Królewski** (Royal Route), which begins with the completely reconstructed **Royal Castle** (open Tues., Thurs., Sat. 10am-2:45pm, Wed., Fri. noon-5:30pm, Sun. 10am-2:30pm), at the northern end of ul. Krakówskie Przedmieście. In front of the castle on plac Zamkowy looms **King Sigismund's Column,** a 1644 monument to the relocation of Poland's capital from Kraków. **Uniwersytet Warszawski** occupies a complex of rebuilt seventeenth-century palaces just north of the intersection of Nowy Świat and al. Jerozolimskie. Fryderyk Chopin lived and composed at the Academy of Fine Arts in the **Pałac Czapski.** Pilgrims can view the urn containing his heart farther down the street at **St. Cross Church.** The Royal Route then continues down Aleje Ujazdowskie, the southern continuation of Krakowskie Przedmieście and Nowy Świat, terminating in the **Park Łazienkowski** at plac Na Rozdrożu. The breathtaking neoclassical **Pałac Łazienkowski** was the summer home of doomed King Stainislaus Poniatowski; it now houses galleries of seventeenth- and eighteenth-century art. (Open Tues.-Sun. 10am-3pm.)

Meticulously manicured trees and an outstanding baroque palace grace the **Wilanów Gardens,** reached by bus #180 and express bus B from ul. Marszałkowska. (Palace open Mon., Wed., and Fri.-Sun. 10am-2:30pm.) Of particular interest at Wilanów is the **Muzeum Plakatu,** Europe's largest poster museum. (Open Tues.-Sun 10am-4pm.)

Ever an element of Polish politics, the Jewish question again came to the fore in the spring of 1983, when the government and Solidarity held competing ceremonies on the anniversary of the Warsaw Ghetto uprising—the only surviving leader of the uprising attended the Solidarity observance. The government ceremony was held in the beautifully reconstructed **synagogue** at ul. Twarda 6. (Open Thurs. 10am-3pm and Sat. 9am-noon.) Other enlightening expressions of the history of

Polish Jewry are the **Ghetto Uprising Monument** on ul. Zamenhofa, and the **Jewish Cemetery** on ul. Okopowa.

Warsaw is home to excellent bazaars: **Rozyckiego** on ul. Targowa (open daily, tram #7 from the center), **Perski Jarmark,** a large flea market in the Ochota quarter (open Sun. 9am-6pm), and another flea market at the **Hala Mirowska** on ul. Marchlewskiego, a couple blocks north of the central train station.

Entertainment

Much of Warsaw's social life revolves around its *winiarnie* (wine cellars) and *kawiarnie* (cafes). During the summer months outdoor cafes spring up everywhere. The most popular are those on the Market Square in the old town.

Fukier, on Rynek Starego Miasta in the *stare miasto.* A premier wine cellar for the past 300 years. Filled with smoke and Poles. Open Mon.-Sat. until 10pm.

U Hopfera, ul. Kràkowskie Przedmieście 53, next to the Aeroclub. Another fine Warsaw winery. Open 9am-2am.

Gwiazdeczka, Piwna 40, in the old town. A favorite meeting place for students, with an airy back courtyard. Principally a cafe, but serves drinks too. Open until 10pm.

Café St. Michała, ul. Freta 4. Worth a visit as much for the pastries and sandwiches as for the locals and artists who make the place their hangout. Janos, the amiable polyglot manager, is a good source of local history. Open daily until 9pm.

Akwarium, ul. Emilii Plater 49, behind the Pałac Kultury. The best place in the city for live music, especially jazz.

Hybrydy, ul. Kniewskiego 7-9, near the commercial district. A disco popular with students. **Stodoła,** ul. Batorego 10 (bus D from the train station), is also regularly crowded. Both open July-Aug. Tues.-Sun. Sept.-May Sat.-Sun.

Daily classical concerts are held in the **Gallery of Sculptures** in the Pomaranczarnia near the Pałac Łazienkowski. (Ticket inquiries at the palace or gallery.) The **Pomnik Chopina** (Chopin Monument) nearby is the setting for Sunday performances by some of Poland's most distinguished artists. (May-Oct. noon, 4pm, and 5pm.) **Teatr Wielki,** Warsaw's main opera and ballet hall, hosts performances twice per week, except during July. The **Filharmonia Narodowa** (National Philharmonic Orchestra) gives regular concerts in its hall on ul. Jasna, north of the train station. For information and tickets for all kinds of performances, visit **Kasy Teatralne** at ul. Jerozolimskie 25. (Open Mon.-Fri. 10:30am-6pm.)

The climax of any Chopin pilgrimage to Poland will be the composer's birthplace at **Zelazowa Wola,** just 32 miles west of Warsaw. From June 1 to September 30 ORBIS runs excursions (every Sun.; bus leaves Hotel Forum at 9am; 2500 zł).

Toruń

Toruń is a modest, quiet town which calls itself the City of Copernicus. At ul. Kopernika 17 you can visit **Dom Kopernika,** the house where the renowned astronomer was born. The **museum** in the **Ratusz** (town hall) has a collection of medieval stained glass windows, but is worth visiting just to see the interior. The bell tower of the Ratusz offers a bird's-eye view of the old town. A bit of Pisa in Poland, Toruń's **Leaning Tower** tips precariously over admiring tourists. If you missed it coming into town, make sure to take in the panoramic view of the old town from the other side of the Vistula River.

The **ORBIS** office, ul. Żeglarska 31 (upstairs), will provide you with brochures on Toruń, Copernicus, etc. There is an ALMATUR **youth hostel** at ul. Gagarina 21 (tel. 214 44); From ul. Odrodzenie take bus #15 4 or 5 stops. (1900zł with ISIC card, 2400zł without. Open July 6-Sept. 6.) Another youth hostel is on ul. Podmurna 4 (tel. 235 53; juniors 300zł, seniors 600zł). The campground **Tramp** (tel. 241 87) is within walking distance of the train station, or take any bus one stop.

Probably the best food in town can be had in the restaurant of the **Helios Hotel,** ul. Kraszewskiego 1-3. In the old town at the **Pizzeria,** ul. Różana 3, you can get a slice of pizza, soup, and a drink for 200zł. For liquid refreshment try the **Kawiarnia Pod Atlantem,** ul. Sw. Ducha 3. Student clubs like the **Interclub/Odnowa,** ul. Gagarina, can be found on the university *miasteczko* (campus).

Gdańsk

If Solidarity was the consummate expression of the Polish spirit, then Gdańsk—its birthplace and always its most active center—ought to be the consummate Polish city. Yet Gdańsk's history sets it apart from the rest of the country. As a port city and a major partner in the Hanseatic League, Gdańsk has always been in close contact with foreign countries. Throughout much of its history it was not Gdańsk at all, but the German city of Danzig. The 1919 Treaty of Versailles changed that; Hitler's desire to "correct" this situation was a significant factor in his decision to begin World War II in Poland.

Although traces of German rule remain—most notably in the architecture and in gravestone inscriptions—the most compelling edifice in Gdańsk today is distinctively Polish: the striking monument at the gates of the Lenin Shipyard in honor of workers who died in the 1970 uprising against the economic policies of Party First Secretary Gomułka. If you have come in search of signs of the Solidarity movement, you will have to look beneath the paint that now covers *Solidarność* grafitti.

Orientation and Practical Information

Gdańsk, situated on the Baltic Sea, is Poland's principal port. Ferries connect the city to Finland and Sweden, and frequent trains and flights link the city with the rest of the country. Most of Gdańsk's points of interest are in the *główne miasto* (main town).

Tourist Offices: A helpful information office sits directly opposite the train station at ul. Heweliusza 8 (tel. 31 03 38). Open Mon.-Fri. 9am-3pm. **ORBIS** is in the Hotel Monopol on pl. Gorkiego (tel. 31 14 66), and in the Hotel Hevelius at ul. Heweliusza 22 (tel. 31 47 77). International tickets, general city information, and IUS cards. Open Mon.-Fri. 10am-4pm. **ALMATUR** is at Długi Targ 11 (tel. 31 78 01), in the center of town. Open Mon.-Fri. 9am-3pm.

American Express: At the Hevelius **ORBIS** office. For mail pickup and lost checks only. No wired money or check sales. Closest full-service office is in Berlin.

Currency Exchange: An invariable national rate at banks and major hotels.

Post Office: Ul. Pocztowa and ul. Długa, in the center of town. Open Mon.-Fri. 8am-8pm, Sat. 9am-1pm.

Telephones: At the post office. **Telephone code:** 058.

Flights: The **airport** is 14 miles away at Rębiechowo. Buses #131, 110, and 162 connect it with the train station. The **LOT** office is at ul. Wały Jagiellońskie 2-4 (tel. 31 11 61). Open in summer Mon.-Fri. 8am-7pm, Sat. 9am-3pm; off-season Mon.-Fri. only.

Trains: Get off at **Gdańsk Głowny,** ul. Wały Jagiellońskie, near the old town. Information, probably not in English (tel. 31 11 12).

Ferries: The terminal at **Nowy Port** is reached by electric train or tram #10. To Stockholm (US$60) and Helsinki (2 per week, US$70). Check with ORBIS for schedules and tickets.

Emergencies: Police (tel. 997). **Ambulance** (tel. 999).

Hitchhiking: To Warsaw go to ul. Elblącka (near the stadium) and walk down the road.

Accommodations and Camping

Besides being a beautiful city, Gdańsk has Poland's most popular beach and is consequently very crowded in summer. It's a very wise idea to arrive with vouchers and/or reservations. For help in finding a room, try **Biuro Zakwaterowań,** at ul. Elzbietańska 10-11 (tel. 31 26 34), across from the train station. (Open daily 7:30am-7pm.)

Schronisko Młodzieżowe (IYHF), ul. Wałowa 21 (tel. 31 34 61), a 5-min. walk from the train station. The most convenient of 6 area hostels. Dingy and crowded, but tolerable. Singles 300zł, doubles available. Lockout 10am-5pm. Curfew 10pm.

Schronisko Młodzieżowe (IYHF), ul. Dzierzynskiego 11 (tel. 41 41 08). Take tram #8 from the station. Not much more comfortable, less convenient. Lockout 10am-5pm. Curfew 10pm.

International Student Hostel (ALMATUR), location changes annually; check with the ALMATUR office. Students 600zł, others 1200zł. Open July-Aug.

Camping: Gdańsk-Jelitkowo, ul. Jelitkowska (tel. 53 27 31). From Oliwa station, take tram #5 or 8 to the last stop, then go left 100m. Primitive, but large and usually has space. 50zł per person, no charge per tent. 2-person bungalows 1400zł. Open June 1-Sept. 15. **Gdańsk-Brzeźno,** ul. Marksa 234 (tel. 56 65 31), is open mid-May to Oct. 31.

Food

Gdańsk is always well-supplied with fish during the summer. On the walkway over the river you can often get fresh fish toasted in batter—delicious and absurdly cheap.

Bar Mleczny Neptun, ul. Długa 32-34. A cafeteria-style milk bar where you won't pay more than 100zł for a meal. Open Mon.-Sat. 7am-7pm, Sun. 9am-4pm.

Palowa, ul. Długa 47, in the basement of the town hall. A popular cafeteria run by the Gdańsk students' union. All kinds of food 50-70zł. Open Wed.-Sun. 10am-midnight.

Pod Wieżą, ul. Piwna 50-51. Traditional Polish cuisine at reasonable prices. Open Tues.-Sun. 1-10pm.

Pod Łososiem, ul. Szeroka 54. This 400-year-old restaurant is the most elegant in Gdańsk. House specialty grilled salmon 800zł. Open 11am-11pm; hot dishes served after 1pm.

Sights and Entertainment

Gdańsk's market square, **Długi Targ,** is the center of town. The restoration work that's been done here is extraordinary—it's impossible to tell which facades are original and which have been restored. The **Dwór Artusa,** just opposite the Neptune Fountain, served as headquarters for the Hanseatic League; its original sixteenth-century facade looms over the square. One block north is Gdańsk's grandest church, the **Kosciól Mariacki.** Almost completely rebuilt after the destruction of World War II, it suffered a more recent indignity under martial law when the building was tear-gassed during Sunday Mass. Climb the steeple for a panorama of the city. A trip up the tower of the **Town Hall** includes a series of photographs of Gdańsk just after the war. (Open Tues. 10am-3:30pm, Thurs. 10am-4pm, Sat. 2-5:30pm, Sun. 11am-3:30pm.) **Ul. Mariacka,** behind the Mariacki Cathedral, is perhaps Gdańsk's most beautiful street, with exquisite examples of Hanseatic architecture.

On the island of **Westerplatte** you can see the place where the first shots of World War II were fired. Boats to Westerplatte leave from ul. Wartka 4 (May 15-Sept. 30, 12 per day). The **Lenin Shipyard** and the **monument** to the 1970 uprising are north of the center of town, near ul. Jaracza.

Its no secret that the Gdańsk area enjoys more sunshine than any other in the country. Consensus labels **Stogi Beach** the city's best. To get there, take tram #9 or 11 (direction: Stogi) from the train station to the end, then follow ul. Nowotna and the hordes. The beach at **Sopot** is considered more chic; take the electric train to Sopot and follow the crowds. Some recommend staying out of the water because of the pollution.

Students in Gdańsk frequent clubs—sometimes disco, sometimes jazz. **Kameralna,** ul. Długa 57, is popular. **Flisak,** on ul. Chlebnicka, is a small, quiet hangout for local art students. The **Rudy Kot,** ul. Garncarska 18-20, has disco every other night.

Every year during the first two weeks of August, Gdańsk becomes a huge street fair, the **Jarmark Dominikański.** The **Jantar Jazz Festival** which visits the city during July and August is followed directly by the September **Polish Film Festival,** held in the NOT building next to the Hotel Hevelius. Nearby Sopot hosts a **Music Festival** at the end of August. In Oliwa there is an **Organ Music Festival** in July and August.

Between Gdańsk and Toruń lies **Malbork,** former headquarters of the Teutonic Knights. Whether you see the castle from the train or stroll around it, its sheer size will not fail to impress you.

Poznań

Poznań is half-way between Warsaw and Berlin in more ways than one. Known as Posen to its Prussian (1793-1918) and German (1939-45) rulers, the town betrays its Germanic past in its local dialect, cuisine, and architecture. Look, for example, at the fifteenth-century merchant homes lining the **old marketplace.** The sixteenth-century Renaissance **Ratusz** (town hall) in the middle of the marketplace houses a **museum** (open noon-6pm) detailing the town's history. Just off the old marketplace, down Świętojańska St., look for the moving baroque **Fary** (parish church).

In 1956 workers demonstrating against high food prices were met with armed force and at least 250 people were killed. This painful incident is commemorated by an imposing **monument** in the park at the intersection of ul. Stalingradzka and ul. Czerwonej Armii. The recorded explanation in the tourist information box wasn't working in 1987; get a Polish friend to explain the monument's symbolism.

For coffee and ice cream, the **Sukiennicza** cafe across from the Ratusz blends a smokeless atmosphere, rare in Poland, with pleasant turn-of-the-century decor. Next door, **Miodosytnia u Rajców** attracts a student crowd for its mead (honey liqueur) and hot mulled wine. **Bistro u Dylla** serves respectable main dishes (150-450zł).

The old town is up ul. Dworcowa, right onto ul. Zwierzyniecka (which turns into ul. Czerwonej Armii) as far as plac Wiosny Ludów, and finally left onto ul. Szkolna to the old marketplace. The **BOC** office in the Hotel Poznań, plac Henryka Dąbrowskiego 1 (tel. 33 02 81 or 33 09 41), will register you, change money, and find you private accommodations (singles 4900zł, doubles 7100zł). There is a **youth hostel** at ul. Obornicka 94a (tel. 23 24 31; singles 3500zł, doubles 5400zł; take bus #68 from the train station). To get to the **campground** in Strzeszynek take bus #106 from intersection of ul. Jarosława and ul. S Żeromskiego.

Wrocław

Better known to many by its German name Breslau, this city's dual past is claimed by both Poles and Germans. The city is in fact the capital of Silesia, which once encompassed what is today southwestern Poland and northwestern Czechoslovakia. The **Ostrów Tumski** (Cathedral Island) is the oldest and most picturesque section of town. Sneak into the main building of the University of Wrocław on ul. Grodzka, and peek into the dreamy baroque **Aula Leopoldina** (Leopold Hall). Whether or not you are familiar with Polish history, a visit to the **Panorama Racławicka** is worth the experience. Lining the inside of a round building on ul. Purkiniego, this 120-meter circular painting recounts one of the final battles before Poland lost independence in the late eighteenth century.

The **Biuro Usług Turystycznych Odrą,** ul. Świerczewskiego 98 (tel. 44 41 01; open Mon.-Fri. 9am-5pm, Sat. 9am-2pm), will find you a room (singles 2300-3000zł, doubles 3700-4500zł). In July and August there is a **youth hostel** at ul. Wittiga, Osiedle Biskupina, DS "T"-19 (tel. 48 42 51; singles 600zł).

At the **Caffe Pizzeria Rancho,** ul. Szewska 59, you can get kiełbasa pizza and a drink for 210zł. **Zorba,** hidden away in the middle of the Rynek, is a tiny Greek restaurant with great food (full meal 600zł). It's easy to get tickets to the **opera,** ul. Świdnicka 35 (ticket office open Mon. 10am-2pm, Tues.-Fri. 10am-7pm). The best student clubs are the **ACK Pałacyk,** ul. Kościuszki 34 and the **Rura Jazz Club,** ul. Łazienna 4. Every June the **Jazz nad Odrą** (Jazz on the Oder) festival attracts listeners from all over the world.

Kraków

Kraków is beautiful, a jewel among European cities, and unlike most of Poland, it miraculously escaped the destruction of World War II. Although its lovely buildings now suffer the effects of pollution, Kraków remains the undisputed architectural capital of Poland and home to one of Europe's oldest universities. The abundance of theaters and cabarets and the city's many parks make Kraków a wonderful city to visit.

Orientation and Practical Information

Kraków lies in southern Poland, 100km from the Czech border. Trains and airplanes connect the city with others in Poland and throughout Eastern Europe. Kraków is sprawling, but most sights and services are located in the *stare miasto* (old town). For a map of the city, try ORBIS offices or hotels.

Tourist Offices: COIT (Tourist Information Office), ul. Pawia 6 (tel. 22 04 71 or 22 60 91). Follow the row of grocery stores from the train or bus station. Pick up *Co, Gdzie, Kiedy,* a booklet of information on sights and accommodations (in Polish, but the staff will help translate). Open Mon.-Fri. 8am-8pm, Sat. 8am-6pm, Sun. 8am-noon. **ORBIS,** in The Hotel Cracovia, al. Puszkina 1 (tel. 22 47 46 or 22 46 32). Open Mon.-Fri. 8am-8pm, Sat.-Sun. 8am-4pm. **ALMATUR,** Rynek Główny 7-8, in the back (tel. 21 51 30). The very helpful English-speaking director will pile on the Tatry Mountains information, as well as tips on Kraków. Open Mon.-Fri. 10am-4pm.

Budget Travel: ALMATUR (see Tourist Offices). IUS and ISIC cards and straight answers.

American Express: At the **ORBIS** office in The Hotel Cracovia (see Tourist Offices). Mail held and lost checks replaced, but no wired money accepted and no traveler's checks sold. Nearest full-service office is in Vienna.

Currency Exchange: Same rate at any hotel, bank, or tourist office.

Post Office: At Westerplatte and Bohaterów Stalingradu for Poste Restante. Open Mon.-Sat. 8am-8pm. Also a branch opposite the train station. Open Mon.-Fri. 8am-8:30pm, Sat. 8am-8pm.

Telephones: At either post office. Open 24 hours. **Telephone code:** 0-signal-12.

Trains: Get off at **Kraków Główny** on pl. Kolejowy, a 10-min. walk from the center of town. Information (tel. 22 41 82 or 22 22 48). Ticket sales at train station or at ORBIS, Rynek Główny 41 (tel. 22 40 35 or 22 19 23). Open Mon.-Fri. 8am-7pm, Sat. 9am-1pm.

Buses: PKS station opposite the train station. Several buses per day to Oświęcim, Nowy Sącz, and Częstochowa. Ticket office #6 (tel. 933) sells tickets to Zakopane and the Tatry Mountains.

Flights: The **airport** is 16km away in Balice. Downtown **LOT** office is at ul. Basztowa 15 (tel. 22 50 76 or 22 70 78). From the train station take bus #208 (40 min., 27zł). A LOT bus leaves 1 hr. before flights from the LOT office (20 min., 80zł).

Emergencies: Police (tel. 997). **Ambulance** (tel. 999).

Consulate: U.S., ul. Stolarska 9 (tel. 22 97 64). Library open Mon.-Fri. noon-5pm.

Cultural Centers: Klub Międzynarodowej Prasy i Ksiazki, the national press and book club, has a reading room at Mały Rynek 4-5. The **Institut Français** features expositions and films in French during the academic year and a library with current French periodicals. Open Sept.-July Mon.-Fri. 9am-8pm.

Accommodations, Camping, and Food

For help finding rooms to let, consult **Biuro Zakwaterowań** at ul. Pawia 8 (tel. 22 19 21), next to the tourist office. (Singles 2850zł, doubles 4360zł; open Mon.-Fri. 7am-9pm, Sat. 1-7pm.) The **Wawel Tourist** (tel. 22 15 09), next door, will put you up in one of their hotels (singles 4030zł, doubles 6140zł; open Mon.-Fri. 9am-3pm, Sat. 9am-5pm).

Schronisko Młodzieżowe (IYHF), ul. Oleandry 4 (tel. 33 82 22). Take tram #17 or 18. Gets crowded—you may find yourself sleeping on straw mats on the floor. Juniors 400zł, seniors 800zł. Lockout 10am-5pm. Curfew 10pm.

International Student Hotel (ALMATUR), al. Planu 6-letniego 62 (tel. 37 00 11). Try to reserve ahead. Members 1900zł, nonmembers 2700zł. Open July 1-Sept. 15.

PTTK Dom Turysty, Westerplatte 15-16 (tel. 22 95 66), near the train station. Medium-priced and comfortable. Beds in 8-bed dorms 1300zł, singles 4220zł, doubles 6000zł.

Camping: Camping Krak, ul. Radzikowskiego 99 (tel. 37 21 22). Take tram #8 or 12 to Fizyków and walk north, or take bus #208. Bungalows 700zł per person, 600zł per tent. Open May 15-Sept. 15.

Kraków has more street food than any other Polish city; try the diamond-shaped *oszczypecki* (lumps of smoked sheep cheese), *obwarzanki* (like a soft pretzel), or *zapiekanki* (pizza bread with mushrooms and melted cheese).

Balaton, ul. Grodzka 37. Great Hungarian cuisine always attracts crowds. Try the *placki ziemniaczane po węgiersku* (Hungarian potato pancakes) or the *gulasz* (goulash). Open daily 9am-10:30pm.

Staropolska, ul. Sienna 4. Traditional Polish fare. You can't go wrong with the *obiad firmowy* (suggested menu) for 600zł. Open daily 9am-11pm.

Piccolo Pizza, ul. Szewska 14. Try the mushroom pizza (105zł)—that's all they sell. **Pizza Włoska,** on the Planty near the train station, serves something a little closer to the Italian original.

Wierzynek, Rynek Główny 15. Local cuisine at its most elegant. Popular with 14th-century monarchs. Entrees 1000-1200zł. Open daily 9am-11pm. Reservations and neat dress suggested.

Kawiarnia u Zalipanek, ul. Szweska 24. A delightful cafe decorated by local folk artists. Good for breakfast—*jajecznica na maśle* (scrambled eggs; 134zł) are the house specialty.

Austropol/Alvorado, Rynek Główny 30. *The* place for ice cream on the Rynek. Don't miss the courtyard in back.

Sights

At the center of the old town is the **Rynek Główny,** one of the most beautiful market squares in Europe. The **Kosciól Mariacki,** in its northeastern corner, is a richly decorated cathedral, with a 500-year-old altarpiece carved by Wit Stwosz. At noon, the altarpiece is opened with a fanfare; an unfinished trumpet call is sounded in memory of the thirteenth-century trumpeter whose throat was split by a Tartar arrow as he warned the town of an attack. Diagonally across the square stands the lonely **Ratusz** (town hall tower), spared when the rest of the building was torn down in 1820. Dividing the Rynek in half, the Italianate **Sukiennice** (Cloth Hall) is as mercantile now as it was in guild times. The ground floor is an enormous souvenir shop; upstairs, the **Muzeum Narodowe** (National Museum) houses eighteenth- and nineteenth-century Polish classics. (Open Mon. and Fri.-Sun. 10am-4pm, Thurs. noon-6pm.) During the academic year, Polish students gather at the **statue** of Adam Mickiewicz, Poland's most celebrated Romantic poet.

The **Zamek Wawelski** (Wawel Castle) is the finest surviving piece of Renaissance architecture in Poland. Begun in the tenth century and largely rebuilt during the sixteenth, the castle has served alternately as cathedral and fortress. Its 71 chambers house an eclectic grouping of paintings and furniture, a magnificent series of sixteenth-century tapestries woven in Brussels by royal commission, and a series of eight tapestries from Arras depicting the story of Noah's Ark. An English guidebook is available. (Open Tues., Thurs., and Sat.-Sun. 10am-3pm; Wed., Fri. noon-6pm.) Beneath Wawel hill is the **Smocza Jama** (Dragon's Den), home to Kraków's fire-breathing mascot.

Kraków has a number of excellent small museums. Religious art from the fifteenth to eighteenth centuries is housed in the **Kamienica Szolayskich,** plac Szczepański 9. (Open Mon., Wed. and Sat.-Sun. 8am-4pm, Tues. 10am-6pm.) The **Zbiory Czartoryskich,** ul. Sw. Jana 19, has a fine collection of paintings from the Renaissance to the eighteenth century, including Leonardo da Vinci's *Lady with the Ermine* and Rembrandt's *Landscape with the Good Samaritan.* (Open Mon.-Tues. and Sat.-Sun. 8am-4pm, Fri. 10am-6pm.) For a break from high art, visit the **gallery** at ul. Sw. Jana 14, home to a permanent exhibit of work by Kraków's irreverent cartoonist, Andrzej Mieczko; see if you can enlist a translator. (Open Mon.-Sat. 10am-5pm.)

While America's oldest university was counting off its 350th year in 1986, Kraków's **Jagiellonian University,** the second-oldest in Eastern Europe after Prague, was already comfortably over 600. Among the school's distinguished alumni is Nicholas Copernicus. Retrace some of his steps through the **Collegium Maius,** the university's oldest building (15th century) with a lovely Gothic courtyard and vaulted walkway. (Open Mon.-Sat. noon-1pm, to groups only—join or form one.)

Surrounding the old town is the **Planty,** a delightful green park in the place of the old town walls. A section of walls still stands at the **Brama Floriańska** (Florian's Gate) in front of which sits the **Barbakan,** a robust sample of the city's old fortifications.

South of the center, and reached by trams #6, 8, 10, 18, and 19, lies **Kazimierz,** the Jewish quarter of Kraków from about 1500. You can still see the signs of what was once a large and vital community; along the streets called Estery, Izaaka, Józefa, and Jakuba you'll find holes left by *mezuzot* on many doorposts, and a number of buildings that look suspiciously like synagogues. Poland's oldest synagogue, the **Stara Synagoga,** at Szeroka 40, is now a museum. (Open Wed.-Thurs. and Sat.-Sun. 9am-3pm, Fri. 11am-6pm.) The friendly staff will direct you to other relics of Jewish culture in the area.

Entertainment

Student clubs are especially popular in Kraków. Most are open from about 8pm to midnight or 1am, and charge a minimal cover fee. **Pod Jaszczurami,** Rynek Główny 8, often has good jazz and on weekend nights a disco that fills up early. The **Rotunda,** ul. Oleandry 1, has a well-known disco as well as frequent concerts. The walls of **Jama Michalika,** Floriańska 45, Kraków's best known cafe, are covered with political caricatures; there's often a cabaret in the evenings. Political and social satire thrive in the cabaret in the **Piwnica Pod Baranami.** Tickets can be hard to come by. Bring a translator!

Kraków's eight repertory companies are renowned for their brilliant performances, though not all companies perform in the summer. The best is said to be **Teatr Stary,** ul. Jagiellońska 1. If you're lucky enough to visit from September through May, don't miss **Cricot 2,** an avant-garde group that performs in the Gothic cellars of the **Pałac Krzysztofory** at ul. Sczcepańska 2. Many of Poland's best musicians live in Kraków; the **Filharmonia Krakówska** plays regularly in its hall at ul. Zwierzyniecka 2. There are often classical performances in the courtyard of the Wawel Cathedral.

Near Kraków

Words cannot describe the Holocaust. Only the evidence displayed at the **Auschwitz** and **Birkenau** concentration camps can begin to portray the suffering of the millions murdered here by the Nazis. Prisoners were originally kept at **Konzentra-**

zionlager Auschwitz I; begin your visit with the film shot here by the Soviet Army on January 27, 1945. The camp itself has been left as it was found that day; barracks and crematoria now house moving displays of evidence of the Nazi atrocities and exploitation. An excellent English guidebook (15zł) is available at the entrance. (Open June-Aug. 8am-7pm; May and Sept. 8am-6pm; April and Oct. Tues.-Sun. 8am-5pm; March and Nov. Tues.-Sun. 8am-4pm; Dec.-Feb. 8am-3pm. Free.) **Konzentrazionlager Auschwitz II-Birkenau,** 3km from the original camp, was constructed later in the war. The endless rows of gas chambers and crematoria have similarly been left untouched since 1945. From the watch tower at the entrance, you can get a vision of the enormity of the largest Nazi death camp; at the opposite end of the camp, there is a pond still gray from the tons of ashes deposited there four decades ago. (Always open.)

The camps are located in the industrial town of Oświęcim, 61km southwest of Kraków. There is a **Dom Turysty** in the main building at the entrance to Auschwitz I. (600zł per person.) Buses to Oświęcim leave about once per hour; by train, travel directly (3 per day) or transfer in Trzebinia. Signs mark the way from Oświęcim to the camps. From June 1 to September 30 the **ORBIS** office in the Hotel Cracovia (tel. 22 28 85) offers trips to Oświęcim (Tues., Thurs., and Sat.; 1400zł).

A fascinating daytrip from Kraków is a visit to the 1000-year-old salt mine at **Wieliczka,** 13km southeast of the city. One hundred meters underground, pious Poles have carved an immense 20-chapel complex in salt. The **Chapel of the Blessed Kings,** with a delicate seventeenth-century salt altar, five salt chandeliers, bas-reliefs, and a salt version of the *Last Supper,* is the highlight of the tour. (Mine open April-Oct. daily 8am-6pm; Nov.-March daily 8am-4pm; last tour 1½ hr. before closing. Visit by guided tour only: Mon. 170zł, Tues.-Sun. 230zł.) Trains travel from Kraków to the station at Wieliczka Rynek (hourly, 25 min.); buses also make the trip frequently. From the train station, follow the *do kopalni* signs. The same ORBIS office leads excursions to Wieliczka in summer (Tues., Thurs., and Sat.; 1100zł).

As Mecca is to Muslims, so **Częstochowa** is to Catholic Poles. Every year hundreds of thousands of Poles and foreigners go on pilgrimages to pay homage to the most sacred of Polish icons, the **Black Madonna.** (Monastery housing the icon open 6am-noon.) The story goes that during the seventeenth-century Swedish invasion of Poland, the icon miraculously shed tears, giving the Poles the strength to turn back the Swedes.

Częstochowa is easily accessible from Kraków by bus or train. From the train or bus station, walk up al. Najświętszej Maryi Panny to the monastery. In summer, contact **ALMATUR,** ul. Zawadzkiego 29, DS1 (tel. 541 06), about student accommodations.

Tatry Mountains

Directly south of Kraków, the Tatry Mountains rise to 2500-meter peaks. **Zakopane** is the uninteresting center of the region, an important transportation hub and the best place to collect alpine information. The town is connected to Katowice and Kraków by bus and rail, and to Warsaw by a direct train. Once in Zakopane, you can get maps and hiking tips from the **Tatry Center,** ul. Chałubinskiego 44 (open unreliably daily 9am-9pm), or **TPT Tatry,** ul. Kościuszki 7 (open daily 8am-8pm). For information on **mountain shelters,** contact the **Biuro Obsługi Ruchu Turystycznego (PTTK),** ul. Krupówki 37. They run most of the refuges in the region; the Kraków ALMATUR office runs several as well. Shelters are ordinarily a day's hike apart.

There are several excellent shorter hikes from Zakopane. To reach the summit of **Giewont** (1090m) from central Zakopane, follow ul. Kaprusie then ul. Strążyska, and finally the red signs through the Dolina (valley) Strążyska to the top (ascent 4½ hr.). To trek through the **Dolina Kościeliska** to the **Hala Ornak mountain shelter,** take a bus from ul. Kościuzki to Kiry (bus ½ hr., hike 2 hr.). One of the most popular and beautiful destinations is the mountain lake of **Morskie Oko** and its lovely shelter, the oldest in the region; take a bus (1 hr.) from Zakopane and then hike 1 mile.

If you must spend the night in Zakopane, the office on the second floor of **ORBIS,** ul. Krupówki 22, next to the post office, will arrange for a place in a private home. (Open Mon.-Fri. 8am-4pm, Sat. 9am-2pm, Sun. 9-11am.) In the event that their listings are booked, they'll know if the **DW ZAK** ALMATUR student hostel at ul. Heleny Marusarzówny 15 (tel. (0165) 57 06) still exists. During weekends and vacations Zakopane is very crowded; fortunately the **Camping Pod Krokwią,** ul. Zeromskiego, across the street from the base of the ski jump, usually has space. (Open May-Aug.)

To the east of Zakopane and far off the tourist track lies the modest provincial capital of **Nowy Sącz.** The middle of the market square is graced by the beautiful neo-Renaissance **Town Hall,** where classical concerts are held throughout the year. The **museum** in the fifteenth-century **Gotycki Dom** is a good place to compare seventeenth-century Orthodox icons to Catholic sculpture from the same period. **Stary Sącz** is an older settlement upstream whose streets still look much the same as they did centuries ago. From Nowy Sącz, take bus #8, 10, or 21 (reservations recommended). The town's most important sight is the **Klasztor PP. Klarysek,** a convent founded by Queen Kinga after the Tartars ravaged her country. The Romanesque ruins house an art gallery with exhibitions by local artists. (Open Mon.-Fri. 10am-1pm and 3-6pm.) Bus #14 will carry you from the train station to the **Skansen Ethnographic Park,** off ul. Kasprzaka, an open-air museum showing traditional wooden huts, some decorated with wall paintings, from as far back as the fourteenth century. (Open May-Sept. Mon.-Fri. 10am-4pm, Sat.-Sun. 10am-5pm. Admission 10zł.) For accommodations in Nowy Sącz, try the **PTTK Hostel and Camping** at ul. Jamnicka 2. (Take bus #14.) **Camping Przystań Piaski** is situated in the woods 5km from town. For more information and a map of the city, or to arrange a stay in a private home, contact the **Biuro Zakwaterowań,** ul. Długosza (tel. (0181) 211 07).

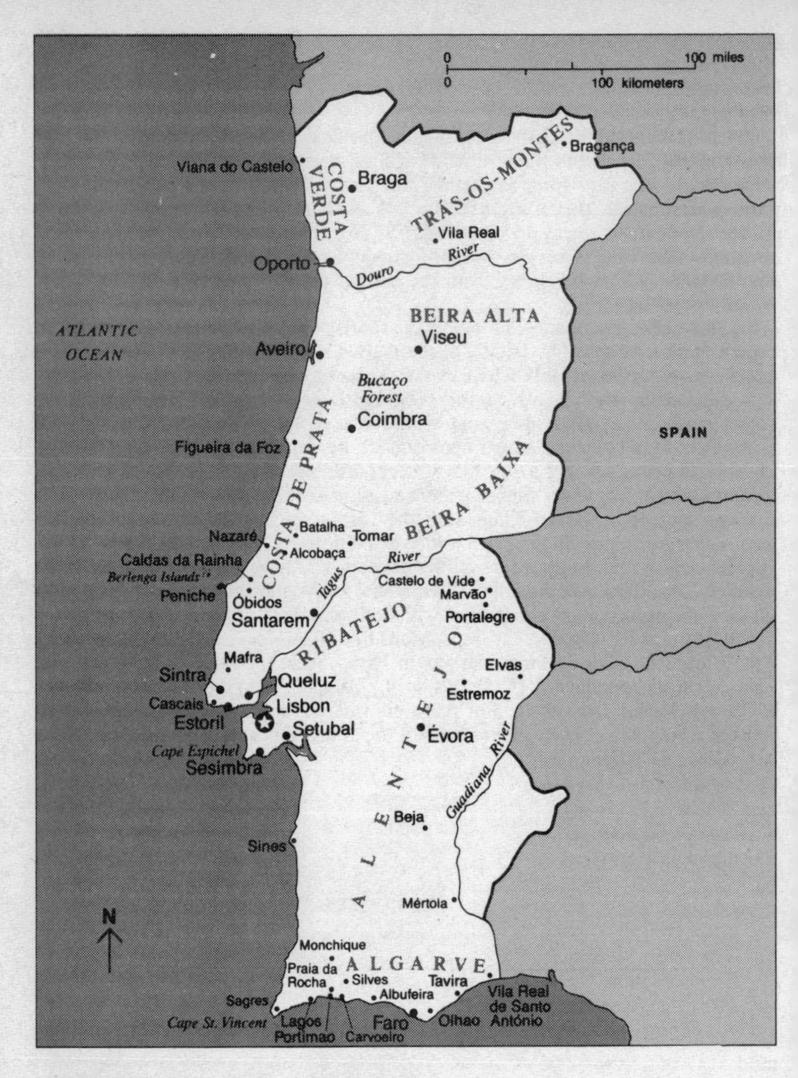

PORTUGAL

US$1 = 143 escudos ($)	**100$ = US$0.70**
CDN$1 = 108$	**100$ = CDN$0.92**
UK£1 = 234$	**100$ = UK£0.43**
AUS$1 = 101$	**100$ = AUS$0.99**

Portugal has always known the sea intimately. Still today, in almost every fishing village, the rowing in of the catch at dusk takes on an aura of ritual. Centuries ago, Portuguese explorers realized that the Atlantic Ocean did not swallow the sun every evening. They quickly built on this knowledge with vanguard navigational and shipbuilding techniques to sail formerly uncharted waters, sending Vasco de Gama forging around the Cape of Good Hope and Magellan around the world. Portugal's fifteenth century, known as the Age of Discovery, is remembered today in *fado* (folk ballads).

By 1580, Portugal had exhausted both its resources and its royal line. After minimal resistance, the Spaniard Philip II claimed the Portuguese throne; independence was not regained until 1640, when, in alliance with England, enormous architectural projects were undertaken. The 1755 earthquake brought most of these to the ground. When Napoleon invaded in 1807, King Pedro III moved the court of the crumbling empire to Brazil. A parliamentary monarchy was established in 1910, only to be overthrown by a 1926 military coup.

Antonio Salazar then ran the country for 40 years, building the economy through the exploitation of a domestic peasantry and profitable colonial holdings in Africa. These colonies gained independence in 1974, setting off a rush of immigration into economically unhealthy Portugal and toppling Salazar's goverment. Since 1974, Portugal has seen 17 governments, each stumped by the underdeveloped country's economic woes. In 1986, Portugal became the newest member of the EEC, which promised US$700 million in aid over the next 10 years; but Anibal Silva was, in April 1987, temporarily forced out of office because of public dissatisfaction with the economy—only to be re-elected in July.

For travelers, the sick economy means that local beer and wine are as cheap as water, and a full meal can cost as litle as 500$. Each year sun worshipers migrate to the sands, cliffs, and sparkling waters of the Algarve; fewer visit the rougher northern coast. The north abounds in notable architecture: Coimbra and Oporto have beautiful Romanesque churches, while the area north of the River Douro is dotted with Roman and Visigothic ruins. In the center and south are massive fortresses testifying to Moorish occupation. Lisbon is the center of the indigenous Manueline style, an exuberant ornamentation that embraces elements of the lands and cultures discovered afar by the great explorers.

For more coverage of this enchanting country than we can provide here, consult *Let's Go: Spain, Portugal, and Morocco.*

Transportation

Eurail and InterRail passes are valid on the Portuguese national train system, **Caminhos de Ferro Portugueses (CFP);** passholders must pay a supplement on express trains. Trains are best between Lisbon and the Algarve, and on the Oporto-Coimbra-Lisbon line. Otherwise, stick to the buses, which are faster and more frequent, if slightly more expensive. **Rodoviária Nacional** is the largest company, providing virtually nationwide service; many smaller local companies keep Rodoviária honest.

Cycling is good for getting around in Portugal; distances are short and the climate mild—except during the summer in the Alentejo and Algarve, where it's desert-like. You can have similar freedom at a higher price in a car (20,000-25,000$ per week), although gasoline prices (160$ per liter), narrow roads, and notoriously rash drivers may deter you.

Except in heavily touristed areas, hitchhiking in Portugal is slow. Few people own cars, and no one has insurance that covers hitchers—an effective discouragement for drivers and hitchers alike.

Practical Information

A dense and efficient national network of regional and municipal tourist offices welcomes visitors to Portugal. In just about every small town accustomed to tourists, you'll find bureaus with English-speaking staff happy to help with accommodations.

Portuguese is a Romance language, most similar to Spanish, but more or less accessible to those with a background in French or Italian and an English-Portuguese dictionary. Most Portuguese can understand, though not speak, Spanish. In the southern and central provinces, where tourism is heaviest, many people speak English or French as a second language.

Women traveling alone may encounter difficulties in Portugal. You'll very likely encounter inordinate amounts of male attention, which, though annoying, is rarely dangerous. If a situation becomes uncomfortable, don't get flustered; a look of supreme disgust is far more effective.

Portuguese currency is in *escudos* and *centavos;* the "$" sign is used as a decimal point. Inflation is high, so expect the *escudo* prices here to shift considerably.

As in most of southern Europe, work prospects for travelers are grim, although there is a demand for native English speakers as teachers. Also, EEC citizens may be able to work legally in this member country by 1988. Looking for work during the grape harvest (late Sept.) is possible but quixotic.

Still a strongly Catholic country, much of Portugal's community activity centers around a variety of religious festivals. Two of the most important commemorate the appearances of the Virgin in **Fátima** (May 12 and Oct. 12). The intervening months host numerous lesser festivities. **Holy Week** in April brings processions and crowds to Braga; Easter Sunday marks the beginning of the Portuguese bullfighting season (here, the bullfight is a bloodless art). Festivals in honor of local patron saints are called *romarías* and are accompanied by pilgrimages, village fairs, and, often, make-shift amusement parks. The following dates are official public holidays when everything in Portugal is closed: New Year's Day, Carnival Tuesday, Good Friday and Easter Sunday (March 3, and April 17 and 19 in 1987), Liberty Day (April 25), Labor Day (May 1), Camões, or National Day (June 10), Corpus Christi, Assumption (Aug. 15), First Republic Day (Oct. 5), All Saints Day (Nov. 1), Restoration of Independence (Dec. 1), Immaculate Conception (Dec. 8), and Christmas (Dec. 24-25).

Shops are usually open Monday through Friday from 9am to 1pm and from 3 to 7pm, and Saturday morning. Normal banking hours are Monday through Friday from 8:30am to 11:45 and 1 to 2:45pm. Remember that Portugal is in a different time zone from Spain; clocks are set one hour earlier. Post offices in larger towns are open Monday through Friday from 9am to 7pm and Saturday from 9am to 12:30pm. In smaller towns they close for lunch and weekends. Poste Restante is held at central post offices; pick-up costs 20$ per item. Post offices also house telephone offices, which in larger cities remain open until 11:30pm or midnight. To use pay phones (except for international calls), put a 2.50$, 5$, or 25$ coin into the trough on top of the phone and then dial. Long-distance calls require the appropriate area code. The *credifone* system, using magnetic cards similar to credit cards, is now available in most of Portugal. You can purchase the card at locations posted on the booths themselves. For an international operator, dial 098. For emergencies anywhere in the country, dial 115.

Accommodations and Camping

You'll seldom have trouble finding a place to stay in Portugal; if you do, local tourist offices will often help. Hotels are rated on a five-star system, the lower end of which is accessible to the budget traveler. Pensions (*pensões*), also affordable, are rated on a three-star system. An inexpensive option in small towns or heavily traveled areas is a *quarto* (room) in a private home. Look in house windows for signs, or check the list at the tourist office. Such rooms are often cheaper and more comfortable than *pensões,* but less easy to find. Double rooms with one bed, known as a *casal* ("marriage bed") are usually significantly cheaper than two-bed doubles.

Portugal currently has 14 IYHF youth hostels, known in Portuguese as *pousadas de juventude*—not to be confused with other *pousadas,* which are government-run luxury accommodations in places of historic interest or natural beauty. In most youth hostels, IYHF cards are required; prices range from 500-600$ per night, usually including breakfast. Linen is often furnished (free) on request.

Most of Portugal's campgrounds *(parques de campismo)* are located along the Atlantic coast, although many significant interior cities have them as well. Pick up e guide *Roteira Campista* from the National Tourist Office in your country or Lisbon, or write to the **Federação Portuguesa de Campismo,** Rua Voz do Operio, Lisbon (tel. 86 23 50). For information on campsites throughout Portugal, ntact **Orbitur,** Av. Almirante Gago Coutinho, 25d, Lisbon (tel. 89 23 41). (Open on.-Fri. 9am-12:30pm and 2:30-6pm.) Where there are no official campsites, unofial camping is usually acceptable.

ood

Portuguese restaurant prices shouldn't drive you to fairs and markets. A good eal anywhere costs 400-600$, and in small towns and student restaurants complete eals cost as little as 300$. *Marisquerias* specialize in seafood, *churrasquerias* in oiled chicken and meat. Portions are usually enormous, and one entree often feeds o people. If you are traveling alone or can't agree on a dish, ask for a half-portion *neia dose). Snack bars* offer lighter fare than restaurants but more protein than *stelarias* (pastry shops) or *cafeterias* (coffee shops). *Bars* provide a little of everying—coffee, alcohol, light food, and more.

Fish is a specialty here. Try *peixe espada grelhado* (grilled swordfish) or *bacalhau* odfish). *Carne de porco á alentejana* (pork made with clams in a coriander sauce) a meat favorite. *Cozido á Portuguesa,* vegetable stew with token bits of pork, is staple at economy restaurants. Outside of and even in the major cities, vegetarian staurants are scarce, but most places offer at least omelettes and salads. The price bread and butter is not included in the price of the meal. Breakfast (bread and ffee) is usually served from 8 to 10am; lunch from noon to 2pm, and dinner from to 10pm.

Wine is perhaps Portugal's most endearing product. For centuries, British imrters have monopolized the trade in port wine exported from Oporto, the city at gave its name to both the wine and the country. Farther south, the Dão Valley oduces hearty reds and whites with a plump, fruity bouquet, while the northern inho region puts out a slightly effervescent *vinho verde* ("green wine"), which goes ry well with fish.

Bar and cafe parlance is specialized, and learning it is a sure way to endear yourlf to the Portuguese; a cup of delicious black coffee is called a *bica* (not to be consed with a *pica,* a marijuana cigarette); *café com leite* (coffee with milk) is often ferred to as *galão;* and a small glass of draft beer is known as a *fino* or *canha,* hile a mug is a *caneca.* (*Sagres* is among the best.)

entral Portugal

isbon (Lisboa)

The scent and rhythm of the sea pervade this ancient port city, filling the narrow bbled streets and energizing the wide avenues that course among the hills. The rtuguese capital is no longer the European center that it was during the glorious afaring days of the fifteenth century, and the disastrous earthquake of 1755 deroyed much of the medieval city. But the character of Lisbon remains intact, and ough residents look back on former grandeur with nostalgia, modern-day Lisbon no less vibrant for it. Beautiful as Lisbon is, it is the friendliness of the *Lisboetas* at will stick in your memory—the cynicism and impatience of modern culture ve been slow to reach this corner of the world.

rientation and Practical Information

Capital of Portugal, coastal Lisbon is also its major transport hub. Train and bus es from all directions converge here. The heart of Lisbon is the **Praça dos Res-**

tauradores in the **Baixa** (lower city). A few blocks to the west lies the **Bairro A**
(upper city), accessible by elevator, funicular, or foot. North of Restauradores
the new business district, reached by **Avenida da Liberdade.** East of Baixa sprea
the **Alfama,** Lisbon's medieval quarter. Six kilometers west of the center is **Belé**
famous for its Manueline monuments.

Tourist Offices: Municipal and National, Palacio da Foz, Praça dos Restauradores (tel. 36 36 43). Not terribly friendly, but does provide accommodations service and maps. Open Mon.-Fri. 9:30am-5:30pm, closed Sat.-Sun. There is also a 24-hour service with currency exchange at the Santa Apolónia station.

Budget Travel: Tagus, Praça de Londres, 9b (tel. 88 49 57). Metro: Alameda. BIGE and flights to Madeira. Open Mon.-Fri. 9am-1pm and 2:30-6pm.

American Express: Star Travel Service, Av. Sidónio Pais, 4 (tel. 53 98 71). Metro: Parque. Mail held, checks sold, cardholders' personal checks cashed. (Open Mon.-Fri. 9am-7pm.)

Currency Exchange: At the airport and Santa Apolónia station. Long lines at station on weekends. Both open 24 hours. Normal banking hours are Mon.-Fri. 8:30am-11:45am and 1-2:45pm.

Post Office: Correio, Praça do Comércio. Open Mon.-Fri. 9am-7pm for stamps and telegrams. Poste Restante (20$ per item) around the corner at Rua do Arsenal, 27. Open Mon.-Fri. 9am-5pm. The office on Praça dos Restauradores is open daily 8am-midnight. **Postal Code:** 1100.

Telephones: Praça D. Pedro IV, 68. Open daily 8am-11pm. The post office on Praça dos Restauradores has telephones as well. **Telephone code:** 01.

Flights: From the airport, the Linha Verde express bus will bring you to the center of town (180$), as will the less expensive local bus #44 or 45, which you can catch at stops along Av. República or Av. Liberdade.

Trains: 4 stations handle traffic in and out of Lisbon. **Rossio** handles the Sintra and western lines. **Santa Apolónia** is for all international, northern, and eastern lines. **Cais de Sodré** serves Estoril and Cascais. **Barreiro** carriages go to the southeast and south (Algarve). If you arrive at Santa Apolónia station, bus #9 or 9a (from the water side of the station) will take you to Praça dos Restauradores. Arriving at Cais de Sodré station, a 15-min. walk or bus #1, 2, 32, 44, or 45 will do the same. Rossio station is just a block away. To reach Barreiro you must ferry across Rio Tejo; boats leave from Praça do Comércio (15 min., 80$, free if you're coming from the south into Lisbon). Accurate and friendly information on all trains at Rossio station. Open daily 8am-11pm.

Buses: Rodoviária Nacional, Av. Casal Ribeiro, 18 (tel. 57 77 15).

Public Transportation: On city buses the conductor will charge you about 85$, depending on the route. A **Tourist Ticket,** good for 7 days' travel on **CARRIS** buses, trolleys, and subways, costs 1000$ and can be purchased at CARRIS booths in most network train stations (open 8am-8pm). The **Metro** covers only part of the city, but is very fast (35$ per ride, 300$ for a book of 10 tickets). Trolleys are 35$, on longer trips 85$.

Emergencies: Police or **Ambulance** (tel. 115 or 36 61 41).

Medical Assistance: British Hospital, Rua Saraiva de Carvalho, 49 (tel. 60 20 20, at night 60 37 85).

Embassies: U.S., Av. das Forças Armadas (tel. 72 56 00). **Canada,** Rua Rosa Araújo, 2 (tel. 56 25 47). **U.K.,** Rua de São Domingo à Lapa, 37 (tel. 66 11 91). **Australia,** Av. da Liberdade, 244 (tel. 53 91 08). Nationals from **New Zealand** should contact the British Embassy. **Spain,** Rua do Salitre, 1 (tel. 37 28 31). **Morocco,** Avda. João Crisótomo, 66 (tel. 52 16 44).

Bookstore: Livraria Clássica Editora, Praça dos Restauradores, 17. Wide selection of English books.

Hitchhiking: Lots of competition, especially in Aug. South, take the ferry from Praça do Comércio to Cacilhas, then start on the Setúbal road. North, take bus #8, 21, 44, 45, or 53 to the Rotonda do Aeroporto. To Spain, take the Autoestrada do Porto; continue on it if traveling to Galicia, or get off at the junction with the road to Badajoz (about 30km from Lisbon) for Andalusia or Madrid.

:commodations and Camping

/ou should have no trouble getting a single for around 1000$ or a double for und 1500 to 1800$. Most places have only double beds and charge quite a bit re than half for single occupancy. The vast majority of *pensões* are in the center he city on **Avenida da Liberdade** and adjacent side streets. For a quieter and re interesting location try the city's **Castelo** (castle) and **Bairro Alto** districts, h only a 10-minute walk from the center; women may be uncomfortable in these as at night. Don't hesitate to turn off the main avenues for inexpensive places, ecially on **Rua dos Correiros** and the streets around **Praça de Figueira.**

Pousada de Juventude Catalazete (IYHF), on Estrada Marginal in Oeiras (tel. 243 06 38). Take a train from Cais de Sodré station to Oeiras, then walk east along the beach (20 min.) until you see the old fortress in which the hostel is housed. An excellent place. 650$. Breakfast included; other meals 320$. Lockout 10:30am-6pm. Curfew 11pm. Open year-round.

Pousada de Juventude de Lisboa (IYHF), Rua Andrade Corvo, 46 (tel. 53 26 96). More centrally located, near American Express. Metro: Picoas, or take bus #44 from Cais de Sodré or Rossio to Praça Saldanha. Hostel is 2 blocks south on Av. Pereira Melo and 2 blocks east on Rua Andrade Corvo. Not the homiest of hostels. Cooking facilities. 650$. Breakfast included. Lockout 10:30am-6pm. Curfew midnight. Open year-round.

Pensão Imperial, Praça dos Restauradores, 79 (tel. 32 01 66). Up quite a few stairs, but right in the heart of things, with friendly management. Doubles 1500$. Doubles with shower 2200$.

Pensão Campos, Rua Jardim do Regedor, 24 (tel. 32 05 60), on the pedestrian street at the southeast end of Praça dos Restauradores. Small, run by a sweet family. Doubles 2200$.

Pensão Ninho de Águias, Costa do Castelo, 74 (tel. 86 03 91). A flowering garden and stupendous views. Worth reserving or calling ahead. Singles 1800$; doubles 2200$, with shower 2900$, with bath 3300$. Breakfast included.

Pensão Londres, Rua Dom Pedro V, 53 (tel. 36 55 23). Take the funicular from Praça dos Restauradores, then walk to the right. A large place, near parks and inexpensive restaurants. Doubles 2150$; also triples, quads, and quints. Breakfast included.

Hotel Suisso Atlântico, Rua da Gloria, 3-19 (tel. 36 17 13), in the Bairro Alto. A nice splurge with modern rooms. Singles with bath 3100$, doubles with bath 4000$.

Camping: Parque Nacional de Turismo e Campismo (tel. 70 44 13). Lisbon's municipal facility. Take bus #14 from Praça de Figueira. Swimming pool, reasonably priced supermarket. Open year-round. **Costa da Caporica,** reached by direct bus from Praça de Espanha (5km, 15 min.). Beautiful beaches and plenty of shade; bungalows available.

od

.isbon probably has the least expensive restaurants of any capital in Western Eue. You can stuff yourself with delicious food, drink gallons of beer or wine, gorge rself on tempting desserts and still pay less than 600$. Hundreds of restaurants located in the **Baixa,** especially along **Rua dos Correiros** and **Rua das Portas Santo Antão** parallel to Avenida da Liberdade. Food here is generally inexpen-, though quality can vary. Lunch is usually served only from noon to 2pm, and ner from 7 to 10pm. Most restaurants close on Sunday, and many close during /.

'o fix your own meals, shop at the **Mercado Ribeira,** outside the Cais de Sodré. en Mon.-Sat. until 2pm.) The market in **Cascais** is held on Wednesday morn-s.

Restaurante Inhaca, Rua das Portas de Santo Antão, 8-10. Tall stacks of crabs and mounds of shrimp in the window; excellent *açorda de mariscos* (seafood stew) 550$. Open Mon.-Sat. 9am-11pm.

Restaurante Gloria, Rua da Gloria, 39. Generous if mundane fare, with entrees starting at 300$. Open daily 8am-11pm.

Cervejaria da Trindade, Rua Nova da Trindade, 20c. Once a convent, this spacious building retains its beautiful tiled walls and garden. *Carne de porco á alentejana* (pork with clams) is a house specialty (1750$)—wash it down with *mista* (mixed light and dark beer). Other entrees 500-800$. Open Thurs.-Tues. 9am-10pm.

Casa de Pasto de Francisco Cardoso, Rua de O Século, 244, off Rua Dom Pedro V. Friendly, intimate. Try the homemade sangria and cornbread. Good entrees 380-650$. Open Mon.-Sat. noon-10pm.

Mestre André, Calçadinha de Sto. Estevão, 6, off Rua dos Remédios. Their deliciously tender *lingua de ternera* (veal tongue with mashed potatoes) will win over even the skeptical (325$). Less daring but still delicious is the *salada roxa,* a fish salad (380$). Open Mon.-Sat. noon-3pm and 7pm-midnight.

Restaurante Macrobiótico, rua Primero de Dezembro, 47, near Rossio. Cafeteria-style health food. Tasty entrees and sandwiches 125-400$. So popular you may want to wait until after peak meal hours. Open Mon.-Fri. 9am-7pm, Sat. 9am-1pm. Well-stocked health food store attached.

Sights

The **Alfama** is, in the words of local author Alexandre Herculano, "A labyrin confused, heaped up, multi-colored, and re-twisted—an anthill of souls." Origina a Visigothic settlement and then a fashionable Saracen enclave, the Alfama beca the noisy popular section of town that it is today after the Christians took ov Eighteenth-century town planners did not dare try to sort out this turbulent br of balconies, archways, terraces, and courtyards. It would be absurd to suggest itinerary for the Alfama, since you're sure to get lost. If you happen to pass look into **San Miguel,** probably the finest of the many churches here; **Largo do S vador, 22,** a noble's sixteenth-century mansion; and the busy **Rua de São Ped** There are reports that the Alfama is prone to crime, so use reasonable caution a consider leaving handbags and cameras elsewhere while you explore.

Bordering on the Alfama is **Miradouro de Santa Luzia,** an intimate square tiles and grapevines with a splendid view of the Alfama and the harbor below. F ther along are the magnificent ruins of **Castelo São Jorge,** the fortress that has do nated the city for 1500 years. The ancient walls—really an endless series of st terraces—enclose lovely gardens, streams, and white peacocks. This is the best pl to watch the sunset. From downtown take bus #37 (Castelo) or trolley # (Graça).

Near the center of town, the Romanesque **Sé** (cathedral) is worth a visit for ambulatory and tombs. **Praça de Comércio,** lined with classical buildings in the b Pombal style, is entered from the north through a massive baroque arch. A w straight up the *praça* leads to the **Rossio,** the city's principal square, embellish with bronze fountains and a statue of Dom Pedro IV atop a giant Corinthian c umn. Just beyond, elegant **Avenida da Liberdade** leads to the formal **Parque uardo VII.**

The **Bairro Alto** is a fascinating area, with art nouveau coffeehouses, hundr of bookshops, and quiet parks and squares. Take the elevator on Rua Santa Ju (15$) for a fabulous view of the city. You'll find yourself near the ruins of the la fourteenth-century **Carmo Church,** now housing an archeological museum. Near is the **Church of São Roque;** the impressive baroque interior is notable mainly its rich Italianate **Chapel of St. John the Baptist,** exuberantly decorated with an thyst, porphyry, and lapis lazuli. Beyond the church, off Rua Dom Pedro, are th of the city's most beautiful parks: **São Pedro de Alcantara Belvedere, Praça do Pr cipe Real,** and the tropical **Jardim Botânico.**

Because the 1755 earthquake destroyed so much of the city, Lisbon's most nowned architecture is concentrated in its outskirts, in the **Belém** section. Fr Praça do Comércio, take tram #15, 16, or 17 and get off at the **Museu Nacio dos Coches** (Coach Museum). (Open Tues.-Sun. 10am-6:30pm. Admission 150 The nearby **Mosteiro dos Jerônimos** (Hieronymite Monastery) is the finest exam anywhere of the Manueline style, with its intricately carved cloisters. Not far fr here, at the edge of the water, stands the **Torre de Belém,** an elegant and impos fortress—Gothic inside, Renaissance outside. Both these places look most beautiful toward sunset, when the stone takes on a rich glow the color of white wine.

There are several outstanding museums in Lisbon. The **Museu Nacional de Arte Antigua,** on Rua das Janelas Verdes, houses Portuguese primitives and paintings by Bosch, Dürer, and Holbein the Elder. To reach the museum, take bus #40 or trolley #19 from Praça da Figueira. (Open Tues.-Wed. and Fri.-Sat. 10am-5pm, Thurs. and Sun. 10am-7pm. Admission 50$; students and everyone on Sun. free.) The **Museu Gulbenkian,** at Praça de Espanha, has an excellent collection, once belonging to an Armenian oil millionaire, which spans from ancient times to the most avant-garde of Portuguese art. (Open Tues.-Fri. and Sun. 10am-5pm, Sat. 10am-7pm. Admission 40$, students 20$.) The **Museu de Arte Popular** (Folk Art Museum), Av. Marginal, Belém, has a fairly interesting collection of traditional Portuguese art. (Open Tues.-Sun. 10am-12:30pm and 2-5pm.) The **Fundação Espiritu Santo Silva,** Largo Portas do Sol, near the Alfama, is a splendid decorative arts museum. (Open Tues.-Sat. 10am-1pm and 2:30-5pm. Obligatory guided tour in Portuguese, French, or English. Free, but tip the guide 50$ per person.)

Entertainment

In Lisbon, cafe life centers around the *fado,* ballads full of nostalgia for the past, recounting tales of lost loves and bygone glory. These songs alternately lull their listeners into silence and rouse them into drunken frenzy. The best *fado* in the city can be heard at **Sr. Vinho,** Meio a Lapa, 18 (tel. 67 26 81), and at **Patio das Cantigas,** Rua São Caetano, 27; both have a minimum of around 1000$. More touristy, but cheaper, is **Parreirinha d'Alfama,** on Largo Charfaris de Dentro (tel. 86 82 09), with an 800$ minimum. Most *fado* starts around 9:30pm, but gets much better about two hours later when the tour groups start to leave, and goes on well into the morning. Taxi drivers are usually a good source of information on the non-touristy *fado* shows.

For a more relaxing atmosphere, try the **Café Brasileira,** Rua Garrett, 120-122, in the Bairro Alto. This coffee shop was frequented by nineteenth-century authors such as Eça de Queirós. (Open until 9pm.) For live music, try **O Berro,** Rua da Esperança, 158 (tel. 66 55 68), near the Parliament. For disco, head for **Rock Rendez-Vous,** Rua da Beneficência, 175 (tel. 77 44 02). Metro: Praça de Espanha. **Memorial,** Rua Gustavo de Matos Sequeira, 42a (tel. 66 88 91), is a gay bar with dancing. (Open Tues.-Sun. 10pm-2am.)

The **Feira Popular** amusement park (Metro: Entre Campos) throngs with Portuguese of all ages every night from May to September until 1am. (Admission 75$.) More transient celebrations include the **International Fair of Lisbon,** held in Alcântara in June.

You can find listings not only for all fairs and concerts, but also for movies, plays, and bullfights, in the newspaper *Sete,* available at kiosks; the tourist office keeps a copy on hand and they'll help you translate. Portuguese theater is performed at the **Teatro Nacional de Maria II,** Praça Pedro IV (tel. 32 27 46). Tickets range from 300 to 2000$, with a 50% discount for students. Opera season (Oct.-June) fills the **Teatro São Carlos,** Rua Serpa Pinto; tickets are 400-2000$. Concerts of all descriptions are held in the **Congress Palace of Estoril,** and the **Gulbenkian Foundation** sponsors classical and jazz concerts.

Near Lisbon

Fifteen kilometers from Rossio station on the Sintra train line (75$) is **Queluz,** an eighteenth-century palace, enclosing delightful gardens and endless rooms. (Open Wed.-Mon. 10am-5pm. Admission 50$.)

Sintra is the fairy-tale city of Portugal, with fanciful palaces and a thick magical forest. After Lord Byron dubbed it "glorious Eden" and sang its charms in his "Childe Harold," Sintra became a must for nineteenth-century English travelers taking the grand tour. The **Palácio Nacional** was built on the foundations of a Moorish castle; its extraordinary conical chimneys are the early fifteenth-century additions of King John I, while the striking ornamentation of the right wing windows is unmistakably Manueline. (Open Thurs.-Tues. 10am-6pm; last ticket sold 4:45pm. Admission 150$, students free.) The town's other principal attractions are clustered more than 500m above the center on **Mount Pena.** Hike, thumb, or taxi (1200$ round-trip) up the 3km of winding access road to the **Palácio da Pena** (admission 150$), a massive palace built over an old Hieronymite monastery. This gorgeous but confusing mish-mash of styles dubbed "Wagnerian fantasy" is surrounded by Pena Park, with its 3000 botanical species from all over the world. Finally, there's the impressive **Castelo** captured from the Moors in the twelfth century by the first Portuguese king, Alfonso Henriques. Sintra's **Turismo** (tel. 293 11 57) is located at Praça da Republica, 19, across from the post office. For an inexpensive meal, try the **Casa de Avó** near the fire station. Sintra, 25km north of Lisbon, is accessible by train from the Rossio station (4 per hr.).

Cabo da Roça, the westernmost point of continental Europe, can be reached by bus from Sintra (20 min.); get off at Cruz da Azoia and walk 3km downhill to the Cabo, or take the direct bus from Cascais. The view from the lighthouse is unforgettable.

The waters around Lisbon have been given over to shipping, and the nearest beaches, **Cascais** and **Estoril,** are 20km away. Despite a big tourist buildup, the two towns are still pleasant with their turn-of-the-century villas and verdant gardens. For *pensões* in Cascais, try **Pensão Le Biarritz,** Av. do Ultramar (tel. 28 22 16). For a special meal go to **Pereira,** Rua Bela Vista, 30. In Estoril stay at **Costa,** Rua de Olivença, 2 (tel. 268 16 99). The **Maryluz,** Rua Maestro Lacerda, 13 (tel. 268 27 40), is a fine second choice.

Ribatejo

The Ribatejo ("Bank of the Tagus") is known throughout Portugal as the primary pastureland for Arabian horses and great black bulls. The *festa brava,* the region's great biannual celebration, occurs during the first week of July and the first week of October in the small community of **Vila Franca de Xira,** a 32-kilometer train ride north of Lisbon. Festivities revolve around countless bullfights and the *corrida,* the running of the bulls, when *campinos* in traditional garb chase the enraged animals down the main street.

The tranquil medieval township of **Tomar,** 90 minutes by train from Lisbon, graces the banks of the winding River Nabão with its sumptuous parks and brightly colored houses. Most of Tomar's numerous architectural monuments date from the period when it served as the successive headquarters of the notorious Knights Templar and the Knights of Christ, both renowned for their exploratory voyages and conquests during Portugal's Age of Discovery. The **Convento de Cristo** dominates the cityscape from its beautifully preserved hilltop fortress. The convent's polygonal **Templars' Rotunda,** modeled after the Holy Sepulchre in Jerusalem, is highlighted by magnificent Manueline windows on the west wall. The adjacent **Claustro dos Felipes** is Portugal's finest Renaissance piece. (Complex open March-Sept. daily 9:30am-12:30pm and 2-6pm; Oct.-Feb. daily 9:30am-12:30pm and 2-5pm.) Life in Tomar revolves around its handsome main square, **Praça Republica,** which is commanded by the fifteenth-century Gothic **Church of São João Baptista** and linked by the town's delightful main street, **Rua Serpa Pinto.**

From Tomar's train or bus station, walk straight down the street in front of the station until you reach Av. do Candido Madureira; Tomar's **Turismo** (tel. 332 37) is two blocks to your left. (Open Mon.-Fri. 9:30am-12:30pm and 2-6pm, Sat.-Sun. 10am-1pm and 3-6pm.) The cheapest rooms in town are at the **Pensão Nuno Alvares,** Av. D. Nuno Alvares Pereira, 3 (tel. 328 73; singles 800$, doubles 1200$). The **Residêncial União,** Rua Serpa Pinto, 94 (tel. 328 31), is comfortable and centrally located. (Singles 1750$, doubles 2500$.)

vora

The town of Évora rises proudly from a parched plain punctuated by tough cork d olive trees. Coveted by a succession of empires, its labyrinthine streets shelter erything from a Roman temple to a Renaissance palace. But above all, Évora ınds as Portugal's foremost medieval showpiece, with beautifully preserved, color- tile facades on ancient whitewashed walls, all tucked away in a tangle of winding eets and topped off by balconies hung with potted plants and caged canaries. If u have time to visit only a few places in Portugal, make Évora one of them.

rientation and Practical Information

Évora, 150km east of Lisbon, is reached five times per day by trains from the pital's Barreiro Station. Three trains each day roll in from Faro. **Praça do Giraldo** Évora's central square.

Tourist Office: Turismo, Praça do Giraldo, 73. English-speaking and helpful. Open April-Oct. daily 9am-7pm; Nov.-March daily 9:30am-6pm.

Post Office: Rua de Olivença. Open Mon.-Fri. 8:30am-6:30pm. **Postal code:** 7001.

Telephones: In the post office, with same hours. **Telephone code:** 066.

Trains: Station is a 1½-km hike (no buses) from Praça do Giraldo: Follow Rua de Dr. Baronha, which becomes Rua da Republica, to the praça.

Buses: Rodoviária Nacional, Rua da República, below São Francisco Church. To Lisbon (5 per day, 3½ hr., 650$) and Faro (1 per day, 900$). Information: (tel. 221 21).

Emergencies: Police or **Ambulance** (tel. 115); Police headquarters at Rua Francisco Soares Lusitania (tel. 220 22).

Medical Assistance: Hospital, Rua do Valasco (tel. 221 33).

Hitchhiking: To Lisbon, go to the edge of Rua Serpa Pinto, at the ancient walls. It's not easy.

ccommodations, Camping, and Food

Finding a room in Évora is rarely a problem. Prices become more flexible during e off-season; try bargaining for 10 to 20% off.

Pousada de Juventude (IYHF), Rua de Corredoura, 32 (tel. 250 43). From Praça do Giraldo, walk down Rua João de Deus, then under the aqueduct onto Rua de Aviz, and take the 2nd right. An excellent hostel, very clean, with a cheerful warden. Members 500$. Breakfast included. Reception open May-Sept. 9-10am and 7-11pm; Oct.-April 9-10am and 5:30-10:30pm.

Pensão Os Manueis, Rua do Raimundo, 35 (tel. 228 61), around the corner from Turismo. Sunny and clean. Singles 1000$; doubles 1500$, with bath 2000$.

Pensão Policarpo, Rua da Freira de Baixo, 16 (tel. 224 24), behind the cathedral in a quiet, picturesque part of town. A former ducal palace. Singles 1300$, with bath 1600$; doubles 2200$, with bath 2400$.

Camping: Campground is on **Estrada das Alcáçovas** (tel. 232 16). Open mid-Jan. to mid-Nov.

Every weekday morning there is a **public market** in the small square behind São ancisco Church and in front of the public gardens.

Restaurante Pastor, Rua 5 de Outobro, 21. Behind the green door you'll find a boisterous tavern and hearty meals for 400-550$.

Restaurant Repas, Praça Primeiro de Maio, 19, near São Francisco Church. Very cheap food in a bar-type atmosphere. Grilled lamb chops, fried potatoes, and rice 460$. Half portions available. Open daily 8am-10pm.

Restaurante Faísca, Rua do Raimundo, 33, around the corner from Turismo, downstairs from Pensão Os Manueis. Tasty entrees from $350. Open Mon.-Sat. 8am-10pm.

Sights and Entertainment

From Praça do Giraldo walk down Rua 5 de Outobro, with its charming til houses, to the colossal twelfth-century **Sé** (cathedral). Inside the entrance to t right are beautiful cloisters. (Open Tues.-Sun. 9am-noon and 2-5pm. Admissi 100$.) From here you can climb the ramparts for an excellent view of the tov Next door is the **Museu d'Évora,** housed in an old bishop's palace, and containi everything from Roman artifacts to sixteenth-century Portuguese paintings. (Op Tues.-Sun. 10am-12:30pm and 2-5pm. Admission 150$, students free.) Across frc the museum is Évora's most famous monument, the second-century Roman **Tem of Diana.** Facing the temple is the **Church of São João Evangelista,** the town's be concealed treasure. The church adjoins the **Cadavel Palace** and is still the priv property of the Cadavel family. Apply to the palace caretaker to view the chur (85$).

The most perverse of Évora's sights is the **Capela de Ossos** (Chapel of Bon in the **Church of São Francisco.** Above the door an inscription reads: "*Nos os que a qui estamos / Pelos vossos esperamos.*" ("Our own bones here awaiting li Your own bones and you to die"—poetic *Let's Go* translation.) The chapel was co structed with the remains of some 5000 monks and nuns as a less than subtle minder of human mortality. (Admission 25$.)

On a more cheerful note, the **Feira de São João** (June 23-July 2) marks the arri of summer in Évora. The climax, with a bullfight, fireworks, and dancing all nig is the **Feast of São Pedro** (June 29). Évora's most popular cafe/beer hangout is t **Portugal,** Rua João de Deus, 55.

Algarve

The Algarve is indeed as wonderful as everyone says it is—though "everyon is exactly the problem here. But despite recent development and increasing touris the Algarve remains attractive. You'll find clear skies throughout the summer, steady breeze to keep temperatures bearable, and 200km of perfect beaches and s cluded coves, with fine gold sand everywhere. Look for untouristed spots outsi resort areas (Lagos, Faro, and Albufeira); try between Lagos and Sagres. It's usua not hard to get to remote beaches, since **Rodoviária Nacional** has local buses ever where. For longer hauls, the train is cheaper and more sensible; it runs inland, co necting major coastal cities. 14 trains per day run from Lagos to Vila Real de San António. Trains run several times per day from Lisbon (5 hr.) to Tunis, then bran west toward Lagos or east toward Vila Real.

Due to the tourist traffic, English has practically become a second language he and *pensões* can be hard to find in the most popular cities. For high season acco modations (July-Aug.), consider making a reservation by writing ahead with a 20 deposit, sending a postcard, or even calling. *Quartos* (rooms to let) abound. If y arrive without accommodations, tourist offices and managers of full *residências* w usually help find a place. Expect to pay 1000-1500$ for a double without priva bath. For longer stays (at least several weeks), apartments with cooking faciliti can always be found; again, a Turismo branch can set you up. Freelance campi is tolerated only in isolated areas where there are no campgrounds.

Food, especially fish, is excellent. Specialties include *sardinhas assadas* (grill sardines), *caldeira* (a chowder of fish and shellfish), *cataplana* (ham, clams, and sa sage), and *lulhinas* (squid), often cooked in its own ink.

For information on festivities, special events, trendy clubs and nudist beach pick up a copy of the *Algarve News* (60$) or *Algarve Magazine* (125$), available tourist offices. While topless sunbathing is the fashion here, bottomless is offensi to the locals, not to mention illegal. **Hospitals** at Faro, Lagos, and Portimão ha 24-hour emergency wards.

To leave the Algarve for Spain, take the train to Vila Real de Santo António, the end of the Portuguese coastal line. From there take the ferry across the River Guadiana to Ayamonte. During the summer, ferries run from 8am to 8pm and cost 60$. You can change money at **Turismo** next to customs after hours until 11pm; escudos are nearly worthless in Spain.

Lagos

Founded by the Romans as Lacobrigia, Lagos rose to prominence under the Moors when it became the center of trade between Portugal and North Africa. Today, Lagos offers all the advantages of a well-developed beach resort yet maintains a measure of local flavor.

The 1755 earthquake destroyed most of Lagos's old sector. Only the **Church of Santo António** and the **Regional Museum** remain. The church's modest facade conceals an interior extraordinary for the richness of its woodwork; the vaulted ceiling is done in the customary false perspective. Adjoining the church, the Regional Museum's collection includes the usual costumes, weapons, and handicrafts. (Both open Tues.-Sun. 9am-12:30pm and 2-5pm. Admission 50$.)

Lagos's main attractions are the splendid nearby beaches surrounded by weathered orange and yellow cliffs. One of the loveliest is **Praia Dona Ana,** whose sculpted cliffs and grottos are featured on half the postcards of the Algarve. Forty-five-minute motorboat cruises visit the grottos (2000$, up to 6 passengers); you might convince your skipper to drop you at a secluded spot and retrieve you a few hours later—but watch the tides. In summer, Lagos's streets are alive until the wee hours of the morning; the **Praça Gil Eanes** and adjoining streets are lined with colorful cafes. The **Café Gil Eanes** on the *praça* is a popular gay spot.

Train and bus stations are both on the eastern edge of town. Follow the main avenue by the water, going west, until you reach Rua Portas de Portugal and bear right. This will take you to Praça Gil Eanes; from here follow the signs to **Turismo** on Largo Marquez de Pombal (tel. 630 31). (Open daily 9am-7pm.) Lagos has a good variety of accommodations, and it's easy to find a room in a private home for 1000-1200$ per person; ask at Turismo or at any *residência* for a referral. **Pensão Caravela,** Rua 25 de Abril, 8 (tel. 633 61), rents pleasant rooms surrounding a central courtyard. Reservations are accepted with a 20% deposit. (Singles 1700$; doubles 2000$, with bath 2200$. Breakfast included.) A bit cheaper and very comfortable is **Os Reis** at Rua Candido dos Reis, 54 (tel. 630 82). (Singles 1200-1500$, doubles 1800-2000$.) For camping visit **Trinidade** (tel. 629 31) at Praia Dona Ana, or peaceful **Camping Valverde** (tel. 692 11) at the beautiful beach 4km west of Praia da Luz. (Both 200$ per person, 200$ per tent.)

Restaurants can be found around the Praça Gil Eanes and along the Rua 25 de Abril. Try **Restaurante Veneza,** Rua 25 de Abril, 73, or **Costinho,** Rua Soeiro la Costa, 6, a tiny family-run place with fresh fish on an open grill outside. **Churrasqueira A Balança,** Soeiro da Costa, 31, has great food by the kilo. **Ao Natural,** Rua Silva Lopes, 29, is a new, Dutch-run, European-staffed veggie dive with a huge selection of fruit drinks and a good salad bar. (All open daily noon-2pm and 7-10pm. Meals 500-800$.)

Sagres

For fewer tourists, lower prices, and more beautiful scenery than you'll find elsewhere in the Algarve, head for the **Sagres Peninsula** in the extreme southwestern corner of Portugal. Here the powerful Atlantic winds bring cooler temperatures, which keep some of the crowds away.

The town of Sagres, surrounded by beaches, remains the peaceful home of the **Fortaleza** (fortress), once the school of navigation built by Prince Henry the Navigator and attended by Vasco da Gama, Magellan, Dias, and Cabral. The view from the cliffside edifice is exquisite. A half-hour film of Henry's story is shown indoors five times per day in summer. (English version at 3:45pm. Admission 5$.)

Beyond the fortress walls, the sea is likely to be the highlight of a stay in Sagres. The two main beaches flanking the fortress are beautiful, though heavily buffeted by Atlantic winds. The most popular spot among backpackers is the small but beautifully sheltered beach around the rocks beyond the main beach on the west side of the fortress. Off the main road between Lagos and Sagres (and served by direct buses) are good beaches at **Salema** and **Burgau.** One kilometer east of the nearby village of Vila do Bispo, the road turns off for the secluded beaches of **Igrina** and **Martinhal.** Buses run between Lagos and Sagres 12 times per day (1 hr., 250$). The best spot to thumb out of Sagres is from in front of the GALP station.

The Fortaleza houses Sagres's **tourist office** (tel. 641 25), little more than a brochure stand. (Officially open daily 10am-6pm.) Also in the fortress is Sagres's renowned **pousada de juventude (IYHF)** (tel. 641 29). The widespread fame of the hostel stems from its thriving social scene. Previous problems with the water supply have apparently been solved. (Members 910$, nonmembers 2910$. Breakfast and dinner included. Lock-out until 7pm. Curfew 11pm. The 3-night maximum is enforced when the place is packed.) Sagres also abounds in rooms to let. (Singles and doubles average 600-1000$, triples average 1500-1700$.) The police tend to interrupt anyone camping freelance on the beach or in the fields.

During the day, the youth hostel crowd loiters at **Café Conchinha.** Upstairs is an excellent restaurant (fresh fried sardines 250$). In the evening, young folk cross the street to lubricate their throats at **A Lanterna,** a German-run bar where Led Zeppelin may soothe the sunburnt soul. The **Last Chance Saloon** is another popular watering hole. Good restaurants include **A Nascimento** and the **Cafe-Atlantico Bar,** located along the main street; both specialize in seafood dishes (400-600$).

Cape Saint Vincent (Cabo de São Vicente)

Once revered as the end of the world, Cape St. Vincent crowns the southwestern tip of Europe. To sail beyond the visible expanse of ocean, it was believed, was to plunge over the edge into nothingness. Looking out over the Cape, the concept becomes immediately clear—the sheer cliff face of the continent drops vertically hundreds of feet into the ocean. A more definite and dramatic end to the world could not be imagined until the fifteenth century. Standing at the tip of the cape, the second most powerful **lighthouse** in Europe projects its beam 60 miles out to sea; ask at the gate for a tour. You can hike the 6km from Sagres, or a taxi will take you for about 800$; ask in the main square in Sagres.

Halfway to the cape lies the beautiful, well-sheltered beach of **Beliche.** But the best-kept secret of the Algarve remains the enormous wind-blown crescent of sand and freelance campground at **Carrapateira,** 16km to the north. To get there, take the road (turn-off at Vila do Bispo) or the bus for Aljezur to the small village of Carrapateira, and then proceed a kilometer down the small dirt road to the coast. At the top of the road, marking the turn-off, is the **Restaurante Corbrita,** where you can indulge in a generous feast of freshly caught fish grilled on an open-air barbecue (300-600$, usually about 5:30pm).

Faro

The Algarve's capital and largest city, Faro is the starting point for many northern Europeans' holidays in the sun. Yet tourists have not overrun Faro; it's a large city, and its marvelous beach, floating on an islet outside the town, helps the jaded forget their lot. To reach the beach, take bus #16 from the stop in front of **Turismo,**

Rua da Misericórdia, 8-12 (tel. 254 04). (Open July-Aug. daily 9am-10pm; Sept.-June daily 9am-7pm.)

For lodgings, try **Residência Pinto,** Rua Primeiro de Maio, 27 (tel. 228 20), just up from the Faro Hotel. (Singles 1200$, doubles 1500$. Showers included.) Cheaper, but equally pleasant is the **Casa Emilia,** Rua Reitor Teixeira Guedes, 21 (tel. 233 52), a 5-minute walk up the Rua de San Antonio and then to your left. (Singles 1000$, doubles 1450$.) A good roast chicken dinner goes for 325$ (take-out 650$ per kilo) at the **Fim do Mundo Restaurant,** Rua Vasco da Gama, 53, off Praça Ferreira de Almeida. **Cozinherio,** Rua Filipe Alistao, 30, is a low-key establishment dishing out generous portions of good food for 300-500$.

There is an **American Express** representative office at Rua Conselheiro Bivar, 36 (tel. 251 25); they sell traveler's checks and hold mail, but cannot accept wired money. (Open Mon.-Fri. 9am-12:30pm and 2-6pm.)

Northern Portugal

Nazaré

In spite of the tourists that flock here every summer, **Nazaré** has maintained a traditional way of life based on the sea: When the crowds leave the beach at dusk, the locals pull in their nets and wash and prepare sardines on large screens. The local **Turismo** is at Rua de Mouzinho de Albuquerque, 72 (tel. 461 20). (Open July-Sept. daily 9am-12:30pm and 2-5pm; Oct.-June daily 9am-12:30pm and 2-5:30pm.) From the bus station take a right onto the avenue that fronts the beach, then right again onto Praça Souza Oliveira and keep right as the street turns uphill. For rooms try the **Pensão Nazarense,** Rua de Mouzinho de Albuquerque, 48 (tel. 461 88), near the tourist office. (Singles 800$, doubles 1500$. Breakfast included.) There is a pleasant **campground** 3km uphill from town. You can buy a whole barbecued chicken for 300 to 400$ beside the bus station, or sit down for sardines (with salad and potatoes, 260$) at tiny **Casa Santos,** Rua Dr. José Maria Carvalho, Jr., 19.

Five kilometers south of Nazaré is one of the most beautiful youth hostels anywhere. On a hill above **Alfeizerão,** the **IYHF pousada de juventude** (tel. 981 06) is clean and rustic, with polished floors, acres of gardens, and exceedingly friendly managers. The hostel is accessible from São Martinho (in turn accessible from Nazaré) by bus; get off at Alfeizerão and walk up the path for about 25 minutes. (500$. Breakfast included; other meals 350$.)

Near Nazaré

The stately monasteries in **Alcobaça** and **Batalha** are not to be missed. The **Monastery of Santa Maria,** in Alcobaça, contains the exquisitely sculpted tombs of Inês de Castro and Dom Pedro, in addition to vast and cavernous living quarters, kitchens, and chapter-houses. (Complex open April-Sept. Tues.-Sun. 9am-7pm; Oct.-March Tues.-Sun. 9am-5pm. Admission 150$, students free.) Outside Alcobaça, **Museu do Vinho** will teach you everything you ever wanted to know about the history, production, and consumption of Portuguese wine. (Open Mon.-Fri. 9:30am-12:30pm and 2-5:30pm.) Batalha's **Monastery of Santa Maria da Victória** is full of soaring Gothic arches and ornate Manueline tracery. Frequent buses connect Alcobaça and Batalha with Peniche and Nazaré.

Obidos, also connected to the coast by frequent buses, remains a tiny medieval stronghold surrounded by high walls. The only inexpensive lodgings are in private rooms (about 1000$ per person). **Turismo,** Rua Direita (tel. 952 31) can help. (Open in summer daily 9:30am-8pm; in winter 9:30am-6pm.)

Figueira da Foz and Aveiro

Though less dazzling in its northern reaches, the Costa de Prata extends beyond Nazaré as far as Espinho. **Figueira da Foz** is a brilliant beach with town attached. **Turismo** is on Av. 25 de Abril (tel. 226 10). (Open in summer daily 9am-midnight; in winter daily 9am-7pm.) Another branch is in nearby Buarcos (tel. 250 19). The clean beach, more than 3km long and 500m wide, is a 20-minute hike from the train station, or you can take the bus marked *"Caminho do Ferro-Buarcos"* (30$). There's plenty of space to unroll your sleeping bag, but if you prefer to keep the sand out of your belongings, you'll probably opt for the *pensões* in town (around 1000$ per person). Cheap places are concentrated along Rua Bernardo Lopes; the best is **Pensão Peninsular** at #35 (tel. 223 20). The **Rancho,** Rua Miguel Bombarda, 40, offers delicious main dishes in the 250 to 400$ range. If you'd like to eat fish with those who caught them, visit inexpensive **Casa Santos** on Rua do Cotovelo, off Praça 8 de Maio. A notch up is **Restaurante O Escondidinho,** Rua Dinis, 62, serving both Portuguese and Goanese Indian dishes for 380 to 560$. (Open daily 11:30am-3pm and 6pm-midnight.)

Aveiro, 62km farther north, is not quite the Venice of Portugal, as its residents boast, but it does have canals and a prosperous fishing industry. Bar and cafe crawling in Aveiro is almost as popular as the beaches near **San Jacinto** and the northern reaches of Aveiro's lagoon. Official **camping** is 8km away in the **Parque Nacional das Dunas de São Jacinto,** an area of sand dunes and scrub pine accessible by bus-and-ferry combination through **Barra** from a stop in front of **Turismo** (Turismo has schedules). Barra's best (and only) pension, the **Jardim** (tel. 36 17 45), rents rooms for about 1000$ per person. Outside of Aveiro, your best budget bet is free-lance camping on the beaches.

Coimbra

Coimbra is a town of steep, tiered streets winding above the River Mondego. Founded in 1290 (and subsequently transferred for several centuries back and forth between Coimbra and Lisbon), the university here has long been Portugal's foremost center of learning. For two weeks at the end of May, Coimbra also becomes the country's biggest party as the **Student Festival** erupts with concerts, folk dancing, and street music. During the **Fiestas da Rainha Santa** (the first week of July in even-numbered years), the festooned streets echo with the efforts of all types of choral groups.

In the center of town is the **Santa Cruz Monastery,** founded in 1131 but not finished until the sixteenth century; the Renaissance pulpit (1522) is one of the great masterpieces of Portuguese sculpture. Climb the stairs under the Moorish **Arco de Almedina** into the upper district of the city and the **Old University,** with its library, museum, and chapel. The gem of the complex is the **library,** built by D. João IV between 1717 and 1728 in a sort of Chinese baroque. The neighboring **Machado de Castro Museum** is justly famous for its superb Gothic sculptures and seventeenth-century polychrome figures. (Open Tues.-Sun. 10am-12:30pm and 2-4:40pm. Admission 150$, students free.)

Coimbra's **Turismo** (tel. (039) 255 76) is situated two blocks east of the "A" station on the triangular Largo da Portagem—walk along Av. Emidio Navarro, keeping the River Mondego on your right. (Open Mon.-Fri. 9am-7pm, Sun.-Sat. 9am-12:30pm and 2-5:30pm.) Cheap but sleazy *pensões* can be found on Rua da Sota, near Coimbra "A" station. A better idea is to cross Largo da Portagem onto Av. Navarro, overlooking the river, where **Residência Parque** at #42 (tel. 292 02), **Pensão Universal,** and **Pensão Jardim** offer neat singles and doubles for 1000$ and 1600$, respectively.

A wonderful **open-air market** is held off Rua Olimpio Nicolau Rui Fernando (Mon.-Sat. 8am-3pm). Try the area around the station for inexpensive restaurants, as well as the neighborhood west of Praça 8 de Maio and Largo da Portagem. Near the university on Praça da Republica are many student haunts with cheap food. Try **Democrática,** on Travessa da Rua Nova, off Rua da Sofia, a popular place where meals cost 500$ or less. After dinner, the pub **Diligéncia,** down the street, attracts Coimbra's most unrestrained *fado* singers. Across the river, in a red building at Av. João Regra, 32, is **O Alfredo,** a popular place serving big portions of outstanding regional dishes; try *arroz de lamprea* (rice with lamprey). (Entrees 600-800$.)

Coimbra is on the main coastal rail line north from Lisbon, and is a junction point for the rail line to Salamanca. Get off at centrally located Coimbra "A."

Oporto (Porto)

Portugal's second-largest city, Oporto is known not for its beauty, but for the sweet taste of its wine. The city was first extensively developed by the British during the War of the Spanish Succession: When England and Portugal allied against Spain and France, Whig patriots and profiteers promoted the drinking of Port instead of French claret. The 80-odd Port houses on the southern bank of the River Douro still play a major role in the city's economy.

Orientation and Practical Information

Situated on a dramatic gorge cut by the River Douro, Oporto lies 6km from the sea, on the main rail line up from Lisbon and down from Valença do Minho. An east-west line brings in travelers from Salamanca and other points in Spain.

The hub of Oporto is **Avenida dos Aliados,** a wide avenue bordered to the north by **Praça General H. Delgado** and to the south by **Praça da Liberdade.** But the most alluring part of town is the **Ribeira** (river district), where three of Europe's most graceful bridges span the gorge.

Tourist Office: Turismo, Rua dos Fenianos, 25 (tel. 31 27 40), 4 blocks from São Bento Station, beside City Hall. Open Mon.-Fri. 9am-7pm, Sat. 9am-4pm, Sun. 10am-1pm.

American Express: Star Travel Service, Av. dos Aliados, 210 (tel. 236 89). Holds mail. All financial services. Open Mon.-Fri. 9am-12:30pm and 2-6pm.

Currency Exchange: Banco Borges & Irmão, in the Brasília shopping center, keeps late hours: Mon.-Fri. 3-8pm. Take bus #2 from Praça da Liberdade. Hotels are fine for pesetas-to-escudos exchanges, but have poor rates for other currencies.

Post Office: Praça General H. Delgado, across from Turismo. Open for stamps Mon.-Fri. 9am-7pm; Poste Restante daily 8am-10pm. **Postal code:** 4000.

Telephones: Praça da Liberdade, 62. Open daily 8am-11:30pm. Also at the post office. Open daily 8am-11:30pm. **Telephone code:** 02.

Trains: São Bento Station (tel. 227 22), for routes north and inland. **Campanhã Station** (tel. 56 41 41), for southern and international routes. To Coimba (14 per day, 440$) and Lisbon (10 per day, 920$).

Buses: Rodoviária Nacional. For destinations to the south, Rua de Alexandre Herculano, 366 (tel. 269 54). To travel north, Praça D. Filipa de Lencastre, 1 block west of Av. dos Aliados.

Emergencies: Police or **Ambulance** (tel. 115).

Medical Assistance: Hospital de Santo António, Rua Prof. Vicente José de Carvalho (tel. 252 41).

Consulates: U.S., Rua Júlio Dinis, 826 (tel. 31 62 00). **U.K.,** Av. de Boavista, 3072 (tel. 68 47 89). There are no Australian or New Zealand consulates in Oporto, but Spanish multiple-entry visas allow those from Down Under to cross the border any number of times.

Bookstore: Livraría Diario de Notícias, Rua Sá da Bandeira, 5, near São Bento Station, has the best selection of English books. Open Mon.-Fri. 9am-12:30pm and 2:30-7pm, Sat. 9am-1pm; closed Sat. in summer.

Laundry: Penguin, in the Brasília shopping center. Open Mon.-Sat. 10am-midnight.

Accommodations and Camping

Most of the city's *pensões* are situated west of Avenida dos Aliados. Though plentiful, they fill by late afternoon in July and August.

Pousada de Juventude do Porto (IYHF), Rua Rodrigues Lobo, 95 (tel. 655 35). Take bus #3, 19 or 20 from Praça da Liberdade about 2km to Rua Júlio Dinis. This hostel draws rave reviews but is very crowded in the summer. 650$ per person. Breakfast included. Lockout 10am-6pm. Curfew 11pm.

Residencial Porto Rico, Rua do Almada, 237 (tel. 31 87 85). Friendly landlady and cramped, if cheap, rooms. Singles 1000$, doubles 2000$, with bath 2500$.

Residência Novo Mundo, Rua Conde de Vizela, 92 (tel. 254 03), off Rua Clérigos. Somewhat dark, but acceptable. Doubles 1200-1600$.

Pensão Monumental, Av. dos Aliados, 151 (tel. 239 64), smack in the middle of town. Roomy singles 1400$, doubles 1800$. Breakfast included.

Pensão dos Aliados, Rua Elísio de Melo, 27 (tel. 248 53), just west of Av. dos Aliados. Quite luxurious. Singles 1300$, doubles 1700$. Doubles with bath 2600$. Breakfast included.

Camping: Parque de Prelada (tel. 626 16), 5km from the beach. Take bus #6 from Praça da Liberdade. 170$ per person, 90$ per tent. Open year-round.

Food

The most colorful and inexpensive restaurants are along the river on Cais de Ribeira and adjacent Rua de Cima do Muro, atop a wall.

Luar Regional, Rua da Bainharia, 4. Descend into a misty cellar for the most typical regional dishes, including *tripas.* Entrees 280-350$.

Boa Nova, Muro dos Bacalhoeiros, 115. Still pours wine from huge, wooden barrels. Entrées 330-450$.

Café Mira-Douro, Rua de Cima do Muro, 2, by the bridge. Entrees 400-500$, served on an outdoor terrace. Open Thurs.-Tues. 8am-2am.

Brasileira, Rua do Bonjardim, 18. A bit more expensive; enjoy traditional coffee and pastry or sandwiches amid a mixture of art deco and turn-of-the-century Edwardian. Very popular. Open daily 7am-10pm.

Sights

Just south of São Bento Station rises Oporto's great **Sé** (Cathedral), a ponderous, fortified Romanesque structure whose heavy granite foundations, thick walls, and tiny windows enclose a gloomy interior. (Open daily 9am-12:30pm and 3-6pm.) West of the cathedral, at the intersection of Rua da Bolsa and Rua do Comércio do Porto, stands the **Bolsa** (Stock Exchange), built in the early nineteenth century (follow signs from Rua Mouzinho da Silveira). A tour of the interior is worthwhile, if only to view the extraordinary pseudo-Moorish hall modeled after Granada's Alhambra. (Open Mon.-Fri. 9am-noon and 2:30-5pm.) South of the Bolsa, the **Ribeira** (esplanade) stretches along the river, skirted by a marvelous quay filled with shops and restaurants. Nearby, have a look into the **Church of São Francisco,** which shelters one of the most elaborate gilded wood interiors in all Portugal. Take tram #1 from here for further views of the Ribeira and river; it goes all the way to **Foz do Douro,** Oporto's beach community. Oporto's most characteristic monument, the ornate **Torre dos Clérigos,** offers a panorama of the city from atop its 240 steps. (Open Mon.-Fri. 7:30-9:30am, 10:30am-noon and 3:30-8pm, Sun. 10:30am-3pm and 8:30-10:30pm. Admission 25$.)

No visit to Oporto would be complete without a stop at some of the many **bodegas** (wine lodges) where port is stored and bottled. Most of the lodges are across the bridge from the Ribeira, in **Vila Nova da Gaia.** Of the 15 lodges offering free tours and sampling, the major ones, such as **Cintra, Vasconcellos** and **Sandeman** have the most dependable hours (normally, daily 10am-5pm, though Sandeman (the best) is closed Sat.-Sun.).

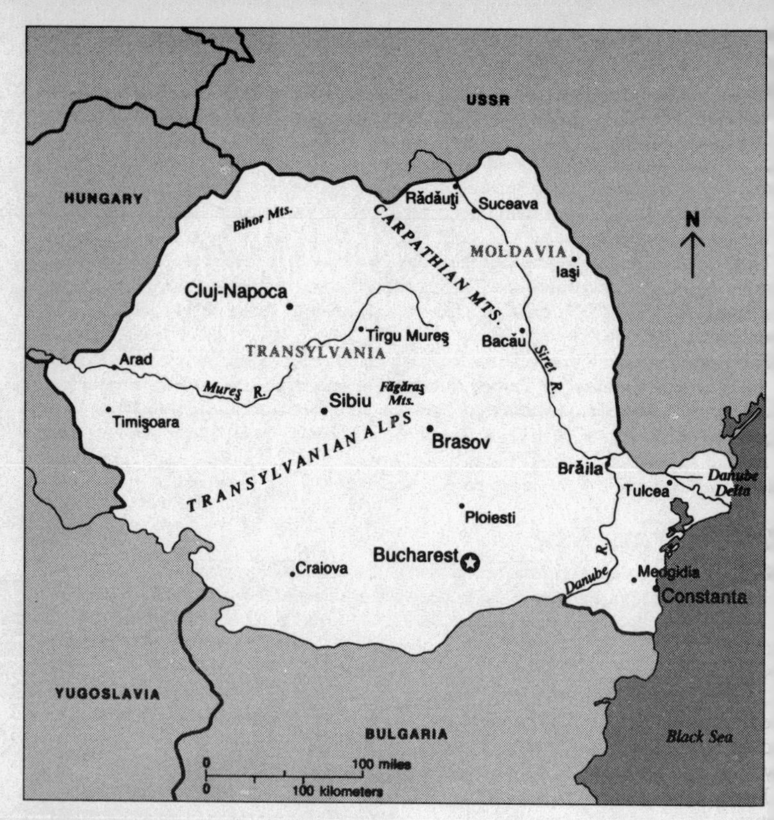

ROMANIA

US$1 = 10.08 lei **10 lei = US$0.99**
UK£1 = 16.43 lei **10 lei = UK£0.61**

More than any other country in Eastern Europe, Romania gives you the sensation of being in a different world. Perhaps no other country in Europe offers such a feel for life as the locals live it. Your daily experiences will reflect the challenges that constantly confront Romanians—getting even the simplest food is a time-consuming chore. Don't expect spectacular sights here, and prepare yourself to do without many of the amenities that you take absolutely for granted.

Once the easternmost province of the Roman Empire, Romania has been a thorn in the side of every imperial power in the region, fighting bitterly for centuries against both Hapsburg and Turk. In 1859, the medieval republics of Transylvania, Wallachia, and Moldavia united to form Romania. The communist revolution took place at the end of World War II. Today, Romania is the most independent partner in the Warsaw Pact. Unlike other areas of Eastern Europe, it is free of a Soviet Army presence, openly criticizes the Soviet presence in Afghanistan, and is the only Warsaw Pact country that participated in the 1984 Olympics.

Romania today is the poorest nation in Europe; a situation that results from a self-imposed austerity. Life was easier in the 1970s, but Romania incurred a large foreign debt, which the government resolved to abolish during the 1980s—since then, it is estimated, there has been a 20-30% drop in living standards. Nearly everyıg produced is exported; what you see are the leftovers. During the first half of decade, Romania halved its foreign debt, and the hard times appeared to be ling. But radioactive contamination from Chernobyl slowed the export of pro-e in 1986-87, and things remain shaky at best. Compounding Romania's eco-nic woes is an autocratic government; Premier Nicolae Ceauşescu was less recep- to Soviet talk of reform than any other Warsaw Pact leader, and his wife-and-dent-successor Elena is seen to hold the same opinions, only more strongly.

Though Romania promotes tourism, the government reserves its tender loving e for wealthy package tourists. Desperate for foreign currencies, the government devalued them 100%, making prices comparable to those in Switzerland and ndinavia.

For a sense of the Romanian culture, past and present, read the relaxed account Ian Matley, *Romania: A Profile.* Among the nation's great authors is novelist . Caragiale; his *Sketches and Stories* is an excellent anthology, translated into glish by E.D. Tappe. Works of the twentieth-century poet Tudor Arghezi are nslated by Michael Impey. Finally, for a taste of the socialist realist school as ced in Romania, try the more recent works of Mihael Sadoveanu.

anning Your Trip

If entering by train, you must get a visa in advance. To apply to the Romanian bassy in your home country's capital city, gather the following package of materi- together: (1) your passport; (2) a letter explaining your reasons for going to Ro-nia and the duration of your stay; (3) a stamped, self-addressed envelope so your ssport can be returned to you; (4) US$13. The visa will normally be issued in to 20 days; for US$5 there is a rush service that usually requires only two to days. Visas can be obtained much more quickly in Eastern Europe (US$20), d can be issued on the spot in Yugoslavia. You can obtain a visa at the border you enter by plane, car, or tour bus, but the process can take hours.

The required currency exchange is US$10 for each day that your visa is valid. u will have no trouble spending this amount—unless you camp and live on bread d water. It's a good idea to get a visa for several days longer than you plan to y, as visa extensions are a hassle. To transit the country, you must exchange $20. International trains are scheduled such that your stay will straddle mid-ht.

If you enter from Yugoslavia, watch your luggage to make sure that it is not used the many Yugoslavians who smuggle Romanian money into the country. The in will be searched centimeter by centimeter, although Westerners' bags generally only a cursory poke. Books on Romania, language phrasebooks, and Romanian-glish dictionaries may be confiscated.

Most toiletry articles are practically unavailable. Bring twice as much toilet paper you think you will need, as the food may give you diarrhea.

ansportation

Hitchhiking (*autostop*) is the best way to travel unless you have a car or InterRail ss. Drivers expect a payment equivalent to 50-100% of the bus fare for the jour-y. Many drivers refuse payment from Westerners, but no one holds out long ainst Kent cigarettes or other treasures. On major roads women can often get ide in three to ten minutes; poorer rural regions are not as good, but still decent. manian women do hitch alone, but a single woman is advised to take the usual cautions. A wave of the hand, rather than a thumb, is the recognized sign.

Buying train tickets is the straw that can break the traveler's back; you can buy kets only two hours before departure—not always enough time to get through crushing lines. Tickets are sold in advance at the Agence de Voyage, C.F.R., ually located in the center of town. This means mobs of vacationing Romanians hour-plus lines. You must wait first in a typically enormous information line to find out at which ticket window to line up or to ask any questions. A copy of Thomas Cook timetable can save you hours of agony.

There are three types of trains; *Rapid, accelerat,* and *personal. Rapid* and *accel* levy a small surcharge, but are worth it: A 3½-hour ride by *rapid* train can t 13 hours by *personal* train.

Buying international tickets is especially troublesome; try to get through or ret tickets before you enter the country. Western travelers wanting an internatic ticket must go first to the information line and request a form saying that they w a ticket for a certain train on a certain day. Then they must go to a special casl and pay in Western currency before getting in a similarly long ticket line. The an 80% markup on tickets to the West (including Yugoslavia); it's cheaper faster to buy a domestic ticket to the last stop on the border, and then simply rem on the train. After you cross the frontier, the new conductor will often gladly you another ticket for whatever currency you have. Budapest-bound trains may Romania through either Arad or Oradea; you'll need to specify which when buy a ticket.

Use the extensive local bus system only when trains are not available. Buses cheaper than trains, but usually packed. Look for the signs for *autogară* (bus stati in each town. Before venturing off, it's wise to ask for a copy of the bus sched (*"Aşi dorii mersul autobuzelor, vă rog"*).

Practical Information

ONT is the Romanian national tourist bureau, with offices throughout the co try. Their information about the price and availabilty of cheap accommodati is not always reliable. ONT offices in expensive hotels are often more useful t the main offices. **BTT,** the youth travel agency, is designed for organized gro and will be utterly befuddled by your presence. Their youth hotels cost 300 lei Westerners. If you want to try your luck in getting an IUS card (25% disco on international rail tickets), bring an Eastern European friend and cross your gers.

The black market in Romania is enticing, especially in light of the high pri However, the small savings are probably not worth the risk. "Economic crim are the one thing for which Westerners will do time in jail—from several we to several years depending on the amounts involved and the nature of the trans tion. Money changed illegally cannot always be used for accommodations, never for international transportation. If you decide to take the risk, change a sn amount (bring US$10 bills) and with a different person each time, so that the offe is less grave if you are caught. The going rate is reportedly 600% of the offi rate. About the only place in which you will be approached is Bucharest.

Waiting is a way of life in Romania. Especially in Bucharest, expect long li in which short tempers are often provoked to violence. You might receive noth more than an irate and incomprehensible tirade from the official behind the wind (or the salesperson behind the counter), accompanied by screams and shouts fr people behind you. To avoid this problem, try to find a person in the line who spe some English. If necessary, allow the person behind you to go ahead while you c lect your wits. Above all, do not relinquish your place in line. In buying goods services, remember that prices for Westerners are sometimes different than pri for Romanians.

Gifts for everyone you deal with can make your travels somewhat less rou Some call it bribery, but it's more akin to a tip for quicker service in a country wh waiting is the norm. **Kent cigarettes** are the best; in Romania a pack sells for m than 50 lei and cars will emergency brake for them. Showing a pack of Kents n help you get service in a restaurant or a hotel room.

The Romanian language is a Romance language; travelers familiar with Fren Italian, Spanish, or Portuguese can usually decipher public signs. Spoken Roman has been considerably more influenced by the surrounding Balkan languages, a is a trial for the average visitor. In Transylvania, German and Hungarian are wid

en. Throughout the country, French is the second language for the older gener-
ı, and English for younger people. If you use Russian, address the person in
lish first.
heft is a problem. Keep doors locked, and watch your baggage at all times.
nt your change and politely request an explanation of the bill if things seem
ng. Traveling for women is fairly hassle-free. If something does happen, a calm
and firm voice is usually sufficient to end any harassment.
eople work full days Monday through Friday, shorter hours on Saturday and
lay. National holidays are New Year's Day (Jan. 1), May Day (May 1), and
Day of Liberation from Fascism (Aug. 23). The day following each of these
so a holiday. Romania is in the same time zone as Bulgaria and one hour ahead
'ugoslavia and Hungary.

commodations

ring either a tent or a pile of money. Campgrounds cost 40 to 50 lei per person.
galows are a relatively cheap alternative (about 145 lei), but are often full in
ummer. One solution is to take an overnight train, but these always incur the
of theft. Get the tourist map called *Popasuri Turistice* (in French), which lists
campgrounds. Sites are crowded, and bathrooms may be filthy. Camping cou-
and hotel coupons are no longer honored, despite signs to the contrary.
ne price of youth hotels has quadrupled in recent years to 300 lei. Hotels actu-
cost less and are more likely to have space for Westerners. Hotel prices start
:0 lei for a single, and 340 lei for a double. Doubling up is difficult because very
people travel alone in Romania. You won't find rooms for rent in private homes;
llegal to stay in the home of a Romanian citizen unless he or she is a first cousin
loser.
you decide to bypass ONT and find your own hotel room, you must pay in
f you book the room through ONT, you must pay in Western currency.

od

e U.S. Department of State for Eastern Europe and Yugoslavia has stated
t food currently available in Romania is not in any way contaminated by
lout from the 1986 Chernobyl disaster.

much for the good news—finding food is what makes travel in Romania so
usting. In some cities you will wait on line (sometimes for hours) virtually every
you want a drink or a bite to eat. Lines are worst in Bucharest. Even after
nat trouble, what you get may make you ill. Bring non-perishable food with
Your best strategy is to buy food anytime you see a shop without a mile-long
Unless you can boil milk, stay away from it. Ready-to-eat cheese is not avail-
and most meat is suspect. In outdoor markets you can buy root vegetables
about three types of fruit (often half-spoiled). Bread is often stale; pretzel sticks,
etimes found in bread stores and kiosks, are a better bet. People on a sugar-only
will be delighted; desserts are available everywhere in *cofetărie* for about 4 lei
e.
ne only drink widely available is beer, and "soda" that tastes like medicine (3
Fruit juice is not available in any form. It's a good idea to carry a water bottle.
e are taps in train stations and spaced regularly along major roads. Wines of
Murfatlar region, near the Black Sea, are world-famous, but always ask the price
lvance; a bottle can cost 70 lei (about the cost of food for 2), even in a cheap
urant. A good, cheap local drink is *ţuică* (plum brandy), traditionally taken
ght up.
prepared to spend up to two hours for every restaurant meal. You *may* be
to speed things up by passing the waiter some money (try 5 lei) or laying a
of Kent cigarettes in plain sight. Many restaurants serve only one choice a
–a full meal consisting of a meat, potato, vegetable or rice, and bread (about

5 lei). Only expensive restaurants have menus, provide napkins, and serve wa Restaurants are generally open from 7am to 9pm.

Take heart—the Romanians are healthy and well-nourished. The food is th It just requires perseverance to get it.

Bucharest (Bucureşti)

Because of the French influence during the 1920s and 1930s, Bucharest has b called "the Paris of the East." It does have a modest copy of the Arc de Tri phe—but there the resemblance ends. The queues which permeate the country come unbearable here. Don't make Bucharest your only stop in Romania, or will come away with nothing but memories of grey walls, dusty boulevards, endless lines.

Orientation and Practical Information

Bucharest is situated in southeastern Romania, 70km north of the Danube the Bulgarian border. Direct trains connect the city with Istanbul, Belgrade, all East European capitals.

Armed with a city map from the train station, head east on **Calea Griviţei** take a right onto **Calea Victoriei,** which leads to the sights and tourist spots if turn right. A short walk on Strada Biserica Amzei, the continuation of Griv brings you to **Bulevardul Magheru** (which becomes Bd. Bălcescu and then 1848), the main artery in Bucharest. Tram #87 from the station to Piaţa Rom will take you to Bd. Magheru.

Tourist Offices: ONT has two offices. The cantankerous agent in the office at the Gara de Nord may quote false prices to steer you into a hotel, and will do little to help you until you've booked a hotel room. For more reliable help, go to the main office, Bd. Magheru 7 (tel. 14 51 60). Maps, information on sights and scheduled events in Bucharest, and on accommodations and camping throughout the country. Open Mon.-Sat. 7:30am-9:30pm, Sun. 7:30am-3pm, but tourist information available only Mon.-Fri. 8am-4pm. When these offices are closed, try one of the fancy hotels near the train station for maps.

Budget Travel: BTT, Str. Oneşti 4-6 (tel. 14 05 66), at the 2nd traffic light to the right of ONT. Intended for groups, but if you are very lucky you may be able to get an IUS card Open Mon.-Fri. 8am-5pm, Sat. 8am-1:30pm.

American Express: At the Bd. Magheru ONT office. Only if you've lost checks; no checks sold, no wired money accepted (mail arriving in 1987 was postmarked 1985!).

Currency Exchange: Any ONT office.

Post Office: Str. Matei Millo, off Calea Victoriei. Open daily 7am-midnight. Jam-packed daily 9am-7pm. Poste Restante here is unreliable. **Postal code:** 70154.

Telephones: International calls may be made from Calea Victoriei 37, near the theaters. No collect calls. Pay phones, when working, take a 1 lei coin and lots of perseverance.

Flights: Otopeni Airport (tel. 33 31 37), 16km away, handles international traffic. **Băneasa Airport** for domestic flights. The TAROM bus from Otopeni will let you off near the Hotel Intercontinental on Bd. Magheru. Buses to Otopeni leave from the TAROM office every 1 2 hr. (15 lei). Buy tickets on bus. Băneasa is connected with Piaţa Romană by trams #131 and 331. Airplane tickets must be bought at the **TAROM** office, Str. Brezoianu 10, 2nd floor (tel. 33 00 33), south of Bd. Gheorgiu-Dej, between Calea Victoriei and Cişmigiu Park. Open Mon.-Sat. 7am-7pm, Sun. 8am-1pm.

Trains: Gara de Nord (tel. 052) is the principal station; it's unlikely that you'll have to visit **Basarab, Băneasa,** or **Obor.** Domestic tickets can be purchased in advance at the **Agence de Voyage, CFR,** Str. Brezoianu 10, 1st floor (tel. 13 26 44), 2 blocks south of Bd. Gheorgiu-Dej and between Calea Victoriei and Cişmigiu Park. Use the TAROM entrance. No domestic information in English. Expect a bone-crushing 1- to 3-hr. wait, unless you show up at 7am Open Mon.-Sat. 7am-8pm, Sun. 7am-1pm. International tickets must be purchased here (takes ½-2 hr.). Currency desk (and sale of international tickets) closed 1-2pm. You may be inspired to walk upstairs to the TAROM office, or to give up and hitchhike.

Buses: Three stations serve Bucharest. **Filaret,** Piaţa Gării Filaret 1 (tel. 41 06 92), and **Rahova,** Şos. Alexandriei 164 (tel. 80 47 95), are both in the southern suburbs, while **Băneasa,** Str. I. Ionesiu de la Brad 5 (tel. 79 56 45), is well to the north. All are madhouses.

Ferries: Navrom, Bd. Dinicu Golescu 38 (tel. 16 74 54), near the train station, runs boats on the Danube.

Public Transportation: Travel in the city is provided by a network of buses (3.50 lei), trolley buses (3 lei), and trams (2 lei). Tickets are available at kiosks near most stops. All lines are clearly marked on the ONT map. Buses are extremely packed on busy routes—people literally hang out the doors. If you do get on, hold on to your valuables. Two lines of the new **Metro** are in operation (use 1 lei coins at the entrance). The entire system shuts down around 11:30pm.

Taxis: 6 lei for flag drop plus 9 lei per km.

Emergencies: Police (tel. 055 or 061), but better to call the U.S. Embassy, 24 hours.

Medical Assistance: Clinica Batiştei, Tudor Arghezi 28, behind the Hotel Intercontinental, is the only hospital authorized to treat foreigners.

Pharmacies: Those at Bd. Magheru 18 (tel. 14 61 16), and in the train station are open 24 hours.

Embassies: U.S., Tudor Arghezi 7-9 (tel. 12 40 40), 1 block behind Hotel Intercontinental. Claims not to hold mail, but you can try your luck; also register yourself at the consulate next door, Str. Snagov 25 (tel. 11 45 93). Open Mon.-Fri. 8am-5pm. **Canada,** Nicolae Iorga 36 (tel. 50 63 30), near Piaţa Romană. Open Mon.-Fri. 9am-5pm. **U.K.,** Str. Jules Michelet 24 (tel. 11 16 34). Open Mon.-Thurs. 8:30am-5pm, Fri. 8am-1pm. **New Zealand,** 1010 Viena, Lugeck 1 (tel. 52 66 36). Citizens of **Australia** should contact the embassy in Beograd, Yugoslavia or the British Embassy. **Bulgaria,** Str. Rabat 5 (tel. 33 21 50). Open Mon.-Fri. 8:30am-12:30pm and 2-5pm. 10-day wait for visa. **Czechoslovakia,** Str. Ion Ghica 11. Visas at Str. M. Eminescu 124, bloc A, apt. 12, 5th floor (tel. 11 92 06). Open Mon.-Fri. 7:45am-4:30pm. **Hungary,** Str. Alexandru Sahia 63 (tel. 15 82 73). Open Mon.-Thurs. 8am-4:30pm, Fri. 8am-3:30pm. The main ONT office can process a Hungarian visa for you in 1 day for US$4.

Hitchhiking: The street map lists all tram lines; to head north, take any tram to either airport. For the Black Sea and Constanţa, take tram #13 east from Piaţa Unirii. For Giurgiu and Bulgaria, take tram #12 from Piaţa Unirii. For Piteşti and western Romania, take tram #13 west from Piaţa Unirii.

Accommodations and Camping

Ask first at the main ONT office about **Camping Băneasa,** near the airport of the same name. ONT officials may be reluctant to send you there, just as they may be reluctant to book you a cheaper hotel room; their job is to make sure that Westerners with money spend it in the big hotels.

Category II hotels are the accommodations option most likely to have space; but they're expensive. (Singles US$22-24, doubles US$36, triples US$50, all including breakfast.) Most cluster around the train station; **Hotel Griviţei** and **Hotel Bucegi** are slightly nicer than others. If you are lucky enough to find a room that you like and is available, take it; you don't have to book through ONT. **Hotel Cişmigiu,** Bd. Gheorgiu-Dej 18 (tel. 14 74 10), **Hotel Muntenia,** Str. Academiei 21 (tel. 14 60 10), and **Hotel Carpaţi,** Str. Matei Millo 16 (tel. 15 76 90) are all within several blocks of one another in the center of town, just east of Cişmigiu Park. Call ahead.

During the school year (early Sept.-late June), male travelers wandering among the university buildings, should watch for foreign student dormitories (their cars have license plates starting with "5-B"). Romanian students are not allowed to host foreigners, but there are many English-speaking male students from Arab and African countries who will gladly offer hospitality. Try the dormitories of the **Polytechnic Institute** near the Grozăveşti Metro. You might prefer to hitch up to the cheap accommodations in Snagov (see Near Bucharest), or leave on a night train (the one time when a personal train is useful).

Food

Expect to wait in line constantly; all the problems of scarcity are magnified in this crowded capital.

Restaurant Bucegi, on the 1st floor of the hotel next to the Gara de Nord and crowded with locals. Kill a wait for a train with a 50 lei meal.

Hanul Manuc, Str. 30 Decembrie 62. Romanian cuisine in a beautifully restored nineteenth-century manor, near the southern end of Calea Victoriei. Meals about 60 lei.

Monte Carlo, in the center of Cişmigiu Park overlooking the rowboats on the lake. Meals about 50 lei. Open until 10pm.

Self-Service, Hotel Intercontinental, at 4-6 N. Bd. Bălcescu (southern end), in the basement. Jam-packed at meal times. Open 7am-10pm.

Hotel-Restaurant Griviţa, Calea Griviţei 130, near train station. Serves small pizzas (22 lei) and omelettes at breakfast.

Hotel Restaurant Ambassador, Bd. Magheru 10, across from ONT. Entirely Western, but an abundance of food. Meat entrees 40-70 lei, but spaghetti only 20 lei. Open daily 7am-10pm.

Sights

You can see the remnants of old Bucharest by covering the circuit formed by **Calea Victoriei, Strada Lipscani,** and **Bulevardul Magheru.** Most of the elegant buildings making up the palace on **Piaţa Victoriei** are now government offices, but visit the extensive collection of Western and Romanian art at the **Art Museum of the Romanian Socialist Republic** (open Tues.-Sun. 10am-6pm) on Str. Ştirbei Vodă. A number of private art collections are now concentrated in the **Museum of Art,** farther down Calea Victoriei at #111.

Continue your tour south through **Strada Lipscani,** a traditional center of merchants and shopping crowds. Even farther south, past the **open-air market** at Piaţa Unirii, are the excavations of an old Roman settlement retrieved from below Str. 30 Decembrie, and the **Church of the Patriarchy,** home of the Romanian Orthodoxy. Try to catch a 10am Sunday service here, at the **Creţulescu Church,** Calea Victoriei 47, or at any one of the more frequented Byzantine churches in the southern part of the city.

Although there is no substitute for traveling through the countryside of Moldavia or Maramureş to discover Romanian folklore, the open-air **Village Museum** in Parcul Herăstrău houses peasant dwellings from all regions of Romania. Take trolley #82. (Open Tues.-Sun. 9am-6pm.) The **National History Museum,** Calea Victoriei 12, has an authentic parchment dated September 20, 1459—the earliest use of the name "Bucureşti" in any written document. The parchment, curiously enough, bears the signature of Vlad Dracula.

Bucharest is a city of parks. Wander through well-groomed central **Cişmigiu Park,** a few blocks west of Calea Victoriei, or the picturesque **Herăstrău Park** to the north. These are not just refuges from the summer heat, but focal points for much of the city's social life. Elderly pensioners, young couples, soccer players, and backgammon and chess whizzes are everywhere. You can also join the crowds at **Parcul Studenţilor** on Lacul Tei, where you can play volleyball and basketball or sunbathe. Take bus #35 or trolley #86 or 90 to the end and follow signs. (Admission 5 lei. Some form of student ID required.)

Bucharest is within an easy bus or trolley ride of an arc of lakes, most of which are in parks and recreations areas. En route to the airport are the shaded walks and zoo of **Băneasa Forest.** Farther yet are three monasteries, each in a pleasant park—**Snagov, Caldaruşani,** and **Ţiganeşti.**

Entertainment

At the **Student Club of Bucharest University,** Calea Plevnei 61, behind the Opera, you can mix with Romanian students, many of whom speak English. Another popuar nightspot for Bucharest's youth is the **Architects Club,** Str. Academiei 2-4, near he Hotel Intercontinental. As a foreign student, you must first get the approval of the Institute of Architecture (near the Club). The club's program changes daily, alternating between disco, jazz, theater performances, and film. During the summer, here are nightly performances in the theaters clustered on Calea Victoriei north of Bd. Gheorghiu. (Tickets 10-20 lei.) Buy tickets at the *casa de billete,* 48 Calea Victoriei (9am-1pm and 2-8pm for **Theater Ţandarica;** 10am-1pm and 4:30-7:30pm or **Theater Giulesti**).

At other times of the year, you can check at ONT for information on excellent performances by the **Romanian Philharmonic,** the **Operas,** and the **Operetta Theater.** The **National Theater** at Bd. Bălcescu 2, **C. Wottara,** Bd. Magheru 20 (tel. 15 93 02), and the **Bulandra Theater** on Str. Mągureanu are the most renowned. Seasons run from mid-October to late March. Tickets are sold for the following week's performance on Saturday at the individual box office of each theater. Bucharest also has the only **Jewish State Theater** in Europe. It is located at Str. Iuliu Barasch 15 and performs throughout the summer. The shows are in Yiddish, with simultaneous headphone translations in Romanian.

Near Bucharest

When Bucharest gets to be too much, take a daytrip to **Snagov.** This tiny village is half an hour north of Bucharest by car, and an easy hitch; buses run only on Sunday. During the summer, hordes descend upon Snagov Park, 5km west of Snagov village, where you can swim in the somewhat dirty lake or rent a rowboat to **Snagov Monastery** (½-hr. row each way, 11 lei rental for 1½ hr.). Accommodations in Snagov are considerably cheaper than any in Bucharest (bungalows by the lake 115 lei). There is no market, but the restaurant serves tasty meals for 60 lei.

Transylvania

For centuries, Hungarians, Romanians, Russians, and Turks have fought over the rich Transylvanian plateaus in northwestern Romania. The evidence remains—villages built around fortified churches, towns encircling castles, and citadel ruins standing on nearly every hill. Romania's Hungarians (the largest minority group at 10% of the population) are concentrated here. Many people speak more German or Hungarian than Romanian, and Romanian Orthodox churches share the skyline with Lutheran steeples.

Cluj-Napoca

If you were dropped into this Transylvanian town, chances are you'd guess that you were in Hungary; every other person speaks nearly perfect Hungarian. Yet Cluj-Napoca is one of Romania's most important cultural, educational, and industrial centers. The **History Museum of Transylvania,** Str. Emil Isac 2, has excellent architectural and sculptural exhibits documenting the area's history. The Gothic **Reform Church,** Str. M. Kogălniceanu, dates from the fifteenth century. The once-Gothic **Franciscan Monastery,** Str. Emil Zola, one of the oldest buildings in town, was remodeled in the baroque style in 1728. Over 10,000 species of plants thrive at the **Botanical Gardens,** Str. Republicii 42.

Cluj-Napoca is on the railway line between Bucharest and Budapest. Two **trains** per day run from Braşov (3 hr.) and Bucharest (8 hr.). The train station is in the extreme northern section of town; to get to the center, catch almost any bus down Str. Horea to the **Piaţa Libertăţii.** The **ONT** office, Str. Şincai 2 (tel. 217 78), and **CFR,** the railway agency, at Piaţa Libertăţii (tel. 122 12), are located within minutes of each other in the town center. At Str. Horea 29 is **Hotel Central-Melody** (tel. 174 65), and at #3-5 is **Hotel Astoria.** Two kilometers south on road 1 is **Făget Campground. Lacto-Vegetarian,** Piaţa Libertăţii 12, has good, cheap food.

Braşov

At the foot of Mt. Tîmpa, Braşov is one of the most beautiful cities in Romania. A good base for excursions to the Carpathian Mountains, Braşov is small enough to get around and large enough to harbor several interesting monuments from its mercantile past. Visit the arresting **Black Church** on Curtea Bisericii Negre, one of the most representative structures of Gothic architecture in Romania. Its nineteenth-century calliope has 4000 pipes and 4 keyboards; check for organ concerts (3 lei). Also interesting is the thirteenth-century **St. Bartholomew Church,** Str. Lungă 251.

Braşov has only two category II hotels: **Hotel Carpaţi-Sport** (tel. 428 40), behind the Hotel Carpaţi at Str. Maiakovsky 3, and **Turist Hotel,** at Str. Karl Marx 32 (tel. 400 20); both may not have room for Westerners. (Singles 240 lei, doubles 290 lei.) The closest camping area is at **Dîrşte,** 8km from Braşov toward Bucharest, set in a beautiful wooded area. More convenient for sight-seeing is campground **Cetatea Rîşnov,** in Rîşnov, southwest of Braşov on road 73. The pedestrian zone on Strada Republicii has restaurants to suit all budgets.

Braşov is north of Bucharest on the rail line to Budapest. Five *rapid* **trains** per day run from Bucharest (2½ hr.). Several trains per day connect Braşov with Sibiu (3 hr. *accelerat*) and Cluj-Napoca (5 hr. *rapid*). Braşov's **ONT** office, Blvd. Gh. Gheorghiu-Dej 9, in the Hotel Carpaţi (tel. 442 86), distributes maps and will help find accommodations. To reach it, take bus #4 from the train station for about six stops. (Open daily 7:30am-10pm.)

The most famous Romanian may be Dracula, Prince of Wallachia from 1456 to 1462, who isn't known here as a vampire, but rather as Vlad Ţepeş, "The Impaler." Ţepeş lived in the **Castle of Bran,** 28km southwest of Braşov. He earned his reputation when he refused to pay the traditional dues imposed on Romania by the Ottoman Empire. To punish him, the Turks sent a force which Vlad outwitted and then slaughtered. To discourage further incursions, the Prince of Wallachia then impaled the heads of the dead Turks on spikes and set them around the walls of his capital. The familiar story of Dracula the vampire is a fictional concoction of the Irish writer Bram Stoker, and has not a grain of truth. (Castle open Tues.-Sun. 9am-6pm. Admission 6 lei, students 3 lei.)

Just as scenic is the thirteenth-century **Peasant Citadella** overlooking Rîşnov. (Open Tues.-Sun. 10am-4pm. Admission 4 lei, students 1.50 lei.) A stairway up to the citadel begins at the Casa de Cultură on Piaţa 23 August. If you go down through the woods on the other side, you'll find a pool, restaurant, and campground. One train (around noon) leaves from Braşov to Rîşnov, where you can catch a bus to Bran.

Forty-four kilometers south of Braşov, the mountain resort of **Sinaia** sits in northern Wallachia on the Prahova Valley. The beautiful setting has earned it the nickname "Pearl of the Carpathians." The **Sinaia Monastery** has two elaborately frescoed churches from the seventeenth and nineteenth centuries. A former summer residence of the Romanian royal family, **Peleş Castle** is a rich confection of every conceivable style. There is excellent hiking and skiing in the hills above the town. Just north of the town is campground **Vada Cerbului.** Ten kilometers away on the same road is **Izvorul Rece,** the only category II hotel in town.

Sinaia is one hour from Braşov by *rapid* train. Hitchhiking along E-15 is faster than taking the train.

Sibiu and the Făgăraş Mountains

The heart of Transylvania, Sibiu is an old administrative center from the days of the Austro-Hungarian Empire, and one of the few towns in Romania with well-preserved medieval architecture. The excellent exhibits at the **Bruckenthal Museum,** Piaţa Republicii 4, include an extensive collection of Titians and Van Dycks. (Open Tues.-Sun. 10am-6pm. Admission 12 lei.) If you are staying at the campsite, visit the **Museum of Folk Crafts** across the road. (Open May-Oct.)

The friendly **ONT** staff in **Hotel Bulevard,** Piaţa Unirii, 10 (tel. 121 40) is more helpful than the staff in the main ONT office across the street. All four hotels in Sibiu are category I (singles US$30-35, doubles US$45-50), so take bus T-1 (3 per hr.) 4km south to campground **Dumbrava.** The food situation is equally grim. If you're lucky, the **Lacto Bar** midway between the ONT and Piaţa Republici will have yogurt (1 lei) and omelettes (8 lei).

Sibiu is the point of access for the **Făgăras Mountains,** with some of the highest and least crowded hiking routes in the Carpathians. The most spectacular routes are east of Sibiu, south of the railway route toward Braşov. At **Librăria Dacia Trăian,** Nicolae Bălcescu 2 in Piaţa Republicii, ask for *Munţii Făgăraşului Hartă Turistică,* a map with a very detailed hiking guide in German (10 lei). Ask at the crowded **CFR train agency** (across and down the street at #6) about the several daily local trains destined for Braşov that stop in villages near the trail heads. From the villages **Sebeş-Olt** and **Porumbecu de Jos** you can hike to **Suru** (2283m) and **Negoiu** (2535m) in seven or eight hours. Another **Dumbrava** campground is 20km south of Bîlea Lake on road 7. With the exception of the final approaches, the gradient of these trails is moderate; the view of the Wallachian plains to the south and the Transylvanian plateau to the north will make up for any exhaustion. August and September are the ideal months for climbing in this area; during the rest of the year, expect capricious weather.

Three *accelerat* trains per day connect Sibiu to Bucharest (4½ hr., 100 lei). Stay off the 13½ hr. *personal* train. Trains also run to Cluj-Napoca and Braşov.

Moldavia

Situated in the mountains of northeastern Romania, this former republic is now famous chiefly for the **Bukovina Monasteries.** Erected five centuries ago, the monasteries of **Voroneţ, Humor, Suceviţa, Arbore,** and **Moldoviţa** have unusual and well-preserved exterior frescoes. They are tough to visit unless you have a car or are hitchhiking; there is no train, and bus connections are inconvenient.

Suceava is the transport hub and former capital of Moldavia. The **ONT** office is at 2A Str. Nicolae Bălcescu (tel. 173 39), and the **Agenţia de Voiaj, CFR,** is nearby at #8 (tel. 143 35). Hotels are expensive; you'd do better at the **Ştrand** campground, south on road 2 at Km 450, or at the **Adîncata** campground, west on road 29. There are more campgrounds near the Suceviţa and Moldoviţa monasteries.

Two *rapid* trains per day connect Suceava to Bucharest. During the summer, ticket lines from Bucharest to Moldavia can be three hours long, so consider hitching or flying (daily flights from Bucharest, 292 lei).

Black Sea Coast

The stretch between the three arms of the Danube from Tulcea to the Black Sea is a world of natural and artificial canals cutting their way through miles of roads—a 1676-square-mile paradise for anglers, birdwatchers, and adventurers equipped with small boats. This huge ecosystem undergoes perceptible changes within a single lifetime; 40 meters of land are created every year.

During the summer the coast is jam packed; on the bright side, many tourist personnel speak English. Three trains per day run from Bucharest to Constanţa (56 lei), but the summer ticket lines are unbearably long, so consider hitchhiking or flying (several flights from Bucharest to Constanţa, 184 lei).

Tulcea is the gateway to the **Danube Delta,** the northern half of the coast. There is still a noticeable presence from the days of the Ottoman Empire here in the form of a sizable Turkish population and a few conspicuous mosques in the downtown skyline. The **ONT,** 2 Gării-Faleză St. (tel. (914) 147 20), in the Hotel Delta, organizes daily eight-hour excursions through the delta (tickets about US$30, departure 10am). (Open Mon.-Sat. 8am-8pm, Sun. 8am-3pm.) The **Hotel Delta** and **Hotel**

Egreta, Str. Păcii 1 (tel. 171 03), both charge 200 lei per person. Alternatively, you can equip yourself with a good map of the delta from the ONT and take a regular passenger boat east to **Maliuc.** There, you can rent a small rowboat from the **Hotel Salcia** (Category II), and stay at the adjacent **campground.** Thirty-two kilometers southeast of Tulcea by road is another campground, **Pelicanul,** near the old fishing village of **Murighiol.**

Tulcea is five hours from Bucharest via Megidia by fast train, and four hours from Constanţa by slow train.

There are no affordable hotels in Constanţa, and ONT will send you to **Mamaia,** which has five Category II hotels. (In high season singles US$23.50, doubles US$29; low season singles US$15.50, doubles US$20.) The **ONT** in Mamaia is located in the Hotel Bucureşti (tel. 317 80). Extremely crowded resorts take over south of Mamaia. Sixteen campgrounds provide accommodations, but are generally booked well in advance.

SPAIN

US$1 = 122 pesetas (ptas)	**100ptas = US$0.82**
CDN$1 = 92.5ptas	**100ptas = CDN$1.08**
UK£1 = 199.19ptas	**100ptas = UK£0.50**
AUS$1 = 86.76ptas	**100ptas = AUS$1.15**

Bullfights, red wine, and dancing gypsies conjure up an image of Spain that is woefully inadequate. This unbelievably diverse country is full of surprises, and when you've had your first glass of wine, you've just opened the doors to this vast cultural cornucopia. Basque terrorism illustrates the strong-headedness of Spain's autonomous regions, and the different languages of these regions—*catalán, gallego,* and *euskera*—define their cultural distinctions. The plains of Andalusia (where it does not often, in fact, rain) are about as distinct from the lush mountains of Galicia as Andaluces are from Gallegos.

Modern Spain dates from 1492, the year that Granada was seized from the Moors and the *Reconquista* of the Iberian peninsula made complete. With Carlos V's establishment of the powerful Hapsburg dynasty in Madrid and the important role that Spain assumed during the Counter Reformation, the country joined the ranks of the greatest European powers. The plunder of gold and jewels that the *conquistadores* brought back from the Americas made the nation one of Europe's wealthiest. The death of the last Hapsburg monarch in the early eighteenth century climaxed a century of decline, and Spaniards no longer involved themselves in the politics of northern Europe. The nineteenth century saw the rise of regionalist movements, often with a working class flavor, and increasing domestic strife led to the bloody Spanish Civil War in the late 1930s. Francisco Franco emerged from the war as the country's dictatorial leader, and remained so until his death in the '70s. King Juan Carlos has since done a remarkable job of leading Spain into democracy; free elections in 1981 and 1982 and EEC membership in 1986 have all brought the country more securely into the fold of European democracies. Prime Minister Felipe González currently leads a Socialist government that is beleaguered by opposition from the left on the issues of anti-abortion laws, university admission policies, and, most importantly, a large U.S. military presence. Separatist terrorists, particularly from the Basque country, also remain active. *El País,* the Madrid daily, is a good way for Spanish-speakers to keep abreast of current events.

Spain's literary tradition ranges from the anonymous *Poema de Mío Cid* to Cervantes through to modern playwright Federico García Lorca. And some of Europe's most influential art has developed here: The baroque mannerisms of El Greco, the elegance of Velázquez, the politics of Goya, and the innovation of Picasso, Dalí, and Miró.

If Spain exercises its magic on you, consult *Let's Go: Spain Portugal, and Morocco* for more detailed coverage than we can provide here.

Transportation

RENFE, the national railroad system, will cause you problems mainly at the border, where you must change to trains with Spain's unique track gauge. Once you're across the border, the best (and most expensive) trains are called *Talgo;* these are usually twice the price of other trains, and require a reservation, as well as a significant supplement for railpass and BIGE holders. Next in RENFE's pecking order are the *electro* and *TER,* both quite comfortable, but stopping more often. *Expreso* and *rápido* also travel with reasonable speed and efficiency. Finally, somnolent *tranvía, semi-directo, correo,* and *ferrobús* trains stop everywhere—great for a lesson in rural Spanish train station architecture. To avoid getting on the wrong train it's useful to note the difference between *cercanías,* trains primarily for the area around the point of departure, and *largos recorridos,* which are longer-distance trains; the latter are usually better trains with cabins rather than rows of seats. *Largos recorridos* require a reservation of railpass and BIGE holders. Whatever their speed, Spanish trains are a travel bargain: second-class fares are usually only 3-4ptas per kilometer. Additionally, just about everyone gets a price cut on *días azules* ("blue days"), about three out of four days over the course of the year; they are prominently indicated on RENFE calendars. In addition, the company offers the Tarjeta Joven for people aged 12 to 26. For 2000ptas you receive a 50% discount on all trains, from May through December; trips must be over 100km. In addition, you get one free round-trip long distance train ticket—worth more than Tarjeta Joven costs. Both Eurail and InterRail are valid in Spain. RENFE stations are often fairly distant from the city center. The company has downtown offices in all significant cities and towns. We list these in most cases; you might also check a local telephone directory. Many travel agencies are hooked in to RENFE's computerized ticket reservation system; purchase your tickets here to avoid exasperating lines at the station.

Bus travel in Spain is often even less expensive than train, but considering the pace and number of local stops, it's usually good only for shorter excursions; express buses and longer distances may cost more than trains, but are more convenient along some routes (Valencia-Málaga, for instance). Spain has no national bus line, so check with a number of different *empresas* (companies) to determine which has the most direct route to your destination. The various *empresas* usually coordinate their routes with each other, so making connections shouldn't be difficult.

Rental cars are considerably less expensive than in other European countries, but gas costs about US$3.50 per gallon. Taxis are indispensable for quick dashes to train stations or returning from a night on the town after public transportation has stopped; most rides are under 350ptas.

Hitching will generally get you wherever you want to go—maybe today, maybe *mañana.* Terrorist violence has exercised a curb on Spanish hospitality. Backpacks are a great help, as they make you look legitimate—like the many university students who rely on hitching to get home to see their families on weekends. If you're tidy and look decent, your chances of a ride are *much* better. Money is never expected, though inviting your driver to coffee or *tapas* is an appreciated sign of gratitude. Northern areas are relatively good, as is the Mediterranean coast. Castile is only fair; hitching out of Madrid—in any direction—is nearly impossible. Andalusia is the worst part of the country; rides are infrequent and the sun can be broiling.

Biking is possible in Spain, but not necessarily enjoyable. Spain is very mountainous in parts, and the weather—especially in summer—can be extreme. Moreover, roads are not designed to facilitate cycling, and drivers often act rashly towards cyclists. Good bicycle shops are harder to find here than in other European countries.

Iberia, the national airline, has flights to all major cities in Spain, with most one-way fares ranging from 7000 to 9000ptas. For some cities, like Barcelona and Tenerife, cheaper night fares *(tarifas nocturnas)* are available; to the Balearic Islands, the airfare is actually less than that for the ferry.

Practical Information

Just about every town in Spain that receives visitors has an **oficina de turismo** (often known simply as "turismo") that distributes city maps, lists of accommodations, and general information about the town; many offices will also help you find accommodations. Hours are generally long, and in larger cities often include a Sunday session.

Spanish is a child of Latin, and is very similar to other Romance languages in syntax, grammar, and vocabulary. Some people speak English, though you may have more luck with a Romance cousin—Italian, Portuguese, and French, in that order. Spanish (*castellano*) is the official language of the whole country. Other languages are official only in the regions where they are spoken, and regional patriotism runs high. Various dialects of *catalán* (which is *not* a dialect of Spanish) are spoken in and around Catalonia, Valencia, and the Balearic Islands. *Euskera* or Basque, the only non-Romance language in the country, is spoken in the Basque region, and *gallego,* closer to Portuguese, is the tongue of northwest Galicia. In Spanish, double "l" is pronounced like "y"; "j" like "h"; and soft "c" and "z" become "th" in most of the country . Pocket Spanish-English dictionaries are widely available.

Women may be made to feel uncomfortable by excessive or unwelcome male attention. Many admirers may not understand annoyance or anger at their advances. In most cases, the best answer is no answer; any reply may be interpreted as willingness to prolong the encounter. If a situation becomes genuinely threatening, a tirade (in any language) or screaming, especially in the presence of onlookers, may be necessary. *Let's Go* lists emergency, police, and consulate phone numbers in many cities.

During August, inland cities are deserted and coastal regions jammed, both with Spanish tourists and northern Europeans on package tours.

Spain's climate is as varied as its geography. Hot summers and long, fairly cold winters characterize the large and arid interior plateau *(meseta).* The Mediterranean coast, protected by mountain ranges, enjoys generally balmy weather year-round, while the verdant northern provinces bordering the Cantabrian Sea and the Atlantic offer mild and humid weather with a mixture of sun, mist, and fine rain. Summer will be hot all over, though less so in the northern Basque Country and Galicia. Winter brings tourist crowds to the Costa del Sol, the islands, and the mountain resort areas; the weather elsewhere shouldn't be prohibitively cold. Autumn, with its long sunny days, is a wonderful time—especially in Castile, Andalusia, the Mediterranean Coast, and the islands. Spring runs a close second.

Inflation in Spain is considerable; you can expect peseta prices that we quote here to rise by 20% or more by 1988. Spain's entrance in the EEC has brought *IVA (Im-*

puesto al Valor Añadido), a 6% tax on all commercial transactions. Work prospects beyond *intercambio* arrangements (an exchange of services for room and board) and teaching English are grim, even for members of Common Market countries. For both *intercambio* and official work, resort areas, where English skills are an asset are the best places to look.

The Fiesta de San Fermín, held in Pamplona from July 7 to 14 and better known as the **Running of the Bulls,** is Spain's wildest celebration. The **Semana Santa** (Holy Week) celebrations in April bring about some great shows; especially in Andalusia, cities and towns strive to outdo one another for the most ardent displays of adoration throughout the week between Palm Sunday and Easter. Lest this evoke a mood too somber for the pagan tourist, Seville's **Feria de Abril** follows on the heels of Holy Week. Valencia's **Las Fallas** (literally "the bonfires") is a week of fireworks, floral parades, and dancing in the streets. On the last night, great wooden effigies *(ninots)* are set ablaze in a custom dating from the Middle Ages.

Banks, shops, and offices shut down on legal and religious holidays in Spain: New Year's Day; Epiphany (Jan. 6); Saint Joseph's Day (March 29); Maundy Thursday, Good Friday, and Easter Sunday; May Day (May 1); Corpus Christi (June 18); Feast of Santiago (July 25); Feast of the Assumption (Aug. 15); Independence Day (Oct. 12); Feast of the Immaculate Conception (Dec. 8); and Christmas (Dec. 25). Some of these religious celebrations are no longer legal holidays, but business slows down anyway and sometimes stops altogether.

Spanish workdays ordinarily start at 9am, stop at 1pm for a three-hour *siesta,* and recommence at 4pm until 8pm. On Saturday, places are usually open only in the morning, and Sunday is a day of *descanso* for everything but a few indispensables (some tourist offices among them). Most banks are open Monday through Friday from 9am to 2pm and Saturday from 9am to 1pm. All pharmacies post a list of 24-hour pharmacies and emergency numbers. Post offices *(Correos)* are open from 9am to 2pm, and some reopen from 4 to 7pm; telegrams may be sent from 8am to 10pm at the post office or by phone on a 24-hour basis (consult the phone book for the regional phone number). Stamps (*sellos)* are also sold at some tobacco shops (look for the burnt-orange tobacco-leaf sign). The name for Poste Restante in Spanish is *Lista de Correos.* Although cities the size of Madrid, Barcelona, or Granada have a telephone office *(telefónica)* for long distance calls, you can dial direct from anywhere to anywhere—if you have enough change. You can purchase telephone credit cards at the *telefónica* and use them in specially equipped payphones. If you wish to place a collect call *(cobro revertido),* you must use the *telefónica.* Anywhere in Spain, you can dial 003 for information and 008 for operator assistance. In an emergency, dial 091.

Accommodations and Camping

Spanish hotels are a great bargain, but like any bargain, you have to arrive early to get in on it, at least in summer. Hotels in Spain come in a number of nationally regulated styles and sizes. In ascending order of amenities and prices, the categories are: *fondas, casas de huéspedes, pensiones, hostales* or *hostales-residencias* (rated on a 3-star system), and *hoteles* (rated on a 5-star system). Prices are fixed for every room according to the facilities, but these are applied at the discretion of the manager and can be undercut, though not legally exceeded. There are also a number of subtleties that can affect lodging prices. Breakfast is obligatory in some places, and hot showers *(duchas calientes)* often cost extra (100-200ptas). One of your major considerations in choosing a room—and perhaps your biggest problem in Spanish cities in the summer—will be to steer clear of noise and heat. Look for places on side streets or take a room as high up as possible without being right under the roof.

If for some reason you have trouble when it comes time to pay the bill, request an *hoja oficial de reclamación,* which vigilant regional governments require be produced on demand. Most arguments will end there; all complaints must be forwarded to the authoritites and hotel owners caught overcharging are severely penalized.

Spain has over 100 official youth hostels *(albergues de la juventud* or *albergues juveniles).* Conditions vary considerably, but many are quite comfortable and cheap (around 350ptas per night) with reasonable rates for meals. IYHF cards are usually required; other regulations are enforced with varying degrees of rigidity. Sheets are not generally required.

Campgrounds in Spain are also regulated by the government. Category makes little difference in price, but facilities are usually substantially better at Class I sites than at lower-ranked grounds. University dorms or *colegios mayores* sometimes have overnight lodging, and are ideal for longer stays. Unregistered rooms in private homes *(casas particulares)* are an excellent accommodations alternative, particularly in the popular tourist cities during summer, or in very small towns with no hotels. Ask at local bars or tourist offices, or look for signs in the windows of homes.

Food

You'll find yourself gorging on a variety of national staples, including *callos con chorizo* (tripe served with tasty red sausage), *cocido* (a stew of meat, chick peas, potatoes, and bacon), *tortilla española* (potato omelette), and the ubiquitous *paella* (steamed saffron-flavored rice with chicken stock and an assortment of seafood).

With so many distinct regional cultures, it's not surprising that Spain should have an endless repertoire of dishes. Anywhere you go, you'll be lured by the seafood *(mariscos),* and especially by shellfish. In the north you'll find *bacalao* (cod), *calamares* (squid, often fried in chewy rings), *sardinas* (grilled or charbroiled sardines), and perhaps most famous of all, *angulas* (baby eels). In Galicia treat yourself to shellfish *a La Gallega* (hot and spicy with chili powder and paprika in an orange-red sauce). Order *santiaguinos* (spider crabs) or *gambas* (large shrimp), or try *vieiras* and *mejillones* (fresh-water scallops and fresh-water mussels, respectively). In the eastern provinces you'll hunger after *langosta catalana* and *langosta Ibiza,* lobster specialties. *Sopa de pescado* (fish soup) and *zarzuela* (assorted fish stew) are everywhere.

There's plenty to consume beyond ocean fare, too. Try *fabada,* a bean stew, in the Asturias region in the north. If you want to splurge in Castile, order *cochinillo asado al horno* (roast suckling pig). *Gazpacho,* a hot-weather cold soup, is the specialty of Andalusian kitchens. It's made of ground cucumbers, tomatoes, peppers, onions in vinegar, olive oil, and garlic. For a gastronomic adventure, head to Majorca for *lenguas de cerdo con salsa de granada* (pig tongue with pomegranate).

Spaniards start their day with a breakfast *(desayuno)* of coffee and bread or *churros,* curly rope-shaped dough, deep-fried and sprinkled with sugar or dipped in chocolate. Spanish coffee *(café)* is heavily toasted, thick and plenty strong. *Café solo* is a small cup of espresso; a *cortado* is a *solo* with a dash of milk; *café con leche* is espresso with a good quantity of warm steamed milk—similar to the French *café au lait.* If you prefer a lighter brew, ask for *café largo de agua;* it will be served in a larger cup, with a little extra hot water. *Almuerzo* is a light meal taken around 11:30am. Dinner *(comida)* is taken between 1 and 4pm. Supper *(cena),* which does not begin until 7 or 8pm, is preceded by *tapas* around 5 or 6pm; most places continue serving until 11pm or midnight.

For *comida* and *cena,* all cafeterias and the cheaper restaurants are required to offer a *menú de la casa* (house menu) or *menú del día* (menu of the day), also known as a *menú turístico,* consisting of soup or appetizer, one or two main courses, bread, dessert, and ¼-liter of wine or mineral water. These are a bargain if you're hungry, but limit your opportunity for experimentation. *Menús* average about 600-650ptas. In addition, many restaurants offer cheap, fixed-price *cubiertos* (set meals) or *platos combinados* (combination plates, main course, and side dishes on a single plate, plus bread and sometimes beverage). It's customary to tip 5-10% for good service.

If the late supper schedule seems cruel and unusual, *tapas* (hors d'oeuvres) and *bocadillos* (sandwiches) can provide relief. After work Spaniards make for the local bars and *mesones* or *tascas* to meet friends and to munch on these delightful tidbits.

Large portions are available as *raciones* (rations), which make an excellent cheap, light meal.

Cena, comida, and *tapas* are almost always washed down with a glass of wine (*vino blanco* is white, *vino tinto* is red, and a *chato* is a glass of red wine), or beer *(cerveza).* Beer is served in bottles or on draft, in either a small glass *(caña)* or a tall one *(tubo). Aguila, Estrella,* and *San Miguel* are excellent national brands; *Voll-damm* (Catalonia) and *Alhambra* (Andalusia) are fine regional brews. *Rioja* is a world-renowned wine-growing region, with especially good reds; there are innumerable fine regional wines. *Sangria* is made of red wine, sugar, brandy, seltzer, and peaches. Another native beverage you may want to try is sherry *(jeréz),* from the city of the same name.

Castile (Castilla)

Windswept plateaus, medieval walled cities, and tall Romanesque belfries rising from yellow fields emblazon themselves as images of Castile, the region geographically and symbolically at the heart of Spain. In the Middle Ages, Castilians played a crucial role in the *Reconquista,* the 800-year-long war to push the Muslims to the south. Centuries later, Spanish writers appalled by their country's defeat in the Spanish-American War turned to the landscape of Castile in their search for the essence of Spain.

Most parts of Castile have a distinct cuisine, but two tasty dishes are common to the entire region: *sopa castellana* (a soup made with garlic, ham, eggs, and bread), and *cocido castellano* (a stew made with beef, ham, potatoes, *chorizo,* carrots, and garlic). Pork and mutton are prepared in a variety of succulent dishes.

Madrid

Madrid has a tempo all its own: The dry air of the sun-scorched Castilian plain crackles with its cosmopolitan crowds. If you are overwhelmed by the illuminated shop windows along the Gran Vía and the unrelenting elegance of Paseo de la Castellana, retreat to Old Madrid. Its tangle of side streets south and east of Plaza Mayor and Puerta del Sol may be the only place in the city where a gypsy can sidle up to the bar beside a businessperson. Spend half a day in the Prado Museum, then sit a spell on the steps leading down to the lake in lush Retiro Park. The city begins to live it up as the sun goes down. Year-round, Madrid teems with cultural events, and after concert, play, or film, you can choose among literally hundreds of *tapas* bars and an endless, varied array of nightspots.

Orientation and Practical Information

Madrid sits just about at the center of Spain, and is connected to every corner of the country by rail and bus.

Downtown Madrid fits between two parks: the **Casa de Campo** in the west, and the **Parque del Retiro** in the east. In the middle lies the **Puerta del Sol,** a large square which is Spain's geographic heart—notice the "Km 0" marker on the sidewalk in front of the police station. Many major streets intersect at this square, although the **Gran Vía,** Madrid's main east-west artery and principal commercial thoroughfare, runs a bit to the north.

Greater Madrid is huge and sprawling, but an efficient metro and a dense network of buses will whisk you all over the city. The free map available at the tourist office should be a sufficient guide; better maps (such as Baedeker's) are available at kiosks. Scattered throughout the center of town are **Columnas Informativas,** which look like telephone booths and contain indexed maps of the city.

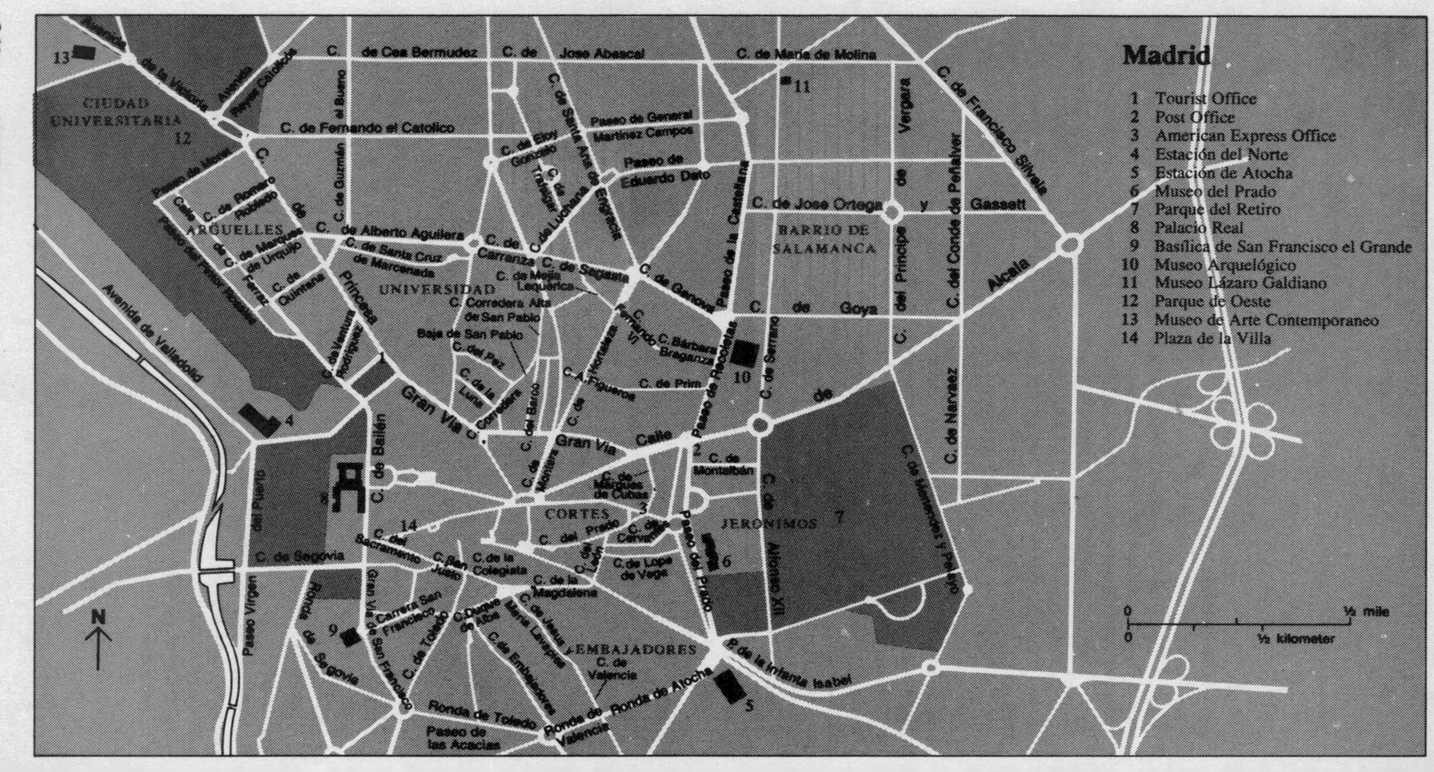
Madrid
1 Tourist Office
2 Post Office
3 American Express Office
4 Estación del Norte
5 Estación de Atocha
6 Museo del Prado
7 Parque del Retiro
8 Palacio Real
9 Basílica de San Francisco el Grande
10 Museo Arqueológico
11 Museo Lázaro Galdiano
12 Parque de Oeste
13 Museo de Arte Contemporaneo
14 Plaza de la Villa
CIUDAD UNIVERSITARIA
ARGUELLES
UNIVERSIDAD
BARRIO DE SALAMANCA
CORTES
JERONIMOS
EMBAJADORES
C. de Cea Bermudez
C. de Jose Abascal
C. de Maria de Molina
C. de Fernando el Catolico
C. de Alberto Aguilera
C. de Jose Ortega y Gassett
C. de Goya
C. de Bailén
Gran Via
Calle de Alcala
Paseo de Recoletas
Paseo de la Castellana
Paseo del Prado
C. de Serrano
C. de Narvaez
C. de Francisco Silvela
Avenida de Valladolid
Ronda de Toledo
Ronda de Atocha
Ronda de Valencia
C. de Segovia
Paseo Virgen del Puerto
N
0 ½ mile
0 ½ kilometer

Summer visitors should be warned that Madrid is nearly deserted during August much of the city's populace, including many of its restaurateurs, leave for vacation Like any major city, Madrid has its dangerous areas. Walking alone after 1am in the following areas would be a mistake: Plaza Dos de Mayo, Puerta del Sol, C. Preciados, and C. Montera.

Tourist Offices: Nacional, C. Princesa, 1, Pl. de España (tel. 241 23 25). Metro: Pl. de España. Open Mon.-Fri. 9am-7pm, Sat. 10am-2pm. Another branch at Barasas Airport (tel. 205 86 56), open Mon.-Fri. 8am-8pm, Sat. 8am-1pm. **Municipal,** Pl. Mayor (tel. 266 54 77). Metro: Sol. Open Mon.-Fri. 10am-1:30pm and 4-7pm, Sat. 9:30am-1:30pm. For information about less popular museums, call the **Oficina de Museos,** Palacio Real (tel. 248 74 04).

Student Travel Office: Viajes TIVE. Central office, C. Fernando el Católico, 88 (tel. 401 90 11). Metro: Quevedo. Branch office, José Ortega y Gasset, 71 (tel. 401 95 01). Metro: Lista. Some English spoken at both. Both open Mon.-Fri. 9am-2pm, Sat. 9am-1pm.

American Express: Pl. de las Cortes, 2 (tel. 429 28 75), off Carrera de San Jerónimo. Open Mon.-Fri. 9am-5:30pm, Sat. 9am-noon.

Currency Exchange: Banks open Mon.-Fri. 9am-2pm, Sat. 9am-1pm. At Barasas Airport, open 24 hours. At Chamartín train station, open daily 8am-10pm. Every El Corte Inglés store has a currency exchange office charging a 1% commission on currency, 2% on traveler's checks.

Post Office: Palacio de Comunicaciones, Pl. de la Cibeles. Open Mon.-Sat. 9am-10pm, including telegraphs and stamps; Poste Restante open Mon.-Fri. 9am-2pm and 4-6pm, Sat. 9am-2pm. Door H remains open Sun. 8am-10pm for telegrams, telex, etc. **Postal code:** 28070.

Telephones: Gran Vía, 28 (entrance on C. de Fuencarral). Open Mon.-Sat. 9am-10pm, Sun. 10am-2pm and 5-9pm. The Palacio de Comunicaciones has a comfortable office for long-distance calls, open daily 8am-1am (enter on Paseo del Prado). **Telephone code:** 91.

Trains: Chamartín (the main station) is located far to the north. Metro: Charmartín, train from Atocha (see next listing), bus #27, or M-6 to Pl. de Castilla; then bus #80 to the station. To Burgos, Basque Country, Cantabrian Coast, Catalonia, and France. **Atocha** is located south of the Prado. Metro: Atocha, or bus #6, 14, 19, 27, or 45. To Andalusia and Toledo. Both Chamartín and Atocha Stations service Ávila, Alicante, Guadalajara, Segovia, Valencia, and Lisbon. **Norté,** also called **Príncipe Pío.** Metro: Norté, or bus Circular #1 or 46. To Barcelona, Seville, Granada, Galicia, Salamanca, and Santiago de Compostela. Information (tel. 733 30 00, 24 hours). **RENFE,** Alcalá, 44 (tel. 222 76 09). Open Mon.-Fri. 8am-2:30pm and 4-7pm, Sat. 8am-1:30pm. Chamartín and Atocha ticket offices open daily 9am-9pm; Norté ticket office open daily 9am-7pm.

Inter-City Buses: Estación Sur de Autobuses, Canarias, 17 (tel. 468 42 00). Metro: Palos de Moguer. There are 8 bus stations in Madrid, almost all with numerous bus companies and destinations.

Public Transportation: The several lines of the **metro** subway system emanate more or less from the Puerta del Sol and operate daily 6:30am-1:30am. (50ptas per trip, 10-trip ticket 410ptas.) Check the map at each entrance; inside they are few and far between. Pick up a free map at one of the booths. Buses are usually faster but slightly more expensive. **Red buses** run from 5:30am-11pm or 2am, depending on the line; the circle line runs 24 hours. (55ptas per trip, 80ptas including transfer, 10-ride card excluding transfers 500ptas.) More comfortable, air-conditioned **yellow microbuses** (look for prefix "M") are also available. (65ptas per ride, 20-ticket book 1300ptas.) Multiple-ride cards for both types of buses available at all municipal tourist offices. **Taxis** cost an initial 80ptas plus 38ptas per additional km. Airport fee adds 150ptas, 20ptas per piece of luggage.

Airport: Barasas Airport (tel. 205 43 72 for arrivals). **Iberia,** main office at Pl. de Canovas, 4 (tel. 411 25 45). Open Mon.-Fri. 9am-7pm, Sat. 9am-2pm.

Baggage Check: Lockers at Chamartín and Atocha train stations (100ptas per day; lockers fit large backpacks), Estación Sur de Autobuses, and the air terminal beneath Pl. de Colón.

Emergencies: Police (tel. 091 or 092); headquarters, Puerta del Sol (tel. 221 65 16). **Ambulance** (tel. 252 32 64).

Medical Assistance: Hospital Anglo-Americano, Pl. del Marqués de Salamanca, 9-bajo, Parque Metropolitano (tel. 431 22 29). Metro: Moncloa, or bus Circular.

Pharmacies: To find pharmacies open after 8pm dial 098 or check listings in newspapers *El País* or *ABC.*

Women's Center: Librería de Mujeres, C. San Cristóbal, 17, near Pl. Mayor.

Rape Hotline: Tel. 274 01 10. **VD/Abortion:** Tel. 730 49 01.

Embassies: U.S., C. Serrano, 75 (tel. 276 34 00; in emergencies tel. 276 32 29). **Canada,** C. Núñez de Balboa, 35 (tel. 431 43 00). **U.K.,** C. Fernando el Santo, 16 (tel. 419 15 28). **Australia,** Paseo de la Castellana, 143 (tel. 279 85 01). Travelers from **New Zealand** should contact the British Embassy.

Cultural Centers: American, Marqués de Villa Magna, 8 (tel. 435 69 22). Library open in summer Mon.-Fri. noon-7pm. **British,** C. Almagro, 5 (tel. 419 12 50). Library open in summer Mon.-Fri. 9am-1pm and 3-6pm; in winter Mon.-Thurs. 9am-7pm, Fri. 9am-2pm.

English Bookstores: Turner English Bookshop, C. Génova, 3, on Pl. de Santa Barbara. Metro: Alonso Martinez. English literature and *Let's Go* books as well. Open Mon.-Fri. 9:30am-2pm and 5-8pm, Sat. 10am-2pm.

Laundry: Lavandería Marcenado, C. Marcenado, 15 (tel. 416 68 71). Metro: Prosperidad. 5kg washed and dried for 500ptas. **Lavandería Maryland,** Melendéz Valdés, 52 (tel. 243 30 41). Metro: Argüelles. Self-service. 5kg washed and dried for 550ptas. Near Santa Cruz de Marcenado youth hostel.

Swimming Pools (Piscinas Municipales): Outdoor, Casa de Campo (tel. 463 00 50). Metro: El Lago. Open 10am-8pm. Admission 200ptas. **Indoor,** Pl. de Cebada (tel. 265 00 31). Metro: Latina. Open Sept.-July Mon.-Fri. 10am-6pm, Sat. 10am-8pm, Sun. 10am-3pm. Admission 200ptas.

Moped/Motorcycle Rental: Motocicletas Antonio Castro, C. Conde Duque, 13 (tel. 242 06 57), at Santa Cruz de Marcenado. A great way to see Madrid. Starting from 1350ptas plus 12% VAT per day and all gas used (9am-8pm). Must have valid driver's license, passport, and be at least 18. Open Mon.-Fri. 8:30am-2pm and 5-8pm, Sat. 9am-1:30pm.

Hitchhiking: By road from Madrid, N-II (northeast) to Barcelona and Zaragosa; N-III (east) to Cuenca and Valencia; N-IV (south) to Aranjuez, Andalusia, Alicante, and Cádiz; N-VI (northwest) to Ávila, Segovia, and Salamanca; E-4 (west) to Extremadura and Portugal; and 401 (southeast) to Toledo. For information on routes, dial 441 72 22.

Accommodations and Camping

Tourist offices in Madrid will not arrange accommodations, but don't worry—there are more than enough rooms. Both hostels are scheduled to reopen after renovations in September 1987.

Albergue Juvenil (IYHF), C. Santa Cruz de Marcenado, 28 (tel. 247 45 32), off C. de Serrano Jover, between C. de la Princesa and C. de Alberto Aguilera. Metro: Argüelles. Hold on tight to your belongings. Otherwise, nice facilities and a fine location. 600ptas per night, ages over 25 670ptas. Curfew 12:30am.

Albergue Juvenil Richard Schirrman (IYHF), Casa de Campo (tel. 463 56 99). Metro: El Lago. Turn left immediately as you exit metro station El Lago, then turn left again, and walk 1km on the unpaved rocky footpath along the metro tracks. Then cross over small concrete footbridge. Turn left at sign reading "Albergue Juvenil." In a park close to the lake and municipal swimming pool; solo travelers might feel uneasy about the trek at night. Rooms are open during the day and very clean. 425ptas per night, ages over 25 525ptas. Lunch and dinner 400ptas. Curfew 1am.

The numerous budget accommodations between Puerta del Sol and the Palacio Real are close to the major sights. The area between Puerta del Sol and the Atocha station is home to some of Madrid's cheapest dives, but is not especially safe. Accommodations along the Gran Vía are plentiful and usually quite comfortable, though higher-priced and much noisier than those elsewhere.

Hostal-Residencia Jeyma, C. Arenal, 24 (tel. 248 77 43). Metro: Opera. A little rickety. Talkative and friendly owner. Singles 636ptas, doubles 1272ptas. Showers 150ptas.

Hostal Mairu, C. Espejo, 2, south of Teatro Real (tel. 247 30 88). Metro: Opera. Morgue-like atmosphere, but you can't argue the prices: singles 670ptas, doubles 1200ptas, warm showers 150ptas. 3 singles, 9 doubles, but fills up quickly and has some long-term residents.

Casa de Huespedes Jaén, Costanilla de los Angeles, 8 (tel. 242 34 63), off Pl. de Santo Domingo, 1 block from C. Arenal. Metro: Santo Domingo or Callao. Cramped, noisy rooms but the price is right, especially if you're with company. Singles 700ptas, doubles 1200ptas, triples 1500ptas. Showers 150ptas.

Hostal Residencia Miño, C. Arenal, 16, 2nd floor (tel. 231 50 79). Metro: Opera or Sol. Plant-lined balconies, TV room. Singles with bathroom 2000ptas, doubles with bathroom 2600ptas. **Hostal Alicante,** next door, has similar prices.

Hostal-Residencia Malagueña, C. Preciados, 35 (tel. 248 52 33), between Pl. de Santo Domingo and Pl. del Callao. Metro: Callao. Friendly manager. Big, clean, well-lit rooms. Singles 900ptas, doubles 1500ptas, triples 2000ptas. Showers 200ptas.

Hostal Residencia Cruz-Sol, Pl. de Santa Cruz, 6, 3rd floor (tel. 232 71 97), a stone's throw from the east side of Pl. Mayor. Metro: Sol. Highly recommended. Spacious rooms, most with wrought-iron balconies overlooking the chiming Church of Sta. Cruz. Owner is an upstanding Galician *caballero.* Doubles for single use 1000ptas, doubles 1350ptas. Hot showers 150ptas (100ptas for stays over 1 night). On the 2nd floor is **Hostal Santa Cruz** (tel. 522 24 41), with higher ceilings and prices. Doubles with shower 2320ptas.

Hostal Residencia Pinariega, C. Santiago, 1, 1st floor (tel. 248 08 19). Metro: Sol. Springy beds but friendly management. Rooms not facing street are a bit gloomy. For a hot shower, ask Paco to turn on the *agua caliente.* Singles 1100ptas, doubles 1400ptas.

Hostal Residencia Paz, C. Flora, 4 (tel. 247 30 47), off C. Arenal by Pl. Isabel II. Metro: Opera. Delightful owners and large rooms. Singles 1300ptas, doubles 1500ptas. If full, try **Hostal Residencia Portugal** on the ground floor (tel. 248 76 26). Portuguese management seems to have a funky fetish for purple. Singles 1100ptas, doubles 1900ptas.

Hostal Residencia Mondragón, Carrera San Jerónimo, 32, 4th floor (tel. 429 68 16). Metro: Sol. Little old lady keeps the place clean. Singles 900ptas, doubles 1600ptas. Showers 150ptas. On the 5th floor is **Hostal Aguilar** (tel. 429 59 26), a good place to go to if you arrive late at night; with 50 rooms, they're likely to have a vacancy. Spartan hallways, but golden bedspreads. Singles with bathroom 1600ptas, doubles with bathroom 2700ptas. There are several other *hostales* in the building, similar in price and value.

Pensión Mollo, C. de Atocha, 104 (tel. 228 71 76), a bit up the street from the station. Metro: Atocha or Antón Martín. Dark, steep staircase. Singles 700ptas, doubles 1500ptas. Showers 175ptas.

Hotel Sud-Americana, Paseo del Prado, 12 (tel. 429 25 64), across from the Prado. Metro: Atocha or Antón Martín. Fine rooms. Singles 1300-1700ptas, doubles 2200ptas. Showers 200ptas. **Hostal Corona,** below (tel. 429 25 43), is under very personable management. Singles 1300ptas, doubles 2200ptas. Showers 200ptas.

Hostal El Pinar, C. Isabel la Católica, 19 (tel. 247 32 82), just off Gran Vía. Metro: Plaza de España. Recently redecorated, clean, with wildly colorful bathrooms. Singles 1100ptas, doubles 1900ptas. Showers 150ptas.

Hostal Margarita, Gran Vía, 50 (tel. 247 35 49). Metro: Callao. A homey, comfortable place run by a Cuban woman. Singles 1100ptas, with private shower 1500ptas, doubles with private shower 2200-2500ptas. **Hostal Lauria** (tel. 241 91 82) also has large, clean rooms. Singles 2000ptas, doubles 3000ptas; both with private bath.

Camping

There are about a dozen campsites within 50km of Madrid; the tourist offices have information on all of them. **Camping Madrid** (tel. 202 28 35) is on the Carretera Madrid-Burgos (km 7). Take the metro to Pl. de Castilla, then bus #129 to Iglesia de los Dominicos. (225ptas per person, 210ptas per tent.) **Camping Osuna** (tel. 741 05 10) is on the Ajalvir-Vicálvaro road (km 15.5). Take the metro to Canillejas, then bus #105 to Avda. de Logroño. (275ptas per person, 225ptas per tent.)

Food

Travelers who go hungry in Madrid display extraordinary ingenuity: There are countless bars, *mesones,* and cafés serving *tapas* and scrumptious pastries. Much of Madrid's cuisine has been influenced by that of other regions; still, there are many deserving local specialties such as *cocido madrileño* (sausage, chickpea, and potato stew) and tripe Madrid-style, with wine, cognac, sausage, and ham.

Madrid's student quarter, **Argüelles,** is a fine place to eat and drink cheaply and meet people. It starts at the intersection of Calle de la Princesa, Alberto Aguilera, and Marqués de Urquijo (metro: Argüelles or Moncloa, or bus Circular #1, 12, or 61). While university is in session (Sept.-June), students crowd the bars—try Calle Princesa from noon to 2:30pm and from 8 to 11pm. There is also a swarm of budget restaurants between San Bernardo, Fuencarral, and Gran Vía. Near Puerta del Sol, explore Calle Ventura de la Vega, off San Jerónimo.

For picnics and cooking, fresh meat, produce, wine, and bread are available at **Mercado de San Miguel** off the northwest corner of Plaza Mayor. (Open Mon.-Sat. 9am-3pm and 5:30-7:30pm.) Bear in mind that many restaurants close in July and August.

Casa Mingo, Paseo de la Florida, 2 (tel. 247 79 18). Metro: Norte. The interior is dark, the walls stacked with wine barrels, the clientele loyal. Specialty is roast chicken (520ptas) and Asturian *sidra* (cider; 185ptas). Open Sun.-Fri. 1-11:30pm.

La Gata Flora, C. de los Dos de Mayo, 1, at C. San Vincente Ferrer. Metro: Noviciado or Tribunal. Good Italian restaurant run by friendly Argentines. Yellow bohemian interior. *Cappelletti al pesto* gets high marks. Most dishes 450-590ptas. Open Sun.-Thurs. 2-4pm and 8:30pm-12:30am, Fri.-Sat. 2-4pm and 8:30pm-1:30am.

Museo del Jamón, Carrera San Jerónimo, 6 (tel. 521 03 46), off Puerta del Sol. Metro: Sol. Famous for its ham. Iberian ham sandwiches 80ptas, ½ baked chicken 300ptas. Open Mon.-Sat. 1pm-2am, Sun. 1-9pm. Three other locations: Gran Vía, 72 (tel. 241 20 23); Paseo del Prado, 44 (tel. 230 43 85); and Atocha, 54 (tel. 227 07 16).

Restaurante Toscana, C. Manuel Fernández y González, 10-17 (tel. 429 55 74). Metro: Seville or Sol. House specialty is *morcillo* (incredibly tender veal) with fries 800ptas. Open Mon. 8pm-midnight, Tues.-Sat. noon-4pm and 8pm-midnight.

Café Comercial, Glorieta de Bilbao, 7. Metro: Bilbao. High-ceilinged, traditional cafe-restaurant once frequented by artists and republican aviators alike. Sandwiches from 125ptas. Also serves lunch and *tapas.* Open daily 11am-midnight.

Foster's Hollywood, C. Velźquez, 80 (tel. 435 61 28). Metro: Nuñez de Balboa. The ½-lb. burgers are the best in Madrid. With baked potato or fries and salad 525ptas. Open daily 1pm-2am.

Restaurante Sobrino Botín, C. Cuchilleros, 17 (tel. 266 42 17), off southwest corner of Pl. Mayor. Metro: Sol or Opera. The oldest restaurant in Spain (1725); Hemingway called it one of the best in the world. House menu of gazpacho, roast suckling pig, ice cream, and wine 2410ptas. Two sittings for dinner: 8 and 10:30pm, reservations required. Open daily 1-4pm and 8pm-12:30am.

Sights

The **Museo del Prado,** one of the world's greatest and oldest art galleries, contains over 3000 paintings from all over Europe, many of them collected by Spanish kings between the fifteenth and eighteenth centuries. The collection is enormous; try to make several visits. You might want to concentrate on the works of the Spanish masters—Goya, Velázquez, and El Greco. Velázquez's *Las Meninas* (The Maids of Honor) has come alive after its recent restoration. The couple reflected on the background mirror are Philip IV and his wife Mariana; their *real* portraits face the painter from the next room. (Open May-Oct. Tues.-Sat. 9am-7pm, Sun. 9am-2pm; Nov.-April Tues.-Sat. 10am-5pm, Sun. 10am-2pm. Admission 400ptas, students free.) Your ticket to the Prado also admits you to the nearby **Casón del Buen Retiro,** on C. Alfonso XXII, where you can see Picasso's famous *Guernica.* During the Spanish Civil War, scores of civilians were killed when Guernica, a small town in the Basque Country, was mercilessly bombed by German airplanes. Supposedly, when asked by Nationalist officials whether he had painted the picture, Picasso answered, "No, you did." He gave the canvas to New York's Museum of Modern Art with the request that it be returned to Spain only when democracy was restored. *Guernica* arrived in Madrid in the fall of 1981, and remains so controversial that the painting is protected by a glass case. (Open Tues.-Sat. 9am-6:45pm, Sun. 9am-1:45pm.)

The **Palacio Real** confronts the visitor with a vision of pomp and splendor, by virtue of its sheer size, huge and elegant facade, and aloofness from the city's hustle and bustle. There's a lot to see: The required guided tour (in English, about 2 hr.) will show you an endless collection of porcelain, tapestries, furniture, chandeliers, armor, and paintings. Don't miss the gadgetry of medieval combat in the **Armería.** (Open—except during royal visits—Mon.-Sat. 10am-12:45pm and 4-5:45pm, Sun. 10am-12:45pm. Comprehensive ticket 400ptas.) The palace faces the Plaza de Oriente and is enclosed on the northern side by the well-kept **Jardines de Sabatini,** where parents take their children on autumn afternoon promenades, and Madrid's street people come to wash their clothes. Behind the palace is the lush and spotless **Campo del Moro.** King Juan Carlos opened the *campo* to the public in the summer of 1977; this is a fine site for a royal picnic. (Open daily 9:30am-8pm; only one gate of access, on Paseo de la Virgen del Puerto.)

The **Parque del Retiro** is 353 acres of green in the heart of the city, with elegant gardens and woods, fountains, botanical collections, a lake where you can rent a rowboat, and the **Palacio de Cristal,** a glass structure housing varying cultural exhibits. (Metro: Retiro.) **Casa de Campo,** to the northwest, has woods, shaded lanes, a municipal pool, an excellent zoo, and an amusement park. More than ten times the size of Retiro, this park makes the city seem like a minor development on the outskirts of the forest. (Metro: Lagos or Batán, or take bus #33.) In the university section, the **Parque del Oeste** boasts the **Temple of Debod,** an authentic Egyptian temple donated by Nasser as a token of gratitude; Spanish archeologists had helped in the relocation of other temples during the construction of the Aswan Dam. In summer, plays and concerts are held on the stage behind the temple.

The **Museo de la Academia Real de Bellas Artes de San Fernando,** C. Alcalá, 13 (tel. 232 15 46), has just reopened its first-rate salons to the public. (Metro: Sol or Sevilla.) Its carefully selected collection includes Goya's haunting *Casa de Locos* (Madhouse) and carnavalesque *Entierro de la Sardina* (Sardina's Burial). (Open Tues.-Sat. 10am-noon and 4-7pm. Admission 200ptas.)

Plaza Mayor, a handsome seventeenth-century square built by Philip III for celebrations, competitions, and *autos-da-fé,* is filled with shops, markets, restaurants, and summer and Christmas festivities. Located in the most picturesque part of Old Madrid, it isn't far from smaller and quieter **Plaza de la Villa,** where you can see Madrid's **Casa de la Villa** (City Hall). South of the Plaza Mayor is the seventeenth-century **Catedral de San Isidro,** dedicated to Madrid's patron saint. The nearby **Church of San Francisco** is built on the site where, legend has it, Saint Francis built a convent in the thirteenth century.

The little-known **Museo Sorolla,** C. General Martínez Campos, 37, Chamberí (tel. 460 15 84), was the home and studio of the celebrated nineteenth-century Spanish painter. (Metro: Iglesia or Rubén Darío, or bus #5, 16, or 61. Open Sept.-July Tues.-Sun. 10am-2pm. Admission 200ptas, students free.) The **Museo Lázaro Galdiano,** C. Serrano, 112 (tel. 261 80 64), housed in a turn-of-the-century palace, has a wonderful collection of *objets d'art,* paintings (English art is well represented), and antiques. (Metro: Serrano. Open Sept.-July Tues.-Sun. 10am-2pm. Admission 150ptas.) For a sense of Spain's past—stretching back to prehistory—visit the **Museo Arqueológico Nacional,** C. Serrano, 13 (tel. 403 65 59). A life-size reproduction of the prehistoric cave paintings in Altamira is especially interesting. (Metro: Serrano. Open Tues.-Sun. 9:15am-1:45pm. Admission 200ptas, students free.) The **Museo Español de Arte Contemporáneo,** C. Juan de Herrera, 2 (tel. 449 71 50), displays an excellent collection by major twentieth-century Spanish artists, including works by Picasso, Miró, and Dali. (Metro: Moncloa. Open Tues.-Sat. 10am-6pm, Sun. 10am-3pm. Admission 200ptas, students free.) For a great view of the city, head to the top of the Edificio España at the **Plaza de España.**

For more exhaustive coverage of Madrid's treasures that we can offer here, turn to *Let's Go: Spain, Portugal, and Morocco.*

ntertainment

Every evening of the week *madrileños* are out in search of amusement, often head-g for the bars and *mesones* right after work. Streets begin to fill around 9:30pm ith people on their way to the cinema or theater, or simply taking an after-dinner roll. Late-night entertainment often means bar-hopping, a social, relatively sober perience—a *copa de vino* in animated surroundings here and there. There are ore bars on Calle de Alcalá in Madrid than in all of Norway. The cafes along **aseo de Recoletos, Plaza de Santa Bárbara, Plaza Mayor,** and the mall between ıerta del Sol and Callao are excellent hangouts. In summer, the tree-lined boule-ırd strip formed by Paseos del Prado is covered by *terrazas* or *chiringuitos,* where u can see all sorts of performers while sipping some *horchata.* Self-proclaimed ›st-modern *madrileños* and *madrileñas* have their haunt at the nameless *terraza* Paseo de la Castellana, 21. Lost Americans hang out at **Viva Madrid,** C. Manuel ernández y Gonazález, 7, near Pl. de Santa Ana. (Open daily noon-1:30am.)

Guía del Ocio (60ptas at any kiosk) offers complete listings of everything going . The *Villa de Madrid,* available free from kiosks selling bus tickets, lists all of e open-air theater, films, and concerts sponsored by the city; in July and August, ere are free cultural activities nightly in the major plazas, the **Parque del Retiro,** ıd the **Casa de Campo.** For foreign films, check the **Filmoteca,** C. Princesa, 1 (tel. 7 16 57), or the **Alphaville,** C. Princesa, 15 (tel. 248 45 24). In the summer, the **eranos de la Villa** attracts top performers from all over the world.

For live music outside of the major concert centers, try the jazz at **Café Central,** . del Angel, 10 (tel. 468 08 44). **La Fidula,** C. Huertas, 57 (tel. 429 29 47), has ve classical music, as does the **Conservatorio Superior de Música,** Pl. Isabel II ar the Palacio Real. The latter often presents free student performances, profes-onal traveling orchestras, and celebrated soloists; for dates and tickets ask at the sk inside. **Manuela,** at C. San Vicente Ferrer, 29, is good for folk music. Though tertaining, flamenco in Madrid tends to be tourist-oriented and wildly expensive. ry **Arco de Cuchilleros,** C. Cuchilleros, 7 (tel. 266 58 67), just off Pl. Mayor. The itarists are emotional and the dancers are proud stampers, but the cover charge ncluding first drink) is 1900ptas. Subsequent drinks, alcoholic or not, are 700ptas. wo shows per day (10:30pm and 12:30am). *Madrileños* say that the most authentic amenco lives at **Torres Bermejas,** C. Mesonero Romano, 11 (tel. 232 33 22). Discos e popular but can be expensive. Many have "afternoon" sessions (usually 7-10pm; lmission 250-700ptas) and "night" sessions (11:30pm-3:30am; admission up to 200ptas). Rates are higher on weekends, and men are usually charged 200ptas ore than women; check out the **Malasaña** (metro: Bilbao) and **Dos de Mayo** netro: Tribunal) areas. For salsa and Brazilian music, try **Oba Oba,** C. Jaco-etrezo, 4 (metro: Callao). **Bocaccio,** C. Marqués de la Ensenada, 16 (tel. 419 10 3; metro: Colón), and **El Baile,** C. Reina, 2 (metro: Gran Vía), are also highly commended. Gay nightlife in Madrid is concentrated around the Chueca area. ry **Elle et Lui,** Travesía de Parada, 6 (open daily 7pm-2:30am), or, for women nly, **Ella's,** at C. San Dimas. (Metro: Noviciados; open Mon.-Sat. 10pm-5am.)

No trip to Spain is complete without witnessing a bullfight. Outside the **Festival f San Isidro** (mid- to late May), *corridas* are usually every other Sunday. Keep our eyes open for posters in bars and cafés (especially on C. de la Victoria, off Carr-a San Jerónimo), or inquire at either ticket office listed below. The **Plaza de las entas,** C. de Alcalá, 237, northeast of central Madrid, is the biggest bullring in e country. (Metro: Ventas, or bus #21, 53, or 110.) Tickets are usually available n the Saturday before and the Sunday of the bullfight, at C. de la Victoria, 3, off arrera San Jerónimo, east of Puerta del Sol (metro: Sol), and the Plaza de Toros netro: Ventas). Seats cost 225-660ptas. Try to read up on bullfighting before you , or take someone along who knows about *toros,* otherwise you'll miss the many uances of the spectacle.

Near Madrid

Aranjuez, 49km south of Madrid (205ptas by train), was once the summer hau of Bourbon monarchs, but now seems to belong to tourists. Take a bus to the **Pala Real** from the station (45ptas) to see a terrific collection of pianos, finely work Vatican mosaics, sixteenth-century chandeliers from La Granja, and Flemish tap tries, in addition to the Oriental porcelain room, Chinese print room, and a gau copy of the Alhambras Mozarabic smoking room. (Open Wed.-Mon. 10am-1 and 3-6pm. Admission 175ptas.) Stay at the **Hostal Rusiñol,** C. San Antonio, (tel. 891 01 55; singles 700ptas, doubles 1300ptas).

The massive, white granite monastery of **El Escorial** claims a mountainside c hour northwest of Madrid by train (250ptas). Built as Philip II's retreat, the re complex commemorates the defeat of the French on August 10, 1557, feast of t town's patron saint, San Lorenzo. The royal pantheon, lined with jade, gray marb and bronze, preserves the remains of the greatest Spanish rulers, from Phillip on. A combination ticket (350ptas) admits you to the palace, new museum, pa theon, library, and the Prince's Cottage, one kilometer downhill. Those with ti on their hands should take the bus (1 per day, 240ptas) to **Santa Cruz del Va de los Cuidos.** The 150-meter granite cross (dedicated to the victims of the Span Civil War) commands a tremendous view of the Castilian plain. El Escorial's **tour office,** Floridablanca, 10, may be able to help you with rooms, but in summer thir are tight. Reserve ahead, or plan on returning to Madrid. **Hostal Vasco,** Plaza San ago, 11 (tel. 890 16 19), uphill from the town center, has clean and colorful roo and a seascaped restaurant. (Singles 1000ptas, doubles with bath 1700ptas.)

Segovia

Segovia is Castile at its best—splendid golden churches and twisting alleywa filled with the smell of *sopa castellana* (a rich garlic soup of sausages, bread, a eggs) and *lomo de cerdo* (slabs of roast suckling pig). Don't dash past the massi Roman aqueduct, the cathedral, and the stunning Alcázar in a quick daytrip; Seg via's cool plazas after sundown are the real attraction.

Orientation and Practical Information

Segovia lies 88km northwest of Madrid on the rail line to Valladolid and Galic **Plaza Mayor,** next to the cathedral, is the center of town.

Tourist Office: Oficina de Turismo, Pl. Mayor, 10 (tel. 43 03 28), in front of the bus stop. Information on accommodations, inter-city buses, trains, and sights—all including prices—is posted outside the door, but step inside to collect their useful map. Open Mon.-Fri. 9am-2pm and 4-6pm, Sat. 9am-2pm, closed Sun.

Post Office: Pl. del Doctor Laguna, 5. Most services open Mon.-Fri. 9am-2pm and 5-7pm, Sat. 9am-2pm. Poste Restante (enter in rear) open Mon.-Sat. 9am-2pm. **Postal Code:** 40006.

Telephones: Pl. de los Huertos, down Cronista Lecea. Open Mon.-Fri. 9am-3pm. **Telephone code:** 911.

Trains: Paseo Conde de Sepúlveda (tel. 42 15 63), southeast of the center. Walk along the Paseo and turn right onto Avda. Fernández Ladreda, or take bus #3. Trains to Madrid (9 per day, 2½ hr, 450ptas), and Valladolid via Medina del Campo (3 per day, 2¾ hr., 550ptas).

Buses: At Paseo de Sepúlveda and Avda. Fernández Ladreda (tel. 42 77 25). Buses to La Granja (9 per day), Madrid (4 per day, 1¾ hr.), Valladolid (4 per day), and Avila (2 per day).

Emergencies: Police (tel. 091); headquarters at C. Perucho, 2 (tel. 43 12 12). **Ambulance** (tel. 43 01 00).

Medical Assistance: Casa de Socorro, Arias Dávila, 3 (tel. 43 41 41).

Accommodations, Camping, and Food

Finding somewhere to sleep in Segovia is seldom a problem, even in August. The area surrounding Plaza Mayor is the best place to look.

Albergue Juvenil (IYHF), Paseo Conde de Sepúlveda (tel. 42 00 27), between the bus and train stations. A great place to stay—quiet, uncrowded, close to town, few rules, and no lockout. 500ptas. Open mid-Oct. to mid-Aug.

Casa de Huéspedes Aragon, Pl. Mayor, 4 (tel. 43 35 27), across from the tourist office. Gloomy stairwell hides clean rooms. Singles 700ptas, triples 1500ptas. **Casa Cubo** (tel. 43 63 86), upstairs, is dirtier and cheaper. Singles 600ptas, doubles 850ptas. Showers 200ptas.

Hostal Sol Cristina, C. Obispo Quesada, 40 (tel. 42 75 13), not far from Pl. Mayor. Bright rooms match owner's disposition. Singles 1000ptas, doubles 1900ptas. Showers 200ptas.

Camping: Camping Acueducto, 2km out of town on the road to La Granja (tel. 42 50 00). 225ptas per person, 225ptas per tent. Open June-Sept.

Menús del día in Segovia are usually a great bargain, and often include delicious regional specialties. Try **Mesón del Campesino,** C. de Infanta Isabel, 12, with a superb *menú* (600ptas) and even cheaper combination plates (170-390ptas). **Bar El Turel,** Santa Columba, 3, off Pl. del Azoguejo has a great view of the aqueduct, an enormous key ring collection, and cheap *platos* (250-500ptas). **Mesón Candido,** across the plaza, is only for those budget-blasters in search of the ultimate in Spanish cuisine (*menú* 150ptas).

Sights and Entertainment

The imposing **acueducto romano** (Roman aqueduct) has been moving water for over two millennia. View it at its maximum height (30m) from **Plaza del Azoguejo,** or catch its profile from the steps on the left side of the plaza.

The city's position at the confluence of the Rivers Eresma and Clamores has led people to compare Segovia to a sailing ship, with the **Alcázar** (fortress) as its majestic bow. The fortress commands a stellar view of Segovia and the surrounding plain; inside is a collection of medieval weaponry and several spectacular handcrafted ceilings. (Open April-Sept. daily 10am-7pm; Oct.-March daily 10am-6pm. Admission 125ptas, students 75ptas.)

The **catedral,** quite new by Spanish standards, is a massive late Gothic edifice. Note the strictly geometric *Entombment* sculpture by Juan de Juni, and the beautiful cloister saved from the destroyed former cathedral. (Open April-Sept. daily 9am-7pm; Oct.-March Mon.-Fri. 9:30am-1pm and 3-6pm, Sat.-Sun. 9:30am-6pm. Admission 100ptas, students 75ptas.) A good number of Romanesque churches dot the streets of Segovia; among the most outstanding are **San Esteban, San Millán, San Lorenzo, San Juan de los Caballeros,** and **La Trinidad.** (All open during mass only.)

Nighttime activity focuses on Plaza Mayor and the surrounding sidestreets. Hit the trendy **Pub Oja Blanca** or **Cafe Jeyma** in the Plaza, or relax at the **Oasis Bar** down C. Isabela de la Católica. On the second Saturday and Sunday in February, the women of Segovia symbolically take over the town's administration during the Fiesta de Santa Asueda in **Zamarramala,** 1km away, reenacting a botched attack on the Alcázar when the women of the town tried to seduce the garrison guards. There is a running of the bulls in **Cuéllar,** 46km north of Segovia on the last Sunday in August.

Near Segovia

The **Marble Rooms,** the **Throne Room** and the **Japanese Room** of **La Granja de San Ildefonso,** 11km from Segovia, are all elegantly furnished, and sections of the gardens in the immediate vicinity of the palace are well-manicured. The tourist office in Segovia can tell you when the magnificent fountains will be turned on. Buses connect Segovia and La Granja (9 per day, 25 min., 65ptas). (Palace open Mon.-Fri. 10am-1:30pm and 3-4:30pm. Admission 300ptas, students 250ptas.)

Avila

Avila is a near-perfect eleventh-century walled city set against the backdrop of the snow-capped ridge of the Sierra de Gredos. Here and there throughout town are little carved images of bulls and hogs, reminders of a Celtiberian culture much older than Alfonso's fortifications. Of the two immutable Avilian fixtures—the fortified walls and Santa Teresa de Jesús—it is the mystic's presence which is felt most strongly today. Reformer of the Carmelite order, author of *Path to Sainthood,* and founder of 17 convents, Santa Teresa was elected a Doctor of the Church in 1970. Every October the city spends a full week celebrating her, with fairs and parades of "giants" (figures with large heads). In the middle of July, **Summer Fiestas** are held, with exhibitions and bullfights.

The town is best seen from the highway to Salamanca by the Cuatro Postes. For a closer encounter, climb the walls along the *parador* on Pl. Concepción Arenal. The **catedral,** with its red-splotched interior and stone relief works, is actually embedded in the walls. The small **museo de la catedral** has a fine collection of gold and silver work and medieval paintings, including a small El Greco. (Cathedral open May-Sept. daily 8am-1pm and 3-7pm; Oct.-April 8am-1pm and 3-5pm. Free. Museum open May-Sept. daily 10am-1pm and 3-5pm. Admission 75ptas.) The **Convento de San José** is the first founded by Santa Teresa. The **Convento de Santa Teresa** was built on the site of her birth; she later had quite a few mystical experiences at the **Convento de la Encarnación.**

Avila's **oficina de turismo** is at Pl. de la Catedral, 4 (tel. (918) 21 13 87). From the train station, follow Av. José Antonio to C. de Isaac Peral and turn left on C. del Duque de Alba to Pl. de Santa Teresa (15 min.). (Open in summer Mon.-Fri. 8am-3pm, Sat. 9am-1:30pm, closed Sun.; in winter Mon.-Fri. 8am-3pm and 4-6pm, Sat. 9am-2pm, closed Sun.) Few visitors stay overnight, so rooms are easy to find. Try **Fonda La Abulense,** C. Estrada, 11 (tel. (918) 21 14 95), for nice, clean rooms and a friendly owner. (Singles 800ptas, doubles 1400ptas. Showers 150ptas.) Downstairs, **fonda Valdeverde** (tel. 21 19 70) has similar prices, but some rooms lack ventilation. **Hostal Continental,** Pl. de la Catedral, 6 (tel. 21 15 02), may have lumpy beds, but the showers are incredibly strong and hot, even late at night. (Singles 1350ptas, doubles 2200ptas, with bath 2450ptas; 150-200ptas less in off-season.)

Food in Avila means roast veal (*ternera asada* or *ternera de Avila*) and *yemas,* a local confection made of egg yolks. Try **Vinos/Comidas,** C. Martin Carramolino, 14, off C. Caballeros, just off Pl. de la Victoria, for rock-bottom prices. *Paella* 200ptas, *pollo en salsa* (chicken in sauce) 250ptas. (Open daily 1-4pm and 9-11:15pm.) **Bar Palomar,** at corner of C. Vara del Rey and C. Tomás L. de Victorias (tel. 21 31 04) is a favorite spot for *cochinillo asado* (roast pork, 600ptas). (Open Sun.-Fri. 1-4pm and 8:30-11pm, Sat. 1-4pm.) The **market** is on C. Comuneros de Castilla near Pl. de la Victoria and open daily from 9:30am to 2pm and from 4 to 7pm.

Trains bound for Salamanca from Madrid stop in Avila. From Segovia, you'll have to take a bus.

Salamanca

Salamanca is an architectural tapestry woven in sandstone, with Roman, Romanesque, Gothic, Renaissance, and baroque structures all crafted in the golden stone. Salamanca is perhaps best known for its university, the oldest in Spain. If you're interested in studying in Spain, consider the university's programs for foreigners. Though Salamanca doesn't have the Costa del Sol's beaches or Madrid's big city bustle, the student *morida* is second to none.

Orientation and Practical Information

Salamanca is due west of Segovia, to which it's connected by bus, and northwest of Madrid and Avila, with direct rail and bus connections to both.

The train station is a 20-minute walk or a short bus ride from **Plaza Mayor,** the center of town. **Ruá Mayor** connects the plaza with the university and cathedral area. **Calle de España** (Gran Vía) runs parallel to Mayor. Salamanca is small and you can get around easily on foot, but tangled streets make the tourist office's map indispensable.

Tourist Offices: National, C. de España, 39-41 (tel. 24 37 30). Excellent polyglot services. Open Mon.-Fri. 9:30am-2pm and 4:30-9pm, Sat. 9:30am-2pm, closed Sun. **Municipal,** Pl. Mayor (tel. 21 83 42). More of an information booth—get your map and go to the National. Open Mon.-Fri. 10am-1:30pm and 5-7pm, closed Sat.-Sun. **Student Travel Office: Vrajes Juventus,** Pl. Libertad, 4 (tel. 21 74 07), just north of Pl. Mayor. BIGE tickets and cheap surf deals (1 week Costa del Sol from 11,600ptas, transport included). Open Mon.-Fri. 10am-2pm and 4:30-8pm, Sat. 10:30am-2pm.

Post Office: C. de España, 25. Open Mon.-Fri. 9am-2pm and 4-6pm, Sat. 9am-2pm. **Postal Code:** 37008.

Telephones: Pl. Peña Primera, 2, off C. de Torres Villarroel. Open Mon.-Sat. 9am-1pm and 5-9pm. **Telephone code:** 923.

Trains: Avda. Estación de Ferrocarril. To reach Pl. Mayor, take the bus that runs in front of the station to Pl. del Mercado, next to Mayor. Or turn left as you exit the station down Avda. Estación de Ferrocarril to Pl. de España, and turn onto C. Azafranal (20 min.). Information (tel. 22 57 42). To Madrid (3½ hr., 975ptas), Avila, and Seville.

Buses: Avda. Filiberto Villalobos, 79 (tel. 23 67 17). Take bus labeled "Plaza del Mercado" to reach the center of town. Buses to Madrid (10 per day, 1079ptas), Barcelona, Seville (4 per day, 2565ptas), and Avila (2 hr., 470ptas).

Emergencies: Police (tel. 091); headquarters at Carretera Ciudad Rodrigo, a.k.a. N-620 (tel. 21 51 05). **Ambulance** (tel. 24 09 16).

Medical Assistance: Hospital Clínico, Paseo San Vicente (tel. 23 22 00).

Accommodations and Camping

Hotels and pensions are plentiful in Salamanca. There are lots of *fondas* around **Plaza Mayor,** and on **Calle Meléndez** just below; beds run about 600ptas per person.

Pensión Barez, C. Meléndez, 19 (tel. 21 74 95). A homey place kept sparkling clean. 600ptas per person. Showers 125ptas.

Fonda Lucero, C. Meléndez, 23 (tel. 21 55 41). A good deal if you can get an airy front room. Good place for meeting Spanish students. 600ptas per person. Hot showers 200ptas.

Hostal-Residencia Colón, Pl. de la Libertad, 10 (tel. 21 99 10), just north of Pl. Mayor. Reasonable rooms with Escher floor tiles. Singles 900ptas, doubles 1600ptas. Showers 200ptas.

Camping: Don Quijote, 4km out of town on the road to Aldealengua. 250ptas per person and per tent. Open July-Sept. **Regio** (tel. 20 02 50), 4km out of town along the road to Madrid, is open year-round, costs a bit more, and has a pool.

Food

Eating in Salamanca shouldn't be too hard on your budget. Some of the cheapest bar/restaurants are on **Calle Méndez Meléndez** or on **Ci Libreros,** by the university. Substantial meals will set you back no more than 375ptas. Try the *jeta,* a local *tapas* of skin from the mouth of a pig. The **Plaza del Mercado** has a market for produce and picnic makings.

Comedor Universitario, C. Peñuelas de San Blas. A bland but cheap student mensa. Student cards not checked. Full meals 250-300ptas. Open Oct.-May.

Mesón Cervantes, Pl. Mayor, 15, first floor. A stoic likeness of Cervantes reminds students of their work. Great *platos combinados* 340ptas at the long wooden benches, 50ptas more outside on the terrace. Open daily 1-4pm and 7:30-11pm.

El Drogstore, C. Condes de Crespo Rascón. A student tradition; ask anyone for directions. Good for late-night junk food and *horchata.* Open 24 hours.

El Candil, C. Aguilera, 10, off C. Amarillo. A cozy dining room hidden behind a crowded *tapas* bar. Always full despite the prices: *menú de la casa* 1200ptas. Popular with Spanish families. Open 1-4pm and 8-10pm.

Sights and Entertainment

Plaza Mayor, considered by many the most beautiful main square in Spain, was built by Philip II and is a fine place for admiring both architecture and passersby. Between the arches are carved medallions of famous Spaniards, from El Cid and Cervantes to Franco. The **Town Hall** is the large, handsome building in the center of the square.

The **university,** the focal point of Salamanca, is entered from Patio de las Escuelas, off C. Libreros. The facade is one of the best examples of Spanish Plateresque, a style named after the silversmith's intricate art. Look for the small frog carved on a skull in the facade's right pilaster; students claim it gives them good luck on exams. Don't miss the **Escuelas Menores,** across the plaza, with its *Cielo de Salamanca* (Sky of Salamanca), a fifteenth-century fresco of the signs of the zodiac. (Both buildings open Mon.-Fri. 9:30am-1:30pm and 4-6:30pm, Sat. 9:30am-1:30pm and 4:30-6:30pm, Sun. and holidays 10am-1pm. Admission 150ptas, free with university ID but not ISIC.)

The **New Cathedral**'s beautiful Plateresque facades and lovely cloister by Alberto Churriguera are next door to the Romanesque **Old Cathedral,** which has an amazing Nicolás Florentino altarpiece that tells the story of the Virgin Mary in 53 scenes. In the apocalyptic cupola, angels separate out the sinners. The "degree chapel," once the site of final exams for the university's degree candidates, seems a fitting place for divinely inspired essays. (Open June-Sept. daily 10am-2pm and 4-6pm, Oct.-May daily 9:30am-1:30pm and 3:30-6pm. Admission 75ptas.)

The **Casa de las Conchas** (House of Shells) was decorated with chiseled conch shells as a monument to the shells brought back by pilgrims to Santiago de Compostela. Unfortunately, it blocks the view of the splendid baroque **Clerecía** across the street; fervent Jesuit residents once offered to dispense large sums of money if the house would be torn down.

In the center of the **Puente Romano,** a 2000-year-old Roman bridge spanning the River Tormes, stands the **Toro Ibérico,** a huge headless granite bull. The view from the opposite side of the bridge is magnificent.

Salamanca hums at night with the animated ruminations of its libated educated. Before dinner, students collect *tapas* and beer in the area between Plaza del Mercado and Plaza San Julián. Later, crowds gather to gander on Plaza Mayor; **Café Novelty,** at the northeast corner, is the oldest in the city. **El Puerto de Chus,** at Plaza San Julián, is known as one of the best late-night spots; other late-night bars line C. Meléndez and C. Isaac de Peyra. Read posters at the **Colegio Mayor** (Palacio de Anaya) or ask at the tourist office to learn about the most current student happenings.

Burgos

Tranquil and conservative, Burgos is the site of one of Spain's most magnificent cathedrals and the city most closely associated with El Cid, Castile's real-life epic hero. Legendary as the liberator of Valencia from the Moors, El Cid is honored by a colossal statue in Plaza del General Primo de Rivera. Burgos also considers itself among the most purely Castilian cities in Spain; the clipped and exquisite Spanish of its residents will make you stand up and take notice.

Orientation and Practical Information

Burgos lies 250km due north of Madrid, connected by rail to Madrid, Valladolid, ilbao (with connections to France), and Calatayud, on the Madrid-Barcelona line. The city spreads on both sides of the River Arlanzón. The bus and train stations re on the southern side; everything else of interest on the other bank.

Tourist Office: Oficina de Turismo, Pl. Alonso Martínez, 7 (tel. 20 31 25). Hotel and sights information posted in the window. From the train station, cross the bridge straight ahead and go right along the river bank. Enter through the Arco de Santa María, and from Pl. del Rey San Fernando to the right of cathedral entrance, continue straight up C. Paloma and C. Laín Calvo, until you reach Pl. Alonso Martínez. Open Mon.-Fri. 8am-3pm and 4:30-6:30pm, Sat. 9am-2pm.

Budget Travel: Viajes TIVE, on Pl. San Juan in the Casa de Cultura (tel. 20 98 81). BIGE and good advice. Open Mon.-Fri. 9am-2pm.

Post Office: Pl. Conde de Castro, 1 (tel. 26 27 50), just across the river. Stamps and Poste Restante open Mon.-Fri. 9am-2pm and 4-6pm, Sat. 9am-2pm.

Telephones: C. de San Lesmes, 18, off Pl. España, but around the side of the building. Open Mon.-Sat. 9am-1pm and 5-9pm. **Telephone code:** 947.

Trains: Station is at the end of Avda. Conde Guadalhorce (tel. 20 35 60), across the river from Pl. Castilla (15 min. on foot). 12 trains per day to Madrid, 4 to Barcelona, 12 to San Sebastián and the French border, and many more. Information open daily 7am-1pm. 24-hr. baggage check (100ptas). **RENFE** is at C. Moneda, 21 (tel. 20 90 31). Open Mon.-Fri. 9am-1pm and 4-7pm, Sat. 9am-1pm.

Buses: C. Miranda, 4-6 (tel. 26 55 65), off Pl. Vega, across the river from the cathedral. 5 buses per day to Madrid, 2 to Barcelona, 1 to San Sebastián, 1 to Valladolid, 1 to León; 2-4 per week to Paris and London (10% discount to students with Linebus Co.), and many others.

Emergencies: Police (tel. 091). Headquarters at C. Merced, 11 (tel. 20 21 38).

Medical Assistance: Casa de Socorro, C. Conde de Vallellano, 4 (tel. 26 14 10), at C. Ramón y Cajal, near the post office.

Laundry: Lavomatique, C. Moneda, 18. Open daily 9am-1pm and 5-8pm.

Accommodations, Camping, and Food

Burgos offers its visitors lots of respectable and fairly cheap places to stay. Look round Plaza José Antonio for the more respectable, Plaza de Vega for the cheaper.

Albergue Juvenil (IYHF), C. General Vigón (tel. 22 03 62). Walk out Avda. de los Reyes Católicos, and take a left at the intersection. The hostel is in a *colegio* on the right. Members 450ptas, breakfast included; nonmembers 600ptas. Open July-Aug.

Hostal Victoria, C. San Juan, 3 (tel. 20 15 42), off C. Laín Calvo, just around the corner from the tourist office. Bright rooms with character. Singles 700ptas, doubles 1200ptas. Showers 150ptas.

Hostal García, C. Santander, 1 (tel. 20 55 53). Reasonable rooms run by an unassuming family. Singles 800ptas, doubles 1400ptas; perhaps negotiable.

Fonda Fontaneda, C. Concepción, 14 (tel. 20 80 35), a block from Pl. de Vega. Religious effigies adorn the walls. Doubles 1250ptas.

Camping: Most reasonable and pleasant is **Fuentes Blancas** (tel. 22 10 16), 3km east of downtown near the Cartuja de Miraflores monastery. Take the bus which leaves on the hr. from Pl. Primo de Rivera (42ptas). 225ptas per person, 175ptas per tent. Open April-Sept.

Burgos, in the middle of one of Spain's richest agricultural regions, has staggeringly good food. Try any lamb or pork dish, *morcilla de Burgos* (blood sausage), or the city's famed *queso fresco* (cream cheese); do so outside the touristy neighborhood surrounding the cathedral. The smoky neighborhood **Bar-Restaurante Casa Constan,** Avda. el Cid Campeador, 2 (tel. 20 88 49), at C. Hortelanos, includes surprisingly good seafood for landlocked Burgos in its 525ptas *menú.* (Open daily for meals 1-3:30pm and 9-11:30pm.) The next best thing to the supermarket is **Bar la Moneda,** C. Moneda, 13, where you can get hot dogs (75ptas) and cheap *raciones* (45-60ptas); ample *platos combinados* 250-375ptas. You'll find some cheap *menus* around Plaza de Vega; **Restaurante Casa Pepe,** C. de San Cosme, 22 (tel. 20 61 05), is simple and no-frills with a 500ptas *menu.* For a little bit of style, head back over the river to **Restaurante Casa Ojeda,** C. Victoria, 5, next to Pl. Calvo Sotelo. This local favorite serves 600ptas *combinados* in the downstairs bar/cafeteria, and exquisite food upstairs in the restaurant. (House specialty—roast lamb—1300ptas. Entrees 800-1200ptas. Open daily 1-4pm and 9-11:30pm.) Look for Burgos's daily **market** on C. Miranda by the bus station.

Sights and Entertainment

Burgos's landmark will always be its **cathedral,** a majestic Gothic structure topped by two lacy stone spires. Built during the thirteenth and fifteenth centuries, it features exemplary Gothic and Plateresque architecture and artwork. Notice the glorious vaulting, complete with glass sections, over the main crossing, and the octagonal Capilla del Condestable, behind the main altar. The *capilla mayor,* in the center of the church, contains the tombs of El Cid and his wife, while the famous *Cofre del Cid,* the box in which his remains were found, hangs against a side wall. The cathedral **museum** counts among its treasures an auburn-haired *Magdalena* attributed to da Vinci. Ask the souvenir vendor in the back to see it. (Open daily 10am-1:30pm and 4-6:30pm. Admission to museum and chapels 150ptas, students 100ptas.)

A few steps across Plaza de Santa María stands the **Santa María Arch,** erected as a gateway to the walled city and later decorated with the busts of Burgos's favorites: a guardian angel, Emperor Charles V, and, *rigurosamente,* El Cid. The Gothic **Church of San Nicolás** contains a unique stone ornamental *reredos* depicting the saint's life.

Past the fifteenth-century **Casa del Cordón** on C. Santander (where Columbus once met with Ferdinand and Isabella, and Philip the Fair expired after a trying game of handball, leaving his wife Juana the Mad utterly insane), you'll find the **Museo Marceliano Santa María** in the ruins of a monastery on Pl. San Juan, containing the Burgalese painter's vaguely impressionist Castilian landscapes and portraits of his contemporaries. (Open Tues.-Sat. 10am-2pm and 5-8pm, Sun. 10am-2pm. Admission 25ptas.) Across the river, the **Museo Arqueológico** houses Gothic, Moorish, and Roman artifacts from Burgos and environs. (Open Tues.-Sun. 10am-1:30pm and 5-7pm. Admission 150ptas.)

The **Museo-Monasterio de las Huelgas Reales,** 1km west of Burgos, was a summer palace for Castilian monarchs and later a convent for Cistercian nuns. It contains royal sepulchers and a collection of medieval clothing, plus several beautiful rooms and a Romanesque cloister. (Open Tues.-Sat. 11am-2pm and 4-6pm, Sun. 11am-2pm. Admission 150ptas, including Spanish tour; students free.) Three kilometers east of Burgos is the **Cartuja de Miraflores,** a Carthusian monastery representing the peak of the Isabeline style. The abbey church houses the ornate tombs of King John II, his wife, Isabel of Portugal, and Don Alfonso, her brother who died as a child. (Open Mon.-Sat. 10:15am-3pm and 4-7pm, Sun. 11:20am-12:30pm, 1-3pm, and 4-7pm. Free.) To get there, take the Fuentes Blancas bus from Plaza Primo de Rivera (1 per hr., 42ptas), or walk along lovely Paseo de la Quintra.

People-watching is a veritable sport in this city, and the best takes place along elegant **Paseo del Espolón,** by the river. The younger crowd is more likely to hang out on pub-lined **Plaza Huerto del Rey,** a block from Calle Paloma, or along Calle San Juan. Some popular places there include **Distrito,** C. San Juan, 22, and **Ibiza,** C. San Juan, 43. Burgos's major festival is held annually in late June, in honor of the city's patron saints Peter and Paul.

.eón

León still likes to remind the world that it had had 24 kings before Castile had ws. Though this blue and airy city reached its peak in the eleventh century, it's ill remarkably appealing. One of the outstanding attractions is the colossal **Cathe-ral,** a thirteenth-century Gothic extravaganza with so many resplendent stained lass windows that the walls have required reinforcements. (Open Mon.-Sat. 0:30am-1pm and 4-6pm, Sun. 10:30am-1pm. Admission to museum 150ptas.) An-ther is the **Basilica of San Isidro,** a Romanesque structure whose pantheon is oated with vibrant, perfectly preserved frescoes from the twelfth century. (Open Iay-Sept. Mon.-Fri. 9am-2pm and 3:30-8pm, Sat. 10am-noon; Oct.-April Mon.-'ri. 10am-1:30pm and 4-6pm, Sat. 10am-noon. Admission 150ptas.)

The **Oficina de Turismo** (tel. (987) 23 70 82) is at Pl. de Regla, 3, in front of ne cathedral. (Open Mon.-Fri. 9am-2pm and 4-6pm, Sat. 9am-1pm, closed Sun.) **lesidencia Juvenil Infanta Doña Sancha,** C. de la Corredera, 2 (tel. (987) 20 22 1), is a clean, modern university dorm used as a hotel in the summer. (500ptas er person, 600ptas for ages 26 and older. Open June-Sept.) Cheap *pensiones* are ocated on Avda. de Roma, which branches to the left from the plaza across the iver from the train station. **Hostal-Residencia Guzmán el Bueno,** López Castrillón, (tel. (987) 23 64 12), has large modern rooms. (Singles 1100ptas, doubles 1700ptas. howers 250ptas.) For cheap eats, try **La Cepedana,** C. Mariano D. Berrueta, 11, ıst off C. del Generalísimo near the cathedral, or its next-door neighbors. (All have *nenús* for 400-450ptas.) **Restaurant Fornos,** C. del Cid off C. del Generalísimo, has xcellent food for 325-650ptas.

León is on a direct rail line to Avila (1220ptas) and Madrid (1695ptas). No trains un to Salamanca—take the bus (1230ptas).

Toledo

Toledo flourished during one of the most auspicious periods in Spanish history. The medieval *convivencia*—peaceful coexistence and collaboration among Chris-ians, Muslims, and Jews—has left behind a dignified and slightly mystical walled ity. Toledo's monuments crowd together in a dizzying anarchy of periods and tyles, held together in a medieval matrix of sagging houses, churches, synagogues, nd mosques. The city that El Greco portrayed in a few of his rare landscapes has hanged little over the years.

Orientation and Practical Information

Toledo is an easy daytrip from Madrid, but try to stay overnight to avoid the rowds. No Castilian city is as labyrinthine as Toledo, so ask for the large poster nap (with monuments in 3-D and an El Greco monk on the back) at Turismo; it's vorlds better than the small one in the Toledo brochure.

Tourist Office: Turismo, on the north side of town, just outside Puerta de Bisagra (tel. 22 08 43). The bus from the train station stops in front. Some English spoken. Open Mon.-Fri. 9am-3pm and 4-6pm, Sat. 9am-1:30pm.

Post Office: C. de los Clérigos Menores, 2, off C. de la Plata. Open Mon.-Fri. 9am-2pm and 4-6pm; Poste Restante Mon.-Fri. 9am-2pm. **Postal Code:** 45001.

Telephones: C. de la Plata, 18. Visa card accepted for calls of 500ptas minimum value. Open Mon.-Sat. 9am-1pm and 5-9pm. **Telephone code:** 925.

Train Station: Paseo de la Rosa (tel. 22 30 99), across the Puente del Safont. Trains leave every 1-2 hr. to Aranjuez (230ptas) and Madrid's Atocha Station (380ptas). Connections to Avila in Madrid. The bus marked "Santa Bárbara" runs from the station to the central Pl. de Zocodover—45ptas will save you a 20-min. uphill trek.

Bus Station: In the Zona de Nominada Safón, just northwest of the Puente de Azarquiel outside the old city. **Continental/Galiano** (tel. 22 29 61) to Madrid (every hr., 360ptas). **Samar Bus Co.** to La Mancha, also frequently.

Emergencies: Police (tel. 091). Headquarters at Pl. del Ayuntamiento (tel. 22 34 07).

Medical Assistance: Seguridad Social, Avda. Barver (tel. 22 55 00).

Accommodations, Camping, and Food

Most tourists make Toledo a daytrip from Madrid, so you should have little trouble finding a room.

Residencia Juvenil (IYHF): Castillo de San Servando (tel. 22 45 54). Uphill on the left from the train station; across the Puente Viejo from the center of town. A castle from without and a palace from within. Comfy TV room, beautiful pool. Members only. 410ptas per person. Sheets 185ptas. Breakfast 85ptas; lunch 415ptas, dinner 440ptas. 1am curfew. Open year-round.

Fonda Segovia, C. Recoletos, 4 (tel. 21 11 24), just off C. de la Sillería (off Pl. de Zocodover). Clean, refreshingly quiet rooms. Doubles and triples 675ptas per person. Showers included, but don't expect hot water.

Pensión Descalzos, C. de los Descalzos, 30 (tel. 22 28 88), just inside the southern walls east of Pl. del Tránsito, near the Casa del Greco. Brand new and spacious. May soon have a second story with good views. Singles 700ptas, doubles 1300ptas, with bath 2000ptas. Hot showers included.

Fonda Lumbreras, C. Juan Labrador, 7 (tel. 22 15 71), near the Alcázar. Adequate rooms, but many noisy kids in this family-run establishment. Doubles 1200ptas, triples and quads 1800ptas. Showers 150ptas. **Hostal Residencia Labrador** at #16 (tel. 22 26 20) has singles for 1166ptas, doubles with shower 2120ptas, with bath 2544ptas.

Camping: Camping El Greco (tel. 21 35 37) is 1½km from town on the road to Madrid. **Camping Circo Romano,** Circo Romano, 21 (tel. 22 04 42), is closer to the old city. Both charge about 275ptas per person, 275ptas per tent. The latter has a great pool—450ptas to enter (550ptas on weekends).

Food in Toledo is tough on the budget. At **Restaurante Bisagra,** C. Real del Arrabal, 14, just within the Puerta Nueva de Bisagra, you can eat *platos combinados,* such as fried chicken with fries, for 425ptas. (Open daily 1-4pm and 8:30pm-1am.) **El Nido,** Pl. de la Magdalena, 5, just south of Pl. de Zocodover, has a 650ptas three-course *menu,* wine included. (Open daily 1-4pm and 8-11pm.) Excellent *pollo ajillo* (garlic chicken) is only 475ptas at **Restaurante La Cubana,** Paseo de la Rosa, 2 (tel. 22 00 88), in front of the Puente Viejo de Alcántara. (Open daily 1-5pm and 7-11pm.) **Restaurant Sinaí,** C. de los Reyes Católicos, 7, across from the Sinagoga de Santa María la Blanca, is run by an amicable English-speaking Moroccan who claims to be the only Jew resident in Toledo since the 1500s. Try the lamb kebab and couscous for 800ptas. (Open Wed.-Mon. 10am-7pm.) Sit on the terrace at **Restaurante Chirón,** Puerta del Cambrión, 1 (tel. 22 01 50), off Paseo de Recaredo on the west side of the city. The menu is expensive, but *not* if you order the Navarra trout (500ptas), which is out of this world. (Open July daily 10am-4pm and 8pm-midnight; Sept.-June daily 10am-11pm.)

Sights

Although religious harmony deteriorated over the centuries, artifacts of Christian, Muslim, and Jewish origin continue to complement one another in Toledo, often within the same building.

The **catedral** is a rich and complex banquet of architectural styles that will take hours to explore. Admission to the church is free but a 250ptas fee is charged for admission to the treasure, the *coro,* the chapterhouse, the Kings' Chapel, and the sacristy. The museum annex contains paintings by such old masters as El Greco and Caravaggio. (Open July-Aug. daily 10:30am-1pm and 3:30-7pm; Sept.-June until 6pm.)

Domenico Theotocopuli, alias El Greco, is in part responsible for Toledo's image as an entrancing, mysterious place. His tempestuous skies and expressive, almost tortured-looking portraits have come to be identified with this city. El Greco canvasses lurk at every turn—many of his paintings have not left Toledo since the sixteenth century. The modest Mudéjar **Church of San Tomé** houses one of El Greco's best known works, *El entierro del Conde de Orgaz* (*The Burial of Count Orgaz*), a subtle meeting of heaven and earth. (Open in summer Tues.-Sat. 10am-1:45pm and 3:30-6:45pm, Sun. 10am-1:45pm; in winter Tues.-Sat. 10am-1:45pm and 3:30-5:45pm, Sun. 10am-1:45pm. Admission 150ptas.) The so-called **Casa del Greco,** at C. S. Levi, 3, stands at best only close to where the painter lived. Nevertheless, it is a fine example of Toledo's sixteenth-century secular architecture and twentieth-century tourist allure. Get here very early to avoid crowds. (Open in summer Tues.-Sat. 10am-1:45pm and 3:30-5:45pm, Sun. 10am-1:45pm; in winter Tues.-Sat. 10am-1:45pm and 4-5:45pm, Sun. 10am-1:45pm. Admission 200ptas.) The **Museo de Santa Cruz,** at C. Cervantes, 3, houses a well-organized and mercifully undertouristed collection of tapestries and paintings, including works by El Greco. (Open Mon.-Sat. 10am-6:30pm, Sun. 10am-2pm. Admission 200ptas, students free.)

Two synagogues are all that remain of what was once the largest Jewish community in Spain. The **Sinagoga del Tránsito,** constructed in the fourteenth century by Samuel Ha-Levi, treasurer to Peter I of Castile, has wonderful Mudéjar decorations and an *artesonado* ceiling. Three rooms house the **Museo Sefardí** and its collection of Sephardic manuscripts, inscriptions, amulets, and sarcophagus lids. (Open Tues.-Sat. 10am-1:45pm and 3:30-5:45pm, Sun. 10am-1:45pm. Admission 200ptas.) The nearby **Sinagoga de Santa María la Blanca** was built to function as a synagogue, looks like a mosque, and was for many years a church. (Open in summer daily 10am-2pm and 3:30-7pm; in winter daily 10am-2pm and 3:30-6pm. Admission 50ptas.)

Reminders of the Muslim presence in Toledo are visible near the **Puerta del Sol,** a fourteenth-century Mudéjar gate. The **Mezquita del Cristo de la Luz** has been both a Muslim and a Christian place of worship. The tenth-century mosque, built on the site of a Visigothic church, is the only building in Toledo to survive from the pre-Christian era. The Visigothic columns support arches inspired by the mosque at Córdoba. Nearby is the church of **Santiago del Arrabal,** an outstanding Mudéjar temple.

The **Alcázar** commands Toledo's skyline. Little remains of the original thirteenth-century structure, last used for practical purposes during the Spanish Civil War, when 538 rebels sought its refuge. Today the fortress is a painful reminder of years of war and dictatorship. (Open March-Aug. daily 9:30am-7pm; Sept.-Oct. daily 9:30am-6:30pm; Nov.-Feb. daily 9:30am-6pm. Admission 100ptas.)

Near Toledo

A virtually impregnable hilltop town, **Cuenca** perches on high, surrounded by swift-flowing rivers and towering mountains. The city's confined quarters are responsible for Cuenca's famed **Casas Colgadas** (Hanging Houses), dangling as precariously over the banks of the River Huécar today as they did six centuries ago. The footbridge some 60m above the river affords the best view. Cuenca also possesses the only Gothic-Anglo-Norman **catedral** in Spain, dominating Plaza Mayor. The **Museo de Arte Abstracto,** a museum of modern Spanish painters, demonstrates decisively that Spanish modern art did not stop with Picasso. (Open Tues.-Fri. 11am-2pm and 4-6pm, Sat. 11am-2pm and 4-10pm, Sun. 11am-2pm.) Less compelling is the **Museo Arqueológico.** (Open Tues.-Fri. 10am-2pm and 4-6pm, Sun. 10am-2pm. Admission 25ptas.)

The **tourist office,** C. Dalmacio García Izcara, 9 (tel. (966) 22 22 31) can help with accommodations. (Open Mon.-Fri. 9am-2pm and 4-6pm, Sat. 9am-2pm.) The **Hostería Central,** on C. Alonso Chirino (tel. (966) 21 15 11) is passable. (Singles 675ptas, doubles 950ptas.) For food, look along Calle Cervantes or Calle República Argentina in the old city.

Andalusia (Andalucía)

The colorful customs and sights that most foreigners associate with Spain—flamenco, bullfights, sunny coastal resorts, white-washed houses hung with flowers—are mainly characteristic of Andalusia, much to the Andalusians's pride and other Spaniards's chagrin. Scenes of poverty and desolation, however, often counter the flashy attractions, for Andalusia is one of Spain's poorest regions.

Seville (Sevilla)

Seville's whitewashed grace, jasmined balconies, and exotic parks may convince you that romantic cities still exist. Held by Romans, Moors, and the Catholic Kings, Seville has never failed to spark the imagination of newcomers. Jean Cocteau included it in his trio of magic cities. St. Teresa denounced it as the work of the Devil. *Carmen, Don Giovanni,* the *Barber of Seville,* and Dostoevsky's *Grand Inquisitor* are only a few of the artistic works inspired by the metropolis. Whether or not the Moorish historian al-Saqundi was right in proclaiming that even the milk of birds can be found here, the sweetness of Seville still seduces the unwary traveler with an enchantment tough to dispel.

Orientation and Practical Information

Seville is situated in far southwestern Spain, 100km upriver from the coast. The city is a major travel hub with lines west to Portugal, south to Cádiz, and east to Córdoba and Madrid.

The River Guadalquivir runs approximately north-south through Seville. Most of the city, including the old quarter of **Barrio de Santa Cruz,** is on the east bank, while the **Barrio de Triana,** the old gypsy quarter, lies on the west bank. Between the two train stations, running north-south, is the main street, **Avenida de la Constitución,** with the famous cathedral and Giralda Tower. Look for the cathedral's conspicuous bell tower to get your bearings; the tourist office, the major sights, the post office, and banks are all concentrated in this area.

Tourist Office: Oficina de Turismo, Avda. de la Constitución, 21b (tel. 22 14 04), 1 block south of the cathedral. Very helpful staff. Excellent map and brochures. Open April-Sept. Mon.-Sat. 9am-7pm, Sun. 9:30am-1:30pm; Oct.-March Mon.-Sat. 9am-7pm, closed Sun.

Budget Travel: Viajes TIVE, Avda. Reina Mercedes, 53 (tel. 61 31 88). BIGE and good advice. Open Mon.-Fri. 9am-2pm and 4-6pm.

American Express: Viajes Alhambra TTE, Coronel Segui, 3 (tel. 21 29 23), just north of Pl. Nueva. Mail held, cardholders' checks cashed, traveler's checks sold. Exchange currency at a bank—they rake in 2% here. Open Mon.-Fri. 9am-1pm and 4-8pm, Sat. 9am-1pm.

Post Office: Avda. de la Constitución, 32 (tel. 22 88 80). Stamps sold Mon.-Fri. 9am-9pm, Sat. 9am-2pm. Poste Restante open Mon.-Fri. 9am-8pm, Sat. 10am-2pm. **Postal Code:** 41001.

Telephones: Pl. Nueva, 3. Open Mon.-Fri. 9am-1pm and 5-9pm, Sat. 9am-noon. **Telephone code:** 054.

Flights: Airport (tel. 31 61 11). Iberia office in town at C. Almirante Lobo (tel. 22 89 01). 10 buses per day (250ptas) run between the Iberia office and the airport.

Trains: Estación de Córdoba, Pl. de Armas, 56 (tel. 22 88 17), just off C. Marqués de Paradas on the west side of the city, is the city's principal terminal. **Estación de Cádiz,** C. San Bernardo, 13 (tel. 23 22 55), on the east side, just off C. Menéndez y Pelayo, has some regional and coastal service, including trains to and from Cádiz. **RENFE,** C. de Zaragoza, 29 (tel. 23 19 24).

Buses: Main Station, C. José María Osborne, 11 (tel. 41 71 11), has service to most of Andalusia, plus Barcelona and Madrid. Luggage storage 45ptas per day.

Laundry: Lavandería Robledo, C. F. Sánchez Bedoya, 18. One block south of the cathedral off Avda. de la Constitución. 2-hr. service; 5kg washed and dried for 750ptas. Open Mon.-Fri. 10am-2pm and 5-8pm, Sat. 10am-2pm.

Emergencies: Police (tel. 091); headquarters at Pl. de la Gavidia (tel. 22 88 40).

Medical Assistance: Casa de Socorro, C. Jesús del Gran Poder, 34 (tel. 22 47 60 or 38 24 61). English spoken at **Hospital Universitario,** Avda. Dr. Fedriani (tel. 37 84 00).

Consulates: U.K., Pl. Nueva, 8 (tel. 22 88 75).

ccommodations and Camping

Seville has ample cheap lodgings for as little as 600ptas per person. The best area search is the Barrio de Santa Cruz, especially in the streets off **Calle Mateos Gago.** so try the Plaza de Curtidores and the Plaza de Pilatos, in the Barrios de la Puerta d de Carmona to the north. Calle de San Eloy, in the city's commercial district, lined with *hostales* at generally higher prices. Pedro del Torro and Gravina, both st east of the Córdoba Station, are chock full o' cheap places. During *Semana nta* (Holy Week) and the *Feria de Abril* (April Fair) rates more than double and servations are necessary. In low season, you can bargain; "official prices" exist be lowered.

Albergue Juvenil Fernando el Santo (IYHF), C. Isaac Peral, 2 (tel. 61 31 50). Take bus #19 or walk the 2km out of town. Inconvenient and mostly filled with local students. Members 550ptas, nonmembers 650ptas. No curfew. Open year-round.

Hostal-Residencia Monreal, Rodrigo Caro 8 (tel. 21 41 66). A place with character and an excellent location in the Barrio de Santa Cruz. Singles 800ptas, doubles 1600ptas. Showers included.

Hostal Bienvenido, C. Archeros, 14 (tel. 41 36 55), near the Pl. de los Curtidores. Simple, clean rooms. English spoken. 750ptas per person. Showers 150ptas.

Hostal Virgen de los Reyes, C. Alvarez Quintero, 31 (tel. 21 48 51), west of the cathedral's Moorish gate. Clean student quarters with terraces, kitchen facilities, and TV. Singles 1000ptas, doubles 1800ptas. Showers included.

Hostal La Gloria, C. de San Eloy, 58 (tel. 22 26 73). Sunny rooms with pristine baths. Singles 1000ptas, doubles 1800ptas. Showers included.

Fonda Ramos, C. de San Eloy, 45 (tel. 22 69 38). Colorful hodgepodge with low prices and matching quality. 600ptas per person. Showers 100ptas.

Camping: The area's 3 campsites are the **Sevilla** (tel. 51 43 79), 6km out on Carretera de Córdoba, the **Wilson** (tel. 72 08 28), 8km out on the Carretera de Cádiz, and the **Club de Campo** (tel. 72 02 50), right nearby. Most charge about 250ptas per person and are open year-round. Seville has more facilities.

ood

Food is generally expensive by Spanish standards, but you can still find enjoyable d cheap meals. Get groceries at the **Mercadillo de Triana,** just across the Puente Isabel II from the main part of the city. Indistinguishable cheap restaurants clus- on C. del Marqués de Paradas, near the Pl. de Armas train station.

Rincón San Eloy, C. de San Eloy, 24 (tel. 22 25 04). Barking waiters amidst old wine barrels in a typical courtyard. Various *platos* 400ptas, *menú* 490ptas. Meals served daily 1:30-4pm and 9-11pm.

Bar Pizzeria "El Artesano," C. Mateus Gago, 9 (tel. 21 38 58). Drinkers from the *bodega* across the street file in for Spanish-style pizzas, some with goat's cheese (250-500ptas). Open daily noon-midnight.

Los Gallegos, Carpio, 3 (tel. 21 40 11), an alley off the Campaña. Plentiful fare and plenty greasy. Popular with local families. Main dishes 290-380ptas, *menú del día* 495ptas. Open Thurs.-Tues.

Jalea Real, Sor Angela de la Cruz, 37, near the Pl. de la Encarnación. Excellent vegetarian selection. *Menú* 550ptas. Open Mon.-Fri. 1-5pm and 8pm-midnight, Sat. 1-5pm.

Sights and Entertainment

In 1401, the Catholics razed the greatest of the Almohad mosques in Seville an built, on the same spot, a church "so great that those who come after us will tak us for madmen." From the street, the **Cathedral** seems unimpressive; you must g inside to get a sense of its dimensions. Massive pillars support the vaulted roof, an the wealth of treasure is fabulous beyond belief. Only St. Peter's in Rome and S Paul's in London are larger. The ponderous gold and black coffin bearers at th entrance allegedly carry the tomb of Christopher Columbus. The reliquaries contai remains of saints and apostles, and the walls are hung with relatively minor work by major artists including Murillo, Goya, Luis de Vargas, and others. The **Giralc** was the minaret of the Almohad mosque. The Christians made only modest alte ations to it: A belfry was added, as was a weather vane whose gyrations inspir the tower's name. The austerity of the Almohad sect is apparent in the clean lin and simplicity of ornamentation. From the top, there's a good view of the city acro the barbed spires and buttresses of the roof. (Cathedral and tower open daily Ma Sept. Mon.-Sat. 10:30am-1:30pm and 4:30-6:30pm, Sun. 10:30am-1pm; Oct.-Apr Mon.-Sat. 10:30am-1pm and 4-6pm, Sun. 10:30am-1pm. Admission 125ptas. N shorts allowed.)

On the other side of the **Lonja Palace,** a sixteenth-century structure now hon to maps and documents relating to the discovery of the New World, is the **Alcáza** a magnificent fourteenth-century Mudéjar palace with both Gothic and Mooris features. Almost as stunning as the intricate tilework in the palace's interior a the resplendent gardens outside. (Open daily 9am-12:45pm and 3-5:45pm. Admi sion 125ptas.) Built in 1540 by the Marquis of Tarifa, the **Casa de Pilatos,** on th plaza of the same name, is now home to the Duke of Medinaceli. The building another fine example of Mudéjar architecture. (Open May-Sept. daily 9am-8pn Oct.-April daily 9am-7pm. Admission 200ptas.)

The **Museo Provincial de Bellas Artes,** in the former Convento de la Merce on Pl. del Museo, has a collection of Spanish masters second only to the Prado i Madrid. In a sixteenth-century Andalusian palace and a connected church, th open-air galleries are richly perfumed with the flowers from the patio, and hold a amazing collection of Murillo and Valdés Leal, plus a few works by Velázquez, Zu barán, and others. (Open Tues.-Fri. 10am-2pm and 4-7pm, Sat.-Sun. 10am-2pn Admission 250ptas.) More works by Murillo and Valdés Leal can be seen in th church **Hospital de la Caridad,** on C. Temprado, parallel to the Paseo de Coló (Open daily 9:30am-1:30pm and 4-7pm. Admission 100ptas.) The **Museo de Ar Contemporáneo,** C. Santo Tomás, 5, exhibits the vanguard of twentieth-centu Spanish art. (Open Tues.-Fri. 10am-2pm and 5-8pm, Sat.-Sun 10am-2pm. Admi sion 250ptas.)

If you tire of the art, architecture, and withering heat, escape to a tiled benc in one of Seville's many shady retreats, such as the **Parque María Luisa,** or th **Jardines de Murillo.** In front of the Córdoba Station, in the middle of the mo intolerable traffic, are the banks of the Guadalquivir, where you can rent rowboa or paddleboats in summer (230ptas per hr.).

To experience the local *sevillana* brand of *flamenco* music and dancing, drop in **La Garrocha,** on C. Salado in Barrio de los Remedios, where highly talented patro dance. For a quieter evening, make your way to **La Carbonería,** C. Levies, 18, ne C. Menéndez y Pelayo; the place has a long tradition of fostering young artists Seville. Sample local wine amidst the 5-meter high vats of **Casa Morales,** one bloc west of the cathedral on C. Garcia de Vinuesa. In the Barrio Sta. Cruz, wand from the lively local hangout **La Gitanilla,** C. Xímenez de Enciso, 11, up to th Pl. de los Venerables and the **Hostería de Laurel. Tibus II,** on C. Descalyos, is lesbian club. Gay bars are abundant on **C. Trastamara.**

Seville's **Semana Santa** (Holy Week) festival is internationally famous for its processions of barefoot, hooded penitents carrying candles or supporting resplendent floats. The city explodes in the **Feria de Abril** (April Fair), a week-long festival with origins in a popular revolt against foreign influences in the nineteenth century. Based in the *casetas* (pavilions) of the fairground in Triana, the party rages through Seville with circuses, folklore displays, and bullfights.

Near Seville

About 100km southwest of Seville, on the southern part of Spain's Atlantic coast, is a world of rural villages famous for their winemaking. There are some fine beaches here, but heavy industry and even heavier winds mar the easily accessible ones. Perhaps the best way to see the region is to head inland following the **Ruta de los Pueblos Blancos** (Route of the White Villages), a string of towns running from the Costa de la Luz, around Gibraltar, to the Costa del Sol. There are no particular "white villages"; the name simply refers to those towns inland from the coast, all basically undiscovered by the region's many beachgoers. An automobile or a patient thumb are good for exploring the region; bus service to and from major Andalusian towns is quite good.

Untouristed **Jerez de la Frontera,** 20km from the port of Cádiz on the Seville-Cádiz rail line, produces some of the world's finest sherries. You can sample *jerez* (sherry) for free by taking a tour of a *bodega,* the warehouse where it lies fermenting; most of the main ones, including **Sandeman, González Byas,** and **Pedro Domecq** offer guided tours. (Usually open Mon.-Sat. 9am-1pm.) Pick up a map showing locations at one of the travel agencies in town, or at the **tourist office** at Alameda Cristina, 7 (just off the north end of José Primo de Rivera). The best time to appreciate winemaking here is during the **Fiestas de la Vendimia,** the celebration of the season's harvest during the second week of September. Other attractions include the **Museo de los Relojes** (Clock Museum), with an interesting collection of antique time pieces, and the sixteenth-century baroque **Church of Santo Domingo.** Look around calle Medina for a place to spend the night or your lunch money.

Only 19km away is spectacular **Arcos de la Frontera,** a labyrinthine white village on top of a harsh promontory. Undercut on three sides by the River Guadalete, this village is a maze of alleyways, medieval ruins, and stone arches. The fifteenth-century Church of Santa Mariá, on Pl. de España, is magnificent. Climb to the top for an unforgettable view, and pick up provisions from the **market;** but find lodgings at the bottom, in **Huéspedes Galvín,** off C. Corredera by the Caja de Ahorros de Ronda, or at **Fonda Las Cuevas,** also off C. Corredera near the Banco de Vizcaya. Buses travel frequently between Arcos de la Frontera and Jerez.

Ronda

The German poet Rainer Maria Rilke once settled in Ronda in search of inspiration. He chose well: The town is perched on a rocky massif split by a thousand-foot gorge, el Tajo, that channels the River Guadelevin. Ronda's old city, on the eastern side of the ravine, is a natural fortress whose towering cliff walls are graced with Roman, Moorish, and medieval Christian monuments.

Orientation and Practical Information

Ronda lies amidst the isolated hills of the Serrania de Ronda, 104km northwest of Málaga. In town, three bridges span the breathtaking gorge. The eighteenth-century **Puente Nuevo,** connects the **Ciudad** (old quarter) with the **Mercadillo** (new quarter). The main *paseo* of the city is the Carrera Espinel, which runs perpendicular to **Calle Jerez,** the street that connects the old and new quarters.

Tourist Office: Oficina de Turismo, Pl. de España (tel. 87 12 72). Maps and meager information. Open daily 10am-2pm and 4-7pm.

Post Office: C. Virgen de la Paz, 20 (tel. 87 25 57). Stamps and Poste Restante open Mon.-Fri. 9am-2pm, Sat. 9am-1pm. **Postal Code:** 29400.

Telephones: At the post office. **Telephone code:** 952.

Trains: Station is on Avda. Andalucía (tel. 87 16 73). To get to Pl. de España from the station, walk along Avda. de Andalucía towards Alameda del Tajo, the city park; turn left on C. Molino, and then right onto C. Nueva. Direct to Algeciras (4 per day, 2 hr., 450ptas), or to Bobadilla for connections to Seville (975ptas), Málaga (570ptas), and Granada (795ptas). **RENFE** ticket office, C. Infantes, 20 (tel. 87 16 62). Open Mon.-Fri. 10am-2pm.

Buses: Station is at Avda. Concepción García Redondo, 2. For Pl. de España, follow train station directions. **Empresa los Amarillos** (tel. 87 22 64) goes to Seville (4 per day, 770ptas) and Málaga (3 per day, 655ptas). **Empresa Comes** (tel. 87 19 92) to Jerez (4 per day, 685ptas) and Cádiz (1 per day, 851ptas).

Emergencies: Police, C. Espinel, 39 (tel. 87 13 70).

Medical Assistance: First Aid (tel. 87 97 73). **Municipal Hospital,** Capitán Cortés (tel. 87 23 44).

Accommodations and Food

Budget accommodations more than meet the healthy tourist demand. Calle Sevilla, perpendicular to Avenida Andalucía, contains the highest concentration, starting with the somewhat rundown **Fonda Nuestra Señora de Lourdes** at #16 (tel. 87 10 32; 500ptas; showers 150ptas). Next door, **Hostal La Purísima** (tel. 87 10 50) is a little neater (700ptas; showers 100ptas). For well-lit rooms and a pleasant tiled courtyard, try **Hostal Morales,** at #51 (tel. 87 15 38; singles 800ptas, doubles 1500ptas; showers included).

There are lots of places to eat inexpensively in Ronda. Basic fare can be had at **Las Cañas,** on Avda. Duque de la Victoria, 2, of Pl. de Socorro (*menú* 450ptas). **Cervecería Marisquería El Patio,** C. Espinel, 100, has a festive patio overflowing with flowers. (*Menú del día* 550ptas. Open Thurs.-Tues.) **Todo Natural,** C. Marina, 1, off Pl. del Socorro, serves amazing vegetarian fare, including large salad plates (375ptas) and a *menú* that changes daily (400ptas). Kill for the chocolate and orange mousse. (Open Mon.-Sat. noon-10:30pm.) A former prison, **Bodega Flamenca,** inside an arch of the Puente Nuevo (entrance from a stairway off Pl. de España), is great for drinks and *tapas.* (Open June-Sept. daily 10:30am-7:30pm.)

Sights

Ronda's tremendous gorge is a sight in itself. Construction of the **Puente Nuevo** (New Bridge), finished in 1735, killed one head architect and caused another to commit suicide. Across the bridge in the **Ciudad** (old quarter), a colonnaded walkway leads to the **Palacio del Marqués de Salvatierra,** a Renaissance palace whose floor sparkles with ceramic tiles. (Open Fri.-Wed. 10am-2pm and 4-7pm. Admission 150ptas.) Facing the carved Incas of the palace facade, the **Casa del Rey Moro** promises to remain closed for restoration in 1988. Descending the winding stone steps, Ronda's two remaining bridges come into view, as well as the **Baños Arabes** (Arabian sauna baths). (Open Tues.-Sun 10am-2pm and 4-7pm. Free.) At the center of the old quarter, the asymmetrical **cathedral,** with heavy Moorish influence, looks out over a refreshing plaza with gardens. At night, **Las Catacumbas,** a tavern in the bowels of the cathedral, becomes a worldly nightspot with terrific sangria.

Back in the new quarter, visit the **Plaza de Toros,** Spain's first bullring, dating from 1784. The **Museo Taurino** inside takes you through the history of the two great bullfighting dynasties of Ronda: that of Pedro Romero, considered the founder of modern bullfighting, born in 1755; and that of Cayetano Ordoñez, immortalized as the matador in Hemingway's *The Sun Also Rises.* They fought here. They were good. (Open daily 9am-7pm. Admission 120ptas.) Bullfights are held during the *Feria de Ronda* in early September.

Córdoba

Perhaps nowhere else does Spain's diverse heritage present itself so tangibly as in Córdoba. The Roman bridge, and scattered pillars and ramparts testify to the city's importance in Roman times, as do the names of some of its citizens: the philosopher and dramatist Seneca, and his nephew the poet Lucan. The Arab occupation brought the **Mezquita** (mosque) and the town's greatest prosperity; for a time Córdoba, with its vast library, was one of the largest cities in medieval Europe. Today, Córdoba captures the essence of Andalusia: Whitewashed houses along narrow streets hide serene patios, and the strains of *cante jondo* still resound from time to time.

Orientation and Practical Information

Córdoba is at the top of the Andalusian triangle (with Seville and Granada), about halfway between Madrid and Gibraltar. Most sights, monuments, and accommodations are clustered in the **Judería,** a maze of narrow winding streets that was once the city's Jewish quarter. This area lies between the Plaza de las Tendillas and the Río Guadalquivir. North of the plaza is the new city, home to the train station and the various bus lines.

Tourist Office: Provincial, C. Torrijos, 10 (tel. (957) 47 12 35), on the west side of the Mezquita; enter through the Palacio de Congresos y Exposiciones. Well-staffed and informative. Open Mon-Sat. 9:30am-2:30pm, closed Sun. **Municipal,** Pl. de Juda Levi (tel. 29 07 40), 2 blocks west of the Mezquita. Open Mon.-Fri. 8:30am-3pm, Sat. 10am-1pm, closed Sun.

Post Office: C. Cruz Conde, 15 (tel. 47 82 67). Open for stamps and Poste Restante Mon.-Fri. 9am-2pm and 4-6pm, Sat. 9am-2pm. **Postal code:** 14001.

Telephones: Pl. de las Tendillas, 7. Open Mon.-Fri. 9am-1:30pm and 5-9pm. **Telephone code:** 957.

Flights: Iberia, Ronda de los Tejares, 3 (tel. 47 12 27). Open Mon.-Fri. 9am-1pm and 4-7pm, Sat. 9am-1pm.

Trains: Station is on Avda. de América (tel. 47 82 21), on the north side of town. To reach the Judería, follow Avda. Gran Capitán (to your left exiting the station) to its conclusion, then weave your way through the ensuing maze in approximately the same direction: The Judería begins within a few blocks and extends down to the river. *Consigna* (luggage storage) in Café Sagitario, across the street, until 10pm (100ptas). **RENFE,** Ronda de los Tejares, 3 (tel. 47 58 84). Open Mon.-Fri. 9am-2pm and 4:30-7pm.

Buses: Transportes Ureña, Avda. de Cervantes, 22 (tel. 47 23 52). To Seville (2 per day, 2 hr., 710ptas). **Alsina-Graells Sur,** Avda. Medina Azahara, 29 (tel. 23 64 74). To Granada (4 per day, 3 hr., 1095ptas) and Málaga (2 per day, 3½hr., 885ptas). **Autocares Priego,** Paseo de la Victoria, 29 (tel. 29 01 58). To Madrid (3 per day, 6 hr., 2010ptas).

Emergencies: Police (tel. 091); headquarters at Campo Madres de Dios, 5 (tel. 25 14 14).

Medical Assistance: At Avda. República Argentina, 4 (tel. 23 46 46).

Laundry: Cordobesas, Dalmacia, 3 (tel. 26 98 54), visible off C. Barros, midway between Tendillas and the Mezquita. 5kg for 700ptas. Open Mon.-Fri. 9:30am-1:30pm and 5-8:30pm, Sat. 9:30am-1pm.

Accommodations, Camping, and Food

Cheap accommodations are plentiful, especially in the Judería. Many of the *casas de huéspedes* and *hostales* here have traditional Moorish patios. Some of the cleanest and cheapest (about 900ptas per person) are on Calle Rey Heredia, northeast of the Mezquita: **La Milagrosa** at #12 (tel. 47 33 17), and **Rey Heredia** at #26 (tel. 47 41 82). For an extra 200-400ptas you can live like a Moorish monarch. Also worth checking out is the area around the Plaza del Potro, east of the cathedral.

Huéspedes Martinez Rücker, Martinez Rücker, 14 (tel. 47 25 62), just west of the Mezquita. Staff keeps the rooms spotless. 800ptas per person. Showers 100ptas.

Fonda Maestre, C. Romero Barros, 16 (tel. 47 53 95), between C. San Fernando and the Pl. del Potro. Closest thing Córdoba has to a relaxed youth hostel. Large patio, clean rooms, kitchen, and laundry facilities. Singles 900ptas, doubles 1500ptas. Showers included.

Hostal-Residencia Séneca, C. Conde y Luque, 7 (tel. 47 32 34), 2 blocks north of the Mezquita. Very clean, with a beautiful Moorish patio complete with a lively singing canary. Singles 1215ptas, doubles 2430ptas. Showers and breakfast included.

Camping: Campamento Municipal de Turismo, Carretera Córdoba-Villaviciosa (tel. 27 50 48). 275ptas per person and per tent. Open year-round.

To eat cheaply in Córdoba, stay away from the Mezquita. The mosque attracts high-priced eateries like Muhammad did followers. Branch out into the Judería. The best place is the austere-looking **Bar-Restaurante Carmona,** located on tiny Menéndez y Pelayo, between Paseo de la Victoria and Avda. del Grán Capitán. The 350ptas *menú especial* is served daily (1-4pm and 8:30-10:30pm). A little off the beaten path, **Restaurante Lalala,** C. Cruz del Rastro, 3, along the river, features indoor and outdoor dining, with a wide choice of *menús* for 400-500ptas. (Open daily 8am-4pm and 7pm-midnight.) North of the Mezquita on C. Buen Pastor, **Bar-Mesón Rafaé** is popular with locals and proud of its *rabo de toro* (bull's tail stew; 325ptas). (Open Wed.-Mon. 9am-10:30pm.)

Sights and Entertainment

No group of camera-flashing tourists could subvert the majesty of Córdoba's **Mezquita (Mosque**). Begun in 785, the structure was intended to surpass all other mosques in sheer grandeur. It took over two centuries to nurture this airy forest of 850 marble, alabaster, and stone pillars, many of which were taken from the Visigothic cathedral originally on the site. Off to one side is the *mirhab* (prayer niche), with the richest mosaics in Spanish Islamic art. (Open April-Sept. daily 10:30am-1:30pm and 4-7pm; Oct.-March daily 10:30am-1:30pm and 3:30-5:30pm. Admission Mon.-Sat. 200ptas; free Sun. mornings.)

The **Alcázar** is more than just an important military monument; there are several Roman mosaics, manicured gardens, and terraced goldfish ponds. (Open May-Sept. daily 9:30am-1:30pm and 5-8pm; Oct.-April 9:30am-1:30pm and 4-7pm. Admission 100ptas.) Córdoba's **Synagogue,** on C. de los Judíos, marked by a statue of Maimonides, is a sad reminder of the expulsion and genocide of Spanish Jewry. (Open May-Sept. Tues.-Sat. 10am-2pm and 6-8pm, Sun. 10am-1:30pm; Oct.-April Tues.-Sat. 10am-2pm and 5-7pm, Sun. 10am-1:30pm. Contributions requested.) Almost next door is the **Museo Municipal de Arte Cordobés y Taurino,** a museum devoted to *la corrida* with galleries devoted to the *tauromaquía* of the Córdoban legends Lagartijo, Guerrita, and Manolete. A copy of Manolete's tomb is exhibited beneath the stretched hide of his nemesis, Islero. (Open May-Sept. Tues.-Sat. 9:30am-1:30pm and 5-8pm, Sun. 9:30am-1:30pm; Oct.-April Tues.-Sat. 9:30am-1:30pm and 4-7pm. Admission 100ptas.) If you pass through the **Plaza del Potro,** look for the inn described by Cervantes in *Don Quixote.*

The Jewish quarter around the Mezquita, especially on C. de la Luna, is great for *tapas* and bar-hopping. The local wines, from Montilla and Moriles, are superb. Try a light, dry *fino* or a sweet *Pedro Ximénez;* a bottle of either costs about 400ptas. For an enjoyable diversion, head to **Bodegas Campos,** in an alley off C. Lineros (near the Plaza del Potro), to taste wine and read the famous signatures on the barrels.

Those seeking more Moorish *mirhabs* should go to the **Medina Azahara,** 8km northwest of Seville. Constructed in the tenth century by Abderraman III as a gift to his favorite of many wives, the palace ruins have only recently been restored. **Autotransportes San Sebastian,** C. de la Bodega, runs buses to the turnoff, 2km from the ruins; to return, you must flag a bus or hitch. (Open May-Sept. Tues.-Sat. 10am-2pm and 6-8pm, Sun. 10am-1:30pm; Oct.-April Tues.-Sat. 10am-2pm and 4-6pm, Sun. 10am-1:30pm. Admission 250ptas.)

Granada

The Muslim rulers of Granada adored and adorned this provincial capital. Boabdil, its last Arab king, on being forced to leave his beloved city, turned around on the site now called the *Suspiro del Moro* (Sigh of the Moor) and, according to a sexist but memorable proverb, "cried like a woman for what he could not defend like a man." Ignore the low apartments of Granada and look up: The majestic clay-red Alhambra palace looms against the Sierra Nevada, Europe's sunniest ski slopes. And the refreshing coastline is also nearby.

Orientation and Practical Information

Granada forms the southeastern vertex of the "Andalusian Triangle" (Sevilla-Córdoba-Granada). The Sierra Nevada range separates it from the Costa del Sol. The visitor's center is **Plaza Nueva,** framed by a handful of handsome Renaissance buildings. **Gran Vía de Colón** and **Calle de los Reyes Católicos** intersect at **Plaza de Isabel la Católica,** just south of Plaza Nueva.

Tourist Office: C. de Libreros, 2 (tel. 22 10 22), between the southeast corner of the cathedral and Pl. Bib-Rambla. Informative bulletin boards posted in window in off-hours. Open Mon.-Fri. 10am-1pm and 4-7pm, Sat. 10am-1pm.

Budget Travel: Viages TIVE, Martinez Campo, 21 (tel. 27 92 50). BIGE tickets and assorted travel info. Open Mon.-Fri. 9:30am-2pm.

American Express: Viajes Bonal, Avda. Calvo Sotelo, 19 (tel. 27 63 12), at the western end of Gran Vía de Colón. Mail held, checks sold, and cardholders' personal checks cashed, but no wired money accepted. Open Mon.-Fri. 9:30am-1:30pm and 5-8pm.

Post Office: Puerta Real, at the southern opening to C. de los Reyes Católicos (tel. 22 48 35). General services open Mon.-Fri. 9am-2pm and 4-6pm, Sat. 9am-2pm. **Postal Code:** 18070

Telephones: C. de los Reyes Católicos, 55, 2 blocks north of Pl. Isabel Católica. Open daily 9am-1pm and 5-9pm. **Telephone code:** 958.

Flights: Airport information (tel. 23 33 22). **Iberia,** Pl. de Isabel la Católica, 2 (tel. 22 75 92). Open Mon.-Fri. 9am-1:15pm and 4-7:15pm.

Trains: Station on Avda. Andaluces, off Calvo Sotelo (tel. 23 34 08). Take bus #4, 5, 9, or 11 to the center of town. Dilapidated shack with "Camas" sign to right of the exit will store bags for the day (100ptas). **RENFE,** C. de los Reyes Católicos, 63 (tel. 22 34 97). Open Mon.-Fri. 8am-2:30pm.

Buses: Alsina Graells, Camino de Ronda, 97 (tel. 25 13 58), near the intersection with C. Emperatriz Eugenia. To Córdoba, Seville, the Sierra Nevada, and the Costa del Sol. Get a list of destinations and times at the tourist office to avoid the lines here.

Emergencies: Police, C. Duquesa, 21 (tel. 27 83 00).

Medical Assistance: Casa de Socorro, Lepanto, 3 (tel. 22 15 44).

Hitchhiking: The Tourist Office will tell you which buses to take to the outskirts of town.

Accommodations, Camping, and Food

Granada's **Colegio Emperador Carlos (IYHF),** Camino de Ronda, 171 (tel. 27 26 38), is a five-minute walk from the train station; follow the tracks away from town, under the bridge, and up onto the left side to the white arch that says *"Junta de Andalucía Instalaciones Deportivas";* when locked, go around back. (Members 450ptas, ages over 25, 550ptas; nonmembers 700ptas. Open year-round.) The best private accommodations, despite the constant roar of passing tour buses, are along Cuesta de Gomérez, about a five-minute walk from the Alhambra; interior rooms are less noisy. **Hostal-Residencia Gomérez,** at #10 (tel. 22 44 37), is kept sparkling clean by its young proprietor. (Singles 650ptas, doubles 1000ptas. Showers 90ptas.) At #21, **Hostal Britz** (tel. 22 36 52) borders the plaza with firm beds. (Singles 850ptas, doubles 1400ptas. Showers included.) Closer to the train station is **Hostal-**

Residencia San Joaquin, Mano de Hierro, 14 (tel. 28 28 79), a former fifteenth-century palace. (900ptas per person. Showers included.) **Camping** is available at five locations near Granada, all of which charge about 275ptas per person and per tent. **Sierra Nevada** (tel. 27 09 56), on Carretera de Madrid, offers the best facilities and services, and is open year-round.

The area around Plaza Nueva is full of restaurants offering cheap and filling *platos combinados* or *menús del día.* **Restaurante-Bar-Café Boabdil,** C. Corpus Christi, 2 (tel. 22 81 36), is popular with locals for its filling *menús* (500ptas and up). **La Nueva Bodega,** C. Cetti Merién, up from the cathedral, offers *bocadillos* for less than 100ptas and *menús* from 425-950ptas. For fantastic atmosphere, venture into the **Albayzín,** the old Arab quarter, where most bars serve meals for about 500ptas. Try the *media barca* (half boat), a fried fish platter for two (600ptas), on the outdoor tables of the freshest *freiduría* in Spain: **El Ladrillo,** Placeta de Fatima, off C. Pages. For dessert, try a delicious *café blanco y negro* (165ptas) at **Gran Café-Bar Granada,** a graceful old landmark on the Puerta Real.

Sights and Entertainment

Framed by the silvery backdrop of the Sierra Nevada, the **Alhambra** (red castle—actually the Moorish monarch's royal palace), is a haunting combination of beauty and bloodshed, the foremost tribute to the turbulent eight-century Moorish occupation of Spain. The numerous courtyards and rooms inside the palaces of the **Casa Real** are among the finest examples of Mudéjar art and architecture anywhere in the world. Don't miss the spooky baths below. Your ticket enables you to roam the extensive gardens and visit the **Generalife,** the summer retreat of the sultans. The **Museo de Bellas Artes** in the **Palacio de Carlos V** has a good collection of oils and polychrome sculpture. (Complex open March-Sept. daily 9:30am-7:45pm; Oct.-April daily 9:30am-5:15pm. Admission 350ptas, Sun. 4-7pm free. Some rooms closed for restoration.)

The **Cathedral** (entrance on Gran Vía) is the first purely Renaissance cathedral in Spain. Begun 30 years after the Christian reconquest of the city, the ornate church, intended to outshine the Alhambra, does not even rise out of its shadow. Go early to see the oil paintings; the lighting is so poor that by late afternoon they are nearly indistinguishable. The **Capilla Real** (Royal Chapel), reached by a separate entrance, contains the elaborate tomb of Ferdinand and Isabella, along with Isabella's splendid private art collection. (Both open daily March.-Sept. 11am-1pm and 4-7pm; Oct.-April 11am-1pm and 3:30-6pm. Admission for each 150ptas, Sun. morning free.)

To reach the Albayzín, take city bus #7 from beside the Cathedral and get off at C. de Pages on top of the hill. From here walk down C. Agua through the **Puerta Arabe,** an old gate to the city. The terrace adjacent to the Church of San Nicolás affords the best view of the Alhambra in all Granada—try to come at sunset. The nearby **Church of San Salvador,** built on the site of the Albayzín's most important mosque, still preserves a *patio árabe.* Solo travelers should exert caution in the Albayzín after dark.

Corpus Christi celebrations include festivities, processions, and bullfights. The **International Festival** which runs from mid-June to mid-July features classical ballet in the gardens of the Generalife, and concerts in the Renaissance palace on the Cerro del Sol. For less cultural diversion, stick to the student pubs around the university, in the area bounded by C. Pedro Antonio de Alarcón, Callejón de Nevot, and C. de Melchor Almargo.

A word of advice: avoid the **Gypsy Caves of Sacromonte.** This tourist trap is home to whitewashed grottoes full of gypsies shaking in rhythm in a poor imitation of flamenco. Money is expected.

Near Granada

Glistening above the Alhambra is the **Sierra Nevada,** the tallest range in Iberia; the peaks of **Mulhacén** (3481m) and **Veleta** (3470m) are snow-covered most of the year. Although not essential, a car makes travel in the Sierra Nevada much easier. In Granada, try **ATESA,** Pl. de los Cuchilleros (tel. 22 56 65), which charges about 2300ptas per day plus 19ptas per kilometer. During the summer you can drive up to the peak of Veleta and down the other side to **Capileira,** in the southern valley of the **Alpujarras.** This hike is a good 25km among rock-strewn meadows with only wild goats and a few birds for company. Even in summer temperatures plummet to near-freezing at night and the wind is severe, so plan accordingly. The best map of the region, printed by the Federación Española de Montañismo, is available at bookstores and newsstands in Granada (350ptas).

A daily bus for a mid-Veleta ski station/restaurant leaves from in front of the Palacio de la Disputación on the Carretera de Genil at 9am; from the restaurant, it's a breathtaking three hours to Veleta's summit. The bus returns to Granada at 5pm (380ptas round-trip). There is an expensive hotel at the peak, the **Peñones San Francisco** (tel. 48 01 22; 2500ptas per person; full board). During ski season (Nov. to mid-May), lifts and equipment rentals operate in the area.

Costa del Sol

Having learned to use beauty for profit, the Costa del Sol is showing the strains of its trade. Artifice covers once-natural charms, and chic promenades and hotels seal off whitewashed towns from the shoreline. Nearing Málaga and its famous resorts to the southwest, water washes almost entirely against concrete. Still, pockets of beautiful coastline do survive. Northeast of Málaga, the hills dip straight into the ocean and the road coils around splendid vistas of surf pounding against rock face. For wayfarers weary of cathedrals, even the packaged sun of the Costa del Sol may prove welcome relief.

June and September are the best times to visit, when summer is in town but hordes of vacationers aren't. In July and August, be prepared for crammed lodgings and beaches, and higher prices (*temporada alta,* when rooms are often double the normal price, is usually mid-June to mid-Sept.). Consider making reservations, arriving early in the day, asking around for private homes with rooms to let (*casas particulares*), or sleeping on the beach at the outskirts of town—a practice winked at in less elegant resorts, but not advisable for women alone. The coastal rail line connects Málaga to Torremolinos and Fuengirola. Private bus lines (railpasses not valid) make the rest of the connections; they're inexpensive and run often, so you can make stops wherever you feel so inclined. With patience, hitching will get you somewhere, but it isn't a good idea for women alone.

Málaga

Like Cinderella's stepmother, Málaga is ugly and harsh, yet crucial to the story: Its transportation network plays a vital role in serving the Costa del Sol. Still, this cosmopolitan port has inspired sensitive souls like native son Picasso and Nobel laureate Vicente Aleixandre, who called Málaga *la ciudad del paraíso,* the city of paradise. The palm-lined **Paseo del Parque** will take you below the **Alcazaba,** a Moorish palace whose fortified walls enclose fragrant gardens and an archeological museum. (Open Mon.-Sat. 10am-1pm and 5-8pm, Sun. 10am-2pm. Admission 20ptas.) The lofty **Gibralfaro Castle** crowns a nearby hill, with fine views of the sprawling city below. (Open daily sunrise-sunset. Free.) Also worth a visit is the **Museo de Bellas Artes,** San Augustín, 6, which houses a wealth of mosaics, sculptures, and paintings, including works by Murillo, Rivera, and Picasso. (Open year-round, 10am-1:30pm and 5-6pm. Admission 250ptas, EEC students free.)

Málaga's **Oficina de Turismo** is at C. Marqués de Larios, 5 (tel. (952) 21 34 45). (Open Mon.-Sat. 9am-2pm and 4-8pm.) The **Residencia Juvenil Mediterráneo**

(IYHF), Plaza de Pio XII (tel. (952) 30 85 00), has fine facilities and a lively pub; take bus #18 to the last stop. (450ptas with IYHF card. Curfew 11pm, but last bus 8pm. Open year-round.) There are plenty of accommodations north of the Paseo del Parque and Alameda Principal. Try the **Hostal-Residencia Lampérez,** C. Santa María, 6 (tel. (952) 21 94 84). (Singles 800ptas, doubles 1600ptas. Showers 150ptas). The **La Cancela** Restaurant, C. Denís Belgrano, 3, just off C. Granada, is pleasant and relatively cheap (great *gazpacho,* 100ptas).

The **RENFE** office on C. Strachen (tel. (952) 21 31 22), is less crowded and more convenient than the **train station** at C. Cuarteles (tel. (952) 31 25 00). (RENFE open Mon.-Fri. 9am-1:30pm and 4:30-7:30pm.) Buses to Nerja, Seville, Granada, Córdoba, and Almería leave from the **Alsina Graells** office, Pl. de Toros Vieja, 14 (tel. (952) 31 04 00). Buses to Marbella, Ronda, and Algeciras depart from **Empresa Portillo,** C. Córdoba, 7 (tel. (952) 22 73 00).

East of Málaga lies **Nerja,** a relaxed coastal resort with great beaches about 15 minutes by foot to either side of town. The town is popular and expensive, so accommodations may not be easy to find; ask at the various bars for *casas particulares.* Five kilometers east of the town lie the tremendous, cathedral-like **Cuevas de Nerja,** filled with eerie rock formations. The most stunning chambers lie just beyond a stage on which music and ballet performances take place in late July and early August. (Open May to mid-Sept. daily 10am-9:30pm; mid-Sept. to April daily 10am-1:30pm and 4-7pm. Admission 150ptas.) Buses to the caves run hourly from Nerja (50ptas). From here, a 1½-kilometer trek down the small coastal road will take you to the tiny village of **Maro** and a little cove by the cliffs—unfortunately, not undiscovered.

If you're tired of the sleek and the chic, hop on any bus heading east. Close to Nerja, **Salobreña,** still typically Spanish, commands a lovely outcrop only 10 minutes from the beach. **Pension Arreda,** on C. Nueva, has rooms for 700ptas per person, including showers and a view of the castle at the top. **Camping Peñon** (tel. 61 02 07) is on the beach (275ptas per person and per tent; open April-Oct.). For isolated sandy beaches, head for the **Cabo de Gata** (Cape of the Cat), about 100 kilometers northeast of Nerja. Only attempt this with a few days free and a willingness to camp on beaches—buses seldom run and rooms are scarce.

Marbella

Marbella accommodates highbrows and hippies with equal grace, and the twisting streets of its eastern section, brilliant with flowers, will help you forget the highrise hotels. **Plaza de los Naranjos** is particularly pleasant—a shady square filled with orange trees and the soothing sound of a fountain. The **Oficina de Turismo** is at Avda. Miguel Cano, 1 (tel. (952) 77 14 42); from the bus station on Avda. Ricardo Sorano, take a left, then a right just before the park. Their indexed map is a lifesaver. (Open Mon.-Fri. 9:30am-1pm and 5-7:30pm, Sat. 10am-1pm.)

Marbella is a popular place, especially during late July and August; without reservations, arrive early and cross your fingers. Bars often know of residents renting rooms for the night. The best place to find *hostales* and *fondas* is in the old section behind Avda. Ramón y Cajal. Try looking on **Calle Ancha** and its continuation, **Calle San Francisco.** On **Calle Aduar,** parallel and two blocks west, the **Pensión Aduar** is the best of several alternatives; the back overflows with flowers, and the manager is friendly. (Singles 1100ptas, doubles 1800ptas. Showers 150ptas.) **Pensión Luisa,** C. San Francisco, 6 (tel. (952) 77 08 40), has big, clean beds (singles 1000ptas, doubles 2000ptas) and also offers roof space (400ptas per person). **Albergue Juvenil Africa (IYHF),** C. Trapiche, 2 (tel. (952) 77 14 91), just above C. San Francisco, is a beautiful place but often fills with Spanish school groups. Very full in July and August. (700ptas. Breakfast included. Strict 11pm curfew. Open year-round.) For the cheapest *menú de la casa* in town (350ptas), try **Bar el Gallo,** C. Lobatas, 40. **Bar Taurino,** towards the top of C. San Francisco, has a great *tortilla* for 300ptas, and attracts lots of young people. (Open March-Sept.) **Restaurante Sol y Sombra,** C. Tetuán, 7, offers somewhat expensive but fresh seafood dishes (500ptas).

Gibraltar and Algeciras

Timeless, resolute, and severe, the solid rock of **Gibraltar** thrusts its mountainous profile out of the Mediterranean. Inhabited by an eccentric enclave of British nationals, Gibraltar was cut off from all contact with Spain for two decades; the fervid colonial pride of Her Majesty's loyal subjects affords a glimpse of a time when Britain ruled the waves. In 1985, the Spanish government opened its frontier gates, ending almost 20 years of isolation for the peninsula. Anyone with a passport may now travel freely to and from the Rock. Gibraltar uses pounds sterling, but Spanish pesetas are widely accepted.

Gibraltar's **tourist office** has branches on Mackintosh Sq. (tel. 755 55) and Cathedral Sq. (tel. 764 00). (Both open July-Aug. Mon.-Fri. 8am-3:30pm, Sat. 9am-1pm, closed Sun.; Sept.-June Mon.-Fri. 8:45am-5:30pm, closed Sat.-Sun.) The cheapest beds in town are at the **Toc H Hostel** on Lime Wall Rd. (tel. 734 31). Beds for £3.50 per night, but it's a spartan sort of place, and almost always full. The **Queen's Hotel** on 1 Boyd Street (facing the cable car station) usually has rooms available (singles £14, doubles £10, with bath £11, with sea view £15). Camping is illegal on the Rock but discreet questions to local youth might clue you in to overnight shelters in abandoned bunkers and houses.

The principal attraction of the port town of **Algeciras** is its proximity to Africa, 13km across the Strait of Gibraltar. Clean, inexpensive accommodations are found along C. José Santacana, one block inland. Buses should run between Algeciras and Gibraltar every half hour, but check with the tourist office. The **tourist office** and travel agencies also provide information about ferry services to Tangier in Morocco and Ceuta. (Tickets to Tangiers 2550ptas, to Ceuta 1100ptas.) U.S., Canadian, and British citizens need only their passports to enter Morocco and stay for 90 days.

The Mediterranean Coast

Valencia

Valencia prizes its *huertas* (orchards) of citrus fruit trees, which flourish despite the arid conditions. This provincial capital, the third largest city in Spain, is a trove of museums, ancient monuments, and buildings, all with a distinctly Moorish and nautical flavor. The regional language is *valenciano,* a dialect of Catalan, but residents speak *castellano* (Spanish) as well. The best time to visit is during the festival of Las Fallas (March 12-19), one of the grandest celebrations in Spain.

Orientation and Practical Information

Frequent trains connect Valencia to Madrid, Barcelona, Alicante, and Andalusia; buses travel between these cities as well. Valencia, on the Mediterranean, is also a major access point for flights and ferries to the Balearic Islands.

It's most convenient to arrive by train, as Valencia's Estació del Nord, is very near **Plaça del País Valencià,** the center of town. The city sprawls for miles, but most visitors will be interested in the area running from this *plaça* north to the **River Turia.** The tourist-office map is useful, though not indexed; for an indexed map, inquire at newsstands for the *Bayarri* street plan (350ptas).

Tourist Offices: Pl. del País Valencià, 1 (tel. 351 04 17). Open Mon.-Fri. 9am-1:30pm and 4:30-7pm, Sat. 9am-1:30pm. Other offices on Avda. Catalunya (tel. 369 79 32), in the train station, and at the airport (tel. 153 03 25).

Budget Travel: Viajes TIVE, C. Mar, 54 (tel. 352 28 01). BIGE tickets, RENFE *tarjeta joven* (discount card), ferry information, and general advice. Open Mon.-Fri. 8am-3pm, Sat. 8am-1pm.

American Express: Viajes Meliá, C. Paz, 41 (tel. 352 26 42). Mail held, traveler's checks sold, and cardholders' personal checks cashed. Cannot exchange currency or accept wired money. Open Mon.-Fri. 9:30am-1:30pm and 4:30-8pm, Sat. 9am-1:30pm.

Post Office: Pl. del País Valencià, 24. For stamps, open Mon.-Fri. 9am-2pm and 4-6pm, Sat. 9am-2pm. Poste Restante open Mon.-Sat. 9am-8pm. **Telegrams** open Mon.-Fri. 8am-midnight, Sat.-Sun. 8am-10pm. **Postal code:** 14600.

Telephones: Pl. del País Valencià, 27. Open Mon.-Sat. 9am-1pm and 5-9pm. **Telephone code:** 96.

Trains: Estació del Nord, very near the central Pl. del País Valencià. Information (tel. 351 36 12). Ticket office at Pl. de Alfonso el Magnánimo, 2. To Barcelona (11 per day, 6 hr., 1545ptas), Madrid (8 per day, 6 hr., 1665ptas), Alicante (12 per day, 4 hr., 795ptas).

Buses: Estació Central, Avda. de Menéndez Pidal, 13 (tel. 349 72 22), 25 min. from the center of town. Bus #8 connects with Pl. del País Valencià. **Municipal,** booth in Pl. del País Valencià. One fare 55ptas.

Ferries: Transmediterránea (Aucona), Avda. Manuel Soto Ingeniero, 15 (tel. 367 07 04). Service to the Balearic and Canary Islands. You can also buy tickets (day of departure only, 4480ptas) at the port office in the Estació Marítima (tel. 367 39 72). **Flebasa** (tel. 340 09 55) has service to Ibiza from Denia, to the south (in summer 6 per week, 3 hr., 4300ptas, including free Valencia-Denia transport on Ubesa coaches).

Emergencies: Police (tel. 091); headquarters at Gran Vía de Ramón y Cajal, 40 (tel. 351 08 62).

Medical Assistance: First Aid, Pl. de América, 6 (tel. 322 22 39). **Hospital Provincal,** Avda. Cid Con Tres Cruces (tel. 379 16 00).

Consulate: U.S., C. de Ribera, 3 (tel. 351 69 73).

Laundry: C. Barmes, 7, west of Pl. Mercat. Bring change (wash 250ptas, dry 25ptas for 6 min.) and your own detergent. Open Mon.-Sat. 8am-8pm.

Accommodations

Cheap *fondas* and *casas de huéspedes,* most charging about 650ptas per person, are scattered around the old city near the **Placa del Mercat.** For cleaner, more expensive lodging (around 800ptas per single and up), try **Plaça del País Valencià** and the area to the northeast, off Calle Barcas. The area between **Plaça Redonda** and **Plaça Tetuán** requires more walking but has cheaper rooms.

Colegio Mayor La Paz (IYHF), Avda. del Puerto, 69 (tel. 369 01 52). Take bus #19; access is difficult. Quads only. 425ptas per person. Closed 1:30-4:30pm. Curfew 10pm.

Hostal del Rincón, C. Carda, 11 (tel. 331 60 83), just past Pl. del Mercat. Clean rooms and an animated proprietor. Singles 675ptas, doubles 1325ptas. Showers 185ptas.

Hospedería El Comercio, C. de las Botellas, around the corner from Hostal del Rincón. Dark and rundown—the spongy beds will swallow you up. Singles 600ptas, doubles 1200ptas. Showers 150ptas.

Hostal Universal, C. Barcas, 5 (tel. 351 53 84), just off Pl. del País Valencià. A convenient but noisy location. Three floors of tired but basic, clean rooms. Singles 954ptas, doubles 1590ptas. Showers 150ptas.

Food

Valencia is the birthplace of both *paella* and *orxata de chufas,* and the most authentic setting for sampling them. *Paella* is saffron-flavored rice loaded with meat, poultry, or seafood. Preparation requires much time, patience, and a special pan. *Orxata* is a refreshing drink on a hot day—it comes from the *chufa* or earth-almond. Elsewhere in Spain *orxata* is *orxata,* but here you can get it *granizada* (with crushed ice) or *líquida* (straight up).

Near the train station, stop at **Freiduría Duero,** C. Xátiva, 12, a local favorite and unofficially the cholesterol capital of the world, with a wide range of *platos* (450-500ptas) and *bocadillos* (160ptas). **Bar La Rotunda,** on Pl. Redonda, serves a

525ptas *menú* that includes *paella* and their breezy terrace. The cheapest place in town may be **Casa Eliseo,** C. Conde Montornés, in the student quarter, where good food in a basic dining room costs just 375ptas. (Open Mon.-Sat. 1-4pm and 8:30-11pm.) Also, the **mercat,** on Pl. del Mercat, offers mass quantities of fresh food at low prices. (Open Mon.-Sat. 8am-2pm, Fri. 8am-2pm and 5:30-8pm.)

Sights and Entertainment

From the center of town rises the Gothic and neoclassical **Seu,** (Metropolitan Cathedral). Its tower, the **Micalet,** offers a far-reaching panorama; from here, Victor Hugo counted 300 bell towers, though he must have been suffering from vertigo—there are actually no more than 100. The inside of the cathedral is notable for its cool simplicity and beautiful, six-panel altarpiece. The **Museu de la Seu** (Cathedral Museum) claims, among other lesser treasures, two large Goyas and one of Spain's several "authentic" Holy Grails. (Open June-Sept. Mon.-Sat. 10am-1pm and 4-7pm, Sun. 10am-1pm; March-May and Oct.-Nov. Mon.-Sat. 10am-1pm and 4-6pm, Sun. 10am-1pm; Dec.-Feb. daily 10am-1pm. Admission 50ptas.) Nearby is the **Llotja de la Seda,** the former silk exchange, with its handsome twisting pillars. The upper chambers house a masterfully sculpted ceiling which you can reach from the Orange Court by stairway. (Open Tues.-Fri. 10am-2pm and 4-6pm, Sat.-Sun. 10am-1pm. Free.)

The **Carrer dels Cavallers** is lined with the former residences of Valencia's nobility. From there, C. Serrans leads through the **Torres dels Serrans** (Watchmen's Towers), the fortified entrance to the city, and over the now defunct River Túria. Some distance to the right is the **Museu de Belles Arts** (Fine Arts Museum), with an excellent collection of Valencian "primitives" (fourteenth- to sixteenth-century religious paintings), Spanish masterpieces, a Bosch triptych, and a Van Dyck portrait. Here you can view a Velázquez self-portrait and the best pooch Goya ever painted, in his *Doña Joaquina Candado.* (Open Tues.-Sat. 10am-2pm and 4-6pm, Sun. 10am-2pm. Admission 200ptas, students free.) Nearby are some of Valencia's loveliest public gardens: the **Jardins del Real** (open daily 8am-sundown, free) with their small zoo; and the more tranquil, neoclassical **Jardì Monteforte,** featuring ivied arbors and a lily pond (open daily 10am-sundown, free).

Returning along Via Puente de la Pasarela, you'll see the beautiful **Glorieta** gardens. A short walk takes you past the wild facade of the **Palau del Marqués de Dos Aigües,** the brainstorm of Hipólito Rovira. Inside is one of Spain's finest ceramic collections, as well as numerous works by Picasso. (Open Tues.-Sat. 10am-2pm and 4-6pm, Sun. 10am-2pm. Admission 200ptas, students free.) Down the street, the museum adjoining the lovely sixteenth-century **Església del Patriarca** (Partriarch's Church) has an array of paintings by El Greco, Caravaggio, and others. (Open in summer daily 11am-1pm, in winter Sat.-Sun. only. Admission 50ptas.)

The **Museu Faller** (Fallas Museum), Pl. de Monteolivete, 4, is on the other side of the city, but worth the trip. It houses all the *ninots* (effigies made for *Las Fallas*) worthy of salvation from the flames. Only one is chosen each year. (Open Oct.-July Tues.-Sun. 10am-2pm and 4-7pm; Aug.-Sept. Tues.-Sun. 10am-2pm. Admission 50ptas.) Don't miss the **Museu Històric** (Historical Museum) in the **Casa de la Ciutat** (Town Hall) on Pl. del País Valencià. The lavish marble interior of the building is beautiful, particularly the **Saló de Festes** (Banquet Hall), and the exhibit is interesting.

In the fourteenth century, the so-called *Tribunal de Aigües* (Water Court) was instituted to settle disputes concerning water rights. If you're in town on a Thursday, you can still watch their proceedings; they conduct business by the Apostle's Door of the cathedral in Plaça de la Mare de Déu.

The best entertainment in Spain happens the week of March 12 to 19, when Valencia erupts in festivities that rival even Pamplona's San Fermin. This outrageous annual excess, known as **Las Fallas,** includes parades, fireworks, and street dancing. All the neighborhoods compete to see who can build the most elaborate and satirical *papier-mâché* effigy; at midnight on March 19 the *ninots* are simultaneously set ablaze in one final, clamorous, orgiastic celebration.

During **Semana Santa** (Holy Week), monks ride on platforms depicting biblical scenes. In June, the **Festival of Corpus Christi** features *rocas,* magnificently ornate coaches which serve as theatrical stages. Festivities continue in summer with the **Fira de Juliol,** July 15 to 31, featuring fireworks, cultural events, and *batallas de flors* (flower wars) in which citizens assault each other with flowers.

In summer, most nightlife centers around **Platja el Saler,** 14km away; unfortunately bus service ceases at 9pm. **Platja de la Malva-Rosa** is hot year round and can be reached by bus #1 or 2, both of which run until 1:30am. In town, the district of **Barri del Carme,** to the north of the *mercat,* boasts cafes and pubs such as **Café Behemios** on C. Bolsería, 36. Avenida Blasco Ibáñez and the streets **San Bult** and **En Blanch,** near Plaza Tetuán exude university *ambient* (atmosphere). Gay men might like **Balkis,** C. Dr. Monserrat, 23; lesbian women meet at **Carnaby Club,** C. Poeta Liern, 17.

Near Valencia

The Second Punic War was declared over **Sagunto,** 25km north of Valencia. The town is rich in Roman ruins, most of which lie on the hill just above. The **Museu Arqueològic,** under the shadow of a well-preserved **Teatro Romano** (Roman Theater), has a small collection of sculptures, friezes, and coins. Crowning Sagunto's hilltop are the ramparts of a medieval **castell,** which extend for an entire kilometer across the ancient acropolis. The view from the ramparts is superb, spanning the huddled town and the dark green of the *huerta,* marred only by the mammoth steel works. (Museum, theater, and castle open Tues.-Sat. 10am-2pm and 5-6pm, Sun. 10am-2pm. Admission to castle 200ptas.) For further information and advice on accommodations, visit **Turisme,** C. Autonomia, 2 (tel. 246 12 30), in the Ayuntamiento. (Open Mon.-Sat. 8am-2pm.)

Levante and **Las Arenas** beaches are polluted and overcrowded, but the **Saler** bus (from Pl. Porta del Mar by the Glorieta on C. General Palanca) will take you to a beautiful, though crowded, pine-bordered strand of the same name, 14km from the center, with an excellent campground right by the beach. Just next to it extends the lovely **Albufera,** Spain's largest lagoon, cut off from the sea by a thin strip of sand.

Xàtiva was the birthplace of the painter José de Ribera and two popes, Calixtus III and Alexander VI. Its two hilltop **castells,** the Romanesque **Church of St. Philip,** and numerous Gothic buildings and fountains merit a visit. Xàtiva has its own variation of *paella* and, on Fridays and Sundays, an open market animates the Plaça del Mercat. Nocturnal attractions include the **Pub Tulay,** C. Obispos 2, with its affable and informative proprietor. Xàtiva is accessible from Valencia by train (2 hr., 250ptas).

Alicante

A beautiful, well-planned city, Alicante is the surprise of the southern coast. Beyond polished pedestrian pavements lie the crowded streets of the old city at the foot of an imposing *castillo.* With beautiful (but busy) beaches nearby and cheap accommodations, Alicante is a great stopover between Valencia and Andalusia.

Orientation and Practical Information

Crows make it from Valencia to Alicante in about 125km; trains take the 200-kilometer coastal route along the overdeveloped Costa Blanca. A train line inland to Albacete, and eventually Madrid, begins at Alicante. The Esplanade de España stretches along the waterfront, in front of the mazed streets of the old quarter, which extends up to the foot of the dominant *castillo.* In 1987, all six-digit telephone numbers were changed to seven-digit numbers beginning with "5."

Tourist Offices: Oficina de Turismo, Esplanada de España, 2 (tel. 521 22 85). Open Mon.-Fri. 9am-2pm and 5-7pm, Sat. 9am-1pm. Another office near the bus station at C. Portugal, 17 (tel. 522 38 02). Open Mon.-Fri. 9am-1pm and 4:30-7:30pm, Sat. 9am-1pm. A **provincial tourist office** is on Pl. de l'Ajuntament, near the waterfront.

Post Office: Pl. de Gabriel Miró. Open for stamps and Poste Restante Mon.-Sat. 9am-2pm and 4-6pm. **Telegram** services open Mon.-Fri. 8am-9pm, Sat.-Sun. 9am-7pm. **Postal code:** 03000.

Telephones: Avda. de la Constitución, 10. Open Mon.-Fri. 9am-1pm and 5-8pm, Sat. 9am-1pm. **Telephone code:** 96.

Trains: Estación Término, Avda. Salamanca (tel. 522 01 27), for RENFE long-distance service to Valencia and Barcelona, Murcia and Andalusia, and Albacete and Madrid (250ptas). **Estación de la Marina,** Avda. Villajoyosa (tel. 526 27 31), for local FEVE service to Benidorm, Calpe, and Denia. Take bus C-1 from Pl. de España.

Buses: Station is on C. Portugal (tel. 522 07 00). Direct buses to Madrid, Benidorm, and Valencia; and along the Costa Blanca.

Ferries: Flebasa boats for Ibiza leave from Denia to the north (6 per week, 3 hr., 4300ptas, including free bus-feeder service aboard Ubesa coaches). In Alicante (tel. 522 21 88), in Denia (tel. 578 40 11).

Emergencies: Police (tel. 091); headquarters at C. Médico Pascual Pérez, 33 (tel. 521 13 13).

Medical Assistance: Hospital Provincal, C. General Elizaicin (tel. 520 10 00).

Accommodations, Camping, and Food

There seems to be a *pensión* on every corner in Alicante, but many are filled with seedy characters. For reputable lodgings, try Calle San Francisco, Calle San Ferdinando, and Rambla Méndez Núñez.

Residencia Juvenil "Lucentum" (IYHF), Avda. de Orihuela, 97 (tel. 528 12 11), 2km from town. Take bus B or E. 8-bed rooms in a converted prison. 550ptas. Showers and breakfast included. Midnight curfew.

Pensión Castillo, C. Barón de Finestrat (tel. 521 25 52). Great English-speaking family runs this immaculate *pensión.* Terrific meals, too. Singles 600ptas, doubles 1000ptas. Showers 100ptas. Open May-Oct.

Casa Miguel, C. Quintana, 4 (tel. 520 78 55), by the market. Gruff management; shabby, but cheap rooms. Singles 400ptas, doubles 800ptas. Showers 100ptas.

Camping: Camping Bahía, 4km away aboard bus C-1. 250ptas per person. Open May-Oct.

The best food options in Alicante are the deteriorating family-run places as far away from the Esplanade as you can get. Try **Restaurante Pedro,** C. de Bazán (tel. 521 55 90), for large three-course *menus* for 500ptas. (Open daily 1-4pm and 8-11pm.) Also good is **Comidas Rafaela,** off C. Mayor, with a charming view of the Church of St. Mary and a 500ptas *menú.* (Open daily 1-3:30pm). The cheapest food is at **La Chuleta,** C. de General Sanjurjo, off Pl. San Cristóbal, with a 450ptas *menú.* (Open daily 1-4pm and 7-10pm.)

Sights and Entertainment

With drawbridges, moats, tunnels, and secret passageways, the **Castillo de Santa Bárbara** is not just another castle—nor is the view from the top just another view; take the elevator (75ptas) up from the shorefront. (Open mid-June to Sept. Mon.-Fri. 9am-9pm, Sat. 9am-2pm; Oct. to mid-June Mon.-Fri. 9am-7:30pm, Sat. 9am-2pm.) The **Cathedral of San Nicolás de Bari** is typical of the severe Renaissance architectural styles in Spain and has a nice cloister with intricately carved doors. The impressive **Museo Colección "Arte del Siglo XX"** on C. Mayor has outstanding works by Picasso, Braque, Calder, and Miró. (Open May-Sept. Tues.-Sun. 10:30am-1:30pm and 6-9pm; Oct.-April Tues.-Sun. 10am-1pm and 5-8pm.)

By day, **Playa San Juan** is popular and gorgeous—a body-covered ribbon of white with a sandy-bottomed, seaweed-free shorefront. To reach the beach, take bus C-1 from Alicante.

By night, try the clubs at **San Juan** if you have a car, or dance at the neon **Discoteca Bugatti** on C. San Fernando. Gay men might enjoy the **Memphis** disco. From June 21 to 29, the **Festival of San Juan** breaks loose with dancing, spectacular nightly fireworks, and effigy competitions.

The beaches that form the **Costa Blanca,** up the coast from Alicante, are often infernos of pan-European tourism, but true beach fanatics shouldn't miss these stretches of sand and sunbathers. **Denia** and **Calpe** retain their fishing-port atmospheres, but avoid **Benidorm.** It's nasty.

Catalonia (Catalunya)

No portion of Spain retains as intact a regional identity as Catalonia. During the Middle Ages, when the concept of "Spain" was still farfetched, Catalans were writing mystical treatises and amorous poetry, erecting serene Romanesque churches high in the Pyrenees, and ruling a maritime empire that encompassed a fair part of the Mediterranean. Centuries later, the Catalan reputation for industriousness and innovation received a healthy boost from the region's feet-first leap into the age of the steam engine, and prosperity hasn't stopped yet. Franco tried to homogenize the country by outlawing regional languages, but the Catalans held their tongues; Franco's death in 1975 restored the region's autonomy and initiated a flourishing of the Catalan culture.

Catalans are fiercely proud of their culture and their famous artists have become folk heroes. Two of the best-known are Antonio Gardí, who designed the famous Saguada Familia, and Joan Miró, the modern artist who died in 1983. If you've never seen Miró's work, you will here—the ubiquitous blue starfish logo of "la Caixa" is taken from a Miró tapestry which the bank commissioned. Another major cultural rallying point is their language, which is not a dialect of Spanish. While the region is officially bilingual, Catalan is always used in the local governments, and throughout the region Spanish signs that haven't been changed to Catalan probably have stickers on them that say "El Catalá, es losa de tots" ("Catalan, it's for everyone"). The region now has its own television station, and Catalan will be one of the four official languages at the 1992 Olympic Games in Barcelona.

Barcelona

La Vanguardia is the name of the city's newspaper, and the vanguard is exactly where Barcelonans are used to finding themselves, for they are residents of Spain's most progressive city. Culturally innovative and politically savvy, Barcelona is the home of the wildly imaginative *moderninsta* buildings that sprung up from the Catalan Renaixença (renaissance) around the turn of this century. Its strategic position at the gateway to Europe make it an ideal stopping point for travelers, who will no doubt become enchanted with the sculpted Barri Gòtic streets and elegant boulevards of the Eixample.

Orientation and Practical Information

Barcelona, on Spain's Mediterranean coast 200km from the French border and due east of Madrid, is Spain's second most important transport hub; most traffic to and from the rest of Europe passes through here. Southern France is surprisingly close; Madrid five to eight hours away.

Maintaining your bearings in Barcelona is easy. **Plaça de Catalunya** is the city's center; from here, the **Rambles** and **Via Laietana** run straight to the harbor. The

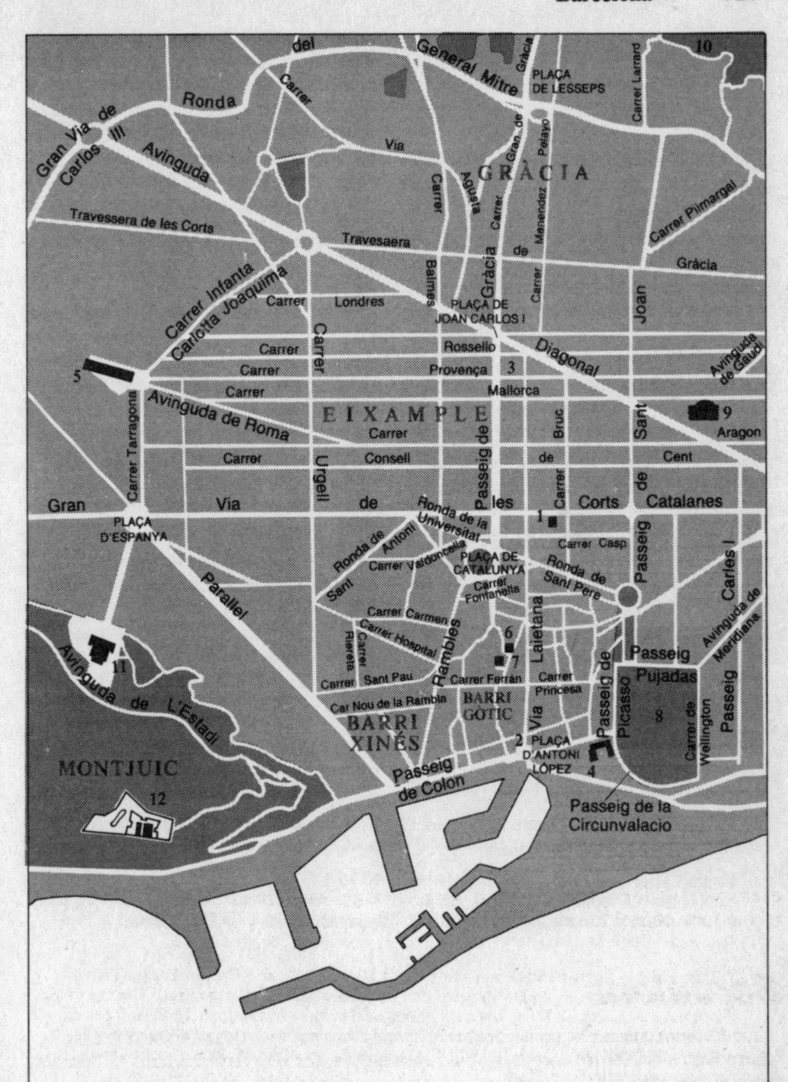

Barcelona

1 Tourist Office
2 Post Office
3 American Express Office
4 Estació de Franca
5 Estació Sants-Central
6 Catedral
7 Palau de la Generalitat
8 Parc de la Ciutadella
9 Temple Expiatori de la Sagrada Familia
10 Parc Güell
11 Palau Nacional
12 Castell de Montjuic

0 1 mile
0 1 kilometer

Barri Gòtic, centered around the cathedral and **Plaça Sant Jaume,** lies in between. On the other side of Plaça de Catalunya, **Gran Via de les Corts Catalanes** cuts broadly across the city, marking the beginning of the **Eixample,** which extends to **Avinguda Diagonal. Passeig de Gràcia** cuts between these two boulevards, leading toward the **Gràcia** quarter; **Tibidabo** lies farther in this direction. The hill of **Montjuïc** rises to the south. Be careful with your personal belongings when walking around Barcelona—always watch your wallet and avoid carrying a purse. The area between Plaça Sant Jaume and the port can be particularly dangerous at night; the other side of the Rambles should be avoided entirely. The Plaça Reial gets especially wild at night with drunks and hash dealers.

Place names in Barcelona are given primarily in Catalan, with most public instructions available in both languages. When looking for an address, make sure you have it in the language of your map (e.g. *Carrer del Banys Nous* is Catalan for *Calle de los Baños Nuevos*). We list all names in Catalan.

Tourist Offices: Gran Via de les Corts Catalanes, 658 (tel. 301 74 43), 3 blocks from Passeig de Gràcia near Pl. de Catalunya. Good help and lots of maps; information on all parts of Spain. Open Mon.-Fri. 9am-7pm, Sat. 9am-2pm. Another branch at Estació Sants-Central (tel. 410 25 94), opposite RENFE information (open daily 8am-10pm; airport). Summer offices at Columbus Monument (Pl. Portal de la Pau) and Plaça Pablo Neruda (near Sagrada Familia). **Municipal Information Office** (tel. 010), in the Ajuntament on Pl. Sant Jaume. Great for finding out what's on. Open Mon.-Fri. 8am-8pm, Sat. 8am-2pm, closed Sun.

Budget Travel: TIVE-Officina de Tourisme Juvenil, C. de Gravina, 1 (tel. 302 06 82), a block from Plaça de la Universitat, off C. Pelai. Check here first for cheap buses and flights, student IDs, and youth hostel cards. Often busy. Open Mon.-Fri. 9am-1pm and 4-5:30pm, Sat. 9am-noon.

American Express: Passeig de Gràcia, 101 (tel. 217 17 50), at Carrer Rosselló. Metro: Diagonal (L3, L5). Mail held. All banking services. Open Mon.-Fri. 9:30am-6pm, Sat. 10am-noon.

Currency Exchange: El Coute Inglés, Pl. de Catalunya, open Mon.-Sat. 10am-8pm. Offices at train stations open daily until 10pm.

Post Office: Pl. d'Antoni López, at the bottom of Via Laietana. Stamps (in basement) sold Mon.-Sat. 8:30am-10pm, Sun. 10am-noon; **Poste Restante** at window #17 open Mon.-Fri. 9am-9pm, Sat. 9am-2pm. **Postal code:** 08000.

Telephones: C. de Fontanella, 4, right off Pl. de Catalunya. Open Mon.-Sat. 8:30am-9pm. Also at Estació Sants-Central, open daily 7:45am-10:45pm. **Telephone code:** 93.

Flights: Airport at El Prat de Llobregat (tel. 370 10 11), 10km away. Trains to and from Estació Sants-Central every 20 min. 6:15am-11pm (15 min., 120ptas). **Iberia** (tel. 301 39 93 for information), Rambla de Catalunya, 18, on the corner of Gran Via. Open Mon.-Fri. 9am-1pm and 4-7pm, Sat. 9am-1pm.

Trains: Estació Sants-Central, uptown (Metro L3 and L5), and **Estació França-Termino,** down by the harbor on Avda. Marqués de l'Argentera (Metro: Barceloneta). Use the first if you have a choice; it's safer, has more trains, and is more convenient. To Paris 3 per day (9290ptas), Madrid 7-8 per day (*rápido* 3400ptas), and connections to just about everywhere. At Sants, **RENFE** information (tel. 322 41 42), open daily 6:30am-10:30pm. Lockers (100ptas per day) open daily 7am-11pm.

Buses: Julia, Pl. Universitat, 12 (tel. 318 38 95), and **VIA Tourisme,** C. de Pau Claris, 117 (tel. 302 56 75), have coaches to Lisbon (8000ptas), London (11,650ptas), Paris (7600ptas), Brussels (9125ptas), and Munich (12,850ptas). **Alsina Graells,** Ronda Universitat, 4 (tel. 302 65 45), serves Andorra (1350ptas). **Sarfa,** Passeig Colóm, 3 (tel. 315 35 08), near the harbor, runs 12 buses per day along the Costa Brava.

Ferries: The **Estació Maritima** (tel. 301 25 98), at the Drassanes Metro stop on line 3. **Transmediterránea,** Via Laietana, 2 (tel. 319 82 12), sails to the Balearics. Open Mon.-Fri. 9am-1pm and 5-7pm, Sat. 9am-noon.

Public Transportation: The 4 lines of the **Metro** cover the entire metropolitan area; Plaça de Catalunya is the system hub. Rides cost 50ptas Mon.-Sat., 55ptas on Sun.; 10-ride cards are 295ptas. The Metro operates 5am-11pm, Sat.-Sun. 5am-1am. **FFCC** commuter trains often operate as part of the Metro system. **Buses** extend the system farther ("N" lines run all night) and cost 55ptas Mon.-Sat., 60ptas on Sun. 345ptas entitles you to 10 bus or Metro rides, 490ptas to 10 of each. Information (tel. 336 00 00).

Emergencies: Police (tel. 091); headquarters at Via Laietana, 43. **Ambulance** (tel. 300 04 22).

Medical Assistance: Hospital Clínico, C. Casanova, 143 (tel. 254 25 80).

Pharmacies: *La Vanguardia* publishes a daily list of 24-hour pharmacies.

Consulates: U.S., Via Laietana, 33 (tel. 319 95 50; 24 hours). **U.K.,** Avda. Diagonal, 477 (tel. 322 21 51). **Canada,** Via Augusta, 125 (tel. 209 06 34). **France,** Passeig de Gràcia, 11B (tel. 317 81 50). For visas you need 2 photos and 1000ptas. Takes about 24 hours. Open Mon.-Fri. 8:30am-12:30pm. Often a line in summer.

Gay Center: Front d'Alliberament Gai de Catalunya (FAGC), Villarroel, 62 (tel. 318 43 55).

Bookstores: Librería Francesa, Passeig de Gràcia, 91. Good selection of English books; *Let's Go* guides too. Open Mon.-Fri. 9:30am-1:30pm and 4:30-7:30pm, Sat. 9:30am-1:30pm.

Laundry: Lavamar, C. Ample, 51 (tel. 315 39 57), by the post office. Open Mon.-Fri. 9am-2pm and 4-8pm, Sat. 9am-2pm; up to 900ptas for 5kg.

Swimming Pools: The 2 on Montjüic are open June-Sept. Mon.-Fri. 10am-3:30pm, Sat.-Sun. 10am-3pm (150ptas).

Hitchhiking: To hitch north to France (A17 via La Junquera), take bus #62 from Pl. Tetuán (on Gran Via) to Avda. Meridiana, beyond Pl. de les Glóries. For Valencia (A7) or Madrid (A2), catch bus #6 or 15 from Pl. de Joan Carlos along Avda. Diagonal to Pl. Francesco Maciá, where the *autopista* access begins. The German organization **Mitfahrzentrale** has a Barcelona office, C. de Provença, 214 (tel. 253 22 07), which pairs rides with riders. **Compasco,** C. Ribas, 31 (tel. 246 69 08), performs a similar service.

Accommodations and Camping

Barcelona's youth hostels are very good, although a bit far from the center. Cheap hotels abound in the narrow streets around the Rambles, but be careful; some are filthy. Rooms in the Eixample are likely to be both more spacious and clean.

Hostal de Joves (IYHF), Passeig Pujades, 29 (tel. 300 31 04), across from Parc de la Ciutadella. Metro: Arc de Triomf (L1). Friendly atmosphere and kitchen facilities. Unisex bedrooms and showers. 435ptas with breakfast (no IYHF card required). 5-day maximum stay. Reception open 8-10am and 3pm-midnight. Rooms closed 10am-3pm. Midnight curfew.

Hostal Verge de Montserrat (IYHF), Passeig Nostra Senyora de Coll, 49-51 (tel. 213 86 33), beyond Parc Güell. Take bus #28 from Pl. de Catalunya, or Metro L3 to Pl. Lesseps, then bus #25. Worth the 20-30 min. commute. A renovated Neo-Moorish villa, full of colored tiles and stained glass, overlooking the city. IYHF card required (1800ptas at reception). 500ptas per night. Breakfast included. Curfew midnight-2am.

Casa de Huéspedes Mari-Luz, C. Palau, 4 (tel. 317 34 63). Metro: Jaume I (L4) or Liceu (L3). C. de Ferran runs between Pl. Sant Jaume and the Rambles; 1 block from Sant Jaume, C. de l'Ensenyança cuts toward the harbor, and becomes C. Palau after 300m. An exceptionally friendly and very popular place—Mari-Luz will go out of her way to help you. 800ptas per person; ask about stays of 15 days or longer. New hot showers. Around the corner at C. Ferran, 31, **Pensión Fernando** (tel. 301 79 93) is almost as good a deal, though it lacks Mari-Luz's charm. 800ptas per person. Showers included, but not always hot.

Hostal Noya, Rambla de Canaletas, 133 (tel. 301 48 31), just off Pl. de Catalunya. Metro: Catalunya (L1, L3). Well worth it if you can get a room with a view of the Rambles. Clean and personable. 800ptas per person. **Hostal Canaletas** (tel. 301 56 60), upstairs, is cheaper and just as good. Singles 600-700ptas, doubles 1200-1400ptas.

Hostal-Residencia Pintor, C. Gignás, 25 (tel. 315 47 08), by the post office. Metro: Correos (L3). Very large rooms, most with balconies. Friendly management. Singles 848ptas, doubles 1696ptas. Hot showers free.

Hotel Kabul, Pl. Reial, 17 (tel. 318 51 90), off the Rambles. Metro: Liceu (L3). A slightly run down private hostel in a dubious area. Lockers available. 450ptas per night. Cheap meals. Open 24 hours.

Residencia Australia, Ronda Universitat, 11 (tel. 317 41 77). Metro: Catalunya (L1, L3) or Universitat (L1). Run by an English-speaking woman who cares: heat in winter, boards under the mattresses. Try to make reservations. Singles 1236ptas, doubles 1802ptas.

Pensión L'Isard, C. Tallers, 82 (tel. 302 51 83), off Pl. Universitat. Metro: Universitat (L1). Clean rooms with alcoves next to the balconies. Singles 1060ptas, doubles 2120ptas.

Hostal-Residencia Lausanne, Avda. Porta de l'Angel, 24 (tel. 302 11 39), near Pl. de Catalunya. Metro: Catalunya (L1, L3). Great rooms and a charming proprietor. Singles 990ptas, doubles 1450ptas.

Hostal-Residencia Oliva, Passeig de Gràcia, 32 (tel. 317 50 87). Metro: Passeig de Gràcia (L3, L4). Beautiful, *modernista* elevator takes you up to clean, simple rooms with a great view. Singles 1272ptas, doubles with shower 2625ptas.

Camping: Most campgrounds lie about 15km outside the city along highway C245 in Gavá. Here you'll find **Albatross** (tel. 662 20 31; 415ptas per person); **Tres Estrellas** (tel. 662 11 16; 340ptas per person); and **Gavá** (220ptas per person, open year-round). From Plaça Universitat (the Gran Via side), take the UC bus to Castelldefels (last bus at 9:45pm, 100ptas).

Food

Finding a good, cheap restaurant in Barcelona is tough. The Barri Gòtic and the area between the Rambles and Ronda Sant Antoni's is your best bet. Try *faves a la catalana,* a lima bean dish, or roasted *butifarra* (Catalonian sausage). "La Boqueria," or the Mercat de Sant Josep, just off Rambla Sant Josep, is Barcelona's best **mercado.** (Open Mon.-Sat. 7:30am-3pm and 6-8pm.)

Casa José, Pl. Sant Josep Oriol, 10 (tel. 302 40 20), between C. del Pi and C. Boquería. A legend—the dizzying set of *menús* (300ptas, 310ptas, 350ptas, 500ptas) and large servings of *paella* (335ptas; 25-min. wait) are all great deals. Sometimes a line. Open Sun.-Fri. 1-4:30pm and 8pm-midnight.

Restaurante Ambos Mundos, Pl. Reial, 10 (tel. 317 01 66), across from the entrance of the Rambles. 500ptas *menú,* as well as regional specialities like *butifarra con judías* and *paella* (600ptas). Open Wed.-Mon. 8am-2:30am.

Sitjas, C. de Sitjas, 3 (tel. 317 29 72), a block in from Rambla de Canaletas. Good food at an unbeatable price—350ptas *menú.* Open Mon.-Sat. 1-4pm and 8-11pm.

Pizzeria Rivolta, C. de l'Hospital, 116 (tel. 329 35 15), a couple blocks from Rambla de Sant Josep. Won'ta rivolta you. Picks up during the night with Catalan separatists and hard rockers. Pizzas start at 300ptas. Open Tues.-Sat. 1-4pm and 8pm-1am, later on Fri.-Sat.

Bar-Restaurante La Concha, C. Escudellers, 42, off the lower Rambles. Liquor on one side of the room, a fish counter on the other. *Menú* 400ptas. Open daily 7am-1:30am; dinner from 8pm.

Can Conesa, Llibreteria, 1, on the corner of Pl. Sant Jaume. Some of the best hot *bocadillos* in Barcelona, 100-250ptas. Open Mon.-Sat. 8am-9:30pm.

Restaurant Les Corts Catalanes, Gran Via de les Corts Catalanes, 603 (tel. 301 03 76), 1 block from Passeig de Gràcia. Behind the awnings proclaiming "*Vida Sana*" (healthy life) is a delicious vegetarian restaurant and delicatessen, serving everything from pasta to an original vegetable lasagna. Four course *menú* 595ptas. Open Mon.-Sat. 9am-4pm and 8-11pm, Sun. noon-11:30pm.

El Viejo Pop, Gran Via de les Corts Catalanes, 635, across from the tourist office. Pizza and sandwiches 300-370ptas. 450ptas *menú.* A hangout for students and young professionals. Open Mon.-Thurs. 8am-1am, Fri. 8am-2:30am, Sat. 11am-2:30am. Closed Sun. during July and Aug.

Sights

More than 2000 years of fervent cultural activity has adorned Barcelona with everything from Roman sculptures to the splash of modern paintings, and enough museums for a month of Sundays.

A good place to start is on the **Rambles,** the tree-lined boulevard that descends from Plaça de Catalunya to the **Columbus Monument** on the waterfront. The sights on the street that W. Somerset Maugham described as the most beautiful in the world are human: bird-vendors, gypsies, sidewalk artists, and street musicians. Inanimate exhibits include the priceless art collection of the **Colección Cambó** in the

Palau de la Virreina, at Rambles, 99. (Open Tues.-Sat. 10am-2pm and 4:30-9pm, Sun. 10am-2pm. Admission 200ptas.)

Through the honeycomb of alleys in the **Barri Gòtic** looms the Gothic **cathedral,** built on fourth-century Paleochristian ruins. Its cloister shelters a small museum and a dozen plump white geese. Behind the cathedral, on C. dels Comtes, stands the **Palau Reial,** Royal Palace of the Counts of Barcelona, with a major collection of polychromed wood statues housed in the **Museu Frederic Marés.** (Open Tues.-Sat. 9am-2pm and 4-7pm, Sun. 9am-2pm. Admission 85ptas, students free.) Cool down in the subterranean excavations of a Roman settlement at nearby **Museu de l'Història de la Ciutat.** (Open Tues.-Sat. 9am-2pm and 4-8pm, Sun. 9am-1:30pm. Admission 85ptas, students free, everyone free on Sun.) Then wind your way through the streets to **Plaça de Sant Jaume,** with the **Ajuntament,** (Barcelona's government) and the **Palau de la Generalitat,** with its beautiful facade on C. del Bisbe.

Fewer visitors venture across Via Laietana to the streets around the Gothic church of **Santa María del Mar,** a monument to Barcelona's great age as a sea power in the fourteenth century. The **Museu Picasso,** nearby at C. de Montcada, 15, houses such masterpieces as the *Harlequin* (1917) and the *Maids of Honor* series (1957). (Open Tues.-Sat. 9:30am-1:30pm and 4-8:30pm, Sun. 9:30am-1:30pm, Mon. 4-8:30pm. Admission 190ptas, students free.) The **Parc de la Ciutadella,** beyond the museum, is second home to half of Barcelona's schoolchildren and site of the **Museu d'Art Modern** and the **Parc Zoològic,** with a dolphin and killer whale (orca) show. (Museum open Tues.-Sat. 9am-7:30pm, Sun. 9am-2pm, Mon. 3-7:30pm. Admission 110ptas, students free. Zoo open daily 9:30am-7:30pm. Admission 400ptas.)

The broad, elegant streets of the **Eixample** were laid out in 1859 in a burst of nineteenth-century progressivism that also razed city walls. The imaginative touch of *chaflanes* (the slanted corners of each block) was a feature of Ildefons Cerdà's plan, which won a competition. Scattered throughout the Eixample are many *modernista* buildings built during the Catalan Renaixença at the beginning of this century. The most ambitious of these is Gaudí's **Temple Expiatori de la Sagrada Família,** filling a block between C. de Provença and C. de Mallorca (Metro: Sagrada Família, L5). The otherworldly towers and bits of walls which have been completed after 103 years' work give only a hint of Gaudí's vision, one that seemingly rejected every hint of flat surfaces and instead took its inspiration from the shapes of plants and animals. If the building is ever completed, it will look like the model in the crypt; in the meantime, don't pass up the chance to climb or be lifted to the towers, and wander amid the bridges, steps, and crannies of the facade, each and every one of them an art nouveau vision. (Site open in summer daily 8am-9pm; in winter daily 8am-7pm. Admission 250ptas. Elevator runs daily 10am-1:45pm and 3-7:45pm; 75ptas.) More *modernista* buildings can be found on Passeig de Gràcia; most striking must be Gaudí's **Casa Batilló** at #43, which looks like a building in which Hansel and Gretl might be trapped. Next door at #41, Puig i Cadafelch opted for a more cubical pattern. The disjunction is such that the block is known as the *manzana de la discordia* (block of disagreement). Up the street at Passeig de Gràcia, 92, you'll find **Casa Milá,** which looks like it's going to melt into the sidewalk. The ironwork and chimneys are a good example of the freedom Gaudí gave the artisans who worked on his buildings. Take bus #24 from here to the **Parc Güell,** which exemplifies Gaudí's ideas about city planning. The project floundered, but two guard houses, decorated with extravagant tiles and sensual shapes, give you an idea of what it would have been. (Open daily 10am-8pm. Free.) Visit the small **Museu Gaudí** (open in summer Mon.-Thurs. 11am-1:30pm and 4:30-7:30pm, Fri. 11am-1:30pm, Sun. and holidays 10am-2pm and 4-7pm; admission 50ptas).

If you think Gaudí's gaudy, escape to the green parks of **Montjuïc,** where Barcelona will stage a few of the events of the 1992 Olympics. From Plaça d'Espanya, head past the **Fonts Luminoses** (Illuminated Fountains, in operation in summer Thurs. and Sat.-Sun. 9pm-midnight, in winter Sat.-Sun. 8-11pm) and up an almost endless flight of stairs to the **Palau Nacional.** The **Museu d'Art de Catalunya,** housed here, holds a magnificent collection of Catalan Romanesque and Gothic art, including frescoes removed from Pyrenean chapels. (Open Tues.-Sun. 9am-2pm.

Admission 190ptas, students, and on Sun. everyone, free.) Close by is the **Poble Espanyol** (Spanish Village), Barcelona's attempt to keep you from visiting the rest of Spain; it displays typical reconstructed buildings from every region. (Open daily 9am-8pm. Admission 250ptas, students 175ptas.) On the other side of the hill, the **Fundaciò Joan Miró,** designed by Josep Lluís Sert, has a wonderful view of Barcelona and a permanent collection of Miró's works, including an extravagant 35-foot high tapestry. The museum is adding two new wings to accommodate visiting exhibits of modern art. (Open Tues.-Sat. 11am-8pm, Sun. 11am-2:30pm. Admission 300ptas, students 150ptas.) Just down the street from here is the top of the *funicular,* which you can get on at the Parallel Metro stop (L3). It costs 55ptas. From the top of the *funicular,* you can take the *teleferique* (115ptas one way, 215ptas round-trip) to the amusement park or the *castell* at the top of the hill.

Entertainment

Barcelona offers an irresistible combination of exuberance and variety—the only problem is the late schedule. Plan on a *paseo* (stroll) until 10 or 11pm, a drink until 1 or 2am, then dancing. For guidance to the thousand things happening daily in the city, check the weekly *Guía del Ocio* (60ptas at a newsstand) or the brochure *Actes a la Ciutat* (free at the tourist office).

The **Gran Teatre del Liceu,** Rambla de Caputxins, 61 (tel. 318 92 77), is one of the world's leading opera houses. (Box office open Sept.-July noon-3pm and 5-10pm.) Classical concert music resounds from fall to spring at the fantastic art nouveau **Palau de la Musica Catalana,** C. Amadeu Vives, near Pl. Urquinaona. (Box office open Mon.-Fri. 11am-1pm and 5-8pm.) Inquire about their series of free concerts. Barcelona has dozens of cinemas. If you don't understand Spanish, check *La Vanguardia's* Cartelená section for movies marked "V.O." (original version), and they'll be subtitled not dubbed. The **Filmoteca,** Travessera de Gràcia, 63 (tel. 201 29 06) offers everything from art films to cult films for only 150ptas. The **Teatre Grec** season, usually beginning in late June, sees more movies, theater, dance, and music. Performances are usually held outdoors. Tickets available at the Palau de la Virreina, Rambla, 99 (tel. 318 85 99; open daily 10am-7pm).

Karma, Pl. Reial, 10 (tel. 302 56 80), combines music (usually rock, Fri.-Sat. at midnight) with tarot card readings and other mysterious attractions. (Open Tues.-Sun. until 4:30am.) A more traditional setting is **Zeleste,** C. Argentenria, 65 (tel. 319 86 41), off Via Laietana near Santa María del Mar, with well-known rock groups and occasional jazz and avant-garde performances, usually beginning around midnight. Local jazz musicians love **La Cova del Drac,** C. Tuset, 30. **Ebano,** C. Roger de Flor, 114 (tel. 232 89 17), has huge African photos on the walls, serves a large and potent African cocktail (450ptas), and plays a mixture of African, Spanish, and American music. Open Tues.-Sun. until 5am; cover charge 600ptas. A good gay place with dancing is **Keops,** C. Bruc, 62, in the Eixample. A real Barcelona institution is the **Bodega Bohemia,** C. Lancaster, 2 (tel. 302 50 61), near Avda. Parallel—a dance hall with all kinds of people dancing to all kinds of music. (Open nightly from 10:30pm.) You'll often hear mentioned in the same breath **El Molino,** C. Vila Vilá, 99, at Avda. Parallel (tel. 241 63 83), a music hall whose show has changed little in 50 years—part music, part comedy, part burlesque. (Tues.-Sun. 2 shows per night, usually around 11pm and 1am; 1000ptas.)

Don't miss a chance to watch a *sardana,* Catalonia's regional dance; participants young and old join hands and dance in a circle around their belongings. The best chances are Saturday and Sunday at around 7pm in front of the cathedral, Sunday at 7pm in Pl. de Sant Jaume, and Saturday at noon on C. Porta de l'Angel, in front of the Galerías Preciados department store. (During Aug., only the Galerías Preciados happens.)

Bulls are dispatched regularly in Barcelona's bullring, **Las Arenas.** Look for posters—fights are usually on weekends. Tickets are sold at an office at C. Muntaner, 24 (tel. 253 38 21), parallel to Passeig de Gràcia. (Open daily 10am-1pm and 4:30-7pm.) Any tickets left are sold at the ring an hour before opening.

Big festivals in Barcelona include the **Fiesta de Sant Jordi** (April 22), when loved ones exchange books and roses in celebration of Catalonia's patron saint, and, the **Feast of the Virgen de la Merced** (Sept. 24).

Near Barcelona

Like huge bubbles of frozen steam, the gigantic boulders of **Montserrat** surround Catalunya's spiritual center, the monastery that houses *La Virgen de Montserrat* and some 80 Benedictine monks. (Open daily 6-10:30am and noon-6:30pm.) Two museums nearby keep tourists happy with religious treasures and paintings from the Catalan *Renaixença.* (Open in summer daily 10am-2pm and 3:30-6pm. Admission 125ptas.) From the top of a nearby funicular you can walk to the hermitage of **Sant Joan** along a path with spectacular views of the monastery and the valley. Montserrat can be easily reached by bus or train from Barcelona. **Auto/Transporte Julia,** Pl. Universitat, 12 (tel. 318 72 38), has two buses per day (at 8 and 9am, 266ptas one way, 532ptas round-trip). Much more fun, however, is the **Ferrocarrils de Catalunya,** whose trains leave from Pl. Espanya and make a connection with a cable car at **Aeri de Montserrat** (825ptas round-trip). Trains leave Barcelona at 9:10 and 11am.

Golden-hued rocks and pine trees hanging over shady coves make up the **Costa Brava** ("Untamed Coast"). **Tossa,** on the southern edge of the Costa Brava, offers a good mix of history and natural beauty. The narrow cobblestoned streets of the **Vila Vella** provide spectacular views of nearby coves. The **tourist office** at the bus terminal has a helpful map. (Open Mon.-Sat. 9am-8pm, Sun. 10am-2pm and 5-8pm in summer.) Try staying at **Pensiò Montserrat,** C. Sant Telmo, 12 (tel. 34 01 48), for 750ptas per person. From Barcelona take RENFE trains to Blanes, then catch a bus to Tossa. Up the coast, the inland town of **Palafrugell** provides a good base for exploring the nearby beaches of Tamariu, Calella, and Llafranc. Stay here at **Pensiò Ramirez,** C. Sant Sebastià, 29 (tel. 30 00 43). Buses to the beach and Gevona leave from C. Torres Jonama, 33 (tel. 30 06 23). Don't miss the Dalí museum in **Figueras,** where you can stay at the newly renovated **IYHF youth hostel,** C. Anicet de Paglés, 2 (tel. 50 12 13), just beyond the **tourist office** (tel. 50 31 55) on Plaça del Sol. (Tourist office open Mon.-Sat. 9am-1pm and 3-6pm.) Artists and musicians head for **Cadaqués,** the small whitewashed village east of Figueres that was home to Salvador Dalí.

Balearic Islands (Illes Balears)

More sun-kissed than a Florida orange, the islands of Majorca, Minorca, and Ibiza seduce thousands of vacationing Europeans with their gorgeous beaches and scenic terrain. A massive summertime influx of Northern Europeans has taken its toll: A large portion of Majorca is now encased in concrete, and the jet-set crowd is leading Ibiza similarly astray. Minorca remains the most traditional and least crowded of the trio, but is also the hardest to do on a budget.

Tourist offices can help you find a room. Camping, official or illegal, is practically non-existent on Majorca and Minorca, but Ibiza has five sites.

You can reach the islands by both boat and plane. Budget travel offices can help you find cheap charter flights or a *tarifa-mini:* an advance-purchase, no-refund-or-exchange round-trip ticket that saves about 40% off the regular round-trip fare. Both require advance bookings in the summer. You can decide to go at the last minute and pay less on the **Transmediterránea** ferries, which travel daily from Barcelona and Valencia to Palma and the other islands (8 hr., 4500ptas). **Flebasa Lines** runs ferries from Denia, between Alicante and Valencia, to Ibiza Sant Antoni (3 hr., 4500ptas). In conjunction with **Ubesa Buses,** Flebasa Lines has service from Madrid for 5900ptas (Ubesa at C. Jaime Conquistador, 6). (See Practical Information in Barcelona, Valencia, and Alicante for specifics.) Traveling between islands is cheaper and quicker by air (20 min., 3125ptas for Palma to Maó or Ibiza; make reservation at least a week ahead in summer). Lots of buses help you get around on the islands, and bike or moped rental as well as hitchhiking, which is safe and fairly easy, will get you to the less-crowded beaches.

Majorca (Mallorca)

The largest of the Balearic Islands, Majorca eagerly absorbs the stream of tourists who pour each summer into **Palma.** Plagued by flashy discos and flashier patrons, Palma should be visited as quickly as possible. The **Transmediterránea** ferries, Muelle Viejo, 5 (tel. 72 67 40), actually arrive at Muelle de Pelaires, from which bus #1 runs to the center of town (60ptas); bus #17 will bring you in from the airport (120ptas). **Iberia,** Passeig de Born, 10 (tel. 28 69 66 or 46 34 00), will book cheap inter-island travel.

The city's principal street, at right angles to the harbor, is Passeig de Born, which meets Avinguda Rei Jaume III at Plaça Pio XIII. The national tourist office, **Oficina d'Informació i Turisme,** Auda Rey Jaime III, 10 (tel. 71 22 16), has reams of pamphlets, transportation information, and can help you with accommodations. (Open Mon.-Fri. 9am-1:30pm and 4:30-7:30pm, Sat. 9am-1pm.)

The **Alberg Juvenil Platja de Palma (IYHF),** C. Costa Brava, 13 (tel. 26 08 92), 8km out of Palma in El Arenal, is immaculate, spacious, and only two blocks from the beach. Call before taking bus #15 from Pl. España (65ptas). (Members 500ptas, non-members 600ptas. Open Dec.-Oct.) **Hostal Goya,** C. Estanco, 7 (tel. 71 21 34), has simple rooms and a high turnover. (600ptas per person. Showers included.) **Hostal la Paz,** C. Salas, 5 (tel. 71 50 10), is also likely to have vacancies. (Clean, if dark, singles 600-700ptas, doubles 1200ptas.) Two pretty **hostales** are on C. General Barceló, 8: **Hostal Residencia Pons** (tel. 72 26 58) has cool singles for 650ptas and doubles for 1100ptas, and the friendly owners at **Hostal Residencia Palma** (tel. 72 44 17) will rent singles for 800ptas and doubles for 1100-1300ptas (showers included).

Just up the street, try **La Viña,** C. General Barceló, 6 (tel. 72 11 45), where a hearty meal of *mallorquín* costs 375ptas. **Restaurante Yate Rizz,** Passeig de Born, 2, has a little more glitter, and the friendly cooks make filling **combinados.** (**Menú** 400ptas; Open in summer daily noon-3:30pm and 8-10:30pm; in winter Mon.-Sat. only.) Cheap **bocadillos** are at **Bodega Casa Payesa,** C. de Molineros, just off C. San Miguel. The Plaça Gomila and El Terreno neighborhoods abound with hopping bars and discos, but the most chic are in Cala Mayor. Take buses #3, 20, 21, or 22 to all three areas. The popular **Casablanca,** C. Frederico Garcia Lorca, 23, off Pl. Gomila, serves good drinks. (Open Thurs.-Tues. 7:30pm-sunrise.) Closer to town and more sedate, the Es Jonquet neighborhood, under the windmills off calle San Magin, harbors several fine clubs and bars.

The island's efficient and extensive bus service makes travel easy. Fringed by the jagged Serra de Tramontana, the northwestern coast is lined with beautiful beaches, rustic villages, and lemon and olive groves. The quiet village of **Valldemosa,** 18km north of Palma, is where Chopin and his mistress George Sand spent an amorous winter in the monastery of the **Cartuja Real.** The museum (300ptas) contains Chopin memorabilia and hosts an annual piano concert in late July. The narrow road hugs the contour of the mountains up to **Sóller;** at times you think you're going to plunge into the sea below. Just before Sóller, a road winds down to the beach at **Sa Calobra;** have the bus drop you off at the top and hitch down.

Sóller is connected to Palma by train, so it's crowded. The monastery at **Lluc,** however, about 18km up the coast, offers a cool and peaceful retreat from the burning bodies on the beaches. Home of **La Virgen de Lluc,** a 700-year-old carved image, the monastery has comfortable beds for 850ptas a person. The monks (tel. 51 70 25) will show you where to camp if no beds are available.

Explore the eastern coast from **Alcúdia,** built on the site of the Roman city Pollentia. The idyllic youth hostel, **Albergue Victoria** (IYHF), Carretera Cabo Pinar, 4 (tel. 54 53 95), 4km east of town, is just 50m from an empty beach and tucked up against good hiking territory. (595ptas. Open mid-June-Sept.) **Puerto Alcudia** has a friendly and helpful **tourist office,** Calle V. Moreno, 2 (tel. 54 63 71), on the waterfront near the telephone kiosk. (Open daily 10am-1pm and 4:30-10pm). **Hostal Vista Alegre,** C. V. Moreno, 22 (tel. 54 69 77), right at the port, is clean, and some rooms overlook the water. (100ptas per person.) **Hostal C'an Toni,** next door (tel. 54 50 08), is a bit more expensive. (Doubles with bath 2000ptas.) The **Restaurante El Anda** keeps you cool with palm fronds and serves a 500ptas *menú.* Frequent buses connect Alcúdia with Palma (5 per day, 265ptas.)

If you want to stay in **Puerto Cristo** after viewing the famous **Cuevas del Drach,** try **Pension Orient** on the Plaza del Carmen. (Singles 1000ptas, doubles 1500ptas.) Local fare is served up at **C'an Marti,** C. del Puerto, 96 (tel. 57 07 48), with a 450ptas *menú.*

The southeastern corner of the island offers peace and quiet, miles of unspoiled beaches (including the nudist beach **Es Trenc**), and great spots for unofficial camping. Take the infrequent bus bound for Colonia Sant Jordi.

Minorca (Menorca)

Minorca's isolated beaches and whitewashed towns are spared both the glitter of Ibiza and the package tourists of Majorca. While you'll probably want to head straight for the shimmering sands, set aside some time to explore the Bronze Age remains in the interior of the island.

Maó (Mahón in Spanish) is the island's capital and the birthplace of mayonnaise. From the airport, you'll have to take a taxi into the city (500ptas). If you arrive at the port (Transmediterránea, tel. 36 29 50), walk up the staircase that climbs the palisades. The **tourist office** (tel. 36 37 90) is on the Plaça de l'Esplanada, where most of the buses to the beaches stop. (Open in summer Mon.-Fri. 9am-2pm and 5-7pm, Sat. 9am-2pm; in winter Mon.-Sat. 9am-2pm.) The best place to sleep is **Hostal Orsi,** Carrer Infanta, 19 (tel. 36 47 51), where the hard-working and friendly owners keep bright rooms. (Singles 975ptas, doubles 1950ptas.) For cheaper rooms, try **Casa Huéspedes Company,** C. del Rosari, 27 (tel. 36 22 67). (700ptas per person.) Minorca is short on restaurants that serve cheap anything. For a full meal, try **La Huerta,** Carrer de Joan Ramis, 64 (tel. 36 28 85), with a 550ptas *menu.* **Majestic Café,** Pl. del Príncep, 5, features a variety of salads, mixed plates, and brochettes for under 500ptas. (Open Mon.-Fri. 8:30am-3:30pm and 7-10pm, Sat. 9:30am-3pm.)

Buses to Ciutadella, on the other side of the island, leave from the **TMSA** on C. José M. Quadundo, 7 (tel. 36 03 61). Ciutadella is a convenient base for exploring nearby beaches, such as Cala Blanca and Cala Santandria, or prehistoric sites like Torre Trencada or the **Naveta dels Tudons,** a burial chamber that is the oldest building in Europe. Buses also leave for the beaches at Es Grau, Punta Prima, Cala'n Porter, and Son Bou.

Ibiza (Eivissa)

A one-time haven for artists and hippies, Ibiza has become a flashy fashion center for the rich. The city at the center of this mayhem is Eivissa; the **tourist office** is on Paseo Vara del Rey, 13 (tel. 30 19 00). Start your hunt for a room at **Hostal Las Nieves,** C. Juan de Austria, 18 (tel. 31 58 22), or **Hostal Juanito,** across the street at #17 (same phone). (Singles 750ptas, doubles 1500ptas.) Otherwise, try any one of the four *hostales* along C. Bartolomé Vicente Ramón, one block over. Camping is a good alternative; closest to town is **Garbí** (tel. 30 52 82), less than 2km away on the road to Platja d'En Bossa. (Open April-Sept.)

The narrow alleys of the *d'alt vila* (old town) will take you to the **cathedral** and **castle,** both of which have a spectacular view of the city and the surrounding environs. Also visit the **Puig des Molins,** a seventh-century B.C.E. Carthaginian necropolis with over 4000 tombs cut into the rocks. (Museum open Mon.-Sat. 4-7pm. Admission 60ptas, students free.)

At night, Carrer Major in the Sa Penya erupts with disco neon and expensive fashion. Escape the scene at **Tavern Ibiza,** Carrer de la Virgen, 20, with 125ptas beers.

The closest beaches are Las Salinas and the Platja Es Cavallet; buses leave from Avda. Isidor Malabich. Buses also go to Sant Antoni and Santa Eulalia, both of which are close to better beaches.

Pyrenees (Pirineos)

The northern province of Aragon, an independent kingdom from the eleventh to the fifteenth centuries, sweeps from dusty plains to the most spectacular peaks in the Spanish Pyrenees. Lush mountain valleys such as Ansó and Hecho are stunning gateways into France. The Parque Nacional de Ordesa harbors some of the most spectacular scenery in Europe, with wonderful opportunities for mountain hiking and climbing. The main problem is access, but careful use of infrequent buses and some hitchhiking should get you up and into the hills. **Aldecar,** Avda. Jacetania, 60, in Jaca (tel. (974) 36 07 81), rents small cars for 1500ptas per day plus 15ptas per kilometer.

Jaca, once the capital of Aragon, is now a popular retreat for outdoor enthusiasts. Only 29km from France, the town is a great base for exploring nearby Ordesa; the well-stocked **tourist office,** Avda. Regimiento Galicia (tel. 36 00 98), just south of the park, has information. (Open July-Sept. 15 Mon.-Fri. 9am-2pm and 4-8pm, Sat. 9am-2pm; Sept. 16-June Mon.-Fri. 9:30am-1:30pm and 4:30-7pm. Sat. 10am-1pm.) The **train station,** at the other end of town off C. Juan XXII, has daily trains to Zaragora, Madrid, and Sabinañigo, where buses connect to Ordesa. Trains also go north to Canfranc and the ski areas.

Rooms are readily available at Jaca, except during late July and early August in odd-numbered years, when the **Folklore Festival** is held. To reach the **Residencia Juvenil de Vacaciones,** Avda. Perimentral (tel. (974) 36 10 32), walk down the stairs at the foot of C. Ferrenal; the hostel is pleasant, with two to four beds per room and lots of showers. (600ptas. Open Jan.-Sept.) In town, the best rooms are at **Pensión Vivas,** C. Gil Berges (tel. (974) 36 05 31), off C. Mayor. (Singles 700ptas, doubles 1000ptas.) More expensive, but more likely to have room, is **Hostal Galindo,** C. Mayor, 45 (tel. (974) 36 15 67). (Singles 875ptas, doubles 1650ptas, with private bath 1950ptas.) The best campsite, **Peña Oroel** (tel. (974) 36 02 15), 3½km out of town towards Sabiñanigo, has first-rate facilities. (310ptas per person, 310ptas per tent. Open March-Oct.) **Camping Victoria** (tel. (974) 36 03 23) is only 1¾km away on Highway C-134. (225ptas per person, 120ptas per tent. Open year-round.) Jaca's best food is happily its least expensive. **Restaurante La Fragua,** C. Gil Berges, 4, grills delicious pork, lamb, and beef on a former blacksmith's forge. (Meals 345-450ptas. Open Thurs.-Tues. noon-3:30pm and 7-11:30pm.)

Jaca's Romanesque **Cathedral** (ca. 1063) is the earliest of its kind in Spain, a legacy of Jaca's role as a stop on the medieval pilgrimage route to Santiago, while the pentagonal **Castillo de San Pedro** is the only intact *ciudadela* in the country. Those seen, break camp for the **Parque Nacional de Ordesa,** a valley etched in stone by the Río Araraz. You'll find some of the most rugged and beautiful scenery in the entire Pyrenees, complete with giant poplar trees, rushing streams, and sheer canyon walls towering 1000m above the valley floor. To reach the park, take the train from Jaca to Sabiñanigo, and catch the one daily bus to Torla, a village 9km from the park entrance. Accommodations in Torla are expensive.

To enjoy the park thoroughly and safely, you'll need a lot more information than we can provide here; consult the tourist office in Jaca, the ranger station at the parking lot/trailhead in the park, and the red *Cartographic Guide to Ordesa, Vignemale, and Monte Perdido* (275ptas), stocked by Jaca bookstores. Camping in the park is prohibited, but many *refugios* (mountain huts) offer shelter; these are free if there are no facilities, a few hundred pesetas otherwise. All huts are clearly marked on trail maps. If you're not equipped to make an overnight visit to the park, you might want to take the seven-hour **Soaso Circle** trail, an exhausting but exhilarating hike.

In the winter, the slopes near Jaca provide good skiing for significantly less money than those in the Alps. At the Jaca tourist office, ask for the pamphlet *Ski Aragon.* For information on ski conditions (in Spanish) dial 22 56 56.

Northern Lleida holds the spectacular **Parc Nacional d'Aigüestortes i Estany de Sant Maurici,** about 100km east of Ordesa. The area was sculpted by a glacier that left rock-strewn fields, valleys of soft tundra, crashing waterfalls, and serene lakes in its wake. Four *refugios* provide the park's accommodations—camping is illegal. From the west side, get to Aigüestortes from Vall de Bot, one of the best places to see Romanesque architecture in the Pyrenees. Buses to the park leave Barcelona daily and arrive in Espot, on the east side of the park.

Basque Country (País Vasco, Euskadi)

The rain in Spain does *not* fall mainly on the plain; the rugged hills and mountains of this region and, unfortunately, the sandy beaches as well, get the lion's share of precipitation. These provinces are green, forested, and for the most part unspoiled. The Basques enjoy being a people apart. The origin of their language *euskera* (prohibited during Franco's reign) is still debated. Some claim it is the original human language; scholars have been able to find similarities to it only in the Caucasus in inner Asia. Half a million Basques have managed to raise bilingual signposts and establish the three provinces of the Basque Country (Vizcaya, Guipúzcoa, and Alava) as an autonomous community since Franco's death in 1975. Still, a large part is not content with this, and an extremist fringe called *ETA* has a small-scale civil war going with the *Guardia Civil,* continuing the centuries-old Basque struggle for separation. Madrid won't let go easily, especially since the region includes some of the richest and most industrially developed areas in Spain.

Two areas of more peaceful Basque divergence from the Spanish mainstream are sports and cooking. *Pelota* (jai alai) was born here; to Basques, this lightning-fast game is both a sport and a cultural symbol. Basque cooking is famous for its richness and variety, and has influenced Spanish cuisine; *Bacalao a la vizcaína* (salt cod in a tomato sauce), and *chipirones en su tinta* (cuttlefish in its own ink) have become popular throughout the Iberian peninsula.

San Sebastián (Donostia)

San Sebastián seems to have been created as the perfect summer playground. Neither high prices nor sirens in the night can keep European tourists away from this showpiece of a city. San Sebastián has traditionally been favored as a summer haunt for vacationing Spaniards and as a target for ETA autonomy pitches. But while the deluge of visitors submerges local culture during July and August, men come out in September to play *pelota* on the walls of the breakwaters, and fishermen mend their nets near the *puerto.*

Orientation and Practical Information

Just a few kilometers inside Spain, San Sebastián is a convenient stopover on the way to or from France; all direct Paris-Madrid trains pass through the city.

The broad, elegant **Avenida de la Libertad,** San Sebastián's major artery, bisects the peninsula. The city was destroyed by fire in 1813, so even the **parte antigua** (old quarter) below Monte Urgull is relatively recent. The new city, south of Avda. de la Libertad, faces west to the scallop-shaped Bahía and its two beautiful beaches, La Concha and Ondarreta. San Sebastián is small enough to be negotiated by foot.

Tourist Offices: Oficina de Gobierno Vasco, C. Andia, 13 (tel. 42 62 82), on the corner of C. Miramar at Pl. de Cervantes, on the beach. Most helpful, with information on the city and the Basque Country. Ask for help if you're desperate for a room. Open July-Sept. Mon.-Fri. 9:30am-1:30pm and 4-7pm, Sat. 9am-1pm; Oct.-June Mon.-Fri. 9:30am-1:30pm and 4-6pm. **Centro de Atracción y Turismo,** C. Reina Regente (tel. 42 10 02), at the end of Alameda de Boulevard where the first bridge crosses the river. A municipal office; not as helpful, but they do have a list of *casas particulares.* Open Mon.-Fri. 9am-2pm and 3:30-7:30pm, Sat. 9am-2pm.

Budget Travel: Viajes TIVE, Avda. Ategorrieta, 9 (tel. 27 69 34), across the river. Tips for cheap travel and IYHF cards (1800ptas). Open Mon.-Fri. 8am-2pm, Sat. 8am-noon.

Post Office: C. Urdaneta, 9 (tel. 46 49 14), near the cathedral. Open for stamps Mon.-Fri. 9am-8pm, Sat. 9am-2pm. Poste Restante Mon.-Fri. 9am-1pm and 4-6pm, Sat. 9am-2pm. **Postal code:** 20000.

Telephones: Avda. de la Libertad, 26. Open Mon.-Fri. 9am-1pm and 5-9pm. **Telephone code:** 943.

Airport: Near Fuenterrabía, about 25km away (tel. 64 22 40). Aviaco flights to Madrid (2 per day, 9710ptas), and Barcelona (daily, 10,310ptas).

Trains: Main station is on the east side of the river. To reach the center of town, cross the Puente (bridge) María Cristina, and turn right, continuing along the river to the next bridge, Santa Catalina, where you'll hit Avda. de la Libertad. 5 trains per day to Madrid, 2 to Portugal via Salamanca, 2 to Valencia and Alicante. Frequent *tranvías* to the border at Irún/Hendaye (80ptas) and to Pamplona. **RENFE** is on Avda. de Francia (tel. 28 35 99). **Estación de Amara,** to the west at Pl. Easo, has 2 private lines, Vascongado (tel. 45 01 31) and Topo (tel. 46 18 52); travel to Guernica/Bermeo on Vascongado.

Buses: Most leave from Pl. Pío XII (walk down Avda. Sancho el Sabio); offices are clustered nearby. **Pesa,** Avda. Sancho el Sabio, 33 (tel. 46 39 74), has service to Lequeitio several times per day. **Continental Auto,** Avda. Sancho el Sabio, 31 (tel. 46 90 74), drives to Madrid (3 per day, 2410ptas). **Viajes Abril** (tel. 45 26 88), in the same office, will book you for Paris. Around the corner at Paseo de Vizcaya, 16, **RENFE Bus** (tel. 46 80 87) goes to Burgos; **La Roncalesa** (tel. 46 10 64) makes it to Pamplona (3 per day); and **Turytrans** (tel. 46 23 60) zips to Bilbao (7 per day) and Santander (3-4 per day). A French company, **ATCRB,** will pick you up in the parking lot for Biarritz and Bayonne.

Emergencies: Police (tel. 091); headquarters at C. Larramendi (tel. 45 00 00). **Ambulance** (tel. 27 22 22).

Medical Assistance: Casa de Socorro, C. Easo, 39 (tel. 46 41 20).

Laundry: Lavomatique, C. Iñigo, 12, in the old city. Open Mon.-Fri. 10am-2pm and 4-8pm, Sat. 10am-3pm, Sun. 11am-2pm.

Baggage Check: C. Easo, near corner of C. Urdaneta. 100ptas per day. Open July-Sept. daily 10am-2pm and 4-8pm.

Hitchhiking: For all but the closest destinations go to Avda. de Carlos I, between Pl. de Pío XII and the main highway.

Accommodations and Camping

Getting a room here in July or August is like trying to break down a wall with your head, *and* prices are exorbitant, *and* singles are nonexistent. The only way to get into the hostel is to be there when reception opens at 10am. Otherwise, get a list of *casas particulares* and *fondas* from the tourist office, then call ahead until you find a room; it's not worth dragging your stuff around the city just to get turned down everywhere. Many people sleep on the beach at *La Concha.* If it rains you can move under the walkway.

Residencia Juvenil Anoeta (IYHF), Ciudad Deportiva Anoeta (tel. 45 29 70), behind the track. Walk 20 min. or catch Amara-Anoeta bus along C. Urbieta. Crowded in summer, so reserve early in the morning. 625ptas with breakfast. IYHF card required but can be purchased (1850ptas). Reception open 10am-noon and 4-7pm. 2am curfew.

Pensión La Perla, C. Loyola, 10 (tel. 42 81 23), 1 block north of the cathedral. Nice people, spacious rooms, high ceilings, attractive beds. One single 1400ptas, doubles 2530ptas. Rates lower in winter.

Pensión Urkia, C. Urbieta, 12 (tel. 42 44 36), around the corner from La Perla, is run by that owner's sister. Equally friendly and a good deal. 1200ptas per person.

Pensión Donostiarra, C. Easo, 12 (tel. 46 79 45), up the street from the baggage check. Cheerful and bright. Singles 1400ptas, doubles 2200ptas.

Hostal-Residencia Easo, C. San Bartolomé, 24 (tel. 46 68 92). Up-to-date, well-kept. Doubles 2440ptas, with private bath 2700ptas. 200-300ptas less in winter.

Hostal Gran Bahía, C. Embeltran, 16 (tel. 42 38 38), in the *parte antigua.* Big, fairly clean rooms. Doubles 2000-2400ptas. Showers 150ptas.

Camping: Camping Igueldo (tel. 21 45 02), 5km west of town. Bus "Barrio de Igueldo" leaves 13 times per day (5 Sun.) from Alameda de Boulevard, 22 (40ptas, last bus 10pm). 265ptas per person, 170ptas per tent. Open May-Sept.

Food

San Sebastián may be seafood heaven, but at these prices, those crustaceans are probably safe from you. Even *menús* here cost about 800ptas. Try a meal of *tapas* instead: the bars in the old city lay out an array of enticing tidbits. Try them with *Txacoli,* the strong regional wine. Most *tapas* bars will let you help yourself; the bill is calculated later by the number of toothpicks on your plate.

The area around the port is full of merchants selling shrimp in little egg cups and periwinkles in paper cones for 100ptas. Should you find you've merely whetted your appetite, head for **Mariscos Kaia el Puerto,** Paseo del Muelle (Pasealekua), 1, to get seafood by the kilo. (Open 10am-2pm and 5-9:30pm.) For other fresh food, there's a **market** on Alameda de Boulevard and another a block north of the cathedral off C. Loyola. (Both open Mon.-Fri. 7:30am-2pm and 5-7:30pm, Sat. 7:30am-2pm.)

La Barranquesa, C. Larramendi, 21. A smoky neighborhood basement restaurant. Specialties include *lengua en salsa* (cow's tongue in sauce) and *txiperones* (squid in its own ink). The excellent 445ptas *menú* includes more traditional fare. Open Mon.-Sat.

Bar-Restaurant Soterotxo, Paseo del Muelle, 7 (under an awning). The best of the seafood places by the port. *Paella* 550ptas, *menú* 775ptas. If they're closed, don't despair; there's plenty of competition nearby.

Restaurante Morgan, Narrika Kalea, 7, in the *parte antigua.* A favorite of Basque gourmets. Exquisite food a bargain at 1200ptas for the *menú.* Dinner served nightly 9-10:30pm.

Sights and Entertainment

The most spectacular sight of all is San Sebastián itself and the green mountains and thundering ocean that surround it. The view of the city is most spectacular after dark, when the entire bay of Santa Clara Island is lit by banks of floodlights. To enjoy the view, you can take the funicular to the top of **Monte Igueldo** (every 15 min.; in summer daily 10am-10pm, in winter daily 11am-6 or 8pm; 45ptas one way), where there is also an **amusement park;** take the Igueldo bus to get to the base of the mountain. At the end of the walkway skirting the mountain, a *plaza* that overlooks the ocean becomes a musical instrument when waves force air and water through seven tubes of different lengths. Closer to the city is **Monte Urgull,** at the tip of the peninsula; you can climb to its summit or walk the **Paseo Nuevo,** a wind-whipped road that rounds the peninsula.

Basque slogans cover the government buildings at **Plaza de la Constitución;** the authorities tried to plant a tree in the center, but residents keep carving the bark off in symbolic protest. **Museo San Telmo,** with its fascinating collection of Basque artifacts and fine arts, rests in an old Dominican monastery on Pl. Zuloaga, curiously ignored by tourists. The collection is an interesting and varied representation of the development of a national artistic character, from prehistoric *steles* (funerary stones) to José María Sert's epic murals. (Open June-Sept. Tues.-Sat. 9am-9pm, Sun. 9am-2pm; Oct.-May Tues.-Sat. 10am-1:30pm and 3-7pm, Sun. 10am-1:30pm. Admission 150ptas, students free.)

By evening, crowds fill the streets and bars of the *parte antigua,* especially along **Calbetón Kalea.** Later, flashier nightlife centers around **Plaza de Zaragoza** and the nearby beachfront. Most discotheques stay open every night until sunrise and cost 1000-1200ptas, either as a cover charge (which includes 1 drink) or in the cost of the alcohol. Everything opens at 11:30pm, but don't go before 2 or 3am unless you want to dance with your shadow. **Bataplan,** below the beachfront sidewalk on Paseo de la Concha, is the city's leading discotheque; others are within striking distance. For live music, try **Be Bop Bar,** at Paseo de Salamanca, 3, where there are often jazz jam sessions. There are any number of student cafes along **Calle de los Reyes Católicos** and surrounding streets.

The city hosts an international **Jazz Festival** the third week in July, the **Euskal Jaiak** (Basque Feasts) and the **San Sebastián International Film Festival** in September (the former the week of Sept. 8, the latter toward the end of the month), and beginning August 14, **San Sebastián's Grand Week,** which includes an international fireworks contest.

Near San Sebastián

Fuenterrabía (Hondarribía in Basque), is right on the French border; you can stay at the excellent **Juan Sebastián Elcano Hostel (IYHF),** 100m from the beach on Carretera del Faro (tel. 64 15 50). (300ptas, IYHF card a must. 11pm curfew. Open year-round.) Camp below the hostel, at nearby **Jaizkebel** (tel. 64 16 79) or at **Faro de Higuer** (tel. 64 10 08). (Both 240ptas per person, 170ptas per tent.) Regular buses run from San Sebastián.

In the other direction, and also accessible by bus from San Sebastián, lovely **Lequeitio** (or Lekeito) sits on a wide bay with a small island. When the tide goes out, the whole expanse becomes a great beach, and you can wade out to explore the island. It's easiest to stay in a *casa particular* (around 1500ptas); let the friendly staff of the **tourist office** at Arranegiko Zabala, 10 (tel. 684 22 72), help you find one. (Open June 15-Sept. 15 Mon.-Sat. 10am-1:30pm and 5-8pm, Sun. 10am-1pm; Oct.-May Mon.-Sat. 9am-2pm and 4:30-7:30pm.)

The German bombing of **Guernica** (Gernika) on April 26, 1937 inspired Picasso's famous painting of the same name. You can also see the **Tree of Guernica,** symbol of Basque nationalism. Guernica is reached by slow Vascongado train from San Sebastián, or, better, by bus from Lequeitio.

Pamplona (Iruña)

The capital of the medieval kingdom of Navarra performs a spectacular quick-change act for the **Fiesta de San Fermín,** a.k.a. **The Running of the Bulls** (July 7-14), Spain's most wildly celebrated festival and Pamplona's sole but irresistible attraction. Immortalized by Hemingway in *The Sun Also Rises,* the Fiesta is a 24-hour orgy of singing, dancing, and parades, the highlight of which is the *encierro,* Europe's most unusual party game. Each morning at 8am young men in white with red sashes and scarves and foolhardy male tourists (women seldom run) dart in front of the bulls along the streets leading to the bullring. The idea is to run alongside a bull without its noticing you for a couple meters. Once the bulls are safely past, a crowd forms inside the arena where more terrified animals, with sawed-off horns, are let loose on this drunken, human mass. After the carnage, the party returns to the streets, although the bulls are fought that evening in the *corrida.* People are gored and stampeded, but the past 60 years have seen only 12 bull-related fatalities (and several more party-related ones). San Fermín must be watching benevolently over the city where he was martyred by being dragged by bulls.

You will not sleep in a bed in Pamplona during the Fiesta unless you are extraordinarily lucky. Write to or check with **Turismo,** C. Duque de Ahumada, 3 (tel. (948) 22 07 41) for *casas particulares,* which start at 1000-1200ptas per person. (Tourist office open April-Sept. Mon.-Fri. 9am-9pm, Sat. 9am-2pm; Oct.-March Mon.-Fri. 9am-2pm and 4-7pm, Sat. 9am-2pm.) Otherwise, brave the long, long line, stash your pack at the bus station, C. Conde Oliveto, 2, past Pl. del Principe de Viana (75-100ptas), and prepare to sack out in a park. Avoid filthy and unsafe **Plaza del Castillo;** head instead for the green grass on the other side of the bullring. You might also try commuting (4 buses per day) from **Camping Ezcaba** (tel. (948) 33 03 15), 7km away. (275ptas per person, 195ptas per tent.) For a swim and shower in Pamplona, take the 20-minute walk to the **municipal swimming pool,** in the bend of the river below the old city. (Open June-Sept. daily 10:30am-9pm. Admission 80ptas, 235ptas during Fiesta.)

During the Fiesta, Calle Navarrería is a particularly heavy-duty party spot, though nothing competes with the complete blowout in Plaza del Castillo, as the blighted trees and stains on the pavement testify. For food, C. San Nicolás and C. San Gregorio are the best places to look. If your bus breaks down in Pamplona—the only reason to stay here the other 51 weeks of the year—look for cheap lodging in one of the places along C. San Nicolás and C. San Gregorio. The best of the stretch is **Fonda La Montañesa,** C. San Gregorio, 2 (tel. 22 43 80), with clean and well-kept rooms (800ptas per person). You'll find slightly more expensive but much more elegant rooms at **Casa Huéspedes Santa Cecilia,** C. Navarrería, 17 (tel. 22 22 30; 1000ptas per person).

Bus #9 connects the train station at Rochapea (tel. (948) 12 69 81) with the end of Paseo de Sarasate. The large bus station offers excellent connections to Madrid, Zaragoza, San Sebastián, Jaca, and many villages in the Pyrenees.

Galicia

Frequently veiled by a misty drizzle, Galicia is a Celtic land where bleating *gaitas* (bagpipes) are heard in rolling green hills. Here narrow, pitted roads weave through dense woods, along valleys patched with stone-walled farms, and past slate-roofed fishing villages set beside long, white beaches. Galicians continue to speak their native tongue, *Gallego,* a language closer to Portuguese than to Castilian. Buses here are more expensive but more expedient than trains, and are the only way to reach many coastal and hillside towns.

Santiago de Compostela

With the discovery of the remains of St. James (Santiago) more than 1100 years ago, this city became a major destination for pilgrimages. In 1130 an enterprising monk wrote the *Codex Calixtinus,* a sort of *Let's Go: Santiago,* which detailed the least dangerous routes, the best accommodations, and the safest drinking water along the way.

Orientation and Practical Information

Santiago de Compostela is situated in far northwestern Spain, 100km north of the Portuguese border; the Portuguese coastal rail line continues to Santiago and north to La Coruña. Tracks from León and Zamora (where lines from Salamanca and Medina del Campo converge) join at Orense, where you may have to change trains.

Tourist Office: Turismo, Rúa del Villar, 43 (tel. 58 40 81), in the old town. Generally helpful. Pick up a map here—you'll need it. Open Mon.-Fri. 9am-2pm and 4:30-7pm, Sat. 9am-2pm.

Budget Travel: Viajes TIVE, Rúa del Villar, 35, 2nd floor (tel. 58 15 72). BIGE tickets and competent advice. Open Mon.-Fri. 9am-2pm.

Post Office: Travesía de Fonseca. Open Mon.-Fri. 9am-2pm, Sat. 9am-noon; stamps also available Mon.-Fri. 5-6pm.

Telephones: C. Alfredo Brañas, 2, in the new town. Open Mon.-Sat. 9am-1pm and 5-9pm. **Telephone code:** 981.

Trains: C. del General Franco (tel. 59 60 50). To reach the old town, climb the stairs, bear a bit to the right, and follow C. del General Franco to Pl. de Galicia.

Buses: Estación Central de Autobuses, C. San Cayetano (tel. 58 77 00). Reached from Pl. de Galicia by bus #10 (45ptas). Good connections to Rías Altas and Bajas.

Emergencies: Police (tel. 091); headquarters at Avda. Rodrigo de Padrón (tel. 58 11 10). **Ambulance** (tel. 58 84 90).

Medical Assistance: Hospital General de Galicia, C. Galeras (tel. 58 78 11).

Laundry: Lava-Express, at C. Alfredo Brañas and C. República Salvador. Up to 6kg for 350ptas. Open Mon.-Fri. 9:30am-1:30pm and 4-8pm.

Accommodations, Camping, and Food

Bypass the hawkers at the train station unless you're prepared to investigate and haggle, and start your room search in the old town. Rúa del Villar and Calle Raiña are excellent streets for budget-lodging hunts. **Pensión Lens,** Rúa del Villar, 73 (tel. 58 67 77), run by two sisters, is an excellent value, with low ceilings and oddly placed bathrooms. (800ptas per person.) **Hospedaje Ramos,** C. Raiña, 18 (tel. 58 18 59), also has comfortable rooms. (Singles 750ptas, doubles 1500ptas. Showers included.) **Camping Las Cancelas** (tel. 55 02 66) is not far from the bus station, on Avda. Camino Frances, the main road to Lugo. (Open June-Sept.) Nicer, though farther out, is **Camping Santiago** (tel. 88 80 02), in Piedra Rubia on the road to Finisterre.

Budget eateries fill the old town, particularly along Calle Franco, Calle Raiña, and Calle Algalia Arriba. Be sure to try these Galician delights: *caldo gallego* (a chunky vegetable broth), *pulpo a la gallega* (yummy octopus in orange sauce), and steamed mussels. Also, soak up the cloudy, white *Ribeiro* wine. Most *menus* cost around 500ptas. Galicians sup earlier than most Spaniards, so don't wait until 11pm to find a place for dinner. **Asesiño,** Pl. de la Universidad, 16, is a small place run by three friendly sisters. They bicker constantly, but their cooking is well-known and wonderful—lots of students here. (Open for lunch only, noon-2pm.) **Mesón Caballo Blanco,** C. Pescadería Vieja, 5, is very local and very simple. (*Menu* 500ptas. Open daily 2-4pm and 8-9:30pm.) The **open market** is held between Pl. de San Félix and the Convent of San Agustín. (Mon.-Sat. 8am-2pm.)

Sights and Entertainment

The **catedral** is majestic, a harmonious melding of styles and eras beneath two soaring towers. Just inside the main entrance is the **Pórtico de la Gloria,** one of the outstanding ensembles of Romanesque sculpture in Europe. Executed by Maestro Mateo between 1168 and 1188, it includes a likeness of the sculptor that visitors knock heads with in the hope that some of his genius will rub off. The **Museo do Pobo Galego** (Museum of the Galician People), housed in the Monasterio de Santo Domingo, contains replicas of the *castros* (ancient Celtic ruins) from the nearby countryside, and gives an idea of how Galicians live outside Santiago. (Open Mon.-Sat. 10am-1pm and 4-7pm, Sun. 10am-1pm. Admission 50ptas.)

You might invest 1000ptas in the guided Spanish tour of the city run by the tourist office; it includes admission to several museums and an artist's interpretation of the cathedral's baroque and Romanesque facades. (Tours Mon.-Sat. at 4pm. English tours arranged on request. 4000ptas, up to 5 persons.)

Nearly half of Santiago's population is made up of rowdy students itching to have a good time. Bars and pubs can be found throughout the old town and along Calle Santiago de Chile. **Teteria,** on C. Algalia Arriba, is a beatnik teashop that plays rock music. **Modus Vivendi,** in Plazuela de Feixoo, is an eclectic dungeon that alternates between British invaders and Galician bagpipes. Santiago's **Fiesta** runs July 15-31, climaxing on July 25, St. James's Day. For two weeks, street musicians and haunting figures on stilts roam the streets. Rooms become harder to find and even if you get one, there's no sleeping.

Near Santiago de Compostela

Though Santiago may be the monarch of Galician cities, no landlocked settlement can compare with this region's rugged coastline. The *rías* (inlets), settled by Celts and Vikings from the north, are Spain's answer to the Norwegian fjords. The **Rías Altas** drive their watery fingers into the land from the province of Lugo down to **Cabo Finisterre.** Shrouded in mist and prey to storms, even in summer, the upper *rías* do not attract as many tourists as do other Spanish coastal regions. **La Coruña** is the largest port and the administrative center of the Rías Altas. Well-connected by rail and bus lines to the rest of Galicia, it makes an ideal base for explorations north past the **Cabo Ortegal** and south to **Cabo Finisterre.** The **tourist office** by the harbor at Darseua de la Marina (tel. 22 18 12) issues brochures on both the region and the city itself. Also inquire here about lodgings and bus and train schedules. (Open July-Sept. Mon.-Fri. 10am-1:30pm and 4:30-6pm, Sat. 10:30am-7pm; Oct.-June Mon.-Fri. 10am-1:30pm and 4:30-6pm.)

The **Cabo Finisterre,** once thought to be the end of the world, is the point where the Rías Altas become the **Rías Bajas.** Unlike the coastland farther north, Finisterre is usually dry in the summer, although nights can be chilly. **Camping Ruta Finisterre** has beach-side camping facilities. (265ptas per person, 300ptas per tent.) Following the coast south to **Muros** you come across some of the clearest waters and whitest beaches in Spain. Although the area is fairly popular with Spanish vacationers, there's plenty of sand to go around.

The resident population, tourists, and pollution all increase as you go south, toward the major cities of Pontevedra and Vigo. Nevertheless, the water is warmer in the lower *rías* and the beaches are more accessible than their northern counterparts. **Pontevedra,** an old town built of granite, makes a good base for exploring the Rías Bajas, while **Vigo,** a fast-growing port, is the principal gateway into northern Portugal.

SWEDEN

US$1 = 6.37 kronor (kr)	**1kr = US$0.16**
CDN$1 = 4.83kr	**1kr = CDN$0.21**
UK£1 = 10.39kr	**1kr = UK£0.10**
AUS$1 = 4.53kr	**1kr = AUS$0.22**

Some call Sweden the world's success story, a modern miracle. A policy of strict neutrality has spared Sweden the ravages of two wars, allowing it to bloom into affluence. For the traveler, the high national income unfortunately translates into some of the most expensive supermarket shelves and services in Europe—but there is no price on the magnificent and carefully preserved beauty of the land, richly forested and sparkling with thousands of lakes.

Sweden's sights are off the beaten path, and include a rich and fascinating folk culture as well. In the hilly central province of Dalarna, you'll find Swedish folk music and art, as well as warm hospitality. Hundreds of Swedes make the pilgrimage north to Lapland to soak up the midnight sun, and swim in the clear (and very cold) lakes. But you don't need to go that far to find unspoiled wilderness. Gotland, the island center of the Viking world, offers ruins, thousands of wildflowers, and fine beaches. Uppsala, seat of Sweden's oldest university, is rich in history and tradition, while Göteborg is an exciting port city. And at the center of all this lies elegant Stockholm and its pristine archipelago.

The largest Scandinavian country, Sweden once challenged Russia for supremacy in the Baltic. No longer a military power, Sweden today is noteworthy for its collective identity as a model liberal society, one recently shocked by the assassination of prime minister Olof Palme in the spring of 1986.

Transportation and Practical Information

A reliable network of trains crisscrosses southern Sweden and runs all the way to Narvik in Norway. Trains in Scandinavia are expensive; you should consider buying the 21-day **Nordturist Ticket,** available at any train station or national tourist office in Denmark, Sweden, Norway, or Finland. It costs 1320kr and is good for all state-run trains and ferries, including the ferry between Puttgarten, Germany and Rødby, Denmark. Eurail and InterRail (1380kr) are both valid.

Ask at any train station for a free copy of the schedule for inter-city trains *(snabbtåg)*. The letter "R" enclosed in a box indicates trains that require a 10kr seat reservation, even for railpass holders. Otherwise, reservations are unnecessary, except on popular lines (especially to and from Stockholm) during busy hours (such as Fri. and Sun. afternoons and evenings). Those under 26 can buy a *rabattkort* (85kr) good for 45% off all train fares, except journeys between Friday and Saturday mornings or Sunday and Monday mornings. Those without passes should also avoid these trips, as regular fares are about 20% higher on Fridays and Sundays. Other discounts are available to families and disabled and retired persons. **SAS Airlines** offers a special youth standby fare for those under 26—150kr for all domestic flights. Planes are usually full; try the earliest and latest flights of the day. Hitching in Sweden is slow; try going to the local ASG (freight) terminal in major cities for long distance lifts.

Local tourist offices *(turistbyrå)* are found in almost every town accessible by public transport. They help arrange accommodations, and many book rooms in private homes for a small fee. Only the largest *turistbyrå* can provide information on the whole country—consult the *resebyrå* (travel agencies), found virtually everywhere.

Many Swedes in large cities have an impressive command of English. In rural areas, dialects are such that even Swedes have difficulty understanding each other, and little English is spoken.

Sweden is a nation of festivals. At Midsummer (around June 21), there is dancing around the maypole, drinking, and general euphoria. Dalarna is an especially good place to celebrate. Lucia Day (Dec. 13) marks the start of an equally festive period; the whole country closes down for the Christmas and New Year's period.

Most banks in Sweden remain open until 5pm Monday through Friday; some branches close Friday at 3pm. As is true of most of Scandinavia, many post offices double as banks, and are open Monday through Friday from 9am to 5pm or later, Saturday from 9am to 1pm. Try to exchange checks in large denominations, as there is usually a 10kr commission per check. International telephone calls can be made from post and telephone offices, and from any pay phone. Rates are somewhat cheaper than in Finland or Norway. Anywhere in the country, dial 900 00 for emergency help, 901 20 for information.

Accommodations, Camping, and Food

The **Svenska Turistföreningen (STF)** runs Sweden's excellent youth hostels (*vandrarhem*). They often fill up quickly, though, especially during peak season (mid-June to mid-Aug.), so call at least a day in advance. Bring your own sheets or rent them. Hostels charge IYHF members 35 to 50kr per night, while nonmembers may purchase an International Guest Card. There is no age limit for guests. Of Sweden's 280 hotels, more than 100 are open year-round, but most close for a week or two around Christmas and on New Year's Day. The STF also manages mountain hut accommodations in the northern wilds, and can offer hiking and camping advice. Rooms in private homes (60-100kr per person) can be booked through local tourist offices; many campgrounds (20-50kr per site) also offer accommodations in *stugor* (simple cottages, often with kitchen facilities) for around 50 to 90kr per person. If you don't have an International Camping Card you'll need a Swedish one. (20kr.) A Finnish card is usually valid, and vice-versa. Thanks to *allmänsrätten,* you may camp on unfenced land anywhere in Sweden, though it's customary to stay at least 100m from private homes and to ask the owner for permission.

Clogs and caviar come cheap in Sweden, but it's hard to fill up on either. To keep your budget in decent shape, rely on supermarkets, open-air markets, and indoor markets—the best quality is found in the latter two, the lowest prices in the first. Swedes eat light open-faced sandwiches on the ruffly crackers called *knäckebröd,* on paper-thin *flatbröd,* or on dark, dense, delicious *fullkornsbröd.* Pile on some mild Swedish cheese—*riddarost, greve,* or *västerbotten*—or one of the varieties of seasoned cream cheese *(kryddost).* For breakfast, try some *filmjölk,* a kind of rich yogurt, on your cereal (great with freshly picked berries). You can pick your own berries; cloudberries and gooseberries grow everywhere.

The cost of restaurant meals can be held down somewhat if you order the specialty of the day *(dagens rätt),* usually offered weekdays between 11am and 3pm (30-50kr). Swedish specialties worth trying are *pannkakor med lingonsylt* (pancakes with lingonberry jam), *pytt i panna* (a potato, onion, and meat hash), and *renskav* (delicious reindeer stew).

Blodpudding (blood and fat sausage) is Sweden's cheapest food, but many foreigners detest it. Sweden's long coastline and clean lakes make for an abundance of excellent seafood, often available along harbors and in marketplaces. Try huge fresh *räkor,* peeling shrimp (120kr per kg), and shiny smoked kippers (75kr per kg). Seafood salads in a mayonnaise base make great sandwich toppings; shrimp salad usually runs about 100kr per kilogram.

Beer comes in three grades and three prices: *lättöl* has very little alcohol; *folköl* is the government's middle-strength beer, and *starköl* is strong and expensive. *Akvavit* (the "water of life") is Sweden's hard liquor—to be accompanied by *surströmming* (aged fish). All forms of alcohol are extremely expensive; heavy government taxes bring beer prices to at least 12kr per bottle, 15 to 35kr for a large draft beer in a pub.

Gothenburg (Göteborg)

Carl Milles's gigantic bronze Poseidon bares his muscles in the middle of Götaplatsen, the city's art center, and the sea god's domain extends far beyond. Enormous crates preside over the harbor as travelers arrive from the rest of Scandinavia, Britain, and Germany. Seafarers auction their catch weekday mornings at 7am at the Fiskhamnen. There's even a "fish church" (Feskekörka), on the fish square (Fisketorget).

Orientation and Practical Information

Gothenburg is one of the country's two principal ports of entry, and the most convenient access point for those traveling to and from Norway. Rail lines extend north and south, as well as east to Stockholm.

Tourist Offices: Main tourist office, Bassargatan 10 (tel. (031) 10 07 40). Follow the canal from the ferry terminal. From the train and bus stations, walk a few blocks down Larmgatan. Open late June to mid-Aug. daily 10am-8pm; early to mid-June daily 10am-6pm; mid-Aug. to May Mon.-Fri. 10am-6pm, Sat. 10am-2pm. **Branch** at Östra Nordstan mall (tel. (031) 15 07 05), across the street from the train station. Open Mon.-Fri. 9:30am-6pm, Sat. 9am-3pm. Both offices give out maps and book rooms.

Ferries: To Harwich, England and Newcastle, England with *DFDS Seaways* (tel (031) 17 20 50). June-Aug. 670kr to Newcastle, 15% reduction for those under 26. To Frederikshavn, Denmark; Kiel, West Germany; and Oslo, Norway (June-Aug. only) with *Stena Line* (tel. (031) 452 43 66). June-Aug. 110kr to Frederikshavn (free with railpass). Fares drop significantly in the off-season. Take tram #3 from the main train station to the ferry terminal.

Public Transportation: Gothenburg's excellent bus and tram system can be used most easily with a 24-hour pass (21kr). The **Göteborg Card** is a good value, combining free public transportation, sightseeing trips, and discounts (24-hr. 70kr; 48-hr. 105kr; 72-hr. 135kr).

Bike Rental: At the tourist office. 50kr per day, including a first-day bag lunch; 40kr without lunch.

Telephone code: 031.

Accommodations, Camping, and Food

Both tourist offices book rooms in **private homes** for a 20kr fee. (Singles 100kr, doubles and larger 75kr per person.) Otherwise, you must rely on the four IYHF *vandrarhem* for cheap accommodations; all are quite nice. The gigantic, modern **Ostkupan (IYHF)** is at Mejerigatan 2 (tel. (031) 40 10 50 or 44 61 63), near the Liseberg amusement park. Take bus #64 direct from Södrehamngatan along the canal; or take tram #5 from Kungsportsplatsen to St. Sigfridsplan, then bus #62 or 64 to Gräddgatan. You'll find a sauna, kitchen, and laundry facilities. (50kr. Open early June-late Aug. 7:30am-10:30pm.) The hostel at **Partille (IYHF)** (tel. 44 61 63) is less fancy, but also less likely to be full; take bus #501 or 503 from the Heden bus station, or walk down Kungs Aveny from the main tourist office (about 5 min.). **Torrekulla Turiststation (IYHF)** (tel. (031) 95 14 95) is in a nature reserve 30 minutes from town. Take one of the Kållered buses (#710-715) from Heden bus station or bus #730, 731, or 732 from the train station (12kr), and follow the hostel signs 20 minutes through the hills. (40-50kr. Unexceptional breakfast 28kr. Open Jan. to mid-Dec.) **Kungälus Vandrarhem (IYHF)** (tel. (030) 31 89 00) is also distant. Take bus #301-4 to Eriksdal and walk towards the fortress. The most convenient campsite, at **Kärralund** (tel. 25 27 61), fills up fast. Take tram #5 to Welandergatan. (55kr per tent.) Otherwise try the campground at **Askim** (tel. 28 62 61), 10km out of town; take tram #1 or 2 to Linneplatsen, then bus #82 for Särö. Both campsites are near sandy beaches.

Leonis, Kungsport 32, has a good salad bar (32kr). (Open Mon.-Sat. 11am-7pm, Sun. noon-4pm.) The fancy **Golden Days** restaurant at Södrahamngatan 31 puts off the ritz Monday after 6pm with a *gravad lax* (pickled salmon) and potatoes special at 16kr. (Daily lunch specials 30-40kr.) The cafeteria at **Chalmers Technical College** serves a reasonable lunch year-round on weekdays (you needn't be a student). Take tram #6 or 7 from Brunnsparken. For lighter, more elegant fare, try the coffee, waffles, and warm sandwiches at **Drottning Kristinas Jaktslott,** Otterhällegatan 16, a former "hunting castle" of the queen. (Open June-Aug. Mon.-Fri. 11am-4pm; Sept.-May daily 11am-4pm.) The vegetarian restaurant **Annorlunda,** Lillakorsgaten 2, has a very good *dagens rätt* (30kr). (Open Mon.-Fri. 11am-5pm, Sat. 11am-4pm.) For groceries head to the basement of **Domus,** Kongsportavenyn 28, five minutes from the tourist office.

Sights and Entertainment

The best way to appreciate Gothenburg's intimate relationship with the sea is to take a tour on one of the *Paddan* sightseeing boats: You'll glide past parks and old houses, go under bridges so low that you have to duck, and venture out into the harbor, with its shipyards and enormous floating docks. Tours leave from the canal across from the main tourist office (in summer 10am-5pm, 55 min., 30kr). To visit **Elfsborg,** a seventeenth-century island fortress, board the *M/S Snäckeskär* at Stenpiren (mid-May to mid-Aug. 7 per day, 35kr).

Though Gothenburg is a bustling city of almost half a million, its parks are pretty and restful. **Slottsskogen** has lakes, birds, and a children's zoo; take tram #1 or 2. Just beyond are the **Botanical Gardens,** with collections from around the world. The **Röhsska Museum of Arts and Crafts,** Vasagatan 37-39, exhibits traditional as well as contemporary crafts. Take tram #5 to Valand. (Open May-Aug. Mon.-Fri. noon-4pm, Sun. 11am-5pm; Sept.-April Tues. and Thurs.-Sat. noon-4pm, Sun. 11am-5pm, Wed. noon-4pm and 6-9pm.)

Become a child again at **Liseberg,** the largest amusement park in Scandinavia. The roller coaster is nearly a mile long. (Admission late June to mid-Aug. 20kr; mid-Aug. to late June 15kr. Save money with ticket booklets.)

Near Gothenburg

The countryside around Gothenburg is marvelous, especially along the coast and Kungälv archipelago. **Kungälv,** site of a famous fifteenth-century fortress, is accessible by bike or bus from Nils Ericsonsplatsen (the main bus station), near the train station. **Marstrand,** an island slightly to the north of Kungälv, offers tranquil beaches. Excursion boats leave from Skeppsbron Monday through Saturday, and from Stenpiren on Sunday. (Fare Tues.-Sun. 30kr one way, 58kr round-trip, Mon. 25kr one way, 50kr round-trip.) For the best beaches, though, head to **Askimsbadet,,** near the campsite (see above), or to **Vallda Sandö,** 34km to the south, accessible by bus #15 from Nils Ericsonsplatsen.

Stockholm

Cobblestone streets to bold contemporary design; midnight cabarets to opera; Rembrandt to toy museums. Arriving in Stockholm is like entering a huge candy store: everything looks so good that you can't decide what you want. The center of the city is never far from the peaceful islands of the outlying 24,000-string *skärgård* (archipelago), where the urban bustle fades to a quiet buzz.

Orientation and Practical Information

Stockholm is situated on Sweden's east coast, about eight rail hours due east from Oslo, a similar distance northeast from Gothenburg. The city is connected to Turku, Helsinki, and Mariehamn (Åland) in Finland by daily ferries; steamers also shuttle back and forth to Gdańsk, Poland.

Tourist Offices: Stockholm Tourist Office, in Sverige huset, across from Hamngatan 27, entrance on Kungsträdgården (tel. 789 20 00, Sat.-Sun. tel. 789 24 17). T-bana: Kungsträdgården. One of the best equipped in Europe. Accommodations booked for a 15kr fee. *What to See and Do In and Around Stockholm* (15kr) is particularly useful. Open mid-June to mid-Aug. Mon.-Fri. 8:30am-6pm, Sat.-Sun. 8am-5pm; mid-Aug. to mid-June Mon.-Fri. 9am-5pm, Sat.-Sun. 9am-2pm. **Hotellcentralen,** at the train station (tel. 24 08 80), distributes city maps and lists of accommodations, and books beds at hostels (10kr) and hotels (15kr). Very friendly. Open June-Aug. daily 8am-9pm; Sept.-May Mon.-Fri. 8:30am-4:45pm. **Svenska Turistföreningen (STF),** Vasagatan 48 (tel. 790 32 00). T-bana: T-Centralen. Your best source of information for hiking or camping; they run the country's hostels, maintain cabins along hiking trails in the north, and run guided expeditions. Open May-July Mon.-Fri. 9am-6pm; Aug. Mon.-Fri. 9am-5:30pm; Sept.-Apr. Mon.-Fri. 9am-5pm. **International Youth Center,** Valhallavägen 142 (tel. 63 43 89). T-bana: Karlaplan. An amazing range of freebies: cook, mend your clothes, use the darkroom, take a shower, rent bikes (12kr per hr., 30kr per day), and get information on where to stay. Open Mon.-Sat. 1-9pm. A second branch with fewer magical powers has opened on Skeppsholmen, right behind the af Chapman (tel. 21 45 48). Open Mon.-Fri. 9am-5pm.

Budget Travel: SFS-Resebyrå, Kungsgatan 4 (tel. 34 01 80). BIGE, and cheap charter flights south. Open Mon. and Thurs. 10am-6pm; Tues., Wed., and Fri. 10am-5pm. **Transalpino,** Birger Jarlsgatan 13. T-bana: Östermalmstorg. Open Mon.-Fri. 10am-5:30pm.

American Express: Resebyra, Birger Jarlsgatan 1 (tel. 22 88 60). T-bana: Östermalmstorg. Mail held and checks sold and replaced, but no currency exchange and no wired money accepted. Open Mon.-Fri. 9am-5pm, Sat. 10am-1pm. Check-replacement at **Avis,** Sveavägen 61 (tel. 34 99 10). Open Mon.-Fri. 7:30am-6pm, Sat.-Sun. 9am-3pm.

Currency Exchange: When banks (generally open Mon.-Fri. 9:30am-3pm) are closed, go to Centralstation. Open daily 8am-9pm.

Post Office: Vasagatan 28-34, near Centralstation. Open Mon.-Fri. 8am-8pm, Sat. 9am-1pm. Also a branch at Centralstation. Open Mon.-Fri. 7am-9pm, Sat. 9am-1pm.

Telephones: Visit **Telecenter,** Skeppsbron 2 (tel. 902 00). Open daily 8am-midnight. Also a telephone office at Centralstation (tel. 10 64 39). Open Mon.-Fri. 8am-8pm, Sat. 9am-1pm. **Information:** 901 40. **Telephone code:** 08.

Flights: Gray Flygbussar buses travel between Stockholm's **Arlanda Airport** and Centralstation (28kr).

Trains: Sprawling **Centralstation** (T-bana: T-Centralen) is Stockholm's principal gateway. Walk a few blocks northeast to reach the tourist office. Station lockers not safe. 4 trains per day to Copenhagen (8-9 hrs., 312kr), 3 per day to Oslo (5-9 hrs., 337kr).

Ferries: Silja Line, Kungsgatan 2 (tel. 22 21 40), and **Viking Line,** Stureplan 8 (tel. 23 58 55), both sail to Helsinki daily. 240kr, Silja line free for Eurailpass.

Public Transportation: It's very pleasant to walk around Stockholm's downtown area, but for longer trips you may want to use Storstockholms Lokaltrafik's excellent network of buses and subways (*tunnelbana*). Look for the letter "T" indicating entrances to stations. A ride within a single zone costs 7kr, with intrazone transfers allowed for one hour. The central zone encompasses all of downtown. Purchase 10-trip tickets for 40kr, or you can buy an SL Tourist card: a 24-hour pass for the central zone costs 21kr; one that covers all zones (including buses and trains) is 38kr. Both options grant one free trip on the ferry to Djurgården from Slussen or Nybroplan. If you're planning on some heavy sightseeing, consider the tourist office's **Stockholmskortet,** which covers all mass transit, many bus and boat excursions, and offers free admission to many museums and attractions: 1 day 66kr, 2 days 112kr, 3 days 168kr, 4 days 224kr. Even if you stay for just 2 weeks, consider getting SL's monthly card (190kr); for an extra 100kr you also get free boat travel in the archipelago. All of these passes are available at the tourist office, Hotellcentralen, and Pressbyrå kiosks. **SL Information:** (tel. 23 60 00).

Bike Rental: Paddel och Pedal: Slipgatan 10 (tel. 68 33 66). T-bana: Hornstull. Rents 3- and 5- and 10-speed bicycles for 40kr per 24 hrs., 150kr per week, with saddlebags.

Boat and Canoe Rental: Skepp o Hoj, Djurgårdsbron (tel. 60 57 57). Boats and canoes 27kr for first hr., 18kr each following hr., 90kr per day. Boat rentals begin as early as April (depending on weather) and end in Sept. Daily 9am-10pm.

Emergencies: Police or **Ambulance** (tel. 900 00). Police headquarters at Agnesgatan 33-37 (tel. 769 30 00).

Pharmacy: Apotek C. W. Sheele, Klarabergsgatan 64 (tel. 21 89 34). Open 24 hours.

Women's Center: Kvinnohuset, Snickarbacken 10 (tel. 10 08 00). A meeting place for feminists, with a rape crisis center.

Lesbian Center: (tel. 10 76 57).

Gay Center: Riksförbundet För Sexuellt Likaberättigande (RFSL), Hornsgatan 18-20 (tel. 84 55 76; help line 84 56 66).

Embassies: U.S., Strandvägen 101 (tel. 783 53 00). **Canadian,** Tegelbacken 4 (tel. 23 79 20). **U.K.,** Skarpögatan 6-8 (tel. 67 01 40). **Australian,** Sergelstorg 12 (tel. 24 46 60). Travelers from **New Zealand** should contact the British Embassy. **GDR,** Bragevägen 2 (tel. 23 50 30). **Poland,** Karlavägen 35 (tel. 11 41 32; visas, tel. 21 27 70).

Cultural Center: Alternativ Stad, Stockholmshuset, Götgatan 26 (tel. 43 70 51). T-bana: Slussen. A bookstore/cafe, and center for progressive movements. Information on work camps, cooperative foodstores, and similar enterprises. Bookstore open Mon.-Fri. 9am-5pm; inquire for times of meetings, special events.

Bookstore: Bok Akademien, Mäster Samuelsgatan 32, has a good selection of English books.

Laundry: Tvättomaten at Västmannagatan 61 (tel. 34 64 80). Wash and dry, including soap, 38kr. You can also wash your clothes at the International Youth Center, 10kr.

Accommodations and Camping

Stockholm is popular, so try to arrive as early in the day as possible. If you get in late, ask at the Hotellcentralen or the tourist office. As in all of Scandinavia, hotel rooms are expensive.

Hostels

Hostels in Stockholm are plentiful and varied—everything from converted dance academies to old ships. The Swedish word for hostel is *vandrarhem.*

af Chapman (IYHF), is a fully-rigged nineteenth-century sailing ship (tel. 20 57 05) majestically moored off the island of Skeppsholmen, across from Gamla Stan, a 5-min. walk from downtown. Very popular—arrive early in the morning, and always call ahead to make sure there's space. 4- to 8-bed cabins. No sleeping bags. Members 50kr, nonmembers 70kr. Linen 20kr. Reception closed noon-3pm. Curfew 1am; lockout 9am-4pm. Open March to mid-Dec.

Hantverkshuset (IYHF), Skeppsholmen (tel. 20 25 06), just behind af Chapman. Not as much fun, but bigger rooms and lockers. Call ahead. Members 50kr, nonmembers 70kr. Linen 20kr. No curfew, but reception closed noon-3pm. Open year-round.

Zinken Hostel (IYHF), Pipmakargränd 2A (tel. 58 50 11 or 68 57 86). From T-bana: Hornstull, follow Horngatan east, turn right at the Teleskolan Building (#103), go down 2 sets of stairs in back, then follow path. Bright and cheery; many families. Laundry (20kr) and kitchens. Doubles, triples, and quads. Members 50kr, nonmembers 70kr. Linen 22kr. Reception open 7am-11pm. Open year-round.

International Youth Center, Valhallavägen 142 (tel. 63 43 89). T-bana: Karlaplan. Big, informal dorms; friendly and casual. 35kr plus 10kr registration fee first night, 35kr per night thereafter. Linen 15kr. Laundry 10kr. Open June-Aug. Hostel: Mon.-Sat. 1pm-1am, Sun. 6pm-1am; Information Center: Mon.-Sat. 1-9pm.

Columbus Hostel, Tjärhovsgatan 11 (tel. 44 17 17). T-bana: Tjärhovsgatan. Nice management and good clean facilities in an old building. Access to kitchen 6-10am and 4-10pm. 65kr in multi-bedded rooms. No curfew or lock-out. Check-in 4pm. Open year-round.

Hotell Frescati, Professorslingan 13-15 (tel. 15 79 96). T-bana: Universitetet. All double rooms, some with private bath. Singles 132kr, doubles 132kr. Open June-Aug. Reception open 24 hrs.

Dans Akademien, Döbelnsgatan 56 (tel. 31 31 18). T-bana: Rådmansgatan. A dancing school in winter—the mirrors make the 3 mixed rooms look larger than they are. Crowded and casual. Kitchen. One of the last places to fill up. 55kr. Linen 20kr. Open July to mid-Aug. 7am-1pm and 4pm-midnight.

Kista Inter-Railpoint, Jyllandsgatan 16 (tel. 752 65 46). T-bana: Kista. Associated with YMCA—small and informal. Sports facilities and kitchens. 50kr. Linen 15kr. Open mid-July to mid-Aug. 7:30-10am and 6pm-midnight.

Sommar hyr (Summer rent), Körsbärsvägen in the Forum, 4c (tel. 16 61 09). T-bana: Tekniska Högskolan. For those planning a longer stay in Stockholm: weekly rates. Open mid-May to mid-Sept. Mon.-Fri. 1-4pm.

Hotels

Hotell Jerum, Studentbacken 21 (tel. 63 53 80). T-bana: Gärdet, or bus #62. Big, clean, and simple. Singles with bath 230kr, doubles with bath 275kr, triples with bath 335kr. Breakfast included. Open June-Aug. Reception open 24 hrs.

Gustavsvikshemmet, Västmannagatan 15 (tel. 21 44 50). T-bana: Odenplan. Brightly furnished though small rooms, friendly folks. Singles 200kr, doubles 280kr. Kitchen facilities.

Camping

Though it's technically legal to sack out in one of Stockholm's many parks, those near the center are not especially safe.

Bredäng Camping, 10km southwest from the city center (tel. 97 70 71), near the coast. Take T-bana #13 or 15 to Bredäng and walk 5-10 min. Crowded and dirty. 30kr per person; no charge per tent. Open May-Sept. 6am-11pm; Oct.-April 7am-10pm.

Ängby Camping, on Lake Mälaren (tel. 37 04 20), also about 10km out. Take T-bana #17 or 18 to Ängbyplan, then walk 10 min. Good facilities and lake swimming. 30kr per person; no charge per tent. Open June-Aug. 6am-11pm.

Food

Stockholm's best deals are at lunch, when most restaurants offer a *dagens rätt* for 25 to 30kr. Put together an inspired picnic in the basement of **Åhléns** on Klarabergsgatan near Sergels Torg (open Mon.-Sat. 9:30am-8pm, Sun. noon-8pm), or at **Östermalms Saluhall** (an indoor market). (Open Mon. 10am-6pm, Tues.-Fri. 9am-6pm, Sat. 9am-3pm.) Outdoor markets feature fresh fruit at both **Östermalmstorg** and **Hötorget;** also at Hötorget is the underground **Hötorgshallen,** with fresh produce. There's a supermarket at T-bana: Östermalmstorg (open Mon.-Fri. 8am-8pm, Sat. 9am-6pm, Sun. noon-4pm). If you're after the elusive Swedish cuisine, look for restaurants advertising *husmans kost.*

Örtagården, Nybrogatan 31, right on Östermalmstorget. Delicious vegetarian food. The 45kr buffet is one of the best bargains around; Sat.-Sun. and Mon.-Fri. after 5pm, it costs 60kr. Open Mon.-Fri. 10:30am-11:30pm, Sat. 11am-6pm, Sun. noon-6pm.

Lyktan, Teatergatan 6, behind the Grand Hotel (located at Södra Blasieholmshamnen 8). An entree, plus all-you-can-eat salad and bread 33-37kr; without entree, 27kr. Open Mon.-Fri. 11am-9pm.

La Brochette, Storgatan 27. An expensive French restaurant in the evenings, but a great value for lunch (except for drinks). Their *quiche Lorraine,* served with a great salad, is delicious. 36-46kr. Open Mon.-Fri. 11am-4pm and 5pm-midnight.

Magnus Ladulås, Österlånggatan 26, in Gamla Stan. Swedish cuisine. The *dagens varmrätt* for lunch is an especially good value at 36kr (11am-2:30pm). Coffee 5kr. Open Mon.-Fri. 11am-11pm, Sat. 5-11pm.

The Huset (Tea House), Kungsträdgården, around the corner from the Opera House, right behind the statue of Charles XII. This outdoor cafe under the shade of giant elm trees is Stockholm's friendliest outdoor meeting place. Good coffee and pastries for 12kr. Open in summer.

Sights

The **Gamla Stan** quarter is Stockholm's ancient heart, and it still beats. At the northwest corner sits the eighteenth-century **Royal Palace,** where the guard changes daily (Mon.-Sat. noon, Sun. 1pm). Inside the palace, the magnificent **apartments** and **Royal Armory** deserve a visit. Don't miss the royal carriages and coronation dresses in the Armory. (Apartments open May-Aug. Tues.-Sat. 10am-3pm, Sun. noon-3pm; Sept.-Dec. Tues.-Sun. noon-3pm; Jan.-April Tues.-Sat. noon-3pm. Admission 10kr, children 5kr. Royal Armory open May-Aug. Mon.-Fri. 10am-4pm, Sat.-Sun. 11am-4pm; Sept.-April Tues.-Fri. 10am-4pm, Sat.-Sun. 11am-4pm. Admission 10kr, children 5kr.) Right beside the palace soars Stockholm's 700-year-old **Storkyrkan** (Cathedral), with its famous fifteenth-century wooden sculpture of St. George and the Dragon. (Open 9am-4pm.) Down Storkyrkbrinken towards the water, the seventeenth-century **Riddarhuset** (House of Nobles) contains the relics of Sweden's former first estate. (Open Mon.-Fri. 11:30am-12:30pm. Admission 5kr, children 3kr.) Don't miss **Stortorget,** a friendly square with charming architecture, and **Mårten Trotzigs Gränd,** the narrowest alleyway in Stockholm, just off Västerlänggatan.

Symbol of Stockholm, **Stadshuset** (City Hall) was built only in 1911. Nineteen million mosaic tiles make the Golden Hall especially attractive. Nobel Prize winners attend a banquet in their honor here. (Guided tours Mon.-Sat. 10am, Sun. 10am and noon. Tower open May-Sept. 10am-3pm. Admission 5kr, children free.)

Visit **Skeppsholmen,** the island east of Gamla Stan, to see Stockholm's two finest art museums; both can be reached by T-bana to Kungsträdgården. The **National Museum,** just before the bridge to the island, has a fascinating collection of decorative arts and European paintings, including some Rembrandts and a Renoir. No backpacks allowed in the museum. (Open Wed.-Sun. 10am-4pm, Tues. 10am-9pm. Admission 20kr, students 10kr, ages under 16 free; free for all Tues. Concerts late June-Aug. Tues. 8pm; galleries close at 5pm on concert days.) The **Moderna Museet** in the center of Skeppsholmen, has an excellent collection of American and European modern art—everything from Picassos to a sculpture of a goat wearing a rubber tire. The outdoor cafe often sponsors rock concerts in the evenings. (Open Tues.-Fri. 11am-9pm, Sat.-Sun. 11am-5pm. Admission 15kr, students 7kr; free Thurs.)

Djurgården, east of Skeppsholmen, is Stockholm's pleasure island, reached by bus #44 or 47 from the center, by foot from attractive harborside Strandvägen, or by ferry from Nybroplan or Slussen (7kr; free with SL Tourist Card). Call 14 08 30 for information on archipelago ferries. You can spend the whole day walking amid the greenery or visiting the many museums (see *Stockholm This Week* for current exhibits and hours). The **Wasa,** a seventeenth-century warship dug up in 1961, is on exhibit in a super-humidified shell. The ship traveled only about 10 minutes on its first voyage; while attempting to salute the king, the sailors rolled too many cannons to one side, causing the vessel to capsize. (Open early June to mid-Aug. daily 9:30am-7pm; mid-Aug. to early June daily 10am-5pm. Admission 15kr, students 7kr, children 5kr.) **Gröna Lund** is Stockholm's Tivoli—but more expensive and a touch seedy. (Open early June to mid-Aug. Mon.-Sat. 1pm-midnight; mid-Aug. to mid-Sept. and mid-April to early June Tues.-Fri. 7pm-midnight, Sat. 1pm-midnight, Sun. 1-9pm. Admission 20kr, children 9kr.) **Kulturhuset,** Sergels Torg 3, is Stockholm's popular cultural center. Try your creative talents working with clay, wool, or leather in the studios, or enjoy a concert or poetry-reading—check their program. (Exhibit and studio areas open Mon. 11am-6pm, Tues. 11am-10pm, Wed.-Fri. 11am-6pm, Sat.-Sun. 11am-5pm. Everything in this modern pleasure palace is free.)

Entertainment

Wander past the pubs and jazz clubs of Gamla Stan, or simply listen to the street musicians on a sunny summer night. There are free concerts or theater in different city parks nearly every night—Kungsträdgården often features rock. On Djurgården, you'll find concerts and dancing throughout the summer at Skansen or Gröna Lund. For something different, set sail Tuesday and Thursday 7:30-11pm on the old *S.S. Blidsösund,* with live music and sometimes dinner. The price varies, but it is usually reasonable. Call 22 18 40 for information on cultural events in Stockholm.

Stampen, Stora Nygatan 5 (tel. 20 57 93), in Gamla Stan. Great traditional jazz in a cozy setting. Cover 50kr. Open daily 7pm-1am. Music starts around 9pm.

Mosebacke Etablissement, Mosebacke Torg 3 (tel. 41 90 20). T-bana: Slussen. A pub with a beautiful terrace overlooking the city from the bluffs of Söder. Often live music (from jazz to rhapsodies to opera), outdoor dancing, singers, and poets. Cover 30-50kr; free in summer. Open in summer daily at 11am; in winter Fri.-Sat. 8pm-1am, Sun. midnight-5pm.

Tre Backar, Tegnérgatan 14 (tel. 31 31 38). T-bana: Rådmansgatan. The first floor is a quiet library where you can read Swedish books; downstairs there's lively rock music, drinks, and *croque monsieur* sandwiches. Open daily 7pm-midnight.

Klubb Timmy, Timmermansgatan 24 (tel. 84 80 30), not to be confused with Tim's Restaurant. A cozy gay club sponsored by RFSL. Open Mon. 8-11pm, Tues.-Thurs. 8-11:30pm, Fri.-Sat. 9pm-1:30am.

Near Stockholm

With 24,000 islands in Stockholm's **skärgården** (archipelago), you'll have to pick and choose. A trip can take an afternoon or a week—boat connections are good, and hostels or camping provide accommodations. The tourist office will sell you a **Båtluffarekort** entitling you to 16 days travel, beginning on a Saturday, on boats run by Waxholmsbolaget (125kr, available June-Aug. only).

Beautiful places have beautiful names, and for some **Drottningholm,** currently the royal residence, is the sweetest-sounding word in Swedish. This elegant palace on the water boasts baroque gardens, an English-style park, and beautiful interiors. Featured in Bergman's *The Magic Flute,* the palace's **theater** is reason enough to visit Sweden. Performances are still given using the original stage machinery, and the hourly tours in English can be delightfully dramatic, with wind and thunder effects included. (Opera and ballet performances, May-Sept.) **Kina slott** is Drottningholm's Asian pavilion, with charming *objets d'art* from China and Japan. Boats to Drottningholm depart from Stadshusbron, near the City Hall, every half hour (1 hr., 33kr, with Stockholmskortet 23kr). (Palace open May-Aug. Mon.-Sat. 11am-4:30pm, Sun. noon-4:30pm; Sept. Mon.-Fri. 1-3:30pm, Sat.-Sun. 12-3:30pm. Admission 10kr, children 5kr. Theater open May-Aug. Mon.-Sat. 11:30am-4:30pm, Sun. 12:30-4:30pm; Sept. daily 12:30-3pm. Admission 17kr, children 8kr. Kina slott open same hours as palace, and also April and Oct. Admission 10kr, children 5kr.)

Another day trip takes you to **Björkö,** the island site of Sweden's oldest city, Birka, a trading outpost for merchants of the Viking era. Nothing remains of the town, but some sandy coves offer pleasant bathing. (Boats run June 9-Aug. 19 Tues.-Thur. and Sat.-Sun.; May 5-June 3 and Aug. 25-Sept. 2 Sat.-Sun. only. 65kr round-trip.)

Gotland

Vacationing Swedes have long come to Gotland for its medieval churches, great beaches, and thousands of wildflowers and seabirds, but foreign travelers keep ignoring this idyllic Baltic island. You can tour the countryside by bike, inhale the fresh salty air and soak up the sun, explore the fortified Hanseatic city of Visby, and even visit Villa Villekulla, the home of Pippi Longstocking.

Ferries sail between Gotland and Oskarhamn, and Gotland and Nynäshamn. (Also between Gotland and Västervik in summer.) A feeder bus from Stockholm to Nynäshamn leaves from Vattugatan (T-bana: Central Station), 90 minutes before ferry departures (30kr). Ferries cost 109kr, except from mid-June to mid-August when they cost 129kr Fri.-Sun. Seniors and children enjoy discounts throughout the year, as do students in the off-season. Call (0498) 605 00 in Gotland for ferry information. Information and bookings for both ferries and accommodations are available at the office of the **Gotland Tourist Association** in Stockholm at Kungsgatan 48 (tel. 23 61 70; open Mon.-Fri. 9:30am-6pm, Sat. 10am-2pm). You can fly youth standby (under 26) from Stockholm to Visby for 150kr, though in summer it's almost impossible to get a flight.

Visby is a perfectly preserved medieval town. Its ancient wall (3.6km long) encloses narrow, winding streets, ruined churches, and chic shops geared to Stockholm vacationers. Visit **Gotlands Fornsal Museum,** Strandgatan 12-14, for an overview of the island's history, including cryptic Viking runes from the eighth century. (Open mid-May to Aug. Mon.-Sun. 11am-5pm; Sept. Mon.-Sun. 1-4pm; Oct. to mid-May Tues.-Fri. 1-3pm, Sat.-Sun. 1-4pm. Adults 10kr, children, students and seniors 5kr, families 20kr.) You can learn about Gotland's geography at the **Nature Museum,** across the street from the tourist office. Good slide shows in English. (Open June-Aug. daily 11am-5pm; Sept.-May Sun. 1-4pm. Admission 5kr; students, children, and seniors 2kr.)

The **tourist office, Burmeisterska huset,** Strandgatan 9 (tel. (0498) 109 82), a 10-minute walk left from the ferry terminal, is very helpful. (Open late April-May Mon.-Fri. 8am-5pm, Sat.-Sun. noon-6pm; June to mid-Aug. Mon.-Fri. 8am-8pm, Sat.-Sun. 10am-7pm; mid-Aug. to mid-Sept. Mon.-Fri. 8am-5pm, Sat.-Sun. 10am-4pm.) For friendly knowledgeable advice, stop in at **Visby Resebyrå,** Hamnplan 5 (tel. (0498) 170 50), a seven-minute walk from the ferry terminal. If you want to rent a room in a private home, do so here and not at the tourist office—you'll save up to 30kr (singles 125kr, doubles 105kr per person). Visby's pleasant and friendly **vandrarhem (IYHF),** at Gråbofritidsgård (tel. (0498) 169 33), has a TV and a full kitchen. Take bus #1 from Österport, up the hill through town and outside the wall. (Members 38kr, non-members 58kr. If full, they'll squeeze you onto the floor for 25kr. Lock-out 11pm-5am. Closed 10am-5pm. Open May-Aug.) Campgrounds abound on Gotland, and you can pitch your tent anywhere not too conspicuous. **Kneippbyns Campingplats** (tel. 643 65), 4km south of Visby, is directly on the sea and accessible by bus. (Open May to mid-Sept.)

Tant Grön, Adelsgatan 1B, has great vegetarian food: delicious saffron pancakes (20kr), or an enormous salad with soup (35kr). (Open in summer Mon.-Fri. 10am-6pm, Sat. 10am-1pm; in winter Mon.-Fri. 11am-2pm.) Admire a crumbling church ruin over excellent pastry and bottomless cups of coffee at **Saint Hans Konditori,** St. Hansplan 2; they serve large meals from 34kr (10% discount for seniors) and metamorphose into a mellow nightspot, sometimes with live folk music. (Open April-Aug. Mon.-Sat. 8am-11pm, Sun. 9am-11pm. Midnight coffee bar Sat.-Sun. midnight-4am.) **Burmeister,** Strandgatan, next-door to the tourist office, has live outdoor music and a nightly disco in the summer (10pm-2am; cover 45kr). Every second or third evening in July and August, Visby hosts the **Ruinspel,** a mystic opera festival among the ruins; tickets (47-95kr) are often booked long in advance, but try the festival office, Tranhusgatan 47 (tel. (0498) 110 68).

Cycling is the best way to explore Gotland's flat terrain. The bike rental shops on the quay open when the first night ferries come in. When she visits Gotland, Queen Silvia rents a bike at **Hyr Hoj Här** (tel. (0498) 141 33; open May-Sept. Mon.-Sun. 5am-7pm). (23-28kr.) You can also rent tandems (150kr per day), or "camping bicycles," which come with a cart, tent, cooking gear, and foam sleeping pad (550kr 2 people per week; 450kr per 5 days.) If biking doesn't float your boat, you might invest in a **Gotlandskortet,** which entitles you to unrestricted bus travel for three days, plus admission to six museums (60kr, ages 16 and under 30kr).

Near Visby, the church at **Bro** incorporates ancient picture stones on its walls, while the one at **Dalhem** shows off original stained glass. South of Visby, a boat tour departs from Klintehamn to the delightful **Stora Karlsö Islands,** formed naturally upon a coral reef and featuring a Stone Age archeological dig, unusual wildflowers, and thousands of nesting razorbills and guillemots (birds). (Ferries mid-May to mid-Aug. 90kr one way, ages 7-17 60kr. You must book before you go; call (0498) 405 67 for complete information.) Farther south, inspect the medieval crucifix in the church at **Öja.** At **Hoburgen,** there are magnificent limestone cliffs.

North of Visby you can visit the quiet beach at **Brissund,** only 10km out of town, or the famous **Lummelunda Caves**—Sweden's largest (adults 20kr, children 12kr). There's a **vandrarhem (IYHF)** in Lummelunda with kitchen facilities (tel. (0498) 730 43). (Members 38kr, nonmembers 58kr. Open early May-late Aug.) At Lickershamn, you can view the large limestone formations called *rauks.*

Military installations extend to the northern tip of Gotland. Non-Swedish citizens are forbidden access to this area, as well as to the islands of Gotska Sandön and Fårö (where Ingmar Bergman keeps his summer home). There are some exceptions; one such allows for a visit to the excellent **Bungemuseet** (Bunge Cultural Museum) in Fårösund, where traditional crafts are demonstrated in antique cottages. (Open mid-May to June Mon.-Fri. 10am-2pm, Sat.-Sun. noon-4pm; June and Aug. Mon.-Sun. 10am-6pm; July Mon.-Sun. 10am-8pm. Adults 10kr, children 5kr.)

Uppsala

Once the cradle of Swedish civilization, Uppsala now shelters the soaring twin spires of the country's finest cathedral, where Swedish monarchs were baptized, married, and buried. The royalty may have moved to Stockholm, but the 40,000 students of Sweden's oldest university didn't—and guess who's more likely to join you for a drink.

Uppsala's stately **cathedral** is the ecclesiastical seat and coronation church of Sweden, as well as the largest church in Scandinavia. (Open June-Aug. daily 8am-8pm; Sept.-May daily 8am-6pm.) The **Gustavianum,** between the cathedral and the main university building, houses four small museums: the Victoria Museum of Egyptology, the Nordic History Museum, the Museum of Antiquity, and the fascinating Anatomical Theater, where the general public could witness dissections of criminals, provided they attended the funeral immediately afterwards. (Open late June to mid-Aug. daily 11am-3pm. Anatomical Theater open in winter by request. Admission 3kr per museum, 10kr for all four.) **Uppsala Castle** is up the hill from the university; tours now pace the site of former intrigue, abdication, and murder. (Open late April-Aug. daily 11am-4pm; Sept. daily 11am-2pm.)

Pre-Christian monarchs are buried at **Gamla Uppsala,** the original city. Today little remains except huge burial mounds and **Uppsala Church,** one of Sweden's oldest. (Open May-Aug. daily 8am-8pm.) Take bus #24 from Dragarbrunnsgatan (7kr, free transfers 1kr). The gardens and residence of **Carl Linnaeus,** pioneer of modern botany, are at Svartbacksgatan 27. In honor of Uppsala's 700th birthday in 1986, the **Jubileumslinje** (bus #700) was instituted to run between the cathedral, the castle, and Gamla Uppsala, providing Swedish/English commentary en route. A 30kr ticket, available at the tourist office or on #700 buses, entitles you to 24 hours of bus service and admission to the sites.

The **tourist office,** Smedsgränd 7 (tel. (018) 11 75 00), finds rooms in private homes (about 85kr) for a 15kr fee. (Open May-Aug. Mon.-Fri. 9am-6pm, Sat. 9am-2pm; Aug.-May Mon.-Fri. 9am-5pm.) There's also a branch at the cathedral. (Open late May-Aug. Mon.-Fri. 9am-7pm, Sat. 9am-6pm, Sun. 12:30-5pm.) **Sunnerstå Herrgård (IYHF),** Sunnerstavägen 24 (tel. (018) 32 42 20), offers double rooms but is distant; take bus #20 from Östra Ågatan on the east side of the river or bus #50 from Dragarbrunnsgata after 6pm and weekends. You can swim in Lake Mälaren nearby. (Members 45kr, nonmembers 65kr. Lockout 10am-5pm. Open May-Aug.) Not quite as nice but closer to town is **Fritidsgården Gläntan (IYHF),** Norbyvägen 46 (tel. (018) 10 80 60). Take bus #6 or 7 from Stora Torget (the central square), bus #52 evenings and on weekends. (Members 38kr, nonmembers 58kr. Open mid-June to mid-Aug. 8-10am and 5-11pm.) Right on the river is **Fyris Camping** (tel. (018) 13 23 33). (June-Aug. tents 25kr, huts 200kr; Sept.-May heated huts 160kr.) Rent bikes at **Gulle Villan,** Stadstrad Gärden (tel. (018) 16 16 40), south of the tourist office. (28kr for 24 hr. Open June-Aug.)

All students at the university belong to "nations," corresponding to their home districts in Sweden. The nations are the center of social life; during the academic year, any university ID will gain you admission to parties and meals. Only a few nations are open in summer, usually for lunch (11am-3pm, about 25-30kr), or as discos at night. To find out what's on, check the bulletin board in the library, Carolina Rediviva—walk to the left as you enter. Students frequent **Cafe Ubbo,** behind the main university building. (*Dagens rätt* 20kr. Open Sept. to mid-June 8am-5pm; mid-June to Aug. Mon.-Fri. 8am-3pm.) For picnic fixings, visit the **Saluhallen,** the indoor market on St. Eriks Torg, the little square behind the cathedral. (Open July-Aug. Mon.-Fri. 9:30am-6pm, Sat. 9:30am-1pm; Sept.-June Mon.-Fri. only.) **Ahimsa,** a vegetarian restaurant between St. Eriks Torg and Fyris Torg, offers a fantastic daily special for 28kr, students 25kr. (Open Mon.-Fri. 11:30am-3pm, Sat. noon-4pm.) Students come to **Ofrandahls,** Sysslomansgatan 5, for coffee and pastry. Try an *arraksboll,* flavored with *punch,* the after-dinner drink of choice in the region. (Open Mon.-Fri. 9am-9pm, Sat. 9am-4pm.)

A boat trip on Lake Mälaren is a fine way to pass a sunny afternoon. Head out to **Skokloster** (70kr round-trip), a baroque castle (open May-Sept. daily noon-4pm; admission 10kr); or **Sigtuna,** a well-preserved medieval town (50kr one way). With money you can even reach Stockholm by water (8 hr., 120kr). Uppsala is also connected to Stockholm by frequent trains (40 min., 32kr, Fri. and Sun. 40kr).

Dalarna

An old Ingmar Bergman movie goes by the title *Wild Strawberries* in English. The Swedish title, *Smultronstället* (place of the wild strawberries), holds two meanings: A place of the elusive fruit, or a secret place where one goes to commune with nature, one's self, and one's significant other. Dalarna is Sweden's *smultronställe.* Scores of Swedes summer here in the woods in neat red and white farmhouses. The region lies about 3½ hours northwest of Stockholm; one rail line extends through Uppsala to Leksand, Tällberg, Råttvik, and Mora, while another connects to Falun (3-4 trains per day on each).

Swedes flock to **Leksand,** a small town on Lake Siljan, to take part in the ancient **Midsummer** festivities—the raising of the maypole, the procession of richly decorated "church boats," folk musicians and costumes, and drinking and dancing that lasts all night. The annual **Musik vid Siljan Festival** is a celebration of folk music (July 2-10 in 1988). **Himlaspelet,** a traditional play with music, recounts the adventures of Mats, a young man who realizes that paradise is really his farm in Dalarna. (Late July. Programs in English.)

Accommodations are packed in summer, so call ahead. The **Turistbyrå,** Norsgatan (tel. (0247) 803 00), a five-minute walk from the train station along Källberget, will find you a room in a private home for 70-80kr and a 20kr fee. (Open in summer Mon.-Sat. 9am-9pm, Sun. 1-9pm; in winter Mon.-Fri. 9am-7pm, Sat. 9am-1pm.) Just down the street, **Utesport,** Norsgatan 17 (tel. (0247) 116 58), can rent you a bike. The **IYHF youth hostel** in Lisselby (tel. (0247) 101 86) is a 15-minute walk from the Leksand train station. (Members 45kr, nonmembers 62kr. Open May to mid-Sept.) A 20-minute walk north on the road toward Tällberg will bring you to **camping** (tel. (0247) 112 01) at Orsandbaden. (30kr per tent.)

From Leksand's quay there are convenient and beautiful boat connections to all the towns along Siljan on the *Gustaf Wasa.* Rättvik (40kr), and Mora (55kr) are two possible destinations; a special combination boat and train return ticket to Mora costs 65kr. For more information, call (0247) 116 09, or talk to the tourist office.

The idyllic village of **Tällberg** is famed among Swedes for its excellent handicrafts, sold and displayed at **Klockargården.** Enjoy Tällberg's hilltop view over Siljan from the shop's **Kaffestuga** (open in summer daily 10am-10pm). Buses and trains travel the 14km between Leksand and Tällberg; it's also an easy bike ride with rewarding views. On the way, you'll pass the village of **Hjortnäs,** whose lakeside dancing area is popular on Wednesday and Sunday evenings in summer. For another good look at the lake, head out toward **Siljansnäs** by bus or bike, and turn left after Västanviks Camping on the road marked **Granberg.** The road up is a favorite haunt of local moose.

Few towns are as beautifully situated as **Rättvik,** tucked into the wooded hills at the edge of Siljan, 20 minutes by train north of Leksand. Rättvik is very active during the Musik vid Siljan Festival (see above). During the **Bingsjö Spelmansstämma** ("Player's Convention"), some 30,000 people from all over the world gather at a private farm in Bingsjö, 40km from Rättvik, and set up impromptu groups playing everything from Swedish folk songs to bluegrass. (July 2-10.) The helpful **tourist office** (tel. (0248) 109 10), just across from the train station, books rooms in private homes or in a *stugor* (cabin) for a 20kr fee. (Singles 85kr, doubles 150kr, triples 180kr, quads 240kr. Call at least a day in advance. Open in summer Mon.-Sat. 9am-9pm, Sun. 1-9pm; otherwise Mon.-Fri. 9am-5pm, Sat. 9am-1pm.) The new **IYHF youth hostel** (tel. (0248) 105 66), is in a wooded setting behind the tourist office. (Members 50kr, nonmembers 70kr.) **Rättviksparken Campingplats** (tel. (0248) 102 51) is open year-round; walk 15 minutes along Centralgatan to the left of the tourist office. (25kr per tent. 4-bed cabins 160kr.) **Siljansbadets Campingplats** (tel. (0248) 106 45) is on the lakefront. (20kr per tent. Cottages 120kr. Open mid-June to mid-Sept.) You can rent a canoe, bicycle, or windsurf board at **Siljansbadet** or at **Sörlins Sport,** Storgatan 1 (tel. (0248) 103 33).

In-town attractions include **Rättviks Gammelgård,** a re-creation of a Dalarna farm, with local handicrafts and a fine cafe. Walk 10 minutes out of the center towards Sjurberg. (Open mid-June to mid-Aug. Mon.-Sat. 11am-6pm, Sun. 12:30-6pm.) **Handverksbyen,** a 15-minute walk along the road to Gärdeby, offers coffee, cakes, and handicrafts in a traditional setting. Or stop in next to the tourist office for coffee, pastry, and sandwiches at the popular **Fricks Konditoria,** outlet of the famous Fricks bakery. (Open Mon.-Fri. 8am-10pm, Sat. 9am-10pm, Sun. 10am-9pm.)

An enormous meteorite created the large valley of which Lake Siljan is just a small part. Bike 20km north of Rättvik to Boda to see **Styggforsen,** a waterfall and geological outcrop resulting from the prehistoric collision. The 7km trip to **Vikarbyen** is another good option; a tradional Swedish summer cattle farm *(fäbod)* and a ceramic works await inspection. If the simple, ancient lifestyle of the *fäbod* intrigues you, consider working on one. Write to Ärteråsens Fäbodar, hos Furudal-Orebygdens Turistförening, Furudal (tel. (0258) 100 69). Handicrafts and cooking classes are offered as well. Fans of traditional dance should not miss the **Rättviksdansen** international dance festival, held during the first week of August of even-numbered years.

Head north to **Mora** for even more beautiful scenery and tons of blueberries, lingonberries, and *svamp* (mushrooms). The **tourist office** (tel. (0250) 265 50), 15 minutes from the station on the lakefront, will find you a bed in a **private home** for a 20kr fee. (Open in summer Mon.-Sat. 9am-9pm, Sun. 1-9pm.) Some beds are available for 70kr in *stugor* (cottages). You'll need your own sleeping bag or sheets.

Sweden's greatest modern image-maker, **Carl Larsson,** was a lifelong lover of Dalarna's countryside. Visit his home in Sundborn, 12km north of Falun (on the Borlänge-Gävle bus line) for a taste of the best in turn-of-the-century Swedish design. (Open May-Sept. Mon.-Sat. 10am-5pm, Sun. 1-5pm.) Sundborn makes a nice bike ride from Falun; call the Falun tourist office (tel. (023) 836 37) for help finding a bike.

In winter Dalarna offers fine cross-country skiing, as well as hills and ski jumps. Contact the tourist offices for information.

Lapland (Lappland)

For many "Southerners"—anyone living south of the Arctic Circle—Lapland consists of towering pine trees, herds of moose and reindeer, and thick snow blotting the North Star. All this is only half the truth. Thanks to the Gulf Stream, summers are warm—in the 70°s F by day—and, instead of enormous mountains, marshes and flatlands predominate. Swedish Lapland is the most accessible part of Lapland, which also stretches across Finland and Norway. Two train lines run north, and the most heavily traveled one from Stockholm through Boden to Gällivare has service 2 or 3 times per day. The inland line, going from Östersund through Jokkmokk to Gällivare is more scenic, but sends only one train per day in each direction. SAS's special youth standby fare—150kr from Stockholm to any point in Sweden—is the cheapest way to the north of Scandinavia. Buses are the only public transport to the smaller villages and into the national parks. Request bus and train schedules in stations and tourist bureaus; *Inlandsbanen Tidtabeller* is quite helpful and *Turisttrafik i Fjällen* provides a rough outline of every route in the area. Hitchhikers and cyclists will have to deal with intermittent summer showers.

The only way to get right up into the mountains is on foot. Bring your own food and supplies; good equipment, a topographical map, and a compass are essential for extended trips; this is rugged country and there may be snow as late as July. You don't need camping equipment to enjoy the mountains; it's easy to reach the mountain tourist stations, which make great bases for day hikes from most towns. If you plan to hike or camp, contact **Svenska Turistföreningen** in Stockholm (see Tourist Offices under Practical Information) for maps, advice, and information about their mountain huts and 2300km of trails. The STF huts are in high demand in summer; contact the local tourist offices to make arrangements.

The most popular months for hiking and camping are July and August, despite the hordes of mosquitoes. Swedes swear by the *Jungle Oil* brand of mosquito repellent. Late August or early September may be the ideal time for a visit. Earlier or later in the year, many of the mountain huts are closed. Lapland's national parks, all of which are noted on the maps, are particularly good for camping, though at some you may be restricted to official sites. **Sareks** requires advanced mountaineering experience, complete equipment, and familiarity with Swedish conditions; **Padjelanta** and **Stora Sjöfallet** are more accessible, yet wild enough for most. Wherever you go, be aware that even heavily-used hiking routes traverse real wilderness. Plan your route, and leave it with someone before you set off. Do not take short-cuts in Lapland; everything on the tundra looks alike, and you can lose your sense of direction easily.

Lapland specialties include reindeer meat and smoked cod. Golden cloudberries (*hjorntron*) grow throughout Lapland, but only in Sweden is it legal to pick them. You'll find them in the marshes, and as a topping on waffles and pancakes.

Jokkmokk means "bend in the stream" in Lapp, but more geographically exciting is its location as first town north of the Arctic Circle on the inland railway. Coming in on the train, you'll be able to purchase an official, gold-embossed "I've crossed the Arctic Circle" certificate for 15kr. The town is the nexus of all camping and hiking in the area. The **tourist office,** Porjusvägen 4 (tel. (0971) 121 40), will happily furnish you with keys to *stugor* (wilderness huts), or find you a private room in town (70-75kr per person). (Open mid-May to Aug. daily 9am-9pm; Sept. to mid-May daily 8am-noon and 1-4pm.) The **IYHF youth hostel,** Borgargatan 2 (tel. (0971) 119 77), on the outskirts of town, has a comfortable sitting room, a full kitchen, and laundry facilities. (Members 50kr, nonmembers 70kr. Reception open until 9pm. Call in advance. Open mid-June to mid-Aug.) **Jokkmokk Camping** (tel. (0971) 123 70) charges 40kr per tent.

Buses run from Jokkmokk to **Kvikkjokk,** right near the rugged **Sareks National Park** (2 per day, 51kr). This is an excellent starting point for real wilderness experience. Guided tours leave from the mountain station (mid-June to Aug.). Kvikkjokk has accommodations in **Kvikkjokk Fjällstation** (tel. (0971) 210 22) for about 90kr per person.

Gällivare, an old Lapp center, is today the site of Sweden's premier alpine skiing competition, the Lapland Cup. In summer the town is a convenient base from which to explore Lapland's wilderness. The midnight sun lasts from early June to mid-July. The **tourist office** (tel. (0970) 186 63) is at Storgatan 16; from the train station, turn left, then right. (Open in summer 9am-10pm.) The **IYHF youth hostel** (tel. (0970) 143 80) is a five-minute walk from the station; walk over the tracks, then cross the bridge on your left. (50kr. Sauna 5kr. Kitchen and laundry facilities. Open mid-May to mid-Sept. Call for reservations.) Gällivare's **campground** is 1½km from the station, next to a pleasant mosquito pond. (30kr per tent. Bikes 35kr per day.) **Polar Turism** (tel. (0970) 600 50), in nearby Killingi, can arrange a variety of hiking and rafting adventures, as well as rent snowmobiles and snowshoes in winter.

Kiruna, a dull mining town and the northernmost municipality in Sweden, sits amid vast wilderness. Kiruna has the world's largest underground iron ore mine; during the summer the tourist office arranges daily coach tours to the mine at 10am, noon, 2pm, and 4pm. The **tourist office,** Hjalmar Lundbohmsvägen 52 (tel. (0980) 188 80), is 10 minutes from the station past the hill and park, across from the Town Hall. They offer free maps, and will book rooms in **private homes.** (Singles 120kr, doubles 150kr, triples 180kr, quads 200kr; fee included. Office open mid-June to mid-Aug. Mon.-Sat. 9am-8pm, Sun. 1-8pm; mid-Aug. to mid-June Mon.-Fri. 10am-4pm.) There is also a summer branch office by the train station. (Open 8am-9pm.) The **IYHF youth hostel** (tel. (0980) 171 95) is about 1km north of the train station; go right as you exit. Book one day in advance—it fills up. (45kr. Kitchen facilities. Open July-Aug.) **Gult Hus** (tel. (0980) 114 51) on Parkgatan offers a kitchen and TV room (singles 85kr, doubles 170kr). **Kiruna Camping** (tel. (0980) 131 00) is a

15-minute hike from the train station (35kr per tent). **Mat och Mums,** in the swimming hall downtown, has a very good *dagens rätt* for 32kr. (Open Mon.-Fri. 10am-11pm, Sat. 11am-11pm, Sun. 1-8pm.) There are several grocery stores in the town center.

Spectacular trails leave from **Nikkolaukta,** 66km from Kiruna. The cafe here is popular with the Lapps waiting for ferries to Padjelanta, where they breed reindeer in the summer. Linger over a cup of tea and a waffle with cloudberry sauce. Buses link Kiruna to **Karesuando** (2 per day, 177kr), from which you can continue to Kautokeino, Norway, and Kilpisjärvi, Finland. Remember that Finland is one time zone ahead when consulting bus schedules. For further information on nearby areas, turn to the Norway and Finland chapters.

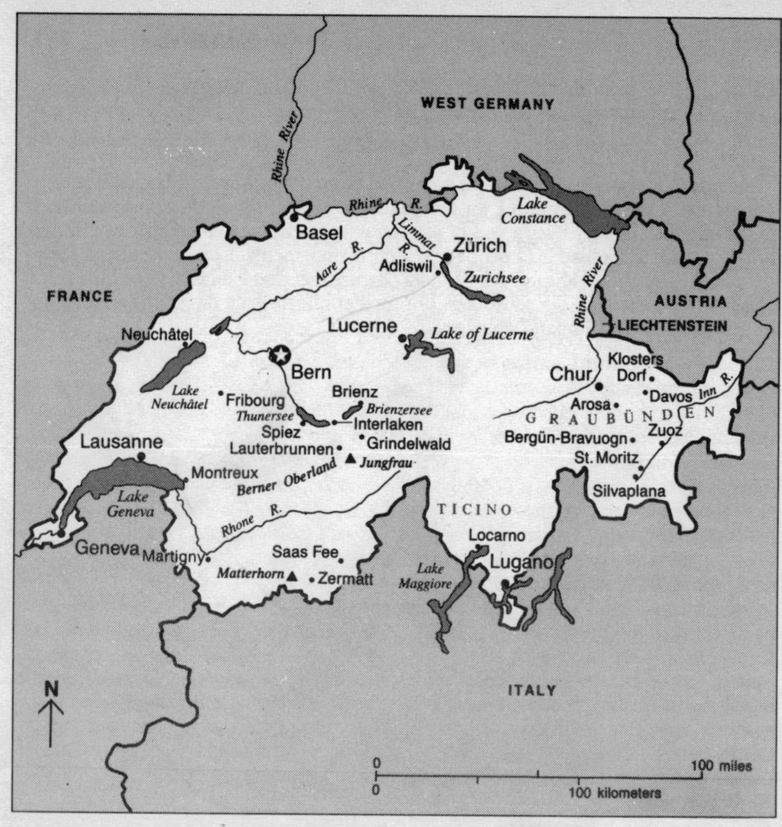

SWITZERLAND

US$1 = 1.49 francs (SFr) — **1SFr = US $0.67**
CDN$1 = 1.15SFr — **1SFr = CDN $0.87**
UK£1 = 2.44SFr — **1SFr = UK£0.41**
AUS $1 = 1.07SFr — **1SFr = AUS $0.93**

Landlocked Switzerland sits on the rooftop of Europe. Covering well over half of Swiss territory, the Swiss Alps are the logical vacation spot for skiers, hikers, and mountain climbers alike. The Berner Oberland and the legendary Matterhorn are only two of the best-known landmarks in a stunning countryside that is universally appealing. Centers for world commerce and banking, Switzerland's major cities are more staid than spectacular.

Split by long impassable mountains and united neither by language or religion, it is curious that Switzerland is a nation at all. It is in fact a confederation of largely autonomous cantons, initiated in 1291 and steadily augmented until the early nineteenth century. Switzerland has enjoyed its famous neutrality since 1815, guarding it through two World Wars and into the present day: It is a member of neither NATO, the EEC, nor even the UN.

Transportation

Getting around Switzerland is extremely easy. Federal and private railways, and yellow post buses, which serve many of the remote villages, keep time as well as

Swiss watches. Both Eurail and InterRail passes are valid in Switzerland, though only on state-run railways. Approximately 40% of the train service in Switzerland is on private lines; on these, as well as on national lines, fares are frighteningly expensive. The trip from Zürich to Geneva will set you back 45SFr.

Those planning to spend much time in the country should consider the myriad "Holiday" plans. The **Swiss Holiday Card** costs 145SFr for four days, 170SFr for eight days, 205SFr for 15 days; and 285SFr for one month, all second class; ages 6 to 16 years pay half-price. This pass gives unlimited travel on all government-operated railways, all lake steamers, and most private railways and postal buses, but only a 25-50% discount on the most expensive mountain railways and cable cars. The **Half-Fare Travel Card** (55SFr for 15 days, 70SFr for 1 month, ages 6-25 35SFr for 1 month) entitles you to 50% off all trips on federal and private railroads, postal buses, and steamers. **Day Cards**—four-day (125SFr) or 10-day (240SFr)—give you free travel on all federal and some private railroads. The days need not be consecutive. Finally, each of the 23 cantons of Switzerland has its own **Regional Holiday Season Ticket** for 38-134SFr, depending on the region. Regional tickets are valid for 15 days, of which five not necessarily consecutive days can be used for free travel, and the remaining 10 for half-fare travel. Ages 6-15 years pay half-fare; Swiss Holiday Card or Half-Fare Travel Card holders get a 20% discount. Most of these passes can be purchased abroad through the Swiss National tourist office for 5-10% less than the cost in the country itself.

Steamers ply many of the larger lakes. Again, fares are no bargain, but a Eurailpass often merits free passage, InterRail holders get 50% off, and a Swiss Holiday Card almost always entitles you to free travel.

Hitching in Switzerland is difficult, because the narrow mountain roads carry mostly local traffic going short distances. Despite the hills, cycling is an enjoyable and increasingly popular way to see the country. Bicycles can be rented at most train stations (12SFr per day, 9SFr for ticket holders) and returned to any station. Cross-country walking is the most enjoyable way to see Switzerland.

Practical Information

Tourist offices in Switzerland are just about everywhere. They can always find rooms and provide information on outdoor activities. Local offices have maps of skiing and hiking trails, or you can get a guidebook and map from the **Association of Swiss Hiking Trails,** Schweizer Wanderwege, Im Hirshalm 49, 4125 Riehen, Switzerland, (tel. (061) 49 15 35). Many towns have their own Alpine societies which the tourist office can direct you to. Skiing costs, but if you go during low-season weeks in the winter you can get by without breaking the bank.

Switzerland is officially quatrilingual. French is spoken in the west; Italian in the south; Romansch (a language of Latin origin) in the Engadin and Graubünden cantons; and Swiss-German, a dialect nearly incomprehensible to other German speakers, everywhere else. Whatever language people speak first, they often speak at least two others, including English.

Shops and offices are closed on the standard Christian holidays, and on August 1, Switzerland's Independence Day. Most stores are open Monday through Friday 8am to 6:30pm (with a break from noon to 2pm) and Saturday mornings. Dialing 191 connects you with an English-speaking operator; dial 117 anywhere in the country to reach the police in an emergency, or 144 to summon an ambulance. International phone calls can be made from PTT offices and post offices. The **country code** for Switzerland is 41.

Let's Go includes the country of Liechtenstein at the end of the Switzerland chapter.

Accommodations, Camping, and Food

International federation and private youth hostels are the only "budget" options in many parts of Switzerland. **IYHF** hostels (7-15SFr) require membership cards.

Inexpensive hotels are rare, but expensive ones often have a few bathless rooms which they will rent for a very low price, especially in the evening. In rural areas, guesthouses and *Zimmer* (rooms in private homes—look for *Zimmerfrei* signs) are reasonably priced. There are over 1200 clean and efficient campgrounds in Switzerland. Urban campgrounds are often far from town, but rural camping is a wonderful way to enjoy the countryside. Freelance camping along roads and in public areas is forbidden, but a quiet rest-stop or parking lot is fine for trailers and camping vehicles.

The Swiss are not culinary daredevils, but restaurant meals as a rule are well-prepared and satisfying. There is a good selection of gourmet and delicatessen food, as well as many **Coop** and **Migros** grocery stores. Sample your way through the various smoked meats, herbal cheeses, and fruit-studded breads. Remember, too, that Switzerland provides innumerable gorgeous settings for picnics. Cafeterias in cities offer tasty, inexpensive dishes during the day, but often have stand-up dining only.

In French Switzerland, try the cheese specialties: *Fondue* is always excellent, as is *raclette* (melted cheese served with pickled onions and boiled new potatoes). In the German section, the food is heartier: Try *Züricher Geschnetzeltes,* veal strips in a delicious cream sauce, and *Rösti,* almost-hashbrowned potato with onion. Swiss restaurant and hotel prices include a service charge, so tipping is not necessary.

German Switzerland

Zürich

Prosperous and opulent, Zürich is the quintessential banker's town. "The gnomes of Europe" was former British Prime Minister Harold Wilson's epithet for Zürich's bankers, who pervade world banking as they do their city. Zürich was also the seat of the Reformation in German Switzerland; today wealth and strong Protestant sentiments live a self-satisfied coexistence. Tristan Tzara and his fellow dadaists of the Cabaret Voltaire made Zürich one of the avant-garde capitals of Europe, and even James Joyce managed to flourish here. A large student population enlivens this otherwise quiet city.

Orientation and Practical Information

Zürich sits on the northern tip of the Zürichsee (lake) with the River Limmat dividing it into two roughly equal parts. Exceptionally efficient public trams serve all parts of town; cost varies with distance (less than 5 stops, 1SFr). The 24-hour *Tageskarte* is a bargain at 5SFr.

Tourist Offices: Bahnhofplatz 15 (tel. 211 40 00). Exit to the right from the station (under the big red "Globus" sign) and turn left on Bahnhofplatz. For 3 to 5SFr, the staff will help you find rooms. Get a free copy of the weekly *Zürich News,* and information about their "Meet the Swiss" program: They will match you with a Zürich family who will invite you to their home for a typical Swiss dinner, for tea, or just to chat. (You don't have to speak German and it's free, but you must be in Zürich for at least 3 days.) Open March-Oct. Mon.-Fri. 8am-10pm, Sat.-Sun. 8am-8:30pm; Nov.-Feb. Mon.-Thurs. 8am-8pm, Fri. 8am-10pm, Sat.-Sun. 9am-6pm. Also at the **airport** terminal A (tel. 816 25 34; open daily 11am-8pm) and terminal B (tel. 816 35 11; open daily 8am-5pm).

Budget Travel: SSR, Leonhardstr. 10 (tel. 47 29 55). Across the river from the station and up the hill to the left. Open Mon. 1-6pm, Tues.-Fri. 10am-6pm, Sat. 10am-noon. BIGE tickets across the street, same hours. Information on budget ski packages and excursions at **SSR,** Bäckerstr. 52 (tel. 242 30 00).

American Express: Bahnhofstr. 20 (tel. 211 83 70). Mail held. All banking services. Open Mon.-Fri. 8:30am-5:30pm, Sat. 8:30am-noon.

Currency Exchange: At the train station. Open daily 6:30am-11:30pm.

Post Office: At the station, the Fraumünster, and on Kasernenstr. 95-99. All open Mon.-Fri. 7:30am-6:30pm, Sat. 7:30-11am. Mail held at: Sihlpost, Kasernenstr., Postlagernde Briefe, CH-8021 Zürich; counter remains open until 11pm, but a .50SFr fee is charged after 6:30pm.

Telephones: At the train station. Open daily 7am-10:30pm. **Telephone code:** 01.

Flights: Over 100 trains per day connect the international airport with the Hauptbahnhof (10 min., 4.20SFr, railpasses valid).

Trains: Information (tel. 211 50 10).

Bike Rental: At the baggage counter (*Gepäckexpedition Fly-Gepäck*) in the east end of the station. 9SFr per day and 51SFr per week for rail ticket holders, 12SFr per day and 66SFr per week otherwise. Open daily 6am-10pm.

Emergencies: Police (tel. 117). **Ambulance** (tel. 144). **Medical Emergency** (tel. 47 47 00).

Consulates: U.S., Zollikerstr. 141 (tel. 55 25 66). **U.K.,** Dufourstr. 56 (tel. 47 15 20).

Laundry: MM Speed-Wash, 4 locations throughout Zürich: Müllerstr. 55, Mattengasse 29, Weinberstr. 37, and Friesstr. 4. Open Mon.-Sat. 7am-10pm, Sun. 10:30am-10pm.

Hitchhiking: For Basel, Geneva, Paris, or Bonn, take tram #4 from the station to the end (Werdhölzli). To Lucerne, Italy, Chur, and Austria, take tram #5 or 14 to Bahnhof Wiedikon and walk 1 block down Schimmelstr. to Silhölzli. For Munich, take tram #14 to Milchbuck, walk to Schaffhauserstr., toward St. Gallen and St. Margarethen. **Mitfahrzentrale** is at tel. 241 04 04.

Accommodations and Camping

Hotels in Zürich are expensive, but the hostels are a good value.

Jugendherberge Zürich (IYHF), Mutschellenstr. 114 (tel. 45 35 44). Take tram #7 to Morgental and follow the signs (5 min.). Huge and modern, it's often filled with groups. Kitchen facilities, jukebox, and kiosk. Members 15SFr, nonmembers 22SFr. Showers, breakfast, and mandatory sheet rental included. Adequate dinner 7SFr (6-7:30pm). Reception open 6-10am and 2pm-1am; rooms closed 10am-5pm, though day-room always open. Curfew 1am. Open year-round.

Foyer Hottingen, Hottingerstr. 31 (tel. 47 93 15). Take tram #3 from Bahnhofplatz to Hottingerplatz. Women and families only. Tidy, cheerful rooms of 1-6 beds, in a semi-religious atmosphere. Kitchen facilities. 16-20SFr in dorm rooms, 28SFr per person in smaller rooms. Midnight curfew. Open year-round.

Glockenhof, Sihlstr. 33 (tel. 221 36 73), next to the more expensive *Hotel* Glockenhof (10 min. from the station). A local YMCA with a limited number of rooms, for men only. Spartan and rather depressing. Singles 30SFr, doubles 50SFr. Dinner 8.30SFr.

Hinterer Sternen, Freieckgasse 7 (tel. 251 32 68), off Bellevueplatz. Take tram #11 from Bahnhofstr. to Bellevueplatz. Fairly clean and centrally located; not much more. Singles 35SFr, doubles 50SFr. Showers included.

Marthahaus, Zähringerstr. 36 (tel. 251 27 57), across the river from the station. Dormitory rooms with 6 beds, mostly for women, but some for men. Full by 2pm in the summer. 22SFr per person with breakfast.

Camping: Camping Seebucht, Seestr. 559 (tel. 482 16 12), far from the center, but attractively located on the shore of the Zürichsee. Take the train to Wollishofen and walk 15 min., or ride bus #61 or 65 from Bürkliplatz, on the lake at the end of Bahnhofstr., to Grenzsteig. 4SFr per person plus 6-8SFr per tent. Open early May-late Sept.

Food

Zürich has over 1300 restaurants, but don't overlook the numerous *Würstli* stands, where you can buy any type of sausage, fresh bread, and trimmings from around 3SFr. Pick up the free brochure *Zürich on a Budget: Meals for Less Than 10SF* at the tourist office. Zürich has two excellent university mensas open to all.

Mensa der Universität Zürich, Rämistr. 71. Take tram #6 from Bahnhofplatz to ETH Zentrum, or walk. To return to town, take the tram on Tannenstr. Good meals 5SFr with ISIC, 7.20SFr without. Open Mon.-Fri. 7:30am-8pm, Sat. 7:30am-1pm; lunch served 11am-1:30pm, dinner 5:15-7:30pm.

Mensa Polyterrasse, Rämistr. 101, nearby. Most people prefer the food at this mensa. *Menus* 4.20-7SFr, *a la carte* 9.40SFr. Open mid-Sept. to mid-July Mon.-Thurs. 11:15am-1:30pm and 5:30-7:30pm, Fri. 11:15am-1:30pm and 5:30-7:15pm, Sat. 11:30am-1pm; mid-July to mid-Sept. open for lunch only. The university cafe upstairs offers lighter fare and a wonderful view of Zürich and the Alps. Open Mon.-Fri. 6:45am-9pm, Sat. 7:30am-1:15pm.

Rheinfelder Bierhaus, Marktgasse 19, in the Altstadt. Terrific food, huge portions, and full meals starting at 8SFr. Always filled with raucous, fun-loving locals. Open daily 9am-midnight.

Schifflände, Schifflände 18, in the Altstadt, has delicious meals for 8-12SFr and a constant crowd of students. Cafe, bar, and restaurant open Mon.-Fri. 7am-2am, Sat.-Sun. 5pm-2am. A casual disco in the basement is free on weeknights and 10SFr on weekends. Late-service fee applies after 11:45pm.

Vier Linden, Gemeindestr. 48, near the Foyer Hottingen Hotel. Good vegetarian food in a pastel dining room. 2 *menus:* 15SFr with dessert, 12SFr without. Open Mon.-Fri. 6am-9pm, Sat. 7am-5pm.

Sights and Entertainment

Despite the boring banks and the exclusive, expensive shops, **Bahnhofstrasse** is a colorful artery, adorned with flags and lime trees as it runs toward the Zürichsee. The **Altstadt** (old city) starts near the River Limmat; its finest edifice is the **Fraumünster** on Stadthaus Quai Strasse, an austere Gothic cathedral enlivened by the vibrant windows of Marc Chagall and Augusto Giacometti. (Open May-Sept. Mon.-Sat. 10am-12:30pm and 2-5pm; March-April and Oct. daily 10am-noon and 2-5pm; Nov.-Feb. daily 10am-noon and 2-4pm.) Across the river lies the **Grossmünster,** a Romanesque cathedral which was a center of the Reformation under Huldrych Zwingli, Zürich's answer to John Calvin. (Open April-Sept. Mon.-Fri. 10am-6pm, Sat. 10am-5pm, Sun. after services until 6pm; Oct.-March daily 10am-4pm.)

The second floor of the **Kunsthaus,** on Rämistrasse at Heimplatz, holds works of Picasso, Chagall, Klee, Mondrian, as well as of the expressionist, dadaist, and surrealist schools. (Open Mon. 2-5pm, Tues.-Fri. 10am-9pm, Sat.-Sun. 10am-5pm. Admission 2SFr, students 1SFr; free Mon. and Fri. 5-9pm.) James Joyce, a resident of Zürich for many years, is still here—in the **Fluntern Cemetery.** (Open May-Aug. daily 7am-7pm; March-April and Sept.-Oct. daily 7am-6pm; Nov.-Feb. daily 8am-5pm. Take tram #5 or 6 to the terminus (Zoo).) The **Kunstgewerbe Museum,** Austellung Str. 60, exhibits applied and commercial art from the eighteenth century to the present. (Open Tues.-Fri. 10am-6pm, Wed. 10am-9pm, Sat.-Sun. 10am-noon and 2-5pm. Admission 3SFr, students 1.50SFr, children free.)

Most of Zürich's nightlife revolves around Niederdorfstrasse and Limmatquai with its bars, clubs, and musicians. Many establishments charge a 2SFr tax or double drink prices after midnight. Popular with students is **Casa Bar,** Münstergasse 30, a small, crowded pub with good live jazz. Come early, or you may end up standing in the doorway. (Open daily 7pm-2am.) Zürich's new-wave and fashion followers hang out at **Bar Odeon,** which is also popular among gays, toward the end of Limmatquai. (Open Mon.-Sat. 7am-2am, Sun. 11am-2am.) For intense disco activity, go to **Let's Go,** Feldstr. 8180 in Bülach, on the outskirts of the city. Wear orange and bop 'til you drop. (Open daily until 2am.)

Near Zürich

Boat trips on the **Zürichsee** range from short jaunts (1½ hr.) stopping at little villages along the way (7.80SFr), to a "grand tour" (4 hr., 20SFr; free with Eurailpass, half-price with InterRail). All boats leave from Bürkliplatz. Boats from the Landesmuseum (6.80SFr; railpasses not valid) sail down the Limmat through Zürich, past the elegant, frescoed facades of the guildhouses. For more information on boat excursions, ask for the *Zürichsee* brochure at the tourist office.

Basel (Bâle)

Situated on the Rhine at the intersection of Germany, France, and Switzerland, Basel is a bustling metropolis and home of Switzerland's oldest university. Although an industrial center, Basel preserves a lovely central city and retains a rich cultural tradition.

The **Altstadt** (old city) is a curious mélange of twisted cobblestoned streets and sleek galleries and boutiques. Walking tours, which retrace the steps of the scholar Erasmus, depart from **Münsterplatz,** 500m east of the tourist office, on the river. (Sun.-Mon. 2:30pm, 6SFr.) Erasmus is buried at Basel's eleventh-century **Münster** (cathedral), which also has a spectacular view of the Rhine from the terrace in back. The beautifully restored **Rathaus** (City Hall) is on **Marktplatz,** around which much of the medieval city is clustered. **Totengässlein** leads from Marktplatz past rich patrician homes and guildhouses to the thirteenth-century **Peterskirche.**

Of the 27 museums in Basel, be sure you see the **Kunstmuseum,** St. Alban-Graben 16, down Rittergasse from the Münster. In addition to numerous works by Hans Holbein the Younger, the museum houses a large collection of cubist art. Entire rooms full of works by Picasso, Dalí, Braque, and Gris adjoin masterpieces by Klee, Kandinsky, Mondrian, Léger, and Delaunay, bought by a far-sighted museum director when Hitler's Germany deemed them "decadent." (Open Tues.-Sun. 10am-5pm. Admission 3SFr, students 2SFr, free Sun.) Basel's famous **Zoo** is next to the train station. A zoo and park rolled into one; the residents of its *Affenhaus* (monkey house) are particularly captivating. (Open daily 8am-6pm. Admission 6SFr.) Beginning the Monday after Ash Wednesday, all of Basel takes to the streets to celebrate **Fasnacht,** a three-day festival of parades and parties (in 1988, February 22-24); revelers wear masks to scare away the spirits of winter. The **International Art Fair of Twentieth-Century Art** will be in Basel June 15-20, 1988.

The **Verkehrsbüro,** Blumenrain 2 (tel. (061) 25 50 50), offers a free city map and information in English on Basel's history, museums, and accommodations. (Open Mon.-Wed. and Fri. 8:30am-6pm, Thurs. 8:30am-9pm, Sat. 8:30am-1pm.) To get there from the train station, take tram #1 to Schifflände stop; the office is on the river, near the bridge. Basel's **Jugendherberge (IYHF),** St. Alban-Kirchrain 10 (tel. (061) 23 05 72), by the river, is new, large, and friendly. From the station, take tram #1 one stop, then tram #3 two stops. (13.50SFr in 8-bed rooms, 20SFr in smaller private rooms. Breakfast 4.50SFr, dinner 6.50SFr. Open in summer 7am-12:30am; in winter 7am-11:30pm. Closed Dec. 24-Jan. 3.) Only five minutes from the station, **Hotel Steinenschanze,** Steinengraben 69 (tel. (061) 23 53 53), is comfortable, with a helpful management. (Singles 50SFr, doubles 75SFr; students 30SFr per person for the first 3 nights in both singles and doubles.) The nearest **camping** is in **Reinach,** 10km from town on highway 18, "Waldhort," (tel. (061) 76 64 29; open March-Oct.). For good, simple fare try the **Restaurant zum Stadtkeller,** Marktgasse 11, just down the street from the tourist office. **Gift Hüttli,** Schneidergasse 11, is quaint with wood paneling and full dinners for 8-12SFr.

Lucerne (Luzern)

With the Alps and the Vierwaldstätter See as its backdrop, Lucerne is spectacular. Brightly colored wall paintings, an art form that flourished in the late sixteenth century, decorate its narrow streets and colorful squares—some of the best are on **Weinmarkt** and **Hirschenplatz.** The city is ideal for boat trips and excursions to Mt. Rigi, Mt. Pilatus, and Mt. Titlis. Lucerne is 90 minutes by train southeast of Basel, and a similar distance south of Zürich and east of Berne.

A walk along the river affords a great view of the old city. The **Kapellbrücke** (1333) is decorated with scenes from Swiss history, and runs by the **Water Tower**—a symbol of the city. The shorter **Spreuerbrücke** is adorned with Kaspar Meglinger's eerie *Totentanz* (*Dance of Death*) paintings. For a bird's-eye view of Lucerne and the Alps, climb the medieval fortifications with their numerous towers. (Open May-Oct.) Don't miss **Das Löwendenkmal** (the lion monument), a huge lion carved into the face of a rock dedicated to the Swiss mercenaries of Versailles. Mark Twain dubbed it "the saddest and most compassionate piece of rock on earth;" from Schweizerhofquai turn left on Löwenstrasse and follow the signs. In the **Am Rhyn Haus,** next to the Altes Rathaus, you can see a small but interesting collection of late Picasso works. (Open April-Oct. daily 10am-6pm; Nov.-March Fri.-Sun. 11am-noon and 2-5pm. Admission 2SFr, students .50SFr.)

Richard Wagner lived in the nearby village of **Tribschen** from 1866 to 1872, and his former home has been converted into a museum with memorabilia and an instrument display. (Open May to mid-Oct. Tues.-Sat. 9am-noon and 2-6pm, Sun. 10:30am-noon and 2-5pm; mid-Oct. to April Tues., Thurs., Sat. 9am-noon and 2-6pm, Sun. 10:30am-noon and 2-5pm. Admission 3SFr.) Bus #6 or 7 travels to Tribschen from Lucerne's train station.

Steamers ply the sparkling waters of the Vierwaldstätter See; half- or full-day excursions can be combined with mountain hiking or strolls along the lake. (10-30SFr round-trip, free with Eurailpass, 50% off with InterRail. Boats depart from Lucerne near the train station.) Take the train to Engelberg and then four cable cars up **Mt. Titlis.** The glacier is open for hiking in the summer, and there is good skiing in the winter.

Lucerne's world-renowned **International Festival of Music** will hold its 50th Jubilee in 1988. The celebration will include a first-time restaging of the Medieval Easter plays *(Osterfest Spiele)* at the Weinmarkt fountain, March 18-26. A classical music festival will be held Aug. 17-Sept. 10, 1988. Contact the Central Booking Office at Box 424, 6002 Lucerne (tel. 23 52 72), or Dailey-Thorpe Inc., 315 W. 57th St., New York, NY 10019, for information and tickets. The equally renowned **International Rowing Championships** will be held on the **Rotsee** in mid-July, 1988.

The **Information Office** (tel. (041) 51 71 71) is located next to the station on Frankenstr. 1. They will help you get a room for a 2.50-3.50SFr fee. (Open Mon.-Fri. 8am-noon, 2-6pm, Sat. 9am-noon. Closed Sun. and holidays.) **SSR,** Mariahlfgasse 3 (tel. (041) 51 13 02), handles budget travel. (Open Mon. 1:30-6pm, Tues.-Fri. 9:30am-noon and 1:30-6pm, Sat. 9:30am-noon.) **Telephones** and the **post office** are to the left of the station on Bahnhofstr. (Open Mon.-Sat. 7am-9pm, Sun. telephones only 8am-9pm.) The **train station** (tel. (041) 21 33 11) has a **currency exchange** (open Mon.-Fri. 7:30am-9pm, Sat.-Sun. 7:30am-7:30pm) and **bicycle rental** at the luggage desk (9SFr per day with railpass or ticket, 12SFr without.)

Though far from town, the cheapest beds are at the **Jugendherberge Am Rotsee (IYHF),** Sedelstr. 12 (tel. (041) 36 88 00). Take bus #1 to Schlossberg, then follow Friedentalstr. (10 min.); or take bus #18 to Gopplismoos. Laundry facilities. (17SFr, breakfast included. Reception open 5-10pm. Curfew 11:30pm. Open year-round.) **Touristen Hotel Luzern,** St. Karliquai 12 (tel. (041) 51 24 74), on the river, 15 minutes from the station, has large rooms and helpful management. (30SFr per person in rooms with 3 bunkbeds, doubles 72SFr; students 10% less. Reception open June-Aug. 7am-9pm; Sept.-May 7:30am-noon and 4-9pm.) **Camping Lido,** Lido str. (tel. (041) 31 21 46), has a fantastic location on the Lido beach, a 30-minute walk from the station. Cross the Seebrücke and turn right along the quay, or take bus #2 toward Verkehrshaus. Tennis, pool, and other sports facilities nearby. (4.80SFr per person, 2SFr per tent. Open in summer only.) To get to **Camping Horw** "Steinibachried" (tel. (041) 475 58), take bus #20 from the station to **Horw Rank** (20 min.). (4.60SFr per person, 2SFr per tent. Open year-round 8am-10pm.)

You can buy groceries along the quays every day; a particularly good selection of produce is available on market days (Tues. and Sat.). There's a **Migros** market at Hertensteinstr. 44. (Open Mon.-Wed. and Fri.-Sat. 8am-6:30pm, Thurs. 8am-9pm.) **Schlüsselstube,** Franziskanerplatz 12, specializes in Yugoslavian and Swiss food (8-17SFr). **Wirtshaus Zur Schmiede,** on Pilatusplatz, serves dinners composed, not surprisingly, of *Würste* (sausage) for 10-15SFr. **Bristol-Vegetarian Restaurant,** nearby at Obergrund 3, offers a wide variety of vegetarian dishes for 6-15SFr. Although nightlife in Lucerne is basically colorless, **Zum Storchen,** on Kornmarktplatz, is fun. (Open Mon.-Sat. 8:30pm-12:30am.)

Berne (Bern)

Capital of Switzerland, Berne is a calm, beautiful city, lined with seventeenth-century arcades and dotted with colorful fountains. The story goes that the city got its name when its founder, Berchtold of Zahringen, was advised by his counsels to go on a hunt, and to name his city after the first catch. The famed beast was a bear; today the heraldic animal of the city is everywhere.

Practical Information

Tourist Office: Verkehrsbüro, on the ground floor in the train station complex (tel. 22 76 76). Very helpful and efficient. Pick up a map and the valuable pamphlet *This Week in Berne.* They make room reservations; when closed, check their board for hotel availability. Open May-Sept. Mon.-Sat. 8am-8:30pm, Sun. 9am-8:30pm; Oct.-April Mon.-Sat. 8am-6:30pm, Sun. 10am-5pm.

Budget Travel: SSR, Hallerstr. 4 (tel. 24 03 12), behind the university. Take bus #12 to Universität. BIGE tickets and other discounts. Open Mon.-Fri. 10am-6pm.

American Express: Bubenberg 11 (tel. (031) 22 94 01). Mail held 1 month. All banking services. Open Mon.-Fri. 8:30am-6pm, Sat. 9am-noon.

Currency Exchange: At the train station. Open daily 6:10am-10pm.

Post Office: Schanzenpost 1. Open Mon.-Fri. 7:30am-6:30pm, Sat. 7:30-11am. Limited services daily until 11pm.

Telephones: At the train station. Open Mon.-Sat. 6:30am-10:30pm, Sun. 7am-10:30pm. **Telephone code:** 031.

Trains: Information (tel. 21 11 11).

Transportation: For all buses and street cars of the **SVB** (tel. (031) 22 14 44), buy a Touristen-Karte (3SFr for 1 day, 5SFr for 2 days) available at the station or at Bubenbergplatz 5.

Emergencies: Police (tel. 117). **Ambulance** (tel. 144).

Embassies: U.S., Jubiläumstr. 93 (tel. 43 70 11). **Canada,** Kirchenfeldstr. 88 (tel. 44 63 81). **U.K.,** Thunstr. 50 (tel. 44 50 21). **Australia,** Alpenstr. 29 (tel. 43 01 43). Travelers from **New Zealand** should consult their consulate in Geneva. **France,** Schosshaldenstr. 46 (tel. (031) 43 24 24). All tourists to France must now have a visa. Open Mon.-Fri. 8:30-noon for visas. **Spain,** Brunnadernstr. 43 (tel. 44 04 12).

Hitchhiking: For Geneva and Lausanne, take bus #11 to terminus Brückfeld. For Interlaken and Lucerne, take tram #5 to terminus Ostring. For the Autobahn north, take bus #20 to terminus Wyler.

Accommodations and Camping

The hotel situation is bleak. Unless you stay at the youth hostel, you will pay at least 40SFr for a single. Guesthouses a few miles from town, though, offer rooms for 20-30SFr. The tourist office has information on these, and will help you with hotel reservations.

Jugendhaus (IYHF), Weihergasse 4 (tel. 22 63 16), near the river and below the Houses of Parliament (10 min. from the station). Take the stairs down to the river from near the Bundesterrasse. A fine riverside hostel, clean, with balconies. Crowded, but they'll try to make room (mattress-on-the-floor) if full. Laundry facilities. Members 8SFr, nonmembers 15SFr. Small breakfast 4SFr, lunch or dinner 7SFr. Open 7-9:30am and 5pm-midnight; revelers pay a 1SFr "tax" 10pm-midnight.

Camping: Camping Eichholz, Strandweg 49 (tel. 54 26 02), take tram #9 to terminus Wabern. Rooms (not tents) 10SFr, to be divided by number of people in room, plus 3.80SFr per person. Open May-Sept. **Camping Eymatt** (tel. 36 15 01). Take postal bus Bern-Hinterkappelen in front of the station and get off at Eymatt. 4SFr per person, 4.20SFr per tent. Open year-round. **Camping Kappelenbrücke** (tel. (031) 36 10 07), 12km from Bern on the Aare river. Modern facilities and warm management in a quiet location. Bus and train station 2km nearby. 4.40SFr per person, 4SFr per tent. Open Jan. 15-Nov. 1.

Food

It's best to do your own shopping. The selection is especially good on market days—Tuesday and Saturday at **Bärenplatz** and Thursday at **Waisenhausplatz. Migros** and **Coop** supermarkets are near the train station.

Mensa der Universität, Gesellschaftstr. 2, past Hochschulstr., northwest of the station. Take bus #12 to Universität stop. A good university cafeteria. 6SFr, students 4.50SFr. Open Mon.-Thurs. 11:30am-1:45pm and 5:45-7:30pm, Fri. 11:30am-1:45pm and 5:45-7:15pm.

Vegetaris, Neuengasse 15. A large vegetarian menu with daily special 5-12SFr. Open Mon. 10am-9pm, Tues.-Fri. 7:30am-9pm, Sat. 11am-2pm.

Gfeller am Bärenplatz, Bärenplatz 10. A pleasant, simple restaurant with an outdoor cafe opposite a flower market, and a cheaper self-service upstairs. Popular with local students. Meals 8-15SFr. Open Mon.-Wed. and Fri. 6:30am-8pm, Thurs. 6:30am-10pm, Sat. 6:30am-6pm.

Sights and Entertainment

The best introduction to Berne is the walking tour described on the tourist office map. The cobblestoned route takes you past the **clock tower** with its famous moving figures. Shows start four minutes before each hour; tours of the tower's interior are given daily May-October at 4:30pm. (3SFr; tickets available at the tourist office.) From there continue on to Kramgasse 49, **Albert Einstein's house** from 1902 to 1909. A look-alike of the genius sells postcards and books. (Open Tues.-Fri. 10am-5pm, Sat. 10am-4pm. Free.) A small alleyway a few blocks down leads to the **cathedral,** a fine example of Swiss Gothic architecture. (Open Mon.-Sat. 10am-noon and 2-5pm, Sun. 11am-noon and 2-5pm.) Across the river are the **Bärengraben** (bear pits), whose residents will perform tricks for you (make circular motions with your finger to engage one) for a bribe. The **Rosengarten** (past the Bärengraben) allows a magnificent view of the old city and the River Aare. Tours of Switzerland's **Parliamentsgebäude** (Parliament) are a great introduction to the country's political system. (Tours hourly 9am-4pm, except when Parliament is in session; ask at the tourist office about visiting an assembly.)

Berne offers many fine museums, several of them grouped together at **Helvetiaplatz** (across the Kirchenfeldbrücke). Take Tram #3 or 5 to Helvetiaplatz. The **Bernisches Historische Museum** exhibits colorful Flemish tapestries and replicas of rural Swiss rooms. (Open June-Sept. Tues.-Sun. 10am-5pm; Oct.-May Mon. 10am-noon and 2-5pm, Tues. and Thurs.-Sat. 9am-noon and 2-5pm, Wed. 9am-noon and 5-9pm. Admission 3SFr, free Sat.) The **Kunstmuseum** features 2000 of Paul Klee's works, some fine impressionist works, and a comprehensive collection of regional art. (Open Tues. 10am-9pm, Wed.-Sun. 10am-5pm. Admission depends on the exhibits visited. Not more than 3SFr.) The **Swiss Alpine Museum**'s collection of maps and old hiking equipment will interest visiting hillwalkers. In addition, it has several exhibits on the flora and fauna of the Alps. (Open Mon. 2-5pm, Tues.-Sun. 10am-noon and 2-5pm. Admission 1SFr.)

Berne's most famous nighttime haunt is the **Kornhauskeller,** Kornhausplatz 18 (tel. 22 11 33). From the outside, this former grain vault looks stark, but the interior has been transformed into a huge beer cellar with live music. (Cover 5SFr, less if you eat. Open Tues.-Sun. until 11pm.)

Near Berne

The **Schwarzsee** (Black Lake) appears black because of the volcanic rock beneath its surface. In summer, daily postal buses leave the train station at 1:30pm, if the weather permits and enough people want to take the trip, and return at 6pm. (20SFr round-trip, free with Swiss Holiday Pass.) Alternatively, you can take the train (8SFr one way, 16SFr round-trip) or hitch to **Fribourg** (not to be confused with Freiburg im Breisgau), a twelfth-century town that was for centuries the home and refuge of German Swiss Catholicism. The river through Fribourg marks the traditional boundary between the French- and German-speaking regions of Switzerland. Notice the names of places to the left and right of the river to see just how abrupt a boundary it was. The **auberge de jeunesse (IYHF)** is at 61, av. Général Guisan (tel. (037) 26 28 98). (Open March-Oct. 5-10pm. Family rooms available. 7SFr per person per night.) Another worthwhile excursion is the trip to **Murten,** a medieval town with arcades and a massive stone castle. In summer, there are boat trips around the **Murtensee.** Take the direct bus to Murten, or take the train to Kerzers and transfer (18SFr round-trip, railpasses valid).

Interlaken and the Berner Oberland

Snow-capped mountain peaks disappearing into the clouds, cool mountain lakes, the jingle of cowbells breaking the perfect silence—this is where Heidi and Toblerone come true. The mighty triad of **Mönch, Eiger,** and **Jungfrau,** with the rest of the Oberland mountain range, dwarf the idyllic countryside below. In summer, the land turns beautiful shades of green and offers countless walking, climbing, biking, and boating opportunities; in winter, the Berner Oberland is dazzling white and popular with skiers. You'll get the most out of the region by walking. Some of the trails are rugged, especially above the tree line, but all are well-marked and well-maintained. You will notice that the yellow signs measure time rather than distance; find out how you compare to the Swiss grandparents on whose walking speed the times are supposedly based. As always, the Alps can be brutal; hike only with adequate clothing, preparation, and a good topographical map. For general planning, the free Jungfrau region map, available at train stations and tourist offices, should suffice. For information about winter sports, general activities, and inexpensive package deals for longer stays, write to the Interlaken Tourist Office, Höheweg 37, CH-3800 Interlaken.

Interlaken

Interlaken is an hour by train from Berne, and is both a starting point for trains to the surrounding mountains and a central point for train connections throughout Switzerland. The town is situated between both the Brienzersee and the Thunersee, and offers access to both lakes. It is heavily touristed; stores selling watches and Swiss army knives (all advertised in English) line the streets, and in winter few of the people you meet will be Swiss.

You'll probably arrive at **Westbahnhof,** where there is a currency exchange, and a branch tourist office which will trade you a map of the town for 1SFr. (Open June-Sept. Mon.-Sat. 7:30am-noon and 1:30-7pm, Sun. 7:30am-noon and 1:30-6:30pm; Oct.-May Mon.-Sat. 7:30am-noon and 1:30-6pm, Sun. 8am-noon and 2-6pm.) There is a tourist information computer on the station platform which gives a lot of general information in three languages. **Ostbahnhof** is used by trains to and from Lucerne, and private railways. The main **tourist office** (tel. (036) 22 21 21), on Höheweg in the Hotel Metropol, offers a room-finding service, currency exchange, maps, and railway/boat schedules. They can be brusque if you're not interested in expensive excursion tickets. (Open June-Sept. Mon.-Fri. 8am-noon and 1:30-7pm, Sat. 8am-noon and 1:30-5pm, Sun. 4-6pm; Oct.-May Mon.-Fri. 8am-noon and 2-6pm, Sat. 8am-noon.) Ask for their list of rooms in private homes if you'll be staying at least three days. (20-30SFr per person per night.) The **post office** is on Höheweg, 5 minutes from the Westbahnhof. The **telephone office** is next door (open May-Sept. daily 7am-9:30pm; Oct.-April Mon.-Sat. 7am-9pm, Sun. 9am-1pm and 5-9pm). You can rent a moped or bike to tour the area at **A. Balmer,** 27 Rosenstr. (tel. (036) 22 42 88). Mopeds cost 30SFr per day, bikes 10SFr per day. (Open Mon.-Fri. 7:30am-noon and 1:30-6:30pm, Sat. 7:30am-noon.)

To escape the high costs, proceed to **Balmer's Herberge,** Hauptstr. 23 in Matten (tel. (036) 22 19 61), a 15-minute walk from either station. Follow the blue signs from the center of town to Grindelwald-Lauterbrünnen. Although dominated by English-speaking travelers in the summer, this hostel receives guests from around the world. Balmer's is understandably popular for its myriad conveniences: currency exchange, bike rental, laundry and kitchen facilities, inexpensive meals, films on videotape, music, television, table tennis, safe deposit boxes, reading room, weight room, a small store, no curfew, and no membership requirements. Once you arrive at Balmer's, sign in and return at 5pm, when beds are assigned. You must sign in again each morning between 7 and 9am. (Dorm beds 12SFr, doubles 25SFr. Showers 1SFr. Breakfast included.) If full, they'll usually offer mattresses on the floor for 8SFr, which makes the place look like a scene from Dickens' *Oliver Twist.* Cheap excursions for hiking and skiing are available through Balmer's as well. If all this doesn't appeal to you, try **Jugendherberge Bönigen (IYHF)** (tel. (036) 22 43 53), accessible by bus #1 from either station. IYHF members only. (12SFr, showers and breakfast included.) **Hotel Spiess,** at Jungfraustr. (tel. (036) 22 25 51), off Höheweg, is friendly, but space is limited, so call ahead. (Singles and doubles 25SFr per person.) The modern **Hotel Tell,** Hauptstr. 49 in Matten (tel. (036) 22 18 25), just down the street from Balmer's, offers spotless, well-furnished singles for 45SFr, doubles for 70SFr; all rooms have baths, and breakfast is included. **Camping** is farther down Hauptstrasse in Matten at **Jungfraublick** (tel. (036) 22 44 14; 5SFr per person, plus 5SFr per tent; open Dec.-Sept.), at **Camping Sackgut,** 15 minutes from the station on Brienzstrasse (tel. (036) 22 44 34; 4SFr per person, 4SFr per tent; open May 1-Sept. 30), or at **Manor Farm** (tel. (036) 22 22 64), a huge place at Neuhaus on the Thunersee (5SFr per person plus 10SFr per tent).

Restaurants are expensive, so you might want to visit the **Coop** across from the Westbahnhof or the **Migros** right down Höheweg. On Tuesday mornings there is a **market** on Jungfraustr. Otherwise, try the *raclette* (from 7SFr) at **Des Alpes** or the great cheese fondue (12.50SFr) at the posh **Im Gade** (both on Höheweg). Nightlife on Höheweg is fairly active, mainly due to the large number of young people. A popular spot is **Buddy's,** a small and usually crowded English pub that serves cheap beer until 12:30am. The crowd then moves to **Johnny's Dancing Club** on Höheweg. (Cover on weekends. Open until 2am.)

Schiller's **Wilhelm Tell** is staged annually from late June through early September on Thursday and Saturday at 8:15pm (rain or shine) in a huge outdoor amphitheater a bit south of the city. The play has been performed for 75 years, and incorporates horses and cows which are paraded through the streets before the performance begins. Performances are in German; you can buy an English synopsis. Contact **Tellbüro,** Bahnhofstr. 5 (tel. (036) 22 37 23), or the tourist office for information and tickets. (8-25SFr. Disabled access.)

Lakes

Both the **Brienzersee** to the east and the **Thunersee** to the west are lined with classic Swiss towns and scenery. Steamers on the lakes can get you nearly any place you want to go. (Eurailpasses valid, InterRail 50% off; day cards July-Aug. 26SFr, Sept.-June 19SFr.)

The medieval architecture of **Spiez,** a 20-min. train ride from Interlaken on the Thunersee, culminates in its **castle,** which juts into the lake amidst thatched cottages and vineyards. (Open April-Oct. Mon. 2-6pm, Tues.-Sun. 9:30am-noon and 2-6pm.) Another fun boat trip on the Thunersee (½ hr.) takes you to the **Beatushöhlen,** prehistoric caves with interesting rock formations. (Open April-Oct. daily 9am-5pm. Admission 5SFr.) The **tourist office,** Thunstr. 4 (tel. (033) 54 72 56) has more information on lake trips. There is a small **Jugendherberge (IYHF)** in Faulensee at Quellenhofweg 66 (tel. (033) 54 19 88). (12SFr. Curfew 10pm. Open Jan.-Oct.)

Brienz, on the Brienzersee, makes a great daytrip from Interlaken (20 min.). There you'll find the new **Ballenberg Swiss Open-Air Museum,** a 50-acre country park in which rural dwellings from every region of Switzerland are on display, and Swiss artisans are busily at work. The park is about an hour's walk from the train station, but a regular bus (5.20SFr round-trip) connects the two. (Open June-Sept. daily 9:30am-5:30pm; April-May and Oct. daily 10am-5pm. Admission 8SFr, students 4SFr.) The **Brienz Rothorn Bahn,** a small open train, snakes up the Rothorn and operates from June 7 to the end of September. (26SFr one way; you can hike down.) Stop in at the **Information Office** (tel. (036) 51 32 42) across from the train station. (Open Mon.-Fri. 8am-noon and 2-6pm, Sat. 8am-noon; July-Aug. Sat. also 2-5pm.) The train station also rents **bicycles** (6SFr per 4 hr., 7SFr per day, and an additional 2SFr if you don't have a train ticket). There is a **Jugendherberge (IYHF)** on Strandweg 10 in Brienz (tel. (036) 51 11 52), on the lake. (9.60SFr. Breakfast 3.50SFr, dinner 6.50SFr. Check-in 5-6pm and 7-8pm. Curfew 10:30pm. Open March and May to mid-Nov.) Along the same stretch are two campgrounds: **Camping Seegärtli** (tel. (036) 51 13 51; 5.50SFr per person plus 2-4SFr per tent; open summer only), and **Camping Aaregg** (tel. (036) 51 18 43; 4.40SFr per person plus 2SFr per tent; open year-round). Boat and canoe rentals are available here too.

Another excursion on the Brienzersee is to **Giessbach Falls,** where you can climb for hours beside the cascade, and then walk the peaceful path to **Iseltwald.** You can camp in Iseltwald at **Camping du Lac** (tel. (036) 45 11 48; 3.50SFr per person plus 2SFr per tent; open May-Sept.).

Valleys

There are two major valleys of the Berner Oberland: Lauterbrünnen to the southwest and Grindelwald to the southeast. Both valleys become busier and considerably more expensive during ski season. On the plus side, the ski areas abound with dishwashing, bartending, etc. . . . jobs. It's best to look immediately after the first heavy snowfalls, usually in December. Hourly trains on a private railway run to each valley from Interlaken Ostbahnhof (8.40SFr round-trip to Lauterbrünnen, 12.80SFr to Grindelwald). Hitchhiking is possible, as long as you walk from Interlaken to Wilderswil to avoid the local traffic. The private mountain railways and cable cars that lace the mountains are outrageously priced. For information on skiing, see the end of this section.

Though tourist-filled, **Grindelwald,** beneath the north face of the **Eiger,** is a skier and climber's town par excellence. There is a small information counter at the train station. The main **Verkehrsbüro** (tel. (036) 53 12 12), up the street and on the right in the Sportzentrum, can find you rooms in private homes for stays of more than a week. (Open July-Aug. Mon.-Sat. 8am-noon and 2-6pm; Sept.-June Mon.-Fri. 9am-noon and 2-6pm, Sat. 9am-noon and 2-5pm.)

The **Jugendherberge Die Weid (IYHF)** (tel. (036) 53 10 09) is a 20-minute climb up Terrassenweg (take the right fork from the train station), in a beautiful old wooden house with a spectacular view. The warm management will recommend shops that rent equipment for skiing and hiking. Come early and write your name on the list to reserve a place, then check in 4:30-6:30pm. Small rooms, some with balconies. (10.30SFr, showers and sleep-sack included. Breakfast 4SFr, dinner 7SFr. Curfew 10pm.) If it's full, try the **Naturfreundehaus,** also on Terrassenweg (tel. (036) 53 13 33). **Hotel Sonnenberg,** uphill on Sonnenweg (tel. (036) 53 10 15), has singles for 41SFr and doubles for 85SFr. There are five **campgrounds** in Grindelwald. Try **Sand** (tel. (036) 53 29 23) at Grindelwald-Grund; walk left from behind the station and take the first right. (4.20SFr per person, 1SFr per tent. Open year-round.) You can also hike through town toward the glacier tip and turn right to **Camping Gletscherdorf** (tel. (036) 53 14 29), a small campground with a spectacular view of the mountains. Clean facilities. (4SFr per person, 2.50SFr per tent. Open year-round.) On the outskirts of town, there are also several *Zimmerfrei* (rooms in private homes). Restaurants are fairly expensive; for a do-it-yourself meal, buy provisions from the **Coop** across from the tourist office. Grindelwald has a self-service **laundromat** next to Gasthof Steinbock in the center of town. (Wash 1.40SFr, dry 1SFr, soap 1SFr. Open 24 hours.)

Climb or ride the lift to the **First** mountain for breathtaking views. (18.40SFr one way, 27.20SFr round-trip.) Alternatively, you can make your way to the summit of the **Männlichen** for a spectacular view of the Eiger, the Mönch, and Jungfrau; take the cable car from the Grindelwald-Grund station to Männlichen (34.20SFr round-trip). From Männlichen the cable car runs down to **Wengen** (13.40SFr one way), a steep little village in which small electric flatcars carry goods brought up by helicopter and train. Wengen is a major center for winter sports and hosts the world's longest and most challenging downhill race every year in January. If you want to stay in Wengen, stop by the **information booth** at the train station (tel. (036) 55 14 14; open until 8:30pm). **Chalet Schweizerheim** (tel. (036) 55 15 81) has quiet rooms from 25SFr, breakfast included.

Lauterbrünnen means "pure springs," but the most dramatic water here sails down the sheer walls of the narrow, glacier-cut valley. The **Verkehrsbüro** (tel. (036) 55 19 55) is right above the train station. (Open Mon.-Sat. 8am-noon and 2-6pm. Stay at the **Matratzenlager Stocki,** (tel. (036) 55 17 54), through the underpass to Stocki from the train station. Rows of mattresses fill large rooms, but kitchens and showers are clean. (In summer 7SFr; in winter 8SFr. Open Jan.-Oct.) **Camping Schützenbach** (tel. (036) 55 12 68) offers showers, laundry facilities, and kitchen use. (4.80SFr per person, 4SFr per tent; 9SFr in a dorm room, 13SFr in a 4-bunk room. Open year-round.) Follow the signs towards Trümmelbach from the station (15 min.). **Camping Jungfrau** (tel. (036) 55 16 38), straight up the main street from the station toward the large waterfall, has kitchens, showers, lounges, snack bar, and cheap beds. (4.80SFr per person, 2.40SFr per tent; 11SFr per person in a dorm room. Open year-round.)

To reach the higher villages, catch a cable car (hourly 7am-5pm) from **Stechelberg,** a one-hour walk from Lauterbrünnen. (A postal bus also runs hourly 7am-5pm; 7.20SFr round-trip.) There is a **Naturfreundehaus** (Alpenhof, tel. (036) 55 12 02) in Stechelberg (8SFr; breakfast 3SFr, dinner 8SFr), and also a **Coop** and **post office** (both open Mon.-Fri. 8am-noon and 2-5pm, Sat. 8-11am). From Stechelberg you can hike and/or take cable cars to the tiny village of **Gimmelwald,** where there is a **Jugendherberge (IYHF)** (tel. (036) 55 17 04). It's small, so call ahead. (Members 5.50SFr, nonmembers 12.50SFr. Showers 1SFr. No breakfast. Curfew 10pm.) You can also get to **Mürren,** and the top of the **Schilthorn.**

Perhaps the most stunning trip you can make in this area—or in all of Switzerland—is the ascent of the **Jungfraujoch** (3454m). Trains start at Interlaken's Ostbahnhof and travel to either Grindelwald or Lauterbrünnen. From either town trains continue to **Kleine Scheidegg** (28.20SFr round-trip). Kleine Scheidegg can also be reached by four-hour hikes from Grindelwald or Lauterbrünnen. If you take the 6:40am or 7:40am train from Interlaken, the Jungfraubahn from Klein Scheidegg to the Jungfraujoch will cost you 51SFr; otherwise the fare is 95SFr. Eurailpasses aren't valid on this private railway, but Swiss rail passes entitle you to a 25% discount. While you may pay through the nose to ride this train, workers at the turn of the century paid with their lives in laying the track. The rail is chiseled out of solid mountain and goes right through the Eiger and Mönch. You'll have little to see as the train makes its way through the mountain, but two huge "windows" have been cut. The first window exposes the infamous North Face of the Eiger; the second stop offers an incredible view of the **Eismeer** glacier. At the summit, you'll be rewarded with a once-in-a-lifetime spectacle: a panorama stretching to the Black Forest in Germany. Included in the price are visits to the **Ice Palace** (a maze cut into the ice), and the **Sphinx** scientific station. The Jungfraujoch can be very disappointing on a cloudy day—call (036) 55 10 22 for a weather forecast. Even in midsummer, the summit is extremely cold and the line to the elevator which takes you to the Sphinx is often an hour long; bring warm clothing and, unless you're wealthy, food.

Skiing

There are 4 types of **ski passes** for the Oberland; the Jungfrau Region pass is the most extensive (44SFr per day). Prices go down the longer you stay; seven-day passes cost 194SFr. The Kleine Scheidegg/Männlichen pass (36SFr per day) covers more trails than you'd tire of in a week. Ski rental is available throughout the valleys; skis, boots, and poles rent for about 35SFr the first day, less each day thereafter. The **ski schools** in Grindelwald (tel. (036) 53 20 21) and Wengen (tel. (036) 55 20 22) have information on classes. Information on weather and ski conditions is at (036) 23 18 18.

In Interlaken, **Balmer's Herberge** offers daily packages (open to anyone) that include ski rental, transportation, and ski passes. You'll save anywhere from 10-40SFr. Cross-country skiing is much cheaper; rental is a standard 18SFr per day and trails are open to everyone for free.

Zermatt and the Matterhorn

The Matterhorn is an ornery giant, its peak often shrouded in thick clouds; the best time to catch a glimpse is at dawn or dusk. To climb this beast you need a mountain of money; hiring a guide costs over 500SFr. You also need to know what you're doing. The best time to climb the Matterhorn is from mid-July to mid-September. The trip to the top takes two days—the first takes you to **Hörnli Hütte,** the camp at the foot of the Matterhorn; the rest of the distance is covered on the second day. If you're tempted to try your skill without a guide, spend an hour studying the inscriptions on graves of would-be climbers in the cemetery across from the church; they all read *Bergtod* (mountain death). Information on other hikes for the experienced and the novice alike is available at the **Mountaineering Office** (tel. (028) 67 34 56), near the tourist office. (Open July-Sept. Mon.-Fri. 8:30am-noon and 4:30-7pm, Sat. 4:30-7pm, Sun. 10am-noon and 4:30-7pm.) Be warned that when the map says "steep ascent," it means it. Even on day hikes, bring warm clothing, plenty of food, and rain gear.

The day hike from Zermatt to Hörnli Hütte is particularly scenic, even if you don't plan to continue on. It's possible to ride the *téléferique* as far as Schwarzsee (12.50SFr one way, 20SFr round-trip) and then hike the rest of the way (2-3 hr., depending on the depth of the snow). The famed **Gornergratbahn** will lift you to 3100m and phenomenal panoramas, but it is expensive. (26SFr one way, 42SFr round-trip; 25% off with Swiss Holiday Card, 50% with InterRail, no discount with Eurailpass.) Zermatt has more summer ski trails than any other Alpine resort. An all-day lift ticket costs 40SFr, and equipment rental will run about 35SFr. There are also numerous cross-country ski trails (20SFr per day). Rent your equipment as close as possible to the *téléferique* (follow the river toward Winkelmatten). There is a **summer ski school** (tel. (028) 67 24 56) next to the post office. For **alpine rescue,** call (028) 67 22 82.

In Zermatt, the strictly run **Jugendherberge (IYHF)** (tel. (028) 67 23 20) is clean and comfortable, and it pipes Alpine yodeling tunes into the bedrooms. From the train station, walk down the main street, turn left at the church, and follow the yellow signs for 10 minutes. (9.75SFr. Breakfast 4SFr; dinner 6.50SFr. Open June-Oct. and mid-Dec. to April 7:30-9am and 5-8pm.) The proprietor of the **Hotel Bahnhof** (tel. (028) 67 24 06), to your left as you exit the station, will tell you where and when you can see the Matterhorn best. A lovely kitchen downstairs complements the cozy, rustic rooms. (Dorm beds 16-18SFr, singles 25SFr, doubles 40-46SFr.) **Camping Matterhorn Zermatt,** at the entrance to the town, charges 5.50SFr per person. (Open June-Sept.)

The **Coop** supermarket is right across the street from the station. Cafes are expensive, but cheese fondue goes for 14SFr, and *raclette* is usually a good deal at 5SFr. Zermatt's oldest restaurant, the **Café du Pont,** next to a rushing river at the end of the main street, serves hearty Alpine fare. (Open daily 9am-midnight.)

To reach Zermatt, take the private railway from Visp or Brig. (17 trains per day; 1½ hr.; Eurail invalid, InterRail 50% reduction.)

Uncrowded **Saas Fee,** one valley east of Zermatt, marks the end of the great *cirque* of the Alps that begins in Chamonix. This wonderful town, banned to automobiles, is a paradise in summer or winter. Though you can't see the tilted pyramid of the Matterhorn, the brilliant ice of the overhanging Feegletscher and the stark majesty of 4000m peaks more than compensate for its absence. If you're coming from Zermatt, you can take the train or hitch to **Stalden** and then take the bus from there to Saas Fee (9.70SFr one way, 13SFr round-trip). From Visp or Brig, you must reserve a place from the post office, or call the train station information office at Brig (tel. (028) 23 19 01). The price from Visp is 12.60SFr one way, 20SFr round-trip; from Brig, 14.20SFr one way, 22.40SFr round-trip. Hitching directly to Saas Fee is possible but difficult. Cable cars travel from the town to **Längfluh** and **Felskinn** (17SFr to ascend, 12SFr to descend; 22SFr round-trip). A one-day pass for summer skiing costs 34-36SFr; there are fewer trails open here than in Zermatt.

The **tourist office,** located in front of the bus station, will help with maps and room reservations. (Open Mon.-Sat. 8am-noon and 2-6pm; also Sun. 11am-noon and 5-6pm during the winter and summer high seasons.) Five minutes' walk from the bus station is a **Jugendherberge (IYHF)** (tel. (028) 57 27 24); go right as you exit the station, past the parking lot, and follow the yellow arrows. Reception next door at Hôtel Mascotte. The hostel's rooms (4-8 beds) are very comfortable and have private showers. (10SFr. Breakfast 5SFr; dinner 10SFr. Prices higher in winter.) When the hostel is full, try the **Feehof Garni** (tel. (028) 57 23 08) at 26-34SFr per person, depending on the season. For a bite to eat, sample the *Gschwelti mit Käse* (small potatoes served with a variety of cheeses; 6.50SFr) in the **Restaurant Vieux Chalet** on the main street.

French Switzerland

Geneva (Genève)

Geneva remains the international city it has been for centuries, epitomizing the Swiss neutrality which has welcomed such diverse visitors as Lenin and Borges. The birthplace of the Red Cross and once home to the League of Nations, Geneva today is the European base of the U.N. and a favoured neutral ground for negotiating belligerents. Diplomats and the executives of innumerable corporations fill Geneva's offices, though seldom its spotless streets.

Orientation and Practical Information

At the westernmost tip of Switzerland, on the shores of Lac Léman, Geneva draws traffic from its own country, from France, and from Italy. Trains arrive at the **Gare Cornavin;** the *vieille ville* (old town) and the bustling shopping district are on the opposite bank of the Rhône. The tourist office maps aren't very good; look for the one published by Crédit Suisse.

Tourist Office: Office de Tourisme, in the train station (tel. 45 52 00). Very friendly: They will load you with free maps and brochures and help you find accommodations. Open in summer daily 8am-10pm; shorter hours at other times.

Budget Travel: SSR, 3, rue Vignier (tel. 29 97 33). BIGE and charters. Open Mon. 1-5:30pm, Tues.-Fri. 9:30am-5pm, Sat. 9:30am-12:30pm.

American Express: 7, rue du Mont-Blanc (tel. 31 76 00). Mail held 2 months. All banking services. Open Mon.-Fri. 8:30am-5:30pm, Sat. 9am-noon.

Trains: Gare Cornavin (tel. 31 64 50). **Currency Exchange:** Open Mon.-Fri. 5:15am-10:45pm, Sat.-Sun. 5:15am-8:45pm. **Telephones:** Open daily 7am-10:30pm. **Telephone code:** 022. **Bike Rental** at the luggage check, starting at 12SFr per day. Open daily 7am-midnight.

Post Office: 18, rue du Mont Blanc. Open Mon.-Fri. 7:30am-noon and 1:45-6pm, Sat. 7:30-11am.

Flights: Information (tel. 98 11 22). Trains leave Gare Cornavin every 10 minutes (9am-11pm) for **Cointrin Airport** (3.40SFr).

Public Transportation: Rides of 3 or fewer stops along routes marked in dark red cost SRr0.90. For 1.50SFr you get a 1-hr. ticket, and 6SFr will allow you to use the system all day.

Ferries: To Lausanne (3 hr., 31SFr round-trip) and Montreux (4 hr., 38SFr round-trip). Information (tel. 26 35 35).

Emergencies: Police (tel. 117). **Ambulance** (tel. 144).

Medical Assistance: There are walk-in clinics throughout the city; the one at 21, rue Chantepoulet (tel. 31 21 20) is convenient. For medical referrals, call 20 25 11.

Consulates: U.S., 1-3 av. de la Paix (tel. 33 55 37). **Canada,** 10a, av. de Budé (tel. 33 90 00). **U.K.,** 37-39, rue de Vermont (tel. 34 38 00). **Australia,** 56-58, rue de Moillebeau (tel. 34 62 00). **New Zealand,** 28a, chemin du Petit-Saconnex (tel. 34 95 30). **Spain,** 7, rue Pestalozzi (tel. 34 46 04). **France,** 11, rue J. Imbert-Galloix (tel. 29 62 11).

Bookstore: Librairie des Amateurs, 15, Grand' Rue, in the old town, has secondhand books in English. Open Mon.-Fri. 9am-12:30pm and 2-7pm, Sat. 9am-12:30pm and 2-5pm.

Laundry: 61, bd. St-Georges, 5 min. from the hostel. Wash 3.20-4SFr, dry 1SFr, soap SFr0.20.

Hitchhiking: Take bus #5 from the station to pl. Albert Thomas. For lifts call **Auto-Stop,** 2, crêt de Champel (tel. 46 79 39). Open Mon.-Tues. and Thurs.-Fri. 3-7pm, Wed. noon-4pm.

Accommodations and Camping

Be sure to ask for the tourist office's brochure *Youth Accommodation.*

Auberge de Jeunesse (IYHF), 28-30, rue Rothschild (tel. 32 62 60). Take bus 4/44 (direction Jardin Botanique) to the second stop. Turn right before the Renault garage onto Rothschild (2 min). A brand new hostel that will undoubtedly impress you. 15SFr per person. Breakfast included. Open in summer 6:30-10am and 4-11pm; otherwise 7-10am and 5-10pm.

Hôme St-Pierre, Petershöfli, 4, cour St-Pierre (tel. 28 37 07), right by the cathedral. Women only. Excellent location but a bit dumpy. Small, so call ahead. Free laundry. Dorm beds 8SFr, doubles 12SFr, singles 16SFr. Showers included. Breakfast 5SFr.

Hotel de l'Etoile, 17, Vieux-Grenadiers (tel. 28 72 08). Take bus #1 or 44 to Plaine de Plainpalais. Comfortable rooms in a renovated building. Singles 40SFr, with bath 45SFr; doubles 60SFr, with bath 70SFr. Breakfast 6SFr.

Le Prince, 16, rue des Voisins (tel. 29 85 44), near the Hotel de L'Etoile. Take bus #1 or 11 to Plaine de Plainpalais. Somewhat shabby. Rooms with color TV. Singles 50SFr, with shower 65SFr; doubles 65SFr, with shower 75SFr.

Camping: Camping D'Hermance (tel. 51 14 83). Take bus #9 to Hermance. Geneva's best. 5.50SFr per person, 2SFr per tent.

Food

Geneva's international flavor permeates its restaurants. You can eat everything here from sushi to American fast food.

Le Zofage (restaurant universitaire), 6, rue des Voisins, off place des Philosophes, near the university. One of the cheapest spots in town to placate your stomach, though institutional. *Plat du jour* (8SFr) comes with salad, bread, and clamor. Open Sun.-Fri. 7am-midnight, Sat. 7am-2am.

Restaurant Manora, 4, rue Cornavin, attached to La Placette department store, not far from the station. Large, pleasant, self-service. Very popular, especially for its desserts. Great *plats du jour* (6-12SFr). Open Mon.-Sat. 7am-11pm, Tues. 8am-11pm.

Tutti Frutti, 21, av. du Mail. Italian and vegetarian specialities. Full meals 10-15SFr. Open Mon.-Sat. noon-2pm and 6-10pm, Sun. 6-10pm.

Pizzeria Pizzaiolo, 29, pl. du Bourg de Four, in the heart of the old town. Tasty, enormous meals at low prices. Open Mon.-Sat. noon-2pm and 7-11pm.

Sights

Climb the north tower of John Calvin's church, the **Cathédrale de St-Pierre,** for a view of the winding streets and flower-bedecked homes of Geneva's old section. (Cathedral open June-Sept. daily 9am-7pm; March-May and Oct. daily 9am-noon and 2-6pm; Nov.-Feb. daily 9am-noon and 2-5pm. Free. Tower open daily 11:30am-5:30pm except when cathedral closes for lunch.)

Most of the city's museums are in the old town. The **Musée d'Art et d'Histoire,** 2, rue Charles-Galland, prides itself on its eclecticism: Exhibits range from ancient Greek vases to Dadaist art. (Open Tues.-Sun. 10am-5pm. Free.) The **Musée d'Instruments Anciens de Musique,** 23, rue Lefort, nearby, contains beautiful stringed instruments. (Open Tues. 3-6pm, Thurs. 10am-noon and 3-6pm, Fri. 8-10pm. Admission 1SFr, students free.) The **Petit-Palais,** 2, terrasse St-Victor, houses a wonderful collection of modern art in a nineteenth-century palace. Classical music echoes through its five floors, and in the second *sous-sol* you can see Geneva's ancient ramparts. (Open Mon. 2-6pm, Tues.-Sun. 10am-noon and 2-6pm. Admission 5SFr, students 3.50SFr.) Attend an assembly at the **United Nations,** take a guided tour, or stroll through the lovely garden. (Open July-Aug. 9am-5:15pm, Sept.-June 9am-noon and 2-5:15pm.)

Geneva's **lakefront** is beautiful. The audacious **Jet d'Eau** (known as "Calvin's bidet" to irreverent foreigners) is the world's tallest fountain. Don't miss the manicured **Jardin Anglais,** with its famous **Horloge Fleurie,** a large clock adorned with flowers, erected in homage to Geneva's clock industry. Two fine beaches front the lake: **Paquis Plage,** at quai du Mont-Blanc (.50SFr), and **Genève Plage** (4SFr). **Ferry tours** of the lake are great fun (10-17SFr).

Entertainment

Pick up *This Week in Geneva,* an invaluable guide to activities both before and after dark, free at the tourist office. Nightlife in Geneva during the summer centers around the cafes and quays, though these tend to be expensive. **Place Bourg-du-Four,** below St-Pierre in the old town, is popular; **Le Clémence,** at #20, is one of its most popular locales. **Quai Gustave-Ador,** with its outdoor musicians and ice cream shops, is another favorite.

Every August, Geneva celebrates itself during the **Fêtes de Genève.** Three days of international musical and artistic celebration culminate in boat shows and a fabulous fireworks display. On Saturdays from June through September, free **organ recitals** are held at St-Pierre. If you come during the first week in August, you'll enjoy the three-day **Fête de Genève,** Geneva's raucous annual affair. The **Fête du Bois de la Batie** in October is also fun. Homesick U.S. citizens and other merrymakers should be in Geneva for the **Fourth of July,** when the local U.S. expatriate community throws a big bash.

Lausanne

On the shores of Lac Léman at the foot of towering Alpine peaks, Lausanne is the headquarters of the International Olympic Committee. In summer, the Quai d'Ouchy is the spot for sailers, swimmers, and waterskiers. But Lausanne was once the seat of bishops, and its old sections retain an ecclesiastical, medieval air.

Lausanne is a short train (or boat) ride from Geneva and Montreux, its neighbors on Lac Léman. The town's streets are incredibly steep, so take advantage of the efficient and inexpensive bus system.

The rue Cité Devant and rue Cité Derrière comprise the heart of the old city. These medieval streets lead to the *pièce de résistance,* the Gothic **Cathédrale.** Famed for its rose window, it's one of the outstanding monuments of Switzerland. (Open March-Sept. Mon.-Fri. 7am-7pm, Sat. 8am-6pm, Sun. 11:30am-6pm; Oct.-Feb. daily 7am-5:30pm. Tower open Mon.-Sat. 9-11:30am and 1:30-5pm, Sun. 2-5pm.) The **Château Sainte Maire,** the bishop's official residence, is a short walk up from the cathedral and has a large and sunny terrace, which offers a good view of Lac Léman. **Place de la Palud,** nearby, has a large fountain where young people congregate. **Place St-François,** a small, quaint shopping district, is also a good spot for people-watching; the **Church of St-François** has brilliantly colored stained glass windows and a fifteenth-century steeple.

Those with a taste for the bizarre will enjoy the **Collection de l'Art Brut,** 11, av. des Bergières. This small museum is devoted to the artwork of eccentric criminals and others suffering from psychological disorders. Jean Dubuffet, the collector, believed that art is at its best when it no longer remembers its name. (Open Tues.-Fri. 10am-noon and 2-6pm, Sat.-Sun. 2-6pm. Admission 5SFr, students 3SFr.) The **Musée Olympique,** 18, av. Ruchonnet, presents the philosophy and history of the Olympics Games. (Open Tues.-Sat. 9am-noon and 2-6pm, Sun.-Mon. 2-6pm. Free.) The **quai de Belgique** is a lakeside promenade flanked by flowers, immaculate gardens, small fountains, and benches. Nature-lovers will also enjoy the statues and placid ponds of the **Parc du Denantou** at the end of quai d'Ouchy.

The **office de tourisme,** 2, av. de Rhodanie (tel. (021) 27 73 21), is located across from the lake, in Ouchy. Take the metro from the train station to the last stop (1.50SFr) and walk 100 yards to the right. (Open daily 8am-6pm.) **SSR,** 20, bd. de Grancy (tel. 9021) 27 56 27), has valuable information on budget travel and discount airline tickets. (Open Mon.-Fri. 9:30am-5:30pm.) Lausanne's comfortable and modern **auberge de jeunesse (IYHF),** 1, chemin de Muguet (tel. (021) 26 57 82), near Ouchy, looks out to the lake and mountains. Take bus #1 (direction La Maladière) to Le Reposoir, then follow the signs. (Members only. 14SFr. Breakfast included. Reception open 5-10pm. 11:30pm curfew. Cheapest dinner in Lausanne 8SFr.) The **Logements Prés de Vidy,** 36, chemin du Bois-de-Vaux (tel. (021) 24 24 79), charges 18SFr per person or 28SFr per double in a lakeside setting. Take bus #1 to La Maladière. (Breakfast 5SFr. Open July-Aug. 8am-noon and 5pm-midnight; Sept.-June 9-11am and 7-10pm.) Nearby, **Camping de Vidy-Lausanne,** 3, chemin du Camping (tel. (021) 24 20 31) charges 5SFr per person (students 4.50SFr) plus 4SFr per tent. (Open year-round.) You can also camp in the hills above Lausanne; ask at the tourist office.

Restaurants are expensive, so morning produce **markets** come in handy: Monday and Thursday on blvd. de Grancy, Tuesday and Friday on rue du Petit-Chêne, and the largest, on Wednesday and Saturday, at pl. de la Riponne and pl. de la Palud in the old city. The **Restaurant Universitaire,** 1, rue de la Barre, near the château, serves daily *menus* for 5SFr. Take bus #16 from pl. St.-François. (Student ID required. Open year-round 11:30am-1:30pm.) **Pinte Besson,** 4, rue de l'Ale, has turned out fondue (9.50SFr) since its grand opening in 1780. Aside from a cheese plate *(croute au fromage)* and a few sandwiches, it's still the only thing served. (Open Mon.-Sat. 7:30am-midnight.) Finally, **Restaurant Lavaux,** 2, rue Neuve, serves filling and inexpensive meals. (Open Mon.-Sat. 7:30am-midnight, Sun. 8am-10pm.)

Montreux

Popular resort and retirement place of the wealthy, Montreux is also host to hordes of footloose young people attracted by its various music festivals. The most famous is the **Montreux Jazz Festival,** to be held July 2 to 17 in 1988, featuring jazz, gospel, blues, big band, and salsa. Tickets cost 55SFr to 75SFr, depending on artist and seat. Write well in advance for information and tickets to Festival du Jazz, Case 97, CH-1820 Montreux, or call (021) 63 12 12. They require payment in full before they will reserve your tickets, which you pick up when you get to town. From late August to October 12, the **Classical Music Festival** comes to Montreux. Write to Festival de Musique, Case 124, CH-1820 Montreux for information (tickets 20-120SFr). In the United States, write to Daily-Thorp Inc., 315 W. 57th St., New York, NY 10019, or call 212-307-1555 for information. Once or twice per week during June, July, and September, and occasionally during August, free concerts—everything from yodeling to rock—are held in the pavilion of the Rouvenaz.

When the festivals are gone, Montreux is refreshingly peaceful. The lakeside promenade is overgrown with exotic tropical plants, and offers a spectacular view of the mountains in the distance. The lake itself is home to swans and sailors alike, and is absolutely magnificent at sunset. An hour away by foot lies the **Château de Chillon,** a remarkably well-preserved thirteenth-century fortress, complete with prison, torture chamber, weapons room, and terrific views. Lord Byron immortalized it in *The Prisoner of Chillon.* (Open June-Oct. daily 9am-5:45pm; Nov.-Feb. daily 10am-noon and 1:30-4:45pm; March-May daily 10am-noon and 1:30-4:45pm. Admission 3.50SFr, students 3SFr.)

Montreux's **office de tourisme,** 5, rue du Théâtre (tel. (021) 63 12 12), is on the lake. Go out of the train station onto av. des Alpes, cross the street, descend the steps to your right, and walk to your left—you'll see the signs. (Open June-Sept. Mon.-Sat. 8am-noon and 1-6pm, Sun. 9am-noon; Oct.-May Mon.-Fri. 8am-noon and 2-6pm, Sat. 8am-noon.) The **Auberge de Jeunesse Haut Lac (IYHF),** 8, passage de l'Auberge (tel. (021) 63 49 34), is a 30-minute walk along the lake to your left, or take bus #1 (direction Villeneuve) and get off at the Hotel Bristol; if your train stops at Montreux's Territet station, get off, as the hostel is only three minutes away. Spotlessly clean with very comfortable rooms, this centrally located hostel fills quickly, especially in July. Call ahead and reserve, or arrive well before 5pm. (Members only. 14.20SFr. Breakfast included; lunch or dinner 8SFr. Open 7-9am and 5-10pm. Flexible curfew.) Right downtown, the **Hôtel Elite,** 25, av. du Casino (tel. (021) 63 67 33), is inexpensive and respectable. (Rooms start at 30SFr per person with breakfast.) In nearby **Villeneuve** there is luxurious lakeside camping at **Les Horizons Bleues** (tel. (021) 60 15 47; 3.40SFr per person; open April-Sept.; closes at 10pm). Also in Villeneuve is **Camping Plage** (tel. (021) 60 14 11; 5SFr per person, 4SFr per tent; open May-Sept.). During the Jazz Festival, Montreux offers free camping to ticket holders in Villeneuve. **La Locanda,** 44, ruelle du Trait, off av. du Casino, is a clean, cheerful restaurant with a pleasant atmosphere and great Italian dishes for 10-22SFr. (Open Mon.-Sat. noon-2pm and 7-11:30pm.)

Near Montreux

Southeast of Montreux lies **Leysin,** a major resort in the Dents du Midi mountain range. A spectacular cog railway climbs from Aigle up to the town, at 2200m. (All railpasses valid.) Overnight visitors can get a **Carte de Séjour** from the tourist office (tel. 34 22 44); it entitles them to use of an outdoor swimming pool, mini-golf, tennis courts, and ice-skating rink. The **Club Vagabond** (tel. (025) 34 13 21) also serves as headquarters for the International School of Mountaineering. On the premises is a lively bar (happy hour 5-7:30pm) and disco. Rooms with 3-4 beds and terrace are 19SFr in summer and 24SFr in winter. Excellent dinners for 12SFr. Take the cog railway to Feydey and follow the signs.

In winter, Leysin is littered with skiers. Lift tickets start at 25SFr per day; equipment rental starts at 20SFr per day.

Graubünden (Grisons)

Graubünden is the largest but least populous of the Swiss cantons, stretching from the source of the Rhine in the west to the River Inn in the southeastern region known as the Engadin. It is a symbol of the cultural heterogeneity of Switzerland;

from valley to valley the language changes from German to Romansch to Italian, with a wide range of dialects in between. Even the architecture alters drastically: In the east the houses are decorated plaster; to the south homes are stone and have a Mediterranean look; to the west they are wooden and raised on stilts.

A few developed resorts such as St. Moritz bring winter tourism, high prices, and large crowds. However in most of the region, and throughout most of the year, cattle own the roads and glacial plains. Seasonality is of the utmost importance here; prices and hours depend on the time of year. High season runs December through March (reservations absolutely necessary) and peaks again in July and August. In May and early June virtually everything shuts down.

Chur

About 25km south of Liechtenstein, Chur is a good base for excursions into the surrounding mountains. The largest city in Graubünden, Chur retains the small-town custom of completely closing down between noon and 3pm. The twelfth-century Romanesque **cathedral** has beautiful stained glass windows and a tremendous altarpiece. In summer, outdoor plays and concerts enliven the **Hofplatz,** in front of the cathedral. There are 150 valleys to explore, and the knowledgeable staff at the **tourist office,** Ottostr. 6, Bahnhofplatz (tel. 22 18 18), will help you plan a route. (Open Mon. 1:30-6:30pm, Tues.-Fri. 9am-noon and 1:30-6pm, Sat. 9am-noon.)

Chur's rustic, clean **Jugendherberge (IYHF),** Berggasse 28 (tel. 22 65 63), is about 20 minutes from the train station; walk up Bahnhofstr., turn left on Ouaderstr., walk to the end and turn left onto Leo-Str., bear right at the fork onto Lürlibadstr., and bear right again at the next fork onto Berggasse. The rooms are cramped, with beds literally side by side. (12.30SFr. Sheets, showers, and breakfast included. 10pm curfew. Open Feb.-Nov. 7-10am and 5-10pm.) The **Hotel Franziskaner,** Unteregasse (tel. 22 12 61), is a 10-minute walk from the train station. Take Bahnhofstr., turn left on Grabenstr., take another left after the park, and then follow Unteregasse around the bend. Each of the clean, pleasant rooms has a sink; the cheerful dining room downstairs serves inexpensive meals. (Singles 30SFr, doubles 60SFr, with private shower 70-90SFr. Showers 3.50SFr. Breakfast included.) **Camp Au** (tel. 24 22 83) is a modern and well-equipped campground; take bus #3 marked "Obere Au" (runs until 7pm) to the end of the line. (4.20SFr per person plus 3SFr per tent. Open year-round.) The **Grill-Pizzeria Zur Eiche,** Grabenstr. 39, two blocks west of the post office, serves tasty Italian and Swiss dishes (8-15SFr) on a street lined with cafes and outdoor restaurants. (Open Mon.-Fri. 11am-2pm and 5pm-midnight, Sat.-Sun. 10am-midnight.) There's a **Vilan** supermarket two blocks from the station toward town. (Open Mon.-Fri. 9am-6pm, Sat. 9am-4pm.) The train station has **lockers** (2SFr for 24 hours), **bicycle rental** (12SFr per day, 9SFr with ticket; open daily but 1 day's notice needed to rent a bike), and a **currency exchange** booth that keeps erratic hours. **Post office** and **telephones** are to the right as you exit the station. (Open Mon.-Fri. 8:30am-noon and 2-6pm, Sat. 9am-noon.) Chur's **telephone code** is 081.

Near Chur

The well-known and well-heeled resorts of Arosa, Davos, and Klosters offer great access to spectacular hiking in summer; in winter, the glitterati come to show off their fur coats and to ski.

Arosa, an internationally famous health resort on the Obersee, is beautiful and fresh. In the summer, hiking, tennis, golf, riding, rowing, and swimming are among the athletic options. In winter there are 80km of excellent downhill ski trails as well as 40km of cross-country trails. The little red train of the Rhätische Bahn leaves Chur almost hourly for the hour-long ride to Arosa, taking you over enormous wooded gorges and past endless waterfalls. (Eurail and InterRail valid.) The **tourist**

office (tel. (081) 31 16 21) is a 15-minute walk up from the station. (Open Mon.-Fri. 8am-noon and 2-6pm, Sat. 8am-noon; early July-late Aug. also Sat. 2-4pm.) The local **Jugendherberge (IYHF)** is on Hubelstr. (tel. (081) 31 13 97), down the hill. (10SFr; in winter 11SFr. Breakfast 4SFr; dinner 8SFr. Lockout 9am-5pm. 10pm curfew. Closed May to mid-June and Nov. to mid-Dec.) **Camping** (tel. (081) 31 23 77) is at the southern end of town. (5SFr per person plus 2SFr per tent. Open mid-June to mid-Oct.) **Café Gloor,** toward the end of the main street, has a lovely balcony overlooking the mountains. (Open daily 8:30am-6pm.)

High in Alpine meadows, **Klosters** is filled with wooden-balconied houses and ringed with mountains laced with hiking trails. The **tourist office** (tel. (083) 418 77) is one block from the train station. Take a right on the main road opposite the station and follow the signs. (Open Mon.-Fri. 8am-noon and 2-6pm, Sat. 8am-noon; July-Aug. also Sat. 2-4pm.) If you're staying in Klosters, get a *tourist card* which entitles you to reductions and discounts. A **Coop** grocery store is a good alternative to costly meals; turn right as you leave the train station and walk 25m. (Open Mon.-Fri. 8am-12:30pm and 1:30-6:30pm, Sat. 8am-12:30pm and 1:30-4pm.) SSR operates the **Student Hotel Chesa Selfranga** (tel. (083) 412 55), about a 30-minute walk south of the train station; pick up a map at the train information counter. (10SFr per person, 11SFr in winter.) From **Klostersdorf,** a three-minute train ride from Klosters, a cable car ascends the **Madrisa** for great summer hiking; in the winter, continue up to the ski lifts of the Madrisa area. A ski pass for the six lifts in this area is 31SFr per day. Winter ski specials are offered by the tourist office; also ask at the Chesa Selfranga. Rental prices are 18SFr for cross-country, 28SFr for downhill. The **Swiss Ski School of Graubünden** (tel. (083) 413 80) has an office in Klosters on the Hauptstr. and can help with lessons. More advanced skiers will enjoy the cable car to the Gotschna area. Skipasses covering both the Gotschna and Madrisa lifts start at 40SFr per day. Mountain bikes can be rented from **Doerfji Sport,** Landstr. (tel. (083) 444 50), in the summer months. (35SFr per day, 75SFr for 3 days.)

Davos is another place whose jet-set reputation shouldn't put you off. Divided into Davos-Dorf and Davos-Platz, the town has excellent downhill and cross-country ski slopes. Information and **currency exchange** are in the Davos-Dorf station. (Open daily 6:50am-8:50pm.) The main **tourist office,** Promenade 67 (tel. (083) 351 35), is in the center of town. Another branch is in Davos-Dorf at Bahnhofstr. 7. (Both open Mon.-Fri. 8am-noon and 1:45-6pm, Sat. 8am-noon and 1:45-5pm.) The **Höhwald (IYHF)** (tel. (083) 514 84) in Davos-Wolfgang (train stop Davos-Dorf) is an elegant chalet on the lakeshore. (10SFr. Sheets included. No washing facilities. Breakfast 4SFr; dinner 7SFr. Kitchen use 1SFr. Open 7-9am and 5-10pm. 10pm curfew. Closed late April to mid-June and Nov.) For more luxury, try the **Hotel Terminus,** at the train station, Davos-Platz (tel. (083) 37751), a nice hotel where dormitory-type beds (in a large clean room with individual closets) occupy the extra rooms. Prices increase in the winter, but ask about special ski weeks. (Dorm bed 22SFr with breakfast in summer; 42SFr in winter with breakfast and one additional meal.) For great skiing, start up the **Parsenn bahn** to the lifts above Davos-Dorf. You can eventually ski over to Klosters and enjoy their runs as well. Lift passes for the entire area cost about 45SFr per day. Cross-country rentals run about 18SFr per day, downhill rentals 28SFr. Prices go down after the first day.

Set on a mountain stream between Chur and St. Moritz, the unspoiled Romansch village of **Bergün** is very different from the worldly resorts nearby. Cows roam cobblestone streets and houses are adorned with *Ecker-fenster* (triangular windows). The **tourist office** (tel. (081) 73 11 52) offers friendly advice and good hiking maps; they can also put you up in a primitive sleeping hall for 6 to 8SFr. (Open June-Aug. daily 8am-noon and 3-6pm; Sept.-June Mon.-Fri. only.) Bergün's cheapest private accommodations are at the **Hotel Albula** (tel. (081) 73 11 26), which has small, neat rooms. (Singles and doubles 30SFr. Breakfast included.)

Well worth the half-hour walk from Bergün is tiny, secluded **Latsch,** spectacularly set on a cliff overlooking the valley. From Latsch, it's a 45-minute walk along a narrow road overlooking the valley to the even tinier town of **Stuls.** The thirteenth-century church here, with its painted walls and ceiling, is a minuscule but elegant Romanesque structure. The beautiful **Tours Valley** starts by Bergün and follows the River Tours into the mountains; you can walk its length in about two hours.

St. Moritz

St. Moritz is above all a famous tourist town, as evidenced by the exclusive shops, luxury hotels, and prohibitively high prices. The friendly **tourist office,** p. Mauritius (tel. 331 47), sells detailed maps of the area (10SFr and 19.80SFr), provides advice on trails, and makes free room reservations. (Open Mon.-Fri. 9am-noon and 2-6pm, Sat. 9am-noon and sometimes 2-5pm.) The **information booth** at the train station will exchange money and help you find a room. (Open daily 6:40am-8pm.) Bike rentals are also available at the station (8SFr per day, 6SFr with a railpass). The bus station (on the hillside above the train station) has a **post office** (open Mon.-Fri. 7:45am-noon and 1:45-6:15pm, Sat. 7:45-11am), **lockers** (1SFr), and a **telephone office** (open Mon.-Fri. 7:30am-8:45pm, Sat. 7:30am-7:45pm, Sun. 8am-noon and 3:30-7:45pm). Send mail to Postlagernde Briefe, CH-7500 St. Moritz. The **telephone code** in and around St. Moritz is 082.

The **Jugendherberge Stille (IYHF),** via Surpunt, 60 (tel. 339 69), is modern, luxurious, and immaculate, with only four beds per room. From the station, take the bus to "Sonne" stop or walk around the lake (30 min.); go right as you exit the station, toward the lake, and follow the signs. (13SFr. Sheets and showers included. Breakfast 4SFr; dinner 7SFr. 10pm curfew. Open June 15-Oct. 31 and Dec. 15-April 30.) **Hotel Bernina,** via dal Bagn (tel. 360 22), has large, clean, comfortable rooms. (Singles 35SFr, with bath 45SFr; doubles 70SFr, with bath 90SFr.) For campers, the **Olympiaschanze** (tel. 340 90) is a 45-minute walk or short bus ride south of the station. (4.40SFr per person plus 6SFr per tent. Open year-round.)

Restaurants in St. Moritz are expensive. Plan a picnic and buy your groceries at the **Coop.** (Open Mon.-Thurs. 8am-noon and 1:30-6:30pm, Fri. 8am-noon and 1:30-8pm, Sat. 8am-noon.) The **Hotel Hauser,** in the center of town, is fairly inexpensive. (Open daily 7:30am-9pm.) **Restaurant Valentin,** p. dal Mulin 4, serves a filling tourist menu on sidewalk tables for 12-15SFr. (Open Mon.-Sat.) A variety of dishes can be had at **Au Réduit,** p. Mauritius, a cafe in the modern mall next to the tourist office. (Meals 9-18SFr.)

Near St. Moritz

Most of the towns in Engadin are good daytrips along the train routes from St. Moritz; Eurail and InterRail are valid. **Zuoz,** 30 minutes by train from St. Moritz, is an enchanting melange of Romansch houses, fountains, and carved troughs, the best-preserved in Engadin. The **church,** via Maistra, has sweet-smelling pine pews and hymnals written in Romansch. Down the street, the **tourist office** (tel. 715 10) helps with hiking suggestions and rents bicycles for 12SFr per day. (Open July-Sept. Mon.-Fri. 8:30am-noon and 2-6pm, Sat. 8:30am-noon; Oct.-Nov. Mon.-Fri. 8:30am-noon and 2-6pm.) **Frau Walther** (tel. 713 64), right across from the tourist office, rents singles, doubles, and a triple with a library for 25SFr per person.

Sulsana, on the banks of the Valember, has a **Jugendherberge (IYHF)** (tel. 711 05). From station Cinuos-Chel (5km from Zuoz), turn left and walk 1km back along the main road. This simple, friendly farmhouse, the oldest youth hostel in Switzerland, offers a mattress in the straw, but you must bring your own sleeping bag. (4SFr. Open June-Sept. until 10pm.) **Pontresina** has a slightly less rugged youth hostel; the **Jugendherberge (IYHF)** (tel. 672 23), across from the train station. (12SFr. Open June to mid-Oct. and mid-Nov. to April.) The **Hotel Post** (tel. 663 18) rents inexpensive private rooms. Post buses run hourly between St. Moritz and Pontresina.

From Pontresina southeast, you won't find much in the way of lodging, but drive or take the train on the **Passo del Bernina** route in the direction of Tirano (Italy);

the Rhaetian Railways' Bernina Express (Eurail valid) runs through the Alps at staggering heights. For fantastic hiking, get off at the **Morteratsch** railroad stop and walk up a steep and rocky path (40 min. each way) to the **Chünetta** lookout. Or take the nearby flat but equally rocky path toward the **Morteratschgletscher** (30 min. each way). To combine these two into a single one-hour hike, go halfway toward Morteratschgletscher, follow the sign on the right to Chünetta, then come back down to the station. If you want to continue from Morteratsch, take the train farther to **Diavolezza,** where a cable car (17SFr round-trip) takes you up to one of Europe's most famous glacial panoramas—and spectacular winter skiing. At 4049m, the **Piz Bernina** dominates these mountain peaks. You can also walk up to where the cable car stops (a 3-hr. hike).

Southwest of St. Moritz are the villages of Silvaplana, Sils, Maloja, and Soglio, all along the **Bregaglia Valley,** which leads to Italy. Post buses connect these towns (40 min. each way; St. Moritz-Maloja 8.20SFr round-trip, St. Moritz-Sils 5.80SFr round-trip. Railpasses valid.) The resort town of **Sils** lies on a windy plain between the lakes of Silvaplana and Sils, nestled among imposing mountains. Its 90km of cross-country trails and its six ski lifts make Sils a popular stopover for skiers. The village is divided into two parts; **Sils Maria** includes the **Nietzsche House** (tel. 453 69), near Hotel Edelweiss, where the philosopher spent his summers. (Open in summer Tues.-Sun. 11am-noon and 4-6pm; in winter Tues.-Sun. 4-6pm.) The **tourist office** (tel. 452 37) is in the same building as the Cantonal Bank. (Open Mon.-Fri. 8:30am-noon and 2-6pm, Sat. 9-11am and 3-5pm.) **Sils Baseglia,** at the edge of the water, has a **Ferienlager** (tel. 451 16), the cheapest accommodations in town. (Rooms 24SFr, with breakfast and dinner 34SFr. Open in winter only.) **Sils im Domleschg** has a **youth hostel (IYHF),** at Burg Ehrenfels (tel. 81 15 18), 10 minutes from Sils. (10SFr breakfast included. 10pm curfew. Open April-Oct.)

Situated at the entrance of the Bregaglia valley, **Maloja** lies in an incredible wind tunnel. Some days, you can witness the *Malojaschlange,* a fog condensed into the shape of an enormous snake. The **tourist office** (tel. 431 88) will help with rooms, hikes, and everything else. (Open Mon.-Fri. 8am-noon and 2-6pm, Sat. 8am-noon.) The rustic **Jugendherberge (IYHF),** across from the train station (tel. 432 58), is a convenient place to stay. (10SFr. Lockout 9:30am-4:30pm. 10pm curfew. Open July-Oct. and Dec.-May.) The hotels here are the cheapest in Engandin; rooms with breakfast start at 30SFr per person. **Camping Curtivac** (tel. 431 81) is on the lake just outside of town. (4SFr per person. Open mid-June to late Aug.) Maloja is the starting point for many hikes to neighboring towns; the two-hour walk to Sils, through the mountains above the lake, is especially beautiful.

Ski rental prices are standard throughout the region at about 40SFr per day for downhill equipment, 20SFr for cross-country. Skiing in Zuoz is predominantly easy, St. Moritz has a little of everything, and Diavolezza has mostly advanced runs. The **Swiss Ski School of Engadin** in the St. Moritz tourist office can help you. Ski passes for the entire area run at about 35SFr per adult and 27SFr for children. 3-day passes cost 93SFr and 63SFr.

On the border of Italy, 22km farther down the valley, lies **Soglio,** a tiny Swiss-Italian village considered by some the most beautiful village in Switzerland. Accessible by post bus from Promontogno, Soglio charms visitors with its narrow, crooked streets and ancient houses.

Ticino

Snow caps the mountain tops in the winter, but people in Ticino shed their wooly sweaters, hang up their ski boots, and sail and swim under a warm southern sun the rest of the year. A combination of Swiss efficiency and Italian *dolce vita* make this area special. Lugano and Locarno are the major resort towns, but you can find solitude in the secluded villages along Lago di Lugano and Lago Maggiore. Italian is the official language of the region, but many people also speak German, English, or French. A **Regional Holiday Season Ticket** is good for seven consecutive days of travel on everything from lake steamers to trains to cable cars in Ticino. Ask at railway or tourist offices. (60SFr, ages under 16 30SFr.) The **telephone code** for both Lugano and Locarno is 091.

Lugano

In Lugano, Alpine peaks tower over bronze church domes, narrow cobblestone streets, and lush vegetation. Start your explorations at the sixteenth-century **Cathedral of San Lorenzo,** between the station and the lake. Set high on a hill, it offers a fine view of the city, as well as a masterful Renaissance facade. The **Cathedral of Santa Maria degli Angioli** has a celebrated crucifixion scene by Bernardino Luini. From here, walk along the lake or take bus #2 to the **Thyseen-Bornemisza Gallery** in Villa Favorita, Castagnola, one of the outstanding private collections in Europe, with works by Duccio, Raphael, Titian, Rembrandt, Rubens, Velázquez, and El Greco. (Open mid-April to mid-Nov. 10am-5pm. Admission 8SFr, students 4SFr.) Funiculars climb **Monte San Salvatore** and **Monte Bre,** both of which offer a splendid panorama of the Bernese and Valaise Alps and the Monte Rosa. (San Salvatore funicular runs only mid-March to mid-Nov. Both 11SFr round-trip.)

The busy **tourist office,** riva Giocondo Albertolli, 5 (tel. 21 46 64), makes hotel reservations and provides maps of the surrounding area. (Open Easter-Oct. Mon.-Fri. 8am-noon and 2-6pm, Sat. 9am-noon and 2-5pm; otherwise Mon.-Fri. only.) Hotel information is also available at the train station. The charming **albergho per la gioventù (IYHF)** in Crocifisso-Lugano (tel. 56 27 28), is a short ride on bus #5 to Crocifisso (follow the signs from there), or a 25-minute uphill walk from the station. There's a swimming pool, and the owner's collection of exotic plants and flowers is great. (12SFr. Sheets 2SFr. Breakfast 4SFr. Reception open all day. 10pm curfew. Open mid-March to Oct.) Women can stay in the **Casa della Giovane,** Corso Elvezia 34 (tel. 22 95 53), a building with spotless rooms. (15SFr per person; open only in summer. The mensa here serves good, inexpensive meals.) Another alternative is the **Hotel Montarina,** via Montarina, 1 (tel. (091) 56 72 72), to the right as you exit the train station. (Dorm beds 12SFr, singles 25-35SFr, doubles 50SFr. Breakfast 5SFr. Reception open until 9pm. No curfew. Open March.-Nov.) Two blocks from the tourist office, behind the park, is **Garni del Parco,** viale Cattaneo, 17 (tel. (091) 22 82 38), with cheerful, clean rooms for 25SFr per person, breakfast included. The **Ristorante Analcoolico,** on via Pestalozzi near piazza d'Indipendenza, serves Italian food and vegetarian dishes, but no alcohol. (Open daily 8am-11pm.) You can get a decent meal at the self-service side of **Mövenpick Restaurant,** viale Cattaneo 25. (Open daily 8am-11pm. Pasta, drinks, and dessert for less than 10SFr.) At night, join the local youth at the **Bar Argentino,** piazza Riforma.

Locarno

Locarno shares the climate, charms, and tropical splendor of Lugano, but lacks the crowds. The town's landmark and symbol, the **Madonna del Sasso** (Madonna of the Rock), can be reached by funicular (every 15 min., 4SFr round-trip). (Open daily 6:45am-7pm.) The **Museo d'Arte Moderna** in the Castello Visconti houses a good collection of Dadaist work. (Open Tues.-Sun. 10am-noon and 2-5pm. Admission 3SFr.) To reach Locarno's **tourist office,** viale F. Balli, 2 (tel. 31 86 33), take the main road heading toward the lake as you exit the train station. (Open April-Oct. Mon.-Fri. 8am-7pm, Sat.-Sun. 9am-noon and 2-6pm; Nov.-March Mon.-Fri. 8am-noon and 2-6pm.) There are no hostels. The **Gottardo** (tel. 33 44 54), on the hillside above the station, has singles from 35SFr, doubles from 56SFr, and studios with kitchens for 40-50SFr per person, depending on the season. The **Miralago** (tel. 33 60 32), below the station, charges 35SFr per person. The **Hotel Vecchia Locarno** (tel. 31 65 02), near p. Grande, has restored rooms in an old building off the *piazza.* (Singles 40SFr with bath and breakfast; 32SFr in low season.) The **Coop** on the p. Grande has a wide selection of groceries. (Open Mon.-Fri. 8am-6:30pm, Sat. 7:30am-5pm.) Also on p. Grande, the **Ristorante Svizzero** is good for Italian cuisine. (Open daily 11:30am-10pm.)

Perhaps the most striking section of the region is the **Valle Maggia,** a sparsely populated valley of forests and pastures. Visit tranquil **Bosco Gurin,** a rustic village with waterfalls, old wooden houses, and the only German-speaking populace in Ticino. The town is reached by bus from Cevio (13.80SFr round-trip). Don't miss the boat trip (12.40SFr) to **Brissago Island,** a vast botanical garden of fragrant subtropical plants, palms, and stone promenades. (Open April-Oct. daily 9am-6pm. Admission 3SFr.)

Liechtenstein

Liechtenstein uses Swiss Currency.

Protected by the surrounding mountains, the tiny Alpine principality of Liechtenstein is famous chiefly for its postage stamps, wines, and royal family, whose portrait graces postcards throughout the country. The language here is a dialect of German and the currency is Swiss, but the people have enjoyed the status of a sovereign territory since 1806. In a castle tucked away in the forest high above the vineyards of Vaduz, the capital city, lives the Count of Liechtenstein with his family. The main train station is in **Schaan,** but post buses run frequently between the 11 towns. Schaan's **tourist office** is on Landstr. 9 (tel. (075) 265 65), in the Postillion-Reisen A6 office. (Open Mon.-Thurs. 8:30am-noon and 1:30-6pm, Fri. 8:30am-noon and 1:30-7pm, Sat. 9am-noon.) Schaan also has the only **youth hostel (IYHF)** in Liechtenstein, at Untere Rüttigasse 6 (tel. (075) 250 22). Take the post bus "Vaduz" from either station and request the Hotel Mühle stop; from there, take a left on Marianumstr., then follow the orange signs. (Seniors 16SFr, juniors 13SFr. Showers, sheets, and breakfast included. Dinner 9SFr. Private rooms for longer stays run 18-20SFr. Reception open mid-Dec. to Oct. Mon.-Fri. 7-10am and 5-10pm, Sat.-Sun. 6-10pm.)

Vaduz is the capital and largest town of Liechtenstein. The **Kunsthalle,** Städtle 37, next to the tourist office, exhibits paintings collected in Vienna by the Princes of Liechtenstein. (Open Nov.-March daily 10am-noon and 2-5:30pm; April-Oct. 10am-noon, and 1-5:30pm. Admission 3SFr, students 1SFr.) The world-famous **Postage Stamp Museum,** near the tourist office, features rare stamps from Liechtenstein and other countries. (Open daily 10am-noon and 2-6pm. Free.) Stamp collectors will also have a field day at the **post office** (open Mon.-Fri. 8am-noon, and 1:45-6:30pm, Sat. 8-11am).

The main **tourist office** (tel. (075) 214 43) is in Vaduz, just across the street from the post office/bus stop. They will help you find a room, and will provide maps and general information for the entire principality; the *Wanderkarte Vaduz und Umgebung* (1.50SFr) lists many hiking routes. (Open Mon.-Fri. 8am-noon and 1:30-5:30pm, Sat. 9am-noon and 1-4pm.) Don't forget to get a Souvenir Passport Stamp from the tourist office for 1SFr. The train stations in Buchs and Sargans (both in Switzerland) exchange money and rent **bikes.** (Open daily 6am-8:30pm. Bikes 6SFr for 4 hr., 9SFr for 4-12 hr., and 12SFr for 12-24 hr.)

If the youth hostel in Schaan is full, try **Gasthof Au,** Austr. (tel. (075) 211 17). Follow Städtle Str. to simple rooms and inexpensive meals at the restaurant/outdoor beer garden. (Singles 25SFr, doubles 45SFr, triples 66SFr. Breakfast included. Open Dec.-Oct.) **Camping** is best at **Meierhof, Vaduz Süd** (tel. (075) 218 36). Follow signs to Triesen and Malbun; it's about2km from the center. (4SFr per person, 4SFr per tent. Showers 0.20SFr. Pool available 2SFr. Open year-round.) For hearty fare and delicate pastries, try **Cafe Wolf,** on the main street. Meals run 6-12SFr. (Open Tues.-Sun. 7am-11pm.) The community of **Triesenberg** has a large collection of historical and architectural exhibits from the original thirteenth-century settlers in the **Walser Museum,** Dorfzentrum. (Open Tues.-Sat. 1:30-5:30pm, Sun. 2-5pm. Admission 2SFr, students 1SFr.) The mountain resort of **Malbun** has good skiing at an affordable price. Contact the Malbun **Kurverwaltung** (tel. (075) 265 77) for information on ski week packages (365SFr for 7 days of room and board). Ski passes for six lifts (covering quite a few slopes) cost 24SFr per day, 15SFr for children. Week passes cost 85SFr.

From **Steg** or **Malbun** you can continue on up to the **Pfälzerhute.** There are Alpine huts scattered throughout the principality, with varying conveniences, prices, and opening times. Of the three campgrounds in Liechtenstein, the one in **Bendern** (tel. (075) 314 65) is the cheapest and most convenient, with cooking facilities and an indoor swimming pool; take the bus to Bendern. (3.50SFr per person.) Also worth a look is **Balzers,** Liechtenstein's southernmost and sleepiest village, and the site of **Gutenberg Castle,** which rises abruptly on a vine-covered hill and commands a panoramic view.

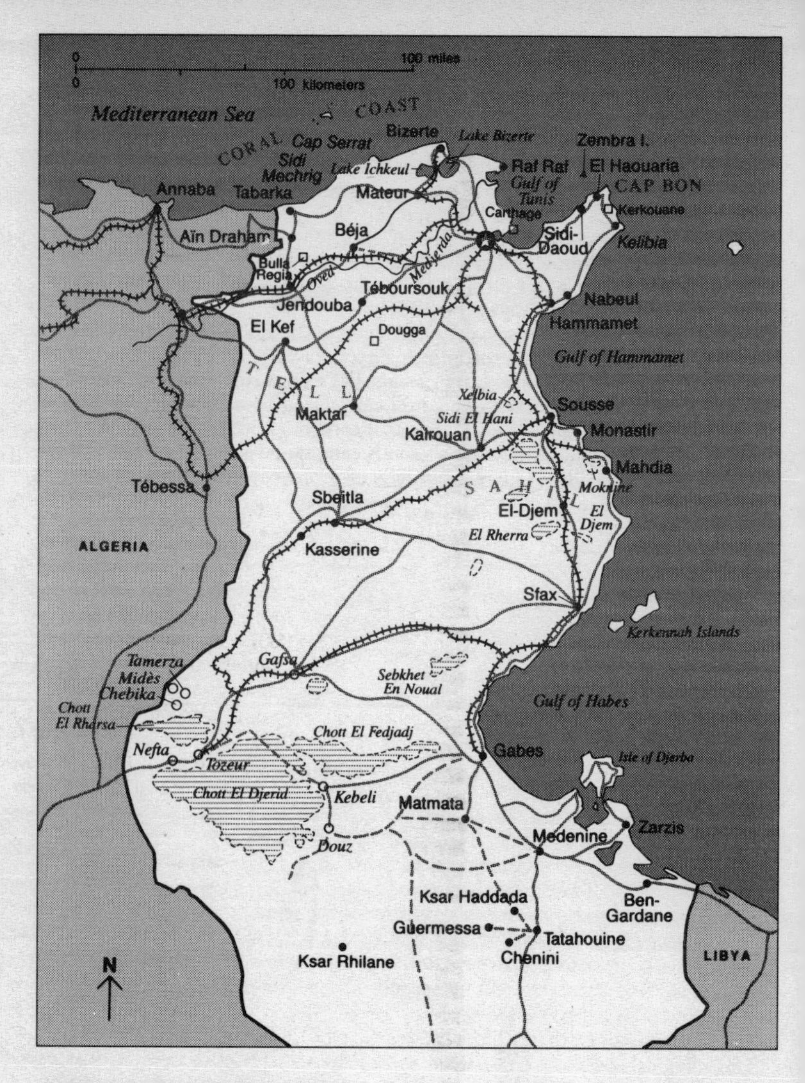

TUNISIA

US$1 = 0.65 dinar (D)
UK£1 = 1.06D

1D = US$1.53
1D = UK£0.94

When Queen Dido of Phoenicia was exiled from Tyre in the ninth century B.C.E., she sailed to Carthage to found a nation "rich in wealth and harsh in the pursuit of war." Thousands of years later, Tunisia's people are far from wealthy, and little is harsh in this gentlest of Arab lands. Tunisia's spectacular ancient sights, long, sandy beaches, vast open spaces, remote green oases, and secluded desert villages will whet even the most jaded traveler's appetite for adventure. However, mass tourism of the package holiday variety dominates the Tunisian travel scene (particularly in summer), and a visit to the larger resorts along the coast will leave you wondering where the Tunisians are. But don't despair—the least bit of effort to get away fom the European crowds reveals a most hospitable and curious people, proud of their country and protective of its Islamic/North African culture.

Relieved of 75 years of French colonial rule in 1956, Tunisia is a study in the attempt to equate a fledgling nation's identity with that of one individual. By most accounts, President-for-Life Habib Bourguiba has served Tunisia well; the country is a model of civic freedoms and social emancipation in the Arab world. But with the President hitting his mid-80s, the country's political situation is growing increasingly turbulent. Crackdowns in June, 1987 were officially aimed at the fundamentalist and allegedly Teheran-backed Islamic Tendency Movement, but critics maintain that suppression of the labor movement, the independent press, and the secular opposition parties signal a wider retreat from liberalism. Whichever path Tunisia takes in the ensuing year, its beaches, ruins, and oases are sure to survive, as is the endearing warmth of its people.

Getting There and Transportation

The cheapest transport between Europe and Tunisia is passenger ferry. There is one ferry per week between Tunis and Trapani (L67,400), Palermo (L108,000), Cagliari (L80,400), and Genoa (L49,000) in Italy, and Marseille, France (630F). Hydrofoils run between Kelibia, east of Tunis on Cap Bón, and Trapani, Sicily, every other day, weather permitting (53D, or L55,000). For travel from Tunisia, book at least one week in advance (especially in late summer) at the Tirrenia Ticket Office, 122, rue de Yougoslavie, in Tunis. For those under 26, **Tunis Air** offers a 50% reduction on flights from most European capitals. (Fares run US$150-175.) It's possible to enter from Algeria by bus, train, or thumb. Train fare from Tunis to Algiers is 20.600D, from Tunis to the Algeria/Morocco border 32D. Because of the ongoing dispute over the Spanish Sahara, traveling from Morocco to Algeria may not be feasible. (See the Morocco chapter for more details.) There are flights to Tunis from Casablanca (88.500D) and Cairo (108D).

Public transportation on major routes within Tunisia is inexpensive and efficient. The 100km from Tunis to Sousse is covered in 2½ hours and costs 2.700D. Buses predominate, especially on smaller routes. Trains connect major cities on the east coast, but don't cover much of the country. Long distance taxis *(louages)* usually offer prices competitive with those of buses and trains on major routes. They leave as soon as they have five people. Generally, *louages* run between specific cities, usually marked on a sign on the roof of the vehicle. For men, hitchhiking can be a fine way of getting around, since Tunisians tend to be eager to talk to foreigners. The going can be slow off the main routes, as cars are small and journeys short. Car rental, though not cheap, is the best option for reaching the oases and desert villages in the south; expect to pay about 220D for one week, with unlimited mileage.

Practical Information

No visa is required of U.S. citizens for visits to Tunisia of up to four months, or for Canadian or British citizens for visits of up to three months. Australian and New Zealand citizens can obtain a visa (1D) for seven days at the point of entry, but should obtain a tourist visa from a consulate abroad for a longer stay.

The best source of information in Tunisia is the **ONTT**, the national tourist service, with offices in all major cities. ONTT publishes a free, pocket-sized gem, the *Tunisia Practical Guide,* with addresses of tourist offices, hotels, car rental agencies, and a wealth of practical information of interest to visitors. In many cities you'll find the local information office—the **Syndicat d'Initiative**—a very helpful supplement to ONTT. Although the official language is Arabic, almost everyone speaks some French, and many tourist personnel speak some English.

In winter, average temperatures in the north hover in the mid-50°F; nights can be especially chilly. In the south in the summer, expect scorching daytime temperatures (above 100°F). Low humidity makes the heat surprisingly bearable, but also speeds dehydration. Especially in the desert, wear loose clothing and a hat, and drink plenty of fluids. Tap water north of Gabes is generally potable, but elsewhere bottled water (120ml per liter) is a wise precaution.

Islam and nationalism are the major forces shaping Tunisian life; the major celebrations each year mark Ramadan, and the birthday of Habib Bourguiba (Aug. 3). The month of Ramadan has a major impact on all aspects of daily life. Shops and services generally close by early afternoon, most restaurants remain closed during daylight hours, and, particularly in smaller communities, eating, drinking, or smoking before sunset is offensive to locals. In larger towns, some tourist restaurants remain open; elsewhere, you can usually buy canned goods and bread in corner shops. Ramadan takes place from April 18 to May 18 in 1988.

You can't buy dinars before you get to Tunisia, since it's illegal to import or export them. When leaving you can only reconvert 30% of your initial exchange, *so save your receipts.* The dinar is divided into 1000 millimes; minor sums are expressed as tens or hundreds of millimes (ml). Banks are open for exchange in summer (mid-June to mid-Sept.) Monday through Friday from 7:30 to 11am; otherwise Monday through Thursday from 8 to 11am and 2 to 4:15pm, Friday from 8 to 11am and 1:30 to 3:15pm. During Ramadan banks are open Monday through Friday from 8 to 11:30am and 1 to 2:30pm; long lines are the norm. After hours, all airports and most large tourist hotels will exchange cash, but the latter may not accept traveler's checks.

All major post offices accept Poste Restante (you'll pay 100-120ml per letter), but many will only hold mail for two weeks. The American Express representative in Tunis will not hold mail. Overseas telephone and telegraph offices are also found at the central post offices; expect a few hours' wait to call collect. The emergency number throughout Tunisia is 197.

Accommodations, Camping, and Food

The ONTT rates hotels on a four-star scale: No-star, one-star, and two-star hotels (outside of Tunis) are in the budget range. No-stars run 1 to 4D per person, one-stars 5 to 7D, and two-stars 8 to 10D. Cheap hotels charge a fixed rate per person; more expensive places tack on a supplement of about 30% for singles. Tunisia's network of IYHF youth hostels and youth centers (about 25, all listed in the *Practical Guide*) charge about 1 to 1.500D per night, but they are often incoveniently located and are rarely frequented by Western travelers; membership cards are never required. Women traveling alone should avoid the cheapest hotels and all hostels; these are generally all male, and harassment can occur. There are few organized campgrounds, though most youth hostels allow camping on the grounds for a few hundred millimes. Freelance camping is possible almost anywhere and particularly common on the beaches, but you shouldn't camp alone—there have been problems with theft. It's a good idea to get permission from the local police or National Guard office before you pitch a tent in a prominent place.

Tunisian cooking reflects the country's competing foreign influences, mixing North African and French cuisines. *Couscous* and potatoes are the usual starches. Vegetables, mostly tomatoes, cucumbers, onions, and olives, are finely chopped and marinated in olive oil, vinegar, and lemon juice for *mechovia,* Tunisia's national salad. *Brik à l'oeuf* is an egg and potatoes (and often a vegetable or cheese) wrapped in pastry and deep-fried so the yolk is still runny. Popular beverages include lemonade, *thé vert* (mint tea), and *café au lait.* Although Islam frowns upon alcohol, beer (600ml per bottle) and wine (under 2D per bottle) are widely served.

Tunis

Tunis is the heart of Tunisia in every sense. Its *medina* is vibrant and vast, and, while the *souks* of Old Tunis are touristy, the ruins of Carthage, the beautiful village of Sidi Bou Said, and the National Museum of the Bardo all make Tunis and environs worth several days of your time. Don't be deceived by the Parisian facade of the new city; a great deal of North Africa hides around each corner.

Orientation and Practical Information

The downtown section of the new city was laid down by the French in their beloved colonial checkerboard fashion. **Avenue Habib Bourguiba** and **avenue de France** stretch from the water's edge to the gates of the medina, an immense labyrinth whose navigation requires a good map and much patience.

Tourist Office: ONTT, at the corner of av. Bourguiba and av. Muhammad V. Sullen, noteworthy for its free map, *Tunisia Practical Guide,* and the rudeness of some of the staff. Open mid-June to mid-Sept. Mon.-Sat. 7:30am-1:30pm and 4-7pm, Sun. 9am-noon; mid-Sept. to mid-June Mon.-Sat. 8:30am-1pm and 3-6pm, Sun. 9am-noon; Ramadan 8:30am-2:30pm and 3-6pm, Sun. 9am-noon. For better service, try the ONTT office at the **train station.** (Same hours.)

American Express: Carthage Tours, 59, av. Bourguiba. Checks sold and replaced, but no client mail service and no wired money accepted. Open Mon.-Sat. 7am-7pm, Sun. 9am-noon.

Currency Exchange: Société Tunisienne de Banque, next door to the Africa Hotel on av. Bourguiba, and the bank exchange at the train station are both open extended hours. Also at the airport (open 24 hours) and the port.

Post Office: 30, av. Charles de Gaulle. 120ml per letter for Poste Restante. Open Mon.-Thurs. 7:30am-12:30pm and 5-7pm, Fri.-Sat. 7:30am-1:30pm, Sun. 9-11am.

Telephones: 29, rue Jemal Abdel Nasser, around the corner. Open 24 hours. **Telephone code:** 01.

Flights: From the **Tunis-Carthage International Airport** (tel. 23 60 00), take bus #35 downtown (300ml). Taxis should charge 2D.

Trains: Gare SNCFT, pl. de la Barcelone (tel. 24 44 40), near the center of town.

Buses: Gare Routière Sud (tel. 49 52 55) serves the south. Walk down av. de Carthage to the end and turn right. **Gare Routière Nord,** Bab Saadoun—you guessed it. Take bus #3 from av. Bourguiba.

Ferries: Ferries land at the port of **La Goulette,** 1km from the stop of the TGM commuter train to downtown (250ml).

Emergencies: Police (tel. 197). **Ambulance** (tel. 190 or 34 12 50).

Embassies: U.S., 114, av. de la Liberté (tel. 23 25 66). **Canada,** 3, rue Didon (tel. 28 65 77). **U.K.,** 5, pl. de la Victoire (tel. 24 51 00). Citizens of **Australia** and **New Zealand** should contact the British Embassy. **Algeria,** 18, rue de Niger (tel. 28 31 66). Visas required for citizens of the US, Canada, Australia, and New Zealand. 9.500D and 4 photos.

Accommodations and Food

Tunis has plenty of inexpensive hotels, but the cheapest are sleazy and unsafe. In summer, start your search early in the morning. **Hôtel Cirta,** 42, rue Charles de Gaulle (tel. 24 15 82), has an affable manager and clean rooms. (Singles 3D, doubles 6D. Hot or cold showers 500ml.) Rue Charles de Gaulle begins at av. de France, two blocks from the entrance to the medina. Off rue Charles de Gaulle toward av. Bourguiba is the **Hôtel Commodore,** 17, rue d'Allemagne (tel. 24 49 41)—a cut above, with almost spotless rooms. (Singles with private shower 5.750D, with private bath 6.900D; doubles with shower 8D, with bath 10.500D.) **Hotel de Suisse,** 5, rue de Suisse (tel. 24 38 21), in a narrow alley off rue de Hollande near the train station, is clean and cheap. (Singles 3.500D, doubles 6D, with bath 8D. Showers

500ml.) **Victoria Hotel,** 72 ave. Farhat Hached (tel. 24 18 94), across the street directly in front of the train station, is also a pleasant place with helpful management. (Singles 5.500D; doubles 8D, with bath 9D.)

Restaurant Les Palmiers, 11, rue d'Egypte, off av. de la Liberté, a 10-minute walk from av. Bourguiba, serves outstanding dishes for 1D and below. **Restaurant de la Poste,** 7, rue d'Angleterre, is a lively place with free-flowing beers. Dishes run 1.500-2D, beers 600ml. **Restaurant Neptune,** 3, rue de Caire, across from the Hôtel Africa on a narrow street, serves a good three-course meal for 1.600D. On the same street at #6 and #9 are two other cheap eateries, restaurants **du Caire** and **Ennil.** For a splurge, try **M'Rabet,** in the center of the *medina* (souk Et-Trouk), complete with Arab music and belly dancing.

Sights

Rather than searching in Tunis for amusement, you'd do better to catch a commuter train to the cafes of Sidi Bou Said or the beaches of La Marsa, both minutes away. Die-hard city slickers should stroll down **avenue Habib Bourguiba,** where once graceful French colonial town houses elbow third-rate modern skyscrapers, to the entrance to the **medina** (old city). The vast maze of **souks** (market streets) provides an interesting taste of Arab life, but many of the byways have become infested with tacky tourist emporia. Avoid the main tourist strip, the rue Jamaa ez Zitounia, to the left; instead, take the right hand entrance, the **route de la Kasbah,** where the shoppers are Tunisian. You may want to stop in at the **Grande Mosquée.** (Open to non-Muslims Sat.-Thurs. 8am-noon. Dress conservatively and brush off those who offer to guide you for money.) It's most rewarding to get as far from the beaten track as you can; if you keep right, you'll eventually reach the **Bab Souika,** which is in the most authentic Arab neighborhood in Tunis.

Tunis does have one outstanding attraction: the **Bardo Museum,** which has helped itself to the greatest hits of the ruins that dot the country, assembling the finest collection of Roman mosaics in the world. Also here are giant marble sandals, leering bronze household gods, and a parade of dyspeptic emperors' heads—the collection will add much to subsequent visits to the sites. To reach the museum, take bus #3 from av. Bourguiba or #3 or 4 from Bab Souika. (Open Tues.-Sun. 9:30am-4:30pm. Admission 1D, students free.)

Near Tunis

Three worthwhile towns lie less than an hour from downtown Tunis on the TGM commuter line, which begins at the head of av. Bourguiba: Carthage, Sidi Bou Said, and La Marsa. **Carthage** has unfortunately never lived up to its reputation; travel guides ever since Virgil have lamented the gap between the glorious myth of the city that fired the hopes and fears of the ancients, and the sad reality of its annihilation by the Romans in 146 B.C.E. The powerful Punic metropolis was once the world's greatest naval power and its second mightiest city, eclipsed only by Rome. Carthage's most famous general, Hannibal, led an army of men and elephants over the Alps to attack and defeat Rome. Fired by its conservative senator Cato, Rome counter-attacked, razed the city, and sowed its ruins with salt. The ruins that inspired Aeneas are *very* ruined; if you take the train directly to the Carthage-Hannibal stop, you can see the best preserved site—the second-century C.E. **Baths of Antonius.** Up the road are the **Roman Villas** and the **archeological gardens,** a Punic necropolis. (Both sites open in summer daily 8am-7pm; in winter daily 8am-5pm. Admission 1D, students free.)

Two stops farther on the same rail line is **Sidi Bou Said,** a shining village perched on a promontory. The white and blue houses and bohemian outdoor cafes here seduced André Gide and Paul Klee. If you call ahead, you may be lucky enough to stay at the **Pension Sidi Bou Fares** (tel. 27 09 48), just above the main square, which has eight spotless rooms with stone floors, all around a lovely courtyard shaded by fig trees. (Singles 8.500D, doubles 13D, triples 18D.) Off the square, the **Restau-**

rant Chergui has another beautiful courtyard, and delicious food at low prices; try the *tajine de fromage* (1.200D) or *couscous poulet* (1.200D). Sidi Bou Said comes alive in the evenings; its cafes are easily the most lively in Tunisia. The **Café des Nattes,** right on the main square, is best for people-watching; the multi-level **Café Chabaana** down the street is a fine place for clifftop views of the sea. **La Marsa,** the last stop on the TGM, has the best beach near Tunis. Near the beach, **Les Palmiers** serves delicious crepes (1.500-2.300D).

Across the bay from Tunis, jagged mountains jut up from the sea to form the **Cap Bón Peninsula.** While the cities of Hammamet and Nabeul attract waves of European vacationers, the northern end of the peninsula offers pleasant beaches and a relaxed way of life. It borders on miraculous that **Hammamet** has become one of the largest resorts on the Mediterranean and still retains much of its pristine coastal beauty. Development wasn't oriented toward the budget traveler; **Hotel Alya** (tel. 802 18) charges 12.500D for singles in July and August, 17D for doubles (prices are nearly halved in winter). **Ideal Camping,** right in town, is only 800ml per person and 350ml per tent. **Nabeul,** just north of Hammamet, is the ceramics and tile center of Tunisia, and boasts a bevy of budget beds. The **IYHF youth hostel** (tel. 855 47) has musty dorms that are often filled with youth groups, but its beachside location and dedicated staff compensate. (2D. Half pension 3.200D, full pension 4.700D. Excellent food.) If they're full, there's always an extra mattress in the courtyard. In town, the pleasant **Pension les Roses** (tel. 855 70) costs 4.500D per person in summer, 3D in winter (shower 500ml). The **Pension les Hafsides** (tel. 858 23) is spotless and particularly friendly. (5.500D per person in summer; 4.500D in winter; bath and breakfast included.)

Kelibia, El Haouania, Sidi Daoud, Karbou, and other quiet villages to the north of Cap Bón offer pleasant beaches and fewer tourists. In windswept **Kelibia,** there is a cramped **Maison des Jeunes (IYHF)** (tel. 961 05), 3km from the bus station, beneath a craggy hilltop fortress. A little closer to town, the **Hotel Florida** (tel. 962 48) has good rooms. (Rooms with private shower 7D per person. Tasty 4-course dinner 2.500D.) **Hôtel En-Nassim** (tel. 962 45), next door, has bungalows, with bath, for 5D per person. The white beach of El Mansoura is 2km farther north.

Northern Tunisia

Bizerte, the coastal center of northern Tunisia, is too hard working to have time to primp for visitors. But an earthy old port that comes alive at night, two good hostels, and the proximity of spectacular beaches make this a fine base for the serious sunbather. The **Remel Youth Hostel (IYHF)** (tel. (02) 408 04), 4km south of town on the route to Tunis, is ramshackle, but it has character and a warden that likes Anglophones; best of all, just through the trees is idyllic Remel Beach. Take the Tunis-bound bus or bus #8 bound for Menzel Djmal, and ask the driver to let you off at Remel Plage. (900ml. Open March-Jan.) Closer to town, next to the municipal pool and the Palais du Congrès, is the **Maison des Jeunes** (tel. (02) 316 08), with clean five-person rooms on a large courtyard (2D). The Remel hostel is probably safer for women, and has more character to boot. North of town is the Corniche Beach, lined with ugly tourist hotels with expensive bike (2D per hr.) and windsurfer (5D per hr.) rental. 10km north of Bizerte lies Cap Blanc, the northernmost point in Africa.

Perhaps the most spectacular beach in Tunisia is at **Raf Raf,** along the coast between Tunis and Bizerte. The water is pure emerald and the thin crescent of sand stretches for miles around a craggy islet in the middle of the bay. Few tourists have been let in on the secret; there is no riff raff at Raf Raf. From either Bizerte or Tunis, take one of the frequent buses to Ras Djebel (about 1 hr. from either city), then catch a local bus down to the beach. You can rent a straw hut on the beach for 3D per day (not the safest), or try the pricey **Hotel Dalia** (tel. 476 68; singles 9D, doubles 12D).

More charming than Bizerte is the tiny fishing village of **Tabarka,** only a few miles from the Algerian border. Its beautiful beaches are complemented by rolling mountains and waters that teem with colorful marine life. You can take scuba lessons from the **Yachting Club** (1-week course 60D). Across the street, the marine store rents mask, snorkel, and fins (3.500D per day, if you haggle)—a wise investment. The comfortable **Hôtel de France,** av. Bourguiba (tel. 445 77), has very clean and airy rooms. (Singles 6-10.500D, doubles 7.500-15D, depending on season. Breakfast and dinner included.) On the same street is the musty but perfectly clean and less expensive **Hôtel Corail** (tel. 444 55), with doubles for 6D. Both fill up by noon, so come early.

The ancient fortified town of **El Kef** is one of the most appealing in the country, thanks to its untarnished authenticity and well-preserved monuments. The narrow cobbled alleys of the *medina* are carved into a craggy hill, surveyed by a commanding fortress at the summit. The brand new **Hotel Medina** (tel. (08) 20 214) is spotless and a bargain at 2D per person. The funky **Hotel La Source** (tel. 213 97) has a pleasant aura of faded elegance, and a quad (10D) fit for a Sultan. (Singles with shower 4D, doubles with shower 5D.) The **IYHF youth hostel** (tel. 203 67), 2km out of town, does not merit the trek. (2D per person.)

Near Le Kef are the two best preserved and most dazzling Roman ruins in Tunisia. **Bulla Regia** seems disappointing at first, but only because its treasures are underground. Well-heeled Romans built a teeming city here in the second century, then duplicated it underground to escape from the summer heat. Most of the upper levels were destroyed in a seventh-century earthquake, but the many treasures below were spared, including mosaic floors that remain almost completely intact. If you understand French, a guided tour is a good deal; don't pay more than 1D. (Open daily 8am-6pm. Admission 1D, students free.) The marked, 3-kilometer road to Bulla is 6km from the ugly industrial city of Jendouba.

Dougga is as well-endowed above as Bulla is below. From its temple to its toilets, this former agricultural city still stands in recognizable form; indeed it was inhabited as recently as a century ago. The **Capitol** is a stunning monument, widely held to be the most impressive Roman ruin in North Africa, but don't miss the remains of the once-thriving **brothel.** The Romans erected a giant marble phallus to mark the spot, but prudish tourist authorities withdrew it several years ago. (Admission 1D, students 500ml.)

The six kilometers between Dougga and the farming village of **Teboursouk** can be traversed only by foot or thumb. Just below Teboursouk, the charming, two-star **Hotel Thugga** has clean, cool rooms. (Singles 9D, doubles 13D. Showers and breakfast included.)

Sahil

Tunisia's central plain, the olive-bearing Sahil, stretches to the eastern Mediterranean coast and embraces both landlocked Kairouan, one of Islam's holiest cities, and the chic seaside resort of Sousse, where discos outnumber mosques three to one.

Seven pilgrimages to **Kairouan** are considered equivalent to one trip to Mecca in absolving a devout Muslim of worldly sins. The average tourist pilgrimage is only a few hours long, and consists of a daytrip by bus from one of the coastal cities. Buses run from Sousse (1½ hr., 1.540D) and Tunis (3 hr., 2.450D) until late afternoon; *louages* then continue service until 8 or 9pm. The immense **Sidi Oqba Mosque,** which dates from the seventh century, is the oldest Islamic monument in the world. (Open daily 8am-12:30pm and 4:30-6pm.) Visit the two *zaouias* (mausoleums) of *sidi* (Islamic saints). **Zaouia Sidi Abid el Ghariani,** near the tourist office, has a striking courtyard with black and white striped arches. (Open daily 8am-6pm.) The *zaouia* on the opposite side of town holds **Abou Zama,** better known as Sidi Sahab, or St. Barber (he always carried hairs of the prophet Muhammad). His mausoleum has remarkable painted tile walls and carved cedar and stucco ceilings. (Open daily 8am-12:30pm and 4:30-6pm; Ramadan daily 7am-noon.) Stop in at the **ONTT office,** pl. des Martyres (tel. 217 97), facing the gateway to the *medina,* and buy a *required* combined admission ticket to the major sights for 600ml. (Open Sat.-Thurs. 8am-5:30pm, Fri. 8am-noon.) They can also tell you how to get to the large blockhouse **IYHF youth hostel** (tel. (07) 203 09), where dormitory beds are 2D. **Hôtel Marhala** (tel. (07) 207 36) is a converted monastery in the center of the *medina.* (3.500D per person. Not recommended for women traveling alone.) **Sabra** (tel. (07) 202 60), next to the tourist office, is less ascetic, and safer for women. (Singles 3.500D, doubles 6D, triples 9D.)

Sousse has been an important harbor town for millenia. The **Grand Mosque** is open to those who dress respectfully. (Open Sat.-Thurs. 9am-2pm. Admission 300ml; purchase tickets at the *syndicat.*) Next door, you can scale the tower of the **Ribat,** an imposing fortified monastery. (Open Tues.-Sun. 9am-noon and 3-6:30pm. Admission 800ml.) From this point you can see (or rock) the **Kasbah,** or defensive fortress, at the opposite corner of the *medina,* which today houses an **Archeological Museum** with a collection of mosaics that rivals that in the Bardo. (Open Tues.-Sun. 9am-noon and 3-6:30pm. Admission 1D.) Be sure to explore Sousse's *medina,* one of the largest and best preserved in the country. Both the **ONTT office** and **Syndicat d'Initiative** provide information and city maps, and are centrally located on pl. Farhat Hached. To stay in the **IYHF youth hostel,** off bd. Taib M'hiri (tel. (03) 212 69), take bus #1 from pl. Farhat Hached or walk 2km from the center of town. (2D per person.) **Hôtel Ahla** (tel. (03) 205 70) is in a great location, just inside the old city walls next to the Grand Mosque. (Rooms 4D per person.)

Hourly commuter trains (4.100D) run south along the coast to **Monastir,** birthplace of President Habib Bourguiba and site of his mausoleum, as well as of a magnificient eighth-century **Ribat.** At **Mahdia,** 50km farther south, the immense, fortified **Borj el-Kebir** dominates the peninsula where the old town is located, effectively separating the delightful *medina* from a solitary lighthouse on the tip of windblown Cape Africa. (Open in summer daily 7:30am-1:30pm and 3-8pm; in winter daily 9am-6pm. Admission 1D.) Stay at the **Hotel Jazira** in the *medina;* clean, and with some rooms overlooking the water, it's an incredible bargain at 2D per person (showers 500ml). Just 42km inland from Mahdia, El Djem claims a **Colosseum** even grander than its counterpart in Rome. El Djem is on the rail line and main road from Sousse to Sfax.

Farther south is the prosperous industrial city of **Sfax,** a jumping-off point for travelers heading to the **Kerkennah Islands.** Only a short ferry ride from the mainland, these islands attract those looking for remote, quiet surroundings. The cheapest beds along the stretch of beach at Side Frej are the **Kastil's** single bungalows. (5D per person.) The **Hotel Cercina** next door serves excellent grilled mullet. There are up to six ferries per day (500ml) from the Bassin des Voliers, just a few blocks from downtown Sfax.

Southern Tunisia

Southern Tunisia has many faces, including the endless sand dunes of the Great Eastern Erg of the Sahara, the stark, jagged Ksour Mountains, the salt flats of the Chott el Djerid, and, perhaps most spectacularly, the explosions of green oasis foliage. If you want to explore any of the remote regions of the Sahara, bring a hat, plenty of water, and allow yourself at least a week—you'll be glad you did.

Though a combination of public transport and hitching can take you to some of the most isolated spots, this option is viable only for those prepared to wait hours for the rare *louage* or passing pick-up. If you assemble a group, renting a car for three days (about 180D with unlimited mileage) or a full week (about 240D) becomes affordable. Despite the claims of the companies which run expensive Land Rover tours of the south (160D per person per week, from Gabes), a Renault 4, the standard cheap rental car, can reliably rattle along all but the worst roads; be sure to bring a jack, spare tire, and lots of water.

The huge coastal oasis of **Gabes** is a good starting point; it's at the southern terminus of the rail system, has plenty of cheap restaurants and hotels, and is a good place to team up with other travelers or begin hopping buses and *louages* to the more remote villages.

A three-hour bus-and-ferry journey from Gabes will take you to the palm-studded **Isle of Djerba,** the island of the Lotus Eaters of Homeric fame. In **Houmt-Souk,** the island's main city, you can stay at an excellent **IYHF youth hostel** (tel. 506 19) in a newly renovated seventeenth-century *funduq* (caravanserai). (Members only. 1.500D per person.) The **Marhala** (tel. 501 46) and **Arischa** (tel. 503 84) hotels are also beautifully restored *funduqs,* at double the price. Djerba has one of the oldest Jewish communities in the world; visit **La Ghriba Synagogue** in the village of **Er-Riadh** (bus #14 from Houmt-Souk). Join the tourists along the beautiful beaches of the northeastern shore (bus #11), or hang out at the waterside **youth hostel** in the village of Aghir (bus #10 or 11; 2D per person).

Inland from Gabes lies **Matmata,** where the local Berber population has evolved elaborate underground dwellings to counter the harsh environment. You can stay at the **Marhala** (tel. 300 15), a complex of pit houses converted into a hotel. You may recognize the place—the bar scene from *Star Wars* was shot here. (Singles 3D, doubles 4.800D. Breakfast included.) Buses run twice per day (10km) to **Tamerzet,** an untouristed Berber village without accommodations.

The villages around the large and uninteresting towns of **Medenine** and **Tatahouine** in southeastern Tunisia feature an equally peculiar architectural tradition: pigeonhole-shaped *ghorfa* dwellings which have been stacked for centuries to form a giant human honeycomb. The most beautiful of the *ghorfa* communities is the tiny Berber village of **Chenini,** but the villages of **Ksar Jouama** and **Douriat** are also worth a visit. All these villages lack accommodations, but there is a *ghorfa* complex serving as a hotel in **Ksar Haddada,** just out of the town of Ghomrassen. (Tel. 696 05; 4.500D.)

Farther inland, on the southwestern corner of the Chott el-Djerid and the northern reaches of the Sahara, the small oasis of **Douz** provides a base for exploration of the surrounding desert. The **Marhala** hotel (tel. 15) in Douz has an excellent pool. Across the Chott, passable in the summer when the marshy lake dries into a salt flat, the oasis gems of Tozeur and Nefta support lush, cool palmeries. The old city of **Tozeur** is worth exploring for the unusual geometric patterns in its 500-year-old sunbaked brick walls. **Nefta's** *corbeille* is an enormous rocky basin where hot and cold springs nurture a vibrant garden. The town is also a center of Sufism (Islamic mysticism) in Tunisia. Both have cheap accommodations. **Gafsa,** farther north, is an unattractive but more accessible oasis town, served by direct buses from Gabes and Sfax. The town's greatest attraction is the two Roman pools still in use as swimming holes.

Perhaps the most spectacular oases are the relatively inaccessible trio of **Tamerza, Midès,** and **Chebika,** nestled against the Algerian border. Rent a car in Tozeur or Gafsa, or catch a bus to the nearby mining town of Redeyef and a *louage* from there. It's worth the trip; cool waterfalls, shady palms, spectacular gorges, and abandoned villages set against dramatic mountain backdrops await.

TURKEY

US$1 = 920 lire (TL)
CDN$1 = 700TL
UK £1 = 1523TL
AUS$1 = 675TL

1000TL = US$1.09
1000TL = CDN$1.43
1000TL = UK£0.66
100oTL = AUS$1.48

Only 3% of Turkey's vast land mass lies on the European continent, which is fitting, for this country bears little resemblance to those in the rest of this book. For the adventurous traveler, it's a gold mine. The Aegean coast, though a lot busier than it was three years ago, is less commercialized than the Greek islands, while the long Mediterranean coast offers even less touristed beaches, and archeological remnants of obscure civilizations—the Lycians and the Pamphylians. Istanbul is a teasing taste of the Orient which may whet your appetite for travel inland, where await the Seljuk and Arab monuments at Konya, Urfa, and Diyarbakir, the bizarre moonscape of Cappadocia, with its Byzantine cave-churches, and the Armenian ruins and natural beauty of Eastern Turkey. To top it all off, Turkey is relatively inexpensive compared to Europe, and Turkish people, especially in the less touristed areas, are unbelievably (even, to some, suspiciously) hospitable. For the most part, the hospitality is entirely sincere. Be prepared to be offered small gifts (maybe even livestock), and endless cups of *çay* (tea.)

Asia Minor has shifted back and forth between western and eastern cultures. From this turmoil emerged some of the most influential contributors to the western heritage. The Hittites overran Asia Minor in the Third Millenium B.C.E. and created a society with a government and laws learned from their eastern neighbors the Sumerians. The Hittites also discovered how to forge iron and developed the Indo-European language that became the root of most European languages. Later, Greek cities on the Aegean coast—Miletus, Ephesus, Pergammon, and Smyrna—contributed as much to Greek culture as Greece proper. Meanwhile, St. Paul, St. Peter, and St. John spent their later years in Asia Minor, building the religion that would grip Eruope for the next 1500 years. In the eleventh century, another militaristic people from the East, the Seljuk Turks, gradually chipped away at the last remnant of Roman rule, the Byzantine Empire.

The most recent empire to rule in Turkey was the Ottoman, from the fifteenth century to the end of World War I. They left the country in a mess, rife with corruption and lagging far behind the industrial West. That modern Turkey exists at all is a tribute to the heroics of Mustafa Kemal Atatürk, who led forces to expel the British, French, Greek, and Russian armies that had moved in to carve up the spoils. Atatürk also dragged Turkey into the Western world, abolishing the Caliphate, westernizing the alphabet, and laying the framework for a democratic political system.

One person can only do so much, though. Outside of Istanbul and a few other large cities, traditional Islamic customs and attitudes prevail, and liberal democracy is far from established. In the late 1970s, another of several experiments in democracy began to falter when extremist terrorist street warfare literally laid siege to Istanbul, and the military stepped in. Martial law is almost fully repealed: Elections held in 1983 ushered in the right-wing party of Prime Minister Özal. The leader of the opposition is still in enforced exile, but his party has just recently been reinstated, and Turkey is slowly and hesitatingly having another go at democracy. The most important item on the Turkish agenda remains the country's ambiguous national identity—should Turks consider themselves Eastern, or Western? One of the crucial partners of NATO, with a manpower contribution second only to that of the U.S., Turkey sends millions of guest workers to Western Europe annually, and is politicking vigorously for admission to the EEC. On the other hand, Islam has enjoyed a resurgency since the 1980 military coup, and Özal has forged much closer economic and diplomatic ties with the Arab countries than had any of the predecessors. Turkey, it must suffice to say, is Turkish.

The Istanbul Art and Culture Festival welcomes a large variety of foreign musical and theatrical groups, as well as local folk groups, from June 20 through July 15 each summer. In late September, the wine harvest brings local folk dancing and wine tasting to Cappadocia. On weekends in Konya from May through October, the traditional *Cirit Oyunu* game (a sort of jousting on horseback) is enacted. If you're in Turkey in the winter, don't miss the Mevlana Commemorative Ceremonies in Konya, held in mid-December, when the dervishes perform their mystical dances, or the hilarious camel wrestling contests in Selcuk, near Kuşadasi, on January 15 and 16.

If you'd like to indulge in some Turkish literature, try the work of Yaşar Kemal, whose novel, *Memed, My Hawk,* won the author great acclaim, including nominations for the Nobel Prize. Najim Hikmet has published in translation and is widely considered to be the greatest modern Turkish poet. If you'd like to read about Turkey, Homer's *Iliad* is just about the best fiction there is; Steven Runciman's *Byzantine Civilisation,* Lord Kinross's *The Ottoman Centuries,* and Bernard Lewis's *The Emergence of Modern Turkey* are all readable, comprehensive histories. Also highly recommended is Herbert Muller's *The Loom of History.*

For more detailed coverage of Istanbul and Turkey's Aegean and Mediterranean coasts, consult those chapters in *Let's Go: Greece and Turkey.*

Getting There

Perhaps the cheapest way to reach Turkey is by long-distance bus. **Euroways Eurolines** provides service from London for £118. Their office is at 52 Grosvenor Gardens, Victoria (tel. 730 82 35). Euroways also runs from Paris; contact VIA International, 8 Pl. Stalingrad (tel. 42 05 12 10). However you arrive from Europe, you'll pass through Bulgaria, for which you need a transit visa (usually US$20), obtainable at Bulgarian diplomatic missions.

BIGE/Transalpino fares are slightly less bus fares, but are only available to those under 26. Eurail and InterRail are invalid in Turkey. Avoid taking the train to Turkey from Greece; the journey is an excruciating 38-hour odyssey, only two-thirds of which is spent in motion. If you have a railpass you want to use, take the train as far as Alexandroupolis and hitch or get a bus from there; this way you'll avoid the Greco-Turkish border games. If you're trying to hitch to Turkey from Greece, try to make it in one ride from Alexandroupolis; there isn't much traffic. Also be careful that you don't get your driver's car stamped into your passport, or you'll have all sorts of trouble explaining that you didn't sell "your" car on the black market. You are *not* permitted to walk across the border, but must be in some form of conveyance.

The ferries that sail between the Greek islands in the eastern Aegean and the nearby Turkish shore are a popular way to enter Turkey. Boats run from Samos to Kuşadasi (3-7 per week, about US$25 one way), Rhodes to Marmaris (6 per week, about US$20 one way), and Chios to Çeşme (July 15-Sept. 15, 6 per week, US$15-20 one way). For many of the cruisings, you must turn in your passport the night before. Be prepared for the Turkish port tax—usually around $US8. Check the Northeast Aegean and Dodecanese section of the Greece chapter in this book for more information.

Turkish Airlines (THY) has regular service to Turkey from European and Middle Eastern countries, and offers discounts of 60% on European flights and 10% on domestic flights to students under 28 years of age; everyone under 22 is entitled to a 25% discount. THY also offers a discount of 50% to those under 26 (students up to 31) on its flights to and from Middle Eastern countries. In London and other European capitals, you can often find deals in the travel classifieds of local newspapers and by consulting budget travel agents.

Many travelers cross Turkey on the way to other Asian countries. By far the greatest obstacle to overland travel is the required transit visa for Iran. In 1987, citizens of all English-speaking countries except Australia and New Zealand were being refused visas. Australian and New Zealanders were reporting at least three-month waits, with no guarantee of success. Travelers who've come overland from Southeast Asia report that the situation is a little hairy. Most buses to the east depart directly from Ankara (see Buses under Practical Information in Ankara). Iraqi and Syrian visas are much easier to obtain (you must, though, exchange US$100 or the equivalent at the Syrian border). Buses originate in Ankara, but you can catch them in Antakya or Gaziantep for Syria and in Mardin for Iraq. Flights may be your only way to the subcontinent, but be prepared to pay dearly; prices in 1987 were 218,000TL Istanbul-Karachi—with a 50% discount for ages under 26.

Transportation

Getting around in Turkey is a budget traveler's dream. Buses are quick, efficient, modern (usually Mercedes Benzes), and most importantly, cheap—about 500TL per hour of travel. All bus companies are private, and you can often chisel 10-15% off the price if you bargain; mentioning that you're a student often helps. **Varan Tours** buses, though slightly more expensive, are wonderfully comfortable for longer trips (they're air-conditioned), and faster.

Train travel in Turkey is leisurely—that is to say, slow. This has its good side, though: When a bus would drop you off at your destination at 3am, an overnight train lets you stretch out and sleep until a decent hour. Furthermore, train fares are even lower than bus fares, and students get a 10% discount on top of that. First class seats, about 500TL more expensive, give you plenty of empty seats except on frequently traveled routes. There are no trains along the western coast.

Dolmuş (shared taxis), usually minibuses or vans, fill any gaps left by the remarkably comprehensive bus system, and also follow fixed routes. They are more expensive than buses (about 600TL per hr. of travel), and leave whenever they fill up (*dolma* means "stuffed," and they're not kidding). You can get on and off whenever you like—salvation for the weary hitchhiker.

Hitchhiking in Turkey is easy and interesting. If you're hiking between towns, locals invariably offer rides. For long distances between major cities, truckers will be your best bet. If you're asked to pay for the ride, offer half of the bus fare. The hitching signal is a waving hand.

If you want to get to the east of Turkey without suffering a 36-hour bus ride (50 or more hr. by train), consider the low domestic fares of Turkish Airlines: Istanbul to Ankara 40,000TL, to Diyarbakir or Erzurum 50,000TL, and to Trabzon or Van

54,000TL. There is a 10% discount for married couples (or couples who claim to be married).

There is no ferry system along the west coast except for a **Turkish Maritime Line** boat from Istanbul to Izmir (1 per week year-round, increasing to 3 per week July-Sept.; 6000TL one way, lowest class). The Black Sea boat from Istanbul to Trabzon passes by some of the most beautiful scenery in Turkey (8500TL). It leaves Istanbul at 5:30pm on Monday and is frequently booked, so make reservations as soon as you arrive in the city. There is a 10% student discount on all fares.

Practical Information

Though neither the slickest nor the most efficient, the Turkish government tourist offices and tourist police exist all the same, in most major cities and resort areas. Some English, or other European language, is spoken. They will help find accommodations and often provide the usual slew of other services. In places without an official office, travel agents sometimes serve the same function.

The exchange figures listed at the head of this chapter were recorded at research time; we suggest that you use them to obtain an estimate of the dollar price of our listings (these usually remain reasonably stable). The black market exchange rate is only slightly better than the official rate (5%). If you're coming from Greece, spend your *drachmae* before arriving; the few banks that change *drachmae* invariably give an absurd rate. Try not to run out of money while you're in Turkey; although having money wired to Turkey is getting easier, especially in Istanbul, the difficulties involved in getting transfers elsewhere can be extraordinary.

Avoid drugs in Turkey. The horror stories of lengthy prison sentences and dealer-informers are true; embassies are absolutely helpless in all cases. The minimum sentence for possession of even the smallest quantity is sixteen months. Turkish law also provides for "guilt by association;" those in the company of a person caught are subject to prosecution. As for the foolish notion of smuggling: Anything looking remotely like a backpacker gets searched with a fine-tooth comb arriving back in Europe from Turkey.

Another thing to be careful of is accidentally taking antiques out of the country. Make sure that the curious souvenir you picked up at a bazaar isn't an antique. Exporting them is a jailable offense, even if you claim you had no idea.

Women traveling in Turkey may have a less pleasant experience than men. Off the Aegean and Mediterranean coasts and outside of Istanbul, most Turkish women are veiled and are rarely seen in public. In central and eastern Turkey, you will be stared at perpetually and approached very frequently. If you feel threatened, getting visibly and loudly angry, particularly in a public place, is likely to be an effective deterrent. Or better yet, say you're going to the police; Turks are very afraid of the police, and in these situations, the police almost always side with the foreigner.

Some people speak English in the big cities, but they're few and far between in the provinces. German is useful, even among rural populations, because many people have relatives who have lived and worked in Germany. Remember that in Turkey a raise of the chin followed by a closing of the eyes means "no," and that a wave of the hand up and down means "come here." Perhaps one of the most useful gestures in Turkey is done by putting your palm flat on your chest. This is a polite way of refusing an offer—and the Turks seem to be forever offering visitors things, especially tea.

Toiletries are cheap and readily available in Turkey; tampons can't always be found in the east. You should always carry toilet paper, and expect to encounter quite a number of pit toilets.

Turkey is a large country with a widely varying **climate.** In the summer months, the Aegean and Mediterranean coasts are hot, with average daily temperatures around 32°C. The swimming season from Bodrum south, and all along the Mediterranean coast, lasts from early May well into October. On the Black Sea coast (Istanbul included), the swimming season is shorter (June-early Sept.), and fall brings considerable rainfall; winters aren't especially cold on this coast, but are usually pretty wet. As you move inland, the climate becomes more extreme; the area around Urfa is regularly above 40°C in the summer, while the area north of Van is kept relatively cool because of the high altitude. In the winter, the situation switches, and Urfa is quite temperate while most of central and eastern Anatolia is bitter cold and experiences heavy snowfall.

Everything closes on the national **holidays:** January 1, April 23, May 19, August 30, and October 29. During Ramadan (April 18-May 18 in 1988), pious Muslims will not eat, drink, smoke, or travel between dawn and sunset. You'd hardly notice it in Istanbul, Ankara, and the coastal resort towns, but elsewhere things really slow down. It's a lot easier to get hotel rooms during this period, even at resorts. Large celebrations mark Ramadan's conclusion, known as Bayram, when it's practically impossible to get bus and train tickets and hotel rooms. There's a second Bayram festivity from July 25 to July 30; things become similarly hectic. Museums, archeological sites, and monuments are generally open from 9am to 5pm; many close on Monday. Most cost 500TL, on weekends 250TL; students get in free. Museums, cinemas, and concerts usually cost students 50% less. Despite the enormous area of Turkey, it is all within the same time zone—three hours ahead of Greenwich Mean Time in the summer, two ahead in the winter.

Shops in Turkey are generally open Monday through Saturday from 9am to 1pm and 2 to 7pm. Government offices are open Monday through Friday 8:30am to 12:30pm and 1:30pm to 5pm. Banks are open Monday through Friday 8:30am to noon and 1:30 to 5:30pm. Food stores, open bazaars, and pharmacies tend to have longer hours. Haggling in shops, over accommodations, and over less regulated transportation fares is common practice and often has great results if you're persistent enough.

To call collect you have to wait from one to two hours for the call to be placed; calls must be made from post offices. Costs are upwards of 10,000TL for three minutes to North America. Post offices (PTTs) are typically open Monday through Friday from 8:30am to noon and 1 to 5:30pm; central post offices in larger towns keep longer hours, sometimes around the clock—but for international mail and phone calls or Poste Restante, you should go during the weekday. Poste Restante should be addressed *Merkez Postanesi.*

Accommodations, Camping, and Food

Turkish hotels are classified in four categories, but the majority are unclassified, and it is these that you'll most likely frequent. Budget accommodation averages 2000-2500TL per person on the Aegean coast, 1000-1500TL in the east. On the Aegean coast your best bets are pensions and private boarding houses; in the east you'll have to resort to drab and dingy hotels, often without showers. Most Turkish towns have a *hamam,* or bathhouse, where you can get a wonderful steam bath for 700-1000TL. *Hamami* schedule different times for men and women. You can also clean off at any mosque. Camping is widespread in Turkey, and there are cheap campgrounds throughout the country (100TL per person at most places). Freelance camping is possible, but the police are usually quite strict, and there are few beaches accessible by road that haven't got some sort of campground on them already.

Turkey is one of the few places where eating cheaply still entitles you to sample a great variety of carefully prepared dishes. Restaurants are called *lokanta;* a meal with beer should cost you 2000TL. There are always numerous stands selling *şiş* or *döner kebab* for 500TL. In restaurants, it's customary to go to the kitchen yourself and choose after seeing everything. Look for *tarhana çorbasi,* a tomato-yogurt soup; *erişteli çorba,* a tomato-base noodle soup; different varieties of *pilav* (rice); *pilaki,* navy beans in a tomato sauce, often with pieces of meat added; and *dolma,* stuffed vegetables served hot or cold and usually filled with chopped meat, rice, onions, and seasoning. Salads, available almost everywhere, include *çoban salatasi* (cucumber and tomato salad) and *karişik salata* (mixed salad)—both very spicy. Turkish yogurt and *zeytin* (olives) are terrific. For the main course, there's almost always *döner kebab* (slices cut from a leg of lamb roasting on a spit) and *şiş kebab* (skewered chunks of lamb), or fish if you're near the sea. *Pide* is a distant relative of pizza: flat bread served with your choice of eggs, meat, tomatoes, cheese, or spices. Or try *köfte,* spicy meatballs. *Bira* (beer) is very popular; *efes-pilsen* and *tekel beyaz* are light, while *tekel siyah* is dark; all are fairly good and around 400TL per liter. Wine is generally available only in fancy restaurants, except in the wine-producing areas of Cappadocia and Izmir and in coastal resort towns, where it's a real bargain. *Raki,* a licorice-flavored spirit, is the powerful national liquor.

Northwestern Turkey

Istanbul

The sight of minarets against a misty orange sunset, the sound of the evening call to prayer, the smell of fish, charcoal, spice, and rosewater—Istanbul is a feast for the senses. There's something ambiguously but unmistakably Eastern about this city, which has been the capital of two world empires, the Byzantine and the Ottoman. Aya Sofya, the St. Peter's of early Christianity, is here, but the city is only as Western as its great mosques, the Sultanahmet and Süleymaniye. Poised between two pasts, Istanbul is also poised between two presents. Men smoke *nargiles* (water pipes) while their sons listen to transistor radios, and office clerks clad in business suits share the streets with scarved women in traditional garb. Istanbul's pollution and chaos may be a bit overwhelming, but its rich heritage and present-day vitality will easily captivate you.

Orientation and Practical Information

Turkey's largest city, situated in the northwestern corner of the country, straddles the Bosphorus Strait, the ever-strategic passage from the Black Sea out to the Sea of Marmara, the Dardanelles, and the Aegean.

Waterways divide Istanbul into three parts: The **Golden Horn** (Haliç) estuary splits the European half of the city in two; the **Bosphorus Strait** (Boğaziçi) separates these sections from the Asian sector. Almost all historical sites, markets, and older quarters are located on the southern bank of the Golden Horn. The **Sultanahmet** quarter, right by the Aya Sofya, is the center for budget travelers. The name of the appropriate quarter is about all you need when using public transportation or asking directions. The tourist office provides a free map, but you may want to invest in one of the detailed maps sold in bookstores. Don't try walking everywhere; familiarize yourself with the dense network of buses and *dolmuş.*

Tourist Offices: In Sultanahmet, hidden across Divan Yolu Cad., from the Sultan Pub (tel. 5 224 903); at Karaköy Maritime Station (tel. 1 495 776); at the Hilton Hotel Arcade, Taksim (tel. 1 330 592); and at the International Terminal of the airport (tel. 5 737 399). All are well-informed, helpful, and stock good maps. All offices open daily 9am-5pm.

Budget Travel: Gençtur, 15 Yerebatan Cad., 3rd floor (tel. 5 265 409), right in the center of Sultanahmet. Very helpful. They sell ISIC cards, distribute maps (free), provide Poste Restante service, and organize paid workcamps throughout Turkey. Open Mon.-Fri. 9am-6pm, Sat. 9am-1:30pm.

Seventur Travel Shop, 2-C Alemdar Cad. (tel. 5 124 183), next to the Aya Sofya, also provides a Poste Restante service. Other travel agencies in Sultanahmet are not licensed and may sell you bogus tickets.

American Express: Hilton Hotel lobby, 91 Cumhuriyet Cad. (tel. 1 410 274). Mail held (US$3 pick-up charge for those without AmEx card or traveler's checks). No currency exchange. Open daily 8:30am-8pm. **Koç American Bank,** 233 Cumhuriyet Cad., accepts wired money. Open Mon.-Fri. 9:30am-12:30pm and 1:30-3pm.

Currency Exchange: Banks open Mon.-Fri. 9am-noon and 1:30-4pm. **Imar Bankasi** on Divan Yolu Cad. charges no commission on traveler's checks. The airport exchange booth is open 24 hours; the Karaköy Maritime Station booth is open for late ships. Small shops in Sultanahmet give good rates, but accept only cash.

Post Offices: Marked with a yellow "PTT" sign. The **Central Post Office** at 25 Yeni Postane Çokak, as well as the **Bakirköy** and **Beyoğlu** branches offer 24-hour stamp, telephone, and telegraph services. To send packages abroad, go to **Kadiköy, Beyazit,** or **Tophane** (on Rithim Cad.). Poste Restante at the Central Post Office, but it is extremely crowded; have mail sent to American Express or Gençtur (see Budget Travel, above).

Telephones: At the **Central Post Office** or the **Taksim** branch. Buy *büyük* (large) *jetons* and throw them into the machines as fast as you can. Collect calls can also be made from here (1-hr. wait). Open 24 hours. Use *küçük* (small) *jetons* for local calls. Sometimes phone numbers in Istanbul are listed only with six digits—there should be seven. The first digit is always either 1, 3, or 5; 1 for the north side of the Horn, 3 for the Asian side of the Bosphorus, and 5 for the south side of the Horn.

Flights: Yeşiköy Airport (tel. 5 731 331), for domestic flights, and **Atatürk Airport** (tel. 5 733 500), for international flights, are both connected to Aksaray by THY Airlines bus ("Uçak Servisi;" every 30 min., 550TL), and municipal bus #96 (less frequently, 150TL). To reach Sultanahmet from the bus stop, walk toward the big traffic intersection, turn right onto Ordu Cad. and continue for 2km, or hop aboard any bus on Ordu Cad.

Trains: Trains for Europe leave from **Sirkeci Station** (tel. 5 270 051). Daily departures to Munich, Belgrade, Sofia, Athens, and Edirne. **Haydarpaşa Station** (tel. 3 360 475), on the Asian side, is for Asia-bound domestic traffic. Ferries connect the station with Karaköy pier #7 every 30 min.

Buses: All buses leave from the chaotic **Topkapi Bus Terminal.** The terminal, which isn't on any map for some unfathomable reason, is just beyond the city walls on Millet Cad. From Sultanahmet, take any bus which has "Topkapi" on the side panel. All bus companies, both domestic and international, have offices at Topkapi, and many have offices in Sultanahmet as well. According to the tourist police, only **Bosfor Turizm** (tel. 1 432 525) and **Varan Tours** are licensed to operate throughout Western Europe. These two and **Derya Turism** are licensed for Greece. Most bus companies are authorized to go to Eastern Europe. Unlicensed companies may offer substantial discounts for Western Europe and abandon their passengers in Eastern Europe. Neither tourist authorities nor common sense can explain how these "unlicensed" outfits stay in business. We recommend that you try the cheapest lines, and that you expect delays, inefficiency, licensing problems, and/or border hassles with all carriers. Whichever company you travel choose, you must obtain a Bulgarian transit visa *in advance* (usually overnight). Only some companies will handle this for you. Agencies downtown are clustered on Hüdavendigâr Cad., behind the Sirkeci Railway Station in Sultanahmet, and on Izmar Cad., off Ordu Cad. to the left just before the Aksaray intersection.

Ferries: Turkish Maritime Lines ticket office on the waterfront at Karaköy (tel. 1 440 207), just west of the Haydarpaşa ferry terminal. Cheapest fare to Izmir for a *koltuk* (pullman, but it also means "armpit") is US$11, to Trabzon US$14. Boat stops en route; meals are not included.

Public Transportation: Bus tickets (150TL, students 80TL) can be bought in kiosks and at larger bus stops marked *"Plantonluk."* Hawkers charge an extra 10TL. Frequent service 6:30am-10:30pm. Read the sign on the side of the bus and ask the driver for particular quarters. Going to Sultanahmet from the north, the sign will usually include Beyazit; from the west, it will usually include Eminönü. *Dolmuş* (shared taxis) run fixed routes and cost about 200TL. They are minibuses or old, large cars, and have *dolmuş* on a sign on the roof. *Dolmuş* stops are indicated by a large "D" on a blue sign.

Police: Tel. 1 666 666; they may not speak English. **Tourist Police,** on Mimar Kemalettin Cad., near Sirkeci Railway Station (tel. 5 274 503). Help if you've been burgled or swindled. Open daily 9am-6pm; phone line open 24 hours.

Medical Assistance: American Hospital Admiral Bristol Hastanesi, Nişantaş, Güzelbahçe Sokak (tel. 1 486 030), or **German Hospital,** Siraselviler Cad., Taksim (tel. 1 438 100).

Consulates: U.S., 106 Meşrutiyet Cad., Tepebaşi (tel. 1 513 602). **U.K.,** 34 North Meşrutiyet Cad. (tel. 1 447 540). **Bulgaria,** 15 Yildisposta Cad., Gayrettepe (tel. 1 662 605). Open Mon.-Fri. 9am-noon. **Iran,** Ankara Cad., Cağaloğlu (tel. 5 120 090). **Iraq,** Teşvikiye Cad., Teşvikiye (tel. 1 605 020). **Syria,** 3 Silahtar Cad. (tel. 1 482 735).

Bookstore: Ayda, 80 Divan Yolu Cad. The best selection of guidebooks and foreign newspapers in Sultanahmet. Open daily 8am-8pm.

Hitchhiking: Best place to get a ride is the **Londra Mocamp** (see Accommodations). Mon.-Wed. are the best days for finding trucks bound for central Europe.

Accommodations

Istanbul's budget accommodations are concentrated in the **Sultanahmet** district, something of a backpackers' ghetto. You'll be within easy reach of all downtown Istanbul and the most important sights. Prices range from 1500TL in a dorm room or on a rooftop to 6000TL for a single; anywhere else in Istanbul that's this cheap is also seedy and dirty. If you're able to spend a little more, you might look at third- and fourth-class hotels in the adjacent Laleli and Aksaray districts.

Yücelt Youth Hostel (IYHF), 6 Caferiye Sok. (tel. 5 224 790), in Sultanahmet. Clean, crowded rooms and large patio. The library and Turkish bath are more frill than function. Doubles 6500TL, dorm beds 2250TL.

Sultan Tourist Hostel, Yerebatan Cad. (tel. 5 207 676). Immaculate rooms. Management caters to backpackers. Doubles 8000TL, triples, quads, and dorms 3000TL per person. Hot showers 500TL.

Topkapi Hostel, at Işakpaşa Cad. and Kutlugün Şok. (tel. 5 272 433). Down the hill from the entrance to Topkapi Palace. Friendly and quiet. Dorm bed 2000TL, covered rooftop (closed in winter) 1500TL.

Hotel Popüler, at Küçükayasofya Cad. and Yeğen Sok. (tel. 5 274 709), a few blocks south of the Blue Mosque. Well-removed from "Hotel Row" and decorated with carpets and various knick-knacks. Doubles 8000TL; worth the splurge.

Londra Mocamp, on the airport road, 1km from the airport. Stay here only if you're stuck at the airport. Facilities include cafeteria, bar, and pool. 1700TL per person, 1275TL per tent.

Food

From the sandwich stands in the streets to the elegant seafood restaurants on the Bosphorus, the variety of food in Istanbul is great, the quality is high, and the cost reasonable. While Sultanahmet is the best place to stay, it is decidedly *not* the best place to eat—you'll do much better in the Eminönü market quarter between the Grand Bazaar and the New Mosque, or in the Tepebasi quarter. There are several popular, inexpensive restaurants with music at night along the **Çiçek Pasaji,** an alleyway north of Istiklal Cad. in the Galatasaray district. You might also take an excursion up the Bosphorus (bus #25A from Eminönü) to the seafood restaurants at Sariyer or Rumeli Kavaği. The ubiquitous *kebab* stands are good for a quick, filling, stand-up lunch (600-800TL). A complete meal at a cheap *lokanta* shouldn't run you more than 1200TL. Although eating out is so economical that buying your own food seems a waste of time, you might try the **open-air fruit markets.** Two are centrally located—one in Galatasaray, and another in the Misir (Egyptian) Bazaar, near the New Mosque.

Sultanahmet: The restaurants along **Divan Yolu** are good, but overpriced by Istanbul standards. The cheapest, **Sultanahmet Köftecisi,** caters to a more Turkish crowd. If you're really on a shoestring, go to **Öz Karadeniz,** 61 Tigarethane Cad.; turn left on Çatal Çeşme Sok. from Yerebatan Cad. Also try **Metin Lokanta,** Cankurtaren Meydan. Follow the Topkapi Palace wall south past Topkapi Hostel.

Galata Bridge: Descend the staircase on the northern side of the bridge and sit down to a seafood meal at any of the restaurants (2000-4000TL). The Golden Horn waves roll right up to you. The beer house at the bottom of the staircase serves the cheapest beer in town (400TL). Smoke *nargiles* or play backgammon next door.

Çamlica: On the Asian side. A bit of an ordeal to get here, but worth it for the fairy-tale garden and view of Istanbul (on clear days). Take the ferry from Eminönü to Üsküdar and hop on bus #11, 11A, 11B, 11E, 11M, or 11U. Ask the driver to drop you off at Çamlica and take a taxi or walk 1½km to the top of the hill, the tallest in Istanbul. Brass tables, fireplace, and candlelight. Omelettes 800TL, full meals 2000TL.

Sights

Aya Sofya, built in 537 by the Emperor Justinian, is unquestionably one of the world's greatest churches. It was Constantinople's cathedral for 900 years, and then served as a mosque after the Turkish conquest in 1453 until 1935, when Atatürk made it into a museum. The enormous dome was the largest in the world until St. Peter's was built. Unfortunately, most of the celebrated mosaics have been removed to be incorporated into a mosaic museum which doesn't yet exist. (Open Sun.-Fri. 9:30am-4pm. Admission Mon.-Fri. 1000TL, Sat.-Sun. 500TL. ISIC cardholders get free admission to this and all other Istanbul sights.)

Sultan Ahmet I built the **Sultanahmet Camii** (Blue Mosque) nearly 1100 years after the construction of Aya Sofya in a clear attempt to outdo Justinian. Many believe he succeeded. The mosque's silhouette is unforgettable, and the interior is glorified by the deep blue of Iznik tiles. The elegant minarets were the focus of some concern for Islamic religious leaders of the day—they didn't want the Sultan to exceed the number of minarets at Mecca. Ahmet boldly avoided religious controversy by providing the money and workers necessary to erect a seventh minaret at Mecca. You may visit the mosque at any time except during prayers; modest dress is required. English-speaking Turks often loiter around the entrance during the day, eager to give potentially instructive freelance tours. Agree on the fee, if any, before the tour. Heading northwest you'll pass by the ancient **Hippodrome** and the sixteenth-century **Ibrahim Paşa Palace,** a beautifully exhibited museum of Turkish and Islamic art.

By returning to Divan Yolu and heading west you'll pass the **Kapali Çarşi,** one of the world's largest covered markets. Prices are relatively high, and in any case, the price you're first quoted will be 300-400% too high. Faulty and shoddy wares are rampant—the brightly-colored *kayseri* rugs, for instance, are worthless. If you plan to buy a rug, first visit the Carpet Museum near the Blue Mosque. Leather is a bargain, though you should examine quality carefully and be prepared to haggle. The older part of the bazaar includes an interesting book market that opens up to a shady tea garden beside the **Beyazit Mosque,** Istanbul's oldest. (The Kapali Çarşi is open daily 9am-7pm.)

The other mosque that you should be sure to visit is the **Süleymaniye,** considered by many to be the most beautiful mosque in Istanbul. The adjacent *türbes* (mausoleums) of Suleyman the Magnificent and his wife, Roxalena, are even more splendid than the mosque itself. Walk down to the Horn from the Süleymaniye and you'll pass the tiny mosque of **Rüstem-Paşa,** notable for its splendid interior tiling. A mandatory stop for lovers of Byzantine art is the fantastically preserved **Kariye Camii,** a long way up Fevzipaşa Cad. near Edirne Gate, best reached by *dolmuş* or bus #39 or 86 from Sultanahmet. Once a Byzantine church, then a mosque, and finally a museum, the building has superb fourteenth-century frescoes and mosaics. (Open daily 9:30am-4:30pm. Admission 250TL.)

One of Istanbul's great attractions is the **Topkapi Saray,** the palace of the Ottoman sultans. You can spend a whole afternoon here among the exhibits of gold, diamonds, jade, emeralds, ornate miniatures, and fine Oriental porcelain. The elegant terraces offer wonderful views of the city. Guided tours of the **Harem** run three times per day (500TL). (Palace open Wed.-Mon. 9:30am-5pm. Admission 400TL.)

Istanbul's other great museums are down the hill from Topkapi—enter the gate marked "Archeological Museums." Inside you'll find the **Cinili Kiosk,** a lovely pleasure palace that is now a museum of Turkish tiles. The **Museum of the Ancient Orient** has a terrific collection of Hittite, Babylonian, Sumerian, Assyrian, and Egyptian artifacts, including a tablet from the Hammurabi code and a peace treaty between a Hittite ruler and the Egyptian Pharaoh Ramses II. The **Archeological Museum** (labeled only in Turkish and French) has a fantastic collection of Greek,

Hellenic, and Roman marbles and bronzes, including the alleged sarcophagus of Alexander the Great. (Complex open daily 9:30am-5pm. Admission 500TL.)

For a solid historical background of Istanbul's sights, get *Strolling Through Istanbul* by Sumner-Boyd and Freely (10,000TL), or the more compact *Istanbul: A Brief Guide to the City,* by the same authors (4000TL).

Entertainment

Most western tourists hang out at the bars in Sultanahmet. Beers run 500-600TL. Places close at 11pm, except for **Yörük,** which stays open until 2am. There is a corny but free sound-and-light show at the Blue Mosque every night (June-Sept. only). Check the schedule posted at the Sultanahmet Tourist Office for shows in English. Avoid the expensive night clubs off Istiklal Cad.; you'll be endlessly harrassed by members of the opposite sex. In the same area, though, you might enjoy food and wine at restaurants that sometimes feature gypsy dancers.

A Turkish bath might sound alluring, but *hamams* in Sultanahmet are overpriced and have poor service. Wait until you visit Edirne or Bursa for some beautiful Ottoman baths.

During the **Istanbul Festival** (June 20-July 21), orchestras, ballet companies, and folk dance ensembles perform throughout the city. You must purchase tickets at the Atatürk Kültür Merkezi facing Taksim Square. Inquire at the tourist office for more information.

Near Istanbul

Ferries depart from the Eminönü end of the Galata Bridge for the **Princes' Isles,** stopping at four of the nine islands of this little suburban archipelago; you'll find all of them tainted only slightly, if at all, by the dirt and noise of Istanbul. Although some prefer the quieter atmosphere of **Burgazada** and **Heybeliada, Büyükada** is the largest and most scenic of the islands, and has the best swimming in the Istanbul area.

Just as scenic is a boat tour zig-zagging up the **Bosphorus** to the Black Sea and back, leaving twice per day from pier #4. You might consider getting off at any one stop and catching the ferry on its return trip.

If you're traveling west by train, stop in **Edirne,** just across the border from Greece in European Turkey. Capital of the Ottoman Empire from 1363 to 1453, Edirne contains some masterpieces of Ottoman architecture.

Bursa

Osman, the founder of the Ottoman dynasty, conquered Bursa in 1322, and his son, Orhan, decided to make it his capital. Bursa is now a crowded city with nothing to see save the Ottoman buildings from the period before 1363, when the capital moved to Edirne.

From Istanbul, three ferries per day travel from Kabataş, near the Dolmabahçe Palace, to Yalova, on the south coast of the Sea of Marmaris; buses for Bursa await the ferry (1½ hr.). Direct buses from Istanbul's Topkapi Station also travel to Bursa (4 hr.). From the bus station, take a *dolmuş* to the *heykel* (statue) on Atatürk Cad. Bursa's **tourist office,** Atatürk Cad. (tel. 21 23 59), downstairs at the fountain, is helpful and English-speaking. (Open July-Aug. daily 8am-5:30pm; Sept.-June Mon.-Fri. 8am-5:30pm, closed Sat.-Sun.)

Inexpensive hotels line Tahtakale Cad., parallel to and one block uphill from Atatürk Cad. Try either the **Hotel Uğur,** at #27 (tel. 21 19 89) or the **Otel Marmara,** at #31A (tel. 21 20 97). Both charge 3000TL for doubles. *Iskender kebab,* an excellent kebab dish with a sauce of tomatoes, yogurt, and garlic, originated in Bursa; two or three restaurants around town still serve the dish. The best place for budget restaurants is the area around Inönü Cad., between the *heykel* and the first set of traffic lights.

One block west of the tourist office is the **Ulu Camii.** This great mosque, built in the fifteenth century, has a beautiful *mirhab* (a niche indicating the direction of Mecca), and a carved, wooden *minbar* (pulpit) which scholars believe represents an astrological chart. On the lighter side, the mosque is also famous for its puppets. To this day, puppet shows featuring Hacivat—the clever one—and Karagöz—the innocent one—are performed throughout Turkey. A small theater here puts on shows nightly during the **Bursa Festival** in July.

Yeşil Camii (Green Mosque), the most famous religious monument in Bursa and one of the most beautiful Ottoman mosques anywhere, is distinguished by lavish blue and green tile work symbolizing the heavens. Before leaving, ask the custodian to show you the sumptuously tiled Sultan's section in the gallery just above the entrance. Across the way, the same striking turquoise tiles cover the exterior of **Yeşil Türbe** (Green Mausoleum), the interior of which is tiled in deeper shades. (Mausoleum open Tues.-Sun. 8am-5pm. Admission Mon.-Fri. 200TL, Sat.-Sun. 100TL.) At the other end of town, on a hill in Çerkirge (take a *dolmuş* from Atatürk Cad.), is the **Murat Camii,** famous for its two-story architecture. The upper floor was a theological school, the lower was, and still is, a mosque. The Byzantine pillars on the upper story were reused by Ottoman conquerors.

Bursa's Turkish baths of fresh spring water are famous. On the way to Çerkirge is the sixteenth-century **Yeni Kaplica** baths, where men and women can bathe together in private rooms. For a change of pace, ride Bursa's cable car to the alpine slopes of **Ulu Dağ.** *Dolmuş* marked *"teleferik"* leave from behind the *heykel.* (Cable car runs every hour on the hour 9am-10pm to the mid-station, and on the ½-hr. 9:30am-9:30pm to the top.) Ask at the tourist office about ski rental during the ski season, which lasts from December through April.

Thirty kilometers off the Yalova-Bursa highway is **Iznik,** the ancient city of Nicaea. Still enclosed in its ancient walls, Iznik lies on a lake with bungalows (4000TL for 2).

Aegean Coast

In many ways the least Turkish part of Turkey, the Aegean coast is also the most heavily visited. This area was the cultural center of Greek civilization after the classical age, during the Hellenistic period of Alexander and his successors. It then became the core of the Roman province of Asia Minor, and was the last part of Turkey to fall to the Ottoman Empire, in the fourteenth and fifteenth centuries. In fact, but for the efforts of Atatürk's forces in the 1920s, the coastline would today be part of Greece. The Western influence is clear everywhere—bikinis and suntan oil rule the beaches, and commercialism has marred the larger towns of Kuşadasi and Marmaris.

Whether or not you've come for the traditional Turkey, the Aegean coast has everything over the Greek islands just offshore—better preserved and more interesting ruins, thinner crowds, lower prices, and a more beautiful landscape. And scads of ferry companies are more than happy to get you there, as are Istanbul bus drivers.

North Coast

The Aegean coast north of Izmir is neither as historically interesting nor as naturally spectacular as the stretch to the south. Australians and New Zealanders often make the pilgrimage to the battlefield of **Gallipoli.** From Istanbul this involves a bus ride to Gelibolu, then a *dolmuş,* and finally a taxi to the site. Hourly ferries cross the Dardanelles from Çanakkale; cheapest of all is the tour from Çanakkale offered by **Troyanzac** travel agency (2500TL). Further south, don't miss the ruins at **Pergamon,** near the modern town of **Bergama.** In its heyday during the late Hellenistic period, Pergamon boasted a library of 200,000 volumes. In Bergama, you can stay at the **Park Hotel,** near the station. (Doubles 2750TL.) However, **Pergamon Pension** occupies a 150-year-old Italian house, and has a nicer ambience. Hot showers included. (2500TL per person.) The resort town of **Foça** is south of Bergama; three buses per day connect it to Izmir.

Due east of Izmir is the town of **Çeşme,** popular among Turkish tourists and very congested during the summer. Frequent minibuses run from Izmir's Konak station to Çeşme (1½ hr.). You can stay at the **Işik Pansiyon,** Müftü Sok. (tel. 263 05; doubles 5000TL), or at any of the slightly more expensive places that line this street and Bağlar Cad. There are **campsites** all along the penninsula; buses run to Ilica, Altinkum, and south along the beach. As long as you're reasonably far from a campsite, freelance camping is no problem. If you're in the area in late June, call 267 68 and ask about the musical offerings of Çeşme's **International Festival.** Boats connect Çeşme with the Greek island of Chios six days per week during the summer (US$15-20 one way).

Izmir, Turkey's third-largest city, is a worthwhile stopover and well connected by bus to the rest of Turkey. The **tourist office** (tel. 14 21 47) is in the Büyük Efes hotel; a *dolmuş* runs from the bus station. (Open June-Sept. Mon.-Fri. 8:30am-6pm, Sat.-Sun. 9am-5pm; Oct.-May closed Sun.) **Akso Oteli** and others along Anafartalar Cad., in the bustling market area, offer cheap if somewhat grimy rooms (doubles 2000TL). The **Bayburt Oteli,** on 1370 Sok. (tel. 12 20 13), merits a splurge (doubles 6600TL). Anafartalar Cad. is also the best place to look for a good, cheap meal. The sights in town are the **bazaar**—more authentic and less expensive than Istanbul's—and **American Express** at 2b, NATO Arkesi Talapaşa Blv. (tel. 21 79 27). There is also a **US Consulate** (tel. 13 13 69) and a **British Consulate** (tel. 21 17 95).

Take the opportunity to see an archeological excavation in process at **Sardis,** once the capital of the Lydian kingdom (7th and 6th centuries B.C.E.). The Lydians are thought to have invented dice and, more significantly, coinage. The few remaining columns of the massive **Temple of Artemis** and a second-century C.E. **synagogue** are among the most interesting of the ruins, which are currently being excavated by American archeologists who will answer visitors' questions. Sardis is 1½ hr. from Izmir along the bus route to Şart; ask to be let off, as the bus may not stop otherwise.

Kuşadasi and Surrounding Sites

In summer, Kuşadasi's proximity to the Greek island of Samos and its place in the itinerary of many Aegean cruise ships swell the town to a touristy mess. Those traveling from or to Greece should note that the Samos-Kuşadasi crossing is the most expensive (US$25 one way, US$30 round-trip, US$45 open return). Kuşadasi's popularity, however unfortunate, is deserved—it is the best base for visits to four of Turkey's most interesting ancient sites: Priene, Miletus, Didyma, and the incomparable Ephesus. Bear with Kuşadasi just as long as it takes to see these sites; for natural beauty or for a more genuine glimpse of Turkish life, head either east or south.

Kuşadasi's **tourist office** (tel. (636) 11 03), right on the waterfront, will give you maps, bus and *dolmuş* schedules, and a list of the town's pensions. (Open April-Nov. 7am-8pm; Dec.-March Mon.-Fri. 8:30am-noon and 1-5:30pm.) Accommodations here are expensive by Turkish standards. To reach the pension area, either go up Yali Cad. (the street running parallel to the water to the left of Kervanseray Hotel, if facing the water) and then turn left up the hill, or turn right up the hill at the end of Teyyare Cad. and at the police watchtower take the right fork up the hill along Aslanlar Cad. **Pension Su,** 13 Aslanlar Cad. (tel. 14 53), is cheap and clean, with friendly management. (Singles 2300TL, doubles 3200TL.) One block uphill is **Şafak Pension** (tel. 17 64), popular with backpackers (doubles 3200TL). **Hotel Rose** (tel. 11 11), nearby, has a cozy lounge and budget roof beds (2000TL, doubles

5600TL). **Camping Önder** (tel. 24 13) and **Yat Camping** (tel. 13 33) are 2 to 3km north of town on the Selçuk-Izmir road. (Both 980TL per person, 560TL per tent.)

For cheap sustenance in Kuşadasi, try one of the numerous *pide* shops near the bus station; **Konya Pide Salonu,** on Kahramanlar Cad., 50m beyond the station, is good (400-500TL). Across from the bus station,**Merkez Restaurant** has good food and fewer tourists than the waterfront. For interesting, delicious Turkish delicacies try **Kuşadasi Tandir Çorba Salonu,** 24 Saglik Cad. The menu includes *kuzu tandir* (half a sheep's head) for 1000TL, and *paça* (sheep's feet soup—really good!) for 300TL. Turn left at the police watertower; it's on the right, about two blocks down.

The **post office, telephone office,** and **police station** are up the main drag from the waterfront on Barbaros Heyrettin Cad. Continue up this road, which becomes Kahramanlar Cad., about 400m to reach the **bus station,** with connections to Istanbul (5 per day), frequent connections to Izmir via Selçuk, and connections south to Bodrum. *Dolmuş* leave from this station for Selçuk and Söke.

The most compelling reason to visit Kuşadasi is **Ephesus** (Efes), once a seaside city of 250,000 and capital of the Roman province of Asia Minor. The site extends over 2000 acres, and is the most impressive set of ancient ruins from this period. The city saw its golden age from the reign of Alexander to the Rome of early Christianity; Ephesus was the site of one of the first Christian communities. The money for a guided tour would be much better spent on a guidebook; *Ephesus: The Way It Was,* by Dr. Ü. Önen, is a good one. The ruins are near **Selçuk,** a nondescript town 17km from Kuşadasi. To get to the site, take a Selçuk *dolmuş* from Kuşadasi; it will drop you off at the turn-off to the site, about 2km from Selçuk. From there it is a 1-kilometer walk to the admission stand. (Open June-Aug. daily 8am-7pm; Sept.-May Mon.-Fri. 9am-noon and 1-5pm. Admission 1000TL, weekends 500TL.)

Ephesus lies in ruins today because of the continually receding waters of the Aegean; the city's location was changed several times before the swamps created by the silt of the river Caÿster became infested with malaria, killing the populace. From the entrance on the Kuşadasi-Selçuk road, you'll see to your left the almost intact **Vedius Gymnasium,** the rough equivalent of a high school. This is just the suburbs; through the main entrance, the colonnaded **Arcadian Street** leads to the **Grand Theater,** which once sat 24,000. The **Marble Road,** the best preserved street on the site, leads from the theater past the **Agora,** the main square of the city, to the **Library of Celsius,** whose reconstructed facade gives some idea of what the city must once have been like. Continue uphill to the **Temple of Hadrian** and the **Fountain of Trajan,** each of which would be centerpieces at most archeological sites. Be sure to bring water along; the unshaded site can get unbearably hot by 10am on a summer day.

The helpful **tourist office** at Selçuk has a complete list of pensions. **Erol Pension** (tel. 16 22) is the cleanest and has hot showers; it's one block back from the clock tower and two blocks to the left. The **Epheseus Museum** exhibits artifacts from the site. (Open daily 8:30am-6:30pm. Admission Mon.-Fri. 500TL, Sat.-Sun. 250TL). Also here are the remains of the **Basilica of St. John,** containing the tomb of St. John the Theologian, and the scant ruins of the **Temple of Artemis,** one of seven wonders of the ancient world. Selçuk also offers bus connections to Izmir and to Denizli, where you change for or from Pamukkale.

The other three sites of interest—Priene, Miletus, Didyma—are arranged in a row south of Kuşadasi. *Dolmuş* reach the sites from Kuşadasi via Söke. All three are open daily from 8:30am to 7pm; off-season 8:30am-5pm. (Admission Mon.-Fri. 400TL, Sat.-Sun. 200TL).

Priene was designed by Pytheos—architect, sculptor, and man of letters—and is nestled on the slopes of Mt. Mykale, high above the surrounding plains. The walls, Byzantine church, theater, stadium, gymnasium, and various sanctuaries of Greek and Roman gods, are all overshadowed by the Temple of Athena, once revered as the paradigm of all Ionic architecture. Priene is the oldest surviving example of a Hellenic metropolis in which the streets were laid out in a grid pattern.

From Priene, wave down any *dolmuş* going south to get to **Miletus,** an ancient harbor which is now landlocked. The superbly well preserved theater, originally set at the water's edge, seats 25,000 spectators.

Farther south is the Sanctuary of Apollo at **Didyma,** ranked as the third-largest sacred structure in the Hellenic world. The oracle here was almost as esteemed as her/his counterpart in Delphi. The graceful columns and extensive foundations still give a sense of the mammoth proportions of the original edifice: It was 120m long and composed of more than 100 columns.

Pamukkale and Aphrodisias

One of the most extraordinary natural wonders in a country of great natural beauty, **Pamukkale** is also a great place to wind down after a hard week of visiting ruins or braving Istanbul's crowds. Take an eastbound bus from Selçuk to Denizli (3½ hr.) and from there one of the frequent *dolmuş* to Pamukkale. Pamukkale's Turkish name means "Cotton Castle" and refers to the spectacular chalk-white cliffs upon which the present-day resort is built: Dripping slowly down the face of a mountainside, heated thermal waters formed multiple semicircular terraces, the edges of which spill over into petrified white cascades of stalactites. Legend has it that the formations are actually cotton (the area's principal crop) that solidified after being left out to dry by giants. In any case, the cliffs are spectacular, and the warm springs a joy to swim in year-round. Sleep in the sleepy village at the foot of the cliffs, not in the motel complexes at the top. **Kervansaray Pension** (tel. (6218) 12 09) is quiet and has a swimming pool (2500TL per person). Other good places with the same prices are **Halley Pension** and **Gold Star Pension.** For camping, try **Kur Tur** (tel. 10 29) by the red springs 3km away at Karahayit. (1500TL per person; frequent *dolmuş* travel to village). The **Pizzeria Restaurant** serves outstanding Italian pizza (1000TL) and regular Turkish food, but their dorm rooms are noisy.

At the top of the cliffs the ancient Roman ruins of **Hierapolis** include a theater, a temple of Apollo, a hole spouting poisonous carbonic gases, a Christian basilica, and Roman baths. The Roman bath complex is now an **archeological museum.** (Open Tues.-Sun. 9am-noon and 1:30-5pm. Admission Mon.-Fri. 400TL, Sat.-Sun. 200TL.) Within the grounds of the Pamukkale Motel is the **Sacred Fountain,** a pool of warm spring water with scattered Roman ruins lying on its floor. (Open daily 8:30am-6:30pm. Admission 500TL.) Three kilometers away at Karahayit is a hot, technicolor red spring. You can bathe in a series of pools leading from the springs. (Admission 500TL.)

For a less hedonistic expedition, visit the ruins at **Aphrodisias,** an important center for the arts after the fall of Pergamon in the second century B.C.E. The site, still under excavation, promises to produce some of Turkey's finest archeological finds. Particularly worth seeing are the most complete surviving Greek **stadium,** with a seating capacity of 30,000, and the elegant **Temple of Aphrodite.** Aphrodisias lies by the village of Geyre, near the village of Karacusu. From Pamukkale, take a bus to Nazilli, on the Izmir-Denizli road, and then two *dolmuş*. Transport from Kuşadasi is much easier; take a *dolmuş* to Selçuk and then a bus to the site. The first bus leaves Selçuk at 9:45am, the last leaves Aphrodisias at 5pm.

Bodrum

Bodrum, south of Izmir and across a narrow channel from the Greek island of Kos, is one of the prettiest resorts in Turkey, with picturesque harbors extending from both sides of a medieval castle. The town is a popular summer hang-out for Turkey's artists, intellectuals, and well-heeled city dwellers.

Dominating Bodrum from its strategic waterfront position stands the **Kale,** reputedly the world's best-preserved Crusader castle, constructed by the notorious Order of the Knights of St. John during the fifteenth and sixteenth centuries. Today, the structure houses the **Museum of Underwater Archeology,** a fascinating collection of artifacts from ancient shipwrecks, excavated from sites along the Turkish coast. (Open Tues.-Sun. 8:30am-5pm. Admission Mon.-Fri. 500TL, Sat.-Sun. 250TL.) Bodrum is built on top of Halicarnassus, capital of the pre-Hellenic kingdom of Caria and birthplace of Herodotus, one of the first historians. The most famous ruins are those of one of the seven wonders of the world, the **Mausoleum,** or tomb of King Mausolus, who reigned in the fourth century B.C.E. Follow the signs from Neyzen Tevfik up Haman Sok. onto Turgut Reis Cad.

The **tourist office** (tel. (6141) 10 91) is next to the castle. They can provide you with complete accommodations listings and a lousy map. (Open May-Sept. daily 8:30am-7pm; Oct.-April Mon.-Fri. 8:30am-noon and 1:30-5:30pm.) Accommodations in the summer are expensive, but—except for singles—plentiful. Often there are rooms to let in private homes; look for signs reading "*Oda Var.*" Pensions charge between 6000 and 10,000TL for a double, and few will bargain in summer. The cheaper pensions are located along the right bay (facing the water) before the yacht harbor, and along the middle of the left bay, before the Halikarnas Hotel, and up the hill. In town, **Yilmaz Pansiyon,** Cumhuriyet Cad. (tel. 13 63), has an excellent view of the harbor and is redolent of baking ice cream cones. (Doubles 6000TL) **Durak Pansiyon** (tel. 24 02), off Cumhuriyet Cad. near the end, is one of the few places that takes singles (2500TL per person). On the other side of town, off Neyzen Teufik, **Amca** and **Belmi pensions** are good, but more expensive.

Bodrum is known for its outstanding if expensive seafood restaurants. Try **Orhan's #7,** in the covered alley off Kale Cad. **Sokkali Ali Doksan Restaurant,** 15 Kale Cad., doesn't serve fish, but is cheap, good, and always packed. At night, Cumhuriyet Cad. is the place to be for cheap *kebab* stalls, bars, discos, ice cream stalls, and cafes. **Fiesta** has deliciously fresh sandwiches. From the international phones by the castle (with your back to the castle), take your farthest right; it's on the left side. (Open daily noon-11pm.) For live Turkish music, have a few drinks at the **Mavi Bar,** near the end of Cumhuriyet Cad.

Frequent buses connect Bodrum with Söke and Marmaris. Boats connect Bodrum with Kos (June-Aug. daily; May-Sept. 1 per week; 11,000TL one way). There are also ferries to Datça during the summer (6000TL one way). Inquire at any travel agent. **Karya Tours** and **Flama Tours,** both on the waterfront, are particularly good and efficient.

The reason behind the throng of tourists in Bodrum is the peninsula of the same name. *Dolmuş motorlari* boats leave Bodrum harbor daily in the summer at around 11am, visit beaches and coves inaccessible by car, and return in the evening (2500TL). **Gümbet Beach,** 3km out of Bodrum town, is the most popular beach in the area; you can camp at **Setaş Camping** for 1500TL. On the beach at **Bitez,** one cove further from town, bars have built docks out over the water so that you can have your drink and work on your tan at the same time. **Gümüşlük,** at the end of the peninsula, makes another fine day trip from Bodrum, or you can stay at either **Mindos Pansiyon** (doubles 6000TL) or **Ali Baba Camping** (700TL per person).

Mediterranean Coast

From Marmaris in the west to Antakya near the Syrian border, this 800-kilometer stretch of coastline offers everything from lively resorts to unexplored, inaccessible beaches. The main drawback are the high summer temperatures—usually over 100°F in July and August—that make it less pleasant than the Aegean.

West of Antalya are the great beaches at Ölü Deniz, the archeological site of Xanthos, the ancient port and desert-like beach at Patara, and the seaside villages of Kalkan and Kaş. Between Antalya and Alanya there is less scenery and more tourists, but also the Roman sites of Perge, Aspendos, and Side. After Alanya tourists are virtually non-existant and the coastline becomes mountainous again, before flattening into a hot, dusty coastal strip which extends to the Biblical cities of Tarsus and Antakya (Antioch), on the Syrian border.

Marmaris and the Datça Peninsula

The next resort south of Bodrum, tacky **Marmaris** is overdeveloped and has a dirty beach. The area around Marmaris, though, is quite picturesque, with wooded mountains lining the coast. The **tourist office,** by the water, has a helpful English-speaking staff who can provide you with a map. (Open June-Sept. daily 8:30am-5:30pm; Oct.-May Mon.-Fri. only.) **Yaşar Pansiyon,** by the bus station (tel. 20 77), doesn't look like much, but has spotless rooms (2000TL per person). Also try **Kordon Pansiyon,** 8 Kemeralti Mah. (tel. 47 62), one block north of the post office (3000TL per person). Cheaper, but cramped and noisy, is **Star Pansiyon** (tel. 17 77). Look for the sign at the public fountain (2000TL per person). Eat at **Ay Yildiz Restaurant,** by the public fountain. For breakfast or drinks in the evening, go to **Kemal's Hangout** on the yacht harbor.

Marmaris is well-connected to Rhodes by ferry (Mon.-Sat. at 8:30am, 17,000TL one way, 20,000TL same day round-trip, 30,000TL open round-trip). You can purchase tickets at any travel agent. Frequent buses run between Marmaris and Bodrum or Fethiye.

Don't stay in Marmaris any longer than you have to; instead, head out to the stunningly beautiful **Datça Peninsula.** The Pamukkale bus company travels between Marmaris and the little village of Datça (10 per day, 2 hr.). At Datça, stay either at the **Huzur Pansiyon** (tel. 10 52), up the hill, or at **Yali Pansiyon** (tel. 10 59), above the hardware store. Both charge 2000TL per person. You can camp on the beach, either officially at **Ilica Camping** (1000TL per person), or unofficially anywhere else. Feridun, the owner of the campground, might take you on a wild boar hunt. In the likely event that you don't catch anything, settle for the good food at the **Denizati Restaurant,** nearby. Thirty kilometers east of Datça along the main road is the well-run but touristy **Aktur Camping** (tel. 11 67; 1350TL per person, 900TL per tent).

Right at the end of the Datça Peninsula sits the Hellenistic site of **Knidos,** a major attraction in ancient times for its statue of Aphrodite. The statue unfortunately no longer exists, but the site is still interesting and notable for its beautiful location on a bluff above the sea. While you're out here, try the excellent *balik çorba* (fish soup) at the **Fisherman Restaurant.** Knidos is approachable by land along a tortuous 40-kilometer road from Datça—a *dolmuş* will take you only as close as the village of **Yaziköy,** 7km short of the ruins. Taxis make the trip for 15,000 to 20,000TL. **Karya Tours** (tel. (6141) 17 59) runs excursion boats from Bodrum for US$24.

The ruins of **Caunos,** near the town of **Dalyan,** lie between Marmaris and Fethiye. Each year, archeologists uncover more rock tombs and temples on the site; some predict that it will soon rival Ephesus in importance and scale. For the time being, it is relatively undiscovered and blessed with a verdant natural setting which itself is worth a visit. Boats run from Dalyan to Caunos and carry on to the beach (8000TL round-trip); it is often possible to arrange to camp overnight and be picked up the next day. Staying at one of Dalyan's many pensions or camping by Lake Köycegiz are other options, but both involve sharing the night with swarms of mosquitoes.

Fethiye to Kaş

The small modern port of Fethiye is not the pristine coastal village you've been looking for. Nonetheless, it harbors some striking Lycian rock tombs, and offers a variety of excursions. The **tourist office** on the waterfront provides free maps and pension listings. (Open May-Sept. daily 8:30am-7pm; Oct.-April Mon.-Fri. 8:30am-5:30pm.) Stay at **Ülgen Pension** on Cumhuriyet Mah. (tel. 34 91; 2000TL per person). Excursion boats leave from the harbor for the so-called **Twelve Island Tour,** which hops around the archipelago of the Bay of Fethiye (full day, 4000TL). There are also tours to Xantos, Letoon, and Patara, to Caunos and Dalyon, and to Ölü

Deniz and St. Nicolas Island. Inquire at the tourist office or at Big Tur, 30 Atatürk Cad.

Don't fritter your time away in Fethiye when you could be lounging on the outrageously fine beaches of **Ölü Deniz,** 14km away. This sandy lagoon can be reached by frequent shared taxis and less frequent *dolmuş* vans from Fethiye. Here is a hedonistic ritual site extraordinaire. Sun and swim all day, then dance the night away at any of the campsites' free discos (Derya, Deniz, Sun Kamping, Moon Disco, until 2-3am). All this without ever having to deal with tourist shops, hustlers, or carpet dealers. You can change money at the grocery store behind Derya Camping, but rates are better in Fethiye. **Ölü Deniz Camping** (tel. 12 50), 300m to the right as you face the sea, has a small patch of beach (camping 1000TL per person, bungalows for two 6000TL). Two kilometers to the left, over a ridge, is the **municipal campground** with a huge beach and plenty of shady pine trees (1500TL per tent, 300TL per person). **Kumsal Motel** charges only 500TL for sleeping on the roof; **Deniz Camping** has a dormitory (1500TL per bed), roof (1000TL per person), and bungalows (5000TL per person including breakfast). Most people eat in the overpriced campground cafeterias; it's cheaper to buy groceries in Fethiye. **Pirate's Inn,** 100m up the road to Fethiye, has deliciously interesting food.

Between Kalkan and Fethiye are two historical sites and a marvelous beach. **Xanthos,** the ancient Lycian capital, has the best examples of Lycian rock tombs and funeral monuments. Fifteen kilometers from Xanthos, on a desert-like beach, are the ruins of **Patara.** This ancient Lycian port was the seat of the Roman governor to Lycia, the site of an oracle to Apollo, and the birthplace of St. Nicolas (otherwise known as Santa Claus). The ruins include a necropolis, the triumphant Arch of Mettius Modestus, Roman baths, a Christian basilica, a temple, a theater, and a granary. But nothing can beat the 17-kilometer stretch of deserted, sandy beach. Sleeping on the beach is prohibited, but **St. Nikolas Pension** and **Golden Pension** are both excellent (2000TL per person). The dirty **campsite** charges only 500TL per tent. Any bus from Fethiye to Kalkan will drop you at the turn-off to Patara, from which it's a 6-kilometer walk or an easy hitch.

Kalkan, between Fethiye and Kaş, is a picture-postcard Turkish fishing village. The tiny harbor is enclosed by a graceful breakwater and surrounded by a huddle of austere old stone mansions with handsome balconies. Unfortunately, Kalkan is slowly becoming infected with Mediterranean coast commercialism. Accommodations are relatively expensive, but food is reasonable and quite good. **Yilmaz Pansiyon** is clean and well-decorated (doubles and triples with bath 6000TL, 1500TL to sleep on pillows and couch in the hall, 1000TL for roof). **Kervan Han Pansiyon** has friendly management and a spacious terrace (2500TL per person, 1500TL on the terrace). **Smile Restaurant,** near the waterfront, serves the best food. **Höyük Bar,** underneath Yilmaz Pansiyon, plays the Grateful Dead and sets their tables with tie-dye tablecloths. Purchase Turkish pants here; Kalkan is famous for its tailors.

Kaş is a great place to waste an entire month. It seems that all who come here stay longer than originally planned, seduced by the serpentine coastline and genuine hospitality. The staff at the **tourist office** on Cumhuriyet Cad. (tel. 12 38) may not speak English. (Open late April-Sept. daily 8am-8pm; Oct.-April daily 8:30am-5:30pm.) Most of the travel agencies on the waterfront offer the same excursions, but shop around for prices. The **Mini Pension** is spotlessly clean (doubles 5000TL). **Kisnet Pansiyon** and the hippyish **Peace Pansiyon** are also good and have terraces you can sleep on (doubles 5000TL, 1000TL on terrace). All three of these are located up Uzun Çarşi Cad. **Kaş Kamping,** on Hastane Cad. past the hospital, has a fantastic seaside location next to a lovely Greek theater, but very mediocre facilities and too many rocks (1000TL per person). Eat in **Derya Restaurant,** in the covered alley running from the old bus station to Cumhuriyet Cad., where you can pile your plate with appetizers for 1500TL.

An excellent day trip takes you to **Kekova,** a partially submerged Lycian city about 3½ hours east by boat. In summer the fare is about 4000TL, but at other times you should be able to find someone to take you for less. The trip (plan on spending about 12 hr.) includes Byzantine ruins and two nearby fishing villages, one lying under a cliff honeycombed with Lycian tombs. Another possible day trip is to Santa Claus country. He was born in Patara, became famous for gift-giving, was appointed Bishop of Myra, and was later martyred. You can visit Santa's tomb at the **Christian Basilica** in **Denre;** his bones—except his jaw and teeth which are at the Archaeological Museum in Antalya—were stolen and taken to Italy 1000 years ago. Buses running from Kaş to Antalya stop in Denre. You can sometimes visit the Greek island of **Kastelorizo** (40 min.), but you can't officially cross into Greece here (inquire at Kaş Sea Tours at the harbor).

Antalya and Alanya

Antalya, a rough 4½ hour bus ride from Kaş, is a dull city with mediocre beaches; come here only to visit the great ruined Roman cities to the east. Connections to major Turkish cities are possible by Turkish Airlines and Turkish Maritime Lines, as well as by bus. To get to the main **tourist office** (tel. (311) 117 47) from the bus station, follow Kazim Özalp Cad. toward town, turn right onto Cumhuriyet Cad., and go 100m past the statue of Atatürk. (Open in summer Mon.-Fri. 8am-9pm, Sat.-Sun. 8am-7:30pm; off-season daily 8am-5:30pm.) The best pensions are in the old city, southeast of the yacht harbor. You can stay cheaply in old Ottoman homes; one of the nicest is **Adler Pansiyon** at Barbaros Mah. and Civelek Sok. (3000TL per person). Signs point you from the bus station to the bohemian **Sima Pension** (rooms 3000TL per person, dorm bed 2500TL, mat on roof 1500TL).

East of Antalya stretches the ancient Roman province of **Pamphylia.** Several important and only partially excavated sites exist in this area. If you're heading out, first visit Antalya's **Archeological Museum** on Kenan Evren Bulvari at the western end of town, which houses many of the artifacts found thus far. (Open Tues.-Sat. 9am-noon and 1:30-6pm.) Then buy *Pamphilia: An Archeological Guide* (3000TL), which is more informative and better translated than most of its kind; it includes plans of the sites.

At **Perge,** 16km from Antalya, a theater decorated with beautiful marble reliefs, a long colonnaded avenue, and a stadium all conjure up images of the city as it was in its heyday. (Open daily 8:30am-6pm. Admission Mon.-Fri. 500TL, Sat.-Sun. 250TL.) To get here from Antalya take a *dolmuş* to Aksu from the central *dolmuş* station, then walk 2km. Much more impressive are the ruins at **Aspendos,** 49km from Antalya. No imaginative reconstruction is necessary here, thanks to the efforts of the Seljuk Turks, who preserved the site and used it as a pilgrimage way station. The huge theater is one of the best preserved in the world; even the stage is almost completely intact.

Alanya is an unabashed resort town with dirty beaches. If you can't change buses quickly enough, try the simple but clean **Yayla Palas** (2500TL per person); from the main coastal road, walk east past the PTT and turn right, taking the right fork up the hill to Yayla Palas. Buses from Antalya to Alanya leave every one to two hours.

Silifke and Mersin

Five buses per day cover the rough road between Alanya and Silifke (7 hr.). Consider breaking the trip at **Anamur** (5 hr.), a dusty town close to a long beach on which you can camp, a medieval castle, and the Roman site of Anamurium. **Silifke** is useful mainly for its bus connections to the east and inland to Konya or Ankara, and for its proximity to the port of **Taşucu,** a departure point for northern Cyprus. There is no reason to linger in Silifke or in any of the crowded beach towns between here and Mersin.

The caves of **Cennet ve Cehennem** (Heaven and Hell) are about 20km east of Silifke; take a bus heading towards Mersin, get off at the Narlikuyu Museum and walk 3km uphill. The grandest of the three caves is Heaven; Hell is just that. You'll need a lamp (and unfortunately, a guide—they own the lamps), but you should be able to arrange an impromptu tour for 1000TL; have the guide show you the twelfth-century Armenian chapel as well. You can stay by the Narlikuyu Museum (3000TL per person) or at the beach campground 4km farther east.

Mersin is Turkey's largest Mediterranean port, of note to travelers for its ferry connections to northern Cyprus. The Friday boat to Cyprus continues to Lattakia, Syria (17500TL); Syrian visas are available in Istanbul and Ankara. The **Turkish Maritime Lines** (Denizyollari) office is on the waterfront just across from the tourist office. The **tourist office** can help you find lodgings (tel. (741) 163 58; open daily 8:30am-5:30pm). **Hotel Doğan,** 11 Buyuk Hamam Sok. (tel. (741) 217 50), a few blocks inland from the large mosque, lets doubles for 2600TL.

Antakya

Antakya dominates the fertile Turkish province of Hatay, bordered to the east and south by Syria and only annexed to Turkey in a 1939 plebiscite. Breezes from the sea and the surrounding mountains make Antakya a welcome respite from the summer heat of eastern Turkey and Syria. The main square, Atatürk Meydani, lies right by the river. Here you'll find the **Archeological Museum,** which exhibits finds from Antakya's past as Antioch, one of the largest cities of the Hellenistic and Roman Mediterranean. The collection of late Roman mosaics is famous throughout the world. (Open Mon. 1:30-5:30pm, Tues.-Sun. 8:30am-noon and 1:30-5:30pm. Admission Mon.-Fri. 500TL, Sat.-Sun. 250TL.) Wander through the bustling **market,** northeast of the main bridge, and through the winding alleys of the **old city,** southeast of the bridge. Two kilometers from the center of town along the road to Reyhanli is St. Peter's church, where St. Peter drew together the first congregation and decided to name the new religion "Christianity." (Open Tues.-Sun. 8am-noon and 1:30-6:30pm. Admission 400TL.)

From Atatürk Meydani head down Atatürk Cad. to the **tourist office** (open Mon.-Fri.). Returning to Atatürk Meydani, cross the bridge and you'll see **Otel Saray** diagonally to the right (tel. (891) 254 37; doubles 3300TL). Antakya's **bus station** is located off Hurriyet Cad., which runs south to the main bridge. The most frequent connections are to Gaziantep and Mersin; buses also run to Ankara and Istanbul. If you have a Syrian visa, you can take a bus directly to Aleppo (Halep in Turkish), 100km away (7000TL). You must exchange US$100 at the border. Daily buses also run to Jordan (Ürdün in Turkish; 14,000TL).

The **Hatay coast** is most interesting south of the resort of Assuz. From here the road separates lush farmland and mountain ridges from a deserted gravel beach. A new road (scheduled for 1988) will follow the beach all the way to Samandağ. Inquire at the tourist office about *dolmuş.* **Gaziantep,** 200km northeast of Antakya, is a city of 450,000 in the center of Turkey's pistachio-growing region. It's not very interesting, but has the best bus connections to the Middle East. Daily **buses** run to Aleppo (7000TL), Damascus (7000TL), Lattakia (7000TL), Baghdad (15,000TL), Saudi Arabia (25,000TL), and Jordan. Hitching into these countries is also quite easy from here. During the Hajj (most of July and Aug.), non-Muslims cannot enter Saudi Arabia.

Central Turkey

The forbidding Anatolian plateau, stretching for mile after rugged mile, was the first part of Turkey to be civilized; neolithic sites dot the area surrounding Ankara, Turkey's capital. Konya, once the capital of the Seljuk Empire, offers a variety of handsome mosques and tombs. But unless you're a real history enthusiast, skip this otherwise unexciting region for Cappadocia and Eastern Turkey.

Konya

Konya was the twelfth-century capital of the Seljuk sultans and has been Turkey's religious center since the thirteenth century, when Mevlana taught here. Founder of the famous order of Whirling Dervishes, Mevlana believed spiritual perfection and union with the divine could be achieved through the ecstatic dance. In 1925 Atatürk dissolved the order and today the dervishes dance only once a year (Dec. 12-17 in 1987); during this week performances take place twice per day (tickets start at 2000TL).

You can spot the thirteenth-century **Mevlana Tekke** by its remarkable enameled green tower. Inside the complex, originally a kind of monastery, are the *türbes* of Mevlana and other dervishes and an interesting museum exhibiting prayer rugs, musical instruments, elaborately decorated garments, and beautifully calligraphed Korans. (Open Tues.-Sun. 8:30am-6pm, Mon. 3-6pm. Admission 500TL.) Konya's other major attractions are on or around Alaadin Tepesi (Aladdin Hill), several hundred yards up Hükümet Cad. **Alaadin Camii,** near the hilltop, is a very plain thirteenth-century mosque in the Syrian Seljuk style (closed in 1987 for restoration). Note the pieces of Roman and Byzantine columns incorporated on the facade, and the interwoven black and white marble which matches that on the **Karatay Medresi** below the mosque across the street. The Karatay, originally a thirteenth-century theological school, now houses a collection of blue Seljuk tiles. The Seljuks studied astrology through the reflection of the night sky off the pool in the main chamber. Several blocks away, the **Archeological Museum** houses interesting classical and Hellenistic art, with one outstanding piece: a third-century sarcophagus illustrating the labors of Hercules. (Open Tues.-Sun. 8am-noon and 1:30-5:30pm. Admission 400TL.) While in Konya, be sure to spend some time wandering in the enchantingly chaotic **market,** between the Aziziye Mosque and the **post office** (open 24 hours) on Alaadin Cad.

Get a map of the city from the **tourist office** on Mevlana Cad., the main street (tel. (331) 110 74) next to the Mevlana Tekke. (Open in summer daily 9am-6pm; off-season 9am-5pm.) A *Kilim* (woven rug) hangs in every room at the **Yeşil Bursa Hotel,** 8 Keçeci Sok. (tel. (331) 128 14); head southwest from the Selimiye Mosque (doubles 4000TL, showers 400TL). You'll find much cleaner rooms at the new **Hotel Tur,** 13 Eş'ârizade Sok. (tel. (331) 198 25), around the corner east of the tourist office (doubles 6000TL).

Buses run 10 times per day between Konya and the Mediterranean town of Silifke (5 hr.), even more frequently to and from Ankara (5 hr.), and 15 times per day to Izmir. Nightime buses run to and from Istanbul. If you arrive at the bus station during the day, take a mini-bus marked "Mevlana" to the center; at night you can try a conveyance unique to Konya, a three-wheeled cart. Both leave from behind the station. After midnight, you'll have to take a taxi.

Near Konya

The basis of Turkey's claim to being one of the birthplaces of civilization lies at **Çatalhöyük,** near the town of Çümra, 50km south of Konya on the Silifke road. An advanced neolithic community, Çatalhöyük vies with Jericho for the title "world's first city." Its famous cave drawings and all artifacts have been removed to Ankara and Holland and little remains but a few crumbling walls. The tour isn't really worth it, but the guidebook on sale at Mevlana is. Take a bus from the Eski Garage near Pira Paşa Mosque to Çümra (45 min.), then a taxi the remaining distance (4500TL round-trip).

Every half hour a municipal bus leaves from Alaadin Cad. to the isolated village of **Sille,** with numerous rock-dwellings and a fourth-century church. Inquire at the tourist office about an excursion to **Karadağ,** a mountain top with several crumbling churches dating from Roman times.

Ankara

Like Washington, Bonn, or Canberra, Ankara is the capital but not the first city. The city's modernity surprises those arriving from its primitive countryside. Pleasant and less touristed than Istanbul, Ankara has a handful of interesting sights, and a tremendous museum. It's also a transportation hub for travel east and south, and home to all the embassies in Turkey.

Orientation and Practical Information

Although it's quicker to travel between Istanbul and Ankara by bus (6 hr., 4000TL), the overnight train may be more convenient and comfortable (departs at about 9pm, 11 hr., 2600TL). There are also connections to Izmir, Konya, Cappadocia, Erzurum, other Turkish cities, and Iran, Syria, and Jordan.

Try to arrive with a map; this city of two million is huge and confusing. **Kizilay** and **Yenişehir** are the central districts.

Tourist Office: Main office at 33 Gazi Kemal Bulvari (tel. 230 19 11). Take bus #65 from Ulus. There is a more helpful office in Ulus, at 4 Istanbul Cad. Both offices open in summer Mon.-Fri. 8:30am-5:30pm, Sat. 8:30am-5pm, Sun. 8:30am-2pm; off-season Mon.-Fri. 8:30am-5:30pm.

American Express: 7 Cinnah Cad. (tel. 167 73 34). Take bus #13 which stops across from the Ulus post office. Mail held. Wired money not accepted. Open Mon.-Fri. 9am-6pm, Sat. 9am-1pm.

Post Office: PTT, on Atatürk Bulvari in Ulus. Open 24 hours. Poste Restante open daily 9am-5pm.

Telephones: At the post office. Open 24 hours. Also at the bus and train stations. **Telephone code:** 4.

Buses: Ankara's station is enormous. Take bus #16 from the station to Ulus. Buses begin here for destinations throughout Turkey. Frequent departures to Istanbul, Izmir, Konya, Sivas, and Erzurum. Buses also run to Nevşehir and Ürgüp every hr. until 8pm. Daily buses to Teheran (20,000TL), Baghdad (22,000TL), and Aleppo, Syria (12,500TL). To Pakistan and India you can reportedly change buses in Teheran.

Embassies: All embassies in Ankara are south of Hurriyet Sq., along Atatürk Bul. **U.S.,** 110 Atatürk Bul. (tel. 126 54 70). **Canada,** 75 Nenehatun Cad. (tel. 127 58 03). **U.K.,** 46a Şehit Ersan Cad. (tel. 127 43 10). **Australia,** 83 Nenehatun Cad. (tel. 128 67 15). Travelers from **New Zealand** should contact the British mission. **Bulgaria,** 124 Atatürk Bul. (tel. 126 74 55). **Iran,** 10 Tahran Cad. (tel. 127 43 20). **Iraq,** 11 Turan Emeksiz Sok. (tel. 126 61 18). **Jordan,** 18 Dede Korkut Sok. (tel. 139 42 30). **Syria,** 7 Abdullah Cevdet Sok. (tel. 139 45 88). The embassy of **Northern Cyprus** is at 20 Incirli Sok. (tel. 137 95 38).

Bookstore: If you've come this far, you probably have an interest in Turkish culture and literature. There's a great bookstore on the northeast side of Hurriyet Sq., **Tarhan Kitabevi.** The learned gentleman who works here can guide you through a good sample of contemporary Turkish writing in translation.

Hitchhiking: Ankara is a good place to hitch a ride on a truck either east or west, as it lies on the main Istanbul-Teheran highway. To head east, try the Bayindir Baraji Mocamp, Kayaş (tel. 19 41 61), 15km east of the city. Any bus to Kirikkale or Yozgut, or a long-distance bus to Samsun, Trabzon, or Erzurum, will get you there. Going west, your best bet is the Kervansaray Susuzköy Mocamp, 22km west of town on the Istanbul highway. Likewise, any buses to Kazam or Kizilcahamam or the Istanbul bus will get you there.

Accommodations and Food

Budget accommodations in Ankara aren't very good, as it's not really a tourist town. The best place to look is in the **Ulus** district, at the north end of Atatürk Bulvari. Avoid places right on the main road; they're noisy and cater to the clientele of the seamy nightclubs below. First try the **Şehir Palas Oteli,** 10 Şan Sok. (tel 10 84 14), just off Anafartalar Cad. (2000TL per person). **Hotel Pinar,** 14 Hisar Parki Cad. (tel. 311 89 51), has dirty bathrooms but friendly management (doubles 4200TL). If this is full, walk downhill two blocks and take a left on Hal Önü Sok. to **Sahil Palas Oteli** (tel. 10 69 35), with slightly cramped doubles for 4800TL.

The **Yeni Karpiç Restaurant,** in the mall diagonally across from the main post office, is a bit expensive, but offers fantastic food and a patio setting (steak and mushrooms 2200TL). If you turn right off Atatürk Bul. just after the post office, you'll come to Ankara's big **food market,** where you'll find everything from sugared almonds to live chickens.

Sights

From the tourist office, turn right and you'll come to Atatürk Bulvari, the main north-south boulevard. Almost any bus going north will take you to **Ulus,** the older section of town. Near the southern end of the citadel that dominates the old town, you'll find the fantastic **Anadolu Medeniyetleri Muzesi** (Museum of Anatolian Civilizations). Take a taxi (500TL) or walk up the hill past Ulus Meydani and the equestrian statue of Atatürk, turn right onto Hisarparki Cad., and right again onto Ipek Street. The museum's outstanding neolithic and Hittite collections are the primary reason for a visit to Ankara. The setting is unique: A restored Ottoman *han* and *bedesten* (covered bazaar), its halls populated by canaries, houses a collection of artifacts that trace all of Anatolian history. (Open Tues.-Sun. 8:30am-12:30pm and 1:30-5:30pm. Admission 500TL.) While in the area, stroll through the **bazaar,** the town-within-a-town inside the citadel walls, and the **Alâeddin Mosque.**

Don't leave Ankara without visiting **Anit Kabir,** the tomb of Atatürk. Its sheer size and the museum of Atatürk's personal effects will give you a sense of Turkey's immense reverence for its national hero. The site is in a large park west of the tourist office (a 25-min. walk from Kizilay). The southbound #63 bus on Atatürk Cad. will take you to the southern entrance of the park, where the mausoleum is. (Open Tues.-Sun. 9am-12:30pm and 1:30-5pm.)

Other sights in Ankara include the **Temple of Augustus,** built in 25 B.C.E. over the site of earlier temples to Cybele, an Anatolian fertility god, and to the Phrygian moon god, but later converted into a Byzantine church. Nearby are **Haci Bazram Mosque,** the **Ethnographic Museum,** the old parliament, and the zoo.

Near Ankara

If you're headed east from Ankara, don't miss the sprawling ruins of **Hattusas,** the Hittite capital, some 200km from Ankara off the highway to Samsun. The first people to smelt iron, the Hittites conquered Anatolia in around 1700 B.C.E. and the Assyrians fled to the southeast. United under a central authority at Hattusas, the Hittites vied with the Egyptians for control of the fertile lands of Mesopotamia. The western Sea People razed Hattusas shortly after 1200 B.C.E., but archeologists have unearthed enough to provide a fair representation of the city. Along the 9-kilometer wall encircling Hattusas, the **Yerkasi,** a 70-meter-long tunnel/gate, merits a special visit. Be sure to stroll through the **Büyükmabet** ("Big Temple"), from whose inner sanctum the Hittite high priest ruled the empire. To enter the chamber, subjects had to cross a drawbridge over two pools of water. Your admission ticket (500TL, students 50TL) is also valid for **Yazilikaya,** an open-air temple where the Hittite pantheon is represented in bas-relief. Yazilikaya lies 2km south of Hattusas.

To get to Hattusas, take a bus to Sungurlu (1500TL) and then a *dolmuş* to Boğazkale, right next to the site (500TL); the alternative is hiring a taxi for 5000TL. You need at least half a day to walk through the site. There is a small campsite midway between Hattusas and Yazilikaya. Sungurlu has several cheap hotels.

Cappadocia

The ancient province of Cappadocia is the most interesting part of Turkey's central plateau. Beautifully eroded volcanic formations create a striking landscape of cone-shaped monoliths and fairy chimneys clustered in valleys and along ridges. The soft volcanic rock that eroded to form these bizarre geological configurations is also responsible for Cappadocia's many fascinating historical remains: When Christians arrived here in the sixth century, they carved houses, churches, and entire cities out of the rock. The result is an extraordinary blend of natural and built environments, with architecture as marvelous as its surroundings. The central area of the province is defined by the triangle formed by the city of Nevşehir and the smaller towns of Avanos and Ürgüp, about 300km southeast of Ankara.

Nevşehir

Most buses stop in ugly Nevşehir, though some visit Ürgüp and Avanos as well. In addition to the Ankara bus, a bus departs every morning for Konya, Mersin, and Tarsus, and overnight rides go to Izmir and Istanbul. Though Nevşehir is not an interesting place, it is the center of the region's *dolmuş* routes. Go to the **tourist office** (tel. (4851) 11 37), 600m down Aksaray Cad. from the bus station—follow the signs. They can help you contact a student guide who will take you to the sites for less than the travel agencies charge. They'll also provide a map of Nevşehir and the region, showing all *dolmuş* routes and stations. (Open in summer daily 8:30am-noon and 1:30-6pm; off-season Mon.-Fri. 9:30am-5:30pm.) One *dolmuş* route runs to the underground city of Kaymakli and Derinkuyu on its way to Niğde. Another goes to Üçhisar Göreme and the Open-Air Museum and Ürgüp. A third goes to Avanos. A fourth travels to Aksaray, where you can catch a bus to Konya or the Mediterranean coast. Municipal buses also run nine times per day at regularly scheduled times (check at the tourist office) between Nevşehir and Ürgüp, for less than the *dolmuş*. Guided tours offered by travel agencies generally cost the same whether from Nevşehir, Göreme, or Ürgüp (7500TL per person). Hitching around the triangle is very easy during the summer; there is also the expensive option of hiring a taxi or private car for the day.

Don't stay in Nevşehir unless you have to; check to see if your bus also stops at Ürgüp (most do). If you're stuck in Nevşehir, stay at the **Otel Sunar Palas,** 2 Belediye Cad. (tel. 14 44); follow Aksaray St. and turn right after Akbank. (1300TL per person.)

Kaymakli and Derinkuyu

These two extensive underground cities are both south of Nevşehir, on the road to Niğde; the first is 20km away, the second 29km. Both are fun places to spend a couple of hours, particularly if you've brought a flashlight or candle and can imagine yourself a pioneering archeologist or a ninth-century Christian fleeing quickly and silently into the maze of tunnels away from Arab marauders. Over centuries of purges, Christians living in neighboring towns bored this intricate tunnel system to escape from their homes directly into the hidden refuge below. The size of Kaymakli—miles of tunnels, five levels burrowing down hundreds of feet—is boggling; Derinkuyu is almost twice as big, with escape tunnels (now blocked) 5 to 6km long, and one passage believed to lead back to Kaymakli. In both cities, the tunnels were deliberately built low and narrow to hamper the progress of invaders and twentieth-century tourists. The tunnels are very poorly marked, and you won't have explored extensively until you get lost at least once—just head in the "up" direction and listen for other tourists.

In the tunnels, see if you can distinguish the kitchens from churches, the bedrooms from stables. Even during the hottest days it's cool and damp down below, so you might want to bring a sweater. Try to plan your return from Derinkuyu by 4pm and from Kaymakli by 4:30pm; later, *dolmuş* are rare. You may be able to hitch with other tourists. (Both sites open daily 8:30am-noon and 1:30-6pm. Admission 500TL.)

Göreme

The name Göreme refers to three things, which can make for some confusion: the general area of Göreme Valley, the cluster of churches known as the Göreme Open-Air Museum, and the town of Göreme, sometimes called **Avçilar.** The last is a small village right in the center of Cappadocia; its proximity to the open air museums of Göreme and Zelve, as well as its many fine and inexpensive pensions, make it a good base. If you're offered a cheap spot on a roof, be sure to have a warm sleeping bag; like the rest of Cappadocia, Göreme gets pretty cool at night.

If you want to experience cave-dwelling with the comfort of a hotel, try **Peri's Pension** (tel. (4857) 11 36), where rooms are in a giant rock cone. Rooms on the lower level (without windows) are cooler and cost less (1500TL per person). Their bar, also carved into the rock, has authentic and tasteful Cappadocian decoration and frequent *saz* music. The **Köse Pension and Camping** is a friendly travelers' place run by a Turkish man and his affable Scots wife. Camp here (500TL per person) but don't stay in the filthy rooms. **Halil Pansion,** on the opposite side of town (tel. (4857) 10 30), is carved out of a rock cliff (2000TL per person).

The most impressive concentration of sights in the region is at the **Göreme Open-Air Museum,** 1km out of Göreme village on the Ürgüp road. The churches here are the legacy of Cappadocian Christianity in the Byzantine Empire. St. Basil, who lived in the fourth century, founded one of the first Christian monasteries here, setting down religious tenets which greatly influenced the teachings of St. Benedict, and thus spread throughout the Western monastic movement. The monks of Cappadocia built the majority of the churches in Göreme between the fourth and tenth centuries, and inhabited the area until the formation of the modern Turkish Republic, when all Anatolian Christians were traded to Greece for the Muslims living there. The remaining churches are remarkable for their frescoes, which span most of the Byzantine era, and though often vandalized, provide a comprehensive history of that era of Christian art. The earliest frescoes are simple crosses and Christian symbols such as the palm tree and the fish, usually done in red and dating from the three or four hundred years after Basil's death. For a time thereafter, during the iconoclastic period, all representations were deemed idolatrous; the designs are uniquely geometrical. Finally, toward the end of the first millenium, the Byzantine Renaissance began, and sophisticated religious portraits became the rule. From this period (11th to 13th centuries) come the most impressive Göreme frescoes. These are found in the **Barbara Kilise, Elmali Kilise** (Church of the Apple), **Çarikli Kilise** (Church of the Sandal), and **Karanlik Kilise,** whose darkness has done a particularly good job of preserving the frescoes. (Open daily 8:30am-noon and 1:30-6pm. Admission 700TL.) The **bank** and **post office** here are open the same hours as the site.

Near Göreme

The road north from Göreme to Avanos leads past the lesser site of the Christian sanctuary at Çavuşin to the much more interesting **Zelve Valley,** a city carved into the pink rock which carbon-14 dating and tattered Elvis Presley posters show to have been inhabited as late as the early 1950s. Though its frescoes don't compare with those at the Open-Air Museum, its caverns are much more extensive. (Open daily 8am-5:30pm. Admission 500TL.)

A few kilometers farther, the landscape switches from Dalí and pop surrealism to something reminiscent of Ansel Adams's American Southwest. The potters of

Alvanos have been throwing the red, iron-rich Cappadocian clay since time immemorial.

Ürgüp

The town of Ürgüp lies 20km east of Nevşehir and is a pleasant base for exploring the area; the Göreme Open-Air Museum and Zelve are both convenient. A bus runs nine times per day to Nevşehir; most of the long-distance buses to and from Nevşehir also call here, and there are *dolmuş* and buses (slightly cheaper) to Kayseri for connections to the east.

The Ürgüp **tourist office** is on Kayseri Cad., inside the garden. (Open June-Aug. daily 8am-6pm; Sept.-May Mon.-Fri. 8am-5pm.) Next door is a tiny **Archeological Museum.** Take your choice between Ürgüp's two cheap pensions. The management can be strange at the **Erciyes Pension** (tel. 12 06), and you have to walk through a cornfield to get to the bathroom at the **Güzelgöz** (tel. 10 94). Both charge 1500TL per person (showers 500TL), and are located downhill from the bus station (follow the signs). **Seymen Pansiyon,** just before the road to Nevşehir, has comfortable rooms downstairs and a cool sitting room full of folksy knick-knacks (3000TL per person, showers and breakfast included). The **Cappadocia Restaurant** has the usual assortment of stews, soups, and vegetables at a good price.

The tourist agencies at Ürgüp organize a daily tour of the region for 7500TL per person without a guide (5 persons min.) and 10,000TL per person with a guide. The nine-hour tour is very comprehensive, but a little rushed; you may find yourself too frazzled to appreciate anything by the latter half of the day. The tour visits the castles at Üçhisar, the underground city at Kaymakli, the Göreme Open-Air Museum, and the rock dwellings at Zelve, as well as numerous other "photo stops"-cum-souvenir stands along the way. Count on about 2000TL extra per person for entrance fees to the sites.

Near Ürgüp

The small village of **Ortahisar** clusters around a tall fortress hewn out of volcanic rock. If you hike around the area to the south of the village you'll come across scores of abandoned rock dwellings and several rock churches, the best of which are decorated with frescoes from the tenth and eleventh centuries. Ortahisar does not lie on the main Nevşehir-Ürgüp bus route, but is only 2km from the main road, along a turn-off some 6km from Ürgüp.

Üçhisar is a slightly larger village, similarly built at the foot of a craggy fortress. Because it is on a hill, the town, and to an even greater extent the fortress, commands fantastic views of the whole Göreme Valley. Üçhisar is also the site of a pleasant and inexpensive pension, the **Maison du Rêve,** on the opposite side of the castle from the town; follow the signs. (Rooms 3000TL per person. Hot showers and breakfast included.) Occasional *dolmuş* leave from the town square to Nevşehir, but it's much more reliable to walk 1km to the main road and flag down the Nevşehir-Ürgüp bus.

Once capital of the short-lived Kingdom of Cappadocia and later, as Caesarea, of the Roman province of the same name, **Kayseri** today doesn't really seem part of the region. The unremarkable twentieth-century Turkish-modern **bus station** is Kayseri's *raison d'être* for most travelers. You can get here from Ürgüp on a *dolmuş.* Buses run to Samsun, Sivas, Erzurum, Mersin, and Diyarbakir. There are also frequent buses to Ankara and Istanbul, though from Cappadocia you'd be better off going to Nevşehir to travel west. To get to Nemrut Daği, you have to take a bus from here to Malatya. If you'd like to stay in Kayseri, try **Hotel Hunat** and **Hotel Dilek,** next door to one another behind Hunat Mosque.

Eastern Turkey

As you travel eastward in Turkey, there's a point at which things change. There are no more English or German stop signs, not many more English or Germans, and the land itself seems immense and not a little daunting. The line where you turn from traveler to swashbuckler begins somewhere near Cappadocia, running from Samsun in the north to Adana in the south.

Some caveats are in order for travel here, and some myths need to be dispelled. The bad news first. Women will not feel comfortable alone, and even when traveling in pairs should wear long pants or skirts, long-sleeved blouses, and scarves over their heads. Travelers should bring some toiletries, notably toilet paper and tampons. The climate here is typically continental, and not gentle. Gaziantep, Urfa, Diyarbakir, and Mardin are hot as hell in the summer, with daytime temperatures above 45°C. Conversely, much of the northeastern end of Turkey is periodically cut off in the winter. Hakkâri is virtually inaccessible from November through March, and everywhere northeast of Konya is *cold.* As for language, if English doesn't work, try German. Many soldiers come from the Western half of the country, and are likely to speak a foreign language. Tourist offices in the east run hot and cold, but have been improving in past years as the government realizes the potential for tourism here. Just about every town large enough to stop in has a bank, but you should carry U.S. dollars, as cash or small-denomination traveler's checks. Also, food in eastern Turkey tends to be a little unsanitary; always walk into the kitchen to inspect the meat.

There is no such thing as a picturesque town in eastern Turkey—the cities are usually dusty, concrete, and ugly, and the villages picturesque only to those impervious to their abject poverty. The beauty of the region lies in the harsh steppe lands and the jagged peaks of the countryside, and in the experience—for here is something truly different, not packaged like the tourist office's folk dances in Istanbul, but genuinely of another world. There are some off-putting things you may hear about travel here: It's not safe, no one speaks English, there are hostile soldiers everywhere, and so forth. Much of this is untrue. Expect to be stared at, but if anything, you'll tire of excessive friendliness rather than malevolence. Traveling in the east can be one of the best parts of your stay in Turkey—for more information, ask around while you're in Istanbul; you'll likely find many people who've just been and will be able to tempt you further with tales of beautiful Armenian churches at Akdamar and Ani, gorgeous scenery at Kars and Hakkâri, the bizarre heads at Nemrut Daği, and the beautiful palace at Doğubayazit.

You should know something about the Kurdish population in Turkey, since published information about them is practically prohibited by the Turkish government. East of Adiyaman you start to find a lot of Kurds, and their numbers grow as you approach the Iranian border. The Kurds are a nation without a state, stretching over eastern Turkey and northern Iran into Afghanistan. They speak a distinct language that combines features of Turkish, Latin, and Farsi, and have a long history of violent struggle against those who have opposed the formation of an independent Kurdistan. The center of the separatist struggle in Turkey is in the extreme southeast, in the wild Hakkâri region. Government figures put the number of arrested dissidents (the Kurdish Party is also socialist, which doesn't help their cause) at around 100 per year, but Hakkâri locals estimate that at least half again that number are killed annually in fighting between the villagers and the army. The situation does not really affect the foreign traveler, but you should be aware of it, especially if you want to travel southeast of Van.

Nemrut Daği

Nemrut Daği (the "ğ" is unpronounced) is the most heavily visited spot in eastern Turkey, and with good reason. Huge funerary statues of the Commagene Empire (the faces alone are 1m high) sit atop the summit of the 2150-meter peak. The Commagene Empire was founded in the first century B.C.E. by Mithridates, whose son, Antiochus, is believed to be buried under the mound on the summit. The monument may be Turkey's finest: colossal statues built at the foot of a 50m-high tomb on an almost inaccessible peak. The statues are of the Commagene gods, hybrids of Greek and Persian deities. The glaring eagles, majestic lions, and severe human figures gaze over the mountainous landscape. Be sure to take plenty of warm clothing; the summit is chillingly cold at night even in the dead of summer.

The most common way to get up the mountain is from the town of **Kahta,** 70km away, on the road between Malatya and Urfa; from there minibuses make the rest of the trip, either in the middle of the night to make it by sunrise, or in the afternoon for the sunset. Kahta is full of tour hustlers; shop around before you commit yourself, and feel free to bargain. They generally charge about 30,000TL round-trip, 35,000TL for a slightly longer route which goes by **Eski Kale,** the old capital of the Commagene Empire; a Roman bridge over the refreshing waters of the River Cendere; and an unimpressive funerary mound of the princesses and queens of the Empire. Tour prices are the same regardless of the number of passengers; the maximum is 10. The best place to whip together a group is at one of Kahta's four hotels. The 2½-hour trip up the recently paved road is only possible May through October.

At the friendly **Merhaba Hotel,** students get a substantial discount (roof 1500TL, doubles with bath 7000TL); non-students pay twice as much. Head toward town from the bus station and look for the sign. At the turnoff for Merhaba Hotel you'll see **Ipek Palas Hotel** (tel. 11 25) above a tea house. (1000TL per person.)

The more adventurous can tackle the mountain from the small Kurdish village of **Eski Kahta,** 25km closer to the summit. This method of ascending consumes both time and money: 1000TL for a *dolmuş* from Kahta to Eski Kahta, and then 7000TL per person for rental of a guide and horse for the 10- to 12-hour ascent and descent.

An easier journey is from the north, via **Malatya,** acity of several hundred thousand people, impossible to avoid if you're coming to Nemrut from the west. Buses connect it to Kayseri, Ankara, and Diyarbakir. The Malatya **tourist office,** right at the bus station, springs into action the moment you arrive. They will shepherd you onto their tour, which goes up the north side of the mountain via the villages of Tepehan and Büyüköz. The tour leaves at least once per day from the central tourist office (right at the main square) and returns the next morning. (8300TL per person includes bed, dinner, and breakfast at the summit.) The bus winds up a dirt road, through streams and past beautiful scenery, for six hours, ending at a small Kurdish village 25 minutes below the summit. You can stay in a Kurdish mud hut, but it gets so crowded with tourists that you may have to sleep in a tent outside. If you camp yourself and either bring your own food or eat at the restaurant, you save 3000TL. When you add up the bus fare from Malatya to Kahta, the night's stay, and the evening meal, you're still a little short of the cost of the northern ascent, but the Malatya route is more of an adventure.

Continuing over the other side of the mountain may sound attractive, but it's hard to find vehicles with space, and you don't want to get stuck hiking at midday during summer. If you have to stay in Malatya, try the **Otel Mimar Sinan.** From the bus station, head into town and turn left 1½ blocks past the main tourist office (doubles 2600TL).

Urfa (Şanliurfa)

The city of Urfa sits in the borderlands of Turkey, only 50km from the Syrian frontier. Accordingly, Urfa has a distinctly Arab flavor—and is hot enough to fry eggs throughout the long summer. It's definitely worth a stop, though, for its distinctive atmosphere, its attractive religious complex, and its fascinating bazaar.

One of the best things about Urfa is the sprawling **covered market.** There are shops selling spices, shops selling shoes, shops selling sheep—say *that* five times. At the back of the market is a row of rug and *kilim* shops without the usual hard sell and with good prices. The market is at the far end of Sarayönü Cad., which then curves to the right past the food market and all the water vendors. Two hundred meters farther, at the foot of the citadel, is a spring that the Greeks called Callirhoe, which now feeds the **pools of sacred carp** next to the lovely gardens of the **Hasan Paşa** and **Mevlut Halil** mosques. Nearby at the foot of the castle you can sip water from the spring where Abraham was born.

The **bus station** is about a kilometer out of town; to get to the center, head toward the castle and take a left through the middle of the cemetery. The **tourist office** (tel. (8711) 24 67) is on your right, 20m before the intersection with the town's main road, Sarayönü Caddesi. The office is friendly, if a little useless; they can show you their photos of the town, and will offer you a town plan. (Open Mon.-Fri. only.) Look for accommodations between the market and the castle. **Park Otel,** 101 Göl Cad. (tel. (8711) 10 95), has a fantastic illuminated view from its terrace. (Terrace 1600TL, doubles 3800TL.) Cleaner and more centrally located is the **Lale Oteli,** 11 Kişla Cad. (tel. (8711) 16 42), two left turns from the tourist office. (Doubles 3850TL.) The little *pastanesi* at 131 Sarayönü Cad. serves delicious lasagne-like *börek* for a criminally low price. Head south along Saranyönü Cad. to get to the post office and most of the sights.

Near Urfa

The road south from Urfu to the Syrian border passes through Sultantepe, an unimpressive Assyrian archeological site which has, however, provided scholars with a good deal of what is known about the Assyrian culture. Thirty-three kilometers from Urfa a road leads 11km to the left to the modern village of **Altinbaşuk,** site of the ancient town of **Harran.** This odd village, easily recognizable for its unique beehive-like dwellings, is where Abraham and Lot stopped on their way from Ur to Canaan (they were, presumably, lost). No hotels remain, but there are the ruins of a castle and a Seljuk/Kurdish mosque built on the foundations of a Roman university. To get to Harran, you must hire a taxi (6000TL) or a *dolmuş* (8000TL), both of which will wait for you at the site.

Diyarbakir

Diyarbakir rises like some medieval fortress of evil from the barren south Anatolian plain, its huge black walls visible for miles. The walls are largely the work of the Seljuks, who are also responsible for the city's **Ulu Camii** (Great Mosque). Just north of the mosque is the **Hasan Paşa Hani** (caravanserai), now full of carpet shops. Across from here and a few blocks in is the **bazaar.** In the southwest part of the city is the Byzantine **Meryam Ana Church,** rebuilt several times since the fourth century. Southwest of here is a good section of the city wall to climb and walk along. At the other end of the city, close to the Bitlis Gate, is the ancient Byzantine **citadel.**

The main street, **Izzet Paşa Caddesi,** runs from Bitlis Gate in the east to Mardin Gate in the south. It intersects the road in from the bus station and Urfa Gate at the site of the huge Ulu Camii. Nearby is Gazi Caddesi, on which there is a **post office,** and several **banks.** Buses run frequently to Urfa and Malatya, and less frequently to Van. The **bus station** is 3km northwest of town; *dolmuş* will take you into town or stop along the way near the **tourist office** on Lise Cad. (tel. (831) 121 78). Try the **Otel Şenol** at Gazi Cad. and Manav Sok. (tel. (831) 231 05), with an air-conditioned lobby. (Doubles 3000TL.) South on Gazi Cad. at the *dolmuş* station is **Özgür Lokantasi,** with a chicken and herbal rice dish for 700TL.

100km south of Diyarbakir is the desert city of Mardin, which is uninteresting but the only connection point to the **Deyrulzafaran Monastery.** The seat of the Syrian patriarchy from the fourth century until 1922, the monastery is now inhabited by only one monk and a handful of students. They still speak Aramaic, the language that Jesus spoke. *Dolmuş* from the station on Gazi Cad. leave for Mardin, from which you must take a taxi 8km to the site (3000TL round-trip).

Lake Van

The gorgeous turquoise waters of Lake Van reflect for 360km around the snow-covered peak of Süphan Daği with a splendor you may have thought was reserved for postcards. Camping on or near Lake Van's gravel beaches allows you to enjoy cool breezes and Van's strange, sudsy water—you can even wash your clothes without any soap. The restaurant at the boat launch for Akdamar will let you camp for 500TL per person. Six kilometers east of there (37km west of the city of Van) is the more serene **Cafer Camping** (1000TL per tent; no showers).

One especially attractive Armenian church is on the tiny island of **Akdamar,** 43km west of Van off the south coast of the lake. The **Church of the Holy Cross,** built in the tenth century, boasts beautifully sculptured friezes, and the island itself is perfect for swimming. A boat runs there when it fills (800TL round-trip). Admission to the church is 400TL. Any bus heading to Van from the west will pass by the island. From Van you can take a *dolmuş.*

The dusty city of **Van** lies 5km away from the water. The **bus station** is 2km outside of town; most bus companies offer free transportation to and from the city center. Buses run to Diyarbakir and all other points west, Ağri, and Hakkâri. The friendly and attentive **tourist office** (tel. (061) 136 75) is at the east end of the main drag by the traffic circle. Right on Cumhuriyet Cad. at #118 is the clean **Otel Nuh** (tel. (061) 110 45; 1000TL per person). **Hotel Sibel,** 71 Küçük Camii Civari (tel. (061) 15 40), is much more attractive but a bit dirty. Turn off the main drag at Iş Bank and continue on the street veering slightly to the right when you reach the dead-end; it's just before Hotel Tekin. (Doubles 2600TL.)

From the intersection of Cumhuriyet Cad. and Iskele Cad. you can take a *dolmuş* 4km to the stunning **citadel** and **ancient city.** The ruin was once the capital of the Urartian Empire. The Urartians, who descended from the northeastern steppes to fill the vacuum left by the declining Hittite Empire, reached their peak between 900 and 700 B.C.E., but suffered numerous defeats at the hands of the Assyrians, and finally fell to the Scythians in the sixth century B.C.E. The most extensive collection of Urartian artifacts rests in the museum in Ankara. The small **Archeological Museum** in Van houses an interesting array of artifacts. (Open daily 8am-noon and 1:30-5:30pm. Admission 400TL.) The Urartians were succeeded at Van by the Armenians, who lived in this region and north as far as Kars from the eighth or ninth century B.C.E.; the Armenian Empire reached its height between 862 and 1045 C.E., and there are Armenian fortifications from this period as far southwest as Anamur, on the Mediterranean coast. The empire enjoyed a renaissance of sorts with the rise of Georgian power in the thirteenth and fourteenth centuries, and then became a province of the Ottoman Empire. With the collapse of the Ottomans after World War I, the Armenians allied with the Russians in an effort to establish an independent state once again. Turkish nationalists, allied with the British, feared a Bolshevik presence in the Middle East; they defeated the Russo/Armenian army in 1920, and, according to surviving Armenians, proceeded to massacre the Armenian population. Turks will claim that the massacre was a peasant retaliation against Armenian raids and that the Turkish army came to *save* the remaining Armenians by transporting them abroad. What actually went on is still a subject of hot debate.

At present any publications about Armenian history or culture are discouraged in Turkey; even tourist brochures with descriptions of Armenian ruins don't mention the word Armenian. At any rate, there are still a good number of Armenian buildings, particularly the beautifully decorated churches, in the area between Van and Kars.

Near Van

Around **Tatvan,** an uninteresting little place at the western end of the lake, only two things are worth seeing: the ruins of Ahlat, and the crater lake of Nemrut Gölü. **Ahlat,** 38km north of Tatvan, was populated first by the Armenians, and then by a succession of peoples until it was abandoned under Ottoman rule a couple of hundred years ago. Today the ghost town on the lakeshore is beautiful and spooky, particularly the ornately carved Seljuk and Ottoman tombs. Just to the north of Tatvan another **Nemrut Daği** rises 3000m into the sky, this one without any Commagene statues, but with a breathtaking **crater lake** at 2400m. Almost 7km in diameter, the lake's north shore is formed by stupendous cliffs hundreds of meters high. There are no roads from Tatvan, so you have to climb up on foot. *Dolmuş* run from Tatvan to the villages of Ahlat and Adilcevaz.

Two hundred kilometers south of Van lies the town of **Hakkâri,** set among beautifully rugged mountains. The town itself services a large military base and is not too interesting, but the bus ride through spectacular mountain passes makes the journey worthwhile. Though officials will never talk about it, the mountain area is the home of Kurdish guerillas who clash periodically with Turkish soldiers stationed there. Camping outside of town can be dangerous, but if you stay in one of Hakkâri's two hotels, you shouldn't have any problems. If you have time, stop off at the village of **Güzelsu,** dominated by the seventeenth-century Ottoman castle of **Hoşap.**

Ağri and Mount Ararat

Ağri is a nasty place without redemption, but is necessary for bus connections to Doğubayazit, which sits at the foot of majestic Ağri Daği (Mount Ararat), the legendary resting place of Noah's Ark. Buses run from Ağri to Van and Erzurum, as well as to Doğubayazit. Don't buy a ticket from or to Doğubayazit from anywhere but Ağri—though you may save 100-200TL, you will also have to wait in Ağri for up to four hours for a connection.

The dirty little town of **Doğubayazit** wouldn't normally be of any interest, but the perpetual view of the mountain and the palace of **Işak Paşa** make it one of eastern Turkey's most noteworthy stops. The palace was built by an eccentric Ottoman feudal lord in the late eighteenth century on what must be the only spot within 100km from which you can't see Mt. Ararat. Still, the partially ruined palace is great to visit; check out the harem and the mosque and climb the Uruartian fortress across the ravine for a fantastic view. The palace is a 5-kilometer trek uphill from town, or you can take a *dolmuş,* which runs all morning until noon (100TL each way). (Palace open Tues.-Sun. 8am-5pm. Admission 600TL.)

Mount Ararat is 500m taller than Mont Blanc, and the net height from the plain to the summit is as great as you'll find anywhere outside of the Himalayas. If you fancy climbing it (for experienced climbers only), you first need permission from the capitol building in Ankara. Contact the Turkish embassy in your home country before you leave. Trek Travel Agency in town will hire you a guide for US$43 per day. You might instead contact freelance guide Yavuz Selim Karakuşla, who speaks fluent English and can be found at the Hotel Erzurum during the summer.

In Doğubayazit, the **Hotel Erzurum,** near the end of town on the road to the palace, has clean rooms (1500TL per person). Nearer the center, the **Dumlupinar Lokantasi** serves a variety of freshly prepared meals for the usual low prices. A **post office** and a few banks can be found in the town center.

Kars

Kars is another one of those ugly eastern Turkish towns, and the only reason you want to visit is to see the ancient Armenian capital of Ani. Stay in Kars at either the **Otel Nur Saray** (1500TL per person) or the considerably more spartan **Hayat Oteli** (1000TL per person), both on Fayik Bey Cad. The **Çobanoğlu Kahvesi,** near the Hotel Temel, occasionally features improvisational *aşik* (guitar) players (8:30-11:30pm; 200TL).

To visit **Ani,** you must first get permission from the Kars **tourist office,** off Fayik Bey Cad.; turn just after the Bağ Kur sign. (Open in summer daily 8am-noon and 1:30-5:30pm; in winter when they feel like it.) In the morning you might run into enough people to hire a *dolmuş* economically (22,000TL), or you can take the bus. (Mon.-Fri. at 6:30am; returns from Ani at 4pm; it may make an extra trip at midday but don't count on it.) Alternatively, you could visit one of the luxury hotels and try to hitch a ride on one of the tour buses. A soldier guides you around the site (photographs forbidden); the Soviet Union lies just across the ravine of the River Arpa. At Ani, be sure and see the **cathedral,** a fine example of Armenian architecture, and the smaller but better preserved **Church of St. Gregory** (one of three) on a bluff at the extreme eastern end of the town, about 500m from the cathedral. (Admission to site 1000TL.)

Black Sea Coast

You could easily miss Turkey's longest and least visited coast, but that would be a mistake. Industrial cities and fishing villages punctuate gravel or narrow sandy beaches that you share not with sunbathers but with creeping ivy and a few fishing boats pulled up on shore. Cool Russian breezes and lush scenery also provide relief from the heat of other coasts. Many of the cities here were major trading ports in ancient times, especially when Arab invasions blocked the southern silk route; numerous Byzantine structures remain, especially around Trabzon. Today a highway follows the coast closely, so you can scan from your vehicle and choose where you want to explore. Hotels are available only in the larger cities, but campsites appear every 50km or so.

Though geographically part of central Turkey, **Amasya** has been historically tied to the Black Sea since it was capital of the Pontus Kingdom. The Pontics conquered most of Asia Minor from their Black Sea homeland, but later fell to the Roman war machine. Surrounded by mountains and castles, Amasya is a gem of a city with a beautifully restored Ottoman home, the **Hazeranlar Konaği,** in the old town, and some Pontic rock tombs. Stay at the **Hotel Aydin,** 86 Mustafa Kemal Cad. (1000TL per person), or the more spacious **Konfor Palas Oteli,** in a courtyard on the river (doubles 2250TL).

Sinop is one of the few touristed towns on the Black Sea. Visit the medieval castle walls running through the city and the **Balatlar Church,** a ruined Byzantine religious compound. There is a **tourist office** (tel. (3761) 19 96) at the harbor. A few blocks away on Orta Yol is the nondescript **Karahan Oteli** (1000TL per person). East of Sinop is the large port city of **Samsun,** 85km after which (just short of Ünye) are **Europa Camping** (2000TL per tent) and a pension (doubles 4000TL). Between Fatsa and Ordu, the black cliffs of the Yasum peninsula plunge into green water. Particularly pleasant villages on the peninsula are **Bolaman, Yazilköy,** and **Caka.** In the fishing village of **Mersin,** 26km west of Trabzon, **Mersin Turistik Tesisleri** might give you a free camping spot by their outdoor night club.

Trabzon is a fascinating city with several churches left from the Trebizond Kingdom, an offshoot of the Byzantine Empire founded by Alexis Comneni in 1204. The **tourist office,** right on the main square, is extremely helpful and can recommend truly tranquil villages along the coast. (Open in summer daily 8am-7:30pm; off-season daily 8am-5:30pm.) A good place to stay is the **Şirin Otel** (tel. (031) 154

45), two blocks east of the tourist office. From in front of the tourist office, buses leave at 9am and 10am for **Sumela Monastery,** one of Turkey's most spectacular sights (1000TL round-trip). Established in 385 C.E., this cliffside monastery reached its zenith in the late Middle Ages, when it comprised 72 rooms and an immense library. Little remains behind the four-story facade except for the main chapel, covered with frescoes inside and out. (Monastery open daily 9am-5pm. Admission to park 100TL; to monastery 500TL.) Trabzon is well connected by bus (about 1 per hr.) with Ankara, Istanbul, and Samsun, and with other cities at least once per day. A more interesting transit option is **Turkish Maritime Line**'s two-day ferry from Istanbul which hugs the Black Sea coast. (1 boat per week, 8500TL.)

The segment of coast east of Trabzon is the shangri-la of Turkey; the air is moist and plants seem to sprout from everything. East of Trabzon (30km) is a friendly fishing village, **Kalezik;** you can camp under a rock overhang below a Byzantine castle. Farther along, **Rize** is the center of Turkey's tea industry. The highway finally turns inland at **Hopa,** where you can catch the Artvin Ekspres bus to Kars (4500TL).

USSR

US$1 = 0.64 rubles (R)
CDN$1 = 0.48R
UK£1 = 1.04R

1R = US$1.58
1R = CDN$2.08
1R = UK£0.96

The Soviet Union defies comprehension. No other country evokes such conflicting images of youth and age, great diversity and crushing monotony, power and relative poverty. You'll meet Soviets who despise their system, others who swear by the Great October Socialist Revolution, and still others (perhaps the majority) who devote their concern to the demands of daily life.

The country's enigmatic character stems partly from its abrupt and incomplete entrance into the twentieth century: Few cashiers have computers; most still use an abacus. Indeed, the medieval empire of the tsars extended well into this century, and the country's development has been retarded twice since by the World Wars, which claimed the lives of over 20 million Soviet citizens. A determination not to forget these wars pervades every level of Soviet society. Moreover, associations with the past are everywhere—from Catherine the Great's ornate palace in Pushkin and the great mosques of central Asia to the sign on Nevsky Prospekt in Leningrad warning passersby of the danger of German shelling, and the World War II movies constantly shown on TV. A genuine curiosity to learn more about the country's past will often be rewarded by a friendly conversation.

Foreigners who to imagine the Soviets as a people entrapped by an oppressive government may be surprised. The Soviets are a patriotic people, whether as a result of indoctrination or a profoundly sentimental love of country. Most obey the pervasive petty regulations with a remarkable consistency and proudly describe the merits of their lives. By acknowledging this pride you will put yourself in a fine position to break down the veneer that separates members of two vastly disparate societies. Travelers to the Soviet Union tell of chance encounters blooming into long friendships, of uniquely helpful and hospitable people. Recent travelers report that the much-heralded reforms have led to a noticeably more friendly and relaxed atmosphere in public places.

Russia clearly predominates among the 15 Soviet republics, with the greatest population, largest cities, and the ethnic majority in the Kremlin. However, behind the title "Soviet" is a world of diverse peoples, languages, and distinctly non-Soviet histories. The Ukraine, though similar to Russia, holds fiercely to its separate language and history. Estonia, Latvia, and Lithuania, on the Baltic, are much more Nordic, and are further distinguished by the predominance of the Lutheran and Catholic Churches. Black Sea resorts such as Odessa, Sochi, and Yalta are crowded with *dachas* where Soviet gentry sunbathe. In the republic of Uzbekistan, you can see the ancient trading cities of Samarkand and Bukhara, as well as the modern capital city Tashkent. The republics of Georgia and Armenia, wedged between the Black and Caspian Seas, have the highest living standards in the USSR. And in harsh, mineral-rich Siberia, cities such as Bratsk and Irkutsk have come to life in the last few decades. Non-Russian peoples do study Russian in school, but courses are conducted variably in Russian or in the native tongue. Political affairs in the non-Russian republics are also often conducted in the native languages.

Planning Your Trip

A visit to the Soviet Union requires careful advance planning. Visas are required: To obtain one, you first must have a day-by-day itinerary confirmed and approved by one of the two Soviet travel bureaus—**Intourist,** or the more youth-oriented **Sputnik.** In capitals such as Washington and London you can normally obtain a visa within two weeks, but it is wise to submit your visa application at least one month in advance of your planned arrival in the USSR. In Scandinavian countries, you can get Soviet visas in as little as nine days. Confirmation of itineraries also takes a number of weeks; begin your planning three or four months in advance, six months or more if you will be designing an independent itinerary. Your first step should be to obtain a copy of Intourist's pamphlet *Visiting the USSR,* which contains general information pertinent to all travel in the country, and specific information about three of your options—Intourist tours, independent travel, and car-camping trips. Write to Intourist at one of the addresses listed in our appendix.

Group Tours

The group tour is still the only economical and reasonably convenient way to visit the Soviet Union. Don't be put off by the name. It is possible and advisable to miss group excursions and meals, and to see cities on your own. If your guide tries to dissuade you from skipping your tour, be firm—tell him or her you're not coming and set off on your own (though you are not permitted to leave the city limits).

The tours offered by **Scandinavian Student Travel Service (SSTS)** in conjunction with Sputnik are the best deal. Leaving in the summer only, they consist of pre-set itineraries departing on fixed dates and include meals, full sightseeing programs, often a "youth-group meeting" (basically a party thrown in your honor by a student or worker's union), accommodation in two- or three-bed rooms, and transportation within the country. Transportation to or from Moscow is not included. Sputnik can change planned excursions and even the number of days that your group will be visiting each city. Prices in 1987 ranged from about US$265 for seven days in Moscow and Leningrad to about US$1095 for a trans-Siberian extravaganza. Your company will be mostly American and some European young people, and you'll save a chunk over an Intourist tour.

You can book SSTS tours in the U.S. through **STN**, and in Canada through **Travel CUTS.** Depending on exchange rates, you may be able to save some money by buying their tours in Europe, or by dealing directly with SSTS and paying in Danish kroner. To do so, contact SSTS in Copenhagen at Hauchsvej 17, DK-1825 Copenhagen V, Denmark (tel. (01) 21 47 40). You must take care of your visa on your own on SSTS and most other tours. **Travela,** Mannerheimintie 5 (tel. 62 41 01), in Helsinki, Finland, runs four-day bus tours to Leningrad (about US$200) and five-day (excluding travel-time) train tours to Moscow (about US$300). Price includes all the same things as the SSTS tours plus transportation. Travela requires a completed visa application and a photocopy of your entire passport at least 21 days before your departure date.

Independent Travel

Independent travel is a useful option if you want to visit someone, or if a group arrangement does not permit you to stay in a place of particular interest long enough, but it is expensive. Choose an Intourist-approved travel agent (their brochure, *Visiting the USSR,* lists them) who will make arrangements with Intourist. All payment must be made in advance in Western currency, and it is nearly impossible to receive any refund if your plans change; you'll end up paying about US$100 per extra day.

Getting There

Both the Intourist and Sputnik tours start in the Soviet Union; you must arrange your own transportation into and out of the country. SSTS tours start and finish at the airports of the first and last cities of the itinerary and are synchronized with SSTS flights to and from Copenhagen and London. In 1987, SSTS airfare between Moscow and Copenhagen was about US$140 each way.

Independent travel to the Soviet Union costs considerably less. Rail travel from Finland is an excellent option if your tour begins in Leningrad; Helsinki is only six hours away. Traveling to Moscow from Helsinki or Eastern Europe is problematic. Moscow is so distant from any border that you will have to enter the country one day ahead of your group if you want to meet them when the tour is scheduled to start; ordinarily, your visa is valid only from day one of your tour. If you anticipate traveling by train to Moscow, inquire with Intourist and the nearest Soviet Embassy. Flying from Eastern Europe is possible, but significantly more expensive than SSTS flights.

Practical Information

Each morning, your Soviet guide will have a lecture ready to offer you in the comfort of the tour bus. Use these excursions for sights that are out of town or otherwise hard to reach on your own, or to bypass admission lines, which are often long. Otherwise, consider setting off on your own with a map and some determination; you may see quantitatively fewer sights, but the qualitative leap is well worth it.

Once on your own, or with only a couple of others, there will be a greater chance of Soviets approaching you. Most Soviets are keenly interested in anything Western, and your attire and general manners will instantly betray you as such. Hospitality exists even in the largest cities; travelers who have simply asked the way to the Metro from a Soviet citizen have been known to receive their own personal walking tour of literary Moscow. The possibility of getting into trouble with the authorities has in the past made many people standoffish, but *glasnost* seems to have caused a remarkable thaw. Women should be aware that replying to a Russian man can be construed as agreeing to a date. But never worry—when you decide you've had enough, saying *ostantye* (leave me alone) resolutely will solve your problems.

Many younger Soviets have studied English, though their conversational ability may be poor. In general, you'll have to take the initiative by learning some Russian if you hope to communicate with Soviets. At the very least, learn the alphabet before arriving in the country; record the Cyrillic alphabet table from a good dictionary. This will enable you to piece together street signs and use public transport. More doors will open if you speak even the worst conceivable Russian. Soviets will be less shy if you conform somewhat to their standard of behavior; loudness, abrasiveness, and casual manners are offensive.

Many of those who approach you may be blackmarketeers. Some are less than obvious at first but will soon express interest in your blue jeans, backpack, tennis shoes, or anything else visibly Western. Often you will be approached with a comically urgent "Do you have *anything* to sell?" A good indication of a blackmarketeer is an excellent command of English. More subtle dealers may befriend you, offer to show you the city sights, and even try to buy you dinner. After you've incurred an emotional or financial debt, they may bring up some small favors you could do for them. Such ulterior motives are unfortunately a very real and frequent dimension of acquaintances begun on the street. Answer unreasonable requests with an adamant "*nyet*" (no), but don't avoid all relations just for the sake of safety.

You may find it hard to comply with the rules governing the currency black market. Though you'll be approached often, and it will begin to seem as if *everybody* deals on the sly, there are unarguable reasons for avoiding such transactions. Depending on the gravity of your offense, you could be deported or thrown into jail. Finally, there is the practical consideration that all you'll receive is rubles, and most of the things you'll want to purchase will be found only in *beriyozki* (Western currency shops).

Exchanges not involving money are generally tolerated, as is gift-giving. If you do want to trade anything, you should be aware that personal stereos and T-shirts are very popular, as are (unripped) designer jeans. American and European cigarettes have become almost a second currency. Taxi drivers often prefer them to rubles, and, for getting into crowded restaurants, a pack of American cigarettes makes an unbeatable bribe. You can buy Western cigarettes in *beriyozki.* Chewing gum is a great thing to bring from the West—all children know the words "chewing gum" and will ask you for it constantly.

Once you recognize the need for some caution, it is probably safe to assume that most of those you meet are genuinely interested in talking to you. A visit to a *banya* (public bath) provides an opportunity to meet and chat casually with Soviet citizens from every walk of life. Older Russians will happily show you how to properly beat yourself with the birch twigs provided. Virtually every Soviet town has a *banya;* these range from one-room wooden huts in the villages to three-story palaces in the major cities.

In any case, if you do make Soviet friends, keep the fact private. Mentioning their names to your group leader can get them into trouble with the authorities. Be considerate of the Soviets you are with. The consequences of misbehavior (even just suspected) can be serious for them.

Every floor in Russian hotels has its own *dezhurnaya* in charge of handing you your keys, supervising the kitchen (when there is one), and—if they're friendly—offering other small services such as a needle and thread to sew your things. Don't ever take anything from a Soviet hotel room, as *dezhurnayas* know exactly how many towels, sheets, etc., you had (they must pay for anything missing). Travelers who "borrowed" a towel have been followed to the airport. Statues and other monuments abound in the Soviet Union. Be *very* respectful; if you sit even at a statue's pedestal, the police or concerned *babushkas* (old women) will chase you away on grounds of *nekulturnost* (not being "cultured" enough).

Don't bring rubles into the country—they'll be confiscated if found and you may not be allowed to enter. Declare all your currency and valuables at the border. You will be given a Customs Declaration Form on which to list the amount of each currency you have; you should also list your major valuables. Remember that you must take with you any valuables you list when you leave the country. While in the USSR, you can exchange your money for rubles at state banks and in many Intourist hotels. When converting foreign currency into rubles, you must produce your customs form. You will then be given a State Bank Certificate, on which the amount of exchange will be listed. You cannot export rubles; when leaving the country, you must show your Customs Form and all State Bank Certificates in order to exchange your unused rubles back into foreign currency; you cannot re-convert more rubles than you legally exchanged. Keep all receipts from *beriyozki* so that you can prove that no Western cash disappeared through illegal means. Undeclared money, along with rubles, is liable to confiscation.

If you fly in with your group, you may well be waved through customs. But Soviet customs can be harrowing, even if you have nothing to hide. Your reading material should not be explicitly or even implicitly anti-Soviet. Russian books not in circulation in the USSR are considered illegal and will be confiscated, as will letters and manuscripts written by or intended for Soviet citizens. Western newspapers and magazines will usually be confiscated.

Icons, old samovars, and books published before 1977 will all prove difficult to get out of the country. You'll need a permit which will take time to process, if granted at all, and there is a 100% duty charge. Pleas of ignorance and appeals to an embassy cannot keep these items from being confiscated at the border. Military clothing, including items such as army belts, popular in trades with young Russians, are considered "ammunition" and will also be confiscated.

The government limits your freedom of movement to a 25km radius around the city you're visiting. Essentially, this means you must stay within city limits, unless you are on an Intourist day-tour or have some form of approval from Intourist. With Soviet friends and in a car, you can probably get away with a trip into the countryside, but remember that, if caught, you risk prompt deportation, and probable refusal of a visa the next time you'd like to visit the country.

The reliability of mail service in and out of the Soviet Union fluctuates. Delivery time can be as short as 10 days, as long as three to four weeks, or the item may just be lost. The authorities selectively read mail going in both directions, so you should not write anything offensive or incriminating. If you want to receive mail but do not know where you'll be staying, have it addressed Poste Restante, K-600, "Intourist" Hotel, 3/5 Gorky St., Moscow, USSR; or Poste Restante, C-400, "Oktiabrskaya" Hotel, Leningrad, USSR. To mail items out, take them unwrapped to the Central Telegraph Office at 6 Gorky St. in Moscow, or the Intourist Hotel nearby; they will be wrapped and mailed while you wait. Bring receipts with you, and leave price tags on to facilitate matters.

Telephones cost 2 kopeks (they take 1- and 2-kopek pieces). These coins are very rare, and it is a custom for citizens to ask one another for the pieces—a courtesy which will cheerfully be done for you at a later date. In some phone booths you must press the button marked "OTBET" when your call is answered. Soviet phones are unreliable and you may have to search to find one that works. Long distance calls must be made from a telegraph office or your hotel room. Calls to North America cost 6 rubles per minute (3-min. minimum), calls to Europe 3 rubles per minute. You cannot call collect. It's easiest to call from a hotel, but you may book in advance at the Central Telephone Office or make a same-day call there after waiting about 45 minutes. If you don't speak Russian you'll need to find someone in the waiting room who can let you know which booth to go to when your call is announced. To be reached quickly in an emergency, leave the number of your tour group with someone at home. Your embassy should be able to find you if they have this number. If traveling independently, leave a copy of your itinerary with the embassy, along with your name, address, date and place of birth, and passport number.

Food

You don't go to the Soviet Union for the food; eating well here is a challenge. Intourist and Sputnik hotels normally offer well-prepared but boring meals. Inexpensive cafeterias known as *stolovaia* serve dirt-cheap food, which is just about that tasty. They do offer an opportunity to rub elbows with the average Soviet, whose salary makes culinary exploration impossible. *Kafes* are one step up, and usually offer a decent chicken dish for around 2 rubles; ask for the waiter's recommendation. Be sure to have at least one meal at a really fine restaurant. US$25 to 30 is about the most you can spend—wine, vodka, champagne, and caviar included. Make reservations, or arrive very early (before 5pm you'll rarely encounter a line). If you take neither of these precautions, a pack of cigarettes can be useful.

Try to sample the offerings of street vendors. Ice cream *(morozhenoye)* is great here. Flavors other than vanilla are rare; asking for *shokolad* will get you powdered chocolate on top. The bland, meat-filled pastries known as *pirozhki* can make a light meal. Wash them down with either *pivo* (beer) or *kyas* (a pungent, brown drink made from fermented rye bread), both sold at summer sidewalk stands and served in a communal glass. For a mere 3 kopeks you can have a glass of *gazirovannaya voda* (mineral water), sold from the ubiquitous vending machines. And then there's always Pepsi (42K per bottle). In general, try something when you see it, as stands are usually portable and pop up only briefly before selling out. Be sure to try Russian chocolate; the best kind regularly available in *beriyozki* is called Troika.

Laws passed in 1985 forbid the sale of all liquors except beer before 2pm (foreign-currency bars are exempt from these regulations), and the number of bottles on the shelves has dropped considerably of late. Still, vodka is an integral part of almost every involved meal. Try to join in the fun if the opportunity arises, though you may despair of keeping up. *Russkaya* and *Zubrovka* are the best brands, and *Stolichnaya* and *Moskovskaya* are very well known, but the generic brand is usually quite satisfactory. A fine selection of vodkas and wines is available in *beriyozki.* Try Georgian wines (*Aligote* and *Arbatskaia* in particular). Intourist's foreign-currency bars (usually one at every Intourist hotel) are great places to stock up on foreign luxuries. Bring small bills and coins, or you might get change in a combination of Swiss francs, British pounds, and chewing gum.

Moscow (Moskva)

The sprawling city of Moscow sits on the edge of Europe and in the heart of Russia, the largest republic in the Soviet Union. The city's size alone numbs: eight million people crammed into thousands of nearly identical housing units in an area exceeding 600,000 acres. From the Tsar's Bell in the Kremlin, the largest in the world, to the star-topped skyscrapers, Moscow is overwhelming.

First mentioned in historical chronicles in 1147, Moscow has since been inextricably linked with the history of the Russian people. In fact, it was once common to refer to the Russian state as Muscovy, and to its inhabitants as Muscovites. Moscow is the historical seat of both the Orthodox Church and the Tsarist empire. Peter I, hot on the trail of Western progress, moved the capital to St. Petersburg in 1712, although he and his successors never deigned to be crowned there. In March 1918, the new Soviet government moved the capital back to *Matushka Moskva* (Mother Moscow), and the country was ruled from the Kremlin once again.

Orientation and Practical Information

Moscow is structured more-or-less like a web, with the Kremlin at the center. The city is enormous; four blocks can easily translate into a very long walk. The Moskva, Moscow's handsome river, has so many curves that it is not terribly helpful in finding one's way around the city.

Tourist Offices: Intourist Hotel, Ul. Gor'kovo 3-5, 1 block from Red Square. Connected, but with a separate entrance to the left, is the **Central Excursion Bureau** (tel. 203 69 62). Excellent resource center; arrange trips within and outside Moscow here. Tourist visas extended here. Theater tickets, but usually only same-day performances. Everything must be paid for in Western currency. Open daily 9am-noon and 1-9pm. **Central Intourist Office** is at Prospekt Marksa 16 (tel. 229 42 06). Open daily 9am-6pm. **Sputnik,** Ul. Kosygina 15, at the Orlyonok Hotel. Open daily 9am-6pm.

American Express: Sadovaya-Kudrinskaya Ul. 21a (tel. 254 43 05), near Ul. Gor'kovo. No currency exchange, but will hold mail, replace stolen or lost checks or credit cards, and sell traveler's checks to cardholders. Open Mon.-Fri. 9am-5:30pm.

Post Office: Moscow Central Telegraph, Ul. Gor'kovo 7, a few blocks from the Kremlin. Change machines, and **telephones.** Open Mon.-Fri. 8am-2pm and 3-9pm, Sat. 8am-7pm, Sun. 9am-7pm. Another branch, often less crowded, at Prospekt Kalinina, near Dom Knigi.

Public Transportation: If you're not familiar with the Cyrillic alphabet, the 9 lines of the **Metro** won't be easy to navigate. *Vkhod* and *Vykhod* mean entrance and exit respectively, while *Vykhod v gorod* indicates an exit to the street and *Perekhod* a passage to a different line and often to a different station altogether. For identifying the names of the stations, some people find counting letters the easiest method. (You can't do this by counting the letters in the Romanized version of the names—a Cyrillic letter is often translated as 2 Roman letters.) Above ground, stations are marked by a large, illuminated "M." Operates 6am-1am. A metro map is available at street kiosks for 6k. Fare is 5k, distance unlimited; there are change machines at all stations. **Lost and found:** Tel. 222 20 85 (for items lost in metro) and 233 00 18, ext. 139 (for items lost in a trolley, tram, or bus).

Taxis: (tel. 225 00 00 or 227 00 40). If you don't speak Russian, wave down a taxi on the street, or go to a hotel service desk for help.

Emergencies: Police (tel. 02). **Ambulance** (tel. 03). **Fire** (tel. 01). No coins needed from pay phones. Also try the U.S. Embassy's emergency number (tel. 252 24 51).

Train and Plane Tickets: Intourist Main Office, Ul. Petroyka 15, to the right of Bolshoi Theater. The office is inside the courtyard of building #15; enter underneath the archway on Ul. Petrovka. Open Mon.-Fri. 9am-6pm.

Medical Assistance: Walk-in medical care available at the U.S. Embassy (tel. 252 24 51, ext. 247.) Open Mon.-Fri. 9-10am.

Embassies: U.S., Ul. Chaikovskovo 19-23 (tel. 252 24 51 through 252 24 59). Get off at metro Barrikadnaya. Open Mon.-Fri. 9am-1pm and 2-6pm. **Canada,** Starokonyushenny per. 23 (tel. 241 91 55). Open Mon.-Fri. 8:30am-1pm and 2-5pm. **U.K.,** Nab. Morisa Toreza 14 (tel. 231 85 11). Open Mon.-Fri. 9am-12:30pm and 2:30-6pm. **Australia,** Kropotkinsky per. 13 (tel. 246 50 11). **New Zealand,** Ul. Vorovskovo 44 (tel. 290 34 85).

Food

Restaurants

Moscow's restaurants are the best in the Soviet Union, but are plagued by crowds. Try to adopt an early eating schedule; even average restaurants and cafes have long lines after 5pm. Reservations are recommended for the restaurants we list; call, or have hotel personnel assist you. Prices run 20-25 rubles for a good dinner, complete with vodka and, often, caviar. Menus are generally written only in Cyrillic. Look for the *bylochnaya* (bakery), *pirozhki* (stand-up cafeteria with sandwiches and drinks), and *gastronom* (food store).

Aragvi, Ul. Gor'kovo 6 (tel. 229 37 62). Turn right exiting metro Prospekt Marksa; Ul. Gor'kovo is at the first intersection. Georgian cuisine. Became famous during the days of Stalin, Georgia's native son. Specialties include *satsivi* (cold chicken in a walnut sauce), *suluguni* (fried cheese), and *shashlyk* (shish-kebab). Have a bottle of *Mukuzani* or *Tsinandali* with your meal.

Uzbekistan, Neglinnaya ul. 29 (tel. 294 60 53). Metro: Pushkinskaya. A hangout for homesick Uzbeks, Kazakhs, and Tadzhiks. Noisy and always crowded. Try *tkhumdulma* (boiled egg with a fried meat patty) or one of the soups, followed by *shashlyk* Uzbek style. Be sure to try the specially prepared Uzbek bread, baked on the premises.

Rossiya Hotel, Moskoretskaya nab. 1 (tel. 298 41 33), the modern edifice that looms over St. Basil's Cathedral. Ask for the restaurant on the 21st floor. The view more than compensates for the slow (but English-speaking) service. Try one of the mushroom appetizers. Fairly expensive by Moscow standards, but careful ordering can fill you up for 8-10 rubles.

Slavyansky Bazar, Ul. Dvadtsat' Piatovo Oktyabrya 17 (tel. 221 18 72). This old Moscow landmark used to be a favorite of wealthy Moscow merchants and the intelligentsia. Start off with a shot of vodka, *osetrina* (sturgeon), or *ikra* (caviar), and follow it up with *bliny, bifshteksy,* or chicken and *shampanskoye* (champagne).

Praga, Ul. Arbat 2 (tel. 290 61 71). Metro: Arbatskaya. Luxurious open-air roof terrace with a splendid view of the Kremlin. Good food.

Budapest, Ul. Petroyka 2 (tel. 221 40 44). Metro: Ploshchad' Sverdlova. Elegant chandeliers and pink walls. Wide choice of mainly Hungarian but also other European dishes; entertainment nightly after 7pm. Hungarian beefsteak is tasty but unadventurous.

Mezhdunarodnaya, corner of Ul. 1905 Goda and Krasnopresnenskaya nab. (tel. 253 23 83). Metro: Kransnopresnenskaya, then bus #4. This most modern of the Moscow hotels often offers a tasty lunchtime buffet.

Cafes

There are a number of cafes in Moscow that serve inexpensive food and drink, as well as the traditional assortment of coffee and pastry.

Kafe Moskva, Ul. Gor'kovo 6, near the Intourist Hotel and Red Square. Popular with Muscovites; expect a long line.

Kafe Kosmos, Ul. Gor'kovo, across from the central post office. Nice place to meet young Russians. Open 11am-4pm and 5-11pm.

Kafe Ptitsa, Ploshchad' Sovetskaya 6. Try the cold chicken and red wine. Open 11am-10:30pm.

Kafe u Nikitskikh Vorot, Ul. Gertsena 17, next to the Mayakovsky Theater. Cozy ambience enhanced by old Shalyapin records. Popular. Cover (5 rubles) includes a main dish and a drink. Open until 11pm.

Kafe Stoleshniki, on Stoleshnikov per. between Pushkinskaya ul. and Ul. Gor'kovo. Noteworthy for its intimate atmosphere—bare brick walls and candlelight. 5 ruble cover includes a dish and a drink. Open until 11pm.

Kafe Ogni Moskvy, on the 15th floor of the Hotel Moskva, 1 block from Red Square. Good cheap food and a terrific view. Fills fast (the cafe, not you).

Kafe Shchokoladnitsa, on Ul. Dimitrova. Metro: Oktyabr'skaya. Distinctive desserts. Try *bliny* (pancakes) with plum filling and chocolate sauce (the place's name means "chocolate").

Kafe Tourist, Ul. Kirova 20. Metro: Kirovskaya/Turgenevskaya. The office and *pirozhki* are all right, but the hippies who congregate here are what set it apart.

Sights

Lenin's omnipresence, in the form of billboards, statues, and fond memories, strikes most visitors to Moscow. The greatest pilgrimage a patriotic Soviet can make is to **Lenin's Mausoleum** on **Red Square,** the center of downtown Moscow. The red granite structure houses the preserved remains of the famous leader. You can get an Intourist escort and skip to the front of the line, but spending time in the line (1 hr., at least) is an excellent way to take part in a ritual of Soviet life. Shorts and cameras are not permitted, and a respectful attitude is expected; the guards will ask tourists to take their hands out of their pockets. (Open Tues.-Thurs. and Sat. 9am-1pm, Sun. 9am-2pm.) After exiting, take time to contemplate the graves of Josef Stalin, John Reed (the only American buried in the Kremlin wall), and other Soviet notables, including Maxim Gorky and Yuri Gagarin (the first person in space).

If this expedition leaves you eager for more Lenin memorabilia, there is no better place than the **Central Lenin Museum.** Containing everything from his Mercedes to his study, the detailed museum is located at Ploshchad Revolyutsii 2, just off Red Square. The half-hour film, though in Russian, is worth seeing for the footage of Lenin's speeches. (Open mid-May to mid-Sept. Tues.-Sun. 10am-6pm; mid-Sept. to mid-May Tues.-Thurs. 11am-7:30pm, Fri.-Sun. 10am-6:30pm.) Next door is the large, red **Historical Museum,** Moscow's oldest. This vast collection of coins, robes, and implements stretches from prehistoric times to the present. Not always the most interesting of exhibits—whole rooms are devoted to the history of Finnish-Soviet cultural relations, for example. (Open Thurs.-Mon. 10am-6pm, Wed. 10am-7pm.)

Across Red Square from the museum stands the Soviet Union's most distinctive structure, **St. Basil's Cathedral** (Pokrovsky sobor). Legend has it that after the cathedral was completed, Ivan the Terrible had the architects' eyes gouged out to ensure that they would never build one more beautiful. The interior, now a museum, is less impressive than the overwhelming exterior, but still merits a quick visit. (Times subject to change, but posted clearly in front.)

The power and centralization commonly attributed to the Soviet Union find their most succinct expression in Moscow's 69-acre centerpiece. Surrounded by a 2-kilometer-long wall up to 20m high and 10m thick, the **Kremlin** seems to forbid all visitors; but overcome your instincts and enter, for this is the one sight in Moscow not to be missed. A tour guide or detailed guidebook is advisable amid the sprawling cluster of buildings. Chief attractions include an impressive series of Russian Orthodox cathedrals. The **Annunciation Cathedral,** with an iconostasis by the great painters Andrei Rublyev and Theophan the Greek, stands near the **Archangel Cathedral,** where Ivan the Terrible and other tsars are buried. Not far away is the huge **Assumption Cathedral,** where all the tsars were crowned; Ivan the Terrible's custom-made coronation throne still resides proudly by the south portal. Less ceremoniously, Napoleon set up his stables here. Take time to visit the interiors of the magnificent, ornate buildings. (Open Fri.-Wed. 10am-7pm; arrive 1 hr. before closing time. Purchase an admission ticket at the kiosk next to the Archangel: 45k.) The very plain **Church of the Twelve Apostles** was patriarch Nikon's seventeenth-century answer to the extravagant sixteenth-century madness of St. Basil's. The **Armory Museum,** just inside Borovitsky Gate, includes goblets, gowns, and carriages in a luxurious collection initiated as a resting place for the treasures of Muscovite princes. Gem connoisseurs should not miss the museum's **Diamond Fund,** which houses Catherine the Great's incredible crown of 5000 diamonds. (Separate admission required.)

Unlike the ancient hearts of most European nations, the Kremlin still beats. The imposing yellow **Grand Kremlin Palace,** where the Supreme Soviet meets (note all the black sedans outside), can be admired from outside only, but the modern **Palace of Congresses** is open for ballet and opera performances throughout the summer. It is in this huge room that the Party meets every five years to set its agenda. (Shorts and large bags are prohibited inside the Kremlin complex; you can check bags near the gate.) Leaving the Kremlin from Trinity Gate, next to the Palace, you enter **Alexandrovsky Gardens.** At their northern end, the eternal flame of the **Tomb of the Unknown Soldier** flickers in memory of the country's 20 million lost in World War II. On Saturday afternoons, hundreds of brides, following a special after-hours tour of the Lenin Mausoleum, file past to lay bouquets on the tomb and take wedding pictures.

For the best views of the Kremlin, walk behind St. Basil's, across the bridge and along the far bank of the River Moskva, or take a ride on one of the sightseeing boats—they stop at every bridge along the way (every 20 min., 45k). Guided tour boats leave from Rossiya Hotel (behind St. Basil's) Monday, Wednesday, and Friday at 3:30pm (2 hr., 3.50R). From Park Kultury Metro station, cross **Krimsky Most** bridge to get to **Gorky Park,** Moscow's amusement park, where out-of-towners and young Muscovites come in droves on summer afternoons to promenade and relax. Huge outdoor speakers play modern Soviet music day in and day out, and in winter the paths in Gorky Park are flooded to create a park-wide ice rink; skates are available for rental. On weekends, there is an admission charge of 30k. **Izmailovsky Park** is farther from the city center, and so visited by fewer tourists. (Metro: Izmailovskaya.) In summer both parks have tent **circuses** that are less polished but more traditional than Moscow's famous Old and New Circuses. Tickets for all of them must be purchased in advance at your hotel service bureau or a street kiosk.

Be sure to ride the **Metro,** much more than just the most efficient means of transportation in Moscow. Each station is adorned with original artwork and fantastic chandeliers. **Ploshchad Revolyutsii** will chill the blood of any well-meaning capitalist; **Mayakovskaya** is a veritable museum piece.

For a taste of the average Muscovite's life take the Metro out of the city center to a random stop and stroll among the apartment and shopping complexes. The southwestern region of town (Metro: Yugozapadnaya) is mostly housing projects. Step off at Universitet Metro station to walk around the grounds of **Moscow State University.** The entire university is contained within a single Stalinist edifice; to appreciate fully the structure's size, you must see it at close range. You need a pass to enter the university premises, but talking to a guard (try to do it in Russian, however broken) may get you in. Nearby is a viewing area from where you can see the **Luzhniki Sports Complex** and all of Moscow behind it. Sticking out like a sore thumb is **Lenin Stadium,** second largest in the world, and site of the 1980 Olympics. On the hills is a ski jump used by skiers even in summer. On the way back, stop off at Kropotkinskaya Ploshchad'. Nearby is the **Moscow Swimming Pool,** a heated outdoor pool, open year-round. If you go for a swim, do not leave your Western clothes, shoes, and valuables in a vulnerable spot. In winter, the steam rising from the pool makes it difficult to see anything—young Muscovite couples sometimes take advantage of this, as there are few places they can go for privacy.

A stroll along **Kropotkinskaya** provides an opportunity to view some nineteenth-century homes of the aristocracy and intelligentsia. At #11 is the **Lev Tolstoy Museum;** nearby at Ul. Lva Tolstovo 21 is the **Lev Tolstoy House-Museum,** the mansion where Tolstoy lived and worked from 1882-1901. The latter, containing the writer's perfectly preserved study, is more interesting, but both are worth seeing. (Museum open Tues.-Sun. 10am-6pm. House-Museum open in summer Tues.-Sun. 10am-5:30pm; in winter Tues.-Sun. 10am-3pm; closed the last Fri. of every month.) Moscow has museums to commemorate all the great Soviet writers, including **Chekhov's House-Museum,** at Sadovaya-Kudrinskaya 6, **Dostoevsky's Flat-Museum,** at Ul. Dostoevskovo 2, and **Gorky's Flat-Museum** at Ul. Kachalova 6/2. The Gorky Flat-Museum is particularly interesting because of the interior design; the main staircase is designed to project the feeling and movement of waves on the sea.

A major tourist excursion for Soviets from other republics is to the **Exhibition of Economic Achievements,** an immense park with dozens of pavilions detailing progress made in education, technology, and medicine. Especially interesting is the **Kosmos** exhibit, with a model of Yuri Gagarin's space ship. Located on Prospekt Mira, the park is best reached by riding the Metro to VDNKh. West of the park is luxurious **Ostankino Palace,** now a museum of serf art. (Open in summer daily 10am-5pm; in winter daily 10am-2pm.)

The **Tretyakov Art Gallery** (Metro: Novokuznetskaya) houses a superb collection of Russian and Soviet art under its traditional peaked roofs. Look for the fifteenth-century icons of Andrei Rublyev, the magnificent historical paintings and portraits of Repin, the lush madness of Vrubel, and the Russian impressionist works of Valentin Serov and Isaac Levitan. (Unfortunately, most of the rooms will be under restoration for several years. Open Tues.-Sun. 10am-8pm. Admission 40k.) The **Pushkin Museum of Fine Arts** on Volkhonka St. 12 (Metro: Kropotkinskaya) has a fair collection of Western art (including copies of the Winged Victory and other famous statues), intended to educate Soviet citizens about places they can't go. (Open Tues.-Sat. 10am-8pm, Sun. 10am-6pm; closed the last Tues. of every month. Admission 40k.)

The **Novodevichy Convent,** located several blocks from the Sportivnaya Metro station, has an illustrious past. Here Boris Godunov ingeniously planned his election as Tsar in 1598, and Napoleon set up a provisional depot. The scars on the wall remain, but **Smolensky Cathedral** is strikingly beautiful; church services are still held twice per day in the refectory, the long red and white building to the right of the entrance. Exact times are posted on the front door, but since services are often over two hours long, you can be reasonably sure that by arriving at 8am or 6pm you will witness at least part of one. The convent's cemetery lies nearby with the graves of Gogol, Chekhov, Stanislavsky, Khrushchev, and Mayakovsky. Avoid visiting the convent on Sundays, when tour buses crowd up to the door. (Convent open Wed.-Mon. 10:30am-5:30pm; closed the first Mon. of each month. Cemetery closed to virtually everyone; try dressing in Soviet clothes, carrying flowers, and sobbing profusely.) Or visit any other modern cemetery—the gravestones are either statues or engraved with the image of the deceased, and are a veritable museum.

Another placid sight that offers a great break from the tourist mainstream is the **Kolomenskoye Summer Residence** of the Tsars. Situated on a wooded rise above the River Moskva, this collection of buildings is a short walk from the Kolomenskaya Metro station. Peter the Great's log cabin (1702) and Bratsk Prison, where the persecuted Archpriest Avvakum wrote his final work, have been moved here from Archangelsk and Siberia, respectively.

Another pleasant walk away from the tourist mainstream begins behind the huge Rossiya Cinema, which looms over Pushkin Square (Metro: Pushkinskaya); walk along this park-like boulevard, and, using it as a reference point, stray off into adjacent byways and neighborhoods. Turn right on Ul. Zhdanova, for example, and up to the left you'll find a venerable old monastery that probably welcomes no more than 10 foreign visitors a year. There's a small square nearby with a statue of Lenin and benches where you can sit and contemplate the sunset over the onion dome of an Orthodox church or chat with a Soviet friend. Ul. Gertsena, leading up to the Nikitskiye Gates, is also in a very pretty area. The Tchaikovsky conservatory is on this street as well (notice the notes on the fence—his best hits).

To get a real feeling for Russian culture, visit an Orthodox service. Of the churches still in use, one seventeenth-century jewel is the **Church of St. Nicholas** on the corner of Komsomolsky Prospekt and Ul. Frunze. Daily services are at 9:30am and 6pm; women must cover their heads, and all should dress and act discreetly. Try also the **Troitskaya Church** at Lenin Hills (close to Moscow State University). There is an active **synagogue** at Ul. Arkhopova 8. If you're in Moscow during a Jewish holiday, be sure to visit—you'll be surprised by the celebrating throngs.

Moscow's **beriozkas** (foreign-currency shops) are well-stocked, with good buys on fur from Siberia (rabbit and wolf), amber necklaces from the Baltic coast, and hand-painted boxes from the villages of Palekh, Kholui, and Mstere. The Hotel Rossiya at Moskvoretskaya Naberezhnaya houses a large *beriozka;* also try the one in the Mezhdunarodnaya Hotel (which even has a supermarket; take the Metro to Krasnopresnenskaya, then bus #4). The complex resembles nothing so much as an American mall (it was, in fact, built by Americans). (Open daily 9am-2pm and 3-8pm; bring your passport). **Prospekt Kalinina** is Moscow's most glamorous retail boulevard. At the **Melodiya** record store, Prospekt Kalinina 40, you can find hard-to-get Russian classics and records by popular Soviet artists. **Dom Knigi,** Prospekt Kalinina 26, has a wide selection of books in many languages, as well as colorful propaganda posters. The **Plakati** poster store, on Ul. Arbat, around the corner from the Praga Restaurant, has an even better selection. A visit to the mammoth **GUM** department store, more like an Asian bazaar than a retail store, will prove memorable even if you don't find anything to buy. This unique institution is situated in Red Square directly across from the Lenin Mausoleum. If you want to buy any antiques, samovars, or paintings, be sure to get an export permit (see Practical Information in the country introduction). Or save yourself the headache and buy such things at the *beriozkas.*

Entertainment

It is not true that Moscow has no nightlife—it's simply hard for foreigners to find. There are two popular anonymous **bars** that sit side-by-side on Leningradsky Prospekt between Ul. Pravdy and Ul. Raskavoy, across from the Belorusskaya Metro station; another colorful place is behind the Bolshoi Theater on Ul. Petrovka just before Stoleshnikov Per. The really adventurous can strike out for a **disco** where the young beautiful people go. From Kashirskaya Metro, go right down the highway several blocks to the movie theater. The Kafe Druzhba is on the little street going past to the left of the theater; the disco is above it (ask any young person for help). The disco is crowded, the music mostly foreign—but it's a place few tourists ever go. Also go into a Soviet **beer hall,** where there are beer vending machines, piles of shrimp, and Soviet workers. Ask for the nearest Pivny Zal (there's one not far from the Rossiya movie theater).

Pushkin Square on Ulitsa Gor'kovo, with its monument to Russia's greatest poet, is a gathering place for everybody, including students; flanking the monument is the Izvestiya building, a famous example of Soviet architecture of the 1920s. The small park containing the monument to Karl Marx, across from the Bolshoi Theater, is another good place to meet young Russians. In the evenings, students and young people congregate and stroll up and down the first few blocks of Ulitsa Gor'kovo.

We have heard that the **Kafe Sadko,** on Pushkinskaya Ul. is a popular gay hangout; also try **Kafe Artisticheskoye** on Proezd Khudozhestvennovo Teatra. If your Russian is up to it, Soviet cinema is well worth a visit (tickets 25-40k). Two of the bigger cinemas are **Rossiya,** Pushkinskaya Ploshchad' (tel. 299 04 41) and **Oktyabr'** on Prospekt Kalimina 42 (tel. 202 11 11). For old films, go to **Poytornovo Fil'ma** on Ul. Gertsena 23/9 (tel. 290 42 28). Films are listed in *Kinonedelya.* **Illynzion,** at the beginning of Ul. Volodarskovo, near the State Library of Foreign Literature, often screens foreign-language films.

Moscow can be a bargain paradise for theater and ballet buffs, who need pay only a few rubles to see world-famous companies. At the top of the list are the **Bolshoi Ballet** and the **Moscow Art Theater** (better known by the acronym **MKGAT**), with a new home on Tverskoy Bulvar and tradition going back 90 years to the days of Stanislavsky, Chekhov, and the young Gorky. Located at Ploshchad' Sverdlova 2, this glamorous hall holds a fairly small audience, so order tickets early through a hotel. Local companies go on tour between mid-July and mid-September, and there may be no visitors performing. Ballet and opera run throughout the summer at the Kremlin's **Palace of Congresses.** Moscow youth prefer the more experimental and avant-garde Sovremennik and Taganka companies. The **Sovremennik Theater** is located at Chistoprudny Bulvar 19a (tel. 297 18 19); the **Taganka Theater of Drama and Comedy** stands at Ul. Chkalova 76 (tel. 272 63 00). Performances are, naturally, in Russian.

If Moscow's famed **Obraztsov Puppet Theater** is in town, don't miss it. Also check out the unique **Gypsy Theater** in the Hotel Sovietskaya at Leningradsky Prospekt 32/2, and the program at the **Tchaikovsky Concert Hall.** Tickets to most of these events are available at sidewalk kiosks and in Intourist hotel service bureaus. Try the **Intourist Hotel Travel Bureau** at Ul. Gor'kovo 3 early in the morning of the day you want to see a performance; although they often sell out sooner than the kiosks, their information is centralized—and in English. The National Hotel has a helpful service bureau; if you encounter trouble entering the building without a pass, tell the attendant you're going to the *beriozka* or the bathroom. In general, if you are told an event is sold out, be persistent and look elsewhere. Small gifts may make an uncooperative cashier more resourceful, and you can sometimes get a ticket in front of the theater before curtain time.

Moscow's **Old** and **New Circuses** are both famous and worthy of their reputations. The former is more traditional, located at Tsvetnoy Bulvar 13 (tel. 221 58 80), while the more dazzling New Circus thrills its spectators at Prospekt Vernadskovo 7 (tel. 130 96 76).

If you're in Moscow during an international soccer game, you'll see how popular the sport is here. The local teams **Dinamo, Spartak, TsSka,** and smaller **Torpedo** also bring out fans, but real cheering is reserved for international games (held at Lenin Stadium: Metro Sportivnaya). The complex also has two ice rinks that host frequent hockey games in winter. TsSka is one of the best teams in the world, though they aren't as exciting to watch as Canadians—as many young Muscovites will tell you.

Near Moscow

There are scores of fascinating sights beyond the 25-kilometer limit of your visa. If something in the great beyond interests you, the legal solution is the Central Exursion Bureau (see Orientation and Practical Information). They'll prepare the visa n about a day and charge a flat rate for the excursion, including transportation. If a Russian acquaintance offers to take you in a personal car, you must decide whether it is worth the risk.

Zagorsk, about 160km from Moscow, has one of the Soviet Union's few remaining active monasteries. There are several beautiful cathedrals (including one with a turquoise dome studded with golden stars), which in some cases have original iconostases (icon screens) by Rublyev and his followers. The one-day Intourist tour to Zagorsk, including a stop at Pereslavl, leaves Fri. 9:15am from the Intourist Hotel (23R).

The trip you should try hardest to make is to **Suzdal.** Located 230km from Moscow, Suzdal once flaunted a church for every four of its inhabitants. Though a number of churches have been lost, at least five monasteries still stand along the lazy overgrown banks of the town's river, in a pastoral setting of distinctly Russian beauty. You can visit Suzdal and nearby Vladimir (which also has a fine church) on an Intourist tour for 30R (including lunch). Tours leave Sunday at 8am from the Intourist Hotel and last 15 hours.

Leningrad

Most Westerners, if forced to take up residence in the Soviet Union, would probably choose cool, aristocratic Leningrad as their home. Inextricably linked to the major events of Soviet history, Leningrad (formerly St. Petersburg) cannot escape the shadow of its imperial past. Physically, at least, Leningrad has been the city of the tsars since Peter the Great founded it and moved the capital here from Moscow in 1712 to provide greater contact with the West. Many of the major baroque and neoclassical buildings, well-designed streets, and landscaped parks are the work of French and Italian architects.

In addition to supporting the court's glamorous social and cultural life, St. Petersburg became Russia's main gateway for the importation of science and ideas from the West. Perhaps the most influential Western idea to take root in Leningrad was Marxism in the 1870s; it was ultimately responsible for the birth of the Bolshevik Revolution here in 1917. In 1944 Leningrad was awarded the title of "Hero City" for its citizenry's strength during a 900-day German siege in which 650,000 Leningraders died.

Orientation and Practical Information

Leningrad is in the northwestern Soviet Union, just a half-dozen rail hours from Helsinki, Finland. Traveling from Helsinki to Leningrad independently to meet your tour group is fairly simple; tours to Leningrad are also available in Helsinki. (See Helsinki for more details.)

Leningrad was built in the swampy delta of the **River Neva,** and the city is laced with canals. The historical heart of the city lies at the Peter and Paul Fortress, where Peter the Great made his first settlement in 1703. Cut by canals, Leningrad's major avenues fan out from this point. Among them is **Nevsky Prospekt,** the city's principal thoroughfare.

Tourist Office: Intourist Service Bureau, in the Leningrad Hotel, Progovskaya Naberezhnaya 7. Excursions leave daily for Petrodvorets, and several times per week for Pavlosvsk and Pushkin.

Currency Exchange: In the Hotel Astoria, Ul. Gertsena 39 (across from Gorky Park). Centrally located. Open daily 9:30am-12:30pm, 4:30-6pm, and 6:30-8:30pm. Try also the **Exchange Bank** on Ul. Brodskovo 4 (off Nevsky Prospekt). Open Mon.-Fri. 8:30am-1pm, 2-6pm, and 6:30-8pm.

Post Office: Ul. Soyuza Sviazi 9. Open Mon.-Sat. 9am-9pm, Sun. 10am-8pm; telegrams taken next door at #15. Mail sent to the **Poste Restante** address given in the chapter introduction may be picked up at Nevsky Prospekt 6. Also on Nevsky Prospekt 42. Open Mon.-Sat. 9am-12:30pm, and 1-8pm.

Telephones: Ul. Gertsena 3/5.

Public Transportation: An efficient **Metro,** buses, and trolleys keep Leningrad moving 6am-1am. 5k fare; bus tickets bought on board with correct change, trolley tickets sold at kiosks.

Emergencies: Police (tel. 02). **Ambulance** (tel. 03). **Fire** (tel. 01).

Consulate: U.S., Ul. Petra Lavrova 15 (tel. 274 82 35). The only one in town.

Food

Leningrad may not have quite the array of top-rated restaurants that Moscow does, but travelers can still turn to a number of excellent options here. Restaurants usually close at 11pm, and reservations are often advisable.

Leningrad tap water troubles some stomachs, and the bottled variety tastes funny. You can get foreign brands of mineral water at Intourist hotels.

Sadko, corner of Nevsky and Ul. Brodskovo (tel. 2100 36 57). Traditional Russian cuisine. Takes its reputation as Leningrad's "best" rather seriously. A great place for that 'bye-'bye-to-the-USSR dinner party: great vodka, good Georgian wine, champagne, caviar, and chocolate ice cream. Expect to spend 20R apiece. Reservations recommended. Open noon-11:30pm.

Kavkazky, Nevsky Prospekt 25 (tel. 311 39 77). Specializes in Caucasian cuisine. Try *kharcho* soup (a Georgian gazpacho), entrees of *shashlyk (shish-kebab), chakhombili* (chicken in a spicy sauce), or the *cherbureki* (cakes of mutton, rice, and parsley). Friendly management. Open noon-6pm and 7-11pm.

Baku, on Ul. Sadovaya between Nevsky and Ul. Rakova. Azerbaidjan cuisine; bottom floor less formal than the top. Recommended are a cold appetizer of *satsivi* (chicken in a heavy spice sauce with red onions), *basturma* (a kind of shish-kebab), and cold coffee with ice cream in it. About 20R. To make reservations, come in the morning and bring ID. Open noon-5pm and 7pm-midnight.

Metropol, Ul. Sadovaya 22, directly across from the south side of Gostiny Dvor. Traditional Russian cuisine. Not quite as full of foreign tourists as Sadko—a better place to meet Russians. Delicious chicken kiev—rumored to be the best in Leningrad. For reservations, drop by in the morning. Open noon-midnight.

Kafe Druzhba, Nevsky Prospekt 15. No one outstanding dish, but very popular with Soviets. Open noon-10pm.

Kafe Morozhenoye, Nevsky Prospekt 24, opposite the Kavkazky Restaurant. Leningrad's nicest and most popular ice-cream parlor. Faded elegance and pastel green walls. Ice cream 35k for 200 grams, with a glass of champagne 2.50R. Almost always a line. Open daily 10am-2pm and 3-10pm.

Sever, Nevsky Prospekt 44-46, downstairs. The place to go in town for pastry.

Sights

For a splendid overview of the city, climb to the dome of **St. Isaac's Cathedral** on Isaakyevskaya Square, a massive example of nineteenth-century civic-religious architecture; its dome is covered with 100kg of pure gold. The murals and mosaics inside are by some of Russia's greatest artists. (Museum open Thurs.-Mon. 11am-7pm, Tues. 11am-5pm. Colonnades open Thurs.-Mon. 11am-4pm, Tues. 11am-3pm. Admission to museum 50k, students 25k; to colonnades 30k, students 20k.) Nearby, on **Decembrists' Square** overlooking the Neva, Falconet's **Monument to Peter the Great** inspired Pushkin's famous poem, *The Bronze Horseman.*

Inside the **Peter and Paul Fortress** notice the artful transformation of wood into marble, and the icons illustrating the divine right of the tsars. Beyond the archway that leads out to the Neva are plaques commemorating the terrible floods that have repeatedly devastated Leningrad, including the one in 1824 that Pushkin commemorated. In 1717, the fortress was turned into a political prison where many revolutionaries were jailed, including Dostoevsky, Gorky, and Alexander Ulyanov,

Lenin's older brother. (Open June-Aug. Thurs.-Mon. 10am-6pm, Tues. 10am-4pm; Sept.-May Thurs.-Mon. 11am-6pm, Tues. 11am-4pm; closed the last Tues. of each month. Admission 40k.)

Get acquainted with **Nevsky Prospekt** via a tram or bus trip, or better, walk up one side and down the other. Try not to look too conspicuously foreign or you will have speculators/black marketeers constantly accosting you. Few other streets have played such a prominent role in Russian literature. The **Dom Knigi** at #28 is interesting for its array of anti-Western posters and its wealth of books in Russian; both at very cheap prices. (Open Mon.-Sat. 10am-8pm.) Farther along, near the Moscow Railway Station, you'll find an immense food market on **Ligovsky Prospekt,** where farmers hustle their produce. There is also a large covered market at **Ploshchad' Mira.** At the end of the *Prospekt,* near the entrance to the Alexander Nevsky Lavra (monastery), are two **cemeteries** where many nineteenth-century luminaries are buried, including Tchaikovsky, Lomonosov, and Dostoevsky. To get inside the cemeteries you have to buy a ticket to the tomb museum. (Open daily 11am-7pm.)

Along the banks of the Neva, the smaller River Moika, and the Griboedov and Fontanka Canals, you can escape the bustle of Nevsky Prospekt. A promenade along the **Palace Embankment** of the Neva toward the **Summer Gardens** will take you past many former embassies and beautiful examples of nineteenth-century neoclassical architecture. Stop to contemplate the diversity of Leningrad's many churches; the Slavic revival gingerbread of the **Church of the Bleeding Savior,** a rough copy of St. Basil's in Moscow's Red Square; the monumental **Our Lady of Kazan Cathedral,** modeled on St. Peter's in Rome and now the **Museum of the History of Religion and Atheism** (both these churches border the Griboedov Canal); and the baroque grace of the **Nikolsky Cathedral,** near the confluence of the Griboedov and Kriukov Canals. The Museum of the History of Religion and Atheism has guided tours (Thurs.-Tues. 11am-6pm every 10-20 min., 1½ hr.). Set in a bend of the Neva is the **Smolny Institute,** originally a convent complex designed by Rastrelli, centering around the dramatic **Cathedral of the Resurrection** that combines Russian and baroque characteristics; in 1917, the complex served as the nerve center of the revolutionary forces. Another pleasant walk is along the outside of the Peter and Paul Fortress; cross to **Vassily Island,** and to the Palace Embankment. There is a popular beach here, where, for lack of space, people tan themselves standing up.

Even if the rest of the city were nonexistent, the **Hermitage** alone would merit a week-long visit to Leningrad. Located in the magnificent, luxurious **Winter Palace,** former residence of the tsars, this collection of art unquestionably ranks among the world's finest. In Spanish works, it is surpassed only by the Prado in Madrid, while in Dutch paintings (especially Rembrandts) it is first. The museum also holds Flemish masters, above all Rubens, and works of da Vinci, Michelangelo, and Titian. Finally, the impressionist and twentieth-century collections are also first-rate. The Hermitage collection started with Catherine the Great's collection of 24 paintings; it now includes 2,400,000 items, kept in about 1000 rooms. The building itself is a paragon of extravagance; before you immerse yourself in the art, take in the main halls where the Tsar reigned and entertained, especially the awesome **Malachite Hall,** where the Provisional Government held its last meeting before the revolution exploded around it. If you're lucky, the Tsar's private apartments, complete with family portraits and a nursery, will be open. The main entrance is from the Embankment. Inside a back entrance (on the Palace Square side) is a fine *beriozka* selling art books. (Open June-Sept. Tues.-Sun. 9:30am-10:30pm; Oct.-May Tues.-Sun. 10:30am-5:30pm). Try and go with a group; the lines can be eternally long.

The **Russian Museum** is a lesser-known gem, but a gem nonetheless. The collection includes ancient icons (by Rublyev, Theophan the Greek, and others), and works by the greatest Russian artists of the eighteenth and nineteenth centuries (including Levitsky, Shchedrin, Perov, Bryulloy, Repin, Kramskoy, and Aivazovsky). The museum also has a major collection of Soviet art, past and present. (Open Wed.-Mon. 10am-6pm. Admission 50k, students 15k.) For what is probably the best poster collection in the Soviet Union, go to **Plakat** on Lermontovsky Prospekt, across from the Soyetskaya Hotel. Take the metro to Baltiiskaya Station, cross the bridge, and go up on Lermontovsky Prospekt. (Store open Mon.-Sat. 10am-7pm.) The **Literary Museum of the Institute of Russian Literature** contains a collection of manuscripts, portraits, and other memorabilia connected with such great Russian writers as Tolstoy, Dostoevsky, Gorky, Lermontov, and Gogol. Among the smaller literary museums is the beautifully preserved **Pushkin Apartment,** Moika Embankment 12, where the author died of his dueling wounds. (Open Wed.-Sun. 11am-5:30pm, Mon. 11am-4pm.) The **Dostoevsky Museum** is in the writer's last apartment at Kuznechny Lane 5/2. Here, Dostoevsky wrote his last masterpiece, *The Brothers Karamazov.* On display also are the writer's hadwritten notes for various novels, and the family apartments. Dostoevsky's study is preserved as it was when he died; the clock on the table points to the exact hour of his death. (Open Tues.-Sun. 10:30am-6:30pm; closed the last Wed. of each month. Admission 25k, students 10k.)

Many of the more than 500,000 victims of the seige of Leningrad are buried in the **Piskarevskoye Memorial Cemetery,** under the inscription "No one is forgotten, nothing is forgotten." Leningrad required a complete rebuilding after this tragedy, and a visit to the cemetery is one way to grasp the suffering endured. It's far from the center of town, so you may want to join an Intourist excursion.

Entertainment

The city is usually quiet by 11pm. Although they are picturesque against the midnight-sun summer sky, Leningrad's raised drawbridges may mean you won't be able to get home until 5am; they rise promptly at 1am and the Metro quits at 12:45am.

The **White Nights Festival** prolongs Leningrad's theater and entertainment season through the end of July. The major company is the **Kirov Opera and Ballet,** housed in Theater Square in the former **Mariinsky Theater,** which witnessed the classic performances of Pavlova and Shalyapin and where all the famous Russian operas were premiered. Nowadays the ballet is probably better here than the opera; try to see one of the Tchaikovsky standards. A good modern ballet company is the **Leningrad Ballet Ensemble,** which dances to both classical and contemporary music. To obtain tickets, go to Hotel Moskva early in the morning of the day you want to see a performance. (Metro: Ploshchad' A. Nevskovo.) Find out what is available, order tickets, and pick them up at the same place at 6pm. Tickets are often available at kiosks and ticket tables near St. Isaac's Cathedral or along Nevsky Prospekt. For more placid entertainment, take a boat ride up and down the River Neva. Tours leave across from the Hermitage. A 1½-hour ride costs 1R. On solid ground, try the English-language movies at **Kino Barri Kada,** on the corner of Ul. Gertsen and Nevsky Prospekt. (Shows at 10am, 4pm, and 6pm; 25k during the day; 40k at night and on holidays.)

Near Leningrad

Leningrad is surrounded by a string of sumptuous eighteenth-century summer palaces and estates which, though badly damaged during the war, are being restored to their former beauty. All are accessible by bus, electric train, or better yet, a hydrofoil ride on the Bay of Finland. (Check with your guide or hotel Service Bureau for details.) **Petrodvorets** is the Versailles-style palace estate of golden fountains and waterfalls begun by Peter the Great; you can skip the palace interior but follow the sound of shrieks and giggles to the "joke fountains" which, activated by one mis-step, suddenly drench their unwitting victims. (Palace open Tues.-Sun. 11am-6pm; closed the last Tues. of each month.) Hydrofoils leave between 9am and 8pm from a dock in front of the Winter Palace (every 20-25 min., 35-min. trip, 1.80 rubles).

The town of **Pushkin,** formerly Tsarskoe Selo ("Tsar Village"), has a huge parks system, the lyceum where Pushkin studied, and the country's most important Pushkin exhibit. The **Pavlovsk Palace** down the road has a fascinating architectural history of continual rebuilding and enlarging by Catherine the Great's dissatisfied descendants. Elizabeth I, Catherine's daughter, once wrote in her diary that she was tempted to tear it all down and start over. The war settled the matter; restoration has now lasted 10 years and is far from complete. Rastrelli's huge facade is once again in place, and the surrounding parks are wonderful.

If you're interested in what the country *dacha* of a leading nineteenth-century painter looks like, take the trip out to the **Penates** of Ilia Repin. To buy a one-day Intourist tour of any of the above places, go to Hotel Leningradskaya on Ploshchad Lenina. (Metro: Leningradskaya.)

Uzbekistan

Tuborg beer may be readily available at the Intourist foreign-currency bars and Aeroflot may have replaced camel caravans across the desert, but the Uzbek Soviet Socialist Republic is still very much an Asian land. Centuries ago, cities like **Samarkand** and **Bukhara** were important stops on the fabled silk trade route between China and Europe, and, though modern in many ways, they still preserve exotic bazaars where you can purchase aromatic spices and delicious dry fruits. Turbans may not be the rage in the boulevards of sprawling **Tashkent,** the republic's capital and one of the largest cities in the country, but many still wear colorful striped dress which bespeaks the region's traditions. Geographically closer to Kabul and Teheran than to Moscow, Uzbekistan is a fascinating and clearly non-Russian Soviet republic.

When the Russians entered Uzbekistan in 1868, they found the remnants of a great civilization. There had flourished men such as Muhammad ibn-Muza al-Khuwarizmi, one of the founders of algebra (the word "algorithm" is derived from his name), and Avicenna, the famous scientist and physician. The hordes of Genghis Khan brought about a 100-year decline, but Tamerlane—of Philip Marlowe fame—managed to establish a powerful if short-lived empire in the fourteenth century. With the advent of Soviet rule in the 1920s, Islam lost ground. Women symbolically burned their veils in 1927, and most mosques and *madrasahs* were reduced to mere architectural monuments. Today many Uzbeks compare their standard of living with that of some of their neighbors to the south—such as Pakistan—and find much to smile about.

You'll find Uzbeks a much warmer people than Moscow and Leningrad residents. Both children and adults will often approach you with a friendly *"otkuda?"* ("where are you from?"). Warmer still than the populace is the average summer temperature; the heat, at least, is very dry. To make things even more interesting, tap water is not safe to drink. Anti-diarrhea pills will prove a blessing. Bottled water is generally available, but it is always carbonated, hardly ever cold (ice is made from tap water), and tastes funny. In Uzbekistan, Intourist's foreign-currency bars will prove to be veritable oases in the desert. Atmosphere is usually nil and you'll probably run into more ugly-tourist types than you'll care to remember, but nowhere else will you find such delicacies as Vichy water, good cold beer, ginger ale, and orange juice; remember to bring small bills and change.

With its Middle Eastern and Indian overtones, Uzbek food will probably be more exciting than Russian, but Sputnik hotels specialize in serving the same repast day in and day out. To add some spice to your life, visit the bazaars. Moscow residents are normally astonished at the variety and prices (some fruits are a quarter the price here), and will often ship large amounts of produce home. You probably won't be as thrilled, but there are usually some good buys (watermelons, dried apricots, almonds); wash all fruit before consumption.

It's possible to travel from Moscow to Uzbekistan by train, but in summer the trip is an exercise in masochism. Flying time is about four hours from Moscow, five from Leningrad. Tashkent is three hours ahead of Moscow time, Samarkand and Bukhara two hours ahead.

Tashkent

Never the possessor of glorious architecture like Samarkand and Bukhara, Tashkent saw its treasure trove of monuments further diminished after an earthquake *and* a hurricane struck the city in 1966. The authorities took these events in stride, and soon set out to rebuild the city with the help of architects from all over the Soviet Union. With its shady boulevards, squares and fountains, the capital of Uzbekistan is not unpleasant, but hardly merits a special trip. Nonetheless, both Sputnik and Intourist often include Tashkent on their tours to Uzbekistan (they'll probably fill time by taking you to a factory). Oddly enough, the fifth largest city in the Soviet Union has a relaxed, small-town atmosphere—a perfect place to unwind after heavy sightseeing elsewhere.

Tashkent's old-town—what's left of it—spans several blocks of modest, unexciting sixteenth-century houses. Its one remarkable monument is the **Barak Khan Madrasah,** a handsome sixteenth-century building that presently houses the Muslim Religious Board for Central Asia and Kazakhstan. This institution receives students from as far away as Bulgaria and North Africa. Right across the street is an active mosque.

The residents of Tashkent are justifiably more proud of the modern districts of town. Sprawling **Lenin Square** features not only some attractive buildings and a statue of you-know-who looking slightly fatter than usual, but also a huge, wonderfully refreshing fountain. The statue in the **Square of the Friendship of Nations** commemorates Uzbek families who welcomed into their homes Russian children displaced by Hitler's army. Tashkent boasts a **Museum of Applied Arts** worth visiting. The exhibit features lots of Uzbek folk art, including some beautiful rugs; there is also an array of Russian icons and paintings.

Samarkand

Industrial plants, educational establishments, progressive blocks of flats—but who cares? Your guide will probably want you to see modern Samarkand, but don't let him or her distract your attention from the splendid, ancient architecture of one of the oldest cities on earth. Samarkand is not 2500 years old for nothing. The little village that Alexander the Great conquered in ancient times became Tamerlane's imperial capital in the fourteenth century. While architects erected geometrical domes, astronomers like Ulug Bek explored the heavens, and poets praised Samarkand as "the paradise of the universe." Of the 63 mosques that existed before the revolution, only two are still operating, but Samarkand remains a privileged spot for exploring the achievements of Islam.

Samarkand's jewel is no doubt the splendid architectural ensemble of **Registan.** Students of theology, mathematics, astronomy, and other subjects called these three beautiful *madrasahs* home. **Ulug Bek's Madrasah,** the oldest of the three, dates from the fifteenth century. Some two hundred years later, architects erected the **Shir Dor Madrasah** ("madrasah with the tigers") as a delicate mirror image of the first edifice. Finally, also in the seventeenth century, the **Tillia Kari Madrasah** ("golden madrasah") was built to complete this masterpiece of equilibrium and serene artifice. On hot days, the square is a shady, refreshing place to sit.

Several notables are buried in the **Gur Emir Mausoleum,** including Tamerlane and his grandson, Ulug Bek. Don't miss the beautifully decorated interior, and take time to visit the narrow, dusty streets surrounding the mausoleum; they are a world apart from the modern buildings on the main streets. The mosques and mausoleums of **Shadi Zinda** can easily occupy a couple of hours of your time. Although it has never been confirmed, Muhammad's second cousin is allegedly buried here, and Shadi Zinda, like Mecca, is one of the holy places of Islam. Various members of Samarkand's nobility are also buried here.

Ulug Bek, who ruled in Samarkand from age fifteen, was one of the great astronomers of all times. His **observatory,** dug up by archeologists in 1908, is excellent proof of the sophistication that science had achieved in fifteenth-century Samarkand. **Ulug**

Bek's Museum merits a five-minute visit at the most, unless you have a strong interest in the man.

Samarkand's residents are proud of their **Opera and Ballet Theater,** across from the Intourist Hotel. Performers are not top notch, but tickets are cheap (1.50 rubles). The **sound and light show** at Registan is pretty at first, but soon becomes monotonous. Shows are in Russian, Uzbek, English, and other languages on alternate nights, but the show loses little without the narrative.

The best restaurants in Samarkand are either out of the range of public transport, or are underground establishments that cannot be listed in a guidebook (try asking around the bazaar). The restaurant at **Hotel Samarkand** is decidedly unadventurous, but the prices are reasonable. Take the elevator to the eleventh-floor outdoor bar, where an almost all-Soviet crowd is eager to speak with you (though you must break the ice). For a lesson in cultural sincretism, observe how the dancers combine elegant Uzbek arm movements with frantic rock music.

Bukhara

The mosques and *madrasahs* may be centuries old, but little Bukhara has all the atmosphere of a pioneer town. The townsfolk happily speak of new factories and irrigation projects, while the desert, gray and dusty, seems to lurk at every street corner. The city's ancient domes and minarets seem quite content to share their space with lots of glowing sunflowers. Iranian influence is strongest here; many people speak Farsi.

For a town this size, there's quite a lot to see. The 46-meter-high **Kalyan Minaret** is the town's best-known landmark. Erected more than 800 years ago to call the faithful to prayer, in the eighteenth and nineteenth centuries it served a more down-to-earth purpose: Prisoners sentenced to death were thrown to their deaths from the minaret's top. Among the other buildings in the square, the **Mir Arab Madrasah** is a rarity—a functioning *madrasah.*

The assertive **Ark** (fortress) is Bukhara's oldest archeological monument, and presently houses the **Historical Museum.** The exhibits here are not particularly fascinating, but don't miss the emir's holiday robe, just one of seven layers of clothing he wore.

At the Central Park of Culture and Rest you'll find the handsome **Mausoleum of Ismail Samani,** built in the ninth and tenth centuries. Ordinary bricks were used to create all kinds of magical patterns. Equally magical were the answers given by the *mullahs* to the questions left by the faithful in the bricks, always accompanied by some money. It's a good idea to come here more than once, as the color of the building varies with the position of the sun; it's at its best and most romantic in the moonshine.

The **Chor Minor** exhibits clearly the influence of Indian architecture. Its four solidly planted minarets represent what all Muslim men supposedly strive for: land, wealth, strength, and women. The emirs of Bukhara built the **Royal Summer Palace** in the nineteenth century on the outskirts of town. The palace combines both Oriental and European architectural styles, and presently houses the **Museum of Decorative and Applied Arts.** Uzbek brides flock here to contemplate themselves in the mirror of the 40 reflections, which allegedly will preserve their youth forever.

YUGOSLAVIA

US$1 = 781 dinar (Din)	**1000Din = US$1.28**
CDN$1 = 595Din	**1000Din = CDN$1.68**
UK£1 = 1300Din	**1000Din = UK£0.77**
AUS$1 = 559Din	**1000Din = AUS$1.79**

Because inflation in Yugoslavia runs at 130% per year, *Let's Go* presents all prices in U.S. dollars. Because the dinar devalues against the dollar as it inflates, these prices should remain more constant.

The Adriatic's clear blue water and the blue-gray woods of Bosnia's mountains contribute to Yugoslavia's inspiring landscape. However, it is the combination of this natural splendor with an extraordinary political situation that makes Yugoslavia such an enthralling place to visit. The West regards Yugoslavia as Eastern, and the East considers it a Western relative, but Yugoslavia is unique. The Communist Party is the only legal party, yet freedom of speech and of movement is substantial. With an abundance of goods and services, Yugoslavia is almost as amenable to travel as Greece or Italy. At the same time, you can meet visiting Eastern Europeans in a setting where they can speak freely.

Yugoslavia is a federation of six republics: Bosnia-Herzegovina, Croatia, Macedonia, Montenegro, Serbia, and Slovenia. After the fifteenth century, much of the country was occupied by the Ottomans, and in the early twentieth century Croatia,

Slovenia, and Bosnia-Herzegovia were held by Austria-Hungary. Slavic nationalism erupted in 1914 with the assassination in Sarajevo of Archduke Ferdinand, heir to the Austro-Hungarian throne. A new pan-Slavic state—named Yugoslavia—eventually emerged out of World War I, yet violent regional rivalry, chiefly between Serbia and Croatia, continued to rock the country. Wide support of the Communist Party finally united the six republics in the 1930s, and Josip Broz Tito emerged as Yugoslavia's overwhelmingly popular national leader during World War II.

After breaking with Stalinism in 1948, Yugoslavia steered an innovative path which the world watches with interest. Worker self-management is being tried on a scale larger than anywhere else in the world, but inefficiency, underemployment, and a massive foreign debt threaten the faltering economy. Between 1986 and 1987, dinar prices more than doubled (inflation runs at 130%). Because Western currencies rose about 50% against the dinar, the foreigner encountered a real inflation of at least 50% for many items. Prices for transportation and some foods can still produce a smile, but accommodations will eat into your budget. The Alps cost a fraction of their Western counterparts, and the Adriatic Coast is still cheap compared to Italy, but is now slightly more expensive than Greece. In 1987, the budget traveler could live fairly well on US$15-20 per day.

Rebecca West's pre-Tito *Black Lamb, Gray Falcon* is an evocative travel journal that can help you unravel Yugoslavia's complex history. In Yugoslavian bookstores you're likely to run across *The Pasha's Concubine and Other Tales* by Bosnian Nobel laureate Ivo Andrić. Before you leave home, try to find Andrić's *The Bridge on The Drina,* or works by Dobrica Ćosić (such as *The Time of Death*). Duško Doder's *The Yugoslavs* is an interesting discussion of the Yugoslavian sociological puzzle. If you have the opportunity, see the award-winning *When Father Was Away on Business,* an enlightening look at post-World War II Yugoslavia. If you're going to be staying in Yugoslavia for several months, pick up the *Rough Guide To Yugoslavia.*

Transportation

Buses and trains are cheap at about US$1 per hour of scheduled travel. InterRail is valid, and in 1987, Beogradtours sold discount tickets to IUS and ISIC cardholders, but only on trains to Hungary.

The main international train lines from points west pass through Ljubljana, Zagreb, Belgrade, and Skopje. Train lines from Zagreb wend their way to the ports of Split and Rijeka. Two southern routes—Belgrade to Bar, and to Kardeljevo via Sarajevo—link the interior to the coast, and both are tortuous. Trains run late; add an extra hour for every four on the schedule. Pick up the useful schedule book *Red Vožnje 1988-89* for US$1 at major train stations. During the school vacation in July and August, transport can be hellishly crowded. Definitely remember to buy a seat reservation (*rezervacija sedišta*) every time you buy a train ticket.

On buses, you are guaranteed a seat with a ticket. It is generally impossible, however, to buy an advance ticket for a bus which does not originate in the city you are in; you must wait until the bus arrives before finding out whether any seats are available. It's a good idea to jot down your request in advance. *Dolazak* means "arrival;" *polazak* or *odlazak* means "departure."

Ferries are much more comfortable than buses, but cost twice as much. **Jadroagent** ferries link major ports with Greece, and **Jadrolinija** runs local ferries. Boat offices on every wharf sell tickets and hand out schedules. Service is reduced 75% in winter. Zadar, Split, Dubrovnik, and Bar all have sailings to Italian ports. For more information, see the regional introduction to the coast.

JAT, Yugoslav Airlines, connects all major cities. All domestic flights cost about US$20, and 25% youth discounts are theoretically available. In summer, you must reserve five to ten days in advance, but you can check for cancellations. In winter, two days is usually enough. From each Yugoslavian airport, you can take a JAT shuttle bus to the center of town (US$1.15 one way).

Hitchhiking is slow, even on the main Zagreb-Belgrade highway. If you're transiting the country, consider waiting for a ride that will take you all the way to the opposite border. Cyclists may be discouraged by the narrow roads and furious drivers. There are also many roads with uneven, unpaved surfaces.

Practical Information

Britons need no visa to enter Yugoslavia. U.S. citizens and Canadians can pick up a visa at the border with no wait. Australians may be able to get a visa at the border but are advised by the Yugoslavian government to obtain it in advance. New Zealanders must obtain a visa in advance. You're allowed to bring in 5000Din on a first visit and 2000Din on each additional visit in a given year. Exchange rates are the same everywhere in Yugoslavia, so don't hesitate to change money at the border. Because the rate changes weekly, you profit by changing only small amounts of money at a time. It is possible to exchange dinars back into lire in Italy, but only at a considerable loss. In Beograd, visas are conveniently issued on the spot for all Eastern European countries except East Germany, Bulgaria, and Poland; visas for these countries take one to six days.

Tourist offices (**turist biro**) are located throughout Yugoslavia. **Karavan,** the official youth travel organization, has offices in Belgrade, Zagreb, and Skopje, and provides information on youth discounts. Each branch sells ISIC cards to students, and YIEE and IUS cards to anyone under 26. IUS cards are of limited use in Yugoslavia, but are useful in East European countries.

Yugoslavia uses three languages and two alphabets. Serbo-Croatian will get you by everywhere. Bring a Serbo-Croatian phrasebook with dictionary; *Serbo-Croatian for Foreigners* is good. German is also widely understood. In Serbia and Macedonia, the Cyrillic alphabet is used. Saying "hvala" constantly (VA-lah, meaning "thank you") will win you many friends.

A woman traveling alone will receive many stares and suggestive remarks, but will generally be quite safe. The situation becomes less comfortable as you travel south and inland—Kosovo in particular can be unpleasant.

Many street addresses include the word *trg* (pronounced terg), which means "square." Street names on signs often differ from names on maps by "-va" or "-a" because of grammatical declensions.

Local calls required a 10 dinar coin in 1987. Anywhere in the country, dial 92 for **police** (*milicija*), and 94 for an **ambulance.** The **country code** for Yugoslavia is 38.

Stores are generally abundantly stocked. Tampons, however, can be hard to find. It's also a good idea to carry toilet paper. Public bathrooms are found in restaurants and cost up to US$0.30. Offices keep long hours; usually Monday through Friday from 8am to 6pm, Saturday 8:30am to 1:30pm. Many stores stay open on weekdays from 8am to 8pm, with shorter hours on weekends, but the hotter regions of the country may have a noon to 6pm siesta, with stores reopening in the evening for several hours. Little besides restaurants is open from Saturday noon to Monday 8am.

Banks and many shops are closed for three to five days during national holidays. These include New Year's Day, May Day (International Labor Day; May 1), Fighter's Day (July 4), and Republic Day (Nov. 29). In Serbia only, Fighter's Day runs into The Day of the Uprising of 1941 (July 7), and shops and offices stay shut for the entire week. Major seasonal cultural events include the **Dubrovačke Ljetne Igre** (Dubrovnik Summer Festival), **Ohridsko Ljeto** (Ohrid Summer), and **Splitsko Ljeto** (Split Summer). All feature concerts, opera, ballet, folklore, and theater during July and August.

Accommodations

Sobe (rooms to let; often advertised as *zimmer*) are a terrific way to go in Yugoslavia, but prices are rising fast. In 1987, rooms cost about US$7-8 per person (showers included). Pick up the brochure *Private Accommodations Rates* at a major tourist office. It lists virtually all of the offices that arrange rooms, and is especially useful for the islands along the coast. In the most popular waterfront cities, crowds of room-letters greet travelers at transportation terminals. Asking prices can invariably be bargained down. Singles are expensive and hard to find, so try to team up. It's a good idea to check your luggage at the *garderoba* in stations and see the room first. Official agencies often raise the prices by up to 50% unless you stay three nights or more. Only official places can give you a card for each night, though only about half of them do it. If you run afoul of the police with no cards at all, you'll probably get fined, but you're not likely to be checked.

In 1987, **IYHF hostels** cost US$4 virtually everywhere in Yugoslavia. Some are dirty and unpleasant, lacking amenities such as hot water. From July 1 through August, you can stay in *studentski domovi,* university dormitories that serve as hostels during summer vacation. They are sometimes centrally located, and almost always cleaner and more pleasant than hostels, but cost US$7-8 per person in doubles. Most tourist information offices will call ahead to hostels and dorms for you to check on space and current prices.

Organized campgrounds, usually open from April or May to September or October, are found throughout the country. They are listed and described in the brochure *Camping-Yugoslavia,* available from major tourist offices. Rates vary from US$1-8 per person and US$0-5 per tent. Freelance camping is illegal, and the prohibition is generally enforced.

Avoid hotels unless you're really desperate. In large cities, a single in a C-class hotel can cost as much as US$30.

Food

Regional cuisine varies with the region's history of foreign influence. Slovene food is practically Austrian, Croatian has Hungarian overtones, and Serbian, Bosnian, Montenegran, and Macedonian exhibit a strong Turkish influence. *Ćevapčići* (grilled meatballs, US$1-2) are the best-known Yugoslavian specialty. Other grilled favorites are *ražnjići* (pork kebabs) and *pljeskavica* (hamburger patty). *Mousaka,* layered eggplant or potato with ground meat, is a scrumptious Serbian specialty; *purica s mlincima* (turkey with pasta), is a Croatian favorite. Yogurt can be poured on any casserole, and is served with *kapama* (stewed lamb, spinach, and onions). Try the almost universally loved *kajmak,* made by stacking layers of cream taken off fresh milk. Along the coast, try *lignje* (squid) especially with black risotto, or *pršut* (smoked Dalmatian ham).

For a cheap and convenient meal, grab something from a kiosk. Found everywhere, *burek* is a delicious layered filo pie filled with *sirom* (cheese) or *meso* (meat). Honey-soaked pastries and ice cream are sold in ubiquitous *slastičarna.* As delightful as Italian ice, Yugoslavian *sladoled* (ice cream) is only US$0.15 for each small scoop.

In a restaurant, the main dish alone averages US$4. Vegetables cost US$1 extra each, but soup is cheap at US$0.50 a bowl. Self-service cafeterias (often labeled *ekspres*) lack ambiance but are great deals. You see what you are ordering, and pay only US$1-2 for meat and vegetable. Eating places are generally open daily from about 11am to 10 or 11pm, but a better selection of food is often available from noon to 2pm and 7 to 9pm. Go to the outdoor market (at least one in every city) for fresh produce. (US$1-2 per kg of fruit.) Undiluted fruit juice comes primarily in bottles.

By far the most common drink in restaurants is the locally brewed *pivo* (beer), but you may prefer *vino* (wine), either *crno* (red) or *belo* (white). Tap water is usually drinkable. Liquor is good and cheap. Try the local favorites: *šljivovica* (plum brandy), or *vinjak* (local cognac), *kajsijevaă* (apricot brandy), or *klekovaă* (plum and berry brandy). A service charge is almost always included in the bill, so there's no need to tip.

Croatia (Hrvatska)

Croatia achieved regional unity not as the result of ethnic or social bonds but simply through historical happenstance—the various towns in the region were the only ones able to repel Turkish invasions five centuries ago. Upper Croatia reveals Slavic influences and traits left by Austrian rule (most people speak German), while numerous outposts along the rugged Dalmatian and Istrian coasts betray a colorful Roman and Venetian past.

Zagreb

Zagreb is Yugoslavia's second-largest city, and the political and spiritual center of Croatia. One of the wealthier cities in Yugoslavia, Zagreb is a happy medium between the overdeveloped coastal resorts and the poverty of the southeast.

Orientation and Practical Information

Zagreb is situated 120km south of the Austrian border, on the main Europe-Greece rail line through Yugoslavia. Trains leave hourly for Ljubljana (2 hr., US$2) and Belgrade (6 hr., US$1.20). The dead-end rail fork to Split (2 per day, 8½ hr., US$3.50) begins here; connections to Budapest (6¾ hr.) leave daily at 8am.

Zagreb is a convenient city for travelers; most sights and services are within walking distance of the train station. From the station, a series of parks stretches almost to the main square, **Trg Republike.** Walk along the left side of the parks to get to the tourist office. Just beyond Trg Republike are the cobblestoned streets and cafes of the **stari grad** (old town). The bus depot is 1km to the right of the train station. Trams connect the two frequently.

Tourist Office: Turistički Informativni Centar (TIC), Trg Nikole Zrinjskog 14 (tel. 41 18 83 or 44 18 80). Not a very helpful staff. Open daily 8am-6pm. The Generalturist office next door may answer questions, although its main function is booking flights and hotels.

Budget Travel: Karavan-Naromtravel, Tomašićeva 3 (tel. 41 12 80), 2 blocks west of Trg Republike. For information, they refer you back to the TIC. IUS cards US$3.50. Open Mon.-Fri. 7:30am-6pm, Sat. 8am-1pm.

American Express: Atlas, Zrinjevac 17 (tel. 42 76 23). Mail held, but for cash transactions see Practical Information in the chapter introduction. Open Mon.-Fri. 8am-7pm, Sat. 9am-1pm.

Post Office: Branimirova 4, just to the right as you exit the train station. Open Mon.-Fri. 9am-10pm, Sat. 9am-7pm, Sun. 1-8pm. Same hours for Poste Restante, which should be addressed to Post Office 2 for this office. The central post office is at Jurišičeva 13 (tel. 27 71 12), 1 block east of Trg Republike. **Postal code:** 41000.

Telephones: Branimirova 2, and Jurišičeva 13, next to post offices listed above. International calling hours 8am-10pm.

Flights: Airport is 27km southeast of town near Velika Gorica. A 20-min. shuttle bus ride (US$1.10) takes you to the city air terminal at Grgurova, right next to the train station. Information (tel. 51 22 22).

Trains: All arrive and depart **Glavni Željeznički Kolodvor,** Tomislavova 12. Information (tel. 27 22 44).

Buses: Autobuski Kolodvor, Marina Držića (tel. 51 50 37). Buses to Plitvice and Kumrovec.

Emergencies: Police (tel. 92). **Ambulance** (tel. 94).

Medical Assistance: At Dordićeva 26.

Pharmacy: Central Pharmacy, Trg Republike 3 (tel. 27 63 05). Open 24 hours.

Consulates: U.S., Braće Kavurića 2 (tel. 44 48 00). American Cultural Center is in the same building, but enter at Zrinjevac 13 (open Mon.-Fri. 1:30-7pm). **U.K.,** Ilica 12 (tel. 42 48 88). Open Mon.-Fri. 8am-2pm.

Women's Center: At the Tresnjaka Community Center. A rape and crisis hotline is scheduled to be in operation from Jan. 1988.

Hitchhiking: To Kumrovec and Austrian Alps, take tram #1 or 11 out Ilica from Trg Republike. To the Plitvice Lakes and the coast, take tram #5 from the bus station to the end and catch bus #108 to Avenija Borisa Kidriča. To Ljubljana and the Slovenian Alps, take tram #4 from the train station to Avenija Ljubljanska and go right. To Belgrade, take tram #6 from the train or bus station to Avenija Beogradska and go left.

Accommodations, Camping, and Food

The **Omladinski Turistički Centar (IYHF),** Petrinjska 77 (tel. 43 49 64) is convenient, inexpensive, and a great place to meet other travelers. From the train station, go right (east) one block, turn left onto Petrinjska, and walk two blocks. (Members US$4, nonmembers US$6, in rooms of 6 beds. US$8 per person for doubles or triples. Curfew 1am. Open year-round.) If you want a private room, the **Generalturist** Office at Zrinjskoga 18 (tel. 42 59 66) is the only branch of Generalturist that can book them. (Singles US$20, doubles US$30. Generalturist open Mon.-Fri. 7am-6pm, Sat. 7am-1pm.) **Studentski Centar,** Savska 25 (tel. 27 86 11), about seven blocks west of the train station, rents dorm rooms to travelers from July through September for about US$8. Take tram #14 from Trg Republike to the intersection of Savska and Vodnikova.

You'll have little problem finding tasty and inexpensive eats in Zagreb. Try the simple fare at Zagreb's **Splendid Express** cafeterias, at Zrinjskoga 15 (tel. 42 77 15; US$0.70-1.25; open daily 7am-8pm). Share tables with the locals and sample *ćevapčići* (US$2.15) at **Somun,** Petrinjska 25 (tel. 43 08 90), three blocks from the hostel. Four blocks west of Trg Republike, **Medulić** at Medulićeva 2 has extensive menus, both vegetarian and carnivorous.

Sights and Entertainment

Begin with a look at the **stari grad** (old town). Climbing the steps from Trg Republike, you'll pass the **Katedrala** on your right. To the left are narrow cobblestone streets and the **Church of Sveti Marko,** which houses several works by Yugoslavia's most famous sculptor, Ivan Meštrović. His workshop, **Atelje Meštrović,** is nearby at Mletačka 8 (tel. 44 50 75; open Wed.-Sun. 10am-1pm, Tues. 10am-1pm and 5-7pm). Visit the **Galerija Primitivne Umjetnosti** (Gallery of Primitive Art), Ćirilometodska 3, for a look at Yugoslav native art. (Tel. 44 32 94. Open daily 11am-1pm and 5-8pm.)

The cafes along **Tkalčićeva** in the old town are the best place to meet Zagreb's trendsetters. **Sunčani Sat** at #27 and **Club Z** at #16 are very popular, but look for **Pivnica Melin** tucked in behind Ikalčićeva at Kozarska 19, where you can sink into pillowed chairs while the breeze blows flower petals into your lap. (Open Mon.-Sat. 9am-midnight, Sun. 6pm-midnight.) Try to be in Zagreb during the last week of July for the **International Folklore Festival,** a premier gathering of European folk dance troupes and singing groups. Free performances are held at Trg Katerina, in the old town at 8pm, and at Trg Republike at 9pm. Check with the tourist office for details.

Near Zagreb

If the omnipresence of Marshall Tito in pictures, monuments, and namesakes has aroused your curiosity, a visit to his birthplace at **Kumrovec,** 47km north of Zagreb, will be worthwhile. His childhood home has been transformed into a museum and memorial. (Open daily 8am-6pm.) Overlooking the small town is another **museum** dedicated to Yugoslavia's "national liberation struggle." (Open Tues.-Sun. 9am-noon and 3-6pm.) Buses travel to Kumrovec from platform #7 in Zagreb's main bus station (4 per day, 1 hr., US$1.35); trains also make the journey (3 per day, 90 min.).

Plitvice Lakes (Plitvička Jezera)

About mid-way between Zagreb and Zadar, the **Plitvice Lakes National Park** is one of the most beautiful regions in Yugoslavia—or anywhere. Waterfalls as high as 75m connect the park's 16 sparkling clear lakes, some reserved for swimming or trout fishing. A network of well-marked paths guides pedestrians over and under the falls and through thick forests.

Buses pass the park almost hourly from Zagreb (6am-8pm, 2½ hr., US$3) and Zadar (6am-6pm, 3½ hr., US$4). All buses stop at *ulaz* (entrance) 1, but you can request to stop at *ulaz* 2, 2½km away, for nicer terrain. The most spectacular series of falls, **Slap Plitvice,** are between the two entrances, closer to *ulaz* 2, and marked "e" and "f" on park signs. If you have several days and would like to hike the full length of the park, descend to the right from *ulaz* 1 to the lowest and most peaceful of the lakes. It's often easier to depart the parks from *ulaz* 1, as harried bus drivers may choose not to stop for one extra passenger at *ulaz* 2. (Park admission US$6.50, students US$3.50.)

Private rooms are provided by the **tourist information offices** at either entrance, though those near *ulaz* 1 are less of a hike (3-5km). Facilities are modern and generally well-maintained; Category II rooms are perfectly adequate. Freelance **camping** is frowned upon, but there's plenty of space in which to lose yourself on the hillsides above the Zagreb-Zadar road. Organized campsites dominated by caravans are situated near each *ulaz.*

There are **supermarkets** (open daily 8am-4pm) and **self-service restaurants** (open daily 10am-6pm) at both entrances. After a long day of hiking, splurge amid the country-inn atmosphere of the **Restauracija Lička Kuća,** opposite *ulaz* 1. For more information on excursions, contact the **Plitvice Lakes Information Office** in Zagreb at Tomislavov Trg 19 (tel. (041) 44 24 48), along the western edge of the parks, to the left as you look from the train station; in Belgrade at Makedonska 7 (tel. (011) 32 64 06). (Both open Mon.-Fri. 7am-3pm, Sat. 8am-1pm.) Cheap one-day excursions are easy for "round-trip" expeditions (US$10, park admission included); inquire at the information offices above, or at the tourist office in Zadar.

Slovenia

From the Istrian coast to the Julian Alps, Slovenia comprises one of the most varied and beautiful regions in the country. Bordered on two sides by Austria and Italy, Slovenia shares its neighbors' Western atmosphere, but not their expense.

Ljubljana

Snow-capped Alps ring Ljubljana, the capital of Slovenia and Western culture's gateway to Yugoslavia.

Orientation and Practical Information

Ljubljana is situated just 40km inside Yugoslavia, near the Austrian border. A major rail junction between the main north-south and east-west lines, it is easily accessible from Italy, Austria, Hungary, and other parts of Yugoslavia.

The train and bus stations stand side-by-side near the center of town. From either, turn right, then left at Miklošičeva Cesta, which will lead you directly into the central **Prešerna Trg.** Beyond this square lie the **Tromostovje** (Three Bridges) over the river Ljubljanica; cross one and you'll find yourself in the **old town,** snug at the base of the castle hill.

Tourist Office: Turistično Informacijski Center (TIC), Titova Cesta 11 (tel. 21 54 12). From Prešernov Trg, turn up Čopova ulica (away from the river) through the pedestrian mall to Titova; TIC is across the street on your right. One of the best and friendliest in the country. Room-finding service, maps, plus lots of good information on Slovenia and Yugoslavia. Get the monthly calendar (in English). Open April-Sept. Mon.-Fri. 8am-9pm, Sat.-Sun. 8am-noon and 5-8pm; Oct.-March Mon.-Fri. 8am-7pm, Sat.-Sun. 8am-noon and 4-7pm.

Budget Travel: Center Za Mladinski Turizam (Mladi Turist), Celovška 49 (tel. 32 18 97). Take bus #1 or 3 from Titova Cesta. Information for Yugoslavian students only, but sells IUS cards (US$3.50). Open Mon. 8am-2pm, Tues.-Thurs. 8am-2pm and 4-6pm, Fri. 8am-2pm.

American Express: Atlas, Mestni Trg (tel. 22 27 11), in the old city 1 block from the river. Mail held and check sales, but no cabled money. Open Mon.-Fri. 8am-7pm.

Post Office: PTT, Cigaletova 15, 3 blocks to the right as you exit the train station. Open 24 hours. **Postal code:** 61000.

Telephones: PTT, Pražakova 3, next to the post office. Open Mon.-Fri. 7am-8pm, Sat. 7am-2pm, Sun. 7am-1pm. Main office (Copova 11) is by the TIC. **Telephone code:** 061.

Emergencies: Police (tel. 92); headquarters at Prešernova 18. **Ambulance** (tel. 94).

Medical Assistance: Bohoričeva, or call 32 30 60.

Women's Center: Contact Lilith at **SKUC,** in the student cultural center at Kersnikova 4, third floor (tel. 21 65 90). Magnus, at the same address, has information on gay and lesbian activities and nightlife.

Pharmacy: Prešernova 5 (tel. 31 19 44), or Miklošičeva 24 (tel. 31 45 88). One of these two is always open.

Laundromat: Pralinca. Several on Vrtača near the intersection with Prešernova Cesta in southwest Ljubljana, 5 blocks from the river. You must leave clothes overnight. Open 7am-3pm.

Hitchhiking: To Bled, take bus #1 to last stop. To the coast, walk out of town along Tržaška.

Accommodations, Camping, and Food

Arrive early in the day as Ljubljana has no hostel and few hotels. From July through September, however, cheap empty dorm rooms (US$8 per person in doubles) are available from TIC. The **Dom Učencev Tabor,** Vidovdanska 7 (tel. 32 10 67), 5 blocks south of the train station, is large and well-managed. **Dijaški Dom Ivana Cankarja** is 3 blocks further south, at Poljanska 26-28 (tel. 32 35 50). Catch bus #6 or 8 on Titova Cesta to get to **Autocamp Ježica,** Titova 260a (tel. 37 13 82), near the river. (US$8 per person, no charge per tent. Open May-Sept.) **Private rooms** are available from TIC, but they fill quickly. (Singles US$7, doubles US$12.50.)

Facing the old city and the three bridges, take a right and you'll find reasonably priced riverfront restaurants. Follow the river (south) three blocks to **Pizzeria Ljubljanski Dvor** at Dvorni Trg, and get a wood-oven pizza for only US$2.50. Five blocks further south is the elegant **Pri Vitezu** (tel. 21 83 03). (House specialties US$3.50-4. Open Mon.-Sat. noon-11:30pm, Sun. 1-10pm. Women alone may want to go in daytime.) Bargain entrees await around the corner from the TIC at **Daj Dam,** Cankarjeva 2. Choose your food in the serving line but sit down to order. (Entrees US$0.60-1.00.) There is a large **outdoor market** in the old town. Turn left after crossing any of the three bridges. (Go Mon.-Sat. before 2pm.)

Sights and Entertainment

During the day, walk up Studentovska from the outdoor market to the castle for a panorama of the city. The castle is closed indefinitely, however, for remodeling. Worth visiting is the **Muzej Ljudske Revolucije Slovenije** (Slovenian Museum of the People's Revolution) at Celovška 23 (tel. 32 39 71), near the budget travel office; it contains permanent exhibitions on the Yugoslavian revolution during World War II. (Open Tues.-Fri. 10am-7pm, Sat.-Sun. 10am-1pm and 3-6pm. Admission US$0.16.)

The popular cafes lining Stari Trg, the main street of the old town, offer a relaxing vantage point for people-watching. Throughout the year, evenings in Ljubljana are alive with concerts and theater. The **Simfonični Orkester Slovenske Filharmonije** (Slovenian Symphony Orchestra) performs regularly at the modern Cankarjev Dom. (Tickets as low as US$1.) The city hosts an annual jazz festival in late June, and its annual **Mednarodni Poletni Festival** (late June-Aug.) features ballet on odd-numbered years, and opera on even-numbered years.

Near Ljubljana

About 50km south of Ljubljana, **Postojnska Jama** (Postojna Cave) makes a great daytrip. Twenty-seven kilometers in length, with plunging depths and fantastic stalactite formations, the cave is spectacular. Daily tours begin every half hour in the summer, less frequently at other times of the year; from May to September, the last tour begins at 6pm, at 5pm in April and October, and at 1:30pm from November to February (3pm on Sun.). The town of **Postojna** lies on the main rail line from Italy, halfway between Trieste and Ljubljana, and is also accessible by bus from the latter. The **Turist-Biro,** Tržaška 4 (tel. (067) 210 77), provides information on the cave, and can help you find private accommodations (doubles US$10).

Julian Alps (Julijske Alpe)

The Alps in Yugoslavia are just as stunning as those in neighboring countries. Prices a mere fraction of those in Austria and Switzerland make these peaks one of the best budget highs in Europe. Yugoslavia's biggest inland resort, **Bled** can be either a daytrip from Ljubljana or a base for excursions into the mountains. Buses run from Ljubljana (hourly, 1½ hr., US$1.50), but the train stops in Lesce, 5km away. The **Youth Hostel Bledec (IYHF)** is 300m uphill from the bus station at Grajska 17 (tel. (064) 782 30 or 31 21 85); follow signs for the *grad.* (US$8 with breakfast but no hot water. Curfew 10pm. Open year-round.) For a hot shower, splash at the Hotel Park on the lake. (Swim and shower US$3. Open daily 7am-7pm.) For private rooms, walk down Prešernova 400m from the bus station and take a right on Ljubljanska to **Kompas,** Ljubljanska 7 (tel. (064) 772 35). (Singles US$8, doubles US$12. Open Mon.-Sat. 7:30am-8pm.) A left from Prešernova onto Ljubljanska will take you to **Alpetour** at #13 (tel. (064) 775 75), a room-finding agency with similar rates. (US$1 less if not July-Aug.) **Camping Zaka,**on the opposite side of the lake, 2km from the town (tel. (064) 779 32), has its own beach; follow the path around either side of the lake. (US$7 per person, no charge per tent. Open May-Sept.) There's usually space there, but if not, try **Camping Šobec** (tel. (064) 782 89), 2½km from Bled off the road to Lesce. (US$7 per person, no charge per tent. Open May-Sept.)

Because Bled caters to groups, meal prices tend to be higher here than in cities like Ljubljana. You can dine on trout at **Gostišče Rikli,** Riklijeva 9, near the hostel, but the cheapest place in town is the **Hram** pizzeria next to the Hotel Park (pizza with egg, US$3). Hikers can load up at the **market** in the same building as the tourist office. (Closed Sun.) Any boat by the lake will take you to the tiny island in the middle (US$2.50 round-trip), from which there is a lovely view of the Alps. Hike up to the church at the hilltop to make a wish and ring the church bell.

To find out what the mountains offer, pick up a copy of *An Alpinen Guide* (free) from one of three tourist offices: in Bled, the **Turistično Društvo,** Ljubljanska 4 (tel. (064) 774 09), across the street from the Hotel Park in the Kazina building (open May-Sept. Mon.-Sat. 8am-8pm; Oct.-April Mon.-Sat. 8am-5pm); in Ljubljana, the

Planinska Zveza Slovenije, Dvoržakova 9 (tel. 31 25 53), near the post office, or the **Alpetour Office,** Šubićeva 1 (tel. 21 11 18).

You can take an early morning bus to **Pokljuka,** and hike 16km back to Bled through lush vegetation, or stay there to ascend **Mt. Triglav,** Yugoslavia's highest peak (2864m). The most common itinerary includes a six-hour hike, an overnight stay at the Planika hut (2408m), then a one-and-a-half-hour climb to the summit and five-hour return to Pokljuka. The slopes of **Mt. Vogel** and the trails around **Lake Bohinj** are also popular destinations.

Between December and April, skiers can choose from among several Julian resorts. **Zatrnik,** 8km from Bled, offers 16-kilometer downhill trails. **Vogel,** 30km away from Bled, offers even more, including an 8-kilometer trail. **Pokljuka** is especially good for cross-country skiing, and **Kranjska hora,** 28km from Bled, has what may be the best skiing facilities in Slovenia. (Lift tickets US$7.50 per day.) A special ski bus from Bled travels to the first three of these resorts (US$1-1.30); to get to Kranskja hora, take the bus to the Lesce-Bled train station and then another bus to Kranskja hora. Private rooms are plentiful in Kranskja hora, but check at the Bled tourist office about availability during ski season. Equipment can be rented at Generalturist or Kompas in Bled, and on the mountain at Kranskja hora; downhill gear costs about US$8, cross-country US$5.

Bosnia and Herzegovina

Mountainous Bosnia-Hercegovina lies in the center of Yugoslavia, west of Serbia and separated from the Adriatic by southern Croatia. Ruled by the Ottomans for 400 years, the region is still 40% Muslim. The works of Ivo Andrić provide exhilarating insight into the region, and are all the more interesting if you read them here.

Bus travel is excruciatingly slow (40km per hr.), but fascinating; the tunneled train line from Belgrade through Sarajevo to the coast will shelter you from both the landscape and the local color. However you travel in summer, be sure to make seat reservations at least one day in advance.

Sarajevo

Site of the 1984 Winter Olympics, Sarajevo evinces the strong Middle Eastern dimension of Yugoslavian culture. With 85 mosques, countless Turkish restaurants, and a colorful bazaar, the city will help you forget the bland modern buildings of lowland Yugoslavia.

Orientation and Practical Information

There are only a few direct trains per day to Sarajevo from Zagreb (8 hr., US$4) and Belgrade (8 hr., US$4), and four indirect ones for which you'll have to change at Osijek. All these trains are destined for Kardeljevo (3½ hr., US$2), which is 2½ hours from Dubrovnik by bus. The bus from Dubrovnik to Sarajevo (5 per day, US$6) takes seven hours. Buses also connect Sarajevo with Beograd (4 per day) and Zagreb (2 per day). Tram #1 in front of the train station (buy ticket in kiosk and validate on board) takes you 2½km to **Baščaršija,** the lively center of the old city.

Tourist Offices: Turistički Informativni Biro, Jugoslovenske Narodne Armije 50 (tel. 251 51), near the old city. Eager to help. Free city maps and information about the region. Open Mon.-Sat. 7am-9pm, first Sun. of month 8am-2pm. **Unis-Tourist,** Vase Miškina 16 (tel. 231 40), near the old city. The only agency in town that books private rooms (doubles only, US$19). Open Mon.-Sat. 7am-9pm.

Post Office: Obala Vojvode Stepe 8, on the river, a few hundred meters downstream from the Princip Bridge. Open Mon.-Sat. 7am-8pm. **Postal code:** 71000.

Telephones: In post office #5, Vojvode Putnika 100. Take tram #3 to Hotel Beograd and ask. Open 24 hours. **Telephone Code:** 071.

Trains: Željeznička stanica, at Stanični Trg 14.

Buses: Autobuska stanica, at Kruševačka 9.

Emergencies: Police (tel. 92). **Ambulance** (tel. 94).

Hitchhiking: To Jahorina and Belgrade, walk out of town from the old town hall. For Mostar and the coast, take tram #2 from Baščaršija; get off just before the terminus at Čengić-vila and go out Džemala Bijedića.

Accommodations, Camping, and Food

Student dorms are the best value. If closed try the hostels, but arrive early during summer. Go to Unis-Tourist for private rooms.

Dom Odmora Mladost BIH Trebević (IYHF), on Sarajevo's favorite mountain (tel. 53 59 21). Take bus #38 from the Princip Bridge. Still the youth hostel of choice; even though it's far away. Closed for repairs in 1987, but call to see if it has reopened.

Youth Hostel (IYHF), Zadrugina 17 (tel. 361 63), 10 min. from the stations. From Kranjčevića, the street in front of the bus and train stations, go left, and then take the first left onto Brodska. Take the first right (unmarked) onto Tešanjska and follow the road uphill to Kalemova #16. Unpleasant bathrooms and unreliable hot water. US$6 per person. Lockout 9am-2pm. 11pm curfew. Open year-round.

Studentski Dom Mladen Stojanović, Radićeva 4d (tel. 333 40). Located midway between the bus station and the old city. From the bus station, take tram #1 to the Skenderija stop. Walk 2 blocks along the river and turn left onto Radićeva. Beautiful rooms, private bathrooms, lots of hot water. Shared rooms US$10. Singles US$15, doubles US$17. Open July-Oct. 3.

Studentski Dom Bratstvo-Jedinstvo, Aleja Branka Bujića 2 (tel. 61 21 86). Far from the center, but cheaper than Mladen Stojanović. Open July-Aug.

Camping Ilidža (tel. 62 14 36), 10km out of town. Take tram #3 to the end and follow signs. US$2 per person, US$2 per tent.

The main square in the Baščaršija is filled with grills that specialize in *ćevapčići.* Across from the mosque at 33 Baščaršija, **Cevabožinica Baščaršija** serves delicious *ćevapčići* for only US$0.50. (Open daily 8am-9pm.) On the other side of the mosque is **Aščinica Baščaršija,** where you can fill a plate with four different entrees for only US$1.50-2.50. Throughout Sarajevo you can find **burek**-type meat pies under various names for about US$0.50.

Sights and Entertainment

Most of Sarajevo's interesting sights are within a five-minute walk of the Baščaršija. Next to the small shops in this old Turkish quarter stands the **Gazi-Husrevbegova Džamija,** Yugoslavia's largest mosque. The mosque was constructed in the sixteenth century by Ajem Esir Ali, who moved on to become the chief architect in Constantinople. Let the caretaker know you speak English, and he'll offer you a tape explaining the history of the mosque. Sarajevo's older mosques are museums, open from 7am to 7pm (7am-9pm in summer), but closed at prayer time. The **Srpska Pravoslavna Crkva** (Serbian Orthodox Church), at Maršala Tita 87, presents another side of Sarajevo's unique religious and cultural history; the **museum** next door houses an interesting collection of icons. (Open Mon.-Sat. 8am-5:30pm, Sun. 10am-noon. Admission US$0.35.)

Before the Olympics, Sarajevo was best known for its role in the start of World War I. Near the eighteenth-century **Principov Most** (Princip Bridge), the Bosnian student Gavrilo Princip assassinated Austrian Archduke Franz Ferdinand. On the corner next to the bridge, where JNA St. meets the river, are a pair of footprints in the pavement, supposedly marking the spot where Princip stood as he shot the locally despised Austrian ruler. Cross the Princip Bridge and follow signs 300m to the **Trebevićka Žičara** (cable car), which will carry you to the top of the mountain for a beautiful panorama of Sarajevo's minarets and red-tiled roofs. (Open daily 10am-8pm. US$0.45 round-trip.)

In the evening, join the crowds on Sarajevo's promenade, **Vase Miškina,** which leads into the heart of the old town.

Near Sarajevo

Would-be Olympians can ski during the winter months on **Mount Jahorina,** 30km southeast of Sarajevo. A shuttle bus departs from the stop 75m uphill from Princip Bridge. (US$6 for an all-day lift; US$7.50 per day for skis and boots; US$4 per day for cross-country equipment. For information call 80 01 26 or ask at the tourist office. Other Olympic facilities are scattered throughout the Sarajevo area; many are open to the public.

Jajce, 157km northwest of Sarajevo near the route to Zagreb, is worth a detour. Jajce is one of the oldest towns in Bosnia, and was its capital in the fifteenth century. Hundreds of years later, Josip Tito chose it as the site of the November 1943 assembly where the modern state of Yugoslavia was formed; the **Muzej AVNOJ** (Museum of the Anti-Fascist Council) commemorates that event. A well-preserved **medieval fortress** presides over the town's waterfall. **Unis-Tourist** and the **Turistički Biro,** both near the bus station, can arrange private accommodations. A few kilometers to the north of town on the shores of the Plivina Jezera, there is a well-equipped **campground** (tel. 336 74; US$1.50 per person, US$1 per tent).

Three hours away in **Mostar,** the famous **bridge** straddling the hillsides is lovely indeed, but the small town offers little else to the tourist. The bridge is 2km from the train and bus station. Stop here for a few hours en route inland, or make it a daytrip from Sarajevo; there are no buses from Mostar to Dubrovnik.

The Coast

The cliffs, beaches, islands, and coves of Yugoslavia's coast are simply breathtaking. Basically a mountain range hidden beneath the waves, the hundreds of islands resemble nothing so much as ridges and peaks. The ancient cities of Split and Dubrovnik combine the beauty of medieval hill towns with enticing waters. But don't remain on shore; explore coves and beaches on the islands of Hvar, Korčula, and others.

The history of the coastal region is as complicated as it is fascinating. The area has always been a meeting point between the great Mediterranean empires and the landlocked peoples migrating to the coast. After passing through the hands of Greece and Rome, much of the coast settled in for several hundred years as part of the Venetian mercantile empire. As a result, many of the towns along the coast are tiny architectural gems bearing the unmistakable imprint of Venice's style. For a readable account of the area's tortured history, try Rebecca West's *Black Lamb, Gray Falcon.*

The coast is the breadwinner of Yugoslavia's tourist industry, and life here is easy for the traveler. Many tourist personnel speak English, and signs are in the Roman alphabet. The waters are warm enough for swimming, but the weather not unbearably hot. If your budget can accommodate the ferries, then take them. Traveling by land is scenic, but the long bus rides can turn you into a basket case.

Jadroagent runs a ferry that passes through Rijeka, Rab, Zadar, Split, Hvar, Korčula, Dubrovnik, Bar, and Corfu and Igoumenitsa in Greece. (Rijeka-Split US$16, Split-Dubrovnik US$15, Dubrovnik-Bar US$12.50. US$2-7 cheaper from mid-April to mid-June and Oct.-Dec.) **Jadrolinija**'s local ferries connect the coast with nearby islands.

Camping on Yugoslavia's beaches is rigorously prohibited. Official campsites, which in July and August resemble parking lots, are all along the coast. There are

20 youth hostels on the Adriatic, though they vary widely in comfort and beach access. Private rooms seem to be available everywhere, but their prices are rising fast. Look for *sobe* or *Zimmer* signs. Some monasteries will provide accommodations, or let you camp on their grounds.

Rijeka to Split

Use the crowded port of **Rijeka** (the largest in Yugoslavia) only as a base for excursions along the northern Adriatic coast. Walk about five blocks to your right as you leave the train station to reach the bus station. The **Jadrolinija** office at Obala Jugoslavenske Mornarice 16 (tel. 227 58), two blocks to the right of the bus station, provides information about all ferries. (Open 5:30am-5pm.) If you miss the last boat out of town, arrange for a private room (singles US$12.50, doubles US$21.50) with **Kvarner Express** (tel. 306 17), one block inland of the Jadrolinija office. (Open Mon.-Sat. 7:30am-8pm.) Rijeka is somewhat redeemed by its **beach,** only 15 minutes away by bus #2 (from anywhere along the coastal road). Get off at Pecina and follow the crowds.

The wooded islands offshore are the least crowded on Yugoslavia's coast. Direct services to **Cres** run once daily year-round from Rijeka (US$3.80), hourly during the summer from Brestova, 45km west of Rijeka. Cross the bridge to go to Cres's main port of Mali Lošinj, and try either **Kvarner Express** or **Lošinjplov** for private rooms. (Singles US$12.50, doubles US$21.50; 20% higher July-Aug.) Direct ferries from Rijeka to Porozine run once per day (US$0.25). **Senj,** 69km south of Rijeka, is good for a short break. Hike around its medieval castles and fortress, used to defend against Venetians. From Senj, you can catch a ferry to the island **Krk** (2 per day) and then another ferry to **Rab** (4 per day), another island complete with medieval architecture and good beaches.

Split

Split was originally a prodigious waterfront palace which the Roman emperor Diocletian had built for his retirement before his abdication in 305 C.E. Over the centuries following the Empire's fall, local residents moved into the palace's innumerable rooms. The palace halls have become streets, and its rooms are now houses. Brought to the attention of architects through Robert Adams's detailed study in 1757, the singular blend of styles at Split had a profound effect on Georgian architecture.

Orientation and Practical Information

Split is situated just about at the midpoint of the Yugoslav coast, and is the terminus of the coastal rail line from Zagreb (7 per day, 8½ hr., US$3.70) and Rijeka (6 per day, 7 hr., US$4). Split is a major port for both intracoastal service and connections to Italy, and an important bus hub with direct service to all major Yugoslav cities. Buses from Rijeka run eight times per day (8 hr., US$9).

East to west (right to left as you face inland) are the ferry terminal, the bus depot, and the train station. Farther to the west is the outdoor produce market and the city's boardwalk, which borders Diocletian's Palace.

Tourist Office: Turistički Biro, Titova 12 (tel. 421 42), along the waterfront near the palace. Not a happy crew. Provides information only about private accommodations. City maps US$1. Open in summer Mon.-Sat. 7am-8pm, Sun. 7am-noon; in winter Mon.-Sat. 8am-8pm, closed Sun.

American Express: Atlas, Preporoda 7 (tel. 430 55), just inside the Roman walls to the right of the tourist office. Mail held and money changed. For other cash transactions, see Practical Information in the chapter introduction. Open Mon.-Sat. 7am-9pm.

Post Office: Lavčevića 9. Walk along the waterfront from the bus station, take a right at the edge of the old city walls, continue to the first main street and then go left. Open Mon.-Fri. 8am-8pm, Sat. 8am-7pm, Sun. 8am-noon. **Postal code:** 58000.

Telephones: In the post office. Open daily 7am-9:45pm. **Telephone code:** 058.

Ferries: The information office in the ferry terminal on the harbor sells tickets and distributes schedules for all routes out of Split.

Hitchhiking: For Dubrovnik, take bus #15 or 60 to Lovrijenac and start there. For the north coastal road, take bus #2 or 37 to Sućurac and head away from town.

Accommodations, Camping, and Food

The tourist office has access to **private rooms,** though the various agencies scattered along the waterfront are likely to be more helpful. (Singles US$8, doubles US$10.50; 20% higher July-Aug.) Invariably, you'll be approached outside one of the transport terminals by hawkers offering *sobe;* leave your pack in a locker, in case the rooms are unacceptable. The average asking price per person in a double is US$10, but you can easily bargain down to US$8, or even less if you are staying more than two nights. Solo travelers need to pair up or pay about US$11.50.

Watch the crowds on the boardwalk from the riverfront **Restaurant Adrijana.** (Grilled entrees from US$3. Open daily 7am-midnight.) A few blocks away and up the hill from the water is the **Bastion Self-Service,** Marmontova 9, the cheapest place in town. (Open daily 7am-10pm.) For inexpensive and unusual pastries, go to **Minosa** at 10 Bosanska in the old town. (Pastries from US$0.25. Open 6am-10pm.) Split's **open-air market** lies on the harbor west of the transport terminals.

Sights

The **Dioklecijanova Palata** (Diocletian's Palace) is the centerpiece of the traveler's Split. (Open daily 8am-7pm. Admission US$0.70.) The **Bronze Gate** on the south near the water leads through the fascinating cavernous cellars beneath the former imperial apartments, and into a courtyard, the **Peristyle.** Just inside the Peristyle, a black sphinx still guards **Diocletian's Mausoleum,** since transformed into the **Cathedral of Sveti Duje;** the church's interior walls are covered with elaborate stone sculpture and wood carvings.

The **Arheološki Muzej,** northwest of the palace at Zrinjsko-Frankopanska 13, houses many of the castle's Roman artifacts, including several interesting mosaics. (Open Tues.-Sat. 9am-1pm and 4-6pm, Sun. 10am-noon. Admission US$0.20, students US$0.10.) The **Galerija Meštrović** houses a sizable body of work by Yugoslavia's premier twentieth-century sculptor, Ivan Meštrović. To reach his former home and studio, walk 2km west along the coastal road, or take bus #12 to Moše Pijade 44. (Open daily 10am-7pm.) You probably won't want to spend much time indoors in this metropolis. To escape the city, take bus #37 20km west to the coastal town of **Trogir.**

Split to Dubrovnik

Yugoslavia's largest and most famous islands dot the waters south of Split. Their coasts are rock, pebble, and occasionally sand, and the water is a startingly clear blue-green; you might even find a secluded spot—if you're persistent. Ferries leave Split for Šolta, Brač, Hvar, and Korčula; smaller islands can be reached by local boats from these four.

One hour away, **Brač** is an easy daytrip from Split; ferries run hourly (US$3 one way). Its main town, **Supetar,** is jammed all summer, but has one of Brač's few official campgrounds. Try **Turističko Društvo** (tel. 480 65) in the town of Sutivan, or **Jadran Agency** (tel. 63 12 60; open 8am-10pm) in Supetar for private rooms. (Singles US$8.50, doubles US$14.50.) **Bol,** on the island's south side, has fine but crowded beaches. Two kilometers west is the even more popular **Zlatni Rat,** with a good beach. Less built up than Brač, **Šolta** is also an hour from Split, although ferries run only five times per day.

Seven ferries per day travel to the island of **Hvar,** depositing you either in the port of Vira, or in Stari Grad, 20km east. An early afternoon bus runs between the two towns. The town of Hvar is dominated by fortifications built during the time of Napoleon, though the town walls date to Venetian rule, as early as the thirteenth century. During the seventeenth century, Hvar's citizens started what is now the oldest communal theater in Europe, still in fine condition. The **Turist Biro** has private rooms but only for stays of three days or more in season; ask first for the Category III accommodations. Look for *sobe* (rooms to let) signs. **Camping Vira** is near the port (US$7.50 per person, no charge per tent). For a bit more privacy, you can make daytrips via taxi boat to the **Pakleni Otoci** ("Islands of Hell"), off Hvar.

The ferry to **Stari Grad** will leave you 2km from town, which lies at the tip of a long inlet. From the landing, take the path to the left along the water to town or take the bus (US$0.25) via an inland road. Along the seaside path, note the uncrowded flat boulders on which you can sun. Most people take the bus to town, miss this area, and then make do at the crowded pebble beach near Hotel Helios on the right side of the inlet. For rooms, try the friendly people at **Rija Vri Kred,** a tiny office to the left of the inlet, next to the big red building. (Open daily 7am-9pm. Singles US$8, doubles US$13.) Campers can hike to nearby **Plantaža** and **Bunarić** (the closer of the two). (Both US$1.35 per person, US$1.15 per tent.) You can rent bicycles at **Neptune** near the Rija Vri Kred (US$6.50 per day). **Restaurant Tri Palme,** between the bus drop-off point and Neptune, is the least expensive in town, but shopping at the **outdoor market** may be a better option.

Sućuraj, at the eastern tip of the island, is small and less crowded than Hvar's other towns. Connected to Drvenik on the mainland by an hourly ferry (US$0.60), Sućuraj is easily reached by those coming from Kardeljevo. A local bus makes the three-hour trip to the island's other towns twice per day. The Turističko Društvo just off the ferry dock can find you rooms (doubles US$15).

Unless you take the ferry from Split to **Vela Luka,** with its pebble beaches, the best way to get to the island of **Korčula** is to take the bus to **Orebić** on the Pelješac Peninsula (90km west of Dubrovnik), and make the short hop across the channel to Korčula Town from there. If you're coming from Sarajevo to Kardeljevo, take the ferry (US$3) to **Trpanj,** and then bus to Orebić. Korčula, the birthplace of Marco Polo, has pebble beaches and a cathedral with works by Tintoretto. At **Putnik Marko Polo** (tel. 810 67), you can find doubles as cheap as US$8 (30% higher in July and Aug.). **Solitudo** campground, in nearby Sveti Antun, is home to nude beaches. (US$7.50 per person, US$5 per tent; open April-Oct.) The best restaurant on the island is **Adio Mare,** in Grad, at the beginning of Marko Polo street; a full meal featuring exquisite fish and wine costs US$10. In the evenings, you can stroll around Grad's narrow streets lined with pleasant cafes and galleries. The peninsula of **Pelješac** is a fine spot to rest if you're in no hurry to get to Korčula. Mid-way between the mainland and Orebić, **Jancina** and **Trpanj** offer secluded beaches and coves.

From Trstenik on Pelješac, you can take a ferry to **Mljet** island (2 per day, 4 in high season, US$3.50) where unspoiled nature is protected in a national park.

Dubrovnik

George Bernard Shaw called Dubrovnik "the pearl of the Adriatic, a paradise on earth," and, indeed, it may be one of the most beautiful cities you'll ever see. Meander down winding alleys in the Venetian Old City, or swim amid magnificent scenery. Though Dubrovnik is already Yugoslavia's most touristed spot, its Old City is being restored to attract even more travelers. If you wander away from the crowds, you too may find a piece of heaven.

Orientation and Practical Information

Dubrovnik can be reached by ferry, plane, and bus, but not by train. The bus to or from Split runs through breathtaking scenery (4½ hr., US$6.50). From the bus station, tram #1, 2, 6, or 8, or a scenic hike down Maršala Tita will take you to **Pile** (Old City), 3km away. From the ferry dock at Gruž, take tram #1.

Tourist Office: Turistički Informativni Centar (TIC), Poljana Paška Miličevića 1 (tel. 263 54). Just inside the west gate of the Old City. Pick up map and excellent information booklet (free). Books private rooms: singles US$17, doubles US$25. Open Mon.-Sat. 9am-9pm.

American Express: Atlas, Pile 1 (tel. 273 33), by the bus stop just outside the west gate of the Old City. Mail held and checks sold and replaced. No wired money accepted. Open daily 7:30am-9pm.

Post Office: Maršala Tita 16, 150m west of the Old City's west gate. Open in summer Mon.-Sat. 7am-10pm, Sun. 8am-noon; off-season Mon.-Sat. 7am-9pm. **Postal code:** 50000.

Telephones: At the post office. Open in summer daily 7am-10pm; off-season Mon.-Sat. 7am-9pm, Sun. 7am-8pm. **Telephone code:** 050.

Flights: Buses (US$1) run between the airport and the city air terminal at Maršala Tita 87, next to the bus station. Buses leave 1½ hr. before each JAT departure. For tickets and information, try the **JAT** office at Maršala Tita 7, outside the Old City's west gate. To Belgrade US$18.50, to Zagreb US$21.

Buses: Several per day to Bar, Split, and Sarajevo, among others. Buses leave hourly for Kardeljevo, (2-2½ hr., US$3), the closest rail station.

Ferries: Dubrovnik's Gruž harbor handles traffic to ports all along the Adriatic. **Adriatica** has service to and from the Italian ports of Bari (June-Sept. 3-4 per week; Oct.-May 3 per month; 8 hr., US$67), Venice and Trieste via Split (June-Sept. 3 per month, 15 hr., US$67), Ancona via Split (June-Sept. 6 per month; Oct.-May 3 per month; 14 hr., US$62), and Rimini (June-Sept. 1 per week, 22 hr., US$62). Sept.-May prices drop approximately US$20. **Jadrolinija** runs 4 boats per week from Dubrovnik to Corfu and Igoumenitsa in Greece (US$50). Remember that you must pay for your ferry transportation to non-Yugoslav ports in Western currency. **Jadroagent,** Gruška Obala 63 (tel. 234 64), between the port and the bus station, has international ferry schedules and sells tickets. Open Mon.-Fri. 7am-1pm and 2-7pm, Sat. 7am-noon, Sun. 8-10am. **Jadrolinija,** nearby at Gruška Obala 74 (tel. 230 68), handles schedules and tickets for ferries up and down the Yugoslav coast. Open Mon.-Sat. 7am-1pm and 2-7pm, Sun. 8am-noon. Ferries run to Bar (2 per week, 4 hr., US$12.50) and to Rijeka (6 per week, 22 hr., US$21.40-25), passing through Korčula, Hvar, and Split (9 hr., US$15).

Emergencies: Police (tel. 92); *Milicija* headquarters at Maršala Tita 75, 1km west of the Old City. **Ambulance** (tel. 94).

Medical Assistance: Medicinski Center, Maršala Tita 61 (tel. 326 77).

Hitchhiking: From the Old City walk past the cable car station (*Žičara*) to the main highway, Jadranska Magistrala. Toward the northwest is Split, southeast is Kotor.

Accommodations and Camping

Dubrovnik has more private rooms than any other city in Yugoslavia. However, during the big Dubrovnik Festival in July and August, things may become desperate, so arrive early in the day. Average asking price among the crowd greeting travelers at the bus station and dock is US$10 for a single, and US$17 for a double, but you can often bargain. Ask if the room is close to the Old City or on a bus route. Freelance camping is illegal and non-compliants are fined heavily.

Ferijalni Savez Jugoslavije (IYHF), Vinka Segestrana 3 (tel. 232 41). From the bus station, go right and walk uphill on Put Republike, take the first right, and then go left onto Maršala Tita. Take the first street uphill (right), then a sharp right onto Oktobarske Revolucije, and follow the signs. Members US$4, nonmembers US$5. Curfew 1pm. Open May-Sept.

Dubrovnik-Tourist, Put Republike 5A (tel. 321 08). 2nd building on the right from bus station. Books private rooms. Singles US$11.50, doubles US$13. Open Mon.-Sat. 7am-9pm, Sun. 8am-noon.

Kvarner Express, Gruška Obala 69 (tel. 227 72). Convenient to the pier at Gruz. Singles US$12, doubles US$17. Open Mon.-Sat. 7am-9pm, Sun. 3-8pm.

Camping Solitude (tel. 202 47), less than 3km west of the bus station. Take bus #4 or 6 from the Old City or from near the bus station. Enjoys a commanding position on Lapad. Space for 1500—unlikely to fill, unlikely to be tranquil. US$6.50 per person, US$2.50 per tent. Open year-round.

Food

The Old City is the place to go, but eating anywhere in Dubrovnik is expensive. For a splurge, dine at the elegant restaurants along Ulica Prijeko, parallel to the main promenade street, Placa. Entrees average US$6, but go as low as US$2.50. Bargains are located on the other side of Placa. Cheapest is the self-service restaurant at Lučarica 2. (Most entrees US$2. Open 8am-10pm.) Nearby are **Jug,** at Izmedu Ploča 6 (tel. 262 53; entrees US$2.50-4), and slightly spiffier **Cavtat,** at Ploče (tel. 274 49; entrees US$4-6; open 9am-11pm). If stuck in the port area, go to **Restaurant Primorka,** N. Tesle 10, on the waterfront on the Lapad side. The outdoor **market** is midway between the pier and the bus station.

Sights

Everywhere in the Old City signs beckon you to ascend the **City Walls** (open daily 9am-7:30pm; admission US$0.65). Walk on the oceanfront side, where you can soak in the sounds of the waves and the bustle of city life simultaneously. If you wish to restrict your museum visits to one, make it the **Maritime Museum** in St. John's Fortress on the eastern edge of the Old City. Its artifacts give an idea of Dubrovnik's heyday in the sixteenth century. (Open daily 9am-2pm. Admission US$0.80.) Just before exiting the Old City through the west gate, turn right to visit the **Franciscan Monastery** and peaceful **cloisters** (open daily 9am-noon and 2-4pm; admission US$0.80). Inside the entrance is the oldest European **pharmacy,** founded in 1317. In the northeast corner of the Old City is the **Dominican Cloister and Museum,** with a polyptych by Titian. (Open Mon.-Sat. 9am-noon and 2-6pm. Admission US$0.80.) In the treasury of the **cathedral** look for the work by Raphael. (Open Mon.-Sat. 9am-noon and 2-6pm. Admission US$0.80.)

Dubrovnik's biggest attraction, though, is the sea. Bring shoes and US$0.35 to the stony hotel beaches at either end of Dubrovnik. The adventurous can swim around the city walls as others gawk from above. (Look along Od Margarite for unmarked exits leading to the water.) A water shuttle (2 per hr., 7am-7pm, US$1.35 round-trip) runs to **Lokrum Island,** with sometimes deserted beaches to the right (as you get off the boat) and nude swimming 500m to the left.

A daily Jadrolinija ferry from Gruž harbor connects Dubrovnik with the **Elaphite Islands** (Koločep, Lopud, and Šipan) and the island of **Miljet,** a half hour away. **Hotel Koločep** (tel. 242 44) can arrange private rooms. On Lopud try **Atlas** (tel. 870 15). Doubles US$11 at both.

Entertainment

In the evening, everyone cruises the streets of the Old City. Join the crowds on the main promenade, or explore the alleys where local children play. Six **open-air cinemas** operate in summer (US$1). Look for movie posters just inside the west gate of Old City. From July 10 through August 25, the **Dubrovnik Festival** fills the city with ballet, opera, symphonic and chamber concerts, plays, and folk dances (tickets US$6-8). Year-round concerts in the sixteenth-century **Rector's Palace** are usually US$8, but if you wait until a half hour before the music starts, you can sit on ledges 10m above the stage for only US$1.50.

Montenegro (Crna Gora)

The Montenegran coast south of Dubrovnik loses much of the tourist whitewash of its more prosperous northern counterpart. Unbrellas and locals fill identical, occasionally littered beaches. There are no islands, few English-speakers, and predominately Cyrillic signs. The old sections of towns along this coast were almost uniformly devastated by a 1979 earthquake.

As is the case farther north, buses are cheap and reliable, but tiring and less scenic. In July and August always make reservations as far in advance as possible to avoid getting stuck in a little coastal town because of infrequent connections. **Jadrolinija** runs a ferry from Dubrovnik to Bar (mid-April to mid-Oct. 2 per week, 4 hr., US$12.50).

One hour south of Dubrovnik by bus and near the entrance to the Gulf of Kotor is **Herceg-Novi** with its seventeenth-century Franciscan monastery and eleventh-century Orthodox Savina monastery. The very helpful **Boka** tourist office is in the bus station. One hour farther south is **Kotor.** (Frequent buses to Bar and Budva; July-Aug. 1 bus per day to Skopje.) Streets are piled with rubble and many houses are uninhabited, but you can still visit the well-restored twelfth-century **cathedral,** with its gold and silver objects, carved fourteenth-century altar, and paintings by Veronese. (Admission US$0.40, students US$0.20.) Above the town, explore the battlements that wind their way up the mountainside; these sixteenth-century fortifications were a *tour de force* of defense technology in their day. The **tourist office** is 10 minutes from the bus station and close to the beach. For private rooms, **Montenegro Express** offers doubles for US$13, 20% more in July and August. (Open Mon.-Sat. 7am-8pm.) In the red booth next to the outdoor market, **Putnik** offers singles and doubles for US$6 per person. (Open daily 8am-1pm and 6-8pm.)

Still farther south is **Budva,** where rock beaches start virtually from the bus station. (Frequent buses to Bar and Kotor.) Large signs prohibit anyone from entering the earthquake-shattered old town; the first restored street was scheduled to re-open in July 1987. On Maršala Tita are the **Turist Biro** (tel. 414 14; open daily 6am-10pm), **Putnik** (open daily 8am-noon and 5-7pm), and **Kompas** (open daily 7am-9pm). All offer only expensive doubles, for about US$17.

Five hours from Dubrovnik is **Bar,** the most important coastal town in Montenegro. Frequent buses run north to Budva and Dubrovnik. The bus and train stations are 1½km from the center. From the bus station, go left on the main road and turn left at the light. The **turist biro** is at Maršala Tita (tel. 275 44), across from the bus stop. (Open Mon.-Fri. 7am-noon and 6-8pm, Sat.-Sun. 8am-noon.) They can book rooms, but the friendlier people at **Kompas,** 14, Crnog. Brig. (tel. 273 64), 1km down the road, are a better bet. Take the red bus to Šušanj or walk down Maršala Tita until you pass the campground after the bridge. Rooms cost US$8 per person. (Open daily 7am-8pm.) Look for rooms on your own up Nikole Lekiča, across the street. **Campground Šušanj** is a good place to meet Eastern Europeans, but the showers have no walls. (US$2 per person.) The rooms-to-let clustered here and the campground are both only one minute from the beach.

Bar is the southernmost point in Yugoslavia to hop a ferry to Italy. **Ferry offices** are clustered to the right of the bus station, along the beach. **Prekookeanska Plovidba,** 4A, Obala 13. Jula (tel. 223 66), sells tickets to Bari, Italy. (Late July-early Sept. 3 per week; May-Oct. 2 per week; March-Dec. 1 per week. July-Aug. US$47; Sept.-June US$34.) Jadrolinija ferries run to Corfu and Igoumenitsa in Greece (in summer 2 per week, US$40; off-season 1 per week, US$34).

About five trains per day make the spectacular trip from Bar to Belgrade. The trip is a true adventure, passing through an unbelievable number of tunnels, spectacular mountain scenery, and the heart-pounding **Morača Canyon.** In Titograd, take a detour north to hike and camp in **Durmitor National Park** (going through Nikšić). An even more exciting option is to get off the train at **Mojkovac** (70km north of Titograd) to visit the spectacular **Tara Canyon,** second largest in the world (after the Grand). There is no organized campground near the 1200-meter gorge, but there's plenty of opportunity for freelancing.

Unbelievable scenes take place in late summer, when Belgrade-bound trains pull into Montenegro stations and screaming hordes board like refugees escaping war. Reservations are made 10 days in advance, so you may have to scramble. In July and August you can take an early-morning train to Skopje. Otherwise you have to change in Titograd for a bus to Skopje, which passes through gorge-ous **Rugovo Gorge.** Stay away from the 18-hour train ride from Bar to Skopje, with a post-midnight connection in the middle of nowhere.

Your Adriatic journey southward ends in **Ulcinj,** a half hour from Bar by bus and 16km from the Albanian border. Get a map from the bus station (staff knows German but not English), which is 1½km from the old town and the **turist biro.** There is allegedly a **Bratstvo-Jedinstvo hostel (IYHF)** (tel. (085) 818 57) in Ulcinj. (Open May-Sept.) Four kilometers south of Ulcinj, **Velika Plaža** (Great Beach) is just that, satisfying beach bums from all over for 12 splendid kilometers. The first couple of kilometers on the road to the beach are full of signs for rooms (*sobe*) (about US$8 per person). The bus from Apoteka takes you to the nearest campgrounds, **Nep tun** (tel. 818 88; US$6 per person; open April-Oct.). You can hike the last 5km to **Bojana,** where nudist campgrounds provide a stolid defense against any potential Albanian aggression.

Serbia and Macedonia

Serbia comprises about 40% of Yugoslavia's area—the entire eastern half as far south as Macedonia. The strongest province since medieval times, Serbia spearheaded Yugoslavia's unification in the twentieth century, and Belgrade is the capital of both province and nation. History has not been so kind to Macedonian ambitions, except for the singular exploits of Alexander the Great. Following five centuries of rule by the Ottomans and then the Balkan Wars of 1911-13, Macedonia was split into three parts, within political jurisdiction of Greece, Bulgaria, and Yugoslavia. Despite division, modern-day Yugoslavian Macedonia deserves a stopover for the outdoor recreation activities around Lake Ohrid and the nearby Šar Mountains.

Cyrillic is the dominant alphabet in Serbia (bring along an alphabet for transliterating), but English is commonly studied. Macedonian is a distinct Slavic language, somewhat similar to Bulgarian, and also uses the Cyrillic alphabet.

A few trains per day travel the main rail line between Belgrade, Skopje, and Thessaloniki, Greece, and one mid-afternoon train connects Bitola and Florina, Greece. This somewhat limited train service makes the very crowded bus system all the more important. Get your tickets and reservations as far in advance as possible.

Belgrade (Beograd)

The dismaying discovery that there is little affordable accommodation may turn you right off the place. But if you can see past the ugly grey architecture, you might come to enjoy the concerts, bookstores, and other cultural attractions of this bustling capital.

Orientation and Practical Information

Belgrade lies in eastern Yugoslavia, 60km from the Romanian border, straddling the River Sava at its junction with the Danube. All long-distance trains to and from Greece, Austria, and Italy stop here. Belgrade is also Yugoslavia's principal hub for service to Hungary, Romania, and Bulgaria, and the best jumping-off point for visits to the monasteries in the Serbian countryside.

Belgrade's train and bus stations are located next to one another on Trg Bratstva i Jedinstva. Pick up a city map, complete with bus and tram routes and scores of addresses and telephone numbers, at the tourist office inside the train station. The **River Sava** separates **stari grad** (old city) from **Novi Beograd.** The center of the old city is a 20-minute uphill walk from the station; go up the street by the Putnik and Lasta tourist agencies and take the first left onto Balkanska, which takes you to **Terazije.** You can also take bus #34. The main tourist office is to your left in the underpass by the Albanlja Palace. To the right, Terazije leads to **Kneza Milǒsa** (embassy row).

Tourist Offices: Turistički Informativni Centar, Knez Mihailova 48 (tel. 63 53 43). The largest tourist office in Yugoslavia. Wonderfully patient and knowledgeable English-speaking staff. Pick up the excellent map and *Beogradscope,* a monthly calendar of events. Open daily 8am-8pm. Other less extensive offices at the train station (tel. 64 62 40), and the airport (tel. 60 23 26); both open Mon.-Sat. 7am-9pm.

Budget Travel: Karavan-Naromtravel, Takovska 12 (tel. 33 30 55). From the JAT city terminal, go right on Bulevar Revolucije and then the second right onto Takovska. Sales office for Naromtravel, Yugoslavia's student travel organization. Sells YIEE, ISIC, and IUS cards; the latter is important if you're continuing into Eastern Europe. Open Mon.-Sat. 8am-7pm. **Discount Rail Tickets: Beogradtours,** Milovana Milovanovića 5. Across from the station, past the Putnik office. IUS cardholders get 30% reductions on tickets to Hungary. InterRail cards renewed here in the morning only. Open Mon.-Fri. 8:30am-7pm, Sat. 9am-noon.

American Express: Atlas, Zmaj Jovina 10 (tel. 18 36 71). The only office in Yugoslavia that can receive wired money and cash personal checks. Pick up mail at Moše Pijade 11 (tel. 34 14 71), 3 blocks from main tourist office. Both open Mon.-Fri. 8am-8pm, Sat. 8am-3pm.

Post Office: PTT, Takovska 2 (tel. 34 34 81), 2 blocks from JAT city terminal. Open daily 8am-8pm. **Poste Restante** open Mon.-Fri. 7am-7pm, Sat. 8am-2pm. **Postal code:** 11000 for Beograd, 11101 for Poste Restante at this office.

Telephones: PTT, Zmaj Jovina 17, at the corner of V. Čarapića, near Trg Republike. Open 24 hours. Also at main post office. **Telephone code:** 011.

Flights: All land at **Aerodrom Beograd** in Surčin, 35 min. west of the city. For information call 60 23 26. **JAT** buses (tel. 64 27 33) leave the airport every ½ hr. 4:30am-11pm, stop outside the train station, and end up at the JAT city air terminal by St. Mark's Cathedral and the Tašmajdan Park on Bulevar Revolucije. After taking a right onto Bulevar Revolucije, go straight ahead, turn left at the Trg Marksa i Engelsa, and you'll be at Terazije; the tourist office is at the opposite end of this street. Another JAT office at Maršala Tita 18 (tel. 64 27 33). Fares within Yugoslavia approximately US$20.

Trains: Central Station is on Trg Bratstva i Jedinstva. Take bus #34 to the old city or follow walking directions above. Information in Serbo-Croatian (tel. 64 58 22). 3 trains per day to Budapest and Athens. 1 train per day to Munich, Paris, Rome, Vienna, and Prague. Trains to and from Romania at Đure Đakovica 39, in northeast Belgrade.

Buses: Main station is next to the train station (tel. 62 47 51 or 62 70 49). No international service.

Emergencies: Police (tel. 92). **Ambulance** (tel. 94).

Medical Assistance: Dom Zdravlja "Boris Kidrič," Pasterova 1 (tel. 68 37 55).

Pharmacy: Prvi Maj, Maršala Tita 9. Open 24 hours.

Embassies: U.S., Kneza Miloša 50 (tel. 64 56 22; open Mon.-Fri. 7am-noon). **Canada,** Kneza Miloša 75 (tel. 64 46 66; open Mon.-Thurs. 7:30am-4pm, Fri. 7:30am-1pm). **U.K.,** General Ždanova 46 (tel. 64 50 55; open Mon.-Fri. 8am-12:30pm). **Australia,** Čika Ljubina 13 (tel. 62 46 55; open Mon. and Wed. 7:30am-5:30pm, Tues. and Thurs.-Fri. 7:30am-1:45pm). **New Zealand** affairs handled by the British Embassy. **Albania,** Kneza Miloša 56 (tel. 64 68 64; open Mon.-Fri. 9am-2pm). **Bulgaria,** Birčaninova 26 (tel. 64 62 22; open Mon.-Fri. 7am-2pm). Visas issued while you wait, US$18. **Czechoslovakia,** Bulevar Revolucije 22 (tel. 33 15 73; open Mon.-Fri. 9am-noon). Visas issued while you wait, US$15 and 2 photos. **Hungary,** Ivana Milutinovića 74 (tel. 444 04 72; open Mon.-Fri. 9am-noon). Visas issued while you wait, US$12 and 2 photos. **Poland,** Kneza Miloša 38 (tel. 64 57 96; open Mon.-Fri. 8am-noon). Visas take 1-3 days, US$13 and 2 photos. **Romania,** Kneza Miloša 70 (tel. 64 60 71). Visas issued while you wait, US$20. Information in French.

American Center: At the beginning of Čika Ljubina, off Knez Mihailova, next to embassy. Open Mon.-Sat. 9am-5pm. **English Library,** Knez Mihailova, 20 min. from the American Center, towards Kalemegdan. Periodicals and air conditioning. Open Mon.-Fri. 10am-5pm.

Women's Center: Contact Źena I Druśtvo through Studentski Kulturni Centar, Maršala Tita 46 (tel. 68 23 51).

Bookstore: The shop at Prodavniza 1, above the tourist office, has a good selection of paperbacks and dictionaries. Another shop on the opposite side of the same building has a good selection of travel guides and phrasebooks. Open Mon.-Sat. 8am-8pm.

Hitchhiking: For Zagreb and Ljubljana, take bus #601 from the Sava Center in Novi Beograd out as far as it goes on the *auto-put* (expressway). For Skopje and points south, take bus #38 as far as it goes on *auto-put* Stevana Prvovenčanog. Lots of luck.

Accommodations and Camping

To avoid paying US$30-45 for a hotel room, arrive early in the day; even then you may join the exodus of frustrated travelers on the night train out of Belgrade.

Youth Guest House "Mladost" (IYHF), Bulevar JNA (Jugoslovenske Narodne Armije) 56a (tel. 46 53 24). Clean and cheap and an English-speaking staff, but ½ hr. from the center of town. Take tram #9 or 10 from the train station and ask someone for the stop "Mladost" or "Kapetan Zaviića," the street you follow 2 blocks to Bulevar JNA. Members US$6, non-members US$7. Breakfast included. Open year-round 24 hours. Closed for repairs in 1987, but scheduled to re-open Jan. 1, 1988.

Studentski Dom: Rifat Burdževića, Milana Rakića 38 (tel. 41 14 54). Get the information office to set this one up. US$7 per person. Often full even in early morning. Open July-Aug. only.

Lasta, Trg Bratstva i Jedinstva 1a (tel. 64 12 51), 1 min. from train station. Arranges private rooms. Singles US$15, doubles US$17, triples US$33.

Camping: Camping Košutnjak, Kneza Višeslava 17 (tel. 55 69 61). Take bus #53 south from station near tourist office to Kiro-vljeva St. and walk 3 blocks. Pitch your tent far from the restaurant, whence music blares well into the morning. US$1.50 per person, US$1 per tent. **Camping National,** Bežanijska Kosa 1a (tel. 69 35 09), in Novi Beograd (take bus #601), costs US$3.30 per person, US$1.30 per tent. Both open year-round.

Food

Belgrade may be short on good budget accommodations, but its many inexpensive restaurants will easily soothe frayed nerves. Across from the train station a number of places sell freshly roasted chicken (US$2 for half a chicken). For a typical Serbian dish, try *pasulj*—beans, cooked generally with ribs (*sa suvim rebrima*). A dinner along enchanting **Skadarska Ulica** would alone make the trip to Belgrade worthwhile. After 8pm, talented folk musicians turn this street into a fairyland.

Cheaper than restaurants, the carry-outs near the fountain on Skadarska sell scrumptious *lepinja* (hot bread filled with *kajmak* cheese or *goulash*) for US$0.50. Down the street, follow this up with US$0.40. worth of *sardele* (a paper cone filled with deep-fried sardines), or pick up a *pljeskavica* (US$1.15).

Dva Jelena (Two Deer), Skadaska 32. Good views from the center of the promenade. Or try **Ima Dana,** at #38, and **Tri Šešira** (Three Deer), at #29. Each serves tender grilled specialties for US$4.

Klub Književnika, ulica Francuska, 10m under the National Theater. Excellent food—both grilled meat and home-cooked dishes (up to US$6). In the summer, tables in a beautiful garden. Bohemian atmosphere; many well-known people come here.

? Cafe, 7 Jula St. #6, near Kneza Mihaila, across the street from the city's main church. The oldest continuously operating (since 1823) cafe-restaurant in Belgrade. The owner was once sued by the church; apprehension about whether he would remain open produced the question mark. Come here for libation or for Serbian cuisine served on low wooden tables. Full meals with drink US$6.

Vuk, Vuka Karadžića, a couple of blocks from the ? Cafe. Its sign is in Cyrillic (BYK), but the menu is translated into English. Try Serbian specialties such as stuffed zucchini or peppers (US$1.35).

Self-Service Kasina, Terazije 25, right near the main tourist office. Belgrade's best prices. A wide variety of already prepared dishes. Most main courses about US$1.35.

Sights and Entertainment

At the end of the Terazije on Trg Republike stands the **Narodni Muzej** (National Museum), a mammoth collection of prehistoric artifacts, icons, frescoes, and paintings from Serbian and European schools. Discoveries from the neolithic settlement at Lepenski Vir and works by Yugoslavia's best known sculptor, Ivan Meštrović are also displayed here. The National Museum's **Galerija Fresaka** (Gallery of Frescoes), near Kalemegdan Park at Cara Uroša 20, houses faithful copies of the vivid and dramatic medieval works found in various Serbian and Macedonian Orthodox monasteries. (Both open Tues.-Wed. and Fri.-Sat. 10am-5pm, Thurs. 10am-7pm, Sun. 10am-2pm. Admission US$0.75, students US$0.35.)

Six blocks northwest of the tourist office is **Kalemegdan.** A fortress in Roman times, this is now a beautiful park, with an observatory, several museums, a zoo, four discotheques, and a breathtaking view of the confluence of Sava and Danube.

Modern Yugoslavia is a fascinating example of ethnic coexistence; for an interesting official interpretation of the nation's struggles, visit the **Muzej Revolucije Naroda i Narodnosti Jugoslavije** (Museum of the Revolution of the Nations and Nationalities of Yugoslavia), at Trg Marksa i Engelsa 11. (Open Tues.-Wed. and Fri.-Sat. 10am-5pm, Thurs. 10am-7pm, Sun. 10am-2pm. Admission US$1.35, students US$0.65.) More insight into Yugoslavia's turbulent history is offered in the presentations of the world-war liberation struggles in the **Vojni Muzej** (Military Museum) in the Kalemegdan Park. (Open Tues.-Wed. and Fri.-Sat. 10am-5pm, Thurs. 10am-7pm, Sun. 10am-2pm. Admission US$1.35, students US$0.65.)

Whether you have dinner there or not, carouse down **Skadarska Ulica** some evening. A nineteenth-century haunt of artists and bohemians, the so-called "Skadarlija" has had its original cobblestones and atmosphere restored. **Ada Ciganlija,** an island in River Sava, has restaurants on houseboats. On the New Belgrade side, they are not easy to get to (taxi is the best), but you are on the water, and fun goes on far later into the night.

Every Tuesday evening, **Kolo,** an excellent Yugoslav folk song and dance group, performs at Belgrade's foremost concert hall, the **Kolarac People's University** at Studentski Trg 5. On Monday and Thursday nights throughout the year, classical music concerts are held at the **Galerija Srpske Akademije Nauka i Umetnosti** (Gallery of the Serbian Academy of Sciences and Arts), Knez Mihailova 35. The **Narodno Pozorište** (National Theater) has opera, ballet, and drama performances. During the summer, outdoor concerts are held regularly in **Kalemegdan Park.** The monthly *Beogradscope* includes comprehensive listings of cultural events in and around town; most are very inexpensive (less than US$1.50.)

Skopje

Skopje is the capital of Macedonia, and the first major Yugoslav city on the train route linking Greece with northern Europe. A major trade center during the Roman and Ottoman Empires, the city was almost completely destroyed by a 1963 earthquake, and the newly-constructed buildings pale in comparison. The train station is 1½km from the bus station (walk 3 blocks to river, then cross the third bridge); the bus station is conveniently downhill from the bazaar.

If you're traveling by bus in July or August, your first move once in Skopje should be to get a bus ticket and reservation for your departure because of the crowds passing through Skopje for Ohrid. Pick up a map at the information booth in the train station. The main **Turistička Agencija** (tel. 22 34 29), 100m from the bus station, has a few rooms to let for US$5. (Open daily 8am-8pm.) The **Karavan Youth Trave Office,** Gradski trgovinski center "bb" (tel. 21 32 13) is in the shopping center be hind Maršala Tita Square. They sell IUS, YIEE, and ISIC cards, and give informa tion on discount air tickets. **The Youth Hostel Blagoje Šošolčev (IYHF)** 25, Prole (tel. 23 38 66), is sociable, neat (even the pit toilets are clean), and extremely conve nient. From the train station, head toward the river and take your second left ont Prolet. (Members US$2 in rooms of 6, nonmembers US$6; doubles US$4 an US$7.) In July and August, try the student dorms in the southwestern part of th city, all near or on Ivo Ribar-Lola avenue: **K. J. Pitu** at Ribar 58 (tel. 23 53 60 and **Goce Delčev** at Taftalidže II (tel. 25 30 21). Beds at both US$3.

Most of Skopje's historical sights are within easy walking distance of the bus sta tion. As you exit to the left, less than 100m on your right will be the fifteenth-centur **Daut-pašin Amam** (Turkish bath). (Open Mon.-Fri. 8am-7pm, Sat. 9am-1pm. Ad mission US$0.40, students US$0.20.) As you enter the old bazaar from the baths bear left up the main street to the **Church of Sveti Spas,** with a fantastically-carvec walnut iconostasis (altar screen). (Open Mon.-Sat. 7am-7pm. Admission US$0.40 students US$0.20, complete with English-speaking guide.) On the same hill is th **Mustafa-pašina džamija** (Mustafa Pasha mosque), the large **Kuršumli han** (Turkish inn), and the **Macedonian Archeological Museum.**

In the bazaar, you'll find a lot of *skara* that serve cooked meats with a side o green peppers. Across the river are inexpensive self-service restaurants: **Ishrana,** a Ive Lole Ribara 11, and **Pelister** at Maršala Tita 50. Entrees at either cost around US$1. (Both open daily 6:30am-9:30pm.)

The **telephone code** in Skopje is 091.

Lake Ohrid (Ohridsko Ezero)

Four-million-year-old Lake Ohrid lies in the extreme southwest corner of Yugo slavia; indeed, part of it belongs to Albania. Its age and depth have contributed to ward making it the refuge of fish known elsewhere only through fossils. Forty By zantine churches and several fine beaches and campsites grace its shores.

Ten buses per day connect the town of Ohrid with Skopje (US$3). The quickest route (2½ hr.) is via Titov Veles. The longer but more scenic western route (4½ hr.) travels through Yugoslavia's second-highest mountains—the **Šar Planina** range. The slowest and least exciting way to Ohrid is by train to Bitola and then by bus to the town.

Next to Ohrid's bus station, you'll find the **Turističko Društvo** at Partizanska 3 (tel. (096) 224 94). Besides furnishing maps of the Ohrid area (US$0.40) and information on Macedonia, they can place you in private homes. (Open daily 7am-9pm. Rooms US$5-8 per person.) The crowd at the bus station offers rooms for US$7-8. **Youth Hostel Mladost** (tel. (096) 216 26) is 2km from town and dirty. You can eat rare Lake Ohrid trout on the rooftop in **Letnica** restaurant (across from the bus station) for US$3.50; the self-service section of Letnica costs only US$1-2.50 for meat and vegetable. (Open daily 6am-10pm.)

Ohrid was an important stop on the Roman road, Via Egnatia. When the Slavs took possession of the area in the ninth century, they developed a university which became an important center of Slavic culture and literacy. In the upper part of the town, don't miss the **Church of Sveti Kliment.** Its 600-year-old frescoes have recently been cleaned and are in superb condition. (Open Tues.-Sun. 8am-noon and 3-7pm. Admission US$0.40, students US$0.20.) The **Church of Sveti Jovan,** perched on a cliff above the lake in the neighboring village of Kaneo, finds its way onto most posters of Lake Ohrid; below, there is a picturesque though packed beach. In the center of Ohrid's old town is the famous **Sveta Sofija,** where performances of the **Festival Ohridsko Leto** (mid-July through late Aug.) and the **Balkan Festival,** an exhibition of international folk dancing (first week in July; tickets US$3) are held.

The exquisitely adorned monastery of **Sveti Naum** is right against the Albanian border. Take the bus 29km along the lakeshore from Ohrid (6 per day, 1 hr., US$1) or a ferry (4 per week, US$3 round-trip). Try to get to the town for a Sunday morning service, or better yet on July 3, the saint's feast day. Hundreds sing, dance, and eat, accompanied by traditional music.

Lake Ohrid's waters are murky, and cooler than those on the Adriatic, but refreshing nonetheless. Take the local bus to Hotel Gorica (2km), or walk south (left from bus station) along the waters until you hear people swimming behind the bushes.

Between Ohrid and Sveti Naum is the fishing village of **Pestani.** Nearby are two campgrounds, **Elešec** and **Gradište,** both with lovely mountain scenery and clean, relatively uncrowded beaches. (Both US$2 per person, US$2.50 per tent.) Southeast of Lake Ohrid is **Prespansko Ezero** (Lake Prespa), 158m higher. Located partly in Greece and partly in Albania, Lake Prespa also offers clear water and sandy beaches. Campgrounds are located at **Krani** (US$1.50 per person, US$2 per tent) and **Resen** (US$2 per person, US$2 per tent).

Macedonian folk music is the best in Yugoslavia. Back in Ohrid for the evening, head for the **Hotel Riviera,** just off the waterfront, where locals sit and drink in the patio listening to traditional tunes and occasional contemporary ones. Other hotels and the restaurant **Orient** also occasionally offer these musical evenings.

Congratulations to all those who used this book in alphabetical order. Here is your chance to start all over again: Albania is across the lake.

Appendix

National Tourist Offices

Austrian National Tourist Office

U.S.: 500 Fifth Ave., Suite 2009-2022, New York, NY 10110. Tel. (212) 944-6880.
Canada: 2 Bloor St. East, Suite 3330, Toronto, Ontario M4W 1A8. Tel. (416) 967-3381.
Great Britain: 30 Saint George St., London W1R 0AL. Tel. (01) 629 04 61.
Australia: 19th Floor, No. 1 York St., Sydney NSW 2000. Tel. (02) 241 19 16.

Belgian National Tourist Office

U.S.: 745 Fifth Ave., Suite 7104, New York, NY 10151. Tel. (212) 758-8130.
Great Britain: 38 Dover St., London W1X 3RB. Tel. (01) 499 53 79.

Čedok (Czechoslovakia)

U.S.: 10 East 40th St., Suite 1902, New York, NY 10016. Tel. (212) 689-9720.

Danish Tourist Board

U.S.: 655 Third Ave., 18th floor, New York, NY 10017. Tel. (212) 949-2333.
Canada: P.O. Box 115, Station N, Toronto, Ontario M8V 3S4. Tel. (416) 823-9620.
Great Britain: Sceptre House, 169-173 Regent St., London W1R 8PY. Tel. (01) 734 26 37.
Australia: 60 Market St., P.O. Box 4531, Melbourne, Victoria 3001. Tel. (03) 62 33 63.

Egyptian Tourist Authority

U.S.: 630 Fifth Ave., New York, NY 10111. Tel. (212) 246-6960.
Canada: Place Bonaventure, 40 Frontenac, P.O. Box 304, Montréal, Québec H5A 1B4. Tel. (514) 861-4420.
Great Britain: 168 Piccadilly, London W1. Tel. (01) 493 52 82.

Finnish Tourist Board

U.S.: 655 Third Ave., 18th floor, New York, NY 10017. Tel. (212) 949-2333.
Canada: 1200 Bay St., Suite 604, Toronto, Ontario M5R 2A5. Tel. (416) 964-0159.
Great Britain: 66-68 Haymarket, London SW1Y 4RF. Tel. (01) 839 40 48.

French Government Tourist Office

U.S.: 610 Fifth Ave., New York, NY 10020-2452. Tel. (212) 757-1125.
Canada: 1 Dundas St. West, Suite 2405, Box 8, Toronto, Ontario M5G 1Z3. Tel. (416) 593-4723.
Great Britain: 178 Piccadilly, London W1V OAL. Tel. (01) 493 65 94.
Australia: Kindersley House, 33 Bligh St., Sydney NSW 2000. Tel. (02) 231 52 44.

West German National Tourist Office

U.S.: 747 Third Ave., New York, NY 10017. Tel. (212) 308-3300.
Canada: 2 Fundy, P.O. Box 417, Place Bonaventure, Montréal, Québec H5A 1B8. Tel. (514) 878-9885.
Great Britain: 61 Conduit St., London W1R 0EN. Tel. (01) 734 26 00.
Australia: Lufthansa House, 12th floor, 143 Macquarie St., Sydney NSW 2000. Tel. (02) 221 10 08.

British Tourist Authority

U.S.: 40 West 57th St., 3rd floor, New York, NY 10019. Tel. (212) 581-4700.
Canada: 94 Cumberland St., Suite 600, Toronto, Ontario M5R 3N3. Tel. (416) 925-6326.
Australia: 171 Clarence St., Sydney NSW 2000. Tel. (02) 29 86 27.

Greek National Tourist Organization

U.S.: Olympic Tower, 645 Fifth Ave., New York, NY 10022. Tel. (212) 421-5777.
Canada: 1233 rue de la Montagne, Suite 101, Montréal, Québec H3G 1Z2. Tel. (514) 871-1535.
Great Britain: 195-197 Regent St., London W1R 8DR. Tel. (01) 734 59 97.
Australia: 51-57 Pitt St., Sydney NSW 2000. Tel. (02) 241 1663

IBUSZ (Hungary)

U.S.: 630 Fifth Ave., Suite 2455, New York, NY 10111. Tel. (212) 582-7412.
Great Britain: Danube Travel, Ltd., 6 Conduit St., London W1R 9TG. Tel. (01) 493 02 63.

Icelandic Tourist Board
U.S.: 655 Third Ave., 18th Floor, New York, NY 10017. Tel. (212) 949-2333.

Irish Tourist Board
U.S.: 757 Third Ave., New York, NY 10017. Tel. (212) 418-0800.
Canada: 10 King St. East, Toronto, Ontario M5C 1C3. Tel. (416) 364-1301.
Great Britain: 150 New Bond St., London W1Y 0AQ. Tel. (01) 493 32 01.
Australia: MLC Centre, 36th Level, Martin Place, Sydney NSW 2000. Tel. (02) 232 71 77.

Israeli Government Tourist Office
U.S.: 350 Fifth Ave., New York, NY 10118. Tel. (212) 560-0650.
Canada: 180 Bloor St. West, Toronto, Ontario M5S 2V6. Tel. (416) 964-3784.
Great Britain: 18 Great Marlborough St., London. Tel. (01) 434 36 51.

Italian Government Tourist Office
U.S.: 630 Fifth Ave., Suite 1565, Rockefeller Center, New York, NY 10111. Tel. (212) 245-4822.
Canada: 3 Place Ville Marie, 56 Plaza, Montréal, Québec. H3B 2E3. Tel. (514) 866-7667.
Great Britain: 1 Princes St., London W1R 8AY. Tel. (01) 408 12 54.

Embassy of Jordan Information Counselor
U.S.: 2319 Wyoming Ave. NW, Washington, D.C. 20008. Tel. (202) 265-1606.
Canada: 100 Bronson Avenue, Suite 701, Ottawa, Ontario K1R 6G8. Tel. (613) 238-8090.
Great Britain: 6 Upper Phillimore Gardens, London W8 7HB. Tel. (01) 937 36 85.
Australia: 29 Roebuck St., Red Hill Act. 2603, Canberra. Tel. (062) 95 99 51.

Luxèmbourg National Tourist Office
U.S.: 801 Second Ave., New York, NY 10017. Tel. (212) 370-9850.
Great Britain: 36-37 Piccadilly, London W1V 9PA. Tel. (01) 434 28 00.

Moroccan National Tourist Office
U.S.: 20 East 46th St., Suite 1201, New York, NY 10017. Tel. (212) 557-2520.
Canada: 2001 rue Université, Suite 1460, Montréal, Québec H3A 2A6. Tel. (514) 842-8111.
Great Britain: 174 Regent St., London W1R GHB. Tel. (01) 437 00 73.

Netherlands Tourist Office
U.S.: 355 Lexington Ave., 21st floor, New York, NY 10017. Tel. (212) 370-7367.
Canada: 25 Adelaide St. East, Suite 710, Toronto, Ontario M5C 1Y2. Tel. (416) 363-1577.
Great Britain: Egginton House, 25-28 Buckingham Gate, London SW1E 6LD. Tel. (01) 630 04 51.

Norwegian Tourist Office
U.S.: 655 Third Ave., 18th floor, New York, NY 10017. Tel. (212) 949-2333.
Great Britain: 20 Pall Mall, London SW1Y 5NE. Tel (01) 839 26 50.

ORBIS (Poland)
U.S.: 500 Fifth Ave., New York, NY 10110. Tel. (212) 391-0844.
Great Britain: 82 Mortimer St., London W1N 7DE. Tel. (01) 637 49 71.

Portuguese National Tourist Office
U.S.: 548 Fifth Ave., New York, NY 10036. Tel. (212) 354-4403.
Great Britain: New Bond St. House, 1-5 New Bond St., London, W1Y ONP. Tel. (01) 493 38 73.

Romanian National Tourist Office
U.S.: 573 Third Ave., New York, NY 10016. Tel. (212) 697-6971.

National Tourist Office of Spain
U.S.: 665 Fifth Ave., New York, NY 10022. Tel. (212) 759-8822.
Canada: 60 Bloor St. West, Suite 201, Toronto, Ontario M4W 3B8. Tel. (416) 961-3131.
Great Britain: 57-58 Saint James St., London SW1A 1LD. Tel. (01) 499 11 69.

Swedish National Tourist Office
U.S.: 655 Third Ave., 18th floor, New York, NY 10017. Tel. (212) 949-2333.
Great Britian: 3 Cork St., London W1X 1HA. Tel. (01) 437 58 16.

Swiss National Tourist Office

U.S.: 608 Fifth Ave., New York, NY 10020. Tel. (212) 757-5944.
Canada: P.O. Box 215, Commerce Court, Toronto, Ontario M5L 1E8. Tel. (416) 868-0584.
Great Britain: Swiss Centre, 1 New Coventry St., London W1V 8EE. Tel. (01) 734 19 21.
Australia: 203-233 New South Head Road, P.O. Box 82, Edgecliffe, Sydney NSW 2027.

Tunisian Tourist Office

U.S.: Embassy of Tunisia, Cultural Section, 2408 Massachusetts Ave. NW, Washington, D.C. 20008. Tel. (202) 234-6650.
Canada: Embassy of Tunisia, Cultural Section, 515 Oscannor St., Ottawa, Ontario. Tel. (613) 237-0330.
Great Britain: Tunisian National Tourist Office, 7a Stafford St., London W1X 3PG. Tel. (01) 493 75 23.

Turkish Culture and Information Office

U.S.: 821 United Nations Plaza, New York, NY 10017. Tel. (212) 687-2194.
Great Britain: 170-173 Piccadilly, First Floor, London W1 VDD. Tel. (01) 734 86 81.

Intourist (USSR)

U.S.: 630 Fifth Ave., Suite 868, New York, NY 10111. Tel. (212) 757-3884.
Canada: 1801 McGill College Ave., Montreal, Quebec H3A 2N4. Tel. (514) 849-6394.
Great Britain: 292 Regent St., London W1R 6QL. Tel. (01) 631 12 82.

Yugoslav National Tourist Office

U.S.: 630 Fifth Ave., Suite 280, New York, NY 10111. Tel. (212) 757-2801.
Great Britain: 143 Regent St., London W1. Tel. (01) 734 52 43.

INDEX

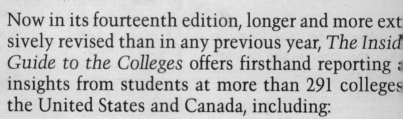

Readership Survey

In order to suit your travel needs better, it helps us to know a little about you.

1. Age ______ 2. Please Circle: Male Female
3. Are you a college student? Yes No College Year: Fr. So. Jr. Sr.
4. Household Income: $15,000 or below $15,000-$25,000 $25,000-$50,000 $50,000-$100,000 $100,000 or above
5. Circle all modes of transportation you plan to use. Underline the primary one: rented car leased car purchased car bus train bicycle motorcycle hitching
6. Country of origin__________ 7. Length of stay _____ (number of weeks)
8. How much do you plan to spend on your trip exclusive of airfare?
   $400-$800 $800-$1200 $1200-$1600
   $1600-$2000 $2000-$2800 over $2800
9. How many dollars worth of traveler's checks will you bring?
   <$100, $100-250, $250-500, $500-750, $750-1000, $1000-1500 >$1500
10. Circle forms of accommodations you will be using. Underline the primary one: hostels, budget hotels, hotels, campgrounds, camper, other
11. Average amount of money spent per day on accommodations? ________
12. From which city will you leave? NY BOS LA SF Miami Dallas Chicago Other
13. How many rolls of film will you use? <5 5-10 >10
14. Type of camera you are using? 110-Instamatic 35mm-Instamatic Instant (Polaroid) 35mm SLR
15. Will you carry? backpack knapsack (daypack) suitcase other
16. Approximate percentage of trip spent in major cities? 10 25 50 75 100
17. Number the following sections of the book in order of importance:
   Practical Information ____ Accommodations ____ Food ____
   Sights ____ Travelers with Children ____ Disabled Travelers ____
   Dietary concerns ____ Gay and Lesbian Travelers ____
18. How many people are you traveling with? ____
19. Season in which you will begin travel: spring summer fall winter
20. Primary reason for travel: study work pleasure
21. Please circle all places you plan to visit. Underline your first destination:
   Alaska Austria Belgium Bulgaria Czechoslovakia Denmark E. Germany Egypt Finland France Great Britain Greece Hawaii Hungary Iceland Ireland Israel Italy Jordan Luxembourg Mexico Morocco Netherlands N. Ireland Norway Poland Portugal Romania Scotland Spain Sweden Switzerland Turkey USA USSR W. Germany Yugoslavia
22. Where did you buy this book? bookstore ___ college bookstore ___ other ___

Please return to:

Readership Survey, Dept. E, Harvard Student Agencies, Inc.
Thayer Hall-B, Harvard University,
Cambridge, MA 02138